THE MACMILLAN DICTIONARY OF QUOTATIONS

THE MACMILLAN DICTIONARY OF QUOTATIONS

CHARTWELL
BOOKS, INC.

This edition published in 2000 by Chartwell Books, Inc.
A division of Book Sales Inc.
114 Northfield Avenue
Edison, NJ 08837

ISBN: 0-7858-1191-5

Published by arrangement with and permission of
IDG Books Worldwide, Inc.
919 E. Hillsdale Blvd., Suite 400
Foster City, CA 94404

Liberty of Congress Cataloging-in-Publication Data
Macmillan dictionary of quotations.

p. cm.
Includes Index.
ISBN 0-7858-1191-5
1. Quotations. 2. Quotations, English. I. Macmillan Publishing Company. II. Title: Dictionary of quotations.
PN6081.M27 1989
082---dc20 89-12237 CIP

Printed in the United States of America

• Contents

Acknowledgments

Editors

John Daintith
Hazel Egerton
Rosalind Fergusson
Anne Stibbs
Edmund Wright

Contributors

Graham Betts
Elizabeth Bonham
Deborah Chapman
Sue Cope
Eve Daintith
Joan Gallagher
Joanna Gosling
Jock Graham
Lawrence Holden
Valerie Illingworth
Alan Isaacs
Amanda Isaacs
Stephen Jones
Elizabeth Martin
Jennifer Monk
David Pickering
Ruth Salomon
Jessica Scholes
Gwynneth Shaw
Mary Shields
Kate Smith
Brenda Tomkins
Jean Wright

• Introduction

This dictionary is a compilation of more than 20,000 quotations selected for their interest, relevance, or wit. It combines, in a single volume, *Biographical entries*—quotations by people—and *Thematic entries*—quotations about topics. We hope that this will enable the user to look up sayings or comments by certain authors as well as finding quotations on certain subjects.

Most of the thematic entries are on the subjects that one would expect—**life, death, love, hate, sex**, etc. Perhaps less predictable are the more topical themes, including **pollution, healthy living**, and **feminism**. These entries also have cross references to related topics—a reader interested in **adultery** may find extra guidance by reading the entries on **sex, unfaithfulness**, and even **marriage**!

The thematic quotations are largely *about* the topic under which they are listed. In choosing these quotations we have been guided by two different rules. One is that they should be familiar —the quotations that many people know—or, at least, half remember. Like idioms and proverbs, they are an intrinsic part of the English language. As Dr Johnson said in his *Dictionary*, "Every quotation contributes something to the stability and enlargement of the language." The other criterion is that the quotations should be relevant—they should say something perceptive or amusing about the topic. For this reason we have also included many writings or sayings that are probably not familiar, but perhaps ought to be. In this we have been guided by Anatole France: "When a thing has been said, and said well, have no scruple. Take it and copy it." However, we have made no judgments about what is being said. Indeed, one of the interesting features of this method of organization is the juxtaposition of different opinions.

As well as quotations *about* subjects we have included a number of quotations that are *examples* of the theme. Under **epitaphs** for instance, quotations about epitaphs are given together with examples of epitaphs. Similar themes include **last words,**

execution, boasts, telegrams, misquotations, insults, compliments, and **repartee**. A reader wishing to insult or compliment someone can look up the relevant theme and be guided by experts.

There are about 150 biographical entries, ranging from Woody Allen to W. B. Yeats. As our selection of suitable biographical topics will not be everyone's choice, perhaps we ought to explain how we have chosen them. The main criterion for inclusion has been "quotability", irrespective of any other merit. This accounts for the appearance of **Woody Allen** and **Dorothy Parker** as well as **Shakespeare, Byron,** and **Wordsworth**. We have also included sayings by a number of people in American public life —mostly presidents, but also other politicians.

In addition to the thematic and biographical entries there are entries for **Biblical quotations, Proverbs, Nursery Rhymes**, and quotations by that productive author known as "Anon" (*see* **Anonymous**).

Within each thematic entry the quotations are arranged alphabetically by author. For the first appearance of an author within an entry, a brief biographical note and important dates are given. If the author has more than one quotation under an entry, the biographical note is not repeated. The quotation is also followed by an explanatory note if one is needed and by the source, if it is known.

As far as possible, we have tried to give sources for all the quotations in the book. This has not always been possible; many quotations, which we have labeled "Attrib.", are sayings or remarks generally ascribed to a person but without an identifiable source. There are also problems in attributing some quotations. Some are widely ascribed to two or more people. For these we have included explanatory notes after the quotation. Another problem is that of co-authors, such as Lennon and McCartney. In these cases the quotations are included under the first named, with a cross reference from the second. This does not, of course, imply that one is in any way more important.

The example of Mae West typifies another difficulty. Many of her sayings are lines from films; therefore the author should, strictly speaking, be the script writer. However, remarks such as "Come up and see me (sometime)" are so closely associated with her that it would be perverse not to include them under her name.

Yet another problem involves such quotations as those of Goldwyn and Spooner, who almost certainly never made some of the remarks attributed to them. We decided to include these, if only because they are too good to leave out. Some indication of the difficulties in attributing quotations is given by the reaction of one person we telephoned about a quotation. "Yes," she said, "it is often said to be by me, but I was only repeating something I heard years ago." And the difficulty in selection is illustrated by her next remark. “But I have said lots of other clever things that nobody has noticed.”

The policy on spelling also needs some comment. According to George Bernard Shaw, “Britain and America are two countries separated by the same language.” In this book the thematic headwords, the biographies, and the notes use American spelling. The quotations themselves are reproduced as they were written—British spellings for British quotations; American spellings for American quotations. Translations are reproduced in American spelling unless a standard translation is being used.

There are two indexes at the back of the book. One is a key word/key phrase index to help the reader to locate particular quotations. The other is an author index to help locate quotations by particular speakers and writers.

We hope that these indexes will make the book a useful work of reference but, above all, we hope that it will be an enjoyable and informative book to read and browse through. Many people have helped in the preparation of this dictionary—their names are listed under **Contributors** on the Acknowledgments page. We would also like to thank Philip Turner of Macmillan for suggesting many quotations and for his encouragement and help in producing this book.

The Editors

A

ABILITY

1 One should oblige everyone to the extent of one's ability. One often needs someone smaller than oneself.

Jean de La Fontaine (1621–95) French poet. *Fables*, II, 'Le Lion et le Rat'

2 Intelligence is quickness to apprehend as distinct from ability, which is capacity to act wisely on the thing apprehended.

A. N. Whitehead (1861–1947) British philosopher. *Dialogues*, 135

ABOLITION

See Civil War, slavery

ABORTION

1 Some women behave like harlots; when they feel the life of a child in their wombs, they induce herbs or other means to cause miscarriage, only to perpetuate their amusement and unchastity. Therefore I shall deprive them from everlasting life and send them to everlasting death.

Bridget of Sweden (1303–73) *Revelations*, Vol. VII

2 For those in the courtroom who were hearing the opinion for the first time, that answer could not come soon enough. The wait seemed interminable, but finally Justice Blackmun read: 'This right of privacy . . . is broad enough to encompass a woman's decision whether or not to terminate her pregnancy.' This privacy right to abortion, the opinion further noted, was grounded in either the "Fourteenth Amendment's concept of personal liberty or . . . in the Ninth Amendment's reservation of rights to the people." A palpable sigh of relief went through the courtroom. That was the crux of the opinion – the victory for pro-choice forces, as it were. The Court had ruled that a woman's right to abortion was constitutionally protected.

Marian Faux US writer. Referring to a Supreme Court decision in the Roe v. Wade case concerning the right to abortion.

3 The greatest destroyer of peace is abortion because if a mother can kill her own child what is left for me to kill you and you to kill me? There is nothing between.

Mother Teresa (1910–) Yugoslavian missionary in Calcutta. *Nobel Peace Prize Lecture*

4 To hinder a birth is merely speedier man-killing; nor does it matter whether you take away a life that is born, or destroy one that is coming to the birth. That is a man which is going to be one; you have the fruit already in its seed.

Tertullian (c. 160–c. 225) Carthaginian father of the church. *Apologeticus*, IX

5 If a man come near unto a damsel, . . . and she conceives by him, and she says, 'I have conceived by thee;' and he replies, 'Go then to the old woman and apply to her that she may procure thee miscarriage;'
And the damsel goes to the old woman and applies to her that she may procure her miscarriage; and the old woman brings her some Banga or Shaêta, or Ghnâna or Fraspâta, or some other of the drugs that produce miscarriage and the man says, 'Cause thy fruit to perish!' and she causes her fruit to perish; the sin is on the head of all three, the man, the damsel, and the old woman.

The Zend-Avesta (c. 550 BC) *The Vendidad*, XV:2

ABSENCE

See also presence, separation

1 Long absent, soon forgotten.

Proverb

2 Out of sight, out of mind.

Proverb

3 When the cat's away, the mice will play.

Proverb

4 Absence makes the heart grow fonder,
Isle of Beauty, Fare thee well!

Thomas Haynes Bayly (1797–1839) British writer. *Isle of Beauty*

5 What's become of Waring
Since he gave us all the slip?

Robert Browning (1812–89) British poet. *Waring*

6 Absence is to love what wind is to fire; it extinguishes the small, it inflames the great.

Bussy-Rabutin (Roger de Rabutin, Comte de Bussy; 1618–93) French soldier and writer. *Histoire amoureuse des Gaules*

7 What's the good of a home, if you are never in it?

George Grossmith (1847–1912) British singer and comedian. *The Diary of a Nobody*, Ch. 1

8 Has anybody here seen Kelly?
Kelly from the Isle of Man?

C. W. Murphy (19th century) British songwriter. *Has Anybody Here Seen Kelly?*

9 We seek him here, we seek him there,
Those Frenchies seek him everywhere.
Is he in heaven? – Is he in hell?
That damned elusive Pimpernel?

Baroness Orczy (1865–1947) British novelist. *The Scarlet Pimpernel*, Ch. 12

10 Why art thou silent! Is thy love a plant
Of such weak fibre that the treacherous air
Of absence withers what was once so fair?

William Wordsworth (1770–1850) British poet. *Miscellaneous Sonnets*, III

ABSENT MINDEDNESS

1 I liked the store detective who said he'd seen a lot of people who were so confused that they'd stolen things, but never one so confused that they'd paid twice.

Baroness Phillips Director of the Association for the Prevention of Theft in Shops. *The Sunday Telegraph*, 14 Aug 1977

ABSTINENCE

See also alcohol, self-denial, sex, smoking

1 If you resolve to give up smoking, drinking and loving, you don't actually live longer; it just seems longer.

Anonymous

2 He neither drank, smoked, nor rode a bicycle. Living frugally, saving his money, he died early, surrounded by greedy relatives. It was a great lesson to me.

John Barrymore (1882–1942) US actor. *The Stage*, Jan 1941 (J. P. McEvoy)

3 Teetotallers lack the sympathy and generosity of men that drink.
W. H. Davies (1871–1940) British poet. *Shorter Lyrics of the 20th Century, Introduction*

4 It was a brilliant affair; water flowed like champagne.
William M. Evarts (1818–1901) US lawyer and statesman. Describing a dinner given by US President Rutherford B. Hayes (1877–81), an advocate of temperance. Attrib.

5 Mr Mercaptan went on to preach a brilliant sermon on that melancholy sexual perversion known as continence.
Aldous Huxley (1894–1964) British novelist. *Antic Hay*, Ch. 18

6 My experience through life has convinced me that, while moderation and temperance in all things are commendable and beneficial, abstinence from spiritous liquors is the best safeguard of morals and health.
Robert E. Lee (1807–70) US general. Letter, 9 Dec 1869

7 The few bad poems which occasionally are created during abstinence are of no great interest.
Wilhelm Reich (1897–1957) Austrian-born US psychiatrist. *The Sexual Revolution*

8 The people who are regarded as moral luminaries are those who forego ordinary pleasures themselves and find compensation in interfering with the pleasures of others.
Bertrand Russell (1872–1970) British philosopher. *Sceptical Essays*

9 Lastly (and this is, perhaps, the golden rule), no woman should marry a teetotaller, or a man who does not smoke.
Robert Louis Stevenson (1850–94) Scottish writer. *Virginibus Puerisque*

10 Though in silence, with blighted affection, I pine,
Yet the lips that touch liquor must never touch mine!
G. W. Young (19th century) British writer. *The Lips That Touch Liquor*

ACADEMICS

See also education, intellectuals

1 A professor is one who talks in someone else's sleep.
W. H. Auden (1907–73) British poet. Attrib.

2 First come I; my name is Jowett.
There's no knowledge but I know it.
I am Master of this college:
What I don't know isn't knowledge.
H. C. Beeching (1859–1919) British academic. Referring to Benjamin Jowett, master of Balliol College, Oxford. *The Masque of Balliol*

3 A professor is a gentleman who has a different opinion.
August Bier (1861–1949) Aphorism

4 If there weren't so many professors, medicine would be much easier.
August Bier Aphorism

5 It's no use trying to be *clever* – we are all clever here; just try to be *kind* – a little kind.
F. J. Foakes Jackson (1855–1941) British academic. Advice given to a new don at Jesus College, Cambridge. Noted in A. C. Benson's Commonplace Book

6 Like so many ageing college people, Pnin had long ceased to notice the existence of students on the campus.
Vladimir Nabokov (1899–1977) Russian-born US novelist. *Pnin*, Ch. 3

7 The successful teacher is no longer on a height, pumping knowledge at high pressure into passive receptacles. . . . He is a senior student anxious to help his juniors.
William Osler (1849–1919) Canadian physician. *The Student Life*

8 I am the Dean of Christ Church, Sir:
There's my wife; look well at her.
She's the Broad and I'm the High;
We are the University.
Cecil Arthur Spring-Rice (1859–1918) British diplomat. *The Masque of Balliol*

ACCIDENTS

See also chance, disaster, misfortune

1 ACCIDENT n. An inevitable occurrence due to the action of immutable natural laws.
Ambrose Bierce (1842–c. 1914) US writer and journalist. *The Devil's Dictionary*

2 The Act of God designation on all insurance policies; which means, roughly, that you cannot be insured for the accidents that are most likely to happen to you.
Alan Coren (1938–) British humorist and writer. *The Lady from Stalingrad Mansions*, 'A Short History of Insurance'

3 Accidents will occur in the best-regulated families.
Charles Dickens (1812–70) British novelist. *David Copperfield*, Ch. 28

4 My good man, I'm not a strawberry.
Edward VII (1841–1910) King of the United Kingdom. Rebuking a footman who had spilt cream on him. *The Last Country Houses* (C. Aslat)

5 Here's another fine mess you've gotten me into.
Oliver Hardy (1892–1957) US film comedian. Catchphrase; said to Stan Laurel

6 Heard there was a party. Came.
Beatrice Lillie (Constance Sylvia Munston, Lady Peel; 1898–) Canadian-born British actress. On arriving breathlessly at a friend's house seeking help after a car crash. Attrib.

7 O Diamond! Diamond! thou little knowest the mischief done!
Isaac Newton (1642–1727) British scientist. Said to a dog that set fire to some papers, representing several years' work, by knocking over a candle. *Wensley-Dale . . . a Poem* (Thomas Maude)

8 Knocked down a doctor? With an ambulance? How could she? It's a contradiction in terms.
N. F. Simpson (1919–) British dramatist. *One-Way Pendulum*, I

9 The chapter of accidents is the longest chapter in the book.
John Wilkes (1725–97) British politician. Attrib. in *The Doctor* (Southey), Vol. IV

ACCUSATION

See also responsibility

1 I do not know the method of drawing up an indictment against an whole people.
Edmund Burke (1729–97) British politician. *Speech on Conciliation with America* (House of Commons, 22 Mar 1775)

2 Never make a defence or apology before you be accused.
Charles I (1600–49) King of England. Letter to Lord Wentworth, 3 Sept 1636

3 . . . a disciple and limb of the fiend, called the Pucelle, that used false enchantments and sorcery.
John of Lancaster, Duke of Bedford (1389–1435) Brother of Henry V. Referring to Joan of Arc. *Proceeding and Ordinances of the Privy Council* (ed. N. H. Nicolas), Vol. IV

4 *J'accuse.*
I accuse.
Émile Zola (1840–1902) French novelist. Title of an open letter to the French President, denouncing the French army's conduct in the Dreyfus affair. *L'Aurore*, 13 Jan 1898

ACHESON, Dean Gooderham

(1893–1971) US lawyer and statesman. Noted for his strong stance against Soviet expansionism, he was prominent in the development of the Truman Doctrine, the Marshall Plan, and NATO.

Quotations about Acheson

1 Washington's number 1 number 2 man.

Anonymous

2 Not only did he not suffer fools gladly; he did not suffer them at all.

Lester Pearson (1897–1972) Canadian statesman. *Time*, 25 Oct 1971

Quotations by Acheson

3 It hasn't taken Winston long to get used to American ways. He hadn't been an American citizen for three minutes before attacking an ex-secretary of state!

At a ceremony in 1963 to make Churchill an honorary American citizen, Churchill obliquely attacked Acheson's reference to Britain losing an empire. *Randolph Churchill* (K. Halle)

4 It is worse than immoral, it's a mistake.

Describing the Vietnam war. *See also* BOULAY DE LA MEURTHE. Quoted by Alistair Cooke in his radio program *Letter from America*

5 I will undoubtedly have to seek what is happily known as gainful employment, which I am glad to say does not describe holding public office.

Remark made on leaving his post as secretary of state, 1952; he subsequently returned to private legal practice

6 Great Britain has lost an Empire and has not yet found a role.

Speech, Military Academy, West Point, 5 Dec 1962

7 A memorandum is written not to inform the reader but to protect the writer.

Attrib.

ACHIEVEMENT

See also effort, success

1 Every man who is high up likes to feel that he has done it himself; and the wife smiles, and lets it go at that. It's our only joke. Every woman knows that.

J. M. Barrie (1860–1937) British playwright. *Peter Pan*

2 It is all very well to be able to write books, but can you waggle your ears?

J. M. Barrie Speaking to H. G. Wells. *Barrie: The Story of A Genius* (J. A. Hamerton)

3 Ye shall know them by their fruits. Do men gather grapes of thorns, or figs of thistles?
Even so every good tree bringeth forth good fruit; but a corrupt tree bringeth forth evil fruit.
A good tree cannot bring forth evil fruit, neither can a corrupt tree bring forth good fruit.
Every tree that bringeth not forth good fruit is hewn down, and cast into the fire.
Wherefore by their fruits ye shall know them.

Bible: Matthew 7:16–20

4 One never notices what has been done; one can only see what remains to be done. . . .

Marie Curie (1867–1934) Polish chemist. Letter to her brother, 18 Mar 1894

5 We never do anything well till we cease to think about the manner of doing it.

William Hazlitt (1778–1830) British essayist. *On Prejudice*

6 Well, we knocked the bastard off!

Edmund Hillary (1919–) New Zealand mountaineer. On first climbing Mount Everest (with Tenzing Norgay), 29 May 1953. *Nothing Venture, Nothing Win*

7 Anybody can be Pope; the proof of this is that I have become one.

John XXIII (1881–1963) Italian-born pope. Attrib.

8 I do not want to die . . . until I have faithfully made the most of my talent and cultivated the seed that was placed in me until the last small twig has grown.

Käthe Kollwitz (1867–1945) German sculptor and graphic artist. *Diaries and Letters*, 15 Feb 1915

9 For, as I suppose, no man in this world hath lived better than I have done, to achieve that I have done.

Thomas Malory (1400–71) English writer. *Morte d'Arthur*, Bk. XVII, Ch. 16

10 Log-cabin to White House.

W. M. Thayer (1820–98) US writer. The title of his biography of James Garfield, US president

11 To achieve great things we must live as though we were never going to die.

Marquis de Vauvenargues (1715–47) French soldier and writer. *Réflexions et maximes*

ACTING

See also action, actors, cinema, criticism, plays, theater

1 Theatre director: a person engaged by the management to conceal the fact that the players cannot act.

James Agate (1877–1947) British theater critic. Attrib.

2 Never work with animals or children.

Anonymous Show business maxim.

3 Can't act, can't sing, slightly bald. Can dance a little.

Anonymous Report on Fred Astaire's first screen test.

4 For the theatre one needs long arms; it is better to have them too long than too short. An *artiste* with short arms can never, never make a fine gesture.

Sarah Bernhardt (Sarah Henriette Rosine Bernard; 1844–1923) French actress. *Memories of My Life*, Ch. 6

5 Just know your lines and don't bump into the furniture.

Noël Coward (1899–1973) British dramatist. Advice for actors. Attrib.

6 Nothing to be fixed except your performance.

Noël Coward Replying to a telegram from the actress Gertrude Lawrence – 'Nothing wrong that can't be fixed' – referring to her part in Coward's play *Private Lives*. *Noël Coward and his Friends*

7 Pray to God and say the lines.

Bette Davis (Ruth Elizabeth Davis; 1908– US film star. Advice to the actress Celeste Holm. Attrib.

8 It is easier to get an actor to be a cowboy than to get a cowboy to be an actor.

John Ford (Sean O'Feeney; 1895–1973) US film director. Attrib.

9 It is. But not as hard as farce.

Edmund Gwenn (1875–1959) British actor. On his deathbed, in reply to the comment 'It must be very hard' *Time*, 30 Jan 1984

10 Acting is therefore the lowest of the arts, if it is an art at all.

George Moore (1852–1933) Irish writer and art critic. *Mummer-Worship*

11 The art of acting consists in keeping people from coughing.

Ralph Richardson (1902–83) British actor. *The Observer*

12 In music, the punctuation is absolutely strict, the bars and the rests are absolutely defined. But

our punctuation cannot be quite strict, because we have to relate it to the audience. In other words, we are continually changing the score.
Ralph Richardson *The Observer Magazine*, 'Tynan on Richardson', 18 Dec 1977

13 Speak the speech, I pray you, as I pronounced it to you, trippingly on the tongue; but if you mouth it, as many of your players do, I had as lief the town-crier spoke my lines. Nor do not saw the air too much with your hand, thus; but use all gently: for in the very torrent, tempest, and – as I may say – whirlwind of passion, you must acquire and beget a temperance, that may give it smoothness. O! it offends me to the soul to hear a robustious periwig-pated fellow tear a passion to tatters, to very rags, to split the ears of the groundlings, who for the most part are capable of nothing but inexplicable dumb-shows and noise: I would have such a fellow whipped for o'erdoing Termagant; it out-herods Herod: pray you, avoid it.
William Shakespeare (1564–1616) English dramatist. *Hamlet*, III:2

14 Imagination! imagination! I put it first years ago, when I was asked what qualities I thought necessary for success upon the stage.
Ellen Terry (1847–1928) British actress. *The Story of My Life*, Ch. 2

15 Ladies, just a little more virginity, if you don't mind.
Herbert Beerbohm Tree (1853–1917) British actor and theater manager. Directing a group of sophisticated actresses. *Smart Aleck* (H. Teichmann)

ACTION

See also acting

1 Barking dogs seldom bite.
Proverb

2 Doing is better than saying.
Proverb

3 Easier said than done.
Proverb

4 Footprints on the sands of time are not made by sitting down.
Proverb

5 Saying is one thing, and doing another.
Proverb

6 Let's meet, and either do, or die.
Francis Beaumont (1584–1616) English dramatist. *See also* BURNS *The Island Princess*, II:2

7 He who desires but acts not, breeds pestilence.
William Blake (1757–1827) British poet. *See also* BEAUMONT *The Marriage of Heaven and Hell*, 'Proverbs of Hell'

8 Liberty's in every blow!
Let us do or die!
Robert Burns (1759–96) Scottish poet. *Scots, Wha Hae*

9 Deliberation is the work of many men. Action, of one alone.
Charles De Gaulle (1890–1970) French general and statesman. *War Memoirs*, Vol. 2

10 No action is in itself good or bad, but only such according to convention.
W. Somerset Maugham (1874–1965) British novelist. *A Writer's Notebook*

11 Suit the action to the word, the word to the action; with this special observance, that you o'erstep not the modesty of nature.
William Shakespeare (1564–1616) English dramatist. *Hamlet*, III:2

12 Thy wish was father, Harry, to that thought.
William Shakespeare *Henry IV, Part 2*, IV:5

13 If to do were as easy as to know what were good to do, chapels had been churches, and poor men's cottages princes' palaces.
William Shakespeare *The Merchant of Venice*, I:2

14 So many worlds, so much to do,
So little done, such things to be.
Alfred, Lord Tennyson (1809–92) British poet. *In Memoriam A.H.H.*, LXXIII

15 It's dogged as does it. It ain't thinking about it.
Anthony Trollope (1815–82) British novelist. *Last Chronicle of Barset*, Ch. 61

ACTORS

See also acting, cinema, criticism, plays, theater

1 O God, send me some good actors – cheap.
Lilian Baylis (1874–1937) British theater owner and producer. *The Guardian*, 1 Mar 1976

2 An actor's a guy who, if you ain't talking about him, ain't listening.
Marlon Brando (1924–) US film star. *The Observer*, 'Sayings of the Year', Jan 1956

3 Never meddle with play-actors, for they're a favoured race.
Miguel de Cervantes (1547–1616) Spanish novelist. *Don Quixote*, Pt. II, Ch. 11

4 Bogart's a helluva nice guy till 11.30 p.m. After that he thinks he's Bogart.
Dave Chausen US restaurateur. *The Filmgoer's Book of Quotes* (L. Halliwell)

5 Chaplin is no business man – all he knows is that he can't take anything less.
Samuel Goldwyn (Samuel Goldfish; 1882–1974) Polish-born US film producer. Attrib.

6 Actors should be treated like cattle.
Alfred Hitchcock (1889–1980) British film director. Said in clarification of a remark attributed to him, 'Actors are like cattle' Attrib.

7 At one time I thought he wanted to be an actor. He had certain qualifications, including no money and a total lack of responsibility.
Hedda Hopper (1890–1966) US writer. *From Under My Hat*

8 She looked as though butter wouldn't melt in her mouth – or anywhere else.
Elsa Lanchester (1902–86) British-born US actress. Referring to Maureen O'Hara. Attrib.

9 *Romance on the High Seas* was Doris Day's first picture; that was before she became a virgin.
Oscar Levant (1906–72) US pianist and actor. *Memoirs of an Amnesiac*

10 Scratch an actor and you'll find an actress.
Dorothy Parker (1893–1967) US writer. Attrib.

11 They didn't act like people and they didn't act like actors. It's hard to explain. They acted more like they knew they were celebrities and all. I mean they were good, but they were *too* good.
J. D. Salinger (1919–) US novelist. *The Catcher in the Rye*, Ch. 17

12 Goodbye Norma Jean
Though I never knew you at all
You had the grace to hold yourself
While those around you crawled.
They crawled out of the woodwork
And they whispered into your brain
Set you on the treadmill
And made you change your name.
Bernie Taupin (1913–) British songwriter. Lyrics for a song by Elton John about Marilyn Monroe. *Candle in the Wind*

13 Ah, every day dear Herbert becomes *de plus en plus Oscarié*. It is a wonderful case of nature imitating art.

Oscar Wilde (1854–1900) Irish-born British dramatist. Referring to Beerbohm Tree's unconscious adoption of some of the mannerisms of a character he was playing in one of Wilde's plays. *Great Theatrical Disasters* (G. Brandreth)

ADAMS, John Quincy

(1767–1848) Sixth president of the USA (1825–29). As secretary of state to President James Monroe (1817–25), he formulated the Monroe Doctrine opposing foreign intervention in American affairs.

Quotations about Adams

1 A man must be a born fool who voluntarily engages in controversy with Mr Adams on a question of fact. I doubt whether he was ever mistaken in his life.

Henry Clay (1777–1852) US politician. Remark, 1823

2 He is no literary old gentleman, but a bruiser, and loves the melee.

Ralph Waldo Emerson (1803–82) US poet and essayist. *Journal*

Quotations by Adams

3 Think of your forefathers! Think of your posterity!

Speech, Plymouth, Massachusetts, 22 Dec 1802

4 I inhabit a weak, frail, decayed tenement; battered by the winds and broken in on by the storms, and, from all I can learn, the landlord does not intend to repair.

Said during his last illness. Attrib.

ADAPTABILITY

1 Remember that to change your mind and follow him who sets you right is to be none the less free than you were before.

Marcus Aurelius (121–180 AD) Roman emperor. *Meditations*, Bk. VIII, Ch. 16

2 Mahomet made the people believe that he would call a hill to him . . . when the hill stood still, he was never a whit abashed, but said, 'If the hill will not come to Mahomet, Mahomet will go to the hill.'

Francis Bacon (1561–1626) English philosopher. Often misquoted as 'If the mountain will not come to Mohammed' *Essays*, 'Of Boldness'

3 President Robbins was so well adjusted to his environment that sometimes you could not tell which was the environment and which was President Robbins.

Randall Jarrell (1914–65) US author. *Pictures from an Institution*, Pt. I, Ch. 4

4 As time requireth, a man of marvellous mirth and pastimes, and sometimes of as sad gravity, as who say: a man for all seasons.

Robert Whittington (16th century) English writer. Referring to Sir Thomas More; after Erasmus. *Vulgaria*, Pt. II, 'De constructione nominum'

ADDICTION

1 Cocaine isn't habit-forming. I should know – I've been using it for years.

Tallulah Bankhead (1903–68) US actress. *Pentimento* (Lillian Hellman), 'Theatre'

2 OPIATE. An unlocked door in the prison of
Identity. It leads into the jail yard.

Ambrose Bierce (1842–c. 1914) US writer and journalist. *The Devil's Dictionary*

3 I'll die young, but it's like kissing God.

Lenny Bruce (1923–66) US comedian. *The Routledge Dictionary of Quotations* (Robert Andrews)

4 'For me,' said Sherlock Holmes, 'there still remains the cocaine bottle.'

Arthur Conan Doyle (1859–1930) British writer, creator of Sherlock Holmes. *The Sign of Four*, 'The Strange Story of Jonathan Small'

5 There is only one reason why men become addicted to drugs, they are weak men. Only strong men are cured, and they cure themselves.

Martin H. Fischer (1879–1962) *Fischerisms* (Howard Fabing and Ray Marr)

6 Every form of addiction is bad, no matter whether the narcotic be alcohol or morphine or idealism.

Carl Gustav Jung (1875–1961) Swiss psychoanalyst. *Memories, Dreams, Reflections*, Ch. 12

7 Turn on, tune in, drop out.

Timothy Leary (1920–) Hippie guru. Title of lecture, 1967

ADDISON, Joseph

(1672–1719) British essayist. A Whig politician, he entered parliament in 1708. Addison contributed numerous essays to the *Tatler* and was cofounder (with Richard Steele) of *The Spectator* (1711).

Quotations about Addison

1 Whoever wishes to attain an English style, familiar but not coarse and elegant but not ostentatious, must give his days and nights to the volumes of Addison.

Samuel Johnson (1709–84) British lexicographer. *Lives of the Poets*

2 A parson in a tye-wig.

Bernard Mandeville (?1670–1733) Dutch-born British doctor, writer, and wit. Remark

Quotations by Addison

3 Pray consider what a figure a man would make in the republic of letters.

Ancient Medals

4 'Tis not in mortals to command success,
But we'll do more, Sempronius; we'll deserve it.

Cato, I:2

5 And if the following day, he chance to find
A new repast, or an untasted spring,
Blesses his stars, and thinks it luxury.

Cato, I:4

6 The woman that deliberates is lost.

Cato, IV:1

7 When vice prevails, and impious men bear sway,
The post of honour is a private station.

Cato, IV:1

8 What pity is it
That we can die but once to serve our country!

Cato, IV:4

9 A reader seldom peruses a book with pleasure until he knows whether the writer of it be a black man or a fair man, of a mild or choleric disposition, married or a bachelor.

The Spectator, 1

10 Thus I live in the world rather as a Spectator of mankind, than as one of the species, by which means I have made myself a speculative statesman, soldier, merchant, and artisan, without ever meddling with any practical part of life.

The Spectator, 1

11 Nothing is capable of being well set to music that is not nonsense.

The Spectator, 18

12 The infusion of a China plant

sweetened with the pith of an Indian cane.
The Spectator, 69

13 *Sir Roger* told them, with the air of a man who would not give his judgment rashly, that 'much might be said on both sides'.
Sir Roger de Coverley was a fictional archetype of the old-fashioned and eccentric country squire. *The Spectator*, 122

14 I have often thought, says Sir Roger, it happens very well that Christmas should fall out in the Middle of Winter.
The Spectator, 269

15 The Hand that made us is divine.
The Spectator, 465

16 A woman seldom asks advice until she has bought her wedding clothes.
The Spectator, 475

17 We are always doing something for posterity, but I would fain see posterity do something for us.
The Spectator, 583

18 I have but ninepence in ready money, but I can draw for a thousand pounds.
Comparing his ability to make conversation and to write. *Life of Johnson* (Boswell)

19 See in what peace a Christian can die.
Last words

ADDRESSES

1 Addresses are given to us to conceal our whereabouts.
Saki (Hector Hugh Munro; 1870–1916) British writer. *Cross Currents*

2 Three addresses always inspire confidence, even in tradesmen.
Oscar Wilde (1854–1900) Irish-born British dramatist. *The Importance of Being Earnest*, III

ADMIRATION

See also compliments, love, respect, praise, wonder

1 Miss J. Hunter Dunn, Miss J. Hunter Dunn,
Furnish'd and burnish'd by Aldershot sun.
John Betjeman (1906–84) British poet. *A Subaltern's Love Song*

2 Here's looking at you, kid.
Humphrey Bogart (1899–1957) US film star. *Casablanca*

3 A fool always finds a greater fool to admire him.
Nicolas Boileau (1636–1711) French writer. *L'Art poétique*, I

4 There is a garden in her face,
Where roses and white lilies grow;
A heav'nly paradise is that place,
Wherein all pleasant fruits do flow.
There cherries grow, which none may buy
Till 'Cherry ripe' themselves do cry.
Thomas Campion (1567–1620) English poet. *Fourth Book of Airs*

5 Pretty amazing.
HRH the Princess Diana (1961–) British Royal. When asked what her first impression was of Prince Charles. Remark, 1981

6 No, it did a lot of other things, too.
James Joyce (1882–1941) Irish novelist. When a young man asked, 'May I kiss the hand that wrote Ulysses?' *James Joyce* (R. Ellman)

7 I do think better of womankind than to suppose they care whether Mister John Keats five feet high likes them or not.
John Keats (1795–1821) British poet. Letter to Benjamin Bailey, 18 July 1818

8 'There is a report that Piso is dead; it is a great loss; he was an honest man, who deserved to live longer; he was intelligent and agreeable, resolute and courageous, to be depended upon, generous and faithful.' Add: 'provided he is really dead'.
Jean de La Bruyère (1645–96) French satirist. *See also* VOLTAIRE *Les Caractères*

9 On Richmond Hill there lives a lass,
More sweet than May day morn,
Whose charms all other maids surpass,
A rose without a thorn.
Leonard MacNally (1752–1820) Irish dramatist and poet. *The Lass of Richmond Hill*

10 Many a man has been a wonder to the world, whose wife and valet have seen nothing in him that was even remarkable. Few men have been admired by their servants.
Michel de Montaigne (1533–92) French essayist. *Essais*, III

11 Charlie is my darling, my darling, my darling,
Charlie is my darling, the young Chevalier.
Baroness Nairne (1766–1845) Scottish songwriter. Referring to Bonnie Prince Charlie. *Charlie is my Darling*

12 Not to admire, is all the art I know
To make men happy, and to keep them so.
Alexander Pope (1688–1744) British poet. *Imitations of Horace*, 'To Mr. Murray'

13 Where'er you walk, cool gales shall fan the glade,
Trees, where you sit, shall crowd into a shade:
Where'er you tread, the blushing flow'rs shall rise,
And all things flourish where you turn your eyes.
Alexander Pope *Pastorals*, 'Summer'

14 But search the land of living men,
Where wilt thou find their like agen?
Walter Scott (1771–1832) Scottish novelist. *Marmion*, I

15 The barge she sat in, like a burnish'd throne,
Burn'd on the water. The poop was beaten gold;
Purple the sails, and so perfumed that
The winds were love-sick with them; the oars were silver,
Which to the tune of flutes kept stroke and made
The water which they beat to follow faster,
As amorous of their strokes. For her own person,
It beggar'd all description.
William Shakespeare (1564–1616) English dramatist. *Antony and Cleopatra*, II:2

16 Age cannot wither her, nor custom stale
Her infinite variety. Other women cloy
The appetites they feed, but she makes hungry
Where most she satisfies.
William Shakespeare *Antony and Cleopatra*, II:2

17 'A was a man, take him for all in all,
I shall not look upon his like again.
William Shakespeare *Hamlet*, I:2

18 Who is Silvia? What is she,
That all our swains commend her?
Holy, fair, and wise is she.
William Shakespeare *The Two Gentlemen of Verona*, IV:2

19 He was a great patriot, a humanitarian, a loyal friend – provided, of course, that he really is dead.
Voltaire (François-Marie Arouet; 1694–1778) French writer. Giving a funeral oration. *See also* DE LA BRUYÈRE Attrib.

20 The sweetest thing that ever grew

Beside a human door!

William Wordsworth (1770–1850) British poet. *Lucy Gray*

ADOLESCENCE

See age

ADULTERY

See also marriage, sex, unfaithfulness

1 What men call gallantry, and gods adultery,
Is much more common where the climate's sultry.

Lord Byron (1788–1824) British poet. *Don Juan*, I

2 I have looked on a lot of women with lust. I've committed adultery in my heart many times. God recognises I will do this and forgives me.

Jimmy Carter (1924–) US statesman and president. Remark

3 Sara could commit adultery at one end and weep for her sins at the other, and enjoy both operations at once.

Joyce Cary (1888–1957) British novelist. *The Horse's Mouth*, Ch. 8

4 I say I don't sleep with married men, but what I mean is that I don't sleep with happily married men.

Britt Ekland (1942–) Swedish film actress. Attrib.

5 You know, of course, that the Tasmanians, who never committed adultery, are now extinct.

W. Somerset Maugham (1874–1965) British novelist. *The Bread-Winner*

6 Madame, you must really be more careful. Suppose it had been someone else who found you like this.

Duc de Richelieu (1766–1822) French statesman. Discovering his wife with her lover. *The Book of Lists* (D. Wallechinsky)

7 With all my heart. Whose wife shall it be?

John Horne Tooke (1736–1812) British clergyman, politician, and etymologist. Replying to the suggestion that he take a wife. Attrib.

ADVENTURE

1 To die will be an awfully big adventure.

J. M. Barrie (1860–1937) British novelist and dramatist. *Peter Pan*, III

2 . . . we owe something to extravagance, for thrift and adventure seldom go hand in hand. . . .

Jennie Jerome Churchill (1854–1921) US-born British hostess and writer. *Pearson's*, 'Extravagance'

3 Marriage is the only adventure open to the cowardly.

Voltaire (François-Marie Arouet; 1694–1778) French writer. *Thoughts of a Philosopher*

ADVERSITY

See misfortune

ADVERTISING

1 Any publicity is good publicity.

Proverb

2 It pays to advertise.

Anonymous Already current by c. 1912 when Cole Porter used it as the title of an early song.

3 Advertising is the most fun you can have with your clothes on.

Jerry Della Femina (1936–) Advertising executive. *From those wonderful folks who gave you Pearl Harbor*

4 Half the money I spend on advertising is wasted, and the trouble is I don't know which half.

Viscount Leverhulme (1851–1925) British industrialist. *Confessions of an Advertising Man* (D. Ogilvy)

5 Freedom of the press in Britain is freedom to print such of the proprietor's prejudices as the advertisers don't object to.

Hannen Swaffer (1879–1962) British journalist. Attrib.

ADVICE

1 A good scare is worth more than good advice.

Proverb

2 Don't teach your grandmother to suck eggs.

Proverb

3 He that has no children brings them up well.

Proverb

4 He that has no wife, beats her oft.

Proverb

5 Never eat at a place called Mom's. Never play cards with a man called Doc. Never go to bed with a woman whose troubles are greater than your own.

Nelson Algren (1909–81) US novelist and short story writer. *A Walk on the Wild Side*

6 Remember that to change your mind and follow him who sets you right is to be none the less free than you were before.

Marcus Aurelius (121–180 AD) Roman emperor. *Meditations*, Bk. VIII, Ch. 16

7 Dyb-dyb-dyb.

Robert Baden-Powell (1857–1941) British soldier and founder of the Boy Scouts. Wolf-Cub chant meaning 'Do your best'

8 Advice is seldom welcome; and those who want it the most always like it the least.

Earl of Chesterfield (1694–1773) English statesman. Letter to his son, 29 Jan 1748

9 Do not criticize your government when out of the country. Never cease to do so when at home.

Winston Churchill (1874–1965) British statesman. Attrib.

10 Perhaps one of the only positive pieces of advice that I was ever given was that supplied by an old courtier who observed: 'Only two rules really count. Never miss an opportunity to relieve yourself; never miss a chance to sit down and rest your feet.'

Edward VIII (1894–1972) British sovereign. *A King's Story*

11 Your business is to put me out of business.

Dwight D. Eisenhower (1890–1969) US general and statesman. Addressing a graduating class at a university. *Procession* (J. Gunther)

12 This judgment I have of you, that you will not be corrupted with any manner of gift and that you will be faithful to the state, and that, without respect of my private will, you will give me that counsel that you think best.

Elizabeth I (1533–1603) Queen of England. To William Cecil, 1558

13 I intended to give you some advice but now I remember how much is left over from last year unused.

George Harris (1844–1922) US congressman. Said when addressing students at the start of a new academic year. *Braude's Second Encyclopedia* (J. Braude)

14 On my twenty-first birthday my father said, 'Son, here's a million dollars. Don't lose it.'

Larry Niven (1938–) US science-fiction writer. When asked 'What is the best advice you have ever been given?' Attrib.

15 One gives nothing so freely as advice.

Duc de la Rochefoucauld (1613–80) French writer. *Maximes*, 110

16 Cromwell, I charge thee, fling away ambition:
By that sin fell the angels; how can man then,
The image of his Maker, hope to win by't?
Love thyself last: cherish those hearts that hate thee;
Corruption wins not more than honesty.
Still in thy right hand carry gentle peace,
To silence envious tongues: be just, and fear not.
Let all the ends thou aim'st at be thy country's,
Thy God's, and truth's: then if thou fall'st O Cromwell!
Thou fall'st a blessed martyr.

William Shakespeare (1564–1616) English dramatist. *Henry VIII*, III:2

17 If to do were as easy as to know what were good to do, chapels had been churches, and poor men's cottages princes' palaces.

William Shakespeare *The Merchant of Venice*, I:2

18 Only do always in health what you have often promised to do when you are sick.

Sigismund (1368–1437) Holy Roman Emperor. His advice on achieving happiness. *Biographiana*, Vol. I

19 Don't tell your friends their social faults, they will cure the fault and never forgive you.

Logan Pearsall Smith (1865–1946) US writer. *Afterthoughts*

20 No one wants advice – only corroboration.

John Steinbeck (1902–68) US novelist.

21 It's queer how ready people always are with advice in any real or imaginary emergency, and no matter how many times experience has shown them to be wrong, they continue to set forth their opinions, as if they had received them from the Almighty!

Annie Sullivan (1866–1936) US teacher of the handicapped. Letter, 12 June 1887

22 I have lived some thirty years on this planet, and I have yet to hear the first syllable of valuable or even earnest advice from my seniors.

Henry David Thoreau (1817–62) US writer. *Walden*, 'Economy'

23 Are you in trouble? Do you need advice? Write to Miss Lonelyhearts and she will help.

Nathaniel West (Nathan Weinstein; 1903–40) US novelist. *Miss Lonelyhearts*

AFFECTATION

See also ostentation

1 Don't you sit there and sigh gal like you was Lady Nevershit.

Arnold Wesker (1932–) British dramatist. *Roots*, III

2 She keeps on being Queenly in her own room with the door shut.

Edith Wharton (1862–1937) US novelist. *The House of Mirth*, Bk. II, Ch. 1

AFRICA

1 When a white man in Africa by accident looks into the eyes of a native and sees the human being (which it is his chief preoccupation to avoid), his sense of guilt, which he denies, fumes up in resentment and he brings down the whip.

Doris Lessing (1919–) British novelist, brought up in Rhodesia. *The Grass is Singing*, Ch. 8

2 There is always something new out of Africa.

Pliny the Elder (Gaius Plinius Secundus; 23–79 AD) Roman scholar. *Natural History*, VIII

3 Crossing Piccadilly Circus.

Joseph Thomson (1858–95) Scottish explorer. His reply when asked by J. M. Barrie what was the most hazardous part of his expedition to Africa. *J. M. Barrie* (D. Dunbar)

AFTERLIFE

See also heaven

1 CLOV. Do you believe in the life to come?
HAMM. Mine was always that.

Samuel Beckett (1906–) Irish novelist and dramatist. *Endgame*

2 That which is the foundation of all our hopes and of all our fears; all our hopes and fears which are of any consideration: I mean a Future Life.

Joseph Butler (1692–1752) British churchman. *The Analogy of Religion*, Introduction

3 We have no reliable guarantee that the afterlife will be any less exasperating than this one, have we?

Noël Coward (1899–1973) British dramatist. *Blithe Spirit*, I

4 We sometimes congratulate ourselves at the moment of waking from a troubled dream; it may be so the moment after death.

Nathaniel Hawthorne (1804–64) US novelist and writer. *American Notebooks*

5 Work and pray, live on hay,
You'll get pie in the sky when you die.

Joe Hill (1879–1915) Swedish-born US songwriter. *The Preacher and the Slave*

6 Death is nothing at all. I have only slipped away into the next room. I am I and you are you. Whatever we were to each other, that we are still. Call me by my old familiar name, speak to me in the easy way you always use. Put no difference into your tone, wear no forced air of solemnity or sorrow .... What is death but negligible accident? Why should I be out of mind because I am out of sight? I am waiting for you, for an interval, somewhere very near just around the corner. All is well.

Henry Scott Holland (1847–1918) British Anglican clergyman. Attrib.

7 Is there another life? Shall I awake and find all this a dream? There must be, we cannot be created for this sort of suffering.

John Keats (1795–1821) British poet. Letter, 1820

8 My doctrine is: Live that thou mayest desire to live again – that is thy duty – for in any case thou wilt live again!

Friedrich Wilhelm Nietzsche (1844–1900) German philosopher. *Eternal Recurrence*

9 After your death you will be what you were before your birth.

Arthur Schopenhauer (1788–1860) German philosopher. *Parerga and Paralipomena*

10 The dread of something after death –
The undiscover'd country, from whose bourn
No traveller returns.

William Shakespeare (1564–1616) English dramatist. *Hamlet*, III:1

11 I am going a long way
With these thou seest – if indeed I go
(For all my mind is clouded with a doubt) –
To the island-valley of Avilion;
Where falls not hail, or rain, or any snow,
Nor ever wind blows loudly; but it lies

Deep-meadow'd, happy, fair with orchard lawns
And bowery hollows crown'd with summer sea,
Where I will heal me of my grievous wound.

Alfred, Lord Tennyson (1809–92) British poet. *Idylls of the King*, 'The Passing of Arthur'

12 One world at a time.

Henry David Thoreau (1817–62) US writer. On being asked his opinion of the hereafter. Attrib.

AGE

See also longevity, old age, youth

1 Never too late to learn.

Proverb

2 There's many a good tune played on an old fiddle.

Proverb

3 Years ago we discovered the exact point the dead center of middle age. It occurs when you are too young to take up golf and too old to rush up to the net.

Franklin P. Adams (1881–1960) US journalist and humorist. *Nods and Becks*

4 An adult is one who has ceased to grow vertically but not horizontally.

Anonymous

5 You've reached middle age when all you exercise is caution.

Anonymous

6 All evil comes from the old. They grow fat on ideas and young men die of them.

Jean Anouilh (1910–87) French dramatist. *Catch as Catch Can*

7 I am past thirty, and three parts iced over.

Matthew Arnold (1822–88) British poet and critic. Letter to A. H. Clough, 12 Feb 1853

8 Age will not be defied.

Francis Bacon (1561–1626) English philosopher. *Essays*, 'Of Regiment of Health'

9 A man that is young in years may be old in hours, if he have lost no time.

Francis Bacon *Essays*, 'Of Youth and Age'

10 The only thing I regret about my past life is the length of it. If I had my past life over again I'd make all the same mistakes – only sooner.

Tallulah Bankhead (1903–68) US actress. *The Times*, 28 July 1981

11 What is an adult? A child blown up by age.

Simone de Beauvoir (1908–86) French writer. *La Femme rompue*

12 If thou hast gathered nothing in thy youth, how canst thou find any thing in thine age?

Bible: Ecclesiasticus 25:3

13 And all the days of Methuselah were nine hundred sixty and nine years: and he died.

Bible: Genesis 5:27

14 No man also having drunk old wine straightway desireth new: for he saith, The old is better.

Bible: Luke 5:39

15 Old age is . . . a lot of crossed off names in an address book.

Ronald Blythe (1922–) British author. *The View in Winter*

16 Being now come to the years of discretion.

The Book of Common Prayer *Order of Confirmation*

17 Therefore I summon age
To grant youth's heritage.

Robert Browning (1812–89) British poet. *Rabbi ben Ezra*, XIII

18 Ah well, perhaps one has to be very old before one learns how to be amused rather than shocked.

Pearl Buck (1892–1973) US novelist. *China, Past and Present*, Ch. 6

19 A lady of a 'certain age', which means
Certainly aged.

Lord Byron (1788–1824) British poet. *Don Juan*, VI

20 Man arrives as a novice at each age of his life.

Nicolas Chamfort (1741–94) French writer and wit. *Caractères et anecdotes*, 576

21 A man is as old as he's feeling,
A woman as old as she looks.

Mortimer Collins (1827–76) British writer. *The Unknown Quantity*

22 Pushing forty? She's clinging on to it for dear life.

Ivy Compton-Burnett (1884–1969) British novelist. Attrib.

23 When a middle-aged man says in a moment of weariness that he is half dead, he is telling the literal truth.

Elmer Davis (1890–1958) US journalist. *By Elmer Davis*, 'On not being Dead, as Reported'

24 Middle age is youth without its levity,
And age without decay.

Daniel Defoe (1660–1731) English journalist and writer.

25 The years that a woman subtracts from her age are not lost. They are added to the ages of other women.

Diane de Poitiers (1499–1566) Attrib.

26 Youth is a blunder; manhood a struggle; old age a regret.

Benjamin Disraeli (1804–81) British statesman. *Coningsby*, Bk. III, Ch. 1

27 I am resolved to grow fat and look young till forty, and then slip out of the world with the first wrinkle and the reputation of five-and-twenty.

John Dryden (1631–1700) British poet and dramatist. *The Maiden Queen*, III

28 Men are but children of a larger growth;
Our appetites as apt to change as theirs,
And full as craving too, and full as vain.

John Dryden *All for Love*, IV

29 The years between fifty and seventy are the hardest. You are always being asked to do things, and you are not yet decrepit enough to turn them down.

T. S. Eliot (1888–1965) US-born British poet and dramatist. *Time*, 23 Oct 1950

30 Here I am, an old man in a dry month,
Being read to by a boy, waiting for rain.

T. S. Eliot *Gerontion*

31 *Si jeunesse savait; si vieillesse pouvait.*
If only youth knew, if only age could.

Henri Estienne (1528–98) French scholar. *Les Prémices*

32 At sixteen I was stupid, confused, insecure and indecisive. At twenty-five I was wise, self-confident, prepossessing and assertive. At forty-five I am stupid, confused, insecure and indecisive. Who would have supposed that maturity is only a short break in adolescence?

Jules Feiffer (1929–) US writer, cartoonist, and humorist. *The Observer*, 3 Feb 1974

33 Though the Jazz Age continued, it became less and less an affair of youth. The sequel was like a children's party taken over by the elders.

F. Scott Fitzgerald (1896–1940) US novelist. *The Crack-Up*

34 At twenty years of age, the will reigns; at thirty, the wit; and at forty, the judgement.
Benjamin Franklin (1706–90) US scientist and statesman. *Poor Richard's Almanack*

35 A diplomat is a man who always remembers a woman's birthday but never remembers her age.
Robert Frost (1875–1963) US poet. Attrib.

36 She may very well pass for forty-three
In the dusk, with a light behind her!
W. S. Gilbert (1836–1911) British dramatist. *Trial by Jury*

37 'Old Cary Grant fine. How you?'
Cary Grant (Archibald Leach; 1904–86) British-born US film star. Replying to a telegram sent to his agent inquiring: 'How old Cary Grant?' *The Filmgoer's Book of Quotes* (Leslie Halliwell)

38 We do not necessarily improve with age: for better or worse we become more like ourselves.
Peter Hall (1930–) British theater director. *The Observer*, 'Sayings of the Week', 24 Jan 1988

39 You will recognize, my boy, the first sign of old age: it is when you go out into the streets of London and realize for the first time how young the policemen look.
Seymour Hicks (1871–1949) British actor-manager. *They Were Singing* (C. Pulling)

40 Middle age is when your age starts to show around the middle.
Bob Hope (1904–) British-born US comedian.

41 What do the ravages of time not injure? Our parents' age (worse than our grandparents') has produced us, more worthless still, who will soon give rise to a yet more vicious generation.
Horace (Quintus Horatius Flaccus; 65–8 BC) Roman poet. *Odes*, III

42 I think middle age is the best time, if we can escape the fatty degeneration of the conscience which often sets in at about fifty.
W. R. Inge (1860–1954) British churchman and writer. *Observer*, 8 June 1930

43 Whenever a man's friends begin to compliment him about looking young, he may be sure that they think he is growing old.
Washington Irving (1783–1859) US writer. *Bracebridge Hall*, 'Bachelors'

44 It is sobering to consider that when Mozart was my age he had already been dead for a year.
Tom Lehrer (1928–) US university teacher and songwriter. *An Encyclopedia of Quotations about Music* (N. Shapiro)

45 Will you still need me, will you still feed me
When I'm sixty-four?
John Lennon (1940–80) British rock musician. *When I'm Sixty-Four* (with Paul McCartney)

46 The four stages of man are infancy, childhood, adolescence and obsolescence.
Art Linkletter (1912–) Canadian-born US radio and television personality. *A Child's Garden of Misinformation*, 8

47 I am just turning forty and taking my time about it.
Harold Lloyd (1893–1971) US silent-film comedian. Reply when, aged 77, he was asked his age. *The Times*, 23 Sept 1970

48 Growth is a greater mystery than death. All of us can understand failure, we all contain failure and death within us, but not even the successful man can begin to describe the impalpable elations and apprehensions of growth.
Norman Mailer (1923–) US writer. *Advertisements for Myself*

49 But at my back I always hear
Time's winged chariot hurrying near;
And yonder all before us lie
Deserts of vast eternity.
Andrew Marvell (1621–78) English poet. *To His Coy Mistress*

50 A man is only as old as the woman he feels.
Groucho Marx (Julius Marx; 1895–1977) US comedian. Attrib.

51 I am old enough to be – in fact am – your mother.
A. A. Milne (1882–1956) British writer. *Belinda*

52 How soon hath Time, the subtle thief of youth,
Stolen on his wing my three-and-twentieth year!
John Milton (1608–74) English poet. *Sonnet*: 'On Being Arrived at the Age of Twenty-three'

53 Do you think my mind is maturing late,
Or simply rotted early?
Ogden Nash (1902–71) US poet. *Lines on Facing Forty*

54 At 50, everyone has the face he deserves.
George Orwell (Eric Blair; 1903–50) British novelist. Last words in his manuscript notebook, 17 Apr 1949.

55 Each generation imagines itself to be more intelligent than the one that went before it, and wiser than the one that comes after it.
George Orwell Book Review

56 From forty to fifty a man is at heart either a stoic or a satyr.
Arthur Pinero (1855–1934) British dramatist. *The Second Mrs Tanqueray*, I

57 Life Begins at Forty.
William B. Pitkin (1878–1953) US professor in journalism. Book title

58 One of the pleasures of middle age is to *find out* that one WAS right, and that one was much righter than one knew at say 17 or 23.
Ezra Pound (1885–1972) US poet. *ABC of Reading*, Ch. 1

59 Inexperience is what makes a young man do what an older man says is impossible.
Herbert V. Prochnow (1897–) US writer. *Satuday Evening Post*, 4 Dec 1948

60 You know, by the time you reach my age, you've made plenty of mistakes if you've lived your life properly
Ronald Reagan (1911–) US politician and president. *The Observer*, 'Sayings of the Week', 8 Mar 1987

61 As we get older we do not get any younger.
Seasons return, and today I am fifty-five,
And this time last year I was fifty-four,
And this time next year I shall be sixty-two.
Henry Reed (1914–86) British poet and dramatist. *A Map of Verona*, 'Chard Whitlow'

62 It is fun to be in the same decade with you.
Franklin D. Roosevelt (1882–1945) US Democratic president. After Churchill had congratulated him on his 60th birthday. *The Hinge of Fate* (Winston S. Churchill), Ch. 4

63 Don't trust anyone over thirty.
Jerry Rubin (1938–) US 'yippie' leader. *Listening to America* (S. B. Flexner)

64 I have always felt that a woman has the right to treat the subject of her age with ambiguity until, perhaps, she passes into the realm of over ninety. Then it is better she be candid with herself and with the world.
Helena Rubinstein (1882–1965) Polish-born US cosmetics manufacturer. *My Life for Beauty*, Pt. I, Ch. 1

65 The young have aspirations that

never come to pass, the old have reminiscences of what never happened.
Saki (Hector Hugh Munro; 1870–1916) British writer. *Reginald at the Carlton*

66 The young man who has not wept is a savage, and the old man who will not laugh is a fool.
George Santayana (1863–1952) US philosopher. *Dialogues in Limbo*, Ch. 3

67 When I was young, I was told: 'You'll see, when you're fifty. I am fifty and I haven't seen a thing.
Erik Satie (1866–1925) French composer. From a letter to his brother. *Erik Satie* (Pierre-Daniel Templier), Ch. 1

68 Thou hast nor youth nor age;
But, as it were, an after-dinner's sleep,
Dreaming on both.
William Shakespeare (1564–1616) English dramatist. *Measure for Measure*, III:1

69 Doth not the appetite alter? A man loves the meat in his youth that he cannot endure in his age.
William Shakespeare *Much Ado About Nothing*, II:3

70 Crabbed age and youth cannot live together:
Youth is full of pleasure, age is full of care;
Youth like summer morn, age like winter weather;
Youth like summer brave, age like winter bare.
William Shakespeare *The Passionate Pilgrim*, XII

71 All that the young can do for the old is to shock them and keep them up to date.
George Bernard Shaw (1856–1950) Irish dramatist and critic. *Fannie's First Play*

72 It's a funny thing about that bust. As time goes on it seems to get younger and younger.
George Bernard Shaw Referring to a portrait bust sculpted for him by Rodin. *More Things I Wish I'd Said* (K. Edwards)

73 One's prime is elusive. You little girls, when you grow up, must be on the alert to recognize your prime at whatever time of your life it may occur. You must then live it to the full.
Muriel Spark (1918–) British novelist. *The Prime of Miss Jean Brodie*, Ch. 1

74 The mark of the immature man is that he wants to die nobly for a cause, while the mark of the mature man is that he wants to live humbly for one.
Wilhelm Stekel (1868–1940) Viennese psychiatrist. *The Catcher in the Rye* (J. D. Salinger), Ch. 24

75 Men come of age at sixty, women at fifteen.
James Stephens (1882–1950) Irish novelist. *The Observer*, 'Sayings of the Week', 1 Oct 1944

76 I was born old and get younger every day. At present I am sixty years young.
Herbert Beerbohm Tree (1853–1917) British actor and theater manager. *Beerbohm Tree* (Hesketh Pearson)

77 Life begins at forty.
Sophie Tucker (Sophia Abuza; 1884–1966) Russian-born US singer. Attrib.

78 From birth to age eighteen, a girl needs good parents. From eighteen to thirty-five, she needs good looks. From thirty-five to fifty-five, she needs a good personality. From fifty-five on, she needs good cash.
Sophie Tucker Attrib.

79 There are no old men any more. *Playboy* and *Penthouse* have between them made an ideal of eternal adolescence, sunburnt and saunaed, with the grey dorianed out of it.
Peter Ustinov (1921–) British actor. *Dear Me*, Ch. 18

80 It is charming to totter into vogue.
Horace Walpole (1717–97) British writer. Letter to G. A. Selwyn, 1765

81 In a man's middle years there is scarcely a part of the body he would hesitate to turn over to the proper authorities.
E. B. White (1899–) US journalist and humorist. *The Second Tree from the Corner*, 'A Weekend with the Angels'

82 No woman should ever be quite accurate about her age. It looks so calculating.
Oscar Wilde (1854–1900) Irish-born British dramatist. *The Importance of Being Earnest*, III

83 One should never trust a woman who tells one her real age. A woman who would tell one that, would tell one anything.
Oscar Wilde *A Woman of No Importance*, I

84 The older one grows the more one likes indecency.
Virginia Woolf (1882–1941) British novelist. *Monday or Tuesday*

85 My heart leaps up when I behold
A rainbow in the sky:
So was it when my life began;
So is it now I am a man;
So be it when I shall grow old,
Or let me die!
The Child is Father of the Man;
And I could wish my days to be
Bound each to each by natural piety.
William Wordsworth (1770–1850) British poet. *My Heart Leaps Up*

86 One that is ever kind said yesterday:
'Your well-belovèd's hair has threads of grey,
And little shadows come about her eyes.'
W. B. Yeats (1865–1939) Irish poet. *The Folly of Being Comforted*

87 Where, where but here have Pride and Truth,
That long to give themselves for wage,
To shake their wicked sides at youth
Restraining reckless middle age?
W. B. Yeats *On hearing that the Students of our New University have joined the Agitation against Immoral Literature*

88 Though leaves are many, the root is one;
Through all the lying days of my youth
I swayed my leaves and flowers in the sun;
Now I may wither into the truth.
W. B. Yeats *The Coming of Wisdom with Time*

89 Wine comes in at the mouth
And love comes in at the eye;
That's all we shall know for truth
Before we grow old and die.
W. B. Yeats *A Drinking Song*

90 Be wise with speed,
A fool at forty is a fool indeed.
Edward Young (1683–1765) British poet. *Love of Fame*, II

AGGRAVATION

1 This is adding insult to injuries.
Edward Moore (1712–57) British dramatist. *The Foundling*, V

2 The point is that nobody likes having salt rubbed into their wounds, even if it is the salt of the earth.
Rebecca West (Cicely Isabel Fairfield; 1892–1983) British novelist and journalist. *The Salt of the Earth*, Ch. 2

AGREEMENT

1 My cousin Francis and I are in

perfect accord – he wants Milan, and so do I.

Charles V (1500–58) Holy Roman Emperor. Referring to his dispute with Francis I of France over Italian territory. *The Story of Civilization* (W. Durant), Vol. 5

2 I am always of the opinion with the learned, if they speak first.

William Congreve (1670–1729) British Restoration dramatist. *Incognita*

3 'My idea of an agreeable person,' said Hugo Bohun, 'is a person who agrees with me.'

Benjamin Disraeli (1804–81) British statesman. *Lothair*, Ch. 35

4 We seldom attribute common sense except to those who agree with us.

Duc de la Rochefoucauld (1613–80) French writer. *Maximes*, 347

5 Our agenda is now exhausted. The secretary general is exhausted. All of you are exhausted. I find it comforting that, beginning with our very first day, we find ourselves in such complete unanimity.

Paul Henri Spaak (1899–1972) Belgian statesman. Concluding the first General Assembly meeting of the United Nations.

6 Ah! don't say you agree with me. When people agree with me I always feel that I must be wrong.

Oscar Wilde (1854–1900) Irish-born British dramatist. *The Critic as Artist*, Pt. 2

7 If two men on the same job agree all the time, then one is useless. If they disagree all the time, then both are useless.

Darryl F. Zanuck (1902–79) US film producer. *The Observer*, 'Sayings of the Week', 23 Oct 1949

AGRICULTURE

See also countryside

1 We plough the fields, and scatter
The good seed on the land,
But it is fed and watered
By God's Almighty Hand.
He sends the snow in winter,
The warmth to swell the grain,
The breezes and the sunshine,
And soft refreshing rain.

Jane Montgomery Campbell (1817–78) British hymn writer. Hymn

2 Three acres and a cow.

Jesse Collings (1831–1920) British politician. Slogan used in his land-reform propaganda

3 Is my team ploughing,
That I was used to drive?

A. E. Housman (1859–1936) British scholar and poet. *A Shropshire Lad*, 'Bredon Hill'

4 'O Mary, go and call the cattle home,
And call the cattle home,
And call the cattle home,
Across the sands of Dee.'
The western wind was wild and dank with foam,
And all alone went she.

Charles Kingsley (1819–75) British writer. *The Sands of Dee*

5 This bread I break was once the oat,
This wine upon a foreign tree
Plunged in its fruit;
Man in the day or wind at night
Laid the crops low, broke the grape's joy.

Dylan Thomas (1914–53) Welsh poet. *This bread I break*

AIDS

1 Everywhere I go I see increasing evidence of people swirling about in a human cesspit of their own making.

James Anderton (1932–) British Chief Constable of Greater Manchester. Referring to AIDS

2 It could be said that the Aids pandemic is a classic own-goal scored by the human race against itself.

Princess Anne (1950–) The Princess Royal, only daughter of Elizabeth II. Remark, Jan 1988

3 My message to the businessmen of this country when they go abroad on business is that there is one thing above all they can take with them to stop them catching AIDS, and that is the wife.

Edwina Currie (1946–) British politician. *The Observer*, 15 Feb 1987

4 We're all going to go crazy, living this epidemic every minute, while the rest of the world goes on out there, all around us, as if nothing is happening, going on with their own lives and not knowing what it's like, what we're going through. We're living through war, but where they're living it's peacetime, and we're all in the same country.

Larry Kramer (1935–) US dramatist and novelist. *The Normal Heart*

ALCOHOL

See also abstinence, drinks, drunkenness, public houses

1 A cask of wine works more miracles than a church full of saints.

Italian proverb. Proverb

2 Adam's ale is the best brew.

Proverb

3 A good drink makes the old young.

Proverb

4 First the man takes a drink, then the drink takes a drink, then the drink takes the man.

Proverb

5 He who drinks a little too much drinks much too much.

Proverb

6 Take a hair of the dog that bit you.

Proverb

7 The brewery is the best drugstore.

Proverb

8 There's many a slip 'twixt the cup and the lip.

Proverb

9 When the wine is in, the wit is out.

Proverb

10 If all be true that I do think,
There are five reasons we should drink;
Good wine – a friend – or being dry –
Or lest we should be by and by –
Or any other reason why.

Dean Aldrich (1647–1710) English poet. *Reasons for Drinking*

11 I feel no pain, dear mother, now
But oh, I am so dry!
O take me to a brewery
And leave me there to die.

Anonymous Shanty

12 Mona Lisa cocktail – two of them and you can't get the silly grin off your face.

Anonymous

13 Punch cures the gout, the colic, and the 'tsick
And is by all agreed the very best of physic.

Anonymous English rhyme (18th Century)

14 So who's in a hurry?

Robert Benchley (1889–1945) US humorist. When asked whether he knew that drinking was a slow death. Attrib.

15 He is believed to have liked port, but to have said of claret that 'it would be port if it could'.

Richard Bentley (1662–1742) English academic. *Bentley* (R. C. Jebb)

16 Woe unto them that rise up early in the morning, that they may follow strong drink; that continue until night, till wine inflame them!
Bible: Isaiah 5:11

17 When the ruler of the feast had tasted the water that was made wine, and knew not whence it was: (but the servants which drew the water knew;) the governor of the feast called the bridegroom,
And saith unto him, Every man at the beginning doth set forth good wine; and when men have well drunk, then that which is worse: but thou hast kept the good wine until now.
Bible: John 2:9–10

18 No man also having drunk old wine straightway desireth new: for he saith, The old is better.
Bible: Luke 5:39

19 Wine is a mocker, strong drink is raging: and whosoever is deceived thereby is not wise.
Bible: Proverbs 20:1

20 Look not thou upon the wine when it is red, when it giveth his colour in the cup, when it moveth itself aright.
At the last it biteth like a serpent, and stingeth like an adder.
Bible: Proverbs 23:31–32

21 Drink no longer water, but use a little wine for thy stomach's sake and thine often infirmities.
Bible: I Timothy 5:23

22 . . . while there is more drinking, there is less drunkenness than formerly, and that the increase in drinking is to be laid mainly to the account of the female sex. This latter phase seems to be one of the unexpected results of the emancipation of women.
Charles Booth (1840–1916) British sociologist. *Life and Labour in London*

23 Threre's nought, no doubt, so much the spirit calms
As rum and true religion.
Lord Byron (1788–1824) British poet.

24 The heart which grief hath cankered
Hath one unfailing remedy – the Tankard.
C. S. Calverley (1831–84) British poet. *Beer*

25 Alcohol is like love: the first kiss is magic, the second is intimate, the third is routine. After that you just take the girl's clothes off.
Raymond Chandler (1888–1959) US novelist. *The Long Good-bye*

26 So was hir joly whistle wel y-wet.
Geoffrey Chaucer (c. 1342–1400) English poet. *The Canterbury Tales*, 'The Reve's Tale'

27 I must point out that my rule of life prescribed as an absolutely sacred rite smoking cigars and also the drinking of alcohol before, after, and if need be during all meals and in the intervals between them.
Winston Churchill (1874–1965) British statesman. Said during a lunch with the Arab leader Ibn Saud, when he heard that the king's religion forbade smoking and alcohol. *The Second World War*

28 Apart from cheese and tulips, the main product of the country is advocaat, a drink made from lawyers.
Alan Coren (1938–) British humorist and writer. Referring to Holland. *The Sanity Inspector*, 'All You Need to Know about Europe'

29 Then trust me, there's nothing like drinking
So pleasant on this side the grave;
It keeps the unhappy from thinking,
And makes e'en the valiant more brave.
Charles Dibdin (1745–1814) British actor and dramatist. *Nothing like Grog*

30 'Did you ever taste beer?' 'I had a sip of it once,' said the small servant. 'Here's a state of things!' cried Mr Swiveller . . . . 'She *never* tasted it – it can't be tasted in a sip!'
Charles Dickens (1812–70) British novelist. *The Old Curiosity Shop*, Ch. 57

31 First you take a drink, then the drink takes a drink, then the drink takes you.
F. Scott Fitzgerald (1896–1940) US novelist. *Ackroyd* (Jules Feiffer), '1964, May 7'

32 A good gulp of hot whisky at bedtime – it's not very scientific, but it helps.
Alexander Fleming (1881–1955) British microbiologist. When asked about a cure for colds. News summary, 22 Mar 1954

33 Best while you have it use your breath,
There is no drinking after death.
John Fletcher (1579–1625) English dramatist. With Jonson and others *The Bloody Brother*, II:2

34 And he that will go to bed sober,
Falls with the leaf still in October.
John Fletcher *The Bloody Brother*, II:2

35 A taste for drink, combined with gout,
Had doubled him up for ever.
W. S. Gilbert (1836–1911) British dramatist. *The Gondoliers*, I

36 Let schoolmasters puzzle their brain,
With grammar, and nonsense, and learning,
Good liquor, I stoutly maintain,
Gives genius a better discerning.
Oliver Goldsmith (1728–74) Irish-born British writer. *She Stoops to Conquer*, I

37 He that goes to bed thirsty rises healthy.
George Herbert (1593–1633) English poet. *Jacula Prudentum*

38 Who could have foretold, from the structure of the brain, that wine could derange its functions?
Hippocrates (c. 460–c. 377 BC)

39 Our country has deliberately undertaken a great social and economic experiment, noble in motive and far-reaching in purpose.
Herbert Hoover (1874–1964) US president. Referring to Prohibition. Letter to W.H. Borah, 28 Feb 1928

40 Malt does more than Milton can
To justify God's ways to man.
A. E. Housman (1859–1936) British scholar and poet. *A Shropshire Lad*, 'The Welsh Marches'

41 The sway of alcohol over mankind is unquestionably due to its power to stimulate the mystical faculties of human nature.
William James (1842–1910) US philosopher and psychologist. *The Varieties of Religious Experience*, 'Mysticism'

42 Claret is the liquor for boys; port for men; but he who aspires to be a hero must drink brandy.
Samuel Johnson (1709–84) British lexicographer. *Life of Johnson* (J. Boswell), Vol. III

43 No, Sir; there were people who died of dropsies, which they contracted in trying to get drunk.
Samuel Johnson Scornfully criticizing the strength of the wine in Scotland before the Act of Union in response to Boswell's claim that there had been a lot of drunkenness. *Tour to the Hebrides* (J. Boswell)

44 Come, let me know what it is that makes a Scotchman happy!
Samuel Johnson Ordering for himself a glass of whisky. *Tour to the Hebrides* (J. Boswell)

45 My friends should drink a dozen of Claret on my Tomb.
John Keats (1795–1821) British poet. Letter to Benjamin Bailey, 14 Aug 1819

46 O, for a draught of vintage! that hath been
Cool'd a long age in the deep-delved earth.
John Keats *Ode to a Nightingale*

47 O for a beaker full of the warm South,
Full of the true, the blushful Hippocrene,
With beaded bubbles winking at the brim,
And purple-stained mouth.
John Keats *Ode to a Nightingale*

48 Even though a number of people have tried, no one has yet found a way to drink for a living.
Jean Kerr (1923–) US dramatist. *Poor Richard*

49 I'm so holy that when I touch wine, it turns into water.
Aga Khan III (1877–1957) Muslim leader. Defending drinking alcohol. *Who's Really Who* (Compton Miller)

50 If we heard it said of Orientals that they habitually drank a liquor which went to their heads, deprived them of reason and made them vomit, we should say: 'How very barbarous!'
Jean de La Bruyère (1645–96) French satirist. *Les Caractères*

51 Frenchmen drink wine just like we used to drink water before Prohibition.
Ring Lardner Jnr (1885–1933) American humorist. *Wit's End* (R. E. Drennan)

52 It takes a good deal of physical courage to ride a horse. This, however, I have. I get it at about forty cents a flask, and take it as required.
Stephen Leacock (1869–1944) English-born Canadian economist and humorist. *Literary Lapses*, 'Reflections on Riding'

53 Long quaffing maketh a short lyfe.
John Lyly (1554–1606) English dramatist and novelist. *Euphues*

54 If die I must, let me die drinking in an inn.
Walter Map (c. 1140–c. 1209) Welsh clergyman and writer. *De Nugis Curialium*

55 The tranquilizer of greatest value since the early history of man, and which may never become outdated, is alcohol, when administered in moderation. It possesses the distinct advantage of being especially pleasant to the taste buds.
Nathan Masor (1913–) Attrib.

56 I've made it a rule never to drink by daylight and never to refuse a drink after dark.
H. L. Mencken (1880–1956) US journalist. *New York Post*, 18 Sept 1945

57 No man is genuinely happy, married, who has to drink worse gin than he used to drink when he was single.
H. L. Mencken *Prejudices*, 'Reflections on Monogamy'

58 Then to the spicy nut-brown ale.
John Milton (1608–74) English poet. *L'Allegro*

59 Candy
Is dandy
But liquor
Is quicker.
Ogden Nash (1902–71) US poet. *Hard Lines*, 'Reflection on Ice-Breaking'

60 A torchlight procession marching down your throat.
John L. O'Sullivan (1813–95) US writer. Referring to whisky. *Collections and Recollections* (G. W. E. Russell), Ch. 19

61 Wine is the most healthful and most hygienic of beverages.
Louis Pasteur (1822–95) French scientist. *Études sur le vin*, Pt. I, Ch. 2

62 *In vino veritas.*
Truth comes out in wine.
Pliny the Elder (Gaius Plinius Secundus; 23–79 AD) Roman scholar. *Natural History*, XIV

63 It is WRONG to do what everyone else does – namely, to hold the wine list just out of sight, look for the second cheapest claret on the list, and say, 'Number 22, please'.
Stephen Potter (1900–69) British writer. *One-Upmanship*, Ch. 14

64 A good general rule is to state that the bouquet is better than the taste, and vice versa.
Stephen Potter *One-Upmanship*, Ch. 14

65 It is the unbroken testimony of all history that alcoholic liquors have been used by the strongest, wisest, handsomest, and in every way best races of all times.
George Edward Bateman Saintsbury (1845–1933) British writer and critic. *Notes on a Cellar-Book*

66 People may say what they like about the decay of Christianity; the religious system that produced green Chartreuse can never really die.
Saki (Hector Hugh Munro; 1870–1916) British writer. *Reginald on Christmas Presents*

67 By insisting on having your bottle pointing to the north when the cork is being drawn, and calling the waiter Max, you may induce an impression on your guests which hours of laboured boasting might be powerless to achieve. For this purpose, however, the guests must be chosen as carefully as the wine.
Saki *The Chaplet*

68 It provokes the desire, but it takes away the performance. Therefore much drink may be said to be an equivocator with lechery.
William Shakespeare (1564–1616) English dramatist. *Macbeth*, II:3

69 MACDUFF. What three things does drink especially provoke?
PORTER. Marry, sir, nose-painting, sleep, and urine.
William Shakespeare *Macbeth*, II:3

70 Come, come; good wine is a good familiar creature if it be well used; exclaim no more against it.
William Shakespeare *Othello*, II:3

71 I am only a beer teetotaller, not a champagne teetotaller.
George Bernard Shaw (1856–1950) Irish dramatist and critic. *Candida*

72 Alcohol is a very necessary article . . . It enables Parliament to do things at eleven at night that no sane person would do at eleven in the morning.
George Bernard Shaw *Major Barbara*, II

73 Gin was mother's milk to her.
George Bernard Shaw *Pygmalion*, III

74 Well, then, my stomach must just digest in its waistcoat.
Richard Brinsley Sheridan (1751–1816) British dramatist. On being warned that his drinking would destroy the coat of his stomach. *The Fine Art of Political Wit* (L. Harris)

75 Another little drink wouldn't do us any harm.
Edith Sitwell (1887–1964) British poet and writer. *Façade*, 'Scotch Rhapsody'

76 Selwyn Macgregor, the nicest boy who ever committed the sin of whisky.
Muriel Spark (1918–) British novelist. *The Go-Away Bird*, 'A Sad Tale's Best for Winter'

77 Fifteen men on the dead man's chest

Yo-ho-ho, and a bottle of rum!
Drink and the devil had done for the rest –
Yo-ho-ho, and a bottle of rum!

Robert Louis Stevenson (1850–94) Scottish writer. *Treasure Island*, Ch. 1

78 There are two things that will be believed of any man whatsoever, and one of them is that he has taken to drink.

Booth Tarkington (1869–1946) US novelist. *Penrod*, Ch. 10

79 An alcoholic is someone you don't like who drinks as much as you do.

Dylan Thomas (1914–53) Welsh poet. Attrib.

80 I've had eighteen straight whiskies. I think that's the record... After thirty-nine years, this is all I've done.

Dylan Thomas Attrib.

81 It's a Naive Domestic Burgundy, Without Any Breeding. But I think you'll be Amused by its Presumption.

James Thurber (1894–1961) US humorist. *Men, Women and Dogs*

82 'Joe,' I said, 'was perhaps the first great nonstop literary drinker of the American nineteenth century. He made the indulgences of Coleridge and De Quincey seem like a bit of mischief in the kitchen with the cooking sherry.'

James Thurber *Alarms and Diversions*, 'The Moribundant Life...'

83 Whiskey is the most popular of all the remedies that won't cure a cold.

Jerry Vale *Bartlett's Unfamiliar Quotations* (Leonard Louis Levinson)

84 I prefer temperance hotels – although they sell worse kinds of liquor than any other kind of hotels.

Artemus Ward (Charles Farrar Browne; 1834–67) US humorous writer. *Artemus Ward's Lecture*

85 Across the Street and Into the Bar.

E. B. White (1899–1985) US humorist. Alluding to Hemingway's book 'Across the River and into the Trees' Title of satire on Ernest Hemingway

86 I hadn't the heart to touch my breakfast. I told Jeeves to drink it himself.

P. G. Wodehouse (1881–1975) British humorous novelist. *My Man Jeeves*

87 It was my Uncle George who discovered that alcohol was a food well in advance of modern medical thought.

P. G. Wodehouse *The Inimitable Jeeves*, Ch. 16

88 I must get out of these wet clothes and into a dry Martini.

Alexander Woollcott (1887–1943) US journalist. Also attributed to others. *Reader's Digest*

89 Father, dear father, come home with me now,
The clock in the steeple strikes one.

Henry Clay Work (1832–84) US songwriter. A temperance song. *Come Home, Father*

ALIENATION

1 He called his name Gershom: for he said, I have been a stranger in a strange land.

Bible: Exodus 2:22

2 What is a rebel? A man who says no.

Albert Camus (1913–60) French existentialist writer. *The Rebel*

3 Angry Young Man.

Leslie Paul (1905–) British writer. Book title

ALLEN, Woody

(Allen Stewart Konigsberg; 1935–) US film actor and director. His films include *Play It Again, Sam* (1972), *Annie Hall* (1977), and *The Purple Rose of Cairo* (1985).

1 Is sex dirty? Only if it's done right.

All You've Ever Wanted to Know About Sex

2 It was the most fun I ever had without laughing.

Referring to sex. *Annie Hall*

3 Don't knock it, it's sex with someone you love.

Referring to masturbation. *Annie Hall*

4 I'm short enough and ugly enough to succeed on my own.

Play It Again Sam

5 I'm really a timid person – I was beaten up by Quakers.

Sleeper

6 My brain: it's my second favorite organ.

Sleeper

7 It's not that I'm afraid to die. I just don't want to be there when it happens.

Without Feathers, 'Death (A Play)'

8 The lion and the calf shall lie down together but the calf won't get much sleep.

Without Feathers, 'The Scrolls'

9 And my parents finally realize that I'm kidnapped and they snap into action immediately: they rent out my room.

Woody Allen and His Comedy (E. Lax)

10 I don't want to achieve immortality through my work... I want to achieve it through not dying.

Woody Allen and His Comedy (E. Lax)

11 I want to tell you a terrific story about oral contraception. I asked this girl to sleep with me and she said 'no'.

Woody Allen: Clown Prince of American Humor (Adler and Feinman), Ch. 2

AMBITION

See also desire

1 He who rides a tiger is afraid to dismount.

Proverb

2 *Per ardua ad astra.*
Through endeavour to the stars

Anonymous Motto of the Royal Air Force.

3 Room at the Top.

John Braine (1922–86) British novelist. From Daniel Webster's remark 'There is always room at the top' Book title

4 Ah, but a man's reach should exceed his grasp,
Or what's a heaven for?

Robert Browning (1812–89) British poet. *Andrea del Sarto*

5 Man partly is and wholly hopes to be.

Robert Browning *A Death in the Desert*

6 You seem to have no real purpose in life and won't realize at the age of twenty-two that for a man life means work, and hard work if you mean to succeed....

Jennie Jerome Churchill (1854–1921) US-born British hostess and writer. Letter to Winston Churchill, 26 Feb 1897. *Jennie* (Ralph G. Martin), Vol. II

7 I have found some of the best reasons I ever had for remaining at the bottom simply by looking at the men at the top.

Frank More Colby (1865–1925) US editor. *Essays*, II

8 If thy heart fails thee, climb not at all.
Elizabeth I (1533–1603) Queen of England. Written on a window in reply to Walter RALEIGH's line. *Worthies of England* (Fuller), Vol. I

9 Hitch your wagon to a star.
Ralph Waldo Emerson (1803–82) US poet and essayist. *Society and Solitude,* 'Civilization'

10 I would like to throw an egg into an electric fan.
Oliver Herford (1863–1935) British-born US humorist. When asked if he really had no ambition beyond making people laugh. Attrib.

11 With a suitcase full of clothes and underwear in my hand and an indomitable will in my heart, I set out for Vienna . . . I too hope to become 'something'.
Adolf Hitler (1889–1945) German dictator. *Mein Kampf*

12 I am going to build the kind of nation that President Roosevelt hoped for, President Truman worked for and President Kennedy died for.
Lyndon B. Johnson (1908–73) US statesman. *The Sunday Times,* 27 Dec 1964

13 A slave has but one master; an ambitious man has as many masters as there are people who may be useful in bettering his position.
Jean de La Bruyère (1645–96) French satirist. *Les Caractères*

14 The shades of night were falling fast,
As through an Alpine village passed
A youth, who bore, 'mid snow and ice,
A banner with the strange device,
Excelsior!
Henry Wadsworth Longfellow (1807–82) US poet. Opening of a poem best known as a Victorian drawing-room ballad, and the butt of many music-hall jokes. Excelsior means 'higher' (Latin) *Excelsior*

15 If you would hit the mark, you must aim a little above it;
Every arrow that flies feels the attraction of earth.
Henry Wadsworth Longfellow *Elegiac Verse*

16 If men could regard the events of their own lives with more open minds they would frequently discover that they did not really desire the things they failed to obtain.
André Maurois (Émile Herzog; 1885–1967) French writer. *The Art of Living*

17 Ambition is the grand enemy of all peace.
John Cowper Powys (1872–1963) British novelist. *The Meaning of Culture*

18 Fain would I climb, yet fear I to fall.
Walter Raleigh (1554–1618) English explorer. Written on a window pane. For the reply *see* ELIZABETH I Attrib.

19 'Tis a common proof,
That lowliness is young ambition's ladder,
Whereto the climber-upward turns his face;
But when he once attains the upmost round,
He then unto the ladder turns his back,
Looks in the clouds, scorning the base degrees
By which he did ascend
William Shakespeare (1564–1616) English dramatist. *Julius Caesar,* II:1

20 Ambition should be made of sterner stuff.
William Shakespeare *Julius Caesar,* III:2

21 I have no spur
To prick the sides of my intent, but only
Vaulting ambition, which o'er-leaps itself,
And falls on th' other.
William Shakespeare *Macbeth,* I:7

22 LADY MACBETH. I have given suck, and know
How tender 'tis to love the babe that milks me:
I would, while it was smiling in my face,
Have plucked my nipple from his boneless gums,
And dash'd the brains out, had I so sworn as you
Have done to this.
MACBETH. If we should fail, –
LADY MACBETH. We fail!
But screw your courage to the sticking-place,
And we'll not fail.
William Shakespeare *Macbeth,* I:7

23 Who would not make her husband a cuckold to make him a monarch?
William Shakespeare *Othello,* IV:3

24 And he that strives to touch the stars,
Oft stumbles at a straw.
Edmund Spenser (1552–99) English poet. *The Shepherd's Calendar,* 'July'

25 There is always room at the top.
Daniel Webster (1782–1852) US statesman. When advised not to become a lawyer because the profession was overcrowded. Attrib.

26 Well, good luck to you, kid! I'm going to write the Great Australian Novel.
Patrick White (1912–) British-born Australian novelist. *The Vivisector,* 112

AMERICA

See United States

ANALOGY

See also similarity

1 Though analogy is often misleading, it is the least misleading thing we have.
Samuel Butler (1835–1902) British writer. *Notebooks*

2 She, and comparisons are odious.
John Donne (1573–1631) English poet. *Elegies,* 8, 'The Comparison'

3 She has the smile of a woman who has just dined off her husband.
Lawrence Durrell (1912–) British writer. Referring to the Mona Lisa. Attrib.

4 My mistress' eyes are nothing like the sun;
Coral is far more red than her lips' red.
William Shakespeare (1564–1616) English dramatist. *Sonnet 130*

5 And yet, by heaven, I think my love as rare
As any she belied with false compare.
William Shakespeare *Sonnet 130*

6 Jeeves coughed one soft, low, gentle cough like a sheep with a blade of grass stuck in its throat.
P. G. Wodehouse (1881–1975) British humorous novelist. *The Inimitable Jeeves,* Ch. 13

ANARCHY

1 They that are discontented under *monarchy,* call it *tyranny* ; and they that are displeased with *aristocracy,* call it *oligarchy*: so also, they which find themselves grieved under a *democracy,* call it *anarchy,* which signifies the want of government; and yet I think no man believes, that want of government, is any new kind of government.
Thomas Hobbes (1588–1679) English philosopher. *Leviathan,* Pt. II, Ch. 19

ANCESTRY

See also aristocracy, family

1 I am my own ancestor.
Duc d'Abrantes (1771–1813) French general. Said on being made a duke. Attrib.

2 I can trace my ancestry back to a protoplasmal primordial atomic globule. Consequently, my family pride is something in-conceivable. I can't help it. I was born sneering.
W. S. Gilbert (1836–1911) British dramatist. *The Mikado*, I

3 The difference between us is that my family begins with me, whereas yours ends with you.
Iphicrates (d. 353 BC) Athenian general. Reply to a descendant of Harmodius (an Athenian hero), who had derided Iphicrates for being the son of a cobbler. Attrib.

4 Being Southerners, it was a source of shame to some members of the family that we had no recorded ancestors on either side of the Battle of Hastings.
Harper Lee (1926–) US writer. *To Kill a Mockingbird*, Pt. I, Ch. 1

5 I don't know who my grandfather was; I am much more concerned to know what his grandson will be.
Abraham Lincoln (1809–65) US statesman. Taking part in a discussion on ancestry. Attrib.

ANGELS

1 Its visits,
Like those of angels, short, and far between.
Robert Blair (1699–1746) Scottish poet. *The Grave*

2 In heaven an angel is nobody in particular.
George Bernard Shaw (1856–1950) Irish dramatist and critic. *Man and Superman*, 'Maxims for Revolutionists'

ANGER

1 He could enrage his antagonists by making them feel their own impotence to enrage him.
Anonymous Referring to Henry Cabot Lodge.

2 The man who gets angry at the right things and with the right people, and in the right way and at the right time and for the right length of time, is commended.
Aristotle (384–322 BC) Greek philosopher. *Nicomachean Ethics*, Bk. IV

3 When they heard these things, they were cut to the heart, and they gnashed on him with their teeth.
Bible: Acts 7:54

4 Never go to bed mad. Stay up and fight.
Phyllis Diller (1917–) US writer and comedienne. *Phyllis Diller's Housekeeping Hints*

5 Anger makes dull men witty, but it keeps them poor.
Elizabeth I (1533–1603) Queen of England. *Apophthegms* (Bacon)

6 Anger is one of the sinews of the soul.
Thomas Fuller (1608–61) English historian. *The Holy State and the Profane State*

7 Spleen can subsist on any kind of food.
William Hazlitt (1778–1830) British essayist. *On Wit and Humour*

8 Touch me with noble anger,
And let not women's weapons, water-drops,
Stain my man's cheeks! No, you unnatural hags,
I will have such revenges on you both
That all the world shall – I will do such things, –
What they are yet I know not, – but they shall be
The terrors of the earth. You think I'll weep;
No, I'll not weep:
I have full cause of weeping, but this heart
Shall break into a hundred thousand flaws
Or ere I'll weep. O fool! I shall go mad.
William Shakespeare (1564–1616) English dramatist. *King Lear*, II:4

9 Anger has overpowered him, and driven him to a revenge which was rather a stupid one, I must acknowledge, but anger makes us all stupid.
Johanna Spyri (1827–1901) Swiss writer. *Heidi*, Ch. 23

10 Anger supplies the arms.
Virgil (Publius Vergilius Maro; 70–19 BC) Roman poet. *Aeneid*, Bk. I

ANIMALISM

See also evolution, lust, mankind, sex

1 My brain: it's my second favorite organ.
Woody Allen (Allen Stewart Konigsberg; 1935–) US film actor. *Sleeper*

2 But oh, the farmyard world of sex!
Harley Granville-Barker (1877–1946) British actor and dramatist. *The Madras House*, IV

3 Be a good animal, true to your animal instincts.
D. H. Lawrence (1885–1930) British novelist. *The White Peacock*, Pt. II, Ch. 2

4 It's all this cold-hearted fucking that is death and idiocy.
D. H. Lawrence *Lady Chatterley's Lover*, Ch. 14

5 The soul started at the knee-cap and ended at the navel.
Wyndham Lewis (1882–1957) British novelist. *The Apes of God*, Pt. XII

6 – 'Do you come here often?'
'Only in the mating season.'
Spike Milligan (1918–) British comic actor and author. *The Goon Show*

7 The wren goes to't, and the small gilded fly
Does lecher in my sight.
William Shakespeare (1564–1616) English dramatist. *King Lear*, IV:6

ANIMALS

See also cats, dogs, horses, rabbits

1 There was a young lady of Riga,
Who went for a ride on a tiger;
They returned from the ride
With the lady inside,
And a smile on the face of the tiger.
Anonymous

2 The fox knows many things – the hedgehog one *big* one.
Archilochus (c. 680–c. 640 BC) Greek poet. Attrib.

3 And God said, Let the earth bring forth the living creature after his kind, cattle, and creeping thing, and beast of the earth after his kind: and it was so.
Bible: Genesis 1:24

4 Now the serpent was more subtil than any beast of the field which the Lord God had made.
Bible: Genesis 3:1

5 But the poor man had nothing, save one little ewe lamb, which he had bought and nourished up: and it grew up together with him, and with his children; it did eat of his own meat, and drank of his own cup, and lay in his bosom, and was unto him as a daughter.
Bible: II Samuel 12:3

6 Tiger! Tiger! burning bright

In the forests of the night,
What immortal hand or eye
Could frame thy fearful symmetry?
William Blake (1757–1827) British poet. *Songs of Experience*, 'The Tiger'

7 Rats!
They fought the dogs and killed the cats,
And bit the babies in the cradles.
Robert Browning (1812–89) British poet. *The Pied Piper of Hamelin*

8 And the muttering grew to a grumbling;
And the grumbling grew to a mighty rumbling;
And out of the houses the rats came tumbling.
Robert Browning *The Pied Piper of Hamelin*

9 Wee, sleekit, cow'rin', tim'rous beastie,
O what a panic's in thy breastie!
Robert Burns (1759–96) Scottish poet. *To a Mouse*

10 Whenever you observe an animal closely, you feel as if a human being sitting inside were making fun of you.
Elias Canetti (1905–) Bulgarian-born novelist. *The Human Province*

11 The devil's walking parody
On all four-footed things.
G. K. Chesterton (1874–1936) British writer. *The Donkey*

12 Fools! For I also had my hour;
One far fierce hour and sweet;
There was a shout about my ears,
And palms before my feet.
G. K. Chesterton *The Donkey*

13 Animals are such agreeable friends – they ask no questions, they pass no criticisms.
George Eliot (Mary Ann Evans; 1819–80) British novelist. *Scenes of Clerical Life*, 'Mr Gilfil's Love Story', Ch. 7

14 Mary had a little lamb,
Its fleece was white as snow,
And everywhere that Mary went
The lamb was sure to go.
Sarah Josepha Hale (1788–1879) US writer. *Poems for Our Children*, 'Mary's Little Lamb'

15 'Twould ring the bells of Heaven
The wildest peal for years,
If Parson lost his senses
And people came to theirs,
And he and they together
Knelt down with angry prayers
For tamed and shabby tigers
And dancing dogs and bears,
And wretched, blind, pit ponies,
And little hunted hares.
Ralph Hodgson (1871–1962) British poet. *The Bells of Heaven*

16 The stars grew bright in the winter sky,
The wind came keen with a tang of frost,
The brook was troubled for new things lost,
The copse was happy for old things found,
The fox came home and he went to ground.
John Masefield (1878–1967) British poet. *Reynard the Fox*

17 I never nurs'd a dear gazelle,
To glad me with its soft black eye
But when it came to know me well,
And love me, it was sure to die!
Thomas Moore (1779–1852) Irish poet. *Lalla Rookh*

18 Dogs, like horses, are quadrupeds. That is to say, they have four rupeds, one at each corner, on which they walk.
Frank Muir (1920–) British writer and broadcaster. *You Can't Have Your Kayak and Heat It* (Frank Muir and Denis Norden), 'Ta-ra-ra-boom-de-ay!'

19 The cow is of the bovine ilk;
One end is moo, the other, milk.
Ogden Nash (1902–71) US poet. *The Cow*

20 Nothing can be more obvious than that all animals were created solely and exclusively for the use of man.
Thomas Love Peacock (1785–1866) British novelist. *Headlong Hall*, Ch. 2

21 Don't go into Mr McGregor's garden: your Father had an accident there; he was put in a pie by Mrs McGregor.
Beatrix Potter (1866–1943) British children's writer. *The Tale of Peter Rabbit*

22 *Exit, pursued by a bear.*
William Shakespeare (1564–1616) English dramatist. Stage direction. *The Winter's Tale*, III:3

23 There are two things for which animals are to be envied: they know nothing of future evils, or of what people say about them.
Voltaire (François-Marie Arouet; 1694–1778) French writer. Letter, 1739

24 Let dogs delight to bark and bite,
For God hath made them so;
Let bears and lions growl and fight,
For 'tis their nature too.
Isaac Watts (1674–1748) English theologian and hymn writer. *Divine Songs for Children*, 'Against Quarrelling'

25 Feather-footed through the plashy fen passes the questing vole.
Evelyn Waugh (1903–66) British novelist. *Scoop*, Bk. I, Ch. 1

26 I think I could turn and live with animals, they're so placid and self-contained,
I stand and look at them long and long.
Walt Whitman (1819–92) US poet. *Song of Myself*, 32

ANONYMOUS

This includes a selection of sayings, rhymes, epitaphs, ballads, etc., for which the author is unknown. They are arranged in alphabetical order of the first line. Further anonymous quotations are given under the entries for Nursery Rhymes and Proverbs.

1 Adieu, adieu, kind friends, adieu, adieu, adieu,
I can no longer stay with you, stay with you.
I'll hang my harp on a weeping willow-tree.
And may the world go well with thee.
There is a Tavern in the Town

2 *Ad majorem Dei gloriam.*
To the greater glory of God.
Motto of the Jesuits

3 All human beings are born free and equal in dignity and rights.
Universal Declaration of Human Rights (1948), Article 1

4 All present and correct.
Report by the orderly sergeant to the officer of the day. *King's Regulations (Army).*

5 All who come my grave to see
Avoid damp beds and think of me.
Epitaph of Lydia Eason, St Michael's, Stoke

6 Any officer who shall behave in a scandalous manner, unbecoming the character of an officer and a gentleman shall . . . be cashiered.
The words 'conduct unbecoming the character of an officer' are a direct quotation from the Naval Discipline Act (10 Aug 1860), Article 24. *Articles of War* (1872), *Disgraceful Conduct*, 79

7 Are we downhearted? No!
A favorite expression of the British soldiers during World War I. Attrib.

8 As I sat on a sunny bank,
On Christmas Day in the morning,
I spied three ships come sailing by.
As I sat on a Sunny Bank

9 *Ave Caesar, morituri te salutant.*
Hail Caesar; those who are about to die salute you.
Greeting to the Roman Emperor by gladiators

10 Begone, dull care! I prithee begone from me!
Begone, dull care, you and I shall never agree.
Begone Dull Care

11 Beneath this stone, in hope of Zion,
Doth lie the landlord of the 'Lion'.
His son keeps on the business still,
Resign'd unto the Heavenly will.
Epitaph, Upton-on-Severn churchyard

12 Come landlord, fill the flowing bowl,
Until it doth run over . . .
For tonight we'll merry, merry be,
Tomorrow we'll be sober.
Come, Landlord, Fill the Flowing Bowl

13 Come lasses and lads, get leave of your dads,
And away to the Maypole hie,
For every he has got him a she,
And the fiddler's standing by.
Come Lasses and Lads

14 Conduct . . . to the prejudice of good order and military discipline.
Army Act, 40

15 Dear Sir, Your astonishment's odd:
I am always about in the Quad.
And that's why the tree
Will continue to be,
Since observed by Yours faithfully,
God.
The response to EWER's limerick

16 Early one morning, just as the sun was rising.
I heard a maid singing in the valley below:
'Oh, don't deceive me; Oh, never leave me!
How could you use a poor maiden so?'
Early One Morning

17 Everyman, I will go with thee, and be thy guide.
In thy most need to go by thy side.
Everyman Pt. 1

18 Farewell and adieu to you,
Fair Spanish Ladies,
Farewell and adieu to you, Ladies of Spain.
Spanish Ladies

19 From ghoulies and ghosties and long-leggety beasties
And things that go bump in the night,
Good Lord, deliver us!
Cornish

20 God be in my head,
And in my understanding;
God be in my eyes,
And in my looking;
God be in my mouth,
And in my speaking;
God be in my heart,
And in my thinking;
God be at my end,
And at my departing.
Sarum Missal

21 God rest you merry, gentlemen,
Let nothing you dismay.
God Rest you Merry

22 Greensleeves was all my joy,
Greensleeves was my delight,
Greensleeves was my heart of gold,
And who but Lady Greensleeves.
Greensleeves

23 Ha, ha, ha, you and me,
Little brown jug, don't I love thee!
The Little Brown Jug

24 Hail Mary, full of grace, the Lord is with thee: Blessed art thou among women, and blessed is the fruit of thy womb, Jesus.
Ave Maria, 11th century

25 Here lie I and my four daughters,
Killed by drinking Cheltenham waters.
Had we but stick to Epsom salts,
We wouldn't have been in these here vaults.
Cheltenham Waters

26 Here lie I by the chancel door;
They put me here because I was poor.
The further in, the more you pay,
But here lie I as snug as they.
Epitaph, Devon churchyard

27 Here lies a man who was killed by lightning;
He died when his prospects seemed to be brightening.
He might have cut a flash in this world of trouble,
But the flash cut him, and he lies in the stubble.
Epitaph, Torrington, Devon

28 Here lies a valiant warrior
Who never drew a sword;
Here lies a noble courtier
Who never kept his word;
Here lies the Earl of Leicester
Who governed the estates
Whom the earth could never living love,
And the just heaven now hates.
Attrib. to Ben Jonson in *Collection of Epitaphs* (Tissington), 1857.

29 Here lies father and mother and sister and I,
We all died within the space of one short year;
They all be buried at Wimble, except I,
And I be buried here.
Epitaph, Staffordshire churchyard

30 Here lies Fred,
Who was alive and is dead:
Had it been his father,
I had much rather;
Had it been his brother,
Still better than another;
Had it been his sister,
No one would have missed her;
Had it been the whole generation,
Still better for the nation:
But since 'tis only Fred,
Who was alive and is dead, –
There's no more to be said.
Referring to Frederick, Prince of Wales, eldest son of George II and father of George III. *Memoirs of George II* (Horace Walpole)

31 Here lies my wife,
Here lies she;
Hallelujah!
Hallelujee!
Epitaph, Leeds churchyard

32 Here lies the body of Mary Ann Lowder,
She burst while drinking a seidlitz powder.
Called from the world to her heavenly rest,
She should have waited till it effervesced.
Epitaph

33 Here lies the body of Richard Hind,
Who was neither ingenious, sober, nor kind.
Epitaph

34 Here lies Will Smith – and, what's something rarish,
He was born, bred, and hanged, all in the same parish.
Epitaph

35 Here's a health unto his Majesty . . .
Confusion to his enemies, . . .
And he that will not drink his health,
I wish him neither wit nor wealth,
Not yet a rope to hang himself.
Here's a Health unto his Majesty

36 Here's tae us wha's like us?
Gey few, and they're a' deid.
Scottish toast.

37 Here we come gathering nuts in May
Nuts in May,
. . .

On a cold and frosty morning.
Children's song

38 He that fights and runs away
May live to fight another day.
Musarum Deliciae

39 *Honi soit qui mal y pense.*
Evil be to him who evil thinks.
Motto for the Order of the Garter

40 'How different, how very different from the home life of our own dear Queen!'
Remark about the character of Cleopatra as performed by Sarah Bernhardt

41 I always eat peas with honey
I've done it all my life,
They do taste kind of funny,
But it keeps them on the knife.
Peas

42 If all the world were paper,
And all the sea were ink,
And all the trees were bread and cheese,
What should we do for drink?
If All the World were Paper

43 I feel no pain, dear mother, now
But oh, I am so dry!
O take me to a brewery
And leave me there to die.
Shanty

44 I know two things about the horse,
And one of them is rather coarse.
The Horse

45 I'll sing you twelve O.
Green grow the rushes O.
What is your twelve O?
Twelve for the twelve apostles,
Eleven for the eleven who went to heaven,
Ten for the ten commandments,
Nine for the nine bright shiners,
Eight for the eight bold rangers,
Seven for the seven stars in the sky,
Six for the six proud walkers,
Five for the symbol at your door,
Four for the Gospel makers,
Three for the rivals,
Two, two, the lily-white boys,
Clothed all in green O,
One is one and all alone
And ever more shall be so.
The Dilly Song

46 I met wid Napper Tandy, and he took me by the hand,
And he said, 'How's poor ould Ireland, and how does she stand?'
She's the most disthressful country that iver yet was seen,
For they're hangin' men an' women there for the wearin' o' the Green.
The Wearin' o' the Green

47 In Dublin's fair city, where the girls are so pretty,
I first set my eyes on sweet Molly Malone,
As she wheeled her wheelbarrow, through streets broad and narrow,
Crying, Cockles and mussels! alive, alive, O!

She was a fishmonger, but sure 'twas no wonder,
For so were her father and mother before.
Cockles and Mussels

48 In good King Charles's golden days,
When loyalty no harm meant,
A zealous High Churchman was I,
And so I got preferment.

And this is law, that I'll maintain,
Unto my dying day, Sir,
That whatsoever King shall reign,
I'll be the Vicar of Bray, Sir.
The Vicar of Bray

49 In Scarlet town, where I was born,
There was a fair maid dwellin',
Made every youth cry *Well-a-way!*
Her name was Barbara Allen.

All in the merry month of May,
When green buds they were swellin',
Young Jemmy Grove on his death-bed lay,
For love of Barbara Allen.

So slowly, slowly rase she up,
And slowly she came nigh him,
And when she drew the curtain by –
'Young man, I think you're dyin'!'.
Barbara Allen's Cruelty

50 John Wayne is dead
The hell I am
Inscription on a wall in Bermondsey Antique Market, together with a ghostly denial. *Evening Standard*, 1980

51 *Liberté! Égalité! Fraternité!*
Freedom! Equality! Brotherhood!
Motto for French Revolutionaries

52 Little Willy from his mirror
Licked the mercury right off,
Thinking in his childish error,
It would cure the whooping cough.
At the funeral his mother
Smartly said to Mrs Brown:
''Twas a chilly day for Willie
When the mercury went down'.
Willie's Epitaph

53 Lizzie Borden took an axe
And gave her mother forty whacks;
When she saw what she had done
She gave her father forty-one!
On 4 Aug 1892 in Fall River, Massachusetts, Lizzie Borden was acquitted of the murder of her stepmother and her father.

54 Lo, Hudled up, together Lye
Gray Age, Grene youth, White Infancy.
If Death doth Nature's Laws dispence,
And reconciles All Difference
Tis Fit, One Flesh, One House Should have
One Tombe, One Epitaph, One Grave:
And they that Liv'd and Lov'd Either,
Should Dye and Lye and Sleep together.

Good Reader, whether go or stay
Thou must not hence be Long Away
Epitaph, of William Bartholomew (died 1662), his wife and some of their children, St John the Baptist, Burford

55 Love is blind; friendship closes its eyes.
Proverb

56 Mary Ann has gone to rest,
Safe at last on Abraham's breast,
Which may be nuts for Mary Ann,
But is certainly rough on Abraham.
Epitaph

57 Miss Buss and Miss Beale
Cupid's darts do not feel.
How different from us,
Miss Beale and Miss Buss.
Written about the headmistresses of North London Collegiate School and Cheltenham Ladies' College, respectively

58 My Bonnie lies over the ocean,
My Bonnie lies over the sea,
My Bonnie lies over the ocean,
Oh, bring back my Bonnie to me.
My Bonnie

59 My Love in her attire doth show her wit,
It doth so well become her:
For every season she hath dressings fit,
For winter, spring, and summer.
No beauty she doth miss,
When all her robes are on;
But beauty's self she is,
When all her robes are gone.
Madrigal

60 My name is George Nathaniel Curzon,
I am a most superior person.
My face is pink, my hair is sleek,

I dine at Blenheim once a week.
The Masque of Balliol

61 My sledge and anvil lie declined
My bellows too have lost their wind
My fire's extinct, my forge decayed,
And in the Dust my Vice is laid
My coals are spent, my iron's gone
My Nails are Drove, My Work is done.
An epitaph to William Strange, blacksmith, died 6 June 1746 and buried in Nettlebed churchyard.

62 No one provokes me with impunity.
Motto of the Crown of Scotland

63 Now I am a bachelor, I live by myself and I work at the weaving trade,
And the only only thing that I ever did wrong
Was to woo a fair young maid.

She sighed, she cried, she damned near died: she said 'What shall I do?'
So I took her into bed and covered up her head
Just to save her from the foggy, foggy dew.
Weaver's Song

64 Now I lay me down to sleep,
I pray the Lord my soul to keep.
If I should die before I wake,
I pray the Lord my soul to take.
New England Primer, 1781

65 O Death, where is thy sting-a-ling-a-ling,
O Grave, thy victoree?
The bells of hell go ting-a-ling-a-ling
For you but not for me.
Song of World War I

66 O, Shenandoah, I long to hear you
Away, you rolling river.
Shenandoah

67 O ye'll tak' the high road, and I'll tak' the low road,
And I'll be in Scotland afore ye,
But me and my true love will never meet again,
On the bonnie, bonnie banks o' Loch Lomon'.
The Bonnie Banks o' Loch Lomon'

68 *Per ardua ad astra.*
Hard and high to the stars!
Motto of the Royal Air Force.

69 Please to remember the Fifth of November,
Gunpowder Treason and Plot.
We know no reason why gunpowder treason
Should ever be forgot.
Traditional

70 Sacred to the memory of
Captain Anthony Wedgwood
Accidentally shot by his gamekeeper
Whilst out shooting
'Well done thou good and faithful servant'
Epitaph

71 She was poor but she was honest
Victim of a rich man's game.
First he loved her, then he left her,
And she lost her maiden name.

See her on the bridge at midnight,
Saying 'Farewell, blighted love.'
Then a scream, a splash and goodness,
What is she a-doin' of?

It's the same the whole world over,
It's the poor wot gets the blame,
It's the rich wot gets the gravy.
Ain't it all a bleedin' shame?
She was Poor but she was Honest

72 Since wars begin in the minds of men, it is in the minds of men that the defences of peace must be constructed.
Constitution of UNESCO

73 Some talk of Alexander, and some of Hercules,
Of Hector and Lysander, and such great names as these;
But of all the world's brave heroes there's none that can compare
With a tow, row, row, row, row, row for the British Grenadier.
The British Grenadiers

74 Stranger! Approach this spot with gravity!
John Brown is filling his last cavity.
Epitaph of a dentist

75 Sumer is icumen in,
Lhude sing cuccu!
Groweth sed, and bloweth med,
And springth the wude nu.
Cuckoo Song, c. 1250

76 Swing low sweet chariot,
Comin' for to carry me home,
I looked over Jordan an' what did I see?
A band of Angels coming after me,
Comin' for to carry me home.
Swing Low, Sweet Chariot

77 Swore to be true to each other, true as the stars above;
He was her man, but he done her wrong.
Frankie and Johnny

78 That this house will in no circumstances fight for its King and country.
Motion passed at the Oxford Union, 9 Feb 1933

79 The animals went in one by one,
There's one more river to cross.
One More River

80 The Campbells are comin', oho, oho.
The Campbells are Comin'

81 The fault is great in man or woman
Who steals a goose from off a common;
But what can plead that man's excuse
Who steals a common from a goose?
The Tickler Magazine, 1 Feb 1821

82 The holly and the ivy,
When they are both full grown,
Of all the trees that are in the wood,
The holly bears the crown.
The rising of the sun
And the running of the deer,
The playing of the merry organ,
Sweet singing in the choir.
The Holly and the Ivy

83 The King over the Water.
Jacobite toast

84 The king sits in Dunfermline town
Drinking the blude-red wine.

'I saw the new moon late yestreen
Wi' the auld moon in her arm;
And if we gang to sea master,
I fear we'll come to harm.'

O lang, lang may the ladies sit,
Wi' their fans into their hand,
Before they see Sir Patrick Spens
Come sailing to the strand!
Sir Patrick Spens

85 The rabbit has a charming face;
Its private life is a disgrace.
The Rabbit, 20th century

86 There are twelve months in all the year,
As I hear many men say,
But the merriest month in all the year
Is the merry month of May.
Robin Hood and the Widow's Three Sons

87 There is a lady sweet and kind,
Was never face so pleased my mind;
I did but see her passing by,
And yet I love her till I die.
Passing By

88 There is a tavern in the town,
And there my dear love sits him down,

And drinks his wine 'mid laughter free,
And never, never thinks of me.

Fare thee well, for I must leave thee,
Do not let this parting grieve thee,
And remember that the best of friends must part.
There is a Tavern in the Town

89 There is so much good in the worst of us,
And so much bad in the best of us,
That it hardly becomes any of us
To talk about the rest of us.
Good and Bad

90 There's a wonderful family called Stein,
There's Gert and there's Epp and there's Ein;
Gert's poems are bunk,
Epp's statues are junk,
And no one can understand Ein.

91 There was a faith-healer of Deal,
Who said, 'Although pain isn't real,
If I sit on a pin
And it punctures my skin,
I dislike what I fancy I feel.'

92 There was an old man from Darjeeling,
Who boarded a bus bound for Ealing,
He saw on the door:
'Please don't spit on the floor',
So he stood up and spat on the ceiling.

93 There was an old man of Boulogne
Who sang a most topical song.
It wasn't the words
That frightened the birds,
But the horrible double-entendre.

94 There was a young lady of Riga,
Who went for a ride on a tiger;
They returned from the ride
With the lady inside,
And a smile on the face of the tiger.

95 There was a young man of Japan
Whose limericks never would scan;
When they said it was so,
He replied, 'Yes, I know,
But I always try to get as many words into the last line as ever I possibly can.'

96 There was a young woman called Starkie,
Who had an affair with a darky.
The result of her sins
Was quadruplets, not twins –
One black, and one white, and two khaki.

97 There were three ravens sat on a tree,
They were as black as they might be.
The one of them said to his make,
'Where shall we our breakfast take?'
The Three Ravens

98 There were twa sisters sat in a bour;
Binnorie, O Binnorie!
There came a knight to be their wooer,
By the bonnie milldams o' Binnorie.
Binnorie

99 The sons of the prophet were brave men and bold,
And quite unaccustomed to fear,
But the bravest by far in the ranks of the Shah
Was Abdul the Bulbul Amir.
Abdul the Bulbul Amir

100 Thirty days hath September,
April, June, and November;
All the rest have thirty-one,
Excepting February alone,
And that has twenty-eight days clear
And twenty-nine in each leap year.
Stevins Manuscript, c. 1555

101 This animal is very bad; when attacked it defends itself.
La Ménagerie (P. K. Théodore), 1828

102 This is a rotten argument, but it should be good enough for their lordships on a hot summer afternoon.
A note on a ministerial brief read out by mistake in the House of Lords. *The Way the Wind Blows* (Lord Home), 1976

103 This the grave of Mike O'Day
Who died maintaining his right of way.
His right was clear, his will was strong.
But he's just as dead as if he'd been wrong.
Epitaph

104 'Tom Pearse, Tom Pearse, lend me you grey mare,
All along, down along, out along, lee
For I want for to go to Widdicombe Fair,
Wi' Bill Brewer, Jan Stewer, Peter Gurney, Peter Davey, Dan'l Whiddon, Harry Hawk;
Old Uncle Tom Cobbleigh and all.
Old Uncle Tom Cobbleigh and all.'
Widdicombe Fair

105 Warm summer sun shine kindly here:
Warm summer wind blow softly here:
Green sod above lie light, lie light:
Good-night, Dear Heart: good-night, good-night.
Memorial to Clorinda Haywood, St Bartholomew's, Edgbaston

106 What shall we do with the drunken sailor
Early in the morning?
Hoo-ray and up she rises
Early in the morning.
What shall we do with the Drunken Sailor?

107 When I am dead, and laid in grave,
And all my bones are rotten,
By this may I remembered be
When I should be forgotten.
On a girl's sampler, 1736

108 When Israel was in Egypt land,
Let my people go,
Oppressed so hard they could not stand,
Let my people go.
Go down, Moses,
Way-down in Egypt land,
Tell old Pharaoh
To let my people go.
Negro spiritual

109 Whose Finger do you want on the Trigger When the World Situation Is So Delicate?
Headline from the *Daily Mirror* on the day before the General Election, Oct 1951. *Publish and Be Damned* (Hugh Cudlipp), 1953

110 Ye Highlands and ye Lawlands,
O where hae ye been?
They hae slain the Earl of Murray,
And hae laid him on the green.

He was a braw gallant,
And he rid at the ring;
And the bonny Earl of Murray,
O he might hae been a king!

O lang will his Lady
Look owre the Castle Downe,
Ere she see the Earl of Murray
Come sounding through the town!
The Bonny Earl of Murray

ANSWERS

1 What is truth? said jesting Pilate, and would not stay for an answer.
Francis Bacon (1561–1626) English philosopher. *Essays*, 'Of Truth'

2 Miss not the discourse of the elders: for they also learned of their fathers, and of them thou shalt

learn understanding, and to give answer as need requireth.
Bible: Ecclesiasticus 8:9

3 Answer a fool according to his folly, lest he be wise in his own conceit.
Bible: Proverbs 26:5

4 But answer came there none –
And this was scarcely odd because
They'd eaten every one.
Lewis Carroll (Charles Lutwidge Dodgson; 1832–98) British writer. *Through the Looking-Glass*, Ch. 4

5 Examinations are formidable even to the best prepared, for the greatest fool may ask more than the wisest man can answer.
Charles Caleb Colton (?1780–1832) British clergyman and writer. *Lacon*, Vol. II

6 A timid question will always receive a confident answer.
Lord Darling (1849–1936) British judge. *Scintillae Juris*

7 Yes, 'n' how many years can some people exist
Before they're allowed to be free?
Yes, 'n' how many times can a man turn his head,
Pretending he just doesn't see?
The answer, my friend, is blowin' in the wind.
Bob Dylan (Robert Allen Zimmerman; 1941–) US popular singer. *Blowin' in the Wind*

8 There are innumerable questions to which the inquisitive mind can in this state receive no answer: Why do you and I exist? Why was this world created? Since it was to be created, why was it not created sooner?
Samuel Johnson (1709–84) British lexicographer and writer. *Life of Johnson* (J. Boswell), Vol. III

9 Fortunately, in her kindness and patience, Nature has never put the fatal question as to the meaning of their lives into the mouths of most people. And where no one asks, no one needs to answer.
Carl Gustav Jung (1875–1961) Swiss psychoanalyst. *The Development of Personality*

ANTHROPOMORPHISM

1 The Romans and Greeks found everything human. Everything had a face, and a human voice. Men spoke, and their fountains piped an answer.
D. H. Lawrence (1885–1930) British novelist. *Fantasia of the Unconscious*, Ch. 4

ANTICIPATION

See also expectation

1 A stitch in time saves nine.
Proverb

2 Don't cross the bridge till you get to it.
Proverb

3 The early bird catches the worm.
Proverb

4 Don't count your chickens before they are hatched.
Aesop (6th century BC) Reputed Greek writer of fables. *Fables*, 'The Milkmaid and her Pail'

5 To swallow gudgeons ere they're catched,
And count their chickens ere they're hatched.
Samuel Butler (1612–80) English satirist. *Hudibras*, Pt. II

6 He told me never to sell the bear's skin before one has killed the beast.
Jean de La Fontaine (1621–95) French poet. *Fables*, V, 'L'Ours et les deux Compagnons'

7 To travel hopefully is a better thing than to arrive, and the true success is to labour.
Robert Louis Stevenson (1850–94) Scottish writer. *Virginibus Puerisque*

ANTISEMITISM

See also Jews, prejudice

1 Modern Physics is an instrument of Jewry for the destruction of Nordic science . . . True physics is the creation of the German spirit.
Rudolphe Tomaschek (20th century) German scientist. *The Rise and Fall of the Third Reich* (W. L. Shirer), Ch. 8

APOLOGIES

See also regret

1 Very sorry can't come. Lie follows by post.
Charles Beresford (1846–1919) British naval officer. Reply, by telegram, to a dinner invitation at short notice from Edward, Prince of Wales. *The World of Fashion 1837–1922* (R. Nevill), Ch. 5

2 I should never be allowed out in private.
Randolph Churchill (1911–68) British political journalist. Apologizing to a hostess whose dinner party he had ruined. *Randolph* (B. Roberts)

3 I have two huge lions tearing at my flanks, the so-called Emperor Otto and John, King of England. Both try with all their might to upset the Kingdom of France. I cannot leave the country myself or do without my son here.
Philip II (1165–1223) King of France. Explaining, to Pope Innocent III, his refusal to crusade against the Albigensian heretics.

4 Miss Otis regrets she's unable to lunch today.
Cole Porter (1893–1964) US songwriter. *Hi Diddle Diddle*, Miss Otis Regrets

5 Love means never having to say you're sorry.
Erich Segal (1937–) US writer. *Love Story*

6 Mr. Speaker, I said the honorable member was a liar it is true and I am sorry for it. The honourable member may place the punctuation where he pleases.
Richard Brinsley Sheridan (1751–1816) British dramatist. On being asked to apologize for calling a fellow MP a liar. Attrib.

7 It is a good rule in life never to apologize. The right sort of people do not want apologies, and the wrong sort take a mean advantage of them.
P. G. Wodehouse (1881–1975) British humorous novelist. *The Man Upstairs and Other Stories*

APPEARANCE

See also appearances, beauty, clothes, cosmetics, eyes

1 A man need not look in your mouth to know how old you are.
Proverb

2 Fine feathers make fine birds.
Proverb

3 Handsome is as handsome does.
Proverb

4 You're phoney. Everything about you is phoney. Even your hair – which looks false – is real.
Anonymous US diplomat to the British politician Brendan Bracken during World War II.

5 A homely face and no figure have aided many women heavenward.
Minna Antrim (1861–?) US writer. *Naked Truth and Veiled Allusions*

6 Take a close-up of a woman past sixty! You might as well use a picture of a relief map of Ireland!
Nancy Astor (1879–1964) American-born British politician. When asked for a close-up photograph. Attrib.

7 Your cameraman might enjoy

himself, because my face looks like a wedding cake left out in the rain.
W. H. Auden (1907–73) British-born poet. *W. H. Auden* (H. Carpenter)

8 Like the skins of some small mammal just not large enough to be used as mats.
Max Beerbohm (1872–1956) British writer. Referring to the dramatist Sir Arthur Pinero's eyebrows. *Edward Marsh* (C. Hassall)

9 But if a woman have long hair, it is a glory to her: for her hair is given her for a covering.
Bible: I Corinthians 11:15

10 It is the common wonder of all men, how among so many million of faces, there should be none alike.
Thomas Browne (1605–82) English physician and writer. *Religio Medici*, Pt. II

11 Alas, after a certain age every man is responsible for his face.
Albert Camus (1913–60) French existentialist writer. *The Fall*

12 Ears like bombs and teeth like splinters:
A blitz of a boy is Timothy Winters.
Charles Causley (1917–) British poet and broadcaster. *Timothy Winters*

13 It was a blonde. A blonde to make a bishop kick a hole in a stained-glass window.
Raymond Chandler (1888–1959) US novelist. *Farewell, My Lovely*, Ch. 13

14 It's nothing to be born ugly. Sensibly, the ugly woman comes to terms with her ugliness and exploits it as a grace of nature.
Colette (Sidonie-Gabrielle C.; 1873–1954) French novelist. *Journey for Myself*

15 Sunburn is very becoming – but only when it is even – one must be careful not to look like a mixed grill.
Noël Coward (1899–1973) British dramatist. *The Lido Beach*

16 The ring so worn, as you behold,
So thin, so pale, is yet of gold.
George Crabbe (1754–1832) British poet. *His Mother's Wedding Ring*

17 The most delightful advantage of being bald – one can hear snowflakes.
R. G. Daniels (1916–) British magistrate. *The Observer*, 'Sayings of the Week', 11 July 1976

18 He had but one eye, and the popular prejudice runs in favour of two.
Charles Dickens (1812–70) British novelist. Said by Mr Squeers. *Nicholas Nickleby*, Ch. 4

19 It was not a bosom to repose upon, but it was a capital bosom to hang jewels upon.
Charles Dickens Describing Mrs Merdle. *Little Dorrit*, Bk. I, Ch. 21

20 I am so changed that my oldest creditors would hardly know me.
Henry Stephen Fox (1791–1846) British diplomat. Remark after an illness. Letter from Byron to John Murray, 8 May 1817

21 There is a great difference between painting a face and not washing it.
Thomas Fuller (1608–61) English historian. *Church History*, Bk. VII

22 The flowers that bloom in the spring,
Tra la,
Have nothing to do with the case.
I've got to take under my wing,
Tra la,
A most unattractive old thing,
Tra la,
With a caricature of a face.
W. S. Gilbert (1836–1911) British dramatist. *The Mikado*, II

23 There was always something in her voice that made you think of lorgnettes.
Henry, O. (William Sidney Porter; 1862–1910) US short-story writer. *The Defeat of the City*

24 There's one thing about baldness – it's neat.
Don Herold Attrib.

25 If it's a boy I'll call him John. If it's a girl I'll call her Mary. But if, as I suspect, it's only wind, I'll call it F. E. Smith.
Gordon Hewart (1870–1943) British lawyer. When F. E. Smith commented on the size of his stomach, saying 'What's it to be – a boy or a girl?' Attrib.

26 We tolerate shapes in human beings that would horrify us if we saw them in a horse.
W. R. Inge (1860–1954) British churchman and writer. Attrib.

27 Where's the cheek that doth not fade,
Too much gaz'd at? Where's the maid
Whose lip mature is ever new?
John Keats (1795–1821) British poet. *Fancy*, I

28 It always seemed to me that men wore their beards, like they wear their neckties, for show. I shall always remember Lewis for saying his beard was part of him.
D. H. Lawrence (1885–1930) British novelist. *St Mawr*

29 There was an Old Man with a beard,
Who said, 'It is just as I feared! –
Two Owls and a Hen,
Four Larks and a Wren,
Have all built their nests in my beard!'
Edward Lear (1812–88) British artist and writer. *Book of Nonsense*

30 A smile that snapped back after using, like a stretched rubber band.
Sinclair Lewis (1885–1951) US novelist. Attrib.

31 The Lord prefers common-looking people. That is why he makes so many of them.
Abraham Lincoln (1809–65) US statesman. *Our President* (James Morgan), Ch. 6

32 He looks as if he had been weaned on a pickle.
Alice Roosevelt Longworth (1884–1980) US hostess. Referring to John Calvin Coolidge, US president 1923–29. *Crowded Hours*

33 Dewey looks like the bridegroom on the wedding cake.
Alice Roosevelt Longworth Referring to Thomas E. Dewey. *New York Times*, 25 Feb 1980

34 Gentlemen always seem to remember blondes.
Anita Loos (1891–1981) US novelist. *Gentlemen Prefer Blondes*, Ch. 1

35 In high school and college my sister Mary was very popular with the boys, but I had braces on my teeth and got high marks.
Betty MacDonald (1908–58) US writer. *The Egg and I*, Ch. 2

36 The huge laughing cockroaches on his top lip.
Osip Mandelstam (1891–1938) Russian poet. *Poems* (Stalin Epigram)

37 Smiling encouragement like a clumsy dentist.
Katherine Mansfield (1888–1923) New-Zealand-born British writer. *Bank Holiday*

38 There's a man outside with a big black mustache.
– Tell him I've got one.
Groucho Marx (Julius Marx; 1895–1977) US comedian. *Horse Feathers*

39 I eat like a vulture. Unfortunately the resemblance doesn't end there.
Groucho Marx Attrib.

40 To Crystal, hair was the most important thing on earth. She would

never get married because you couldn't wear curlers in bed.

Edna O'Brien (1936–) Irish novelist. *Winter's Tales*, 8, 'Come into the Drawing Room, Doris'

41 At fifty everyone has the face he deserves.

George Orwell (Eric Blair; 1903–50) British novelist. Final entry in his notebook

42 . . . reminds me of nothing so much as a recently dead fish before it has had time to stiffen.

George Orwell Referring to Clement Attlee. Diary, 19 May 1942

43 Men seldom make passes
At girls who wear glasses.

Dorothy Parker (1893–1967) US writer. Attrib.

44 All I say is, nobody has any business to go around looking like a horse and behaving as if it were all right. You don't catch horses going around looking like people, do you?

Dorothy Parker *Horsie*

45 His voice was intimate as the rustle of sheets.

Dorothy Parker *Dusk before Fireworks*

46 Had Cleopatra's nose been shorter, the whole face of the world would have changed.

Blaise Pascal (1623–62) French philosopher and mathematician. *Pensées*, II

47 To church; and with my mourning, very handsome, and new periwig, make a great show.

Samuel Pepys (1633–1703) English diarist. *Diary*, 31 Mar 1667

48 A smile that floated without support in the air.

Marcel Proust (1871–1922) French novelist. *Remembrance of Things Past*

49 My nose is huge! Vile snub-nose, flat-nosed ass, flat-head, let me inform you that I am proud of such an appendage, since a big nose is the proper sign of a friendly, good, courteous, witty, liberal, and brave man, such as I am.

Edmond Rostand (1868–1918) French poet and dramatist. *Cyrano de Bergerac*, I:1

50 In the spring . . . your lovely Chloë lightly turns to one mass of spots.

Ronald Searle (1920–) British cartoonist. *The Terror of St Trinian's*, Ch. 7

51 Your face, my thane, is as a book where men
May read strange matters. To beguile the time,
Look like the time; bear welcome in your eye,
Your hand, your tongue: look like the innocent flower,
But be the serpent under't.

William Shakespeare (1564–1616) English dramatist. *Macbeth*, I:5

52 Grim-visag'd war hath smooth'd his wrinkl'd front;
And now, instead of mounting barbed steeds,
To fright the souls of fearful adversaries, –
He capers nimbly in a lady's chamber
To the lascivious pleasing of a lute.
But I, that am not shap'd for sportive tricks,
Nor made to court an amorous looking-glass;
I, that am rudely stamp'd, and want love's majesty
To strut before a wanton ambling nymph;
I, that am curtail'd of this fair proportion,
Cheated of feature by dissembling nature,
Deform'd, unfinish'd, sent before my time
Into this breathing world, scarce half made up,
And that so lamely and unfashionable
That dogs bark at me, as I halt by them;
Why, I, in this weak piping time of peace,
Have no delight to pass away the time.

William Shakespeare *Richard III*, I:1

53 Poor soul, the centre of my sinful earth,
Fool'd by these rebel powers that thee array,
Why dost thou pine within and suffer dearth,
Painting thy outward walls so costly gay!
Why so large cost, having so short a lease,
Dost thou upon thy fading mansion spend?

William Shakespeare *Sonnets*, 146

54 For I have sworn thee fair, and thought thee bright,
Who art as black as hell, as dark as night.

William Shakespeare *Sonnets*, 147

55 LORD NORTHCLIFFE. The trouble with you, Shaw, is that you look as if there were famine in the land.
G.B.S. The trouble with you, Northcliffe, is that you look as if you were the cause of it.

George Bernard Shaw (1856–1950) Irish dramatist and critic. Attrib.

56 Why not be oneself? That is the whole secret of a successful appearance. If one is a greyhound why try to look like a Pekinese?

Edith Sitwell (1887–1964) British poet and writer. *Why I Look As I Do.*

57 There is more felicity on the far side of baldness than young men can possibly imagine.

Logan Pearsall Smith (1865–1946) US-born British writer. *Afterthoughts*, 2

58 A short neck denotes a good mind . . . You see, the messages go quicker to the brain because they've shorter to go.

Muriel Spark (1918–) British novelist. *The Ballad of Peckham Rye*, Ch. 7

59 But Shelley had a hyper-thyroid face.

John Collings Squire (1884–1958) British journalist. *Ballade of the Glandular Hypothesis*

60 . . . his nicotine eggyellow weeping walrus Victorian moustache worn thick and long in memory of Doctor Crippen.

Dylan Thomas (1914–53) Welsh poet. *Under Milk Wood*

61 Very hard for a man with a wig to keep order.

Evelyn Waugh (1903–66) British novelist. *Decline and Fall*, Pt. I, Ch. 3

62 Enclosing every thin man, there's a fat man demanding elbow-room.

Evelyn Waugh *Officers and Gentlemen*, Interlude

63 He smiled bunching his fat cheeks like twin rolls of smooth pink toilet paper.

Nathaniel West (Nathan Weinstein; 1903–40) US novelist. *Miss Lonelyhearts*

64 But there are other things than dissipation that thicken the features. Tears, for example.

Rebecca West (Cicely Isabel Fairfield; 1892–1983) British novelist and journalist. *Black Lamb and Grey Falcon*, 'Serbia'

65 Grief has turned her fair.

Oscar Wilde (1854–1900) Irish-born British dramatist. Referring to the fact that a recently-bereaved lady friend had dyed her hair blonde. Attrib.

66 Big chap with a small moustache

and the sort of eye that can open an oyster at sixty paces.
P. G. Wodehouse (1881–1975) British humorous novelist. *The Code of the Woosters*

67 The stationmaster's whiskers are of a Victorian bushiness and give the impression of having been grown under glass.
P. G. Wodehouse *Wodehouse at Work to the End* (Richard Usborne), Ch. 2

APPEARANCES

See also appearance, deception, hypocrisy

1 All that glitters is not gold.
Proverb

2 Appearances are deceptive.
Proverb

3 Never judge from appearances.
Proverb

4 Still waters run deep.
Proverb

5 Things are not always what they seem.
Proverb

6 Vice is often clothed in virtue's habit.
Proverb

7 You can't tell a book by its cover.
Proverb

8 The lamb that belonged to the sheep whose skin the wolf was wearing began to follow the wolf in the sheep's clothing.
Aesop (6th century BC) Reputed Greek writer of fables. *Fables*, 'The Wolf in Sheep's Clothing'

9 The French are wiser than they seem, and the Spaniards seem wiser than they are.
Francis Bacon (1561–1626) English philosopher. *Essays*, 'Of Seeming Wise'

10 The loveliest face in all the world will not please you if you see it suddenly eye to eye, at a distance of half an inch from your own.
Max Beerbohm (1872–1956) British writer. *Zuleika Dobson*

11 No-wher so bisy a man as he ther nas,
And yet he semed bisier than he was.
Geoffrey Chaucer (c. 1342–1400) English poet. Referring to the man of law. *The Canterbury Tales*, Prologue

12 Keep up appearances; there lies the test
The world will give thee credit for the rest.
Charles Churchill (1731–64) British poet. *Night*

13 I may not hope from outward forms to win
The passion and the life, whose fountains are within.
Samuel Taylor Coleridge (1772–1834) British poet. *Dejection: An Ode*

14 Appearances are not held to be a clue to the truth. But we seem to have no other.
Ivy Compton-Burnett (1892–1969) British novelist. *Manservant and Maidservant*

15 Outside, among your fellows, among strangers, you must preserve appearances, a hundred things you cannot do, but inside, the terrible freedom!
Ralph Waldo Emerson (1803–82) US poet and essayist.

16 No man could be so wise as Thurlow looked.
Charles James Fox (1749–1806) British Whig politician. *Lives of the Lord Chancellors* (Campbell), Vol. V

17 Before I applied the pressure bandages to prevent swelling, I took a final look at my work. The woman before me was no longer forty-five but a lovely person with the taut firm beauty of youth.
Dr. Robert Alyn Franklyn *Beauty Surgeon*

18 Ah, pray make no mistake,
We are not shy;
We're very wide awake,
The moon and I.
W. S. Gilbert (1836–1911) British dramatist. *The Mikado*, II

19 She's genuinely bogus.
Christopher Hassall (1912–63) British writer. Referring to Edith Sitwell. Attrib.

20 An' for all 'is dirty 'ide
'E was white, clear white, inside
When 'e went to tend the wounded under fire!
Rudyard Kipling (1865–1936) Indian-born British writer. *Gunga Din*

21 Strip the phoney tinsel off Hollywood and you'll find the real tinsel underneath.
Oscar Levant (1906–72) US pianist and actor. Attrib.

22 Ugliness is a point of view: an ulcer is wonderful to a pathologist.
Austin O'Malley (1858–1932)

23 And you cannot tell by the way a party looks or how he lives in this town, if he has any scratch, because many a party who is around in automobiles, and wearing good clothes, and chucking quite a swell is nothing but a phonus bolonus and does not have any real scratch whatever.
Damon Runyon (1884–1946) US writer. *More than Somewhat*, 'The Snatching of Bookie Bob'

24 Things are entirely what they appear to be and *behind them* . . . there is nothing.
Jean-Paul Sartre (1905–80) French writer. *Nausea*

25 Care I for the limb, the thews, the stature, bulk, and big assemblance of a man! Give me the spirit.
William Shakespeare (1564–1616) English dramatist. *Henry IV, Part Two*, III:2

26 Fairest Cordelia, that art most rich, being poor;
Most choice, forsaken; and most lov'd, despis'd!
William Shakespeare *King Lear*, I:1

27 A man may see how this world goes with no eyes. Look with thine ears: see how yond justice rails upon yond simple thief. Hark, in thine ear: change places; and, handy-dandy, which is the justice, which is the thief?
William Shakespeare *King Lear*, IV:6

28 Through tatter'd clothes small vices do appear;
Robes and furr'd gowns hide all.
William Shakespeare *King Lear*, IV:6

29 Fair is foul, and foul is fair;
Hover through the fog and filthy air.
William Shakespeare *Macbeth*, I:1

30 . . . if ill,
Why hath it given me earnest of success,
Commencing in a truth? I am Thane of Cawdor:
If good, why do I yield to that suggestion
Whose horrid image doth unfix my hair
And make my seated heart knock at my ribs,
Against the use of nature? Present fears
Are less than horrible imaginings;
My thought, whose murder yet is but fantastical,
Shakes so my single state of man that function
Is smother'd in surmise, and nothing is

But what is not.
William Shakespeare *Macbeth*, I:3

31 But I will wear my heart upon my sleeve
For daws to peck at: I am not what I am.
William Shakespeare *Othello*, I:1

32 I am not merry, but I do beguile
The thing I am by seeming otherwise.
William Shakespeare *Othello*, II:1

33 And thus I clothe my naked villany
With odd old ends stol'n forth of holy writ,
And seem a saint when most I play the devil.
William Shakespeare *Richard III*, I:3

34 So may the outward shows be least themselves:
The world is still deceived with ornament.
In law, what plea so tainted and corrupt
But, being season'd with a gracious voice,
Obscures the show of evil? In religion,
What damned error, but some sober brow
Will bless it and approve it with a text,
Hiding the grossness with fair ornament?
There is no vice so simple but assumes
Some mark of virtue on his outward parts.
William Shakespeare *The Merchant of Venice*, III:2

35 Ornament is but the guiled shore
To a most dangerous sea; the beauteous scarf
Veiling an Indian beauty; in a word,
The seeming truth which cunning times put on
To entrap the wisest.
William Shakespeare *The Merchant of Venice*, III:2

36 Our purses shall be proud, our garments poor;
For 'tis the mind that makes the body rich;
And as the sun breaks through the darkest clouds,
So honour peereth in the meanest habit.
William Shakespeare *The Taming of the Shrew*, IV:3

37 Ladies and gentlemen, I stand before you tonight in my green chiffon evening gown, my face softly made up, my fair hair gently waved . . . the Iron Lady of the Western World. Me? A cold war warrior? Well, yes – if that is how they wish to interpret my defence of values, and freedoms fundamental to our way of life.
Margaret Thatcher (1925–) British politician and prime minister. Referring to the nickname 'The Iron Lady' used by the Soviet paper *Red Star*. Speech, Dorking, 31 Jan 1976

38 It is only shallow people who do not judge by appearances.
Oscar Wilde (1854–1900) Irish-born British dramatist. *The Picture of Dorian Gray*, Ch. 2

ARCHITECTURE

See also houses, stately homes

1 Sir Christopher Wren
Said, 'I am going to dine with some men.
If anybody calls
Say I am designing St Paul's.'
Edmund Clerihew Bentley (1875–1956) British writer. *Biography for Beginners*

2 A very stately palace before him, the name of which was Beautiful.
John Bunyan (1628–88) English writer. *The Pilgrim's Progress*, Pt. I

3 . . . a jostling scrum of office buildings so mediocre that the only way you ever remember them is by the frustration they induce – like a basketball team standing shoulder to shoulder between you and the Mona Lisa.
Charles, Prince of Wales (1948–) Eldest son of Elizabeth II. Referring to the buildings surrounding St Paul's Cathedral. Speech, London, 1 Dec 1987

4 Like a carbuncle on the face of an old and valued friend.
Charles, Prince of Wales Referring to a proposed modern extension to the National Gallery. Speech, 1986

5 You have to give this much to the Luftwaffe – when it knocked down our buildings it did not replace them with anything more offensive than rubble. We did that.
Charles, Prince of Wales *The Observer*, 'Sayings of the Week', 6 Dec 1987

6 A modern, harmonic and lively architecture is the visible sign of an authentic democracy.
Walter Gropius (1883–1969) German architect. *The Observer*, 'Sayings of the Week', 8 Dec 1968

7 'Fan vaulting' . . . an architectural device which arouses enormous enthusiasm on account of the difficulties it has all too obviously involved but which from an aesthetic standpoint frequently belongs to the 'Last-supper-carved-on-a-peach-stone' class of masterpiece.
Osbert Lancaster (1908–86) British cartoonist. *Pillar to Post*, 'Perpendicular'

8 What has happened to architecture since the second world war that the only passers-by who can contemplate it without pain are those equipped with a white stick and a dog?
Bernard Levin (1928–) British journalist. *The Times*, 1983

9 Less is more.
Ludwig Mies Van Der Rohe (1886–1969) German-born architect. *New York Herald Tribune*, 1959

10 I declare this thing open – whatever it is.
Prince Philip (1921–) The consort of Queen Elizabeth II. Opening a new annex at Vancouver City Hall. Attrib.

11 When you think of some of the high flats around us, it can hardly be an accident that they are as near as one can get to an architectural representation of a filing cabinet.
Jimmy Reid Leader of the UCS shop stewards. In his address as new Rector of Glasgow University. *The Observer*, 'Sayings of the Week', 30 Apr 1972

12 No person who is not a great sculptor or painter can be an architect. If he is not a sculptor or painter, he can only be a *builder.*
John Ruskin (1819–1900) British art critic and writer. *Lectures on Architecture and Painting*

13 When we build let us think that we build for ever.
John Ruskin *The Seven Lamps of Architecture*, Ch. 6, 'The Lamp of Memory'

14 Architecture in general is frozen music.
Friedrich Wilhelm Joseph von Schelling (1775–1854) German philosopher. *Philosophie der Kunst*

15 When we mean to build,
We first survey the plot, then draw the model;
And when we see the figure of the house,
Then we must rate the cost of the erection;
Which if we find outweighs ability,
What do we then but draw anew the model

In fewer offices, or at last desist
To build at all?
William Shakespeare (1564–1616) English dramatist. *Henry IV, Part 2,* I:3

16 Many of my buildings are condemned now in advance.
Richard Seifert (1910–) British architect. He designed Centre Point, London, and other office block schemes. *The Observer,* 'Sayings of the Week', 6 Aug 1972

17 The architect is a servant, a tailor, who cuts and measures the thin chap or the fat chap and tries to make him comfortable. He is not a reformer.
Basil Spence (1907–76) British architect. *The Observer,* 'Sayings of the Week', 25 Oct 1970

18 It's beige! My color!
Elsie De Wolfe (1865–1950) US designer. On first sighting the Acropolis. *Elsie de Wolfe* (J. Smith)

19 In *Architecture* as in all other *Operative* Arts, the *end* must direct the *Operation.* The *end* is to build well. Well building hath three Conditions. *Commodity, Firmness,* and *Delight.*
Henry Wotton (1568–1639) English poet and diplomat. *Elements of Architecture,* Pt. I

20 Architecture has its political use; publick buildings being the ornament of a country; it establishes a nation, draws people and commerce; makes the people love their native country, which passion is the original of all great actions in a commonwealth.
Christopher Wren (1632–1723) English architect and scientist. *Parentalia*

ARGUMENTS

1 It takes two to make a quarrel.
Proverb

2 Least said soonest mended.
Proverb

3 For every why he had a wherefore.
Samuel Butler (1612–80) English satirist. *Hudibras,* Pt. I

4 Many a long dispute among divines may be thus abridged: It is so. It is not so. It is so. It is not so.
Benjamin Franklin (1706–90) US scientist and statesman. *Poor Richard's Almanack*

5 In every age and clime we see,
Two of a trade can ne'er agree.
John Gay (1685–1732) English poet and dramatist. *Fables*

6 Scholars dispute, and the case is still before the courts.
Horace (Quintus Horatius Flaccus; 65–8 BC) Roman poet. *Ars Poetica c. 8* BC

7 'It's like the question of the authorship of the *Iliad,*' said Mr Cardan. 'The author of that poem is either Homer or, if not Homer, somebody else of the same name.'
Aldous Huxley (1894–1964) British novelist. *Those Barren Leaves,* Pt. V, Ch. 4

8 It takes in reality only one to make a quarrel. It is useless for the sheep to pass resolutions in favour of vegetarianism while the wolf remains of a different opinion.
Dean Inge (1860–1954) British churchman. *Outspoken Essays*

9 Sir, I have found you an argument; but I am not obliged to find you an understanding.
Samuel Johnson (1709–84) British lexicographer. *Life of Johnson* (J. Boswell), Vol. IV

10 Though a quarrel in the streets is a thing to be hated, the energies displayed in it are fine; the commonest man shows a grace in his quarrel.
John Keats (1795–1821) British poet. Letter

11 When men understand what each other mean, they see, for the most part, that controversy is either superfluous or hopeless.
Cardinal Newman (1801–90) British theologian. Sermon, Oxford, Epiphany 1839

12 Quarrels would not last so long if the fault were on only one side.
Duc de la Rochefoucauld (1613–80) French writer. *Maximes,* 496

13 The most savage controversies are those about matters as to which there is no good evidence either way.
Bertrand Russell (1872–1970) British philosopher. *Unpopular Essays*

14 In a false quarrel there is no true valour.
William Shakespeare (1564–1616) English dramatist. *Much Ado About Nothing,* V:1

15 I love argument, I love debate. I don't expect anyone just to sit there and agree with me, that's not their job.
Margaret Thatcher (1925–) British politician and prime minister. *The Times,* 1980

16 I did not know that we had ever quarrelled.
Henry David Thoreau (1817–62) US writer. On being urged to make his peace with God. Attrib.

17 I am, sir for the last time in my life, Your Humble Servant Horace Walpole.
Horace Walpole (1717–97) British writer. Ending a letter written to an uncle with whom he had recently quarrelled. *Horace Walpole* (R. Ketton-Cremes)

18 I am not arguing with you – I am telling you.
James Whistler (1834–1903) US painter. *The Gentle Art of Making Enemies*

19 No question is ever settled
Until it is settled right.
Ella Wheeler Wilcox (1850–1919) US poet. *Settle the Question Right*

ARISTOCRACY

See also ancestry, class, Houses of Parliament, nobility, stately homes, titles

1 One has often wondered whether upon the whole earth there is anything so unintelligent, so unapt to perceive how the world is really going, as an ordinary young Englishman of our upper class.
Matthew Arnold (1822–88) British poet and critic. *Culture and Anarchy,* Ch. 2

2 There are only two kinds of people in the world. Those who are nice to their servants and those who aren't.
Duke of Argyll (1937–) Attrib.

3 I was obviously destined to go down and down when in 1958 my father and brother died within ten days of each other and I became an Earl... Life is much easier, being an Earl. It has changed me a lot. I'm much nastier now.
Earl of Arran (1938–) British publisher. *The Sunday Times,* 15 Jan 1967

4 Like many of the upper class
He liked the sound of broken glass.
Hilaire Belloc (1870–1953) French-born British poet. *See also* Evelyn WAUGH. *New Cautionary Tales,* 'About John'

5 The nobility of England, my lord, would have snored through the Sermon on the Mount.
Robert Bolt (1924–) British playwright. *A Man for All Seasons*

6 ... for the most part the worst instructed, and the least knowing of any of their rank, I ever went amongst.

Gilbert Burnet (1643–1715) Scottish-born English bishop. Referring to the English gentry. *History of My Own Times*, Conclusion

7 Lord Salisbury constitutes himself the spokesman of a class, of the class to which he himself belongs, who 'toil not neither do they spin'

Joseph Chamberlain (1836–1914) British politician. Referring to the aristocracy. Speech, Birmingham, 30 Mar 1883

8 We, my lords, may thank heaven that we have something better than our brains to depend upon.

Earl of Chesterfield (1694–1773) English statesman. Speech, House of Lords. *The Story of Civilization* (W. Durant), Vol. 9

9 Democracy means government by the uneducated, while aristocracy means government by the badly educated.

G. K. Chesterton (1874–1936) British writer. *New York Times*, 1 Feb 1931

10 In the eighteenth century he would have become Prime Minister before he was thirty; as it was he appeared honourably ineligible for the struggle of life.

Cyril Connolly (1903–74) British writer. Referring to the British prime minister Sir Alec Douglas-Home at Eton. *Enemies of Promise*

11 The Stately Homes of England
How beautiful they stand,
To prove the upper classes
Have still the upper hand.

Noël Coward (1899–1973) British dramatist. *Operette*, 'The Stately Homes of England'

12 If human beings could be propagated by cutting, like apple trees, aristocracy would be biologically sound.

J. B. S. Haldane (1892–1964) British geneticist. *The Inequality of Man*, title essay

13 *Honi soit qui mal y pense*
Evil be to him who evil thinks.

Edward III Reputedly said on retrieving the Countess of Salisbury's garter, which had fallen off. Attrib. in later tradition; associated with the foundation of the Order of the Garter (1344)

14 There are no credentials They do not even need a medical certificate. They need not be sound either in body or mind. They only require a certificate of birth – just to prove that they are first of the litter. You would not choose a spaniel on these principles.

David Lloyd George (1863–1945) British Liberal statesman. Budget Speech, 1909

15 A fully equipped Duke costs as much to keep up as two Dreadnoughts, and Dukes are just as great a terror, and they last longer.

David Lloyd George Speech, Limehouse, 30 July 1909

16 An aristocracy in a republic is like a chicken whose head has been cut off: it may run about in a lively way, but in fact it is dead.

Nancy Mitford (1904–73) British writer. *Noblesse Oblige*

17 He is without strict doubt a Hoorah Henry, and he is generally figured as nothing but a lob as far as doing anything useful in this world is concerned.

Damon Runyon (1884–1946) US writer. *Short Takes*, 'Tight Shoes'

18 Kind hearts are more than coronets,
And simple faith than Norman blood.

Alfred, Lord Tennyson (1809–92) British poet. *Lady Clara Vere de Vere*, VI

19 If the French noblesse had been capable of playing cricket with their peasants, their chateaux would never have been burnt.

George Macaulay Trevelyan (1876–1962) British historian. *English Social History*, Ch. XIII

20 My Lord Bath, you and I are now two as insignificant men as any in England.

Robert Walpole (1676–1745) British statesman. Said to William Pulteney, Earl of Bath, when they were promoted to the peerage (1742) *Political & Literary Anecdotes* (W. King)

21 The sound of the English county families baying for broken glass.

Evelyn Waugh (1903–66) British novelist. *See also* Hilaire BELLOC. *Decline and Fall*, Prelude

22 Unlike the male codfish which, suddenly finding itself the parent of three million five hundred thousand little codfish, cheerfully resolves to love them all, the British aristocracy is apt to look with a somewhat jaundiced eye on its younger sons.

P. G. Wodehouse (1881–1975) British humorous novelist. *Wodehouse at Work to the End* (Richard Usborne), Ch. 5

ARMY

See also officers, soldiers, war, weapons

1 Conduct . . . to the prejudice of good order and military discipline.

Anonymous Army Act, 40

2 Oh! the grand old Duke of York
He had ten thousand men;
He marched them up to the top of the hill,
And he marched them down again.
And when they were up they were up,
And when they were down they were down,
And when they were only half way up,
They were neither up nor down.

Anonymous Traditional

3 The chief attraction of military service has consisted and will consist in this compulsory and irreproachable idleness.

Leo Tolstoy (1828–1910) Russian writer. *War and Peace*, Bk. VII, Ch. 1

4 An army is a nation within a nation; it is one of the vices of our age.

Alfred de Vigny (1797–1863) French writer. *Servitude et grandeur militaire*, 1

5 I have got an infamous army, very weak and ill-equipped, and a very inexperienced staff.

Duke of Wellington (1769–1852) British general and statesman. Written at the beginning of the Waterloo campaign. Letter to Lord Stewart, 8 May 1815

6 Ours is composed of the scum of the earth.

Duke of Wellington Of the British army. Remark, 4 Nov 1831

7 The army ages men sooner than the law and philosophy; it exposes them more freely to germs, which undermine and destroy, and it shelters them more completely from thought, which stimulates and preserves.

H. G. Wells (1866–1946) British writer. *Bealby*, Pt. VIII, Ch. 1

ARNOLD, Matthew

(1822–88) British poet and critic, who served for 35 years as inspector of schools.

Quotations about Arnold

1 He is not as handsome as his photographs – or his poetry.

Henry James (1843–1916) US novelist. Letter to Charles Eliot Norton, 31 Mar 1873

2 Arnold is a dandy Isaiah, a poet without passion . . .
George Meredith (1829–1909) British novelist. *Fortnightly Review*, July 1909

Quotations by Arnold

3 Culture being a pursuit of our total perfection by means of getting to know, on all the matters which most concern us, the best which has been thought and said in the world.
Culture and Anarchy, Preface

4 Our society distributes itself into Barbarians, Philistines, and Populace; and America is just ourselves, with the Barbarians quite left out, and the Populace nearly.
Culture and Anarchy, Preface

5 The pursuit of perfection, then, is the pursuit of sweetness and light. . . . He who works for sweetness and light united, works to make reason and the will of God prevail.
Culture and Anarchy, Ch. 1

6 One has often wondered whether upon the whole earth there is anything so unintelligent, so unapt to perceive how the world is really going, as an ordinary young Englishman of our upper class.
Culture and Anarchy, Ch. 2

7 For this class we have a designation which now has become pretty well known, and which we may as well still keep for them, the designation of Philistines.
Referring to the middle class. *Culture and Anarchy*, Ch. 3

8 I often, therefore, when I want to distinguish clearly the aristocratic class from the Philistines proper, or middle class, name the former, in my own mind *the Barbarians*.
Culture and Anarchy, Ch. 3

9 But that vast portion, lastly, of the working-class which, raw and half-developed, has long lain half-hidden amidst its poverty and squalor, and is now issuing from its hiding-place to assert an Englishman's heaven-born privilege of doing as he likes, and is beginning to perplex us by marching where it likes, meeting where it likes, bawling what it likes, breaking what it likes – to this vast residuum we may with great propriety give the name of Populace.
Culture and Anarchy, Ch. 3

10 The sea is calm to-night,
The tide is full, the moon lies fair
Upon the Straits.
Dover Beach

11 And we are here as on a darkling plain
Swept with confused alarms of struggle and flight,
Where ignorant armies clash by night.
Dover Beach

12 Is it so small a thing
To have enjoy'd the sun,
To have lived light in the spring,
To have loved, to have thought, to have done?
Empedocles on Etna

13 Home of lost causes, and forsaken beliefs, and unpopular names, and impossible loyalties!
Referring to Oxford. *Essays in Criticism*, First Series, Preface

14 I am bound by my own definition of criticism: a disinterested endeavour to learn and propagate the best that is known and thought in the world.
Essays in Criticism, First Series, 'Functions of Criticism at the Present Time'

15 A criticism of life under the conditions fixed for such a criticism by the laws of poetic truth and poetic beauty.
Essays in Criticism, Second Series, 'The Study of Poetry'

16 Come, dear children, let us away;
Down and away below.
The Forsaken Merman

17 She left lonely for ever
The kings of the sea.
The Forsaken Merman

18 A wanderer is man from his birth.
He was born in a ship
On the breast of the river of Time.
The Future

19 Wandering between two worlds, one dead,
The other powerless to be born.
The Grande Chartreuse

20 Years hence, perhaps, may dawn an age,
More fortunate, alas! than we,
Which without hardness will be sage,
And gay without frivolity.
The Grande Chartreuse

21 The great apostle of the Philistines, Lord Macaulay.
Joubert

22 Culture, the acquainting ourselves with the best that has been known and said in the world, and thus with the history of the human spirit.
Literature and Dogma, Preface

23 Culture is the passion for sweetness and light, and (what is more) the passion for making them prevail.
Literature and Dogma, Preface

24 The eternal *not ourselves* that makes for righteousness.
Literature and Dogma, Ch. 8

25 It always seems to me that the right sphere for Shelley's genius was the sphere of music, not of poetry.
Maurice de Guérin, Footnote

26 When Byron's eyes were shut in death,
We bow'd our head and held our breath.
He taught us little: but our soul
Had *felt* him like the thunder's roll.
Memorial Verses

27 He spoke, and loos'd our heart in tears.
He laid us as we lay at birth
On the cool flowery lap of earth.
Referring to Wordsworth. *Memorial Verses*

28 Time may restore us in his course
Goethe's sage mind and Byron's force:
But where will Europe's latter hour
Again find Wordsworth's healing power?
Memorial Verses

29 We cannot kindle when we will
The fire which in the heart resides,
The spirit bloweth and is still,
In mystery our soul abides.
Morality

30 Now he is dead! Far hence he lies
In the lorn Syrian town;
And on his grave, with shining eyes,
The Syrian stars look down.
Obermann Once More

31 He will find one English book and one only, where, as in the *Iliad* itself, perfect plainness of speech is allied with perfect nobleness; and that book is the Bible.
On Translating Homer

32 I think it will be found that the grand style arises in poetry, when a noble nature, poetically gifted,

treats with simplicity or with severity a serious subject.
Closing words. *On Translating Homer*

33 Cruel, but composed and bland,
Dumb, inscrutable and grand,
So Tiberius might have sat,
Had Tiberius been a cat.
Poor Matthias

34 Go, for they call you, Shepherd, from the hill.
The Scholar Gipsy

35 All the live murmur of a summer's day.
The Scholar Gipsy

36 Tired of knocking at Preferment's door.
The Scholar Gipsy

37 Before this strange disease of modern life,
With its sick hurry, its divided aims.
The Scholar Gipsy

38 Still nursing the unconquerable hope,
Still clutching the inviolable shade.
The Scholar Gipsy

39 Resolve to be thyself: and know, that he
Who finds himself, loses his misery.
Self-Dependence

40 Others abide our question, Thou art free,
We ask and ask: Thou smilest and art still,
Out-topping knowledge.
Referring to Shakespeare. *Shakespeare*

41 Truth sits upon the lips of dying men.
Sohrab and Rustum

42 Who saw life steadily, and saw it whole:
The mellow glory of the Attic stage.
Sonnets to a Friend

43 And see all sights from pole to pole,
And glance, and nod, and bustle by;
And never once possess our soul
Before we die.
A Southern Night

44 The difference between genuine poetry and the poetry of Dryden, Pope, and all their school, is briefly this: their poetry is conceived and composed in their wits, genuine poetry is conceived and composed in the soul.
Thomas Gray

45 That sweet City with her dreaming spires
She needs not June for beauty's heightening.
Referring to Oxford. *Thyrsis*

46 And sigh that one thing only has been lent
To youth and age in common – discontent.
Youth's Agitations

47 I am past thirty, and three parts iced over.
Letter to A. H. Clough, 12 Feb 1853

ARROGANCE

See also conceit, egotism, pride

1 The need to be right – the sign of a vulgar mind.
Albert Camus (1913–60) French existentialist writer. *Notebooks*, 1935–42.

2 I am sure no man in England will take away my life to make you King.
Charles II (1630–85) King of England. To his brother James following revelation of Popish Plot fabricated by Titus Oates. Attrib.

3 He was like a cock who thought the sun had risen to hear him crow.
George Eliot (Mary Ann Evans; 1819–80) British novelist. *Adam Bede*

4 If this young man expresses himself in terms too deep for *me*,
Why, what a very singularly deep young man this deep young man must be!
W. S. Gilbert (1836–1911) British dramatist. *Patience*, I

5 There, but for the Grace of God, goes God.
Herman J. Mankiewicz (1897–1953) US journalist and screenwriter. Said of Orson Welles in the making of *Citizen Kane*. Also attributed to others. *The Citizen Kane Book*

6 The bullet that is to kill me has not yet been moulded.
Napoleon I (Napoleon Bonaparte; 1769–1821) French emperor. In reply to his brother Joseph, King of Spain, who had asked whether he had ever been hit by a cannonball. Attrib.

7 What His Royal Highness most particularly prides himself upon, is the excellent harvest.
Richard Brinsley Sheridan (1751–1816) British dramatist. Lampooning George IV's habit of taking credit for everything good in England. *The Fine Art of Political Wit* (L. Harris)

8 A LADY. This landscape reminds me of your work.
WHISTLER. Yes madam, Nature is creeping up.
James Whistler (1834–1903) US painter. *Whistler Stories* (D. Seitz)

9 Well, not bad, but there are decidedly too many of them, and they are not very well arranged. I would have done it differently.
James Whistler His reply when asked if he agreed that the stars were especially beautiful one night. Attrib.

10 The Admiral of the Atlantic salutes the Admiral of the Pacific.
Wilhelm II (1859–1941) King of Prussia and Emperor of Germany. Telegram sent to Czar Nicholas II during a naval exercise. *The Shadow of the Winter Palace* (E. Crankshaw)

11 All men think all men mortal, but themselves.
Edward Young (1683–1765) British poet. *Night Thoughts*

ART

See also artists, arts, painting, sculpture

1 The works of art, by being publicly exhibited and offered for sale, are becoming articles of trade, following as such the unreasoning laws of markets and fashion; and public and even private patronage is swayed by their tyrannical influence.
Prince Albert (1819–61) The consort of Queen Victoria. Referring to the Great Exhibition. Speech, Royal Academy Dinner, 3 May 1851

2 The object of art is to give life a shape.
Jean Anouilh (1910–87) French dramatist. *The Rehearsal*

3 The lower one's vitality, the more sensitive one is to great art.
Max Beerbohm (1872–1956) British writer. *Seven Men*, 'Enoch Soames'

4 It would follow that 'significant form' was form behind which we catch a sense of ultimate reality.
Clive Bell (1881–1964) British art critic. *Art*, Pt. I, Ch. 3

5 Art is the only thing that can go on mattering once it has stopped hurting.
Elizabeth Bowen (1899–1973) Irish novelist. *The Heat of the Day*, Ch. 16

6 Art for art's sake.
Victor Cousin (1792–1867) French philosopher. Lecture, Sorbonne, 1818

7 Art is a jealous mistress.
Ralph Waldo Emerson (1803–82) US poet and essayist. *Conduct of Life*, 'Wealth'

8 Works of art, in my opinion, are

the only objects in the material universe to possess internal order, and that is why, though I don't believe that only art matters, I do believe in Art for Art's sake.

E. M. Forster (1879–1970) British novelist. *Art for Art's Sake*

9 No artist is ahead of his time. He *is* his time; it is just that others are behind the times.

Martha Graham (1894–) US dancer and choreographer. *The Observer Magazine*, 8 July 1979

10 . . . I rarely draw what I see. I draw what I feel in my body.

Barbara Hepworth (1903–75) British sculptor. *World of Art Series* (A. M. Hammersmith)

11 In free society art is not a weapon. . . . Artists are not engineers of the soul.

John Fitzgerald Kennedy (1917–63) US statesman. Address at Dedication of the Robert Frost Library, 26 Oct 1963

12 But the Devil whoops, as he whooped of old:
'It's clever, but is it art?'

Rudyard Kipling (1865–1936) Indian-born British writer. *The Conundrum of the Workshops*

13 Art is not a special sauce applied to ordinary cooking; it is the cooking itself if it is good.

W. R. Lethaby (1857–1931) British architect. *Form in Civilization*, 'Art and Workmanship'

14 In other countries, art and literature are left to a lot of shabby bums living in attics and feeding on booze and spaghetti, but in America the successful writer or picture-painter is indistinguishable from any other decent business man.

Sinclair Lewis (1885–1951) US novelist. *Babbitt*, Ch. 14

15 I do not know whether he draws a line himself. But I assume that his is the direction . . . .It makes Disney the most significant figure in graphic art since Leonardo.

David Low (1871–1963) New-Zealand-born newspaper cartoonist. *Walt Disney* (R. Schickel), Ch. 20

16 In England, pop art and fine art stand resolutely back to back.

Colin MacInnes (1914–76) British novelist. *England, Half English*, 'Pop Songs and Teenagers'

17 Art is not a mirror to reflect the world, but a hammer with which to shape it.

Vladimir Mayakovsky (1893–1930) Soviet poet. *The Guardian*, 11 Dec 1974

18 Nothing unites the English like war. Nothing divides them like Picasso.

Hugh Mills (1913–71) British screenwriter. *Prudence and the Pill* (film)

19 To be aristocratic in Art one must avoid polite society.

George Moore (1852–1933) Irish writer and art critic. *Enemies of Promise* (Cyril Connolly), Ch. 15

20 All art deals with the absurd and aims at the simple. Good art speaks truth, indeed *is* truth, perhaps the only truth.

Iris Murdoch (1919–) Irish-born British novelist. *The Black Prince*, 'Bradley Pearson's Foreword'

21 All art constantly aspires towards the condition of music.

Walter Pater (1839–94) British critic. *The Renaissance*, 'The School of Giorgione'

22 When I was their age, I could draw like Raphael, but it took me a lifetime to learn to draw like them.

Pablo Picasso (1881–1973) Spanish painter. Visiting an exhibition of drawings by children. *Picasso: His Life and Work* (Ronald Penrose)

23 The pain passes, but the beauty remains.

Pierre Auguste Renoir (1841–1919) French impressionist painter. Explaining why he still painted when his hands were twisted with arthritis. Attrib.

24 Burnings of people and (what was more valuable) works of art.

A. L. Rowse (1903–) British historian and critic. *Historical Essays* (H. R. Trevor-Roper)

25 Life without industry is guilt, and industry without art is brutality.

John Ruskin (1819–1900) British art critic and writer. *Lectures on Art*, 3, 'The Relation of Art to Morals', 23 Feb 1870

26 Fine art is that in which the hand, the head, and the heart of man go together.

John Ruskin *The Two Paths*, Lecture II

27 The trouble, Mr Goldwyn is that you are only interested in art and I am only interested in money.

George Bernard Shaw (1856–1950) Irish dramatist and critic. Turning down Goldwyn's offer to buy the screen rights of his plays. *The Movie Moguls* (Philip French), Ch. 4

28 A portrait is a picture in which there is something wrong with the mouth.

Eugene Speicher (1883–1962) US painter. Attrib.

29 Skill without imagination is craftsmanship and gives us many useful objects such as wickerwork picnic baskets. Imagination without skill gives us modern art.

Tom Stoppard (1937–) Czech-born British dramatist. *Artist Descending a Staircase*

30 Art is not a handicraft, it is the transmission of feeling the artist has experienced.

Leo Tolstoy (1828–1910) Russian writer. *What is Art?*, Ch. 19

31 What a delightful thing this perspective is!

Paolo Uccello (1397–1475) Italian painter. *Men of Art* (T. Craven)

32 . . . any authentic work of art must start an argument between the artist and his audience.

Rebecca West (Cicely Isabel Fairfield; 1892–1983) British novelist and journalist. *The Court and the Castle*, Pt. I, Ch. 1

33 Art is the imposing of a pattern on experience, and our aesthetic enjoyment is recognition of the pattern.

A. N. Whitehead (1861–1947) British philosopher. *Dialogues*, 228

34 Art never expresses anything but itself.

Oscar Wilde (1854–1900) Irish-born British dramatist. *The Decay of Lying*

35 All Art is quite useless.

Oscar Wilde *The Picture of Dorian Gray*, Preface

36 Art is the most intense mode of individualism that the world has known.

Oscar Wilde *The Soul of Man Under Socialism*

ARTHURIAN LEGEND

1 What were they going to do with the Grail when they found it, Mr Rossetti?

Max Beerbohm (1872–1956) British writer. Caption to a cartoon

2 An arm
Rose up from out the bosom of the lake,
Clothed in white samite, mystic, wonderful.

Alfred, Lord Tennyson (1809–92) British poet. *Idylls of the King*, 'The Passing of Arthur'

3 On either side the river lie
Long fields of barley and of rye,
That clothe the wold and meet the sky;
And thro' the field the road runs by
To many-tower'd Camelot.

Alfred, Lord Tennyson *The Lady of Shalott*, Pt. I

ARTISTS

See also art, painting

1 When Sir Joshua Reynolds died
All Nature was degraded;
The King dropped a tear in the Queen's ear,
And all his pictures faded.
William Blake (1757–1827) British poet. *On Art and Artists*

2 Poets and painters are outside the class system, or rather they constitute a special class of their own, like the circus people and the gipsies.
Gerald Brenan (Edward Fitzgerald Brenan; 1894–1987) British writer. *Thoughts in a Dry Season*, 'Writing'

3 Remember I'm an artist. And you know what that means in a court of law. Next worst to an actress.
Joyce Cary (1888–1957) British novelist. *The Horse's Mouth*, Ch. 14

4 You have no idea what portrait painters suffer from the vanity of their sitters.
Kenneth Clark (1903–83) British art historian. *The Observer*, 29 Mar 1959

5 Beware of the artist who's an intellectual also. The artist who doesn't fit.
F. Scott Fitzgerald (1896–1940) US novelist. *This Side of Paradise*, Bk. II, Ch. 5

6 I don't advise any one to take it up as a business proposition, unless they really have talent, and are crippled so as to deprive them of physical labor.
Grandma Moses (Anna Mary Robertson Moses; 1860–1961) US primitive painter. Referring to painting. *The New York Times*, 'How Do I Paint?', 11 May 1947

7 In a few generations you can breed a racehorse. The recipe for making a man like Delacroix is less well known.
Pierre Auguste Renoir Attrib.

8 I should desire that the last words which I should pronounce in this Academy, and from this place, might be the name of – Michael Angelo.
Joshua Reynolds (1723–92) British portrait painter. Discorse to Students of the Royal Academy, 10 Dec 1790

9 Nobody cares much at heart about Titian, only there is a strange undercurrent of everlasting murmur about his name, which means the deep consent of all great men that he is greater than they.
John Ruskin (1819–1900) British art critic and writer. *The Two Paths*, Lecture II

10 An amateur is an artist who supports himself with outside jobs which enable him to paint. A professional is someone whose wife works to enable him to paint.
Ben Shahn (1898–1969) US artist. Attrib.

11 What is an artist? For every thousand people there's nine hundred doing the work, ninety doing well, nine doing good, and one lucky bastard who's the artist.
Tom Stoppard (1937–) Czech-born British dramatist. *Travesties*, I

12 If Botticelli were alive today he'd be working for *Vogue*.
Peter Ustinov (1921–) British actor. *The Observer*, 'Sayings of the Week', 21 Oct 1962

13 A painter should not paint what he sees, but what will be seen.
Paul Valéry (1871–1945) French poet and writer. *Mauvaises Pensées et Autres*

14 All his own geese are swans, as the swans of others are geese.
Horace Walpole (1717–97) British writer. Referring to Sir Joshua Reynolds. Letter to the Countess of Upper Ossory, 1 Dec 1786

15 An artist is someone who produces things that people don't need to have but that he – for *some reason* – thinks it would be a good idea to give them.
Andy Warhol (Andrew Warhola; 1926–87) US pop artist. *From A to B and Back Again*, 'Atmosphere'

16 No, I ask it for the knowledge of a lifetime.
James Whistler (1834–1903) US painter. Replying to the taunt, during the Ruskin trial, that he was asking a fee of 200 guineas for two days' painting. *Lives of the Wits* (H. Pearson)

17 A living is made, Mr Kemper, by selling something that everybody needs at least once a year. Yes, sir! And a million is made by producing something that everybody needs every day. You artists produce something that nobody needs at any time.
Thornton Wilder (1897–1975) US novelist and dramatist. *The Matchmaker*, II

ARTS

1 Every man's work, whether it be literature or music or pictures or architecture or anything else, is always a portrait of himself.
Samuel Butler (1835–1902) British writer. *The Way of All Flesh*, Ch. 14

2 The artistic temperament is a disease that afflicts amateurs.
G. K. Chesterton (1874–1936) British writer. *Heretics*, Ch. 17

3 No poet, no artist of any sort, has his complete meaning alone. His significance, his appreciation is the appreciation of his relation to the dead poets and artists.
T. S. Eliot (1888–1965) US-born British poet and dramatist. *Tradition and the Individual Talent*

4 Yes, the work comes out more beautiful from a material that resists the process, verse, marble, onyx, or enamel.
Théophile Gautier (1811–72) French poet and critic. *L'Art*

5 A work of art is part of nature seen through a temperament.
André Gide (1869–1951) French novelist. *Protests*

6 The excellence of every art is its intensity, capable of making all disagreeables evaporate, from their being in close relationship with beauty and truth.
John Keats (1795–1821) British poet. Letter to G. and T. Keats, 21 Dec 1817

7 The whole of art is an appeal to a reality which is not without us but in our minds.
Desmond MacCarthy (1877–1952) British writer and theater critic. *Theatre*, 'Modern Drama'

8 For painters, poets and builders have very high flights, but they must be kept down.
Sarah, Duchess of Marlborough (1660–1744) Wife of John Churchill, 1st Duke of Marlborough. Letter to the Duchess of Bedford, 21 June 1734

9 Music begins to atrophy when it departs too far from the dance; . . . poetry begins to atrophy when it gets too far from music.
Ezra Pound (1885–1972) US poet. *ABC of Reading*, 'Warning'

10 The secret of the arts is to correct nature.
Voltaire (François-Marie Arouet; 1694–1778) French writer. *Épîtres*, 'À M. de Verrière'

11 A work of art has an author and yet, when it is perfect, it has

something which is anonymous about it.
Simone Weil (1909–43) French philosopher. *Gravity and Grace*

ASSASSINATION

See also killing, murder

1 If His Majesty shall come by any violent death, it shall be revenged to the utmost upon all Papists.
Anonymous Resolution, House of Commons, 1679

2 Assassination has never changed the history of the world.
Benjamin Disraeli (1804–81) British statesman. Speech, House of Commons, 1 May 1865

3 My fellow citizens, the President is dead, but the Government lives and God Omnipotent reigns.
James A. Garfield (1831–81) US statesman. Speech following the assassination of Lincoln.

4 They really are bad shots.
Charles De Gaulle (1890–1970) French general and statesman. Remark after narrowly escaping death in an assassination attempt. *Ten First Ladies of the World* (Pauline Frederick)

5 Will no one rid me of this turbulent priest?
Henry II (1133–89) King of England. Referring to Thomas Becket, Archbishop of Canterbury; four of Henry's household knights took these words literally, hurried to Canterbury, and killed Becket in the cathedral (Dec 1170) Attrib.

6 A piece of each of us died at that moment.
Michael J. Mansfield (1903–) US senator. Referring to the assassination (22 Nov 1963) of President Kennedy. Speech, Senate, 24 Nov 1963

7 Assassination is the extreme form of censorship.
George Bernard Shaw (1856–1950) Irish dramatist and critic. *The Shewing-Up of Blanco Posnet*, 'The Limits of Toleration'

8 This was the day I was meant not to see.
Margaret Thatcher (1925–) British politician and prime minister. On her feelings the Sunday after she had escaped death in the IRA bomb explosion at the Grand Hotel, Brighton. TV interview, Oct 1984

ASTRONOMY

See also moon, space, stars, sun, universe

1 There is one glory of the sun, and another glory of the moon, and another glory of the stars: for one star differeth from another star in glory.
Bible: I Corinthians 15:41–42

2 ... in my studies of astronomy and philosophy I hold this opinion about the universe, that the Sun remains fixed in the centre of the circle of heavenly bodies, without changing its place; and the Earth, turning upon itself, moves round the Sun.
Galileo Galilei (1564–1642) Italian scientist. Letter to Cristina di Lorena, 1615

3 *Eppur si muove.*
Yet it moves.
Galileo Galilei Referring to the Earth. Remark supposedly made after his recantation (1632) of belief in the Copernican system. Attrib.

4 Astronomy teaches the correct use of the sun and the planets.
Stephen Leacock (1869–1944) English-born Canadian economist and humorist. *Literary Lapses*, 'A Manual of Education'

ATHEISM

See also God, religion

1 An atheist is one point beyond the devil.
Proverb

2 God never wrought miracle to convince atheism, because his ordinary works convince it.
Francis Bacon (1561–1626) English philosopher. *Essays*, 'Of Atheism'

3 For none deny there is a God, but those for whom it maketh that there were no God.
Francis Bacon *Essays*, 'Of Atheism'

4 An atheist is a man who has no invisible means of support.
John Buchan (1875–1940) British politician and writer. Attrib.

5 I am an atheist still, thank God.
Luis Buñuel (1900–83) Spanish film director. *Luis Buñuel: an Introduction* (Ado Kyrou)

6 Wandering in a vast forest at night, I have only a faint light to guide me. A stranger appears and says to me: 'My friend, you should blow out your candle in order to find your way more clearly.' This stranger is a theologian.
Denis Diderot (1713–84) French writer. *Addition aux Pensées philosophiques*

7 An atheist is a man who has no invisible means of support.
Harry Emerson Fosdick (1878–1969) US baptist minister. Attrib.

8 Perhaps if I wanted to be understood or to understand I would bamboozle myself into belief, but I am a reporter; God exists only for leader-writers.
Graham Greene (1904–) British novelist. *The Quiet American*

9 If you don't find a God by five o'clock this afternoon you must leave the college.
Benjamin Jowett (1817–93) British theologian. Responding to a conceited young student's assertion that he could find no evidence for a God. Attrib.

10 I have no need of that hypothesis.
Marquis de Laplace (1749–1827) French mathematician and astronomer. On being asked by Napoleon why he had made no mention of God in his book about the universe, *Mécanique céleste*. *Men of Mathematics* (E. Bell)

11 He was an embittered atheist (the sort of atheist who does not so much disbelieve in God as personally dislike Him).
George Orwell (Eric Blair; 1903–50) British novelist. *Down and Out in Paris and London*, Ch. 30

12 It has been said that the highest praise of God consists in the denial of Him by the atheist, who finds creation so perfect that he can dispense with a creator.
Marcel Proust (1871–1922) French novelist. *À la recherche du temps perdu: Le Côté de Guermantes*

13 The worst moment for an atheist is when he feels grateful and doesn't know who to thank.
Wendy Ward Attrib.

14 By night an atheist half believes a God.
Edward Young (1683–1765) British poet. *Night Thoughts*

AUDEN, W(ystan) H(ugh)

(1907–73) British poet; professor of poetry at Oxford University (1956–61). Auden made his name in the 1930s.

Quotations about Auden

1 We have one poet of genius in Auden who is able to write prolifically, carelessly and exquisitely, nor does he seem to have to pay any price for his inspiration.
Cyril Connolly (1903–74) British journalist. *Enemies of Promise*

2 The high watermark, so to speak,

of Socialist literature is W. H. Auden, a sort of gutless Kipling.
George Orwell (Eric Blair; 1903–50) British novelist. *The Road to Wigan Pier*

Quotations by Auden

3 Yet no one hears his own remarks as prose.
At a Party

4 Political history is far too criminal and pathological to be a fit subject of study for the young. Children should acquire their heroes and villains from fiction.
A Certain World

·5 All sin tends to be addictive, and the terminal point of addiction is what is called damnation.
A Certain World

6 Happy the hare at morning, for she cannot read
The Hunter's waking thoughts.
The Dog Beneath the Skin (with Christopher Isherwood)

7 When I find myself in the company of scientists, I feel like a shabby curate who has strayed by mistake into a drawing-room full of dukes.
The Dyer's Hand

8 The true men of action in our time, those who transform the world, are not the politicians and statesmen, but the scientists. Unfortunately, poetry cannot celebrate them, because their deeds are concerned with things, not persons and are, therefore, speechless.
The Dyer's Hand

9 Man is a history-making creature who can neither repeat his past nor leave it behind.
The Dyer's Hand, 'D. H. Lawrence'

10 Some books are undeservedly forgotten; none are undeservedly remembered.
The Dyer's Hand, 'Reading'

11 No poet or novelist wishes he were the only one who ever lived, but most of them wish they were the only one alive, and quite a number fondly believe their wish has been granted.
The Dyer's Hand, 'Writing'

12 Let us honour if we can
The vertical man
Though we value none
But the horizontal one.
Epigraph for Poems

13 To save your world you asked this man to die:
Would this man, could he see you now, ask why?
Epitaph for an Unknown Soldier

14 Alone, alone, about the dreadful wood
Of conscious evil runs a lost mankind,
Dreading to find its Father.
For the Time Being, 'Chorus'

15 To us he is no more a person
Now but a climate of opinion
In Memory of Sigmund Freud

16 Now Ireland has her madness and her weather still,
For poetry makes nothing happen.
In Memory of W. B. Yeats, II

17 Earth, receive an honoured guest:
William Yeats is laid to rest.
Let the Irish vessel lie
Emptied of its poetry.
In Memory of W. B. Yeats, III

18 It is time for the destruction of error.
The chairs are being brought in from the garden,
The summer talk stopped on that savage coast
Before the storms.
It is time

19 Look, stranger, at this island now
The leaping light for your delight discovers.
Look, Stranger

20 Lay your sleeping head, my love,
Human on my faithless arm.
Lullaby

21 To the man-in-the-street, who, I'm sorry to say
Is a keen observer of life,
The word Intellectual suggests straight away
A man who's untrue to his wife.
Note on Intellectuals

22 God bless the USA, so large,
So friendly, and so rich.
On the Circuit

23 Only those in the last stage of disease could believe that children are true judges of character.
The Orators, 'Journal of an Airman'

24 My Dear One is mine as mirrors are lonely.
The Sea and the Mirror

25 Their fate must always be the same as yours,
To suffer the loss they were afraid of, yes,
Holders of one position, wrong for years.
Since you are going to begin today

26 When it comes, will it come without warning
Just as I'm picking my nose?
Will it knock on my door in the morning,
Or tread in the bus on my toes?
Will it come like a change in the weather?
Will its greeting be courteous or rough?
Will it alter my life altogether?
O tell me the truth about love.
Twelve Songs, XII

27 Our researchers into Public Opinion are content
That he held the proper opinions for the time of year;
When there was peace, he was for peace; when there was war, he went.
The Unknown Citizen

28 If there are any of you at the back who do not hear me, please don't raise your hands because I am also nearsighted.
Starting a lecture in a large hall. In *Book of the Month Club News*, Dec 1946

29 A professor is one who talks in someone else's sleep.
Attrib.

AUDIENCES

1 Long experience has taught me that in England nobody goes to the theatre unless he or she has bronchitis.
James Agate (1877–1947) British theater critic. *See also* Artur SCHNABEL *Ego*, 6

2 Busy yourselves with *this*, you damned walruses, while the rest of us proceed with the libretto.
John Barrymore (1882–1942) US actor. Throwing a fish to a noisy audience. *Try and Stop Me* (B. Cerf)

3 There are two golden rules for an orchestra: start together and finish together. The public doesn't give a damn what goes on in between.
Thomas Beecham (1879–1961) British conductor. *Beecham Stories* (H. Atkins and A. Newman)

4 Ladies and gentlemen, unless the

play is stopped, the child cannot possibly go on.

John Philip Kemble (1757–1823) British tragic actor. Announcement to the audience when the play he was in was continually interrupted by a child crying. *A Book of Anecdotes* (D. George)

5 Those in the cheaper seats clap. The rest of you rattle your jewellery.

John Lennon (1940–80) British rock musician. Remark, Royal Variety Performance, 15 Nov 1963

6 Those people on the stage are making such a noise I can't hear a word you're saying.

Henry Taylor Parker (1867–1934) US music critic. Rebuking some talkative members of an audience, near whom he was sitting. *The Humor of Music* (L. Humphrey)

7 A nice respectable, middle-class, middle-aged maiden lady, with time on her hands and the money to help her pass it . . . Let us call her Aunt Edna . . . Aunt Edna is universal, and to those who feel that all the problems of the modern theatre might be saved by her liquidation, let me add that. . . . She is also immortal.

Terence Rattigan (1911–77) British dramatist. *Collected Plays*, Vol II, Preface

8 I know two kinds of audience only – one coughing and one not coughing.

Artur Schnabel (1882–1951) Austrian concert pianist. *See also* James AGATE *My Life and Music*, Pt. II, Ch. 10

9 I quite agree with you, sir, but what can two do against so many?

George Bernard Shaw (1856–1950) Irish dramatist and critic. Responding to a solitary hiss heard amongst the applause at the first performance of *Arms and the Man* in 1894. *Oxford Book of Literary Anecdotes*

AUSTEN, Jane

(1775–1817) British novelist. Her novels of middle-class life combine humor with perceptive characterization.

Quotations about Austen

1 More can be learnt from Miss Austen about the nature of the novel than from almost any other writer.

Walter Allen (1911–) British author and literary journalist. *The English Novel*

2 That young lady has a talent for describing the involvements and feelings and characters of ordinary life which is to me the most wonderful thing I ever met with.

Walter Scott (1771–1832) Scottish novelist. *Journals*, 14 Mar 1826

3 Jane Austen's books, too, are absent from this library. Just that one omission alone would make a fairly good library out of a library that hadn't a book in it.

Mark Twain (Samuel Langhorne Clemens; 1835–1910) US writer. *Following the Equator*, Pt. II

Quotations by Austen

4 One half of the world cannot understand the pleasures of the other.

Emma, Ch. 9

5 Nobody is healthy in London, nobody can be.

Emma, Ch. 12

6 A man . . . must have a very good opinion of himself when he asks people to leave their own fireside, and encounter such a day as this, for the sake of coming to see him. He must think himself a most agreeable fellow.

Emma, Ch. 13

7 Human nature is so well disposed towards those who are in interesting situations, that a young person, who either marries or dies, is sure to be kindly spoken of.

Emma, Ch. 22

8 The sooner every party breaks up the better.

Emma, Ch. 25

9 Business, you know, may bring money, but friendship hardly ever does.

Emma, Ch. 34

10 One has no great hopes from Birmingham. I always say there is something direful in the sound.

Emma, Ch. 36

11 One of Edward's Mistresses was Jane Shore, who has had a play written about her, but it is a tragedy and therefore not worth reading.

The History of England

12 She was nothing more than a mere good-tempered, civil and obliging young woman; as such we could scarcely dislike her – she was only an Object of Contempt.

Love and Friendship

13 Let other pens dwell on guilt and misery.

Mansfield Park, Ch. 48

14 But are they all horrid, are you sure they are all horrid?

Northanger Abbey, Ch. 6

15 Oh! who can ever be tired of Bath?

Northanger Abbey, Ch. 10

16 A woman, especially if she have the misfortune of knowing anything, should conceal it as well as she can.

Northanger Abbey, Ch. 14

17 One does not love a place the less for having suffered in it unless it has all been suffering, nothing but suffering.

Persuasion, Ch. 20

18 It is a truth universally acknowledged, that a single man in possession of a good fortune must be in want of a wife.

The opening words of the book. *Pride and Prejudice*, Ch. 1

19 She was a woman of mean understanding, little information, and uncertain temper.

Pride and Prejudice, Ch. 1

20 A lady's imagination is very rapid; it jumps from admiration to love, from love to matrimony in a moment.

Pride and Prejudice, Ch. 6

21 Happiness in marriage is entirely a matter of chance.

Pride and Prejudice, Ch. 6

22 It is happy for you that you possess the talent of flattering with delicacy. May I ask whether these pleasing attentions proceed from the impulse of the moment, or are the result of previous study?

Pride and Prejudice, Ch. 14

23 You have delighted us long enough.

Pride and Prejudice, Ch. 18

24 Next to being married, a girl likes to be crossed in love a little now and then.

Pride and Prejudice, Ch. 24

25 One cannot be always laughing at a man without now and then stumbling on something witty.

Pride and Prejudice, Ch. 40

26 For what do we live, but to make sport for our neighbours, and laugh at them in our turn?

Pride and Prejudice, Ch. 57

27 I have been a selfish being all my

life, in practice, though not in principle.
Pride and Prejudice, Ch. 58

28 What dreadful hot weather we have! It keeps me in a continual state of inelegance.
Letter, 18 Sept 1796

29 Mrs Hall of Sherbourne was brought to bed yesterday of a dead child, some weeks before she expected, owing to a fright. I suppose she happened unawares to look at her husband.
Letter, 27 Oct 1798

30 I do not want people to be very agreeable, as it saves me the trouble of liking them a great deal.
Letter, 24 Dec 1798

31 We met . . . Dr Hall in such very deep mourning that either his mother, his wife, or himself must be dead.
Letter to Cassandra Austen, 17 May 1799

32 The little bit (two inches wide) of ivory on which I work with so fine a brush as produces little effect after much labour.
Letter, 16 Dec 1816

AUTHORITARIANISM

See also tyranny

1 *Roma locuta est; causa finita est.*
Rome has spoken; the case is concluded.
St Augustine of Hippo (354–430) Bishop of Hippo. *Sermons*, Bk. I

2 Then cometh the end, when he shall have delivered up the kingdom to God, even the Father; when he shall have put down all rule and all authority and power.
For he must reign, till he hath put all enemies under his feet.
The last enemy that shall be destroyed is death.
Bible: I Corinthians 15:24–26

3 And the Lord said unto Moses, Come up to me into the mount, and be there: and I will give thee tables of stone, and a law, and commandments which I have written; that thou mayest teach them.
Bible: Exodus 24:12

4 Dictators ride to and fro upon tigers which they dare not dismount. And the tigers are getting hungry.
Winston Churchill (1874–1965) British statesman. *While England Slept*

5 I will have this done, so I order it done; let my will replace reasoned judgement.
Juvenal (Decimus Junius Juvenalis; 60–130 AD) Roman satirist. *Satires*, VI

6 Big Brother is watching you.
George Orwell (Eric Blair; 1903–50) British novelist. *Nineteen Eighty-Four*

7 I am painted as the greatest little dictator, which is ridiculous – you always take some consultations.
Margaret Thatcher (1925–) British politician and prime minister. *The Times*, 1983

8 I don't mind how much my ministers talk – as long as they do what I say.
Margaret Thatcher *The Times*, 1987

9 As for being a General, well, at the age of four with paper hats and wooden swords we're all Generals. Only some of us never grow out of it.
Peter Ustinov (1921–) British actor. *Romanoff and Juliet*, I

AUTHORS

See writers

B

BABIES

See also birth, children

1 There is no finer investment for any community than putting milk into babies.
Winston Churchill (1874–1965) British statesman. Radio broadcast, 21 Mar 1943

2 There is no more sombre enemy of good art than the pram in the hall.
Cyril Connolly (1903–74) British journalist. *Enemies of Promise*, Ch. 3

3 Every baby born into the world is a finer one than the last.
Charles Dickens (1812–70) British novelist. *Nicholas Nickleby*, Ch. 36

4 Infants do not cry without some legitimate cause.
Ferrarius (16th century) *The Advancement of Child Health* (A. V. Neale)

5 Other people's babies –
That's my life!
Mother to dozens,
And nobody's wife.
A. P. Herbert (1890–1971) British writer and politician. *A Book of Ballads*, 'Other People's Babies'

6 A loud noise at one end and no sense of responsibility at the other.
Ronald Knox (1888–1957) British Roman Catholic priest. Attrib.

7 We all of us wanted babies – but did we want children?
Eda J. Leshan *How to Survive Children* (Katherine Whitehorn)

BACHELORS

1 I should like to know what is the proper function of women, if it is not to make reasons for husbands to stay at home, and still stronger reasons for bachelors to go out.
George Eliot (Mary Ann Evans; 1819–80) British novelist. *The Mill on the Floss*, Ch. 6

2 Never trust a husband too far, nor a bachelor too near.
Helen Rowland (1876–1950) US writer. *The Rubaiyat of a Bachelor*

3 Bachelor's fare; bread and cheese, and kisses.
Jonathan Swift (1667–1745) Irish-born Anglican priest and writer. *Polite Conversation*, Dialogue 1

BALDNESS

1 The most delightful advantage of being bald – one can hear snowflakes.
R. G. Daniels (1916–) British magistrate. *The Observer*, 'Sayings of the Week', 11 July 1976

BANKHEAD, Tallulah

(1903–68) US actress, famous for her extravagant lifestyle.

Quotations about Bankhead

1 More of an act than an actress.
Anonymous

2 She was always a star, but only intermittently a good actress.
Brendan Gill *The Times*, 4 Aug 1973

3 She was an open, wayward, free, cosmopolitan, liberated, sensuous human being. In thus systematically invading her own privacy she was the first of the modern personalities.
Lee Israel *Miss Tallulah Bankhead*

Quotations by Bankhead

4 I have three phobias which, could I mute them, would make my life as slick as a sonnet, but as dull as ditch water: I hate to go to bed, I hate to get up, and I hate to be alone.
Tallulah, Ch. 1

5 It's one of the tragic ironies of the theater that only one man in it can count on steady work – the night watchman.
Tallulah, Ch. 1

6 I've been called many things, but never an intellectual.
Tallulah, Ch. 15

7 Cocaine isn't habit-forming. I should know – I've been using it for years.
Pentimento (Lillian Hellman), 'Theatre'

8 There is less in this than meets the eye.
Referring to a revival of a play by Maeterlink. *Shouts and Murmurs* (A. Woollcott), 'Capsule Criticism'

9 Don't bother to thank me. I know what a perfectly ghastly season it's been for you Spanish dancers.
Said on dropping fifty dollars into a tambourine held out by a Salvation Army collector. *With Malice Toward All* (D. Hermann)

10 I'm as pure as the driven slush.
The Observer, 'Sayings of the Week', 24 Feb 1957

11 Only good girls keep diaries. Bad girls don't have the time.
Attrib.

BANKS

See also money

1 Banks lend you money as people lend you an umbrella when the sun is shining and want it back when it starts to rain.
Edward Beddington-Behrens (?–1968) *Look Back – Look Forward*, 1963

2 I don't trust a bank that would lend money to such a poor risk.
Robert Benchley (1889–1945) US humorist. To a bank that granted his request for a loan. Attrib.

3 Straighteners, managers and cashiers of the Musical Banks.
Samuel Butler (1835–1902) British writer. *Erewhon*, Ch. 9

4 It is better that a man should tyrannize over his bank balance than over his fellow citizens.
John Maynard Keynes (1883–1946) British economist. *The General Theory of Employment, Interest and Money*, Bk. VI, Ch. 24

5 I cried all the way to the bank.
Liberace (Wladzin Valentino Liberace; 1919–87) US pianist and showman. Said when asked whether he minded being criticized. *Liberace: An Autobiography*, Ch. 2

6 A pleasant old buffer, nephew to a lord,
Who believed that the bank was mightier than the sword,
And that an umbrella might pacify barbarians abroad:
Just like an old liberal
Between the wars.
William Plomer (1903–73) South African poet and novelist. *Father and Son: 1939*

BASEBALL

1 It was not very wonderful that Catherine . . . should prefer cricket, base ball . . . to books.
Jane Austen (1775–1817) British novelist. The first recorded reference to baseball. *Northanger Abbey*, Ch. 3

2 Nice guys finish last.
Leo Durocher (1905–) US baseball player. Reply when asked whether he felt sorry to have beaten such a 'nice bunch of guys' as the New York Giants. Attrib.

3 Well, this year I'm told the team did well because one pitcher had a fine curve ball. I understand that a curve ball is thrown with a deliberate attempt to deceive. Surely that is not an ability we should want to foster at Harvard.
Charles William Eliot (1834–1926) US educator; president of Harvard (1869–1909). Reply when asked why he wished to drop baseball as a college sport. Attrib.

4 Well, that kind of puts the damper on even a Yankee win.
Phil Rizzuto (1918–) US sports commentator. Remark, while commentating on a baseball game involving the New York Yankees, on hearing that Pope Paul VI had died. Attrib.

5 Hello, Joe? It's Frank. Giants three, Dodgers nothing.
Franklin D. Roosevelt (1882–1945) US Democratic president. Telephone call to Joseph Stalin. Attrib. in *The Faber Book of Anecdotes* (where it is said to be 'almost surely apocryphal')

6 That last one sounded kinda high to me.
Babe Ruth (1895–1948) US baseball player. Questioning the umpire about three fast pitches that he had not seen. Attrib.

7 I know, but I had a better year.
Babe Ruth Reply when a club official objected that the salary he was demanding was greater than the US president's. Attrib.

8 Managing is getting paid for home runs someone else hits.
Casey Stengel (1890–1975) US baseball manager. Attrib.

BEAUTY

See also admiration, appearance, compliments

1 A good face is a letter of recommendation.
Proverb

2 Beauty is only skin-deep.
Proverb

3 Beauty is potent but money is omnipotent.
Proverb

4 Small is beautiful.
Proverb

5 My Love in her attire doth show her wit,
It doth so well become her:
For every season she hath dressings fit,
For winter, spring, and summer.
No beauty she doth miss,
When all her robes are on;
But beauty's self she is,
When all her robes are gone.
Anonymous Madrigal

6 There is no excellent beauty that hath not some strangeness in the proportion.
Francis Bacon (1561–1626) English philosopher. *Essays*, 'Of Beauty'

7 Beauty and the lust for learning have yet to be allied.
Max Beerbohm (1872–1956) British writer. *Zuleika Dobson*, Ch. 7

8 Exuberance is Beauty.

William Blake (1757–1827) British poet. *The Marriage of Heaven and Hell*, 'Proverbs of Hell'

9 For beauty being the best of all we know
Sums up the unsearchable and secret aims
Of nature.

Robert Bridges (1844–1930) British poet. *The Growth of Love*

10 Beauty sat with me all the summer day,
Awaiting the sure triumph of her eye;
Nor mark'd I till we parted, how, hard by,
Love in her train stood ready for his prey.

Robert Bridges *The Growth of Love*

11 Incredibly, inordinately, devastatingly, immortally, calamitously, hearteningly, adorably beautiful.

Rupert Brooke (1887–1915) British) poet. Referring to the actress Cathleen Nesbitt. *Rupert Brooke* (C. Hassall)

12 It is better to be first with an ugly woman than the hundredth with a beauty.

Pearl Buck (1892–1973) US novelist. *The Good Earth*, Ch. 1

13 Beauty in distress is much the most affecting beauty.

Edmund Burke (1729–97) British politician. *On the Sublime and Beautiful*, Pt. III

14 She walks in beauty, like the night
Of cloudless climes and starry skies;
And all that's best of dark and bright
Meet in her aspect and her eyes.

Lord Byron (1788–1824) British poet. *She Walks in Beauty*

15 SONYA. I'm not beautiful.
HELEN. You have lovely hair.
SONYA. No, when a woman isn't beautiful, people always say, 'You have lovely eyes, you have lovely hair.'

Anton Chekhov (1860–1904) Russian dramatist. *Uncle Vanya*, III

16 There is nothing ugly; *I never saw an ugly thing in my life:* for let the form of an object be what it may, – light, shade, and perspective will always make it beautiful.

John Constable (1776–1837) British landscape painter. Letter to John Fisher, 23 Oct 1821

17 Love built on beauty, soon as beauty, dies.

John Donne (1573–1631) English poet. *Elegies*, 2, 'The Anagram'

18 One girl can be pretty – but a dozen are only a chorus.

F. Scott Fitzgerald (1896–1940) US novelist. *The Last Tycoon*

19 Against the beautiful and the clever and the successful, one can wage a pitiless war, but not against the unattractive.

Graham Greene (1904–) British novelist. *The Heart of the Matter*

20 Glory be to God for dappled things –
For skies of couple-colour as a brinded cow;
For rose-moles all in stipple upon trout that swim.

Gerard Manley Hopkins (1844–99) British Jesuit and poet. *Pied Beauty*

21 Beauty in things exists in the mind which contemplates them.

David Hume (1711–76) Scottish philosopher. *Essays*, 'Of Tragedy'

22 Beauty is altogether in the eye of the beholder.

Margaret Wolfe Hungerford (c. 1855–97) Irish novelist. Also attributed to the US soldier and writer Lew Wallace (1827–1905). *Molly Bawn*

23 A thing of beauty is a joy for ever:
Its loveliness increases; it will never
Pass into nothingness; but still will keep
A bower quiet for us, and a sleep
Full of sweet dreams, and health, and quiet breathing.

John Keats (1795–1821) British poet. *Endymion*, I

24 'Beauty is truth, truth beauty,' – that is all
Ye know on earth, and all ye need to know.

John Keats *Ode on a Grecian Urn*

25 Was this the face that launch'd a thousand ships
And burnt the topless towers of Ilium?
Sweet Helen, make me immortal with a kiss.

Christopher Marlowe (1564–93) English dramatist. *Doctor Faustus*, V:1

26 Oh, thou art fairer than the evening air
Clad in the beauty of a thousand stars.

Christopher Marlowe *Doctor Faustus*, V:1

27 You're the most beautiful woman I've ever seen, which doesn't say much for you.

Groucho Marx (Julius Marx; 1895–1977) US comedian. *Animal Crackers*

28 Beauty stands
In the admiration only of weak minds
Led captive.

John Milton (1608–74) English poet. *Paradise Regained*, Bk. II

29 I hate that aesthetic game of the eye and the mind, played by these connoisseurs, these mandarins who 'appreciate' beauty. What *is* beauty, anyway? There's no such thing. I never 'appreciate', any more than I 'like'. I love or I hate.

Pablo Picasso (1881–1973) Spanish painter. *Life with Picasso* (Françoise Gilot and Carlton Lake), Ch. 2

30 And when I told them how beautiful you are
They didn't believe me! They didn't believe me!

M. E. Rourke (20th century) US songwriter and lyricist. *They Didn't Believe Me* (song)

31 There are no ugly women, only lazy ones.

Helena Rubinstein (1882–1965) Polish-born US cosmetics manufacturer. *My Life for Beauty*, Pt. II, Ch. 1

32 All she has to do is to walk around and about Georgie White's stage with only a few light bandages on, and everybody considers her very beautiful, especially from the neck down.

Damon Runyon (1884–1946) US writer. *Furthermore*, 'A Very Honourable Guy'

33 Remember that the most beautiful things in the world are the most useless, peacocks and lilies for instance.

John Ruskin (1819–1900) British art critic and writer. *The Stones of Venice*, Vol. I, Ch. 2

34 I always say beauty is only sin deep.

Saki (Hector Hugh Munro; 1870–1916) British writer. *Reginald's Choir Treat*

35 Beauty too rich for use, for earth too dear.

William Shakespeare (1564–1616) English dramatist. *Romeo and Juliet*, I:5

36 From fairest creatures we desire increase,
That thereby beauty's rose might never die.

William Shakespeare *Sonnet 1*

37 Beauty itself doth of itself persuade
The eyes of men without an orator.

William Shakespeare *The Rape of Lucrece*, I

38 For she was beautiful – her beauty made

The bright world dim, and everything beside
Seemed like the fleeting image of a shade.
Percy Bysshe Shelley (1792–1822) British poet. *The Witch of Atlas*, XII

39 Health is beauty, and the most perfect health is the most perfect beauty.
William Shenstone (1714–63) English poet. *Essays on Men and Manners*, 'On Taste'

40 Half light, half shade,
She stood, a sight to make an old man young.
Alfred, Lord Tennyson (1809–92) British poet. *The Gardener's Daughter*

41 But Lancelot mused a little space;
He said, 'She has a lovely face;
God in his mercy lend her grace,
The Lady of Shalott.'
Alfred, Lord Tennyson *The Lady of Shalott*, Pt. IV

42 A woman of so shining loveliness
That men threshed corn at midnight by a tress,
A little stolen tress.
W. B. Yeats (1865–1939) Irish poet. *The Secret Rose*

43 All changed, changed utterly:
A terrible beauty is born.
W. B. Yeats *Easter 1916*

BED

See also idleness, rest, sleep

1 Early to bed and early to rise, makes a man healthy, wealthy and wise.
Proverb

2 Go to bed with the lamb, and rise with the lark.
Proverb

3 It isn't the ecstatic leap across that I deplore, it's the weary trudge home.
Anonymous Referring to single beds.

4 The cool kindliness of sheets, that soon
Smooth away trouble; and the rough male kiss of blankets.
Rupert Brooke (1887–1915) British) poet. *The Great Lover*

5 I'm Burlington Bertie:
I rise at ten-thirty.
W. F. Hargreaves (1846–1919) British songwriter. *Burlington Bertie*

6 I have, all my life long, been lying till noon; yet I tell all young men, and tell them with great sincerity, that nobody who does not rise early will ever do any good.
Samuel Johnson (1709–84) British lexicographer. *Tour to the Hebrides* (J. Boswell)

7 O! it's nice to get up in the mornin',
But it's nicer to stay in bed.
Harry Lauder (Hugh MacLennon; 1870–1950) Scottish music-hall artist. Song

8 Believe me, you have to get up early if you want to get out of bed.
Groucho Marx (Julius Marx; 1895–1977) US comedian. *The Cocoanuts*

9 It was such a lovely day I thought it was a pity to get up.
W. Somerset Maugham (1874–1965) British novelist. *Our Betters*, II

10 And so to bed.
Samuel Pepys (1633–1703) English diarist. *Diary*, 6 May 1660 and *passim*

11 Not to be abed after midnight is to be up betimes.
William Shakespeare (1564–1616) English dramatist. *Twelfth Night*, II:3

12 Early to rise and early to bed makes a male healthy and wealthy and dead.
James Thurber (1894–1961) US humorist. *Fables for Our Time*, 'The Shrike and the Chipmunks'

BEERBOHM, Sir Max

(1872–1936) British writer and caricaturist. His only novel, *Zuleika Dobson* (1911), is set in Oxford.

Quotations about Beerbohm

1 The Incomparable Max.
George Bernard Shaw (1856–1950) Irish dramatist and critic. *Dramatic Opinions and Essays*, Vol. II

2 He has the most remarkable and seductive genius – and I should say about the smallest in the world.
Lytton Strachey (1880–1932) British writer. Letter to Clive Bell, 4 Dec 1917

Quotations by Beerbohm

3 There is always something rather absurd about the past.
1880

4 To give an accurate and exhaustive account of that period would need a far less brilliant pen than mine.
1880

5 Great men are but life-sized. Most of them, indeed, are rather short.
And Even Now

6 I believe the twenty-four hour day has come to stay.
A Christmas Garland, 'Perkins and Mankind'

7 Most women are not so young as they are painted.
A Defence of Cosmetics

8 Anything that is worth doing has been done frequently. Things hitherto undone should be given, I suspect, a wide berth.
Mainly on the Air

9 It is Oxford that has made me insufferable.
More, 'Going back to School'

10 The lower one's vitality, the more sensitive one is to great art.
Seven Men, 'Enoch Soames'

11 The dullard's envy of brilliant men is always assuaged by the suspicion that they will come to a bad end.
Zuleika Dobson

12 It needs no dictionary of quotations to remind me that the eyes are the windows of the soul.
Zuleika Dobson, Ch. 4

13 Women who love the same man have a kind of bitter freemasonry.
Zuleika Dobson, Ch. 4

14 You will find that the woman who is really kind to dogs is always one who has failed to inspire sympathy in men.
Zuleika Dobson, Ch. 6

15 Beauty and the lust for learning have yet to be allied.
Zuleika Dobson, Ch. 7

16 You will think me lamentably crude: my experience of life has been drawn from life itself.
Zuleika Dobson, Ch. 7

17 You cannot make a man by standing a sheep on its hind legs. But by standing a flock of sheep in that position you can make a crowd of men.
Zuleika Dobson, Ch. 9

18 She was one of the people who say, 'I don't know anything about music really, but I know what I like'.
Zuleika Dobson, Ch. 16

19 It's not in support of cricket but as an earnest protest against golf.
Said when giving a shilling towards W. G. Grace's testimonial. *Carr's Dictionary of Extraordinary English Cricketers*

20 Of course we all know that Morris was a wonderful all-round man, but the act of walking round him has always tired me.
Referring to William Morris. *Conversations with Max* (S. N. Behrman)

21 They were a tense and peculiar family, the Oedipuses, weren't they?
Max: A Biography (D. Cecil)

22 What were they going to do with the Grail when they found it, Mr Rossetti?
Caption to a cartoon

BEGINNING

See also prophecy

1 From small beginnings come great things.
Proverb

2 Great oaks from little acorns grow.
Proverb

3 The first step is the hardest.
Proverb

4 No task is a long one but the task on which one dare not start. It becomes a nightmare.
Charles Baudelaire (1821–67) French poet. *My Heart Laid Bare*

5 She looked at him, as one who awakes:
The past was a sleep, and her life began.
Robert Browning (1812–89) British poet. *The Statue and the Bust*

6 The distance doesn't matter; it is only the first step that is difficult.
Marquise du Deffand (Marie de Vichy-Chamrond; 1697–1780) French noblewoman. Referring to the legend of St Denis, who is traditionally believed to have carried his severed head for six miles after his execution. Letter to d'Alembert, 7 July 1763

7 In my beginning is my end.
T. S. Eliot (1888–1965) American-born poet. *Four Quartets*, 'East Coker'

8 With the possible exception of the equator, everything begins somewhere.
Peter Fleming (1907–71) British travel writer. *One's Company*, 1934

9 From today and from this place there begins a new epoch in the history of the world.
Goethe (1749–1832) German poet and dramatist. On witnessing the victory of the French at the battle of Valmy. *The Story of Civilization* (W. Durant), Vol. II

10 'Tis always morning somewhere in the world.
Richard Henry Horne (1803–84) English writer. *Orion*, Bk III, Ch. 2

11 There is an old saying 'well begun is half done' – 'tis a bad one. I would use instead – Not begun at all until half done.
John Keats (1795–1821) British poet. Letter, 1817

12 We stand today on the edge of a new frontier.
John Fitzgerald Kennedy (1917–63) US statesman. Said on his nomination as Presidential candidate. Speech, Democratic Party Convention, 15 July 1960

13 Are you sitting comfortably? Then I'll begin.
Julia S. Lang (1921–) British broadcaster. Introduction to the story in the British children's radio program *Listen with Mother*.

14 If you really want to hear about it, the first thing you'll probably want to know is where I was born and what my lousy childhood was like, and how my parents were occupied and all before they had me, and all that David Copperfield kind of crap.
J. D. Salinger (1919–) US novelist. The opening words of the book. *The Catcher in the Rye*

BELIEF

See also faith

1 Believe nothing of what you hear, and only half of what you see.
Proverb

2 Seeing is believing.
Proverb

3 A cause is like champagne and high heels – one must be prepared to suffer for it.
Arnold Bennett (1867–1931) British novelist. *The Title*

4 Vain are the thousand creeds
That move men's hearts: unutterably vain;
Worthless as wither'd weeds.
Emily Brontë (1818–48) British novelist. *Last Lines*

5 If Jesus Christ were to come today, people would not even crucify him. They would ask him to dinner, and hear what he had to say, and make fun of it.
Thomas Carlyle (1795–1881) Scottish historian and essayist. *Carlyle at his Zenith* (D. A. Wilson)

6 *Action will furnish belief*, – but will that belief be the true one?
This is the point, you know.
Arthur Hugh Clough (1819–61) British poet. *Amours de voyage*, V

7 I believe firmly what I read in the holy Scriptures, and the Creed, called the Apostles', and I don't trouble my head any farther: I leave the rest to be disputed and defined by the clergy, if they please; and if any Thing is in common use with Christians that is not repugnant to the holy Scriptures, I observe it for this Reason, that I may not offend other people.
Erasmus (c. 1467–1536) Dutch humanist. Commenting on the teachings of John Colet. *The Colloquies of Erasmus*, Vol. I

8 The true believer is in a high degree protected against the danger of certain neurotic afflictions; by accepting the universal neurosis he is spared the task of forming a personal neurosis.
Sigmund Freud (1856–1939) Austrian psychoanalyst. *The Future of an Illusion*, Ch. 8

9 There seems to be a terrible misunderstanding on the part of a great many people to the effect that when you cease to believe you may cease to behave.
Louis Kronenberger (1904–80) US writer and literary critic. *Company Manners*

10 Believe it or not.
R. L. Ripley (1893–1949) US writer. Title of newspaper column

11 I believe because it is impossible.
Tertullian (c. 160–225 AD) Carthaginian father of the church. The usual misquotation of 'It is certain because it is impossible.' *De Carne Christi*, V

12 All right, have it your way – you heard a seal bark.
James Thurber (1894–1961) US humorist. Cartoon caption, 'The Seal in the Bedroom'

13 If there were a verb meaning 'to believe falsely', it would not have any significant first person, present indicative.
Ludwig Wittgenstein (1889–1951) Austrian philosopher. *A Certain World* (W. H. Auden)

BELLOC, (Joseph) Hilaire (Pierre)

(1870–1953) French-born British poet, essayist, and historian; Liberal MP for Salford (1906–10). Publications include *Cautionary Tales* (1907) and biographies of major historical figures. He was an ardent Roman Catholic.

Quotations about Belloc

1 He cannot bear isolation or final ethical responsibility; he clings to the Roman Catholic Church; he clung to his French nationality because one nation was not enough for him.

George Bernard Shaw (1856–1950) Irish dramatist and critic. *Lives of the Wits* (H. Pearson)

2 He is conscious of being decrepit and forgetful, but not of being a bore.

Evelyn Waugh (1903–66) British novelist. Diary, 1 May 1945

Quotations by Belloc

3 Child! do not throw this book about;
Refrain from the unholy pleasure
Of cutting all the pictures out!
Preserve it as your chiefest treasure.

The Bad Child's Book of Beasts, 'Dedication'

4 Alas! That such affected tricks
Should flourish in a child of six!

Cautionary Tales, 'Godolphin Horne'

5 The Chief Defect of Henry King
Was chewing little bits of String.

Cautionary Tales, 'Henry King'

6 'Oh, my Friends, be warned by me,
That Breakfast, Dinner, Lunch and Tea
Are all the Human Frame requires . . .'
With that the Wretched Child expires.

Cautionary Tales, 'Henry King'

7 A trick that everyone abhors
In little girls is slamming doors.

Cautionary Tales, 'Rebecca'

8 They died to save their country and they only saved the world.

The English Graves

9 The accursed power which stands on Privilege
(And goes with Women, and Champagne, and Bridge)
Broke – and Democracy resumed her reign:
(Which goes with Bridge, and Women and Champagne).

Epigrams, 'On a Great Election'

10 When I am dead, I hope it may be said:
'His sins were scarlet, but his books were read.'

Epigrams, 'On His Books'

11 I'm tired of Love: I'm still more tired of Rhyme.
But Money gives me pleasure all the Time.

Fatigue

12 Whatever happens, we have got
The Maxim Gun, and they have not.

Referring to African natives. *The Modern Traveller*

13 The Microbe is so very small
You cannot make him out at all.

More Beasts for Worse Children, 'The Microbe'

14 Like many of the upper class
He liked the sound of broken glass.

New Cautionary Tales, 'About John'

15 The fleas that tease in the high Pyrenees.

Tarantella

16 I always like to associate with a lot of priests because it makes me understand anti-clerical things so well.

Letter to E. S. P. Haynes, 9 Nov 1909

17 I am a Catholic. As far as possible I go to Mass every day. As far as possible I kneel down and tell these beads every day. If you reject me on account of my religion, I shall thank God that he has spared me the indignity of being your representative.

Said in his first election campaign. Speech, Salford, 1906

18 Candidates should not attempt more than six of these.

Suggested addition to the Ten Commandments. Attrib.

BENNETT, (Enoch) Arnold

(1867–1931) British novelist. His novels, set in his native Staffordshire, include *Anna of the Five Towns* (1902) and *Clayhanger* (1910).

Quotations about Bennett

1 Bennett – a sort of pig in clover.

D. H. Lawrence (1885–1930) British novelist. Letter to Aldous Huxley, 27 Mar 1928

2 I remember that once, beating his knee with his clenched fist to force the words through his writhing lips, he said, 'I am a nice man.' He was.

W. Somerset Maugham (1874–1965) British novelist. *The Vagrant Mood*

Quotations by Bennett

3 'Ye can call it influenza if ye like,' said Mrs Machin. 'There was no influenza in my young days. We called a cold a cold.'

The Card, Ch. 8

4 The people who live in the past must yield to the people who live in the future. Otherwise the world would begin to turn the other way round.

Milestones

5 Pessimism, when you get used to it, is just as agreeable as optimism.

Things that have Interested Me, 'The Slump in Pessimism'

6 Well, my deliberate opinion is – it's a jolly strange world.

The Title, I

7 Being a husband is a whole-time job. That is why so many husbands fail. They cannot give their entire attention to it.

The Title, I

8 Journalists say a thing that they know isn't true, in the hope that if they keep on saying it long enough it will be true.

The Title, II

9 Good taste is better than bad taste, but bad taste is better than no taste.

The Observer, 'Sayings of the Week', 24 Aug 1930

BEQUESTS

1 When you have told anyone you have left him a legacy the only decent thing to do is to die at once.

Samuel Butler (1835–1902) British writer. *Samuel Butler: A Memoir* (Festing Jones), Vol. 2

2 I'm sorry to hear that, sir, you don't happen to have the shilling about you now, do you?

Tom Sheridan (1775–1817) Son of the dramatist Richard Brinsley Sheridan. To his father, on being told that he was to be cut off in his will with a shilling. *The Fine Art of Political Wit* (L. Harris)

3 The man who leaves money to charity in his will is only giving

away what no longer belongs to him.

Voltaire (François-Marie Arouet; 1694–1778) French writer. Letter, 1769

BETJEMAN, Sir John

(1906–84) British poet; poet laureate (1972–84). Publications include *Collected Poems* (1958), *High and Low* (1976), and a verse autobiography, *Summoned by Bells* (1960).

Quotations about Betjeman

1 By appointment: Teddy Bear to the Nation.

Alan Bell *The Times,* 20 Sept 1982

2 You've no idea how original it was to write like Tennyson in the 1930s, rather than Eliot or Auden.

Lord David Cecil (1902–86) British writer and critic. Remark

3 We invite people like that to tea, but we don't marry them.

Lady Chetwode Lady Chetwode later became Betjeman's mother-in-law. Remark

Quotations by Betjeman

4 Spirits of well-shot woodcock, partridge, snipe
Flutter and bear him up the Norfolk sky.

Death of King George V

5 You ask me what it is I do. Well actually, you know,
I'm partly a liaison man and partly P.R.O.
Essentially I integrate the current export drive
And basically I'm viable from ten o'clock till five.

Executive

6 Phone for the fish knives Norman,
As Cook is a little unnerved;
You kiddies have crumpled the serviettes
And I must have things daintily served.

How to get on in Society

7 I know what I wanted to ask you;
Is trifle sufficient for sweet?

How to get on in Society

8 Rumbling under blackened girders,
Midland, bound for Cricklewood,
Puffed its sulphur to the sunset
where the Land of Laundries stood.
Rumble under, thunder over, train and tram alternate go.

Parliament Hill Fields

9 Come, friendly bombs, and fall on Slough
It isn't fit for humans now.
There isn't grass to graze a cow
Swarm over, Death!
. . .
Come, friendly bombs, and fall on Slough
To get it ready for the plough.
The cabbages are coming now:
The earth exhales.

Slough

10 Miss J. Hunter Dunn, Miss J. Hunter Dunn,
Furnish'd and burnish'd by Aldershot sun.

A Subaltern's Love Song

BETRAYAL

See also treason

1 And he answered and said, He that dippeth his hand with me in the dish, the same shall betray me.
The Son of man goeth as it is written of him: but woe unto that man by whom the Son of man is betrayed! it had been good for that man if he had not been born.
Then Judas, which betrayed him, answered and said, Master, is it I? He said unto him, Thou hast said.

Bible: Matthew 26:23–25

2 Jesus said unto him, Verily I say unto thee, That this night, before the cock crow, thou shalt deny me thrice.
Peter said unto him, Though I should die with thee, yet will I not deny thee. Likewise also said all the disciples.

Bible: Matthew 26:34–35

3 And forthwith he came to Jesus, and said, Hail, master; and kissed him.
And Jesus said unto him, Friend, wherefore art thou come? Then came they, and laid hands on Jesus, and took him.

Bible: Matthew 26:49–50

4 Then Judas, which had betrayed him, when he saw that he was condemned, repented himself, and brought again the thirty pieces of silver to the chief priests and elders,
Saying, I have sinned in that I have betrayed the innocent blood. And they said, What is that to us? see thou to that.

Bible: Matthew 27:3–4

5 Just for a handful of silver he left us,
Just for a riband to stick in his coat.

Robert Browning (1812–89) British poet. *The Lost Leader*

6 It is all right to rat, but you can't re-rat.

Winston Churchill (1874–1965) British statesman. Attrib.

7 I hate the idea of causes, and if I had to choose between betraying my country and betraying my friend, I hope I should have the guts to betray my country.

E. M. Forster (1879–1970) British novelist. *Two Cheers for Democracy,* 'What I Believe'.

8 I'm waiting for the cock to crow.

William Morris Hughes (1864–1952) Australian statesman. Said in parliament, after being viciously critized by a member of his own party. *The Fine Art of Political Wit* (L. Harris)

9 He . . . felt towards those whom he had deserted that peculiar malignity which has, in all ages, been characteristic of apostates.

Lord Macaulay (1800–59) British historian. *History of England,* Vol. I, Ch. 1

10 I owe you everything, Sire, but I believe I can pay some of my debt with this gift – Colbert.

Cardinal Mazarin (1602–61) Italian-born French statesman. Remark to Louis XIV, shortly before Mazarin's death; referring to Jean-Baptiste Colbert

11 I let down my friends, I let down my country. I let down our system of government.

Richard Milhous Nixon (1913–) US president. *The Observer,* 'Sayings of the Week', 8 May 1977

12 *Et tu, Brute?*
You too, Brutus?

William Shakespeare (1564–1616) English dramatist. Said by Julius Caesar. *Julius Caesar,* III:1

13 That pig of a Henry VIII committed such sacrilege by profaning so many ecclesiastical benefices in order to give their goods to those who being so rewarded might stand firmly for the King in the Lower House; and now the King's greatest enemies are those who are enriched by these benefices.

Francis Windebank (1582–1646) English politician. Remark to the Papal envoy, Apr 1635

BIBLE

See also religion

1 He will find one English book and one only, where, as in the *Iliad* itself, perfect plainness of speech is allied with perfect nobleness; and that book is the Bible.

Matthew Arnold (1822–88) British poet and critic. *On Translating Homer*

2 Candidates should not attempt more than six of these.

Hilaire Belloc (1870–1953) French-born British poet. Suggested addition to the Ten Commandments. Attrib.

3 There's a great text in Galatians,
Once you trip on it, entails
Twenty-nine distinct damnations,
One sure, if another fails.

Robert Browning (1812–89) British poet. *Soliloquy of the Spanish Cloister*

4 Isn't God a shit.

Randolph Churchill (1911–68) British political journalist. Evelyn Waugh discovered that Churchill had never read the Bible and persuaded him to do so; this is Churchill's reaction when asked what he thought of it. *Diaries* (E. Waugh)

5 I have spent a lot of time searching through the Bible for loopholes.

W. C. Fields (1880–1946) US comedian. Said during his last illness. Attrib.

6 Had the Bible been in clear straightforward language, had the ambiguities and contradictions been edited out, and had the language been constantly modernised to accord with contemporary taste it would almost certainly have been, or become, a work of lesser influence.

John Kenneth Galbraith (1908–) US economist. *Economics, Peace and Laughter*

7 I am very sorry to know and hear how unreverently that most precious jewel, the Word of God, is disputed, rhymed, sung and jangled in every ale-house and tavern, contrary to the true meaning and doctrine of the same.

Henry VIII (1491–1547) King of England. Commenting on the translation of the Bible into English. Speech, Parliament, 24 Dec 1545

8 We have used the Bible as if it was a constable's handbook – an opium-dose for keeping beasts of burden patient while they are being overloaded.

Charles Kingsley (1819–75) British writer. *Letters to the Chartists*, 2

9 The English Bible, a book which, if everything else in our language should perish, would alone suffice to show the whole extent of its beauty and power.

Lord Macaulay (1800–59) British historian. *Essays and Biographies*, 'John Dryden'. *Edinburgh Review*

10 The number one book of the ages was written by a committee, and it was called The Bible.

Louis B. Mayer (1885–1957) Russian-born US film producer. Comment to writers who had objected to changes in their work. *The Filmgoer's Book of Quotes* (Leslie Halliwell)

11 There's a Bible on that shelf there. But I keep it next to Voltaire – poison and antidote.

Bertrand Russell (1872–1970) British philosopher. *Kenneth Harris Talking To:* 'Bertrand Russell' (Kenneth Harris)

12 The Bible is literature, not dogma.

George Santayana (1863–1952) US philosopher. *Introduction to the Ethics of Spinoza*

13 As society is now constituted, a literal adherence to the moral precepts scattered throughout the Gospels would mean sudden death.

A. N. Whitehead (1861–1947) British philosopher. *Adventures in Ideas*

14 LORD ILLINGWORTH. The Book of Life begins with a man and a woman in a garden.
MRS ALLONBY. It ends with Revelations.

Oscar Wilde (1854–1900) Irish-born British dramatist. *A Woman of No Importance*, I

BIBLICAL QUOTATIONS

Unless otherwise stated, quotations are taken from the *Authorized Version*. The books are given in alphabetical order. *See also* Psalms.

Acts

1 And when he had spoken these things, while they beheld, he was taken up; and a cloud received him out of their sight. 1:9

2 And when the day of Pentecost was fully come, they were all with one accord in one place.
And suddenly there came a sound from heaven as of a rushing mighty wind, and it filled all the house where they were sitting.
And there appeared unto them cloven tongues like as of fire, and it sat upon each of them.
And they were all filled with the Holy Ghost, and began to speak with other tongues, as the Spirit gave them utterance. 2:1–4

3 Others mocking said, These men are full of new wine. 2:13

4 Then Peter said, Silver and gold have I none; but such as I have give I thee: In the name of Jesus Christ of Nazareth rise up and walk. 3:6

5 When they heard these things, they were cut to the heart, and they gnashed on him with their teeth. 7:54

6 And as he journeyed, he came near Damascus: and suddenly there shined round about him a light from heaven:
And he fell to the earth, and heard a voice saying unto him, Saul, Saul, why persecutest thou me?
And he said, Who art thou, Lord? And the Lord said, I am Jesus whom thou persecutest: it is hard for thee to kick against the pricks. 9:3–5

7 And the Lord said unto him, Arise, and go into the street which is called Straight, and enquire in the house of Judas for one called Saul, of Tarsus: for, behold, he prayeth. 9:11

8 But the Lord said unto him, Go thy way: for he is a chosen vessel unto me, to bear my name before the Gentiles, and kings, and the children of Israel. 9:15

9 But Peter took him up, saying, Stand up; I myself also am a man. 10:26

10 Then Peter opened his mouth, and said, Of a truth I perceive that God is no respecter of persons. 10:34

11 And the people gave a shout, saying, It is the voice of a god, and not of a man.
And immediately the angel of the Lord smote him, because he gave not God the glory: and he was eaten of worms, and gave up the ghost. 12:22–23

12 (For all the Athenians and strangers which were there spent their time in nothing else, but either to tell, or to hear some new thing.)
Then Paul stood in the midst of Mars' hill, and said, Ye men of Athens, I perceive that in all things ye are too superstitious.
For as I passed by, and beheld your devotions, I found an altar with this inscription, TO THE UNKNOWN GOD. Whom therefore ye ignorantly worship, him declare I unto you.
God that made the world and all things therein, seeing that he is Lord

of heaven and earth, dwelleth not in temples made with hands 17:21–24

13 For in him we live, and move, and have our being; as certain also of your own poets have said, For we are also his offspring. 17:28

14 And the evil spirit answered and said, Jesus I know, and Paul I know; but who are ye? 19:15

15 And when they heard these sayings, they were full of wrath, and cried out, saying, Great is Diana of the Ephesians. 19:28

16 And now, behold, I go bound in the spirit unto Jerusalem, not knowing the things that shall befall me there. 20:22

17 And the chief captain answered, With a great sum obtained I this freedom. And Paul said, But I was free born. 22:28

18 Then said Paul unto him, God shall smite thee, thou whited wall: for sittest thou to judge me after the law, and commandest me to be smitten contrary to the law? 23:3

19 Then Festus, when he had conferred with the council, answered, Hast thou appealed unto Caesar? Unto Caesar shalt thou go. 25:12

Amos

20 Seek him that maketh the seven stars and Orion, and turneth the shadow of death into the morning, and maketh the day dark with night: that calleth for the waters of the sea, and poureth them out upon the face of the earth: The Lord is his name. 5:8

Colossians

21 Beware lest any man spoil you through philosophy and vain deceit, after the tradition of men, after the rudiments of the world, and not after Christ. 2:8

22 Touch not; taste not; handle not. 2:21

23 Where there is neither Greek nor Jew, circumcision nor uncircumcision, Barbarian, Scythian, bond nor free; but Christ is all, and in all. 3:11

24 Husbands, love your wives, and be not bitter against them. 3:19

25 Fathers, provoke not your children to anger, lest they be discouraged. 3:21

26 Let your speech be alway with grace, seasoned with salt, that ye may know how ye ought to answer every man. 4:6

I Corinthians

27 For after that in the wisdom of God the world by wisdom knew not God, it pleased God by the foolishness of preaching to save them that believe.
For the Jews require a sign, and the Greeks seek after wisdom:
But we preach Christ crucified, unto the Jews a stumblingblock, and unto the Greeks foolishness. 1:21–23

28 But God hath chosen the foolish things of the world to confound the wise; and God hath chosen the weak things of the world to confound the things which are mighty. 1:27

29 But as it is written, Eye hath not seen, nor ear heard, neither have entered into the heart of man, the things which God hath prepared for them that love him. 2:9

30 For the kingdom of God is not in word, but in power. 4:20

31 Meats for the belly, and the belly for meats: but God shall destroy both it and them. Now the body is not for fornication, but for the Lord; and the Lord for the body. 6:13

32 What? know ye not that your body is the temple of the Holy Ghost which is in you, which ye have of God, and ye are not your own? 6:19

33 Let the husband render unto the wife due benevolence: and likewise also the wife unto the husband. 7:3

34 But if they cannot contain, let them marry: for it is better to marry than to burn. 7:9

35 And they that use this world, as not abusing it: for the fashion of this world passeth away. 7:31

36 But he that is married careth for the things that are of the world, how he may please his wife. 7:33

37 Now as touching things offered unto idols, we know that we all have knowledge. Knowledge puffeth up, but charity edifieth. 8:1

38 Who goeth a warfare any time at his own charges? who planteth a vineyard, and eateth not of the fruit thereof? or who feedeth a flock, and eateth not of the milk of the flock? 9:7

39 Know ye not that they which run in a race run all, but one receiveth the prize? So run, that ye may obtain.
And every man that striveth for the mastery is temperate in all things. Now they do it to obtain a corruptible crown; but we an incorruptible.
I therefore so run, not as uncertainly; so fight I, not as one that beateth the air:
But I keep under my body, and bring it into subjection: lest that by any means, when I have preached to others, I myself should be a castaway. 9:24–27

40 All things are lawful for me, but all things are not expedient: all things are lawful for me, but all things edify not. 10:23

41 For the earth is the Lord's, and the fulness thereof. 10:26

42 Conscience, I say, not thine own, but of the other: for why is my liberty judged of another man's conscience? 10:29

43 But if a woman have long hair, it is a glory to her: for her hair is given her for a covering. 11:15

44 Though I speak with the tongues of men and of angels, and have not charity, I am become as sounding brass, or a tinkling cymbal.
And though I have the gift of prophecy, and understand all mysteries, and all knowledge; and though I have all faith, so that I could remove mountains, and have not charity, I am nothing.
And though I bestow all my goods to feed the poor, and though I give my body to be burned, and have not charity, it profiteth me nothing.
Charity suffereth long, and is kind; charity envieth not; charity vaunteth not itself, is not puffed up,
Doth not behave itself unseemly, seeketh not her own, is not easily provoked, thinketh no evil;
Rejoiceth not in iniquity, but rejoiceth in the truth;
Beareth all things, believeth all things, hopeth all things, endureth all things.
Charity never faileth: but whether there be prophecies, they shall fail; whether there be tongues, they shall cease; whether there be knowledge, it shall vanish away.

For we know in part, and we prophesy in part.
But when that which is perfect is come, then that which is in part shall be done away.
When I was a child, I spake as a child, I understood as a child, I thought as a child: but when I became a man, I put away childish things.
For now we see through a glass, darkly; but then face to face: now I know in part; but then shall I know even as also I am known.
And now abideth faith, hope, charity, these three; but the greatest of these is charity. 13:1–13

45 Let all things be done decently and in order. 14:40

46 Then cometh the end, when he shall have delivered up the kingdom to God, even the Father; when he shall have put down all rule and all authority and power.
For he must reign, till he hath put all enemies under his feet.
The last enemy that shall be destroyed is death. 15:24–26

47 If after the manner of men I have fought with beasts at Ephesus, what advantageth it me, if the dead rise not? let us eat and drink; for tomorrow we die.
Be not deceived: evil communications corrupt good manners. 15:32–33

48 There is one glory of the sun, and another glory of the moon, and another glory of the stars: for one star differeth from another star in glory.
So also is the resurrection of the dead. It is sown in corruption; it is raised in incorruption. 15:41–42

49 Behold, I shew you a mystery; We shall not all sleep, but we shall all be changed,
In a moment, in the twinkling of an eye, at the last trump: for the trumpet shall sound, and the dead shall be raised incorruptible, and we shall be changed.
For this corruptible must put on incorruption, and this mortal must put on immortality.
So when this corruptible shall have put on incorruption, and this mortal shall have put on immortality, then shall be brought to pass the saying that is written, Death is swallowed up in victory.
O death, where is thy sting? O grave, where is thy victory? 15:51–55

50 If any man love not the Lord Jesus Christ, let him be Anathema Maranatha.
The grace of our Lord Jesus Christ be with you. 16:22–23

II Corinthians

51 For we walk by faith, not by sight. 5:7

52 Every man according as he purposeth in his heart, so let him give; not grudgingly, or of necessity: for God loveth a cheerful giver. 9:7

53 For though we walk in the flesh, we do not war after the flesh:
For the weapons of our warfare are not carnal, but mighty through God to the pulling down of strong holds. 10:3–4

54 For ye suffer fools gladly, seeing ye yourselves are wise. 11:19

55 And lest I should be exalted above measure through the abundance of the revelations, there was given to me a thorn in the flesh, the messenger of Satan to buffet me, lest I should be exalted above measure. 12:7

Daniel

56 And he changeth the times and the seasons: he removeth kings, and setteth up kings: he giveth wisdom unto the wise, and knowledge to them that know understanding:
He revealeth the deep and secret things: he knoweth what is in the darkness, and the light dwelleth with him. 2:21–22

57 That at what time ye hear the sound of the cornet, flute, harp, sackbut, psaltery, dulcimer, and all kinds of musick, ye fall down and worship the golden image that Nebuchadnezzar the king hath set up:
And whoso falleth not down and worshippeth shall the same hour be cast into the midst of a burning fiery furnace. 3:5–6

58 Shadrach, Meshach, and Abed-nego, answered and said to the king, O Nebuchadnezzar, we are not careful to answer thee in this matter. 3:16

59 Then was Nebuchadnezzar full of fury, and the form of his visage was changed against Shadrach, Meshach, and Abed-nego: therefore he spake, and commanded that they should heat the furnace one seven times more than it was wont to be heated. 3:19

60 He answered and said, Lo, I see four men loose, walking in the midst of the fire, and they have no hurt; and the form of the fourth is like the Son of God. 3:25

61 The same hour was the thing fulfilled upon Nebuchadnezzar: and he was driven from men, and did eat grass as oxen, and his body was wet with the dew of heaven, till his hairs were grown like eagles' feathers, and his nails like birds' claws. 4:33

62 In the same hour came forth fingers of a man's hand, and wrote over against the candlestick upon the plaister of the wall of the king's palace: and the king saw the part of the hand that wrote. 5:5

63 And this is the writing that was written, MENE, MENE, TEKEL, UPHARSIN.
This is the interpretation of the thing: MENE; God hath numbered thy kingdom, and finished it.
TEKEL; Thou art weighed in the balances, and art found wanting.
PERES; Thy kingdom is divided, and given to the Medes and Persians. 5:25–28

64 Then the king commanded, and they brought Daniel, and cast him into the den of lions. Now the king spake and said unto Daniel, Thy God whom thou servest continually, he will deliver thee. 6:16

Deuteronomy

65 I call heaven and earth to witness against you this day, that ye shall soon utterly perish from off the land whereunto ye go over Jordan to possess it; ye shall not prolong your days upon it, but shall utterly be destroyed. 4:26

66 For the Lord thy God bringeth thee into a good land, a land of brooks of water, of fountains and depths that spring out of valleys and hills;
A land of wheat, and barley, and vines, and fig trees, and pomegranates; a land of oil olive, and honey;
A land wherein thou shalt eat bread without scarceness, thou shalt not lack any thing in it; a land whose stones are iron, and out of whose hills thou mayest dig brass.

When thou hast eaten and art full, then thou shalt bless the Lord thy God for the good land which he hath given thee. 8:7–10

67 Take heed to yourselves, that your heart be not deceived, and ye turn aside, and serve other gods, and worship them. 11:16

68 Thou shalt not hearken unto the words of that prophet, or that dreamer of dreams. 13:3

69 I call heaven and earth to record this day against you, that I have set before you life and death, blessing and cursing: therefore choose life, that both thou and thy seed may live. 30:19

70 Be strong and of a good courage, fear not, nor be afraid of them: for the Lord thy God, he it is that doth go with thee; he will not fail thee, nor forsake thee. 31:6

71 He found him in a desert land, and in the waste howling wilderness; he led him about, he instructed him, he kept him as the apple of his eye. 32:10

72 And he buried him in a valley in the land of Moab, over against Beth-peor: but no man knoweth of his sepulchre unto this day. 34:6

73 And there arose not a prophet since in Israel like unto Moses, whom the Lord knew face to face. 34:10

Ecclesiastes

74 Vanity of vanities, saith the Preacher, vanity of vanities; all is vanity.
What profit hath a man of all his labour which he taketh under the sun?
One generation passeth away, and another generation cometh: but the earth abideth for ever. 1:2–4

75 All the rivers run into the sea; yet the sea is not full; unto the place from whence the rivers come, thither they return again.
All things are full of labour; man cannot utter it: the eye is not satisfied with seeing, nor the ear filled with hearing.
The thing that hath been, it is that which shall be; and that which is done is that which shall be done: and there is no new thing under the sun. 1:7–9

76 There is no remembrance of former things; neither shall there be any remembrance of things that are to come with those that shall come after. 1:11

77 And I gave my heart to seek and search out by wisdom concerning all things that are done under heaven: this sore travail hath God given to the sons of man to be exercised therewith.
I have seen all the works that are done under the sun; and, behold, all is vanity and vexation of spirit. 1:13–14

78 For in much wisdom is much grief: and he that increaseth knowledge increaseth sorrow. 1:18

79 I said of laughter, It is mad: and of mirth, What doeth it? 2:2

80 Then I saw that wisdom excelleth folly, as far as light excelleth darkness.
The wise man's eyes are in his head; but the fool walketh in darkness: and I myself perceived also that one event happeneth to them all. 2:13–14

81 To every thing there is a season, and a time to every purpose under the heaven:
A time to be born, and a time to die; a time to plant, and a time to pluck up that which is planted;
A time to kill, and a time to heal; a time to break down, and a time to build up;
A time to weep, and a time to laugh; a time to mourn, and a time to dance;
A time to cast away stones, and a time to gather stones together; a time to embrace, and a time to refrain from embracing;
A time to get, and a time to lose; a time to keep, and a time to cast away;
A time to rend, and a time to sew; a time to keep silence, and a time to speak;
A time to love, and a time to hate; a time of war, and a time of peace. 3:1–8

82 Wherefore I praised the dead which are already dead more than the living which are yet alive.
Yea, better is he than both they, which hath not yet been, who hath not seen the evil work that is done under the sun. 4:2–3

83 Two are better than one; because they have a good reward for their labour.
For if they fall, the one will lift up his fellow: but woe to him that is alone when he falleth; for he hath not another to help him up. 4:9–10

84 And if one prevail against him, two shall withstand him; and a threefold cord is not quickly broken. 4:12

85 Better is a poor and a wise child than an old and foolish king, who will no more be admonished. 4:13

86 Better is it that thou shouldest not vow, than that thou shouldest vow and not pay. 5:5

87 A good name is better than precious ointment; and the day of death than the day of one's birth.
It is better to go to the house of mourning, than to go to the house of feasting: for that is the end of all men; and the living will lay it to his heart. 7:1–2

88 Then I commended mirth, because a man hath no better thing under the sun, than to eat, and to drink, and to be merry: for that shall abide with him of his labour the days of his life, which God giveth him under the sun. 8:15

89 Whatsoever thy hand findeth to do, do it with thy might; for there is no work, nor device, nor knowledge, nor wisdom, in the grave, whither thou goest. 9:10

90 I returned, and saw under the sun, that the race is not to the swift, nor the battle to the strong, neither yet bread to the wise, nor yet riches to men of understanding, nor yet favour to men of skill; but time and chance happeneth to them all.
For man also knoweth not his time: as the fishes that are taken in an evil net, and as the birds that are caught in the snare; so are the sons of men snared in an evil time, when it falleth suddenly upon them. 9:11–12

91 The words of wise men are heard in quiet more than the cry of him that ruleth among fools. 9:17

92 Dead flies cause the ointment of the apothecary to send forth a stinking savour: so doth a little folly him that is in reputation for wisdom and honour. 10:1

93 He that diggeth a pit shall fall into it;

and whoso breaketh an hedge, a serpent shall bite him. 10:8

94 A feast is made for laughter, and wine maketh merry: but money answereth all things. 10:19

95 Curse not the king, no not in thy thought; and curse not the rich in thy bedchamber: for a bird of the air shall carry the voice, and that which hath wings shall tell the matter. 10:20

96 Cast thy bread upon the waters: for thou shalt find it after many days. 11:1

97 If the clouds be full of rain, they empty themselves upon the earth: and if the tree fall toward the south, or toward the north, in the place where the tree falleth, there it shall be. 11:3

98 And further, by these, my son, be admonished: of making many books there is no end; and much study is a weariness of the flesh. 12:12

99 Let us hear the conclusion of the whole matter: Fear God, and keep his commandments: for this is the whole duty of man. 12:13

Ecclesiasticus

100 My son, if thou come to serve the Lord, prepare thy soul for temptation. 2:1

101 Be not curious in unnecessary matters: for more things are shewed unto thee than men understand 3:23

102 Winnow not with every wind, and go not into every way: for so the sinner that hath a double tongue. 5:9

103 Miss not the discourse of the elders: for they also learned of their fathers, and of them thou shalt learn understanding, and to give answer as need requireth. 8:9

104 Forsake not an old friend; for the new is not comparable to him: a new friend is as new wine; when it is old, thou shalt drink it with pleasure. 9:10

105 The physician cutteth off a long disease; and he that is today a king tomorrow shall die. 10:10

106 Desire not a multitude of unprofitable children, neither delight in ungodly sons. 16:1

107 Be not made a beggar by banqueting upon borrowing, when thou hast nothing in thy purse: for thou shalt lie in wait for thine own life, and be talked on. 18:33

108 If thou hast heard a word, let it die with thee; and be bold, it will not burst thee. 19:10

109 If thou hast gathered nothing in thy youth, how canst thou find any thing in thine age? 25:3

110 Leave off first for manners' sake: and be not unsatiable, lest thou offend. 31:17

111 Let thy speech be short, comprehending much in few words; be as one that knoweth and yet holdeth his tongue. 32:8

112 The wisdom of a learned man cometh by opportunity of leisure: and he that hath little business shall become wise.
How can he get wisdom that holdeth the plough, and that glorieth in the goad, that driveth oxen, and is occupied in their labours, and whose talk is of bullocks? 38:24–25

113 Let us now praise famous men, and our fathers that begat us. 44:1

114 Such as did bear rule in their kingdoms, men renowned for their power, giving counsel by their understanding, and declaring prophecies:
Leaders of the people by their counsels, and by their knowledge of learning meet for the people, wise and eloquent in their instructions:
Such as found out musical tunes and recited verses in writing:
Rich men furnished with ability living peaceably in their habitations:
All these were honoured in their generations, and were the glory of their times.
There be of them, that have left a name behind them, that their praises might be reported.
And some there be, which have no memorial; who are perished, as though they had never been; and are become as though they had never been born; and their children after them. 44:3–9

115 Their bodies are buried in peace; but their name liveth for evermore. 44:14

Ephesians

116 That he would grant you, according to the riches of his glory, to be strengthened with might by his Spirit in the inner man;
That Christ may dwell in your hearts by faith; that ye, being rooted and grounded in love,
May be able to comprehend with all saints what is the breadth, and length, and depth, and height;
And to know the love of Christ, which passeth knowledge, that ye might be filled with all the fulness of God.
Now unto him that is able to do exceeding abundantly above all that we ask or think, according to the power that worketh in us,
Unto him be glory in the church by Christ Jesus throughout all ages, world without end. Amen. 3:16–21

117 Wherefore putting away lying, speak every man truth with his neighbour: for we are members one of another.
Be ye angry, and sin not: let not the sun go down upon your wrath:
Neither give place to the devil.
Let him that stole steal no more: but rather let him labour, working with his hands the thing which is good, that he may have to give to him that needeth. 4:25–28

118 Children, obey your parents in the Lord: for this is right. 6:1

119 Finally, my brethren, be strong in the Lord, and in the power of his might.
Put on the whole armour of God, that ye may be able to stand against the wiles of the devil.
For we wrestle not against flesh and blood, but against principalities, against powers, against the rulers of the darkness of his world, against spiritual wickedness in high places.
Wherefore take unto you the whole armour of God, that ye may be able to withstand in the evil day, and having done all, to stand.
Stand therefore, having your loins girt about with truth, and having on the breastplate of righteousness;
And your feet shod with the preparation of the gospel of peace;
Above all, taking the shield of faith,

wherewith ye shall be able to quench all the fiery darts of the wicked.
And take the helmet of salvation, and the sword of the Spirit, which is the word of God. 6:10–17

II Esdras

120 Then had I pity upon your mournings, and gave you manna to eat; so ye did eat angels' bread. 1:19

121 He answered and said unto me, These be they that have put off the mortal clothing, and put on the immortal, and have confessed the name of God: now are they crowned, and receive palms.
Then said I unto the angel, What young person is it that crowneth them, and giveth them palms in their hands?
So he answered and said unto me, It is the Son of God, whom they have confessed in the world. Then began I greatly to commend them that stood so stiffly for the name of the Lord. 2:45–47

122 And he said unto me, If I should ask thee how great dwellings are in the midst of the sea, or how many springs are in the beginning of the deep, or how many springs are above the firmament, or which are the outgoings of paradise:
Peradventure thou wouldest say unto me, I never went down into the deep, nor as yet into hell, neither did I ever climb up into heaven. 4:7–8

123 He answered me, and said, I went into a forest into a plain, and the trees took counsel,
And said, Come, let us go and make war against the sea, that it may depart away before us, and that we may make us more woods.
The floods of the sea also in like manner took counsel, and said, Come, let us go up and subdue the woods of the plain, that there also we may make us another country.
The thought of the wood was in vain, for the fire came and consumed it.
The thought of the floods of the sea came likewise to nought, for the sand stood up and stopped them. 4:13–17

124 Then were the entrances of this world made narrow, full of sorrow and travail: they are but few and evil, full of perils, and very painful.
For the entrances of the elder world were wide and sure, and brought immortal fruit. 7:12–13

125 For the world hath lost his youth, and the times begin to wax old. 14:10

126 And come hither, and I shall light a candle of understanding in thine heart, which shall not be put out, till the things be performed which thou shalt begin to write. 14:25

Esther

127 And the king loved Esther above all the women, and she obtained grace and favour in his sight more than all the virgins; so that he set the royal crown upon her head, and made her queen instead of Vashti. 2:17

Exodus

128 Now there arose up a new king over Egypt, which knew not Joseph. 1:8

129 And when she could not longer hide him, she took for him an ark of bulrushes, and daubed it with slime and with pitch, and put the child therein; and she laid it in the flags by the river's brink. 2:3

130 He called his name Gershom: for he said, I have been a stranger in a strange land. 2:22

131 And the angel of the Lord appeared unto him in a flame of fire out of the midst of a bush: and he looked, and, behold, the bush burned with fire, and the bush was not consumed. 3:2

132 And he said, Draw not nigh hither: put off thy shoes from off thy feet, for the place whereon thou standest is holy ground.
Moreover he said, I am the God of thy father, the God of Abraham, the God of Isaac, and the God of Jacob. And Moses hid his face; for he was afraid to look upon God. 3:5–6

133 And I am come down to deliver them out of the hand of the Egyptians, and to bring them up out of that land unto a good land and a large, unto a land flowing with milk and honey; unto the place of the Canaanites, and the Hittites, and the Amorites, and the Perizzites, and the Hivites, and the Jebusites. 3:8

134 And God said unto Moses, I AM THAT I AM: and he said, Thus shalt thou say unto the children of Israel, I AM hath sent me unto you. 3:14

135 And Moses said unto the Lord, O my Lord, I am not eloquent, neither heretofore, nor since thou hast spoken unto thy servant: but I am slow of speech, and of a slow tongue. 4:10

136 And I will harden Pharaoh's heart, and multiply my signs and my wonders in the land of Egypt. 7:3

137 For they cast down every man his rod, and they became serpents: but Aaron's rod swallowed up their rods. 7:12

138 Your lamb shall be without blemish, a male of the first year: ye shall take it out from the sheep, or from the goats. 12:5

139 And thus shall ye eat it; with your loins girded, your shoes on your feet, and your staff in your hand; and ye shall eat it in haste: it is the Lord's passover.
For I will pass through the land of Egypt this night, and will smite all the firstborn in the land of Egypt, both man and beast; and against all the gods of Egypt I will execute judgment: I am the Lord. 12:11–12

140 And the Egyptians were urgent upon the people, that they might send them out of the land in haste; for they said, We be all dead men. 12:33

141 And the Lord went before them by day in a pillar of a cloud, to lead them the way; and by night in a pillar of fire, to give them light; to go by day and night. 13:21

142 And the children of Israel went into the midst of the sea upon the dry ground: and the waters were a wall unto them on their right hand, and on their left. 14:22

143 Then sang Moses and the children of Israel this song unto the Lord, and spake, saying, I will sing unto the Lord, for he hath triumphed gloriously: the horse and his rider hath he thrown into the sea. 15:1

144 The Lord is a man of war: the Lord is his name. 15:3

145 And when the children of Israel saw it, they said one to another, It is manna: for they wist not what it was. And Moses said unto them, This is the bread which the Lord hath given you to eat. 16:15

146 And mount Sinai was altogether on a smoke, because the Lord descended upon it in fire: and the smoke thereof ascended as the smoke of a furnace, and the whole mount quaked greatly. 19:18

147 I am the Lord thy God, which have brought thee out of the land of Egypt, out of the house of bondage.
Thou shalt have no other gods before me.
Thou shalt not make unto thee any graven image, or any likeness of any thing that is in heaven above, or that is in the earth beneath, or that is in the water under the earth:
Thou shalt not bow down thyself to them, nor serve them: for Lord thy God am a jealous God, visiting the iniquity of the fathers upon the children unto the third and fourth generation of them that hate me;
And shewing mercy unto thousands of them that love me, and keep my commandments.
Thou shalt not take the name of the Lord thy God in vain; for the Lord will not hold him guiltless that taketh his name in vain.
Remember the sabbath day, to keep it holy.
Six days shalt thou labour, and do all thy work:
But the seventh day is the sabbath of the Lord thy God: in it thou shalt not do any work, thou, nor thy son, nor thy daughter, thy manservant, nor thy maidservant, nor thy cattle, nor thy stranger that is within thy gates:
For in six days the Lord made heaven and earth, the sea, and all that in them is, and rested the seventh day: wherefore the Lord blessed the sabbath day, and hallowed it.
Honour thy father and thy mother: that thy days may be long upon the land which the Lord thy God giveth thee.
Thou shalt not kill.
Thou shalt not commit adultery.
Thou shalt not steal.
Thou shalt not bear false witness against thy neighbour.
Thou shalt not covet thy neighbour's house, thou shalt not covet thy neighbour's wife, nor his manservant, nor his maidservant, nor his ox, nor his ass, nor any thing that is thy neighbour's. 20:2–17

148 And if any mischief follow, then thou shalt give life for life,
Eye for eye, tooth for tooth, hand for hand, foot for foot,
Burning for burning, wound for wound, stripe for stripe. 21:23–25

149 Thou shalt not suffer a witch to live. 22:18

150 The first of the firstfruits of thy land thou shalt bring into the house of the Lord thy God. Thou shalt not seethe a kid in his mother's milk. 23:19

151 And the Lord said unto Moses, Come up to me into the mount, and be there: and I will give thee tables of stone, and a law, and commandments which I have written; that thou mayest teach them. 24:12

152 And thou shalt put in the breastplate of judgment the Urim and the Thummim; and they shall be upon Aaron's heart, when he goeth in before the Lord: and Aaron shall bear the judgment of the children of Israel upon his heart before the Lord continually. 28:30

153 And he received them at their hand, and fashioned it with a graving tool, after he had made it a molten calf: and they said, These be thy gods, O Israel, which brought thee up out of the land of Egypt. 32:4

154 And the Lord said unto Moses, I have seen this people, and, behold, it is a stiffnecked people. 32:9

155 Then Moses stood in the gate of the camp, and said, Who is on the Lord's side? let him come unto me. And all the sons of Levi gathered themselves together unto him. 32:26

156 Yet now, if thou wilt forgive their sin —; and if not, blot me, I pray thee, out of thy book which thou hast written. 32:32

157 And he said, Thou canst not see my face: for there shall no man see me, and live. 33:20

158 And it shall come to pass, while my glory passeth by, that I will put thee in a clift of the rock, and will cover thee with my hand while I pass by. 33:22

Ezekiel

159 And thou, son of man, be not afraid of them, neither be afraid of their words, though briers and thorns be with thee, and thou dost dwell among scorpions: be not afraid of their words, nor be dismayed at their looks, though they be a rebellious house. 2:6

160 Son of man, thou dwellest in the midst of a rebellious house, which have eyes to see, and see not; they have ears to hear, and hear not: for they are a rebellious house. 12:2

161 Behold, every one that useth proverbs shall use this proverb against thee, saying, As is the mother, so is her daughter. 16:44–45

162 What mean ye, that ye use this proverb concerning the land of Israel, saying, The fathers have eaten sour grapes, and the children's teeth are set on edge? 18:2

163 Again, when the wicked man turneth away from his wickedness that he hath committed, and doeth that which is lawful and right, he shall save his soul alive. 18:27

164 And he said unto me, Son of man, can these bones live? And I answered, O Lord God, thou knowest.
Again he said unto me, Prophesy upon these bones, and say unto them, O ye dry bones, hear the word of the Lord. 37:3–4

165 So I prophesied as I was commanded: and as I prophesied, there was a noise, and behold a shaking, and the bones came together, bone to his bone. 37:7

166 And the man said unto me, Son of man, behold with thine eyes, and hear with thine ears, and set thine heart upon all that I shall shew thee; for to the intent that I might shew them unto thee art thou brought hither: declare all that thou seest to the house of Israel. 40:4

Ezra

167 The people could not discern the noise of the shout of joy from the noise of the weeping of the people: for the people shouted with a loud shout, and the noise was heard afar off. 3:13

Galatians

168 O foolish Galatians, who hath bewitched you, that ye should not obey the truth, before whose eyes Jesus Christ hath been evidently set forth, crucified among you? 3:1

169 There is neither Jew nor Greek, there is neither bond nor free, there is neither male nor female: for ye are all one in Christ Jesus. 3:28

170 But Jerusalem which is above is free, which is the mother of us all. 4:26

171 For the flesh lusteth against the Spirit, and the Spirit against the flesh: and these are contrary the one to the other: so that ye cannot do the things that ye would. 5:17

172 But the fruit of the Spirit is love, joy, peace, longsuffering, gentleness, goodness, faith,
Meekness, temperance: against such there is no law. 5:22–23

173 Be not deceived: God is not mocked: for whatsoever a man soweth, that shall he also reap.
For he that soweth to his flesh shall of the flesh reap corruption; but he that soweth to the Spirit shall of the Spirit reap life everlasting.
And let us not be weary in well doing: for in due season we shall reap, if we faint not. 6:7–9

Genesis

174 In the beginning God created the heaven and the earth.
And the earth was without form, and void; and darkness was upon the face of the deep. And the Spirit of God moved upon the face of the waters.
And God said, Let there be light: and there was light.
And God saw the light, that it was good: and God divided the light from the darkness.
And God called the light Day, and the darkness he called Night. And the evening and the morning were the first day. 1:1–5

175 Fiat lux. Vulgate 1:3

176 And God called the dry land Earth; and the gathering together of the waters called he Seas: and God saw that it was good.
And God said, Let the earth bring forth grass, the herb yielding seed, and the fruit tree yielding fruit after his kind, whose seed is in itself, upon the earth: and it was so. 1:10–11

177 And God made two great lights: the greater light to rule the day, and the lesser light to rule the night: he made the stars also. 1:16

178 And God said, Let the earth bring forth the living creature after his kind, cattle, and creeping thing, and beast of the earth after his kind: and it was so. 1:24

179 And God said, Let us make man in our image, after our likeness: and let them have dominion over the fish of the sea, and over the fowl of the air, and over the cattle, and over all the earth, and over every creeping thing that creepeth upon the earth.
So God created man in his own image, in the image of God created he him; male and female created he them.
And God blessed them, and God said unto them, Be fruitful, and multiply, and replenish the earth, and subdue it: and have dominion over the fish of the sea, and over the fowl of the air, and over every living thing that moveth upon the earth. 1:26–28

180 And on the seventh day God ended his work which he had made; and he rested on the seventh day from all his work which he had made. 2:2

181 But there went up a mist from the earth, and watered the whole face of the ground.
And the Lord God formed man of the dust of the ground, and breathed into his nostrils the breath of life; and man became a living soul.
And the Lord God planted a garden eastward in Eden; and there he put the man whom he had formed.
And out of the ground made the Lord God to grow every tree that is pleasant to the sight, and good for food; the tree of life also in the midst of the garden, and the tree of knowledge of good and evil.
And a river went out of Eden to water the garden. 2:6–10

182 And the Lord God took the man, and put him into the garden of Eden to dress it and to keep it.
And the Lord God commanded the man, saying, Of every tree of the garden thou mayest freely eat:
But of the tree of the knowledge of good and evil, thou shalt not eat of it: for in the day that thou eatest thereof thou shalt surely die. 2:15–17

183 And the Lord God said, It is not good that the man should be alone; I will make him an help meet for him.
And out of the ground the Lord God formed every beast of the field, and every fowl of the air; and brought them unto Adam to see what he would call them: and whatsoever Adam called every living creature, that was the name thereof. 2:18–19

184 And the Lord God caused a deep sleep to fall upon Adam, and he slept: and he took one of his ribs, and closed up the flesh instead thereof;
And the rib, which the Lord God had taken from man, made he a woman, and brought her unto the man.
And Adam said, This is now bone of my bones, and flesh of my flesh: she shall be called Woman, because she was taken out of Man.
Therefore shall a man leave his father and his mother, and shall cleave unto his wife: and they shall be one flesh.
And they were both naked, the man and his wife, and were not ashamed. 2:21–25

185 Now the serpent was more subtil than any beast of the field which the Lord God had made. 3:1

186 God doth know that in the day ye eat thereof, then your eyes shall be opened, and ye shall be as gods, knowing good and evil.
And when the woman saw that the tree was good for food, and that it was pleasant to the eyes, and a

tree to be desired to make one wise, she took of the fruit thereof, and did eat, and gave also unto her husband with her; and he did eat.
And the eyes of them both were opened, and they knew that they were naked; and they sewed fig leaves together; and made themselves aprons.
And they heard the voice of the Lord God walking in the garden in the cool of the day: and Adam and his wife hid themselves from the presence of the Lord God amongst the trees of the garden. 3:5–8

187 And he said, I heard thy voice in the garden, and I was afraid, because I was naked; and I hid myself.
And he said, Who told thee that thou wast naked? 3:10–11

188 And the man said, The woman whom thou gavest to be with me, she gave me of the tree, and I did eat.
And the Lord God said unto the woman, What is this that thou hast done? And the woman said, The serpent beguiled me, and I did eat.
And the Lord God said unto the serpent, Because thou hast done this, thou art cursed above all cattle, and above every beast of the field; upon thy belly shalt thou go, and dust shalt thou eat all the days of thy life:
And I will put enmity between thee and the woman, and between thy seed and her seed; it shall bruise thy head, and thou shalt bruise his heel.
Unto the woman he said, I will greatly multiply thy sorrow and thy conception; in sorrow thou shalt bring forth children; and thy desire shall be to thy husband, and he shall rule over thee.
And unto Adam he said, Because thou hast hearkened unto the voice of thy wife, and has eaten of the tree, of which I commanded thee, saying, Thou shalt not eat of it: cursed is the ground for thy sake; in sorrow shalt thou eat of it all the days of thy life. 3:12–17

189 In the sweat of thy face shalt thou eat bread, till thou return unto the ground; for out of it wast thou taken: for dust thou art and unto dust shalt thou return.
And Adam called his wife's name Eve; because she was the mother of all living. 3:19–20

190 Abel was a keeper of sheep, but Cain was a tiller of the ground. 4:2

191 And the Lord said unto Cain, Where is Abel thy brother? And he said, I know not: Am I my brother's keeper?
And he said, What hast thou done? the voice of thy brother's blood crieth unto me from the ground. 4:9–10

192 When thou tillest the ground, it shall not henceforth yield unto thee her strength; a fugitive and a vagabond shalt thou be in the earth.
And Cain said unto the Lord, My punishment is greater than I can bear. 4:12–13

193 And the Lord said unto him, Therefore whosoever slayeth Cain, vengeance shall be taken on him sevenfold. And the Lord set a mark upon Cain, lest any finding him should kill him.
And Cain went out from the presence of the Lord, and dwelt in the land of Nod, on the east of Eden. 4:15–16

194 And all the days of Methuselah were nine hundred sixty and nine years: and he died. 5:27

195 The sons of God saw the daughters of men that they were fair; and they took them wives of all which they chose.
And the Lord said, My spirit shall not always strive with man, for that he also is flesh: yet his days shall be an hundred and twenty years.
There were giants in the earth in those days; and also after that, when the sons of God came in unto the daughters of men, and they bare children to them, the same became mighty men which were of old, men of renown. 6:2–4

196 And it repented the Lord that he had made man on the earth, and it grieved him at his heart. 6:6

197 And they went in unto Noah into the ark, two and two of all flesh, wherein is the breath of life.
And they that went in, went in male and female of all flesh, as God had commanded him: and the Lord shut him in.
And the flood was forty days upon the earth; and the waters increased, and bare up the ark, and it was lift up above the earth. 7:15–17

198 And the dove came in to him in the evening; and, lo, in her mouth was an olive leaf pluckt off: so Noah knew that the waters were abated from off the earth. 8:11

199 And the Lord smelled a sweet savour; and the Lord said in his heart, I will not again curse the ground any more for man's sake; for the imagination of man's heart is evil from his youth; neither will I again smite any more every thing living, as I have done.
While the earth remaineth, seedtime and harvest, and cold and heat, and summer and winter, and day and night shall not cease. 8:21–22

200 And surely your blood of your lives will I require; at the hand of every beast will I require it, and at the hand of man; at the hand of every man's brother will I require the life of man.
Whoso sheddeth man's blood, by man shall his blood be shed: for in the image of God made he man. 9:5–6

201 I do set my bow in the cloud, and it shall be for a token of a covenant between me and the earth. 9:13

202 He was a mighty hunter before the Lord: wherefore it is said, Even as Nimrod the mighty hunter before the Lord. 10:9

203 And the whole earth was of one language, and of one speech. 11:1

204 Therefore is the name of it called Babel; because the Lord did there confound the language of all the earth: and from thence did the Lord scatter them abroad upon the face of all the earth. 11:9

205 Now the Lord had said unto Abram, Get thee out of thy country, and from thy kindred, and from thy father's house, unto a land that I will shew thee:
And I will make of thee a great nation, and I will bless thee, and make thy name great; and thou shalt be a blessing:
And I will bless them that bless thee, and curse him that curseth thee: and in thee shall all families of the earth be blessed. 12:1–3

206 But the men of Sodom were wicked and sinners before the Lord exceedingly. 13:13

207 And he will be a wild man; his hand will be against every man, and every man's hand against him; and he shall dwell in the presence of all his brethren. 16:12

208 Is any thing too hard for the Lord? At the time appointed I will return unto thee, according to the time of life, and Sarah shall have a son. 18:14

209 That be far from thee to do after this manner, to slay the righteous with the wicked: and that the righteous should be as the wicked, that be far from thee: Shall not the Judge of all the earth do right? 18:25

210 Then the Lord rained upon Sodom and upon Gomorrah brimstone and fire from the Lord out of heaven. 19:24

211 But his wife looked back from behind him, and she became a pillar of salt. 19:26

212 And Abraham said, My son, God will provide himself a lamb for a burnt offering: so they went both of them together. 22:8

213 And Abraham lifted up his eyes, and looked, and behold behind him a ram caught in a thicket by his horns: and Abraham went and took the ram, and offered him up for a burnt offering in the stead of his son. 22:13

214 And Abraham was old, and well stricken in age: and the Lord had blessed Abraham in all things. 24:1

215 And Jacob said to Rebekah his mother, Behold, Esau my brother a hairy man, and I am a smooth man. 27:11

216 And he dreamed, and behold a ladder set up on the earth, and the top of it reached to heaven: and behold the angels of God ascending and descending on it. 28:12

217 And Jacob awaked out of his sleep, and he said, Surely the Lord is in this place; and I knew it not.
And he was afraid, and said, How dreadful is this place! this is none other but the house of God, and this is the gate of heaven. 28:16–17

218 Leah was tender eyed; but Rachel was beautiful and well favoured. 29:17

219 Now Israel loved Joseph more than all his children, because he was the son of his old age: and he made him a coat of many colours. 37:3

220 And they said one to another, Behold, this dreamer cometh.
Come now therefore, and let us slay him, and cast him into some pit, and we will say, Some evil beast hath devoured him: and we shall see what will become of his dreams. 37:19–20

221 And all his sons and all his daughters rose up to comfort him; but he refused to be comforted; and he said, For I will go down into the grave unto my son mourning. Thus his father wept for him. 37:35

222 And Judah said unto Onan, Go in unto thy brother's wife, and marry her, and raise up seed to thy brother.
And Onan knew that the seed should not be his; and it came to pass, when he went in unto his brother's wife, that he spilled it on the ground, lest that he should give seed to his brother. 38:8–9

223 And the seven thin ears devoured the seven rank and full ears. And Pharaoh awoke, and, behold, it was a dream. 41:7

224 And the famine was sore in the land. 43:1

225 And take your father and your households, and come unto me: and I will give you the good of the land of Egypt, and ye shall eat the fat of the land. 45:18

226 The sceptre shall not depart from Judah, nor a lawgiver from between his feet, until Shiloh come; and unto him shall the gathering of the people be. 49:10

227 His eyes shall be red with wine, and his teeth white with milk. 49:12

228 Issachar is a strong ass couching down between two burdens:
And he saw that rest was good, and the land that it was pleasant; and bowed his shoulder to bear, and became a servant unto tribute. 49:14–15

229 Dan shall be a serpent by the way, an adder in the path, that biteth the horse heels, so that his rider shall fall backward.
I have waited for thy salvation, O Lord. 49:17–18

230 Benjamin shall ravin as a wolf: in the morning he shall devour the prey, and at night he shall divide the spoil. 49:27

Habakkuk

231 But the Lord is in his holy temple: let all the earth keep silence before him. 2:20

Haggai

232 Now therefore thus saith the Lord of hosts; Consider your ways.
Ye have sown much, and bring in little; ye eat, but ye have not enough; ye drink, but ye are not filled with drink; ye clothe you, but there is none warm; and he that earneth wages earneth wages to put it into a bag with holes. 1:5–6

Hebrews

233 God, who at sundry times and in divers manners spake in time past unto the fathers by the prophets,
Hath in these last days spoken unto us by his Son, whom he hath appointed heir of all things, by whom also he made the worlds;
Who being the brightness of his glory, and the express image of his person, and upholding all things by the word of his power, when he had by himself purged our sins, sat down on the right hand of the Majesty on high;
Being made so much better than the angels, as he hath by inheritance obtained a more excellent name than they. 1:1–4

234 For the word of God is quick, and powerful, and sharper than any two-edged sword, piercing even to the dividing asunder of soul and spirit, and of the joints and marrow, and is a discerner of the thoughts and intents of the heart. 4:12

235 By faith the walls of Jericho fell down, after they were compassed about seven days. 11:30

236 (Of whom the world was not worthy:) they wandered in deserts, and in mountains, and in dens and caves of the earth. 11:38

237 Let brotherly love continue. Be not forgetful to entertain strangers: for thereby some have entertained angels unawares. 13:1–2

238 And almost all things are by the law purged with blood; and without shedding of blood is no remission. 9:22

239 Now faith is the substance of things hoped for, the evidence of things not seen. 11:1

240 These all died in faith, not having received the promises, but having seen them afar off, and were persuaded of them, and embraced them, and confessed that they were strangers and pilgrims on the earth. 11:13

241 Esteeming the reproach of Christ greater riches than the treasures in Egypt: for he had respect unto the recompence of the reward. 11:26

Hosea

242 For they have sown the wind, and they shall reap the whirlwind: it hath no stalk: the bud shall yield no meal: if so be it yield, the strangers shall swallow it up. 8:7

243 Sow to yourselves in righteousness, reap in mercy; break up your fallow ground: for it is time to seek the Lord, till he come an rain righteousness upon you.
Ye have plowed wickedness, ye have reaped iniquity; ye have eaten the fruit of lies: because thou didst trust in thy way, in the multitude of thy mighty men. 10:12–13

Isaiah

244 Come now, and let us reason together, saith the Lord: though your sins be as scarlet, they shall be as white as snow; though they be red like crimson, they shall be as wool. 1:18

245 How is the faithful city become an harlot! it was full of judgment; righteousness lodged in it; but now murderers. 1:21

246 And it shall come to pass in the last days, that the mountain of the Lord's house shall be established in the top of the mountains, and shall be exalted above the hills; and all nations shall flow unto it. 2:2

247 And he shall judge among the nations, and shall rebuke many people: and they shall beat their swords into plowshares, and their spears into pruning-hooks: nation shall not lift up sword against nation, neither shall they learn war any more. 2:4

248 For, behold, the Lord, the Lord of hosts, doth take away from Jerusalem and from Judah the stay and the staff, the whole stay of bread, and the whole stay of water,
The mighty man, and the man of war, the judge, and the prophet, and the prudent, and the ancient,
The captain of fifty, and the honourable man, and the counsellor, and the cunning artificer, and the eloquent orator.
And I will give children to be their princes, and babes shall rule over them.
And the people shall be oppressed, every one by another, and every one by his neighbour: the child shall behave himself proudly against the ancient, and the base against the honourable. 3:1–5

249 What mean ye that ye beat my people to pieces, and grind the faces of the poor? saith the Lord God of hosts. 3:15

250 Woe unto them that rise up early in the morning, that they may follow strong drink; that continue until night, till wine inflame them! 5:11

251 Woe unto them that call evil good, and good evil; that put darkness for light, and light for darkness; that put bitter for sweet, and sweet for bitter! 5:20

252 In the year that king Uzziah died I saw also the Lord sitting upon a throne, high and lifted up, and his train filled the temple.
Above it stood the seraphims: each one had six wings; with twain he covered his face, and with twain he covered his feet, and with twain he did fly.
And one cried unto another, and said, Holy, holy, holy, is the Lord of hosts: the whole earth is full of his glory.
And the posts of the door moved at the voice of him that cried, and the house was filled with smoke.
Then said I, Woe is me! for I am undone; because I am a man of unclean lips, and I dwell in the midst of a people of unclean lips: for mine eyes have seen the King, the Lord of hosts.
Then flew one of the seraphims unto me, having a live coal in his hand, which he had taken with the tongs from off the altar:
And he laid it upon my mouth, and said, Lo, this hath touched thy lips; and thine iniquity is taken away, and thy sin purged.
Also I heard the voice of the Lord, saying, Whom shall I send, and who will go for us? Then said I, Here am I; send me. 6:1–8

253 Therefore the Lord himself shall give you a sign; Behold, a virgin shall conceive, and bear a son, and shall call his name Immanuel.
Butter and honey shall he eat, that he may know to refuse the evil, and choose the good. 7:14–15

254 And he shall be for a sanctuary; but for a stone of stumbling and for a rock of offence to both the houses of Israel, for a gin and for a snare to the inhabitants of Jerusalem. 8:14

255 The people that walked in darkness have seen a great light: they that dwell in the land of the shadow of death, upon them hath the light shined.
Thou hast multiplied the nation, and not increased the joy: they joy before thee according to the joy in harvest, and as men rejoice when they divide the spoil.
For thou hast broken the yoke of his burden, and the staff of his shoulder, the rod of his oppressor, as in the day of Midian. 9:2–4

256 For unto us a child is born, unto us a son is given: and the government shall be upon his shoulder: and his name shall be called Wonderful, Counsellor, The mighty God, The everlasting Father, The Prince of Peace.
Of the increase of his government and peace there shall be no end, upon the throne of David, and upon his kingdom, to order it, and to establish it with judgment and with justice from henceforth even for ever. The zeal of the Lord of hosts will perform this. 9:6–7

257 And there shall come forth a rod out of the stem of Jesse, and a Branch shall grow out of his roots:
And the spirit of the Lord shall rest upon him, the spirit of wisdom and understanding, the spirit of coun-

sel and might, the spirit of knowledge and of the fear of the Lord. 11:1–2

258 The wolf also shall dwell with the lamb, and the leopard shall lie down with the kid; and the calf and the young lion and the fatling together: and a little child shall lead them.
And the cow and the bear shall feed; their young ones shall lie down together: and the lion shall eat straw like the ox.
And the sucking child shall play on the hole of the asp, and the weaned child shall put his hand on the cockatrice' den.
They shall not hurt nor destroy in all my holy mountain: for the earth shall be full of the knowledge of the Lord, as the waters cover the sea. 11:6–9

259 Therefore with joy shall ye draw water out of the wells of salvation. 12:3

260 But wild beasts of the desert shall lie there; and their houses shall be full of doleful creatures; and owls shall dwell there, and satyrs shall dance there.
And the wild beasts of the islands shall cry in their desolate houses, and dragons in their pleasant palaces: and her time is near to come, and her days shall not be prolonged. 13:21–22

261 He calleth to me out of Seir, Watchman, what of the night? Watchman, what of the night?
The watchman said, The morning cometh, and also the night: if ye will enquire, enquire ye: return, come. 21:11–12

262 And behold joy and gladness, slaying oxen, and killing sheep, eating flesh, and drinking wine: let us eat and drink; for tomorrow we shall die. 22:13

263 They shall not drink wine with a song; strong drink shall be bitter to them that drink it. 24:9

264 In that day the Lord with his sore and great and strong sword shall punish leviathan the piercing serpent, even leviathan that crooked serpent; and he shall slay the dragon that is in the sea. 27:1

265 For precept must be upon precept, precept upon precept; line upon line, line upon line; here a little, and there a little. 28:10

266 Stay yourselves, and wonder; cry ye out, and cry: they are drunken, but not with wine; they stagger, but not with strong drink. 29:9

267 And though the Lord give you the bread of adversity, and the water of affliction, yet shall not thy teachers be removed into a corner any more, but thine eyes shall see thy teachers. 30:20

268 The wilderness and the solitary place shall be glad for them; and the desert shall rejoice, and blossom as the rose. 35:1

269 Then the eyes of the blind shall be opened, and the ears of the deaf shall be unstopped.
Then shall the lame man leap as an hart, and the tongue of the dumb sing: for in the wilderness shall waters break out, and streams in the desert.
And the parched ground shall become a pool, and the thirsty land springs of water: in the habitation of dragons, where each lay, shall be grass with reeds and rushes. 35:5–7

270 Comfort ye, comfort ye my people, saith your God.
Speak ye comfortably to Jerusalem, and cry unto her, that her warfare is accomplished, that her iniquity is pardoned: for she hath received of the Lord's hand double for all her sins.
The voice of him that crieth in the wilderness, Prepare ye the way of the Lord, make straight in the desert a highway for our God.
Every valley shall be exalted, and every mountain and hill shall be made low: and the crooked shall be made straight, and the rough places plain:
And the glory of the Lord shall be revealed, and all flesh shall see it together: for the mouth of the Lord hath spoken it.
The voice said, Cry. And he said, What shall I cry? All flesh is grass, and all the goodliness thereof is as the flower of the field:
The grass withereth, the flower fadeth: because the spirit of the Lord bloweth upon it: surely the people is grass.
The grass withereth, the flower fadeth: but the word of our God shall stand for ever.
O Zion, that bringest good tidings, get thee up into the high mountain; O Jerusalem, that bringest good tidings, lift up thy voice with strength; lift it up, be not afraid; say unto the cities of Judah, Behold your God! 40:1–9

271 He shall feed his flock like a shepherd: he shall gather the lambs with his arm, and carry them in his bosom, and shall gently lead those that are with young. 40:11

272 The isles saw it, and feared; the ends of the earth were afraid, drew near, and came.
They helped every one his neighbour; and every one said to his brother, Be of good courage. 41:5–6

273 Verily thou art a God that hidest thyself, O God of Israel, the Saviour. 45:15

274 There is no peace, saith the Lord, unto the wicked. 48:22

275 How beautiful upon the mountains are the feet of him that bringeth good tidings, that publisheth peace; that bringeth good tidings of good, that publisheth salvation; that saith unto Zion, Thy God reigneth! 52:7

276 All we like sheep have gone astray; we have turned every one to his own way; and the Lord hath laid on him the iniquity of us all.
He was oppressed, and he was afflicted, yet he opened not his mouth: he is brought as a lamb to the slaughter, and as a sheep before her shearers is dumb, so he openeth not his mouth.
He was taken from prison and from judgment: and who shall declare his generation? for he was cut off out of the land of the living: for the transgression of my people was he stricken. 53:6–8

277 The righteous perisheth, and no man layeth it to heart: and merciful men are taken away, none considering that the righteous is taken away from the evil to come. 57:1

278 Oh that thou wouldest rend the heavens, that thou wouldest come down, that the mountains might flow down at thy presence. 64:1

279 Which say, Stand by thyself, come not near to me; for I am holier than thou. These are a smoke in my nose, a fire that burneth all the day. 65:5

280 For, behold, I create new heavens and a new earth: and the former shall not be remembered, nor come into mind. 65:17

James

281 Blessed is the man that endureth temptation: for when he is tried, he shall receive the crown of life, which the Lord hath promised to them that love him. 1:12

282 Every good gift and every perfect gift is from above, and cometh down from the Father of lights, with whom is no variableness, neither shadow of turning. 1:17

283 Wherefore, my beloved brethren, let every man be swift to hear, slow to speak, slow to wrath:
For the wrath of man worketh not the righteousness of God.
Wherefore lay apart all filthiness and superfluity of naughtiness, and receive with meekness the engrafted word, which is able to save your souls.
But be ye doers of the word, and not hearers only, deceiving your own selves.
For if any be a hearer of the word, and not a doer, he is like unto a man beholding his natural face in a glass:
For he beholdeth himself, and goeth his way, and straightway forgetteth what manner of man he was.
But whoso looketh into the perfect law of liberty, and continueth therein, he being not a forgetful hearer, but a doer of the work, this man shall be blessed in his deed. 1:19–25

284 Even so faith, if it hath not works, is dead, being alone. 2:17

285 Even so the tongue is a little member, and boasteth great things. Behold, how great a matter a little fire kindleth! 3:5

286 But the tongue can no man tame; it is an unruly evil, full of deadly poison. 3:8

287 Submit yourselves therefore to God. Resist the devil, and he will flee from you.
Draw nigh to God, and he will draw nigh to you. Cleanse your hands, ye sinners; and purify your hearts, ye double minded. 4:7–8

288 Grudge not one against another, brethren, lest ye be condemned: behold, the judge standeth before the door. 5:9

289 Let him know, that he which converteth the sinner from the error of his way shall save a soul from death, and shall hide a multitude of sins. 5:20

Jeremiah

290 They have healed also the hurt of the daughter of my people slightly, saying, Peace, peace; when there is no peace. 6:14

291 We looked for peace, but no good came; and for a time of health, and behold trouble! 8:15

292 Can the Ethiopian change his skin, or the leopard his spots? then may ye also do good, that are accustomed to do evil. 13:23

293 And it shall come to pass, if they say unto thee, Whither shall we go forth? then thou shalt tell them, Thus saith the Lord; Such as are for death, to death; and such as are for the sword, to the sword; and such as are for the famine, to the famine; and such as are for the captivity, to the captivity. 15:2

294 In their heat I will make their feasts, and I will make them drunken, that they may rejoice, and sleep a perpetual sleep, and not wake, saith the Lord. 51:39

Job

295 And the Lord said unto Satan, Whence comest thou? Then Satan answered the Lord, and said, From going to and fro in the earth, and from walking up and down in it.
And the Lord said unto Satan, Hast thou considered my servant Job, that there is none like him in the earth, a perfect and an upright man, one that feareth God, and escheweth evil?
Then Satan answered the Lord, and said, Doth Job fear God for nought? 1:7–9

296 Naked came I out of my mother's womb, and naked shall I return thither: the Lord gave, and the Lord hath taken away; blessed be the name of the Lord.
In all this Job sinned not, nor charged God foolishly. 1:21–22

297 Then said his wife unto him, Dost thou still retain thine integrity? curse God, and die. 2:9

298 Let the day perish wherein I was born, and the night in which it was said, There is a man child conceived. 3:3

299 The eye of him that hath seen me shall see me no more: thine eyes are upon me, and I am not. 7:8

300 Wherefore then hast thou brought me forth out of the womb? Oh that I had given up the ghost, and no eye had seen me! 10:18

301 With the ancient is wisdom; and in length of days understanding. 12:12

302 They grope in the dark without light, and he maketh them to stagger like a drunken man. 12:25

303 Man that is born of a woman is of few days, and full of trouble. 14:1

304 Then Job answered and said, I have heard many such things: miserable comforters are ye all. 16:1–2

305 I have said to corruption, Thou art my father: to the worm, Thou art my mother, and my sister. 17:14

306 For I know that my redeemer liveth, and that he shall stand at the latter day upon the earth:
And though after my skin worms destroy this body, yet in my flesh shall I see God. 19:25–26

307 No mention shall be made of coral, or of pearls: for the price of wisdom is above rubies. 28:18

308 I was eyes to the blind, and feet was I to the lame. 29:15

309 What man is like Job, who drinketh up scorning like water? 34:7

310 Then the Lord answered Job out of the whirlwind, and said,
Who is this that darkeneth counsel by words without knowledge?
Gird up now thy loins like a man; for I will demand of thee, and answer thou me.
Where wast thou when I laid the foundations of the earth? declare, if thou hast understanding.
Who hath laid the measures there-

of, if thou knowest? or who hath stretched the line upon it? Whereupon are the foundations thereof fastened? or who laid the corner stone thereof;
When the morning stars sang together, and all the sons of God shouted for joy? 38:1–7

311 Hath the rain a father? or who hath begotten the drops of dew? 38:28

312 Canst thou bind the sweet influences of Pleiades, or loose the bands of Orion? 38:31

313 Deck thyself now with majesty and excellency; and array thyself with glory and beauty. 40:10

314 Canst thou draw out leviathan with an hook? or his tongue with a cord which thou lettest down? 41:1

315 So the Lord blessed the latter end of Job more than his beginning: for he had fourteen thousand sheep, and six thousand camels, and a thousand yoke of oxen, and a thousand she asses. 42:12

John

316 In the beginning was the Word, and the Word was with God, and the Word was God.
The same was in the beginning with God.
All things were made by him; and without him was not any thing made that was made.
In him was life; and the life was the light of men.
And the light shineth in darkness; and the darkness comprehended it not.
There was a man sent from God, whose name was John.
The same came for a witness, to bear witness of the Light, that all men through him might believe.
He was not that Light, but was sent to bear witness of that Light.
That was the true Light, which lighteth every man that cometh into the world.
He was in the world, and the world was made by him, and the world knew him not.
He came unto his own, and his own received him not.
But as many as received him, to them gave he power to become the sons of God, even to them that believe on his name:
Which were born, not of blood, nor of the will of the flesh, the will of man, but of God.
And the Word was made flesh, and dwelt among us, (and we beheld his glory, the glory as of the only begotten of the Father,) full of grace and truth. 1:1–14

317 He it is, who coming after me is preferred before me, whose shoe's latchet I am not worthy to unloose. 1:27

318 The next day John seeth Jesus coming unto him, and saith, Behold the Lamb of God, which taketh away the sin of the world. 1:29

319 Jesus saith unto her, Woman, what have I to do with thee? mine hour is not yet come. 2:4

320 When the ruler of the feast had tasted the water that was made wine, and knew not whence it was: (but the servants which drew the water knew;) the governor of the feast called the bridegroom,
And saith unto him, Every man at the beginning doth set forth good wine; and when men have well drunk, then that which is worse: but thou hast kept the good wine until now. 2:9–10

321 Jesus answered and said unto him, Verily, verily, I say unto thee, Except a man be born again, he cannot see the kingdom of God. 3:3

322 Jesus answered, Verily, verily, I say unto thee, Except a man be born of water and of the Spirit, he cannot enter into the kingdom of God.
That which is born of the flesh is flesh; and that which is born of the Spirit is spirit. 3:5–6

323 The wind bloweth where it listeth, and thou hearest the sound thereof, but canst not tell whence it cometh, and whither it goeth: so is every one that is born of the Spirit. 3:8

324 For God so loved the world, that he gave his only begotten Son, that whosoever believeth in him should not perish, but have everlasting life. 3:16

325 And this is the condemnation, that light is come into the world, and men loved darkness rather than light, because their deeds were evil. 3:19

326 He that hath the bride is the bridegroom: but the friend of the bridegroom, which standeth and heareth him, rejoiceth greatly because of the bridegroom's voice: this my joy therefore is fulfilled.
He must increase, but I must decrease. 3:29–30

327 Jesus answered and said unto her, Whosoever drinketh of this water shall thirst again:
But whosoever drinketh of the water that I shall give him shall never thirst; but the water that I shall give him shall be in him a well of water springing up into everlasting life. 4:13–14

328 Afterward Jesus findeth him in the temple, and said unto him, Behold, thou art made whole: sin no more, lest a worse thing come unto thee. 5:14

329 Verily, verily, I say unto you, He that heareth my word, and believeth on him that sent me, hath everlasting life, and shall not come into condemnation; but is passed from death unto life.
Verily, verily, I say unto you, The hour is coming, and now is, when the dead shall hear the voice of the Son of God: and they that hear shall live. 5:24–25

330 There is a lad here, which hath five barley loaves, and two small fishes: but what are they among so many?
And Jesus said, Make the men sit down. Now there was much grass in the place. So the men sat down, in number about five thousand. 6:9–10

331 And Jesus said unto them, I am the bread of life: he that cometh to me shall never hunger; and he that believeth on me shall never thirst. 6:35

332 All that the Father giveth me shall come to me; and him that cometh to me I will in no wise cast out. 6:37

333 Your fathers did eat manna in the wilderness, and are dead.
This is the bread which cometh down from heaven, that a man may eat thereof, and not die.
I am the living bread which came down from heaven: if any man eat of this bread, he shall live for ever: and the bread that I will give

is my flesh, which I will give for the life of the world. 6:49–51

334 So when they continued asking him, he lifted up himself, and said unto them, He that is without sin among you, let him first cast a stone at her. 8:7

335 She said, No man, Lord. And Jesus said unto her, Neither do I condemn thee: go, and sin no more. 8:11

336 Then spake Jesus again unto them, saying, I am the light of the world: he that followeth me shall not walk in darkness, but shall have the light of life. 8:12

337 And ye shall know the truth, and the truth shall make you free. 8:32

338 He answered and said, Whether he be a sinner or no, I know not: one thing I know, that, whereas I was blind, now I see. 9:25

339 Verily, verily, I say unto you, He that entereth not by the door into the sheepfold, but climbeth up some other way the same is a thief and a robber.
But he that entereth in by the door is the shepherd of the sheep.
To him the porter openeth, and the sheep hear his voice: and he calleth his own sheep by name, and leadeth them out.
And when he putteth forth his own sheep, he goeth before them, and the sheep follow him: for they know his voice. 10:1–4

340 I am the door: by me if any man enter in, he shall be saved, and shall go in and out, and find pasture. 10:9

341 I am the good shepherd: the good shepherd giveth his life for the sheep.
But he that is an hireling, and not the shepherd, whose own the sheep are not, seeth the wolf coming, and leaveth the sheep, and fleeth: and the wolf catcheth them, and scattereth the sheep.
The hireling fleeth, because he is an hireling, and careth not for the sheep. 10:11–13

342 Jesus said unto her, I am the resurrection, and the life: he that believeth in me, though he were dead, yet shall he live. 11:25

343 When Jesus therefore saw her weeping, and the Jews also weeping which came with her, he groaned in the spirit, and was troubled,
And said, Where have ye laid him? They said unto him, Lord, come and see.
Jesus wept. 11:33–35

344 Now is the judgment of this world: now shall the prince of this world be cast out.
And I, if I be lifted up from the earth, will draw all men unto me. 12:31–32

345 Now there was leaning on Jesus' bosom one of his disciples, whom Jesus loved. 13:23

346 In my Father's house are many mansions: if it were not so, I would have told you. I go to prepare a place for you. 14:2

347 Jesus saith unto him, I am the way, the truth, and the life: no man cometh unto the Father, but by me. 14:6

348 If ye love me, keep my commandments.
And I will pray the Father, and he shall give you another Comforter, that he may abide with you for ever;
Even the Spirit of truth; whom the world cannot receive, because it seeth him not, neither knoweth him: but ye know him; for he dwelleth with you, and shall be in you. 14:15–17

349 Peace I leave with you, my peace I give unto you: not as the world giveth, give I unto you. Let not your heart be troubled, neither let it be afraid. 14:27

350 I am the true vine, and my Father is the husbandman. 15:1

351 Greater love hath no man than this, that a man lay down his life for his friends. 15:13

352 Ye have not chosen me, but I have chosen you, and ordained you, that ye should go and bring forth fruit, and that your fruit should remain: that whatsoever ye shall ask of the Father in my name, he may give it you. 15:16

353 But now I go my way to him that sent me; and none of you asketh me, Whither goest thou? 16:5

354 Quo vadis? Vulgate 16:5

355 Nevertheless I tell you the truth; It is expedient for you that I go away: for if I go not away, the Comforter will not come unto you; but if I depart, I will send him unto you. 16:7

356 A woman when she is in travail hath sorrow, because her hour is come: but as soon as she is delivered of the child, she remembereth no more the anguish, for joy that a man is born into the world. 16:21

357 These things I have spoken unto you, that in me ye might have peace. In the world ye shall have tribulation: but be of good cheer; I have overcome the world. 16:33

358 Now Caiaphas was he, which gave counsel to the Jews, that it was expedient that one man should die for the people. 18:14

359 Pilate saith unto him, What is truth? And when he had said this, he went out again unto the Jews, and saith unto them, I find in him no fault at all. 18:38

360 Then cried they all again, saying, Not this man, but Barabbas. Now Barabbas was a robber. 18:40

361 Then came Jesus forth, wearing the crown of thorns, and the purple robe. And Pilate saith unto them, Behold the man! 19:5

362 Ecce homo. Vulgate 19:5

363 Pilate answered, What I have written I have written. 19:22

364 When Jesus therefore saw his mother, and the disciple standing by, whom he loved, he saith unto his mother, Woman, behold thy son!
Then saith he to the disciple, Behold thy mother! And from that hour that disciple took her unto his own home. 19:26–27

365 When Jesus therefore had received the vinegar, he said, It is finished: and he bowed his head, and gave up the ghost. 19:30

366 Consummatum est. Vulgate 19:30

367 Now in the place where he was crucified there was a garden; and in the garden a new sepulchre, wherein was never man yet laid. 19:41

368 The first day of the week cometh

Mary Magdalene early, when it was yet dark, unto the sepulchre, and seeth the stone taken away from the sepulchre.
Then she runneth, and cometh to Simon Peter, and to the other disciple, whom Jesus loved, and saith unto them, They have taken the Lord out of the sepulchre, and we know not where they have laid him. 20:1–2

369 Jesus saith unto her, Woman, why weepest thou? whom seekest thou? She, supposing him to be the gardener, saith unto him, Sir, if thou have borne him hence, tell me where thou hast laid him, and I will take him away.
Jesus saith unto her, Mary. She turned herself, and saith unto him, Rabboni; which is to say, Master.
Jesus saith unto her, Touch me not; for I am not yet ascended to my Father: but go to my brethren, and say unto them, I ascend unto my Father, and your Father; and to my God, and your God. 20:15–17

370 Noli me tangere. Vulgate 20:17

371 The other disciples therefore said unto him, We have seen the Lord. But he said unto them, Except I shall see in his hands the print of the nails, and put my finger into the print of the nails, and thrust my hand into his side, I will not believe. 20:25

372 Then saith he to Thomas, Reach hither thy finger, and behold my hands; and reach hither thy hand, and thrust it into my side: and be not faithless, but believing.
And Thomas answered and said unto him, My Lord and my God.
Jesus saith unto him, Thomas, because thou hast seen me, thou hast believed: blessed are they that have not seen, and yet have believed. 20:27–29

373 So when they had dined, Jesus saith to Simon Peter, Simon, son of Jonas, lovest thou me more than these? He saith unto him, Yea, Lord; thou knowest that I love thee. He saith unto him, Feed my lambs. 21:15

374 He saith unto him the third time, Simon, son of Jonas, lovest thou me? Peter was grieved because he said unto him the third time, Lovest thou me? And he said unto him, Lord, thou knowest all things; thou knowest that I love thee. Jesus saith unto him, Feed my sheep. 21:17

375 Peter seeing him saith to Jesus, Lord, and what shall this man do? Jesus saith unto him, If I will that he tarry till I come, what is that to thee? follow thou me. 21:21–22

I John

376 If we say that we have no sin, we deceive ourselves, and the truth is not in us.
If we confess our sins, he is faithful and just to forgive us our sins, and to cleanse us from all unrighteousness. 1:8–9

377 For all that is in the world, the lust of the flesh, and the lust of the eyes, and the pride of life, is not of the Father, but is of the world. 2:16

378 Beloved, let us love one another: for love is of God; and every one that loveth is born of God, and knoweth God.
He that loveth not knoweth not God; for God is love. 4:7–8

379 There is no fear in love; but perfect love casteth out fear: because fear hath torment. He that feareth is not made perfect in love. 4:18

380 If a man say, I love God, and hateth his brother, he is a liar: for he that loveth not his brother whom he hath seen, how can he love God whom he hath not seen? 4:20

381 Little children, keep yourselves from idols. 5:21

Jonah

382 So the shipmaster came to him, and said unto him, What meanest thou, O sleeper? arise, call upon thy God, if so be that God will think upon us, that we perish not.
And they said every one to his fellow, Come, and let us cast lots, that we may know for whose cause this evil is upon us. So they cast lots, and the lot fell upon Jonah. 1:6–7

383 Now the Lord had prepared a great fish to swallow up Jonah. And Jonah was in the belly of the fish three days and three nights. 1:17

Joshua

384 And the priests that bare the ark of the covenant of the Lord stood firm on dry ground in the midst of Jordan, and all the Israelites passed over on dry ground, until all the people were passed clean over Jordan. 3:17

385 So the people shouted when the priests blew with the trumpets: and it came to pass, when the people heard the sound of the trumpet, and the people shouted with a great shout, that the wall fell down flat, so that the people went up into the city, every man straight before him, and they took the city. 6:20

386 And the princes said unto them, Let them live; but let them be hewers of wood and drawers of water unto all the congregation; as the princes had promised them. 9:21

Jude

387 Mercy unto you, and peace, and love, be multiplied. 2

Judges

388 And when he shewed them the entrance into the city, they smote the city with the edge of the sword; but they let go the man and all his family. 1:25

389 They fought from heaven; the stars in their courses fought against Sisera. 5:20

390 Blessed above women shall Jael the wife of Heber the Kenite be, blessed shall she be above women in the tent.
He asked water, and she gave him milk; she brought forth butter in a lordly dish.
She put her hand to the nail, and her right hand to the workmen's hammer; and with the hammer she smote Sisera, she smote off his head, when she had pierced and stricken through his temples.
At her feet he bowed, he fell, he lay down: at her feet he bowed, he fell: where he bowed, there he fell down dead.
The mother of Sisera looked out at a window, and cried through the lattice, Why is his chariot so long

in coming? why tarry the wheels of his chariots? 5:24–28

391 And the angel of the Lord appeared unto him, and said unto him, The Lord is with thee, thou mighty man of valour. 6:12

392 And he said unto them, Out of the eater came forth meat, and out of the strong came forth sweetness. And they could not in three days expound the riddle. 14:14

393 And the men of the city said unto him on the seventh day before the sun went down, What is sweeter than honey? and what is stronger than a lion? And he said unto them, If ye had not plowed with my heifer, ye had not found out my riddle. 14:18

394 And he smote them hip and thigh with a great slaughter. 15:8

395 And Samson said, With the jawbone of an ass, heaps upon heaps, with the jaw of an ass have I slain a thousand men. 15:16

396 In those days there was no king in Israel, but every man did that which was right in his own eyes. 17:6

I Kings

397 So David slept with his fathers, and was buried in the city of David. 2:10

398 Then the king answered and said, Give her the living child, and in no wise slay it: she is the mother thereof.
And all Israel heard of the judgment which the king had judged; and they feared the king: for they saw that the wisdom of God was in him, to do judgment. 3:27–28

399 And when the queen of Sheba heard of the fame of Solomon concerning the name of the Lord, she came to prove him with hard questions. 10:1

400 But king Solomon loved many strange women, together with the daughter of Pharaoh, women of the Moabites, Ammonites, Edomites, Zidonians, and Hittites. 11:1

401 Get thee hence, and turn thee eastward, and hide thyself by the brook Cherith, that is before Jordan.
And it shall be, that thou shalt drink of the brook; and I have commanded the ravens to feed thee there. 17:3–4

402 But he himself went a day's journey into the wilderness, and came and sat down under a juniper tree: and he requested for himself that he might die; and said, It is enough; now, O Lord, take away my life; for I am not better than my fathers. 19:4

403 And he said, Go forth, and stand upon the mount before the Lord. And, behold, the Lord passed by, and a great and strong wind rent the mountains, and brake in pieces the rocks before the Lord; but the Lord was not in the wind: and after the wind an earthquake; but the Lord was not in the earthquake:
And after the earthquake a fire; but the Lord was not in the fire: and after the fire a still small voice. 19:11–12

404 And say, Thus saith the king, Put this fellow in the prison, and feed him with bread of affliction and with water of affliction, until I come in peace. 22:27

II Kings

405 And it came to pass, as they still went on, and talked, that, behold, there appeared a chariot of fire, and horses of fire, and parted them both asunder; and Elijah went up by a whirlwind into heaven.
And Elisha saw it, and he cried, My father, my father, the chariot of Israel, and the horsemen thereof. And he saw him no more: and he took hold of his own clothes, and rent them in two pieces. 2:11–12

406 And when Jehu was come to Jezreel, Jezebel heard of it; and she painted her face, and tired her head, and looked out at a window. 9:30

407 And they went to bury her: but they found no more of her than the skull, and the feet, and the palms of her hands. 9:35

408 In those days was Hezekiah sick unto death. And the prophet Isaiah the son of Amoz came to him, and said unto him, Thus saith the Lord, Set thine house in order; for thou shalt die, and not live.
Then he turned his face to the wall. 20:1–2

Lamentations

409 And I said, My strength and my hope is perished from the Lord: Remembering mine affliction and my misery, the wormwood and the gall. 3:18–19

410 It is good for a man that he bear the yoke in his youth. 3:27

411 Waters flowed over mine head; then I said, I am cut off. 3:54

Luke

412 And the angel came in unto her, and said, Hail, thou that art highly favoured, the Lord is with thee: blessed art thou among women.
And when she saw him, she was troubled at his saying, and cast in her mind what manner of salutation this should be. 1:28–29

413 And Mary said, My soul doth magnify the Lord,
And my spirit hath rejoiced in God my Saviour.
For he hath regarded the low estate of his handmaiden: for, behold, from henceforth all generations shall call me blessed. 1:46–48

414 He hath shewed strength with his arm; he hath scattered the proud in the imagination of their hearts.
He hath put down the mighty from their seats, and exalted them of low degree.
He hath filled the hungry with good things; and the rich he hath sent empty away. 1:51–53

415 Blessed be the Lord God of Israel; for he hath visited and redeemed his people. 1:68

416 And the child grew, and waxed strong in spirit, and was in the deserts till the day of his shewing unto Israel. 1:80

417 And it came to pass in those days, that there went out a decree from Caesar Augustus, that all the world should be taxed. 2:1

418 And she brought forth her firstborn son, and wrapped him in swaddling clothes, and laid him in a manger; because there was no room for them in the inn. 2:7

419 And there were in the same country shepherds abiding in the field, keeping watch over their flock by night.
And, lo, the angel of the Lord came upon them, and the glory of the Lord shone round about them: and they were sore afraid.
And the angel said unto them, Fear not: for, behold, I bring you good tidings of great joy, which shall be to all people. 2:8–10

420 Glory to God in the highest, and on earth peace, good will toward men. 2:14

421 But Mary kept all these things, and pondered them in her heart. 2:19

422 Lord, now lettest thou thy servant depart in peace, according to thy word:
For mine eyes have seen thy salvation,
Which thou hast prepared before the face of all people;
A light to lighten the Gentiles, and the glory of thy people Israel. 2:29–32

423 And it came to pass, that after three days they found him in the temple, sitting in the midst of the doctors, both hearing them, and asking them questions.
And all that heard him were astonished at his understanding and answers. 2:46–47

424 And the devil, taking him up into an high mountain, shewed unto him all the kingdoms of the world in a moment of time. 4:5

425 And he said unto them, Ye will surely say unto me this proverb, Physician, heal thyself: whatsoever we have heard done in Capernaum, do also here in thy country. 4:23

426 No man also having drunk old wine straightway desireth new: for he saith, The old is better. 5:39

427 And stood at his feet behind him weeping, and began to wash his feet with tears, and did wipe them with the hairs of her head, and kissed his feet, and anointed them with the ointment. 7:38

428 Wherefore I say unto thee, Her sins, which are many, are forgiven; for she loved much: but to whom little is forgiven, the same loveth little. 7:47

429 And he said to the woman, Thy faith hath saved thee; go in peace. 7:50

430 Go your ways: behold, I send you forth as lambs among wolves.
Carry neither purse, nor scrip, nor shoes: and salute no man by the way.
And into whatsoever house ye enter, first say, Peace be to this house.
And if the son of peace be there, your peace shall rest upon it: if not, it shall turn to you again.
And in the same house remain, eating and drinking such things as they give: for the labourer is worthy of his hire. Go not from house to house. 10:3–7

431 And he said unto them, I beheld Satan as lightning fall from heaven. 10:18

432 And Jesus answering said, A certain man went down from Jerusalem to Jericho, and fell among thieves, which stripped him of his raiment, and wounded him, and departed, leaving him half dead.
And by chance there came down a certain priest that way: and when he saw him, he passed by on the other side. 10:30–31

433 But a certain Samaritan, as he journeyed, came where he was: and when he saw him, he had compassion on him,
And went to him, and bound up his wounds, pouring in oil and wine, and set him on his own beast, and brought him to an inn, and took care of him.
And on the morrow when he departed, he took out two pence, and gave them to the host, and said unto him, Take care of him; and whatsoever thou spendest more, when I come again, I will repay thee. 10:33–35

434 And he said, He that shewed mercy on him. Then said Jesus unto him, Go, and do thou likewise. 10:37

435 Woe unto you, lawyers! for ye have taken away the key of knowledge: ye entered not in yourselves, and them that were entering in ye hindered. 11:52

436 Are not five sparrows sold for two farthings, and not one of them is forgotten before God? 12:6

437 And they all with one consent began to make excuse. The first said unto him, I have bought a piece of ground, and I must needs go and see it: I pray thee have me excused.
And another said, I have bought five yoke of oxen, and I go to prove them: I pray thee have me excused.
And another said, I have married a wife, and therefore I cannot come.
So that servant came, and shewed his lord these things. Then the master of the house being angry said to his servant, Go out quickly into the streets and lanes of the city, and bring in hither the poor, and the maimed, and the halt, and the blind. 14:18–21

438 What man of you, having an hundred sheep, if he lose one of them, doth not leave the ninety and nine in the wilderness, and go after that which is lost until he find it?
And when he hath found it, he layeth it on his shoulders, rejoicing.
And when he cometh home, he calleth together his friends and neighbours, saying unto them, Rejoice with me; for I have found my sheep which was lost.
I say unto you, that likewise joy shall be in heaven over one sinner that repenteth, more than over ninety and nine just persons, which need no repentance. 15:4–7

439 And he would fain have filled his belly with the husks that the swine did eat: and no man gave unto him.
And when he came to himself, he said, How many hired servants of my father's have bread enough and to spare, and I perish with hunger!
I will arise and go to my father, and will say unto him, Father, I have sinned against heaven, and before thee,
And am no more worthy to be called thy son: make me as one of thy hired servants.
And he arose, and came to his father. But when he was yet a great way off, his father saw him, and had compassion, and ran, and fell on his neck, and kissed him. 15:16–20

440 And bring hither the fatted calf, and

kill it; and let us eat, and be merry:
For this my son was dead, and is alive again; he was lost, and is found. And they began to be merry. 15:23–24

441 There was a certain rich man, which was clothed in purple and fine linen, and fared sumptuously every day:
And there was a certain beggar named Lazarus, which was laid at his gate, full of sores,
And desiring to be fed with the crumbs which fell from the rich man's table: moreover the dogs came and licked his sores.
And it came to pass, that the beggar died, and was carried by the angels into Abraham's bosom: the rich man also died, and was buried; 16:19–22

442 And when he was demanded of the Pharisees, when the kingdom of God should come, he answered them and said, The kingdom of God cometh not with observation:
Neither shall they say, Lo here! or, lo there! for, behold, the kingdom of God is within you. 17:20–21

443 Remember Lot's wife. 17:32

444 And he saith unto him, Out of thine own mouth will I judge thee, thou wicked servant. Thou knewest that I was an austere man, taking up that I laid not down, and reaping that I did not sow. 19:22

445 And he answered and said unto them, I tell you that, if these should hold their peace, the stones would immediately cry out. 19:40

446 And when they were come to the place, which is called Calvary, there they crucified him, and the malefactors, one on the right hand, and the other on the left. 23:33

447 Then said Jesus, Father, forgive them; for they know not what they do. And they parted his raiment, and cast lots. 23:34

448 But the other answering rebuked him, saying, Dost not thou fear God, seeing thou art in the same condemnation?
And we indeed justly; for we receive the due reward of our deeds: but this man hath done nothing amiss.
And he said unto Jesus, Lord, remember me when thou comest into thy kingdom.
And Jesus said unto him, Verily I say unto thee, Today shalt thou be with me in paradise. 23:40–43

449 And when Jesus had cried with a loud voice, he said, Father, into thy hands I commend my spirit: and having said thus, he gave up the ghost. 23:46

450 And as they were afraid, and bowed down their faces to the earth, they said unto them, Why seek ye the living among the dead? 24:5

451 Saying, The Lord is risen indeed, and hath appeared to Simon.
And they told what things were done in the way, and how he was known of them in breaking of bread. 24:34–35

I Maccabees

452 I perceive therefore that for this cause these troubles are come upon me, and, behold, I perish through great grief in a strange land. 6:13

Malachi

453 Have we not all one father? hath not one God created us? why do we deal treacherously every man against his brother, by profaning the covenant of our fathers? 2:10

454 Behold, I will send my messenger, and he shall prepare the way before me: and the Lord, whom ye seek, shall suddenly come to his temple, even the messenger of the covenant, whom ye delight in: behold, he shall come, saith the Lord of hosts.
But who may abide the day of his coming? and who shall stand when he appeareth? for he is like a refiner's fire, and like fullers' soap. 3:1–2

455 But unto you that fear my name shall the Sun of righteousness arise with healing in his wings; and ye shall go forth, and grow up as calves of the stall. 4:2

Mark

456 And he said unto them, The sabbath was made for man, and not man for the sabbath: Therefore the Son of man is Lord also of the sabbath. 2:27–28

457 And he asked him, What is thy name? And he answered, saying. My name is Legion: for we are many. 5:9

458 And forthwith Jesus gave them leave. And the unclean spirits went out, and entered into the swine: and the herd ran violently down a steep place into the sea, (they were about two thousand;) and were choked in the sea. 5:13

459 For what shall it profit a man, if he sahll gain the whole world, and lose his own soul? Or what shall a man give in exchange for his soul? 8:36–37

460 But when Jesus saw it, he was much displeased, and said unto them. Suffer the little children to come unto me, and forbid them not: for of such is the kingdom of God. 10:14

461 And there came a certain poor widow, and she threw in two mites, which make a farthing. And he called unto him his disciples, and saith unto them, Verily I say unto you, That this poor widow hath cast more in, than all they which have cast into the treasury: For all they did cast in of their abundance; but she of her want did cast in all that she had, even all her living. 12:42–44

462 And he said unto them, Go ye into all the world, and preach the gospel to every creature. 16:15

Matthew

463 Now when Jesus was born in Bethlehem of Judaea in the days of Herod the king, behold, there came wise men from the east to Jerusalem,
Saying, Where is he that is born King of the Jews? for we have seen his star in the east, and are come to worship him.
When Herod the king had heard these things, he was troubled, and all Jerusalem with him. 2:1–3

464 And when they were come into the house, they saw the young child with Mary his mother, and fell down, and worshipped him: and when they had opened their treasures, they presented unto him gifts; gold, and frankincense, and myrrh.
And being warned of God in a

dream that they should not return to Herod, they departed into their own country another way. 2:11–12

465 For this is he that was spoken of by the prophet Esaias, saying, The voice of one crying in the wilderness, Prepare ye the way of the Lord, make his paths straight.
And the same John had his raiment of camel's hair, and a leathern girdle about his loins; and his meat was locusts and wild honey. 3:3–4

466 But when he saw many of the Pharisees and Sadducees come to his baptism, he said unto them, O generation of vipers, who hath warned you to flee from the wrath to come? 3:7

467 And Jesus answering said unto him, Suffer it to be so now: for thus it becometh us to fulfil all righteousness. Then he suffered him.
And Jesus, when he was baptized, went up straightway out of the water: and, lo, the heavens were opened unto him, and he saw the Spirit of God descending like a dove, and lighting upon him:
And lo a voice from heaven, saying, This is my beloved Son, in whom I am well pleased. 3:15–17

468 Then was Jesus led up of the Spirit into the wilderness to be tempted of the devil.
And when he had fasted forty days and forty nights, he was afterward an hungred.
And when the tempter came to him, he said, If thou be the Son of God, command that these stones be made bread.
But he answered and said, It is written, Man shall not live by bread alone, but by every word that proceedeth out of the mouth of God. 4:1–4

469 Jesus said unto him, It is written again, Thou shalt not tempt the Lord thy God.
Again, the devil taketh him up into an exceeding high mountain, and sheweth him all the kingdoms of the world, and the glory of them. 4:7–8

470 From that time Jesus began to preach, and to say, Repent: for the kingdom of heaven is at hand. 4:17

471 And he saith unto them, Follow me, and I will make you fishers of men. 4:19

472 Blessed are the poor in spirit: for theirs is the kingdom of heaven.
Blessed are they that mourn: for they shall be comforted.
Blessed are the meek: for they shall inherit the earth.
Blessed are they which do hunger and thirst after righteousness: for they shall be filled.
Blessed are the merciful: for they shall obtain mercy.
Blessed are the pure in heart: for they shall see God.
Blessed are the peacemakers: for they shall be called the children of God.
Blessed are they which are persecuted for righteousness' sake: for theirs is the kingdom of heaven. 5:3–10

473 Ye are the salt of the earth: but if the salt have lost his savour, wherewith shall it be salted? it is thenceforth good for nothing, but to be cast out, and to be trodden under foot of men.
Ye are the light of the world. A city that is set on an hill cannot be hid.
Neither do men light a candle, and put it under a bushel, but on a candlestick; and it giveth light unto all that are in the house.
Let your light so shine before men, that they may see your good works, and glorify your Father which is in heaven. 5:13–16

474 For verily I say unto you, Till heaven and earth pass, one jot or one tittle shall in no wise pass from the law, till all be fulfilled. 5:18

475 For I say unto you, That except your righteousness shall exceed the righteousness of the scribes and Pharisees, ye shall in no case enter into the kingdom of heaven. 5:20

476 And if thy right eye offend thee, pluck it out, and cast it from thee: for it is profitable for thee that one of thy members should perish, and not that thy whole body should be cast into hell. 5:29

477 But I say unto you, That ye resist not evil: but whosoever shall smite thee on thy right cheek, turn to him the other also.
And if any man will sue thee at the law, and take away thy coat, let him have thy cloke also.
And whosoever shall compel thee to go a mile, go with him twain. 5:39–41

478 But I say unto you, Love your enemies, bless them that curse you, do good to them that hate you, and pray for them which despitefully use you, and persecute you;
That ye may be the children of your Father which is in heaven: for he maketh his sun to rise on the evil and on the good, and sendeth rain on the just and on the unjust.
For if ye love them which love you, what reward have ye? do not even the publicans the same? 5:44–46

479 Be ye therefore perfect, even as your Father which is in heaven is perfect. 5:48

480 But when ye pray, use not vain repetitions, as the heathen do: for they think that they shall be heard for their much speaking.
Be not ye therefore like unto them: for your Father knoweth what things ye have need of, before ye ask him.
After this manner therefore pray ye: Our Father which art in heaven, Hallowed be thy name.
Thy kingdom come. Thy will be done in earth, as it is in heaven.
Give us this day our daily bread.
And forgive us our debts, as we forgive our debtors.
And lead us not into temptation, but deliver us from evil: For thine is the kingdom, and the power, and the glory, for ever. Amen. 6:7–13

481 Lay not up for yourselves treasures upon earth, where moth and rust doth corrupt, and where thieves break through and steal:
But lay up for yourselves treasures in heaven, where neither moth nor rust doth corrupt, and where thieves do not break through nor steal:
For where your treasure is, there will your heart be also. 6:19–21

482 No man can serve two masters: for either he will hate the one, and love the other; or else he will hold to the one, and despise the other. Ye cannot serve God and mammon.
Therefore I say unto you, Take no thought for your life, what ye shall eat, or what ye shall drink; nor yet for your body, what ye shall put on. Is not the life more than meat, and the body than raiment? 6:24–25

483 Behold the fowls of the air: for they sow not, neither do they reap, nor gather into barns; yet your heavenly Father feedeth them.
Are ye not much better than they? Which of you by taking thought can add one cubit unto his stature?
And why take ye thought for raiment? Consider the lilies of the field, how they grow; they toil not, neither do they spin:
And yet I say unto you, That even Solomon in all his glory was not arrayed like one of these.
Wherefore, if God so clothe the grass of the field, which today is, and tomorrow is cast into the oven, shall he not much more clothe you, O ye of little faith?
Therefore take no thought, saying, What shall we eat? or, What shall we drink? or, Wherewithal shall we be clothed? 6:26–31

484 But seek ye first the kingdom of God, and his righteousness; and all these things shall be added unto you.
Take therefore no thought for the morrow: for the morrow shall take thought for the things of itself. Sufficient unto the day is the evil thereof. 6:33–34

485 Judge not, that ye be not judged. 7:1

486 And why beholdest thou the mote that is in thy brother's eye, but considerest not the beam that is in thine own eye? 7:3

487 Give not that which is holy unto the dogs, neither cast ye your pearls before swine, lest they trample them under their feet, and turn again and rend you. 7:6

488 Ask, and it shall be given you; seek, and ye shall find; knock, and it shall be opened unto you:
For every one that asketh receiveth; and he that seeketh findeth; and to him that knocketh it shall be opened. 7:7–8

489 Or what man is there of you, whom if his son ask bread, will he give him a stone? 7:9

490 Enter ye in at the strait gate: for wide is the gate, and broad is the way, that leadeth to destruction, and many there be which go in thereat:
Because strait is the gate, and narrow is the way, which leadeth unto life, and few there be that find it. 7:13–14

491 Beware of false prophets, which come to you in sheep's clothing, but inwardly they are ravening wolves. 7:15

492 Ye shall know them by their fruits. Do men gather grapes of thorns, or figs of thistles?
Even so every good tree bringeth forth good fruit; but a corrupt tree bringeth forth evil fruit.
A good tree cannot bring forth evil fruit, neither can a corrupt tree bring forth good fruit.
Every tree that bringeth not forth good fruit is hewn down, and cast into the fire.
Wherefore by their fruits ye shall know them. 7:16–20

493 Therefore whosoever heareth these sayings of mine, and doeth them, I will liken him unto a wise man, which built his house upon a rock:
And the rain descended, and the floods came, and the winds blew, and beat upon that house; and it fell not: for it was founded upon a rock.
And every one that heareth these sayings of mine, and doeth them not, shall be likened unto a foolish man, which built his house upon the sand:
And the rain descended, and the floods came, and the winds blew, and beat upon that house; and it fell: and great was the fall of it. 7:24–27

494 But the children of the kingdom shall be cast out into outer darkness: there shall be weeping and gnashing of teeth. 8:12

495 And Jesus saith unto him, The foxes have boles, and the birds of the air have nests; but the Son of man hath not where to lay his head. 8:20

496 But Jesus said unto him, Follow me; and let the dead bury their dead. 8:22

497 And his disciples came to him, and awoke him, saying, Lord, save us: we perish.
And he saith unto them, Why are ye fearful, O ye of little faith? Then he arose, and rebuked the winds and the sea; and there was a great calm.
But the men marvelled, saying, What manner of man is this, that even the winds and the sea obey him! 8:25–27

498 Neither do men put new wine into old bottles: else the bottles break, and the wine runneth out, and the bottles perish: but they put new wine into new bottles, and both are preserved. 9:17

499 Heal the sick, cleanse the lepers, raise the dead, cast out devils: freely ye have received, freely give. 10:8

500 And ye shall be hated of all men for my name's sake: but he that endureth to the end shall be saved. 10:22

501 Think not that I am come to send peace on earth: I came not to send peace, but a sword. 10:34

502 He that hath ears to hear, let him hear. 11:15

503 Come unto me, all ye that labour and are heavy laden, and I will give you rest.
Take my yoke upon you, and learn of me; for I am meek and lowly in heart: and ye shall find rest unto your souls.
For my yoke is easy, and my burden is light. 11:28–30

504 O generation of vipers, how can ye, being evil, speak good things? for out of the abundance of the heart the mouth speaketh. 12:34

505 For whosoever shall do the will of my Father which is in heaven, the same is my brother, and sister, and mother. 12:50

506 And he spake many things unto them in parables, saying, Behold, a sower went forth to sow;
And when he sowed, some seeds fell by the way side, and the fowls came and devoured them up:
Some fell upon stony places, where they had not much earth: and forthwith they sprung up, because they had no deepness of earth:
And when the sun was up, they were scorched; and because they had no root, they withered away.
And some fell among thorns; and the thorns sprung up, and choked them:
But other fell into good ground, and brought forth fruit, some an

hundredfold, some sixtyfold, some thirtyfold. 13:3–8

507 And they were offended in him. But Jesus said unto them, A prophet is not without honour, save in his own country, and in his own house. 13:57

508 But when Herod's birthday was kept, the daughter of Herodias danced before them, and pleased Herod.
Whereupon he promised with an oath to give her whatsoever she would ask.
And she, being before instructed of her mother, said, Give me John Baptist's head in a charger. 14:6–8

509 And in the fourth watch of the night Jesus went unto them, walking on the sea.
And when the disciples saw him walking on the sea, they were troubled, saying, It is a spirit; and they cried out for fear.
But straightway Jesus spake unto them, saying, Be of good cheer; it is I; be not afraid. 14:25–27

510 And immediately Jesus stretched forth his hand, and caught him, and said unto him, O thou of little faith, wherefore didst thou doubt? 14:31

511 And besought him that they might only touch the hem of his garment: and as many as touched were made perfectly whole. 14:36

512 And I say also unto thee, That thou art Peter, and upon this rock I will build my church; and the gates of hell shall not prevail against it.
And I will give unto thee the keys of the kingdom of heaven: and whatsoever thou shalt bind on earth shall be bound in heaven: and whatsoever thou shalt loose on earth shall be loosed in heaven. 16:18–19

513 Then said Jesus unto his disciples, If any man will come after me, let him deny himself, and take up his cross, and follow me. 16:24

514 And said, Verily I say unto you, Except ye be converted, and become as little children, ye shall not enter into the kingdom of heaven. 18:3

515 And whoso shall receive one such little child in my name receiveth me.
But whoso shall offend one of these little ones which believe in me, it were better for him that a millstone were hanged about his neck, and that he were drowned in the depth of the sea. 18:5–6

516 For where two or three are gathered together in my name, there am I in the midst of them. 18:20

517 Then came Peter to him, and said, Lord, how oft shall my brother sin against me, and I forgive him? till seven times?
Jesus saith unto him, I say not unto thee, Until seven times: but, Until seventy times seven. 18:21–22

518 Wherefore they are no more twain, but one flesh. What therefore God hath joined together, let not man put asunder. 19:6

519 Jesus said unto him, If thou wilt be perfect, go and sell that thou hast, and give to the poor, and thou shalt have treasure in heaven: and come and follow me.
But when the young man heard that saying, he went away sorrowful: for he had great possessions. 19:21–22

520 Then said Jesus unto his disciples, Verily I say unto you, That a rich man shall hardly enter into the kingdom of heaven.
And again I say unto you, It is easier for a camel to go through the eye of a needle, than for a rich man to enter into the kingdom of God. 19:23–24

521 But many that are first shall be last; and the last shall be first. 19:30

522 And a very great multitude spread their garments in the way; others cut down branches from the trees, and strawed them in the way.
And the multitudes that went before, and that followed, cried, saying, Hosanna to the Son of David: Blessed is he that cometh in the name of the Lord; Hosanna in the highest. 21:8–9

523 And said unto them, It is written, My house shall be called the house of prayer; but ye have made it a den of thieves. 21:13

524 For many are called, but few are chosen. 22:14

525 And he saith unto them, Whose is this image and superscription? They say unto him, Caesar's. Then saith he unto them, Render therefore unto Caesar the things which are Caesar's; and unto God the things that are God's. 22:20–21

526 Jesus said unto him, Thou shalt love the Lord thy God with all thy heart, and with all thy soul, and with all thy mind.
This is the first and great commandment.
And the second is like unto it, Thou shalt love thy neighbour as thyself.
On these two commandments hang all the law and the prophets. 22:37–40

527 Woe unto you, scribes and Pharisees, hypocrites! for ye are like unto whited sepulchres, which indeed appear beautiful outward, but are within full of dead men's bones, and of all uncleanness. 23:27

528 And Jesus said unto them, See ye not all these things? verily I say unto you, There shall not be left here one stone upon another, that shall not be thrown down. 24:2

529 And ye shall hear of wars and rumours of wars: see that ye be not troubled: for all these things must come to pass, but the end is not yet.
For nation shall rise against nation, and kingdom against kingdom: and there shall be famines, and pestilences, and earthquakes, in divers places.
All these are the beginning of sorrows. 24:6–8

530 Immediately after the tribulation of those days shall the sun be darkened, and the moon shall not give her light, and the stars shall fall from heaven, and the powers of the heavens shall be shaken:
And then shall appear the sign of the Son of man in heaven: and then shall all the tribes of the earth mourn, and they shall see the Son of man coming in the clouds of heaven with power and great glory.
And he shall send his angels with a great sound of a trumpet, and they shall gather together his elect from the four winds, from one end of heaven to the other. 24:29–31

531 Heaven and earth shall pass away,

but my words shall not pass away. 24:35

532 And at midnight there was a cry made, Behold, the bridegroom cometh; go ye out to meet him.
Then all those virgins arose, and trimmed their lamps.
And the foolish said unto the wise, Give us of your oil; for our lamps are gone out. 25:6–8

533 And unto one he gave five talents, to another two, and to another one; to every man according to his several ability; and straightway took his journey. 25:15

534 His lord said unto him, Well done, thou good and faithful servant: thou hast been faithful over a few things, I will make thee ruler over many things: enter thou into the joy of thy lord. 25:21

535 For unto every one that hath shall be given, and he shall have abundance: but from him that hath not shall be taken away even that which he hath.
And cast ye the unprofitable servant into outer darkness: there shall be weeping and gnashing of teeth. 25:29–30

536 And before him shall be gathered all nations: and he shall separate them one from another, as a shepherd divideth his sheep from the goats:
And he shall set the sheep on his right hand, but the goats on the left. 25:32–33

537 Then shall the King say unto them on his right hand, Come, ye blessed of my Father, inherit the kingdom prepared for you from the foundation of the world:
For I was an hungred, and ye gave me meat: I was thirsty, and ye gave me drink: I was a stranger, and ye took me in:
Naked, and ye clothed me: I was sick, and ye visited me: I was in prison, and ye came unto me. 25:34–36

538 And the King shall answer and say unto them, Verily I say unto you, Inasmuch as ye have done it unto one of the least of these my brethren, ye have done it unto me. 25:40

539 And he answered and said, He that dippeth his hand with me in the dish, the same shall betray me.
The Son of man goeth as it is written of him: but woe unto that man by whom the Son of man is betrayed! it had been good for that man if he had not been born.
Then Judas, which betrayed him, answered and said, Master, is it I? He said unto him, Thou hast said. 26:23–25

540 And as they were eating, Jesus took bread, and blessed it, and brake it, and gave it to the disciples, and said, Take, eat; this is my body.
And he took the cup, and gave thanks, and gave it to them, saying, Drink ye all of it;
For this is my blood of the new testament, which is shed for many for the remission of sins. 26:26–28

541 Jesus said unto him, Verily I say unto thee, That this night, before the cock crow, thou shalt deny me thrice.
Peter said unto him, Though I should die with thee, yet will I not deny thee. Likewise also said all the disciples. 26:34–35

542 Then saith he unto them, My soul is exceeding sorrowful, even unto death: tarry ye here, and watch with me. 26:38

543 Watch and pray, that ye enter not into temptation: the spirit indeed is willing, but the flesh is weak. 26:41

544 And forthwith he came to Jesus, and said, Hail, master; and kissed him.
And Jesus said unto him, Friend, wherefore art thou come? Then came they, and laid hands on Jesus, and took him. 26:49–50

545 Then said Jesus unto him, Put up again thy sword into his place: for all they that take the sword shall perish with the sword. 26:52

546 Then Judas, which had betrayed him, when he saw that he was condemned, repented himself, and brought again the thirty pieces of silver to the chief priests and elders,
Saying, I have sinned in that I have betrayed the innocent blood. And they said, What is that to us? see thou to that. 27:3–4

547 When Pilate saw that he could prevail nothing, but that rather a tumult was made, he took water, and washed his hands before the multitude, saying, I am innocent of the blood of this just person: see ye to it.
Then answered all the people, and said, His blood be on us, and on our children. 27:24–25

548 And about the ninth hour Jesus cried with a loud voice, saying, Eli, Eli, lama sabachthani? that is to say, My God, my God, why hast thou forsaken me? 27:46

549 Jesus, when he had cried again with a loud voice, yielded up the ghost.
And, behold, the veil of the temple was rent in twain from the top to the bottom; and the earth did quake, and the rocks rent;
And the graves were opened; and many bodies of the saints which slept arose. 27:50–52

550 Teaching them to observe all things whatsoever I have commanded you: and, lo, I am with you alway, even unto the end of the world. Amen. 28:20

Micah

551 Trust ye not in a friend, put ye not confidence in a guide: keep the doors of thy mouth from her that lieth in thy bosom. 7:5

Nehemiah

552 And I said, Should such a man as I flee? and who is there, that, being as I am, would go into the temple to save his life? I will not go in. 6:11

Numbers

553 The Lord bless thee, and keep thee:
The Lord make his face shine upon thee, and be gracious unto thee:
The Lord lift up his countenance upon thee, and give thee peace. 6:24–26

554 Now the man Moses was very meek, above all the men which were upon the face of the earth. 12:3

555 Is it a small thing that thou hast brought us up out of a land that floweth with milk and honey, to kill us in the wilderness, except thou make thyself altogether a prince over us? 16:13

556 And Moses lifted up his hand, and

with his rod he smote the rock twice: and the water came out abundantly, and the congregation drank, and their beasts also. 20:11

557 And the Lord opened the mouth of the ass, and she said unto Balaam, What have I done unto thee, that thou hast smitten me these three times? 22:28

558 But if ye will not do so, behold, ye have sinned against the Lord: and be sure your sin will find you out. 32:23

I Peter

559 Whom having not seen, ye love; in whom, though now ye see him not, yet believing, ye rejoice with joy unspeakable and full of glory. 1:8

560 Being born again, not of corruptible seed, but of incorruptible, by the word of God, which liveth and abideth for ever.
For all flesh is as grass, and all the glory of man as the flower of grass. The grass withereth, and the flower thereof falleth away. 1:23–24

561 Honour all men. Love the brotherhood. Fear God. Honour the king. 2:17

562 Even as Sara obeyed Abraham, calling him lord: whose daughters ye are, as long as ye do well, and are not afraid with any amazement.
Likewise, ye husbands, dwell with them according to knowledge, giving honour unto the wife, as unto the weaker vessel, and as being heirs together of the grace of life; that your prayers be not hindered. 3:6–7

Philippians

563 But made himself of no reputation, and took upon him the form of a servant, and was made in the likeness of men:
And being found in fashion as a man, he humbled himself, and became obedient unto death, even the death of the cross.
Wherefore God also hath highly exalted him, and given him a name which is above every name:
That at the name of Jesus every knee should bow, of things in heaven, and things in earth, and things under the earth. 2:7–10

564 Rejoice in the Lord alway: and again I say, Rejoice. 4:4

565 And the peace of God, which passeth all understanding, shall keep your hearts and minds through Christ Jesus. 4:7

566 Finally, brethren, whatsoever things are true, whatsoever things are honest, whatsoever things are just, whatsoever things are pure, whatsoever things are lovely, whatsoever things are of good report; if there be any virtue; and if there be any praise, think on these things. 4:8

Proverbs

567 A wise man will hear, and will increase learning; and a man of understanding shall attain unto wise counsels:
To understand a proverb, and the interpretation; the words of the wise, and their dark sayings.
The fear of the Lord is the beginning of knowledge: but fools despise wisdom and instruction. 1:5–7

568 Wisdom is the principal thing; therefore get wisdom: and with all thy getting get understanding. 4:7

569 But the path of the just is as the shining light, that shineth more and more unto the perfect day. 4:18

570 For the lips of a strange woman drop as an honeycomb, and her mouth is smoother than oil:
But her end is bitter as wormwood, sharp as a two-edged sword. 5:3–4

571 Wisdom hath builded her house, she hath hewn out her seven pillars. 9:1

572 Stolen waters are sweet, and bread eaten in secret is pleasant. 9:17

573 He that spareth his rod hateth his son: but he that loveth him chasteneth him betimes. 13:24

574 Pride goeth before destruction, and an haughty spirit before a fall. 16:18

575 He that is slow to anger is better than the mighty; and he that ruleth his spirit than he that taketh a city. 16:32

576 Wine is a mocker, strong drink is raging: and whosoever is deceived thereby is not wise. 20:1

577 The hearing ear, and the seeing eye, the Lord hath made even both of them. 20:12

578 Look not thou upon the wine when it is red, when it giveth his colour in the cup, when it moveth itself aright.
At the last it biteth like a serpent, and stingeth like an adder. 23:31–32

579 For thou shalt heap coals of fire upon his head, and the Lord shall reward thee. 25:22

580 As cold waters to a thirsty soul, so is good news from a far country. 25:25

581 Answer a fool according to his folly, lest he be wise in his own conceit. 26:5

582 Boast not thyself of tomorrow; for thou knowest not what a day may bring forth. 27:1

583 Who can find a virtuous woman? for her price is far above rubies
The heart of her husband doth safely trust in her, so that he shall have no need of spoil.
She will do him good and not evil all the days of her life. 31:10–12

Revelations

584 Behold, he cometh with clouds; and every eye shall see him, and they also which pierced him: and all kindreds of the earth shall wail because of him. Even so, Amen.
I am Alpha and Omega, the beginning and the ending, saith the Lord, which is, and which was, and which is to come, the Almighty.
I John, who also am your brother, and companion in tribulation, and in the kingdom and patience of Jesus Christ, was in the isle that is called Patmos, for the word of God, and for the testimony of Jesus Christ.
I was in the Spirit on the Lord's day, and heard behind me a great voice, as of a trumpet,
Saying, I am Alpha and Omega, the first and the last: and, What thou seest, write in a book, and send it unto the seven churches which are in Asia; unto Ephesus, and unto Smyrna, and unto Pergamos, and unto Thyatira, and unto Sardis,

and unto Philadelphia, and unto Laodicea.
And I turned to see the voice that spake with me. And being turned, I saw seven golden candlesticks;
And in the midst of the seven candlesticks one like unto the Son of man, clothed with a garment down to the foot, and girt about the paps with a golden girdle.
His head and his hairs were white like wool, as white as snow; and his eyes were as a flame of fire;
And his feet like unto fine brass, as if they burned in a furnace; and his voice as the sound of many waters.
And he had in his right hand seven stars: and out of his mouth went a sharp twoedged sword: and his countenance was as the sun shineth in his strength. 1:7–16

585 And he shall rule them with a rod of iron; as the vessels of a potter shall they be broken to shivers: even as I received of my Father. 2:27

586 And I saw in the right hand of him that sat on the throne a book written within and on the backside, sealed with seven seals.
And I saw a strong angel proclaiming with a loud voice, Who is worthy to open the book, and to loose the seals thereof? 5:1–2

587 And I beheld, and, lo, in the midst of the throne and of the four beasts, and in the midst of the elders, stood a Lamb as it had been slain, having seven horns and seven eyes, which are the seven Spirits of God sent forth into all the earth. 5:6

588 Saying with a loud voice, Worthy is the Lamb that was slain to receive power, and riches, and wisdom, and strength, and honour, and glory, and blessing. 5:12

589 And I looked, and behold a pale horse: and his name that sat on him was Death, and Hell followed with him. And power was given unto them over the fourth part of the earth, to kill with sword, and with hunger, and with death, and with the beasts of the earth. 6:8

590 And one of the elders answered, saying unto me, What are these which are arrayed in white robes? and whence came they?
And I said unto him, Sir, thou knowest. And he said to me, These are they which came out of great tribulation, and have washed their robes, and made them white in the blood of the Lamb.
Therefore are they before the throne of God, and serve him day and night in his temple: and he that sitteth on the throne shall dwell among them.
They shall hunger no more, neither thirst any more; neither shall the sun light on them, nor any heat.
For the Lamb which is in the midst of the throne shall feed them, and shall lead them unto living fountains of waters: and God shall wipe away all tears from their eyes. 7:13–17

591 And the name of the star is called Wormwood: and the third part of the waters became wormwood; and many men died of the waters, because they were made bitter. 8:11

592 And there was war in heaven: Michael and his angels fought against the dragon; and the dragon fought and his angels,
And prevailed not; neither was their place found any more in heaven.
And the great dragon was cast out, that old serpent, called the Devil, and Satan, which deceiveth the whole world: he was cast out into the earth, and his angels were cast out with him. 12:7–9

593 And that no man might buy or sell, save he that had the mark, or the name of the beast, or the number of his name.
Here is wisdom. Let him that hath understanding count the number of the beast: for it is the number of a man; and his number is Six hundred threescore and six. 13:17–18

594 Behold, I come as a thief. Blessed is he that watcheth, and keepeth his garments, lest he walk naked, and they see his shame.
And he gathered them together into a place called in the Hebrew tongue Armageddon. 16:15–16

595 And there came one of the seven angels which had the seven vials, and talked with me, saying unto me, Come hither; I will shew unto thee the judgment of the great whore that sitteth upon many waters. 17:1

596 And the woman was arrayed in purple and scarlet colour, and decked with gold and precious stones and pearls, having a golden cup in her hand full of abominations and filthiness of her fornication:
And upon her forehead was a name written, MYSTERY, BABYLON THE GREAT, THE MOTHER OF HARLOTS AND ABOMINATIONS OF THE EARTH.
And I saw the woman drunken with the blood of the saints, and with the blood of the martyrs of Jesus: and when I saw her, I wondered with great admiration. 17:4–6

597 And I saw heaven opened, and behold a white horse; and he that sat upon him was called Faithful and True, and in righteousness he doth judge and make war. 19:11

598 And he hath on his vesture and on his thigh a name written, KING OF KINGS, AND LORD OF LORDS. 19:16

599 Blessed and holy is he that hath part in the first resurrection: on such the second death hath no power, but they shall be priests of God and of Christ, and shall reign with him a thousand years.
And when the thousand years are expired, Satan shall be loosed out of his prison,
And shall go out to deceive the nations which are in the four quarters of the earth, Gog and Magog, to gather them together to battle: the number of whom is as the sand of the sea. 20:6–8

600 And I saw a great white throne, and him that sat on it, from whose face the earth and the heaven fled away; and there was found no place for them.
And I saw the dead, small and great, stand before God; and the books were opened: and another book was opened, which is the book of life: and the dead were judged out of those things which were written in the books, according to their works.
And the sea gave up the dead which were in it; and death and hell delivered up the dead which were in them: and they were judged every man according to their works. 20:11–13

601 And I saw a new heaven and a new earth: for the first heaven and the

first earth were passed away; and there was no more sea.
And I John saw the holy city, new Jerusalem, coming down from God out of heaven, prepared as a bride adorned for her husband.
And I heard a great voice out of heaven saying, Behold, the tabernacle of God is with men, and he will dwell with them, and they shall be his people, and God himself shall be with them, and be their God.
And God shall wipe away all tears from their eyes; and there shall be no more death, neither sorrow, nor crying, neither shall there be any more pain: for the former things are passed away.
And he that sat upon the throne said, Behold, I make all things new. And he said unto me, Write: for these words are true and faithful. 21:1–5

602 And he carried me away in the spirit to a great and high mountain, and shewed me that great city, the holy Jerusalem, descending out of heaven from God.
Having the glory of God: and her light was like unto a stone most precious, even like a jasper stone, clear as crystal. 21:10–11

603 And the building of the wall of it was of jasper: and the city was pure gold, like unto clear glass.
And the foundations of the wall of the city were garnished with all manner of precious stones. The first foundation was jasper; the second, sapphire; the third, a chalcedony; the fourth, an emerald;
The fifth, sardonyx; the sixth, sardius; the seventh, chrysolite; the eighth, beryl; the ninth, a topaz; the tenth, a chrysoprasus; the eleventh, a jacinth; the twelfth, an amethyst.
And the twelve gates were twelve pearls; every several gate was of one pearl: and the street of the city was pure gold, as it were transparent glass.
And I saw no temple therein: for the Lord God Almighty and the Lamb are the temple of it.
And the city had no need of the sun, neither of the moon, to shine in it: for the glory of God did lighten it, and the Lamb is the light thereof. 21:18–23

604 And he shewed me a pure river of water of life, clear as crystal, proceeding out of the throne of God and of the Lamb.
In the midst of the street of it, and on either side of the river, was there the tree of life, which bare twelve manner of fruits, and yielded her fruit every month: and the leaves of the tree were for the healing of the nations. 22:1–2

605 He that is unjust, let him be unjust still: and he which is filthy, let him be filthy still: and he that is righteous, let him be righteous still: and he that is holy, let him be holy still.
And, behold, I come quickly; and my reward is with me, to give every man according as his work shall be. 22:11–12

Ruth

606 And Ruth said, Intreat me not to leave thee, or to return from following after thee: for whither thou goest, I will go; and where thou lodgest, I will lodge: thy people shall be my people, and thy God my God:
Where thou diest, will I die, and there will I be buried: the Lord do so to me, and more also, if ought but death part thee and me. 1:16–17

607 And he shall be unto thee a restorer of thy life and a nourisher of thine old age: for thy daughter in law, which loveth thee, which is better to thee than seven sons, hath born him. 4:15

I Samuel

608 Therefore Eli said unto Samuel, Go, lie down: and it shall be, if all thee, that thou shalt say, Speak, Lord; for thy servant heareth.
So Samuel went and lay down in his place. 3:9

609 And it came to pass, when all that knew him beforetime saw that, behold, he prophesied among the prophets, then the people said one to another, What is this that is come unto the son of Kish? Is Saul also among the prophets? 10:11

610 But now thy kingdom shall not continue: the Lord hath sought him a man after his own heart, and the Lord hath commanded him to be captain over his people, because thou hast not kept that which the Lord commanded thee. 13:14

611 And the people said unto Saul, Shall Jonathan die, who hath wrought this great salvation in Israel? God forbid: as the Lord liveth, there shall not one hair of his head fall to the ground; for he hath wrought with God this day. So the people rescued Jonathan, that he died not. 14:45

612 And he took his staff in his hand, and chose him five smooth stones out of the brook, and put them in a shepherd's bag which he had, even in a scrip; and his sling was in his hand: and he drew near to the Philistine. 17:40

613 And the women answered one another as they played, and said, Saul hath slain his thousands, and David his ten thousands. 18:7

614 Then said Saul, I have sinned: return, my son David: for I will no more do thee harm, because my soul was precious in thine eyes this day: behold, I have played the fool, and have erred exceedingly. 26:21

II Samuel

615 Saul and Jonathan were lovely and pleasant in their lives, and in their death they were not divided: they were swifter than eagles, they were stronger than lions. 1:23–24

616 I am distressed for thee, my brother Jonathan: very pleasant hast thou been unto me: thy love to me was wonderful, passing the love of women.
How are the mighty fallen, and the weapons of war perished! 1:26–27

617 But the poor man had nothing, save one little ewe lamb, which he had bought and nourished up: and it grew up together with him, and with his children; it did eat of his own meat, and drank of his own cup, and lay in his bosom, and was unto him as a daughter. 12:3

618 And Nathan said to David, Thou art the man. 12:7

619 And a certain man saw it, and told Joab, and said, Behold, I saw Absalom hanged in an oak. 18:10

620 And the king was much moved, and went up to the chamber over the gate, and wept: and as he went, thus he said, O my son Absalom, my son, my son Absalom! would

God I had died for thee, O Absalom, my son, my son! 18:33

Song of Solomon

621 The song of songs, which is Solomon's.
Let him kiss me with the kisses of his mouth: for thy love is better than wine.
Because of the savour of thy good ointments thy name is as ointment poured forth, therefore do the virgins love thee.
Draw me, we will run after thee: the king hath brought me into his chambers: we will be glad and rejoice in thee, we will remember thy love more than wine: the upright love thee.
I am black, but comely, O ye daughters of Jerusalem, as the tents of Kedar, as the curtains of Solomon.
Look not upon me, because I am black, because the sun hath looked upon me: my mother's children were angry with me; they made me the keeper of the vineyards; but mine own vineyard have I not kept.
Tell me, O thou whom my soul loveth, where thou feedest, where thou makest thy flock to rest at noon: for why should I be as one that turneth aside by the flocks of thy companions?
If thou know not, O thou fairest among women, go thy way forth by the footsteps of the flock, and feed thy kids beside the shepherds' tents.
I have compared thee, O my love, to a company of horses in Pharaoh's chariots. 1:1–9

622 I am the rose of Sharon, and the lily of the valleys.
As the lily among thorns, so is my love among the daughters. 2:1–2

623 He brought me to the banqueting house, and his banner over me was love.
Stay me with flagons, comfort me with apples: for I am sick of love.
His left hand is under my head, and his right hand doth embrace me. 2:4–6

624 The voice of my beloved! behold, he cometh leaping upon the mountains, skipping upon the hills. 2:8

625 My beloved spake, and said unto me, Rise up, my love, my fair one, and come away.
For, lo, the winter is past, the rain is over and gone;
The flowers appear on the earth; the time of the singing of birds is come, and the voice of the turtle is heard in our land. 2:10–12

626 Take us the foxes, the little foxes, that spoil the vines: for our vines have tender grapes. 2:15

627 My beloved is mine, and I am his: he feedeth among the lilies.
Until the day break, and the shadows flee away, turn, my beloved, and be thou like a roe or a young hart upon the mountains of Bether. 2:16–17

628 By night on my bed I sought him whom my soul loveth: I sought him, but I found him not. 3:1

629 Behold, thou art fair, my love, behold, thou art fair; thou hast doves' eyes within thy locks; thy hair is as a flock of goats, that appear from mount Gilead.
Thy teeth are like a flock of sheep that are even shorn, which came up from the washing; whereof every one bear twins, and none is barren among them.
Thy lips are like a thread of scarlet, and thy speech is comely: thy temples are like a piece of a pomegranate within thy locks.
Thy neck is like the tower of David builded for an armoury, whereon there hang a thousand bucklers, all shields of mighty men.
Thy two breasts are like two young roes that are twins, which feed among the lilies.
Until the day break, and the shadows flee away, I will get me to the mountain of myrrh, and to the hill of frankincense.
Thou art all fair, my love; there is no spot in thee. 4:1–7

630 A fountain of gardens, a well of living waters, and streams from Lebanon. 4:15

631 Awake, O north wind; and come, thou south; blow upon my garden, that the spices thereof may flow out. Let my beloved come into his garden, and eat his pleasant fruits. 4:16

632 I am come into my garden, my sister, my spouse: I have gathered my myrrh with my spice; I have eaten my honeycomb with my honey; I have drunk my wine with my milk: eat, O friends; drink, yea, drink abundantly, O beloved.
I sleep, but my heart waketh: it is the voice of my beloved that knocketh, saying, Open to me, my sister, my love, my dove, my undefiled: for my head is filled with dew, and my locks with the drops of the night. 5:1–2

633 My beloved put in his hand by the hole of the door, and my bowels were moved for him. 5:4

634 My beloved is gone down into his garden, to the beds of spices, to feed in the gardens, and to gather lilies.
I am my beloved's, and my beloved is mine: he feedeth among the lilies. 6:2–3

635 Who is she that looketh forth as the morning, fair as the moon, clear as the sun, and terrible as an army with banners? 6:10

636 Return, return, O Shulamite; return, return, that we may look upon thee. What will ye see in the Shulamite? As it were the company of two armies. 6:13

637 How beautiful are thy feet with shoes, O prince's daughter! joints of thy thighs are like jewels, the work of the hands of a cunning workman.
Thy navel is like a round goblet, which wanteth not liquor: thy belly is like an heap of wheat set about with lilies. 7:1–2

638 How fair and how pleasant art thou, O love, for delights! 7:6

639 I am my beloved's, and his desire is toward me. 7:10

640 Who is this that cometh up from the wilderness, leaning upon her beloved? I raised thee up under the apple tree: there thy mother brought thee forth: there she brought thee forth that bare thee. 8:5

641 Make haste, my beloved, and be thou like to a roe or to a young hart upon the mountains of spices. 8:14

I Thessalonians

642 Remembering without ceasing your work of faith, and labour of love, and patience of hope in our Lord

Jesus Christ, in the sight of God and our Father. 1:3

643 For yourselves know perfectly that the day of the Lord so cometh as a thief in the night. 5:2

644 Prove all things; hold fast that which is good. 5:21

II Thessalonians

645 For even when we were with you, this we commanded you, that if any would not work, neither should he eat. 3:10

I Timothy

646 This is a faithful saying, and worthy of all acceptation, that Christ Jesus came into the world to save sinners; of whom I am chief. 1:15

647 This is a true saying, If a man desire the office of a bishop, he desireth a good work.
A bishop then must be blameless, the husband of one wife, vigilant, sober, of good behaviour, given to hospitality, apt to teach;
Not given to wine, no striker, not greedy of filthy lucre; but patient, not a brawler, not covetous. 3:1–3

648 For every creature of God is good, and nothing to be refused, if it be received with thanksgiving. 4:4

649 Drink no longer water, but use a little wine for thy stomach's sake and thine often infirmities. 5:23

650 For we brought nothing into this world, and it is certain we carry nothing out. 6:7

651 For the love of money is the root of all evil: which while some coveted after, they have erred from the faith, and pierced themselves through with many sorrows. 6:10

652 Fight the good fight of faith, lay hold on eternal life, whereunto thou art also called, and hast professed a good profession before many witnesses. 6:12

653 O Timothy, keep that which is committed to thy trust, avoiding profane and vain babblings, and oppositions of science falsely so called. 6:20

II Timothy

654 For God hath not given us the spirit of fear; but of power, and of love, and of a sound mind. 1:7

655 But evil men and seducers shall wax worse and worse, deceiving, and being deceived. 3:13

656 For I am now ready to be offered, and the time of my departure is at hand.
I have fought a good fight, I have finished my course, I have kept the faith:
Henceforth there is laid up for me a crown of righteousness, which the Lord, the righteous judge, shall give me at that day: and not to me only, but unto all them also that love his appearing. 4:6–8

Titus

657 One of themselves, even a prophet of their own, said, The Cretians are alway liars, evil beasts, slow bellies. 1:12

Tobit

658 Be not greedy to add money to money: but let it be as refuse in respect of our child. 5:18

659 Be of good comfort, my daughter; the Lord of heaven and earth give thee joy for this thy sorrow: be of good comfort, my daughter. 7:18

Wisdom

660 For the ear of jealousy heareth all things: and the noise of murmurings is not hid. 1:10

661 For the bewitching of naughtiness doth obscure things that are honest; and the wandering of concupiscence doth undermine the simple mind.
He, being made perfect in a short time, fulfilled a long time. 4:12–13

662 For all men have one entrance into life, and the like going out. 7:6

663 For wisdom is more moving than any motion: she passeth and go through all things by reason of her pureness.
For she is the breath of the power of God, and a pure influence flowing from the glory of the Almighty: therefore can no defiled thing fall into her.
For she is the brightness of the everlasting light, the unspotted mirror of the power of God, and the image of his goodness.
And being but one, she can do all things: and remaining in herself, she maketh all things new: and in all ages entering into holy souls, she maketh them friends of God, and prophets.
For God loveth none but him that dwelleth with wisdom. 7:24–28

664 Wisdom reacheth from one end to another mightily: and sweetly doth she order all things. 8:1

665 For thou hast power of life and death: thou leadest to the gates of hell, and bringest up again.

BIERCE, Ambrose Gwinnett

(1842–?1914) US writer and journalist. His short stories were published in such collections as *In the Midst of Life* (1892). He also compiled *The Devil's Dictionary* (1906).

Quotations about Bierce

1 ... I have heard one young woman declare, 'I can feel him ten feet away!'
George Sterling *American Mercury*, Sept 1925

2 There was nothing of the milk of human kindness in old Ambrose ...
H. L. Mencken (1880–1956) US journalist. *Prejudices*, 'Ambrose Bierce'

Quotations by Bierce

3 *Bore*, n. A person who talks when you wish him to listen.
The Devil's Dictionary

4 *Brain*, n. An apparatus with which we think that we think.
The Devil's Dictionary

5 *Debauchee*, n. One who has so earnestly pursued pleasure that he has had the misfortune to overtake it.
The Devil's Dictionary

6 *Egotist*, n. A person of low taste, more interested in himself than in me.
The Devil's Dictionary

7 *Future*, n. That period of time in which our affairs prosper, our friends are true and our happiness is assured.
The Devil's Dictionary

8 *Marriage*, n. The state or condition

of a community consisting of a master, a mistress and two slaves, making in all two.
The Devil's Dictionary

9 *Patience*, n. A minor form of despair, disguised as a virtue.
The Devil's Dictionary

10 *Peace*, n. In international affairs, a period of cheating between two periods of fighting.
The Devil's Dictionary

BIOGRAPHY

1 The Art of Biography
Is different from Geography.
Geography is about Maps,
But Biography is about Chaps.
Edmund Clerihew Bentley (1875–1956) British writer. *Biography for Beginners*

2 A well-written Life is almost as rare as a well-spent one.
Thomas Carlyle (1795–1881) Scottish historian and essayist. *Critical and Miscellaneous Essays*, 'Richter'

3 History is the essence of innumerable biographies.
Thomas Carlyle *Critical and Miscellaneous Essays*, 'History'

4 Campbell has added another terror to death.
John Singleton Copley (1772–1863) US-born British lawyer. Referring to Lord Campbell's controversial *Lives of the Lord Chancellors* (1845–47), from which Lyndhurst was excluded because he was still alive.

5 There is properly no history; only biography.
Ralph Waldo Emerson (1803–82) US poet and essayist. *Essays*, 'History'

6 Just how difficult it is to write biography can be reckoned by anybody who sits down and considers just how many people know the real truth about his or her love affairs.
Rebecca West (Cicely Isabel Fairfield; 1892–1983) British novelist and journalist. *Vogue* magazine

BIRDS

1 One for sorrow, two for mirth; three for a wedding, four for a birth; five for silver, six for gold; seven for a secret, not to be told; eight for heaven, nine for hell; and ten for the devil's own sel.
Referring to magpies or crows; there are numerous variants. Proverb

2 There were three ravens sat on a tree,
They were as black as they might be.
The one of them said to his make,
'Where shall we our breakfast take?'
Anonymous *The Three Ravens*

3 A robin redbreast in a cage
Puts all Heaven in a rage.
William Blake (1757–1827) British poet. *Auguries of Innocence*

4 That's the wise thrush; he sings each song twice over,
Lest you should think he never could recapture
The first fine careless rapture!
Robert Browning (1812–89) British poet. *Home Thoughts from Abroad*

5 With my cross-bow
I shot the albatross.
Samuel Taylor Coleridge (1772–1834) British poet. *The Rime of the Ancient Mariner*, I

6 It was the Rainbow gave thee birth,
And left thee all her lovely hues.
W. H. Davies (1871–1940) British poet. *The Kingfisher*

7 On a tree by a river a little tom-tit
Sang 'Willow, titwillow, titwillow!'
W. S. Gilbert (1836–1911) British dramatist. *The Mikado*, II

8 If there's one thing above all a vulture can't stand, it's a glass eye.
'Kin' Hubbard (1868–1930) US humorist. Attrib.

9 Thou wast not born for death, immortal Bird!
No hungry generations tread thee down;
The voice I hear this passing night was heard
In ancient days by emperor and clown:
Perhaps the self-same song that found a path
Through the sad heart of Ruth, when sick for home,
She stood in tears amid the alien corn;
The same that oft-times hath
Charm'd magic casements, opening on the foam
Of perilous seas, in faery lands forlorn.
John Keats (1795–1821) British poet. *Ode to a Nightingale*

10 She's only a bird in a gilded cage.
A. J. Lamb (1870–1928) British songwriter. Song title

11 Ye living lamps, by whose dear light
The nightingale does sit so late,
And studying all the summer night,
Her matchless songs does meditate.
Andrew Marvell (1621–78) English poet. *The Mower to the Glow-worms*

12 There were angels dining at the Ritz
And a nightingale sang in Berkeley Square.
Eric Maschwitz (20th century) British songwriter. *A Nightingale Sang in Berkley Square* (song)

13 To hear the lark begin his flight,
And singing startle the dull night,
From his watch-tower in the skies,
Till the dappled dawn doth rise.
John Milton (1608–74) English poet. *L'Allegro*

14 Sweet bird, that shunn'st the noise of folly,
Most musical, most melancholy!
John Milton Referring to the nightingale. *Il Penseroso*

15 Because he spills his seed on the ground.
Dorothy Parker (1893–1967) US writer. On naming her canary 'Onan'; referring to Genesis, 38:9, 'And Onan knew that the seed should not be his; and it came to pass, when he went in unto his brother's wife, that he spilled it on the ground'. *You Might As Well Live* (J. Keats)

16 Hail to thee, blithe Spirit!
Bird thou never wert,
That from Heaven, or near it,
Pourest thy full heart
In profuse strains of unpremeditated art.
Percy Bysshe Shelley (1792–1822) British poet. *To a Skylark*

17 We think caged birds sing, when indeed they cry.
John Webster (1580–1625) English dramatist. *The White Devil*, V:4

18 Ethereal minstrel! pilgrim of the sky!
Dost thou despise the earth where cares abound?
William Wordsworth (1770–1850) British poet. *To a Skylark*

19 O Nightingale, thou surely art
A creature of a 'fiery heart'.
William Wordsworth *O Nightingale*

20 The pious bird with the scarlet breast,
Our little English robin.
William Wordsworth *The Redbreast chasing the Butterfly*

21 Thrice welcome, darling of the spring!
Even yet thou art to me
No bird, but an invisible thing,

A voice, a mystery.
William Wordsworth *To the Cuckoo*

BIRTH

See also babies, life and death

1 It is natural to die as to be born; and to a little infant, perhaps, the one is as painful as the other.
Francis Bacon *Essays*, 'Of Death'

2 Hanging head downwards between cliffs of bone, was the baby, its arms all but clasped about its neck, its face aslant upon its arms, hair painted upon its skull, closed, secret eyes, a diver poised in albumen, ancient and epic, shot with delicate spasms, as old as a Pharaoh in its tomb.
Enid Bagnold (1889–) British writer. *The Door of Life*, Ch. 2

3 A woman when she is in travail hath sorrow, because her hour is come: but as soon as she is delivered of the child, she remembereth no more the anguish, for joy that a man is born into the world.
Bible: John 16:21

4 For all men have one entrance into life, and the like going out.
Bible: Wisdom 7:6

5 My mother groan'd, my father wept,
Into the dangerous world I leapt;
Helpless, naked, piping loud,
Like a fiend hid in a cloud.
William Blake (1757–1827) British poet. *Songs of Experience*, 'Infant Sorrow'

6 For man's greatest crime is to have been born.
Pedro Calderón de la Barca (1600–81) Spanish dramatist. *La Vida es Sueño*, I

7 Parturition is a physiological process – the same in the countess and in the cow.
W. W. Chipman (1866–1950)

8 The history of man for the nine months preceding his birth would, probably, be far more interesting and contain events of greater moment than all the three-score and ten years that follow it.
Samuel Taylor Coleridge (1772–1834) British poet. *Miscellanies, Aesthetic and Literary*

9 If men had to have babies they would only ever have one each.
Diana, Princess of Wales (1961–) Wife of Prince Charles. *The Observer*, 'Sayings of the Week', 29 July 1984

10 Man always dies before he is fully born.
Erich Fromm (1900–80) US psychologist and philosopher. *Man for Himself*, Ch. 3

11 Man's main task in life is to give *birth* to himself.
Erich Fromm *Man for Himself*, Ch. 4

12 Birth may be a matter of a moment. But it is a unique one.
Frédérick Leboyer (1918–) French obstetrician. *Birth Without Violence*

13 I'll simply say here that I was born Beatrice Gladys Lillie at an extremely tender age because my mother needed a fourth at meals.
Beatrice Lillie (Constance Sylvia Munston, Lady Peel; 1898–1989) Canadian-born British actress. *Every Other Inch a Lady*, Ch. 1

14 In men nine out of ten abdominal tumors are malignant; in women nine out of ten abdominal swellings are the pregnant uterus.
Rutherford Morison (1853–1939) *The Practitioner*, Oct 1965

15 MACBETH. I bear a charmed life, which must not yield
To one of woman born.
MACDUFF. Despair thy charm;
And let the angel whom thou still hast serv'd
Tell thee Macduff was from his mother's womb
Untimely ripp'd.
William Shakespeare (1564–1616) English dramatist. *Macbeth*, V:8

16 When we are born we cry that we are come
To this great stage of fools.
William Shakespeare *King Lear*, IV:6

17 The explanation is quite simple. I wished to be near my mother.
James Whistler (1834–1903) US painter. Explaining to a snobbish lady why he had been born in such an unfashionable place as Lowell, Massachusetts. Attrib.

18 Our birth is but a sleep and a forgetting.
William Wordsworth (1770–1850) British poet. *Ode: Intimations of Immortality*

BITTERNESS

1 The dupe of friendship, and the fool of love; have I not reason to hate and to despise myself? Indeed I do; and chiefly for not having hated and despised the world enough.
William Hazlitt (1778–1830) British essayist. *On the Pleasure of Hating*

2 It is very difficult to get up resentment towards persons whom one has never seen.
Cardinal Newman (1801–90) British theologian. *Apologia pro Vita Sua* (1864), 'Mr Kingsley's Method of Disputation'

3 Fie, fie! unknit that threatening unkind brow,
And dart not scornful glances from those eyes,
To wound thy lord, thy king, thy governor.
William Shakespeare (1564–1616) English dramatist. *The Taming of the Shrew*, V:2

4 He gave a deep sigh – I saw the iron enter into his soul!
Laurence Sterne (1713–68) Irish-born British writer. *A Sentimental Journey*, 'The Captive. Paris'

BLAKE, William

(1757–1827) British poet, painter, engraver, and visionary. Blake's mystical engravings and watercolours illustrate such works as *Songs of Innocence* (1789) and the poem *Jerusalem* (1804–20).

Quotations about Blake

1 . . . William Blake's insanity was worth more than the sanity of any number of artistic mediocrities.
Gerald Abraham *Radio Times*, 10 Dec 1937

2 Where other poets use reality as a springboard into space, he uses it as a foothold when he returns from flight.
Arthur Symons (1865–1945) British poet. *William Blake*

Quotations by Blake

3 For everything that lives is holy, life delights in life.
America

4 The strongest poison ever known
Came from Caesar's laurel crown.
Auguries of Innocence

5 Every wolf's and lion's howl
Raises from Hell a human soul.
Auguries of Innocence

6 A truth that's told with bad intent
Beats all the lies you can invent.
Auguries of Innocence

7 Every tear from every eye

Becomes a babe in Eternity.
Auguries of Innocence

8 He who shall teach the child to doubt
The rotting grave shall ne'er get out.
Auguries of Innocence

9 To see a World in a grain of sand,
And a Heaven in a wild flower,
Hold Infinity in the palm of your hand,
And Eternity in an hour.
Auguries of Innocence

10 A robin redbreast in a cage
Puts all Heaven in a rage.
Auguries of Innocence

11 Does the Eagle know what is in the pit
Or wilt thou go ask the Mole?
Can Wisdom be put in a silver rod,
Or love in a golden bowl?
The Book of Thel, 'Thel's Motto'

12 'What,' it will be questioned, 'when the sun rises, do you not see a round disc of fire somewhat like a guinea?' 'O no, no, I see an innumerable company of the heavenly host crying, "Holy, Holy, Holy is the Lord God Almighty!" '
Descriptive Catalogue, 'The Vision of Judgment'

13 Humility is only doubt,
And does the sun and moon blot out.
The Everlasting Gospel

14 Great things are done when men and mountains meet;
This is not done by jostling in the street.
Gnomic Verses

15 He who bends to himself a Joy
Doth the wingèd life destroy;
But he who kisses the Joy as it flies
Lives in Eternity's sunrise.
Gnomic Verses

16 He who would do good to another must do it in Minute Particulars. General Good is the plea of the scoundrel, hypocrite, and flatterer.
Jerusalem

17 I care not whether a man is Good or Evil; all that I care
Is whether he is a Wise Man or a Fool. Go! put off Holiness,
And put on Intellect.
Jerusalem

18 Without Contraries is no progression. Attraction and Repulsion, Reason and Energy, Love and Hate, are necessary to Human existence.
The Marriage of Heaven and Hell, 'The Argument'

19 If the doors of perception were cleansed everything would appear to man as it is, infinite.
The Marriage of Heaven and Hell, 'A Memorable Fancy'

20 Prisons are built with stones of Law, brothels with bricks of Religion.
The Marriage of Heaven and Hell, 'Proverbs of Hell'

21 Sooner murder an infant in its cradle than nurse unacted desires.
The Marriage of Heaven and Hell, 'Proverbs of Hell'

22 In seed time learn, in harvest teach, in winter enjoy.
The Marriage of Heaven and Hell, 'Proverbs of Hell'

23 The cut worm forgives the plough.
The Marriage of Heaven and Hell, 'Proverbs of Hell'

24 What is now proved was once only imagined.
The Marriage of Heaven and Hell, 'Proverbs of Hell'

25 The road of excess leads to the palace of Wisdom.
The Marriage of Heaven and Hell, 'Proverbs of Hell'

26 He who desires but acts not, breeds pestilence.
The Marriage of Heaven and Hell, 'Proverbs of Hell'

27 A fool sees not the same tree that a wise man sees.
The Marriage of Heaven and Hell, 'Proverbs of Hell'

28 Damn braces. Bless relaxes.
The Marriage of Heaven and Hell, 'Proverbs of Hell'

29 Exuberance is Beauty.
The Marriage of Heaven and Hell, 'Proverbs of Hell'

30 Those who restrain Desire, do so because theirs is weak enough to be restrained.
The Marriage of Heaven and Hell, 'Those who restrain Desire . . . '

31 Man has no Body distinct from his Soul; for that called Body is a portion of Soul discerned by the five Senses, the chief inlets of Soul in this age.
The Marriage of Heaven and Hell, 'The Voice of the Devil'

32 Energy is Eternal Delight.
The Marriage of Heaven and Hell, 'The Voice of the Devil'

33 And did those feet in ancient time
Walk upon England's mountains green?
And was the holy lamb of God
On England's pleasant pastures seen?
. . .
I will not cease from mental fight,
Nor shall my sword sleep in my hand,
Till we have built Jerusalem
In England's green and pleasant land.
Better known as the hymn 'Jerusalem', with music by Sir Hubert Parry; not to be confused with Blake's longer poem *Jerusalem*. *Milton*, Preface

34 Mock on, mock on, Voltaire, Rousseau;
Mock on, mock on; 'tis all in vain!
You throw the sand against the wind,
And the wind blows it back again.
Mock on, mock on, Voltaire, Rousseau

35 When Sir Joshua Reynolds died
All Nature was degraded;
The King dropped a tear in the Queen's ear,
And all his pictures faded.
On Art and Artists

36 Love seeketh not itself to please,
Nor for itself hath any care,
But for another gives its ease,
And builds a Heaven in Hell's despair.
Songs of Experience, 'The Clod and the Pebble'

37 Love seeketh only Self to please,
To bind another to its delight,
Joys in another's loss of ease,
And builds a Hell in Heaven's despite.
Songs of Experience, 'The Clod and the Pebble'

38 My mother groan'd, my father wept,
Into the dangerous world I leapt;
Helpless, naked, piping loud,
Like a fiend hid in a cloud.
Songs of Experience, 'Infant Sorrow'

39 Tiger! Tiger! burning bright
In the forests of the night,
What immortal hand or eye
Could frame thy fearful symmetry?
Songs of Experience, 'The Tiger'

40 When the stars threw down their spears,
And watered heaven with their tears,
Did he smile his work to see?

Did he who made the Lamb make thee?
Songs of Experience, 'The Tiger'

41 Piping down the valleys wild,
Piping songs of pleasant glee,
On a cloud I saw a child.
Songs of Innocence, Introduction

42 'Pipe a song about a Lamb!'
So I piped with merry cheer.
Songs of Innocence, Introduction

43 To Mercy, Pity, Peace, and Love
All pray in their distress.
Songs of Innocence, 'The Divine Image'

44 For Mercy has a human heart,
Pity a human face,
And Love, the human form divine,
And Peace, the human dress.
Songs of Innocence, 'The Divine Image'

45 'Twas on a Holy Thursday, their innocent faces clean,
The children walking two and two, in red and blue and green.
Songs of Innocence, 'Holy Thursday'

46 Little Lamb, who made thee?
Dost thou know who made thee?
Songs of Innocence, 'The Lamb'

47 When the green woods laugh with the voice of joy.
Songs of Innocence, 'Laughing song'

48 My mother bore me in the southern wild.
And I am black, but O! my soul is white;
White as an angel is the English child,
But I am black, as if bereav'd of light.
Songs of Innocence, 'The Little Black Boy'

49 Man's Desires are limited by his Perceptions; none can desire what he has not perceived.
There is no Natural Religion

50 The Desire of Man being Infinite, the possession is Infinite, and himself Infinite.
There is no Natural Religion

51 I mock thee not, though I by thee am mockèd;
Thou call'st me madman, but I call thee blockhead.
To Flaxman

52 To generalize is to be an idiot.
Life of Blake (Gilchrist)

BLESSING

See also prayer

1 Matthew, Mark, Luke and John,
The bed be blest that I lie on.
Thomas Ady (17th century) British poet. *A Candle in the Dark*

2 I see the moon,
And the moon sees me;
God bless the moon,
And God bless me.
Anonymous *Gammer Gurton's Garland*

3 Thank you, sister. May you be the mother of a bishop!
Brendan Behan (1923–64) Irish playwright. Said to a nun nursing him on his deathbed. Attrib.

4 The Lord bless thee, and keep thee:
The Lord make his face shine upon thee, and be gracious unto thee:
The Lord lift up his countenance upon thee, and give thee peace.
Bible: Numbers 6:24–26

5 And the peace of God, which passeth all understanding, shall keep your hearts and minds through Christ Jesus.
Bible: Philippians 4:7

6 'God bless us every one!' said Tiny Tim, the last of all.
Charles Dickens (1812–70) British novelist. *A Christmas Carol*

BLINDNESS

See also disability

1 A nod is as good as a wink to a blind horse.
Proverb

2 Men are blind in their own cause.
Proverb

3 My eyes are dim
I cannot see
I have not brought my specs with me.
Anonymous *The Quartermaster's Stores*

4 . . . for three years I have been deprived of my sight. I wish you to learn from my own hand that thanks to the Divine Goodness I have recovered it. I see but as one sees after an operation, that is to say very dimly. Even this is a blessing for one who has had the misfortune to become blind. When I was sightless I cared for nothing, now I want to see everything . . . .
Rosalba Carriera (1675–1757) Letter, 23 Aug 1749

5 My soul is full of whispered song;
My blindness is my sight;
The shadows that I feared so long
Are all alive with light.
Alice Cary (1820–71) *Dying Hymn*

6 How reconcile this world of fact with the bright world of my imagining? My darkness has been filled with the light of intelligence, and behold, the outer day-light world was stumbling and groping in social blindness.
Helen Keller (1880–1968) US writer and lecturer. *The Cry for Justice* (ed. Upton Sinclair)

7 Ask for this great deliverer now, and find him
Eyeless in Gaza at the mill with slaves.
John Milton (1608–74) English poet. *Samson Agonistes*

8 Doth God exact day-labour, light deny'd,
I fondly ask.
John Milton *Sonnet*, 'When I Consider How my Light is Spent'

9 O dark, dark, dark, amid the blaze of noon,
Irrecoverably dark, total eclipse,
Without all hope of day!
John Milton *Samson Agonistes*

10 When I consider how my light is spent
Ere half my days in this dark world and wide,
And that one talent which is death to hide
Lodged with me useless.
John Milton *Sonnet*: 'On his Blindness'

11 Why, in truth, should I not bear gently the deprivation of sight, when I may hope that it is not so much lost as revoked and retracted inwards, for the sharpening rather than the blunting of my mental edge?
John Milton

12 I have only one eye: I have a right to be blind sometimes: I really do not see the signal.
Lord Nelson (1758–1805) British admiral. Remark, Battle of Copenhagen, 2 Apr 1801; Nelson ignored Admiral Parker's order to disengage by placing his telescope to his blind eye; an hour later, he was victorious. *Life of Nelson* Ch. 7 (Robert Southey)

13 He clapped the glass to his sightless eye,
And 'I'm damned if I see it', he said.
Henry John Newbolt (1862–1938) British poet. Referring to Lord Nelson at the Battle of Copenhagen. *Admirals All*

14 And so I betake myself to that

course, which is almost as much as to see myself go into my grave – for which, and all the discomforts that will accompany my being blind, the good God prepare me!

Samuel Pepys (1633–1703) English diarist. The closing words of Pepys's *Diary*; he lived another 34 years and did not go blind. *Diary*, 31 May 1669

15 I have no way, and therefore want no eyes;
I stumbled when I saw.

William Shakespeare (1564–1616) English dramatist. *King Lear*, IV:1

16 In the Country of the Blind, the One-eyed Man is King.

H. G. Wells (1866–1946) British writer. *The Country of the Blind*

BOASTS

1 I have done almost every human activity inside a taxi which does not require main drainage.

Alan Brien (1925–) British critic. *Punch*, 5 July 1972

2 CAPTAIN. I'm never, never sick at sea!
ALL. What never?
CAPTAIN. No, never!
ALL. What, *never?*
CAPTAIN. Hardly ever!

W. S. Gilbert (1836–1911) British dramatist. *HMS Pinafore*, I

3 All my shows are great. Some of them are bad. But they are all great.

Lew Grade (1906–) British impressario. Attrib.

4 If, drunk with sight of power, we loose
Wild tongues that have not Thee in awe,
Such boastings as the Gentiles use,
Or lesser breeds without the Law.

Rudyard Kipling (1865–1936) Indian-born British writer. *Recessional*

5 I can piss the old boy in the snow.

Max Liebermann (1847–1935) German painter. Remark to an artist who said he could not draw General Paul von Hindenburg's face. *Conversations with Stravinsky* (Igor Stravinsky and Robert Craft)

6 Just begin a story with such a phrase as 'I remember Disraeli – poor old Dizz! – once saying to me, in answer to my poke in the eye,' and you will find me and Morpheus off in a corner, necking.

Dorothy Parker (1893–1967) US writer. *The New Yorker*, 22 Oct 1927

7 There are two motives for reading a book: one, that you enjoy it, the other that you can boast about it.

Bertrand Russell (1872–1970) British philosopher. *The Conquest of Happiness*

8 And when we open our dykes, the waters are ten feet deep.

Wilhelmina (1880–1962) Queen of the Netherlands. Replying to a boast by Wilhelm II that his guardsmen were all seven feet tall. Attrib.

BOATS

See also navy, sea

1 There's something wrong with our bloody ships today.

Earl Beatty (1871–1936) British admiral. Remark during Battle of Jutland, 30 May 1916. Attrib.

2 All rowed fast but none so fast as stroke.

Desmond Coke (1879–1931) British writer. Popular misquotation, derived from the passage: 'His blade struck the water a full second before any other . . . until . . . as the boats began to near the winning post, his own was dipping into the water *twice* as often as any other.' *Sandford of Merton*

3 As idle as a painted ship
Upon a painted ocean.

Samuel Taylor Coleridge (1772–1834) British poet. *The Rime of the Ancient Mariner*, I

4 Jolly boating weather,
And a hay harvest breeze,
Blade on the feather,
Shade off the trees
Swing, swing together
With your body between your knees.

William Johnson Cory (1823–92) British schoolmaster and poet. *Eton Boating Song*

5 Fair stood the wind for France
When we our sails advance.

Michael Drayton (1563–1631) English poet. *Agincourt*

6 For you dream you are crossing the Channel, and tossing about in a steamer from Harwich
Which is something between a large bathing machine and a very small second-class carriage.

W. S. Gilbert (1836–1911) British dramatist. *Iolanthe*, II

7 There is nothing – absolutely nothing – half so much worth doing as simply messing about in boats.

Kenneth Grahame (1859–1932) Scottish writer. *The Wind in the Willows*, Ch. 1

8 The little ships, the unforgotten Homeric catalogue of *Mary Jane* and *Peggy IV*, of *Folkestone Belle*, *Boy Billy*, and *Ethel Maud*, of *Lady Haig* and *Skylark* . . . the little ships of England brought the Army home.

Philip Guedalla (1889–1944) British writer. Referring to the evacuation of Dunkirk. *Mr. Churchill*

9 Well: while was fashioning
This creature of cleaving wing,
The Immanent Will that stirs and urges everything

Prepared a sinister mate
For her – so gaily great –
A Shape of Ice, for the time far and dissociate.

And as the smart ship grew
In stature, grace, and hue,
In shadowy silent distance grew the Iceberg too.

Thomas Hardy (1840–1928) British novelist. Referring to the 'Titanic', a luxury passenger ship, thought to be unsinkable because of its special design. It struck an iceberg on its maiden voyage and sank, causing the loss of 1513 lives. *The Convergence of the Twain*

10 No man will be a sailor who has contrivance enough to get himself into a jail; for being in a ship is being in a jail, with the chance of being drowned . . . A man in a jail has more room, better food, and commonly better company.

Samuel Johnson (1709–84) British lexicographer. *Life of Johnson* (J. Boswell), Vol. I

11 I'd like to get you
On a slow boat to China.

Frank Loesser (1910–69) US songwriter. *Slow Boat to China*

12 It was the schooner Hesperus,
That sailed the wintry sea;
And the skipper had taken his little daughter,
To bear him company.

Henry Wadsworth Longfellow (1807–82) US poet. *The Wreck of the Hesperus*

13 Quinquireme of Nineveh from distant Ophir
Rowing home to haven in sunny Palestine,
With a cargo of ivory,
And apes and peacocks,
Sandalwood, cedarwood, and sweet white wine.

John Masefield (1878–1967) British poet. *Cargoes*

14 Dirty British coaster with a salt-caked smoke stack,
Butting through the Channel in the mad March days,
With a cargo of Tyne coal,
Road-rail, pig-lead,

Firewood, iron-ware, and cheap tin trays.

John Masefield *Cargoes*

15 Now the sunset breezes shiver,
And she's fading down the river,
But in England's song for ever
She's the Fighting Téméraire.

Henry John Newbolt (1862–1938) British poet. *The Fighting Téméraire*

16 Only fools and passengers drink at sea.

Alan John Villiers (1903–) Australian naval commander. *The Observer*, 'Sayings of the Week', 28 Apr 1957

BODY

1 A healthy body is the guest-chamber of the soul, a sick, its prison.

Francis Bacon (1561–1626) English philosopher, lawyer, and politician. *Augmentis Scientiarum*, 'Valetudo'

2 DIAPHRAGM, n. A muscular partition separating disorders of the chest from disorders of the bowels.

Ambrose Bierce (1842–c. 1914) US writer and journalist. *The Devil's Dictionary*

3 LIVER, n. A large red organ thoughtfully provided by nature to be bilious with. . . . It was at one time considered the seat of life; hence its name – liver, the thing we live with.

Ambrose Bierce *The Devil's Dictionary*

4 The human body is the only machine for which there are no spare parts.

Hermann M. Biggs (1859–1923) Radio talk

5 I have finally come to the conclusion that a good reliable set of bowels is worth more to a man than any quantity of brains.

Josh Billings *Bartlett's Unfamiliar Quotations* (Leonard Louis Levinson)

6 The body is truly the garment of the soul, which has a living voice; for that reason it is fitting that the body simultaneously with the soul repeatedly sing praises to God through the voice.

Hildegarde von Bingen (1098–1179) Letter to the Prelates of Mainz, c. 1178

7 Man has no Body distinct from his Soul; for that called Body is a portion of Soul discerned by the five Senses, the chief inlets of Soul in this age.

William Blake (1757–1827) British poet. *The Marriage of Heaven and Hell*, 'The Voice of the Devil'

8 My first article of belief is based on the observation, almost universally confirmed in present knowledge, that what happens in our bodies is directed toward a useful end.

Walter B. Cannon (1871–1945) US physiologist. *The Way of an Investigator*, 'Some Working Principles'

9 Of all these questions the one he asks most insistently is about man. How does he walk? How does the heart pump blood? What happens when he yawns and sneezes? How does a child live in the womb? Why does he die of old age? Leonardo discovered a centenarian in a hospital in Florence and waited gleefully for his demise so that he could examine his veins.

Kenneth Clark (1903–83) British historian. Referring to Leonardo da Vinci. *Civilisation*

10 The only bodily organ which is really regarded as inferior is the atrophied penis, a girl's clitoris.

Sigmund Freud (1856–1939) Austrian psychoanalyst. 'The Dissection of the Psychical Personality'

11 When I first gave my mind to vivisection, as a means of discovering the motions and uses of the heart, and sought to discover these from actual inspection, and not from the writings of others, I found the task so truly arduous, so full of difficulties, that I was almost tempted to think with Fracastorius, that the motion of the heart was only to be comprehended by God.

William Harvey (1578–1657) English physician and anatomist. *On the Motion of the Heart and Blood in Animals*, Ch. 1

12 *Orandum est ut sit mens sana in corpore sano.*
Your prayer must be for a sound mind in a sound body.

Juvenal (Decimus Junius Juvenalis; 60–130 AD) Roman satirist. *Satires*, X

13 Skin is like wax paper that holds everything in without dripping.

Art Linkletter (1912–) Canadian-born US radio and television personality. *A Child's Garden of Misinformation*, 5

14 How idiotic civilization is! Why be given a body if you have to keep it shut up in a case like a rare, rare fiddle?

Katherine Mansfield (1888–1923) New Zealand-born British writer. *Bliss and Other Stories*, 'Bliss'

15 The human body . . . indeed is like a ship; its bones being the stiff standing-rigging, and the sinews the small running ropes, that manage all the motions.

Herman Melville (1819–91) US novelist. *Redburn*, Ch. 13

16 The human body is a machine which winds its own springs: the living image of perpetual movement.

Julien Offroy de la Mettrie (1709–51) *L'Homme machine*

17 The abdomen is the reason why man does not easily take himself for a god.

Friedrich Nietzsche (1844–1900) German philosopher. *Beyond Good and Evil*, 141

18 I'd the upbringing a nun would envy and that's the truth. Until I was fifteen I was more familiar with Africa than my own body.

Joe Orton (1933–67) British dramatist. *Entertaining Mr Sloane*, I

19 Happiness is beneficial for the body, but it is grief that develops the powers of the mind.

Marcel Proust (1871–1922) French writer. *À la recherche du temps perdu: Le Temps retrouvé*

20 It is in moments of illness that we are compelled to recognize that we live not alone but chained to a creature of a different kingdom, whole worlds apart, who has no knowledge of us and by whom it is impossible to make ourselves understood: our body.

Marcel Proust *À la recherche du temps perdu: Le Côté de Guermantes*

21 The body is not a permanent dwelling, but a sort of inn (with a brief sojourn at that) which is to be left behind when one perceives that one is a burden to the host.

Seneca (c. 4 BC–65 AD) Roman writer. *Epistulae ad Lucilium*, CXX

22 Our purses shall be proud, our garments poor;
For 'tis the mind that makes the body rich;
And as the sun breaks through the darkest clouds,
So honour peereth in the meanest habit.

William Shakespeare (1564–1616) English dramatist. *The Taming of the Shrew*, IV:3

23 I have finally kum to the konklusion, that a good reliable sett ov bowels iz wurth more tu a man, than enny quantity ov brains.

Henry Wheeler Shaw ('Josh Billings'; 1818–85) *Josh Billings: His Sayings*, Ch. 29

24 Our body is a machine for living. It is organized for that, it is its

nature. Let life go on in it unhindered and let it defend itself, it will do more than if you paralyse it by encumbering it with remedies.
Leo Tolstoy (1828–1910) Russian writer. *War and Peace*, Bk. X, Ch. 29

25 Surgeons and anatomists see no beautiful women in all their lives, but only a ghastly stack of bones with Latin names to them, and a network of nerves and muscles and tissues inflamed by disease.
Mark Twain (Samuel L. Clemens; 1835–1910) US writer. Letter to the *Alta Californian*, San Francisco, 28 May 1867

26 If anything is sacred the human body is sacred.
Walt Whitman (1819–92) US poet. *I Sing the Body Electric*, 8

27 I have said that the soul is not more than the body,
And I have said that the body is not more than the soul,
And nothing, but God, is greater to one than one's self is.
Walt Whitman *Song of Myself*, 48

BOLDNESS

See also courage, danger, frankness, impertinence

1 Boldness, and again boldness, and always boldness!
Georges Jacques Danton (1759–94) French political activist. Speech, French Legislative Committee, 2 Sept 1792

2 Oliver Twist has asked for more.
Charles Dickens (1812–70) British novelist. *Oliver Twist*, Ch. 2

3 If the creator had a purpose in equipping us with a neck, he surely meant us to stick it out.
Arthur Koestler (1905–83) Hungarian-born British writer. *Encounter*, May 1970

BOOK OF COMMON PRAYER, THE

1 Read, mark, learn and inwardly digest.
Collect, 2nd Sunday in Advent

2 All our doings without charity are nothing worth.
Collect, Quinquagesima Sunday

3 We have erred, and strayed from thy ways like lost sheep.
Morning Prayer, General Confession

4 We have left undone those things which we ought to have done; and we have done those things we ought not to have done.
Morning Prayer, General Confession

5 As it was in the beginning, is now, and ever shall be: world without end.
Morning Prayer, Gloria

6 When two or three are gathered together in thy Name thou wilt grant their requests.
Morning Prayer, Prayer of St Chrysostom

7 Defend us from all perils and dangers of this night.
Morning Prayer, Prayer of St Chrysostom

8 All the deceits of the world, the flesh, and the devil.
Morning Prayer, Prayer of St Chrysostom

9 In the hour of death, and in the day of judgement.
Morning Prayer, Prayer of St Chrysostom

10 Give peace in our time, O Lord.
Morning Prayer, Versicles

11 Being now come to the years of discretion.
Order of Confirmation

12 Renounce the devil and all his works.
Publick Baptism of Infants

13 If any of you know cause, or just impediment.
Solemnization of Matrimony

14 Let him now speak, or else hereafter for ever hold his peace.
Solemnization of Matrimony

15 To have and to hold from this day forward, for better for worse, for richer for poorer, in sickness and in health, to love and to cherish, till death us do part.
Solemnization of Matrimony

BOOKS

See also criticism, fiction, literature, novels, publishing, reading, writing

1 Books and friends should be few but good.
Proverb

2 The true system of the World has been recognized , developed and perfected . . . Everything has been discussed and analysed, or at least mentioned.
Jean d'Alembert (1717–83) French philosopher and mathematician. Referring to the *Encyclopédie* (1751–80), which he helped to edit. *Elements of Philosophy*

3 Some books are undeservedly forgotten; none are undeservedly remembered.
W. H. Auden (1907–73) British poet. *The Dyer's Hand*, 'Reading'

4 Some books are to be tasted, others to be swallowed, and some few to be chewed and digested.
Francis Bacon (1561–1626) English philosopher. *Essays*, 'Of Studies'

5 Books must follow sciences, and not sciences books.
Francis Bacon *Proposition touching Amendment of Laws*

6 When I am dead, I hope it may be said:
'His sins were scarlet, but his books were read.'
Hilaire Belloc (1870–1953) French-born British poet. *Epigrams*, 'On His Books'

7 Child! do not throw this book about;
Refrain from the unholy pleasure
Of cutting all the pictures out!
Preserve it as your chiefest treasure.
Hilaire Belloc *The Bad Child's Book of Beasts*, 'Dedication'

8 And further, by these, my son, be admonished: of making many books there is no end; and much study is a weariness of the flesh.
Bible: Ecclesiastes 12:12

9 A best-seller was a book which somehow sold well simply because it was selling well.
Daniel J. Boorstin *The Image*, 'From Shapes to Shadows: Dissolving Forms'

10 I keep my books at the British Museum and at Mudie's.
Samuel Butler (1835–1902) British writer. *The Humour of Homer*, 'Ramblings in Cheapside'

11 'Tis pleasant, sure, to see one's name in print;
A book's a book, although there's nothing in't.
Lord Byron (1788–1824) British poet. *English Bards and Scotch Reviewers*

12 A good book is the purest essence of a human soul.
Thomas Carlyle (1795–1881) Scottish historian and essayist. Speech made in support of the London Library. *Carlyle and the London Library* (F. Harrison)

13 'What is the use of a book,' thought Alice, 'without pictures or conversation?'
Lewis Carroll (Charles Lutwidge Dodgson; 1832–98) British writer. *Alice's Adventures in Wonderland*, Ch. 1

14 Go, litel book, go litel myn tragedie.
O moral Gower, this book I directe
To thee.
Geoffrey Chaucer (c. 1342–1400) English poet. *Troilus and Criseyde*, 5

15 Due attention to the inside of books, and due contempt for the outside, is the proper relation between a man of sense and his books.
Earl of Chesterfield (1694–1773) English statesman. Letter to his son, 10 Jan 1749

16 Books cannot always please, however good;
Minds are not ever craving for their food.
George Crabbe (1754–1832) British poet. *The Borough*, 'Schools'

17 Books, we are told, propose to *instruct* or to *amuse*. Indeed! . . . The true antithesis to knowledge, in this case, is not *pleasure*, but *power*. All that is literature seeks to communicate power; all that is not literature, to communicate knowledge.
Thomas De Quincey (1785–1859) British writer. *Letters to a Young Man*

18 A book is not harmless merely because no one is consciously offended by it.
T. S. Eliot (1888–1965) US-born British poet and dramatist. *Religion and Literature*

19 Books are made not like children but like pyramids . . . and they're just as useless! and they stay in the desert! . . . Jackals piss at their foot and the bourgeois climb up on them.
Gustave Flaubert (1821–80) French novelist. Letter to Ernest Feydeau, 1857

20 Learning hath gained most by those books by which the printers have lost.
Thomas Fuller (1608–61) English historian. *The Holy State and the Profane State*

21 A book may be amusing with numerous errors, or it may be very dull without a single absurdity.
Oliver Goldsmith (1728–74) Irish-born British writer. *The Vicar of Wakefield*, Advertisement

22 Few books today are forgivable.
R. D. Laing (1927–) British psychiatrist. *The Politics of Experience*, Introduction

23 Borrowers of books – those mutilators of collections, spoilers of the symmetry of shelves, and creators of odd volumes.
Charles Lamb (1775–1834) British essayist. *Essays of Elia*, 'The Two Races of Men'

24 Get stewed:
Books are a load of crap.
Philip Larkin (1922–85) British poet. *A Study of Reading Habits*

25 To every man who struggles with his own soul in mystery, a book that is a book flowers once, and seeds, and is gone.
D. H. Lawrence (1885–1930) British novelist. *Phoenix*, 'A Bibliography of D.H.L.'

26 Never judge a cover by its book.
Fran Lebowitz (1950–) US writer. *Metropolitan Life*

27 There can hardly be a stranger commodity in the world than books. Printed by people who don't understand them; sold by people who don't understand them; bound, criticized and read by people who don't understand them; and now even written by people who don't understand them.
Georg Christoph Lichtenberg (1742–99) German physicist and writer. *Aphorisms*

28 He felt about books as doctors feel about medicines, or managers about plays – cynical but hopeful.
Dame Rose Macaulay (1881–1958) British writer. *Crewe Train*, Ch. 8, Pt. 2

29 In recommending a book to a friend the less said the better. The moment you praise a book too highly you awaken resistance in your listener.
Henry Miller (1891–1980) US novelist. *The Books In My Life*

30 Who kills a man kills a reasonable creature, God's image; but he who destroys a good book, kills reason itself, kills the image of God, as it were in the eye.
John Milton (1608–74) English poet. *Areopagitica*

31 A good book is the precious life-blood of a master spirit, embalmed and treasured up on purpose to a life beyond life.
John Milton *Areopagitica*

32 The books one reads in childhood, and perhaps most of all the bad and good bad books, create in one's mind a sort of false map of the world, a series of fabulous countries into which one can retreat at odd moments throughout the rest of life, and which in some cases can even survive a visit to the real countries which they are supposed to represent.
George Orwell (Eric Blair; 1903–50) British novelist. *Riding Down from Bangor*

33 At last, an unprintable book that is readable.
Ezra Pound (1885–1972) US poet. Referring to *Tropic of Cancer* by Henry Miller.

34 An anthology is like all the plums and orange peel picked out of a cake.
Walter Raleigh (1861–1922) British scholar. Letter to Mrs Robert Bridges, 15 Jan 1915

35 I have known her pass the whole evening without mentioning a single book, or *in fact anything unpleasant* at all.
Henry Reed (1914–) British poet and dramatist. *A Very Great Man Indeed*

36 When a new book is published, read an old one.
Samuel Rogers (1763–1855) British poet. Attrib.

37 We all know that books burn – yet we have the greater knowledge that books cannot be killed by fire. People die, but books never die. No man and no force can abolish memory. . . . In this war, we know, books are weapons.
Franklin D. Roosevelt (1882–1945) US Democratic president. Message to American Booksellers Association, 23 Apr 1942

38 If a book is worth reading, it is worth buying.
John Ruskin (1819–1900) British art critic and writer. *Sesame and Lilies*, 'Of Kings' Treasuries'

39 All books are divisible into two classes, the books of the hour, and the books of all time.
John Ruskin *Sesame and Lilies*, 'Of Kings' Treasuries'

40 How long most people would look at the best book before they would give the price of a large turbot for it!
John Ruskin *Sesame and Lilies*, 'Of Kings' Treasuries'

41 A library is thought in cold storage.
Herbert Samuel (1870–1963) British Liberal statesman. *A Book of Quotations*

42 Children . . . have no use for psychology. They detest sociology. They still believe in God, the family, angels, devils, witches, goblins, logic, clarity, punctuation, and other such obsolete stuff . . . When a book is boring, they yawn openly. They don't expect their writer to redeem humanity, but leave to adults such childish illusions.

Isaac Bashevis Singer (1904–) Polish-born US writer. Speech on receiving the Nobel Prize for Literature. *The Observer*, 17 Dec 1978

43 A best-seller is the gilded tomb of a mediocre talent.

Logan Pearsall Smith (1865–1946) US writer. *Afterthoughts*, 'Art and Letters'

44 No furniture so charming as books.

Sydney Smith (1771–1845) British clergyman and essayist. *Memoir* (Lady Holland)

45 Books are good enough in their own way, but they are a mighty bloodless substitute for life.

Robert Louis Stevenson (1850–94) Scottish writer. *Virginibus Puerisque*

46 My brother-in-law wrote an unusual murder story. The victim got killed by a man from another book.

Robert Sylvester (1907–75) US writer. Attrib.

47 Not with blinded eyesight poring over miserable books.

Alfred, Lord Tennyson (1809–92) British poet. *Locksley Hall*

48 A good book is the best of friends, the same to-day and for ever.

Martin Farquhar Tupper (1810–89) British writer. *Proverbial Philosophy*, 'Of Reading'

49 Books, I don't know what you see in them . . . I can understand a person reading them, but I can't for the life of me see why people have to write them.

Peter Ustinov (1921–) British actor. *Photo-Finish*

50 God forbid that any book should be banned. The practice is as indefensible as infanticide.

Rebecca West (Cicely Isabel Fairfield; 1892–1983) British novelist and journalist. *The Strange Necessity*, 'The Tosh Horse'

51 There is no such thing as a moral or an immoral book. Books are well written, or badly written.

Oscar Wilde (1854–1900) Irish-born British dramatist. *The Picture of Dorian Gray*, Preface

BOOK, SONG, AND PLAY TITLES

1 Who's Afraid of Virginia Woolf?

Edward Albee (1928–) US dramatist. Play title

2 Lucky Jim.

Kingsley Amis (1922–) British novelist. Title of novel

3 The Ugly Duckling.

Hans Christian Andersen (1805–75) Danish writer. Story title

4 Eating People Is Wrong.

Malcolm Bradbury (1932–) British academic, novelist, and critic. From a song 'The Reluctant Cannibal' by Michael Flanders and Donald Swann. Book title

5 Room at the Top.

John Braine (1922–86) British novelist. From Daniel Webster's remark 'There is always room at the top'. Book title

6 Tender Is the Night.

F. Scott Fitzgerald (1896–1940) US novelist. From the 'Ode to a Nightingale' (John Keats): 'Already with thee! tender is the night'. Book title

7 When the Kissing Had to Stop.

Constantine FitzGibbon From 'A Toccata at Galuppi's' (Robert Browning): 'What of soul was left, I wonder, when the kissing had to stop'. Book title

8 Diamonds Are Forever.

Ian Fleming (1908–64) British writer. From the advertising slogan 'A Diamond is Forever' for De Beers Consolidated Mines. Book title

9 'Tis Pity She's a whore.

John Ford (c. 1586–c. 1640) English dramatist. Play title

10 Goodbye to All That.

Robert Graves (1895–1985) British poet. Book title

11 A Woman Killed with Kindness.

Thomas Heywood (c. 1574–1641) English dramatist. Play title

12 The Light that Failed.

Rudyard Kipling (1865–1936) Indian-born British writer. Novel title

13 Shoot all the bluejays you want, if you can hit 'em, but remember it's a sin to kill a mockingbird.

Harper Lee (1926–) US writer. *To Kill a Mockingbird*, Pt. II, Ch. 10

14 Sergeant Pepper's Lonely Hearts Club Band.

John Lennon (1940–80) British rock singer. Song title (with Paul McCartney)

15 None But the Lonely Heart.

Richard Llewellyn British writer. Adapted from the English title of Tchaikowsky's song 'None But the Weary Heart' (original words by Goethe). Book title

16 Of Human Bondage.

W. Somerset Maugham (1874–1965) British novelist and doctor. From the title of one of the books in *Ethics* (Spinoza). Book title

17 The Moon and Sixpence.

W. Somerset Maugham From a review of his novel *Of Human Bondage*, 'Like so many young men, was so busy yearning for the moon that he never saw the sixpence at his feet'. (*Times Literary Supplement*) Book title

18 The Heart Is a Lonely Hunter.

Carson McCullers (1917–67) US novelist. From the poem 'The Lonely Hunter' (William Sharp): 'My heart is a lonely hunter that hunts on a lonely hill'. Book title

19 Gone With the Wind.

Margaret Mitchell (1909–49) US novelist. From the poem *Non Sum Qualis Eram* (Ernest Dowson): 'I have forgot much, Cynara! Gone with the wind . . . '. Book title

20 The Moon's a Balloon.

David Niven (1909–83) British actor. From e. e. cummings, '&': 'Who knows if the moon's a balloon, coming out of a keen city in the sky – filled with pretty people?'. Book title

21 A Dance to the Music of Time.

Anthony Powell (1905–) British novelist. From the name of a painting by Nicolas Poussin. Book title

22 A Bridge Too Far.

Cornelius Ryan Lieut. General Sir Frederick Browning said to Field Marshal Montgomery 'But, sir, we may be going a bridge too far'; referring to the airborne attack to capture eleven bridges over the Rhine, including the bridge at Arnhem, prior to the invasion of Germany (1944). Book title

23 Fanny by Gaslight.

Michael Sadleir (1888–1957) British author. Book title

24 Look Homeward, Angel!

Thomas Wolfe (1900–38) US novelist. From 'Lycidas' by John Milton. Book title

BOREDOM

See also bores

1 Nothing happens, nobody comes, nobody goes, it's awful!

Samuel Beckett (1906–) Irish novelist and dramatist. *Waiting for Godot*, I

2 I'm so bored with it all.

Winston Churchill (1874–1965) British statesman. Said to be his last words. *Clementine* (M. Soames)

3 I wanted to be bored to death, as good a way to go as any.

Peter De Vries (1910–) US novelist. *Comfort me with Apples*, Ch. 17

4 Millions long for immortality who do not know what to do with themselves on a rainy Sunday afternoon.

Susan Ertz British novelist and playwright. *Anger in the Sky*

5 You ought not to be ashamed of

being bored. What you ought to be ashamed of is being boring.

Lord Hailsham (1907–) British Conservative politician. *The Observer*, 'Sayings of the Week', 12 Oct 1975

6 Symmetry is tedious, and tedium is the very basis of mourning. Despair yawns.

Victor Hugo (1802–85) French writer. *Les Misérables*, Vol. II, Bk. IV, Ch. 1

7 The effect of boredom on a large scale in history is underestimated. It is a main cause of revolutions, and would soon bring to an end all the static Utopias and the farmyard civilization of the Fabians.

Dean Inge (1860–1954) British churchman. *The End of an Age*, Ch. 6

8 By his very success in inventing labor-saving devices modern man has manufactured an abyss of boredom that only the privileged classes in earlier civilisations have ever fathomed.

Lewis Mumford (1895–) US social philosopher. *The Conduct of Life*

9 Is not life a hundred times too short for us to bore ourselves?

Friedrich Wilhelm Nietzsche (1844–1900) German philosopher. *Jenseits von Gut und Böse*

10 When you're bored with yourself, marry and be bored with someone else.

David Pryce-Jones (1936–) British author and critic. *Owls and Satyrs*

BORES

See also boredom

1 *Bore*, n. A person who talks when you wish him to listen.

Ambrose Bierce (1842–?1914) US writer and journalist. *The Devil's Dictionary*

2 Society is now one polish'd horde,
Form'd of two mighty tribes, the *Bores* and *Bored*.

Lord Byron (1788–1824) British poet. *Don Juan*, XIII

3 Sir, you are like a pin, but without either its head or its point.

Douglas William Jerrold (1803–57) British dramatist. Speaking to a small thin man who was boring him. Attrib.

4 He is not only a bore but he bores for England.

Malcolm Muggeridge (1903–) British writer. Referring to Sir Anthony Eden. In *New-statesmanship* (E. Hyams), 'Boring for England'

5 A bore is a man who, when you ask him how he is, tells you.

Bert Leston Taylor (1866–1921) US journalist. Attrib.

6 Somebody's boring me, I think it's me.

Dylan Thomas (1914–53) Welsh poet. Remark made after he had been talking continuously for some time. *Four Absentees* (Rayner Heppenstall)

7 He is an old bore; even the grave yawns for him.

Herbert Beerbohm Tree (1853–1917) British actor and theater manager. Referring to Israel Zangwill. *Beerbohm Tree* (Hesketh Pearson)

8 A healthy male adult bore consumes each year one and a half times his own weight in other people's patience.

John Updike (1932–) US novelist. *Assorted Prose*, 'Confessions of a Wild Bore'

9 Dear Frank, we believe you; you have dined in every house in London – *once*.

Oscar Wilde (1854–1900) Irish-born British dramatist. Interrupting Frank Harris's interminable account of the houses he had dined at. Attrib.

BORROWING

1 Borrowed garments never fit well.

Proverb

2 I don't trust a bank that would lend money to such a poor risk.

Robert Benchley (1889–1945) US humorist. To a bank that granted his request for a loan. Attrib.

3 Be not made a beggar by banqueting upon borrowing, when thou hast nothing in thy purse: for thou shalt lie in wait for thine own life, and be talked on.

Bible: Ecclesiasticus 18:33

4 One of the mysteries of human conduct is why adult men and women all over England are ready to sign documents which they do not read, at the behest of canvassers whom they do not know, binding them to pay for articles which they do not want, with money which they have not got.

Gerald Hurst (1877–1957) British writer and judge. *Closed Chapters*

5 The human species, according to the best theory I can form of it, is composed of two distinct races, the men who borrow, and the men who lend.

Charles Lamb (1775–1834) British essayist. *Essays of Elia*, 'The Two Races of Men'

6 Borrowers of books – those mutilators of collections, spoilers of the symmetry of shelves, and creators of odd volumes.

Charles Lamb *Essays of Elia*, 'The Two Races of Men'

7 Not everyone is a debtor who wishes to be; not everyone who wishes makes creditors.

François Rabelais (1483–1553) French satirist. *Pantagruel*, Bk. III, Ch. 3

8 Neither a borrower nor a lender be;
For loan oft loses both itself and friend,
And borrowing dulls the edge of husbandry.
This above all: to thine own self be true,
And it must follow, as the night the day,
Thou canst not then be false to any man.

William Shakespeare (1564–1616) English dramatist. *Hamlet*, I:3

9 Thank God, that's settled.

Richard Brinsley Sheridan (1751–1816) British dramatist. Handing one of his creditors an IOU. *Wit, Wisdom, and Foibles of the Great* (C. Shriner)

10 It is not my interest to pay the principal, nor my principle to pay the interest.

Richard Brinsley Sheridan To his tailor when he requested the payment of a debt, or of the interest on it at least. Attrib.

11 My dear fellow, be reasonable; the sum you ask me for is a very considerable one, whereas I only ask you for twenty-five pounds.

Richard Brinsley Sheridan. On being refused a further loan of £25 from a friend to whom he already owed £500. *Literary and Scientific Anecdotes* (W. Keddie)

12 Let us all be happy, and live within our means, even if we have to borrer the money to do it with.

Artemus Ward (Charles Farrar Browne; 1834–67) US humorous writer. *Science and Natural History*

13 I don't owe a penny to a single soul – not counting tradesmen, of course.

P. G. Wodehouse (1881–1975) British humorous novelist. *My Man Jeeves*, 'Jeeves and the Hard-Boiled Egg'

BOSTON

1 A Boston man is the east wind made flesh.
Thomas Gold Appleton (1812–84) US writer. Attrib.

2 And this is good old Boston,
The home of the bean and the cod,
Where the Lowells talk only to Cabots,
And the Cabots talk only to God.
John Collins Bossidy (1860–1928) US writer. Toast at Holy Cross Alumni dinner, 1910

BOUNDARIES

See also neighbours

1 When you think about the defence of England you no longer think of the chalk cliffs of Dover. You think of the Rhine. That is where our frontier lies to-day.
Stanley Baldwin (1867–1947) British statesman. Speech, House of Commons, 30 July 1934

2 Something there is that doesn't love a wall.
Robert Frost (1875–1963) US poet. *North of Boston*, 'Mending Wall'

BOYS

See children, youth

BRAIN

1 *Brain*, n. An apparatus with which we think that we think.
Ambrose Bierce (1842–?1914) US writer and journalist. *The Devil's Dictionary*

2 We, my lords, may thank heaven that we have something better than our brains to depend upon.
Earl of Chesterfield (1694–1773) English statesman. Speech, House of Lords. *The Story of Civilization* (W. Durant), Vol. 9

3 We know the human brain is a device to keep the ears from grating on one another.
Peter De Vries (1910–) US novelist. *Comfort me with Apples*, Ch. 1

4 A man should keep his little brain attic stocked with all the furniture that he is likely to use, and the rest he can put away in the lumber room of his library, where he can get it if he wants it.
Arthur Conan Doyle (1856–1930) British writer. *Five Orange Pips*

5 So this gentleman said a girl with brains ought to do something else with them besides think.
Anita Loos (1891–1981) US novelist. *Gentlemen Prefer Blondes*, Ch. 1

6 I mix them with my brains, sir.
John Opie (1761–1807) British painter. When asked what he mixed his colors with *Self-Help* (Samuel Smiles), Ch. 4

7 If it is for mind that we are seaching the brain, then we are supposing the brain to be much more than a telephone-exchange. We are supposing it a telephone-exchange along with the subscribers as well.
Charles Scott Sherrington (1857–1952) British physiologist. *Man on his Nature*

8 Give me the young man who has brains enough to make a fool of himself!
Robert Louis Stevenson (1850–94) Scottish writer. *Virginibus Puerisque*

9 All the unhappy marriages come from the husbands having brains. What good are brains to a man? They only unsettle him.
P. G. Wodehouse (1881–1975) British humorous novelist. *The Adventures of Sally*

BRAVERY

See courage

BREAD

1 Cast thy bread upon the waters: for thou shalt find it after many days.
Bible: Ecclesiastes 11:1

2 And Jesus said unto them, I am the bread of life: he that cometh to me shall never hunger; and he that believeth on me shall never thirst.
Bible: John 6:35

3 Stolen waters are sweet, and bread eaten in secret is pleasant.
Bible: Proverbs 9:17

4 Here with a Loaf of Bread beneath the Bough,
A Flask of Wine, a Book of Verse – and Thou
Beside me singing in the Wilderness –
And Wilderness is Paradise enow.
Edward Fitzgerald (1809–83) British poet. *The Rubáiyát of Omar Khayyám*

5 Oh! God! that bread should be so dear,
And flesh and blood so cheap!
Thomas Hood (1799–1845) British poet. *The Song of the Shirt*

6 Their learning is like bread in a besieged town: every man gets a little, but no man gets a full meal.
Samuel Johnson (1709–84) British lexicographer and writer. Referring to education in Scotland. *Life of Johnson* (J. Boswell), Vol. II

7 The people long eagerly for just two things – bread and circuses.
Juvenal (Decimus Junius Juvenalis; 60–130 AD) Roman satirist. *Satires*, X

8 Bachelor's fare; bread and cheese, and kisses.
Jonathan Swift (1667–1745) Irish-born Anglican priest and writer. *Polite Conversation*, Dialogue 1

9 This bread I break was once the oat,
This wine upon a foreign tree
Plunged in its fruit;
Man in the day or wind at night
Laid the crops low, broke the grape's joy.
Dylan Thomas (1914–53) Welsh poet. *This bread I break*

BREVITY

See also sermons, speeches, verbosity

1 You lose.
Calvin Coolidge (1872–1933) US President. When a lady at a dinner told him that someone had bet her that she would not get more than two words out of him. Attrib.

2 Good things, when short, are twice as good.
Baltasar Gracián (1601–58) Spanish writer. *The Art of Worldly Wisdom*

3 I strive to be brief, and I become obscure.
Horace (Quintus Horatius Flaccus; 65–8 BC) Roman poet. *Ars Poetica*

4 ?
Victor Hugo (1802–85) French writer. The entire contents of a telegram sent to his publishers asking how *Les Misérables* was selling; the reply was '!'. *The Literary Life* (R. Hendrickson)

5 But the shortest works are always the best.
Jean de La Fontaine (1621–95) French poet. *Fables*, X, 'Les Lapins'

6 Brevity is the soul of lingerie.
Dorothy Parker (1893–1967) US writer. *While Rome Burns* (Alexander Woollcott)

7 Trust the man who hesitates in his speech and is quick and steady in action, but beware of long arguments and long beards.
George Santayana (1863–1952) US philosopher. *Soliloquies in England*, 'The British Character'

8 Brevity is the soul of wit.

William Shakespeare (1564–1616) English dramatist. *Hamlet*, II:2

9 Men of few words are the best men.

William Shakespeare *Henry V*, III:2

10 Nurse unupblown.

Evelyn Waugh (1903–66) British novelist. Cable sent after he had failed, while a journalist serving in Ethiopia, to substantiate a rumor that an English nurse had been blown up in an Italian air raid. *Our Marvelous Native Tongue* (R. Claiborne)

BRIBERY

See also corruption

1 When their lordships asked Bacon
How many bribes he had taken
He had at least the grace
To get very red in the face.

Edmund Clerihew Bentley (1875–1956) British writer. *Baseless Biography*

2 I stuffed their mouths with gold!

Aneurin Bevan (1897–1960) British Labour politician. Explaining how he persuaded doctors not to oppose the introduction of the National Health Service. Attrib.

3 To a shower of gold most things are penetrable.

Thomas Carlyle (1795–1881) Scottish historian and essayist. *History of the French Revolution*, Pt. I, Bk. III, Ch. 7

4 I have often noticed that a bribe . . . has that effect – it changes a relation. The man who offers a bribe gives away a little of his own importance; the bribe once accepted, he becomes the inferior, like a man who has paid for a woman.

Graham Greene (1904–) British novelist. *The Comedians*, Pt. I, Ch. 4

5 Though authority be a stubborn bear, yet he is oft led by the nose with gold.

William Shakespeare (1564–1616) English dramatist. *The Winter's Tale*, IV:3

BRIDGE

1 That is the road we all have to take – over the Bridge of Sighs into eternity.

Soren Kierkegaard (1813–55) Danish philosopher. *Kierkegaard Anthology* (Auden)

2 I stood on the bridge at midnight,
As the clocks were striking the hour.

Henry Wadsworth Longfellow (1807–82) US poet. *The Bridge*

3 Beautiful Railway Bridge of the Silv'ry Tay!
Alas, I am very sorry to say
That ninety lives have been taken away
On the last Sabbath day of 1879,
Which will be remember'd for a very long time.

William McGonagall (1830–1902) Scottish poet. *The Tay Bridge Disaster*

4 London Bridge is broken down,
My fair lady.

Nursery Rhyme *Namby Pamby* (Henry Carey)

5 Like a bridge over troubled water,
I will ease your mind.

Paul Simon (1941–) US singer. *Bridge Over Troubled Water*

BRITAIN

See also British, British Empire, England, Ireland, patriotism, Scotland, Wales

1 Great Britain has lost an Empire and has not yet found a role.

Dean Acheson (1893–1971) US lawyer and statesman. Speech, Military Academy, West Point, 5 Dec 1962

2 A nation of shop-keepers are very seldom so disinterested.

Samuel Adams (1722–1803) US revolutionary leader. Referring to Britain, following the Declaration of Independence, 4 July 1776. Speech, Philadelphia, 1 Aug 1776

3 Land of Hope and Glory, Mother of the Free,
How shall we extol thee, who are born of thee?
Wider still and wider shall thy bounds be set;
God who made thee mighty, make thee mightier yet.

A. C. Benson (1862–1925) British writer. *Land of Hope and Glory*

4 Britain has lived for too long on borrowed time, borrowed money and even borrowed ideas.

James Callaghan (1912–) British politician and prime minister. *The Observer*, 'Sayings of the Week', 3 Oct 1976

5 God save our Gracious King,
Long live our noble King,
God save the King.
Send him victorious,
Happy and glorious.

Henry Carey (c. 1690–1743) English poet and musician. *God Save the King*

6 When the British warrior queen,
Bleeding from the Roman rods,
Sought; with an indignant mien,
Counsel of her country's gods.

William Cowper (1731–1800) British poet. *Boadicea*

7 Britain is not a country that is easily rocked by revolution . . . In Britain our institutions evolve. We are a Fabian Society writ large.

William Hamilton (1917–) Scottish MP. *My Queen and I*, Ch. 9

8 We may be a small island, but we are not a small people.

Edward Heath (1916–) British politician. *The Observer*, 'Sayings of the Week', 21 June 1970

9 We are unable to influence events in the way we want because we do not have the power or will to do so.

Nicholas Henderson (1919–) British diplomat. Referring to Britain; written on ceasing to be ambassador to France. Letter to the foreign secretary, David Owen, 1979

10 Sir, it is not so much to be lamented that Old England is lost, as that the Scotch have found it.

Samuel Johnson (1709–84) British lexicographer. *Life of Johnson* (J. Boswell), Vol. III

11 This is a very fine country to be acutely ill or injured in, but take my advice and do not be old and frail or mentally ill here – at least not for a few years. This is definitely not a good country to be deaf or blind in either.

Keith Joseph (1918–) British politician. *The Observer*, 'Sayings of the Week', 1 July 1973

12 Once, when a British Prime Minister sneezed, men half a world away would blow their noses. Now when a British Prime Minister sneezes nobody else will even say 'Bless You'.

Bernard Levin (1928–) British journalist. *The Times*, 1976

13 Everything that is most beautiful in Britain has always been in private hands.

Malcolm Rifkind (1946–) British politician. *The Observer*, 'Sayings of the Week', 17 Jan 1988

14 When Britain first, at heaven's command,
Arose from out the azure main,
This was the charter of the land,
And guardian angels sung this strain:
'Rule, Britannia, rule the waves;
Britons never will be slaves.'

James Thomson (1700–48) British poet. *Alfred: a Masque*, Act II

15 I should like to help Britain to

become a Third Programme country.
Ellen Cicely Wilkinson (1891–1947) British feminist and politician. *The Observer*, 'Sayings of the Week', 2 Feb 1947

BRITISH

See also Britain, English, Irish, Scots, Welsh

1 A young Scotsman of your ability let loose upon the world with £300, what could he not do? It's almost appalling to think of; especially if he went among the English.
J. M. Barrie (1860–1937) British novelist and dramatist. *What Every Woman Knows*, I

2 There are no countries in the world less known by the British than these selfsame British Islands.
George Henry Borrow (1803–81) British writer. *Lavengro*, Preface

3 The British love permanence more than they love beauty.
Hugh Casson (1910–) British architect. *The Observer*, 'Sayings of the Week', 14 June 1964

4 It must be owned, that the Graces do not seem to be natives of Great Britain; and I doubt, the best of us here have more of rough than polished diamond.
Earl of Chesterfield (1694–1773) English statesman. Letter to his son, 18 Nov 1748

5 The maxim of the British people is 'Business as usual'.
Winston Churchill (1874–1965) British statesman. Speech, Guildhall, 9 Nov 1914

6 They are the only people who like to be told how bad things are – who like to be told the worst.
Winston Churchill Speech, 1921

7 Courtesy is not dead – it has merely taken refuge in Great Britain.
Georges Duhamel (1884–1966) French writer. *The Observer*, 'Sayings of Our Times', 31 May 1953

8 The British won't fight.
Leopoldo Galtieri (1924–) President of Argentina. Referring to the Falklands crisis. Remark to Alexander Haig, US Secretary of State, 10 Apr 1982

9 Of all noxious animals, too, the most noxious is a tourist. And of all tourists the most vulgar, ill-bred, offensive and loathsome is the British tourist.
Francis Kilvert (1840–79) British diarist and clergyman. *Diary*, 5 Apr 1870

10 I would rather be British than just.
Ian Paisley (1926–) Northern Irish politician. *The Sunday Times*, 12 Dec 1971

11 It is beginning to be hinted that we are a nation of amateurs.
Earl of Rosebery (1847–1929) British statesman. Rectorial Address, Glasgow, 16 Nov 1900

12 Other nations use 'force'; we Britons alone use 'Might'.
Evelyn Waugh (1903–66) British novelist. *Scoop*, Bk. II, Ch. 5

BRITISH EMPIRE

1 The British flag has never flown over a more powerful or a more united empire . . . Never did our voice count for more in the councils of nations; or in determining the future destinies of mankind.
George Nathaniel Carson (1859–1925) British politician. Speech, House of Lords, 18 Nov 1918

2 I have not become the King's First Minister in order to preside over the liquidation of the British Empire.
Winston Churchill (1874–1965) British statesman. Speech, Mansion House, 10 Nov 1942

3 The loss of India would mark and consummate the downfall of the British Empire. That great organism would pass at a stroke out of life into history. From such a catastrophe there could be no recovery.
Winston Churchill Speech to Indian Empire Society, London, 12 Dec 1930

4 It is only when you get to see and realize what India is –that she is the strength and the greatness of England – it is only then that you feel that every nerve a man may strain, every energy he may put forward, cannot be devoted to a nobler purpose than keeping tight the cords that hold India to ourselves.
George Curzon (1859–1925) British politician. Speech, Southport, 15 Mar 1893

5 How is the Empire?
George V (1865–1936) King of the United Kingdom. Last words. *The Times*, 21 Jan 1936

6 'Can't' will be the epitaph of the British Empire – unless we wake up in time.
Oswald Mosley (1896–1980) British politician. Speech, Manchester, 9 Dec 1937

7 His Majesty's dominions, on which the sun never sets.
Christopher North (John Wilson; 1785–1854) Scottish writer. *Noctes Ambrosianae*, 20 Apr 1829

8 The Empire is a Commonwealth of Nations.
Earl of Rosebery (1847–1929) British statesman. Speech, Adelaide, 18 Jan 1884

9 We the English seem, as it were, to have conquered and peopled half the world in a fit of absence of mind.
John Robert Seeley (1834–95) British historian. *The Expansion of England*, I

BROWNING, Robert

(1812–89) British poet. *Men and Women* (1855), *Dramatis Personae* (1864), and *The Ring and the Book* (1868–69), were written after his marriage to the poet Elizabeth Barrett, with whom he eloped to Italy in 1846.

Quotations about Browning

1 Browning used words with the violence of a horse-breaker, giving out the scent of a he-goat. But he got them to do their work.
Ford Madox Ford (1873–1939) British novelist. *The March of Literature*

2 He might have passed for a politician, or a financier, or a diplomatist or, indeed, for anything but a poet.
George William Russell (1867–1965) Irish poet and dramatist. *Portraits of the Seventies*

Quotations by Browning

3 So free we seem, so fettered fast we are!
Andrea del Sarto

4 Ah, but a man's reach should exceed his grasp,
Or what's a heaven for?
Andrea del Sarto

5 Why need the other women know so much?
Any Wife to any Husband

6 My sun sets to rise again.
At the 'Mermaid'

7 Best be yourself, imperial, plain and true!
Bishop Blougram's Apology

8 We mortals cross the ocean of this world
Each in his average cabin of a life.
Bishop Blougram's Apology

9 Just when we are safest, there's a sunset-touch,
A fancy from a flower-bell, some one's death,
A chorus-ending from Euripides, –
And that's enough for fifty hopes and fears
As old and new at once as Nature's self,
To rap and knock and enter in our soul.
Bishop Blougram's Apology

10 The grand Perhaps!
Bishop Blougram's Apology

11 All we have gained then by our unbelief
Is a life of doubt diversified by faith,
For one of faith diversified by doubt:
We called the chess-board white, – we call it black.
Bishop Blougram's Apology

12 No, when the fight begins within himself,
A man's worth something.
Bishop Blougram's Apology

13 He said true things, but called them by wrong names.
Bishop Blougram's Apology

14 'Tis the Last Judgment's fire must cure this place,
Calcine its clods and set my prisoners free.
Childe Roland to the Dark Tower Came, XI

15 As for the grass, it grew as scant as hair
In leprosy.
Childe Roland to the Dark Tower Came, XIII

16 I never saw a brute I hated so;
He must be wicked to deserve such pain.
Childe Roland to the Dark Tower Came, XIV

17 Dauntless the slug-horn to my lips I set,
And blew. *Childe Roland to the Dark Tower came.*
Childe Roland to the Dark Tower Came, XXXIV

18 Though Rome's gross yoke
Drops off, no more to be endured,
Her teaching is not so obscured
By errors and perversities,
That no truth shines athwart the lies.
Christmas Eve, XI

19 Such ever was love's way; to rise, it stoops.
A Death in the Desert

20 For I say, this is death, and the sole death,
When a man's loss comes to him from his gain,
Darkness from light, from knowledge ignorance,
And lack of love from love made manifest.
A Death in the Desert

21 Man partly is and wholly hopes to be.
A Death in the Desert

22 How very hard it is
To be a Christian!
Easter-Day, I

23 At last awake
From life, that insane dream we take
For waking now.
Easter-Day, XIV

24 No, at noonday in the bustle of man's worktime
Greet the unseen with a cheer!
Epilogue to Asolando

25 Oh, to be in England
Now that April's there.
Home Thoughts from Abroad

26 And after April, when May follows,
And the whitethroat builds, and all the swallows!
Home Thoughts from Abroad

27 That's the wise thrush; he sings each song twice over,
Lest you should think he never could recapture
The first fine careless rapture!
Home Thoughts from Abroad

28 I sprang to the stirrup, and Joris, and he;
I galloped, Dirck galloped, we galloped all three.
How they brought the Good News from Ghent to Aix

29 Oh, good gigantic smile o' the brown old earth.
James Lee's Wife, VII

30 And, Robert Browning, you writer of plays,
Here's a subject made to your hand!
A Light Woman, XIV

31 Just for a handful of silver he left us,
Just for a riband to stick in his coat.
The Lost Leader

32 Blot out his name, then, record one lost soul more,
One task more declined, one more footpath untrod,
One more devils'-triumph and sorrow for angels,
One wrong more to man, one more insult to God!
The Lost Leader

33 Then let him receive the new knowledge and wait us,
Pardoned in heaven, the first by the throne!
The Lost Leader

34 Where the quiet-coloured end of evening smiles,
Miles and miles.
Love among the Ruins, I

35 She had
A heart – how shall I say? – too soon made glad,
Too easily impressed.
My Last Duchess

36 Never the time and the place
And the loved one all together!
Never the Time and the Place

37 What's come to perfection perishes.
Things learned on earth, we shall practise in heaven.
Works done least rapidly, Art most cherishes.
Old Pictures in Florence, XVII

38 There remaineth a rest for the people of God:
And I have had troubles enough, for one.
Old Pictures in Florence, XVII

39 Suddenly, as rare things will, it vanished.
One Word More, IV

40 God be thanked, the meanest of his creatures
Boasts two soul-sides, one to face the world with,
One to show a woman when he loves her!
One Word More, XVII

41 Hamelin Town's in Brunswick,
By famous Hanover city;
The river Weser, deep and wide,
Washes its wall on the southern side;
A pleasanter spot you never spied.
The Pied Piper of Hamelin

42 Rats!
They fought the dogs and killed the cats,
And bit the babies in the cradles.
The Pied Piper of Hamelin

43 And the muttering grew to a grumbling;
And the grumbling grew to a mighty rumbling;

And out of the houses the rats came tumbling.
The Pied Piper of Hamelin

44 'You threaten us, fellow? Do your worst,
Blow your pipe there till you burst!'
The Pied Piper of Hamelin

45 The year's at the spring,
And day's at the morn;
Morning's at seven;
The hill-side's dew-pearled;
The lark's on the wing;
The snail's on the thorn;
God's in His heaven –
All's right with the world.
Pippa Passes, Pt. I

46 A king lived long ago,
In the morning of the world,
When earth was nigher heaven than now.
Pippa Passes, Pt. I

47 Such grace had kings when the world begun!
Pippa Passes, Pt. I

48 All service ranks the same with God –
With God, whose puppets, best and worst,
Are we: there is no last or first.
Pippa Passes, Pt. I

49 Therefore I summon age
To grant youth's heritage.
Rabbi ben Ezra, XIII

50 How good is man's life, the mere living! how fit to employ
All the heart and the soul and the senses for ever in joy!
Saul, IX

51 Leave the flesh to the fate it was fit for! the spirit be thine!
Saul, XIII

52 Gr-r-r- there go, my heart's abhorrence!
Water your damned flower-pots, do!
Soliloquy of the Spanish Cloister

53 I the Trinity illustrate,
Drinking watered orange-pulp –
In three sips the Arian frustrate;
While he drains his at one gulp.
Soliloquy of the Spanish Cloister

54 There's a great text in Galatians,
Once you trip on it, entails
Twenty-nine distinct damnations,
One sure, if another fails.
Soliloquy of the Spanish Cloister

55 My scrofulous French novel
On grey paper with blunt type!
Soliloquy of the Spanish Cloister

56 She looked at him, as one who awakes:
The past was a sleep, and her life began.
The Statue and the Bust

57 What of soul was left, I wonder, when the kissing had to stop?
A Toccata of Galuppi's

58 What's become of Waring
Since he gave us all the slip?
Waring

BRUTALITY

See cruelty

BUREAUCRACY

1 A memorandum is written not to inform the reader but to protect the writer.
Dean Acheson (1893–1971) US lawyer and statesman. Attrib.

2 I'm surprised that a government organization could do it that quickly.
Jimmy Carter (1924–) US statesman. Visiting Egypt, when told that it took twenty years to build the Great Pyramid. *Presidential Anecdotes* (P. Boller)

3 A committee is a cul-de-sac down which ideas are lured and then quietly strangled.
Barnett Cocks (1907–) British political writer. *New Scientist*, 1973

4 Whatever was required to be done, the Circumlocution Office was beforehand with all the public departments in the art of perceiving – HOW NOT TO DO IT.
Charles Dickens (1812–70) British novelist. *Little Dorrit*, Bk. I, Ch. 10

5 A Royal Commission is a broody hen sitting on a china egg.
Michael Foot (1913–) British Labour politician and journalist. Speech, House of Commons, 1964

6 A difficulty for every solution.
Herbert Samuel (1870–1963) British Liberal statesman. Referring to the Civil Service. Attrib.

7 The working of great institutions is mainly the result of a vast mass of routine, petty malice, self interest, carelessness, and sheer mistake. Only a residual fraction is thought.
George Santayana (1863–1952) US philosopher. *The Crime of Galileo*

8 My life's been a meeting, Dad, one long meeting. Even on the few committees I don't yet belong to, the agenda winks at me when I pass.
Gwyn Thomas (1913–81) British writer. *The Keep*, I

9 The British civil service . . . is a beautifully designed and effective braking mechanism.
Shirley Williams (1930–) British politician. Speech, Royal Institute of Public Administration, 11 Feb 1980

BURKE, Edmund

(1729–97) British politician and political philosopher. He entered parliament as a Whig in 1765. In *Reflections on the Revolution in France* (1790) he condemned the French Revolution.

Quotations about Burke

1 Burke was a damned wrong-headed fellow, through his whole life jealous and obstinate.
Charles James Fox (1749–1806) British Whig politician. Attrib.

2 If a man were to go by chance at the same time with Burke under a shed, to shun a shower, he would say – 'this is an extraordinary man.'
Samuel Johnson (1709–84) British lexicographer. *Life of Johnson* (J. Boswell), Vol. IV

Quotations by Burke

3 Example is the school of mankind, and they will learn at no other.
Letters on a Regicide Peace, letter 1

4 The only infallible criterion of wisdom to vulgar minds – success.
Letter to a Member of the National Assembly

5 There is, however, a limit at which forbearance ceases to be a virtue.
Observations on a Publication, 'The Present State of the Nation'

6 I am convinced that we have a degree of delight, and that no small one, in the real misfortunes and pains of others.
On the Sublime and Beautiful, Pt. I

7 Beauty in distress is much the most affecting beauty.
On the Sublime and Beautiful, Pt. III

8 Vice itself lost half its evil, by losing all its grossness.
Reflections on the Revolution in France

9 But the age of chivalry is gone. That of sophisters, economists, and

calculators, has succeeded; and the glory of Europe is extinguished for ever.
Reflections on the Revolution in France

10 That chastity of honour, that felt a stain like a wound.
Reflections on the Revolution in France

11 Man is by his constitution a religious animal.
Reflections on the Revolution in France

12 Superstition is the religion of feeble minds.
Reflections on the Revolution in France

13 The concessions of the weak are the concessions of fear.
Speech on Conciliation with America (House of Commons, 22 Mar 1775)

14 All government, indeed every human benefit and enjoyment, every virtue, and every prudent act, is founded on compromise and barter.
Speech on Conciliation with America (House of Commons, 22 Mar 1775)

15 The use of force alone is but *temporary*. It may subdue for a moment; but it does not remove the necessity of subduing again: and a nation is not governed, which is perpetually to be conquered.
Speech on Conciliation with America (House of Commons, 22 Mar 1775)

16 I do not know the method of drawing up an indictment against an whole people.
Speech on Conciliation with America (House of Commons, 22 Mar 1775)

17 Kings are naturally lovers of low company.
Speech on the Economical Reform (House of Commons, 11 Feb 1780)

18 The people are the masters.
Speech on the Economical Reform (House of Commons, 11 Feb 1780)

19 And having looked to government for bread, on the very first scarcity they will turn and bite the hand that fed them.
Thoughts and Details on Scarcity

20 When bad men combine, the good must associate; else they will fall one by one, an unpitied sacrifice in a contemptible struggle.
Thoughts on the Cause of the Present Discontents

21 Liberty, too, must be limited in order to be possessed.
Letter to the Sherrifs of Bristol, 1777

22 Among a people generally corrupt, liberty cannot long exist.
Letter to the Sherrifs of Bristol, 1777

23 Nothing is so fatal to religion as indifference, which is, at least, half infidelity.
Letter to William Smith, 29 Jan 1795

24 Somebody has said, that a king may make a nobleman, but he cannot make a gentleman.
Letter to William Smith, 29 Jan 1795

25 The greater the power, the more dangerous the abuse.
Speech, House of Commons, 7 Feb 1771

26 Your representative owes you, not his industry only, but his judgement; and he betrays instead of serving you if he sacrifices it to your opinion.
Speech to the electors of Bristol, 3 Nov 1774

27 He was not merely a chip of the old block, but the old block itself.
Referring to William Pitt the Younger's first speech in the House of Commons, 26 Feb 1781. Remark

28 A thing may look specious in theory, and yet be ruinous in practice; a thing may look evil in theory, and yet be in practice excellent.
Impeachment of Warren Hastings, 19 Feb 1788

29 Dangers by being despised grow great.
Speech, House of Commons, 11 May 1792

BURNS, Robert

(1759–96) Scottish poet. A farmer's son, Burns established his reputation with *Poems, Chiefly in the Scottish Dialect* (1786). He subsequently wrote many songs, notably *Auld Lang Syne*, and the narrative poem *Tam o' Shanter*, all of which made him the national poet of Scotland.

Quotations about Burns

1 The largest soul of all the British lands came among us in the shape of a hard-handed Scottish peasant.
Thomas Carlyle (1795–1881) Scottish historian and poet. *On Heroes, Hero-Worship and the Heroic in History*, Lecture V

2 If you can imagine a Scotch commercial traveller in a Scotch commercial hotel leaning on the bar and calling the barmaid 'Dearie' then you will know the keynote of Burns' verse.
A. E. Housman (1859–1936) British scholar and poet. *Electric Delights* (William Plumer)

Quotations by Burns

3 O Thou! Whatever title suit thee –
Auld Hornie, Satan, Nick, or Clootie.
Address to the Devil

4 Should auld acquaintance be forgot,
And never brought to min'?
Auld Lang Syne

5 We'll tak a cup o' kindness yet,
For auld lang syne.
Auld Lang Syne

6 Gin a body meet a body
Coming through the rye;
Gin a body kiss a body,
Need a body cry?
Coming through the Rye

7 I wasna fou, but just had plenty.
Death and Doctor Hornbrook

8 On ev'ry hand it will allow'd be,
He's just – nae better than he should be.
A Dedication to Gavin Hamilton

9 Here lie Willie Michie's banes;
O Satan, when ye tak him,
Gie him the schoolin' of your weans,
For clever deils he'll mak them!
Epitaph on a Schoolmaster

10 A man's a man for a' that.
For a' that and a' that

11 Green grow the rashes O,
Green grow the rashes O,
The sweetest hours that e'er I spend,
Are spent amang the lasses O!
Green Grow the Rashes

12 John Anderson my jo, John,
When we were first acquent,
Your locks were like the raven,
Your bonnie brow was brent.
John Anderson My Jo

13 Let them cant about decorum
Who have characters to lose.
The Jolly Beggars

14 Man's inhumanity to man
Makes countless thousands mourn!
Man was Made to Mourn

15 My heart's in the Highlands, my heart is not here;
My heart's in the Highlands a-chasing the deer;
Chasing the wild deer, and following the roe,

My heart's in the Highlands, wherever I go.
My Heart's in the Highlands

16 My love is like a red red rose
That's newly sprung in June:
My love is like the melodie
That's sweetly play'd in tune.
A Red, Red Rose

17 Scots, wha hae wi' Wallace bled,
Scots, wham Bruce has aften led,
Welcome to your gory bed,
Or to victorie.
Scots, Wha Hae

18 Liberty's in every blow!
Let us do or die!
Scots, Wha Hae

19 Some hae meat, and canna eat,
And some wad eat that want it,
But we hae meat and we can eat,
And sae the Lord be thankit.
The Selkirk Grace

20 Ah, gentle dames! It gars me greet
To think how mony counsels sweet,
How mony lengthen'd sage advices,
The husband frae the wife despises!
Tam o' Shanter

21 Wee, sleekit, cow'rin', tim'rous beastie,
O what a panic's in thy breastie!
To a Mouse

22 The best laid schemes o' mice an' men
Gang aft a-gley,
An' lea'e us nought but grief an' pain
For promis'd joy.
To a Mouse

23 But yet the light that led astray
Was light from Heaven.
The Vision

24 Ye banks and braes o' bonnie Doon,
How can ye bloom sae fresh and fair?
How can ye chant, ye little birds,
And I sae weary fu' o' care?
Ye Banks and Braes

BUSINESS

See also capitalism

1 In Dublin's fair city, where the girls are so pretty,
I first set my eyes on sweet Molly Malone,
As she wheeled her wheelbarrow, through streets broad and narrow,
Crying, Cockles and mussels! alive, alive, O!
She was a fishmonger, but sure 'twas no wonder,
For so were her father and mother before.
Anonymous *Cockles and Mussels*

2 Who will change old lamps for new ones? . . . new lamps for old ones?
The Arabian Nights (c. 1500) A collection of tales from the East. *The History of Aladdin*

3 You ask me what it is I do. Well actually, you know,
I'm partly a liaison man and partly P.R.O.
Essentially I integrate the current export drive
And basically I'm viable from ten o'clock till five.
John Betjeman (1906–84) British poet. *Executive*

4 Pile it high, sell it cheap.
Sir Jack Cohen (1898–1979) British supermarket trader. Business motto

5 The business of America is business.
Calvin Coolidge (1872–1933) US president. Speech, Washington, 17 Jan 1925

6 Here's the rule for bargains: 'Do other men, for they would do you.'
That's the true business precept.
Charles Dickens (1812–70) British novelist. *Martin Chuzzlewit*, Ch. 11

7 A business that makes nothing but money is a poor kind of business.
Henry Ford (1863–1947) US car manufacturer. Interview

8 No nation was ever ruined by trade.
Benjamin Franklin (1706–90) US scientist and statesman. *Essays*, 'Thoughts on Commercial Subjects'

9 Remember that time is money.
Benjamin Franklin *Advice to a Young Tradesman*

10 There's no such thing as a free lunch.
Milton Friedman (1912–) US economist. Used before Friedman but popularized by him.

11 The salary of the chief executive of the large corporation is not a market award for achievement. It is frequently in the nature of a warm personal gesture by the individual to himself.
John Kenneth Galbraith (1908–) US economist. *Annals of an Abiding Liberal*

12 If you pay peanuts, you get monkeys.
James Goldsmith (1933–) British businessman. Attrib.

13 Where wealth and freedom reign, contentment fails,
And honour sinks where commerce long prevails.
Oliver Goldsmith (1728–74) Irish-born British writer. *The Traveller*

14 Cherry ripe, ripe, ripe, I cry.
Full and fair ones; come and buy.
Robert Herrick (1591–1674) English poet. *Hesperides*, 'Cherry Ripe'

15 When you are skinning your customers, you should leave some skin on to grow so that you can skin them again.
Nikita Khrushchev (1894–1971) Soviet statesman. Said to British businessmen. *The Observer*, 'Sayings of the Week', 28 May 1961

16 . . . content to follow mechanically the lead given by their fathers. They worked shorter hours, and they exerted themselves less to obtain new practical ideas than their fathers had done, and thus a part of England's leadership was destroyed rapidly. In the 'nineties it became clear that in the future Englishmen must take business as seriously as their grandfathers had done, and as their American and German rivals were doing: that their training for business must be methodical, like that of their new rivals, and not merely practical, on lines that had sufficed for the simpler world of two generations ago: and lastly that the time had passed at which they could afford merely to teach foreigners and not learn from them in return.
Alfred Marshall (1842–1924) British economist. Referring to British manufacturers. Memorandum; White Paper, 1908

17 He is the only man who is for ever apologizing for his occupation.
H. L. Mencken (1880–1956) US journalist. Referring to the businessman. *Prejudices*, 'Types of Men'

18 He's a businessman. I'll make him an offer he can't refuse.
Mario Puzo (1920–) US novelist. *The Godfather*

19 A dinner lubricates business.
William Scott (1745–1836) British jurist. *Life of Johnson* (J. Boswell), 1791

20 The customer is always right.
H. Gordon Selfridge (1857–1947) US-born businessman. Slogan adopted at his shops

21 He lends out money gratis, and brings down
The rate of usance here with us in Venice.

If I can catch him once upon the hip,
I will feed fat the ancient grudge I bear him.
He hates our sacred nation, and he rails,
Even there where merchants most do congregate,
On me, my bargains, and my well-won thrift,
Which he calls interest.

William Shakespeare (1564–1616) English dramatist. *The Merchant of Venice*, I:3

22 The big print giveth and the fine print taketh away.

J. Fulton Sheen (1895–1979) US Roman Catholic archbishop. Referring to his contract for a television appearance. Attrib.

23 People of the same trade seldom meet together but the conversation ends in a conspiracy against the public, or in some diversion to raise prices.

Adam Smith (1723–90) Scottish economist. *The Wealth of Nations*

24 You never expected justice from a company, did you? They have neither a soul to lose nor a body to kick.

Sydney Smith (1771–1845) British clergyman and essayist. *Memoir* (Lady Holland)

25 I have heard of a man who had a mind to sell his house, and therefore carried a piece of brick in his pocket, which he shewed as a pattern to encourage purchasers.

Jonathan Swift (1667–1745) Irish-born Anglican priest and writer. *The Drapier's Letters*, 2 (4 Aug 1724)

26 It's just like having a licence to print your own money.

Lord Thomson of Fleet (1894–1976) Canadian-born British newspaper proprietor. Speaking about commercial television. Attrib.

27 All business sagacity reduces itself in the last analysis to a judicious use of sabotage.

Thorstein Bunde Veblen (1857–1929) US social scientist. *The Nature of Peace*

28 The best sun we have is made of Newcastle coal.

Horace Walpole (1717–97) British writer. Letter to Montagu, 15 June 1768

29 If Max gets to Heaven he won't last long. He will be chucked out for trying to pull off a merger between Heaven and Hell . . . after having secured a controlling interest in key subsidiary companies in both places, of course.

H. G. Wells (1866–1946) British writer. Referring to Lord Beaverbrook. *Beaverbrook* (A. J. P. Taylor)

30 For many years I thought what was good for our country was good for General Motors, and vice versa.

Charles Erwin Wilson (1890–1961) US engineer. Said in testimony to the Senate Armed Services Committee, Jan 1953. Attrib.

31 Business underlies everything in our national life, including our spiritual life. Witness the fact that in the Lord's Prayer the first petition is for daily bread. No one can worship God or love his neighbor on an empty stomach.

Woodrow Wilson (1856–1925) US statesman. Speech, New York, 1912

32 If two men on the same job agree all the time, then one is useless. If they disagree all the time, then both are useless.

Darryl F. Zanuck (1902–79) US film producer. *The Observer*, 'Sayings of the Week', 23 Oct 1949

BUTLER, Samuel

(1612–80) English satirist, secretary to George Villiers, 2nd Duke of Buckingham. The satirical poem *Hudibras* (1663–78), a mock romance, is his most famous work.

1 When civil fury first grew high,
And men fell out they knew not why.

Hudibras, Pt. I

2 For every why he had a wherefore.

Hudibras, Pt. I

3 To swallow gudgeons ere they're catched,
And count their chickens ere they're hatched.

Hudibras, Pt. II

4 Love is a boy, by poets styl'd,
Then spare the rod, and spoil the child.

Hudibras, Pt. II

5 Through perils both of wind and limb,
Through thick and thin she follow'd him.

Hudibras, Pt. II

6 Oaths are but words, and words but wind.

Hudibras, Pt. II

7 What makes all doctrines plain and clear?
About two hundred pounds a year.

Hudibras, Pt. III

8 He that complies against his will,
Is of his own opinion still.

Hudibras, Pt. III

9 The souls of women are so small,
That some believe they've none at all.

Miscellaneous Thoughts

BUTTERFLIES

1 Literature and butterflies are the two sweetest passions known to man.

Vladimir Nabokov (1899–1977) Russian-born US novelist. *Radio Times*, Oct 1962

BYRON, George Gordon, 6th Baron

(1788–1824) British poet. The melancholy *Childe Harold's Pilgrimage* (1812) brought him to the attention of literary society. After scandalizing London with his sexual exploits he lived abroad, largely in Italy; his later works include the poetic drama *Manfred* (1817) and the epic satire *Don Juan* (1819–24).

Quotations about Byron

1 When Byron's eyes were shut in death,
We bow'd our head and held our breath.
He taught us little: but our soul
Had *felt* him like the thunder's roll.

Matthew Arnold (1822–88) British poet and critic. *Memorial Verses*

2 If they had said the sun and the moon was gone out of the heavens it could not have struck me with the idea of a more awful and dreary blank in the creation than the words: Byron is dead.

Jane Welsh Carlyle (1801–66) The wife of Thomas Carlyle. Letter to Thomas Carlyle, 1824

3 Mad, bad, and dangerous to know.

Lady Caroline Lamb (1785–1828) The wife of William Lamb. Said of Byron in her journal. *Journal*

Quotations by Byron

4 The 'good old times' – all times when old are good –
Are gone.

The Age of Bronze, I

5 The land self-interest groans from shore to shore,

For fear that plenty should attain the poor.
The Age of Bronze, XIV

6 In short, he was a perfect cavaliero,
And to his very valet seem'd a hero.
Beppo

7 I like the weather, when it is not rainy,
That is, I like two months of every year.
Beppo

8 Maidens, like moths, are ever caught by glare,
And Mammon wins his way where Seraphs might despair.
Childe Harold's Pilgrimage, I

9 Adieu, adieu! my native shore
Fades o'er the waters blue.
Childe Harold's Pilgrimage, I

10 My native Land – Good Night!
Childe Harold's Pilgrimage, I

11 War, war is still the cry, 'War even to the knife!'
Childe Harold's Pilgrimage, I

12 Hereditary bondsmen! know ye not
Who would be free themselves must strike the blow?
Childe Harold's Pilgrimage, I

13 There was a sound of revelry by night,
And Belgium's capital had gather'd then
Her Beauty and her Chivalry, and bright
The lamps shone o'er fair women and brave men.
Childe Harold's Pilgrimage, III

14 On with the dance! let joy be unconfined;
No sleep till morn, when Youth and Pleasure meet
To chase the glowing Hours with flying feet.
Childe Harold's Pilgrimage, III

15 While stands the Coliseum, Rome shall stand;
When falls the Coliseum, Rome shall fall;
And when Rome falls – the World.
Childe Harold's Pilgrimage, IV

16 There is a pleasure in the pathless woods,
There is a rapture on the lonely shore,
There is society, where none intrudes,
By the deep Sea, and music in its roar:
I love not Man the less, but Nature more.
Childe Harold's Pilgrimage, IV

17 The spirit burning but unbent,
May writhe, rebel – the weak alone repent!
The Corsair, II

18 'Tis sweet to hear the watch-dog's honest bark
Bay deep-mouthed welcome as we draw near home;
'Tis sweet to know there is an eye will mark
Our coming, and look brighter when we come.
Don Juan, I

19 What men call gallantry, and gods adultery,
Is much more common where the climate's sultry.
Don Juan, I

20 Man's love is of man's life a thing apart,
'Tis woman's whole existence.
Don Juan, I

21 Man, being reasonable, must get drunk;
The best of life is but intoxication.
Don Juan, II

22 All tragedies are finish'd by a death,
All comedies are ended by a marriage.
Don Juan, III

23 Cost his enemies a long repentance,
And made him a good friend, but bad acquaintance.
Don Juan, III

24 Though sages may pour out their wisdom's treasure,
There is no sterner moralist than Pleasure.
Don Juan, III

25 Agree to a short armistice with truth.
Don Juan, III

26 The isles of Greece, the isles of Greece!
Where burning Sappho loved and sung,
Where grew the arts of war and peace,
Where Delos rose, and Phoebus sprung!
Eternal summer gilds them yet,
But all, except their sun, is set.
Don Juan, III

27 The mountains look on Marathon –
And Marathon looks on the sea:
And musing there an hour alone,
I dream'd that Greece might still be free.
Don Juan, III

28 Nothing so difficult as a beginning
In poesy, unless perhaps the end.
Don Juan, IV

29 I thought it would appear
That there had been a lady in the case.
Don Juan, V

30 The women pardoned all except her face.
Don Juan, V

31 There is a tide in the affairs of women,
Which, taken at the flood, leads –
God knows where.
Don Juan, VI

32 A lady of a 'certain age', which means
Certainly aged.
Don Juan, VI

33 Now hatred is by far the longest pleasure;
Men love in haste, but they detest at leisure.
Don Juan, XIII

34 Society is now one polish'd horde,
Form'd of two mighty tribes, the *Bores* and *Bored.*
Don Juan, XIII

35 'Tis strange – but true; for truth is always strange;
Stranger than fiction: if it could be told,
How much would novels gain by the exchange!
Don Juan, XIV

36 I'll publish, right or wrong:
Fools are my theme, let satire be my song.
English Bards and Scotch Reviewers

37 'Tis pleasant, sure, to see one's name in print;
A book's a book, although there's nothing in't.
English Bards and Scotch Reviewers

38 A man must serve his time to every trade
Save censure – critics all are ready made.
English Bards and Scotch Reviewers

39 With death doomed to grapple,
Beneath this cold slab, he

Who lied in the chapel
Now lies in the Abbey.
Epitaph for William Pitt

40 She walks in beauty, like the night
Of cloudless climes and starry skies;
And all that's best of dark and bright
Meet in her aspect and her eyes.
She Walks in Beauty

41 So, we'll go no more a roving
So late into the night,
Though the heart be still as loving,
And the moon be still as bright.
So, we'll go no more a roving

42 Though the night was made for loving,
And the day returns too soon,
Yet we'll go no more a roving
By the light of the moon.
So, we'll go no more a roving

43 A better farmer ne'er brushed dew from lawn,
A worse king never left a realm undone!
Referring to George III. *The Vision of Judgment,* VIII

44 If I should meet thee
After long years,
How should I greet thee? –
With silence and tears.
When we two parted

45 I awoke one morning and found myself famous.
Remark made after the publication of *Childe Harold's Pilgrimage* (1812) Entry in Memoranda

C

CAESAR

1 *Ave Caesar, morituri te salutant.*
Hail Caesar; those who are about to die salute you.
Anonymous Greeting to the Roman Emperor by gladiators

2 The strongest poison ever known
Came from Caesar's laurel crown.
William Blake (1757–1827) British poet. *Auguries of Innocence*

3 Caesar had his Brutus – Charles the First, his Cromwell – and George the Third – ('Treason,' cried the Speaker) . . . *may profit by their example.* If *this* be treason, make the most of it.
Patrick Henry (1736–99) US statesman. Speech, Virginia Convention, May 1765

4 O mighty Caesar! dost thou lie so low?
Are all thy conquests, glories, triumphs, spoils,
Shrunk to this little measure?
William Shakespeare (1564–1616) English dramatist. *Julius Caesar,* III:1

CAMBRIDGE

See also England, Oxford

1 Oxford is on the whole more attractive than Cambridge to the ordinary visitor; and the traveller is therefore recommended to visit Cambridge first, or to omit it altogether if he cannot visit both.
Karl Baedeker (1801–59) German publisher. *Baedeker's Great Britain,* 'From London to Oxford'

2 The King to Oxford sent a troop of horse,
For Tories own no argument but force:
With equal skill to Cambridge books he sent,
For Whigs admit no force but argument.
William Browne (1692–1774) English physician. A reply to TRAPP. *Literary Anecdotes* (Nichols), Vol. III

3 The young Cambridge group, the group that stood for 'freedom' and flannel trousers and flannel shirts open at the neck, and a well-bred sort of emotional anarchy, and a whispering, murmuring sort of voice, and an ultra-sensitive sort of manner.
D. H. Lawrence (1885–1930) British novelist. *Lady Chatterley's Lover,* Ch. 1

4 Spring and summer did happen in Cambridge almost every year.
Vladimir Nabokov (1899–1977) Russian-born US novelist. *The Real Life of Sebastian Knight,* Ch. 5

5 This is the city of perspiring dreams.
Frederic Raphael (1931–) British author. *The Glittering Prizes: An Early Life,* III

6 The King, observing with judicious eyes
The state of both his universities,
To Oxford sent a troop of horse, and why?
That learned body wanted loyalty;
To Cambridge books, as very well discerning
How much that loyal body wanted learning.
Joseph Trapp (1679–1747) English churchman and academic. Written after George I donated the Bishop of Ely's library to Cambridge; for a reply see BROWNE. *Literary Anecdotes* (Nichols), Vol. III

CAMPING

1 Those who have never dwelt in tents have no idea either of the charm or of the discomfort of a nomadic existence. The charm is purely romantic, and consequently very soon proves to be fallacious.
Vita Sackville-West (Victoria Sackville-West; 1892–1962) British poet and novelist. *Twelve Days,* Ch. 6

CANNIBALISM

1 Eating people is wrong.
Michael Flanders (1922–75) British comedian and songwriter. *The Reluctant Cannibal*

2 If he became convinced tomorrow that coming out for cannibalism would get him the votes he so sorely needs, he would begin fattening a missionary on the White House backyard come Wednesday.
H. L. Mencken (1880–1956) US journalist. Referring to Franklin Roosevelt. *Franklin D. Roosevelt, A Profile* (ed. W. E. Leuchtenburg)

3 The better sort of Ishmaelites have been Christian for many centuries and will not publicly eat human flesh uncooked in Lent, without special and costly dispensation from their bishop.
Evelyn Waugh (1903–66) British novelist. *Scoop,* Bk. II, Ch. 1

CANT

See also hypocrisy, insincerity

1 Ancient sculpture is the true school of modesty. But where the Greeks had modesty, we have cant; where they had poetry, we have cant; where they had patriotism, we have cant; where they had anything that exalts, delights, or adorns humanity, we have nothing but cant, cant, cant.
Thomas Love Peacock (1785–1866) British novelist. *Crotchet Castle,* Ch. 7

CAPITALISM

See also business

1 Capitalism is the exploitation of man by man. Communism is the complete opposite.
Anonymous

2 What mean ye that ye beat my people to pieces, and grind the faces of the poor? saith the Lord God of hosts.
Bible: Isaiah 3:15

3 Pile it high, sell it cheap.
Jack Cohen (1898–1979) British supermarket trader. Business motto

4 It is closing time in the gardens of the West.
Cyril Connolly (1903–74) British journalist. *The Condemned Playground*

5 Property has its duties as well as its rights.
Thomas Drummond (1797–1840) British engineer and statesman. Letter to the Earl of Donoughmore, 22 May 1838

6 If I had to give a definition of capitalism I would say: the process whereby American girls turn into American women.
Christopher Hampton (1946–) British writer and dramatist. *Savages*, Sc. 16

7 It is the unpleasant and unacceptable face of capitalism but one should not suggest that the whole of British industry consists of practices of this kind.
Edward Heath (1916–) British politician and prime minister. Referring to the Lonrho Affair. Speech, House of Commons, 15 May 1973

8 If you want to see the acceptable face of capitalism, go out to an oil rig in the North Sea.
Edward Heath Speech, Edinburgh, 18 Feb 1974

9 . . . militarism . . . is one of the chief bulwarks of capitalism, and the day that militarism is undermined, capitalism will fail.
Helen Keller (1880–1968) US writer and lecturer. *The Story of My Life*

10 We cannot remove the evils of capitalism without taking its source of power: ownership.
Neil Kinnock (1942–) British politician. *Tribune*, 1975

11 Under capitalism we have a state in the proper sense of the word, that is, a special machine for the suppression of one class by another.
Lenin (Vladimir Ilich Ulyanov; 1870–1924) Russian revolutionary leader. *The State and Revolution*, Ch. 5

12 Not every problem someone has with his girlfriend is necessarily due to the capitalist mode of production.
Herbert Marcuse (1898–1979) German-born US philosopher. *The Listener*

13 Capitalist production begets, with the inexorability of a law of nature, its own negation.
Karl Marx (1818–83) German philosopher and revolutionary. *Das Kapital*, Ch. 15

14 Man is the only creature that consumes without producing.
George Orwell (Eric Blair; 1903–50) British novelist. *Animal Farm*, Ch. 1

15 I have gone to war too . . . I am going to fight capitalism even if it kills me. It is wrong that people like you should be comfortable and well fed while all around you people are starving.
Sylvia Pankhurst (1882–1960) British suffragette. *The Fighting Pankhursts* (David Mitchell)

16 Property is theft.
Pierre Joseph Proudhon (1809–65) French socialist. *See also* SHAW *Qu'est-ce que la Propriété?*, Ch. 1

17 Property is organised robbery.
George Bernard Shaw (1856–1950) Irish dramatist and critic. *See also* PROUDHON. *Major Barbara*, Preface

18 Lenin was the first to discover that capitalism 'inevitably' caused war; and he discovered this only when the First World War was already being fought. Of course he was right. Since every great state was capitalist in 1914, capitalism obviously 'caused' the First World War; but just as obviously it had 'caused' the previous generation of Peace.
A. J. P. Taylor (1906–) British historian. *The Origins of the Second World War*, Ch. 6

19 In a country economically backward, the proletariat can take power earlier than in countries where capitalism is advanced.
Leon Trotsky (Lev Davidovich Bronstein; 1879–1940) Russian revolutionary. *Permanent Revolution*

20 The public be damned. I am working for my stockholders.
William Henry Vanderbilt (1821–85) US railroad chief. Refusing to speak to a reporter, who was seeking to find out his views on behalf of the public.

CARE

1 Begone, dull care! I prithee begone from me!
Begone, dull care, you and I shall never agree.
Anonymous *Begone Dull Care*

2 And this the burthen of his song,
For ever us'd to be,
I care for nobody, not I,
If no one cares for me.
Isaac Bickerstaffe (c. 1735–c. 1812) Irish dramatist. *Love in a Village*, I

3 I knew once a very covetous, sordid fellow, who used to say, 'Take care of the pence, for the pounds will take care of themselves.'
Earl of Chesterfield (1694–1773) English statesman. Possibly referring to William Lowndes. Letter to his son, 6 Nov 1747

4 I recommend you to take care of the minutes: for hours will take care of themselves.
Earl of Chesterfield Letter to his son, 6 Nov 1747

5 Mortals, whose pleasures are their only care,
First wish to be imposed on, and then are.
William Cowper (1731–1800) British poet. *The Progress of Error*

6 We are so vain that we even care for the opinion of those we don't care for.
Marie Ebner von Eschenbach (1830–1916) Austrian writer. *Aphorism*

7 Our ingress into the world
Was naked and bare;
Our progress through the world
Is trouble and care.
Henry Wadsworth Longfellow (1807–82) US poet. *Tales of A Wayside Inn*, 'The Student's Tale'

8 Care
Sat on his faded cheek.
John Milton (1608–74) English poet. *Paradise Lost*, Bk. I

9 Sleep that knits up the ravell'd sleave of care,
The death of each day's life, sore labour's bath,
Balm of hurt minds, great nature's second course,
Chief nourisher in life's feast.
William Shakespeare (1564–1616) English dramatist. *Macbeth*, II:2

CAREERS

See professions

CARELESSNESS

1 To lose one parent, Mr Worthing, may be regarded as a misfortune; to lose both looks like carelessness.
Oscar Wilde (1854–1900) Irish-born British dramatist. *The Importance of Being Earnest*, I

CARLYLE, Thomas

(1795–1881) Scottish historian and essayist. *Sartor Resartus*, a philosophical work, appeared in 1836; his subsequent writings include *The French Revolution* (1837) and *Heroes, Hero-Worship and the Heroic in History* (1841).

Quotations about Carlyle

1 It was very good of God to let Carlyle and Mrs Carlyle marry one another and so make only two people miserable instead of four.
Samuel Butler (1835–1902) British writer. Attrib.

2 Carlyle is a poet to whom nature has denied the faculty of verse.
Alfred, Lord Tennyson (1809–92) British poet. Letter to W. E. Gladstone

Quotations by Carlyle

3 A poet without love were a physical and metaphysical impossibility.
Critical and Miscellaneous Essays, 'Burns'

4 A witty statesman said, you might prove anything by figures.
Critical and Miscellaneous Essays, 'Chartism'

5 All reform except a moral one will prove unavailing.
Critical and Miscellaneous Essays, 'Corn Law Rhymes'

6 History is the essence of innumerable biographies.
Critical and Miscellaneous Essays, 'History'

7 A well-written Life is almost as rare as a well-spent one.
Critical and Miscellaneous Essays, 'Richter'

8 Literary men are . . . a perpetual priesthood.
Critical and Miscellaneous Essays, 'The State of German Literature'

9 The three great elements of modern civilization, Gunpowder, Printing, and the Protestant Religion.
Critical and Miscellaneous Essays, 'The State of German Literature'

10 Genius (which means transcendent capacity of taking trouble, first of all).
Frederick the Great, Vol. IV, Ch. 3

11 No great man lives in vain. The history of the world is but the biography of great men.
Heroes and Hero-Worship, 'The Hero as Divinity'

12 The true University of these days is a collection of books.
Heroes and Hero-Worship, 'The Hero as Man of Letters'

13 Burke said that there were Three Estates in Parliament; but, in the Reporters' Gallery yonder, there sat a *Fourth Estate*, more important far than they all.
Heroes and Hero-Worship, 'The Hero as Man of Letters'

14 France was a long despotism tempered by epigrams.
History of the French Revolution, Pt. I, Bk. I, Ch. 1

15 To a shower of gold most things are penetrable.
History of the French Revolution, Pt. I, Bk. III, Ch. 7

16 A whiff of grapeshot.
Describing how Napoleon, early in his career, quelled a minor riot in Paris. *History of the French Revolution*, Pt. I, Bk. V, Ch. 3

17 The seagreen Incorruptible.
Referring to Robespierre. *History of the French Revolution*, Pt. II, Bk. IV, Ch. 4

18 The difference between Orthodoxy or My-doxy and Heterodoxy or Thy-doxy.
History of the French Revolution, Pt. II, Bk. IV, Ch. 2

19 The Public is an old woman. Let her maunder and mumble.
Journal, 1835

20 Respectable Professors of the Dismal Science.
Referring to economics. *Latter-Day Pamphlets*, 1

21 Nature admits no lie.
Latter-Day Pamphlets, 5

22 Captains of industry.
Past and Present, Bk. IV, Ch. 4

23 No man who has once heartily and wholly laughed can be altogether irreclaimably bad.
Sartor Resartus, Bk. I, Ch. 4

CARROLL, Lewis

(Charles Lutwidge Dodgson; 1832–98) British writer and mathematician; author of the children's classics *Alice's Adventures in Wonderland* (1865) and *Through the Looking-Glass* (1872).

1 'What is the use of a book,' thought Alice, 'without pictures or conversation?'
Alice's Adventures in Wonderland, Ch. 1

2 'Curiouser and curiouser!' cried Alice.
Alice's Adventures in Wonderland, Ch. 2

3 'You are old, Father William,' the young man said,
'And your hair has become very white;
And yet you incessantly stand on your head –
Do you think at your age, it is right?'
Alice's Adventures in Wonderland, Ch. 5

4 'If everybody minded their own business,' the Duchess said in a hoarse growl, 'the world would go round a deal faster than it does.'
Alice's Adventures in Wonderland, Ch. 6

5 This time it vanished quite slowly, beginning with the end of the tail, and ending with the grin, which remained some time after the rest of it had gone.
Describing the Cheshire Cat. *Alice's Adventures in Wonderland*, Ch. 6

6 'Then you should say what you mean,' the March Hare went on. 'I do,' Alice hastily replied; 'at least – at least I mean what I say – that's the same thing, you know.'
'Not the same thing a bit!' said the Hatter. 'Why, you might just as well say that 'I see what I eat' is the same thing as 'I eat what I see!"
Alice's Adventures in Wonderland, Ch. 7

7 Twinkle, twinkle, little bat!
How I wonder what you're at!
Up above the world you fly!
Like a teatray in the sky.
Alice's Adventures in Wonderland, Ch. 7

8 'Take some more tea,' the March Hare said to Alice, very earnestly.
'I've had nothing yet,' Alice replied in an offended tone, 'so I can't take more.'
'You mean you can't take *less*,' said the Hatter: 'it's very easy to take *more* than nothing.'
Alice's Adventures in Wonderland, Ch. 7

9 'Off with his head!'
Alice's Adventures in Wonderland, Ch. 8

10 Everything's got a moral, if only you can find it.
Alice's Adventures in Wonderland, Ch. 9

11 Take care of the sense, and the sounds will take care of themselves.
Alice's Adventures in Wonderland, Ch. 9

12 'Reeling and Writhing, of course, to begin with,' the Mock Turtle replied; 'and then the different branches of Arithmetic – Ambition, Distraction, Uglification, and Derision.'
Alice's Adventures in Wonderland, Ch. 9

13 'Will you walk a little faster?' said a whiting to a snail,
'There's a porpoise close behind us, and he's treading on my tail.'
Alice's Adventures in Wonderland, Ch. 10

14 Will you, won't you, will you, won't you, will you join the dance?
Alice's Adventures in Wonderland, Ch. 10

15 Soup of the evening, beautiful Soup!
Said by the Mock Turtle. *Alice's Adventures in Wonderland,* Ch. 10

16 The Queen of Hearts, she made some tarts,
All on a summer day:
The Knave of Hearts, he stole those tarts,
And took them quite away!
Alice's Adventures in Wonderland, Ch. 11

17 'Where shall I begin, please your Majesty?' he asked.
'Begin at the beginning' the King said, gravely, 'and go on till you come to the end: then stop.'
Alice's Adventures in Wonderland, Ch. 11

18 'No, no!' said the Queen. 'Sentence first – verdict afterwards.'
Alice's Adventures in Wonderland, Ch. 12

19 For the Snark *was* a Boojum, you see.
The Hunting of the Snark

20 'Twas brillig, and the slithy toves
Did gyre and gimble in the wabe;
All mimsy were the borogoves,
And the mome raths outgrabe.
Through the Looking-Glass, Ch. 1

21 Now, *here,* you see, it takes all the running *you* can do, to keep in the same place. If you want to get somewhere else, you must run at least twice as fast as that!
Through the Looking-Glass, Ch. 2

22 Tweedledum and Tweedledee
Agreed to have a battle;
For Tweedledum said Tweedledee
Had spoiled his nice new rattle.
Through the Looking-Glass, Ch. 4

23 'Contrariwise,' continued Tweedledee, 'if it was so, it might be; and if it were so, it would be: but as it isn't, it ain't. That's logic.'
Through the Looking-Glass, Ch. 4

24 The Walrus and the Carpenter
Were walking close at hand;
They wept like anything to see
Such quantities of sand:
'If this were only cleared away,'
They said, 'it *would* be grand!'
Through the Looking-Glass, Ch. 4

25 'The time has come,' the Walrus said,
'To talk of many things:
Of shoes – and ships – and sealing-wax –
Of cabbages – and kings –
And why the sea is boiling hot –
And whether pigs have wings.'
Through the Looking-Glass, Ch. 4

26 But answer came there none –
And this was scarcely odd because
They'd eaten every one.
Through the Looking-Glass, Ch. 4

27 The rule is, jam tomorrow and jam yesterday – but never jam today.
Through the Looking-Glass, Ch. 5

28 'They gave it me,' Humpty Dumpty continued thoughtfully, . . . 'for an un-birthday present.'
Through the Looking-Glass, Ch. 6

29 'When *I* use a word,' Humpty Dumpty said in rather a scornful tone, 'it means just what I choose it to mean – neither more nor less.'
Through the Looking-Glass, Ch. 6

30 He's an Anglo-Saxon Messenger – and those are Anglo-Saxon attitudes.
Through the Looking-Glass, Ch. 7

31 It's as large as life, and twice as natural!
Through the Looking-Glass, Ch. 7

32 The Lion looked at Alice wearily. 'Are you animal – or vegetable – or mineral?' he said, yawning at every other word.
Through the Looking-Glass, Ch. 7

33 'Speak when you're spoken to!' the Red Queen sharply interrupted her.
Through the Looking-Glass, Ch. 9

34 'You look a little shy; let me introduce you to that leg of mutton,' said the Red Queen. 'Alice – Mutton; Mutton – Alice.'
Through the Looking-Glass, Ch. 9

CARTER, Jimmy

(1924–) US statesman; governor of Georgia (1970–74) and president (1977–81).

1 I'm surprised that a government organization could do it that quickly.
Visiting Egypt, when told that it took twenty years to build the Great Pyramid. *Presidential Anecdotes* (P. Boller)

CATHOLICISM

See also Christianity, Protestantism, religion

1 A priest is a man who is called Father by everyone except his own children who are obliged to call him Uncle.
Italian proverb

2 *Ad majorem Dei gloriam.*
To the greater glory of God.
Anonymous Motto of the Jesuits

3 I expect you know my friend Evelyn Waugh, who, like you, your Holiness, is a Roman Catholic.
Randolph Churchill (1911–68) British political journalist. Remark made during an audience with the Pope

4 I have a Catholic soul, but a Lutheran stomach.
Erasmus (1466–1536) Dutch humanist, scholar, and writer. Replying to criticism of his failure to fast during Lent. *Dictionnaire Encyclopédique*

5 It is the custom of the Roman Church which I unworthily serve with the help of God, to tolerate some things, to turn a blind eye to some, following the spirit of discretion rather than the rigid letter of the law.
Gregory VII (c. 1020–85) Pope and saint. Letter, 9 Mar 1078

6 The Papacy is not other than the Ghost of the deceased Roman Empire, sitting crowned upon the grave thereof.
Thomas Hobbes (1588–1679) English philosopher. *Leviathan,* Pt. IV, Ch. 37

7 There is no idolatry in the Mass. They believe God to be there, and they adore him.
Samuel Johnson (1709–84) British lexicographer. *Life of Johnson* (J. Boswell), Vol. II

8 We know these new English Catholics. They are the last words in Protest. They are Protestants protesting against Protestantism.
D. H. Lawrence (1885–1930) British novelist. *Phoenix*, 'Review of Eric Gill, *Art Nonsense*'

9 Since God has given us the papacy, let us enjoy it.
Leo X (Giovanni de' Medici; 1475–1521) Pope (1513–21). *Men of Art* (T. Craven)

10 One cannot really be a Catholic and grown-up.
George Orwell (Eric Blair; 1903–50) British novelist. *Collected Essays*

11 I was fired from there, finally, for a lot of things, among them my insistence that the Immaculate Conception was spontaneous combustion.
Dorothy Parker (1893–1967) US writer. *Writers at Work, First Series* (Malcolm Cowley)

12 The Pope! How many divisions has *he* got?
Joseph Stalin (J. Dzhugashvili; 1879–1953) Soviet statesman. When urged by Pierre Laval to tolerate Catholicism in the USSR to appease the Pope, 13 May 1935. When told of this by Churchill, the Pope (Pius XII) replied, 'Tell our brother Joseph that he will meet our divisions in Heaven'. *The Second World War* (W. S. Churchill), Vol. I, Ch. 8

13 Becoming an Anglo-Catholic must surely be a sad business – rather like becoming an amateur conjurer.
John St Loe Strachey (1901–63) British politician. *The Coming Struggle for Power*, Pt. III, Ch. 11

14 'God knows how you Protestants can be expected to have any sense of direction,' she said. 'It's different with us. I haven't been to mass for years, I've got every mortal sin on my conscience, but I know when I'm doing wrong. I'm still a Catholic.
Angus Wilson (1913–) British novelist. *The Wrong Set*, 'Significant Experience'

CATS

See also animals

1 Cruel, but composed and bland,
Dumb, inscrutable and grand,
So Tiberius might have sat,
Had Tiberius been a cat.
Matthew Arnold (1822–88) British poet and critic. *Poor Matthias*

2 Macavity, Macavity, there's no one like Macavity,
There never was a Cat of such deceitfulness and suavity.
He always has an alibi, and one or two to spare:
At whatever time the deed took place – MACAVITY WASN'T THERE!
T. S. Eliot (1888–1965) US-born British poet and dramatist. *Macavity: The Mystery Cat*

3 I have noticed that what cats most appreciate in a human being is not the ability to produce food which they take for granted – but his or her entertainment value.
Geoffrey Household (1900–88) British writer. *Rogue Male*

4 When I observed he was a fine cat, saying, 'why yes, Sir, but I have had cats whom I liked better than this'; and then as if perceiving Hodge to be out of countenance, adding, 'but he is a very fine cat, a very fine cat indeed.'
Samuel Johnson (1709–84) British lexicographer. *Life of Johnson* (J. Boswell), Vol. IV

5 If a fish is the movement of water embodied, given shape, then cat is a diagram and pattern of subtle air.
Doris Lessing (1919–) British novelist. *Particularly Cats*, Ch. 2

6 When I play with my cat, who knows whether she is not amusing herself with me more than I with her?
Michel de Montaigne (1533–92) French essayist. *Essais*, II

7 If a dog jumps onto your lap it is because he is fond of you; but if a cat does the same thing it is because your lap is warmer.
A. N. Whitehead (1861–1947) British philosopher and mathematician. *Dialogues*

CAUTION

See also prudence

1 Better be safe than sorry.
Proverb

2 Don't put all your eggs in one basket.
Proverb

3 He that fights and runs away, may live to fight another day.
Proverb

4 He who sups with the devil should have a long spoon.
Proverb

5 If you trust before you try, you may repent before you die.
Proverb

6 Keep your mouth shut and your eyes open.
Proverb

7 Keep your weather-eye open.
Proverb

8 Look before you leap.
Proverb

9 And all should cry, Beware! Beware!
His flashing eyes, his floating hair!
Weave a circle round him thrice,
And close your eyes with holy dread,
For he on honey-dew hath fed,
And drunk the milk of Paradise.
Samuel Taylor Coleridge (1772–1834) British poet. *Kubla Khan*

10 Chi Wen Tzu always thought three times before taking action. Twice would have been quite enough.
Confucius (K'ung Fu-tzu; 551–479 BC) Chinese philosopher. *Analects*

11 Take example by your father, my boy, and be very careful o' vidders all your life.
Charles Dickens (1812–70) British novelist. *Pickwick Papers*, Ch. 13

12 Don't go into Mr McGregor's garden: your Father had an accident there; he was put in a pie by Mrs McGregor.
Beatrix Potter (1866–1943) British children's writer. *The Tale of Peter Rabbit*

13 The only way to be absolutely safe is never to try anything for the first time.
Magnus Pyke (1908–) British scientist, television personality, and writer. BBC radio program

CENSORSHIP

See also pornography, prudery

1 More to the point, would you allow your gamekeeper to read it?
Anonymous Referring to Mervyn Griffiths-Jones' remark during the *Lady Chatterley's Lover* trial.

2 To defend society from sex is no one's business. To defend it from officiousness is the duty of everyone who values freedom – or sex.
Brigid Brophy (1929–) British novelist and critic. *The Observer*, 'Sayings of the Week', 9 Aug 1970

3 Whenever books are burned men also in the end are burned.
Heinrich Heine (1797–1856) German poet and writer. *Almansor*

4 Mahound shakes his head. 'Your blasphemy, Salman, can't be forgiven. Did you think I wouldn't work it out? To set your words against the Words of God.'
Salman Rushdie (1947–) Indian-born British novelist. *The Satanic Verses*

5 The author of the Satanic Verses book, which is against Islam, the Prophet and the Koran, and all those involved in its publication who were aware of its content, are sentenced to death. I ask all Moslems to execute them wherever they find them.
Ayatolla Ruholla Khomeini (1900–) Iranian Shiite Muslim leader. Speech, 14 Feb 1989

6 I call upon the intellectual community in this country and abroad to stand up for freedom of the imagination, an issue much larger than my book or indeed my life.
Salman Rushdie Press statement, 14 Feb 1989

7 There is in our hands as citizens an instrument to mould the minds of the young and to create great and good and noble citizens for the future.
Edward Shortt (1862–1935) Home Secretary (1919–22); President of the British Board of Film Censors (1929–35). Referring to the British Board of Film Censors. Remark, 1929

8 Censorship is more depraving and corrupting than anything pornography can produce.
Tony Smythe (1938–) Chairman of the National Council for Civil Liberties, Great Britain. *The Observer*, 'Sayings of the Week', 18 Sept 1972

9 God forbid that any book should be banned. The practice is as indefensible as infanticide.
Rebecca West (Cicely Isabel Fairfield; 1892–1983) British novelist and journalist. *The Strange Necessity*, 'The Tosh Horse'

CERTAINTY

See also self-confidence

1 If a man will begin with certainties, he shall end in doubts, but if he will be content to begin with doubts, he shall end in certainties.
Francis Bacon (1561–1626) English philosopher. *The Advancement of Learning*, Bk. I, Ch. 5

2 Of that there is no manner of doubt –
No probable, possible shadow of doubt –
No possible doubt whatever.
W. S. Gilbert (1836–1911) British dramatist. *The Gondoliers*, I

CERVANTES (Saavedra), Miguel de

(1547–1616) Spanish novelist and dramatist; creator of *Don Quixote* (1605; 1615), a satirical romance of chivalry.

Quotations about Cervantes

1 Casting my mind's eye over the whole of fiction, the only absolutely original creation that I can think of is Don Quixote.
W. Somerset Maugham (1874–1965) British novelist. *10 Novels and their Authors*, Ch. 1

2 Cervantes laughed chivalry out of fashion.
Horace Walpole (1717–97) British writer. Letter to Sir Horace Mann, 19 July 1774

Quotations by Cervantes

3 A silly remark can be made in Latin as well as in Spanish.
The Dialogue of the Dogs

4 Take care, your worship, those things over there are not giants but windmills.
Don Quixote, Pt. I, Ch. 8

5 Didn't I tell you, Don Quixote, sir, to turn back, for they were not armies you were going to attack, but flocks of sheep?
Don Quixote, Pt. I, Ch. 18

6 The Knight of the Doleful Countenance.
Sancho Panza describing Don Quixote. *Don Quixote*, Pt. I, Ch. 19

7 Fear has many eyes and can see things underground.
Don Quixote, Pt. I, Ch. 20

8 A leap over the hedge is better than good men's prayers.
Don Quixote, Pt. I, Ch. 21

9 I have always heard, Sancho, that doing good to base fellows is like throwing water into the sea.
Don Quixote, Pt. I, Ch. 23

10 Let them eat the lie and swallow it with their bread. Whether the two were lovers or no, they'll have accounted to God for it by now. I have my own fish to fry.
Don Quixote, Pt. I, Ch. 25

11 A knight errant who turns mad for a reason deserves neither merit nor thanks. The thing is to do it without cause.
Don Quixote, Pt. I, Ch. 25

12 One shouldn't talk of halters in the hanged man's house.
Don Quixote, Pt. I, Ch. 25

13 She isn't a bad bit of goods, the Queen! I wish all the fleas in my bed were as good.
Don Quixote, Pt. I, Ch. 30

14 In me the need to talk is a primary impulse, and I can't help saying right off what comes to my tongue.
Don Quixote, Pt. I, Ch. 30

15 Every man is as Heaven made him, and sometimes a great deal worse.
Don Quixote, Pt. II, Ch. 4

16 The best sauce in the world is hunger.
Don Quixote, Pt. II, Ch. 5

17 Well, now, there's a remedy for everything except death.
Don Quixote, Pt. II, Ch. 10

18 Never meddle with play-actors, for they're a favoured race.
Don Quixote, Pt. II, Ch. 11

19 He's a muddle-headed fool, with frequent lucid intervals.
Sancho Panza describing Don Quixote. *Don Quixote*, Pt. II, Ch. 18

20 There are only two families in the world, my old grandmother used to say, The *Haves* and the *Have-Nots*.
Don Quixote, Pt. II, Ch. 20

21 A private sin is not so prejudicial in the world as a public indecency.
Don Quixote, Pt. II, Ch. 22

22 Tell me what company thou keepest, and I'll tell thee what thou art.
Don Quixote, Pt. II, Ch. 23

23 Good painters imitate nature, bad ones spew it up.
El Licenciado Vidriera

CHANCE

See also luck, opportunity

1 Throw out a sprat to catch a mackerel.
Proverb

2 I returned, and saw under the sun, that the race is not to the swift, nor the battle to the strong, neither yet bread to the wise, nor yet riches to men of understanding, nor

yet favour to men of skill; but time and chance happeneth to them all. For man also knoweth not his time: as the fishes that are taken in an evil net, and as the birds that are caught in the snare; so are the sons of men snared in an evil time, when it falleth suddenly upon them.
Bible: Ecclesiastes 9:11–12

3 Of all the gin joints in all the towns in all the world, she walks into mine!
Humphrey Bogart (1899–1957) US film star. *Casablanca*

4 I shot an arrow into the air,
It fell to earth, I knew not where.
Henry Wadsworth Longfellow (1807–82) US poet. *The Arrow and the Song*

5 Accidental and fortuitous concurrence of atoms.
Lord Palmerston (1784–1865) British statesman. Speech, House of Commons, 1857

6 When you take the bull by the horns . . . what happens is a toss up.
William Pett Ridge (1860–1930) British novelist. *Love at Paddington Green*, Ch. 4

7 I have set my life upon a cast,
And I will stand the hazard of the die.
William Shakespeare (1564–1616) English dramatist. *Richard III*, V:4

CHANDLER, Raymond

(1888–1959) US novelist, famous for his detective stories and thrillers. His detective, Philip Marlowe, first appeared in *The Big Sleep* (1939).

1 It was a blonde. A blonde to make a bishop kick a hole in a stained-glass window.
Farewell, My Lovely, Ch. 13

2 She gave me a smile I could feel in my hip pocket.
Farewell, My Lovely, Ch. 18

3 Alcohol is like love: the first kiss is magic, the second is intimate, the third is routine. After that you just take the girl's clothes off.
The Long Good-bye

4 Down these mean streets a man must go who is not himself mean; who is neither tarnished nor afraid.
The Simple Art of Murder

5 If my books had been any worse I should not have been invited to Hollywood, and if they had been any better I should not have come.
The Life of Raymond Chandler (F. MacShane)

6 When I split an infinitive, god damn it, I split it so it stays split.
Letter to his English publisher

CHANGE

See also conservatism, constancy, progress, transcience

1 Can the Ethiopian change his skin, or the leopard his spots? then may ye also do good, that are accustomed to do evil.
Bible: Jeremiah 13:23

2 All reform except a moral one will prove unavailing.
Thomas Carlyle (1795–1881) Scottish historian and essayist. *Critical and Miscellaneous Essays*, 'Corn Law Rhymes'

3 The time's come: there's a terrific thunder-cloud advancing upon us, a mighty storm is coming to freshen us up. . . . It's going to blow away all this idleness and indifference, and prejudice against work. . . . I'm going to work, and in twenty-five or thirty years' time every man and woman will be working.
Anton Chekhov (1860–1904) Russian dramatist. *Three Sisters*, I

4 Variety's the very spice of life
That gives it all its flavour.
William Cowper (1731–1800) British poet. *The Task*

5 Most women set out to try to change a man, and when they have changed him they do not like him.
Marlene Dietrich (Maria Magdalene von Losch; 1904–) German-born film star. Attrib.

6 Come mothers and fathers
Throughout the land
And don't criticize
What you can't understand.
Bob Dylan (Robert Allen Zimmerman; 1941–) US popular singer. *The Times They Are A-Changin'*

7 The Times They Are A-Changin'.
Bob Dylan Song title

8 Man is so made that he can only find relaxation from one kind of labour by taking up another.
Anatole France (Jacques Anatole François Thibault; 1844–1924) French writer. *The Crime of Sylvestre Bonnard*

9 Most of the change we think we see in life
Is due to truths being in and out of favor.
Robert Frost (1875–1963) US poet. *The Black Cottage*

10 Everything flows and nothing stays.
Heraclitus (c. 535–c. 475 BC) Greek philosopher. *Cratylus* (Plato), 402a

11 You can't step into the same river twice.
Heraclitus *Cratylus* (Plato), 402a

12 Change is not made without inconvenience, even from worse to better.
Richard Hooker (c. 1554–1600) English theologian. *English Dictionary* (Johnson), Preface

13 There is a certain relief in change, even though it be from bad to worse; as I have found in traveling in a stage-coach, that it is often a comfort to shift one's position and be bruised in a new place.
Washington Irving (1783–1859) US writer. *Tales of a Traveller*, 'To the Reader'

14 An old Dutch farmer, who remarked to a companion once that it was not best to swap horses in mid-stream.
Abraham Lincoln (1809–65) US statesman. Speech, 9 June 1864

15 Well, I find that a change of nuisances is as good as a vacation.
David Lloyd George (1863–1945) British Liberal statesman. On being asked how he maintained his cheerfulness when beset by numerous political obstacles. Attrib.

16 The wind of change is blowing through the continent. Whether we like it or not, this growth of national consciousness is a political fact.
Harold Macmillan (1894–1986) British politician and prime minister. Speech, South African Parliament, 3 Feb 1960

17 At last he rose, and twitched his mantle blue:
To-morrow to fresh woods, and pastures new.
John Milton (1608–74) English poet. *Lycidas*

18 Poor old Daddy – just one of those sturdy old plants left over from the Edwardian Wilderness, that can't understand why the sun isn't shining any more.
John Osborne (1929–) British dramatist. *Look Back in Anger*, II:2

19 That which is now a horse, even with a thought
The rack dislimns, and makes it indistinct,

As water is in water.

William Shakespeare (1564–1616) English dramatist. *Antony and Cleopatra*, IV:12

20 Through all the changing scenes of life.

Nahum Tate (1652–1715) Irish-born English poet. *New Version of the Psalms*, 'Through all the Changing'

21 And slowly answer'd Arthur from the barge:
'The old order changeth, yielding place to new,
And God fulfils himself in many ways.'

Alfred, Lord Tennyson (1809–92) British poet. *Idylls of the King*, 'The Passing of Arthur

CHARACTER

1 She's as strong as an ox. She'll be turned into Bovril when she dies.

Margot Asquith (1865–1945) The second wife of Herbert Asquith. Referring to Lady Desborough. *As I Remember*

2 Every man is as Heaven made him, and sometimes a great deal worse.

Miguel de Cervantes (1547–1616) Spanish novelist. *Don Quixote*, Pt. II, Ch. 4

3 He was as fresh as is the month of May.

Geoffrey Chaucer (c. 1342–1400) English poet. Referring to the squire. *The Canterbury Tales*, Prologue

4 Souninge in moral vertu was his speche,
And gladly wolde he lerne, and gladly teche.

Geoffrey Chaucer Referring to the clerk. *The Canterbury Tales*, Prologue

5 From a timid, shy girl I had become a woman of resolute character, who could not longer be frightened by the struggle with troubles.

Anna Dostoevsky (1846–1918) Russian diarist and writer. *Dostoevsky Portrayed by His Wife*

6 What e'r he did was done with so much ease,
In him alone, 'twas Natural to please.

John Dryden (1631–1700) British poet and dramatist. *Absalom and Achitophel*, I

7 A patronizing disposition always has its meaner side.

George Eliot (Mary Ann Evans; 1819–80) British novelist. *Adam Bede*

8 I am a man for whom the outside world exists.

Théophile Gautier (1811–72) French poet and critic. *Journal des Goncourt*, 1 May 1857

9 Talent develops in quiet places, character in the full current of human life.

Goethe (1749–1832) German poet and dramatist. *Torquato Tasso*, I

10 She's genuinely bogus.

Christopher Hassall (1912–63) British writer. Referring to Edith Sitwell. Attrib.

11 . . . a patron of play-actors and a follower of hounds to become a shepherd of souls.

Herbert of Bosham (fl. 1162–86) Chaplain and biographer of Thomas Becket. Referring to Becket. *Vita Sancti Thomae*

12 Strong enough to answer back to desires, to despise distinctions, and a whole man in himself, polished and well-rounded.

Horace (Quintus Horatius Flaccus; 65–8 BC) Roman poet. *Satires*, II

13 A tart temper never mellows with age, and a sharp tongue is the only edged tool that grows keener with constant use.

Washington Irving (1783–1859) US writer. *The Sketch Book*, 'Rip Van Winkle'

14 What is character but the determination of incident? What is incident but the illustration of character?

Henry James (1843–1916) US novelist. *Partial Portraits*, 'The Art of Fiction'

15 He was a vicious man, but very kind to me. If you call a dog *Hervey*, I shall love him.

Samuel Johnson (1709–84) British lexicographer. *Life of Johnson* (J. Boswell), Vol. I

16 A very unclubable man.

Samuel Johnson Referring to Sir John Hawkins. *Life of Johnson* (J. Boswell), Vol. I

17 Rich, noble, lovable, eloquent, handsome, gallant, every way attractive, a little lower than the angels – all these gifts he turned to the wrong side.

Walter Map (c. 1140–c. 1209) Welsh clergyman and writer. Referring to Henry, 'The Young King', eldest son of Henry II. *De Nugis Curialium*, Pt. I, Ch. 1

18 I recognize that I am made up of several persons and that the person that at the moment has the upper hand will inevitably give place to another. But which is the real one? All of them or none?

W. Somerset Maugham (1874–1965) British novelist. *A Writer's Notebook*

19 Monday's child is fair of face,
Tuesday's child is full of grace,
Wednesday's child is full of woe,
Thursday's child has far to go,
Friday's child is loving and giving,
Saturday's child works hard for his living,
And the child that is born on the Sabbath day
Is bonny and blithe, and good and gay.

Nursery Rhyme *Traditions of Devonshire* (A. E. Bray)

20 It is with narrow-souled people as with narrow-necked bottles: the less they have in them, the more noise they make in pouring it out.

Alexander Pope (1688–1744) British poet. *Thoughts on Various Subjects*

21 You can tell a lot about a fellow's character by the way he eats jelly beans.

Ronald Reagan (1911–) US Republican president. *Daily Mail*, 22 Jan 1981

22 Children with Hyacinth's temperament don't know better as they grow older; they merely know more.

Saki (Hector Hugh Munro; 1870–1916) British writer. *Hyacinth*

23 I have long since been aware that your king is a man of the greatest honour and bravery, but he is imprudent.

Saladin (1137–93) Sultan of Egypt and Syria. Referring to Richard I. Remark to the Bishop of Salisbury, 1192

24 There is no such thing as psychological. Let us say that one can improve the biography of the person.

Jean-Paul Sartre (1905–80) French writer. *The Divided Self* (R. D. Laing), Ch. 8

25 A certain person may have, as you say, a wonderful presence: I do not know. What I do know is that he has a perfectly delightful absence.

Idries Shah (1924–) British author. *Reflections*, 'Presence and Absence'

26 His life was gentle; and the elements
So mix'd in him that Nature might stand up
And say to all the world 'This was a man!'

William Shakespeare (1564–1616) English dramatist. Referring to Brutus. *Julius Caesar*, V:5

27 A man of great common sense and good taste, – meaning thereby a man without originality or moral courage.

George Bernard Shaw (1856–1950) Irish dramatist and critic. Referring to Julius Caesar. *Caesar and Cleopatra*, Notes

28 I'm not hard – I'm frightfully soft. But I will not be hounded.
Margaret Thatcher (1925–) British politician and prime minister. *Daily Mail,* 1972

29 He is a man of brick. As if he was born as a baby literally of clay and decades of exposure have baked him to the color and hardness of brick.
John Updike (1932–) US novelist. *Rabbit, Run*

30 There aren't many left like him nowadays, what with education and whisky the price it is.
Evelyn Waugh (1903–66) British novelist. *Decline and Fall,* Pt. I, Ch. 7

31 I've met a lot of hardboiled eggs in my time, but you're twenty minutes.
Billy Wilder (Samuel Wilder; 1906–) Austrian-born US film director. *Ace in the Hole*

32 The Right Stuff.
Tom Wolfe (1931–) US writer. Referring to people involved in the early US space program. Book title

CHARITY

See also generosity, help, parasites, philanthropy

1 Charity begins at home.
Proverb

2 Private patients, if they do not like me, can go elsewhere; but the poor devils in the hospital I am bound to take care of.
John Abernethy (1764–1831) English surgeon. *Memoirs of John Abernethy,* Ch. 5 (George Macilwain)

3 The living need charity more than the dead.
George Arnold (1834–65) US poet and humorist. *The Jolly Old Pedagogue*

4 In charity there is no excess.
Francis Bacon (1561–1626) English philosopher. *Essays,* 'Of Goodness, and Goodness of Nature'

5 Don't bother to thank me. I know what a perfectly ghastly season it's been for you Spanish dancers.
Tallulah Bankhead (1903–68) US actress. Said on dropping fifty dollars into a tambourine held out by a Salvation Army collector. *With Malice Toward All* (D. Hermann)

6 Now as touching things offered unto idols, we know that we all have knowledge. Knowledge puffeth up, but charity edifieth.
Bible: I Corinthians 8:1

7 Though I speak with the tongues of men and of angels, and have not charity, I am become as sounding brass, or a tinkling cymbal.
And though I have the gift of prophecy, and understand all mysteries, and all knowledge; and though I have all faith, so that I could remove mountains, and have not charity, I am nothing.
And though I bestow all my goods to feed the poor, and though I give my body to be burned, and have not charity, it profiteth me nothing.
Charity suffereth long, and is kind; charity envieth not; charity vaunteth not itself, is not puffed up,
Doth not behave itself unseemly, seeketh not her own, is not easily provoked, thinketh no evil;
Rejoiceth not in iniquity, but rejoiceth in the truth;
Beareth all things, believeth all things, hopeth all things, endureth all things.
Charity never faileth: but whether there be prophecies, they shall fail; whether there be tongues, they shall cease; whether there be knowledge, it shall vanish away.
For we know in part, and we prophesy in part.
But when that which is perfect is come, then that which is in part shall be done away.
When I was a child, I spake as a child, I understood as a child, I thought as a child: but when I became a man, I put away childish things.
For now we see through a glass, darkly; but then face to face: now I know in part; but then shall I know even as also I am known.
And now abideth faith, hope, charity, these three; but the greatest of these is charity.
Bible: I Corinthians 13:1–13

8 Or what man is there of you, whom if his son ask bread, will he give him a stone?
Bible: Matthew 7:9

9 But a certain Samaritan, as he journeyed, came where he was: and when he saw him, he had compassion on him,
And went to him, and bound up his wounds, pouring in oil and wine, and set him on his own beast, and brought him to an inn, and took care of him.
And on the morrow when he departed, he took out two pence, and gave them to the host, and said unto him, Take care of him; and whatsoever thou spendest more, when I come again, I will repay thee.
Bible: Luke 10:33–35

10 All our doings without charity are nothing worth.
The Book of Common Prayer *Collect, Quinquagesima Sunday*

11 Charity begins at home, is the voice of the world.
Thomas Browne (1605–82) English physician and writer. *Religio Medici,* Pt. II

12 I have always heard, Sancho, that doing good to base fellows is like throwing water into the sea.
Miguel de Cervantes (1547–1616) Spanish novelist. *Don Quixote,* Pt. I, Ch. 23

13 Charity is the power of defending that which we know to be indefensible. Hope is the power of being cheerful in circumstances which we know to be desperate.
G. K. Chesterton (1874–1936) British writer. *Heretics,* Ch. 12

14 No people do so much harm as those who go about doing good.
Mandell Creighton (1843–1901) British churchman. *Life*

15 Lady Bountiful.
George Farquhar (1678–1707) Irish dramatist. *The Beaux' Strategem,* I:1

16 I'm not interested in the bloody system! Why has he no food? Why is he starving to death?
Bob Geldof (1952–) Irish rock musician. *The Observer,* 'Sayings of the Week', 27 Oct 1985

17 In medicine, charity offers to the poor the gains in medical skill, not the leavings.
Alan Gregg (1890–1957) *The Bampton Lectures*

18 She's the sort of woman who lives for others – you can always tell the others by their hunted expression.
C. S. Lewis (1898–1963) British academic and writer. *The Screwtape Letters*

19 In the field of world policy; I would dedicate this nation to the policy of the good neighbor.
Franklin D. Roosevelt (1882–1945) US Democratic president. First Inaugural Address, 4 Mar 1933

20 When they will not give a doit to relieve a lame beggar, they will lay out ten to see a dead Indian.
William Shakespeare (1564–1616) English dramatist. *The Tempest,* II:2

21 If you see anybody fallen by the

wayside and lying in the ditch, it isn't much good climbing into the ditch and lying by his side.
H. R. L. Sheppard (1880–1937) British clergyman. *Dick Sheppard* (Carolyn Scott)

22 The white man knows how to make everything, but he does not know how to distribute it.
Sitting Bull (c. 1834–90) US Sioux Indian chief. Attrib.

23 You find people ready enough to do the Samaritan, without the oil and twopence.
Sydney Smith (1771–1845) British clergyman and essayist. *Memoir* (Lady Holland)

24 The house which is not opened for charity will be opened to the physician.
The Talmud

25 To keep a lamp burning we have to keep putting oil in it.
Mother Teresa (Agnes Gonxha Bojaxhui; 1910–) Yugoslavian missionary in Calcutta. *Time*, 'Saints Among Us', 29 Dec 1975

26 As for doing good, that is one of the professions which are full.
Henry David Thoreau (1817–62) US writer. *Walden*, 'Economy'

27 I have always depended on the kindness of strangers.
Tennessee Williams (1911–83) US dramatist. *A Streetcar Named Desire*, II:3

CHARM

1 It's a sort of bloom on a woman. If you have it, you don't need to have anything else; and if you don't have it, it doesn't much matter what else you have.
J. M. Barrie (1860–1937) British novelist and dramatist. *What Every Woman Knows*, I

2 All charming people have something to conceal, usually their total dependence on the appreciation of others.
Cyril Connolly (1903–74) British journalist. *Enemies of Promise*, Ch. 16

3 Oozing charm from every pore,
He oiled his way around the floor.
Alan Jay Lerner (1918–86) US songwriter. *My Fair Lady*, II:1

CHASTITY

See also abstinence

1 Give me chastity and continence, but not yet.
St Augustine of Hippo (354–430) Bishop of Hippo. *Confessions*, Bk. VIII, Ch. 7

CHAUCER, Geoffrey

(c. 1342–1400) English poet. *The Canterbury Tales* is a collection of stories told by pilgrims on their way to Canterbury. His other works include the poem *The Book of the Duchess* and *Troilus and Crisayde.*

Quotations about Chaucer

1 Chaucer, notwithstanding the praises bestowed on him, I think obscene and contemptible; he owes his celebrity merely to his antiquity.
Lord Byron (1788–1824) British poet. Attrib.

2 I read Chaucer still with as much pleasure as any of our poets. He is a master of manners and of description and the first tale-teller in the true enlivened, natural way.
Alexander Pope (1688–1744) British poet. Attrib.

Quotations by Chaucer

3 Whan that Aprille with his shoures sote
The droghte of Marche hath perced to the rote.
The Canterbury Tales, Prologue

4 He was a verray parfit gentil knight.
Referring to the knight. *The Canterbury Tales*, Prologue

5 He was as fresh as is the month of May.
Referring to the squire. *The Canterbury Tales*, Prologue

6 Ful wel she song the service divyne,
Entuned in hir nose ful semely.
Referring to the prioress. *The Canterbury Tales*, Prologue

7 A Clerk ther was of Oxenford also,
That un-to logik hadde longe y-go.
The Canterbury Tales, Prologue

8 As lene was his hors as is a rake.
The Canterbury Tales, Prologue

9 Souninge in moral vertu was his speche,
And gladly wolde he lerne, and gladly teche.
Referring to the clerk. *The Canterbury Tales*, Prologue

10 No-wher so bisy a man as he ther nas,
And yet he semed bisier than he was.
Referring to the man of law. *The Canterbury Tales*, Prologue

11 For gold in phisik is a cordial,
Therfore he lovede gold in special.
Referring to the doctor. *The Canterbury Tales*, Prologue

12 She was a worthy womman al hir lyve,
Housbondes at chirche-dore she hadde fyve,
Withouten other companye in youthe.
Referring to the wife of Bath. *The Canterbury Tales*, Prologue

13 The smyler with the knyf under the cloke.
The Canterbury Tales, 'The Knight's Tale'

14 This world nis but a thurghfare ful of wo,
And we ben pilgrimes, passinge to and fro;
Deeth is an ende of every worldly sore.
The Canterbury Tales, 'The Knight's Tale'

15 Tragedie is to seyn a certeyn storie,
As olde bokes maken us memorie,
Of him that stood in greet prosperitee
And is y-fallen out of heigh degree
Into miserie, and endeth wrecchedly.
The Canterbury Tales, 'The Monk's Prologue'

16 Whan that the month in which the world bigan,
That highte March, whan God first maked man.
The Canterbury Tales, 'The Nun's Priest's Tale'

17 Mordre wol out, that see we day by day.
The Canterbury Tales, 'The Nun's Priest's Tale'

18 So was hir joly whistle wel y-wet.
The Canterbury Tales, 'The Reve's Tale'

19 That lyf so short, the craft so long to lerne,
Th' assay so hard, so sharp the conquerynge.
The Parliament of Fowls

20 For of fortunes sharp adversitee
The worst kinde of infortune is this,
A man to have ben in prosperitee,
And it remembren, what is passed is.
Troilus and Criseyde, 3

21 Go, litel book, go litel myn tragedie.
O moral Gower, this book I directe
To thee.
Troilus and Criseyde, 5

CHESTERFIELD, Philip Dormer Stanhope, 4th Earl of

(1694–1773) English statesman and diplomat; author of the famous *Letters* (1774) to his illegitimate son. Appointed ambassador to The Hague in 1728, he subsequently served in Ireland and as secretary of state (1746–48).

Quotations about Chesterfield

1 The only Englishman who ever maintained that the art of pleasing was the first duty in life.
Voltaire (François-Marie Arouet; 1694–1778) French writer. Letter to Frederick the Great, 16 Aug 1774

2 He was a man of much wit, middling sense, and some learning; but as absolutely void of virtue as any Jew, Turk or Heathen that ever lived.
John Wesley (1703–91) British religious leader. *Journal*, 11 Oct 1775

Quotations by Chesterfield

3 Be wiser than other people if you can, but do not tell them so.
Letter to his son, 19 Nov 1745

4 Whatever is worth doing at all is worth doing well.
Letter to his son, 10 Mar 1746

5 An injury is much sooner forgotten than an insult.
Letter to his son, 9 Oct 1746

6 Take the tone of the company you are in.
Letter to his son, 9 Oct 1747

7 Do as you would be done by is the surest method that I know of pleasing.
Letter to his son, 16 Oct 1747

8 I knew once a very covetous, sordid fellow, who used to say, 'Take care of the pence, for the pounds will take care of themselves.'
Possibly referring to William Lowndes. Letter to his son, 6 Nov 1747

9 I recommend you to take care of the minutes: for hours will take care of themselves.
Letter to his son, 6 Nov 1747

10 Advice is seldom welcome; and those who want it the most always like it the least.
Letter to his son, 29 Jan 1748

11 It must be owned, that the Graces do not seem to be natives of Great Britain; and I doubt, the best of us here have more of rough than polished diamond.
Letter to his son, 18 Nov 1748

12 Due attention to the inside of books, and due contempt for the outside, is the proper relation between a man of sense and his books.
Letter to his son, 10 Jan 1749

13 Idleness is only the refuge of weak minds.
Letter to his son, 20 July 1749

14 Women are much more like each other than men: they have, in truth, but two passions, vanity and love; these are their universal characteristics.
Letter to his son, 19 Dec 1749

15 Every woman is infallibly to be gained by every sort of flattery, and every man by one sort or other.
Letter to his son, 16 Mar 1752

16 A chapter of accidents.
Letter to his son, 16 Feb 1753

17 Religion is by no means a proper subject of conversation in a mixed company.
Letter to his godson

18 We, my lords, may thank heaven that we have something better than our brains to depend upon.
Speech, House of Lords. *The Story of Civilization* (W. Durant), Vol. 9

19 Make him a bishop, and you will silence him at once.
When asked what steps might be taken to control the evangelical preacher George Whitefield. Attrib.

20 When your ladyship's faith has removed them, I will go thither with all my heart.
Said to his sister, Lady Gertrude Hotham, when she suggested he go to a Methodist seminary in Wales to recuperate, recommending the views. Attrib.

21 Give Dayrolles a chair.
Said on his deathbed when visited by his godson, Solomon Dayrolles. Last words

CHESTERTON, G(ilbert) K(eith)

(1874–1936) British essayist, novelist, and poet. His detective stories feature the priest Father Brown and his novels include *The Napoleon of Notting Hill* (1904). After conversion to Roman Catholicism (1933) much of his writing was religious.

1 A great deal of contemporary criticism reads to me like a man saying: 'Of course I do not like green cheese: I am very fond of brown sherry.'
All I Survey

2 The modern world . . . has no notion except that of simplifying something by destroying nearly everything.
All I Survey

3 Talk about the pews and steeples
And the cash that goes therewith!
But the souls of Christian peoples
. . .
Chuck it, Smith!
Antichrist, or the Reunion of Christendom

4 The strangest whim has seized me
. . . After all
I think I will not hang myself today.
A Ballade of Suicide

5 'My country, right or wrong' is a thing that no patriot would thing of saying, except in a desperate case. It is like saying 'My mother, drunk or sober.'
The Defendant

6 There is a road from the eye to the heart that does not go through the intellect.
The Defendant

7 The one stream of poetry which is continually flowing is slang.
The Defendant

8 All slang is metaphor, and all metaphor is poetry.
The Defendant

9 The devil's walking parody
On all four-footed things.
The Donkey

10 Fools! For I also had my hour;
One far fierce hour and sweet;
There was a shout about my ears,
And palms before my feet.
The Donkey

11 The rich are the scum of the earth in every country.
The Flying Inn

12 One sees great things from the valley; only small things from the peak.
The Hammer of God

13 The word 'orthodoxy' not only no longer means being right; it practically means being wrong.
Heretics, Ch. 1

14 There is no such thing on earth as

an uninteresting subject; the only thing that can exist is an uninterested person.
Heretics, Ch. 1

15 As enunciated today, 'progress' is simply a comparative of which we have not settled the superlative.
Heretics, Ch. 2

16 We ought to see far enough into a hypocrite to see even his sincerity.
Heretics, Ch. 5

17 Happiness is a mystery like religion, and should never be rationalized.
Heretics, Ch. 7

18 Charity is the power of defending that which we know to be indefensible. Hope is the power of being cheerful in circumstances which we know to be desperate.
Heretics, Ch. 12

19 Carlyle said that men were mostly fools. Christianity, with a surer and more reverend realism, says that they are all fools.
Heretics, Ch. 12

20 A good novel tells us the truth about its hero; but a bad novel tells us the truth about its author.
Heretics, Ch. 15

21 The artistic temperament is a disease that afflicts amateurs.
Heretics, Ch. 17

22 To be clever enough to get all that money, one must be stupid enough to want it.
The Innocence of Father Brown

23 Evil comes at leisure like the disease; good comes in a hurry like the doctor.
The Man who was Orthodox

24 You can only find truth with logic if you have already found truth without it.
The Man who was Orthodox

25 The human race, to which so many of my readers belong.
The Napoleon of Notting Hill, Vol. I, Ch. 1

26 The madman is not the man who has lost his reason. The madman is the man who has lost everything except his reason.
Orthodoxy, Ch. 1

27 The cosmos is about the smallest hole that a man can hide his head in.
Orthodoxy, Ch. 1

28 Reason is itself a matter of faith. It is an act of faith to assert that our thoughts have any relation to reality at all.
Orthodoxy, Ch. 3

29 Mr Shaw is (I suspect) the only man on earth who has never written any poetry.
Referring to George Bernard Shaw. *Orthodoxy*, Ch. 3

30 All conservatism is based upon the idea that if you leave things alone you leave them as they are. But you do not. If you leave a thing alone you leave it to a torrent of change.
Orthodoxy, Ch. 7

31 Angels can fly because they take themselves lightly.
Orthodoxy, Ch. 7

32 Before the Roman came to Rye or out to Severn strode,
The rolling English drunkard made the rolling English road.
The Rolling English Road

33 Smile at us, pay us, pass us; but do not quite forget.
For we are the people of England, that never have spoken yet.
The Secret People

34 Is ditchwater dull? Naturalists with microscopes have told me that it teems with quiet fun.
The Spice of Life

35 He could not think up to the height of his own towering style.
Referring to Tennyson. *The Victorian Age in Literature*, Ch. 3

36 Compromise used to mean that half a loaf was better than no bread. Among modern statesmen it really seems to mean that half a loaf is better than a whole loaf.
What's Wrong with the World

37 Mankind is not a tribe of animals to which we owe compassion. Mankind is a club to which we owe our subscription.
Daily News, 10 Apr 1906

38 Just the other day in the Underground I enjoyed the pleasure of offering my seat to three ladies.
Suggesting that fatness had its consolations. *Das Buch des Lachens* (W. Scholz)

39 There is nothing the matter with Americans except their ideals. The real American is all right; it is the ideal American who is all wrong.
New York Times, 1 Feb 1931

40 Democracy means government by the uneducated, while aristocracy means government by the badly educated.
New York Times, 1 Feb 1931

41 Education is simply the soul of a society as it passes from one generation to another.
The Observer, 'Sayings of the Week', 6 July 1924

42 I want to reassure you I am not this size, really – dear me no, I'm being amplified by the mike.
At a lecture in Pittsburgh. *The Outline of Sanity: A Life of G. K. Chesterton* (S. D. Dale)

43 Am in Birmingham. Where ought I to be?
Telegram to his wife during a lecture tour. *Portrait of Barrie* (C. Asquith)

44 The only way to be sure of catching a train is to miss the one before it.
Vacances à tous prix, 'Le Supplice de l'heure' (P. Daninos)

45 How beautiful it would be for someone who could not read.
Referring to the lights on Broadway. Attrib.

46 A puritan's a person who pours righteous indignation into the wrong things.
Attrib.

47 New roads: new ruts.
Attrib.

CHICAGO

1 This is virgin territory for whorehouses.
Al Capone (1899–1947) Italian-born US gangster. Talking about suburban Chicago. *The Bootleggers* (Kenneth Allsop), Ch. 16

CHILDREN

See also babies, family, innocence of childhood, youth

1 Spare the rod and spoil the child.
Proverb

2 There's only one pretty child in the world, and every mother has it.
Proverb

3 If this was adulthood the only improvement she could detect in her situation was that she could

now eat dessert without eating her vegetables.
Lisa Alther (1944–) US writer. *Kinflicks*

4 It was no wonder that people were so horrible when they started life as children.
Kingsley Amis (1922–) British novelist. *One Fat Englishman*, Ch. 14

5 Only those in the last stage of disease could believe that children are true judges of character.
W. H. Auden (1907–73) British poet. *The Orators*, 'Journal of an Airman'

6 Children sweeten labours, but they make misfortunes more bitter.
Francis Bacon (1561–1626) English philosopher. *Essays*, 'Of Parents and Children'

7 Children have never been very good at listening to their elders, but they have never failed to imitate them.
James Baldwin (1924–87) US writer. *Esquire*, 1960

8 I am married to Beatrice Salkeld, a painter. We have no children, except me.
Brendan Behan (1923–64) Irish playwright. Attrib.

9 I wish I'd been a mixed infant.
Brendan Behan *The Hostage*, II

10 Alas! That such affected tricks
Should flourish in a child of six!
Hilaire Belloc (1870–1953) French-born British poet. *Cautionary Tales*, 'Godolphin Horne'

11 A trick that everyone abhors
In little girls is slamming doors.
Hilaire Belloc *Cautionary Tales*, 'Rebecca'

12 Desire not a multitude of unprofitable children, neither delight in ungodly sons.
Bible: Ecclesiasticus 16:1

13 Unto the woman he said, I will greatly multiply thy sorrow and thy conception; in sorrow thou shalt bring forth children.
Bible: Genesis 3:16

14 But when Jesus saw it, he was much displeased, and said unto them, Suffer the little children to come unto me, and forbid them not: for of such is the kingdom of God.
Bible: Mark 10:14

15 Verily I say unto you, Except ye be converted, and become as little children, ye shall not enter into the kingdom of heaven.
Bible: Matthew 18:3

16 And whoso shall receive one such little child in my name receiveth me.
But whoso shall offend one of these little ones which believe in me, it were better for him that a millstone were hanged about his neck, and that he were drowned in the depth of the sea.
Bible: Matthew 18:5–6

17 He that spareth his rod hateth his son: but he that loveth him chasteneth him betimes.
Bible: Proverbs 13:24

18 You can do anything with children if you only play with them.
Prince Otto von Bismarck (1815–98) German statesman. Attrib.

19 'Twas on a Holy Thursday, their innocent faces clean,
The children walking two and two, in red and blue and green.
William Blake (1757–1827) British poet. *Songs of Innocence*, 'Holy Thursday'

20 I guess that'll hold the little bastards.
Don Carney (1897–1954) US broadcaster. Carney was ending a children's radio show and thought that he was off the air. Attrib.

21 Sometimes when I look at my children I say to myself, 'Lillian, you should have stayed a virgin.'
Mrs Lillian Carter (1898–1983) US mother of president Carter. Remark

22 There is no finer investment for any community than putting milk into babies.
Winston Churchill (1874–1965) British statesman. Radio Broadcast, 21 Mar 1943

23 Boys do not grow up gradually. They move forward in spurts like the hands of clocks in railway stations.
Cyril Connolly (1903–74) British journalist. *Enemies of Promise*, Ch. 18

24 Two things should be cut: the second act and the child's throat.
Noël Coward (1899–1973) British dramatist. Referring to a play featuring a child actor. *The Wit of Noël Coward* (D. Richards)

25 It is only rarely that one can see in a little boy the promise of a man, but one can almost always see in a little girl the threat of a woman.
Alexandre Dumas, fils (1824–95) French writer. Attrib.

26 Anybody who hates children and dogs can't be all bad.
W. C. Fields (1880–1946) US actor. Attrib.

27 To bear many children is considered not only a religious blessing but also an investment. The greater their number, some Indians reason, the more alms they can beg.
Indira Gandhi (1917–84) Indian stateswoman. *New York Review of Books*, 'Indira's Coup' (Oriana Fallaci)

28 Three little maids from school are we,
Pert as a school-girl well can be,
Filled to the brim with girlish glee.
W. S. Gilbert (1836–1911) British dramatist. *The Mikado*, I

29 You may give them your love but not your thoughts.
For they have their own thoughts.
You may house their bodies but not their souls,
For their souls dwell in the house of tomorrow, which you cannot visit, not even in your dreams.
Kahlil Gibran (1883–1931) Lebanese mystic and poet. *The Prophet*, 'On Children'

30 Common morality now treats childbearing as an aberration. There are practically no good reasons left for exercising one's fertility.
Germaine Greer (1939–) Australian-born British writer and feminist.

31 The four eaglets are my four sons who cease not to persecute me even unto death. The youngest of them, whom I now embrace with so much affection, will sometime in the end insult me more grievously and more dangerously than any of the others.
Henry II (1133–89) King of England. Describing a painting of four eaglets preying on their parent. 'The youngest' refers to the future King John. *De Principis Instructione* (Gerald of Wales)

32 The business of being a child interests a child not at all. Children very rarely play at being other children.
David Holloway (1924–) Literary editor. *The Daily Telegraph*, 15 Dec 1966

33 Oh, for an hour of Herod!
Anthony Hope (1863–1933) British novelist. Said at the children's play *Peter Pan* (J. M. Barrie). *J. M. Barrie and the Lost Boys* (A. Birkin)

34 One of the most obvious facts about grown-ups to a child is that they have forgotten what it is like to be a child.

Randall Jarrell (1914–65) US author. *Third Book of Criticism*

35 It is easier for a father to have children than for children to have a real father.

Pope John XXIII (Angelo Roncalli; 1881–1963) Italian churchman. Attrib.

36 A child deserves the maximum respect; if you ever have something disgraceful in mind, don't ignore your son's tender years.

Juvenal (Decimus Junius Juvenalis; 60–130 AD) Roman satirist. *Satires*, XIV

37 The real menace in dealing with a five-year-old is that in no time at all you begin to sound like a five-year-old.

Jean Kerr (1923–) US dramatist. *Please Don't Eat the Daisies*

38 At every step the child should be allowed to meet the real experiences of life; the thorns should never be plucked from his roses.

Ellen Key (Karolina Sofia Key; 1849–1926) Swedish writer. *The Century of the Child*, Ch. 3

39 It is . . . sometimes easier to head an institute for the study of child guidance than it is to turn one brat into a decent human being.

Joseph Wood Krutch (1893–1970) US essayist, critic, and teacher. *If You Don't Mind My Saying*, 'Whom Do We Picket Tonight?'

40 Boys are capital fellows in their own way, among their mates; but they are unwholesome companions for grown people.

Charles Lamb (1775–1834) British essayist. *Essays of Elia*, 'The Old and the New Schoolmaster'

41 A child's a plaything for an hour.

Mary Lamb (1764–1847) Sister of Charles Lamb. *Parental Recollections*

42 Man hands on misery to man.
It deepens like a coastal shelf.
Get out as early as you can,
And don't have any kids yourself.

Philip Larkin (1922–85) British poet. *High Windows*, 'This Be the Verse'

43 Where are the children I might have had? You may suppose I might have wanted them. Drowned to the accompaniment of the rattling of a thousand douche bags.

Malcolm Lowry (1909–57) British novelist. *Under the Volcano*, Ch. 10

44 I love children – especially when they cry, for then someone takes them away.

Nancy Mitford (1904–73) British writer. Attrib.

45 Monday's child is fair of face,
Tuesday's child is full of grace,
Wednesday's child is full of woe,
Thursday's child has far to go,
Friday's child is loving and giving,
Saturday's child works hard for his living,
And the child that is born on the Sabbath day
Is bonny and blithe, and good and gay.

Nursery Rhyme *Traditions of Devonshire* (A. E. Bray)

46 Part of the reason for the ugliness of adults, in a child's eyes, is that the child is usually looking upwards, and few faces are at their best when seen from below.

George Orwell (Eric Blair; 1903–50) British novelist. *Essays*

47 But at three, four, five, and even six years the childish nature will require sports; now is the time to get rid of self-will in him, punishing him, but not so as to disgrace him.

Plato (c. 427 BC–347 BC) Greek philosopher. *Laws*, VII, 794

48 Woe to the land that's govern'd by a child!

William Shakespeare (1564–1616) English dramatist. *Richard III*, II:3

49 Thou cam'st on earth to make the earth my hell.
A grievous burden was thy birth to me;
Tetchy and wayward was thy infancy;
Thy school-days frightful, desperate, wild and furious;
Thy prime of manhood daring, bold, and venturous;
Thy age confirm'd, proud, subtle, sly, and bloody,
More mild, but yet more harmful, kind in hatred;
What comfortable hour canst thou name
That ever grac'd me in thy company?

William Shakespeare *Richard III*, IV:4

50 Parents learn a lot from their children about coping with life.

Muriel Spark (1918–) British novelist. *The Comforters*, Ch. 6

51 There are only two things a child will share willingly – communicable diseases and his mother's age.

Dr Benjamin Spock (1903–) US pediatrician and psychiatrist. Attrib.

52 I have a big house – and I hide a lot.

Mary Ure (1933–75) British actress. Explaining how she coped with her large family of children. Attrib.

53 Never have children, only grandchildren.

Gore Vidal (1925–) US novelist. *Two Sisters*

54 A food is not necessarily essential just because your child hates it.

Katherine Whitehorn (1926–) British journalist. *How to Survive Children*

CHIVALRY

See also courtesy

1 A gentleman is any man who wouldn't hit a woman with his hat on.

Fred Allen (1894–1956) US comedian. Attrib.

2 Even nowadays a man can't step up and kill a woman without feeling just a bit unchivalrous.

Robert Benchley (1889–1945) US humorist. *Chips off the Old Benchley*, 'Down in Front'

3 Somebody has said, that a king may make a nobleman, but he cannot make a gentleman.

Edmund Burke (1729–97) British politician. Letter to William Smith, 29 Jan 1795

4 A Knyght ther was and that a worthy man,
That fro the tyme that he first bigan
To riden out, he loved chivalrie,
Trouthe and honour, fredom and curteisie.
. . .
He was a verray parfit, gentil knyght.

Geoffrey Chaucer (c. 1342–1400) English poet. *The Canterbury Tales*, Prologue

5 Madame, I would have given you another!

Alfred Jarry (1873–1907) French surrealist dramatist. On being reprimanded by a woman for firing his pistol in the vicinity of her child, who might have been killed. *Recollections of a Picture Dealer* (A. Vollard)

6 Some say that the age of chivalry is past, that the spirit of romance is dead. The age of chivalry is never past, so long as there is a wrong left unredressed on earth.

Charles Kingsley (1819–75) British writer. *Life* (Mrs C. Kingsley), Vol. II, Ch. 28

7 For he's one of Nature's Gentlemen, the best of every time.
W. J. Linton (1812–97) British writer. *Nature's Gentleman*

8 It is almost a definition of a gentleman to say that he is one who never inflicts pain.
Cardinal Newman (1801–90) British theologian. *The Idea of a University*, 'Knowledge and Religious Duty'

9 O, young Lochinvar is come out of the west,
Through all the wide Border his steed was the best.
Walter Scott (1771–1832) Scottish novelist. *Marmion*, V

10 So faithful in love, and so dauntless in war,
There never was knight like the young Lochinvar.
Walter Scott *Marmion*, V

11 I have a truant been to chivalry.
William Shakespeare (1564–1616) English dramatist. *Henry IV, Part 1*, V:1

12 Love of honour and honour of love.
Philip Sidney (1554–86) English poet and courtier. Referring to the ideal of chivalry. *English Literature: Mediaeval* (W. P. Ker)

13 A bow-shot from her bower-eaves,
He rode between the barley-sheaves,
The sun came dazzling thro' the leaves
And flamed upon the brazen graves
Of bold Sir Lancelot.
Alfred, Lord Tennyson (1809–92) British poet. *The Lady of Shalott*, Pt. III

CHOICE

1 Any color, so long as it's black.
Henry Ford (1863–1947) US car manufacturer. Referring to the color options offered for the Model-T Ford car. Attrib.

2 Two roads diverged in a wood, and I –
I took the one less traveled by,
And that has made all the difference.
Robert Frost (1875–1963) US poet. *The Road Not Taken*

3 More ways of killing a cat than choking her with cream.
Charles Kingsley (1819–75) British writer. *Westward Ho!*, Ch. 20

4 We have to believe in free will. We've got no choice.
Isaac Bashevis Singer (1904–) Polish-born US writer. *The Times*, 21 June 1982

5 There is no easy popularity in that but I believe people accept there is no alternative.
Margaret Thatcher (1925–) British politician and prime minister. The oft-used phrase 'There is no alternative' led to the acronymic nickname 'TINA'. Speech, Conservative Women's Conference, 21 May 1980

6 I'll have that one, please.
Herbert Beerbohm Tree (1853–1917) British actor and theater manager. In a Post Office, pointing at a stamp in the middle of a sheet. *Beerbohm Tree* (H. Pearson)

CHRISTIANITY

See also Catholicism, Protestantism, religion

1 There is a green hill far away,
Without a city wall,
Where the dear Lord was crucified,
Who died to save us all.
C. F. Alexander (1818–95) British hymn writer. *There is a Green Hill Far Away*

2 Christianity, of course but why journalism?
Arthur Balfour (1848–1930) British statesman. In reply to Frank Harris's remark, '. . . all the faults of the age come from Christianity and journalism'. *Autobiography* (Margot Asquith), Ch. 10

3 Onward, Christian soldiers,
Marching as to war,
With the Cross of Jesus
Going on before.
Sabine Baring-Gould (1834–1924) British author and hymn writer. *Onward Christian Soldiers*

4 Jesus picked up twelve men from the bottom ranks of business and forged them into an organization that conquered the world.
Bruce Barton (1886–1967) US advertising executive. *The Man Nobody Knows: A Discovery of the Real Jesus*

5 The Christian glories in the death of a pagan because thereby Christ himself is glorified.
St Bernard (1090–1153) French monk and theologian. *Richard the Lionheart* (J. Gillingham), Ch. 9

6 Oh mighty soldier, O man of war, at last you have a cause for which you can fight without endangering your soul; a cause in which to win is glorious and for which to die is but gain. Are you a shrewd businessman, quick to see the profits of this world? If you are, I can offer you a bargain which you cannot afford to miss. Take the sign of the cross. At once you will have an indulgence for all the sins which you confess with a contrite heart. The cross is cheap and if you wear it with humility you will find that you have obtained the Kingdom of Heaven.
St Bernard Referring in particular to the second Crusade. *Richard the Lionheart* (J. Gillingham), Ch. 6

7 Beware lest any man spoil you through philosophy and vain deceit, after the tradition of men, after the rudiments of the world, and not after Christ.
Bible: Colossians 2:8

8 Where there is neither Greek nor Jew, circumcision nor uncircumcision, Barbarian, Scythian, bond nor free; but Christ is all, and in all.
Bible: Colossians 3:11

9 Take heed to yourselves, that your heart be not deceived, and ye turn aside, and serve other gods, and worship them.
Bible: Deuteronomy 11:16

10 There is neither Jew nor Greek, there is neither bond nor free, there is neither male nor female: for ye are all one in Christ Jesus.
Bible: Galatians 3:28

11 But the fruit of the Spirit is love, joy, peace, longsuffering, gentleness, goodness, faith, Meekness, temperance: against such there is no law.
Bible: Galatians 5:22–23

12 Therefore the Lord himself shall give you a sign; Behold, a virgin shall conceive, and bear a son, and shall call his name Immanuel. Butter and honey shall he eat, that he may know to refuse the evil, and choose the good.
Bible: Isaiah 7:14–15

13 He shall feed his flock like a shepherd: he shall gather the lambs with his arm, and carry them in his bosom, and shall gently lead those that are with young.
Bible: Isaiah 40:11

14 He it is, who coming after me is preferred before me, whose shoe's latchet I am not worthy to unloose.
Bible: John 1:27

15 The next day John seeth Jesus coming unto him, and saith, Behold the Lamb of God, which taketh away the sin of the world.
Bible: John 1:29

16 Jesus answered and said unto him,

Verily, verily, I say unto thee, Except a man be born again, he cannot see the kingdom of God.
Bible: John 3:3

17 For God so loved the world, that he gave his only begotten Son, that whosoever believeth in him should not perish, but have everlasting life.
Bible: John 3:16

18 Then spake Jesus again unto them, saying, I am the light of the world: he that followeth me shall not walk in darkness, but shall have the light of life.
Bible: John 8:12

19 I am the good shepherd: the good shepherd giveth his life for the sheep.
Bible: John 10:11

20 Jesus said unto her, I am the resurrection, and the life: he that believeth in me, though he were dead, yet shall he live.
Bible: John 11:25

21 Jesus saith unto him, I am the way, the truth, and the life: no man cometh unto the Father, but by me.
Bible: John 14:6

22 But unto you that fear my name shall the Sun of righteousness arise with healing in his wings; and ye shall go forth, and grow up as calves of the stall.
Bible: Malachi 4:2

23 And he said unto them, Go ye into all the world, and preach the gospel to every creature.
Bible: Mark 16:15

24 And Jesus, when he was baptized, went up straightway out of the water: and, lo, the heavens were opened unto him, and he saw the Spirit of God descending like a dove, and lighting upon him:
And lo a voice from heaven, saying, This is my beloved Son, in whom I am well pleased.
Bible: Matthew 3:16–17

25 And he saith unto them, Follow me, and I will make you fishers of men.
Bible: Matthew 4:19

26 Come unto me, all ye that labour and are heavy laden, and I will give you rest.
Take my yoke upon you, and learn of me; for I am meek and lowly in heart: and ye shall find rest unto your souls.
For my yoke is easy, and my burden is light.
Bible: Matthew 11:28–30

27 Then said Jesus unto his disciples, If any man will come after me, let him deny himself, and take up his cross, and follow me.
Bible: Matthew 16:24

28 And said unto them, It is written, My house shall be called the house of prayer; but ye have made it a den of thieves.
Bible: Matthew 21:13

29 And as they were eating, Jesus took bread, and blessed it, and brake it, and gave it to the disciples, and said, Take, eat; this is my body.
And he took the cup, and gave thanks, and gave it to them, saying, Drink ye all of it;
For this is my blood of the new testament, which is shed for many for the remission of sins.
Bible: Matthew 26:26–28

30 But made himself of no reputation, and took upon him the form of a servant, and was made in the likeness of men:
And being found in fashion as a man, he humbled himself, and became obedient unto death, even the death of the cross.
Wherefore God also hath highly exalted him, and given him a name which is above every name:
That at the name of Jesus every knee should bow, of things in heaven, and things in earth, and things under the earth.
Bible: Philippians 2:7–10

31 How very hard it is
To be a Christian!
Robert Browning (1812–89) British poet. *Easter-Day*, I

32 It was just one of those parties which got out of hand.
Lenny Bruce (1925–66) US comedian. Referring to the Crucifixion. *The Guardian*, 10 May 1979

33 If Jesus Christ were to come to-day, people would not even crucify him. They would ask him to dinner, and hear what he had to say, and make fun of it.
Thomas Carlyle (1795–1881) Scottish historian and essayist. *Carlyle at his Zenith* (D. A. Wilson)

34 He who begins by loving Christianity better than Truth will proceed by loving his own sect or church better than Christianity, and end by loving himself better than all.
Samuel Taylor Coleridge (1772–1834) British poet. *Aids to Reflection: Moral and Religious Aphorisms*,

35 We should easily convert even the Turks to the obedience of our gospel, if only we would agree among ourselves and unite in some holy confederacy.
Thomas Cranmer (1489–1556) English churchman. Letter to the Swiss scholar, Joachim Vadian, 1537

36 His Christianity was muscular.
Benjamin Disraeli (1804–81) British statesman. *Endymion*, Bk. 1, Ch. 14

37 Christianity has done a great deal for love by making a sin of it.
Anatole France (Jacques Anatole François Thibault; 1844–1924) French writer. *The Garden of Epicurus*

38 What about it? Do you want to crucify the boy?
Lew Grade (Lewis Winogradsky; 1906–) British film and TV producer. Referring to the revelation that an actor portraying Christ on television was living with a woman to whom he was not married. Attrib.

39 Christianity is part of the Common Law of England.
Matthew Hale (1609–76) English judge. *Historia Placitorum Coronae* (ed. Sollom Emlyn)

40 Tell me the old, old story
Of unseen things above,
Of Jesus and His glory
Of Jesus and His love.
Katherine Hankey (1834–1911) British hymn writer. *Tell Me the Old, Old Story*

41 A local cult called Christianity.
Thomas Hardy (1840–1928) British novelist. *The Dynasts*, I:6

42 The Christian religion not only was at first attended with miracles, but even at this day cannot be believed by any reasonable person without one. Mere reason is insufficient to convince us of its veracity: and whoever is moved by faith to assent to it, is conscious of a continued miracle in his own person, which subverts all the principles of his understanding, and gives him a determination to believe what is most contrary to custom and experience.
David Hume (1711–76) Scottish philosopher. *Essays*, 'Of Miracles'

43 Christianity accepted as given a

metaphysical system derived from several already existing and mutually incompatible systems.

Aldous Huxley (1894–1964) British novelist. *Grey Eminence*, Ch. 3

44 There must be several young women who would render the Christian life intensely difficult to him if only you could persuade him to marry one of them.

C. S. Lewis (1898–1963) British academic and writer. *The Screwtape Letters*

45 Ride on! ride on in majesty!
In lowly pomp ride on to die.

Henry Hart Milman (1791–1868) British poet and historian. *Ride On*

46 Fight the good fight with all thy might,
Christ is thy strength and Christ thy right,
Lay hold on life, and it shall be
Thy joy and crown eternally.

John Monsell (1811–75) British hymn writer. Hymn

47 No kingdom has ever had as many civil wars as the kingdom of Christ.

Baron de Montesquieu (1688–1755) French writer. *Lettres persanes*

48 I call Christianity the one great curse, the one enormous and innermost perversion, the one great instinct of revenge, for which no means are too venomous, too underhand, too underground and too petty – I call it the one immortal blemish of mankind.

Friedrich Wilhelm Nietzsche (1844–1900) German philosopher. *The Antichrist*

49 As with the Christian religion, the worst advertisement for Socialism is its adherents.

George Orwell (Eric Blair; 1903–50) British novelist. *The Road to Wigan Pier*, Ch. 11

50 Christianity has made of death a terror which was unknown to the gay calmness of the Pagan.

Ouida (Marie Louise de la Ramée; 1839–1908) British novelist. *The Failure of Christianity*

51 All hail, the power of Jesus' name!
Let angels prostrate fall.

Edward Perronet (1726–92) British hymn writer. Hymn

52 People may say what they like about the decay of Christianity; the religious system that produced green Chartreuse can never really die.

Saki (Hector Hugh Munro; 1870–1916) British writer. *Reginald on Christmas Presents*

53 If a Jew is fascinated by Christians it is not because of their virtues, which he values little, but because they represent anonymity, humanity without race.

Jean-Paul Sartre (1905–80) French writer. *Anti-Semite and Jew*

54 Whether you think Jesus was God or not, you must admit that he was a first-rate political economist.

George Bernard Shaw (1856–1950) Irish dramatist and critic. *Androcles and the Lion*, Preface, 'Jesus as Economist'

55 Who dreamed that Christ has died in vain?
He walks again on the Seas of Blood,
He comes in the terrible Rain.

Edith Sitwell (1887–1964) British poet and writer. *The Shadow of Cain*

56 The Church's one foundation
Is Jesus Christ her Lord;
She is His new creation
By water and the Word.

Samuel. J. Stone (1839–1901) US hymn writer. Hymn

57 Well, you might try getting crucified and rising again on the third day.

Talleyrand (Charles Maurice de Talleyrand-Périgord; 1754–1838) French politician. When asked what action might impress the French peasantry. Attrib.

58 Christianity is the most materialistic of all great religions.

William Temple (1881–1944) British churchman. *Reading in St John's Gospel*, Vol. I, Introduction

59 And so the Word had breath, and wrought
With human hands the creed of creeds
In loveliness of perfect deeds,
More strong than all poetic thought.

Alfred, Lord Tennyson (1809–92) British poet. *In Memoriam A.H.H.*, XXXVI

60 See how these Christians love one another.

Tertullian (c. 160–225 AD) Carthaginian father of the church. *Apologeticus*, XXXIX

61 The blood of the martyrs is the seed of the Church.

Tertullian Traditional misquotation: more accurately, 'Our numbers increase as often as you cut us down: the blood of Christians is the seed.' *Apologeticus*, L

62 Fraser . . . left his children unbaptized – his wife did it secretly in the washing basin.

Virginia Woolf (1882–1941) British novelist. *Jacob's Room*, Ch. 9

63 A Christian is a man who feels
Repentance on a Sunday
For what he did on Saturday
And is going to do on Monday.

Thomas Russell Ybarra (born 1880) Venezuelan-born US writer. *The Christian*

CHRISTMAS

See also Christianity

1 I have often thought, says Sir Roger, it happens very well that Christmas should fall out in the Middle of Winter.

Joseph Addison (1672–1719) British essayist. *The Spectator*, 269

2 Once in royal David's city
Stood a lowly cattle shed,
Where a Mother laid her Baby
In a manger for His bed:
Mary was that Mother mild,
Jesus Christ her little Child.

C. F. Alexander (1818–95) British hymn writer. *Once in Royal David's City*

3 As I sat on a sunny bank,
On Christmas Day in the morning,
I spied three ships come sailing by.

Anonymous *As I sat on a Sunny Bank*

4 God rest you merry, gentlemen,
Let nothing you dismay.

Anonymous *God Rest you Merry*

5 The holly and the ivy,
When they are both full grown,
Of all the trees that are in the wood,
The holly bears the crown.
The rising of the sun
And the running of the deer,
The playing of the merry organ,
Sweet singing in the choir.

Anonymous *The Holly and the Ivy*

6 I'm dreaming of a white Christmas.

Irving Berlin (1888–) US composer and lyricist. *Holiday Inn*, 'White Christmas'

7 For unto us a child is born, unto us a son is given: and the government shall be upon his shoulder: and his name shall be called Wonderful, Counsellor, The mighty God, The everlasting Father, The Prince of Peace.
Of the increase of his government and peace there shall be no end, upon the throne of David, and upon his kingdom, to order it, and to establish it with judgment and with justice from henceforth even for ever. The zeal of the Lord of hosts will perform this.

Bible: Isaiah 9:6–7

8 And she brought forth her firstborn son, and wrapped him in swaddling

clothes, and laid him in a manger; because there was no room for them in the inn.
Bible: Luke 2:7

9 And there were in the same country shepherds abiding in the field, keeping watch over their flock by night.
And, lo, the angel of the Lord came upon them, and the glory of the Lord shone round about them: and they were sore afraid.
And the angel said unto them, Fear not: for, behold, I bring you good tidings of great joy, which shall be to all people.
Bible: Luke 2:8–10

10 Now when Jesus was born in Bethlehem of Judaea in the days of Herod the king, behold, there came wise men from the east to Jerusalem,
Saying, Where is he that is born King of the Jews? for we have seen his star in the east, and are come to worship him.
When Herod the king had heard these things, he was troubled, and all Jerusalem with him.
Bible: Matthew 2:1–3

11 And when they were come into the house, they saw the young child with Mary his mother, and fell down, and worshipped him: and when they had opened their treasures, they presented unto him gifts; gold, and frankincense, and myrrh.
And being warned of God in a dream that they should not return to Herod, they departed into their own country another way.
Bible: Matthew 2:11–12

12 O little town of Bethlehem,
How still we see thee lie;
Above thy deep and dreamless sleep
The silent stars go by.
Phillips Brooks (1835–93) US Episcopal bishop. *O Little Town of Bethlehem*

13 Christians awake, salute the happy morn,
Whereon the Saviour of the world was born.
John Byrom (1692–1763) British poet and hymn writer. *Hymn for Christmas Day*

14 'Twas the night before Christmas, when all through the house
Not a creature was stirring, not even a mouse;
The stockings were hung by the chimney with care,
In hopes that St Nicholas soon would be there.
Clement Clarke Moore (1779–1863) US writer. In *Troy Sentinel*, 23 Dec 1823, 'A Visit from St. Nicholas'

15 Good King Wenceslas looked out,
On the Feast of Stephen;
When the snow lay round about,
Deep and crisp and even.
John Mason Neale (1818–66) British churchman. *Good King Wenceslas*

16 The first day of Christmas,
My true love sent to me
A partridge in a pear tree.
Nursery Rhyme *Mirth without Mischief*

17 The twelfth day of Christmas,
My true love sent to me
Twelve lords a-leaping,
Eleven ladies dancing,
Ten pipers piping,
Nine drummers drumming,
Eight maids a-milking,
Seven swans a-swimming,
Six geese a-laying,
Five gold rings,
Four colly birds,
Three French hens,
Two turtle doves, and
A partridge in a pear tree.
Nursery Rhyme *Mirth without Mischief*

18 O come all ye faithful,
Joyful and triumphant,
O come ye, O come ye to Bethlehem.
Frederick Oakeley (1802–80) British churchman. Translated from the Latin hymn, *Adeste Fideles*. *O Come All Ye Faithful*

19 It came upon the midnight clear,
That glorious song of old,
From Angels bending near the earth
To touch their harps of gold;
'Peace on the earth; good will to man
From Heaven's all gracious King.'
The world in solemn stillness lay
To hear the angels sing.
E. H. Sears (1810–76) US clergyman. *That Glorious Song of Old*

20 While shepherds watch'd their flocks by night,
All seated on the ground,
The Angel of the Lord came down,
And Glory shone around.
Nahum Tate (1652–1715) Irish-born English poet. *Supplement to the New Version of the Psalms*, 'While Shepherds Watched'

21 At Christmas play and make good cheer,
For Christmas comes but once a year.
Thomas Tusser (1524–80) English farmer. *Five Hundred Points of Good Husbandry*, 'The Farmer's Daily Diet'

22 To perceive Christmas through its wrapping becomes more difficult with every year.
Elwyn Brooks White (1899–1985) US journalist and humorist. *The Second Tree from the Corner*

CHURCH

See also clergy, religion

1 And I say also unto thee, That thou art Peter, and upon this rock I will build my church; and the gates of hell shall not prevail against it.
And I will give unto thee the keys of the kingdom of heaven: and whatsoever thou shalt bind on earth shall be bound in heaven: and whatsoever thou shalt loose on earth shall be loosed in heaven.
Bible: Matthew 16:18–19

2 For where two or three are gathered together in my name, there am I in the midst of them.
Bible: Matthew 18:20

3 And of all plagues with which mankind are curst,
Ecclesiastic tyranny's the worst.
Daniel Defoe (1660–1731) British journalist and writer. *The True-Born Englishman*, Pt. II

4 No Bishop, no King.
James I (1566–1625) King of England. An expression, at a conference on doctrinal reform, of his belief that a non-episcopal form of church government was incompatible with monarchy. Remark, Hampton Court, 14 Jan 1604; reported by William Barlow

5 I laboured nothing more than that the external public worship of God, too much slighted in most parts of this kingdom, might be preserved.
William Laud (1573–1645) Archbishop of Canterbury. Remark at his trial, 12 Mar 1644

6 To arrive at the truth in all things, we ought always to be ready to believe that what seems to us white is black if the hierarchical Church so defines it.
St Ignatius Loyola (1491–1556) Spanish priest. *Spiritual Exercises*

7 We Italians then owe to the Church of Rome and to her priests our having become irreligious and bad, but we owe her a still greater debt, and one that will be the cause of our ruin, namely that the Church

has kept and still keeps our country divided.

Machiavelli (1469–1527) Italian statesman. *Discourses on First Ten Books of Livy*

8 It is hard to tell where MCC ends and the Church of England begins.

J. B. Priestley (1894–1984) British novelist. The MCC is the Marylebone Cricket Club. *New Statesman*, 20 July 1962, 'Topside Schools'

9 The Church should be no longer satisfied to represent only the Conservative Party at prayer.

Agnes Maude Royden (1887–1967) British Congregationalist minister. Speech, London, 16 July 1917

10 The Church exists for the sake of those outside it.

William Temple (1881–1944) British churchman. Attrib.

CHURCHILL, Sir Winston Leonard Spencer

(1874–1965) British statesman and writer, prime minister 1940–45, 1951–55. After service as a war correspondent in the Boer War, he became first Lord of the Admiralty in World War I and led a coalition government in World War II. He was celebrated for his skill as an orator and was the author of several historical books.

Quotations about Churchill

1 It hasn't taken Winston long to get used to American ways. He hadn't been an American citizen for three minutes before attacking an ex-secretary of state!

Dean Acheson (1893–1971) US lawyer and statesman. At a ceremony in 1963 to make Churchill an honorary American citizen, Churchill obliquely attacked Acheson's reference to Britain losing an empire. *Randolph Churchill* (K. Halle)

2 Then comes Winston with his hundred-horse-power mind and what can I do?

Stanley Baldwin (1867–1947) British statesman. *Stanley Baldwin* (G. M. Young), Ch. 11

3 I thought he was a young man of promise; but it appears he was a young man of promises.

Arthur Balfour (1848–1930) British statesman. Said of Winston Churchill on his entry into politics, 1899. *Winston Churchill* (Randolph Churchill), Vol. I

4 He is a man suffering from petrified adolescence.

Aneurin Bevan (1897–1960) British Labour politician. *Aneurin Bevan* (Vincent Brome), Ch. 11

5 The nation had the lion's heart. I had the luck to give the roar.

Winston Churchill (1874–1965) British statesman. Said on his 80th birthday

6 The first time you meet Winston you see all his faults and the rest of your life you spend in discovering his virtues.

Lady Constance Lytton (1869–1923) British suffragette. *Edward Marsh* (Christopher Hassall), Ch. 7

7 Winston has devoted the best years of his life to preparing his impromptu speeches.

F. E. Smith (1872–1930) British lawyer and politician. Attrib.

8 Simply a radio personality who outlived his prime.

Evelyn Waugh (1903–66) British novelist. *Evelyn Waugh* (Christopher Sykes)

Quotations by Churchill

9 Well, the principle seems the same. The water still keeps falling over.

When asked whether the Niagara Falls looked the same as when he first saw them. *Closing the Ring*, Ch. 5

10 I said that the world must be made safe for at least fifty years. If it was only for fifteen to twenty years then we should have betrayed our soldiers.

Closing the Ring, Ch. 20

11 We must have a better word than 'prefabricated'. Why not 'ready-made'?

Closing the Ring, Appendix C

12 The redress of the grievances of the vanquished should precede the disarmament of the victors.

The Gathering Storm, Ch. 3

13 I felt as if I were walking with destiny, and that all my past life had been but a preparation for this hour and this trial.

The Gathering Storm, Ch. 38

14 I have only one purpose, the destruction of Hitler, and my life is much simplified thereby. If Hitler invaded Hell I would make at least a favourable reference to the Devil in the House of Commons.

The Grand Alliance

15 When you have to kill a man it costs nothing to be polite.

Justifying the fact that the declaration of war against Japan was made in the usual diplomatic language. *The Grand Alliance*

16 Before Alamein we never had a victory. After Alamein we never had a defeat.

The Hinge of Fate, Ch. 33

17 By being so long in the lowest form I gained an immense advantage over the cleverest boys . . . I got into my bones the essential structure of the normal British sentence – which is a noble thing.

My Early Life, Ch. 2

18 Headmasters have powers at their disposal with which Prime Ministers have never yet been invested.

My Early Life, Ch. 2

19 So they told me how Mr Gladstone read Homer for fun, which I thought served him right.

My Early Life, Ch. 2

20 Which brings me to my conclusion upon Free Will and Predestination, namely – let the reader mark it – that they are identical.

My Early Life, Ch. 3

21 It is a good thing for an uneducated man to read books of quotations.

My Early Life, Ch. 9

22 Everyone threw the blame on me. I have noticed that they nearly always do. I suppose it is because they think I shall be able to bear it best.

My Early Life, Ch. 17

23 Those who can win a war well can rarely make a good peace and those who could make a good peace would never have won the war.

My Early Life, Ch. 26

24 I have never seen a human being who more perfectly represented the modern conception of a robot.

Referring to the Soviet statesman Molotov. *The Second World War*

25 I must point out that my rule of life prescribed as an absolutely sacred rite smoking cigars and also the drinking of alcohol before, after, and if need be during all meals and in the intervals between them.

Said during a lunch with the Arab leader Ibn Saud, when he heard that the king's religion forbade smoking and alcohol. *The Second World War*

26 In Franklin Roosevelt there died the greatest American friend we have ever known and the greatest champion of freedom who has ever

brought help and comfort from the New World to the Old.
The Second World War

27 In war, resolution; in defeat, defiance; in victory, magnanimity; in peace, goodwill.
Epigram used by Sir Edward Marsh after World War II; used as 'a moral of the work' in Churchill's book. *The Second World War*

28 No one can guarantee success in war, but only deserve it.
Their Finest Hour

29 Wars are not won by evacuations.
Referring to Dunkirk. *Their Finest Hour*

30 When I look back on all these worries I remember the story of the old man who said on his deathbed that he had had a lot of trouble in his life, most of which had never happened.
Their Finest Hour

31 Peace with Germany and Japan on our terms will not bring much rest. . . . As I observed last time, when the war of the giants is over the wars of the pygmies will begin.
Triumph and Tragedy, Ch. 25

32 Dictators ride to and fro upon tigers which they dare not dismount. And the tigers are getting hungry.
While England Slept

33 In defeat unbeatable; in victory unbearable.
Referring to Viscount Montgomery. *Ambrosia and Small Beer* (E. Marsh), Ch. 5

34 You may take the most gallant sailor, the most intrepid airman, or the most audacious soldier, put them at a table together – what do you get? *The sum of their fears.*
Talking about the Chiefs of Staffs system, 16 Nov 1943. *The Blast of War* (H. Macmillan), Ch. 16

35 Don't talk to me about naval tradition. It's nothing but rum, sodomy, and the lash.
Former Naval Person (Sir Peter Gretton), Ch. 1

36 Jellicoe was the only man on either side who could lose the war in an afternoon.
The Observer, 'Sayings of the Week', 13 Feb 1927

37 Everybody has a right to pronounce foreign names as he chooses.
The Observer, 'Sayings of the Week', 5 Aug 1951

38 This is the sort of English up with which I will not put.
The story is that Churchill wrote the comment in the margin of a report in which a Civil Servant had used an awkward construction to avoid ending a sentence with a preposition. An alternative version substitutes 'bloody nonsense' for 'English'. *Plain Words* (E. Gowers), Ch. 9

39 Men will forgive a man anything except bad prose.
Election speech, Manchester, 1906

40 It cannot in the opinion of His Majesty's Government be classified as slavery in the extreme acceptance of the word without some risk of terminological inexactitude.
Speech, House of Commons, 22 Feb 1906

41 *The Times* is speechless and takes three columns to express its speechlessness.
Referring to Irish Home Rule. Speech, Dundee, 14 May 1908

42 He is one of those orators of whom it was well said, 'Before they get up they do not know what they are going to say; when they are speaking, they do not know what they are saying; and when they sit down, they do not know what they have said'.
Referring to Lord Charles Beresford. Speech, House of Commons, 20 Dec 1912

43 The maxim of the British people is 'Business as usual'.
Speech, Guildhall, 9 Nov 1914

44 Labour is not fit to govern.
Election speech, 1920

45 I remember, when I was a child, being taken to the celebrated Barnum's circus, which contained an exhibition of freaks and monstrosities, but the exhibit . . . which I most desired to see was the one described as 'The Boneless Wonder'. My parents judged that that spectacle would be too revolting and demoralising for my youthful eyes, and I have waited 50 years to see the boneless wonder sitting on the Treasury Bench.
Referring to Ramsey MacDonald. Speech, House of Commons, 28 Jan 1931

46 India is a geographical term. It is no more a united nation than the Equator.
Speech, Royal Albert Hall, 18 Mar 1931

47 We have sustained a defeat without a war.
Speech, House of Commons, 5 Oct 1938

48 I cannot forecast to you the action of Russia. It is a riddle wrapped in a mystery inside an enigma.
Broadcast talk, 1 Oct 1939

49 I have nothing to offer but blood, toil, tears and sweat.
On becoming prime minister. Speech, House of Commons, 13 May 1940

50 Victory at all costs, victory in spite of all terror, victory however long and hard the road may be; for without victory there is no survival.
Speech, House of Commons, 13 May 1940

51 We shall not flag or fail. We shall fight in France, we shall fight on the seas and oceans, we shall fight with growing confidence and growing strength in the air, we shall defend our island, whatever the cost may be, we shall fight on the beaches, we shall fight on the landing grounds, we shall fight in the fields and in the streets, we shall fight in the hills; we shall never surrender.
Speech, House of Commons, 4 June 1940

52 This was their finest hour.
Referring to the Dunkirk evacuation. Speech, House of Commons, 18 June 1940

53 The battle of Britain is about to begin.
Speech, House of Commons, 1 July 1940

54 Never in the field of human conflict was so much owed by so many to so few.
Referring to the Battle of Britain pilots. Speech, House of Commons, 20 Aug 1940

55 We are waiting for the long-promised invasion. So are the fishes.
Radio broadcast to the French people, 21 Oct 1940

56 Give us the tools, and we will finish the job.
Referring to Lend-lease, which was being legislated in the USA. Radio Broadcast, 9 Feb 1941

57 You do your worst, and we will do our best.
Addressed to Hitler. Speech, 14 July 1941

58 Do not let us speak of darker days; let us rather speak of sterner days. These are not dark days: these are great days – the greatest days our country has ever lived.
Address, Harrow School, 29 Oct 1941

59 When I warned them that Britain would fight on alone whatever they did, their Generals told their Prime Minister and his divided Cabinet: 'In three weeks England will have her neck wrung like a chicken.'

Some chicken! Some neck!
Referring to the French Government. Speech, Canadian Parliament, 30 Dec 1941

60 This is not the end. It is not even the beginning of the end. But it is, perhaps, the end of the beginning.
Referring to the Battle of Egypt. Speech, Mansion House, 10 Nov 1942

61 I have not become the King's First Minister in order to preside over the liquidation of the British Empire.
Speech, Mansion House, 10 Nov 1942

62 The Almighty in His infinite wisdom did not see fit to create Frenchmen in the image of Englishmen.
Speech, House of Commons, 10 Dec 1942

63 There is no finer investment for any community than putting milk into babies.
Radio Broadcast, 21 Mar 1943

64 There are few virtues which the Poles do not possess and there are few errors they have ever avoided.
Speech, House of Commons, 1945

65 An iron curtain has descended across the Continent.
Address, Westminster College, Fulton, USA, 5 Mar 1946

66 We must build a kind of United States of Europe.
Speech, Zurich, 19 Sept 1946

67 Perhaps it is better to be irresponsible and right than to be responsible and wrong.
Party Political Broadcast, London, 26 Aug 1950

68 To jaw-jaw is better than to war-war.
Speech, Washington, 26 June 1954

69 They are the only people who like to be told how bad things are – who like to be told the worst.
Referring to the British. Speech, 1921

70 An appeaser is one who feeds a crocodile – hoping that it will eat him last.
Attrib.

71 The nation had the lion's heart. I had the luck to give the roar.
Said on his 80th birthday

CINEMA

See also Goldwynisms

1 Hollywood – a place where people from Iowa mistake themselves for movie stars.
Fred Allen (1894–1956) US comedian. Attrib.

2 Garbo Talks!
Anonymous Promotional slogan.

3 What's up, Doc?
Anonymous Used in 'Bugs Bunny' cartoons.

4 If my books had been any worse I should not have been invited to Hollywood, and if they had been any better I should not have come.
Raymond Chandler (1888–1959) US novelist. *The Life of Raymond Chandler* (F. MacShane)

5 Hollywood is a world with all the personality of a paper cup.
Raymond Chandler Attrib.

6 I was born at the age of twelve on a Metro-Goldwyn-Mayer lot.
Judy Garland (Frances Gumm; 1922–69) US film star. *The Observer*, 'Sayings of the Week', 18 Feb 1951

7 I like a film to have a beginning, a middle and an end, but not necessarily in that order.
Jean-Luc Godard (1930–) French film director. Attrib.

8 Photography is truth. And cinema is truth twenty-four times a second.
Jean-Luc Godard *Le Petit Soldat*

9 Why should people go out and pay money to see bad films when they can stay at home and see bad television for nothing?
Samuel Goldwyn (Samuel Goldfish; 1882–1974) Polish-born US film producer. *The Observer*, 'Sayings of the Week', 9 Sept 1956

10 A wide screen just makes a bad film twice as bad.
Samuel Goldwyn Attrib.

11 Strip the phoney tinsel off Hollywood and you'll find the real tinsel underneath.
Oscar Levant (1906–72) US pianist and actor. Attrib.

12 Working for Warner Bros is like fucking a porcupine; it's a hundred pricks against one.
Wilson Mizner (1876–1933) US writer and wit. *Bring on the Empty Horses* (David Niven)

13 In Hollywood, if you don't have happiness you send out for it.
Rex Reed (1938–) US columnist and actor. *Colombo's Hollywood*, 'Hollywood the Bad' (J. R. Colombo)

14 They only got two things right, the camels and the sand.
Lowell Thomas (1892–1981) US author and broadcaster. Referring to the film *Lawrence of Arabia*. Obituary, *The Times*, 29 Aug 1981

15 Take that black box away. I can't act in front of it.
Herbert Beerbohm Tree (1853–1917) British actor and theater manager. Objecting to the presence of the camera while performing in a silent film. *Hollywood: The Pioneers* (K. Brownlow)

16 Thanks to the movies, gunfire has always sounded unreal to me, even when being fired at.
Peter Ustinov (1921–) British actor. *Dear Me*, Ch. 7

17 Me? Tarzan?
Johnny Weissmuller (1904–84) US swimmer and film actor. Reacting to an invitation to play Tarzan. Attrib.

18 It's the biggest train set a boy ever had.
Orson Welles Referring to a Hollywood film studio. Attrib.

19 When you get the personality, you don't need the nudity.
Mae West (1892–1980) US actress. *The Observer*, 'Sayings of the Week', 4 Aug 1968

20 It was like going to the dentist making a picture with her. It was hell at the time, but after it was all over, it was wonderful.
Billy Wilder (1906–) US film director. Referring to Marilyn Monroe. *The Show Business Nobody Knows* (E. Wilson)

21 You can seduce a man's wife there, attack his daughter and wipe your hands on his canary, but if you don't like his movie, you're dead.
Joseph Von Sternberg (1894–1969) Austrian-born film director. Referring to Hollywood. Attrib.

CITIES

See Chicago, London, New York, Paris, places

CIVILIZATION

See also culture

1 Civilization is a method of living, an attitude of equal respect for all men.
Jane Addams (1860–1935) US social worker. Speech, Honolulu, 1933

2 I wish I could bring Stonehenge to Nyasaland to show there was a

time when Britain had a savage culture.

Hastings Banda (1906–) Malawi statesman. *The Observer*, 'Sayings of the Week', 10 Mar 1963

3 The three great elements of modern civilization, Gunpowder, Printing, and the Protestant Religion.

Thomas Carlyle (1795–1881) Scottish historian and essayist. *Critical and Miscellaneous Essays*, 'The State of German Literature'

4 The modern world . . . has no notion except that of simplifying something by destroying nearly everything.

G. K. Chesterton (1874–1936) British writer. *All I Survey*

5 In essence the Renaissance was simply the green end of one of civilization's hardest winters.

John Fowles (1926–) British novelist. *The French Lieutenant's Woman*, Ch. 10

6 I think it would be a good idea.

Mahatma Gandhi (Mohandas Karamchand Gandhi; 1869–1948) Indian national leader. On being asked for his view on Western civilization. Attrib.

7 There is precious little in civilization to appeal to a Yeti.

Edmund Hillary (1919–) New Zealand mountaineer. *The Observer*, 'Sayings of the Week', 3 June 1960

8 In your time we have the opportunity to move not only toward the rich society and the powerful society but upward to the Great Society.

Lyndon B. Johnson (1908–73) US Democratic president. Speech, University of Michigan, May 1964

9 As civilization advances, poetry almost necessarily declines.

Lord Macaulay (1800–59) British historian. *Literary Essays Contributed to the 'Edinburgh Review'*, 'Milton'

10 The degree of a nation's civilization is marked by its disregard for the necessities of existence.

W. Somerset Maugham (1874–1965) British novelist. *Our Betters*, I

11 I regard everything that has happened since the last war as a decline in civilization.

A. L. Rowse (1903–) British historian and critic. *The Observer*, 'Sayings of the Week', 15 June 1975

CLARITY

See also communication, confusion

1 Oh! rather give me commentators plain,
Who with no deep researches vex the brain;
Who from the dark and doubtful love to run,
And hold their glimmering tapers to the sun.

George Crabbe (1754–1832) British poet. *The Parish Register*, 'Baptisms'

2 It's odd how people waiting for you stand out far less clearly than people you are waiting for.

Jean Giraudoux (1882–1944) French dramatist. *Tiger at the Gates*, I

3 When man's whole frame is obvious to a flea.

Alexander Pope (1688–1744) British poet. *The Dunciad*, IV

CLASS

See also aristocracy, equality, public, snobbery

1 Let the cobbler stick to his last.

Proverb

2 There's one law for the rich, and another for the poor.

Proverb

3 You can measure the social caste of a person by the distance between the husband's and wife's apartments.

Alfonso XIII (1886–1941) Spanish monarch. Attrib.

4 I often, therefore, when I want to distinguish clearly the aristocratic class from the Philistines proper, or middle class, name the former, in my own mind *the Barbarians*.

Matthew Arnold (1822–88) British poet and critic. *Culture and Anarchy*, Ch. 3

5 When Adam delved and Eve span,
Who was then the gentleman?

John Ball (d. 1381) English priest. Text of sermon

6 His Lordship may compel us to be equal upstairs, but there will never be equality in the servants' hall.

J. M. Barrie (1860–1937) British novelist and dramatist. *The Admirable Crichton*, I

7 I love the people with their straightforward minds. It's just that their smell brings on my migraine.

Bertolt Brecht (1898–1956) German dramatist. *The Caucasian Chalk Circle*

8 Yet it is better to drop thy friends,
O my daughter, than to drop thy 'H's'.

C. S. Calverley (1831–84) British poet. *Proverbial Philosophy*, 'Of Friendship'

9 One of those refined people who go out to sew for the rich because they cannot bear contact with the poor.

Colette (1873–1954) French novelist. *The Other One*

10 Servants should not be ill. We have quite enough illnesses of our own without them adding to the symptoms.

Lady Diana Cooper (1892–1986) Actress and writer. *Diana Cooper* (Philip Ziegler)

11 I never knew the lower classes had such white skins.

George Nathaniel Curzon (1859–1925) British politician. On seeing soldiers bathing. Attrib.

12 He bade me observe it, and I should always find, that the calamities of life were shared among the upper and lower part of mankind; but that the middle station had the fewest disasters.

Daniel Defoe (1660–1731) British journalist and writer. *Robinson Crusoe*, Pt. I

13 O let us love our occupations,
Bless the squire and his relations,
Live upon our daily rations,
And always know our proper stations.

Charles Dickens (1812–70) British novelist. *The Chimes*, '2nd Quarter'

14 He differed from the healthy type that was essentially middle-class – he never seemed to perspire.

F. Scott Fitzgerald (1896–1940) US novelist. *This Side of Paradise*, Bk. I, Ch. 2

15 Bow, bow, ye lower middle classes!
Bow, bow, ye tradesmen, bow, ye masses!

W. S. Gilbert (1836–1911) British dramatist. *Iolanthe*, I

16 He combines the manners of a Marquis with the morals of a Methodist.

W. S. Gilbert *Ruddigore*, I

17 All shall equal be.
The Earl, the Marquis, and the Dook,
The Groom, the Butler, and the Cook,
The Aristocrat who banks with Coutts,

The Aristocrat who cleans the boots.
W. S. Gilbert *The Gondoliers*, I

18 All the world over, I will back the masses against the classes.
William Ewart Gladstone (1809–98) British statesman. Speech, Liverpool, 28 June 1886

19 Dialect words – those terrible marks of the beast to the truly genteel.
Thomas Hardy (1840–1928) British novelist. *The Mayor of Casterbridge*, Ch. 20

20 '*Bourgeois*,' I observed, 'is an epithet which the riff-raff apply to what is respectable, and the aristocracy to what is decent'.
Anthony Hope (Sir Anthony Hope Hawkins; 1863–1933) British novelist. *The Dolly Dialogues*

21 You may be the most liberal Liberal Englishman, and yet you cannot fail to see the categorical difference between the responsible and the irresponsible classes.
D. H. Lawrence (1885–1930) British novelist. *Kangaroo*, Ch. 1

22 A Social-Democrat must never forget that the proletariat will inevitably have to wage a class struggle for Socialism even against the most democratic and republican bourgeoisie and petty bourgeoisie.
Lenin (Vladimir Ilich Ulyanov; 1870–1924) Russian revolutionary leader. *The State and Revolution*, Ch. 10

23 An Englishman's way of speaking absolutely classifies him
The moment he talks he makes some other Englishman despise him.
Alan Jay Lerner (1918–86) US songwriter. *My Fair Lady*, I:1

24 I'm not interested in classes . . . Far be it from me to foster inferiority complexes among the workers by trying to make them think they belong to some special class. That has happened in Europe but it hasn't happened here yet.
John Llewellyn Lewis (1880–1969) US labor leader. *The Coming of the New Deal* (A. M. Schlesinger, Jnr), Pt. 7, Ch. 25

25 Said Marx: 'Don't be snobbish, we seek to abolish
The 3rd Class, not the 1st.'
Christopher Logue (1926–) British poet and dramatist. *Christopher Logue's ABC*, 'M'

26 The history of all hitherto existing society is the history of class struggles.
Karl Marx (1818–83) German philosopher and revolutionary. *The Communist Manifesto*, 1

27 Mrs. Carey thought there were only four professions for a gentleman, the Army, the Navy, the Law, and the Church. She had added medicine . . . but did not forget that in her young days no one ever considered the doctor a gentleman.
W. Somerset Maugham (1874–1965) British writer and doctor. *Of Human Bondage*, Ch. 33

28 The one class you do *not* belong to and are not proud of at all is the lower-middle class. No one ever describes himself as belonging to the lower-middle class.
George Mikes (1912–87) Hungarian-born British writer. *How to be Inimitable*

29 Only on the third class tourist class passengers' deck was it a sultry overcast morning, but then if you do things on the cheap you must expect these things.
Spike Milligan (1918–) British comic actor and writer. *A Dustbin of Milligan*

30 The worst fault of the working classes is telling their children they're not going to succeed, saying: 'There is a life, but it's not for you'.
John Mortimer (1923–) British lawyer and dramatist. *The Observer*, 'Sayings of the Week', 5 June 1988

31 Actually I vote Labour, but my butler's a Tory.
Lord Mountbatten (1900–79) British admiral. Said to a Tory canvasser during the 1945 election

32 We have nothing to lose but our aitches.
George Orwell (Eric Blair; 1903–50) British novelist. Referring to the middle classes. *The Road to Wigan Pier*, Ch. 13

33 I don't think one 'comes down' from Jimmy's university. According to him, it's not even red brick, but white tile.
John Osborne (1929–) British dramatist. *Look Back in Anger*, II:1

34 Prison will not work until we start sending a better class of people there.
Laurence J. Peter (1919–) Canadian writer. Attrib.

35 You can be in the Horse Guards and still be common, dear.
Terence Rattigan (1911–77) British dramatist. *Separate Tables:* 'Table Number Seven'

36 The Englishman . . . always has in his hands an accurate pair of scales in which he scrupulously weighs up the birth, the rank, and above all, the wealth of the people he meets, in order to adjust his behaviour towards them accordingly.
Jean Rouquet *The Reign of George III* (J. Steven Watson), Ch. 3

37 U and Non-U, An Essay in Sociological Linguistics.
Alan Strode Campbell Ross (1907–78) British professor of linguistics. Essay title, *Noblesse Oblige*, 1956

38 Since every Jack became a gentleman
There's many a gentle person made a Jack.
William Shakespeare (1564–1616) English dramatist. *Richard III*, I:3

39 There are two classes in good society in England. The equestrian classes and the neurotic classes.
George Bernard Shaw (1856–1950) Irish dramatist and critic. *Heartbreak House*

40 We must be thoroughly democratic and patronise everybody without distinction of class.
George Bernard Shaw *John Bull's Other Island*

41 I am a gentleman. I live by robbing the poor.
George Bernard Shaw *Man and Superman*

42 Common people do not pray; they only beg.
George Bernard Shaw *Misalliance*

43 The English have no respect for their language, and will not teach their children to speak it . . . It is impossible for an Englishman to open his mouth, without making some other Englishman despise him.
George Bernard Shaw *Pygmalion*, Preface

44 He's a gentleman: look at his boots.
George Bernard Shaw *Pygmalion*

45 I have to live for others and not for myself; that's middle class morality.
George Bernard Shaw *Pygmalion*

46 It is impossible for one class to appreciate the wrongs of another.
Elizabeth Stanton (1815–1902) US suffragette. *History of Woman Suffrage* (with Susan B. Anthony and Mathilda Gage), Vol. I

47 The charm of Britain has always been the ease with which one can move into the middle class.
Margaret Thatcher (1925–) British politician and prime minister. *The Observer*, 'Sayings of the Week', 27 Oct 1974

48 The ship follows Soviet custom: it

is riddled with class distinctions so subtle, it takes a trained Marxist to appreciate them.

Paul Theroux (1941–) US-born writer. *The Great Railway Bazaar,* Ch. 30

49 For generations the British bourgeoisie have spoken of themselves as gentlemen, and by that they have meant, among other things, a self-respecting scorn of irregular perquisites. It is the quality that distinguishes the gentleman from both the artist and the aristocrat.

Evelyn Waugh (1903–66) British novelist. *Decline and Fall,* Pt. I, Ch. 6

50 No writer before the middle of the 19th century wrote about the working classes other than as grotesque or as pastoral decoration. Then when they were given the vote certain writers started to suck up to them.

Evelyn Waugh Interview. *Paris Review,* 1963

51 Bricklayers kick their wives to death, and dukes betray theirs; but it is among the small clerks and shopkeepers nowadays that it comes most often to the cutting of throats.

H. G. Wells (1866–1946) British writer. *Short Stories,* 'The Purple Pileus'

52 Margaret Thatcher's great strength seems to be the better people know her, the better they like her. But, of course, she has one great disadvantage – she is a daughter of the people and looks trim, as the daughters of the people desire to be. Shirley Williams has such an advantage over her because she's a member of the upper-middle class and can achieve that kitchen-sink-revolutionary look that one cannot get unless one has been to a really good school.

Rebecca West (Cicely Isabel Fairfield; 1892–1983) British novelist and journalist. Said in an interview with Jilly Cooper. *The Sunday Times,* 25 July 1976

53 Really, if the lower orders don't set us a good example, what on earth is the use of them?

Oscar Wilde (1854–1900) Irish-born British dramatist. *The Importance of Being Earnest,* I

54 A very large part of English middle-class education is devoted to the training of servants . . . In so far as it is, by definition, the training of upper servants, it includes, of course, the instilling of that kind of confidence which will enable the upper servants to supervise and direct the lower servants.

Raymond Henry Williams (1921–) British academic and writer. *Culture and Society,* Ch. 3

55 The constitution does not provide for first and second class citizens.

Wendell Lewis Willkie (1892–1944) US lawyer and businessman. *An American Programme,* Ch. 2

CLASSICS

1 They were a tense and peculiar family, the Oedipuses, weren't they?

Max Beerbohm (1872–1956) British writer. *Max: A Biography* (D. Cecil)

2 . . . it a great error to waste young gentlemen's years so long in learning Latin by so tedious a grammar.

Gilbert Burnet (1643–1715) Scottish-born English bishop *The Later Stuarts* (Sir George Clark)

3 So they told me how Mr Gladstone read Homer for fun, which I thought served him right.

Winston Churchill (1874–1965) British statesman. *My Early Life,* Ch. 2

4 Nor can I do better, in conclusion, than impress upon you the study of Greek literature which not only elevates above the vulgar herd, but leads not infrequently to positions of considerable emolument.

Thomas Gaisford (1799–1855) British classicist. Christmas Day Sermon at Oxford. *Reminiscences of Oxford* (Revd W. Tuckwell)

5 To the Greeks the Muse gave native wit, to the Greeks the gift of graceful eloquence.

Horace (Quintus Horatius Flaccus; 65–8 BC) Roman poet. *Ars Poetica*

6 Thou hadst small Latin, and less Greek.

Ben Jonson (1573–1637) English dramatist. *To the Memory of William Shakespeare*

7 The classics are only primitive literature. They belong in the same class as primitive machinery and primitive music and primitive medicine.

Stephen Leacock (1869–1944) English-born Canadian economist and humorist. *Homer and Humbug*

8 Every man with a belly full of the classics is an enemy of the human race.

Henry Miller (1891–1980) US novelist. *Tropic of Cancer,* 'Dijon'

9 Nobody can say a word against Greek: it stamps a man at once as an educated gentleman.

George Bernard Shaw (1856–1950) Irish dramatist and critic. *Major Barbara,* I

10 We were taught as the chief subjects of instruction Latin and Greek. We were taught very badly because the men who taught us did not habitually use either of these languages.

H. G. Wells (1866–1946) British writer. *The New Machiavelli,* Bk. I, Ch. 3

CLASSIFICATION

See also generalizations

1 One of the unpardonable sins, in the eyes of most people, is for a man to go about unlabelled. The world regards such a person as the police do an unmuzzled dog, not under proper control.

T. H. Huxley (1825–95) British biologist. *Evolution and Ethics*

2 The young Cambridge group, the group that stood for 'freedom' and flannel trousers and flannel shirts open at the neck, and a well-bred sort of emotional anarchy, and a whispering, murmuring sort of voice, and an ultra-sensitive sort of manner.

D. H. Lawrence (1885–1930) British novelist. *Lady Chatterley's Lover,* Ch. 1

3 Decades have a delusive edge to them. They are not, of course, really periods at all, except as any other ten years would be. But we, looking at them, are caught by the different name each bears, and give them different attributes, and tie labels on them, as if they were flowers in a border.

Rose Macaulay (1889–1958) British writer. *Told by an Idiot,* Pt. II, Ch. 1

CLEANNESS

1 Bathe early every day and sickness will avoid you.

Indian (Hindustani) proverb

2 Half of the secret of resistance to disease is cleanliness; the other half is dirtiness.

Anonymous

3 Bath twice a day to be really clean,

once a day to be passably clean, once a week to avoid being a public menace.

Anthony Burgess (John Burgess Wilson; 1917–) British novelist. *Mr Enderby*, Pt. I, Ch. 2

4 Man does not live by soap alone, and hygiene, or even health, is not much good unless you can take a healthy view of it – or, better still, feel a healthy indifference to it.

G. K. Chesterton (1874–1936) British writer. *All I Survey*, 'On St. George Revivified'

5 Since the antiseptic treatment has been brought into full operation, and wounds and abscesses no longer poison the atmosphere with putrid exhalations, my wards, though in other respects under precisely the same circumstances as before, have completely changed their character; so that during the last nine months not a single instance of pyaemia, hospital gangrene or erysipelas has occurred in them.

As there appears to be no doubt regarding the cause of this change, the importance of the fact can hardly be exaggerated.

Joseph, Lord Lister (1827–1912) British surgeon. *British Medical Journal*, 2:246, 1867

6 Hygiene is the corruption of medicine by morality.

H. L. Mencken (1880–1956) US journalist and editor. *Prejudices*, 14

7 What separates two people most profoundly is a different sense and degree of cleanliness.

Friedrich Nietzsche (1844–1900) German philosopher. *Beyond Good and Evil*, 271

8 The first possibility of rural cleanliness lies in *water supply*.

Florence Nightingale (1820–1910) British nurse. Letter to Medical Officer of Health, Nov 1891

9 Soap and water and common sense are the best disinfectants.

William Osler (1849–1919) Canadian physician. *Sir William Osler: Aphorisms*, Ch. 5 (William B. Bean)

10 MR PRITCHARD. I must dust the blinds and then I must raise them.
MRS OGMORE-PRITCHARD. And before you let the sun in, mind it wipes its shoes.

Dylan Thomas (1914–53) Welsh poet. *Under Milk Wood*

11 Have you ever taken anything out of the clothes basket because it had become, relatively, the cleaner thing?

Katherine Whitehorn (1926–) British journalist. *The Observer*, 'On Shirts', 1964

CLERGY

See also Church, religion

1 I always like to associate with a lot of priests because it makes me understand anti-clerical things so well.

Hilaire Belloc (1870–1953) French-born British poet. Letter to E. S. P. Haynes, 9 Nov 1909

2 This is a true saying, If a man desire the office of a bishop, he desireth a good work.
A bishop then must be blameless, the husband of one wife, vigilant, sober, of good behaviour, given to hospitality, apt to teach;
Not given to wine, no striker, not greedy of filthy lucre; but patient, not a brawler, not covetous.

Bible: I Timothy 3:1–3

3 Make him a bishop, and you will silence him at once.

Earl of Chesterfield (1694–1773) English statesman. When asked what steps might be taken to control the evangelical preacher George Whitefield. Attrib.

4 It is no accident that the symbol of a bishop is a crook, and the sign of an archbishop is a double-cross.

Dom Gregory Dix (1901–52) British monk. Letter to *The Times*, 3 Dec 1977 (Francis Bown)

5 For clergy are men as well as other folks.

Henry Fielding (1707–54) British novelist. *Joseph Andrews*, Bk. II, Ch. 6

6 He had been a bishop so long that no one knew now what he thought about death, or indeed about anything except the Prayer Book, any change in which he deprecated with determination.

John Galsworthy (1867–1933) British novelist. *Maid in Waiting*

7 That whisky priest, I wish we had never had him in the house.

Graham Greene (1904–) British novelist. *The Power and the Glory*, Pt. I

8 In old time we had treen chalices and golden priests, but now we have treen priests and golden chalices.

John Jewel (1522–71) English bishop. *Certain Sermons Preached Before the Queen's Majesty*

9 A man who is good enough to go to heaven, is good enough to be a clergyman.

Samuel Johnson (1709–84) British lexicographer. *Life of Johnson* (J. Boswell), Vol. II

10 Damn it all, another Bishop dead, –
I verily believe they die to vex me.

Lord Melbourne (1779–1848) British statesman. Attrib.

11 How can a bishop marry? How can he flirt? The most he can say is, 'I will see you in the vestry after service.'

Sydney Smith (1771–1845) British clergyman and essayist. *Memoir* (Lady Holland)

12 I never saw, heard, nor read, that the clergy were beloved in any nation where Christianity was the religion of the country. Nothing can render them popular, but some degree of persecution.

Jonathan Swift (1667–1745) Irish-born Anglican priest and writer. *Thoughts on Religion*

13 There is a certain class of clergyman whose mendicity is only equalled by their mendacity.

Frederick Temple (1821–1902) British churchman. Remark at a meeting of the Ecclesiastical Commissioners. *Years of Endeavour* (Sir George Leveson Gower)

14 But the churchmen fain would kill their church,
As the churches have kill'd their Christ.

Alfred, Lord Tennyson (1809–92) British poet. *Maud*, V

15 If I were a cassowary
On the plains of Timbuctoo,
I would eat a missionary,
Cassock, band, and hymn-book too.

Samuel Wilberforce (1805–73) British churchman. Also attrib. to W. M. Thackeray. Attrib.

CLEVERNESS

1 I never heard tell of any clever man that came of entirely stupid people.

Thomas Carlyle (1795–1881) Scottish historian and essayist. Speech, Edinburgh, 2 Apr 1886

2 It's no use trying to be *clever* – we are all clever here; just try to be *kind* – a little kind.

F. J. Foakes Jackson (1855–1941) British academic. Advice given to a new don at Jesus College, Cambridge. Noted in A. C. Benson's Commonplace Book

3 Be good, sweet maid, and let who can be clever;
Do lovely things, not dream them, all day long;

And so make Life, and Death, and that For Ever,
One grand sweet song.
Charles Kingsley (1819–75) British writer. *A Farewell. To C. E. G.*

4 But the Devil whoops, as he whooped of old:
'It's clever, but is it art?'
Rudyard Kipling (1865–1936) Indian-born British writer. *The Conundrum of the Workshops*

5 The height of cleverness is to be able to conceal it.
Duc de la Rochefoucauld (1613–80) French writer. *Maximes*, 245

6 If I ever felt inclined to be timid as I was going into a room full of people, I would say to myself, 'You're the cleverest member of one of the cleverest families in the cleverest class of the cleverest nation in the world, why should you be frightened?'
Beatrice Webb (1858–1943) British economist and writer. *Portraits from Memory* (Bertrand Russell), 'Sidney and Beatrice Webb'

7 It is never wise to try to appear to be more clever than you are. It is sometimes wise to appear slightly less so.
William Whitelaw (1918–) British politician. *The Observer*, 'Sayings of the Year', 1975

CLOCKS

1 It was a bright cold day in April, and the clocks were striking thirteen.
George Orwell (Eric Blair; 1903–50) British novelist. *Nineteen Eighty-Four*

2 My poor fellow, why not carry a watch?
Herbert Beerbohm Tree (1853–1917) British actor and theater manager. Remark made to a man carrying a grandfather clock. *Beerbohm Tree* (Hesketh Pearson)

3 My grandfather's clock was too large for the shelf.
So it stood ninety years on the floor.
Henry Clay Work (1832–84) US songwriter. *Grandfather's Clock*

4 But it stopped short – never to go again –
When the old man died.
Henry Clay Work *Grandfather's Clock*

CLOTHES

See also appearance, beauty, fashion, nakedness

1 Woollen clothing keeps the skin healthy.
Venetian proverb

2 It is not only fine feathers that make fine birds.
Aesop (6th century BC) Reputed Greek writer of fables. *Fables*, 'The Jay and the Peacock'

3 Gentlemen, it was necessary to abolish the fez, which sat on the heads of our nation as an emblem of ignorance, negligence, fanaticism and hatred of progress and civilization, to accept in its place the hat, the headgear worn by the whole civilized world.
Kemal Ataturk (1880–1938) Founder of the Turkish Republic. Speech, Turkish Assembly, Oct 1927

4 She just wore
Enough for modesty – no more.
Robert Williams Buchanan (1841–1901) British poet and writer. *White Rose and Red*, I

5 I go to a better tailor than any of you and pay more for my clothes. The only difference is that you probably don't sleep in yours.
Clarence Seward Darrow (1857–1938) US lawyer. Reply when teased by reporters about his appearance. *2500 Anecdotes* (E. Fuller)

6 'Good heavens!' said he, 'if it be our clothes alone which fit us for society, how highly we should esteem those who make them.'
Marie Ebner von Eschenbach (1830–1916) Austrian writer. *The Two Countesses*

7 The sense of being well-dressed gives a feeling of inward tranquillity which religion is powerless to bestow.
C. F. Forbes (1817–1911) British writer. *Social Aims* (Emerson)

8 Would you be shocked if I put on something more comfortable?
Jean Harlow (1911–37) US film actress. *Hell's Angels*

9 Those who make their dress a principal part of themselves, will, in general, become of no more value than their dress.
William Hazlitt (1778–1830) British essayist. *On the Clerical Character*

10 A sweet disorder in the dress
Kindles in clothes a wantonness.
Robert Herrick (1591–1674) English poet. *Hesperides*, 'Delight in Disorder'

11 Whenas in silks my Julia goes
Then, then (methinks) how sweetly flows
That liquefaction of her clothes.
Robert Herrick *Hesperides*, 'Upon Julia's Clothes'

12 Fine clothes are good only as they supply the want of other means of procuring respect.
Samuel Johnson (1709–84) British lexicographer. *Life of Johnson* (J. Boswell), Vol. II

13 The uniform 'e wore
Was nothin' much before,
An' rather less than 'arf o' that be'ind.
Rudyard Kipling (1865–1936) Indian-born British writer. *Gunga Din*

14 How do you look when I'm sober?
Ring Lardner Jnr (1885–1933) American humorist. Speaking to a flamboyantly dressed stranger who walked into the club where he was drinking. *Ring* (J. Yardley)

15 Is anything worn beneath the kilt?
No, it's all in perfect working order.
Spike Milligan (1918–) British comic actor and author. *The Great McGonagall Scrapbook*

16 Brevity is the soul of lingerie.
Dorothy Parker (1893–1967) US writer. *While Rome Burns* (Alexander Woollcott)

17 Where did you get that hat?
Where did you get that tile?
James Rolmaz (19th century) British songwriter. *Where Did You Get That Hat?*

18 Not a gentleman; dresses too well.
Bertrand Russell (1872–1970) British philosopher. Referring to Anthony Eden. *Six Men* (A. Cooke)

19 His socks compelled one's attention without losing one's respect.
Saki (Hector Hugh Munro; 1870–1916) British writer. *Ministers of Grace*

20 Costly thy habit as thy purse can buy,
But not express'd in fancy; rich, not gaudy;
For the apparel oft proclaims the man.
William Shakespeare (1564–1616) English dramatist. *Hamlet*, I:3

21 Thou art the thing itself; unaccommodated man is no more but such a poor, bare, forked animal as thou art. Off, off, you lendings! Come; unbutton here.
William Shakespeare *King Lear*, III:4

22 The only man who really needs a tail coat is a man with a hole in his trousers.
John Taylor (20th century) The editor of the *Tailor and Cutter*. *The Observer*, 'Shouts and Murmurs'

23 You can say what you like about long dresses, but they cover a multitude of shins.
Mae West (1892–1980) US actress. *Peel Me a Grape* (J. Weintraub)

24 Hats divide generally into three classes: offensive hats, defensive hats, and shrapnel.
Katherine Whitehorn (1926–) British journalist. *Shouts and Murmurs*, 'Hats'

25 Then the little man wears a shocking bad hat.
Duke of York and Albany (1763–1827) The second son of George III. Referring to Horace Walpole. Attrib.

CLOWNS

See also humor

1 I remain just one thing, and one thing only – and that is a clown. It places me on a far higher plane than any politician.
Charlie Chaplin (Sir Charles Spencer C.; 1889–1977) British film actor. *The Observer*, 'Sayings of the Week', 17 June 1960

2 Send in the Clowns.
Stephen Sondheim (1930–) US composer and lyricist. Song title

CLUBS

1 Mankind is not a tribe of animals to which we owe compassion. Mankind is a club to which we owe our subscription.
G. K. Chesterton (1874–1936) British essayist, novelist, and poet. *Daily News*, 10 Apr 1906

2 I think . . . that it is the best club in London.
Charles Dickens (1812–70) British novelist. Mr Tremlow describing the House of Commons. *Our Mutual Friend*, Bk. II, Ch. 3

3 All I've got against it is that it takes you so far from the club house.
Eric Linklater (1889–1974) Scottish novelist. Referring to golf. *Poet's Pub*, Ch. 3

4 Please accept my resignation. I don't want to belong to any club that will accept me as a member.
Groucho Marx (Julius Marx; 1895–1977) US comedian and film actor. Resigning from the Friar's Club in Hollywood. Attrib.

5 To be an Englishman is to belong to the most exclusive club there is.
Ogden Nash (1902–71) US poet. *England Expects*

COLD WAR

1 Let us not be deceived – we are today in the midst of a cold war.
Bernard Baruch (1870–1965) US financier and presidential adviser. Speech, South Carolina Legislature, 16 Apr 1947

2 An iron curtain has descended across the Continent.
Winston Churchill (1874–1965) British statesman. The phrase 'iron curtain' was originally coined by Joseph Goebbels. Address, Westminster College, Fulton, USA, 5 Mar 1946

3 Now we are in a period which I can characterize as a period of cold peace.
Trygve Lie (1896–1968) Norwegian lawyer. *The Observer*, 'Sayings of the Week', 21 Aug 1949

COLERIDGE, Samuel Taylor

(1772–1834) British poet, chiefly remembered for such works as 'Kubla Khan' (composed in 1797, under the influence of opium) and *The Rime of the Ancient Mariner* (1798). His *Lyrical Ballads* (1798), written with William Wordsworth, was extremely influential.

Quotations about Coleridge

1 A weak, diffusive, weltering, ineffectual man.
Thomas Carlyle (1795–1881) Scottish historian and essayist. Attrib.

2 His face when he repeats his verses hath its ancient glory, an Archangel a little damaged.
Charles Lamb (1775–1834) British essayist. Letter, 26 Apr 1816

Quotations by Coleridge

3 He who begins by loving Christianity better than Truth will proceed by loving his own sect or church better than Christianity, and end by loving himself better than all.
Aids to Reflection: Moral and Religious Aphorisms,

4 If a man could pass through Paradise in a dream, and have a flower presented to him as a pledge that his soul had really been there, and if he found that flower in his hand when he awoke – Aye, and what then?
Anima Poetae

5 The primary imagination I hold to be the living power and prime agent of all human perception, and as a repetition in the finite mind of the eternal act of creation in the infinite I AM.
Biographia Literaria, Ch. 13

6 The Fancy is indeed no other than a mode of memory emancipated from the order of time and space.
Biographia Literaria, Ch. 13

7 Nothing can permanently please, which does not contain in itself the reason why it is so, and not otherwise.
Biographia Literaria, Ch. 14

8 That willing suspension of disbelief for the moment, which constitutes poetic faith.
Biographia Literaria, Ch. 14

9 Our myriad-minded Shakespeare.
Biographia Literaria, Ch. 15

10 A sight to dream of, not to tell!
Christabel, I

11 I may not hope from outward forms to win
The passion and the life, whose fountains are within.
Dejection: An Ode

12 Swans sing before they die – 'twere no bad thing,
Did certain persons die before they sing.
Epigram on a Volunteer Singer

13 On awaking he . . . instantly and eagerly wrote down the lines that are here preserved. At this moment he was unfortunately called out by a person on business from Porlock.
Kubla Khan (preliminary note)

14 In Xanadu did Kubla Khan
A stately pleasure-dome decree:
Where Alph, the sacred river, ran
Through caverns measureless to man
Down to a sunless sea.
Kubla Khan

15 It was a miracle of rare device,
A sunny pleasure-dome with caves of ice!
Kubla Khan

16 A savage place! as holy and enchanted
As e'er beneath a waning moon was haunted
By woman wailing for her demon-lover!
Kubla Khan

17 And all should cry, Beware! Beware!
His flashing eyes, his floating hair!
Weave a circle round him thrice,
And close your eyes with holy dread,
For he on honey-dew hath fed,
And drunk the milk of Paradise.
Kubla Khan

18 Poetry is not the proper antithesis to prose, but to science. Poetry is

opposed to science, and prose to metre.
Lectures and Notes of 1818, I

19 Reviewers are usually people who would have been poets, historians, biographers, . . . if they could; they have tried their talents at one or at the other, and have failed; therefore they turn critics.
Lectures on Shakespeare and Milton, I

20 The faults of great authors are generally excellences carried to an excess.
Miscellanies, 149

21 With Donne, whose muse on dromedary trots,
Wreathe iron pokers into true-love knots.
On Donne's Poetry

22 The most happy marriage I can picture or imagine to myself would be the union of a deaf man to a blind woman.
Recollections (Allsop)

23 If men could learn from history, what lessons it might teach us! But passion and party blind our eyes and the light which experience gives is a lantern on the stern, which shines only on the waves behind us!
Recollections (Allsop)

24 It is an ancient Mariner,
And he stoppeth one of three.
'By thy long grey beard and glittering eye,
Now wherefore stopp'st thou me?'
The Rime of the Ancient Mariner, I

25 The Sun came up upon the left,
Out of the sea came he!
And he shone bright, and on the right
Went down into the sea.
The Rime of the Ancient Mariner, I

26 The ice was here, the ice was there,
The ice was all around:
It cracked and growled, and roared and howled,
Like noises in a swound!
The Rime of the Ancient Mariner, I

27 With my cross-bow
I shot the albatross.
The Rime of the Ancient Mariner, I

28 As idle as a painted ship
Upon a painted ocean.
The Rime of the Ancient Mariner, I

29 The fair breeze blew, the white foam flew,
The furrow followed free;
We were the first that ever burst
Into that silent sea.
The Rime of the Ancient Mariner, II

30 Water, water, every where,
And all the boards did shrink;
Water, water, every where,
Nor any drop to drink.
The Rime of the Ancient Mariner, II

31 Alone, alone, all, all alone,
Alone on a wide wide sea!
And never a saint took pity on
My soul in agony.
The Rime of the Ancient Mariner, IV

32 The many men, so beautiful!
And they all dead did lie:
And a thousand thousand slimy things
Lived on; and so did I.
The Rime of the Ancient Mariner, IV

33 The moving Moon went up the sky,
And no where did abide:
Softly she was going up,
And a star or two beside.
The Rime of the Ancient Mariner, IV

34 Oh sleep! it is a gentle thing,
Beloved from pole to pole!
The Rime of the Ancient Mariner, V

35 Quoth he, 'The man hath penance done,
And penance more will do.'
The Rime of the Ancient Mariner, V

36 Like one, that on a lonesome road
Doth walk in fear and dread,
And having once turned round walks on,
And turns no more his head;
Because he knows, a frightful fiend
Doth close behind him tread.
The Rime of the Ancient Mariner, VI

37 No voice; but oh! the silence sank
Like music on my heart.
The Rime of the Ancient Mariner, VI

38 He prayeth well, who loveth well
Both man and bird and beast.
The Rime of the Ancient Mariner, VII

39 He prayeth best, who loveth best
All things both great and small;
For the dear God who loveth us,
He made and loveth all.
The Rime of the Ancient Mariner, VII

40 A sadder and a wiser man,
He rose the morrow morn.
The Rime of the Ancient Mariner, VII

41 I wish our clever young poets would remember my homely definitions of prose and poetry; that is, prose = words in their best order; – poetry = the best words in the best order.
Table Talk

42 No mind is thoroughly well organized that is deficient in a sense of humour.
Table Talk

43 What comes from the heart, goes to the heart.
Table Talk

44 The misfortune is, that he has begun to write verses without very well understanding what metre is.
Referring to Tennyson. *Table Talk*

45 To see him act, is like reading Shakespeare by flashes of lightning.
Referring to Kean. *Table Talk*

46 I believe the souls of five hundred Sir Isaac Newtons would go to the making up of a Shakespeare or a Milton.
Letter to Thomas Poole, 23 Mar 1801

47 Summer has set in with its usual severity.
Quoted in Lamb's letter to V. Novello, 9 May 1826

COMEDY

1 Tragedy is if I cut my finger. Comedy is if I walk into an open sewer and die.
Mel Brooks (Melvyn Kaminsky; 1926–) US film director. *New Yorker*, 30 Oct 1978

2 All I need to make a comedy is a park, a policeman and a pretty girl.
Charlie Chaplin (Sir Charles Spencer C.; 1889–1977) British film actor. *My Autobiography*

3 Life is a tragedy when seen in close-up, but a comedy in long-shot.
Charlie Chaplin In *The Guardian*, Obituary, 28 Dec 1977

4 Farce is the essential theatre. Farce refined becomes high comedy: farce brutalized becomes tragedy.
Gordon Craig (1872–1966) British actor. *The Story of my Days*, Index

5 Comedy, like sodomy, is an unnatural act.
Marty Feldman (1933–83) British comedian. *The Times*, 9 June 1969

6 We participate in a tragedy; at a comedy we only look.
Aldous Huxley (1894–1964) British novelist. *The Devils of Loudon*, Ch. 11

7 Comedy, we may say, is society protecting itself – with a smile.
J. B. Priestley (1894–1984) British novelist. *George Meredith*

COMFORT

See also endurance, sympathy

1 And always keep a hold of Nurse
For fear of finding something worse.
Hilaire Belloc (1870–1953) British writer. *Cautionary Tales*, 'Jim'

2 The crash of the whole solar and stellar systems could only kill you once.
Thomas Carlyle (1795–1881) Scottish historian and essayist. Letter to John Carlyle, 1831

3 For this relief much thanks. 'Tis bitter cold,
And I am sick at heart.
William Shakespeare (1564–1616) English dramatist. *Hamlet*, I:1

4 I beg cold comfort.
William Shakespeare *King John*, V:7

5 Like a bridge over troubled water,
I will ease your mind.
Paul Simon (1941–) US singer. *Bridge Over Troubled Water*

COMMITMENT

1 In for a penny, in for a pound.
Proverb

2 Never do things by halves.
Proverb

3 One cannot be a part-time nihilist.
Albert Camus (1913–60) French existentialist writer. *The Rebel*

4 Catholics and Communists have committed great crimes, but at least they have not stood aside, like an established society, and been indifferent. I would rather have blood on my hands than water like Pilate.
Graham Greene (1904–) British novelist. *The Comedians*, Pt. III, Ch. 4

5 I love being at the centre of things.
Margaret Thatcher (1925–) British politician and prime minister. *Reader's Digest*, 1984

6 Miss Madeleine Philips was making it very manifest to Captain Douglas that she herself was a career; that a lover with any other career in view need not – as the advertisements say – apply.
H. G. Wells (1866–1946) British writer. *Bealby*, Pt. V, Ch. 5

COMMON MARKET

1 You do not haggle over the price when you are invited to climb onto a lifeboat. You scramble aboard while there is still a seat for you.
Lord Crowther (1907–72) British economist. On the terms of entry into the Common Market. *The Observer*, 'Sayings of the Week', 1 Aug 1971

COMMUNICATION

See also clarity, conversation, language, letter-writing, speech

1 Only connect!
E. M. Forster (1879–1970) British novelist. *Howards End*, Epigraph

2 Unless one is a genius, it is best to aim at being intelligible.
Anthony Hope (Sir Anthony Hope Hawkins; 1863–1933) British novelist. *The Dolly Dialogues*

3 The medium is the message. This is merely to say that the personal and social consequences of any medium . . . result from the new scale that is introduced into our affairs by each extension of ourselves or by any new technology.
Marshall McLuhan (1911–81) Canadian sociologist. *Understanding Media*, Ch. 1

4 And this certainly has to be the most historic phone call ever made.
Richard Milhous Nixon (1913–) US President. Telephone call to astronauts on moon, 20 July 1969.

5 What have we to say to India?
John Ruskin (1819–1900) British art critic and writer. Referring to the completion of the British-Indian cable. Attrib.

COMMUNISM

See also Marxism, Russia, socialism

1 Are you now or have you ever been a member of a godless conspiracy controlled by a foreign power?
Richard Arens (1913–69) US lawyer. Question put to people appearing at hearings of the House of Representatives Committee on Un-American Activities (1947–c. 1957) *The Fifties* (P. Lewis)

2 Russian communism is the illegitimate child of Karl Marx and Catherine the Great.
Clement Atlee (1883–1967) British statesman and Labour prime minister. Speech, 11 Apr 1956

3 Its relationship to democratic institutions is that of the death watch beetle – it is not a Party, it is a conspiracy.
Aneurin Bevan (1897–1960) British Labour politician. Referring to the Communist Party. *Tribune*

4 Communism with a human face.
Alexander Dubček (1921–) Czech statesman. A resolution by the party group in the Ministry of Foreign Affairs, in 1968, referred to Czechoslovak foreign policy acquiring 'its own defined face'. Attrib.

5 The state is not 'abolished', it withers away.
Friedrich Engels (1820–95) German communist. *Anti-Dühring*

6 Every year humanity takes a step towards Communism. Maybe not you, but at all events your grandson will surely be a Communist.
Nikita Khrushchev (1894–1971) Soviet statesman. Said to Sir William Hayter, June 1956

7 Those who wait for that must wait until a shrimp learns to whistle.
Nikita Khruschev Referring to the chances of the Soviet Union rejecting communism. Attrib.

8 Communism is Soviet power plus the electrification of the whole country.
Lenin (Vladimir Ilich Ulyanov; 1870–1924) Russian revolutionary leader. Political slogan of 1920, promoting the program of electrification.

9 In a state worthy of the name there is no liberty. The people want to exercise power but what on earth would they do with it if it were given to them?
Lenin *The State and Revolution*

10 It looks like a duck, walks like a duck, and quacks like a duck.
Joseph R. McCarthy (1908–57) US senator. Suggested method of identifying a communist. Attrib.

11 There's no such thing in Communist countries as a load of old cod's wallop, the cod's wallop is always fresh made.
Robert Morley (1908–) British actor. *Punch*, 20 Feb 1974

12 Between complete Socialism and Communism there is no difference whatever in my mind. Communism is in fact the completion of Socialism; when that ceases to be militant and becomes triumphant, it will be communism.
William Morris (1834–96) English Utopian socialist. Lecture to the Hammersmith Socialist Society, 1893

13 Communism is like prohibition, it's a good idea but it won't work.

Will Rogers (1879–1935) US actor and humorist. *Autobiography*, Nov 1927

14 Nature has no cure for this sort of madness, though I have known a legacy from a rich relative work wonders.

F. E. Smith (1872–1930) British lawyer and politician. Referring to Communism. *Law, Life and Letters* (1927), Vol. II

15 For us in Russia communism is a dead dog, while, for many people in the West, it is still a living lion.

Alexander Solzhenitsyn (1918–) Soviet novelist. *The Listener*, 15 Feb 1979

16 Every communist has a fascist frown, every fascist a communist smile.

Muriel Spark (1918–) British novelist. *The Girls of Slender Means*, Ch. 4

17 The party is the rallying-point for the best elements of the working class.

Joseph Stalin (J. Dzhugashvili; 1879–1953) Soviet statesman. Attrib.

18 Communism continued to haunt Europe as a spectre – a name men gave to their own fears and blunders. But the crusade against Communism was even more imaginary than the spectre of Communism.

A. J. P. Taylor (1906–) British historian. *The Origins of the Second World War*, Ch. 2

19 Lenin's method leads to this: the party organization at first substitutes itself for the party as a whole. Then the central committee substitutes itself for the party organization, and finally a single dictator substitutes himself for the central committee.

Leon Trotsky (Lev Davidovich Bronstein; 1879–1940) Russian revolutionary. *The Communist Parties of Western Europe* (N. McInnes), Ch. 3

COMPANY

1 Company, villainous company, hath been the spoil of me.

William Shakespeare (1564–1616) English dramatist. *Henry IV, Part 1*, III:3

COMPASSION

1 But a certain Samaritan, as he journeyed, came where he was: and when he saw him, he had compassion on him,
And went to him, and bound up his wounds, pouring in oil and wine, and set him on his own beast, and brought him to an inn, and took care of him.
And on the morrow when he departed, he took out two pence, and gave them to the host, and said unto him, Take care of him; and whatsoever thou spendest more, when I come again, I will repay thee.

Bible: Luke 10:33–35

2 Compassion is not a sloppy, sentimental feeling for people who are underprivileged or sick . . . it is an absolutely practical belief that, regardless of a person's background, ability or ability to pay, he should be provided with the best that society has to offer.

Neil Kinnock (1942–) British politician. Maiden speech, House of Commons, 1970

COMPLAINTS

1 You will find in politics that you are much exposed to the attribution of false motives. Never complain and never explain.

Stanley Baldwin, 1st Earl of Bewdley (1867–1947) British Conservative prime minister. Quoting Disraeli. Said to Harold Nicolson, 21 July 1943

2 We have first raised a dust and then complain we cannot see.

Bishop Berkeley (1685–1753) Irish churchman and philosopher. *Principles of Human Knowledge*, Introduction

3 The world is disgracefully managed, one hardly knows to whom to complain.

Ronald Firbank (1886–1926) British novelist. *Vainglory*

4 We was robbed!

Joe Jacobs (1896–1940) US boxing manager. Complaining to the audience when the heavyweight title of Max Schmeling, whom he managed, was passed to Jack Sharkey. Attrib.

5 If you are foolish enough to be contented, don't show it, but grumble with the rest.

Jerome K. Jerome (1859–1927) British humorist. *Idle Thoughts of an Idle Fellow*

6 Nay, Madam, when you are declaiming, declaim; and when you are calculating, calculate.

Samuel Johnson (1709–84) British lexicographer. Commenting on Mrs Thrales's discourse on the price of children's clothes. *Life of Johnson* (J. Boswell), Vol. III

7 I never saw a wild thing
Sorry for itself.
A small bird will drop frozen dead
From a bough
Without every having felt sorry for itself.

D. H. Lawrence (1885–1930) British novelist. *Self Pity*

8 How could God do this to me after all I have done for him?

Louis XIV (1638–1715) French king. On receiving news of the French army's defeat at the Battle of Blenheim. *Saint-Simon at Versailles* (L. Norton)

9 I want to register a complaint. Do you know who sneaked into my room at three o'clock this morning? . . .
– Who? . . .
Nobody, and that's my complaint.

Groucho Marx (Julius Marx; 1895–1977) US comedian. *Monkey Business*

10 I have always been a grumbler. I am designed for the part – sagging face, weighty underlip, rumbling, resonant voice. Money couldn't buy a better grumbling outfit.

J. B. Priestley (1894–1984) British novelist. *The Guardian*, 15 Aug 1984

11 If this is the way Queen Victoria treats her prisoners, she doesn't deserve to have any.

Oscar Wilde (1854–1900) Irish-born British dramatist. Complaining at having to wait in the rain for transport to take him to prison. Attrib.

COMPLIMENTS

See also admiration, beauty, flattery, love, praise

1 Nature made him, and then broke the mould.

Ludovico Ariosto (1474–1533) Italian poet. Referring to Charlemagne's paladin, Roland. *Orlando furioso*

2 It's a sort of bloom on a woman. If you have it, you don't need to have anything else; and if you don't have it, it doesn't much matter what else you have.

J. M. Barrie (1860–1937) British novelist and dramatist. *What Every Woman Knows*, I

3 Miss J. Hunter Dunn, Miss J. Hunter Dunn,
Furnish'd and burnish'd by Aldershot sun.

John Betjeman (1906–84) British poet. *A Subaltern's Love Song*

4 Here's looking at you, kid.

Humphrey Bogart (1899–1957) US film star. *Casablanca*

5 Incredibly, inordinately,
devastatingly, immortally,

calamitously, hearteningly, adorably
beautiful.

Rupert Brooke (1887–1915) British poet. Referring to the actress Cathleen Nesbitt. *Rupert Brooke* (C. Hassall)

6 She walks in beauty, like the night
Of cloudless climes and starry skies;
And all that's best of dark and bright
Meet in her aspect and her eyes.

Lord Byron (1788–1824) British poet. *She Walks in Beauty*

7 There is a garden in her face,
Where roses and white lilies grow;
A heav'nly paradise is that place,
Wherein all pleasant fruits do flow.
There cherries grow, which none
may buy
Till 'Cherry ripe' themselves do cry.

Thomas Campion (1567–1620) English poet. *Fourth Book of Airs*

8 She isn't a bad bit of goods, the Queen! I wish all the fleas in my bed were as good.

Miguel de Cervantes (1547–1616) Spanish novelist. *Don Quixote*, Pt. I, Ch. 30

9 It was a blonde. A blonde to make a bishop kick a hole in a stained-glass window.

Raymond Chandler (1888–1959) US novelist. *Farewell, My Lovely*, Ch. 13

10 If you weren't the best light comedian in the country, all you'd be fit for would be the selling of cars in Great Portland Street.

Noël Coward (1899–1973) British dramatist. To Rex Harrison. Attrib.

11 Here with a Loaf of Bread beneath
the Bough,
A Flask of Wine, a Book of Verse –
and Thou
Beside me singing in the
Wilderness –
And Wilderness is Paradise enow.

Edward Fitzgerald (1809–83) British poet. *The Rubáiyát of Omar Khayyám*

12 He talked on for ever; and you wished him to talk on for ever.

William Hazlitt (1778–1830) British essayist. Referring to Coleridge. *Lectures on the English Poets*, Lecture VIII, 'On the Living Poets'

13 His worst is better than any other person's best.

William Hazlitt *English Literature*, Ch. XIV, 'Sir Walter Scott'

14 Whenever a man's friends begin to compliment him about looking young, he may be sure that they think he is growing old.

Washington Irving (1783–1859) US writer. *Bracebridge Hall*, 'Bachelors'

15 She is Venus when she smiles;
But she's Juno when she walks,
And Minerva when she talks.

Ben Jonson (1573–1637) English dramatist. *The Underwood*, 'Celebration of Charis, V. His Discourse with Cupid'

16 On Richmond Hill there lives a lass,
More sweet than May day morn,
Whose charms all other maids
surpass,
A rose without a thorn.

Leonard MacNally (1752–1820) Irish dramatist and poet. *The Lass of Richmond Hill*

17 Oh, thou art fairer than the evening
air
Clad in the beauty of a thousand
stars.

Christopher Marlowe *Doctor Faustus*, V:1

18 Your eyes shine like the pants of my blue serge suit.

Groucho Marx (Julius Marx; 1895–1977) US comedian. *The Cocoanuts*

19 Most people are such fools that it is really no great compliment to say that a man is above the average.

W. Somerset Maugham (1874–1965) British novelist. *A Writer's Notebook*

20 Charlie is my darling, my darling,
my darling,
Charlie is my darling, the young
Chevalier.

Baroness Nairne (1766–1845) Scottish songwriter. Referring to Bonnie Prince Charlie. *Charlie is my Darling*

21 Pretty witty Nell.

Samuel Pepys (1633–1703) English diarist. Referring to Nell Gwynne. *Diary*, 3 Apr 1665

22 Where'er you walk, cool gales shall
fan the glade,
Trees, where you sit, shall crowd
into a shade:
Where'er you tread, the blushing
flow'rs shall rise,
And all things flourish where you
turn your eyes.

Alexander Pope (1688–1744) British poet. *Pastorals*, 'Summer'

23 I get no kick from champagne.
Mere alcohol doesn't thrill me at all,
So tell me why should it be true
That I get a kick out of you?

Cole Porter (1891–1964) US composer and lyricist. *Anything Goes*, 'I Get a Kick Out of You'

24 It is fun to be in the same decade with you.

Franklin D. Roosevelt (1882–1945) US Democratic president. After Churchill had congratulated him on his 60th birthday. *The Hinge of Fate* (Winston S. Churchill), Ch. 4

25 My doctor said to me afterwards, 'When you were ill you behaved like a true philosopher. Every time you came to yourself you made a joke.' I never had a compliment that pleased me more.

Bertrand Russell (1872–1970) British philosopher. Letter to Jean Nichol, 2 Oct 1921

26 His vocal cords were kissed by God.

Harold Schoenberg (1915–) US music critic. Referring to Luciano Pavarotti. *The Times*, 30 June 1981

27 But search the land of living men,
Where wilt thou find their like agen?

Walter Scott (1771–1832) Scottish novelist. *Marmion*, I

28 The barge she sat in, like a
burnish'd throne,
Burn'd on the water. The poop was
beaten gold;
Purple the sails, and so perfumed
that
The winds were love-sick with them;
the oars were silver,
Which to the tune of flutes kept
stroke and made
The water which they beat to follow
faster,
As amorous of their strokes. For her
own person,
It beggar'd all description.

William Shakespeare (1564–1616) English dramatist. *Antony and Cleopatra*, II:2

29 Age cannot wither her, nor custom
stale
Her infinite variety. Other women
cloy
The appetites they feed, but she
makes hungry
Where most she satisfies.

William Shakespeare *Antony and Cleopatra*, II:2

30 'A was a man, take him for all in
all,
I shall not look upon his like again.

William Shakespeare *Hamlet*, I:2

31 Shall I compare thee to a summer's
day?
Thou art more lovely and more
temperate.
Rough winds do shake the darling
buds of May,
And summer's lease hath all too
short a date.

William Shakespeare *Sonnet 18*

32 Who is Silvia? What is she,
That all our swains commend her?
Holy, fair, and wise is she.

William Shakespeare *The Two Gentlemen of Verona*, IV:2

33 For she was beautiful – her beauty made
The bright world dim, and everything beside
Seemed like the fleeting image of a shade.
Percy Bysshe Shelley (1792–1822) British poet. *The Witch of Atlas*, XII

34 Won't you come into the garden? I would like my roses to see you.
Richard Brinsley Sheridan (1751–1816) British dramatist. Said to a young lady. Attrib. in *The Perfect Hostess*

35 She would rather light candles than curse the darkness, and her glow has warmed the world.
Adlai Stevenson (1900–65) US statesman. Referring to Eleanor Roosevelt. Address, United Nations General Assembly, 9 Nov 1962

36 What, when drunk, one sees in other women, one sees in Garbo sober.
Kenneth Tynan (1927–80) British theater critic. *The Sunday Times*, 25 Aug 1963

37 Of this blest man, let his just praise be given,
Heaven was in him, before he was in heaven.
Izaak Walton (1593–1683) English writer. Referring to Dr Richard Sibbes. Written in a copy of *Returning Backslider* by Richard Sibbes

38 Roses are flowering in Picardy,
But there's never a rose like you.
Frederic Edward Weatherly (1848–1929) British lawyer and songwriter. *Roses of Picardy*

39 The sweetest thing that ever grew
Beside a human door!
William Wordsworth (1770–1850) British poet. *Lucy Gray*

COMPOSERS

See also criticism, music, musicians

1 Too much counterpoint; what is worse, Protestant counterpoint.
Thomas Beecham (1879–1981) British conductor. Said of J. S. Bach
The Guardian 8 Mar 1971

2 Off with you! You're a happy fellow, for you'll give happiness and joy to many other people. There is nothing better or greater than that!
Ludwig van Beethoven (1770–1827) German composer. Said to Franz Liszt when Liszt, aged 11, had visited Beethoven and played for him. *Beethoven: Letters, Journals and Conversations* (M. Hamburger)

3 A master is dead. Today we sing no more.
Johannes Brahms (1833–97) German composer. Stopping a choral rehearsal on hearing of the death of Wagner. *Brahms* (P. Latham)

4 The greatest composers since Beethoven.
Richard Buckle (1916–) British ballet critic. Referring to the Beatles. *The Sunday Times*, 29 Dec 1963

5 The public doesn't want new music: the main thing it demands of a composer is that he be dead.
Arthur Honegger (1892–1955) French composer. Attrib.

6 For instrumental music there is a certain Haydn, who has some peculiar ideas, but he is only just beginning.
Maria Theresa (1717–80) Empress and ruler of the Habsburg dominions. Letter to Archduchess Marie Beatrix, 1772

7 Wagner is the Puccini of music.
J. B. Morton (1893–1979) British journalist. Attrib.

8 Rachmaninov's immortalizing totality was his scowl. He was a six-and-a-half-foot-tall scowl.
Igor Stravinsky (1882–1971) Russian-born US composer. *Conversations with Igor Stravinsky* (Igor Stravinsky and Robert Craft)

9 A good composer does not imitate; he steals.
Igor Stravinsky *Twentieth Century Music* (Peter Yates)

10 Ah, a German and a genius! a prodigy, admit him!
Jonathan Swift (1667–1745) Irish-born Anglican priest and writer. Learning of the arrival of Handel; Swift's last words. Attrib.

COMPROMISE

1 It takes two to tango.
Proverb

2 We know what happens to people who stay in the middle of the road. They get run over.
Aneurin Bevan (1897–1960) Welsh Labour politician. *The Observer*, 9 Dec 1953

3 For the flesh lusteth against the Spirit, and the Spirit against the flesh: and these are contrary the one to the other: so that ye cannot do the things that ye would.
Bible: Galatians 5:17

4 All government, indeed every human benefit and enjoyment, every virtue, and every prudent act, is founded on compromise and barter.
Edmund Burke (1729–97) British politician. *Speech on Conciliation with America* (House of Commons, 22 Mar 1775)

5 Compromise used to mean that half a loaf was better than no bread. Among modern statesmen it really seems to mean that half a loaf is better than a whole loaf.
G. K. Chesterton (1874–1936) British writer. *What's Wrong with the World*

6 That smooth-fac'd gentleman, tickling Commodity,
Commodity, the bias of the world.
William Shakespeare (1564–1616) English dramatist. *King John*, II:1

CONCEIT

See also arrogance, boasts, egotism, pride

1 I'm the greatest!
Muhammad Ali (Cassius Clay; 1942–) US boxer. Remark, often said after his fights

2 A man . . . must have a very good opinion of himself when he asks people to leave their own fireside, and encounter such a day as this, for the sake of coming to see him. He must think himself a most agreeable fellow.
Jane Austen (1775–1817) British novelist. *Emma*, Ch. 13

3 It was prettily devised of Aesop, 'The fly sat upon the axletree of the chariot-wheel and said, what a dust do I raise.'
Francis Bacon (1561–1626) English philosopher. *Essays*, 'Of Vain-Glory'

4 To give an accurate and exhaustive account of that period would need a far less brilliant pen than mine.
Max Beerbohm (1872–1956) British writer. *1880*

5 It seems to be a law of nature that no man ever is loth to sit for his portrait.
Max Beerbohm *Quia Imperfectum*

6 If ever he went to school without any boots it was because he was too big for them.
Ivor Bulmer-Thomas (1905–) British writer and politician. Referring to Harold Wilson. Remark, Conservative Party Conference, 1949

7 Vanity plays lurid tricks with our memory.
Joseph Conrad (Teodor Josef Konrad Korzeniowski; 1857–1924) Polish-born British novelist. *Lord Jim*

8 I know he is, and he adores his maker.

Benjamin Disraeli (1804–81) British statesman. Replying to a remark made in defense of John Bright that he was a self-made man; often also attrib. to Bright referring to Disraeli. *The Fine Art of Political Wit* (L. Harris)

9 We are so vain that we even care for the opinion of those we don't care for.

Marie Ebner von Eschenbach (1830–1916) Austrian writer. *Aphorism*

10 I am the Captain of the *Pinafore*;
And a right good captain too!

W. S. Gilbert (1836–1911) British dramatist. *HMS Pinafore*, I

11 I have a left shoulder-blade that is a miracle of loveliness. People come miles to see it. My right elbow has a fascination that few can resist.

W. S. Gilbert *The Mikado*, II

12 All my shows are great. Some of them are bad. But they are all great.

Lew Grade (Lewis Winogradsky; 1906–) British film and TV producer. *The Observer*, 'Sayings of the Week', 14 Sept 1975

13 Conceit is the finest armour a man can wear.

Jerome K. Jerome (1859–1927) British humorist. *Idle Thoughts of an Idle Fellow*

14 He fell in love with himself at first sight and it is a passion to which he has always remained faithful. Self-love seems so often unrequited.

Anthony Powell (1905–) British novelist. *A Dance to the Music of Time: The Acceptance World*, Ch. 1

15 Self-love is the greatest of all flatterers.

Duc de la Rochefoucauld (1613–80) French writer. *Maximes*, 2

16 You're so vain, you probably think this song is about you.

Carly Simon (1945–) US singer. *You're So Vain*

17 Besides Shakespeare and me, who do you think there is?

Gertrude Stein (1874–1946) US writer. Speaking to a friend she considered knew little about literature. *Charmed Circle* (J. Mellow)

18 The Jews have produced only three originative geniuses: Christ, Spinoza, and myself.

Gertrude Stein *Charmed Circle* (J. Mellow)

19 Vanity dies hard; in some obstinate cases it outlives the man.

Robert Louis Stevenson (1850–94) Scottish writer. *Prince Otto*

20 He would like to destroy his old diaries and to appear before his children and the public only in his patriarchal robes. His vanity is immense!

Sophie Tolstoy (1844–1919) Russian writer. *A Diary of Tolstoy's Wife, 1860–1891*

21 No, no, Oscar, you forget. When you and I are together we never talk about anything except me.

James Whistler (1834–1903) US painter. Cable replying to Oscar Wilde's message: 'When you and I are together we never talk about anything except ourselves'. *The Gentle Art of Making Enemies*

22 Isn't it? I know in my case I would grow intolerably conceited.

James Whistler Replying to the pointed observaton that it was as well that we do not see ourselves as others see us. *The Man Whistler* (H. Pearson)

23 A LADY. I only know of two painters in the world: yourself and Velasquez.
WHISTLER. Why drag in Velasquez?

James Whistler *Whistler Stories* (D. Seitz)

24 I cannot tell you that, madam. Heaven has granted me no offspring.

James Whistler Replying to a lady who had inquired whether he thought genius hereditary. *Whistler Stories* (D. Seitz)

25 Nothing, except my genius.

Oscar Wilde (1854–1900) Irish-born British dramatist. Replying to a US customs official on being asked if he had anything to declare. Attrib.

26 To love oneself is the beginning of a lifelong romance.

Oscar Wilde *An Ideal Husband*, III

27 Who am I to tamper with a masterpiece?

Oscar Wilde Refusing to make alterations to one of his own plays. Attrib.

CONFLICT

See also doublethink, opposites

1 Attack is the best form of defense.

Proverb

2 Fight fire with fire.

Proverb

3 He who lives by the sword dies by the sword.

Proverb

4 Without Contraries is no progression. Attraction and Repulsion, Reason and Energy, Love and Hate, are necessary to Human existence.

William Blake (1757–1827) British poet. *The Marriage of Heaven and Hell*, 'The Argument'

5 No, when the fight begins within himself,
A man's worth something.

Robert Browning (1812–89) British poet. *Bishop Blougram's Apology*

6 Two souls dwell, alas! in my breast.

Johann Wolfgang von Goethe (1749–1832) German poet and dramatist. *Faust*, Pt. I

7 Two loves I have, of comfort and despair,
Which like two spirits do suggest me still;
The better angel is a man right fair,
The worser spirit a woman colour'd ill.

William Shakespeare (1564–1616) English dramatist. *Sonnet 144*

CONFORMITY

See also orthodoxy

1 Who spits against the wind, it falls in his face.

Proverb

2 When in Rome, live as the Romans do: when elsewhere, live as they live elsewhere.

St Ambrose (c. 339–97) Bishop of Milan. Advice to St Augustine

3 If you're not part of the solution, you're part of the problem.

Anonymous

4 Take the tone of the company you are in.

Earl of Chesterfield (1694–1773) English statesman. Letter to his son, 9 Oct 1747

5 Whoso would be a man must be a nonconformist.

Ralph Waldo Emerson (1803–82) US poet and essayist. *Essays*, 'Self-Reliance'

6 Why do you have to be a nonconformist like everybody else?

James Thurber (1894–1961) US humorist. Attrib. Actually a cartoon caption by Stan Hunt in the *New Yorker*

CONFUSION

1 Anyone who isn't confused here doesn't really understand what's going on.

Anonymous Referring to the sectarian problems in Northern Ireland.

2 Well, my deliberate opinion is – it's a jolly strange world.
Arnold Bennett (1867–1931) British novelist. *The Title*, I

3 I can't say I was ever lost, but I was bewildered once for three days.
Daniel Boone (1734–1820) US pioneeer. Reply when asked if he had ever been lost. Attrib.

4 'Curiouser and curiouser!' cried Alice.
Lewis Carroll (Charles Lutwidge Dodgson; 1832–98) British writer. *Alice's Adventures in Wonderland*, Ch. 2

5 This world is very odd we see,
We do not comprehend it;
But in one fact we all agree,
God won't, and we can't mend it.
Arthur Hugh Clough (1819–61) British poet. *Dipsychus*, Bk. II

6 Bewitched, Bothered and Bewildered.
Lorenz Hart (1895–1943) US songwriter. From the musical *Babes in Arms*. Song title

7 I had nothing to offer anybody except my own confusion.
Jack Kerouac (1922–69) US novelist. *On the Road*, Pt. II

8 Confusion is a word we have invented for an order which is not understood.
Henry Miller (1891–1980) US novelist. *Tropic of Cancer*

9 . . . the state of things and the dispositions of men were then such, that a man could not well tell whom he might trust or whom he might fear.
Sir Thomas More (1478–1535) English lawyer and scholar. Refering to England. *The English Works of Sir Thomas More*, Vol. I

10 I don't want you to think I'm not incoherent.
Harold W. Ross (1892–1951) US journalist. *The Years with Ross* (James Thurber)

11 For mine own part, it was Greek to me.
William Shakespeare (1564–1616) English dramatist. *Julius Caesar*, I:2

12 The attempt and not the deed,
Confounds us.
William Shakespeare *Macbeth*, II:2

13 That blessed mood,
In which the burthen of the mystery,
In which the heavy and the weary weight
Of all this unintelligible world,
Is lightened.
William Wordsworth (1770–1850) British poet. *Lines composed a few miles above Tintern Abbey*

CONGREVE, William

(1670–1729) British Restoration dramatist, whose comedies include *Love for Love* (1695) and *The Way of the World* (1700). He also wrote a tragedy, *The Mourning Bride* (1697).

Quotations about Congreve

1 William Congreve is the only sophisticated playwright England has produced; and like Shaw, Sheridan, and Wilde, his nearest rivals, he was brought up in Ireland.
Kenneth Tynan (1927–80) British theater critic. *Curtains*, 'The Way of the World'

2 He spoke of his works as trifles that were beneath him.
Voltaire (François-Marie Arouet; 1694–1778) French writer. *Letters concerning the English nation*

Quotations by Congreve

3 She lays it on with a trowel.
The Double Dealer, III:10

4 See how love and murder will out.
The Double Dealer, IV:6

5 I am always of the opinion with the learned, if they speak first.
Incognita

6 O fie miss, you must not kiss and tell.
Love for Love, II:10

7 I know that's a secret, for it's whispered every where.
Love for Love, III:3

8 Music has charms to soothe a savage breast.
The Mourning Bride, I

9 Heaven has no rage like love to hatred turned,
Nor hell a fury like a woman scorned.
The Mourning Bride, III

10 SHARPER. Thus grief still treads upon the heels of pleasure:
Marry'd in haste, we may repent at leisure.
SETTER. Some by experience find those words mis-plac'd:
At leisure marry'd, they repent in haste.
The Old Bachelor, V:8

11 Courtship to marriage, as a very witty prologue to a very dull Play.
The Old Bachelor, V:10

12 Alack he's gone the way of all flesh.
Squire Bickerstaff Detected, attrib.

13 Say what you will, 'tis better to be left than never to have been loved.
The Way of the World, II:1

14 Lord, what is a lover that it can give? Why one makes lovers as fast as one pleases, and they live as long as one pleases, and they die as soon as one pleases: and then if one pleases one makes more.
The Way of the World, II:4

15 I nauseate walking; 'tis a country diversion, I loathe the country and everything that relates to it.
The Way of the World, IV:4

16 I hope you do not think me prone to any iteration of nuptials.
The Way of the World, IV:12

17 O, she is the antidote to desire.
The Way of the World, IV:14

CONNOLLY, Cyril (Vernon)

(1903–74) British journalist and writer. A contributor to the *New Statesman*, the *Sunday Times*, and other papers, he published several collections of essays, such as *Enemies of Promise* (1938).

Quotations about Connolly

1 Writers like Connolly gave pleasure a bad name.
E. M. Forster (1879–1970) British novelist. Attrib.

2 The key to his behaviour was self-indulgence, which he made almost a rule of life.
Stephen Spender (1909–) British poet. *The Observer*, 10 July 1983

Quotations by Connolly

3 It is closing time in the gardens of the West.
The Condemned Playground

4 A great writer creates a world of his own and his readers are proud to live in it. A lesser writer may entice them in for a moment, but soon he will watch them filing out.
Enemies of Promise, Ch. 1

5 The ape-like virtues without which no one can enjoy a public school.
Enemies of Promise, Ch. 1

6 Literature is the art of writing something that will be read twice; journalism what will be grasped at once.
Enemies of Promise, Ch. 3

7 An author arrives at a good style when his language performs what is required of it without shyness.
Enemies of Promise, Ch. 3

8 As repressed sadists are supposed to become policemen or butchers so those with irrational fear of life become publishers.
Enemies of Promise, Ch. 3

9 Whom the gods wish to destroy they first call promising.
Enemies of Promise, Ch. 3

10 There is no more sombre enemy of good art than the pram in the hall.
Enemies of Promise, Ch. 3

11 All charming people have something to conceal, usually their total dependence on the appreciation of others.
Enemies of Promise, Ch. 16

12 I have always disliked myself at any given moment; the total of such moments is my life.
Enemies of Promise, Ch. 18

13 Boys do not grow up gradually. They move forward in spurts like the hands of clocks in railway stations.
Enemies of Promise, Ch. 18

14 The only way for writers to meet is to share a quick pee over a common lamp-post.
The Unquiet Grave

15 Life is a maze in which we take the wrong turning before we have learnt to walk.
The Unquiet Grave

16 In the sex-war thoughtlessness is the weapon of the male, vindictiveness of the female.
The Unquiet Grave

17 There is no fury like an ex-wife searching for a new lover.
The Unquiet Grave

18 Imprisoned in every fat man a thin one is wildly signalling to be let out.
Similar sentiments have been stated by others. *The Unquiet Grave*

19 Better to write for yourself and have no public, than write for the public and have no self.
Turnstile One (ed. V. S. Pritchett)

20 The man who is master of his passions is Reason's slave.
Turnstile One (ed. V. S. Pritchett)

CONSCIENCE

See also integrity

1 Conscience, I say, not thine own, but of the other: for why is my liberty judged of another man's conscience?
Bible: I Corinthians 10:29

2 All a man can betray is his conscience.
Joseph Conrad *Under Western Eyes*

3 Conscience is the internal perception of the rejection of a particular wish operating within us.
Sigmund Freud (1856–1939) Austrian psychoanalyst. *Totem and Taboo*

4 Conscience is a coward, and those faults it has not strength enough to prevent it seldom has justice enough to accuse.
Oliver Goldsmith (1728–74) Irish-born British writer. *The Vicar of Wakefield*, Ch. 13

5 Those who follow their conscience directly are of my religion; and, for my part, I am of the same religion as all those who are brave and true.
Henri IV (1533–1610) King of France. Henri had become a Roman Catholic, as a political move, in 1576. Letter to M. de Batz, 1577

6 Conscience is the inner voice that warns us somebody may be looking.
H. L. Mencken (1880–1956) US journalist. *A Mencken Chrestomathy*

7 Thus conscience does make cowards of us all;
And thus the native hue of resolution
Is sicklied o'er with the pale cast of thought.
And enterprises of great pith and moment
With this regard their currents turn awry,
And lose the name of action.
William Shakespeare (1564–1616) English dramatist. *Hamlet*, III:1

8 A peace above all earthly dignities,
A still and quiet conscience.
William Shakespeare *Henry VIII*, III:2

9 Foul whisperings are abroad. Unnatural deeds
Do breed unnatural troubles; infected minds
To their deaf pillows will discharge their secrets;
More needs she the divine than the physician.
William Shakespeare *Macbeth*, V:1

10 Give me another horse! bind up my wounds!
Have mercy, Jesu! Soft! I did but dream.
O coward conscience, how dost thou afflict me!
William Shakespeare *Richard III*, V:3

11 My conscience hath a thousand several tongues,
And every tongue brings in several tale,
And every tale condemns me for a villain.
William Shakespeare *Richard III*, V:3

12 Conscience is but a word that cowards use,
Devis'd at first to keep the strong in awe.
William Shakespeare *Richard III*, V:3

CONSERVATION

See ecology

CONSERVATISM

See also change

1 The most conservative man in the world is the British Trade Unionist when you want to change him.
Ernest Bevin (1881–1951) British trade-union leader and politician. Speech, Trade Union Congress, 8 Sept 1927

2 All conservatism is based upon the idea that if you leave things alone you leave them as they are. But you do not. If you leave a thing alone you leave it to a torrent of change.
G. K. Chesterton (1874–1936) British writer. *Orthodoxy*, Ch. 7

3 I love everything that's old: old friends, old times, old manners, old books, old wine.
Oliver Goldsmith (1728–74) Irish-born British writer. *She Stoops to Conquer*, I

4 You can't teach the old maestro a new tune.
Jack Kerouac (1922–69) US novelist. *On the Road*, Pt. I

5 I do not know which makes a man more conservative – to know

nothing but the present, or nothing but the past.

John Maynard Keynes (1883–1946) British economist. *The End of Laisser-Faire*, I

6 What is conservatism? Is it not adherence to the old and tried, against the new and untried?

Abraham Lincoln (1809–65) US statesman. Speech, 27 Feb 1860

7 You can't teach an old dogma new tricks.

Dorothy Parker (1893–1967) US writer. *Wit's End* (R. E. Drennan)

8 The radical invents the views. When he has worn them out, the conservative adopts them.

Mark Twain (Samuel Langhorne Clemens; 1835–1910) US writer. *Notebooks*

CONSTANCY

See also change, conservatism

1 A foolish consistency is the hobgoblin of little minds, adored by little statesmen and philosophers and divines. With consistency a great soul has simply nothing to do.

Ralph Waldo Emerson (1803–82) US poet and essayist. *Essays*, 'Self-reliance'

2 Consistency is contrary to nature, contrary to life. The only completely consistent people are the dead.

Aldous Huxley (1894–1964) British novelist. *Do What you Will*

3 *Plus ça change, plus c'est la même chose.*
The more things change, the more they stay the same.

Alphonse Karr (1808–90) French writer. *Les Guêpes*, Jan 1849

4 For men may come and men may go
But I go on for ever.

Alfred, Lord Tennyson (1809–92) British poet. *The Brook*

5 Still glides the Stream, and shall for ever glide;
The Form remains, the Function never dies.

William Wordsworth (1770–1850) British poet. *The River Duddon*, 'After-Thought'

CONTEMPT

See also ridicule

1 She was nothing more than a mere good-tempered, civil and obliging young woman; as such we could scarcely dislike her – she was only an Object of Contempt.

Jane Austen (1775–1817) British novelist. *Love and Friendship*

2 'You threaten us, fellow? Do your worst,
Blow your pipe there till you burst!'

Robert Browning (1812–89) British poet. *The Pied Piper of Hamelin*

3 It is alarming and also nauseating to see Mr Gandhi, a seditious Middle Temple lawyer, now posing as a fakir of a type well-known in the East, striding half-naked up the steps of the vice-regal palace.

Winston Churchill (1874–1965) British statesman. When Gandhi was released from jail to take part in a conference. Speech, Epping, 23 Feb 1931

4 He looked at me as if I was a side dish he hadn't ordered.

Ring Lardner Jnr (1885–1933) American humorist. Referring to W. H. Taft, US president (1909–13). *The Home Book of Humorous Quotations* (A. K. Adams)

5 Disdain and scorn ride sparkling in her eyes.

William Shakespeare (1564–1616) English dramatist. *Much Ado About Nothing*, III:1

6 Teach not thy lip such scorn, for it was made
For kissing, lady, not for such contempt.

William Shakespeare *Richard III*, I:2

CONTENTMENT

See also happiness, satisfaction

1 Live with the gods. And he does so who constantly shows them that his soul is satisfied with what is assigned to him.

Marcus Aurelius (121–180 AD) Roman emperor. *Meditations*, Bk. V, Ch. 27

2 Sweet Stay-at-Home, sweet Well-content.

W. H. Davies (1871–1940) British poet. *Sweet Stay-at-Home*

3 Here with a Loaf of Bread beneath the Bough,
A Flask of Wine, a Book of Verse – and Thou
Beside me singing in the Wilderness –
And Wilderness is Paradise enow.

Edward Fitzgerald (1809–83) British poet. *The Rubáiyát of Omar Khayyám*

4 I got rhythm,
I got music,
I got my man—
Who could ask for anything more.

Ira Gershwin (1898–1937) US composer. *Girl Crazy*

5 Notwithstanding the poverty of my outside experience, I have always had a significance for myself, and every chance to stumble along my straight and narrow little path, and to worship at the feet of my Deity, and what more can a human soul ask for?

Alice James (1848–92) US diarist. *The Diary of Alice James* (ed. Leon Edel)

6 If I had not been born Perón, I would have liked to be Perón.

Juan Perón (1895–1974) Argentine statesman. *The Observer*, 'Sayings of the Week', 21 Feb 1960

7 Who doth ambition shun
And loves to live i' the sun,
Seeking the food he eats,
And pleas'd with what he gets.

William Shakespeare (1564–1616) English dramatist. *As You Like It*, II:5

8 I earn that I eat, get that I wear, owe no man hate, envy no man's happiness, glad of other men's good, content with my harm.

William Shakespeare *As You Like It*, III:2

9 O, this life
Is nobler than attending for a check,
Richer than doing nothing for a bribe,
Prouder than rustling in unpaid-for silk.

William Shakespeare *Cymbeline*, III:3

10 Nought's had, all's spent,
Where our desire is got without content.
'Tis safer to be that which we destroy,
Than by destruction dwell in doubtful joy.

William Shakespeare *Macbeth*, III:2

CONTRACEPTION

See also sex

1 Vasectomy means not ever having to say you're sorry.

Larry Adler (1914–) US harmonica player and entertainer. Before his vasectomy operation

2 I want to tell you a terrific story about oral contraception. I asked this girl to sleep with me and she said 'no'.

Woody Allen (Allen Stewart Konigsberg; 1935–) US film actor. *Woody Allen: Clown Prince of American Humor* (Adler and Feinman), Ch. 2

3 The best contraceptive is a glass of

cold water: not before or after, but instead.
Anonymous

4 He no play-a da game. He no make-a da rules!
Earl Butz (1909–) US politician. Referring to the Pope's strictures against contraception. Remark, 1974

5 Accidents will occur in the best-regulated families.
Charles Dickens (1812–70) British novelist. *David Copperfield*, Ch. 28

6 The command 'Be fruitful and multiply' was promulgated according to our authorities, when the population of the world consisted of two people.
Dean Inge (1860–1954) British churchman; Dean of St Pauls. *More Lay Thoughts of a Dean*

7 Where are the children I might have had? You may suppose I might have wanted them. Drowned to the accompaniment of the rattling of a thousand douche bags.
Malcolm Lowry (1909–57) British novelist. *Under the Volcano*, Ch. 10

8 I would not like to leave contraception on the long finger too long.
Jack Lynch (1917–) Irish statesman. *Irish Times*, 23 May 1971

9 It is now quite lawful for a Catholic woman to avoid pregnancy by a resort to mathematics, though she is still forbidden to resort to physics and chemistry.
H. L. Mencken (1880–1956) US journalist. *Notebooks*, 'Minority Report'

10 Contraceptives should be used on every conceivable occasion.
Spike Milligan (1918–) British comic actor and author. *The Last Goon Show of All*

11 We want far better reasons for having children than not knowing how to prevent them.
Dora Russell (1894–1986) *Hypatia*, Ch. 4

12 Skullion had little use for contraceptives at the best of times. Unnatural, he called them, and placed them in the lower social category of things along with elastic-sided boots and made-up bow ties. Not the sort of attire for a gentleman.
Tom Sharpe (1928–) British novelist. *Porterhouse Blue*, Ch. 9

13 Protestant women may take the Pill. Roman Catholic women must keep taking the *Tablet*.
Irene Thomas (1920–) British writer and broadcaster. *The Tablet* is a British Roman Catholic newspaper. Attrib.

14 Marriages are not normally made to avoid having children.
Rudolf Virchow (1821–1902) German pathologist. *Bulletin of the New York Academy of Medicine*, 4:995, 1928 (F. H. Garrison)

CONTROVERSY

See argument

CONVERSATION

See also speech

1 I have but ninepence in ready money, but I can draw for a thousand pounds.
Joseph Addison (1672–1719) British essayist. Comparing his ability to make conversation and to write. *Life of Johnson* (Boswell)

2 JOHNSON. Well, we had a good talk.
BOSWELL. Yes, Sir; you tossed and gored several persons.
James Boswell (1740–95) Scottish lawyer and writer. *Life of Johnson*, Vol. II

3 Although there exist many thousand subjects for elegant conversation, there are persons who cannot meet a cripple without talking about feet.
Ernest Bramah (1869–1942) British writer. *The Wallet of Kai Lung*

4 An indigestion is an excellent common-place for two people that never met before.
William Hazlitt (1788–1830) English essayist and journalist. *Literary Remains*, 'The Fight'

5 Questioning is not the mode of conversation among gentlemen.
Samuel Johnson (1709–84) British lexicographer. *Life of Johnson* (J. Boswell), Vol. II

6 If you haven't anything nice to say about anyone, come and sit by me.
Alice Roosevelt Longworth (1884–1980) US hostess. Embroidered on a cushion at her home. *New York Times*, 25 Feb 1980

7 Beware of the conversationalist who adds 'in other words'. He is merely starting afresh.
Robert Morley (1908–) British actor. *The Observer*, 'Sayings of the Week', 6 Dec 1964

8 Ideal conversation must be an exchange of thought, and not, as many of those who worry most about their shortcomings believe, an eloquent exhibition of wit or oratory.
Emily Post (1873–1960) US writer. *Etiquette*, Ch. 6

9 Conversation has a kind of charm about it, an insinuating and insidious something that elicits secrets from us just like love or liquor.
Seneca (c. 4 BC–65 AD) Roman author. *Epistles*

10 BEATRICE. I wonder that you will still be talking, Signior Benedick: nobody marks you.
BENEDICK. What! my dear Lady Disdain, are you yet living?
William Shakespeare (1564–1616) English dramatist. *Much Ado About Nothing*, I:1

11 She speaks poniards, and every word stabs: if her breath were as terrible as her terminations, there were no living near her; she would infect to the north star.
William Shakespeare *Much Ado About Nothing*, II:1

12 Teas,
Where small talk dies in agonies.
Percy Bysshe Shelley (1792–1822) British poet. *Peter Bell the Third*

13 There is no such thing as conversation. It is an illusion. There are intersecting monologues, that is all.
Rebecca West (Cicely Isabel Fairfield; 1892–1983) British novelist and journalist. *There Is No Conversation*, Ch. 1

14 A good listener is not someone who has nothing to say. A good listener is a good talker with a sore throat.
Katherine Whitehorn (1926–) British journalist. Attrib.

15 'What ho!' I said, 'What ho!' said Motty. 'What ho! What ho!' 'What ho! What ho! What ho!' After that it seemed rather difficult to go on with the conversation.
P. G. Wodehouse (1881–1975) British humorous novelist. *Carry On Jeeves*

COOLIDGE, (John) Calvin

(1872–1933) 30th president of the USA (1923–29). A Republican, he served as governor of Massachusetts and as vice-president to Warren G. Harding before succeeding to the presidency.

Quotations about Coolidge

1 He looks as if he had been weaned on a pickle.
Alice Roosevelt Longworth (1884–1980) US hostess. *Crowded Hours*

2 How could they tell?
Dorothy Parker (1893–1967) US writer. On being told that Coolidge had died. *You Might As Well Live* (J. Keats)

Quotations by Coolidge

3 There is no right to strike against the public safety by anybody, anywhere, any time.
Referring to the Boston police strike. Remark, 14 Sept 1919

4 He said he was against it.
Reply when asked what a clergyman had said regarding sin in his sermon. Attrib.

5 The business of America is business.
Speech, Washington, 17 Jan 1925

CORRUPTION

See also bribery, decline

1 Among a people generally corrupt, liberty cannot long exist.
Edmund Burke (1729–97) British politician. Letter to the Sheriffs of Bristol, 1777

2 We have a cancer within, close to the Presidency, that is growing. It is growing daily.
John Dean (1938–) US presidential counsel. Referring to the Watergate scandal. *The White House Transcripts*, 1974

3 . . . no one before Anselm became a bishop or abbot who did not first become the king's man and from his hand receive investiture by the gift of the pastoral staff.
Eadmer (c. 1055–c. 1124) English cleric and historian. *Historia Novorum in Anglia*

4 Corruption, the most infallible symptom of constitutional liberty.
Edward Gibbon (1737–94) British historian. *Decline and Fall of the Roman Empire*, Ch. 21

5 I order you to hold a free election, but forbid you to elect anyone but Richard my clerk.
Henry II (1133–89) King of England. Writ to the electors of the See of Winchester regarding the election of a new bishop; Richard d'Ilchester was one of the king's trusted servants. *Recueil des Historiens des Gaules et de la France*, XIV

6 The hungry sheep look up, and are not fed,
But, swoln with wind and the rank mist they draw,
Rot inwardly, and foul contagion spread.
John Milton (1608–74) English poet. *Lycidas*

7 As killing as the canker to the rose.
John Milton *Lycidas*

8 There will be no whitewash in the White House.
Richard Milhous Nixon (1913–) US president. Referring to the Watergate scandal. Statement, 17 Apr 1973

9 All things can corrupt perverted minds.
Ovid (Publius Ovidius Naso; 43 BC–17 AD) Roman poet. *Tristia*, Bk. II

10 Any institution which does not suppose the people good, and the magistrate corruptible is evil.
Robespierre (1758–94) French lawyer and revolutionary. *Déclaration des Droits de l'homme*, 24 Apr 1793

11 Something is rotten in the state of Denmark.
William Shakespeare (1564–1616) English dramatist. *Hamlet*, I:4

12 For sweetest things turn sourest by their deeds:
Lilies that fester smell far worse than weeds.
William Shakespeare *Sonnet 94*

13 Let none presume
To wear an undeserved dignity.
O! that estates, degrees, and offices
Were not deriv'd corruptly, and that clear honour
Were purchased by the merit of the wearer.
How many then should cover that stand bare;
How many be commanded that command;
How much low peasantry would then be glean'd
From the true seed of honour; and how much honour
Pick'd from the chaff and ruin of the times
To be new varnish'd!
William Shakespeare *The Merchant of Venice*, II:9

14 A reformer is a guy who rides through a sewer in a glass-bottomed boat.
James J. Walker (1881–1946) US politician. Speech, New York, 1928

15 All those men have their price.
Robert Walpole (1676–1745) British statesman. *Memoirs of Sir Robert Walpole* (W. Coxe)

COSMETICS

See also appearance

1 Most women are not so young as they are painted.
Max Beerbohm (1872–1956) British writer. *A Defence of Cosmetics*

2 Wherever one wants to be kissed.
Coco Chanel (1883–1971) French dress designer. When asked where one should wear perfume. *Coco Chanel, Her Life, Her Secrets* (Marcel Haedrich)

3 Waits at the window wearing the face that she keeps in a jar by the door.
John Lennon (1940–80) British rock musician. *Eleanor Rigby*

4 In the factory we make cosmetics. In the store we sell hope.
Charles Revson (1906–75) US business tycoon. *Fire and Ice* (A. Tobias)

COUNTRIES

See nationality, nations, places

COUNTRYSIDE

See also agriculture, ecology, flowers, nature, trees

1 I nauseate walking; 'tis a country diversion, I loathe the country and everything that relates to it.
William Congreve (1670–1729) British Restoration dramatist. *The Way of the World*, IV:4

2 God made the country, and man made the town.
William Cowper (1731–1800) British poet. *The Task*

3 Ever charming, ever new,
When will the landscape tire the view?
John Dyer (1700–58) British poet. *Grongar Hill*

4 . . . the sanctuary and special delight of kings, where, laying aside their cares, they withdraw to refresh themselves with a little hunting; there, away from the turmoils inherent in a court, they breathe the pleasure of natural freedom.
Richard FitzNigel (d. 1198) Treasurer of England and Bishop of London. Referring to the royal forests. *Dialogus de Scaccario*, Bk. I, Ch. 11

5 There is nothing good to be had in the country, or, if there is, they will not let you have it.
William Hazlitt (1778–1830) British essayist. *Observations on Wordsworth's* 'Excursion'

6 When I am in the country I wish to vegetate like the country.
William Hazlitt *On Going a Journey*

7 Here of a Sunday morning
My love and I would lie,
And see the coloured counties,
And hear the larks so high
About us in the sky.
A. E. Housman (1859–1936) British scholar and poet. *A Shropshire Lad*, 'Bredon Hill'

8 Learn from the beasts the physic of the field.
Alexander Pope (1688–1744) English poet. *Essay on Man*

9 It must be generations since anyone but highbrows lived in this cottage . . . I imagine most of the agricultural labourers round here commute from London.
Anthony Powell (1905–) British novelist. *A Dance to the Music of Time: The Kindly Ones*, Ch. 2

10 O, Brignal banks are wild and fair,
  And Gretna woods are green,
And you may gather garlands there
  Would grace a summer queen.
Walter Scott (1771–1832) Scottish novelist. *Rokeby*, III

11 Hath not old custom made this life more sweet
Than that of painted pomp? Are not these woods
More free from peril than the envious court?
Here feel we but the penalty of Adam,
The seasons' difference; as, the icy fang
And churlish chiding of the winter's wind,
Which, when it bites and blows upon my body,
Even till I shrink with cold, I smile and say,
'This is no flattery.'
William Shakespeare (1564–1616) English dramatist. *As You Like It*, II:1

12 Under the greenwood tree
Who loves to lie with me,
And turn his merry note
Unto the sweet bird's throat,
Come hither, come hither, come hither.
Here shall he see
No enemy
But winter and rough weather.
William Shakespeare *As You Like It*, II:5

13 Anybody can be good in the country.
Oscar Wilde (1854–1900) Irish-born British dramatist. *The Picture of Dorian Gray*, Ch. 19

14 One impulse from a vernal wood
May teach you more of man,
Of moral evil and of good,
Than all the sages can.
William Wordsworth (1770–1850) British poet. *The Tables Turned*

COURAGE

See also endurance, heroism, patriotism

1 Because of my title, I was the first to enter here. I shall be the last to go out.
Duchesse d'Alençon (d. 1897) Bavarian-born duchess. Refusing help during a fire, 4 May 1897, at a charity bazaar in Paris. She died along with 120 others. Attrib.

2 The sons of the prophet were brave men and bold,
And quite unaccustomed to fear,
But the bravest by far in the ranks of the Shah
Was Abdul the Bulbul Amir.
Anonymous *Abdul the Bulbul Amir*

3 Who dares, wins.
Anonymous Motto of the British Special Air Service regiment

4 No coward soul is mine,
No trembler in the world's storm-troubled sphere:
I see Heaven's glories shine,
And faith shines equal, arming me from fear.
Emily Brontë (1818–48) British novelist. *Last Lines*

5 Perhaps your fear in passing judgement is greater than mine in receiving it.
Giordano Bruno (1548–1600) Italian philosopher. Said to the cardinals who excommunicated him, 8 Feb 1600. Attrib.

6 And though hard be the task,
'Keep a stiff upper lip.'
Phoebe Cary (1824–71) US poet. *Keep a Stiff Upper Lip*

7 Down these mean streets a man must go who is not himself mean; who is neither tarnished nor afraid.
Raymond Chandler (1888–1959) US novelist. *The Simple Art of Murder*

8 Take a step forward, lads. It will be easier that way.
Erskine Childers (1870–1922) British-born author and Irish patriot. Last words before being executed by firing squad, 24 Nov 1922. *The Riddle of Erskine Childers* (A. Boyle)

9 The Red Badge of Courage.
Stephen Crane (1871–1900) US writer. *Title of novel*

10 I'll bell the cat.
Archibald Douglas (1449–1514) Scottish nobleman. Of his proposed capture of Robert Cochrane (executed 1482); the phrase 'bell the cat' was earlier used by Eustache Deschamps in his *Ballade: Le Chat et les souris*

11 None but the Brave deserves the Fair.
John Dryden (1631–1700) British poet and dramatist. *Alexander's Feast*

12 Courage is the price that Life exacts for granting peace.
Amelia Earhart (1898–1937) US flyer. *Courage*

13 The ability to get to the verge without getting into the war is the necessary art. If you cannot master it, you inevitably get into war. If you try to run away from it, if you are scared to go to the brink, you are lost.
John Foster Dulles (1888–1959) US politician. The origin of the term 'brinkmanship'. *Life*, 16 Jan 1956

14 Come cheer up, my lads! 'tis to glory we steer,
To add something more to this wonderful year;
To honour we call you, not press you like slaves,
For who are so free as the sons of the waves?
Heart of oak are our ships,
Heart of oak are our men:
We always are ready;
Steady, boys, steady;
We'll fight and we'll conquer again and again.
David Garrick (1717–79) British actor and manager. *Heart of Oak*

15 The boy stood on the burning deck
Whence all but he had fled;
The flame that lit the battle's wreck
Shone round him o'er the dead.
Felicia Dorothea Hemans (1793–1835) British poet. *Casabianca*

16 It is better to be the widow of a hero than the wife of a coward.
Dolores Ibarruri (1895–) Spanish politician. Speech, Valencia, 1936

17 It is better to die on your feet than to live on your knees.
Dolores Ibarruri Speech, Paris, 3 Sept 1936

18 . . . we could never learn to be brave and patient, if there were only joy in the world.
Helen Keller (1880–1968) US writer and lecturer. *Atlantic Monthly* (May 1890)

19 Then out spake brave Horatius,
The Captain of the Gate:

'To every man upon this earth
Death cometh soon or late.
And how can man die better
Than facing fearful odds,
For the ashes of his fathers,
And the temples of his Gods?'

Lord Macaulay (1800–59) British historian. *Lays of Ancient Rome,* 'Horatius', 27

20 The stubborn spear-men still made good
Their dark impenetrable wood,
Each stepping where his comrade stood,
The instant that he fell.

Walter Scott (1771–1832) Scottish novelist. *Marmion,* VI

21 Once more unto the breach, dear friends, once more;
Or close the wall up with our English dead.

William Shakespeare (1564–1616) English dramatist. *Henry V,* III:1

22 I dare do all that may become a man;
Who dares do more is none.

William Shakespeare *Macbeth,* I:7

23 Lay on, Macduff;
And damn'd be him that first cries, 'Hold, enough!'

William Shakespeare *Macbeth,* V:5

24 He was a bold man that first eat an oyster.

Jonathan Swift (1667–1745) Irish-born Anglican priest and writer. *Polite Conversation,* Dialogue 2

25 Half a league, half a league,
Half a league onward,
All in the valley of Death
Rode the six hundred.

Alfred, Lord Tennyson (1809–92) British poet. *The Charge of the Light Brigade*

26 Into the jaws of Death,
Into the mouth of Hell.

Alfred, Lord Tennyson *The Charge of the Light Brigade*

27 Fortune favours the brave.

Terence (Publius Terentius Afer; c. 190–159 BC) Roman poet. *Phormio*

28 The three-o'-clock in the morning courage, which Bonaparte thought was the rarest.

Henry David Thoreau (1817–62) US writer. *Walden,* 'Sounds'

COURTESY

See also chivalry, etiquette, manners, respect

1 Civility costs nothing.

Proverb

2 If a man be gracious and courteous to strangers, it shews he is a citizen of the world.

Francis Bacon (1561–1626) English philosopher. *Essays,* 'Of Goodness and Goodness of Nature'

3 The English are polite by telling lies. The Americans are polite by telling the truth.

Malcolm Bradbury (1932–) British academic and novelist. *Stepping Westward,* Bk. II, Ch. 5

4 Courtesy is not dead – it has merely taken refuge in Great Britain.

Georges Duhamel (1884–1966) French writer. *The Observer,* 'Sayings of Our Times', 31 May 1953

COWARD, Sir Noël

(1899–1973) British actor, dramatist, and songwriter. After his first success, *The Vortex* (1924), he wrote a number of comedies, including *Blithe Spirit* (1941) and *Brief Encounter* (1946), both made into films. His songs include *Mad Dogs and Englishmen.*

Quotations about Coward

1 He was his own greatest invention.

John Osborne (1929–) British dramatist. Attrib.

2 He was once Slightly in *Peter Pan,* and has been wholly in Peter Pan ever since.

Kenneth Tynan (1927–80) British theater critic. Attrib.

Quotations by Coward

3 We have no reliable guarantee that the afterlife will be any less exasperating than this one, have we?

Blithe Spirit, I

4 Never mind, dear, we're all made the same, though some more than others.

The Café de la Paix

5 There's always something fishy about the French.

Conversation Piece, I:6

6 Everybody was up to something, especially, of course, those who were up to nothing.

Future Indefinite

7 Sunburn is very becoming – but only when it is even – one must be careful not to look like a mixed grill.

The Lido Beach

8 And though the Van Dycks have to go
And we pawn the Bechstein grand,
We'll stand by the Stately Homes of England.

Operette, 'The Stately Homes of England'

9 The Stately Homes of England
How beautiful they stand,
To prove the upper classes
Have still the upper hand.

Operette, 'The Stately Homes of England'

10 Very flat, Norfolk.

Private Lives

11 Strange how potent cheap music is.

Private Lives

12 Certain women should be struck regularly, like gongs.

Private Lives

13 She refused to begin the 'Beguine'
Tho' they besought her to
And with language profane and obscene
She curs'd the man who taught her to
She curs'd Cole Porter too!

Sigh No More, 'Nina'

14 Dance, dance, dance little lady.

Title of song

15 Don't let's be beastly to the Germans.

Title of song

16 Don't put your daughter on the stage, Mrs Worthington.

Title of song

17 Mad about the boy.

Title of song

18 Mad dogs and Englishmen go out in the mid-day sun.

Title of song

19 Poor Little Rich Girl.

Title of song

20 Twentieth-Century Blues.

Title of song

21 I've over-educated myself in all the things I shouldn't have known at all.

Wild Oats

22 Work is much more fun than fun.

The Observer, 'Sayings of the Week', 21 June 1963

23 Dear 338171 (May I call you 338?).

Starting a letter to T. E. Lawrence, who had retired from public life to become Aircraftsman Ross, 338171. *Letters to T. E. Lawrence*

24 I never realized before that Albert married beneath him.

After seeing a certain actress in the role of Queen Victoria. *Tynan on Theatre* (K. Tynan)

COWARDICE

See also self-preservation

1 Probably a fear we have of facing up to the real issues. Could you say we were guilty of Noël Cowardice?

Peter De Vries (1910–) US novelist. *Comfort me with Apples*, Ch. 8

2 None but a coward dares to boast that he has never known fear.

Marshal Foch (1851–1929) French soldier. Attrib.

3 He led his regiment from behind
He found it less exciting.

W. S. Gilbert (1836–1911) British dramatist. *The Gondoliers*, I

4 When the foeman bares his steel,
Tarantara! tarantara!
We uncomfortable feel.

W. S. Gilbert *The Pirates of Penzance*, II

5 To a surprising extent the war-lords in shining armour, the apostles of the martial virtues, tend not to die fighting when the time comes. History is full of ignominious getaways by the great and famous.

George Orwell (Eric Blair; 1903–50) British novelist. *Who Are the War Criminals?*

6 The summer soldier and the sunshine patriot will, in this crisis, shrink from the service of their country.

Thomas Paine (1737–1809) British writer. *Pennsylvania Journal*, 'The American Crisis'

7 Thus conscience does make cowards of us all;
And thus the native hue of resolution
Is sicklied o'er with the pale cast of thought.

William Shakespeare (1564–1616) English dramatist. *Hamlet*, III:1

8 Some craven scruple
Of thinking too precisely on th' event.

William Shakespeare *Hamlet*, IV:4

9 I dare not fight; but I will wink and hold out mine iron.

William Shakespeare *Henry V*, II:1

10 Cowards die many times before their deaths:
The valiant never taste of death but once.
Of all the wonders that I yet have heard,
It seems to me most strange that men should fear;
Seeing that death, a necessary end,
Will come when it will come.

William Shakespeare *Julius Caesar*, II:2

COWPER, William

(1731–1800) British poet. A lawyer and commissioner of bankrupts, his life was dogged by depression, bouts of insanity, and suicide attempts. His ballad *John Gilpin's Ride* (1783) and the long poem *The Task* (1785) established his reputation; he also translated Homer.

Quotations about Cowper

1 His taste lay in smiling, colloquial, good-natured humour; his melancholy was a black and diseased melancholy, not a grave and rich contemplativeness.

E. Brydges *Recollection of Foreign Travel*

2 That maniacal Calvinist and coddled poet.

Lord Byron (1788–1824) British poet. Attrib.

Quotations by Cowper

3 Regions Caesar never knew
Thy posterity shall sway,
Where his eagles never flew,
None invincible as they.

Boadicea

4 When the British warrior queen,
Bleeding from the Roman rods,
Sought, with an indignant mien,
Counsel of her country's gods.

Boadicea

5 Rome shall perish – write that word
In the blood that she has spilt.

Boadicea

6 We perish'd, each alone:
But I beneath a rougher sea,
And whelm'd in deeper gulphs than he.

The Castaway

7 He found it inconvenient to be poor.

Charity

8 Absence from whom we love is worse than death.

'Hope, like the Short-lived Ray'

9 John Gilpin was a citizen
Of credit and renown,
A train-band captain eke was he
Of famous London town.

John Gilpin

10 To-morrow is our wedding-day,
And we will then repair
Unto the Bell at Edmonton,
All in a chaise and pair.

John Gilpin

11 Now let us sing, Long live the king,
And Gilpin, long live he;
And when he next doth ride abroad,
May I be there to see!

John Gilpin

12 My hat and wig will soon be here,
They are upon the road.

John Gilpin

13 Says John, It is my wedding-day,
And all the world would stare,
If wife should dine at Edmonton,
And I should dine at Ware.

John Gilpin

14 What peaceful hours I once enjoyed!
How sweet their memory still!
But they have left an aching void
The world can never fill.

Olney Hymns, 1

15 Prayer makes the Christian's armour bright;
And Satan trembles when he sees
The weakest saint upon his knees.

Olney Hymns, 29

16 I seem forsaken and alone,
I hear the lion roar;
And every door is shut but one,
And that is Mercy's door.

Olney Hymns, 33

17 God moves in a mysterious way
His wonders to perform;
He plants his footsteps in the sea,
And rides upon the storm.

Olney Hymns, 35

18 The bud may have a bitter taste,
But sweet will be the flower.

Olney Hymns, 35

19 The poplars are felled, farewell to the shade,
And the whispering sound of the cool colonnade!

The Poplar Field

20 Mortals, whose pleasures are their only care,
First wish to be imposed on, and then are.

The Progress of Error

21 For 'tis a truth well known to most,
That whatsoever thing is lost –
We seek it, ere it come to light,
In every cranny but the right.

The Retired Cat

22 God made the country, and man made the town.
The Task

23 England, with all thy faults, I love thee still,
My country.
The Task

24 Variety's the very spice of life
That gives it all its flavour.
The Task

25 While the bubbling and loud-hissing urn
Throws up a steamy column, and the cups,
That cheer but not inebriate, wait on each,
So let us welcome peaceful evening in.
The Task

26 Nature is but a name for an effect
Whose cause is God.
The Task

27 Oh for a lodge in some vast wilderness,
Some boundless contiguity of shade,
Where rumour of oppression and deceit,
Of unsuccessful or successful war,
Might never reach me more!
The Task

28 Mountains interposed
Make enemies of nations, who had else,
Like kindred drops, been mingled into one.
The Task

29 Slaves cannot breathe in England; if their lungs
Receive our air, that moment they are free;
They touch our country, and their shackles fall.
A situation resulting from a judicial decision in 1772. *The Task*

30 Riches have wings, and grandeur is a dream.
The Task

31 Detested sport,
That owes its pleasures to another's pain.
The Task

32 Knowledge dwells
In heads replete with thoughts of other men;
Wisdom in minds attentive to their own.
The Task

33 Society, friendship, and love,
Divinely bestowed upon man,
Oh, had I the wings of a dove,
How soon would I taste you again!
Verses supposed to be written by Alexander Selkirk

34 I am monarch of all I survey,
My right there is none to dispute;
From the centre all round to the sea
I am lord of the fowl and the brute.
Oh, solitude! where are the charms
That sages have seen in thy face?
Better dwell in the midst of alarms,
Than reign in this horrible place.
Verses supposed to be written by Alexander Selkirk

CREATION

1 The Hand that made us is divine.
Joseph Addison (1672–1719) British essayist. *The Spectator*, 465

2 In the beginning God created the heaven and the earth.
And the earth was without form, and void; and darkness was upon the face of the deep. And the Spirit of God moved upon the face of the waters.
And God said, Let there be light: and there was light.
And God saw the light, that it was good: and God divided the light from the darkness.
And God called the light Day, and the darkness he called Night. And the evening and the morning were the first day.
Bible: Genesis 1:1–5

3 And God called the dry land Earth; and the gathering together of the waters called he Seas: and God saw that it was good.
And God said, Let the earth bring forth grass, the herb yielding seed, and the fruit tree yielding fruit after his kind, whose seed is in itself, upon the earth: and it was so.
Bible: Genesis 1:10–11

4 And God made two great lights: the greater light to rule the day, and the lesser light to rule the night: he made the stars also.
Bible: Genesis 1:16

5 And God said, Let the earth bring forth the living creature after his kind, cattle, and creeping thing, and beast of the earth after his kind: and it was so.
Bible: Genesis 1:24

6 And God said, Let us make man in our image, after our likeness: and let them have dominion over the fish of the sea, and over the fowl of the air, and over the cattle, and over all the earth, and over every creeping thing that creepeth upon the earth.
So God created man in his own image, in the image of God created he him; male and female created he them.
And God blessed them, and God said unto them, Be fruitful, and multiply, and replenish the earth, and subdue it: and have dominion over the fish of the sea, and over the fowl of the air, and over every living thing that moveth upon the earth.
Bible: Genesis 1:26–28

7 And the Lord God caused a deep sleep to fall upon Adam, and he slept: and he took one of his ribs, and closed up the flesh instead thereof.
Bible: Genesis 2:21

8 When the stars threw down their spears,
And watered heaven with their tears,
Did he smile his work to see?
Did he who made the Lamb make thee?
William Blake (1757–1827) British poet. *Songs of Experience*, 'The Tiger'

9 Little Lamb, who made thee?
Dost thou know who made thee?
William Blake *Songs of Innocence*, 'The Lamb'

10 Whan that the month in which the world bigan,
That highte March, whan God first maked man.
Geoffrey Chaucer (c. 1342–1400) English poet. *The Canterbury Tales*, 'The Nun's Priest's Tale'

11 'Who *is* the Potter, pray, and who the Pot?'
Edward Fitzgerald (1809–83) British poet. *The Rubáiyát of Omar Khayyám*

12 It took the whole of Creation
To produce my foot, each feather:
Now I hold creation in my foot.
Ted Hughes (1930–) British poet. *The Hawk in the Rain*, 'Hawk Roosting'

13 I cannot forgive Descartes; in all his philosophy he did his best to dispense with God. But he could not avoid making Him set the world in motion with a flip of His thumb; after that he had no more use for God.
Blaise Pascal (1623–62) French philosopher and mathematician. *Pensées*, II

14 'Do you know who made you?'
'Nobody, as I knows on,' said the

child, with a short laugh . . . 'I 'spect I grow'd.'

Harriet Beecher Stowe (1811–96) US novelist. *Uncle Tom's Cabin*, Ch. 20

15 Which beginning of time according to our Chronologie, fell upon the entrance of the night preceding the twenty third day of *Octob.* in the year of the Julian Calendar, 710.

James Ussher (1581–1656) Irish churchman. Referring to the Creation, as described in Genesis, which, he had calculated, took place on 22 Oct 4004 BC. *The Annals of the World*

16 God made everything out of nothing. But the nothingness shows through.

Paul Valéry (1871–1945) French poet and writer. *Mauvaises Pensées et autres*

17 The art of creation
is older than the art of killing.

Andrei Voznesensky (1933–) Soviet poet. *Poem with a Footnote*

CRICKET

See also sport

1 It's not in support of cricket but as an earnest protest against golf.

Max Beerbohm (1872–1956) British writer. Said when giving a shilling towards W. G. Grace's testimonial. *Carr's Dictionary of Extraordinary English Cricketers*

2 I do love cricket – it's so very English.

Sarah Bernhardt (Sarah Henriette Rosine Bernard; 1844–1923) French actress. On seeing a game of football. *Nijinsky* (R. Buckle)

3 They came to see me bat not to see you bowl.

W. G. Grace (1848–1915) British doctor and cricketer. Refusing to leave the field after being bowled first ball in front of a large crowd. Attrib.

4 It's more than a game. It's an institution.

Thomas Hughes (1822–96) British novelist. Referring to cricket. *Tom Brown's Schooldays*, Pt. II, Ch. 7

5 There's a breathless hush in the Close tonight –
Ten to make and the match to win –
A bumping pitch and a blinding light,
An hour to play and the last man in.

Henry John Newbolt (1862–1938) British poet. *Vitaï Lampada*

6 I tend to believe that cricket is the greatest thing that God ever created on earth . . . certainly greater than sex, although sex isn't too bad either.

Harold Pinter (1930–) British playwright. *The Observer*, 5 Oct 1980

7 It requires one to assume such indecent postures.

Oscar Wilde (1854–1900) Irish-born British dramatist. Explaining why he did not play cricket. Attrib.

CRIME

See also theft, murder

1 And surely your blood of your lives will I require; at the hand of every beast will I require it, and at the hand of man; at the hand of every man's brother will I require the life of man.
Whoso sheddeth man's blood, by man shall his blood be shed: for in the image of God made he man.

Bible: Genesis 9:5–6

2 How many crimes committed merely because their authors could not endure being wrong!

Albert Camus (1913–60) French existentialist writer. *The Fall*

3 Thieves respect property; they merely wish the property to become their property that they may more perfectly respect it.

G. K. Chesterton (1874–1936) British writer. Attrib.

4 He is the Napoleon of crime.

Arthur Conan Doyle (1856–1930) British writer. Referring to Professor Moriarty. *The Final Problem*

5 If poverty is the mother of crime, stupidity is its father.

Jean de La Bruyère (1645–96) French satirist. *Les Caractères*

6 Crime, like virtue, has its degrees.

Jean Racine (1639–99) French dramatist. *Phèdre*, IV:2

7 A man who has never gone to school may steal from a freight car, but if he has a university education he may steal the whole railroad.

Franklin D. Roosevelt (1882–1945) US Democratic president. Attrib.

8 I came to the conclusion many years ago that almost all crime is due to the repressed desire for aesthetic expression.

Evelyn Waugh (1903–66) British novelist. *Decline and Fall*, Pt. III, Ch. 1

CRITICISM

See also actors, compliments, insults, poets, writers

1 As a contribution to natural history, the work is negligible.

Anonymous Review of Kenneth Grahame's *The Wind in the Willows* in the *Times Literary Supplement*. *The Life of Kenneth Grahame* (Green)

2 I am bound by my own definition of criticism: a disinterested endeavour to learn and propagate the best that is known and thought in the world.

Matthew Arnold (1822–88) British poet and critic. *Essays in Criticism*, First Series, 'Functions of Criticism at the Present Time'

3 There is less in this than meets the eye.

Tallulah Bankhead (1903–68) US actress. Referring to a revival of a play by Maeterlinck. *Shouts and Murmurs* (A. Woollcott), 'Capsule Criticism'

4 Too much counterpoint; what is worse, Protestant counterpoint.

Thomas Beecham (1879–1961) British conductor. Said of J. S. Bach. *The Guardian*, 8 Mar 1971

5 The musical equivalent of the towers of St Pancras station – neo-Gothic, you know.

Thomas Beecham Referring to Elgar's A Flat Symphony. *Sir Thomas Beecham* (N. Cardus)

6 What can you do with it? – it's like a lot of yaks jumping about.

Thomas Beecham Referring to Beethoven's 7th Symphony. *Beecham Stories* (H. Atkins and A. Newman)

7 I will try to account for the degree of my aesthetic emotion. That, I conceive, is the function of the critic.

Clive Bell (1881–1964) British art critic. *Art*, Pt. II, Ch. 3

8 Of all fatiguing, futile, empty trades, the worst, I suppose, is writing about writing.

Hilaire Belloc (1870–1953) French-born British poet. *The Silence of the Sea*

9 See Hebrews 13:8.

Robert Benchley (1889–1945) US humorist. Criticism of a long-running play; the text is: 'Jesus Christ the same yesterday, and today, and for ever'. Attrib.

10 And why beholdest thou the mote that is in thy brother's eye, but

considerest not the beam that is in thine own eye?
Bible: Matthew 7:3

11 Tallulah Bankhead barged down the Nile last night and sank. As the Serpent of the Nile she proves to be no more dangerous than a garter snake.
John Mason Brown (1900–69) US critic. Referring to her performance as Shakespeare's Cleopatra. *Current Biography*

12 He who discommendeth others obliquely commendeth himself.
Thomas Browne (1605–82) English physician and writer. *Christian Morals*, Pt. I

13 A great deal of contemporary criticism reads to me like a man saying: 'Of course I do not like green cheese: I am very fond of brown sherry.'
G. K. Chesterton (1874–1936) British writer. *All I Survey*

14 To see him act, is like reading Shakespeare by flashes of lightning.
Samuel Taylor Coleridge (1772–1834) British poet. Referring to Kean. *Table Talk*

15 I never realized before that Albert married beneath him.
Noël Coward (1899–1973) British dramatist. After seeing a certain actress in the role of Queen Victoria. *Tynan on Theatre* (K. Tynan)

16 Two things should be cut: the second act and the child's throat.
Noël Coward Referring to a play featuring a child actor. *The Wit of Noël Coward* (D. Richards)

17 This paper will no doubt be found interesting by those who take an interest in it.
John Dalton (1766–1844) British scientist. Said on many occasions when chairing scientific meetings. Attrib.

18 If you hear that someone is speaking ill of you, instead of trying to defend yourself you should say: 'He obviously does not know me very well, since there are so many other faults he could have mentioned'.
Epictetus (c. 60–110 AD) Stoic philosopher. *Enchiridion*

19 He played the King as though under momentary apprehension that someone else was about to play the ace.
Eugene Field (1850–95) US poet and journalist. Referring to Creston Clarke's performance in the role of King Lear. Attrib.

20 It is not good enough to spend time and ink in describing the penultimate sensations and physical movements of people getting into a state of rut, we all know them too well.
John Galsworthy (1867–1933) British novelist. Referring to D. H. Lawrence's *Sons and Lovers*. Letter to Edward Garnett, 13 Apr 1914

21 Funny without being vulgar.
W. S. Gilbert (1836–1911) British dramatist. Referring to Sir Henry Irving's *Hamlet*. Attrib.

22 My dear chap! Good isn't the word!
W. S. Gilbert Speaking to an actor after he had given a poor performance. Attrib.

23 We were as nearly bored as enthusiasm would permit.
Edmund Gosse (1849–1928) British writer and critic. Referring to a play by Swinburne. *Biography of Edward Marsh* (C. Hassall)

24 There are two things which I am confident I can do very well: one is an introduction to any literary work, stating what it is to contain, and how it should be executed in the most perfect manner; the other is a conclusion, shewing from various causes why the execution has not been equal to what the author promised to himself and to the public.
Samuel Johnson (1709–84) British lexicographer. *Life of Johnson* (J. Boswell), Vol. I

25 It is burning a farthing candle at Dover, to shew light at Calais.
Samuel Johnson Referring to the impact of Sheridan's works upon the English language. *Life of Johnson* (J. Boswell), Vol. I

26 You *may* abuse a tragedy, though you cannot write one. You may scold a carpenter who has made you a bad table, though you cannot make a table. It is not your trade to make tables.
Samuel Johnson Referring to the qualifications needed to indulge in literary criticism. *Life of Johnson* (J. Boswell), Vol. I

27 This man I thought had been a Lord among wits; but, I find, he is only a wit among Lords.
Samuel Johnson Referring to Lord Chesterfield. *Life of Johnson* (J. Boswell), Vol. I

28 They teach the morals of a whore, and the manners of a dancing master.
Samuel Johnson Referring to Lord Chesterfield's *Letters*. *Life of Johnson* (J. Boswell), Vol. I

29 Yes, Sir, many men, many women, and many children.
Samuel Johnson When asked by Dr Blair whether any man of their own time could have written the poems of Ossian. *Life of Johnson* (J. Boswell), Vol. I

30 They are forced plants, raised in a hot-bed; and they are poor plants; they are but cucumbers after all.
Samuel Johnson Referring to Gray's *Odes*. *Life of Johnson* (J. Boswell), Vol. IV

31 Difficult do you call it, Sir? I wish it were impossible.
Samuel Johnson On hearing a famous violinist. *Johnsonian Miscellanies* (ed. G. B. Hill), Vol. II

32 The pleasure of criticizing robs us of the pleasure of being moved by some very fine things.
Jean de La Bruyère (1645–96) French satirist. *Les Caractères*

33 They are great parables, the novels, but false art. They are only parables. All the people are *fallen angels* – even the dirtiest scrubs. This I cannot stomach. People are not fallen angels, they are merely people.
D. H. Lawrence (1885–1930) British novelist. Referring to the novels of Dostoyevsky. Letter to J. Middleton Murray and Katherine Mansfield, 17 Feb 1916

34 Nothing but old fags and cabbage-stumps of quotations from the Bible and the rest, stewed in the juice of deliberate, journalistic dirty-mindedness.
D. H. Lawrence Referring to James Joyce. Letter to Aldous Huxley, 15 Aug 1928

35 His verse exhibits . . . something that is rather like Keats's vulgarity with a Public School accent.
F. R. Leavis (1895–1978) British literary critic. Referring to Rupert Brooke. *New Bearings in English Poetry*, Ch. 2

36 I cried all the way to the bank.
Liberace (Wladzin Valentino Liberace; 1919–87) US pianist and showman. Said when asked whether he minded being criticized. *Liberace: An Autobiography*, Ch. 2

37 People who like this sort of thing will find this is the sort of thing they like.
Abraham Lincoln (1809–65) US statesman. A comment on a book. Attrib.

38 His writing bears the same relation to poetry which a Turkey carpet bears to a picture. There are colours in the Turkey carpet out of which a picture might be made. There are words in Mr

Montgomery's writing which, when disposed in certain orders and combinations, have made, and will make again, good poetry. But, as they now stand, they seem to be put together on principle in such a manner as to give no image of anything 'in the heavens above, or in the earth beneath, or in the waters under the earth'.

Lord Macaulay (1800–59) British historian. *Literary Essays Contributed to the 'Edinburgh Review'*, 'Mr. Robert Montgomery's Poems'

39 His imagination resembled the wings of an ostrich. It enabled him to run, though not to soar.

Lord Macaulay *Essays and Biographies*, 'John Dryden'

40 It was a book to kill time for those who like it better dead.

Rose Macaulay (1889–1958) British writer. Attrib.

41 I was so long writing my review that I never got around to reading the book.

Groucho Marx (Julius Marx; 1895–1977) US comedian. Attrib.

42 People ask you for criticism, but they only want praise.

W. Somerset Maugham (1874–1965) British novelist. *Of Human Bondage*, Ch. 50

43 I could eat alphabet soup and *shit* better lyrics.

Johnny Mercer (1909–76) US lyricist and composer. Describing a British musical. Attrib.

44 There are passages in *Ulysses* which can be read only in the toilet – if one wants to extract the full flavor of their content.

Henry Miller (1891–1980) US novelist. *Black Spring*

45 Yea, marry, now it is somewhat, for now it is rhyme; before, it was neither rhyme nor reason.

Thomas More (1478–1535) English lawyer and scholar. On reading an unremarkable book recently rendered into verse by a friend of his. *Apophthegms* (Bacon), 287

46 Prolonged, indiscriminate reviewing of books involves constantly *inventing* reactions towards books about which one has no spontaneous feelings whatever.

George Orwell (Eric Blair; 1903–50) British novelist. *Confessions of a Book Reviewer*

47 Mr Blunden is no more able to resist a quotation than some people are to refuse a drink.

George Orwell Reviewing a book by Edmund Blunden. *Manchester Evening News*, 20 Apr 1944

48 She ran the whole gamut of the emotions from A to B.

Dorothy Parker (1893–1967) US writer. Referring to a performance by Katharine Hepburn on Broadway. Attrib.

49 This is not a novel to be tossed aside lightly. It should be thrown with great force.

Dorothy Parker Book review. *Wit's End* (R. E. Dremman)

50 'Tis hard to say, if greater want of skill
Appear in writing or in judging ill.

Alexander Pope (1688–1744) British poet. *An Essay on Criticism*

51 Damn with faint praise, assent with civil leer,
And, without sneering, teach the rest to sneer.

Alexander Pope *Epistle to Dr. Arbuthnot*

52 I never read anything concerning my work. I feel that criticism is a letter to the public which the author, since it is not directed to him, does not have to open and read.

Rainer Maria Rilke (1875–1926) Austrian poet. *Letters*

53 Very good, but it has its *longueurs*.

Antoine de Rivarol (1753–1801) French writer and wit. Giving his opinion of a couplet by a mediocre poet. *Das Buch des Lachens* (W. Scholz)

54 The Stealthy School of Criticism.

Dante Gabriel Rossetti (1828–82) British painter and poet. Letter to the *Athenaeum*, 1871

55 Wagner has lovely moments but awful quarters of an hour.

Gioacchino Rossini (1792–1868) Italian operatic composer. Remark made to Emile Naumann, April 1867. *Italienische Tondichter* (Naumann)

56 I have seen, and heard, much of Cockney impudence before now; but never expected to hear a coxcomb ask two hundred guineas for flinging a pot of paint in the public's face.

John Ruskin (1819–1900) British art critic and writer. On Whistler's painting 'Nocturne in Black and Gold' Letter, 18 June 1877

57 For I am nothing if not critical.

William Shakespeare (1564–1616) English dramatist. *Othello*, II:1

58 It does not follow . . . that the right to criticize Shakespeare involves the power of writing better plays. And in fact . . . I do not profess to write better plays.

George Bernard Shaw (1856–1950) Irish dramatist and critic. *Three Plays for Puritans*, Preface

59 It is disappointing to report that George Bernard Shaw appearing as George Bernard Shaw is sadly miscast in the part. Satirists should be heard and not seen.

Robert E. Sherwood (1896–1955) US writer and dramatist. Reviewing a Shaw play

60 It had only one fault. It was kind of lousy.

James Thurber (1894–1961) US humorist. Remark made about a play. Attrib.

61 A strange, horrible business, but I suppose good enough for Shakespeare's day.

Victoria (1819–1901) Queen of the United Kingdom. Giving her opinion of *King Lear*. *Living Biographies of Famous Rulers* (H. Thomas)

62 I do not think this poem will reach its destination.

Voltaire (François-Marie Arouet; 1694–1778) French writer. Reviewing Rousseau's poem 'Ode to Posterity'. Attrib.

63 As far as criticism is concerned, we don't resent that unless it is absolutely biased, as it is in most cases.

John Vorster (Balthazar Johannes Vorster; 1915–83) South African politician. *The Observer*, 'Sayings of the Week', 9 Nov 1969

64 My dear fellow a unique evening! I wouldn't have left a turn unstoned.

Arthur Wimperis (1874–1953) British screenwriter. Replying when asked his opinion of a vaudeville show. *Fifty Years of Vaudeville* (E. Short)

65 I saw it at a disadvantage – the curtain was up.

Walter Winchell (1879–1972) US journalist. Referring to a show starring Earl Carroll. *Come to Judgment* (A. Whiteman)

66 Trivial personalities decomposing in the eternity of print.

Virginia Woolf (1882–1941) British novelist. *The Common Reader*, 'Jane Eyre'

67 *Middlemarch*, the magnificent book which with all its imperfections is one of the few English novels for grown up people.

Virginia Woolf *The Common Reader*, 'George Eliot'

68 He is all blood, dirt and sucked sugar stick.

W. B. Yeats (1865–1939) Irish poet. Referring to Wilfred Owen. *Letters on Poetry to Dorothy Wellesley*, Letter, 21 Dec 1936

CRITICS

1 I will try to account for the degree of my aesthetic emotion. That, I conceive, is the function of the critic.
Clive Bell (1881–1964) British art critic. *Art*, Pt. II, Ch. 3

2 A man must serve his time to every trade
Save censure – critics all are ready made.
Lord Byron (1788–1824) British poet. *English Bards and Scotch Reviewers*

3 Reviewers are usually people who would have been poets, historians, biographers, . . . if they could; they have tried their talents at one or at the other, and have failed; therefore they turn critics.
Samuel Taylor Coleridge (1772–1834) British poet. *Lectures on Shakespeare and Milton*, I

4 A good critic is one who narrates the adventures of his mind among masterpieces.
Anatole France (Jacques Anatole François Thibault; 1844–1924) French writer. *The Literary Life*, Preface

5 I sometimes think
His critical judgement is so exquisite
It leaves us nothing to admire except his opinion.
Christopher Fry (1907–) British dramatist. *The Dark is Light Enough*, II

6 Asking a working writer what he thinks about critics is like asking a lamp-post how it feels about dogs.
Christopher Hampton (1946–) British writer and dramatist. *The Sunday Times Magazine*, 16 Oct 1977

7 What is a modern poet's fate?
To write his thoughts upon a slate;
The critic spits on what is done,
Gives it a wipe – and all is gone.
Thomas Hood (1799–1845) British poet. *Alfred Lord Tennyson, A Memoir* (Hallam Tennyson), Vol. II, Ch. 3

8 There is a certain race of men that either imagine it their duty, or make it their amusement, to hinder the reception of every work of learning or genius, who stand as sentinels in the avenues of fame, and value themselves upon giving Ignorance and Envy the first notice of a prey.
Samuel Johnson (1709–84) British lexicographer. *The Rambler*

9 A fly, Sir, may sting a stately horse and make him wince; but one is but an insect, and the other is a horse still.
Samuel Johnson *Life of Johnson* (J. Boswell), Vol. I

10 Dear Roger Fry whom I love as a man but detest as a movement.
Edward Howard Marsh (1872–1953) British civil servant and writer. Roger Fry (1866–1934) was an artist and art critic, who championed the postimpressionists. *Edward Marsh* (Christopher Hassall), Ch. 11

11 Insects sting, not from malice, but because they want to live. It is the same with critics – they desire our blood, not our pain.
Friedrich Wilhelm Nietzsche (1844–1900) German philosopher. *Miscellaneous Maxims and Reflections*

12 Nor in the critic let the man be lost.
Alexander Pope (1688–1744) British poet. *An Essay on Criticism*

13 They will review a book by a writer much older than themselves as if it were an over-ambitious essay by a second-year student . . . It is the little dons I complain about, like so many corgis trotting up, hoping to nip your ankles.
J. B. Priestley (1894–1984) British novelist. *Outcries and Asides*

14 The greater part of critics are parasites, who, if nothing had been written, would find nothing to write.
J. B. Priestley *Outcries and Asides*

15 Pay no attention to what the critics say. No statue has ever been put up to a critic.
Jean Sibelius (1865–1957) Finnish composer. Attrib.

16 Unless the bastards have the courage to give you unqualified praise, I say ignore them.
John Steinbeck (1902–68) US novelist. *A Life in Our Times* (J. K. Galbraith)

17 I doubt that art needed Ruskin any more than a moving train needs one of its passengers to shove it.
Tom Stoppard (1937–) Czech-born British dramatist. *Times Literary Supplement*, 3 June 1977

18 I had another dream the other day about music critics. They were small and rodent-like with padlocked ears, as if they had stepped out of a painting by Goya.
Igor Stravinsky (1882–1971) Russian-born US composer. *The Evening Standard*, 29 Oct 1969

19 A whipper-snapper of criticism who quoted dead languages to hide his ignorance of life.
Herbert Beerbohm Tree (1853–1917) British actor and theater manager. Referring to A. B. Walkley. *Beerbohm Tree* (Hesketh Pearson)

20 A critic is a man who knows the way but can't drive the car.
Kenneth Tynan (1927–80) British theater critic. *New York Times Magazine*, 9 Jan 1966

21 A good drama critic is one who perceives what is happening in the theatre of his time. A great drama critic also perceives what is not happening.
Kenneth Tynan *Tynan Right and Left*, Foreword

CRUELTY

See also hurt, nastiness, violence

1 The wish to hurt, the momentary intoxication with pain, is the loophole through which the pervert climbs into the minds of ordinary men.
Jacob Bronowski (1908–74) British scientist and writer. *The Face of Violence*, Ch. 5

2 Man's inhumanity to man
Makes countless thousands mourn!
Robert Burns (1759–96) Scottish poet. *Man was Made to Mourn*

3 Fear is the parent of cruelty.
J. A. Froude (1818–94) British historian. *Short Studies on Great Subjects*, 'Party Politics'

4 A cruel story runs on wheels, and every hand oils the wheels as they run.
Ouida (Marie Louise de la Ramée; 1839–1908) British novelist. *Wisdom, Wit and Pathos*, 'Moths'

5 I must be cruel only to be kind.
William Shakespeare (1564–1616) English dramatist. *Hamlet*, III:4

6 Whipping and abuse are like laudanum: You have to double the dose as the sensibilities decline.
Harriet Beecher Stowe (1811–96) US novelist. *Uncle Tom's Cabin*, Ch. 20

CULTURE

See also civilization, philistinism

1 Culture, the acquainting ourselves with the best that has been known and said in the world, and thus with the history of the human spirit.
Matthew Arnold (1822–88) British poet and critic. *Literature and Dogma*, Preface

2 Culture is the passion for

sweetness and light, and (what is more) the passion for making them prevail.
Matthew Arnold *Literature and Dogma*, Preface

3 Culture is an instrument wielded by professors to manufacture professors, who when their turn comes will manufacture professors.
Simone Weil (1909–43) French philosopher. *The Need for Roots*

4 Mrs Ballinger is one of the ladies who pursue Culture in bands, as though it were dangerous to meet it alone.
Edith Wharton (1862–1937) US novelist. *Xingu*, Ch. 1

CURIOSITY

See also interfering, wonder

1 Ask no questions and hear no lies.
Proverb

2 Curiosity killed the cat.
Proverb

3 Be not curious in unnecessary matters: for more things are shewed unto thee than men understand.
Bible: Ecclesiasticus 3:23

4 There is no such thing on earth as an uninteresting subject; the only thing that can exist is an uninterested person.
G. K. Chesterton (1874–1936) British writer. *Heretics*, Ch. 1

5 The world is but a school of inquiry.
Michel de Montaigne (1533–92) French essayist. *Essais*, III

6 I ofen looked up at the sky an' assed meself the question – what is the stars, what is the stars?
Sean O'Casey (1884–1964) Irish dramatist. *Juno and the Paycock*, I

7 Curiosity will conquer fear even more than bravery will.
James Stephens (1882–1950) Irish novelist. *The Crock of Gold*

8 Disinterested intellectual curiosity is the life blood of real civilisation.
George Macaulay Trevelyan (1876–1962) British historian *English Social History*, Preface

CURSES

1 Then said his wife unto him, Dost thou still retain thine integrity? curse God, and die.
Bible: Job 2:9

2 Curse the blasted, jelly-boned swines, the slimy, the belly-wriggling invertebrates, the miserable sodding rotters, the flaming sods, the snivelling, dribbling, dithering, palsied, pulseless lot that make up England today.
D. H. Lawrence (1885–1930) British novelist. On a publisher's rejection of *Sons and Lovers*. Letter to Edward Garnett, 3 July 1912

3 Down, down to hell; and say I sent thee thither.
William Shakespeare (1564–1616) English dramatist. *Henry VI*, Pt. 3, V:6

4 A plague o' both your houses!
They have made worms' meat of me.
William Shakespeare *Romeo and Juliet*, III:1

5 Curses are like young chickens, they always come home to roost.
Robert Southey (1774–1843) British poet. *The Curse of Kehama*, Motto

6 'The curse is come upon me,' cried
The Lady of Shalott.
Alfred, Lord Tennyson (1809–92) British poet. *The Lady of Shalott*, Pt. III

7 She has heard a whisper say,
A curse is on her if she stay
To look down to Camelot.
Alfred, Lord Tennyson *The Lady of Shalott*, Pt. II

CUSTOM

See also habit

1 *O tempora! O mores!*
What times! What customs!
Cicero (106–43 BC) Roman orator and statesman. *In Catilinam*, I

2 Custom, then, is the great guide of human life.
David Hume (1711–76) Scottish philosopher. *An Enquiry Concerning Human Understanding*

3 Custom calls me to't.
What custom wills, in all things should we do't,
The dust on antique time would lie unswept,
And mountainous error be too highly heap'd
For truth to o'erpeer.
William Shakespeare (1564–1616) English dramatist. *Coriolanus*, II:3

4 But to my mind, though I am native here
And to the manner born, it is a custom
More honour'd in the breach than the observance.
William Shakespeare *Hamlet*, I:4

CYNICISM

1 One is not superior merely because one sees the world in an odious light.
Vicomte de Chateaubriand (1768–1848) French diplomat and writer. Attrib.

2 Cynicism is an unpleasant way of saying the truth.
Lillian Hellman (1905–84) US dramatist. *The Little Foxes*, I

3 Cynicism is humour in ill-health.
H. G. Wells (1866–1946) British writer. *Short Stories*, 'The Last Trump'

4 A man who knows the price of everything and the value of nothing.
Oscar Wilde (1854–1900) Irish-born British dramatist. Referring to a cynic. *Lady Windermere's Fan*, III

D

DAMNATION

See also devil, hell

1 Blot out his name, then, record one lost soul more,
One task more declined, one more footpath untrod,
One more devils'-triumph and sorrow for angels,
One wrong more to man, one more insult to God!
Robert Browning (1812–89) British poet. *The Lost Leader*

2 You will be damned if you do –
And you will be damned if you don't.
Lorenzo Dow (1777–1834) British churchman. Speaking of Calvinism. *Reflections on the Love of God*

3 Now hast thou but one bare hour to live,
And then thou must be damn'd perpetually!

Stand still, you ever-moving spheres of heaven,
That time may cease, and midnight never come.
Christopher Marlowe (1564–93) English dramatist. *Doctor Faustus,* V:2

4 Ugly hell, gape not! come not, Lucifer!
I'll burn my books!
Christopher Marlowe *Doctor Faustus,* V:2

DANCING

1 On with the dance! let joy be unconfined;
No sleep till morn, when Youth and Pleasure meet
To chase the glowing Hours with flying feet.
Lord Byron (1788–1824) British poet. *Childe Harold's Pilgrimage,* III

2 Will you, won't you, will you, won't you, will you join the dance?
Lewis Carroll (Charles Lutwidge Dodgson; 1832–98) British writer. *Alice's Adventures in Wonderland,* Ch. 10

3 Dance, dance, dance little lady.
Noël Coward (1899–1973) British dramatist. Title of song

4 I have discovered the dance. I have discovered the art which has been lost for two thousand years.
Isadora Duncan (1878–1927) US dancer. *My Life*

5 Any time you're Lambeth way,
Any evening, any day,
You'll find us all doin' the Lambeth walk.
Douglas Furber (1885–1961) British songwriter. *Doin' the Lambeth Walk*

6 The trouble with nude dancing is that not everything stops when the music stops.
Sir Robert Helpmann (1909–86) Australian dancer and choreographer. After the opening night of *Oh, Calcutta!*. *The Frank Muir Book*

7 Sometimes I think that dancing, like youth, is wasted on the young.
Max Lerner (1902–) US author and journalist. *The Unfinished Country*

8 My men, like satyrs grazing on the lawns,
Shall with their goat-feet dance an antic hay.
Christopher Marlowe (1564–93) English dramatist. *Edward the Second,* I:1

9 Come, and trip it as you go
On the light fantastic toe.
John Milton (1608–74) English poet. *L'Allegro*

10 . . . although one may fail to find happiness in theatrical life, one never wishes to give it up after having once tasted its fruits. To enter the School of the Imperial Ballet is to enter a convent whence frivolity is banned, and where merciless discipline reigns.
Anna Pavlova (1881–1931) Russian ballet dancer. *Pavlova: A Biography* (ed. A. H. Franks), 'Pages of My Life'

11 A perpendicular expression of a horizontal desire.
George Bernard Shaw (1856–1950) Irish dramatist and critic. Referring to dancing. *Revolt into Style* (G. Melly)

DANGER

1 Any port in a storm.
Proverb

2 If you play with fire you get burned.
Proverb

3 Defend us from all perils and dangers of this night.
The Book of Common Prayer *Morning Prayer, Prayer of St Chrysostom*

4 Dangers by being despised grow great.
Edmund Burke (1729–97) British politician. Speech, House of Commons, 11 May 1792

5 Of course I realized there was a measure of danger. Obviously I faced the possibility of not returning when first I considered going. Once faced and settled there really wasn't any good reason to refer to it.
Amelia Earhart (1898–1937) US flyer. Referring to her flight in the 'Friendship'. *20 Hours: 40 Minutes – Our Flight in the Friendship,* Ch. 5

6 Believe me! The secret of reaping the greatest fruitfulness and the greatest enjoyment from life is to *live dangerously!*
Friedrich Wilhelm Nietzsche (1844–1900) German philosopher. *Die Fröhliche Wissenschaft,* Bk. IV

7 There's a snake hidden in the grass.
Virgil (Publius Vergilius Maro; 70–19 BC) Roman poet. *Eclogue,* Bk. III

DARKNESS

1 The darkest hour is just before the dawn.
Proverb

2 All colours will agree in the dark.
Francis Bacon (1561–1626) English philosopher. *Essays,* 'Of Unity in Religion'

3 Men fear death, as children fear to go in the dark; and as that natural fear in children is increased with tales, so is the other.
Francis Bacon *Essays,* 'Of Death'

4 In the beginning God created the heaven and the earth.
And the earth was without form, and void; and darkness was upon the face of the deep. And the Spirit of God moved upon the face of the waters.
And God said, Let there be light: and there was light.
And God saw the light, that it was good: and God divided the light from the darkness.
And God called the light Day, and the darkness he called Night. And the evening and the morning were the first day.
Bible: Genesis 1:1–5

5 And this is the condemnation, that light is come into the world, and men loved darkness rather than light, because their deeds were evil.
Bible: John 3:19

6 A blind man in a dark room – looking for a black hat – which isn't there.
Lord Bowen (1835–94) British judge. Characterization of a metaphysician. Attrib.

7 I'm not frightened of the darkness outside. It's the darkness inside houses I don't like.
Shelagh Delaney (1939–) British dramatist. *A Taste of Honey,* I:1

8 The day Thou gavest, Lord, is ended,
The darkness falls at Thy behest.
John Ellerton (1826–93) British churchman. *A Liturgy for Missionary Meetings*

9 Strange, is it not? that of the myriads who
Before us pass'd the door of Darkness through,
Not one returns to tell us of the Road,
Which to discover we must travel too.
Edward Fitzgerald (1809–83) British poet. *The Rubáiyát of Omar Khayyám*

10 Turn up the lights, I don't want to go home in the dark.

O. Henry (William Sidney Porter; 1862–1910) US short-story writer. Quoting a popular song of the time. *O. Henry* (C. A. Smith), Ch. 9

11 I am about to take my last voyage, a great leap in the dark.

Thomas Hobbes (1588–1679) English philosopher.

12 I'm afraid of losing my obscurity. Genuineness only thrives in the dark. Like celery.

Aldous Huxley (1894–1964) British novelist. *Those Barren Leaves,* Pt. I, Ch. 1

13 The dark night of the soul.

St John of the Cross (Juan de Yepes y Alvarez; 1542–91) Spanish churchman and poet. English translation of *Noche obscura del alma,* the title of a poem

14 O dark, dark, dark, amid the blaze of noon,
Irrecoverably dark, total eclipse,
Without all hope of day!

John Milton (1608–74) English poet. *Samson Agonistes*

15 What in me is dark
Illumine, what is low raise and support;
That, to the height of this great argument,
I may assert Eternal Providence,
And justify the ways of God to men.

John Milton *Paradise Lost,* Bk. I

16 Brief and powerless is Man's life; on him and all his race the slow, sure doom falls pitiless and dark.

Bertrand Russell (1872–1970) British philosopher. *Mysticism and Logic,* 'A Free Man's Worship'

17 The bright day is done,
And we are for the dark.

William Shakespeare (1564–1616) English dramatist. *Antony and Cleopatra,* V:2

18 She would rather light candles than curse the darkness, and her glow has warmed the world.

Adlai Stevenson (1900–65) US statesman. Referring to Eleanor Roosevelt. Address, United Nations General Assembly, 9 Nov 1962

DAY AND NIGHT

1 Now the day is over,
Night is drawing nigh,
Shadows of the evening
Steal across the sky.

Sabine Baring-Gould (1834–1924) British author and hymn writer. *The Evening Hymn*

2 He calleth to me out of Seir,
Watchman, what of the night?
Watchman, what of the night?
The watchman said, The morning cometh, and also the night: if ye will enquire, enquire ye: return, come.

Bible: Isaiah 21:11–12

3 The day begins to droop, –
Its course is done:
But nothing tells the place
Of the setting sun.

Robert Bridges (1844–1930) British poet. *Winter Nightfall*

4 Where the quiet-coloured end of evening smiles,
Miles and miles.

Robert Browning (1812–89) British poet. *Love among the Ruins,* I

5 I had a dream, which was not all a dream.
The bright sun was extinguished, and the stars
Did wander darkling in the eternal space,
Rayless, and pathless, and the icy earth
Swung blind and blackening in the moonless air;
Morn came and went – and came, and brought no day,
And men forgot their passions in the dread
Of this their desolation; and all hearts
Were chilled into a selfish prayer for light.

Lord Byron (1788–1824) British poet. *Darkness*

6 Today is the first day of the rest of your life.

Charles Dederich US founder of anti-heroin centers. Attrib.

7 The day Thou gavest, Lord, is ended,
The darkness falls at Thy behest.

John Ellerton (1826–93) British churchman. *A Liturgy for Missionary Meetngs*

8 Awake! for Morning in the Bowl of Night
Has flung the Stone that puts the Stars to Flight:
And Lo! the Hunter of the East has caught
The Sultan's Turret in a Noose of Light.

Edward Fitzgerald (1809–83) British poet. *The Rubáiyát of Omar Khayyám*

9 Tender Is the Night.

F. Scott Fitzgerald (1896–1940) US novelist. From the 'Ode to a Nightingale' (John Keats): 'Already with thee! tender is the night'. Book title

10 The Curfew tolls the knell of parting day,
The lowing herd winds slowly o'er the lea,
The plowman homeward plods his weary way,
And leaves the world to darkness and to me.

Thomas Gray (1716–71) British poet. *Elegy Written in a Country Churchyard*

11 Oh, what a beautiful morning!
Oh, what a beautiful day!

Oscar Hammerstein (1895–1960) US lyricist. From the musical *Oklahoma. Oh, What a Beautiful Morning*

12 Sweet day, so cool, so calm, so bright,
The bridal of the earth and sky.

George Herbert (1593–1633) English poet. *Virtue*

13 The candles burn their sockets,
The blinds let through the day,
The young man feels his pockets
And wonders what's to pay.

A. E. Housman (1859–1936) British scholar and poet. *Last Poems,* 'Eight O'Clock'

14 In the country the darknessof night is friendly and familiar, but in a city, with its blaze of lights, it is unnatural, hostile and menacing. It is like a monstrous vulture that hovers, biding its time.

W. Somerset Maugham (1874–1965) British novelist. *A Writer's Notebook*

15 Under the opening eye-lids of the morn.

John Milton (1608–74) English poet. *Lycidas*

16 Now came still Evening on, and Twilight grey
Had in her sober livery all things clad.

John Milton *Paradise Lost,* Bk. IV

17 Midnight brought on the dusky hour
Friendliest to sleep and silence.

John Milton *Paradise Lost,* Bk. V

18 Three o'clock is always too late or too early for anything you want to do.

Jean-Paul Sartre (1905–80) French writer. *Nausea*

19 Good morrow, masters; put your torches out,
The wolves have prey'd; and look, the gentle day,
Before the wheels of Phoebus, round about
Dapples the drowsy east with spots of grey.

William Shakespeare (1564–1616) English dramatist. *Much Ado About Nothing,* V:3

20 Gallop apace, you fiery-footed steeds,
Towards Phoebus' lodging; such a waggoner
As Phaethon would whip you to the west,
And bring in cloudy night immediately.
Spread thy close curtain, love-performing night! That runaway's eyes may wink, and Romeo
Leap to these arms, untalk'd of and unseen!
Lovers can see to do their amorous rites
By their own beauties; or, if love be blind,
It best agrees with night. Come, civil night,
Thou sober-suited matron, all in black.
William Shakespeare *Romeo and Juliet*, III:2

21 Night's candles are burnt out, and jocund day
Stands tiptoe on the misty mountain tops.
William Shakespeare *Romeo and Juliet*, III:5

22 The principality of the sky lightens now, over our green hill, into spring morning larked and crowed and belling.
Dylan Thomas (1914–53) Welsh poet. *Under Milk Wood*

DEATH

See also afterlife, assassination, drowning, epitaphs, equality in death, execution, funerals, killing, last words, life and death, love and death, memorials, mortality, mourning, murder, obituaries, posterity, suicide

1 After death the doctor.
Proverb

2 A man can die but once.
Proverb

3 A piece of churchyard fits everybody.
Proverb

4 As soon as man is born he begins to die.
Proverb

5 Dead men tell no tales.
Proverb

6 Death defies the doctor.
Proverb

7 Death is the great leveller.
Proverb

8 Death is the poor man's best physician.
Proverb

9 Ever since dying came into fashion, life hasn't been safe.
Proverb

10 Fear of death is worse than death itself.
Proverb

11 Never speak ill of the dead.
Proverb

12 Nothing is certain but death and taxes.
Proverb

13 The good die young.
Proverb

14 The old man has his death before his eyes; the young man behind his back.
Proverb

15 There will be sleeping enough in the grave.
Proverb

16 It's not that I'm afraid to die. I just don't want to be there when it happens.
Woody Allen (Allen Stewart Konigsberg; 1935–) US film actor. *Without Feathers*, 'Death (A Play)'

17 Death is an acquired trait.
Woody Allen *Woody Allen and His Comedy* (E. Lax)

18 God grants an easy death only to the just.
Svetlana Alliluyeva (1926–) Russian writer; daughter of Joseph Stalin. *Twenty Letters to a Friend*

19 Death has got something to be said for it:
There's no need to get out of bed for it;
Wherever you may be,
They bring it to you, free.
Kingsley Amis (1922–) British writer. 'Delivery Guaranteed'

20 As Amr lay on his death-bed a friend said to him: 'You have often remarked that you would like to find an intelligent man at the point of death, and to ask him what his feelings were. Now I ask *you* that question. Amr replied, 'I feel as if heaven lay close upon the earth and I between the two, breathing through the eye of a needle.'
Amr Ibn Al-As (d. 664) Arab conqueror of Egypt. *The Harvest of a Quiet Eye* (Alan L. Mackay)

21 The bells of hell go ting-a-ling-a-ling
For you but not for me.
O Death, where is thy sting-a-ling-a-ling,
O Grave, thy victoree?
Anonymous *See* BIBLE I CORINTHIANS. Song of World War I

22 There is a dignity in dying that doctors should not dare to deny.
Anonymous

23 Swing low sweet chariot,
Comin' for to carry me home,
I looked over Jordan an' what did I see?
A band of Angels coming after me,
Comin' for to carry me home.
Anonymous *Swing Low, Sweet Chariot*

24 He's gone to join the majority.
Petronius Arbiter (1st century AD) Roman satirist. Referring to a dead man. *Satyricon: Cena Trimalchionis*, 42

25 Death must simply become the discreet but dignified exit of a peaceful person from a helpful society that is not torn, not even overly upset by the idea of a biological transition without significance, without pain or suffering, and ultimately without fear.
Philippe Ariès *The Hour of Our Death*

26 Now he is dead! Far hence he lies
In the lorn Syrian town;
And on his grave, with shining eyes,
The Syrian stars look down.
Matthew Arnold (1822–88) British poet and critic. *Obermann Once More*

27 I have often thought upon death, and I find it the least of all evils.
Francis Bacon (1561–1626) English philosopher. *An Essay on Death*

28 I do not believe that any man fears to be dead, but only the stroke of death.
Francis Bacon *An Essay on Death*

29 Men fear death, as children fear to go in the dark; and as that natural fear in children is increased with tales, so is the other.
Francis Bacon *Essays*, 'Of Death'

30 It is natural to die as to be born; and to a little infant, perhaps, the one is as painful as the other.
Francis Bacon *Essays*, 'Of Death'

31 To die will be an awfully big adventure.
J. M. Barrie (1860–1937) British novelist and dramatist. *Peter Pan*, III

32 What I like about Clive
Is that he is no longer alive.
There is a great deal to be said
For being dead.
Edmund Clerihew Bentley (1875–1956) British writer. *Biography for Beginners*

33 Behold, I shew you a mystery; We shall not all sleep, but we shall all be changed,
In a moment, in the twinkling of an eye, at the last trump: for the trumpet shall sound, and the dead shall be raised incorruptible, and we shall be changed.
For this corruptible must put on incorruption, and this mortal must put on immortality.
So when this corruptible shall have put on incorruption, and this mortal shall have put on immortality, then shall be brought to pass the saying that is written, Death is swallowed up in victory.
O death, where is thy sting? O grave, where is thy victory?
Bible: I Corinthians 15:51–55

34 The physician cutteth off a long disease; and he that is today a king tomorrow shall die.
Bible: Ecclesiasticus 10:10

35 Lord, now lettest thou thy servant depart in peace, according to thy word:
For mine eyes have seen thy salvation,
Which thou hast prepared before the face of all people;
A light to lighten the Gentiles, and the glory of thy people Israel.
Bible: Luke 2:29–32

36 For all flesh is as grass, and all the glory of man as the flower of grass. The grass withereth, and the flower thereof falleth away.
Bible: I Peter 1:23–24

37 And I looked, and behold a pale horse: and his name that sat on him was Death, and Hell followed with him. And power was given unto them over the fourth part of the earth, to kill with sword, and with hunger, and with death, and with the beasts of the earth.
Bible: Revelations 6:8

38 Its visits,
Like those of angels, short, and far between.
Robert Blair (1699–1746) Scottish poet. *The Grave*

39 In the hour of death, and in the day of judgement.
The Book of Common Prayer *Morning Prayer, Prayer of St Chrysostom*

40 Any amusing deaths lately?
Maurice Bowra (1898–1971) British scholar. Attrib.

41 We all labour against our own cure, for death is the cure of all diseases.
Thomas Browne (1605–82) English physician and writer. *Religio Medici*

42 I am not so much afraid of death, as ashamed thereof, 'tis the very disgrace and ignominy of our natures.
Thomas Browne *Religio Medici*

43 With what shift and pains we come into the World we remember not; but 'tis commonly found no easy matter to get out of it.
Thomas Browne *Christian Morals*, Pt. II

44 For I say, this is death, and the sole death,
When a man's loss comes to him from his gain,
Darkness from light, from knowledge ignorance,
And lack of love from love made manifest.
Robert Browning (1812–89) British poet. *A Death in the Desert*

45 It is important what a man still plans at the end. It shows the measure of injustice in his death.
Elias Canetti (1905–) Bulgarian-born novelist. *The Human Province*

46 Days and moments quickly flying,
Blend the living with the dead;
Soon will you and I be lying
Each within our narrow bed.
Edward Caswall (1814–78) British hymn writer. Hymn

47 He had been, he said, a most unconscionable time dying; but he hoped that they would excuse it.
Charles II (1630–85) King of England. *History of England* (Macaulay), Vol. I, Ch. 4

48 I am ready to meet my Maker. Whether my Maker is prepared for the ordeal of meeting me is another matter.
Winston Churchill (1874–1965) British statesman.

49 I am ready to meet my Maker. Whether my Maker is ready for the ordeal of meeting me is another matter.
Winston Churchill On his 75th birthday. Speech, 30 Nov 1949

50 Death . . . a friend that alone can bring the peace his treasures cannot purchase, and remove the pain his physicians cannot cure.
Charles C. Colton (c. 1780–1843) *Lacon*, Vol. II, Ch. 110

51 Alack he's gone the way of all flesh.
William Congreve (1670–1729) British Restoration dramatist. *Squire Bickerstaff Detected*, attrib.

52 We perish'd, each alone:
But I beneath a rougher sea,
And whelm'd in deeper gulphs than he.
William Cowper (1731–1800) British poet. *The Castaway*

53 There is only one ultimate and effectual preventive for the maladies to which flesh is heir, and that is death.
Harvey Cushing (1869–1939) US surgeon. *The Medical Career and Other Papers*, 'Medicine at the Crossroads'

54 He'd make a lovely corpse.
Charles Dickens (1812–70) British novelist. *See also* GOLDSMITH *Martin Chuzzlewit*, Ch. 25

55 Because I could not stop for Death,
He kindly stopped for me;
The carriage held but just ourselves
And Immortality.
Emily Dickinson (1830–86) US poet. *The Chariot*

56 Our journey had advanced;
Our feet were almost come
To that odd fork in Being's road,
Eternity by term.
Emily Dickinson *Our Journey had Advanced*

57 Death be not proud, though some have called thee
Mighty and dreadful, for, thou art not so.
John Donne (1573–1631) English poet. *Holy Sonnets*, 10

58 Any man's death diminishes me, because I am involved in Mankind; And therefore never send to know for whom the bell tolls; it tolls for thee.
John Donne *Devotions*, 17

59 Sin brought death, and death will disappear with the disappearance of sin.
Mary Baker Eddy (1821–1910) US religious leader. *Science and Health, with Key to the Scriptures*

60 So death, the most terrifying of ills, is nothing to us, since so long as we exist, death is not with us; but when death comes, then we do not exist. It does not then concern either the living or the dead, since for the former it is not, and the latter are no more.

Epicurus (341 BC–270 BC) Greek philosopher. *Letter to Menoeceus*

61 Death is my neighbour now.

Edith Evans (1888–1976) British actress. Said a week before her death. BBC radio interview, 14 Oct 1976

62 It hath been often said, that it is not death, but dying, which is terrible.

Henry Fielding (1707–54) British novelist. *Amelia*, Bk. III, Ch. 4

63 Strange, is it not? that of the myriads who
Before us pass'd the door of Darkness through,
Not one returns to tell us of the Road,
Which to discover we must travel too.

Edward Fitzgerald (1809–83) British poet. *The Rubáiyát of Omar Khayyám*

64 In vain we shall penetrate more and more deeply the secrets of the structure of the human body, we shall not dupe nature; we shall die as usual.

Bernard de Fontenelle (1657–1757) French philosopher. *Dialogues des morts*, Dialogue V

65 He hath shook hands with time.

John Ford (c. 1586–c. 1640) English dramatist. *The Broken Heart*, V:2

66 Death destroys a man, the idea of Death saves him.

E. M. Forster (1879–1970) British novelist. *Howards End*, Ch. 27

67 Dere's no more work for poor old Ned,
He's gone whar de good niggers go.

Stephen Foster (1826–64) US composer of popular songs. *Uncle Ned*

68 If Mr Selwyn calls again, shew him up: if I am alive I shall be delighted to see him; and if I am dead he would like to see me.

Henry Fox (1705–74) British politician. Said during his last illness. George Selwyn was known for his morbid fascination for dead bodies. *George Selwyn and his Contemporaries* (J. H. Jesse), Vol. III

69 Why fear death? It is the most beautiful adventure in life.

Charles Frohman (1860–1915) US theater producer. Said before going down with the liner *Lusitania*, alluding to 'To die will be an awfully big adventure' from Barrie's *Peter Pan*, which Frohman had produced. *J. M. Barrie and the Lost Boys* (A. Birkin)

70 Something lingering, with boiling oil in it, I fancy.

W. S. Gilbert (1836–1911) British dramatist. *The Mikado*, II

71 I am told he makes a very handsome corpse, and becomes his coffin prodigiously.

Oliver Goldsmith (1728–74) Irish-born British writer. *See also* DICKENS. *The Good-Natured Man*, I

72 The doctors found, when she was dead –
Her last disorder mortal.

Oliver Goldsmith *Elegy on Mrs. Mary Blaize*

73 Can storied urn or animated bust
Back to its mansion call the fleeting breath?
Can honour's voice provoke the silent dust,
Or flatt'ry soothe the dull cold ear of death?

Thomas Gray (1716–71) British poet. *Elegy Written in a Country Churchyard*

74 Here rests his head upon the lap of Earth
A youth to fortune and to fame unknown.
Fair Science frown'd not on his humble birth,
And Melancholy mark'd him for her own.

Thomas Gray *Elegy Written in a Country Churchyard*

75 My friend, the artery ceases to beat.

Albrecht von Haller *The Harvest of a Quiet Eye* (Alan L. Mackay)

76 Grieve not that I die young. Is it not well
To pass away ere life hath lost its brightness?

Lady Flora Hastings (1806–39) British poet. *Swan Song*

77 Once you're dead, you're made for life.

Jimi Hendrix (1942–70) US rock musician. Attrib.

78 Death is still working like a mole,
And digs my grave at each remove.

George Herbert (1593–1633) English poet. *Grace*

79 Anno domini – that's the most fatal complaint of all in the end.

James Hilton (1900–54) British novelist. *Good-bye, Mr Chips*, Ch. 1

80 Death is nothing at all. I have only slipped away into the next room. I am I and you are you. Whatever we were to each other, that we are still. Call me by my old familiar name, speak to me in the easy way you always use. Put no difference into your tone, wear no forced air of solemnity or sorrow... What is death but negligible accident? Why should I be out of mind because I am out of sight? I am waiting for you, for an interval, somewhere very near just around the corner. All is well.

Henry Scott Holland (1847–1918) British Anglican clergyman. Attrib.

81 It is the duty of a doctor to prolong life. It is not his duty to prolong the act of dying.

Lord Thomas Horder (1871–1955) Speech, House of Lords, Dec 1936

82 Death... It's the only thing we haven't succeeded in completely vulgarizing.

Aldous Huxley (1894–1964) British novelist. *Eyeless in Gaza*, Ch. 31

83 You mean what everybody means nowadays... Ignore death up to the last moment; then, when it can't be ignored any longer, have yourself squirted full of morphia and shuffle off in a coma.

Aldous Huxley *Time Must Have a Stop*, Ch. 26

84 Our civilization is founded on the shambles, and every individual existence goes out in a lonely spasm of helpless agony.

William James (1842–1910) US psychologist and philosopher. *Varieties of Religious Experience*

85 I die because I do not die.

St John of the Cross (Juan de Yepes y Alvarez; 1542–91) Spanish churchman and poet. *Coplas del alma que pena por ver a dios*

86 I am able to follow my own death step by step. Now I move softly towards the end.

Pope John XXIII (Angelo Roncalli; 1881–1963) Italian churchman. Remark made two days before he died. *The Guardian*, 3 June 1963

87 It matters not how a man dies, but how he lives. The act of dying is not of importance, it lasts so short a time.

Samuel Johnson (1709–84) British lexicographer. *Life of Johnson* (J. Boswell), Vol. II

88 Above ground I shall be food for kites; below I shall be food for mole-crickets and ants. Why rob one to feed the other?

Juang-zu (4th century BC) Chinese Taoist philosopher. When asked on his deathbed what his wishes were regarding the disposal of his body. *Famous Last Words* (B. Conrad)

89 God finally caught his eye.

George S. Kaufman (1889–1961) US dramatist. Referring to a dead waiter. *George S. Kaufman and the Algonquin Round Table* (S. Meredith)

90 Darkling I listen; and, for many a time
I have been half in love with easeful Death,
Call'd him soft names in many a mused rhyme,
To take into the air my quiet breath;
Now more than ever seems it rich to die,
To cease upon the midnight with no pain,
While thou art pouring forth thy soul abroad
In such an ecstasy!

John Keats (1795–1821) British poet. *Ode to a Nightingale*

91 I shall soon be laid in the quiet grave – thank God for the quiet grave – O! I can feel the cold earth upon me – the daisies growing over me – O for this quiet – it will be my first.

John Keats In a letter to John Taylor by Joseph Severn, 6 Mar 1821

92 Teach me to live, that I may dread
The grave as little as my bed.

Thomas Ken (1637–1711) English bishop. *An Evening Hymn*

93 In the long run we are all dead.

John Maynard Keynes (1883–1946) British economist. *Collected Writings*, 'A Tract on Monetary Reform'

94 That is the road we all have to take – over the Bridge of Sighs into eternity.

Soren Kierkegaard (1813–55) Danish philosopher. *Kierkegaard Anthology* (Auden)

95 O pity the dead that are dead, but cannot make
the journey, still they moan and beat
against the silvery adamant walls of life's exclusive city.

D. H. Lawrence (1885–1930) British novelist. *The Houseless Dead*

96 The dead don't die. They look on and help.

D. H. Lawrence Letter

97 I detest life-insurance agents. They always argue that I shall some day die, which is not so.

Stephen Leacock (1869–1944) English-born Canadian economist and humorist. *Literary Lapses*

98 There is a Reaper whose name is Death,
And, with his sickle keen,
He reaps the bearded grain at a breath,
And the flowers that grow between.

Henry Wadsworth Longfellow (1807–82) US poet. *The Reaper and the Flowers*

99 Death is better than disease.

Henry Wadsworth Longfellow *Christus: A Mystery*, Pt. II, Sect. 1

100 There is . . . no death . . . There is only . . . *me . . . me . . . who is going to die . . .*

André Malraux (1901–76) French writer and statesman. *The Royal Way*

101 It is the only disease you don't look forward to being cured of.

Herman J. Mankiewicz (1897–1953) US journalist and screenwriter. Referring to death. *Citizen Kane*

102 Cut is the branch that might have grown full straight,
And burned is Apollo's laurel-bough,
That sometime grew within this learned man.

Christopher Marlowe (1564–93) English dramatist. *Doctor Faustus*, Epilogue

103 The grave's a fine and private place,
But none, I think, do there embrace.

Andrew Marvell (1621–78) English poet. *To His Coy Mistress*

104 Either he's dead or my watch has stopped.

Groucho Marx (Julius Marx; 1895–1977) US comedian. *A Day at the Races*

105 My husband is dead.
– I'll bet he's just using that as an excuse.
I was with him to the end.
– No wonder he passed away.
I held him in my arms and kissed him.
– So it was murder!

Groucho Marx *Duck Soup*

106 Dying is a very dull, dreary affair. And my advice to you is to have nothing whatever to do with it.

W. Somerset Maugham (1874–1965) British novelist. *Escape from the Shadows* (Robin Maugham)

107 Dying is the most hellishly boresome experience in the world! Particularly when it entails dying of 'natural causes'.

W. Somerset Maugham *The Two Worlds of Somerset Maugham* (Wilmon Menard), Ch. 22

108 Alas! Lord and Lady Dalhousie are dead, and buried at last,
Which causes many people to feel a little downcast.

William McGonagall (1830–1902) Scottish poet. *The Death of Lord and Lady Dalhousie*

109 Whom the gods love dies young.

Menander (c. 341–c. 290 BC) Greek dramatist. *Dis Exapaton*

110 One dies only once, and it's for such a long time!

Molière (Jean Baptiste Poquelin; 1622–73) French dramatist. *Le Dépit amoureux*, V:3

111 Oh well, no matter what happens, there's always death.

Napoleon I (Napoleon Bonaparte; 1769–1821) French emperor. Attrib.

112 And in the happy no-time of his sleeping
Death took him by the heart.

Wilfred Owen (1893–1918) British poet. *Asleep*

113 Christianity has made of death a terror which was unknown to the gay calmness of the Pagan.

Ouida (Marie Louise de la Ramée; 1839–1908) British novelist. *The Failure of Christianity*

114 It costs me never a stab nor squirm
To tread by chance upon a worm.
'Aha, my little dear,' I say,
'Your clan will pay me back one day.'

Dorothy Parker (1893–1967) US writer. *Sunset Gun*, 'Thought for a Sunshiny Morning'

115 Many men on the point of an edifying death would be furious if they were suddenly restored to life.

Cesare Pavese (1908–50) Italian writer.

116 Dying
is an art, like everything else.
I do it exceptionally well.

Sylvia Plath (1932–63) US writer. *Lady Lazarus*

117 I mount! I fly!
O grave! where is thy victory?
O death! where is thy sting?

Alexander Pope (1688–1744) British poet. See BIBLE: I Corinthians. *The Dying Christian to his Soul*

118 Here am I, dying of a hundred good symptoms.

Alexander Pope *Anecdotes by and about Alexander Pope* (Joseph Spence)

119 How often are we to die before we go quite off this stage? In every

friend we lose a part of ourselves, and the best part.
Alexander Pope Letter to Jonathan Swift, 5 Dec 1732

120 Death is the greatest kick of all, that's why they save it for last.
Robert Raisner British writer. *Graffiti*, 'Death'

121 The hero is strangely akin to those who die young.
Rainer Maria Rilke (1875–1926) Austrian poet. *Duineser Elegien*, VI

122 I shall have more to say when I am dead.
Edwin Arlington Robinson (1869–1935) US poet. *John Brown*

123 When I am dead, my dearest,
Sing no sad songs for me;
Plant thou no roses at my head,
Nor shady cypress tree:
Be the green grass above me
With showers and dewdrops wet;
And if thou wilt, remember,
And if thou wilt, forget.
Christina Rossetti (1830–74) British poet. *When I am Dead*

124 He who pretends to look on death without fear lies. All men are afraid of dying, this is the great law of sentient beings, without which the entire human species would soon be destroyed.
Jean-Jacques Rousseau (1712–78) French philosopher. *Julie, or the New Eloise*

125 Death is the privilege of human nature,
And life without it were not worth our taking.
Nicholas Rowe (1674–1718) English dramatist. *The Fair Penitent*, V:1

126 In the post-mortem room we witness the final result of disease, the failure of the body to solve its problems, and there is an obvious limit to what one can learn about normal business transactions from even a daily visit to the bankruptcy court.
W. Russell, Lord Brain *Canadian Medical Association Journal*, 83:349, 1960

127 Ain't It Grand to Be Bloomin' Well Dead?
Leslie Sarony (1897–1985) British entertainer and writer. Song title

128 To that dark inn, the grave!
Walter Scott (1771–1832) Scottish novelist. *The Lord of the Isles*, VI

129 His morning walk was beneath the elms in the churchyard; 'for death,' he said, 'had been his next-door neighbour for so many years, that he had no apology for dropping the acquaintance.'
Walter Scott *The Legend of Montrose*, Introduction

130 I have a rendezvous with Death
At some disputed barricade.
Alan Seeger (1888–1916) US poet. *I Have a Rendezvous with Death*

131 Death is a punishment to some, to some a gift, and to many a favour.
Seneca (c. 4 BC–AD 65) Roman writer. *Hercules Oetaeus*

132 I will be
A bridegroom in my death, and run into 't
As to a lover's bed.
William Shakespeare (1564–1616) English dramatist. *Antony and Cleopatra*, IV:12

133 If thou and nature can so gently part,
The stroke of death is as a lover's pinch,
Which hurts, and is desir'd.
William Shakespeare *Antony and Cleopatra*, V:2

134 He had rather
Groan so in perpetuity, than be cured
By the sure physician, death.
William Shakespeare *Cymbeline*

135 The rest is silence.
William Shakespeare *Hamlet*, V:2

136 But thoughts, the slaves of life, and life, time's fool,
And time, that takes survey of all the world,
Must have a stop.
William Shakespeare *Henry IV, Part One*, V:4

137 I care not; a man can die but once; we owe God a death.
William Shakespeare *Henry IV, Part Two*, III:2

138 His nose was as sharp as a pen, and 'a babbl'd of green fields.
William Shakespeare Referring to Falstaff on his deathbed. *Henry V*, II:3

139 Why, he that cuts off twenty years of life
Cuts off so many years of fearing death.
William Shakespeare *Julius Caesar*, III:1

140 O mighty Caesar! dost thou lie so low?
Are all thy conquests, glories, triumphs, spoils,
Shrunk to this little measure?
William Shakespeare *Julius Caesar*, III:1

141 Nothing in his life
Became him like the leaving it: he died
As one that had been studied in his death
To throw away the dearest thing he ow'd
As 'twere a careless trifle.
William Shakespeare *Macbeth*, I:4

142 Ay, but to die, and go we know not where;
To lie in cold obstruction, and to rot;
This sensible warm motion to become
A kneaded clod; and the delighted spirit
To bathe in fiery floods or to reside
In thrilling region of thick-ribbed ice.
William Shakespeare *Measure for Measure*, III:1

143 Dar'st thou die?
The sense of death is most in apprehension,
And the poor beetle, that we tread upon,
In corporal sufferance finds a pang as great
As when a giant dies.
William Shakespeare *Measure for Measure*, III:1

144 If I must die,
I will encounter darkness as a bride,
And hug it in mine arms.
William Shakespeare *Measure for Measure*, III:1

145 Be not afraid, though you do see me weapon'd;
Here is my journey's end, here is my butt,
And very sea-mark of my utmost sail.
William Shakespeare *Othello*, V:2

146 The worst is death, and death will have his day.
William Shakespeare *Richard II*, III:2

147 Of comfort no man speak:
Let's talk of graves, of worms, and epitaphs;
Make dust our paper, and with rainy eyes
Write sorrow on the bosom of the earth.
Let's choose executors, and talk of wills.

William Shakespeare *Richard II*, III:3

148 A dateless bargain to engrossing death!

William Shakespeare *Romeo and Juliet*, V:3

149 Full fathom five thy father lies;
Of his bones are coral made;
Those are pearls that were his eyes;
Nothing of him that doth fade
But doth suffer a sea-change
Into something rich and strange.

William Shakespeare *The Tempest*, I:2

150 He that dies pays all debts.

William Shakespeare *The Tempest*, III:2

151 After all, what *is* death? Just nature's way of telling us to slow down.

Dick Sharples *In Loving Memory*, Yorkshire Television, 1979

152 Death is the veil which those who live call life:
They sleep, and it is lifted.

Percy Bysshe Shelley (1792–1822) British poet. *Prometheus Unbound*, III

153 It is a modest creed, and yet
Pleasant if one considers it,
To own that death itself must be,
Like all the rest, a mockery.

Percy Bysshe Shelley *The Sensitive Plant*, III

154 I cannot forgive my friends for dying: I do not find these vanishing acts of theirs at all amusing.

Logan Pearsall Smith (1865–1946) US writer. *Trivia*

155 I do really think that death will be marvellous . . . If there wasn't death, I think you couldn't go on.

Stevie Smith (Florence Margaret Smith; 1902–71) British poet. *The Observer*, 9 Nov 1969

156 Death must be distinguished from dying, with which it is often confused.

Sydney Smith (1771–1845) British clergyman, essayist, and wit. *The Smith of Smiths* (Pearson)

157 The whole of his life had prepared Podduyev for living, not for dying.

Alexander Solzhenitsyn (1918–) Soviet novelist. *Cancer Ward*, Pt. I, Ch. 8

158 My name is death; the last best friend am I.

Robert Southey (1774–1843) British poet. *Carmen Nuptiale: The Lay of the Laureate*, 'The Dream'

159 Sleep after toil, port after stormy seas,
Ease after war, death after life does greatly please.

Edmund Spenser (1552–99) English poet. *The Faerie Queene*, I:9

160 Under the wide and starry sky
Dig the grave and let me lie.
Glad did I live and gladly die,
– And I laid me down with a will.
This is the verse you grave for me:
'Here he lies where he longed to be;
Home is the sailor, home from sea,
And the hunter home from the hill.'

Robert Louis Stevenson (1850–94) Scottish writer. *Underwoods*, Bk. I, 'Requiem'

161 It is impossible that anything so natural, so necessary, and so universal as death, should ever have been designed by Providence as an evil to mankind.

Jonathan Swift (1667–1745) Irish-born Anglican priest and writer. 'Thoughts on Religion'

162 Even so, in death the same unknown will appear as ever known to me. And because I love this life, I know I shall love death as well. The child cries out when from the right breast the mother takes it away, in the very next moment to find in the left one its consolation.

Rabindranath Tagore (1861–1941) Indian poet and philosopher. *Gitanjali*

163 Row upon row with strict impunity
The headstones yield their names to the element.

Allen Tate (1899–) US poet. *Ode to the Confederate Dead*

164 A day less or more
At sea or ashore,
We die – does it matter when?

Alfred, Lord Tennyson (1809–92) British poet. *The Revenge*, XI

165 I, born of flesh and ghost, was neither
A ghost nor man, but mortal ghost.
And I was struck down by death's feather.

Dylan Thomas (1914–53) Welsh poet. *Before I knocked*

166 After the first death, there is no other.

Dylan Thomas *A Refusal to Mourn the Death, by Fire, of a Child in London*

167 Do not go gentle into that good night,
Old age should burn and rave at close of day;
Rage, rage, against the dying of the light.

Dylan Thomas *Do not go gentle into that good night*

168 And Death Shall Have No Dominion.

Dylan Thomas Title of poem

169 There is not any book
Or face of dearest look
That I would not turn from now
To go into the unknown
I must enter, and leave, alone,
I know not how.

Edward Thomas (1878–1917) British poet. *Lights Out*

170 Death is the price paid by life for an enhancement of the complexity of a live organism's structure.

Arnold Toynbee (1889–1975) British historian. *Life After Death*

171 Go and try to disprove death. Death will disprove you, and that's all!

Ivan Turgenev (1818–83) Russian novelist. *Fathers and Sons*, Ch. 27

172 All right, my lord creator, Don Miguel, you too will die and return to the nothing whence you came. God will cease to dream you!

Miguel de Unamuno y Jugo (1864–1936) Spanish writer. *Mist*

173 While I thought that I was learning how to live, I have been learning how to die.

Leonardo da Vinci (1452–1519) Italian artist. *Notebooks*

174 The human race is the only one that knows it must die, and it knows this only through its experience. A child brought up alone and transported to a desert island would have no more idea of death than a cat or a plant.

Voltaire (François-Marie Arouet; 1694–1778) French writer and philosopher. *The Oxford Book of Death* (D. J. Enright)

175 There's no repentance in the grave.

Isaac Watts (1674–1748) English theologian and hymn writer. *Divine Songs for Children*, 'Solemn Thoughts of God and Death'

176 For he who lives more lives than one
More deaths than one must die.

Oscar Wilde (1854–1900) Irish-born British dramatist. *The Ballad of Reading Gaol*, III:37

177 Dead! and . . . never called me mother.
Mrs Henry Wood (1814–87) British novelist. *East Lynne* (dramatized version; the words do not occur in the novel)

178 Three years she grew in sun and shower,
Then Nature said, 'A lovelier flower
On earth was never sown;
This child I to myself will take;
She shall be mine, and I will make
A Lady of my own.
William Wordsworth (1770–1850) British poet. *Three Years she Grew*

179 We are laid asleep
In body, and become a living soul:
While with an eye made quiet by the power
Of harmony, and the deep power of joy,
We see into the life of things.
William Wordsworth *Lines composed a few miles above Tintern Abbey*

DEBAUCHERY

See also animalism, lust, pleasure, sex

1 A fool bolts pleasure, then complains of moral indigestion.
Minna Antrim (1861–?) US writer. *Naked Truth and Veiled Allusions*

2 A great many people have come up to me and asked how I manage to get so much work done and still keep looking so dissipated.
Robert Benchley (1889–1945) US humorist. *Chips off the Old Benchley*, 'How to Get Things Done'

3 *Debauchee*, n. One who has so earnestly pursued pleasure that he has had the misfortune to overtake it.
Ambrose Bierce (1842–?1914) US writer and journalist. *The Devil's Dictionary*

4 So, we'll go no more a roving
So late into the night,
Though the heart be still as loving,
And the moon be still as bright.
Lord Byron (1788–1824) British poet. *So, we'll go no more a roving*

5 I've over-educated myself in all the things I shouldn't have known at all.
Noël Coward (1899–1973) British dramatist. *Wild Oats*

6 My problem lies in reconciling my gross habits with my net income.
Errol Flynn (1909–59) Australian actor. Attrib.

7 No one ever suddenly became depraved.
Juvenal (Decimus Junius Juvenalis; 60–130 AD) Roman satirist. *Satires*, II

8 We're poor little lambs who've lost our way,
Baa! Baa! Baa!
We're little black sheep who've gone astray,
Baa-aa-aa!
Gentleman-rankers out on the spree,
Damned from here to Eternity,
God ha' mercy on such as we,
Baa! Yah! Bah!
Rudyard Kipling (1865–1936) Indian-born British writer. *Gentleman-Rankers*

9 Some things can't be ravished. You can't ravish a tin of sardines.
D. H. Lawrence (1885–1930) British novelist. *Lady Chatterley's Lover*

10 Home is heaven and orgies are vile
But you need an orgy, once in a while.
Ogden Nash (1902–71) US poet. *Home, 99.44/100% Sweet Home*

11 Once: a philosopher; twice: a pervert!
Voltaire (François-Marie Arouet; 1694–1778) French writer. Turning down an invitation to an orgy, having attended one the previous night for the first time. Attrib.

DEBT

See borrowing

DECEPTION

See also appearances, hypocrisy, insincerity, lying

1 To deceive oneself is very easy.
Proverb

2 Beware of false prophets, which come to you in sheep's clothing, but inwardly they are ravening wolves.
Bible: Matthew 7:15

3 Almost every man wastes part of his life in attempts to display qualities which he does not possess, and to gain applause which he cannot keep.
Samuel Johnson (1709–84) British lexicographer. *The Rambler*

4 You can fool some of the people all the time and all the people some of the time; but you can't fool all the people all the time.
Abraham Lincoln (1809–65) US statesman. Attrib.

5 Lord, Lord, how this world is given to lying! I grant you I was down and out of breath; and so was he; but we rose both at an instant, and fought a long hour by Shrewsbury clock.
William Shakespeare (1564–1616) English dramatist. *Henry IV, Part 1*, V:4

6 I want that glib and oily art
To speak and purpose not; since what I well intend,
I'll do't before I speak.
William Shakespeare *King Lear*, I:1

7 False face must hide what the false heart doth know.
William Shakespeare *Macbeth*, I:7

8 Sigh no more, ladies, sigh no more,
Men were deceivers ever;
One foot in sea, and one on shore,
To one thing constant never.
Then sigh not so,
But let them go,
And be you blithe and bonny,
Converting all your sounds of woe
Into Hey nonny, nonny.
William Shakespeare *Much Ado About Nothing*, II:3

9 If she be false, O! then heaven mocks itself.
I'll not believe it.
William Shakespeare *Othello*, III:3

10 You can fool too many of the people too much of the time.
James Thurber (1894–1961) US humorist. *Fables for Our Time*, 'The Owl Who Was God'

11 I have invented an invaluable permanent invalid called Bunbury, in order that I may be able to go down into the country whenever I choose.
Oscar Wilde (1854–1900) Irish-born British dramatist. *The Importance of Being Earnest*, I

DECISION

See also determination

1 I'm Gonna Wash That Man Right Out of My Hair.
Oscar Hammerstein II (1895–1960) US lyricist. *South Pacific*, Title of song

2 Tender-handed stroke a nettle,
And it stings you for your pains;
Grasp it like a man of mettle,
And it soft as silk remains.
Aaron Hill (1685–1750) British poet and dramatist. *Verses Written on Window*

3 Like all weak men he laid an exaggerated stress on not changing one's mind.
W. Somerset Maugham (1874–1965) British novelist. *Of Human Bondage*, Ch. 37

4 If someone tells you he is going to make 'a realistic decision', you immediately understand that he has resolved to do something bad.

Mary McCarthy (1912–) US novelist. *On the Contrary*

5 This is the night
That either makes me or fordoes me quite.

William Shakespeare (1564–1616) English dramatist. *Othello*, V:1

DECLINE

1 And though the Van Dycks have to go
And we pawn the Bechstein grand,
We'll stand by the Stately Homes of England.

Noël Coward (1899–1973) British dramatist. *Operette*, 'The Stately Homes of England'

2 That's Why the Lady Is a Tramp.

Lorenz Hart (1895–1943) US songwriter. From the musical *Babes in Arms*. Song title

3 It is the logic of our times,
No subject for immortal verse –
That we who lived by honest dreams
Defend the bad against the worse.

C. Day Lewis (1904–72) British poet. *Where are the War Poets?*

4 From morn
To noon he fell, from noon to dewy eve,
A summer's day, and with the setting sun
Dropped from the zenith, like a falling star.

John Milton (1608–74) English poet. *Paradise Lost*, Bk. I

5 Macmillan seemed, in his very person, to embody the national decay he supposed himself to be confuting. He exuded a flavour of moth-balls.

Malcolm Muggeridge (1903–) British writer. *Tread Softly For You Tread on My Jokes*, 'England, whose England'

6 It is only a step from the sublime to the ridiculous.

Napoleon I (Napoleon Bonaparte; 1769–1821) French emperor. Remark following the retreat from Moscow, 1812. Attrib.

7 We have on our hands a sick man – a very sick man.

Nicholas I (1796–1855) Tsar of Russia. Referring to Turkey, the 'sick man of Europe'; said to Sir G. H. Seymour, British envoy to St Petersburg, Jan 1853. Attrib.

8 Now there are fields where Troy once was.

Ovid (Publius Ovidius Naso; 43 BC–17 AD) Roman poet. *Heroides*, Bk. I

9 There may have been disillusionments in the lives of the medieval saints, but they would scarcely have been better pleased if they could have foreseen that their names would be associated nowadays chiefly with racehorses and the cheaper clarets.

Saki (Hector Hugh Munro; 1870–1916) British writer. *Reginald at the Carlton*

10 O! what a noble mind is here o'erthrown:
The courtier's, soldier's, scholar's, eye, tongue, sword;
The expectancy and rose of the fair state,
The glass of fashion, and the mould of form,
The observed of all observers, quite, quite, down!
And I, of ladies most deject and wretched,
That suck'd the honey of his music vows,
Now see that noble and most sovereign reason,
Like sweet bells jangled, out of tune and harsh;
That unmatch'd form and figure of blown youth,
Blasted with ecstasy: O! woe is me,
To have seen what I have seen, see what I see!

William Shakespeare (1564–1616) English dramatist. *Hamlet*, III:1

11 What must the king do now? Must he submit?
The king shall do it: must he be depos'd?
The king shall be contented: must he lose
The name of king? o' God's name, let it go.
I'll give my jewels for a set of beads,
My gorgeous palace for a hermitage,
My gay apparel for an almsman's gown,
My figur'd goblets for a dish of wood,
My sceptre for a palmer's walking staff,
My subjects for a pair of carved saints,
And my large kingdom for a little grave,
A little little grave, an obscure grave;
Or I'll be buried in the king's highway,
Some way of common trade, where subjects' feet
May hourly trample on their sovereign's head;
For on my heart they tread now whilst I live;
And buried once, why not upon my head?

William Shakespeare *Richard II*, III:3

12 You may my glories and my state depose,
But not my griefs; still am I king of those.

William Shakespeare *Richard II*, IV:1

13 I shall be like that tree; I shall die from the top.

Jonathan Swift (1667–1745) Irish-born Anglican priest and writer. Predicting his own mental decline, on seeing a tree with a withered crown. *Lives of the Wits* (H. Pearson)

14 I dreamed there would be Spring no more,
That Nature's ancient power was lost.

Alfred, Lord Tennyson (1809–92) British poet. *In Memoriam A.H.H.*, LXIX

15 The difference between our decadence and the Russians' is that while theirs is brutal, ours is apathetic.

James Thurber (1894–1961) US humorist. *The Observer*, 'Sayings of the Week', 5 Feb 1961

16 I started at the top and worked my way down.

Orson Welles (1915–85) US film actor. *The Filmgoer's Book of Quotes* (Leslie Halliwell)

17 Plain living and high thinking are no more.

William Wordsworth (1770–1850) British poet. *Sonnets*, 'O friend! I know not'

18 Milton! thou shouldst be living at this hour:
England hath need of thee; she is a fen
Of stagnant waters: altar, sword, and pen,
Fireside, the heroic wealth of hall and bower,
Have forfeited their ancient English dower
Of inward happiness.

William Wordsworth *Sonnets*, 'Milton! thou shouldst'

DEFEAT

See also loss

1 If it is a blessing, it is certainly very well disguised.

Winston Churchill (1874–1965) British statesman. Said to his wife after his defeat in the

1945 general election, when she said that it was a blessing in disguise. *Memoirs of Richard Nixon* (R. Nixon)

2 As always, victory finds a hundred fathers, but defeat is an orphan.
Count Galeazzo Ciano (1903–44) Italian Foreign Minister. Diary entry, 9 Sept 1942

3 'Tis better to have fought and lost,
Than never to have fought at all.
Arthur Hugh Clough (1819–61) British poet. *Peschiera*

4 Of all I had, only honour and life have been spared.
Francis I (1494–1547) King of France. Referring to his defeat at the Battle of Pavia, 24 Feb 1525; usually misquoted as 'All is lost save honour.' Letter to Louise of Savoy (his mother), 1525

5 Sire you no longer have an army.
Wilhelm Groener (1867–1939) German general. Said to the Emperor Wilhelm II of Germany, 9 Nov 1918

6 A man can be destroyed but not defeated.
Ernest Hemingway (1899–1961) US novelist. *The Old Man and the Sea*

7 As an English General has very truly said, 'The German army was stabbed in the back'.
Paul von Hindenburg (1847–1934) German Field Marshal and President. Referring to Germany's defeat in World War I; it is not known whom Hindenburg was quoting. Statement to a Reichstag Committee, 18 Nov 1918

8 The war situation has developed not necessarily to Japan's advantage.
Hirohito (1901–89) Japanese head of state. Announcing Japan's surrender, 15 Aug 1945

9 We wuz robbed – We should have stood in bed.
Joe Jacobs (1896–1940) US boxing manager. After Max Schmeling's defeat by Jack Sharkey. *Strong Cigars and Lovely Women* (J. Lardner)

10 Woe to the vanquished.
Livy (Titus Livius; 59 BC–17 AD) Roman historian. *History*, V:48

11 When I am dead and opened, you shall find 'Calais' lying in my heart.
Mary I (1516–58) Queen of England. *Chronicles* (Holinshed), III

12 I brought myself down. I gave them a sword and they stuck it in and they twisted it with relish. And I guess if I'd been in their position I'd have done the same thing.
Richard Milhous Nixon (1913–) US President. TV interview, 19 May 1977

13 Every man meets his Waterloo at last.
Wendell Phillips (1811–84) US reformer. Speech, Brooklyn, 1 Nov 1859

14 Of the two lights of Christendom, one has been extinguished.
Aeneas Silvius (1405–64) Bishop of Trieste. Remark on hearing of the fall of Constantinople to the Turks (29 May 1453)

15 Well, I have one consolation, No candidate was ever elected ex-president by such a large majority!
William Howard Taft (1857–1930) US statesman. Referring to his disastrous defeat in the 1912 presidential election. Attrib.

16 It is the beginning of the end.
Talleyrand (Charles Maurice de Talleyrand-Périgord; 1754–1838) French politician. Referring to Napoleon's defeat at Borodino, 1813. Attrib.

17 Please understand that there is no one depressed in *this* house; we are not interested in the possibilities of defeat; they do not exist.
Victoria (1819–1901) Queen of the United Kingdom. Referring to the Boer War; said to Balfour. *Life of Salisbury* (Lady G. Cecil)

18 Another year! – another deadly blow!
Another mighty empire overthrown!
And we are left, or shall be left, alone.
William Wordsworth (1770–1850) British poet. Napoleon defeated Prussia at the Battles of Jena and Auerstädt, 14 Oct 1806. *Sonnets*, 'Another year!'

DEFENSE

See also war

1 The only defence is in offence, which means that you have to kill more women and children more quickly than the enemy if you want to save yourselves.
Stanley Baldwin (1867–1947) British statesman. Speech, Nov 1932

2 Preparing for suicide is not a very intelligent means of defence.
Bruce Kent (1929–) British campaigner for nuclear disarmament. *The Observer*, 'Sayings of the Week', 10 Aug 1986

3 The best immediate defense of the United States is the success of Great Britain defending itself.
Franklin D. Roosevelt (1882–1945) US Democratic president. At press conference, 17 Dec 1940. *Their Finest Hour* (Winston S. Churchill), Ch. 28

4 Truth telling is not compatible with the defence of the realm.
George Bernard Shaw (1856–1950) Irish dramatist and critic. *Heartbreak House*

DEFIANCE

See also rebellion

1 The defiance of established authority, religious and secular, social and political, as a world-wide phenomenon may well one day be accounted the outstanding event of the last decade.
Hannah Arendt (1906–75) German-born US philosopher and historian. *Crises of the Republic*, 'Civil Disobedience'

2 In war, resolution; in defeat, defiance; in victory, magnanimity; in peace, goodwill.
Winston Churchill (1874–1965) British statesman. Epigram used by Sir Edward Marsh after World War II; used as 'a moral of the work' in Churchill's book. *The Second World War*

3 My father made the most part of you almost out of nothing.
Mary I (1516–58) Queen of England. Reply when threatened, during the reign of Edward VI, because of her Catholicism. *The Earlier Tudors* (J. D. Mackie)

4 The poorest man may in his cottage bid defiance to all the forces of the Crown. It may be frail – its roof may shake – the wind may blow through it – the storm may enter – the rain may enter – but the King of England cannot enter! – all his force dares not cross the threshold of the ruined tenement!
William Pitt the Elder (1708–78) British statesman. *Statesmen in the Time of George III* (Lord Brougham), Vol. I

DELIGHT

1 Look, stranger, at this island now
The leaping light for your delight discovers.
W. H. Auden (1907–73) British poet. *Look, Stranger*

2 Whosoever is delighted in solitude is either a wild beast or a god.
Francis Bacon (1561–1626) English philosopher. *Essays*, 'Of Friendship'

3 Studies serve for delight, for ornament, and for ability.
Francis Bacon *Essays*, 'Of Studies'

4 Energy is Eternal Delight.
William Blake (1757–1827) British poet. *The Marriage of Heaven and Hell*, 'The Voice of the Devil'

5 I am convinced that we have a

degree of delight, and that no small one, in the real misfortunes and pains of others.

Edmund Burke (1729–97) British politician. *On the Sublime and Beautiful*, Pt. I

6 Oh! don't you remember sweet Alice, Ben Bolt,
Sweet Alice, whose hair was so brown,
Who wept with delight when you gave her a smile,
And trembled with fear at your frown?

Thomas Dunn English (1819–1902) US lawyer and writer. *Ben Bolt*

7 Ay, in the very temple of delight
Veil'd Melancholy has her sovran shrine.
Though seen of none save him whose strenuous tongue
Can burst Joy's grape against his palate fine.

John Keats *Ode on Melancholy*

8 Teach us delight in simple things,
And mirth that has no bitter springs;
Forgiveness free of evil done,
And love to all men 'neath the sun!

Rudyard Kipling (1865–1936) Indian-born British writer. *The Children's Song*

9 To business that we love we rise betime,
And go to't with delight.

William Shakespeare (1564–1616) English dramatist. *Antony and Cleopatra*, IV:4

10 What a piece of work is a man! How noble in reason! how infinite in faculties! in form and moving, how express and admirable! in action, how like an angel! in apprehension, how like a god! the beauty of the world! the paragon of animals! And yet, to me, what is this quintessence of dust? Man delights not me – no, nor woman neither.

William Shakespeare *Hamlet*, II:2

11 He has occasional flashes of silence, that make his conversation perfectly delightful.

Sydney Smith (1771–1845) British clergyman and essayist. Referring to Lord Macaulay. *Memoir* (Lady Holland)

12 What a delightful thing this perspective is!

Paolo Uccello (1397–1475) Italian painter. *Men of Art* (T. Craven)

13 In *Architecture* as in all other *Operative* Arts, the *end* must direct the *Operation*. The *end* is to build well. Well building hath three Conditions. *Commodity, Firmness*, and *Delight*.

Henry Wotton (1568–1639) English poet and diplomat. *Elements of Architecture*, Pt. I

DELUSION

1 But yet the light that led astray
Was light from Heaven.

Robert Burns (1759–96) Scottish poet. *The Vision*

2 Take care, your worship, those things over there are not giants but windmills.

Miguel de Cervantes (1547–1616) Spanish novelist. *Don Quixote*, Pt. I, Ch. 8

3 Didn't I tell you, Don Quixote, sir, to turn back, for they were not armies you were going to attack, but flocks of sheep?

Miguel de Cervantes *Don Quixote*, Pt. I, Ch. 18

4 Take the life-lie away from the average man and straight away you take away his happiness.

Henrik Ibsen (1828–1906) Norwegian dramatist. *The Wild Duck*, V

5 Many people have delusions of grandeur but you're deluded by triviality.

Eugène Ionesco (1912–) French dramatist. *Exit the King*

6 Is this a dagger I see before me,
The handle toward my hand? Come, let me clutch thee:
I have thee not, and yet I see thee still.
Art thou not, fatal vision, sensible
To feeling as to sight? or art thou but
A dagger of the mind, a false creation,
Proceeding from the heat-oppressed brain?

William Shakespeare (1564–1616) English dramatist. *Macbeth*, II:1

DEMOCRACY

See also class, government, majority, public, republic

1 Democracy means government by discussion but it is only effective if you can stop people talking.

Clement Attlee (1883–1967) British statesman and Labour prime minister. *Anatomy of Britain* (Anthony Sampson)

2 A democracy must remain at home in all matters which affect the nature of her institutions . . . We do not want the racial antipathies or national antagonisms of the Old World translated to this continent, as they will should we become a part of European politics. The people of this country are overwhelmingly for a policy of neutrality.

William Edgar Borah (1865–1940) US senator. Radio broadcast, 22 Feb 1936

3 A committee is an animal with four back legs.

John Le Carré (1931–) British writer. *Tinker, Tailor, Soldier, Spy*

4 One man shall have one vote.

John Cartwright (1740–1824) British writer. *People's Barrier Against Undue Influence*

5 Democracy means government by the uneducated, while aristocracy means government by the badly educated.

G. K. Chesterton (1874–1936) British writer. *New York Times*, 1 Feb 1931

6 Democracy is the wholesome and pure air without which a socialist public organisation cannot live a full-blooded life.

Mikhail Gorbachov (1931–) Soviet statesman. Report to 27th Party Congress. Speech, 25 Feb, 1986

7 Some comrades apparently find it hard to understand that democracy is just a slogan.

Mikhail Gorbachov *The Observer*, 'Sayings of the Week', 1 Feb 1987

8 Democracy is only an experiment in government, and it has the obvious disadvantage of merely counting votes instead of weighing them.

Dean Inge (1860–1954) British churchman. *Possible Recovery?*

9 The vote is the most powerful instrument ever devised by man for breaking down injustice and destroying the terrible walls which imprison men because they are different from other men.

Lyndon B. Johnson (1908–73) US statesman. Address on signing Voting Rights Bill, Washington, DC, 6 Aug 1965

10 A democracy is a state which recognises the subjecting of the minority to the majority.

Lenin (Vladimir Ilich Ulyanov; 1870–1924) Russian revolutionary leader. *The State and The Revolution*

11 No man is good enough to govern another man without that other's consent.

Abraham Lincoln (1809–65) US statesman. Speech, 1854

12 The ballot is stronger than the bullet.
Abraham Lincoln Speech, 19 May 1856

13 This country, with its institutions, belongs to the people who inhabit it. Whenever they shall grow weary of the existing government, they can exercise their constitutional right of amending it, or their revolutionary right to dismember or overthrow it.
Abraham Lincoln First Inaugural Address, 4 Mar 1861

14 . . . that government of the people, by the people, and for the people, shall not perish from the earth.'
Abraham Lincoln Speech, 19 Nov 1863, dedicating the national cemetery on the site of the Battle of Gettysburg

15 Man's capacity for evil makes democracy necessary and man's capacity for good makes democracy possible.
Reinhold Niebuhr (1892–) US churchman. Quoted by Anthony Wedgwood Benn in *The Times*, 18 Jul 1977

16 Democracy passes into despotism.
Plato (429–347 BC) Greek philosopher. *Republic*, Bk. 8

17 I think if the people of this country can be reached with the truth, their judgment will be in favor of the many, as against the privileged few.
Eleanor Roosevelt (1884–1962) US writer and lecturer. *Ladies' Home Journal*

18 We must be the great arsenal of democracy.
Franklin D. Roosevelt (1882–1945) US Democratic president. Broadcast address to Forum on Current Problems, 29 Dec 1940

19 We must be thoroughly democratic and patronise everybody without distinction of class.
George Bernard Shaw (1856–1950) Irish dramatist and critic. *John Bull's Other Island*

20 Democracy substitutes election by the incompetent many for appointment by the corrupt few.
George Bernard Shaw *Man and Superman*, 'Maxims for Revolutionists'

21 It's not the voting that's democracy; it's the counting.
Tom Stoppard (1937–) Czech-born British dramatist. *Jumpers*

22 A committee should consist of three men, two of whom are absent.
Herbert Beerbohm Tree (1853–1917) British actor and theater manager. *Beerbohm Tree* (H. Pearson)

23 I shall not vote because I do not aspire to advise my sovereign on the choice of her servants.
Evelyn Waugh (1903–66) British novelist. *A Little Order*

24 Democracy means simply the bludgeoning of the people by the people for the people.
Oscar Wilde (1854–1900) Irish-born British dramatist. *The Soul of Man under Socialism*

25 The world must be made safe for democracy.
Woodrow Wilson (1856–1925) US statesman. Address to Congress, asking for a declaration of war, 2 Apr 1917

DENIAL

1 I am the spirit that always denies.
Goethe (1749–1832) German poet and dramatist. *Faust*, Pt. I

2 No, I am no one's contemporary – ever.
That would have been above my station . . .
How I loathe that other with my name.
He certainly never was me.
Osip Mandelstam (1891–1938) Russian poet. *Poems*, No. 141

3 I am not a crook.
Richard Milhous Nixon (1913–) US president. Attrib., 17 Nov 1973

4 He would, wouldn't he?
Mandy Rice-Davies (1944–) British call girl. Of Lord Astor, when told that he had repudiated her evidence at the trial of Stephen Ward, 29 June 1963, during the Profumo scandal

5 There was no impropriety whatsoever in my acquaintanceship with Miss Keeler.
John Profumo (1915–) British politician. Speech, House of Commons, 22 Mar 1963

DEPARTURE

See also dismissal, parting

1 Come, dear children, let us away;
Down and away below.
Matthew Arnold (1822–88) British poet and critic. *The Forsaken Merman*

2 She left lonely for ever
The kings of the sea.
Matthew Arnold *The Forsaken Merman*

3 Once I leave, I leave. I am not going to speak to the man on the bridge, and I am not going to spit on the deck.
Stanley Baldwin, 1st Earl of Bewdley (1867–1947) British Conservative prime minister. Statement to the Cabinet, 28 May 1937

4 Adieu, adieu! my native shore
Fades o'er the waters blue.
Lord Byron (1788–1824) British poet. *Childe Harold's Pilgrimage*, I

5 My native Land – Good Night!
Lord Byron *Childe Harold's Pilgrimage*, I

6 Let us go then, you and I,
When the evening is spread out against the sky
Like a patient etherized upon a table.
T. S. Eliot (1888–1965) US-born British poet and dramatist. *The Love Song of J. Alfred Prufrock*

7 And they are gone: aye, ages long ago
These lovers fled away into the storm.
John Keats (1795–1821) British poet. *The Eve of Saint Agnes*, XLII

8 She's leaving home after living alone for so many years.
John Lennon (1940–80) British rock musician. *She's Leaving Home* (with Paul McCartney)

9 When I leave it I never dare look back lest I turn into a pillar of salt and the conductor throw me over his left shoulder for good luck.
Frank Sullivan (1892–) US humorist. Attrib.

DESIRE

See also hunger, lust, thirst

1 Were the world all mine
From the sea to the Rhine
I'd give it all
If so be the Queen of England
Lay in my arms.
Anonymous Referring to Eleanor of Aquitaine. *Wandering Scholars* (Helen Waddell); a free translation of *Carmina Burana* (ed. Schmeller), 108a

2 Those who restrain Desire, do so because theirs is weak enough to be restrained.
William Blake (1757–1827) British poet. *The Marriage of Heaven and Hell*, 'Those who restrain Desire . . . '

3 Sooner murder an infant in its cradle than nurse unacted desires.
William Blake *The Marriage of Heaven and Hell*, 'Proverbs of Hell'

4 Man's Desires are limited by his Perceptions; none can desire what he has not perceived.
William Blake *There is no Natural Religion*

5 A sight to dream of, not to tell!
Samuel Taylor Coleridge (1772–1834) British poet. *Christabel*, I

6 O, she is the antidote to desire.
William Congreve (1670–1729) British Restoration dramatist. *The Way of the World*, IV:14

7 Someday I'll wish upon a star.
E. Y. Harburg (1896–1981) US songwriter. From the musical *The Wizard of Oz*. *Over the Rainbow*

8 Somewhere over the rainbow,
Way up high:
There's a land that I heard of
Once in a lullaby.
E. Y. Harburg From the musical *The Wizard of Oz*. *Over the Rainbow*

9 Ship me somewheres east of Suez, where the best is like the worst,
Where there aren't no Ten Commandments, an' a man can raise a thirst:
For the temple-bells are callin', an' it's there that I would be
By the old Moulmein Pagoda, looking lazy at the sea.
Rudyard Kipling (1865–1936) Indian-born British writer. *The Road to Mandalay*

10 All I want is a room somewhere,
Far away from the cold night air;
With one enormous chair . . .
Oh, wouldn't it be loverly?
Alan Jay Lerner (1918–86) US songwriter. *My Fair Lady*, I:1

11 There is wishful thinking in Hell as well as on earth.
C. S. Lewis (1898–1963) British academic and writer. *The Screwtape Letters*, Preface

12 There is nothing like desire for preventing the thing one says from bearing any resemblance to what one has in mind.
Marcel Proust (1871–1922) French novelist. *À la recherche du temps perdu: Le Côté de Guermantes*

13 Appetite comes with eating.
François Rabelais (1483–1553) French satirist. *Gargantua*, Bk. I, Ch. 5

14 That she belov'd knows nought that knows not this:
Men prize the thing ungain'd more than it is.
William Shakespeare (1564–1616) English dramatist. *Troilus and Cressida*, I:2

15 There are two tragedies in life. One is to lose your heart's desire. The other is to gain it.
George Bernard Shaw (1856–1950) Irish dramatist and critic. *Man and Superman*, IV

16 Desire is the very essence of man.
Benedict Spinoza (Baruch de Spinoza; 1632–77) Dutch philosopher. *Ethics*

17 And pluck till time and times are done
The silver apples of the moon
The golden apples of the sun.
W. B. Yeats (1865–1939) Irish poet. *The Song of Wandering Aengus*

DESPAIR

See also sorrow

1 Despair is better treated with hope, not dope.
Richard Asher (1912–) *Lancet*, I:954, 1958

2 And about the ninth hour Jesus cried with a loud voice, saying, Eli, Eli, lama sabachthani? that is to say, My God, my God, why hast thou forsaken me?
Bible: Matthew 27:46

3 The name of the slough was Despond.
John Bunyan (1628–88) English writer. *The Pilgrim's Progress*, Pt. I

4 A castle called Doubting Castle, the owner whereof was Giant Despair.
John Bunyan *The Pilgrim's Progress*, Pt. I

5 Because I do not hope to turn again
Because I do not hope
Because I do not hope to turn.
T. S. Eliot (1888–1965) US-born British poet and dramatist. *Ash-Wednesday*

6 Not, I'll not, carrion comfort, Despair, not feast on thee;
Not untwist – slack they may be – these last strands of man
In me or, most weary, cry *I can no more*. I can;
Can something, hope, wish day come, not choose not to be.
Gerard Manley Hopkins (1844–99) British Jesuit and poet. *Carrion Comfort*

7 Don't despair, not even over the fact that you don't despair.
Franz Kafka (1883–1924) Czech novelist. *Diary*

8 O! that I were as great
As is my grief, or lesser than my name,
Or that I could forget what I have been,
Or not remember what I must be now.
William Shakespeare (1564–1616) English dramatist. *Richard II*, III:3

9 I shall despair. There is no creature loves me;
And if I die, no soul will pity me:
Nay, wherefore should they, since that I myself
Find in myself no pity to myself?
William Shakespeare *Richard III*, V:3

10 The mass of men lead lives of quiet desperation.
Henry David Thoreau (1817–62) US writer. *Walden*, 'Economy'

DESTINY

See also purpose

1 What must be, must be.
Proverb

2 Whatever may happen to you was prepared for you from all eternity; and the implication of causes was from eternity spinning the thread of your being.
Marcus Aurelius (121–180 AD) Roman emperor. *Meditations*, Bk. X, Ch. 5

3 Everything that happens happens as it should, and if you observe carefully, you will find this to be so.
Marcus Aurelius *Meditations*, Bk. IV, Ch. 10

4 . . . it was ordained that the winding ivy of a Plantagenet should kill the true tree itself.
Francis Bacon (1561–1626) English philosopher. Referring to the execution (1499) of Perkin Warbeck, who claimed to be Edward V's brother, and the Earl of Warwick, the true heir of the house of York. *The Life of Henry VII*

5 I felt as if I were walking with destiny, and that all my past life had been but a preparation for this hour and this trial.
Winston Churchill (1874–1965) British statesman. *The Gathering Storm*, Ch. 38

6 Which brings me to my conclusion upon Free Will and Predestination, namely – let the reader mark it – that they are identical.
Winston Churchill *My Early Life*, Ch. 3

7 'Tis all a Chequer-board of Nights and Days
Where Destiny with Men for Pieces plays:
Hither and thither moves, and mates, and slays,
And one by one back in the Closet lays.
Edward Fitzgerald (1809–83) British poet. *The Rubáiyát of Omar Khayyám*, XLIX

8 The Moving Finger writes; and, having writ,
Moves on: nor all thy Piety nor Wit
Shall lure it back to cancel half a Line,

Nor all thy Tears wash out a Word of it.
Edward Fitzgerald *The Rubáiyát of Omar Khayyám*, LI

9 And that inverted Bowl we call The Sky,
Whereunder crawling coop't we live and die,
Lift not thy hands to *It* for help – for It
Rolls impotently on as Thou or I.
Edward Fitzgerald *The Rubáiyát of Omar Khayyám*, LII

10 Drink! for you know not whence you came, nor why:
Drink! for you know not why you go, nor where.
Edward Fitzgerald *The Rubáiyát of Omar Khayyám*, LXXIV

11 Tempt not the stars, young man, thou canst not play
With the severity of fate.
John Ford (c. 1586–c. 1640) English dramatist. *The Broken Heart*, I:3

12 Anatomy is destiny.
Sigmund Freud (1856–1939) Austrian psychoanalyst.

13 Never let success hide its emptiness from you, achievement its nothingness, toil its desolation. And so . . . keep alive the incentive to push on further, that pain in the soul which drives us beyond ourselves . . . Do not look back. And do not dream about the future, either. It will neither give you back the past, nor satisfy your other daydreams. Your duty, your reward – your destiny – are *here* and *now*.
Dag Hammarskjöld (1905–61) Swedish secretary-general of the United Nations. *Markings*

14 I go the way that Providence dictates with the assurance of a sleepwalker.
Adolf Hitler (1889–1945) German dictator. Referring to his successful reoccupation of the Rhineland, despite advice against the attempt. Speech, Munich, 15 Mar 1936

15 Do not try to find out – we're forbidden to know – what end the gods have in store for me, or for you.
Horace (Quintus Horatius Flaccus; 65–8 BC) Roman poet. *Odes*, I

16 Who can foretell for what high cause
This darling of the Gods was born?
Andrew Marvell (1621–78) English poet. *The Picture of Little T.C. in a Prospect of Flowers*

17 And yet the order of the acts is planned,
The way's end destinate and unconcealed.
Alone. Now is the time of Pharisees.
To live is not like walking through a field.
Boris Pasternak (1890–1960) Russian Jewish poet and novelist. *Hamlet* (trans. Henry Kamen)

18 We may become the makers of our fate when we have ceased to pose as its prophets.
Karl Popper (1902–) Austrian-born British philosopher. *The Observer*, 28 Dec 1975

19 Man never found the deities so kindly
As to assure him that he'd live tomorrow.
François Rabelais (1483–1553) French satirist. *Pantagruel*, Bk. III, Ch. 2

20 There's a divinity that shapes our ends,
Rough-hew them how we will.
William Shakespeare (1564–1616) English dramatist. *Hamlet*, V:2

21 There is a tide in the affairs of men,
Which, taken at the flood, leads on to fortune;
William Shakespeare *Julius Caesar*, III:3

22 As flies to wanton boys are we to th' gods –
They kill us for their sport.
William Shakespeare *King Lear*, IV:1

23 The wheel is come full circle.
William Shakespeare *King Lear*, V:3

24 The ancient saying is no heresy:
Hanging and wiving goes by destiny.
William Shakespeare *The Merchant of Venice*, II:9

25 Who can control his fate?
William Shakespeare *Othello*, V:2

26 O! I am Fortune's fool.
William Shakespeare *Romeo and Juliet*, III:1

27 One God, one law, one element,
And one far-off divine event,
To which the whole creation moves.
Alfred, Lord Tennyson (1809–92) British poet. *In Memoriam A.H.H.*, CXXXI

28 I embrace the purpose of God and the doom assigned.
Alfred, Lord Tennyson *Maud*, III

29 We are merely the stars' tennis-balls, struck and bandied
Which way please them.
John Webster (1580–1625) English dramatist. *The Duchess of Malfi*, V:4

30 Every bullet has its billet.
William III (1650–1702) King of England. *Journal* (John Wesley), 6 June 1765

DETERMINATION

See also endurance, inflexibility, persistence, stubbornness

1 He who hesitates is lost.
Proverb

2 Where there's a will there's a way.
Proverb

3 There is no such thing as a great talent without great will-power.
Honoré de Balzac (1799–1850) French novelist. *La Muse du département*

4 Let us determine to die here, and we will conquer.
There is Jackson standing like a stone wall. Rally behind the Virginians.
Barnard Elliot Bee (1824–61) US soldier. Said at the First Battle of Bull Run, 1861; hence Gen Thomas Jackson's nickname, 'Stonewall Jackson'. *Reminiscences of Metropolis* (Poore), II

5 By God, O King, I will neither go nor hang!
Roger Bigod, Earl of Norfolk (1245–1306) Marshal of England. Reply to Edward I's 'By God, Earl, you shall either go or hang!'; Edward had ordered Norfolk and other barons to invade France from Gascony. *Hemingburgh's Chronicle*, Bk. II

6 We will not go to Canossa.
Bismarck (1815–98) German statesman. A declaration of his anti-Roman Catholic policy; the Emperor Henry IV had submitted to Pope Gregory VII at Canossa, N. Italy, in 1077. Speech, Reichstag, 14 May 1872

7 The Congress will push me to raise taxes and I'll say no, and they'll push, and I'll say no, and they'll push again. And I'll say to them, read my lips, no new taxes.
George Bush (1924–) US politician and president. Speech accepting his nomination as presidential candidate, Republican Party Convention, New Orleans, Aug 1988

8 The spirit burning but unbent,
May writhe, rebel – the weak alone repent!
Lord Byron (1788–1824) British poet. *The Corsair*, II

9 We must just KBO ('Keep Buggering On').
Winston Churchill (1874–1965) British statesman. Remark, Dec 1941. *Finest Hour* (M. Gilbert)

10 I purpose to fight it out on this line, if it takes all summer.
Ulysses Simpson Grant (1822–85) US general. Dispatch to Washington, 11 May 1864

11 Never let success hide its emptiness from you, achievement its nothingness, toil its desolation. And so . . . keep alive the incentive to push on further, that pain in the soul which drives us beyond ourselves . . . Do not look back. And do not dream about the future, either. It will neither give you back the past, nor satisfy your other daydreams. Your duty, your reward – your destiny – are *here* and *now*.
Dag Hammarskjöld (1905–61) Swedish secretary-general of the United Nations. *Markings*

12 I will be conquered; I will not capitulate.
Samuel Johnson (1709–84) British lexicographer. Referring to his illness. *Life of Johnson* (J. Boswell), Vol. IV

13 I have not yet begun to fight.
John Paul Jones (1747–92) Scottish-born US naval commander. Retort when informed that his ship was sinking. *Life and Letters of J. P. Jones* (De Koven), Vol. I

14 Very well, alone.
David Low (1891–1963) British cartoonist. The cartoon showed a British soldier shaking his fist at a hostile sea and a sky full of war planes. Caption to cartoon, *Evening Standard*, 18 June 1940

15 I shall return.
Douglas Macarthur (1880–1964) US general. Message (11 Mar 1942) on leaving Corregidor in the Philippines

16 What though the field be lost?
All is not lost – the unconquerable will,
And study of revenge, immortal hate,
And courage never to submit or yield:
And what is else not to be overcome?
John Milton (1608–74) English poet. *Paradise Lost*, Bk. I

17 Look for me by moonlight;
Watch for me by moonlight;
I'll come to thee by moonlight, though hell should bar the way!
Alfred Noyes (1880–1958) British poet. *The Highwayman*

18 I don't believe I ought to quit because I am not a quitter.
Richard Milhous Nixon (1913–) US President. TV address, 23 Sept 1952

19 *Ils ne passeront pas.*
They shall not pass.
Marshal Pétain (1856–1951) French marshal. Attrib; probably derived from General R.-G. Nivelle's Order of the Day, *'Vous ne les laisserez pas passer'* (June 1916). It is also attributed to the Spanish politician Dolores Ibarruri.

20 My resolution's plac'd, and I have nothing
Of woman in me; now from head to foot
I am marble-constant, now the fleeting moon
No planet is of mine.
William Shakespeare (1564–1616) English dramatist. *Antony and Cleopatra*, V:2

21 I will have my bond.
William Shakespeare *The Merchant of Venice*, III:3

22 Even if the doctor does not give you a year, even if he hesitates about a month, make one brave push and see what can be accomplished in a week.
Robert Louis Stevenson (1850–94) Scottish writer. *Virginibus Puerisque*, Ch. 5

23 We are not now that strength which in old days
Moved earth and heaven; that which we are, we are;
One equal temper of heroic hearts,
Made weak by time and fate, but strong in will
To strive, to seek, to find, and not to yield.
Alfred, Lord Tennyson (1809–92) British poet. *Ulysses*

DEVIL

See also damnation, hell

1 Talk of the devil, and he is bound to appear.
Proverb

2 The devil is not so black as he is painted.
Proverb

3 And the devil, taking him up into an high mountain, shewed unto him all the kingdoms of the world in a moment of time.
Bible: Luke 4:5

4 And he said unto them, I beheld Satan as lightning fall from heaven.
Bible: Luke 10:18

5 And he asked him, What is thy name? And he answered, saying, My name is Legion: for we are many.
Bible: Mark 5:9

6 And the Lord said unto Satan, Whence comest thou? Then Satan answered the Lord; and said, From going to and fro in the earth, and from walking up and down in it.
Bible: Job 1:7

7 And there was war in heaven: Michael and his angels fought against the dragon; and the dragon fought and his angels,
And prevailed not; neither was their place found any more in heaven.
And the great dragon was cast out, that old serpent, called the Devil, and Satan, which deceiveth the whole world: he was cast out into the earth, and his angels were cast out with him.
Bible: Revelations 12:7–9

8 And that no man might buy or sell, save he that had the mark, or the name of the beast, or the number of his name.
Here is wisdom. Let him that hath understanding count the number of the beast: for it is the number of a man; and his number is Six hundred threescore and six.
Bible: Revelations 13:17–18

9 O Thou! Whatever title suit thee – Auld Hornie, Satan, Nick, or Clootie.
Robert Burns (1759–96) Scottish poet. *Address to the Devil*

10 Wherever God erects a house of prayer,
The Devil always builds a chapel there;
And 'twill be found, upon examination,
The latter has the largest congregation.
Daniel Defoe (1660–1731) British journalist and writer. *The True-Born Englishman*, Pt. I

11 It is so stupid of modern civilization to have given up believing in the devil when he is the only explanation of it.
Ronald Knox (1888–1957) British Roman Catholic priest. *Let Dons Delight*

12 It is no good casting out devils. They belong to us, we must accept them and be at peace with them.
D. H. Lawrence (1885–1930) British novelist. *Phoenix*, 'The Reality of Peace'

13 High on a throne of royal state, which far

Outshone the wealth of Ormus and of Ind,
Or where the gorgeous East with richest hand
Showers on her kings barbaric pearl and gold,
Satan exalted sat, by merit raised
To that bad eminence.
John Milton (1608–74) English poet. *Paradise Lost*, Bk. II

14 The devil can cite Scripture for his purpose.
William Shakespeare (1564–1616) English dramatist. *The Merchant of Venice*, I:3

15 Sometimes
The Devil is a gentleman.
Percy Bysshe Shelley (1792–1822) British poet. *Peter Bell the Third*

DIAGNOSIS

1 To avoid delay, please have all your symptoms ready.
Anonymous Notice in an English doctor's waiting-room

2 The fingers should be kept on the pulse at least until the hundredth beat in order to judge of its kind and character; the friends standing round will be all the more impressed because of the delay, and the physician's words will be received with just that much more attention.
Archimathaeus (c. 1100) *The Coming of a Physician to his Patient*

3 A smart mother makes often a better diagnosis than a poor doctor.
August Bier (1861–1949)

4 It is more important to cure people than to make diagnoses.
August Bier

5 DIAGNOSIS, n. A physician's forecast of disease by the patient's pulse and purse.
Ambrose Bierce (1842–c. 1914) US writer and journalist. *The Devil's Dictionary*

6 Physicians must discover the weaknesses of the human mind, and even condescend to humour them, or they will never be called in to cure the infirmities of the body.
Charles Caleb Colton (1780–1832) British clergyman and writer. *Lacon*, 1

7 In diagnosis think of the easy first.
Martin H. Fischer (1879–1962) *Fischerisms* (Howard Fabing and Ray Marr)

8 There are men who would even be afraid to commit themselves to the doctrine that castor oil is a laxative.
Camille Flammarion (1842–1925)

9 The doctor may also learn more about the illness from the way the patient tells the story than from the story itself.
James B. Herrick (1861–1954) *Memories of Eighty Years*, Ch. 8

10 In acute diseases it is not quite safe to prognosticate either death or recovery.
Hippocrates (c. 460–c. 377 BC) Greek physician. *Aphorisms*, II

11 Declare the past, diagnose the present, foretell the future.
Hippocrates (c. 460 BC–c. 357 BC) Greek physician. *Epidemics*

12 Diagnosis precedes treatment.
Russell John Howard (1875–1942) *The Hip* (F. G. St. Clair Strange)

13 Physicians think they do a lot for a patient when they give his disease a name.
Immanuel Kant (1724–1804) German philosopher. Attrib.

14 We are too much accustomed to attribute to a single cause that which is the product of several, and the majority of our controversies come from that.
Baron Justus von Liebig (1803–73)

15 The examining physician often hesitates to make the necessary examination because it involves soiling the finger.
William J. Mayo (1861–1939) US surgeon. *Journal-Lancet*, 35:339, 1915

16 The fact that your patient gets well does not prove that your diagnosis was correct.
Samuel J. Meltzer (1851–1921) Attrib.

17 There is no royal road to diagnosis.
Robert Tuttle Morris (1857–1945) *Doctors versus Folks*, Ch. 4

18 The physician who is attending a patient . . . has to know the cause of the ailment before he can cure it.
Mo-tze (fl. 5th–4th century BC) *Ethical and Political Works*, Bk. IV, Ch. 14

19 The most important requirement of the art of healing is that no mistakes or neglect occur. There should be no doubt or confusion as to the application of the meaning of complexion and pulse. These are the maxims of the art of healing.
Huang Ti (2697–1597 BC) *Nei Ching Su Wên*, Bk. 4, Sect. 13

DIARIES

1 Let diaries, therefore, be brought in use.
Francis Bacon (1561–1626) English philosopher. *Essays*, 'Of Travel'

2 Only good girls keep diaries. Bad girls don't have the time.
Tallulah Bankhead (1903–68) US actress. Attrib.

3 With the publication of his Private Papers in 1952, he committed suicide 25 years after his death.
Lord Beaverbrook (1879–1964) British newspaper owner and politician. Referring to Earl Haig. *Men and Power*

4 I do not keep a diary. Never have. To write a diary every day is like returning to one's own vomit.
Enoch Powell (1912–) British politician. *The Sunday Times*, 6 Nov 1977

5 What is a diary as a rule? A document useful to the person who keeps it, dull to the contemporary who reads it, invaluable to the student, centuries afterwards, who treasures it!
Ellen Terry (1847–1928) British actress. *The Story of My Life*, Ch. 14

6 I always say, keep a diary and some day it'll keep you.
Mae West (1892–1980) US film actress. Attrib.

7 I never travel without my diary. One should always have something sensational to read in the train.
Oscar Wilde (1854–1900) Irish-born British dramatist. *The Importance of Being Earnest*, II

DICKENS, Charles

(1812–70) British novelist. His career began with contributions to magazines using the pen name Boz, *Pickwick Papers* (1837) bringing him sudden fame. His many subsequent novels, all appearing in monthly instalments and depicting the poverty of the working classes in Victorian England, have remained immensely popular.

Quotations about Dickens

1 We were put to Dickens as children but it never quite took. That unremitting humanity soon had me cheesed off.
Alan Bennett (1934–) British playwright. *The Old Country*, II

2 It does not matter that Dickens' world is not life-like; it is alive.
Lord Cecil (1902–86) British writer and critic. *Early Victorian Novelists*

3 One would have to have a heart of stone to read the death of Little Nell without laughing.
Oscar Wilde (1854–1900) Irish-born British dramatist. Lecturing upon Dickens. *Lives of the Wits* (H. Pearson)

Quotations by Dickens

4 'There are strings', said Mr Tappertit, 'in the human heart that had better not be wibrated.'
Barnaby Rudge, Ch. 22

5 This is a London particular . . . A fog, miss.
Bleak House, Ch. 3

6 I expect a judgment. Shortly.
Bleak House, Ch. 3

7 'Old girl,' said Mr Bagnet, 'give him my opinion. You know it.'
Bleak House, Ch. 27

8 It is a melancholy truth that even great men have their poor relations.
Bleak House, Ch. 28

9 O let us love our occupations,
Bless the squire and his relations,
Live upon our daily rations,
And always know our proper stations.
The Chimes, '2nd Quarter'

10 'God bless us every one!' said Tiny Tim, the last of all.
A Christmas Carol

11 'I am a lone lorn creetur,' were Mrs Gummidge's words . . . 'and everythink goes contrairy with me.'
David Copperfield, Ch. 3

12 Barkis is willin'.
David Copperfield, Ch. 5

13 Annual income twenty pounds, annual expenditure nineteen nineteen six, result happiness. Annual income twenty pounds, annual expenditure twenty pounds ought and six, result misery.
David Copperfield, Ch. 12

14 I am well aware that I am the 'umblest person going . . . My mother is likewise a very 'umble person. We live in a numble abode.
Said by Uriah Heep. *David Copperfield*, Ch. 16

15 We are so very 'umble.
David Copperfield, Ch. 17

16 Uriah, with his long hands slowly twining over one another, made a ghastly writhe from the waist upwards.
David Copperfield, Ch. 17

17 Accidents will occur in the best-regulated families.
David Copperfield, Ch. 28

18 I'm Gormed – and I can't say no fairer than that.
David Copperfield, Ch. 63

19 When found, make a note of.
Dombey and Son, Ch. 15

20 There's a young man hid with me, in comparison with which young man I am a Angel. That young man hears the words I speak. That young man has a secret way pecooliar to himself, of getting at a boy, and at his heart, and at his liver.
Said by Magwitch. *Great Expectations*, Ch. 1

21 Now, what I want is Facts . . . Facts alone are wanted in life.
Hard Times, Bk. I, Ch. 1

22 Whatever was required to be done, the Circumlocution Office was beforehand with all the public departments in the art of perceiving – how not to do it.
Little Dorrit, Bk. I, Ch. 10

23 In company with several other old ladies of both sexes.
Said by Mr Meagles. *Little Dorrit*, Bk. I, Ch. 17

24 It was not a bosom to repose upon, but it was a capital bosom to hang jewels upon.
Describing Mrs Merdle. *Little Dorrit*, Bk. I, Ch. 21

25 As she frequently remarked when she made any such mistake, it would be all the same a hundred years hence.
Said by Mrs Squeers. *Martin Chuzzlewit*, Ch. 9

26 Let us be moral. Let us contemplate existence.
Martin Chuzzlewit, Ch. 10

27 Here's the rule for bargains: 'Do other men, for they would do you.' That's the true business precept.
Martin Chuzzlewit, Ch. 11

28 Buy an annuity cheap, and make your life interesting to yourself and everybody else that watches the speculation.
Martin Chuzzlewit, Ch. 18

29 He'd make a lovely corpse.
Martin Chuzzlewit, Ch. 25

30 'She's the sort of woman now,' said Mould, '. . . one would almost feel disposed to bury for nothing: and do it neatly, too!'
Martin Chuzzlewit, Ch. 25

31 He had but one eye, and the popular prejudice runs in favour of two.
Said by Mr Squeers. *Nicholas Nickleby*, Ch. 4

32 When he has learnt that bottinney means a knowledge of plants, he goes and knows 'em. That's our system, Nickleby; what do you think of it?
Said by Mr Squeers. *Nicholas Nickleby*, Ch. 8

33 Every baby born into the world is a finer one than the last.
Nicholas Nickleby, Ch. 36

34 All is gas and gaiters.
Nicholas Nickleby, Ch. 49

35 'Did you ever taste beer?' 'I had a sip of it once,' said the small servant. 'Here's a state of things!' cried Mr Swiveller . . . 'She *never* tasted it – it can't be tasted in a sip!'
The Old Curiosity Shop, Ch. 57

36 Oliver Twist has asked for more.
Oliver Twist, Ch. 2

37 Known by the *sobriquet* of 'The artful Dodger.'
Oliver Twist, Ch. 8

38 'If the law supposes that,' said Mr Bumble . . . 'the law is a ass – a idiot.'
Oliver Twist, Ch. 51

39 The question about everything was, would it bring a blush to the cheek of a young person?
Pondered by Mr Podsnap. *Our Mutual Friend*, Bk. I, Ch. 11

40 I think . . . that it is the best club in London.
Mr Tremlow describing the House of Commons. *Our Mutual Friend*, Bk. II, Ch. 3

41 He'd be sharper than a serpent's tooth, if he wasn't as dull as ditch water.
Our Mutual Friend, Bk. III, Ch. 10

42 Kent, sir – everybody knows Kent – apples, cherries, hops and women.
Pickwick Papers, Ch. 2

43 I wants to make your flesh creep.
Pickwick Papers, Ch. 8

44 'It's always best on these occasions to do what the mob do.'
'But suppose there are two mobs?' suggested Mr Snodgrass.
'Shout with the largest,' replied Mr Pickwick.
Pickwick Papers, Ch. 13

45 Take example by your father, my boy, and be very careful o' vidders all your life.
Pickwick Papers, Ch. 13

46 Poverty and oysters always seem to go together.
Pickwick Papers, Ch. 22

47 Wery glad to see you indeed, and hope our acquaintance may be a long 'un, as the gen'l'm'n said to the fi' pun' note.
Pickwick Papers, Ch. 25

48 Poetry's unnat'ral; no man ever talked poetry 'cept a beadle on boxin' day.
Pickwick Papers, Ch. 33

49 It's my opinion, sir, that this meeting is drunk.
Pickwick Papers, Ch. 33

50 I am afeered that werges on the poetical, Sammy.
Said by Sam Weller. *Pickwick Papers*, Ch. 33

51 Never sign a walentine with your own name.
Said by Sam Weller. *Pickwick Papers*, Ch. 33

52 Put it down a we, my lord, put it down a we!
Pickwick Papers, Ch. 34

53 Miss Bolo rose from the table considerably agitated, and went straight home, in a flood of tears and a Sedan chair.
Pickwick Papers, Ch. 35

54 Anythin' for a quiet life, as the man said wen he took the sitivation at the lighthouse.
Pickwick Papers, Ch. 43

55 A smattering of everything, and a knowledge of nothing.
Sketches by Boz, 'Tales', Ch. 3

56 It was the best of times, it was the worst of times, it was the age of wisdom, it was the age of foolishness, it was the epoch of belief, it was the epoch of incredulity, it was the season of Light, it was the season of Darkness, it was the spring of hope, it was the winter of despair, we had everything before us, we had nothing before us, we were all going direct to Heaven, we were all going direct the other way.
The opening words of the book. *A Tale of Two Cities*, Bk. I, Ch. 1

57 It is a far, far, better thing that I do, than I have ever done; it is a far, far, better rest that I go to, than I have ever known.
A Tale of Two Cities, Bk. II, Ch. 15

DICTATORSHIP

See authoritarianism

DIFFERENCE

See also individuality, opposites, similarity, taste

1 Every man after his fashion.
Proverb

2 Every one to his taste.
Proverb

3 One man's meat is another man's poison.
Proverb

4 There is more than one way to skin a cat.
Proverb

5 There is no accounting for tastes.
Proverb

6 There's nowt so queer as folk.
Proverb

7 All colours will agree in the dark.
Francis Bacon (1561–1626) English philosopher. *Essays*, 'Of Unity in Religion'

8 The only inequalities that matter begin in the mind. It is not income levels but differences in mental equipment that keep people apart, breed feelings of inferiority.
Jacquetta Hawkes (1910–) British archeologist. *New Statesman*, Jan 1957

9 If we cannot now end our differences, at least we can help make the world safe for diversity.
John Fitzgerald Kennedy (1917–63) US statesman. Speech, American University (Washington, DC), 10 June 1963

DIPLOMACY

See also tact

1 Our business is to break with them and yet to lay the breache at their door.
Earl of Arlington (1618–85) Referring to the diplomacy that preceded the third Dutch War (1672–74). *Arlington* (Violet Barbour)

2 We're in the Embassy residence, subject, of course, to some of the discomfiture as a result of a need for, uh, elements of refurbishment and rehabilitation.
Walter Annenberg (1908–) US publisher and diplomat. To Queen Elizabeth II. TV documentary, *Royal Family*

3 It is better for aged diplomats to be bored than for young men to die.
Warren Austin (1877–1962) US politician and diplomat. When asked if he got tired during long debates at the UN. Attrib.

4 An honest broker.
Bismarck (1815–98) German statesman. His professed role in the diplomacy of 1878, including the Congress of Berlin. Speech, Reichstag, 19 Feb 1878

5 To jaw-jaw is better than to war-war.
Winston Churchill (1874–1965) British statesman. Speech, Washington, 26 June 1954

6 An appeaser is one who feeds a crocodile – hoping that it will eat him last.
Winston Churchill Attrib.

7 When you have to kill a man it costs nothing to be polite.
Winston Churchill Justifying the fact that the declaration of war against Japan was made in the usual diplomatic language. *The Grand Alliance*

8 A diplomat is a man who always remembers a woman's birthday but never remembers her age.
Robert Frost (1875–1963) US poet. Attrib.

9 Treaties are like roses and young girls – they last while they last.
Charles De Gaulle (1890–1970) French general and statesman. Attrib.

10 We have stood alone in that which is called isolation – our splendid isolation, as one of our colonial friends was good enough to call it.
George Joachim Goschen (1831–1907) English Conservative politician. Speech, Lewes, 26 Feb 1896

11 I met the great little man, the man who can be silent in several languages.
James Guthrie Harbord (1866–1947) US general. Referring to Colonel House. *Mr Wilson's War* (John Dos Passos), Ch. 3

12 Our kingdom and whatever anywhere is subject to our rule we place at your disposal and commit to your power, that everything may be arranged at your nod, and that the will of your empire may be carried out in all respects. Let there be between us and our peoples an undivided unity of love and peace and safety of commerce, in such a way that to you, who are pre-eminent in dignity, be given the authority of command, and to us the will to obey shall not be lacking.

Henry II (1133–89) King of England. Letter to the Emperor Frederick Barbarossa, 1157

13 Official dignity tends to increase in inverse ratio to the importance of the country in which the office is held.

Aldous Huxley (1894–1964) British novelist. *Beyond the Mexique Bay*

14 We are not about to send American boys nine or ten thousand miles away from home to do what Asian boys ought to be doing for themselves.

Lyndon B. Johnson (1908–73) US Democratic president. Broadcast address, 21 Oct 1964

15 You let a bully come into your front yard, the next day he'll be on your porch.

Lyndon B. Johnson Referring to Vietnam. *Time*, 15 Apr 1984

16 The great nations have always acted like gangsters, and the small nations like prostitutes.

Stanley Kubrick (1928–) US film director. *The Guardian*, 5 June 1963

17 All diplomacy is a continuation of war by other means.

Chou En Lai (1898–1976) Chinese statesman.

18 *La cordiale entente qui existe entre mon gouvernement et le sien.*
The friendly understanding that exists between my government and hers.

Louis Philippe (1773–1850) King of France. Referring to an informal understanding reached between Britain and France in 1843. The more familiar phrase, 'entente cordiale', was first used in 1844. Speech, 27 Dec 1843

19 The reluctant obedience of distant provinces generally costs more than it is worth.

Lord Macaulay (1800–59) British historian. *Historical Essays Contributed to the 'Edinburgh Review'*, 'Lord Mahon's War of the Succession'

20 Let them especially put their demands in such a way that Great Britain could say that she supported both sides.

Ramsey MacDonald (1866–1937) British statesman and prime minister. Referring to France and Germany. *The Origins of the Second Word War* (A. J. P. Taylor), Ch. 3

21 By intermarriage and by every means in his power he bound the two peoples into a firm union.

Walter Map (c. 1140–c. 1209) Welsh cleric and writer. Referring to Henry I of England, and specifically to his marriage (1100) to Matilda, a descendant of the Anglo-Saxon royal family. *De Nugis Curialium*, Pt. V, Ch. 5

22 Austria will astound the world with the magnitude of her ingratitude.

Prince Schwarzenberg (1800–52) Austrian statesman. On being asked whether Austria was under any obligation to Russia for help received previously. *The Fall of the House of Habsburg* (E. Crankshaw)

23 A diplomat these days is nothing but a head-waiter who's allowed to sit down occasionally.

Peter Ustinov (1921–) British actor and dramatist. *Romanoff and Juliet*, I

24 Madam, there are fifty thousand men slain this year in Europe, and not one Englishman.

Robert Walpole (1676–1745) British statesman. Referring to his determination not to involve Britain in the War of Polish Succession (1733–35), despite considerable political pressure. Remark to Queen Caroline, 1734

25 No nation is fit to sit in judgement upon any other nation.

Woodrow Wilson (1856–1925) US statesman. Address, Apr 1915

26 An ambassador is an honest man sent to lie abroad for the good of his country.

Henry Wotton (1568–1639) English poet and diplomat. *Life* (Izaak Walton)

DISABILITY

See also blindness

1 If there are any of you at the back who do not hear me, please don't raise your hands because I am also nearsighted.

W. H. Auden (1907–73) British poet. Starting a lecture in a large hall. In *Book of the Month Club News*, Dec 1946

2 I'm a colored, one-eyed Jew.

Sammy Davis Jnr (1925–) Black US singer. When asked what his handicap was during a game of golf. Attrib.

3 You are not crippled at all unless your mind is in a splint.

Frank Scully *Bartlett's Unfamiliar Quotations* (Leonard Louis Levinson)

4 There are two kinds of deafness. One is due to wax and is curable; the other is not due to wax and is not curable.

William Wilde (1815–76)

DISAPPOINTMENT

See also disillusion, expectation

1 Unhappiness is best defined as the difference between our talents and our expectations.

Edward de Bono (1933–) British physician and writer. *The Observer*, 'Sayings of the Week', 12 June 1977

2 The best laid schemes o' mice an' men
Gang aft a-gley,
An' lea'e us nought but grief an' pain
For promis'd joy.

Robert Burns (1759–96) Scottish poet. *To a Mouse*

3 Mountains will heave in childbirth, and a silly little mouse will be born.

Horace (Quintus Horatius Flaccus; 65–8 BC) Roman poet. *See also* LA FONTAINE *Ars Poetica*

4 A mountain in labour shouted so loud that everyone, summoned by the noise, ran up expecting that she would be delivered of a city bigger than Paris; she brought forth a mouse.

Jean de La Fontaine (1621–95) French poet. *See also* HORACE. *Fables*, V, 'La Montagne qui accouche'

5 Levin wanted friendship and got friendliness; he wanted steak and they offered spam.

Bernard Malamud (1914–) US novelist. *A New Life*, VI

6 Look in my face; my name is Might-have-been.
I am also called No-more, Too-late, Farewell.

Dante Gabriel Rossetti (1828–82) British painter and poet. *The House of Life*, 'A Superscription'

7 Oh, I wish that God had not given me what I prayed for! It was not so good as I thought.

Johanna Spyri (1827–1901) Swiss writer. *Heidi*, Ch. 11

8 He said that he was too old to cry, but it hurt too much to laugh.

Adlai Stevenson (1900–65) US statesman. Said after losing an election, quoting a story told by Abraham Lincoln. Speech, 5 Nov 1952

DISASTER

See also accidents

1 Bad news travels fast.
Proverb

2 Let us hope . . . that a kind of Providence will put a speedy end to the acts of God under which we have been laboring.
Peter De Vries (1910–) US novelist. *The Mackerel Plaza,* Ch. 3

3 An Act of God was defined as *something which no reasonable man could have expected.*
A. P. Herbert (1890–1971) British writer and politician. *Uncommon Law*

4 Beautiful Railway Bridge of the Silv'ry Tay!
Alas, I am very sorry to say
That ninety lives have been taken away
On the last Sabbath day of 1879,
Which will be remember'd for a very long time.
William McGonagall (1830–1902) Scottish poet. *The Tay Bridge Disaster*

DISCONTENT

See also envy

1 And sigh that one thing only has been lent
To youth and age in common – discontent.
Matthew Arnold (1822–88) British poet and critic. *Youth's Agitations*

2 The idiot who praises, with enthusiastic tone,
All centuries but this, and every country but his own.
W. S. Gilbert (1836–1911) British dramatist. *The Mikado,* I

3 So have I loitered my life away, reading books, looking at pictures, going to plays, hearing, thinking, writing on what pleased me best. I have wanted only one thing to make me happy, but wanting that have wanted everything.
William Hazlitt (1778–1830) British essayist. *English Literature,* Ch. XVII, 'My First Acquaintance with Poets'

4 How is it, Maecenas, that no one lives contented with his lot, whether he has planned it for himself or fate has flung him into it, but yet he praises those who follow different paths?
Horace (Quintus Horatius Flaccus; 65–8 BC) Roman poet. *Satires,* I

5 Ever let the fancy roam,
Pleasure never is at home.
John Keats (1795–1821) British poet. *Fancy,* I

6 I am sick o' wastin' leather on these gritty pavin'-stones,
An' the blasted English drizzle wakes the fever in my bones;
Tho' I walks with fifty 'ousemaids outer Chelsea to the Strand,
An' they talks a lot o' lovin', but wot do they understand?
Beefy face an' grubby 'and –
Law! Wot do they understand?
I've a neater, sweeter maiden in a cleaner, greener land!
Rudyard Kipling (1865–1936) Indian-born British writer. *The Road to Mandalay*

7 He disdains all things above his reach, and preferreth all countries before his own.
Thomas Overbury (1581–1613) English poet. *Miscellaneous Works,* 'An Affectate Traveller'

8 When in disgrace with fortune and men's eyes
I all alone beweep my outcast state,
And trouble deaf heaven with my bootless cries,
And look upon myself, and curse my fate,
Wishing me like to one more rich in hope
Featur'd like him, like him with friends possess'd,
Desiring this man's art, and that man's scope,
With what I most enjoy contented least.
William Shakespeare (1564–1616) English dramatist. *Sonnet 29*

9 While not exactly disgruntled, he was far from feeling gruntled.
P. G. Wodehouse (1881–1975) British humorous novelist. *The Code of the Woosters*

10 I'd rather be
A Pagan suckled in a creed outworn;
So might I, standing on this pleasant lea,
Have glimses that would make me less forlorn;
Have sight of Proteus rising from the sea;
Or hear Old Triton blow his wreathed horn.
William Wordsworth (1770–1850) British poet. *Sonnets,* 'The world is too much with us'

DISCOVERY

See also exploration, science, space

1 *Eureka!*
I have found it!
Archimedes (c. 287–212 BC) Greek mathematician. An exclamation of joy supposedly uttered as, stepping into a bath and noticing the water overflowing, he saw the answer to a problem and began the train of thought that led to his principle of buoyancy. Attrib.

2 Look, stranger, at this island now
The leaping light for your delight discovers.
W. H. Auden (1907–73) British poet. *Look, Stranger*

3 Medicinal discovery,
It moves in mighty leaps,
It leapt straight past the common cold
And gave it us for keeps.
Pam Ayres British poet. *Some of Me Poetry,* 'Oh, No, I Got a Cold'

4 They are ill discoverers that think there is no land, when they can see nothing but sea.
Francis Bacon (1561–1626) English philosopher. *The Advancement of Learning,* Bk. II, Ch. 7

5 Upon the whole New Holland, tho' in every respect the most barren country I have seen, is not so bad that between the products of sea and land, a company of people who should have the misfortune of being shipwrecked upon it might support themselves.
Sir Joseph Banks (1744–1820) British scientist. Note, as a participant in Captain Cook's circumnavigation of the world (1768–71), on leaving New South Wales. Journal, Aug 1770

6 At daylight in the morning we discovered a bay, which appeared to be tolerably well sheltered from all winds, into which I resolved to go with the ship.
James Cook (1728–79) British navigator and cartographer. On the discovery of Botany Bay. Journal, 28 Apr 1770

7 Many a man who is brooding over alleged mighty discoveries reminds me of a hen sitting on billiard balls.
J. Chalmers Da Costa (1863–1933) *The Trials and Triumphs of the Surgeon,* Ch. 1

8 We have discovered the secret of life!
Francis Crick (1916–) British scientist. Excitedly bursting into a Cambridge pub with James Watson to celebrate the fact that they had unravelled the structure of DNA. *The Double Helix* (J. D. Watson)

9 None of the great discoveries was made by a 'specialist' or a 'researcher'.
Martin H. Fischer (1879–1962) *Fischerisms* (Howard Fabing and Ray Marr)

10 God could cause us considerable embarrassment by revealing all the secrets of nature to us: we should

not know what to do for sheer apathy and boredom.
Goethe (1749–1832) German poet and dramatist. *Memoirs* (Riemer)

11 Then felt I like some watcher of the skies
When a new planet swims into his ken;
Or like stout Cortez when with eagle eyes
He star'd at the Pacific – and all his men
Look'd at each other with a wild surmise –
Silent, upon a peak in Darien.
John Keats (1795–1821) British poet. *On first looking into Chapman's Homer*

12 I do not know what I may appear to the world, but to myself I seem to have been only like a boy playing on the sea-shore, and diverting myself in now and then finding a smoother pebble or a prettier shell than ordinary, whilst the great ocean of truth lay all undiscovered before me.
Isaac Newton (1642–1727) British scientist. *Isaac Newton* (L. T. More)

13 The people – could you patent the sun?
Jonas E. Salk (1914–) US virologist. On being asked who owned the patent on his polio vaccine. *Famous Men of Science* (S. Bolton)

14 We must also keep in mind that discoveries are usually not made by one man alone, but that many brains and many hands are needed before a discovery is made for which one man receives the credit.
Henry E. Sigerist (1891–1957) *A History of Medicine*, Vol. I, Introduction

15 Discovery consists of seeing what everybody has seen and thinking what nobody has thought.
Albert Szent-Györgyi (1893–) Hungarian-born US biochemist. *The Scientist Speculates* (I. J. Good)

DISCRETION

1 Being now come to the years of discretion.
The Book of Common Prayer *Order of Confirmation*

2 The better part of valour is discretion; in the which better part I have saved my life.
William Shakespeare (1564–1616) English dramatist. *Henry IV, Part One*, V:4

3 We schoolmasters must temper discretion with deceit.
Evelyn Waugh (1903–66) British novelist. *Decline and Fall*, Pt. I, Ch. 1

DISCRIMINATION

See prejudice

DISEASE

1 A disease known is half cured.
Proverb

2 'Pray, Mr. Abernethy, what is a cure for gout?' was the question of an indolent and luxurious citizen. 'Live upon sixpence a day – and earn it,' was the cogent reply.
John Abernethy (1764–1831) English surgeon. *Medical Portrait Gallery*, Vol. II (Thomas J. Pettigrew)

3 We are led to think of diseases as isolated disturbances in a healthy body, not as the phases of certain periods of bodily development.
Sir Clifford Allbutt (1836–1925) *Bulletin of the New York Academy of Medicine*, 4:1000, 1928 (F. H. Garrison)

4 Everywhere I go I see increasing evidence of people swirling about in a human cesspit of their own making.
James Anderton (1932–) British Chief Constable of Greater Manchester. Referring to AIDS

5 Screw up the vise as tightly as possible – you have rheumatism; give it another turn, and that is gout.
Anonymous

6 Once I am sure a patient has terminal cancer I tell them straight, I say, 'Its time to go visit with the grand-children.' They seem to appreciate it.
Anonymous Said by a doctor from New Mexico. *The Encyclopedia of Alternative Medicine and Self-Help* (ed. Malcolm Hulke)

7 Before this strange disease of modern life,
With its sick hurry, its divided aims.
Matthew Arnold *The Scholar Gipsy*

8 Only those in the last stage of disease could believe that children are true judges of character.
W. H. Auden (1907–73) British poet. *The Orators*, 'Journal of an Airman'

9 Cure the disease and kill the patient.
Francis Bacon (1561–1626) English philosopher. *Essays*, 'Of Friendship'

10 The remedy is worse than the disease.
Francis Bacon *Essays*, 'Of Seditions and Troubles'

11 And besought him that they might only touch the hem of his garment: and as many as touched were made perfectly whole.
Bible: Matthew 14:36

12 GOUT, n. A physician's name for the rheumatism of a rich patient.
Ambrose Bierce (1842–c. 1914) US writer and journalist. *The Devil's Dictionary*

13 I suffer from an incurable disease – colour blindness.
Joost de Blank (1908–68) Dutch-born British churchman. Attrib.

14 Diseases crucify the soul of man, attenuate our bodies, dry them, wither them, shrivel them up like old apples make them so many anatomies.
Robert Burton (1577–1640) English scholar and churchman. *The Anatomy of Melancholy*, 1

15 Evil comes at leisure like the disease; good comes in a hurry like the doctor.
G. K. Chesterton (1874–1936) British writer. *The Man who was Orthodox*

16 Life is an incurable disease.
Abraham Cowley (1618–67) English poet. *To Dr Scarborough*

17 There is a dread disease which so prepares its victim, as it were, for death. . . a disease in which death and life are so strangely blended, that death takes a glow and hue of life, and life the gaunt and grisly form of death – a disease which medicine never cured, wealth warded off, or poverty could boast exemption from – which sometimes moves in giant strides, and sometimes at a tardy sluggish pace, but, slow or quick, is ever sure and certain.
Charles Dickens (1812–70) British novelist. *Nicholas Nickleby*, Ch. 49

18 Epidemics have often been more influential than statesmen and soldiers in shaping the course of political history, and diseases may also colour the moods of civilizations.
René and Jean Dubos (1901– ; 1918–) *The White Plague*, Ch. 5

19 Disease is an experience of mortal

mind. It is fear made manifest on the body.

Mary Baker Eddy (1821–1910) US religious reader and scientist. *Science and Health,* Ch. 14

20 To think that a bottle of wine or a truffled pâté, or even a glass of beer, instead of being absorbed and eliminated by the system in the usual manner, should mine its way through the thighs, knees, calves, ankles, and instep, to explode at last in a fiery volcano in one's great toe, seems a mirth-provoking phenomenon to all but him who is immediately concerned.

George Herman Ellwanger (fl. 1897) *Meditations on Gout,* 'The Malady'

21 Time had robbed her of her personal charms, and that scourge of the human race, the gout, was racking her bones and sinews.

Hannah Farnham Lee (1780–1865) Referring to Catherine de Medici. *The Huguenots in France and America*

22 A Chicago Papa is so Mean he Wont let his Little Baby have More than One Measle at a time.

Eugene Field (1850–95) US poet and journalist. *Nonsense for Old and Young,* 'A Mean Man'

23 Many a diabetic has stayed alive by stealing the bread denied him by his doctor.

Martin H. Fischer (1879–1962) *Fischerisms* (Howard Fabing and Ray Marr)

24 Cancer's a Funny Thing:
I wish I had the voice of Homer
To sing of rectal carcinoma,
Which kills a lot more chaps, in fact,
Than were bumped off when Troy was sacked . . .

J. B. S. Haldane (1892–1964) British geneticist. Written while mortally ill with cancer. *JBS* (Ronald Clark)

25 If gentlemen love the pleasant titillation of the gout, it is all one to the Town Pump.

Nathaniel Hawthorne (1804–64) US writer. *The Town Pump*

26 Some people are so sensitive they feel snubbed if an epidemic overlooks them.

Frank (Kin) Hubbard (1868–1930) US humorist and journalist. *Abe Martin's Broadcast*

27 Gout is to the arteries what rheumatism is to the heart.

Henri Huchard (1844–1910) *Lancet,* 1:164, 1967 (D. Evan Bedford)

28 Many suffer from the incurable disease of writing, and it becomes chronic in their sick minds.

Juvenal (Decimus Junius Juvenalis; 60–130 AD) Roman satirist. *Satires,* VII

29 We're all going to go crazy, living this epidemic every minute, while the rest of the world goes on out there, all around us, as if nothing is happening, going on with their own lives and not knowing what it's like, what we're going through. We're living through war, but where they're living it's peacetime, and we're all in the same country.

Larry Kramer (1935–) US dramatist and novelist. *The Normal Heart*

30 It is the only disease you don't look forward to being cured of.

Herman J. Mankiewicz (1897–1953) US journalist and screenwriter. Referring to death. *Citizen Kane*

31 While there are several chronic diseases more destructive to life than cancer, none is more feared.

Charles H. Mayo (1865–1939) US physician. *Annals of Surgery,* 83:357, 1926

32 Fever the eternal reproach to the physicians.

John Milton (1608–74) English poet. *Paradise Lost,* Bk. XI

33 I suffer from the disease of writing books and being ashamed of them when they are finished.

Baron de Montesquieu (1688–1755) French writer. *Pensées diverses*

34 I have Bright's disease and he has mine.

S. J. Perelman Attrib.

35 The Muse but serv'd to ease some friend, not Wife,
To help me through this long disease, my life.

Alexander Pope (1688–1744) British poet. *Epistle to Dr. Arbuthnot*

36 Cur'd yesterday of my disease,
I died last night of my physician.

Matthew Prior (1664–1721) British poet. *The Remedy Worse than the Disease*

37 Diseases are the tax on pleasures.

John Ray (1627–1705) English naturalist. *English Proverbs*

38 The diseases which destroy a man are no less natural than the instincts which preserve him.

George Santayana (1863–1952) Spanish-born US philosopher, poet, and critic. *Dialogues in Limbo,* 3

39 Preachers say, Do as I say, not as I do. But if the physician had the same disease upon him that I have, and he should bid me do one thing, and himself do quite another, could I believe him?

John Selden (1584–1654) English historian. *Table Talk*

40 Disease is not of the body but of the place.

Seneca (c. 4 BC–65 AD) Roman writer. *Epistulae ad Lucilium*

41 Not even remedies can master incurable diseases.

Seneca *Epistulae ad Lucilium*

42 The development of industry has created many new sources of danger. Occupational diseases are socially different from other diseases, but not biologically.

Henry E. Sigerist (1891–1957) *Journal of the History of Medicine and Allied Sciences,* 13:214, 1958

43 The man of the present day would far rather believe that disease is connected only with immediate causes for the fundamental tendency in the modern view of life is always to seek what is most convenient.

Rudolf Steiner (1861–1925) Austrian philosopher, founder of anthroposophy. *The Manifestations of Karma,* Lecture III

44 The old saw is that 'if you drink wine you have the gout, and if you do not drink wine the gout will have you.'

Thomas Sydenham (1624–89) *Works,* 'A Treatise on Gout and Dropsy'

45 Decay and disease are often beautiful, like the pearly tear of the shellfish and the hectic glow of consumption.

Henry David Thoreau (1817–62) US writer. *Journal,* 11 June 1852

46 The art of medicine consists of amusing the patient while Nature cures the disease.

Voltaire (1694–1788) French writer. Attrib.

47 I would like to remind those responsible for the treatment of tuberculosis that Keats wrote his best poems while dying of this disease. In my opinion he would never have done so under the influence of modern chemotherapy.

Arthur M. Walker (1896–1955) *Walkerisms* (Julius L. Wilson)

DISHONOR

1 Not the owner of many possessions will you be right to call happy: he more rightly deserves the name of happy who knows how to use the gods' gifts wisely and to put up with rough poverty, and who fears dishonour more than death.

Horace (Quintus Horatius Flaccus; 65–8 BC) Roman poet. *Odes*, IV

2 You're a disgrace to our family name of Wagstaff, if such a thing is possible.

Groucho Marx (Julius Marx; 1895–1977) US comedian. *Horse Feathers*

3 His honour rooted in dishonour stood,
And faith unfaithful kept him falsely true.

Alfred, Lord Tennyson (1809–92) British poet. *Idylls of the King*, 'Lancelot and Elaine'

DISILLUSION

See also disappointment, innocence of childhood

1 The price one pays for pursuing any profession or calling is an intimate knowledge of its ugly side.

James Baldwin (1924–87) US writer. *Nobody Knows My Name*

2 If you live long enough, you'll see that every victory turns into a defeat.

Simone de Beauvoir (1908–86) French writer. *Tous les hommes sont mortels*

3 The coach has turned into a pumpkin and the mice have all run away.

Lady Bird Johnson (1912–) Wife of Lyndon B. Johnson. Said after Lyndon Johnson gave up the presidency. *The Vantage Point* (Lyndon B. Johnson)

4 I have protracted my work till most of those whom I wished to please have sunk into the grave; and success and miscarriage are empty sounds.

Samuel Johnson (1709–84) British lexicographer. *Dictionary of the English Language*

5 One stops being a child when one realizes that telling one's trouble does not make it better.

Cesare Pavese (1908–50) Italian novelist and poet. *The Business of Living: Diaries 1935–50*

6 Thou wretched, rash, intruding fool, farewell!
I took thee for thy better.

William Shakespeare (1564–1616) English dramatist. *Hamlet*, III:4

DISMISSAL

See also departure

1 You have sat too long here for any good you have been doing. Depart, I say, and let us have done with you. In the name of God, *go!*

Leopold Amery (1873–1955) British statesman. Said to Neville Chamberlain using Cromwell's words. Speech, House of Commons, May 1940

2 You have delighted us long enough.

Jane Austen (1775–1817) British novelist. *Pride and Prejudice*, Ch. 18

3 My language fails
Go out and govern new South Wales.

Hilaire Belloc (1870–1953) British writer. *Cautionary Tales*, 'Lord Lundy'

4 It is not fit that you should sit here any longer... you shall now give place to better men.

Oliver Cromwell (1599–1658) English soldier and statesman. Speech to the Rump Parliament, 20 Apr 1653

5 Take away that fool's bauble, the mace.

Oliver Cromwell Speech dismissing Parliament, 20 Apr 1653

6 Go, and never darken my towels again!

Groucho Marx (Julius Marx; 1895–1977) US comedian. *Duck Soup*

7 There comes a time in every man's life when he must make way for an older man.

Reginald Maudling (1917–77) British politician. Remark made on being replaced in the shadow cabinet by John Davies, his elder by four years. *The Guardian*, 20 Nov 1976

8 We Don't Want To Lose You But We Think You Ought To Go.

Paul Alfred Rubens (1875–1917) British dramatist and songwriter. Title of song

9 Stand not upon the order of your going,
But go at once.

William Shakespeare (1564–1616) English dramatist. *Macbeth*, III:4

10 Dropping the pilot.

John Tenniel (1820–1914) British illustrator and cartoonist. Caption of a cartoon. The cartoon refers to Bismarck's resignation, portraying him as a ship's pilot walking down the gangway of the ship while Wilhelm II watches from the deck. *Punch*, 29 Mar 1890

11 The son of a bitch isn't going to resign on me, I want him fired.

Harry S. Truman (1884–1972) US statesman. To Omar Bradley, when Truman sacked MacArthur from his command of UN forces in Korea, 1951. Attrib.

DISRAELI, Benjamin, 1st Earl of Beaconsfield

(1804–81) British statesman of Italian-Jewish descent, who became Conservative prime minister (1868; 1874–80). He was supported by Queen Victoria, whom he made Empress of India. He also wrote novels, including *Coningsby* (1844) and *Sybil* (1845).

Quotations about Disraeli

1 The soul of Dizzy was a chandelier.

Edmund Clerihew Bentley (1875–1956) British writer. *A Ballad of Souls*

2 He was without any rival whatever, the first comic genius whoever installed himself in Downing Street.

Michael Foot (1913–) British Labour politician and journalist. *Debts of Honour*

3 Disraeli lacked two qualities, failing which true eloquence is impossible. He was never quite in earnest, and he was not troubled by dominating conviction.

Henry Lucy (1843–1924) British journalist. *Sixty Years In The Wilderness*

Quotations by Disraeli

4 Youth is a blunder; manhood a struggle; old age a regret.

Coningsby, Bk. III, Ch. 1

5 Almost everything that is great has been done by youth.

Coningsby, Bk. III, Ch. 1

6 His Christianity was muscular.

Endymion, Bk. 1, Ch. 14

7 'Sensible men are all of the same religion.' 'And pray what is that?' inquired the prince. 'Sensible men never tell.'

Endymion, Bk. I, Ch. 81

8 The blue ribbon of the turf.

Describing the Derby. *Life of Lord George Bentinck*, Ch. 26

9 When a man fell into his anecdotage it was a sign for him to retire from the world.

Lothair, Ch. 28

10 Every woman should marry – and no man.

Lothair, Ch. 30

11 'My idea of an agreeable person,' said Hugo Bohun, 'is a person who agrees with me.'

Lothair, Ch. 35

12 'Two nations; between whom there is no intercourse and no sympathy;

who are as ignorant of each other's habits, thoughts, and feelings, as if they were dwellers in different zones, or inhabitants of different planets; who are formed by a different breeding, are fed by a different food, are ordered by different manners, and are not governed by the same laws.'
'You speak of–' said Egremont, hesitatingly.
'THE RICH AND THE POOR.'
Sybil, Bk. II, Ch. 5

13 Little things affect little minds.
Sybil, Bk. III, Ch. 2

14 A majority is always the best repartee.
Tancred, Bk. II, Ch. 14

15 It destroys one's nerves to be amiable every day to the same human being.
The Young Duke

16 There are three kinds of lies: lies, damned lies and statistics.
Autobiography (Mark Twain)

17 I will not go down to posterity talking bad grammar.
Remark made when correcting proofs of his last parliamentary speech, 31 Mar 1881. *Disraeli* (Blake), Ch. 32

18 I know he is, and he adores his maker.
Replying to a remark made in defense of John Bright that he was a self-made man. *The Fine Art of Political Wit* (L. Harris)

19 Thank you for the manuscript; I shall lose no time in reading it.
His customary reply to those who sent him unsolicited manuscripts. *Irreverent Social History* (F. Muir)

20 I will sit down now, but the time will come when you will hear me.
Maiden Speech, House of Commons, 7 Dec 1837

21 The Continent will not suffer England to be the workshop of the world.
Speech, House of Commons, 15 Mar 1838

22 Thus you have a starving population, an absentee aristocracy, and an alien Church, and in addition the weakest executive in the world. That is the Irish Question.
Speech, House of Commons, 16 Feb 1844

23 The right honourable gentleman caught the Whigs bathing, and walked away with their clothes.
Referring to Sir Robert Peel. Speech, House of Commons, 28 Feb 1845

24 A Conservative government is an organized hypocrisy.
Speech, 17 Mar 1845

25 A precedent embalms a principle.
Speech, House of Commons, 22 Feb 1848

26 He has to learn that petulance is not sarcasm, and that insolence is not invective.
Said of Sir C. Wood. Speech, House of Commons, 16 Dec 1852

27 I am myself a gentleman of the Press, and I bear no other scutcheon.
Speech, House of Commons, 18 Feb 1863

28 The question is this: Is man an ape or an angel? I, my lord, am on the side of the angels.
Speech, 25 Nov 1864

29 Assassination has never changed the history of the world.
Speech, House of Commons, 1 May 1865

30 An author who speaks about his own books is almost as bad as a mother who talks about her own children.
Speech, Glasgow, 19 Nov 1873

31 Lord Salisbury and myself have brought you back peace – but a peace I hope with honour.
Speech, House of Commons, 16 July 1878

32 A sophistical rhetorician inebriated with the exuberance of his own verbosity.
Referring to Gladstone. Speech, 27 July 1878

33 Your dexterity seems a happy compound of the smartness of an attorney's clerk and the intrigue of a Greek of the lower empire.
Speaking to Lord Palmerston. Attrib.

34 If a traveller were informed that such a man was leader of the House of Commons, he may well begin to comprehend how the Egyptians worshipped an insect.
Referring to Lord John Russell. Attrib.

35 Pray remember, Mr Dean, no dogma, no Dean.
Attrib.

36 Nobody is forgotten when it is convenient to remember him.
Attrib.

37 Her Majesty is not a subject.
Responding to Gladstone's taunt that Disraeli could make a joke out of any subject, including Queen Victoria. Attrib.

38 When I meet a man whose name I can't remember, I give myself two minutes; then, if it is a hopeless case, I aways say, And how is the old complaint?
Attrib.

39 She is an excellent creature, but she never can remember which came first, the Greeks or the Romans.
Referring to his wife. Attrib.

40 When I want to read a novel I write one.
Attrib.

41 I am dead: dead, but in the Elysian fields.
Said on his move to the House of Lords. Attrib.

42 No, it is better not. She will only ask me to take a message to Albert.
On his deathbed, declining an offer of a visit from Queen Victoria. Attrib.

DISTRESS

1 To Mercy, Pity, Peace, and Love
All pray in their distress.
William Blake (1757–1827) British poet. *Songs of Innocence*, 'The Divine Image'

2 The superior man is satisfied and composed; the mean man is always full of distress.
Confucius (K'ung Fu-tzu; 551–479 BC) Chinese philosopher. *Analects*

DISTRUST

1 'We stay together, but we distrust one another.'
'Ah, yes . . . but isn't that a definition of marriage?'
Malcolm Bradbury (1932–) British academic and novelist. *The History Man*, Ch. 3

2 Silence is the best tactic for him who distrusts himself.
Duc de la Rochefoucauld (1613–80) French writer. *Maximes*, 79

3 It is more shameful to distrust one's friends than to be deceived by them.
Duc de la Rochefoucauld *Maximes*, 84

4 Trust none;
For oaths are straws, men's faiths are wafer-cakes,
And hold-fast is the only dog, my duck.
William Shakespeare (1564–1616) English dramatist. *Henry V*, II:3

DIVINITY

1 There is surely a piece of divinity in us, something that was before the elements, and owes no homage unto the sun.
Thomas Browne (1605–82) English physician and writer. *Religio Medici*, Pt. II

2 There's such divinity doth hedge a king
That treason can but peep to what it would.
William Shakespeare (1564–1616) English dramatist. *Hamlet*, IV:5

3 There's a divinity that shapes our ends,
Rough-hew them how we will.
William Shakespeare *Hamlet*, V:2

4 They say there is divinity in odd numbers, either in nativity, chance, or death.
William Shakespeare *The Merry Wives of Windsor*, V:1

DIVORCE

See also marriage

DOCTORS

See also health, illness, medicine, remedies

1 A young doctor makes a humpy graveyard.
Proverb

2 Do not dwell in a city whose governor is a physician.
Proverb

3 God heals, and the doctor takes the fee.
Proverb

4 No man is a good physician who has never been sick.
Proverb

5 Physicians' faults are covered with earth, and rich men's with money.
Proverb

6 The presence of the doctor is the beginning of the cure.
Proverb

7 The superior doctor prevents sickness;
The mediocre doctor attends to impending sickness;
The inferior doctor treats actual sickness.
Proverb

8 While doctors consult, the patient dies.
Proverb

9 I am dying with the help of too many physicians.
Alexander the Great (356–323 BC) King of Macedon. Attrib.

10 These are the duties of a physician: First . . . to heal his mind and to give help to himself before giving it to anyone else.
Anonymous Epitaph of an Athenian doctor, 2 AD. *Journal of the American Medical Association*, 189:989, 1964

11 In illness the physician is a father; in convalescence a friend; when health is restored, he is a guardian.
Anonymous Brahmanic saying

12 One physician cures you of the colic; two physicians cure you of the medicine.
Anonymous *Journal of the American Medical Association*, 190:765, 1964 (Vincent J. Derbes)

13 Fifty years ago the successful doctor was said to need three things; a top hat to give him Authority, a paunch to give him Dignity, and piles to give him an Anxious Expression.
Anonymous *Lancet*, 1:169, 1951

14 A physician is nothing but a consoler of the mind.
Petronius Arbiter (1st century AD) Roman satirist. *Satyricon*

15 The blunders of a doctor are felt not by himself but by others.
Ar-Rumi (836–896)

16 My dear old friend King George V always told me that he would never have died but for that vile doctor.
Margot Asquith (1865–1945) Wife of Herbert Asquith. Referring to Lord Dawson of Penn.

17 Give me a doctor partridge-plump,
Short in the leg and broad in the rump,
An endomorph with gentle hands
Who'll never make absurd demands
That I abandon all my vices
Nor pull a long face in a crisis,
But with a twinkle in his eye
Will tell me that I have to die.
W. H. Auden (1907–73) British poet. *Nones*, 'Footnotes to Dr. Sheldon'

18 Doctors and undertakers
Fear epidemics of good health.
Gerald Barzan

19 They answered, as they took their fees,
'There is no cure for this disease.'
Hilaire Belloc (1870–1953) British writer. *Cautionary Tales*, 'Henry King'

20 Physician, heal thyself.
Bible: Luke 4:23

21 If you think that you have caught a cold, call in a good doctor. Call in three good doctors and play bridge.
Robert Benchley (1889–1945) *From Bed to Worse*, 'How to Avoid Colds'

22 BODY-SNATCHER, n. A robber of grave-worms. One who supplies the young physicians with that with which the old physicians have supplied the undertaker.
Ambrose Bierce (1842–c. 1914) US writer and journalist. *The Devil's Dictionary*

23 PHYSICIAN, n. One upon whom we set our hopes when ill and our dogs when well.
Ambrose Bierce *The Devil's Dictionary*

24 You medical people will have more lives to answer for in the other world than even we generals.
Napoleon Bonaparte (1769–1821) French Emperor. *Napoleon in Exile* (Barry O'Meara)

25 As long as men are liable to die and are desirous to live, a physician will be made fun of, but he will be well paid.
Jean de La Bruyère (1645–96) French writer and moralist. *Caractères*

26 The doctors allow one to die, the charlatans kill.
Jean de La Bruyère *Caractères*

27 A skilful leech is better far
Than half a hundred men of war.
Samuel Butler (1612–80) English satirist. *Hudibras*, Pt. I

28 But modern quacks have lost the art,
And reach of life the sacred seat;
They know not how its pulses beat,
Yet take their fee and write their bill,
In barb'rous prose resolved to kill.
Anna Chamber (d. 1777) *Poems, Printed at Strawberry Hill*

29 If the clinician, as observer, wishes to see things as they really are, he must make a *tabula rasa* of his mind and proceed without any preconceived notions whatever.
Jean Martin Charcot (1825–93) French neurologist.

30 Doctors are just the same as lawyers; the only difference is that

lawyers merely rob you, whereas doctors rob you and kill you, too.
Anton Chekhov (1860–1904) Russian dramatist. *Ivanov*, I

31 The skilful doctor treats those who are well but the inferior doctor treats those who are ill.
Ch'in Yueh-jen (c. 225 BC)

32 I have noticed a tendency on the part of an occasional elderly and distinguished man to think that the rules of medical ethics were meant for young fellows just starting out, but not for him.
J. Chalmers Da Costa (1863–1933) *The Trials and Triumphs of the Surgeon*, Ch. 1

33 A fashionable surgeon like a pelican can be recognized by the size of his bill.
J. Chalmers Da Costa *The Trials and Triumphs of the Surgeon*, Ch. 1

34 When a doctor does go wrong he is the first of criminals. He has nerve and he has knowledge.
Arthur Conan Doyle (1856–1930) British writer and creator of Sherlock Holmes. *The Speckled Band*

35 'What sort of doctor is he?'
'Oh, well, I don't known much about his ability; but he's got a very good beside manner!'
George du Maurier (1834–96) British novelist and cartoonist. Caption to cartoon, *Punch*, 15 Mar 1884

36 He had surrendered all reality, all dread and fear, to the doctor beside him, as people do.
William Faulkner (1897–1962) US novelist. *Light in August*, Ch. 17

37 Medicine is the one place where all the show is stripped of the human drama. You, as doctors, will be in a position to see the human race stark naked – not only physically, but mentally and morally as well.
Martin H. Fischer (1879–1962) *Fischerisms* (Howard Fabing and Ray Marr)

38 A doctor must work eighteen hours a day and seven days a week. If you cannot console yourself to this, get out of the profession.
Martin H. Fischer *Fischerisms*

39 DOCTOR: Always preceded by 'the good.' Among men, in familiar conversation, 'Oh! balls, doctor!' Is a wizard when he enjoys your confidence, a jackass when you're no longer on terms. All are materialists: 'You can't probe for faith with a scalpel.'
Gustave Flaubert (1821–80) French novelist. *Dictionary of Accepted Ideas*

40 We anatomists are like the porters in Paris, who are acquainted with the narrowest and most distant streets, but who know nothing of what takes place in the houses!
Bernard Le Bovier de Fontenelle (1657–1757)

41 There are more old drunkards than old doctors.
Benjamin Franklin (1706–90) US scientist and statesman. Attrib.

42 Quacks are the greatest liars in the world except their patients.
Benjamin Franklin Attrib.

43 Physicians, like beer, are best when they are old.
Thomas Fuller (1608–61) English historian. *The Holy State and the Profane State*

44 That physician will hardly be thought very careful of the health of others who neglects his own.
Galen (fl. 2nd century) Greek physician and scholar. *Of Protecting the Health*, Bk. V

45 The patient's ears remorseless he assails;
Murder with jargon where his medicine fails.
Samuel Garth (1661–1719) English physician and poet. *The Dispensary*

46 See, one physician, like a sculler plies,
The patient lingers and by inches dies,
But two physicians, like a pair of oars
Waft him more swiftly to the Stygian shores.
Samuel Garth Attrib.

47 'Is there no hope?' the sick man said,
The silent doctor shook his head,
And took his leave with signs of sorrow,
Despairing of his fee tomorrow.
John Gay (1685–1732) English poet and dramatist.

48 The doctors are always changing their opinions. They always have some new fad.
David Lloyd George (1863–1945) British liberal statesman. After a well- known surgeon recommended that people sleep on their stomachs. *War Diary*, Ch. 36 (Lord Riddell)

49 It is so hard that one cannot really have confidence in doctors and yet cannot do without them.
Johann Wolfgang von Goethe (1749–1832) German poet, dramatist, and scientist.

50 The doctor found, when she was dead,
Her last disorder mortal.
Oliver Goldsmith (1728–74) Irish-born British writer. *Elegy on Mrs. Mary Blaize*

51 It is a distinct art to talk medicine in the language of the non-medical man.
Edward H. Goodman (1879–)

52 The crowd of physicians has killed me.
Hadrian (Publius Aelius Hadrianus; 76 AD–138 AD) Roman emperor. *Essays*, Bk. II (Michel de Montaigne)

53 The consultant's first obligation is to the patient, not to his brother physician.
Burton J. Hendrick (1870–1949)

54 A physician who is a lover of wisdom is the equal to a god.
Hippocrates (c. 460–c. 377 BC) Greek physician. *Decorum*, V

55 Foolish the doctor who despises the knowledge acquired by the ancients.
Hippocrates *Entering the World* (M. Odent)

56 I suppose one has a greater sense of intellectual degradation after an interview with a doctor than from any human experience.
Alice James (1848–92) US diarist. *The Diary of Alice James* (ed. Leon Edel), 27 Sept 1890

57 When people's ill, they comes to I,
I physics, bleeds, and sweats 'em;
Sometimes they live, sometimes they die.
What's that to I? I lets 'em.
John Coakley Lettsom (1744–1815) *On Dr. Lettsom, by Himself*

58 A doctor is a man licensed to make grave mistakes.
Leonard Louis Levinson *Bartlett's Unfamiliar Quotations* (Leonard Louis Levinson)

59 But a doctor who has gone into lonely and discouraged homes, where there was fear for the sick, and no one else at hand to administer remedy, and give hope, can really say, 'I amount to something. I'm worth while.'
Carlton K. Matson (1890–1948) *The Cleveland Press*

60 As he approached the place where a meeting of doctors was being held, he saw some elegant

limousines and remarked, 'The surgeons have arrived.' Then he saw some cheaper cars and said, 'The physicians are here, too.' A few scattered model-T Fords led him to infer that there were pathologists present. And when he saw a row of overshoes inside, under the hat rack, he is reported to have remarked, 'Ah, I see there are laboratory men here.'
William J. Mayo (1861–1939) US surgeon. *The Way of an Investigator*, Ch. 19 (Walter B. Cannon)

61 English physicians kill you, the French let you die.
William Lamb, Lord Melbourne (1779–1848) British statesman. *Queen Victoria*, Ch. 5 (Elizabeth Longford)

62 No doctor takes pleasure in the health even of his friends.
Michel de Montaigne (1533–92) French essayist. *Essais*, I

63 I used to wonder why people should be so fond of the company of their physician, till I recollected that he is the only person with whom one dares to talk continually of oneself, without interruption, contradiction or censure; I suppose that delightful immunity doubles their fees.
Hannah More (1745–1833) English writer. Letter to Horace Walpole, 27 July 1789

64 One must not count upon all of his patients being willing to steal in order to pay doctor's bills.
Robert Tuttle Morris *Doctors Versus Folks*, Ch. 3

65 The most dangerous physicians are those who can act in perfect mimicry of the born physician.
Friedrich Nietzsche (1844–1900) German philosopher. *Human, All Too Human*, Pt. II

66 We doctors have always been a simple trusting folk. Did we not believe Galen implicitly for 1500 years and Hippocrates for more than 2000?
William Osler (1849–1919) Canadian physician.

67 A physician who treats himself has a fool for a patient.
William Osler *Sir William Osler: Aphorisms*, Ch. I (William B. Bean)

68 One of the first duties of the physician is to educate the masses not to take medicine.
William Osler

69 Physicians who care much for the elderly may find their lives slowly shredded to pieces as their seniors pick at them with minor worries magnified by the rapidly diminishing sands. If the telephone should come into common use, this state of affairs would worsen.
Frank Kittredge Paddock (1841–1901) Attrib.

70 Every physician must be rich in knowledge, and not only of that which is written in books; his patients should be his book, they will never mislead him.
Paracelsus (c. 1493–1541) Swiss philosopher and alchemist. *The Book of Tartaric Diseases*, Ch. 13

71 The doctors were very brave about it
Dorothy Parker 1893–1967) US writer. Said after she had been seriously ill. *Journal of the American Medical Association*, 194:211, 1965

72 When the physician said to him, 'You have lived to be an old man,' he said, 'That is because I never employed you as my physician.'
Pausanias (fl. 479 BC) Greek traveler. *Moralia* (Plutarch), 'Sayings of Spartans'

73 If your time hasn't come not even a doctor can kill you.
Meyer A. Perlstein (1902–)

74 Life in itself is short enough, but the physicians with their art, know to their amusement, how to make it still shorter.
Petrarch (1304–74) Italian poet. *Invectives*, Preface, Letter to Pope Clement VI

75 After all, a doctor is just to put your mind at rest.
Petronius (fl. 1st century) Roman satirist. *Satyricon*, 42

76 There is not a doctor who desires the health of his friends; not a soldier who desires the peace of his country.
Philemon (c. 361–c. 263 BC) Greek dramatist. *Fabulae Incertae*, Fragment 46

77 A country doctor needs more brains to do his work passably than the fifty greatest industrialists in the world require.
W. B. Pitkin (1878–1953) *The Twilight of the American Mind*, Ch. 10

78 Who shall decide when doctors disagree?
Alexander Pope (1688–1744) British poet. *Moral Essays*, III

79 Physicians of all men are most happy; what success soever they have, the world proclaimeth, and what fault they commit, the earth covereth.
Francis Quarles (1592–1644) English poet. *Hieroglyphics of the Life of Man*

80 If you want to get out of medicine the fullest enjoyment, be students all your lives.
David Riesman (1867–1940)

81 The best doctor in the world is the Veterinarian. He can't ask his patients what is the matter – he's got to just know.
Will Rogers (1879–1935) US actor and humorist. *The Autobiography of Will Rogers*, 12

82 First they get *on*, then they get *honour*, then they get *honest*.
Humphrey Rolleston (1862–1944) British physician. Referring to physicians. *Confessions of an Advertising Man* (David Ogilvy)

83 They, on the whole, desire to cure the sick; and, – if they are good doctors, and the choice were fairly put to them, – would rather cure their patient and lose their fee, than kill him, and get it.
John Ruskin (1819–1900) British art critic and writer on sociology and economics. *The Crown of Wild Olive*

84 The doctor occupies a seat in the front row of the stalls of the human drama, and is constantly watching, and even intervening in, the tragedies, comedies and tragicomedies which form the raw material of the literary art.
W. Russell, Lord Brain (1895–1966) *The Quiet Art: a Doctor's Anthology*, Foreword (R. Coope)

85 The common people say, that physicians are the class of people who kill other men in the most polite and courteous manner.
John of Salisbury (c. 1115–80) English churchman, philosopher, and scholar. *Polycraticus*, Bk. II, Ch. 29

86 The physician cannot prescribe by letter the proper time for teating or bathing; he must feel the pulse.
Seneca (c. 4 BC–65 AD) Roman writer. *Epistulae ad Lucilium*, XII

87 Make it compulsory for a doctor using a brass plate to have inscribed on it, in addition to the letters indicating his qualifications, the words 'Remember that I too am mortal'.
George Bernard Shaw (1856–1950) Irish dramatist and critic. *The Doctor's Dilemma*, 'Preface on Doctors'

88 The most tragic thing in the world is a sick doctor.
George Bernard Shaw *The Doctor's Dilemma*, I

89 I had rather follow you to your grave than see you owe your life to any but a regular-bred physician.
Richard Brinsley Sheridan (1751–1816) British dramatist. *St. Patrick's Day*, II:4

90 Our doctor would never really operate unless it was necessary. He was just that way. If he didn't need the money, he wouldn't lay a hand on you.
Herb Shriner

91 A young man, in whose air and countenance appeared all the uncouth gravity and supercilious self-conceit of a physician piping hot from his studies.
Tobias Smollett (1721–71) English novelist and journalist. *The Adventures of Peregrine Pickle*, Ch. 42

92 There are worse occupations in the world than feeling a woman's pulse.
Laurence Sterne (1713–68) Irish-born English writer and churchman.

93 . . . the physician . . . is the flower (such as it is) of our civilization.
Robert Louis Stevenson (1850–94) Scottish writer. *Underwoods*, Dedication

94 The best doctors in the world are Doctor Diet,
Doctor Quiet and Doctor Merryman.
Jonathan Swift (1667–1745) Anglo-Irish priest, satirist, and poet.

95 Apollo was held the god of physic and sender of disease. Both were originally the same trade, and still continue.
Jonathan Swift *Thoughts on Various Subjects, Moral and Diverting*

96 An unruly patient makes a harsh physician.
Publilius Syrus (1st century BC) Roman dramatist.

97 This is where the strength of the physician lies, be he a quack, a homeopath or an allopath. He supplies the perennial demand for comfort, the craving for sympathy that every human sufferer feels.
Leo Tolstoy (1828–1910) Russian writer. *War and Peace*, Pt. 9, Ch. 16

98 Mr. Anaesthetist, if the patient can keep awake, surely you can.
Wilfred Trotter (1872–1939) Quoted in *Lancet*, 2:1340, 1965

99 He has been a doctor a year now and has had two patients, no, three, I think – yes, it was three; I attended their funerals.
Mark Twain (Samuel L. Clemens; 1835–1910) US writer.

100 The physicians are the natural attorneys of the poor and the social problems should largely be solved by them.
Rudolf Virchow (1821–1902) German pathologist. *Rudolf Virchow*, 'The Doctor' (Erwin H. Ackernecht)

101 Who are the greatest deceivers? The doctors? And the greatest fools? The patients?
Voltaire (1694–1778) French writer and philosopher.

102 A physician is one who pours drugs of which he knows little into a body of which he knows less.
Voltaire Attrib.

103 By quack I mean imposter not in opposition to but in common with physicians.
Horace Walpole (1717–97) English writer.

104 Doctors are mostly impostors. The older a doctor is and the more venerated he is, the more he must pretend to know everything. Of course, they grow worse with time. Always look for a doctor who is hated by the best doctors. Always seek out a bright young doctor before he comes down with nonsense.
Thornton Wilder (1897–1975) US novelist and dramatist.

105 Doctors are generally dull dogs.
John Wilson (Christopher North) (1785–1854) Scottish poet, essayist, and critic.

DOGS

See also animals

1 A huge dog, tied by a chain, was painted on the wall and over it was written in capital letters 'Beware of the dog.'
Petronius Arbiter (1st century AD) Roman satirist. Latin, *Cave canem. Satyricon: Cena Trimalchionis*, 29

2 The woman who is really kind to dogs is always one who has failed to inspire sympathy in men.
Max Beerbohm (1872–1956) British writer. *Zuleika Dobson*

3 It's the one species I wouldn't mind seeing vanish from the face of the earth. I wish they were like the White Rhino – six of them left in the Serengeti National Park, and all males.
Alan Bennett (1934–) British playwright. Referring to dogs. *Getting On*, I

4 The great pleasure of a dog is that you may make a fool of yourself with him and not only will he not scold you, he will make a fool of himself too.
Samuel Butler (1835–1902) British writer. *Notebooks*

5 'Tis sweet to hear the watch-dog's honest bark
Bay deep-mouthed welcome as we draw near home;
'Tis sweet to know there is an eye will mark
Our coming, and look brighter when we come.
Lord Byron (1788–1824) British poet. *Don Juan*, I

6 Anybody who hates children and dogs can't be all bad.
W. C. Fields (1880–1946) US actor. Attrib.

7 The dog, to gain some private ends,
Went mad and bit the man.
Oliver Goldsmith (1728–74) Irish-born British writer. *Elegy on the Death of a Mad Dog*

8 The man recovered of the bite,
The dog it was that died.
Oliver Goldsmith *Elegy on the Death of a Mad Dog*

9 Stop running those dogs on your page. I wouldn't have them peeing on my cheapest rug.
William Randolph Hearst (1863–1951) US newspaper owner. Referring to the publication of Thurber's drawings by one of his editors. *The Years with Ross* (James Thurber)

10 You ain't nothin' but a hound dog,
Cryin' all the time.
Jerry Leiber (1933–) US songwriter. *Hound Dog* (with Mike Stoller)

11 A door is what a dog is perpetually on the wrong side of.
Ogden Nash (1902–71) US poet. *A Dog's Best Friend Is His Illiteracy*

12 Regardless of what they say about it, we are going to keep it.
Richard Milhous Nixon (1913–) US President. Referring to 'Checkers', a dog given to his daughters. He was defending himself against corruption charges. TV address, 23 Sept 1952

13 I am His Highness' dog at Kew;
Pray tell me sir, whose dog are you?
Alexander Pope (1688–1744) British poet. On the collar of a dog given to Frederick, Prince of Wales

14 That indefatigable and unsavoury engine of pollution, the dog.
John Sparrow (1906–) British lawyer and academic. Letter to *The Times*, 30 Sept 1975

15 I loathe people who keep dogs. They are cowards who haven't got the guts to bite people themselves.
August Strindberg (1849–1912) Swedish dramatist. *A Madman's Diary*

16 Daddy wouldn't buy me a bow-wow, bow-wow.
I've got a little cat
And I'm very fond of that.
Joseph Tabrar (20th century) US songwriter. *Daddy Wouldn't Buy Me A Bow-wow* (song)

DONNE, John

(1573–1631) English poet of the metaphysical school. He was ordained at the age of 43 and was appointed Dean of St Pauls (1621). His verse includes *Divine Poems* (1607) and *Epithalamium* (1613).

Quotations about Donne

1 With Donne, whose muse on dromedary trots,
Wreathe iron pokers into true-love knots.
Samuel Taylor Coleridge (1772–1834) British poet. *On Donne's Poetry*

2 Dr Donne's verses are like the peace of God; they pass all understanding.
James I (1566–1625) King of England.

Quotations by Donne

3 And new Philosophy calls all in doubt,
The Element of fire is quite put out;
The Sun is lost, and th' earth, and no man's wit
Can well direct him where to look for it.
An Anatomy of the World, 205

4 Come live with me, and be my love,
And we will some new pleasures prove
Of golden sands, and crystal brooks,
With silken lines, and silver hooks.
The Bait

5 For God's sake hold your tongue and let me love.
The Canonization

6 But I do nothing upon myself, and yet I am mine own Executioner.
Devotions, 12

7 No man is an Island, entire of itself; every man is a piece of the Continent, a part of the main.
Devotions, 17

8 Any man's death diminishes me, because I am involved in Mankind; And therefore never send to know for whom the bell tolls; it tolls for thee.
Devotions, 17

9 Love built on beauty, soon as beauty, dies.
Elegies, 2, 'The Anagram'

10 She, and comparisons are odious.
Elegies, 8, 'The Comparison'

11 Licence my roving hands, and let them go,
Before, behind, between, above, below.
Elegies, 18, 'Love's Progress'

12 O my America! my new-found-land,
My Kingdom, safeliest when with one man man'd.
Elegies, 19, 'Going To Bed'

13 Go, and catch a falling star,
Get with child a mandrake root,
Tell me, where all past years are,
Or who cleft the Devil's foot.
Go and Catch a Falling Star

14 Death be not proud, though some have called thee
Mighty and dreadful, for, thou art not so.
Holy Sonnets, 10

15 It comes equally to us all, and makes us all equal when it comes. The ashes of an Oak in the Chimney, are no epitaph of that Oak, to tell me how high or how large that was; It tells me not what flocks it sheltered while it stood, nor what men it hurt when it fell. The dust of great persons' graves is speechless too, it says nothing, it distinguishes nothing.
Speaking of Death. *Sermons*, XV

16 Busy old fool, unruly Sun,
Why dost thou thus,
Through windows and through curtains call on us?
The Sun Rising

17 I am two fools, I know,
For loving, and for saying so
In whining Poetry.
The Triple Fool

DOOM

1 Alas, regardless of their doom,
The little victims play!
Thomas Gray (1716–71) British poet. *Ode on a Distant Prospect of Eton College*

2 Brief and powerless is Man's life; on him and all his race the slow, sure doom falls pitiless and dark.
Bertrand Russell (1872–1970) British philosopher. *Mysticism and Logic*, 'A Free Man's Worship'

3 Love alters not with his brief hours and weeks,
But bears it out even to the edge of doom.
If this be error, and upon me prov'd,
I never writ, nor no man ever lov'd.
William Shakespeare (1564–1616) English dramatist. *Sonnet 116*

4 I embrace the purpose of God and the doom assigned.
Alfred, Lord Tennyson (1809–92) British poet. *Maud*, III

DOOMSDAY

1 That at what time ye hear the sound of the cornet, flute, harp, sackbut, psaltery, dulcimer, and all kinds of musick, ye fall down and worship the golden image that Nebuchadnezzar the king hath set up:
And whoso falleth not down and worshippeth shall the same hour be cast into the midst of a burning fiery furnace.
Bible: Daniel 3:5–6

2 Immediately after the tribulation of those days shall the sun be darkened, and the moon shall not give her light, and the stars shall fall from heaven, and the powers of the heavens shall be shaken:
And then shall appear the sign of the Son of man in heaven: and then shall all the tribes of the earth mourn, and they shall see the Son of man coming in the clouds of heaven with power and great glory.
And he shall send his angels with a great sound of a trumpet, and they shall gather together his elect from the four winds, from one end of heaven to the other.
Bible: Matthew 24:29–31

3 'Tis the Last Judgment's fire must cure this place,
Calcine its clods and set my prisoners free.
Robert Browning (1812–89) British poet. *Childe Roland to the Dark Tower Came*, XI

4 Don't wait for the Last Judgement. It takes place every day.
Albert Camus (1913–60) French existentialist writer. *The Fall*

5 When all the world dissolves,
And every creature shall be purified,
All place shall be hell that is not heaven.
Christopher Marlowe (1564–93) English dramatist. *Doctor Faustus*, II:1

DOUBLETHINK

See also conflict, opposites

1 War is Peace, Freedom is Slavery, Ignorance is Strength.
George Orwell (Eric Blair; 1903–50) British novelist. *Nineteen Eighty-Four*

2 Doublethink means the power of holding two contradictory beliefs in one's mind simultaneously, and accepting both of them.
George Orwell *Nineteen Eighty-Four*

DOUBT

See also scepticism, uncertainty

1 If a man will begin with certainties, he shall end in doubts, but if he will be content to begin with doubts, he shall end in certainties.
Francis Bacon (1561–1626) English philosopher. *The Advancement of Learning*, Bk. I, Ch. 5

2 Then saith he to Thomas, Reach hither thy finger, and behold my hands; and reach hither thy hand, and thrust it into my side: and be not faithless, but believing.
And Thomas answered and said unto him, My Lord and my God.
Jesus saith unto him, Thomas, because thou hast seen me, thou hast believed: blessed are they that have not seen, and yet have believed.
Bible: John 20:27–29

3 And immediately Jesus stretched forth his hand, and caught him, and said unto him, O thou of little faith, wherefore didst thou doubt?
Bible: Matthew 14:31

4 He who shall teach the child to doubt
The rotting grave shall ne'er get out.
William Blake (1757–1827) British poet. *Auguries of Innocence*

5 All we have gained then by our unbelief
Is a life of doubt diversified by faith,
For one of faith diversified by doubt:
We called the chess-board white, – we call it black.
Robert Browning (1812–89) British poet. *Bishop Blougram's Apology*

6 His doubts are better than most people's certainties.
Lord Hardwicke (1690–1764) English judge. Referring to Dirleton's *Doubts*. *Life of Johnson* (J. Boswell)

7 Negative Capability, that is, when a man is capable of being in uncertainties, mysteries, doubts, without any irritable reaching after fact and reason.
John Keats (1795–1821) British poet. Letter to G. and T. Keats, 21 Dec 1817

8 The trouble with the world is that the stupid are cocksure and the intelligent full of doubt.
Bertrand Russell (1872–1970) British philosopher. *Autobiography*

9 Those obstinate questionings
Of sense and outward things,
Fallings from us, vanishings;
Blank misgivings of a Creature
Moving about in worlds not realised,
High instincts before which our mortal nature
Did tremble like a guilty thing surprised.
William Wordsworth (1770–1850) British poet. *Ode. Intimations of Immortality*, IX

DOYLE, Sir Arthur Conan

(1856–1930) British writer and creator of the detective Sherlock Holmes. Originally a doctor, he ceased to practise in 1890, devoting himself entirely to his writing. He also wrote books on spiritualism.

1 It is an old maxim of mine that when you have excluded the impossible, whatever remains, however improbable, must be the truth.
The Beryl Coronet

2 You know my method. It is founded upon the observance of trifles.
The Boscombe Valley Mystery

3 The husband was a teetotaller, there was no other woman, and the conduct complained of was that he had drifted into the habit of winding up every meal by taking out his false teeth and hurling them at his wife.
A Case of Identity

4 It has long been an axiom of mine that the little things are infinitely the most important.
A Case of Identity

5 Depend upon it, there is nothing so unnatural as the commonplace.
A Case of Identity

6 It is my belief, Watson, founded upon my experience, that the lowest and vilest alleys of London do not present a more dreadful record of sin than does the smiling and beautiful countryside.
Copper Beeches

7 'Excellent!' I cried. 'Elementary,' said he.
Watson talking to Sherlock Holmes; Holmes's reply is often misquoted as 'Elementary my dear Watson'. *The Crooked Man*

8 'It is my duty to warn you that it will be used against you,' cried the Inspector, with the magnificent fair play of the British criminal law.
The Dancing Men

9 He is the Napoleon of crime.
Referring to Professor Moriarty. *The Final Problem*

10 A man should keep his little brain attic stocked with all the furniture that he is likely to use, and the rest he can put away in the lumber room of his library, where he can get it if he wants it.
Five Orange Pips

11 It is quite a three-pipe problem.
The Red-Headed League

12 An experience of women which extends over many nations and three continents.
The Sign of Four

13 'Is there any point to which you would wish to draw my attention?'
'To the curious incident of the dog in the night-time.'
'The dog did nothing in the night-time.'
'That was the curious incident,' remarked Sherlock Holmes.
The Silver Blaze

14 London, that great cesspool into which all the loungers of the Empire are irresistibly drained.
A Study in Scarlet

15 Mediocrity knows nothing higher than itself, but talent instantly recognizes genius.
The Valley of Fear

DREAMS

1 Dreams and predictions ought to serve but for winter talk by the fireside.
Francis Bacon (1561–1626) English philosopher. *Essays*, 'Of Prophecies'

2 It was a dream of perfect bliss,
Too beautiful to last.
Thomas Haynes Bayly (1797–1839) British writer. *It was a Dream*

3 So I awoke, and behold it was a dream.
John Bunyan (1628–88) English writer. *The Pilgrim's Progress*, Pt. I

4 I do not know whether I was then a man dreaming I was a butterfly, or whether I am now a butterfly dreaming I am a man.
Chuang Tse (*or* Zhuangzi; c. 369–286 BC) Chinese philosopher. *Chuang Tse* (H. A. Giles), Ch. 2

5 The people's prayer, the glad diviner's theme,
The young men's vision, and the old men's dream!
John Dryden (1631–1700) British poet and dramatist. *Absalom and Achitophel*, I

6 Last night I dreamt I went to Manderley again.
Daphne Du Maurier (1907–89) British novelist. *Rebecca*, Ch. 1

7 Underneath the arches
We dream our dreams away.
Bud Flanagan (Robert Winthrop; 1896–1968) British comedian. *Underneath the Arches*

8 Abou Ben Adhem (may his tribe increase!)
Awoke one night from a deep dream of peace,
And saw, within the moonlight in his room,
Making it rich, and like a lily in bloom,
An angel writing in a book of gold: – . . .
Leigh Hunt (1784–1859) British poet. *Abou Ben Adhem and the Angel*

9 Castles in the air – they're so easy to take refuge in. So easy to build, too.
Henrik Ibsen (1828–1906) Norwegian dramatist. *The Master Builder*, III

10 Alas, all the castles I have, are built with air, thou know'st.
Ben Jonson (1573–1637) English dramatist. *Eastward Ho*, II:2

11 All men dream: but not equally. Those who dream by night in the dusty recesses of their minds wake in the day to find that it was vanity: but the dreamers of the day are dangerous men, for they may act their dream with open eyes, to make it possible.
T. E. Lawrence (1888–1935) British soldier and writer. *Seven Pillars of Wisdom*, Ch. 1

12 My Oberon! what visions have I seen!
Methought I was enamour'd of an ass.
William Shakespeare (1564–1616) English dramatist. *A Midsummer Night's Dream*, IV:1

13 I have had a dream, past the wit of man to say what dream it was.
William Shakespeare *A Midsummer Night's Dream*, IV:1

14 The eye of man hath not heard, the ear of man hath not seen, man's hand is not able to taste, his tongue to conceive, nor his heart to report, what my dream was.
William Shakespeare *A Midsummer Night's Dream*, IV:1

15 If we shadows have offended,
Think but this, and all is mended,
That you have but slumber'd here
While these visions did appear.
William Shakespeare *A Midsummer Night's Dream*, V:2

16 Many's the long night I've dreamed of cheese – toasted, mostly.
Robert Louis Stevenson (1850–94) Scottish writer. Said by the castaway Ben Gunn. *Treasure Island*, Ch. 15

17 Dreams are true while they last, and do we not live in dreams?
Alfred, Lord Tennyson (1809–92) British poet. *The Higher Pantheism*

18 I have spread my dreams under your feet.
Tread softly because you tread on my dreams.
W. B. Yeats (1865–1939) Irish poet. *He wishes For The Cloths of Heaven*

DRINKS

See also alcohol, drunkenness, water

1 The infusion of a China plant sweetened with the pith of an Indian cane.
Joseph Addison (1672–1719) British essayist. *The Spectator*, 69

2 Bowen's Beer Makes You Drunk.
Kingsley Amis (1922–) British novelist, poet, and critic. Suggested advertising slogan. *I Like It Here*

3 Look here, Steward, if this is coffee, I want tea; but if this is tea, then I wish for coffee.
Anonymous Cartoon caption, *Punch*, 1902

4 If I had known there was no Latin word for tea I would have let the vulgar stuff alone.
Hilaire Belloc (1870–1953) French-born British poet. Attrib.

5 Drink no longer water, but use a little wine for thy stomach's sake and thine often infirmities.
Bible: I Timothy 5:23

6 The shortest way out of Manchester is notoriously a bottle of Gordon's gin.
William Bolitho (1890–1930) British writer. Attrib.

7 I the Trinity illustrate,
Drinking watered orange-pulp –
In three sips the Arian frustrate;
While he drains his at one gulp.
Robert Browning (1812–89) British poet. *Soliloquy of the Spanish Cloister*

8 I am willing to taste any drink once.
James Cabell (1879–1958) US novelist and journalist. *Jurgen*, Ch. 1

9 That one day this country of ours, which we love so much, will find dignity and greatness and peace again.
Noël Coward (1899–1973) British dramatist. The toast from *Cavalcade*

10 While the bubbling and loud-hissing urn
Throws up a steamy column, and the cups,
That cheer but not inebriate, wait on each,
So let us welcome peaceful evening in.
William Cowper (1731–1800) British poet. *The Task*

11 Gimme a viskey. Ginger ale on the side. And don't be stingy, baby.
Greta Garbo (1905–) Swedish-born US film actress. *Anna Christie*

12 Tea for Two, and Two for Tea.
Otto Harback (1873–1963) US dramatist. From the musical *No! No! Nanette*. Song title

13 This wine is too good for toast-drinking, my dear. You don't want to mix emotions up with a wine like that. You lose the taste.
Ernest Hemingway (1898–1961) US novelist. *The Sun also Rises*

14 One more drink and I'd be under the host.
Dorothy Parker (1893–1967) US writer. *You Might As Well Live* (J. Keats)

15 Coffee which makes the politician wise,
And see through all things with his half-shut eyes.
Alexander Pope (1688–1744) British poet. *The Rape of the Lock*, III

16 Here thou great Anna! whom three realms obey,
Dost sometimes counsel take – and sometimes Tea.
Alexander Pope *The Rape of the Lock*, III

17 Our trouble is that we drink too much tea. I see in this the slow revenge of the Orient, which has diverted the Yellow River down our throats.
J. B. Priestley (1894–1984) British novelist. *The Observer*, 'Sayings of the Week', 15 May 1949

18 It's a Naive Domestic Burgundy without Any Breeding, But I Think You'll be Amused by its Presumption.
James Thurber (1894–1961) US humorist. *Men, Women and Dogs*, cartoon caption

19 I think it must be so, for I have been drinking it for sixty-five years and I am not dead yet.
Voltaire (François-Marie Arouet; 1694–1778) French writer. On learning that coffee was considered a slow poison. Attrib.

DROWNING

See also death

1 The western tide crept up along the sand,
And o'er and o'er the sand,
And round and round the sand,
As far as eye could see.
The rolling mist came down and hid the land:
And never home came she.
Charles Kingsley (1819–75) British writer. *The Sands of Dee*

2 O Lord, methought what pain it was to drown,
What dreadful noise of waters in my ears,
What sights of ugly death within my eyes!
William Shakespeare (1564–1616) English dramatist. *Richard III*, I:4

3 Nobody heard him, the dead man,
But still he lay moaning:
I was much further out than you thought
And not waving but drowning.
Stevie Smith (Florence Margaret Smith; 1902–71) British poet. *Not Waving But Drowning*

DRUGS

1 Medicine cures the man who is fated not to die.
Proverb

2 A drug is that substance which, when injected into a rat, will produce a scientific report.
Anonymous

3 Hark! The herald angels sing
Beecham's pills are just the thing.
Peace on earth and mercy mild;
Two for man and one for child.
Anonymous Apparently the result of a Beecham's advertisement in a hymnbook

4 APOTHECARY, n. The physician's accomplice, undertaker's benefactor and grave worm's provider.
Ambrose Bierce (1842–c. 1914) US writer and journalist. *The Devil's Dictionary*

5 Thou hast the keys of Paradise, oh, just, subtle, and mighty opium!
Thomas De Quincey (1785–1859) British essayist and critic. *Confessions of an English Opium-Eater*, Pt. II

6 Alarmed successively by every fashionable medical terror of the day, she dosed her children with every specific which was publicly advertised or privately recommended. No creatures of their age had taken such quantities of Ching's lozenges, Godbold's elixir, or Dixon's anti-bilious pills. The consequence was, that the dangers, which had at first been imaginary, became real: these little victims of domestic medicine never had a day's health: they looked, and were, more dead than alive.
Maria Edgeworth (1767–1849) British novelist. *Patronage*

7 A man who cannot work without his hypodermic needle is a poor doctor. The amount of narcotic you use is inversely proportional to your skill.
Martin H. Fischer (1879–1962) *Fischerisms* (Howard Fabing and Ray Marr)

8 Half the modern drugs could well be thrown out the window, except that the birds might eat them.
Martin H. Fischer *Fischerisms* (Howard Fabing and Ray Marr)

9 As to diseases, make a habit of two things – to help, or at least to do no harm.
Hippocrates (c. 460 BC–c. 377 BC) Greek physician. *Epidemics*, Bk. I

10 Medicines are nothing in themselves, if not properly used, but the very hands of the gods, if employed with reason and prudence.
Herophilus (fl. 300 BC) Greek physician.

11 No families take so little medicine as those of doctors, except those of apothecaries.
Oliver Wendell Holmes (1809–94) US writer and physician. *Medical Essays*, 'Currents and Counter-Currents in Medical Science'

12 A hundred doses of happiness are not enough: send to the drug-store for another bottle – and, when that is finished, for another. . . There can be no doubt that, if tranquillizers could be bought as easily and cheaply as aspirin they would be consumed, not by the billions, as they are at present, but by the scores and hundreds of billions. And a good, cheap stimulant would be almost as popular.
Aldous Huxley (1894–1963) British writer. *Brave New World Revisited*, Ch. 8

13 What is dangerous about the tranquilizers is that whatever peace of mind they bring is a packaged peace of mind. Where you buy a pill and buy peace with it, you get conditioned to cheap solutions instead of deep ones.
Max Lerner (1902–) Russian-born US teacher, editor, and journalist. *The Unfinished Country*, 'The Assault on the Mind'

14 I will lift up mine eyes unto the pills. Almost everyone takes them, from the humble aspirin to the multi-coloured, king-sized three deckers, which put you to sleep, wake you up, stimulate and soothe you all in one. It is an age of pills.
Malcolm Muggeridge (1903–) British writer and editor. *The New Statesman*, 3 Aug 1962

15 One of the first duties of the physician is to educate the masses not to take medicine.
William Osler (1849–1919) *Sir William Osler: Aphorisms*, Ch. 3 (William B. Bean)

16 Imperative drugging – the ordering of medicine in any and every malady – is no longer regarded as the chief function of the doctor.
William Osler *Aequanimitas, with Other Addresses*, 'Medicine in the Nineteenth Century'

17 The treatment with poison medicines comes from the West.
Huang Ti (The Yellow Emperor; 2697 BC–2597 BC) *Nei Ching Su Wên*, Bk. 4

18 I owe my reputation to the fact that I use digitalis in doses the text books say are dangerous and in cases that the text books say are unsuitable.

Karel Frederik Wenckebach (1864–1940) *Lancet*, 2:633, 1937

DRUNKENNESS

See also alcohol

1 There are more old drunkards than old doctors.

Proverb

2 His mouth has been used as a latrine by some small animal of the night.

Kingsley Amis (1922–) British novelist. Describing a hangover. *Lucky Jim*

3 Come landlord, fill the flowing bowl,
Until it doth run over . . .
For tonight we'll merry, merry be,
Tomorrow we'll be sober.

Anonymous *Come, Landlord, Fill the Flowing Bowl*

4 Lord George-Brown drunk is a better man than the Prime Minister sober.

Anonymous Comparing him with Harold Wilson. *The Times*, 6 Mar 1976

5 What shall we do with the drunken sailor
Early in the morning?
Hoo-ray and up she rises
Early in the morning.

Anonymous *What shall we do with the Drunken Sailor?*

6 Ha, ha, ha, you and me,
Little brown jug, don't I love thee!

Anonymous *The Little Brown Jug*

7 One reason I don't drink is that I want to know when I am having a good time.

Nancy Astor (1879–1964) American-born British politician. Attrib.

8 An alcoholic has been lightly defined as a man who drinks more than his own doctor.

Alvan L. Barach (1895–) *Journal of the American Medical Association*, 181:393, 1962

9 Drunkenness, the ruin of reason, the destruction of strength, premature old age, momentary death.

St. Basil the Great (c. 330–c. 379) Bishop of Caesarea in Cappadocia. *Homilies*, No. XIV, Ch. 7

10 For when the wine is in, the wit is out.

Thomas Becon (1512–67) English Protestant churchman. *Catechism*, 375

11 Others mocking said, These men are full of new wine.

Bible: Acts 2:13

12 Wine is a mocker, strong drink is raging: and whosoever is deceived thereby is not wise.

Bible: Proverbs 20:1

13 Man, being reasonable, must get drunk;
The best of life is but intoxication.

Lord Byron (1788–1824) British poet. *Don Juan*, II

14 It's my opinion, sir, that this meeting is drunk.

Charles Dickens (1812–70) British novelist. *Pickwick Papers*, Ch. 33

15 I am as sober as a Judge.

Henry Fielding (1707–54) British novelist. *Don Quixote in England*, III:14

16 Drink! for you know not whence you came, nor why:
Drink! for you know not why you go, nor where.

Edward Fitzgerald *The Rubáiyát of Omar Khayyám*, LXXIV

17 Drunkenness is never anything but a substitute for happiness. It amounts to buying the dream of a thing when you haven't money enough to buy the dreamed-of thing materially.

André Gide (1869–1951) French novelist and critic. *Journaux*

18 If merely 'feeling good' could decide, drunkenness would be the supremely valid human experience.

William James (1842–1910) US psychologist and philosopher. *Varieties of Religious Experience*

19 A branch of the sin of drunkenness, which is the root of all sins.

James I (1566–1625) King of England. *A Counterblast to Tobacco*

20 A man who exposes himself when he is intoxicated, has not the art of getting drunk.

Samuel Johnson (1709–84) British lexicographer. *Life of Johnson* (J. Boswell), Vol. III

21 Better sleep with a sober cannibal than a drunken Christian.

Herman Melville (1819–91) US novelist. *Moby Dick*, Ch. 3

22 Drunkenness . . . spoils health, dismounts the mind, and unmans men.

William Penn (1644–1718) English founder of Pennsylvania. *Fruits of Solitude*, Maxim 72

23 I am as drunk as a lord, but then, I am one, so what does it matter?

Bertrand Russell (1872–1970) British philosopher. *Bertrand Russell, Philosopher of the Century* (Ralph Schoenman)

24 Drunkenness is temporary suicide the happiness that it brings is merely negative, a momentary cessation of unhappiness.

Bertrand Russell *The Conquest of Happiness*

25 No, thank you, I was born intoxicated.

George William Russell (1867–1935) Irish poet and dramatist. Refusing a drink that was offered him. *10,000 Jokes, Toasts, and Stories* (L. Copeland)

26 Drunkenness is simply voluntary insanity.

Seneca (c. 4 BC–AD 65) Roman writer. *Epistulae ad Lucilium*, LXXXIII

27 But I'm not so think as you drunk I am.

John Collings Squire (1884–1958) British journalist. *Ballade of Soporific Absorption*

28 An alcoholic is someone you don't like who drinks as much as you do.

Dylan Thomas (1914–53) Welsh poet. *Dictionary of 20th Century Quotations* (Nigel Rees)

29 Come, Robert, you shall drink twice while I drink once, for I cannot permit the son in his sober senses to witness the intoxication of his father.

Horace Walpole (1717–97) British writer. Explaining why he filled his son's glass twice for every glass he drank himself. Attrib.

DRYDEN, John

(1631–1700) British poet and dramatist. His play *Marriage à la Mode* (1673) and the verse satire *Absalom and Achitophel* (1681) were highly regarded. He was made poet laureate by Charles II in 1668, but having become a Catholic in 1685, he was deprived of the office by William of Orange on his accession.

Quotations about Dryden

1 He never heartily and sincerely praised any human being, or felt any real enthusiasm for any subject he took up.

John Keble (1792–1866) British poet and clergyman. *Lectures on Poetry*

2 Ev'n copious Dryden wanted, or forgot

The last and greatest art – the art to blot.
Alexander Pope (1688–1744) British poet. *Imitations of Horace*

Quotations by Dryden

3 In pious times, e'r Priest-craft did begin,
Before Polygamy was made a Sin.
Absalom and Achitophel, I

4 What e'r he did was done with so much ease,
In him alone, 'twas Natural to please.
Absalom and Achitophel, I

5 Great Wits are sure to Madness near alli'd
And thin Partitions do their Bounds divide.
Absalom and Achitophel, I

6 Bankrupt of Life, yet Prodigal of Ease.
Absalom and Achitophel, I

7 For Politicians neither love nor hate.
Absalom and Achitophel, I

8 But far more numerous was the Herd of such,
Who think too little, and who talk too much.
Absalom and Achitophel, I

9 A man so various, that he seem'd to be
Not one, but all Mankind's Epitome.
Stiff in Opinions, always in the wrong;
Was Everything by starts, and Nothing long.
Absalom and Achitophel, I

10 Did wisely from Expensive Sins refrain,
And never broke the Sabbath, but for Gain.
Absalom and Achitophel, I

11 During his Office, Treason was no Crime.
The Sons of Belial had a Glorious Time.
Absalom and Achitophel, I

12 Nor is the Peoples Judgment always true:
The Most may err as grosly as the Few.
Absalom and Achitophel, I

13 Beware the Fury of a Patient Man.
Absalom and Achitophel, I

14 The people's prayer, the glad diviner's theme,
The young men's vision, and the old men's dream!
Absalom and Achitophel, I

15 To die for faction is a common evil,
But to be hanged for nonsense is the Devil.
Absalom and Achitophel, II

16 None but the Brave deserves the Fair.
Alexander's Feast

17 Errors, like Straws, upon the surface flow;
He who would search for Pearls must dive below.
All for Love, Prologue

18 Men are but children of a larger growth;
Our appetites as apt to change as theirs,
And full as craving too, and full as vain.
All for Love, IV

19 So sicken waning moons too near the sun,
And blunt their crescents on the edge of day.
Annus Mirabilis

20 By viewing Nature, Nature's handmaid, art,
Makes mighty things from small beginnings grow.
Annus Mirabilis

21 Here lies my wife; here let her lie!
Now she's at rest, and so am I.
Epitaph Intended for Dryden's Wife

22 He was the man who of all modern, and perhaps ancient poets had the largest and most comprehensive soul.
Referring to Shakespeare. *Essay of Dramatic Poesy*

23 He was naturally learned; he needed not the spectacles of books to read nature; he looked inwards, and found her there.
Referring to Shakespeare. *Essay of Dramatic Poesy*

24 If by the people you understand the multitude, the *hoi polloi,* 'tis no matter what they think; they are sometimes in the right, sometimes in the wrong; their judgement is a mere lottery.
Essay of Dramatic Poesy

25 For present joys are more to flesh and blood
Than a dull prospect of a distant good.
The Hind and the Panther, III

26 All humane things are subject to decay,
And, when Fate summons, Monarchs must obey.
Mac Flecknoe

27 I am resolved to grow fat and look young till forty, and then slip out of the world with the first wrinkle and the reputation of five-and-twenty.
The Maiden Queen, III

28 I am to be married within these three days; married past redemption.
Marriage à la Mode, I

29 For, Heaven be thanked, we live is such an age,
When no man dies for love, but on the stage.
Mithridates, Epilogue

30 A man is to be cheated into passion, but to be reasoned into truth.
Religio Laici, Preface

31 Happy the Man, and happy he alone,
He who can call today his own:
He who, secure within, can say,
Tomorrow do thy worst, for I have liv'd today.
Translation of Horace, III

DULLNESS

See also boredom, stupidity

1 He'd be sharper than a serpent's tooth, if he wasn't as dull as ditch water.
Charles Dickens (1812–70) British novelist. *Our Mutual Friend,* Bk. III, Ch. 10

2 He is not only dull in himself, but the cause of dullness in others.
Samuel Foote (1720–77) British actor and dramatist. Parody of a line from Shakespeare's *Henry IV, Part 2*. *Life of Johnson* (J. Boswell)

DUST

1 It was prettily devised of Aesop, 'The fly sat upon the axletree of the chariot-wheel and said, what a dust do I raise.'
Francis Bacon (1561–1626) English philosopher. *Essays,* 'Of Vain-Glory'

2 We have first raised a dust and then complain we cannot see.
Bishop Berkeley (1685–1753) Irish churchman and philosopher. *Principles of Human Knowledge*, Introduction

3 It comes equally to us all, and makes us all equal when it comes. The ashes of an Oak in the Chimney, are no epitaph of that Oak, to tell me how high or how large that was; It tells me not what flocks it sheltered while it stood, nor what men it hurt when it fell. The dust of great persons' graves is speechless too, it says nothing, it distinguishes nothing.
John Donne (1573–1631) English poet. *Sermons*, XV

4 And I will show you something different from either
Your shadow at morning striding behind you,
Or your shadow at evening rising to meet you
I will show you fear in a handful of dust.
T. S. Eliot (1888–1965) US-born British poet and dramatist. *The Waste Land*, 'The Burial of the Dead'

5 Less than the dust beneath thy chariot wheel,
Less than the weed that grows beside thy door,
Less than the rust that never stained thy sword,
Less than the need thou hast in life of me,
Even less am I.
Laurence Hope (Mrs M. H. Nicolson; 1804–1905) British poet and songwriter. *The Garden of Kama and other Love Lyrics from India*, 'Less than the Dust'

6 The dust and silence of the upper shelf.
Lord Macaulay (1800–59) British historian. *Literary Essays Contributed to the 'Edinburgh Review'*, 'Milton'

7 A heap of dust alone remains of thee;
'Tis all thou art, and all the proud shall be!
Alexander Pope (1688–1744) British poet. *Elegy to the Memory of an Unfortunate Lady*

8 Wit that can creep, and pride that licks the dust.
Alexander Pope *Epistle to Dr. Arbuthnot*

9 Fear no more the heat o' th' sun
Nor the furious winter's rages;
Thou thy worldly task hast done,
Home art gone, and ta'en thy wages.
Golden lads and girls all must,
As chimney-sweepers, come to dust.
William Shakespeare (1564–1616) English dramatist. *Cymbeline*, IV:2

DUTY

See also obligation

1 From a very early age, I had imbibed the opinion, that it was every man's duty to do all that lay in his power to leave his country as good as he had found it.
William Cobbett (1763–1835) British journalist and writer. *Political Register*, 22 Dec 1832

2 Do your duty and leave the rest to the Gods.
Pierre Corneille (1606–84) French dramatist. *Horace*, II:8

3 England expects every man will do his duty.
Lord Nelson (1758–1805) British admiral. Signal hoisted prior to the Battle of Trafalgar, 1805.

4 When a stupid man is doing something he is ashamed of, he always declares that it is his duty.
George Bernard Shaw (1856–1950) Irish dramatist and critic. *Caesar and Cleopatra*, III

5 Sunset and evening star,
And one clear call for me!
And may there be no moaning of the bar
When I put out to sea.
Alfred, Lord Tennyson (1809–92) British poet. *Crossing the Bar*

DYLAN, Bob

(Robert Allen Zimmerman; 1941–) US popular singer and songwriter. Originally a member of the 1960s protest movement, producing such albums as *The Times They Are A-changin'* (1964), in the late 1970s his conversion to Christianity led to such religious albums as *Saved* (1980).

1 How many roads must a man walk down
Before you call him a man?
Blowin' in the Wind

2 Yes, 'n' how many years can some people exist
Before they're allowed to be free?
Yes, 'n' how many times can a man turn his head,
Pretending he just doesn't see?
The answer, my friend, is blowin' in the wind.
Blowin' in the Wind

3 She takes just like a woman, yes, she does
She makes love just like a woman, yes, she does
And she aches just like a woman
But she breaks just like a little girl.
Just Like a Woman

4 How does it feel
To be without a home
Like a complete unknown
Like a rolling stone?
Like a Rolling Stone

5 She knows there's no success like failure
And that failure's no success at all.
Love Minus Zero No Limit

6 Hey! Mr Tambourine Man, play a song for me.
I'm not sleepy and there is no place I'm going to.
Mr Tambourine Man

7 Come mothers and fathers
Throughout the land
And don't criticize
What you can't understand
The Times They Are A-Changin'

8 Yeah, some of them are about ten minutes long, others five or six.
On being asked, during an interview, if he would say something about his songs

9 A Hard Rain's A-Gonna Fall.
Song title

E

EARTH

1 Give me a firm place to stand, and I will move the earth.
Archimedes (c. 287–212 BC) Greek mathematician. *On the Lever*

2 He spoke, and loos'd our heart in tears.
He laid us as we lay at birth
On the cool flowery lap of earth.
Matthew Arnold Referring to Wordsworth. *Memorial Verses*

3 The gentleman will please remember that when his half-civilized ancestors were hunting the

wild boar in Silesia, mine were princes of the earth.
Judah Philip Benjamin (1811–84) US politician. Replying to a senator of Germanic origin who had made an antisemitic remark. Attrib.

4 In the beginning God created the heaven and the earth.
And the earth was without form, and void; and darkness was upon the face of the deep. And the Spirit of God moved upon the face of the waters.
And God said, Let there be light: and there was light.
And God saw the light, that it was good: and God divided the light from the darkness.
And God called the light Day, and the darkness he called Night. And the evening and the morning were the first day.
Bible: Genesis 1:1–5

5 And God called the dry land Earth; and the gathering together of the waters called he Seas: and God saw that it was good.
And God said, Let the earth bring forth grass, the herb yielding seed, and the fruit tree yielding fruit after his kind, whose seed is in itself, upon the earth: and it was so.
Bible: Genesis 1:10–11

6 I do set my bow in the cloud, and it shall be for a token of a covenant between me and the earth.
Bible: Genesis 9:13

7 Heaven and earth shall pass away, but my words shall not pass away.
Bible: Matthew 24:35

8 And I saw a great white throne, and him that sat on it, from whose face the earth and the heaven fled away; and there was found no place for them.
And I saw the dead, small and great, stand before God; and the books were opened: and another book was opened, which is the book of life: and the dead were judged out of those things which were written in the books, according to their works.
And the sea gave up the dead which were in it; and death and hell delivered up the dead which were in them: and they were judged every man according to their works.
Bible: Revelations 20:11–13

9 A king lived long ago,
In the morning of the world,
When earth was nigher heaven than now.
Robert Browning (1812–89) British poet. *Pippa Passes*, Pt. I

10 But did thee feel the earth move?
Ernest Hemingway (1899–1961) US novelist. *For Whom the Bell Tolls*, Ch. 13

11 O, for a draught of vintage! that hath been
Cool'd a long age in the deep-delved earth.
John Keats (1795–1821) British poet. *Ode to a Nightingale*

12 The meek do not inherit the earth unless they are prepared to fight for their meekness.
H. J. Laski (1893–1950) British political theorist. Attrib.

13 A heav'n on earth.
John Milton (1608–74) English poet. *Paradise Lost*, Bk. IV

14 Falstaff sweats to death
And lards the lean earth as he walks along.
William Shakespeare (1564–1616) English dramatist. *Henry IV, Part One*, II:2

15 There are more things in heaven and earth, Horatio,
Than are dreamt of in your philosophy.
William Shakespeare *Hamlet*, I:5

16 This royal throne of kings, this sceptred isle,
This earth of majesty, this seat of Mars,
This other Eden, demi-paradise,
This fortress built by Nature for herself
Against infection and the hand of war,
This happy breed of men, this little world,
This precious stone set in the silver sea,
Which serves it in the office of a wall,
Or as a moat defensive to a house,
Against the envy of less happier lands;
This blessed plot, this earth, this realm, this England,
This nurse, this teeming womb of royal kings,
Fear'd by their breed, and famous by their birth.
William Shakespeare *Richard II*, II:1

17 The earth does not argue,
Is not pathetic, has no arrangements,
Does not scream, haste, persuade, threaten, promise,
Makes no discriminations, has no conceivable failures,
Closes nothing, refuses nothing, shuts none out.
Walt Whitman (1819–92) US poet. *To the sayers of words*

18 By the splendour of God I have taken possession of my realm; the earth of England is in my two hands.
William the Conqueror (1027–87) King of England. Said after falling over when coming ashore at Pevensey with his army of invasion. Attrib.

19 A youth to whom was given
So much of earth – so much of heaven,
And such impetuous blood.
William Wordsworth (1770–1850) British poet. *Ruth*

20 Earth has not anything to show more fair:
Dull would he be of soul who could pass by
A sight so touching in its majesty:
The City now doth, like a garment, wear
The beauty of the morning; silent, bare,
Ships, towers, domes, theatres, and temples lie
Open unto the fields, and to the sky;
All bright and glittering in the smokeless air.
William Wordsworth *Sonnets*, 'Composed upon Westminster Bridge'

21 Earth fills her lap with pleasures of her own:
Yearnings she hath in her own natural kind.
William Wordsworth *Ode. Intimations of Immortality*, VI

22 Ethereal minstrel! pilgrim of the sky!
Dost thou despise the earth where cares abound?
William Wordsworth *To a Skylark*

EATING

1 Then I commended mirth, because a man hath no better thing under the sun, than to eat, and to drink, and to be merry: for that shall abide with him of his labour the days of his life, which God giveth him under the sun.
Bible: Ecclesiastes 8:15

2 And behold joy and gladness, slaying oxen, and killing sheep, eating flesh, and drinking wine: let

us eat and drink; for tomorrow we shall die.

Bible: Isaiah A similar sentiment is expressed in Corinthians 15:32–33. Often misquoted as 'let us eat, drink, and be merry'. 22:13

3 For even when we were with you, this we commanded you, that if any would not work, neither should he eat.

Bible: II Thessalonians 3:10

4 Some hae meat, and canna eat,
And some wad eat that want it,
But we hae meat and we can eat,
And sae the Lord be thankit.

Robert Burns (1759–96) Scottish poet. *The Selkirk Grace*

5 Let them eat the lie and swallow it with their bread. Whether the two were lovers or no, they'll have accounted to God for it by now. I have my own fish to fry.

Miguel de Cervantes (1547–1616) Spanish novelist. *Don Quixote*, Pt. I, Ch. 25

6 Don't eat too many almonds; they add weight to the breasts.

Colette (1873–1954) French novelist. *Gigi*

7 To eat well in England you should have breakfast three times a day.

W. Somerset Maugham (1874–1965) British novelist. Attrib.

8 One should eat to live, not live to eat.

Molière (Jean Baptiste Poquelin; 1622–73) French dramatist. *L'Avare*, III:2

9 I think I could eat one of Bellamy's veal pies.

William Pitt the Younger (1759–1806) British statesman. Last words. Attrib.

10 My advice if you insist on slimming: Eat as much as you like – just don't swallow it.

Harry Secombe (1921–) Welsh singer, actor, and comedian. *Daily Herald*, 5 Oct 1962

11 3RD FISHERMAN. Master, I marvel how the fishes live in the sea.
1ST FISHERMAN. Why, as men do a-land – the great ones eat up the little ones.

William Shakespeare (1564–1616) English dramatist. *Pericles*, II:1

ECOLOGY

See also environment

1 Over increasingly large areas of the United States, spring now comes unheralded by the return of the birds, and the early mornings are strangely silent where once they were filled with the beauty of bird song.

Rachel Carson (1907–64) US biologist. *The Silent Spring*

2 As cruel a weapon as the cave man's club, the chemical barrage has been hurled against the fabric of life.

Rachel Carson *The Silent Spring*

3 Man has been endowed with reason, with the power to create, so that he can add to what he's been given. But up to now he hasn't been a creator, only a destroyer. Forests keep disappearing, rivers dry up, wild life's become extinct, the climate's ruined and the land grows poorer and uglier every day.

Anton Chekhov (1860–1904) Russian dramatist. *Uncle Vanya*, I

4 It will be said of this generation that it found England a land of beauty and left it a land of beauty spots.

Cyril Joad (1891–1953) British writer and broadcaster. *The Observer*, 'Sayings of Our Times', 31 May 1953

5 We are living beyond our means. As a people we have developed a life-style that is draining the earth of its priceless and irreplaceable resources without regard for the future of our children and people all around the world.

Margaret Mead (1901–78) US anthropologist. *Redbook*, 'The Energy Crisis – Why Our World Will Never Again Be the Same.'

6 I became an ecologist long before I heard the word.

Francisco Mendes (1944–88) Brazilian rubber tapper and ecological campaigner. Remark

7 We are wealthy and wasteful but this can't go on. If we don't eat dog biscuits, we could end up eating our dog instead.

Magnus Pyke (1908–) British scientist, television personality, and writer. *The Observer*, 'Sayings of the Week', 12 Jan 1975

ECONOMICS

1 Don't spoil the ship for a ha'porth of tar.

Proverb

2 Save water – bath with a friend.

Anonymous British slogan

3 John Stuart Mill
By a mighty effort of will
Overcame his natural bonhomie
And wrote 'Principles of Political Economy'.

Edmund Clerihew Bentley (1875–1956) British writer. *Biography for Beginners*

4 Respectable Professors of the Dismal Science.

Thomas Carlyle (1795–1881) Scottish historian and essayist. Referring to economists. *Latter-Day Pamphlets*, 1

5 Provided that the City of London remains as at present, the Clearing-house of the World.

Joseph Chamberlain (1836–1914) British politician. Speech, Guildhall, London, 19 Jan 1904

6 There is only a certain sized cake to be divided up, and if a lot of people want a larger slice they can only take it from others who would, in terms of real income, have a smaller one.

Stafford Cripps (1889–1952) British Labour politician. Speech, Trade Union Congress, 7 Sept 1948

7 Daily many warantis come to me of paiementz . . . of much more than all youre revenuz wold come to, thowe they were not assigned afore . . . the which warrantes yf I shuld paye hem, youre Household, chambre and warderope and youre werkes, shuld be unservid and unpaide and yf I paye hem not, I renne in grete indignation of my lordes and grete sclandre, noyse and maugre of all youre peple.

Lord Cromwell (c. 1394–1456) Treasurer of England. *Rotuli Parliamentorum*, Vol. IV

8 Annual income twenty pounds, annual expenditure nineteen nineteen six, result happiness. Annual income twenty pounds, annual expenditure twenty pounds ought and six, result misery.

Charles Dickens (1812–70) British novelist. *David Copperfield*, Ch. 12

9 All races have produced notable economists, with the exception of the Irish who doubtless can protest their devotion to higher arts.

John Kenneth Galbraith (1908–) US economist. *The Age of Uncertainty*, Ch. 1

10 When every blessed thing you hold
Is made of silver, or of gold,
You long for simple pewter.
When you have nothing else to wear
But cloth of gold and satins rare,
For cloth of gold you cease to care –
Up goes the price of shoddy.

W. S. Gilbert (1836–1911) British dramatist. *The Gondoliers*, I

11 Having a little inflation is like being a little pregnant.

Leon Henderson (1895–1986) US economist. Attrib.

12 Did y'ever think, Ken, that making a speech on economics is a lot like pissing down your leg? It seems hot to you, but it never does to anyone else.

Lyndon B. Johnson (1908–73) US Democratic president. *A Life in Our Times*

13 In the long run we are all dead.

John Maynard Keynes (1883–1946) British economist. *Collected Writings*, 'A Tract on Monetary Reform'

14 I will not be a party to debasing the currency.

John Maynard Keynes On refusing to pay more than a small tip on having his shoes polished, while on a visit to Africa. *John Maynard Keynes* (C. Hession)

15 Practical men, who believe themselves to be quite exempt from any intellectual influences, are usually the slaves of some defunct economist. Madmen in authority, who hear voices in the air, are distilling their frenzy from some academic scribbler of a few years back.

John Maynard Keynes *The General Theory of Employment, Interest and Money*, Bk. VI, Ch. 24

16 Inflation in the Sixties was a nuisance to be endured, like varicose veins or French foreign policy.

Bernard Levin (1928–) British journalist. *The Pendulum Years*, 'Epilogue'

17 Population, when unchecked, increases in a geometrical ratio. Subsistence only increases in an arithmetical ratio.

Thomas Robert Malthus (1766–1834) British clergyman and economist. *Essays on the Principle of Population*

18 A nation is not in danger of financial disaster merely because it owes itself money.

Andrew William Mellon (1855–1937) US financier. Attrib.

19 Recession is when a neighbor loses his job; depression is when you lose yours.

Ronald Reagan (1911–) US politician and president. *The Observer*, 'Sayings of the Week', 26 Oct 1980

20 If all economists were laid end to end, they would not reach a conclusion.

George Bernard Shaw (1856–1950) Irish dramatist and critic. Attrib.

21 Give me a one-handed economist! All my economists say, 'on the one hand . . . on the other.

Harry S. Truman (1884–1972) US statesman. *Presidential Anecdotes* (P. Boller)

22 From now, the pound is worth 14 per cent or so less in terms of other currencies. It does not mean, of course, that the pound here in Britain, in your pocket or purse or in your bank, has been devalued.

Harold Wilson (1916–) British politician and prime minister. Speech after devaluation of the pound, 20 Nov 1967

23 One man's wage rise is another man's price increase.

Harold Wilson *The Observer*, 'Sayings of the Week', 11 Jan 1970

EDITORS

See also books, journalism, newspapers, publishing

1 Where were you fellows when the paper was blank?

Fred Allen (1894–1956) US comedian. Said to writers who heavily edited one of his scripts. Attrib.

2 Have you heard? The Prime Minister has resigned and Northcliffe has sent for the King.

Anonymous Said by a member of Lord Northcliffe's staff; at the height of his career, Northcliffe owned, among other newspapers, *The Times*, *The Observer*, the *Daily Mail*, the *Daily Mirror*, and the *London Evening News*. *Northcliffe, An Intimate Biography* (Hamilton Fyfe)

3 He made righteousness readable.

James Bone (1872–1962) British journalist. Referring to C. P. Scott, former editor of *The Manchester Guardian*. Attrib.

4 An editor is one who separates the wheat from the chaff and prints the chaff.

Adlai Stevenson (1900–65) US statesman. *The Stevenson Wit*

EDUCATION

See also academics, classics, examinations, indoctrination, learning, punishment

1 Soon learned, soon forgotten.

Proverb

2 They know enough who know how to learn.

Henry Brooks Adams (1838–1918) US historian. *The Education of Henry Adams*

3 But above all things I strive to train them to be useful to the Holy Church of God and for the glory of your kingdom.

Alcuin (c. 735–804) English theologian. Referring to his school at Tours. Letter to Charlemagne, c. 796

4 . . . all the youth now in England of free men, who are rich enough to be able to devote themselves to it, be set to learn as long as they are not fit for any other occupation, until they are able to read English writing well.

Alfred the Great (849–901) King of Wessex *Cura Pastoralis*, Preface

5 I wish I could have a little tape-and-loudspeaker arrangement sewn into the binding of this magazine, to be triggered off by the light reflected from the reader's eyes on to this part of the page, and set to bawl out at several bels: MORE WILL MEAN WORSE.

Kingsley Amis (1922–) British novelist, poet, and critic. Discussing the idea that many students are unable to get university places. *Encounter*, July 1960

6 A maiden at college, named Breeze,
Weighed down by B.A.s and M.D.s
Collapsed from the strain.
Said her doctor, 'It's plain
You are killing yourself by degrees!'

Anonymous

7 My object will be, if possible to form Christian men, for Christian boys I can scarcely hope to make.

Thomas Arnold (1795–1842) British educator. Letter on appointment as Headmaster of Rugby, 1828

8 What we must look for here is, first, religious and moral principles; secondly, gentlemanly conduct; thirdly, intellectual ability.

Thomas Arnold Address to the Scholars at Rugby

9 I remember when I was young, in the north, they went to the grammar school little children: they came from thence great lubbers: always learning, and little profiting: learning without book everything, understanding within the book little or nothing.

Roger Ascham (1515–68) *The Scholemaster*

10 Universities incline wits to sophistry and affectation.

Francis Bacon (1561–1626) English philosopher. *Valerius Terminus of the Interpretation of Nature*, Ch. 26

11 Studies serve for delight, for ornament, and for ability.

Francis Bacon *Essays*, 'Of Studies'

12 It is Oxford that has made me insufferable.

Max Beerbohm (1872–1956) British writer. *More*, 'Going back to School'

13 Broad of Church and broad of mind,
Broad before and broad behind,
A keen ecclesiologist,
A rather dirty Wykehamist.

John Betjeman (1906–84) British poet. *The Wykehamist*

14 The dread of beatings,
Dread of Being Late
And greatest dread of all, the dread of games.

John Betjeman *Summoned by Bells*

15 The education of the doctor which goes on after he has his degree is, after all, the most important part of his education.

John Shaw Billings (1838–1913) *Boston Medical and Surgical Journal*, 1894

16 My students are dismayed when I say to them, 'Half of what you are taught as medical students will in ten years have been shown to be wrong, and the trouble is, none of your teachers knows which half.'

C. Sidney Burwell (1893–1967) *British Medical Journal*, 1956 (G.W. Pickering)

17 Learning is good in and of itself . . . the mothers of the Jewish ghettoes of the east would pour honey on a book so the children would know that learning is sweet. And the parents who settled hungry Kansas would take their children in from the fields when a teacher came.

George Bush (1924–) US politician and president. Speech accepting his nomination as presidential candidate, Republican Party Convention, New Orleans, Aug 1988

18 The true University of these days is a collection of books.

Thomas Carlyle (1795–1881) Scottish historian and essayist. *Heroes and Hero-Worship*, 'The Hero as Man of Letters'

19 'Reeling and Writhing, of course, to begin with,' the Mock Turtle replied; 'and then the different branches of Arithmetic – Ambition, Distraction, Uglification, and Derision.'

Lewis Carroll (Charles Lutwidge Dodgson; 1832–98) British writer. *Alice's Adventures in Wonderland*, Ch. 9

20 This is to seyn, to syngen and to rede,
As smale children doon in hire childhede.

Geoffrey Chaucer (c. 1342–1400) English poet. *The Canterbury Tales*, 'The Prioress's Tale'

21 His English education at one of the great public schools had preserved his intellect perfectly and permanently at the stage of boyhood.

G. K. Chesterton (1874–1936) British writer. *The Man Who Knew Too Much*

22 Education is simply the soul of a society as it passes from one generation to another.

G. K. Chesterton *The Observer*, 'Sayings of the Week', 6 July 1924

23 Headmasters have powers at their disposal with which Prime Ministers have never yet been invested.

Winston Churchill (1874–1965) British statesman. *My Early Life*, Ch. 2

24 The ape-like virtues without which no one can enjoy a public school.

Cyril Connolly (1903–74) British journalist. *Enemies of Promise*, Ch. 1

25 When he has learnt that bottinney means a knowledge of plants, he goes and knows 'em. That's our system, Nickleby; what do you think of it?

Charles Dickens (1812–70) British novelist. Said by Mr Squeers. *Nicholas Nickleby*, Ch. 8

26 I pay the schoolmaster, but 'tis the schoolboys that educate my son.

Ralph Waldo Emerson (1803–82) US poet and essayist. *Journal*

27 Public schools are the nurseries of all vice and immorality.

Henry Fielding (1707–54) British novelist. *Joseph Andrews*, Bk. III, Ch. 5

28 The great doctors all got their education off dirt pavements and poverty – not marble floors and foundations.

Martin H. Fischer (1879–1962) *Fischerisms* (Howard Fabing and Ray Marr)

29 It is not that the Englishman can't feel – it is that he is afraid to feel. He has been taught at his public school that feeling is bad form. He must not express great joy or sorrow, or even open his mouth too wide when he talks – his pipe might fall out if he did.

E. M. Forster (1879–1970) British novelist. *Abinger Harvest* 'Notes on the English character'

30 They go forth into it with well-developed bodies, fairly developed minds, and undeveloped hearts.

E. M. Forster Referring to public schoolboys going into the world. *Abinger Harvest*, 'Notes on the English Character'

31 Spoon feeding in the long run teaches us nothing but the shape of the spoon.

E. M. Forster *The Observer*, 'Sayings of the Week', 7 Oct 1951

32 We keep the students within view of their parents; we save them many toils and long foreign journeys; we protect them from robbers. They used to be pillaged while travelling abroad; now, they may study at small cost and short wayfaring, thanks to our liberality.

Frederick II (1194–1250) Holy Roman Emperor. Foundation charter of Naples University

33 A teacher is paid to teach, not to sacrifice rats and hamsters.

Edward A. Gall (1906–) *Journal of Medical Education*, 36:275, 1961

34 To the University of Oxford I acknowledge no obligation; and she will as cheerfully renounce me for a son, as I am willing to disclaim her for a mother. I spent fourteen months at Magdalen College: they proved the fourteen months the most idle and unprofitable of my whole life.

Edward Gibbon (1737–94) British historian. *Autobiography*

35 Let schoolmasters puzzle their brain,
With grammar, and nonsense, and learning,
Good liquor, I stoutly maintain,
Gives genius a better discerning.

Oliver Goldsmith (1728–74) Irish-born British writer. *She Stoops to Conquer*, I

36 Education made us what we are.

Claude-Adrien Helvétius (1715–71) French philosopher. *Discours* XXX, Ch. 30

37 A good clinical teacher is himself a Medical School.

Oliver Wendell Holmes (1809–94) US writer and physician. *Medical Essays*, 'Scholastic and Bedside Teaching'

38 The bedside is always the true center of medical teaching.

Oliver Wendell Holmes *Medical Essays*, 'Scholastic and Bedside Teaching'

39 The most essential part of a student's instruction is obtained, as

I believe, not in the lecture room, but at the beside.

Oliver Wendell Holmes *Medical Essays*, 'Scholastic and Bedside Teaching'

40 And seek for truth in the groves of Academe.

Horace (Quintus Horatius Flaccus; 65–8 BC) Roman poet. *Epistles*, II

41 Those of us who have the duty of training the rising generation of doctors . . . must not inseminate the virgin minds of the young with the tares of our own fads. It is for this reason that it is easily possible for teaching to be too 'up to date'. It is always well, before handing the cup of knowledge to the young, to wait until the froth has settled.

Robert Hutchison (1871–1960) *British Medical Journal*, 1925

42 You sought the last resort of feeble minds with classical educations. You became a schoolmaster.

Aldous Huxley (1894–1964) British novelist and essayist. *Antic Hay*

43 Some experience of popular lecturing had convinced me that the necessity of making things plain to uninstructed people was one of the very best means of clearing up the obscure corners in one's own mind.

T. H. Huxley (1825–95) British biologist. *Man's Place in Nature*, Preface

44 Any attempt to reform the university without attending to the system of which it is an integral part is like trying to do urban renewal in New York City from the twelfth story up.

Ivan Illich (1926–) Austrian sociologist. *Deschooling Society*, Ch. 3

45 In teaching the medical student the primary requisite is to keep him awake.

Chevalier Jackson (1865–1958) *The Life of Chevalier Jackson*, Ch. 16

46 His mind must be strong indeed, if, rising above juvenile credulity, it can maintain a wise infidelity against the authority of his instructors, and the bewitching delusions of their theories.

Thomas Jefferson (1743–1826) US statesman. Letter to Dr. Caspar Wistar, 21 June 1807

47 It is no matter what you teach them first, any more than what leg you shall put into your breeches first.

Samuel Johnson (1709–84) British lexicographer. *Life of Johnson* (J. Boswell), Vol. I

48 There is now less flogging in our great schools than formerly, but then less is learned there; so that what the boys get at one end they lose at the other.

Samuel Johnson *Life of Johnson* (J. Boswell), Vol. II

49 There mark what ills the scholar's life assail
Toil, envy, want, the patron, and the jail.

Samuel Johnson *Vanity of Human Wishes*

50 I find the three major administrative problems on a campus are sex for the students, athletics for the alumni and parking for the faculty.

Clark Kerr (1911–) US educator. *Time*, 17 Nov 1958

51 Nothing would more effectively further the development of education than for all flogging pedagogues to learn to educate with the head instead of with the hand.

Ellen Key (Karolina Sofia Key; 1849–1926) Swedish writer. *The Century of the Child*, Ch. 3

52 If every day in the life of a school could be the last day but one, there would be little fault to find with it.

Stephen Leacock (1869–1944) English-born Canadian economist and humorist. *College Days*, 'Memories and Miseries of a Schoolmaster'

53 Four times, under our educational rules, the human pack is shuffled and cut – at eleven-plus, sixteen-plus, eighteen-plus and twenty-plus – and happy is he who comes top of the deck on each occasion, but especially the last. This is called Finals, the very name of which implies that nothing of importance can happen after it. The British postgraduate student is a lonely forlorn soul . . . for whom nothing has been real since the Big Push.

David Lodge (1935–) British author. *Changing Places*, Ch. 1

54 Whenever I look in the glass or see a photograph of myself, I am reminded of Petrarch's simple statement 'Nothing is more hideous than an old schoolmaster'!

G. W. Lyttelton *The Lyttelton Hart-Davis Letters*, 11 Apr 1956

55 If you educate a man you educate a person, but if you educate a woman you educate a family.

Ruby Manikan (20th century) Indian Church leader. *The Observer*, 'Sayings of the Week', 30 Mar 1947

56 . . . the rustics vie with each other in bringing up their ignoble and degenerate offspring to the liberal arts.

Walter Map (c. 1140–c. 1209) Welsh cleric and writer. Drawing a comparison with the aristocracy, who were 'too poud or too lazy to put their children to learning'. *De Nugis Curialium*, Pt. I, Ch. 10

57 A gentleman need not know Latin, but he should at least have forgotten it.

Brander Matthews (1852–1929) US writer. Attrib.

58 There are two objects of medical education: To heal the sick, and to advance the science.

Charles H. Mayo (1865–1939) *Collected Papers of the Mayo Clinic and Mayo Foundation*, 18:1093, 1926

59 A whale ship was my Yale College and my Harvard.

Herman Melville (1819–91) US novelist. *Moby Dick*, Ch. 24

60 One tongue is sufficient for a woman.

John Milton (1608–74) English poet. On being asked whether he would allow his daughters to learn foreign languages. Attrib.

61 And if education is always to be conceived along the same antiquated lines of a mere transmission of knowledge, there is little to be hoped from it in the bettering of man's future. For what is the use of transmitting knowledge if the individual's total development lags behind?

Maria Montessori (1870–1952) Italian doctor and educator. *The Absorbent Mind*

62 We teachers can only help the work going on, as servants wait upon a master.

Maria Montessori *The Absorbent Mind*

63 Discussion in class, which means letting twenty young blockheads and two cocky neurotics discuss something that neither their teacher nor they know.

Vladimir Nabokov (1899–1977) Russian-born US novelist. *Pnin*, Ch. 6

64 Every schoolmaster after the age of 49 is inclined to flatulence, is apt to swallow frequently, and to puff.

Harold Nicolson (1886–1968) British writer. *The Old School*

65 The schoolteacher is certainly underpaid as a childminder, but ludicrously overpaid as an educator.

John Osborne (1929–) British dramatist. *The Observer*, 'Sayings of the Week', 21 July 1985

66 I desire no other epitaph – no

hurry about it, I may say – than the statement that I taught medical students in the wards, as I regard this as by far the most useful and important work I have been called upon to do.
William Osler (1849–1919) Canadian physician. *Aequanimitas, with Other Addresses*, 'The Fixed Period'

67 I have learned since to be a better student, and to be ready to say to my fellow students 'I do not know.'
William Osler *Aequanimitas, with Other Addresses*, 'After Twenty-Five Years'

68 School yourself to demureness and patience. Learn to innure yourself to drudgery in science. Learn, compare, collect the facts.
Ivan Pavlov (1849–1936) Russian physiologist. *Bequest to the Academic Youth of Soviet Russia*, 27 Feb 1936

69 He was sent, as usual, to a public school, where a little learning was painfully beaten into him, and from thence to the university, where it was carefully taken out of him.
Thomas Love Peacock (1785–1866) British novelist. *Nightmare Abbey*, Ch. 1

70 'Tis education forms the common mind,
Just as the twig is bent, the tree's inclined.
Alexander Pope (1688–1744) British poet. *Moral Essays*, I

71 A man who has never gone to school may steal from a freight car, but if he has a university education he may steal the whole railroad.
Franklin D. Roosevelt (1882–1945) US Democratic president. Attrib.

72 But, good gracious, you've got to educate him first.
You can't expect a boy to be vicious till he's been to a good school.
Saki (Hector Hugh Munro; 1870–1916) British writer. *Reginald in Russia*

73 For every person wishing to teach there are thirty not wanting to be taught.
W. C. Sellar (1898–1951) British humorous writer. *And Now All This*

74 No profit grows where is no pleasure ta'en;
In brief, sir, study what you most affect.
William Shakespeare (1564–1616) English dramatist. *The Taming of the Shrew*, I:1

75 A learned man is an idler who kills time by study.
George Bernard Shaw (1856–1950) Irish dramatist and critic. *Man and Superman*

76 There is nothing on earth intended for innocent people so horrible as a school. It is in some respects more cruel than a prison. In a prison, for example, you are not forced to read books written by the warders and the governor.
George Bernard Shaw *Parents and Children*

77 He who can, does. He who cannot, teaches.
George Bernard Shaw *Man and Superman*, 'Maxims for Revolutionists'

78 Educated: in the holidays from Eton.
Osbert Sitwell (1892–1969) British writer. Entry in *Who's Who*

79 Indeed one of the ultimate advantages of an education is simply coming to the end of it.
B. F. Skinner (1904–) US psychologist. *The Technology of Teaching*

80 Education is what survives when what has been learned has been forgotten.
B. F. Skinner *New Scientist*, 21 May 1964, 'Education in 1984'

81 To me education is a leading out of what is already there in the pupil's soul. To Miss Mackay it is a putting in of something that is not there, and that is not what I call education, I call it intrusion. . . .
Muriel Spark (1918–) British novelist. *The Prime of Miss Jean Brodie*, Ch. 2

82 Education . . . has produced a vast population able to read but unable to distinguish what is worth reading.
George Macaulay Trevelyan (1876–1962) British historian. *English Social History*, Ch. 18

83 Soap and education are not as sudden as a massacre, but they are more deadly in the long run.
Mark Twain (Samuel Langhorne Clemens; 1835–1910) US writer. *The Facts concerning the Recent Resignation*

84 People at the top of the tree are those without qualifications to detain them at the bottom.
Peter Ustinov (1921–) British actor. Attrib.

85 I expect you'll be becoming a schoolmaster sir. That's what most of the gentlemen does sir, that gets sent down for indecent behaviour.
Evelyn Waugh (1903–66) British novelist. *Decline and Fall*, Prelude

86 We class schools you see, into four grades: Leading School, First-rate School, Good School, and School.
Evelyn Waugh *Decline and Fall*, Pt. I, Ch. 1

87 We schoolmasters must temper discretion with deceit.
Evelyn Waugh *Decline and Fall*, Pt. I, Ch. 1

88 That's the public-school system all over. They may kick you out, but they never let you down.
Evelyn Waugh *Decline and Fall*, Pt. I, Ch. 3

89 Anyone who has been to an English public school will always feel comparatively at home in prison.
Evelyn Waugh *Decline and Fall*, Pt. III, Ch. 4

90 Assistant masters came and went . . . . Some liked little boys too little and some too much.
Evelyn Waugh *A Little Learning*

91 Medical education is not completed at the medical school: it is only begun.
William H. Welch (1850–1934) *Bulletin of the Harvard Medical School Association*, 3:55, 1892

92 The battle of Waterloo was won on the playing fields of Eton.
Duke of Wellington (1769–1852) British general. Attrib.

93 A very large part of English middle-class education is devoted to the training of servants . . . In so far as it is, by definition, the training of upper servants, it includes, of course, the instilling of that kind of confidence which will enable the upper servants to supervise and direct the lower servants.
Raymond Henry Williams (1921–) British academic and writer. *Culture and Society*, Ch. 3

EFFORT

See also work

1 If a job's worth doing, it's worth doing well.
Proverb

2 Energy is Eternal Delight.
William Blake (1757–1827) British poet. *The Marriage of Heaven and Hell*, 'The Voice of the Devil'

3 I have nothing to offer but blood, toil, tears and sweat.
Winston Churchill (1874–1965) British statesman. On becoming prime minister. Speech, House of Commons, 13 May 1940

4 A world where nothing is had for nothing.
Arthur Hugh Clough (1819–61) British poet. *The Bothie of Tober-na-Vuolich*, Bk. VIII, Ch. 5

5 As is the case in all branches of art, success depends in a very large measure upon individual initiative and exertion, and cannot be achieved except by dint of hard work.
Anna Pavlova (1881–1931) Russian ballet dancer. *Pavlova: A Biography* (ed. A. H. Franks), 'Pages of My Life'

6 And here is the lesson I learned in the army. If you want to do a thing badly, you have to work at it as though you want to do it well.
Peter Ustinov (1921–) British actor. *Dear Me*, Ch. 8

7 Please do not shoot the pianist. He is doing his best.
Oscar Wilde (1854–1900) Irish-born British dramatist. *Impressions of America*, 'Leadville'

EGOTISM

See also arrogance, conceit, pride, selfishness

1 Against whom?
Alfred Adler (1870–1937) Austrian psychiatrist. Said when he heard that an egocentric had fallen in love. *Some of My Best Friends* (J. Bishop), 'Exponent of the Soul'

2 No poet or novelist wishes he were the only one who ever lived, but most of them wish they were the only one alive, and quite a number fondly believe their wish has been granted.
W. H. Auden (1907–73) British poet. *The Dyer's Hand*, 'Writing'

3 *Egotist*, n. A person of low taste, more interested in himself than in me.
Ambrose Bierce (1842–?1914) US writer and journalist. *The Devil's Dictionary*

4 Someone said of a very great egotist: 'He would burn your house down to cook himself a couple of eggs.
Nicolas Chamfort (1741–94) French writer. *Caractères et anecdotes*

5 An author who speaks about his own books is almost as bad as a mother who talks about her own children.
Benjamin Disraeli (1804–81) British statesman. Speech in Glasgow, 19 Nov 1873

6 If the Almighty himself played the violin, the credits would still read 'Rubinstein, God, and Piatigorsky', in that order.
Jascha Heifetz (1901–87) Russian-born US violinist. Whenever Heifetz played in trios with Arthur Rubinstein (piano) and Gregor Piatigorsky (cello), Rubinstein always got top billing. *Los Angeles Times*, 29 Aug 1982

7 One had rather malign oneself than not speak of oneself at all.
Duc de la Rochefoucauld (1613–80) French writer. *Maximes*, 138

8 As who should say 'I am Sir Oracle,
And when I ope my lips let no dog bark'.
William Shakespeare (1564–1616) English dramatist. *The Merchant of Venice*, I:1

9 A pompous woman of his acquaintance, complaining that the head-waiter of a restaurant had not shown her and her husband immediately to a table, said, 'We had to tell him who we were.' Gerald, interested, enquired, 'And who were you?'
Edith Sitwell (1887–1964) British poet and writer. *Taken Care Of*, Ch. 15

10 No man thinks there is much ado about nothing when the ado is about himself.
Anthony Trollope (1815–82) British novelist. *The Bertrams*, Ch. 27

11 I am the only person in the world I should like to know thoroughly.
Oscar Wilde (1854–1900) Irish-born British dramatist. *Lady Windermere's Fan*, II

EINSTEIN, Albert

(1879–1955) German physicist who became a Swiss citizen (1901) and later a US citizen (1940). His theory of relativity revolutionized scientific thought. He was persuaded to write to President Roosevelt to warn him that Germany could possibly make an atomic bomb.

Quotations about Einstein

1 Einstein – the greatest Jew since Jesus. I have no doubt that Einstein's name will still be remembered and revered when Lloyd George, Foch and William Hohenzollern share with Charlie Chaplin that ineluctable oblivion which awaits the uncreative mind.
J. B. S. Haldane (1892–1964) British genetist. *Daedalus or Science and the Future*

2 The genius of Einstein leads to Hiroshima.
Pablo Picasso (1881–1973) Spanish painter. *Life with Picasso* (Françoise Gilot and Carlton Lake)

Quotations by Einstein

3 Science without religion is lame, religion without science is blind.
Out of My Later Years

4 If you want to find out anything from the theoretical physicists about the methods they use, I advise you to stick closely to one principle: Don't listen to their words fix your attention on their deeds.
The World As I See It

5 God is subtle but he is not malicious.
Inscribed over the fireplace in the Mathematical Institute, Princeton. It refers to Einstein's objection to the quantum theory. *Albert Einstein* (Carl Seelig), Ch. 8

6 God does not play dice.
Einstein's objection to the quantum theory, in which physical events can only be known in terms of probabilities. It is sometimes quoted as 'God does not play dice with the Universe'. *Albert Einstein, Creator and Rebel* (B. Hoffman), Ch. 10

7 If only I had known, I should have become a watchmaker.
Reflecting on his role in the development of the atom bomb. *New Statesman*, 16 Apr 1965

8 Common sense is the collection of prejudices acquired by age eighteen.
Scientific American, Feb 1976

9 A theory can be proved by experiment; but no path leads from experiment to the birth of a theory.
The Sunday Times, 18 July 1976

10 As far as the laws of mathematics refer to reality, they are not certain, and as far as they are certain, they do not refer to reality.
The Tao of Physics (F. Capra), Ch. 2

11 I never think of the future. It comes soon enough.
Interview, 1930

EISENHOWER, Dwight D(avid)

(1890–1969) US general and statesman. President (1953–61) during the Cold War and the period of anticommunist witch hunts led by Senator McCarthy. In World War II he became supreme commander and was responsible for the D-day invasion of Europe.

Quotations about Eisenhower

1 Roosevelt proved a man could be president for life; Truman proved anybody could be president; and Eisenhower proved we don't need a president.
Anonymous

2 As an intellectual he bestowed upon the games of golf and bridge all the enthusiasm and perseverance that he withheld from books and ideas.
Emmet John Hughes *The Ordeal of Power*

3 The best clerk I ever fired.
Douglas Macarthur (1880–1964) US general. Attrib.

Quotations by Eisenhower

4 Whatever America hopes to bring to pass in this world must first come to pass in the heart of America.
Inaugural address, 1953

5 There is one thing about being President – nobody can tell you when to sit down.
The Observer, 'Sayings of the Week', 9 Aug 1953

6 Your business is to put me out of business
Addressing a graduating class at a university. *Procession* (J. Gunther)

ELIOT, T(homas) S(tearns)

(1888–1965) US-born British poet and dramatist. He worked as a bank clerk before publication of his *Prufrock and Other Observations* (1917). *The Waste Land* (1922) established his reputation, which was confirmed by his *Four Quartets* (1935–41). His verse dramas include *Murder in the Cathedral* (1935) and *The Cocktail Party* (1949).

Quotations about Eliot

1 He likes to look on the bile when it is black.
Aldous Huxley (1894–1964) British novelist and essayist. *Ambrosia and Small Beer* (E. Marsh)

2 He is very yellow and glum. Perfect manners. Dyspeptic, ascetic, eclectic. Inhibitions. Yet obviously a nice man and a great poet.
Harold Nicolson (1886–1968) British writer. *Diary*, 2 May 1932

Quotations by Eliot

3 Because I do not hope to turn again
Because I do not hope
Because I do not hope to turn.
Ash-Wednesday

4 We can say of Shakespeare, that never has a man turned so little knowledge to such great account.
The Classics and the Man of Letters (lecture)

5 Hell is oneself;
Hell is alone, the other figures in it
Merely projections. There is nothing to escape from
And nothing to escape to. One is always alone.
The Cocktail Party, I:3

6 Time present and time past
Are both perhaps present in time future,
And time future contained in time past.
Four Quartets, 'Burnt Norton'

7 Human kind
Cannot bear very much reality.
Four Quartets, 'Burnt Norton'

8 Here I am, an old man in a dry month,
Being read to by a boy, waiting for rain.
Gerontion

9 We are the hollow men
We are the stuffed men
Leaning together
Headpiece filled with straw.
The Hollow Men

10 This is the way the world ends
Not with a bang but a whimper.
The Hollow Men

11 Let us go then, you and I,
When the evening is spread out against the sky
Like a patient etherized upon a table.
The Love Song of J. Alfred Prufrock

12 In the room the women come and go
Talking of Michelangelo.
The Love Song of J. Alfred Prufrock

13 I have measured out my life with coffee spoons.
The Love Song of J. Alfred Prufrock

14 I grow old . . . I grow old . . .
I shall wear the bottoms of my trousers rolled.
The Love Song of J. Alfred Prufrock

15 Shall I part my hair behind? Do I dare to eat a peach?
I shall wear white flannel trousers, and walk upon the beach.
I have heard the mermaids singing, each to each.
The Love Song of J. Alfred Prufrock

16 Macavity, Macavity, there's no one like Macavity,
There never was a Cat of such deceitfulness and suavity.
He always has an alibi, and one or two to spare:
At whatever time the deed took place – MACAVITY WASN'T THERE!
Macavity: The Mystery Cat

17 I am aware of the damp souls of the housemaids
Sprouting despondently at area gates.
Morning at the Window

18 The last temptation is the greatest treason:
To do the right deed for the wrong reason.
Murder in the Cathedral, I

19 The winter evening settles down
With smell of steaks in passageways.
Preludes

20 'Put your shoes at the door, sleep, prepare for life.'
The last twist of the knife.
Rhapsody on a Windy Night

21 Birth, and copulation, and death.
That's all the facts when you come to brass tacks.
Sweeney Agonistes, 'Fragment of an Agon'

22 The host with someone indistinct
Converses at the door apart,
The nightingales are singing near
The Convent of the Sacred Heart.
Sweeney among the Nightingales

23 No poet, no artist of any sort, has his complete meaning alone. His significance, his appreciation is the appreciation of his relation to the dead poets and artists.
Tradition and the Individual Talent

24 Poetry is not a turning loose of emotion, but an escape from emotion; it is not the expression of personality, but an escape from personality.
Tradition and the Individual Talent

25 April is the cruellest month, breeding
Lilacs out of the dead land, mixing
Memory and desire, stirring
Dull roots with spring rain.
The Waste Land, 'The Burial of the Dead'

26 I read, much of the night, and go south in the winter.
The Waste Land, 'The Burial of the Dead'

27 And I will show you something different from either
Your shadow at morning striding behind you,
Or your shadow at evening rising to meet you
I will show you fear in a handful of dust.
The Waste Land, 'The Burial of the Dead'

ELIZABETH I

(1533–1603) Queen of England. The daughter of Henry VIII and Anne Boleyn, she established the Protestant Church in England and had her Catholic cousin, Mary, Queen of Scots, beheaded. The Elizabethan age was one of greatness for England.

Quotations about Elizabeth I

1 The queen did fish for men's souls, and had so sweet a bait that no one could escape her network.
Christopher Hatton Attrib.

2 As just and merciful as Nero and as good a Christian as Mahomet.
John Wesley (1703–91) British religious leader. *Journal,* 29 Apr 1768

Quotations by Elizabeth I

3 Though God hath raised me high, yet this I count the glory of my crown: that I have reigned with your loves.
The Golden Speech, 1601

4 Madam I may not call you; mistress I am ashamed to call you; and so I know not what to call you; but howsoever, I thank you.
Writing to the wife of the Archbishop of Canterbury, expressing her disapproval of married clergy. *Brief View of the State of the Church* (Harington)

5 God may pardon you, but I never can.
To the Countess of Nottingham. *History of England under the House of Tudor* (Hume), Vol. II, Ch. 7

6 Good-morning, gentlemen both.
When addressing a group of eighteen tailors. *Sayings of Queen Elizabeth* (Chamberlin)

7 I will make you shorter by a head.
Sayings of Queen Elizabeth (Chamberlin)

8 Must! Is *must* a word to be addressed to princes? Little man, little man! thy father, if he had been alive, durst not have used that word.
Said to Robert Cecil, on her death bed. *A Short History of the English People* (J. R. Green), Ch. 7

9 If thy heart fails thee, climb not at all.
Written on a window in reply to Sir Walter RALEIGH's line. *Worthies of England* (Fuller), Vol. I

10 I know I have the body of a weak and feeble woman, but I have the heart and stomach of a King, and of a King of England too.
Speech at Tilbury on the approach of the Spanish Armada

11 All my possessions for a moment of time.
Last words

EMBARRASSMENT

1 The question about everything was, would it bring a blush to the cheek of a young person?
Charles Dickens (1812–70) British novelist. Pondered by Mr Podsnap. *Our Mutual Friend,* Bk. I, Ch. 11

2 He really needs to telephone, but he's too embarrassed to say so.
Dorothy Parker (1893–1967) US writer. When a man asked to go to the men's room. *You Might As Well Live* (J. Keats)

3 Dentopedology is the science of opening your mouth and putting your foot in it. I've been practising it for years.
Prince Philip (1921–) The consort of Queen Elizabeth II. Attrib.

4 Man is the only animal that blushes. Or needs to.
Mark Twain (Samuel Langhorne Clemens; 1835–1910) US writer. *Following the Equator,* heading of Ch. 27

EMERSON, Ralph Waldo

(1803–82) US poet and essayist ordained in 1829, his book *Nature* (1836) contained his transcendental philosophy. He expressed his optimistic humanism in *Representative Men* (1850) and the *Conduct of Life* (1860).

Quotations about Emerson

1 I could readily see in Emerson a gaping flaw. It was the insinuation that had he lived in those days when the world was made, he might have offered some valuable suggestions.
Herman Melville (1819–91) US novelist. Attrib.

2 Emerson is one who lives instinctively on ambrosia – and leaves everything indigestible on his plate.
Friedrich Nietzsche (1844–1900) German philosopher. Attrib.

Quotations by Emerson

3 A person seldom falls sick, but the bystanders are animated with a faint hope that he will die.
Conduct of Life, 'Considerations by the Way'

4 Art is a jealous mistress.
Conduct of Life, 'Wealth'

5 The louder he talked of his honor, the faster we counted our spoons.
Conduct of Life, 'Worship'

6 The religions we call false were once true.
Essays, 'Character'

7 Nothing great was ever achieved without enthusiasm.
Essays, 'Circles'

8 A Friend may well be reckoned the masterpiece of Nature.
Essays, 'Friendship'

9 There is properly no history; only biography.
Essays, 'History'

10 All mankind love a lover.
Essays, 'Love'

11 The reward of a thing well done is to have done it.
Essays, 'New England Reformers'

12 Every man is wanted, and no man is wanted much.
Essays, 'Nominalist and Realist'

13 In skating over thin ice, our safety is in our speed.
Essays, 'Prudence'

14 Whoso would be a man must be a nonconformist.
Essays, 'Self-Reliance'

15 A foolish consistency is the hobgoblin of little minds, adored by little statesmen and philosophers and divines. With consistency a great soul has simply nothing to do.
Essays, 'Self-reliance'

16 To be great is to be misunderstood.
Essays, 'Self-Reliance'

17 What is a weed? A plant whose virtues have not been discovered.
Fortune of the Republic

18 Talent alone cannot make a writer. There must be a man behind the book.
Goethe

19 I pay the schoolmaster, but 'tis the schoolboys that educate my son.
Journal

20 The book written against fame and learning has the author's name on the title-page.
Journal

21 Old age brings along with its uglinesses the comfort that you will soon be out of it, – which ought to be a substantial relief to such discontented pendulums as we are.
Journal

22 Every hero becomes a bore at last.
Representative Men, 'Uses of Great Men'

23 Hitch your wagon to a star.
Society and Solitude, 'Civilization'

24 We boil at different degrees.
Society and Solitude, 'Eloquence'

25 America is a country of young men.
Society and Solitude, 'Old Age'

26 If a man make a better mouse-trap than his neighbor, though he build his house in the woods, the world will make a beaten path to his door.
Attrib.

EMOTION

See also passion, sentimentality

1 There is a road from the eye to the heart that does not go through the intellect.
G. K. Chesterton (1874–1936) British writer. *The Defendant*

2 'There are strings', said Mr Tappertit, 'in the human heart that had better not be wibrated.'
Charles Dickens (1812–70) British novelist. *Barnaby Rudge*, Ch. 22

3 Grief and disappointment give rise to anger, anger to envy, envy to malice, and malice to grief again, till the whole circle be completed.
David Hume (1711–76) Scottish philosopher. *A Treatise of Human Nature*

4 The intellect is always fooled by the heart.
Duc de la Rochefoucauld (1613–80) French writer. *Maximes*, 102

5 Light breaks where no sun shines;
Where no sea runs, the waters of the heart
Push in their tides.
Dylan Thomas (1914–53) Welsh poet. *Light breaks where no sun shines*

6 Pure and complete sorrow is as impossible as pure and complete joy.
Leo Tolstoy (1828–1910) Russian writer. *War and Peace*, Bk. XV, Ch. 1

EMPIRE

1 Great Britain has lost an Empire and has not yet found a role.
Dean Acheson (1893–1971) US lawyer and statesman. Speech, Military Academy, West Point, 5 Dec 1962

2 The day of small nations has long passed away. The day of Empires has come.
Joseph Chamberlain (1836–1914) British politician. Speech, Birmingham, 12 May 1904

3 How is the Empire?
George V (1865–1936) King of the United Kingdom. Last words. *The Times*, 21 Jan 1936

4 An empire founded by war has to maintain itself by war.
Baron de Montesquieu (1688–1755) French writer. *Considérations sur les causes de la grandeur et de la décadence des romains*, Ch. 8

5 Providence has given to the French the empire of the land, to the English that of the sea, and to the Germans that of the air.
Jean Paul Richter (Johann Paul Friedrich Richter; 1763–1825) German novelist. Quoted by Thomas Carlyle

6 This agglomeration which was called and which still calls itself the Holy Roman Empire was neither holy, nor Roman, nor an empire.
Voltaire (François-Marie Arouet; 1694–1778) French writer. *Essai sur les moeurs et l'esprit des nations*, LXX

ENCOURAGEMENT

1 Just at this moment we are suffering a national defeat comparable to any lost military campaign, and what is more it is self-inflicted . . . I think it is about time we pulled our finger out.
Prince Philip (1921–) The consort of Queen Elizabeth II. Speech to businessmen, 17 Oct 1961

ENDING

1 All good things must come to an end.
Proverb

2 All's well that ends well.
Proverb

3 This is the way the world ends
Not with a bang but a whimper.
T. S. Eliot (1888–1965) US-born British poet and dramatist. *The Hollow Men*

4 We'll to the woods no more,
The laurels all are cut.
A. E. Housman (1859–1936) British scholar and poet. *Last Poems*, Introductory

5 The Last Hurrah.
Edwin O'Connor (1918–68) US writer. Book title

6 So goodbye, dear, and amen.
Cole Porter (1891–1964) US composer and lyricist. *Jubilee*, 'Just One of Those Things'

7 That but this blow
Might be the be-all and the end-all here –
But here upon this bank and shoal of time –
We'd jump the life to come.
William Shakespeare (1564–1616) English dramatist. *Macbeth*, I:7

8 The bright day is done,
And we are for the dark.
William Shakespeare *Antony and Cleopatra*, V:2

9 Jack shall have Jill;
Nought shall go ill;
The man shall have his mare again,
And all shall be well.
William Shakespeare *A Midsummer Night's Dream*, III:2

10 Ring out, wild bells, to the wild sky,
The flying cloud, the frosty light:
The year is dying in the night;
Ring out, wild bells, and let him die.
Alfred, Lord Tennyson (1809–92) British poet. *In Memoriam A.H.H.*, CVI

ENDURANCE

See also comfort, courage, determination, misfortune, suffering

1 Even a worm will turn.
Proverb

2 The last straw breaks the camel's back.
Proverb

3 What can't be cured, must be endured.
Proverb

4 Nothing happens to any man that he is not formed by nature to bear.
Marcus Aurelius (121–180 AD) Roman emperor. *Meditations,* Bk. V, Ch. 18

5 Through the night of doubt and sorrow
Onward goes the pilgrim band,
Singing songs of expectation,
Marching to the Promised Land.
Sabine Baring-Gould (1834–1924) British author and hymn writer. *Through the Night of Doubt and Sorrow*

6 In the fell clutch of circumstance,
I have not winced nor cried aloud;
Under the bludgeonings of chance
My head is bloody, but unbowed.
William Ernest Henley (1849–1903) British writer. *Echoes,* IV, 'Invictus. In Mem. R.T.H.B.'

7 . . . we could never learn to be brave and patient, if there were only joy in the world.
Helen Keller (1880–1968) US writer and lecturer. *Atlantic Monthly* (May 1890)

8 Job endured everything – until his friends came to comfort him, then he grew impatient.
Soren Kierkegaard (1813–55) Danish philosopher. *Journal*

9 Sorrow and silence are strong, and patient endurance is godlike.
Henry Wadsworth Longfellow (1807–82) US poet. *Evangeline*

10 Know how sublime a thing it is
To suffer and be strong.
Henry Wadsworth Longfellow *The Light of Stars*

11 It is not miserable to be blind; it is miserable to be incapable of enduring blindness.
John Milton (1608–74) English poet.

12 The weariest nights, the longest days, sooner or later must perforce come to an end.
Baroness Orczy (1865–1947) British novelist. *The Scarlet Pimpernel,* Ch. 22

13 No pain, no palm; no thorns, no throne; no gall, no glory; no cross, no crown.
William Penn (1644–1718) English preacher. *No Cross, No Crown*

14 The Muse but serv'd to ease some friend, not Wife,
To help me through this long disease, my life.
Alexander Pope (1688–1744) British poet. *Epistle to Dr. Arbuthnot*

15 The pain passes, but the beauty remains.
Pierre Auguste Renoir (1841–1919) French impressionist painter. Explaining why he still painted when his hands were twisted with arthritis. Attrib.

16 Does the road wind up-hill all the way?
Yes, to the very end.
Will the day's journey take the whole long day?
From morn to night, my friend.
Christina Rossetti (1830–74) British poet. *Up-Hill*

17 Had we lived, I should have had a tale to tell of the hardihood, endurance, and courage of my companions which would have stirred the heart of every Englishman. These rough notes and our dead bodies must tell the tale.
Captain Robert Falcon Scott (1868–1912) British explorer. *Message to the Public*

18 I am tied to the stake, and I must stand the course.
William Shakespeare (1564–1616) English dramatist. *King Lear,* III:7

19 The worst is not,
So long as we can say, 'This is the worst.'
William Shakespeare *King Lear,* IV:1

20 Men must endure
Their going hence, even as their coming hither:
Ripeness is all.
William Shakespeare *King Lear,* V:2

21 Still have I borne it with a patient shrug,
For sufferance is the badge of all our tribe.
William Shakespeare *The Merchant of Venice,* I:3

22 For there was never yet philosopher
That could endure the toothache patiently.
William Shakespeare *Much Ado About Nothing,* V:1

23 Let's talk sense to the American people. Let's tell them the truth, that there are no gains without pains.
Adlai Stevenson (1900–65) US statesman. Speech, Chicago, 26 July 1952

24 If you can't stand the heat, get out of the kitchen.
Harry S. Truman (1884–1972) US statesman. Perhaps proverbial in origin, possibly echoes the expression 'kitchen cabinet'. *Mr Citizen,* Ch. 15

25 O you who have borne even heavier things, God will grant an end to these too.
Virgil (Publius Vergilius Maro; 70–19 BC) Roman poet. *Aeneid,* Bk. I

26 Maybe one day we shall be glad to remember even these hardships.
Virgil *Aeneid,* Bk. I

27 I sing of arms and the man who first from the shores
of Troy came destined an exile to Italy and the
Lavinian beaches, much buffeted he on land and on
the deep by force of the gods because of fierce
Juno's never-forgetting anger.
Virgil Referring to Aeneas. *Aeneid,* Bk. I

28 Much in sorrow, oft in woe,
Onward, Christians, onward go.
Henry Kirke White (1785–1806) British poet. A hymn, better known in its later form, 'Oft in danger, oft in woe'

ENEMIES

1 Better a thousand enemies outside the house than one inside.
Arabic proverb

2 But I say unto you, That ye resist not evil: but whosoever shall smite thee on thy right cheek, turn to him the other also.
And if any man will sue thee at the law, and take away thy coat, let him have thy cloke also.
And whosoever shall compel thee to go a mile, go with him twain.
Bible: Matthew 5:39–41

3 But I say unto you, Love your enemies, bless them that curse you, do good to them that hate you, and pray for them which despitefully use you, and persecute you;
That ye may be the children of your Father which is in heaven: for he maketh his sun to rise on the evil and on the good, and sendeth rain on the just and on the unjust.
For if ye love them which love you,

what reward have ye? do not even the publicans the same?
Bible: Matthew 5:44–46

4 Even a paranoid can have enemies.
Henry Kissinger (1923–) German-born US politician and diplomat. *Time*, 24 Jan 1977

5 They made peace between us; we embraced, and we have been mortal enemies ever since.
Alain-René Lesage (1668–1747) French writer. *Le Diable boiteux*, Ch. 3

6 You must hate a Frenchman as you hate the devil.
Lord Nelson (1758–1805) British admiral. *Life of Nelson* (Southey), Ch. 3

7 My near'st and dearest enemy.
William Shakespeare (1564–1616) English dramatist. *Henry IV, Part 1*, III:2

8 The only good Indians I ever saw were dead.
Philip H. Sheridan (1831–88) US general. *The People's Almanac 2* (D. Wallechinsky)

9 He makes no friend who never made a foe.
Alfred, Lord Tennyson (1809–92) British poet. *Idylls of the King*, 'Lancelot and Elaine'

10 I should be like a lion in a cave of savage Daniels.
Oscar Wilde (1854–1900) Irish-born British dramatist. Explaining why he would not be attending a function at a club whose members were hostile to him. Attrib.

ENGLAND

See also Britain, Cambridge, English, London, Oxford, patriotism

1 The quality of Mersey is not strained.
Anonymous Referring to the polluted condition of the River Mersey. *Sunday Graphic*, 14 Aug 1932

2 A great ship which sailed for many a day in the sea of prosperity is that plenteous realm, the realm of England. The forecastle of this ship is the clergy, prelates, religious, and priests; the hindcastle is the barony, the king with his nobles; the body of the ship is the commons, merchants, craftsmen and labourers.
Anonymous From a sermon preached in the reign of Henry V (1413–22). *Literature and Pulpit in Medieval England* (G. R. Owst)

3 Oh! who can ever be tired of Bath?
Jane Austen (1775–1817) British novelist. *Northanger Abbey*, Ch. 10

4 One has no great hopes from Birmingham. I always say there is something direful in the sound.
Jane Austen *Emma*, Ch. 36

5 Come, friendly bombs, and fall on Slough
It isn't fit for humans now.
There isn't grass to graze a cow
Swarm over, Death!
. . .
Come, friendly bombs, and fall on Slough
To get it ready for the plough.
The cabbages are coming now:
The earth exhales.
John Betjeman (1906–84) British poet. *Slough*

6 And did those feet in ancient time
Walk upon England's mountains green?
And was the holy lamb of God
On England's pleasant pastures seen?
. . .
I will not cease from mental fight,
Nor shall my sword sleep in my hand,
Till we have built Jerusalem
In England's green and pleasant land.
William Blake (1757–1827) British poet. Better known as the hymn 'Jerusalem', with music by Sir Hubert Parry; not to be confused with Blake's longer poem *Jerusalem*. *Milton*, Preface

7 The smoke of their foul dens
Broodeth on Thy Earth as a black pestilence,
Hiding the kind day's eye. No flower, no grass there groweth,
Only their engines' dung which the fierce furnace throweth.
Wilfred Scawen Blunt (1840–1922) British poet. Describing a northern town. *Satan Absolved: a Victorian Mystery*

8 A population sodden with drink, steeped in vice, eaten up by every social and physical malady, these are the denizens of Darkest England amidst whom my life has been spent.
William Booth (1829–1912) British preacher and founder of the Salvation Army. *In Darkest England, and the Way Out*

9 England is the mother of parliaments.
John Bright (1811–89) British radical politician. Speech, Birmingham, 18 Jan 1865

10 For England's the one land, I know,
Where men with Splendid Hearts may go;
And Cambridgeshire, of all England,
The shire for Men who Understand.
Rupert Brooke (1887–1915) British poet. *The Old Vicarage, Grantchester*

11 A pulse in the eternal mind, no less
Gives somewhere back the thoughts by England given.
Her sights and sounds; dreams happy as her day;
And laughter, learnt of friends; and gentleness,
In hearts at peace, under an English heaven.
Rupert Brooke *The Soldier*

12 Oh, to be in England
Now that April's there.
Robert Browning (1812–89) British poet. *Home Thoughts from Abroad*

13 Without class differences, England would cease to be the living theatre it is.
Anthony Burgess (John Burgess Wilson; 1917–) British novelist. *The Observer*, 'Sayings of the Week', 26 May 1985

14 In England there are sixty different religions, and only one sauce.
Domenico Caracciolo (1715–89) Governor of Sicily. Attrib.

15 This could have occurred nowhere but in England, where men and sea interpenetrate, so to speak.
Joseph Conrad (Teodor Josef Konrad Korzeniowski; 1857–1924) Polish-born British novelist. *Youth*

16 Very flat, Norfolk.
Noël Coward (1899–1973) British dramatist. *Private Lives*

17 Regions Caesar never knew
Thy posterity shall sway,
Where his eagles never flew,
None invincible as they.
William Cowper (1731–1800) British poet. *Boadicea*

18 There are many things in life more worthwhile than money. One is to be brought up in this our England which is still the envy of less happy lands.
Lord Denning (1899–) British judge. *The Observer*, 'Sayings of the Week', 4 Aug 1968

19 Kent, sir – everybody knows Kent – apples, cherries, hops and women.
Charles Dickens (1812–70) British novelist. *Pickwick Papers*, Ch. 2

20 The Continent will not suffer England to be the workshop of the world.
Benjamin Disraeli (1804–81) British statesman. Speech, House of Commons, 15 Mar 1838

21 England is the paradise of women,

the purgatory of men, and the hell of horses.

John Florio (c. 1553–1625) English lexicographer. *Second Fruits*

22 Living in England, provincial England, must be like being married to a stupid but exquisitely beautiful wife.

Margaret Halsey (1910–) US writer. *With Malice Toward Some*

23 All of Stratford, in fact, suggests powdered history –add hot water and stir and you have a delicious, nourishing Shakespeare.

Margaret Halsey *With Malice Toward Some*

24 Dr Johnson's morality was as English an article as a beefsteak.

Nathaniel Hawthorne (1804–64) US novelist and writer. *Our Old Home*, 'Lichfield and Uttoxeter'

25 Those only can care intelligently for the future of England to whom the past is dear.

Dean Inge (1860–1954) British churchman. *Assessments and Anticipations*

26 Pass a law to give every single wingeing bloody Pommie his fare home to England. Back to the smoke and the sun shining ten days a year and shit in the streets. Yer can have it.

Thomas Keneally (1935–) Australian novelist. *The Chant of Jimmy Blacksmith*

27 Winds of the World, give answer!
They are whimpering to and fro –
And what should they know of England who only England know?

Rudyard Kipling (1865–1936) Indian-born British writer. *The English Flag*

28 It was one of those places where the spirit of aboriginal England still lingers, the old savage England, whose last blood flows still in a few Englishmen, Welshmen, Cornishmen.

D. H. Lawrence (1885–1930) British novelist. *St Mawr*

29 And suddenly she craved again for the more absolute silence of America. English stillness was so soft, like an inaudible murmur of voices, of presences.

D. H. Lawrence *St Mawr*

30 In an English ship, they say, it is poor grub, poor pay, and easy work; in an American ship, good grub, good pay, and hard work. And this is applicable to the working populations of both countries.

Jack London (1876–1916) US novelist. *The People of the Abyss*, Ch. 20

31 In no country, I believe, are the marriage laws so iniquitous as in England, and the conjugal relation, in consequence, so impaired.

Harriet Martineau (1802–76) British writer. *Society in America*, Vol. III, 'Marriage'

32 In England there is only silence or scandal.

André Maurois (Émile Herzog; 1885–1967) French writer. Attrib.

33 When people say England, they sometimes mean Great Britain, sometimes the United Kingdom, sometimes the British Isles, – but never England.

George Mikes (1912–87) Hungarian-born British writer. *How to be an Alien*

34 It was twenty-one years ago that England and I first set foot on each other. I came for a fortnight; I have stayed ever since.

George Mikes *How to be Inimitable*

35 When you see how in this happy country the lowest and poorest member of society takes an interest in all public affairs; when you see how high and low, rich and poor, are all willing to declare their feelings and convictions; when you see how a carter, a common sailor, a beggar is still a man, nay, even more, an Englishman – then, believe me, you find yourself very differently affected from the experience you feel when staring at our soldiers drilling in Berlin.

Karl Philipp Moritz (1756–93) German Lutheran pastor. Reaction to a by-election at Westminster. Letter to a friend, 1782

36 A family with the wrong members in control – that, perhaps, is as near as one can come to describing England in a phrase.

George Orwell (Eric Blair; 1903–50) British novelist. *The Lion and the Unicorn*, 'The Ruling Class'

37 There can hardly be a town in the South of England where you could throw a brick without hitting the niece of a bishop.

George Orwell *The Road to Wigan Pier*, Ch. 7

38 Damn you, England. You're rotting now, and quite soon you'll disappear.

John Osborne (1929–) British dramatist. Letter in *Tribune*, Aug 1961

39 There'll always be an England
While there's a country lane,
Wherever there's a cottage small
Beside a field of grain.

Clarke Ross Parker (1914–74) British songwriter. *There'll Always Be an England*

40 It is now apparent that this great, this powerful, this formidable Kingdom is considered only as a province of a despicable Electorate.

William Pitt the Elder (1708–78) British statesman. Referring to Hanover, which Pitt accused George II of favoring over England. Speech, House of Commons, 10 Dec 1742

41 The real fact is that I could no longer stand their eternal cold mutton.

Cecil Rhodes (1853–1902) South African statesman. Explaining why he had left his friends in England and come to South Africa. *Cecil Rhodes* (G. le Sueur)

42 My God! this is a wonderful land and a faithless one; for she has exiled, slain, destroyed and ruined so many Kings, so many rulers, so many great men, and she is always diseased and suffering from differences, quarrels and hatred between her people.

Richard II (1365–99) King of England. Attrib. remark, Tower of London, 21 Sept 1399

43 England is the paradise of individuality, eccentricity, heresy, anomalies, hobbies, and humors.

George Santayana (1863–1952) US philosopher. *Soliloquies in England*, 'The British Character'

44 This royal throne of kings, this sceptred isle,
This earth of majesty, this seat of Mars,
This other Eden, demi-paradise,
This fortress built by Nature for herself
Against infection and the hand of war,
This happy breed of men, this little world,
This precious stone set in the silver sea,
Which serves it in the office of a wall,
Or as a moat defensive to a house,
Against the envy of less happier lands;
This blessed plot, this earth, this realm, this England,
This nurse, this teeming womb of royal kings,
Fear'd by their breed, and famous by their birth.

William Shakespeare (1564–1616) English dramatist. *Richard II*, II:1

45 Well, I cannot last ever; but it was always yet the trick of our English nation, if they have a good thing, to make it too common.

William Shakespeare *Henry IV, Part Two*, I:2

46 If I were asked at this moment for a summary opinion of what I have seen in England, I might probably say that its political institutions present a detail of corrupt practices, of profusion, and of personal ambition, under the mask of public spirit very carelessly put on, more disgusting than I should have expected.... On the other hand, I should admit very readily that I have found the great mass of the people richer, happier, and more respectable than any other with which I am acquainted.

L. Simond French traveler and diarist. *Journal of a Tour and Residence in Great Britain during 1810 and 1811 by a French Traveller*

47 The English take their pleasures sadly after the fashion of their country.

Duc de Sully (1560–1641) French statesman. *Memoirs*

48 They say that men become attached even to Widnes.

A. J. P. Taylor (1906–) British historian. *The Observer*, 15 Sept 1963

49 Yes. I remember Adlestrop –
The name, because one afternoon
Of heat the express train drew up there
Unwontedly. It was late June.

Edward Thomas (1878–1917) British poet. *Adlestrop*

50 You never find an Englishman among the underdogs – except in England of course.

Evelyn Waugh (1903–66) British novelist. *The Loved One*

ENGLISH

See also British, nationality

1 An Englishman's home is his castle.

Proverb

2 An Englishman's word is his bond.

Proverb

3 That typically English characteristic for which there is no English name – *esprit de corps*.

Frank Ezra Adcock (1886–1968) British classicist. Presidential address

4 The English instinctively admire any man who has no talent and is modest about it.

James Agate (1877–1947) British theater critic. Attrib.

5 But of all nations in the world the English are perhaps the least a nation of pure philosophers.

Walter Bagehot (1826–77) British economist and journalist. *The English Constitution*, 'The Monarchy'

6 They came from three very powerful nations of the Germans; that is, from the *Saxones*, *Angli*, and *Iutae*.

St Bede (The Venerable Bede; c. 673–735 AD) English churchman and historian. Referring to the Anglo-Saxon invaders of Britain. *Historia Ecclesiastica*, Bk. I

7 I like the English. They have the most rigid code of immorality in the world.

Malcolm Bradbury (1932–) British academic and novelist. *Eating People is Wrong*, Ch. 5

8 The wish to spread those opinions that we hold conducive to our own welfare is so deeply rooted in the English character that few of us can escape its influence.

Samuel Butler (1835–1902) British writer. *Erewhon*, Ch. 20

9 The most dangerous thing in the world is to make a friend of an Englishman, because he'll come sleep in your closet rather than spend 10 shillings on a hotel.

Truman Capote (1924–84) US novelist. *The Observer*, 'Sayings of the Week', 24 Mar 1968

10 Thirty millions, mostly fools.

Thomas Carlyle (1795–1881) Scottish historian and essayist. When asked what the population of England was. Attrib.

11 He's an Anglo-Saxon Messenger – and those are Anglo-Saxon attitudes.

Lewis Carroll (Charles Lutwidge Dodgson; 1832–98) British writer. *Through the Looking-Glass*, Ch. 7

12 All the faces here this evening seem to be bloody Poms.

Charles, Prince of Wales (1948–) Eldest son of Elizabeth II. Remark at Australia Day dinner, 1973

13 Smile at us, pay us, pass us; but do not quite forget.
For we are the people of England, that never have spoken yet.

G. K. Chesterton (1874–1936) British writer. *The Secret People*

14 The wealth of our island may be diminished, but the strength of mind of the people cannot easily pass away... We cannot lose our liberty, because we cannot cease to think.

Humphry Davy (1778–1829) British chemist. Letter to Thomas Poole, 28 Aug 1807

15 O that Ocean did not bound our style
Within these strict and narrow limits so:
But that the melody of our sweet isle
Might now be heard to Tiber, Arne, and Po:
That they might know how far Thames doth outgo
The music of declined Italy.

Michael Drayton (1563–1631) English poet. Referring to the English Language. *The Reign of Elizabeth* (J. B. Black), Ch. 8

16 It is said, I believe, that to behold the Englishman at his *best* one should watch him play tip-and-run.

Ronald Firbank (1886–1926) British novelist. *The Flower Beneath the Foot*, Ch. 14

17 *Non Angli sed Angeli*
Not Angles, but angels.

Gregory I (540–604) Pope and saint. On seeing some children in the slave market in Rome, and being told that they were Angles. Attrib.

18 ... it takes a great deal to produce ennui in an Englishman and if you do, he only takes it as convincing proof that you are well-bred.

Margaret Halsey (1910–) US writer. *With Malice Toward Some*

19 The attitude of the English... toward English history reminds one a good deal of the attitude of a Hollywood director toward love.

Margaret Halsey *With Malice Toward Some*

20 ... the English think of an opinion as something which a decent person, if he has the misfortune to have one, does all he can to hide.

Margaret Halsey *With Malice Toward Some*

21 The English (it must be owned) are rather a foul-mouthed nation.

William Hazlitt (1778–1830) British essayist. *On Criticism*

22 The Englishman never enjoys himself except for a noble purpose.

A. P. Herbert (1890–1971) British writer and politician. *Uncommon Law*

23 When two Englishmen meet, their first talk is of the weather.

Samuel Johnson (1709–84) British lexicographer. *The Idler*

24 The English people on the whole are surely the *nicest* people in the world, and everyone makes everything so easy for everybody else, that there is almost nothing to resist at all.

D. H. Lawrence (1885–1930) British novelist. *Dull London*

25 England is . . . a country infested with people who love to tell us what to do, but who very rarely seem to know what's going on.

Colin MacInnes (1914–76) British novelist. *England, Half English,* 'Pop Songs and Teenagers'

26 An Englishman, even if he is alone, forms an orderly queue of one.

George Mikes (1912–87) Hungarian-born British writer. *How to be an Alien*

27 Continental people have sex life; the English have hot-water bottles.

George Mikes *How to be an Alien*

28 English women are elegant until they are ten years old, and perfect on grand occasions.

Nancy Mitford (1904–73) British writer. *The Wit of Women* (L. and M. Cowan)

29 The English are busy; they don't have time to be polite.

Baron de Montesquieu (1688–1755) French writer. *Pensées diverses*

30 It has to be admitted that we English have sex on the brain, which is a very unsatisfactory place to have it.

Malcolm Muggeridge (1903–) British writer. *The Observer,* 'Sayings of the Decade', 1964

31 England is a nation of shopkeepers.

Napoleon I (Napoleon Bonaparte; 1769–1821) French emperor. Attrib.

32 To be an Englishman is to belong to the most exclusive club there is.

Ogden Nash (1902–71) US poet. *England Expects*

33 But Lord! to see the absurd nature of Englishmen, that cannot forbear laughing and jeering at everything that looks strange.

Samuel Pepys (1633–1703) English diarist. *Diary,* 27 Nov 1662

34 Remember that you are an Englishman, and have consequently won first prize in the lottery of life.

Cecil Rhodes (1853–1902) South African statesman. *Dear Me* (Peter Ustinov), Ch. 4

35 The English have no respect for their language, and will not teach their children to speak it . . . It is impossible for an Englishman to open his mouth, without making some other Englishman despise him.

George Bernard Shaw (1856–1950) Irish dramatist and critic. *Pygmalion,* Preface

36 I think for my part one half of the nation is mad – and the other not very sound.

Tobias Smollett (1721–71) British novelist. *The Adventures of Sir Launcelot Greaves,* Ch. 6

37 I cannot but conclude the bulk of your natives to be the most pernicious race of little odious vermin that nature ever suffered to crawl upon the surface of the earth.

Jonathan Swift (1667–1745) Irish-born Anglican priest and writer. *Gulliver's Travels,* 'Voyage to Brobdingnag', Ch. 6

38 The national sport of England is obstacle-racing. People fill their rooms with useless and cumbersome furniture, and spend the rest of their lives in trying to dodge it.

Herbert Beerbohm Tree (1853–1917) British actor and theater manager. *Beerbohm Tree* (Hesketh Pearson)

ENTHUSIASM

1 If many people follow your enthusiastic endeavours, perhaps a new Athens might be created in the land of the Franks, or rather a much better one.

Alcuin (c. 735–804) English theologian. Letter to Charlemagne, Mar 799

2 How can I take an interest in my work when I don't like it?

Francis Bacon (1909–) British painter. *Francis Bacon* (Sir John Rothenstein)

3 It is unfortunate, considering that enthusiasm moves the world, that so few enthusiasts can be trusted to speak the truth.

Arthur Balfour (1848–1930) British statesman. Letter to Mrs Drew, 1918

4 Nothing great was ever achieved without enthusiasm.

Ralph Waldo Emerson (1803–82) US poet and essayist. *Essays,* 'Circles'

5 The love of life is necessary to the vigorous prosecution of any undertaking.

Samuel Johnson (1709–84) British lexicographer. *The Rambler*

6 Don't clap too hard – it's a very old building.

John Osborne (1929–) British dramatist. *The Entertainer*

7 Every man loves what he is good at.

Thomas Shadwell (1642–92) English dramatist. *A True Widow,* V:1

8 To business that we love we rise betime,
And go to't with delight.

William Shakespeare (1564–1616) English dramatist. *Antony and Cleopatra,* IV:4

ENVIRONMENT

See also ecology

1 Irritations of the eyes, which are caused by smoke, over-heating, dust, or similar injury, are easy to heal; the patient being advised first of all to avoid the irritating causes . . . For the disease ceases without the use of any kind of medicine, if only a proper way of living be adopted.

Aetios (c. 535) *Tetrabiblon,* Sermo II

2 The first Care in building of Cities, is to make them airy and well perflated; infectious Distempers must necessarily be propagated amongst Mankind living close together.

John Arbuthnot (1667–1735) Scottish physician and satirist. *An Essay Concerning the Effects of Air on Human Bodies*

3 One cannot assess in terms of cash or exports and imports an imponderable thing like the turn of a lane or an inn or a church tower or a familiar skyline.

John Betjeman (1906–84) British poet. Referring to a plan to site a new London airport in the Vale of Aylesbury. *The Observer,* 'Sayings of the Week', 20 July 1969

4 They improvidentially piped growing volumes of sewage into the sea, the healing virtues of which were advertised on every railway station.

Robert Cecil (1913–) British writer. Referring to seaside resorts. *Life in Edwardian England*

5 A physician is obligated to consider more than a diseased organ, more even than the whole man – he must view the man in his world.

Harvey Cushing (1869–1939) US surgeon. *Man Adapting,* Ch. 12 (René J. Dubos)

6 It can be said that each civilization has a pattern of disease peculiar to it. The pattern of disease is an expression of the response of man to his total environment (physical, biological, and social); this response is, therefore, determined by anything that affects man himself or his environment.

René J. Dubos (1901–) *Industrial Medicine and Surgery*, 30:369, 1961

7 I say that it touches a man that his blood is sea water and his tears are salt, that the seed of his loins is scarcely different from the same cells in a seaweed, and that of stuff like his bones are coral made. I say that a physical and biologic law lies down with him, and wakes when a child stirs in the womb, and that the sap in a tree, uprushing in the spring, and the smell of the loam, where the darkness, and the path of the sun in the heaven, these are facts of first importance to his mental conclusions, and that a man who goes in no consciousness of them is a drifter and a dreamer, without a home or any contact with reality.

Donald Culross Peattie (1898–1964) *An Almanac for Moderns*, 'April First'

8 If sunbeams were weapons of war, we would have had solar energy long ago.

George Porter (1920–) British chemist. *The Observer*, 'Sayings of the Week', 26 Aug 1973

9 The emergence of intelligence, I am convinced, tends to unbalance the ecology. In other words, intelligence is the great polluter. It is not until a creature begins to manage its environment that nature is thrown into disorder.

Clifford D. Simak (1904–) US journalist. *Shakespeare's Planet*

10 It is obvious that the best qualities in man must atrophy in a standing-room-only environment.

Stewart L. Udall (1920–) US politician. *The Quiet Crisis*, 13

ENVY

See also discontent, jealousy

1 Better be envied than pitied.

Proverb

2 The rich man has his motor car,
His country and his town estate.
He smokes a fifty-cent cigar
And jeers at Fate.

F. P. Adams (1881–1960) US journalist. *The Rich Man*

3 Yet though my lamp burns low and dim,
Though I must slave for livelihood –
Think you that I would change with him?
You bet I would!

F. P. Adams *The Rich Man*

4 I am sure the grapes are sour.

Aesop (6th century BC) Reputed Greek writer of fables. *Fables*, 'The Fox and the Grapes'

5 Moral indignation is in most cases 2 per cent moral, 48 per cent indignation and 50 per cent envy.

Vittorio de Sica (1901–) Italian-born French actor. *The Observer*, 'Sayings of the Decade', 1961

6 Fools may our scorn, not envy raise,
For envy is a kind of praise.

John Gay (1685–1732) English poet and dramatist. *Fables*

7 A physician ought to be extremely watchful against covetousness, for it is a vice imputed, justly or unjustly, to his Profession.

Thomas Gisborne (1758–1846) *The Duties of Physicians*

8 The man with toothache thinks everyone happy whose teeth are sound.

George Bernard Shaw (1856–1950) Irish dramatist and critic. *Man and Superman*

9 Whenever a friend succeeds, a little something in me dies.

Gore Vidal (1925–) US novelist. *The Sunday Times Magazine*, 16 Sept 1973

10 Never having been able to succeed in the world, he took his revenge by speaking ill of it.

Voltaire (François-Marie Arouet; 1694–1778) French writer. *Zadig*, Ch. 4

EPITAPHS

1 Hereabouts died a very gallant gentleman, Captain L. E. G. Oates of the Inniskilling Dragoons. In March 1912, returning from the Pole, he walked willingly to his death in a blizzard, to try and save his comrades, beset by hardships.

E. L. Atkinson (1882–1929) British naval officer. Epitaph on memorial in the Antarctic.

2 Earth, receive an honoured guest
William Yeats is laid to rest
Let the Irish vessel lie
Emptied of its poetry.

W. H. Auden (1907–73) British poet. *In Memory of W. B. Yeats*

3 I've played everything but the harp.

Lionel Barrymore (1848–1954) US actor. When asked what words he would like engraved on his tombstone. Attrib.

4 She sleeps alone at last.

Robert Benchley (1889–1945) US humorist. Suggested epitaph for an actress. Attrib.

5 His was the sort of career that made the Recording Angel think seriously about taking up shorthand.

Nicolas Bentley (1907–78) British cartoonist and writer. Attrib.

6 When Sir Joshua Reynolds died
All Nature was degraded;
The King dropped a tear in the Queen's ear,
And all his pictures faded.

William Blake (1757–1827) British poet. *On Art and Artists*

7 With death doomed to grapple,
Beneath this cold slab, he
Who lied in the chapel
Now lies in the Abbey.

Byron, George Gordon, 6th Baron (1788–1824) British poet. *Epitaph for William Pitt*

8 Here lies my wife; here let her lie!
Now she's at rest, and so am I.

John Dryden (1631–1700) British poet and dramatist. *Epitaph Intended for Dryden's Wife*

9 To me it shall be a full satisfaction both for the memorial of my name, and for the glory also, if when I shall let my last breath, it be engraven upon my marble tomb, 'Here lieth Elizabeth, who reigned a virgin and died a virgin'.

Elizabeth I (1533–1603) Queen of England. Reply to a petition from the House of Commons, 6 Feb 1559

10 Here Skugg
Lies snug
As a bug
In a rug.

Benjamin Franklin (1706–90) US scientist. An epitaph for a squirrel, 'skugg' being a dialect name for the animal. Letter to Georgiana Shipley, 26 Sept 1772

11 The body of
Benjamin Franklin, printer,
(Like the cover of an old book,
Its contents worn out,
And stript of its lettering and gilding)
Lies here, food for worms!
Yet the work itself shall not be lost,
For it will, as he believed, appear once more
In a new
And more beautiful edition,
Corrected and amended
By its Author!

Benjamin Franklin Suggestion for his own epitaph.

12 Is life a boon?
If so, it must befall
That Death, whene'er he call,

Must call too soon.

W. S. Gilbert (1836–1911) British dramatist. The lines are written on Arthur Sullivan's memorial in the Embankment gardens. *The Yeoman of the Guard,* I

13 Here rests his head upon the lap of Earth
A youth to fortune and to fame unknown.
Fair Science frown'd not on his humble birth,
And Melancholy mark'd him for her own.

Thomas Gray (1716–71) British poet. *Elegy Written in a Country Churchyard*

14 Their name, their year, spelt by the unlettered muse,
The place of fame and elegy supply:
On many a holy text around she strews,
That teach the rustic moralist to die.

Thomas Gray *Elegy Written in a Country Churchyard*

15 He gave to Mis'ry all he had, a tear,
He gain'd from Heav'n ('twas all he wish'd) a friend.

Thomas Gray *Elegy Written in a Country Churchyard*

16 John Brown's body lies a-mouldering in the grave,
His soul is marching on!

Charles Sprague Hall (19th century) US songwriter. The song commemorates the American hero who died in the cause of abolishing slavery. *John Brown's Body*

17 To Oliver Goldsmith, A Poet, Naturalist, and Historian, who left scarcely any style of writing untouched, and touched none that he did not adorn.

Samuel Johnson (1709–84) British lexicographer. Epitaph on Goldsmith. *Life of Johnson* (J. Boswell), Vol. III

18 In lapidary inscriptions a man is not upon oath.

Samuel Johnson *Life of Johnson* (J. Boswell), Vol. II

19 Here lies Joseph, who failed in everything he undertook.

Joseph II (1741–90) Holy Roman Emperor. Suggesting his own epitaph when reflecting upon the disappointment of his hopes for reform. Attrib.

20 Nowhere probably is there more true feeling, and nowhere worse taste, than in a churchyard – both as regards the monuments and the inscriptions. Scarcely a word of true poetry anywhere.

Benjamin Jowett (1817–93) British theologian. *Letters of B. Jowett* (Abbott and Campbell)

21 Over my dead body!

George S. Kaufman (1889–1961) US dramatist. On being asked to suggest his own epitaph. *The Algonquin Wits* (R. Drennan)

22 Here lies one whose name was writ in water.

John Keats (1795–1821) British poet. Suggesting his own epitaph (recalling a line from *Philaster* by Beaumont and Fletcher). *Life of Keats* (Lord Houghton), Ch. 2

23 'There is a report that Piso is dead; it is a great loss; he was an honest man, who deserved to live longer; he was intelligent and agreeable, resolute and courageous, to be depended upon, generous and faithful.' Add: 'provided he is really dead'.

Jean de La Bruyère (1645–96) French satirist. *Les Caractères*

24 Go, stranger, and tell the Lacedaemonians that here we lie, obedient to their commands.

Leonidas (died 480 BC) King of Sparta. Epitaph over the tomb in which he and his followers were buried after their defeat at Thermopylae.

25 Maybe it would have been better if neither of us had been born.

Napoleon I (Napoleon Bonaparte; 1769–1821) French emperor. Said while looking at the tomb of the philosopher Jean-Jacques Rousseau, whose theories had influenced the French Revolution. *The Story of Civilization* (W. Durant), Vol. II

26 Beneath this slab
John Brown is stowed.
He watched the ads
And not the road.

Ogden Nash (1902–71) US poet. *Lather as You Go*

27 For all the Brothers were valiant, and all the Sisters virtuous.

Margaret, Duchess of Newcastle (1624–74) Second wife of William Cavendish. Epitaph in Westminster Abbey

28 A certain versifier, a false one, said, 'Just as England has been filthy with the defiler John, so now the filth of Hell is fouled by his foul presence'; but it is dangerous to write against a man who can easily do you wrong.

Matthew Paris (fl. 1235–50) Chronicler. Referring to King John of England (r. 1199–1216); this quotation is better known in the form used by J. R. Green in his *Short History of the English People* (1875): 'Foul as it is, Hell itself is defiled by the fouler presence of King John.'. *Chronica Majora,* 1216

29 He lies below, correct in cypress wood,
And entertains the most exclusive worms.

Dorothy Parker (1893–1967) US writer. *Epitaph for a Very Rich Man*

30 The poor son-of-a-bitch!

Dorothy Parker Quoting from *The Great Gatsby* on paying her last respects to F. Scott Fitzgerald. *Thalberg: Life and Legend* (B. Thomas)

31 In wit a man; simplicity a child.

Alexander Pope (1688–1744) British poet. *Epitaph on Mr. Gay*

32 There died a myriad,
And of the best, among them,
For an old bitch gone in the teeth,
For a botched civilization . . .

Ezra Pound (1885–1972) US poet. *Hugh Selwyn Mauberley*

33 Died some, pro patria,
non 'dulce' non 'et decor'

Ezra Pound *Hugh Selwyn Mauberley*

34 At last God caught his eye.

Harry Secombe (1921–) Welsh comedian. Suggested epitaph for a head waiter. *Punch,* May 1962

35 What can you say about a 25-year-old girl who died? That she was beautiful? And brilliant. That she loved Mozart and Bach. And the Beatles. And me.

Erich Segal (1937–) US writer. *Love Story*

36 Alas, poor Yorick! I knew him, Horatio: a fellow of infinite jest, of most excellent fancy.

William Shakespeare (1564–1616) English dramatist. *Hamlet,* V:1

37 Here lies our sovereign lord the King
Whose promise none relies on;
He never said a foolish thing,
Or ever did a wise one.

John Wilmot, Earl of Rochester (1647–80) British poet. For a reply see CHARLES II. *The King's Epitaph*

38 *Si monumentum requiris, circumspice.*
If you seek my monument, look around you.

Christopher Wren (1632–1723) English architect. Inscription in St Paul's Cathedral, London

39 Under bare Ben Bulben's head
In Drumcliff churchyard Yeats is laid
. . .
On limestone quarried near the spot
By his command these words are cut:

W. B. Yeats (1865–1939) Irish poet. *Under Ben Bulben,* VI

40 All who come my grave to see

Avoid damp beds and think of me.
Epitaph of Lydia Eason, St Michael's, Stoke

41 Beneath this stone, in hope of Zion,
Doth lie the landlord of the 'Lion'.
His son keeps on the business still,
Resign'd unto the Heavenly will.
Epitaph, Upton-on-Severn churchyard

42 He died as he lived – at sea.
Anonymous On Ramsay Macdonald who died during a cruise.

43 Her body dissected by fiendish men,
Her bones anatomized,
Her soul, we trust, has risen to God,
Where few physicians rise.
Epitaph of Ruth Sprague

44 Here lie I and my four daughters,
Killed by drinking Cheltenham waters.
Had we but stick to Epsom salts,
We wouldn't have been in these here vaults.
Cheltenham Waters

45 Here lie I by the chancel door;
They put me here because I was poor.
The further in, the more you pay,
But here lie I as snug as they.
Epitaph, Devon churchyard

46 Here lies a man who was killed by lightning;
He died when his prospects seemed to be brightening.
He might have cut a flash in this world of trouble,
But the flash cut him, and he lies in the stubble.
Epitaph, Torrington, Devon

47 Here lies a valiant warrior
Who never drew a sword;
Here lies a noble courtier
Who never kept his word;
Here lies the Earl of Leicester
Who governed the estates
Whom the earth could never living love,
And the just heaven now hates.
Attrib. to Ben Jonson in *Collection of Epitaphs* (Tissington), 1857.

48 Here lies father and mother and sister and I,
We all died within the space of one short year;
They all be buried at Wimble, except I,
And I be buried here.
Epitaph, Staffordshire churchyard

49 Here lies Fred,
Who was alive and is dead:
Had it been his father,
I had much rather;
Had it been his brother,
Still better than another;
Had it been his sister,
No one would have missed her;
Had it been the whole generation,
Still better for the nation:
But since 'tis only Fred,
Who was alive and is dead, –
There's no more to be said.
Referring to Frederick, Prince of Wales (d. 1751), eldest son of George II and father of George III. *Memoirs of George II* (Horace Walpole)

50 Here lies my wife,
Here lies she;
Hallelujah!
Hallelujee!
Epitaph, Leeds churchyard

51 Here lies the body of Mary Ann Lowder,
She burst while drinking a seidlitz powder.
Called from the world to her heavenly rest,
She should have waited till it effervesced.
Epitaph

52 Here lies the body of Richard Hind,
Who was neither ingenious, sober, nor kind.
Epitaph

53 Here lies Will Smith – and, what's something rarish,
He was born, bred, and hanged, all in the same parish.
Epitaph

54 Mary Ann has gone to rest,
Safe at last on Abraham's breast,
Which may be nuts for Mary Ann,
But is certainly rough on Abraham.
Epitaph

55 My sledge and anvil lie declined
My bellows too have lost their wind
My fire's extinct, my forge decayed,
And in the Dust my Vice is laid
My coals are spent, my iron's gone
My Nails are Drove, My Work is done.
An epitaph to William Strange, blacksmith, died 6 June 1746 and buried in Nettlebed churchyard.

56 Pain was my portion;
Physic was my food;
Groans my devotion;
Drugs did me no good.
Epitaph at Oldbury-on-Severn, England

57 Sacred to the memory of
Captain Anthony Wedgwood
Accidentally shot by his gamekeeper
Whilst out shooting
'Well done thou good and faithful servant'
Epitaph

58 Stranger! Approach this spot with gravity!
John Brown is filling his last cavity.
Epitaph of a dentist

59 This the grave of Mike O'Day
Who died maintaining his right of way.
His right was clear, his will was strong.
But he's just as dead as if he'd been wrong.
Epitaph

60 Warm summer sun shine kindly here:
Warm summer wind blow softly here:
Green sod above lie light, lie light:
Good-night, Dear Heart: good-night, good-night.
Memorial to Clorinda Haywood, St Bartholomew's, Edgbaston

EQUALITY

See also class, feminism, human rights

1 A cat may look at a king.
Proverb

2 All cats are gray in the dark.
Proverb

3 Equality may perhaps be a right, but no power on earth can ever turn it into a fact.
Honoré de Balzac (1799–1850) French novelist. *La Duchesse de Langeais*

4 From the point of view of sexual morality the aeroplane is valuable in war in that it destroys men and women in equal numbers.
Ernest William Barnes (1874–1953) British clergyman and mathematician. *Rise of Christianity*

5 What makes equality such a difficult business is that we only want it with our superiors.
Henry Becque (1837–99) French dramatist. *Querelles littéraires*

6 When security and equality are in conflict, it will not do to hesitate a moment. Equality must yield.
Jeremy Bentham (1748–1832) British philosopher. *Principles of Legislation*

7 All service ranks the same with God –
With God, whose puppets, best and worst,

Are we: there is no last or first.

Robert Browning (1812–89) British poet. *Pippa Passes*, Pt. I

8 The terrorist and the policeman both come from the same basket.

Joseph Conrad (Teodor Josef Konrad Korzeniowski; 1857–1924) Polish-born British novelist. *The Secret Agent*, Ch. 4

9 The majestic egalitarianism of the law, which forbids rich and poor alike to sleep under bridges, to beg in the streets, and to steal bread.

Anatole France (Jacques Anatole François Thibault; 1844–1924) French writer. *The Red Lily*, Ch. 7

10 Men are made by nature unequal. It is vain, therefore, to treat them as if they were equal.

J. A. Froude (1818–94) British historian. *Short Studies on Great Subjects*, 'Party Politics'

11 That all men are equal is a proposition to which, at ordinary times, no sane individual has ever given his assent.

Aldous Huxley (1894–1964) British novelist. *Proper Studies*

12 A just society would be one in which liberty for one person is constrained only by the demands created by equal liberty for another.

Ivan Illich (1926–) Austrian sociologist. *Tools for Conviviality*

13 Fair Shares for All, is Labour's Call.

Douglas Jay (1907–) British Labour politician. Slogan, Battersea North by-election, June 1946

14 Your levellers wish to level *down* as far as themselves; but they cannot bear levelling *up* to themselves.

Samuel Johnson (1709–84) British lexicographer. *Life of Johnson* (J. Boswell), Vol. I

15 It is better that some should be unhappy than that none should be happy, which would be the case in a general state of equality.

Samuel Johnson *Life of Johnson* (J. Boswell), Vol. III

16 I have a dream that one day this nation will rise up, live out the true meaning of its creed: we hold these truths to be self-evident, that all men are created equal.

Martin Luther King (1929–68) US Black civil-rights leader. He used the words 'I have a dream' in a number of speeches. Speech, Washington, 27 Aug 1963

17 Every man a king but no man wears a crown.

Huey Long (1893–1935) US demagogue. Quoting William Jennings Bryan. Slogan, 1928

18 Never descend to the ways of those above you.

George Mallaby (1902–78) British diplomat and writer. *From My Level*

19 Every man who comes to England is entitled to the protection of the English law, whatever oppression he may heretofore have suffered, and whatever may be the colour of his skin, whether it is black or whether it is white.

Lord Mansfield (1705–93) British judge and politician. From the judgment in the case of James Somersett, a fugitive negro slave (May 1772); it established the principle that slaves enjoyed the benefits of freedom while in England.

20 This isn't going to be a good country for any of us to live in until it's a good country for all of us to live in.

Richard Milhous Nixon (1913–) US president. *The Observer*, 'Sayings of the Week', 29 Sep 1968

21 All animals are equal but some animals are more equal than others.

George Orwell (Eric Blair; 1903–50) British novelist. *Animal Farm*, Ch. 10

22 In America everybody is of the opinion that he has no social superiors, since all men are equal, but he does not admit that he has no social inferiors.

Bertrand Russell (1872–1970) British philosopher. *Unpopular Essays*

23 I think the King is but a man as I am: the violet smells to him as it doth to me.

William Shakespeare (1564–1616) English dramatist. *Henry V*, IV:1

24 What infinite heart's ease
Must kings neglect, that private men enjoy!
And what have kings that privates have not too,
Save ceremony, save general ceremony?

William Shakespeare *Henry V*, IV:1

25 I was born free as Caesar; so were you:
We both have fed as well, and we can both
Endure the winter's cold as well as he:
For once, upon a raw and gusty day,
The troubl'd Tiber chafing with her shores,
Caesar said to me, 'Dar'st thou, Cassius, now,
Leap in with me into this angry flood,
And swim to yonder point?' Upon the word,
Accoutred as I was, I plunged in,
And bade him follow . . .
But ere we could arrive the point propos'd,
Caesar cried, 'Help me, Cassius, or I sink!'
I, as Aeneas, our great ancestor,
Did from the flames of Troy upon his shoulder
The old Anchises bear, so from the waves of Tiber
Did I the tired Caesar. And this man
Is now become a god.

William Shakespeare *Julius Caesar*, I:2

26 Hath not a Jew eyes? Hath not a Jew hands, organs, dimensions, senses, affections, passions, fed with the same food, hurt with the same weapons, subject to the same diseases, healed by the same means, warmed and cooled by the same winter and summer, as a Christian is? If you prick us, do we not bleed? If you tickle us, do we not laugh? If you poison us, do we not die? And if you wrong us, shall we not revenge?

William Shakespeare *The Merchant of Venice*, III:1

27 Life levels all men: death reveals the eminent.

George Bernard Shaw (1856–1950) Irish dramatist and critic. *Maxims for Revolutionists*

28 This is a movie, not a lifeboat.

Spencer Tracy (1900–67) US film star. Defending his demand for equal billing with Katherine Hepburn. Attrib.

29 Everybody should have an equal chance – but they shouldn't have a flying start.

Harold Wilson (1916–) British politician and prime minister. *The Observer*, 'Sayings of the Year', 1963

Equality in death

See also death, equality

30 It comes equally to us all, and makes us all equal when it comes. The ashes of an Oak in the Chimney, are no epitaph of that Oak, to tell me how high or how large that was; It tells me not what flocks it sheltered while it stood, nor what men it hurt when it fell. The dust of great persons' graves is speechless too, it says nothing, it distinguishes nothing.

John Donne (1573–1631) English poet. *Sermons*, XV

31 Pale Death kicks his way equally

into the cottages of the poor and the castles of kings.
Horace (Quintus Horatius Flaccus; 65–8 BC) Roman poet. *Odes*, I

32 A heap of dust alone remains of thee;
'Tis all thou art, and all the proud shall be!
Alexander Pope (1688–1744) British poet. *Elegy to the Memory of an Unfortunate Lady*

33 Thersites' body is as good as Ajax'
When neither are alive.
William Shakespeare (1564–1616) English dramatist. *Cymbeline*, IV:2

34 Indeed this counsellor
Is now most still, most secret, and most grave,
Who was in life a foolish prating knave.
William Shakespeare *Hamlet*, III:4

ERROR

1 It is time for the destruction of error.
The chairs are being brought in from the garden,
The summer talk stopped on that savage coast
Before the storms.
W. H. Auden (1907–73) British poet. *It is time*

2 The weak have one weapon: the errors of those who think they are strong.
Georges Bidault (1899–1983) French statesman. *The Observer*, 1962

3 We have erred, and strayed from thy ways like lost sheep.
The Book of Common Prayer *Morning Prayer, General Confession*

4 There are few virtues which the Poles do not possess and there are few errors they have ever avoided.
Winston Churchill (1874–1965) British statesman. Speech, House of Commons, 1945

5 Errors, like Straws, upon the surface flow;
He who would search for Pearls must dive below.
John Dryden (1631–1700) British poet and dramatist. *All for Love*, Prologue

6 Nor is the Peoples Judgment always true:
The Most may err as grosly as the Few.
John Dryden *Absalom and Achitophel*, I

7 Riddle of destiny, who can show
What thy short visit meant, or know
What thy errand here below?
Charles Lamb (1775–1834) British essayist. *On an Infant Dying as soon as Born*

8 It is one thing to show a man that he is in an error, and another to put him in possession of truth.
John Locke (1632–1704) English philosopher. *An Essay Concerning Human Understanding*, Bk. IV, Ch. 7

9 A new maxim is often a brilliant error.
Chrétien Guillaume de Lamoignonde Malesherbes (1721–94) French statesman. *Pensées et maximes*

10 Love's perfect blossom only blows
Where noble manners veil defect.
Angels may be familiar; those
Who err each other must respect.
Coventry Patmore (1823–96) British poet. *The Angel in the House*, Bk. I, Prelude 2

11 To err is human, to forgive, divine.
Alexander Pope (1688–1744) British poet. *An Essay on Criticism*

ESCAPE

1 The view that a peptic ulcer may be the hole in a man's stomach through which he crawls to escape from his wife has fairly wide acceptance.
J. A. D. Anderson (1926–) *A New Look at Social Medicine*

2 I bet you a hundred bucks he ain't in here.
Charles Bancroft Dillingham (1868–1934) US theatrical manager. Referring to the escapologist Harry Houdini; said at his funeral, while carrying his coffin. Attrib.

3 He can run, but he can't hide.
Joe Louis (Joseph Louis Barrow; 1914–81) US boxer. Referring to the speed for which his coming opponent, Billy Conn, was renowned. Attrib.

4 CLEOPATRA: Lord of lords!
O infinite virtue! com'st thou smiling from
The world's great snare uncaught?
ANTONY: My nightingale,
We have beat them to their beds.
William Shakespeare (1564–1616) English dramatist. *Antony and Cleopatra*, IV:8

ETERNITY

See also immortality, time

1 Kiss till the cow comes home.
Francis Beaumont (1584–1616) English dramatist. *Scornful Lady*, II:2

2 As it was in the beginning, is now, and ever shall be: world without end.
The Book of Common Prayer *Morning Prayer, Gloria*

3 Thou, silent form, dost tease us out of thought
As doth eternity: Cold Pastoral!
John Keats (1795–1821) British poet. *Ode on a Grecian Urn*

4 Eternity's a terrible thought. I mean, where's it going to end?
Tom Stoppard (1937–) Czech-born British dramatist. *Rosencrantz and Guildenstern Are Dead*, II

ETIQUETTE

See also manners

1 Phone for the fish knives Norman,
As Cook is a little unnerved;
You kiddies have crumpled the serviettes
And I must have things daintily served.
John Betjeman (1906–84) British poet. *How to get on in Society*

2 He is the only man since my dear husband died, to have the effrontery to kiss me on the lips.
Elizabeth the Queen Mother (1900–) British Royal. Referring to president Carter. Attrib.

3 'It is very pleasant dining with a bachelor,' said Miss Matty, softly, as we settled ourselves in the counting-house. 'I only hope it is not improper; so many pleasant things are!'
Elizabeth Gaskell (1810–65) British novelist. *Cranford*, Ch. 4

4 It's all right, Arthur. The white wine came up with the fish.
Herman J. Mankiewicz (1897–1953) US journalist and screenwriter. After vomiting at the table of a fastidious host. Attrib.

5 At a dinner party one should eat wisely but not too well, and talk well but not too wisely.
W. Somerset Maugham (1874–1965) British novelist. *A Writer's Notebook*

6 We could not lead a pleasant life,
And 'twould be finished soon,
If peas were eaten with the knife,
And gravy with the spoon.
Eat slowly: only men in rags
And gluttons old in sin
Mistake themselves for carpet bags
And tumble victuals in.
Walter Alexander Raleigh (1861–1922) British scholar. *Laughter from a Cloud*, 'Stans puer ad mensam'

7 'How did you think I managed at dinner, Clarence?' 'Capitally!' 'I had a knife and two forks left at the end,' she said regretfully.
William Pett Ridge (1860–1930) British novelist. *Love at Paddington Green*, Ch. 6

8 I think she must have been very strictly brought up, she's so desperately anxious to do the wrong thing correctly.
Saki (Hector Hugh Munro; 1870–1916) British writer. *Reginald on Worries*

EUROPE

See also Britain, England, France, Germany, Ireland, Russia, Scotland, Switzerland, Venice, Wales

1 The countries of western Europe are no longer in a position to protect themselves individually.
Konrad Adenauer (1876–1967) West German chancellor. Speech, May 1953

2 Rome's just a city like anywhere else. A vastly overrated city, I'd say. It trades on belief just as Stratford trades on Shakespeare.
Anthony Burgess (John Burgess Wilson; 1917–) British novelist. *Mr Enderby*, Pt. II, Ch. 2

3 But the age of chivalry is gone. That of sophisters, economists, and calculators, has succeeded; and the glory of Europe is extinguished for ever.
Edmund Burke (1729–97) British politician. *Reflections on the Revolution in France*

4 While stands the Coliseum, Rome shall stand;
When falls the Coliseum, Rome shall fall;
And when Rome falls – the World.
Lord Byron (1788–1824) British poet. *Childe Harold's Pilgrimage*, IV

5 We must build a kind of United States of Europe.
Winston Churchill (1874–1965) British statesman. Speech, Zurich, 19 Sept 1946

6 Apart from cheese and tulips, the main product of the country is advocaat, a drink made from lawyers.
Alan Coren (1938–) British humorist and writer. Referring to Holland. *The Sanity Inspector*, 'All You Need to Know about Europe'

7 Holland . . . lies so low they're only saved by being dammed.
Thomas Hood (1799–1845) British poet. *Up the Rhine*

8 It's not enough to be Hungarian, you must have talent too.
Alexander Korda (Sandor Kellner; 1893–1956) Hungarian-born British film director. *Alexander Korda* (K. Kulik)

9 In Western Europe there are now only small countries – those that know it and those that don't know it yet.
Théo Lefèvre (1914–73) Belgian prime minister. *The Observer*, 'Sayings of the Year', 1963

10 The only lasting solution is that Europe itself should gradually find its way to an internal equilibrium and a limitation of armaments by political appeasement.
11th Marquess of Lothian (1882–1940) British politician. Letter to *The Times*, 4 May 1934

11 I am inclined to notice the ruin in things, perhaps because I was born in Italy.
Arthur Miller (1915–) US dramatist. *A View from the Bridge*, I

12 Austria is Switzerland speaking pure German and with history added.
J. E. Morpurgo (1918–) British writer and academic. *The Road to Athens*

13 Providence has given to the French the empire of the land, to the English that of the sea, and to the Germans that of the air.
Jean Paul Richter (Johann Paul Friedrich Richter; 1763–1825) German novelist. Quoted by Thomas Carlyle

14 The people of Crete unfortunately make more history than they can consume locally.
Saki (Hector Hugh Munro; 1870–1916) British writer. *The Jesting of Arlington Stringham*

15 We are part of the community of Europe and we must do our duty as such.
Marquess of Salisbury (1830–1903) British statesman. Speech, Caernarvon, 11 Apr 1888

16 We're from Madeira, but perfectly respectable, so far.
George Bernard Shaw (1856–1950) Irish dramatist and critic. *You Never Can Tell*, I

17 This going into Europe will not turn out to be the thrilling mutual exchange supposed. It is more like nine middle-aged couples with failing marriages meeting in a darkened bedroom in a Brussels hotel for a Group Grope.
E. P. Thompson (1924–) British historian. On the Europe debate, *Sunday Times*, 27 Apr 1975

18 Every place I look at I work out the cubic feet, and I say it will make a good warehouse or it won't. Can't help myself. One of the best warehouses I ever see was the Vatican in Rome.
Arnold Wesker (1932–) British dramatist. *Chips with Everything*, I:6

19 That Europe's nothin' on earth but a great big auction, that's all it is.
Tennessee Williams (1911–83) US dramatist. *Cat on a Hot Tin Roof*, I

EVIL

See also good and evil, sin, vice

1 *Honi soit qui mal y pense.*
Evil be to him who evil thinks.
Anonymous Motto for the Order of the Garter

2 It takes a certain courage and a certain greatness even to be truly base.
Jean Anouilh (1910–87) French dramatist. *Ardele*

3 The fearsome word-and-thought-defying *banality of evil.*
Hannah Arendt (1906–75) German-born US philosopher and historian. *Eichmann in Jerusalem: A Report on the Banality of Evil*

4 Wherefore I praised the dead which are already dead more than the living which are yet alive.
Yea, better is he than both they, which hath not yet been, who hath not seen the evil work that is done under the sun.
Bible: Ecclesiastes 4:2–3 sun

5 But evil men and seducers shall wax worse and worse, deceiving, and being deceived.
Bible: II Timothy 3:13

6 And this is the condemnation, that light is come into the world, and men loved darkness rather than light, because their deeds were evil.
Bible: John 3:19

7 And when the thousand years are expired, Satan shall be loosed out of his prison,
And shall go out to deceive the nations which are in the four quarters of the earth, Gog and Magog, to gather them together to battle: the number of whom is as the sand of the sea.
Bible: Revelations 20:7–8

8 I never saw a brute I hated so;

He must be wicked to deserve such pain.
Robert Browning (1812–89) British poet. *Childe Roland to the Dark Tower Came*, XIV

9 The belief in a supernatural source of evil is not necessary; men alone are quite capable of every wickedness.
Joseph Conrad (Teodor Josef Konrad Korzeniowski; 1857–1924) Polish-born British novelist. *Under Western Eyes*, Part 2

10 There's a young man hid with me, in comparison with which young man I am a Angel. That young man hears the words I speak. That young man has a secret way pecooliar to himself, of getting at a boy, and at his heart, and at his liver.
Charles Dickens (1812–70) British novelist. Said by Magwitch. *Great Expectations*, Ch. 1

11 Something nasty in the woodshed.
Stella Gibbons (1902–) British poet and novelist. *Cold Comfort Farm*

12 The disease of an evil conscience is beyond the practice of all the physicians of all the countries in the world.
William E. Gladstone (1809–98) British statesman. Speech, Plumstead, 1878

13 But evil is wrought by want of thought,
As well as want of heart!
Thomas Hood (1799–1845) British poet. *The Lady's Dream*

14 He who passively accepts evil is as much involved in it as he who helps to perpetrate it.
Martin Luther King (1929–68) US Black civil-rights leader. *Stride Towards Freedom*

15 Farewell remorse! All good to me is lost;
Evil, be thou my Good.
John Milton (1608–74) English poet. *Paradise Lost*, Bk. IV

16 Take thy beak from out my heart, and take thy form from off my door!
Quoth the Raven, 'Nevermore.'
Edgar Allan Poe (1809–49) US poet and writer. *The Raven*

17 There is scarcely a single man sufficiently aware to know all the evil he does.
Duc de la Rochefoucauld (1613–80) French writer. *Maximes*, 269

18 She is a smart old broad. It is a pity she is so nefarious.
Damon Runyon (1884–1946) US writer. *Runyon à la carte*, 'Broadway Incident'

19 Friends, Romans, countrymen, lend me your ears
I come to bury Caesar, not to praise him.
The evil that men do lives after them;
The good is oft interred with their bones.
William Shakespeare (1564–1616) English dramatist. *Julius Caesar*, III:2

20 Wisdom and goodness to the vile seem vile;
Filths savour but themselves.
William Shakespeare *King Lear*, IV:2

21 Oftentimes, to win us to our harm,
The instruments of darkness tell us truths;
Win us with honest trifles, to betray's
In deepest consequence.
William Shakespeare *Macbeth*, I:3

22 The raven himself is hoarse
That croaks the fatal entrance of Duncan
Under my battlements. Come, you spirits
That tend on mortal thoughts! unsex me here,
And fill me from the crown to the toe top full
Of direst cruelty; make thick my blood,
Stop up the access and passage to remorse,
That no compunctious visitings of nature
Shake my fell purpose, nor keep peace between
The effect and it! Come to my woman's breasts,
And take my milk for gall, you murdering ministers,
Wherever in your sightless substances
You wait on nature's mischief! Come, thick night,
And pall thee in the dunnest smoke of hell,
That my keen knife see not the wound it makes,
Nor heaven peep through the blanket of the dark,
To cry 'Hold, hold!'
William Shakespeare *Macbeth*, I:5

23 And therefore, since I cannot prove a lover,
To entertain these fair well-spoken days,
I am determined to prove a villain,
And hate the idle pleasures of these days.
William Shakespeare *Richard III*, I:1

EVOLUTION

See also survival

1 An ape is ne'er so like an ape
As when he wears a doctor's cape.
Proverb

2 Descended from the apes? My dear, we will hope it is not true. But if it is, let us pray that it may not become generally known.
Anonymous Remark by the wife of a canon of Worcester Cathedral. *Man's Most Dangerous Myth, The Fallacy of Race* (F. Ashley Montagu)

3 A hen is only an egg's way of making another egg.
Samuel Butler (1835–1902) British writer. *Life and Habit*, VIII

4 Some call it Evolution
And others call it God.
William H. Carruth (1859–1924) *Each in His Own Tongue*

5 From an evolutionary point of view, man has stopped moving, if he ever did move.
Pierre Teilhard de Chardin (1881–1955) French Jesuit and paleontologist. *The Phenomenon of Man*, Postscript

6 I confess freely to you I could never look long upon a Monkey, without very Mortifying Reflections.
William Congreve (1670–1729) English Restoration dramatist. Letter to John Dennis, 10 July 1695

7 Man is developed from an ovule, about the 125th of an inch in diameter, which differs in no respect from the ovules of other animals.
Charles Darwin (1809–82) British life scientist. *The Descent of Man*, Ch. 1

8 We must, however, acknowledge, as it seems to me, that man with all his noble qualities, still bears in his bodily frame the indelible stamp of his lowly origin.
Charles Darwin Closing words. *Descent of Man*, Ch. 21

9 We will now discuss in a little more detail the struggle for existence.
Charles Darwin *Origin of Species*, Ch. 3

10 I have called this principle, by which each slight variation, if useful,

is preserved, by the term of Natural Selection.
Charles Darwin *Origin of Species,* Ch. 3

11 The expression often used by Mr Herbert Spencer of the Survival of the Fittest is more accurate, and is sometimes equally convenient.
Charles Darwin *Origin of Species,* Ch. 3

12 The question is this: Is man an ape or an angel? I, my lord, am on the side of the angels.
Benjamin Disraeli (1804–81) British statesman. Speech, 25 Nov 1864

13 How like us is that ugly brute, the ape!
Ennius (239 BC–169 BC) Roman poet. *On the Nature of the Gods,* I (Cicero)

14 I am, in point of fact, a particularly haughty and exclusive person, of pre-Adamite ancestral descent. You will understand this when I tell you that I can trace my ancestry back to a protoplasmal primordic atomic globule.
William S. Gilbert (1836–1911) British dramatist and comic writer. *The Mikado,* I

15 Philip is a living example of natural selection. He was as fitted to survive in this modern world as a tapeworm in an intestine.
William Golding (1911–) British novelist. *Free Fall,* Ch. 2

16 I am quite sure that our views on evolution would be very different had biologists studied genetics and natural selection before and not after most of them were convinced that evolution had occurred.
J. B. S. Haldane (1892–1964) British geneticist.

17 Everything from an egg.
William Harvey (1578–1657) English physician. *De Generatione Animalium,* Frontispiece

18 The probable fact is that we are descended not only from monkeys but from monks.
Elbert G. Hubbard (1856–1915) US writer and editor. *A Thousand and One Epigrams*

19 I asserted – and I repeat – that a man has no reason to be ashamed of having an ape for his grandfather. If there were an ancestor whom I should feel shame in recalling it would rather be a *man* – a man of restless and versatile intellect – who, not content with an equivocal success in his own sphere of activity, plunges into scientific questions with which he has no real acquaintance, only to obscure them by an aimless rhetoric, and distract the attention of his hearers from the real point at issue by eloquent digressions and skilled appeals to religious prejudice.
T. H. Huxley (1825–95) British biologist. Replying to Bishop WILBERFORCE in the debate on Darwin's theory of evolution at the meeting of the British Association at Oxford. No transcript was taken at the time: the version above is commonly quoted. After hearing Wilberforce's speech, and before rising himself, Huxley is said to have remarked, 'The Lord has delivered him into my hands!'. Speech, 30 June 1860

20 Evolution is far more important than living.
Ernst Jünger *The Rebel,* Ch. 3 (Albert Camus)

21 We are very slightly changed
From the semi-apes who ranged
India's prehistoric clay.
Rudyard Kipling (1865–1936) Indian-born British writer. *General Summary*

22 Never neglect the history of a missed menstrual period.
Rutherford Morrison (1853–1939) *The Practitioner,* Oct 1965

23 The tide of evolution carries everything before it, thoughts no less than bodies, and persons no less than nations.
George Santayana (1863–1952) Spanish-born US philosopher, poet, and critic. *Little Essays,* 44

24 We have been God-like in our planned breeding of our domesticated plants and animals, but we have been rabbit-like in our unplanned breeding of ourselves.
Arnold Toynbee (1889–1975) British historian. *National Observer,* 10 June 1963

25 And, in conclusion, I would like to ask the gentleman . . . whether the ape from which he is descended was on his grandmother's or his grandfather's side of the family.
Samuel Wilberforce (1805–73) British churchman. In a debate on Darwin's theory of evolution at the annual meeting of the British Association of the Advancement of Science held 30 June 1860 in Oxford. *See* HUXLEY.

EXAMINATIONS

See also education

1 Examinations are formidable even to the best prepared, for the greatest fool may ask more than the wisest man can answer.
Charles Caleb Colton (?1780–1832) British clergyman and writer. *Lacon,* Vol. II

2 Do not on any account attempt to write on both sides of the paper at once.
W. C. Sellar (1898–1951) British humorous writer. *1066 And All That,* Test Paper 5

3 If silicon had been a gas I should have been a major-general.
James Whistler (1834–1903) US painter. Referring to his failure in a West Point chemistry examination. *English Wits* (L. Russell)

EXAMPLE

1 Practise what you preach.
Proverb

2 Example is the school of mankind, and they will learn at no other.
Edmund Burke (1729–97) British politician. *Letters on a Regicide Peace,* letter 1

3 Do as you would be done by is the surest method that I know of pleasing.
Earl of Chesterfield (1694–1773) English statesman. Letter to his son, 16 Oct 1747

4 What you do not want done to yourself, do not do to others.
Confucius (K'ung Fu-tzu; 551–479 BC) Chinese philosopher. *Analects*

5 When the President does it, that means it is not illegal.
Richard Milhous Nixon (1913–) US president. TV interview, 19 May 1977

6 Men are not hanged for stealing horses, but that horses may not be stolen.
George Saville (1633–95) English statesman. *Political, Moral and Miscellaneous Thoughts and Reflections*

7 A precedent embalms a principle.
William Scott (1745–1836) British jurist. An opinion given while Advocate-General. Attrib.; also quoted by Benjamin Disraeli (1848)

8 Preachers say, Do as I say, not as I do. But if the physician had the same disease upon him that I have, and he should bid me do one thing, and himself do quite another, could I believe him?
John Selden (1584–1654) English historian. *Table Talk*

9 Do not, as some ungracious pastors do,
Show me the steep and thorny way to heaven,
Whiles, like a puff'd and reckless libertine,
Himself the primrose path of dalliance treads
And recks not his own rede.
William Shakespeare (1564–1616) English dramatist. *Hamlet,* I:3

10 *Dans ce pays-ci, il est bon de tuer de temps en temps un amiral pour encourager les autres.*
In this country it is good to kill an admiral from time to time, to encourage the others.
Voltaire (François-Marie Arouet; 1694–1778) French writer. Referring to England: Admiral Byng was executed for failing to defeat the French at Minorca (1757). *Candide*, Ch. 23

EXCELLENCE

See also superiority

1 Whatever is worth doing at all is worth doing well.
Earl of Chesterfield (1694–1773) English statesman. Letter to his son, 10 Mar 1746

2 The danger chiefly lies in acting well,
No crime's so great as daring to excel.
Charles Churchill (1731–64) British poet. *Epistle to William Hogarth*

3 If you had been mine when you were seven you would have been the crème de la crème.
Muriel Spark (1918–) British novelist. *The Prime of Miss Jean Brodie*, Ch. 2

4 The best is the enemy of the good.
Voltaire (François-Marie Arouet; 1694–1778) French writer. *Dictionnaire philosophique*, 'Art dramatique'

EXCESS

See also moderation

1 *L'embarras des richesses.*
A superfluity of good things.
Abbé Lénor Jean d'Allainval (1700–53) French dramatist. Play title

2 Nothing in excess.
Anonymous

3 What fun it would be to be poor, as long as one was *excessively* poor! Anything in excess is most exhilarating.
Jean Anouilh (1910–87) French dramatist. *Ring Round the Moon*

4 The road of excess leads to the palace of Wisdom.
William Blake (1757–1827) British poet. *The Marriage of Heaven and Hell*, 'Proverbs of Hell'

5 I would remind you that extremism in the defence of liberty is no vice. And let me remind you also that moderation in the pursuit of justice is no virtue!
Barry Goldwater (1904–) US politician. Speech, San Francisco, 17 July 1964

6 No part of the walls is left undecorated. From everywhere the praise of the Lord is drummed into you.
Nikolaus Pevsner (Bernhard Leon; 1902–83) German-born British art historian. *London, except the Cities of London and Westminster*

7 In baiting a mouse-trap with cheese, always leave room for the mouse.
Saki (Hector Hugh Munro; 1870–1916) British writer. *The Square Egg*

8 'Tis not the drinking that is to be blamed, but the excess.
John Selden (1584–1654) English historian. *Table Talk*

9 The lady doth protest too much, methinks.
William Shakespeare (1564–1616) English dramatist. *Hamlet*, III:2

10 It out-herods Herod.
William Shakespeare *Hamlet*, III:2

11 Well said; that was laid on with a trowel.
William Shakespeare *As You Like It*, I:2

12 To gild refined gold, to paint the lily,
To throw a perfume on the violet,
To smooth the ice, or add another hue
Unto the rainbow, or with taper-light
To seek the beauteous eye of heaven to garnish,
Is wasteful and ridiculous excess.
William Shakespeare *King John*, IV:2

13 Heat not a furnace for your foe so hot
That it do singe yourself. We may outrun
By violent swiftness that which we run at,
And lose by over-running.
William Shakespeare *Henry VIII*, I:1

14 Extreme *busyness*, whether at school or college, kirk or market, is a symptom of deficient vitality.
Robert Louis Stevenson (1850–94) Scottish writer. *Virginibus Puerisque*

15 Battering the gates of heaven with storms of prayer.
Alfred, Lord Tennyson (1809–92) British poet. *St Simeon Stylites*

16 Moderation is a fatal thing, Lady Hunstanton. Nothing succeeds like excess.
Oscar Wilde (1854–1900) Irish-born British dramatist. *A Woman of No Importance*, III

17 ... belching from daily excess he came hiccupping to the war.
William of Malmesbury (c. 1080–c. 1143) English cleric and historian. Referring to Philip I of France. *Gesta Regum*, Bk. II

EXCUSES

1 Oh no, thank you, I only smoke on special occasions.
Anonymous Labour minister dining with King George VI, when offered a cigar.

2 If you please, ma'am, it was a very little one.
Captain Frederick Marryat (1792–1848) British novelist. Said by the nurse to excuse the fact that she had had an illegitimate baby. *Mr. Midshipman Easy*, Ch. 3

3 But I wasn't kissing her. I was whispering in her mouth.
Chico Marx (1886–1961) US comedian. When his wife caught him kissing a chorus girl. *The Marx Brothers Scrapbook* (G. Marx and R. Anobile)

4 Tell him I've been too fucking busy – or vice versa.
Dorothy Parker (1893–1967) US writer. When asked why she had not delivered her copy on time. *You Might As Well Live* (J. Keats)

5 Had I been brighter, the ladies been gentler, the Scotch been weaker, had the gods been kinder, had the dice been hotter, this could have been a one-sentence story: Once upon a time I lived happily ever after.
Mickey Rooney (1920–) US actor. Attrib.

6 I am as drunk as a lord, but then, I am one, so what does it matter?
Bertrand Russell (1872–1970) British philosopher. *Bertrand Russell, Philosopher of the Century* (Ralph Schoenman)

EXECUTION

See also last words, martyrdom, punishment

1 The parliament intended to have hanged him; and he expected no less, but resolved to be hanged with the Bible under one arm and Magna Carta under the other.
John Aubrey (1626–97) English antiquary. David Jenkins (1582–1663), a Welsh judge and royalist, was imprisoned by parliament (1645–60). *Brief Lives*, 'David Jenkins'

2 It's time for me to enjoy another pinch of snuff. Tomorrow my hands will be bound, so as to make it impossible.
Jean Sylvain Bailly (1736–93) French astronomer. Said on the evening before his execution. *Anekdotenschatz* (H. Hoffmeister)

3 And almost all things are by the law purged with blood; and without shedding of blood is no remission.
Bible: Hebrews 9:22

4 And when they were come to the place, which is called Calvary, there they crucified him, and the malefactors, one on the right hand, and the other on the left.
Bible: Luke 23:33

5 'Off with his head!'
Lewis Carroll (Charles Lutwidge Dodgson; 1832–98) British writer. *Alice's Adventures in Wonderland*, Ch. 8

6 I die a Christian, according to the Profession of the Church of England, as I found it left me by my Father.
Charles I (1600–49) King of England. Speech on the scaffold, 30 Jan 1649

7 Thou wilt show my head to the people: it is worth showing.
Georges Jacques Danton (1759–94) French political activist. Said as he mounted the scaffold, 5 Apr 1794. *French Revolution* (Carlyle), Bk. VI, Ch. 2

8 It is a far, far, better thing that I do, than I have ever done; it is a far, far, better rest that I go to, than I have ever known.
Charles Dickens (1812–70) British novelist. Said by Sydney Carton. *A Tale of Two Cities*, Bk. II, Ch. 15

9 To die for faction is a common evil,
But to be hanged for nonsense is the Devil.
John Dryden (1631–1700) British poet and dramatist. *Absalom and Achitophel*, II

10 This year, that is to mean ye 18 day of February, the Duke of Clarence and second brother to the king, then being prisoner in ye Tower, was secretly put to death and drowned in a barrel of malvesye within the said Tower.
Robert Fabyan (d. 1513) English chronicler. This account is apocryphal and reflects popular rumour. *Chronicle*

11 Oh let that day from time be blotted quite,
And let belief of't in next age be waived.
In deepest silence th'act concealed might,
So that the Kingdom's credit might be saved.

But if the Power Divine permitted this,
His Will's the law and ours must acquiesce.
Lord Thomas Fairfax (1612–71) General. Referring to the execution of Charles I. *The Faber Book of English History in Verse* (Kenneth Baker)

12 Son of Saint Louis, ascend to heaven.
Abbé Edgeworth de Firmont (1745–1807) Irish-born confessor to Louis XVI. Said to Louis XVI as he climbed up to the guillotine. Attrib.

13 Let them bestow on every airth a limb;
Then open all my veins, that I may swim
To thee, my Maker! in that crimson lake;
Then place my parboiled head upon a stake –
Scatter my ashes – strew them in the air; –
Lord! since thou know'st where all these atoms are,
I'm hopeful thou'lt recover once my dust,
And confident thou'lt raise me with the just.
James Graham (1612–50) Scottish general. Lines written on the window of his jail the night before his execution.

14 And in that journey was Owen Tudor taken and brought unto Haverfordwest, and he was beheaded at the market place, and his head set upon the highest grice of the market cross, and a mad woman combed his hair and washed away the blood of his face, and she got candles and set about him burning more than a hundred.
William Gregory (d. 1467) Chronicler. Owen Tudor was the grandfather of Henry VII. *Gregory's Chronicle*

15 And have they fixed the where and when?
And shall Trelawny die?
Here's twenty thousand Cornish men
Will know the reason why!
R. S. Hawker (1803–75) British poet. Referring to the imprisonment (1688) of Trelawny, Bishop of Bristol, by James II. *Song of the Western Men*

16 They hang us now in Shrewsbury jail:
The whistles blow forlorn,
And trains all night groan on the rail
To men that die at morn.
A. E. Housman (1859–1936) British scholar and poet. *A Shropshire Lad*, 'Reveillé'

17 O holy simplicity!
John Huss (Jan Hus; c. 1369–1415) Bohemian religious reformer. On noticing a peasant adding a faggot to the pile at his execution. *Apophthegmata* (Zincgreff-Weidner), Pt. III

18 Depend upon it, Sir, when a man knows he is to be hanged in a fortnight, it concentrates his mind wonderfully.
Samuel Johnson (1709–84) British lexicographer. *Life of Johnson* (J. Boswell), Vol. III

19 If we are to abolish the death penalty, I should like to see the first step taken by our friends the murderers.
Alphonse Karr (1808–90) French writer. *Les Guêpes*, Jan 1849

20 'For they're hangin' Danny Deever, you can hear the Dead March play,
The Regiment's in 'ollow square – they're hangin' 'im to-day;
They've taken of 'is buttons off an' cut 'is stripes away,
An' they're hangin' Danny Deever in the mornin'.'
Rudyard Kipling (1865–1936) Indian-born British writer. *Danny Deever*

21 Be of good comfort, Master Ridley, and play the man; we shall this day light such a candle, by God's grace, in England as I trust shall never be put out.
Hugh Latimer (1485–1555) English churchman. Said to Nicholas Ridley as they were about to be burnt at the stake for heresy. *Famous Last Words* (B. Conrad)

22 He nothing common did or mean
Upon that memorable scene,
But with his keener eye
The axe's edge did try.
Andrew Marvell (1621–78) English poet. Referring to the execution of Charles I. *An Horatian Ode upon Cromwell's Return from Ireland*

23 Do not hack me as you did my Lord Russell.
Duke of Monmouth (1649–85) An illegitimate son of Charles II. Said to the headsman before his execution. *History of England* (Macaulay), Vol. I, Ch. 5

24 I cumber you goode Margaret muche, but I woulde be sorye, if it shoulde be any lenger than to morrowe, for it is S. Thomas evin and the vtas of Sainte Peter and therefore to morowe longe I to goe to God, it were a daye very meete and conveniente for me. I neuer liked your maner towarde me better then when you kissed me laste for I loue when doughterly loue and deere charitie hathe no laisor to looke to worldely curtesye. Fare well my deere childe and praye for me, and I shall for you and all your friendes that we maie merily meete in heaven.

Thomas More (1478–1535) English lawyer and scholar. Last letter to Margaret Roper, his daughter, on the eve of his execution on 6 July 1535

25 I pray you, Master Lieutenant, see me safe up, and for coming down let me shift for myself.

Thomas More On climbing onto the scaffold prior to his execution. *Life of Sir Thomas More* (William Roper)

26 Pluck up thy spirits, man, and be not afraid to do thine office; my neck is very short; take heed therefore thou strike not awry, for saving of thine honesty.

Thomas More Said to the headsman. *Life of Sir Thomas More* (Roper)

27 This hath not offended the king.

Thomas More Said as he drew his beard aside before putting his head on the block

28 The sight of it gave me infinite pleasure, as it proved that I was in a civilized society.

Mungo Park (1771–1806) Scottish explorer. Remark on finding a gibbet in an unexplored part of Africa. Attrib.

29 I went out to Charing Cross, to see Major-general Harrison hanged, drawn, and quartered; which was done there, he looking as cheerful as any man could do in that condition.

Samuel Pepys (1633–1703) English diarist. *Diary*, 13 Oct 1660

30 The world itself is but a large prison, out of which some are daily led to execution.

Walter Raleigh (1554–1618) English explorer. Said after his trial for treason, 1603. Attrib.

31 Even such is Time, that takes in trust
Our youth, our joys, our all we have,
And pays us but with age and dust;
Who in the dark and silent grave,
When we have wandered all our ways,
Shuts up the story of our days;
But from this earth, this grave, this dust,
My God shall raise me up, I trust.

Walter Raleigh Written on the night before his execution. Attrib.

32 So the heart be right, it is no matter which way the head lies.

Walter Raleigh On laying his head on the executioner's block. Attrib.

33 Tis a sharp remedy, but a sure one for all ills.

Walter Raleigh Referring to the executioner's axe just before he was beheaded. Attrib.

34 If you give me six lines written by the most honest man, I will find something in them to hang him.

Cardinal Richelieu (1585–1642) French statesman. Exact wording uncertain. Attrib.

35 *'O liberté! O liberté! Que de crimes on commet en ton nom!'*
Oh liberty! Oh liberty! What crimes are committed in thy name!

Madame Roland (1754–93) French revolutionary. Said as she mounted the steps of the guillotine. Attrib.

36 I will burn, but this is a mere incident. We shall continue our discussion in eternity.

Michael Servetus (1511–53) Spanish physician and theologian. Comment to the judges of the Inquisition after being condemned to be burned at the stake as a heretic. *Borges: A Reader* (E. Monegal)

37 FIRST CLOWN: What is he that builds stronger than either the mason, the shipwright, or the carpenter?
SECOND CLOWN: The gallows-maker; for that frame outlives a thousand tenants.

William Shakespeare (1564–1616) English dramatist. *Hamlet*, V:1

38 Then, with that faint fleeting smile playing about his lips, he faced the firing squad; erect and motionless, proud and disdainful, Walter Mitty, the undefeated, inscrutable to the last.

James Thurber (1894–1961) US humorist. *My World and Welcome to It*, 'The Secret Life of Walter Mitty'

EXISTENCE

1 Dear Sir, Your astonishment's odd:
I am always about in the Quad.
And that's why the tree
Will continue to be,
Since observed by Yours faithfully,
God.

Anonymous The response to KNOX's limerick

2 Let us be moral. Let us contemplate existence.

Charles Dickens (1812–70) British novelist. *Martin Chuzzlewit*, Ch. 10

3 As far as we can discern, the sole purpose of human existence is to kindle a light in the darkness of mere being.

Carl Gustav Jung (1875–1961) Swiss psychoanalyst. *Memories, Dreams, Reflections*, Ch. 11

4 There once was a man who said 'God
Must think it exceedingly odd
If he find that this tree
Continues to be
When there's no one about in the Quad.'

Ronald Knox (1888–1957) British Roman Catholic priest. For a reply, *see* ANONYMOUS. Attrib.

5 I know perfectly well that I don't want to do anything; to do something is to create existence – and there's quite enough existence as it is.

Jean-Paul Sartre (1905–80) French writer. *Nausea*

EXPECTATION

See also anticipation, disappointment, hope

1 We joined the Navy to see the world,
And what did we see? We saw the sea.

Irving Berlin (1888–) US composer and lyricist. *Follow the Fleet*, 'We Saw the Sea'

2 For there is good news yet to hear and fine things to be seen,
Before we go to Paradise by way of Kensal Green.

G. K. Chesterton (1874–1936) British writer. *The Rolling English Road*

3 As I know more of mankind I expect less of them, and am ready now to call a man *a good man*, upon easier terms than I was formerly.

Samuel Johnson (1709–84) British lexicographer. *Life of Johnson* (J. Boswell), Vol. IV

4 This dumb ox will fill the whole world with his bellowing.

Albertus Magnus (c. 1200–80) German bishop. Referring to his pupil Thomas Aquinas, whose nickname was 'The Dumb Ox'. *Aquinas* (A. Kenny)

5 Dear Mary, We all knew you had it in you.

Dorothy Parker (1893–1967) US writer. Telegram sent to a friend on the successful outcome of her much-publicized pregnancy

6 'Blessed is the man who expects nothing, for he shall never be disappointed' was the ninth beatitude.

Alexander Pope (1688–1744) British poet. Letter to Fortescue, 23 Sept 1725

7 See yon pale stripling! when a boy,
A mother's pride, a father's joy!

Walter Scott (1771–1832) Scottish novelist. *Rokeby*, III

8 Gomer Owen who kissed her once by the pig-sty when she wasn't looking and never kissed her again although she was looking all the time.
Dylan Thomas (1914–53) Welsh poet. *Under Milk Wood*

EXPEDIENCY

1 Half a loaf is better than no bread.
Proverb

2 The end justifies the means.
Proverb

3 The shoemaker's son always goes barefoot.
Proverb

4 You can't make an omelette without breaking eggs.
Proverb

5 And my parents finally realize that I'm kidnapped and they snap into action immediately: they rent out my room.
Woody Allen (Allen Stewart Konigsberg; 1935–) US film actor. *Woody Allen and His Comedy* (E. Lax)

6 I would rather be an opportunist and float than go to the bottom with my principles round my neck.
Stanley Baldwin (1867–1947) British statesman. Attrib.

7 Now Caiaphas was he, which gave counsel to the Jews, that it was expedient that one man should die for the people.
Bible: John 18:14

8 Nobody is forgotten when it is convenient to remember him.
Benjamin Disraeli (1804–81) British statesman. Attrib.

9 You can't learn too soon that the most useful thing about a principle is that it can always be sacrificed to expediency.
W. Somerset Maugham (1874–1965) British novelist. *The Circle*, III

10 No man is justified in doing evil on the ground of expediency.
Theodore Roosevelt (1858–1919) US Republican president. *The Strenuous Life*

11 Well, a widow, I see, is a kind of sinecure.
William Wycherley (1640–1716) English dramatist. *The Plain Dealer*, V:3

EXPERIENCE

See also history, past

1 A young physician fattens the churchyard.
Proverb

2 Experience is the best teacher.
Proverb

3 Experience is the mother of science.
Proverb

4 Experience is the mother of wisdom.
Proverb

5 Live and learn.
Proverb

6 Practice makes perfect.
Proverb

7 Experience is a good teacher, but she sends in terrific bills.
Minna Antrim (1861–?) US writer. *Naked Truth and Veiled Allusions*

8 One should try everything once, except incest and folk-dancing.
Arnold Bax (1883–1953) British composer. *Farewell to My Youth*

9 You will think me lamentably crude: my experience of life has been drawn from life itself.
Max Beerbohm (1872–1956) British writer. *Zuleika Dobson*, Ch. 7

10 Experience isn't interesting till it begins to repeat itself – in fact, till it does that, it hardly *is* experience.
Elizabeth Bowen (1899–1973) Irish novelist. *The Death of the Heart*, Pt. I, Ch. 1

11 When all is said and done, no literature can outdo the cynicism of real life; you won't intoxicate with one glass someone who has already drunk up a whole barrel.
Anton Chekhov (1860–1904) Russian dramatist. Letter, 1887

12 If men could learn from history, what lessons it might teach us! But passion and party blind our eyes and the light which experience gives is a lantern on the stern, which shines only on the waves behind us!
Samuel Taylor Coleridge (1772–1834) British poet. *Recollections* (Allsop)

13 An experience of women which extends over many nations and three continents.
Arthur Conan Doyle (1856–1930) British writer. *The Sign of Four*

14 How many roads must a man walk down
Before you call him a man?
Bob Dylan (Robert Allen Zimmerman; 1941–) US popular singer. *Blowin' in the Wind*

15 As for me, I see no such great cause why I should either be fond to live or fear to die. I have had good experience of this world, and I know what it is to be a subject and what to be a sovereign. Good neighbours I have had, and I have met with bad: and in trust I have found treason.
Elizabeth I (1533–1603) Queen of England. Speech to Parliament, 1586

16 What experience and history teach is this – that people and governments never have learned anything from history, or acted on principles deduced from it.
Hegel (1770–1831) German philosopher. *Philosophy of History*, Introduction

17 A moment's insight is sometimes worth a life's experience.
Oliver Wendell Holmes (1809–94) US writer. *The Professor at the Breakfast Table*, Ch. 10

18 Experience is never limited, and it is never complete; it is an immense sensibility, a kind of huge spider-web of the finest silken threads suspended in the chamber of consciousness, and catching every air-borne particle in its tissue.
Henry James (1843–1916) US novelist. *Partial Portraits*, 'The Art of Fiction'

19 Nothing ever becomes real till it is experienced – even a proverb is no proverb to you till your life has illustrated it.
John Keats (1795–1821) British poet. Letter to George and Georgiana Keats, 19 Mar 1819

20 He was what I often think is a dangerous thing for a statesman to be – a student of history; and like most of those who study history, he learned from the mistakes of the past how to make new ones.
A. J. P. Taylor (1906–) British historian. Referring to Napoleon III. *The Listener*, 6 June 1963

21 Nourishing a youth sublime
With the fairy tales of science, and the long result of Time.
Alfred, Lord Tennyson (1809–92) British poet. *Locksley Hall*

22 All experience is an arch wherethro'
Gleams that untravelled world, whose margin fades

For ever and for ever when I move.
Alfred, Lord Tennyson *Ulysses*

23 You don't set a fox to watching the chickens just because he has a lot of experience in the hen house.
Harry S. Truman (1884–1972) US statesman. Referring to Vice-President Nixon's nomination for President. Speech, 30 Oct 1960

24 I have learned
To look on nature, not as in the hour
Of thoughtless youth; but hearing oftentimes
The still, sad music of humanity.
William Wordsworth (1770–1850) British poet. *Lines composed a few miles above Tintern Abbey*

EXPERTS

1 By studying the masters – not their pupils.
Niels Henrik Abel (1809–29) Norwegian mathematician. When asked how he had become a great mathematician so quickly. *Men of Mathematics* (E. T. Bell)

2 Patients consult so-called authorities. And I have become one also. Yet, we don't know more than the others. We are only the prey of hypochondriacs.
August Bier (1861–1949) Aphorism

3 An expert is a man who has made all the mistakes, which can be made, in a very narrow field.
Niels Bohr (1885–1962) Danish physicist. Attrib.

4 An expert is someone who knows some of the worst mistakes that can be made in his subject, and how to avoid them.
Werner Heisenberg (1901–76) German physicist. *Physics and Beyond*

5 An accomplished man to his fingertips.
Horace (Quintus Horatius Flaccus; 65–8 BC) Roman poet. *Satires*, I

6 One who limits himself to his chosen mode of ignorance.
Elbert Hubbard (1856–1915) US writer and editor.

7 Specialist – A man who knows more and more about less and less.
William James Mayo (1861–1934) US surgeon. Also attributed to Nicholas Butler

8 The trouble with specialists is that they tend to think in grooves.
Elaine Morgan (1920–) British writer. *The Descent of Woman*, Ch. 1

EXPLANATIONS

1 You will find in politics that you are much exposed to the attribution of false motives. Never complain and never explain.
Stanley Baldwin, 1st Earl of Bewdley (1867–1947) British Conservative prime minister. Quoting Disraeli. Said to Harold Nicolson, 21 July 1943

2 The doggie in front has suddenly gone blind, and the other one has very kindly offered to push him all the way to St Dunstan's.
Noël Coward (1899–1973) British dramatist. To a small child, who asked what two dogs were doing together in the street. St Dunstan's is a British institution for the blind. *Two Hands Clapping* (K. Tynan)

3 Never explain: your friends don't need it and your enemies won't believe it.
Victor Grayson (1881–?1920) British Labour politician. Attrib.

4 I am one of those unfortunates to whom death is less hideous than explanations.
D. B. Wyndham Lewis (1891–1969) British journalist and writer. *Welcome to All This*

5 There is occasions and causes why and wherefore in all things.
William Shakespeare (1564–1616) English dramatist. *Henry V*, V:1

EXPLOITATION

1 Thus the devil played at chess with me, and yielding a pawn, thought to gain a queen of me, taking advantage of my honest endeavours.
Thomas Browne (1605–82) English physician and writer. *Religio Medici*, Pt. I

2 Mortals, whose pleasures are their only care,
First wish to be imposed on, and then are.
William Cowper (1731–1800) British poet. *The Progress of Error*

3 I should be trading on the blood of my men.
Robert E. Lee (1807–70) US general. Refusing to write his memoirs. *Nobody Said It Better* (M. Ringo)

EXPLORATION

See also discovery

1 The fair breeze blew, the white foam flew,
The furrow followed free:
We were the first that ever burst
Into that silent sea.
Samuel Taylor Coleridge (1772–1834) British poet. *The Rime of the Ancient Mariner*, II

2 Go West, young man, and grow up with the country.
Horace Greeley (1811–72) US politician and journalist. Also attributed to the US writer John Soule (1815–91), *Terre Haute* (Indiana) *Express*, 1851. *Hints toward Reform*

3 Nothing easier. One step beyond the pole, you see, and the north wind becomes a south one.
Robert Edwin Peary (1856–1920) US explorer. Explaining how he knew he had reached the North Pole. Attrib.

4 Had we lived, I should have had a tale to tell of the hardihood, endurance, and courage of my companions which would have stirred the heart of every Englishman. These rough notes and our dead bodies must tell the tale.
Captain Robert Falcon Scott (1868–1912) British explorer. *Message to the Public*

5 Dr Livingstone, I presume?
Henry Morton Stanley (1841–1904) British explorer. On finding David Livingstone at Ujiji on Lake Tanganyika, Nov 1871. *How I found Livingstone*, Ch. 11

EXTRAORDINARY

1 Little minds are interested in the extraordinary; great minds in the commonplace.
Elbert Hubbard (1856–1915) US writer. *Roycroft Dictionary and Book of Epigrams*

EXTRAVAGANCE

See also excess, luxury, money, ostentation, thrift, waste

1 Riches are for spending.
Francis Bacon (1561–1626) English philosopher. *Essays*, 'Of Expense'

2 All progress is based upon a universal innate desire on the part of every organism to live beyond its income.
Samuel Butler (1835–1902) British writer. *Notebooks*

3 He sometimes forgets that he is Caesar, but I always remember that I am Caesar's daughter.
Julia (39 BC–AD 14) Daughter of Augustus. Replying to suggestions that she should live in the simple style of her father, which contrasted with her own extravagance. *Saturnalia* (Macrobius)

4 All decent people live beyond their incomes nowadays, and those who aren't respectable live beyond other

people's. A few gifted individuals manage to do both.

Saki (Hector Hugh Munro; 1870–1916) British writer. *The Match-Maker*

5 I suppose that I shall have to die beyond my means.

Oscar Wilde (1854–1900) Irish-born British dramatist. When told that an operation would be expensive. He is also believed to have said 'I am dying beyond my means' on accepting a glass of champagne as he lay on his deathbed. *Life of Wilde* (Sherard)

EYES

See also appearance

1 The eyes are the window of the soul.

Proverb

2 Our sight is the most perfect and most delightful of all our senses. It fills the mind with the largest variety of ideas, converses with its objects at the greatest distance, and continues the longest in action without being tired or satiated with its proper enjoyments.

Joseph Addison (1672–1719) British essayist. *The Spectator*, 411

3 It needs no dictionary of quotations to remind me that the eyes are the windows of the soul.

Max Beerbohm (1872–1956) British writer. *Zuleika Dobson*, Ch. 4

4 The eye of him that hath seen me shall see me no more: thine eyes are upon me, and I am not.

Bible: Job 7:8

5 That youthful sparkle in his eyes is caused by his contact lenses, which he keeps highly polished.

Sheilah Graham Referring to Ronald Reagan. *The Times*, 22 Aug 1981

6 Jeepers Creepers – where'd you get them peepers?

Johnny Mercer (1909–76) US lyricist and composer. *Jeepers Creepers*

7 Who formed the curious texture of the eye,
And cloath'd it with the various tunicles,
And texture exquisite; with chrystal juice
Supply'd it, to transmit the rays of light?

Henry Needler (1685–1760) *A Poem to Prove the Certainty of a God*

8 Out vile jelly!
Where is thy lustre now?

William Shakespeare (1564–1616) English dramatist. Spoken by Cornwall as he puts out Gloucester's remaining eye. *King Lear*, III:7

F

FACTS

See also truth

1 Now, what I want is Facts . . .
Facts alone are wanted in life.

Charles Dickens (1812–70) British novelist. *Hard Times*, Bk. I, Ch. 1

2 Facts are not science – as the dictionary is not literature.

Martin H. Fischer (1879–1962) *Fischerisms* (Howard Fabing and Ray Marr)

3 Facts do not cease to exist because they are ignored.

Aldous Huxley (1894–1964) British novelist. *Proper Studies*

4 Facts are ventriloquists' dummies. Sitting on a wise man's knee they may be made to utter words of wisdom; elsewhere they say nothing or talk nonsense.

Aldous Huxley *Time Must Have A Stop*

5 Once a newspaper touches a story, the facts are lost forever, even to the protagonists.

Norman Mailer (1923–) US writer. *The Presidential Papers*

6 Its primary office is the gathering of news. At the peril of its soul it must see that the supply is not tainted. Neither in what it gives, nor in what it does not give, nor in the mode of presentation, must the unclouded face of truth suffer wrong. Comment is free but facts are sacred.

C. P. Scott (1846–1932) British journalist. *Manchester Guardian*, 6 May 1926

7 Facts speak louder than statistics.

Geoffrey Streatfield (1897–1978) British lawyer. *The Observer*, 'Sayings of the Week', 19 Mar 1950

8 The Doctor said that Death was but
A scientific fact.

Oscar Wilde (1854–1900) *The Ballad of Reading Gaol*

FAILURE

See also success

1 A miss is as good as a mile.

Proverb

2 Well, back to the old drawing board.

Peter Arno (1904–68) US cartoonist. Caption to a cartoon of people leaving a crashed plane. *New Yorker*

3 Dear Randolph, utterly unspoiled by failure.

Noël Coward (1899–1973) British dramatist. Referring to Randolph Churchill. Attrib.

4 She knows there's no success like failure
And that failure's no success at all.

Bob Dylan (Robert Allen Zimmerman; 1941–) US popular singer. *Love Minus Zero No Limit*

5 Here lies Joseph, who failed in everything he undertook.

Joseph II (1741–90) Holy Roman Emperor. Suggesting his own epitaph when reflecting upon the disappointment of his hopes for reform. Attrib.

6 Show me a good and gracious loser and I'll show you a failure.

Knute Rockne (1888–1931) US football coach. Attrib.

7 Like a dull actor now
I have forgot my part and I am out,
Even to a full disgrace.

William Shakespeare (1564–1616) English dramatist. *Coriolanus*, V:3

8 Failure? Do you remember what Queen Victoria once said? 'Failure? – the possibilities do not exist.'

Margaret Thatcher (1925–) British politician and prime minister. Queen Victoria had been speaking about the Boer War. TV news interview, at start of Falklands War, 5 Apr 1982

9 The crime is not to avoid failure. The crime is not to give triumph a chance.

Huw Wheldon (1916–86) British broadcaster and TV executive. Advice given to television producers. Attrib.

FAIRIES

See also supernatural

1 Every time a child says 'I don't believe in fairies' there is a little

fairy somewhere that falls down dead.

J. M. Barrie (1860–1937) British novelist and dramatist. *Peter Pan*

2 When the first baby laughed for the first time, the laugh broke into a thousand pieces and they all went skipping about, and that was the beginning of fairies.

J. M. Barrie *Peter Pan*

3 Do you believe in fairies? Say quick that you believe. If you believe, clap your hands!

J. M. Barrie *Peter Pan*

4 There are fairies at the bottom of our garden.

Rose Fyleman (1877–1957) British writer. *Fairies and Chimneys*

5 In a hole in the ground there lived a hobbit.

J. R. R. Tolkien (1892–1973) British writer. *The Hobbit*, Ch. 1

FAIRNESS

1 Never give a sucker an even break.

W. C. Fields (1880–1946) US comedian. Film title

2 We are reasonable. We have always been reasonable. We are noted for our sweet reasonableness.

The Rev. Ian Paisley (1926–) British politician. *The Observer*, 'Sayings of the Week', 11 May 1975

FAITH

See also belief, faithfulness, God, religion

1 Faith will move mountains.

Proverb

2 For we walk by faith, not by sight.

Bible: II Corinthians 5:7

3 Now faith is the substance of things hoped for, the evidence of things not seen.

Bible: Hebrews 11:1

4 These all died in faith, not having received the promises, but having seen them afar off, and were persuaded of them, and embraced them, and confessed that they were strangers and pilgrims on the earth.

Bible: Hebrews 11:13

5 By faith the walls of Jericho fell down, after they were compassed about seven days.

Bible: Hebrews 11:30

6 Even so faith, if it hath not works, is dead, being alone.

Bible: James 2:17

7 The prayer of faith shall save the sick.

Bible: James 5:15

8 And Jesus said unto them, I am the bread of life: he that cometh to me shall never hunger; and he that believeth on me shall never thirst.

Bible: John 6:35

9 And his disciples came to him, and awoke him, saying, Lord, save us: we perish.
And he saith unto them, Why are ye fearful, O ye of little faith? Then he arose, and rebuked the winds and the sea; and there was a great calm.

Bible: Matthew 8:25–26

10 Fight the good fight of faith, lay hold on eternal life, whereunto thou art also called, and hast professed a good profession before many witnesses.

Bible: I Timothy 6:12

11 For I am now ready to be offered, and the time of my departure is at hand.
I have fought a good fight, I have finished my course, I have kept the faith:
Henceforth there is laid up for me a crown of righteousness, which the Lord, the righteous judge, shall give me at that day: and not to me only, but unto all them also that love his appearing.

Bible: II Timothy 4:6–8

12 I feel no need for any other faith than my faith in human beings.

Pearl Buck (1892–1973) US novelist. *I Believe*

13 The prayer that reforms the sinner and heals the sick is an absolute faith that all things are possible to God – a spiritual understanding of Him, an unselfed love.

Mary Baker Eddy (1821–1910) US religious leader. *Science and Health, with Key to the Scriptures*

14 It's only a paper moon,
Sailing over a cardboard sea,
But it wouldn't be make-believe
If you believed in me.

E. Y. Harburg (1898–1981) US lyricist. *The Great Magoo*, 'It's Only a Paper Moon'

15 And I said to the man who stood at the gate of the year: 'Give me a light that I may tread safely into the unknown'. And he replied: 'Go out into the darkness and put your hand into the hand of God. That shall be to you better than light and safer than a known way.'

Minnie Louise Haskins (1875–1957) US writer. Remembered because it was quoted by George VI in his Christmas broadcast, 1939. *The Desert*, Introduction

16 So long as the body is affected through the mind, no audacious device, even of the most manifestly dishonest character, can fail of producing occasional good to those who yield it an implicit or even a partial faith.

Oliver Wendell Holmes (1809–94) US writer and physician. *Medical Essays*, 'Homoeopathy and its Kindred Delusions'

17 If I said that God did not send me, I should condemn myself; truly God did send me.

St Joan of Arc (c. 1412–31) French patriotic leader. Said at her trial

18 My dear child, you must believe in God in spite of what the clergy tell you.

Benjamin Jowett (1817–93) British theologian. *Autobiography* (Asquith), Ch. 8

19 Booth died blind and still by faith he trod,
Eyes still dazzled by the ways of God.

Vachel Lindsay (1879–1931) US poet. *General William Booth Enters Heaven*

20 Be a sinner and sin strongly, but more strongly have faith and rejoice in Christ.

Martin Luther (1483–1546) German Protestant. Letter to Melanchthon

21 Faith may be defined briefly as an illogical belief in the occurrence of the improbable.

H. L. Mencken (1880–1956) US journalist. *Prejudices*, 'Types of Men'

22 It takes a long while for a naturally trustful person to reconcile himself to the idea that after all God will not help him.

H. L. Mencken *Notebooks*, 'Minority Report'

23 Lead, kindly Light, amid the encircling gloom,
Lead thou me on;
The night is dark, and I am far from home,
Lead thou me on.

Cardinal Newman (1801–90) British theologian. *Lead Kindly Light*

24 Nothing in life is more wonderful than faith – the one great moving force which we can neither weigh in the balance nor test in the crucible.

Sir William Osler (1849–1919) Canadian physician. *British Medical Journal*, 1:1470, 1910

25 God and the Doctor we alike adore
But only when in danger, not before;
The danger o'er, both are alike requited,
God is forgotten, and the Doctor slighted.

Robert Owen (1771–1838) British social reformer. Epigram

26 Even such is Time, that takes in trust
Our youth, our joys, our all we have,
And pays us but with age and dust;
Who in the dark and silent grave,
When we have wandered all our ways,
Shuts up the story of our days;
But from this earth, this grave, this dust,
My God shall raise me up, I trust.

Walter Raleigh (1554–1618) English explorer. Written on the night before his execution. Attrib.

27 *Dieu et mon droit.*
God and my right.

Richard I Motto on the royal arms of Great Britain; originally used as a war-cry, Sept 1198

28 A miracle is an event which creates faith. Frauds deceive. An event which creates faith does not deceive; therefore it is not a fraud, but a miracle.

George Bernard Shaw (1856–1950) Irish dramatist and critic. *St Joan*

29 'Tis not the dying for a faith that's so hard, Master Harry – every man of every nation has done that – 'tis the living up to it that is difficult.

William Makepeace Thackeray (1811–63) British novelist. *Henry Esmond*, Ch. 6

30 Life is doubt, and faith without doubt is nothing but death.

Miguel de Unamuno y Jugo (1864–1936) Spanish writer and philosopher. *Poesías*

31 There can be no scientific dispute with respect to faith, for science and faith exclude one another.

Rudolf Virchow (1821–1902) German pathologist. *Disease, Life, and Man*, 'On Man'

32 Faith consists in believing when it is beyond the power of reason to believe. It is not enough that a thing be possible for it to be believed.

Voltaire (François-Marie Arouet; 1694–1778) French writer. *Questions sur l'encyclopédie*

FAITHFULNESS

See also loyalty

1 It is better to be unfaithful than faithful without wanting to be.

Brigitte Bardot (1934–) French film actress. *The Observer*, 'Sayings of the Week', 18 Feb 1968

2 Through perils both of wind and limb,
Through thick and thin she follow'd him.

Samuel Butler (1612–80) English satirist. *Hudibras*, Pt. II

3 I have been faithful to thee, Cynara! in my fashion.

Ernest Dowson (1867–1900) British lyric poet. *Non Sum Qualis Eram Bonae Sub Regno Cynarae*

4 We only part to meet again.
Change, as ye list, ye winds; my heart shall be
The faithful compass that still points to thee.

John Gay (1685–1732) English poet and dramatist. *Sweet William's Farewell*

5 But I'm always true to you, darlin', in my fashion,
Yes, I'm always true to you, darlin', in my way.

Cole Porter (1893–1964) US songwriter. *Kiss Me, Kate*, 'Always True to You in My Fashion'

6 God pardon all oaths that are broke to me!
God keep all vows unbroke are made to thee!

William Shakespeare (1564–1616) English dramatist. *Richard II*, IV:1

7 O heaven! were man
But constant, he were perfect.

William Shakespeare *Two Gentlemen of Verona*, V:4

FALL

See also months, seasons

1 Season of mists and mellow fruitfulness,
Close bosom-friend of the maturing sun;
Conspiring with him how to load and bless
With fruit the vines that round the thatch-eaves run.

John Keats (1795–1821) British poet. *To Autumn*

FALSENESS

1 It is impossible that a man who is false to his friends and neighbours should be true to the public.

Bishop Berkeley (1685–1753) Irish churchman and philosopher. *Maxims Concerning Patriotism*

2 Beware of false prophets, which come to you in sheep's clothing, but inwardly they are ravening wolves.

Bible: Matthew 7:15

3 The religions we call false were once true.

Ralph Waldo Emerson (1803–82) US poet and essayist. *Essays*, 'Character'

4 True and False are attributes of speech, not of things. And where speech is not, there is neither Truth nor Falsehood.

Thomas Hobbes (1588–1679) English philosopher. *Leviathan*, Pt. I, Ch. 4

5 Vain wisdom all, and false philosophy.

John Milton (1608–74) English poet. *Paradise Lost*, Bk. II

6 False face must hide what the false heart doth know.

William Shakespeare (1564–1616) English dramatist. *Macbeth*, I:7

7 Neither a borrower nor a lender be;
For loan oft loses both itself and friend,
And borrowing dulls the edge of husbandry.
This above all: to thine own self be true,
And it must follow, as the night the day,
Thou canst not then be false to any man.

William Shakespeare *Hamlet*, I:3

FAME

See also popularity, posterity, reputation

1 I agree with you that the name of Spiro Agnew is not a household name. I certainly hope that it will become one within the next couple of months.

Spiro T. Agnew (1918–) US Republican politician. TV interview, 8 Aug 1968

2 A celebrity is a person who works hard all his life to become known, then wears dark glasses to avoid being recognized.

Fred Allen (1894–1956) US comedian. *Treadmill to Oblivion*

3 Fame is like a river, that beareth

up things light and swollen, and drowns things weighty and solid.
Francis Bacon (1561–1626) English philosopher. *Essays*, 'Of Praise'

4 I should like one of these days to be so well known, so popular, so celebrated, so famous, that it would permit me . . . to break wind in society, and society would think it a most natural thing.
Honoré de Balzac (1799–1850) French novelist. Attrib.

5 The celebrity is a person who is known for his well-knownness.
Daniel J. Boorstin (1914–) US writer. *The Image*, 'From Hero to Celebrity: The Human Pseudo-event'

6 A best-seller was a book which somehow sold well simply because it was selling well.
Daniel J. Boorstin *The Image*, 'From Shapes to Shadows: Dissolving Forms'

7 I awoke one morning and found myself famous.
Lord Byron (1788–1824) British poet. Remark made after the publication of *Childe Harold's Pilgrimage* (1812). Entry in Memoranda

8 I don't care what you say about me, as long as you say *something* about me, and as long as you spell my name right.
George M. Cohan (1878–1942) US entertainer. *George M. Cohan* (J. McCabe)

9 Being a star has made it possible for me to get insulted in places where the average Negro could never hope to get insulted.
Sammy Davis Jnr (1925–) Black US singer. *Yes I Can*

10 If a man make a better mouse-trap than his neighbor, though he build his house in the woods, the world will make a beaten path to his door.
Ralph Waldo Emerson (1803–82) US poet and essayist. Attrib.

11 A big man has no time really to do anything but just sit and be big.
F. Scott Fitzgerald (1896–1940) US novelist. *This Side of Paradise*, Bk. III, Ch. 2

12 Fame is sometimes like unto a kind of mushroom, which Pliny recounts to be the greatest miracle in nature, because growing and having no root.
Thomas Fuller (1608–61) English historian. *The Holy State and the Profane State*

13 I'm into pop because I want to get rich, get famous and get laid.
Bob Geldof (1952–) Irish-born pop singer. Attrib.

14 Fame is a powerful aphrodisiac.
Graham Greene (1904–) British novelist. *Radio Times*, 10 Sept 1964

15 Every man has a lurking wish to appear considerable in his native place.
Samuel Johnson (1709–84) British lexicographer. Letter to Sir Joshua Reynolds. *Life of Johnson* (J. Boswell), Vol. II

16 One of the drawbacks of Fame is that one can never escape from it.
Nellie Melba (Helen Porter Mitchell; 1861–1931) Australian soprano. *Melodies and Memories*

17 Fame is the spur that the clear spirit doth raise
(That last infirmity of noble mind)
To scorn delights, and live laborious days.
John Milton (1608–74) English poet. *Lycidas*

18 'What are you famous *for*?'
'For nothing. I am just famous.'
Iris Murdoch (1919–) Irish-born British novelist. *The Flight from the Enchanter*

19 I'm never going to be famous . . . I don't do anything. Not one single thing. I used to bite my nails, but I don't even do that any more.
Dorothy Parker (1893–1967) US writer. *The Little Hours*

20 If you have to tell them who you are, you aren't anybody.
Gregory Peck (1916–) US film star. Remarking upon the failure of anyone in a crowded restaurant to recognize him. *Pieces of Eight* (S. Harris)

21 Cannes is where you lie on the beach and stare at the stars – or vice versa.
Rex Reed (1938–) US columnist and actor. Attrib.

22 The more you are talked about, the more you will wish to be talked about. The condemned murderer who is allowed to see the account of his trial in the Press is indignant if he finds a newspaper which has reported it inadequately. . . . Politicians and literary men are in the same case.
Bertrand Russell (1872–1970) British philosopher. *Human Society in Ethics and Politics*

23 Love of fame is the last thing even learned men can bear to be parted from.
Tacitus (c. 55–c. 120 AD) Roman historian. *Histories*, IV, 6

24 He had a genius for backing into the limelight.
Lowell Thomas (1892–1981) US author. Referring to T. E. Lawrence. *Lawrence of Arabia*

25 To famous men all the earth is a sepulchre.
Thucydides (c. 460–c. 400 BC) Greek historian and general. *History of the Peloponnesian War*, Bk. II, Ch. 43

26 The only man who wasn't spoilt by being lionized was Daniel.
Herbert Beerbohm Tree (1853–1917) British actor and theater manager. *Beerbohm Tree* (Hesketh Pearson)

27 When I pass my name in such large letters I blush, but at the same time instinctively raise my hat.
Herbert Beerbohm Tree *Beerbohm Tree* (Hesketh Pearson)

28 Even the youngest of us will know, in fifty years' time, exactly what we mean by 'a very Noel Coward sort of person'.
Kenneth Tynan (1927–80) British critic. *Curtains*

29 In the future, everyone will be famous for 15 minutes.
Andy Warhol (Andrew Warhola; 1926–87) US pop artist. Attrib.

30 There is only one thing in the world worse than being talked about, and that is not being talked about.
Oscar Wilde (1854–1900) Irish-born British dramatist. *The Picture of Dorian Gray*, Ch. 1

FAMILIARITY

1 Familiarity breeds contempt.
Proverb

2 No man is a hero to his valet.
Anne-Marie Bigot de Cornuel (1605–94) French society hostess. *Lettres de Mlle Aissé*, 13 Aug 1728

3 I've grown accustomed to the trace
Of something in the air,
Accustomed to her face.
Alan Jay Lerner (1918–86) US songwriter. *My Fair Lady*, II:6

4 I have been here before.
But when or how I cannot tell:
I know the grass beyond the door,
The sweet keen smell,
The sighing sound, the lights around the shore.
Dante Gabriel Rossetti (1828–82) British painter and poet. *Sudden Light*

5 He began to think the tramp a fine, brotherly, generous fellow. He was also growing accustomed to something – shall I call it an

olfactory bar – that had hitherto kept them apart.
H. G. Wells (1866–1946) British writer. *Bealby*, Pt. VI, Ch. 3

FAMILY

See also children

1 Blood is thicker than water.
Proverb

2 Every family has a skeleton in the cupboard.
Proverb

3 Like father, like son.
Proverb

4 The family that prays together stays together.
Proverb

5 There's a black sheep in every flock.
Proverb

6 Sir Walter, being strangely surprised and put out of his countenance at so great a table, gives his son a damned blow over the face. His son, as rude as he was, would not strike his father, but strikes over the face the gentleman that sat next to him and said 'Box about: 'twill come to my father anon'.
John Aubrey (1626–97) English antiquary. *Brief Lives*, 'Sir Walter Raleigh'

7 He that hath wife and children hath given hostages to fortune; for they are impediments to great enterprises, either of virtue or mischief.
Francis Bacon (1561–1626) English philosopher. *See also* LUCAN *Essays*, 'Of Marriage and Single Life'

8 The joys of parents are secret, and so are their griefs and fears.
Francis Bacon *Essays*, 'Of Parents and Children'

9 Fathers, provoke not your children to anger, lest they be discouraged.
Bible: Colossians 3:21

10 Behold, every one that useth proverbs shall use this proverb against thee, saying, As is the mother, so is her daughter.
Bible: Ezekiel 16:44–45

11 The sort of place everyone should send his mother-in-law for a month, all expenses paid.
Ian Botham (1955–) British cricketer. Referring to Pakistan. BBC Radio 2 interview, Mar 1984

12 Parents are the last people on earth who ought to have children.
Samuel Butler (1835–1902) British writer. *Notebooks*

13 I love all my children, but some of them I don't like.
Lillian Carter (1902–) The mother of Jimmy Carter. In *Woman*, 9 Apr 1977

14 If one is not going to take the necessary precautions to avoid having parents one must undertake to bring them up.
Quentin Crisp (1910–) British model, publicist, and writer. *The Naked Civil Servant*

15 Fate chooses your relations, you choose your friends.
Jacques Delille (1738–1813) French abbé and poet. *Malheur et pitié*, I

16 There are times when parenthood seems nothing but feeding the mouth that bites you.
Peter De Vries (1910–) US novelist. *Tunnel of Love*

17 It is a melancholy truth that even great men have their poor relations.
Charles Dickens (1812–70) British novelist. *Bleak House*, Ch. 28

18 Come mothers and fathers
Throughout the land
And don't criticize
What you can't understand.
Bob Dylan (Robert Allen Zimmerman; 1941–) US popular singer. *The Times They Are A-Changin'*

19 What a marvellous place to drop one's mother-in-law!
Marshal Foch (1851–1929) French soldier. Remark on being shown the Grand Canyon. Attrib.

20 The mother-child relationship is paradoxical and, in a sense, tragic. It requires the most intense love on the mother's side, yet this very love must help the child grow away from the mother and to become fully independent.
Erich Fromm (1900–80) US psychologist and philosopher.

21 Possessive parents rarely live long enough to see the fruits of their selfishness.
Alan Garner (1934–) British writer. *The Owl Service*

22 My father was frightened of his mother. I was frightened of my father, and I'm damned well going to make sure that my children are frightened of me.
George V (1865–1936) King of the United Kingdom (1910–36). Attrib.

23 And so do his sisters, and his cousins and his aunts!
His sisters and his cousins,
Whom he reckons up by dozens,
And his aunts!
W. S. Gilbert (1836–1911) British dramatist. *HMS Pinafore*, I

24 LEONTINE. An only son, sir, might expect more indulgence.
CROAKER. An only father, sir, might expect more obedience.
Oliver Goldsmith (1728–74) Irish-born British writer. *The Good-Natured Man*, I

25 A person may be indebted for a nose or an eye, for a graceful carriage or a voluble discourse, to a great-aunt or uncle, whose existence he has scarcely heard of.
William Hazlitt (1778–1830) British essayist. *On Personal Character*

26 Good families are generally worse than any others.
Anthony Hope (Sir Anthony Hope Hawkins; 1863–1933) British novelist. *The Prisoner of Zenda*, Ch. 1

27 But there, everything has its drawbacks, as the man said when his mother-in-law died, and they came down upon him for the funeral expenses.
Jerome K. Jerome (1859–1927) British humorist. *Three Men in a Boat*, Ch. 3

28 I was the seventh of nine children. When you come from that far down you have to struggle to survive.
Robert Kennedy (1925–68) US politician. *The Kennedy Neurosis* (B. G. Clinch)

29 A poor relation – is the most irrelevant thing in nature.
Charles Lamb (1775–1834) British essayist. *Last Essays of Elia*, 'Poor Relations'

30 They fuck you up, your mum and dad.
They may not mean to, but they do.
They fill you with the faults they had
And add some extra, just for you.
Philip Larkin (1922–85) British poet. *This be the Verse*

31 Far from being the basis of the good society, the family, with its

narrow privacy and tawdry secrets, is the source of all our discontents.
Edmund Leach (1910–) British social anthropologist. In the BBC Reith Lectures for 1967. Lecture reprinted in *The Listener*

32 I have a wife, I have sons: all of them hostages given to fate.
Lucan (Marcus Annaeus Lucanus; 39–65 AD) Roman poet. *See also* BACON *Works*, VII

33 A group of closely related persons living under one roof; it is a convenience, often a necessity, sometimes a pleasure, sometimes the reverse; but who first exalted it as admirable, an almost religious ideal?
Rose Macaulay (1889–1958) British writer. *The World My Wilderness*, Ch. 20

34 You're a disgrace to our family name of Wagstaff, if such a thing is possible.
Groucho Marx (Julius Marx; 1895–1977) US comedian. *Horse Feathers*

35 Few misfortunes can befall a boy which bring worse consequences than to have a really affectionate mother.
W. Somerset Maugham (1874–1965) British novelist. *A Writer's Notebook*

36 The sink is the great symbol of the bloodiness of family life. All life is bad, but family life is worse.
Julian Mitchell (1935–) British writer. *As Far as You Can Go*, Pt. I, Ch. 1

37 I cumber you goode Margaret muche, but I woulde be sorye, if it shoulde be any lenger than to morrowe, for it is S. Thomas evin and the vtas of Sainte Peter and therefore to morowe longe I to goe to God, it were a daye very meete and conveniente for me. I neuer liked your maner towarde me better then when you kissed me laste for I loue when doughterly loue and deere charitie hathe no laisor to looke to worldely curtesye. Fare well my deere childe and praye for me, and I shall for you and all your friendes that we maie merily meete in heaven.
Thomas More (1478–1535) English lawyer and scholar. Last letter to Margaret Roper, his daughter, on the eve of his execution on 6 July 1535

38 Children aren't happy with nothing to ignore,
And that's what parents were created for.
Ogden Nash (1902–71) US poet. *The Parents*

39 And Her Mother Came Too.
Ivor Novello (David Ivor Davies; 1893–1951) British actor, composer, and dramatist. Title of song

40 There was an old woman who lived in a shoe,
She had so many children she didn't know what to do;
She gave them some broth without any bread;
She whipped them all soundly and put them to bed.
Nursery Rhyme *Gammer Gurton's Garland*

41 The worst misfortune that can happen to an ordinary man is to have an extraordinary father.
Austin O'Malley (1858–1932) US writer.

42 Men are generally more careful of the breed of their horses and dogs than of their children.
William Penn (1644–1718) English preacher. *Some Fruits of Solitude, in Reflections and Maxims relating to the conduct of Humane Life*, Pt. I, No 52

43 Parents are sometimes a bit of a disappointment to their children. They don't fulfil the promise of their early years.
Anthony Powell (1905–) British novelist. *A Buyer's Market*

44 All men are brothers, but, thank God, they aren't all brothers-in-law.
Anthony Powell *A Dance to the Music of Time: At Lady Molly's*, Ch. 4

45 Who has not watched a mother stroke her child's cheek or kiss her child *in a certain way* and felt a nervous shudder at the possessive outrage done to a free solitary human soul?
John Cowper Powys (1872–1963) British novelist. *The Meaning of Culture*

46 For there is no friend like a sister
In calm or stormy weather;
To cheer one on the tedious way,
To fetch one if one goes astray,
To lift one if one totters down,
To strengthen whilst one stands.
Christina Rossetti (1830–74) British poet. *Goblin Market*

47 Two mothers-in-law.
Lord John Russell (1792–1878) British statesman. His answer when asked what he would consider a proper punishment for bigamy. *Anekdotenschatz* (H. Hoffmeister)

48 It is a wise father that knows his own child.
William Shakespeare (1564–1616) English dramatist. *The Merchant of Venice*, II:2

49 There is only one person an English girl hates more than she hates her elder sister; and that is her mother.
George Bernard Shaw (1856–1950) Irish dramatist and critic. *Man and Superman*

50 That dear octopus from whose tentacles we never quite escape, nor in our innermost hearts never quite wish to.
Dodie Smith (1896–) British dramatist and novelist. *Dear Octopus*

51 I wish either my father or my mother, or indeed both of them, as they were in duty both equally bound to it, had minded what they were about when they begot me.
Laurence Sterne (1713–68) Irish-born British writer. *Tristram Shandy*

52 The greatest destroyer of peace is abortion because if a mother can kill her own child what is left for me to kill you and you to kill me? There is nothing between.
Mother Teresa (1910–) Yugoslavian missionary in Calcutta. *Nobel Peace Prize Lecture*

53 If a man's character is to be abused, say what you will, there's nobody like a relation to do the business.
William Makepeace Thackeray (1811–63) British novelist. *Vanity Fair*, Ch. 19

54 All happy families resemble one another, each unhappy family is unhappy in its own way.
Leo Tolstoy (1828–1910) Russian writer. *Anna Karenina*, Pt. I, Ch. 1

55 No man is responsible for his father. That is entirely his mother's affair.
Margaret Turnbull (fl. 1920s–1942) US writer. *Alabaster Lamps*

56 Parents are the bones on which children sharpen their teeth.
Peter Ustinov (1921–) British actor. *Dear Me*

57 'Parents are strange,' said Amy, 'for their age.'
Amanda Vail (Warren Miller; 1921–66) US writer. *Love Me Little*

58 Don't hold your parents up to contempt. After all, you are their son, and it is just possible that you may take after them.
Evelyn Waugh (1903–66) British novelist. *The Tablet*, 9 May 1951

59 The thing that impresses me most about America is the way parents obey their children.

Duke of Windsor (1894–1972) King of the United Kingdom; abdicated 1936. *Look Magazine*, 5 Mar 1957

60 It is no use telling me that there are bad aunts and good aunts. At the core they are all alike. Sooner or later, out pops the cloven hoof.

P. G. Wodehouse (1881–1975) British humorous novelist. *The Code of the Woosters*

FANATICISM

1 Defined in psychological terms, a fanatic is a man who consciously over-compensates a secret doubt.

Aldous Huxley (1894–1964) British novelist. *Vulgarity in Literature*, Ch. 4

2 Fanatics have their dreams,
wherewith they weave
A paradise for a sect.

John Keats (1795–1821) British poet. *The Fall of Hyperion*, I

3 You are never dedicated to something you have complete confidence in. No one is fanatically shouting that the sun is going to rise tomorrow. They *know* it's going to rise tomorrow. When people are fanatically dedicated to political or religious faiths or any other kind of dogmas or goals, it's always because these dogmas or goals are in doubt.

Robert T. Pirsig (1928–) US writer. *Zen and the Art of Motorcycle Maintenance*, Pt. II, Ch. 13

FASCISM

See also Hitler, Nazism

1 *Il Duce ha sempre ragione.*
The Duce is always right.

Anonymous Fascist Slogan

2 The crafty, cold-blooded, black-hearted Italian.

Winston Churchill (1874–1965) British statesman. Referring to Benito Mussolini. Radio broadcast, 9 Feb 1941

3 With a suitcase full of clothes and underwear in my hand and an indomitable will in my heart, I set out for Vienna . . . I too hope to become 'something'.

Adolf Hitler (1889–1945) German dictator. *Mein Kampf*

4 It was no secret that this time the revolution would have to be bloody . . . When we spoke of it, we called it 'The Night of the Long Knives'.

Adolf Hitler Referring to the liquidation of the leadership of the SA. Speech, Reichstag, 13 July 1934

5 The final solution of the Jewish problem.

Adolf Hitler *The Final Solution* (G. Geitlinger).

6 Before the organization of the Blackshirt movement free speech did not exist in this country.

Oswald Mosley (1896–1980) British politician. Selections from the *New Statesman, This England*, Pt. I

7 I should be pleased, I suppose, that Hitler has carried out a revolution on our lines. But they are Germans. So they will end by ruining our idea.

Benito Mussolini (1883–1945) Italian dictator. *Benito Mussolini* (C. Hibbert), Pt. II, Ch. 1

8 Fascism is a religion; the twentieth century will be known in history as the century of Fascism.

Benito Mussolini On Hitler's seizing power. *Sawdust Caesar* (George Seldes), Ch. 24

9 The keystone of the Fascist doctrine is its conception of the State, of its essence, its functions, and its aims. For Fascism the State is absolute, individuals and groups relative.

Benito Mussolini *Fascism, Doctrine and Institutions*

10 I could have transformed this gray assembly hall into an armed camp of Blackshirts, a bivouac for corpses. I could have nailed up the doors of Parliament.

Benito Mussolini Referring to the Fascist march on Rome, which had resulted in Mussolini becoming prime minister (31 Oct 1922). Speech, Chamber of Deputies, 16 Nov 1922

11 Fascism is not an article for export.

Benito Mussolini Report in the German press, 1932

12 Every communist has a fascist frown, every fascist a communist smile.

Muriel Spark (1918–) British novelist. *The Girls of Slender Means*, Ch. 4

13 Fascism means war.

John St Loe Strachey (1901–63) British politician. Slogan, 1930s

FASHION

See also clothes

1 Why, Madam, do you know there are upward of thirty yards of bowels squeezed underneath that girdle of your daughter's? Go home and cut it; let Nature have fair play, and you will have no need of my advice.

John Abernethy (1764–1831) English surgeon. Advice to a lady who took her tightly laced daughter to him. *Memoirs of John Abernethy*, Ch. 33 (George Macilwain)

2 No perfumes, but very fine linen, plenty of it, and country washing.

'Beau' Brummell (George Bryan Brummell; 1778–1840) British dandy. *Memoirs* (Harriette Wilson), Ch. 2

3 Fashion is architecture: it is a matter of proportions.

Coco Chanel (1883–1971) French dress designer. *Coco Chanel, Her Life, Her Secrets* (Marcel Haedrich)

4 One had as good be out of the world, as out of the fashion.

Colley Cibber (1671–1757) British actor and dramatist. *Love's Last Shift*, II

5 The Englishman's dress is like a traitor's body that hath been hanged, drawn, and quartered, and is set up in various places; his codpiece is in Denmark, the collar of his doublet and the belly in France; the wing and narrow sleeve in Italy; the short waist hangs over a Dutch butcher's stall in Utrecht; his huge slops speak Spanishly. . . . And thus we that mock every nation for keeping of one fashion, yet steal patches from every one of them to piece out our pride.

Thomas Dekker (c. 1570–1632) English writer. *Seven Deadly Sins of London*

6 I walk down the Strand
With my gloves on my hand,
And I walk down again
With them off.

W. F. Hargreaves (1846–1919) British songwriter. *Burlington Bertie*

7 There are few who would not rather be taken in adultery than in provincialism.

Aldous Huxley (1894–1964) British novelist. *Antic Hay*, Ch. 10

8 I haven't the slightest idea where fashions in pathology are born. . . . Possibly some of my older readers dimly recollect the days when modish scientists declared that the only dependable method of relieving a toothache was a clean, conclusive appendectomy. Then the whistle blew for the quarter, the two teams changed goals, and it developed that if you had a pain in your side it

was high time your teeth came out . . . . Only one point is clear: it's better to be dead, or even perfectly well, than to suffer from the wrong affliction. The man who owns up to affliction. The man who owns up to arthritis in a beriberi year is as lonely as a woman in a last month's dress.

Ogden Nash (1902–71) US poet. *Saturday Evening Post*, 14 Oct 1933

9 Her frocks are built in Paris but she wears them with a strong English accent.

Saki (Hector Hugh Munro; 1870–1916) British writer. *Reginald on Women*

10 For an idea ever to be fashionable is ominous, since it must afterwards be always old-fashioned.

George Santayana (1863–1952) US philosopher. *Winds of Doctrine*, 'Modernism and Christianity'

11 Fashions, after all, are only induced epidemics.

George Bernard Shaw (1856–1950) Irish dramatist and critic. *Doctor's Dilemma*, Preface

FAT

See obesity

FATE

See also destiny

1 The rich man has his motor car,
His country and his town estate.
He smokes a fifty-cent cigar
And jeers at Fate.

F. P. Adams (1881–1960) US journalist. *The Rich Man*

2 And it shall come to pass, if they say unto thee, Whither shall we go forth? then thou shalt tell them, Thus saith the Lord; Such as are for death, to death; and such as are for the sword, to the sword; and such as are for the famine, to the famine; and such as are for the captivity, to the captivity.

Bible: Jeremiah 15:2

3 The wind bloweth where it listeth, and thou hearest the sound thereof, but canst not tell whence it cometh, and whither it goeth: so is every one that is born of the Spirit.

Bible: John 3:8

4 No, it is not only our fate but our business to lose innocence, and once we have lost that, it is futile to attempt a picnic in Eden.

Elizabeth Bowen (1899–1973) Irish novelist. In *Orion III*, 'Out of a Book'

5 Leave the flesh to the fate it was fit for! the spirit be thine!

Robert Browning (1812–89) British poet. *Saul*, XIII

6 Each man the architect of his own fate.

Appius Caecus (4th–3rd century BC) Roman statesman. *De Civitate* (Sallust), Bk. I

7 All humane things are subject to decay,
And, when Fate summons, Monarchs must obey.

John Dryden (1631–1700) British poet and dramatist. *Mac Flecknoe*

8 Tempt not the stars, young man, thou canst not play
With the severity of fate.

John Ford (c. 1586–c. 1640) English dramatist. *The Broken Heart*, I:3

9 Sandy lost his last ache. In the moment of freedom he saw life and the world as a blessed gift and stood at the heart of what seemed the creative intention. He knew the feeling quite well. It came back to him, like a memorable scent suddenly encountered, peat smoke or wild thyme, but, where the scent was tethered, it took wing. As his eyes lifted with it, they set Allan on his course over the hills and in that moment Sandy wished the lad well, through time and chance. No man gets away from his reckoning, but with luck he may learn how to face it.

Neil Gunn (1891–1973) Scottish writer. *Blood Hunt*

10 It matters not how strait the gate,
How charged with punishments the scroll,
I am the master of my fate:
I am the captain of my soul.

William Ernest Henley (1849–1903) British writer. *Echoes*, IV, 'Invictus. In Mem. R.T.H.B.'

11 Many men would take the death-sentence without a whimper to escape the life-sentence which fate carries in her other hand.

T. E. Lawrence (1888–1935) British soldier and writer. *The Mint*, Pt. I, Ch. 4

12 Rummidge . . . had lately suffered the mortifying fate of most English universities of its type (civic redbrick): having competed strenuously for fifty years with two universities chiefly valued for being old, it was, at the moment of drawing level, rudely overtaken in popularity and prestige by a batch of universities chiefly valued for being new.

David Lodge (1935–) British author. *Changing Places*, Ch. 1

13 I have a wife, I have sons: all of them hostages given to fate.

Lucan (Marcus Annaeus Lucanus; 39–65 AD) Roman poet. *See also* BACON *Works*, VII

14 But she was of the world where the fairest things have the worst fate. Like a rose, she has lived as long as roses live, the space of one morning.

François de Malherbe (1555–1628) French poet. *Consolation à M. du Périer*

15 We may become the makers of our fate when we have ceased to pose as its prophets.

Karl Popper (1902–) Austrian-born British philosopher. *The Observer*, 28 Dec 1975

16 For man is man and master of his fate.

Alfred, Lord Tennyson (1809–92) British poet. *Idylls of the King*, 'The Marriage of Geraint'

17 Oh, Vanity of vanities!
How wayward the decrees of Fate are;
How very weak the very wise,
How very small the very great are!

William Makepeace Thackeray (1811–63) British novelist. *Vanitas Vanitatum*

FATHERS

See family

FEAR

1 In the Nineteenth Century men lost their fear of God and acquired a fear of microbes.

Anonymous

2 It is a miserable state of mind to have few things to desire and many things to fear.

Francis Bacon (1561–1626) English philosopher. *Essays*, 'Of Empire'

3 Men fear death, as children fear to go in the dark; and as that natural fear in children is increased with tales, so is the other.

Francis Bacon *Essays*, 'Of Death'

4 And thou, son of man, be not afraid of them, neither be afraid of their words, though briers and thorns be with thee, and thou dost dwell

among scorpions: be not afraid of their words, nor be dismayed at their looks, though they be a rebellious house.
Bible: Ezekiel 2:6

5 There is no fear in love; but perfect love casteth out fear: because fear hath torment. He that feareth is not made perfect in love.
Bible: I John 4:18

6 For God hath not given us the spirit of fear; but of power, and of love, and of a sound mind.
Bible: II Timothy 1:7

7 Fear has many eyes and can see things underground.
Miguel de Cervantes (1547–1616) Spanish novelist. *Don Quixote*, Pt. I, Ch. 20

8 You may take the most gallant sailor, the most intrepid airman, or the most audacious soldier, put them at a table together – what do you get? *The sum of their fears.*
Winston Churchill (1874–1965) British statesman. Talking about the Chiefs of Staffs system, 16 Nov 1943. *The Blast of War* (H. Macmillan), Ch. 16

9 Like one, that on a lonesome road
Doth walk in fear and dread,
And having once turned round walks on,
And turns no more his head;
Because he knows, a frightful fiend
Doth close behind him tread.
Samuel Taylor Coleridge (1772–1834) British poet. *The Rime of the Ancient Mariner*, VI

10 I'm not frightened of the darkness outside. It's the darkness inside houses I don't like.
Shelagh Delaney (1939–) British dramatist. *A Taste of Honey*, I:1

11 I wants to make your flesh creep.
Charles Dickens (1812–70) British novelist. *Pickwick Papers*, Ch. 8

12 And I will show you something different from either
Your shadow at morning striding behind you,
Or your shadow at evening rising to meet you
I will show you fear in a handful of dust.
T. S. Eliot (1888–1965) US-born British poet and dramatist. *The Waste Land*, 'The Burial of the Dead'

13 When you suffer an attack of nerves you're being attacked by the nervous system. What chance has a man got against a system?
Russell Hoban (1925–) US writer and illustrator. *The Lion of Boaz-Jachin and Jachin-Boaz*, Ch. 13

14 Let me assert my firm belief that the only thing we have to fear is fear itself.
Franklin D. Roosevelt (1882–1945) US Democratic president. First Inaugural Address, 4 Mar 1933

15 MACBETH. I am afraid to think what I have done;
Look on't again I dare not.
LADY MACBETH. Infirm of purpose!
Give me the daggers. The sleeping and the dead
Are but as pictures; 'tis the eye of childhood
That fears a painted devil. If he do bleed
I'll gild the faces of the grooms withal;
For it must seem their guilt.
William Shakespeare (1564–1616) English dramatist. *Macbeth*, II:2

16 I had else been perfect,
Whole as the marble, founded as the rock,
As broad and general as the casing air,
But now I am cabin'd, cribb'd, confin'd, bound in
To saucy doubts and fears.
William Shakespeare *Macbeth*, II:4

17 To be thus is nothing;
But to be safely thus.
William Shakespeare *Macbeth*, III:1

18 The devil damn thee black, thou cream-faced loon!
Where gott'st thou that goose look?
William Shakespeare *Macbeth*, V:3

19 A lion among ladies is a most dreadful thing; for there is not a more fearful wild-fowl than your lion living.
William Shakespeare *A Midsummer Night's Dream*, III:1

20 By the apostle Paul, shadows tonight
Have struck more terror to the soul of Richard
Than can the substance of ten thousand soldiers.
William Shakespeare *Richard III*, V:3

21 Fear lent wings to his feet.
Virgil (Publius Vergilius Maro; 70–19 BC) Roman poet. *Aeneid*, Bk. VIII

22 He had one peculiar weakness; he had faced death in many forms but he had never faced a dentist. The thought of dentists gave him just the same sick horror as the thought of Socialism.
H. G. Wells (1866–1946) British writer. *Bealby*, Pt. VIII, Ch. 1

23 By night an atheist half believes a God.
Edward Young (1683–1765) British poet. *Night Thoughts*

FEMINISM

See also equality, sexes, women

1 Old-fashioned ways which no longer apply to changed conditions are a snare in which the feet of women have always become readily entangled.
Jane Addams (1860–1935) US social worker. In *Newer Ideals of Peace*, 'Utilization of Women in City Government'

2 WOMEN'S RIGHTS NOW
Yes Dear
Anonymous Exchange of graffiti

3 A woman needs a man like a fish needs a bicycle.
Anonymous Graffiti

4 Burn your bra!
Anonymous Feminist slogan

5 Men their rights and nothing more; women their rights and nothing less.
Susan B. Anthony (1820–1906) US editor. *The Revolution*, Motto

6 . . . there never will be complete equality until women themselves help to make laws and elect lawmakers.
Susan B. Anthony In *The Arena*, (May 1897) 'The Status of Women, Past, Present and Future'

7 There is a tide in the affairs of women,
Which, taken at the flood, leads – God knows where.
Lord Byron (1788–1824) British poet. *Don Juan*, VI

8 Nothing would induce me to vote for giving women the franchise. I am not going to be henpecked into a question of such importance.
Winston Churchill (1874–1965) British statesman. *The Amazing Mr Churchill* (Robert Lewis Taylor)

9 From a timid, shy girl I had become a woman of resolute character, who

could not longer be frightened by the struggle with troubles.
Anna Dostoevsky (1846–1918) Russian diarist. *Dostoevsky Portrayed by His Wife*

10 The extension of women's rights is the basic principle of all social progress.
Charles Fourier (1772–1837) French social reformer. *Théorie des Quatre Mouvements*

11 The great question . . . which I have not been able to answer, despite my thirty years of research into the feminine soul, is 'What does a woman want'?
Sigmund Freud (1856–1939) Austrian psychoanalyst. *Psychiatry in American Life* (Charles Rolo)

12 Where young boys plan for what they will achieve and attain, young girls plan for whom they will achieve and attain.
Charlotte Perkins Gilman (1860–1935) US writer. *Women and Economics*, Ch. 5

13 Mother is the dead heart of the family, spending father's earnings on consumer goods to enhance the environment in which he eats, sleeps and watches the television.
Germaine Greer (1939–) Australian-born British writer and feminist. *The Female Eunuch*

14 Women fail to understand how much men hate them.
Germaine Greer *The Female Eunuch*

15 I know you do not make the laws but I also know that you are the wives and mothers, the sisters and daughters of those who do . . .
Angelina Grimké (1805–79) US writer. *The Anti-Slavery Examiner* (Sep 1836), 'Appeal to the Christian Women of the South'

16 . . . the emancipation of women is practically the greatest egoistic movement of the nineteenth century, and the most intense affirmation of the right of the self that history has yet seen . . .
Ellen Key (Karolina Sofia Key; 1849–1926) Swedish writer. *The Century of the Child*, Ch. 2

17 The First Blast of the Trumpet Against the Monstrous Regiment of Women.
John Knox (c. 1514–72) Scottish religious reformer. Title of Pamphlet, 1558

18 Can anything be more absurd than keeping women in a state of ignorance, and yet so vehemently to insist on their resisting temptation?
Vicesimus Knox (1752–1821) British essayist. *Liberal Education*, Vol. I, 'On the Literary Education of Women'

19 Other books have been written by men physicians . . . One would suppose in reading them that women possess but one class of physical organs, and that these are always diseased. Such teaching is pestiferous, and tends to cause and perpetuate the very evils it professes to remedy.
Mary Ashton Livermore (c. 1820–1905) US writer. *What Shall We Do with Our Daughters?*, Ch. 2

20 I'm furious about the Women's Liberationists. They keep getting up on soapboxes and proclaiming that women are brighter than men. That's true, but it should be kept very quiet or it ruins the whole racket.
Anita Loos (1891–1981) US novelist. *The Observer*, 'Sayings of the Year', 30 Dec 1973

21 . . . is it to be understood that the principles of the Declaration of Independence bear no relation to half of the human race?
Harriet Martineau (1802–76) British writer. *Society in America*, Vol. III, 'Marriage'

22 The only way a woman can marry now is to agree to become a charwoman, regardless of her education and skills.
Margaret Mead (1901–78) US anthropologist.

23 Women's Liberation is just a lot of foolishness. It's the men who are discriminated against. They can't bear children. And no one's likely to do anything about that.
Golda Meir (1898–1978) Israeli stateswoman. Attrib.

24 The most important thing women have to do is to stir up the zeal of women themselves.
John Stuart Mill (1806–73) British philosopher. Letter to Alexander Bain, 14 July 1869

25 . . . the rumblings of women's liberation are only one pointer to the fact that you already have a discontented work force. And if conditions continue to lag so far behind the industrial norm and the discomfort increases, you will find . . . that you will end up with an inferior product.
Elaine Morgan (1920–) British writer. *The Descent of Woman*, Ch. 11

26 No *man*, not even a doctor, ever gives any other definition of what a nurse should be than this – 'devoted and obedient.' This definition would do just as well for a porter. It might even do for a horse. It would not do for a policeman.
Florence Nightingale (1820–1910) British nurse. *Notes on Nursing*

27 The vote, I thought, means nothing to women. We should be armed.
Edna O'Brien (1936–) Irish novelist. Quoted as epigraph to *Fear of Flying* (Erica Jong), Ch. 16

28 . . . if civilisation is to advance at all in the future, it must be through the help of women, women freed of their political shackles, women with full power to work their will in society. It was rapidly becoming clear to my mind that men regarded women as a servant class in the community, and that women were going to remain in the servant class until they lifted themselves out of it.
Emmeline Pankhurst (1858–1928) British suffragette. *My Own Story*

29 Women had always fought for men, and for their children. Now they were ready to fight for their own human rights. Our militant movement was established.
Emmeline Pankhurst *My Own Story*

30 We have taken this action, because as women . . . we realize that the condition of our sex is so deplorable that it is our duty even to break the law in order to call attention to the reasons why we do so.
Emmeline Pankhurst Speech in court, 21 Oct 1908. *Shoulder to Shoulder* (ed. Midge Mackenzie)

31 Give women the vote, and in five years there will be a crushing tax on bachelors.
George Bernard Shaw (1856–1950) Irish dramatist. *Man and Superman*, Preface

32 The prolonged slavery of women is the darkest page in human history.
Elizabeth Stanton (1815–1902) US suffragette. *History of Woman Suffrage* (with Susan B. Anthony and Mathilda Gage), Vol. I

33 Womanhood is the great fact in her life; wifehood and motherhood are but incidental relations.
Elizabeth Stanton *History of Woman Suffrage* (with Susan B. Anthony and Mathilda Gage), Vol. I

34 *Declaration of Sentiments:* . . . We

hold these truths to be self-evident: that all men and women are created equal . . .

Elizabeth Stanton *History of Woman Suffrage* (with Susan B. Anthony and Mathilda Gage), Vol. I

35 I do, and I also wash and iron them.

Denis Thatcher (1915–) British businessman, husband of Margaret Thatcher. Replying to the question 'Who wears the pants in this house?'. *Times* (Los Angeles), 21 Apr 1981

36 I owe nothing to Women's Lib.

Margaret Thatcher (1925–) British politician and prime minister. *The Observer*, 1 Dec 1974

37 The battle for women's rights has been largely won.

Margaret Thatcher *The Guardian*, 1982

38 The Queen is most anxious to enlist every one who can speak or write to join in checking this mad, wicked folly of 'Woman's Rights', with all its attendant horrors, on which her poor feeble sex is bent, forgetting every sense of womanly feeling and propriety.

Victoria (1819–1901) Queen of England. Letter to Sir Theodore Martin, 29 May 1870

39 The thought could not be avoided that the best home for a feminist was in another person's lab.

James Dewey Watson (1928–) US geneticist. *The Double Helix*, Ch. 2

40 People call me a feminist whenever I express sentiments that differentiate me from a doormat or a prostitute.

Rebecca West (1892–) British novelist. Attrib.

41 Women have always been the guardians of wisdom and humanity which makes them natural, but usually secret, rulers. The time has come for them to rule openly, but together with and not against men.

Charlotte Wolff (1904–) German-born British writer. *Bisexuality: A Study*, Ch. 2

42 Women have served all these centuries as looking-glasses possessing the magic and delicious power of reflecting the figure of man at twice its natural size.

Virginia Woolf (1882–1941) British novelist. *A Room of One's Own*

43 The *divine right* of husbands, like the divine right of kings, may, it is hoped, in this enlightened age, be contested without danger.

Mary Wollstonecraft (1759–97) British writer. *A Vindication of the Rights of Woman*, Ch. 3

44 I do not wish them to have power over men; but over themselves.

Mary Wollstonecraft Referring to women. *A Vindication of the Rights of Woman*, Ch. 4

45 A king is always a king – and a woman always a woman: his authority and her sex ever stand between them and rational converse.

Mary Wollstonecraft *A Vindication of the Rights of Woman*, Ch. 4

FERTILITY

1 The moon is nothing
But a circumambulating aphrodisiac
Divinely subsidized to provoke the world
Into a rising birth-rate.

Christopher Fry (1907–) British dramatist. *The Lady's Not for Burning*

FICTION

See also books, literature, novels, writing

1 Science fiction is no more written for scientists than ghost stories are written for ghosts.

Brian Aldiss (1925–) British science-fiction writer. *Penguin Science Fiction*, Introduction

2 Sometimes I don't know whether Zelda and I are real or whether we are characters in one of my novels.

F. Scott Fitzgerald (1896–1940) US novelist. Said of himself and his wife. *A Second Flowering* (Malcolm Cowley)

3 There are many reasons why novelists write, but they all have one thing in common – a need to create an alternative world.

John Fowles (1926–) British novelist. *The Sunday Times Magazine*, 2 Oct 1977

4 Cynics have claimed there are only six basic plots Frankenstein and My Fair Lady are really the same story.

Leslie Halliwell (1929–) British film consultant. *Filmgoer's Book of Quotes*, 1973

5 Casting my mind's eye over the whole of fiction, the only absolutely original creation I can think of is Don Quixote.

W. Somerset Maugham (1874–1965) British novelist. *10 Novels and Their Authors*, Ch. 1

FIGHT

1 Fight fire with fire.

Proverb

2 And did those feet in ancient time
Walk upon England's mountains green?
And was the holy lamb of God
On England's pleasant pastures seen?
. . .
I will not cease from mental fight,
Nor shall my sword sleep in my hand,
Till we have built Jerusalem
In England's green and pleasant land.

William Blake (1757–1827) British poet. Better known as the hymn 'Jerusalem', with music by Sir Hubert Parry; not to be confused with Blake's longer poem *Jerusalem*. *Milton*, Preface

3 No, when the fight begins within himself,
A man's worth something.

Robert Browning (1812–89) British poet. *Bishop Blougram's Apology*

4 The only time in his life he ever put up a fight was when we asked him for his resignation.

Georges Clemenceau (1841–1929) French statesman. Referring to Marshal Joffre. *Here I Lie* (A.M. Thomson)

5 Ulster will fight; Ulster will be right.

Randolph Churchill (1849–95) British Conservative politician. Letter, 7 May 1886

6 We have sustained a defeat without a war.

Winston Churchill (1874–1965) Speech, House of Commons, 5 Oct 1938

7 There are some of us . . . who will fight, fight, fight, and fight again to save the party we love.

Hugh Gaitskell After his policy for a nuclear deterrent had been defeated. Speech, Labour Party conference, Scarborough, 3 Oct 1960

8 Come cheer up, my lads! 'tis to glory we steer,
To add something more to this wonderful year;
To honour we call you, not press you like slaves,
For who are so free as the sons of the waves?
Heart of oak are our ships,
Heart of oak are our men:
We always are ready;
Steady, boys, steady;
We'll fight and we'll conquer again and again.

David Garrick (1717–79) British actor and manager. *Heart of Oak*

9 You cannot fight against the future. Time is on our side.

William Ewart Gladstone (1809–98) British statesman. Advocating parliamentary reform. Speech, 1866

10 I purpose to fight it out on this line, if it takes all summer.

Ulysses Simpson Grant (1822–85) US general. Dispatch to Washington, 11 May 1864

11 Every position must be held to the last man: there must be no retirement. With our backs to the wall, and believing in the justice of our cause, each one of us must fight on to the end.

Earl Haig (1861–1928) British general. Order to the British Army, 12 Apr 1918

12 We don't want to fight, but, by jingo if we do,
We've got the ships, we've got the men, we've got the money too.
We've fought the Bear before, and while Britons shall be true,
The Russians shall not have Constantinople.

George William Hunt (c. 1829–1904) British writer. *We Don't Want to Fight*

13 I have not yet begun to fight.

John Paul Jones (1747–92) Scottish-born US naval commander. Retort when informed his ship was sinking. *Life and Letters of J. P. Jones* (De Koven), Vol. I

14 To give and not to count the cost;
To fight and not to heed the wounds;
To toil and not to seek for rest;
To labour and not ask for any reward
Save that of knowing that we do Thy will.

St Ignatius Loyola (1491–1556) Spanish priest. *Prayer for Generosity*

15 Fight the good fight with all thy might,
Christ is thy strength and Christ thy right,
Lay hold on life, and it shall be
Thy joy and crown eternally.

John Monsell (1811–75) British hymn writer. Hymn

16 We are not ashamed of what we have done, because, when you have a great cause to fight for, the moment of greatest humiliation is the moment when the spirit is proudest.

Christabel Pankhurst (1880–1958) British suffragette. Speech, Albert Hall, London, 19 Mar 1908

17 I dare not fight; but I will wink and hold out mine iron.

William Shakespeare (1564–1616) English dramatist. *Henry V*, II:1

18 There is such a thing as a man being too proud to fight.

Woodrow Wilson (1856–1925) US statesman. Address to foreign-born citizens, 10 May 1915

19 Nor law, nor duty bade me fight,
Nor public men, nor cheering crowds,
A lonely impulse of delight
Drove to this tumult in the clouds;
I balanced all, brought all to mind,
The years to come seemed waste of breath,
A waste of breath the years behind
In balance with this life, this death.

W. B. Yeats (1865–1939) Irish poet. *An Irish Airman Foresees his Death*

FIRE

1 All things, oh priests, are on fire . . . . The eye is on fire; forms are on fire; eye-consciousness is on fire; impressions received by the eye are on fire.

Buddha (Gautama Siddhartha; c. 563–c. 483 BC) Indian religious teacher. *The Fire Sermon*

2 The fire, mean time, walks in a broader gross,
To either hand his wings he opens wide:
He wades the streets, and straight he reaches cross,
And plays his longing flames on th'other side.

At first they warm, then scorch, and then they take:
Now with long necks from side to side they feed:
At length, grown strong, their Mother fire forsake,
And a new collony of flames succeed.

John Dryden (1631–1700) British poet and dramatist. *Annus Mirabilis*

3 Billy, in one of his nice new sashes,
Fell in the fire and was burnt to ashes;
Now, although the room grows chilly,
I haven't the heart to poke poor Billy.

Harry Graham (1874–1936) British writer. *Ruthless Rhymes for Heartless Homes*, 'Tender-Heartedness'

4 Whatsoever might be the extent of the private calamity, I hope it will not interfere with the public business of the country.

Richard Brinsley Sheridan (1751–1816) British dramatist. On learning, while in the House of Commons, that his Drury Lane Theatre was on fire. *Memoirs of Life of the R. Hon. Richard Brinsley Sheridan* (T. Moore)

5 A man may surely be allowed to take a glass of wine by his own fireside.

Richard Brinsley Sheridan As he sat in a coffeehouse watching his theater burn down. *Memoirs of the Life of the Rt. Hon. Richard Brinsley Sheridan* (T. Moore)

6 Arson, after all, is an artificial crime. . . . A large number of houses deserve to be burnt.

H. G. Wells (1866–1946) British writer. *The History of Mr Polly*, Pt. X, Ch. 1

FIRST IMPRESSIONS

1 First impressions are the most lasting.

Proverb

2 There is a lady sweet and kind,
Was never face so pleased my mind;
I did but see her passing by,
And yet I love her till I die.

Anonymous *Passing By*

3 Harris, I am not well; pray get me a glass of brandy.

George IV (1762–1830) King of the United Kingdom. On seeing Caroline of Brunswick for the first time. *Diaries* (Earl of Malmesbury)

4 You have sent me a Flanders mare.

Henry VIII (1491–1547) King of England. Said on meeting his fourth wife, Anne of Cleves, for the first time. Attrib.

5 First feelings are always the most natural.

Louis XIV (1638–1715) French king. Repeated by Mme de Sévigné

6 Who ever loved, that loved not at first sight?

Christopher Marlowe (1564–93) English dramatist. *Hero and Leander*, I

7 Mistrust first impulses; they are nearly always good.

Talleyrand (Charles Maurice de Talleyrand-Périgord; 1754–1838) French politician. Sometimes attrib. to Count Montrond. Attrib.

FISH

See also fishing, food

1 Fish die belly-upward and rise to the surface; it is their way of falling.

André Gide (1869–1951) French novelist. *Journals*

2 Oysters are more beautiful than any religion . . . There's nothing in Christianity or Buddhism that quite matches the sympathetic unselfishness of an oyster.

Saki (Hector Hugh Munro; 1870–1916) British writer. *The Match-Maker*

FISHING

See also sport

1 Fly fishing may be a very pleasant amusement; but angling or float fishing I can only compare to a stick and a string, with a worm at one end and a fool at the other.

Samuel Johnson (1709–84) British lexicographer. Attrib. in *Instructions to Young Sportsmen* (Hawker)

2 Angling is somewhat like poetry, men are to be born so.

Izaak Walton (1593–1683) English writer. *The Compleat Angler,* Ch. 1

3 We may say of angling as Dr Boteler said of strawberries, 'Doubtless God could have made a better berry, but doubtless God never did.'

Izaak Walton *The Compleat Angler,* Ch. 5

4 Let the blessing of St Peter's Master be . . . upon all that are lovers of virtue; and dare trust in His providence; and be quiet; and go a-Angling.

Izaak Walton *The Compleat Angler,* Ch. 21

5 Angling may be said to be so like the mathematics, that it can never be fully learnt.

Izaak Walton *The Compleat Angler,* Epistle to the Reader

FITZGERALD, Edward

(1809–83) British poet and translator. His translation of *The Rubáiyát of Omar Khayyám* was a free adaption of the 12th-century Persian original.

1 Taste is the feminine of genius.

Letter to J. R. Lowell, Oct 1877

2 Awake! for Morning in the Bowl of Night
Has flung the Stone that puts the Stars to Flight:
And Lo! the Hunter of the East has caught
The Sultan's Turret in a Noose of Light.

The Rubáiyát of Omar Khayyám (1st edn.), I

3 Come, fill the Cup, and in the Fire of Spring
The Winter Garment of Repentance fling:
The Bird of Time has but a little way
To fly – and Lo! the Bird is on the Wing.

The Rubáiyát of Omar Khayyám (1st edn.), VII

4 The Wine of Life keeps oozing drop by drop,
The Leaves of Life keep falling one by one.

The Rubáiyát of Omar Khayyám (4th edn.), VIII

5 Here with a Loaf of Bread beneath the Bough,
A Flask of Wine, a Book of Verse – and Thou
Beside me singing in the Wilderness –
And Wilderness is Paradise enow.

The Rubáiyát of Omar Khayyám (1st edn.), XI

6 Ah, take the Cash in hand and waive the Rest;
Oh, the brave Music of a *distant* Drum!

The Rubáiyát of Omar Khayyám (1st edn.), XII

7 The Worldly Hope men set their Hearts upon
Turns Ashes – or it prospers; and anon,
Like Snow upon the Desert's dusty face,
Lighting a little Hour or two – is gone.

The Rubáiyát of Omar Khayyám (1st edn.), XIV

8 I sometimes think that never blows so red
The Rose as where some buried Caesar bled;
That every Hyacinth the Garden wears
Dropt in her Lap from some once lovely Head.

The Rubáiyát of Omar Khayyám (1st edn.), XVIII

9 Ah, my Belovéd, fill the Cup that clears
TO-DAY of past Regrets and Future Fears:
To-morrow! – Why, To-morrow I may be
Myself with Yesterday's Sev'n thousand Years.

The Rubáiyát of Omar Khayyám (1st edn.), XX

10 One thing is certain, that Life flies;
One thing is certain, and the Rest is Lies;
The Flower that once has blown for ever dies.

The Rubáiyát of Omar Khayyám (1st edn.), XXVI

11 I came like Water, and like Wind I go.

The Rubáiyát of Omar Khayyám (1st edn.), XXVIII

12 Ah, fill the Cup: – what boots it to repeat
How Time is slipping underneath our Feet:
Unborn tomorrow, and dead yesterday,
Why fret about them if today be sweet!

The Rubáiyát of Omar Khayyám (1st edn.), XXXVII

13 'Tis all a Chequer-board of Nights and Days
Where Destiny with Men for Pieces plays:
Hither and thither moves, and mates, and slays,
And one by one back in the Closet lays.

The Rubáiyát of Omar Khayyám (1st edn.), XLIX

14 The Moving Finger writes; and, having writ,
Moves on: nor all thy Piety nor Wit
Shall lure it back to cancel half a Line,
Nor all thy Tears wash out a Word of it.

The Rubáiyát of Omar Khayyám (1st edn.), LI

15 And that inverted Bowl we call The Sky,
Whereunder crawling coop't we live and die,
Lift not thy hands to *It* for help – for It
Rolls impotently on as Thou or I.

The Rubáiyát of Omar Khayyám (1st edn.), LII

16 'Who *is* the Potter, pray, and who the Pot?'

The Rubáiyát of Omar Khayyám (1st edn.), LX

17 Strange, is it not? that of the myriads who
Before us pass'd the door of Darkness through,
Not one returns to tell us of the Road,
Which to discover we must travel too.

The Rubáiyát of Omar Khayyám (4th edn.), LXIV

18 Drink! for you know not whence you came, nor why:
Drink! for you know not why you go, nor where.

The Rubáiyát of Omar Khayyám (4th edn.), LXXIV

FITZGERALD, F(rancis) Scott (Key)

(1896–1940) US novelist. His first successful novel was the autobiographical *This Side of Paradise* (1920). This was followed by *The Great Gatsby* (1925) and *Tender is the Night* (1934) before he declined into alcoholism.

Quotations about Fitzgerald

1 Fitzgerald was an alcoholic, a spendthrift and a superstar playboy

possessed of a beauty and a glamour that only a Byron could support without artistic ruination.

Anthony Burgess (1917–) British novelist and critic. *The Observer*, 7 Feb 1982

2 The poor son-of-a-bitch!

Dorothy Parker (1893–1967) US writer. Quoting from *The Great Gatsby* on paying her last respects to Fitzgerald. *Thalberg: Life and Legend* (B. Thomas)

Quotations by Fitzgerald

3 In the real dark night of the soul it is always three o'clock in the morning.

See ST JOHN OF THE CROSS *The Crack-Up*

4 Though the Jazz Age continued, it became less and less an affair of youth. The sequel was like a children's party taken over by the elders.

The Crack-Up

5 fitzgerald. The rich are different from us.
hemingway. Yes, they have more money.

The Crack-Up, 'Notebooks, E'

6 I entertained on a cruising trip that was so much fun that I had to sink my yacht to make my guests go home.

The Crack-Up, 'Notebooks, K'

7 One of those men who reach such an acute limited excellence at twenty-one that everything afterward savors of anti-climax.

The Great Gatsby, Ch. 1

8 I was one of the few guests who had actually been invited. People were not invited – they went there.

The Great Gatsby, Ch. 3

9 One girl can be pretty – but a dozen are only a chorus.

The Last Tycoon

10 He differed from the healthy type that was essentially middle-class – he never seemed to perspire.

This Side of Paradise, Bk. I, Ch. 2

11 Beware of the artist who's an intellectual also. The artist who doesn't fit.

This Side of Paradise, Bk. II, Ch. 5

12 'I know myself,' he cried, 'but that is all.'

This Side of Paradise, Bk. II, Ch. 5

13 A big man has no time really to do anything but just sit and be big.

This Side of Paradise, Bk. III, Ch. 2

14 First you take a drink, then the drink takes a drink, then the drink takes you.

Ackroyd (Jules Feiffer), '1964, May 7'

15 Sometimes I don't know whether Zelda and I are real or whether we are characters in one of my novels.

Said of himself and his wife. *A Second Flowering* (Malcolm Cowley)

16 All good writing is *swimming under water* and holding your breath.

Letter to Frances Scott Fitzgerald

FLATTERY

See also compliments, insincerity, praise, servility

1 Imitation is the sincerest form of flattery.

Proverb

2 It is happy for you that you possess the talent of flattering with delicacy. May I ask whether these pleasing attentions proceed from the impulse of the moment, or are the result of previous study?

Jane Austen (1775–1817) British novelist. *Pride and Prejudice*, Ch. 14

3 A rich man's joke is always funny.

Thomas Edward Brown (1830–97) British poet. *The Doctor*

4 Every woman is infallibly to be gained by every sort of flattery, and every man by one sort or other.

Earl of Chesterfield (1694–1773) English statesman. Letter to his son, 16 Mar 1752

5 Madam, before you flatter a man so grossly to his face, you should consider whether or not your flattery is worth his having.

Samuel Johnson (1709–84) British lexicographer. *Diary and Letters* (Mme D'Arblay), Vol. I, Ch. 2

6 Be advised that all flatterers live at the expense of those who listen to them.

Jean de La Fontaine (1621–95) French poet. *Fables*, I, 'Le Corbeau et le Renard'

7 It is always pleasant to be urged to do something on the ground that one can do it well.

George Santayana (1863–1952) US philosopher. *Letters*

8 I will praise any man that will praise me.

William Shakespeare (1564–1616) English dramatist. *Antony and Cleopatra*, II:6

9 He that loves to be flattered is worthy o' the flatterer.

William Shakespeare *Timon of Athens*, I:1

10 Flattery is all right so long as you don't inhale.

Adlai Stevenson (1900–65) US statesman. Attrib.

11 'Tis an old maxim in the schools,
That flattery's the food of fools;
Yet now and then your men of wit
Will condescend to take a bit.

Jonathan Swift (1667–1745) Irish-born Anglican priest and writer. *Cadenus and Vanessa*

FLOWERS

See also gardens

1 She wore a wreath of roses,
The night that first we met.

Thomas Haynes Bayly (1797–1839) British writer. *She Wore a Wreath of Roses*

2 Just now the lilac is in bloom
All before my little room.

Rupert Brooke (1887–1915) British poet. *The Old Vicarage, Grantchester*

3 Unkempt about those hedges blows
An unofficial English rose.

Rupert Brooke *The Old Vicarage, Grantchester*

4 Tiptoe through the tulips with me.

Al Dubin (20th century) US songwriter. From the musical, *Gold Diggers of Broadway*. *Tiptoe Through the Tulips*

5 I sometimes think that never blows so red
The Rose as where some buried Caesar bled;
That every Hyacinth the Garden wears
Dropt in her Lap from some once lovely Head.

Edward Fitzgerald (1809–83) British poet. *The Rubáiyát of Omar Khayyám* (1st edn.), XVIII

6 Their smiles,
Wan as primroses gather'd at midnight
By chilly finger'd spring.

John Keats (1795–1821) British poet. *Endymion*, IV

7 Good God, I forgot the violets!

Walter Savage Landor (1775–1864) British poet and writer. Having thrown his cook out of an open window onto the flowerbed below. *Irreverent Social History* (F. Muir)

8 And I will make thee beds of roses
And a thousand fragrant posies.

Christopher Marlowe (1564–93) English dramatist. *The Passionate Shepherd to his Love*

9 Gather the flowers, but spare the buds.
Andrew Marvell (1621–78) English poet. *The Picture of Little T.C. in a Prospect of Flowers*

10 'Tis the last rose of summer
Left blooming alone;
All her lovely companions
Are faded and gone.
Thomas Moore (1779–1852) Irish poet. *Irish Melodies*, ''Tis the Last Rose'

11 Say it with flowers.
Patrick O'Keefe (1872–1934) US advertising agent. Slogan for Society of American Florists

12 They are for prima donnas or corpses – I am neither.
Arturo Toscanini (1867–1957) Italian conductor. Refusing a floral wreath at the end of a performance. *The Elephant that Swallowed a Nightingale* (C. Galtey)

13 But as we went along there were more and yet more and there at last under the boughs of the trees, we saw that there was a long belt of them along the shore, about the breadth of a country turnpike road. I never saw daffodils so beautiful they grew among the mossy stones about and about them, some rested their heads upon these stones as on pillow for weariness and the rest tossed and reeled and danced and seemed as if they verily laughed with the wind that blew upon them over the lake.
Dorothy Wordsworth (1771–1855) British diarist and sister of William Wordsworth. *The Grasmere Journals*, 15 Apr 1802

14 I wandered lonely as a cloud
That floats on high o'er vales and hills,
When all at once I saw a crowd,
A host, of golden daffodils.
William Wordsworth 1770–1850 British poet. *I Wandered Lonely as a Cloud*

15 Thou unassuming common-place
Of Nature.
William Wordsworth *To the Daisy*

FLYING

See also travel

1 From the point of view of sexual morality the aeroplane is valuable in war in that it destroys men and women in equal numbers.
Ernest William Barnes (1874–1953) British clergyman and mathematician. *Rise of Christianity*

2 Of course I realized there was a measure of danger. Obviously I faced the possibility of not returning when first I considered going. Once faced and settled there really wasn't any good reason to refer to it.
Amelia Earhart (1898–1937) US flyer. Referring to her flight in the 'Friendship'. *20 Hours: 40 Minutes – Our Flight in the Friendship*, Ch. 5

3 Had I been a man I might have explored the Poles or climbed Mount Everest, but as it was my spirit found outlet in the air. . . .
Amy Johnson (1903–41) British flyer. *Myself When Young* (ed. Margot Asquith)

4 I feel about airplanes the way I feel about diets. It seems to me that they are wonderful things for other people to go on.
Jean Kerr (1923–) US dramatist. *The Snake Has All the Lines*, 'Mirror, Mirror, on the Wall'

5 A man with wings large enough and duly attached might learn to overcome the resistance of the air, and conquering it succeed in subjugating it and raise himself upon it.
Leonardo da Vinci (1452–1519) Italian artist. *Flight of Birds*

6 There are only two emotions in a plane: boredom and terror.
Orson Welles (1915–85) US film actor. *The Observer*, 'Sayings of the Week', 12 May 1985

7 Nor law, nor duty bade me fight,
Nor public men, nor cheering crowds,
A lonely impulse of delight
Drove to this tumult in the clouds;
I balanced all, brought all to mind,
The years to come seemed waste of breath,
A waste of breath the years behind
In balance with this life, this death.
W. B. Yeats (1865–1939) Irish poet. *An Irish Airman Foresees his Death*

FOOD

See also etiquette, greed, obesity

1 A meal without flesh is like feeding on grass.
Indian proverb

2 An apple-pie without some cheese is like a kiss without a squeeze.
Proverb

3 Bread is the staff of life.
Proverb

4 Eat to live and not live to eat.
Proverb

5 The nearer the bone, the sweeter the flesh.
Proverb

6 I always eat peas with honey
I've done it all my life,
They do taste kind of funny,
But it keeps them on the knife.
Anonymous *Peas*

7 There is no such thing as a free lunch.
Anonymous Often attributed to Milton Friedman.

8 Carnation milk is the best in the land;
Here I sit with a can in my hand –
No tits to pull, no hay to pitch,
You just punch a hole in the son of a bitch.
Anonymous Referring to a brand of canned milk.

9 'Tis not *her* coldness, father,
That chills my labouring breast;
It's that confounded cucumber
I've eat and can't digest.
R. H. Barham ('Thomas Ingoldsby') (1788–1845) British humorous writer. *The Ingoldsby Legends*, 'The Confession'

10 'Oh, my Friends, be warned by me,
That Breakfast, Dinner, Lunch and Tea
Are all the Human Frame requires . . .'
With that the Wretched Child expires.
Hilaire Belloc (1870–1953) French-born British poet. *Cautionary Tales*, 'Henry King'

11 The Chief Defect of Henry King
Was chewing little bits of String.
Hilaire Belloc *Cautionary Tales*, 'Henry King'

12 I know what I wanted to ask you;
Is trifle sufficient for sweet?
John Betjeman (1906–84) British poet. *How to get on in Society*

13 And when the children of Israel saw it, they said one to another, It is manna: for they wist not what it was. And Moses said unto them, This is the bread which the Lord hath given you to eat.
Bible: Exodus 16:15

14 There is a lad here, which hath five barley loaves, and two small fishes: but what are they among so many? And Jesus said, Make the men sit down. Now there was much grass in

the place. So the men sat down, in number about five thousand.

Bible: John 6:9–10

15 Your fathers did eat manna in the wilderness, and are dead.
This is the bread which cometh down from heaven, that a man may eat thereof, and not die.
I am the living bread which came down from heaven: if any man eat of this bread, he shall live for ever: and the bread that I will give is my flesh, which I will give for the life of the world.

Bible: John 6:49–51

16 EAT, v.i. To perform successively (and successfully) the functions of mastication, humectation, and deglutition.

Ambrose Bierce (1842–c. 1914) US writer and journalist. *The Devil's Dictionary*

17 I'm a man
More dined against than dining.

Maurice Bowra (1898–1971) British scholar. *Summoned by Bells* (J. Betjeman)

18 A good Kitchen is a good Apothicaries shop.

William Bullein (d. 1576) *The Bulwark Against All Sickness*

19 Some hae meat, and canna eat,
And some wad eat that want it,
But we hae meat and we can eat,
And sae the Lord be thankit.

Robert Burns (1759–96) Scottish poet. *The Selkirk Grace*

20 The Queen of Hearts, she made some tarts,
All on a summer day:
The Knave of Hearts, he stole those tarts,
And took them quite away!

Lewis Carroll (Charles Lutwidge Dodgson; 1832–98) British writer. *Alice's Adventures in Wonderland*, Ch. 11

21 Soup of the evening, beautiful Soup!

Lewis Carroll Said by the Mock Turtle. *Alice's Adventures in Wonderland*, Ch. 10

22 One should eat to live, not live to eat.

Cicero (106 BC–43 BC) Roman orator and statesman. *Rhetoricorum*, LV

23 Don't eat too many almonds; they add weight to the breasts

Colette (1873–1954) French novelist. *Gigi*

24 To eat is human, to digest divine.

Charles T. Copeland (1860–1952)

25 Do you *know* what breakfast cereal is made of? It's made of all those little curly wooden shavings you find in pencil sharpeners!

Roald Dahl (1916–) British writer. *Charlie and the Chocolate Factory*, Ch. 27

26 It's a very odd thing –
As odd as can be –
That whatever Miss T eats
Turns into Miss T.

Walter De La Mare (1873–1956) British poet. *Miss T*

27 A good eater must be a good man; for a good eater must have a good digestion, and a good digestion depends upon a good conscience.

Benjamin Disraeli, Lord Beaconsfield (1804–81) British statesman. *The Young Duke*

28 Bouillabaisse is only good because cooked by the French, who, if they cared to try, could produce an excellent and nutritious substitute out of cigar stumps and empty matchboxes.

Norman Douglas (1868–1952) British novelist. *Siren Land*, 'Rain on the Hills'

29 The winter evening settles down
With smell of steaks in passageways.

T. S. Eliot (1888–1965) US-born British poet and dramatist. *Preludes*

30 The way to a man's heart is through his stomach.

Fanny Fern (1811–72) US writer. *Willis Parton*

31 Oh! The roast beef of England.
And old England's roast beef.

Henry Fielding (1707–54) British novelist. *The Grub Street Opera*, III:3

32 First need in the reform of hospital management? That's easy! The death of all dietitians, and the resurrection of a French chef.

Martin H. Fischer (1879–1962) *Fischerisms* (Howard Fabing and Ray Marr)

33 With my little stick of Blackpool rock,
Along the Promenade I stroll.
It may be sticky but I never complain,
It's nice to have a nibble at it now and again.

George Formby (1905–61) British comedian. *With My Little Stick of Blackpool Rock*

34 I eat to live, to serve, and also, if it so happens, to enjoy, but I do not eat for the sake of enjoyment.

Mahatma Gandhi (Mohandas Karamchand Gandhi; 1869–1948) Indian national leader. Attrib.

35 Take your hare when it is cased . . .

Hannah Glasse (18th century) English writer. Often misquoted as, 'First catch your hare' and wrongly attributed to Mrs Beaton. *The Art of Cookery Made Plain and Easy*, Ch. 1

36 The best number for a dinner party is two – myself and a dam' good head waiter.

Nubar Gulbenkian (1896–1972) Turkish oil magnate. Attrib.

37 Food is so fundamental, more so than sexuality, aggression, or learning, that it is astounding to realize the neglect of food and eating in depth psychology.

James Hillman *Womansize* (Kim Chernin)

38 But one day, one cold winter's day,
He screamed out, 'Take the soup away!'

Heinrich Hoffman (1809–74) German writer. *Struwwelpeter*, 'Augustus'

39 This was a good dinner enough, to be sure; but it was not a dinner to *ask* a man to.

Samuel Johnson (1709–84) British lexicographer. *Life of Johnson* (J. Boswell), Vol. I

40 It is as bad as bad can be: it is ill-fed, ill-killed, ill-kept, and ill-drest.

Samuel Johnson About the roast mutton at an inn. *Life of Johnson* (J. Boswell), Vol. IV

41 A cucumber should be well sliced, and dressed with pepper and vinegar, and then thrown out, as good for nothing.

Samuel Johnson *Tour to the Hebrides* (J. Boswell)

42 I hate a man who swallows it, affecting not to know what he is eating. I suspect his taste in higher matters.

Charles Lamb (1775–1834) British essayist. Referring to food. *Essays of Elia*, 'Grace before Meat'

43 Some things can't be ravished. You can't ravish a tin of sardines.

D. H. Lawrence (1885–1930) British novelist. *Lady Chatterley's Lover*

44 Any two meals at a boarding-house are together less than two square meals.

Stephen Leacock (1869–1944) English-born Canadian economist and humorist. *Literary Lapses*, 'Boarding-House Geometry'

45 They dined on mince, and slices of quince,
Which they ate with a runcible spoon;
And hand in hand, on the edge of the sand,

They danced by the light of the moon.
Edward Lear (1812–88) British artist and writer. *The Owl and the Pussy-Cat*

46 Food is an important part of a balanced diet.
Fran Lebowitz (1950–) US writer. *Metropolitan Life*, 'Food for Thought and Vice Versa'

47 I told my doctor I get very tired when I go on a diet, so he gave me pep pills. Know what happened? I ate faster.
Joe E. Lewis

48 The Chinese do not draw any distinction between food and medicine.
Lin Yutang (1895–) *The Importance of Living*, Ch. 9, Sect. 7

49 You can't make a soufflé rise twice.
Alice Roosevelt Longworth (1884–1980) US hostess. Referring to Dewey's nomination, in 1948. Attrib.

50 This piece of cod passes all understanding.
Edwin Lutyens (1869–1944) British architect. Comment made in a restaurant. Attrib.

51 To eat well in England you should have breakfast three times a day.
W. Somerset Maugham (1874–1965) British novelist. Attrib.

52 Kissing don't last: cookery do!
George Meredith (1828–1909) British novelist. *The Ordeal of Richard Feverel*, Ch. 28

53 What I say is that, if a fellow really likes potatoes, he must be a pretty decent sort of fellow.
A. A. Milne (1882–1956) British writer. *Not That It Matters*

54 One should eat to live, not live to eat.
Molière (Jean Baptiste Poquelin; 1622–73) French dramatist *L'Avare*, III:2

55 Some breakfast food manufacturer hit upon the simple notion of emptying out the leavings of carthorse nosebags, adding a few other things like unconsumed portions of chicken layer's mash, and the sweepings of racing stables, packing the mixture in little bags and selling them in health food shops.
Frank Muir (1920–) British writer and broadcaster. *Upon My Word!*

56 An army marches on its stomach.
Napoleon I (Napoleon Bonaparte; 1769–1821) French emperor. Attrib.

57 Old Mother Hubbard
Went to the cupboard,
To fetch her poor dog a bone;
But when she got there
The cupboard was bare
And so the poor dog had none.
Nursery Rhyme *The Comic Adventures of Old Mother Hubbard and Her Dog*

58 I have often seen the King consume four plates of different soups, a whole pheasant, a partridge, a large plate of salad, two big slices of ham, a dish of mutton in garlic sauce, a plateful of pastries followed by fruit and hard-boiled eggs. The King and Monsieur greatly like hard-boiled eggs.
Duchess of Orleans (1652–1722) Sister-in-law to Louis XIV. Letter, ?1682

59 I think I could eat one of Bellamy's veal pies.
William Pitt the Younger (1759–1806) British statesman. Last words. Attrib.

60 The vulgar boil, the learned roast an egg.
Alexander Pope (1688–1744) British poet. *Satires and Epistles of Horace Imitated*, Bk II

61 To the old saying that man built the house but woman made of it a 'home' might be added the modern supplement that woman accepted cooking as a chore but man has made of it a recreation.
Emily Post (1873–1960) US writer. *Etiquette*, Ch. 34

62 Dinner at the Huntercombes' possessed 'only two dramatic features – the wine was a farce and the food a tragedy'.
Anthony Powell (1905–) British novelist. *A Dance to the Music of Time: The Acceptance World*, Ch. 4

63 Great restaurants are, of course, nothing but mouth-brothels. There is no point in going to them if one intends to keep one's belt buckled.
Frederic Raphael (1931–) British author. *The Sunday Times Magazine*, 25 Sep 1977

64 The thought of two thousand people crunching celery at the same time horrified me.
George Bernard Shaw (1856–1950) Irish dramatist and critic. Explaining why he had turned down an invitation to a vegetarian gala dinner. *The Greatest Laughs of All Time* (G. Lieberman)

65 Many's the long night I've dreamed of cheese – toasted, mostly.
Robert Louis Stevenson (1850–94) Scottish writer. Said by the castaway Ben Gunn. *Treasure Island*, Ch. 15

66 He was a bold man that first eat an oyster.
Jonathan Swift (1667–1745) Irish-born Anglican priest and writer. *Polite Conversation*, Dialogue 2

67 Kitchen Physic is the best Physic.
Jonathan Swift *Polite Conversation*, Dialogue 2

68 Illness isn't the only thing that spoils the appetite.
Ivan Turgenev (1818–83) Russian novelist and dramatist. *A Month in the Country*, IV

69 The ancient Egyptians used to set large cones of perfumed ointment, which must often have been made with olive oil, upon their heads at dinner parties; as the atmosphere warmed up the cones would gradually melt and deliciously drizzle scented oil down their hair and faces and over their bodies.
Margaret Visser South African writer. *Much Depends on Dinner*

70 Yes, cider and tinned salmon are the staple diet of the agricultural classes.
Evelyn Waugh (1903–66) British novelist. *Scoop*, Bk. I, Ch. 1

71 I saw him even now going the way of all flesh, that is to say towards the kitchen.
John Webster (1580–1625) English dramatist. *Westward Hoe*, II:2

72 You breed babies and you eat chips with everything.
Arnold Wesker (1932–) British dramatist. *Chips with Everything*, I:2

73 If I had the choice between smoked salmon and tinned salmon, I'd have it tinned. With vinegar.
Harold Wilson (1916–) British politician and prime minister. *The Observer*, 'Sayings of the Week', 11 Nov 1962

FOOLISHNESS

See also gullibility, ignorance, stupidity, wisdom and foolishness

1 A fool and his money are soon parted.
Proverb

2 A fool at forty is a fool indeed.
Proverb

3 A fool believes everything.
Proverb

4 Better be a fool than a knave.
Proverb

5 Empty vessels make the greatest sound.
Proverb

6 Fools build houses, and wise men buy them.
Proverb

7 Fools live poor to die rich.
Proverb

8 There's no fool like an old fool.
Proverb

9 Give not that which is holy unto the dogs, neither cast ye your pearls before swine, lest they trample them under their feet, and turn again and rend you.
Bible: Matthew 7:6

10 Answer a fool according to his folly, lest he be wise in his own conceit.
Bible: Proverbs 26:5

11 The world is made up for the most part of fools and knaves.
Duke of Buckingham (1628–87) English politician. *To Mr Clifford, on his Humane Reason*

12 He's a muddle-headed fool, with frequent lucid intervals.
Miguel de Cervantes (1547–1616) Spanish novelist. Sancho Panza describing Don Quixote. *Don Quixote*, Pt. II, Ch. 18

13 The wisest fool in Christendom.
Henri IV (1553–1610) King of France. Referring to James I of England. Attrib.

14 Mix a little foolishness with your serious plans: it's lovely to be silly at the right moment.
Horace (Quintus Horatius Flaccus; 65–8 BC) Roman poet. *Odes*, IV

15 Fools are in a terrible, overwhelming majority, all the wide world over.
Henrik Ibsen (1828–1906) Norwegian dramatist. *An Enemy of the People*, IV

16 You cannot fashion a wit out of two half-wits.
Neil Kinnock (1942–) British politician. *The Times*, 1983

17 No creature smarts so little as a fool.
Alexander Pope (1688–1744) British poet. *Epistle to Dr. Arbuthnot*

18 Lord, what fools these mortals be!
William Shakespeare (1564–1616) English dramatist. *A Midsummer Night's Dream*, III:2

19 LEAR. Dost thou call me fool, boy?
FOOL. All thy other titles thou hast given away; that thou was born with.
William Shakespeare *King Lear*, I:4

20 The portrait of a blinking idiot.
William Shakespeare *The Merchant of Venice*, II:9

21 He was a bold man that first eat an oyster.
Jonathan Swift (1667–1745) Irish-born writer. Polite conversation, Dialogue 2

FOOTBALL

See also sport

1 Professional football is no longer a game. It's a war. And it brings out the same primitive instincts that go back thousands of years.
Malcolm Allison *The Observer*, 'Sayings of the Week', 14 Mar 1973

2 I do love cricket – it's so very English.
Sarah Bernhardt (Sarah Henriette Rosine Bernard; 1844–1923) French actress. On seeing a game of soccer. *Nijinsky* (R. Buckle)

3 . . . wherein is nothing but beastly fury and extreme violence, whereof proceedeth hurt; and consequently rancour and malice do remain with them that be wounded.
Thomas Elyot (?1450–1522) English diplomat. Referring to football. *Boke called the Governour*

4 No one ever taught me and I can't teach anyone. If you can't explain it, how can you take credit for it?
Red Grange (1903–) US football player. Referring to his talent for eluding tackles. Remark

5 The goal stands up, the keeper
Stands up to keep the goal.
A. E. Housman (1859–1936) British scholar and poet. *A Shropshire Lad*, 'Bredon Hill'

6 Winning isn't everything, but wanting to win is.
Vince Lombardi (1913–70) US football coach. Remark

7 The goal was scored a little bit by the hand of God, another bit by the head of Maradona.
Diego Maradona (1960–) Argentinian soccer player. Referring to a goal he scored against England in the 1986 World Cup quarter-final; although scored illegally with the hand, the referee allowed it to stand. *The Observer*, 'Sayings of the Week', 28 Dec 1986

8 I loathed the game . . . it was very difficult for me to show courage at it. Football, it seemed to me, is not really played for the pleasure of kicking a ball about, but is a species of fighting.
George Orwell (Eric Blair; 1903–50) British novelist. *Such, Such Were The Joys*

9 The streets were full of footballs.
Samuel Pepys (1633–1703) English diarist. *Diary*, 2 Jan 1665

10 A man who had missed the last home match of 't 'United' had to enter social life on tiptoe in Bruddersford.
J. B. Priestley (1894–1984) British novelist and dramatist. *The Good Companions*

11 Football isn't a matter of life and death – it's much more important than that.
Bill Shankly (1914–81) British soccer manager. Attrib.

12 Footeball . . . causeth fighting, brawling, contention, quarrel picking, murder, homicide and great effusion of bloode, as daily experience teacheth.
Philip Stubbes (fl. 1583–91) English puritan pamphleteer. *Anatomie of Abuses*

13 I will not permit thirty men to travel four hundred miles to agitate a bag of wind.
Andrew Dickson White (1832–1918) US educator. Refusing to allow the Cornell American football team to visit Michigan to play a match. *The People's Almanac* (D. Wallechinsky)

FORCE

See also oppression, power politics, violence

1 Do not remove a fly from your friend's forehead with a hatchet.
Anonymous Chinese proverb.

2 Force is not a remedy.
John Bright (1811–89) British radical politician. Speech, Birmingham, 16 Nov 1880

3 The use of force alone is but *temporary*. It may subdue for a moment; but it does not remove the necessity of subduing again: and a nation is not governed, which is perpetually to be conquered.
Edmund Burke (1729–97) British politician. *Speech on Conciliation with America* (House of Commons, 22 Mar 1775)

FORD, Gerald R(udolph)

(1913–) US statesman. In 1973, following Spiro Agnew's resignation, Richard Nixon nominated Ford as vice president. Upon Nixon's resignation in 1974, Ford became president thus assuming presidential office without virtue of popular vote.

Quotations about Ford

1 He looks like the guy in the science fiction movie who is the first to see 'The Creature'.
David Frye Attrib.

2 Jerry Ford is so dumb that he can't fart and chew gum at the same time.
Lyndon B. Johnson (1908–73) US statesman. Sometimes quoted as '. . . can't walk and chew gum'. *A Ford, Not a Lincoln* (R. Reeves), Ch. 1

Quotations by Ford

3 I guess it proves that in America anyone can be President.
Referring to his own appointment as president. *A Ford Not a Lincoln* (R. Reeves), Ch. 4

FORGIVENESS

1 Forgive and forget.
Proverb

2 Let bygones be bygones.
Proverb

3 Come now, and let us reason together, saith the Lord: though your sins be as scarlet, they shall be as white as snow; though they be red like crimson, they shall be as wool.
Bible: Isaiah 1:18

4 I will arise and go to my father, and will say unto him, Father, I have sinned against heaven, and before thee,
And am no more worthy to be called thy son: make me as one of thy hired servants.
And he arose, and came to his father. But when he was yet a great way off, his father saw him, and had compassion, and ran, and fell on his neck, and kissed him.
Bible: Luke 15:18–20

5 Wherefore I say unto thee, Her sins, which are many, are forgiven; for she loved much: but to whom little is forgiven, the same loveth little.
Bible: Luke 7:47

6 Then said Jesus, Father, forgive them; for they know not what they do. And they parted his raiment, and cast lots.
Bible: Luke 23:34

7 But I say unto you, That ye resist not evil: but whosoever shall smite thee on thy right cheek, turn to him the other also.
And if any man will sue thee at the law, and take away thy coat, let him have thy cloke also.
And whosoever shall compel thee to go a mile, go with him twain.
Bible: Matthew 5:39–41

8 Then came Peter to him, and said, Lord, how oft shall my brother sin against me, and I forgive him? till seven times?
Jesus saith unto him, I say not unto thee, Until seven times: but, Until seventy times seven.
Bible: Matthew 18:21–22

9 The cut worm forgives the plough.
William Blake (1757–1827) British poet. *The Marriage of Heaven and Hell*, 'Proverbs of Hell'

10 The women pardoned all except her face.
Lord Byron (1788–1824) British poet. *Don Juan*, V

11 It is the government that should ask me for a pardon.
Eugene Victor Debs (1855–1926) US labor unionist, socialist, and pacifist. When released from prison (1921) on the orders of President Harding after being jailed for sedition (1918). *The People's Almanac* (D. Wallechinsky)

12 Once a woman has forgiven her man, she must not reheat his sins for breakfast.
Marlene Dietrich (Maria Magdalene von Losch; 1904–) German-born film star. *Marlene Dietrich's ABC*

13 God may pardon you, but I never can.
Elizabeth I (1533–1603) Queen of England. To the Countess of Nottingham. *History of England under the House of Tudor* (Hume), Vol. II, Ch. 7

14 Only lies and evil come from letting people off. . . .
Iris Murdoch (1919–) Irish-born British novelist. *A Severed Head*

15 To err is human, to forgive, divine.
Alexander Pope (1688–1744) British poet. *An Essay on Criticism*

16 Think no more of it, John; you are only a child who has had evil counsellors.
Richard I Said at his reconciliation, at Lisieux in May 1294, with his brother John, who had attempted to overthrow him while he was held prisoner in Germany (1193–94). *Histoire de Guillaume le Maréchal*

17 The robb'd that smiles steals something from the thief.
William Shakespeare (1564–1616) English dramatist. *Othello*, I:3

18 Beware of the man who does not return your blow: he neither forgives you nor allows you to forgive yourself.
George Bernard Shaw (1856–1950) Irish dramatist and critic. *Man and Superman*, 'Maxims for Revolutionists'

19 The stupid neither forgive nor forget; the naive forgive and forget; the wise forgive but do not forget.
Thomas Szasz (1920–) US psychiatrist. *The Second Sin*

20 I bear no ill-will against those responsible for this. That sort of talk will not bring her back to life. I know there has to be a plan even though we might not understand it. God is good and we shall meet again.
Gordon Wilson Retired businessman. Speaking of the murder of his daughter, Marie Wilson, in an IRA bombing at the Enniskillen Remembrance Day service, 8 Nov 1987

FORTUNE

1 He that hath wife and children hath given hostages to fortune; for they are impediments to great enterprises, either of virtue or mischief.
Francis Bacon (1561–1626) English philosopher. *See also* LUCAN *Essays*, 'Of Marriage and Single Life'

2 Errors look so very ugly in persons of small means – one feels they are taking quite a liberty in going astray; whereas people of fortune may naturally indulge in a few delinquencies.
George Eliot (Mary Ann Evans; 1819–80) British novelist. *Janet's Repentance*, Ch. 25

3 Fortune, that favours fools.
Ben Jonson (1573–1637) English dramatist. *The Alchemist*, Prologue

4 We need greater virtues to sustain good fortune than bad.
Duc de la Rochefoucauld (1613–80) French writer. *Maximes*, 25

5 When in disgrace with fortune and men's eyes
I all alone beweep my outcast state,
And trouble deaf heaven with my bootless cries,
And look upon myself, and curse my fate,
Wishing me like to one more rich in hope
Featur'd like him, like him with friends possess'd,
Desiring this man's art, and that man's scope,

With what I most enjoy contented least.

William Shakespeare (1564–1616) English dramatist. *Sonnet 29*

6 To be, or not to be – that is the question;
Whether 'tis nobler in the mind to suffer
The slings and arrows of outrageous fortune,
Or to take arms against a sea of troubles,
And by opposing end them? To die, to sleep –
No more; and by a sleep to say we end
The heart-ache and the thousand natural shocks
That flesh is heir to, 'tis a consummation
Devoutly to be wish'd. To die, to sleep;
To sleep, perchance to dream. Ay, there's the rub;
For in that sleep of death what dreams may come,
When we have shuffled off this mortal coil,
Must give us pause.

William Shakespeare *Hamlet*, III:1

7 Fortune favours the brave.

Terence (Publius Terentius Afer; c. 190–159 BC) Roman poet. *Phormio*

FOSTER, S(tephen) C(ollins)

(1826–64) US composer of popular songs, including *My Old Kentucky Home, The Old Folks at Home*, and *O Susanna*. A big earner, but a bigger spender, he died in poverty.

1 Gwine to run all night!
Gwine to run all day!
I bet my money on the bob-tail nag.
Somebody bet on the bay.

Camptown Races

2 Weep no more, my lady,
Oh! weep no more today!
We will sing one song for the old Kentucky Home,
For the old Kentucky Home far away.

My Old Kentucky Home

3 'Way down upon de Swanee Ribber,
Far, far away,
Dere's where my heart is turning ebber:
Dere's where de old folks stay.
All up and down de whole creation
Sadly I roam,
Still longing for de old plantation,
And for de old folks at home.

Old Folks at Home

4 O, Susanna! O, don't you cry for me,
I've come from Alabama, wid my banjo on my knee.

O, Susanna

5 I'm coming, I'm coming,
For my head is bending low
I hear their gentle voices calling,
'Poor old Joe'

Poor Old Joe

6 Dere's no more work for poor old Ned,
He's gone whar de good niggers go.

Uncle Ned

FRANCE

See also Europe, French Revolution, Paris

1 All Gaul is divided into three parts.

Julius Caesar (100–44 BC) Roman general and statesman. *De Bello Gallico*, Vol. I, Ch. 1

2 France was a long despotism tempered by epigrams.

Thomas Carlyle (1795–1881) Scottish historian and essayist. *History of the French Revolution*, Pt. I, Bk. I, Ch. 1

3 They are short, blue-vested people who carry their own onions when cycling abroad, and have a yard which is 3.37 inches longer than other people's.

Alan Coren (1938–) British humorist and writer. *The Sanity Inspector*, 'All You Need to Know about Europe'

4 There's always something fishy about the French.

Noël Coward (1899–1973) British dramatist. *Conversation Piece*, I:6

5 Bouillabaisse is only good because cooked by the French, who, if they cared to try, could produce an excellent and nutritious substitute out of cigar stumps and empty matchboxes.

Norman Douglas (1868–1952) British novelist. *Siren Land*, 'Rain on the Hills'

6 To all Frenchmen: France has lost a battle but France has not lost the war.

Charles De Gaulle (1890–1970) French general and statesman. Proclamation, June 1940

7 A revolutionary France would always rather win a war with General Hoche than lose it with Marshal Soubise.

Charles De Gaulle Speech, London, 1 Apr 1942

8 The French will only be united under the threat of danger. Nobody can simply bring together a country that has 265 kinds of cheese.

Charles De Gaulle Speech, 1951

9 I hate the French because they are all slaves, and wear wooden shoes.

Oliver Goldsmith (1728–74) Irish-born British writer. *Essays*, 'Distresses of a Common Soldier'

10 The best thing I know between France and England is – the sea.

Douglas William Jerrold (1803–57) British dramatist. *Wit and Opinions of Douglas Jerrold*, 'The Anglo-French Alliance'

11 A Frenchman must be always talking, whether he knows anything of the matter or not; an Englishman is content to say nothing, when he has nothing to say.

Samuel Johnson (1709–84) British lexicographer. *Life of Johnson* (J. Boswell), Vol. IV

12 *Allons, enfants, de la patrie,*
Le jour de gloire est arrivé.
Come, children of our native land,
The day of glory has arrived.

Rouget de Lisle (Claude Joseph Rouget de Lisle; 1760–1836) French military engineer and composer. *La Marseillaise* (French national anthem)

13 Yet, who can help loving the land that has taught us
Six hundred and eighty-five ways to dress eggs?

Thomas Moore (1779–1852) Irish poet. *The Fudge Family in Paris*

14 France has more need of me than I have need of France.

Napoleon I (Napoleon Bonaparte; 1769–1821) French emperor. Speech, 31 Dec 1813

15 There's something Vichy about the French.

Ivor Novello (David Ivor Davies; 1893–1951) British actor, composer, and dramatist. *Ambrosia and Small Beer* (Edward Marsh), Ch. 4

16 A mademoiselle from Armenteers,
She hasn't been kissed for forty years,
Hinky, dinky, par-lee-voo.

Edward Rowland (20th century) British songwriter. Armentières was completely destroyed (1918) in World War I. *Mademoiselle from Armentières* (song)

17 They are a loyal, a gallant, a generous, an ingenious, and good-temper'd people as is under heaven – if they have a fault, they are too *serious*.

Laurence Sterne (1713–68) Irish-born British writer. *A Sentimental Journey*, 'The Character. Versailles'

18 I do not dislike the French from the vulgar antipathy between neighbouring nations, but for their insolent and unfounded airs of superiority.

Horace Walpole (1717–97) British writer. Letter to Hannah More, 14 Oct 1787

19 France is a country where the money falls apart in your hands and you can't tear the toilet paper.

Billy Wilder (Samuel Wilder; 1906–) Austrian-born US film director. Attrib.

FRANKLIN, Benjamin

(1706–90) US scientist and statesman. His experiments with a kite established the electrical nature of thunderstorms and enabled him to invent lightning conductors. As a diplomat in Paris he negotiated peace with Britain in 1783.

Quotations about Franklin

1 I succeed him; no one can replace him.

Thomas Jefferson (1743–1826) US statesman. Replying to the question 'Is it you, sir, who replaces Dr Franklin?' Letter, 1791

2 A philosophical Quaker full of mean and thrifty maxims.

John Keats (1795–1821) British poet. Letter, 14 Oct 1818

Quotations by Franklin

3 Remember that time is money.

Advice to a Young Tradesman

4 No nation was ever ruined by trade.

Essays, 'Thoughts on Commercial Subjects'

5 A little neglect may breed mischief, . . . for want of a nail, the shoe was lost; for want of a shoe the horse was lost; and for want of a horse the rider was lost.

Poor Richard's Almanack

6 Some are weather-wise, some are otherwise.

Poor Richard's Almanack

7 Three may keep a secret, if two of them are dead.

Poor Richard's Almanack

8 At twenty years of age, the will reigns; at thirty, the wit; and at forty, the judgement.

Poor Richard's Almanack

9 Dost thou love life? Then do not squander time, for that's the stuff life is made of.

Poor Richard's Almanack

10 Many a long dispute among divines may be thus abridged: It is so. It is not so. It is so. It is not so.

Poor Richard's Almanack

11 What is the use of a new-born child?

Response when asked the same question of a new invention. *Life and Times of Benjamin Franklin* (J. Parton), Pt. IV

12 Man is a tool-making animal.

Life of Johnson (J. Boswell), 7 Apr 1778

13 A lonesome man on a rainy day who does not know how to read.

On being asked what condition of man he considered the most pitiable. *Wit, Wisdom, and Foibles of the Great* (C. Shriner)

14 Here Skugg
Lies snug
As a bug
In a rug.

An epitaph for a squirrel, 'skug' being a dialect name for the animal. Letter to Georgiana Shipley, 26 Sept 1772

15 We must indeed all hang together, or most assuredly, we shall all hang separately.

Remark on signing the Declaration of Independence, 4 July 1776

16 There never was a good war or a bad peace.

Letter to Josiah Quincy, 11 Sept 1783

17 In this world nothing is certain but death and taxes.

Letter to Jean-Baptiste Leroy, 13 Nov 1789

18 The body of
Benjamin Franklin, printer,
(Like the cover of an old book,
Its contents worn out,
And stript of its lettering and gilding)
Lies here, food for worms!
Yet the work itself shall not be lost,
For it will, as he believed, appear
once more
In a new
And more beautiful edition,
Corrected and amended
By its Author!

Suggestion for his own epitaph.

FRANKNESS

See also honesty, sincerity, truth

1 But of all plagues, good Heaven, thy wrath can send,
Save me, oh, save me, from the candid friend.

George Canning (1770–1827) British statesman. *New Morality*

2 I have two very cogent reasons for not printing any list of subscribers; – one, that I have lost all the names, – the other, that I have spent all the money.

Samuel Johnson (1709–84) British lexicographer. Referring to subscribers to his *Dictionary of the English Language*. *Life of Johnson* (J. Boswell), Vol. IV

3 I deny the lawfulness of telling a lie to a sick man for fear of alarming him. You have no business with consequences; you are to tell the truth. Besides, you are not sure what effect your telling him that he is in danger may have. It may bring his distemper to a crisis, and that may cure him. Of all lying, I have the greatest abhorrence of this, because I believe it has been frequently practised on myself.

Samuel Johnson *Life of Johnson* (J. Boswell)

4 The great consolation in life is to say what one thinks.

Voltaire (François-Marie Arouet; 1694–1778) French writer. Letter, 1765

5 On an occasion of this kind it becomes more than a moral duty to speak one's mind. It becomes a pleasure.

Oscar Wilde (1854–1900) Irish-born British dramatist. *The Importance of Being Earnest*, II

FREEDOM

See also human rights, imprisonment

1 Wilkes and Liberty.

Anonymous Slogan of the London mob

2 There is a wind of nationalism and freedom blowing round the world, and blowing as strongly in Asia as elsewhere.

Stanley Baldwin, 1st Earl of Bewdley (1867–1947) British Conservative prime minister. Speech, London, 4 Dec 1934

3 I'll have a fling.

Francis Beaumont (1584–1616) English dramatist. *Rule a Wife and have a Wife*, III:5

4 My policy is to be able to take a ticket at Victoria Station and go anywhere I damn well please.

Ernest Bevin (1881–1951) British trade-union leader and politician. *The Spectator*, 20 Apr 1951

5 And the chief captain answered, With a great sum obtained I this freedom. And Paul said, But I was free born.

Bible: Acts 22:28

6 Conscience, I say, not thine own, but of the other: for why is my liberty judged of another man's conscience?

Bible: I Corinthians 10:29

7 So free we seem, so fettered fast we are!

Robert Browning (1812–89) British poet. *Andrea del Sarto*

8 Liberty, too, must be limited in order to be possessed.

Edmund Burke (1729–97) British politician. Letter to the Sheriffs of Bristol, 1777

9 Hereditary bondsmen! know ye not
Who would be free themselves must strike the blow?

Lord Byron (1788–1824) British poet. *Childe Harold's Pilgrimage*, I

10 England may as well dam up the waters from the Nile with bulrushes as to fetter the step of Freedom, more proud and firm in this youthful land.

Lydia M. Child (1802–80) US abolitionist campaigner. *The Rebels*, Ch. 4

11 But what is Freedom? Rightly understood,
A universal licence to be good.

Hartley Coleridge (1796–1849) British poet. *Liberty*

12 The condition upon which God hath given liberty to man is eternal vigilance.

John Philpot Curran (1750–1817) Irish judge. Speech on the Right of Election of Lord Mayor of Dublin, 10 July 1790

13 Yes, 'n' how many years can some people exist
Before they're allowed to be free?
Yes, 'n' how many times can a man turn his head,
Pretending he just doesn't see?
The answer, my friend, is blowin' in the wind.

Bob Dylan (Robert Allen Zimmerman; 1941–) US popular singer. *Blowin' in the Wind*

14 The eyes of the world are upon you. The hopes and prayers of liberty-loving people everywhere march with you.

Dwight D. Eisenhower (1890–1969) US general and statesman. Order to his troops, 6 June 1944 (D-Day)

15 My people and I have come to an agreement which satisfies us both. They are to say what they please, and I am to do what I please.

Frederick the Great (1712–86) King of Prussia. Attrib.

16 This is Liberty-Hall, gentlemen.

Oliver Goldsmith (1728–74) Irish-born British writer. *She Stoops to Conquer*, II

17 *Laissez faire, laissez passer.*
Liberty of action, liberty of movement.

Jean Claude Vincent de Gournay (1712–59) French economist. Speech, Sept 1758

18 Power is so apt to be insolent and Liberty to be saucy, that they are seldom upon good Terms.

George Saville Halifax (1633–95) English statesman. *Political, Moral, and Miscellaneous Thoughts and Reflections*

19 Liberty is so much latitude as the powerful choose to accord to the weak.

Judge Learned Hand (1872–1961) US judge. Speech, University of Pennsylvania Law School, 21 May 1944

20 The love of liberty is the love of others; the love of power is the love of ourselves.

William Hazlitt (1778–1830) British essayist. *The Times*, 1819

21 I know not what course others may take; but as for me, give me liberty or give me death.

Patrick Henry (1736–99) US statesman. Speech, Virginia Convention, 23 Mar 1775

22 I struck the board, and cried, 'No more;
I will abroad.'
What, shall I ever sigh and pine?
My lines and life are free; free as the road,
Loose as the wind, as large as store.

George Herbert (1593–1633) English poet. *The Collar*

23 'Painters and poets alike have always had licence to dare anything.' We know that, and we both claim and allow to others in their turn this indulgence.

Horace (Quintus Horatius Flaccus; 65–8 BC) Roman poet. *Ars Poetica*

24 *Nullius addictus iurare in verba magistri,*
Quo me cumque rapit tempestas, deferor hospes.
Not bound to swear allegiance to any master, wherever the wind takes me I travel as a visitor.

Horace *Nullius in verba* is the motto of the Royal Society. *Epistles*, I

25 A man should never put on his best trousers when he goes out to battle for freedom and truth.

Henrik Ibsen (1828–1906) Norwegian dramatist. *An Enemy of the People*, V

26 This charter has been forced from the king. It constitutes an insult to the Holy See, a serious weakening of the royal power, a disgrace to the English nation, a danger to all Christendom, since this civil war obstructs the crusade.

Innocent III (1160–1216) Pope. Referring to Magna Carta. Papal Bull, 24 Aug 1215

27 The tree of liberty must be refreshed from time to time with the blood of patriots and tyrants. It is its natural manure.

Thomas Jefferson (1743–1826) US statesman. Letter to W. S. Smith, 13 Nov 1787

28 I have got no further than this: Every man has a right to utter what he thinks truth, and every other man has a right to knock him down for it. Martyrdom is the test.

Samuel Johnson (1709–84) British lexicographer. *Life of Johnson* (J. Boswell), Vol. IV

29 The Liberty of the press is the *Palladium* of all the civil, political and religious rights of an Englishman.

Junius An unidentified writer of letters (1769–72) to the *London Public Advertiser*. *Letters*, 'Dedication'

30 It's often safer to be in chains than to be free.

Franz Kafka (1883–1924) Czech novelist. *The Trial*, Ch. 8

31 Freedom's just another word for nothing left to lose.

Kris Kristofferson (1936–) US film actor and folk musician. *Me and Bobby McGee*

32 It is true that liberty is precious – so precious that it must be rationed.

Lenin (Vladimir Ilich Ulyanov; 1870–1924) Russian revolutionary leader. Attrib.

33 I intend no modification of my oft-expressed personal wish that all men everywhere could be free.

Abraham Lincoln (1809–65) US statesman. Letter to Horace Greeley, 22 Aug 1862

34 Those who deny freedom to others, deserve it not for themselves.

Abraham Lincoln Speech, 19 May 1856

35 Many politicians of our time are in the habit of laying it down as a self-evident proposition, that no people ought to be free till they are fit to use their freedom. The maxim is worthy of the fool in the old story, who resolved not to go into the water till he had learnt to swim. If men are to wait for liberty till they

become wise and good in slavery, they may indeed wait for ever.
Lord Macaulay (1800–59) British historian. *Literary Essays Contributed to the 'Edinburgh Review'*, 'Milton',

36 It would be better that England should be free than that England should be compulsorily sober.
William Connor Magee (1821–91) British clergyman. Speech on the Intoxicating Liquor Bill, House of Lords, 2 May 1872

37 I cannot and will not give any undertaking at a time when I, and you, the people, are not free. Your freedom and mine cannot be separated.
Nelson Mandela (1918–) South African lawyer and politician. Message read by his daughter to a rally in Soweto, 10 Feb 1985

38 Letting a hundred flowers blossom and a hundred schools of thought contend is the policy for promoting the progress of the arts and the sciences.
Mao Tse-Tung (1893–1976) Chinese communist leader. *Quotations from Chairman Mao Tse-Tung*, Ch. 32

39 The liberty of the individual must be thus far limited; he must not make himself a nuisance to other people.
John Stuart Mill (1806–73) British philosopher. *On Liberty*, Ch. 3

40 None can love freedom heartily, but good men; the rest love not freedom, but licence.
John Milton (1608–74) English poet. *Tenure of Kings and Magistrates*

41 . . . always with right reason dwells Twinn'd, and from her hath no dividual being.
John Milton Referring to liberty. *Paradise Lost*, Bk. XII

42 Liberty is the right to do everything which the laws allow.
Baron de Montesquieu (1688–1755) French writer. *L'Esprit des lois*

43 Before the organization of the Blackshirt movement free speech did not exist in this country.
Oswald Mosley (1896–1980) British politician. Selections from the *New Statesman, This England*, Pt. I

44 My government will protect all liberties but one – the liberty to do away with other liberties.
Gustavo Diaz Ordaz (1911–) President of Mexico (1964–1970). Inaugural speech

45 Freedom is the right to tell people what they do not want to hear.
George Orwell (Eric Blair; 1903–50) British novelist. *The Road to Wigan Pier*

46 I sometimes think that the price of liberty is not so much eternal vigilance as eternal dirt.
George Orwell *The Road to Wigan Pier*, Ch. 4

47 We must plan for freedom, and not only for security, if for no other reason than that only freedom can make security secure.
Karl Popper (1902–) Austrian-born British philosopher. *The Open Society and Its Enemies*

48 Now: heaven knows, anything goes.
Cole Porter (1893–1964) US songwriter. *Anything Goes*, title song

49 *Laissez faire, laissez passer.*
Let it be, let it pass.
François Quesnay (1694–1774) French economist. Attrib.

50 In their rules there was only one clause: Do what you will.
François Rabelais (1483–1553) French satirist. Referring to the fictional Abbey of Thélème. *Gargantua*, Bk. I, Ch. 57

51 *'O liberté! O liberté! Que de crimes on commet en ton nom!'*
Oh liberty! Oh liberty! What crimes are committed in thy name!
Madame Roland (1754–93) French revolutionary. Said as she mounted the steps of the guillotine at her execution. Attrib.

52 Man was born free and everywhere he is in chains.
Jean Jacques Rousseau (1712–78) French philosopher. *Du contrat social*, Ch. 1

53 No human being, however great, or powerful, was ever so free as a fish.
John Ruskin (1819–1900) British art critic and writer. *The Two Paths*, Lecture V

54 Man is condemned to be free.
Jean-Paul Sartre (1905–80) French writer. *Existentialism is a Humanism*

55 Liberty means responsibility. That is why most men dread it.
George Bernard Shaw (1856–1950) Irish dramatist and critic. *Man and Superman*, 'Maxims for Revolutionists'

56 You took my freedom away a long time ago and you can't give it back because you haven't got it yourself.
Alexander Solzhenitsyn (1918–) Soviet novelist. *The First Circle*, Ch. 17

57 My definition of a free society is a society where it is safe to be unpopular.
Adlai Stevenson (1900–65) US statesman. Speech, Detroit, Oct. 1952

58 It is by the goodness of God that in our country we have those three unspeakably precious things: freedom of speech, freedom of conscience, and the prudence never to practice either of them.
Mark Twain (Samuel Langhorne Clemens; 1835–1910) US writer. *Following the Equator*, heading of Ch. 20

59 Liberty is the hardest test that one can inflict on a people. To know how to be free is not given equally to all men and all nations.
Paul Valéry (1871–1945) French poet and writer. *Reflections on the World Today*, 'On the Subject of Dictatorship'

60 I never approved either the errors of his book, or the trivial truths he so vigorously laid down. I have, however, stoutly taken his side when absurd men have condemned him for these same truths.
Voltaire Referring to Helvetius's *De L'Esprit*, which was publicly burned in 1758; usually misquoted as 'I disapprove of what you say, but I will defend to the death your right to say it'. *Dictionnaire Philosophique Portatif*, 'Homme'

61 Liberty does not consist in mere declarations of the rights of man. It consists in the translation of those declarations into definite action.
Woodrow Wilson (1856–1924) US statesman. Speech, 4 July 1914

62 Me this unchartered freedom tires;
I feel the weight of chance-desires:
My hopes no more must change their name,
I long for a repose that ever is the same.
William Wordsworth (1770–1850) British poet. *Ode to Duty*

63 We must be free or die, who speak the tongue
That Shakspeare spake; the faith and morals hold
Which Milton held.
William Wordsworth *Sonnets*, 'It is not to be thought of'

64 Two voices are there; one is of the sea,
One of the mountains; each a mighty voice:
In both from age to age thou didst rejoice,
They were thy chosen music, Liberty!
William Wordsworth *Sonnets*, 'Two voices are there'

FRENCH REVOLUTION

See also France, revolution

1 The French Revolution is merely the herald of a far greater and much more solemn revolution, which will be the last . . . The hour has come for founding the Republic of Equals, that great refuge open to every man.

François-Noël Babeuf (1760–97) French revolutionary. *Conjuration des Egaux*

2 Let us take as our emblem green cockades, green the colour of hope!

Camille Desmoulins (1760–94) French Revolutionary leader. *Le Vieux Cordelier*

3 It was the best of times, it was the worst of times, it was the age of wisdom, it was the age of foolishness, it was the epoch of belief, it was the epoch of incredulity, it was the season of Light, it was the season of Darkness, it was the spring of hope, it was the winter of despair, we had everything before us, we had nothing before us, we were all going direct to Heaven, we were all going direct the other way.

Charles Dickens (1812–70) British novelist. The opening words of the book. *A Tale of Two Cities*, Bk. I, Ch. 1

4 How much the greatest event it is that ever happened in the world! and how much the best!

Charles James Fox (1749–1806) British Whig politician. Referring to the fall of the Bastille, 14 July 1789. Letter to Fitzpatrick, 30 July 1789

5 *Rien*
Nothing.

Louis XVI (1754–93) King of France. Diary, 14 July 1789 – the day the Bastille fell

6 No National Assembly ever threatened to be so stormy as that which will decide the fate of the monarchy, and which is gathering in such haste, and with so much distrust on both sides.

Comte de Mirabeau (1749–91) French statesman. Letter, 6 Dec 1788

7 Citizens, we are talking of a republic, and yet Louis lives! We are talking of a republic, and the person of the King still stands between us and liberty.

Robespierre (1758–94) French lawyer and revolutionary. Speech, Convention, 3 Dec 1792

8 Who will dare deny that the Third Estate contains within itself all that is needed to constitute a nation?

Abbé de Sieyès (1748–1836) French churchman. The 'Third Estate' comprised all the French people except the nobility (the First Estate) and the clergy (the Second Estate). *Qu'est-ce que le Tiers État?* (pamphlet, Jan 1789)

9 It is still too early to form a final judgement on the French Revolution.

George Macaulay Trevelyan Speech, National Book League, 30 May 1945

10 There has been reason to fear that the Revolution may, like Saturn, devour each of her children one by one.

Pierre Vergniaud (1753–93) French revolutionary. Said at his trial, Nov 1793. Attrib.

11 Bliss was it in that dawn to be alive,
But to be young was very heaven!

William Wordsworth (1770–1850) British poet. *The Prelude*, XI

12 That which sets
. . . The budding rose above the rose full blown.

William Wordsworth *The Prelude*, XI

13 Not in Utopia, – subterranean fields, –
Or some secreted island, Heaven knows where!
But in the very world, which is the world
Of all of us, – the place where, in the end,
We find our happiness, or not at all!

William Wordsworth *The Prelude*, XI

FRIENDS

See also enemies, friendship

1 Books and friends should be few but good.

Proverb

2 Forsake not an old friend; for the new is not comparable to him: a new friend is as new wine; when it is old, thou shalt drink it with pleasure.

Bible: Ecclesiasticus 9:10

3 Cost his enemies a long repentance,
And made him a good friend, but bad acquaintance.

Lord Byron (1788–1824) British poet. *Don Juan*, III

4 Tell me what company thou keepest, and I'll tell thee what thou art.

Miguel de Cervantes (1547–1616) Spanish novelist. *Don Quixote*, Pt. II, Ch. 23

5 Have no friends not equal to yourself.

Confucius (K'ung Fu-tzu; 551–479 BC) Chinese philosopher. *Analects*

6 *Changez vos amis.*
Change your friends.

Charles De Gaulle (1890–1970) French general and statesman. Replying to the complaint by Jacques Soustelle that he was being attacked by his own friends. Attrib.

7 Fate chooses your relations, you choose your friends.

Jacques Delille (1738–1813) French abbé and poet. *Malheur et pitié*, I

8 A Friend may well be reckoned the masterpiece of Nature.

Ralph Waldo Emerson (1803–82) US poet and essayist. *Essays*, 'Friendship'

9 If a man does not make new acquaintance as he advances through life, he will soon find himself left alone. A man, Sir, should keep his friendship in constant repair.

Samuel Johnson (1709–84) British lexicographer. *Life of Johnson* (J. Boswell), Vol. I

10 Friends are God's apology for relations.

Hugh Kingsmill (1889–1949) British writer. *God's Apology* (R. Ingrams)

11 I get by with a little help from my friends.

John Lennon (1940–80) British rock musician. *With a Little Help from My Friends* (with Paul McCartney)

12 He's an oul' butty o' mine – oh, he's a darlin' man, a daarlin' man.

Sean O'Casey (1884–1964) Irish dramatist. *Juno and the Paycock*, I

13 It is more shameful to distrust one's friends than to be deceived by them.

Duc de la Rochefoucauld (1613–80) French writer. *Maximes*, 84

14 A friend should bear his friend's infirmities,
But Brutus makes mine greater than they are.

William Shakespeare (1564–1616) English dramatist. *Julius Caesar*, IV:3

15 If it is abuse – why one is always sure to hear of it from one damned good-natured friend or other!

Richard Brinsley Sheridan (1751–1816) British dramatist. *The Critic*, I

16 Associate yourself with men of good quality if you esteem your own

reputation; for 'tis better to be alone than in bad company.
George Washington (1732–99) US statesman. *Rules of Civility*

FRIENDSHIP

See also friends, love and friendship

1 A friend in need is a friend indeed.
Proverb

2 A good friend is my nearest relation.
Proverb

3 A hedge between keeps friendship green.
Proverb

4 God defend me from my friends; from my enemies I can defend myself.
Proverb

5 Love is blind; friendship closes its eyes.
Proverb

6 The best of friends must part.
Proverb

7 There is no such thing as a free lunch.
Anonymous Often attributed to Milton Friedman.

8 Do not remove a fly from your friend's forehead with a hatchet.
Anonymous Chinese proverb.

9 Old friends are generally the refuge of unsociable persons.
Max Beerbohm (1872–1956) British writer. *The Incomparable Max* (C. S. Roberts)

10 Two are better than one; because they have a good reward for their labour.
For if they fall, the one will lift up his fellow: but woe to him that is alone when he falleth; for he hath not another to help him up.
Bible: Ecclesiastes 4:9–10

11 A faithful friend is the medicine of life.
Bible: Ecclesiasticus 6:16

12 Saul and Jonathan were lovely and pleasant in their lives, and in their death they were not divided: they were swifter than eagles, they were stronger than lions.
Bible: II Samuel 1:23–24

13 Louis, I think this is the beginning of a beautiful friendship.
Humphrey Bogart (1899–1957) US film star. The last words of the film. *Casablanca*

14 I've noticed your hostility towards him . . . I ought to have guessed you were friends.
Malcolm Bradbury (1932–) British academic and novelist. *The History Man*, Ch. 7

15 I don't trust him. We're friends.
Bertolt Brecht (1898–1956) German dramatist. *Mother Courage*, III

16 Should auld acquaintance be forgot,
And never brought to min'?
Robert Burns (1759–96) Scottish poet. *Auld Lang Syne*

17 We'll tak a cup o' kindness yet,
For auld lang syne.
Robert Burns *Auld Lang Syne*

18 Only solitary men know the full joys of friendship. Others have their family – but to a solitary and an exile his friends are everything.
Willa Cather (1873–1947) US writer and poet. *Shadows On the Rock*

19 Two may talk together under the same roof for many years, yet never really meet; and two others at first speech are old friends.
Mary Catherwood (1847–1901) US writer. *Mackinac and Lake Stories*, 'Marianson'

20 A woman can become a man's friend only in the following stages – first an acquaintance, next a mistress, and only then a friend.
Anton Chekhov (1860–1904) Russian dramatist. *Uncle Vanya*, II

21 There is nothing in the world I wouldn't do for Hope, and there is nothing he wouldn't do for me . . . We spend our lives doing nothing for each other.
Bing Crosby (Harry Lillis Crosby; 1904–77) US singer. Referring to Bob Hope. *The Observer*, 'Sayings of the Week', 7 May 1950

22 It is not so much our friends' help that helps us as the confident knowledge that they will help us.
Epicurus (341–270 BC) Greek philosopher.

23 These are called the pious frauds of friendship.
Henry Fielding (1707–54) British novelist. *Amelia*, Bk. III, Ch. 4

24 That which you love most in him (a friend) may be clearer in his absence.
Kahil Gibran (1883–1931) Lebanese mystic poet and novelist. *The Prophet*

25 Always, Sir, set a high value on spontaneous kindness. He whose inclination prompts him to cultivate your friendship of his own accord, will love you more than one whom you have been at pains to attach to you.
Samuel Johnson (1709–84) British lexicographer. *Life of Johnson* (J. Boswell), Vol. IV

26 Sir, I look upon every day to be lost, in which I do not make a new acquaintance.
Samuel Johnson *Life of Johnson* (J. Boswell), Vol. IV

27 Greater love than this, he said, no man hath that a man lay down his wife for a friend. Go thou and do likewise. Thus, or words to that effect, saith Zarathustra, sometime regius professor of French letters to the University of Oxtail.
James Joyce (1882–1941) Irish novelist. *Ulysses*

28 Friendship is unnecessary, like philosophy, like art . . . . It has no survival value; rather it is one of those things that give value to survival.
C. S. Lewis (1898–1963) British academic and writer. *The Four Loves, Friendship*

29 Two buttocks of one bum.
T. Sturge Moore (1870–1944) British poet and illustrator. Referring to Hilaire Belloc and G. K. Chesterton.

30 To like and dislike the same things, that is indeed true friendship.
Sallust (Gaius Sallustius Crispus; c. 86–c. 34 BC) Roman historian and politician. *Bellum Catilinae*

31 As in a soul remembering my good friends.
William Shakespeare (1564–1616) English dramatist. *Richard II*, II:3

32 I might give my life for my friend, but he had better not ask me to do up a parcel.
Logan Pearsall Smith (1865–1946) US writer. *Trivia*

FROST, Robert Lee

(1875–1963) US poet, whose collections *Boy's Will* (1913) and *North of Boston* (1914) brought him considerable acclaim.

1 Most of the change we think we see in life
Is due to truths being in and out of favor.
The Black Cottage

2 No tears in the writer, no tears in the reader.
Collected Poems, Preface

3 Home is the place where, when you have to go there,
They have to take you in.
The Death of the Hired Man

4 Forgive, O Lord, my little jokes on Thee
And I'll forgive Thy great big one on me.
In the clearing, 'Cluster of Faith'

5 Something there is that doesn't love a wall.
North of Boston, 'Mending Wall'

6 My apple trees will never get across
And eat the cones under his pines, I tell him.
He only says, 'Good fences make good neighbors.'
North of Boston, 'Mending Wall'

7 Two roads diverged in a wood, and I –
I took the one less traveled by,
And that has made all the difference.
The Road Not Taken

8 The woods are lovely, dark, and deep,
But I have promises to keep,
And miles to go before I sleep,
And miles to go before I sleep.
Stopping by Woods on a Snowy Evening

9 Writing free verse is like playing tennis with the net down.
Speech, Milton Academy, 17 May 1935

10 A diplomat is a man who always remembers a woman's birthday but never remembers her age.
Attrib.

11 Poetry is what gets lost in translation.
Attrib.

FUN

See humor

FUNERALS

See also death

Most of the people who will walk after me will be children, so make the beat keep time with short steps.
Hans Christian Andersen (1805–75) Danish writer. Planning the music for his funeral.
Hans Christian Andersen (R. Godden)

2 This is the last time that I will take part as an amateur.
Daniel-François-Esprit Auber (1782–1871) French composer. Said at a funeral. *Das Buch des Lachens* (W. Scholz)

3 When we attend the funerals of our friends we grieve for them, but when we go to those of other people it is chiefly our own deaths that we mourn for.
Gerald Brenan (Edward Fitzgerald Brenan; 1894–1987) British writer. *Thoughts in a Dry Season,* 'Death'

4 'If you don't go to other men's funerals,' he told Father stiffly, 'they won't go to yours.'
Clarence Shepard Day (1874–1935) US writer. *Life With Father,* 'Father plans'

5 I bet you a hundred bucks he ain't in here.
Charles Bancroft Dillingham (1868–1934) US theatrical manager. Referring to the escapologist Harry Houdini; said at his funeral, while carrying his coffin. Attrib.

6 When I die I want to decompose in a barrel of porter and have it served in all the pubs in Dublin.
J. P. Donleavy (1926–) US novelist. *The Ginger Man*

7 Many funerals discredit a physician.
Ben Jonson (1572–1637) English dramatist.

8 My friends should drink a dozen of Claret on my Tomb.
John Keats (1795–1821) British poet. Letter to Benjamin Bailey, 14 Aug 1819

9 Why should I go? She won't be there.
Arthur Miller (1915–) US dramatist. When asked if he would attend Marilyn Monroe's funeral. Attrib.

10 It proves what they say, give the public what they want to see and they'll come out for it.
Red Skelton (Richard Bernard Skelton; 1913–) US actor and comedian. Said while attending the funeral in 1958 of Hollywood producer Harry Cohn. It has also been attributed to Samuel Goldwyn while attending Louis B. Mayer's funeral in 1957.

11 How Henry would have loved it!
Ellen Terry (1847–1928) British actress. Referring to Sir Henry Irving's funeral. *Yesterdays* (Robert Hitchens)

12 Evan the Death presses hard with black gloves on the coffin of his breast in case his heart jumps out.
Dylan Thomas (1914–53) Welsh poet. *Under Milk Wood*

13 Not a drum was heard, not a funeral note,
As his corse to the rampart we hurried.
Charles Wolfe (1791–1823) Irish poet. *The Burial of Sir John Moore at Corunna,* I

14 We carved not a line, and we raised not a stone –
But we left him alone with his glory.
Charles Wolfe *The Burial of Sir John Moore at Corunna,* VIII

FURY

1 Heaven has no rage like love to hatred turned,
Nor hell a fury like a woman scorned.
William Congreve (1670–1729) British Restoration dramatist. *The Mourning Bride,* III

2 There is no fury like an ex-wife searching for a new lover.
Cyril Connolly (1903–74) British journalist. *The Unquiet Grave*

3 Beware the Fury of a Patient Man.
John Dryden (1631–1700) British poet and dramatist. *Absalom and Achitophel,* I

4 Patience and passage of time do more than strength and fury.
Jean de La Fontaine (1621–95) French poet. *Fables,* II, 'Le Lion et le Rat'

FUTILITY

See also purpose

1 Why buy a cow when milk is so cheap?
Proverb

2 Why keep a dog and bark yourself?
Proverb

3 You can't get blood out of a stone.
Proverb

4 Mock on, mock on, Voltaire, Rousseau;
Mock on, mock on; 'tis all in vain!
You throw the sand against the wind,
And the wind blows it back again.
William Blake (1757–1827) British poet. *Mock on, mock on, Voltaire, Rousseau*

5 A man who has pedalled twenty-five thousand miles on a stationary bicycle has not circled the globe. He has only garnered weariness.
Paul Eldridge *Horns of Glass*

6 It's but little good you'll do a-watering the last year's crop.
George Eliot (Mary Ann Evans; 1819–80) British novelist. *Adam Bede*

7 So we beat on, boats against the

current, borne back ceaselessly into the past.
F. Scott Fitzgerald (1896–1940) US novelist. *The Great Gatsby*

8 He is very fond of making things which he does not want, and then giving them to people who have no use for them.
Anthony Hope (Sir Anthony Hope Hawkins; 1863–1933) British novelist. *The Dolly Dialogues*

9 He's a real Nowhere Man,
Sitting in his Nowhere Land,
Making all his nowhere plans for nobody.
Doesn't have a point of view,
Knows not where he's going to,
Isn't he a bit like you and me?
John Lennon (1940–80) British rock musician. *Nowhere Man* (with Paul McCartney)

10 I'm not going to re-arrange the furniture on the deck of the *Titanic*.
Rogers Morton (1914–79) US government official. Refusing attempts to rescue President Ford's re-election campaign, 1976. Attrib.

11 'Tis not necessary to light a candle to the sun.
Algernon Sidney (1622–83) English statesman. *Discourses concerning Government*, Ch. 2

12 People talking without speaking,
People listening without hearing,
People writing songs that voices never shared.
Paul Simon (1941–) US singer. *Sound of Silence*

13 All dressed up, with nowhere to go.
William Allen White (1868–1944) US writer. Referring to the Progressive Party, after Theodore Roosevelt's withdrawal from the 1916 US Presidential election

FUTURE

See also past, present, promises, prophecy, time

1 Tomorrow never comes.
Proverb

2 Years hence, perhaps, may dawn an age,
More fortunate, alas! than we,
Which without hardness will be sage,
And gay without frivolity.
Matthew Arnold (1822–88) British poet and critic. *The Grande Chartreuse*

3 I have a vision of the future, chum.
The workers' flats in fields of soya beans
Tower up like silver pencils.
John Betjeman (1906–84) British poet.

4 Boast not thyself of tomorrow; for thou knowest not what a day may bring forth.
Bible: Proverbs 27:1

5 *Future*, n. That period of time in which our affairs prosper, our friends are true and our happiness is assured.
Ambrose Bierce (1842–?1914) US writer. *The Devil's Dictionary*

6 Not a future. At least not in Europe. America's different, of course, but America's really only a kind of Russia. You've no idea how pleasant it is not to have any future. It's like having a totally efficient contraceptive.
Anthony Burgess (John Burgess Wilson; 1917–) British novelist. *Honey for the Bears*, Pt. II, Ch. 6

7 Like the Mississippi, it just keeps rolling along. Let it roll. Let it roll on full flood, inexorable, irresistible, benignant, to broader lands and better days.
Winston Churchill (1874–1965) British statesman. Referring to co-operation with the US. Speech, House of Commons, 20 Aug 1940

8 I never think of the future. It comes soon enough.
Albert Einstein (1879–1955) German-born US physicist. Interview, 1930

9 This is the way the world ends
Not with a bang but a whimper
T. S. Eliot (1888–1965) US born British poet and dramatist. *The Hollow Men*

10 The time of our Ford.
Aldous Huxley (1894–1964) British novelist. *Brave New World*, Ch. 3

11 The future will one day be the present and will seem as unimportant as the present does now.
W. Somerset Maugham (1874–1965) British novelist. *The Summing Up*

12 I have seen the future and it works.
Lincoln Steffens (1866–1936) US journalist. Speaking to Bernard Baruch after visiting the Soviet Union, 1919. *Autobiography*, Ch. 18

13 Live Now, Pay Later.
Jack Trevor Story (1917–) British novelist. Title of screenplay

14 The future is made of the same stuff as the present.
Simone Weil (1909–43) French philosopher. *On Science, Necessity, and the Love of God* (ed. Richard Rees), 'Some Thoughts on the Love of God'

15 The Shape of Things to Come.
H. G. Wells (1866–1946) British writer. Book title

G

GAMBLING

1 This is the temple of Providence where disciples still hourly mark its ways and note the system of its mysteries. Here is the one God whose worshippers prove their faith by their works and in their destruction still trust in Him.
F. H. Bradley (1846–1924) British philosopher. Referring to Monte Carlo. *Aphorisms*

2 Horse sense is a good judgement which keeps horses from betting on people.
W. C. Fields (1880–1946) US comedian. Attrib.

GAMES

See sport and games

GARDENS

See also flowers

1 Mary, Mary, quite contrary,
How does your garden grow?
With silver bells and cockle shells,
And pretty maids all in a row.
Anonymous *Tommy Thumb's Pretty Song Book*

2 God Almighty first planted a garden. And indeed it is the purest of human pleasures.
Francis Bacon (1561–1626) English philosopher. *Essays*, 'Of Gardens'

3 But there went up a mist from the earth, and watered the whole face of the ground.
And the Lord God formed man of the dust of the ground, and breathed into his nostrils the breath of life; and man became a living soul.
And the Lord God planted a garden eastward in Eden; and there he put the man whom he had formed.
And out of the ground made the Lord God to grow every tree that is

pleasant to the sight, and good for food; the tree of life also in the midst of the garden, and the tree of knowledge of good and evil.
And a river went out of Eden to water the garden.
Bible: Genesis 2:6–10

4 A garden is a lovesome thing, God wot!
Thomas Edward Brown (1830–97) British poet. *My Garden*

5 To get the best results you must talk to your vegetables.
Charles, Prince of Wales (1948–) Eldest son of Elizabeth II. *The Observer*, 'Sayings of the Week', 28 Sept 1986

6 God the first garden made, and the first city Cain.
Abraham Cowley (1618–67) English poet. *The Garden*

7 The kiss of sun for pardon,
The song of the birds for mirth –
One is nearer God's Heart in a garden
Than anywhere else on earth.
Dorothy Gurney (1858–1932) British poet. *The Lord God Planted a Garden*

8 Oh, Adam was a gardener, and God who made him sees
That half a proper gardener's work is done upon his knees,
So when your work is finished, you can wash your hands and pray
For the Glory of the Garden, that it may not pass away!
Rudyard Kipling (1865–1936) Indian-born British writer. *The Glory of the Garden*

9 A little thin, flowery border, round, neat, not gaudy.
Charles Lamb (1775–1834) British essayist. Letter to Wordsworth, June 1806

10 I have a garden of my own,
But so with roses overgrown,
And lilies, that you would it guess
To be a little wilderness.
Andrew Marvell (1621–78) English poet. *The Nymph Complaining for the Death of her Fawn*

GARFIELD, James A(bram)

(1831–81) US statesman. He became Republican President (1881) after a military career. He was assassinated.

1 My fellow citizens, the President is dead, but the Government lives and God Omnipotent reigns.
Speech following the assassination of Lincoln.

GENERALIZATIONS

See also classification

1 To generalize is to be an idiot.
William Blake (1757–1827) British poet. *Life of Blake* (Gilchrist)

2 All generalizations are dangerous, even this one.
Alexandre Dumas, fils (1824–95) French writer. Attrib.

3 The tendency of the casual mind is to pick out or stumble upon a sample which supports or defines its prejudices, and then to make it representative of a whole class.
Walter Lippmann (1889–1974) US editor and writer. *Public Opinion*

4 Any general statement is like a check drawn on a bank. Its value depends on what is there to meet it.
Ezra Pound (1885–1972) US poet. *ABC of Reading*, Ch. 2

GENERALS

1 War is too important to be left to the generals.
Georges Clemenceau (1841–1929) French statesman. A similar remark is attributed to Talleyrand. Attrib.

2 Oh! he is mad, is he? Then I wish he would bite some other of my generals.
George II (1683–1760) King of Great Britain and Ireland. Replying to advisors who told him that General James Wolfe was mad. Attrib.

3 I didn't fire him because he was a dumb son of a bitch, although he was, but that's not against the law for generals. If it was, half to three-quarters of them would be in jail.
Harry S. Truman (1884–1972) US statesman. Referring to General MacArthur. *Plain Speaking* (Merle Miller)

4 Dead battles, like dead generals, hold the military mind in their dead grip.
Barbara W. Tuchman (1912–) US editor and writer. *August 1914*, Ch. 2

5 As for being a General, well, at the age of four with paper hats and wooden swords we're all Generals. Only some of us never grow out of it.
Peter Ustinov (1921–) British actor. *Romanoff and Juliet*, I

6 It is not the business of generals to shoot one another.
Duke of Wellington (1769–1852) British general and statesman. Refusing an artillery officer permission to fire upon Napoleon himself during the Battle of Waterloo, 1815. Attrib.

GENERATIONS

1 *Inque brevi spatio mutantur saecla animantum*
Et quasi cursores vitai lampada tradunt.
The generations of living things pass in a short time, and like runners hand on the torch of life.
Lucretius (Titus Lucretius Carus; c. 99–55 BC) Roman philosopher. *On the Nature of the Universe*, II

2 Each generation imagines itself to be more intelligent than the one that went before it, and wiser than the one that comes after it.
George Orwell (Eric Blair; 1903–50) British novelist. Book Review

3 That's what you are. That's what you all are. All of you young people who served in the war. You are a lost generation.
Gertrude Stein (1874–1946) US writer. *A Moveable Feast* (E. Hemingway)

GENEROSITY

See also charity, gifts, kindness, parasites

1 Every man according as he purposeth in his heart, so let him give; not grudgingly, or of necessity: for God loveth a cheerful giver.
Bible: II Corinthians 9:7

2 Heal the sick, cleanse the lepers, raise the dead, cast out devils: freely ye have received, freely give.
Bible: Matthew 10:8

3 Experience was to be taken as showing that one might get a five-pound note as one got a light for a cigarette; but one had to check the friendly impulse to ask for it in the same way.
Henry James (1843–1916) US novelist. *The Awkward Age*

4 In the first place, I have only five guineas in my pocket; and in the second, they are very much at your service.
Lord Peterborough (1658–1735) English military and naval commander. Persuading an angry mob that he was not the Duke of Marlborough, notorious for his meanness. *Dictionary of National Biography*

5 I am not in the giving vein to-day.
William Shakespeare (1564–1616) English dramatist. *Richard III*, IV:2

GENIUS

See also talent, talent and genius

1 Genius is an infinite capacity for taking pains.
Proverb

2 Genius (which means transcendent capacity of taking trouble, first of all).
Thomas Carlyle (1795–1881) Scottish historian and essayist. *Frederick the Great*, Vol. IV, Ch. 3

3 Great Wits are sure to Madness near alli'd
And thin Partitions do their Bounds divide.
John Dryden (1631–1700) British poet and dramatist. *Absalom and Achitophel*, I

4 Genius is one per cent inspiration and ninety-nine per cent perspiration.
Thomas Edison (1847–1931) US inventor. Attrib.

5 True genius walks along a line, and, perhaps, our greatest pleasure is in seeing it so often near falling, without being ever actually down.
Oliver Goldsmith (1728–74) Irish-born British writer. *The Bee*, 'The Characteristics of Greatness'

6 Most of the knowledge and much of the genius of the research worker lie behind his selection of what is worth observing. It is a crucial choice, often determining the success or failure of months of work, often differentiating the brilliant discoverer from the . . . plodder.
Alan Gregg (1890–1957) *The Furtherance of Medical Research*

7 The true genius is a mind of large general powers, accidentally determined to some particular direction.
Samuel Johnson (1709–84) British lexicographer. *Lives of the English Poets*, 'Cowley'

8 A genius! For thirty-seven years I've practiced fourteen hours a day, and now they call me a genius!
Pablo Sarasate (1844–1908) Spanish violinist and composer. On being hailed as a genius by a critic. Attrib.

9 When a true genius appears in the world, you may know him by this sign, that the dunces are all in confederacy against him.
Jonathan Swift (1667–1745) Irish-born Anglican priest and writer. *Thoughts on Various Subjects*

GERMANY

See also Europe, Hitler, Nazism, World War II

1 Hamelin Town's in Brunswick,
By famous Hanover city;
The river Weser, deep and wide,
Washes its wall on the southern side;
A pleasanter spot you never spied.
Robert Browning (1812–89) British poet. *The Pied Piper of Hamelin*

2 Don't let's be beastly to the Germans.
Noël Coward (1899–1973) British dramatist. *Title of song*

3 *Deutschland, Deutschland über alles.*
Germany, Germany before all else.
Heinrich Hoffmann von Fallersleben (1798–1876) German poet. German national anthem

4 Germany will be either a world power or will not be at all.
Adolf Hitler (1889–1945) German dictator. *Mein Kampf*, Ch. 14

5 How appallingly thorough these Germans always managed to be, how emphatic! In sex no less than in war – in scholarship, in science. Diving deeper than anyone else and coming up muddier.
Aldous Huxley (1894–1964) British novelist.

6 All free men, wherever they may live, are citizens of Berlin. And therefore, as a free man, I take pride in the words *Ich bin ein Berliner.*
John Fitzgerald Kennedy (1917–63) US statesman. Speech, City Hall, West Berlin, 26 June 1963

7 The German Empire has become a world empire.
Wilhelm II (1859–1941) King of Prussia and Emperor of Germany. Speech, Berlin, 18 Jan 1896

8 America . . . is the prize amateur nation of the world. Germany is the prize professional nation.
Woodrow Wilson (1856–1925) US statesman. Speech, Aug 1917. *Mr Wilson's War* (John Dos Passos), Pt. III, Ch. 13

GIBBON, Edward

(1737–94) British historian whose monumental *The History of the Decline and Fall of the Roman Empire* (1776–88) caused considerable controversy for its treatment of Christianity.

Quotations about Gibbon

1 Gibbon is an ugly, affected, disgusting fellow, and poisons our literary club for me. I class him among infidel wasps and venomous insects.
James Boswell (1740–95) Scottish lawyer and writer. *Diary*, 1779

2 Johnson's style was grand, Gibbon's elegant. Johnson marched to kettle-drums and trumpets. Gibbon moved to flutes and hautboys.
George Colman the Younger (1762–1836) British dramatist. *Random Records*

Quotations by Gibbon

3 To the University of Oxford I acknowledge no obligation; and she will as cheerfully renounce me for a son, as I am willing to disclaim her for a mother. I spent fourteen months at Magdalen College: they proved the fourteen months the most idle and unprofitable of my whole life.
Autobiography

4 Crowds without company, and dissipation without pleasure.
Referring to London. *Autobiography*

5 The romance of *Tom Jones*, that exquisite picture of human manners, will outlive the palace of the Escurial and the imperial eagle of the house of Austria.
Autobiography

6 The various modes of worship, which prevailed in the Roman world, were all considered by the people as equally true; by the philosopher, as equally false; and by the magistrate, as equally useful. And thus toleration produced not only mutual indulgence, but even religious concord.
Decline and Fall of the Roman Empire, Ch. 2

7 The principles of a free constitution are irrecoverably lost, when the legislative power is nominated by the executive.
Decline and Fall of the Roman Empire, Ch. 3

8 His reign is marked by the rare advantage of furnishing very few

materials for history; which is, indeed, little more than the register of the crimes, follies, and misfortunes of mankind.
Referring to the reign of Antoninus Pius. *Decline and Fall of the Roman Empire*, Ch. 3

9 Corruption, the most infallible symptom of constitutional liberty.
Decline and Fall of the Roman Empire, Ch. 21

10 All that is human must retrograde if it does not advance.
Decline and Fall of the Roman Empire, Ch. 71

GIFTS

See also generosity, materialism

1 Every good gift and every perfect gift is from above, and cometh down from the Father of lights, with whom is no variableness, neither shadow of turning.
Bible: James 1:17

2 Heal the sick, cleanse the lepers, raise the dead, cast out devils: freely ye have received, freely give.
Bible: Matthew 10:8

3 'They gave it me,' Humpty Dumpty continued thoughtfully, . . . 'for an un-birthday present.'
Lewis Carroll (Charles Lutwidge Dodgson; 1832–98) British writer. *Through the Looking-Glass*, Ch. 6

4 The manner of giving is worth more than the gift.
Pierre Corneille (1606–84) French dramatist. *Le Menteur*, I:1

5 If one doesn't get birthday presents it can remobilize very painfully the persecutory anxiety which usually follows birth.
Henry Reed (1914–) British poet and dramatist. *The Primal Scene, as it were*

GILBERT, Sir William Schwenk

(1836–1911) British dramatist and comic writer. His comic verse published as *Bab Ballads* (1896) preceded his libretti for 14 comic operas written for Arthur Sullivan's music.

1 He led his regiment from behind
He found it less exciting.
The Gondoliers, I

2 Of that there is no manner of doubt –
No probable, possible shadow of doubt –
No possible doubt whatever.
The Gondoliers, I

3 A taste for drink, combined with gout,
Had doubled him up for ever.
The Gondoliers, I

4 All shall equal be.
The Earl, the Marquis, and the Dook,
The Groom, the Butler, and the Cook,
The Aristocrat who banks with Coutts,
The Aristocrat who cleans the boots.
The Gondoliers, I

5 When every blessed thing you hold
Is made of silver, or of gold,
You long for simple pewter.
When you have nothing else to wear
But cloth of gold and satins rare,
For cloth of gold you cease to care –
Up goes the price of shoddy.
The Gondoliers, I

6 I'm called Little Buttercup – dear Little Buttercup,
Though I could never tell why.
HMS Pinafore, I

7 I am the Captain of the *Pinafore*;
And a right good captain too!
HMS Pinafore, I

8 captain. I'm never, never sick at sea!
all. What never?
captain. No, never!
all. What, *never?*
captain. Hardly ever!
HMS Pinafore, I

9 And so do his sisters, and his cousins and his aunts!
His sisters and his cousins,
Whom he reckons up by dozens,
And his aunts!
HMS Pinafore, I

10 I always voted at my party's call,
And I never thought of thinking for myself at all.
HMS Pinafore, I

11 Stick close to your desks and never go to sea,
And you all may be Rulers of the Queen's Navee!
HMS Pinafore, I

12 When I was a lad I served a term
As office boy to an Attorney's firm.
I cleaned the windows and I swept the floor,
And I polished up the handle of the big front door.
I polished up that handle so carefullee
That now I am the Ruler of the Queen's Navee!
HMS Pinafore, I

13 For he might have been a Roosian,
A French, or Turk, or Proosian,
Or perhaps Ital-ian!
But in spite of all temptations
To belong to other nations,
He remains an Englishman!
HMS Pinafore, II

14 I see no objection to stoutness, in moderation.
Iolanthe, I

15 Bow, bow, ye lower middle classes!
Bow, bow, ye tradesmen, bow, ye masses!
Iolanthe, I

16 When I went to the Bar as a very young man,
(Said I to myself – said I),
I'll work on a new and original plan,
(Said I to myself – said I).
Iolanthe, I

17 The prospect of a lot
Of dull MPs in close proximity,
All thinking for themselves is what
No man can face with equanimity.
Iolanthe, I

18 The Law is the true embodiment
Of everything that's excellent.
It has no kind of fault or flaw,
And I, my lords, embody the Law.
Iolanthe, I

19 I often think it's comical
How Nature always does contrive
That every boy and every gal
That's born into the world alive
Is either a little Liberal
Or else a little Conservative!
Iolanthe, II

20 The House of Peers, throughout the war,
Did nothing in particular,
And did it very well.
Iolanthe, II

21 For you dream you are crossing the Channel, and tossing about in a steamer from Harwich –
Which is something between a large bathing machine and a very small second-class carriage.
Iolanthe, II

22 Pooh-Bah (Lord High Everything Else)
The Mikado, Dramatis Personae

23 A wandering minstrel I –
A thing of shreds and patches,
Of ballads, songs and snatches,

And dreamy lullaby!
The Mikado, I

24 I can trace my ancestry back to a protoplasmal primordial atomic globule. Consequently, my family pride is something in-conceivable. I can't help it. I was born sneering.
The Mikado, I

25 As some day it may happen that a victim must be found
I've got a little list – I've got a little list
Of society offenders who might well be underground,
And who never would be missed – who never would be missed!
The Mikado, I

26 The idiot who praises, with enthusiastic tone,
All centuries but this, and every country but his own.
The Mikado, I

27 Three little maids from school are we,
Pert as a school-girl well can be,
Filled to the brim with girlish glee.
The Mikado, I

28 Ah, pray make no mistake,
We are not shy;
We're very wide awake,
The moon and I.
The Mikado, II

29 My object all sublime
I shall achieve in time –
To let the punishment fit the crime –
The punishment fit the crime.
The Mikado, II

30 The billiard sharp whom any one catches,
His doom's extremely hard –
He's made to dwell –
In a dungeon cell
On a spot that's always barred.
And there he plays extravagant matches
In fitless finger-stalls
On a cloth untrue
With a twisted cue
And elliptical billiard balls.
The Mikado, II

31 I have a left shoulder-blade that is a miracle of loveliness. People come miles to see it. My right elbow has a fascination that few can resist.
The Mikado, II

32 Something lingering, with boiling oil in it, I fancy.
The Mikado, II

33 The flowers that bloom in the spring,
Tra la,
Have nothing to do with the case.
I've got to take under my wing,
Tra la,
A most unattractive old thing,
Tra la,
With a caricature of a face.
The Mikado, II

34 On a tree by a river a little tom-tit
Sang 'Willow, titwillow, titwillow!'
The Mikado, II

35 If this young man expresses himself in terms too deep for *me*,
Why, what a very singularly deep young man this deep young man must be!
Patience, I

36 Poor wandering one!
Though thou hast surely strayed,
Take heart of grace,
Thy steps retrace,
Poor wandering one!
The Pirates of Penzance, I

37 I am the very model of a modern Major-General,
I've information vegetable, animal and mineral,
I know the kings of England, and I quote the fights historical,
From Marathon to Waterloo, in order categorical.
The Pirates of Penzance, I

38 About binomial theorems I'm teeming with a lot of news,
With many cheerful facts about the square on the hypoteneuse.
The Pirates of Penzance, I

39 When the foeman bares his steel,
Tarantara! tarantara!
We uncomfortable feel.
The Pirates of Penzance, II

40 When constabulary duty's to be done –
A policeman's lot is not a happy one.
The Pirates of Penzance, II

41 He combines the manners of a Marquis with the morals of a Methodist.
Ruddigore, I

42 Is life a boon?
If so, it must befall
That Death, whene'er he call,
Must call too soon.
The lines are written on Arthur Sullivan's memorial in the Embankment gardens. *The Yeoman of the Guard*, I

43 I have a song to sing O!
Sing me your song, O!
The Yeoman of the Guard, I

44 It's a song of a merryman, moping mum,
Whose soul was sad, and whose glance was glum,
Who sipped no sup, and who craved no crumb,
As he sighed for the love of a ladye.
The Yeoman of the Guard, I

45 She may very well pass for forty-three
In the dusk, with a light behind her!
Trial by Jury

46 Sir, I view the proposal to hold an international exhibition at San Francisco with an equanimity bordering on indifference.
Gilbert, His Life and Strife (Hesketh Pearson)

47 My dear chap! Good isn't the word!
Speaking to an actor after he had given a poor performance. Attrib.

48 Funny without being vulgar.
Referring to Sir Henry Irving's *Hamlet*. Attrib.

GIRLS

See children

GLORY

1 What price Glory?
Maxwell Anderson (1888–1959) US playwright. Play title

2 Fools! For I also had my hour;
One far fierce hour and sweet;
There was a shout about my ears,
And palms before my feet.
G. K. Chesterton (1874–1936) British writer. *The Donkey*

3 May God deny you peace but give you glory!
Miguel de Unamuno y Jugo (1864–1936) Spanish writer. Closing words. *The Tragic Sense of Life*

4 *Sic transit gloria mundi.*
Thus the glory of the world passes away.
Thomas à Kempis (Thomas Hemmerken; c. 1380–1471) German monk. *The Imitation of Christ*, I

5 Wi' a hundred pipers an' a', an' a'.
Carolina Nairne (1766–1845) Scottish songwriter. A romantic glorification of the 1745 Jacobite Rebellion. *The Hundred Pipers*

6 A brittle glory shineth in this face:
As brittle as the glory is the face.
William Shakespeare (1564–1616) English dramatist. *Richard II*, IV:1

7 'Hurrah! hurrah! we bring the Jubilee!
Hurrah! hurrah! the flag that makes you free!'
So we sang the chorus from Atlanta to the sea
As we were marching through Georgia.

Henry Clay Work (1832–84) US songwriter. Commemorating the march (Nov–Dec 1864) by a Union army under General Sherman through Confederate Georgia. *Marching Through Georgia*

GOD

See also atheism, creation, faith, prayer, religion

1 Not only is there no God, but try getting a plumber on weekends.

Woody Allen (1937–) US film actor, writer, and director. *Getting Even*, 'My Philosophy'

2 God be in my head,
And in my understanding;
God be in my eyes,
And in my looking;
God be in my mouth,
And in my speaking;
God be in my heart,
And in my thinking;
God be at my end,
And at my departing.

Anonymous *Sarum Missal*

3 He didn't love God, he just fancied him.

Anonymous Referring to W. H. Auden.

4 Every man thinks God is on his side. The rich and powerful know that he is.

Jean Anouilh (1910–87) French dramatist. *The Lark*

5 It were better to have no opinion of God at all, than such an opinion as is unworthy of him.

Francis Bacon (1561–1626) English philosopher. *Essays*, 'Of Superstition'

6 I know I am God because when I pray to him I find I'm talking to myself.

Peter Barnes (1931–) British playwright. *The Ruling Class*

7 Then Peter opened his mouth, and said, Of a truth I perceive that God is no respecter of persons.

Bible: Acts 10:34

8 For in him we live, and move, and have our being; as certain also of your own poets have said, For we are also his offspring.

Bible: Acts 17:28

9 Seek him that maketh the seven stars and Orion, and turneth the shadow of death into the morning, and maketh the day dark with night: that calleth for the waters of the sea, and poureth them out upon the face of the earth: The Lord is his name.

Bible: Amos 5:8

10 For the kingdom of God is not in word, but in power.

Bible: I Corinthians 4:20

11 And he changeth the times and the seasons: he removeth kings, and setteth up kings: he giveth wisdom unto the wise, and knowledge to them that know understanding:
He revealeth the deep and secret things: he knoweth what is in the darkness, and the light dwelleth with him.

Bible: Daniel 2:21–22

12 Be strong and of a good courage, fear not, nor be afraid of them: for the Lord thy God, he it is that doth go with thee; he will not fail thee, nor forsake thee.

Bible: Deuteronomy 31:6

13 Let us hear the conclusion of the whole matter: Fear God, and keep his commandments: for this is the whole duty of man.

Bible: Ecclesiastes 12:13

14 I am the Lord thy God, which have brought thee out of the land of Egypt, out of the house of bondage.
Thou shalt have no other gods before me.
Thou shalt not make unto thee any graven image, or any likeness of any thing that is in heaven above, or that is in the earth beneath, or that is in the water under the earth:
Thou shalt not bow down thyself to them, nor serve them: for Lord thy God am a jealous God, visiting the iniquity of the fathers upon the children unto the third and fourth generation of them that hate me;
And shewing mercy unto thousands of them that love me, and keep my commandments.
Thou shalt not take the name of the Lord thy God in vain; for the Lord will not hold him guiltless that taketh his name in vain.
Remember the sabbath day, to keep it holy.
Six days shalt thou labour, and do all thy work:
But the seventh day is the sabbath of the Lord thy God: in it thou shalt not do any work, thou, nor thy son, nor thy daughter, thy manservant, nor thy maidservant, nor thy cattle, nor thy stranger that is within thy gates:
For in six days the Lord made heaven and earth, the sea, and all that in them is, and rested the seventh day: wherefore the Lord blessed the sabbath day, and hallowed it.
Honour thy father and thy mother: that thy days may be long upon the land which the Lord thy God giveth thee.
Thou shalt not kill.
Thou shalt not commit adultery.
Thou shalt not steal.
Thou shalt not bear false witness against thy neighbour.
Thou shalt not covet thy neighbour's house, thou shalt not covet thy neighbour's wife, nor his manservant, nor his maidservant, nor his ox, nor his ass, nor any thing that is thy neighbour's.

Bible: Exodus 20:2–17

15 And he said, Thou canst not see my face: for there shall no man see me, and live.

Bible: Exodus 33:20

16 And he said, Go forth, and stand upon the mount before the Lord. And, behold, the Lord passed by, and a great and strong wind rent the mountains, and brake in pieces the rocks before the Lord; but the Lord was not in the wind: and after the wind an earthquake; but the Lord was not in the earthquake:
And after the earthquake a fire; but the Lord was not in the fire: and after the fire a still small voice.

Bible: I Kings 19:11–12

17 Man has learned to cope with all questions of importance without recourse to God as a working hypothesis.

Dietrich Bonhoeffer (1906–45) German theologian. *Letters and Papers from Prison*, 8 June 1944

18 A God who let us prove his existence would be an idol.

Dietrich Bonhoeffer *No Rusty Swords*

19 God's gifts put man's best gifts to shame.

Elizabeth Barrett Browning (1806–61) British poet. *Sonnets from the Portuguese*, XXVI

20 Since the order of the world is shaped by death, mightn't it be better for God if we refuse to believe in Him, and struggle with all

our might against death without raising our eyes towards the heaven where He sits in silence?

Albert Camus (1913–60) French existentialist writer. *The Plague*, II, Ch. 7

21 Isn't God a shit.

Randolph Churchill (1911–68) British political journalist. Evelyn Waugh discovered that Churchill had never read the Bible and persuaded him to do so; this is Churchill's reaction when asked what he thought of it. *Diaries* (E. Waugh)

22 Thou shalt have one God only; who
Would be at the expense of two?

Arthur Hugh Clough (1819–61) British poet. *The Latest Decalogue*, 1

23 God moves in a mysterious way
His wonders to perform;
He plants his footsteps in the sea,
And rides upon the storm.

William Cowper (1731–1800) British poet. *Olney Hymns*, 35

24 It is the final proof of God's omnipotence that he need not exist in order to save us.

Peter De Vries (1910–) US novelist. *The Mackerel Plaza*, Ch. 2

25 God is subtle but he is not malicious.

Albert Einstein (1879–1955) German-born US physicist. Inscribed over the fireplace in the Mathematical Institute, Princeton. It refers to Einstein's objection to the quantum theory. *Albert Einstein* (Carl Seelig), Ch. 8

26 At bottom God is nothing more than an exalted father.

Sigmund Freud (1856–1939) Austrian psychoanalyst. *Totem and Taboo*

27 O worship the King, all glorious above!
O gratefully sing his power and his love!
Our Shield and Defender – the Ancient of Days,
Pavilioned in splendour, and girded with praise.

Robert Grant (1779–1838) British hymn writer. Hymn

28 Holy, holy, holy, Lord God Almighty!
Early in the morning our song shall rise to thee.

Reginald Heber (1783–1826) British bishop and hymn writer. *Holy, Holy, Holy*

29 The world is charged with the grandeur of God.

Gerard Manley Hopkins (1844–99) British Jesuit and poet. *God's Grandeur*

30 Mine eyes have seen the glory of the coming of the Lord:
He is trampling out the vintage where the grapes of wrath are stored.

Julia Ward Howe (1819–1910) US writer. *Battle Hymn of the American Republic*

31 Operationally, God is beginning to resemble not a ruler but the last fading smile of a cosmic Cheshire cat.

Julian Huxley (1887–1975) British biologist. *Religion without Revelation*

32 The chess-board is the world; the pieces are the phenomena of the universe; the rules of the game are what we call the laws of Nature. The player on the other side is hidden from us. We know that his play is always fair, just, and patient. But also we know, to our cost, that he never overlooks a mistake, or makes the smallest allowance for ignorance.

T. H. Huxley (1825–95) British biologist. *Lay Sermons*, 'A Liberal Education'

33 An honest God is the noblest work of man.

Robert G. Ingersoll (1833–99) US lawyer and agnostic. *Gods*

34 Man proposes but God disposes.

Thomas à Kempis (Thomas Hemmerken; c. 1380–1471) German monk. *The Imitation of Christ*, I

35 A man with God is always in the majority.

John Knox (c. 1514–72) Scottish religious reformer. Inscription, Reformation Monument, Geneva, Switzerland

36 There once was a man who said 'God
Must think it exceedingly odd
If he finds that this tree
Continues to be
When there's no one about in the Quad.'

Ronald Knox (1888–1957) Roman Catholic priest and author. Attrib.

37 Dear Sir, Your astonishment's odd:
I am always about in the Quad.
And that's why the tree
Will continue to be,
Since observed by Yours faithfully,
God.

Anonymous The response to KNOX's limerick

38 What God does, He does well.

Jean de La Fontaine (1621–95) French poet. *Fables*, IX, 'Le Gland et la Citrouille'

39 I have no need of that hypothesis.

Marquis de Laplace (1749–1827) French mathematician and astronomer. On being asked by Napoleon why he had made no mention of God in his book about the universe, *Mécanique céleste*. *Men of Mathematics* (E. Bell)

40 Though the mills of God grind slowly, yet they grind exceeding small;
Though with patience He stands waiting, with exactness grinds He all.

Friedrich von Logau (1604–55) German poet and writer. *Sinngedichte*, III

41 God is the immemorial refuge of the incompetent, the helpless, the miserable. They find not only sanctuary in His arms, but also a kind of superiority, soothing to their macerated egos; He will set them above their betters.

H. L. Mencken (1880–1956) US journalist. *Notebooks*, 'Minority Report'

42 There's a Friend for little children
Above the bright blue sky,
A Friend who never changes,
Whose love will never die.

Albert Midlane (1825–1909) British hymn writer. Hymn

43 Let us with a gladsome mind
Praise the Lord, for he is kind,
For his mercies ay endure,
Ever faithful, ever sure.

John Milton (1608–74) English poet. *Psalm*

44 What in me is dark
Illumine, what is low raise and support;
That, to the height of this great argument,
I may assert Eternal Providence,
And justify the ways of God to men.

John Milton *Paradise Lost*, Bk. I

45 God is dead: but considering the state the species Man is in, there will perhaps be caves, for ages yet, in which his shadow will be shown.

Friedrich Wilhelm Nietzsche (1844–1900) German philosopher. *Die Fröhliche Wissenschaft*, Bk. III

46 God is a gentleman. He prefers blondes.

Joe Orton (1933–67) British dramatist. *Loot*, II

47 One on God's side is a majority.

Wendell Phillips (1811–84) US reformer. Speech, Brooklyn, 1 Nov 1859

48 God is really only another artist. He invented the giraffe, the elephant, and the cat. He has no real style, He just goes on trying other things.

Pablo Picasso (1881–1973) Spanish painter. *Life with Picasso* Ch. 1 (Françoise Gilot and Carlton Lake),

49 God can stand being told by

Professor Ayer and Marghanita Laski that He doesn't exist.

J. B. Priestley (1894–1984) British novelist. *The Listener*, 1 July 1965, 'The BBC's Duty to Society'

50 Write down that they hope they serve God; and write God first; for God defend but God should go before such villains!

William Shakespeare (1564–1616) English dramatist. *Much Ado About Nothing*, IV:2

51 But already it is time to depart, for me to die, for you to go on living; which of us takes the better course, is concealed from anyone except God.

Socrates (469–399 BC) Athenian philosopher. *Apology* (Plato)

52 In the days of my youth I remembered my God!
And He hath not forgotten my age.

Robert Southey (1774–1843) British poet. *The Old Man's Comforts, and how he Gained them*

53 God heard the embattled nations shout
Gott strafe England and God save the King.
Good God, said God,
I've got my work cut out.

John Collings Squire (1884–1958) British journalist. *1914*

54 Yet her conception of God was certainly not orthodox. She felt towards Him as she might have felt towards a glorified sanitary engineer; and in some of her speculations she seems hardly to distinguish between the Deity and the Drains.

Lytton Strachey (1880–1932) British writer. *Eminent Victorians*, 'Florence Nightingale'

55 It is a mistake to assume that God is interested only, or even chiefly, in religion.

William Temple (1881–1944) British archbishop. Attrib.

56 If God did not exist, it would be necessary to invent Him.

Voltaire (François-Marie Arouet; 1694–1778) French writer. *Épîtres*, 'À l'auteur du livre des trois Imposteurs'

57 If God made us in His image, we have certainly returned the compliment.

Voltaire *Le Sottisier*

58 It now appears that research underway offers the possibility of establishing the existence of an agency having the properties and characteristics ascribed to the religious concept of God.

Dr. Evan Harris Walker Theoretical physicist.

GOLDSMITH, Oliver

(1728–74) Irish-born British writer, dramatist, and poet. He is remembered for his novel *The Vicar of Wakefield* (1776) and the play *She Stoops to Conquer* (1773) in addition to a considerable amount of verse.

Quotations about Goldsmith

1 No man was more foolish when he had not a pen in his hand, or more wise when he had.

Samuel Johnson (1709–84) British lexicographer. *The Life of Johnson* (J. Boswell)

2 An inspired idiot.

Horace Walpole (1717–97) British writer. Attrib.

Quotations by Goldsmith

3 True genius walks along a line, and, perhaps, our greatest pleasure is in seeing it so often near falling, without being ever actually down.

The Bee, 'The Characteristics of Greatness'

4 As writers become more numerous, it is natural for readers to become more indolent.

The Bee, 'Upon Unfortunate Merit'

5 To a philosopher no circumstance, however trifling, is too minute.

The Citizen of the World

6 Ill fares the land, to hast'ning ills a prey,
Where wealth accumulates, and men decay;
Princes and lords may flourish, or may fade;
A breath can make them, as a breath has made;
But a bold peasantry, their country's pride,
When once destroy'd, can never be supplied.

The Deserted Village

7 In arguing too, the parson own'd his skill,
For e'en though vanquish'd, he could argue still;
While words of learned length, and thund'ring sound
Amazed the gazing rustics rang'd around,
And still they gaz'd, and still the wonder grew,
That one small head could carry all he knew.

The Deserted Village

8 Man wants but little here below,
Nor wants that little long.

Edwin and Angelina, or the Hermit

9 The doctor found, when she was dead,
Her last disorder mortal.

Elegy on Mrs. Mary Blaize

10 The dog, to gain some private ends,
Went mad and bit the man.

Elegy on the Death of a Mad Dog

11 The man recovered of the bite,
The dog it was that died.

Elegy on the Death of a Mad Dog

12 I hate the French because they are all slaves, and wear wooden shoes.

Essays, 'Distresses of a Common Soldier'

13 The true use of speech is not so much to express our wants as to conceal them.

Essays, 'The Use of Language'

14 Friendship is a disinterested commerce between equals; love, an abject intercourse between tyrants and slaves.

The Good-Natured Man, I

15 We must touch his weaknesses with a delicate hand. There are some faults so nearly allied to excellence, that we can scarce weed out the fault without eradicating the virtue.

The Good-Natured Man, I

16 LEONTINE. An only son, sir, might expect more indulgence.
CROAKER. An only father, sir, might expect more obedience.

The Good-Natured Man, I

17 I am told he makes a very handsome corpse, and becomes his coffin prodigiously.

The Good-Natured Man, I

18 Silence is become his mother tongue.

The Good-Natured Man, II

19 I love everything that's old: old friends, old times, old manners, old books, old wine.

She Stoops to Conquer, I

20 In my time, the follies of the town crept slowly among us, but now they travel faster than a stagecoach.

She Stoops to Conquer, I

21 Let schoolmasters puzzle their brain,
With grammar, and nonsense, and learning,
Good liquor, I stoutly maintain,
Gives genius a better discerning.
She Stoops to Conquer, I

22 This is Liberty-Hall, gentlemen.
She Stoops to Conquer, II

23 Where wealth and freedom reign, contentment fails,
And honour sinks where commerce long prevails.
The Traveller

24 Laws grind the poor, and rich men rule the law.
The Traveller

25 A book may be amusing with numerous errors, or it may be very dull without a single absurdity.
The Vicar of Wakefield, Advertisement

26 I . . . chose my wife, as she did her wedding gown, not for a fine glossy surface, but such qualities as would wear well.
The Vicar of Wakefield, Preface

27 I was ever of opinion, that the honest man who married and brought up a large family, did more service than he who continued single and only talked of population.
The Vicar of Wakefield, Ch. 1

28 Let us draw upon content for the deficiencies of fortune.
The Vicar of Wakefield, Ch. 3

29 When lovely woman stoops to folly,
And finds too late that men betray,
What charm can soothe her melancholy,
What art can wash her guilt away?
The Vicar of Wakefield, Ch. 9

30 Conscience is a coward, and those faults it has not strength enough to prevent it seldom has justice enough to accuse.
The Vicar of Wakefield, Ch. 13

31 There is no arguing with Johnson; for when his pistol misses fire, he knocks you down with the butt end of it.
Life of Johnson (J. Boswell)

32 As I take my shoes from the shoemaker, and my coat from the tailor, so I take my religion from the priest.
Life of Johnson (J. Boswell)

GOLDWYNISMS

Sayings attributed to Samuel Goldwyn (Samuel Goldfish; 1882–1974), the Polish-born US film producer. Most are apocryphal. *See also* cinema, mixed metaphors

Quotations about Goldwyn

1 You always knew where you were with Goldwyn – nowhere.
F. Scott Fitzgerald (1896–1940) US novelist. *Some Sort of Epic Grandeur*

2 The trouble, Mr. Goldwyn, is that you are only interested in art and I am only interested in money.
George Bernard Shaw (1856–1950) Irish dramatist and critic. Turning down Goldwyn's offer to buy the screen rights of his plays. *The Movie Moguls* (Philip French), Ch. 4

Quotations by Goldwyn

3 Let's have some new clichés.
The Observer, 'Sayings of the Week', 24 Oct 1948

4 Too caustic? To hell with cost; we'll make the picture anyway.

5 We're overpaying him but he's worth it.

6 What we want is a story that starts with an earthquake and works its way up to a climax.

7 I am willing to admit that I may not always be right, but I am never wrong.

8 I don't care if it doesn't make a nickel, I just want every man, woman, and child in America to see it!
Referring to his film *The Best Years of Our Lives.*

9 A wide screen just makes a bad film twice as bad.

10 For years I have been known for saying 'Include me out'; but today I am giving it up for ever.
Address, Balliol College, Oxford, 1 Mar 1945

11 In two words: im - possible.
Attrib.

12 Anybody who goes to see a psychiatrist ought to have his head examined.

13 Every director bites the hand that lays the golden egg.

14 I'll give you a definite maybe.

15 A verbal contract isn't worth the paper it's written on.

16 You ought to take the bull between the teeth.

17 We have all passed a lot of water since then.

18 I read part of it all the way through.

19 If Roosevelt were alive he'd turn in his grave.

20 It's more than magnificent – it's mediocre.

21 'Why only twelve?' 'That's the original number.' 'Well, go out and get thousands.'
Referring to the number of disciples while filming a scene for *The Last Supper.*

22 Yes, I'm going to have a bust made of them.
Replying to an admiring comment about his wife's hands.

23 Tell me, how did you love my picture?

24 The trouble with this business is the dearth of bad pictures.

25 Why should people go out and pay money to see bad films when they can stay at home and see bad television for nothing?

Other examples

Not all Goldwynisms were said by Goldwyn. Here is a selection of remarks that could have been by him, but were, in fact, said by others.

26 The Jews and Arabs should sit down and settle their differences like good Christians.
Warren Austin (1877–1962) US politician and diplomat. Attrib.

27 All my shows are great. Some of them are bad. But they are all great.
Lew Grade (Lewis Winogradsky; 1906–) British film and TV producer. *The Observer*, 'Sayings of the Week', 14 Sept 1975

28 What about it? Do you want to crucify the boy?
Lew Grade Referring to the revelation that an actor portraying Christ on television was living with a woman to whom he was not married. Attrib.

29 Once you're dead, you're made for life.
Jimi Hendrix (1942–70) US rock musician. Attrib.

30 We have to believe in free will. We've got no choice.

Isaac Bashevis Singer (1904–) Polish-born US writer. *The Times*, 21 June 1982

GOLF

See also sport

1 It's not in support of cricket but as an earnest protest against golf.

Max Beerbohm (1872–1956) British writer. Said when giving a shilling towards W. G. Grace's testimonial. *Carr's Dictionary of Extraordinary English Cricketers*

2 I find it more satisfying to be a bad player at golf. The worse you play, the better you remember the occasional good shot.

Nubar Gulbenkian (1896–1972) Turkish oil magnate. *The Daily Telegraph*, obituary, 12 Jan 1972

3 Golf may be played on Sunday, not being a game within the view of the law, but being a form of moral effort.

Stephen Leacock (1869–1944) English-born Canadian economist and humorist. *Other Fancies*, 'Why I refuse to play Golf'

4 All I've got against it is that it takes you so far from the club house.

Eric Linklater (1889–1974) Scottish novelist. Referring to golf. *Poet's Pub*, Ch. 3

5 Golf is a good walk spoiled.

Mark Twain (Samuel Langhorne Clemens; 1835–1910) US writer. Attrib.

GOOD

See also good and evil, righteousness, virtue

1 Men have never been good, they are not good, they never will be good.

Karl Barth (1886–1968) Swiss Protestant theologian. *Time*, 12 Apr 1954

2 He who would do good to another must do it in Minute Particulars.
General Good is the plea of the scoundrel, hypocrite, and flatterer.

William Blake (1757–1827) British poet. *Jerusalem*

3 *Summum bonum.*
The greatest good.

Cicero (106–43 BC) Roman orator and statesman. *De Officiis*, I

4 Nice guys finish last.

Leo Durocher (1905–) US baseball player. Reply when asked whether he felt sorry to have beaten such a 'nice bunch of guys' as the New York Giants. Attrib.

5 What is a weed? A plant whose virtues have not been discovered.

Ralph Waldo Emerson (1803–82) US poet and essayist. *Fortune of the Republic*

6 Would to God that we might spend a single day really well!

Thomas à Kempis (Thomas Hemmerken; c. 1380–1471) German monk. *The Imitation of Christ*, I

7 Teach us delight in simple things,
And mirth that has no bitter springs;
Forgiveness free of evil done,
And love to all men 'neath the sun!

Rudyard Kipling (1865–1936) Indian-born British writer. *The Children's Song*

8 The greatest pleasure I know, is to do a good action by stealth, and to have it found out by accident.

Charles Lamb (1775–1834) British essayist. *The Athenaeum*, 'Table Talk by the late Elia', 4 Jan 1834

9 Goodness does not more certainly make men happy than happiness makes them good.

Walter Savage Landor (1775–1864) British poet and writer. *Imaginary Conversations*, 'Lord Brooke and Sir Philip Sidney'

10 Dowel, Dobet and Dobest.

William Langland (c. 1330–c. 1400) English poet. Do well, Do better, and Do Best: three concepts central to the search for Truth in *Piers Plowman*, in which they appear as allegorical characters. *The Vision of Piers Plowman*

11 Much benevolence of the passive order may be traced to a disinclination to inflict pain upon oneself.

George Meredith (1828–1909) British novelist. *Vittoria*, Ch. 42

12 Abashed the devil stood,
And felt how awful goodness is.

John Milton (1608–74) English poet. *Paradise Lost*, Bk. IV

13 The good is the beautiful.

Plato (429–347 BC) Greek philosopher. *Lysis*

14 Do good by stealth, and blush to find it fame.

Alexander Pope (1688–1744) British poet. *Epilogue to the Satires*, Dialogue I

15 Sweet are the uses of adversity,
Which like the toad, ugly and venomous,
Wears yet a precious jewel in his head;
And this our life, exempt from public haunt,
Finds tongues in trees, books in the running brooks,
Sermons in stones, and good in everything.

William Shakespeare (1564–1616) English dramatist. *As You Like It*, II:1

16 How far that little candle throws his beams!
So shines a good deed in a naughty world.

William Shakespeare *The Merchant of Venice*, V:1

17 Nothing can harm a good man, either in life or after death.

Socrates (469–399 BC) Athenian philosopher. *Apology* (Plato)

18 – My goodness those diamonds are lovely!
Goodness had nothing whatever to do with it.

Mae West (1892–1980) US actress. Used in 1959 as the title of the first volume of her autobiography. *Diamond Lil*, film 1932

19 You shouldn't say it is not good. You should say you do not like it; and then, you know, you're perfectly safe.

James Whistler (1834–1903) US painter. *Whistler Stories* (D. Seitz)

GOOD AND EVIL

See also evil, good, virtue and vice

1 There is so much good in the worst of us,
And so much bad in the best of us,
That it hardly becomes any of us
To talk about the rest of us.

Anonymous *Good and Bad*

2 Good can imagine Evil; but Evil cannot imagine Good.

W. H. Auden (1907–73) British poet. *A Certain World: A Commonplace Book*

3 Evil comes at leisure like the disease; good comes in a hurry like the doctor.

G. K. Chesterton (1874–1936) British writer. *The Man who was Orthodox*

4 The good die early, and the bad die late.

Daniel Defoe (1660–1731) British journalist and writer. *Character of the late Dr. Annesley*

5 A good man can be stupid and still be good. But a bad man must have brains.

Maxim Gorky (Aleksei Maksimovich Peshkov; 1868–1936) Russian writer. *The Lower Depths*

6 The web of our life is of a mingled yarn, good and ill together.

William Shakespeare (1564–1616) English dramatist. *All's Well that Ends Well*, IV:3

7 Then the liars and swearers are fools, for there are liars and swearers enow to beat the honest men and hang up them.
William Shakespeare *Macbeth*, IV:2

8 O! the more angel she,
And you the blacker devil.
William Shakespeare *Othello*, V:2

9 The good die first,
And they whose hearts are dry as summer dust
Burn to the socket.
William Wordsworth (1770–1850) British poet. *The Excursion*

GOSSIP

See also secrecy

1 A tale never loses in the telling.
Proverb

2 Don't wash your dirty linen in public.
Proverb

3 Listeners never hear good of themselves.
Proverb

4 No names, no pack-drill.
Proverb

5 There's no smoke without fire.
Proverb

6 Throw dirt enough, and some will stick.
Proverb

7 Walls have ears.
Proverb

8 How these curiosities would be quite forgot, did not such idle fellows as I am put them down.
John Aubrey (1626–97) English antiquary. *Brief Lives*, 'Venetia Digby'

9 No one gossips about other people's secret virtues.
Bertrand Russell (1872–1970) British philosopher. *On Education*

10 Her first economic drive will be to replace X-ray by hearsay.
Gwyn Thomas (1913–81) British writer. *The Keep*, II

11 I remember that a wise friend of mine did usually say, 'that which is everybody's business is nobody's business'.
Izaak Walton (1593–1683) English writer. *The Compleat Angler*, Ch. 2

GOVERNMENT

See also democracy, Houses of Parliament, monarchy, opposition, politicians, politics

1 I will undoubtedly have to seek what is happily known as gainful employment, which I am glad to say does not describe holding public office.
Dean Acheson (1893–1971) US lawyer and statesman. Remark made on leaving his post as secretary of state, 1952; he subsequently returned to private legal practice

2 The danger is not that a particular class is unfit to govern. Every class is unfit to govern.
Lord Acton (1834–1902) British historian. Letter to Mary Gladstone, 1881

3 The Austrian Government . . . is a system of despotism tempered by casualness.
Victor Adler (1852–1918) Austrian socialist. Speech, International Socialist Congress, Paris, 17 July 1889

4 Whose Finger do you want on the Trigger When the World Situation Is So Delicate?
Anonymous Headline from the *Daily Mirror* on the day before the General Election, Oct 1951. *Publish and Be Damned* (Hugh Cudlipp), 1953

5 Where some people are very wealthy and others have nothing, the result will be either extreme democracy or absolute oligarchy, or despotism will come from either of those excesses.
Aristotle (384–322 BC) Greek philosopher. *Politics*, Bk. IV

6 One to mislead the public, another to mislead the Cabinet, and the third to mislead itself.
Herbert Henry Asquith (1852–1928) British statesman. Explaining why the War Office kept three sets of figures. *The Price of Glory* (Alastair Horne), Ch. 2

7 My language fails
Go out and govern new South Wales.
Hilaire Belloc (1870–1953) British writer. *Cautionary Tales*, 'Lord Lundy'

8 The object of government in peace and in war is not the glory of rulers or of races, but the happiness of the common man.
Lord Beveridge (1879–1963) British economist. *Social Insurance*

9 Too bad all the people who know how to run the country are busy driving cabs and cutting hair.
George Burns (1896–) US comedian.

10 You had better have one King than five hundred.
Charles II (1630–85) King of England. Remark after dissolving the Oxford Parliament, 28 Mar 1681; he did not summon parliament again

11 A small acquaintance with history shows that all Governments are selfish and the French Governments more selfish than most.
David Eccles (1904–) British politician. *The Observer*, 'Sayings of the Year', 29 Dec 1962

12 The king's council was wont to be chosen of the great princes, and of the greatest lords of the land, both spiritual and temporal. . . . Wherethrough, when they came together they were so occupied with their own matters that they attended but little, and other whiles nothing, to the king's matters.
John Fortescue (c. 1394–1476) English jurist. *The Governance of England*

13 He was uniformly of an opinion which, though not a popular one, he was ready to aver, that the right of governing was not property but a trust.
Charles James Fox (1749–1806) British Whig politician. Referring to William Pitt's plans for parliamentary reform. *C.J. Fox* (J. L. Hammond)

14 The principles of a free constitution are irrecoverably lost, when the legislative power is nominated by the executive.
Edward Gibbon (1737–94) British historian. *Decline and Fall of the Roman Empire*, Ch. 3

15 A government that is big enough to give you all you want is big enough to take it all away.
Barry Goldwater (1904–) US politician. *Bachman's Book of Freedom Quotations* (M. Ivens and R. Dunstan)

16 We at no time stand so highly in our estate royal as in the time of Parliament, wherein we as head and you as members are conjoined and knit together into one body politic.
Henry VIII (1491–1547) King of England. Speech to a deputation from the House of Commons, 31 Mar 1543

17 They that are discontented under *monarchy*, call it *tyranny* ; and they that are displeased with *aristocracy*, call it *oligarchy*: so also, they which find themselves grieved under a *democracy*, call it *anarchy*, which signifies the want of government;

and yet I think no man believes, that want of government, is any new kind of government.
Thomas Hobbes (1588–1679) English philosopher. *Leviathan*, Pt. II, Ch. 19

18 I would not give half a guinea to live under one form of government rather than another. It is of no moment to the happiness of an individual.
Samuel Johnson (1709–84) British lexicographer. *Life of Johnson* (J. Boswell), Vol. II

19 Any cook should be able to run the country.
Lenin (Vladimir Ilich Ulyanov; 1870–1924) Russian revolutionary leader. *The First Circle* (Alexander Solzhenitsyn)

20 What is our task? To make Britain a fit country for heroes to live in.
David Lloyd George (1863–1945) British Liberal statesman. Speech, 24 Nov 1918

21 Government has no other end but the preservation of property.
John Locke (1632–1704) English philosopher. *Second Treatise on Civil Government*

22 The Commons, faithful to their system, remained in a wise and masterly inactivity.
James Mackintosh (1765–1832) Scottish lawyer, philosopher, and historian. *Vindiciae Gallicae*

23 Every country has the government it deserves.
Joseph de Maistre (1753–1821) French monarchist. *Lettres et Opuscules Inédits*, 15 Aug 1811

24 The worst government is the most moral. One composed of cynics is often very tolerant and human. But when fanatics are on top there is no limit to oppression.
H. L. Mencken (1880–1956) US journalist. *Notebooks*, 'Minority Report'

25 One day the don't-knows will get in, and then where will we be?
Spike Milligan (1918–) British comic actor and author. Attributed remark made about a pre-election poll

26 The rights of parliament should be preserved sacred and inviolable, wherever they are found. This kind of government, once so universal all over Europe, is now almost vanished from amongst the nations thereof. Our king's dominions are the only supporters of this noble Gothic constitution, save only what little remains may be found thereof in Poland.
William Molyneux (1656–98) Irish politician. *The Case of Ireland's being Bound by Acts of Parliament in England stated* (Pamphlet, 1698)

27 Do you not know, my son, with how little wisdom the world is governed?
Axel Oxenstierna (1583–1654) Swedish statesman. Letter to his son, 1648

28 Government, even in its best state, is but a necessary evil; in its worst state, an intolerable one.
Thomas Paine (1737–1809) British writer. *Common Sense*, Ch. 1

29 As to religion, I hold it to be the indispensable duty of government to protect all conscientious professors thereof, and I know of no other business which government hath to do therewith.
Thomas Paine *Common Sense*, Ch. 4

30 Let the people think they govern and they will be governed.
William Penn (1644–1718) English preacher. *Some Fruits of Solitude*, 337

31 We live under a government of men and morning newspapers.
Wendell Phillips (1811–84) US reformer. *Address: The Press*

32 Parliaments are the great lie of our time.
Konstantin Pobedonostsev (1827–1907) Russian jurist and Procurator of the Holy Synod. *Moskovskii Sbornik*

33 Secrecy is the first essential in affairs of the State.
Cardinal Richelieu (1585–1642) French statesman. *Testament Politique*, Maxims

34 I don't make jokes – I just watch the government and report the facts.
Will Rogers (1879–1935) US actor and humorist. *Saturday Review*, 'A Rogers Thesaurus', 25 Aug 1962

35 Hansard is history's ear, already listening.
Herbert Samuel (1870–1963) British Liberal statesman. *The Observer*, 'Sayings of the Week', 18 Dec 1949

36 Parliament is the longest running farce in the West End.
Cyril Smith (1928–) British Liberal politician. *The Times*, 23 Sept 1977

37 It would be desirable if every government, when it comes to power, should have its old speeches burned.
Philip Snowden (1864–1937) British politician. *Biography* (C. E. Bechafer Roberts)

38 The foundation of the government of a nation must be built upon the rights of the people, but the administration must be entrusted to experts.
Sun Yat-sen (1867–1925) Chinese revolutionary leader. *The Three Principles of the People*

39 Accidentally.
Talleyrand (Charles Maurice de Talleyrand-Périgord; 1754–1838) French politician. Replying, during the reign of Louis Philippe, to the query 'How do you think this government will end?' *The Wheat and the Chaff* (F. Mitterand)

40 The English nation is the only one on earth which has successfully regulated the power of its kings by resisting them; and which, after repeated efforts, has established that beneficial government under which the Prince, all powerful for good, is restrained from doing ill.
Voltaire (François-Marie Arouet; 1694–1778) French writer. *Lettres philosophiques*

41 Governments needs to have both shepherds and butchers.
Voltaire *Notebooks*

42 Many people consider the things which government does for them to be social progress, but they consider the things government does for others as socialism.
Earl Warren (1891–1971) US lawyer. *Peter's Quotations* (Laurence J. Peter)

43 The people's government, made for the people, made by the people, and answerable to the people.
Daniel Webster (1782–1852) US statesman. Second speech on Foote's resolution, 26 Jan 1830

44 If people behaved in the way nations do they would all be put in straitjackets.
Tennessee Williams (1911–83) US dramatist. BBC interview

GRAMMAR

See also language, words

1 'Whom are you?' said he, for he had been to night school.
George Ade (1866–1944) US dramatist and humorist. *Bang! Bang!: The Steel Box*

2 When I split an infinitive, god damn it, I split it so it stays split.
Raymond Chandler (1888–1959) US novelist. Letter to his English publisher

3 By being so long in the lowest form I gained an immense advantage over the cleverest boys . . . I got into my bones the essential structure of the normal British sentence – which is a noble thing.

Winston Churchill (1874–1965) British statesman. *My Early Life*, Ch. 2

4 This is the sort of English up with which I will not put.

Winston Churchill The story is that Churchill wrote the comment in the margin of a report in which a Civil Servant had used an awkward construction to avoid ending a sentence with a preposition. An alternative version substitutes 'bloody nonsense' for 'English'. *Plain Words* (E. Gowers), Ch. 9

5 I will not go down to posterity talking bad grammar.

Benjamin Disraeli (1804–81) British statesman. Remark made when correcting proofs of his last parliamentary speech, 31 Mar 1881. *Disraeli* (Blake), Ch. 32

6 Grammar, which can govern even kings.

Molière (Jean Baptiste Poquelin; 1622–73) French dramatist. *Les Femmes savantes*, II:6

7 I am the Roman Emperor, and am above grammar.

Sigismund (1368–1437) Holy Roman Emperor. Responding to criticism of his Latin. Attrib.

8 Try taking a couple of aspirates.

F. E. Smith (1872–1930) British lawyer and politician. Replying to the Labour MP J. H. Thomas who had complained that he "ad a 'eadache'. Attrib.

9 Why care for grammar as long as we are good?

Artemus Ward (Charles Farrar Browne; 1834–67) US humorous writer. *Pyrotechny*

10 Subjunctive to the last, he preferred to ask, 'And that, sir, would be the Hippodrome?'

Alexander Woollcott (1887–1943) US journalist. *While Rome Burns*, 'Our Mrs Parker'

GRANT, Ulysses Simpson

(1822–85) US general who became a Republican President (1869–77). As supreme commander of the Federal armies he defeated the Confederates.

Quotations about Grant

1 When Grant once gets possession of a place, he holds on to it as if he had inherited it.

Abraham Lincoln (1809–65) US statesman. Letter, 22 June 1864

2 Grant stood by me when I was crazy and I stood by him when he was drunk.

William Sherman (1820–91) US general and president. *Abraham Lincoln: The War Years* (Carl Sandburg)

Quotations by Grant

3 No terms except unconditional and immediate surrender can be accepted. I propose to move immediately upon your works.

Message to opposing commander, Simon Bolivar Buckner, during siege of Fort Donelson, 16 Feb 1862.

4 I purpose to fight it out on this line, if it takes all summer.

Dispatch to Washington, 11 May 1864

5 Let us have peace.

On accepting nomination. Letter, 29 May 1868

6 I know no method to secure the repeal of bad or obnoxious laws so effective as their stringent execution.

Inaugural address, 4 Mar 1869

7 Let no guilty man escape, if it can be avoided . . . No personal considerations should stand in the way of performing a public duty.

Referring to the Whiskey Ring. Indorsement of a letter, 29 July 1875

GRATITUDE

1 Let me say that the credit belongs to the boys in the back rooms. It isn't the man who sits in the limelight like me who should have the praise. It is not the men who sit in prominent places. It is the men in the back rooms.

Lord Beaverbrook (Maxwell Aitken; 1879–1964) Canadian-born politician and newspaper proprietor. From the song 'The Boys in the Back Room', sung by Marlene Dietrich in the film *Destry Rides Again*.

2 Got no check books, got no banks. Still I'd like to express my thanks – I got the sun in the mornin' and the moon at night.

Irving Berlin (1888–) US composer and lyricist. *Annie Get Your Gun*, 'I Got the Sun in the Mornin''

3 There are minds so impatient of inferiority that their gratitude is a species of revenge, and they return benefits, not because recompense is a pleasure, but because obligation is a pain.

Samuel Johnson (1709–84) British lexicographer. *The Rambler*

4 When the messenger who carried the last sheet to Millar returned, Johnson asked him, 'Well, what did he say?' – 'Sir (answered the messenger), he said, thank God I have done with him.' – 'I am glad (replied Johnson, with a smile) that he thanks God for anything.'

Samuel Johnson After the final page of his *Dictionary* had been delivered. *Life of Johnson* (J. Boswell)

5 Thank-you, music-lovers.

Spike Jones (1911–65) US popular musician. Catchphrase

6 Thank heaven for little girls,
For little girls get bigger every day.

Alan Jay Lerner (1918–86) US lyricist and playwright. *Gigi*, 'Thank Heaven for Little Girls'

7 Too kind, too kind.

Florence Nightingale (1820–1910) British nurse. When given the Order of Merit on her deathbed. Attrib.

8 Thank me no thankings, nor proud me no prouds.

William Shakespeare (1564–1616) English dramatist. *Romeo and Juliet*, III:5

GRAVE

1 Now he is dead! Far hence he lies
In the lorn Syrian town;
And on his grave, with shining eyes,
The Syrian stars look down.

Matthew Arnold (1822–88) British poet and critic. *Obermann Once More*

2 Behold, I shew you a mystery; We shall not all sleep, but we shall all be changed,
In a moment, in the twinkling of an eye, at the last trump: for the trumpet shall sound, and the dead shall be raised incorruptible, and we shall be changed.
For this corruptible must put on incorruption, and this mortal must put on immortality.
So when this corruptible shall have put on incorruption, and this mortal shall have put on immortality, then shall be brought to pass the saying that is written, Death is swallowed up in victory.
O death, where is thy sting? O grave, where is thy victory?

Bible: I Corinthians 15:51–55

3 Whatsoever thy hand findeth to do, do it with thy might; for there is no work, nor device, nor knowledge, nor wisdom, in the grave, whither thou goest.

Bible: Ecclesiastes 9:10

4 A little rule, a little sway,

A sunbeam in a winter's day,
Is all the proud and mighty have
Between the cradle and the grave.

John Dyer (1700–58) British poet. *Grongar Hill*

5 The boast of heraldry, the pomp of pow'r,
And all that beauty, all that wealth e'er gave,
Awaits alike th' inevitable hour,
The paths of glory lead but to the grave.

Thomas Gray (1716–71) British poet. *Elegy Written in a Country Churchyard*

6 John Brown's body lies a-moldering in the grave,
His soul is marching on!

Charles Sprague Hall (19th century) US songwriter. The song commemorates the American hero who died in the cause of abolishing slavery. *John Brown's Body*

7 Death is still working like a mole,
And digs my grave at each remove.

George Herbert (1593–1633) English poet. *Grace*

8 I shall soon be laid in the quiet grave – thank God for the quiet grave – O! I can feel the cold earth upon me – the daisies growing over me – O for this quiet – it will be my first.

John Keats (1795–1821) British poet. In a letter to John Taylor by Joseph Severn, 6 Mar 1821

9 Teach me to live, that I may dread
The grave as little as my bed.

Thomas Ken (1637–1711) English bishop. *An Evening Hymn*

10 Art is long, and Time is fleeting,
And our hearts, though stout and brave,
Still, like muffled drums, are beating
Funeral marches to the grave.

Henry Wadsworth Longfellow (1807–82) US poet. *See also* HIPPOCRATES *A Psalm of Life*

11 The grave's a fine and private place,
But none, I think, do there embrace.

Andrew Marvell (1621–78) English poet. *To His Coy Mistress*

12 She is far from the land where her young hero sleeps,
And lovers are round her, sighing:
But coldly she turns from their gaze, and weeps,
For her heart in his grave is lying.

Thomas Moore (1779–1852) Irish poet. *Irish Melodies*, 'She is Far'

13 To that dark inn, the grave!

Walter Scott (1771–1832) Scottish novelist. *The Lord of the Isles*, VI

14 Under the wide and starry sky
Dig the grave and let me lie.
Glad did I live and gladly die,
– And I laid me down with a will.
This is the verse you grave for me:
'Here he lies where he longed to be;
Home is the sailor, home from sea,
And the hunter home from the hill.'

Robert Louis Stevenson (1850–94) Scottish writer. *Underwoods*, Bk. I, 'Requiem'

15 He is an old bore; even the grave yawns for him.

Herbert Beerbohm Tree (1853–1917) British actor and theater manager. Referring to Israel Zangwill. *Beerbohm Tree* (Hesketh Pearson)

GREATNESS

1 A truly great man never puts away the simplicity of a child.

Chinese proverb

2 The dullard's envy of brilliant men is always assuaged by the suspicion that they will come to a bad end.

Max Beerbohm (1872–1956) British writer. *Zuleika Dobson*

3 Great men are but life-sized. Most of them, indeed, are rather short.

Max Beerbohm *And Even Now*

4 Great things are done when men and mountains meet;
This is not done by jostling in the street.

William Blake (1757–1827) British poet. *Gnomic Verses*

5 Nothing grows well in the shade of a big tree.

Constantin Brancusi (1876–1957) Romanian sculptor. Refusing Rodin's invitation to work in his studio. *Compton's Encyclopedia*

6 No great man lives in vain. The history of the world is but the biography of great men.

Thomas Carlyle (1795–1881) Scottish historian and essayist. *Heroes and Hero-Worship*, 'The Hero as Divinity'

7 To be great is to be misunderstood.

Ralph Waldo Emerson (1803–82) US poet and essayist. *Essays*, 'Self-Reliance'

8 The world's great men have not commonly been great scholars, nor great scholars great men.

Oliver Wendell Holmes (1809–94) US writer. *The Autocrat of the Breakfast Table*, Ch. 6

9 If I am a great man, then a good many of the great men of history are frauds.

Bonar Law (1858–1923) British statesman. Attrib.

10 You are one of the forces of nature.

Jules Michelet (1798–1874) French historian. From a letter received by Dumas. *Memoirs*, Vol. VI, Ch. 138 (Alexandre Dumas)

11 To be alone is the fate of all great minds – a fate deplored at times, but still always chosen as the less grievous of two evils.

Arthur Schopenhauer (1788–1860) German philosopher. *Aphorismen zur Lebensweisheit*

12 Some are born great, some achieve greatness, and some have greatness thrust upon 'em.

William Shakespeare (1564–1616) English dramatist. *Twelfth Night*, II:5

13 'My name is Ozymandias, king of kings:
Look on my works, ye Mighty, and despair!'

Percy Bysshe Shelley (1792–1822) British poet. *Ozymandias*

14 Oh, Vanity of vanities!
How wayward the decrees of Fate are;
How very weak the very wise,
How very small the very great are!

William Makepeace Thackeray (1811–63) British novelist. *Vanitas Vanitatum*

15 A great city is that which has the greatest men and women.

Walt Whitman (1819–92) US poet. *Song of the Broad-Axe*, 5

GREECE

1 To the Greeks the Muse gave native wit, to the Greeks the gift of graceful eloquence.

Horace (Quintus Horatius Flaccus; 65–8 BC) Roman poet. *Ars Poetica*

2 Ancient sculpture is the true school of modesty. But where the Greeks had modesty, we have cant; where they had poetry, we have cant; where they had patriotism, we have cant; where they had anything that exalts, delights, or adorns humanity, we have nothing but cant, cant, cant.

Thomas Love Peacock (1785–1866) British novelist. *Crotchet Castle*, Ch. 7

GREED

See also food, materialism, obesity

1 Give him an inch and he'll take a yard.
Proverb

2 Kill not the goose that lays the golden egg.
Proverb

3 The eye is bigger than the belly.
Proverb

4 He that eats till he is sick must fast till he is well.
Hebrew proverb

5 Beware that you do not lose the substance by grasping at the shadow.
Aesop (6th century BC) Reputed Greek writer of fables. *Fables*, 'The Dog and the Shadow'

6 GLUTTON, n. A person who escapes the evils of moderation by committing dyspepsia.
Ambrose Bierce (1842–c. 1914) US writer and journalist. *The Devil's Dictionary*

7 But answer came there none –
And this was scarcely odd because
They'd eaten every one.
Lewis Carroll (Charles Lutwidge Dodgson; 1832–98) British writer. *Through the Looking-Glass*, Ch. 4

8 Gluttony is an emotional escape, a sign something is eating us.
Peter De Vries (1910–) US novelist. *Comfort me with Apples*, Ch. 7

9 More die in the United States of too much food than of too little.
John Kenneth Galbraith (1908–) US economist. *The Affluent Society*, Ch. 9

10 The mountain sheep are sweeter,
But the valley sheep are fatter;
We therefore deemed it meeter
To carry off the latter.
Thomas Love Peacock (1785–1866) British novelist. *The Misfortunes of Elphin*, Ch. 11, 'The War-Song of Dinas Vawr'

11 These citizens are always willing to bet that what Nicely-Nicely dies of will be over-feeding and never anything small like pneumonia, for Nicely-Nicely is known far and wide as a character who dearly loves to commit eating.
Damon Runyon (1884–1946) US writer. *Take it Easy*, 'Lonely Heart'

12 Wealth is like sea-water; the more we drink, the thirstier we become; and the same is true of fame.
Arthur Schopenhauer (1788–1860) German philosopher. *Parerga and Paralipomena*

13 He hath eaten me out of house and home.
William Shakespeare (1564–1616) English dramatist. *Henry IV, Part Two*, II:1

GREETINGS

1 Take me to your leader.
Anonymous Customary line spoken by Martian invaders.

2 I met Curzon in Downing Street, from whom I got the sort of greeting a corpse would give to an undertaker.
Stanley Baldwin, 1st Earl of Bewdley (1867–1947) British Conservative prime minister. After he became prime minister in 1933. Attrib.

3 I thought I told you to wait in the car.
Tallulah Bankhead (1903–68) US actress. When greeted by a former admirer after many years. Attrib.

4 *Atque in perpetuum, frater, ave atque vale.*
And for ever, brother, hail and farewell!
Catullus (c. 84–c. 54 BC) Roman poet. *Carmina*, CI

5 Wery glad to see you indeed, and hope our acquaintance may be a long 'un, as the gen'l'm'n said to the fi' pun' note.
Charles Dickens (1812–70) British novelist. *Pickwick Papers*, Ch. 25

6 Dr Livingstone, I presume?
Henry Morton Stanley (1841–1904) British explorer. On finding David Livingstone at Ujiji on Lake Tanganyika, Nov 1871. *How I found Livingstone*, Ch. 11

7 Lafayette, we are here!
C. E. Stanton (1859–1933) US colonel. The Marquis de Lafayette (1757–1834) aided the colonists in the US War of Independence. Address at Lafayette's grave, Paris, 4 July 1917

GRIEF

1 For in much wisdom is much grief: and he that increaseth knowledge increaseth sorrow.
Bible: Ecclesiastes 1:18

2 The heart which grief hath cankered
Hath one unfailing remedy – the Tankard.
C. S. Calverley (1831–84) British poet. *Beer*

3 One often calms one's grief by recounting it.
Pierre Corneille (1606–84) French dramatist. *Polyeucte*, I:3

4 Grief and disappointment give rise to anger, anger to envy, envy to malice, and malice to grief again, till the whole circle be completed.
David Hume (1711–76) Scottish philosopher. *A Treatise of Human Nature*

5 What's gone and what's past help
Should be past grief.
William Shakespeare (1564–1616) English dramatist. *The Winter's Tale*, III:2

6 Indescribable, O queen, is the grief you bid me to renew.
Virgil (Publius Vergilius Maro; 70–19 BC) Roman poet. The opening words of Aeneas' account to Dido of the fall of Troy. *Aeneid*, Bk. II

7 Grief has turned her fair.
Oscar Wilde (1854–1900) Irish-born British dramatist. Referring to the fact that a recently-bereaved lady friend had dyed her hair blonde. Attrib.

GUIDANCE

See also leadership

1 Everyman, I will go with thee, and be thy guide.
In thy most need to go by thy side.
Anonymous *Everyman* Pt. 1

2 Wandering in a vast forest at night, I have only a faint light to guide me. A stranger appears and says to me: 'My friend, you should blow out your candle in order to find your way more clearly.' This stranger is a theologian.
Denis Diderot (1713–84) French writer. *Addition aux Pensées philosophiques*

3 A little onward lend thy guiding hand
To these dark steps, a little further on.
John Milton (1608–74) English poet. *Samson Agonistes*

GUILT

See also conscience, regret

1 It is quite gratifying to feel guilty if you haven't done anything wrong: how noble! Whereas it is rather hard and certainly depressing to admit guilt and to repent.
Hannah Arendt (1906–75) German-born US philosopher and historian. *Eichmann in Jerusalem*, Ch. 15

2 Alone, alone, about the dreadful wood
Of conscious evil runs a lost mankind,
Dreading to find its Father.
W. H. Auden (1907–73) British poet. *For the Time Being*, 'Chorus'

3 When Pilate saw that he could prevail nothing, but that rather a tumult was made, he took water, and washed his hands before the multitude, saying, I am innocent of the blood of this just person: see ye to it.
Then answered all the people, and said, His blood be on us, and on our children.
Bible: Matthew 27:24–25

4 Then, my lord, be his blood on your own conscience. You might have saved him if you would. I cannot pardon him because I dare not.
Charles II (1630–85) King of England. Reply to the Earl of Essex, who had protested St Oliver Plunket's innocence of the treason for which he had been sentenced to death. *The Later Stuarts* (Sir George Clark)

5 The many men, so beautiful!
And they all dead did lie:
And a thousand thousand slimy things
Lived on; and so did I.
Samuel Taylor Coleridge (1772–1834) British poet. *The Rime of the Ancient Mariner*, IV

6 St. Thomas, guard for me my kingdom! To you I declare myself guilty of that for which others bear the blame.
Henry II (1133–89) King of England. Said at the outbreak of the Great Rebellion, 1173–74; one of Henry's first actions was to perform a public penance for Thomas Becket's murder. *Chronique de la guerre entre les Anglois et les Ecossais en 1173 et 1174* (Jordan Fantosme)

7 Love bade me welcome; yet my soul drew back,
Guilty of dust and sin.
George Herbert (1593–1633) English poet. *Love*

8 You will put on a dress of guilt
and shoes with broken high ideals.
Roger McGough (1937–) British poet. *Comeclose and Sleepnow*

9 I am alone the villain of the earth,
And feel I am so most.
William Shakespeare (1564–1616) English dramatist. *Antony and Cleopatra*, IV:6

10 I have heard,
That guilty creatures sitting at a play
Have by the very cunning of the scene
Been struck so to the soul that presently
They have proclaim'd their malefactions;
For murder, though it have no tongue, will speak
With most miraculous organ.
William Shakespeare *Hamlet*, II:2

11 The lady doth protest too much, methinks.
William Shakespeare *Hamlet*, III:2

12 O! my offence is rank, it smells to heaven.
William Shakespeare *Hamlet*, III:3

13 Suspicion always haunts the guilty mind;
The thief doth fear each bush an officer.
William Shakespeare *Henry VI*, Pt. 3, V:6

14 A little water clears us of this deed.
William Shakespeare *Macbeth*, II:2

15 I am in blood
Stepp'd in so far that, should I wade no more,
Returning were as tedious as go o'er.
William Shakespeare *Macbeth*, III:4

16 Out, damned spot! out, I say!
William Shakespeare *Macbeth*, V:1

17 Here's the smell of the blood still.
All the perfumes of Arabia will not sweeten this little hand.
William Shakespeare *Macbeth*, V:1

18 MACBETH. Canst thou not minister to a mind diseas'd,
Pluck from the memory a rooted sorrow,
Raze out the written troubles of the brain,
And with some sweet oblivious antidote
Cleanse the stuff'd bosom of that perilous stuff
Which weighs upon the heart?
DOCTOR. Therein the patient
Must minister to himself.
MACBETH. Throw physic to the dogs; I'll none of it.
William Shakespeare *Macbeth*, V:3

GULLIBILITY

See also foolishness, impressionability

1 There's a sucker born every minute.
Phineas Barnum (1810–91) US showman. Attrib.

2 When lovely woman stoops to folly,
And finds too late that men betray,
What charm can soothe her melancholy,
What art can wash her guilt away?
Oliver Goldsmith (1728–74) Irish-born British writer. *The Vicar of Wakefield*, Ch. 9

3 Man is a dupable animal. Quacks in medicine, quacks in religion, and quacks in politics know this, and act upon that knowledge.
Robert Southey (1774–1843) British poet. *The Doctor*, Ch. 87

H

HABIT

See also custom

1 Old habits die hard.
Proverb

2 Habit is a great deadener.
Samuel Beckett (1906–) Irish novelist and dramatist. *Waiting for Godot*, III

3 Curious things, habits. People themselves never knew they had them.
Agatha Christie (1891–1976) British detective-story writer. *Witness for the Prosecution*

4 Men's natures are alike; it is their habits that carry them far apart.
Confucius (K'ung Fu-tzu; 551–479 BC) Chinese philosopher. *Analects*

5 They do those little personal things people sometimes do when they think they are alone in railway carriages; things like smelling their own armpits.
Jonathan Miller (1934–) British doctor and television and stage director. *Beyond the Fringe*

HALF MEASURES

1 Two half-truths do not make a truth, and two half-cultures do not make a culture.
Arthur Koestler (1905–83) Hungarian-born British writer. *The Ghost in the Machine*, Preface

2 I'm not really a Jew; just Jew-ish, not the whole hog.
Jonathan Miller (1934–) British doctor and television and stage director. *Beyond the Fringe*

HANGOVERS

1 Take a hair of the dog that bit you.
Proverb

2 His mouth has been used as a latrine by some small animal of the night.
Kingsley Amis (1922–) British novelist. Describing a hangover. *Lucky Jim*

HAPPINESS

See also contentment, laughter, pleasure

1 One joy scatters a hundred griefs.
Chinese proverb

2 If you haven't been happy very young, you can still be happy later on, but it's much harder. You need more luck.
Simone de Beauvoir (1908–86) French writer. *The Observer*, 'Sayings of the Week', 19 May 1975

3 The greatest happiness of the greatest number is the foundation of morals and legislation.
Jeremy Bentham (1748–1832) British philosopher. *See also* HUTCHESON *The Commonplace Book*

4 There was a jolly miller once,
Lived on the river Dee;
He worked and sang from morn till night;
No lark more blithe than he.
Isaac Bickerstaffe (c. 1735–c. 1812) Irish dramatist. *Love in a Village*, I

5 When the green woods laugh with the voice of joy.
William Blake (1757–1827) British poet. *Songs of Innocence*, 'Laughing song'

6 In every adversity of fortune, to have been happy is the most unhappy kind of misfortune.
Boethius (c. 480–524) Roman statesman, philosopher, and scholar. *The Consolation of Philosophy*

7 Happiness is a mystery like religion, and should never be rationalized.
G. K. Chesterton (1874–1936) British writer. *Heretics*, Ch. 7

8 To marvel at nothing is just about the one and only thing, Numicius, that can make a man happy and keep him that way.
Horace (Quintus Horatius Flaccus; 65–8 BC) Roman poet. *Epistles*, I

9 Not the owner of many possessions will you be right to call happy: he more rightly deserves the name of happy who knows how to use the gods' gifts wisely and to put up with rough poverty, and who fears dishonour more than death.
Horace *Odes*, IV

10 The Politics of Joy.
Hubert H. Humphrey (1911–78) US Democratic vice-president. Campaign slogan, 1964

11 That action is best, which procures the greatest happiness for the greatest numbers.
Francis Hutcheson (1694–1746) Scottish philosopher. *See also* BENTHAM *Inquiry into the Original of our Ideas of Beauty and Virtue*, Treatise II, 'Concerning Moral Good and Evil'

12 Happiness is like coke - something you get as a by-product in the process of making something else.
Aldous Huxley (1894–1964) British novelist. *Point Counter Point*

13 That all who are happy, are equally happy, is not true. A peasant and a philosopher may be equally *satisfied*, but not equally *happy*. Happiness consists in the multiplicity of agreeable consciousness.
Samuel Johnson (1709–84) British lexicographer. *Life of Johnson* (J. Boswell), Vol. II

14 . . . because happiness is not an ideal of reason but of imagination.
Immanuel Kant (1724–1804) German philosopher. *Grundlegung zur Metaphysik der Sitten*, II

15 well archy the world is full of ups and downs but toujours gai is my motto.
Don Marquis (1878–1937) US journalist. *archy and mehitabel*

16 Ask yourself whether you are happy, and you cease to be so.
John Stuart Mill (1806–73) British philosopher. *Autobiography*, Ch. 5

17 When a small child . . . I thought that success spelled happiness. I was wrong. Happiness is like a butterfly which appears and delights us for one brief moment, but soon flits away.
Anna Pavlova (1881–1931) Russian ballet dancer. *Pavlova: A Biography* (ed. A. H. Franks), 'Pages of My Life'

18 And we suddenly know, what heaven we're in,
When they begin the beguine.
Cole Porter (1893–1964) US songwriter. *Jubilee*, 'Begin the Beguine'

19 We are never so happy nor so unhappy as we imagine.
Duc de la Rochefoucauld (1613–80) French writer. *Maximes*, 49

20 Happiness is not best achieved by those who seek it directly.
Bertrand Russell (1872–1970) British philosopher. *Mysticism and Logic*

21 Every time I talk to a savant I feel quite sure that happiness is no longer a possibility. Yet when I talk with my gardener, I'm convinced of the opposite.
Bertrand Russell Attrib.

22 One is happy as a result of one's own efforts, once one knows the necessary ingredients of happiness – simple tastes, a certain degree of courage, self denial to a point, love of work, and, above all, a clear conscience. Happiness is no vague dream, of that I now feel certain.
George Sand (Aurore Dupin, Baronne Dudevant; 1804–76) French novelist. *Correspondence*, Vol. V

23 Happiness is the only sanction of life; where happiness fails, existence remains a mad and lamentable experiment.
George Santayana (1863–1952) US philosopher. *The Life of Reason*

24 Oh! how bitter a thing it is to look into happiness through another man's eyes.
William Shakespeare (1564–1616) English dramatist.

25 A lifetime of happiness: no man alive could bear it: it would be hell on earth.
George Bernard Shaw (1856–1950) Irish dramatist and critic. *Man and Superman*, I

26 Mankind are always happy for having been happy, so that if you make them happy now, you make them happy twenty years hence by the memory of it.
Sydney Smith (1771–1845) British clergyman and essayist. *Elementary Sketches of Moral Philosophy*

27 A man is happy so long as he chooses to be happy and nothing can stop him.
Alexander Solzhenitsyn (1918–) Soviet novelist. *Cancer Ward*

28 There is no duty we so much

underrate as the duty of being happy.
Robert Louis Stevenson (1850–94) Scottish writer. *Virginibus Puerisque*

29 Happiness is an imaginary condition, formerly often attributed by the living to the dead, now usually attributed by adults to children, and by children to adults.
Thomas Szasz (1920–) US psychiatrist. *The Second Sin*

30 If you want to be happy, be.
Leo Tolstoy (1828–1910) Russian writer. *Kosma Prutkov*

31 Happiness is no laughing matter.
Richard Whately (1787–1863) British churchman. *Apophthegms*

32 Happy Days Are Here Again.
Jack Yellen (1892–) US lyricist. Used by Roosevelt as a campaign song in 1932. Song title

33 The hell with it. Who never knew the price of happiness will not be happy.
Yevgeny Yevtushenko (1933–) Soviet poet. *Lies*

HASTE

See also impetuosity

1 Don't throw the baby out with the bathwater.
Proverb

2 First come, first served.
Proverb

3 Haste makes waste.
Proverb

4 More haste, less speed.
Proverb

5 'Will you walk a little faster?' said a whiting to a snail,
'There's a porpoise close behind us, and he's treading on my tail.'
Lewis Carroll (Charles Lutwidge Dodgson; 1832–98) British writer. *Alice's Adventures in Wonderland*, Ch. 10

6 In skating over thin ice, our safety is in our speed.
Ralph Waldo Emerson (1803–82) US poet and essayist. *Essays*, 'Prudence'

7 Slow and steady wins the race.
Robert Lloyd (1733–64) British poet. *The Hare and the Tortoise*

8 For fools rush in where angels fear to tread.
Alexander Pope (1688–1744) British poet. *An Essay on Criticism*

9 Never before have we had so little time in which to do so much.
Franklin D. Roosevelt (1882–1945) US Democratic president. Radio address, 23 Feb 1942

10 If it were done when 'tis done, then 'twere well
It were done quickly.
William Shakespeare (1564–1616) English dramatist. *Macbeth*, I:7

11 Wisely and slow; they stumble that run fast.
William Shakespeare *Romeo and Juliet*, II:3

12 He sows hurry and reaps indigestion.
Robert Louis Stevenson (1850–94) Scottish writer. *An Apology for Idlers*

13 Hurry! I never hurry. I have no time to hurry.
Igor Stravinsky (1882–1971) Russian-born US composer. Responding to his publisher's request that he hurry his completion of a composition. Attrib.

HATE

See also bitterness, love and hate

1 I do not love thee, Doctor Fell,
The reason why I cannot tell;
But this alone I know full well,
I do not love thee, Doctor Fell.
Thomas Brown (1663–1704) English satirist. Translation of Martial's *Epigrams*

2 Gr-r-r- there go, my heart's abhorrence!
Water your damned flower-pots, do!
Robert Browning (1812–89) British poet. *Soliloquy of the Spanish Cloister*

3 It does not matter much what a man hates, provided he hates something.
Samuel Butler (1835–1902) British writer. *Notebooks*

4 I am free of all prejudice. I hate everyone equally.
W. C. Fields (1880–1946) US actor. Attrib.

5 We can scarcely hate any one that we know.
William Hazlitt (1778–1830) British essayist. *On Criticism*

6 If you hate a person, you hate something in him that is part of yourself. What isn't part of ourselves doesn't disturb us.
Hermann Hesse (1877–1962) German novelist and poet. *Demian*, Ch. 6

7 With a heavy step Sir Matthew left the room and spent the morning designing mausoleums for his enemies.
Eric Linklater (1889–1974) Scottish novelist. *Juan in America*, Prologue

8 Few people can be happy unless they hate some other person, nation or creed.
Bertrand Russell (1872–1970) British philosopher. Attrib.

9 An intellectual hatred is the worst.
W. B. Yeats (1865–1939) Irish poet. *A Prayer for My Daughter*

HAZLITT, William

(1778–1830) British essayist and journalist. His collections of writings include *Lectures on the English Poets* (1818) and *The Spirit of the Age* (1825).

Quotations about Hazlitt

1 He is your only good damner, and if I am ever damned I should like to be damned by him.
John Keats (1795–1821) British poet. Attrib.

2 He is not a proper person to be admitted into respectable society, being the most perverse and malevolent creature that ill-luck has thrown my way.
William Wordsworth (1770–1850) British poet. Letter to B. R. Haydon, Apr 1817

Quotations by Hazlitt

3 The least pain in our little finger gives us more concern and uneasiness than the destruction of millions of our fellow-beings.
American Literature, 'Dr Channing'

4 If the world were good for nothing else, it is a fine subject for speculation.
Characteristics

5 Man is an intellectual animal, and therefore an everlasting contradiction to himself. His senses centre in himself, his ideas reach to the ends of the universe; so that he is torn in pieces between the two, without a possibility of its ever being otherwise.
Characteristics

6 His sayings are generally like women's letters; all the pith is in the postscript.
Referring to Charles Lamb. *Conversations of Northcote*

7 He writes as fast as they can read,

and he does not write himself down.
English Literature, Ch. XIV, 'Sir Walter Scott'

8 His worst is better than any other person's best.
English Literature, Ch. XIV, 'Sir Walter Scott'

9 So have I loitered my life away, reading books, looking at pictures, going to plays, hearing, thinking, writing on what pleased me best. I have wanted only one thing to make me happy, but wanting that have wanted everything.
English Literature, Ch. XVII, 'My First Acquaintance with Poets'

10 You will hear more good things on the outside of a stagecoach from London to Oxford than if you were to pass a twelvemonth with the undergraduates, or heads of colleges, of that famous university.
The Ignorance of the Learned

11 He talked on for ever; and you wished him to talk on for ever.
Referring to Coleridge. *Lectures on the English Poets,* Lecture VIII, 'On the Living Poets'

12 A nickname is the heaviest stone that the devil can throw at a man.
Nicknames

13 There is nothing good to be had in the country, or, if there is, they will not let you have it.
Observations on Wordsworth's 'Excursion'

14 The greatest offence against virtue is to speak ill of it.
On Cant and Hypocrisy

15 Those who make their dress a principal part of themselves, will, in general, become of no more value than their dress.
On the Clerical Character

16 The English (it must be owned) are rather a foul-mouthed nation
On Criticism

17 We can scarcely hate any one that we know.
On Criticism

18 There is an unseemly exposure of the mind, as well as of the body.
On Disagreeable People

19 No young man believes he shall ever die.
On the Feeling of Immortality in Youth

20 One of the pleasantest things in the world is going on a journey; but I like to go by myself.
On Going a Journey

21 When I am in the country I wish to vegetate like the country.
On Going a Journey

22 To great evils we submit; we resent little provocations.
On Great and Little Things

23 There is not a more mean, stupid, dastardly, pitiful, selfish, spiteful, envious, ungrateful animal than the public. It is the greatest of cowards, for it is afraid of itself.
On Living to Oneself

24 The art of pleasing consists in being pleased.
On Manner

25 A person may be indebted for a nose or an eye, for a graceful carriage or a voluble discourse, to a great-aunt or uncle, whose existence he has scarcely heard of.
On Personal Character

26 The dupe of friendship, and the fool of love; have I not reason to hate and to despise myself? Indeed I do; and chiefly for not having hated and despised the world enough.
On the Pleasure of Hating

27 We never do anything well till we cease to think about the manner of doing it.
On Prejudice

28 The most fluent talkers or most plausible reasoners are not always the justest thinkers.
On Prejudice

29 Rules and models destroy genius and art.
On Taste

30 The love of liberty is the love of others; the love of power is the love of ourselves.
The Times, 1819

31 Spleen can subsist on any kind of food.
On Wit and Humour

32 Well, I've had a happy life.
Last words

HEALTH

See also doctors, illness, medicine, remedies

1 Health is better than wealth.
Proverb

2 Health is the first of all liberties, and happiness gives us the energy which is the basis of health.
Henri Amiel (1821–81) Swiss philosopher and writer. *Journal intime,* 3 Apr 1865

3 In sickness, respect health principally; and in health, action. For those that put their bodies to endure in health, may in most sicknesses, which are not very sharp, be cured only with diet and tendering.
Francis Bacon (1561–1626) English philosopher. *Essays,* 'Of Regiment of Health'

4 Health indeed is a precious thing, to recover and preserve which, we undergo any misery, drink bitter potions, freely give our goods: restore a man to his health, his purse lies open to thee.
Robert Burton (1577–1640) English scholar and explorer. *The Anatomy of Melancholy,* Pt. III, Sect. 1

5 There is no finer investment for any community than putting milk into babies. Healthy citizens are the greatest asset any contry can have.
Winston Churchill (1874–1965) British statesman. Radio broadcast, 21 Mar 1943

6 Safeguard the health both of body and soul.
Cleobulus

7 Doctors are always working to preserve our health and cooks to destroy it, but the latter are the more often successful.
Denis Diderot (1713–84) French philosopher and writer.

8 The health of a people is really the foundation upon which all their happiness and all their power as a State depend.
Benjamin Disraeli (1804–81) British statesman. Speech, 23 June 1877

9 We're all of us ill in one way or another:
We call it health when we find no symptom
Of illness. Health is a relative term.
T. S. Eliot (1888–1965) US-born British poet and dramatist. *The Family Reunion,* I:3

10 Give me health and a day, and I will make the pomp of emperors ridiculous.
Ralph Waldo Emerson (1803–82) US poet and essayist. *Nature,* Ch. 3

11 HEALTHY. Too much health, the cause of illness.
Gustave Flaubert (1821–80) French novelist. *Dictionary of Accepted Ideas*

12 A wise man ought to realize that health is his most valuable possession.
Hippocrates (c. 460 BC–c. 377 BC) Greek physician. *A Regimen for Health*, 9

13 If I had my way I'd make health catching instead of disease.
Robert G. Ingersoll (1833–99) US lawyer and agnostic.

14 We drink one another's health and spoil our own.
Jerome K. Jerome (1859–1927) British humorous writer. *Idle Thoughts of an Idle Fellow*, 'On Eating and Drinking'

15 O health! health! the blessing of the rich! the riches of the poor! who can buy thee at too deare a rate, since there is no enjoying this world, without thee?
Ben Jonson (1573–1637) English dramatist. *Volpone*, II:2

16 Perfect health, like perfect beauty, is a rare thing; and so, it seems, is perfect disease.
Peter Mere Latham (1789–1875) US poet and essayist. *General Remarks on the Practice of Medicine*, Ch. 10, Pt. ii

17 Good health is an essential to happiness, and happiness is an essential to good citizenship.
Charles H. Mayo (1865–1939) US physician. *Journal of the American Dental Association*, 6:505, 1919

18 Health is a precious thing, and the only one, in truth, which deserves that we employ in its pursuit not only time, sweat, trouble, and worldly goods, but even life; inasmuch as without it life comes to be painful and oppressive to us . . . As far as I am concerned, no road that would lead us to health is either arduous or expensive.
Michel de Montaigne (1533–92) French essayist and moralist. *Essais*, II

19 Without health life is not life; it is unlivable. . . . Without health, life spells but languor and an image of death.
François Rabelais (c. 1483–1553) French humanist and satirist. *Pantagruel*, Bk. IV, Prologue

20 To preserve one's health by too strict a regime is in itself a tedious malady.
Duc François de La Rochefoucauld (1613–80) French writer. *Maxims*, 623

21 All health is better than wealth.
Walter Scott (1771–1832) Scottish novelist. *Familiar Letters*, Letter to C. Carpenter, 4 Aug 1812

22 'Tis healthy to be sick sometimes.
Henry David Thoreau (1817–62) US writer.

23 Look to your health: and if you have it, praise God, and value it next to a good conscience; for health is the second blessing that we mortals are capable of; a blessing that money cannot buy.
Izaak Walton (1593–1683) English writer. *The Compleat Angler*, Pt. I, Ch. 21

24 Gold that buys health can never be ill spent.
John Webster and Thomas Dekker (c. 1580–c. 1625; c. 1572–c. 1632) English dramatists. *Westward Ho!*, V

25 Talk health. The dreary, never-ending tale
Our mortal maladies is worn and stale;
You cannot charm or interest or please
By harping on that minor chord, disease.
Say you are well, or all is well with you,
And God shall hear your words and make them true.
Ella Wheeler Wilcox (1850–1919) US poet. *Speech*

26 Health – silliest word in our language, and one knows well the popular idea of health the English country gentleman galloping after a fox – the unspeakable in full pursuit of the uneatable.
Oscar Wilde (1854–1900) Irish-born British writer and wit. *A Woman of No Importance*, I

HEALTHY LIVING

See also doctors, illness, medicine, remedies

1 A little with quiet is the only diet.
Proverb

2 An apple a day keeps the doctor away.
Proverb

3 Early to bed, and early to rise, makes a man healthy, wealthy and wise.
Proverb

4 Health is better than wealth.
Proverb

5 Wash your hands often, your feet seldom, and your head never.
Proverb

6 Fresh air impoverishes the doctor.
Danish proverb

7 The healthy die first.
Italian proverb

8 Better lose a supper than have a hundred physicians.
Spanish proverb

9 Health and cheerfulness mutually beget each other.
Joseph Addison (1672–1719) English essayist. *The Spectator*, no. 387

10 Diet cures more than the lancet.
Anonymous

11 I have two doctors – my left leg and my right.
Anonymous

12 Who lives medically lives miserably.
Anonymous *Anatomy of Melancholy* (Robert Burton)

13 It is a fact that not once in all my life have I gone out for a walk. I have been taken out for walks; but that is another matter.
Max Beerbohm (1872–1956) British writer. *Going Out of a Walk*

14 The ancient Inhabitants of this Island were less troubled with Coughs when they went naked, and slept in Caves and Woods, than Men now in Chambers and Feather-beds.
Thomas Browne (1605–82) English physician and writer. *A Letter to a Friend*

15 I answer 20 000 letters a year and so many couples are having problems because they are not getting the right proteins and vitamins.
Barbara Cartland (1902–) British romantic novelist. *The Observer*, 'Sayings of the Week', 31 Aug 1986

16 Those who think they have not time for bodily exercise will sooner or later have to find time for illness.
Edward Stanley, Earl of Derby (1826–93) British statesman. *The Conduct of Life*, address at Liverpool College, 20 Dec 1873

17 To avoid sickness, eat less, to prolong life, worry less.
Chu Hui Weng *Bulletin of the New York Academy of Medicine*, 4:985, 1928 (F.H. Garrison)

18 Exercise and temperance can preserve something of our early strength even in old age.
Cicero (106 BC–43 BC) Roman orator and statesman. *An Old Age*, X

19 The strongest possible piece of advice I would give to any young woman is: Don't screw around, and don't smoke.

Edwina Currie (1946–) British politician. *The Observer*, 'Sayings of the Week', 3 Apr 1988

20 Better to hunt in fields for health unbought,
Than fee the doctor for a nauseous draught.

John Dryden (1631–1700) English poet and dramatist. *To Sir G. Kneller*

21 Exercise is bunk. If you are healthy, you don't need it: if you are sick you shouldn't take it.

Henry Ford (1863–1947) US industrialist. Attrib.

22 Fat people who want to reduce should take their exercise on an empty stomach and sit down to their food out of breath.... Thin people who want to get fat should do exactly the opposite and never take exercise on an empty stomach.

Hippocrates (c. 460 BC–c. 377 BC) Greek physician. *A Regimen for Health*, IV

23 Whenever I feel like exercise, I lie down until the feeling passes.

Robert M. Hutchins (1899–1977) US educator. Attrib.

24 One swears by wholemeal bread, one by sour milk; vegetarianism is the only road to salvation of some, others insist not only on vegetables alone, but on eating those raw. At one time the only thing that matters is calories; at another time they are crazy about vitamins or about roughage.
The scientific truth may be put quite briefly; eat moderately, having an ordinary mixed diet, and don't worry.

Robert Hutchison (1871–1960) *Newcastle Medical Journal*, Vol. 12, 1932

25 Healthy people are those who live in healthy homes on a healthy diet; in an environment equally fit for birth, growth work, healing, and dying.... Healthy people need no bureaucratic interference to mate, give birth, share the human condition and die.

Ivan Illich (1926–) Austrian sociologist. *Medical Nemesis*

26 The deviation of man from the state in which he was originally placed by nature seems to have proved to him a prolific source of diseases.

Edward Jenner (1749–1823) *An Inquiry into the Causes and Effects of the Variolae Vaccinae, or Cow-Pox*

27 *Orandum est ut sit mens sana in corpore sano.*
Your prayer must be for a sound mind in a sound body.

Juvenal (Decimus Junius Juvenalis; 60–130 AD) Roman satirist. *Satires*, X

28 The Greeks understood that mind and body must develop in harmonious proportions to produce a creative intelligence. And so did the most brilliant intelligence of our earliest days – Thomas Jefferson – when he said, not less than two hours a day should be devoted to exercise.
If the man who wrote the Declaration of Independence, was Secretary of State, and twice President, could give it two hours, our children can give it ten or fifteen minutes.

John F. Kennedy (1917–63) US statesman. Address to the National Football Foundation, 5 Dec 1961

29 The average, healthy, well-adjusted adult gets up at seven-thirty in the morning feeling just plain terrible.

Jean Kerr (1923–) US dramatist, screenwriter and humorist. *Please Don't Eat the Daisies*, 'Where Did You Put the Aspirin?'

30 Joy and Temperance and Repose
Slam the door on the doctor's nose.

Henry Wadsworth Longfellow (1807–82) US poet. *The Sinngedichte of Friedrich von Logau*

31 Some breakfast food manufacturer hit upon the simple notion of emptying out the leavings of carthorse nosebags, adding a few other things like unconsumed portions of chicken layer's mash, and the sweepings of racing stables, packing the mixture in little bags and selling them in health food shops.

Frank Muir (1920–) British writer and broadcaster. *Upon My Word!*

32 Medicine is a collection of uncertain prescriptions, the results of which, taken collectively, are more fatal than useful to mankind. Water, air, and cleanliness are the chief articles in my pharmacopeia.

Napoleon I (Napoleon Bonaparte; 1769–1821) French emperor.

33 Patients should have rest, food, fresh air, and exercise – the quadrangle of health.

William Osler (1849–1919) Canadian physician. *Sir William Osler: Aphorisms*, Ch. 3 (William B. Bean)

34 Diet away your stress, tension and anxiety; a new commonsense plan for the control of low blood sugar related disorders, including overeating and obesity, migraine headaches, alcoholism, mental disturbances, hypoglycemia and hyperactivity.

J. Daniel Palm US physician. Extract from book cover

35 Attention to health is the greatest hindrance to life.

Plato (428 BC–347 BC) Greek philosopher.

36 A man ought to handle his body like the sail of a ship, and neither lower and reduce it much when no cloud is in sight, nor be slack and careless in managing it when he comes to suspect something is wrong.

Plutarch (c. 46–c. 120) Greek biographer and essayist. *Moralia*, 'Advice about Keeping Well'

37 I'll purge, and leave sack, and live cleanly, as a nobleman should do.

William Shakespeare (1564–1616) English dramatist. *Henry IV, Part 1*, V:4

38 Use your health even to the point of wearing it out. That is what it is for. Spend all you have before you die, and do not outlive yourself.

George Bernard Shaw (1856–1950) Irish dramatist and critic. *The Doctor's Dilemma*, 'Preface on Doctors'

39 When you are so poor that you cannot afford to refuse eighteenpence from a man who is too poor to pay you any more, it is useless to tell him that what he or his sick child needs is not medicine, but more leisure, better clothes, better food, and a better drained and ventilated house.

George Bernard Shaw *The Doctor's Dilemma*, 'Preface on Doctors'

40 I am convinced digestion is the great secret of life.

Sydney Smith (1771–1845) English clergyman, essayist, and wit. *Letters*, to Arthur Kinglake

41 The preservation of health is a duty. Few seem conscious that there is such a thing as physical morality.

Herbert Spencer (1820–1903) British philosopher.

42 The proverb warns that, 'You should not bite the hand that feeds you.' But maybe you should, if it prevents you from feeding yourself.

Thomas Szasz (1920–) US psychiatrist. *The Second Sin*, 'Control and Self-control'

43 Early to rise and early to bed

makes a man healthy and wealthy and dead.

James Thurber (1894–1961) US writer, humorist and cartoonist. *Fables of Our Time*, 'The Shrike and the Chipmunks'

44 The twentieth century will be remembered chiefly, not as an age of political conflicts and technical inventions, but as an age in which human society dared to think of the health of the whole human race as a practical objective.

Arnold Toynbee (1889–1975) British historian.

45 Regimen is superior to medicine.

Voltaire (François-Marie Arouet; 1694–1778) French writer and philospher. *A Philosophical Dictionary*, 'Physicians'

46 One knows so well the popular idea of health. The English country gentleman galloping after a fox – the unspeakable in full pursuit of the uneatable.

Oscar Wilde (1856–1900) Irish-born British poet and dramatist. *A Woman of No Importance*, I

HEART

1 God be in my head,
And in my understanding;
God be in my eyes,
And in my looking;
God be in my mouth,
And in my speaking;
God be in my heart,
And in my thinking;
God be at my end,
And at my departing.

Anonymous *Sarum Missal*

2 We cannot kindle when we will
The fire which in the heart resides,
The spirit bloweth and is still,
In mystery our soul abides.

Matthew Arnold (1822–88) British poet and critic. *Morality*

3 Absence makes the heart grow fonder,
Isle of Beauty, Fare thee well!

Thomas Haynes Bayly (1797–1839) British writer. *Isle of Beauty*

4 When they heard these things, they were cut to the heart, and they gnashed on him with their teeth.

Bible: Acts 7:54

5 The proud, the cold untroubled heart of stone,
That never mused on sorrow but its own.

Thomas Campbell (1777–1844) British poet. *Pleasures of Hope*, I

6 What comes from the heart, goes to the heart.

Samuel Taylor Coleridge (1772–1834) British poet. *Table Talk*

7 I love thee for a heart that's kind –
Not for the knowledge in thy mind.

W. H. Davies (1871–1940) British poet. *Sweet Stay-at-Home*

8 'There are strings', said Mr Tappertit, 'in the human heart that had better not be wibrated.'

Charles Dickens (1812–70) British novelist. *Barnaby Rudge*, Ch. 22

9 The way to a man's heart is through his stomach.

Fanny Fern (1811–72) US writer. *Willis Parton*

10 But evil is wrought by want of thought,
As well as want of heart!

Thomas Hood (1799–1845) British poet. *The Lady's Dream*

11 I am certain of nothing but the holiness of the heart's affections and the truth of imagination – what the imagination seizes as beauty must be truth – whether it existed before or not.

John Keats (1795–1821) British poet. Letter to Benjamin Bailey, 22 Nov 1817

12 My heart aches, and a drowsy numbness pains
My sense.

John Keats *Ode to a Nightingale*

13 My heart is a lonely hunter that hunts on a lonely hill.

Fiona Macleod (William Sharp; 1856–1905) Scottish poet and writer. *The Lonely Hunter*

14 My heart shall be thy garden.

Alice Meynell (1847–1922) British poet. *The Garden*

15 I still love you, but in politics there is no heart, only head.

Napoleon I (Napoleon Bonaparte; 1769–1821) French emperor. Referring to his divorce, for reasons of state, from the Empress Josephine (1809). *Bonaparte* (C. Barnett)

16 The heart has its reasons which reason does not know.

Blaise Pascal (1623–62) French philosopher and mathematician. *Pensées*, IV

17 So the heart be right, it is no matter which way the head lies.

Walter Raleigh (1554–1618) English explorer. On laying his head on the executioner's block. Attrib.

18 The intellect is always fooled by the heart.

Duc de la Rochefoucauld (1613–80) French writer. *Maximes*, 102

19 If thou didst ever hold me in thy heart,
Absent thee from felicity awhile,
And in this harsh world draw thy breath in pain,
To tell my story.

William Shakespeare (1564–1616) English dramatist. *Hamlet*, V:2

20 My strength is as the strength of ten,
Because my heart is pure.

Alfred, Lord Tennyson (1809–92) British poet. *Sir Galahad*

21 Great thoughts come from the heart.

Marquis de Vauvenargues (1715–47) French soldier and writer. *Réflexions et maximes*

22 Nature never did betray
The heart that loved her.

William Wordsworth (1770–1850) British poet. *Lines composed a few miles above Tintern Abbey*

23 The wind blows out of the gates of the day,
The wind blows over the lonely of heart,
And the lonely of heart is withered away.

W. B. Yeats (1865–1939) Irish poet. *The Land of Heart's Desire*

HEAVEN

See also afterlife

1 And he dreamed, and behold a ladder set up on the earth, and the top of it reached to heaven: and behold the angels of God ascending and descending on it.

Bible: Genesis 28:12

2 And Jacob awaked out of his sleep, and he said, Surely the Lord is in this place; and I knew it not.
And he was afraid, and said, How dreadful is this place! this is none other but the house of God, and this is the gate of heaven.

Bible: Genesis 28:16–17

3 In my Father's house are many mansions: if it were not so, I would have told you. I go to prepare a place for you.

Bible: John 14:2

4 Then let him receive the new knowledge and wait us,

Pardoned in heaven, the first by the throne!
Robert Browning (1812–89) British poet. *The Lost Leader*

5 Work and pray, live on hay,
You'll get pie in the sky when you die.
Joe Hill (1879–1915) Swedish-born US songwriter. *The Preacher and the Slave*

6 Even the paradise of fools is not an unpleasant abode while it is inhabitable.
Dean Inge (1860–1954) British churchman. Attrib.

7 Probably no invention came more easily to man than Heaven.
Georg Christoph Lichtenberg (1742–99) German physicist and writer. *Aphorisms*

8 A heav'n on earth.
John Milton (1608–74) English poet. *Paradise Lost*, Bk. IV

9 Glorious things of thee are spoken,
Zion, city of our God.
John Newton (1725–1807) British hymn writer. *Glorious Things*

10 For observe, that to hope for Paradise is to live in Paradise, a very different thing from actually getting there.
Vita Sackville-West (Victoria Sackville-West; 1892–1962) British poet and novelist. *Passenger to Tehran*, Ch. 1

11 I expect no very violent transition.
Catharine Maria Sedgwick (1789–1867) US writer. Comparing heaven with her hometown of Stockbridge, Massachussetts. *Edie* (Jean Stein)

12 If you go to Heaven without being naturally qualified for it you will not enjoy yourself there.
George Bernard Shaw (1856–1950) Irish dramatist and critic. *Man and Superman*

13 Heaven, as conventionally conceived, is a place so inane, so dull, so useless, so miserable, that nobody has ever ventured to describe a whole day in heaven, though plenty of people have described a day at the seaside.
George Bernard Shaw *Misalliance*, Preface

14 Shall shine the traffic of Jacob's ladder
Pitched between Heaven and Charing Cross.
Francis Thompson (1859–1907) British poet. *The Kingdom of God*

15 Grant me paradise in this world;
I'm not so sure I'll reach it in the next.
Tintoretto (Jacopo Robusti; 1518–94) Venetian painter. Arguing that he be allowed to paint the *Paradiso* at the doge's palace in Venice, despite his advanced age. Attrib.

16 There is a happy land,
Far, far away,
Where saints in glory stand,
Bright, bright as day.
Andrew John Young (1885–1971) Scottish poet. *There is a Happy Land*

HELL

See also damnation, devil

1 Every wolf's and lion's howl
Raises from Hell a human soul.
William Blake (1757–1827) British poet. *Auguries of Innocence*

2 Abandon hope, all ye who enter here.
Dante Alighieri (1265–1321) Italian poet. The inscription at the entrance to Hell. *Divine Comedy, Inferno*, III

3 Hell is oneself;
Hell is alone, the other figures in it
Merely projections. There is nothing to escape from
And nothing to escape to. One is always alone.
T. S. Eliot (1888–1965) US-born British poet and dramatist. *The Cocktail Party*, I:3

4 Long is the way
And hard, that out of hell leads up to light.
John Milton (1608–74) English poet. *Paradise Lost*, Bk. II

5 Which way I fly is Hell; myself am Hell;
And, in the lowest deep, a lower deep
Still threat'ning to devour me opens wide,
To which the Hell I suffer seems a Heaven.
John Milton *Paradise Lost*, Bk. IV

6 Hell is other people.
Jean-Paul Sartre (1905–80) French philosopher and writer. *Huis clos*

7 Hell is a city much like London –
A populous and smoky city.
Percy Bysshe Shelley (1792–1822) British poet. *Peter Bell the Third*

8 The way down to Hell is easy.
Virgil (Publius Vergilius Maro; 70–19 BC) Roman poet. *Aeneid*, Bk. VI

HELP

See also charity, support

1 Every little helps.
Proverb

2 Many hands make light work.
Proverb

3 One good turn deserves another.
Proverb

4 Scratch my back and I'll scratch yours.
Proverb

5 Too many cooks spoil the broth.
Proverb

6 Two heads are better than one.
Proverb

7 Bind up their wounds – but look the other way.
W. S. Gilbert (1836–1911) British dramatist. *Princess Ida*, III

8 People must help one another; it is nature's law.
Jean de La Fontaine (1621–95) French poet. *Fables*, VIII, 'L'Âne et le Chien'

HEMINGWAY, Ernest

(1898–1961) US novelist, who lived for much of his life in Paris. His first successful novel was *The Sun Also Rises* (1926); subsequent novels include *A Farewell to Arms* (1929) and *For Whom the Bell Tolls* (1940). He was a keen sportsman and admirer of bullfighting.

Quotations about Hemingway

1 He is the bully on the Left Bank, always ready to twist the milksop's arm.
Cyril Connolly (1903–74) British journalist. *The Observer*, 24 May 1964

2 He has a capacity for enjoyment so vast that he gives away great chunks to those about him, and never even misses them . . . . He can take you to a bicycle race and make it raise your hair.
Dorothy Parker (1893–1967) US writer. *New Yorker*, 30 Nov 1929

Quotations by Hemingway

3 Bullfighting is the only art in which the artist is in danger of death and in which the degree of brilliance in the performance is left to the fighter's honor.
Death in the Afternoon, Ch. 9

4 But did thee feel the earth move?
For Whom the Bell Tolls, Ch. 13

5 If you are lucky enough to have lived in Paris as a young man, then wherever you go for the rest of your life, it stays with you, for Paris is a moveable feast.
A Moveable Feast, Epigraph

6 A man can be destroyed but not defeated.
The Old Man and the Sea

7 Because I am a bastard.
When asked why he had deserted his wife for another woman. *Americans in Paris* (B. Morton)

8 Poor Faulkner. Does he really think big emotions come from big words? He thinks I don't know the ten-dollar words. I know them all right. But there are older and simpler and better words, and those are the ones I use.
In response to a jibe by William FAULKNER
Attrib.

HEREDITY

1 What mean ye, that ye use this proverb concerning the land of Israel, saying, The fathers have eaten sour grapes, and the children's teeth are set on edge?
Bible: Ezekiel 18:2

HEROISM

See also courage, endurance, patriotism, war

1 Some talk of Alexander, and some of Hercules,
Of Hector and Lysander, and such great names as these;
But of all the world's brave heroes there's none that can compare
With a tow, row, row, row, row, row for the British Grenadier.
Anonymous *The British Grenadiers*

2 Superman, disguised as Clark Kent, mild-mannered reporter for a great metropolitan newspaper, fights a never-ending battle for truth, justice, and the American way.
Anonymous Hence the description 'Mild-mannered Clark Kent'. Introduction to radio series

3 They died to save their country and they only saved the world.
Hilaire Belloc (1870–1953) French-born British poet. *The English Graves*

4 ANDREA. Unhappy the land that has no heroes.
GALILEO. No, unhappy the land that needs heroes.
Bertolt Brecht (1898–1956) German dramatist. *Galileo*, 13

5 In short, he was a perfect cavaliero,
And to his very valet seem'd a hero.
Lord Byron (1788–1824) British poet. *Beppo*

6 Every hero becomes a bore at last.
Ralph Waldo Emerson (1803–82) US poet and essayist. *Representative Men*, 'Uses of Great Men'

7 I'm a hero with coward's legs. I'm a hero from the waist up.
Spike Milligan (1918–) British comic actor and author. *Puckoon*

8 Being a hero is about the shortest-lived profession on earth.
Will Rogers (1879–1935) US actor and humorist. *Saturday Review*, 'A Rogers Thesaurus', 25 Aug 1962

9 I think continually of those who were truly great –
The names of those who in their lives fought for life,
Who wore at their hearts the fire's centre.
Stephen Spender (1909–) British poet. *I Think Continually of Those Who Were Truly Great*

HISTORIANS

See also history

1 A good historian is timeless; although he is a patriot, he will never flatter his country in any respect.
François Fénelon (1651–1715) French writer and prelate. Letter to M. Dacier

2 The historian must have . . . some conception of how men who are not historians behave. Otherwise he will move in a world of the dead.
E. M. Forster (1879–1970) British novelist. *Abinger Harvest*, 'Captain Edward Gibbon'

3 History repeats itself; historians repeat each other.
Philip Guedalla (1889–1944) British writer. Attrib.

4 Great abilities are not requisite for an Historian . . . Imagination is not required in any high degree.
Samuel Johnson (1709–84) British lexicographer. *Life of Johnson* (J. Boswell), Vol. I

5 History is too serious to be left to historians.
Iain Macleod (1913–70) British politician. *The Observer*, 'Sayings of the Week', 16 July 1961

6 And even I can remember
A day when the historians left blanks in their writings,
I mean for things they didn't know.
Ezra Pound (1885–1972) US poet. *Cantos*, XIII

7 A historian is a prophet in reverse.
Friedrich von Schlegel (1772–1829) German diplomat, writer, and critic. *Das Athenäum*

8 Historians are like deaf people who go on answering questions that no one has asked them.
Leo Tolstoy (1828–1910) Russian writer. *A Discovery of Australia*, 'Being an Historian' (Manning Clark)

HISTORY

See also experience, historians, past

1 History repeats itself.
Proverb

2 Political history is far too criminal and pathological to be a fit subject of study for the young. Children should acquire their heroes and villains from fiction.
W. H. Auden (1907–73) British poet. *A Certain World*

3 Man is a history-making creature who can neither repeat his past nor leave it behind.
W. H. Auden *The Dyer's Hand*, 'D. H. Lawrence'

4 All things from eternity are of like forms and come round in a circle.
Marcus Aurelius (121–180 AD) Roman emperor. *Meditations*, Bk. II, Ch. 14

5 History does not repeat itself. Historians repeat each other.
Arthur Balfour (1848–1930) British Conservative prime minister. Attrib.

6 History is the essence of innumerable biographies.
Thomas Carlyle (1795–1881) Scottish historian and essayist. *Critical and Miscellaneous Essays*, 'History'

7 No great man lives in vain. The history of the world is but the biography of great men.
Thomas Carlyle *Heroes and Hero-Worship*, 'The Hero as Divinity'

8 The history of every country begins in the heart of a man or woman.
Willa Cather (1873–1947) US writer and poet. *O Pioneers!*, Pt. II, Ch. 4

9 History is philosophy teaching by examples.
Dionysius of Halicarnassus (40–8 BC) Greek historian. *Ars rhetorica*, XI:2

10 History is an endless repetition of the wrong way of living.
Lawrence Durrell (1912–) British novelist. *The Listener*, 1978

11 History teaches us that men and nations behave wisely once they have exhausted all other alternatives.
Abba Eban (1915–) Israeli politician. *The Observer*, 'Sayings of the Week', 20 Dec 1970

12 There is properly no history; only biography.
Ralph Waldo Emerson (1803–82) US poet and essayist. *Essays*, 'History'

13 History is more or less bunk. It's tradition. We don't want tradition. We want to live in the present and the only history that is worth a tinker's damn is the history we make today.
Henry Ford (1863–1947) US car manufacturer. *Chicago Tribune*, 25 May 1916

14 There are moments in history when brooding tragedy and its dark shadows can be lightened by recalling great moments of the past.
Indira Gandhi (1917–84) Indian stateswoman. Letter to Richard Nixon, 16 Dec 1971

15 History never looks like history when you are living through it. It always looks confusing and messy, and it always feels uncomfortable.
John W. Gardner (1912–) US writer. *No Easy Victories*

16 His reign is marked by the rare advantage of furnishing very few materials for history; which is, indeed, little more than the register of the crimes, follies, and misfortunes of mankind.
Edward Gibbon (1737–94) British historian. Referring to the reign of Antoninus Pius. *Decline and Fall of the Roman Empire*, Ch. 3

17 A history of humanity to the present time in which Shakespeare is not mentioned and Jesus is dismissed in a page carelessly, as if not worth contempt, shocks me.
Frank Harris (1856–1931) British editor and writer. Referring to H. G. Wells' writing. *My Life*

18 It is not the neutrals or the lukewarm who make history.
Adolf Hitler (1889–1945) German dictator. Speech, Berlin, 23 Apr 1933

19 What we know of the past is mostly not worth knowing. What is worth knowing is mostly uncertain. Events in the past may roughly be divided into those which probably never happened and those which do not matter.
Dean Inge (1860–1954) British churchman. *Assessments and Anticipations*, 'Prognostications'

20 It takes a great deal of history to produce a little literature.
Henry James (1843–1916) US novelist. *Life of Nathaniel Hawthorne*, Ch. 1

21 'History', Stephen said, 'is a nightmare from which I am trying to awake'.
James Joyce (1882–1941) Irish novelist. *Ulysses*

22 If the science of medicine is not to be lowered to the rank of a mere mechanical profession it must preoccupy itself with its history. The pursuit of the development of the human mind, this is the role of the historian.
Maximilien-Paul-Émile Littré (1801–81) French lexicographer and philosopher.

23 Hegel says somewhere that all great events and personalities in world history reappear in one fashion or another. He forgot to add: the first time as tragedy, the second as farce.
Karl Marx (1818–83) German philosopher and revolutionary. *The Eighteenth Brumaire of Louis Napoleon*

24 The history of medicine does not depart from the history of the people.
James G. Mumford (1863–1914)

25 Think of it, soldiers; from the summit of these pyramids, forty centuries look down upon you.
Napoleon I (Napoleon Bonaparte; 1769–1821) French emperor. Speech before the Battle of the Pyramids, 21 July 1798.

26 It is impossible to write ancient history because we do not have enough sources, and impossible to write modern history because we have far too many.
Charles Pierre Péguy (1873–1914) French writer. *Clio*

27 There is no history of mankind, there are only many histories of all kinds of aspects of human life. And one of these is the history of political power. This is elevated into the history of the world.
Karl Popper (1902–) Austrian-born British philosopher. *The Open Society and Its Enemies*

28 ... we mutally agreed to call it *The First World War* in order to prevent the millennium folk from forgetting that the history of the world was the history of war.
Lieut-Col. Charles A'Court Repington (1858–1925) British soldier and journalist. Diary, 10 Sept 1918

29 Progress, far from consisting in change, depends on retentiveness. Those who cannot remember the past are condemned to repeat it.
George Santayana (1863–1952) US philosopher. *The Life of Reason*

30 The history of the World is the World's court of justice.
Friedrich von Schiller (1759–1805) German dramatist. Lecture, Jena, 26 May 1789

31 I have looked upon the face of Agamemnon.
Heinrich Schliemann (1822–90) German archaeologist. On discovering a gold death mask at an excavation in Mycenae. *The Story of Civilization* (W. Durant), Vol. 2

32 History is past politics, and politics present history.
John Robert Seeley (1834–95) British historian. Quoting the historian E. A. Freeman. *The Growth of British Policy*

33 The Cavaliers (Wrong but Wromantic) and the Roundheads (Right but Repulsive).
W. C. Sellar (1898–1951) British humorous writer. *1066 And All That*

34 1066 And All That.
W. C. Sellar Book title

35 The Roman Conquest was, however, a *Good Thing*, since the Britons were only natives at the time.
W. C. Sellar *1066 And All That*

36 Napoleon's armies used to march on their stomachs, shouting: 'Vive l'intérieur!'
W. C. Sellar *1066 And All That*

37 America became top nation and history came to a full stop.
W. C. Sellar *1066 And All That*

38 When in the chronicle of wasted time
I see descriptions of the fairest wights.
William Shakespeare (1564–1616) English dramatist. *Sonnet 106*

39 History gets thicker as it approaches recent times.
A. J. P. Taylor (1906–) British historian. *English History, 1914–1945*, Bibliography

40 All our ancient history, as one of

our wits remarked, is no more than accepted fiction.
Voltaire (François-Marie Arouet; 1694–1778) French writer. *Jeannot et Colin*

41 Indeed, history is nothing more than a tableau of crimes and misfortunes.
Voltaire *L'Ingénu*, Ch. 10

42 Anything but history, for history must be false.
Robert Walpole (1676–1745) British statesman. *Walpoliana*

43 The greater part of what passes for diplomatic history is little more than the record of what one clerk said to another clerk.
George Malcolm Young (1882–1959) British historian. *Victorian England: Portrait of an Age*

HITLER, Adolf

(1889–1945) German dictator, who became president of the Nazi party in 1921 and chancellor of Germany in 1933. His campaign of world conquest led to World War II, defeat and disgrace for Germany, and his own suicide.

Quotations about Hitler

1 The people Hitler never understood, and whose actions continued to exasperate him to the end of his life, were the British.
Alan Bullock (1914–) British academic and historian. *Hitler, A Study in Tyranny*, Ch. 8

2 Hitler showed surprising loyalty to Mussolini, but it never extended to trusting him.
Alan Bullock *Hitler, A Study in Tyranny*, Ch. 11

3 I have only one purpose, the destruction of Hitler, and my life is much simplified thereby. If Hitler invaded Hell I would make at least a favourable reference to the Devil in the House of Commons.
Winston Churchill (1874–1965) British statesman. *The Grand Alliance*

4 The Italians will laugh at me; every time Hitler occupies a country he sends me a message.
Benito Mussolini (1883–1945) Italian dictator. *Hitler* (Alan Bullock), Ch. 8

5 That garrulous monk
Benito Mussolini Referring to Hitler. *The Second World War* (W. Churchill)

6 I wouldn't believe Hitler was dead, even if he told me so himself.
Hjalmar Schacht (1877–1970) German banker. Attrib.

7 A racing tipster who only reached Hitler's level of accuracy would not do well for his clients.
A. J. P. Taylor (1906–) British historian. *The Origins of the Second World War*, Ch. 7

8 Germany was the cause of Hitler just as much as Chicago is responsible for the *Chicago Tribune*.
Alexander Woollcott (1887–1943) US writer and critic. Woollcott died after the broadcast. Radio broadcast, 1943

Quotations by Hitler

9 All those who are not racially pure are mere chaff.
Mein Kampf, Ch. 2

10 Only constant repetition will finally succeed in imprinting an idea on the memory of the crowd.
Mein Kampf, Ch. 6

11 The broad mass of a nation... will more easily fall victim to a big lie than to a small one.
Mein Kampf, Ch. 10

12 Germany will be either a world power or will not be at all.
Mein Kampf, Ch. 14

13 In starting and waging a war it is not right that matters, but victory.
The Rise and Fall of the Third Reich (W. L. Shirer), Ch. 16

14 The essential thing is the formation of the political will of the nation: that is the starting point for political action.
Speech, Dusseldorf, 27 Jan 1932

15 I go the way that Providence dictates with the assurance of a sleepwalker.
Referring to his successful re-occupation of the Rhineland, despite advice against the attempt. Speech, Munich, 15 Mar 1936

16 When Barbarossa commences, the world will hold its breath and make no comment.
Referring to the planned invasion of the USSR, Operation Barbarossa, which began on 22 June 1941. Attrib.

17 Is Paris burning?
Referring to the liberation of Paris, 1944

HOLINESS

1 'Twas on a Holy Thursday, their innocent faces clean,
The children walking two and two, in red and blue and green.
William Blake (1757–1827) British poet. *Songs of Innocence*, 'Holy Thursday'

2 For everything that lives is holy, life delights in life.
William Blake *America*

3 I am certain of nothing but the holiness of the heart's affections and the truth of imagination – what the imagination seizes as beauty must be truth – whether it existed before or not.
John Keats (1795–1821) British poet. Letter to Benjamin Bailey, 22 Nov 1817

HOLISTIC MEDICINE

1 A careful physician..., before he attempts to administer a remedy to his patient, must investigate not only the malady of the man he wishes to cure, but also his habits when in health, and his physical constitution.
Cicero (106 BC–43 BC) Roman orator and statesman. *On the Orator*, II

2 A bodily disease, which we look upon as whole and entire within itself, may, after all, but but a symptom of some ailment in the spiritual part.
Nathaniel Hawthorne (1804–64) US novelist and writer. *The Scarlet Letter*, Ch. 10

3 Natural forces are the healers of disease.
Hippocrates (c. 460 BC–c. 377 BC) Greek physician. *Epidemics*, VI

4 When the minds of the people are closed and wisdom is locked out they remain tied to disease. Yet their feelings and desires should be investigated and made known, their wishes and ideas should be followed; and then it becomes apparent that those who have attained spirit and energy are flourishing and prosperous, while those perish who lose their spirit and energy.
Huang Ti (2697 BC–2597 BC) Chinese emperor, known as 'The Yellow Emperor'. *Nei Ching Su Wên*, Bk. 4, Sect. 13

5 Knowledge indeed is a desirable, a lovely possession, but I do not scruple to say that health is more so. It is of little consequence to store the mind with science if the body be permitted to become debilitated. If the body be feeble, the mind will not be strong.
Thomas Jefferson (1743–1826) US statesman. Letter to Thomas M. Randolph, Jr., 27 Aug 1786

6 Are you sick, or are you sullen?
Samuel Johnson (1709–84) English lexicographer and writer. Letter to James Boswell, 5 Nov 1784

7 Body and soul cannot be separated for purposes of treatment, for they are one and indivisible. Sick minds must be healed as well as sick bodies.
C. Jeff Miller (1874–1936) *Surgery, Gynecology & Obstetrics*, 52:488, 1931

8 The cure of many diseases is unknown to the physicians of Hellas, because they are ignorant of the whole, which ought to be studied also; for the part can never be well unless the whole is well. . . . This is the great error of our day in the treatment of the human body, that the physicians separate the soul from the body.
Plato (c. 427 BC–347 BC) Greek philosopher. *Charmides*

9 Well in body
But sick in mind.
Plautus (c. 254 BC–184 BC) Roman dramatist. *Epidicus*, I:2

10 The body must be repaired and supported, if we would preserve the mind in all its vigour.
Pliny the Younger (Gaius Plinius Caecilius Secundus; 62 AD–c. 113 AD) Roman writer. *Epistles*, I, 9

11 The human body is like a bakery with a thousand windows. We are looking into only one window of the bakery when we are investigating one particular aspect of a disease.
Béla Schick (1877–1967) Hungarian-born US physician. *Aphorisms and Facetiae of Béla Schick*, 'Early Years' (I. J. Wolf)

12 Disease has social as well as physical, chemical, and biological causes.
Henry E. Siegrist (1891–1957)

HOME

See also homesickness, travel

1 East, west, home's best.
Proverb

2 Home is where the heart is.
Proverb

3 A House Is Not a Home.
Polly Adler (1900–62) US madam. Title of memoirs

4 Home is home, though it be never so homely.
John Clarke (fl. 1639) English scholar. *Paroemiologia Anglo-Latina*

5 Home is the place where, when you have to go there,
They have to take you in.
Robert Frost (1875–1963) US poet. *The Death of the Hired Man*

6 What's the good of a home, if you are never in it?
George Grossmith (1847–1912) British singer and comedian. *The Diary of a Nobody*, Ch. 1

7 In fact there was but one thing wrong with the Babbitt house; it was not a home.
Sinclair Lewis (1885–1951) US novelist. *Babbitt*, Ch. 2

8 A man travels the world over in search of what he needs and returns home to find it.
George Moore (1852–1933) Irish writer and art critic. *The Brook Kerith*, Ch. 11

9 Keep the Home Fires Burning.
Ivor Novello (David Ivor Davies; 1893–1951) British actor, composer, and dramatist. Title of song (written with Lena Guilbert Ford)

10 Mid pleasures and palaces though we may roam,
Be it ever so humble, there's no place like home;
. . .
Home, home, sweet, sweet home!
There's no place like home! there's no place like home!
John Howard Payne (1791–1852) US actor and dramatist. *Clari, or the Maid of Milan*

11 Home-keeping youth have ever homely wits.
William Shakespeare (1564–1616) English dramatist. *The Two Gentlemen of Verona*, I:1

12 Seek home for rest,
For home is best.
Thomas Tusser (1524–80) English farmer. *Five Hundred Points of Good Husbandry*, 'Instructions to Housewifery'

13 Look Homeward, Angel!
Thomas Wolfe (1900–38) US novelist. From 'Lycidas' by John Milton. Book title

HOMESICKNESS

See also home, nostalgia

1 They say there's bread and work for all,
And the sun shines always there:
But I'll not forget old Ireland,
Were it fifty times as fair.
Helen Selina Blackwood (1807–67) British poet. *Lament of the Irish Emigrant*

2 Weep no more, my lady,
Oh! weep no more today!
We will sing one song for the old Kentucky Home,
For the old Kentucky Home far away.
Stephen Foster (1826–64) US composer of popular songs. *My Old Kentucky Home*

3 'Way down upon de Swanee Ribber,
Far, far away,
Dere's where my heart is turning ebber:
Dere's where de old folks stay.
All up and down de whole creation
Sadly I roam,
Still longing for de old plantation,
And for de old folks at home.
Stephen Foster *Old Folks at Home*

4 Oh give me a home where the buffalo roam,
Where the deer and the antelope play,
Where seldom is heard a discouraging word
And the skies are not cloudy all day.
Brewster Higley (19th century) US songwriter. *Home on the Range*

5 The accent of one's birthplace lingers in the mind and in the heart as it does in one's speech.
Duc de la Rochefoucauld (1613–80) French writer. *Maximes*, 342

6 Breathes there the man, with soul so dead,
Who never to himself hath said,
This is my own, my native land!
Whose heart hath ne'er within him burn'd,
As home his footsteps he hath turn'd
From wandering on a foreign strand!
Walter Scott (1771–1832) Scottish novelist. *The Lay of the Last Minstrel*, VI

7 In home-sickness you must keep moving – it is the only disease that does not require rest.
H. de Vere Stacpoole (1863–1931) Irish-born novelist. *The Bourgeois*

8 Good-bye Piccadilly, Farewell Leicester Square;
It's a long, long way to Tipperary, but my heart's right there!
Harry Williams (1874–1924) British songwriter. Written with Jack Judge (1878–1938). *It's a Long Way to Tipperary*

9 I travelled among unknown men
In lands beyond the sea;
Nor, England! did I know till then
What love I bore to thee.
William Wordsworth (1770–1850) British poet. *I Travelled among Unknown Men*

HOMOSEXUALITY

See also sex

1 Out of the closets and into the streets.
Anonymous Slogan for US Gay Liberation Front

2 But the men of Sodom were wicked and sinners before the Lord exceedingly.
Bible: Genesis 13:13

3 If God had meant to have homosexuals he would have created Adam and Bruce.
Anita Bryant US singer. Attrib.

4 I became one of the stately homos of England.
Quentin Crisp (c. 1910–) British model, publicist, and writer. *The Naked Civil Servant*

5 The . . . problem which confronts homosexuals is that they set out to win the love of a 'real' man. If they succeed, they fail. A man who 'goes with' other men is not what they would call a real man.
Quentin Crisp *The Naked Civil Servant*

6 Why didn't you bring him with you? I should be delighted to meet him.
Lady (Maud) 'Emerald' Cunard (1872–1948) American-born society figure in Britain. To Somerset Maugham, who said he was leaving a dinner party early 'to keep his youth'. *Emerald and Nancy* (D. Fielding)

7 I am the Love that dare not speak its name.
Lord Alfred Douglas (1870–1945) British writer and poet. *Two Loves*

8 It is a perfectly ordinary little case of a man charged with indecency with four or five guardsmen.
Mervyn Griffith-Jones (1909–78) British lawyer. Attrib. in *This England* (Michael Bateman)

9 There's nothing wrong with going to bed with somebody of your own sex. People should be very free with sex – they should draw the line at goats.
Elton John (1947–) British rock pianist and singer.

10 The 'homo' is the legitimate child of the 'suffragette'.
Wyndham Lewis (1882–1957) British novelist. *The Art of Being Ruled*, Pt. VIII, Ch. 4

11 Well, he looks like a man.
Abraham Lincoln (1809–65) US statesman. On catching sight of Walt Whitman for the first time. Attrib.

12 This sort of thing may be tolerated by the French, but we are British – thank God.
Lord Montgomery (1887–1976) British field marshal. Comment on a bill to relax the laws against homosexuals. *Daily Mail*, 27 May 1965

13 If Michelangelo had been straight, the Sistine Chapel would have been wallpapered.
Robin Tyler US comedienne. Speech to gay-rights rally, Washington, 9 Jan 1988

HONESTY

See also frankness, integrity, sincerity, truth

1 An honest man's word is as good as his bond.
Proverb

2 Honesty is the best policy.
Proverb

3 It is impossible that a man who is false to his friends and neighbours should be true to the public.
Bishop Berkeley (1685–1753) Irish churchman and philosopher. *Maxims Concerning Patriotism*

4 You see, I always divide people into two groups. Those who live by what they know to be a lie, and those who live by what they believe, falsely, to be the truth.
Christopher Hampton (1946–) British writer and dramatist. *The Philanthropist*, Sc. 6

5 Though I be poor, I'm honest.
Thomas Middleton (1580–1627) English dramatist. *The Witch*, III:2

6 To make your children *capable of honesty* is the beginning of education.
John Ruskin (1819–1900) British art critic and writer. *Time and Tide*, Letter VIII

7 To be honest, as this world goes, is to be one man pick'd out of ten thousand.
William Shakespeare (1564–1616) English dramatist. *Hamlet*, II:2

8 I thank God I am as honest as any man living that is an old man and no honester than I.
William Shakespeare *Much Ado About Nothing*, III:5

9 O wretched fool!
That liv'st to make thine honesty a vice.
O monstrous world! Take note, take note, O world!
To be direct and honest is not safe.
William Shakespeare *Othello* III:3

10 Though I am not naturally honest, I am so sometimes by chance.
William Shakespeare *The Winter's Tale*, IV:3

11 Ha, ha! what a fool Honesty is! and Trust his sworn brother, a very simple gentleman!
William Shakespeare *The Winter's Tale*, IV:3

12 Father, I cannot tell a lie. I did it with my little hatchet.
George Washington (1732–99) US statesman. Attrib.

13 Honesty is the best policy; but he who is governed by that maxim is not an honest man.
Richard Whately (1787–1863) British churchman. *Apophthegms*

14 It is a terrible thing for a man to find out suddenly that all his life he has been speaking nothing but the truth.
Oscar Wilde (1854–1900) Irish-born British dramatist. *The Importance of Being Earnest*, III

15 If you do not tell the truth about yourself you cannot tell it about other people.
Virginia Woolf (1882–1941) British novelist. *The Moment and Other Essays*

HONEY

1 For the Lord thy God bringeth thee into a good land, a land of brooks of water, of fountains and depths that spring out of valleys and hills;
A land of wheat, and barley, and vines, and fig trees, and pomegranates; a land of oil olive, and honey;
A land wherein thou shalt eat bread without scarceness, thou shalt not lack any thing in it; a land whose stones are iron, and out of whose hills thou mayest dig brass.
When thou hast eaten and art full, then thou shalt bless the Lord thy God for the good land which he hath given thee.
Bible: Deuteronomy 8:7–10

2 Stands the Church clock at ten to three?
And is there honey still for tea?
Rupert Brooke (1887–1915) British poet. *The Old Vicarage, Grantchester*

3 The Owl and the Pussy-Cat went to sea
In a beautiful pea-green boat,

They took some honey, and plenty of money,
Wrapped up in a five-pound note.

Edward Lear (1812–88) British artist and writer. *The Owl and the Pussy-Cat*

4 How doth the little busy bee
Improve each shining hour,
And gather honey all the day
From every opening flower!

Isaac Watts (1674–1748) English theologian and hymn writer. *Divine Songs for Children*, 'Against Idleness and Mischief'

HONOR

See also titles

1 And they were offended in him. But Jesus said unto them, A prophet is not without honour, save in his own country, and in his own house.

Bible: Matthew 13:57

2 That chastity of honour, that felt a stain like a wound.

Edmund Burke (1729–97) British politician. *Reflections on the Revolution in France*

3 Tell me not, Sweet, I am unkind,
That from the nunnery
Of thy chaste breast and quiet mind
To war and arms I fly.

True, a new mistress now I chase,
The first foe in the field;
And with a stronger faith embrace
A sword, a horse, a shield.

Yet this inconstancy is such
As thou too shalt adore;
I could not love thee, Dear, so much,
Loved I not Honour more.

Richard Lovelace (1618–58) English poet. *To Lucasta, Going to the Wars*

4 Remember, men, we're fighting for this woman's honor; which is probably more than she ever did.

Groucho Marx (Julius Marx; 1895–1977) US comedian. *Duck Soup*

5 Honour pricks me on. Yea, but how if honour prick me off when I come on? How then? Can honour set to a leg? No. Or an arm? No. Or take away the grief of a wound? No. Honour hath no skill in surgery, then? No. What is honour? A word. What is in that word? Honour. What is that honour? Air.

William Shakespeare (1564–1616) English dramatist. *Henry IV, Part One*, V:1

6 I like not such grinning honour as Sir Walter hath: give me life; which if I can save, so; if not, honour comes unlooked for, and there's an end.

William Shakespeare *Henry IV, Part One*, V:3

7 Well, honour is the subject of my story.
I cannot tell what you and other men
Think of this life: but, for my single self,
I had as lief not be as live to be
In awe of such a thing as I myself.

William Shakespeare *Julius Caesar*, I:2

8 For Brutus is an honourable man;
So are they all, all honourable men.

William Shakespeare *Julius Caesar*, III:2

9 I once had a sparrow alight upon my shoulder for a moment while I was hoeing in a village garden, and I felt that I was more distinguished by that circumstance than I should have been by any epaulet I could have worn.

Henry David Thoreau (1817–62) US writer. *Walden*, 'Winter Visitors'

10 Brothers all
In honour, as in one community,
Scholars and gentlemen.

William Wordsworth (1770–1850) British poet. *The Prelude*, IX

HOOD, Thomas

(1799–1845) British poet. His collection *Odes and Addresses* (1825) was followed by several volumes of humorous verse and such political poems as *The Story of the Shirt* (1843).

1 The sedate, sober, silent, serious, sad-coloured sect.

Referring to the Quakers. *The Doves and the Crows*

2 Ben Battle was a soldier bold,
And used to war's alarms:
But a cannon-ball took off his legs,
So he laid down his arms!

Faithless Nelly Gray

3 For here I leave my second leg,
And the Forty-second Foot!

Faithless Nelly Gray

4 The love that loves a scarlet coat
Should be more uniform.

Faithless Nelly Gray

5 His death, which happen'd in his berth,
At forty-odd befell:
They went and told the sexton, and
The sexton toll'd the bell.

Faithless Sally Brown

6 I remember, I remember,
The house where I was born,
The little window where the sun
Came peeping in at morn;
He never came a wink too soon,
Nor brought too long a day,
But now, I often wish the night
Had borne my breath away!

I Remember

7 I remember, I remember,
The fir trees dark and high;
I used to think their slender tops
Were close against the sky:
It was a childish ignorance,
But now 'tis little joy
To know I'm farther off from heav'n
Than when I was a boy.

I Remember

8 But evil is wrought by want of thought,
As well as want of heart!

The Lady's Dream

9 For that old enemy the gout
Had taken him in toe!

Lieutenant Luff

10 No warmth, no cheerfulness, no healthful ease,
No comfortable feel in any member –
No shade, no shine, no butterflies, no bees,
No fruits, no flowers, no leaves, no birds, –
November!

No!

11 O! men with sisters dear,
O! men with mothers and wives!
It is not linen you're wearing out,
But human creatures' lives!

The Song of the Shirt

12 Oh! God! that bread should be so dear,
And flesh and blood so cheap!

The Song of the Shirt

13 Holland . . . lies so low they're only saved by being dammed.

Up the Rhine

14 What is a modern poet's fate?
To write his thoughts upon a slate;
The critic spits on what is done,
Gives it a wipe – and all is gone.

Alfred Lord Tennyson, A Memoir (Hallam Tennyson), Vol. II, Ch. 3

15 There are three things which the public will always clamour for, sooner or later: namely, Novelty, novelty, novelty.

Announcement of *Comic Annual*, 1836

HOOVER, Herbert Clark

(1874–1964) US statesman and Republican President (1929–33).

Quotations about Hoover

1 Facts to Hoover's brain are as water to a sponge; they are absorbed into every tiny interstice.
Bernard Baruch (1870–1965) US financier and presidential adviser. *Herbert Hoover: American Quaker* (D. Hinshaw)

2 Hoover, if elected, will do one thing that is almost incomprehensible to the human mind: he will make a great man out of Coolidge.
Clarence Darrow (1857–1938) US lawyer. Remark during the presidential campaign, 1932

Quotations by Hoover

3 The American system of rugged individualism.
Speech, New York, 22 Oct 1928

4 Older men declare war. But it is youth that must fight and die.
Speech, Republican National Convention, Chicago, 27 June 1944

HOPE

See also ambition, expectation, desire, optimism

1 A drowning man will clutch at a straw.
Proverb

2 Hope for the best.
Proverb

3 It is a long lane that has no turning.
Proverb

4 While there's life there's hope.
Proverb

5 Hope is the physician of each misery.
Irish proverb

6 Comin' in on a Wing and a Prayer.
Harold Adamson (1906–) US songwriter. Film and song title

7 Still nursing the unconquerable hope,
Still clutching the inviolable shade.
Matthew Arnold (1822–88) British poet and critic. *The Scholar Gipsy*

8 Charity is the power of defending that which we know to be indefensible. Hope is the power of being cheerful in circumstances which we know to be desperate.
G. K. Chesterton (1874–1936) British writer. *Heretics*, Ch. 12

9 That one day this country of ours, which we love so much, will find dignity and greatness and peace again.
Noël Coward (1899–1973) British dramatist. The toast from *Cavalcade*

10 People will not readily bear pain unless there is hope.
Michael Edwards (1930–) South African businessman. Speech, 2 July 1980

11 He that lives upon hope will die fasting.
Benjamin Franklin (1706–90) US scientist and statesman. *The Way to Wealth*

12 Confidence and hope do be more good than physic.
Galen (fl. 2nd century) Greek physician.

13 While there is life, there's hope,' he cried;
'Then why such haste?' so groaned and died.
John Gay (1685–1732) English poet and dramatist. *Fables*

14 Death is the greatest evil, because it cuts off hope.
William Hazlitt (1778–1830) British essayist and journalist. *Characteristics*, 35

15 Hope is necessary in every condition. The miseries of poverty, sickness, of captivity, would, without this comfort, be insupportable.
Samuel Johnson (1709–84) English lexicographer and writer. *The Rambler*, 67

16 The first qualification for a physician is hopefulness.
James Little (1836–85) US physician.

17 After all, tomorrow is another day.
Margaret Mitchell (1909–49) US novelist. The closing words of the book. *Gone with the Wind*

18 Always give the patient hope, even when death seems at hand.
Ambroise Paré (c. 1517–90) French surgeon.

19 Hope springs eternal in the human breast;
Man never is, but always to be blest.
Alexander Pope (1688–1744) British poet. *An Essay on Man*, I

20 For hope is but the dream of those that wake.
Matthew Prior (1664–1721) British poet. *Solomon*, II

21 The miserable have no other medicine
But only hope.
William Shakespeare (1564–1616) English dramatist. *Measure for Measure*, III:1

22 The doctor says there is no hope, and as he does the killing he ought to know.
Gaspar Zavala y Zamora (d. 1813) *El Triunfo del Amor y de la Amistad*, II:8

HORACE

(Quintus Horatius Flaccus; 65–8 BC) Roman poet. His *Odes* and *Epistles* portray Roman life in considerable detail.

1 'Painters and poets alike have always had licence to dare anything.' We know that, and we both claim and allow to others in their turn this indulgence.
Ars Poetica

2 I strive to be brief, and I become obscure.
Ars Poetica

3 You will have written exceptionally well if, by skilful arrangement of your words, you have made an ordinary one seem original.
Ars Poetica

4 Many terms which have now dropped out of favour, will be revived, and those that are at present respectable will drop out, if usage so choose, with whom resides the decision and the judgement and the code of speech.
Ars Poetica

5 Scholars dispute, and the case is still before the courts.
Ars Poetica

6 Mountains will heave in childbirth, and a silly little mouse will be born.
Ars Poetica

7 He always hurries to the main event and whisks his audience into the middle of things as though they knew already.
Ars Poetica

8 To the Greeks the Muse gave native wit, to the Greeks the gift of graceful eloquence.
Ars Poetica

9 I'm aggrieved when sometimes even excellent Homer nods.
Ars Poetica

10 Not gods, nor men, nor even

booksellers have put up with poets' being second-rate.
Ars Poetica

11 Let it be kept till the ninth year, the manuscript put away at home: you may destroy whatever you haven't published; once out, what you've said can't be stopped.
Ars Poetica

12 To save a man's life against his will is the same as killing him.
Ars Poetica

13 *Nullius addictus iurare in verba magistri,*
Quo me cumque rapit tempestas, deferor hospes.
Not bound to swear allegiance to any master, wherever the wind takes me I travel as a visitor.
Nullius in verba is the motto of the Royal Society. *Epistles*, I

14 The happy state of getting the victor's palm without the dust of racing.
Epistles, I

15 If possible honestly, if not, somehow, make money.
Epistles, I

16 Let me remind you what the wary fox said once upon a time to the sick lion: 'Because those footprints scare me, all directed your way, none coming back.'
Epistles, I

17 We are just statistics, born to consume resources.
Epistles, I

18 Believe each day that has dawned is your last. Some hour to which you have not been looking forward will prove lovely. As for me, if you want a good laugh, you will come and find me fat and sleek, in excellent condition, one of Epicurus' herd of pigs.
Epistles, I

19 To marvel at nothing is just about the one and only thing, Numicius, that can make a man happy and keep him that way.
Epistles, I

20 You may drive out nature with a pitchfork, yet she'll be constantly running back.
Epistles, I

21 They change their clime, not their frame of mind, who rush across the sea. We work hard at doing nothing: we look for happiness in boats and carriage rides. What you are looking for is here, is at Ulubrae, if only peace of mind doesn't desert you.
Epistles, I

22 For it is your business, when the wall next door catches fire.
Epistles, I

23 If you believe Cratinus from days of old, Maecenas, (as you must know) no verse can give pleasure for long, nor last, that is written by drinkers of water.
Epistles, I

24 And seek for truth in the groves of Academe.
Epistles, II

25 Hard to train to accept being poor.
Odes, I

26 And if you include me among the lyric poets, I'll hold my head so high it'll strike the stars.
Odes, I

27 Pale Death kicks his way equally into the cottages of the poor and the castles of kings.
Odes, I

28 Life's short span forbids us to enter on far-reaching hopes.
Odes, I

29 Drop the question what tomorrow may bring, and count as profit every day that Fate allows you.
Odes, I

30 Do not try to find out – we're forbidden to know – what end the gods have in store for me, or for you.
Odes, I

31 While we're talking, time will have meanly run on: pick today's fruits, not relying on the future in the slightest.
Odes, I

32 *Carpe diem*
Seize the day.
Odes, I

33 When things are steep, remember to stay level-headed.
Odes, II

34 *Dulce et decorum est pro patria mori.*
It is a sweet and seemly thing to die for one's country.
Odes, III

35 Force, if unassisted by judgement, collapses through its own mass.
Odes, III

36 Undeservedly you will atone for the sins of your fathers.
Odes, III

37 What do the ravages of time not injure? Our parents' age (worse than our grandparents') has produced us, more worthless still, who will soon give rise to a yet more vicious generation.
Odes, III

38 My life with girls has ended, though till lately I was up to it and soldiered on not ingloriously; now on this wall will hang my weapons and my lyre, discharged from the war.
Odes, III

39 I have executed a memorial longer lasting than bronze.
Odes, III

40 That I make poetry and give pleasure (if I give pleasure) are because of you.
Odes, IV

41 Not to hope for things to last for ever, is what the year teaches and even the hour which snatches a nice day away.
Odes, IV

42 Many brave men lived before Agamemnon's time; but they are all, unmourned and unknown, covered by the long night, because they lack their sacred poet.
Odes, IV

43 Not the owner of many possessions will you be right to call happy: he more rightly deserves the name of happy who knows how to use the gods' gifts wisely and to put up with rough poverty, and who fears dishonour more than death.
Odes, IV

44 Mix a little foolishness with your serious plans: it's lovely to be silly at the right moment.
Odes, IV

45 How is it, Maecenas, that no one lives contented with his lot, whether he has planned it for himself or fate has flung him into it, but yet he praises those who follow different paths?
Satires, I

46 An accomplished man to his finger-tips.
Satires, I

47 Strong enough to answer back to desires, to despise distinctions, and a whole man in himself, polished and well-rounded.
Satires, II

HORROR

1 Ideal mankind would abolish death, multiply itself million upon million, rear up city upon city, save every parasite alive, until the accumulation of mere existence is swollen to a horror.
D. H. Lawrence (1885–1930) British novelist. *St Mawr*

2 I have a horror of sunsets, they're so romantic, so operatic.
Marcel Proust (1871–1922) French novelist. *À la recherche du temps perdu: Sodome et Gomorrhe*

3 I have supp'd full with horrors.
William Shakespeare (1564–1616) English dramatist. *Macbeth*, V:5

4 He had one peculiar weakness; he had faced death in many forms but he had never faced a dentist. The thought of dentists gave him just the same sick horror as the thought of Socialism.
H. G. Wells (1866–1946) British writer. *Bealby*, Pt. VIII, Ch. 1

HORSES

See also animals, hunting, sport

1 When I appear in public people expect me to neigh, grind my teeth, paw the ground and swish my tail – none of which is easy.
Princess Anne (1950–) The Princess Royal, only daughter of Elizabeth II. *The Observer*, 'Sayings of the Week', 22 May 1977

2 I know two things about the horse,
And one of them is rather coarse.
Anonymous *The Horse*

3 I sprang to the stirrup, and Joris, and he;
I galloped, Dirck galloped, we galloped all three.
Robert Browning (1812–89) British poet. *How they brought the Good News from Ghent to Aix*

4 As lene was his hors as is a rake.
Geoffrey Chaucer (c. 1342–1400) English poet. *The Canterbury Tales*, Prologue

5 The blue ribbon of the turf.
Benjamin Disraeli (1804–81) British statesman. Describing the Derby. *Life of Lord George Bentinck*, Ch. 26

6 Gwine to run all night!
Gwine to run all day!
I bet my money on the bob-tail nag.
Somebody bet on the bay.
Stephen Foster (1826–64) US composer of popular songs. *Camptown Races*

7 They say princes learn no art truly, but the art of horsemanship. The reason is, the brave beast is no flatterer. He will throw a prince as soon as his groom.
Ben Jonson (1573–1637) English dramatist. *Timber, or Discoveries made upon Men and Matter*

8 It takes a good deal of physical courage to ride a horse. This, however, I have. I get it at about forty cents a flask, and take it as required.
Stephen Leacock (1869–1944) English-born Canadian economist and humorist. *Literary Lapses*, 'Reflections on Riding'

9 To confess that you are totally Ignorant about the Horse, is social suicide: you will be despised by everybody, especially the horse.
W. C. Sellar (1898–1951) British humorous writer. *Horse Nonsense*

10 A horse! a horse ! my kingdom for a horse.
William Shakespeare (1564–1616) English dramatist. *Richard III*, V:4

HOSPITALITY

1 A constant guest is never welcome.
Proverb

2 Fish and guests smell in three days.
Proverb

3 The guest who outstays his fellow-guests loses his overcoat.
Chinese proverb

4 The first day a guest, the second day a guest, the third day a calamity.
Indian proverb

5 I'd rather be a host than a guest. As Beerbohm wonderfully observed, a happy host makes a sad guest.
Harold Acton (1904–) British writer. *The Times*, 18 Apr 1970

6 Let brotherly love continue.
Be not forgetful to entertain strangers: for thereby some have entertained angels unawares.
Bible: Hebrews 13:1–2

7 Come again when you can't stay so long.
Walter Sickert (1860–1942) British painter. Said to Denton Welch. *Horizon*, 'Sickert at St. Peter's' (D. Welch)

HOSPITALS

1 So it was all modern and scientific and well-arranged. You could die very nearly as privately in a modern hospital as you could in the Grand Central Station, and with much better care.
Stephen Vincent Benét (1898–1943) US writer. *Tales of Our Time*, 'No Visitors'

2 Our hospital organization has grown up with no plan, with no system; it is unevenly distributed over the country . . . I would rather be kept alive in the efficient if cold altruism of a large hospital than expire in a gush of warm sympathy in a small one.
Aneurin Bevan (1897–1960) British Labour politician. Introducing the National Health Service Bill. Speech, House of Commons, 30 Apr 1946

3 It has been considered from the point of view of the hygienist, the physician, the architect, the tax-payer, the superintendents, and the nurse, but of the several hundred books, pamphlets, and articles on the subject with which I am acquainted, I do not remember to have seen one from the point of view of the patient.
John Shaw Billings (1838–1913) *Public Health Reports*, 1874–75

4 One of the most difficult things to contend with in a hospital is the assumption on the part of the staff that because you have lost your gall bladder you have also lost your mind.
Jean Kerr (1923–) US dramatist, screenwriter, and humorist. *Please Don't Eat the Daisies*, 'Operation Operation'

5 If you are hidebound with prejudice, if your temper is sentimental, you can go through the wards of a hospital and be as ignorant of man at the end as you were at the beginning.
W. Somerset Maugham (1874–1965) British novelist and doctor. *The Summing Up*

6 The sooner patients can be removed from the depressing

influence of general hospital life the more rapid their convalescence.

Charles H. Mayo (1865–1939) US physician. *Journal-Lancet*, 36:1, 1916

7 'She says, if you please, sir, she only wants to be let die in peace.' 'What! and the whole class to be disappointed, impossible! Tell her she can't be allowed to die in peace; it is against the rules of the hospital!'

John Fisher Murray (1811–65) *The World of London*

8 It may seem a strange principle to enunciate as the very first requirement in a Hospital that it should do the sick no harm.

Florence Nightingale (1820–1910) British nurse. *Notes on Hospitals*, Preface

9 Here, at whatever hour you come, you will find light and help and human kindness.

Albert Schweitzer (1875–1965) Franco-German medical missionary, theologian, philosopher, and organist. Inscribed on the lamp outside his jungle hospital at Lambaréné

HOUSES

See also architecture, home, stately homes

1 Houses are built to live in and not to look on; therefore let use be preferred before uniformity, except where both may be had.

Francis Bacon (1561–1626) English philosopher. *Essays*, 'Of Building'

2 A hundred and fifty accurate reproductions of Anne Hathaway's cottage, each complete with central heating and garage.

Osbert Lancaster (1908–86) British cartoonist. *Pillar to Post*, 'Stockbrokers Tudor'

3 A house is a machine for living in.

Le Corbusier (Charles-Édouard Jeanneret; 1887–1965) Swiss-born French architect. *Towards an Architecture*

4 They're all made out of ticky-tacky, and they all look just the same.

Malvina Reynolds (1900–78) US folksinger and songwriter. *Little Boxes*, song describing a housing scheme built in the hills south of San Francisco. *Little Boxes*

5 It's 'aving 'ouses built by men, I believe, makes all the work and trouble.

H. G. Wells (1866–1946) British writer. *Kipps*, Bk. III, Ch. 1

HOUSES OF PARLIAMENT

See also aristocracy, government, politics

1 This is a rotten argument, but it should be good enough for their lordships on a hot summer afternoon.

Anonymous A note on a ministerial brief read out by mistake in the House of Lords. *The Way the Wind Blows* (Lord Home), 1976

2 The House of Lords is like a glass of champagne that has stood for five days.

Clement Attlee (1883–1967) British statesman and Labour prime minister. Attrib.

3 A severe though not unfriendly critic of our institutions said that 'the cure for admiring the House of Lords was to go and look at it.'

Walter Bagehot (1826–77) British economist and journalist. *The English Constitution*, 'The House of Lords'

4 A lot of hard-faced men who look as if they had done very well out of the war.

Stanley Baldwin (1867–1947) British statesman. Referring to the first House of Commons elected after World War I (1918). *Economic Consequences of the Peace* (J. M. Keynes), Ch. 5

5 The House of Lords is the British Outer Mongolia for retired politicians.

Tony Benn (1925–) British politician. Speech, 11 Feb 1962

6 I have been, though unworthy, a member of this House in six or seven Parliaments, yet never did I see the House in so great confusion. This is more fit for a grammar school than a Court of Parliament.

Robert Cecil, 1st Earl of Salisbury (1563–1612) English statesman. Speech, House of Commons, 24 Nov 1601

7 Well, since I see all the birds are flown, I do expect from you that you shall send them unto me as soon as they return hither.

Charles I (1600–49) King of England. On entering the House of Commons to arrest five MPs. Remark, 4 Jan 1642

8 Better than a play.

Charles II (1630–85) King of England. Referring to House of Lords debate on the Divorce Bill. Attrib.

9 I think . . . that it is the best club in London.

Charles Dickens (1812–70) British novelist. Mr Tremlow describing the House of Commons. *Our Mutual Friend*, Bk. II, Ch. 3

10 I am dead: dead, but in the Elysian fields.

Benjamin Disraeli (1804–81) British statesman. Said on his move to the House of Lords. Attrib.

11 The House of Lords is a model of how to care for the elderly.

Frank Field (1942–) British politician. *The Observer*, 24 May 1981

12 There are kings enough in England. I am nothing there, I am old and want rest and should only go to be plagued and teased there about that D—d House of Commons.

George II (1683–1760) King of Great Britain and Ireland. George II's reply when urged to leave Hanover and return to England. Letter from the Earl of Holderness to the Duke of Newcastle, 3 Aug 1755

13 The House of Peers, throughout the war,
Did nothing in particular,
And did it very well.

W. S. Gilbert (1836–1911) British dramatist. *Iolanthe*, II

14 I have neither eye to see, nor tongue to speak here, but as the House is pleased to direct me.

William Lenthall (1591–1662) English parliamentarian. Said on 4 Jan 1642 in the House of Commons when asked by Charles I if he had seen five MPs whom the King wished to arrest. It was a succinct restatement of the Speaker's traditional role. *Historical Collections* (Rushworth)

15 Mr Balfour's Poodle.

David Lloyd George (1863–1945) British Liberal statesman. Referring to the House of Lords and its in-built Conservative majority; said in reply to a claim that it was 'the watchdog of the nation'. Remark, House of Commons, 26 June 1907

16 Every man has a House of Lords in his own head. Fears, prejudices, misconceptions – those are the peers, and they are hereditary.

David Lloyd George Speech, Cambridge, 1927

17 The British, being brought up on team games, enter their House of Commons in the spirit of those who would rather be doing something else. If they cannot be playing golf or tennis, they can at least pretend that politics is a game with very similar rules.

Cyril Northcote Parkinson (1919–) British historian and writer. *Parkinson's Law*, Ch. 2

18 The House of Lords must be the only institution in the world which is kept efficient by the persistent absenteeism of most of its members.

Herbert Samuel (1870–1963) British Liberal statesman. *News Review*, 5 Feb 1948

19 A life peer is like a mule – no

pride of ancestry, no hope of posterity.
Lord Shackleton (1911–) British politician, businessman, and life peer. Attrib.

20 The House of Lords is a perfect eventide home.
Mary Stocks (1891–1975) British politician and writer. *The Observer*, 'Sayings of the Week', 4 Oct 1970

21 The House of Lords, an illusion to which I have never been able to subscribe – responsibility without power, the prerogative of the eunuch throughout the ages.
Tom Stoppard (1937–) Czech-born British dramatist. *Lord Malquist and Mr Moon*, Pt. VI, Ch. 1

22 You must build your House of Parliament upon the river: so . . . that the populace cannot exact their demands by sitting down round you.
Duke of Wellington (1769–1852) British general and statesman. *Words on Wellington* (Sir William Fraser)

HOUSEWORK

See also woman's role

1 Housekeeping ain't no joke.
Louisa May Alcott (1832–88) US novelist. *Little Women*, Pt. I

2 Our motto: Life is too short to stuff a mushroom.
Shirley Conran (1932–) Designer and journalist. *Superwoman*, Epigraph

3 There was no need to do any housework at all. After the first four years the dirt doesn't get any worse.
Quentin Crisp (c. 1910–) British model, publicist, and writer. *The Naked Civil Servant*

4 Cleaning your house while your kids are still growing
Is like shoveling the walk before it stops snowing.
Phyllis Diller (1917–) US writer and comedienne. *Phyllis Diller's Housekeeping Hints*

HOUSMAN, A(lfred) E(dward)

(1859–1936) British scholar and poet. His own verse collections include *A Shropshire Lad* (1896) and *Last Poems* (1922).

Quotations about Housman

1 A prim, old-maidish, rather second-rate, rather tired, rather querulous person.
A. C. Benson (1862–1925) British writer. *Dianes*

Quotations by Housman

2 We'll to the woods no more,
The laurels all are cut.
Last Poems, Introductory

3 The candles burn their sockets,
The blinds let through the day,
The young man feels his pockets
And wonders what's to pay.
Last Poems, 'Eight O'Clock'

4 They say my verse is sad: no wonder;
Its narrow measure spans
Tears of eternity, and sorrow,
Not mine, but man's.
Last Poems, 'Fancy's Knell'

5 Even when poetry has a meaning, as it usually has, it may be inadvisable to draw it out . . . Perfect understanding will sometimes almost extinguish pleasure.
The Name and Nature of Poetry

6 Loveliest of trees, the cherry now
Is hung with bloom along the bough,
And stands about the woodland ride
Wearing white for Eastertide.
A Shropshire Lad, '1887'

7 They hang us now in Shrewsbury jail:
The whistles blow forlorn,
And trains all night groan on the rail
To men that die at morn.
A Shropshire Lad, 'Reveillé'

8 Look not in my eyes, for fear
They mirror true the sight I see,
And there you find your face too clear
And love it and be lost like me.
A Shropshire Lad, 'March'

9 Here of a Sunday morning
My love and I would lie,
And see the coloured counties,
And hear the larks so high
About us in the sky.
A Shropshire Lad, 'Bredon Hill'

10 Is my team ploughing,
That I was used to drive?
A Shropshire Lad, 'Bredon Hill'

11 The goal stands up, the keeper
Stands up to keep the goal.
A Shropshire Lad, 'Bredon Hill'

12 On Wenlock Edge the wood's in trouble;
His forest fleece the Wrekin heaves;
The gale, it plies the saplings double,
And thick on Severn snow the leaves.
A Shropshire Lad, 'The Welsh Marches'

13 East and west on fields forgotten
Bleach the bones of comrades slain,
Lovely lads and dead and rotten;
None that go return again.
A Shropshire Lad, 'The Welsh Marches'

14 Into my heart an air that kills
From yon far country blows:
What are those blue remembered hills,
What spires, what farms are those?
A Shropshire Lad, 'The Welsh Marches'

15 With rue my heart is laden
For golden friends I had,
For many a rose-lipt maiden
And many a lightfoot lad.
A Shropshire Lad, 'The Welsh Marches'

16 Malt does more than Milton can
To justify God's ways to man.
A Shropshire Lad, 'The Welsh Marches'

HUMAN CONDITION

See also human nature, life, mankind

1 A wanderer is man from his birth.
He was born in a ship
On the breast of the river of Time.
Matthew Arnold (1822–88) British poet and critic. *The Future*

2 Thou hast created us for Thyself, and our heart is not quiet until it rests in Thee.
St Augustine of Hippo (354–430) Bishop of Hippo. *Confessions*, Bk. I, Ch. 1

3 Man that is born of a woman is of few days, and full of trouble.
Bible: Job 14:1

4 In real life, of course, it is the hare who wins. Every time. Look around you. And in any case it is my contention that Aesop was writing for the tortoise market . . . Hares have no time to read. They are too busy winning the game.
Anita Brookner (1928–) British novelist. *Hotel du Lac*

5 We mortals cross the ocean of this world
Each in his average cabin of a life.
Robert Browning (1812–89) British poet. *Bishop Blougram's Apology*

6 The human race, to which so many of my readers belong.
G. K. Chesterton (1874–1936) British writer. *The Napoleon of Notting Hill*, Vol. I, Ch. 1

7 If God were suddenly condemned to live the life which he has inflicted on men, He would kill Himself.
Alexandre Dumas, fils (1824–95) French writer. *Pensées d'album*

8 Every man is wanted, and no man is wanted much.
Ralph Waldo Emerson (1803–82) US poet and essayist. *Essays*, 'Nominalist and Realist'

9 The world is a beautiful place
to be born into
if you don't mind some people dying
all the time
or maybe only starving
some of the time
which isn't half so bad
if it isn't you.
Laurence Ferlinghetti (1919–) US poet. *Pictures of the Gone World*

10 The management of fertility is one of the most important functions of adulthood.
Germaine Greer (1939–) Australian-born British writer and feminist.

11 Oh wearisome condition of humanity!
Born under one law, to another bound.
Fulke Greville (1554–1628) English poet and politician. *Mustapha*, V:6

12 The condition of man . . . is a condition of war of everyone against everyone.
Thomas Hobbes (1588–1679) English philosopher. *Leviathan*, Pt. I, Ch. 4

13 No arts; no letters; no society; and which is worst of all, continual fear and danger of violent death; and the life of man, solitary, poor, nasty, brutish, and short.
Thomas Hobbes *Leviathan*, Pt. I, Ch. 13

14 Fade far away, dissolve, and quite forget
What thou among the leaves hast never known,
The weariness, the fever, and the fret,
Here, where men sit and hear each other groan.
John Keats (1795–1821) British poet. *Ode to a Nightingale*

15 Man hands on misery to man.
It deepens like a coastal shelf.
Get out as early as you can,
And don't have any kids yourself.
Philip Larkin (1922–85) British poet. *High Windows*, 'This Be the Verse'

16 Every man carries the entire form of human condition.
Michel de Montaigne (1533–92) French essayist and moralist. *Essays*, 'Of repentance'

17 Solomon Grundy,
Born on a Monday,
Christened on Tuesday,
Married on Wednesday,
Took ill on Thursday,
Worse on Friday,
Died on Saturday,
Buried on Sunday.
This is the end
Of Solomon Grundy.
Nursery Rhyme *The Nursery Rhymes of England* (J. O. Halliwell)

18 There, but for a typographical error, is the story of my life.
Dorothy Parker (1893–1967) US writer. At a Hallowe'en party, when someone remarked, 'They're ducking for apples'. *You Might As Well Live* (J. Keats)

19 Created half to rise, and half to fall;
Great lord of all things, yet a prey to all;
Sole judge of truth, in endless error hurl'd;
The glory, jest, and riddle of the world!
Alexander Pope (1688–1744) British poet. *An Essay on Man*, II

20 The universe is so vast and so ageless that the life of one man can only be justified by the measure of his sacrifice.
V. A. Rosewarne (1916–1940) British pilot. Inscribed on the portrait of the 'Young Airman' in the RAF Museum. Letter to his mother, 1940

21 Brief and powerless is Man's life; on him and all his race the slow, sure doom falls pitiless and dark.
Bertrand Russell (1872–1970) British philosopher. *Mysticism and Logic*, 'A Free Man's Worship'

22 All the world's a stage,
And all the men and women merely players;
They have their exits and their entrances;
And one man in his time plays many parts,
His acts being seven ages.
William Shakespeare (1564–1616) English dramatist. *As You Like It*, II:7

23 Farewell, a long farewell, to all my greatness!
This is the state of man: to-day he puts forth
The tender leaves of hopes: to-morrow blossoms
And bears his blushing honours thick upon him;
The third day comes a frost, a killing frost,
And when he thinks, good easy man, full surely
His greatness is a-ripening, nips his root,
And then he falls, as I do.
William Shakespeare *Henry VIII*, III:2

24 When we are born, we cry that we are come
To this great stage of fools.
William Shakespeare *King Lear*, IV:6

25 We have to believe in free-will. We've got no choice.
Isaac Bashevis Singer (1904–) Polish-born US novelist. *The Times*, 21 June 1982

26 But what am I?
An infant crying in the night:
An infant crying for the light:
And with no language but a cry.
Alfred, Lord Tennyson (1809–92) British poet. *In Memoriam A.H.H.*, LIV

27 Man has given a false importance to death
Any animal plant or man who dies
adds to Nature's compost heap
becomes the manure without which
nothing could grow nothing could be created
Death is simply part of the process.
Peter Weiss (1916–82) German novelist and dramatist. *Marat/Sade*, I:12

28 For what human ill does not dawn seem to bean alternative?
Thornton Wilder (1897–1975) US novelist and dramatist. *The Bridge of San Luis Rey*

HUMAN NATURE

See also mankind

1 We are usually the best men when in the worst health.
Proverb

2 Human nature is so well disposed towards those who are in interesting situations, that a young person, who either marries or dies, is sure to be kindly spoken of.
Jane Austen (1775–1817) British novelist. *Emma*, Ch. 22

3 A man's nature runs either to herbs, or to weeds; therefore let him seasonably water the one, and destroy the other.
Francis Bacon (1561–1626) English philosopher. *Essays*, 'Of Nature in Men'

4 There is in human nature generally more of the fool than of the wise.
Francis Bacon *Essays*, 'Of Boldness'

5 Nature is often hidden, sometimes overcome, seldom extinguished.
Francis Bacon *Essays*, 'Of Nature in Men'

6 Nature, to be commanded, must be obeyed.
Francis Bacon *Novum Organum*

7 There is no surer way of calling the worst out of anyone than that of taking their worst as being their true selves; no surer way of bringing out the best than by only accepting that as being true of them.
E. F. Benson (1867–1940) British novelist. *Rex*

8 I got disappointed in human nature as well and gave it up because I found it too much like my own.
J. P. Donleavy (1926–) US novelist. *Fairy Tales of New York*

9 A man so various, that he seem'd to be
Not one, but all Mankind's Epitome.
Stiff in Opinions, always in the wrong;
Was Everything by starts, and Nothing long.
John Dryden (1631–1700) British poet and dramatist. *Absalom and Achitophel*, I

10 A person seldom falls sick, but the bystanders are animated with a faint hope that he will die.
Ralph Waldo Emerson (1803–82) US poet and essayist. *Conduct of Life*, 'Considerations by the Way'

11 You may drive out nature with a pitchfork, yet she'll be constantly running back.
Horace (Quintus Horatius Flaccus; 65–8 BC) Roman poet. *Epistles*, I

12 Most human beings have an almost infinite capacity for taking things for granted.
Aldous Huxley (1894–1964) British novelist. *Themes and Variations*

13 We need more understanding of human nature, because the only real danger that exists is man himself . . . We know nothing of man, far too little. His psyche should be studied because we are the origin of all coming evil.
Carl Gustav Jung (1875–1961) Swiss psychoanalyst. BBC television interview

14 Out of the crooked timber of humanity no straight thing can ever be made.
Immanuel Kant (1724–1804) German philosopher. *Idee zu einer allgemeinen Geschichte in weltbürgerlicher Absicht*

15 Scenery is fine – but human nature is finer.
John Keats (1795–1821) British poet. Letter to Benjamin Bailey, 13 Mar 1818

16 Upon the whole I dislike mankind: whatever people on the other side of the question may advance, they cannot deny that they are always surprised at hearing of a good action and never of a bad one.
John Keats Letter, 1820

17 No absolute is going to make the lion lie down with the lamb unless the lamb is inside.
D. H. Lawrence (1885–1930) British novelist. *The Later D. H. Lawrence*

18 Our humanity rests upon a series of learned behaviors, woven together into patterns that are infinitely fragile and never directly inherited.
Margaret Mead (1901–78) US anthropologist. *Male and Female*, Ch. 9

19 In the misfortune of our best friends we always find something which is not displeasing to us.
Duc de la Rochefoucauld (1613–80) French writer. *Maximes*, 99

20 'Tis the way of all flesh.
Thomas Shadwell (1642–92) English dramatist. *The Sullen Lovers*, V:2

21 A rarer spirit never
Did steer humanity; but you, gods, will give us
Some faults to make us men.
William Shakespeare (1564–1616) English dramatist. *Antony and Cleopatra*, V:1

22 Get thee to a nunnery: why wouldst thou be a breeder of sinners? I am myself indifferent honest; but yet I could accuse me of such things that it were better my mother had not borne me. I am very proud, revengeful, ambitious; with more offences at my beck than I have thoughts to put them in, imagination to give them shape, or time to act them in. What should such fellows as I do crawling between heaven and earth? We are arrant knaves, all; believe none of us.
William Shakespeare *Hamlet*, III:1

23 How all occasions do inform against me,
And spur my dull revenge! What is a man,
If his chief good and market of his time
Be but to sleep and feed? a beast, no more.
Sure he that made us with such large discourse,
Looking before and after, gave us not
That capability and god-like reason
To fust in us unus'd.
William Shakespeare *Hamlet*, IV:4

24 Virtue! a fig! 'tis in ourselves that we are thus, or thus. Our bodies are our gardens, to the which our wills are gardeners.
William Shakespeare *Othello*, I:3

25 It is part of human nature to hate the man you have hurt.
Tacitus (c. 55–c. 120 AD) Roman historian. *Agricola*, 42

26 It is not the ape, nor the tiger in man that I fear, it is the donkey.
William Temple (1881–1944) British churchman. Attrib.

27 . . . use thought only to justify their injustices, and speech only to conceal their thoughts.
Voltaire (François-Marie Arouet; 1694–1778) French writer. Referring to men. *Dialogue*, 'Le Chapon et la poularde'

28 The earth does not argue,
Is not pathetic, has no arrangements,
Does not scream, haste, persuade, threaten, promise,
Makes no discriminations, has no conceivable failures,
Closes nothing, refuses nothing, shuts none out.
Walt Whitman (1819–92) US poet. *To the sayers of words*

HUMAN RIGHTS

See also equality, freedom, race

1 All human beings are born free and equal in dignity and rights.
Anonymous *Universal Declaration of Human Rights* (1948), Article 1

2 *Liberté! Égalité! Fraternité!*
Freedom! Equality! Brotherhood!
Anonymous Motto for French Revolutionaries

3 We hold these truths to be self-evident: that all men are created equal; that they are endowed by their Creator with certain unalienable rights; that among these

are life, liberty, and the pursuit of happiness.

Thomas Jefferson (1743–1826) US statesman. Declaration of American Independence, 4 July 1776

4 A bill of rights is what the people are entitled to against every government on earth, general or particular and what no just government should refuse to rest on inference.

Thomas Jefferson Letter to James Madison, 20 Dec 1787

5 The poorest he that is in England hath a life to live as the greatest he.

Thomas Rainborowe (d. 1648) English soldier and vice-admiral. *Life of Rainborowe* (Peacock)

6 We look forward to a world founded upon four essential human freedoms. The first is freedom of speech and expression – everywhere in the world. The second is freedom of every person to worship God in his own way – everywhere in the world. The third is freedom from want . . . everywhere in the world. The fourth is freedom from fear . . . anywhere in the world.

Franklin D. Roosevelt (1882–1945) US Democratic president. Speech to Congress, 6 Jan 1941

7 Freedom is an indivisible word. If we want to enjoy it, and fight for it, we must be prepared to extend it to everyone, whether they are rich or poor, whether they agree with us or not, no matter what their race or the color of their skin.

Wendell Lewis Willkie (1892–1944) US lawyer and businessman. *One World*, Ch. 13

8 None ought to be lords or landlords over another, but the earth is free for every son and daughter of mankind to live free upon.

Gerrard Winstanley (c. 1609–c. 1660) English radical. Letter to Lord Fairfax, 1649

HUMILITY

See also service, servility

1 Blessed are the meek: for they shall inherit the earth.

Bible: Matthew 5:5

2 Humility is only doubt,
And does the sun and moon blot out.

William Blake (1757–1827) British poet. *The Everlasting Gospel*

3 I do not consider it an insult but rather a compliment to be called an agnostic. I do not pretend to know where many ignorant men are sure.

Clarence Seward Darrow (1857–1938) US lawyer. Remark during the trial (1925) of John Scopes for teaching the theory of evolution in school.

4 It is difficult to be humble. Even if you aim at humility, there is no guarantee that when you have attained the state you will not be proud of the feat.

Bonamy Dobrée (1891–) British scholar and writer. *John Wesley*

5 There for three days, before the castle gate, he laid aside all his royal gear; barefoot and wearing coarse wool, he stood pitifully, and did not stop begging for our apostolic help and compassion, until he had moved everyone there, or who heard tell of this, to great reverence and pity.

Gregory VII (c. 1020–85) Pope and saint. Referring to the excommunicated Emperor Henry IV's submission at Canossa, N Italy; he received absolution on 28 Jan 1077. Letter

6 Less than the dust beneath thy chariot wheel,
Less than the weed that grows beside thy door,
Less than the rust that never stained thy sword,
Less than the need thou hast in life of me,
Even less am I.

Laurence Hope (Mrs M. H. Nicolson; 1804–1905) British poet and songwriter. *The Garden of Kama and other Love Lyrics from India*, 'Less than the Dust'

7 The meek do not inherit the earth unless they are prepared to fight for their meekness.

H. J. Laski (1893–1950) British political theorist. Attrib.

8 The humble and meek are thirsting for blood.

Joe Orton (1933–67) British dramatist. *Funeral Games*, I

9 Because there's no fourth class.

George Santayana (1863–1952) US philosopher. On being asked why he always traveled third class. *Living Biographies of the Great Philosophers* (H. Thomas)

10 I too had thoughts once of being an intellectual, but I found it too difficult.

Albert Schweitzer (1875–1965) French Protestant theologian, philosopher, and physician. Remark made to an African who refused to perform a menial task on the grounds that he was an intellectual. Attrib.

11 Take physic, pomp;
Expose thyself to feel what wretches feel.

William Shakespeare (1564–1616) English dramatist. *King Lear*, III:4

12 We have the highest authority for believing that the meek shall inherit the Earth; though I have never found any particular corroboration of this aphorism in the records of Somerset House.

F. E. Smith (1872–1930) British lawyer and politician. *Contemporary Personalities*, 'Marquess Curzon'

13 When I survey the wondrous Cross,
On which the Prince of Glory died,
My richest gain I count but loss
And pour contempt on all my pride.

Isaac Watts (1674–1748) English theologian and hymn writer. *When I Survey the Wondrous Cross*

14 Gentle Jesus, meek and mild,
Look upon a little child;
Pity my simplicity,
Suffer me to come to thee.

Charles Wesley (1707–88) British religious leader. *Hymns and Sacred Poems*

HUMOR

See also laughter, nonsense, puns

1 I have a fine sense of the ridiculous, but no sense of humor.

Edward Albee (1928–) US dramatist. *Who's Afraid of Virginia Woolf?*, I

2 Little Willy from his mirror
Licked the mercury right off,
Thinking in his childish error,
It would cure the whooping cough.
At the funeral his mother
Smartly said to Mrs Brown:
''Twas a chilly day for Willie
When the mercury went down'.

Anonymous *Willie's Epitaph*

3 Mary had a little lamb. The doctor fainted.

Anonymous

4 There's a wonderful family called Stein,
There's Gert and there's Epp and there's Ein;
Gert's poems are bunk,
Epp's statues are junk,
And no one can understand Ein.

Anonymous

5 There was an old man from Darjeeling,
Who boarded a bus bound for Ealing,
He saw on the door:
'Please don't spit on the floor',

So he stood up and spat on the ceiling.
Anonymous

6 It is easier to be a lover than a husband, for the same reason that it is more difficult to show a ready wit all day long than to produce an occasional *bon mot.*
Honoré de Balzac (1799–1850) French novelist. Attrib.

7 The marvellous thing about a joke with a double meaning is that it can only mean one thing.
Ronnie Barker (1929–) British comedian. *Sauce,* 'Daddie's Sauce'

8 I do most of my work sitting down; that's where I shine.
Robert Benchley (1889–1945) US humorist. Attrib.

9 'What great cause is he identified with?' 'He's identified . . . with the great cause of cheering us all up.'
Arnold Bennett (1867–1931) British writer. *The Card*

10 The world would not be in such a snarl, had Marx been Groucho instead of Karl.
Irving Berlin (Israel Baline; 1888–) US composer. Telegram to Groucho Marx on his seventy-first birthday

11 It's a good deed to forget a poor joke.
Brendan Bracken (1901–58) British newspaper publisher and politician. *The Observer,* 'Sayings of the Week', 17 Oct 1943

12 Do you know why God withheld the sense of humour from women?
That we may love you instead of laughing at you.
Mrs Patrick Campbell (1865–1940) British actress. To a man. *The Life of Mrs Pat* (M. Peters)

13 All I need to make a comedy is a park, a policeman and a pretty girl.
Charlie Chaplin (Sir Charles Spencer C.; 1889–1977) British film actor. *My Autobiography*

14 A joke's a very serious thing.
Charles Churchill (1731–64) British poet. *The Ghost,* Bk. IV

15 Men will confess to treason, murder, arson, false teeth, or a wig. How many of them will own up to a lack of humor?
Frank More Colby (1865–1925) US editor. *Essays,* I

16 No mind is thoroughly well organized that is deficient in a sense of humour.
Samuel Taylor Coleridge (1772–1834) British poet. *Table Talk*

17 Total absence of humour renders life impossible.
Colette (1873–1954) French novelist. *Chance Acquaintances*

18 No visit to Dove Cottage, Grasmere, is complete without examining the outhouse where Hazlitt's father, a Unitarian minister of strong liberal views, attempted to put his hand up Dorothy Wordsworth's skirt.
Alan Coren (1938–) British humorist and writer. *All Except the Bastard,* 'Bohemia'

19 Dear 338171 (May I call you 338?).
Noël Coward (1899–1973) British dramatist. Starting a letter to T. E. Lawrence who had retired from public life to become Aircraftsman Brown, 338171. *Letters to T. E. Lawrence*

20 Miss Bolo rose from the table considerably agitated, and went straight home, in a flood of tears and a Sedan chair.
Charles Dickens (1812–70) British novelist. *Pickwick Papers,* Ch. 35

21 It . . . was full of dry rot. An unkind visitor said the only reason Menabilly still stood was that the woodworm obligingly held hands.
Daphne Du Maurier (1907–89) British novelist. Interview – referring to her own house in Cornwall upon which Manderley in *Rebecca* was based

22 A different taste in jokes is a great strain on the affections.
George Eliot (Mary Ann Evans; 1819–80) British novelist. *Daniel Deronda*

23 Comedy, like sodomy, is an unnatural act.
Marty Feldman (1933–83) British comedian. *The Times,* 9 June 1969

24 As for the Freudian, it is a very low, Central European sort of humour.
Robert Graves (1895–1985) British poet and novelist. *Occupation: Writer*

25 Funny peculiar, or funny ha-ha?
Ian Hay (John Hay Beith; 1876–1952) British novelist and dramatist. *The Housemaster,* III

26 A hair in the head is worth two in the brush.
Oliver Herford (1863–1935) British-born US humorist.

27 His foe was folly and his weapon wit.
Anthony Hope (Sir Anthony Hope Hawkins; 1863–1933) British novelist. Written for the inscription on the memorial to W. S. Gilbert, Victoria Embankment, London.

28 Wembley, adj. Suffering from a vague *malaise.* 'I feel a bit w. this morning.'
Paul Jennings (1918–) British humorous writer. *The Jenguin Pennings,* 'Ware, Wye, Watford'

29 Every man has, some time in his life, an ambition to be a wag.
Samuel Johnson (1709–84) British lexicographer. *Diary and Letters* (Mme D'Arblay), Vol. III, Ch. 46

30 The desire of the moth for the star.
James Joyce (1882–1941) Irish novelist. Commenting on the interruption of a music recital when a moth flew into the singer's mouth. *James Joyce* (R. Ellmann)

31 'When I makes tea I makes tea,' as old mother Grogan said. 'And when I makes water I makes water'.
James Joyce *Ulysses*

32 The essence of any blue material is timing. If you sit on it, it becomes vulgar.
Danny La Rue (Daniel Patrick Carroll; 1928–) British entertainer. Attrib.

33 The landlady of a boarding-house is a parallelogram – that is, an oblong angular figure, which cannot be described, but which is equal to anything.
Stephen Leacock (1869–1944) English-born Canadian economist and humorist. *Literary Lapses,* 'Boarding-House Geometry'

34 The coarse joke proclaims that we have here an animal which finds its own animality either objectionable or funny.
C. S. Lewis (1898–1963) British academic and writer. *Miracles*

35 One morning I shot an elephant in my pajamas.
How he got into my pajamas I'll never know.
Groucho Marx (Julius Marx; 1895–1977) US comedian *Animal Crackers*

36 I could dance with you till the cows come home. Better still, I'll dance with the cows and *you* come home.
Groucho Marx *Duck Soup*

37 Go – and never darken my towels again.
Groucho Marx *Duck Soup*

38 I don't have a photograph, but you can have my footprints. They are upstairs in my socks.
Groucho Marx *A Night At the Opera*

39 The strains of Verdi will come back

to you tonight, and Mrs Claypool's check will come back to you in the morning.
Groucho Marx *A Night at the Opera*

40 Please accept my resignation. I don't want to belong to any club that will accept me as a member.
Groucho Marx Resigning from the Friar's Club in Hollywood. Attrib.

41 Impropriety is the soul of wit.
W. Somerset Maugham (1874–1965) British novelist. *The Moon and Sixpence*, Ch. 4

42 Dr Strabismus (Whom God Preserve) of Utrecht is carrying out research work with a view to crossing salmon with mosquitoes. He says it will mean a bite every time for fishermen.
J. B. Morton (1893–1979) British journalist. *By the Way*, 'January Tail-piece'

43 It is not for nothing that, in the English language alone, to accuse someone of trying to be funny is highly abusive.
Malcolm Muggeridge (1903–) British writer. *Tread Softly For You Tread on My Jokes*

44 Oh, don't worry about Alan . . . Alan will always land on somebody's feet.
Dorothy Parker (1893–1967) US writer. Said of her husband on the day their divorce became final. *You Might As Well Live* (J. Keats), Pt. IV, Ch. 1

45 He bit his lip in a manner which immediately awakened my maternal sympathy, and I helped him bite it.
S. J. Perelman (1904–79) US humorous writer. *Crazy Like a Fox*, 'The Love Decoy'

46 I have Bright's disease and he has mine.
S. J. Perelman Attrib.

47 A case of the tail dogging the wag.
S. J. Perelman Having escaped with some difficulty from the persistent attentions of some prostitutes in the street. *Another Almanac of Words at Play* (W. Epsy)

48 Attic wit.
Pliny the Elder (Gaius Plinius Secundus; 23–79 AD) Roman scholar. *Natural History*, II

49 True wit is nature to advantage dress'd;
What oft was thought, but ne'er so well express'd.
Alexander Pope (1688–1744) British poet. *An Essay on Criticism*

50 Comedy, we may say, is society protecting itself – with a smile.
J. B. Priestley (1894–1984) British novelist. *George Meredith*

51 A comedian can only last till he either takes himself serious or his audience takes him serious.
Will Rogers (1879–1935) US actor and humorist. Newspaper article, 1931

52 Everything is funny, as long as it's happening to somebody else.
Will Rogers *The Illiterate Digest*

53 The cook was a good cook, as cooks go; and as cooks go she went.
Saki (Hector Hugh Munro; 1870–1916) British writer. *Reginald on Besetting Sins*

54 Napoleon's armies used to march on their stomachs, shouting: 'Vive l'intérieur!'
W. C. Sellar (1898–1951) British humorous writer. *1066 And All That*

55 I am not only witty in myself, but the cause that wit is in other men. I do here walk before thee like a sow that hath overwhelm'd all her litter but one.
William Shakespeare (1564–1616) English dramatist. *Henry IV, Part Two*, I:2

56 A jest's prosperity lies in the ear
Of him that hears it, never in the tongue
Of him that makes it.
William Shakespeare *Love's Labour's Lost*, V:2

57 You wait here and I'll bring the etchings down.
James Thurber (1894–1961) US humorist. Cartoon caption

58 Wall is the name – Max Wall. My father was the Great Wall of China. He was a brick.
Max Wall (1908–) British comedian. Opening line of one of his acts

59 It's hard to be funny when you have to be clean.
Mae West (1892–1980) US actress. *The Wit and Wisdom of Mae West* (ed. J. Weintraub)

60 He spoke with a certain what-is-it in his voice, and I could see that, if not actually disgruntled, he was far from being gruntled.
P. G. Wodehouse (1881–1975) British humorous novelist. *The Code of the Woosters*

61 Humour is the first of the gifts to perish in a foreign tongue.
Virginia Woolf (1882–1941) British novelist. *The Common Reader*

HUNGER

See also desire, food, thirst

1 Hunger is the best sauce.
Proverb

2 Poverty is an anomaly to rich people. It is very difficult to make out why people who want dinner do not ring the bell.
Walter Bagehot (1826–77) British economist and journalist. *Literary Studies*, II

3 When he told men to love their neighbour, their bellies were full. Nowadays things are different.
Bertolt Brecht (1898–1956) German dramatist. *Mother Courage*, II

4 The best sauce in the world is hunger.
Miguel de Cervantes (1547–1616) Spanish novelist. *Don Quixote*, Pt. II, Ch. 5

5 If only it were as easy to banish hunger by rubbing the belly as it is to masturbate.
Diogenes (412–322 BC) Greek philosopher. *Lives and Opinions of Eminent Philosophers* (Diogenes Laertius)

6 They that die by famine die by inches.
Matthew Henry (1662–1714) English nonconformist minister. *Exposition of the Old and New Testaments*

7 The war against hunger is truly mankind's war of liberation.
John Fitzgerald Kennedy (1917–63) US statesman. Speech, World Food Congress, 4 June 1963

8 A hungry stomach has no ears.
Jean de La Fontaine (1621–95) French poet. *Fables*, IX, 'Le Milan et le Rossignol'

9 I came home . . . hungry as a hunter.
Charles Lamb (1775–1834) British essayist. Letter to Coleridge, Apr 1800

10 Let them eat cake.
Marie-Antoinette (1755–93) Queen of France. On being told that the people had no bread to eat; in fact she was repeating a much older saying. Attrib.

HUNTING

See also sport

1 Happy the hare at morning, for she cannot read
The Hunter's waking thoughts.
W. H. Auden (1907–73) British poet. *The Dog Beneath the Skin* (with Christopher Isherwood)

2 Spirits of well-shot woodcock, partridge, snipe
Flutter and bear him up the Norfolk sky.
John Betjeman (1906–84) British poet. *Death of King George V*

3 Detested sport,

That owes its pleasures to another's pain.

William Cowper (1731–1800) British poet. *The Task*

4 Wild animals never kill for sport. Man is the only one to whom the torture and death of his fellow-creatures is amusing in itself.

J. A. Froude (1818–94) British historian. *Oceana*, Ch. 5

5 D'ye ken John Peel with his coat so gay?
D'ye ken John Peel at the break of the day?
D'ye ken John Peel when he's far far away
With his hounds and his horn in the morning?

'Twas the sound of his horn called me from my bed,
And the cry of his hounds has me oft-times led;
For Peel's view-hollo would waken the dead,
Or a fox from his lair in the morning.

John Woodcock Graves (1795–1886) British poet, huntsman, and songwriter. *John Peel*

6 It is very strange, and very melancholy, that the paucity of human pleasures should persuade us ever to call hunting one of them.

Samuel Johnson (1709–84) British lexicographer. *Johnsonian Miscellanies* (ed. G. B. Hill), Vol. I

7 Most of their discourse was about hunting, in a dialect I understand very little.

Samuel Pepys (1633–1703) English diarist. *Diary*, 22 Nov 1663

8 It isn't mere convention. Everyone can see that the people who hunt are the right people and the people who don't are the wrong ones.

George Bernard Shaw (1856–1950) Irish dramatist and critic. *Heartbreak House*

9 But He was never, well,
What I call
A Sportsman;
For forty days
He went out into the desert
– And never shot anything.

Osbert Sitwell (1892–1969) British writer. *Old Fashioned Sportsmen*

10 The English country gentleman galloping after a fox – the unspeakable in full pursuit of the uneatable.

Oscar Wilde (1854–1900) Irish-born British dramatist. *A Woman of No Importance*, I

HURT

See also cruelty, insensitivity, nastiness, suffering

1 Those have most power to hurt us that we love.

Francis Beaumont (1584–1616) English dramatist. *The Maid's Tragedy*, V:6

2 Mrs Montagu has dropt me. Now, Sir, there are people whom one should like very well to drop, but would not wish to be dropped by.

Samuel Johnson (1709–84) British lexicographer. *Life of Johnson* (J. Boswell), Vol. IV

3 It takes your enemy and your friend, working together, to hurt you to the heart; the one to slander you and the other to get the news to you.

Mark Twain (Samuel Langhorne Clemens; 1835–1910) US writer. *Following the Equator*

4 We flatter those we scarcely know,
We please the fleeting guest,
And deal full many a thoughtless blow
To those who love us best.

Ella Wheeler Wilcox (1850–1919) US poet. *Life's Scars*

HUXLEY, Aldous

(1894–1964) British novelist and essayist. His novels include *Antic Hay* (1923), *Point Counter Point* (1928), *Brave New World* (1932), and *Eyeless in Gaza* (1936). His non-fiction includes *The Doors of Perception* (1954).

Quotations about Huxley

1 Mr. Huxley is perhaps one of those people who have to perpetrate thirty bad novels before producing a good one.

T. S. Eliot (1888–1965) US-born British poet and dramatist. Attrib.

2 Like a piece of litmus paper he has always been quick to take the colour of his times.

Anonymous *The Observer*, Profile, 27 Feb 1949

Quotations by Huxley

3 Thanks to words, we have been able to rise above the brutes; and thanks to words, we have often sunk to the level of the demons.

Adonis and the Alphabet

4 Since Mozart's day composers have learned the art of making music throatily and palpitatingly sexual.

Along the Road, 'Popular music'

5 Christlike in my behaviour,
Like every good believer,
I imitate the Saviour,
And cultivate a beaver.

Antic Hay, Ch. 4

6 He was only the Mild and Melancholy one foolishly disguised as a complete Man.

Antic Hay, Ch. 9

7 There are few who would not rather be taken in adultery than in provincialism.

Antic Hay, Ch. 10

8 Mr Mercaptan went on to preach a brilliant sermon on that melancholy sexual perversion known as continence.

Antic Hay, Ch. 18

9 Lady Capricorn, he understood, was still keeping open bed.

Antic Hay, Ch. 21

10 Official dignity tends to increase in inverse ratio to the importance of the country in which the office is held.

Beyond the Mexique Bay

11 The time of our Ford.

Brave New World, Ch. 3

12 The proper study of mankind is books.

Chrome Yellow

13 We participate in a tragedy; at a comedy we only look.

The Devils of Loudon, Ch. 11

14 Consistency is contrary to nature, contrary to life. The only completely consistent people are the dead.

Do What you Will

15 Thought must be divided against itself before it can come to any knowledge of itself.

Do What You Will

16 People will insist . . . on treating the *mons Veneris* as though it were Mount Everest.

Eyeless in Gaza, Ch. 30

17 Death . . . It's the only thing we haven't succeeded in completely vulgarizing.

Eyeless in Gaza, Ch. 31

18 A million million spermatozoa,
All of them alive:

Out of their cataclysm but one poor Noah
Dare hope to survive.
Fifth Philosopher's Song

19 Christianity accepted as given a metaphysical system derived from several already existing and mutually incompatible systems.
Grey Eminence, Ch. 3

20 The quality of moral behaviour varies in inverse ratio to the number of human beings involved.
Grey Eminence, Ch. 10

21 'Bed,' as the Italian proverb succinctly puts it, 'is the poor man's opera.'
Heaven and Hell

22 I can sympathize with people's pains, but not with their pleasures. There is something curiously boring about somebody else's happiness.
Limbo, 'Cynthia'

23 She was a machine-gun riddling her hostess with sympathy.
Mortal Coils, 'The Gioconda Smile'

24 Most of one's life . . . is one prolonged effort to prevent oneself thinking.
Mortal Coils, 'Green Tunnels'

25 She was one of those indispensables of whom one makes the discovery, when they are gone, that one can get on quite as well without them.
Mortal Coils, 'Nuns at Luncheon'

26 Happiness is like coke - something you get as a by-product in the process of making something else.
Point Counter Point

27 There is no substitute for talent. Industry and all the virtues are of no avail.
Point Counter Point

28 Silence is as full of potential wisdom and wit as the unhewn marble of great sculpture.
Point Counter Point

29 A bad book is as much a labour to write as a good one; it comes as sincerely from the author's soul.
Point Counter Point

30 That all men are equal is a proposition to which, at ordinary times, no sane individual has ever given his assent.
Proper Studies

31 Those who believe that they are exclusively in the right are generally those who achieve something.
Proper Studies

32 Facts do not cease to exist because they are ignored.
Proper Studies

33 Most human beings have an almost infinite capacity for taking things for granted.
Themes and Variations

34 I'm afraid of losing my obscurity. Genuineness only thrives in the dark. Like celery.
Those Barren Leaves, Pt. I, Ch. 1

35 'It's like the question of the authorship of the *Iliad,*' said Mr Cardan. 'The author of that poem is either Homer or, if not Homer, somebody else of the same name.'
Those Barren Leaves, Pt. V, Ch. 4

36 How appallingly thorough these Germans always managed to be, how emphatic! In sex no less than in war – in scholarship, in science. Diving deeper than anyone else and coming up muddier.

37 Knowledge is proportionate to being. . . . You know in virtue of what you are.
Time Must Have a Stop, Ch. 26

38 The aristocratic pleasure of displeasing is not the only delight that bad taste can yield. One can love a certain kind of vulgarity for its own sake.
Vulgarity in Literature, Ch. 4

39 Defined in psychological terms, a fanatic is a man who consciously over-compensates a secret doubt.
Vulgarity in Literature, Ch. 4

HYPOCHONDRIA

1 He that is uneasy at every little pain is never without some ache.
Proverb

2 An imaginary ailment is worse than a disease.
Yiddish proverb

3 A story circulated about a man who had decided gradually to give up everything that scientists have linked to cancer.
The first week, he cut out smoked fish and charcoal steaks.
The second week, he cut out smoking.
The third week, he cut out having relations with women.
The fourth week, he cut out drinking.
The fifth week, he cut out paper dolls.
Anonymous *The Boston Herald*, 4 Sept 1965

4 I only take money from sick people.
Pierre Bretonneau (1778–1862) Comment to a hypochondriac. *Bulletin of the New York Academy of Medicine*, 5:154, 1929

5 Hypochondriacs squander large sums of time in search of nostrums by which they vainly hope they may get more time to squander.
Charles C. Colton (1780–1832) British churchman and writer. *Lacon*, 2

6 Nothing is more fatal to *Health*, than an *over Care* of it.
Benjamin Franklin (1706–90) US statesman and scientist. *Poor Richard's Almanack*, 1760

7 If man thinks about his physical or moral state he usually discovers that he is ill.
Johann Wolfgang von Goethe (1749–1832) German poet, dramatist and scientist. *Spruche in Prosa*, Pt. I, Bk. II

8 This state I call the hypochondriac affection in men, and the hysteric in women . . . is a sort of walking dream, which, though a person be otherwise in sound health, makes him feel symptoms of every disease; and, though innocent, yet fills his mind with the blackest horrors of guilt.
William Heberden (1710–1801) *Commentaries on the History and Cure of Diseases*, Ch. 49

9 I never read a patent medicine advertisement without being impelled to the conclusion that I am suffering from the particular disease therein dealt with in its most virulent form.
Jerome K. Jerome (1859–1927) British humorous writer. *Three Men in a Boat*, Ch. 1

10 Dear Doctor (said he one day to a common acquaintance, who lamented the tender state of his *inside*), do not be like the spider, man; and spin conversation thus incessantly out of thy own bowels.
Samuel Johnson (1709–84) English lexicographer and writer. *Johnsonian Miscellanies*, Vol. I, 'Recollections of Dr. Johnson by Miss Reynolds' (G. B. Hill)

11 Hypochondria torments us not only with causeless irritation with the things of the present; not only with groundless anxiety on the score of future misfortunes entirely of our

own manufacture; but also with unmerited self-reproach for our own past actions.
Arthur Schopenhauer (1788–1860) German philosopher. *Parerga und Paralipomena*, Vol. II, Ch. 26

12 People who are always taking care of their health are like misers, who are hoarding a treasure which they have never spirit enough to enjoy.
Laurence Sterne (1713–68) Irish-born English writer and churchman. Attrib.

13 He destroys his health by labouring to preserve it.
Virgil (Publius Vergilius Maro; 70 BC–19 BC) Roman poet. *Aeneid*, Bk. XII

14 The imaginary complaints of indestructible old ladies.
E. B. White (1899–) US journalist and humorous writer. *Harper's Magazine*, Nov 1941

HYPOCRISY

See also cant, example, insincerity

1 All are not saints that go to church.
Proverb

2 It is the wisdom of the crocodiles, that shed tears when they would devour.
Francis Bacon (1561–1626) English philosopher. *Essays*, 'Of Wisdom for a Man's Self'

3 But when he saw many of the Pharisees and Sadducees come to his baptism, he said unto them, O generation of vipers, who hath warned you to flee from the wrath to come?
Bible: Matthew 3:7

4 Woe unto you, scribes and Pharisees, hypocrites! for ye are like unto whited sepulchres, which indeed appear beautiful outward, but are within full of dead men's bones, and of all uncleanness.
Bible: Matthew 23:27

5 Prisons are built with stones of Law, brothels with bricks of Religion.
William Blake (1757–1827) British poet. *The Marriage of Heaven and Hell*, 'Proverbs of Hell'

6 God be thanked, the meanest of his creatures
Boasts two soul-sides, one to face the world with,
One to show a woman when he loves her!
Robert Browning (1812–89) British poet. *One Word More*, XVII

7 Man is the only animal that can remain on friendly terms with the victims he intends to eat until he eats them.
Samuel Butler (1835–1902) British writer. *Notebooks*

8 The smyler with the knyf under the cloke.
Geoffrey Chaucer (c. 1342–1400) English poet. *The Canterbury Tales*, 'The Knight's Tale'

9 We ought to see far enough into a hypocrite to see even his sincerity.
G. K. Chesterton (1874–1936) British writer. *Heretics*, Ch. 5

10 The book written against fame and learning has the author's name on the title-page.
Ralph Waldo Emerson (1803–82) US poet and essayist. *Journal*

11 Man is the only animal that learns by being hypocritical. He pretends to be polite and then, eventually, he *becomes* polite.
Jean Kerr (1923–) US dramatist. *Finishing Touches*

12 Hypocrisy is the most difficult and nerve-racking vice that any man can pursue; it needs an unceasing vigilance and a rare detachment of spirit. It cannot, like adultery or gluttony, be practised at spare moments; it is a whole-time job.
W. Somerset Maugham (1874–1965) British novelist. *Cakes and Ale*, Ch. 1

13 For neither man nor angel can discern
Hypocrisy, the only evil that walks
Invisible, except to God alone.
John Milton (1608–74) English poet. *Paradise Lost*, Bk. III

14 Hypocrisy is the homage paid by vice to virtue.
Duc de la Rochefoucauld (1613–80) French writer. *Maximes*, 218

15 O villain, villain, smiling, damned villain!
My tables, – meet it is I set it down,
That one may smile, and smile, and be a villain;
At least I'm sure it may be so in Denmark.
William Shakespeare (1564–1616) English dramatist. *Hamlet*, I:5

16 To put an antic disposition on.
William Shakespeare *Hamlet*, I:5

17 I speak of peace, while covert enmity
Under the smile of safety wounds the world.
William Shakespeare *Henry IV, Part Two*, Induction, 9

18 Well, whiles I am a beggar, I will rail
And say there is no sin but to be rich;
And being rich, my virtue then shall be
To say there is no vice but beggary.
William Shakespeare *King John*, II:1

19 Thou rascal beadle, hold thy bloody hand!
Why dost thou lash that whore? Strip thine own back;
Thou hotly lust'st to use her in that kind
For which thou whipp'st her.
William Shakespeare *King Lear*, IV:6

20 Come not, when I am dead,
To drop thy foolish tears upon my grave,
To trample round my fallen head,
And vex the unhappy dust thou wouldst not save.
Alfred, Lord Tennyson (1809–92) British poet. *Come Not, When I Am Dead*

21 I sit on a man's back, choking him and making him carry me, and yet assure myself and others that I am very sorry for him and wish to ease his lot by all possible means – except by getting off his back.
Leo Tolstoy (1828–1910) Russian writer. *What Then Must We Do?*, Ch. 16

22 I hope you have not been leading a double life, pretending to be wicked and being really good all the time. That would be hypocrisy.
Oscar Wilde (1854–1900) Irish-born British dramatist. *The Importance of Being Earnest*, II

23 A Christian is a man who feels
Repentance on a Sunday
For what he did on Saturday
And is going to do on Monday.
Thomas Russell Ybarra (born 1880) Venezuelan-born US writer. *The Christian*

I

IDEALISM

1 Of myself I must say this, I never was any greedy, scraping grasper, nor a strait fast-holding prince, nor yet a waster; my heart was never set on wordly goods, but only for my subjects' good.

Elizabeth I Speech to a deputation from the House of Commons (the Golden Speech), 30 Nov 1601

2 If a man hasn't discovered something that he would die for, he isn't fit to live.

Martin Luther King (1929–68) US Black civil-rights leader. Speech, Detroit, 23 June 1963

3 If you can talk with crowds and keep your virtue,
Or walk with Kings – nor lose the common touch,
If neither foes nor loving friends can hurt you,
If all men count with you, but none too much;
If you can fill the unforgiving minute
With sixty seconds' worth of distance run,
Yours is the Earth and everything that's in it,
And – which is more – you'll be a Man my son!

Rudyard Kipling (1865–1936) Indian-born British writer. *If*

4 Ideal mankind would abolish death, multiply itself million upon million, rear up city upon city, save every parasite alive, until the accumulation of mere existence is swollen to a horror.

D. H. Lawrence (1885–1930) British novelist. *St Mawr*

5 Imagine there's no heaven
It's easy if you try
No help below us
Above us only sky
Imagine all the people
Living for today.

John Lennon (1940–80) British rock musician. *Imagine*

6 Let It Be.

John Lennon Title of song, written with Paul McCartney

7 An idealist is one who, on noticing that a rose smells better than a cabbage, concludes that it will also make better soup.

H. L. Mencken (1880–1956) US journalist. *Sententiae*

8 Oh, life is a glorious cycle of song,
A medley of extemporanea;
And love is a thing that can never go wrong
And I am Marie of Roumania.

Dorothy Parker (1893–1967) US writer. *Enough Rope*, 'Comment'

9 Do not despair
For Johnny head-in-air;
He sleeps as sound
As Johnny underground.

John Sleigh Pudney (1909–77) British poet and writer. *For Johnny*

10 A radical is a man with both feet firmly planted in the air.

Franklin D. Roosevelt (1882–1945) US Democratic president. Broadcast, 26 Oct 1939

11 If a woman like Eva Peron with no ideals can get that far, think how far I can go with all the ideals that I have.

Margaret Thatcher (1925–) British politician and prime minister. *The Sunday Times*, 1980

IDEAS

See also opinions

1 Paradoxes are useful to attract attention to ideas.

Mandell Creighton (1843–1901) British churchman. *Life and Letters*

2 What was once thought can never be unthought.

Friedrich Dürrenmatt (1921–) Swiss writer. *The Physicists*

3 A stand can be made against invasion by an army; no stand can be made against invasion by an idea.

Victor Hugo (1802–85) French writer. *Histoire d'un Crime*, 'La Chute'

4 Many ideas grow better when transplanted into another mind than in the one where they sprang up.

Oliver Wendell Holmes Jnr (1841–1935) US jurist.

5 You cannot endow even the best machine with initiative. The jolliest steam-roller will not plant flowers.

Walter Lippmann (1889–1974) US editor and author. *A Preface to Politics*

6 Society goes on and on and on. It is the same with ideas.

Ramsey MacDonald (1866–1937) British statesman and prime minister. Speech, 1935

7 An idea isn't responsible for the people who believe in it.

Don Marquis (1878–1937) US journalist. *New York Sun*

8 A society made up of individuals who were all capable of original thought would probably be unendurable. The pressure of ideas would simply drive it frantic.

H. L. Mencken (1880–1956) US journalist. *Notebooks*, 'Minority Report'

9 Man is ready to die for an idea, provided that idea is not quite clear to him.

Paul Eldridge *Horns of Glass*

IDLENESS

See also bed, laziness, leisure, unemployment

1 The dreadful burden of having nothing to do.

Nicolas Boileau (1636–1711) French writer. *Épîtres*, XI

2 Idleness is only the refuge of weak minds.

Earl of Chesterfield (1694–1773) English statesman. Letter to his son, 20 July 1749

3 I don't think necessity is the mother of invention – invention, in my opinion, arises directly from idleness, possibly also from laziness. To save oneself trouble.

Agatha Christie (1891–1976) British detective-story writer. *An Autobiography*

4 What is this life if, full of care,
We have no time to stand and stare?

W. H. Davies (1871–1940) British poet. *Leisure*

5 . . . many thousands of idle persons are within this realm which, being no way to be set on work, be either mutinous and seek alteration in the state or at least very burdensome to the common wealth and often fall to pilfering and thieving and other lewdness, whereby all the prisons of the land are daily pestered and stuffed full of them.

Richard Hakluyt (c. 1552–1616) Geographer. *Particular Discourse of Western Planting*

6 It is impossible to enjoy idling thoroughly unless one has plenty of work to do.

Jerome K. Jerome (1859–1927) British humorist. *Idle Thoughts of an Idle Fellow*

7 I like work; it fascinates me. I can sit and look at it for hours. I love to keep it by me; the idea of getting rid of it nearly breaks my heart.

Jerome K. Jerome *Three Men in a Boat*, Ch. 15

8 We would all be idle if we could.

Samuel Johnson (1709–84) British lexicographer. *Life of Johnson* (J. Boswell), Vol. III

9 The affluent society has made everyone dislike work, and come to think of idleness as the happiest life.

Geoffrey Keynes (1887–) British surgeon and literary scholar. *The Observer*, 25 Oct 1981

10 Young people ought not to be idle. It is very bad for them.

Margaret Thatcher (1925–) British politician and prime minister. *The Times*, 1984

11 I am happiest when I am idle. I could live for months without performing any kind of labor, and at the expiration of that time I should feel fresh and vigorous enough to go right on in the same way for numerous more months.

Artemus Ward (Charles Farrar Browne; 1834–67) US humorous writer. *Pyrotechny*

12 For Satan finds some mischief still
For idle hands to do.

Isaac Watts (1674–1748) English theologian and hymn writer. *Divine Songs for Children*, 'Against Idleness and Mischief'

IGNORANCE

See also foolishness, innocence, innocence of childhood, stupidity

1 He that knows little, often repeats it.

Proverb

2 He that knows nothing, doubts nothing.

Proverb

3 What you don't know can't hurt you.

Proverb

4 Happy the hare at morning, for she cannot read
The Hunter's waking thoughts.

W. H. Auden (1907–73) British poet. *The Dog Beneath the Skin* (with Christopher Isherwood)

5 *Ignoramus*, *n*. A person unacquainted with certain kinds of knowledge familiar to yourself, and having certain other kinds that you know nothing about.

Ambrose Bierce *The Devil's Dictionary*

6 I don't even know what street Canada is on.

Al Capone (1899–1947) US gangster. Attrib.

7 It is the tragedy of the world that no one knows what he doesn't know – and the less a man knows, the more sure he is that he knows everything.

Joyce Cary (1888–1957) British novelist. *Art and Reality*

8 She is an excellent creature, but she never can remember which came first, the Greeks or the Romans.

Benjamin Disraeli (1804–81) British statesman. Referring to his wife. Attrib.

9 To each his suff'rings, all are men,
Condemn'd alike to groan;
The tender for another's pain,
Th' unfeeling for his own.
Yet ah! why should they know their fate?
Since sorrow never comes too late,
And happiness too swiftly flies.
Thought would destroy their paradise.
No more; where ignorance is bliss,
'Tis folly to be wise.

Thomas Gray (1716–71) British poet. *Ode on a Distant Prospect of Eton College*

10 Alas, regardless of their doom,
The little victims play!

Thomas Gray *Ode on a Distant Prospect of Eton College*

11 I wish you would read a little poetry sometimes. Your ignorance cramps my conversation.

Anthony Hope (Sir Anthony Hope Hawkins; 1863–1933) British novelist. *The Dolly Dialogues*

12 Ignorance is preferable to error; and he is less remote from the truth who believes nothing, than he who believes what is wrong.

Thomas Jefferson (1743–1826) US statesman. *Notes on the State of Virginia*

13 Ignorance, madam, pure ignorance.

Samuel Johnson (1709–84) British lexicographer. His reply on being questioned, by a lady reader of his *Dictionary*, why he had incorrectly defined 'pastern' as the 'knee' of a horse. *Life of Johnson* (J. Boswell), Vol. I

14 Nothing in the world is more dangerous than sincere ignorance and conscientious stupidity.

Martin Luther King (1929–68) US Black civil-rights leader. *Strength To Love*

15 The ignorant man always adores what he cannot understand.

Cesare Lombroso (1853–1909) Italian criminologist. *The Man of Genius*, Pt. III, Ch. 3

16 I count religion but a childish toy,
And hold there is no sin but ignorance.

Christopher Marlowe (1564–93) English dramatist. *The Jew of Malta*, Prologue

17 His ignorance was an Empire State Building of ignorance. You had to admire it for its size.

Dorothy Parker (1893–1967) US writer. Referring to Harold Ross. Attrib.

18 From ignorance our comfort flows,
The only wretched are the wise.

Matthew Prior (1664–1721) British poet. *To the Hon. Charles Montague*

19 He hath never fed of the dainties that are bred in a book; he hath not eat paper, as it were; he hath not drunk ink; his intellect is not replenished.

William Shakespeare (1564–1616) English dramatist. *Love's Labour's Lost*, IV:2

20 He that is robb'd, not wanting what is stol'n,
Let him not know't, and he's not robb'd at all.

William Shakespeare *Othello*, III:3

21 What you don't know would make a great book.

Sydney Smith (1771–1845) British clergyman and essayist. *Memoir* (Lady Holland)

22 Somebody else's ignorance is bliss.

Jack Vance (1916–) US writer. *Star King*

23 Ignorance is like a delicate exotic fruit; touch it, and the bloom is gone.

Oscar Wilde (1854–1900) Irish-born British dramatist. *The Importance of Being Earnest*, I

ILLEGITIMACY

1 I was born in 1896, and my parents were married in 1919.

J. R. Ackerley (1896–1967) British writer. The opening words of the book. *My Father and Myself* (1968)

2 If you please, ma'am, it was a very little one.

Captain Frederick Marryat (1792–1848) British novelist. Said by the nurse to excuse the fact that she had had an illegitimate baby. *Mr. Midshipman Easy*, Ch. 3

3 It serves me right for putting all my eggs in one bastard.

Dorothy Parker (1893–1967) US writer. Said on going into hospital to get an abortion. *You Might as Well Live* (J. Keats), Pt. II, Ch. 3

4 There are no illegitimate children – only illegitimate parents.
Léon R. Yankwich US lawyer. Decision, State District Court, Southern District of California, Jun 1928, quoting the journalist O. O. McIntyre

ILLNESS

See also doctors, health, medicine, remedies

1 Feed a cold and starve a fever.
Commonly interpreted as meaning that one should eat with a cold but not with a fever. An alternative explanation is that if one 'feeds' a cold, by not taking care of it, one will end up having to deal with a fever. Proverb

2 Sickness is felt, but health not at all.
Proverb

3 Sickness soaks the purse.
Proverb

4 Sickness tells us what we are.
Proverb

5 If you are too smart to pay the doctor, you had better be too smart to get ill.
African (Transvaal) proverb

6 Coughs and sneezes spread diseases.
Wartime health slogan in the UK, c. 1942
Anonymous *Dictionary of 20th Century Quotations* (Nigel Rees)

7 For want of timely care
Millions have died of medicable wounds.
John Armstrong (1710–79) English physician and poet. *Art of Preserving Health*

8 Nor bring to see me cease to live,
Some doctor full of phrase and fame,
To shake his sapient head, and give
The ill he cannot cure a name.
Matthew Arnold (1822–88) British poet and critic. 'A Wish'

9 Across the wires the electric message came:
'He is no better, he is much the same.'
Alfred Austin (1835–1913) British poet. Generally attrib. to Austin but there is no definite evidence that he wrote it. *On the Illness of the Prince of Wales*

10 Physicians of the utmost fame,
Were called at once; but when they came
They answered, as they took their fees,
'There is no Cure for this Disease.'
Hilaire Belloc (1870–1953) French-born British poet. *Bartlett's Unfamiliar Quotations* (Leonard Louis Levinson)

11 'Ye can call it influenza if ye like,' said Mrs Machin. 'There was no influenza in my young days. We called a cold a cold.'
Arnold Bennett (1867–1931) British novelist. *The Card*, Ch. 8

12 Be not slow to visit the sick: for that shall make thee to be beloved.
Bible: Ecclesiasticus 7:35

13 They that be whole need not a physician, but they that are sick.
Bible: Matthew 9:12

14 INDIGESTION, n. A disease which the patient and his friends frequently mistake for deep religious conviction and concern for the salvation of mankind. As the simple Red Man of the western wild put it, with, it must be confessed, a certain force: 'Plenty well, no pray; big bellyache, heap God.'
Ambrose Bierce (1842–c. 1914) US writer and journalist. *The Devil's Dictionary*

15 A long illness seems to be placed between life and death, in order to make death a comfort both to those who die and to those who remain.
Jean de La Bruyère (1645–96) *Caractères*, Ch. 11

16 I reckon being ill as one of the greatest pleasures of life, provided one is not too ill and is not obliged to work till one is better.
Samuel Butler (1835–1902) British writer. *The Way of All Flesh*, Ch. 80

17 Most of those evils we poor mortals know
From doctors and imagination flow.
Charles Churchill (1731–64) English poet. *The Prophecy of Famine*

18 Physicians, when the cause of disease is discovered, consider that the cure is discovered.
Cicero (106 BC–43 BC) Roman orator and statesman. Attrib.

19 I don't have ulcers; I give them.
Harry Cohn (1891–1958) US film producer.

20 My message to the businessmen of this country when they go abroad on business is that there is one thing above all they can take with them to stop them catching Aids, and that is the wife.
Edwina Currie (1946–) British politician. *The Observer*, 'Sayings of the Week', 15 Feb 1987

21 Too late for fruit, too soon for flowers.
Walter De La Mare (1873–1956) British poet. On being asked, as he lay seriously ill, whether he would like some fruit or flowers. Attrib.

22 To be too conscious is an illness – a real thorough-going illness.
Fyodor Mikhailovich Dostoevsky (1821–81) Russian writer. *Notes from Underground*, 1

23 Disease can carry its ill-effects no farther than mortal mind maps out the way . . . Disease is an image of thought externalized . . . We classify disease as error, which nothing but Truth or Mind can heal . . . Disease is an experience of so-called mortal mind. It is fear made manifest on the body.
Mary Baker Eddy (1821–1910) US religious leader. *Science and Health, with Key to the Scriptures*

24 The multitude of the sick shall not make us deny the existence of health.
Ralph Waldo Emerson (1803–82) US poet and essayist. *The Conduct of Life*, 'Worship'

25 It is dainty to be sick if you have leisure and convenience for it.
Ralph Waldo Emerson *Journals*, Vol. V

26 A weary thing is sickness and its pains!
Euripides (484 BC–406 BC) Greek dramatist. *Hippolytus*, 176

27 Much of the world's work, it has been said, is done by men who do not feel quite well. Marx is a case in point.
John Kenneth Galbraith (1908–) US economist. *The Age of Uncertainty*, Ch. 3

28 If you start to think about your physical or moral condition, you usually find that you are sick.
Johann Wolfang von Goethe (1749–1832) German poet and dramatist. *Sprüche in Prosa*, Pt. I, Bk. II

29 Hungry Joe collected lists of fatal diseases and arranged them in alphabetical order so that he could put his finger without delay on any one he wanted to worry about.
Joseph Heller (1923–) US novelist. *Catch-22*, Ch. 17

30 For that old enemy the gout
Had taken him in toe!
Thomas Hood (1799–1845) British poet. *Lieutenant Luff*

31 Indigestion is charged by God with enforcing morality on the stomach.
Victor Hugo (1802–85) French poet, novelist, and dramatist. *Les Misérables*, 'Fantine', Bk. III, Ch. 7

32 If he my next-door neighbour is to

be allowed to let his children go unvaccinated, he might as well be allowed to leave strychnine lozenges about in the way of mine.

T. H. Huxley (1825–95) British biologist. *Method and Results*, 'Administrative Nihilism'

33 In scarcely any house did only one die, but all together, man and wife with their children and household, traversed the same road, the road of death . . . I leave the parchment for the work to be continued in case in the future any human survivor should remain, or someone of the race of Adam should be able to escape this plague and continue what I have begun.

John of Clyn Irish friar. Recording the effects of the Black Death in Kilkenny. *Annals of Ireland*

34 How few of his friends' houses would a man choose to be at when he is sick.

Samuel Johnson (1709–84) British lexicographer. *Life of Johnson* (J. Boswell), Vol. IV

35 Cough: A convulsion of the lungs, vellicated by some sharp serosity.

Samuel Johnson *Dictionary of the English Language*

36 Illness makes a man a scoundrel.

Samuel Johnson Letter to Fanny Burney, Jan 1788

37 Oh what can ail thee, knight at arms
Alone and palely loitering;
The sedge has wither'd from the lake,
And no birds sing.

John Keats (1795–1821) British poet. *La Belle Dame Sans Merci*

38 How sickness enlarges the dimensions of a man's self to himself.

Charles Lamb (1775–1834) British essayist. *Last Essays of Elia*, 'The Convalescent'

39 To be sick is to enjoy monarchal prerogatives.

Charles Lamb *Last Essays of Elia*, 'The Convalescent'

40 There are things which will not be defined, and Fever is one of them. Besides, when a word had passed into everyday use, it is too late to lay a logical trap for its meaning, and think to apprehend it by a definition.

Peter Mere Latham (1789–1875) US poet and essayist. *General Remarks on the Practice of Medicine*, Ch. 10, Pt. 1

41 I am only half there when I am ill, and so there is only half a man to suffer. To suffer in one's whole self is so great a violation, that it is not to be endured.

D. H. Lawrence (1885–1930) British novelist. Letter to Catherine Carswell, 16 Apr 1916

42 The most important thing in illness is never to lose heart.

Nikolai Lenin (Vladimir Ilyich Ulyanov; 1870–1924) Russian Communist leader. *The Secret of Soviet Strength*, Bk. II, Ch. 3, Sect. 2 (Hewlett Johnson)

43 Medicine makes sick patients, for doctors imagine diseases, as mathematics makes hypochondriacs and theology sinners.

Martin Luther (1483–1546) German Protestant reformer.

44 One who is ill has not only the right but also the duty to seek medical aid.

Maimonides (Moses ben Maimon; 1135–1204) Spanish-born Jewish philosopher and physician.

45 Disease makes men more physical, it leaves them nothing but body.

Thomas Mann (1875–1955) German novelist. *The Magic Mountain*, 4

46 Unfortunately, only a small number of patients with peptic ulcer are financially able to make a pet of an ulcer.

William James Mayo (1861–1934) US surgeon. *Journal of the American Medical Association*, 79:19, 1922

47 Illness is in part what the world has done to a victim, but in a larger part it is what the victim has done with his world, and with himself.

Karl Menninger (1893–) US psychiatrist. *Illness as Metaphor*, Ch. 6 (Susan Sontag)

48 Confirmed dispepsia is the apparatus of illusions.

George Meredith (1828–1909) British novelist. *The Ordeal of Richard Feverel*

49 She didn't fear death itself, welcoming release from her long struggle between mind and body.

Mary Jane Moffat and Charlotte Painter *Womansize* (Kim Chernin)

50 The sick are the greatest danger for the healthy; it is not from the strongest that harm comes to the strong, but from the weakest.

Friedrich Nietzsche (1844–1900) German philosopher. *Genealogy of Morals*, Essay 3

51 The patient suffered from chronic remunerative appendicitis.

Delbert H. Nickson (1890–1951)

52 When meditating over a disease, I never think of finding a remedy for it, but, instead, a means of preventing it.

Louis Pasteur (1822–95) French scientist. Address to the Fraternal Association of Former Students of the École Centrale des Arts et Manufactures, Paris, 15 May 1884

53 Thence I walked to the Tower; but Lord! how empty the streets are and how melancholy, so many poor sick people in the streets full of sores . . . in Westminster, there is never a physician and but one apothecary left, all being dead.

Samuel Pepys (1633–1703) English diarist. Written during the Great Plague – the last major outbreak of bubonic plague in England, and the worst since the Black Death of 1348. Diary, 16 Sept 1665

54 I've got Bright's disease and he's got mine.

S. J. Perelman (1904–79) US humorous writer. Attrib.

55 Confront disease at its first stage.

Aulus Flaccus Persius (34–62 AD) Roman satirist. *Satires*, III

56 They do certainly give very strange and new-fangled names to diseases.

Plato (c. 427 BC–347 BC) Greek philosopher. *Republic*, III

57 Once Antigonis was told his son, Demetrius, was ill, and went to see him. At the door he met some young beauty. Going in, he sat down by the bed and took his pulse. 'The fever,' said Demetrius, 'has just left me.' 'Oh, yes,' replied the father, 'I met it going out at the door.'

Plutarch (c. 46 AD– c. 120 AD) Greek biographer and essayist. *Bartlett's Unfamiliar Quotations* (Leonard Louis Levinson)

58 Here am I dying of a hundred good symptoms.

Alexander Pope (1688–1744) English poet. Said to George Lyttleton, 15 May 1744

59 He dies every day who lives a lingering life.

Pierrard Poullet (fl. 1590) *La Charité*

60 Every man who feels well is a sick man neglecting himself.

Jules Romains (1885–1972) French writer. *Knock, ou le triomphe de la médecine*

61 The problem of economic loss due to sickness . . . a very serious matter for many families with and without incomes, and therefore, an unfair burden upon the medical profession.

Franklin D. Roosevelt (1882–1945) US Democratic President. Address on the Problems of Economic and Social Security, 14 Nov 1934

62 When I look back upon the past, I can only dispel the sadness which falls upon me by gazing into that happy future when the infection will be banished. . . . The conviction that such a time must inevitably sooner or later arrive will cheer my dying hour.

Ignaz Semmelweis (1818–65) Hungarian physician. Semmelweis had discovered that it was the physicians who spread childbirth fever amongst patients, but he was not believed. *Etiology*, Foreword

63 Only do always in health what you have often promised to do when you are sick.

Sigismund (1368–1437) Holy Roman Emperor. His advice on achieving happiness. *Biographiana*, Vol. I

64 Illness is the night-side of life, a more onerous citizenship. Everyone who is born holds dual citizenship, in the kingdom of the well and in the kingdom of the sick. Although we all prefer to use only the good passport, sooner or later each of us is obliged, at least for a spell, to identify ourselves as citizens of that other place.

Susan Sontag (1933–) US novelist and essayist. *Illness as Metaphor*

65 We are so fond of one another because our ailments are the same.

Jonathan Swift (1667–1745) Anglo-Irish priest, poet, and satirist. Letter to Stella, 1 Feb 1711

66 The medicine increases the disease.

Virgil (Publius Vergilius Maro; 70 BC–19 BC) Roman poet. *Aeneid*, Bk. XII

67 Nor do I in any way approve of the modern sympathy with invalids. I consider it morbid. Illness of any kind is hardly a thing to be encouraged in others.

Oscar Wilde (1856–1900) Irish-born British poet and dramatist. *The Importance of Being Earnest*, I

68 Most of the time we think we're sick, it's all in the mind.

Thomas Wolfe (1900–38) US novelist. *Look Homeward, Angel*, Pt. I, Ch. 1

69 Considering how common illness is, how tremendous the spiritual change that it brings, how astonishing, when the lights of health go down, the undiscovered countries that are then disclosed, what wastes and deserts of the soul a slight attack of influenza brings to view, what precipices and lawns sprinkled with bright flowers a little rise of temperature reveals, what ancient and obdurate oaks are uprooted in us by the act of sickness, how we go down into the pit of death and feel the waters of annihilation close above our heads and wake thinking to find ourselves in the presence of the angels and the harpers when we have a tooth out and come to the surface in the dentist's arm-chair and confuse his 'Rinse the mouth – rinse the mouth' with the greeting of the Deity stooping from the floor of Heaven to welcome us – when we think of this, as we are so frequently forced to think of it, it becomes strange indeed that illness has not taken its place with love and battle and jealousy among the prime themes of literature.

Virginia Woolf (1882–1941) British writer. *The Moment and Other Essays*, 'On Being Ill'

ILLUSIONS

1 The visible universe was an illusion or, more precisely, a sophism. Mirrors and fatherhood are abominable because they multiply it and extend it.

Jorge Luis Borges (1899–1986) Argentinian writer. *Ficciones*, 'Tlon, Uqbar, Orbis Tertius'

2 Religion is an illusion and it derives its strength from the fact that it falls in with our instinctual desires.

Sigmund Freud (1856–1939) Austrian psychoanalyst. *New Introductory Lectures on Psychoanalysis*, 'A Philosophy of Life'

3 If we take in our hand any volume; of divinity or school metaphysics, for instance; let us ask, *Does it contain any abstract reasoning concerning quantity or number?* No. *Does it contain any experimental reasoning, concerning matter of fact and existence?* No. Commit it then to the flames: for it can contain nothing but sophistry and illusion.

David Hume (1711–76) Scottish philosopher. *An Enquiry Concerning Human Understanding*

4 I've looked at life from both sides now
From win and lose and still somehow
It's life's illusions I recall
I really don't know life at all.

Joni Mitchell (1945–) Singer and songwriter. *Both Sides Now*

5 The House of Lords, an illusion to which I have never been able to subscribe – responsibility without power, the prerogative of the eunuch throughout the ages.

Tom Stoppard (1937–) Czech-born British dramatist. *Lord Malquist and Mr Moon*, Pt. VI, Ch. 1

IMAGE

1 That at what time ye hear the sound of the cornet, flute, harp, sackbut, psaltery, dulcimer, and all kinds of musick, ye fall down and worship the golden image that Nebuchadnezzar the king hath set up:
And whoso falleth not down and worshippeth shall the same hour be cast into the midst of a burning fiery furnace.

Bible: Daniel 3:5–6

2 And God said, Let us make man in our image, after our likeness: and let them have dominion over the fish of the sea, and over the fowl of the air, and over the cattle, and over all the earth, and over every creeping thing that creepeth upon the earth.
So God created man in his own image, in the image of God created he him; male and female created he them.
And God blessed them, and God said unto them, Be fruitful, and multiply, and replenish the earth, and subdue it: and have dominion over the fish of the sea, and over the fowl of the air, and over every living thing that moveth upon the earth.

Bible: Genesis 1:26–28

3 It is bad enough to be condemned to drag around this image in which nature has imprisoned me. Why should I consent to the perpetuation of the image of this image?

Plotinus (205–270 AD) Egyptian-born Greek philosopher. Refusing to have his portrait painted. Attrib.

4 A photograph is not only an image (as a painting is an image), an interpretation of the real; it is also a trace, something directly stencilled off the real, like a footprint or a death mask.

Susan Sontag (1933–) US novelist and essayist. *On Photography*

5 If God made us in His image, we

have certainly returned the compliment.

Voltaire *Le Sottisier*

IMAGINATION

1 The primary imagination I hold to be the living power and prime agent of all human perception, and as a repetition in the finite mind of the eternal act of creation in the infinite I AM.

Samuel Taylor Coleridge (1772–1834) British poet. *Biographia Literaria*, Ch. 13

2 The Fancy is indeed no other than a mode of memory emancipated from the order of time and space.

Samuel Taylor Coleridge *Biographia Literaria*, Ch. 13

3 Art is ruled uniquely by the imagination.

Benedetto Croce (1866–1952) Italian philosopher. *Esthetic*, Ch. 1

4 Imagination is more important than knowledge.

Albert Einstein (1879–1955) German-born US physicist. *On Science*

5 She has no imagination and that means no compassion.

Michael Foot (1913–) British Labour politician and journalist. Referring to Margaret Thatcher. Attrib.

6 Were it not for imagination, Sir, a man would be as happy in the arms of a chambermaid as of a Duchess.

Samuel Johnson (1709–84) British lexicographer. *Life of Johnson* (J. Boswell), Vol. III

7 I am certain of nothing but the holiness of the heart's affections and the truth of imagination – what the imagination seizes as beauty must be truth – whether it existed before or not.

John Keats (1795–1821) British poet. Letter to Benjamin Bailey, 22 Nov 1817

8 Children do not give up their innate imagination, curiosity, dreaminess easily. You have to love them to get them to do that.

R. D. Laing (1927–) British psychiatrist. *The Politics of Experience*, Ch. 3

9 Picture yourself in a boat on a river
with tangerine trees and marmalade skies.
Somebody calls you, you answer quite slowly a girl with kaleidoscope eyes.

John Lennon (1940–80) British rock musician. *Lucy in the Sky with Diamonds* (with Paul McCartney)

10 Imagine there's no heaven
It's easy if you try
No help below us
Above us only sky
Imagine all the people
Living for today.

John Lennon (1940–80) British rock musician. *Imagine*

11 His imagination resembled the wings of an ostrich. It enabled him to run, though not to soar.

Lord Macaulay (1800–59) British historian. *Essays and Biographies*, 'John Dryden'. *Edinburgh Review*

12 Imagination and fiction make up more than three quarters of our real life.

Simone Weil *Gravity and Grace*

IMITATION

See also originality

1 A lotta cats copy the Mona Lisa, but people still line up to see the original.

Louis Armstrong (1900–71) US jazz trumpeter. When asked whether he objected to people copying his style. Attrib.

2 Imitation is the sincerest form of flattery.

Charles Caleb Colton (?1780–1832) British clergyman and writer. *Lacon*, Vol. I

3 When people are free to do as they please, they usually imitate each other.

Eric Hoffer (1902–) US writer. *The Passionate State of Mind*

4 A mere copier of nature can never produce anything great.

Joshua Reynolds (1723–92) British portrait painter. Discourse to Students of the Royal Academy, 14 Dec 1770

5 He who resolves never to ransack any mind but his own, will be soon reduced, from mere barrenness, to the poorest of all imitations; he will be obliged to imitate himself, and to repeat what he has before often repeated.

Joshua Reynolds Discourse to Students of the Royal Academy, 10 Dec 1774

6 Of all my verse, like not a single line;
But like my title, for it is not mine.
That title from a better man I stole;
Ah, how much better, had I stol'n the whole!

Robert Louis Stevenson (1850–94) Scottish writer. *Underwoods*, Foreword

7 You will, Oscar, you will.

James Whistler (1834–1903) US painter. Replying to Oscar Wilde's exclamation 'I wish I had said that!'. Attrib.

IMMATURITY

1 Politics are usually the executive expression of human immaturity.

Vera Brittain (1893–1970) British writer and feminist. *The Rebel Passion*

2 The mark of the immature man is that he wants to die nobly for a cause, while the mark of the mature man is that he wants to live humbly for one.

Wilhelm Stekel (1868–1940) Viennese psychiatrist. *The Catcher in the Rye* (J. D. Salinger), Ch. 24

3 Another unsettling element in modern art is that common symptom of immaturity, the dread of doing what has been done before.

Edith Wharton (1862–1937) US novelist. *The Writing of Fiction*, Ch. 1

IMMORTALITY

See also eternity, mortality, posterity

1 I don't want to achieve immortality through my work . . . I want to achieve it through not dying.

Woody Allen (Allen Stewart Konigsberg; 1935–) US film actor. *Woody Allen and His Comedy* (E. Lax)

2 One cannot live for ever by ignoring the price of coffins.

Ernest Bramah (1868–1942) British writer. *Kai Lung Unrolls His Mat*

3 No young man believes he shall ever die.

William Hazlitt (1778–1830) British essayist. *On the Feeling of Immortality in Youth*

4 He had decided to live for ever or die in the attempt.

Joseph Heller (1923–) US novelist. *Catch-22*, Ch. 3

5 I detest life-insurance agents; they always argue that I shall some day die, which is not so.

Stephen Leacock (1869–1944) English-born Canadian economist and humorist. *Literary Lapses*, 'Insurance. Up to Date'

6 Stuck with placards for 'Deathless', that bitter beer that tastes sweet to its drinkers.

Rainer Maria Rilke (1875–1926) Austrian poet. *Duineser Elegien*, X

7 But thy eternal summer shall not fade,

Nor lose possession of that fair thou ow'st,
Nor shall death brag thou wander'st in his shade,
When in eternal lines to time thou grow'st;
So long as men can breathe, or eyes can see,
So long lives this, and this gives life to thee.

William Shakespeare (1564–1616) English dramatist. *Sonnets*, 18

8 We feel and know that we are eternal.

Benedict Spinoza (Baruch de Spinoza; 1632–77) Dutch philosopher. *Ethics*

9 A slumber did my spirit seal;
I had no human fears:
She seemed a thing that could not feel
The touch of earthly years.

No motion has she now, no force;
She neither hears nor sees;
Rolled round in earth's diurnal course,
With rocks, and stones, and trees.

William Wordsworth (1770–1850) British poet. *A Slumber did my Spirit seal*

IMPERFECTION

See also mistakes, perfection, weakness

1 Accidents will happen in the best regulated families.

Proverb

2 No man is infallible.

Proverb

3 To err is human.

Proverb

4 Watch and pray, that ye enter not into temptation: the spirit indeed is willing, but the flesh is weak.

Bible: Matthew 26:41

5 He has his talents, his vast and cultivated mind, his vivid imagination, his independence of soul and his high-souled principles of honour. But then – ah, these Buts! Saint Preux never kicked the fireirons, nor made puddings in his tea cup.

Jane Welsh Carlyle (1801–66) The wife of Thomas Carlyle. Referring to her husband. Letter to a friend, July 1821

6 When you have faults, do not fear to abandon them.

Confucius (K'ung Fu-tzu; 551–479 BC) Chinese philosopher. *Analects*

7 Even imperfection itself may have its ideal or perfect state.

Thomas De Quincey (1785–1859) British writer. *Murder Considered as one of the Fine Arts*

8 We must touch his weaknesses with a delicate hand. There are some faults so nearly allied to excellence, that we can scarce weed out the fault without eradicating the virtue.

Oliver Goldsmith (1728–74) Irish-born British writer. *The Good-Natured Man*, I

9 I'm aggrieved when sometimes even excellent Homer nods.

Horace (Quintus Horatius Flaccus; 65–8 BC) Roman poet. *Ars Poetica*

10 People often say that, by pointing out to a man the faults of his mistress, you succeed only in strengthening his attachment to her, because he does not believe you; yet how much more so if he does!

Marcel Proust (1871–1922) French novelist. *À la recherche du temps perdu: Du côté de chez Swann*

11 We only confess our little faults to persuade people that we have no large ones.

Duc de la Rochefoucauld (1613–80) French writer. *Maximes*, 327

12 If we had no faults of our own, we would not take so much pleasure in noticing those of others.

Duc de la Rochefoucauld *Maximes*, 31

13 Oh. I have got lots of human weaknesses, who hasn't?

Margaret Thatcher (1925–) British politician and prime minister. *The Times*, 1983

14 We are none of us infallible – not even the youngest of us.

William Hepworth Thompson (1810–86) British academic. Referring to G. W. Balfour, who was a junior fellow of Trinity College at the time. *Collections and Recollections* (G. W. E. Russell), Ch. 18

IMPERIALISM

See politics

IMPERTINENCE

See also boldness, frankness, rudeness

1 Shut the door, Wales.

'Beau' Brummell (George Bryan Brummell; 1778–1840) British dandy. Said to the Prince of Wales. Attrib.

2 He has to learn that petulance is not sarcasm, and that insolence is not invective.

Benjamin Disraeli (1804–81) British statesman. Said of Sir C. Wood. Speech, House of Commons, 16 Dec 1852

3 Must! Is *must* a word to be addressed to princes? Little man, little man! thy father, if he had been alive, durst not have used that word.

Elizabeth I (1533–1603) Queen of England. Said to Robert Cecil, on her death bed. *A Short History of the English People* (J. R. Green), Ch. 7

IMPETUOSITY

See also haste, spontaneity

1 In me the need to talk is a primary impulse, and I can't help saying right off what comes to my tongue.

Miguel de Cervantes (1547–1616) Spanish novelist. *Don Quixote*, Pt. I, Ch. 30

2 There are some who speak one moment before they think.

Jean de La Bruyère (1645–96) French satirist. *Les Caractères*

3 Celerity is never more admir'd
Than by the negligent.

William Shakespeare (1564–1616) English dramatist. *Antony and Cleopatra*, III:7

4 When a prisoner sees the door of his dungeon open he dashes for it without stopping to think where he shall get his dinner.

George Bernard Shaw (1856–1950) Irish dramatist and critic. *Back to Methuselah*, Preface

5 A youth to whom was given
So much of earth – so much of heaven,
And such impetuous blood.

William Wordsworth (1770–1850) British poet. *Ruth*

IMPORTANCE

See also triviality

1 Are not five sparrows sold for two farthings, and not one of them is forgotten before God?

Bible: Luke 12:6

2 Not to be sneezed at.

George Colman, the Younger (1762–1836) British dramatist. *Heir-at-Law*, II:1

3 In heaven an angel is nobody in particular.

George Bernard Shaw (1856–1950) Irish dramatist and critic. *Man and Superman*, 'Maxims for Revolutionists'

4 Art and religion first; then philosophy; lastly science. That is the order of the great subjects of life, that's their order of importance.
Muriel Spark (1918–) British novelist. *The Prime of Miss Jean Brodie*, Ch. 2

5 If this is God's world there are no unimportant people.
George Thomas (1909–) British politician. Remark, in a television interview

IMPOSSIBILITY

See also possibility

1 The only way of finding the limits of the possible is by going beyond them into the impossible.
Arthur C. Clarke (1917–) British science-fiction writer. *The Lost Worlds of 2001*

2 However, one cannot put a quart in a pint cup.
Charlotte Perkins Gilman (1860–1935) US writer. *The Living of Charlotte Perkins Gilman*

3 You can't make soufflé rise twice.
Alice Roosevelt Longworth (1884–1980) US hostess. *Mr. Republican* a biography of Robert A. Taft (James T. Patterson)

IMPRESSIONABILITY

See also gullibility

1 She had
A heart – how shall I say? – too soon made glad,
Too easily impressed.
Robert Browning (1812–89) British poet. *My Last Duchess*

2 Like a cushion, he always bore the impress of the last man who sat on him.
David Lloyd George (1863–1945) British Liberal statesman. Referring to Lord Derby. Attrib. in *The Listener*, 7 Sep 1978. This remark is also credited to Earl Haig

3 They'll take suggestion as a cat laps milk.
William Shakespeare (1564–1616) English dramatist. *The Tempest*, II:1

4 I am a feather for each wind that blows.
William Shakespeare *The Winter's Tale*, I:3

5 Give me a girl at an impressionable age, and she is mine for life.
Muriel Spark (1918–) British novelist. *The Prime of Miss Jean Brodie*, Ch. 1

IMPRISONMENT

See also freedom, oppression, slavery

1 And say, Thus saith the king, Put this fellow in the prison, and feed him with bread of affliction and with water of affliction, until I come in peace.
Bible: I Kings 22:27

2 A robin redbreast in a cage
Puts all Heaven in a rage.
William Blake (1757–1827) British poet. *Auguries of Innocence*

3 O! dreadful is the check – intense the agony
When the ear begins to hear, and the eye begins to see;
When the pulse begins to throb – the brain to think again –
The soul to feel the flesh, and the flesh to feel the chain.
Emily Brontë (1818–48) British novelist. *The Prisoner*

4 Thirty years' imprisonment is . . . a declaration of society's intellectual bankruptcy in the field of penology.
Lord Foot (1905–) British politician. *The Observer*, 'Sayings of the Week', 9 Mar 1969

5 Who but my father would keep such a bird in a cage?
Henry, Prince of Wales (1594–1612) First-born son of James I. Referring to Sir Walter Raleigh, who was imprisoned in the Tower of London for treason from 1603. Remark

6 She's only a bird in a gilded cage.
A. J. Lamb (1870–1928) British songwriter. Song title

7 Stone walls do not a prison make,
Nor iron bars a cage.
Richard Lovelace (1618–58) English poet. *To Althea, from Prison*

8 Is not this house as nigh heaven as my own?
Thomas More (1478–1535) English lawyer and scholar. Referring to the Tower of London; More was imprisoned here, and in 1535 executed, for treason arising from his defiance of Henry VIII's religious policies. *Life of Sir Thomas More* (Roper)

9 Come, let's away to prison;
We two alone will sing like birds i' the cage:
When thou dost ask me blessing, I'll kneel down,
And ask of thee forgiveness: and we'll live,
And pray, and sing, and tell old tales, and laugh
At gilded butterflies, and hear poor rogues
Talk of court news; and we'll talk with them too,
Who loses, and who wins; who's in, who's out;
And take upon 's the mystery of things,
As if we were God's spies; and we'll wear out,
In a wall'd prison, packs and sets of great ones
That ebb and flow by the moon.
William Shakespeare (1564–1616) English dramatist. *King Lear*, V:3

10 I have been studying how I may compare
This prison where I live unto the world.
William Shakespeare *Richard II*, V:5

11 Forget the outside world. Life has different laws in here. This is Campland, an invisible country. It's not in the geography books, or the psychology books or the history books. This is the famous country where ninety-nine men weep while one laughs.
Alexander Solzhenitsyn (1918–) Soviet novelist. *The Love-Girl and the Innocent*, I:3

12 We think caged birds sing, when indeed they cry.
John Webster (1580–1625) English dramatist. *The White Devil*, V:4

13 I never saw a man who looked
With such a wistful eye
Upon that little tent of blue
Which prisoners call the sky.
Oscar Wilde (1854–1900) Irish-born British dramatist. *The Ballad of Reading Gaol*, I:3

14 The Governor was strong upon
The Regulations Act:
The Doctor said that Death was but
A scientific fact:
And twice a day the Chaplain called,
And left a little tract.
Oscar Wilde *The Ballad of Reading Gaol*, III:3

15 Something was dead in each of us,
And what was dead was Hope.
Oscar Wilde *The Ballad of Reading Gaol*, III:31

16 I know not whether Laws be right,
Or whether Laws be wrong;
All that we know who lie in gaol
Is that the wall is strong;
And that each day is like a year,
A year whose days are long.
Oscar Wilde *The Ballad of Reading Gaol*, V:1

17 If this is the way Queen Victoria treats her prisoners, she doesn't deserve to have any.
Oscar Wilde Complaining at having to wait in the rain for transport to take him to prison. Attrib.

IMPROBABILITY

1 It is an old maxim of mine that when you have excluded the impossible, whatever remains, however improbable, must be the truth.
Arthur Conan Doyle (1856–1930) British writer. *The Beryl Coronet*

2 Faith may be defined briefly as an illogical belief in the occurrence of the improbable.
H. L. Mencken (1880–1956) US journalist. *Prejudices*, 'Types of Men'

3 If this were play'd upon a stage now, I could condemn it as an improbable fiction.
William Shakespeare (1564–1616) English dramatist. *Twelfth Night*, III:4

IMPROVEMENT

See also progress

1 He so improved the city that he justly boasted that he found it brick and left it marble.
Augustus (63 BC–14 AD) Roman emperor. Referring to Rome. *The Lives of the Caesars* (Suetonius), 'Augustus'

2 I've got to admit it's getting better. It's a little better all the time.
John Lennon (1940–80) British rock musician. *Getting Better* (with Paul McCartney)

3 It is a stupidity second to none, to busy oneself with the correction of the world.
Molière (Jean Baptiste Poquelin; 1622–73) French dramatist. *Le Misanthrope*, I:1

INATTENTION

1 Thank you for the manuscript; I shall lose no time in reading it.
Benjamin Disraeli (1804–81) British statesman. His customary reply to those who sent him unsolicited manuscripts. *Irreverent Social History* (F. Muir)

2 That should assure us of at least forty-five minutes of undisturbed privacy.
Dorothy Parker (1893–1967) US writer. Pressing a button marked NURSE during a stay in hospital. *The Algonquin Wits* (R. Drennan)

3 Donsmanship . . . 'the art of criticizing without actually listening'.
Stephen Potter (1900–69) British writer. *Lifemanship*, Ch. 6

4 I murdered my grandmother this morning.
Franklin D. Roosevelt (1882–1945) US Democratic president. His habitual greeting to any guest at the White House he suspected of paying no attention to what he said. *Ear on Washington* (D. McClellan)

INCOMPETENCE

1 This island is almost made of coal and surrounded by fish. Only an organizing genius could produce a shortage of coal and fish in Great Britain at the same time.
Aneurin Bevan (1897–1960) British Labour politician. Speech, Blackpool, 18 May 1945

2 The grotesque chaos of a Labour council – a *Labour* council – hiring taxis to scuttle around a city handing out redundancy notices to its own workers.
Neil Kinnock (1942–) British politician. Attacking militant members in Liverpool. Speech, Labour Party Conference, Bournemouth, 1985

3 He really deserves some sort of decoration . . . a medal inscribed 'For Vaguery in the Field'.
John Osborne (1929–) British dramatist. *Look Back in Anger*, I

4 Work is accomplished by those employees who have not yet reached their level of incompetence.
Laurence J. Peter (1919–) Canadian writer. *The Peter Principle*

5 Madame, there you sit with that magnificent instrument between your legs, and all you can do is *scratch* it!
Arturo Toscanini (1867–1957) Italian conductor. Rebuking an incompetent woman cellist. Attrib.

6 His ideas of first-aid stopped short at squirting soda-water.
P. G. Wodehouse (1881–1975) British humorous novelist. *My Man Jeeves*, 'Doing Clarence a Bit of Good'

INCONSTANCY

1 The hearts
That spaniel'd me at heels, to whom I gave
Their wishes, do discandy, melt their sweets
On blossoming Caesar.
William Shakespeare (1564–1616) English dramatist. *Antony and Cleopatra*, IV:10

INCONVENIENCE

1 Death and taxes and childbirth! There's never any convenient time for any of them!
Margaret Mitchell (1909–49) US novelist. *Gone with the Wind*

INCORRUPTIBILITY

1 Behold, I shew you a mystery; We shall not all sleep, but we shall all be changed,
In a moment, in the twinkling of an eye, at the last trump: for the trumpet shall sound, and the dead shall be raised incorruptible, and we shall be changed.
For this corruptible must put on incorruption, and this mortal must put on immortality.
So when this corruptible shall have put on incorruption, and this mortal shall have put on immortality, then shall be brought to pass the saying that is written, Death is swallowed up in victory.
O death, where is thy sting? O grave, where is thy victory?
Bible: I Corinthians 15:51–55

2 The seagreen Incorruptible.
Thomas Carlyle (1795–1881) Scottish historian and essayist. Referring to Robespierre. *History of the French Revolution*, Pt. II, Bk. IV, Ch. 4

INDECENCY

1 A private sin is not so prejudicial in the world as a public indecency.
Miguel de Cervantes (1547–1616) Spanish novelist. *Don Quixote*, Pt. II, Ch. 22

2 I expect you'll be becoming a schoolmaster sir. That's what most of the gentlemen does sir, that gets sent down for indecent behaviour.
Evelyn Waugh (1903–66) British novelist. *Decline and Fall*, Prelude

3 The older one grows the more one likes indecency.
Virginia Woolf (1882–1941) British novelist. *Monday or Tuesday*

INDECISION

See also uncertainty

1 I will have nothing to do with a man who can blow hot and cold with the same breath.
Aesop (6th century BC) Reputed Greek writer of fables. *Fables*, 'The Man and the Satyr'

2 She didn't say yes,
She didn't say no.
Otto Harbach (1873–1963) US lyricist. *The Cat and the Fiddle*, 'She Didn't Say Yes'

3 But I am pigeon-liver'd, and lack gall
To make oppression bitter, or ere this

I should have fatted all the region kites
With this slave's offal. Bloody, bawdy villain!
Remorseless, treacherous, lecherous, kindless villain!

William Shakespeare (1564–1616) English dramatist. *Hamlet*, II:2

4 I must have a prodigious quantity of mind; it takes me as much as a week, sometimes, to make it up.

Mark Twain (Samuel Langhorne Clemens; 1835–1910) US writer. *The Innocents Abroad*, Ch. 7

INDEPENDENCE

See also self-reliance, society

1 I'm short enough and ugly enough to succeed on my own.

Woody Allen (Allen Stewart Konigsberg; 1935–) US film actor. *Play It Again Sam*

2 I am the cat that walks alone.

Lord Beaverbrook (Maxwell Aitken; 1879–1964) Canadian-born politician and newspaper proprietor. *Beaverbrook* (A. J. P. Taylor)

3 When in the course of human events, it becomes necessary for one people to dissolve the political bonds which have connected them with another, and to assume among the powers of the earth the separate and equal station to which the laws of nature and of Nature's God entitle them, a decent respect to the opinions of mankind requires that they should declare the causes which impel them to the separation.

Thomas Jefferson (1743–1826) US statesman. Declaration of Independence, Preamble

4 I think it much better that . . . every man paddle his own canoe.

Captain Frederick Marryat (1792–1848) British novelist. *Settlers in Canada*, Ch. 8

INDIFFERENCE

See also insensitivity

1 But what is past my help is past my care.

Francis Beaumont (1584–1616) English dramatist. With John Fletcher. *The Double Marriage*, I:1

2 Nothing is so fatal to religion as indifference, which is, at least, half infidelity.

Edmund Burke (1729–97) British politician. Letter to William Smith, 29 Jan 1795

3 Sir, I view the proposal to hold an international exhibition at San Francisco with an equanimity bordering on indifference.

W. S. Gilbert (1836–1911) British dramatist. *Gilbert, His Life and Strife* (Hesketh Pearson)

4 It's no go the picture palace, it's no go the stadium,
It's no go the country cot with a pot of pink geraniums,
It's no go the Government grants, it's no go the elections,
Sit on your arse for fifty years and hang your hat on a pension.

Louis MacNeice (1907–63) Irish-born British poet. *Bagpipe Music*

5 At length the morn and cold indifference came.

Nicholas Rowe (1674–1718) English dramatist. *The Fair Penitent*, I:1

6 I don't care a twopenny damn what becomes of the ashes of Napoleon Bonaparte.

Duke of Wellington (1769–1852) British general and statesman. Attrib.

7 I hear it was charged against me that I sought to destroy institutions,
But really I am neither for nor against institutions.

Walt Whitman (1819–92) US poet. *I Hear It was Charged against Me*

INDIGNATION

1 A puritan's a person who pours righteous indignation into the wrong things.

G. K. Chesterton (1874–1936) British writer. Attrib.

2 Moral indignation is in most cases 2 percent moral, 48 percent indignation and 50 percent envy.

Vittorio De Sica (1901–74) Italian film director. *The Observer*, 1961

3 An orgy looks particularly alluring seen through the mists of righteous indignation.

Malcolm Muggeridge (1903–) British writer. *The Most of Malcolm Muggeridge*, 'Dolce Vita in a Cold Climate'

4 Wrongdoing can only be avoided if those who are not wronged feel the same indignation at it as those who are.

Solon (6th century BC) Athenian statesman. *Greek Wit* (F. Paley)

INDIVIDUALITY

See also difference, opinions, taste

1 Here's tae us wha's like us?
Gey few, and they're a' deid.

Anonymous Scottish toast.

2 Nature made him, and then broke the mould.

Ludovico Ariosto (1474–1533) Italian poet. Referring to Charlemagne's paladin, Roland. *Orlando furioso*

3 It is the common wonder of all men, how among so many million of faces, there should be none alike.

Thomas Browne (1605–82) English physician and writer. *Religio Medici*, Pt. II

4 . . . a bore, a bounder and a prig. He was intoxicated with his own youth and loathed any milieu which he couldn't dominate. Certainly he had none of a gentleman's instincts, strutting about Peace Conferences in Arab dress.

Henry Channon (1897–1958) British writer. Referring to T. E. Lawrence. Diary, 25 May 1935

5 We boil at different degrees.

Ralph Waldo Emerson (1803–82) US poet and essayist. *Society and Solitude*, 'Eloquence'

6 What many men desire! that 'many' may be meant
By the fool multitide, that choose by show,
Not learning more than the fond eye doth teach;
Which pries not to the interior; but, like the martlet,
Builds in the weather on the outward wall,
Even in the force and road of casualty.
I will not choose what many men desire,
Because I will not jump with common spirits
And rank me with the barbarous multitude.

William Shakespeare (1564–1616) English dramatist. *The Merchant of Venice*, II:9

INDOCTRINATION

See also education

1 Their teacher had advised them not to read Tolstoy novels, because they were very long and would easily confuse the clear ideas which they had learned from reading critical studies of him.

Alexander Solzhenitsyn (1918–) Soviet novelist. *The First Circle*, Ch. 40

2 This universal, obligatory force-feeding with lies is now the most agonizing aspect of existence in our country – worse than all our

material miseries, worse than any lack of civil liberties.
Alexander Solzhenitsyn *Letter to Soviet Leaders*, 6

3 For us, the tasks of education in socialism were closely integrated with those of fighting. Ideas that enter the mind under fire remain there securely and for ever.
Leon Trotsky (Lev Davidovich Bronstein; 1879–1940) Russian revolutionary. *My Life*, Ch. 35

INDULGENCE

1 Love is a boy, by poets styl'd, Then spare the rod, and spoil the child.
Samuel Butler (1612–80) English satirist. *Hudibras*, Pt. II

2 Children, in general, are overclothed and overfed. To these causes, I impute most of their diseases.
William Cadogan (1711–97) *Essays upon Nursing and Management of Children*

3 Every luxury was lavished on you – atheism, breast-feeding, circumcision. I had to make my own way.
Joe Orton (1933–67) British dramatist. *Loot*, I

INDUSTRIAL RELATIONS

See also diplomacy, strikes

1 British management doesn't seem to understand the importance of the human factor.
Charles, Prince of Wales (1948–) Eldest son of Elizabeth II. Speech, Parliamentary and Scientific Committee lunch, 21 Feb 1979

2 Industrial relations are like sexual relations. It's better between two consenting parties.
Vic Feather (1908–76) British trade-union leader. *Guardian Weekly*, 8 Aug 1976

3 I tell you, the only safeguard of order and discipline in the modern world is a standardised worker with interchangeable parts. That would solve the entire problem of management.
Jean Giraudoux (1882–1944) French dramatist. *The Madwoman of Chaillot*

4 It might be said that it is the ideal of the employer to have production without employees and the ideal of the employee is to have income without work.
E. F. Schumacher (1911–77) German-born economist. *The Observer*, 'Sayings of the Week', 4 May 1975

INEQUALITY

1 There is always inequality in life. Some men are killed in a war and some men are wounded and some men never leave the country – Life is unfair.
John Fitzgerald Kennedy (1917–63) US statesman. Speech, 21 Mar 1962

INEVITABILITY

1 Nothing is inevitable until it happens.
A. J. P. Taylor (1906–) British historian. *The Daily Telegraph*, 7 Jan 1980

INFALLIBILITY

1 Accidents will happen in the best regulated families.
Proverb

2 The only infallible criterion of wisdom to vulgar minds – success.
Edmund Burke (1729–97) British politician. *Letter to a Member of the National Assembly*

3 It is an infallible sign of the second-rate in nature and intellect to make use of everything and everyone.
Ada Beddington Leverson (1862–1933) British writer. *The Limit*

4 We are none of us infallible – not even the youngest of us.
William Hepworth Thompson (1810–86) British academic. Referring to G. W. Balfour, who was a junior fellow of Trinity College at the time. *Collections and Recollections* (G. W. E. Russell), Ch. 18

INFERIORITY

See also equality, mediocrity

1 I just met X in the street, I stopped for a moment to exchange ideas, and now I feel like a complete idiot.
Heinrich Heine (1797–1856) German poet and writer. *Autant en apportent les mots* (Pedrazzini)

2 Wherever an inferiority complex exists, there is a good reason for it. There is always something inferior there, although not just where we persuade ourselves that it is.
Carl Gustav Jung (1875–1961) Swiss psychoanalyst. Interview, 1943

3 It is an infallible sign of the second-rate in nature and intellect to make use of everything and everyone.
Ada Beddington Leverson (1862–1933) British writer. *The Limit*

4 There's no such thing as a bad Picasso, but some are less good than others.
Pablo Picasso (1881–1973) Spanish painter. *Come to Judgment* (A. Whitman)

5 Few persons who ever sat for a portrait can have felt anything but inferior while the process is going on.
Anthony Powell (1905–) British novelist. *The Observer*, 9 Jan 1983

6 No one can make you feel inferior without your consent.
Eleanor Roosevelt (1884–1962) US writer and lecturer. *This is My Story*

7 A king of shreds and patches.
William Shakespeare (1564–1616) English dramatist. *Hamlet*, III:4

INFINITY

1 The Desire of Man being Infinite, the possession is Infinite, and himself Infinite.
William Blake (1757–1827) British poet. *There is no Natural Religion*

2 I cannot help it; – in spite of myself, infinity torments me.
Alfred de Musset (1810–57) French dramatist and poet. *L'Espoir en Dieu*

INFLATION

1 Now a double scotch is about the size of a small scotch before the war, and a single scotch is nothing more than a dirty glass.
Lora Dundee (1902–) British politician. *The Observer*, 'Sayings of the Decade', 1960

INFLEXIBILITY

See also determination, stubbornness

1 Whenever you accept our views we shall be in full agreement with you.
Moshe Dayan (1915–81) Israeli general. Said to Cyrus Vance during Arab-Israeli negotiations. *The Observer*, 'Sayings of the Week', 14 Aug 1977

2 You cannot shake hands with a clenched fist.
Indira Gandhi (1917–84) Indian stateswoman. Remark at a press conference, New Delhi, 19 Oct 1971

3 U-turn if you want to. The lady's not for turning.
Margaret Thatcher (1925–) British politician and prime minister. Speech, Conservative Conference, 1980

4 Minds like beds always made up, (more stony than a shore)

unwilling or unable.

William Carlos Williams (1883–1963) US poet. *Patterson,* I, Preface

INFLUENCE

See also inspiration, power

1 Though Rome's gross yoke
Drops off, no more to be endured,
Her teaching is not so obscured
By errors and perversities,
That no truth shines athwart the lies.

Robert Browning (1812–89) British poet. *Christmas Eve,* XI

2 How to Win Friends and Influence People.

Dale Carnegie (1888–1955) US lecturer and writer. Book title

3 In the councils of government, we must guard against the acquisition of unwarranted influence, whether sought or unsought, by the military-industrial complex. The potential for the disastrous rise of misplaced power exists and will persist.

Dwight D. Eisenhower (1890–1969) US president. Farewell address, 17 Jan 1961

4 The proper time to influence the character of a child is about a hundred years before he is born.

Dean Inge (1860–1954) British churchman. *The Observer,* 21 June, 1929

5 We have met too late. You are too old for me to have any effect on you.

James Joyce (1882–1941) Irish novelist. On meeting W. B. Yeats. *James Joyce* (R. Ellmann)

6 Practical men, who believe themselves to be quite exempt from any intellectual influences, are usually the slaves of some defunct economist. Madmen in authority, who hear voices in the air, are distilling their frenzy from some academic scribbler of a few years back.

John Maynard Keynes (1883–1946) British economist. *The General Theory of Employment, Interest and Money,* Bk. VI, Ch. 24

7 The great man . . . walks across his century and leaves the marks of his feet all over it, ripping out the dates on his goloshes as he passes.

Stephen Leacock (1869–1944) English-born Canadian economist and humorist. *Literary Lapses,* 'The Life of John Smith'

8 So you're the little woman who wrote the book that made this great war!

Abraham Lincoln (1809–65) US statesman. Said on meeting Harriet Beecher Stowe, the author of *Uncle Tom's Cabin* (1852), which stimulated opposition to slavery before the US Civil War. *Abraham Lincoln: The War Years* (Carl Sandburg), Vol. II, Ch. 39

9 Peace! impudent and shameless Warwick, peace;
Proud setter up and puller down of kings.

William Shakespeare (1564–1616) English dramatist. *Henry VI,* Pt. 3, III:3

10 I will shake my little finger – and there will be no more Tito. He will fall.

Joseph Stalin (J. Dzhugashvili; 1879–1953) Soviet statesman. Said to Khrushchev. Attrib.

11 Athens holds sway over all Greece; I dominate Athens; my wife dominates me; our newborn son dominates her.

Themistocles (c. 528–462 BC) Athenian statesman. Explaining an earlier remark to the effect that his young son ruled all Greece. Attrib.

12 The hand that rocks the cradle
Is the hand that rules the world.

William Ross Wallace (1819–81) US poet and songwriter. *John o'London's Treasure Trove*

13 I took the right sow by the ear.

Robert Walpole Commenting on his perception that, to influence George II, the correct woman to cultivate was Queen Caroline, not any of the King's mistresses – a mistake made by his political opponents. Remark to a friend, c. 1734

14 The man who can dominate a London dinner-table can dominate the world.

Oscar Wilde (1854–1900) Irish-born British dramatist. Attrib. by R. Aldington in his edition of Wilde

INGRATITUDE

1 Never look a gift horse in the mouth.

Proverb

2 And having looked to government for bread, on the very first scarcity they will turn and bite the hand that fed them.

Edmund Burke (1729–97) British politician. *Thoughts and Details on Scarcity*

3 Our gratitude to most benefactors is the same as our feeling for dentists who have pulled our teeth. We acknowledge the good they have done and the evil from which they have delivered us, but we remember the pain they occasioned and do not love them very much.

Nicolas Chamfort (1741–94) French writer. *Maximes et pensées*

4 Blow, blow, thou winter wind,
Thou art not so unkind
As man's ingratitude.

William Shakespeare (1564–1616) English dramatist. *As You Like It,* II:7

5 Ingratitude, thou marble-hearted fiend,
More hideous when thou show'st thee in a child
Than the sea-monster!

William Shakespeare *King Lear* I:4

6 I hate ingratitude more in a man
Than lying, vainness, babbling drunkenness,
Or any taint of vice whose strong corruption
Inhabits our frail blood.

William Shakespeare *Twelfth Night,* III:4

INJUSTICE

1 Give a dog a bad name and hang him.

Proverb

2 He who was strongest got most, and everyone held on to what he had seized as if by right.

Anonymous Referring to the anarchy of King Stephen's reign, 1135–1154. *Chronicon Monasterii de Bello*

3 . . . hanged privily by night or in the luncheon hour.

Anonymous Referring to abuses of the procedure for trying clerics. *From Domesday Book to Magna Carta* (A. L. Poole)

4 Those who have had no share in the good fortunes of the mighty often have a share in their misfortunes.

Bertolt Brecht (1898–1956) German dramatist. *The Caucasian Chalk Circle*

5 When one has been threatened with a great injustice, one accepts a smaller as a favour.

Jane Welsh Carlyle (1801–66) The wife of Thomas Carlyle. *Journal,* 21 Nov 1855

6 'No, no!' said the Queen. 'Sentence first – verdict afterwards.'

Lewis Carroll (Charles Lutwidge Dodgson; 1832–98) British writer. *Alice's Adventures in Wonderland,* Ch. 12

7 I feel as a horse must feel when the beautiful cup is given to the jockey.

Edgar Degas (1934–17) French artist. On seeing one of his pictures sold at auction. Attrib.

8 To disarm the strong and arm the weak would be to change the social order which it's my job to preserve. Justice is the means by which established injustices are sanctioned.
Anatole France (Jacques Anatole François Thibault; 1844–1924) French writer. *Crainquebille*

9 Undeservedly you will atone for the sins of your fathers.
Horace (Quintus Horatius Flaccus; 65–8 BC) Roman poet. *Odes*, III

10 We was robbed!
Joe Jacobs (1896–1940) US boxing manager. Complaining to the audience when the heavyweight title of Max Schmeling, whom he managed, was passed to Jack Sharkey. Attrib.

11 How could God do this to me after all I have done for him?
Louis XIV (1638–1715) French king. On receiving news of the French army's defeat at the Battle of Blenheim. *Saint-Simon at Versailles* (L. Norton)

12 The government burns down whole cities while the people are forbidden to light lamps.
Mao Tse-Tung (1893–1976) Chinese communist leader. Attrib.

13 I am a man
More sinn'd against than sinning.
William Shakespeare (1564–1616) English dramatist. *King Lear*, III:2

14 That in the captain's but a choleric word
Which in the soldier is flat blasphemy.
William Shakespeare *Measure for Measure*, II:2

15 He was quite sure that he had been wronged. Not to be wronged is to forgo the first privilege of goodness.
H. G. Wells (1866–1946) British writer. *Bealby*, Pt. IV, Ch. 1

16 There is something utterly nauseating about a system of society which pays a harlot 25 times as much as it pays its Prime Minister, 250 times as much as it pays its Members of Parliament, and 500 times as much as it pays some of its ministers of religion.
Harold Wilson (1916–) British politician and prime minister. Referring to the case of Christine Keeler. Speech, House of Commons, June 1963

INNOCENCE

See also conscience, ignorance, innocence of childhood

1 Now I am ashamed of confessing that I have nothing to confess.
Fanny Burney (Frances Burney D'Arblay; 1752–1840) British novelist. *Evelina*, Letter 59

2 Now my innocence begins to weigh me down.
Jean Racine (1639–99) French dramatist. *Andromaque*, III:1

3 'But the Emperor has nothing on at all!' cried a little child.
Hans Christian Andersen (1805–75) Danish writer. *The Emperor's New Clothes*

4 No, it is not only our fate but our business to lose innocence, and once we have lost that, it is futile to attempt a picnic in Eden.
Elizabeth Bowen (1899–1973) Irish novelist. In *Orion III*, 'Out of a Book'

5 Ralph wept for the end of innocence, the darkness of man's heart, and the fall through the air of the true, wise friend called Piggy.
William Golding (1911–) British novelist. *Lord of the Flies*, Ch. 12

6 I remember, I remember,
The fir trees dark and high;
I used to think their slender tops
Were close against the sky:
It was a childish ignorance,
But now 'tis little joy
To know I'm farther off from heav'n
Than when I was a boy.
Thomas Hood (1799–1845) British poet. *I Remember*

7 Credulity is the man's weakness, but the child's strength.
Charles Lamb (1775–1834) British essayist. *Essays of Elia*, 'Witches and other Night Fears'

8 I'd the upbringing a nun would envy and that's the truth. Until I was fifteen I was more familiar with Africa than my own body.
Joe Orton (1933–67) British dramatist. *Entertaining Mr Sloane*, I

9 He hath a person and a smooth dispose
Fram'd to make a woman false.
The Moor is of a free and open nature,
That thinks men honest that but seem to be so.
William Shakespeare (1564–1616) English dramatist. *Othello*, I:3

10 What judgment shall I dread, doing no wrong?
William Shakespeare *The Merchant of Venice*, IV:1

11 And the wild boys innocent as strawberries.
Dylan Thomas (1914–53) Welsh poet. *The hunchback in the park*

12 There was a time when meadow, grove, and stream,
The earth, and every common sight,
To me did seem
Apparelled in celestial light,
The glory and the freshness of a dream.
William Wordsworth (1770–1850) British poet. *Ode. Intimations of Immortality*, I

INNOVATION

See also conservatism, novelty, originality, progress

1 He that will not apply new remedies must expect new evils: for time is the greatest innovator.
Francis Bacon (1561–1626) English philosopher. *Essays*, 'Of Innovations'

2 I once knew a chap who had a system of just hanging the baby on the clothes line to dry and he was greatly admired by his fellow citizens for having discovered a wonderful innovation on changing a diaper.
Damon Runyon (1884–1946) US writer. *Short Takes*, 'Diaper Dexterity'

INNUENDO

See also meaning

1 There was an old man of Boulogne
Who sang a most topical song.
It wasn't the words
That frightened the birds,
But the horrible double-entendre.
Anonymous

2 I'm one of the ruins that Cromwell knocked about a bit.
Marie Lloyd (1870–1922) British music-hall singer. Song title

3 Where more is meant than meets the ear.
John Milton (1608–74) English poet. *Il Penseroso*

INSENSITIVITY

See also hurt, indifference

1 Has anyone here been raped and speaks English?
Anonymous Said to have been shouted by a television journalist to a group of Belgian civilians waiting to be evacuated from the Congo in 1960

2 Miss Buss and Miss Beale

Cupid's darts do not feel.
How different from us,
Miss Beale and Miss Buss.

Anonymous Written about the headmistresses of North London Collegiate School and Cheltenham Ladies' College, respectively

3 'There's been an accident' they said,
'Your servant's cut in half; he's dead!'
'Indeed!' said Mr Jones, 'and please
Send me the half that's got my keys.'

Harry Graham (1874–1936) British writer. *Ruthless Rhymes for Heartless Homes*, 'Mr. Jones'

4 Just as the meanest and most vicious deeds require spirit and talent, so even the greatest deeds require a certain insensitiveness which on other occasions is called stupidity.

Georg Christoph Lichtenberg (1742–99) German physicist and writer. *Aphorisms*

5 One would have to have a heart of stone to read the death of Little Nell without laughing.

Oscar Wilde (1854–1900) Irish-born British dramatist. Lecturing upon Dickens. *Lives of the Wits* (H. Pearson)

INSIGNIFICANCE

See also triviality

1 There are some people who leave impressions not so lasting as the imprint of an oar upon the water.

Kate Chopin (1851–1904) US writer. *The Awakening*, Ch. 34

2 We are the hollow men
We are the stuffed men
Leaning together
Headpiece filled with straw.

T. S. Eliot (1888–1965) US-born British poet. *The Hollow Men*

3 She was one of those indispensables of whom one makes the discovery, when they are gone, that one can get on quite as well without them.

Aldous Huxley (1894–1964) British novelist. *Mortal Coils*, 'Nuns at Luncheon'

4 We are nothing; less than nothing, and dreams. We are only what might have been, and must wait upon the tedious shores of Lethe millions of ages before we have existence, and a name.

Charles Lamb (1775–1834) British essayist. In Greek mythology, Lethe was a river in the underworld, whose waters were drunk by souls about to be reborn in order to forget their past lives. *Essays of Elia*, 'Dream Children'

INSINCERITY

See also cant, hypocrisy

1 Experience teaches you that the man who looks you straight in the eye, particularly if he adds a firm handshake, is hiding something.

Clifton Fadiman (1904–) US writer. *Enter, Conversing*

2 He who praises everybody praises nobody.

Samuel Johnson (1709–84) British lexicographer. *Life of Johnson* (J. Boswell), Vol. III

3 Whatever he may promise me he will break everything to get a regular income from his parliament.

Louis XIV (1638–1715) King of France. Referring to Charles II of England. Letter to Barillon, 1680

4 Went to hear Mrs Turner's daughter . . . play on the harpsichon; but, Lord! it was enough to make any man sick to hear her; yet was I forced to commend her highly.

Samuel Pepys (1633–1703) English diarist. *Diary*, 1 May 1663

5 Most friendship is feigning, most loving mere folly.

William Shakespeare (1564–1616) English dramatist. *As You Like It*, II:7

6 My nose bleeds for you.

Herbert Beerbohm Tree (1853–1917) British actor and theater manager. *Beerbohm Tree* (H. Pearson)

INSOLENCE

1 *Patron.* Commonly a wretch who supports with insolence, and is paid with flattery.

Samuel Johnson (1709–84) British lexicographer. *Dictionary of the English Language*

2 Sir, the insolence of wealth will creep out.

Samuel Johnson *Life of Johnson* (J. Boswell), Vol. III

3 I do not dislike the French from the vulgar antipathy between neighbouring nations, but for their insolent and unfounded airs of superiority.

Horace Walpole (1717–97) British writer. Letter to Hannah More, 14 Oct 1787

INSPIRATION

1 A spur in the head is worth two in the heel.

Proverb

2 Ninety per cent of inspiration is perspiration.

Proverb

3 Inspiration is the act of drawing up a chair to the writing desk.

Anonymous

4 I dare not alter these things; they come to me from above.

Alfred Austin (1835–1913) British poet. When accused of writing ungrammatical verse. *A Number of People* (E. Marsh)

5 That I make poetry and give pleasure (if I give pleasure) are because of you.

Horace (Quintus Horatius Flaccus; 65–8 BC) Roman poet. *Odes*, IV

6 Deprivation is for me what daffodils were for Wordsworth.

Philip Larkin (1922–85) British poet. Interview in *The Observer*

7 Biting my truant pen, beating myself for spite:
'Fool!' said my Muse to me, 'look in thy heart and write.'

Philip Sidney (1554–86) English poet and courtier. Sonnet, *Astrophel and Stella*

8 I did not write it. God wrote it. I merely did his dictation.

Harriet Beecher Stowe (1811–96) US novelist. Referring to *Uncle Tom's Cabin*. Attrib.

9 The true God, the mighty God, is the God of ideas.

Alfred de Vigny (1797–1863) French writer. *La Bouteille à la mer*

INSULTS

See also actors, criticism, politicians, rudeness

1 Sticks and stones may break my bones, but words will never hurt me.

Proverb

2 Quite so. But I have not been on a ship for fifteen years and they still call me 'Admiral'. Italian admiral to whom Eva Peron had complained that she had been called a 'whore' on an Italian visit.

Anonymous

3 TO HELL WITH YOU. OFFENSIVE LETTER FOLLOWS.

Anonymous Telegram to Sir Alec Douglas-Home

4 Lloyd George could not see a belt without hitting below it.

Margot Asquith (1865–1945) The second wife of Herbert Asquith. *The Autobiography of Margot Asquith*

5 An imitation rough diamond.
Margot Asquith *As I Remember*

6 No. The 't' is silent – as in 'Harlow'.
Margot Asquith When Jean Harlow asked whether the 't' was pronounced in 'Margot'. .

7 She was a woman of mean understanding, little information, and uncertain temper.
Jane Austen (1775–1817) British novelist. *Pride and Prejudice*, Ch. 1

8 I thought he was a young man of promise; but it appears he was a young man of promises.
Arthur Balfour (1848–1930) British statesman. Said of Winston Churchill on his entry into politics, 1899. *Winston Churchill* (Randolph Churchill), Vol. I

9 Don't bother to thank me. I know what a perfectly ghastly season it's been for you Spanish dancers.
Tallulah Bankhead (1903–68) US actress. Said on dropping fifty dollars into a tambourine held out by a Salvation Army collector. *With Malice Toward All* (D. Hermann)

10 Busy yourselves with *this*, you damned walruses, while the rest of us proceed with the libretto.
John Barrymore (1882–1942) US actor. Throwing a fish to a noisy audience. *Try and Stop Me* (B. Cerf)

11 He's a kind of musical Malcolm Sargent.
Sir Thomas Beecham (1879–1961) British conductor. Referring to Herbert von Karajan. *Beecham Stories* (H. Atkins and A. Newman)

12 I have known many an instance of a man writing a letter and forgetting to sign his name, but this is the only instance I have ever known of a man signing his name and forgetting to write the letter.
Henry Ward Beecher (1813–87) US Congregational minister. Said on receiving a note containing the single word: 'Fool'. *The Best Stories in the World* (T. Masson)

13 Of course we all know that Morris was a wonderful all-round man, but the act of walking round him has always tired me.
Max Beerbohm (1872–1956) British writer. Referring to William Morris. *Conversations with Max* (S. N. Behrman)

14 I really enjoy only his stage directions; the dialogue is vortical, and, I find, fatiguing. It is like being harangued . . . He uses the English language like a truncheon.
Max Beerbohm *Conversation with Max* (S. N. Behrens)

15 Come in, you Anglo-Saxon swine
And drink of my Algerian wine.
'Twill turn your eyeballs black and blue,
And damn well good enough for you.
Brendan Behan (1923–64) Irish playwright. Painted as an advert on the window of a Paris café (the owner of which could not speak English). *My Life with Brendan* (B. Behan)

16 So boring you fall asleep halfway through her name.
Alan Bennett (1934–) British playwright and actor. Referring to the Greek writer Arianna Stassinopoulos. *The Observer*, 18 Sept 1983

17 Listening to a speech by Chamberlain is like paying a visit to Woolworths; everything in its place and nothing over sixpence.
Aneurin Bevan (1897–1960) Welsh Labour politician. In *Tribune*

18 He is a man suffering from petrified adolescence.
Aneurin Bevan Referring to Winston Churchill. *Aneurin Bevan* (Vincent Brome), Ch. 11

19 I mock thee not, though I by thee am mockèd;
Thou call'st me madman, but I call thee blockhead.
William Blake (1757–1827) British poet. *To Flaxman*

20 If there is anyone here whom I have not insulted, I beg his pardon.
Johannes Brahms (1833–97) German composer. Said on leaving a gathering of friends. *Brahms* (P. Latham)

21 Listen, dear, you couldn't write fuck on a dusty venetian blind.
Coral Brown (1913–) Australian-born actress. To a Hollywood writer who had criticized the writer Alan Bennett. Attrib.

22 Who's your fat friend?
'Beau' Brummell (George Bryan Brummell; 1778–1840) British dandy. Referring to George, Prince of Wales. *Reminiscences* (Gronow)

23 If ever he went to school without any boots it was because he was too big for them.
Ivor Bulmer-Thomas (1905–) British writer and politician. Referring to Harold Wilson. Remark, Conservative Party Conference, 1949

24 A lady of a 'certain age', which means
Certainly aged.
Lord Byron (1788–1824) British poet. *Don Juan*, VI

25 You dirty double-crossing rat!
James Cagney (1899–1986) US actor. Usually misquoted by impressionists as 'You dirty rat'. *Blonde Crazy*

26 That's not writing, that's typing.
Truman Capote (1924–84) US writer. Referring to the writer Jack Kerouac. Attrib.

27 Macaulay is well for a while, but one wouldn't *live* under Niagara.
Thomas Carlyle (1795–1881) Scottish historian and essayist. *Notebook* (R. M. Milnes)

28 Respectable Professors of the Dismal Science.
Thomas Carlyle Referring to economists. *Latter-Day Pamphlets*, 1

29 There goes a woman who knows all the things that can be taught and none of the things that cannot be taught.
Coco Chanel (1883–1971) French dress designer. *Coco Chanel, Her Life, Her Secrets* (Marcel Haedrich)

30 An injury is much sooner forgotten than an insult.
Earl of Chesterfield (1694–1773) English statesman. Letter to his son, 9 Oct 1746

31 If you were my wife, I'd drink it.
Winston Churchill (1874–1965) British statesman. Replying to Lady Astor who had said, 'If you were my husband, I'd put poison in your coffee.' *Nancy Astor and Her Friends* (E. Langhorne)

32 He is like a female llama surprised in her bath.
Winston Churchill Referring to Charles de Gaulle. Attrib.

33 And you, madam, are ugly. But I shall be sober in the morning.
Winston Churchill Replying Bessie Braddock MP who told him he was drunk. Attrib.

34 The only time in his life he ever put up a fight was when we asked him for his resignation.
Georges Clemenceau (1841–1929) French statesman. Referring to Marshal Joffre. *Here I Lie* (A.M. Thomson)

35 America is the only nation in history which miraculously has gone directly from barbarism to degeneration without the usual interval of civilization.
Georges Clemenceau Attrib.

36 The Cat, the Rat, and Lovell our dog
Rule all England under a hog.
William Collingbourne (d. 1484) English landowner. The cat was Sir William Catesby; the rat Sir Richard Ratcliffe; the dog Lord Lovell, who had a dog on his crest. The wild boar refers to the emblem of Richard III. *Chronicles* (R. Holinshed), III

37 Pushing forty? She's clinging on to it for dear life.

Ivy Compton-Burnett (1884–1969) British novelist. Attrib.

38 If you weren't the best light comedian in the country, all you'd be fit for would be the selling of cars in Great Portland Street.

Noël Coward (1899–1973) British dramatist. To Rex Harrison. Attrib.

39 How strange, when I saw you acting in *The Glorious Adventure* I laughed all the time.

Noël Coward To Lady Diana Cooper who said she had not laughed once at his comedy *The Young Idea*. *The Noel Coward Diaries*

40 Not even a public figure. A man of no experience. And of the utmost insignificance.

Lord Curzon (1859–1925) British politician. Referring to Stanley Baldwin on his appointment as Prime Minister. *Curzon: The Last Phase* (Harold Nicolson)

41 I see – she's the original good time that was had by all.

Bette Davis (Ruth Elizabeth Davis; 1908–) US film star. Referring to a starlet of the time. *The Filmgoer's Book of Quotes* (Leslie Halliwell)

42 Your dexterity seems a happy compound of the smartness of an attorney's clerk and the intrigue of a Greek of the lower empire.

Benjamin Disraeli (1804–81) British statesman. Speaking to Lord Palmerston. Attrib.

43 I know he is, and he adores his maker.

Benjamin Disraeli Replying to a remark made in defense of John Bright that he was a self-made man; often also attrib. to Bright referring to Disraeli. *The Fine Art of Political Wit* (L. Harris)

44 He was like a cock who thought the sun had risen to hear him crow.

George Eliot (Mary Ann Evans; 1819–80) British novelist. *Adam Bede*

45 Good-morning, gentlemen both.

Elizabeth I (1533–1603) Queen of England. When addressing a group of eighteen tailors. *Sayings of Queen Elizabeth* (Chamberlin)

46 The nicest old lady I ever met.

William Faulkner (1897–1962) US novelist. Referring to Henry James. *The Battle and the Books* (E. Stone)

47 He has never been known to use a word that might send the reader to the dictionary.

William Faulkner Referring to Ernest HEMINGWAY. Attrib.

48 A semi-house-trained polecat.

Michael Foot (1913–) British Labour politician. Referring to Norman Tebbitt. Speech, House of Commons

49 He is not only dull in himself, but the cause of dullness in others.

Samuel Foote (1720–77) British actor and dramatist. Parody of a line from Shakespeare's *Henry IV, Part 2*. *Life of Johnson* (J. Boswell)

50 He looks like the guy in a science fiction movie who is the first to see the Creature.

David Frye (1934–) US impressionist and comedian. Referring to president Ford. Attrib.

51 Harris, I am not well; pray get me a glass of brandy.

George IV (1762–1830) King of the United Kingdom. On seeing Caroline of Brunswick for the first time. *Diaries* (Earl of Malmesbury)

52 She may very well pass for forty-three
In the dusk, with a light behind her!

W. S. Gilbert (1836–1911) British dramatist. *Trial by Jury*

53 Philip is a living example of natural selection. He was as fitted to survive in this modern world as a tapeworm in an intestine.

William Golding (1911–) British novelist. *Free Fall*, Ch. 2

54 The reason so many people showed up at his funeral was because they wanted to make sure he was dead.

Samuel Goldwyn (1882–1974) Polish-American film producer. Referring to Louis B. Mayer, often attributed to others. *Hollywood Rajah* (B. Crowther)

55 I met the great little man, the man who can be silent in several languages.

James Guthrie Harbord (1866–1947) US general. Referring to Colonel House. *Mr Wilson's War* (John Dos Passos), Ch. 3

56 If, sir, I possessed the power of conveying unlimited sexual attraction through the potency of my voice, I would not be reduced to accepting a miserable pittance from the BBC for interviewing a faded female in a damp basement.

Gilbert Harding (1907–60) British broadcaster. Said to Mae West's manager, who suggested that he should be more 'sexy' when interviewing her. *Gilbert Harding by His Friends*

57 Like being savaged by a dead sheep.

Denis Healey (1917–) British Labour politician. Referring to the attack launched by Geoffrey Howe upon his Budget proposals. *The Listener*, 21 Dec 1978

58 She approaches the problem of our country with all the one-dimensional subtlety of a comic strip.

Denis Healey Referring to Margaret Thatcher. Speech, House of Commons, 22 May 1979

59 Silly Billy!

Denis Healey Catchphrase invented for him by the impressionist, Mike Yarwood, and then sometimes used by him

60 If the Almighty himself played the violin, the credits would still read 'Rubinstein, God, and Piatigorsky', in that order.

Jascha Heifetz (1901–87) Russian-born US violinist. Whenever Heifetz played in trios with Arthur Rubinstein (piano) and Gregor Piatigorsky (cello), Rubinstein always got top billing. *Los Angeles Times*, 29 Aug 1982

61 You have sent me a Flanders mare.

Henry VIII (1491–1547) King of England. Said on meeting his fourth wife, Anne of Cleves, for the first time. Attrib.

62 Do you call that thing under your hat a head?

Ludwig Holberg (1684–1754) Danish dramatist. Reply to the jibe, 'Do you call that thing on your head a hat?'. *Anekdotenschatz* (H. Hoffmeister)

63 I wish you would read a little poetry sometimes. Your ignorance cramps my conversation.

Anthony Hope (Sir Anthony Hope Hawkins; 1863–1933) British novelist. *The Dolly Dialogues*

64 In a disastrous fire in President Reagan's library both books were destroyed. And the real tragedy is that he hadn't finished coloring one.

Jonathan Hunt (1938–) New Zealand politician. *The Observer*, 30 Aug 1981

65 You sought the last resort of feeble minds with classical educations. You became a schoolmaster.

Aldous Huxley (1894–1964) British novelist and essayist. *Antic Hay*

66 The trouble with Senator Long is that he is suffering from halitosis of the intellect. That's presuming Emperor Long has an intellect.

Harold L. Ickes (1874–1952) US Republican politician. *The Politics of Upheaval* (A. M. Schlesinger Jnr), Pt. II, Ch. 14

67 Many people have delusions of grandeur but you're deluded by triviality.

Eugène Ionesco (1912–) French dramatist. *Exit the King*

68 Sir, you are like a pin, but without either its head or its point.

Douglas William Jerrold (1803–57) British dramatist. Speaking to a small thin man who was boring him. Attrib.

69 Jerry Ford is so dumb that he can't fart and chew gum at the same time.

Lyndon B. Johnson (1908–73) US statesman. Sometimes quoted as '. . . can't walk and chew gum'. *A Ford, Not a Lincoln* (R. Reeves), Ch. 1

70 A very unclubable man.

Samuel Johnson (1709–84) British lexicographer. Referring to Sir John Hawkins. *Life of Johnson* (J. Boswell), Vol. I

71 I do not care to speak ill of any man behind his back, but I believe the gentleman is an *attorney*.

Samuel Johnson *Life of Johnson* (J. Boswell), Vol. II

72 Sir, your wife, under pretence of keeping a bawdy-house, is a receiver of stolen goods.

Samuel Johnson An example of the customary badinage between travelers on the Thames. *Life of Johnson* (J. Boswell), Vol. IV

73 Sir, there is no settling the point of precedency between a louse and a flea.

Samuel Johnson When Maurice Morgann asked him who he considered to be the better poet – Smart or Derrick. *Life of Johnson* (J. Boswell), Vol. IV

74 No, Sir; there were people who died of dropsies, which they contracted in trying to get drunk.

Samuel Johnson Scornfully criticizing the strength of the wine in Scotland before the Act of Union in response to Boswell's claim that there had been a lot of drunkenness. *Tour to the Hebrides* (J. Boswell)

75 Come, let me know what it is that makes a Scotchman happy!

Samuel Johnson Ordering for himself a glass of whisky. *Tour to the Hebrides* (J. Boswell)

76 Calumnies are answered best with silence.

Ben Jonson (1573–1637) English dramatist. *Volpone*, II:2

77 They travel best in gangs, hanging around like clumps of bananas, thick skinned and yellow.

Neil Kinnock (1942–) British politician. Referring to Tory critics. *The Observer*, 'Sayings of the Week', 22 Feb 1987

78 She only went to Venice because somebody told her she could walk down the middle of the street.

Neil Kinnock Referring to Margaret Thatcher who attended a meeting in Venice just before the 1987 election. Speech, Leeds, 9 June 1987

79 She looked as though butter wouldn't melt in her mouth – or anywhere else.

Elsa Lanchester (1902–86) British-born US actress. Referring to Maureen O'Hara. Attrib.

80 Oh, well, you play Bach *your* way. I'll play him *his*.

Wanda Landowska (1877–1959) Hungarian harpsichordist. Remark to fellow musician. Attrib.

81 He looked at me as if I was a side dish he hadn't ordered.

Ring Lardner Jnr (1885–1933) American humorist. Referring to W. H. Taft, US president (1909–13). *The Home Book of Humorous Quotations* (A. K. Adams)

82 Play us a medley of your hit.

Oscar Levant (1906–72) US pianist and actor. Replying to George Gershwin's barb 'If you had it all over again, would you fall in love with yourself?'. Attrib.

83 I'm sure he had a fork in the other.

Ada Beddington Leverson (1862–1933) British writer. Reply when told by Oscar Wilde of a devoted *apache* (Parisian gangster) who used to follow him with a knife in one hand. Attrib.

84 A Catholic layman who has never been averse to giving advice to the Pope, or indeed anybody else who he thought might be in need of it.

Bernard Levin (1928–) British journalist. Referring to Norman St John Stevas. *The Pendulum Years*

85 She's the sort of woman who lives for others – you can always tell the others by their hunted expression.

C. S. Lewis (1898–1963) British academic and writer. *The Screwtape Letters*

86 When they circumcised Herbert Samuel they threw away the wrong bit.

David Lloyd George (1863–1945) British Liberal statesman. Attrib. in *The Listener*, 7 Sept 1978

87 Like a cushion, he always bore the impress of the last man who sat on him.

David Lloyd George Referring to Lord Derby. Attrib. in *The Listener*, 7 Sep 1978. This remark is also credited to Earl Haig

88 The Right Hon. gentleman has sat so long on the fence that the iron has entered his soul.

David Lloyd George Referring to Sir John Simon. Attrib.

89 Dewey looks like the bridegroom on the wedding cake.

Alice Roosevelt Longworth (1884–1980) US hostess. Referring to Thomas E. Dewey. *New York Times*, 25 Feb 1980

90 He looks as if he had been weaned on a pickle.

Alice Roosevelt Longworth Referring to John Calvin Coolidge, US president 1923–29. *Crowded Hours*

91 The answer is in the plural and they bounce.

Edwin Lutyens (1869–1944) British architect. Attrib.

92 There, but for the Grace of God, goes God.

Herman J. Mankiewicz (1897–1953) US journalist and screenwriter. Said of Orson Welles in the making of *Citizen Kane*. Also attributed to others. *The Citizen Kane Book*

93 From the moment I picked up your book until I laid it down, I was convulsed with laughter. Some day I intend reading it.

Groucho Marx (Julius Marx; 1895–1977) US comedian and film actor. *The Last Laugh* (S. J. Perelman)

94 Go, and never darken my towels again!

Groucho Marx *Duck Soup*

95 I have forgotten more law than you ever knew, but allow me to say, I have not forgotten much.

John Maynard (1602–90) English judge. Replying to Judge Jeffreys' suggestion that he was so old he had forgotten the law.

96 You are the pits.

John McEnroe (1959–) US tennis player. To an umpire at Wimbledon, 1981. *The Sunday Times*, 24 June 1984

97 And I don't feel the attraction of the Kennedys at all . . . I don't think they are Christians; they may be Catholics but they are not Christians, in my belief anyway.

Mary McCarthy (1912–) US novelist. *The Observer*, 14 Oct 1979

98 I think I'm thoroughly in favour of Mrs. Thatcher's visit to the Falklands. I find a bit of hesitation, though, about her coming back.

John Mortimer (1923–) British lawyer and dramatist. *Any Questions?* (BBC radio program)

99 He is not only a bore but he bores for England.

Malcolm Muggeridge (1903–) British writer. Referring to Sir Anthony Eden. In *New-statesmanship* (E. Hyams), 'Boring for England'

100 Peel's smile: like the silver plate on a coffin.

Daniel O'Connell (1775–1847) Irish politician. Referring to Sir Robert Peel; quoting J. P. Curran (1750–1817). *Hansard*, 26 Feb 1835

101 Pearls before swine.

Dorothy Parker (1893–1967) US writer. Clare Booth Luce, going through a door with her, said, 'Age before beauty'. *You Might As Well Live* (J. Keats)

102 You know, she speaks eighteen languages. And she can't say 'No' in any of them.

Dorothy Parker Speaking of an acquaintance. Attrib.

103 Where does she find them?

Dorothy Parker In reply to a remark, 'Anyway, she's always very nice to her inferiors'. *Lyttelton Hart-Davis Letters*

104 It is with narrow-souled people as with narrow-necked bottles: the less they have in them, the more noise they make in pouring it out.

Alexander Pope (1688–1744) British poet. *Thoughts on Various Subjects*

105 Dinner at the Huntercombes' possessed 'only two dramatic features – the wine was a farce and the food a tragedy'.

Anthony Powell (1905–) British novelist. *A Dance to the Music of Time: The Acceptance World*, Ch. 4

106 I remember coming across him at the Grand Canyon and finding him peevish, refusing to admire it or even look at it properly. He was jealous of it.

J. B. Priestley (1894–1984) British novelist. Referring to George Bernard Shaw. *Thoughts In the Wilderness*

107 My god, they've shot the wrong person!

James Pryde (1866–1941) British artist. At the unveiling of a statue to Nurse Edith Cavell. Attrib.

108 Not a gentleman; dresses too well.

Bertrand Russell (1872–1970) British philosopher. Referring to Anthony Eden. *Six Men* (A. Cooke)

109 He had a smile like a razor-blade.

Anthony Sampson (1926–) British writer and journalist. *The Changing Anatomy of Britain*

110 Thou whoreson zed! thou unnecessary letter!

William Shakespeare (1564–1616) English dramatist. *King Lear*, II:2

111 You are not worth the dust which the rude wind
Blows in your face.

William Shakespeare *King Lear*, IV:2

112 I enjoyed talking to her, but thought *nothing* of her writing. I considered her 'a beautiful little knitter'.

Edith Sitwell (1887–1964) British poet and writer. Referring to Virginia Woolf. Letter to G. Singleton

113 I do not want Miss Mannin's feelings to be hurt by the fact that I have never heard of her. . . . At the moment I am debarred from the pleasure of putting her in her place by the fact that she has not got one.

Edith Sitwell Referring to the novelist Ethel Mannin. *Façades* (J. Pearson)

114 It proves what they say, give the public what they want to see and they'll come out for it.

Red Skelton (Richard Bernard Skelton; 1913–) US actor and comedian. Said while attending the funeral in 1958 of Hollywood producer Harry Cohn. It has also been attributed to Samuel Goldwyn while attending Louis B. Mayer's funeral in 1957.

115 He has occasional flashes of silence, that make his conversation perfectly delightful.

Sydney Smith (1771–1845) British clergyman and essayist. Referring to Lord Macaulay. *Memoir* (Lady Holland)

116 Okie use' to mean you was from Oklahoma. Now it means you're scum. Don't mean nothing itself, it's the way they say it.

John Steinbeck (1902–68) US novelist. *The Grapes of Wrath*, Ch. 18

117 I cannot but conclude the bulk of your natives to be the most pernicious race of little odious vermin that nature ever suffered to crawl upon the surface of the earth.

Jonathan Swift (1667–1745) Irish-born Anglican priest and writer. *Gulliver's Travels*, 'Voyage to Brobdingnag', Ch. 6

118 There is a certain class of clergyman whose mendicity is only equalled by their mendacity.

Frederick Temple (1821–1902) British churchman. Remark at a meeting of the Ecclesiastical Commissioners. *Years of Endeavour* (Sir George Leveson Gower)

119 It's too late to apologize.

Arturo Toscanini (1867–1957) Italian conductor. Retort to the insult 'Nuts to you!' shouted at him by a player he had just ordered from the stage during rehearsal. *The Humor of Music* (L. Humphrey)

120 He is an old bore; even the grave yawns for him.

Herbert Beerbohm Tree (1853–1917) British actor and theater manager. Referring to Israel Zangwill. *Beerbohm Tree* (Hesketh Pearson)

121 Forty years ago he was Slightly in Peter Pan, and you might say that he has been wholly in Peter Pan ever since.

Kenneth Tynan (1927–80) British critic. Referring to Noel Coward. *Curtains*

122 A diplomat these days is nothing but a head-waiter who's allowed to sit down occasionally.

Peter Ustinov (1921–) British actor and dramatist. *Romanoff and Juliet*, I

123 A triumph of the embalmer's art.

Gore Vidal (1925–) US novelist. Referring to Ronald Reagan. *The Observer*, 26 Apr 1981

124 A typical triumph of modern science to find the only part of Randolph that was not malignant and remove it.

Evelyn Waugh (1903–66) British novelist. Remarking upon the news that Randolph Churchill had had a noncancerous lung removed. Attrib.

125 Simply a radio personality who outlived his prime.

Evelyn Waugh Referring to Winston Churchill. *Evelyn Waugh* (Christopher Sykes)

126 You're a fine woman, Lou. One of the finest women that ever walked the streets.

Mae West (1892–1980). US actress. *She Done Him Wrong*, film 1933

127 Every other inch a gentleman.

Rebecca West (1892–1983) British writer. Attrib.

128 Perhaps not, but then you can't call yourself a great work of nature.

James Whistler (1834–1903) US painter. Responding to a sitter's complaint that his portrait was not a great work of art. *Whistler Stories* (D. Seitz)

129 I do not mind the Liberals, still less do I mind the Country Party, calling me a bastard. In some circumstances I am only doing my job if they do. But I hope you will not publicly call me a bastard, as some bastards in the Caucus have.

Gough Whitlam (1916–) Australian statesman. Speech to the Australian Labor Party, 9 June 1974

130 Dear Frank, we believe you; you have dined in every house in London – *once*.

Oscar Wilde (1854–1900) Irish-born British dramatist. Interrupting Frank Harris's interminable account of the houses he had dined at. Attrib.

131 You have Van Gogh's ear for music.
Billy Wilder (Samuel Wilder; 1906–) Austrian-born US film director. Said to Cliff Osmond. Attrib.

132 I have always said about Tony that he immatures with age.
Harold Wilson (1916–) British politician and prime minister. Referring to Anthony Wedgwood Benn. *The Chariot of Israel*

133 She missed the last Lobby briefing, I hear. At the vet's with hard pad, no doubt.
Harold Wilson Referring to a woman journalist he disliked. Attrib.

134 If I had had to choose between him and a cockroach as a companion for a walking-tour, the cockroach would have had it by a short head.
P. G. Wodehouse (1881–1975) British humorous novelist. *My Man Jeeves*, 'The Spot of Art'

135 There is absolutely nothing wrong with Oscar Levant that a miracle cannot fix.
Alexander Woollcott (1887–1943) US writer and critic. *The Vicious Circle* (M. C. Harriman)

136 Then the little man wears a shocking bad hat.
Duke of York and Albany (1763–1827) The second son of George III. Referring to Horace Walpole. Attrib.

INSURANCE

1 The Act of God designation on all insurance policies; which means, roughly, that you cannot be insured for the accidents that are most likely to happen to you.
Alan Coren (1938–) British humorist and writer. *The Lady from Stalingrad Mansions*, 'A Short History of Insurance'

2 I detest life-insurance agents. They always argue that I shall some day die, which is not so.
Stephen Leacock (1869–1944) English-born Canadian economist and humorist. *Literary Lapses*

INTEGRATION

See prejudice

INTEGRITY

See also honesty, morality, principles, righteousness, self, sincerity

1 Be so true to thyself, as thou be not false to others.
Francis Bacon (1561–1626) English philosopher. *Essays*, 'Of Wisdom for a Man's Self'

2 Caesar's wife must be above suspicion.
Julius Caesar (100–44 BC) Roman general and statesman. Said in justification of his divorce from Pompeia, after she was unwittingly involved in a scandal. *Lives*, 'Julius Caesar' (Plutarch)

3 I cannot and will not cut my conscience to fit this year's fashions, even though I long ago came to the conclusion that I was not a political person and could have no comfortable place in any political group.
Lillian Hellman (1905–84) US dramatist. Letter to the US House of Representatives Committee on Un-American Activities, *The Nation*, 31 May 1952

4 Integrity without knowledge is weak and useless, and knowledge without integrity is dangerous and dreadful.
Samuel Johnson (1709–84) British lexicographer. *Rasselas*, Ch. 41

5 It is necessary to the happiness of man that he be mentally faithful to himself. Infidelity does not consist in believing, or in disbelieving, it consists in professing to believe what one does not believe.
Thomas Paine (1737–1809) British writer. *The Age of Reason*, Pt. I

6 Neither a borrower nor a lender be;
For loan oft loses both itself and friend,
And borrowing dulls the edge of husbandry.
This above all: to thine own self be true,
And it must follow, as the night the day,
Thou canst not then be false to any man.
William Shakespeare (1564–1616) English dramatist. *Hamlet*, I:3

7 My strength is as the strength of ten,
Because my heart is pure.
Alfred, Lord Tennyson (1809–92) British poet. *Sir Galahad*

INTELLECT

See also intelligence, mind, thinking

1 Hercule Poirot tapped his forehead. 'These little grey cells, It is 'up to them' – as you say over here.'
Agatha Christie (1890–1976) British detective-story writer. *The Mysterious Affair at Styles*

2 We should take care not to make the intellect our god; it has, of course, powerful muscles, but no personality.
Albert Einstein (1879–1955) German-born US physicist. *Out of My Later Life*, 51

3 The voice of the intellect is a soft one, but it does not rest till it has gained a hearing.
Sigmund Freud (1856–1939) Austrian psychoanalyst. *The Future of an Illusion*

4 Another great Advantage of Deformity is, that it tends to the Improvement of the Mind. A man, that cannot shine in his Person, will have recourse to his Understanding: and attempt to adorn that Part of him, which alone is capable of ornament.
William Hay (1695–1755) *Essay on Deformity*

5 Man is an intellectual animal, and therefore an everlasting contradiction to himself. His senses centre in himself, his ideas reach to the ends of the universe; so that he is torn in pieces between the two, without a possibility of its ever being otherwise.
William Hazlitt (1778–1830) British essayist. *Characteristics*

6 We are thinking beings, and we cannot exclude the intellect from participating in any of our functions.
William James (1842–1910) US psychologist and philosopher. *Varieties of Religious Experience*

7 The highest intellects, like the tops of mountains, are the first to catch and to reflect the dawn.
Lord Macaulay (1800–59) British historian. *Historical Essays Contributed to the 'Edinburgh Review'*, 'Sir James Mackintosh'

8 The higher the voice the smaller the intellect.
Ernest Newman (1868–1959) British music critic. Attrib.

9 Intellect is invisible to the man who has none.
Arthur Schopenhauer (1788–1860) German philosopher. *Aphorismen zur Lebensweisheit*

INTELLECTUALS

See also academics

1 An intellectual is a man who doesn't know how to park a bike.
Spiro Agnew (1918–) US politician. Attrib.

2 To the man-in-the-street, who, I'm sorry to say
Is a keen observer of life,

The word Intellectual suggests straight away
A man who's untrue to his wife.
W. H. Auden (1907–73) British poet. *Note on Intellectuals*

3 I've been called many things, but never an intellectual.
Tallulah Bankhead (1903–68) US actress. *Tallulah*, Ch. 15

4 The intellectuals' chief cause of anguish are one another's works.
Jacques Barzun (1907–) US writer. *The House of Intellect*

5 Intellectuals are people who believe that ideas are of more importance than values. That is to say, their own ideas and other people's values.
Gerald Brenan (Edward Fitzgerald Brenan; 1894–1987) British writer. *Thoughts in a Dry Season*, 'Life'

6 An intellectual is someone whose mind watches itself.
Albert Camus (1913–60) French existentialist writer. *Notebooks*, 1935–42

7 I muse how men of wit can so hardly use that gift they hold.
Elizabeth I (1533–1603) Queen of England. Speech to a delegation from parliament, 5 Nov 1566

8 There is, however, a pathological condition which occurs so often, in such extreme forms, and in men of such pre-eminent intellectual ability, that it is impossible not to regard it as having a real association with such ability. I refer to gout.
Havelock Ellis (1859–1939) British psychologist. *A Study of British Genius*, Ch. 8

9 Beware of the artist who's an intellectual also. The artist who doesn't fit.
F. Scott Fitzgerald (1896–1940) US novelist. *This Side of Paradise*, Bk. II, Ch. 5

10 You will hear more good things on the outside of a stagecoach from London to Oxford than if you were to pass a twelvemonth with the undergraduates, or heads of colleges, of that famous university.
William Hazlitt (1778–1830) British essayist. *The Ignorance of the Learned*

11 I too had thoughts once of being an intellectual, but I found it too difficult.
Albert Schweitzer (1875–1965) French Protestant theologian, philosopher, and physician. Remark made to an African who refused to perform a menial task on the grounds that he was an intellectual. Attrib.

12 The trouble with me is, I belong to a vanishing race. I'm one of the intellectuals.
Robert E. Sherwood (1896–1955) US writer and dramatist. *The Petrified Forest*

13 Do you think it pleases a man when he looks into a woman's eyes and sees a reflection of the British Museum Reading Room?
Muriel Spark (1918–) British novelist. *The Wit of Women* (L. and M. Cowan)

14 What is a highbrow? It is a man who has found something more interesting than women.
Edgar Wallace (1875–1932) British thriller writer. Interview

15 Pointy-headed intellectuals who can't park their bicycles straight.
George Wallace (1919–) US politician. Attrib., often repeated

INTELLIGENCE

See also intellect, knowledge, mind, perception, thinking, understanding, wisdom

1 He's very clever, but sometimes his brains go to his head.
Margot Asquith (1865–1945) The second wife of Herbert Asquith. Referring to F. E. Smith. *As I Remember*

2 He has a brilliant mind until he makes it up.
Margot Asquith Referring to Sir Stafford Cripps. *The Wit of the Asquiths*

3 The intelligent are to the intelligentsia what a man is to a gent.
Stanley Baldwin (1867–1947) British statesman. Attrib.

4 I never heard tell of any clever man that came of entirely stupid people.
Thomas Carlyle (1795–1881) Scottish historian and essayist. Speech, Edinburgh, 2 Apr 1886

5 Common sense is in medicine the master workman.
Peter Mere Latham (1789–1875) US poet and essayist. *General Remarks on the Practice of Medicine*, Ch. 5

6 No one ever went broke underestimating the intelligence of the American people.
H. L. Mencken (1880–1956) US journalist. Attrib.

7 A really intelligent man feels what other men only know.
Baron de Montesquieu (1688–1755) French writer. *Essai sur les causes qui peuvent affecter les esprits et les caractères*

8 The more intelligence one has the more people one finds original. Commonplace people see no difference between men.
Blaise Pascal (1623–62) French philosopher and mathematician. *Pensées*, I

9 The height of cleverness is to be able to conceal it.
Duc de la Rochefoucauld (1613–80) French writer. *Maximes*, 245

10 Intelligence is quickness to apprehend as distinct from ability, which is capacity to act wisely on the thing apprehended.
A. N. Whitehead (1861–1947) British philosopher. *Dialogues*, 135

11 All the unhappy marriages come from the husbands having brains. What good are brains to a man? They only unsettle him.
P. G. Wodehouse (1881–1975) British humorous novelist. *The Adventures of Sally*

INTERFERING

See also curiosity

1 'If everybody minded their own business,' the Duchess said in a hoarse growl, 'the world would go round a deal faster than it does.'
Lewis Carroll (Charles Lutwidge Dodgson; 1832–98) British writer. *Alice's Adventures in Wonderland*, Ch. 6

INTERRUPTIONS

1 On awaking he . . . instantly and eagerly wrote down the lines that are here preserved. At this moment he was unfortunately called out by a person on business from Porlock.
Samuel Taylor Coleridge (1772–1834) British poet. *Kubla Khan* (preliminary note)

2 As I was saying the other day.
Luis Ponce de Léon (1527–91) Spanish monk. Said on resuming a lecture interrupted by five years' imprisonment

3 Mr Wordsworth is never interrupted.
Mary Wordsworth (1770–1850) Wife of William Wordsworth. Rebuking John Keats for interrupting a long monologue by William Wordsworth. Attrib.

INTRIGUE

1 Ay, now the plot thickens very much upon us.
Duke of Buckingham (1628–87) English politician. *The Rehearsal*, III:1

2 Everybody was up to something,

especially, of course, those who were up to nothing.

Noël Coward (1899–1973) British dramatist. *Future Indefinite*

3 Work on,
My medicine, work! Thus credulous fools are caught.

William Shakespeare (1564–1616) English dramatist. *Othello*, IV:1

INTRODUCTIONS

1 'You look a little shy; let me introduce you to that leg of mutton,' said the Red Queen. 'Alice – Mutton; Mutton – Alice.'

Lewis Carroll (Charles Lutwidge Dodgson; 1832–98) British writer. *Through the Looking-Glass*, Ch. 9

2 Do you suppose I could buy back my introduction to you?

Groucho Marx (Julius Marx; 1895–1977) US comedian. *Monkey Business*

INVECTIVE

1 He was the only man I knew who could make a curse sound like a caress.

Michael Foot (1913–) British Labour politician and journalist. Referring to Aneurin Bevan. *Aneurin Bevan 1897–1945*

INVENTION

See also science

1 If a man make a better mouse-trap than his neighbor, though he build his house in the woods, the world will make a beaten path to his door.

Ralph Waldo Emerson (1803–82) US poet and essayist. Attrib.

2 His absent-minded scientist, Dr. Strabismus (whom God Preserve) of Utrecht, had to his credit a list of inventions that included 'a leather grape', 'a revolving wheelbarrow', 'a hollow glass walking stick for keeping very small flannel shirts in', 'waterproof onions', 'a bottle with its neck in the middle', 'false teeth for swordfish', and 'a foghorn sharpener'.

Bernard Levin ((1928–) British journalist. Obituary of J. B. Morton. *The Observer*, 13 May 1979

INVITATIONS

See also summons

1 Anyone for tennis?

Anonymous

2 Come with me to the Casbah.

Charles Boyer (1899–1978) US film actor. Often quoted, but not actually in the film. *Algiers*

3 'Will you walk into my parlour?' said a spider to a fly:
''Tis the prettiest little parlour that ever you did spy.'

Mary Howitt (1799–1888) British writer. *The Spider and the Fly*

4 If you haven't anything nice to say about anyone, come and sit by me.

Alice Roosevelt Longworth (1884–1980) US hostess. Embroidered on a cushion at her home. *New York Times*, 25 Feb 1980

5 Come into the garden, Maud,
For the black bat, night, has flown,
Come into the garden, Maud,
I am here at the gate alone.

Alfred, Lord Tennyson (1809–92) British poet. *Maud*, I

6 I always did like a man in uniform. And that one fits you grand. Why don't you come up sometime and see me?

Mae West (1892–1980) US actress. Often misquoted as 'Come up and see me some time *She Done Him Wrong*, film 1933

IRELAND

See also Britain, Irish

1 I met wid Napper Tandy, and he took me by the hand,
And he said, 'How's poor ould Ireland, and how does she stand?'
She's the most disthressful country that iver yet was seen,
For they're hangin' men an' women there for the wearin' o' the Green.

Anonymous *The Wearin' o' the Green*

2 In Dublin's fair city, where the girls are so pretty,
I first set my eyes on sweet Molly Malone,
As she wheeled her wheelbarrow, through streets broad and narrow,
Crying, Cockles and mussels! alive, alive, O!

She was a fishmonger, but sure 'twas no wonder,
For so were her father and mother before.

Anonymous *Cockles and Mussels*

3 Our day will come.

Tiocfaidh Ar La

Anonymous Slogan of the IRA

4 We are all Home Rulers today.

Anonymous *The Times*, 26 Mar 1919

5 Ulster will fight; Ulster will be right.

Randolph Churchill (1849–95) British Conservative politician. Letter, 7 May 1886

6 By yesterday morning British troops were patrolling the streets of Belfast. I fear that once Catholics and Protestants get used to our presence they will hate us more than they hate each other.

Richard Crossman (1907–74) British politician. *Diaries*, 17 Aug 1969

7 Thus you have a starving population, an absentee aristocracy, and an alien Church, and in addition the weakest executive in the world. That is the Irish Question.

Benjamin Disraeli (1804–81) British statesman. Speech, House of Commons, 16 Feb 1844

8 I never met anyone in Ireland who understood the Irish question, except one Englishman who had only been there a week.

Keith Fraser (1867–1935) British politician. Speech, House of Commons, May 1919

9 It seems that the historic inability in Britain to comprehend Irish feelings and sensitivities still remains.

Charles Haughey (1925–) Irish statesman. Speech, Feb 1988

10 Worth seeing? yes; but not worth going to see.

Samuel Johnson (1709–84) British lexicographer. Referring to the Giant's Causeway. *Life of Johnson* (J. Boswell), Vol. III

11 Ireland is the old sow that eats her farrow.

James Joyce (1882–1941) Irish novelist. *A Portrait of the Artist as a Young Man*, Ch. 5

12 It is a symbol of Irish art. The cracked looking glass of a servant.

James Joyce *Ulysses*

13 The problem with Ireland is that it's a country full of genius, but with absolutely no talent.

Hugh Leonard (1926–) Irish dramatist. Said during an interview. *The Times*, Aug 1977

14 The harp that once through Tara's halls
The soul of music shed,
Now hangs as mute on Tara's walls
As if that soul were fled. –
So sleeps the pride of former days,
So glory's thrill is o'er;

And hearts, that once beat high for praise,
Now feel that pulse no more.

Thomas Moore (1779–1852) Irish poet. *Irish Melodies*, 'The Harp that Once'

15 It is a city where you can see a sparrow fall to the ground, and God watching it.

Conor Cruise O'Brien (1917–) Irish diplomat and writer. Referring to Dublin. Attrib.

16 When a man takes a farm from which another has been evicted, you must show him . . . by leaving him severely alone, by putting him into a moral Coventry, by isolating him from his kind as if he were a leper of old – you must show him your detestation of the crimes he has committed.

Charles Stewart Parnell (1846–91) Member of Parliament and champion of Irish Home Rule. The first person to be so treated was a Captain Boycott – hence the verb, 'to boycott'. Speech, Ennis, 19 Sept 1880

17 No man has a right to fix the boundary of the march of a nation; no man has a right to say to his country – thus far shalt thou go and no further.

Charles Stewart Parnell Speech at Cork, 21 Jan 1885

18 I will drive a coach and six horses through the Act of Settlement.

Stephen Rice (1637–1715) English politician. *State of the Protestants of Ireland* (W. King), Ch. 3

19 The English should give Ireland home rule – and reserve the motion picture rights.

Will Rogers (1879–1935) US actor and humorist. *Autobiography* (published posthumously)

20 Before Irish Home Rule is conceded by the Imperial Parliament, England as the predominant member of the three kingdoms will have to be convinced of its justice and equity.

Lord Rosebery (1847–1929) British statesman. Speech, House of Lords, 11 Mar 1894

21 The moment the very name of Ireland is mentioned, the English seem to bid adieu to common feeling, common prudence, and common sense, and to act with the barbarity of tyrants, and the fatuity of idiots.

Sydney Smith (1771–1845) British clergyman and essayist. *The Letters of Peter Plymley*

22 I would have liked to go to Ireland, but my grandmother would not let me. Perhaps she thought I wanted to take the little place.

Wilhelm II (1859–1941) King of Prussia and Emperor of Germany. Queen Victoria was his grandmother. *Carson* (H. Montgomery Hyde), Ch. 9

IRISH

See also British, Ireland

1 Put an Irishman on the spit, and you can always get another Irishman to baste him.

Proverb

2 Other people have a nationality. The Irish and the Jews have a psychosis.

Brendan Behan (1923–64) Irish playwright. *Richard's Cork Leg*, I

3 The English and Americans dislike only *some* Irish – the same Irish that the Irish themselves detest, Irish writers – the ones that *think*.

Brendan Behan *Richard's Cork Leg*, I

4 Not in vain is Ireland pouring itself all over the earth. . . . The Irish, with their glowing hearts and reverent credulity, are needed in this cold age of intellect and skepticism.

Lydia M. Child (1802–80) US abolitionist campaigner. *Letters from New York*, Vol. I, No. 33, 8 Dec 1842

5 All races have produced notable economists, with the exception of the Irish who doubtless can protest their devotion to higher arts.

John Kenneth Galbraith (1908–) US economist. *The Age of Uncertainty*, Ch. 1

6 Irish Americans are about as Irish as Black Americans are African.

Bob Geldof (1952–) Irish rock musician. *The Observer*, 'Sayings of the Week', 22 Jun 1986

7 The Irish are a fair people; – they never speak well of one another.

Samuel Johnson (1709–84) British lexicographer. *Life of Johnson* (J. Boswell), Vol. II

8 The Irish don't know what they want and are prepared to fight to the death to get it.

Sidney Littlewood (1895–1967) President of The Law Society. Speech, 13 Apr 1961

9 Gladstone spent his declining years trying to guess the answer to the Irish Question; unfortunately, whenever he was getting warm, the Irish secretly changed the question.

W. C. Sellar (1898–1951) British humorous writer. *1066 And All That*

10 For howbeit the Irish might do very good Service, being a People removed from the Scottish, as well in Affections as Religion; yet it is not safe to train them up more than needs must in the military Way.

Thomas Wentworth (1593–1641) English statesman. Letter to King Charles I, from Ireland, 28 July 1638

IRON

1 An iron curtain has descended across the Continent.

Winston Churchill (1874–1965) British statesman. The phrase 'iron curtain' was originally coined by Joseph Goebbels. Address, Westminster College, Fulton, USA, 5 Mar 1946

2 The Right Hon. gentleman has sat so long on the fence that the iron has entered his soul.

David Lloyd George (1863–1945) British Liberal statesman. Referring to Sir John Simon. Attrib.

3 Under the spreading chestnut tree
The village smithy stands;
The smith, a mighty man is he,
With large and sinewy hands;
And the muscles of his brawny arms
Are strong as iron bands.

Henry Wadsworth Longfellow (1807–82) US poet. *The Village Blacksmith*

4 He gave a deep sigh – I saw the iron enter into his soul!

Laurence Sterne (1713–68) Irish-born British writer. *A Sentimental Journey*, 'The Captive. Paris'

IRREVOCABILITY

1 The die is cast.

Julius Caesar (100–44 BC) Roman general and statesman. Said on crossing the Rubicon (49 BC) at the start of his campaign against Pompey. Attrib.

2 What's done cannot be undone. To bed, to bed, to bed.

William Shakespeare (1564–1616) English dramatist. *Macbeth*, V:1

3 The Gods themselves cannot recall their gifts.

Alfred, Lord Tennyson (1809–92) British poet. *Tithonus*

ISLAM

1 Unlike Christianity, which preached a peace that it never achieved, Islam unashamedly came with a sword.

Steven Runciman (1903–) British academic and diplomat. *A History of the Crusades*, 'The First Crusade'

J

JACKSON, Andrew

(1767–1845) US statesman and soldier. A hero of the War of 1812, he served as US president from 1829 to 1937.

Quotations about Jackson

1 Where is there a chief magistrate of whom so much evil has been predicted, and from whom so much good has come?
Thomas H. Benton *30 Years in the U.S. Senate*, Vol. I

2 He was too generous to be frugal, too kindhearted to be thrifty, too honest to live above his means.
Vernon Parrington (1871–1929) *Main Currents in American Thought*, Vol. I, Bk. II

Quotations by Jackson

3 Elevate them guns a little lower.
Order given while watching the effect of the US artillery upon the British lines at the battle of New Orleans. Attrib.

JAMES, Henry

(1843–1916) US novelist, who spent much of his life in Europe (from 1876 in England). *Roderick Hudson* (1875), his first successful novel, was followed by *Washington Square* (1881), *The Bostonians* (1886), *The Turn of the Screw* (1898), *The Ambassadors* (1903), and several others.

Quotations about James

1 Henry James has a mind so fine that no idea could violate it.
T. S. Eliot (1888–1965) US-born British poet and dramatist. Attrib.

2 Henry James was one of the nicest old ladies I ever met.
William Faulkner (1897–1962) US novelist. Attrib.

3 The work of Henry James has always seemed divisible by a simple dynastic arrangement into three reigns. James I, James II, and the Old Pretender.
Philip Guedalla (1889–1944) British writer. *Collected Essays*, 'Men of Letters: Mr. Henry James'

Quotations by James

4 Live all you can; it's a mistake not to. It doesn't so much matter what you do in particular, so long as you have your life. If you haven't had that what *have* you had?
The Ambassadors, Bk. V, Ch. 2

5 Experience was to be taken as showing that one might get a five-pound note as one got a light for a cigarette; but one had to check the friendly impulse to ask for it in the same way.
The Awkward Age

6 It takes a great deal of history to produce a little literature.
Life of Nathaniel Hawthorne, Ch. 1

7 He was unperfect, unfinished, inartistic; he was worse than provincial – he was parochial.
Referring to Thoreau. *Life of Nathaniel Hawthorne*, Ch. 4

8 To kill a human being is, after all, the least injury you can do him.
My Friend Bingham

9 The only obligation to which in advance we may hold a novel, without incurring the accusation of being arbitrary, is that it be interesting.
Partial Portraits, 'The Art of Fiction'

10 Experience is never limited, and it is never complete; it is an immense sensibility, a kind of huge spider-web of the finest silken threads suspended in the chamber of consciousness, and catching every air-borne particle in its tissue.
Partial Portraits, 'The Art of Fiction'

11 What is character but the determination of incident? What is incident but the illustration of character?
Partial Portraits, 'The Art of Fiction'

12 The superiority of one man's opinion over another's is never so great as when the opinion is about a woman.
The Tragic Muse, Ch. 9

13 Nurse, take away the candle and spare my blushes.
On being informed, while confined to his bed, that he had been awarded the Order of Merit. *The American Treasury* (C. Fadiman)

14 Summer afternoon – summer afternoon; to me those have always been the two most beautiful words in the English language.
A Backward Glance (Edith Wharton), Ch. 10

15 So it has come at last, the distinguished thing.
Referring to his own death. *A Backward Glance* (Edith Wharton), Ch. 14

JAZZ

1 Though the Jazz Age continued, it became less and less an affair of youth. The sequel was like a children's party taken over by the elders.
F. Scott Fitzgerald (1896–1940) US novelist. *The Crack-Up*

2 The basic difference between classical music and jazz is that in the former the music is always greater than its performance – whereas the way jazz is performed is always more important than what is being played.
André Previn (1929–) German-born US conductor. *An Encyclopedia of Quotations about Music* (Nat Shapiro)

3 Jazz will endure just as long as people hear it through their feet instead of their brains.
John Philip Sousa (1854–1932) US composer, conductor, and writer. Attrib.

JEALOUSY

1 For the ear of jealousy heareth all things: and the noise of murmurings is not hid.
Bible: Wisdom 1:10

2 Jealousy is no more than feeling alone among smiling enemies.
Elizabeth Bowen (1899–1973) Irish novelist. *The House in Paris*

3 It is with jealousy as with the gout. When such distempers are in the blood, there is never any security against their breaking out; and that often on the slightest occasions, and when least suspected.
Henry Fielding (1707–54) English writer. *Tom Jones*, Bk. II, Ch. 3

4 The others were only my wives.

But you, my dear, will be my widow.
Sacha Guitry (1885–1957) French actor and dramatist. Allaying his fifth wife's jealousy of his previous wives. *Speaker's and Toastmaster's Handbook* (J. Brawle)

5 The secret of my success is that no woman has ever been jealous of me.
Elsa Maxwell (1883–1963) US songwriter, broadcaster, and actress. *The Natives were Friendly* (Noël Barber)

6 CLEOPATRA: If she first meet the curled Antony,
He'll make demand of her, and spend that kiss
Which is my heaven to have. Come, thou mortal wretch,
With thy sharp teeth this knot intrinsicate
Of life at once untie; poor venomous fool,
Be angry, and dispatch. O! couldst thou speak,
That I might hear thee call great Caesar ass
Unpolicied.
CHARMIAN: O eastern star!
CLEOPATRA: Peace! peace!
William Shakespeare (1564–1616) English dramatist. *Antony and Cleopatra*, V:2

7 I do not know the man I should avoid
So soon as that spare Cassius. He reads much;
He is a great observer, and he looks
Quite through the deeds of men; he loves no plays,
As thou dost, Antony; he hears no music;
Seldom he smiles, and smiles in such a sort
As if he mock'd himself, and scorn'd his spirit,
That could be mov'd to smile at anything.
Such men as he be never at heart's ease,
Whiles they behold a greater than themselves,
And therefore are they very dangerous.
William Shakespeare *Julius Caesar*, I:2

8 O, beware, my lord, of jealousy;
It is the green-ey'd monster which doth mock
The meat it feeds on.
William Shakespeare *Othello*, III:3

9 O curse of marriage,
That we can call these delicate creatures ours,
And not their appetites! I had rather be a toad,
And live upon the vapour of a dungeon,
Than keep a corner in the thing I love
For others' uses.
William Shakespeare *Othello*, III:3

10 Jealous souls will not be answer'd so;
They are not ever jealous for the cause,
But jealous for they are jealous.
William Shakespeare *Othello*, III:4

11 He hath a daily beauty in his life.
That makes me ugly.
William Shakespeare *Othello*, V:1

12 She is your treasure, she must have a husband;
I must dance bare-foot on her wedding day,
And, for your love to her, lead apes in hell.
William Shakespeare *The Taming of the Shrew*, II:1

JEFFERSON, Thomas

(1743–1826) US statesman; the third President (1801–09). He was the chief author of the Declaration of Independence.

Quotations about Jefferson

1 His attachment to those of his friends whom he could make useful to himself was thoroughgoing and exemplary.
John Quincy Adams (1767–1848) Sixth president of the USA. *Diary*, 29 July 1836

2 A gentleman of thirty-two who could calculate an eclipse, survey an estate, tie an artery, plan an edifice, try a cause, break a horse, dance a minuet, and play the violin.
James Parton *Life of Thomas Jefferson*, Ch. 19

Quotations by Jefferson

3 When in the course of human events, it becomes necessary for one people to dissolve the political bonds which have connected them with another, and to assume among the powers of the earth the separate and equal station to which the laws of nature and of Nature's God entitle them, a decent respect to the opinions of mankind requires that they should declare the causes which impel them to the separation.
Declaration of Independence, Preamble

4 We hold these truths to be sacred and undeniable; that all men are created equal and independent, that from that equal creation they derive rights inherent and inalienable, among which are the preservation of life, and liberty, and the pursuit of happiness.
Declaration of Independence (original draft)

5 We hold these truths to be self-evident: that all men are created equal; that they are endowed by their Creator with certain unalienable rights; that among these are life, liberty, and the pursuit of happiness.
Declaration of Independence, 4 July 1776

6 A little rebellion now and then is a good thing.
Letter to James Madison, 30 Jan 1787

7 The tree of liberty must be refreshed from time to time with the blood of patriots and tyrants. It is its natural manure.
Letter to W. S. Smith, 13 Nov 1787

JEWELRY

1 Don't ever wear artistic jewelry; it wrecks a woman's reputation.
Colette (1873–1954) French novelist. *Gigi*

2 Diamonds Are Forever.
Ian Fleming (1908–64) British writer. From the advertising slogan 'A Diamond is Forever' for De Beers Consolidated Mines. Book title

JEWS

See also Nazism, prejudice, race, religion

1 His Majesty's Government views with favour the establishment in Palestine of a national home for the Jewish people . . .
Arthur Balfour (1848–1930) British statesman. The so-called 'Balfour Declaration'. Letter to Lord Rothschild, 2 Nov 1917

2 Other people have a nationality. The Irish and the Jews have a psychosis.
Brendan Behan (1923–64) Irish playwright. *Richard's Cork Leg*, I

3 The gentleman will please remember that when his half-civilized ancestors were hunting the

wild boar in Silesia, mine were princes of the earth.

Judah Philip Benjamin (1811–84) US politician. Replying to a senator of Germanic origin who had made an antisemitic remark. Attrib.

4 Now the Lord had said unto Abram, Get thee out of thy country, and from thy kindred, and from thy father's house, unto a land that I will shew thee:
And I will make of thee a great nation, and I will bless thee, and make thy name great; and thou shalt be a blessing:
And I will bless them that bless thee, and curse him that curseth thee: and in thee shall all families of the earth be blessed.

Bible: Genesis 12:1–3

5 I'm Super-jew!

Lenny Bruce (1923–66) US satirist. Jumping from a window; he got away with a broken leg. *The Observer*, 21 Aug 1966

6 How odd
Of God
To choose
The Jews.

William Norman Ewer (1885–1976) British writer. For a reply see Cecil BROWNE

7 But not so odd
As those who choose
A Jewish God,
But spurn the Jews.

Cecil Browne In reply to EWER (above)

8 It is extremely difficult for a Jew to be converted, for how can he bring himself to believe in the divinity of – another Jew?

Heinrich Heine (1797–1856) German poet and writer. Attrib.

9 The final solution of the Jewish problem.

Adolf Hitler (1889–1945) German dictator. *The Final Solution* (G. Geitlinger)

10 For me this is a vital litmus test: no intellectual society can flourish where a Jew feels even slightly uneasy.

Paul Johnson (1928–) British editor. *The Sunday Times Magazine*, 6 Feb 1977

11 The very best that is in the Jewish blood: a faculty for pure disinterestedness, and warm, physically warm love, that seems to make the corpuscles of the blood glow.

D. H. Lawrence (1885–1930) British novelist. *Kangaroo*, Ch. 6

12 Since my daughter is only half-Jewish, could she go in the water up to her knees?

Groucho Marx (Julius Marx; 1895–1977) US comedian. When excluded from a beach club on racial grounds. *The Observer*, 21 Aug 1977

13 Pessimism is a luxury that a Jew never can allow himself.

Golda Meir (1898–1978) Russian-born Israeli stateswoman. *The Observer*, 'Sayings of the Year', 29 Dec 1974

14 There are not enough prisons and concentration camps in Palestine to hold all the Jews who are ready to defend their lives and property.

Golda Meir Speech, 2 May 1940

15 I'm not really a Jew; just Jew-ish, not the whole hog.

Jonathan Miller (1934–) British doctor and television and stage director. *Beyond the Fringe*

16 And furthermore did you know that behind the discovery of America there was a Jewish financier?

Mordecai Richler (1931–) Canadian novelist. *Cocksure*, Ch. 24

17 Doctor, my doctor, what do you say – let's put the id back in yid!

Philip Roth (1933–) US novelist. *Portnoy's Complaint*

18 A Jewish man with parents alive is a fifteen-year-old boy, and will remain a fifteen-year-old boy till they die.

Philip Roth *Portnoy's Complaint*

19 I believe that the Jews have made a contribution to the human condition out of all proportion to their numbers: I believe them to be an immense people. Not only have they supplied the world with two leaders of the stature of Jesus Christ and Karl Marx, but they have even indulged in the luxury of following neither one nor the other.

Peter Ustinov (1921–) British actor. *Dear Me*, Ch. 19

20 The law of dislike for the unlike will always prevail. And whereas the unlike is normally situated at a safe distance, the Jews bring the unlike into the heart of *every milieu*, and must there defend a frontier line as large as the world.

Israel Zangwill (1864–1926) British writer. *Speeches, Articles and Letters*, 'The Jewish Race'

21 No Jew was ever fool enough to turn Christian unless he was a clever man.

Israel Zangwill *Children of the Ghetto*, Ch. 1

JOHNSON, Lyndon B(aines)

(1908–73) US statesman. He became Democratic President from 1963 to 69. His increased involvement in the Vietnam war made him unpopular.

Quotations about Johnson

1 An extraordinarily gifted president who was the wrong man from the wrong place at the wrong time under the wrong circumstances.

Eric F. Goldman *The Tragedy of Lyndon Johnson*, Ch. 18

2 Lyndon acts like there was never going to be a tomorrow.

Lady Bird Johnson (1912–) Wife of Lyndon B. Johnson. Attrib.

3 Kennedy promised, Johnson delivered.

Arthur Schlesinger Jnr (1917–) US historian, educator, and author. *The Observer*, 20 Nov 1983

Quotations by Johnson

4 Jerry Ford is so dumb that he can't fart and chew gum at the same time.

Sometimes quoted as '. . . can't walk and chew gum'. *A Ford, Not a Lincoln* (R. Reeves), Ch. 1

5 If you're in politics and you can't tell when you walk into a room who's for you and who's against you, then you're in the wrong line of work.

The Lyndon Johnson Story (B. Mooney)

6 I am going to build the kind of nation that President Roosevelt hoped for, President Truman worked for and President Kennedy died for.

The Sunday Times, 27 Dec 1964

7 I'd much rather have that fellow inside my tent pissing out, than outside my tent pissing in.

When asked why he retained J. Edgar Hoover at the FBI. *Guardian Weekly*, 18 Dec 1971

JOHNSON, Samuel

(1709–84) British lexicographer and writer. His *Dictionary of the English Language* appeared in 1755. The moral fable *Rasselas* (1759) was followed by *The Lives of the English Poets* (1781). His close friend James Boswell wrote his celebrated biography, *Boswell's Life of Johnson* (1791).

Quotations about Johnson

1 There is no arguing with Johnson, for when his pistol misses fire, he knocks you down with the butt of it.
Oliver Goldsmith (1728–74) Irish-born British writer. *Life of Johnson* (J. Boswell)

2 That great Cham of Literature, Samuel Johnson.
Tobias Smollett (1721–71) British novelist. Letter to John Wilkes, 16 Mar 1759

3 Johnson made the most brutal speeches to living persons; for though he was good-natured at bottom he was ill-natured at top.
Horace Walpole (1717–97) British writer. *Letters*

Quotations by Johnson

4 Every quotation contributes something to the stability or enlargement of the language.
Dictionary of the English Language

5 But these were the dreams of a poet doomed at last to wake a lexicographer.
Dictionary of the English Language

6 I am not yet so lost in lexicography, as to forget that words are the daughters of earth, and that things are the sons of heaven. Language is only the instrument of science, and words are but the signs of ideas: I wish, however, that the instrument might be less apt to decay, and that signs might be permanent, like the things which they denote.
Dictionary of the English Language

7 I have protracted my work till most of those whom I wished to please have sunk into the grave; and success and miscarriage are empty sounds.
Dictionary of the English Language

8 *Dull.* 8. To make dictionaries is dull work.
Dictionary of the English Language

9 *Excise.* A hateful tax levied upon commodities.
Dictionary of the English Language

10 *Lexicographer.* A writer of dictionaries, a harmless drudge.
Dictionary of the English Language

11 *Net.* Anything reticulated or decussated at equal distances, with interstices between the intersections.
Dictionary of the English Language

12 *Oats.* A grain, which in England is generally given to horses, but in Scotland supports the people.
Dictionary of the English Language

13 *Patron.* Commonly a wretch who supports with insolence, and is paid with flattery.
Dictionary of the English Language

14 When the messenger who carried the last sheet to Millar returned, Johnson asked him, 'Well, what did he say?' – 'Sir (answered the messenger), he said, thank God I have done with him.' – 'I am glad (replied Johnson, with a smile) that he thanks God for anything.'
After the final page of his *Dictionary* had been delivered. *Life of Johnson* (J. Boswell)

15 When two Englishmen meet, their first talk is of the weather.
The Idler

16 Pleasure is very seldom found where it is sought; our brightest blazes of gladness are commonly kindled by unexpected sparks.
The Idler

17 We are inclined to believe those whom we do not know because they have never deceived us.
The Idler

18 A Scotchman must be a very sturdy moralist who does not love Scotland better than truth.
Journey to the Western Islands of Scotland, 'Col'

19 The reciprocal civility of authors is one of the most risible scenes in the farce of life.
Life of Sir Thomas Browne

20 The true genius is a mind of large general powers, accidentally determined to some particular direction.
Lives of the English Poets, 'Cowley'

21 I am disappointed by that stroke of death, which has eclipsed the gaiety of nations and impoverished the public stock of harmless pleasure.
Epitaph on David Garrick. *Lives of the English Poets*, 'Edmund Smith'

22 We are perpetually moralists, but we are geometricians only by chance. Our intercourse with intellectual nature is necessary; our speculations upon matter are voluntary, and at leisure.
Lives of the English Poets, 'Milton'

23 There are minds so impatient of inferiority that their gratitude is a species of revenge, and they return benefits, not because recompense is a pleasure, but because obligation is a pain.
The Rambler

24 I have laboured to refine our language to grammatical purity, and to clear it from colloquial barbarisms, licentious idioms, and irregular combinations.
The Rambler

25 The love of life is necessary to the vigorous prosecution of any undertaking.
The Rambler

26 Almost every man wastes part of his life in attempts to display qualities which he does not possess, and to gain applause which he cannot keep.
The Rambler

27 There is a certain race of men that either imagine it their duty, or make it their amusement, to hinder the reception of every work of learning or genius, who stand as sentinels in the avenues of fame, and value themselves upon giving Ignorance and Envy the first notice of a prey.
The Rambler

28 Human life is everywhere a state in which much is to be endured, and little to be enjoyed.
Rasselas, Ch. 11

29 Marriage has many pains, but celibacy has no pleasures.
Rasselas, Ch. 26

30 Integrity without knowledge is weak and useless, and knowledge without integrity is dangerous and dreadful.
Rasselas, Ch. 41

31 Madam, before you flatter a man so grossly to his face, you should

consider whether or not your flattery is worth his having.
Diary and Letters (Mme D'Arblay), Vol. I, Ch. 2

32 Every man has, some time in his life, an ambition to be a wag.
Diary and Letters (Mme D'Arblay), Vol. III, Ch. 46

33 If the man who turnips cries,
Cry not when his father dies,
'Tis a proof that he had rather
Have a turnip than his father.
Johnsonian Miscellanies (ed. G. B. Hill), Vol. I

34 GOLDSMITH. Here's such a stir about a fellow that has written one book, and I have written many.
JOHNSON. Ah, Doctor, there go two-and-forty sixpences you know to one guinea.
Referring to Beattie's *Essay on Truth*. *Johnsonian Miscellanies* (ed. G. B. Hill), Vol. I

35 It is very strange, and very melancholy, that the paucity of human pleasures should persuade us ever to call hunting one of them.
Johnsonian Miscellanies (ed. G. B. Hill), Vol. I

36 Was there ever yet anything written by mere man that was wished longer by its readers, excepting *Don Quixote, Robinson Crusoe,* and the *Pilgrim's Progress*?
Johnsonian Miscellanies (ed. G. B. Hill), Vol. I

37 A man is in general better pleased when he has a good dinner upon his table, than when his wife talks Greek.
Johnsonian Miscellanies (ed. G. B. Hill), Vol. II

38 A tavern chair is the throne of human felicity.
Johnsonian Miscellanies (ed. G. B. Hill), Vol. II

39 The only sensual pleasure without vice.
Referring to music. *Johnsonian Miscellanies* (ed. G. B. Hill), Vol. II

40 Difficult do you call it, Sir? I wish it were impossible.
On hearing a famous violinist. *Johnsonian Miscellanies* (ed. G. B. Hill), Vol. II

41 What is written without effort is in general read without pleasure.
Johnsonian Miscellanies (ed. G. B. Hill), Vol. II

42 Love is the wisdom of the fool and the folly of the wise.
Johnsonian Miscellanies (ed. G. B. Hill), Vol. II

43 In my early years I read very hard. It is a sad reflection, but a true one, that I knew almost as much at eighteen as I do now.
Life of Johnson (J. Boswell), Vol. I

44 It is incident to physicians, I am afraid, beyond all other men, to mistake subsequence for consequence.
Life of Johnson (J. Boswell), Vol. I

45 He was a vicious man, but very kind to me. If you call a dog *Hervey*, I shall love him.
Life of Johnson (J. Boswell), Vol. I

46 I'll come no more behind your scenes, David; for the silk stockings and white bosoms of your actresses excite my amorous propensities.
Said to the actor-manager David Garrick. *Life of Johnson* (J. Boswell), Vol. I

47 A man may write at any time, if he will set himself doggedly to it.
Life of Johnson (J. Boswell), Vol. I

48 Is not a Patron, my Lord, one who looks with unconcern on a man struggling for life in the water, and, when he has reached ground, encumbers him with help? The notice which you have been pleased to take of my labours, had it been early, had been kind; but it has been delayed till I am indifferent, and cannot enjoy it; till I am solitary, and cannot impart it; till I am known, and do not want it.
Letter to Lord Chesterfield, 7 Feb 1755. *Life of Johnson* (J. Boswell), Vol. I

49 A fly, Sir, may sting a stately horse and make him wince; but one is but an insect, and the other is a horse still.
Referring to critics. *Life of Johnson* (J. Boswell), Vol. I

50 This man I thought had been a Lord among wits; but, I find, he is only a wit among Lords.
Referring to Lord Chesterfield. *Life of Johnson* (J. Boswell), Vol. I

51 They teach the morals of a whore, and the manners of a dancing master.
Referring to Lord Chesterfield's *Letters*. *Life of Johnson* (J. Boswell), Vol. I

52 There are two things which I am confident I can do very well: one is an introduction to any literary work, stating what it is to contain, and how it should be executed in the most perfect manner; the other is a conclusion, shewing from various causes why the execution has not been equal to what the author promised to himself and to the public.
Life of Johnson (J. Boswell), Vol. I

53 Ignorance, madam, pure ignorance.
His reply on being questioned, by a lady reader of his *Dictionary*, why he had defined 'pastern' as the 'knee' of a horse. *Life of Johnson* (J. Boswell), Vol. I

54 If a man does not make new acquaintance as he advances through life, he will soon find himself left alone. A man, Sir, should keep his friendship in constant repair.
Life of Johnson (J. Boswell), Vol. I

55 The booksellers are generous liberal-minded men.
Life of Johnson (J. Boswell), Vol. I

56 No man will be a sailor who has contrivance enough to get himself into a jail; for being in a ship is being in a jail, with the chance of being drowned . . . A man in a jail has more room, better food, and commonly better company.
Life of Johnson (J. Boswell), Vol. I

57 BOSWELL. I do indeed come from Scotland, but I cannot help it . . .
JOHNSON. That, Sir, I find, is what a very great many of your countrymen cannot help.
Life of Johnson (J. Boswell), Vol. I

58 Yes, Sir, many men, many women, and many children.
When asked by Dr Blair whether any man of their own time could have written the poems of Ossian. *Life of Johnson* (J. Boswell), Vol. I

59 You *may* abuse a tragedy, though you cannot write one. You may scold a carpenter who has made you a bad table, though you cannot make a table. It is not your trade to make tables.
Referring to the qualifications needed to indulge in literary criticism. *Life of Johnson* (J. Boswell), Vol. I

60 He is the richest author that ever grazed the common of literature.
Referring to Dr John Campbell. *Life of Johnson* (J. Boswell), Vol. I

61 Great abilities are not requisite for an Historian . . . Imagination is not required in any high degree.
Life of Johnson (J. Boswell), Vol. I

62 Norway, too, has noble wild prospects; and Lapland is remarkable for prodigious noble wild prospects. But, Sir, let me tell you, the noblest prospect which a Scotchman ever sees, is the high road that leads him to England!
Life of Johnson (J. Boswell), Vol. I

63 A man ought to read just as

inclination leads him; for what he reads as a task will do him little good.
Life of Johnson (J. Boswell), Vol. I

64 But if he does really think that there is no distinction between virtue and vice, why, Sir, when he leaves our houses let us count our spoons.
Life of Johnson (J. Boswell), Vol. I

65 Truth, Sir, is a cow, which will yield such people no more milk, and so they are gone to milk the bull.
Referring to sceptics. *Life of Johnson* (J. Boswell), Vol. I

66 Your levellers wish to level *down* as far as themselves; but they cannot bear levelling *up* to themselves.
Life of Johnson (J. Boswell), Vol. I

67 It is no matter what you teach them first, any more than what leg you shall put into your breeches first.
Referring to the education of children. *Life of Johnson* (J. Boswell), Vol. I

68 It is burning a farthing candle at Dover, to shew light at Calais.
Referring to the impact of Sheridan's works upon the English language. *Life of Johnson* (J. Boswell), Vol. I

69 A woman's preaching is like a dog's walking on his hinder legs. It is not done well; but you are surprised to find it done at all.
Life of Johnson (J. Boswell), Vol. I

70 This was a good dinner enough, to be sure; but it was not a dinner to *ask* a man to.
Life of Johnson (J. Boswell), Vol. I

71 I refute it *thus*.
Replying to Boswell's contention that they were unable to refute Bishop Berkeley's theory of matter, by kicking a large stone with his foot. *Life of Johnson* (J. Boswell), Vol. I

72 A very unclubable man.
Referring to Sir John Hawkins. *Life of Johnson* (J. Boswell), Vol. I

73 That all who are happy, are equally happy, is not true. A peasant and a philosopher may be equally *satisfied*, but not equally *happy*. Happiness consists in the multiplicity of agreeable consciousness.
Life of Johnson (J. Boswell), Vol. II

74 Our tastes greatly alter. The lad does not care for the child's rattle, and the old man does not care for the young man's whore.
Life of Johnson (J. Boswell), Vol. II

75 Shakespeare never had six lines together without a fault. Perhaps you may find seven, but this does not refute my general assertion.
Life of Johnson (J. Boswell), Vol. II

76 Why, Sir, most schemes of political improvement are very laughable things.
Life of Johnson (J. Boswell), Vol. II

77 There is no idolatry in the Mass. They believe God to be there, and they adore him.
Life of Johnson (J. Boswell), Vol. II

78 It matters not how a man dies, but how he lives. The act of dying is not of importance, it lasts so short a time.
Life of Johnson (J. Boswell), Vol. II

79 That fellow seems to me to possess but one idea, and that is a wrong one.
Life of Johnson (J. Boswell), Vol. II

80 I do not care to speak ill of any man behind his back, but I believe the gentleman is an *attorney*.
Life of Johnson (J. Boswell), Vol. II

81 The triumph of hope over experience.
Referring to the hasty remarriage of an acquaintance following the death of his first wife, with whom he had been most unhappy. *Life of Johnson* (J. Boswell), Vol. II

82 Every man has a lurking wish to appear considerable in his native place.
Letter to Sir Joshua Reynolds. *Life of Johnson* (J. Boswell), Vol. II

83 I would not give half a guinea to live under one form of government rather than another. It is of no moment to the happiness of an individual.
Life of Johnson (J. Boswell), Vol. II

84 Sir, I perceive you are a vile Whig.
Speaking to Sir Adam Fergusson. *Life of Johnson* (J. Boswell), Vol. II

85 A man who is good enough to go to heaven, is good enough to be a clergyman.
Life of Johnson (J. Boswell), Vol. II

86 Much may be made of a Scotchman, if he be *caught* young.
Referring to Lord Mansfield. *Life of Johnson* (J. Boswell), Vol. II

87 ELPHINSTON. What, have you not read it through? . . .
JOHNSON. No, Sir, do *you* read books *through?*
Life of Johnson (J. Boswell), Vol. II

88 Read over your compositions, and where ever you meet with a passage which you think is particularly fine, strike it out.
Recalling the advice of a college tutor. *Life of Johnson* (J. Boswell), Vol. II

89 The woman's a whore, and there's an end on't.
Referring to Lady Diana Beauclerk. *Life of Johnson* (J. Boswell), Vol. II

90 The Irish are a fair people; – they never speak well of one another.
Life of Johnson (J. Boswell), Vol. II

91 There are few ways in which a man can be more innocently employed than in getting money.
Life of Johnson (J. Boswell), Vol. II

92 He was dull in a new way, and that made many people think him *great*.
Referring to the poet Thomas Gray. *Life of Johnson* (J. Boswell), Vol. II

93 I think the full tide of human existence is at Charing-Cross.
Life of Johnson (J. Boswell), Vol. II

94 A man will turn over half a library to make one book.
Life of Johnson (J. Boswell), Vol. II

95 Patriotism is the last refuge of a scoundrel.
Life of Johnson (J. Boswell), Vol. II

96 Their learning is like bread in a besieged town: every man gets a little, but no man gets a full meal.
Referring to education in Scotland. *Life of Johnson* (J. Boswell), Vol. II

97 Knowledge is of two kinds. We know a subject ourselves, or we know where we can find information upon it.
Life of Johnson (J. Boswell), Vol. II

98 Politics are now nothing more than a means of rising in the world.
Life of Johnson (J. Boswell), Vol. II

99 In lapidary inscriptions a man is not upon oath.
Life of Johnson (J. Boswell), Vol. II

100 There is now less flogging in our great schools than formerly, but then less is learned there; so that what the boys get at one end they lose at the other.
Life of Johnson (J. Boswell), Vol. II

101 When men come to like a sea-life, they are not fit to live on land.
Life of Johnson (J. Boswell), Vol. II

102 There is nothing which has yet been contrived by man, by which so much happiness is produced as by a good tavern or inn.
Life of Johnson (J. Boswell), Vol. II

103 Questioning is not the mode of conversation among gentlemen.
Life of Johnson (J. Boswell), Vol. II

104 Fine clothes are good only as they supply the want of other means of procuring respect.
Life of Johnson (J. Boswell), Vol. II

105 If a madman were to come into this room with a stick in his hand, no doubt we should pity the state of his mind; but our primary consideration would be to take care of ourselves. We should knock him down first, and pity him afterwards.
Life of Johnson (J. Boswell), Vol. III

106 Consider, Sir, how should you like, though conscious of your innocence, to be tried before a jury for a capital crime, once a week.
Life of Johnson (J. Boswell), Vol. III

107 We would all be idle if we could.
Life of Johnson (J. Boswell), Vol. III

108 No man but a blockhead ever wrote, except for money.
Life of Johnson (J. Boswell), Vol. III

109 It is better that some should be unhappy than that none should be happy, which would be the case in a general state of equality.
Life of Johnson (J. Boswell), Vol. III

110 A man who has not been in Italy, is always conscious of an inferiority, from his not having seen what it is expected a man should see. The grand object of travelling is to see the shores of the Mediterranean.
Life of Johnson (J. Boswell), Vol. III

111 'Why Sir, it is much easier to say what it is not. We all *know* what light is; but it is not easy to *tell* what it is.'
When asked, 'What is poetry'. *Life of Johnson* (J. Boswell), Vol. III

112 Nay, Madam, when you are declaiming, declaim; and when you are calculating, calculate.
Commenting on Mrs Thrales's discourse on the price of children's clothes. *Life of Johnson* (J. Boswell), Vol. III

113 Sir, it is not so much to be lamented that Old England is lost, as that the Scotch have found it.
Life of Johnson (J. Boswell), Vol. III

114 To Oliver Goldsmith, A Poet, Naturalist, and Historian, who left scarcely any style of writing untouched, and touched none that he did not adorn.
Epitaph on Goldsmith. *Life of Johnson* (J. Boswell), Vol. III

115 If I had no duties, and no reference to futurity, I would spend my life in driving briskly in a post-chaise with a pretty woman.
Life of Johnson (J. Boswell), Vol. III

116 Depend upon it, Sir, when a man knows he is to be hanged in a fortnight, it concentrates his mind wonderfully.
Life of Johnson (J. Boswell), Vol. III

117 When a man is tired of London, he is tired of life; for there is in London all that life can afford.
Life of Johnson (J. Boswell), Vol. III

118 He who praises everybody praises nobody.
Life of Johnson (J. Boswell), Vol. III

119 Round numbers are always false.
Life of Johnson (J. Boswell), Vol. III

120 All argument is against it; but all belief is for it.
Of the ghost of a dead person. *Life of Johnson* (J. Boswell), Vol. III

121 Seeing Scotland, Madam, is only seeing a worse England.
Life of Johnson (J. Boswell), Vol. III

122 A country governed by a despot is an inverted cone.
Life of Johnson (J. Boswell), Vol. III

123 I am willing to love all mankind, *except an American.*
Life of Johnson (J. Boswell), Vol. III

124 Sir, the insolence of wealth will creep out.
Life of Johnson (J. Boswell), Vol. III

125 All censure of a man's self is oblique praise. It is in order to shew how much he can spare.
Life of Johnson (J. Boswell), Vol. III

126 Were it not for imagination, Sir, a man would be as happy in the arms of a chambermaid as of a Duchess.
Life of Johnson (J. Boswell), Vol. III

127 There are innumerable questions to which the inquisitive mind can in this state receive no answer: Why do you and I exist? Why was this world created? Since it was to be created, why was it not created sooner?
Life of Johnson (J. Boswell), Vol. III

128 Claret is the liquor for boys; port for men; but he who aspires to be a hero must drink brandy.
Life of Johnson (J. Boswell), Vol. III

129 A man who exposes himself when he is intoxicated, has not the art of getting drunk.
Life of Johnson (J. Boswell), Vol. III

130 Worth seeing? yes; but not worth going to see.
Referring to the Giant's Causeway. *Life of Johnson* (J. Boswell), Vol. III

131 I have got no further than this: Every man has a right to utter what he thinks truth, and every other man has a right to knock him down for it. Martyrdom is the test.
Life of Johnson (J. Boswell), Vol. IV

132 They are forced plants, raised in a hot-bed; and they are poor plants; they are but cucumbers after all.
Referring to Gray's *Odes*. *Life of Johnson* (J. Boswell), Vol. IV

133 A Frenchman must be always talking, whether he knows anything of the matter or not; an Englishman is content to say nothing, when he has nothing to say.
Life of Johnson (J. Boswell), Vol. IV

134 Sir, your wife, under pretence of keeping a bawdy-house, is a receiver of stolen goods.
An example of the customary badinage between travellers on the Thames. *Life of Johnson* (J. Boswell), Vol. IV

135 Depend upon it that if a man talks of his misfortunes there is something in them that is not disagreeable to him; for where there is nothing but pure misery there never is any recourse to the mention of it.
Life of Johnson (J. Boswell), Vol. IV

136 Mrs Montagu has dropt me. Now, Sir, there are people whom one should like very well to drop, but

would not wish to be dropped by.
Life of Johnson (J. Boswell), Vol. IV

137 Classical quotation is the *parole* of literary men all over the world.
Life of Johnson (J. Boswell), Vol. IV

138 I have two very cogent reasons for not printing any list of subscribers; – one, that I have lost all the names, – the other, that I have spent all the money.
Referring to subscribers to his *Dictionary of the English Language*. *Life of Johnson* (J. Boswell), Vol. IV

139 Always, Sir, set a high value on spontaneous kindness. He whose inclination prompts him to cultivate your friendship of his own accord, will love you more than one whom you have been at pains to attach to you.
Life of Johnson (J. Boswell), Vol. IV

140 Resolve not to be poor: whatever you have, spend less. Poverty is a great enemy to human happiness; it certainly destroys liberty, and it makes some virtues impracticable and others extremely difficult.
Life of Johnson (J. Boswell), Vol. IV

141 I hate a fellow whom pride, or cowardice, or laziness drives into a corner, and who does nothing when he is there but sit and *growl*; let him come out as I do, and *bark*.
Life of Johnson (J. Boswell), Vol. IV

142 How few of his friends' houses would a man choose to be at when he is sick.
Life of Johnson (J. Boswell), Vol. IV

143 There is a wicked inclination in most people to suppose an old man decayed in his intellects. If a young or middle-aged man, when leaving a company, does not recollect where he laid his hat, it is nothing; but if the same inattention is discovered in an old man, people will shrug up their shoulders, and say, 'His memory is going.'
Life of Johnson (J. Boswell), Vol. IV

144 Sir, there is no settling the point of precedency between a louse and a flea.
When Maurice Morgann asked him who he considered to be the better poet – Smart or Derrick. *Life of Johnson* (J. Boswell), Vol. IV

145 When I observed he was a fine cat, saying, 'why yes, Sir, but I have had cats whom I liked better than this'; and then as if perceiving Hodge to be out of countenance, adding, 'but he is a very fine cat, a very fine cat indeed.'
Life of Johnson (J. Boswell), Vol. IV

146 My dear friend, clear your *mind* of cant . . . You may *talk* in this manner; it is a mode of talking in Society: but don't *think* foolishly.
Life of Johnson (J. Boswell), Vol. IV

147 As I know more of mankind I expect less of them, and am ready now to call a man *a good man*, upon easier terms than I was formerly.
Life of Johnson (J. Boswell), Vol. IV

148 If a man were to go by chance at the same time with Burke under a shed, to shun a shower, he would say – 'this is an extraordinary man.'
Referring to Edmund Burke. *Life of Johnson* (J. Boswell), Vol. IV

149 It is as bad as bad can be: it is ill-fed, ill-killed, ill-kept, and ill-drest.
About the roast mutton at an inn. *Life of Johnson* (J. Boswell), Vol. IV

150 Milton, Madam, was a genius that could cut a Colossus from a rock; but could not carve heads upon cherry-stones.
When Miss Hannah More had wondered why Milton could write the epic *Paradise Lost* but only very poor sonnets. *Life of Johnson* (J. Boswell), Vol. IV

151 Sir, I have found you an argument; but I am not obliged to find you an understanding.
Life of Johnson (J. Boswell), Vol. IV

152 No man is a hypocrite in his pleasures.
Life of Johnson (J. Boswell), Vol. IV

153 Dublin, though a place much worse than London, is not so bad as Iceland.
Letter to Mrs Christopher Smart. *Life of Johnson* (J. Boswell), Vol. IV

154 Sir, I look upon every day to be lost, in which I do not make a new acquaintance.
Life of Johnson (J. Boswell), Vol. IV

155 I will be conquered; I will not capitulate.
Referring to his illness. *Life of Johnson* (J. Boswell), Vol. IV

156 A cow is a very good animal in the field; but we turn her out of a garden.
Responding to Boswell's objections to the expulsion of six Methodists from Oxford University. *The Personal History of Samuel Johnson* (C. Hibbert)

157 A lawyer has no business with the justice or injustice of the cause which he undertakes, unless his client asks his opinion, and then he is bound to give it honestly. The justice or injustice of the cause is to be decided by the judge.
Tour to the Hebrides (J. Boswell)

158 I have, all my life long, been lying till noon; yet I tell all young men, and tell them with great sincerity, that nobody who does not rise early will ever do any good.
Tour to the Hebrides (J. Boswell)

159 I am always sorry when any language is lost, because languages are the pedigree of nations.
Tour to the Hebrides (J. Boswell)

160 No, Sir; there were people who died of dropsies, which they contracted in trying to get drunk.
Scornfully criticizing the strength of the wine in Scotland before the Act of Union in response to Boswell's claim that there had been a lot of drunkenness. *Tour to the Hebrides* (J. Boswell)

161 A cucumber should be well sliced, and dressed with pepper and vinegar, and then thrown out, as good for nothing.
Tour to the Hebrides (J. Boswell)

162 Come, let me know what it is that makes a Scotchman happy!
Ordering for himself a glass of whisky. *Tour to the Hebrndes* (J. Boswell)

163 I am sorry I have not learned to play at cards. It is very useful in life: it generates kindness and consolidates society.
Tour to the Hebrides (J. Boswell)

164 Fly fishing may be a very pleasant amusement; but angling or float fishing I can only compare to a stick and a string, with a worm at one end and a fool at the other.
Attrib. in *Instructions to Young Sportsmen* (Hawker)

JOKES

1 Housekeeping ain't no joke.
Louisa May Alcott (1832–88) US novelist. *Little Women*, Pt. I

2 A rich man's joke is always funny.
Thomas Edward Brown (1830–97) British poet. *The Doctor*

3 He cannot bear old men's jokes. That is not new. But now he begins to think of them himself.
Max Frisch (1911–) Swiss dramatist and novelist. *Sketchbook 1966–71*

4 Forgive, O Lord, my little jokes on Thee
And I'll forgive Thy great big one on me.
Robert Frost (1875–1963) US poet. *In the clearing*, 'Cluster of Faith'

5 I don't make jokes – I just watch the government and report the facts.
Will Rogers (1879–1935) US actor and humorist. *Saturday Review*, 'A Rogers Thesaurus', 25 Aug 1962

JONSON, Ben

(1573–1637) English dramatist and poet. His plays include *Volpone* (1606), *The Alchemist* (1610), and *Bartholomew Fair* (1614); he published two collections of verse.

Quotations about Jonson

1 He invades authors like a monarch and what would be theft in other poets, is only victory in him.
John Dryden (1631–1700) British poet and dramatist. *Essay of Dramatic Poesy*

2 O Rare Ben Jonson.
John Young Epitaph in Westminster Abbey

Quotations by Jonson

3 Fortune, that favours fools.
The Alchemist, Prologue

4 Neither do thou lust after that tawney weed tobacco.
Bartholomew Fair, II:6

5 Alas, all the castles I have, are built with air, thou know'st.
Eastward Ho, II:2

6 Ods me, I marvel what pleasure or felicity they have in taking their roguish tobacco. It is good for nothing but to choke a man, and fill him full of smoke and embers.
Every Man in His Humour, III:5

7 Drink to me only with thine eyes,
And I will pledge with mine;
Or leave a kiss but in the cup,
And I'll not look for wine.
The thirst that from the soul doth rise
Doth ask a drink divine;
But might I of Jove's nectar sup,
I would not change for thine.

I sent thee late a rosy wreath,
Not so much honouring thee,
As giving it a hope that there
It could not wither'd be.
The Forest, IX, 'To Celia'

8 They say princes learn no art truly, but the art of horsemanship. The reason is, the brave beast is no flatterer. He will throw a prince as soon as his groom.
Timber, or Discoveries made upon Men and Matter

9 Talking and eloquence are not the same: to speak, and to speak well, are two things.
Timber, or Discoveries made upon Men and Matter

10 Thou hadst small Latin, and less Greek.
To the Memory of William Shakespeare

11 He was not of an age, but for all time!
To the Memory of William Shakespeare

12 Sweet Swan of Avon!
To the Memory of William Shakespeare

13 She is Venus when she smiles;
But she's Juno when she walks,
And Minerva when she talks.
The Underwood, 'Celebration of Charis, V. His Discourse with Cupid'

14 Good morning to the day: and, next, my gold! –
Open the shrine, that I may see my saint.
Volpone, I:1

15 Calumnies are answered best with silence.
Volpone, II:2

16 Come, my Celia, let us prove,
While we can, the sports of love,
Time will not be ours for ever,
He, at length, our good will sever.
Volpone, III:6

JOURNALISM

See also editors, media, newspapers

1 *Punch* – the official journal of dentists' waiting rooms.
The Times, 7 Oct 1981

2 Have you noticed that life, real honest to goodness life, with murders and catastrophes and fabulous inheritances, happens almost exclusively in newspapers?
Jean Anouilh (1910–87) French dramatist. *The Rehearsal*

3 What the proprietorship of these papers is aiming at is power, and power without responsibility – the prerogative of the harlot through the ages.
Stanley Baldwin (1867–1947) British statesman. Attacking the press barons Lords Rothermere and Beaverbrook. It was first used by KIPLING *See also* DEVONSHIRE.
Speech, election rally, 18 Mar 1931

4 Christianity, of course but why journalism?
Arthur Balfour (1848–1930) British statesman. In reply to Frank Harris's remark, '. . . all the faults of the age come from Christianity and journalism'. *Autobiography* (Margot Asquith), Ch. 10

5 If you want to make mischief come and work on my papers.
Lord Beaverbrook (1879–1964) British newspaper owner and politician. Inviting Anthony Howard to join his staff. *Radio Times*, 27 June 1981

6 Who's in charge of the clattering train?
Lord Beaverbrook Attrib.

7 Go out and speak for the inarticulate and the submerged.
Lord Beaverbrook *Somerset Maugham* (E. Morgan)

8 Because he shakes hands with people's hearts.
Lord Beaverbrook On being asked why the sentimental writer Godfrey Winn was paid so much. *Somerset Maugham* (E. Morgan)

9 Journalists say a thing that they know isn't true, in the hope that if they keep on saying it long enough it will be true.
Arnold Bennett (1867–1931) British novelist. *The Title*, II

10 No news is good news; no journalists is even better.
Nicolas Bentley (1907–78) British cartoonist and writer. Attrib.

11 I read the newspaper avidly. It is my one form of continuous fiction.
Aneurin Bevan (1897–1960) British Labour politician. *The Observer*, 'Sayings of the Week', 3 Apr 1960

12 There is a bias in television journalism. It is not against any particular party or point of view – it is a bias against *understanding*.
John Birt (1944–) British TV executive. This launched a series of articles written jointly with Peter Jay. *The Times*, 28 Feb 1975

13 When a dog bites a man that is not news, but when a man bites a dog that is news.
John B. Bogart (1845–1920) US journalist. Sometimes attributed to Charles Dana and Amos Cummings. Attrib.

14 Journalism is the only job that requires no degrees, no diplomas and no specialised knowledge of any kind.
Patrick Campbell (1913–80) British humorous writer and editor. *My Life and Easy Times*

15 Journalism largely consists of saying 'Lord Jones is dead' to people who never knew Lord Jones was alive.
G. K. Chesterton (1874–1936) British writer. Attrib.

16 Literature is the art of writing something that will be read twice; journalism what will be grasped at once.
Cyril Connolly (1903–74) British journalist. *Enemies of Promise*, Ch. 3

17 I hesitate to say what the functions of the modern journalist may be; but I imagine that they do not exclude the intelligent anticipation of facts even before they occur.
Lord Curzon (1859–1925) British politician. Speech, House of Commons, 29 Mar 1898

18 Good God, that's done it. He's lost us the tarts' vote.
Duke of Devonshire (1895–1950) Conservative politician. Referring to Stanley BALDWIN's attack on newspaper proprietors; recalled by Harold Macmillan. Attrib.

19 I am myself a gentleman of the Press, and I bear no other scutcheon.
Benjamin Disraeli (1804–81) British statesman. Speech, House of Commons, 18 Feb 1863

20 Backward ran sentences until reeled the mind.
Wolcott Gibbs (1902–58) US writer. Parodying the style of *Time* magazine. *More in Sorrow*

21 I'm not allowed to say how many planes joined the raid but I counted them all out and I counted them all back.
Brian Hanrahan (1949–) British journalist. Reporting a British air attack in the opening phase of the Falklands War. BBC broadcast, 1 May 1982

22 Good taste is, of course, an utterly dispensable part of any journalist's equipment.
Michael Hogg *Daily Telegraph*, 2 Dec 1978

23 Editor: a person employed by a newspaper whose business it is to separate the wheat from the chaff and to see that chaff is printed.
'Kin' Hubbard (1868–1930) US humorist. *A Thousand and One Epigrams*

24 Blood sport is brought to its ultimate refinement in the gossip columns.
Bernard Ingham (1932–) British journalist. *The Observer*, 'Sayings of the Week', 28 Dec 1986

25 The Liberty of the press is the *Palladium* of all the civil, political and religious rights of an Englishman.
Junius An unidentified writer of letters (1769–72) to the *London Public Advertiser*. *Letters*, 'Dedication'

26 Newspapers always excite curiosity. No one ever lays one down without a feeling of disappointment.
Charles Lamb (1775–1834) British essayist. *Last Essays of Elia*, 'Detached Thoughts on Books and Reading'

27 On the whole I would not say that our Press is obscene. I would say that it trembles on the brink of obscenity.
Lord Longford (1905–) British politician and social reformer. *The Observer*, 'Sayings of the Year', 1963

28 . . . more attentive to the minute hand of history than to the hour hand.
Desmond Macarthy (1887–1952) British writer and theater critic. Referring to journalism. *Curtains* (K. Tynan)

29 The gallery in which the reporters sit has become a fourth estate of the realm.
Lord Macaulay (1800–59) British historian. Referring to the press gallery in the House of Commons. *Historical Essays Contributed to the 'Edinburgh Review'*, Hallam's 'Constitutional History'

30 Once a newspaper touches a story, the facts are lost forever, even to the protagonists.
Norman Mailer (1923–) US writer. *The Presidential Papers*

31 A good newspaper, I suppose, is a nation talking to itself.
Arthur Miller (1915–) US dramatist. *The Observer*, 'Sayings of the Week', 26 Nov 1961

32 SIXTY HORSES WEDGED IN A CHIMNEY
The story to fit this sensational headline has not turned up yet.
J. B. Morton (1893–1979) British journalist. *The Best of Beachcomber*, 'Mr Justice Cocklecarrot: Home Life'

33 A reporter is a man who has renounced everything in life but the world, the flesh, and the devil.
David Murray (1888–1962) British journalist. *The Observer*, 'Sayings of the Week', 5 July 1931

34 We live under a government of men and morning newspapers.
Wendell Phillips (1811–84) US reformer. *Address: The Press*

35 The *New Yorker* will not be edited for the old lady from Dubuque.
Harold W. Ross (1892–1951) US journalist. Attrib.

36 Its primary office is the gathering of news. At the peril of its soul it must see that the supply is not tainted. Neither in what it gives, nor in what it does not give, nor in the mode of presentation, must the unclouded face of truth suffer wrong. Comment is free but facts are sacred.
C. P. Scott (1846–1932) British journalist. *Manchester Guardian*, 6 May 1926

37 He's someone who flies around from hotel to hotel and thinks the most interesting thing about any story is the fact that he has arrived to cover it.
Tom Stoppard (1937–) Czech-born British dramatist. Referring to foreign correspondents. *Night and Day*, I

38 MILNE. No matter how imperfect things are, if you've got a free press everything is correctable, and without it everything is conceivable.
RUTH. I'm with you on the free press. It's the newspapers I can't stand.
Tom Stoppard *Night and Day*, I

39 Freedom of the press in Britain is freedom to print such of the proprietor's prejudices as the advertisers don't object to.
Hannen Swaffer (1879–1962) British journalist. Attrib.

40 The only qualities essential for real success in journalism are rat-like cunning, a plausible manner, and a little literary ability.
Nicholas Tomalin (1931–73) British journalist. *The Sunday Times Magazine*, 26 Oct 1969

41 Journalism – an ability to meet the challenge of filling the space.
Rebecca West (Cicely Isabel Fairfield; 1892–1983) British novelist and journalist. *The New York Herald Tribune*, 22 April 1956

42 There is much to be said in favour of modern journalism. By giving us the opinions of the uneducated, it

keeps us in touch with the ignorance of the community.
Oscar Wilde (1854–1900) Irish-born British dramatist. *The Critic as Artist*, Pt. 2

43 You cannot hope
to bribe or twist,
thank God! the
British journalist.

But, seeing what
the man will do
unbribed, there's
no occasion to.

Humbert Wolfe (1886–1940) British poet. *The Uncelestial City*, Bk. I, 'Over the Fire'

44 Rock journalism is people who can't write interviewing people who can't talk for people who can't read.
Frank Zappa (1940–) US rock musician. Attrib.

JOY

1 One joy scatters a hundred griefs.
Proverb

2 On with the dance! let joy be unconfined;
No sleep till morn, when Youth and Pleasure meet
To chase the glowing Hours with flying feet.
Lord Byron (1788–1824) British poet. *Childe Harold's Pilgrimage*, III

3 I remember, I remember,
The fir trees dark and high;
I used to think their slender tops
Were close against the sky:
It was a childish ignorance,
But now 'tis little joy
To know I'm farther off from heav'n
Than when I was a boy.
Thomas Hood (1799–1845) British poet. *I Remember*

4 A thing of beauty is a joy for ever:
Its loveliness increases; it will never
Pass into nothingness; but still will keep
A bower quiet for us, and a sleep
Full of sweet dreams, and health, and quiet breathing.
John Keats (1795–1821) British poet. *Endymion*, I

5 . . . we could never learn to be brave and patient, if there were only joy in the world.
Helen Keller (1880–1968) US writer and lecturer. *Atlantic Monthly* (May 1890)

6 Silence is the perfectest herald of joy: I were but little happy if I could say how much.
William Shakespeare (1564–1616) English dramatist. *Much Ado About Nothing*, II:1

JUDGMENT

1 And this is the writing that was written, MENE, MENE, TEKEL, UPHARSIN.
This is the interpretation of the thing: MENE; God hath numbered thy kingdom, and finished it.
TEKEL; Thou art weighed in the balances, and art found wanting.
PERES; Thy kingdom is divided, and given to the Medes and Persians.
Bible: Daniel 5:25–28

2 Grudge not one against another, brethren, lest ye be condemned: behold, the judge standeth before the door.
Bible: James 5:9

3 And he saith unto him, Out of thine own mouth will I judge thee, thou wicked servant. Thou knewest that I was an austere man, taking up that I laid not down, and reaping that I did not sow.
Bible: Luke 19:22

4 Judge not, that ye be not judged.
Bible: Matthew 7:1

5 And why beholdest thou the mote that is in thy brother's eye, but considerest not the beam that is in thine own eye?
Bible: Matthew 7:3

6 And I saw a great white throne, and him that sat on it, from whose face the earth and the heaven fled away; and there was found no place for them.
And I saw the dead, small and great, stand before God; and the books were opened: and another book was opened, which is the book of life: and the dead were judged out of those things which were written in the books, according to their works.
And the sea gave up the dead which were in it; and death and hell delivered up the dead which were in them: and they were judged every man according to their works.
Bible: Revelations 20:11–13

7 No man can justly censure or condemn another, because indeed no man truly knows another.
Thomas Browne (1605–82) English physician and writer. *Religio Medici*, Pt. II

8 Your representative owes you, not his industry only, but his judgement; and he betrays instead of serving you if he sacrifices it to your opinion.
Edmund Burke (1729–97) British politician. Speech to the electors of Bristol, 3 Nov 1774

9 You shall judge of a man by his foes as well as by his friends.
Joseph Conrad (Teodor Josef Konrad Korzeniowski; 1857–1924) Polish-born British novelist. *Lord Jim*, Ch. 34

10 Judge not the play before the play be done.
John Davies (1569–1626) English jurist. *Respice Finem*

11 Force, if unassisted by judgement, collapses through its own mass.
Horace (Quintus Horatius Flaccus; 65–8 BC) Roman poet. *Odes*, III

12 Let me remind you of the old maxim: people under suspicion are better moving than at rest, since at rest they may be sitting in the balance without knowing it, being weighed together with their sins.
Franz Kafka (1883–1924) Czech novelist. *The Trial*, Ch. 8

13 Consider what you think justice requires, and decide accordingly. But never give your reasons; for your judgement will probably be right, but your reasons will certainly be wrong.
Lord Mansfield (1705–93) British judge and politician. Advice given to a new colonial governor. *Lives of the Chief Justices* (Campbell), Ch. 40

14 Everyone complains of his memory, but no one complains of his judgement.
Duc de la Rochefoucauld (1613–80) French writer. *Maximes*, 89

JUSTICE

See also injustice, judgment, law, lawyers

1 The place of justice is a hallowed place.
Francis Bacon (1561–1626) English philosopher. *Essays*, 'Of Judicature'

2 When I came back to Dublin, I was court-martialled in my absence and sentenced to death in my absence, so I said they could shoot me in my absence.
Brendan Behan (1923–64) Irish playwright. *The Hostage*, I

3 Then the king answered and said, Give her the living child, and in no

wise slay it: she is the mother thereof.
And all Israel heard of the judgment which the king had judged; and they feared the king: for they saw that the wisdom of God was in him, to do judgment.
Bible: I Kings 3:27–28

4 It is better that ten guilty persons escape than one innocent suffer.
William Blackstone (1723–80) British jurist. *Commentaries on the Laws of England*, Bk. IV, Ch. 27

5 The rain it raineth on the just
And also on the unjust fella:
But chiefly on the just, because
The unjust steals the just's umbrella.
Charles Bowen (1835–94) British judge. *Sands of Time* (Walter Sichel)

6 Justice is being allowed to do whatever I like. Injustice is whatever prevents my doing it.
Samuel Butler (1835–1902) British writer. *Notebooks*

7 Trial by jury itself, instead of being a security to persons who are accused, will be a delusion, a mockery, and a snare.
Thomas Denman (1779–1854) British judge. Judgment in O'Connell v The Queen, 4 Sept 1844

8 I expect a judgment. Shortly.
Charles Dickens (1812–70) British novelist. *Bleak House*, Ch. 3

9 'It is my duty to warn you that it will be used against you,' cried the Inspector, with the magnificent fair play of the British criminal law.
Arthur Conan Doyle (1856–1930) British writer. *The Dancing Men*

10 Nevertheless, this measure is to be common to all the nation, whether Englishmen, Danes or Britons, and every province of my dominion to the end that poor men and rich may possess what they rightly acquire and that a thief may not find a place to bring what he has stolen.
Edgar (944–75) King of England. Law, 962/63

11 Let justice be done, though the world perish.
Ferdinand I (1503–64) Holy Roman Emperor. Attrib.

12 Ah, colonel, all's fair in love and war, you know.
Nathan Bedford Forrest (1821–77) Confederate general. Remark to a captured enemy officer who had been tricked into surrendering. *A Civil War Treasury* (B. Botkin)

13 Let no guilty man escape, if it can be avoided . . . No personal considerations should stand in the way of performing a public duty.
Ulysses Simpson Grant (1822–85) US general. Referring to the Whiskey Ring. Indorsement of a letter, 29 July 1875

14 Justice should not only be done, but should manifestly and undoubtedly be seen to be done.
Gordon Hewart (1870–1943) British lawyer and politician. *The Chief* (R. Jackson)

15 I have come to regard the law courts not as a cathedral but rather as a casino.
Richard Ingrams (1937–) British editor. *The Guardian*, 30 July 1977

16 I was not half bloody enough for him who sent me thither.
Judge Jeffreys (George, Baron J.; 1648–89) English Chief Justice and Lord Chancellor. Referring to his 'Bloody Assizes' following Monmouth's rebellion (1685). Remark made later (Apr 1689) to the chaplain of the Tower of London

17 Consider, Sir, how should you like, though conscious of your innocence, to be tried before a jury for a capital crime, once a week.
Samuel Johnson (1709–84) British lexicographer. *Life of Johnson* (J. Boswell), Vol. III

18 A lawyer has no business with the justice or injustice of the cause which he undertakes, unless his client asks his opinion, and then he is bound to give it honestly. The justice or injustice of the cause is to be decided by the judge.
Samuel Johnson *Tour to the Hebrides* (J. Boswell)

19 Justice is the constant and perpetual wish to render to every one his due.
Justinian I (482–565 AD) Byzantine emperor. *Institutes*, I

20 Justice is such a fine thing that we cannot pay too dearly for it.
Alain-René Lesage (1668–1747) French writer. *Crispin rival de son maître*, IX

21 I'm arm'd with more than complete steel –
The justice of my quarrel.
Christopher Marlowe (1564–93) English dramatist. Play also attributed to others. *Lust's Dominion*, IV:3

22 In England, Justice is open to all, like the Ritz hotel.
James Mathew (1830–1908) British judge. Also attrib. to Lord Darling. *Miscellany-at-Law* (R. E. Megarry)

23 Justice must not only be seen to be done but has to be seen to be believed.
J. B. Morton (1893–1979) British journalist. Attrib.

24 Justice is so subtle a thing, to interpret it one has only need of a heart.
José Garcia Oliver *The Spanish Civil War*

25 A judge is not supposed to know anything about the facts of life until they have been presented in evidence and explained to him at least three times.
Hubert Lister Parker (1900–72) Lord Chief Justice of England. *The Observer*, 'Sayings of the Week', 12 Mar 1961

26 The hungry judges soon the sentence sign,
And wretches hang that jury-men may dine.
Alexander Pope (1688–1744) British poet. *The Rape of the Lock*, III

27 The love of justice in most men is simply the fear of suffering injustice.
Duc de la Rochefoucauld (1613–80) French writer. *Maximes*, 78

28 A man who is good enough to shed his blood for the country is good enough to be given a square deal afterwards. More than that no man is entitled to, and less than that no man shall have.
Theodore Roosevelt (1858–1919) US Republican president. Speech at the Lincoln Monument, Springfield, Illinois, 4 June 1903

29 Haste still pays haste, and leisure answers leisure;
Like doth quit like, and Measure still for Measure.
William Shakespeare (1564–1616) English dramatist. *Measure for Measure*, V:1

30 This is a British murder inquiry and some degree of justice must be seen to be more or less done.
Tom Stoppard (1937–) Czech-born British dramatist. *Jumpers*, II

31 Under a government which imprisons any unjustly, the true place for a just man is also a prison.
Henry David Thoreau (1817–62) US writer. *Civil Disobedience*

K

KEATS, John

(1795–1821) British poet. Trained as a doctor, he devoted most of his short life to poetry. *Endymion* (1818) was attacked by the critics but he eventually established his reputation with *La Belle Dame Sans Merci* (1820), *Ode to a Nightingale* (1820), and other works. He died in Rome of tuberculosis.

Quotations about Keats

1 Here is Jonny Keats' piss-a-bed poetry. No more Keats, I entreat.
Lord Byron (1788–1824) British poet. Letter to the publisher John Murray, 12 Oct 1821

2 I see a schoolboy when I think of him
With face and nose pressed to a sweetshop window.
W. B. Yeats (1865–1939) Irish poet. Attrib.

Quotations by Keats

3 Bright star, would I were steadfast as thou art.
Bright Star

4 A thing of beauty is a joy for ever:
Its loveliness increases; it will never
Pass into nothingness; but still will keep
A bower quiet for us, and a sleep
Full of sweet dreams, and health, and quiet breathing.
Endymion, I

5 Their smiles,
Wan as primroses gather'd at midnight
By chilly finger'd spring.
Endymion, IV

6 St Agnes' Eve – Ah, bitter chill it was!
The owl, for all his feathers, was a-cold;
The hare limp'd trembling through the frozen grass,
And silent was the flock in woolly fold.
The Eve of Saint Agnes, I

7 The Beadsman, after thousand aves told,
For aye unsought-for slept among his ashes cold.
The Eve of Saint Agnes, I

8 Soft adorings from their loves receive
Upon the honey'd middle of the night.
The Eve of Saint Agnes, VI

9 The music, yearning like a God in pain.
The Eve of Saint Agnes, VII

10 He play'd an ancient ditty, long since mute,
In Provence call'd, 'La belle dame sans mercy'.
The Eve of Saint Agnes, XXXIII

11 And they are gone: aye, ages long ago
These lovers fled away into the storm.
The Eve of Saint Agnes, XLII

12 Fanatics have their dreams, wherewith they weave
A paradise for a sect.
The Fall of Hyperion, I

13 The poet and the dreamer are distinct,
Diverse, sheer opposite, antipodes.
The one pours out a balm upon the world,
The other vexes it.
The Fall of Hyperion, I

14 Ever let the fancy roam,
Pleasure never is at home.
Fancy, I

15 Where's the cheek that doth not fade,
Too much gaz'd at? Where's the maid
Whose lip mature is ever new?
Fancy, I

16 Four seasons fill the measure of the year;
There are four seasons in the mind of men.
Four Seasons

17 O aching time! O moments big as years!
Hyperion, I

18 As when, upon a trancèd summer-night,
Those green-rob'd senators of mighty woods,
Tall oaks, branch-charmèd by the earnest stars,
Dream, and so dream all night without a stir.
Hyperion, I

19 Oh what can ail thee, knight at arms
Alone and palely loitering;
The sedge has wither'd from the lake,
And no birds sing.
La Belle Dame Sans Merci

20 La belle Dame sans Merci
Hath thee in thrall!
La Belle Dame Sans Merci

21 Love in a hut, with water and a crust,
Is – Love, forgive us! – cinders, ashes, dust;
Love in a palace is perhaps at last
More grievous torment than a hermit's fast.
Lamia, II

22 Do not all charms fly
At the mere touch of cold philosophy?
Lamia, II

23 Souls of poets dead and gone,
What Elysium have ye known,
Happy field or mossy cavern,
Choicer than the Mermaid Tavern?
Have ye tippled drink more fine
Than mine host's Canary wine?
Lines on the Mermaid Tavern

24 Thou still unravish'd bride of quietness,
Thou foster-child of silence and slow time.
Ode on a Grecian Urn

25 Heard melodies are sweet, but those unheard
Are sweeter; therefore, ye soft pipes, play on.
Ode on a Grecian Urn

26 Thou, silent form, dost tease us out of thought
As doth eternity: Cold Pastoral!
Ode on a Grecian Urn

27 'Beauty is truth, truth beauty,' – that is all
Ye know on earth, and all ye need to know.
Ode on a Grecian Urn

28 For ever warm and still to be enjoy'd,
For ever panting and for ever young;
All breathing human passion far above,
That leaves a heart high-sorrowful and cloy'd,

A burning forehead, and a parching tongue.
Ode on a Grecian Urn

29 No, no, go not to Lethe, neither twist
Wolf's-bane, tight-rooted, for its poisonous wine.
Ode on Melancholy

30 Nor let the beetle, nor the death-moth be
Your mournful Psyche.
Ode on Melancholy

31 Ay, in the very temple of delight
Veil'd Melancholy has her sovran shrine.
Though seen of none save him whose strenuous tongue
Can burst Joy's grape against his palate fine.
Ode on Melancholy

32 My heart aches, and a drowsy numbness pains
My sense.
Ode to a Nightingale

33 O, for a draught of vintage! that hath been
Cool'd a long age in the deep-delved earth.
Ode to a Nightingale

34 O for a beaker full of the warm South,
Full of the true, the blushful Hippocrene,
With beaded bubbles winking at the brim,
And purple-stained mouth.
Ode to a Nightingale

35 Fade far away, dissolve, and quite forget
What thou among the leaves hast never known,
The weariness, the fever, and the fret,
Here, where men sit and hear each other groan.
Ode to a Nightingale

36 Thou wast not born for death, immortal Bird!
No hungry generations tread thee down;
The voice I hear this passing night was heard
In ancient days by emperor and clown:
Perhaps the self-same song that found a path
Through the sad heart of Ruth, when sick for home,
She stood in tears amid the alien corn;
The same that oft-times hath
Charm'd magic casements, opening on the foam
Of perilous seas, in faery lands forlorn.
Ode to a Nightingale

37 Darkling I listen; and, for many a time
I have been half in love with easeful Death,
Call'd him soft names in many a mused rhyme,
To take into the air my quiet breath;
Now more than ever seems it rich to die,
To cease upon the midnight with no pain,
While thou art pouring forth thy soul abroad
In such an ecstasy!
Ode to a Nightingale

38 Much have I travell'd in the realms of gold,
And many goodly states and kingdoms seen.
On first looking into Chapman's Homer

39 Then felt I like some watcher of the skies
When a new planet swims into his ken;
Or like stout Cortez when with eagle eyes
He star'd at the Pacific – and all his men
Look'd at each other with a wild surmise –
Silent, upon a peak in Darien.
On first looking into Chapman's Homer

40 It keeps eternal whisperings around
Desolate shores, and with its mighty swell
Gluts twice ten thousand Caverns.
On the Sea

41 A drainless shower
Of light is poesy; 'tis the supreme of power;
'Tis might half slumb'ring on its own right arm.
Sleep and Poetry

42 Season of mists and mellow fruitfulness,
Close bosom-friend of the maturing sun;
Conspiring with him how to load and bless
With fruit the vines that round the thatch-eaves run.
To Autumn

43 Where are the songs of Spring? Ay, where are they?
To Autumn

44 O soft embalmer of the still midnight.
To Sleep

45 Turn the key deftly in the oiled wards,
And seal the hushed casket of my soul.
To Sleep

46 Here lies one whose name was writ in water.
Suggesting his own epitaph (recalling a line from *Philaster* by Beaumont and Fletcher). *Life of Keats* (Lord Houghton), Ch. 2

47 A long poem is a test of invention which I take to be the Polar star of poetry, as fancy is the sails, and imagination the rudder.
Letter to Benjamin Bailey, 8 Oct 1817

48 I am certain of nothing but the holiness of the heart's affections and the truth of imagination – what the imagination seizes as beauty must be truth – whether it existed before or not.
Letter to Benjamin Bailey, 22 Nov 1817

49 O for a life of sensations rather than of thoughts!
Letter to Benjamin Bailey, 22 Nov 1817

50 Negative Capability, that is, when a man is capable of being in uncertainties, mysteries, doubts, without any irritable reaching after fact and reason.
Letter to G. and T. Keats, 21 Dec 1817

51 The excellence of every art is its intensity, capable of making all disagreeables evaporate, from their being in close relationship with beauty and truth.
Letter to G. and T. Keats, 21 Dec 1817

52 There is an old saying 'well begun is half done' – 'tis a bad one. I would use instead – Not begun at all until half done.
Letter, 1817

53 We hate poetry that has a palpable design upon us – and if we do not agree, seems to put its hand in its breeches pocket. Poetry should be great and unobtrusive, a thing which enters into one's soul, and does not startle or amaze it with itself, but with its subject.
Letter to J. H. Reynolds, 3 Feb 1818

54 If poetry comes not as naturally as

leaves to a tree it had better not come at all.
Letter to John Taylor, 27 Feb 1818

55 Scenery is fine – but human nature is finer.
Letter to Benjamin Bailey, 13 Mar 1818

56 Axioms in philosophy are not axioms until they are proved upon our pulses; we read fine things but never feel them to the full until we have gone the same steps as the author.
Letter to J. H. Reynolds, 3 May 1818

57 I am in that temper that if I were under water I would scarcely kick to come to the top.
Letter to Benjamin Bailey, 21 May 1818

58 I do think better of womankind than to suppose they care whether Mister John Keats five feet high likes them or not.
Letter to Benjamin Bailey, 18 July 1818

59 I think I shall be among the English Poets after my death.
Letter to George and Georgiana Keats, 14 Oct 1818

60 I never can feel certain of any truth but from a clear perception of its beauty.
Letter to George and Georgiana Keats, 16 Dec 1818–4 Jan 1819

61 Nothing ever becomes real till it is experienced – even a proverb is no proverb to you till your life has illustrated it.
Letter to George and Georgiana Keats, 19 Mar 1819

62 My friends should drink a dozen of Claret on my Tomb.
Letter to Benjamin Bailey, 14 Aug 1819

63 Give me books, fruit, French wine and fine weather and a little music out of doors, played by somebody I do not know.
Letter to Fanny Keats, 29 Aug 1819

64 Love is my religion – I could die for that.
Letter to Fanny Brawne, 13 Oct 1819

65 Though a quarrel in the streets is a thing to be hated, the energies displayed in it are fine; the commonest man shows a grace in his quarrel.
Letter

66 I go among the fields and catch a glimpse of a stoat or a fieldmouse peeping out of the withered grass – the creature hath a purpose and its eyes are bright with it. I go amongst the buildings of a city and I see a man hurrying along – to what? the Creature has a purpose and his eyes are bright with it.
Letter, 1819

KENNEDY, John Fitzgerald

(1917–63) US statesman; the first Roman Catholic President (1961–63). His liberal New Frontier policies were cut short by his assassination.

Quotations about Kennedy

1 The enviably attractive nephew who sings an Irish ballad for the company and then winsomely disappears before the table-clearing and dishwashing begin.
Lyndon B. Johnson (1908–73) US statesman. *A Political Education* (H. McPherson)

2 Kennedy the politician exuded that musk odour which acts as an aphrodisiac to many women.
Theodore H. White (1906–64) British novelist. *In Search of History*

Quotations by Kennedy

3 It was involuntary. They sank my boat.
Responding to praise of his courage while serving in the US navy against the Japanese in World War II. *Nobody Said It Better* (M. Ringo)

4 I can't see that it's wrong to give him a little legal experience before he goes out to practice law.
On being criticized for making his brother Robert attorney general. *Nobody Said It Better* (M. Ringo)

5 I guess this is the week I earn my salary.
Comment made during the Cuban missile crisis. *Nobody Said It Better* (M. Ringo)

6 We must use time as a tool, not as a couch.
The Observer, 'Sayings of the Week', 10 Dec 1961

7 The United States has to move very fast to even stand still.
The Observer, 'Sayings of the Week', 21 July 1963

8 The worse I do, the more popular I get.
Referring to his popularity following the failure of the US invasion of Cuba. *The People's Almanac* (D. Wallechinsky)

KILLING

See also assassination, death, murder, suicide

1 Difficult as it may be to cure, it is always easy to poison and to kill.
Elisha Bartlett (1804–55) *Philosophy of Medical Science*, Pt. II, Ch. 16

2 And Samson said, With the jawbone of an ass, heaps upon heaps, with the jaw of an ass have I slain a thousand men.
Bible: Judges 15:16

3 Euthanasia is a long, smooth-sounding word, and it conceals its danger as long, smooth words do, but the danger is there, nevertheless.
Pearl Buck (1892–1973) US novelist. *The Child Who Never Grew*, Ch. 2

4 Thou shalt not kill; but needst not strive
Officiously to keep alive.
Arthur Hugh Clough (1819–61) British poet. *The Latest Decalogue*, 11

5 To save a man's life against his will is the same as killing him.
Horace (Quintus Horatius Flaccus; 65–8 BC) Roman poet. *Ars Poetica*

6 To kill a human being is, after all, the least injury you can do him.
Henry James (1843–1916) US novelist. *My Friend Bingham*

7 Killing
Is the ultimate simplification of life.
Hugh MacDiarmid (Christopher Murray Grieve; 1892–1978) Scottish poet. *England's Double Knavery*

8 . . . there's no difference between one's killing and making decisions that will send others to kill. It's exactly the same thing, or even worse.
Golda Meir (1898–1978) Russian-born Israeli stateswoman. *L'Europeo* (Oriana Fallaci)

9 Kill a man, and you are a murderer. Kill millions of men, and you are a conqueror. Kill everyone, and you are a god.
Jean Rostand (1894–1977) French biologist and writer. *Pensées d'un biologiste*

10 Yet each man kills the thing he loves,
By each let this be heard,
Some do it with a bitter look,
Some with a flattering word.
The coward does it with a kiss,
The brave man with a sword!
Oscar Wilde (1854–1900) Irish-born British dramatist. *The Ballad of Reading Gaol*, I:7

KINDNESS

See also charity, generosity

1 A word of kindness is better than a fat pie.
Russian proverb

2 Pleasant words are as an honeycomb, sweet to the soul, and health to the bones.
Bible: Proverbs 16:24

3 Recompense injury with justice, and recompense kindness with kindness.
Confucius (K'ung Fu-tzu; 551–479 BC) Chinese philosopher. *Analects*

4 I love thee for a heart that's kind –
Not for the knowledge in thy mind.
W. H. Davies (1871–1940) British poet. *Sweet Stay-at-Home*

5 In the sick room, ten cents' worth of human understanding equals ten dollars' worth of medical science.
Martin H. Fischer (1879–1962) *Fischerisms* (Howard Fabing and Ray Marr)

6 True kindness presupposes the faculty of imagining as one's own the suffering and joy of others.
André Gide (1869–1951) French writer.

7 The natural dignity of our work, its unembarrassed kindness, its insight into life, its hold on science – for these privileges, and for all that they bring with them, up and up, high over the top of the tree, the very heavens open, preaching thankfulness.
Stephen Paget (1855–1926) *Confessio Medici*, Epilogue

8 The purpose of human life is to serve and to show compassion and the will to help others.
Albert Schweitzer (1875–1965) Franco-German medical missionary, theologian, philosopher, and organist. *The Schweitzer Album*

9 People pay the doctor for his trouble; for his kindness they still remain in his debt.
Seneca (c. 4 BC–65 AD) Roman writer and statesman.

10 Yet do I fear thy nature;
It is too full o' th' milk of human kindness
To catch the nearest way.
William Shakespeare (1564–1616) English dramatist. *Macbeth*, I:5

11 This is a way to kill a wife with kindness.
William Shakespeare *The Taming of the Shrew*, IV:1

12 So many gods, so many creeds,
So many paths that wind and wind,
While just the art of being kind
Is all the sad world needs.
Ella Wheeler Wilcox (1850–1919) US poet. *The World's Need*

13 That best portion of a good man's life,
His little, nameless, unremembered acts
Of kindness and of love.
William Wordsworth (1770–1850) British poet. *Lines composed a few miles above Tintern Abbey*

KINGS AND KINGDOMS

See also monarchy, royalty

1 That this house will in no circumstances fight for its King and country.
Anonymous Motion passed at the Oxford Union, 9 Feb 1933

2 For the kingdom of God is not in word, but in power.
Bible: I Corinthians 4:20

3 Better is a poor and a wise child than an old and foolish king, who will no more be admonished.
Bible: Ecclesiastes 4:13

4 Curse not the king, no not in thy thought; and curse not the rich in thy bedchamber: for a bird of the air shall carry the voice, and that which hath wings shall tell the matter.
Bible: Ecclesiastes 10:20

5 God save our Gracious King,
Long live our noble King,
God save the King.
Send him victorious,
Happy and glorious.
Henry Carey (c. 1690–1743) English poet and musician. *God Save the King*

6 'Twixt kings and tyrants there's this difference known;
Kings seek their subjects' good: tyrants their own.
Robert Herrick (1591–1674) English poet. *Hesperides*, 'Kings and Tyrants'

7 Pale Death kicks his way equally into the cottages of the poor and the castles of kings.
Horace (Quintus Horatius Flaccus; 65–8 BC) Roman poet. *Odes*, I

8 If you can talk with crowds and keep your virtue,
Or walk with Kings – nor lose the common touch,
If neither foes nor loving friends can hurt you,
If all men count with you, but none too much;
If you can fill the unforgiving minute
With sixty seconds' worth of distance run,
Yours is the Earth and everything that's in it,
And – which is more – you'll be a Man my son!
Rudyard Kipling (1865–1936) Indian-born British writer. *If*

9 A pious man is one who would be an atheist if the king were.
Jean de La Bruyère (1645–96) French satirist. *Les Caractères*

10 Grammar, which can govern even kings.
Molière (Jean Baptiste Poquelin; 1622–73) French dramatist. *Les Femmes savantes*, II:6

11 No kingdom has ever had as many civil wars as the kingdom of Christ.
Baron de Montesquieu (1688–1755) French writer. *Lettres persanes*

12 The poorest man may in his cottage bid defiance to all the forces of the Crown. It may be frail – its roof may shake –the wind may blow through it – the storm may enter – the rain may enter – but the King of England cannot enter! – all his force dares not cross the threshold of the ruined tenement!
William Pitt the Elder (1708–78) British statesman. *Statesmen in the Time of George III* (Lord Brougham), Vol. I

13 I think the King is but a man as I am: the violet smells to him as it doth to me.
William Shakespeare (1564–1616) English dramatist. *Henry V*, IV:1

14 This royal throne of kings, this sceptred isle,
This earth of majesty, this seat of Mars,
This other Eden, demi-paradise,
This fortress built by Nature for herself
Against infection and the hand of war,
This happy breed of men, this little world,
This precious stone set in the silver sea,
Which serves it in the office of a wall,
Or as a moat defensive to a house,
Against the envy of less happier lands;
This blessed plot, this earth, this realm, this England,
This nurse, this teeming womb of royal kings,

Fear'd by their breed, and famous by their birth.
William Shakespeare *Richard II*, II:1

15 It is folly of too many to mistake the echo of a London coffee-house for the voice of the kingdom.
Jonathan Swift (1667–1745) Irish-born Anglican priest and writer. *The Conduct of the Allies*

16 I wanted to be an up-to-date king. But I didn't have much time.
Duke of Windsor (1894–1972) King of the United Kingdom; abdicated 1936. *The Observer*, 'Sayings of the Week', 18 Jan 1970

KIPLING, (Joseph) Rudyard

(1865–1936) Indian-born British writer and poet. His verse collection *Barrack Room Ballads and Other Verses* (1892) included the well-known poems 'If' and 'Gunga Din'. Other works were the *Jungle Books* (1894, 1895), *Kim* (1901), and the children's books *Just So Stories* (1902) and *Puck of Pook's Hill* (1906).

Quotations about Kipling

1 I doubt that the infant monster has any more to give.
Henry James (1843–1916) US novelist. *Letters*, Vol. 3

2 Kipling has done more than any other since Disraeli to show the world that the British race is sound to the core and that rust and dry rot are strangers to it.
Cecil Rhodes (1853–1902) South African statesman. *Rhodes: A Life* (J. G. MacDonald)

Quotations by Kipling

3 Oh, East is East, and West is West, and never the twain shall meet.
The Ballad of East and West

4 And a woman is only a woman, but a good cigar is a smoke.
The Betrothed

5 Teach us delight in simple things,
And mirth that has no bitter springs;
Forgiveness free of evil done,
And love to all men 'neath the sun!
The Children's Song

6 But the Devil whoops, as he whooped of old:
'It's clever, but is it art?'
The Conundrum of the Workshops

7 For they're hangin' Danny Deever, you can hear the Dead March play,
The Regiment's in 'ollow square – they're hangin' 'im to-day;
They've taken of 'is buttons off an' cut 'is stripes away,
An' they're hangin' Danny Deever in the mornin'.
Danny Deever

8 Winds of the World, give answer!
They are whimpering to and fro –
And what should they know of England who only England know?
The English Flag

9 When the Himalayan peasant meets the he-bear in his pride,
He shouts to scare the monster, who will often turn aside.
But the she-bear thus accosted rends the peasant tooth and nail
For the female of the species is more deadly than the male.
The Female of the Species

10 So 'ere's to you, Fuzzy-Wuzzy, at your 'ome in the Soudan;
You're a pore benighted 'eathen but a first-class fightin' man;
An' 'ere's to you, Fuzzy-Wuzzy, with your 'ayrick 'ead of 'air –
You big black boundin' beggar – for you broke a British square!
Fuzzy-Wuzzy

11 We're poor little lambs who've lost our way,
Baa! Baa! Baa!
We're little black sheep who've gone astray,
Baa-aa-aa!
Gentleman-rankers out on the spree,
Damned from here to Eternity,
God ha' mercy on such as we,
Baa! Yah! Bah!
Gentleman-Rankers

12 Oh, Adam was a gardener, and God who made him sees
That half a proper gardener's work is done upon his knees,
So when your work is finished, you can wash your hands and pray
For the Glory of the Garden, that it may not pass away!
The Glory of the Garden

13 The uniform 'e wore
Was nothin' much before,
An' rather less than 'arf o' that be'ind.
Gunga Din

14 An' for all 'is dirty 'ide
'E was white, clear white, inside
When 'e went to tend the wounded under fire!
Gunga Din

15 Though I've belted you an' flayed you,
By the livin' Gawd that made you,
You're a better man than I am, Gunga Din!
Gunga Din

16 If you can keep your head when all about you
Are losing theirs and blaming it on you.
If

17 If you can talk with crowds and keep your virtue,
Or walk with Kings – nor lose the common touch,
If neither foes nor loving friends can hurt you,
If all men count with you, but none too much;
If you can fill the unforgiving minute
With sixty seconds' worth of distance run,
Yours is the Earth and everything that's in it,
And – which is more – you'll be a Man my son!
If

18 Asia is not going to be civilized after the methods of the West. There is too much Asia and she is too old.
Life's Handicap, 'The Man Who Was'

19 The Light that Failed.
Novel title

20 The Saxon is not like us Normans.
His manners are not so polite.
But he never means anything serious till he talks about justice and right,
When he stands like an ox in the furrow with his sullen set eyes on your own,
And grumbles, 'This isn't fair dealing,' my son, leave the Saxon alone.
Norman and Saxon

21 The silliest woman can manage a clever man; but it needs a very clever woman to manage a fool.
Plain Tales from the Hills, 'Three and – an Extra'

22 If, drunk with sight of power, we loose
Wild tongues that have not Thee in awe,
Such boastings as the Gentiles use,
Or lesser breeds without the Law.
Recessional

23 On the road to Mandalay
Where the flyin'-fishes play.
The Road to Mandalay

24 I am sick o' wastin' leather on these gritty pavin'-stones,

An' the blasted English drizzle wakes the fever in my bones;
Tho' I walks with fifty 'ousemaids outer Chelsea to the Strand,
An' they talks a lot o' lovin', but wot do they understand?
Beefy face an' grubby 'and –
Law! Wot do they understand?
I've a neater, sweeter maiden in a cleaner, greener land!
The Road to Mandalay

25 Ship me somewheres east of Suez, where the best is like the worst,
Where there aren't no Ten Commandments, an' a man can raise a thirst:
For the temple-bells are callin', an' it's there that I would be –
By the old Moulmein Pagoda, looking lazy at the sea.
The Road to Mandalay

26 Being kissed by a man who didn't wax his moustache was – like eating an egg without salt.
Soldiers Three, 'The Gadsbys, Poor Dear Mamma'

27 No one thinks of winter when the grass is green!
A St Helena Lullaby

28 Oh, it's Tommy this, an' Tommy that, an' 'Tommy, go away';
But it's 'Thank you, Mister Atkins,' when the band begins to play.
Tommy

29 It's Tommy this, an' Tommy that, an' 'Chuck him out, the brute!'
But it's 'Saviour of 'is country' when the guns begin to shoot.
Tommy

30 They shut the road through the woods
Seventy years ago.
Weather and rain have undone it again,
And now you would never know
There was once a road through the woods.
The Way Through the Woods

31 Take up the White Man's burden –
And reap his old reward:
The blame of those ye better,
The hate of those ye guard.
The White Man's Burden

32 I've just read that I am dead. Don't forget to delete me from your list of subscribers.
Writing to a magazine that had mistakenly published an announcement of his death. *Anekdotenschatz* (H. Hoffmeister)

33 A Soldier of the Great War Known unto God.
The words he selected to be inscribed on the headstones of the graves of unknown soldiers when he was literary adviser for the Imperial War Graves Commission, 1919. *Silent Cities* (ed. Gavin Stamp)

34 Words are, of course, the most powerful drug used by mankind.
Speech, 14 Feb 1923

35 Power without responsibility – the prerogative of the harlot throughout the ages.
Better known for its subsequent use by BALDWIN Attrib.

KISSING

1 What of soul was left, I wonder, when the kissing had to stop?
Robert Browning (1812–89) British poet. *A Toccata of Galuppi's*

2 When the Kissing Had to Stop.
Constantine FitzGibbon From 'A Toccata of Galuppi's' (Robert Browning). Book title

3 Jenny kissed me when we met,
Jumping from the chair she sat in;
Time, you thief, who love to get
Sweets into your list, put that in:
Say I'm weary, say I'm sad,
Say that health and wealth have missed me,
Say I'm growing old, but add,
Jenny kissed me.
Leigh Hunt (1784–1859) British poet. Writing about Jane Carlyle. *Rondeau*

4 Being kissed by a man who didn't wax his moustache was – like eating an egg without salt.
Rudyard Kipling (1865–1936) Indian-born British writer. A similar remark is attributed to the US poet Madison Julius Cawein (1865–1914). *Soldiers Three*, 'The Gadsbys, Poor Dear Mamma'

5 But I wasn't kissing her. I was whispering in her mouth.
Chico Marx (1886–1961) US comedian. When his wife caught him kissing a chorus girl. *The Marx Brothers Scrapbook* (G. Marx and R. Anobile)

6 A kiss without a moustache, they said then, is like an egg without salt; I will add to it: and it is like Good without Evil.
Jean-Paul Sartre (1905–80) French writer. *Words*

KNOWLEDGE

See also learning, self-knowledge, wisdom

1 Knowledge is the mother of all virtue; all vice proceeds from ignorance.
Proverb

2 Learning is a treasure which accompanies its owner everywhere.
Chinese proverb

3 *Nam et ipsa scientia potestas est.*
Knowledge itself is power.
Francis Bacon (1561–1626) English philosopher. *Religious Meditations*, 'Of Heresies'

4 I have taken all knowledge to be my province.
Francis Bacon Letter to Lord Burleigh, 1592

5 For all knowledge and wonder (which is the seed of knowledge) is an impression of pleasure in itself.
Francis Bacon *The Advancement of Learning*, Bk. I, Ch. 1

6 For in much wisdom is much grief: and he that increaseth knowledge increaseth sorrow.
Bible: Ecclesiastes 1:18

7 And the Lord God took the man, and put him into the garden of Eden to dress it and to keep it.
And the Lord God commanded the man, saying, Of every tree of the garden thou mayest freely eat:
But of the tree of the knowledge of good and evil, thou shalt not eat of it: for in the day that thou eatest thereof thou shalt surely die.
Bible: Genesis 2:15–17

8 Now as touching things offered unto idols, we know that we all have knowledge. Knowledge puffeth up, but charity edifieth.
Bible: I Corinthians 8:1

9 Not many people know that.
Michael Caine (1933–) British actor. Attrib., often repeated

10 There goes a woman who knows all the things that can be taught and none of the things that cannot be taught.
Coco Chanel (1883–1971) French dress designer. *Coco Chanel, Her Life, Her Secrets* (Marcel Haedrich)

11 Learning without thought is labor lost; thought without learning is perilous.
Confucius (K'ung Fu-tzu; 551–479 BC) Chinese philosopher. *Analects*

12 Knowledge dwells
In heads replete with thoughts of other men;

Wisdom in minds attentive to their own.
William Cowper (1731–1800) British poet. *The Task*

13 A smattering of everything, and a knowledge of nothing.
Charles Dickens (1812–70) British novelist. *Sketches by Boz*, 'Tales', Ch. 3

14 A man should keep his little brain attic stocked with all the furniture that he is likely to use, and the rest he can put away in the lumber room of his library, where he can get it if he wants it.
Arthur Conan Doyle (1856–1930) British writer. *Five Orange Pips*

15 For lust of knowing what should not be known,
We take the Golden Road to Samarkand.
James Elroy Flecker (1884–1915) British poet. *Hassan*, V:2

16 I am the very model of a modern Major-General,
I've information vegetable, animal and mineral,
I know the kings of England, and I quote the fights historical,
From Marathon to Waterloo, in order categorical.
W. S. Gilbert (1836–1911) British dramatist. *The Pirates of Penzance*, I

17 In arguing too, the parson own'd his skill,
For e'en though vanquish'd, he could argue still;
While words of learned length, and thund'ring sound
Amazed the gazing rustics rang'd around,
And still they gaz'd, and still the wonder grew,
That one small head could carry all he knew.
Oliver Goldsmith (1728–74) Irish-born British writer. *The Deserted Village*

18 The clever men at Oxford
Know all that there is to be knowed.
But they none of them know one half as much
As intelligent Mr Toad.
Kenneth Grahame (1859–1932) Scottish writer. *The Wind in the Willows*, Ch. 10

19 It is the province of knowledge to speak and it is the privilege of wisdom to listen.
Oliver Wendell Holmes (1809–94) US writer. *The Poet at the Breakfast Table*, Ch. 10

20 Knowledge is proportionate to being . . . You know in virtue of what you are.
Aldous Huxley (1894–1964) British novelist. *Time Must Have a Stop*, Ch. 26

21 If a little knowledge is dangerous, where is the man who has so much as to be out of danger?
T. H. Huxley (1825–95) British biologist. *On Elementary Instruction in Physiology*

22 There was never an age in which useless knowledge was more important than in our own.
Cyril Joad (1891–1953) British philosopher and broadcaster. *The Observer*, 'Sayings of the Week', 30 Sept 1951

23 All knowledge is of itself of some value. There is nothing so minute or inconsiderable, that I would not rather know it than not.
Samuel Johnson (1709–84) British lexicographer. *Life of Johnson* (J. Boswell)

24 Integrity without knowledge is weak and useless, and knowledge without integrity is dangerous and dreadful.
Samuel Johnson *Rasselas*, Ch. 41

25 In my early years I read very hard. It is a sad reflection, but a true one, that I knew almost as much at eighteen as I do now.
Samuel Johnson *Life of Johnson* (J. Boswell), Vol. I

26 Knowledge is of two kinds. We know a subject ourselves, or we know where we can find information upon it.
Samuel Johnson *Life of Johnson* (J. Boswell), Vol. II

27 The greater our knowledge increases the more our ignorance unfolds.
John Fitzgerald Kennedy (1917–63) US statesman. Speech, Rice University, 12 Sept 1962

28 A study of history shows that civilizations that abandon the quest for knowledge are doomed to disintegration.
Bernard Lovell (1913–) British astronomer and writer. *The Observer*, 'Sayings of the Week', 14 May 1972

29 Knowledge advances by steps, and not by leaps.
Lord Macaulay (1800–59) British historian. *Essays and Biographies*, 'History'.

30 We have learned the answers, all the answers:
It is the question that we do not know.
Archibald MacLeish (1892–1982) US poet and dramatist. *The Hamlet of A. Macleish*

31 Teach thy tongue to say 'I do not know.'
Maimonides (Moses ben Maimon; 1135–1204) Spanish-born Jewish philosopher and physician.

32 There is no counting the names, that surgeons and anatomists give to the various parts of the human body . . . I wonder whether mankind could not get along without all those names, which keep increasing every day, and hour, and moment . . . But people seem to have a great love for names; for to know a great many names seems to look like knowing a good many things.
Herman Melville (1819–91) US novelist. *Redburn*, Ch. 13

33 A little learning is a dangerous thing;
Drink deep, or taste not the Pierian spring:
There shallow draughts intoxicate the brain,
And drinking largely sobers us again.
Alexander Pope (1688–1744) British poet. *An Essay on Criticism*

34 Our knowledge can only be finite, while our ignorance must necessarily be infinite.
Karl Popper (1902–) Austrian-born British philosopher. *Conjectures and Refutations*

35 His had been an intellectual decision founded on his conviction that if a little knowledge was a dangerous thing, a lot was lethal.
Tom Sharpe (1928–) British novelist. *Porterhouse Blue*, Ch. 18

36 These things shall be! A loftier race
Than e'er the world hath known shall rise,
With flame of freedom in their souls,
And light of knowledge in their eyes.
John Addington Symonds (1840–93) British art historian. Hymn

37 Beware you be not swallowed up in books! An ounce of love is worth a pound of knowledge.
John Wesley (1703–91) British religious leader. *Life of Wesley* (R. Southey), Ch. 16

38 'I dunno,' Arthur said. 'I forget what I was taught. I only remember what I've learnt.'
Patrick White (1912–) British-born Australian novelist. *The Solid Mandala*, Ch. 2

39 I have drunk ale from the Country of the Young
And weep because I know all things now.
W. B. Yeats (1865–1939) Irish poet. *He Thinks of his Past Greatness*

L

LABOR

1 The little bit (two inches wide) of ivory on which I work with so fine a brush as produces little effect after much labour.
Jane Austen (1775–1817) British novelist. Letter, 16 Dec 1816

2 Children sweeten labours, but they make misfortunes more bitter.
Francis Bacon (1561–1626) English philosopher. *Essays*, 'Of Parents and Children'

3 Come unto me, all ye that labour and are heavy laden, and I will give you rest.
Take my yoke upon you, and learn of me; for I am meek and lowly in heart: and ye shall find rest unto your souls.
For my yoke is easy, and my burden is light.
Bible: Matthew 11:28–30

4 Jones – (who, I'm glad to say,
Asked leave of Mrs J. –)
Daily absorbs a clay
After his labours.
C. S. Calverley (1831–84) British poet. *Ode to Tobacco*

5 Man is so made that he can only find relaxation from one kind of labour by taking up another.
Anatole France (Jacques Anatole François Thibault; 1844–1924) French writer. *The Crime of Sylvestre Bonnard*

6 To give and not to count the cost;
To fight and not to heed the wounds;
To toil and not to seek for rest;
To labour and not ask for any reward
Save that of knowing that we do Thy will.
St Ignatius Loyola (1491–1556) Spanish priest. *Prayer for Generosity*

LA BRUYERE, Jean de

(1645–96) French satirist. He served in the household of the Prince of Condé and wrote one book of lasting merit, *Les Caractères de Théophraste, avec les caractères ou les moeurs de ce siècle* (1688).

1 A pious man is one who would be an atheist if the king were.
Les Caractères

2 The majority of men devote the greater part of their lives to making their remaining years unhappy.
Les Caractères

3 There are some who speak one moment before they think.
Les Caractères

4 The pleasure of criticizing robs us of the pleasure of being moved by some very fine things.
Les Caractères

5 Liberality lies less in giving liberally than in the timeliness of the gift.
Les Caractères

6 There are only three events in a man's life; birth, life, and death; he is not conscious of being born, he dies in pain, and he forgets to live.
Les Caractères

7 Women run to extremes; they are either better or worse than men.
Les Caractères

8 One must laugh before one is happy, or one may die without ever laughing at all.
Les Caractères

9 Party loyalty lowers the greatest of men to the petty level of the masses.
Les Caractères

10 There exist some evils so terrible and some misfortunes so horrible that we dare not think of them, whilst their very aspect makes us shudder; but if they happen to fall on us, we find ourselves stronger than we imagined, we grapple with our ill luck, and behave better than we expected we should.
Les Caractères

11 If poverty is the mother of crime, stupidity is its father.
Les Caractères

12 'There is a report that Piso is dead; it is a great loss; he was an honest man, who deserved to live longer; he was intelligent and agreeable, resolute and courageous, to be depended upon, generous and faithful.' Add: 'provided he is really dead'.
Les Caractères

13 If we heard it said of Orientals that they habitually drank a liquor which went to their heads, deprived them of reason and made them vomit, we should say: 'How very barbarous!'
Les Caractères

14 To endeavour to forget anyone is a certain way of thinking of nothing else.
Les Caractères

15 A slave has but one master; an ambitious man has as many masters as there are people who may be useful in bettering his position.
Les Caractères

16 The shortest and best way to make your fortune is to let people see clearly that it is in their interests to promote yours.
Les Caractères

LAMB, Charles

(1775–1834) British essayist. He is best remembered for his *Essays of Elia* (1822).

Quotations about Lamb

1 Charles Lamb I sincerely believe to be in some considerable degree insane. A more pitiful, rickety, gasping, staggering, stammering tomfool I do not know.
Thomas Carlyle (1795–1881) Scottish historian and essayist. Attrib.

2 Charles Lamb, a clever fellow certainly, but full of villainous and abortive puns when he miscarries of every minute.
Thomas Moore (1779–1852) Irish poet. *Diary*, 4 Apr 1823

Quotations by Lamb

3 Nothing is to me more distasteful than that entire complacency and satisfaction which beam in the countenances of a new-married couple.
Essays of Elia, 'A Bachelor's Complaint of Married People'

4 We are nothing; less than nothing, and dreams. We are only what might have been, and must wait upon the tedious shores of Lethe millions of ages before we have existence, and a name.

In Greek mythology, Lethe was a river in the underworld, whose waters were drunk by souls about to be reborn in order to forget their past lives. *Essays of Elia,* 'Dream Children'

5 I hate a man who swallows it, affecting not to know what he is eating. I suspect his taste in higher matters.

Referring to food. *Essays of Elia,* 'Grace before Meat'

6 I have been trying all my life to like Scotchmen, and am obliged to desist from the experiment in despair.

Essays of Elia, 'Imperfect Sympathies'

7 Man is a gaming animal. He must always be trying to get the better in something or other.

Essays of Elia, 'Mrs Battle's Opinions on Whist'

8 In everything that relates to science, I am a whole Encyclopaedia behind the rest of the world.

Essays of Elia, 'The Old and the New Schoolmaster'

9 Boys are capital fellows in their own way, among their mates; but they are unwholesome companions for grown people.

Essays of Elia, 'The Old and the New Schoolmaster' people

10 The human species, according to the best theory I can form of it, is composed of two distinct races, the men who borrow, and the men who lend.

Essays of Elia, 'The Two Races of Men'

11 Borrowers of books – those mutilators of collections, spoilers of the symmetry of shelves, and creators of odd volumes.

Essays of Elia, 'The Two Races of Men'

12 Credulity is the man's weakness, but the child's strength.

Essays of Elia, 'Witches and other Night Fears'

13 I love to lose myself in other men's minds. When I am not walking, I am reading; I cannot sit and think. Books think for me.

Last Essays of Elia, 'Detached Thoughts on Books and Reading'

14 Newspapers always excite curiosity. No one ever lays one down without a feeling of disappointment.

Last Essays of Elia, 'Detached Thoughts on Books and Reading'

15 A poor relation – is the most irrelevant thing in nature.

Last Essays of Elia, 'Poor Relations'

16 It is a pistol let off at the ear; not a feather to tickle the intellect.

Referring to the nature of a pun. *Last Essays of Elia,* 'Popular Fallacies'

17 How sickness enlarges the dimensions of a man's self to himself.

Last Essays of Elia, 'The Convalescent'

18 The greatest pleasure I know, is to do a good action by stealth, and to have it found out by accident.

The Athenaeum, 'Table Talk by the late Elia', 4 Jan 1834

19 I have had playmates, I have had companions
In my days of childhood, in my joyful schooldays –
All, all are gone, the old familiar faces.

The Old Familiar Faces

20 Riddle of destiny, who can show
What thy short visit meant, or know
What thy errand here below?

On an Infant Dying as soon as Born

21 Damn the age. I'll write for antiquity.

Referring to his lack of payment for the *Essays of Elia. English Wits* (L. Russell)

22 Dr Parr . . . asked him, how he had acquired his power of smoking at such a rate? Lamb replied, 'I toiled after it, sir, as some men toil after virtue.'

Memoirs of Charles Lamb (Talfourd)

23 I came home . . . hungry as a hunter.

Letter to Coleridge, Apr 1800

24 Separate from the pleasure of your company, I don't much care if I never see another mountain in my life.

Letter to William Wordsworth, 30 Jan 1801

25 A little thin, flowery border, round, neat, not gaudy.

Letter to Wordsworth, June 1806

26 This very night I am going to leave off tobacco! Surely there must be some other world in which this unconquerable purpose shall be realized. The soul hath not her generous aspirings implanted in her in vain.

Letter to Thomas Manning, 26 Dec 1815

LAMBS

1 When the stars threw down their spears,
And watered heaven with their tears,
Did he smile his work to see?
Did he who made the Lamb make thee?

William Blake (1757–1827) British poet. *Songs of Experience,* 'The Tiger'

2 Little Lamb, who made thee?
Dost thou know who made thee?

William Blake *Songs of Innocence,* 'The Lamb'

3 Mary had a little lamb,
Its fleece was white as snow,
And everywhere that Mary went
The lamb was sure to go.

Sarah Josepha Hale (1788–1879) US writer. *Poems for Our Children,* 'Mary's Little Lamb'

4 We're poor little lambs who've lost our way,
Baa! Baa! Baa!
We're little black sheep who've gone astray,
Baa-aa-aa!
Gentleman-rankers out on the spree,
Damned from here to Eternity,
God ha' mercy on such as we,
Baa! Yah! Bah!

Rudyard Kipling (1865–1936) Indian-born British writer. *Gentleman-Rankers*

5 No absolute is going to make the lion lie down with the lamb unless the lamb is inside.

D. H. Lawrence (1885–1930) British novelist. *The Later D. H. Lawrence*

LAND

1 They are ill discoverers that think there is no land, when they can see nothing but sea.

Francis Bacon (1561–1626) English philosopher. *The Advancement of Learning,* Bk. II, Ch. 7

2 Man has been endowed with reason, with the power to create, so that he can add to what he's been given. But up to now he hasn't been a creator, only a destroyer. Forests keep disappearing, rivers dry up, wild life's become extinct, the climate's ruined and the land grows poorer and uglier every day.

Anton Chekhov (1860–1904) Russian dramatist. *Uncle Vanya,* I

3 When the white man came we had the land and they had the Bibles; now they have the land and we have the Bibles.

Dan George (1899–1982) Canadian Indian chief. Attrib.

4 We are as near to heaven by sea as by land.

Humphrey Gilbert (c. 1539–83) English navigator. Remark made shortly before he went down with his ship *Squirrel*. *A Book of Anecdotes* (D. George)

LANGUAGE

See also class, communication, grammar, Goldwynisms, malapropisms, mixed metaphors, opera, pronunciation, speech, spoonerisms, style, words, writing

1 The Greeks Had a Word for It.

Zoë Akins (1886–1958) US dramatist. Play title

2 The sciences were transmitted into the Arabic language from different parts of the world; by it they were embellished and penetrated the hearts of men, while the beauties of the language flowed in their veins and arteries.

Al-Biruni (973–1048) Arabic scholar. *Kitab as-Saidana*

3 Nouns of multitude (e.g., a pair of shoes, a gaggle of geese, a pride of lions) . . . : a rash of dermatologists, a hive of allergists, a scrub of interns, a chest of phthisiologists, or, a giggle of nurses, a flood of urologists, a pile of proctologists, and eyeful of ophthalmologists; or, a whiff of anesthesiologists, a staff of bacteriologists, a cast of orthopedic rheumatologists, a gargle of laryngologists.

Anonymous *Journal of the American Medical Association*, 190:392, 1964

4 The modern haematologist, instead of describing in English what he can see, prefers to describe in Greek what he can't.

Richard Asher (1912–) *Lancet*, 2:359, 1959

5 Well I ask you? When you take your family on holiday, do you say 'I am taking my gregarious egalitarian sibling group with me'?

Richard Asher *Lancet*, 2:359, 1959

6 A vocabulary that would take the feathers off a hoody crow.

Lillian Beckwith (1916–) US writer. *Lightly Poached*

7 Therefore is the name of it called Babel; because the Lord did there confound the language of all the earth: and from thence did the Lord scatter them abroad upon the face of all the earth.

Bible: Genesis 11:9

8 The cliché is dead poetry. English, being the language of an imaginative race, abounds in clichés, so that English literature is always in danger of being poisoned by its own secretions.

Gerald Brenan (Edward Fitzgerald Brenan; 1894–1987) British writer. *Thoughts in a Dry Season*, 'Literature'

9 'Take some more tea,' the March Hare said to Alice, very earnestly.
'I've had nothing yet,' Alice replied in an offended tone, 'so I can't take more.'
'You mean you can't take *less*,' said the Hatter: 'it's very easy to take *more* than nothing.'

Lewis Carroll (Charles Lutwidge Dodgson; 1832–98) British writer. *Alice's Adventures in Wonderland*, Ch. 7

10 A silly remark can be made in Latin as well as in Spanish.

Miguel de Cervantes (1547–1616) Spanish novelist. *The Dialogue of the Dogs*

11 I speak Spanish to God, Italian to women, French to men, and German to my horse.

Charles V (1500–58) Holy Roman Emperor. Attrib.

12 And for ther is so greet diversitee
in English and in wryting of our tonge
So preye I God that noon miswryte thee
Ne thee mismetre for defaute of tonge.
And red wherso thou be, or elles songe,
That thou be understonde, I God beseche.

Geoffrey Chaucer (c. 1343–1400) English poet. *Troilus and Criseyde*

13 The one stream of poetry which is continually flowing is slang.

G. K. Chesterton (1874–1936) British writer. *The Defendant*

14 All slang is metaphor, and all metaphor is poetry.

G. K. Chesterton *The Defendant*

15 I don't hold with abroad and think that foreigners speak English when our backs are turned.

Quentin Crisp (c. 1910–) British model, publicist, and writer. *The Naked Civil Servant*

16 Bring on the empty horses!

Michael Curtiz (1888–1962) Hungarian-born US film director. Said during the filming of *The Charge of the Light Brigade*. Curtiz, who was not noted for his command of the English language, meant 'riderless horses'. When people laughed at his order he became very angry, shouting, 'You think I know fuck-nothing, when I know fuck-all!' David Niven used the remark as the title of his second volume of autobiography about his experiences in the film industry. *Bring on the Empty Horses* (David Niven)

17 Imagine the Lord talking French! Aside from a few odd words in Hebrew, I took it completely for granted that God had never spoken anything but the most dignified English.

Clarence Shepard Day (1874–1935) US writer. *Life With Father*, 'Father interferes'

18 Rushing from his laboratory and meeting a curator he embraced him exclaiming, 'I have just made a great discovery. I have separated the sodium ammonium protartrate with two salts of opposite action on the plane of polarization of light. The dextro-salt is in all respects identical with the dextroprotartrate. I am so happy and so overcome by such nervous excitement that I am unable again to place my eye to the polarization instrument.'

Alexander Findlay Referring to Louis Pasteur. *Chemistry in the Service of Man*

19 You must learn to talk clearly. The jargon of scientific terminology which rolls off your tongues is mental garbage.

Martin H. Fischer (1879–1962) *Fischerisms* (Howard Fabing and Ray Marr)

20 A master of the English language does not need to exaggerate; an illiterate almost always does.

Lord Hailsham (1907–) British Conservative politician. *The Observer* 'Sayings of the Week', 16 March 1975

21 What is the prose for God?

Harley Granville-Barker (1877–1946) British actor and dramatist. *Waste*, I

22 I would never use a long word, even, where a short one would answer the purpose. I know there are professors in this country who 'ligate' arteries. Other surgeons only tie them, and it stops the bleeding just as well.

Oliver Wendell Holmes (1809–94) US writer and physician. *Medical Essays*, 'Scholastic and Bedside Teaching'

23 I am not yet so lost in lexicography, as to forget that words are the daughters of earth,

and that things are the sons of heaven. Language is only the instrument of science, and words are but the signs of ideas: I wish, however, that the instrument might be less apt to decay, and that signs might be permanent, like the things which they denote.

Samuel Johnson (1709–84) British lexicographer. *Dictionary of the English Language*

24 I have laboured to refine our language to grammatical purity, and to clear it from colloquial barbarisms, licentious idioms, and irregular combinations.

Samuel Johnson *The Rambler*

25 I am always sorry when any language is lost, because languages are the pedigree of nations.

Samuel Johnson *Tour to the Hebrides* (J. Boswell)

26 The baby doesn't understand English and the Devil knows Latin.

Ronald Knox (1888–1957) British Roman Catholic priest. Said when asked to conduct a baptism service in English. *Ronald Knox* (Evelyn Waugh), Pt. I, Ch. 5

27 There are things which will not be defined, and Fever is one of them. Besides, when a word had passed into everyday use, it is too late to lay a logical trap for its meaning, and think to apprehend it by a definition.

Peter Mere Latham (1789–1875) US poet and essayist. *General Remarks on the Practice of Medicine*, Ch. 10, Pt. 1

28 The contraction of his obicular, the lateral obtusion of his sense centres, his night fears, his stomach trouble, the polyencephalitic condition of his youth, and above all the heredity of his old father and young mother, combined to make him an hysterico-epileptic type, traceable in the paranoic psychoses evident in all he wrote.

Cesare Lombroso (1853–1909) Italian criminologist. Referring to Émile Zola. *Paris Was Yesterday* (Janet Flanner)

29 A man of true science . . . uses but few hard words, and those only when none other will answer his purpose; whereas the smatterer in science . . . thinks, that by mouthing hard words, he proves that he understands hard things.

Herman Melville (1819–91) US novelist. *White Jacket*, Ch. 63

30 If the English language had been properly organized . . . then there would be a word which meant both 'he' and 'she', and I could write, 'If John or Mary comes heesh will want to play tennis,' which would save a lot of trouble.

A. A. Milne (1882–1956) British writer. *The Christopher Robin Birthday Book*

31 Most of their discourse was about hunting, in a dialect I understand very little.

Samuel Pepys (1633–1703) English diarist. *Diary*, 22 Nov 1663

32 I include 'pidgin-English' . . . even though I am referred to in that splendid language as 'Fella belong Mrs Queen'.

Prince Philip (1921–) The consort of Queen Elizabeth II. Speech, English-Speaking Union Conference, Ottawa, 29 Oct 1958

33 Life is too short to learn German.

Richard Porson (1759–1808) British classicist. *Gryll Grange* (T. L. Peacock), Ch. 3

34 The language of the men of medicine is a fearful concoction of sesquipedalian words, numbered by thousands.

Frederick Saunders (1807–1902)

35 Honi soie qui mal y pense ('Honey, your silk stocking's hanging down').

W. C. Sellar (1898–1951) British humorous writer. *1066 And All That*

36 The language I have learn'd these forty years,
My native English, now I must forego;
And now my tongue's use is to me no more
Than an unstringed viol or a harp.

William Shakespeare (1564–1616) English dramatist. *Richard II*, I:3

37 O! know, sweet love, I always write of you,
And you and love are still my argument;
So all my best is dressing old words new,
Spending again what is already spent.

William Shakespeare *Sonnets*, 76

38 You taught me language; and my profit on't
Is, I know how to curse: the red plague rid you
For learning me your language!

William Shakespeare *The Tempest*, I:2

39 England and America are two countries separated by the same language.

George Bernard Shaw (1856–1950) Irish dramatist and critic. Attrib.

40 Language grows out of life, out of its needs and experiences . . . *Language* and *knowledge* are indissolubly connected; they are interdependent. Good work in language presupposes and depends on a real knowledge of things.

Annie Sullivan (1866–1936) US teacher of the handicapped. Speech, American Association to Promote the Teaching of Speech to the Deaf, July 1894

41 A foreign swear-word is practically inoffensive except to the person who has learned it early in life and knows its social limits.

Paul Theroux (1941–) US-born writer. *Saint Jack*, Ch. 12

42 The most attractive sentences are not perhaps the wisest, but the surest and soundest.

Henry David Thoreau (1817–62) US writer. *Journal*, 1842

43 I am not like a lady at the court of Versailles, who said: 'What a dreadful pity that the bother at the tower of Babel should have got language all mixed up, but for that, everyone would always have spoken French.

Voltaire (François-Marie Arouet; 1694–1778) French writer. Letter to Catherine the Great, Empress of Russia, 26 May 1767

44 We should constantly use the most common, little, easy words (so they are pure and proper) which our language affords.

John Wesley (1703–91) British religious leader. Advice for preaching to 'plain people'. Attrib.

45 We dissect nature along lines laid down by our native language . . . Language is not simply a reporting device for experience but a defining framework for it.

Benjamin Lee Whorf (1897–1941) US linguist. *New Directions in the Study of Language* (ed. Hoyer), 'Thinking in Primitive Communities'

LAST WORDS

Not always the actual last words said, but including remarks made when dying. Many are apocryphal, hence the fact that some people have more than one set of attributed 'last words'. *See also* death, execution

1 A lot of people, on the verge of death, utter famous last words or stiffen into attitudes, as if the final stiffening in three days' time were not enough; they will have ceased to exist three days' hence, yet they still want to arouse admiration and adopt a pose and tell a lie with their last gasp.

Henry de Montherlant (1896–1972) French novelist. *Explicit Mysterum*

2 I inhabit a weak, frail, decayed tenement; battered by the winds and broken in on by the storms, and, from all I can learn, the landlord does not intend to repair.

John Quincy Adams (1767–1848) Sixth president of the USA. Said during his last illness. Attrib.

3 See in what peace a Christian can die.

Joseph Addison (1672–1719) British essayist.

4 *Ave Caesar, morituri te salutant.*
Hail Caesar; those who are about to die salute you.

Anonymous Greeting to the Roman Emperor by gladiators

5 Jakie, is it my birthday or am I dying?

Viscountess Nancy Astor (1879–1964) American-born British politician. To her son on her death bed He replied: 'A bit of both, Mum'.

6 How were the receipts today in Madison Square Garden?

Phineas Taylor Barnum (1810–91) US showman.

7 I am ready to die for my Lord, that in my blood the Church may obtain liberty and peace.

Thomas Becket (c. 1118–70) English churchman. One version of his last words. *Vita S. Thomae, Cantuariensis Archiepiscopi et Martyris* (Edward Grim)

8 Thank you, sister. May you be the mother of a bishop!

Brendan Behan (1923–64) Irish playwright. Said to a nun nursing him on his deathbed. Attrib.

9 When Jesus therefore had received the vinegar, he said, It is finished: and he bowed his head, and gave up the ghost.

Bible: John 19:30

10 And when Jesus had cried with a loud voice, he said, Father, into thy hands I commend my spirit: and having said thus, he gave up the ghost.

Bible: Luke 23:46

11 Jesus, when he had cried again with a loud voice, yielded up the ghost.
And, behold, the veil of the temple was rent in twain from the top to the bottom; and the earth did quake, and the rocks rent;
And the graves were opened; and many bodies of the saints which slept arose.

Bible: Matthew 27:50–52

12 *Et tu, Brute?*
You too, Brutus?

Julius Caesar (100–44 BC) Roman general and statesman.

13 All right, then, I'll say it: Dante makes me sick.

Lope Félix de Vega Carpio (1562–1635) Spanish dramatist and poet. On being informed he was about to die. Attrib.

14 I realize that patriotism is not enough. I must have no hatred or bitterness towards anyone.

Edith Cavell (1865–1915) British nurse. Before her execution by the Germans in 1915.

15 A Subject and a Sovereign are clean different things.

Charles I (1600–49) King of England. Speech on the scaffold, 30 Jan 1649

16 Let not poor Nelly starve.

Charles II (1630–85) King of England. Referring to Nell Gwynne. Said on his death bed

17 He had been, he said, a most unconscionable time dying; but he hoped that they would excuse it.

Charles II *History of England* (Macaulay), Vol. I, Ch. 4

18 Give Dayrolles a chair.

Earl of Chesterfield (1694–1773) English statesman. Said on his deathbed when visited by his godson, Solomon Dayrolles. Last words

19 Take a step forward, lads. It will be easier that way.

Erskine Childers (1870–1922) British-born author and Irish patriot. Last words before being executed by firing squad, 24 Nov 1922. *The Riddle of Erskine Childers* (A. Boyle)

20 I'm so bored with it all.

Winston Churchill (1874–1965) British statesman. Said to be his last words. *Clementine* (M. Soames)

21 Goodnight, my darlings. I'll see you tomorrow.

Noël Coward (1899–1973) British dramatist. *The Life of Noel Coward* (C. Lesley)

22 It much grieves me that I should be noted a traitor when I always had your laws on my breast, and that I should be a sacramentary. God he knoweth the truth, and that I am of the one and the other guiltless.

Thomas Cromwell (c. 1485–1540) English statesman. On being condemned to death for treason and heresy. Letter to Henry VIII, 30 June 1540

23 Nurse, it was I who discovered that leeches have red blood.

Baron Georges Cuvier (1769–1832) French zoologist. On his deathbed when the nurse came to apply leeches. *The Oxford Book of Death* (D. Enright)

24 Too late for fruit, too soon for flowers.

Walter De La Mare (1873–1956) British poet. On being asked, as he lay seriously ill, whether he would like some fruit or flowers. Attrib.

25 No, it is better not. She will only ask me to take a message to Albert.

Benjamin Disraeli (1804–81) British statesman. On his deathbed, declining an offer of a visit from Queen Victoria.

26 Shakespeare, I come!

Theodore Dreiser (1871–1945) US novelist. His intended last words. *The Constant Circle* (S. Mayfield)

27 Goodbye, my friends, I go on to glory.

Isadora Duncan (1878–1927) US dancer and choreographer. She was strangled when her long scarf became entangled in the wheel of a sports car. Attrib.

28 All my possessions for a moment of time.

Elizabeth I (1533–1603) Queen of England.

29 Must! Is *must* a word to be addressed to princes? Little man, little man! thy father, if he had been alive, durst not have used that word.

Elizabeth I Said to Robert Cecil, on her death bed. *A Short History of the English People* (J. R. Green), Ch. 7

30 Death is my neighbour now.

Edith Evans (1888–1976) British actress. Said a week before her death. BBC radio interview, 14 Oct 1976

31 I have no pain, dear mother, now;
But oh! I am so dry:
Just moisten poor Jim's lips once more;
And, mother, do not cry!

Edward Farmer (1809–76) British writer. A typical sentimental verse of the time. *The Collier's Dying Child*

32 Now I'll have *eine kleine Pause.*

Kathleen Ferrier (1912–53) British contralto. Said shortly before her death. *Am I Too Loud?* (Gerald Moore)

33 I have spent a lot of time searching through the Bible for loopholes.

W. C. Fields (1880–1946) US comedian. Said during his last illness. Attrib.

34 It is high time for me to depart, for

at my age I now begin to see things as they really are.
Bernard de Fontenelle (1657–1757) French philosopher. Remark on his deathbed. *Anekdotenschatz* (H. Hoffmeister)

35 I feel nothing, apart from a certain difficulty in continuing to exist.
Bernard de Fontenelle Remark on his deathbed. *Famous Last Words* (B. Conrad)

36 I die happy.
Charles James Fox (1749–1806) British Whig politician. *Life and Times of C. J. Fox* (Russell), Vol. III

37 Why fear death? It is the most beautiful adventure in life.
Charles Frohman (1860–1915) US theater producer. Said before going down with the liner *Lusitania,* alluding to 'To die will be an awfully big adventure' from Barrie's *Peter Pan,* which Frohman had produced. *J. M. Barrie and the Lost Boys* (A. Birkin)

38 We are all going to Heaven, and Vandyke is of the company.
Thomas Gainsborough (1727–88) British painter. *Thomas Gainsborough* (Boulton), Ch. 9

39 Bugger Bognor.
George V (1865–1936) King of the United Kingdom. His alleged last words, when his doctor promised him he would soon be well enough to visit Bognor Regis.

40 How is the Empire?
George V Last words. *The Times,* 21 Jan 1936

41 We are as near to heaven by sea as by land.
Humphrey Gilbert (c. 1539–83) English navigator. Remark made shortly before he went down with his ship *Squirrel.* *A Book of Anecdotes* (D. George)

42 *Mehr Licht!*
More light!
Goethe (1749–1832) German poet and dramatist. Attrib. last words. In fact he asked for the second shutter to be opened, to allow more light in.

43 It is. But not as hard as farce.
Edmund Gwenn (1875–1959) British actor. On his deathbed, in reply to the comment 'It must be very hard'. *Time,* 30 Jan 1984

44 Well, I've had a happy life.
William Hazlitt (1778–1830) British essayist.

45 You might make that a double.
Neville Heath (1917–46) British murderer. Comment made when offered a drink before his execution. Attrib.

46 Only one man ever understood me. . . . And he didn't understand me.
Hegel (1770–1831) German philosopher. Said on his deathbed. *Famous Last Words* (B. Conrad)

47 God will pardon me. It is His trade.
Heinrich Heine (1797–1856) German poet and writer. *Journal* (Edmond and Charles Goncourt), 23 Feb 1863

48 Turn up the lights, I don't want to go home in the dark.
O. Henry (William Sidney Porter; 1862–1910) US short-story writer. Quoting a popular song of the time. *O. Henry* (C. A. Smith), Ch. 9

49 I am about to take my last voyage, a great leap in the dark.
Thomas Hobbes (1588–1679) English philosopher.

50 If heaven had granted me five more years, I could have become a real painter.
Hokusai (1760–1849) Japanese painter. Said on his deathbed. *Famous Last Words* (B. Conrad)

51 On the contrary!
Henrik Ibsen (1828–1906) Norwegian dramatist. His nurse had just remarked that he was feeling a little better. *True Remarkable Occurrences* (J. Train)

52 So it has come at last, the distinguished thing.
Henry James (1843–1916) US novelist. *A Backward Glance* (Edith Wharton), Ch. 14

53 Above ground I shall be food for kites; below I shall be food for mole-crickets and ants. Why rob one to feed the other?
Juang-zu (4th century BC) Chinese Taoist philosopher. When asked on his deathbed what his wishes were regarding the disposal of his body. *Famous Last Words* (B. Conrad)

54 Don't give up the ship.
James Lawrence (1781–1813) US naval officer. As he lay dying in his ship, the US frigate *Chesapeake,* during the battle with the British frigate *Shannon.*

55 It's all been rather lovely.
John Le Mesurier (1912–83) British actor. *The Times,* 15 Nov 1983

56 Why are you weeping? Did you imagine that I was immortal?
Louis XIV (1638–1715) French king. Noticing as he lay on his deathbed that his attendants were crying. *Louis XIV* (V. Cronin)

57 *Tête d'Armée.*
Chief of the Army.
Napoleon I (Napoleon Bonaparte; 1769–1821) French emperor. Last words. Attrib.

58 I do not have to forgive my enemies, I have had them all shot.
Ramón Maria Narváez (1800–68) Spanish general and political leader. Said on his deathbed, when asked by a priest if he forgave his enemies. *Famous Last Words* (B. Conrad)

59 Kiss me, Hardy.
Lord Nelson (1758–1805) British admiral. Spoken to Sir Thomas Hardy, captain of the *Victory,* during the Battle of Trafalgar, 1805.

60 Too kind, too kind.
Florence Nightingale (1820–1910) British nurse. When given the Order of Merit on her deathbed. Attrib.

61 I am just going outside and may be some time.
Capt. Lawrence Oates (1880–1912) British soldier and explorer. Before leaving the tent and vanishing into the blizzard on the ill-fated Antarctic expedition (1910–12). Oates was afraid that his lameness would slow down the others. *Journal* (R. F. Scott), 17 Mar 1912

62 Die, my dear Doctor, that's the last thing I shall do!
Lord Palmerston (1784–1865) British statesman.

63 I am curious to see what happens in the next world to one who dies unshriven.
Pietro Perugino (1446–1523) Italian painter. Giving his reasons for refusing to see a priest as he lay dying. Attrib.

64 Oh, my country! How I leave my country!
William Pitt the Younger (1759–1806) British statesman.

65 I think I could eat one of Bellamy's veal pies.
William Pitt the Younger

66 I have not told half of what I saw.
Marco Polo (c. 1254–1324) Venetian traveler. *The Story of Civilization* (W. Durant), Vol. I

67 Here am I, dying of a hundred good symptoms.
Alexander Pope (1688–1744) British poet. *Anecdotes by and about Alexander Pope* (Joseph Spence)

68 I owe much; I have nothing; the rest I leave to the poor.
François Rabelais (1483–1553) French satirist.

69 Ring down the curtain, the farce is over.
François Rabelais

70 I am going in search of a great perhaps.
François Rabelais

71 My dear hands. Farewell, my poor hands.
Sergei Rachmaninov (1873–1943) Russian composer. On being informed that he was dying from cancer. *The Great Pianists* (H. Schonberg)

72 I have a long journey to take, and must bid the company farewell.
Walter Raleigh (1554–1618) English explorer. *Sir Walter Raleigh* (Edward Thompson), Ch. 26

73 So little done, so much to do.
Cecil Rhodes (1853–1902) South African statesman.

74 You can keep the things of bronze and stone and give me one man to remember me just once a year.
Damon Runyon (1884–1946) US writer.

75 Dear World, I am leaving you because I am bored. I am leaving you with your worries. Good luck.
George Sanders (1906–72) British film actor. Suicide note

76 Everybody has got to die, but I have always believed an exception would be made in my case. Now what?
William Saroyan (1908–81) US dramatist. *Time,* 16 Jan 1984

77 At last I am going to be well!
Paul Scarron (1610–60) French poet. As he lay dying. Attrib.

78 Nonsense, they couldn't hit an elephant at this distance
John Sedgwick (1813–64) US general. In response to a suggestion that he should not show himself over the parapet during the Battle of the Wilderness. Attrib.

79 His nose was as sharp as a pen, and 'a babbl'd of green fields.
William Shakespeare (1564–1616) English dramatist. Referring to Falstaff on his deathbed. *Henry V,* II:3

80 Thank heavens the sun has gone in and I don't have to go out and enjoy it.
Logan Pearsall Smith (1865–1946) US writer.

81 Crito, we owe a cock to Aesculapius; please pay it and don't let it pass.
Socrates (469–399 BC) Athenian philosopher. Before his execution by drinking hemlock. *Phaedo* (Plato), 118

82 Beautifully done.
Stanley Spencer (1891–1959) British artist. Said to the nurse who had injected him, just before he died. *Stanley Spencer, a Biography* (Maurice Collis), Ch. 19

83 If this is dying, I don't think much of it.
Lytton Strachey (1880–1932) British writer. *Lytton Strachey* (Michael Holroyd), Pt. V, Ch. 17

84 Ah, a German and a genius! a prodigy, admit him!
Jonathan Swift (1667–1745) Irish-born Anglican priest and writer. Learning of the arrival of Handel.

85 I did not know that we had ever quarrelled.
Henry David Thoreau (1817–62) US writer. On being urged to make his peace with God. Attrib.

86 God bless . . . God damn.
James Thurber (1894–1961) US humorist.

87 Even in the valley of the shadow of death, two and two do not make six.
Leo Tolstoy (1828–1910) Russian writer. Refusing to reconcile himself with the Russian Orthodox Church as he lay dying.

88 I have had no real gratification or enjoyment of any sort more than my neighbor on the next block who is worth only half a million.
William Henry Vanderbilt (1821–85) US railroad chief. *Famous Last Words* (B. Conrad)

89 Dear me, I believe I am becoming a god. An emperor ought at least to die on his feet.
Vespasian (9–79 AD) Roman emperor. *Lives of the Caesars* (Suetonius)

90 Either that wall paper goes, or I do.
Oscar Wilde (1854–1900) Irish-born British dramatist. As he lay dying in a drab Paris bedroom. *Time,* 16 Jan 1984

91 I expect I shall have to die beyond my means
Oscar Wilde On accepting a glass of champagne on his deathbed.

92 I haven't got time to be tired.
Wilhelm I (1797–1888) King of Prussia and Emperor of Germany. Said during his last illness

93 Now God be praised, I will die in peace.
James Wolfe (1727–59) British general. After being mortally wounded at the Battle of Quebec, 1759. *Historical Journal of Campaigns, 1757–60* (J. Knox), Vol. II

94 Germany was the cause of Hitler just as much as Chicago is responsible for the *Chicago Tribune.*
Alexander Woollcott (1887–1943) US writer and critic. Woollcott died after the broadcast. Radio broadcast, 1943

LATIN

1 A silly remark can be made in Latin as well as in Spanish.
Miguel de Cervantes (1547–1616) Spanish novelist. *The Dialogue of the Dogs*

2 Thou hadst small Latin, and less Greek.
Ben Jonson (1573–1637) English dramatist. *To the Memory of William Shakespeare*

3 The baby doesn't understand English and the Devil knows Latin.
Ronald Knox (1888–1957) British Roman Catholic priest. Said when asked to conduct a baptism service in English. *Ronald Knox* (Evelyn Waugh), Pt. I, Ch. 5

4 A gentleman need not know Latin, but he should at least have forgotten it.
Brander Matthews (1852–1929) US writer. Attrib.

5 Television? No good will come of this device. The word is half Greek and half Latin.
C. P. Scott (1846–1932) British journalist. Attrib.

6 We were taught as the chief subjects of instruction Latin and Greek. We were taught very badly because the men who taught us did not habitually use either of these languages.
H. G. Wells (1866–1946) British writer. *The New Machiavelli,* Bk. I., Ch. 3

7 Don't quote Latin; say what you have to say, and then sit down.
Duke of Wellington (1769–1852) British general and statesman. Advice to a new Member of Parliament. Attrib.

LAUGHTER

See also happiness, humor

1 Laugh and grow fat.
Proverb

2 Laugh before breakfast, you'll cry before supper.
Proverb

3 Laughter is the best medicine.
Proverb

4 A good laugh and a long sleep are the best cures in the doctor's book.
Irish proverb

5 I make myself laugh at everything, so that I do not weep.
Beaumarchais (1732–99) French dramatist. *Le Barbier de Séville,* I:2

6 I said of laughter, It is mad: and of mirth, What doeth it?
Bible: Ecclesiastes 2:2

7 The most wasted of all days is that on which one has not laughed.
Nicolas Chamfort (1741–94) French writer. *Maximes et pensées*

8 One must laugh before one is happy, or one may die without ever laughing at all.
Jean de La Bruyère (1645–96) French satirist. *Les Caractères*

9 Laughter is pleasant, but the exertion is too much for me.
Thomas Love Peacock (1785–1866) British novelist. Said by the Hon. Mr Listless. *Nightmare Abbey*, Ch. 5

10 Born with the gift of laughter and a sense that the world was mad.
Rafael Sabatini (1875–1950) Italian-born novelist. *Scaramouche*

11 I live in a constant endeavour to fence against the infirmities of ill health, and other evils of life, by mirth.
Laurence Sterne (1713–68) Irish-born English writer and churchman. *Tristram Shandy*, Dedication

12 Laugh, and the world laughs with you;
Weep, and you weep alone,
For the sad old earth must borrow its mirth,
But has trouble enough of its own.
Ella Wheeler Wilcox (1850–1919) US poet. *Solitude*

LAW

See also crime, justice, lawyers

1 A judge knows nothing unless it has been explained to him three times.
Proverb

2 Every dog is allowed one bite.
Proverb

3 Every one is innocent until he is proved guilty.
Proverb

4 Possession is nine points of the law.
Proverb

5 The law does not concern itself about trifles.
Proverb

6 Human law is law only by virtue of its accordance with right reason, and by this means it is clear that it flows from Eternal law. In so far as it deviates from right reason it is called an Unjust law; and in such a case, it is no law at all, but rather an assertion of violence.
St Thomas Aquinas (1225–74) Italian theologian. *Summa Theologiae*

7 One of the Seven was wont to say: 'That laws were like cobwebs; where the small flies were caught, and the great brake through.'
Francis Bacon (1561–1626) English philosopher. *See also* SHENSTONE, SOLON, SWIFT *Apothegms*

8 Every law is an evil, for every law is an infraction of liberty.
Jeremy Bentham (1748–1832) British philosopher. *An Introduction to the Principles of Morals and Legislation*

9 The good of the people is the chief law.
Cicero (106–43 BC) Roman orator and statesman. *De Legibus*, III

10 The law of the realm cannot be changed but by Parliament.
Edward Coke (1552–1634) English lawyer and politician. Dictum, in the case *Articuli Cleri*, 1605

11 The Law of England is a very strange one; it cannot compel anyone to tell the truth. . . . But what the Law can do is to give you seven years for not telling the truth.
Lord Darling (1849–1936) British judge. *Lord Darling* (D. Walker-Smith), Ch. 27

12 'If the law supposes that,' said Mr Bumble . . . , 'the law is a ass – a idiot.'
Charles Dickens (1812–70) British novelist. *Oliver Twist*, Ch. 51

13 We must face the fact that the United Nations is not yet the international equivalent of our own legal system and the rule of law.
Anthony Eden (1897–1977) British statesman and prime minister. Speech, House of Commons, 1 Nov 1956

14 The majestic egalitarianism of the law, which forbids rich and poor alike to sleep under bridges, to beg in the streets, and to steal bread.
Anatole France (Jacques Anatole François Thibault; 1844–1924) French writer. *The Red Lily*, Ch. 7

15 When I went to the Bar as a very young man,
(Said I to myself – said I),
I'll work on a new and original plan,
(Said I to myself – said I).
W. S. Gilbert (1836–1911) British dramatist. *Iolanthe*, I

16 The Law is the true embodiment
Of everything that's excellent.
It has no kind of fault or flaw,
And I, my lords, embody the Law.
W. S. Gilbert *Iolanthe*, I

17 There's no better way of exercising the imagination than the study of law. No poet ever interpreted nature as freely as a lawyer interprets truth.
Jean Giraudoux (1882–1944) French dramatist. *Tiger at the Gates*, I

18 Laws grind the poor, and rich men rule the law.
Oliver Goldsmith (1728–74) Irish-born British writer. *The Traveller*

19 I know no method to secure the repeal of bad or obnoxious laws so effective as their stringent execution.
Ulysses Simpson Grant (1822–85) US president. Inaugural address, 4 Mar 1869

20 The Common Law of England has been laboriously built about a mythical figure – the figure of 'The Reasonable Man'.
A. P. Herbert (1890–1971) British writer and politician. *Uncommon Law*

21 In *this* country, my Lords, . . . the individual subject . . . 'has nothing to do with the laws but to obey them.'
Bishop Samuel Horsley (1733–1806) British bishop. House of Lords, 13 Nov 1795

22 Oh, Mr. President, do not let so great an achievement suffer from any taint of legality.
Philander Chase Knox (1853–1921) US lawyer and politician. Responding to Theodore Roosevelt's request for legal justification of his acquisition of the Panama Canal Zone. *Violent Neighbours* (T. Buckley)

23 In university they don't tell you that the greater part of the law is learning to tolerate fools.
Doris Lessing (1919–) British novelist. *Martha Quest*, Pt. III, Ch. 2

24 No brilliance is needed in the law. Nothing but common sense, and relatively clean finger nails.
John Mortimer (1923–) British lawyer and dramatist. *A Voyage Round My Father*, I

25 Laws were made to be broken.
Christopher North (John Wilson; 1785–1854) Scottish writer. *Noctes Ambrosianae*, 24 May 1830

26 Let us consider the reason of the case. For nothing is law that is not reason.
John Powell (1645–1713) English judge. Coggs v. Bernard, 2 Lord Raymond, 911

27 Any institution which does not suppose the people good, and the magistrate corruptible is evil.
Robespierre (1758–94) French lawyer and revolutionary. *Déclaration des Droits de l'homme*, 24 Apr 1793

28 Every law is a contract between

the king and the people and therefore to be kept.

John Selden (1584–1654) English historian. *Table Talk*

29 Ignorance of the law excuses no man; not that all men know the law, but because 'tis an excuse every man will plead, and no man can tell how to confute him.

John Selden *Table Talk*

30 We must not make a scarecrow of the law,
Setting it up to fear the birds of prey,
And let it keep one shape, till custom make it
Their perch and not their terror.

William Shakespeare (1564–1616) English dramatist. *Measure for Measure*, II:1

31 Let him look to his bond.

William Shakespeare *The Merchant of Venice*, III:1

32 Wrest once the law to your authority:
To do a great right, do a little wrong.

William Shakespeare *The Merchant of Venice*, IV:1

33 Still you keep o' th' windy side of the law.

William Shakespeare *Twelfth Night*, III:4

34 Laws are generally found to be nets of such a texture, as the little creep through, the great break through, and the middle-sized are alone entangled in.

William Shenstone (1714–63) British poet. *See also* BACON, SOLON; SWIFT *Essays on Men, Manners, and Things*, 'On Politics'

35 Laws are like spider's webs: if some poor weak creature come up against them, it is caught; but a bigger one can break through and get away.

Solon (6th century BC) Athenian statesman. *See also* BACON, SHENSTONE; SWIFT *Lives of the Eminent Philosophers* (Diogenes Laertius), I

36 Laws are like cobwebs, which may catch small flies, but let wasps and hornets break through.

Jonathan Swift (1667–1745) Irish-born Anglican priest and writer. *See also* BACON, SHENSTONE, SOLON. *A Tritical Essay upon the Faculties of the Mind*

37 Everybody talks of the constitution, but all sides forget that the constitution is extremely well, and would do very well, if they would but let it alone.

Horace Walpole (1717–97) British writer. Letter to Sir Horace Mann, 1770

LAWRENCE, D(avid) H(erbert)

(1885–1930) British novelist. The son of a coalminer, he earned his reputation with the autobiographical *Sons and Lovers* (1913). Subsequent novels include *Women in Love* (1921), *Kangaroo* (1923), and *Lady Chatterley's Lover* (1928).

Quotations about Lawrence

1 Interesting, but a type I could not get on with. Obsessed with self. Dead eyes and a red beard, long narrow face. A strange bird.

John Galsworthy (1867–1933) British novelist. *Life and Letters* (edited by H. V. Marriot)

2 For Lawrence, existence was one long convalescence, it was as though he were newly reborn from a mortal illness every day of his life.

Aldous Huxley (1894–1964) British novelist. *The Olive Tree*

Quotations by Lawrence

3 You must always be a-waggle with LOVE.

Bibbles

4 The English people on the whole are surely the *nicest* people in the world, and everyone makes everything so easy for everybody else, that there is almost nothing to resist at all.

Dull London

5 To the Puritan all things are impure, as somebody says.

Etruscan Places, 'Cerveteri'

6 The Romans and Greeks found everything human. Everything had a face, and a human voice. Men spoke, and their fountains piped an answer.

Fantasia of the Unconscious, Ch. 4

7 The refined punishments of the spiritual mode are usually much more indecent and dangerous than a good smack.

Fantasia of the Unconscious, Ch. 4

8 Morality which is based on ideas, or on an ideal, is an unmitigated evil.

Fantasia of the Unconscious, Ch. 7

9 When Eve ate this particular apple, she became aware of her own womanhood, mentally. And mentally she began to experiment with it. She has been experimenting ever since. So has man. To the rage and horror of both of them.

Fantasia of the Unconscious, Ch. 7

10 O pity the dead that are dead, but cannot make
the journey, still they moan and beat against the silvery adamant walls of life's exclusive city.

The Houseless Dead

11 How beastly the bourgeois is especially the male of the species.

How beastly the bourgeois is

12 You may be the most liberal Liberal Englishman, and yet you cannot fail to see the categorical difference between the responsible and the irresponsible classes.

Kangaroo, Ch. 1

13 And all lying mysteriously within the Australian underdark, that peculiar, lost weary aloofness of Australia. There was the vast town of Sydney. And it didn't seem to be real, it seemed to be sprinkled on the surface of a darkness into which it never penetrated.

Kangaroo, Ch. 1

14 The very best that is in the Jewish blood: a faculty for pure disinterestedness, and warm, physically warm love, that seems to make the corpuscles of the blood glow.

Kangaroo, Ch. 6

15 We have all lost the war. All Europe.

The Ladybird, 'The Ladybird'

16 The young Cambridge group, the group that stood for 'freedom' and flannel trousers and flannel shirts open at the neck, and a well-bred sort of emotional anarchy, and a whispering, murmuring sort of voice, and an ultra-sensitive sort of manner.

Lady Chatterley's Lover, Ch. 1

17 It's all this cold-hearted fucking that is death and idiocy.

Lady Chatterley's Lover, Ch. 14

18 But tha mun dress thysen, an' go back to thy stately homes of England, how beautiful they stand. Time's up! Time's up for Sir John, an' for little Lady Jane! Put thy shimmy on, Lady Chatterley!

Lady Chatterley's Lover, Ch. 15

19 Water is H_2O, hydrogen two parts, oxygen one,

but there is also a third thing, that makes it water
and nobody knows what that is.
Pansies, 'The Third Thing'

20 It always seemed to me that men wore their beards, like they wear their neckties, for show. I shall always remember Lewis for saying his beard was part of him.
St Mawr

21 The modern pantheist not only sees the god in everything, he takes photographs of it.
St Mawr

22 It was one of those places where the spirit of aboriginal England still lingers, the old savage England, whose last blood flows still in a few Englishmen, Welshmen, Cornishmen.
St Mawr

23 Ideal mankind would abolish death, multiply itself million upon million, rear up city upon city, save every parasite alive, until the accumulation of mere existence is swollen to a horror.
St Mawr

24 And suddenly she craved again for the more absolute silence of America. English stillness was so soft, like an inaudible murmur of voices, of presences.
St Mawr

25 You may have my husband, but not my horse. My husband won't need emasculating, and my horse I won't have you meddle with. I'll preserve one last male thing in the museum of this world, if I can.
St Mawr

26 There's nothing so artificial as sinning nowadays. I suppose it once was real.
St Mawr

27 One realizes with horror, that the race of men is almost extinct in Europe. Only Christ-like heroes and woman-worshipping Don Juans, and rabid equality-mongrels.
Sea and Sardinia, Ch. 3

28 A snake came to my water-trough
On a hot, hot day, and I in pyjamas for the heat,
To drink there.
Snake

29 And so, I missed my chance with one of the lords
Of life.
And I have something to expiate;
A pettiness.
Snake

30 When I read Shakespeare I am struck with wonder
That such trivial people should muse and thunder
In such lovely language.
When I Read Shakespeare

31 Be a good animal, true to your animal instincts.
The White Peacock, Pt. II, Ch. 2

32 No absolute is going to make the lion lie down with the lamb unless the lamb is inside.
The Later D. H. Lawrence

33 Away with all ideals. Let each individual act spontaneously from the for ever incalculable prompting of the creative wellhead within him. There is no universal law.
Phoenix, Preface to 'All Things are Possible' by Leo Shostov

34 Russia will certainly inherit the future. What we already call the greatness of Russia is only her pre-natal struggling.
Phoenix, Preface, 'All Things are Possible' by Leo Shostov

35 Pornography is the attempt to insult sex, to do dirt on it.
Phoenix, 'Pornography and Obscenity'

36 It is no good casting out devils. They belong to us, we must accept them and be at peace with them.
Phoenix, 'The Reality of Peace'

37 Neither can you expect a revolution, because there is no new baby in the womb of our society. Russia is a collapse, not a revolution.
Phoenix, 'The Good Man'

38 I am a man, and alive . . . For this reason I am a novelist. And being a novelist, I consider myself superior to the saint, the scientist, the philosopher, and the poet, who are all great masters of different bits of man alive, but never get the whole hog.
Phoenix, 'Why the Novel Matters'

39 We know these new English Catholics. They are the last words in Protest. They are Protestants protesting against Protestantism.
Phoenix, 'Review of Eric Gill, *Art Nonsense*'

40 To every man who struggles with his own soul in mystery, a book that is a book flowers once, and seeds, and is gone.
Phoenix, 'A Bibliography of D.H.L.'

41 I like to write when I feel spiteful: it's like having a good sneeze.
Letter to Lady Cynthia Asquith, Nov 1913

42 They are great parables, the novels, but false art. They are only parables. All the people are *fallen angels* – even the dirtiest scrubs. This I cannot stomach. People are not fallen angels, they are merely people.
Referring to the novels of Dostoyevsky. Letter to J. Middleton Murray and Katherine Mansfield, 17 Feb 1916

43 I am only half there when I am ill, and so there is only half a man to suffer. To suffer in one's whole self is so great a violation, that it is not to be endured.
Letter to Catherine Carswell, 16 Apr 1916

44 The dead don't die. They look on and help.
Letter

45 I'm not sure if a mental relation with a woman doesn't make it impossible to love her. To know the *mind* of a woman is to end in hating her. Love means the pre-cognitive flow . . . it is the honest state before the apple.
Letter to Dr Trigant Burrow, 3 Aug 1927

LAWYERS

See also law

1 He that is his own lawyer has a fool for a client.
Proverb

2 A lawyer never goes to law himself.
Proverb

3 A lawyer's opinion is worth nothing unless paid for.
Proverb

4 Lawyers are the only persons in whom ignorance of the law is not punished.
Jeremy Bentham (1748–1832) British philosopher. Attrib.

5 Woe unto you, lawyers! for ye have taken away the key of knowledge: ye entered not in yourselves, and them that were entering in ye hindered.
Bible: Luke 11:52

6 A client is fain to hire a lawyer to

keep from the injury of other lawyers – as Christians that travel in Turkey are forced to hire Janissaries, to protect them from the insolencies of other Turks.

Samuel Butler (1835–1902) British writer. *Prose Observations*

7 Hence it comes about that there is scarcely a man learned in the laws to be found in the realm who is not noble or sprung of noble lineage.

Sir John Fortescue (c. 1394–c. 1476) Chief justice of the King's Bench. *The Governance of England*

8 I do not care to speak ill of any man behind his back, but I believe the gentleman is an *attorney*.

Samuel Johnson (1709–84) British lexicographer. *Life of Johnson* (J. Boswell), Vol. II

9 A lawyer with his briefcase can steal more than a thousand men with guns.

Mario Puzo (1920–) US novelist. *The Godfather*

10 CADE. There shall be in England seven halfpenny loaves sold for a penny; the three-hooped pot shall have ten hoops; and I will make it felony to drink small beer. All the realm shall be in common, and in Cheapside shall my palfrey go to grass. And when I am king, – as king I will be, – . . . there shall be no money; all shall eat and drink on my score; and I will apparel them all in one livery, that they may agree like brothers, and worship me their lord.
DICK. The first thing we do, let's kill all the lawyers.

William Shakespeare (1564–1616) English dramatist. *Henry VI*, Pt. 2, IV:2

11 It is a very salutary check for a judge to realise that if he does say something silly it is liable to get into the papers.

Mr Justice Templeman (1920–) British judge. *Observer*, 20 Aug 1978

LAZINESS

See also bed, idleness

1 You can tell a British workman by his hands. They are always in his pockets.

Anonymous *Quote Unquote* (radio program), 26 June 1980

2 We grow old more through indolence, than through age.

Christina of Sweden (1626–89) Swedish queen. *Maxims (1660–1680)*

3 I make no secret of the fact that I would rather lie on a sofa than sweep beneath it. But you have to be efficient if you're going to be lazy.

Shirley Conran (1932–) Designer and journalist. *Superwoman*, 'The Reason Why'

4 I get my exercise acting as a pallbearer to my friends who exercise.

Chauncey Depew (1834–1928) US politician.

5 The only exercise I get is when I take the studs out of one shirt and put them in another.

Ring Lardner Jnr (1885–1933) US humorist. *Bartlett's Unfamiliar Quotations* (Leonard Louis Levinson)

6 Happy is the man with a wife to tell him what to do and a secretary to do it.

Lord Mancroft (1917–) British businessman and writer. *The Observer*, 'Sayings of the Week', 18 Dec 1966

7 Alas! The hours we waste in work
And similar inconsequence,
Friends, I beg you do not shirk
Your daily task of indolence.

Don Marquis (1878–1937) US journalist. *The Almost Perfect State*

8 For one person who dreams of making fifty thousand pounds, a hundred people dream of being left fifty thousand pounds.

A. A. Milne (1882–1956) British writer. *If I May*, 'The Future'

9 It is better to have loafed and lost than never to have loafed at all.

James Thurber (1894–1961) US humorist. *Fables for Our Time*, 'The Courtship of Arthur and Al'

10 'Tis the voice of the sluggard, I heard him complain:
'You have waked me too soon, I must slumber again.'

Isaac Watts (1674–1748) English theologian and hymn writer. *The Sluggard*

LEADERSHIP

See also guidance

1 I know that the right kind of political leader for the Labour Party is a desiccated calculating machine.

Aneurin Bevan (1897–1960) Welsh Labour politician. Usually regarded as a gibe at Hugh Gaitskell. Speech during Labour Party Conference, 29 Sept 1954

2 The trouble in modern democracy is that men do not approach to leadership until they have lost the desire to lead anyone.

Lord Beveridge (1879–1963) British economist. *The Observer*, 'Sayings of the Week', 15 Apr 1934

3 And he shall rule them with a rod of iron; as the vessels of a potter shall they be broken to shivers: even as I received of my Father.

Bible: Revelations 2:27

4 Captains of industry.

Thomas Carlyle (1795–1881) Scottish historian and essayist. *Past and Present*, Bk. IV, Ch. 4

5 As the Prime Minister put it to me . . . he saw his role as being that of Moses.

Peter Jay (1937–) British economist and broadcaster. Referring to a conversation with James Callaghan. *Guardian Weekly*, 18 Sept 1977

6 Let me pass, I have to follow them, I am their leader.

Alexandre Auguste Ledru-Rollin (1807–74) French lawyer and politician. Trying to force his way through a mob during the Revolution of 1848, of which he was one of the chief instigators. A similar remark is attributed to Bonar Law. *The Fine Art of Political Wit* (L. Harris)

7 Lions led by donkeys.

Erich Ludendorff (1865–1937) German general. Referring to British troops in World War I. Attrib.

8 Only one man in a thousand is a leader of men – the other 999 follow women.

Groucho Marx (Julius Marx; 1895–1977) US comedian. *News Review*

9 A leader who doesn't hesitate before he sends his nation into battle is not fit to be a leader.

Golda Meir (1898–1978) Russian-born Israeli stateswoman. *As Good as Golda* (ed. Israel and Mary Shenker)

10 No general in the midst of battle has a great discussion about what he is going to do if defeated.

David Owen (1938–) British politician. *The Observer*, 'Sayings of the Week', 6 June 1987

11 Out great captain's captain.

William Shakespeare (1564–1616) English dramatist. *Othello*, II:1

12 We were not born to sue, but to command.

William Shakespeare *Richard II*, I:1

13 A constant effort to keep his party together, without sacrificing either principle or the essentials of basic strategy, is the very stuff of

political leadership. Macmillan was canonised for it.
Harold Wilson (1916–) British politician and prime minister. *Final Term: The Labour Government 1974–76*

LEARNING

See also education, knowledge

1 I learned just by going around. I know all about Kleenex factories, and all sorts of things.
Princess Anne (1950–) The Princess Royal, only daughter of Elizabeth II. Attrib.

2 What we have to learn to do, we learn by doing.
Aristotle (384–322 BC) Greek philosopher. *Nicomachean Ethics*, Bk. II

3 Miss not the discourse of the elders: for they also learned of their fathers, and of them thou shalt learn understanding, and to give answer as need requireth.
Bible: Ecclesiasticus 8:9

4 Read, mark, learn and inwardly digest.
The Book of Common Prayer *Collect, 2nd Sunday in Advent*

5 An art can only be learned in the workshop of those who are winning their bread by it.
Samuel Butler (1835–1902) British writer. *Erewhon*, Ch. 20

6 LIBOV ANDREEVNA. Are you still a student?
TROFIMOV. I expect I shall be a student to the end of my days.
Anton Chekhov (1860–1904) Russian dramatist. *The Cherry Orchard*, I

7 I am always ready to learn although I do not always like being taught.
Winston Churchill (1874–1965) British statesman. *The Observer*, 9 Nov 1952

8 In the traditional method the child must say something that he has merely learned. There is all the difference in the world between having something to say, and having to say something.
John Dewey (1859–1952) US philosopher and educator. *Dewey On Education*

9 Remember that even the learned ignorance of a nomenclature is something to have mastered, and may furnish pegs to hang facts upon which would otherwise have strewed the floor of memory in loose disorder.
Oliver Wendell Holmes (1809–94) US writer and physician. *Medical Essays*, 'The Young Practitioner'

10 It is the true nature of mankind to learn from mistakes, not from example.
Fred Hoyle (1915–) British astronomer. *Into Deepest Space*

11 Thus men of more enlighten'd genius and more intrepid spirit must compose themselves to the risque of public censure, and the contempt of their jealous contemporaries, in order to lead ignorant and prejudic'd minds into more happy and successful methods.
John Jones (1729–91) Introductory lecture to his course in surgery

12 . . . that is what learning is. You suddenly understand something you've understood all your life, but in a new way.
Doris Lessing (1919–) British novelist. *The Four-Gated City*

13 You will have to learn many tedious things, . . . which you will forget the moment you have passed your final examination, but in anatomy it is better to have learned and lost than never to have learned at all.
W. Somerset Maugham (1874–1965) British writer and doctor. Given as advice to first-year medical students. *Of Human Bondage*, Ch. 54

14 The safest thing for a patient is to be in the hands of a man engaged in teaching medicine. In order to be a teacher of medicine the doctor must always be a student.
Charles H. Mayo (1865–1939) US physician. *Proceedings of the Staff Meetings of the Mayo Clinic*, 2:233, 1927

15 He intended, he said, to devote the rest of his life to learning the remaining twenty-two letters of the alphabet.
George Orwell (Eric Blair; 1903–50) British novelist. *Animal Farm*, Ch. 9

16 For where is any author in the world
Teaches such beauty as a woman's eye?
Learning is but an adjunct to oneself.
William Shakespeare (1564–1616) English dramatist. *Love's Labour's Lost*, IV:3

17 Not with blinded eyesight poring over miserable books.
Alfred, Lord Tennyson (1809–92) British poet. *Locksley Hall*

18 One impulse from a vernal wood
May teach you more of man,
Of moral evil and of good,
Than all the sages can.
William Wordsworth (1770–1850) British poet. *The Tables Turned*

19 Some for renown, on scraps of learning dote,
And think they grow immortal as they quote.
Edward Young (1683–1765) British poet. *Love of Fame*, I

LEISURE

See also idleness, merrymaking, pleasure, rest

1 The wisdom of a learned man cometh by opportunity of leisure: and he that hath little business shall become wise.
How can he get wisdom that holdeth the plough, and that glorieth in the goad, that driveth oxen, and is occupied in their labours, and whose talk is of bullocks?
Bible: Ecclesiasticus 38:24–25

2 We are closer to the ants than to the butterflies. Very few people can endure much leisure.
Gerald Brenan *Thoughts in a Dry Season*

3 Hey! Mr Tambourine Man, play a song for me.
I'm not sleepy and there is no place I'm going to.
Bob Dylan (Robert Allen Zimmerman; 1941–) US popular singer. *Mr Tambourine Man*

4 I am interested in leisure in the way that a poor man is interested in money. I can't get enough of it.
Prince Philip (1921–) The consort of Queen Elizabeth II. Attrib.

5 If all the year were playing holidays, To sport would be as tedious as to work.
William Shakespeare (1564–1616) English dramatist. *Henry IV, Part One*, I:2

6 Days off.
Spencer Tracy (1900–67) US film star. Explaining what he looked for in a script. Attrib.

LETTER-WRITING

See also communication

1 . . . a habit the pleasure of which increases with practice, but becomes more urksome with neglect.
Abigail Adams (1744–1818) US feminist. Letter to her daughter, 8 May 1808

2 Someone, somewhere, wants a letter from you.
Anonymous British Post Office slogan

3 When he wrote a letter, he would put that which was most material in the postscript, as if it had been a by-matter.
Francis Bacon (1561–1626) English philosopher. *See also* HAZLITT. *Essays*, 'Of Cunning'

4 His sayings are generally like women's letters; all the pith is in the postscript.
William Hazlitt (1778–1830) British essayist. Referring to Charles Lamb. *See also* BACON *Conversations of Northcote*

LEXICOGRAPHY

1 To finish is both a relief and a release from an extraordinarily pleasant prison.
Dr. Robert Burchfield (1923–) New Zealand editor. On completing the supplements to the Oxford English Dictionary. *The Observer*, 'Sayings of the Week', 11 Sept 1986

2 Like Webster's Dictionary
We're Morocco bound.
Johnny Burke (1908–64) US songwriter. Song, 'Road to Morocco' from the film *The Road to Morocco*

3 The responsibility of a dictionary is to record a language, not set its style.
Philip Babcock Gove (1902–72) US dictionary editor. Letter to *Life Magazine*, 17 Nov 1961

4 But these were the dreams of a poet doomed at last to wake a lexicographer.
Samuel Johnson (1709–84) British lexicographer. *Dictionary of the English Language*

5 I have protracted my work till most of those whom I wished to please have sunk into the grave; and success and miscarriage are empty sounds.
Samuel Johnson *Dictionary of the English Language*

6 *Lexicographer.* A writer of dictionaries, a harmless drudge.
Samuel Johnson *Dictionary of the English Language*

7 *Dull.* 8. To make dictionaries is dull work.
Samuel Johnson (1709–84)

8 I've been in *Who's Who*, and I know what's what, but this is the first time I ever made the dictionary.
Mae West (1892–1980) US actress. On having a life-jacket named after her. Attrib.

LIARS

See lying

LIBERALISM

1 You Liberals think that goats are just sheep from broken homes.
Malcolm Bradbury (1932–) British academic and novelist. *After Dinner Game* (with Christopher Bigsby)

2 To be absolutely honest, what I feel really bad about is that I don't feel worse. There's the ineffectual liberal's problem in a nutshell.
Michael Frayn (1933–) British journalist and writer. *The Observer*, 8 Aug 1965

3 The permissive society has been allowed to become a dirty phrase. A better phrase is the civilized society.
Roy Jenkins (1920–) British Liberal Democrat politician (formerly a Labour Home Secretary). Speech, Abingdon, 19 July 1969

4 When a liberal is abused, he says: Thank God they didn't beat me. When he is beaten, he thanks God they didn't kill him. When he is killed, he will thank God that his immortal soul has been delivered from its mortal clay.
Lenin (Vladimir Ilich Ulyanov; 1870–1924) Russian revolutionary leader. Lenin heard this characterization at a meeting, and repeated it with approval. *The Government's Falsification of the Duma and the Tasks of the Social-Democrats*, 'Proletary', Dec 1906

5 A pleasant old buffer, nephew to a lord,
Who believed that the bank was mightier than the sword,
And that an umbrella might pacify barbarians abroad:
Just like an old liberal
Between the wars.
William Plomer (1903–73) South African poet and novelist. *Father and Son: 1939*

LIE

1 Without lies humanity would perish of despair and boredom.
Anatole France (Jacques Anatole François Thibault; 1844–1922) French writer. *The Bloom of Life*, 1922

LIFE

See also afterlife, human condition, life and death, mortality, purpose, time, world-weariness

1 Life begins at forty.
Proverb

2 Life is just a bowl of cherries.
Proverb

3 Life is sweet.
Proverb

4 Is it so small a thing
To have enjoy'd the sun,
To have lived light in the spring,
To have loved, to have thought, to have done?
Matthew Arnold (1822–88) British poet and critic. *Empedocles on Etna*

5 Before this strange disease of modern life,
With its sick hurry, its divided aims.
Matthew Arnold *The Scholar Gipsy*

6 Who saw life steadily, and saw it whole:
The mellow glory of the Attic stage.
Matthew Arnold *Sonnets to a Friend*

7 Remember that no man loses any other life than this which he now lives, nor lives any other than this which he now loses.
Marcus Aurelius (121–180 AD) Roman emperor. *Meditations*, Bk. II, Ch. 14

8 The universe is transformation; our life is what our thoughts make it.
Marcus Aurelius *Meditations*, Bk. IV, Ch. 3

9 The present life of men on earth, O king, as compared with the whole length of time which is unknowable to us, seems to me to be like this: as if, when you are sitting at dinner with your chiefs and ministers in wintertime, . . . one of the sparrows from outside flew very quickly through the hall; as if it came in one door and soon went out through another. In that actual time it is indoors it is not touched by the winter's storm; but yet the tiny period of calm is over in a moment, and having come out of the winter it soon returns to the winter and slips out of your sight. Man's life appears to be more or less like this; and of what may follow it, or what preceded it, we are absolutely ignorant.
St Bede (The Venerable Bede; c. 673–735 AD) English churchman and historian. *Ecclesiastical History of the English People*, Bk. II, Ch. 13

10 Life is rather like a tin of sardines – we're all of us looking for the key.
Alan Bennett (1934–) British playwright. *Beyond the Fringe*

11 Your whole life is on the other side

of the glass. And there is nobody watching.
Alan Bennett *The Old Country*, I

12 A man of sixty has spent twenty years in bed and over three years eating.
Arnold Bennett (1867–1931) British novelist. *Bartlett's Unfamiliar Quotations* (Leonard Louis Levinson)

13 One should not exaggerate the importance of trifles. Life, for instance, is much too short to be taken seriously.
Nicolas Bentley (1907–78) British cartoonist and writer. Attrib.

14 Life is a partial, continuous, progressive, multiform and conditionally interactive self-realization of the potentialities of atomic electron states.
John Desmond Bernal (1901–71) *The Origin of Life*

15 For everything that lives is holy, life delights in life.
William Blake (1757–1827) British poet. *America*

16 At last awake
From life, that insane dream we take
For waking now.
Robert Browning (1812–89) British poet. *Easter-Day*, XIV

17 How good is man's life, the mere living! how fit to employ
All the heart and the soul and the senses for ever in joy!
Robert Browning *Saul*, IX

18 Life is one long process of getting tired.
Samuel Butler (1835–1902) British writer. *Notebooks*

19 Life is the art of drawing sufficient conclusions from insufficient premises.
Samuel Butler *Notebooks*

20 To live is like love, all reason is against it, and all healthy instinct for it.
Samuel Butler *Notebooks*

21 Is life worth living? This is a question for an embryo, not for a man.
Samuel Butler *Notebooks*

22 It's as large as life, and twice as natural!
Lewis Carroll (Charles Lutwidge Dodgson; 1832–98) British writer *Through the Looking-Glass*, Ch. 7

23 Living is a sickness from which sleep provides relief every sixteen hours. It's a palliative. The remedy is death.
Nicolas Chamfort (1741–94) French writer and wit.

24 Life is a tragedy when seen in close-up, but a comedy in long-shot.
Charlie Chaplin (Sir Charles Spencer C.; 1889–1977) British film actor. In *The Guardian*, Obituary, 28 Dec 1977

25 For there is good news yet to hear and fine things to be seen,
Before we go to Paradise by way of Kensal Green.
G. K. Chesterton (1874–1936) British writer. *The Rolling English Road*

26 Life is a maze in which we take the wrong turning before we have learnt to walk.
Cyril Connolly (1903–74) British journalist. *The Unquiet Grave*

27 Magnificently unprepared
For the long littleness of life.
Frances Cornford (1886–1960) British poet. *Rupert Brooke*

28 Life is an incurable Disease.
Abraham Cowley (1618–67) English poet. *Pindarique Odes*, 'To Dr. Scarborough', VI

29 Life was a funny thing that occurred on the way to the grave.
Quentin Crisp (c. 1910–) British model, publicist, and writer. *The Naked Civil Servant*

30 What a fine comedy this world would be if one did not play a part in it!
Denis Diderot (1713–84) French writer. *Letters to Sophie Volland*

31 People do not live nowadays – they get about ten percent out of life.
Isadora Duncan (1878–1927) US dancer. *This Quarter Autumn*, 'Memoirs'

32 'Put your shoes at the door, sleep, prepare for life.'
The last twist of the knife.
T. S. Eliot (1888–1965) US-born British poet and dramatist. *Rhapsody on a Windy Night*

33 I have measured out my life with coffee spoons.
T. S. Eliot *The Love Song of J. Alfred Prufrock*

34 Pain and death are a part of life. To reject them is to reject life itself.
Havelock Ellis (1859–1939) British psychologist. *On Life and Sex: Essays of Love and Virtue*, 2

35 One thing is certain, that Life flies;
One thing is certain, and the Rest is Lies;
The Flower that once has blown for ever dies.
Edward Fitzgerald (1809–83) British poet. *The Rubáiyát of Omar Khayyám* (1st edn.), XXVI

36 Personal relations are the important thing for ever and ever, and not this outer life of telegrams and anger.
E. M. Forster (1879–1970) British novelist. *Howards End*

37 Between
Our birth and death we may touch understanding
As a moth brushes a window with its wing.
Christopher Fry (1907–) British dramatist. *The Boy with a Cart*

38 Life is a jest; and all things show it.
I thought so once; but now I know it.
John Gay (1685–1732) English poet and dramatist. *My Own Epitaph*

39 I must consider more closely this cycle of good and bad days which I find coursing within myself. Passion, attachment, the urge to action, inventiveness, performance, order all alternate and keep their orbit; cheerfulness, vigor, energy, flexibility and fatigue, serenity as well as desire. Nothing disturbs the cycle for I lead a simple life, but I must still find the time and order in which I rotate.
Johann Wolfgang von Goethe (1749–1832) German poet and dramatist. *The Encyclopedia of Alternative Medicine and Self-Help* (ed. Malcolm Hulke)

40 Life's Little Ironies.
Thomas Hardy (1840–1928) British novelist. Title of book of stories

41 Life is made up of sobs, sniffles and smiles, with sniffles predominating.
O. Henry (William Sydney Porter; 1862–1910) US short-story writer. *The Gifts of the Magi*

42 Life is a fatal complaint, and an eminently contagious one.
Oliver Wendell Holmes (1809–94) US writer and physician. *The Poet at the Breakfast Table*, XII

43 Life is just one damned thing after another.
Elbert Hubbard (1856–1915) US writer. *A Thousand and One Epigrams*

44 Life isn't all beer and skittles.
Thomas Hughes (1822–96) British novelist. *Tom Brown's Schooldays*, Pt. I, Ch. 2

45 Live all you can; it's a mistake not to. It doesn't so much matter what you do in particular, so long as you have your life. If you haven't had that what *have* you had?

Henry James (1843–1916) US novelist. *The Ambassadors*, Bk. V, Ch. 2

46 The art of life is the art of avoiding pain.

Thomas Jefferson (1743–1826) US statesman. Letter to Maria Cosway, 12 Oct 1786

47 Pain is life – the sharper, the more evidence of life.

Charles Lamb (1775–1834) English essayist. Letter to Bernard Barton, 9 Jan 1824

48 Life is something to do when you can't get to sleep.

Fran Lebowitz (1950–) US writer. *The Observer*, 21 Jan 1979

49 Life is like a sewer. What you get out of it depends on what you put into it.

Tom Lehrer (1928–) US university teacher, songwriter, and entertainer. *We will all go together when we go*

50 Life is what happens to you while you're busy making other plans.

John Lennon (1940–80) British rock musician. *Beautiful Boy*

51 Our ingress into the world
Was naked and bare;
Our progress through the world
Is trouble and care.

Henry Wadsworth Longfellow (1807–82) US poet. *Tales of A Wayside Inn*, 'The Student's Tale'

52 The living are just the dead on holiday.

Maurice Maeterlinck (1862–1949) Belgian poet and playwright. Attrib.

53 All interest in disease and death is only another expression of interest in life.

Thomas Mann (1875–1955) German novelist. *The Magic Mountain*, 6

54 And thou wilt give thyself relief, if thou doest every act of thy life as if it were the last.

Marcus Aurelius (121–180 AD) Roman emperor. *Meditations*, Bk. II, Ch. 5

55 Life to me is like boarding-house wallpaper. It takes a long time to get used to it, but when you finally do, you never notice that it's there. And then you hear the decorators are arriving.

Derek Marlowe (1938–) British writer. *A Dandy in Aspic*

56 Life is not living, but living in health.

Martial (c. 40 AD–c. 104 AD) Roman poet. *Epigrams*, VI

57 It is not true that life is one damn thing after another – it's one damn thing over and over.

Edna St. Vincent Millay (1892–1950) US poet. *Letters of Edna St. Vincent Millay*

58 The aim of life is to live, and to live means to be aware, joyously, drunkenly, serenely, divinely aware.

Henry Miller (1891–1980) US novelist. *The Wisdom of the Heart*, 'Creative Death'

59 I've looked at life from both sides now
From win and lose and still somehow
It's life's illusions I recall
I really don't know life at all.

Joni Mitchell (1945–) Singer and songwriter. *Both Sides Now*

60 There are three ingredients in the good life: learning, earning and yearning.

Christopher Darlington Morley (1890–1957) US writer. *Parnassus on Wheels*, Ch. 10

61 Life is just one damned thing after another.

Frank Ward O'Malley (1875–1932) US writer. Attrib.

62 Life is for each man a solitary cell whose walls are mirrors.

Eugene O'Neill (1888–1953) US dramatist. *Lazarus Laughed*

63 Life is perhaps best regarded as a bad dream between two awakenings.

Eugene O'Neill *Marco Millions*

64 Our lives are merely strange dark interludes in the electric display of God the Father.

Eugene O'Neill *Strange Interlude*

65 Most people get a fair amount of fun out of their lives, but on balance life is suffering and only the very young or the very foolish imagine otherwise.

George Orwell (Eric Blair; 1903–50) British novelist. *Shooting an Elephant*

66 Life Begins at Forty.

William B. Pitkin (1878–1953) US professor in journalism. Book title

67 The vanity of human life is like a river, constantly passing away, and yet constantly coming on.

Alexander Pope (1688–1744) British poet. *Thoughts on Various Subjects*

68 A Dance to the Music of Time.

Anthony Powell (1905–) British novelist. From the name of a painting by Nicolas Poussin. Book title

69 Life is not a spectacle or a feast; it is a predicament.

George Santayana (1863–1952) US philosopher. *The Perpetual Pessimist* (Sagittarius and George)

70 There is no cure for birth and death save to enjoy the interval.

George Santayana *Soliloquies in England*, 24, 'War Shrines'

71 It is only in the microscope that our life looks so big. It is an indivisible point, drawn out and magnified by the powerful lenses of Time and Space.

Arthur Schopenhauer (1788–1860) German philosopher. *Parerga and Paralipomena*, 'The Vanity of Existence'

72 O, how full of briers is this
working-day world!

William Shakespeare (1564–1616) English dramatist. *As You Like It*, I:3

73 And so, from hour to hour, we ripe and ripe,
And then, from hour to hour, we rot and rot;
And thereby hangs a tale.

William Shakespeare *As You Like It*, II:7

74 . . . the time of life is short;
To spend that shortness basely were too long.

William Shakespeare *Henry IV, Part 1*, V:2

75 Life is as tedious as a twice-told tale
Vexing the dull ear of a drowsy man.

William Shakespeare *King John*, III:4

76 Tomorrow, and tomorrow, and tomorrow,
Creeps in this petty pace from day to day
To the last syllable of recorded time,
And all our yesterdays have lighted fools
The way to dusty death. Out, out, brief candle!
Life's but a walking shadow, a poor player,
That struts and frets his hour upon the stage,
And then is heard no more; it is a tale
Told by an idiot, full of sound and fury,
Signifying nothing.

William Shakespeare *Macbeth*, V:5

77 I hold the world but as the world, Gratiano;
A stage where every man must play a part,

And mine a sad one.
William Shakespeare *The Merchant of Venice,* I:1

78 Life is a disease; and the only difference between one man and another is the stage of the disease at which he lives.
George Bernard Shaw (1856–1950) Irish dramatist and critic. *Back to Methuselah,* II, 'Gospel of the Brothers Barnabas'

79 Lift not the painted veil which those who live
Call life.
Percy Bysshe Shelley (1792–1822) British poet. *Lift not the Painted Veil*

80 Living well and beautifully and justly are all one thing.
Socrates (469 BC–399 BC) Greek philosopher. *Crito* (Plato)

81 Life is a gamble, at terrible odds – if it was a bet, you wouldn't take it.
Tom Stoppard (1937–) Czech-born British dramatist. *Rosencrantz and Guildenstern Are Dead,* III

82 As our life is very short, so it is very miserable, and therefore
it is well it is short.
Jeremy Taylor (1613–67) English Anglican theologian. *The Rule and Exercise of Holy Dying*

83 To preserve a man alive in the midst of so many chances and hostilities, is as great a miracle as to create him.
Jeremy Taylor *The Rule and Exercise of Holy Dying*

84 A life that moves to gracious ends
Thro' troops of unrecording friends,
A deedful life, a silent voice.
Alfred, Lord Tennyson (1809–92) British poet. *To – , after reading a Life and Letters*

85 Oh, isn't life a terrible thing, thank God?
Dylan Thomas (1914–53) Welsh poet. *Under Milk Wood*

86 For life is but a dream whose shapes return,
Some frequently, some seldom, some by night
And some by day.
James Thomson (1834–82) British poet. *The City of Dreadful Night,* I

87 The world is a comedy to those who think, a tragedy to those who feel.
Horace Walpole (1717–97) British writer. Letter to Sir Horace Mann, 1769

88 I spent the afternoon musing on Life. If you come to think of it, what a queer thing Life is! So unlike anything else, don't you know, if you see what I mean.
P. G. Wodehouse (1881–1975) British humorous novelist. *My Man Jeeves,* 'Rallying Round Old George'

89 When I think of all the books I have read, and of the wise words I have heard spoken, and of the anxiety I have given to parents and grandparents, and of the hopes that I have had, all life weighed in the scales of my own life seems to me preparation for something that never happens.
W. B. Yeats (1865–1939) Irish poet. *Autobiography*

90 We begin to live when we have conceived life as a tragedy.
W. B. Yeats *Autobiography*

91 Never to have lived is best, ancient writers say;
Never to have drawn the breath of life,
never to have looked into the eye of day
The second best's a gay goodnight and quickly turn away.
W. B. Yeats *Oedipus at Colonus*

LIFE AND DEATH

See also death, life

1 The first breath is the beginning of death.
Proverb

2 Dying is as natural as living.
Proverb

3 The thing to remember is that each time of life has its appropriate rewards, whereas when you're dead it's hard to find the light switch. The chief problem about death, incidentally, is the fear that there may be no afterlife – a depressing thought, particularly for those who have bothered to shave. Also, there is the fear that there is an afterlife but no one will know where it's being held. On the plus side, death is one of the few things that can be done as easily lying down.
Woody Allen (Allen Stewart Konigsberg; 1935–) US film actor and director. *Without Feathers,* 'The Early Essays'

4 In my happier days I used to remark on the aptitude of the saying, 'When in life we are in the midst of death'. I have since learnt that it's more apt to say, 'When in death we are in the midst of life'.
Anonymous Said by a survivor from Belsen. *The Oxford Book of Death* (D.J. Enright)

5 Every moment dies a man,
Every moment one and one sixteenth is born.
Charles Babbage (1792–1871) British mathematician. A parody of TENNYSON's *Vision of Sin.* Letter to Tennyson

6 It is as natural to die as to be born; and to a little infant, perhaps, the one is as painful as the other.
Sir Francis Bacon (1561–1626) English philosopher, lawyer, and politician. *Essays,* 'Of Death'

7 Life, the permission to know death.
Djuna Barnes (1892–) US writer. *Nightwood*

8 . . . Human life is mainly a process of filling in time until the arrival of death, or Santa Claus, with very little choice, if any, of what kind of business one is going to transact during the long wait.
Eric Berne *Games People Play,* Ch. 18

9 I call heaven and earth to record this day against you, that I have set before you life and death, blessing and cursing: therefore choose life, that both thou and thy seed may live.
Bible: Deuteronomy 30:19

10 But Jesus said unto him, Follow me; and let the dead bury their dead.
Bible: Matthew 8:22

11 Life itself is but the shadow of death, and souls but the shadows of the living. All things fall under this name. The sun itself is but the dark *simulacrum,* and light but the shadow of God.
Thomas Browne (1605–82) English physician and writer. *The Garden of Cyrus*

12 This world nis but a thurghfare ful of wo,
And we ben pilgrimes, passinge to and fro;
Deeth is an ende of every worldly sore.
Geoffrey Chaucer (c. 1342–1400) English poet. *The Canterbury Tales,* 'The Knight's Tale'

13 Birth, and copulation, and death.
That's all the facts when you come to brass tacks.
T. S. Eliot (1888–1965) US-born British poet and dramatist. *Sweeney Agonistes,* 'Fragment of an Agon'

14 I came like Water, and like Wind I go.
Edward Fitzgerald (1809–83) British poet. *The Rubáiyát of Omar Khayyám* (1st edn.), XXVIII

15 The memory of birth and the expectation of death always lurk within the human being, making him separate from his fellows and consequently capable of intercourse with them.
E. M. Forster (1879–1970) British writer. 'What I Believe'

16 A man is not completely born until he be dead.
Benjamin Franklin (1706–90) US scientist and statesman. *Letters to Miss Hubbard*

17 When he can keep life no longer in, he makes a fair and easie passage for it to go out.
Thomas Fuller (1608–61) English historian. *The Holy State,* Ch. 17

18 The most rational cure after all for the inordinate fear of death is to set a just value on life.
William Hazlitt (1778–1830) British essayist and journalist. *Table Talk,* 'On the Fear of Death'

19 I believe that the struggle against death, the unconditional and self-willed determination to live, is the motive power behind the lives and activities of all outstanding men.
Hermann Hesse (1877–1962) German novelist and poet. *Steppenwolf,* 'Treatise on the Steppenwolf'

20 There are only three events in a man's life; birth, life, and death; he is not conscious of being born, he dies in pain, and he forgets to live.
Jean de La Bruyère (1645–96) French satirist. *Les Caractères*

21 I strove with none; for none was worth my strife;
Nature I loved, and, next to Nature, Art;
I warmed both hands before the fire of life;
It sinks, and I am ready to depart.
Walter Savage Landor (1775–1864) British poet and writer. *I Strove with None*

22 Many men would take the death-sentence without a whimper to escape the life-sentence which fate carries in her other hand.
T. E. Lawrence (1888–1935) British soldier and writer. *The Mint,* Pt. I, Ch. 4

23 If you wish to live, you must first attend your own funeral.
Katherine Mansfield (1888–1923) New-Zealand-born British writer. *Katherine Mansfield* (Antony Alpers)

24 Life is a great surprise. I do not see why death should not be an even greater one.
Vladimir Nabokov (1899–1977) Russian-born US novelist. *Pale Fire,* 'Commentary'

25 Who was it that said the living are the dead on holiday?
Terry Nation *Dr Who,* BBC TV, 1980

26 When a man lies dying, he does not die from the disease alone. He dies from his whole life.
Charles Péguy (1873–1914) *Basic Verities,* 'The Search for Truth'

27 There is no cure for birth and death save to enjoy the interval.
George Santayana (1863–1952) US philosopher. *Soliloquies in England,* 'War Shrines'

28 Fare thee well, great heart!
Ill-weav'd ambition, how much art thou shrunk!
When that this body did contain a spirit,
A kingdom for it was too small a bound;
But now two paces of the vilest earth
Is room enough: this earth, that bears thee dead,
Bears not alive so stout a gentleman.
William Shakespeare (1564–1616) English dramatist. *Henry IV, Part 1,* V:4

29 He hath awakened from the dream of life –
'Tis we, who lost in stormy visions, keep
With phantoms an unprofitable strife,
And in mad trance, strike with our spirit's knife
Invulnerable nothings.
Percy Bysshe Shelley (1792–1822) British poet. *Adonais,* XXXIX

30 If we are aware of what indicates life, which everyone may be supposed to know, though perhaps no one can say that he truly and clearly understands what constitutes it, we at once arrive at the discrimination of death. It is the cessation of the phenomena with which we are so especially familiar – the phenomena of life.
J. G. Smith *Principles of Forensic Medicine*

31 Every moment dies a man,
Every moment one is born.
Alfred, Lord Tennyson (1809–92) British poet. For a parody, *see* BABBAGE *The Vision of Sin*

32 Because there is no difference.
Thales (c. 624–547 BC) Greek philosopher and astronomer. His reply when asked why he chose to carry on living after saying there was no difference between life and death. *The Story of Civilization* (W. Durant), Vol. 2

33 All say, 'How hard it is that we have to die' – a strange complaint to come from the mouths of people who have had to live.
Mark Twain (Samuel L. Clemens; 1835–1910) US writer. *Pudd'nhead Wilson*

34 Science says: 'We must live,' and seeks the means of prolonging, increasing, facilitating and amplifying life, of making it tolerable and acceptable; wisdom says: 'We must die,' and seeks how to make us die well.
Miguel de Unamuno y Jugo (1864–1936) Spanish writer and philosopher. *Essays and Soliloquies,* 'Arbitrary Reflections'

LIGHT

1 And he changeth the times and the seasons: he removeth kings, and setteth up kings: he giveth wisdom unto the wise, and knowledge to them that know understanding:
He revealeth the deep and secret things: he knoweth what is in the darkness, and the light dwelleth with him.
Bible: Daniel 2:21–22

2 Then I saw that wisdom excelleth folly, as far as light excelleth darkness.
The wise man's eyes are in his head; but the fool walketh in darkness: and I myself perceived also that one event happeneth to them all.
Bible: Ecclesiastes 2:13–14

3 In the beginning God created the heaven and the earth.
And the earth was without form, and void; and darkness was upon the face of the deep. And the Spirit of God moved upon the face of the waters.
And God said, Let there be light: and there was light.
And God saw the light, that it was good: and God divided the light from the darkness.
And God called the light Day, and the darkness he called Night. And the

evening and the morning were the first day.
Bible: Genesis 1:1–5

4 And God made two great lights: the greater light to rule the day, and the lesser light to rule the night: he made the stars also.
Bible: Genesis 1:16

5 Then spake Jesus again unto them, saying, I am the light of the world: he that followeth me shall not walk in darkness, but shall have the light of life.
Bible: John 8:12

6 Lord, now lettest thou thy servant depart in peace, according to thy word:
For mine eyes have seen thy salvation,
Which thou hast prepared before the face of all people;
A light to lighten the Gentiles, and the glory of thy people Israel.
Bible: Luke 2:29–32

7 There was a young lady named Bright,
Whose speed was far faster than light;
She set out one day
In a relative way,
And returned home the previous night.
Arthur Henry Reginald Buller (1874–1944) British botanist. *Limerick*

8 Wandering in a vast forest at night, I have only a faint light to guide me. A stranger appears and says to me: 'My friend, you should blow out your candle in order to find your way more clearly.' This stranger is a theologian.
Denis Diderot (1713–84) French writer. *Addition aux Pensées philosophiques*

9 And I said to the man who stood at the gate of the year: 'Give me a light that I may tread safely into the unknown'. And he replied: 'Go out into the darkness and put your hand into the hand of God. That shall be to you better than light and safer than a known way.'
Minnie Louise Haskins (1875–1957) US writer. Remembered because it was quoted by George VI in his Christmas broadcast, 1939. *The Desert,* Introduction

10 Be of good comfort, Master Ridley, and play the man; we shall this day light such a candle, by God's grace, in England as I trust shall never be put out.
Hugh Latimer (1485–1555) English churchman. Said to Nicholas Ridley as they were about to be burned at the stake for heresy. *Famous Last Words* (B. Conrad)

11 Light breaks where no sun shines;
Where no sea runs, the waters of the heart
Push in their tides.
Dylan Thomas (1914–53) Welsh poet. *Light breaks where no sun shines*

LIMBO

1 Wandering between two worlds, one dead,
The other powerless to be born.
Matthew Arnold (1822–88) British poet and critic. *The Grande Chartreuse*

LIMERICKS

A small selection

1 There's a wonderful family called Stein,
There's Gert and there's Epp and there's Ein;
Gert's poems are bunk,
Epp's statues are junk,
And no one can understand Ein.
Anonymous

2 There was a faith-healer of Deal,
Who said, 'Although pain isn't real,
If I sit on a pin
And it punctures my skin,
I dislike what I fancy I feel.'
Anonymous

3 There was an old man from Darjeeling,
Who boarded a bus bound for Ealing,
He saw on the door:
'Please don't spit on the floor,'
So he stood up and spat on the ceiling.
Anonymous

4 There was an old man of Boulogne
Who sang a most topical song.
It wasn't the words
That frightened the birds,
But the horrible double-entendre.
Anonymous

5 There was a young lady of Riga,
Who went for a ride on a tiger;
They returned from the ride
With the lady inside,
And a smile on the face of the tiger.
Anonymous

6 There was a young man of Japan
Whose limericks never would scan;
When they said it was so,
He replied, 'Yes, I know,
But I always try to get as many words into the last line as ever I possibly can.'
Anonymous

7 There was a young lady named Bright,
Whose speed was far faster than light;
She set out one day
In a relative way,
And returned home the previous night.
Arthur Henry Reginald Buller (1874–1944) British botanist. *Limerick*

8 There once was a man who said 'God
Must think it exceedingly odd
If he find that this tree
Continues to be
When there's no one about in the Quad.'
Ronald Knox (1888–1957) British Roman Catholic priest and writer. For a reply, see below. Attrib.

9 Dear Sir, Your astonishment's odd:
I am always about in the Quad.
And that's why the tree
Will continue to be,
Since observed by Yours faithfully,
God.
Anonymous A reply to KNOX.

10 There was an Old Man with a beard,
Who said, 'It is just as I feared! –
Two Owls and a Hen,
Four Larks and a Wren,
Have all built their nests in my beard!'
Edward Lear (1812–88) British artist and writer. *Book of Nonsense*

LINCOLN, Abraham

(1809–65) US statesman and Republican president (1861–65). He achieved freedom for slaves and the prohibition of slavery. He was assassinated a few days after the surrender of the South in the Civil War.

Quotations about Lincoln

1 Lincoln was not a type. He stands alone – no ancestors, no fellows, no successors.
Robert G. Ingersoll (1833–99) US lawyer and agnostic. *Reminiscences of Abraham Lincoln* (Allen T. Rice)

2 Mr Lincoln's soul seems made of

leather, and incapable of any grand or noble emotion.
Anonymous *New York Post,* 1863

Quotations by Lincoln

3 So you're the little woman who wrote the book that made this great war!
Said on meeting Harriet Beecher Stowe, the author of *Uncle Tom's Cabin* (1852), which stimulated opposition to slavery before the US Civil War. *Abraham Lincoln: The War Years* (Carl Sandburg), Vol. II, Ch. 39

4 The Lord prefers common-looking people. That is why he makes so many of them.
Our President (James Morgan), Ch. 6

5 Die when I may, I want it said of me by those who know me best, that I have always plucked a thistle and planted a flower where I thought a flower would grow.
Presidential Anecdotes (P. Boller)

6 I intend no modification of my oft-expressed personal wish that all men everywhere could be free.
Letter to Horace Greeley, 22 Aug 1862

7 If you don't want to use the army, I should like to borrow it for a while. Yours respectfully, A. Lincoln.
Letter to General George B. McClellan, whose lack of activity during the US Civil War irritated Lincoln.

8 No man is good enough to govern another man without that other's consent.
Speech, 1854

9 The ballot is stronger than the bullet.
Speech, 19 May 1856

10 Those who deny freedom to others, deserve it not for themselves.
Speech, 19 May 1856

11 What is conservatism? Is it not adherence to the old and tried, against the new and untried?
Speech, 27 Feb 1860

12 This country, with its institutions, belongs to the people who inhabit it. Whenever they shall grow weary of the existing government, they can exercise their constitutional right of amending it, or their revolutionary right to dismember or overthrow it.
First Inaugural Address, 4 Mar 1861

13 An old Dutch farmer, who remarked to a companion once that it was not best to swap horses in mid-stream.
Speech, 9 June 1864

14 In a larger sense we cannot dedicate, we cannot consecrate, we cannot hallow this ground. The brave men, living and dead, who struggled here, have consecrated it far above our power to add or detract. The world will little note, nor long remember, what we say here, but it can never forget what they did here. It is for us, the living, rather to be dedicated here to the unfinished work which they who fought here have thus far so nobly advanced. It is rather for us to be here dedicated to the great task remaining before us . . . that we here highly resolve that the dead shall not have died in vain, that this nation, under God, shall have a new birth of freedom; and that government of the people, by the people, and for the people, shall not perish from the earth.
Report of Lincoln's address at the dedication (19 Nov 1863) of the national cemetery on the site of the Battle of Gettysburg.

15 You can fool some of the people all the time and all the people some of the time; but you can't fool all the people all the time.
Attrib.

16 People who like this sort of thing will find this is the sort of thing they like.
A comment on a book. Attrib.

17 I can't spare this man; he fights.
Resisting demands for the dismissal of Ulysses Grant. Attrib.

18 Well, he looks like a man.
On catching sight of Walt Whitman for the first time. Attrib.

19 I don't know who my grandfather was; I am much more concerned to know what his grandson will be.
Taking part in a discussion on ancestry. Attrib.

LIQUOR

See alcohol

LITERACY

See also reading, writing

1 The ratio of literacy to illiteracy is constant, but nowadays the illiterates can read and write.
Alberto Moravia (Alberto Pincherle; 1907–) Italian novelist. *The Observer,* 14 Oct 1979

2 To be a well-favoured man is the gift of fortune; but to write and read comes by nature.
William Shakespeare (1564–1616) English dramatist. *Much Ado About Nothing,* III:3

LITERATURE

See also arts, books, criticism, fiction, novels, plays, poetry, poetry and prose, poets, prose, reading, theater, writers, writing

1 Literature is the art of writing something that will be read twice; journalism what will be grasped at once.
Cyril Connolly (1903–74) British journalist. *Enemies of Promise,* Ch. 3

2 A work that aspires, however humbly, to the condition of art should carry its justification in every line.
Joseph Conrad (Teodor Josef Konrad Korzeniowski; 1857–1924) Polish-born British novelist. *The Nigger of the Narcissus,* Preface

3 The reading of all good books is like a conversation with the finest men of past centuries.
René Descartes (1596–1650) French philosopher. *Le Discours de la méthode*

4 Only two classes of books are of universal appeal. The very best and the very worst.
Ford Maddox Ford (1873–1939) British novelist, critic, and poet. *Joseph Conrad*

5 God forbid people should read our books to find the juicy passages.
Graham Greene (1904–) British novelist. *The Observer,* 'Sayings of the Week', 14 Oct 1979

6 He knew everything about literature except how to enjoy it.
Joseph Heller (1923–) US novelist. *Catch-22,* Ch. 8

7 The proper study of mankind is books.
Aldous Huxley (1894–1964) British novelist. *Chrome Yellow*

8 That was the chief difference between literature and life. In books, the proportion of exceptional to commonplace people is high; in reality, very low.
Aldous Huxley *Eyeless in Gaza*

9 Literature flourishes best when it is half a trade and half an art.
Dean Inge (1860–1954) British churchman. *The Victorian Age*

10 It takes a great deal of history to produce a little literature.
Henry James (1843–1916) US novelist. *Life of Nathaniel Hawthorne,* Ch. 1

11 Was there ever yet anything written by mere man that was wished longer by its readers, excepting *Don Quixote, Robinson Crusoe,* and the *Pilgrim's Progress?*
Samuel Johnson (1709–84) British lexicographer. *Johnsonian Miscellanies* (ed. G. B. Hill), Vol. I

12 *Sturm und Drang.*
Storm and stress.
Friedrich Maximilian von Klinger (1752–1831) German dramatist and novelist. Used to designate a late 18th-century literary movement in Germany. Play title

13 Compared with this revolution the Renaissance is a mere ripple on the surface of literature.
C. S. Lewis (1898–1963) British academic and writer. Referring to the appearance of the concept of courtly love in the 12th century. *The Allegory of Love*

14 Our American professors like their literature clear and cold and pure and very dead.
Sinclair Lewis (1885–1951) US novelist. Speech, on receiving the Nobel Prize, 1930

15 Literature is mostly about having sex and not much about having children; life is the other way round.
David Lodge (1935–) British author. *The British Museum is Falling Down,* Ch. 4

16 You understand *Epipsychidion* best when you are in love; *Don Juan* when anger is subsiding into indifference. Why not Strindberg when you have a temperature?
Desmond MacCarthy (1877–1952) British writer and theater critic. *Theatre,* 'Miss Julie and the Pariah'

17 The idea of going to a writers' congress in Moscow is rather like attending a human rights conference in Nazi Germany.
David Markstein Member of the Writers' Guild of Great Britain.

18 Literature and butterflies are the two sweetest passions known to man.
Vladimir Nabokov (1899–1977) Russian-born US novelist. *Radio Times,* Oct 1962

19 Literature is news that STAYS news.
Ezra Pound (1885–1972) US poet. *ABC of Reading,* Ch. 2

20 Great Literature is simply language charged with meaning to the utmost possible degree.
Ezra Pound *How to Read*

21 His most rational response to my attempts at drawing him out about literature and art was 'I adore italics, don't you?'
Siegfried Sassoon (1886–1967) British poet. Referring to Ronald Fairbanks. *Siegfried's Journey*

22 Romanticism is the art of presenting people with the literary works which are capable of affording them the greatest possible pleasure, in the present state of their customs and beliefs.
Classicism, on the other hand, presents them with the literature that gave the greatest possible pleasure to their great-grandfathers.
Stendhal (Henri Beyle; 1783–1842) French novelist. *Racine et Shakespeare,* Ch. 3

23 Something that everybody wants to have read and nobody wants to read.
Mark Twain (Samuel Langhorne Clemens; 1835–1910) US writer. Definition of a classic of literature. Speech at Nineteenth Century Club, New York, 20 Nov 1900

24 '*Language,* man!' roared Parsons; 'why, it's LITERATURE!'
H. G. Wells (1866–1946) British writer. *The History of Mr Polly,* Pt. I, Ch. 3

25 Literature is the orchestration of platitudes.
Thornton Wilder (1897–1975) US novelist and dramatist. *Time* magazine

LLOYD GEORGE

1 He is without malice of any kind; without prejudices, without morals. He has many enemies and no friends. He does not understand what friendship means . . . and yet he is the best man we have got.
F. S. Oliver *The Anvil of War*

LOGIC

See also philosophy

1 *Logic, n.* The art ofthinking and reasoning in strict accordance with the limitations and incapacities of the human understanding.
Ambrose Bierce (1842–?1914) US writer and journalist. *The Devil's Dictionary*

2 'Contrariwise,' continued Tweedledee, 'if it was so, it might be; and if it were so, it would be: but as it isn't, it ain't. That's logic.'
Lewis Carroll (Charles Lutwidge Dodgson; 1832–98) British writer. *Through the Looking-Glass,* Ch. 4

3 A Clerk ther was of Oxenford also,
That un-to logik hadde longe y-go.
Geoffrey Chaucer (c. 1342–1400) English poet. *The Canterbury Tales,* Prologue

4 You can only find truth with logic if you have already found truth without it.
G. K. Chesterton (1874–1936) British writer. *The Man who was Orthodox*

5 Orr was crazy and could be grounded. All he had to do was ask; and as soon as he did, he would no longer be crazy and would have to fly more missions . . .
Yossarian was moved very deeply by the absolute simplicity of this clause of Catch-22 and let out a respectful whistle.
Joseph Heller (1923–) US novelist. *Catch-22*

6 Logical consequences are the scarecrows of fools and the beacons of wise men.
T. H. Huxley (1825–95) British biologist. *Science and Culture,* 'On the Hypothesis that Animals are Automata'

7 The world is everything that is the case.
Ludwig Wittgenstein (1889–1951) Austrian philosopher. *Tractatus Logico-Philosophicus,* Ch. 1

8 Logic must take care of itself.
Ludwig Wittgenstein *Tractatus Logico-Philosophicus,* Ch. 5

LONDON

See also England

1 The streets of London are paved with gold.
Proverb

2 Nobody is healthy in London, nobody can be.
Jane Austen (1775–1817) British novelist. *Emma,* Ch. 12

3 London is a splendid place to live in for those who can get out of it.
Lord Balfour of Burleigh (1884–1967) British financier. Attrib.

4 What a place to plunder!
Gebhard Blücher (1742–1819) Prussian general. Referring to London. Attrib.

5 Where's Troy, and where's the Maypole in the Strand?
Pease, cabbages and turnips once grew where
Now stands New Bond Street and a newer Square;
Such piles of buildings now rise up and down,

London itself seems going out of Town.
Our Fathers crossed from Fulham in a Wherry,
Their sons enjoy a Bridge at Putney Ferry.

James Bramston (c. 1694–1744) British poet. *The Whig Supremacy* (Basil Williams), Ch. 15

6 Let's all go down the Strand.

Harry Castling (19th century) British songwriter. Song title

7 But what is to be the fate of the great wen of all?

William Cobbett (1763–1835) British journalist and writer. A wen is a sebaceous cyst. *Rural Rides*

8 I don't know what London's coming to – the higher the buildings the lower the morals.

Noël Coward (1899–1973) British dramatist. *Law and Order*

9 London, that great cesspool into which all the loungers of the Empire are irresistibly drained.

Arthur Conan Doyle (1856–1930) British writer. *A Study in Scarlet*

10 Strong be thy wallis that about thee standis;
Wise be the people that within thee dwellis;
Fresh be thy ryver with his lusty strandis;
Blithe by thy chirches, wele swonyng be thy bellis;
Riche by they merchauntis in substaunce that excellis;
Fair be their wives, right lovesom, white and small;
Clere by thy virgyns, lusty under kellis:
London, thou art the flour of Cities all.

William Dunbar (1460–1530) Referring to London. *The Earlier Tudors* (J. D. Mackie)

11 This fatal night about ten, began that deplorable fire near Fish Street in London . . . all the sky were of a fiery aspect, like the top of a burning Oven, and the light seen above 40 miles round about for many nights.

John Evelyn (1620–1706) English diarist. The Fire of London (2–5 Sept 1666) began in a bakehouse in Pudding Lane and spread to two-thirds of the city. Diary, 23 Sept 1666

12 It is not the walls that make the city, but the people who live within them. The walls of London may be battered, but the spirit of the Londoner stands resolute and undismayed.

George VI (1895–1952) King of the United Kingdom. Radio broadcast to the Empire, 23 Sept 1940

13 Crowds without company, and dissipation without pleasure.

Edward Gibbon (1737–94) British historian. *Autobiography*

14 The tourists who come to our island take in the Monarchy along with feeding the pigeons in Trafalgar Square.

William Hamilton (1917–) Scottish MP. *My Queen and I*, Ch. 9

15 . . . the illustrious place, built by the skill of the ancient Romans, called throughout the world the great city of London.

Bishop Helmstan of Winchester *Cartularium Saxonicum*

16 I think the full tide of human existence is at Charing-Cross.

Samuel Johnson (1709–84) British lexicographer. *Life of Johnson* (J. Boswell), Vol. II

17 When a man is tired of London, he is tired of life; for there is in London all that life can afford.

Samuel Johnson *Life of Johnson* (J. Boswell), Vol. III

18 Oranges and lemons,
Say the bells of St Clement's.
You owe me five farthings,
Say the bells of St Martin's.
When will you pay me?
Say the bells of Old Bailey.
When I grow rich,
Say the bells of Shoreditch.
When will that be?
Say the bells of Stepney.
I'm sure I don't know,
Says the great bell at Bow.
Here comes a candle to light you to bed,
Here comes a chopper to chop off your head.

Nursery Rhyme *Tommy Thumb's Pretty Song Book*

19 Here out of the window it was a most pleasant sight to see the City from one end to the other with a glory about it, so high was the light of the bonfires, and so thick round the City, and the bells rang everywhere.

Samuel Pepys (1633–1703) English diarist. Describing the celebrations in London at the end of the Commonwealth. Diary, 21 Feb 1660

20 I would sell London, if I could find a suitable purchaser.

Richard I (1157–1199) King of England. Comment while raising money for the third Crusade. *Historia Rerum Anglicarum* (William of Newburgh), Bk. IV, Ch. 5

21 London, that great sea, whose ebb and flow
At once is deaf and loud, and on the shore
Vomits its wrecks, and still howls on for more.

Percy Bysshe Shelley (1792–1822) British poet. *Letter to Maria Gisborne*, I

22 Hell is a city much like London –
A populous and smoky city.

Percy Bysshe Shelley *Peter Bell the Third*

23 Crossing Piccadilly Circus.

Joseph Thomson (1858–95) Scottish explorer. His reply when asked by J. M. Barrie what was the most hazardous part of his expedition to Africa. *J. M. Barrie* (D. Dunbar)

24 Earth has not anything to show more fair:
Dull would he be of soul who could pass by
A sight so touching in its majesty:
The City now doth, like a garment, wear
The beauty of the morning; silent, bare,
Ships, towers, domes, theatres, and temples lie
Open unto the fields, and to the sky;
All bright and glittering in the smokeless air.

William Wordsworth (1770–1850) British poet. *Sonnets*, 'Composed upon Westminster Bridge'

LONELINESS

See also solitude

1 Oh! why does the wind blow upon me so wild? – It is because I'm nobody's child?

Phila Henrietta Case (fl. 1864) British poet. *Nobody's Child*

2 A fav'rite has no friend.

Thomas Gray (1716–71) British poet. *Ode on the Death of a Favourite Cat*

3 Pray that your loneliness may spur you into finding something to live for, great enough to die for.

Dag Hammarskjöld (1905–61) Swedish diplomat. *Diaries*, 1951

4 Waits at the window, wearing the face that she keeps in a jar by the door
Who is it for? All the lonely people, where do they all come from?

All the lonely people, where do they all belong?

John Lennon (1940–80) British rock musician. *Eleanor Rigby* (with Paul McCartney)

5 None But the Lonely Heart.

Richard Llewellyn British writer. Adapted from the English title of Tchaikowsky's song 'None But the Weary Heart' (original words by Goethe). Book title

6 My heart is a lonely hunter that hunts on a lonely hill.

Fiona Macleod (William Sharp; 1856–1905) Scottish poet and writer. *The Lonely Hunter*

7 At the moment of childbirth, every woman has the same aura of isolation, as though she were abandoned, alone.

Boris Pasternak (1890–1950) Russian writer. *Doctor Zhivago*, Ch. 9, Sect. 3

8 To be alone is the fate of all great minds – a fate deplored at times, but still always chosen as the less grievous of two evils.

Arthur Schopenhauer (1788–1860) German philosopher. *Aphorismen zur Lebensweisheit*

9 Don't think you can frighten me by telling me I am alone. France is alone; and God is alone; and what is my loneliness before the loneliness of my country and my God.

George Bernard Shaw (1856–1950) Irish dramatist and critic. *St. Joan*

10 When my bed is empty,
Makes me feel awful mean and blue.
My springs are getting rusty,
Living single like I do.

Bessie Smith (1894–1937) US blues singer. *Empty Bed Blues*

11 Loneliness and the feeling of being unwanted is the most terrible poverty.

Mother Teresa (Agnes Gonxha Bojaxhui; 1910–) Yugoslavian missionary in Calcutta. *Time*, 'Saints Among Us', 29 Dec 1975

12 The hunchback in the park
A solitary mister
Propped between trees and water.

Dylan Thomas (1914–53) Welsh poet. *The Hunchback in the Park*

13 She dwelt among the untrodden ways
Beside the springs of Dove,
A maid whom there were none to praise
And very few to love.

William Wordsworth (1770–1850) British poet. *She Dwelt Among the Untrodden Ways*

14 The wind blows out of the gates of the day,
The wind blows over the lonely of heart,
And the lonely of heart is withered away.

W. B. Yeats (1865–1939) Irish poet. *The Land of Heart's Desire*

LONGEVITY

See also age, life, old age

1 Get up at five, have lunch at nine,
Supper at five, retire at nine.
And you will live to ninety-nine.

Anonymous *Works*, Bk. IV, Ch. 64 (François Rabelais)

2 He that would live for aye, must eat sage in May.

Latin proverb

3 Aging seems to be the only available way to live a long time.

Daniel-François-Esprit Auber (1782–1871) French composer. *Dictionnaire Encyclopédique* (E. Guérard)

4 LONGEVITY, n. Uncommon extension of the fear of death.

Ambrose Bierce (1842–c. 1914) US writer and journalist. *The Devil's Dictionary*

5 People always wonder how I have achieved such a ripe age, and I can only say I never felt the urge to partake of the grape, the grain, or the weed, but I do eat everything.

Mrs Mary Borah Said at the age of 100. *Bartlett's Unfamiliar Quotations* (Leonard Louis Levinson)

6 Despair of all recovery spoils longevity,
And makes men's miseries of alarming brevity.

Lord Byron (1788–1824) British poet. *Don Juan*, II

7 Longevity is the revenge of talent upon genius.

Cyril Connolly (1903–74) British journalist. *Sunday Times*, 19 June 1966

8 There is no short-cut to longevity. To win it is the work of a lifetime, and the promotion of it is a branch of preventive medicine.

Sir James Crichton-Browne (1840–1938) *The Prevention of Senility*

9 Have a chronic disease and take care of it.

Oliver Wendell Holmes (1809–94) US writer and physician. His formula for longevity.

10 Life protracted is protracted woe.

Samuel Johnson (1709–84) English lexicographer and writer. *The Vanity of Human Wishes*

11 Get your room full of good air, then shut up the windows and keep it. It will keep for years. Anyway, don't keep using your lungs all the time. Let them rest.

Stephen Leacock (1869–1944) English-born Canadian economist and humorist. *Literary Lapses*, 'How to Live to be 200'

12 The brain is the organ of longevity.

George Alban Sacher (1917–) *Perspectives in Experimental Gerontology*

13 Do not try to live forever. You will not succeed.

George Bernard Shaw (1856–1950) Irish dramatist and critic. *The Doctor's Dilemma*, 'Preface on Doctors'

14 I smoke almost constantly, sometimes in the middle of the night. And I drink anything I can get my hands on.

Joe Smart On his 100th birthday. *Bartlett's Unfamiliar Quotations* (Leonard Louis Levinson)

15 If you live long enough, the venerability factor creeps in; you get accused of things you never did and praised for virtues you never had.

I. F. Stone (1907–) US writer and publisher. *Peter's Quotations* (Laurence J. Peter)

16 They live ill who expect to live always.

Publilius Syrus (1st century BC) Roman dramatist. *Moral Sayings*, 457

17 Keep breathing.

Sophie Tucker (1884–1966) Russian-born US singer and vaudeville star. Her reply, at the age of 80, when asked the secret of her longevity. Attrib.

LONGFELLOW, Henry Wadsworth

(1807–82) US poet. A professor of modern languages, he traveled widely in Europe. His narrative poems, including *Evangeline* (1847) and *The Song of Hiawatha* (1855), achieved great popularity.

Quotations about Longfellow

1 Longfellow is to poetry what the barrel-organ is to music.

Van Wyck Brooks *The Flowering of New England*

2 The gentleman was a sweet, beautiful soul, but I have entirely forgotten his name.

Ralph Waldo Emerson (1803–82) US poet and essayist. Attending Longfellow's funeral. Attrib.

Quotations by Longfellow

3 I shot an arrow into the air,

It fell to earth, I knew not where.
The Arrow and the Song

4 I stood on the bridge at midnight,
As the clocks were striking the hour.
The Bridge

5 If you would hit the mark, you must aim a little above it;
Every arrow that flies feels the attraction of earth.
Elegiac Verse

6 Sorrow and silence are strong, and patient endurance is godlike.
Evangeline

7 The shades of night were falling fast,
As through an Alpine village passed
A youth, who bore, 'mid snow and ice,
A banner with the strange device,
Excelsior!
Opening of a poem best known as a Victorian drawing-room ballad, and the butt of many music hall jokes. Excelsior means 'higher' (Latin).
Excelsior

8 Know how sublime a thing it is
To suffer and be strong.
The Light of Stars

9 You would attain to the divine perfection,
And yet not turn your back upon the world.
Michael Angelo

10 Art is long, and Time is fleeting,
And our hearts, though stout and brave,
Still, like muffled drums, are beating
Funeral marches to the grave.
See also HIPPOCRATES *A Psalm of Life*

11 There is a Reaper whose name is Death,
And, with his sickle keen,
He reaps the bearded grain at a breath,
And the flowers that grow between.
The Reaper and the Flowers

12 'Wouldst thou' – so the helmsman answered –
'Learn the secret of the sea?
Only those who brave its dangers
Comprehend its mystery!'
The Secret of the Sea

13 Onaway! Awake, beloved!
Opening of the song sung by Chibiabos at Hiawatha's wedding feast; best known in the setting by Coleridge-Taylor. *The Song of Hiawatha,* XI, 'Hiawatha's Wedding-feast'

14 Our ingress into the world
Was naked and bare;
Our progress through the world
Is trouble and care.
Tales of A Wayside Inn, 'The Student's Tale'

15 Ships that pass in the night, and speak each other in passing;
Only a signal shown and a distant voice in the darkness;
So on the ocean of life we pass and speak one another,
Only a look and a voice; then darkness again and a silence.
Tales of a Wayside Inn, 'The Theologian's Tale. Elizabeth'

16 Under the spreading chestnut tree
The village smithy stands;
The smith, a mighty man is he,
With large and sinewy hands;
And the muscles of his brawny arms
Are strong as iron bands.
The Village Blacksmith

17 Looks the whole world in the face,
For he owes not any man.
The Village Blacksmith

18 It was the schooner Hesperus,
That sailed the wintry sea;
And the skipper had taken his little daughter,
To bear him company.
The Wreck of the Hesperus

LOSS

See also defeat, mourning

1 'Tis better to have loved and lost than never to have lost at all.
Samuel Butler (1835–1902) British writer. *The Way of All Flesh,* Ch. 77

2 What's lost upon the roundabouts we pulls up on the swings!
Patrick Reginald Chalmers (1872–1942) British banker and novelist. *Green Days and Blue Days: Roundabouts and Swings*

3 And much more am I sorrier for my good knights' loss than for the loss of my fair queen; for queens I might have enough, but such a fellowship of good knights shall never be together in no company.
Thomas Malory (1400–71) English writer. *Morte d'Arthur,* Bk. XX, Ch. 9

4 There is a ghost
That eats handkerchiefs;
It keeps you company
On all your travels.
Christian Morgenstern (1871–1914) German poet. *Der Gingganz,* 'Gespenst'

5 Where have all the flowers gone?
Young girls picked them every one.
Pete Seeger (1919–) US folksinger and songwriter. *Where Have All the Flowers Gone?*

6 Hast thou no care of me? shall I abide
In this dull world, which in thy absence is
No better than a sty? O! see my women,
The crown o' the earth doth melt. My lord!
William Shakespeare (1564–1616) English dramatist. *Antony and Cleopatra,* IV:13

7 My daughter! O my ducats! O my daughter!
Fled with a Christian! O my Christian ducats!
Justice! the law! my ducats, and my daughter!
William Shakespeare *The Merchant of Venice,* II:8

8 I've lost the only playboy of the western world.
John Millington Synge (1871–1909) Anglo-Irish dramatist. The closing words. *The Playboy of the Western World,* III

9 I've lost one of my children this week.
Joseph Turner (1775–1851) British painter. His customary remark following the sale of one of his paintings. *Sketches of Great Painters* (E. Chubb)

10 To lose one parent, Mr Worthing, may be regarded as a misfortune; to lose both looks like carelessness.
Oscar Wilde (1854–1900) Irish-born British dramatist. *The Importance of Being Earnest,* I

LOVE

See also admiration, love and death, love and friendship, love and hate, love and marriage, lust, passion, sex

1 All is fair in love and war.
Proverb

2 All the world loves a lover.
Proverb

3 Love laughs at locksmiths.
Proverb

4 Love makes the world go round.
Proverb

5 Love me, love my dog.
Proverb

6 Love will find a way.
Proverb

7 Lucky at cards, unlucky in love.
Proverb

8 No love like the first love.
Proverb

9 Salt water and absence wash away love.
Proverb

10 The way to a man's heart is through his stomach.
Proverb

11 True love never grows old.
Proverb

12 When poverty comes in at the door, love flies out of the window.
Proverb

13 In Scarlet town, where I was born,
There was a fair maid dwellin',
Made every youth cry *Well-a-way!*
Her name was Barbara Allen.

All in the merry month of May,
When green buds they were swellin',
Young Jemmy Grove on his death-bed lay,
For love of Barbara Allen.

So slowly, slowly rase she up,
And slowly she came nigh him,
And when she drew the curtain by –
'Young man, I think you're dyin'!'.
Anonymous *Barbara Allen's Cruelty*

14 Greensleeves was all my joy,
Greensleeves was my delight,
Greensleeves was my heart of gold,
And who but Lady Greensleeves.
Anonymous *Greensleeves*

15 There were twa sisters sat in a bour;
Binnorie, O Binnorie!
There came a knight to be their wooer,
By the bonnie milldams o' Binnorie.
Anonymous *Binnorie*

16 Oh, love is real enough, you will find it some day, but it has one arch-enemy – and that is life.
Jean Anouilh (1910–87) French dramatist. *Ardèle*

17 Love is, above all, the gift of oneself.
Jean Anouilh *Ardèle*

18 Tell me about yourself – your struggles, your dreams, your telephone number.
Peter Arno (1904–68) US cartoonist. Caption to a cartoon of a man talking to a woman

19 When it comes, will it come without warning
Just as I'm picking my nose?
Will it knock on my door in the morning,
Or tread in the bus on my toes?
Will it come like a change in the weather?
Will its greeting be courteous or rough?
Will it alter my life altogether?
O tell me the truth about love.
W. H. Auden (1907–73) British poet. *Twelve Songs*, XII

20 We must love one another or die.
W. H. Auden *September 1, 1939*

21 Nuptial love maketh mankind; friendly love perfecteth it; but wanton love corrupteth and embaseth it.
Francis Bacon (1561–1626) English philosopher. *Essays*, 'Of Love'

22 Women who love the same man have a kind of bitter freemasonry.
Max Beerbohm (1872–1956) British writer. *Zuleika Dobson*, Ch. 4

23 Love ceases to be a pleasure, when it ceases to be a secret.
Aphra Behn (1640–89) English novelist and dramatist. *The Lover's Watch*, 'Four o'clock'

24 And the king loved Esther above all the women, and she obtained grace and favour in his sight more than all the virgins; so that he set the royal crown upon her head, and made her queen instead of Vashti.
Bible: Esther 2:17

25 Beloved, let us love one another: for love is of God; and every one that loveth is born of God, and knoweth God.
He that loveth not knoweth not God; for God is love.
Bible: I John 4:7–8

26 There is no fear in love; but perfect love casteth out fear: because fear hath torment. He that feareth is not made perfect in love.
Bible: I John 4:18

27 If a man say, I love God, and hateth his brother, he is a liar: for he that loveth not his brother whom he hath seen, how can he love God whom he hath not seen?
Bible: I John 4:20

28 Greater love hath no man than this, that a man lay down his life for his friends.
Bible: John 15:13

29 Jesus said unto him, Thou shalt love the Lord thy God with all thy heart, and with all thy soul, and with all thy mind.
This is the first and great commandment.
And the second is like unto it, Thou shalt love thy neighbour as thyself.
On these two commandments hang all the law and the prophets.
Bible: Matthew 22:37–40

30 He brought me to the banqueting house, and his banner over me was love.
Stay me with flagons, comfort me with apples: for I am sick of love.
His left hand is under my head, and his right hand doth embrace me.
Bible: Song of Solomon 2:4–6

31 The voice of my beloved! behold, he cometh leaping upon the mountains, skipping upon the hills.
Bible: Song of Solomon 2:8

32 My beloved is mine, and I am his: he feedeth among the lilies.
Until the day break, and the shadows flee away, turn, my beloved, and be thou like a roe or a young hart upon the mountains of Bether.
Bible: Song of Solomon 2:16–17

33 Love seeketh not itself to please,
Nor for itself hath any care,
But for another gives its ease,
And builds a Heaven in Hell's despair.
William Blake (1757–1827) British poet. *Songs of Experience*, 'The Clod and the Pebble'

34 Love seeketh only Self to please,
To bind another to its delight,
Joys in another's loss of ease,
And builds a Hell in Heaven's despite.
William Blake *Songs of Experience*, 'The Clod and the Pebble'

35 I love thee with a love I seemed to lose
With my lost saints – I love thee with the breath,
Smiles, tears, of all my life! – and, if God choose,
I shall but love thee better after death.
Elizabeth Barrett Browning (1806–61) British poet. *Sonnets from the Portuguese*, XLIII

36 Love is also like a coconut which is good while it is fresh, but you have to spit it out when the juice is gone, what's left tastes bitter.
Bertolt Brecht (1898–1956) German dramatist. *Baal*

37 Such ever was love's way; to rise, it stoops.
Robert Browning (1812–89) British poet. *A Death in the Desert*

38 Green grow the rashes O,
Green grow the rashes O,
The sweetest hours that e'er I spend,
Are spent amang the lasses O!

Robert Burns (1759–96) Scottish poet. *Green Grow the Rashes*

39 My love is like a red red rose
That's newly sprung in June:
My love is like the melodie
That's sweetly play'd in tune.

Robert Burns *A Red, Red Rose*

40 Gin a body meet a body
Coming through the rye;
Gin a body kiss a body,
Need a body cry?

Robert Burns *Coming through the Rye*

41 Absence is to love what wind is to fire; it extinguishes the small, it inflames the great.

Bussy-Rabutin (Roger de Rabutin, Comte de Bussy; 1618–93) French soldier and writer. *Histoire amoureuse des Gaules*

42 God is Love – I dare say. But what a mischievous devil Love is!

Samuel Butler (1835–1902) British writer. *Notebooks*

43 Though the night was made for loving,
And the day returns too soon,
Yet we'll go no more a roving
By the light of the moon.

Byron, George Gordon, 6th Baron (1788–1824) British poet. *So, we'll go no more a roving*

44 Of all the girls that are so smart
There's none like pretty Sally;
She is the darling of my heart
And she lives in our alley.

Henry Carey (c. 1690–1743) English poet and musician. *Sally in our Alley*

45 I have fallen in love with all sorts of girls and I fully intend to go on doing so.

Charles, Prince of Wales (1948–) Eldest son of Elizabeth II. *The Observer*, 21 Dec 1975

46 Yes . . . whatever that may mean.

Charles, Prince of Wales On his engagement, when asked whether he was in love. TV news interview, Feb 1981

47 There ain't a lady livin' in the land
As I'd swop for my dear old Dutch!

Albert Chevalier (1861–1923) British music-hall artist. *My Old Dutch*

48 Many a man has fallen in love with a girl in a light so dim he would not have chosen a suit by it.

Maurice Chevalier (1888–1972) French singer and actor. Attrib.

49 Love and a cottage! Eh, Fanny! Ah, give me indifference and a coach and six!

George Colman, the Elder (1732–94) British dramatist. *The Clandestine Marriage*, I:2

50 See how love and murder will out.

William Congreve (1670–1729) British Restoration dramatist. *The Double Dealer*, IV:6

51 Lord, what is a lover that it can give? Why one makes lovers as fast as one pleases, and they live as long as one pleases, and they die as soon as one pleases: and then if one pleases one makes more.

William Congreve *The Way of the World*, II:4

52 Say what you will, 'tis better to be left than never to have been loved.

William Congreve *The Way of the World*, II:1

53 Mad about the boy.

Noël Coward (1899–1973) British dramatist. *Title of song*

54 Love is a sickness full of woes,
All remedies refusing;
A plant that with most cutting grows,
Most barren with best using.
Why so?
More we enjoy it, more it dies;
If not enjoyed, it sighing cries,
Hey ho.

Samuel Daniel (c. 1562–1619) English poet and dramatist. *Hymen's Triumph*, I

55 It has been said that love robs those who have it of their wit, and gives it to those who have none.

Denis Diderot (1713–84) French writer. *Paradoxe sur le comédien*

56 Come live with me, and be my love,
And we will some new pleasures prove
Of golden sands, and crystal brooks,
With silken lines, and silver hooks.

John Donne (1573–1631) English poet. *The Bait*

57 I am two fools, I know,
For loving, and for saying so
In whining Poetry.

John Donne *The Triple Fool*

58 O my America! my new-found-land,
My Kingdom, safeliest when with one man man'd.

John Donne *Elegies*, 19, 'Going To Bed'

59 It seems to me that he has never loved, that he has only imagined that he has loved, that there has been no real love on his part. I even think that he is incapable of love; he is too much occupied with other thoughts and ideas to become strongly attached to anyone earthly.

Anna Dostoevsky (1846–1918) Russian diarist and writer. *Dostoevsky Portrayed by His Wife*

60 And I was desolate and sick of an old passion.

Ernest Dowson (1867–1900) British lyric poet. *Non Sum Qualis Eram Bonae Sub Regno Cynarae*

61 You may not be an angel
'Cause angels are so few,
But until the day that one comes along
I'll string along with you.

Al Dubin (20th century) US songwriter. *Twenty Million Sweethearts*

62 All mankind love a lover.

Ralph Waldo Emerson (1803–82) US poet and essayist. *Essays*, 'Love'

63 Don't you think I was made for you? I feel like you had me ordered – and I was delivered to you – to be worn – I want you to wear me, like a watch-charm or a button hole bouquet – to the world.

Zelda Fitzgerald (1900–48) US writer. Letter to F. Scott Fitzgerald, 1919

64 . . . I don't want to live – I want to love first, and live incidentally . . .

Zelda Fitzgerald Letter to F. Scott Fitzgerald, 1919

65 *Plaisir d'amour ne dure qu'un moment,*
Chagrin d'amour dure toute la vie.
Love's pleasure lasts but a moment;
love's sorrow lasts all through life.

Jean-Pierre Claris de Florian (1755–94) French writer of fables. *Celestine*

66 I'm leaning on a lamp-post at the corner of the street,
In case a certain little lady walks by.

George Formby (1905–61) British comedian. *Leaning on a Lamp-post*

67 Try thinking of love, or something.
Amor vincit insomnia.

Christopher Fry (1907–) British dramatist. *A Sleep of Prisoners*

68 If with me you'd fondly stray,
Over the hills and far away.

John Gay (1685–1732) English poet and dramatist. *The Beggar's Opera*

69 She who has never loved has never lived.

John Gay *Captives*

70 It's a song of a merryman, moping mum,
Whose soul was sad, and whose glance was glum,

Who sipped no sup, and who craved no crumb,
As he sighed for the love of a ladye.
W. S. Gilbert (1836–1911) British dramatist. *The Yeoman of the Guard*, I

71 In love as in sport, the amateur status must be strictly maintained.
Robert Gravés (1895–1985) British poet and novelist. *Occupation: Writer*

72 Love, love, love – all the wretched cant of it, masking egotism, lust, masochism, fantasy under a mythology of sentimental postures, a welter of self-induced miseries and joys, blinding and masking the essential personalities in the frozen gestures of courtship, in the kissing and the dating and the desire, the compliments and the quarrels which vivify its barrenness.
Germaine Greer (1939–) Australian-born British writer and feminist. *The Female Eunuch*

73 If you were the only girl in the world,
And I were the only boy.
George Grossmith the Younger (1874–1935) British singer, actor, and songwriter. *The Bing Boys*, 'If you were the Only Girl' (with Fred Thompson; 1884–1949)

74 Hello, Young Lovers, Wherever You Are.
Oscar Hammerstein (1895–1960) US lyricist. From the musical *The King and I*. Song title

75 A lover without indiscretion is no lover at all.
Thomas Hardy (1840–1928) British novelist. *The Hand of Ethelberta*, Ch. 20

76 'You must sit down,' says Love, 'and taste My meat,'
So I did sit and eat.
George Herbert (1593–1633) English poet. *Love*

77 My love she's but a lassie yet.
James Hogg (1770–1835) Scottish poet and writer. Title of song

78 Pale hands I loved beside the Shalimar,
Where are you now? Who lies beneath your spell?
Laurence Hope (Mrs M. H. Nicolson; 1804–1905) British poet and songwriter. *The Garden of Kama and other Love Lyrics from India*, 'Pale Hands I Loved'

79 Look not in my eyes, for fear
They mirror true the sight I see,
And there you find your face too clear
And love it and be lost like me.
A. E. Housman (1859–1936) British scholar and poet. *A Shropshire Lad*, 'March'

80 I know nothing about platonic love except that it is not to be found in the works of Plato.
Edgar Jepson (1863–1938) British novelist. *EGO 5* (James Agate)

81 Love is like the measles; we all have to go through with it.
Jerome K. Jerome (1859–1927) British humorist. *Idle Thoughts of an Idle Fellow*

82 Love's like the measles – all the worse when it comes late in life.
Douglas William Jerrold (1803–57) British dramatist. *Wit and Opinions of Douglas Jerrold*, 'A Philanthropist'

83 Love is the wisdom of the fool and the folly of the wise.
Samuel Johnson (1709–84) British lexicographer. *Johnsonian Miscellanies* (ed. G. B. Hill), Vol. II

84 Drink to me only with thine eyes,
And I will pledge with mine;
Or leave a kiss but in the cup,
And I'll not look for wine.
The thirst that from the soul doth rise
Doth ask a drink divine;
But might I of Jove's nectar sup,
I would not change for thine.

I sent thee late a rosy wreath,
Not so much honouring thee,
As giving it a hope that there
It could not wither'd be.
Ben Jonson (1573–1637) English dramatist. *The Forest, IX*, 'To Celia'

85 Come, my Celia, let us prove,
While we can, the sports of love,
Time will not be ours for ever,
He, at length, our good will sever.
Ben Jonson *Volpone*, III:6

86 Love me, love my umbrella.
James Joyce (1882–1941) Irish novelist. Attrib.

87 Love in a hut, with water and a crust,
Is – Love, forgive us! – cinders, ashes, dust;
Love in a palace is perhaps at last
More grievous torment than a hermit's fast.
John Keats (1795–1821) British poet. *Lamia*, II

88 Soft adorings from their loves receive
Upon the honey'd middle of the night.
John Keats *The Eve of Saint Agnes*, VI

89 What will survive of us is love.
Philip Larkin (1922–85) British poet. *The Whitsun Weddings*, 'An Arundel Tomb'

90 I love a lassie.
Harry Lauder (Hugh MacLennon; 1870–1950) Scottish music-hall artist. Song title

91 You must always be a-waggle with LOVE.
D. H. Lawrence (1885–1930) British novelist. *Bibbles*

92 I'm not sure if a mental relation with a woman doesn't make it impossible to love her. To know the *mind* of a woman is to end in hating her. Love means the pre-cognitive flow . . . it is the honest state before the apple.
D. H. Lawrence Letter to Dr Trigant Burrow, 3 Aug 1927

93 I loved you, so I drew these tides
of men into my hands and wrote
my will across the sky in stars
to earn you freedom, the seven pillared worthy house, that your eyes
might be shining for me
when we came.
T. E. Lawrence (1888–1935) British soldier and writer. *The Seven Pillars of Wisdom*, Epigraph 'To S.A.'

94 All You Need Is Love.
John Lennon (1940–80) British rock musician. Title of song, written with Paul McCartney

95 If there's anything that you want,
If there's anything I can do,
Just call on me,
And I'll send it along with love from me to you.
John Lennon *From Me to You* (with Paul McCartney)

96 She loves you, yeh, yeh, yeh,
And with a love like that you know you should be glad.
John Lennon *She Loves You* (with Paul McCartney)

97 Finally found a fellow
He says 'Murder!' – he says!
Every time we kiss he says 'Murder!' – he says!
Is that the language of love?
Frank Loesser (1910–69) US songwriter. *Happy Go Lucky*

98 Two souls with but a single thought,
Two hearts that beat as one.
Maria Lovell (1803–77) British actress and dramatist. *Ingomar the Barbarian*, II (transl. of Friedrich Halm)

99 Time was away and somewhere else,
There were two glasses and two chairs

And two people with one pulse.
Louis MacNeice (1907–63) Irish-born British poet. *Meeting Point*

100 Come live with me, and be my love;
And we will all the pleasures prove
That hills and valleys, dales and fields,
Woods or steepy mountain yields.
Christopher Marlowe (1564–93) English dramatist. *The Passionate Shepherd to his Love*

101 Let us roll all our strength and all
Our sweetness up into one ball,
And tear our pleasures with rough strife
Thorough the iron gates of life:
Thus, though we cannot make our sun
Stand still, yet we will make him run.
Andrew Marvell (1621–78) English poet. *To His Coy Mistress*

102 Send two dozen roses to Room 424 and put 'Emily, I love you' on the back of the bill.
Groucho Marx (Julius Marx; 1895–1977) US comedian. *A Night in Casablanca*

103 Because women can do nothing except love, they've given it a ridiculous importance.
W. Somerset Maugham (1874–1965) British novelist. *The Moon and Sixpence*, Ch. 41

104 I loved Kirk so much, I would have skied down Mount Everest in the nude with a carnation up my nose.
Joyce McKinney (1950–) US former beauty queen. Ms McKinney was accused of kidnapping an ex-lover who had rejected her. Evidence in court, 1977

105 My heart shall be thy garden.
Alice Meynell (1847–1922) British poet. *The Garden*

106 Falling out of love is very enlightening. For a short while you see the world with new eyes.
Iris Murdoch (1919–) Irish-born British novelist. *The Observer*, 'Sayings of the Week', 4 Feb 1968

107 When a man is in love he endures more than at other times; he submits to everything.
Friedrich Wilhelm Nietzsche (1844–1900) German philosopher. *The Antichrist*

108 I do not love thee! – no! I do not love thee!
And yet when thou art absent I am sad.
Caroline Elizabeth Sarah Norton (1808–77) British poet. *I Do Not Love Thee*

109 K-K-K-Katy, beautiful Katy,
You're the only g-g-g-girl that I adore,
When the m-m-m-moon shines over the cow-shed,
I'll be waiting at the k-k-k-kitchen door.
Geoffrey O'Hara (1882–1967) Canadian-born US songwriter. *K-K-K-Katy* (song)

110 By the time you swear you're his,
Shivering and sighing,
And he vows his passion is
Infinite, undying –
Lady, make a note of this:
One of you is lying.
Dorothy Parker (1893–1967) US writer. *Unfortunate Coincidence*

111 Every love is the love before
In a duller dress.
Dorothy Parker *Death and Taxes*

112 Love's perfect blossom only blows
Where noble manners veil defect.
Angels may be familiar; those
Who err each other must respect.
Coventry Patmore (1823–96) British poet. *The Angel in the House*, Bk. I, Prelude 2

113 Ye gods! annihilate but space and time.
And make two lovers happy.
Alexander Pope (1688–1744) British poet. *The Art of Sinking in Poetry*, 11

114 I've Got You Under My Skin.
Cole Porter (1893–1964) US songwriter. *Born to Dance*, song title

115 Night and day, you are the one,
Only you beneath the moon and under the sun.
Cole Porter *The Gay Divorcee*, 'Night and Day'

116 Let's Do It; Let's Fall in Love.
Cole Porter *Paris*, song title

117 I have sometimes regretted living so close to Marie . . . because I may be very fond of her, but I am not quite so fond of her company.
Marcel Proust (1871–1922) French novelist. *À la recherche du temps perdu: Sodome et Gomorrhe*

118 There can be no peace of mind in love, since the advantage one has secured is never anything but a fresh starting-point for further desires.
Marcel Proust *À la recherche du temps perdu: À l'ombre des jeunes filles en fleurs*

119 I loved you when you were inconstant. What should I have done if you had been faithful?
Jean Racine (1639–99) French dramatist. *Andromaque*, IV:5

120 If all the world and love were young,
And truth in every shepherd's tongue,
These pretty pleasures might me move
To live with thee, and be thy love.
Walter Raleigh (1554–1618) English explorer. *Answer to Marlow*

121 There are very few people who are not ashamed of having been in love when they no longer love each other.
Duc de la Rochefoucauld (1613–80) French writer. *Maximes*, 71

122 It takes a woman twenty years to make a man of her son, and another woman twenty minutes to make a fool of him.
Helen Rowland (1876–1950) US writer. *Reflections of a Bachelor Girl*

123 To fear love is to fear life, and those who fear life are already three parts dead.
Bertrand Russell (1872–1970) British philosopher. *Marriage and Morals*

124 Of all forms of caution, caution in love is perhaps the most fatal to true happiness.
Bertrand Russell *Marriage and Morals*

125 Every little girl knows about love. It is only her capacity to suffer because of it that increases.
Françoise Sagan (1935–) French writer. *Daily Express*

126 Liszt said to me today that God alone deserves to be loved. It may be true, but when one has loved a man it is very different to love God.
George Sand (Aurore Dupin, Baronne Dudevant; 1804–76) French novelist. *Intimate Journal*

127 When we love animals and children too much we love them at the expense of men.
Jean-Paul Sartre (1905–80) French writer. *The Words*

128 True love's the gift which God has given
To man alone beneath the heaven.
Walter Scott (1771–1832) Scottish novelist. *The Lay of the Last Minstrel*, V

129 The triple pillar of the world transform'd

Into a strumpet's fool.
William Shakespeare (1564–1616) English dramatist. *Antony and Cleopatra,* I:1

130 There's beggary in the love that can be reckon'd.
William Shakespeare *Antony and Cleopatra,* I:1

131 Sir, you have wrestled well, and overthrown
More than your enemies.
William Shakespeare *As You Like It,* I:2

132 We that are true lovers run into strange capers.
William Shakespeare *As You Like It,* II:4

133 It is as easy to count atomies as to resolve the propositions of a lover.
William Shakespeare *As You Like It,* III:2

134 If thou remember'st not the slightest folly
That ever love did make thee run into,
Thou hast not lov'd.
William Shakespeare *As You Like It,* II:4

135 For aught that I could ever read,
Could ever hear by tale or history,
The course of true love never did run smooth.
William Shakespeare *A Midsummer Night's Dream,* I:1

136 Love looks not with the eyes, but with the mind;
And therefore is wing'd Cupid painted blind.
William Shakespeare *A Midsummer Night's Dream,* I:1

137 The lunatic, the lover, and the poet,
Are of imagination all compact.
William Shakespeare *A Midsummer Night's Dream,* V:1

138 OPHELIA. 'Tis brief, my lord.
HAMLET. As woman's love.
William Shakespeare *Hamlet,* III:2

139 Speak, cousin, or, if you cannot, stop his mouth with a kiss.
William Shakespeare *Much Ado About Nothing,* II:1

140 Contempt, farewell! and maiden pride, adieu!
No glory lives behind the back of such.
And, Benedick, love on; I will requite thee,
Taming my wild heart to thy loving hand.
William Shakespeare *Much Ado About Nothing,* III:1

141 I do love nothing in the world so well as you; is not that strange?
William Shakespeare *Much Ado About Nothing,* IV:1

142 She lov'd me for the dangers I had pass'd,
And I lov'd her that she did pity them.
This only is the witchcraft I have us'd.
William Shakespeare *Othello,* I:3

143 Then must you speak
Of one that lov'd not wisely, but too well;
Of one not easily jealous, but, being wrought,
Perplexed in the extreme; of one whose hand,
Like the base Indian, threw a pearl away
Richer than all his tribe.
William Shakespeare *Othello,* V:2

144 OTHELLO. If it were now to die,
'Twere now to be most happy, for I fear
My soul hath her content so absolute
That not another comfort like to this
Succeeds in unknown fate.
DESDEMONIA. The heavens forbid
But that our loves and comforts should increase
Even as our days do grow!
William Shakespeare *Othello,* II:1

145 Excellent wretch! Perdition catch my soul
But I do love thee! and when I love thee not,
Chaos is come again.
William Shakespeare *Othello,* III:3

146 Was ever woman in this humour woo'd?
Was ever woman in this humour won?
William Shakespeare *Richard III,* I:2

147 But, soft! what light through yonder window breaks?
It is the east, and Juliet is the sun.
William Shakespeare *Romeo and Juliet,* II:2

148 It is my lady; O! it is my love;
O! that she knew she were.
William Shakespeare *Romeo and Juliet,* II:2

149 See! how she leans her cheek upon her hand:
O! that I were a glove upon that hand,
That I might touch that cheek.
William Shakespeare *Romeo and Juliet,* II:2

150 With love's light wings did I o'er-perch these walls;
For stony limits cannot hold love out,
And what love can do that dares love attempt.
William Shakespeare *Romeo and Juliet,* II:2

151 It is too rash, too unadvis'd, to sudden;
Too like the lightning, which doth cease to be
Ere one can say it lightens. Sweet, good-night!
This bud of love, by summer's ripening breath,
May prove a beauteous flower when next we meet.
William Shakespeare *Romeo and Juliet,* II:2

152 My bounty is as boundless as the sea,
My love as deep; the more I give to thee,
The more I have, for both are infinite.
William Shakespeare *Romeo and Juliet,* II:2

153 Love goes toward love, as schoolboys from their books;
But love from love, toward school with heavy looks.
William Shakespeare *Romeo and Juliet,* II:2

154 Therefore love moderately: long love doth so;
Too swift arrives as tardy as too slow.
William Shakespeare *Romeo and Juliet,* II:6

155 Give me my Romeo: and, when he shall die,
Take him and cut him out in little stars,
And he will make the face of heaven so fine
That all the world will be in love with night,
And pay no worship to the garish sun.
William Shakespeare *Romeo and Juliet,* III:2

156 A woman's face, with Nature's own hand painted,

Hast thou, the Master Mistress of my passion.
William Shakespeare *Sonnet 20*

157 So true a fool is love that in your will, Though you do anything, he thinks no ill.
William Shakespeare *Sonnets* 57

158 Let me not to the marriage of true minds
Admit impediments. Love is not love
Which alters when it alteration finds,
Or bends with the remover to remove.
O, no! it is an ever-fixed mark,
That looks on tempests and is never shaken.
William Shakespeare *Sonnet 116*

159 Love alters not with his brief hours and weeks,
But bears it out even to the edge of doom.
If this be error, and upon me prov'd,
I never writ, nor no man ever lov'd.
William Shakespeare *Sonnet 116*

160 When my love swears that she is made of truth,
I do believe her, though I know she lies.
William Shakespeare *Sonnets*, 138

161 But love is blind, and lovers cannot see
The pretty follies that themselves commit.
William Shakespeare *The Merchant of Venice*, II:6

162 FALSTAFF. Of what quality was your love, then?
FORD. Like a fair house built upon another man's ground; so that I have lost my edifice by mistaking the place where I erected it.
William Shakespeare *The Merry Wives of Windsor*, II:2

163 But to be paddling palms and pinching fingers,
As now they are, and making practis'd smiles,
As in a looking-glass.
William Shakespeare *The Winter's Tale*, I:2

164 To be wise and love
Exceeds man's might.
William Shakespeare *Troilus and Cressida*, III:2

165 This is the monstruosity in love, lady, that the will is infinite, and the execution confined; that the desire is boundless, and the act a slave to limit.
William Shakespeare *Troilus and Cressida*, III:2

166 I was adored once too.
William Shakespeare *Twelfth Night*, II:1

167 She never told her love,
But let concealment, like a worm i' th' bud,
Feed on her damask cheek. She pin'd in thought;
And with a green and yellow melancholy
She sat like Patience on a monument,
Smiling at grief.
William Shakespeare *Twelfth Night*, II:4

168 Love sought is good, but given unsought is better.
William Shakespeare *Twelfth Night*, III:1

169 Nowadays we don't think much of a man's love for an animal; we laugh at people who are attached to cats. But if we stop loving animals, aren't we bound to stop loving humans too?
Alexander Solzhenitsyn (1918–) Soviet novelist. *Cancer Ward*, Pt. I, Ch. 20

170 A woman despises a man for loving her, unless she returns his love.
Elizabeth Drew Stoddard (1823–1902) US novelist and poet. *Two Men*, Ch. 32

171 I know she likes me,
'Cause she says so.
Eugene Stratton (1861–1918) British music-hall singer. *The Lily of Laguna*

172 I hold it true, whate'er befall;
I feel it, when I sorrow most;
'Tis better to have loved and lost
Than never to have loved at all.
Alfred, Lord Tennyson (1809–92) British poet. *In Memoriam A.H.H.*, XXVII

173 Such a one do I remember, whom to look at was to love.
Alfred, Lord Tennyson *Locksley Hall*

174 The rose was awake all night for your sake,
Knowing your promise to me;
The lilies and roses were all awake,
They sighed for the dawn and thee.
Alfred, Lord Tennyson *Maud*, I

175 O tell her, brief is life but love is long.
Alfred, Lord Tennyson *The Princess*, IV

176 God gives us love. Something to love
He lends us; but, when love is grown
To ripeness that on which it throve
Falls off, and love is left alone.
Alfred, Lord Tennyson *To J.S.*

177 'Tis strange what a man may do, and a woman yet think him an angel.
William Makepeace Thackeray (1811–63) British novelist. *Henry Esmond*, Ch. 7

178 All, everything that I understand, I understand only because I love.
Leo Tolstoy (1828–1910) Russian writer. *War and Peace*, Bk. VII, Ch. 16

179 One can't live on love alone; and I am so stupid that I can do nothing but think of him.
Sophie Tolstoy (1844–1919) Russian writer. *A Diary of Tolstoy's Wife, 1860–1891*

180 Those who have courage to love should have courage to suffer.
Anthony Trollope (1815–82) British novelist. *The Bertrams*, Ch. 27

181 I doubt whether any girl would be satisfied with her lover's mind if she knew the whole of it.
Anthony Trollope *The Small House at Allington*, Ch. 4

182 Walking My Baby Back Home.
Roy Turk (20th century) US songwriter. Title of song

183 Love conquers all things: let us too give in to Love.
Virgil (Publius Vergilius Maro; 70–19 BC) Roman poet. *Eclogue*, Bk. X

184 The boy I love is up in the gallery,
The boy I love is looking now at me.
George Ware (19th century) British songwriter. *The Boy in the Gallery*

185 It is like a cigar. If it goes out, you can light it again but it never tastes quite the same.
Lord Wavell (1883–1950) British field marshal. Attrib.

186 Beware you be not swallowed up in books! An ounce of love is worth a pound of knowledge.
John Wesley (1703–91) British religious leader. *Life of Wesley* (R. Southey), Ch. 16

187 I have found it impossible to carry the heavy burden of responsibility and to discharge my duties as King as I would wish to do without the help and support of the woman I love.
Duke of Windsor (1894–1972) King of the United Kingdom; abdicated 1936. Radio broadcast, 11 Dec 1936

188 'Ah, love, love' he said. 'Is there anything like it? Were you ever in love, Beach?'
'Yes, sir, on one occasion, when I was a young under-footman. But it blew over.'
P. G. Wodehouse (1881–1975) British humorous novelist. *Pigs Have Wings*

189 There is a comfort in the strength of love;
'Twill make a thing endurable, which else
Would overset the brain, or break the heart.
William Wordsworth (1770–1850) British poet. *Michael*, 448

190 Why art thou silent! Is thy love a plant
Of such weak fibre that the treacherous air
Of absence withers what was once so fair?
William Wordsworth *Miscellaneous Sonnets*, III

191 Love fled
And paced upon the mountains overhead
And hid his face amid a crowd of stars.
W. B. Yeats (1865–1939) Irish poet. *When you are Old*

192 But Love has pitched his mansion in
The place of excrement.
W. B. Yeats *Crazy Jane Talks with the Bishop*

193 A pity beyond all telling
Is hid in the heart of love.
W. B. Yeats *The Pity of Love*

LOVE AND DEATH

See also death, love

1 And for bonnie Annie Laurie
I'll lay me doun and dee.
William Douglas (1672–1748) Scottish poet. *Annie Laurie*

2 For, Heaven be thanked, we live in such an age,
When no man dies for love, but on the stage.
John Dryden (1631–1700) British poet and dramatist. *Mithridates*, Epilogue

3 Love is my religion – I could die for that.
John Keats (1795–1821) British poet. Letter to Fanny Brawne, 13 Oct 1819

4 How alike are the groans of love to those of the dying.
Malcolm Lowry (1909–57) British novelist. *Under the Volcano*, Ch. 12

5 It is very rarely that a man loves
And when he does it is nearly always fatal.
Hugh MacDiarmid (Christopher Murray Grieve; 1892–1978) Scottish poet. *The International Brigade*

6 She shall be buried by her Antony:
No grave upon the earth shall clip in it
A pair so famous.
William Shakespeare (1564–1616) English dramatist. *Antony and Cleopatra*, V:2

7 Men have died from time to time, and worms have eaten them, but not for love.
William Shakespeare *As You Like It*, IV:1

8 I kiss'd thee ere I kill'd thee, no way but this,
Killing myself to die upon a kiss.
William Shakespeare *Othello*, V:2

9 Romeo, come forth; come forth, thou fearful man:
Affliction is enamour'd of thy parts,
And thou are wedded to calamity.
William Shakespeare *Romeo and Juliet*, III:3

10 'Tis said that some have died for love.
William Wordsworth (1770–1850) British poet. *'Tis Said that some have Died*

LOVE AND FRIENDSHIP

See also friendship, love

1 Love is blind; friendship closes its eyes.
Proverb

2 Friendship is a disinterested commerce between equals; love, an abject intercourse between tyrants and slaves.
Oliver Goldsmith (1728–74) Irish-born British writer. *The Good-Natured Man*, I

3 Friendship is constant in all other things
Save in the office and affairs of love.
William Shakespeare (1564–1616) English dramatist. *Much Ado About Nothing*, II:1

LOVE AND HATE

See also hate, love

1 Now hatred is by far the longest pleasure;
Men love in haste, but they detest at leisure.
Lord Byron (1788–1824) British poet. *Don Juan*, XIII

2 *Odi et amo.*
I hate and love.
Catullus (c. 84–c. 54 BC) Roman poet. *Carmina*, LXXXV

3 Heaven has no rage like love to hatred turned,
Nor hell a fury like a woman scorned.
William Congreve (1670–1729) British Restoration dramatist. *The Mourning Bride*, III

4 Oh, I have loved him too much to feel no hate for him.
Jean Racine (1639–99) French dramatist. *Andromaque*, II:1

5 If one judges love by its visible effects, it looks more like hatred than like friendship.
Duc de la Rochefoucauld (1613–80) French writer. *Maximes*, 72

6 My only love sprung from my only hate!
Too early seen unknown, and known too late!
William Shakespeare (1564–1616) English dramatist. *Romeo and Juliet*, I:5

LOVE AND MARRIAGE

See also love, marriage

1 Love and marriage, love and marriage,
Go together like a horse and carriage.
Sammy Cahn (Samuel Cohen; 1913–) US songwriter. *Our Town*, 'Love and Marriage'

2 ALMA. I rather suspect her of being in love with him.
MARTIN. Her own husband? Monstrous! What a selfish woman!
Jennie Jerome Churchill (1854–1921) US-born British hostess and writer. *His Borrowed Plumes*

3 Love is moral even without legal marriage, but marriage is immoral without love.
Ellen Key (Karolina Sofia Key; 1849–1926) Swedish writer. *The Morality of Woman and Other Essays*, 'The Morality of Woman'

4 Many a man in love with a dimple makes the mistake of marrying the whole girl.
Stephen Leacock (1869–1944) English-born Canadian economist and humorist. *Literary Lapses*

5 Any one must see at a glance that if men and women marry those whom they do not love, they must love those whom they do not marry.

Harriet Martineau (1802–76) British writer. *Society in America,* Vol. III, 'Marriage'

6 Can't you read? The score demands *con amore,* and what are you doing? You are playing it like married men!

Arturo Toscanini (1867–1957) Italian conductor. Criticizing the playing of an Austrian orchestra during rehearsal. Attrib.

7 The amount of women in London who flirt with their own husbands is perfectly scandalous. It looks so bad. It is simply washing one's clean linen in public.

Oscar Wilde (1854–1900) Irish-born British dramatist. *The Importance of Being Earnest,* I

LOYALTY

See also betrayal, faithfulness, patriotism, support

1 Dog does not eat dog.
Proverb

2 There is honor among thieves.
Proverb

3 You cannot run with the hare and hunt with the hounds.
Proverb

4 Here's a health unto his Majesty . . .
Confusion to his enemies, . . .
And he that will not drink his health,
I wish him neither wit nor wealth,
Nor yet a rope to hang himself.

Anonymous *Here's a Health unto his Majesty*

5 And Ruth said, Intreat me not to leave thee, or to return from following after thee: for whither thou goest, I will go; and where thou lodgest, I will lodge: thy people shall be my people, and thy God my God:
Where thou diest, will I die, and there will I be buried: the Lord do so to me, and more also, if ought but death part thee and me.

Bible: Ruth 1:16–17

6 The State, in choosing men to serve it, takes no notice of their opinions. If they be willing faithfully to serve it, that satisfies.

Oliver Cromwell (1599–1658) English soldier and statesman. Said before the Battle of Marston Moor, 2 July 1644

7 We are all the President's men.

Henry Kissinger (1923–) German-born US politician and diplomat. Said regarding the invasion of Cambodia, 1970. *The Sunday Times Magazine,* 4 May 1975

8 A man who will steal *for* me will steal *from* me.

Theodore Roosevelt (1858–1919) US Republican president. Firing a cowboy who had applied Roosevelt's brand to a steer belonging to a neighboring ranch. *Roosevelt in the Bad Lands* (Herman Hagedorn)

9 Those he commands move only in command,
Nothing in love; now does he feel his title
Hang loose about him, like a giant's robe
Upon a dwarfish thief.

William Shakespeare (1564–1616) English dramatist. *Macbeth,* V:2

10 In the following him, I follow but myself.

William Shakespeare *Othello,* I:1

11 Myn hert ys set and all myn hole entent,
To serve this flour in my most humble wyse
As faythfully as can be thought or ment,
Wythout feynyng or slouthe in my servyse;
For wytt the wele, yt ys a paradyse
To se this floure when yt begyn to sprede,
Wyth colours fressh ennewyd, white and rede.

Duke of Suffolk (1396–1450) English nobleman. Poem dedicated to Margaret of Anjou, Queen of England. *Secular Lyrics of XIVth and XVth Centuries* (ed. R. H. Robbins)

12 He was my crowned King, and if the Parliamentary authority of England set the Crown upon a stock, I will fight for that stock: And as I fought then for him, I will fight for you, when you are established by the said authority.

Earl of Surrey Reply when asked by Henry VII why he had fought for Richard III at the Battle of Bosworth (22 Aug 1485). *Remains Concerning Britain* (W. Camden)

13 If this man is not faithful to his God, how can he be faithful to me, a mere man?

Theodoric (c. 445–526) King of the Ostrogoths. Explaining why he had had a trusted minister, who had said he would adopt his master's religion, beheaded. *Dictionnaire Encyclopédique* (E. Guérard)

14 When I forget my sovereign, may God forget me!

Lord Thurlow (1731–1806) British lawyer. Speech, House of Lords, 15 Dec 1778

15 Had I but served God as diligently as I have served the king, he would not have given me over in my gray hairs.

Cardinal Wolsey (1475–1530) English churchman. Remark to Sir William Kingston. *Negotiations of Thomas Wolsey* (Cavendish)

LUCK

See also chance, superstition

1 A bad penny always turns up.
Proverb

2 A cat has nine lives.
Proverb

3 Finders keepers, losers weepers.
Proverb

4 It is better to be born lucky than rich.
Proverb

5 The devil looks after his own.
Proverb

6 Today we were unlucky. But remember, we have only to be lucky once. You will have to be lucky always.

Anonymous Telephone call from the IRA following their unsuccessful attempt to blow up Margaret Thatcher and other ministers at the Grand Hotel, Brighton, in 1984

7 There, but for the grace of God, goes John Bradford.

John Bradford (c. 1510–55) English Protestant martyr. Said on seeing some criminals being led to execution. Attrib.

8 This is the temple of Providence where disciples still hourly mark its ways and note the system of its mysteries. Here is the one God whose worshippers prove their faith by their works and in their destruction still trust in Him.

F. H. Bradley (1846–1924) British philosopher. Referring to Monte Carlo. *Aphorisms*

9 Fortune, that favours fools.

Ben Jonson (1573–1637) English dramatist. *The Alchemist,* Prologue

10 I am a great believer in luck, and I find the harder I work the more I have of it.

Stephen Leacock (1869–1944) English-born Canadian economist and humorist. *Literary Lapses*

11 The Eskimo had his own explanation. Said he: 'The devil is asleep or having trouble with his wife, or we should never have come back so easily.'

Robert Edwin Peary (1856–1920) US explorer. *The North Pole*

12 We need greater virtues to sustain good fortune than bad.
Duc de la Rochefoucauld (1613–80) French writer. *Maximes*, 25

13 'My aunt was suddenly prevented from going a voyage
in a ship what went down – would you call that a case
of Providential interference?'
'Can't tell: didn't know your aunt.'
Frederick Temple (1821–1902) British churchman. *Memoirs of Archbishop Temple* (Sandford), Vol. II

LUST

See also animalism, desire, love, sex

1 For all that is in the world, the lust of the flesh, and the lust of the eyes, and the pride of life, is not of the Father, but is of the world.
Bible: I John 2:16

2 For the bewitching of naughtiness doth obscure things that are honest; and the wandering of concupiscence doth undermine the simple mind. He, being made perfect in a short time, fulfilled a long time.
Bible: Wisdom 4:12–13

3 Licence my roving hands, and let them go,
Before, behind, between, above, below.
John Donne (1573–1631) English poet. *Elegies*, 18, 'Love's Progress'

4 What is commonly called love, namely the desire of satisfying a voracious appetite with a certain quantity of delicate white human flesh.
Henry Fielding (1707–54) British novelist. *Tom Jones*, Bk. VI, Ch. 1

5 I'll come no more behind your scenes, David; for the silk stockings and white bosoms of your actresses excite my amorous propensities.
Samuel Johnson (1709–84) British lexicographer. Said to the actor-manager David Garrick. *Life of Johnson* (J. Boswell), Vol. I

6 Oh, to be seventy again!
Oliver Wendell Holmes Jr. (1841–1935) US jurist. Said in his eighty-seventh year, while watching a pretty girl. *The American Treasury* (C. Fadiman)

7 Stand close around, ye Stygian set,
With Dirce in one boat conveyed!
Or Charon, seeing, may forget
That he is old and she a shade.
Walter Savage Landor (1775–1864) British poet and writer. In Greek mythology, Dirce, a follower of Dionysius, was killed by her great-nephews Amphion and Zethus because of her mistreatment of their mother Antiope; Charon was the ferryman who transported dead souls across the River Styx to the underworld. *Dirce*

8 Lolita, light of my life, fire of my loins. My sin, my Soul.
Vladimir Nabokov (1899–1977) Russian-born US novelist. *Lolita*

9 Th' expense of spirit in a waste of shame
Is lust in action; and till action, lust
Is perjur'd, murd'rous, bloody, full of blame,
Savage, extreme, rude, cruel, not to trust;
Enjoy'd no sooner but despised straight.
William Shakespeare (1564–1616) English dramatist. *Sonnet 129*

10 . . . kept a hearth-girl in his house who kindled his fire but extinguished his virtue.
Gerald of Wales (c. 1146–c. 1220) Welsh topographer, archdeacon, and writer. Referring to the parish priest. *Gemma Ecclesiastica*

11 Nonconformity and lust stalking hand in hand through the country, wasting and ravaging.
Evelyn Waugh (1903–66) British novelist. *Decline and Fall*, Pt. I, Ch. 5

12 Outside èvery thin girl there is a fat man trying to get in.
Katharine Whitehorn (1928–) British journalist. Attrib.

LUXURY

See also extravagance, wealth

1 It's grand, and ye canna expect to be baith grand and comfortable.
J. M. Barrie (1860–1937) British novelist and dramatist. *The Little Minister*, Ch. 10

2 The saddest thing I can imagine is to get used to luxury.
Charlie Chaplin (Sir Charles Spencer C.; 1889–1977) British film actor. *My Autobiography*

3 In the affluent society no useful distinction can be made between luxuries and necessaries.
John Kenneth Galbraith (1908–) US economist. *The Affluent Society*, Ch. 21

4 Give us the luxuries of life, and we will dispense with its necessities.
John Lothrop Motley (1814–77) US historian and diplomat. Also quoted by Frank Lloyd Wright. *The Autocrat of the Breakfast Table* (O. W. Holmes), Ch. 6

5 How many things I can do without!
Socrates (469–399 BC) Athenian philosopher. Examining the range of goods on sale at a market. *Lives of the Eminent Philosophers* (Diogenes Laertius), II

6 Beulah, peel me a grape.
Mae West (1892–1980) US actress. *I'm No Angel*, film 1933

LYING

See also deception, honesty, truth

1 A liar is worse than a thief.
Proverb

2 The boy cried 'Wolf, wolf!' and the villagers came out to help him.
Aesop (6th century BC) Reputed Greek writer of fables. *Fables*, 'The Shepherd's Boy'

3 It contains a misleading impression, not a lie. I was being economical with the truth.
Robert Armstrong (1913–) British civil servant. Giving evidence on behalf of the British Government in an Australian court case, Nov 1986. Armstrong was, in fact, quoting Edmund Burke (1729–97).

4 She tells enough white lies to ice a wedding cake.
Margot Asquith (1865–1945) The second wife of Herbert Asquith. Referring to Lady Desborough. *As I Remember*

5 Matilda told such Dreadful Lies
It made one Gasp and Stretch one's Eyes.
For every time she shouted 'Fire'
They only answered 'Little Liar' And therefore when her Aunt returned
Matilda, and the House, were Burned.
Hilaire Belloc (1870–1953) French-born British poet. *Cautionary Tales*

6 The moment a man talks to his fellows he begins to lie.
Hilaire Belloc *The Silence of the Sea*

7 Woe unto them that call evil good, and good evil; that put darkness for light, and light for darkness; that put bitter for sweet, and sweet for bitter!
Bible: Isaiah 5:20

8 Nobody speaks the truth when there's something they must have.
Elizabeth Bowen (1899–1973) Irish novelist. *The House in Paris*, Ch. 5

9 A lie can be halfway round the world before the truth has got its boots on.
James Callaghan (1912–) British Labour prime minister. Quoting the Baptist preacher C. H. Spurgeon (19th C), 'A lie travels round the

world while truth is putting on her boots'.
Speech, House of Commons, 1 Nov 1976

10 It cannot in the opinion of His Majesty's Government be classified as slavery in the extreme acceptance of the word without some risk of terminological inexactitude.
Winston Churchill (1874–1965) British statesman. Speech, House of Commons, 22 Feb 1906

11 Whoever would lie usefully should lie seldom.
Lord Hervey (1696–1743) English writer and pamphleteer. *Memoirs of the Reign of George II*, Vol. I

12 The broad mass of a nation . . . will more easily fall victim to a big lie than to a small one.
Adolf Hitler (1889–1945) German dictator. *Mein Kampf*, Ch. 10

13 She's too crafty a woman to invent a new lie when an old one will serve.
W. Somerset Maugham (1874–1965) British novelist. *The Constant Wife*, II

14 It is hard to believe that a man is telling the truth when you know that you would lie if you were in his place.
H. L. Mencken (1880–1956) US journalist. *Prejudices*

15 Unless a man feels he has a good enough memory, he should never venture to lie.
Michel de Montaigne (1533–92) French essayist. Also quoted in *Le Menteur*, IV:5 by Pierre Corneille (1606–84). *Essais*, I

16 He led a double life. Did that make him a liar? He did not feel a liar. He was a man of two truths.
Iris Murdoch (1919–) Irish-born British novelist. *The Sacred and Profane Love Machine*

17 He who does not need to lie is proud of not being a liar.
Friedrich Wilhelm Nietzsche (1844–1900) German philosopher. *Nachgelassene Fragmente*

18 By the time you say you're his,
Shivering and sighing
And he vows his passion is
Infinite, undying –
Lady, make a note of this
One of you is lying.
Dorothy Parker (1893–1967) US writer. *Not So Deep as a Well*

19 It has made more liars out of the American people than Golf.
Will Rogers (1879–1935) US actor and humorist. Referring to income tax. *Saturday Review*, 'A Rogers Thesaurus', 25 Aug 1962

20 I have never but once succeeded in making him tell a lie and that was by a subterfuge. 'Moore,' I said, 'Do you *always* tell the truth?' 'No', he replied. I believe this to be the only lie he ever told.
Bertrand Russell (1872–1970) British philosopher. Referring to George Edward Moore. *Autobiography*

21 For my part, if a lie may do thee grace,
I'll gild it with the happiest terms I have.
William Shakespeare (1564–1616) English dramatist. *Henry IV, Part 1*, V:4

22 Lord, Lord! how subject we old men are to this vice of lying.
William Shakespeare *Henry IV, Part 2*, III:2

23 In our country the lie has become not just a moral category but a pillar of the State.
Alexander Solzhenitsyn (1918–) Soviet novelist. *The Observer*, 'Sayings of the Year', 29 Dec 1974

24 A lie is an abomination unto the Lord and a very present help in trouble.
Adlai Stevenson (1900–65) US statesman. Speech, Jan 1951

25 That a lie which is all a lie may be met and fought with outright,
But a lie which is part a truth is a harder matter to fight.
Alfred, Lord Tennyson (1809–92) British poet. *The Grandmother*

26 There was things which he stretched, but mainly he told the truth.
Mark Twain (Samuel Langhorne Clemens; 1835–1910) US writer. *The Adventures of Huckleberry Finn*, Ch. 1

M

MACHINES

1 One machine can do the work of fifty ordinary men. No machine can do the work of one extraordinary man.
Elbert Hubbard (1856–1915) US writer. *Roycroft Dictionary and Book of Epigrams*

2 The machine threatens all achievement.
Rainer Maria Rilke (1875–1926) Austrian poet. *Die Sonette an Orpheus*, II, 10

3 Our body is a machine for living. It is organized for that, it is its nature. Let life go on in it unhindered and let it defend itself, it will do more than if you paralyse it by encumbering it with remedies.
Leo Tolstoy (1828–1910) Russian writer. *War and Peace*, Bk. X, Ch. 29

4 I see no reason to suppose that these machines will ever force themselves into general use.
Duke of Wellington (1769–1852) British general and statesman. Referring to steam locomotives. *Geoffrey Madan's Notebooks* (J. Gere)

MADNESS

See also psychiatry, psychology

1 Whom God wishes to destroy, he first makes mad.
Proverb

2 Lucid intervals and happy pauses.
Francis Bacon (1561–1626) English philosopher. *The History of the Reign of King Henry VII*

3 I cultivate my hysteria with joy and terror. Now I am always dizzy, and today, January 23, 1862, I experienced a singular premonition, I felt pass over me a breath of wind from the wings of madness.
Charles Baudelaire (1821–67) French poet. *Journaux intimes*, 'Fusées', XVI

4 We all are born mad. Some remain so.
Samuel Beckett (1906–) Irish novelist and dramatist. *Waiting for Godot*, II

5 All of us are mad. If it weren't for the fact every one of us is slightly abnormal, there wouldn't be any point in giving each person a separate name.
Ugo Betti (1892–1953) Italian dramatist. *The Fugitive*, 2

6 A knight errant who turns mad for a reason deserves neither merit nor thanks. The thing is to do it without cause.
Miguel de Cervantes (1547–1616) Spanish novelist. *Don Quixote*, Pt. I, Ch. 25

7 The madman is not the man who has lost his reason. The madman is the man who has lost everything except his reason.
G. K. Chesterton (1874–1936) British writer. *Orthodoxy*, Ch. 1

8 Much Madness is divinest Sense –
To a discerning Eye –
Much Sense – the starkest Madness –
Emily Dickinson (1830–86) US poet. *Poems*, 'Much Madness is Divinest Sense'

9 There is less harm to be suffered in being mad among madmen than in being sane all by oneself.
Denis Diderot (1713–84) French writer and editor. *Supplement to Bougainville's 'Voyage'*

10 There is a pleasure sure
In being mad which none but madmen know.
John Dryden (1631–1700) English poet and dramatist. *The Spanish Friar*, 2

11 Where does one go from a world of insanity?
Somewhere on the other side of despair.
T. S. Eliot (1888–1965) US-born British poet and dramatist. *The Family Reunion*, II:2

12 Sanity is very rare: every man almost, and every woman, has a dash of madness.
Ralph Waldo Emerson (1803–82) US poet and essayist. *Journals*

13 Those whom God wishes to destroy, he first makes mad.
Euripides (c. 480–406 BC) Greek dramatist. *Fragment*

14 It is his reasonable conversation which mostly frightens us in a madman.
Anatole France (Jacques Anatole François Thibault; 1844–1924) French writer.

15 Madness is part of all of us, all the time, and it comes and goes, waxes and wanes.
Otto Friedrich

16 What is madness
To those who only observe, is often wisdom
To those to whom it happens.
Christopher Fry (1907–) British dramatist. *A Phoenix Too Frequent*

17 I saw the best minds of my generation destroyed by madness, starving hysterical naked.
Allen Ginsberg (1926–) US poet. *Howl*

18 The world is so full of simpletons and madmen, that one need not seek them in a madhouse.
Johann Wolfgang von Goethe (1749–1832) German poet, dramatist, and scientist. *Conversations with Goethe*, 17 Mar 1830 (Johann Peter Eckermann)

19 Ordinarily he is insane, but he has lucid moments when he is only stupid.
Heinrich Heine (1797–1856) German poet and writer. Comment about Savoye, appointed ambassador to Frankfurt by Lamartine, 1848

20 Insanity is often the logic of an accurate mind overtaxed.
Oliver Wendell Holmes (1809–94) US writer and physician.

21 Show me a sane man and I will cure him for you.
Carl Gustav Jung (1875–1961) Swiss psychoanalyst. *The Observer*, 19 July 1975

22 Every one is more or less mad on one point.
Rudyard Kipling (1865–1936) Indian-born British writer and poet. *Plain Tales from the Hills*, 'On the Strength of a Likeness'

23 Madness need not be all breakdown. It may also be breakthrough. It is potential liberation and renewal as well as enslavement and existential death.
R. D. Laing (1927–) British psychiatrist. *The Politics of Experience*, Ch. 16

24 Insanity is hereditary – you can get it from your children.
Sam Levinson

25 The world is becoming like a lunatic asylum run by lunatics.
David Lloyd George (1863–1945) British Liberal statesman. *The Observer*, 'Sayings of Our Times', 31 May 1953

26 The great proof of madness is the disproportion of one's designs to one's means.
Napoleon I (Napoleon Bonaparte; 1769–1821) French emperor. *Maxims*

27 Insanity in individuals is something rare – but in groups, parties, nations, and epochs it is the rule.
Friedrich Nietzsche (1844–1900) German philosopher. *Beyond Good and Evil*, Ch. 4

28 Men are so necessarily mad, that not to be mad would amount to another form of madness.
Blaise Pascal (1623–62) French philosopher and mathematician. *Pensées*, 414

29 His father's sister had bats in the belfry and was put away.
Eden Phillpotts (1862–1960) British novelist and dramatist. *Peacock House*, 'My First Murder'

30 Sanity is madness put to good uses; waking life is a dream controlled.
George Santayana (1863–1952) US philosopher and poet.

31 Our occasional madness is less wonderful than our occasional sanity.
George Santayana *Interpretations of Poetry and Religion*

32 I am but mad north-north-west. When the wind is southerly I know a hawk from a handsaw.
William Shakespeare (1564–1616) English dramatist. *Hamlet*, II:2

33 Though this be madness, yet there is method in't.
William Shakespeare *Hamlet*, II:2

34 Madness in great ones must not unwatch'd go.
William Shakespeare *Hamlet*, III:1

35 O, let me not be mad, not mad, sweet heaven!
Keep me in temper; I would not be mad!
William Shakespeare *King Lear*, I:5

36 MACBETH. Canst thou not minister to a mind diseas'd,
Pluck from the memory a rooted sorrow,
Raze out the written troubles of the brain,
And with some sweet oblivious antidote
Cleanse the stuff'd bosom of that perilous stuff
Which weighs upon the heart?
DOCTOR. Therein the patient
Must minister to himself.
MACBETH. Throw physic to the dogs, I'll none of it!
William Shakespeare *Macbeth*, V:3

37 We want a few mad people now. See where the sane ones have landed us!
George Bernard Shaw (1856–1950) Irish dramatist and critic. *Saint Joan*

38 The madman thinks the rest of the world crazy.
Publilius Syrus (1st century BC) Roman dramatist. *Moral Sayings*, 386

39 Whom Fortune wishes to destroy she first makes mad.
Publilius Syrus *Moral Sayings*, 911

40 If you talk to God, you are praying; if God talks to you, you have schizophrenia. If the dead talk to you, you are a spiritualist; if God

talks to you, you are a schizophrenic.
Thomas Szasz (1920–) US psychiatrist. *The Second Sin*

41 When we remember that we are all mad, the mysteries disappear and life stands explained.
Mark Twain (1835–1910) US writer.

42 The way it is now, the asylums can hold the sane people, but if we tried to shut up the insane we should run out of building materials.
Mark Twain *Bartlett's Unfamiliar Quotations* (Leonard Louis Levinson)

43 Men will always be mad and those who think they can cure them are the maddest of all.
Voltaire (François-Marie Arouet; 1694–1778) French writer. Letter, 1762

44 What is madness? To have erroneous perceptions and to reason correctly from them.
Voltaire *Philosophical Dictionary*, 'Madness'

45 I shudder and I sigh to think
That even Cicero
And many-minded Homer were
Mad as the mist and snow.
W. B. Yeats (1865–1939) Irish poet. *Mad as the Mist and Snow*

MAJORITY

See also democracy, minority, public

1 The one pervading evil of democracy is the tyranny of the majority.
Lord Acton (1834–1902) British historian. *The History of Freedom*

2 When great changes occur in history, when great principles are involved, as a rule the majority are wrong.
Eugene V. Debs (1855–1926) US socialist, pacifist, and labor unionist. Speech, 12 Aug 1918

3 'It's always best on these occasions to do what the mob do.'
'But suppose there are two mobs?' suggested Mr Snodgrass.
'Shout with the largest,' replied Mr Pickwick.
Charles Dickens (1812–70) British novelist. *Pickwick Papers*, Ch. 13

4 A majority is always the best repartee.
Benjamin Disraeli (1804–81) British statesman. *Tancred*, Bk. II, Ch. 14

5 The majority has the might – more's the pity – but it hasn't right. . . The minority is always right.
Henrik Ibsen (1828–1906) Norwegian dramatist. *An Enemy of the People*, IV

6 The worst enemy of truth and freedom in our society is the compact majority. Yes, the damned, compact, liberal majority.
Henrik Ibsen *An Enemy of the People*, IV

7 It is time for the great silent majority of Americans to stand up and be counted.
Richard Milhous Nixon (1913–) US president. Election speech, Oct 1970

MALADIES

1 Medical men all over the world having merely entered into a tacit agreement to call all sorts of maladies people are liable to, in cold weather, by one name; so that one sort of treatment may serve for all, and their practice thereby be greatly simplified.
Jane Welsh Carlyle (1801–66) The wife of Thomas Carlyle. Letter to John Welsh, 4 Mar 1837

2 Work is the grand cure of all the maladies and miseries that ever beset mankind.
Thomas Carlyle (1795–1881) Scottish historian and essayist. Speech, Edinburgh, 2 Apr 1886

3 As soon as he ceased to be mad he became merely stupid. There are maladies we must not seek to cure because they alone protect us from others that are more serious.
Marcel Proust (1871–1922) French novelist. *À la recherche du temps perdu: Le Côté de Guermantes*

MALAPROPISMS

Remarks of a type associated with Mrs Malaprop in Sheridan's play *The Rivals*.

1 Our watch, sir, have indeed comprehended two aspicious persons.
William Shakespeare (1564–1616) English dramatist. *Much Ado About Nothing*, III:5

2 Comparisons are odorous.
William Shakespeare *Much Ado About Nothing*, III:5

3 A progeny of learning.
Richard Brinsley Sheridan (1751–1816) British dramatist. *The Rivals*, I

4 Illiterate him, I say, quite from your memory.
Richard Brinsley Sheridan *The Rivals*, II

5 It gives me the hydrostatics to such a degree.
Richard Brinsley Sheridan *The Rivals*, III

6 As headstrong as an allegory on the banks of the Nile.
Richard Brinsley Sheridan *The Rivals*, III

7 He is the very pine-apple of politeness!
Richard Brinsley Sheridan *The Rivals*, III

8 If I reprehend any thing in this world, it is the use of my oracular tongue, and a nice derangement of epitaphs!
Richard Brinsley Sheridan *The Rivals*, III

MANKIND

See also evolution, human condition, human nature, men, misanthropy, philanthropy, public, society, women

1 Pray consider what a figure a man would make in the republic of letters.
Joseph Addison (1672–1719) British essayist. *Ancient Medals*

2 I am a human being: Do not fold, spindle or mutilate.
Anonymous Hippy slogan

3 Either a beast or a god.
Aristotle (384–322 BC) Greek philosopher. *Politics*, Bk. I

4 Man, when perfected, is the best of animals, but, when separated from law and justice, he is the worst of all.
Aristotle *Politics*, Bk. I

5 Whatever this is that I am, it is a little flesh and breath, and the ruling part.
Marcus Aurelius (121–180 AD) Roman emperor. *Meditations*, Bk. II, Ch. 2

6 Is a man a salvage at heart, skinned o'er with fragile Manners? Or is salvagery but a faint taint in the natural man's gentility, which erupts now and again like pimples on an angel's arse?
John Barth (1930–) US novelist and academic. *The Sot-Weed Factor*, 3

7 Drinking when we are not thirsty and making love all year round, madam; that is all there is to distinguish us from other animals.
Beaumarchais (1732–99) French dramatist. *Le Mariage de Figaro*, II:21

8 And God said, Let us make man in our image, after our likeness: and let them have dominion over the fish of the sea, and over the fowl of the air, and over the cattle, and over all the earth, and over every creeping thing that creepeth upon the earth.
So God created man in his own image, in the image of God created he him; male and female created he them.
And God blessed them, and God said unto them, Be fruitful, and multiply, and replenish the earth, and subdue it: and have dominion over the fish of the sea, and over the fowl of the air, and over every living thing that moveth upon the earth.
Bible: Genesis 1:26–28

9 MAN, n. An animal so lost in rapturous contemplation of what he thinks he is as to overlook what he indubitably ought to be.
Ambrose Bierce (1842–c. 1914) US writer and journalist. *The Devil's Dictionary*

10 For Mercy has a human heart,
Pity a human face,
And Love, the human form divine,
And Peace, the human dress.
William Blake (1757–1827) British poet. *Songs of Innocence*, 'The Divine Image'

11 Man's Desires are limited by his Perceptions; none can desire what he has not perceived.
William Blake *There is no Natural Religion*

12 Every animal leaves traces of what it was; man alone leaves traces of what he created.
Jacob Bronowski (1908–74) British scientist and writer. *The Ascent of Man*, Ch. 1

13 Man is a noble animal, splendid in ashes, and pompous in the grave.
Thomas Browne (1605–82) English physician and writer. *Urn Burial*, Ch. 5

14 There is surely a piece of divinity in us, something that was before the elements, and owes no homage unto the sun.
Thomas Browne *Religio Medici*

15 A single sentence will suffice for modern man: he fornicated and read the papers.
Albert Camus (1913–60) French existentialist writer. *The Fall*

16 The true science and the true study of man is man.
Pierre Charron (1541–1603) French theologian and philosopher. *Traité de la sagesse*, Bk. I, Ch. 1

17 Carlyle said that men were mostly fools. Christianity, with a surer and more reverend realism, says that they are all fools.
G. K. Chesterton (1874–1936) British writer. *Heretics*, Ch. 12

18 Man is an exception, whatever else he is. If he is not the image of God, then he is a disease of the dust.
G. K. Chesterton *All Things Considered*, 'Wine When It Is Red'

19 Mankind is not a tribe of animals to which we owe compassion. Mankind is a club to which we owe our subscription.
G. K. Chesterton *Daily News*, 10 Apr 1906

20 Individually, men may present a more or less rational appearance, eating, sleeping and scheming. But humanity as a whole is changeful, mystical, fickle and delightful. Men are men, but Man is a woman.
G. K. Chesterton *The Napoleon of Notting Hill*

21 The evolution of the human race will not be accomplished in the ten thousand years of tame animals, but in the million years of wild animals, because man is and will always be a wild animal.
Charles Darwin (1887–1962) British life scientist. *The Next Ten Million Years*, Ch. 4

22 A wonderful fact to reflect upon, that every human creature is constituted to be that profound secret and mystery to every other.
Charles Dickens (1812–70) British novelist. *A Tale of Two Cities*, 1

23 What is man, when you come to think upon him, but a minutely set, ingenious machine for turning, with infinite artfulness, the red wine of Shiraz into urine.
Isak Dinesen (1885–1962) Danish writer. *Seven Gothic Tales, The Dreamers*

24 Any man's death diminishes me, because I am involved in Mankind; And therefore never send to know for whom the bell tolls; it tolls for thee.
John Donne (1573–1631) English poet. *Devotions*, 17

25 It's a burden to us even to be human beings – men with our own real body and blood; we are ashamed of it, we think it a disgrace and try to contrive to be some sort of impossible generalized man.
Fyodor Mikhailovich Dostoevsky (1821–81) Russian writer. *Notes from Underground*, 2

26 Man is physically as well as metaphysically a thing of shreds and patches, borrowed unequally from good and bad ancestors, and a misfit from the start.
Ralph Waldo Emerson (1803–82) US poet and essayist. *The Conduct of Life*, 'Beauty'

27 Every man has a wild beast within him.
Frederick the Great (1712–86) Prussian king. *Letter to Voltaire*, 1759

28 Man is Nature's sole mistake.
W. S. Gilbert (1836–1911) British dramatist. *Princess Ida*, I

29 Human beings are like timid punctuation marks sprinkled among the incomprehensible sentences of life.
Jean Giraudoux (1882–1944) French dramatist and writer. *Siegfried*, 2

30 On earth there is nothing great but man; in man there is nothing great but mind.
William Hamilton (1788–1856) Scottish philosopher. *Lectures on Metaphysics*

31 The human race will be the cancer of the planet.
Julian Huxley (1887–1975) British biologist.

32 Man as we know him is a poor creature; but he is halfway between an ape and a god and he is travelling in the right direction.
W. R. Inge (1860–1954) British clergyman. *Outspoken Essays: Second Series*, 'Confessio Fidei'

33 There are only two classes of mankind in the world – doctors and patients.
Rudyard Kipling (1865–1936) Indian-born British writer and poet. *A Doctor's Work*, address to medical students at London's Middlesex Hospital, 1 Oct 1908

34 The majority of men devote the greater part of their lives to making their remaining years unhappy.
Jean de La Bruyère (1645–96) French satirist. *Les Caractères*

35 The anthropologist respects history, but he does not accord it a special value. He conceives it as a study complementary to his own: one of them unfurls the range of human

societies in time, the other in space.
Claude Lévi-Strauss (1908–) French anthropologist. *The Savage Mind*

36 Man appears to be the missing link between anthropoid apes and human beings.
Konrad Lorenz (1903–) Austrian zoologist and pioneer of ethology. *The New York Times Magazine*, 11 Apr 1965 (John Pfeiffer)

37 I'll give you my opinion of the human race . . . Their heart's in the right place, but their head is a thoroughly inefficient organ.
W. Somerset Maugham (1874–1965) British novelist. *The Summing Up*

38 Man is a beautiful machine that works very badly. He is like a watch of which the most that can be said is that its cosmetic effect is good.
H. L. Mencken (1880–1956) US journalist and editor. *Minority Report*, 20

39 A human being, he wrote, is a whispering in the steam pipes on a cold night; dust sifted through a locked window; one or the other half of an unsolved equation; a pun made by God; an ingenious assembly of portable plumbing.
Christopher Morley (1890–1957) US writer and journalist. *Human Being*, Ch. 11

40 Clearly, then, the city is not a concrete jungle, it is a human zoo.
Desmond Morris (1928–) British biologist and writer. *The Human Zoo*, Introduction

41 There are one hundred and ninety-three living species of monkeys and apes. One hundred and ninety-two of them are covered with hair. The exception is a naked ape self-named *Homo sapiens*.
Desmond Morris *The Naked Ape*, Introduction

42 He is proud that he has the biggest brain of all the primates, but attempts to conceal the fact that he also has the biggest penis.
Desmond Morris *The Naked Ape*, Introduction

43 Man's the bad child of the universe.
James Oppenheim *Laughter*

44 Man, as he is, is not a genuine article. He is an imitation of something, and a very bad imitation.
P. D. Ouspensky (1878–1947) Russian-born occultist. *The Psychology of Man's Possible Evolution*, Ch. 2

45 The proper study of Mankind is Man.
Alexander Pope (1688–1744) English poet. *An Essay on Man*, Epistle II

46 The human face is indeed, like the face of the God of some Oriental theogony, a whole cluster of faces, crowded together but on different surfaces so that one does not see them all at once.
Marcel Proust (1871–1922) French novelist. *À la recherche du temps perdu: À l'ombre des jeunes filles en fleurs*

47 Man is Heaven's masterpiece.
Francis Quarles (1592–1644) English writer. *Emblems*, Bk. II

48 I wish I loved the Human Race;
I wish I loved its silly face;
I wish I liked the way it walks;
I wish I liked the way it talks;
And when I'm introduced to one
I wish I thought *What Jolly Fun!*
Walter Raleigh (1861–1922) British scholar. *Laughter from a Cloud*, 'Wishes of an Elderly Man'

49 Everything is good when it leaves the Creator's hands; everything degenerates in the hands of man.
Jean Jacques Rousseau (1712–78) French philosopher. Attrib.

50 Man is not a solitary animal, and so long as social life survives, self-realization cannot be the supreme principle of ethics.
Bertrand Russell (1872–1970) British philosopher. *History of Western Philosophy*, 'Romanticism'

51 The mass of mankind is divided into two classes, the Sancho Panzas who have a sense for reality, but no ideals, and the Don Quixotes with a sense for ideals, but mad.
George Santayana (1863–1952) Spanish-born US philosopher, poet, and critic. *Interpretations of Poetry and Religion*, Preface

52 Doctors, priests, magistrates, and officers know men as thoroughly as if they had made them.
Jean-Paul Sartre (1905–80) French philosopher, dramatist, and novelist. *Nausea*, 'Shrove Tuesday'

53 I love mankind – it's people I can't stand.
Charles M. Schultz (1922–) US cartoonist. *Go Fly a Kite, Charlie Brown*

54 After all, for mankind as a whole there are no exports. We did not start developing by obtaining foreign exchange from Mars or the moon. Mankind is a closed society.
E. F. Schumacher (1911–77) German-born economist. *Small is Beautiful, A Study of Economics as if People Mattered*, Ch. 14

55 What a piece of work is a man! How noble in reason! how infinite in faculties! in form and moving, how express and admirable! in action, how like an angel! in apprehension, how like a god! the beauty of the world! the paragon of animals! And yet, to me, what is this quintessence of dust? Man delights not me – no, nor woman neither.
William Shakespeare (1564–1616) English dramatist. *Hamlet*, II:2

56 But man, proud man
Dress'd in a little brief authority,
Most ignorant of what he's most assur'd,
His glassy essence, like an angry ape,
Plays such fantastic tricks before high heaven
As makes the angels weep.
William Shakespeare *Measure for Measure*, II:2

57 How beauteous mankind is! O brave new world
That has such people in't!
William Shakespeare *The Tempest*, V:1

58 You fools of fortune, trencher-friends, time's flies.
William Shakespeare *Timon of Athens*, III:6

59 Physically there is nothing to distinguish human society from the farm-yard except that children are more troublesome and costly than chickens and women are not so completely enslaved as farm stock.
George Bernard Shaw (1856–1950) Irish dramatist and critic. *Getting Married*, Preface

60 Man, unlike any other thing organic or inorganic in the universe, grows beyond his work, walks up the stairs of his concepts, emerges ahead of his accomplishments.
John Steinbeck (1902–68) US novelist. *The Grapes of Wrath*, Ch. 14

61 Glory to Man in the highest! for Man is the master of things.
Charles Swinburne (1837–1909) British poet. *Hymn of Man*

62 The fish in the water is silent, the animal on the earth is noisy, the bird in the air is singing.
But Man has in him the silence of the

sea, the noise of the earth and the music of the air.
Rabindranath Tagore (1861–1941) Indian poet and philosopher. *Stray Birds*, 43

63 I am a man, I count nothing human foreign to me.
Terence (Publius Terentius Afer; c. 190–159 BC) Roman poet. *Heauton Timorumenos*

64 The highest wisdom has but one science – the science of the whole – the science explaining the whole creation and man's place in it.
Leo Tolstoy (1828–1910) Russian writer. *War and Peace*, Bk.V, Ch. 2

65 Man is a museum of diseases, a home of impurities; he comes today and is gone tomorrow; he begins as dirt and departs as stench.
Mark Twain (Samuel L. Clemens; 1835–1910) US writer.

66 The noblest work of God? Man. Who found it out? Man.
Mark Twain *Autobiography*

67 We should expect the best and the worst from mankind, as from the weather.
Marquis de Luc de Clapiers Vauvenargues (1715–47) French moralist. *Reflections and Maxims*, 102

68 One thousand years more. That's all *Homo sapiens* has before him.
H. G. Wells (1866–1946) British writer. *Diary* (Harold Nicolson)

69 If anything is sacred the human body is sacred.
Walt Whitman (1819–92) US poet. *I Sing the Body Electric*, 8

70 But there comes a moment in everybody's life when he must decide whether he'll live among human beings or not – a fool among fools or a fool alone.
Thornton Wilder (1897–1975) US novelist and dramatist. *The Matchmaker*, IV

71 We're all of us guinea pigs in the laboratory of God. Humanity is just a work in progress.
Tennessee Williams (1911–83) US dramatist. *Camino Real*, 12

72 If this belief from heaven be sent,
If such be Nature's holy plan,
Have I not reason to lament
What man has made of man?
William Wordsworth (1770–1850) British poet. *Lines written in Early Spring*

MANNERS

See also courtesy, etiquette

1 Leave off first for manners' sake: and be not unsatiable, lest thou offend.
Bible: Ecclesiasticus 31:17

2 'Speak when you're spoken to!' the Red Queen sharply interrupted her.
Lewis Carroll (Charles Lutwidge Dodgson; 1832–98) British writer. *Through the Looking-Glass*, Ch. 9

3 Don't tell your friends about your indigestion:
'How are you!' is a greeting, not a question.
Arthur Guiterman *A Poet's Proverbs*, 'Of Tact'

4 To Americans English manners are far more frightening than none at all.
Randall Jarrell (1914–65) US author. *Pictures from an Institution*, Pt. I, Ch. 5

5 On the Continent people have good food; in England people have good table manners.
George Mikes (1912–87) Hungarian-born British writer. *How to be an Alien*

6 Good breeding consists in concealing how much we think of ourselves and how little we think of other persons.
Mark Twain (Samuel Langhorne Clemens; 1835–1910) US writer. *Notebooks*

7 Politeness is organised indifference.
Paul Valéry (1871–1945) French poet and writer. *Tel Quel*

8 Manners are especially the need of the plain. The pretty can get away with anything.
Evelyn Waugh (1903–66) British novelist. *The Observer*, 'Sayings of the Year', 1962

9 Manners maketh man.
William of Wykeham (1324–1404) English churchman. Motto of Winchester College and New College, Oxford

MAO TSE-TUNG

(1893–1976) Chinese communist leader. As chairman of the Communist Party, in 1949 he proclaimed the People's Republic of China and in 1966–68 launched the Cultural Revolution. He developed the form of communism known as Maoism.

Quotations about Mao Tse-Tung

1 No Chinese thinker in the period since Confucius has attained the degree of acceptance and authority which Mao has acquired.
C. P. Fitzgerald *Mao Tse-Tung and China*

2 He dominated the room as I have never seen any person do except Charles de Gaulle.
Henry Kissinger (1923–) German-born US politician and diplomat. *Memoirs*

Quotations by Mao Tse-Tung

3 'War is the continuation of politics'. In this sense war is politics and war itself is a political action.
Quotations from Chairman Mao Tse-Tung, Ch. 5

4 We are advocates of the abolition of war, we do not want war; but war can only be abolished through war, and in order to get rid of the gun it is necessary to take up the gun.
Quotations from Chairman Mao Tse-Tung, Ch. 5

5 All reactionaries are paper tigers.
Quotations from Chairman Mao Tse-Tung, Ch. 6

6 Letting a hundred flowers blossom and a hundred schools of thought contend is the policy for promoting the progress of the arts and the sciences.
Quotations from Chairman Mao Tse-Tung, Ch. 32

7 Every Communist must grasp the truth, 'Political power grows out of the barrel of a gun.'
Selected Works, Vol. II, 'Problems of War and Strategy', 6 Nov 1938

8 To read too many books is harmful.
The New Yorker, 7 Mar 1977

9 The atom bomb is a paper tiger which the United States reactionaries use to scare people.
Interview, Aug 1946

10 The government burns down whole cities while the people are forbidden to light lamps.
Attrib.

MARRIAGE

See also adultery, family, love and marriage, unfaithfulness

1 Better be an old man's darling than a young man's slave.
Proverb

2 Marriages are made in heaven.
Proverb

3 Marry in haste, and repent at leisure.
Proverb

4 Marry in Lent, and you'll live to repent.
Proverb

5 Marry in May, rue for aye.
Proverb

6 The first wife is matrimony, the second company, the third heresy.
Proverb

7 EGGHEAD WEDS HOURGLASS.
Anonymous On marriage of playwright Arthur Miller to Marilyn Monroe. *Variety*, headline 1956

8 To marry a man out of pity is folly; and, if you think you are going to influence the kind of fellow who has 'never had a chance, poor devil,' you are profoundly mistaken. One can only influence the strong characters in life, not the weak; and it is the height of vanity to suppose that you can make an honest man of anyone.
Margot Asquith (1865–1945) The second wife of Herbert Asquith. *The Autobiography of Margot Asquith*, Ch. 6

9 I married beneath me – all women do.
Nancy Astor (1879–1964) American-born British politician. *Dictionary of National Biography*

10 It is a truth universally acknowledged, that a single man in possession of a good fortune must be in want of a wife.
Jane Austen (1775–1817) British novelist. The opening words of the book. *Pride and Prejudice*, Ch. 1

11 Happiness in marriage is entirely a matter of chance.
Jane Austen *Pride and Prejudice*, Ch. 6

12 Mrs Hall of Sherbourne was brought to bed yesterday of a dead child, some weeks before she expected, owing to a fright. I suppose she happened unawares to look at her husband.
Jane Austen Letter, 27 Oct 1798

13 Wives are young men's mistresses, companions for middle age, and old men's nurses.
Francis Bacon (1561–1626) English philosopher. *Essays*, 'Of Marriage and Single Life'

14 He was reputed one of the wise men, that made answer to the question, when a man should marry? A young man not yet, an elder man not at all.
Francis Bacon *Essays*, 'Of Marriage and Single Life'

15 I rather think of having a career of my own.
Arthur Balfour (1848–1930) British statesman. When asked whether he was going to marry Margot Tennant. *Autobiography* (Margot Asquith), Ch. 9

16 It is easier to be a lover than a husband, for the same reason that it is more difficult to show a ready wit all day long than to produce an occasional *bon mot*.
Honoré de Balzac (1799–1850) French novelist. Attrib.

17 The majority of husbands remind me of an orangutang trying to play the violin.
Honoré de Balzac *La Physiologie du mariage*

18 No man should marry until he has studied anatomy and dissected at least one woman.
Honoré de Balzac *La Physiologie du mariage*

19 My father argued sair – my mother didna speak,
But she looked in my face till my heart was like to break;
They gied him my hand but my heart was in the sea;
And so auld Robin Gray, he was gudeman to me.
Lady Ann Barnard (1750–1825) British poet. *Auld Robin Gray*

20 Maybe today's successful marriage is when a man is in love with his wife and only one other woman.
Matt Basile US private detective. *The Observer*, 'Sayings of the Week', 31 Aug 1975

21 I think weddings is sadder than funerals, because they remind you of your own wedding. You can't be reminded of your own funeral because it hasn't happened. But weddings always make me cry.
Brendan Behan (1923–64) Irish playwright. *Richard's Cork Leg*, I

22 Being a husband is a whole-time job. That is why so many husbands fail. They cannot give their entire attention to it.
Arnold Bennett (1867–1931) British novelist. *The Title*, I

23 Husbands, love your wives, and be not bitter against them.
Bible: Colossians 3:19

24 Let the husband render unto the wife due benevolence: and likewise also the wife unto the husband.
Bible: I Corinthians 7:3

25 But if they cannot contain, let them marry: for it is better to marry than to burn.
Bible: I Corinthians 7:9

26 But he that is married careth for the things that are of the world, how he may please his wife.
Bible: I Corinthians 7:33

27 And the Lord God said, It is not good that the man should be alone; I will make him an help meet for him.
Bible: Genesis 2:18

28 Wherefore they are no more twain, but one flesh. What therefore God hath joined together, let not man put asunder.
Bible: Matthew 19:6

29 Even as Sara obeyed Abraham, calling him lord: whose daughters ye are, as long as ye do well, and are not afraid with any amazement. Likewise, ye husbands, dwell with them according to knowledge, giving honour unto the wife, as unto the weaker vessel, and as being heirs together of the grace of life; that your prayers be not hindered.
Bible: I Peter 3:6–7

30 *Marriage*, n. The state or condition of a community consisting of a master, a mistress and two slaves, making in all two.
Ambrose Bierce (1842–?1914) US writer and journalist. *The Devil's Dictionary*

31 To have and to hold from this day forward, for better for worse, for richer for poorer, in sickness and in health, to love and to cherish, till death us do part.
The Book of Common Prayer *Solemnization of Matrimony*

32 Splendid couple – slept with both of them.
Maurice Bowra (1898–1971) British academic. Referring to a well-known literary couple. Attrib.

33 'We stay together, but we distrust one another.'
'Ah, yes . . . but isn't that a definition of marriage?'
Malcolm Bradbury (1932–) British academic and novelist. *The History Man*, Ch. 3

34 Most married couples in the end arrive at tolerable arrangements for living – arrangements that may strike others as odd, but which suit them very well.
John Braine (1922–86) British author. Remark, June 1970

35 Ah, gentle dames! It gars me greet
To think how mony counsels sweet,
How mony lengthen'd sage advices,
The husband frae the wife despises!
Robert Burns (1759–96) Scottish poet. *Tam o' Shanter*

36 Marriage is distinctly and repeatedly excluded from heaven. Is this because it is thought likely to mar the general felicity?
Samuel Butler (1835–1902) British writer. *Notebooks*

37 Wedlock – the deep, deep peace of the double bed after the hurly-burly of the chaise-longue.
Mrs Patrick Campbell (Beatrice Stella Tanner; 1865–1940) British actress. *Jennie* (Ralph G. Martin), Vol. II

38 The one advantage about marrying a princess – or someone from a royal family – is that they do know what happens.
Charles, Prince of Wales (1948–) Eldest son of Elizabeth II. Attrib.

39 She was a worthy womman al hir lyve,
Housbondes at chirche-dore she hadde fyve,
Withouten other companye in youthe.
Geoffrey Chaucer (c. 1342–1400) English poet. Referring to the wife of Bath. *The Canterbury Tales*, Prologue

40 An archaeologist is the best husband any woman can have: the older she gets, the more interested he is in her.
Agatha Christie (1891–1976) British detective-story writer. Attrib.

41 The most happy marriage I can picture or imagine to myself would be the union of a deaf man to a blind woman.
Samuel Taylor Coleridge (1772–1834) British poet. *Recollections* (Allsop)

42 SHARPER. Thus grief still treads upon the heels of pleasure:
Marry'd in haste, we may repent at leisure.
SETTER. Some by experience find those words mis-plac'd:
At leisure marry'd, they repent in haste.
William Congreve (1670–1729) British Restoration dramatist. *The Old Bachelor*, V:8

43 Courtship to marriage, as a very witty prologue to a very dull Play.
William Congreve *The Old Bachelor*, V:10

44 I hope you do not think me prone to any iteration of nuptials.
William Congreve *The Way of the World*, IV:12

45 Marriage is a wonderful invention; but then again so is a bicycle repair kit.
Billy Connolly (1942–) British comedian. *The Authorized Version*

46 Dear Mrs A., hooray hooray,
At last you are deflowered
On this as every other day
I love you. Noël Coward.
Noël Coward (1899–1973) British dramatist. Telegram to Gertrude Lawrence on her marriage to Richard S. Aldrich

47 Says John, It is my wedding-day,
And all the world would stare,
If wife should dine at Edmonton,
And I should dine at Ware.
William Cowper (1731–1800) British poet. *John Gilpin*

48 To-morrow is our wedding-day,
And we will then repair
Unto the Bell at Edmonton,
All in a chaise and pair.
William Cowper *John Gilpin*

49 Daisy, Daisy, give me your answer, do!
I'm half crazy, all for the love of you!
It won't be a stylish marriage,
I can't afford a carriage,
But you'll look sweet upon the seat
Of a bicycle made for two!
Harry Dacre (19th century) British songwriter. *Daisy Bell*

50 If a man stays away from his wife for seven years, the law presumes the separation to have killed him; yet according to our daily experience, it might well prolong his life.
Lord Darling (1849–1936) British judge. *Scintillae Juris*

51 This man, she reasons, as she looks at her husband, is a poor fish. But he is the nearest I can get to the big one that got away.
Nigel Dennis (1912–) British writer. *Cards of Identity*

52 The value of marriage is not that adults produce children but that children produce adults.
Peter de Vries (1906–) US writer. *Tunnel of Love*, Ch. 8

53 'Old girl,' said Mr Bagnet, 'give him my opinion. You know it.'
Charles Dickens (1812–70) British novelist. *Bleak House*, Ch. 27

54 Every woman should marry – and no man.
Benjamin Disraeli (1804–81) British statesman. *Lothair*, Ch. 30

55 It destroys one's nerves to be amiable every day to the same human being.
Benjamin Disraeli *The Young Duke*

56 Now one of the great reasons why so many husbands and wives make shipwreck of their lives together is because a man is always seeking for happiness, while a woman is on a perpetual still hunt for trouble.
Dorothy Dix (Elizabeth Meriwether Gilmer; 1861–1951) US journalist and writer. *Dorothy Dix, Her Book*, Ch. 1

57 The husband was a teetotaller, there was no other woman, and the conduct complained of was that he had drifted into the habit of winding up every meal by taking out his false teeth and hurling them at his wife.
Arthur Conan Doyle (1856–1930) British writer. *A Case of Identity*

58 Here lies my wife; here let her lie!
Now she's at rest, and so am I.
John Dryden (1631–1700) British poet and dramatist. *Epitaph Intended for Dryden's Wife*

59 I am to be married within these three days; married past redemption.
John Dryden *Marriage à la Mode*, I

60 So that ends my first experience with matrimony, which I always thought a highly overrated performance.
Isadora Duncan (1878–1927) US dancer. *The New York Times*, 1923

61 Being an old maid is like death by drowning, a really delightful sensation after you cease to struggle.
Edna Ferber (1887–1968) US writer. *Wit's End* (R. E. Drennan), 'Completing the Circle'

62 When widows exclaim loudly against second marriages, I would always lay a wager, that the man, if not the wedding-day, is absolutely fixed on.
Henry Fielding (1707–54) British novelist. *Amelia*, Bk. VI, Ch. 8

63 One fool at least in every married couple.
Henry Fielding *Amelia,* Bk. IX, Ch. 4

64 His designs were strictly honourable, as the phrase is; that is, to rob a lady of her fortune by way of marriage.
Henry Fielding *Tom Jones,* Bk. XI, Ch. 4

65 Composed that monstrous animal a husband and wife.
Henry Fielding *Tom Jones,* Bk. XV, Ch. 9

66 Most marriages don't add two people together. They subtract one from the other.
Ian Fleming (1908–64) British journalist and author. *Diamonds are Forever*

67 Husbands are like fires. They go out when unattended.
Zsa Zsa Gabor (1919–) Hungarian-born US film star. *Newsweek,* 28 Mar 1960

68 A man in love is incomplete until he has married. Then he's finished.
Zsa Zsa Gabor *Newsweek,* 28 Mar 1960

69 Do you think your mother and I should have liv'd comfortably so long together, if ever we had been married?
John Gay (1685–1732) English poet and dramatist. *The Beggar's Opera*

70 No, I shall have mistresses.
George II (1683–1760) King of Great Britain and Ireland. Reply to Queen Caroline's suggestion, as she lay on her deathbed, that he should marry again after her death. *Memoirs of George the Second* (Hervey), Vol. II

71 When you marry your mistress, you create a job vacancy.
James Goldsmith (1933–) British businessman. Attrib.

72 I was ever of opinion, that the honest man who married and brought up a large family, did more service than he who continued single and only talked of population.
Oliver Goldsmith (1728–74) Irish-born British writer. *The Vicar of Wakefield,* Ch. 1

73 I... chose my wife, as she did her wedding gown, not for a fine glossy surface, but such qualities as would wear well.
Oliver Goldsmith *The Vicar of Wakefield,* Preface

74 The trouble with my wife is that she is a whore in the kitchen and a cook in bed.
Geoffrey Gorer (1905–) British writer and anthropologist. *Exploring the English Character*

75 When a woman gets married it is like jumping into a hole in the ice in the middle of winter; you do it once and you remember it the rest of your days.
Maxim Gorky (Aleksei Maksimovich Peshkov; 1868–1936) Russian writer. *The Lower Depths*

76 The concept of two people living together for 25 years without having a cross word suggests a lack of spirit only to be admired in sheep.
A. P. Herbert (1890–1971) British writer and politican. *News Chronicle,* 1940

77 The critical period in matrimony is breakfast-time.
A. P. Herbert *Uncommon Law*

78 Then be not coy, but use your time;
And while ye may, go marry:
For having lost but once your prime,
You may for ever tarry.
Robert Herrick (1591–1674) English poet. *Hesperides,* 'To the Virgins, to Make Much of Time'

79 Marriage has many pains, but celibacy has no pleasures.
Samuel Johnson (1709–84) British lexicographer. *Rasselas,* Ch. 26

80 The triumph of hope over experience.
Samuel Johnson Referring to the hasty remarriage of an acquaintance following the death of his first wife, with whom he had been most unhappy. *Life of Johnson* (J. Boswell), Vol. II

81 Always see a fellow's weak point in his wife.
James Joyce (1882–1941) Irish novelist. *Ulysses*

82 It has been discovered experimentally that you can draw laughter from an audience anywhere in the world, of any class or race, simply by walking on to a stage and uttering the words 'I am a married man'.
Ted Kavanagh (1892–1958) British radio scriptwriter. *News Review,* 10 July 1947

83 Marry those who are single among you, and such as are honest of your men-servants and your maid-servants: if they be poor, God will enrich them of his abundance; for God is bounteous and wise.
Koran Ch. XXIV

84 Suffer the women whom ye divorce to dwell in some part of the houses wherein ye dwell; according to the room and conveniences of the habitations which ye possess; and make them not uneasy, that ye may reduce them to straits.
Koran Ch. LXV

85 Nothing is to me more distasteful than that entire complacency and satisfaction which beam in the countenances of a new-married couple.
Charles Lamb (1775–1834) British essayist. *Essays of Elia,* 'A Bachelor's Complaint of Married People'

86 Same old slippers,
Same old rice,
Same old glimpse of
Paradise.
William James Lampton (1859–1917) British writer. *June Weddings*

87 He married a woman to stop her getting away
Now she's there all day.
Philip Larkin (1922–85) British poet. *Self's The Man*

88 There was I, waiting at the church,
Waiting at the church, waiting at the church,
When I found he'd left me in the lurch,
Lor', how it did upset me! . . .
Can't get away to marry you today –
My wife won't let me.
Fred W. Leigh (19th century) British songwriter. *Waiting at the Church*

89 I'm getting married in the morning!
Ding dong! the bells are gonna chime.
Pull out the stopper!
Let's have a whopper!
But get me to the church on time!
Alan Jay Lerner (1918–86) US songwriter. *My Fair Lady,* II:3

90 A bachelor lives like a king and dies like a beggar.
L. S. Lowry (1887–1976) British painter. Attrib.

91 Being married six times shows a degree of optimism over wisdom, but I am incorrigibly optimistic.
Norman Mailer (1923–) US writer. *The Observer,* 'Sayings of the Week', 17 Jan 1988

92 I am in truth very thankful for not having married at all.
Harriet Martineau (1802–76) British writer. *Harriet Martineau's Autobiography,* Vol. I

93 ... the early marriages of silly children... where... every woman is married before she well knows how serious a matter human life is.
Harriet Martineau *Society in America,* Vol. III, 'Marriage'

94 In no country, I believe, are the marriage laws so iniquitous as in England, and the conjugal relation, in consequence, so impaired.
Harriet Martineau *Society in America,* Vol. III, 'Marriage'

95 When married people don't get on they can separate, but if they're not married it's impossible. It's a tie that only death can sever.
W. Somerset Maugham (1874–1965) British novelist. *The Circle,* III

96 No man is genuinely happy, married, who has to drink worse gin than he used to drink when he was single.
H. L. Mencken (1880–1956) US journalist and editor. *Prejudices,* 'Reflections on Monogamy'

97 Marriage is like a cage; one sees the birds outside desperate to get in, and those inside equally desperate to get out.
Michel de Montaigne (1533–92) French essayist. *Essais,* III

98 Why did He not marry? Could the answer be that Jesus was not by nature the marrying sort?
Hugh Montefiore (1920–) British Anglican clergyman. Speech, Oxford, 26 July 1967

99 It has been said that a bride's attitude towards her betrothed can be summed up in three words: Aisle. Altar. Hymn.
Frank Muir (1920–) British writer and broadcaster. *Upon My Word!* (Frank Muir and Dennis Norden), 'A Jug of Wine'

100 One doesn't have to get anywhere in a marriage. It's not a public conveyance.
Iris Murdoch (1919–) Irish-born British novelist. *A Severed Head*

101 Writing is like getting married. One should never commit oneself until one is amazed at one's luck.
Iris Murdoch *The Black Prince,* 'Bradley Pearson's Foreword'

102 It is now known . . . that men enter local politics solely as a result of being unhappily married.
Cyril Northcote Parkinson (1919–) British historian and writer. *Parkinson's Law,* Ch. 10

103 Marriage may often be a stormy lake, but celibacy is almost always a muddy horse-pond.
Thomas Love Peacock (1785–1866) British novelist. *Melincourt*

104 Sir, I have quarrelled with my wife; and a man who has quarrelled with his wife is absolved from all duty to his country.
Thomas Love Peacock *Nightmare Abbey,* Ch. 11

105 Strange to say what delight we married people have to see these poor fools decoyed into our condition.
Samuel Pepys (1633–1703) English diarist. *Diary,* 25 Dec 1665

106 A loving wife will do anything for her husband except stop criticising and trying to improve him.
J. B. Priestley (1894–1984) British novelist. *Rain on Godshill*

107 When you're bored with yourself, marry and be bored with someone else.
David Pryce-Jones (1936–) British author and critic. *Owls and Satyrs*

108 It doesn't much signify whom one marries, for one is sure to find next morning that it was someone else.
Samuel Rogers (1763–1855) British poet. *Table Talk* (ed. Alexander Dyce)

109 A married couple are well suited when both partners usually feel the need for a quarrel at the same time.
Jean Rostand (1894–1977) French biologist and writer. *Le Mariage*

110 Never feel remorse for what you have thought about your wife; she has thought much worse things about you.
Jean Rostand *Le Mariage*

111 When you see what some girls marry, you realize how they must hate to work for a living.
Helen Rowland (1876–1950) US writer. *Reflections of a Bachelor Girl*

112 Marriage is for women the commonest mode of livelihood, and the total amount of undesired sex endured by women is probably greater in marriage than in prostitution.
Bertrand Russell (1872–1970) British philosopher. *Marriage and Morals*

113 The Western custom of one wife and hardly any mistresses.
Saki (Hector Hugh Munro; 1870–1916) British writer. *Reginald in Russia*

114 It takes two to make a marriage a success and only one a failure.
Herbert Samuel (1870–1963) British Liberal statesman. *A Book of Quotations*

115 Marriage is nothing but a civil contract.
John Selden (1584–1654) English historian. *Table Talk*

116 The world must be peopled. When I said I would die a bachelor, I did not think I should live till I were married.
William Shakespeare (1564–1616) English dramatist. *Much Ado About Nothing,* II:3

117 For a light wife doth make a heavy husband.
William Shakespeare *The Merchant of Venice,* V:1

118 That I have ta'en away this old man's daughter,
It is most true; true, I have married her:
The very head and front of my offending
Hath this extent, no more.
William Shakespeare *Othello,* I:3

119 Kiss me Kate, we will be married o' Sunday.
William Shakespeare *The Taming of the Shrew,* II:1

120 Such duty as the subject owes the prince,
Even such a woman oweth to her husband.
William Shakespeare *The Taming of the Shrew,* V:2

121 MIRANDA. I am your wife, if you will marry me;
If not, I'll die your maid: to be your fellow
You may deny me; but I'll be your servant
Whether you will or no.
FERDINAND. My mistress, dearest;
And thus I humble ever.
MIRANDA. My husband then?
FERDINAND. Ay, with a heart as willing
As bondage e'er of freedom; here's my hand.
MIRANDA. And mine, with my heart in't.
William Shakespeare *The Tempest,* III:1

122 Many a good hanging prevents a bad marriage.
William Shakespeare *Twelfth Night,* I:5

123 My mother married a very good man . . . and she is not at all keen on my doing the same.
George Bernard Shaw (1856–1950) Irish dramatist and critic. *Heartbreak House*

124 Marriage is popular because it combines the maximum of temptation with the maximum of opportunity.

George Bernard Shaw *Man and Superman*

125 It is a woman's business to get married as soon as possible, and a man's to keep unmarried as long as he can.

George Bernard Shaw *Man and Superman*, II

126 Have you not heard
When a man marries, dies, or turns Hindoo,
His best friends hear no more of him?

Percy Bysshe Shelley (1792–1822) British poet. Referring to Thomas Love Peacock, who worked for the East India Company and had recently married. *Letter to Maria Gisborne*, I

127 Be assured on the faith of a monkey that your frog lives in hope.

Jean de Simier The 'monkey' was Elizabeth I's pet name for Simier, who tried unsuccessfully to arrange a marriage between Elizabeth and his master, the Duke of Anjou (the 'frog').

128 Married women are kept women, and they are beginning to find it out.

Logan Pearsall Smith (1865–1946) US writer. *Afterthoughts*, 'Other people'

129 My definition of marriage: . . . it resembles a pair of shears, so joined that they cannot be separated; often moving in opposite directions, yet always punishing anyone who comes between them.

Sydney Smith (1771–1845) British clergyman and essayist. *Memoir* (Lady Holland)

130 A little in drink, but at all times yr faithful husband.

Richard Steele (1672–1729) Dublin-born British essayist. Letter to his wife, 27 Sept 1708

131 Even if we take matrimony at its lowest, even if we regard it as no more than a sort of friendship recognized by the police.

Robert Louis Stevenson (1850–94) Scottish writer. *Virginibus Puerisque*

132 Marriage is a step so grave and decisive that it attracts light-headed, variable men by its very awfulness.

Robert Louis Stevenson *Virginibus Puerisque*

133 Marriage is like life in this – that it is a field of battle, and not a bed of roses.

Robert Louis Stevenson *Virginibus Puerisque*

134 In marriage, a man becomes slack and selfish and undergoes a fatty degeneration of his moral being.

Robert Louis Stevenson *Virginibus Puerisque*

135 Lastly (and this is, perhaps, the golden rule), no woman should marry a teetotaller, or a man who does not smoke.

Robert Louis Stevenson *Virginibus Puerisque*

136 Bachelor's fare; bread and cheese, and kisses.

Jonathan Swift (1667–1745) Irish-born Anglican priest and writer. *Polite Conversation*, Dialogue 1

137 What they do in heaven we are ignorant of; what they do *not* we are told expressly, that they neither marry, nor are given in marriage.

Jonathan Swift *Thoughts on Various Subjects*

138 He that loves not his wife and children, feeds a lioness at home and broods a nest of sorrows.

Jeremy Taylor (1613–67) English Anglican theologian. *Sermons*, 'Married Love'

139 Or when the moon was overhead,
Came two young lovers lately wed;
'I am half sick of shadows,' said
The Lady of Shalott.

Alfred, Lord Tennyson (1809–92) British poet. *The Lady of Shalott*, Pt. II

140 Remember, it is as easy to marry a rich woman as a poor woman.

William Makepeace Thackeray (1811–63) British novelist. *Pendennis*, Ch. 28

141 This I set down as a positive truth. A woman with fair opportunities and without a positive hump, may marry whom she likes.

William Makepeace Thackeray *Vanity Fair*, Ch. 4

142 Every night of her married life she has been late for school.

Dylan Thomas (1914–53) Welsh poet. *Under Milk Wood*

143 It should be a very happy marriage – they are both so much in love with *him*.

Irene Thomas (1920–) British writer. Attrib.

144 Divorce? Never. But murder often!

Sybil Thorndike (1882–1976) British actress. Replying to a query as to whether she had ever considered divorce during her long marriage to Sir Lewis Casson. Attrib.

145 A man should not insult his wife publicly, at parties. He should insult her in the privacy of the home.

James Thurber (1894–1961) US humorist. *Thurber Country*

146 Nearly all marriages, even happy ones, are mistakes: in the sense that almost certainly (in a more perfect world, or even with a little more care in this very imperfect one) both partners might have found more suitable mates. But the real soul-mate is the one you are actually married to.

J. R. R. Tolkien (1892–1973) British writer. Letter to Michael Tolkien, 6–8 Mar 1941

147 Marriage is the only adventure open to the cowardly.

Voltaire (François-Marie Arouet; 1694–1778) French writer. *Thoughts of a Philosopher*

148 I think women are basically quite lazy. Marriage is still a woman's best investment, because she can con some man into supporting her for the rest of his life.

Alan Whicker (1925–) British television broadcaster and writer. *The Observer*, 'Sayings of the Week', 10 Sept 1972

149 And what would happen to my illusion that I am a force for order in the home if I wasn't married to the only man north of the Tiber who is even untidier than I am?

Katherine Whitehorn (1926–) British journalist. *Sunday Best*, 'Husband-Swapping'

150 Twenty years of romance makes a woman look like a ruin; but twenty years of marriage make her something like a public building.

Oscar Wilde (1854–1900) Irish-born British dramatist. *A Woman of No Importance*, I

151 In married life three is company and two is none.

Oscar Wilde *The Importance of Being Earnest*, I

152 The best part of married life is the fights. The rest is merely so-so.

Thornton Wilder (1897–1975) US novelist and dramatist. *The Matchmaker*, II

153 I married the Duke for better or worse but not for lunch.

Duchess of Windsor (Wallis Warfield Simpson; 1896–1986) The wife of the Duke of Windsor (formerly Edward VIII). *The Windsor Story* (J. Bryan III and J. V. Murphy)

154 Of course, I do have a slight advantage over the rest of you. It helps in a pinch to be able to remind

your bride that you gave up a throne for her.

Duke of Windsor (1894–1972) King of the United Kingdom; abdicated 1936. Discussing the maintenance of happy marital relations. Attrib.

155 Marriage isn't a process of prolonging the life of love, but of mummifying the corpse.

P. G. Wodehouse (1881–1975) British humorous novelist. *Bring on the Girls* (with Guy Bolton)

156 Judges, as a class, display, in the matter of arranging alimony, that reckless generosity that is found only in men who are giving away somebody else's cash.

P. G. Wodehouse *Louder and Funnier*

157 I can honestly say that I always look on Pauline as one of the nicest girls I was ever engaged to.

P. G. Wodehouse *Thank You Jeeves*, Ch. 6

MARTYRDOM

See also execution

1 The king has been very good to me. He promoted me from a simple maid to be a marchioness. Then he raised me to be a queen. Now he will raise me to be a martyr.

Anne Boleyn (1507–36) Second wife of Henry VIII. *Notable Women in History* (W. Abbot)

2 To die for a religion is easier than to live it absolutely.

Jorge Luis Borges (1899–1986) Argentinian writer. *Labyrinthes*

3 'Dying for an idea,' again, sounds well enough, but why not let the idea die instead of you?

Wyndham Lewis (1882–1957) British novelist. *The Art of Being Ruled*, Pt. I, Ch. 1

4 I look on martyrs as mistakes
But still they burned for it at stakes.

John Masefield (1878–1967) British poet. *The Everlasting Mercy*

5 I will burn, but this is a mere incident. We shall continue our discussion in eternity.

Michael Servetus (1511–53) Spanish physician and theologian. Comment to the judges of the Inquisition after being condemned to be burned at the stake as a heretic. *Borges: A Reader* (E. Monegal)

6 It is a heretic that makes the fire,
Not she which burns in 't.

William Shakespeare (1564–1616) English dramatist. *The Winter's Tale*, II:3

MARXISM

See also Communism, socialism

1 The Marxist analysis has got nothing to do with what happened in Stalin's Russia; it's like blaming Jesus Christ for the Inquisition in Spain.

Tony Benn (1925–) British politician. *The Observer*, 27 Apr 1980

2 I was a man who was lucky enough to have discovered a political theory, a man who was caught up in the whirlpool of Cuba's political crisis long before becoming a fully fledged Communist . . . discovering Marxism . . . was like finding a map in the forest.

Fidel Castro (1926–) Cuban statesman. Speech, Chile, 18 Nov 1971

3 Karl Marx wasn't a Marxist all the time. He got drunk in the Tottenham Court Road.

Michael Foot (1913–) British Labour politician and journalist. *Behind The Image* (Susan Barnes)

4 Much of the world's work, it has been said, is done by men who do not feel quite well. Marx is a case in point.

John Kenneth Galbraith (1908–) US economist. *The Age of Uncertainty*, Ch. 3

5 He is the apostle of class-hatred, the founder of a Satanic anti-religion, which resembles some religions in its cruelty, fanaticism and irrationality.

Dean Inge (1860–1954) British churchman. Referring to Karl Marx. *Assessments and Anticipations*

6 Marxian Socialism must always remain a portent to the historians of Opinion – how a doctrine so illogical and so dull can have exercised so powerful and enduring an influence over the minds of men, and, through them, the events of history.

John Maynard Keynes (1883–1946) British economist. *The End of Laisser-Faire*, III

7 A Social-Democrat must never forget that the proletariat will inevitably have to wage a class struggle for Socialism even against the most democratic and republican bourgeoisie and petty bourgeoisie.

Lenin (Vladimir Ilich Ulyanov; 1870–1924) Russian revolutionary leader. *The State and Revolution*, Ch. 10

8 Marxism is like a classical building that followed the Renaissance; beautiful in its way, but incapable of growth.

Harold Macmillan (1894–1986) British politician and prime minister. Speech to the Primrose League, 29 Apr 1981

9 From each according to his abilities, to each according to his needs.

Karl Marx (1818–83) German philosopher and revolutionary. *Criticism of the Gotha Programme*

10 Capitalist production begets, with the inexorability of a law of nature, its own negation.

Karl Marx *Das Kapital*, Ch. 15

11 The history of all hitherto existing society is the history of class struggles.

Karl Marx *The Communist Manifesto*, 1

12 The workers have nothing to lose but their chains. They have a world to gain. Workers of the world, unite.

Karl Marx *The Communist Manifesto*, 4

13 The dictatorship of the proletariat.

Karl Marx Attrib.

14 All I know is that I am not a Marxist.

Karl Marx Attrib.

15 Property is theft.

Pierre Joseph Proudhon (1809–65) French socialist. *See also* SHAW *Qu'est-ce que la Propriété?*, Ch. 1

16 And what a prize we have to fight for: no less than the chance to banish from our land the dark divisive clouds of Marxist socialism.

Margaret Thatcher (1925–) British politician and prime minister. Speech, Scottish Conservative Conference, 1983

17 The ship follows Soviet custom: it is riddled with class distinctions so subtle, it takes a trained Marxist to appreciate them.

Paul Theroux (1941–) US-born writer. *The Great Railway Bazaar*, Ch. 30

MASCULINITY

See also men

1 It makes me feel masculine to tell you that I do not answer questions like this without being paid for answering them.

Lillian Hellman (1905–84) US dramatist. When asked by *Harper's* magazine when she felt most masculine; this question had already been asked of several famous men. *Reader's Digest*, July 1977

2 You may have my husband, but not

my horse. My husband won't need emasculating, and my horse I won't have you meddle with. I'll preserve one last male thing in the museum of this world, if I can.
D. H. Lawrence (1885–1930) British novelist. *St Mawr*

MATERIALISM

See also greed, money, wealth

1 Benefits make a man a slave.
Proverb

2 Thinking to get at once all the gold that the goose could give, he killed it, and opened it only to find – nothing.
Aesop (6th century BC) Reputed Greek writer of fables. *Fables*, 'The Goose with the Golden Eggs'

3 You don't want no pie in the sky when you die,
You want something here on the ground while you're still around.
Muhammad Ali (Cassius Clay; 1942–) US heavyweight boxer. Attrib.

4 Jesus said unto him, If thou wilt be perfect, go and sell that thou hast, and give to the poor, and thou shalt have treasure in heaven: and come and follow me.
But when the young man heard that saying, he went away sorrowful: for he had great possessions.
Bible: Matthew 19:21–22

5 They say unto him, Caesar's. Then saith he unto them, Render therefore unto Caesar the things which are Caesar's; and unto God the things that are God's.
Bible: Matthew 22:21

6 The gentleman's name that met him was Mr Worldly Wiseman.
John Bunyan (1628–88) English writer. *The Pilgrim's Progress*, Pt. I

7 Maidens, like moths, are ever caught by glare,
And Mammon wins his way where Seraphs might despair.
Lord Byron (1788–1824) British poet. *Childe Harold's Pilgrimage*, I

8 For gold in phisik is a cordial,
Therfore he lovede gold in special.
Geoffrey Chaucer (c. 1342–1400) English poet. Referring to the doctor. *The Canterbury Tales*, Prologue

9 To be clever enough to get all that money, one must be stupid enough to want it.
G. K. Chesterton (1874–1936) British writer. *The Innocence of Father Brown*

10 I never hated a man enough to give him diamonds back.
Zsa Zsa Gabor (1919–) Hungarian-born US film star. *The Observer*, 'Sayings of the Week', 28 Aug 1957

11 Increase of material comforts, it may be generally laid down, does not in any way whatsoever conduce to moral growth.
Mahatma Gandhi (Mohandas Karamchand Gandhi; 1869–1948) Indian national leader. Obituary, *News Chronicle*

12 What female heart can gold despise?
What cat's averse to fish?
Thomas Gray (1716–71) British poet. *Ode on the Death of a Favourite Cat*

13 Man must choose whether to be rich in things or in the freedom to use them.
Ivan Illich (1926–) Austrian sociologist. *Deschooling Society*, Ch. 4

14 In a consumer society there are inevitably two kinds of slaves: the prisoners of addiction and the prisoners of envy.
Ivan Illich *Tools for Conviviality*

15 The almighty dollar, that great object of universal devotion throughout our land, seems to have no genuine devotees in these peculiar villages.
Washington Irving (1783–1859) US writer. *Wolfert's Roost*, 'The Creole Village'

16 Good morning to the day: and, next, my gold! –
Open the shrine, that I may see my saint.
Ben Jonson (1573–1637) English dramatist. *Volpone*, I:1

17 The spread of personal ownership is in harmony with the deepest instincts of the British people. Few changes have done more to create one nation.
Nigel Lawson (1932–) British politician. Speech, Jan 1988

18 Kissing your hand may make you feel very very good but a diamond and safire bracelet lasts forever.
Anita Loos (1891–1981) US novelist. *Gentlemen Prefer Blondes*, Ch. 4

19 When an American heiress wants to buy a man, she at once crosses the Atlantic. The only really materialistic people I have ever met have been Europeans.
Mary McCarthy (1912–) US novelist. *On the Contrary* 1962

20 Years ago a person, he was unhappy, didn't know what to do with himself – he'd go to church, start a revolution – *something*. Today you're unhappy? Can't figure it out? What is the salvation? Go shopping.
Arthur Miller (1915–) US dramatist. *The Price*, I

21 Why is it no one ever sent me yet
One perfect limousine, do you suppose?
Ah no, it's always just my luck to get
One perfect rose.
Dorothy Parker (1893–1967) US writer. *One Perfect Rose*

22 Diamonds Are A Girl's Best Friend.
Leo Robin (1899–) US songwriter. *Gentlemen Prefer Blondes*, song title

23 Bell, book, and candle, shall not drive me back,
When gold and silver becks me to come on.
William Shakespeare (1564–1616) English dramatist. *King John*, III:3

24 The want of a thing is perplexing enough, but the possession of it is intolerable.
John Vanbrugh (1664–1726) English architect and dramatist. *The Confederacy*, I:2

25 Conspicuous consumption of valuable goods is a means of reputability to the gentleman of leisure.
Thorstein Bunde Veblen (1857–1929) US social scientist. *The Theory of the Leisure Class*

26 What do you not drive human hearts into, cursed craving for gold!
Virgil (Publius Vergilius Maro; 70–19 BC) Roman poet. *Aeneid*, Bk. III

27 There's something about a crowd like that that brings a lump to my wallet.
Eli Wallach (1915–) US actor. Remarking upon the long line of people at the box office before one of his performances. Attrib.

28 A gold rush is what happens when a line of chorus girls spot a man with a bank roll.
Mae West (1892–1980) US actress. *Klondike Annie*, film 1936

MATHEMATICS

See also numbers

1 All science requires mathematics
Roger Bacon (c. 1214–c. 1292) English monk, scholar, and scientist. *Opus Maius*, Pt. IV

2 What is algebra exactly; is it those three-cornered things?
J. M. Barrie (1860–1937) British novelist and dramatist. *Quality Street*, II

3 I never could make out what those damned dots meant.
Lord Randolph Churchill (1849–95) British Conservative politician. Referring to decimal points. *Lord Randolph Churchill* (W. S. Churchill)

4 As far as the laws of mathematics refer to reality, they are not certain, and as far as they are certain, they do not refer to reality.
Albert Einstein (1879–1955) German-born US physicist. *The Tao of Physics* (F. Capra), Ch. 2

5 When we reach the sphere of mathematics we are among processes which seem to some the most inhuman of all human activities and the most remote from poetry. Yet it is here that the artist has fullest scope for his imagination.
Havelock Ellis (1859–1939) British sexologist. *The Dance of Life*, 1923

6 The mathematician has reached the highest rung on the ladder of human thought.
Havelock Ellis *The Dance of Life*, 1923

7 There is no 'royal road' to geometry.
Euclid (c. 300 BC) Greek mathematician. Said to Ptolemy I when asked if there were an easier way to solve theorems. *Comment on Euclid* (Proclus)

8 *Quod erat demonstrandum.*
Which was to be proved.
Euclid Hence, of course, Q.E.D. *Elements*, I:5

9 About binomial theorems I'm
teeming with a lot of news,
With many cheerful facts about the
square on the hypoteneuse.
W. S. Gilbert (1836–1911) British dramatist. *The Pirates of Penzance*, I

10 One has to be able to count, if only so that at fifty one doesn't marry a girl of twenty.
Maxim Gorky (Aleksei Maksimovich Peshkov; 1868–1936) Russian writer. *The Zykovs*

11 Once I had learnt my twelve times table (at the age of three) it was downhill all the way.
Fred Hoyle (1915–) British astronomer.

12 MORIARTY. How are you at Mathematics?
HARRY SECOMBE. I speak it like a native.
Spike Milligan (1918–) British comic actor and author. *The Goon Show*

13 The only way I can distinguish
proper from improper fractions
Is by their actions.
Ogden Nash (1902–71) US poet. *Ask Daddy, He Won't Know*

14 One geometry cannot be more true than another; it can only be more convenient. Geometry is not true, it is advantageous.
Robert T. Pirsig (1928–) US writer. *Zen and the Art of Motorcycle Maintenance*, Pt. III, Ch. 22

15 Let no one ignorant of mathematics enter here.
Plato (429–347 BC) Greek philosopher. Inscription written over the entrance to the Academy. *Biographical Encyclopedia* (I. Asimov)

16 The true spirit of delight, the exaltation, the sense of being more than Man, which is the touchstone of the highest excellence is to be found in mathematics as surely as in poetry.
Bertrand Russell (1872–1970) British philosopher. *Mysticism and Logic*

17 Mathematics, rightly viewed, possesses not only truth by supreme beauty – a beauty cold and austere like that of sculpture.
Bertrand Russell *Mysticism and Logic*

18 Mathematics may be defined as the subject in which we never know what we are talking about, nor whether what we are saying is true.
Bertrand Russell *Mysticism and Logic*

19 Pure mathematics consists entirely of assertions to the effect that, if such and such a proposition is true of *anything*, then such and such another proposition is true of that thing. It is essential not to discuss whether the first proposition is really true, and not to mention what the anything is, of which it is supposed to be true.
Bertrand Russell *Mysticism and Logic*

20 Mathematics possesses not only truth, but supreme beauty –a beauty cold and austere, like that of sculpture.
Bertrand Russell *The Study of Mathematics*

21 I like mathematics because it is *not* human and has nothing particular to do with this planet or with the whole accidental universe – because, like Spinoza's God, it won't love us in return.
Bertrand Russell Letter to Lady Ottoline Morrell, Mar 1912

22 It is with medicine as with mathematics: we should occupy our minds only with what we continue to know; what we once knew is of little consequence.
Charles Augustin Sainte-Beuve (1804–69) French critic.

23 I knew a mathematician who said 'I do not know as much as God. But I know as much as God knew at my age'.
Milton Shulman (1925–) Canadian writer, journalist, and critic. *Stop The Week*, BBC Radio 4

24 Numbers constitute the only universal language.
Nathaniel West (1903–40) US novelist and scriptwriter. *Miss Lonelyhearts*

25 Mathematics is thought moving in the sphere of complete abstraction from any particular instance of what it is talking about.
A. N. Whitehead (1861–1947) British philosopher. *Science and the Modern World*

MATRIMONY

See marriage

MATURITY

1 At sixteen I was stupid, confused, insecure and indecisive. At twenty-five I was wise, self-confident, prepossessing and assertive. At forty-five I am stupid, confused, insecure and indecisive. Who would have supposed that maturity is only a short break in adolescence?
Jules Feiffer (1929–) US writer, cartoonist, and humorist. *The Observer*, 3 Feb 1974

2 At twenty years of age, the will reigns; at thirty, the wit; and at forty, the judgement.
Benjamin Franklin (1706–90) US scientist and statesman. *Poor Richard's Almanack*

MEANING

See also purpose, words

1 'Then you should say what you mean,' the March Hare went on. 'I do,' Alice hastily replied; 'at least – at least I mean what I say – that's the same thing, you know.'
'Not the same thing a bit!' said the Hatter. 'Why, you might just as well

say that 'I see what I eat' is the same thing as 'I eat what I see!"
Lewis Carroll (Charles Lutwidge Dodgson; 1832–98) British writer. *Alice's Adventures in Wonderland*, Ch. 7

2 Take care of the sense, and the sounds will take care of themselves.
Lewis Carroll *Alice's Adventures in Wonderland*, Ch. 9

3 'When *I* use a word,' Humpty Dumpty said in rather a scornful tone, 'it means just what I choose it to mean – neither more nor less.'
Lewis Carroll *Through the Looking-Glass*, Ch. 6

4 Where in this small-talking world can I find
A longitude with no platitude?
Christopher Fry (1907–) British dramatist. *The Lady's Not for Burning*, III

5 The least of things with a meaning is worth more in life than the greatest of things without it.
Carl Gustav Jung (1875–1961) Swiss psychoanalyst. *Modern Man in Search of a Soul*

MEDIA

1 A spirit of national masochism prevails, encouraged by an effete corps of impudent snobs who characterize themselves as intellectuals.
Spiro T. Agnew (1918–) US Republican politician. Speech, New Orleans, 19 Oct 1969

2 In the United States today we have more than our share of the nattering nabobs of negativism. They have formed their own 4-H Club – the 'hopeless, hysterical hypochondriacs of history.'
Spiro T. Agnew Speech, San Diego, 11 Sept 1970

3 An everyday story of country folk.
Anonymous Introductory announcement. *The Archers*, BBC radio series

4 Broadcasting is really too important to be left to the broadcasters and somehow we must find some new way of using radio and television to allow us to talk to each other.
Anthony Wedgwood Benn (1925–) British Labour politician. Speech, c. 1970

5 The wriggling ponces of the spoken word.
D. G. Bridson (?–1980) British radio producer. Referring to disc jockeys. Attrib.

6 Media is a word that has come to mean bad journalism.
Graham Greene (1904–) British novelist. *Ways of Escape*

7 If, sir, I possessed the power of conveying unlimited sexual attraction through the potency of my voice, I would not be reduced to accepting a miserable pittance from the BBC for interviewing a faded female in a damp basement.
Gilbert Harding (1907–60) British broadcaster. Said to Mae West's manager, who suggested that he should be more 'sexy' when interviewing her. *Gilbert Harding by His Friends*

8 The gift of broadcasting is, without question, the lowest human capacity to which any man could attain.
Sir Harold Nicolson (1886–1968) British writer and politician. *The Observer*, 5 Jan 1947

MEDICINE

See also doctors, health, illness, nurses, remedies

1 Nature, time and patience are the three great physicians.
Bulgarian proverb

2 Medicine can only cure curable diseases, and then not always.
Chinese proverb

3 Dermatology is the best speciality. The patient never dies – and never gets well.
Anonymous

4 If every man would mend a man, then all the world would be mended.
Anonymous

5 If I were summing up the qualities of a good teacher of medicine, I would enumerate human sympathy, moral and intellectual integrity, enthusiasm, and ability to talk, in addition, of course, to knowledge of his subject.
Anonymous

6 The deficiencies which I think good to note . . . I will enumerate . . . . The first is the discontinuance of the ancient and serious diligence of Hippocrates, which used to set down a narrative of the special cases of his patients, and how they proceeded, and how they were judged by recovery or death.
Francis Bacon (1561–1626) English philosopher, lawyer, and politician. *The Advancement of Learning*, Bk. II

7 The poets did well to conjoin Music and Medicine in Apollo: because the office of medicine is but to tune this curious harp of man's body and to reduce it to harmony.
Francis Bacon *The Advancement of Learning*, Bk. II

8 Medicine is a science which hath been, as we have said, more professed than laboured, and yet more laboured than advanced; the labour having been, in my judgment, rather in a circle than in progression.
Francis Bacon *Advancement of Learning*, Bk. II

9 The prime goal is to alleviate suffering, and not to prolong life. And if your treatment does not alleviate suffering, but only prolongs life, that treatment should be stopped.
Christian Barnard (1922–) South African surgeon.

10 With certain limited exceptions, the laws of physical science are positive and absolute, both in their aggregate, and in their elements – in their sum, and in their details; but the ascertainable laws of the science of life are approximative only, and not absolute.
Elisha Bartlett (1804–55) *Philosophy of Medical Science*, Pt. II, Ch. 2

11 Of all the lessons which a young man entering upon the profession of medicine needs to learn, this is perhaps the first – that he should resist the fascination of doctrines and hypotheses till he has won the privilege of such studies by honest labor and faithful pursuit of real and useful knowledge.
William Beaumont (1785–1853) US physician. *Notebook*

12 Medicine is like a woman who changes with the fashions.
August Bier (1861–1949) Aphorism

13 GRAVE, n. A place in which the dead are laid to await the coming of the medical student.
Ambrose Bierce (1842–c. 1914) US writer and journalist. *The Devil's Dictionary*

14 HOMEOPATHY, n. A school of medicine midway between Allopathy and Christian Science. To the last both the others are distinctly inferior, for Christian Science will cure imaginary diseases, and they can not.
Ambrose Bierce *The Devil's Dictionary*

15 Every hospital should have a plaque

in the physicians' and students' entrances: 'There are some patients whom we cannot help, there are none whom we cannot harm.'
Arthur L. Bloomfield (1888–1962) Personal communication after iatrogenic tragedy, c. 1930–36

16 Medicine . . . the only profession that labours incessantly to destroy the reason for its own existence.
Sir James Bryce (1838–1922) British liberal politician, historian, and ambassador to the USA. Address, 23 Mar 1914

17 Among the arts, medicine, on account of its eminent utility, must always hold the highest place.
Henry Thomas Buckle (1821–62) *Miscellaneous and Posthumous Works*, Vol. II

18 Vaccination is the medical sacrament corresponding to baptism.
Samuel Butler (1835–1902) British writer.

19 Medical men all over the world having merely entered into a tacit agreement to call all sorts of maladies people are liable to, in cold weather, by one name; so that one sort of treatment may serve for all, and their practice thereby be greatly simplified.
Jane Welsh Carlyle (1801–66) The wife of Thomas Carlyle. Letter to John Welsh, 4 Mar 1837

20 Quackery gives birth to nothing; gives death to all things.
Thomas Carlyle (1795–1881) Scottish essayist and historian. *Heroes and Hero-Worship*

21 The Art of Medicine is in need really of reasoning, . . . for this is a conjectural art. However, in many cases not only does conjecture fail, but experience as well.
Celsus (25 BC–50 AD) Roman encyclopedist. *De re medicina*

22 It is obvious that we cannot instruct women as we do men in the science of medicine; we cannot carry them into the dissecting room.
Walter Channing Remarks on the Employment of Females as Practitioners in Midwifery, by a Physician

23 The whole imposing edifice of modern medicine is like the celebrated tower of Pisa – slightly off balance.
Charles, Prince of Wales (1948–) Eldest son of Elizabeth II.

24 Nature heals, under the auspices of the medical profession.
Haven Emerson (1874–1957) Lecture

25 To a physician, each man, each woman, is an amplification of one organ.
Ralph Waldo Emerson (1803–82) US poet and essayist. *Bartlett's Unfamiliar Quotations* (Leonard Louis Levinson)

26 Homeopathy is insignificant as an act of healing, but of great value as criticism on the hygeia or medical practice of the time.
Ralph Waldo Emerson *Essays* (Second Series), 'Nominalist and Realist'

27 In the hands of the discoverer, medicine becomes a heroic art . . . wherever life is dear he is a demigod.
Ralph Waldo Emerson *Uncollected Lectures*, 'Resources'

28 Anatomy is to physiology as geography to history; it describes the theatre of events.
Jean Fernel (1497–1558) *On the Natural Part of Medicine*, Ch. 1

29 Patience is the best medicine.
John Florio (1553–1625) English lexicographer and translator. *First Frutes*

30 Study sickness while you are well.
Thomas Fuller (1654–1734) English physician and writer. *Gnomologia*

31 Medicine absorbs the physician's whole being because it is concerned with the entire human organism.
Johann Wolfgang von Goethe (1749–1832) German poet, dramatist and scientist.

32 A well chosen anthology is a complete dispensary of medicine for the more common mental disorders, and may be used as much for prevention as cure.
Robert Graves (1895–1985) British poet and novelist. *On English Poetry*, Ch. 29

33 Comedy is medicine.
Trevor Griffiths (1935–) *Comedians*, I

34 The foundation of the study of Medicine, as of all scientific inquiry, lies in the belief that every natural phenomenon, trifling as it may seem, has a fixed and invariable meaning.
Sir William Withey Gull (1816–90) *Published Writings*, 'Study of Medicine'

35 Medicine is as old as the human race, as old as the necessity for the removal of disease.
Heinrich Haeser (1811–84) *Lehrbuch der Geschichte der Medizin*, Erste Periode

36 Solving the mysteries of heaven has not given birth to as many abortive findings as has the quest into the mysteries of the human body. When you think of yourselves as scientists, I want you always to remember everything you learn from me will probably be regarded tomorrow as the naive confusions of a pack of medical aborigines. Despite all our toil and progress, the art of medicine still falls somewhere between trout casting and spook writing.
Ben Hecht (1894–1964) *Miracle of the Fifteen Murderers*

37 I swear by Apollo the physician, by Asclepius, by Health, by Panacea and by all the gods and goddesses, making them my witnesses, that I will carry out, according to my ability and judgment, this oath and this indenture. To hold my teacher in this art equal to my own parents; to make him partner in my livelihood; when he is in need of money to share mine with him; to consider his family as my own brothers and to teach them this art, if they want to learn it, without fee or indenture; to impart precept, oral instruction, and all other instruction to my own sons, the sons of my teacher, and to indentured pupils who have taken the physician's oath, but to nobody else. I will use treatment to help the sick according to my ability and judgment, but never with a view to injury and wrong-doing. Neither will I administer a poison to anybody when asked to do so, nor will I suggest such a course. Similarly, I will not give a woman a pessary to cause abortion. But I will keep pure and holy both in my life and my art. I will not use the knife, not even, verily, on sufferers from stone but I will give place to such as are craftsmen therein. Into whatsoever houses I enter, I will enter to help the sick, and I will abstain from all intentional wrong-doing and harm, especially from abusing the bodies of man or woman, bond or free. And whatsoever I shall see or hear in the course of my profession, as well as outside my profession in my intercourse with men, if it be what should not be published abroad, I will never divulge holding such things to be holy secret. Now if I carry out this oath, and break it not, may I gain for ever reputation

among all men for my life and for my art; but if I transgress it and forswear myself, may the opposite befall me.

Hippocrates (c. 460 BC–c. 357 BC) Greek physician. *The Hippocratic Oath*

38 Life is short, the Art long, opportunity fleeting, experience treacherous, judgment difficult. The physician must be ready, not only to do his duty himself, but also to secure the co-operation of the patient, of the attendants and of externals.

Hippocrates *Aphorisms*, I, 1

39 The art has three factors, the disease, the patient, and physician. The physician is the servant of the art. The patient must co-operate with the physician in combating the disease.

Hippocrates *Epidemics*, I

40 A miracle drug is any drug that will do what the label says it will do.

Eric Hodgins (1899–1971) US writer and editor. *Episode*

41 Homeopathy . . . a mingled mass of perverse ingenuity, of tinsel erudition, of imbecile credulity, and of artful misrepresentation, too often mingled in practice . . . with heartless and shameless imposition.

Oliver Wendell Holmes (1809–94) US writer and physician. *Medical Essays*, 'Homeopathy and Its Kindred Delusions'

42 It is so hard to get anything out of the dead hand of medical tradition!

Oliver Wendell Holmes *Medical Essays*, 'Currents and Counter-Currents in Medical Science'

43 The truth is, that medicine, professedly founded on observation, is as sensitive to outside influences, political, religious, philosophical, imaginative, as is the barometer to the changes of atmospheric density.

Oliver Wendell Holmes *Medical Essays*, 'Currents and Counter-Currents in Medical Science'

44 *Nature*, in medical language, as opposed to Art, means trust in the reactions of the living system against ordinary normal impressions. *Art*, in the same language, as opposed to Nature, means an intentional resort to extraordinary abnormal impressions for the relief of disease.

Oliver Wendell Holmes *Medical Essays*, 'Currents and Counter-Currents in Medical Science'

45 The lancet was the magician's wand of the dark ages of medicine.

Oliver Wendell Holmes *Medical Essays*, 'Some of My Early Teachers'

46 It is unnecessary – perhaps dangerous – in medicine to be too clever.

Sir Robert Hutchison (1871–1960) *Lancet*, 2:61, 1938

47 The only sure foundations of medicine are, an intimate knowledge of the human body, and observation on the effects of medicinal substances on that.

Thomas Jefferson (1743–1826) US statesman. Letter to Dr. Caspar Wistar, 21 June 1807

48 Fasting is a medicine.

St John Chrysostom (c. 345–407) Bishop of Constantinopole and Doctor of the Church. *Homilies on the Statutes*, III

49 No costs have increased more rapidly in the last decade than the cost of medical care. And no group of Americans has felt the impact of these sky-rocketing costs more than our older citizens.

John F. Kennedy (1917–63) US statesman. Address on the 25th Anniversary of the Social Se curity Act, 14 Aug 1960

50 One of the most difficult things to contend with in a hospital is the assumption on the part of the staff that because you have lost your gall bladder you have also lost your mind.

Jean Kerr (1923–) US dramatist. *Please Don't Eat the Daisies*

51 The ultimate indignity is to be given a bedpan by a stranger who calls you by your first name.

Maggie Kuhn (1905–) US writer and social activist. *The Observer*, 20 Aug 1978

52 Medicine is a strange mixture of speculation and action. We have to cultivate a science and to exercise an art. The calls of science are upon our leisure and our choice; the calls of practice are of daily emergence and necessity.

Peter Mere Latham (1789–1875) US poet and essayist. *Diseases of the Heart*

53 The practice of physic is jostled by quacks on the one side, and by science on the other.

Peter Mere Latham *Collected Works*, Vol. I, 'In Memoriam' (Sir Thomas Watson)

54 In the old-fashioned days when a man got sick he went to the family doctor and said he was sick. The doctor gave him a bottle of medicine. He took it home and drank it and got well.
On the bottle was written, 'Three times a day in water.' The man drank it three times a day the first day, twice the second day, and once the third day. On the fourth day he forgot it. But that didn't matter. He was well by that time . . . .
Such medicine was, of course, hopelessly unscientific, hopelessly limited. Death could beat it round every corner. But it was human, gracious, kindly.

Stephen Leacock (1869–1944) English-born Canadian economist and humorist. *The Leacock Roundabout*, 'The Doctor and the Contraption'

55 When you buy a pill and buy peace with it you get conditioned to cheap solutions instead of deep ones.

Max Lerner (1902–) US author and journalist. *The Unfinished Country*

56 Medicine is not a lucrative profession. It is a divine one.

John Coakley Lettsom (1744–1815) Letter to a friend, 6 Sept 1791

57 Medicine makes people ill, mathematics makes them sad and theology makes them sinful.

Martin Luther (1483–1546) German Protestant reformer.

58 Medical practice is not knitting and weaving and the labor of the hands, but it must be inspired with soul and be filled with understanding and equipped with the gift of keen observation; these together with accurate scientific knowledge are the indispensable requisites for proficient medical practice.

Maimonides (Moses ben Maimon; 1135–1204) Spanish-born Jewish philosopher and physician. *Bulletin of the Institute of the History of Medicine*, 3:555, 1935

59 Medicine is a conjectural art.

Jean Nicolas Corvisart des Marets (1755–1821)

60 Medicine heals doubts as well as diseases.

Karl Marx (1796–1877) German philosopher, economist, and revolutionary. *Bulletin of the New York Academy of Medicine* (F. H. Garrison)

61 The prevention of disease today is one of the most important factors in the line of human endeavor.

Charles H. Mayo (1865–1939) US surgeon. *Collected Papers of the Mayo Clinic and Mayo Foundation*, 5:17, 1913

62 The aim of medicine is to prevent disease and prolong life, the ideal of medicine is to eliminate the need of a physician.

William J. Mayo (1861–1939) US physician. *National Education Association: Proceedings and Addresses*, 66:163, 1928

63 Medicine may be defined as the art or the science of keeping a patient quiet with frivolous reasons for his illness and amusing him with remedies good or bad until nature kills him or cures him.

Gilles Ménage (1613–92) *Ménagiana*, Pt. III

64 The aim of medicine is surely not to make men virtuous; it is to safeguard and rescue them from the consequences of their vices.

H. L. Mencken (1880–1956) US journalist and editor. *Prejudices*, 'Types of Men: the Physician'

65 Medicine is for the patient. Medicine is the people. It is not for the profits.

George Merck (1894–1957)

66 I wasn't driven into medicine by a social conscience but by rampant curiosity.

Jonathan Miller (1936–) British writer and doctor.

67 GERONTE. It was very clearly explained, but there was just one thing which surprised me – that was the positions of the liver and the heart. It seemed to me that you got them the wrong way about, that the heart should be on the left side, and the liver on the right.

SGANARELLE. Yes, it used to be so but we have changed all that. Everything's quite different in medicine nowadays.

Molière (Jean-Baptiste Poquelin; 1622–73) French dramatist. *Le Médecin malgré lui*, II:4

68 The art of medicine is my discovery. I am called Help-Bringer throughout the world, and all the potency of herbs is known to me.

Ovid (Publius Ovidius Naso; 43 BC–17 AD) Roman poet. Spoken by Apollo. *Metamorphoses*

69 The art of medicine is generally a question of time.

Ovid *Remedia Amoris*

70 Medicine sometimes snatches away health, sometimes gives it.

Ovid *Tristia*

71 A hospital should also have a recovery room adjoining the cashier's office.

Francis O'Walsh *Bartlett's Unfamiliar Quotations* (Leonard Louis Levinson)

72 Medicine is not only a science; it is also an art. It does not consist of compounding pills and plasters; it deals with the very processes of life, which must be understood before they may be guided.

Paracelsus (c. 1493–1541) Swiss physician and alchemist. *Die grosse Wundarznei*

73 The art of healing comes from nature not from the physician. Therefore the physician must start from nature, with an open mind.

Paracelsus *Seven Defenses*, Ch. 4

74 Experiment alone crowns the efforts of medicine, experiment limited only by the natural range of the powers of the human mind. Observation discloses in the animal organism numerous phenomena existing side by side, and interconnected now profoundly, now indirectly, or accidentally. Confronted with a multitude of different assumptions the mind must *guess* the real nature of this connection.

Ivan Pavlov (1849–1936) Russian physiologist. *Experimental Psychology and Other Essays*, Pt. X

75 This basis of medicine is sympathy and the desire to help others, and whatever is done with this end must be called medicine.

Frank Payne (1840–1910) *English Medicine in the Anglo-Saxon Times*

76 Medicine is not yet liberated from the medieval idea that disease is the result of sin and must be expiated by mortification of the flesh.

Sir George W. Pickering (1904–) *Resident Physician*, II (No. 9): 71, 1965

77 Medicine is an art, and attends to the nature and constitution of the patient, and has principles of action and reason in each case.

Plato (427 BC–347 BC) Greek philosopher. *Gorgias*

78 And this is what the physician has to do, and in this the art of medicine consists: for medicine may be regarded generally as the knowledge of the loves and desires of the body, and how to satisfy them or not; and the best physician is he who is able to separate fair love from foul, or to convert one into the other; and he who knows how to eradicate and how to implant love, whichever is required, and can reconcile the most hostile elements in the constitution and make them loving friends, is a skilful practitioner.

Plato *Symposium*

79 The first staggering fact about medical education is that after two and a half years of being taught on the assumption that everyone is the same, the student has to find out for himself that everyone is different, which is really what his experience has taught him since infancy. And the second staggering fact about medical education is that after being taught for two and half years not to trust any evidence except that based on the measurements of physical science, the student has to find out for himself that all important decisions are in reality made, almost at unconscious level, by that most perfect and complex of computers the human brain, about which he has as yet learnt almost nothing, and will probably go on learning nothing to the end of his course – this computer which can take in and analyse an incredible number of data in an extremely short time. And the data are mostly not of the hard crude type with which that simple fellow the scientist has to deal, but are of a much more subtle, human, and interesting character, each tinted in its own colours of personality and emotion. All this the student has to discover for himself which his teachers strangely pretend to believe that the secrets of medicine are revealed only to those whose biochemical background is beyond reproach.

Sir Robert Platt (1900–) *British Medical Journal*, 2:551, 1965

80 Medicine, to produce health, has to examine disease.

Plutarch (c. 46–c. 120) Greek biographer and essayist. *Lives*, 'Demetrius', I

81 Medicine for the dead is too late.

Quintilian (Marcus Fabius Quintilianus; c. 35 AD–c. 96 AD) Roman rhetorician and teacher.

82 Truth in medicine is an unattainable goal, and the art as described in books is far beneath the knowledge of an experienced and thoughtful physician.

Rhazes (Ar-Razi; c. 865–c. 928) Persian physician and philosopher. *History of Medicine* (Max Neuburger)

83 In treating a patient, let your first

thought be to strengthen his natural vitality.
Rhazes

84 The first cry of pain through the primitive jungle was the first call for a physician . . . Medicine is a natural art, conceived in sympathy and born of necessity; from instinctive procedures developed the specialized science that is practised today.
Victor Robinson (1886–1947) *The Story of Medicine*

85 Medicine is a noble profession but a damn bad business.
Humphrey Rolleston (1862–1944) British physician. Attrib.

86 Medicine is an occupation for slaves.
Benjamin Rush (c. 1745–1813) *Autobiography*

87 It is with medicine as with mathematics: we should occupy our minds only with what we continue to know; what we once knew is of little consequence.
Charles Augustin Sainte-Beuve (1804–69) French critic.

88 After twenty years one is no longer quoted in the medical literature. Every twenty years one sees a republication of the same ideas.
Béla Schick (1877–1967) Austrian pediatrician. *Aphorisms and Facetiae of Béla Schick*, 'Early Years' (I.J. Wolf)

89 Not even medicine can master incurable diseases.
Seneca (c. 4 BC–65 AD) Roman writer and statesman. *Epistulae ad Lucilium*, XCIV

90 By medicine life may be prolonged, yet death
Will seize the doctor too.
William Shakespeare (1564–1616) English dramatist and poet. *Cymbeline*, V:5

91 Optimistic lies have such immense therapeutic value that a doctor who cannot tell them convincingly has mistaken his profession.
George Bernard Shaw (1856–1950) Irish dramatist and critic. *Misalliance*, Preface

92 Medical science is as yet very imperfectly differentiated from common curemongering witchcraft.
George Bernard Shaw *The Doctor's Dilemma*, 'Preface on Doctors'

93 . . . the department of witchcraft called medical science.
George Bernard Shaw *The Philanderer*

94 The very popular hunting for 'Fathers' of every branch of medicine and every treatment is, therefore, rather foolish; it is unfair not only to the mothers and ancestors but also to the obstetricians and midwives.
Henry E. Sigerist (1891–1957) *A History of Medicine*, Vol. I, Introduction

95 *Prevention* of disease must become the goal of every physician.
Henry E. Sigerist *Medicine and Human Welfare*, Ch. 3

96 I've already had medical attention – a dog licked me when I was on the ground.
Neil Simon (1927–) US playwright. *Only When I Laugh* (screenplay)

97 Medicine can never abdicate the obligation to care for the patient and to teach patient care.
Maurice B. Strauss (1904–74) *Medicine*, 43:19, 1964

98 If they are not interested in the care of the patient, in the phenomena of disease in the sick, they should not be in the clinical department of medicine, since they cannot teach students clinical medicine.
Maurice B. Strauss *Medicine*, 43:619, 1964

99 The art of medicine was to be properly learned only from its practice and its exercise.
Thomas Sydenham (1624–89) *Medical Observations*, Dedicatory Epistle

100 Formerly, when religion was strong and science weak, men mistook magic for medicine, now, when science is strong and religion weak, men mistake medicine for magic.
Thomas Szasz (1920–) US psychiatrist. *The Second Sin*

101 The history of medicine is a story of amazing foolishness and amazing intelligence.
Jerome Tarshis

102 Human beings, yes, but not surgeons.
Rudolph Virchow (1821–1902) German pathologist. Answering a query as to whether human beings could survive appendectomy, which had recently become a widespread practice. *Anekdotenschatz* (H. Hoffmeister)

103 He preferred to know the power of herbs and their value for curing purposes, and, heedless of glory, to exercise that quiet art.
Virgil (Publius Vergilius Maro; 70 BC–19 BC) Roman poet. *Aeneid*

104 The art of medicine consists of amusing the patient while Nature cures the disease.
Voltaire (François Marie Arouet; 1694–1778) French writer and philosopher.

105 Medical education is not completed at the medical school: it is only begun.
William H. Welch (1850–1934) *Bulletin of the Harvard Medical School Association*, 3:55, 1892

MEDIOCRITY

See also inferiority

1 Only mediocrity can be trusted to be always at its best.
Max Beerbohm (1872–1956) British writer. *Conversations with Max* (S.N. Behrman)

2 The world is made of people who never quite get into the first team and who just miss the prizes at the flower show.
Jacob Bronowski (1908–74) British scientist and writer. *The Face of Violence*, Ch. 6

3 Mediocrity knows nothing higher than itself, but talent instantly recognizes genius.
Arthur Conan Doyle (1856–1930) British writer. *The Valley of Fear*

4 Only the mediocre are always at their best.
Jean Giraudoux (1882–1944) French dramatist. Attrib.

5 Some men are born mediocre, some men achieve mediocrity, and some men have mediocrity thrust upon them. With Major Major it had been all three.
Joseph Heller (1923–) US novelist. *Catch-22*, Ch. 9

6 Women want mediocre men, and men are working to be as mediocre as possible.
Margaret Mead (1901–78) US anthropologist. *Quote Magazine*, 15 May 1958

7 With first-rate sherry flowing into second-rate whores,
And third-rate conversation without one single pause:
Just like a couple
Between the wars.
William Plomer (1903–73) South African poet and novelist. *Father and Son: 1939*

8 It isn't evil that is ruining the earth, but mediocrity. The crime is not that Nero played while Rome burned, but that he played badly.
Ned Rorem (1923–) US composer and writer. *The Final Diary*

9 Much of a muchness.
John Vanbrugh (1664–1726) English architect and dramatist. *The Provok'd Husband,* I:1

MELANCHOLY

See also despair, sorrow

1 Nothing's so dainty sweet as lovely melancholy.
Francis Beaumont (1584–1616) English dramatist. *The Nice Valour,* III:3

2 All my joys to this are folly,
Naught so sweet as Melancholy.
Robert Burton (1577–1640) English scholar and explorer. *Anatomy of Melancholy,* Abstract

3 If there is a hell upon earth, it is to be found in a melancholy man's heart.
Robert Burton *Anatomy of Melancholy,* Pt. I

4 Twentieth-Century Blues.
Noël Coward (1899–1973) British dramatist. *Title of song*

5 I am aware of the damp souls of the housemaids
Sprouting despondently at area gates.
T. S. Eliot (1888–1965) US-born British poet and dramatist. *Morning at the Window*

6 I am in that temper that if I were under water I would scarcely kick to come to the top.
John Keats (1795–1821) British poet. Letter to Benjamin Bailey, 21 May 1818

7 Ay, in the very temple of delight
Veil'd Melancholy has her sovran shrine.
Though seen of none save him whose strenuous tongue
Can burst Joy's grape against his palate fine.
John Keats *Ode on Melancholy*

8 My heart aches, and a drowsy numbness pains
My sense.
John Keats *Ode to a Nightingale*

9 Heavy thoughts bring on physical maladies; when the soul is oppressed so is the body.
Martin Luther (1483–1546) German Protestant reformer. *Table-Talk,* Sect. DCXLV, 'Of Temptation and Tribulation'

10 Wrapt in a pleasing fit of melancholy.
John Milton (1608–74) English poet. *Comus*

11 Where glowing embers through the room
Teach light to counterfeit a gloom,
Far from all resort of mirth,
Save the cricket on the hearth.
John Milton *Il Penseroso*

12 I was told I am a true cosmopolitan. I am unhappy everywhere.
Stephen Vizinczey (1933–) Hungarian-born British writer. *The Guardian,* 7 Mar 1968

MELBOURNE, William Lamb, Viscount

(1779–1848) British statesman. Whig prime minister (1934; 1835–41). His marriage to Lady Caroline Ponsonby (1805) ended in divorce after her affair with Lord Byron.

Quotations about Melbourne

1 He is nothing more than a sensible, honest man who means to do his duty to the Sovereign and his country, instead of the ignorant man he pretends to be.
Sydney Smith (1771–1845) British clergyman and essayist. Attrib.

2 He is the person who makes us feel safe and comfortable.
Victoria (1819–1901) Queen of the United Kingdom. *Journal,* 4 July 1838

Quotations by Melbourne

3 Now, is it to lower the price of corn, or isn't it? It is not much matter which we say, but mind, we must all say *the same.*
Said at a cabinet meeting. *The English Constitution* (Bagehot), Ch. 1

4 What I want is men who will support me when I am in the wrong.
Replying to someone who said he would support Melbourne as long as he was in the right. *Lord M.* (Lord David Cecil)

5 For God's sake, ma'am, let's have no more of that. If you get the English people into the way of making kings, you'll get them into the way of *un*making them.
Advising Queen Victoria against granting Prince Albert the title of King Consort. *Lord M.* (Lord David Cecil)

6 I like the Garter; there is no damned merit in it.
Lord Melbourne (H. Dunckley), 'On the Order of the Garter'

7 I wish I was as cocksure of anything as Tom Macaulay is of everything.
Preface to Lord Melbourne's Papers (Earl Cowper)

8 Nobody ever did anything very foolish except from some strong principle.
The Young Melbourne (Lord David Cecil)

9 Damn it all, another Bishop dead, – I verily believe they die to vex me.
Attrib.

10 While I cannot be regarded as a pillar, I must be regarded as a buttress of the church, because I support it from the outside.
Attrib.

11 Things have come to a pretty pass when religion is allowed to invade the sphere of private life.
Attrib.

MEMORIALS

See also epitaphs, memory, obituaries, reputation

1 When I am dead, and laid in grave,
And all my bones are rotten,
By this may I remembered be
When I should be forgotten.
Anonymous On a girl's sampler, 1736

2 You must not miss Whitehall. At one end you will find a statue of one of our kings who was beheaded; at the other the monument to the man who did it. This is just an example of our attempts to be fair to everybody.
Edward Appleton (1892–1965) British physicist. Referring to Charles I and Cromwell. Speech, Stockholm, 1 Jan 1948

3 All your better deeds
Shall be in water writ, but this in marble.
Francis Beaumont (1584–1616) English dramatist. *The Nice Valour,* V:3

4 Such as did bear rule in their kingdoms, men renowned for their power, giving counsel by their understanding, and declaring prophecies:
Leaders of the people by their counsels, and by their knowledge of learning meet for the people, wise and eloquent in their instructions:
Such as found out musical tunes and recited verses in writing:
Rich men furnished with ability living peaceably in their habitations:
All these were honoured in their generations, and were the glory of their times.
There be of them, that have left a name behind them, that their praises might be reported.
And some there be, which have no memorial; who are perished, as though they had never been; and are

become as though they had never been born; and their children after them.
Bible: Ecclesiasticus 44:3–9

5 Their bodies are buried in peace; but their name liveth for evermore.
Bible: Ecclesiasticus 44:14

6 They shall grow not old, as we that are left grow old:
Age shall not weary them, nor the years condemn.
At the going down of the sun and in the morning
We will remember them.
Laurence Binyon (1869–1943) British poet. *Poems For the Fallen*

7 John Brown's body lies a-moldering in the grave,
His soul is marching on!
Charles Sprague Hall (19th century) US songwriter. The song commemorates the American hero who died in the cause of abolishing slavery. *John Brown's Body*

8 I have executed a memorial longer lasting than bronze.
Horace (Quintus Horatius Flaccus; 65–8 BC) Roman poet. *Odes*, III

9 In a larger sense we cannot dedicate, we cannot consecrate, we cannot hallow this ground. The brave men, living and dead, who struggled here, have consecrated it far above our power to add or detract. The world will little note, nor long remember, what we say here, but it can never forget what they did here. It is for us, the living, rather to be dedicated here to the unfinished work which they who fought here have thus far so nobly advanced. It is rather for us to be here dedicated to the great task remaining before us . . . that we here highly resolve that the dead shall not have died in vain, that this nation, under God, shall have a new birth of freedom; and that government of the people, by the people, and for the people, shall not perish from the earth.
Abraham Lincoln (1809–65) US statesman. Report of Lincoln's address at the dedication (19 Nov 1863) of the national cemetery on the site of the Battle of Gettysburg.

10 The monument sticks like a fishbone
in the city's throat.
Robert Lowell (1917–77) US poet. *For the Union Dead*

11 In Flanders fields the poppies blow
Between the crosses, row on row,
That mark our place.
John McCrae (1872–1918) Canadian poet and doctor. *In Flanders Fields*, 'Ypres Salient', 3 May 1915

12 The shrill demented choirs of wailing shells
And buglers calling for them from sad shires.
Wilfred Owen (1893–1918) British poet. *Anthem for Doomed Youth*

13 I was told that the Chinese said they would bury me by the Western Lake and build a shrine to my memory. I have some slight regret that this did not happen, as I might have become a god, which would have been very *chic* for an atheist.
Bertrand Russell (1872–1970) British philosopher. *The Autobiography of Bertrand Russell*, Vol. II, Ch. 3

14 Who will remember, passing through this gate
The unheroic dead who fed the guns?
Who shall absolve the foulness of their fate –
Those doomed, conscripted, unvictorious ones?
Siegfried Sassoon (1886–1967) British poet. *On Passing the New Menin Gate*

15 Men's evil manners live in brass: their virtues
We write in water.
William Shakespeare (1564–1616) English dramatist. *Henry VIII*, IV:2

16 I met a traveller from an antique land
Who said: Two vast and trunkless legs of stone
Stand in the desert.
Percy Bysshe Shelley (1792–1822) British poet. Referring to the legs of a broken statue of the Pharaoh Rameses II (1301–1234 BC; Greek name, Ozymandias). *Ozymandias*

17 Move Queen Anne? Most certainly not! Why it might some day be suggested that *my* statue should be moved, which I should much dislike.
Victoria (1819–1901) Queen of the United Kingdom. Said at the time of her Diamond Jubilee (1897), when it was suggested that the statue of Queen Anne should be moved from outside St. Paul's. *Men, Women and Things* (Duke of Portland), Ch. 5

MEMORY

See also memorials, nostalgia, past

1 Memories are hunting horns whose sound dies on the wind.
Guillaume Apollinaire (Wilhelm de Kostrowitzky; 1880–1918) Italian-born French poet. *Cors de Chasse*

2 I have more memories than if I were a thousand years old.
Charles Baudelaire (1821–67) French poet. *Spleen*

3 Time whereof the memory of man runneth not to the contrary.
William Blackstone (1723–80) British jurist. *Commentaries on the Laws of England*, Bk. I, Ch. 18

4 Memory is the thing you forget with.
Alexander Chase *Perspectives*

5 Am in Birmingham. Where ought I to be?
G. K. Chesterton (1874–1936) British writer. Telegram to his wife during a lecture tour. *Portrait of Barrie* (C. Asquith)

6 When I meet a man whose name I can't remember, I give myself two minutes; then, if it is a hopeless case, I always say, And how is the old complaint?
Benjamin Disraeli (1804–81) British statesman. Attrib.

7 I have forgot much, Cynara! gone with the wind,
Flung roses, roses riotously with the throng.
Ernest Dowson (1867–1900) British lyric poet. *Non Sum Qualis Eram Bonae Sub Regno Cynarae*

8 Oh! don't you remember sweet Alice, Ben Bolt,
Sweet Alice, whose hair was so brown,
Who wept with delight when you gave her a smile,
And trembled with fear at your frown?
Thomas Dunn English (1819–1902) US lawyer and writer. *Ben Bolt*

9 To endeavour to forget anyone is a certain way of thinking of nothing else.
Jean de La Bruyère (1645–96) French satirist. *Les Caractères*

10 Oh, yes I remember it well.
Alan Jay Lerner (1918–86) US lyricist and playwright. *Gigi*, 'I Remember It Well'

11 I never forget a face, but I'll make an exception in your case.
Groucho Marx (Julius Marx; 1895–1977) US comedian. *The Guardian*, 18 June 1965

12 The sigh of midnight trains in empty stations . . .
The smile of Garbo and the scent of roses
These foolish things

Remind me of you.
Eric Maschwitz (1901–69) British songwriter. Song

13 What a strange thing is memory, and hope; one looks backward, the other forward. The one is of today, the other is the Tomorrow. Memory is history recorded in our brain, memory is a painter, it paints pictures of the past and of the day.
Grandma Moses (Anna Mary Robertson Moses; 1860–1961) US primitive painter. *Grandma Moses, My Life's History* (ed. Aotto Kallir), Ch. 1

14 The taste was that of the little crumb of madeleine which on Sunday mornings at Combray . . . , when I used to say good-day to her in her bedroom, my aunt Léonie used to give me, dipping it first in her own cup of real or of lime-flower tea.
Marcel Proust (1871–1922) French novelist. *À la recherche du temps perdu: Du côté de chez Swann*

15 Thanks For the Memory.
Leo Robin (1899–) US songwriter. *Big Broadcast*, song title

16 Everyone complains of his memory, but no one complains of his judgement.
Duc de la Rochefoucauld (1613–80) French writer. *Maximes*, 89

17 Remember me when I am gone away,
Gone far away into the silent land.
Christina Rossetti (1830–74) British poet. *Remember*

18 Better by far you should forget and smile
Than that you should remember and be sad.
Christina Rossetti *Remember*

19 To expect a man to retain everything that he has ever read is like expecting him to carry about in his body everything that he has ever eaten.
Arthur Schopenhauer (1788–1860) German philosopher. *Parerga and Paralipomena*

20 Old men forget; yet all shall be forgot,
But he'll remember, with advantages,
What feats he did that day.
William Shakespeare (1564–1616) English dramatist. *Henry V*, IV:3

21 Music, when soft voices die,
Rose leaves, when the rose is dead,
Are heaped for the beloved's bed;
And so thy thoughts, when thou art gone,
Love itself shall slumber on.
Percy Bysshe Shelley (1792–1822) British poet. *To –*

22 There are three things I always forget. Names, faces and—the third I can't remember.
Italo Svevo (Ettore Schmitz; 1861–1928) Italian writer. Attrib.

23 As a perfume doth remain
In the folds where it hath lain,
So the thought of you, remaining
Deeply folded in my brain,
Will not leave me: all things leave me:
You remain.
Arthur Symons (1865–1945) British poet. *Memory*

24 I suppose that the high-water mark of my youth in Columbus, Ohio, was the night the bed fell on my father.
James Thurber (1894–1961) US humorist. *My Life and Hard Times*, Ch. 1

25 The nice thing about having memories is that you can choose.
William Trevor (1928–) British writer. *Matilda's England*

26 Memories are like mulligatawny soup in a cheap restaurant. It is best not to stir them.
P. G. Wodehouse (1881–1975) British humorous novelist. *Bring on the Girls* (with Guy Bolton)

MEN

See also mankind, marriage, masculinity, marriage, sexes, women

1 One cannot be always laughing at a man without now and then stumbling on something witty.
Jane Austen (1775–1817) British novelist. *Pride and Prejudice*, Ch. 40

2 A man's a man for a' that.
Robert Burns (1759–96) Scottish poet. *For a' that and a' that*

3 All men are rapists and that's all they are. They rape us with their eyes, their laws and their codes.
Marilyn French (1929–) US novelist. *The Women's Room*

4 A man . . . is *so* in the way in the house!
Elizabeth Gaskell (1810–65) British novelist. *Cranford*, Ch. 1

5 Probably the only place where a man can feel really secure is in a maximum security prison, except for the imminent threat of release.
Germaine Greer (1939–) Australian-born British writer and feminist. *The Female Eunuch*

6 I'm Gonna Wash That Man Right Out of My Hair.
Oscar Hammerstein II (1895–1960) US lyricist. *South Pacific*, Title of song

7 How beastly the bourgeois is
especially the male of the species.
D. H. Lawrence (1885–1930) British novelist. *How beastly the bourgeois is*

8 One realizes with horror, that the race of men is almost extinct in Europe. Only Christ-like heroes and woman-worshipping Don Juans, and rabid equality-mongrels.
D. H. Lawrence *Sea and Sardinia*, Ch. 3

9 Why can't a woman be more like a man?
Men are so honest, so thoroughly square;
Eternally noble, historically fair.
Alan Jay Lerner (1918–86) US songwriter. *My Fair Lady*, II:4

10 A sick man is as wayward as a child . . .
Mary Russell Mitford (1787–1855) British writer. *Julian*, I:1

11 He may have hair upon his chest
But, sister, so has Lassie.
Cole Porter (1891–1964) US composer and lyricist. *Kiss Me Kate*, 'I Hate Men'

12 He was formed for the ruin of our sex.
Tobias Smollett (1721–71) British novelist. *Roderick Random*, Ch. 22

13 Sometimes I think if there was a third sex men wouldn't get so much as a glance from me.
Amanda Vail (Warren Miller; 1921–66) US writer. *Love Me Little*, Ch. 6

14 A man in the house is worth two in the street.
Mae West (1892–1980) US actress. *Belle of the Nineties*, film 1934

MENTAL ILLNESS

1 The wish to hurt, the momentary intoxication with pain, is the loophole through which the pervert climbs into the minds of ordinary men.
Jacob Bronowski (1908–74) British mathematician and scientist. *The Face of Violence*, Ch. 5

2 If you are physically sick, you can elicit the interest of a battery of physicians; but if you are mentally sick, you are lucky if the janitor comes around.

Martin H. Fischer (1879–1962) *Fischerisms* (Howard Fabing and Ray Marr)

3 When a man lacks mental balance in pneumonia he is said to be delirious. When he lacks mental balance without the pneumonia, he is pronounced insane by all smart doctors.

Martin H. Fischer *Fischerisms* (Howard Fabing and Ray Marr)

4 Schizophrenic behaviour is a special strategy that a person invents in order to live in an unlivable situation.

R. D. Laing (1927–) British psychiatrist.

5 A body seriously out of equilibrium, either with itself or with its environment, perishes outright. Not so a mind. Madness and suffering can set themselves no limit.

George Santayana (1863–1952) Spanish-born US philosopher, poet, and critic. *The Life of Reason: Reason in Common Sense*, 2

MERCY

1 And he said, He that shewed mercy on him. Then said Jesus unto him, Go, and do thou likewise.

Bible: Luke 10:37

2 I seem forsaken and alone,
I hear the lion roar;
And every door is shut but one,
And that is Mercy's door.

William Cowper (1731–1800) British poet. *Olney Hymns*, 33

3 Everyone knows that I act in everything with kindness and mercy, for I am forcing Rouen into submission by starvation, not by fire, sword or bloodshed.

Henry V (1387–1422) King of England. Remark to an envoy from Rouen, 1418

4 The quality of mercy is not strain'd;
It droppeth as the gentle rain from heaven
Upon the place beneath. It is twice blest;
It blesseth him that gives and him that takes.

William Shakespeare (1564–1616) English dramatist. *The Merchant of Venice*, IV:1

5 And her face so sweet and pleading, yet with sorrow pale and worn,
Touched his heart with sudden pity – lit his eye with misty light;
'Go, your lover lives!' said Cromwell; 'Curfew shall not ring tonight!'

Rose Hartwick Thorpe (1850–1939) US poet and novelist. *Curfew Shall Not Ring Tonight*

MERIT

1 A good dog deserves a good bone.

Proverb

2 I don't deserve this, but I have arthritis, and I don't deserve that either.

Jack Benny (Benjamin Kubelsky; 1894–1974) US actor. Said when accepting an award. Attrib.

3 But many that are first shall be last; and the last shall be first.

Bible: Matthew 19:30

4 GOLDSMITH. Here's such a stir about a fellow that has written one book, and I have written many.
JOHNSON. Ah, Doctor, there go two-and-forty sixpences you know to one guinea.

Samuel Johnson (1709–84) British lexicographer. Referring to Beattie's *Essay on Truth*. *Johnsonian Miscellanies* (ed. G. B. Hill), Vol. I

5 I guess this is the week I earn my salary.

John Fitzgerald Kennedy (1917–63) US statesman. Comment made during the Cuban missile crisis. *Nobody Said It Better* (M. Ringo)

6 Use every man after his desert, and who shall scape whipping?

William Shakespeare (1564–1616) English dramatist. *Hamlet*, II:2

7 I wasn't lucky. I deserved it.

Margaret Thatcher (1925–) British politician and prime minister. Said after receiving school prize, aged nine. Attrib.

8 The Rise of the Meritocracy.

Michael Young (1915–) British political writer. Book title

MERRYMAKING

See also parties, pleasure

1 Come lasses and lads, get leave of your dads,
And away to the Maypole hie,
For every he has got him a she,
And the fiddler's standing by.

Anonymous *Come Lasses and Lads*

2 There was a sound of revelry by night,
And Belgium's capital had gather'd then
Her Beauty and her Chivalry, and bright
The lamps shone o'er fair women and brave men.

Lord Byron (1788–1824) British poet. *Childe Harold's Pilgrimage*, III

3 We have heard the chimes at midnight.

William Shakespeare (1564–1616) English dramatist. *Henry IV, Part Two*, III:2

4 Dost thou think, because thou art virtuous, there shall be no more cakes and ale?

William Shakespeare *Twelfth Night*, II:3

5 You must wake and call me early, call me early, mother dear;
To-morrow 'ill be the happiest time of all the glad New-year;
Of all the glad New-year, mother, the maddest merriest day;
For I'm to be Queen o' the May, mother, I'm to be Queen o' the May.

Alfred, Lord Tennyson (1809–92) British poet. *The May Queen*

6 I love such mirth as does not make friends ashamed to look upon one another next morning.

Izaak Walton (1593–1683) English writer. *The Compleat Angler*, Ch. 5

METAPHYSICS

See also philosophy

1 A blind man in a dark room – looking for a black hat – which isn't there.

Lord Bowen (1835–94) British judge. Characterization of a metaphysician. Attrib.

2 Metaphysics is the finding of bad reasons for what we believe upon instinct; but to find these reasons is no less an instinct.

F. H. Bradley (1846–1924) British philosopher. *Appearance and Reality*, Preface

3 We used to think that if we knew one, we knew two, because one and one are two. We are finding that we must learn a great deal more about 'and'.

Arthur Eddington (1882–1944) British astronomer. *The Harvest of a Quiet Eye* (A. L. Mackay)

4 The unrest which keeps the never stopping clock of metaphysics going is the thought that the non-existence of the world is just as possible as its existence.

William James (1842–1910) US psychologist and philosopher. *Some Problems of Philosophy*

5 In other words, apart from the

known and the unknown, what else is there?
Harold Pinter (1930–) British dramatist. *The Homecoming*, II

MILTON, JOHN

(1608–74) English poet. His poems include *L'Allegro* and *Il Penseroso* (1632) and the great epics *Paradise Lost* (1667) and *Paradise Regained* (1671).

1 Who kills a man kills a reasonable creature, God's image; but he who destroys a good book kills reason itself, kills the image of God, as it were in the eye.
Areopagitica

2 A good book is the precious life-blood of a master spirit, embalmed and treasured up on purpose to a life beyond life.
Areopagitica

3 Hence, vain deluding Joys,
The brood of Folly without father bred!
Il Penseroso

4 Far from all resort of mirth,
Save the cricket on the hearth.
Il Penseroso

5 Or sweetest Shakespeare, Fancy's child, Warble his native wood-notes wild.
L'Allegro

6 Fame is the spur that the clear spirit doth raise ...
Lycidas

7 Of Man's first disobedience, and the fruit
Of that forbidden tree, whose mortal taste
Brought death into the World, and all our woe . . .
Paradise Lost, Bk. I

8 Care
Sat on his faded cheek.
Paradise Lost, Bk. I

9 Long is the way
And hard, that out of hell leads up to light.
Paradise Lost, Bk. II

10 Let us with a gladsome mind
Praise the Lord, for he is kind
For his mercies ay endure
Ever faithful, ever sure.
Psalm

11 When I consider how my light is spent
Ere half my days in this dark world and wide,
And that one talent which is death to hide
Lodged with me useless.
Sonnet: 'On his Blindness'

MIND

See also intellect, intelligence, thinking

1 *Brain*, n. An apparatus with which we think that we think.
Ambrose Bierce (1842–?1914) US writer and journalist. *The Devil's Dictionary*

2 A great many open minds should be closed for repairs.
Toledo Blade

3 The brain is not an organ to be relied upon. It is developing monstrously. It is swelling like a goitre.
Aleksandr Blok (1880–1921) Russian poet.

4 As long as our brain is a mystery, the universe, the reflection of the structure of the brain, will also be a mystery.
Santiago Ramón y Cajal (1852–1934) Spanish scientist. *Charlas de Café*

5 We know the human brain is a device to keep the ears from grating on one another.
Peter De Vries (1910–) US novelist. *Comfort me with Apples*, Ch. 1

6 Minds like bodies, will often fall into a pimpled, ill-conditioned state from mere excess of comfort.
Charles Dickens (1812–70) British novelist. *Barnaby Rudge*, Ch. 7

7 The mind is an iceberg it floats with only 17 of its bulk above water.
Sigmund Freud (1856–1939) Austrian psychoanalyst. *Bartlett's Unfamiliar Quotations* (Leonard Louis Levinson)

8 The conscious mind may be compared to a fountain playing in the sun and falling back into the great subterranean pool of subconscious from which it rises.
Sigmund Freud *Bartlett's Unfamiliar Quotations* (Leonard Louis Levinson)

9 My life and work has been aimed at one goal only: to infer or guess how the mental apparatus is constructed and what forces interplay and counteract in it.
Sigmund Freud *Life and Work of Sigmund Freud* (E. Jones)

10 The remarkable thing about the human mind is its range of limitations.
Celia Green *The Decline and Fall of Science*, 'Aphorisms'

11 We have rudiments of reverence for the human body, but we consider as nothing the rape of the human mind.
Eric Hoffer (1902–) US writer. *Bartlett's Unfamiliar Quotations* (Leonard Louis Levinson)

12 Little minds are interested in the extraordinary; great minds in the commonplace.
Elbert Hubbard (1856–1915) US writer and editor. *Roycroft Dictionary and Book of Epigrams*

13 What we think and feel and are is to a great extent determined by the state of our ductless glands and our viscera.
Aldous Huxley (1894–1964) British writer. *Music at Night*, 'Meditation on El Greco'

14 The natural course of the human mind is certainly from credulity to scepticism.
Thomas Jefferson (1743–1826) US statesman. Letter to Dr. Caspar Wistar, 21 June 1807

15 Bodily decay is gloomy in prospect, but of all human contemplations the most abhorrent is body without mind.
Thomas Jefferson Letter to John Adams, 1 Aug 1816

16 The pendulum of the mind oscillates between sense and nonsense, not between right and wrong.
Carl Gustav Jung (1875–1961) Swiss psychoanalyst. *Memories, Dreams, Reflections*, Ch. 5

17 You should pray for a healthy mind in a healthy body.
Juvenal (c. 60–130 AD) Roman satirist. *Satires*, X

18 The highest function of *mind* is its function of messenger.
D. H. Lawrence (1885–1930) British writer. *Kangaroo*, Ch. 16

19 And the mind must sweat a poison
. . . that, discharged not thence
Gangrenes the vital sense
And makes disorder true.
It is certain we shall attain
No life till we stamp on all
Life the tetragonal
Pure symmetry of the brain.
C. Day Lewis (1904–72) British poet. *Collected Poems 1929–1933*

20 The mind like a sick body can be healed and changed by medicine.
Lucretius (c. 96 BC–55 BC) Roman philosopher and poet. *On the Nature of Things*, III

21 A mind not to be changed by place or time.
The mind is its own place, and in itself
Can make a Heaven of Hell, a Hell of Heaven.
John Milton (1608–74) English poet. *Paradise Lost,* Bk. I

22 The mind has great influence over the body, and maladies often have their origin there.
Molière (Jean Baptiste Poquelin; 1622–73) French dramatist. *Love's the Best Doctor,* III

23 It is good to rub and polish our brain against that of others.
Michel de Montaigne (1533–92) French essayist and moralist. *Essays,* Bk. I

24 A sick mind cannot endure any harshness.
Ovid (Publius Ovidius Naso; 43 BC–17 AD) Roman poet. *Epistulae ex Ponto,* Bk. I

25 That's the classical mind at work, runs fine inside but looks dingy on the surface.
Robert T. Pirsig (1928–) US writer. *Zen and the Art of Motorcycle Maintenance,* Pt. III, Ch. 25

26 Mind is ever the ruler of the universe.
Plato (429 BC–347 BC) Greek philosopher. *Philebus*

27 Happiness is beneficial for the body, but it is grief that develops the powers of the mind.
Marcel Proust (1871–1922) French novelist. *À la recherche du temps perdu: Le Temps retrouvé,* Ch. 3

28 Our minds are lazier than our bodies.
Duc François de la Rochefoucauld (1613–80) French writer. *Bartlett's Unfamiliar Quotations* (Leonard Louis Levinson)

29 The dogma of the Ghost in the Machine.
Gilbert Ryle (1900–76) British philosopher. *The Concept of Mind,* Ch. 1

30 If it is for mind that we are seaching the brain, then we are supposing the brain to be much more than a telephone-exchange. We are supposing it a telephone-exchange along with the subscribers as well.
Charles Scott Sherrington (1857–1952) British physiologist. *Man on his Nature*

31 Once we are destined to live out our lives in the prison of our mind, our one duty is to furnish it well.
Peter Ustinov (1921–) British actor, director, and writer. *Dear Me,* Ch. 20

32 Mind over matter.
Virgil (Publius Vergilius Maro; 70 BC–19 BC) Roman poet. *Aeneid,* Bk. VI

33 When people will not weed their own minds, they are apt to be overrun with nettles.
Horace Walpole (1717–97) British writer. Letter to Lady Ailesbury, 10 July 1779

34 The mind can also be an erogenous zone.
Raquel Welch (Raquel Tejada; 1940–) US film star. *Colombo's Hollywood* (J. R. Colombo)

35 At 83 Shaw's mind was perhaps not quite as good as it used to be, but it was still better than anyone else's.
Alexander Woollcott (1887–1943) US journalist. Referring to George Bernard Shaw. *While Rome Burns*

36 Strongest minds
Are often those of whom the noisy world
Hears least.
William Wordsworth (1770–1850) British poet. *The Excursion*

MINORITY

See also majority

1 What's a cult? It just means not enough people to make a minority.
Robert Altman (1922–) US film director. *The Observer,* 1981

2 The majority has the might – more's the pity – but it hasn't right. . . . The minority is always right.
Henrik Ibsen (1828–1906) Norwegian dramatist. *An Enemy of the People,* IV

3 Minorities . . . are almost always in the right.
Sydney Smith (1771–1845) British clergyman and essayist. *The Smith of Smiths* (H. Pearson), Ch. 9

MIRACLES

1 It was a miracle of rare device,
A sunny pleasure-dome with caves of ice!
Samuel Taylor Coleridge (1772–1834) British poet. *Kubla Khan*

2 Miracles are laughed at by a nation that reads thirty million newspapers a day and supports Wall Street.
Finley Peter Dunne (1867–1936) US journalist. *Mr. Dooley's Opinions,* 1900

3 Of course, before we *know* he is a saint, there will have to be miracles.
Graham Greene (1904–) British novelist. *The Power and the Glory,* Pt. IV

4 The Christian religion not only was at first attended with miracles, but even at this day cannot be believed by any reasonable person without one. Mere reason is insufficient to convince us of its veracity: and whoever is moved by faith to assent to it, is conscious of a continued miracle in his own person, which subverts all the principles of his understanding, and gives him a determination to believe what is most contrary to custom and experience.
David Hume (1711–76) Scottish philosopher. *Essays,* 'Of Miracles'

5 Whatever a man prays for, he prays for a miracle. Every prayer reduces itself to this: 'Great God grant that twice two be not four.'
Ivan Turgenev (1818–83) Russian novelist. *Prayer*

MISANTHROPY

See also mankind, philanthropy

1 What though the spicy breezes
Blow soft o'er Ceylon's isle;
Though every prospect pleases,
And only man is vile . . .
Reginald Heber (1783–1826) British bishop and hymn writer. *From Greenland's Icy Mountains*

2 I've always been interested in people, but I've never liked them.
W. Somerset Maugham (1874–1965) British novelist. *The Observer,* 'Sayings of the Week', 28 Aug 1949

3 A young, earnest American brought up the subject of nuclear warfare which, he said might well destroy the entire human race. 'I can't wait' P. G. Wodehouse murmured.
Malcolm Muggeridge (1903–) British writer. *Tread Softly for You Tread On My Jokes*

4 I love mankind – it's people I can't stand.
Charles M. Schultz (1922–) US cartoonist. *Go Fly a Kite, Charlie Brown*

5 Other people are quite dreadful. The only possible society is oneself.
Oscar Wilde (1854–1900) Irish-born British dramatist. *An Ideal Husband,* III

MISERY

1 Resolve to be thyself: and know, that he
Who finds himself, loses his misery.
Matthew Arnold (1822–88) British poet and critic. *Self-Dependence*

2 Misery acquaints a man with strange bedfellows.
William Shakespeare (1564–1616) English dramatist. *The Tempest*, II:2

3 A still small voice spake unto me,
'Thou art so full of misery,
Were it not better not to be?'
Alfred, Lord Tennyson (1809–92) British poet. *The Two Voices*

4 I always say that, next to a battle lost, the greatest misery is a battle gained.
Duke of Wellington *Diary* (Frances, Lady Shelley)

MISFORTUNE

See also accidents, curses, sorrow, suffering

1 Drink wine, and have the gout; drink no wine, and have the gout too.
Proverb

2 It is easy to bear the misfortunes of others.
Proverb

3 It never rains but it pours.
Proverb

4 Prosperity doth best discover vice; but adversity doth best discover virtue.
Francis Bacon (1561–1626) English philosopher. *Essays*, 'Of Adversity'

5 Calamities are of two kinds. Misfortune to ourselves and good fortune to others.
Ambrose Bierce (1842–?1914) US writer and journalist. *The Devil's Dictionary*

6 There remaineth a rest for the people of God:
And I have had troubles enough, for one.
Robert Browning (1812–89) British poet. *Old Pictures in Florence*, XVII

7 Tragedie is to seyn a certeyn storie,
As olde bokes maken us memorie,
Of him that stood in greet prosperitee
And is y-fallen out of heigh degree
Into miserie, and endeth wrecchedly.
Geoffrey Chaucer (c. 1342–1400) English poet. *The Canterbury Tales*, 'The Monk's Prologue'

8 For of fortunes sharp adversitee
The worst kinde of infortune is this,
A man to have ben in prosperitee,
And it remembren, what is passed is.
Geoffrey Chaucer *Troilus and Criseyde*, 3

9 A chapter of accidents.
Earl of Chesterfield (1694–1773) English statesman. Letter to his son, 16 Feb 1753

10 'I am a lone lorn creetur,' were Mrs Gummidge's words . . . 'and everythink goes contrairy with me.'
Charles Dickens (1812–70) British novelist. *David Copperfield*, Ch. 3

11 Life is mostly froth and bubble;
Two things stand like stone,
Kindness in another's trouble,
Courage in your own.
Adam Lindsay Gordon (1833–70) Australian poet. *Ye Wearie Wayfarer*, Fytte 8

12 Depend upon it that if a man talks of his misfortunes there is something in them that is not disagreeable to him; for where there is nothing but pure misery there never is any recourse to the mention of it.
Samuel Johnson (1709–84) British lexicographer. *Life of Johnson* (J. Boswell), Vol. IV

13 There exist some evils so terrible and some misfortunes so horrible that we dare not think of them, whilst their very aspect makes us shudder; but if they happen to fall on us, we find ourselves stronger than we imagined, we grapple with our ill luck, and behave better than we expected we should.
Jean de La Bruyère (1645–96) French satirist. *Les Caractères*

14 I never knew any man in my life who could not bear another's misfortunes perfectly like a Christian.
Alexander Pope (1688–1744) British poet. *Thoughts on Various Subjects*

15 We are all strong enough to bear the misfortunes of others.
Duc de la Rochefoucauld (1613–80) French writer. *Maximes*, 19

16 In the misfortune of our best friends, we always find something which is not displeasing to us.
Duc de la Rochefoucauld *Maximes*, 99

17 When sorrows come, they come not single spies,
But in battalions!
William Shakespeare (1564–1616) English dramatist. *Hamlet*, IV:5

18 This is the excellent foppery of the world, that, when we are sick in fortune, often the surfeits of our own behaviour, we make guilty of our disasters the sun, the moon, and stars.
William Shakespeare *King Lear*, I:2

19 Misery acquaints a man with strange bedfellows.
William Shakespeare *The Tempest*, II:2

MISOGYNY

See also women

1 I'd be equally as willing
For a dentist to be drilling
Than to ever let a woman in my life.
Alan Jay Lerner (1918–86) US songwriter. *My Fair Lady*, I:2

2 How can I possibly dislike a sex to which Your Majesty belongs?
Cecil Rhodes (1853–1902) South African statesman. Replying to Queen Victoria's suggestion that he disliked women. *Rhodes* (Lockhart)

3 Would you have me speak after my custom, as being a professed tyrant to their sex?
William Shakespeare (1564–1616) English dramatist. *Much Ado About Nothing*, I:1

MISQUOTATION

1 Had I been present at the Creation, I would have given some useful hints for the better ordering of the universe.
Alfonso the Wise (c. 1221–84) King of Castile and Léon. Referring to the complicated Ptolemaic model of the universe. Often quoted as, 'Had I been consulted I would have recommended something simpler'. Attrib.

2 We have ways of making men talk.
Anonymous Film catchphrase, often repeated as 'We have ways of making you talk'. *Lives of a Bengal Lancer*

3 That's one small step for man, one giant leap for mankind.
Neil Armstrong (1930–) US astronaut. Said on stepping onto the moon. Often quoted as, 'small step for a man . . . ' (which is probably what he intended). Remark, 21 July 1969

4 I have seldom spoken with greater regret, for my lips are not yet unsealed. Were these troubles over I would make a case, and I guarantee that not a man would go into the Lobby against us.

Stanley Baldwin (1867–1947) British statesman. Referring to the Abyssinian crisis; usually misquoted as 'My lips are sealed'. Speech, House of Commons, 10 Dec 1935

5 And behold joy and gladness, slaying oxen, and killing sheep, eating flesh, and drinking wine: let us eat and drink; for tomorrow we shall die.

Bible: Isaiah 22:13 A similar sentiment is expressed in Corinthians 15:32–33. Often misquoted as 'let us eat, drink, and be merry'.

6 So when they continued asking him, he lifted up himself, and said unto them, He that is without sin among you, let him first cast a stone at her.

Bible: John 8:7 Often misquoted as 'cast the first stone'.

7 Then said Jesus unto him, Put up again thy sword into his place: for all they that take the sword shall perish with the sword.

Bible: Matthew 26:52 Often misquoted as 'They that live by the sword shall die by the sword'.

8 Pride goeth before destruction, and an haughty spirit before a fall.

Bible: Proverbs 16:18 Often misquoted as 'Pride goeth before a fall'.

9 Play it, Sam. Play 'As Time Goes By.'

Humphrey Bogart (1899–1957) US film star. Often misquoted as 'Play it again, Sam'. *Casablanca*

10 You dirty double-crossing rat!

James Cagney (1899–1986) US actor. Usually misquoted by impressionists as 'You dirty rat'. *Blonde Crazy*

11 War is the continuation of politics by other means.

Karl von Clausewitz (1780–1831) Prussian general. The usual misquotation of 'War is nothing but a continuation of politics with the admixture of other means'. *Vom Kriege*

12 'Excellent!' I cried. 'Elementary,' said he.

Arthur Conan Doyle (1856–1930) British writer. Watson talking to Sherlock Holmes; Holmes's reply is often misquoted as 'Elementary my dear Watson'. *The Crooked Man*

13 I got there fustest with the mostest.

Nathan Bedford Forrest (1821–77) Confederate general. Popular misquotation of his explanation of his success in capturing Murfreesboro; his actual words were, 'I just took the short cut and got there first with the most men'. *A Civil War Treasury* (B. Botkin)

14 I never said, 'I want to be alone.' I only said, 'I want to be *left* alone.' There is all the difference.

Greta Garbo (1905–) Swedish-born US film star. *Garbo* (John Bainbridge)

15 Take your hare when it is cased . . .

Hannah Glasse (18th century) English writer. Often misquoted as, 'First catch your hare' and wrongly attributed to Mrs Beaton. *The Art of Cookery Made Plain and Easy*, Ch. 1

16 Once I built a rail-road,
Now it's done.
Brother, can you spare a dime?

E. Y. Harburg (1898–1981) US lyricist. Often quoted as 'Buddy can you spare a dime'. *New Americana*, 'Brother Can You Spare a Dime'

17 I am happy now that Charles calls on my bedchamber less frequently than of old. As it is, I now endure but two calls a week and when I hear his steps outside my door I lie down on my bed, close my eyes, open my legs and think of England.

Lady Alice Hillingdon (1857–1940) Wife of 2nd Baron Hillingdon. Often mistakenly attributed to Queen Victoria. *Journal* (1912)

18 Jerry Ford is so dumb that he can't fart and chew gum at the same time.

Lyndon B. Johnson (1908–73) US statesman. Sometimes quoted as '. . . can't walk and chew gum'. *A Ford, Not a Lincoln* (R. Reeves), Ch. 1

19 Misquotations are the only quotations that are never misquoted.

Hesketh Pearson (1887–1964) British biographer. *Common Misquotations*

20 A widely-read man never quotes accurately . . . Misquotation is the pride and privilege of the learned.

Hesketh Pearson *Common Misquotations*

21 Alas, poor Yorick! I knew him, Horatio: a fellow of infinite jest, of most excellent fancy.

William Shakespeare (1564–1616) English dramatist. Often misquoted as 'I knew him well'. *Hamlet*, V:1

22 I always did like a man in uniform. And that one fits you grand. Why don't you come up sometime and see me?

Mae West (1892–1980) US actress. Often misquoted as 'Come up and see me some time' *She Done Him Wrong*, film 1933

MISTAKES

See also imperfection

1 Two wrongs do not make a right.

Proverb

2 It is worse than immoral, it's a mistake.

Dean Acheson (1893–1971) US lawyer and statesman. Describing the Vietnam war. *See also* BOULAY DE LA MEURTHE. Quoted by Alistair Cooke in his radio program *Letter from America*

3 The weak have one weapon: the errors of those who think they are strong.

Georges Bidault (1899–1983) French statesman. *The Observer*, 1962

4 It is worse than a crime, it is a blunder.

Antoine Boulay de la Meurthe (1761–1840) French politician. *See also* ACHESON. Referring to the summary execution of the Duc d'Enghien by Napoleon, 1804. Attrib.

5 I guess that'll hold the little bastards.

Don Carney (1897–1954) US broadcaster. Carney was ending a children's radio show and thought that he was off the air. Attrib.

6 The medical errors of one century constitute the popular faith of the next.

Alonzo Clark (1807–87)

7 I beseech you, in the bowels of Christ, think it possible you may be mistaken.

Oliver Cromwell (1599–1658) English soldier and statesman. Letter to the General Assembly of the Church of Scotland, 3 Aug 1650

8 Better send them a Papal Bull.

Lord Curzon (1859–1925) British politician. Written in the margin of a Foreign Office document. The phrase 'the monks of Mount Athos were violating their vows' had been misprinted as '. . . violating their cows'. *Life of Lord Curzon* (Ronaldshay), Vol. III, Ch. 15

9 What we call experience is often a dreadful list of ghastly mistakes.

J. Chalmers Da Costa (1863–1933) *The Trials and Triumphs of the Surgeon*, Ch. 1

10 Yes, once – many, many years ago. I thought I had made a wrong decision. Of course, it turned out that I had been right all along. But I was wrong to have *thought* that I was wrong.

John Foster Dulles (1888–1959) US politician. On being asked whether he had ever been wrong. *Facing the Music* (H. Temianka)

11 Pardon me, madam, but *I* am my brother.

Karl Gustav Jacob Jacobi (1804–51) German mathematician. On being mistaken by a lady for his brother. *Men of Mathematics* (M. H. Jacobi)

12 Erratum. In my article on the Price of Milk, 'Horses' should have read 'Cows' throughout.
J. B. Morton (1893–1979) British journalist. *The Best of Beachcomber*

13 The man who makes no mistakes does not usually make anything.
Edward John Phelps (1822–1900) US lawyer and diplomat. Speech, Mansion House, London, 24 Jan 1899

14 A man should never be ashamed to own he has been in the wrong, which is but saying, in other words, that he is wiser to-day than he was yesterday.
Alexander Pope (1688–1744) British poet. *Thoughts on Various Subjects*

15 To err is human, to forgive, divine.
Alexander Pope *An Essay on Criticism*

16 The follies which a man regrets the most in his life, are those which he didn't commit when he had the opportunity.
Helen Rowland (1876–1950) US writer. *Guide To Men*

17 What time is the next swan?
Leo Slezak (1873–1946) Czechoslovakian-born tenor. When the mechanical swan left the stage without him during a performance of *Lohengrin*. *What Time Is the Next Swan?* (Walter Slezak)

18 We often discover what *will* do, by finding out what will not do; and probably he who never made a mistake never made a discovery.
Samuel Smiles (1812–1904) British writer. *Self-Help*, Ch. 11

19 Human blunders usually do more to shape history than human wickedness.
A. J. P. Taylor (1906–) British historian. *The Origins of the Second World War*, Ch. 10

20 Well, if I called the wrong number, why did you answer the phone?
James Thurber (1894–1961) US humorist. Cartoon caption

21 If we had more time for discussion we should probably have made a great many more mistakes.
Leon Trotsky (Lev Davidovich Bronstein; 1879–1940) Russian revolutionary. *My Life*

22 The physician can bury his mistakes, but the architect can only advise his client to plant vines.
Frank Lloyd Wright (1869–1959) US architect. *New York Times Magazine*, 4 Oct 1953

MISTRUST

See also suspicion, trust

1 After shaking hands with a Greek, count your fingers.
Proverb

2 While I see many hoof-marks going in, I see none coming out.
Aesop (6th century BC) Reputed Greek writer of fables. *Fables*, 'The Lion, the Fox, and the Beasts'

3 The lion and the calf shall lie down together but the calf won't get much sleep.
Woody Allen (Allen Stewart Konigsberg; 1935–) US film actor. *Without Feathers*, 'The Scrolls'

4 The louder he talked of his honor, the faster we counted our spoons.
Ralph Waldo Emerson (1803–82) US poet and essayist. *Conduct of Life*, 'Worship'

5 Let me remind you what the wary fox said once upon a time to the sick lion: 'Because those footprints scare me, all directed your way, none coming back.'
Horace (Quintus Horatius Flaccus; 65–8 BC) Roman poet. *Epistles*, I

6 But if he does really think that there is no distinction between virtue and vice, why, Sir, when he leaves our houses let us count our spoons.
Samuel Johnson (1709–84) British lexicographer. *Life of Johnson* (J. Boswell), Vol. I

7 *Quis custodiet ipsos custodes?*
Who is to guard the guards themselves?
Juvenal (Decimus Junius Juvenalis; 60–130 AD). Roman satirist. *Satires*, VI

8 Ye diners-out from whom we guard our spoons.
Lord Macaulay (1800–59) British historian. Letter to Hannah Macaulay, 29 June 1831

9 Everyone likes a kidder, but no one lends him money.
Arthur Miller (1915–) US dramatist. *Death of a Salesman*

10 Let me have men about me that are fat;
Sleek-headed men, and such as sleep o' nights.
Yon Cassius has a lean and hungry look;
He thinks too much. Such men are dangerous.
William Shakespeare (1564–1616) English dramatist. *Julius Caesar*, I:2

11 An ally has to be watched just like an enemy.
Leon Trotsky (Lev Davidovich Bronstein; 1879–1940) Russian revolutionary. *Expansion and Coexistence* (A. Ulam)

12 *Equo ne credite, Teucri.*
Quidquid id est timeo Danaos et dona ferentis.
Do not trust the horse, Trojans.
Whatever it is, I fear the Greeks even when they bring gifts.
Virgil (Publius Vergilius Maro; 70–19 BC) Roman poet. *Aeneid*, Bk. II

MIXED METAPHORS

See also Goldwynisms

1 If you open that Pandora's Box you never know what Trojan 'orses will jump out.
Ernest Bevin (1881–1951) British trade-union leader and politician. Referring to the Council of Europe. *Ernest Bevin and the Foreign Office* (Sir Roderick Barclay)

2 Every director bites the hand that lays the golden egg.
Samuel Goldwyn (Samuel Goldfish; 1882–1974) Polish-born US film producer. Attrib.

3 You ought to take the bull between the teeth.
Samuel Goldwyn Attrib.

4 Mr Speaker, I smell a rat; I see him forming in the air and darkening the sky; but I'll nip him in the bud.
Boyle Roche (1743–1807) British politician. Attrib.

MODERATION

See also excess

1 Eat and drink measurely, and defy the mediciners.
Proverb

2 Moderation in all things.
Proverb

3 Temperance is the best physic.
Proverb

4 You can have too much of a good thing.
Proverb

5 I have changed my ministers, but I have not changed my measures; I am still for moderation and will govern by it.
Anne (1665–1714) Queen of Great Britain To members of the new Tory ministry, Jan 1711

6 By God, Mr Chairman, at this

moment I stand astonished at my own moderation!

Clive of India (1725–74) British soldier and governor of Bengal. Reply during Parliamentary Inquiry, 1773

7 Eat not to dullness; drink not to elevation.

Benjamin Franklin (1706–90) US scientist and statesman. *Autobiography*, Ch. 5

8 Moderation is a virtue only in those who are thought to have an alternative.

Henry Kissinger (1923–) German-born US politician and diplomat. *The Observer*, 24 Jan 1982

9 What have I gained by health? intolerable dullness. What by early hours and moderate meals? – a total blank.

Charles Lamb (1775–1834) British essayist. Letter to William Wordsworth, 22 Jan 1830

10 Temperance is the love of health, or the inability to overindulge.

Duc de La Rochefoucauld (1613–80) French writer. *Maxims*, No. 583

11 Not too much zeal.

Talleyrand (Charles Maurice de Talleyrand-Périgord; 1754–1838) French politician. Attrib.

12 Moderation is a fatal thing, Lady Hunstanton. Nothing succeeds like excess.

Oscar Wilde (1854–1900) Irish-born British dramatist. *A Woman of No Importance*, III

MODESTY

1 His modesty amounts to deformity.

Margot Asquith (1865–1945) The second wife of Herbert Asquith. Referring to her husband. *As I Remember*

2 I should never have entered the church on that day, though it was an important feast, could I have known the Pope's intention in advance.

Charlemagne (742–814) Holy Roman Emperor. Referring to his coronation as emperor, 25 Dec 800. Attrib.

3 Nurse, take away the candle and spare my blushes.

Henry James (1843–1916) US novelist. On being informed, while confined to his bed, that he had been awarded the Order of Merit. *The American Treasury* (C. Fadiman)

4 It was involuntary. They sank my boat.

John Fitzgerald Kennedy (1917–63) US statesman. Responding to praise of his courage while serving in the US navy against the Japanese in World War II. *Nobody Said It Better* (M. Ringo)

5 In some remote regions of Islam it is said, a woman caught unveiled by a stranger will raise her skirt to cover her face.

Raymond Mortimer (1895–) British literary critic and writer. *Colette*

6 If you want people to think well of you, do not speak well of yourself.

Blaise Pascal (1623–62) French philosopher and mathematician. *Pensées*, I

7 A lot of men who have accepted – or had imposed upon them in boyhood – the old English public school styles of careful modesty in speech, with much understatement, have behind their masks an appalling and impregnable conceit of themselves. If they do not blow their own trumpets it is because they feel you are not fit to listen to the performance.

J. B. Priestley (1894–1984) British novelist. *Outcries and Asides*

8 Be modest! It is the kind of pride least likely to offend.

Jules Renard (1894–1910) French writer. *Journal*

9 . . . the nuns who never take a bath without wearing a bathrobe all the time. When asked why, since no man can see them, they reply 'Oh, but you forget the good God.'

Bertrand Russell (1872–1970) British philosopher. *The Basic Writings*, Pt. II, Ch. 7

10 I have often wished I had time to cultivate modesty . . . But I am too busy thinking about myself.

Edith Sitwell (1887–1964) British poet and writer. *The Observer*, 'Sayings of the Week', 30 Apr 1950

MONARCHY

See also royalty

1 *Rex illiteratus, asinus coronatus.*
An unlettered king is a crowned ass.

Anonymous

2 The best reason why Monarchy is a strong government is that it is an intelligible government. The mass of mankind understand it, and they hardly anywhere in the world understand any other.

Walter Bagehot (1826–77) British economist and journalist. *The English Constitution*, 'The Monarchy'

3 The Sovereign has, under a constitutional monarchy such as ours, three rights – the right to be consulted, the right to encourage, the right to warn.

Walter Bagehot *The English Constitution*, 'The Monarchy'

4 God grant him peace and happiness but never understanding of what he has lost.

Stanley Baldwin (1867–1947) British politician and prime minister. Referring to Edward VIII's abdication.

5 That the king can do no wrong, is a necessary and fundamental principle of the English constitution.

William Blackstone (1723–80) British jurist. *Commentaries on the Laws of England*, Bk. III, Ch. 17

6 The king never dies.

William Blackstone *Commentaries on the Laws of England*, Bk. I, Ch. 7

7 I would rather hew wood than be a king under the conditions of the King of England.

Charles X (1757–1836) King of France. *Encyclopaedia Britannica*

8 There is no middle course between the throne and the scaffold.

Charles X Said to Talleyrand, who is said to have replied 'You are forgetting the post-chaise'. Attrib.

9 Magna Charta is such a fellow, that he will have no sovereign.

Edward Coke (1552–1634) English lawyer and politician. Speaking on the Lords Amendment to the Petition of Right, 17 May 1628. *Hist. Coll.* (Rushworth), I

10 The influence of the Crown has increased, is increasing, and ought to be diminished.

John Dunning (1731–83) British lawyer and politician. Motion passed by the House of Commons, 1780

11 There will soon be only five kings left – the Kings of England, Diamonds, Hearts, Spades and Clubs.

Farouk I (1920–65) The last king of Egypt. Remark made to Lord Boyd-Orr

12 Kings govern by means of popular assemblies only when they cannot do without them.

Charles James Fox (1749–1806) British Whig politician. Attrib.

13 I did not usurp the crown, but was duly elected.

Henry IV (1367–1413) King of England. Reply when accused by Richard Frisby, a Franciscan on trial for plotting (1402) to overthrow him. *Eulogium Historiarum*

14 I will govern according to the

common weal, but not according to the common will.
James I (1566–1625) King of England. *History of the English People* (J. R. Green)

15 A constitutional king must learn to stoop.
Leopold II (1835–1909) King of the Belgians. Instructing Prince Albert, the heir apparent, to pick up some papers that had fallen onto the floor. *The Mistress* (Betty Kelen)

16 *L'État c'est moi.*
I am the State.
Louis XIV (1638–1715) French king. Attrib.

17 There is something behind the throne greater than the King himself.
William Pitt the Elder (1708–78) British statesman. Speech, House of Lords, 2 Mar 1770

18 The right divine of kings to govern wrong.
Alexander Pope (1688–1744) British poet. *The Dunciad*, IV

19 A king is a thing men have made for their own sakes, for quietness' sake. Just as if in a family one man is appointed to buy the meat.
John Selden (1584–1654) English historian. *Table Talk*

20 There's such divinity doth hedge a king
That treason can but peep to what it would.
William Shakespeare (1564–1616) English dramatist. *Hamlet*, IV:5

21 Uneasy lies the head that wears a crown.
William Shakespeare *Henry IV, Part Two*, III:1

22 Every subject's duty is the King's; but every subject's soul is his own.
William Shakespeare *Henry V*, IV:1

23 Not all the water in the rough rude sea
Can wash the balm from an anointed king;
The breath of worldly men cannot depose
The deputy elected by the Lord.
William Shakespeare *Richard II*, III:2

24 The king reigns, and the people govern themselves.
Louis Adolphe Thiers (1797–1877) French statesman and historian. In an unsigned article attributed to Thiers. *Le National*, 20 Jan 1830

25 As guardian of His Majesty's conscience.
Lord Thurlow (1731–1806) British lawyer. Speech, House of Lords, 1779

26 The monarchy is a labour-intensive industry.
Harold Wilson (1916–) British politician and prime minister. *The Observer*, 13 Feb 1977

27 The king reigns, but does not govern.
Jan Zamoyski (1541–1605) Grand chancellor of Poland. Speech, Polish Parliament, 1605

MONEY

See also bribery, economics, extravagance, greed, materialism, thrift, wealth

1 Easy come, easy go.
Proverb

2 Out of debt, out of danger.
Proverb

3 Take care of the pence, and the pounds will take care of themselves.
Proverb

4 I can't afford to waste my time making money.
Jean Louis Rodolphe Agassiz (1807–73) Swiss naturalist. When asked to give a lecture for a fee. Attrib.

5 Business, you know, may bring money, but friendship hardly ever does.
Jane Austen (1775–1817) British novelist. *Emma*, Ch. 34

6 Money is like muck, not good except it be spread.
Francis Bacon (1561–1626) English philosopher. *See also* MURCHISON. *Essays*, 'Of Seditions and Troubles'

7 Money, it turned out, was exactly like sex, you thought of nothing else if you didn't have it and thought of other things if you did.
James Baldwin (1924–87) US writer. *Nobody Knows My Name*

8 I'm tired of Love: I'm still more tired of Rhyme.
But Money gives me pleasure all the Time.
Hilaire Belloc (1870–1953) French-born British poet. *Fatigue*

9 A feast is made for laughter, and wine maketh merry: but money answereth all things.
Bible: Ecclesiastes 10:19

10 For the love of money is the root of all evil: which while some coveted after, they have erred from the faith, and pierced themselves through with many sorrows.
Bible: I Timothy 6:10

11 Straighteners, managers and cashiers of the Musical Banks.
Samuel Butler (1835–1902) British writer. *Erewhon*, Ch. 9

12 It has been said that the love of money is the root of all evil. The want of money is so quite as truly.
Samuel Butler *Erewhon*, Ch. 20

13 What makes all doctrines plain and clear?
About two hundred pounds a year.
Samuel Butler *Hudibras*, Pt. III

14 It is a kind of spiritual snobbery that makes people think that they can be happy without money.
Albert Camus (1913–60) French existentialist writer. *Notebooks*, 1935–1942

15 Where large sums of money are concerned, it is advisable to trust nobody.
Agatha Christie (1891–1976) British detective-story writer. *Endless Night*, Bk. II, Ch. 15

16 How pleasant it is to have money.
Arthur Hugh Clough (1819–61) British poet. *Dipsychus*, Bk. I

17 But then one is always excited by descriptions of money changing hands. It's much more fundamental than sex.
Nigel Dennis (1912–) British writer. *Cards of Identity*

18 Buy an annuity cheap, and make your life interesting to yourself and everybody else that watches the speculation.
Charles Dickens (1812–70) British novelist. *Martin Chuzzlewit*, Ch. 18

19 Ah, take the Cash in hand and waive the Rest;
Oh, the brave Music of a *distant* Drum!
Edward Fitzgerald (1809–83) British poet. *The Rubáiyát of Omar Khayyám* (1st edn.), XII

20 It is only the poor who pay cash, and that not from virtue, but because they are refused credit.
Anatole France (Jacques Anatole François Thibault; 1844–1924) French writer. *A Cynic's Breviary* (J. R. Solly)

21 Money differs from an automobile, a mistress or cancer in being equally important to those who have it and those who do not.
John Kenneth Galbraith (1908–) US economist. Attrib.

22 If possible honestly, if not, somehow, make money.
Horace (Quintus Horatius Flaccus; 65–8 BC) Roman poet. *Epistles*, I

23 We all know how the size of sums of money appears to vary in a remarkable way according as they are being paid in or paid out.
Julian Huxley (1887–1975) British biologist. *Essays of a Biologist*, 5

24 There are few ways in which a man can be more innocently employed than in getting money.
Samuel Johnson (1709–84) British lexicographer. *Life of Johnson* (J. Boswell), Vol. II

25 You don't seem to realize that a poor person who is unhappy is in a better position than a rich person who is unhappy. Because the poor person has hope. He thinks money would help.
Jean Kerr (1923–) US dramatist. *Poor Richard*

26 Clearly money has something to do with life
– In fact, they've a lot in common, if you enquire:
You can't put off being young until you retire.
Philip Larkin (1922–85) British poet. *Money*

27 For I don't care too much for money,
For money can't buy me love.
John Lennon (1940–80) British rock musician. *Can't Buy Me Love* (with Paul McCartney)

28 What's a thousand dollars? Mere chicken feed. A poultry matter.
Groucho Marx (Julius Marx; 1895–1977) US comedian. *The Cocoanuts*

29 Do they allow tipping on the boat?
– Yes, sir.
Have you got two fives?
– Oh, yes, sir.
Then you won't need the ten cents I was going to give you.
Groucho Marx *A Night at the Opera*

30 Money is like a sixth sense without which you cannot make a complete use of the other five.
W. Somerset Maugham (1874–1965) British novelist. *Of Human Bondage*, Ch. 51

31 Money can't buy friends, but you can get a better class of enemy.
Spike Milligan (1918–) British comic actor and author. *Puckoon*, Ch. 6

32 Money is like manure. If you spread it around it does a lot of good. But if you pile it up in one place it stinks like hell.
Clint Murchison Jnr (1895–1969) US industrialist. Following BACON *Time Magazine*, 16 June 1961

33 Some people's money is merited
And other people's is inherited.
Ogden Nash (1902–71) US poet. *The Terrible People*

34 Check enclosed.
Dorothy Parker (1893–1967) US writer. Giving her version of the two most beautiful words in the English language. Attrib.

35 Money is good for bribing yourself through the inconveniences of life.
Gottfried Reinhardt (1911–) Austrian film producer. *Picture*, 'Looks Like We're Still in Business' (Lillian Ross)

36 My boy . . . always try to rub up against money, for if you rub up against money long enough, some of it may rub off on you.
Damon Runyon (1884–1946) US writer. *Furthermore*, 'A Very Honourable Guy'

37 He that wants money, means, and content, is without three good friends.
William Shakespeare (1564–1616) English dramatist. *As You Like It*, III:2

38 I can get no remedy against this consumption of the purse; borrowing only lingers and lingers it out, but the disease is incurable.
William Shakespeare *Henry IV, Part Two*, I:2

39 Put money in thy purse.
William Shakespeare *Othello*, I:3

40 Lack of money is the root of all evil.
George Bernard Shaw (1856–1950) Irish dramatist and critic. *Man and Superman*, 'Maxims for Revolutionists.'

41 The trouble, Mr Goldwyn is that you are only interested in art and I am only interested in money.
George Bernard Shaw Turning down Goldwyn's offer to buy the screen rights of his plays. *The Movie Moguls* (Philip French), Ch. 4

42 Nothing links man to man like the frequent passage from hand to hand of cash.
Walter Richard Sickert (1860–1942) British impressionist painter. *A Certain World* (W. H. Auden)

43 Pieces of eight!
Robert Louis Stevenson (1850–94) Scottish writer. *Treasure Island*, Ch. 10

44 I think I could be a good woman if I had five thousand a year.
William Makepeace Thackeray (1811–63) British novelist. *Vanity Fair*, Ch. 36

45 No one would have remembered the Good Samaritan if he'd only had good intentions. He had money as well.
Margaret Thatcher (1925–) British politician and prime minister. Television interview, 1980

46 The easiest way for your children to learn about money is for you not to have any.
Katherine Whitehorn (1926–) British journalist. *How to Survive Children*

47 You can be young without money but you can't be old without it.
Tennessee Williams (1911–83) US dramatist. *Cat on a Hot Tin Roof*, I

48 All these financiers, all the little gnomes of Zürich and the other financial centres, about whom we keep on hearing.
Harold Wilson (1916–) British politician and prime minister. Speech, House of Commons, 12 Nov 1956

MONTHS

See also autumn, spring, summer, winter

1 March comes in like a lion and goes out like a lamb.
Proverb

2 Ne'er cast a clout till May be out.
Proverb

3 The cuckoo comes in April, and stays the month of May; sings a song at midsummer, and then goes away.
Proverb

4 Thirty days hath September,
April, June, and November;
All the rest have thirty-one,
Excepting February alone,
And that has twenty-eight days clear
And twenty-nine in each leap year.
Anonymous *See also* GRAFTON Stevins Manuscript, c. 1555

5 There are twelve months in all the year,
As I hear many men say,
But the merriest month in all the year
Is the merry month of May.
Anonymous *Robin Hood and the Widow's Three Sons*

6 And after April, when May follows,

And the whitethroat builds, and all
the swallows!

Robert Browning (1812–89) British poet. *Home Thoughts from Abroad*

7 Whan that Aprille with his shoures
sote
The droghte of Marche hath perced
to the rote.

Geoffrey Chaucer (c. 1342–1400) English poet. *The Canterbury Tales*, Prologue

8 April is the cruellest month,
breeding
Lilacs out of the dead land, mixing
Memory and desire, stirring
Dull roots with spring rain.

T. S. Eliot (1888–1965) US-born British poet and dramatist. *The Waste Land*, 'The Burial of the Dead'

9 Thirty days hath November,
April, June and September,
February hath twenty-eight alone,
And all the rest have thirty-one.

Richard Grafton (d. c. 1572) English chronicler and printer. *Abridgement of the Chronicles of England*, Introduction

10 No warmth, no cheerfulness, no
healthful ease,
No comfortable feel in any member –
No shade, no shine, no butterflies,
no bees,
No fruits, no flowers, no leaves, no
birds, –
November!

Thomas Hood (1799–1845) British poet. *No!*

11 February, fill the dyke
With what thou dost like.

Thomas Tusser (1524–80) English farmer. *Five Hundred Points of Good Husbandry*, 'February's Husbandry'

12 Sweet April showers
Do spring May flowers.

Thomas Tusser *Five Hundred Points of Good Husbandry*, 'April's Husbandry'

MOON

See also astronomy, space, universe

1 I saw the new moon late yestreen
Wi' the auld moon in her arm;
And if we gang to sea master;
I fear we'll come to harm.

Anonymous The 'new moon in the old moon's arms' is generally regarded as a sign of bad weather. Sir Patrick Spens

2 The moving Moon went up the sky,
And no where did abide:
Softly she was going up,
And a star or two beside.

Samuel Taylor Coleridge (1772–1834) British poet. *The Rime of the Ancient Mariner*, IV

3 who knows if the moon's
a balloon, coming out of a keen city
in the sky – filled with pretty
people?

e. e. cummings (1894–1962) US poet. Used for the title and epigraph of David Niven's first volume of autobiography, *The Moon's a Balloon*, about his experiences in the film industry.

4 So sicken waning moons too near
the sun,
And blunt their crescents on the
edge of day.

John Dryden (1631–1700) British poet and dramatist. *Annus Mirabilis*

5 For years politicians have promised
the moon, I'm the first one to be
able to deliver it.

Richard Milhous Nixon (1913–) US president. Radio message to astronauts on the moon, 20 Jul 1969

6 Oh! shine on, shine on, harvest
moon
Up in the sky.
I ain't had no lovin'
Since April, January, June or July.

Jack Norworth (1879–1959) US vaudeville comedian and songwriter. *Shine On, Harvest Moon* (song)

MORALITY

See also integrity, principles, righteousness

1 In his own way each man must struggle, lest the moral law become a far-off abstraction utterly separated from his active life.

Jane Addams (1860–1935) US social worker. *Twenty Years at Hull House*

2 No morality can be founded on authority, even if the authority were divine.

A. J. Ayer (1910–) British philosopher. *Essay on Humanism*

3 Morality's not practical. Morality's a gesture. A complicated gesture learnt from books.

Robert Bolt (1924–) British playwright. *A Man for All Seasons*

4 The propriety of some persons seems to consist in having improper thoughts about their neighbours.

F. H. Bradley (1846–1924) British philosopher. *Aphorisms*

5 Moral indignation is in most cases 2 percent moral, 48 percent indignation and 50 percent envy.

Vittorio De Sica (1901–74) Italian film director. *The Observer*, 1961

6 What is moral is what you feel good after, and what is immoral is what you feel bad after.

Ernest Hemingway (1899–1961) US novelist. *Death in the Afternoon*

7 The quality of moral behaviour varies in inverse ratio to the number of human beings involved.

Aldous Huxley (1894–1964) British novelist. *Grey Eminence*, Ch. 10

8 Finally, there is an imperative which commands a certain conduct immediately . . . This imperative is Categorical . . . This imperative may be called that of Morality.

Immanuel Kant (1724–1804) German philosopher. *Grundlegung zur Metaphysik der Sitten*, II

9 Morality which is based on ideas, or on an ideal, is an unmitigated evil.

D. H. Lawrence (1885–1930) British novelist. *Fantasia of the Unconscious*, Ch. 7

10 We know no spectacle so ridiculous as the British public in one of its periodical fits of morality.

Lord Macaulay (1800–59) British historian. *Literary Essays Contributed to the Edinburgh Review*, 'Moore's Life of Lord Byron'

11 It is a public scandal that gives offence, and it is no sin to sin in secret.

Molière (Jean Baptiste Poquelin; 1622–73) French dramatist. *Tartuffe*, IV:5

12 Morality in Europe today is herd-morality.

Friedrich Wilhelm Nietzsche (1844–1900) German philosopher. *Jenseits von Gut und Böse*

13 We have, in fact, two kinds of morality side by side; one which we preach but do not practise, and another which we practise but seldom preach.

Bertrand Russell (1872–1970) British philosopher. *Sceptical Essays*

14 All universal moral principles are idle fancies.

Marquis de Sade (1740–1814) French novelist. *The 120 Days of Sodom*

15 Without doubt the greatest injury . . . was done by basing morals on myth, for sooner or later myth is recognized for what it is, and disappears. Then morality loses the foundation on which it has been built.

Herbert Samuel (1870–1963) British Liberal statesman. Romanes Lecture, 1947

16 Morality consists in suspecting

other people of not being legally married.
George Bernard Shaw (1856–1950) Irish dramatist and critic. *The Doctor's Dilemma*

17 He never does a proper thing without giving an improper reason for it.
George Bernard Shaw *Major Barbara*, III

18 The so-called new morality is too often the old immorality condoned.
Lord Shawcross (1902–) British Labour politician and lawyer. *The Observer*, 17 Nov 1963

19 'Twas Peter's drift
To be a kind of moral eunuch.
Percy Bysshe Shelley (1792–1822) British poet. *Peter Bell the Third*

20 If your morals make you dreary, depend upon it, they are wrong.
Robert Louis Stevenson (1850–94) Scottish writer. *Across the Plains*

21 Victorian values . . . were the values when our country became great.
Margaret Thatcher (1925–) British politician and prime minister. Television interview, 1982

22 Morals are an acquirement – like music, like a foreign language, like piety, poker, paralysis – no man is born with them.
Mark Twain (Samuel Langhorne Clemens; 1835–1910) US writer. *Seventieth Birthday*

MORTALITY

See also death, equality in death, human condition, immortality, life, life and death, time, transience

1 All men are mortal.
Proverb

2 Mortality, behold and fear!
What a change of flesh is here!
Francis Beaumont (1584–1616) English dramatist. *On the Tombs in Westminster Abbey*

3 That lyf so short, the craft so long to lerne,
Th' assay so hard, so sharp the conquerynge.
Geoffrey Chaucer (c. 1342–1400) English poet. *See also* HIPPOCRATES *The Parliament of Fowls*

4 What argufies pride and ambition?
Soon or late death will take us in tow:
Each bullet has got its commission,
And when our time's come we must go.
Charles Dibdin (1745–1814) British actor and dramatist. *Each Bullet has its Commission*

5 All humane things are subject to decay,
And, when Fate summons, Monarchs must obey.
John Dryden (1631–1700) British poet and dramatist. *Mac Flecknoe*

6 The Wine of Life keeps oozing drop by drop,
The Leaves of Life keep falling one by one.
Edward Fitzgerald (1809–83) British poet. *The Rubáyát of Omar Khayyám* (4th edn.), VIII

7 Is life a boon?
If so, it must befall
That Death, whene'er he call,
Must call too soon.
W. S. Gilbert (1836–1911) British dramatist. The lines are written on Arthur Sullivan's memorial in the Embankment gardens. *The Yeoman of the Guard*, I

8 I was not unaware that I had begotten a mortal.
Goethe (1749–1832) German poet and dramatist. On learning of his son's death. *The Story of Civilization* (W. Durant), Vol. X

9 Man wants but little here below,
Nor wants that little long.
Oliver Goldsmith (1728–74) Irish-born British writer. *Edwin and Angelina, or the Hermit*

10 The boast of heraldry, the pomp of pow'r,
And all that beauty, all that wealth e'er gave,
Awaits alike th' inevitable hour,
The paths of glory lead but to the grave.
Thomas Gray (1716–71) British poet. *Elegy Written in a Country Churchyard*

11 I expect to pass through this world but once; any good thing therefore that I can do, or any kindness that I can show to any fellow-creature, let me do it now; let me not defer or neglect it, for I shall not pass this way again.
Stephen Grellet (1773–1855) French-born US missionary. Attrib. *Treasure Trove* (John o'London)

12 The life so short, the craft so long to learn.
Hippocrates (c. 460–c. 377 BC) Greek physician. Describing medicine. It is often quoted in Latin as *Ars longa, vita brevis,* and interpreted as 'Art lasts, life is short'. *See also* CHAUCER. *Aphorisms*, I

13 Life's short span forbids us to enter on far-reaching hopes.
Horace (Quintus Horatius Flaccus; 65–8 BC) Roman poet. *Odes*, I

14 Art is long, and Time is fleeting,
And our hearts, though stout and brave,
Still, like muffled drums, are beating
Funeral marches to the grave.
Henry Wadsworth Longfellow (1807–82) US poet. *See also* HIPPOCRATES *A Psalm of Life*

15 *Inque brevi spatio mutantur saecla animantum*
Et quasi cursores vitai lampada tradunt.
The generations of living things pass in a short time, and like runners hand on the torch of life.
Lucretius (Titus Lucretius Carus; c. 99–55 BC) Roman philosopher. *On the Nature of the Universe*, II

16 Fear no more the heat o' th' sun
Nor the furious winter's rages;
Thou thy worldly task hast done,
Home art gone, and ta'en thy wages.
Golden lads and girls all must,
As chimney-sweepers, come to dust.
William Shakespeare (1564–1616) English dramatist. *Cymbeline*, IV:2

17 Our revels now are ended. These our actors,
As I foretold you, were all spirits, and
Are melted into air, into thin air;
And, like the baseless fabric of this vision,
The cloud-capp'd towers, the gorgeous palaces,
The solemn temples, the great globe itself,
Yea, all which it inherit, shall dissolve,
And, like this insubstantial pageant faded,
Leave not a rack behind. We are such stuff
As dreams are made on; and our little life
Is rounded with a sleep.
William Shakespeare *The Tempest*, IV:1

18 Old and young, we are all on our last cruise.
Robert Louis Stevenson (1850–94) Scottish writer. *Virginibus Puerisque*

19 The woods decay, the woods decay and fall,
The vapours weep their burthen to the ground,
Man comes and tills the field and lies beneath,
And after many a summer dies the swan.
Alfred, Lord Tennyson (1809–92) British poet. *Tithonus*

20 A power is passing from the earth
To breathless Nature's dark abyss;
But when the great and good depart,
What is it more than this –

That Man who is from God sent forth,
Doth yet again to God return? –
Such ebb and flow must ever be,
Then wherefore should we mourn?

William Wordsworth (1770–1850) British poet. Referring to Charles James Fox, the hero of the liberal Whigs, who died in 1806. *Lines on the Expected Dissolution of Mr. Fox*

21 The clouds that gather round the setting sun
Do take a sober colouring from an eye
That hath kept watch o'er man's mortality.

William Wordsworth *Ode. Intimations of Immortality*, XI

22 I am moved to pity, when I think of the brevity of human life, seeing that of all this host of men not one will still be alive in a hundred years' time.

Xerxes (d. 465 BC) King of Persia. On surveying his army.

23 That is no country for old men. The young
In one another's arms, birds in the trees
– Those dying generations – at their song,
The salmon-falls, the mackerel-crowded seas,
Fish, flesh, or fowl, commend all summer long
Whatever is begotten, born, and dies.

W. B. Yeats (1865–1939) Irish poet. *Sailing to Byzantium*, I

24 Man wants but little, nor that little long.

Edward Young (1683–1765) British poet. *Night Thoughts*

MOTHERS

See family, women

MOTIVE

See also purpose

1 Never ascribe to an opponent motives meaner than your own.

J. M. Barrie (1860–1937) British novelist and dramatist. Speech, St Andrews, 3 May 1922

2 The last temptation is the greatest treason:
To do the right deed for the wrong reason.

T. S. Eliot (1888–1965) US-born British poet and dramatist. *Murder in the Cathedral*, I

3 Because it is there.

George Mallory (1886–1924) British mountaineer. Answer to the question 'Why do you want to climb Mt. Everest?'. *George Mallory* (D. Robertson)

4 Nobody ever did anything very foolish except from some strong principle.

Lord Melbourne (1779–1848) British statesman. *The Young Melbourne* (Lord David Cecil)

5 The heart has its reasons which reason does not know.

Blaise Pascal (1623–62) French philosopher and mathematician. *Pensées*, IV

6 Men are rewarded and punished not for what they do, but rather for how their acts are defined. This is why men are more interested in better justifying themselves than in better behaving themselves.

Thomas Szasz (1920–) US psychiatrist. *The Second Sin*

MOUNTAINS

1 Mountains interposed
Make enemies of nations, who had else,
Like kindred drops, been mingled into one.

William Cowper (1731–1800) British poet. *The Task*

2 Separate from the pleasure of your company, I don't much care if I never see another mountain in my life.

Charles Lamb (1775–1834) British essayist. Letter to William Wordsworth, 30 Jan 1801

3 Mountains are the beginning and the end of all natural scenery.

John Ruskin (1819–1900) British art critic and writer. *Modern Painters*, Vol. IV

4 They say that if the Swiss had designed these mountains they'd be rather flatter.

Paul Theroux (1941–) US-born writer. Referring to the Alps. *The Great Railway Bazaar*, Ch. 28

MOURNING

See also death, loss, regret, sorrow

1 We met . . . Dr Hall in such very deep mourning that either his mother, his wife, or himself must be dead.

Jane Austen (1775–1817) British novelist. Letter to Cassandra Austen, 17 May 1799

2 I am distressed for thee, my brother Jonathan: very pleasant hast thou been unto me: thy love to me was wonderful, passing the love of women.
How are the mighty fallen, and the weapons of war perished!

Bible: II Samuel 1:26–27

3 With proud thanksgiving, a mother for her children,
England mourns for her dead across the sea.

Laurence Binyon (1869–1943) British poet. In response to the slaughter of World War I. *Poems For the Fallen*

4 MEDVEDENKO. Why do you wear black all the time?
MASHA. I'm in mourning for my life, I'm unhappy.

Anton Chekhov (1860–1904) Russian dramatist. *The Seagull*, I

5 There's a one-eyed yellow idol to the north of Khatmandu,
There's a little marble cross below the town;
There's a broken-hearted woman tends the grave of Mad Carew
And the Yellow God forever gazes down.

J. Milton Hayes (1884–1940) British writer. *The Green Eye of the Yellow God*

6 What we call mourning for our dead is perhaps not so much grief at not being able to call them back as it is grief at not being able to want to do so.

Thomas Mann (1875–1955) German novelist. *The Magic Mountain*

7 In a cavern, in a canyon,
Excavating for a mine
Dwelt a miner, Forty-niner,
And his daughter, Clementine.
Oh, my darling, Oh, my darling, Oh, my darling Clementine!
Thou art lost and gone for ever, dreadful sorry, Clementine.

Percy Montrose (19th century) US songwriter. *Clementine*

8 She is far from the land where her young hero sleeps,
And lovers are round her, sighing:
But coldly she turns from their gaze, and weeps,
For her heart in his grave is lying.

Thomas Moore (1779–1852) Irish poet. *Irish Melodies*, 'She is Far'

9 O, wither'd is the garland of the war,
The soldier's pole is fall'n! Young boys and girls
Are level now with men. The odds is gone,
And there is nothing left remarkable

Beneath the visiting moon.
William Shakespeare (1564–1616) English dramatist. *Antony and Cleopatra*, IV:13

10 But I have that within which passes show –
these but the trappings and the suits of woe.
William Shakespeare *Hamlet*, I:2

11 Alas, poor Yorick! I knew him, Horatio: a fellow of infinite jest, of most excellent fancy.
William Shakespeare Often misquoted as 'I knew him well'. *Hamlet*, V:1

12 If thou didst ever hold me in thy heart,
Absent thee from felicity awhile,
And in this harsh world draw thy breath in pain,
To tell my story.
William Shakespeare *Hamlet*, V:2

13 And my poor fool is hang'd! No, no, no life!
Why should a dog, a horse, a rat have life,
And thou no breath at all? Thou'lt come no more,
Never, never, never, never.
William Shakespeare *King Lear*, V:3

14 I weep for Adonais – he is dead!
O, weep for Adonais! though our tears
Thaw not the frost which binds so dear a head!
Percy Bysshe Shelley (1792–1822) British poet. Prompted by the death of Keats. *Adonais*, I

15 A lady asked me why, on most occasions, I wore black. 'Are you in mourning?'
'Yes.'
'For whom are you in mourning?'
'For the world.'
Edith Sitwell (1887–1964) British poet and writer. *Taken Care Of*, Ch. 1

16 Home they brought her warrior dead.
She nor swoon'd, nor utter'd cry:
All her maidens, watching said,
'She must weep or she will die.'
Alfred, Lord Tennyson (1809–92) British poet. *The Princess*, VI

MURDER

See also assassination, crime, killing

1 Lizzie Borden took an axe
And gave her mother forty whacks;
When she saw what she had done
She gave her father forty-one!
Anonymous On 4 Aug 1892 in Fall River, Massachusetts, Lizzie Borden was acquitted of the murder of her stepmother and her father.

2 And the Lord said unto Cain, Where is Abel thy brother? And he said, I know not: Am I my brother's keeper?
And he said, What hast thou done? the voice of thy brother's blood crieth unto me from the ground.
Bible: Genesis 4:9–10

3 I've been accused of every death except the casualty list of the World War.
Al Capone (1899–1947) Italian-born US gangster. *The Bootleggers* (Kenneth Allsop), Ch. 11

4 Mordre wol out, that see we day by day.
Geoffrey Chaucer (c. 1342–1400) English poet. *The Canterbury Tales*, 'The Nun's Priest's Tale'

5 See how love and murder will out.
William Congreve (1670–1729) British Restoration dramatist. *The Double Dealer*, IV:6

6 Murder considered as one of the Fine Arts.
Thomas De Quincey (1785–1859) British writer. Essay title

7 I made a remark a long time ago. I said I was very pleased that television was now showing murder stories, because it's bringing murder back into its rightful setting – in the home.
Alfred Hitchcock (1889–1980) British film director. *The Observer*, 'Sayings of the Week', 17 Aug 1969

8 It takes two to make a murder. There are born victims, born to have their throats cut.
Aldous Huxley (1894–1963) British novelist. *Point Counter Point*

9 Murder, like talent, seems occasionally to run in families.
G. H. Lewes (1817–78) British philosopher and writer. *The Physiology of Common Life*, Ch. 12

10 Murder most foul, as in the best it is;
But this most foul, strange, and unnatural.
William Shakespeare (1564–1616) English dramatist. *Hamlet*, I:5

11 Put out the light, and then put out the light.
If I quench thee, thou flaming minister,
I can again thy former light restore,
Should I repent me; but once put out thy light,
Thou cunning'st pattern of excelling nature,
I know not where is that Promethean heat
That can thy light relume.
William Shakespeare *Othello*, V:2

12 I met Murder on the way –
He had a mask like Castlereagh.
Percy Bysshe Shelley (1792–1822) British poet. Viscount Castlereagh (1769–1822) was British foreign secretary (1812–22); he was highly unpopular and became identified with such controversial events as the Peterloo massacre of 1819. *The Mask of Anarchy*, 5

13 Other sins only speak; murder shrieks out.
John Webster (1580–1625) English dramatist. *The Duchess of Malfi*, IV:2

MUSEUMS

1 The Arab who builds himself a hut out of the marble fragments of a temple in Palmyra is more philosophical than all the curators of the museums in London, Munich or Paris.
Anatole France (Jacques Anatole François Thibault; 1844–1924) French writer. *The Crime of Sylvestre Bonnard*

2 If there was a little room somewhere in the British Museum that contained only about twenty exhibits and good lighting, easy chairs, and a notice imploring you to smoke, I believe I should become a museum man.
J. B. Priestley (1894–1984) British novelist. *Self-Selected Essays*, 'In the British Museum'

3 There is in the British Museum an enormous mind. Consider that Plato is there cheek by jowl with Aristotle; and Shakespeare with Marlowe. This great mind is hoarded beyond the power of any single mind to possess it.
Virginia Woolf (1882–1941) British novelist. *Jacob's Room*, Ch. 9

MUSIC

See also criticism, musicians, opera, singing

1 Music helps not the toothache.
Proverb

2 Nothing is capable of being well set to music that is not nonsense.
Joseph Addison (1672–1719) British essayist. *The Spectator*, 18

3 The music teacher came twice each

week to bridge the awful gap between Dorothy and Chopin.
George Ade (1866–1944) US dramatist and humorist. Attrib.

4 Brass bands are all very well in their place – outdoors and several miles away.
Thomas Beecham (1879–1961) British conductor. Attrib.

5 The English may not like music – but they absolutely love the noise it makes.
Thomas Beecham *The Wit of Music* (L. Ayre)

6 The sound of the harpsichord resembles that of a bird-cage played with toasting-forks.
Thomas Beecham Attrib.

7 A musicologist is a man who can read music but can't hear it.
Thomas Beecham *Beecham Remembered* (H. Procter-Gregg)

8 When I composed that, I was conscious of being inspired by God Almighty. Do you think I can consider your puny little fiddle when He speaks to me?
Ludwig van Beethoven (1770–1827) German composer. Said when a violinist complained that a passage was unplayable. *Music All Around Me* (A. Hopkins)

9 *Fiddle, n.* An instrument to tickle human ears by function of a horse's tail on the entrails of a cat.
Ambrose Bierce (1842–?1914) US writer and journalist. *The Devil's Dictionary*

10 Down South where I come from you don't go around hitting too many white keys.
Eubie Blake (1883–1983) US pianist and ragtime composer. When asked why his compositions contained so many sharps and flats. Attrib.

11 Piping down the valleys wild,
Piping songs of pleasant glee,
On a cloud I saw a child.
William Blake (1757–1827) British poet. *Songs of Innocence*, Introduction

12 'Pipe a song about a Lamb!'
So I piped with merry cheer.
William Blake *Songs of Innocence*, Introduction

13 No one really understood music unless he was a scientist, her father had declared, and not just a scientist, either, oh, no, only the real ones, the theoreticians, whose language was mathematics.
Pearl Buck (1892–1973) US novelist. *The Goddess Abides*, Pt. I

14 Music has charms to soothe a savage breast.
William Congreve (1670–1729) British Restoration dramatist. *The Mourning Bride*, I

15 Strange how potent cheap music is.
Noël Coward (1899–1973) British dramatist. *Private Lives*

16 Music is the arithmetic of sounds as optics is the geometry of light.
Claude Debussy (1862–1918) French composer. Attrib.

17 Music was invented to confirm human loneliness.
Lawrence Durrell (1912–) British novelist. *Clea*

18 Beethoven's Fifth Symphony is the most sublime noise that has ever penetrated into the ear of man.
E. M. Forster (1879–1970) British novelist. *Howards End*, Ch. 5

19 The hills are alive with the sound of music
With the songs they have sung
For a thousand years.
Oscar Hammerstein (1895–1960) US lyricist. *The Sound of Music*, title song

20 I do not see any reason why the devil should have all the good tunes.
Rowland Hill (1744–1833) British clergyman. Attrib.

21 Never compose anything unless the not composing of it becomes a positive nuisance to you.
Gustav Holst (1874–1934) British composer. Letter to W. G. Whittaker

22 I accepted the offer without prompting. I sat down at the piano and quickly lost myself in Schumann's songs, grateful for their power to soothe and to strengthen. If music was difficult enough, its technical demands drove everything else from the mind. But even when it was easy, music's patterning shaped the emotions, pushed uncertainty and apprehension into the formal order of theme development, reprise, dissonance and resolution. Even sad passages were optimistic, reassuring. Music proclaimed an orderly universe, promised a better place. I moved from Schumann to folk songs, then to hymns.
Ellen Hunnicutt US writer. *Suite for Calliope*

23 Since Mozart's day composers have learned the art of making music throatily and palpitatingly sexual.
Aldous Huxley (1894–1964) British novelist. *Along the Road*, 'Popular music'

24 The only sensual pleasure without vice.
Samuel Johnson (1709–84) British lexicographer. Referring to music. *Johnsonian Miscellanies* (ed. G. B. Hill), Vol. II

25 Heard melodies are sweet, but those unheard
Are sweeter; therefore, ye soft pipes, play on.
John Keats (1795–1821) British poet. *Ode on a Grecian Urn*

26 There's sure no passion in the human soul,
But finds its food in music.
George Lillo (1693–1739) English dramatist. *Fatal Curiosity*, I:2

27 Music, Maestro, Please.
Herb Magidson (20th century) US songwriter. Song title

28 Music is not written in red, white and blue. It is written in the heart's blood of the composer.
Nellie Melba (Helen Porter Mitchell; 1861–1931) Australian soprano. *Melodies and Memories*

29 Music creates order out of chaos; for rhythm imposes unanimity upon the divergent, melody imposes continuity upon the disjointed, and harmony imposes compatibility upon the incongruous.
Yehudi Menuhin (1916–) US-born British violinist. *The Sunday Times*, 10 Oct 1976

30 The melting voice through mazes running;
Untwisting all the chains that tie
The hidden soul of harmony.
John Milton (1608–74) English poet. *L'Allegro*

31 The song that we hear with our ears is only the song that is sung in our hearts.
Ouida (Marie Louise de la Ramée; 1839–1908) British novelist. *Wisdom, Wit and Pathos*, 'Ariadne'

32 What a terrible revenge by the culture of the Negroes on that of the whites.
Ignacy Paderewski (1860–1941) Polish pianist, composer, and statesman. Referring to jazz. Attrib.

33 Music is your own experience, your thoughts, your wisdom. If you don't live it, it won't come out of your horn.

Charlie Parker (1920–55) US black jazz musician. *Hear Me Talkin' to Ya* (Nat Shapiro and Nat Hentoff)

34 Music and women I cannot but give way to, whatever my business is.

Samuel Pepys (1633–1703) English diarist. *Diary*, 9 Mar 1666

35 The basic difference between classical music and jazz is that in the former the music is always greater than its performance – whereas the way jazz is performed is always more important than what is being played.

André Previn (1929–) German-born conductor. *An Encyclopedia of Quotations about Music* (Nat Shapiro)

36 Seated one day at the organ,
I was weary and ill at ease,
And my fingers wandered idly
Over the noisy keys.
. . .
But I struck one chord of music,
Like the sound of a great Amen.

Adelaide Anne Procter (1825–64) British poet. Better known in the setting by Sir Arthur Sullivan. *Legends and Lyrics*, 'A Lost Chord'

37 I have already heard it. I had better not go: I will start to get accustomed to it and finally like it.

Nikolai Rimsky-Korsakov (1844–1908) Russian composer. Referring to music by Debussy. *Conversations with Stravinsky* (Robert Craft and Igor Stravinsky)

38 Give me a laundry-list and I'll set it to music.

Gioacchino Rossini (1792–1868) Italian operatic composer. Attrib.

39 To be played with both hands in the pocket.

Erik Satie (1866–1925) French composer. Direction on one of his piano pieces. *The Unimportance of Being Oscar* (O. Levant)

40 The sonatas of Mozart are unique; they are too easy for children, and too difficult for artists.

Artur Schnabel (1882–1951) Austrian concert pianist. *An Encyclopedia of Quotations about Music* (Nat Shapiro)

41 I am never merry when I hear sweet music.

William Shakespeare (1564–1616) English dramatist. *The Merchant of Venice*, V:1

42 The man that hath no music in himself,
Nor is not mov'd with concord of sweet sounds,
Is fit for treasons, stratagems, and spoils.

William Shakespeare *The Merchant of Venice*, V:1

43 If music be the food of love, play on,
Give me excess of it, that, surfeiting,
The appetite may sicken and so die.

William Shakespeare *Twelfth Night*, I:1

44 I wish the Government would put a tax on pianos for the incompetent.

Edith Sitwell (1887–1964) British poet and writer. *Letters, 1916–1964*

45 Jazz will endure just as long as people hear it through their feet instead of their brains.

John Philip Sousa (1854–1932) US composer, conductor, and writer. Attrib.

46 I don't write modern music. I only write good music.

Igor Stravinsky (1882–1971) Russian-born US composer. To journalists on his first visit to America, 1925.

47 My music is best understood by children and animals.

Igor Stravinsky *The Observer*, 'Sayings of the Week', 8 Oct 1961

48 Music that gentlier on the spirit lies,
Than tir'd eyelids upon tir'd eyes.

Alfred, Lord Tennyson (1809–92) British poet. *The Lotos-Eaters*, 'Choric Song'

49 Oh I'm a martyr to music.

Dylan Thomas (1914–53) Welsh poet. *Under Milk Wood*

50 The cello is not one of my favourite instruments. It has such a lugubrious sound, like someone reading a will.

Irene Thomas (1920–) British writer. Attrib.

51 God tells me how he wants this music played – and you get in his way.

Arturo Toscanini (1867–1957) Italian conductor. *Etude* (Howard Tubman)

52 When I play on my fiddle in Dooney,
Folk dance like a wave of the sea.

W. B. Yeats (1865–1939) Irish poet. *The Fiddler of Dooney*

MUSICIANS

See also composers, critics, singers

1 Musicians don't retire; they stop when there's no more music in them.

Louis Armstrong (1900–71) US jazz trumpeter. *The Observer*, 'Sayings of the Week', 21 Apr 1968

2 Of all musicians, flautists are most obviously the ones who know something we don't know.

Paul Jennings (1918–) British humorous writer. *The Jenguin Pennings*, 'Flautists Flaunt Afflatus'

3 The conductor has the advantage of not seeing the audience.

André Kostalenetz (1903–80) Russian-born conductor. Attrib.

4 You see, our fingers are circumcised, which gives it a very good dexterity, you know, particularly in the pinky.

Itzhak Perlman (1945–) Israeli violinist. Responding to an observation that many great violinists are Jewish. *Close Encounters* (M. Wallace)

5 My dear hands. Farewell, my poor hands.

Sergei Rachmaninov (1873–1943) Russian composer. On being informed that he was dying from cancer. *The Great Pianists* (H. Schonberg)

6 Sometimes I think, not so much am I a pianist, but a vampire. All my life I have lived off the blood of Chopin.

Arthur Rubinstein (1887–1982) Polish-born US pianist. Attrib.

7 When a piece gets difficult make faces.

Artur Schnabel (1882–1951) Austrian concert pianist. Advice given to the pianist Vladimir Horowitz. *The Unimportance of Being Oscar* (O. Levant)

8 The notes I handle no better than many pianists. But the pauses between the notes – ah, that is where the art resides.

Artur Schnabel *Chicago Daily News*, 11 June 1958

9 He was the only pianist I have ever seen who did not grimace. That is a great deal.

Igor Stravinsky (1882–1971) Russian-born US composer. Referring to Rachmaninov. *Conversations with Igor Stravinsky* (Igor Stravinsky and Robert Craft)

MYTHS

1 Science must begin with myths, and with the criticism of myths.

Karl Popper (1902–) Austrian-born British philosopher. *British Philosophy in the Mid-Century* (ed. C. A. Mace)

2 A myth is, of course, not a fairy story. It is the presentation of facts belonging to one category in the idioms appropriate to another. To explode a myth is accordingly not to deny the facts but to re-allocate them.
Gilbert Ryle (1900–76) British philosopher. *The Concept of Mind,* Introduction

N

NAKEDNESS

1 My Love in her attire doth show her wit,
It doth so well become her:
For every season she hath dressings fit,
For winter, spring, and summer.
No beauty she doth miss,
When all her robes are on;
But beauty's self she is,
When all her robes are gone.
Anonymous Madrigal

2 Nakedness is uncomely as well in mind, as body.
Francis Bacon (1561–1626) English philosopher. *Essays,* 'Of Simulation and Dissimulation'

3 And he said, I heard thy voice in the garden, and I was afraid, because I was naked; and I hid myself.
And he said, Who told thee that thou wast naked?
Bible: Genesis 3:10–11

4 Naked came I out of my mother's womb, and naked shall I return thither: the Lord gave, and the Lord hath taken away; blessed be the name of the Lord.
Bible: Job 1:21

5 Lives there the man that can figure a naked Duke of Windlestraw addressing a naked House of Lords?
Thomas Carlyle (1795–1881) Scottish historian and essayist. *Sartor Resartus,* Bk. I, Ch. 9

6 a pretty girl who naked is
is worth a million statues.
e. e. cummings (1894–1962) US poet. *Collected Poems,* 133

7 No woman so naked as one you can see to be naked underneath her clothes.
Michael Frayn (1933–) British journalist and writer. *Constructions*

8 The trouble with nude dancing is that not everything stops when the music stops.
Robert Helpmann (1909–86) Australian dancer and choreographer. After the opening night of *Oh, Calcutta!*. *The Frank Muir Book*

9 How idiotic civilization is! Why be given a body if you have to keep it shut up in a case like a rare, rare fiddle?
Katherine Mansfield (1888–1923) New-Zealand-born British writer. *Bliss and Other Stories,* 'Bliss'

10 JOURNALIST. Didn't you have anything on?
M. M. I had the radio on.
Marilyn Monroe (Norma-Jean Baker; 1926–62) US film star. Attrib

NAMES

1 Ball . . . how very singular.
Thomas Beecham (1879–1961) British conductor. To a man called Ball. *Sir Thomas Beecham* (N. Cardus)

2 I don't like your Christian name. I'd like to change it.
Thomas Beecham To his future wife. She replied, 'You can't, but you can change my surname.' Attrib.

3 And Adam called his wife's name Eve; because she was the mother of all living.
Bible: Genesis 3:20

4 Bossom? What an extraordinary name. Neither one thing nor the other!
Winston Churchill (1874–1965) British statesman. Referring to Sir Alfred Bossom MP. *Immortal Jester* (L. Frewin)

5 Known by the *sobriquet* of 'The artful Dodger.'
Charles Dickens (1812–70) British novelist. *Oliver Twist,* Ch. 8

6 I'm called Little Buttercup – dear Little Buttercup,
Though I could never tell why.
W. S. Gilbert (1836–1911) British dramatist. *HMS Pinafore,* I

7 A nickname is the heaviest stone that the devil can throw at a man.
William Hazlitt (1778–1830) British essayist. *Nicknames*

8 Dr. Simpson's first patient, a doctor's wife in 1847, had been so carried away with enthusiasm that she christened her child, a girl, 'Anaesthesia'.
Elizabeth Longford (1906–) British writer. *Queen Victoria,* Ch. 17

9 No, Groucho is not my real name. I'm breaking it in for a friend.
Groucho Marx (Julius Marx; 1895–1977) US comedian. Attrib.

10 Regardless of what they say about it, we are going to keep it.
Richard Milhous Nixon (1913–) US President. Referring to 'Checkers', a dog given to his daughters. He was defending himself against corruption charges. TV address, 23 Sept 1952

11 JAQUÉS. I do not like her name.
ORLANDO. There was no thought of pleasing you when she was christened.
William Shakespeare (1564–1616) English dramatist. *As You Like It,* III:2

12 O Romeo, Romeo! wherefore art thou Romeo?
William Shakespeare *Romeo and Juliet,* II:2

13 What's in a name? That which we call a rose
By any other name would smell as sweet.
William Shakespeare *Romeo and Juliet,* II:2

14 People of wealth and rank never use ugly names for ugly things. Apoplexy is an affection of the head; paralysis is nervousness; gangrene is pain and inconvenience in the extremities.
Sydney Smith (1771–1845) British churchman, essayist, and writer. Letter to Mrs Holland, Jan 1844

15 'It's giving girls names like that', said Buggins, 'that nine times out of ten makes 'em go wrong. It unsettles 'em. If ever I was to have a girl, if ever I was to have a dozen girls, I'd call 'em all Jane.'
H. G. Wells (1866–1946) British writer. Referring to the name Euphemia. *Kipps,* Bk. I, Ch. 4

NARCOTICS

1 There is no flying without wings.
French proverb

2 Opium is pleasing to Turks, on account of the agreeable delirium it produces.

Edmund Burke (1729–97) British politician. *On the Sublime and Beautiful*, 'On Taste'

3 Laudanum gave me repose, not sleep; but you, I believe, know how divine this repose is, what a spot of enchantment, a green spot of fountain and flowers and trees in the very heart of a waste of sands.

Samuel Taylor Coleridge (1772–1834) British poet.

4 Opium gives and takes away. It defeats the steady habit of exertion; but it creates spasms of irregular exertion! It ruins the natural power of life; but it develops preternatural paroxysms of intermitting power.

Thomas De Quincey (1785–1859) English essayist and critic. *Confessions of an English Opium-Eater*, Pt. II

5 Opium . . . the Creator himself seems to prescribe, for we often see the scarlet poppy growing in the cornfields, as if it were foreseen that whatever there is hunger to be fed there must also be pain to be soothed.

Oliver Wendell Holmes (1809–94) US writer and physician. *Medical Essays*, 'Currents and Counter-Currents in Medical Science'

6 Science and art are only too often a superior kind of dope, possessing this advantage over booze and morphia: that they can be indulged in with a good conscience and with the conviction that, in the process of indulging, one is leading the 'higher life'.

Aldous Huxley (1894–1964) British writer. *Ends and Means*, 'Beliefs'

7 Two great European narcotics, alcohol and Christianity.

Friedrich Wilhelm Nietzsche (1844–1900) German philosopher. *The Twilight of the Idols*, 'Things the Germans Lack'

8 To tell the story of Coleridge without the opium is to tell the story of Hamlet without mentioning the Ghost.

Leslie Stephen (1832–1904) British critic. *Hours in a Library*, 'Coleridge'

NASH, Ogden

(1902–71) US poet. He wrote many books of satirical verse, including *I'm a Stranger Here Myself* (1938) and *Collected Verse* (1961).

1 The cow is of the bovine ilk;
One end is moo, the other, milk.

The Cow

2 A door is what a dog is perpetually on the wrong side of.

A Dog's Best Friend Is His Illiteracy

3 To be an Englishman is to belong to the most exclusive club there is.

England Expects

4 Women would rather be right than reasonable.

Frailty, Thy Name Is a Misnomer

5 Home is heaven and orgies are vile
But you need an orgy, once in a while.

Home, 99.44 100% Sweet Home

6 Beneath this slab
John Brown is stowed.
He watched the ads
And not the road.

Lather as You Go

7 Do you think my mind is maturing late,
Or simply rotted early?

Lines on Facing Forty

8 Children aren't happy with nothing to ignore,
And that's what parents were created for.

The Parents

9 I prefer to forget both pairs of glasses and pass my declining years saluting strange women and grandfather clocks.

Peekaboo, I Almost See You

10 I think that I shall never see
A billboard lovely as a tree.
Perhaps unless the billboards fall,
I'll never see a tree at all.

Song of the Open Road

NASTINESS

See also cruelty, hurt

1 But are they all horrid, are you sure they are all horrid?

Jane Austen (1775–1817) British novelist. *Northanger Abbey*, Ch. 6

2 I do not want people to be very agreeable, as it saves me the trouble of liking them a great deal.

Jane Austen Letter, 24 Dec 1798

3 There is an unseemly exposure of the mind, as well as of the body.

William Hazlitt (1778–1830) British essayist. *On Disagreeable People*

4 Because I am a bastard.

Ernest Hemingway (1899–1961) US novelist. When asked why he had deserted his wife for another woman. *Americans in Paris* (B. Morton)

5 He was one of those born neither to obey nor to command, but to be evil to the commander and the obeyer alike. Perhaps there was nothing in life that he had much wanted to do, except to shoot rabbits and hit his father on the jaw, and both these things he had done.

John Masefield (1878–1967) British poet. *The Bird of Dawning*

6 One of the worst things about life is not how nasty the nasty people are. You know that already. It is how nasty the nice people can be.

Anthony Powell (1905–) British novelist. *A Dance to the Music of Time: The Kindly Ones*, Ch. 4

7 I can't see that she could have found anything nastier to say if she'd thought it out with both hands for a fortnight.

Dorothy L. Sayers (1893–1957) British writer. *Busman's Holiday*, 'Prothalamion'

8 'I grant you that he's not two-faced,' I said. 'But what's the use of that when the one face he has got is so peculiarly unpleasant?'

C. P. Snow (1905–80) British novelist. *The Affair*, Ch. 4

9 Malice is like a game of poker or tennis; you don't play it with anyone who is manifestly inferior to you.

Hilde Spiel (1911–) Austrian writer. *The Darkened Room*

NATIONALISM

1 Nationalism is an infantile disease. It is the measles of mankind.

Albert Einstein (1879–1955) German-born US physicist. *Einstein: A Study in Simplicity* (Edwin Muller)

NATIONALITY

See also Americans, British

1 The French are wiser than they seem, and the Spaniards seem wiser than they are.

Francis Bacon (1561–1626) English philosopher. *Essays*, 'Of Seeming Wise'

2 He was born an Englishman and remained one for years.

Brendan Behan (1923–64) Irish playwright. *The Hostage*, I

3 PAT. He was an Anglo-Irishman.
MEG. In the blessed name of God, what's that?
PAT. A Protestant with a horse.
Brendan Behan *The Hostage*, I

4 One of themselves, even a prophet of their own, said, The Cretians are alway liars, evil beasts, slow bellies.
Bible: Titus 1:12

5 England is a paradise for women, and hell for horses: Italy a paradise for horses, hell for women.
Robert Burton (1577–1640) English scholar and explorer. *Anatomy of Melancholy*, Pt. III

6 The Almighty in His infinite wisdom did not see fit to create Frenchmen in the image of Englishmen.
Winston Churchill (1874–1965) British statesman. Speech, House of Commons, 10 Dec 1942

7 For he might have been a Roosian,
A French, or Turk, or Proosian,
Or perhaps Ital-ian!
But in spite of all temptations
To belong to other nations,
He remains an Englishman!
W. S. Gilbert (1836–1911) British dramatist. *HMS Pinafore*, II

8 The Saxon is not like us Normans.
His manners are not so polite.
But he never means anything serious till he talks about justice and right,
When he stands like an ox in the furrow with his sullen set eyes on your own,
And grumbles, 'This isn't fair dealing,' my son, leave the Saxon alone.
Rudyard Kipling (1865–1936) Indian-born British writer. *Norman and Saxon*

9 Great artists have no country.
Alfred de Musset (1810–57) French dramatist and poet. *Lorenzaccio*, I:5

10 I am not an Athenian or a Greek, but a citizen of the world.
Socrates (469–399 BC) Athenian philosopher. *Of Banishment* (Plutarch)

11 Men of England! You wish to kill me because I am a Frenchman. Am I not punished enough in not being born an Englishman?
Voltaire (François-Marie Arouet; 1694–1778) French writer. Addressing an angry London mob who desired to hang him because he was a Frenchman. Attrib.

12 We are all American at puberty; we die French.
Evelyn Waugh (1903–66) British novelist. *Diaries*, 'Irregular Notes', 18 July 1961

NATIONS

See also places

1 The day of small nations has long passed away. The day of Empires has come.
Joseph Chamberlain (1836–1914) British politician. Speech, Birmingham, 12 May 1904

2 What kind of people do they think we are?
Winston Churchill (1874–1965) British statesman. Referring to the Japanese. Speech to US Congress, 26 Dec 1941

3 The nations which have put mankind and posterity most in their debt have been small states – Israel, Athens, Florence, Elizabethan England.
Dean Inge (1860–1954) British churchman. *Wit and Wisdom of Dean Inge* (ed. Marchant)

4 This agglomeration which was called and which still calls itself the Holy Roman Empire was neither holy, nor Roman, nor an empire.
Voltaire (François-Marie Arouet; 1694–1778) French writer. *Essai sur les moeurs et l'esprit des nations*, LXX

NATURE

See also animals, birds, countryside, ecology, fish, flowers, human nature, insects, science

1 Nature is better than a middling doctor.
Chinese proverb

2 All things are artificial, for nature is the art of God.
Thomas Browne (1605–82) English physician and writer. *Religio Medici*, Pt. I

3 Oh, good gigantic smile o' the brown old earth.
Robert Browning (1812–89) British poet. *James Lee's Wife*, VII

4 Ye banks and braes o' bonnie Doon,
How can ye bloom sae fresh and fair?
How can ye chant, ye little birds,
And I sae weary fu' o' care?
Robert Burns (1759–96) Scottish poet. *Ye Banks and Braes*

5 There is a pleasure in the pathless woods,
There is a rapture on the lonely shore,
There is society, where none intrudes,
By the deep Sea, and music in its roar:
I love not Man the less, but Nature more.
Lord Byron (1788–1824) British poet. *Childe Harold's Pilgrimage*, IV

6 Nature admits no lie.
Thomas Carlyle (1795–1881) Scottish historian and essayist. *Latter-Day Pamphlets*, 5

7 Is ditchwater dull? Naturalists with microscopes have told me that it teems with quiet fun.
G. K. Chesterton (1874–1936) British writer. *The Spice of Life*

8 Nature is but a name for an effect
Whose cause is God.
William Cowper (1731–1800) British poet. *The Task*

9 Nature can do more than physicians.
Oliver Cromwell (1599–1658) English soldier and statesman.

10 All my life through, the new sights of Nature made me rejoice like a child.
Marie Curie (1867–1934) Polish chemist. *Pierre Curie*

11 By viewing Nature, Nature's handmaid, art,
Makes mighty things from small beginnings grow.
John Dryden (1631–1700) British poet and dramatist. *Annus Mirabilis*

12 All Nature wears one universal grin.
Henry Fielding (1707–54) British novelist. *Tom Thumb the Great*, I:1

13 Whatever Nature has in store for mankind, unpleasant as it may be, men must accept, for ignorance is never better than knowledge.
Enrico Fermi (1901–54) *Atoms in the Family* (Laura Fermi)

14 Here's good advice for practice: go into partnership with nature; she does more than half the work and asks none of the fee.
Martin H. Fischer (1879–1962) *Fischerisms* (Howard Fabing and Ray Marr)

15 The spectacular advances made in therapeutics by industry during recent years tend to make us forget the medicinal value of plants. Their usefulness is far from negligible; their active principles are manifold and well-balanced.
Paul Fruictier *Grandmother's Secrets* (Jean Palaiseul)

16 Natural science does not simply describe and explain nature, it is

part of the interplay between nature and ourselves.

Werner Heisenberg (1901–76) German physicist. *Physics and Philosophy*

17 We must turn to nature itself, to the observations of the body in health and disease to learn the truth.

Hippocrates (c. 460 BC–c. 377 BC) Greek physician.

18 Man's chief goal in life is still to become and stay human, and defend his achievements against the encroachment of nature.

Eric Hoffer (1902–) US writer and philosopher. *The Temper of Our Time*, 'The Return of Nature'

19 Nature is a benevolent old hypocrite; she cheats the sick and the dying with illusions better than any anodynes.

Oliver Wendell Holmes (1809–94) US writer and physician. *Medical Essays*, 'The Young Practitioner'

20 The axis of the earth sticks out visibly through the center of each and every town or city.

Oliver Wendell Holmes *The Autocrat of the Breakfast Table*, Ch. 6

21 Though you drive away Nature with a pitchfork she always returns.

Horace (Quintus Horatius Flaccus; 65 BC–8 BC) Roman poet. *Epistles*, I

22 Nature is as wasteful of promising young men as she is of fish spawn.

Richard Hughes (1900–) British novelist and playwright. *The Fox in the Attic*

23 The whole of nature is a conjugation of the verb to eat, in the active and the passive.

Dean Inge (1860–1954) British churchman. *Outspoken Essays*

24 In nature there are neither rewards nor punishments – there are consequences.

Robert G. Ingersoll (1833–99) US lawyer and agnostic. *Lectures & Essays*, 'Some Reasons Why'

25 Anything green that grew out of the mould
Was an excellent herb to our fathers of old.

Rudyard Kipling (1865–1936) Indian-born British writer. *Grandmother's Secrets* (Jean Palaiseul)

26 Gentlemen know that fresh air should be kept in its proper place – out of doors – and that, God having given us indoors and out-of-doors, we should not attempt to do away with this distinction.

Rose Macaulay (1889–1958) British writer. *Crewe Train*, Pt. I, Ch. 5

27 Nature is very consonant and conformable with herself.

Isaac Newton (1642–1727) British scientist. *Opticks*, Bk. III

28 It is far from easy to determine whether she has proved a kind parent to man or a merciless stepmother.

Pliny the Elder (Gaius Plinius Secundus; 23–79 AD) Roman scholar. *Natural History*, VII

29 Nature abhors a vacuum.

François Rabelais (1483–1553) French satirist. Attrib.

30 O mickle is the powerful grace that lies in herbs, plants, stones and their true qualities.

William Shakespeare (1564–1616) English dramatist and poet. *Romeo and Juliet*, II

31 Are God and Nature then at strife
That Nature lends such evil dreams?
So careful of the type she seems,
So careless of the single life.

Alfred, Lord Tennyson (1809–92) British poet. *In Memoriam A.H.H.*

32 Nature has always had more power than education.

Voltaire (François Marie Arouet; 1694–1778) French writer and philosopher. *Vie de Molière*

33 Nature is usually wrong.

James Whistler (1834–1903) US painter. *The Gentle Art of Making Enemies*

34 After you have exhausted what there is in business, politics, conviviality, and so on – have found that none of these finally satisfy, or permanently wear – what remains? Nature remains.

Walt Whitman (1819–92) US poet. *Specimen Days*, 'New Themes Entered Upon'

35 A vacuum is a hell of a lot better than some of the stuff that nature replaces it with.

Tennessee Williams (1911–83) US dramatist. *Cat On A Hot Tin Roof*

36 Nature never did betray
The heart that loved her.

William Wordsworth (1770–1850) British poet. *Lines composed a few miles above Tintern Abbey*

37 Earth fills her lap with pleasures of her own:
Yearnings she hath in her own natural kind.

William Wordsworth *Ode. Intimations of Immortality*, VI

38 Another race hath been, and other palms are won.
Thanks to the human heart by which we live,
Thanks to its tenderness, its joys and fears,
To me the meanest flower that blows can give
Thoughts that do often lie too deep for tears.

William Wordsworth *Ode. Intimations of Immortality*, IX

39 Come forth into the light of things,
Let Nature be your Teacher.

William Wordsworth *The Tables Turned*

40 O chestnut tree, great rooted blossomer,
Are you the leaf, the blossom or the bole?
O body swayed to music; O brightening glance,
How can we know the dancer from the dance?

W. B. Yeats (1865–1939) Irish poet. *Among School Children*

NAVY

See also boats, officers, sea, war

1 We joined the Navy, to see the world
And what did we see? We saw the sea.

Irving Berlin (Israel Baline; 1888–) US composer. Song

2 The Royal Navy of England has ever been its greatest defence and ornament; it is its ancient and natural strength, the floating bulwark of the island.

Willian Blackstone (1723–80) British jurist. *Commentaries on the Laws of England*, Bk. I, Ch. 13

3 Ye Mariners of England
That guard our native seas,
Whose flag has braved, a thousand years,
The battle and the breeze –
Your glorious standard launch again
To match another foe!
And sweep through the deep,
While the stormy winds do blow, –
While the battle rages loud and long,
And the stormy winds do blow.

Thomas Campbell (1777–1844) British poet. *Ye Mariners of England*

4 It is upon the navy under the Providence of God that the safety, honour, and welfare of this realm do chiefly attend.

Charles II (1630–1685) King of England. Articles of War

5 Don't talk to me about naval tradition. It's nothing but rum, sodomy, and the lash.
Winston Churchill (1874–1965) British statesman. *Former Naval Person* (Sir Peter Gretton), Ch. 1

6 The British navy always travels first class.
Lord Fisher (1841–1920) British admiral. *The Second World War,* Vol. 1 (W. Churchill)

7 I do not say the French cannot come, I only say they cannot come by sea.
John Jervis, Earl St Vincent (1735–1823) British admiral. Remark to the Cabinet, 1803

8 There were gentlemen and there were seamen in the navy of Charles the Second. But the seamen were not gentlemen; and the gentlemen were not seamen.
Lord Macaulay (1800–59) British historian. *History of England,* Vol. I, Ch. 3

9 England's chief defence depends upon the navy being always ready to defend the realm against invasion.
Philip II (1527–98) King of Spain. Philip, as husband of Mary I, was King-Consort of England (1554–58). Submission to the Privy Council

10 Most men were in fear that the French would invade, but I was always of another opinion, for I always said that, whilst we had a fleet in being, they would not dare to make an attempt.
Earl of Torrington English admiral. Justifying his refusal to give battle to a numerically superior French fleet; when subsequently ordered to do so, he was defeated off Beachy Head (10 July 1690). *The Later Stuarts* (Sir George Clark)

11 The Fleet's lit up. It is like fairyland; the ships are covered with fairy lights.
Thomas Woodroofe (1899–1978) British radio broadcaster. Said during commentary at the Coronation Review of the Royal Navy, May 1937

NAZISM

See also fascism, Germany, Hitler, Jews, World War II

1 *Ein Reich, Ein Volk, Ein Führer.*
One Realm, One People, One Leader
Anonymous Slogan of the Nazi Party; first used at Nuremberg, Sept 1934

2 I herewith commission you to carry out all preparations with regard to . . . a *total solution* of the Jewish question, in those territories of Europe which are under German influence.
Hermann Goering (1893–1946) German leader. *The Rise and Fall of the Third Reich* (William Shirer)

3 Our movement took a grip on cowardly Marxism and from it extracted the meaning of socialism. It also took from the cowardly middle-class parties their nationalism. Throwing both into the cauldron of our way of life there emerged, as clear as a crystal, the synthesis – German National Socialism.
Hermann Goering Speech, Berlin, 9 Apr 1933

4 *Kraft durch Freude.*
Strength through joy.
Robert Ley (1890–1945) German Nazi. German Labour Front slogan

5 The former allies had blundered in the past by offering Germany too little, and offering even that too late, until finally Nazi Germany had become a menace to all mankind.
Allan Nevins (1890–1971) US historian. *Current History,* May 1935

6 In Germany, the Nazis came for the Communists and I didn't speak up because I was not a Communist. Then they came for the Jews and I didn't speak up because I was not a Jew. Then they came for the labor unionists and I didn't speak up because I was not a labor unionist. Then they came for the Catholics and I was a Protestant so I didn't speak up. Then they came for me . . . By that time there was no one to speak up for anyone.
Martin Niemöller (1892–1984) German pastor. *Concise Dictionary of Religious Quotations* (W. Neil)

NECESSITY

1 Beggars can't be choosers.
Proverb

2 Necessity is the mother of invention.
Proverb

3 Needs must when the devil drives.
Proverb

4 Necessity hath no law.
Oliver Cromwell (1599–1658) English soldier and statesman. Speech, Parliament, 12 Sept 1654

5 Necessity is the plea for every infringement of human freedom. It is the argument of tyrants; it is the creed of slaves.
William Pitt the Younger (1759–1806) British statesman. Speech, House of Commons, 18 Nov 1783

6 O, reason not the need! Our basest beggars
Are in the poorest thing superfluous.
Allow not nature more than nature needs,
Man's life is cheap as beast's.
William Shakespeare (1564–1616) English dramatist. *King Lear,* II:4

7 The art of our necessities is strange,
That can make vile things precious.
William Shakespeare *King Lear,* III:2

8 Teach thy necessity to reason thus:
There is no virtue like necessity.
William Shakespeare *Richard II,* I:3

9 I am sworn brother, sweet,
To grim Necessity, and he and I
Will keep a league till death.
William Shakespeare *Richard II,* V:1

10 Necessity knows no law.
Publilius Syrus (1st century BC) Roman dramatist. Attrib.

11 I find no hint throughout the universe
Of good or ill, of blessing or of curse;
I find alone Necessity Supreme.
James Thomson (1834–82) British poet. *The City of Dreadful Night,* XIV

NEGLECT

1 A little neglect may breed mischief, . . . for want of a nail, the shoe was lost; for want of a shoe the horse was lost; and for want of a horse the rider was lost.
Benjamin Franklin (1706–90) US scientist and statesman. *Poor Richard's Almanack*

2 The general idea, of course, in any first-class laundry is to see that no shirt or collar ever comes back twice.
Stephen Leacock (1869–1944) English-born Canadian economist and humorist. *Winnowed Wisdom,* Ch. 6

3 The dust and silence of the upper shelf.
Lord Macaulay (1800–59) British historian. *Literary Essays Contributed to the 'Edinburgh Review',* 'Milton'

4 What time he can spare from the

adornment of his person he devotes to the neglect of his duties.
William Hepworth Thompson (1810–86) British academic. Referring to the Cambridge Professor of Greek, Sir Richard Jebb. *With Dearest Love to All* (M. R. Bobbit), Ch. 7

NEIGHBORS

See also boundaries

1 Love your neighbor, yet pull not down your hedge.
Proverb

2 Thou shalt love thy neighbour as thy self.
Bible: Matthew 22:39

3 My apple trees will never get across
And eat the cones under his pines, I tell him.
He only says, 'Good fences make good neighbours.'
Robert Frost (1875–1963) US poet. *North of Boston*, 'Mending Wall'

4 For it is your business, when the wall next door catches fire.
Horace (Quintus Horatius Flaccus; 65–8 BC) Roman poet. *Epistles*, I

5 Try to keep peace with your neighbours. I have loved war too much; do not copy me in that nor in my extravagance.
Louis XIV (1638–1715) French king. Remark to his great-grandson, the future Louis XV

NEPOTISM

1 The son-in-law also rises.
Anonymous Referring to the film maker Louis B. Mayer promoting David Selznick, his daughter's husband.

2 I am against government by crony.
Harold L. Ickes (1874–1952) US Republican politician. Comment on his resignation as Secretary of the Interior (1946) after a dispute with President Truman

3 I can't see that it's wrong to give him a little legal experience before he goes out to practice law.
John Fitzgerald Kennedy (1917–63) US statesman. On being criticized for making his brother Robert attorney general. *Nobody Said It Better* (M. Ringo)

NEUROSIS

See also psychiatry, psychology

1 The psychotic person knows that two and two make five and is perfectly happy about it; the neurotic person knows that two and two make four, but is terribly worried about it.
Anonymous

2 A mistake which is commonly made about neurotics is to suppose that they are interesting. It is not interesting to be always unhappy, engrossed with oneself, malignant and ungrateful, and never quite in touch with reality.
Cyril Connolly (1903–74) British journalist and writer. *The Unquiet Grave*, Pt. II

3 A man should not strive to eliminate his complexes, but to get into accord with them: they are legitimately what directs his conduct in the world.
Sigmund Freud (1856–1939) Austrian psychoanalyst.

4 There are those who have tried to dismiss his story with a flourish of the Union Jack, a psycho-analytical catchword or a sneer; it should move our deepest admiration and pity. Like Shelley and like Baudelaire, it may be said of him that he suffered, in his own person, the neurotic ills of an entire generation.
Christopher Isherwood (1904–86) British novelist. Referring to T. E. Lawrence. *Exhumations*

5 Neurosis is always a substitute for legitimate suffering.
C. G. Jung (1875–1961) Swiss psychologist.

6 This is, I think, very much the Age of Anxiety, the age of the neurosis, because along with so much that weighs on our minds there is perhaps even more that grates on our nerves.
Louis Kronenberger (1904–) US writer, critic, and editor. *Company Manners*, 'The Spirit of the Age'

7 Modern neurosis began with the discoveries of Copernicus. Science made man feel small by showing him that the earth was not the center of the universe.
Mary McCarthy (1912–) US novelist. *On the Contrary*, 'Tyranny of the Orgasm'

8 Neurotic means he is not as sensible as I am, and psychotic means he's even worse than my brother-in-law.
Karl Menninger (1893–) US psychiatrist.

9 Freud is all nonsense; the secret of neurosis is to be found in the family battle of wills to see who can refuse longest to help with the dishes. The sink is the great symbol of the bloodiness of family life. All life is bad, but family life is worse.
Julian Mitchell (1935–) British writer and dramatist. *As Far as You Can Go*, I, Ch. 1

10 Neurosis has an absolute genius for malingering. There is no illness which it cannot counterfeit perfectly . . . If it is capable of deceiving the doctor, how should it fail to deceive the patient?
Marcel Proust (1871–1922) French novelist. *À la recherche du temps perdu: Le Côté de Guermantes*

11 The 'sensibility' claimed by neurotics is matched by their egotism; they cannot abide the flaunting by others of the sufferings to which they pay an ever increasing attention in themselves.
Marcel Proust *À la recherche du temps perdu: Le Côté de Guermantes*

12 Everything great in the world is done by neurotics; they alone founded our religions and created our masterpieces.
Marcel Proust *The Perpetual Pessimist* (Sagittarius and George)

13 Work and love – these are the basics. Without them there is neurosis.
Theodor Reik

14 Neurosis is the way of avoiding non-being by avoiding being.
Paul Tillich (1886–1965) German-born US theologian. *The Courage to Be*

NEWSPAPERS

See also journalism

1 Top people take The Times.
Anonymous Advertisement

2 *The Times* has made many ministries.
Walter Bagehot (1826–77) British economist and journalist. *The English Constitution*, 'The Cabinet'

3 Deleted by French censor.
James Gordon Bennett (1841–1918) US newspaper owner and editor. Used to fill empty spaces in his papers during World War I when news was lacking. *Americans in Paris* (B. Morton)

4 Price of Herald three cents daily. Five cents Sunday. Bennett.
James Gordon Bennett Telegram to William Randolph Hearst, when he heard that Hearst was trying to buy his paper. *The Life and Death of the Press Barons* (P. Brandon)

5 Reading someone else's newspaper is like sleeping with someone else's wife. Nothing seems to be precisely in the right place, and when you find what you are looking for, it is not clear then how to respond to it.
Malcolm Bradbury (1932–) British academic and novelist. *Stepping Westward*, Bk. I, Ch. 1

6 *The Times* is speechless and takes three columns to express its speechlessness.
Winston Churchill (1874–1965) British statesman. Referring to Irish Home Rule. Speech, Dundee, 14 May 1908

7 I believe it has been said that one copy of *The Times* contains more useful information than the whole of the historical works of Thucydides.
Richard Cobden (1804–65) British politician. Speech, Manchester, 27 Dec 1850

8 Small earthquake in Chile. Not many dead.
Claud Cockburn Put forward as an example of a dull newspaper headline. *I Claud*

9 Nothing is news until it has appeared in *The Times*.
Ralph Deakin (1888–1952) Foreign News Editor of *The Times*. Attrib.

10 All the news that's fit to print.
Adolph Simon Ochs (1858–1935) US newspaper publisher. The motto of the *New York Times*

11 Well, there are only two posh papers on a Sunday – the one you're reading and this one.
John Osborne (1929–) British dramatist. *Look Back in Anger*, I

12 Written by office boys for office boys.
Marquess of Salisbury (1830–1903) British statesman. Reaction to the launch of the *Daily Mail*, 1896. *Northcliffe, an Intimate Biography* (Hamilton Fyfe), Ch. 4

13 The *Pall Mall Gazette* is written by gentlemen for gentlemen.
William Makepeace Thackeray (1811–63) British novelist. *Pendennis*, Ch. 32

14 '*The Beast* stands for strong mutually antagonistic governments everywhere', he said. 'Self-sufficiency at home, self-assertion abroad.'
Evelyn Waugh (1903–66) British novelist. *Scoop*, Bk. I, Ch. 1

15 News is what a chap who doesn't care much about anything wants to read. And it's only news until he's read it. After that it's dead.
Evelyn Waugh *Scoop*, Bk. I, Ch. 5

16 They were not so much published as carried screaming into the street.
H. G. Wells (1866–1946) British writer. *War In the Air*

NEW YORK

1 When an American stays away from New York too long something happens to him. Perhaps he becomes a little provincial, a little dead and afraid.
Sherwood Anderson (1876–1941) US writer. *Letters*

2 . . . New York . . . that unnatural city where every one is an exile, none more so than the American.
Charlotte Perkins Gilman (1860–1935) US writer. *The Living of Charlotte Perkins Gilman*

3 When people come together, flowers always flourish – the air is rich with the aroma of a new spring.
Take New York, the dynamic metropolis. What makes New York so special?
It's the invitation of the Statue of Liberty – give me your tired, your poor, your huddled masses who yearn to breathe free.
Not restricted to English only.
Jesse Jackson (1941–) US politician. Speech, Democratic Party Convention, Atlanta, July 1988

4 I like to walk around Manhattan, catching glimpses of its wild life, the pigeons and cats and girls.
Rex Todhunter Stout (1886–1975) US writer. *Three Witnesses*, 'When a Man Murders'

5 One belongs to New York instantly. One belongs to it as much in five minutes as in five years.
Thomas Wolfe (1900–38) US novelist. *The Web and the Rock*

NIETZSCHE, Friedrich Wilhelm

(1844–1900) German philosopher. His rejection of all religion and his glorification of the superman in *Thus Spake Zarathustra* (1883–92) influenced Nazi philosophy in Germany.

Quotations about Nietzsche

1 Nietzsche . . . was a confirmed Life Force worshipper. It was he who raked up the Superman, who is as old as Prometheus.
George Bernard Shaw (1856–1950) Irish dramatist and critic. *Man and Superman*, Act 3

Quotations by Nietzsche

2 When a man is in love he endures more than at other times; he submits to everything.
The Antichrist

3 God created woman. And boredom did indeed cease from that moment – but many other things ceased as well! Woman was God's *second* mistake.
The Antichrist

4 I call Christianity the one great curse, the one enormous and innermost perversion, the one great instinct of revenge, for which no means are too venomous, too underhand, too underground and too petty – I call it the one immortal blemish of mankind.
The Antichrist

5 God is dead: but considering the state the species Man is in, there will perhaps be caves, for ages yet, in which his shadow will be shown.
Die Fröhliche Wissenschaft, Bk. III

6 Believe me! The secret of reaping the greatest fruitfulness and the greatest enjoyment from life is to *live dangerously!*
Die Fröhliche Wissenschaft, Bk. IV

7 As an artist, a man has no home in Europe save in Paris.
Ecce Homo

8 My time has not yet come either; some are born posthumously.
Ecce Homo

9 My doctrine is: Live that thou mayest desire to live again – that is thy duty – for in any case thou wilt live again!
Eternal Recurrence

10 Do you really believe that the sciences would ever have originated and grown if the way had not been prepared by magicians, alchemists, astrologers and witches whose promises and pretensions first had to create a thirst, a hunger, a taste for *hidden* and *forbidden* powers? Indeed, infinitely more had to be *promised* than could ever be fulfilled in order that anything at all might

be fulfilled in the realms of knowledge.
The Gay Science

11 The thought of suicide is a great source of comfort: with it a calm passage is to be made across many a bad night.
Jenseits von Gut und Böse

12 Morality in Europe today is herd-morality.
Jenseits von Gut und Böse

13 Is not life a hundred times too short for us to bore ourselves?
Jenseits von Gut und Böse

14 In the philosopher there is nothing whatever impersonal; and, above all, his morality bears decided and decisive testimony to *who he is* – that is to say, to the order of rank in which the innermost drives of his nature stand in relation to one another.
Jenseits von Gut und Böse

15 Insects sting, not from malice, but because they want to live. It is the same with critics – they desire our blood, not our pain.
Miscellaneous Maxims and Reflections

16 He who does not need to lie is proud of not being a liar.
Nachgelassene Fragmente

17 I teach you the Superman. Man is something that is to be surpassed.
Thus Spake Zarathustra

18 To show pity is felt as a sign of contempt because one has clearly ceased to be an object of *fear* as soon as one is pitied.
The Wanderer and His Shadow

NIGHT

1 It's one of the tragic ironies of the theater that only one man in it can count on steady work – the night watchman.
Tallulah Bankhead (1903–68) US actress. *Tallulah*, Ch. 1

2 In the beginning God created the heaven and the earth.
And the earth was without form, and void; and darkness was upon the face of the deep. And the Spirit of God moved upon the face of the waters.
And God said, Let there be light: and there was light.
And God saw the light, that it was good: and God divided the light from the darkness.
And God called the light Day, and the darkness he called Night. And the evening and the morning were the first day.
Bible: Genesis 1:1–5

3 There was a sound of revelry by night,
And Belgium's capital had gather'd then
Her Beauty and her Chivalry, and bright
The lamps shone o'er fair women and brave men.
Lord Byron (1788–1824) British poet. *Childe Harold's Pilgrimage*, III

4 So, we'll go no more a roving
So late into the night,
Though the heart be still as loving,
And the moon be still as bright.
Lord Byron *So, we'll go no more a roving*

5 The Summer hath his joys,
And Winter his delights.
Though Love and all his pleasures are but toys,
They shorten tedious nights.
Thomas Campion (1567–1620) English poet. *Now Winter Nights Enlarge*

6 It ain't a fit night out for man or beast.
W. C. Fields (1880–1946) US actor. *The Fatal Glass of Beer*

7 I remember, I remember,
The house where I was born,
The little window where the sun
Came peeping in at morn;
He never came a wink too soon,
Nor brought too long a day,
But now, I often wish the night
Had borne my breath away!
Thomas Hood (1799–1845) British poet. *I Remember*

8 Ships that pass in the night, and speak each other in passing;
Only a signal shown and a distant voice in the darkness;
So on the ocean of life we pass and speak one another,
Only a look and a voice; then darkness again and a silence.
Henry Wadsworth Longfellow (1807–82) US poet. *Tales of a Wayside Inn*, 'The Theologian's Tale. Elizabeth'

9 The thought of suicide is a great source of comfort: with it a calm passage is to be made across many a bad night.
Friedrich Wilhelm Nietzsche (1844–1900) German philosopher. *Jenseits von Gut und Bose*

10 The weariest nights, the longest days, sooner or later must perforce come to an end.
Baroness Orczy (1865–1947) British novelist. *The Scarlet Pimpernel*, Ch. 22

11 Come into the garden, Maud,
For the black bat, night, has flown,
Come into the garden, Maud,
I am here at the gate alone.
Alfred, Lord Tennyson (1809–92) British poet. *Maud*, I

NIXON, Richard Milhous

(1913–) US president. A republican, he became president in 1969 and was responsible for ending the US commitment in Vietnam (1973). He was forced to resign after the Watergate scandal (1974), but was pardoned by his successor, President Ford.

Quotations about Nixon

1 President Nixon's motto was, if two wrongs don't make a right, try three.
Norman Cousins *Daily Telegraph*, 17 July 1969

2 Nixon is the kind of politician who would cut down a redwood tree and then mount the stump to make a speech for conservation.
Adlai Stevenson (1900–65) US statesman. Attrib.

Quotations by Nixon

3 There can be no whitewash at the White House.
Referring to the Watergate scandal. *The Observer*, 'Sayings of the Week', 30 Dec 1973

4 I let down my friends, I let down my country. I let down our system of government.
The Observer, 'Sayings of the Week', 8 May 1977

5 You won't have Nixon to kick around any more, gentlemen. This is my last Press Conference.
After losing the election for governorship of California. Press conference, 2 Nov 1962

6 Let us begin by committing ourselves to the truth, to see it like it is and to tell it like it is, to find the truth, to speak the truth and live with the truth. That's what we'll do.
Accepting their nomination as presidential candidate. Speech, Republican Convention, Miami, 8 Aug 1968

7 It is time for the great silent majority of Americans to stand up and be counted.
Election speech, Oct 1970

8 This is the greatest week in the history of the world since the creation.
Said when men first landed on the moon. Attrib., 24 July 1969

9 I am not a crook.
Attrib., 17 Nov 1973

NOBILITY

See also aristocracy, honor

1 There is surely a piece of divinity in us, something that was before the elements, and owes no homage unto the sun.
Thomas Browne (1605–82) English physician and writer. *Religio Medici*, Pt. II

2 Real nobility is based on scorn, courage, and profound indifference.
Albert Camus (1913–60) French existentialist writer. *Notebooks*

3 *Noblesse oblige.*
Nobility has its own obligations.
Duc de Lévis (1764–1830) French writer and soldier. *Maximes et Réflexions*

4 The high sentiments always win in the end, the leaders who offer blood, toil, tears and sweat always get more out of their followers than those who offer safety and a good time. When it comes to the pinch, human beings are heroic.
George Orwell (Eric Blair; 1903–50) British novelist. *The Art of Donald McGill*

5 This was the noblest Roman of them all.
All the conspirators save only he
Did that they did in envy of great Caesar.
William Shakespeare (1564–1616) English dramatist. *Julius Caesar*, V:5

6 His life was gentle, and the elements
So mixed in him that Nature might stand up
And say to all the world, 'This was a man!'
William Shakespeare *Julius Caesar*, V:5

7 Thou hast a grim appearance, and thy face
Bears a command in't; though thy tackle's torn,
Thou show'st a noble vessel. What's thy name?
William Shakespeare *Coriolanus*, IV:5

8 There is
One great society alone on earth:
The noble living and the noble dead.
William Wordsworth (1770–1850) British poet. *The Prelude*, XI

9 Thy soul was like a star, and dwelt apart.
William Wordsworth *Sonnets*, 'Milton! thou shouldst'

NONCOMMITMENT

1 We know what happens to people who stay in the middle of the road. They get run over.
Aneurin Bevan (1897–1960) British Labour politician. *The Observer*, 'Sayings of the Week', 9 Dec 1953

2 Let them eat the lie and swallow it with their bread. Whether the two were lovers or no, they'll have accounted to God for it by now. I have my own fish to fry.
Miguel de Cervantes (1547–1616) Spanish novelist. *Don Quixote*, Pt. I, Ch. 25

3 The Right Hon. gentleman has sat so long on the fence that the iron has entered his soul.
David Lloyd George (1863–1945) British Liberal statesman. Referring to Sir John Simon. Attrib.

NONSENSE

See also humor

1 If all the world were paper,
And all the sea were ink,
And all the trees were bread and cheese,
What should we do for drink?
Anonymous *If All the World were Paper*

2 If ever there was a case of clearer evidence than this of persons acting in concert together, this case is that case.
William Arabin (1773–1841) British judge. *Arabinesque at Law* (Sir R. Megarry)

3 The fleas that tease in the high Pyrenees.
Hilaire Belloc (1870–1953) French-born British poet. *Tarantella*

4 What happens to the hole when the cheese is gone?
Bertolt Brecht (1898–1956) German dramatist. *Mother Courage*, VI

5 Twinkle, twinkle, little bat!
How I wonder what you're at!
Up above the world you fly!
Like a teatray in the sky.
Lewis Carroll (Charles Lutwidge Dodgson; 1832–98) British writer. *Alice's Adventures in Wonderland*, Ch. 7

6 For the Snark *was* a Boojum, you see.
Lewis Carroll *The Hunting of the Snark*

7 'Twas brillig, and the slithy toves
Did gyre and gimble in the wabe;
All mimsy were the borogoves,
And the mome raths outgrabe.
Lewis Carroll *Through the Looking-Glass*, Ch. 1

8 Now, *here*, you see, it takes all the running *you* can do, to keep in the same place. If you want to get somewhere else, you must run at least twice as fast as that!
Lewis Carroll *Through the Looking-Glass*, Ch. 2

9 'The time has come,' the Walrus said,
'To talk of many things:
Of shoes – and ships – and sealing-wax –
Of cabbages – and kings –
And why the sea is boiling hot –
And whether pigs have wings.'
Lewis Carroll *Through the Looking-Glass*, Ch. 4

10 Colourless green ideas sleep furiously.
Noam Chomsky (1928–) US academic linguist. Used by Chomsky to demonstrate that an utterance can be grammatical without having meaning. *Syntactic Structures*

11 Go, and catch a falling star,
Get with child a mandrake root,
Tell me, where all past years are,
Or who cleft the Devil's foot.
John Donne (1573–1631) English poet. *Go and Catch a Falling Star*

12 Gertrude Stein is the mama of dada.
Clifton Fadiman (1904–) US writer. Attrib.

13 So she went into the garden to cut a cabbage-leaf; to make an apple-pie; and at the same time a great she-bear, coming up the street, pops its head into the shop. 'What! no soap?' So he died, and she very imprudently married the barber; and there were present the Picninnies, and the Joblillies, and the Garyalies, and the grand Panjandrum himself, with the little round button at top, and they all fell to playing the game of catch as catch can, till the gun powder ran out at the heels of their boots.
Samuel Foote (1720–77) British actor and dramatist. Nonsense composed to test the actor Charles Macklin's claim that he could memorize anything.

14 If the man who turnips cries,

Cry not when his father dies,
'Tis a proof that he had rather
Have a turnip than his father.

Samuel Johnson (1709–84) British lexicographer. *Johnsonian Miscellanies* (ed. G. B. Hill), Vol. I

15 Three quarks for Muster Mark!

James Joyce (1882–1941) Irish novelist. The word quark has since been adopted by physicists for hypothetical elementary particles. *Finnegans Wake*

16 Lord Ronald said nothing; he flung himself from the room, flung himself upon his horse and rode madly off in all directions.

Stephen Leacock (1869–1944) English-born Canadian economist and humorist. *Nonsense Novels*, 'Gertrude the Governess'

17 On the Coast of Coromandel
Where the early pumpkins blow,
In the middle of the woods
Lived the Yonghy-Bonghy-Bò.

Edward Lear (1812–88) British artist and writer. *The Courtship of the Yonghy-Bonghy-Bò*

18 The Dong! – the Dong!
The wandering Dong through the forest goes!
The Dong! – the Dong!
The Dong with a luminous Nose!

Edward Lear *The Dong with a Luminous Nose*

19 Far and few, far and few,
Are the lands where the Jumblies live;
Their heads are green, and their hands are blue,
And they went to sea in a sieve.

Edward Lear *The Jumblies*

20 He has many friends, laymen and clerical.
Old Foss is the name of his cat:
His body is perfectly spherical,
He weareth a runcible hat.

Edward Lear *Nonsense Songs*, Preface

21 The Owl and the Pussy-Cat went to sea
In a beautiful pea-green boat,
They took some honey, and plenty of money,
Wrapped up in a five-pound note.

Edward Lear *The Owl and the Pussy-Cat*

22 Serve up in a clean dish, and throw the whole out of the window as fast as possible.

Edward Lear *To make an Amblongus Pie*

23 As I was going up the stair
I met a man who wasn't there.
He wasn't there again to-day.
I wish, I wish he'd stay away.

Hughes Mearns (1875–1965) US writer. *The Psychoed*

24 I'm walking backwards till Christmas.

Spike Milligan (1918–) British comic actor and author. *The Goon Show*

NORMALITY

1 She always says she dislikes the abnormal, it is so obvious. She says the normal is so much more simply complicated and interesting.

Gertrude Stein (1874–1946) US writer. *The Autobiography of Alice B. Toklas*

2 My suit is pale yellow. My nationality is French, and my normality has been often subject to question.

Tennessee Williams (1911–83) US dramatist. *Camino Real*, Block 4

NOSTALGIA

See also homesickness, memory, past, regret

1 Were we closer to the ground as children, or is the grass emptier now?

Alan Bennett (1934–) British playwright. *Forty Years On*

2 Play it, Sam. Play 'As Time Goes By.'

Humphrey Bogart (1899–1957) US film star. Often misquoted as 'Play it again, Sam'. *Casablanca*

3 Stands the Church clock at ten to three?
And is there honey still for tea?

Rupert Brooke (1887–1915) British poet. *The Old Vicarage, Grantchester*

4 John Anderson my jo, John,
When we were first acquent,
Your locks were like the raven,
Your bonnie brow was brent.

Robert Burns (1759–96) Scottish poet. *John Anderson My Jo*

5 The 'good old times' – all times when old are good –
Are gone.

Lord Byron (1788–1824) British poet. *The Age of Bronze*, I

6 Nothing recalls the past so potently as a smell.

Winston Churchill (1874–1965) British statesman. *My Early Life*

7 What peaceful hours I once enjoyed!
How sweet their memory still!
But they have left an aching void
The world can never fill.

William Cowper (1731–1800) British poet. *Olney Hymns*, 1

8 I'm sitting on the stile, Mary,
Where we sat, side by side.

Countess of Dufferin (1807–67) British poet. *Lament of the Irish Emigrant*

9 Despair abroad can always nurse pleasant thoughts of home.

Christopher Fry (1907–) British dramatist. *A Phoenix Too Frequent*

10 I remember, I remember,
The house where I was born,
The little window where the sun
Came peeping in at morn;
He never came a wink too soon,
Nor brought too long a day,
But now, I often wish the night
Had borne my breath away!

Thomas Hood (1799–1845) British poet. *I Remember*

11 Into my heart an air that kills
From yon far country blows:
What are those blue remembered hills,
What spires, what farms are those?

A. E. Housman (1859–1936) British scholar and poet. *A Shropshire Lad*, 'The Welsh Marches'

12 With rue my heart is laden
For golden friends I had,
For many a rose-lipt maiden
And many a lightfoot lad.

A. E. Housman *A Shropshire Lad*, 'The Welsh Marches'

13 I have had playmates, I have had companions
In my days of childhood, in my joyful schooldays –
All, all are gone, the old familiar faces.

Charles Lamb (1775–1834) British essayist. *The Old Familiar Faces*

14 . . . the glamour
Of childish days is upon me, my manhood is cast
Down in the flood of remembrance, I weep like a child for the past.

D. H. Lawrence (1885–1930) British novelist. *Piano*

15 Yesterday, all my troubles seemed so far away.

John Lennon (1940–80) British rock musician. *Yesterday* (with Paul McCartney)

16 For love that time was not as love is nowadays.

Thomas Malory (1400–71) English writer. *Morte d'Arthur*, Bk. XX, Ch. 3

17 Oft in the stilly night,
Ere Slumber's chain has bound me,

Fond Memory brings the light
Of other days around me;
The smiles, the tears,
Of boyhood's years,
The words of love then spoken;
The eyes that shone,
Now dimmed and gone,
The cheerful hearts now broken!

Thomas Moore (1779–1852) Irish poet. *National Airs*, 'Oft in the Stilly Night'

18 Fings Ain't Wot They Used T'Be.

Frank Norman (1931–) British dramatist and broadcaster. Title of musical

19 Before the war, and especially before the Boer War, it was summer all the year round.

George Orwell (Eric Blair; 1903–50) British novelist. *Coming Up for Air*, Pt. II, Ch. 1

20 They spend their time mostly looking forward to the past.

John Osborne (1929–) British dramatist. *Look Back in Anger*, II:1

21 The earth's about five thousand million years old. Who can afford to live in the past?

Harold Pinter (1930–) British dramatist. *The Homecoming*

22 Come to me in the silence of the night;
Come in the speaking silence of a dream;
Come with soft rounded cheeks and eyes as bright
As sunlight on a stream;
Come back in tears,
O memory, hope, love of finished years.

Christina Rossetti (1830–74) British poet. *Echo*

23 We have seen better days.

William Shakespeare (1564–1616) English dramatist. *Timon of Athens*, IV:2

24 And the stately ships go on
To their haven under the hill;
But O for the touch of a vanish'd hand,
And the sound of a voice that is still!

Alfred, Lord Tennyson (1809–92) British poet. *Break, Break, Break*

25 For now I see the true old times are dead,
When every morning brought a noble chance,
And every chance brought out a noble knight.

Alfred, Lord Tennyson *Idylls of the King*, 'The Passing of Arthur'

26 Dear as remembered kisses after death,
And sweet as those by hopeless fancy feign'd
On lips that are for others: deep as love,
Deep as first love, and wild with all regret;
O Death in Life, the days that are no more.

Alfred, Lord Tennyson *The Princess*, IV

27 *Mais où sont les neiges d'antan?*
But where are the snows of yesteryear?

François Villon (1431–85) French poet. *Ballade des dames du temps jadis*

28 Where are the boys of the Old Brigade?

Frederic Edward Weatherly (1848–1929) British lawyer and songwriter. *The Old Brigade*

29 Sweet childish days, that were as long
As twenty days are now.

William Wordsworth (1770–1850) British poet. *To a Butterfly, I've Watched You Now*

NOTHING

1 Nothing can be created out of nothing.

Lucretius (Titus Lucretius Carus; c. 99–55 BC) Roman philosopher. *On the Nature of the Universe*, I

2 Nothing will come of nothing. Speak again.

William Shakespeare (1564–1616) English dramatist. *King Lear*, I:1

NOVELS

See also books, criticism, fiction, literature, writers, writing

1 My scrofulous French novel
On grey paper with blunt type!

Robert Browning (1812–89) British poet. *Soliloquy of the Spanish Cloister*

2 A good novel tells us the truth about its hero; but a bad novel tells us the truth about its author.

G. K. Chesterton (1874–1936) British writer. *Heretics*, Ch. 15

3 When I want to read a novel I write one.

Benjamin Disraeli (1804–81) British statesman. Attrib.

4 Yes – oh dear, yes – the novel tells a story.

E. M. Forster (1879–1970) British novelist. *Aspects of the Novel*, Ch. 2

5 The romance of *Tom Jones*, that exquisite picture of human manners, will outlive the palace of the Escurial and the imperial eagle of the house of Austria.

Edward Gibbon (1737–94) British historian. *Autobiography*

6 Historians tell the story of the past, novelists the story of the present.

Edmond de Goncourt (1822–96) French novelist. *Journal*

7 The only obligation to which in advance we may hold a novel, without incurring the accusation of being arbitrary, is that it be interesting.

Henry James (1843–1916) US novelist. *Partial Portraits*, 'The Art of Fiction'

8 It's an odd thing, but now one knows it's profoundly moral and packed with deep spiritual significance a lot of the old charm seems to have gone.

Osbert Lancaster (1908–86) British cartoonist. Referring to *Lady Chatterley's Lover*, after the obscenity trial. Caption to cartoon in the *Daily Express*

9 Far too many relied on the classic formula of a beginning, a muddle, and an end.

Philip Larkin (1922–85) British poet. Referring to modern novels. *New Fiction*, 15 (Jan 1978)

10 I am a man, and alive . . . For this reason I am a novelist. And being a novelist, I consider myself superior to the saint, the scientist, the philosopher, and the poet, who are all great masters of different bits of man alive, but never get the whole hog.

D. H. Lawrence (1885–1930) British novelist. *Phoenix*, 'Why the Novel Matters'

11 I would sooner read a time-table or a catalogue than nothing at all. They are much more entertaining than half the novels that are written.

W. Somerset Maugham (1874–1965) British novelist. *The Summing Up*

12 An interviewer asked me what book I thought best represented the modern American woman. All I could think of to answer was: *Madame Bovary*.

Mary McCarthy (1912–) US novelist. *On the Contrary*

13 People think that because a novel's invented, it isn't true. Exactly the reverse is the case. Biography and memoirs can never be wholly true, since they cannot include every

conceivable circumstance of what happened. The novel can do that.
Anthony Powell (1905–) British novelist. *A Dance to the Music of Time: Hearing Secret Harmonies*, Ch. 3

14 The detective novel is the art-for-art's-sake of yawning Philistinism.
V. S. Pritchett (1900–) British short-story writer. *Books in General*, 'The Roots of Detection'

15 It is the sexless novel that should be distinguished: the sex novel is now normal.
George Bernard Shaw (1856–1950) Irish dramatist and critic. *Table-Talk of G.B.S.*

16 A novel is a mirror walking along a main road.
Stendhal (Henri Beyle; 1783–1842) French novelist. *Le rouge et le noir*, Ch. 49

17 A novel is a static thing that one moves through; a play is a dynamic thing that moves past one.
Kenneth Tynan (1927–80) British theater critic. *Curtains*

18 The novel being dead, there is no point to writing made-up stories. Look at the French who will not and the Americans who cannot.
Gore Vidal (1925–) US novelist. *Myra Breckinridge*, Ch. 2

NOVELTY

See also conservatism, innovation, progress

1 All the rivers run into the sea; yet the sea is not full; unto the place from whence the rivers come, thither they return again.
All things are full of labour; man cannot utter it: the eye is not satisfied with seeing, nor the ear filled with hearing.
The thing that hath been, it is that which shall be; and that which is done is that which shall be done: and there is no new thing under the sun.
Bible: Ecclesiastes 1:7–9

2 Most of the change we think we see in life
Is due to truths being in and out of favour.
Robert Frost (1875–1963) US poet. *The Black Cottage*

3 There are three things which the public will always clamour for, sooner or later: namely, Novelty, novelty, novelty.
Thomas Hood (1799–1845) British poet. Announcement of *Comic Annual*, 1836

4 It is the customary fate of new truths to begin as heresies and to end as superstitions.
T. H. Huxley (1825–95) British biologist. *The Coming of Age of the Origin of Species*

5 New opinions are always suspected, and usually opposed, without any other reason but because they are not already common.
John Locke (1632–1704) English philosopher. *An Essay Concerning Human Understanding*, dedicatory epistle

6 Rummidge . . . had lately suffered the mortifying fate of most English universities of its type (civic redbrick): having competed strenuously for fifty years with two universities chiefly valued for being old, it was, at the moment of drawing level, rudely overtaken in popularity and prestige by a batch of universities chiefly valued for being new.
David Lodge (1935–) British author. *Changing Places*, Ch. 1

7 There are no new truths, but only truths that have not been recognized by those who have perceived them without noticing.
Mary McCarthy (1912–) US novelist. *On the Contrary*

8 There is always something new out of Africa.
Pliny the Elder (Gaius Plinius Secundus; 23–79 AD) Roman scholar. *Natural History*, VIII

9 All great truths begin as blasphemies.
George Bernard Shaw (1856–1950) Irish dramatist and critic. *Annajanska*

10 If we do not find anything pleasant, at least we shall find something new.
Voltaire (François-Marie Arouet; 1694–1778) French writer. *Candide*, Ch. 17

NUCLEAR WEAPONS

See also weapons

1 Ban the bomb.
Anonymous Slogan of nuclear disarmament campaigners

2 Better red than dead.
Anonymous Slogan of the British nuclear disarmament movement

3 Now we are all sons of bitches.
Kenneth Bainbridge (1904–) US physicist. After the first atomic test. *The Decision to Drop the Bomb*

4 If you carry this resolution and follow out all its implications and do not run away from it you will send a Foreign Minister, whoever he may be, naked into the conference chamber.
Aneurin Bevan (1897–1960) British Labour politician. Opposing a motion advocating unilateral nuclear disarmament. Speech, Labour Party Conference, 3 Oct 1957

5 The way to win an atomic war is to make certain it never starts.
Omar Nelson Bradley (1893–1981) US general. *The Observer*, 'Sayings of the Week', 20 Apr 1952

6 The Bomb brought peace but man alone can keep that peace.
Winston Churchill (1874–1965) British statesman. Speech, House of Commons, 16 Aug 1945

7 If only I had known, I should have become a watchmaker.
Albert Einstein (1879–1955) German-born US physicist. Reflecting on his role in the development of the atom bomb. *New Statesman*, 16 Apr 1965

8 Surely the right course is to test the Russians, not the bombs.
Hugh Gaitskell (1906–63) British Labour politician. *The Observer*, 'Sayings of the Week', 23 June 1957

9 We thus denounce the false and dangerous program of the arms race, of the secret rivalry between peoples for military superiority.
John Paul II (Karol Wojtyla; 1920–) Polish pope (1978–). *The Observer*, 'Sayings of the Week', 19 Dec 1976

10 Preparing for suicide is not a very intelligent means of defence.
Bruce Kent (1929–) British campaigner for nuclear disarmament. *The Observer*, 'Sayings of the Week', 10 Aug 1986

11 Hitherto man had to live with the idea of death as an individual; from now onward mankind will have to live with the idea of its death as a species.
Arthur Koestler (1905–83) Hungarian-born British writer. Referring to the development of the atomic bomb. *Peter's Quotations* (Laurence J. Peter)

12 The statesmen of the world who boast and threaten that they have Doomsday weapons are far more dangerous, and far more estranged from 'reality', than many of the people on whom the label 'psychotic' is affixed.
R. D. Laing (1927–) British psychiatrist. *The Divided Self*, Preface

13 At first it was a giant column that

soon took the shape of a supramundane mushroom.

William L. Laurence (1888–1977) US journalist. Referring to the explosion of the first atomic bomb, over Hiroshima, 6 Aug 1945. *The New York Times*, 26 Sept 1945

14 The atom bomb is a paper tiger which the United States reactionaries use to scare people.

Mao Tse-Tung (1893–1976) Chinese communist leader. Interview, Aug 1946

15 As a military man who has given half a century of active service, I say in all sincerity that the nuclear arms race has no military purpose. Wars cannot be fought with nuclear weapons; their existence only adds to our perils because of the illusions which they have generated.

Earl Mountbatten of Burma (1900–79) British admiral and statesman. Speech, Strasbourg, 11 May 1979

16 I am become death, the destroyer of worlds.

J. Robert Oppenheimer (1904–67) US physicist. Quoting Vishnu from the *Gita*, at the first atomic test in New Mexico, 16 July 1945. Attrib.

17 We knew the world would not be the same.

J. Robert Oppenheimer After the first atomic test. *The Decision to Drop the Bomb*

18 It was on this issue, the nuclear defence of Britain, on which I left the Labour Party, and on this issue I am prepared to stake my entire political career.

David Owen (1938–) British politician. *The Observer*, 'Sayings of the Week', 9 Nov 1986

19 Building up arms is not a substitute for diplomacy.

Samuel Pisar (1929–) Polish-born US writer and lawyer. *Of Blood and Hope*

20 You may reasonably expect a man to walk a tightrope safely for ten minutes; it would be unreasonable to do so without accident for two hundred years.

Bertrand Russell (1872–1970) British philosopher. On the subject of nuclear war between the USA and the USSR. *The Tightrope Men* (D. Bagley)

21 There is no evil in the atom; only in men's souls.

Adlai Stevenson (1900–65) US statesman. Speech, Hartford, Connecticut, 18 Sept 1952

22 Man has wrested from nature the power to make the world a desert or to make the deserts bloom. There is no evil in the atom, only in men's souls.

Adlai Stevenson Speech, 18 Sept 1952

23 For Hon. Members opposite the deterrent is a phallic symbol. It convinces them that they are men.

George Wigg (1900–76) British politician. *The Observer*, 'Sayings of the Week', 8 Mar 1964

24 A bigger bang for a buck.

Charles E. Wilson (1890–1961) US Republican politician. On the hydrogen bomb test at Bikini, 1954. *Political Dictionary* (W. Safire)

NUISANCE

1 Never compose anything unless the not composing of it becomes a positive nuisance to you.

Gustav Holst (1874–1934) British composer. Letter to W. G. Whittaker

2 Well, I find that a change of nuisances is as good as a vacation.

David Lloyd George (1863–1945) British Liberal statesman. On being asked how he maintained his cheerfulness when beset by numerous political obstacles. Attrib.

NUMBERS

See also mathematics, statistics

1 I'll sing you twelve O.
Green grow the rushes O.
What is your twelve O?
Twelve for the twelve apostles,
Eleven for the eleven who went to heaven,
Ten for the ten commandments,
Nine for the nine bright shiners,
Eight for the eight bold rangers,
Seven for the seven stars in the sky,
Six for the six proud walkers,
Five for the symbol at your door,
Four for the Gospel makers,
Three for the rivals,
Two, two, the lily-white boys,
Clothed all in green O,
One is one and all alone
And ever more shall be so.

Anonymous *The Dilly Song*

2 Round numbers are always false.

Samuel Johnson (1709–84) British lexicographer. *Life of Johnson* (J. Boswell), Vol. III

3 No, I don't know his telephone number. But it was up in the high numbers.

John Maynard Keynes (1883–1946) British economist. Attrib.

4 One, two,
Buckle my shoe;
Three, four,
Knock at the door.

Nursery Rhyme *Songs for the Nursery*

5 No, it is a very interesting number, it is the smallest number expressible as a sum of two cubes in two different ways.

Srinivasa Ramanujan (1887–1920) Indian mathematician. The mathematician G. H. Hardy had referred to the number – 1729 – as 'dull'. *Collected Papers of Srinivasa Ramanujan*

6 Oh, quite easy! The Septuagint minus the Apostles.

Arthur Woollgar Verrall (1851–1912) British classicist. Reply to a person who thought the number 58 difficult to remember

NURSERY RHYMES

A selection is given here. The form used is that most commonly used today – not the one in the original publication.

1 A frog he would a-wooing go,
Heigh ho! says Rowley,
A frog he would a-wooing go,
Whether his mother would let him or no.
With a rowley, powley, gammon and spinach,
Heigh ho! says Anthony Rowley.

Melismata (Thomas Ravenscroft)

2 All the birds of the air
Fell a-sighing and a-sobbing,
When they heard the bell toll
For poor Cock Robin.

Tommy Thumb's Pretty Song Book

3 As I was going to St Ives,
I met a man with seven wives.
Each wife had seven sacks
Each sack had seven cats,
Each cat had seven kits,
How many were going to St Ives?

Mother Goose's Quarto

4 Baa, baa, black sheep,
Have you any wool?
Yes, sir, yes, sir,
Three bags full;
One for the master,
And one for the dame,
And one for the little boy
Who lives down the lane.

Tommy Thumb's Pretty Song Book

5 Bobby Shafto's gone to sea,
Silver buckles on his knee;
He'll come back and marry me,
Bonny Bobby Shafto!

Songs for the Nursery

6 Boys and girls come out to play,
The moon doth shine as bright as day.

Useful Transactions in Philosophy (William King)

7 Come, let's to bed
Says Sleepy-head;
Tarry a while, says Slow;
Put on the pan;
Says Greedy Nan,
Let's sup before we go.
Gammer Gurton's Garland (R. Christopher)

8 Curly locks, Curly locks,
Wilt thou be mine?
Thou shalt not wash dishes
Nor yet feed the swine,
But sit on a cushion
And sew a fine seam,
And feed upon strawberries,
Sugar and cream.
Infant Institutes

9 Ding dong, bell,
Pussy's in the well.
Who put her in?
Little Johnny Green.
Who pulled her out?
Little Tommy Stout.
Mother Goose's Melody

10 Doctor Foster went to Gloucester
In a shower of rain:
He stepped in a puddle,
Right up to his middle,
And never went there again.
The Nursery Rhymes of England (J. O. Halliwell)

11 Eena, meena, mina, mo,
Catch a nigger by his toe;
If he hollers, let him go,
Eena, meena, mina, mo.
Games and Songs of American Children (Newell)

12 Georgie Porgie, pudding and pie,
Kissed the girls and made them cry;
When the boys came out to play,
Georgie Porgie ran away.
The Nursery Rhymes of England (J. O. Halliwell)

13 Goosey, goosey gander,
Whither shall I wander?
Upstairs and downstairs
And in my lady's chamber.
Gammer Gurton's Garland (R. Christopher)

14 Hey diddle diddle,
The cat and the fiddle,
The cow jumped over the moon;
The little dog laughed
To see such sport,
And the dish ran away with the
spoon.
Mother Goose's Melody

15 Hickory, dickory, dock,
The mouse ran up the clock.
The clock struck one,
The mouse ran down,
Hickory, dickory, dock.
Tommy Thumb's Pretty Song Book

16 Hot cross buns!
Hot cross buns!
One a penny, two a penny,
Hot cross buns!
Christmas Box

17 How many miles to Babylon?
Three score miles and ten.
Can I get there by candle-light?
Yes, and back again.
If your heels are nimble and light,
You may get there by candle-light.
Songs for the Nursery

18 Humpty Dumpty sat on a wall,
Humpty Dumpty had a great fall.
All the king's horses,
And all the king's men,
Couldn't put Humpty together again.
Gammer Gurton's Garland (R. Christopher)

19 Hush-a-bye, baby, on the tree top,
When the wind blows the cradle will
rock;
When the bough breaks the cradle
will fall,
Down will come baby, cradle, and all.
Mother Goose's Melody

20 I had a little nut tree,
Nothing would it bear
But a silver nutmeg
And a golden pear;
The King of Spain's daughter
Came to visit me,
And all for the sake
Of my little nut tree.
Newest Christmas Box

21 I had a little pony,
His name was Dapple Grey;
I lent him to a lady
To ride a mile away.
She whipped him, she lashed him,
She rode him through the mire;
I would not lend my pony now,
For all the lady's hire.
Poetical Alphabet

22 I love sixpence, jolly little sixpence,
I love sixpence better than my life;
I spent a penny of it, I lent a penny
of it,
And I took fourpence home to my
wife.
Gammer Gurton's Garland (R. Christopher)

23 I'm the king of the castle,
Get down you dirty rascal.
Brand's Popular Antiquities

24 Jack and Jill went up the hill
To fetch a pail of water;
Jack fell down and broke his crown,
And Jill came tumbling after.
Mother Goose's Melody

25 Jack Sprat could eat no fat,
His wife could eat no lean,
And so between them both you see,
They licked the platter clean.
Paroemiologia Anglo-Latina (John Clark)

26 Ladybird, ladybird,
Fly away home,
Your house is on fire
And your children all gone.
Tommy Thumb's Pretty Song Book

27 Little Bo-peep has lost her sheep,
And can't tell where to find them;
Leave them alone, and they'll come
home,
Bringing their tails behind them.
Gammer Gurton's Garland (R. Christopher)

28 Little Boy Blue,
Come blow your horn,
The sheep's in the meadow,
The cow's in the corn.
Famous Tommy Thumb's Little Story Book

29 Little Jack Horner
Sat in the corner,
Eating a Christmas pie;
He put in his thumb,
And pulled out a plum,
And said, What a good boy am I!
Namby Pamby (Henry Carey)

30 Little Miss Muffet
Sat on a tuffet,
Eating her curds and whey;
There came a big spider,
Who sat down beside her
And frightened Miss Muffet away.
Songs for the Nursery

31 Little Tommy Tucker,
Sings for his supper:
What shall we give him?
White bread and butter
How shall he cut it
Without a knife?
How will he be married
Without a wife?
Tommy Thumb's Pretty Song Book

32 London Bridge is broken down,
My fair lady.
Namby Pamby (Henry Carey)

33 Monday's child is fair of face,
Tuesday's child is full of grace,
Wednesday's child is full of woe,
Thursday's child has far to go,
Friday's child is loving and giving,
Saturday's child works hard for his
living,
And the child that is born on the Sab-
bath day
Is bonny and blithe, and good and
gay.
Traditions of Devonshire (A. E. Bray)

34 My mother said that I never should
Play with the gypsies in the wood;

If I did, she would say,
Naughty girl to disobey.
Come Hither (Walter de la Mare)

35 Old Mother Hubbard
Went to the cupboard,
To fetch her poor dog a bone;
But when she got there
The cupboard was bare
And so the poor dog had none.
The Comic Adventures of Old Mother Hubbard and Her Dog

36 One, two,
Buckle my shoe;
Three, four,
Knock at the door.
Songs for the Nursery

37 Pat-a-cake, pat-a-cake, baker's man,
Bake me a cake as fast as you can;
Pat it and prick it, and mark it with B,
Put it in the oven for baby and me.
The Campaigners (Tom D'Urfey)

38 Peter Piper picked a peck of pickled pepper;
A peck of pickled pepper Peter Piper picked;
If Peter Piper picked a peck of pickled pepper,
Where's the peck of pickled pepper Peter Piper picked?
Peter Piper's Practical Principles of Plain and Perfect Pronunciation

39 Polly put the kettle on,
Polly put the kettle on,
Polly put the kettle on,
We'll all have tea.
Sukey take it off again,
Sukey take it off again,
Sukey take it off again,
They've all gone away.
Traditional

40 Pussy cat, pussy cat, where have you been?
I've been to London to look at the queen.
Pussy cat, pussy cat, what did you there?
I frightened a little mouse under her chair.
Songs for the Nursery

41 Ride a cock-horse to Banbury Cross,
To see a fine lady upon a white horse;
Rings on her fingers and bells on her toes,
And she shall have music wherever she goes.
Gammer Gurton's Garland (R. Christopher)

42 Ring-a-ring o'roses,
A pocket full of posies,
A-tishoo! A-tishoo!
We all fall down.
Mother Goose (Kate Greenway)

43 Round and round the garden
Like a teddy bear;
One step, two step,
Tickle you under there!
Traditional

44 Rub-a-dub-dub,
Three men in a tub,
And who do you think they be?
The butcher, the baker,
The candlestick-maker,
And they all sailed out to sea.
Christmas Box

45 See-saw, Margery Daw,
Jacky shall have a new master;
Jacky shall have but a penny a day,
Because he can't work any faster.
Mother Goose's Melody

46 Simple Simon met a pieman,
Going to the fair;
Says Simple Simon to the pieman,
Let me taste your ware.
Says the pieman to Simple Simon,
Show me first your penny;
Says Simple Simon to the pieman,
Indeed I have not any.
Simple Simon (Chapbook Advertisement)

47 The king was in his counting-house,
Counting out his money;
The queen was in the parlour,
Eating bread and honey.
The maid was in the garden,
Hanging out the clothes,
When down came a blackbird,
And pecked off her nose.
Tommy Thumb's Pretty Song Book

48 Solomon Grundy,
Born on a Monday,
Christened on Tuesday,
Married on Wednesday,
Took ill on Thursday,
Worse on Friday,
Died on Saturday,
Buried on Sunday.
This is the end
Of Solomon Grundy.
The Nursery Rhymes of England (J. O. Halliwell)

49 The first day of Christmas,
My true love sent to me
A partridge in a pear tree.
Mirth Without Mischief

50 The twelfth day of Christmas,
My true love sent to me
Twelve lords a-leaping,
Eleven ladies dancing,
Ten pipers piping,
Nine drummers drumming,
Eight maids a-milking,
Seven swans a-swimming,
Six geese a-laying,
Five gold rings,
Four colly birds,
Three French hens,
Two turtle doves, and
A partridge in a pear tree.
Mirth Without Mischief

51 The lion and the unicorn
Were fighting for the crown;
The lion beat the unicorn
All round about the town.
Useful Transactions in Philosophy (William King)

52 The Queen of Hearts
She made some tarts,
All on a summer's day;
The Knave of Hearts
He stole the tarts,
And took them clean away.
The European Magazine

53 There was a crooked man, and he walked a crooked mile,
He found a crooked sixpence against a crooked stile:
He bought a crooked cat, which caught a crooked mouse,
And they all lived together in a little crooked house.
The Nursery Rhymes of England (J. O. Halliwell)

54 There was an old woman
Lived under a hill,
And if she's not gone
She lives there still.
Academy of Complements

55 There was an old woman who lived in a shoe,
She had so many children she didn't know what to do;
She gave them some broth without any bread;
She whipped them all soundly and put them to bed.
Gammer Gurton's Garland (R. Christopher)

56 Thirty days hath September,
April, June, and November;
All the rest have thirty-one,
Excepting February alone
And that has twenty-eight days clear
And twenty-nine in each leap year.
Abridgement of the Chronicles of England (Richard Grafton)

57 This is the farmer sowing his corn,
That kept the cock that crowed in the morn,
That waked the priest all shaven and shorn,
That married the man all tattered and torn,
That kissed the maiden all forlorn,

That milked the cow with the crumpled horn,
That tossed the dog,
That worried the cat,
That killed the rat,
That ate the corn,
That lay in the house that Jack built.
Nurse Truelove's New-Year-Gift

58 This little piggy went to market,
This little piggy stayed at home,
This little piggy had roast beef,
This little piggy had none,
And this little piggy cried, Wee-wee-wee-wee-wee,
I can't find my way home.
The Famous Tommy Thumb's Little Story Book

59 Three blind mice, see how they run!
They all run after the farmer's wife,
Who cut off their tails with a carving knife,
Did you ever see such a thing in your life,
As three blind mice?
Deuteromelia (Thomas Ravenscroft)

60 Tinker,
Tailor,
Soldier,
Sailor,
Rich man,
Poor man,
Beggarman,
Thief.
Popular Rhymes and Nursery Tales (J. O. Halliwell)

61 Tom, he was a piper's son,
He learned to play when he was young,
And all the tune that he could play
Was 'Over the hills and far away'.
Tom, The Piper's Son

62 Tom, Tom, the piper's son,
Stole a pig and away he run;
The pig was eat
And Tom was beat,
And Tom went howling down the street.
Tom, The Piper's Son

63 Two little dicky birds,
Sitting on a wall;
One named Peter,
The other named Paul,
Fly away, Peter!
Fly away, Paul!
Come back, Peter!
Come back, Paul!
Mother Goose's Melody

64 Wee Willie Winkie runs through the town
upstairs and downstairs and in his nightgown,
Rapping at the window, crying through the lock,
Are the children all in bed? It's past eight o'clock.
Whistle-Binkie (W. Miller)

65 What are little boys made of?
Frogs and snails
And puppy-dogs' tails,
That's what little boys are made of.
What are little girls made of?
Sugar and spice
And all that's nice,
That's what little girls are made of.
Nursery Rhymes (J. O. Halliwell)

66 What is your fortune, my pretty maid?
My face is my fortune, sir, she said.
Then I can't marry you, my pretty maid.
Nobody asked you, sir, she said.
Archaeologia Cornu-Britannica (William Pryce)

67 Where are you going to, my pretty maid?
I'm going a-milking, sir, she said.
Archaeologia Cornu-Britannica (William Pryce)

68 Who killed Cock Robin?
I, said the Sparrow,
With my bow and arrow,
I killed Cock Robin.
Who saw him die?
I, said the Fly,
With my little eye,
I saw him die.
Tommy Thumb's Pretty Song Book

69 Yankee Doodle came to town,
Riding on a pony;
He stuck a feather in his cap
And called it macaroni.
Gammer Gurton's Garland (R. Christopher)

NURSES

1 Too often a sister puts all her patients back to bed as a housewife puts all her plates back in the plate-rack – to make a generally tidy appearance.
Richard Asher (1912–) *British Medical Journal*

2 If th' Christyan Scientists had some science an' th' doctors more Christyanity, it wudden't make anny diff'rence which ye called in – If ye had a good nurse.
Finley Peter Dunne (1867–1936) US humorist and journalist. *Mr. Dooley's Opinions*, 'Christian Science'

3 It's better to be sick than nurse the sick. Sickness is single trouble for the sufferer: but nursing means vexation of the mind, and hard work for the hands besides.
Euripides (484 BC–406 BC) Greek dramatist. *Hippolytus*

4 . . . a good nurse is of more importance than a physician.
Hannah Farnham Lee (1780–1865) *The Log-Cabin; or, the World Before You*

5 The trained nurse has given nursing the human, or shall we say, the divine touch, and made the hospital desirable for patients with serious ailments regardless of their home advantages.
Charles H. Mayo (1865–1939) US physician. *Collected Papers of the Mayo Clinic and Mayo Foundation*

6 No *man*, not even a doctor, ever gives any other definition of what a nurse should be than this – 'devoted and obedient.' This definition would do just as well for a porter. It might even do for a horse. It would not do for a policeman.
Florence Nightingale (1820–1910) British nurse. *Notes on Nursing*

7 The trained nurse has become one of the great blessings of humanity, taking a place beside the physician and the priest, and not inferior to either in her mission.
William Osler (1849–1919) Canadian physician. *Aequanimitas, with Other Addresses*, 'Nurse and Patient'

8 *Talk of the patience of Job*, said a Hospital nurse, *Job was never on night duty.*
Stephen Paget (1855–1926) *Confessio Medici*, Ch. 6

9 That person alone is fit to nurse or to attend the bedside of a patient, who is cool-headed and pleasant in his demeanour, does not speak ill of any body, is strong and attentive to the requirements of the sick, and strictly and indefatigably follows the instructions of the physician.
Sushruta (5th century BC) *Sushruta-Samhitá*, 'Sutrastánam', Ch. 34

O

OBEDIENCE

1 Children, obey your parents in the Lord: for this is right.
Bible: Ephesians 6:1

2 'She still seems to me in her own way a person born to command,' said Luce . . .
'I wonder if anyone is born to obey,' said Isabel.
'That may be why people command rather badly, that they have no suitable material to work on.'
Ivy Compton-Burnett (1892–1969) British novelist. *Parents and Children,* Ch. 3

3 It is much safer to obey than to rule.
Thomas à Kempis (Thomas Hemmerken; c. 1380–1471) German monk. *The Imitation of Christ,* I

4 My mother said that I never should
Play with the gypsies in the wood;
If I did, she would say,
Naughty girl to disobey.
Nursery Rhyme *Come Hither* (Walter de la Mare)

5 Every good servant does not all commands.
William Shakespeare (1564–1616) English dramatist. *Cymbeline,* V:1

6 'Forward the Light Brigade!'
Was there a man dismay'd?
Not tho' the soldier knew
Some one had blunder'd:
Their's not to make reply,
Their's not to reason why,
Their's but to do and die:
Into the valley of Death
Rode the six hundred.
Alfred, Lord Tennyson (1809–92) British poet. *The Charge of the Light Brigade*

OBESITY

See also food, greed

1 Outside every fat man there is an even fatter man trying to close in.
Kingsley Amis (1922–) British novelist. *See also* CONNOLLY, ORWELL *One Fat Englishman,* Ch. 3

2 A fat paunch never bred a subtle mind.
Anonymous

3 Who's your fat friend?
'Beau' Brummell (George Bryan Brummell; 1778–1840) British dandy. Referring to George, Prince of Wales. *Reminiscences* (Gronow)

4 Just the other day in the Underground I enjoyed the pleasure of offering my seat to three ladies.
G. K. Chesterton (1874–1936) British writer. Suggesting that fatness had its consolations. *Das Buch des Lachens* (W. Scholz)

5 I want to reassure you I am not this size, really – dear me no, I'm being amplified by the mike.
G. K. Chesterton At a lecture in Pittsburgh. *The Outline of Sanity: A Life of G. K. Chesterton* (S. D. Dale)

6 Imprisoned in every fat man a thin one is wildly signalling to be let out.
Cyril Connolly (1903–74) British journalist. *See also* AMIS, ORWELL. *The Unquiet Grave*

7 Obesity is a mental state, a disease brought on by boredom and disappointment.
Cyril Connolly *The Unquiet Grave,* I

8 The one way to get thin is to re-establish a purpose in life.
Cyril Connolly *The Unquiet Grave,* 1

9 O fat white woman whom nobody loves,
Why do you walk through the fields in gloves . . .
Missing so much and so much?
F. M. Cornford (1886–1960) British poet. *To a Fat Lady Seen from a Train*

10 That dark day when a man decides he must wear his belt under instead of over his cascading paunch.
Peter De Vries (1910–) US novelist. *Consenting Adults,* 1980

11 I see no objection to stoutness, in moderation.
W. S. Gilbert (1836–1911) British dramatist. *Iolanthe,* I

12 I'm fat, but I'm thin inside. Has it ever struck you that there's a thin man inside every fat man, just as they say there's a statue inside every block of stone?
George Orwell (Eric Blair; 1903–50) British novelist. *See also* AMIS, CONNOLLY *Coming Up For Air,* Pt. I, Ch. 3

13 My advice if you insist on slimming: Eat as much as you like – just don't swallow it.
Harry Secombe (1921–) Welsh singer, actor, and comedian. *Daily Herald,* 5 Oct 1962

14 Falstaff sweats to death
And lards the lean earth as he walks along.
William Shakespeare (1564–1616) English dramatist. *Henry IV, Part One,* II:2

15 I have more flesh than another man, and therefore more frailty.
William Shakespeare *Henry IV, Part One,* III:3

16 Enclosing every thin man, there's a fat man demanding elbow-room.
Evelyn Waugh (1903–66) British novelist. *Officers and Gentlemen,* Interlude

17 Outside every thin girl there is a fat man trying to get in.
Katharine Whitehorn (1928–) British journalist. Attrib.

18 She fitted into my biggest armchair as if it had been built round her by someone who knew they were wearing armchairs tight about the hips that season.
P. G. Wodehouse (1881–1975) British humorous novelist. *My Man Jeeves,* 'Jeeves and the Unbidden Guest'

19 The Right Hon. was a tubby little chap who looked as if he had been poured into his clothes and had forgotten to say 'When!'
P. G. Wodehouse *Very Good Jeeves!,* 'Jeeves and the Impending Doom'

OBITUARIES

See also death, epitaphs, memorials

1 He caused castles to be built
Which were a sore burden to the poor,
A hard man was the king
And took from his subjects many marks
In gold and many more hundreds of pounds in silver.
These sums he took by weight from his people,
Most unjustly and for little need.
He was sunk in greed
And utterly given up to avarice.
He set apart a vast deer preserve
and imposed laws concerning it.
Whoever slew a hart or a hind
Was to be blinded.
He forbade the killing of boars
Even as the killing of harts.

For he loved the stags as dearly
As though he had been their father.
Hares, also, he decreed should go unmolested.
The rich complained and the poor lamented,
But he was too relentless to care though all might hate him,
And they were compelled, if they wanted
To keep their lives and their lands
And their goods and the favour of the king,
To submit themselves wholly to his will.
Alas! that any man should bear himself so proudly
And deem himself exalted above all other men!
May Almighty God shew mercy to his soul
And pardon him his sins.

Anonymous Written on the death of William the Conqueror. The Peterborough Chronicle (part of *The Anglo-Saxon Chronicle*)

2 I have never killed a man, but I have read many obituaries with a lot of pleasure.

Clarence Darrow (1857–1938) US lawyer. *Medley*

3 With the newspaper strike on I wouldn't consider it.

Bette Davis (Ruth Elizabeth Davis; 1908–) US film star. When told that a rumor was spreading that she had died. *Book of Lists* (I. Wallace)

4 He will be looked upon by posterity as a brave bad man.

Edward Hyde, Earl of Clarendon (1609–74) English statesman and historian. Referring to Cromwell. *History of the Great Rebellion*

5 I've just read that I am dead. Don't forget to delete me from your list of subscribers.

Rudyard Kipling (1865–1936) Indian-born British writer. Writing to a magazine that had mistakenly published an announcement of his death. *Anekdotenschatz* (H. Hoffmeister)

6 John Le Mesurier wishes it to be known that he conked out on November 15th. He sadly misses family and friends.

John Le Mesurier (1912–83) British actor. His death announcement. *The Times*, 15 Nov 1983

7 You should have known that it was not easy for me to die. But, tell me, were my obituaries good?

Makarios (Mikhail Christodoulou Mouskos; 1913–77) Cypriot archbishop, patriarch, and statesman.

8 At social gatherings he was liable to engage in heated and noisy arguments which could ruin a dinner party, and made him the dread of hostesses on both sides of the Atlantic. The tendency was exacerbated by an always generous, and occasionally excessive alcoholic intake.

Malcolm Muggeridge (1903–) British writer. Referring to Randolph Churchill. *The Times*, 7 June 1968

9 . . . that great lover of peace, a man of giant stature who moulded, as few other men have done, the destinies of his age.

Jawaharlal Nehru (1889–1964) First Indian prime minister. Referring to Stalin. Obituary tribute, Indian Parliament, 9 Mar 1953

10 In these days a man is nobody unless his biography is kept so far posted up that it may be ready for the national breakfast-table on the morning after his demise.

Anthony Trollope (1815–82) British novelist. *Doctor Thorne*, Ch. 25

11 Reports of my death are greatly exaggerated.

Mark Twain (Samuel Langhorne Clemens; 1835–1910) US writer. On learning that his obituary had been published. Cable to the Associated Press

OBJECTIVITY

See also perspective, subjectivity

1 Thus I live in the world rather as a Spectator of mankind, than as one of the species, by which means I have made myself a speculative statesman, soldier, merchant, and artisan, without ever meddling with any practical part of life.

Joseph Addison (1672–1719) British essayist. *The Spectator*, 1

2 *Sir Roger* told them, with the air of a man who would not give his judgment rashly, that 'much might be said on both sides'.

Joseph Addison Sir Roger de Coverley was a fictional archetype of the old-fashioned and eccentric country squire. *The Spectator*, 122

3 Only reason can convince us of those three fundamental truths without a recognition of which there can be no effective liberty: that what we believe is not necessarily true; that what we like is not necessarily good; and that all questions are open.

Clive Bell (1881–1964) British art critic. *Civilization*, Ch. 5

OBLIGATION

See also duty

1 The debt which cancels all others.

Charles Caleb Colton (?1780–1832) British clergyman and writer. *Lacon*, Vol. II

2 We are so much bounden to the See of Rome that we cannot do too much honour to it . . . for we received from that See our Crown Imperial.

Henry VIII (1491–1547) King of England. Remark to Thomas More

3 It is the nature of men to be bound by the benefits they confer as much as by those they receive.

Machiavelli (1469–1527) Italian statesman. *The Prince*

OBLIVION

1 Many brave men lived before Agamemnon's time; but they are all, unmourned and unknown, covered by the long night, because they lack their sacred poet.

Horace (Quintus Horatius Flaccus; 65–8 BC) Roman poet. *Odes*, IV

2 No, no, go not to Lethe, neither twist
Wolf's-bane, tight-rooted, for its poisonous wine.

John Keats (1795–1821) British poet. *Ode on Melancholy*

3 Annihilating all that's made
To a green thought in a green shade.

Andrew Marvell (1621–78) English poet. *The Garden*

OBSCENITY

1 Obscenity is such a tiny kingdom that a single tour covers it completely.

Heywood Brown *Shake Well Before Using* (Bennett Cerf) 1948

OBSESSIONS

1 I have three phobias which, could I mute them, would make my life as slick as a sonnet, but as dull as ditch water: I hate to go to bed, I hate to get up, and I hate to be alone.

Tallulah Bankhead (1903–68) US actress. *Tallulah*, Ch. 1

2 'Mad' is a term we use to describe a man who is obsessed with one idea and nothing else.

Ugo Betti (1892–1953) Italian dramatist. *Struggle Till Dawn*, 1

3 *Papyromania* – compulsive accumulation of papers . . .
Papyrophobia – abnormal desire for 'a clean desk'.
Laurence J. Peter (1919–) Canadian writer. *The Peter Principle*, Glossary

OBSTRUCTION

1 I'll put a spoke among your wheels.
Francis Beaumont (1584–1616) English dramatist. *The Mad Lover*, III:6

2 If any of you know cause, or just impediment.
The Book of Common Prayer *Solemnization of Matrimony*

3 If there are obstacles, the shortest line between two points may be the crooked one.
Bertolt Brecht (1898–1956) German dramatist. *Galileo*

4 There was only one catch and that was Catch-22, which specified that a concern for one's own safety in the face of dangers that were real and immediate was the process of a rational mind.
Joseph Heller (1923–) US novelist. *Catch-22*, Ch. 5

OCCUPATIONS

See also doctors, lawyers, nurses, police

1 A priest sees people at their best, a lawyer at their worst, but a doctor sees them as they really are.
Proverb

2 Every man to his trade.
Proverb

3 Jack of all trades, master of none.
Proverb

4 Old soldiers never die, they simply fade away.
Proverb

5 Once a parson always a parson.
Proverb

6 Sailors have a port in every storm.
Proverb

7 Medicine would be the ideal profession if it did not involve giving pain.
Samuel Hopkins Adams (1871–1958) US politician. *The Health Master*, Ch. 3

8 After quitting radio I was able to live on the money I saved on aspirins.
Fred Allen (1894–1956) US comedian.

9 CLINICIAN. learns less and less about more and more until he knows nothing about everything.
RESEARCHER. learns more and more about less and less until he knows everything about nothing.
Anonymous

10 The work of a Prime Minister is the loneliest job in the world.
Stanley Baldwin (1867–1947) British statesman. Speech, 9 Jan 1927

11 The ugliest of trades have their moments of pleasure. Now, if I were a grave-digger, or even a hangman, there are some people I could work for with a great deal of enjoyment.
Douglas William Jerrold (1803–57) British dramatist. *Wit and Opinions of Douglas Jerrold*, 'Ugly Trades'

12 When I caught a glimpse of Rita
Filling in a ticket in her little white book
In a cap she looked much older
And the bag across her shoulder
Made her look a little like a military man
Lovely Rita Meter Maid.
John Lennon (1940–80) British rock musician. *Lovely Rita* (with Paul McCartney)

13 What do you want to be a sailor for? There are greater storms in politics than you'll ever find at sea. Piracy, broadsides, blood on the deck – you'll find them all in politics.
David Lloyd George (1863–1945) British Liberal statesman. Remark to Julian Amery. *The Observer*, 2 Jan 1966

14 He did not know that a keeper is only a poacher turned outside in, and a poacher a keeper turned inside out.
Charles Kingsley (1819–75) British writer. *The Water Babies*, Ch. 1

15 Under the spreading chestnut tree
The village smithy stands;
The smith, a mighty man is he,
With large and sinewy hands;
And the muscles of his brawny arms
Are strong as iron bands.
Henry Wadsworth Longfellow (1807–82) US poet. *The Village Blacksmith*

16 I have nothing against undertakers personally. It's just that I wouldn't want one to bury my sister.
Jessica Mitford (1917–) British writer. Attrib. in *Saturday Review*, 1 Feb 1964

17 If I didn't start painting, I would have raised chickens.
Grandma Moses (Anna Mary Robertson Moses; 1860–1961) US primitive painter. *Grandma Moses, My Life's History* (ed. Aotto Kallir), Ch. 3

18 Tinker,
Tailor,
Soldier,
Sailor,
Rich man,
Poor man,
Beggarman,
Thief.
Nursery Rhyme *Popular Rhymes and Nursery Tales* (J. O. Halliwell)

19 A doctor who doesn't say too many foolish things is a patient half-cured, just as a critic is a poet who has stopped writing verse and a policeman a burglar who has retired from practice.
Marcel Proust (1871–1922) French novelist. *À la recherche du temps perdu: Le Côté de Guermantes*

20 Everybody hates house-agents because they have everybody at a disadvantage. All other callings have a certain amount of give and take; the house-agent simply takes.
H. G. Wells (1866–1946) British writer. *Kipps*, Bk. III, Ch. 1

21 The best careers advice to give to the young is 'Find out what you like doing best and get someone to pay you for doing it.'
Katherine Whitehorn (1926–) British journalist. *The Observer*, 1975

OFFICERS

See also army, navy, soldiers, war

1 Any officer who shall behave in a scandalous manner, unbecoming the character of an officer and a gentleman shall . . . be cashiered.
Anonymous The words 'conduct unbecoming the character of an officer' are a direct quotation from the Naval Discipline Act (10 Aug 1860), Article 24. *Articles of War* (1872), *Disgraceful Conduct*, 79

2 If Kitchener was not a great man, he was, at least, a great poster.
Margot Asquith (1865–1945) The second wife of Herbert Asquith. *Kitchener: Portrait of an Imperialist* (Sir Philip Magnus), Ch. 14

3 In defeat unbeatable; in victory unbearable.
Winston Churchill (1874–1965) British statesman. Referring to Viscount Montgomery. *Ambrosia and Small Beer* (E. Marsh), Ch. 5

4 Jellicoe was the only man on either

side who could lose the war in an afternoon.
Winston Churchill *The Observer*, 'Sayings of the Week', 13 Feb 1927

5 War is too important to be left to the generals.
Georges Clemenceau (1841–1929) French statesman. A similar remark is attributed to Talleyrand. Attrib.

6 When I was a lad I served a term
As office boy to an Attorney's firm.
I cleaned the windows and I swept the floor,
And I polished up the handle of the big front door.
I polished up that handle so carefullee
That now I am the Ruler of the Queen's Navee!
W. S. Gilbert (1836–1911) British dramatist. *HMS Pinafore*, I

7 Stick close to your desks and never go to sea,
And you all may be Rulers of the Queen's Navee!
W. S. Gilbert *HMS Pinafore*, I

8 LUDENDORFF. The English soldiers fight like lions.
HOFFMANN. True. But don't we know that they are lions led by donkeys.
Max Hoffmann (1869–1927) German general. Referring to the performance of the British army in World War I. *The Donkeys* (A. Clark)

9 I can't spare this man; he fights.
Abraham Lincoln (1809–65) US statesman. Resisting demands for the dismissal of Ulysses Grant. Attrib.

10 The Nelson touch.
Lord Nelson (1758–1805) British admiral. Diary, 9 Oct 1805

11 Nelson, born in a fortunate hour for himself and for his country, was always in his element and always on his element.
George Macaulay Trevelyan (1876–1962) British historian. *History of England*, Bk. V, Ch. 5

12 I didn't fire him because he was a dumb son of a bitch, although he was, but that's not against the law for generals. If it was, half to three-quarters of them would be in jail.
Harry S. Truman (1884–1972) US statesman. Referring to General MacArthur. *Plain Speaking* (Merle Miller)

13 I don't know what effect these men will have on the enemy, but, by God, they frighten me.
Duke of Wellington (1769–1852) British general and statesman. Referring to his generals. Attrib.

14 It is not the business of generals to shoot one another.
Duke of Wellington Refusing an artillery officer permission to fire upon Napoleon himself during the Battle of Waterloo, 1815. Attrib.

15 Not upon a man from the colonel to the private in a regiment – both inclusive. We may pick up a marshal or two perhaps; but not worth a damn.
Duke of Wellington Said during the Waterloo campaign, when asked whether he anticipated any desertions from Napoleon's army. *Creevey Papers*, Ch. X

16 I used to say of him that his presence on the field made the difference of forty thousand men.
Duke of Wellington Referring to Napoleon. *Notes of Conversations with the Duke of Wellington* (Stanhope), 2 Nov 1831

OLD AGE

See also age, longevity

1 Grey hairs are death's blossoms.
Proverb

2 You can't teach an old dog new tricks.
Proverb

3 All would live long, but none would be old.
Proverb

4 Man fools himself. He prays for a long life, and he fears an old age.
Chinese proverb

5 Forty is the old age of youth; fifty is the youth of old age.
French proverb

6 Old men are twice children.
Greek proverb

7 Dying while young is a boon in old age.
Yiddish proverb

8 Nobody hears old people complain because people think that's all old people do. And that's because old people are gnarled and sagged and twisted into the shape of a complaint.
Edward Albee (1928–) US dramatist. *The American Dream*

9 As men draw near the common goal
Can anything be sadder
Than he who, master of his soul,
Is servant to his bladder?
Anonymous *The Speculum*, Melbourne, 1938

10 Everyone faces at all times two fateful possibilities: one is to grow older, the other not.
Anonymous

11 The principal objection to old age is that there's no future in it.
Anonymous

12 You are getting old when the gleam in your eyes is from the sun hitting your bifocals.
Anonymous

13 It's a sign of age if you feel like the day after the night before and you haven't been anywhere.
Anonymous

14 When you are forty, half of you belongs to the past . . . And when you are seventy, nearly all of you.
Jean Anouilh (1910–87) French dramatist.

15 When men desire old age, what else do they desire but prolonged infirmity?
St Augustine (354–430) Bishop of Hippo in North Africa. *Of the Catechizing of the Unlearned*, XVI

16 I will never be an old man. To me, old age is always fifteen years older than I am.
Bernard Baruch (1870–1965) US financier and presidential adviser. *The Observer* 'Sayings of the Week', 21 Aug 1955

17 An old man looks permanent, as if he had been born an old man.
H. E. Bates (1905–74) British novelist. *Death In Spring*

18 . . . no one ever speaks of 'a beautiful old woman'.
Simone de Beauvoir (1908–86) French writer. *The Coming of Age*

19 Tidy the old into tall flats.
Desolation at fourteen storeys
becomes a view.
Alan Bennet (1934–) British playwright. *Forty Years On*

20 Tranquillity comes with years, and that horrid thing which Freud calls sex is expunged.
E. F. Benson (1867–1940) British novelist. *Mapp and Lucia*

21 Now all the world she knew is dead
In this small room she lives her days.
The wash-hand stand and single bed
Screened from the public gaze.
John Betjeman (1906–84) British poet. *A Few Late Chrysanthemums*, 'House of Rest'

22 Better is a poor and a wise child than an old and foolish king, who will no more be admonished.
Bible: Ecclesiastes 4:13

23 With the ancient is wisdom; and in length of days understanding.
Bible: Job 12:12

24 To be old is to be part of a huge and ordinary multitude . . . the reason why old age was venerated in the past was because it was extraordinary.
Ronald Blythe (1922–) British author. *The View in Winter*

25 Old age takes away from us what we have inherited and gives us what we have earned.
Gerald Brenan (Edward Fitzgerald Brenan; 1894–1987) British writer. *Thoughts in a Dry Season*, 'Life'

26 I smoke 10 to 15 cigars a day, at my age I have to hold on to something.
George Burns (1896–) US comedian. Attrib.

27 As a white candle
In a holy place,
So is the beauty
Of an aged face.
Joseph Campbell (1879–1944) Irish poet. *The Old Woman*

28 'You are old, Father William,' the young man said,
'And your hair has become very white;
And yet you incessantly stand on your head –
Do you think at your age, it is right?'
Lewis Carroll (Charles Lutwidge Dodgson; 1832–98) British writer. *See also* Robert SOUTHEY. *Alice's Adventures in Wonderland*, Ch. 5

29 I'll keep going till my face falls off.
Barbara Cartland (1902–) British romantic novelist. *The Observer*, 'Sayings of the Week', 17 Aug 1975

30 Old age is the out-patients' department of purgatory.
Lord Cecil (1869–1956) British politician. *The Cecils of Hatfield House* (David Cecil)

31 I prefer old age to the alternative.
Maurice Chevalier (1888–1972) French singer and actor. Attrib.

32 Old-age, a second child, by Nature curs'd
With more and greater evils than the first,
Weak, sickly, full of pains; in ev'ry breath
Railing at life, and yet afraid of death.
Charles Churchill (1731–64) British poet. *Gotham*, I

33 I am ready to meet my Maker. Whether my Maker is ready for the ordeal of meeting me is another matter.
Winston Churchill (1874–1965) British statesman. On his 75th birthday. Speech, 30 Nov 1949

34 Dead birds don't fall out of their nests.
Winston Churchill When someone told him that his trouser fly-buttons were undone. Attrib.

35 It is not by muscle, speed, or physical dexterity that great things are achieved, but by reflection, force of character, and judgement; in these qualities old age is usually not only not poorer, but is even richer.
Cicero (106–43 BC) Roman orator and statesman. *On Old Age*, VI

36 Oh to be seventy again.
Georges Clemenceau (1841–1929) French statesman. Remark on his eightieth birthday, noticing a pretty girl in the Champs Elysées. *Ego 3* (James Agate)

37 So, perhaps, I may escape otherwise than by death the last humiliation of an aged scholar, when his juniors conspire to print a volume of essays and offer it to him as a sign that they now consider him senile.
Robin George Collingwood (1889–1943) British philosopher and archaeologist. *Autobiography*

38 A man is as old as he's feeling,
A woman as old as she looks.
Mortimer Collins (1827–76) British writer. *The Unknown Quantity*

39 Body and mind, like man and wife, do not always agree to die together.
Charles C. Colton (c. 1780–1832) British churchman and writer. *Lacon*, Vol. I, Ch. 324

40 Old age is a shipwreck.
Charles De Gaulle (1890–1970) French general and president. *The Life of Arthur Ransome* (H. Brogan)

41 When a man fell into his anecdotage it was a sign for him to retire from the world.
Benjamin Disraeli (1804–81) British statesman. *Lothair*, Ch. 28

42 In 1716 he had a paralytic stroke which was followed by senile decay. The story is famous of the broken man, hobbling to gaze at Kneller's portrait which showed him in the full splendour of manhood and murmuring, 'That was once a man'.
T. Charles Edwards and Brian Richardson Referring to John Churchill, First Duke of Marlborough. *They Saw it Happen*

43 I grow old . . . I grow old . . .
I shall wear the bottoms of my trousers rolled.
T. S. Eliot (1888–1965) US-born British poet and dramatist. *The Love Song of J. Alfred Prufrock*

44 Shall I part my hair behind? Do I dare to eat a peach?
I shall wear white flannel trousers, and walk upon the beach.
I have heard the mermaids singing, each to each.
T. S. Eliot *The Love Song of J. Alfred Prufrock*

45 Old age brings along with its uglinesses the comfort that you will soon be out of it, – which ought to be a substantial relief to such discontented pendulums as we are.
Ralph Waldo Emerson (1803–82) US poet and essayist. *Journal*

46 All diseases run into one, old age.
Ralph Waldo Emerson *Journals*

47 He cannot bear old men's jokes. That is not new. But now he begins to think of them himself.
Max Frisch (1911–) Swiss dramatist and novelist. *Sketchbook 1966–71*

48 No skill or art is needed to grow old; the trick is to endure it.
Johann Wolfgang von Goethe (1749–1832) German poet, dramatist and scientist.

49 The first sign of his approaching end was when my old aunts, while undressing him, removed a toe with one of his socks.
Graham Greene (1904–) British novelist. *Travels With My Aunt*

50 Time goes by: reputation increases, ability declines.
Dag Hammarskjöld (1905–61) Swedish diplomat. *Diaries*, 1964

51 And now in age I bud again,
After so many deaths I live and write;
I once more smell the dew and rain,
And relish versing; O, my only Light,
It cannot be
That I am he
On whom Thy tempests fell all night.
George Herbert (1593–1633) English poet. *The Flower*

52 Some people reach the age of 60 before others.

Lord Hood (1910–) British civil servant. *The Observer*, 'Sayings of the Week', 23 Feb 1969

53 The misery of a child is interesting to a mother, the misery of a young man is interesting to a young woman, the misery of an old man is interesting to nobody.

Victor Hugo (1802–85) French poet, novelist, and dramatist. *Les Misérables*, 'Saint Denis'

54 The ageing man of the middle twentieth century lives, not in the public world of atomic physics and conflicting ideologies, of welfare states and supersonic speed, but in his strictly private universe of physical weakness and mental decay.

Aldous Huxley (1894–1964) British writer. *Themes and Variations*, 'Variations on a Philosopher'

55 It is so comic to hear oneself called old, even at ninety I suppose!

Alice James (1848–92) US diarist. Letter to William James, 14 June 1889. *The Diary of Alice James* (ed. Leon Edel)

56 There is a wicked inclination in most people to suppose an old man decayed in his intellects. If a young or middle-aged man, when leaving a company, does not recollect where he laid his hat, it is nothing; but if the same inattention is discovered in an old man, people will shrug up their shoulders, and say, 'His memory is going.'

Samuel Johnson (1709–84) British lexicographer. *Life of Johnson* (J. Boswell), Vol. IV

57 A medical revolution has extended the life of our elder citizens without providing the dignity and security those later years deserve.

John F. Kennedy (1917–63) US statesman. Acceptance speech, Democratic National Convention, Los Angeles, 15 July 1960

58 Prolonged and costly illness in later years robs too many of our elder citizens of pride, purpose and savings.

John F. Kennedy *Message to Congress on the Nation's Health Needs*, 27 Feb 1962

59 Perhaps being old is having lighted rooms
Inside your head, and people in them, acting.
People you know, yet can't quite name.

Philip Larkin (1922–85) British poet. *The Old Fools*

60 A 'Grand Old Man'. That means on our continent any one with snow white hair who has kept out of jail till eighty.

Stephen Leacock (1869–1944) English-born Canadian economist and humorist. *The Score and Ten*

61 Old age is woman's hell.

Ninon de Lenclos (1620–1705) French courtesan. Attrib.

62 Only stay quiet while my mind remembers
The beauty of fire from the beauty of embers.

John Masefield (1878–1967) British poet. *On Growing Old*

63 From the earliest times the old have rubbed it into the young that they are wiser than they, and before the young had discovered what nonsense this was they were old too, and it profited them to carry on the imposture.

W. Somerset Maugham (1874–1965) British novelist. *Cakes and Ale*, Ch. 9

64 When you have loved as she has loved you grow old beautifully.

W. Somerset Maugham *The Circle*

65 What makes old age hard to bear is not the failing of one's faculties, mental and physical, but the burden of one's memories.

W. Somerset Maugham *Points of View*, Ch. 1

66 Growing old is a bad habit which a busy man has no time to form.

André Maurois (Émile Herzog; 1885–1967) French writer. *The Ageing American*

67 Being seventy is not a sin.

Golda Meir (1898–1978) Russian-born Israeli stateswoman. *Reader's Digest* (July 1971), 'The Indestructible Golda Meir'

68 Old age puts more wrinkles in our minds than on our faces.

Michel de Montaigne (1533–92) French essayist. *Essays*, Bk. III, Ch. 2, 'Of Repentance'

69 Old age is an island surrounded by death.

Juan Montalvo

70 A ready means of being cherished by the English is to adopt the simple expedient of living a long time. I have little doubt that if, say, Oscar Wilde had lived into his nineties, instead of dying in his forties, he would have been considered a benign, distinguished figure suitable to preside at a school prize-giving or to instruct and exhort scoutmasters at their jamborees. He might even have been knighted.

Malcolm Muggeridge (1903–) British writer. *Tread Softly for you Tread on my Jokes*

71 I prefer to forget both pairs of glasses and pass my declining years saluting strange women and grandfather clocks.

Ogden Nash (1902–71) US poet. *Peekaboo, I Almost See You*

72 Senescence begins
And middle age ends,
The day your descendants,
Outnumber your friends.

Ogden Nash

73 Age only matters when one is ageing. Now that I have arrived at a great age, I might just as well be twenty.

Pablo Picasso (1881–1973) Spanish painter. *The Observer, Shouts and Murmurs*, 'Picasso in Private' (John Richardson)

74 See how the world its veterans rewards!
A youth of frolics, an old age of cards.

Alexander Pope (1688–1744) British poet. *Moral Essays*, II

75 Growing old is like being increasingly penalized for a crime you haven't committed.

Anthony Powell (1905–) British novelist. *A Dance to the Music of Time: Temporary Kings*, Ch. 1

76 As you get older you become more boring and better behaved.

Simon Raven (1927–) British writer. *The Observer* 'Sayings Of the Week', 22 Aug 1976

77 Darling, I am growing old,
Silver threads among the gold.

Eben Rexford (1848–1916) British songwriter. *Silver Threads Among the Gold*

78 Age seldom arrives smoothly or quickly. It's more often a succession of jerks.

Jean Rhys (1894–1979) Dominican-born British novelist. *The Observer*, 'Sayings of the Week', 25 May 1975

79 If you want to be a dear old lady at seventy, you should start early, say about seventeen.

Maude Royden (1876–1956)

80 As I grow older and older,
And totter towards the tomb,
I find that I care less and less
Who goes to bed with whom.

Dorothy L. Sayers (1893–1957) British writer. *That's Why I Never Read Modern Novels*

81 Old age is a disease which we cannot cure.
Seneca (c. 4 BC–65 AD) Roman author and statesman. *Epistulae ad Lucilium*, CVIII

82 Last scene of all,
That ends this strange eventful history,
Is second childishness and mere oblivion;
Sans teeth, sans eyes, sans taste, sans every thing.
William Shakespeare (1564–1616) English dramatist. *As You Like It*, II:7

83 For mine own part, I could be well content
To entertain the lag-end of my life
With quiet hours.
William Shakespeare *Henry IV, Part 1*, V:1

84 I know thee not, old man: fall to thy prayers;
How ill white hairs become a fool and jester!
I have long dream'd of such a kind of man,
So surfeit-swell'd, so old, and so profane.
William Shakespeare *Henry IV, Part 2*, V:5

85 I am a very foolish, fond old man,
Fourscore and upward, not an hour more or less;
And, to deal plainly,
I fear I am not in my perfect mind.
William Shakespeare *King Lear*, IV:7

86 I have liv'd long enough.
My way of life
Is fall'n into the sear, the yellow leaf;
And that which should accompany old age,
As honour, love, obedience, troops of friends,
I must not look to have.
William Shakespeare *Macbeth*, V:3

87 Doth not the appetite alter? A man loves the meat in his youth that he cannot endure in his age.
William Shakespeare *Much Ado About Nothing*, II:3

88 You and I are past our dancing days.
William Shakespeare *Romeo and Juliet*, I:5

89 That time of year thou mayst in me behold
When yellow leaves, or none, or few, do hang
Upon those boughs which shake against the cold,
Bare ruin'd choirs, where late the sweet birds sang.
William Shakespeare *Sonnet 73*

90 Old men are dangerous; it doesn't matter to them what is going to happen to the world.
George Bernard Shaw (1856–1950) Irish dramatist and critic. *Heartbreak House*

91 The denunciation of the young is a necessary part of the hygiene of older people, and greatly assists the circulation of their blood.
Logan Pearsall Smith (1865–1946) US writer. *All Trivia*, 'Last Words'

92 You are old, Father William, the young man cried,
The few locks which are left you are grey;
You are hale, Father William, a hearty old man,
Now tell me the reason, I pray.
Robert Southey (1774–1843) British poet. *The Old Man's Comforts, and how he Gained them*
See also Lewis CARROLL

93 Being over seventy is like being engaged in a war. All our friends are going or gone and we survive amongst the dead and the dying as on a battlefield.
Muriel Spark (1918–) British novelist. *Memento Mori*, Ch. 4

94 There are so few who can grow old with a good grace.
Richard Steele (1672–1729) Irish-born English essayist and dramatist. *The Spectator*, 263

95 A man is as old as his arteries.
Thomas Sydenham (1624–89) *Bulletin of the New York Academy of Medicine*, 4:993, 1928 (F. H. Garrison)

96 The greatest problem about old age is the fear that it may go on too long.
A. J. P. Taylor (1906–) British historian. *Observer* 'Sayings of the Week', 1 Nov 1981

97 Sleeping as quiet as death, side by wrinkled side, toothless, salt and brown, like two old kippers in a box.
Dylan Thomas (1914–53) Welsh poet. *Under Milk Wood*

98 Old age is the most unexpected of all the things that happen to a man.
Leon Trotsky (Lev Davidovich Bronstein; 1879–1940) Russian revolutionary. *Diary in Exile*, 8 May 1935

99 Man can have only a certain number of teeth, hair and ideas; there comes a time when he necessarily loses his teeth, hair and ideas.
Voltaire (François-Marie Arouet; 1694–1778) French writer and philosopher. *Philosophical Dictionary*

100 The gods bestowed on Max the gift of perpetual old age.
Oscar Wilde (1854–1900) Irish-born British dramatist. Referring to Max Beerbohm. Attrib.

101 It is a terrible thing for an old woman to outlive her dogs.
Tennessee Williams (1911–83) US dramatist. *Camino Real*

102 He was either a man of about a hundred and fifty who was rather young for his years or a man of about a hundred and ten who had been aged by trouble.
P. G. Wodehouse (1881–1975) British humorous novelist. *Wodehouse at Work to the End* (Richard Usborne), Ch. 6

103 The wiser mind
Mourns less for what age takes away
Than what it leaves behind.
William Wordsworth (1770–1850) British poet. *The Fountain*

104 Provoke
The years to bring the inevitable yoke.
William Wordsworth *Ode. Intimations of Immortality*, VIII

105 When you are old and gray and full of sleep,
And nodding by the fire, take down this book,
And slowly read, and dream of the soft look
Your eyes had once, and of their shadows deep . . .
W. B. Yeats (1865–1939) Irish poet. *When you are Old*

106 An aged man is but a paltry thing
A tattered coat upon a stick, unless
Soul clap its hands and sing.
W. B. Yeats *Sailing to Byzantium*

107 I pray – for fashion's word is out
And prayer comes round again –
That I may seem, though I die old,
A foolish passionate man.
W. B. Yeats *A Prayer for Old Age*

ONE-UPMANSHIP

See also snobbery, superiority

1 Keeping up with the Joneses was a full-time job with my mother and father. It was not until many years later when I lived alone that I

realized how much cheaper it was to drag the Joneses down to my level.
Quentin Crisp (c. 1910–) British model, publicist, and writer. *The Naked Civil Servant*

2 *How to be one up* – how to make the other man feel that something has gone wrong, however slightly.
Stephen Potter (1900–69) British writer. *Lifemanship*, Introduction

3 There is no doubt that basic weekendmanship should contain some reference to Important Person Play.
Stephen Potter *Lifemanship*, Ch. 2

OPERA

See also music, singing

1 Opera is like a husband with a foreign title: expensive to support, hard to understand, and therefore a supreme social challenge.
Cleveland Amory NBC TV, 6 Apr 1960

2 I do not mind what language an opera is sung in so long as it is a language I don't understand.
Edward Appleton (1892–1965) British physicist. *The Observer*, 'Sayings of the Week,' 28 Aug 1955

3 No good opera plot can be sensible, for people do not sing when they are feeling sensible.
W. H. Auden (1907–73) British poet. *Time*, 29 Dec 1961

4 The opera isn't over till the fat lady sings.
Dan Cook US journalist. *Washington Post*, 13 June 1978

5 People are wrong when they say the opera isn't what it used to be. It is what it used to be. That's what's wrong with it.
Noël Coward (1899–1973) British dramatist. *Design for Living*

6 Opera is when a guy gets stabbed in the back and instead of bleeding he sings.
Ed Gardener *Duffy's Tavern* (American radio show)

7 Opera in English, is, in the main, just about as sensible as baseball in Italian.
H. L. Mencken (1880–1956) US journalist. *The Frank Muir Book* (Frank Muir)

8 I sometimes wonder which would be nicer – an opera without an interval, or an interval without an opera.
Ernest Newman (1868–1959) British music critic. *Berlioz, Romantic and Classic*, (ed. Peter Heyworth)

9 His vocal cords were kissed by God.
Harold Schoenberg (1915–) US music critic. Referring to Luciano Pavarotti. *The Times*, 30 June 1981

10 Our mistake, you see, was to write interminable large operas, which had to fill an entire evening . . . And now along comes someone with a one- or two-act opera without all that pompous nonsense . . . that was a happy reform.
Giuseppe Verdi (1813–1901) Italian composer. Referring to Mascagni.

11 Tenors are noble, pure and heroic and get the soprano. But baritones are born villains in opera. Always the heavy and never the hero.
Leonard Warren (1911–60) US baritone singer. *The New York World Telegram*, 13 Feb 1957

12 Like German opera, too long and too loud.
Evelyn Waugh (1903–66) British novelist. Giving his opinions of warfare after the Battle of Crete, 1941. Attrib.

13 An unalterable and unquestioned law of the musical world required that the German text of French operas sung by Swedish artists should be translated into Italian for the clearer understanding of English speaking audiences.
Edith Wharton (1862–1937) US novelist. *The Age of Innocence*, Bk. I, Ch. 1

OPERATIONS

1 Lose a leg rather than life.
Proverb

2 Exploratory operation: a remunerative reconnaissance.
Anonymous

3 The operation was successful – but the patient died.
Anonymous

4 I never say of an operation that it is without danger.
August Bier (1861–1949)

5 The feasibility of an operation is not the *best* indication for its performance.
Henry, Lord Cohen of Birkenhead (1900–) Annals of the Royal College of Surgeons of England 6:3, 1950

6 Surgery does the ideal thing – it separates the patient from his disease. It puts the patient back to bed and the disease in a bottle.
Logan Clendening (1884–1945) *Modern Methods of Treatment*, Ch. 1

7 But after all, when all is said and done, the king of all topics is operations.
Irvin S. Cobb (1876–1944) US humorist and journalist. *Speaking of Operations*

8 Or, take a surgical operation.
In consultation with the doctor and the surgeon,
In going to bed in the nursing home,
In talking to the matron you are still the subject,
The centre of reality. But, stretched on the table,
You are a piece of furniture in a repair shop
For those who surround you, the masked actors;
All there is of you is your body
All the 'you' is withdrawn.
T. S. Eliot (1888–1965) US-born British poet and dramatist. *The Cocktail Party*, I:1

9 The practice of medicine is a thinker's art the practice of surgery a plumber's.
Martin H. Fischer (1879–1962) Aphorism

10 Surgery is the ready motion of steady and experienced hands.
Galen (fl. 2nd century) Greek physician and scholar. *Definitiones Medicae*, XXXV

11 Before undergoing a surgical operation arrange your temporal affairs – you may live.
Remy de Gourmont (1858–1915)

12 Speaking of the importance of draining abscesses he referred to the time when he was called to Balmoral to operate upon Queen Victoria for an axillary abscess and playfully said, 'Gentlemen, I am the only man who has ever stuck a knife in the Queen.'
J. R. Leeson Referring to Joseph Lister. *Lister as I Knew Him*

13 The greatest triumph of surgery today . . . lies in finding ways for avoiding surgery.
Robert Tuttle Morris (1857–1945) *Doctors Versus Folks*, Ch. 3

14 Anybody who is anybody seems to be getting a lift – by plastic surgery these days. It's the new world wide craze that combines the satisfactions of psychoanalysis,

massage, and a trip to the beauty salon.

Eugenia Sheppard (20th century) *New York Herald-Tribune,* 24 Feb 1958

15 The operation wasn't bad. I quite enjoyed the trip up from my room to the operating parlors, as a closely confined person does enjoy any sort of outing. The morphine had loosened my tongue, and while we waited in the corridor for the surgeon to arrive, the orderly and I let down our hair and had a good chat about fishing tackle.

E. B. White (1899–) US journalist and humorous writer. *The Second Tree from the Corner,* 'A Weekend with the Angels'

16 Ah well, I suppose I shall have to die beyond my means.

Oscar Wilde (1856–1900) Irish-born British writer and wit. On being told the cost of an operation.

OPINIONS

See also ideas

1 A man's opinion on tramcars matters; his opinion on Botticelli matters; his opinion on all things does not matter.

G. K. Chesterton (1874–1936) British writer. *Heretics*

2 Science is the father of knowledge, but opinion breeds ignorance.

Hippocrates (c. 460 BC–c. 377 BC) Greek physician. *The Canon Law,* IV

3 They that approve a private opinion, call it opinion; but they that mislike it, heresy: and yet heresy signifies no more than private opinion.

Thomas Hobbes (1588–1679) English philosopher. *Leviathan,* Pt. I, Ch. 11

4 The superiority of one man's opinion over another's is never so great as when the opinion is about a woman.

Henry James (1843–1916) US novelist. *The Tragic Muse,* Ch. 9

5 'Tis with our judgments as our watches, none
Go just alike, yet each believes his own.

Alexander Pope (1688–1744) British poet. *An Essay on Criticism*

6 The average man's opinions are much less foolish than they would be if he thought for himself.

Bertrand Russell (1872–1970) British philosopher. *Autobiography*

7 It is folly of too many to mistake the echo of a London coffee-house for the voice of the kingdom.

Jonathan Swift (1667–1745) Irish-born Anglican priest and writer. *The Conduct of the Allies*

8 So many men, so many opinions.

Terence (Publius Terentius Afer; c. 190–159 BC) Roman poet. *Phormio*

9 I agree with no man's opinion. I have some of my own.

Ivan Turgenev (1818–83) Russian novelist. *Fathers and Sons,* Ch. 13

10 It is just when opinions universally prevail and we have added lip service to their authority that we become sometimes most keenly conscious that we do not believe a word that we are saying.

Virginia Woolf (1882–1941) British novelist. *The Common Reader*

OPPORTUNITY

See also present

1 All's grist that comes to the mill.

Proverb

2 Every dog has his day.

Proverb

3 Hoist your sail when the wind is fair.

Proverb

4 Make hay while the sun shines.

Proverb

5 Nothing ventured, nothing gained.

Proverb

6 Opportunity seldom knocks twice.

Proverb

7 Strike while the iron is hot.

Proverb

8 Whenever you fall, pick up something.

Oswald Theodore Avery (1877–1955) Canadian bacteriologist. Attrib.

9 A wise man will make more opportunities than he finds.

Francis Bacon (1561–1626) English philosopher. *Essays,* 'Of Ceremonies and Respects'

10 Cast thy bread upon the waters: for thou shalt find it after many days.

Bible: Ecclesiastes 11:1

11 Let him now speak, or else hereafter for ever hold his peace.

The Book of Common Prayer *Solemnization of Matrimony*

12 Healing is a matter of time, but it is sometimes also a matter of opportunity.

Hippocrates (c. 460 BC–c. 377 BC) Greek physician. *Precepts,* I

13 Opportunities are usually disguised as hard work, so most people don't recognise them.

Ann Landers (1918–) US journalist. Attrib.

14 One can present people with opportunities. One cannot make them equal to them.

Rosamond Lehmann (1901–) British novelist. *The Ballad and the Source*

15 There is no security in this life. There is only opportunity.

Douglas MacArthur (1880–1964) US general. *MacArthur, His Rendezvous with History* (Courtney Whitney)

16 Equality of opportunity means equal opportunity to be unequal.

Iain Macleod (1913–70) British politician. *Way Of Life* (John Boyd Carpenter)

17 Grab a chance and you won't be sorry for a might have been.

Arthur Ransome (1884–1967) British novelist. *We didn't mean to go to Sea*

18 There is a tide in the affairs of men
Which, taken at the flood, leads on to fortune;
Omitted, all the voyage of their life
Is bound in shallows and in miseries.
On such a full sea are we now afloat,
And we must take the current when it serves,
Or lose our ventures.

William Shakespeare (1564–1616) English dramatist. *Julius Caesar,* IV:3

19 Why, then the world's mine oyster,
Which I with sword will open.

William Shakespeare *The Merry Wives of Windsor,* II:2

20 A man who never missed an occasion to let slip an opportunity.

George Bernard Shaw (1856–1950) Irish dramatist and critic. Referring to Lord Rosebery. Attrib.

21 I missed the chance of a lifetime, too. Fifty lovelies in the rude and I'd left my Bunsen burner home.

Dylan Thomas (1914–53) Welsh poet. *Portrait of the Artist as a Young Dog,* 'One Warm Saturday'

22 Never miss a chance to have sex or appear on television.

Gore Vidal (1925–) US novelist. Attrib.

OPPOSITES

See also conflict, difference, doublethink

1 It takes all sorts to make a world.
Proverb

2 The poet and the dreamer are distinct,
Diverse, sheer opposite, antipodes.
The one pours out a balm upon the world,
The other vexes it.
John Keats (1795–1821) British poet. *The Fall of Hyperion,* I

3 Oh, East is East, and West is West, and never the twain shall meet.
Rudyard Kipling (1865–1936) Indian-born British writer. *The Ballad of East and West*

4 The sublime and the ridiculous are often so nearly related that it is difficult to class them separately. One step above the sublime makes the ridiculous; and one step above the ridiculous makes the sublime again.
Thomas Paine (1737–1809) British writer. *The Age of Reason,* Pt. 2

5 Roses have thorns, and silver fountains mud;
Clouds and eclipses stain both moon and sun,
And loathsome canker lives in sweetest bud.
All men make faults.
William Shakespeare (1564–1616) English dramatist. *Sonnets,* 35

OPPOSITION

See also government, politics

1 It has been said that England invented the phrase, 'Her Majesty's Opposition'.
Walter Bagehot (1826–77) British economist and journalist. *See* HOBHOUSE *The English Constitution,* 'The Monarchy'

2 The duty of an opposition is to oppose.
Lord Randolph Churchill (1849–95) British Conservative politician. *Lord Randolph Churchill* (W. S. Churchill)

3 When I invented the phrase 'His Majesty's Opposition' he paid me a compliment on the fortunate hit.
John Cam Hobhouse (1786–1869) British politician. Speaking about Canning. *Recollections of a Long Life,* II, Ch. 12

4 One fifth of the people are against everything all the time.
Robert Kennedy (1925–68) US politician. *The Observer,* 'Sayings of the Week', 10 May 1964

5 . . . I have spent many years of my life in opposition and I rather like the role.
Eleanor Roosevelt (1884–1962) US writer and lecturer. Letter to Bernard Baruch, 18 Nov 1952

6 The tragedy of the Police State is that it always regards all opposition as a crime, and there are no degrees.
Lord Vansittart (1881–1957) British politician. Speech, House of Lords, June 1947

OPPRESSION

See also imprisonment, indoctrination, power politics, slavery, tyranny

1 When Israel was in Egypt land,
Let my people go,
Oppressed so hard they could not stand,
Let my people go.
Go down, Moses,
Way-down in Egypt land,
Tell old Pharaoh
To let my people go.
Anonymous Negro spiritual

2 Christ in this country would quite likely have been arrested under the Suppression of Communism Act.
Joost de Blank (1908–68) Dutch-born British churchman. Referring to South Africa. *The Observer,* 'Sayings of the Week', 27 Oct 1963

3 The enemies of Freedom do not argue; they shout and they shoot.
Dean Inge (1860–1954) British churchman. *The End of an Age,* Ch. 4

4 If you want a picture of the future, imagine a boot stamping on a human face – for ever.
George Orwell (Eric Blair; 1903–50) British novelist. *Nineteen Eighty-Four*

5 In the first days of the revolt you must kill: to shoot down a European is to kill two birds with one stone, to destroy an oppressor and the man he oppresses at the same time: there remain a dead man, and a free man.
Jean-Paul Sartre (1905–80) French writer. *The Wretched of the Earth* (F. Fanon), Preface

OPTIMISM

See also hope

1 After a storm comes a calm.
Proverb

2 Every cloud has a silver lining.
Proverb

3 It's an ill wind that blows nobody any good.
Proverb

4 It will all come right in the wash.
Proverb

5 Look on the bright side.
Proverb

6 No news is good news.
Proverb

7 Nothing so bad but it might have been worse.
Proverb

8 The darkest hour is just before the dawn.
Proverb

9 Tomorrow is another day.
Proverb

10 When one door shuts, another opens.
Proverb

11 While there's life there's hope.
Proverb

12 Are we downhearted? No!
Anonymous A favorite expression of the British soldiers during World War I. Attrib.

13 What's the use of worrying?
It never was worth while,
So, pack up your troubles in your old kit-bag,
And smile, smile, smile.
George Asaf (George H. Powell; 1880–1951) US songwriter. *Pack up Your Troubles in Your Old Kit-bag*

14 Let other pens dwell on guilt and misery.
Jane Austen (1775–1817) British novelist. *Mansfield Park,* Ch. 48

15 A Scout smiles and whistles under all circumstances.
Robert Baden-Powell (1857–1941) British soldier and founder of the Boy Scouts. *Scouting for Boys*

16 *Future,* n. That period of time in which our affairs prosper, our friends are true and our happiness is assured.
Ambrose Bierce (1842–?1914) US writer and journalist. *The Devil's Dictionary*

17 My sun sets to rise again.
Robert Browning (1812–89) British poet. *At the 'Mermaid'*

18 No, at noonday in the bustle of man's worktime

Greet the unseen with a cheer!
Robert Browning *Epilogue to Asolando*

19 The pessimist is the man who believes things couldn't possibly be worse, to which the optimist replies 'Oh yes they could.'
Vladimir Bukovsky (1942–) Russian writer and scientist. *The Guardian Weekly*, 10 July 1977

20 Don't you know each cloud contains
Pennies from Heaven?
Johnny Burke (1908–64) US songwriter. *Pennies from Heaven*

21 The optimist proclaims we live in the best of all possible worlds; and the pessimist fears this is true.
James Cabell (1879–1958) US novelist and journalist. *The Silver Stallion*

22 We are not downhearted. The trouble is, we cannot understand what is happening to our neighbours.
Joseph Chamberlain (1836–1914) British politician. Speech, 1906

23 Like the Mississippi, it just keeps rolling along. Let it roll. Let it roll on full flood, inexorable, irresistible, benignant, to broader lands and better days.
Winston Churchill (1874–1965) British statesman. Referring to co-operation with the US. Speech, House of Commons, 20 Aug 1940

24 The place where optimism most flourishes is the lunatic asylum.
Havelock Ellis (1859–1939) British sexologist. *The Dance of Life*, Ch. 3

25 Optimism is the content of small men in high places.
F. Scott Fitzgerald (1896–1940) US novelist. *The Crack-Up*

26 Let us draw upon content for the deficiencies of fortune.
Oliver Goldsmith (1728–74) Irish-born British playwright. *The Vicar of Wakefield*, Ch. 3

27 The corn is as high as an elephant's eye.
Oscar Hammerstein II (1895–1960) US lyricist. *Oklahoma!*, 'Oh, What a Beautiful Mornin''

28 Optimism: A kind of heart stimulant – the digitalis of failure.
Elbert G. Hubbard (1856–1915) *The Roycroft Dictionary*

29 Two men look out through the same bars:
One sees the mud, and one the stars.
Frederick Langbridge (1849–1923) British religious writer. *A Cluster of Quiet Thoughts*

30 An optimist is a guy that never had much experience.
Don Marquis (1878–1937) US journalist. *archy and mehitabel*

31 The Power of Positive Thinking.
Norman Vincent Peale (1899–) US clergyman and writer. Book title

32 The worst is not
So long as we can say 'This is the worst'.
William Shakespeare (1564–1616) English dramatist. *King Lear*, IV:1

33 Now is the winter of our discontent
Made glorious summer by this sun of York.
William Shakespeare *Richard III*, I:1

34 Life may change, but it may fly not;
Hope may vanish, but can die not;
Truth be veiled, but still it burneth;
Love repulsed, – but it returneth!
Percy Bysshe Shelley (1792–1822) British poet. *Hellas*, I

35 The latest definition of an optimist is one who fills up his crossword puzzle in ink.
Clement King Shorter (1857–1926) British journalist and critic. *The Observer*, 'Sayings of the Week', 22 Feb 1925

36 I am an optimist, unrepentant and militant. After all, in order not to be a fool an optimist must know how sad a place the world can be. It is only the pessimist who finds this out anew every day.
Peter Ustinov (1921–) British actor. *Dear Me*, Ch. 9

37 All is for the best in the best of possible worlds.
Voltaire (François-Marie Arouet; 1694–1778) French writer. *Candide*, Ch. 30

38 We are all in the gutter, but some of us are looking at the stars.
Oscar Wilde (1854–1900) Irish-born British dramatist. *Lady Windermere's Fan*, III

39 I'm an optimist, but I'm an optimist who carries a raincoat.
Harold Wilson (1916–) British politician and prime minister. Attrib.

40 Nor greetings where no kindness is, nor all
The dreary intercourse of daily life,
Shall e'er prevail against us, or disturb
Our cheerful faith, that all which we behold
Is full of blessings.
William Wordsworth (1770–1850) British poet. *Lines composed a few miles above Tintern Abbey*

ORDER

1 'Where shall I begin, please your Majesty?' he asked.
'Begin at the beginning' the King said, gravely, 'and go on till you come to the end: then stop.'
Lewis Carroll (Charles Lutwidge Dodgson; 1832–98) British writer. *Alice's Adventures in Wonderland*, Ch. 11

2 Order is heaven's first law.
Alexander Pope (1688–1744) British poet. *An Essay on Man*, IV

3 How sour sweet music is
When time is broke and no proportion kept!
So is it in the music of men's lives.
William Shakespeare (1564–1616) English dramatist. *Richard II*, V:5

4 O, when degree is shak'd,
Which is the ladder of all high designs,
The enterprise is sick!
William Shakespeare *Troilus and Cressida*, I:3

5 The heaven themselves, the planets, and this centre
Observe degree priority, and place,
Insisture, course, proportion, season, form,
Office, and custom, in all line of order.
William Shakespeare *Troilus and Cressida*, I:3

6 Take but degree away, untune that string,
And, hark! what discord follows; each thing meets
In mere oppugnancy.
William Shakespeare *Troilus and Cressida*, I:3

7 A place for everything, and everything in its place.
Samuel Smiles (1812–1904) British writer. *Thrift*, Ch. 5

ORIGINALITY

See also imitation, innovation

1 Anything that is worth doing has been done frequently. Things hitherto undone should be given, I suspect, a wide berth.
Max Beerbohm (1872–1956) British writer. *Mainly on the Air*

2 An original writer is not one who imitates nobody, but one whom nobody can imitate.
Vicomte de Chateaubriand (1768–1848) French diplomat and writer. *Génie du Christianisme*

3 A thought is often original, though you have uttered it a hundred times.
Oliver Wendell Holmes (1809–94) US writer. *The Autocrat of the Breakfast Table*, Ch. 1

4 All good things which exist are the fruits of originality.
John Stuart Mill (1806–73) British philosopher. *On Liberty*, Ch. 3

5 Nothing has yet been said that's not been said before.
Terence (Publius Terentius Afer; c. 190–159 BC) Roman poet. *Eunuchus*, Prologue

6 Another unsettling element in modern art is that common symptom of immaturity, the dread of doing what has been done before.
Edith Wharton (1862–1937) US novelist. *The Writing of Fiction*, Ch. 1

ORTHODOXY

See also conformity

1 The difference between Orthodoxy or My-doxy and Heterodoxy or Thy-doxy.
Thomas Carlyle (1795–1881) Scottish historian and essayist. A similar remark is attributed to the British churchman William Warburton (1698–1779). *History of the French Revolution*, Pt. II, Bk. IV, Ch. 2

2 The word 'orthodoxy' not only no longer means being right; it practically means being wrong.
G. K. Chesterton (1874–1936) British writer. *Heretics*, Ch. 1

3 Worldly wisdom teaches that it is better for the reputation to fail conventionally than to succeed unconventionally.
John Maynard Keynes (1883–1946) British economist. *The General Theory of Employment, Interest and Money*, Bk. IV, Ch. 12

ORWELL, George

(Eric Blair; 1903–50) British novelist. His books include *The Road to Wigan Pier* (1937), *Animal Farm* (1945), and *Nineteen Eighty-Four* (1949).

Quotations about Orwell

1 He could not blow his nose without moralising on the state of the handkerchief industry.
Cyril Connolly (1903–74) British journalist. *The Evening Colonnade*

2 He was a kind of saint, and in that character, more likely in politics to chastise his own side than the enemy.
V. S. Pritchett (1900–) British short-story writer. *New Statesman*, 1950

Quotations by Orwell

3 Man is the only creature that consumes without producing.
An allegory of the Marxist analysis of capitalism, with man representing the capitalist. *Animal Farm*, Ch. 1

4 Four legs good, two legs bad.
Animal Farm, Ch. 3

5 War is war. The only good human being is a dead one.
Animal Farm, Ch. 4

6 He intended, he said, to devote the rest of his life to learning the remaining twenty-two letters of the alphabet.
Animal Farm, Ch. 9

7 All animals are equal but some animals are more equal than others.
Animal Farm, Ch. 10

8 The high sentiments always win in the end, the leaders who offer blood, toil, tears and sweat always get more out of their followers than those who offer safety and a good time. When it comes to the pinch, human beings are heroic.
The Art of Donald McGill

9 I'm fat, but I'm thin inside. Has it ever struck you that there's a thin man inside every fat man, just as they say there's a statue inside every block of stone?
Coming Up For Air, Pt. I, Ch. 3

10 Before the war, and especially before the Boer War, it was summer all the year round.
Coming Up for Air, Pt. II, Ch. 1

11 Prolonged, indiscriminate reviewing of books involves constantly *inventing* reactions towards books about which one has no spontaneous feelings whatever.
Confessions of a Book Reviewer

12 He was an embittered atheist (the sort of atheist who does not so much disbelieve in God as personally dislike Him).
Down and Out in Paris and London, Ch. 30

13 Probably the Battle of Waterloo *was* won on the playing-fields of Eton, but the opening battles of all subsequent wars have been lost there.
The Lion and the Unicorn, 'England, Your England'

14 A family with the wrong members in control – that, perhaps, is as near as one can come to describing England in a phrase.
The Lion and the Unicorn, 'The Ruling Class'

15 Who controls the past controls the future. Who controls the present controls the past.
Nineteen Eighty-Four

16 If you want a picture of the future, imagine a boot stamping on a human face – for ever.
Nineteen Eighty-Four

17 Big Brother is watching you.
Nineteen Eighty-Four

18 War is Peace, Freedom is Slavery, Ignorance is Strength.
Nineteen Eighty-Four

19 Doublethink means the power of holding two contradictory beliefs in one's mind simultaneously, and accepting both of them.
Nineteen Eighty-Four

20 In our time, political speech and writing are largely the defence of the indefensible.
Politics and the English Language

21 The books one reads in childhood, and perhaps most of all the bad and good bad books, create in one's mind a sort of false map of the world, a series of fabulous countries into which one can retreat at odd moments throughout the rest of life, and which in some cases can even survive a visit to the real countries which they are supposed to represent.
Riding Down from Bangor

22 It is brought home to you . . . that it is only because miners sweat their guts out that superior persons can remain superior.
The Road to Wigan Pier, Ch. 2

23 I sometimes think that the price of liberty is not so much eternal vigilance as eternal dirt.
The Road to Wigan Pier, Ch. 4

24 We may find in the long run that tinned food is a deadlier weapon than the machine-gun.
The Road to Wigan Pier, Ch. 6

25 There can hardly be a town in the

South of England where you could throw a brick without hitting the niece of a bishop.
The Road to Wigan Pier, Ch. 7

26 As with the Christian religion, the worst advertisement for Socialism is its adherents.
The Road to Wigan Pier, Ch. 11

27 To the ordinary working man, the sort you would meet in any pub on Saturday night, Socialism does not mean much more than better wages and shorter hours and nobody bossing you about.
The Road to Wigan Pier, Ch. 11

28 The higher-water mark, so to speak, of Socialist literature is W. H. Auden, a sort of gutless Kipling.
The Road to Wigan Pier, Ch. 11

29 We have nothing to lose but our aitches.
Referring to the middle classes. *The Road to Wigan Pier*, Ch. 13

30 The quickest way of ending a war is to lose it.
Second Thoughts on James Burnham

31 Most people get a fair amount of fun out of their lives, but on balance life is suffering and only the very young or the very foolish imagine otherwise.
Shooting an Elephant

32 Serious sport has nothing to do with fair play. It is bound up with hatred, jealousy, boastfulness, disregard of all rules and sadistic pleasure in witnessing violence; in other words it is war minus the shooting.
The Sporting Spirit

33 To a surprising extent the war-lords in shining armour, the apostles of the martial virtues, tend not to die fighting when the time comes. History is full of ignominious getaways by the great and famous.
Who Are the War Criminals?

34 He is pretty certain to come back into favour. One of the surest signs of his genius is that women dislike his books.
Referring to Conrad. *New English Weekly*, 23 Jul 1936

35 Each generation imagines itself to be more intelligent than the one that went before it, and wiser than the one that comes after it.
Book Review

36 At 50, everyone has the face he deserves.
Last words in his manuscript notebook, 17 Apr 1949.

OSTENTATION

See also affectation

1 That's it, baby, if you've got it, flaunt it.
Mel Brooks (Melvyn Kaminsky; 1926–) US film director. *The Producers*

2 The possession of a book becomes a substitute for reading it.
Anthony Burgess (John Burgess Wilson; 1917–) British novelist. *New York Times Book Review*

3 Wealth has never been a sufficient source of honor in itself. It must be advertised, and the normal medium is obtrusively expensive goods.
John Kenneth Galbraith (1908–) US economist. *The Affluent Society*, Ch. 7

4 When I meet those remarkable people whose company is coveted, I often wish they would show off a little more.
Desmond MacCarthy (1877–1952) British writer and theater critic. *Theatre*, 'Good Talk'

5 She's like the old line about justice – not only must be done but must be seen to be done.
John Osborne (1929–) British dramatist. *Time Present*, I

6 With the great part of rich people, the chief employment of riches consists in the parade of riches.
Adam Smith (1723–90) Scottish economist. *The Wealth of Nations*

OXFORD

See also education, England

1 Home of lost causes, and forsaken beliefs, and unpopular names, and impossible loyalties!
Matthew Arnold (1822–88) British poet and critic. *Essays in Criticism*, First Series, Preface

2 That sweet City with her dreaming spires
She needs not June for beauty's heightening.
Matthew Arnold *Thyrsis*

3 Oxford is on the whole more attractive than Cambridge to the ordinary visitor; and the traveller is therefore recommended to visit Cambridge first, or to omit it altogether if he cannot visit both.
Karl Baedeker (1801–59) German publisher. *Baedeker's Great Britain*, 'From London to Oxford'

4 . . . a young man with so superior a voice that he might have been to Oxford twice.
Vernon Bartlett (1894–) British journalist and writer. *And Now, Tomorrow*

5 It is Oxford that has made me insufferable.
Max Beerbohm (1872–1956) British writer. *More*, 'Going back to School'

6 The King to Oxford sent a troop of horse,
For Tories own no argument but force:
With equal skill to Cambridge books he sent,
For Whigs admit no force but argument.
William Browne (1692–1774) English physician. A reply to TRAPP *Literary Anecdotes* (Nichols), Vol. III

7 It is a secret in the Oxford sense: you may tell it to only one person at a time.
Oliver Franks (1905–) British philosopher and administrator. *Sunday Telegraph*, 30 Jan 1977

8 To the University of Oxford I acknowledge no obligation; and she will as cheerfully renounce me for a son, as I am willing to disclaim her for a mother. I spent fourteen months at Magdalen College: they proved the fourteen months the most idle and unprofitable of my whole life.
Edward Gibbon (1737–94) British historian. *Autobiography*

9 Oxford had not taught me, nor had any other place or person, the value of liberty as an essential condition of excellence in human things.
William Ewart Gladstone (1809–98) British statesman. Gladstone graduated from Oxford in 1831.

10 The clever men at Oxford
Know all that there is to be knowed.
But they none of them know one half as much
As intelligent Mr Toad.
Kenneth Grahame (1859–1932) Scottish writer. *The Wind in the Willows*, Ch. 10

11 I often think how much easier the world would have been to manage if

Herr Hitler and Signor Mussolini had been at Oxford.
Viscount Halifax (1881–1959) British politician. Speech, York, 4 Nov 1937

12 Cambridge sees Oxford as the Latin quarter of Cowley.
Marjorie Knight Letter to *Daily Telegraph*, 15 Aug 1979

13 Very nice sort of place, Oxford, I should think, for people that like that sort of place.
George Bernard Shaw (1856–1950) Irish dramatist and critic. *Man and Superman*, II

14 The King, observing with judicious eyes
The state of both his universities,
To Oxford sent a troop of horse, and why?
That learned body wanted loyalty;
To Cambridge books, as very well discerning
How much that loyal body wanted learning.
Joseph Trapp (1679–1747) English churchman and academic. Written after George I donated the Bishop of Ely's library to Cambridge; for reply see BROWNE *Literary Anecdotes* (Nichols), Vol. III

15 Oxford is, and always has been, full of cliques, full of factions, and full of a particular non-social snobbiness.
Mary Warnock (1924–) British philosopher and educator. *The Observer*, 2 Nov 1980

16 We think of Cambridge as a little town and Oxford as a hive of industry, but they aren't that different.
Katherine Whitehorn (1926–) British journalist. *The Observer*, 14 Jan 1979

P

PAIN

1 I feel no pain, dear mother, now
But oh, I am so dry!
O take me to a brewery
And leave me there to die.
Anonymous Shanty

2 There was a faith-healer of Deal,
Who said, 'Although pain isn't real,
If I sit on a pin
And it punctures my skin,
I dislike what I fancy I feel.'
Anonymous

3 The wish to hurt, the momentary intoxication with pain, is the loophole through which the pervert climbs into the minds of ordinary men.
Jacob Bronowski (1908–74) British scientist and writer. *The Face of Violence*, Ch. 5

4 Detested sport,
That owes its pleasures to another's pain.
William Cowper (1731–1800) British poet. *The Task*

5 Corporal punishment is as humiliating for him who gives it as for him who receives it; it is ineffective besides. Neither shame nor physical pain have any other effect than a hardening one . . .
Ellen Key (Karolina Sofia Key; 1849–1926) Swedish writer. *The Century of the Child*, Ch. 8

6 Much benevolence of the passive order may be traced to a disinclination to inflict pain upon oneself.
George Meredith (1828–1909) British novelist. *Vittoria*, Ch. 42

7 The pain passes, but the beauty remains.
Pierre Auguste Renoir (1841–1919) French impressionist painter. Explaining why he still painted when his hands were twisted with arthritis. Attrib.

8 Pleasure is nothing else but the intermission of pain.
John Selden (1584–1654) English historian. *Table Talk*

9 O Lord, methought what pain it was to drown,
What dreadful noise of waters in my ears,
What sights of ugly death within my eyes!
William Shakespeare (1564–1616) English dramatist. *Richard III*, I:4

PAINTING

See also art, artists

1 One picture is worth ten thousand words.
Frederick R. Barnard Ascribed to Chinese origin. *Printer's Ink*, 8 Dec 1921

2 Buy old masters. They fetch a better price than old mistresses.
Lord Beaverbrook (1879–1964) Canadian-born British newspaper proprietor. Attrib.

3 *Painting, n.* The art of protecting flat surfaces from the weather and exposing them to the critic.
Ambrose Bierce (1842–?1914) US writer and journalist. *The Devil's Dictionary*

4 Good painters imitate nature, bad ones spew it up.
Miguel de Cervantes (1547–1616) Spanish novelist. *El Licenciado Vidriera*

5 The day is coming when a single carrot, freshly observed, will set off a revolution.
Paul Cézanne (1839–1906) French postimpressionist painter. Attrib.

6 It's either easy or impossible.
Salvador Dali (1904–1989) Spanish painter. Reply when asked if he found it hard to paint a picture. Attrib.

7 I do not paint a portrait to look like the subject, rather does the person grow to look like his portrait.
Salvador Dali Spanish painter. Attrib.

8 Never mind about my soul, just make sure you get my tie right.
James Joyce (1882–1941) Irish novelist. Responding to the painter Patrick Tuohy's assertion that he wished to capture Joyce's soul in his portrait of him. *James Joyce* (R. Ellmann)

9 If people only knew as much about painting as I do, they would never buy my pictures.
Edwin Landseer (1802–73) British painter and sculptor. Said to W. P. Frith. *Landseer the Victorian Paragon* (Campbell Lennie), Ch. 12

10 I mix them with my brains, sir.
John Opie (1761–1807) British painter. When asked what he mixed his colors with. *Self-Help* (Samuel Smiles), Ch. 4

11 A picture has been said to be something between a thing and a thought.
Samuel Palmer (1805–81) British landscape painter. *Life of Blake* (Arthur Symons)

12 If I like it, I say it's mine. If I don't I say it's a fake.
Pablo Picasso (1881–1973) Spanish painter. When asked how he knew which paintings were his. *The Sunday Times*, 10 Oct 1965

13 I paint objects as I think them, not as I see them.
Pablo Picasso Attrib.

14 Painting is a blind man's profession. He paints not what he sees, but what he feels, what he tells himself about what he has seen.
Pablo Picasso *Journals* (Jean Cocteau), 'Childhood'

15 It's better like that, if you want to kill a picture all you have to do is to hang it beautifully on a nail and soon you will see nothing of it but the frame. When it's out of place you see it better.
Pablo Picasso Explaining why a Renoir in his apartment was hung crooked. *Picasso: His Life and Work* (Ronald Penrose)

16 It is bad enough to be condemned to drag around this image in which nature has imprisoned me. Why should I consent to the perpetuation of the image of this image?
Plotinus (205–270 AD) Egyptian-born Greek philosopher. Refusing to have his portrait painted. Attrib.

17 I just keep painting till I feel like pinching. Then I know it's right.
Pierre Auguste Renoir (1841–1919) French impressionist painter. Explaining how he achieved such lifelike flesh tones in his nudes. Attrib.

18 Every time I paint a portrait I lose a friend.
John Singer Sargent (1856–1925) US portrait painter. Attrib.

19 Portraits of famous bards and preachers, all fur and wool from the squint to the kneecaps.
Dylan Thomas (1914–53) Welsh poet. *Under Milk Wood*

20 My business is to paint not what I know, but what I see.
Joseph Turner (1775–1851) British painter. Responding to a criticism of the fact that he had painted no portholes on the ships in a view of Plymouth. *Proust: The Early Years* (G. Painter)

PARADISE

See heaven

PARASITES

1 Many a man who thinks to found a home discovers that he has merely opened a tavern for his friends.
Norman Douglas (1868–1952) British novelist. *South Wind*, Ch. 24

2 A free-loader is a confirmed guest. He is the man who is always willing to come to dinner.
Damon Runyon (1884–1946) US writer. *Short Takes*, 'Free-Loading Ethics'

3 So, naturalist observe, a flea
Hath smaller fleas that on him prey,
And these have smaller fleas to bite 'em.
And so proceed *ad infinitum*.
Jonathan Swift (1667–1745) Irish-born Anglican priest and writer. *On Poetry*

4 But was there ever dog that praised his fleas?
W. B. Yeats (1865–1939) Irish poet. *To a Poet, who would have me Praise certain Bad Poets, Imitators of His and Mine*

PARENTS

See also family

1 The law of heredity is that all undesirable traits come from the other parent.
Anonymous

2 I like children. I never gave them a second thought when I was making them, but I like them very much.
Jake Thackeray Interview with Frank Kempe. *North Devon Herald*, 6 Sept 1979

PARIS

See also France

1 The last time I saw Paris, her heart was warm and gay,
I heard the laughter of her heart in every street café.
Oscar Hammerstein II (1895–1960) US lyricist. *Lady Be Good*, 'The Last Time I Saw Paris'

2 If you are lucky enough to have lived in Paris as a young man, then wherever you go for the rest of your life, it stays with you, for Paris is a moveable feast.
Ernest Hemingway (1899–1961) US novelist. *A Moveable Feast*, Epigraph

3 Paris is worth a mass.
Henri IV (1553–1610) King of France. Said on entering Paris (March 1594), having secured its submission to his authority by becoming a Roman Catholic. Attrib.

4 Is Paris burning?
Adolf Hitler (1889–1945) German dictator. Referring to the liberation of Paris, 1944

5 As an artist, a man has no home in Europe save in Paris.
Friedrich Wilhelm Nietzsche (1844–1900) German philosopher. *Ecce Homo*

6 I love Paris in the springtime.
Cole Porter (1893–1964) US composer and lyricist. *Can-Can*, 'I Love Paris'

7 Paris Loves Lovers.
Cole Porter *Silk Stockings*

PARKER, Dorothy (Rothschild)

(1893–1967) US writer and wit. Her New York circle in the 1920s included Ogden Nash and James Thurber. She is best known for her short stories, sketches, and poems; her books include *Not So Deep As a Well* (1936).

Quotations about Parker

1 She has put into what she has written a voice, a state of mind, an era, a few moments of human experience that nobody else has conveyed.
Edmund Wilson (1895–1972) US critic and writer. Attrib.

2 She is a combination of Little Nell and Lady Macbeth.
Alexander Woollcott (1887–1943) US journalist. *While Rome Burns*

Quotations by Parker

3 Razors pain you
Rivers are damp;
Acids stain you;
And drugs cause cramp.
Guns aren't lawful;
Nooses give;
Gas smells awful;
You might as well live.
Enough Rope, 'Resumé'

4 He lies below, correct in cypress wood,
And entertains the most exclusive worms.
Epitaph for a Very Rich Man

5 All I say is, nobody has any business to go around looking like a horse and behaving as if it were all right. You don't catch horses going around looking like people, do you?
Horsie

6 How do people go to sleep? I'm afraid I've lost the knack. I might try busting myself smartly over the temple with the nightlight. I might repeat to myself, slowly and soothingly, a list of quotations beautiful from minds profound; if I can remember any of the damn things.
The Little Hours

7 I'm never going to be famous . . . I don't do anything. Not one single

thing. I used to bite my nails, but I don't even do that any more.
The Little Hours

8 Why is it no one ever sent me yet
One perfect limousine, do you suppose?
Ah no, it's always just my luck to get
One perfect rose.
One Perfect Rose

9 Sorrow is tranquillity remembered in emotion.
Sentiment

10 It costs me never a stab nor squirm
To tread by chance upon a worm.
'Aha, my little dear,' I say,
'Your clan will pay me back one day.'
Sunset Gun, 'Thought for a Sunshiny Morning'

11 By the time you swear you're his,
Shivering and sighing,
And he vows his passion is
Infinite, undying –
Lady, make a note of this:
One of you is lying.
Unfortunate Coincidence

12 That should assure us of at least forty-five minutes of undisturbed privacy.
Pressing a button marked NURSE during a stay in hospital. *The Algonquin Wits* (R. Drennan)

13 The poor son-of-a-bitch!
Quoting from *The Great Gatsby* on paying her last respects to F. Scott Fitzgerald. *Thalberg: Life and Legend* (B. Thomas)

14 If all the young ladies who attended the Yale promenade dance were laid end to end, no one would be the least surprised.
While Rome Burns (Alexander Woollcott)

15 Brevity is the soul of lingerie.
While Rome Burns (Alexander Woollcott)

16 This is not a novel to be tossed aside lightly. It should be thrown with great force.
Book review. *Wit's End* (R. E. Dremman)

17 A list of authors who have made themselves most beloved and therefore, most comfortable financially, shows that it is our national joy to mistake for the first-rate, the fecund rate.
Wit's End (R. E. Drennan)

18 You can't teach an old dogma new tricks.
Wit's End (R. E. Drennan)

19 I was fired from there, finally, for a lot of things, among them my insistence that the Immaculate Conception was spontaneous combustion.
Writers at Work, First Series (Malcolm Cowley)

20 This is on me.
Suggesting words for tombstone. *You Might As Well Live* (J. Keats), Pt. I, Ch. 5

21 It serves me right for putting all my eggs in one bastard.
Said on going into hospital to get an abortion. *You Might as Well Live* (J. Keats), Pt. II, Ch. 3

22 Oh, don't worry about Alan . . . Alan will always land on somebody's feet.
Said of her husband on the day their divorce became final. *You Might As Well Live* (J. Keats), Pt. IV, Ch. 1

23 How could they tell?
Reaction to news of the death of Calvin Coolidge, US President 1923–29; also attributed to H. L. Mencken. *You Might As Well Live* (J. Keats)

24 Dear Mary, We all knew you had it in you.
Telegram sent to a friend on the successful outcome of her much-publicized pregnancy

25 You can lead a whore to culture but you can't make her think.
Speech to American Horticultural Society

26 You know, she speaks eighteen languages. And she can't say 'No' in any of them.
Speaking of an acquaintance. Attrib.

27 Men seldom make passes
At girls who wear glasses.
Attrib.

28 Check enclosed.
Giving her version of the two most beautiful words in the English language. Attrib.

29 She ran the whole gamut of the emotions from A to B.
Referring to a performance by Katharine Hepburn on Broadway. Attrib.

30 Excuse my dust.
Her own epitaph

PAROCHIALISM

See also self-interest, selfishness

1 This fellow did not see further than his own nose.
Jean de La Fontaine (1621–95) French poet. *Fables*, III, 'Le Renard et le Bouc'

2 A broken head in Cold Bath Fields produces a greater sensation among us than three pitched battles in India.
Lord Macaulay (1800–59) British historian. Speech, 10 July 1833

3 'That is well said,' replied Candide, 'but we must cultivate our garden.'
Voltaire (François-Marie Arouet; 1694–1778) French writer. *Candide*, Ch. 30

PARTIES

See also society

1 I'll tell you what game we'll play. We're done with Humiliate the Host . . . and we don't want to play Hump the Hostess . . . We'll play a round of Get the Guests.
Edward Albee (1928–) US playwright. *Who's Afraid of Virginia Woolf?*

2 The sooner every party breaks up the better.
Jane Austen (1775–1817) British novelist. *Emma*, Ch. 25

3 And bring hither the fatted calf, and kill it; and let us eat, and be merry: For this my son was dead, and is alive again; he was lost, and is found. And they began to be merry.
Bible: Luke 15:23–24

4 ELYOT. Delightful parties Lady Bundle always gives, doesn't she?
AMANDA. Entrancing. Such a dear old lady.
ELYOT. And so gay. Did you notice her at supper blowing all those shrimps through her ear trumpet.
Noël Coward (1899–1973) British dramatist. *Private Lives*

5 I entertained on a cruising trip that was so much fun that I had to sink my yacht to make my guests go home.
F. Scott Fitzgerald (1896–1940) US novelist. *The Crack-Up*, 'Notebooks, K'

6 I was one of the few guests who had actually been invited. People were not invited – they went there.
F. Scott Fitzgerald *The Great Gatsby*, Ch. 3

7 HE. Have you heard it's in the stars
Next July we collide with Mars?
SHE. Well, did you evah! What a swell party this is.
Cole Porter (1893–1964) US songwriter. *High Society* 'Well, Did You Evah!'

8 Certainly, there is nothing else here to enjoy.
George Bernard Shaw (1856–1950) Irish dramatist and critic. Said at a party when his hostess asked him whether he was enjoying himself. *Pass the Port* (Oxfam)

9 'So like one's first parties' said Miss

Runcible 'being sick with other people singing.'
Evelyn Waugh (1903–66) British novelist. *Vile Bodies*

10 She had heard someone say something about an Independent Labour Party, and was furious that she had not been asked.
Evelyn Waugh *Vile Bodies*

11 The Life and Soul, the man who will never go home while there is one man, woman or glass of anything not yet drunk.
Katherine Whitehorn (1926–) British journalist. *Sunday Best*, 'Husband-Swapping'

12 He would give them his every imitation from 'Eton and Oxford' to the flushing of the lavatory cistern, and so, perhaps, carry the evening through.
Angus Wilson (1913–) British novelist. *A Bit Off the Map*

13 This party is a moral crusade, or it is nothing.
Harold Wilson (1916–) British politician and prime minister. Speech, 1962

PARTING

See also departure, greetings, separation

1 Adieu, adieu, kind friends, adieu, adieu, adieu,
I can no longer stay with you, stay with you.
I'll hang my harp on a weeping willow-tree.
And may the world go well with thee.
Anonymous *There is a Tavern in the Town*

2 There is a tavern in the town,
And there my dear love sits him down,
And drinks his wine 'mid laughter free,
And never, never thinks of me.

Fare thee well, for I must leave thee,
Do not let this parting grieve thee,
And remember that the best of friends must part.
Anonymous *There is a Tavern in the Town*

3 Farewell and adieu to you,
Fair Spanish Ladies
Farewell and adieu to you, Ladies of Spain.
Anonymous *Spanish Ladies*

4 Forty years on, when afar and asunder
Parted are those who are singing today.
E. E. Bowen (1836–1901) British writer. *Forty Years On* (the Harrow school song)

5 Parting is all we know of heaven,
And all we need of hell.
Emily Dickinson (1830–86) US poet. *My Life Closed Twice Before its Close*

6 Since there's no help, come let us kiss and part –
Nay, I have done, you get no more of me;
And I am glad, yea glad with all my heart
That thus so cleanly I myself can free.
Michael Drayton (1563–1631) English poet. *Sonnets*, 61

7 But tha mun dress thysen, an' go back to thy stately homes of England, how beautiful they stand. Time's up! Time's up for Sir John, an' for little Lady Jane! Put thy shimmy on, Lady Chatterley!
D. H. Lawrence (1885–1930) British novelist. *Lady Chatterley's Lover*, Ch. 15

8 It was not like your great and gracious ways!
Do you, that have nought other to lament,
Never, my Love, repent
Of how, that July afternoon,
You went,
With sudden, unintelligible phrase, –
And frightened eye,
Upon your journey of so many days,
Without a single kiss or a good-bye?
Coventry Patmore (1823–96) British poet. *The Unknown Eros*, Bk. I, 'Departure'

9 It is seldom indeed that one parts on good terms, because if one were on good terms one would not part.
Marcel Proust (1871–1922) French novelist. *À la recherche du temps perdu: La Prisonnière*

10 Good night, good night! Parting is such sweet sorrow
That I shall say good night till it be morrow.
William Shakespeare (1564–1616) English dramatist. *Romeo and Juliet*, II:2

11 Farewell! thou art too dear for my possessing,
And like enough thou know'st thy estimate:
The charter of thy worth gives thee releasing;
My bonds in thee are all determinate.
William Shakespeare *Sonnet 87*

12 Good-by-ee! – good-bye-ee!
Wipe the tear, baby dear, from your eye-ee.
Tho' it's hard to part, I know,
I'll be tickled to death to go.
Don't cry-ee! – don't sigh-ee!
There's a silver lining in the sky-ee! –
Bonsoir, old thing! cheerio! chin-chin!
Nahpoo! Toodle-oo! Good-bye-ee!
R. P. Weston (20th century) British songwriter. *Good-bye-ee!* (with Bert Lee)

PASSION

See also emotion, love

1 Asthma is a disease that has practically the same symptoms as passion except that with asthma it lasts longer.
Anonymous

2 The man who is master of his passions is Reason's slave.
Cyril Connolly (1903–74) British journalist. *Turnstile One* (ed. V. S. Pritchett)

3 A man who has not passed through the inferno of his passions has never overcome them.
Carl Gustav Jung (1875–1961) Swiss psychoanalyst. *Memories, Dreams, Reflections*, Ch. 9

4 For ever warm and still to be enjoy'd,
For ever panting and for ever young;
All breathing human passion far above,
That leaves a heart high-sorrowful and cloy'd,
A burning forehead, and a parching tongue.
John Keats (1795–1821) British poet. *Ode on a Grecian Urn*

5 It is with our passions as it is with fire and water, they are good servants, but bad masters.
Roger L'Estrange (1616–1704) English journalist and writer. *Aesop's Fables*, 38

6 And hence one master-passion in the breast,
Like Aaron's serpent, swallows up the rest.
Alexander Pope (1688–1744) British poet. *An Essay on Man*, II

7 The ruling passion, be it what it will
The ruling passion conquers reason still.
Alexander Pope *Moral Essays*, III

8 Passion, you see, can be destroyed by a doctor. It cannot be created.
Peter Shaffer (1926–) British dramatist. *Equus*, II:35

9 Give me that man
That is not passion's slave, and I will wear him
In my heart's core, ay, in my heart of heart,
As I do thee.
William Shakespeare (1564–1616) English dramatist. *Hamlet*, III:2

10 So I triumphed ere my passion, sweeping thro' me, left me dry,
Left me with the palsied heart, and left me with the jaundiced eye.
Alfred, Lord Tennyson (1809–92) British poet. *Locksley Hall*

11 Strange fits of passion have I known:
And I will dare to tell,
But in the lover's ear alone,
What once to me befell.
William Wordsworth (1770–1850) British poet. *Strange Fits of Passion*

PAST

See also experience, future, history, memory, nostalgia, present, regret, time

1 Even God cannot change the past.
Agathon (c. 446–401 BC) Athenian poet and playwright. *Nicomachean Ethics* (Aristotle), VI

2 There is always something rather absurd about the past.
Max Beerbohm (1872–1956) British writer. *1880*

3 A king lived long ago,
In the morning of the world,
When earth was nigher heaven than now.
Robert Browning (1812–89) British poet. *Pippa Passes*, Pt. I

4 Study the past, if you would divine the future.
Confucius (K'ung Fu-tzu; 551–479 BC) Chinese philosopher. *Analects*

5 The past is a foreign country: they do things differently there.
L. P. Hartley (1895–1972) British novelist. *The Go-Between*

6 Why doesn't the past decently bury itself, instead of sitting and waiting to be admitted by the present?
D. H. Lawrence (1885–1930) British novelist. *St. Mawr*

7 Yesterday, all my troubles seemed so far away.
John Lennon (1940–80) British rock musician. *Yesterday* (with Paul McCartney)

8 Look back, and smile at perils past.
Walter Scott (1771–1832) Scottish novelist. *The Bridal of Triermain*, Introduction

9 The past is the only dead thing that smells sweet.
Edward Thomas (1878–1917) British poet. *Early One Morning*

10 Keep off your thoughts from things that are past and done;
For thinking of the past wakes regret and pain.
Arthur Waley (1889–1966) British poet and translator. Translation from the Chinese of Po-Chü-I. *Resignation*

11 The past, at least, is secure.
Daniel Webster (1782–1852) US statesman. Speech, US Senate, 26 Jan 1830

12 Each has his past shut in him like the leaves of a book known to him by heart and his friends can only read the title.
Virginia Woolf (1882–1941) British novelist. *Jacob's Room*

PATIENCE

See also endurance, persistence

1 A watched pot never boils.
Proverb

2 Everything comes to him who waits.
Proverb

3 First things first.
Proverb

4 Patience is a virtue.
Proverb

5 Rome was not built in a day.
Proverb

6 We must learn to walk before we can run.
Proverb

7 Wait and see.
Herbert Henry Asquith (1852–1928) British statesman. In various speeches, 1910

8 *Patience*, n. A minor form of despair, disguised as a virtue.
Ambrose Bierce (1842–?1914) US writer and journalist. *The Devil's Dictionary*

9 The bud may have a bitter taste,
But sweet will be the flower.
William Cowper (1731–1800) British poet. *Olney Hymns*, 35

10 Beware the Fury of a Patient Man.
John Dryden (1631–1700) British poet and dramatist. *Absalom and Achitophel*, I

11 And now before us stands the last problem that must be solved and will be solved. It is the last territorial claim which I have to make in Europe, but it is the claim from which I will not recede and which, God willing, I will make good... With regard to the problem of the Sudeten Germans, my patience is now at an end.
Adolf Hitler (1889–1945) German dictator. Speech, Berlin, 26 Sept 1938

12 Patience and passage of time do more than strength and fury.
Jean de La Fontaine (1621–95) French poet. *Fables*, II, 'Le Lion et le Rat'

13 Though patience be a tired mare, yet she will plod.
William Shakespeare (1564–1616) English dramatist. *Henry V*, II:1

14 Very well, I can wait.
Arnold Schoenberg (1874–1951) German composer. Replying to a complaint that his violin concerto would need a musician with six fingers. Attrib.

15 It is very strange... that the years teach us patience; that the shorter our time, the greater our capacity for waiting.
Elizabeth Taylor (1912–75) British writer. *A Wreath of Roses*, Ch. 10

PATIENTS

1 Every invalid is a physician.
Irish proverb

2 The sick man is the garden of the physicians.
Swahili proverb

3 It is not a case we are treating; it is a living, palpitating, alas, too often suffering fellow creature.
John Brown (1810–82) *Lancet*, 1:464, 1904

4 Never forget that it is not a pneumonia, but a pneumonic man who is your patient. Not a typhoid fever, but a typhoid man.
Sir William Withey Gull (1816–90) *Published Writings*, Memoir II

5 Keep a watch also on the faults of the patients, which often make them lie about the taking of things prescribed.
Hippocrates (c. 460 BC–c. 377 BC) Greek physician. *Decorum*, 14

6 Once in a while you will have a patient of sense, born with the gift of observation, from whom you may learn something.
Oliver Wendell Holmes (1809–94) US writer and physician. *Medical Essays*, 'The Young Practitioner'

7 What I call a good patient is one

who, having found a good physician, sticks to him till he dies.
Oliver Wendell Holmes (1809–94) US writer and physician. *Medical Essays*, 'The Young Practitioner'

8 The most important person in the operating theatre is the patient.
Russell John Howard (1875–1942) *The Hip*, Ch. 3 (F. G. St. Clair Strange)

9 Effective health care depends on self-care; this fact is currently heralded as if it were a discovery . . . The medicalization of early diagnosis not only hampers and discourages preventative health-care but it also trains the patient-to-be to function in the meantime as an acolyte to his doctor. He learns to depend on the physician in sickness and in health. He turns into a life-long patient.
Ivan Illich (1926–) Austrian sociologist. *Medical Nemesis*

10 Treat the man who is sick and not a Greek name.
Abraham Jacobi (1830–1919) *Bulletin of the New York Academy of Medicine*, 4:1003, 1928

11 Never believe what a patient tells you his doctor has said.
Sir William Jenner (1815–98) English physician and pathologist.

12 God help the patient.
Lord Mansfield (1705–93) English judge and politician.

13 Keep up the spirits of your patient with the music of the viol and the psaltery, or by forging letters telling of the death of his enemies or (if he be a cleric) by informing him that he has been made a bishop.
Henri de Mondeville *Bartlett's Unfamiliar Quotations* (Leonard Louis Levinson)

14 It is the patient rather than the case which requires treatment.
Robert Tuttle Morris (1857–1945) *Doctors versus Folks*, Ch. 2

15 The sick man is a parasite of society. In certain cases it is indecent to go on living. To continue to vegetate in a state of cowardly dependence upon doctors and special treatments, once the meaning of life, the right to life has been lost, ought to be regarded with the greatest contempt by society.
Friedrich Nietzsche (1844–1900) German philosopher. *The Twilight of the Idols*, 'Skirmishes in a War with the Age'

16 The treatment of a disease may be entirely impersonal; the care of a patient must be completely personal.
Francis Weld Peabody (1881–1927) *The Care of the Patient*

17 First, the patient, second the patient, third the patient, fourth the patient, fifth the patient, and then maybe comes science. We first do everything for the patient; science can wait, research can wait.
Béla Schick (1877–1967) Austrian pediatrician. *Aphorisms and Facetiae of Béla Schick* (I. J. Wolf)

18 The real work of a doctor . . . is not an affair of health centres, or public clinics, or operating theatres, or laboratories, or hospital beds. These techniques have their place in medicine, but they are not medicine. The essential unit of medical practice is the occasion when, in the intimacy of the consulting room or sick room, a person who is ill, or believes himself to be ill, seeks the advice of a doctor whom he trusts. This is a consultation and all else in the practice of medicine derives from it.
Sir James Calvert Spence (1892–1954) *The Purpose and Practice of Medicine*, Ch. 18

19 The patient has been so completely taken to pieces that nobody is able to look on him again as a whole being. He is no longer an individual man but a jumble of scientific data.
Kenneth Walker *The Circle of Life*, I, Ch. 1

PATRIOTISM

See also homesickness, loyalty, war

1 What pity is it
That we can die but once to serve our country!
Joseph Addison (1672–1719) British essayist. *Cato*, IV:4

2 Speak for England.
Leopold Amery (1873–1955) British statesman. Shouted to Arthur Greenwood, Labour Party spokesman, before he began to speak in a House of Commons debate immediately preceding the declaration of war, 2 Sept 1939

3 I know my own heart to be entirely English.
Anne (1665–1714) Drawing a contrast with her predecessor, the Dutch William III. Speech on opening parliament, 1702

5 Your country needs you!
Anonymous World War I recruiting slogan

6 That this House will in no circumstances fight for its King and Country.
Anonymous A motion, 9 Feb 1933, debated in the Oxford University Union. It was carried by 275 votes to 153.

7 The *Daily Mirror* does not believe that patriotism had to be proved in blood. Especially someone else's blood.
Anonymous Referring to the Falklands War. *Daily Mirror*, Apr 1982

8 'My country, right or wrong' is a thing that no patriot would think of saying, except in a desperate case. It is like saying 'My mother, drunk or sober.'
G. K. Chesterton (1874–1936) British writer. *The Defendant*

9 Be England what she will,
With all her faults, she is my country still.
Charles Churchill (1731–64) British poet. *The Farewell*

10 England, with all thy faults, I love thee still,
My country.
William Cowper (1731–1800) British poet. *The Task*

11 The tocsin you hear today is not an alarm but an alert: it sounds the charge against our enemies. To conquer them we must dare, and dare again, and dare for ever; and thus will France be saved
Georges Jacques Danton (1759–94) French political activist. Speech, Paris, 2 Sept 1792

12 Our country! In her intercourse with foreign nations, may she always be in the right; but our country, right or wrong.
Stephen Decatur (1779–1820) US naval officer. Speech, Norfolk, Virginia, Apr 1816

13 I have never understood why one's affections must be confined, as once with women, to a single country.
John Kenneth Galbraith (1908–) US economist. *A Life in our Times*

14 Anyone who wants to carry on the war against the outsiders, come with me. I can't offer you either honors or wages; I offer you hunger, thirst, forced marches, battles and death. Anyone who loves his country, follow me.
Giuseppe Garibaldi (1807–82) Italian general and political leader. *Garibaldi* (Guerzoni)

15 That kind of patriotism which consists in hating all other nations.
Elizabeth Gaskell (1810–65) British novelist. *Sylvia's Lovers*, Ch. 1

16 Born and educated in this country I glory in the name of Briton.
George III (1738–1820) King of Great Britain and Ireland. Speech on opening parliament, 18 Nov 1760

17 I only regret that I have but one life to lose for my country.
Nathan Hale (1755–76) US revolutionary hero. Speech before his execution, 22 Sept 1776

18 *Dulce et decorum est pro patria mori.*
It is a sweet and seemly thing to die for one's country.
Horace (Quintus Horatius Flaccus; 65–8 BC) Roman poet. Odes, III

19 Unlike so many who find success, she remained a 'dinkum hard-swearing Aussie' to the end.
Arnold Haskell (1903–80) English writer on ballet. Referring to Dame Nellie Melba. *Waltzing Matilda*

20 We don't want to fight, but, by jingo if we do,
We've got the ships, we've got the men, we've got the money too.
We've fought the Bear before, and while Britons shall be true,
The Russians shall not have Constantinople.
George William Hunt (c. 1829–1904) British writer. *We Don't Want to Fight*

21 One of the great attractions of patriotism – it fulfils our worst wishes. In the person of our nation we are able, vicariously, to bully and to cheat. Bully and cheat, what's more, with a feeling that we are profoundly virtuous.
Aldous Huxley (1894–1964) British novelist. *Eyeless in Gaza*

22 I have often heretofore ventured my life in defence of this nation; and I shall go as far as any man in preserving it in all its just rights and liberties.
James II (1633–1701) Address to the Privy Council on becoming King (1685).

23 Patriotism is the last refuge of a scoundrel.
Samuel Johnson (1709–84) British lexicographer. *Life of Johnson* (J. Boswell), Vol. II

24 And so, my fellow Americans: ask not what your country can do for you – ask what you can do for your country. My fellow citizens of the world: ask not what America will do for you, but what together we can do for the freedom of man.
John Fitzgerald Kennedy (1917–63) US statesman. Inaugural address, 20 Jan 1961

25 Those who prate about Blimpish patriotism in the mode of Margaret Thatcher are also the ones who will take millions off the caring services of this country.
Neil Kinnock (1942–) British politician. Speech, Labour Party Conference, Brighton, 1983

26 I would die for my country . . . but I would not let my country die for me.
Neil Kinnock Speech on nuclear disarmament, 1987

27 My principle is: France before everything.
Napoleon I (Napoleon Bonaparte; 1769–1821) French emperor. Letter to Eugène Beauharnais, 23 Aug 1810

28 Patriotism is often an arbitrary veneration of real estate above principles.
G. J. Nathan (1882–1958) US drama critic. *Testament of a Critic*

29 'Take my drum to England, hang et by the shore,
Strike et when your powder's runnin' low;
If the Dons sight Devon, I'll quit the port o' Heaven,
An' drum them up the Channel as we drummed them long ago.'
Henry John Newbolt (1862–1938) British poet. *Drake's Drum*

30 But cared greatly to serve God and the King,
And keep the Nelson touch.
Henry John Newbolt *Minora Sidera*

31 The old Lie: *Dulce et decorum est Pro patria mori.*
Wilfred Owen (1893–1918) British poet. *Dulce et decorum est*

32 If I were an American, as I am an Englishman, while a foreign troop was landed in my country, I never would lay down my arms, – never – never – never!
William Pitt the Elder (1708–78) British statesman. Speech, House of Lords, 18 Nov 1777

33 There is no room in this country for hyphenated Americanism.
Theodore Roosevelt (1858–1919) US Republican president. Speech, New York, 12 Oct 1915

34 There can be no fifty-fifty Americanism in this country. There is room here for only one hundred per cent Americanism.
Theodore Roosevelt Speech, Saratoga, 19 July 1918

35 Patriots always talk of dying for their country and never of killing for their country.
Bertrand Russell (1872–1970) British philosopher. *The Autobiography of Bertrand Russell*

36 We few, we happy few, we band of brothers;
For he to-day that sheds his blood with me
Shall be my brother; be he ne'er so vile
This day shall gentle his condition:
And gentlemen in England, now a-bed
Shall think themselves accurs'd they were not here,
And hold their manhoods cheap whiles any speaks
That fought with us upon Saint Crispin's day.
William Shakespeare (1564–1616) English dramatist. *Henry V*, IV:3

37 Not that I lov'd Caesar less, but that I lov'd Rome more.
William Shakespeare *Julius Caesar*, III:2

38 You'll never have a quiet world till you knock the patriotism out of the human race.
George Bernard Shaw (1856–1950) Irish dramatist and critic. *O'Flaherty V.C.*

39 True patriotism is of no party.
Tobias Smollett (1721–71) British novelist. *The Adventures of Sir Launcelote Greaves*

40 I vow to thee, my country – all earthly things above –
Entire and whole and perfect, the service of my love.
Cecil Arthur Spring-Rice (1859–1918) British diplomat. *I Vow to Thee, My Country*

41 Patriotism to the Soviet State is a revolutionary duty, whereas patriotism to a bourgeois State is treachery.
Leon Trotsky (Lev Davidovich Bronstein; 1879–1940) Russian revolutionary. *Disputed Barricade* (Fitzroy Maclean)

42 I was born an American; I will live an American; I shall die an American.
Daniel Webster (1782–1852) US statesman. Speech, US Senate, 17 July 1850

43 'Shoot, if you must, this old gray head,
But spare your country's flag,' she said.

A shade of sadness, a blush of shame,
Over the face of the leader came.

John Greenleaf Whittier (1807–92) US poet. *Barbara Frietchie*

44 There is one certain means by which I can be sure never to see my country's ruin; I will die in the last ditch.

William III (1650–1702) King of Great Britain. *History of England* (Hume)

PATRONAGE

See also promotion

1 *Patron.* Commonly a wretch who supports with insolence, and is paid with flattery.

Samuel Johnson (1709–84) British lexicographer. *Dictionary of the English Language*

2 Is not a Patron, my Lord, one who looks with unconcern on a man struggling for life in the water, and, when he has reached ground, encumbers him with help? The notice which you have been pleased to take of my labours, had it been early, had been kind; but it has been delayed till I am indifferent, and cannot enjoy it; till I am solitary, and cannot impart it; till I am known, and do not want it.

Samuel Johnson Letter to Lord Chesterfield, 7 Feb 1755. *Life of Johnson* (J. Boswell), Vol. I

PEACE

See also war and peace

1 'Here you are–don't lose it again.'

Anonymous Caption to cartoon showing a wounded soldier handing over 'victory and peace in Europe'. *Daily Mirror*, 8 May 1945

2 The wolf also shall dwell with the lamb, and the leopard shall lie down with the kid; and the calf and the young lion and the fatling together: and a little child shall lead them.

And the cow and the bear shall feed; their young ones shall lie down together: and the lion shall eat straw like the ox.

And the sucking child shall play on the hole of the asp, and the weaned child shall put his hand on the cockatrice' den.

They shall not hurt nor destroy in all my holy mountain: for the earth shall be full of the knowledge of the Lord, as the waters cover the sea.

Bible: Isaiah 11:6–9

3 There is no peace, saith the Lord, unto the wicked.

Bible: Isaiah 48:22

4 Peace I leave with you, my peace I give unto you: not as the world giveth, give I unto you. Let not your heart be troubled, neither let it be afraid.

Bible: John 14:27

5 *Peace*, n. In international affairs, a period of cheating between two periods of fighting.

Ambrose Bierce (1842–?1914) US writer and journalist. *The Devil's Dictionary*

6 Give peace in our time, O Lord.

The Book of Common Prayer *Morning Prayer*, Versicles

7 Don't tell me peace has broken out.

Bertolt Brecht (1898–1956) German dramatist. *Mother Courage*, VIII

8 I believe it is peace for our time . . . peace with honour.

Neville Chamberlain (1869–1940) British statesman. Broadcast after Munich Agreement, 1 Oct 1938

9 Anythin' for a quiet life, as the man said wen he took the sitivation at the lighthouse.

Charles Dickens (1812–70) British novelist. *Pickwick Papers*, Ch. 43

10 Lord Salisbury and myself have brought you back peace – but a peace I hope with honour.

Benjamin Disraeli (1804–81) British statesman. Speech, House of Commons, 16 July 1878

11 Let us have peace.

Ulysses Simpson Grant (1822–85) US general. On accepting nomination. Letter, 29 May 1868

12 Arms alone are not enough to keep the peace – it must be kept by men.

John Fitzgerald Kennedy (1917–63) US president. *The Observer*, 'Sayings of the Decade', 1962

13 And who will bring white peace
That he may sleep upon his hill again?

Vachel Lindsay (1879–1931) US poet. *Abraham Lincoln Walks at Midnight*

14 Peace is indivisible.

Maxim Litvinov (1876–1951) Russian statesman. Speech to the League of Nations, 1 July 1936

15 I would make great sacrifices to preserve peace. . . . But if a situation were to be forced upon us, in which peace could only be preserved by the surrender of the great and beneficent position Britain has won by centuries of heroism and achievement . . . I say emphatically that peace at that price would be a humiliation intolerable for a great country like ours to endure.

David Lloyd George (1863–1945) British Liberal statesman. *British Documents* (Gooch and Temperley), Vol. VII

16 The issues are the same. We wanted peace on earth, love, and understanding between everyone around the world. We have learned that change comes slowly.

Paul McCartney (1943–) British rock musician. *The Observer*, 'Sayings of the Week', 7 June 1987

17 Roll up that map: it will not be wanted these ten years.

William Pitt the Younger (1759–1806) British statesman. On learning that Napoleon had won the Battle of Austerlitz. Attrib.

18 Nation shall speak peace unto nation.

Montague John Rendall (1862–1950) British schoolmaster. Motto of BBC, 1927

19 When peace has been broken anywhere, the peace of all countries everywhere is in danger.

Franklin D. Roosevelt (1882–1945) US Democratic president. Radio broadcast, 3 Sept 1939

20 Here, where the world is quiet;
Here, where all trouble seems
Dead winds' and spent waves' riot
In doubtful dreams of dreams.

Algernon Charles Swinburne (1837–1909) British poet. *The Garden of Proserpine*

21 We are the true peace movement.

Margaret Thatcher (1925–) British politician and prime minister. *The Times*, 1983

22 And I shall have some peace there, for peace comes dropping slow,
Dropping from the veils of the morning to where the cricket sings.

W. B. Yeats (1865–1939) Irish poet. *The Lake Isle of Innisfree*

PEERAGE

1 The House of Lords has lost, at the age of 91, one of its most picturesque personalities in the Earl of Morton. He had a great gift for silence, and during all the years that he attended at Westminster as

a Scottish representative peer his voice was never heard in debate.
Anonymous *The Times* (obituary)

2 I have heard it said of the 'backwoods' peer that he had three qualities. He knew how to kill a fox, he knew how to get rid of a bad tenant, and he knew how to discard an unwanted mistress. A man who possesses these three qualities would certainly have something to contribute to the work of the House.
Lord Winster Speech, House of Lords

PEOPLE

1 Most of the people who will walk after me will be children, so make the beat keep time with short steps.
Hans Christian Andersen (1805–75) Danish writer. Planning the music for his funeral. *Hans Christian Andersen* (R. Godden)

2 The good of the people is the chief law.
Cicero (106–43 BC) Roman orator and statesman. *De Legibus*, III

3 When the People contend for their Liberty, they seldom get anything by their Victory but new masters.
Lord Halifax (1633–95) English statesman. *Political, Moral, and Miscellaneous Thoughts and Reflections*

4 When people are free to do as they please, they usually imitate each other.
Eric Hoffer (1902–) US writer. *The Passionate State of Mind*

5 Many people believe that they are attracted by God, or by Nature, when they are only repelled by man.
Dean Inge *More Lay Thoughts of a Dean*

6 People must help one another; it is nature's law.
Jean de La Fontaine (1621–95) French poet. *Fables*, VIII, 'L'Âne et le Chien'

7 . . . that government of the people, by the people, and for the people, shall not perish from the earth.
Abraham Lincoln (1809–65) US President. Speech, 19 Nov 1863, dedicating the national cemetery on the site of the Battle of Gettesburg

8 I've always been interested in people, but I've never liked them.
W. Somerset Maugham (1874–1965) British novelist. *The Observer*, 'Sayings of the Week', 28 Aug 1949

9 The right people are rude. They can afford to be.
W. Somerset Maugham *Our Betters*, II

10 People who need people are the luckiest people in the world.
Bob Merrill (Robert Merrill; 1890–1977) US lyricist and composer. *People Who Need People*

11 It is with narrow-souled people as with narrow-necked bottles: the less they have in them, the more noise they make in pouring it out.
Alexander Pope (1688–1744) British poet. *Thoughts on Various Subjects*

12 I think if the people of this country can be reached with the truth, their judgment will be in favor of the many, as against the privileged few.
Eleanor Roosevelt (1884–1962) US writer and lecturer. *Ladies' Home Journal*

13 They didn't act like people and they didn't act like actors. It's hard to explain. They acted more like they knew they were celebrities and all. I mean they were good, but they were *too* good.
J. D. Salinger (1919–) US novelist. *The Catcher in the Rye*, Ch. 17

14 Hell is other people.
Jean-Paul Sartre (1905–80) French philosopher and writer. *Huis clos*

15 If people behaved in the way nations do they would all be put in straitjackets.
Tennessee Williams (1911–83) US dramatist. BBC interview

PERCEPTION

1 If the doors of perception were cleansed everything would appear to man as it is, infinite.
William Blake (1757–1827) British poet. *The Marriage of Heaven and Hell*, 'A Memorable Fancy'

2 Man's Desires are limited by his Perceptions; none can desire what he has not perceived.
William Blake *There is no Natural Religion*

3 'What,' it will be questioned, 'when the sun rises, do you not see a round disc of fire somewhat like a guinea?' 'O no, no, I see an innumerable company of the heavenly host crying, 'Holy, Holy, Holy is the Lord God Almighty!"
William Blake *Descriptive Catalogue*, 'The Vision of Judgment'

4 I saw it, but I did not realize it.
Elizabeth Peabody (1804–94) US educator. Giving a Transcendentalist explanation for her accidentally walking into a tree. *The Peabody Sisters of Salem* (L. Tharp)

PERFECTION

See also imperfection

1 The pursuit of perfection, then, is the pursuit of sweetness and light. . . . He who works for sweetness and light united, works to make reason and the will of God prevail.
Matthew Arnold (1822–88) British poet and critic. *Culture and Anarchy*, Ch. 1

2 Be ye therefore perfect, even as your Father which is in heaven is perfect.
Bible: Matthew 5:48

3 The year's at the spring,
And day's at the morn;
Morning's at seven;
The hill-side's dew-pearled;
The lark's on the wing;
The snail's on the thorn;
God's in His heaven –
All's right with the world.
Robert Browning (1812–89) British poet. *Pippa Passes*, Pt. I

4 What's come to perfection perishes.
Things learned on earth, we shall practise in heaven.
Works done least rapidly, Art most cherishes.
Robert Browning *Old Pictures in Florence*, XVII

5 You would attain to the divine perfection,
And yet not turn your back upon the world.
Henry Wadsworth Longfellow (1807–82) US poet. *Michael Angelo*

6 Perfection has one grave defect; it is apt to be dull.
W. Somerset Maugham (1874–1965) British novelist. *The Summing Up*

7 The essence of being human is that one does not seek perfection.
George Orwell (1903–50) British novelist. *Shooting an Elephant*, 'Reflections on Gandhi'

8 Whoever thinks a faultless piece to see,
Thinks what ne'er was, nor is, nor e'er shall be.
Alexander Pope (1688–1744) British poet. *An Essay on Criticism*

9 Everything's Coming Up Roses.
Stephen Sondheim (1930–) US composer and lyricist. Song title

10 Finality is death. Perfection is finality. Nothing is perfect. There are lumps in it.
James Stephens (1882–1950) Irish novelist. *The Crock of Gold*

PERSISTENCE

See also determination, endurance, patience

1 If the mountain will not come to Mahomet, Mahomet must go to the mountain.
Proverb

2 Never say die.
Proverb

3 Slow but sure wins the race.
Proverb

4 And ye shall be hated of all men for my name's sake: but he that endureth to the end shall be saved.
Bible: Matthew 10:22

5 If at first you don't succeed,
Try, try again.
William Edward Hickson (1803–70) British educator. *Try and Try Again*

6 A man may write at any time, if he will set himself doggedly to it.
Samuel Johnson (1709–84) British lexicographer. *Life of Johnson* (J. Boswell), Vol. I

7 The drop of rain maketh a hole in the stone, not by violence, but by oft falling.
Hugh Latimer (1485–1555) English churchman. *See also* LUCRETIUS; OVID Sermon preached before Edward VI

8 Keep right on to the end of the road.
Harry Lauder (Hugh MacLennon; 1870–1950) Scottish music-hall artist. Song title

9 You persisted for a certain number of years like a stammer. You were a *stammer*, if you like, of Space-Time.
Wyndham Lewis (1882–1957) British novelist. *The Human Age*, 'The Childermass'

10 Constant dripping hollows out a stone.
Lucretius (Titus Lucretius Carus; c. 99–55 BC) Roman philosopher. *On the Nature of the Universe*, I. *See also* LATIMER; OVID

11 Dripping water hollows out a stone, a ring is worn away by use.
Ovid (Publius Ovidius Naso; 43 BC–17 AD) Roman poet. *See also* LATIMER; LUCRETIUS *Epistulae Ex Ponto*, Bk. IV

12 I am a kind of burr; I shall stick.
William Shakespeare (1564–1616) English dramatist. *Measure for Measure*, IV:3

PERSPECTIVE

See also objectivity

1 'Tis distance lends enchantment to the view,
And robes the mountain in its azure hue.
Thomas Campbell (1777–1844) British poet. *Pleasures of Hope*, I

2 One sees great things from the valley; only small things from the peak.
G. K. Chesterton (1874–1936) British writer. *The Hammer of God*

3 Fleas know not whether they are upon the body of a giant or upon one of ordinary size.
Walter Savage Landor (1775–1864) British poet and writer. *Imaginary Conversations*, 'Southey and Porson'

4 Everything must be taken seriously, nothing tragically.
Louis Adolphe Thiers (1797–1877) French statesman and historian. Speech, French National Assembly, 24 May 1873

PERSUASION

1 There is a holy, mistaken zeal in politics, as well as religion. By persuading others we convince ourselves.
Junius An unidentified writer of letters (1769–72) to the *London Public Advertiser*. Letter, 19 Dec 1769

2 For a priest to turn a man when he lies a-dying, is just like one that has a long time solicited a woman, and cannot obtain his end; at length makes her drunk, and so lies with her.
John Selden (1584–1654) English historian. *Table Talk*

3 The President spends most of his time kissing people on the cheek in order to get them to do what they ought to do without getting kissed.
Harry S. Truman (1884–1972) US statesman. *The Observer*, 'Sayings of the Week', 6 Feb 1949

4 They will conquer, but they will not convince.
Miguel de Unamuno y Jugo (1864–1936) Spanish writer. Referring to the Franco rebels. Attrib.

PERVERSITY

See also petulance, stubbornness

1 If it's heaven for climate, it's hell for company.
J. M. Barrie (1860–1937) British novelist and dramatist. *The Little Minister*, Ch. 3

2 Never the time and the place
And the loved one all together!
Robert Browning (1812–89) British poet. *Never the Time and the Place*

3 For 'tis a truth well known to most,
That whatsoever thing is lost –
We seek it, ere it come to light,
In every cranny but the right.
William Cowper (1731–1800) British poet. *The Retired Cat*

4 Let's find out what everyone is doing,
And then stop everyone from doing it.
A. P. Herbert (1890–1971) British writer and politician. *Let's Stop Somebody*

5 I had never had a piece of toast
Particularly long and wide,
But fell upon the sanded floor,
And always on the buttered side.
James Payn (1830–98) British writer and editor. *Chambers's Journal*, 2 Feb 1884

6 Adam was but human – this explains it all. He did not want the apple for the apple's sake, he wanted it only because it was forbidden.
Mark Twain (Samuel Langhorne Clemens; 1835–1910) US writer. *Pudd'nhead Wilson's Calendar*, Ch. 2

PESSIMISM

1 Pessimism, when you get used to it, is just as agreeable as optimism.
Arnold Bennett (1867–1931) British novelist. *Things that have Interested Me*, 'The Slump in Pessimism'

2 Scratch a pessimist, and you find often a defender of privilege.
Lord Beveridge (1879–1963) British economist. *The Observer*, 'Sayings of the Week', 17 Dec 1943

3 The optimist proclaims we live in the best of all possible worlds; and the pessimist fears this is true.
James Cabell (1879–1958) US novelist and journalist. *The Silver Stallion*

4 He who despairs over an event is a coward, but he who holds hopes for the human condition is a fool.
Albert Camus (1913–60) French existentialist writer. *The Rebel*

5 A Hard Rain's A-Gonna Fall.
Bob Dylan (Robert Allen Zimmerman; 1941–) US popular singer. Song title

6 Only the man who finds everything wrong and expects it to get worse is thought to have a clear brain.

John Kenneth Galbraith (1908–) US economist. *The Age of Uncertainty*

7 We all agree that pessimism is a mark of superior intellect.

John Kenneth Galbraith *The Observer*, 'Sayings of the Week', 3 Apr 1977

8 Sleep is good, death is better; but of course, the best thing would be never to have been born at all.

Heinrich Heine (1797–1856) German poet and writer. *Morphine*

9 Nothing makes me more pessimistic than the obligation not to be pessimistic.

Eugène Ionesco (1912–) French dramatist. Attrib.

10 Nothing to do but work,
Nothing to eat but food,
Nothing to wear but clothes,
To keep one from going nude.

Benjamin Franklin King (1857–94) American humorist. *The Pessimist*

11 If we see light at the end of the tunnel it is the light of an oncoming train.

Robert Lowell (1917–77) US poet. *Day by Day*

12 How many pessimists end up by desiring the things they fear, in order to prove that they are right.

Robert Mallet (1915–) French writer. *Apostilles*

13 A pessimist is a man who looks both ways before crossing a one-way street.

Laurence J. Peter (1919–) Canadian writer. *Peter's Quotations*

14 It is not, nor it cannot come to good.

William Shakespeare (1564–1616) English dramatist. *Hamlet*, I:2

PETULANCE

See also perversity, stubbornness

1 She refused to begin the 'Beguine'
Tho' they besought her to
And with language profane and obscene
She curs'd the man who taught her to
She curs'd Cole Porter too!

Noël Coward (1899–1973) British dramatist. *Sigh No More*, 'Nina'

2 He has to learn that petulance is not sarcasm, and that insolence is not invective.

Benjamin Disraeli (1804–81) British statesman. Said of Sir C. Wood. Speech, House of Commons, 16 Dec 1852

3 I am the emperor, and I want dumplings.

Ferdinand I (1793–1875) Emperor of Austria. *The Fall of the House of Habsburg* (E. Crankshaw)

4 I hate a fellow whom pride, or cowardice, or laziness drives into a corner, and who does nothing when he is there but sit and *growl*; let him come out as I do, and *bark*.

Samuel Johnson (1709–84) British lexicographer. *Life of Johnson* (J. Boswell), Vol. IV

PHILANTHROPY

1 Sometimes give your services for nothing. . . . And if there be an opportunity of serving one who is a stranger in financial straits, give full assistance to all such. For where there is love of man, there is also love of the art.

Hippocrates (c. 460 BC–c. 377 BC) Greek physician. *Precepts*, Sect. VI

PHILISTINISM

See also arts, books, culture

1 For this class we have a designation which now has become pretty well known, and which we may as well still keep for them, the designation of Philistines.

Matthew Arnold (1822–88) British poet and critic. Referring to the middle class. *Culture and Anarchy*, Ch. 3

2 The great apostle of the Philistines, Lord Macaulay.

Matthew Arnold *Joubert*

3 The finest collection of frames I ever saw.

Humphry Davy (1778–1829) British chemist. When asked what he thought of the Paris art galleries. Attrib.

4 When I hear anyone talk of Culture, I reach for my revolver.

Hermann Goering (1893–1946) German leader. Attrib. to Goering but probably said by Hanns Johst

5 I've never been in there . . . but there are only three things to see, and I've seen color reproductions of all of them.

Harold W. Ross (1892–1951) US journalist. Referring to the Louvre. *A Farewell to Arms* (Ernest Hemingway)

6 All my wife has ever taken from the Mediterranean – from that whole vast intuitive culture – are four bottles of Chianti to make into lamps, and two china condiment donkeys labelled Sally and Peppy.

Peter Shaffer (1926–) British dramatist. *Equus*, I:18

7 Particularly against books the Home Secretary is. If we can't stamp out literature in the country, we can at least stop it being brought in from outside.

Evelyn Waugh (1903–66) British novelist. *Vile Bodies*, Ch. 2

8 Listen! There never was an artistic period. There never was an Art-loving nation.

James Whistler (1834–1903) US painter. Attrib.

PHILOSOPHERS

See also philosophy

1 All are lunatics, but he who can analyze his delusion is called a philosopher.

Ambrose Bierce (1842–c. 1914) US writer and journalist. *Epigrams*

2 There is nothing so absurd but some philosopher has said it.

Cicero (106–43 BC) Roman orator and statesman. *De Divinatione*, II

3 To a philosopher no circumstance, however trifling, is too minute.

Oliver Goldsmith (1728–74) Irish-born British writer. *The Citizen of the World*

4 Philosophers never balance between profit and honesty, because their decisions are general, and neither their passions nor imaginations are interested in the objects.

David Hume (1711–76) Scottish philosopher. *A Treatise of Human Nature*

5 I doubt if the philosopher lives, or ever has lived, who could know himself to be heartily despised by a street boy without some irritation.

T. H. Huxley (1825–95) British biologist. *Evolution and Ethics*

6 The philosophers have only interpreted the world in various ways; the point is to change it.

Karl Marx (1818–1883) German philosopher and revolutionary. *Theses on Feuerbach*

7 In the philosopher there is nothing whatever impersonal; and, above all, his morality bears decided and decisive testimony to *who he is* – that is to say, to the order of rank

in which the innermost drives of his nature stand in relation to one another.
Friedrich Wilhelm Nietzsche (1844–1900) German philosopher. *Jenseits von Gut und Böse*

8 Not to care for philosophy is to be a true philosopher.
Blaise Pascal (1623–62) French philosopher and mathematician. *Pensées*, I

9 Nowadays there are no serious philosophers who are not looking forward to the pension to which their involvement with the subject entitles them.
Anthony Quinton (1925–) British philosopher. *Thoughts and Thinkers*

10 Three passions, simple but overwhelmingly strong, have governed my life: the longing for love, the search for knowledge, and unbearable pity for the suffering of mankind.
Bertrand Russell (1872–1970) British philosopher. *The Autobiography of Bertrand Russell*, Prologue

11 Philosophers are as jealous as women. Each wants a monopoly of praise.
George Santayana (1863–1952) US philosopher. *Dialogues In Limbo*

12 For there was never yet philosopher
That could endure the toothache patiently.
William Shakespeare (1564–1616) English dramatist. *Much Ado About Nothing*, V:1

13 The philosopher is Nature's pilot. And there you have our difference; to be in hell is to drift; to be in heaven is to steer.
George Bernard Shaw (1856–1950) Irish dramatist and critic. *Man and Superman*

14 There are now-a-days professors of philosophy but not philosophers.
Henry David Thoreau (1817–62) US writer. *Walden*, 'Economy'

15 A philosopher of imposing stature doesn't think in a vacuum. Even his most abstract ideas are, to some extent, conditioned by what is or what is not known in the time when he lives.
A. N. Whitehead (1861–1947) British philosopher. *Dialogues*

PHILOSOPHY

See also logic, metaphysics, philosophers

1 The principles of logic and metaphysics are true simply because we never allow them to be anything else.
A. J. Ayer (1910–) British philosopher. *Language, Truth and Logic*

2 Philosophy, like medicine, has plenty of drugs, few good remedies, and hardly any specific cures.
Nicolas Chamfort (1741–94) French writer and wit. *Maximes et pensées*

3 The formula 'Two and two make five' is not without its attractions.
Fedor Mikhailovich Dostoevsky (1821–81) Russian novelist. *Notes from the Underground*

4 If we take in our hand any volume; of divinity or school metaphysics, for instance; let us ask, *Does it contain any abstract reasoning concerning quantity or number?* No. *Does it contain any experimental reasoning, concerning matter of fact and existence?* No. Commit it then to the flames: for it can contain nothing but sophistry and illusion.
David Hume (1711–76) Scottish philosopher. *An Enquiry Concerning Human Understanding*

5 We are perpetually moralists, but we are geometricians only by chance. Our intercourse with intellectual nature is necessary; our speculations upon matter are voluntary, and at leisure.
Samuel Johnson (1709–84) British lexicographer. *Lives of the English Poets*, 'Milton'

6 I refute it *thus.*
Samuel Johnson Replying to Boswell's contention that they were unable to refute Bishop Berkeley's theory of matter, by kicking a large stone with his foot. *Life of Johnson* (J. Boswell), Vol. I

7 There are innumerable questions to which the inquisitive mind can in this state receive no answer: Why do you and I exist? Why was this world created? Since it was to be created, why was it not created sooner?
Samuel Johnson *Life of Johnson* (J. Boswell), Vol. III

8 Do not all charms fly
At the mere touch of cold philosophy?
John Keats (1795–1821) British poet. *Lamia*, II

9 Axioms in philosophy are not axioms until they are proved upon our pulses; we read fine things but never feel them to the full until we have gone the same steps as the author.
John Keats Letter to J. H. Reynolds, 3 May 1818

10 The Power of Positive Thinking.
Norman Vincent Peale (1899–) US clergyman and writer. Book title

11 Zen and the Art of Motorcycle Maintenance.
Robert M. Pirsig (1929–) US writer. Book title

12 There will be no end to the troubles of states, or indeed, my dear Glaucon, of humanity itself, till philosophers become kings in this world, or till those we now call kings and rulers really and truly become philosophers.
Plato (429–347 BC) Greek philosopher. *Republic*, Bk. 5

13 We thought philosophy ought to be patient and unravel people's mental blocks. Trouble with doing that is, once you've unravelled them, their heads fall off.
Frederic Raphael (1931–) British author. *The Glittering Prizes: A Double Life*, III:2

14 Matter . . . a convenient formula for describing what happens where it isn't.
Bertrand Russell (1872–1970) British philosopher. *An Outline of Philosophy*

15 To teach how to live without certainty and yet without being paralysed by hesitation is perhaps the chief thing that philosophy, in our age, can do for those who study it.
Bertrand Russell *The History of Western Philosophy*

16 The point of philosophy is to start with something so simple as to seem not worth stating, and to end with something so paradoxical that no one will believe it.
Bertrand Russell *Logic and Knowledge*

17 Science is what you know, philosophy is what you don't know.
Bertrand Russell

18 Philosophy is the replacement of category-habits by category-disciplines.
Gilbert Ryle (1900–76) British philosopher. *The Concept of Mind*, Introduction

19 It is a great advantage for a system of philosophy to be substantially true.
George Santayana (1863–1952) US philosopher. *The Unknowable*

20 Because he is the highest vertebrate he can do what no other vertebrate can do: when, out of whatever desire and knowledge may

be his, he makes a choice, he can say 'I will.' . . . And knowing how and why he says 'I will', he comes to his own as a philosopher.

Homer W. Smith (1895–1962) *From Fish to Philosopher*, Ch. 13

21 Philosophy is the product of wonder.

A. N. Whitehead (1861–1947) British philosopher. *Nature and Life*, Ch. 1

22 The safest general characterization of the European philosophical tradition is that it consists of a series of footnotes to Plato.

A. N. Whitehead (1861–1947) British philosopher. *Process and Reality*

23 My advice to you is not to inquire why or whither, but just enjoy your ice-cream while it's on your plate, – that's my philosophy.

Thornton Wilder (1897–1975) US novelist and dramatist. *The Skin of Our Teeth*, I

24 Philosophy, as we use the word, is a fight against the fascination which forms of expression exert upon us.

Ludwig Wittgenstein (1889–1951) Austrian philosopher. *The Blue Book*

25 Philosophy is not a theory but an activity.

Ludwig Wittgenstein *Tractatus Logico-Philosophicus*, Ch. 4

PHOTOGRAPHY

1 Photography can never grow up if it imitates some other medium. It has to walk alone; it has to be itself.

Berenice Abbott (1898–) US photographer. *Infinity*, 'It Has to Walk Alone'

2 Tony made my nose look wonderful, but everyone thought I'd had it fixed by plastic surgery.

Princess Alexandra (1936–) Cousin of Queen Elizabeth II. Referring to a portrait by Lord Snowdon

3 The camera cannot lie. But it can be an accessory to untruth.

Harold Evans (1928–) British journalist. *Pictures on a Page*

4 As far as I knew, he had never taken a photograph before, and the summit of Everest was hardly the place to show him how.

Edmund Hillary (1919–) New Zealand mountaineer. Referring to Tenzing Norgay, his companion on the conquest of Mt Everest (1953). *High Adventure*

5 The modern pantheist not only sees the god in everything, he takes photographs of it.

D. H. Lawrence (1885–1930) British novelist. *St Mawr*

6 I have for instance among my purchases . . . several original Mona Lisas and all painted (according to the Signature) by the great artist Kodak.

Spike Milligan (1918–) British comic actor and author. *A Dustbin of Milligan*, 'Letters to Harry Secombe'

7 A photograph is not only an image (as a painting is an image), an interpretation of the real; it is also a trace, something directly stencilled off the real, like a footprint or a death mask.

Susan Sontag (1933–) US novelist and essayist. *On Photography*

PITY

1 For Mercy has a human heart,
Pity a human face,
And Love, the human form divine,
And Peace, the human dress.

William Blake (1757–1827) British poet. *Songs of Innocence*, 'The Divine Image'

2 If a madman were to come into this room with a stick in his hand, no doubt we should pity the state of his mind; but our primary consideration would be to take care of ourselves. We should knock him down first, and pity him afterwards.

Samuel Johnson (1709–84) British lexicographer. *Life of Johnson* (J. Boswell), Vol. III

3 To show pity is felt as a sign of contempt because one has clearly ceased to be an object of *fear* as soon as one is pitied.

Friedrich Wilhelm Nietzsche (1844–1900) German philosopher. *The Wanderer and His Shadow*

4 Above all I am not concerned with Poetry. My subject is War, and the pity of War. The Poetry is in the pity.

Wilfred Owen (1893–1918) British poet. *Poems*, Preface

5 Three passions, simple but overwhelmingly strong, have governed my life: the longing for love, the search for knowledge, and unbearable pity for the suffering of mankind.

Bertrand Russell (1872–1970) British philosopher. *The Autobiography of Bertrand Russell*, Prologue

PLACES

See also Britain, Europe

1 All roads lead to Rome.

Proverb

2 See Naples and die.

Proverb

3 This is beautiful downtown Burbank.

Anonymous Catchphrase in the TV comedy series, *Rowan and Martin's Laugh-In*.

4 I went to New Zealand but it was closed.

Anonymous

5 The shortest way out of Manchester is notoriously a bottle of Gordon's gin.

William Bolitho (1890–1930) British writer. Attrib.

6 Three words made peace and union in South Africa: 'methods of barbarism'.

Louis Botha (1862–1919) South African statesman. *Life of Campbell-Bannerman* (J. A. Spender)

7 The sort of place everyone should send his mother-in-law for a month, all expenses paid.

Ian Botham (1955–) British cricketer. Referring to Pakistan. BBC Radio 2 interview, Mar 1984

8 For Cambridge people rarely smile,
Being urban, squat, and packed with guile.

Rupert Brooke (1887–1915) British) poet. *The Old Vicarage, Grantchester*

9 Nothing and no one can destroy the Chinese people. They are relentless survivors. They are the oldest civilized people on earth. Their civilization passes through phases but its basic characteristics remain the same. They yield, they bend to the wind, but they never break.

Pearl Buck (1892–1973) US novelist. *China, Past and Present*, Ch. 1

10 I don't even know what street Canada is on.

Al Capone (1899–1947) US gangster. Attrib.

11 Hollywood is a world with all the personality of a paper cup.

Raymond Chandler (1888–1959) US novelist. Attrib.

12 India is a geographical term. It is no more a united nation than the Equator.

Winston Churchill (1874–1965) British statesman. Speech, Royal Albert Hall, 18 Mar 1931

13 There are few virtues which the Poles do not possess and there are few errors they have ever avoided.
Winston Churchill Speech, House of Commons, 1945

14 Oh what a pity were the greatest and most virtuous of kings, of that real virtue which makes the greatest of princes, to be measured by the yardstick of Versailles!
Jean-Baptiste Colbert (1619–83) French statesman. Letter to Louis XIV, 28 Sept 1665

15 I believe that the earthly Paradise lies here, which no one can enter except by God's leave. I believe that this land which your Highnesses have commanded me to discover is very great, and that there are many other lands in the south of which there have never been reports.
Christopher Columbus (1451–1506) Italian navigator. From the narrative of his third voyage, on which he discovered South America

16 Latins are tenderly enthusiastic. In Brazil they throw flowers at you. In Argentina they throw themselves.
Marlene Dietrich (Maria Magdalene von Losch; 1904–) German-born film star. *Newsweek*, 24 Aug 1959

17 I find it hard to say, because when I was there it seemed to be shut.
Clement Freud (1924–) British Liberal politician and broadcaster. On being asked for his opinion of New Zealand. Similar remarks have been attributed to others. BBC radio, 12 Apr 1978

18 From Greenland's icy mountains,
From India's coral strand,
Where Afric's sunny fountains
Roll down their golden sand.
Reginald Heber (1783–1826) British bishop and hymn writer. *From Greenland's Icy Mountains*

19 Dublin, though a place much worse than London, is not so bad as Iceland.
Samuel Johnson (1709–84) British lexicographer. Letter to Mrs Christopher Smart. *Life of Johnson* (J. Boswell), Vol. IV

20 Liverpool is the pool of life.
Carl Jung (1875–1961) Swiss psychologist. Attrib.

21 Asia is not going to be civilized after the methods of the West. There is too much Asia and she is too old.
Rudyard Kipling (1865–1936) Indian-born British writer. *Life's Handicap*, 'The Man Who Was'

22 On the road to Mandalay
Where the flyin'-fishes play.
Rudyard Kipling *The Road to Mandalay*

23 And all lying mysteriously within the Australian underdark, that peculiar, lost weary aloofness of Australia. There was the vast town of Sydney. And it didn't seem to be real, it seemed to be sprinkled on the surface of a darkness into which it never penetrated.
D. H. Lawrence (1885–1930) British novelist. *Kangaroo*, Ch. 1

24 Don't let it be forgot
That once there was a spot
For one brief shining moment that was known
As Camelot.
Alan Jay Lerner (1918–86) US lyricist and playwright. *Camelot*

25 So you're going to Australia! Well, I made twenty thousand pounds on my tour there, but of course *that* will never be done again. Still, it's a wonderful country, and you'll have a good time. What are you going to sing? All I can say is – sing 'em muck! It's all they can understand!
Nellie Melba (Helen Porter Mitchell; 1861–1931) Australian soprano. Speaking to Clara Butt. *Clara Butt: Her Life Story* (W. H. Ponder)

26 I shook hands with a friendly Arab . . . I still have my right hand to prove it.
Spike Milligan (1918–) British comic actor and author. *A Dustbin of Milligan*, 'Letters to Harry Secombe'

27 That bastard of the Versailles treaty.
Vyacheslav Mikhailovich Molotov (1890–1986) Soviet statesman. Referring to Poland.

28 Jerusalem the golden,
With milk and honey blest,
Beneath thy contemplation
Sink heart and voice opprest.
John Mason Neale (1818–66) British churchman. *Jerusalem the Golden*

29 The Great White Way.
Albert Bigelow Paine (1861–1937) US writer. Later used as a name for Broadway. Book title

30 Once a jolly swagman camped by a billy-bong,
Under the shade of a coolibah tree,
And he sang as he sat and waited for his billy-boil,
'You'll come a-waltzing, Matilda, with me.'
Andrew Barton Paterson (1864–1941) Australian journalist and poet. *Waltzing Matilda*

31 The whole city is arrayed in squares just like a chess-board, and disposed in a manner so perfect and masterly that it is impossible to give a description that should do it justice.
Marco Polo (c. 1254–1324) Venetian traveler. Referring to Kublai Khan's capital, Cambaluc (later Peking). *The Book of Marco Polo*

32 Even the Hooligan was probably invented in China centuries before we thought of him.
Saki (Hector Hugh Munro; 1870–1916) British writer. *Reginald on House-Parties*

33 Great God! this is an awful place.
Captain Robert Falcon Scott (1868–1912) British explorer. Referring to the South Pole. *Journal*, 17 Jan 1912

34 The South African Police would leave no stone unturned to see that nothing disturbed the even terror of their lives.
Tom Sharpe (1928–) British novelist. *Indecent Exposure*, Ch. 1

35 Cusins is a very nice fellow, certainly: nobody would ever guess that he was born in Australia.
George Bernard Shaw (1856–1950) Irish dramatist and critic. *Major Barbara*, I

36 Perhaps it is God's will to lead the people of South Africa through defeat and humiliation to a better future and a brighter day.
Jan Smuts (1870–1950) South African statesman and general. Speaking to Boer delegates at the peace conference that ended the Boer War. Speech, Vereeniging, 31 May 1902

37 The Japanese have perfected good manners and made them indistinguishable from rudeness.
Paul Theroux (1941–) US-born writer. *The Great Railway Bazaar*, Ch. 2

38 I'm Charley's aunt from Brazil, where the nuts come from.
Brandon Thomas (1856–1914) British actor and dramatist. *Charley's Aunt*, I

39 Oh, Calcutta!
Kenneth Tynan From the French expression, 'Oh quel cul t'as' ('what a lovely arse you've got'). Play title

PLAYS

See also acting, actors, criticism, literature, Shakespeare, theatre, writers, writing

1 Now a whole is that which has a beginning, a middle, and an end.
Aristotle (384–322 BC) Greek philosopher. Referring specifically to the dramatic form of tragedy. *Poetics*, Ch. 7

2 One of Edward's Mistresses was Jane Shore, who has had a play

written about her, but it is a tragedy and therefore not worth reading.
Jane Austen (1775–1817) British novelist. *The History of England*

3 In the theatre the audience want to be surprised – but by things that they expect.
Tristan Bernard (1866–1947) French dramatist. *Contes, Repliques et Bon Mots*

4 Prologues precede the piece – in mournful verse;
As undertakers – walk before the hearse.
David Garrick (1717–79) British actor and manager. *Apprentice*, Prologue

5 I'd say award winning plays are written only for the critics.
Lew Grade (Lewis Winogradsky; 1906–) British film and TV producer. *The Observer*, 'Sayings of the Week', 18 Oct 1970

6 Oh, for an hour of Herod!
Anthony Hope (1863–1933) British novelist. Said at the children's play *Peter Pan* (J. M. Barrie). *J. M. Barrie and the Lost Boys* (A. Birkin)

7 He always hurries to the main event and whisks his audience into the middle of things as though they knew already.
Horace (Quintus Horatius Flaccus; 65–8 BC) Roman poet. *Ars Poetica*

8 The weasel under the cocktail cabinet.
Harold Pinter (1930–) British playwright. Reply when asked what his plays were about. *Anger and After* (J. Russell Taylor)

9 I think you would have been very glad if I had written it.
Alexis Piron (1689–1773) French poet and dramatist. Discussing Voltaire's *Sémiramis* with him after its poor reception on the first night. *Cyclopaedia of Anecdotes* (K. Arvine)

10 Depending upon shock tactics is easy, whereas writing a good play is difficult. Pubic hair is no substitute for wit.
J. B. Priestley (1894–1984) British novelist. *Outcries and Asides*

11 My soul; sit thou a patient looker-on;
Judge not the play before the play is done:
Her plot hath many changes, every day
Speaks a new scene; the last act crowns the play.
Francis Quarles (1592–1644) English poet. *Epigram, Respice Finem*

12 Rehearsing a play is making the word flesh. Publishing a play is reversing the process.
Peter Shaffer (1926–) British dramatist. *Equus*, Note

13 If it be true that good wine needs no bush, 'tis true that a good play needs no epilogue.
William Shakespeare (1564–1616) English dramatist. *As You Like It*, Epilogue

14 The play's the thing
Wherein I'll catch the conscience of the King.
William Shakespeare *Hamlet*, II:2

15 A good many inconveniences attend play-going in any large city, but the greatest of them is usually the play itself.
Kenneth Tynan (1927–80) British theater critic. *New York Herald Tribune*

16 A novel is a static thing that one moves through; a play is a dynamic thing that moves past one.
Kenneth Tynan *Curtains*

17 The play was a great success, but the audience was a disaster.
Oscar Wilde (1854–1900) Irish-born British dramatist. Referring to a play that had recently failed. Attrib.

PLEASURE

See also debauchery, happiness, leisure, merry-making

1 No pleasure without pain.
Proverb

2 And if the following day, he chance to find
A new repast, or an untasted spring,
Blesses his stars, and thinks it luxury.
Joseph Addison (1672–1719) British essayist. *Cato*, I:4

3 One half of the world cannot understand the pleasures of the other.
Jane Austen (1775–1817) British novelist. *Emma*, Ch. 9

4 Then I commended mirth, because a man hath no better thing under the sun, than to eat, and to drink, and to be merry: for that shall abide with him of his labour the days of his life, which God giveth him under the sun.
Bible: Ecclesiastes 8:15

5 He who bends to himself a Joy
Doth the wingèd life destroy;
But he who kisses the Joy as it flies
Lives in Eternity's sunrise.
William Blake (1757–1827) British poet. *Gnomic Verses*

6 He said once to myself that he was no atheist but he could not think God would make a man miserable only for taking a little pleasure out of the way.
Gilbert Burnet (1643–1715) English bishop and historian. Referring to Charles II. *History of My Own Times*

7 Pleasure after all is a safer guide than either right or duty.
Samuel Butler (1835–1902) British writer. *The Way of All Flesh*, Ch. 19

8 Though sages may pour out their wisdom's treasure,
There is no sterner moralist than Pleasure.
Lord Byron (1788–1824) British poet. *Don Juan*, III

9 In Xanadu did Kubla Khan
A stately pleasure-dome decree:
Where Alph, the sacred river, ran
Through caverns measureless to man
Down to a sunless sea.
Samuel Taylor Coleridge (1772–1834) British poet. *Kubla Khan*

10 It was a miracle of rare device,
A sunny pleasure-dome with caves of ice!
Samuel Taylor Coleridge *Kubla Khan*

11 Nothing can permanently please, which does not contain in itself the reason why it is so, and not otherwise.
Samuel Taylor Coleridge *Biographia Literaria*, Ch. 14

12 For present joys are more to flesh and blood
Than a dull prospect of a distant good.
John Dryden (1631–1700) British poet and dramatist. *The Hind and the Panther*, III

13 The art of pleasing consists in being pleased.
William Hazlitt (1778–1830) British essayist. *On Manner*

14 People must not do things for fun. We are not here for fun. There is no reference to fun in any Act of Parliament.
A. P. Herbert (1890–1971) British writer and politician. *Uncommon Law*

15 Pleasure is very seldom found where it is sought; our brightest

blazes of gladness are commonly kindled by unexpected sparks.
Samuel Johnson (1709–84) British lexicographer. *The Idler*

16 No man is a hypocrite in his pleasures.
Samuel Johnson *Life of Johnson* (J. Boswell), Vol. IV

17 If I had no duties, and no reference to futurity, I would spend my life in driving briskly in a post-chaise with a pretty woman.
Samuel Johnson *Life of Johnson* (J. Boswell), Vol. III

18 Give me books, fruit, French wine and fine weather and a little music out of doors, played by somebody I do not know.
John Keats (1795–1821) British poet. Letter to Fanny Keats, 29 Aug 1819

19 I love the gay Eastertide, which brings forth leaves and flowers; and I love the joyous song of the birds, re-echoing through the copse. But I also love to see, amidst the meadows, tents and pavilions spread; it gives me great joy to see, drawn up on the field, knights and horses in battle array.
Bertrand le Born French troubadour.

20 Life would be tolerable, were it not for its amusements.
George Cornewall Lewis (1806–63) British statesman and writer. *The Perpetual Pessimist* (Sagittarius and George)

21 A little of what you fancy does you good.
Marie Lloyd (1870–1922) British music-hall singer. Song title

22 Who loves not wine, woman and song,
Remains a fool his whole life long.
Martin Luther (1483–1546) German Protestant. Attrib.

23 My candle burns at both ends;
It will not last the night;
But ah, my foes, and oh my friends –
It gives a lovely light!
Edna St Vincent Millay (1892–1950) US poet. *A Few Figs from Thistles*, 'First Fig'

24 To sport with Amaryllis in the shade,
Or with the tangles of Neaera's hair.
John Milton (1608–74) English poet. *Lycidas*

25 Hence, vain deluding Joys,
The brood of Folly without father bred!
John Milton *Il Penseroso*

26 Great lords have their pleasures, but the people have fun.
Baron de Montesquieu (1688–1755) French writer. *Pensées diverses*

27 It was great fun,
But it was just one of those things.
Cole Porter (1891–1964) US composer and lyricist. *Jubilee*, 'Just One of Those Things'

28 It's delightful, it's delicious, it's de-lovely.
Cole Porter *Red, Hot and Blue*, 'It's De-Lovely'

29 I wish thee as much pleasure in the reading, as I had in the writing.
Francis Quarles (1592–1644) English poet. *Emblems*, 'To the Reader'

30 A life of pleasure requires an aristocratic setting to make it interesting.
George Santayana (1863–1952) US philosopher. *Life of Reason*, 'Reason in Society'

31 Pleasures are all alike simply considered in themselves . . . He that takes pleasure to hear sermons enjoys himself as much as he that hears plays.
John Selden (1584–1654) English historian. *Table Talk*

32 Pleasure is nothing else but the intermission of pain.
John Selden *Table Talk*

33 A Good Time Was Had by All.
Stevie Smith (Florence Margaret Smith; 1902–71) British poet. Book title

34 Everyone is dragged on by their favourite pleasure.
Virgil (Publius Vergilius Maro; 70–19 BC) Roman poet. *Eclogue*, Bk. II

35 All the things I really like to do are either immoral, illegal, or fattening.
Alexander Woollcott (1887–1943) US journalist. Attrib.

36 Pleasures newly found are sweet
When they lie about our feet.
William Wordsworth (1770–1850) British poet. *To the Small Celandine*

POETRY

See also criticism, inspiration, literature, poetry and prose, poets

1 For this reason poetry is something more philosophical and more worthy of serious attention than history.
Aristotle (384–322 BC) Greek philosopher. *Poetics*, Ch. 9

2 A criticism of life under the conditions fixed for such a criticism by the laws of poetic truth and poetic beauty.
Matthew Arnold (1822–88) British poet and critic. *Essays in Criticism*, Second Series, 'The Study of Poetry'

3 I think it will be found that the grand style arises in poetry, when a noble nature, poetically gifted, treats with simplicity or with severity a serious subject.
Matthew Arnold Closing words. *On Translating Homer*

4 The difference between genuine poetry and the poetry of Dryden, Pope, and all their school, is briefly this: their poetry is conceived and composed in their wits, genuine poetry is conceived and composed in the soul.
Matthew Arnold *Thomas Gray*

5 Now Ireland has her madness and her weather still,
For poetry makes nothing happen.
W. H. Auden (1907–73) British poet. *In Memory of W. B. Yeats*, II

6 A verbal art like poetry is reflective. It stops to think. Music is immediate, it goes on to become.
W. H. Auden (1907–) British poet. Attrib.

7 Poetry makes nothing happen, it survives
In the valley of its saying.
W. H. Auden (1907–73) British poet. *In Memory of W. B. Yeats*

8 It is not possible for a poet to be a professional. Poetry is essentially an amateur activity.
Lord Barrington (1908–) British barrister and peer. Speech, House of Lords, 23 Nov 1978

9 Too many people in the modern world view poetry as a luxury, not a necessity like petrol. But to me it's the oil of life.
John Betjeman (1906–84) British poet. *The Observer*, 'Sayings of the Year', 1974

10 Poetry is as much a part of the universe as mathematics and physics. It is not a cleverer device or recreation, unless the Eternal is clever.
Edmund Blunden (1896–1974) British poet. Speech on his election as Professor of Poetry at Oxford University, 1966

11 Masefield's sonnets? Ah yes. Very nice. Pure Shakespeare. Masefield's 'Reynard the Fox'? Very nice, too. Pure Chaucer. Masefield's 'Everlasting Mercy'? H'm. Yes. Pure Masefield.
Robert Bridges (1844–1930) British poet. *Twenty-Five* (Beverley Nichols)

12 Nothing so difficult as a beginning
In poesy, unless perhaps the end.
Lord Byron (1788–1824) British poet. *Don Juan*, IV

13 I have nothing to say, I am saying it, and that is poetry.
John Cage (1912–) US composer. In *The Sunday Times* (quoted by Cyril Connolly), 10 Sept 1972

14 For the godly poet must be chaste himself, but there is no need for his verses to be so.
Catullus (c. 84–c. 54 BC) Roman poet. *Carmina*, XVI

15 That willing suspension of disbelief for the moment, which constitutes poetic faith.
Samuel Taylor Coleridge (1772–1834) British poet. *Biographia Literaria*, Ch. 14

16 Poetry's unnat'ral; no man ever talked poetry 'cept a beadle on boxin' day.
Charles Dickens (1812–70) British novelist. *Pickwick Papers*, Ch. 33

17 I am afeered that werges on the poetical, Sammy.
Charles Dickens Said by Sam Weller. *Pickwick Papers*, Ch. 33

18 Poetry is not a turning loose of emotion, but an escape from emotion; it is not the expression of personality, but an escape from personality.
T. S. Eliot (1888–1965) US-born British poet and dramatist. *Tradition and the Individual Talent*

19 All one's inventions are true, you can be sure of that. Poetry is as exact a science as geometry.
Gustave Flaubert (1821–80) French novelist. Letter to Louise Colet, 14 Aug 1853

20 We all write poems; it is simply that poets are the ones who write in words.
John Fowles (1926–) British novelist. *The French Lieutenant's Woman*, Ch. 19

21 Writing free verse is like playing tennis with the net down.
Robert Frost (1875–1963) US poet. Speech, Milton Academy, 17 May 1935

22 Poetry is the language in which man explores his own amazement.
Christopher Fry (1907–) British dramatist. *Time*, 3 Apr 1950

23 Rightly thought of there is poetry in peaches . . . even when they are canned.
Harley Granville-Barker (1877–1946) British actor and dramatist. *The Madras House*, I

24 If Galileo had said in verse that the world moved, the Inquisition might have let him alone.
Thomas Hardy (1840–1928) British novelist. *The Later Years of Thomas Hardy* (F. E. Hardy)

25 It's hard to say why writing verse
Should terminate in drink or worse.
A. P. Herbert (1890–1971) British writer and politician. *Punch*, 'Lines for a Worldly Person'

26 Even when poetry has a meaning, as it usually has, it may be inadvisable to draw it out . . . Perfect understanding will sometimes almost extinguish pleasure.
A. E. Housman (1859–1936) British scholar and poet. *The Name and Nature of Poetry*

27 If a line of poetry strays into my memory, my skin bristles so that the razor ceases to act.
A. E. Housman Lecture, *The Name and Nature of Poetry*, Cambridge, 9 May 1933

28 'Why Sir, it is much easier to say what it is not. We all *know* what light is; but it is not easy to *tell* what it is.'
Samuel Johnson (1709–84) British lexicographer. When asked, 'What is poetry'. *Life of Johnson* (J. Boswell), Vol. III

29 A drainless shower
Of light is poesy; 'tis the supreme of power;
'Tis might half slumb'ring on its own right arm.
John Keats (1795–1821) British poet. *Sleep and Poetry*

30 A long poem is a test of invention which I take to be the Polar star of poetry, as fancy is the sails, and imagination the rudder.
John Keats Letter to Benjamin Bailey, 8 Oct 1817

31 We hate poetry that has a palpable design upon us – and if we do not agree, seems to put its hand in its breeches pocket. Poetry should be great and unobtrusive, a thing which enters into one's soul, and does not startle or amaze it with itself, but with its subject.
John Keats Letter to J. H. Reynolds, 3 Feb 1818

32 If poetry comes not as naturally as leaves to a tree it had better not come at all.
John Keats Letter to John Taylor, 27 Feb 1818

33 When power narrows the areas of man's concern, poetry reminds him of the richness and diversity of his existence.
John Fitzgerald Kennedy (1917–63) US statesman. Address at Dedication of the Robert Frost Library, 26 Oct 1963

34 Deprivation is for me what daffodils were for Wordsworth.
Philip Larkin (1922–85) British poet. Interview in *The Observer*

35 Perhaps no person can be a poet, or can even enjoy poetry, without a certain unsoundness of mind.
Lord Macaulay (1800–59) British historian. *Literary Essays Contributed to the 'Edinburgh Review'*, 'Milton'

36 Poem me no poems.
Rose Macaulay (1889–1958) British writer. *Poetry Review*, Autumn 1963

37 Poetry is a comforting piece of fiction set to more or less lascivious music.
H. L. Mencken (1880–1956) US journalist. *Prejudices*, 'The Poet and his Art'

38 Verse libre; a device for making poetry easier to read and harder to write.
H. L. Mencken *A Book of Burlesques*

39 Blest pair of Sirens, pledges of Heaven's joy,
Sphere-born harmonious sisters, Voice and Verse.
John Milton (1608–74) English poet. *At a Solemn Music*

40 Rhyme being no necessary adjunct or true ornament of poem or good verse, in longer works especially, but the invention of a barbarous age, to set off wretched matter and lame metre.
John Milton *Paradise Lost*, The Verse. Preface to 1668 ed.

41 The troublesome and modern bondage of Rhyming.
John Milton *Paradise Lost*, The Verse. Preface to 1668 ed.

42 . . . poetry, 'The Cinderella of the Arts.'
Harriet Monroe (1860–1936) US poet and editor. *Famous American Women* (Hope Stoddard), 'Harriet Monroe'

43 Above all I am not concerned with Poetry. My subject is War, and the pity of War. The Poetry is in the pity.
Wilfred Owen (1893–1918) British poet. *Poems*, Preface

44 Curst be the verse, how well so'er
it flow,
That tends to make one worthy man
my foe.
Alexander Pope (1688–1744) British poet. *Epistle to Dr. Arbuthnot*

45 For three years, out of key with his time,
He strove to resuscitate the dead art
Of poetry to maintain 'the sublime'
In the old sense. Wrong from the start.
Ezra Pound (1885–1972) US poet. *Pour l'élection de son sépulcre*

46 It is a perfectly possible means of overcoming chaos.
I. A. Richards (1893–1979) British critic. *Science and Poetry*

47 A sonnet is a moment's monument, –
Memorial from the Soul's eternity
To one dead deathless hour.
Dante Gabriel Rossetti (1828–82) British painter and poet. *The House of Life*, Introduction

48 What is poetry? The suggestion, by the imagination, of noble grounds for the noble emotions.
John Ruskin (1819–1900) British art critic and writer. *Modern Painters*, Vol. III

49 Poetry is the achievement of the synthesis of hyacinths and biscuits.
Carl Sandburg (1878–1967) US author and poet. *Atlantic Monthly*

50 The truest poetry is the most feigning.
William Shakespeare (1564–1616) English dramatist. *As You Like It*, III:3

51 The poet's eye, in a fine frenzy
rolling,
Doth glance from heaven to earth,
from earth to heaven;
And as imagination bodies forth
The forms of things unknown, the
poet's pen
Turns them to shapes, and gives to
airy nothing
A local habitation and a name.
William Shakespeare *A Midsummer Night's Dream*, V:1

52 The lunatic, the lover, and the
poet,
Are of imagination all compact.
William Shakespeare *A Midsummer Night's Dream*, V:1

53 Not marble, nor the gilded
monuments
Of princes, shall outlive this powerful
rhyme.
William Shakespeare *Sonnet 55*

54 Poetry is the record of the best and happiest moments of the happiest and best minds.
Percy Bysshe Shelley (1792–1822) British poet. *A Defence of Poetry*

55 One of the purposes of poetry is to show the dimensions of man that are, as Sir Arthur Eddington said 'midway in scale between the atom and the star.'
Edith Sitwell (1887–1964) British poet and writer. *Rhyme and Reason*

56 My poems are hymns of praise to the glory of life.
Edith Sitwell *Collected Poems*, 'Some Notes on My Poetry'

57 It is as unseeing to ask what is the *use* of poetry as it would be to ask what is the use of religion.
Edith Sitwell *The Outcasts*, Preface

58 Poetry ennobles the heart and the eyes and unveils the meaning of things upon which the heart and the eyes dwell.
Edith Sitwell *Rhyme and Reason*

59 A man does not write poems about what he knows, but about what he does not know.
Robin Skelton (1925–) British academic. *Teach Yourself Poetry*

60 These poems, with all their crudities, doubts, and confusions, are written for the love of Man and in praise of God, and I'd be a damn' fool if they weren't.
Dylan Thomas (1914–53) Welsh poet. *Collected Poems*, Note

61 Having verse set to music is like looking at a painting through a stained glass window.
Paul Valéry (1871–1945) French poet and writer. Attrib.

62 There are no poetic ideas; only poetic utterances.
Evelyn Waugh (1903–66) British novelist. *Books On Trial*

63 Hence no force however great can stretch a cord however fine into an horizontal line which is accurately straight: there will always be a bending downwards.
William Whewell (1794–1866) British philosopher and mathematician. An example of unintentional versification. *Elementary Treatise on Mechanics* (1819 edition), Ch. 4

64 No one will ever get at my verses who insists upon viewing them as a literary performance.
Walt Whitman (1819–92) US poet. *A Backward Glance O'er Travel'd Roads*

65 I would rather have written those lines than take Quebec.
James Wolfe (1727–59) British general. Referring to Gray's Elegy, on the eve of the Battle of Quebec, 1759. Attrib.

66 Poetry is the spontaneous overflow of powerful feelings: it takes its origin from emotion recollected in tranquillity.
William Wordsworth (1770–1850) British poet. *Lyrics Ballads*, Preface

67 Out of the quarrel with others we make rhetoric; out of the quarrel with ourselves we make poetry.
W. B. Yeats (1865–1939) Irish poet. *Essay*

68 Too true, too sincere. The Muse prefers the liars, the gay and warty lads.
W. B. Yeats Referring to the poetry of James Reed. *The Long Week End* (Robert Graves and Alan Hodge)

POETRY AND PROSE

See also poetry, prose

1 Poetry is not the proper antithesis to prose, but to science. Poetry is opposed to science, and prose to metre.
Samuel Taylor Coleridge (1772–1834) British poet. *Lectures and Notes of 1818*, I

2 I wish our clever young poets would remember my homely definitions of prose and poetry; that is, prose = words in their best order; – poetry = the best words in the best order.
Samuel Taylor Coleridge *Table Talk*

3 Prose on certain occasions can bear a great deal of poetry: on the other hand, poetry sinks and swoons under a moderate weight of prose.
Walter Savage Landor (1775–1864) British poet and writer. *Imaginary Conversations*, 'Archdeacon Hare and Walter Landor'

4 For to write good prose is an affair of good manners. It is, unlike

verse, a civil art. . . . Poetry is baroque.
W. Somerset Maugham (1874–1965) British novelist. *The Summing Up*

5 Poetry is to prose as dancing is to walking.
John Wain (1925–) British novelist and poet. Talk, BBC radio, 13 Jan 1976

6 The poet gives us his essence, but prose takes the mould of the body and mind entire.
Virginia Woolf (1882–1941) British novelist. *The Captain's Death Bed*, 'Reading'

7 There neither is, nor can be, any *essential* difference between the language of prose and metrical composition.
William Wordsworth (1770–1850) British poet. *Lyrical Ballads*, Preface

8 O'CONNOR. How are you?
W.B.Y. Not very well, I can only write prose today.
W. B. Yeats (1865–1939) Irish poet. Attrib.

POETS

See also Byron, criticism, poetry, Shakespeare, writers

1 It always seems to me that the right sphere for Shelley's genius was the sphere of music, not of poetry.
Matthew Arnold (1822–88) British poet and critic. *Maurice de Guérin*, Footnote

2 He spoke, and loos'd our heart in tears.
He laid us as we lay at birth
On the cool flowery lap of earth.
Matthew Arnold Referring to Wordsworth. *Memorial Verses*

3 Time may restore us in his course
Goethe's sage mind and Byron's force:
But where will Europe's latter hour
Again find Wordsworth's healing power?
Matthew Arnold *Memorial Verses*

4 He was so fair that they called him *the lady of* Christ's College.
John Aubrey *Brief Lives*, 'John Milton'

5 Earth, receive an honoured guest:
William Yeats is laid to rest.
Let the Irish vessel lie
Emptied of its poetry.
W. H. Auden (1907–73) British poet. *In Memory of W. B. Yeats*, III

6 I agree with one of your reputable critics that a taste for drawing rooms has spoiled more poets than ever did a taste for gutters.
Thomas Beer (1889–1940) US author. *The Mauve Decade*

7 Poets and painters are outside the class system, or rather they constitute a special class of their own, like the circus people and the gipsies.
Gerald Brenan (Edward Fitzgerald Brenan; 1894–1987) British writer. *Thoughts in a Dry Season*, 'Writing'

8 The Fleshly School of Poetry.
Robert Williams Buchanan (1841–1901) British poet and writer. Referring to Swinburne, William Morris, D. G. Rossetti, etc. Title of article in the *Contemporary Review*, Oct 1871

9 A poet without love were a physical and metaphysical impossibility.
Thomas Carlyle (1795–1881) Scottish historian and essayist. *Critical and Miscellaneous Essays*, 'Burns'

10 He could not think up to the height of his own towering style.
G. K. Chesterton (1874–1936) British writer. Speaking of Tennyson. *The Victorian Age in Literature*, Ch. 3

11 A true poet does not bother to be poetical. Nor does a nursery gardener scent his roses.
Jean Cocteau (1889–1963) French poet and artist. *Professional Secrets*

12 With Donne, whose muse on dromedary trots,
Wreathe iron pokers into true-love knots.
Samuel Taylor Coleridge (1772–1834) British poet. *On Donne's Poetry*

13 The misfortune is, that he has begun to write verses without very well understanding what metre is.
Samuel Taylor Coleridge Referring to Tennyson. *Table Talk*

14 A poet is not a public figure. A poet should be read and not seen.
C. Day Lewis (1904–72) British poet. *The Observer*, 'Sayings of the Week', 7 Jan 1968

15 Immature poets imitate; mature poets steal.
T. S. Eliot (1888–1965) US-born British poet and dramatist. *Philip Massinger*

16 *Hugo – hélas!*
André Gide (1869–1951) French novelist. Replying to an inquiry as to whom he considered the finest poet of the 19th century. *André Gide–Paul Valéry Correspondence 1890–1942*

17 Poets should never marry. The world should thank me for not marrying you.
Maud Gonne (1866–1953) Irish patriot and philanthropist. Said to W. B. Yeats. Attrib.

18 To be a poet is a condition rather than a profession.
Robert Graves (1895–1985) British poet and novelist. *Horizon*

19 Most poets are dead by their late twenties.
Robert Graves *The Observer*, 11 Nov 1962

20 Shelley and Keats were the last English poets who were at all up to date in their chemical knowledge.
J. B. S. Haldane (1892–1964) British geneticist. *Daedalus or Science and the Future*

21 He talked on for ever; and you wished him to talk on for ever.
William Hazlitt (1778–1830) British essayist. Referring to Coleridge. *Lectures on the English Poets*, Lecture VIII, 'On the Living Poets'

22 Not gods, nor men, nor even booksellers have put up with poets' being second-rate.
Horace (Quintus Horatius Flaccus; 65–8 BC) Roman poet. *Ars Poetica*

23 Sir, there is no settling the point of precedency between a louse and a flea.
Samuel Johnson (1709–84) British lexicographer. When Maurice Morgann asked him who he considered to be the better poet – Smart or Derrick. *Life of Johnson* (J. Boswell), Vol. IV

24 He was dull in a new way, and that made many people think him *great*.
Samuel Johnson Referring to the poet Thomas Gray. *Life of Johnson* (J. Boswell), Vol. II

25 Milton, Madam, was a genius that could cut a Colossus from a rock; but could not carve heads upon cherry-stones.
Samuel Johnson When Miss Hannah More had wondered why Milton could write the epic *Paradise Lost* but only very poor sonnets. *Life of Johnson* (J. Boswell), Vol. IV

26 Walt Whitman who laid end to end words never seen in each other's company before outside of a dictionary.
David Lodge (1935–) British author. *Changing Places*, Ch. 5

27 When one hears of a poet past thirty-five he seems somehow unnatural and obscene.
H. L. Mencken *Prejudices*

28 The courage of the poet is to keep ajar the door that leads to madness.
Christopher Morley (1890–1957) US writer and journalist. *Inward Ho*

29 Popular poets are the parish priests of the Muse, retailing her ancient divinations to a long since converted public.
George Santayana (1863–1952) US philosopher. *The Life of Reason*, 'Reason in Art'

30 For ne'er
Was flattery lost on poet's ear:
A simple race! they waste their toil
For the vain tribute of a smile.
Walter Scott (1771–1832) Scottish novelist. *The Lay of the Last Minstrel*, IV

31 There have been many most excellent poets that have never versified, and now swarm many versifiers that need never answer to the name of poets.
Philip Sidney (1554–86) English poet and courtier. *The Defence of Poesy*

32 The poet speaks to all men of that other life of theirs that they have smothered and forgotten.
Edith Sitwell (1887–1964) British poet and writer. *Rhyme and Reason*

33 People sometimes divide others into those you laugh at and those you laugh with. The young Auden was someone you could laugh-at-with.
Stephen Spender (1909–) British poet. Address, W. H. Auden's memorial service, Oxford, 27 Oct 1973

34 The poet is the priest of the invisible.
Wallace Stevens (1879–1955) US poet. *Opus Posthumous*, 'Adagio'

35 The poet may be used as the barometer, but let us not forget he is also part of the weather.
Lionel Trilling (1905–75) US critic. *The Liberal Imagination*

36 I hate the whole race . . . There is no believing a word they say – your professional poets, I mean – there never existed a more worthless set than Byron and his friends for example.
Duke of Wellington (1769–1852) British general and statesman. Lady Salisbury's diary, 26 Oct 1833

37 All poets who when reading from their own works experience a choking feeling are major. For that matter, all poets who read from their own works are major, whether they choke or not.
Elwyn Brooks White (1899–1985) US journalist and humorist. *How to Tell a Major Poet from a Minor Poet*

38 That William Blake
Who beat upon the wall
Till Truth obeyed his call.
W. B. Yeats (1865–1939) Irish poet. *An Acre of Grass*

39 He is the handsomest man in England, and he wears the most beautiful shirts.
W. B. Yeats Referring to Rupert Brooke. Attrib.

POLICE

1 I have never seen a situation so dismal that a policeman couldn't make it worse.
Brendan Behan (1923–64) Irish playwright. Attrib.

2 Gentlemen, get the thing straight once and for all. The policeman isn't there to *create* disorder, the policeman is there to *preserve* disorder.
Richard J. Daley (1902–76) US Democratic politician and mayor of Chicago. Said during anti-Vietnam war riots at the 1968 Democratic Convention. Attrib.

3 When constabulary duty's to be done –
A policeman's lot is not a happy one.
W. S. Gilbert (1836–1911) British dramatist. *The Pirates of Penzance*, II

4 Why can't the police be equipped with fast-acting tranquilliser darts or pellets? If it works with rhinos, why not with robbers?
U. Light Letter to *The Observer*, 21 Jan 1979

5 Policemen are numbered in case they get lost.
Spike Milligan (1918–) British comic actor and author. *The Last Goon Show of All*

6 A thing of duty is a boy for ever.
Flann O'Brien (Brian O'Nolan; 1911–66) Irish novelist and journalist. About policemen always seeming to be young-looking. *The Listener*, 24 Feb 1977

7 Reading isn't an occupation we encourage among police officers. We try to keep the paper work down to a minimum.
Joe Orton (1933–67) British dramatist. *Loot*, II

8 Policemen, like red squirrels, must be protected.
Joe Orton *Loot*

9 My father didn't create you to arrest me.
Lord Peel (1829–1912) British politician. Protesting against his arrest by the police, recently established by his father. Attrib.

10 One always has the air of someone who is lying when one speaks to a policeman.
Charles-Louis Philippe (1874–1909) French novelist. *Les Chroniques du canard sauvage*

11 (If you want to know the time) Ask a p'liceman.
E. W. Rogers (1864–1913) Song Title

12 P. C. Attila Rees, ox-broad, barge-booted, stamping out of Handcuff House in a heavy, beef-red huff, blackbrowed under his damp helmet . . . and lumbering down towards the strand to see that the sea is still there.
Dylan Thomas (1914–53) Welsh poet. *Under Milk Wood*

POLITENESS

1 Politeness is only one half good manners and the other half good lying.
Mary Wilson Little Attrib.

2 I was far too polite to ask.
Gore Vidal (1925–) US novelist. When asked whether the first person he had slept with was male or female. Attrib.

POLITICIANS

See also Churchill, compliments, government, Hitler, Houses of Parliament, insults, politics

1 The G.O.M., when his life ebbs out,
Will ride in a fiery chariot,
And sit in state
On a red-hot plate
Between Pilate and Judas Iscariot.
Anonymous Gladstone, known as the Grand Old Man, was blamed for the death of General Gordon at Khartoum. *The Faber Book of English History in Verse* (Kenneth Baker)

2 The Iron Lady of British politics is seeking to revive the cold war.
Anonymous Commenting on a speech by Margaret Thatcher. *Red Star*, 23 Jan 1976

3 Margaret Thatcher is David Owen in drag.
Anonymous *The Rhodesia Herald*, 8 Aug 1979

4 Would you buy a used car from this man?
Anonymous Referring to Richard Nixon.

5 Lord George-Brown drunk is a better man than the Prime Minister sober.
Anonymous Comparing him with Harold Wilson. *The Times*, 6 Mar 1976

6 It is fitting that we should have

buried the Unknown Prime Minister by the side of the Unknown Soldier.

Herbert Henry Asquith (1852–1928) British statesman. Said at Bonar Law's funeral, 5 Nov 1923. Attrib.

7 He always has his arm round your waist and his eye on the clock.

Margot Asquith (1865–1945) The second wife of Herbert Asquith. *As I Remember*

8 You'll never get on in politics, my dear, with *that* hair.

Viscountess Nancy Astor (1879–1964) American-born British politician. Attrib.

9 You have no right whatever to speak on behalf of the Government. Foreign Affairs are in the capable hands of Ernest Bevin. His task is quite sufficiently difficult without the embarrassment of irresponsible statements of the kind which you are making . . . a period of silence on your part would be welcome.

Clement Attlee (1883–1967) British Labour prime minister. Letter to Harold Laski, Chairman of the Labour Party, 20 Aug 1945. *British Political Facts 1900–75*

10 No man has come so near our definition of a constitutional statesman – the powers of a first-rate man and the creed of a second-rate man.

Walter Bagehot (1826–77) British economist and journalist. *Historical Essays*, 'The Character of Sir Robert Peel'

11 He believes, with all his heart and soul and strength, that there *is* such a thing as truth; he has the soul of a martyr with the intellect of an advocate.

Walter Bagehot Referring to Gladstone. *Historical Essays*, 'Mr Gladstone'

12 Of all the politicians I ever saw
The least significant was Bonar Law.
Unless it was MacDonald, by the way:
Or Baldwin – it's impossible to say.

Hilaire Belloc (1870–1953) French-born British poet. *The Faber Book of English History in Verse* (Kenneth Baker)

13 He therefore was at strenuous pains
To atrophy his puny brains
And registered success in this
Beyond the dreams of avarice
Till when he had at last become
Blind, paralytic, deaf and dumb
Insensible and cretinous
He was admitted ONE OF US.

Hilaire Belloc *The Statesman*

14 If I rescued a child from drowning, the Press would no doubt headline the story 'Benn grabs child'.

Tony Benn (1925–) British politician. *The Observer*, 'Sayings of the Week', 2 Mar 1975

15 We are not just here to manage capitalism but to change society and to define its finer values.

Tony Benn Speech, Labour Party Conference, 1 Oct 1975

16 I am on the right wing of the middle of the road and with a strong radical bias.

Tony Benn Attrib.

17 Mr Lloyd George spoke for a hundred and seventeen minutes, in which period he was detected only once in the use of an argument.

Arnold Bennett (1867–1931) British writer. *Things That Have Interested Me*, 'After the March Offensive'

18 A dessicated calculating machine.

Aneurin Bevan (1897–1960) British Labour politician. Referring to Hugh Gaitskell. *Hugh Gaitskell* (W. T. Rodgers)

19 There is no reason to attack the monkey when the organ-grinder is present.

Aneurin Bevan The 'monkey' was Selwyn Lloyd; the 'organ-grinder' was Harold Macmillan. Speech, House of Commons

20 She is trying to wear the trousers of Winston Churchill.

Leonid Brezhnev (1906–82) Soviet statesman. Referring to Margaret Thatcher. Speech, 1979

21 Most British statesmen have either drunk too much or womanized too much. I never fell into the second category.

Lord George Brown (1914–85) British Labour politician. *The Observer*, 11 Nov 1974

22 I think the Prime Minister has to be a butcher, and know the joints. That is perhaps where I have not been quite competent enough in knowing the ways that you cut up a carcass.

R. A. Butler (1902–82) British Conservative politician. Television interview, June 1966

23 For the purposes of recreation he has selected the felling of trees, and we may usefully remark that his amusements, like his politics, are essentially destructive. . . . The forest laments in order that Mr Gladstone may perspire.

Randolph Churchill (1849–95) British Conservative politician. Speech, Blackpool, 24 Jan 1884

24 Their worst misfortune was his birth; their next worst – his death.

Winston Churchill (1874–1965) British statesman. Referring to Lenin. *The World Crisis*

25 I have never seen a human being who more perfectly represented the modern conception of a robot.

Winston Churchill Referring to the Soviet statesman Molotov. *The Second World War*

26 In Franklin Roosevelt there died the greatest American friend we have ever known and the greatest champion of freedom who has ever brought help and comfort from the New World to the Old.

Winston Churchill *The Second World War*

27 I remember, when I was a child, being taken to the celebrated Barnum's circus, which contained an exhibition of freaks and monstrosities, but the exhibit . . . which I most desired to see was the one described as 'The Boneless Wonder'. My parents judged that that spectacle would be too revolting and demoralising for my youthful eyes, and I have waited 50 years to see the boneless wonder sitting on the Treasury Bench.

Winston Churchill (1874–1965) British statesman. Referring to Ramsey MacDonald. Speech, House of Commons, 28 Jan 1931

28 He is like a female llama surprised in her bath.

Winston Churchill Referring to Charles de Gaulle. Attrib.

29 The Happy Warrior of Squandermania.

Winston Churchill Referring to Lloyd George. Attrib.

30 In the eighteenth century he would have become Prime Minister before he was thirty; as it was he appeared honourably ineligible for the struggle of life.

Cyril Connolly (1903–74) British writer. Referring to the British prime minister Sir Alec Douglas-Home at Eton. *Enemies of Promise*

31 I do not choose to run for President in 1928.

Calvin Coolidge (1872–1933) US president. Announcement in 1927

32 President Nixon's motto was, if two wrongs don't make a right, try three.

Norman Cousins (1915–) US editor and author. *Daily Telegraph*, 17 July 1979

33 Dear Randolph, utterly unspoiled by failure.
Noël Coward (1899–1973) British dramatist. Referring to Randolph Churchill. Attrib.

34 a politician is an arse upon which everyone has sat except a man
e. e. cummings (1894–1962) US poet. *A Politician*

35 In private conversation he tries on speeches like a man trying on ties in his bedroom to see how he would look in them.
Lionel Curtis (1872–1955) British writer. Referring to Winston Churchill. Letter to Nancy Astor, 1912

36 Not even a public figure. A man of no experience. And of the utmost insignificance.
Lord Curzon (1859–1925) British politician. Referring to Stanley Baldwin on his appointment as Prime Minister. *Curzon: The Last Phase* (Harold Nicolson)

37 When I was a boy I was told that anybody could become President of the United States. I am beginning to believe it.
Clarence Darrow (1857–1938) US lawyer. Attrib.

38 Since a politician never believes what he says, he is surprised when others believe him.
Charles De Gaulle (1890–1970) French general and statesman. Attrib.

39 In order to become the master, the politician poses as the servant.
Charles De Gaulle Attrib.

40 I have come to the conclusion that politics are too serious a matter to be left to the politicians.
Charles De Gaulle Attrib.

41 . . . a great master of gibes and flouts and jeers.
Benjamin Disraeli (1804–81) British statesman. Referring to Lord Salisbury. Speech, House of Commons, 5 Aug 1874

42 Gladstone, like Richelieu, can't write. Nothing can be more unmusical, more involved or more uncouth than all his scribblement.
Benjamin Disraeli Letter, 3 Oct 1877

43 If a traveller were informed that such a man was leader of the House of Commons, he may well begin to comprehend how the Egyptians worshipped an insect.
Benjamin Disraeli Referring to Lord John Russell. Attrib.

44 There are two problems in my life. The political ones are insoluble and the economic ones are incomprehensible.
Alec Douglas-Home (1903–) British statesman. Speech, Jan 1964

45 He is used to dealing with estate workers. I cannot see how anyone can say he is out of touch.
Lady Caroline Douglas-Home (1937–) Daughter of Alec Douglas-Home. Referring to her father's suitability for his new role as prime minister. *Daily Herald*, 21 Oct 1963 (Jon Akass)

46 For Politicians neither love nor hate.
John Dryden (1631–1700) British poet and dramatist. *Absalom and Achitophel*, I

47 The difference between being an elder statesman
And posing successfully as an elder statesman
Is practically negligible.
T. S. Eliot (1888–1965) US-born British poet and dramatist. *The Elder Statesman*

48 I always voted at my party's call,
And I never thought of thinking for myself at all.
W. S. Gilbert (1836–1911) British dramatist. *HMS Pinafore*, I

49 The prospect of a lot
Of dull MPs in close proximity,
All thinking for themselves is what
No man can face with equanimity.
W. S. Gilbert *Iolanthe*, I

50 This cardinal is the person who rules both the king and the entire kingdom.
Sebastian Giustiniani Venetian ambassador to England. Referring to Cardinal Wolsey. *Wolsey* (A. F. Pollard)

51 Nothing pleased him more than to be styled the arbitrator of the affairs of Christendom.
Sebastian Giustiniani Referring to Cardinal Wolsey. *Letters and Papers of Henry VIII*, Vol. III

52 Count not his broken pledges as a crime
He MEANT them, HOW he meant them – at the time.
Kensal Green Referring to David Lloyd George. *The Faber Book of English History in Verse* (Kenneth Baker)

53 A sad day this for Alexander
And many another dead commander.
Jealousy's rife in heroes' hall –
Winston Churchill has bluffed them all.
Kensal Green *The Faber Book of English History in Verse* (Kenneth Baker)

54 His fame endures; we shall not quite forget
The name of Baldwin till we're out of debt.
Kensal Green *The Faber Book of English History in Verse* (Kenneth Baker)

55 This man has a nice smile, but he has got iron teeth.
Andrei Gromyko (1909–) Soviet politician. In proposing Mikhail Gorbachev for the post of Soviet Communist Party leader. Speech, 1985

56 'Do you pray for the senators, Dr Hale?' 'No, I look at the senators and I pray for the country.'
Edward Everett Hale (1822–1909) US author and clergyman. *New England Indian Summer* (Van Wyck Brooks)

57 For the past few months she has been charging about like some bargain-basement Boadicea.
Denis Healey (1917–) British Labour politician. Referring to Margaret Thatcher. *Observer*, 'Sayings of the Week', 7 Nov 1982

58 I am the Gromyko of the Labour party.
Denis Healey Alluding to Andrei Gromyko (1909–), Soviet statesman who was foreign minister from 1957 to 1985. Attrib.

59 There is one statesman of the present day, of whom I always say that he would have escaped making the blunders that he has made if he had only ridden more in omnibuses.
Arthur Helps (1813–75) British historian. *Friends in Council*

61 She is the Enid Blyton of economics. Nothing must be allowed to spoil her simple plots.
Richard Holme (1936–) British campaigner for electoral reform. Referring to Margaret Thatcher. Speech, Liberal Party Conference, 10 Sept 1980

62 He would rather follow public opinion than lead it.
Harry Hopkins (1890–1946) US politician. Referring to Roosevelt. Attrib.

63 A politician rises on the backs of his friends . . . but it is through his enemies he will have to govern afterwards.
Richard Hughes (1900–76) British writer. *The Fox in the Attic*

64 Walpole was a minister given by the King to the people:—Pitt was a minister given by the people to the King.
Samuel Johnson (1709–84) British lexicographer. *Life of Johnson* (J. Boswell)

65 If a man were to go by chance at

the same time with Burke under a shed, to shun a shower, he would say – 'this is an extraordinary man.'

Samuel Johnson Referring to Edmund Burke. *Life of Johnson* (J. Boswell), Vol. IV

66 Do you realize the responsibility I carry? I'm the only person standing between Nixon and the White House.

John Fitzgerald Kennedy (1917–63) US statesman. Said to Arthur Schlesinger, 13 Oct 1960; Richard Nixon was the Republican candidate in the 1960 US Presidential election. *A Thousand Days* (Arthur M. Schlesinger, Jnr)

67 This goat-footed bard, this half-human visitor to our age from the hag-ridden magic and enchanted woods of Celtic antiquity.

John Maynard Keynes (1883–1946) British economist. Referring to Lloyd George. *Essays and Sketches in Biography*

68 Political renegades always start their career of treachery as 'the best men of all parties' and end up in the Tory knackery.

Neil Kinnock (1942–) British politician. Speech, Welsh Labour Party Conference, 1985

69 Politicians are the same everywhere. They promise to build bridges even where there are no rivers.

Nikita Khrushchev (1894–1971) Soviet statesman. Attrib., Oct 1960

70 We will bury you.

Nikita Khrushchev Said at a reception at the Kremlin, 26 Nov 1956

71 We have heard of people being thrown to the wolves, but never before have we heard of a man being thrown to the wolves with a bargain on the part of the wolves that they would not eat him.

Bonar Law (1858–1923) British statesman. Referring to the fact that the then war minister, Col Seely, had offered his resignation. Speech, House of Commons, Mar 1914

72 Look at that man's eyes. You will hear more of him later.

Bonar Law Referring to Mussolini. Attrib.

73 Poor Bonar can't bear being called a liar. Now I don't mind.

David Lloyd George (1863–1945) British Liberal statesman. Referring to Bonar Law, prime minister 1922–23. *Stanley Baldwin* (G. M. Young)

74 He saw foreign policy through the wrong end of a municipal drainpipe.

David Lloyd George Referring to Neville Chamberlain. *The Fine Art of Political Wit* (Harris), Ch. 6

75 A politician is a person with whose politics you don't agree; if you agree with him he is a statesman.

David Lloyd George Attrib.

76 A savage old Nabob, with an immense fortune, a tawny complexion, a bad liver and a worse heart.

Lord Macaulay (1800–59) British historian. Referring to Clive of India (1725–74). *Historical Essays*, 'Lord Clive'

77 I am MacWonder one moment and MacBlunder the next.

Harold Macmillan (1894–1986) British politician and prime minister. *Daily Telegraph*, 15 Nov 1973

78 If people want a sense of purpose they should get it from their archbishop. They should certainly not get it from their politicians.

Harold Macmillan *The Life of Politics* (H. Fairlie)

79 When you're abroad you're a statesman: when you're at home you're just a politician.

Harold Macmillan Speech, 1958

80 So restless Cromwell could not cease
In the inglorious arts of peace.

Andrew Marvell (1621–78) English poet. *An Horatian Ode upon Cromwell's Return from Ireland*

81 It is very unfair to expect a politician to live in private up to the statements he makes in public.

W. Somerset Maugham (1874–1965) British novelist. *The Circle*

82 Sit down, man. You're a bloody tragedy.

James Maxton (1885–1946) Scottish Labour leader. Said to Ramsay MacDonald when he made his last speech in Parliament. Attrib.

83 The rogue elephant among British prime ministers.

Dr Kenneth Morgan (1934–) British historian. Referring to Lloyd George. *Life of David Lloyd George*

84 The proper memory for a politician is one that knows when to remember and when to forget.

John Morley (1838–1923) British statesman. *Recollections*

85 I am not and never have been, a man of the right. My position was on the left and is now in the centre of politics.

Oswald Mosley (1896–1980) British politician. *The Times*, 26 Apr 1968

86 Argue as you please, you are nowhere, that grand old man, the Prime Minister, insists on the other thing.

Lord Northcote (1818–87) British statesman. Referring to Gladstone; the phrase, and its acronym GOM, became his nickname – temporarily reversed to MOG ('Murderer of Gordon') in 1885, after the death of General Gordon at Khartoum. Speech, Liverpool, 12 Apr 1882

87 . . . reminds me of nothing so much as a recently dead fish before it has had time to stiffen.

George Orwell (Eric Blair; 1903–50) British novelist. Referring to Clement Attlee. Diary, 19 May 1942

88 How could they tell?

Dorothy Parker (1893–1967) US writer. Reaction to news of the death of Calvin Coolidge, US President 1923–29; also attributed to H. L. Mencken. *You Might As Well Live* (J. Keats)

89 A statesman is a politician who places himself at the service of the nation. A politician is a statesman who places the nation at his service.

Georges Pompidou (1911–74) French statesman. *The Observer*, 'Sayings of the Year', 30 Dec 1973

90 All political lives, unless they are cut off in mid-stream at a happy juncture, end in failure.

Enoch Powell (1912–) British politician. *Sunday Times*, 6 Nov 1977

91 Above any other position of eminence, that of Prime Minister is filled by fluke.

Enoch Powell *The Observer*, 'Sayings of the Week', 8 Mar 1987

92 A number of anxious dwarfs trying to grill a whale.

J. B. Priestley (1894–1984) British novelist. *Outcries and Asides*

93 There was no impropriety whatsoever in my acquaintanceship with Miss Keeler.

John Profumo (1915–) British politician. Speech, House of Commons, 22 Mar 1963

94 Coolidge is a better example of evolution than either Bryan or Darrow, for he knows when not to talk, which is the biggest asset the monkey possesses over the human.

Will Rogers (1879–1935) US actor and humorist. *Saturday Review*, 'A Rogers Thesaurus', 25 Aug 1962

95 Stalin hates the guts of all your top people. He thinks he likes me better, and I hope he will continue to do so.

Franklin D. Roosevelt (1882–1945) US Democratic president. *The Hinge of Fate* (Winston S. Churchill), Ch. 11

96 Our great democracies still tend to think that a stupid man is more likely to be honest than a clever man, and our politicians take advantage of this prejudice by pretending to be even more stupid than nature has made them.

Bertrand Russell (1872–1970) British philosopher. *New Hopes for a Changing World*

97 . . . a man who, with all his great qualities, was unable to decide a general principle of action, or to ensure that when decided on it should be carried out by his subordinates.

Marquess of Salisbury (1830–1903) British statesman. Referring to Benjamin Disraeli. *Chapters of Autobiography* (A. J. Balfour)

98 Get thee glass eyes,
And, like a scurvy politician, seem
To see the things thou dost not.

William Shakespeare (1564–1616) English dramatist. *King Lear*, IV:6

99 He knows nothing; and he thinks he knows everything. That points clearly to a political career.

George Bernard Shaw (1856–1950) Irish dramatist and critic. *Major Barbara*, III

100 The Right Honourable gentleman is indebted to his memory for his jests, and to his imagination for his facts.

Richard Brinsley Sheridan (1751–1816) British dramatist. Replying to a speech in the House of Commons. Attrib.

101 I will not accept if nominated, and will not serve if elected.

General William Sherman (1820–91) US politician and president. Replying to a request that he accept the Republican presidential nomination. Attrib.

102 He was the Messiah of the new age, and his crucifixion was yet to come.

George Edward Slocombe (1894–1963) British journalist. Referring to Woodrow Wilson and his visit to the Versailles conference. *Mirror to Geneva*

103 All politicians have vanity. Some wear it more gently than others.

David Steel (1938–) British politician. *The Observer*, 'Sayings of the Week', 14 July 1985

104 Nixon is the kind of politician who would cut down a redwood tree, then mount the stump for a conservation speech.

Adlai Stevenson (1900–65) US statesman. Attrib.

105 A politician is a statesman who approaches every question with an open mouth.

Adlai Stevenson Also attrib. to Arthur Goldberg. *The Fine Art of Political Wit* (L. Harris)

106 Whoever could make two ears of corn or two blades of grass to grow upon a spot of ground where only one grew before would deserve better of mankind and do more essential service to his country than the whole race of politicians put together.

Jonathan Swift (1667–1745) Irish-born Anglican priest and writer. *Gulliver's Travels*, 'Voyage to Brobdingnag', Ch. 7

107 With favour and fortune fastidiously blest,
He's loud in his laugh and he's coarse in his jest;
. . .
Though I name not the wretch you know who I mean –
'Tis the cur dog of Britain and spaniel of Spain.

Jonathan Swift Referring to Sir Robert Walpole. *Two Character Studies*

108 A master of improvised speech and improvised policies.

A. J. P. Taylor (1906–) British historian. Referring to Lloyd George. *English History 1914–1945*

109 I hope Mrs Thatcher will go until the turn of the century looking like Queen Victoria.

Norman Tebbitt (1931–) British Conservative politician. *The Observer*, 'Sayings of the Week', 17 May 1987

110 I owe nothing to Women's Lib.

Margaret Thatcher (1925–) British politician and prime minister. *The Observer*, 1 Dec 1974

111 Ladies and gentlemen, I stand before you tonight in my green chiffon evening gown, my face softly made up, my fair hair gently waved . . . the Iron Lady of the Western World. Me? A cold war warrior? Well, yes – if that is how they wish to interpret my defence of values, and freedoms fundamental to our way of life.

Margaret Thatcher Referring to the nickname 'The Iron Lady' used by the Soviet paper *Red Star*. Speech, Dorking, 31 Jan 1976

112 In politics, if you want anything said, ask a man; if you want anything done, ask a woman.

Margaret Thatcher *The Changing Anatomy of Britain* (Anthony Sampson)

113 If a woman like Eva Peron with no ideals can get that far, think how far I can go with all the ideals that I have.

Margaret Thatcher *The Sunday Times*, 1980

114 I'd punch him in the snoot.

William Hale 'Big Bill' Thompson (1867–1944) US politician and Mayor of Chicago. His reaction if ever King George V were to come to Chicago. Attrib.

115 I like old Joe Stalin. He's a good fellow but he's a prisoner of the Politburo. He would make certain agreements but they won't let him keep them.

Harry S. Truman (1884–1972) US statesman. *News Review*, 24 June 1948

116 A politician is a man who understands government, and it takes a politician to run a government. A statesman is a politician who's been dead ten or fifteen years.

Harry S. Truman *New York World Telegram and Sun*, 12 Apr 1958

117 Introducing Super-Mac.

Vicky (Victor Weisz; 1913–66) German-born British cartoonist. Cartoon caption depicting Harold Macmillan as Superman. *Evening Standard*, 6 Nov 1958

118 The danger to the country, to Europe, to her vast Empire, which is involved in having all these great interests entrusted to the shaking hand of an old, wild, and incomprehensible man of 82½, is very great!

Victoria (1819–1901) Queen of the United Kingdom. Reaction to Gladstone's fourth and last appointment as prime minister, 1892. Letter to Lord Lansdowne, 12 Aug 1892

119 He speaks to Me as if I was a public meeting.

Victoria Referring to Gladstone. *Collections and Recollections* (G. W. E. Russell), Ch. 14

120 I cannot bring myself to vote for a woman who has been voice-trained to speak to me as though my dog has just died.

Keith Waterhouse (1929–) British journalist and novelist. Referring to Margaret Thatcher. Attrib.

121 The fate of a nation has often depended upon the good or bad digestion of a prime minister.

Voltaire (François-Marie Arouet; 1694–1778) French writer and philosopher. *Bartlett's Unfamiliar Quotations* (Leonard Louis Levinson)

122 I have lived long enough in the world, Sir, . . . to know that the safety of a minister lies in his having the approbation of this House. Former ministers, Sir, neglected this, and therefore they fell; I have always made it my first study to obtain it, and therefore I hope to stand.

Robert Walpole (1717–97) British statesman. Speech, House of Commons, 21 Nov 1739

123 Politicians can forgive almost anything in the way of abuse; they can forgive subversion, revolution, being contradicted, exposed as liars, even ridiculed, but they can never forgive being ignored.

Auberon Waugh (1939–) British novelist and critic. *The Observer*, 11 Oct 1981

124 It is a pity, as my husband says, that more politicians are not bastards by birth instead of vocation.

Katherine Whitehorn (1926–) British journalist. *The Observer*, 1964

125 Every time Mr Macmillan comes back from abroad, Mr Butler goes to the airport and grips him warmly by the throat.

Harold Wilson (1916–) British politician and prime minister. Attrib.

POLITICS

See also Communism, democracy, diplomacy, government, Houses of Parliament, monarchy, opposition, politicians, power politics, socialism

1 When the political columnists say 'Every thinking man' they mean themselves and when the candidates appeal to 'Every intelligent voter' they mean everybody who is going to vote for them.

Franklin P. Adams (1881–1960) US journalist and humorist. *Nods And Becks*

2 Practical politics consists in ignoring facts.

Henry Brooks Adams (1838–1918) US historian. *The Education of Henry Adams*, 1907

3 Politics, as a practice, whatever its professions, has always been the systematic organisation of hatreds.

Henry Brooks Adams *The Education of Henry Adams*

4 *Algérie Française.*

Algeria is French.

Anonymous Slogan of the opponents of Algerian independence

5 Don't tell my mother I'm in politics – she thinks I play the piano in a whorehouse.

Anonymous US saying.

6 No Popery, No Slavery.

Anonymous Slogan of the London MPs at the Oxford Parliament (Mar 1681)

7 No wonder Harold is back in form – every Labour politician feels more at home attacking his own party's politics.

Anonymous Referring to Harold Wilson. Cartoon caption, *Punch*, 31 Jan 1973

8 He warns the heads of parties against believing their own lies.

John Arbuthnot (1667–1735) Scottish writer and physician. *The Art of Political Lying*

9 Man is by nature a political animal.

Aristotle (384–322 BC) Greek philosopher. *Politics*, Bk. I

10 We believe in a League system in which the whole world should be ranged against an aggressor.

Clement Attlee (1883–1967) British statesman and Labour prime minister. Speech, House of Commons, 11 Mar 1935

11 I am a Tory Anarchist, I should like everyone to go about doing just as he pleased – short of altering any of the things to which I have grown accustomed.

Max Beerbohm (1872–1956) British writer. Attrib.

12 The connection between humbug and politics is too long established to be challenged.

Ronald Bell British politician. Speech, 5 Dec 1979

13 The accursed power which stands on Privilege
(And goes with Women, and Champagne, and Bridge)
Broke – and Democracy resumed her reign:
(Which goes with Bridge, and Women and Champagne).

Hilaire Belloc (1870–1953) French-born British poet. *Epigrams*, 'On a Great Election'

14 Every Briton is at heart a Tory – especially every British Liberal.

Arnold Bennett (1867–1931) British novelist. *Journal*

15 Politics is a blood sport.

Aneurin Bevan (1897–1960) British Labour politician. *My Life with Nye* (Jennie Lee)

16 No attempt at ethical or social seduction can eradicate from my heart a deep burning hatred for the Tory Party... So far as I am concerned they are lower than vermin.

Aneurin Bevan Speech, Manchester, 4 July 1949

17 We know what happens to people who stay in the middle of the road. They get run over.

Aneurin Bevan *The Observer*, 9 Dec 1953

18 And you call that statesmanship. I call it an emotional spasm.

Aneurin Bevan Speech, Labour Party Conference, 3 Oct 1957

19 I know that the right kind of political leader for the Labour Party is a desiccated calculating machine.

Aneurin Bevan Usually regarded as a gibe at Hugh Gaitskell. Speech during Labour Party Conference, 29 Sept 1954

20 Not while I'm alive, he ain't.

Ernest Bevin (1881–1951) British Labour politician. When told that Aneurin Bevan was 'his own worst enemy'. Also attributed to others. *Aneurin Bevan* (M. Foot)

21 Politics is not an exact science.

Bismarck (1815–98) German statesman. Speech, Prussian Chamber, 18 Dec 1863

22 Politics is not a science... but an art.

Bismarck Speech, Reichstag, 15 Mar 1884

23 Faction is to party what the superlative is to the positive: party is a political evil and faction is the worst of all parties.

Bolingbroke, Henry St John, Viscount (1678–1751) British politician and writer. *The Patriot King*

24 Politics are usually the executive expression of human immaturity.

Vera Brittain (1893–1970) British writer and feminist. *The Rebel Passion*

25 Most British statesmen have either drunk too much or womanised too much. I never fell into the second category.

Lord George-Brown (1914–) British peer and businessman. Attrib.

26 Voodoo economics.

George Bush (1924–) US statesman. Referring to Ronald Reagan's economic policies. Remark during the 1980 presidential election campaign

27 Politics is the art of the possible.

R. A. Butler (1902–82) British Conservative politician. Often attrib. to Butler but used earlier by others, including Bismarck. *The Art of the Possible*, Epigraph

28 The healthy stomach is nothing if

not conservative. Few radicals have good digestions.
Samuel Butler (1835–1902) British writer. *Notebooks*

29 I don't think that other people in the world would share the view that there is mounting chaos.
James Callaghan (1912–) British politician and prime minister. Referring to increasing industrial unrest in Britain; generally misquoted as 'Crisis? What crisis?'. Remark, 10 Jan 1979

30 I am not made for politics because I am incapable of wishing for, or accepting the death of my adversary.
Albert Camus (1913–60) French existentialist writer. *The Rebel*

31 What a genius the Labour Party has for cutting itself in half and letting the two parts writhe in public.
Cassandra (William Neil Cannon; 1910–67) Irish journalist. *The Daily Mirror*

32 Labour is not fit to govern.
Winston Churchill (1874–1965) British statesman. Election speech, 1920

33 It is alarming and also nauseating to see Mr Gandhi, a seditious Middle Temple lawyer, now posing as a fakir of a type well-known in the East, striding half-naked up the steps of the vice-regal palace.
Winston Churchill When Gandhi was released from gaol to take part in a conference. Speech, Epping, 23 Feb 1931

34 If it is a blessing, it is certainly very well disguised.
Winston Churchill Said to his wife after his defeat in the 1945 general election, when she said that it was a blessing in disguise. *Memoirs of Richard Nixon* (R. Nixon)

35 Would a special relationship between the United States and the British Commonwealth be inconsistent with our over-riding loyalty to the World Organization?
Winston Churchill Speech, 5 Mar 1946

36 Do not criticize your government when out of the country. Never cease to do so when at home.
Winston Churchill Attrib.

37 The disastrous element in the Labour party is its intellectuals.
George Norman Clark (1890–1979) British historian. *A Man of the Thirties* (A. L. Rowse)

38 The good Lord has only ten.
Georges Clemenceau (1841–1929) French politician. On President Wilson's Fourteen Points (1918). Attrib.

39 My home policy? I wage war. My foreign policy? I wage war. Always, everywhere, I wage war.
Georges Clemenceau Speech to the Chamber of Deputies, 8 Mar 1918

40 I do not choose to run for President in 1928.
Calvin Coolidge (1872–1933) US President. Remark to newsmen, 2 Aug 1927

41 We now are, as we always have been, decidedly and conscientiously attached to what is called the Tory, and which might with more propriety be called the Conservative, party.
John Wilson Croker (1780–1857) British Tory politician. The first use of the term 'Conservative Party'. In *Quarterly Review*, Jan 1830

42 Pity it is that the folly of one brainsick Pole – or, to say better, of one witless fool – should be the ruin of so great a family.
Thomas Cromwell (c. 1485–1540) English statesman. Referring to the denunciation of Reginald Pole (the King's cousin) for siding with the Pope in the disputes of the English Reformation. Letter to Michael Throgmorton (Pole's confidant), Sept 1537

43 I myself have become a Gaullist only little by little.
Charles De Gaulle (1890–1970) French general and statesman. *The Observer*, 'Sayings of the Year', 29 Dec 1963

44 The right honourable gentleman caught the Whigs bathing, and walked away with their clothes.
Benjamin Disraeli (1804–81) British statesman. Referring to Sir Robert Peel. Speech, House of Commons, 28 Feb 1845

45 A Conservative government is an organized hypocrisy.
Benjamin Disraeli Speech, 17 Mar 1845

46 During the last few weeks I have felt that the Suez Canal was flowing through my drawing room.
Clarissa Eden (1920–85) Wife of Anthony Eden. Said during the Suez crisis of 1956. Attrib.

47 Our long national nightmare is over. Our constitution works.
Gerald Ford (1913–) US president. On being sworn in as President after the resignation of Richard Nixon. Speech, 9 Aug 1974

48 All terrorists, at the invitation of the Government, end up with drinks at the Dorchester.
Hugh Gaitskell (1906–63) British Labour politician. Letter to *The Guardian*, 23 Aug 1977 (Dora Gaitskell)

49 There are some of us . . . who will fight, fight, fight, and fight again to save the party we love.
Hugh Gaitskell After his policy for a nuclear deterrent had been defeated. Speech, Labour Party conference, Scarborough, 3 Oct 1960

50 There are times in politics when you must be on the right side and lose.
John Kenneth Galbraith (1908–) US economist. *The Observer*, 'Sayings of the Week', 11 Feb 1968

51 Few things are as immutable as the addiction of political groups to the ideas by which they have once won office.
John Kenneth Galbraith *The Affluent Society*, Ch. 13

52 There is just one rule for politicians all over the world. Don't say in Power what you say in Opposition: if you do you only have to carry out what the other fellows have found impossible.
John Galsworthy (1867–1933) British novelist. *Maid in Waiting*

53 It isn't worth a pitcher of warm spit.
John Nance Garner (1868–1937) US Democratic vice-president. Referring to the Vice-Presidency; sometimes 'piss' is substituted for 'spit'. Attrib.

54 Today 23 years ago dear Grandmama died. I wonder what she would have thought of a Labour Government.
George V (1865–1936) King of the United Kingdom On the formation of the first Labour Government. Diary, 22 Jan 1924

55 I often think it's comical
How Nature always does contrive
That every boy and every gal
That's born into the world alive
Is either a little Liberal
Or else a little Conservative!
W. S. Gilbert (1836–1911) British dramatist. *Iolanthe*, II

56 It does no harm to throw the occasional man overboard, but it does not do much good if you are steering full speed ahead for the rocks.
Ian Gilmour (1926–) British Conservative politician. Said after being sacked as Deputy Foreign Secretary. *Time*, Sept 1981

57 In your heart you know he's right.
Barry M. Goldwater (1909–) US Republican politician. Election slogan; his opponents retaliated with 'In your guts you know he's nuts!'

58 If the British public falls for this, I say it will be stark, staring bonkers.
Lord Hailsham (1907–) British Conservative politician. Referring to Labour policy in the 1964 general-election campaign. Press conference, Conservative Central Office, 12 Oct 1964

59 A great party is not to be brought down because of a scandal by a woman of easy virtue and a proved liar.
Lord Hailsham Referring to the Profumo affair, in BBC interview, 13 June 1963. *The Pendulum Years*, Ch. 3 (Bernard Levin)

60 America's present need is not heroics but healing, not nostrums but normalcy.
Warren G. Harding (1865–1923) US President. Speech, Boston, May 1920

61 Their Europeanism is nothing but imperialism with an inferiority complex.
Denis Healey (1917–) British Labour politician. Referring to the policies of the Conservative party. *The Observer*, 'Sayings of the Week', 7 Oct 1962

62 I warn you there are going to be howls of anguish from the 80,000 people who are rich enough to pay over 75% on the last slice of their income.
Denis Healey Speech, Labour Party Conference, 1 Oct 1973

63 Nor would it be in the interests of the Community that its enlargement should take place except with the full-hearted consent of the Parliament and people of the new member countries.
Edward Heath (1916–) British politician and prime minister. Speech to the Franco-British Chamber of Commerce, Paris, 5 May 1970

64 This would, at a stroke, reduce the rise in prices, increase productivity and reduce unemployment.
Edward Heath Press release from Conservative Central Office, 16 June 1970

65 We were returned to office to change the course of history of this nation – nothing less. If we are to achieve this task we will have to embark on a change so radical, a revolution so quiet and yet so total, that it will go far beyond the programme for a parliament to which we are committed and on which we have already embarked, far beyond the decade and way into the 80s.
Edward Heath Speech, Conservative Party Conference, Oct 1970

66 I perceive that that man hath the sow by the right ear.
Henry VIII (1491–1547) King of England. Referring to Cranmer. Letter to Edward Foxe and Stephen Gardiner, 3 Aug 1529

67 Never judge a country by its politics. After all, we English are quite honest by nature, aren't we?
Alfred Hitchcock (1889–1980) British film director. *The Lady Vanishes*

68 The essential thing is the formation of the political will of the nation: that is the starting point for political action.
Adolf Hitler (1889–1945) German dictator. Speech, Düsseldorf, 27 Jan 1932

69 We are challenged with a peace-time choice between the American system of rugged individualism and a European philosophy of diametrically opposed doctrines – doctrines of paternalism and state socialism.
Herbert Hoover (1874–1964) US Republican president. Campaign speech, New York City, 22 Oct 1928

70 The grass will grow in the streets of a hundred cities, a thousand towns; the weeds will overrun the fields of millions of farms if that protection is taken away.
Herbert Hoover Campaign speech, 31 Oct 1932

71 You can't adopt politics as a profession and remain honest.
Louis McHenry Howe (1871–1936) US diplomat. Speech, Columbia University, 17 Jan 1933

72 The Politics of Joy.
Hubert H. Humphrey (1911–78) US Democratic vice-president. Campaign slogan, 1964

73 For in the case of nutrition and health, just as in the case of education, the gentleman in Whitehall really does know better what is good for people than the people know themselves.
Douglas Jay (1907–) British Labour politician. *The Socialist Case*

74 Fair Shares for All, is Labour's Call.
Douglas Jay Slogan, Battersea North by-election, June 1946

75 A mission to explain.
Peter Jay (1937–) British journalist and broadcaster. Explaining his philosophy for a new breakfast-television company. Said on many occasions

76 Breaking the mould of British politics.
Roy Jenkins (1920–) British Liberal Democrat politician (formerly a Labour Home Secretary). Referring to the establishment of the Social Democratic Party.

77 If you're in politics and you can't tell when you walk into a room who's for you and who's against you, then you're in the wrong line of work.
Lyndon B. Johnson (1908–73) US statesman. *The Lyndon Johnson Story* (B. Mooney)

78 Sir, I perceive you are a vile Whig.
Samuel Johnson (1709–84) British lexicographer. Speaking to Sir Adam Fergusson. *Life of Johnson* (J. Boswell), Vol. II

79 Why, Sir, most schemes of political improvement are very laughable things.
Samuel Johnson *Life of Johnson* (J. Boswell), Vol. II

80 Politics are now nothing more than a means of rising in the world.
Samuel Johnson *Life of Johnson* (J. Boswell), Vol. II

81 Mothers all want their sons to grow up to become president, but they don't want them to become politicians in the process.
John Fitzgerald Kennedy (1917–63) US statesman. Attrib.

82 What is objectionable, what is dangerous about extremists is not that they are extreme but that they are intolerant.
Robert Kennedy (1925–68) US politician. *The Pursuit of Justice*

83 Proportional Representation, I think, is fundamentally counter-democratic.
Neil Kinnock (1942–) British politician. *Marxism Today*, 1983

84 The idea that there is a model Labour voter, a blue-collar council house tenant who belongs to a union and has 2.4 children, a five-year-old car and a holiday in Blackpool, is patronizing and politically immature.
Neil Kinnock Speech, 1986

85 Party loyalty lowers the greatest of men to the petty level of the masses.
Jean de La Bruyère (1645–96) French satirist. *Les Caractères*

86 States, like men, have their growth,

their manhood, their decrepitude, their decay.

Walter Savage Landor (1775–1864) British poet and writer. *Imaginary Conversations*, 'Pollio and Calvus'

87 If it were necessary to give the briefest possible definition of imperialism we should have to say that imperialism is the monopoly stage of capitalism.

Lenin (Vladimir Ilich Ulyanov; 1870–1924) Russian revolutionary leader. *Imperialism, the Highest Stage of Capitalism*, Ch. 7

88 Politicians tend to live *in character* and many a public figure has come to imitate the journalism which describes him.

Walter Lippmann (1889–1974) US editor and writer. *A Preface to Politics*

89 The only lasting solution is that Europe itself should gradually find its way to an internal equilibrium and a limitation of armaments by political appeasement.

11th Marquess of Lothian (1882–1940) British politician. Letter to *The Times*, 4 May 1934

90 In every age the vilest specimens of human nature are to be found among demagogues.

Lord Macaulay (1800–59) British historian. *History of England*, Vol. I, Ch. 5

91 Forever poised between a cliché and an indiscretion.

Harold Macmillan (1894–1986) British politician and prime minister. Referring to a Foreign Secretary's life. *Newsweek*, 30 Apr 1956

92 I thought the best thing to do was to settle up these little local difficulties, and then turn to the wider vision of the Commonwealth.

Harold Macmillan (1894–1986) British politician and prime minister. Referring to resignation of ministers. Attrib., London Airport, 7 Jan 1958

93 There are three groups that no prime minister should provoke: the Treasury, the Vatican, and the National Union of Mineworkers.

Harold Macmillan First used by Stanley Baldwin. Attrib.

94 Selling the family silver.

Harold Macmillan Referring to privatization of profitable nationalized industries. Speech, House of Lords, 1986

95 In politics, as in grammar, one should be able to tell the substantives from the adjectives. Hitler was a substantive; Mussolini only an adjective. Hitler was a nuisance. Mussolini was bloody. Together a bloody nuisance.

Salvador de Madariaga y Rogo (1886–1978) Spanish diplomat and writer. Attrib.

96 Every intellectual attitude is latently political.

Thomas Mann (1875–1955) German novelist. *The Observer*, 11 Aug 1974

97 All reactionaries are paper tigers.

Mao Tse-Tung (1893–1976) Chinese communist leader. *Quotations from Chairman Mao Tse-Tung*, Ch. 6

98 PORTEOUS. Shouldn't I have been Prime Minister, Clare?
LADY KITTY. Prime Minister? You haven't the brain, you haven't the character.
CHAMPION-CHENY. Cheek, push and a gift of the gab will serve very well instead, you know.

W. Somerset Maugham (1874–1965) British novelist. *The Circle*

99 McCarthyism is Americanism with its sleeves rolled.

Joseph R. McCarthy (1908–57) US senator. Speech, 1952

100 The expression 'positive neutrality' is a contradiction in terms. There can be no more positive neutrality than there can be a vegetarian tiger.

V. K. Krishna Menon (1897–) Indian barrister and writer. *The New York Times*, 18 Oct 1960

101 One has to be a lowbrow, a bit of a murderer, to be a politician, ready and willing to see people sacrificed, slaughtered for the sake of an idea, whether a good one or a bad one.

Henry Miller (1891–1980) US novelist. *Writers at Work*

102 Any party which takes credit for the rain must not be surprised if its opponents blame it for the drought.

Dwight W. Morrow (1873–1931) US politician. Speech, Oct 1930

103 We cannot change our policy now. After all, we are not political whores.

Benito Mussolini (1883–1945) Italian dictator. *Hitler* (Alan Bullock), Ch. 8

104 I still love you, but in politics there is no heart, only head.

Napoleon I (Napoleon Bonaparte; 1769–1821) French emperor. Referring to his divorce, for reasons of state, from the Empress Josephine (1809). *Bonaparte* (C. Barnett)

105 I'll speak for the man, or against him, whichever will do him most good.

Richard Milhous Nixon (1913–) US president. When agreeing to support a politician

106 I don't give a shit about the lira.

Richard Milhous Nixon Remark, 23 June 1972 (tape transcript)

107 I don't give a shit what happens. I want you all to stonewall it, let them plead the Fifth Amendment, cover-up or anything else, if it'll save it, save the plan.

Richard Milhous Nixon Referring to the Watergate cover-up. In conversation, 22 Mar 1973 (tape transcript)

108 We are fed up with fudging and nudging, with mush and slush.

David Owen (1938–) British politician. Speech, Labour Party Conference, Blackpool, 2 Oct 1980

109 In our time, political speech and writing are largely the defence of the indefensible.

George Orwell (Eric Blair; 1903–50) British novelist. *Politics and the English Language*

110 I gave up politics when I discovered that I would rather be a poet than a prime minister.

John Pardoe (1934–) British politician. BBC Radio 4, 2 April 1980

111 One of those ideas was that man was not born to go down on his belly before the state.

Alan Paton (1903–88) South African novelist. Speech at the last meeting of the South African Liberal party, 1968; referring to the party's principles

112 As these two, the kingdom and the priesthood, are brought together by divine mystery, so are their two heads, by the force of mutual loves; the King may be found in the Roman pontiff, and the Roman pontiff be found in the King.

St Peter Damian (1007–72) Bishop of Ostia. Written just after the enthronement of Pope Alexander II (1061). *Disceptatio synodalis*

113 All political lives, unless they are cut off in mid-stream at a happy juncture, end in failure, because that is the nature of politics and of human affairs.

Enoch Powell (1912–) British politician. *Joseph Chamberlain*

114 Like the sorry tapping of Neville

Chamberlain's umbrella on the cobblestones of Munich.
Ronald Reagan (1911–) US politician and president. Referring to President Carter's foreign policy

115 I used to say that politics was the second lowest profession and I have come to know that it bears a great similarity to the first.
Ronald Reagan *The Observer*, 13 May 1979

116 Please assure me that you are all Republicans!
Ronald Reagan Addressing the surgeons on being wheeled into the operating theater for an emergency operation after an assassination attempt. *Presidential Anecdotes* (P. Boller)

117 Remember this, Griffin. The revolution eats its own. Capitalism re-creates itself.
Mordecai Richler (1931–) Canadian novelist. *Cocksure*, Ch. 22

118 The more you read about politics, you got to admit that each party is worse than the other.
Will Rogers (1879–1935) US actor and humorist. *Saturday Review*, 'A Rogers Thesaurus', 25 Aug 1962

119 England elects a Labour Government. When a man goes in for politics over here, he has no time to labor, and any man that labors has no time to fool with politics. Over there politics is an obligation; over here it's a business.
Will Rogers *Autobiography*, Ch. 14

120 I am reminded of four definitions. A radical is a man with both feet firmly planted – in the air; a conservative is a man with two perfectly good legs who, however, has never learned to walk; a reactionary is a somnambulist walking backwards; a liberal is a man who uses his legs and his hands at the behest of his head.
Franklin D. Roosevelt (1882–1945) US Democratic president. Radio broadcast, 26 Oct 1939

121 You have to clean your plate.
Lord Rosebery (1847–1929) British statesman. Said to the Liberal Party. Speech, Chesterfield, 16 Dec 1901

122 Revolutionary spirits of my father's generation waited for Lefty. Existentialist heroes of my youth waited for Godot. Neither showed up.
Theodore Roszak (1933–) US writer and editor. *Unfinished Animal*

123 We're eyeball to eyeball and I think the other fellow just blinked.
Dean Rusk (1909–) US Democratic politician. In conversation with journalist during Cuban Missile Crisis, 24 Oct 1962. *Political Dictionary* (W. Safire)

124 An Englishman has to have a Party, just as he has to have trousers.
Bertrand Russell (1872–1970) British philosopher. Letter to Maurice Amos MP, 16 June 1936

125 The collection of prejudices which is called political philosophy is useful provided that it is not called philosophy.
Bertrand Russell *The Observer*, 'Sayings of the Year', 1962

126 History is past politics, and politics present history.
John Robert Seeley (1834–95) British historian. Quoting the historian E. A. Freeman. *The Growth of British Policy*

127 No matter how thin you slice it, it's still baloney.
Alfred E. Smith (1873–1944) US politician. Campaign speeches, 1936

128 If Her Majesty stood for Parliament – if the Tory Party had any sense and made Her its leader instead of that grammar school twit Heath – us Tories, mate, would win every election we went in for.
Johnny Speight (1920–) British television scriptwriter. *Till Death Do Us Part*

129 The Republican form of Government is the highest form of government; but because of this it requires the highest type of human nature – a type nowhere at present existing.
Herbert Spencer (1820–1903) British philosopher. *Essays*, 'The Americans'

130 The tasks of the party are . . . to be cautious and not allow our country to be drawn into conflicts by warmongers who are accustomed to have others pull the chestnuts out of the fire for them.
Joseph Stalin (J. Dzhugashvili; 1879–1953) Soviet statesman. Speech, 8th Congress of the Communist Party, 6 Jan 1941

131 Disdain is the wrong word, but perhaps affection is too strong a word.
David Steel (1938–) British politician. Referring to his attitude to the Liberal party. *The Observer*, 'Sayings of the Week', 22 Sept 1985

132 Go back to your constituencies and prepare for government!
David Steel Speech to party conference, 1985

133 I sense that the British electorate is now itching to break out once and for all from the discredited straight-jacket of the past.
David Steel *The Times*, 2 June 1987

134 An independent is a guy who wants to take the politics out of politics.
Adlai Stevenson (1900–65) US statesman. *The Art Of Politics*.

135 Politics is perhaps the only profession for which no preparation is thought necessary.
Robert Louis Stevenson (1850–94) Scottish writer. *Familiar Studies of Men and Books*, 'Yoshida-Torajiro'

136 Socialists treat their servants with respect and then wonder why they vote Conservative.
Tom Stoppard (1937–) Czech-born British dramatist. *Lord Malquist and Mr Moon*, Pt. V, Ch. 1

137 A balanced state of well-modulated dis-satisfaction.
Eduard, Count von Taaffe (1833–95) Austrian Prime Minister (1868–70, 1879–93). Referring to his policy towards nationalistic tensions within the Austro-Hungarian Empire. Remark

138 Revolts, republics, revolutions, most
No graver than a schoolboy's barring out.
Alfred, Lord Tennyson (1809–92) British poet. *The Princess*, Conclusion

139 Britain is no longer in the politics of the pendulum, but of the ratchet.
Margaret Thatcher (1925–) British politician and prime minister. Speech, Institute of Public Relations, 1977

140 I can trust my husband not to fall asleep on a public platform and he usually claps in the right places.
Margaret Thatcher *Observer*, 20 Aug 1978

141 One does wish that there were a few more women in parliament. Then one could be less conspicuous oneself.
Margaret Thatcher *The Observer*, 6 May 1979

142 Any woman who understands the problems of running a home will be nearer to understanding the problems of running a country.
Margaret Thatcher *The Observer*, 8 May 1979

143 There is no easy popularity in that

but I believe people accept there is no alternative.

Margaret Thatcher The oft-used phrase 'There is no alternative' led to the acronymic nickname 'TINA'. Speech, Conservative Women's Conference, 21 May 1980

144 Looking around the House, one realizes that we are all minorities now.

Jeremy Thorpe (1929–) British politician. After a General Election which resulted in no clear majority for any party. Speech, House of Commons, 6 Mar 1974

145 Politics is the art of preventing people from taking part in affairs which properly concern them.

Paul Valéry (1871–1945) French poet and writer. *Tel quel*

146 In vain will such a minister, or the foul dregs of his power, the tools of despotism and corruption, preach up 'the spirit of concord . . .' They have sent the spirit of discord through the land and I will prophesy it will never be distingushed but by the extinction of their power.

John Wilkes (1725–97) British politician. Part of a libellous article on George III's speech (which was drafted by George Grenville, the 'minister') at the opening of parliament. This article led to a celebrated legal battle, and launched his career as a champion of the common man against overbearing government. *North Briton*, 45 (23 Apr 1763)

147 Every dog is allowed one bite, but a different view is taken of a dog that goes on biting all the time. He may not get his licence returned when it falls due.

Harold Wilson (1916–) British politician and prime minister. Referring to opposition within his own party. Speech, 2 Mar 1967

148 For socialists, going to bed with the Liberals is like having oral sex with a shark.

Larry Zolf (1934–) Canadian TV journalist and writer.

POLLUTION

See ecology, environment

POMPOSITY

1 A bit like God in his last years, the Alderman.

Gwyn Thomas (1913–) British writer *The Keep*, I

POPE, Alexander

(1688–1744) British poet. His witty and satirical poems include the mock-heroic *The Rape of the Lock* (1712), the mock epic *The Dunciad* (1728), and the philosophical *An Essay on Man* (1733).

Quotations about Pope

1 The wicked asp of Twickenham.

Lady Mary Wortley Montagu (1689–1762) English writer. Attrib.

2 In Pope I cannot read a line,
But with a sigh I wish it mine;
When he can in one couplet fix
More sense than I can do in six:
It gives me such a jealous fit,
I cry, 'Pox take him and his wit!'

Jonathan Swift (1667–1745) Irish-born Anglican priest and writer. *On the Death of Dr. Swift*

Quotations by Pope

3 Ye gods! annihilate but space and time.
And make two lovers happy.

The Art of Sinking in Poetry, 11

4 The right divine of kings to govern wrong.

The Dunciad, IV

5 When man's whole frame is obvious to a flea

The Dunciad, IV

6 I mount! I fly!
O grave! where is thy victory?
O death! where is thy sting?

The Dying Christian to his Soul

7 A heap of dust alone remains of thee;
'Tis all thou art, and all the proud shall be!

Elegy to the Memory of an Unfortunate Lady

8 Line after line my gushing eyes o'erflow,
led through a sad variety of woe.

Eloisa to Abelard

9 You beat your pate, and fancy wit will come;
Knock as you please, there's nobody at home.

Epigram

10 Do good by stealth, and blush to find it fame.

Epilogue to the Satires, Dialogue I

11 Ask you what provocation I have had?
The strong antipathy of good to bad.

Epilogue to the Satires, Dialogue II

12 Yes; I am proud, I must be proud to see
Men not afraid of God, afraid of me.

Epilogue to the Satires, Dialogue II

13 The Muse but serv'd to ease some friend, not Wife,
To help me through this long disease, my life.

Epistle to Dr. Arbuthnot

14 Damn with faint praise, assent with civil leer,
And, without sneering, teach the rest to sneer.

Epistle to Dr. Arbuthnot

15 Curst be the verse, how well so'er it flow,
That tends to make one worthy man my foe.

Epistle to Dr. Arbuthnot

16 Wit that can creep, and pride that licks the dust.

Epistle to Dr. Arbuthnot

17 No creature smarts so little as a fool.

Epistle to Dr. Arbuthnot

18 In wit a man; simplicity a child.

Epitaph on Mr. Gay

19 Nature, and Nature's laws lay hid in night:
God said, *Let Newton be!* and all was light.

For a reply, *see* SQUIRE *Epitaphs*, 'Intended for Sir Isaac Newton'

20 'Tis hard to say, if greater want of skill
Appear in writing or in judging ill.

An Essay on Criticism

21 'Tis with our judgments as our watches, none
Go just alike, yet each believes his own.

An Essay on Criticism

22 Of all the causes which conspire to blind
Man's erring judgment, and misguide the mind,
What the weak head with strongest bias rules,
Is Pride, the never-failing vice of fools.

An Essay on Criticism

23 A little learning is a dangerous thing;
Drink deep, or taste not the Pierian spring:
There shallow draughts intoxicate the brain,

And drinking largely sobers us again.
An Essay on Criticism

24 Whoever thinks a faultless piece to see,
Thinks what ne'er was, nor is, nor e'er shall be.
An Essay on Criticism

25 True wit is nature to advantage dress'd;
What oft was thought, but ne'er so well express'd.
An Essay on Criticism

26 True ease in writing comes from art, not chance,
As those move easiest who have learn'd to dance.
'Tis not enough no harshness gives offence,
The sound must seem an echo to the sense.
An Essay on Criticism

27 Fondly we think we honour merit then,
When we but praise ourselves in other men.
An Essay on Criticism

28 To err is human, to forgive, divine.
An Essay on Criticism

29 For fools rush in where angels fear to tread.
An Essay on Criticism

30 Words are like leaves; and where they most abound,
Much fruit of sense beneath is rarely found.
An Essay on Criticism

31 Nor in the critic let the man be lost.
An Essay on Criticism

32 Hope springs eternal in the human breast;
Man never is, but always to be blest.
An Essay on Man, I

33 Created half to rise, and half to fall;
Great lord of all things, yet a prey to all;
Sole judge of truth, in endless error hurl'd;
The glory, jest, and riddle of the world!
An Essay on Man, II

34 Know then thyself, presume not God to scan,
The proper study of Mankind is Man.
An Essay on Man, II

35 And hence one master-passion in the breast,
Like Aaron's serpent, swallows up the rest.
An Essay on Man, II

36 That true self-love and social are the same;
That virtue only makes our bliss below;
And all our knowledge is, ourselves to know.
An Essay on Man, IV

37 Order is heaven's first law.
An Essay on Man, IV

38 Not to admire, is all the art I know
To make men happy, and to keep them so.
Imitations of Horace, 'To Mr. Murray'

39 To observations which ourselves we make.
We grow more partial for th' observer's sake.
Moral Essays, I

40 'Tis education forms the common mind,
Just as the twig is bent, the tree's inclined.
Moral Essays, I

41 Most women have no characters at all.
Moral Essays, II

42 Men, some to business, some to pleasure take;
But every woman is at heart a rake.
Moral Essays, II

43 Woman's at best a contradiction still.
Moral Essays, II

44 See how the world its veterans rewards!
A youth of frolics, an old age of cards.
Moral Essays, II

45 The ruling passion, be it what it will
The ruling passion conquers reason still.
Moral Essays, III

46 Who shall decide when doctors disagree?
Moral Essays, III

47 Where'er you walk, cool gales shall fan the glade,
Trees, where you sit, shall crowd into a shade:
Where'er you tread, the blushing flow'rs shall rise,
And all things flourish where you turn your eyes.
Pastorals, 'Summer'

48 What dire offence from am'rous causes springs,
What mighty contests rise from trivial things.
The Rape of the Lock, I

49 Here thou great Anna! whom three realms obey,
Dost sometimes counsel take – and sometimes Tea.
The Rape of the Lock, III

50 Not louder shrieks to pitying heav'n are cast,
When husbands, or when lap-dogs breathe their last.
The Rape of the Lock, III

51 The hungry judges soon the sentence sign,
And wretches hang that jury-men may dine.
The Rape of the Lock, III

52 Coffee which makes the politician wise,
And see through all things with his half-shut eyes.
The Rape of the Lock, III

53 The vulgar boil, the learned roast an egg.
Satires and Epistles of Horace Imitated, Bk II

54 A man should never be ashamed to own he has been in the wrong, which is but saying, in other words, that he is wiser to-day than he was yesterday.
Thoughts on Various Subjects

55 It is with narrow-souled people as with narrow-necked bottles: the less they have in them, the more noise they make in pouring it out.
Thoughts on Various Subjects

56 When men grow virtuous in their old age, they only make a sacrifice to God of the devil's leavings.
Thoughts on Various Subjects

57 I never knew any man in my life who could not bear another's misfortunes perfectly like a Christian.
Thoughts on Various Subjects

58 The vanity of human life is like a river, constantly passing away, and yet constantly coming on.
Thoughts on Various Subjects

59 Here am I, dying of a hundred good symptoms.
Anecdotes by and about Alexander Pope (Joseph Spence)

60 'Blessed is the man who expects

nothing, for he shall never be disappointed' was the ninth beatitude.

Letter to Fortescue, 23 Sept 1725

61 How often are we to die before we go quite off this stage? In every friend we lose a part of ourselves, and the best part.

Letter to Jonathan Swift, 5 Dec 1732

62 I am His Highness' dog at Kew; Pray tell me sir, whose dog are you?

On the collar of a dog given to Frederick, Prince of Wales

POPULARITY

See also fame

1 Do not let that trouble Your Excellency; perhaps the greetings are intended for me.

Ludwig van Beethoven (1770–1827) German composer. Said when walking with Goethe, when Goethe complained about greetings from passers-by. *Thayer's Life of Beethoven* (E. Forbes)

2 Everybody hates me because I'm so universally liked.

Peter De Vries (1910–) US novelist. *The Vale of Laughter*, Pt. I

3 Popularity is a crime from the moment it is sought; it is only a virtue where men have it whether they will or no.

Lord Halifax (1633–95) English statesman. *Political, Moral and Miscellaneous Thoughts and Reflections*

4 Popularity? It's glory's small change.

Victor Hugo (1802–85) French writer. *Ruy Blas*, III

5 The worse I do, the more popular I get.

John Fitzgerald Kennedy (1917–63) US statesman. Referring to his popularity following the failure of the US invasion of Cuba. *The People's Almanac* (D. Wallechinsky)

6 We're more popular than Jesus Christ now. I don't know which will go first. Rock and roll or Christianity.

John Lennon (1940–80) British rock musician. *The Beatles Illustrated Lyrics*

7 He's liked, but he's not well liked.

Arthur Miller (1915–) US dramatist. *Death of a Salesman*, I

8 He hasn't an enemy in the world, and none of his friends like him.

Oscar Wilde (1854–1900) Irish-born British dramatist. Said of G. B. Shaw. *Sixteen Self Sketches* (Shaw), Ch. 17

POPULAR MUSIC

1 Rock'n'roll is part of a pest to undermine the morals of the youth of our nation. It . . . brings people of both races together.

Anonymous Statement by the North Alabama Citizens' Council in the 1950s

2 Listen kid, take my advice, never hate a song that has sold half a million copies.

Irving Berlin (Israel Baline; 1888–) Russian-born US composer. Giving advice to Cole Porter. Attrib.

3 Do they merit vitriol, even a drop of it? Yes, because they corrupt the young, persuading them that the mature world, which produced Beethoven and Schweitzer, sets an even higher value on the transient anodynes of youth than does youth itself. . . . They are the Hollow Men. They are electronic lice.

Anthony Burgess (1917–) British novelist. Referring to disc jockeys. *Punch*, 20 Sept 1967

4 Canned music is like audible wallpaper.

Alistair Cooke (1908–) British-born US broadcaster. Attrib.

5 Strange how potent cheap music is.

Noël Coward (1899–1973) British dramatist. *Private Lives*

6 I think popular music in this country is one of the few things in the twentieth century that have made giant strides in reverse.

Bing Crosby (Harry Lillis Crosby; 1904–77) US singer. Interview, *This Week*

7 Yeah, some of them are about ten minutes long, others five or six.

Bob Dylan (Robert Allen Zimmerman; 1941–) US songwriter. On being asked in an interview, to say something about his songs. Attrib.

8 We're more popular than Jesus Christ now. I don't know which will go first, Rock and Roll or Christianity.

John Lennon (1940–80) British rock musician. *The Beatles Illustrated Lyrics*

9 What a terrible revenge by the culture of the Negroes on that of the Whites.

Ignacy Paderewski (1860–1941) Polish pianist. Referring to jazz. Attrib.

10 Every popular song has at least one line or sentence that is perfectly clear – the line that fits the music.

Ezra Pound (1885–1972) US poet and critic. Attrib.

11 Jazz will endure just as long as people hear it through their feet instead of their brains.

John Philip Sousa (1854–1932) US composer, conductor, and writer. Attrib.

PORNOGRAPHY

See also censorship, prudery, sex

1 This is the kind of show that gives pornography a bad name.

Clive Barnes (1927–) British-born theater and ballet critic. Reviewing *Oh, Calcutta!*. Attrib.

2 I don't think pornography is very harmful, but it is terribly, terribly boring.

Noël Coward (1899–1973) British dramatist. *The Observer*, 'Sayings of the Week', 24 Sept 1972

3 Pornography is the attempt to insult sex, to do dirt on it.

D. H. Lawrence (1885–1930) British novelist. *Phoenix*, 'Pornography and Obscenity'

4 It is heartless and it is mindless and it is a lie.

John McGahern (1934–) British writer. *The Pornographer*

5 Its avowed purpose is to excite sexual desire, which, I should have thought, is unnecessary in the case of the young, inconvenient in the case of the middle aged, and unseemly in the old.

Malcolm Muggeridge (1903–) British writer. *Tread Softly For You Tread On My Jokes*, 1966

6 *Lady Chatterley's Lover* is a book that all Christians might read with profit.

John Robinson (1919–83) Bishop of Woolwich. Said in the court case against Penguin Books. Attrib.

7 Don't be daft. You don't get any pornography on there, not on the telly. Get filth, that's all. The only place you get pornography is in yer Sunday papers.

Johnny Speight (1920–) British television scriptwriter. *Till Death Do Us Part*

PORTER, Cole

(1893–1964) American songwriter and composer, noted for his witty lyrics. He wrote scores for such musicals as *Kiss Me Kate* (1953), *High Society* (1956), and *Can-Can* (1959).

1 Now: heaven knows, anything goes.

Anything Goes, title song

2 I've Got You Under My Skin.
Born to Dance, song title

3 I love Paris in the springtime.
Can-Can, 'I Love Paris'

4 Night and day, you are the one,
Only you beneath the moon and under the sun.
The Gay Divorcee, 'Night and Day'

5 Miss Otis regrets she's unable to lunch today.
Hi Diddle Diddle, Miss Otis Regrets

6 HE. Have you heard it's in the stars
Next July we collide with Mars?
SHE. Well, did you evah! What a swell party this is.
High Society 'Well, Did You Evah!'

7 And we suddenly know, what heaven we're in,
When they begin the beguine.
Jubilee, 'Begin the Beguine'

8 But I'm always true to you, darlin', in my fashion,
Yes, I'm always true to you, darlin', in my way.
Kiss Me, Kate, 'Always True to You in My Fashion'

9 Let's Do It; Let's Fall in Love.
Paris, song title

10 Who Wants to Be a Millionaire? I don't.
Who Wants to be a Millionaire?, title song

POSSIBILITY

See also impossibility

1 The grand Perhaps!
Robert Browning (1812–89) British poet. *Bishop Blougram's Apology*

2 Your If is the only peace-maker; much virtue in If.
William Shakespeare (1564–1616) English dramatist. *As You Like It,* V:4

POSTERITY

See also death, fame, future, immortality, reputation

1 Think of your forefathers! Think of your posterity!
John Quincy Adams (1767–1848) Sixth president of the USA. Speech, Plymouth, Massachusetts, 22 Dec 1802

2 We are always doing something for posterity, but I would fain see posterity do something for us.
Joseph Addison (1672–1719) British essayist. *The Spectator,* 583

3 Let us honour if we can
The vertical man
Though we value none
But the horizontal one.
W. H. Auden (1907–73) British poet. *Epigraph for Poems*

4 Posterity is as likely to be wrong as anybody else.
Heywood Brown *Sitting on the World*

5 When a man is in doubt about this or that in his writing, it will often guide him if he asks himself how it will tell a hundred years hence.
Samuel Butler (1835–1902) British writer. *Notebooks*

6 I think I shall be among the English Poets after my death.
John Keats (1795–1821) British poet. Letter to George and Georgiana Keats, 14 Oct 1818

7 A writer's ambition should be to trade a hundred contemporary readers for ten readers in ten years' time and for one reader in a hundred years' time.
Arthur Koestler (1905–83) Hungarian-born British writer. *New York Times Book Review,* 1 Apr 1951

8 Damn the age. I'll write for antiquity.
Charles Lamb (1775–1834) British essayist. Referring to his lack of payment for the *Essays of Elia. English Wits* (L. Russell)

9 Now I'm dead in the grave with my lips moving
And every schoolboy repeating my words by heart.
Osip Mandelstam (1891–1938) Russian poet. *Poems,* No. 306

10 My time has not yet come either; some are born posthumously.
Friedrich Wilhelm Nietzsche (1844–1900) German philosopher. *Ecce Homo*

POUND, Ezra

(1885–1972) US poet and critic. His poetry includes *Hugh Selwyn Mauberly* (1920) and *The Pisan Cantos* (1925–69). His support for Mussolini led to his confinement in a US mental hospital (1946–58).

Quotations about Pound

1 To me Pound remains the exquisite showman minus the show.
Ben Hecht *Pounding Ezra*

2 I confess I am seldom interested in what he is saying, but only in the way he says it.
T. S. Eliot (1888–1965) US-born British poet and dramatist. *The Dial,* 'Isolated superiority'

Quotations by Pound

3 Music begins to atrophy when it departs too far from the dance; . . . poetry begins to atrophy when it gets too far from music.
ABC of Reading, 'Warning'

4 One of the pleasures of middle age is to *find out* that one WAS right, and that one was much righter than one knew at say 17 or 23.
ABC of Reading, Ch. 1

5 Literature is news that STAYS news.
ABC of Reading, Ch. 2

6 Any general statement is like a check drawn on a bank. Its value depends on what is there to meet it.
ABC of Reading, Ch. 2

7 Winter is icummen in,
Lhude sing Goddamm,
Raineth drop and staineth slop
And how the wind doth ramm!
Sing: Goddamm.
Ancient Music

8 And even I can remember
A day when the historians left blanks in their writings,
I mean for things they didn't know.
Cantos, XIII

9 Bah! I have sung women in three cities,
But it is all the same;
And I will sing of the sun.
Cino

10 The difference between a gun and a tree is a difference of tempo. The tree explodes every spring.
Criterion, July 1937

11 Great Literature is simply language charged with meaning to the utmost possible degree.
How to Read

12 For three years, out of key with his time,
He strove to resuscitate the dead art
Of poetry to maintain 'the sublime'
In the old sense. Wrong from the start.
Pour l'élection de son sépulcre

POVERTY

See also hunger, poverty and wealth

1 From clogs to clogs is only three generations.
Proverb

2 Hunger is the best sauce.
Proverb

3 Poverty is not a crime.
Proverb

4 To some extent, if you've seen one city slum you've seen them all.
Spiro Agnew (1918–) US politician. Election speech, Detroit, 18 Oct 1968

5 When you have learnt all that Oxford can teach you, go and discover why, with so much wealth in Britain, there continues to be so much poverty and how poverty can be cured.
Edward Caird (1835–1908) British philosopher and theologian. Said to Lord Beveridge

6 To be poor and independent is very nearly an impossibility.
William Cobbett (1763–1835) British journalist and writer. *Advice to Young Men*

7 He found it inconvenient to be poor.
William Cowper (1731–1800) British poet. *Charity*

8 Poverty and oysters always seem to go together.
Charles Dickens (1812–70) British novelist. *Pickwick Papers*, Ch. 22

9 There's no scandal like rags, nor any crime so shameful as poverty.
George Farquhar (1678–1707) Irish dramatist. *The Beaux' Strategem*, I:1

10 The very poor are unthinkable and only to be approached by the statistician and the poet.
E. M. Forster (1879–1970) British novelist. *Howards End*

11 It is only the poor who are forbidden to beg.
Anatole France (Jacques Anatole François Thibault; 1844–1924) French writer. *Crainquebille*

12 For every talent that poverty has stimulated, it has blighted a hundred.
John W. Gardner (1912–) US writer. *Excellence*

13 No sir, tho' I was born and bred in England, I can dare to be poor, which is the only thing now-a-days men are asham'd of.
John Gay (1685–1732) English poet and dramatist. *Polly*

14 Is it possible that my people live in such awful conditions? . . . I tell you, Mr Wheatley, that if I had to live in conditions like that I would be a revolutionary myself.
George V (1865–1936) King of the United Kingdom. On being told Mr Wheatley's life story. *The Tragedy of Ramsay MacDonald* (L. MacNeill Weir), Ch. 16

15 Let not Ambition mock their useful toil,
Their homely joys, and destiny obscure;
Nor Grandeur hear with a disdainful smile,
The short and simple annals of the poor.
Thomas Gray (1716–71) British poet. *Elegy Written in a Country Churchyard*

16 People who are much too sensitive to demand of cripples that they run races ask of the poor that they get up and act just like everyone else in society.
Michael Harrington (1928–) US socialist and writer. *The Other America*

17 I want there to be no peasant in my kingdom so poor that he is unable to have a chicken in his pot every Sunday.
Henri IV (1553–1610) King of France. *Hist. de Henry le Grand* (Hardouin de Péréfixe)

18 Seven cities warr'd for Homer, being dead,
Who, living, had no roof to shroud his head.
Thomas Heywood (c. 1574–1641) English dramatist. *The Hierarchy of the Blessed Angels*

19 Oh! God! that bread should be so dear,
And flesh and blood so cheap!
Thomas Hood (1799–1845) British poet. *The Song of the Shirt*

20 Hard to train to accept being poor.
Horace (Quintus Horatius Flaccus; 65–8 BC) Roman poet. *Odes*, I

21 It is easy enough to say that poverty is no crime. No; if it were men wouldn't be ashamed of it. It is a blunder, though, and is punished as such. A poor man is despised the whole world over.
Jerome K. Jerome (1859–1927) British humorist. *Idle Thoughts of an Idle Fellow*

22 This Administration here and now declares unconditional war on poverty in America.
Lyndon B. Johnson (1908–73) US statesman. State of the Union message, 8 Jan 1964

23 Resolve not to be poor: whatever you have, spend less. Poverty is a great enemy to human happiness; it certainly destroys liberty, and it makes some virtues impracticable and others extremely difficult.
Samuel Johnson (1709–84) British lexicographer. *Life of Johnson* (J. Boswell), Vol. IV

24 The misfortunes of poverty carry with them nothing harder to bear than that it exposes men to ridicule.
Juvenal (Decimus Junius Juvenalis; 60–130 AD) Roman satirist. *Satires*, III

25 It's not easy for people to rise out of obscurity when they have to face straitened circumstances at home.
Juvenal *Satires*, III

26 We're really all of us bottomly broke.
I haven't had time to work in weeks.
Jack Kerouac (1922–69) US novelist. *On the Road*, Pt. I

27 The trouble with being poor is that it takes up all your time.
William de Kooning Attrib.

28 Few, save the poor, feel for the poor.
Letitia Landon (1802–38) British poet and novelist. *The Poor*

29 I (Who Have Nothing).
Jerry Leiber (1933–) US songwriter. Credited to 'Donida; Leiber, Stoller, Mogol'. Song title

30 Look at me: I worked my way up from nothing to a state of extreme poverty.
Groucho Marx (Julius Marx; 1895–1977) US comedian. *Monkey Business*

31 The forgotten man at the bottom of the economic pyramid.
Franklin D. Roosevelt (1882–1945) US Democratic president. Speech on radio, 7 Apr 1932

32 The poor don't know that their function in life is to exercise our generosity.
Jean-Paul Sartre (1905–80) French writer. *Words*

33 The heart of the matter, as I see it, is the stark fact that world poverty is primarily a problem of two million villages, and thus a problem of two thousand million villagers.

E. F. Schumacher (1911–77) German-born economist. *Small is Beautiful, A Study of Economics as if People Mattered,* Ch. 13

34 CUSINS. Do you call poverty a crime?

UNDERSHAFT. The worst of all crimes. All the other crimes are virtues beside it.

George Bernard Shaw (1856–1950) Irish dramatist and critic. *Major Barbara,* IV

35 Disease creates poverty and poverty disease. The vicious circle is closed.

Henry E. Sigerist (1891–1957) *Medicine and Human Welfare,* Ch. 1

36 Moving through the silent crowd
Who stand behind dull cigarettes,
These men who idle in the road,
I have the sense of falling light.

They lounge at corners of the street
And greet friends with a shrug of the shoulder
And turn their empty pockets out,
The cynical gestures of the poor.

Stephen Spender (1909–) British poet. *Unemployed*

37 . . . the poor are our brothers and sisters . . . people in the world who need love, who need care, who have to be wanted.

Mother Teresa (Agnes Gonxha Bojaxhui; 1910–) Yugoslavian missionary in Calcutta. *Time,* 'Saints Among Us', 29 Dec 1975

38 I have achieved poverty with distinction, but never poverty with dignity; the best I can manage is dignity with poverty.

Dylan Thomas (1914–53) Welsh poet. Letter to Henry Treece

39 It is very good, sometimes, to have nothing. I want society, not me, to have places to sit in and beds to lie in; and who wants a hatstand of his very own?

Dylan Thomas *Dylan Thomas: Poet of His People* (Andrew Sinclair)

40 There were times my pants were so thin I could sit on a dime and tell if it was heads or tails.

Spencer Tracy (1900–67) US film star. *Spencer Tracy* (L. Swindell)

41 As for the virtuous poor, one can pity them, of course, but one cannot possibly admire them.

Oscar Wilde (1854–1900) Irish-born British dramatist. *The Soul of Man under Socialism*

42 But I, being poor, have only my dreams;
I have spread my dreams under your feet;
Tread softly because you tread on my dreams.

W. B. Yeats (1865–1939) Irish poet. *He Wishes for the Cloths of Heaven*

POVERTY AND WEALTH

See also money, poverty, wealth

1 She was poor but she was honest
Victim of a rich man's game.
First he loved her, then he left her,
And she lost her maiden name.

See her on the bridge at midnight,
Saying 'Farewell, blighted love.'
Then a scream, a splash and goodness,
What is she a-doin' of?

It's the same the whole world over,
It's the poor wot gets the blame,
It's the rich wot gets the gravy.
Ain't it all a bleedin' shame?

Anonymous *She was Poor but she was Honest*

2 There was a certain rich man, which was clothed in purple and fine linen, and fared sumptuously every day:
And there was a certain beggar named Lazarus, which was laid at his gate, full of sores,
And desiring to be fed with the crumbs which fell from the rich man's table: moreover the dogs came and licked his sores.
And it came to pass, that the beggar died, and was carried by the angels into Abraham's bosom: the rich man also died, and was buried;
And in hell he lift up his eyes, being in torments, and seeth Abraham afar off, and Lazarus in his bosom.

Bible: Luke 16:19–23

3 There are only two families in the world, my old grandmother used to say, The *Haves* and the *Have-Nots.*

Miguel de Cervantes (1547–1616) Spanish novelist. *Don Quixote,* Pt. II, Ch. 20

4 'Two nations; between whom there is no intercourse and no sympathy; who are as ignorant of each other's habits, thoughts, and feelings, as if they were dwellers in different zones, or inhabitants of different planets; who are formed by a different breeding, are fed by a different food, are ordered by different manners, and are not governed by the same laws.'
'You speak of. –' said Egremont, hesitatingly
'THE RICH AND THE POOR.'

Benjamin Disraeli (1804–81) British statesman. *Sybil,* Bk. II, Ch. 5

5 Errors look so very ugly in persons of small means – one feels they are taking quite a liberty in going astray; whereas people of fortune may naturally indulge in a few delinquencies.

George Eliot (Mary Ann Evans; 1819–80) British novelist. *Janet's Repentance,* Ch. 25

6 Whereas it has long been known and declared that the poor have no right to the property of the rich, I wish it also to be known and declared that the rich have no right to the property of the poor.

John Ruskin (1819–1900) British art critic and writer. *Unto this Last,* Essay III

7 When the rich wage war it is the poor who die.

Jean-Paul Sartre (1905–80) French writer. *The Devil and the Good Lord*

8 As long as men are men, a poor society cannot be too poor to find a right order of life, nor a rich society too rich to have need to seek it.

R. H. Tawney (1880–1962) British economist and historian. *The Acquisitive Society*

9 If the rich could hire other people to die for them, the poor could make a wonderful living.

Yiddish proverb

POWER

See also influence leadership, responsibility

1 Divide and rule.

Proverb

2 He who pays the piper calls the tune.

Proverb

3 Power tends to corrupt, and absolute power corrupts absolutely. Great men are almost always bad men . . . There is no worse heresy than that the office sanctifies the holder of it.

Lord Acton (1834–1902) British historian. Often misquoted as 'Power corrupts . . . '. Letter to Bishop Mandell Creighton, 5 Apr 1887

4 A friend in power is a friend lost.

Henry Brooks Adams (1838–1918) US historian. *The Education of Henry Adams*

5 Nothing destroyeth authority so

much as the unequal and untimely interchange of power pressed too far, and relaxed too much.
Francis Bacon (1561–1626) English philosopher. *Essays*, 'Of Empire'

6 He did not care in which direction the car was travelling, so long as he remained in the driver's seat.
Lord Beaverbrook (1879–1964) Canadian-born British newspaper proprietor. Referring to Lloyd George. *New Statesman*, 14 June 1963

7 The strongest poison ever known
Came from Caesar's laurel crown.
William Blake (1757–1827) British poet. *Auguries of Innocence*

8 The greater the power, the more dangerous the abuse.
Edmund Burke (1729–97) British politician. Speech, House of Commons, 7 Feb 1771

9 The less people know about what is really going on, the easier it is to wield power and authority.
Charles, Prince of Wales (1948–) Eldest son of Elizabeth II. *The Observer*, 'Sayings of the Week', 2 Mar 1975

10 In the councils of government, we must guard against the acquisition of unwarranted influence, whether sought or unsought, by the military-industrial complex. The potential for the disastrous rise of misplaced power exists and will persist.
Dwight D. Eisenhower (1890–1969) US president. Farewell address, 17 Jan 1961

11 Just as the moon receives its light from the sun, . . . so the royal power takes all its reputation and prestige from the pontifical power.
Innocent III (1160–1216) Pope. Letter to recteurs of Tuscany, 1198

12 All I have, I would have given gladly not to be standing here today.
Lyndon B. Johnson (1908–73) US Democratic president. Following the assassination of President Kennedy. Speech to Congress, 27 Nov 1963

13 Son, they are all my helicopters.
Lyndon B. Johnson Johnson was moving towards the wrong helicopter and an officer said to him, 'Your helicopter is over there'. Attrib.

14 My opinion is, that power should always be distrusted, in whatever hands it is placed.
Sir William Jones (1746–1794) British jurist, linguist and orientalist. Letter to Lord Althorpe, 5 Oct 1782

15 I looked around at the little fishes present and said, 'I'm the Kingfish.'
Huey Long (1893–1935) US demagogue. *The Politics of Upheaval* (A. Schlesinger Jr)

16 Power? It's like a dead sea fruit; when you achieve it, there's nothing there.
Harold Macmillan (1894–1986) British politician and prime minister. Attrib.

17 The power of kings and magistrates is nothing else, but what only is derivative, transformed and committed to them in trust from the people to the common good of them all, in whom the power yet remains fundamentally, and cannot be taken from them, without a violation of their natural birthright.
John Milton (1608–74) English poet. *The Tenure of Kings and Magistrates*

18 I am become death, the destroyer of worlds.
J. Robert Oppenheimer (1904–67) US physicist. Quoting Vishnu from the *Gita*, at the first atomic test in New Mexico, 16 July 1945. Attrib.

19 Religions, which condemn the pleasures of sense, drive men to seek the pleasures of power. Throughout history power has been the vice of the ascetic.
Bertrand Russell (1872–1970) British philosopher. *New York Herald-Tribune Magazine*, 6 May 1938

20 How long a time lies in one little word!
Four lagging winters and four wanton springs
End in a word; such is the breath of kings.
William Shakespeare (1564–1616) English dramatist. *Richard II*, I:3

21 Is not the king's name twenty thousand names?
Arm, arm, my name! A puny subject strikes
At thy great glory.
William Shakespeare *Richard II*, III:2

22 You don't have power if you surrender all your principles – you have office.
Ron Todd Trade union leader. Remark, June 1988

23 The machine is running away with *him* as it ran away with *me*.
Wilhelm II (1859–1941) King of Prussia and Emperor of Germany. Referring to Hitler. Remark to Sir Robert Bruce-Lockhart and Sir John Wheeler-Bennett, 27 Aug 1939

POWER POLITICS

See also force, oppression, violence, weapons

1 Let no one expect us to disarm unilaterally. We are not a naive people.
Yuri Andropov (1914–83) Soviet statesman and president. Speech, Central Committee of the Soviet Communist Party, 22 Nov 1982

2 Whatever happens, we have got
The Maxim Gun, and they have not.
Hilaire Belloc (1870–1953) French-born British poet. Referring to African natives. *The Modern Traveller*

3 Covenants without the sword are but words and of no strength to secure a man at all.
Thomas Hobbes (1588–1679) English philosopher. *Leviathan*, Pt. II, Ch. 17

4 You cannot control a free society by force.
Robert Mark (1917–) British police commissioner. *The Observer*, 'Sayings of the Week', 25 July 1976

5 Do not hit at all if it can be avoided, but never hit softly.
Theodore Roosevelt (1858–1919) US Republican president. *Autobiography*

6 O! it is excellent
To have a giant's strength, but it is tyrannous
To use it like a giant.
William Shakespeare (1564–1616) English dramatist. *Measure for Measure*, II:2

PRACTICALITY

1 I have no dress except the one I wear every day. If you are going to be kind enough to give me one, please let it be practical and dark so that I can put it on afterwards to go to the laboratory.
Marie Curie (1867–1934) Polish chemist. Referring to a wedding dress. Letter to a friend

2 What would you do with it? It is full of leprosy.
Father Damien (Joseph de Veuster; 1840–89) Belgian Roman Catholic missionary. When asked on his deathbed whether he would leave another priest his mantle, like Elijah. *Memoirs of an Aesthete* (H. Acton)

3 The Arab who builds himself a hut out of the marble fragments of a temple in Palmyra is more philosophical than all the curators of the museums in London, Munich or Paris.
Anatole France (Jacques Anatole François Thibault; 1844–1924) French writer. *The Crime of Sylvestre Bonnard*

4 Talk to him of Jacob's ladder, and he would ask the number of the steps.
Douglas William Jerrold (1803–57) British dramatist. *Wit and Opinions of Douglas Jerrold,* 'A Matter-of-fact Man'

5 Don't carry away that arm till I have taken off my ring.
Lord Raglan (1788–1855) British field marshal. Request immediately after his arm had been amputated following the battle of Waterloo. *Dictionary of National Biography*

6 Very well, then I shall not take off my boots.
Duke of Wellington (1769–1852) British general and statesman. Responding to the news, as he was going to bed, that the ship in which he was traveling seemed about to sink. Attrib.

PRAGMATISM

1 The pragmatist knows that doubt is an art which has to be acquired with difficulty.
Charles Sanders Pierce *Collected Papers*

PRAISE

See also admiration, boasts, compliments, flattery

1 Self-praise is no recommendation.
Proverb

2 If I were not Alexander, I would be Diogenes.
Alexander the Great (356–323 BC) King of Macedon. Plutarch, *Life of Alexander,* Bk. XIV

3 Just as it is always said of slander that something always sticks when people boldly slander, so it might be said of self-praise (if it is not entirely shameful and ridiculous) that if we praise ourselves fearlessly, something will always stick.
Francis Bacon (1561–1626) English philosopher. *The Advancement of Learning*

4 Let us now praise famous men, and our fathers that begat us.
Bible: Ecclesiasticus 44:1

5 Watch how a man takes praise and there you have the measure of him.
Thomas Burke (1886–1945) British writer. *T. P.'s Weekly,* 8 June 1928

6 The advantage of doing one's praising for oneself is that one can lay it on so thick and exactly in the right places.
Samuel Butler (1835–1902) British writer. *The Way of All Flesh,* Ch. 34

7 Fondly we think we honour merit then,
When we but praise ourselves in other men.
Alexander Pope (1688–1744) British poet. *An Essay on Criticism*

8 To refuse praise reveals a desire to be praised twice over.
Duc de la Rochefoucauld (1613–80) French writer. *Maximes,* 149

PRAYER

See also Christianity, faith, God, religion

1 Hail Mary, full of grace, the Lord is with thee: Blessed art thou among women, and blessed is the fruit of thy womb, Jesus.
Anonymous *Ave Maria,* 11th century

2 From ghoulies and ghosties and long-leggety beasties
And things that go bump in the night,
Good Lord, deliver us!
Anonymous Cornish saying

3 O Lord! thou knowest how busy I must be this day: if I forget thee, do not thou forget me.
Lord Astley (1579–1652) English Royalist general. Prayer before taking part in the Battle of Edgehill. *Memoires* (Sir Philip Warwick)

4 *Da mihi castitatem et continentiam, sed noli modo.*
Give me chastity and continence, but not yet.
St Augustine of Hippo (354–430) Bishop of Hippo. *Confessions*

5 O God, send me some good actors – cheap.
Lilian Baylis (1874–1937) British theater owner and producer. *The Guardian,* 1 Mar 1976

6 *Pray, v.* To ask that the rules of the universe be annulled on behalf of a single petitioner, confessedly unworthy.
Ambrose Bierce (1842–?1914) US writer and journalist. *The Devil's Dictionary*

7 But when ye pray, use not vain repetitions, as the heathen do: for they think that they shall be heard for their much speaking.
Be not ye therefore like unto them: for your Father knoweth what things ye have need of, before ye ask him.
After this manner therefore pray ye: Our Father which art in heaven, Hallowed be thy name.
Thy kingdom come. Thy will be done in earth, as it is in heaven.
Give us this day our daily bread.
And forgive us our debts, as we forgive our debtors.
And lead us not into temptation, but deliver us from evil: For thine is the kingdom, and the power, and the glory, for ever. Amen.
Bible: Matthew 6:7–13

8 To Mercy, Pity, Peace, and Love
All pray in their distress.
William Blake (1757–1827) British poet. *Songs of Innocence,* 'The Divine Image'

9 When two or three are gathered together in thy Name thou wilt grant their requests.
The Book of Common Prayer *Morning Prayer, Prayer of St Chrysostom*

10 A leap over the hedge is better than good men's prayers.
Miguel de Cervantes (1547–1616) Spanish novelist. *Don Quixote,* Pt. I, Ch. 21

11 He prayeth well, who loveth well
Both man and bird and beast.
Samuel Taylor Coleridge (1772–1834) British poet. *The Rime of the Ancient Mariner,* VII

12 He prayeth best, who loveth best
All things both great and small;
For the dear God who loveth us,
He made and loveth all.
Samuel Taylor Coleridge *The Rime of the Ancient Mariner,* VII

13 'Does God always answer prayer?' the cardinal was asked. 'Yes' he said. 'And sometimes the answer is – 'No'.'
Alistair Cooke (1908–) British writer and broadcaster. *Letter from America* (BBC radio)

14 Prayer makes the Christian's armour bright;
And Satan trembles when he sees
The weakest saint upon his knees.
William Cowper (1731–1800) British poet. *Olney Hymns,* 29

15 The idea that He would take his attention away from the universe in order to give me a bicycle with three speeds is just so unlikely I can't go along with it.
Quentin Crisp (?1910–) British model, publicist, and writer. *The Sunday Times,* 18 Dec 1977

16 Some day when you have time, look into the business of prayer, amulets, baths and poultices, and discover for yourself how much valuable therapy the profession has cast on the dump.
Martin H. Fischer (1879–1962) *Fischerisms* (Howard Fabing and Ray Marr)

17 The most odious of concealed narcissisms – prayer.
John Fowles (1926–) British novelist. *The Aristos*

18 Forgive, O Lord, my little jokes on Thee
And I'll forgive Thy great big one on me.
Robert Frost (1875–1963) US poet. *In the clearing*, 'Cluster of Faith'

19 Religion's in the heart, not in the knees.
Douglas William Jerrold (1803–57) British dramatist. *The Devil's Ducat*, I.2

20 Your cravings as a human animal do not become a prayer just because it is God whom you must ask to attend to them.
Dag Hammarskjöld (1905–61) Swedish diplomat. *Markings*

21 The Beadsman, after thousand aves told,
For aye unsought-for slept among his ashes cold.
John Keats (1795–1821) British poet. *The Eve of Saint Agnes*, I

22 If thou may not continually gather thyself together, do it some time at least once a day, morning or evening.
Thomas à Kempis (1380–1471) German monk and writer. *The Imitation of Christ*, 1

23 Better to enjoy and suffer than sit around with folded arms. You know the only true prayer? Please God, lead me into temptation.
Jennie Lee (1904–) British politician and writer. *My Life with Nye*

24 Arise, O Lord, plead Thine own cause; remember how the foolish man reproacheth Thee daily; the foxes are wasting Thy vineyard, which Thou hast given to Thy Vicar Peter, the boar out of the wood doth waste it, and the wild beast of the field doth devour it.
Leo X (Giovanni de' Medici; 1475–1521) Pope (1513–21). Papal Bull, *Exsurge, Domine*, Preface

25 Nowhere can man find a quieter or more untroubled retreat than in his own soul.
Marcus Aurelius (Marcus Aurelius Antoninus; 121–180) Roman emperor and Stoic philosopher. *Meditations*, 4

26 Our dourest parsons, who followed the nonconformist fashion of long extemporary prayers, always seemed to me to be bent on bullying God. After a few 'beseech thees' as a mere politeness, they adopted a sterner tone and told Him what they expected from Him and more than hinted He must attend to His work.
J. B. Priestley (1894–1984) British novelist. *Outcries and Asides*

27 I am just going to pray for you at St Paul's, but with no very lively hope of success.
Sydney Smith (1771–1845) British clergyman and essayist. On meeting an acquaintance. *The Smith of Smiths* (H. Pearson), Ch. 13

28 If thou shouldst never see my face again,
Pray for my soul. More things are wrought by prayer
Than this world dreams of.
Alfred, Lord Tennyson (1809–92) British poet. *Idylls of the King*, 'The Passing of Arthur'

29 Whatever a man prays for, he prays for a miracle. Every prayer reduces itself to this: 'Great God grant that twice two be not four.'
Ivan Turgenev (1818–83) Russian novelist. *Prayer*

PRECOCITY

See also children, youth

1 When you were quite a little boy somebody ought to have said 'hush' just once.
Mrs Patrick Campbell (1865–1940) British actress. Letter to George Bernard Shaw, 1 Nov 1912

2 One of those men who reach such an acute limited excellence at twenty-one that everything afterward savors of anti-climax.
F. Scott Fitzgerald (1896–1940) US novelist. *The Great Gatsby*, Ch. 1

3 Thank you, madam, the agony is abated.
Lord Macaulay (1800–59) British historian. Replying, aged four, to a lady who asked if he had hurt himself. *Life and Letters of Macaulay* (Trevelyan), Ch. 1

4 So wise so young, they say, do never live long.
William Shakespeare (1564–1616) English dramatist. *Richard III*, III:1

PREJUDICE

See also equality, feminism, Jews, objectivity, race, racism, religion, subjectivity

1 I am a Catholic. As far as possible I go to Mass every day. As far as possible I kneel down and tell these beads every day. If you reject me on account of my religion, I shall thank God that he has spared me the indignity of being your representative.
Hilaire Belloc (1870–1953) French-born British poet. Said in his first election campaign. Speech, Salford, 1906

2 Mother is far too clever to understand anything she does not like.
Arnold Bennett (1867–1931) British novelist. *The Title*

3 Don't half-quote me to reinforce your own prejudices.
Brian Clark (1932–) British playwright. *Kipling*

4 Common sense is the collection of prejudices acquired by age eighteen.
Albert Einstein (1879–1955) German-born US physicist. *Scientific American*, Feb 1976

5 I am free of all prejudice. I hate everyone equally.
W. C. Fields (1880–1946) US actor. Attrib.

6 My corns ache, I get gouty, and my prejudices swell like varicose veins.
James Gibbons Huneker (1860–1921) *Old Fogy*, Ch. 1

7 Since my daughter is only half-Jewish, could she go in the water up to her knees?
Groucho Marx (Julius Marx; 1895–1977) US comedian. When excluded from a beach club on racial grounds. *The Observer*, 21 Aug 1977

8 Vegetarians have wicked, shifty eyes, and laugh in a cold and calculating manner. They pinch little children, steal stamps, drink water, favour beards . . . wheeze, squeak, drawl and maunder.
J. B. Morton (1893–1979) British journalist. *By the Way*, '4 June'

9 Why bastard? wherefore base?
When my dimensions are as well compact,
My mind as generous, and my shape as true,
As honest madam's issue? Why brand they us
With base? with baseness? bastardy? base, base?
Who in the lusty stealth of nature take
More composition and fierce quality
Than doth, within a dull, stale, tired bed,
Go to creating a whole tribe of fops,
Got 'tween asleep and wake?
William Shakespeare (1564–1616) English dramatist. *King Lear*, I:2

10 I will buy with you, sell with you, talk with you, walk with you, and so following; but I will not eat with you, drink with you, nor pray with you. What news on the Rialto?
William Shakespeare *The Merchant of Venice*, I:3

11 How like a fawning publican he looks!
I hate him for he is a Christian;
William Shakespeare *The Merchant of Venice*, I:3

12 Mislike me not for my complexion,
The shadow'd livery of the burnish'd sun,
To whom I am neighbour and near bred.
William Shakespeare *The Merchant of Venice*, II:1

13 I'll refer me to all things of sense,
Whether a maid so tender, fair, and happy,
So opposite to marriage that she shunn'd
The wealthy curled darlings of our nation,
Would ever have, to incur a general mock,
Run from her guardage to the sooty bosom
Of such a thing as thou.
William Shakespeare *Othello*, I:2

14 . . . I *too well* know its truth, from experience, that whenever any poor Gipsies are encamped anywhere and crimes and robberies &c. occur, it is invariably laid to their account, which is shocking; and if they are always looked upon as vagabonds, how *can* they become good people?
Victoria (1819–1901) Queen of the United Kingdom. Journal, 29 Dec 1836

15 I do not intend to prejudge the past.
William Whitelaw (1918–) British politician. Said on arriving in Ulster as Minister for Northern Ireland. *The Times*, 3 Dec 1973

16 No Jewish blood runs among my blood,
but I am as bitterly and hardly hated by every anti-semite
as if I were a Jew. By this
I am a Russian.
Yevgeny Yevtushenko (1933–) Soviet poet. *Babi Yar*

PRESENT

See also future, opportunity, past, time

1 No time like the present.
Proverb

2 The past was nothing to her; offered no lesson which she was willing to heed. The future was a mystery which she never attempted to penetrate. The present alone was significant . . . .
Kate Chopin (1851–1904) US writer. *The Awakening*, Ch. 15

3 I have learned to live each day as it comes, and not to borrow trouble by dreading tomorrow. It is the dark menace of the future that makes cowards of us.
Dorothy Dix (Elizabeth Meriwether Gilmer; 1861–1951) US journalist and writer. *Dorothy Dix, Her Book*, Introduction

4 Happy the Man, and happy he alone,
He who can call today his own:
He who, secure within, can say,
Tomorrow do thy worst, for I have liv'd today.
John Dryden (1631–1700) British poet and dramatist. *Translation of Horace*, III

5 Ah, my Belovéd, fill the Cup that clears
TO-DAY of past Regrets and Future Fears:
To-morrow! – Why, To-morrow I may be
Myself with Yesterday's Sev'n thousand Years.
Edward Fitzgerald (1809–83) British poet. *The Rubáiyát of Omar Khayyám* (1st edn.), XX

6 Gather ye rosebuds while ye may,
Old time is still a-flying:
And this same flower that smiles today
Tomorrow will be dying.
Robert Herrick (1591–1674) English poet. *Hesperides*, 'To the Virgins, to Make Much of Time'

7 Believe each day that has dawned is your last. Some hour to which you have not been looking forward will prove lovely. As for me, if you want a good laugh, you will come and find me fat and sleek, in excellent condition, one of Epicurus' herd of pigs.
Horace (Quintus Horatius Flaccus; 65–8 BC) Roman poet. *Epistles*, I

8 *Carpe diem.*
Seize the day.
Horace *Odes*, I

9 Drop the question what tomorrow may bring, and count as profit every day that Fate allows you.
Horace *Odes*, I

10 While we're talking, time will have meanly run on: pick today's fruits, not relying on the future in the slightest.
Horace *Odes*, I

11 We live in stirring times – tea-stirring times.
Christopher Isherwood (1904–86) British novelist. *Mr Norris Changes Trains*

12 Redeem thy mis-spent time that's past;
Live this day, as if 'twere thy last.
Thomas Ken (1637–1711) English bishop. *A Morning Hymn*

13 What is love? 'Tis not hereafter;
Present mirth hath present laughter;
What's to come is still unsure.
In delay there lies no plenty,
Then come kiss me, sweet and twenty;
Youth's a stuff will not endure.
William Shakespeare (1564–1616) English dramatist. *Twelfth Night*, II:3

PRESIDENTS

1 In Franklin Roosevelt there died the greatest American friend we have ever known and the greatest champion of freedom who has ever brought help and comfort from the New World to the Old.
Winston Churchill (1874–1965) British politician and prime minister. *The Second World War*

2 When I was a boy I was told that anybody could become President of the United States. I am beginning to believe it.
Clarence Darrow (1857–1938) US lawyer. Attrib.

3 There is one thing about being President – nobody can tell you when to sit down.
Dwight D. Eisenhower (1890–1969) US general and statesman. *The Observer*, 'Sayings of the Week', 9 Aug 1953

4 He looks like the guy in a science fiction movie who is the first to see the Creature.
David Frye (1934–) US impressionist and comedian. Referring to president Ford. Attrib.

5 My fellow citizens, the President is dead, but the Government lives and God Omnipotent reigns.
James A. Garfield (1831–81) US statesman. Speech following the assassination of Lincoln.

6 He would rather follow public opinion than lead it.
Harry Hopkins (1890–1946) US politician. Referring to Roosevelt. Attrib.

7 President Robbins was so well adjusted to his environment that sometimes you could not tell which was the environment and which was President Robbins.
Randall Jarrell (1914–65) US author. *Pictures from an Institution*, Pt. I, Ch. 4

8 Power is the ultimate aphrodisiac.
Henry Kissinger (1923–) German-born US politician and diplomat. *The Guardian*, 28 Nov 1976

9 He looked at me as if I was a side dish he hadn't ordered.
Ring Lardner Jnr (1885–1933) American humorist. Referring to W. H. Taft, US president (1909–13). *The Home Book of Humorous Quotations* (A. K. Adams)

10 He looks as if he had been weaned on a pickle.
Alice Roosevelt Longworth (1884–1980) US hostess. Referring to John Calvin Coolidge, US president 1923–29. *Crowded Hours*

11 Here, indeed, was his one really notable talent. He slept more than any other President, whether by day or by night. . . . Nero fiddled, but Coolidge only snored. . . . He had no ideas, and he was not a nuisance.
H. L. Mencken (1880–1956) US journalist. Referring to President Coolidge. *American Mercury*, 1933

12 How could they tell?
Dorothy Parker (1893–1967) US writer. Reaction to news of the death of Calvin Coolidge, US President 1923–29; also attributed to H. L. Mencken. *You Might As Well Live* (J. Keats)

13 My fellow Americans, I am pleased to tell you that I have signed legislation to outlaw Russia for ever. We begin bombing in five minutes.
Ronald Reagan (1911–) US Republican president. When asked to do a microphone test. Recording, 13 Aug 1984

14 You know that nobody is strongminded around a President . . . it is always: 'yes sir', 'no sir' (the 'no sir' comes when he asks whether you're dissatisfied).
George Edward Reedy (1917–) US government official. *The White House* (ed. R. Gordon Hoxie)

15 Would you buy a second-hand car from this man?
Mort Sahl (1926–) US political comedian. Referring to President Nixon. Attrib.

16 Power corrupts, but lack of power corrupts absolutely.
Adlai Stevenson (1900–65) US statesman. *The Observer*, Jan 1963

17 He said that he was too old to cry, but it hurt too much to laugh.
Adlai Stevenson Said after losing an election, quoting a story told by Abraham Lincoln. Speech, 5 Nov 1952

18 Log-cabin to White House.
W. M. Thayer (1820–98) US writer. The title of his biography of James Garfield, US president

19 While I'd rather be right than president, at any time I'm ready to be both.
Norman M. Thomas (1884–1968) US politician. Referring to his lack of success in presidential campaigns. The expression 'I'd rather be right than president' is also attributed to the US politician Henry Clay (1777–1852). *Come to Judgment* (A. Whitman)

20 The President spends most of his time kissing people on the cheek in order to get them to do what they ought to do without getting kissed.
Harry S. Truman (1884–1972) US statesman. *The Observer*, 'Sayings of the Week', 6 Feb 1949

21 Any American who is prepared to run for President should automatically, by definition, be disqualified from ever doing so.
Gore Vidal (1925–) US novelist. Attrib.

22 A writer of crook stories ought never to stop seeking new material.
Edgar Wallace (1875–1932) British thriller writer. Said when a candidate for Parliament. *The Long Weekend* (Alan Hodge)

PRESS

See journalism, newspapers

PRIDE

See also arrogance, conceit, egotism, self-respect

1 Pride goeth before destruction, and an haughty spirit before a fall.
Bible: Proverbs Often misquoted as 'Pride goeth before a fall'. 16:18

2 He that is down needs fear no fall;
He that is low, no pride.
John Bunyan (1628–88) English writer. *The Pilgrim's Progress*, 'Shepherd Boy's Song'

3 The virtue of pride, which was once the beauty of mankind, has given place to that fount of all ugliness, Christian humility.
Max Ernst (1891–) German surrealist painter. Attrib.

4 When the Lord sent me forth into the world, He forbade me to put off my hat to any high or low.
George Fox (1624–91) English religious leader. *Journal*

5 And if you include me among the lyric poets, I'll hold my head so high it'll strike the stars.
Horace (Quintus Horatius Flaccus; 65–8 BC) Roman poet. *Odes*, I

6 We are not ashamed of what we have done, because, when you have a great cause to fight for, the moment of greatest humiliation is the moment when the spirit is proudest.
Christabel Pankhurst (1880–1958) British suffragette. Speech, Albert Hall, London, 19 Mar 1908

7 Yes; I am proud, I must be proud to see
Men not afraid of God, afraid of me.
Alexander Pope (1688–1744) British poet. *Epilogue to the Satires*, Dialogue II

8 Of all the causes which conspire to blind
Man's erring judgment, and misguide the mind,
What the weak head with strongest bias rules,
Is Pride, the never-failing vice of fools.
Alexander Pope *An Essay on Criticism*

9 There is false modesty, but there is no false pride.
Jules Renard (1894–1910) French writer. *Journal*

10 Let pride be taught by this rebuke,
How very mean a thing's a Duke;
From all his ill-got honours flung,
Turn'd to that dirt from whence he sprung.
Jonathan Swift (1667–1745) Irish-born Anglican priest and writer. Referring to the Duke of Marlborough. *A Satirical Elegy on the Death of a Late Famous General*

11 The French want no-one to be their *superior*. The English want *inferiors*. The Frenchman constantly raises his eyes above him with anxiety. The Englishman lowers his beneath him with satisfaction. On either side it is pride, but understood in a different way.
Alexis de Tocqueville (1805–59) French writer, historian, and politician. *Voyage en Angleterre et en Irlande de 1835*, 18 May

12 We cannot bring ourselves to believe it possible that a foreigner should in any respect be wiser than ourselves. If any such point out to us our follies, we at once claim

those follies as the special evidences of our wisdom.

Anthony Trollope (1815–82) British novelist. *Orley Farm*, Ch. 18

PRIME MINISTERS

1 It hasn't taken Winston long to get used to American ways. He hadn't been an American citizen for three minutes before attacking an ex-secretary of state!

Dean Acheson (1893–1971) US lawyer and statesman. At a ceremony in 1963 to make Churchill an honorary American citizen, Churchill obliquely attacked Acheson's reference to Britain losing an empire. *Randolph Churchill* (K. Halle)

2 You have sat too long here for any good you have been doing. Depart, I say, and let us have done with you. In the name of God, *go!*

Leopold Amery (1873–1955) British statesman. Said to Neville Chamberlain using Cromwell's words. Speech, House of Commons, May 1940

3 He believes, with all his heart and soul and strength, that there *is* such a thing as truth; he has the soul of a martyr with the intellect of an advocate.

Walter Bagehot (1826–77) British economist and journalist. Referring to Gladstone. *Historical Essays*, 'Mr Gladstone'

4 Then comes Winston with his hundred-horse-power mind and what can I do?

Stanley Baldwin (1867–1947) British statesman. *Stanley Baldwin* (G. M. Young), Ch. 11

5 I thought he was a young man of promise; but it appears he was a young man of promises.

Arthur Balfour (1848–1930) British statesman. Said of Winston Churchill on his entry into politics, 1899. *Winston Churchill* (Randolph Churchill), Vol. I

6 She is trying to wear the trousers of Winston Churchill.

Leonid Brezhnev (1906–82) Soviet statesman. Referring to Margaret Thatcher. Speech, 1979

7 He was not merely a chip of the old block, but the old block itself.

Edmund Burke (1729–97) British politician. Referring to William Pitt the Younger's first speech in the House of Commons, 26 Feb 1781. Attrib.

8 Mr Macmillan is the best prime minister we have.

R. A. Butler (1902–82) British Conservative politician. Often quoted in the form above. In fact, Butler simply answered 'Yes' to the question 'Would you say that this is the best prime minister we have?'. Interview, London Airport, Dec 1955

9 Politics and the fate of mankind are shaped by men without ideals and without greatness. Men who have greatness within them don't go in for politics.

Albert Camus (1913–60) French existentialist writer. *Notebooks*, 1935–42

10 Pitt is to Addington
As London is to Paddington.

George Canning (1770–1827) British statesman. *The Oracle*

11 The seagreen Incorruptible.

Thomas Carlyle (1795–1881) Scottish historian and essayist. Referring to Robespierre. *History of the French Revolution*, Pt. II, Bk. IV, Ch. 4

12 She is clearly the best man among them.

Barbara Castle (1910–) British politician. Referring to Margaret Thatcher. *The Castle Diaries*

13 You seem to have no real purpose in life and won't realize at the age of twenty-two that for a man life means work, and hard work if you mean to succeed.

Jennie Jerome Churchill (1854–1921) US-born British hostess and writer. Letter to Winston Churchill, 26 Feb 1897. *Jennie* (Ralph G. Martin), Vol. II

14 An old man in a hurry.

Lord Randolph Churchill (1849–95) British Conservative politician. Referring to Gladstone. Speech, June 1886

15 So they told me how Mr Gladstone read Homer for fun, which I thought served him right.

Winston Churchill (1874–1965) British statesman. *My Early Life*, Ch. 2

16 In private conversation he tries on speeches like a man trying on ties in his bedroom to see how he would look in them.

Lionel Curtis (1872–1955) British writer. Referring to Winston Churchill. Letter to Nancy Astor, 1912

17 Not even a public figure. A man of no experience. And of the utmost insignificance.

Lord Curzon (1859–1925) British politician. Referring to Stanley Baldwin on his appointment as Prime Minister. *Curzon: The Last Phase* (Harold Nicolson)

18 He is used to dealing with estate workers. I cannot see how anyone can say he is out of touch.

Lady Caroline Douglas-Home (1937–) Daughter of Alec Douglas-Home. Referring to her father's suitability for his new role as prime minister. *Daily Herald*, 21 Oct 1963 (Jon Akass)

19 I know he is, and he adores his maker.

Benjamin Disraeli (1804–81) British statesman. Replying to a remark made in defense of John Bright that he was a self-made man; often also attrib. to Bright referring to Disraeli. *The Fine Art of Political Wit* (L. Harris)

20 A sophistical rhetorician inebriated with the exuberance of his own verbosity.

Benjamin Disraeli Referring to Gladstone. Speech, 27 July 1878

21 She has no imagination and that means no compassion.

Michael Foot (1913–) British Labour politician and journalist. Referring to Margaret Thatcher. Attrib.

22 For the past few months she has been charging about like some bargain-basement Boadicea.

Denis Healey (1917–) British Labour politician. Referring to Margaret Thatcher. *Observer*, 'Sayings of the Week', 7 Nov 1982

23 Once, when a British Prime Minister sneezed, men half a world away would blow their noses. Now when a British Prime Minister sneezes nobody else will even say 'Bless You'.

Bernard Levin (1928–) British journalist. *The Times*, 1976

24 Poor Bonar can't bear being called a liar. Now I don't mind.

David Lloyd George (1863–1945) British Liberal prime minister. Referring to Bonar Law, prime minister 1922–23. *Stanley Baldwin* (G. M. Young)

25 The rogue elephant among British prime ministers.

Dr Kenneth Morgan (1934–) British historian. Referring to Lloyd George. *Life of David Lloyd George*

26 Macmillan seemed, in his very person, to embody the national decay he supposed himself to be confuting. He exuded a flavour of moth-balls.

Malcolm Muggeridge (1903–) British writer. *Tread Softly For You Tread on My Jokes*, 'England, whose England'

27 Argue as you please, you are nowhere, that grand old man, the Prime Minister, insists on the other thing.

Lord Northcote (1818–87) British statesman. Referring to Gladstone; the phrase, and its acronym GOM, became his nickname – temporarily reversed to MOG ('Murderer of Gordon') in 1885, after the death of General Gordon at Khartoum. Speech, Liverpool, 12 Apr 1882

28 Above any other position of eminence, that of Prime Minister is filled by fluke.

Enoch Powell (1912–) British politician. *The Observer*, 'Sayings of the Week', 8 Mar 1987

29 Not a gentleman; dresses too well.

Bertrand Russell (1872–1970) British philosopher. Referring to Anthony Eden. *Six Men* (A. Cooke)

30 I hope Mrs Thatcher will go until the turn of the century looking like Queen Victoria.

Norman Tebbitt (1931–) British Conservative politician. *The Observer*, 'Sayings of the Week', 17 May 1987

31 Introducing Super-Mac.

Vicky (Victor Weisz; 1913–66) German-born British cartoonist. Cartoon caption depicting Harold Macmillan as Superman. *Evening Standard*, 6 Nov 1958

32 The danger to the country, to Europe, to her vast Empire, which is involved in having all these great interests entrusted to the shaking hand of an old, wild, and incomprehensible man of 82½, is very great!

Victoria (1819–1901) Queen of the United Kingdom. Reaction to Gladstone's fourth and last appointment as prime minister, 1892. Letter to Lord Lansdowne, 12 Aug 1892

33 He speaks to Me as if I was a public meeting.

Victoria Referring to Gladstone. *Collections and Recollections* (G. W. E. Russell), Ch. 14

34 Margaret Thatcher's great strength seems to be the better people know her, the better they like her. But, of course, she has one great disadvantage – she is a daughter of the people and looks trim, as the daughters of the people desire to be. Shirley Williams has such an advantage over her because she's a member of the upper-middle class and can achieve that kitchen-sink-revolutionary look that one cannot get unless one has been to a really good school.

Rebecca West (Cicely Isabel Fairfield; 1892–1983) British novelist and journalist. Said in an interview with Jilly Cooper. *The Sunday Times*, 25 July 1976

35 Then the little man wears a shocking bad hat.

Duke of York and Albany (1763–1827) The second son of George III. Referring to Horace Walpole. Attrib.

PRINCIPLES

See also integrity, morality

1 It is easier to fight for one's principles than to live up to them.

Alfred Adler (1870–1937) Austrian psychiatrist. *Alfred Adler* (P. Bottome)

2 Ethics and Science need to shake hands.

Richard Clarke Cabot (1868–1939) *The Meaning of Right and Wrong*, Introduction

3 If one sticks too rigidly to one's principles one would hardly see anybody.

Agatha Christie (1891–1976) British detective-story writer. *Towards Zero*, I

4 Whenever two good people argue over principles, they are both right.

Marie Ebner von Eschenbach (1830–1916) Austrian writer. *Aphorism*

5 Well, sir, you never can tell. That's a principle in life with me, sir, if you'll excuse my having such a thing, sir.

George Bernard Shaw (1856–1950) Irish dramatist and critic. *You Never Can Tell*, II

6 It is often easier to fight for principles than to live up to them.

Adlai Stevenson (1900–65) US statesman. Speech, New York, 27 Aug 1952

PRIVACY

1 Private faces in public places
Are wiser and nicer
Than public faces in private places.

W. H. Auden (1907–73) British-born poet. *Marginalia*

2 The house of every one is to him as his castle and fortress.

Edward Coke (1552–1634) English lawyer and politician. *Semayne's Case*

3 I never said, 'I want to be alone.' I only said, 'I want to be *left* alone.' There is all the difference.

Greta Garbo (1905–) Swedish-born US film star. *Garbo* (John Bainbridge)

4 The poorest man may in his cottage bid defiance to all the forces of the Crown. It may be frail – its roof may shake – the wind may blow through it – the storm may enter – the rain may enter – but the King of England cannot enter! – all his force dares not cross the threshold of the ruined tenement!

William Pitt the Elder (1708–78) British statesman. *Statesmen in the Time of George III* (Lord Brougham), Vol. I

5 This is a free country, madam. We have a right to share your privacy in a public place.

Peter Ustinov (1921–) British actor. *Romanoff and Juliet*, I

PROCRASTINATION

1 Never put off till tomorrow what you can do today.

Proverb

2 Put off the evil hour as long as you can.

Proverb

3 The road to hell is paved with good intentions.

Proverb

4 Give me chastity and continence, but not yet.

St Augustine of Hippo (354–430) Bishop of Hippo. *Confessions*, Bk. VIII, Ch. 7

5 Procrastination is the thief of time.

Edward Young (1683–1765) British poet. *Night Thoughts*

PROGRESS

See also change, conservatism, improvement, innovation, novelty, technology

1 We've made great medical progress in the last generation. What used to be merely an itch is now an allergy.

Anonymous

2 Surely every medicine is an innovation, and he that will not apply new remedies, must expect new evils.

Sir Francis Bacon (1561–1626) English philosopher, lawyer, and politician. *Essays*, 'Of Innovations'

3 The Coming of Post-Industrial Society.

Daniel Bell (1919–) US sociologist. Book title

4 The people who live in the past must yield to the people who live in the future. Otherwise the world would begin to turn the other way round.

Arnold Bennett (1867–1931) British novelist. *Milestones*

5 Progress is
The law of life, man is not man as yet.

Robert Browning (1812–89) British poet. *Paracelsus*, 5

6 All progress is based upon a universal innate desire on the part of every organism to live beyond its income.

Samuel Butler (1835–1902) British writer. *Notebooks*

7 Disease is very old, and nothing about it has changed. It is we who change, as we learn to recognize what was formerly imperceptible.

Jean Martin Charcot (1825–93) *De l'expectation en médecine*

8 As enunciated today, 'progress' is simply a comparative of which we have not settled the superlative.

G. K. Chesterton (1874–1936) British writer. *Heretics*, Ch. 2

9 New roads: new ruts.

G. K. Chesterton Attrib.

10 What we call progress is the exchange of one nuisance for another nuisance.

Havelock Ellis (1859–1939) British sexologist. Attrib.

11 All that is human must retrograde if it does not advance.

Edward Gibbon (1737–94) British historian. *Decline and Fall of the Roman Empire*, Ch. 71

12 You cannot fight against the future. Time is on our side.

William Ewart Gladstone (1809–98) British statesman. Advocating parliamentary reform. Speech, 1866

13 And if the Russian word 'perestroika' has easily entered the international lexicon, this is due to more than just interest in what is going on in the Soviet Union. Now the whole world needs restructuring i.e. progressive development, a fundamental change.

Mikhail Gorbachov (1931–) Soviet statesman. *Perestroika*

14 In your time we have the opportunity to move not only toward the rich society and the powerful society but upward to the Great Society.

Lyndon B. Johnson (1908–73) US Democratic president. Speech, University of Michigan, May 1964

15 Human salvation lies in the hands of the creatively maladjusted.

Martin Luther King (1929–68) US Black civil-rights leader. *Strength to Love*

16 One step forward, two steps back. . . . It happens in the lives of individuals, and it happens in the history of nations and in the development of parties.

Lenin (Vladimir Ilich Ulyanov; 1870–1924) Russian revolutionary leader. *One Step Forward, Two Steps Back*

17 If I have seen further it is by standing on the shoulders of giants.

Isaac Newton (1642–1727) British scientist. Letter to Robert Hooke, 5 Feb 1675

18 You can't say civilization don't advance, however, for in every war they kill you a new way.

Will Rogers (1879–1935) US actor and humorist. *Autobiography*, Ch. 12

19 Organic life, we are told, has developed gradually from the protozoon to the philosopher, and this development, we are assured, is indubitably an advance. Unfortunately it is the philosopher, not the protozoon, who gives us this assurance.

Bertrand Russell (1872–1970) British philosopher. *Mysticism and Logic*, Ch. 6

20 Man's 'progress' is but a gradual discovery that his questions have no meaning.

Antoine de Saint-Exupéry (1900–44) French novelist and aviator. *The Wisdom of the Sands*

21 Progress, far from consisting in change, depends on retentiveness. Those who cannot remember the past are condemned to repeat it.

George Santayana (1863–1952) US philosopher. *The Life of Reason*

22 To slacken the tempo . . . would mean falling behind. And those who fall behind get beaten . . . .

We are fifty or a hundred years behind the advanced countries. We must make good this distance in ten years. Either we do it, or they crush us.

Joseph Stalin (J. Dzhugashvili; 1879–1953) Soviet statesman.

23 In England we have come to rely upon a comfortable time lag of fifty years or a century intervening between the perception that something ought to be done and a serious attempt to do it.

H. G. Wells (1866–1946) British writer. *The Work, Wealth and Happiness of Mankind*

PROMISCUITY

See also sex

1 I see – she's the original good time that was had by all.

Bette Davis (Ruth Elizabeth Davis; 1908–) US film star. Referring to a starlet of the time. *The Filmgoer's Book of Quotes* (Leslie Halliwell)

2 Lady Capricorn, he understood, was still keeping open bed.

Aldous Huxley (1894–1964) British novelist. *Antic Hay*, Ch. 21

3 The woman's a whore, and there's an end on't.

Samuel Johnson (1709–84) British lexicographer. Referring to Lady Diana Beauclerk. *Life of Johnson* (J. Boswell), Vol. II

4 The whore, and the whoremonger, shall ye scourge with a hundred stripes.

Koran Ch. XXIV

5 You mustn't think I advocate perpetual sex. Far from it. Nothing nauseates me more than promiscuous sex in and out of season.

D. H. Lawrence (1885–1930) British novelist. Letter to Lady Ottoline Morrell, 20 Dec 1928

6 You were born with your legs apart. They'll send you to the grave in a Y-shaped coffin.

Joe Orton (1933–67) British dramatist. *What the Butler Saw*, I

7 You know, she speaks eighteen languages. And she can't say 'No' in any of them.

Dorothy Parker (1893–1967) US writer. Speaking of an acquaintance. Attrib.

8 Your idea of fidelity is not having more than one man in the bed at the same time . . . . You're a whore, baby, that's all, just a whore, and I don't take whores in taxis.

Frederick Raphael (1931–) British writer. *Darling* (film)

9 I have made love to ten thousand women.

Georges Simenon (1903–) Belgian novelist. Interview with *Die Tat*, 1977

10 I'm glad you like my Catherine. I like her too. She ruled thirty million people and had three thousand lovers. I do the best I can in two hours.

Mae West (1892–1980) US actress. After her performance in *Catherine the Great*. Speech from the stage

PROMISES

1 On my honour I promise that I will

do my best . . . to do my duty to God and the King . . . to help other people at all times . . . to obey the Scout Law.
Robert Baden-Powell (1857–1941) British soldier and founder of the Boy Scouts. The Scout's oath. *Scouting for Boys*

2 Better is it that thou shouldest not vow, than that thou shouldest vow and not pay.
Bible: Ecclesiastes 5:5

3 I do set my bow in the cloud, and it shall be for a token of a covenant between me and the earth.
Bible: Genesis 9:13

4 The rule is, jam tomorrow and jam yesterday – but never jam today.
Lewis Carroll (Charles Lutwidge Dodgson; 1832–98) British writer. *Through the Looking-Glass*, Ch. 5

5 If you feed people just with revolutionary slogans they will listen today, they will listen tomorrow, they will listen the day after tomorrow, but on the fourth day they will say 'To hell with you!'
Nikita Khrushchev (1894–1971) Soviet statesman. Attrib.

6 A promise made is a debt unpaid.
Robert William Service (1874–1958) Canadian poet. *The Cremation of Sam McGee*

7 Jam today, and men aren't at their most exciting: Jam tomorrow, and one often sees them at their noblest.
C. P. Snow (1905–80) British novelist. *The Two Cultures and the Scientific Revolution*, 4

8 Promises and pie-crust are made to be broken.
Jonathan Swift (1667–1745) Irish-born Anglican priest and writer. *Polite Conversation*, Dialogue 1

PROMOTION

See also patronage

1 Tired of knocking at Preferment's door.
Matthew Arnold (1822–88) British poet and critic. *The Scholar Gipsy*

2 He had said he had known many kicked down stairs, but he never knew any kicked up stairs before.
Lord Halifax (1633–95) English statesman. *Original Memoirs* (Burnet)

3 Every time I make an appointment, I make one ungrateful person and a hundred with a grievance.
Louis XIV (1638–1715) French king. *Siècle de Louis XIV* (Voltaire), Ch. 26

4 The Thane of Cawdor lives; why do you dress me
In borrow'd robes?
William Shakespeare (1564–1616) English dramatist. *Macbeth*, I:3

PROMPTNESS

1 Liberality lies less in giving liberally than in the timeliness of the gift.
Jean de La Bruyère (1645–96) French satirist. *Les Caractères*

2 Punctuality is the politeness of kings.
Louis XVIII (1755–1824) French king. Attrib.

3 Better never than late.
George Bernard Shaw (1856–1950) Irish dramatist and critic. Responding to an offer by a producer to present one of Shaw's plays, having earlier rejected it. *The Unimportance of Being Oscar* (Oscar Levant)

4 He gives twice who gives promptly.
Publilius Syrus (1st century BC) Roman dramatist. Attrib.

5 Punctuality is the virtue of the bored.
Evelyn Waugh (1903–66) British novelist. *Diaries*, 'Irregular Notes', 26 Mar 1962

PRONUNCIATION

See also class, language, speech, spelling

1 The 't' is silent as in Harlow.
Margot Asquith (1865–1945) The 2nd wife of Herbert Asquith. Referring to her name being mispronounced by Jean Harlow.

2 Everybody has a right to pronounce foreign names as he chooses.
Winston Churchill (1874–1965) British statesman. *The Observer*, 'Sayings of the Week', 5 Aug 1951

3 To correct an Englishman's pronunciation is to imply that he is not quite a gentleman.
George Bernard Shaw (1856–1950) Irish dramatist and critic. When chairman of the BBC's committee on standard pronunciation

4 Oh my God! Remember you're in Egypt. The *skay* is only seen in Kensington.
Herbert Beerbohm Tree (1853–1917) British actor and theater manager. To a leading lady. *Beerbohm Tree* (Hesketh Pearson)

5 They spell it Vinci and pronounce it Vinchy; foreigners always spell better than they pronounce.
Mark Twain (Samuel Langhorne Clemens; 1835–1910) US writer. *The Innocents Abroad*, Ch. 19

PROOF

1 One swallow does not make a summer.
Proverb

2 Fifty million Frenchmen can't be wrong.
Anonymous

3 What is now proved was once only imagined.
William Blake (1757–1827) British poet. *The Marriage of Heaven and Hell*, 'Proverbs of Hell'

4 If a man could pass through Paradise in a dream, and have a flower presented to him as a pledge that his soul had really been there, and if he found that flower in his hand when he awoke – Aye, and what then?
Samuel Taylor Coleridge (1772–1834) British poet. *Anima Poetae*

5 Of course, before we *know* he is a saint, there will have to be miracles.
Graham Greene (1904–) British novelist. *The Power and the Glory*, Pt. IV

6 If only I could get down to Sidcup! I've been waiting for the weather to break. He's got my papers, this man I left them with, it's got it all down there, I could prove everything.
Harold Pinter (1930–) British dramatist. *The Caretaker*, I

7 Some circumstantial evidence is very strong, as when you find a trout in the milk.
Henry David Thoreau (1817–62) US writer. *Journal*, 1850

PROPAGANDA

1 Propaganda is that branch of the art of lying which consists in nearly deceiving your friends without quite deceiving your enemies.
F. M. Cornford (1886–1960) British poet. *New Statesman*, 15 Sept 1978

2 The greater the lie, the greater the chance that it will be believed.
Adolf Hitler (1889–1945) German dictator. *Mein Kampf*

3 The propagandist's purpose is to make one set of people forget that certain other sets of people are human.
Aldous Huxley (1894–1964) British novelist and essayist. *The Olive Tree*

4 I give you bitter pills in sugar

coating. The pills are harmless, the poison is in the sugar.
Stanislaw Lec *Unkempt Thoughts*

5 Comrade Napoleon is always right.
George Orwell (Eric Blair; 1903–50) British novelist. *Animal Farm*

6 I wonder if we could contrive . . . some magnificent myth that would in itself carry conviction to our whole community.
Plato (429–347 BC) Greek philosopher. *Republic*, Bk. 5

7 Why is propaganda so much more successful when it stirs up hatred than when it tries to stir up friendly feeling?
Bertrand Russell (1872–1970) British philosopher. *The Conquest of Happiness*

PROPHECY

See also beginning, future

1 'I saw the new moon late yestreen
Wi' the auld moon in her arm;
And if we gang to sea master,
I fear we'll come to harm.'
Anonymous *Sir Patrick Spens*

2 If we do not now dare everything, the fulfillment of that prophecy, recreated from the Bible in song by a slave, is upon us: *God gave Noah the rainbow sign, No more water, the fire next time!*
James Baldwin (1924–87) US novelist. *The Fire Next Time*

3 And there arose not a prophet since in Israel like unto Moses, whom the Lord knew face to face.
Bible: Deuteronomy 34:10

4 A hopeful disposition is not the sole qualification to be a prophet.
Winston Churchill (1874–1965) British statesman. Speech, House of Commons, 10 Apr 1927

5 I am signing my death warrant.
Michael Collins (1890–1922) Irish nationalist. Said on signing the agreement with Great Britain, 1921, that established the Irish Free State. He was assassinated in an ambush some months later. *Peace by Ordeal* (Longford), Pt. 6, Ch. 1

6 Fasten your seatbelts. It's going to be a bumpy night.
Bette Davis (Ruth Elizabeth Davis; 1908–) US film star. *All About Eve*

7 I can see her in about ten years from now on the yacht of a Greek petrol millionaire.
Charles de Gaulle (1890–1970) French general and president. Referring to Jackie Kennedy after the assassination of President Kennedy. Attrib.

8 I will sit down now, but the time will come when you will hear me.
Benjamin Disraeli (1804–81) British statesman. Maiden Speech, House of Commons, 7 Dec 1837

9 The lamps are going out over all Europe; we shall not see them lit again in our lifetime.
Lord Grey (1862–1933) British statesman. Remark made on 3 Aug 1914, the eve of World War I.

10 You ain't heard nothin' yet, folks.
Al Jolson (Asa Yoelson; 1886–1950) US actor and singer. In the film *The Jazz Singer*, July 1927. *The Jazz Singer*

11 You can't make a soufflé rise twice.
Alice Roosevelt Longworth (1884–1980) US hostess. Referring to Dewey's nomination, in 1948. Attrib.

12 We have had our last chance. If we do not devise some greater and more equitable system, Armageddon will be at our door.
Douglas Macarthur (1880–1964) US General. Broadcast, 2 Sept 1945

13 *Après nous le déluge.*
After us the deluge.
Madame de Pompadour (1721–64) The mistress of Louis XV of France. After the Battle of Rossbach, 1757

14 As I look ahead, I am filled with foreboding. Like the Roman, I seem to see 'the River Tiber foaming with much blood'.
Enoch Powell (1912–) British politician. Talking about immigration. Speech in Birmingham, 20 Apr 1968

15 Beware the ides of March.
William Shakespeare (1564–1616) English dramatist. *Julius Caesar*, I:2

16 Be bloody, bold, and resolute; laugh to scorn
The power of man, for none of woman born
Shall harm Macbeth.
William Shakespeare *Macbeth*, IV:1

17 Macbeth shall never vanquish'd be until
Great Birnam wood to high Dunsinane hill
Shall come against him.
William Shakespeare *Macbeth*, IV:1

18 It will be years – and not in my time – before a woman will lead the party or become Prime Minister.
Margaret Thatcher (1925–) British politician and prime minister. Said when she was minister for health. Speech, 1974

19 Mr Turnbull had predicted evil consequences . . . and was now doing the best in his power to bring about the verification of his own prophecies.
Anthony Trollope (1815–82) British novelist. *Phineas Finn*, Ch. 25

20 I see wars, horrible wars, and the Tiber foaming with
much blood.
Virgil (Publius Vergilius Maro; 70–19 BC) Roman poet. Part of the Sibyl's prophecy to Aeneas, foretelling his difficulties in winning a home in Italy. *Aeneid*, Bk. VI

PROSE

See also books, criticism, fiction, literature, novels, poetry and prose, writing

1 Yet no one hears his own remarks as prose.
W. H. Auden (1907–73) British poet. *At a Party*

2 I could also have stepped into a style much higher than this in which I have here discoursed, and could have adorned all things more than here I have seemed to do, but I dare not. God did not play in convincing of me, the devil did not play in tempting of me neither did I play when I sunk into a bottomless pit, when the pangs of hell caught hold upon me; wherefore I may not play in my relating of them, but be plain and simple, and lay down the thing as it was.
John Bunyan (1628–88) Referring to literary style. *Grace Abounding to the Chief of Sinners*, Preface

3 Men will forgive a man anything except bad prose.
Winston Churchill (1874–1965) British statesman. Election speech, Manchester, 1906

4 . . . the pulpit was the cradle of English prose.
A. G. Little (1863–1945) British historian. *English Historical Review*, xlix (1934)

5 It has been said that good prose should resemble the conversation of a well-bred man.
W. Somerset Maugham (1874–1965) British novelist and doctor. *The Summing Up*

6 Good heavens! I have been talking

prose for over forty years without realizing it.

Molière (Jean Baptiste Poquelin; 1622–73) French dramatist. *Le Bourgeois Gentilhomme*, II:4

PROSPERITY

1 The American economy is not going to be able to prosper unless Americans regard as necessities what other people look on as luxuries.

Wendell Wilkie *One World*

PROTESTANTISM

See also Catholicism, Christianity, religion

1 The three great elements of modern civilization, Gunpowder, Printing, and the Protestant Religion.

Thomas Carlyle (1795–1881) Scottish historian and essayist. *Critical and Miscellaneous Essays*, 'The State of German Literature'

2 A single friar who goes counter to all Christianity for a thousand years must be wrong.

Charles V (1500–58) Holy Roman Emperor. Referring to Martin Luther. Remark, Diet of Worms, 19 Apr 1521

3 I shall never be a heretic, I may err in dispute; but I do not wish to decide anything finally; on the other hand, I am not bound by the opinions of men.

Martin Luther (1483–1546) German Protestant. Letter to the chaplain to the Elector of Saxony, 28 Aug 1518

4 If I had heard that as many devils would set on me in Worms as there are tiles on the roofs, I should none the less have ridden there.

Martin Luther Referring to the Diet of Worms. *Luthers Sammtliche Schriften*

5 Anyone who can be proved to be a seditious person is an outlaw before God and the emperor; and whoever is the first to put him to death does right and well.

Martin Luther Referring to the 'Peasants' War', an uprising (1524–25) of peasants in Germany partly inspired by Luther's teachings. *Against the Robbing and Murdering Hordes of Peasants* (Broadsheet, May 1525)

6 The chief contribution of Protestantism to human thought is its massive proof that God is a bore.

H. L. Mencken (1880–1956) US journalist. *Notebooks*, 'Minority Report'

7 'You're a Christian?' 'Church of England,' said Mr Polly. 'Mm,' said the employer, a little checked. 'For good all round business work, I should have preferred a Baptist.'

H. G. Wells (1866–1946) British writer. *The History of Mr Polly*, Pt. III, Ch. 1

8 Take heed of thinking. *The farther you go from the church of Rome, the nearer you are to God.*

Henry Wotton (1568–1639) English poet and diplomat. *Reliquiae Wottonianae* (Izaak Walton)

PROUST, Marcel

(1871–1922) French novelist. His masterpiece was a series of partly autobiographical novels, *À la recherche du temps perdu* (1913–27), which give a detailed portrait of the life of his time.

Quotations about Proust

1 Reading Proust is like bathing in someone else's dirty water.

Alexander Woollcott Attrib.

Quotations by Proust

2 The taste was that of the little crumb of madeleine which on Sunday mornings at Combray . . . , when I used to say good-day to her in her bedroom, my aunt Léonie used to give me, dipping it first in her own cup of real or of lime-flower tea.

À la recherche du temps perdu: Du côté de chez Swann

3 People often say that, by pointing out to a man the faults of his mistress, you succeed only in strengthening his attachment to her, because he does not believe you; yet how much more so if he does!

À la recherche du temps perdu: Du côté de chez Swann

4 The human face is indeed, like the face of the God of some Oriental theogony, a whole cluster of faces, crowded together but on different surfaces so that one does not see them all at once.

À la recherche du temps perdu: À l'ombre des jeunes filles en fleurs

5 There can be no peace of mind in love, since the advantage one has secured is never anything but a fresh starting-point for further desires.

À la recherche du temps perdu: À l'ombre des jeunes filles en fleurs

6 As soon as one is unhappy one becomes moral.

À la recherche du temps perdu: À l'ombre des jeunes filles en fleurs

7 A PUSHING LADY. What are your views on love?

MME LEROI. Love? I make it constantly but I never talk about it.

À la recherche du temps perdu: Le Côté de Guermantes

8 It has been said that the highest praise of God consists in the denial of Him by the atheist, who finds creation so perfect that he can dispense with a creator.

À la recherche du temps perdu: Le Côté de Guermantes

9 A doctor who doesn't say too many foolish things is a patient half-cured, just as a critic is a poet who has stopped writing verse and a policeman a burglar who has retired from practice.

À la recherche du temps perdu: Le Côté de Guermantes

10 Neurosis has an absolute genius for malingering. There is no illness which it cannot counterfeit perfectly . . . If it is capable of deceiving the doctor, how should it fail to deceive the patient?

À la recherche du temps perdu: Le Côté de Guermantes

11 As soon as he ceased to be mad he became merely stupid. There are maladies we must not seek to cure because they alone protect us from others that are more serious.

À la recherche du temps perdu: Le Côté de Guermantes

12 His hatred of snobs was a derivative of his snobbishness, but made the simpletons (in other words, everyone) believe that he was immune from snobbishness.

À la recherche du temps perdu: Le Côté de Guermantes

13 There is nothing like desire for preventing the thing one says from bearing any resemblance to what one has in mind.

À la recherche du temps perdu: Le Côté de Guermantes

14 Good-bye, I've barely said a word to you, it is always like that at parties, we never see the people, we never say the things we should like to say, but it is the same everywhere in this life. Let us hope

that when we are dead things will be better arranged.
À la recherche du temps perdu: Sodome et Gomorrhe

15 I have sometimes regretted living so close to Marie . . . because I may be very fond of her, but I am not quite so fond of her company.
À la recherche du temps perdu: Sodome et Gomorrhe

16 I have a horror of sunsets, they're so romantic, so operatic.
À la recherche du temps perdu: Sodome et Gomorrhe

17 It is seldom indeed that one parts on good terms, because if one were on good terms one would not part.
À la recherche du temps perdu: La Prisonnière

18 One of those telegrams of which M. de Guermantes had wittily fixed the formula: 'Cannot come, lie follows'.
À la recherche du temps perdu: Le Temps retrouvé

19 Happiness is beneficial for the body, but it is grief that develops the powers of the mind.
À la recherche du temps perdu: Le Temps retrouvé

20 Everything great in the world is done by neurotics; they alone founded our religions and created our masterpieces.
The Perpetual Pessimist (Sagittarius and George)

PROVERBS

A selection of the commonest proverbs and other sayings is given here. The proverbs are arranged in alphabetical order.

1 A bad penny always turns up.

2 A bad workman always blames his tools.

3 A bird in the hand is worth two in the bush.

4 Absence makes the heart grow fonder.

5 A cask of wine works more miracles than a church full of saints.
Italian proverb

6 A cat has nine lives.

7 A cat may look at a king.

8 Accidents will happen in the best regulated families.

9 A chain is no stronger than its weakest link.

10 A constant guest is never welcome.

11 Actions speak louder than words.

12 Adam's ale is the best brew.

13 A dimple in the chin, a devil within.

14 A drowning man will clutch at a straw.

15 A fool and his money are soon parted.

16 A fool at forty is a fool indeed.

17 A fool believes everything.

18 A friend in need is a friend indeed.

19 After a storm comes a calm.

20 After shaking hands with a Greek, count your fingers.

21 A good dog deserves a good bone.

22 A good drink makes the old young.

23 A good face is a letter of recommendation.

24 A good friend is my nearest relation.

25 A good scare is worth more than good advice.

26 A hedge between keeps friendship green.

27 A judge knows nothing unless it has been explained to him three times.

28 A lawyer never goes to law himself.

29 A lawyer's opinion is worth nothing unless paid for.

30 A liar is worse than a thief.

31 All are not saints that go to church.

32 All cats are grey in the dark.

33 All good things must come to an end.

34 All is fair in love and war.

35 All men are mortal.

36 All roads lead to Rome.

37 All's grist that comes to the mill.

38 All's well that ends well.

39 All that glitters is not gold.

40 All the world loves a lover.

41 All work and no play makes Jack a dull boy.

42 Although there exist many thousand subjects for elegant conversation, there are persons who cannot meet a cripple without talking about feet.
Chinese proverb

43 A man can die but once.

44 A man is as old as he feels, and a woman as old as she looks.

45 A man of straw is worth a woman of gold.

46 A meal without flesh is like feeding on grass.
Indian proverb

47 A miss is as good as a mile.

48 An apple a day keeps the doctor away.

49 An apple-pie without some cheese is like a kiss without a squeeze.

50 An atheist is one point beyond the devil.

51 An Englishman's home is his castle.

52 An Englishman's word is his bond.

53 An honest man's word is as good as his bond.

54 An hour in the morning is worth two in the evening.

55 A nod is as good as a wink to a blind horse.

56 Any port in a storm.

57 Any publicity is good publicity.

58 A penny saved is a penny earned.

59 A piece of churchyard fits everybody.

60 Appearances are deceptive.

61 A priest sees people at their best, a lawyer at their worst, but a doctor sees them as they really are.

62 A rainbow in the morning is the shepherd's warning; a rainbow at night is the shepherd's delight.

63 Ask a silly question and you'll get a silly answer.

64 Ask no questions and hear no lies.

65 A spur in the head is worth two in the heel.

66 As soon as man is born he begins to die.

67 A still tongue makes a wise head.

68 A stitch in time saves nine.

69 A tale never loses in the telling.

70 A trouble shared is a trouble halved.

71 A truly great man never puts away the simplicity of a child.
Chinese proverb

72 Attack is the best form of defence.

73 A watched pot never boils.

74 A woman's place is in the home.

75 A woman's work is never done.

76 A young physician fattens the churchyard.

77 Bad news travels fast.

78 Barking dogs seldom bite.

79 Beauty is in the eye of the beholder.

80 Beauty is only skin-deep.

81 Beauty is potent but money is omnipotent.

82 Beggars can't be choosers.

83 Believe nothing of what you hear, and only half of what you see.

84 Benefits make a man a slave.
Arabic proverb

85 Better a lie that heals than a truth that wounds.

86 Better an egg today than a hen tomorrow.

87 Better a thousand enemies outside the house than one inside.
Arabic proverb

88 Better be a fool than a knave.

89 Better be an old man's darling than a young man's slave.

90 Better be envied than pitied.

91 Better be safe than sorry.

92 Better late than never.

93 Birds of a feather flock together.

94 Blood is thicker than water.

95 Books and friends should be few but good.

96 Borrowed garments never fit well.

97 Bread is the staff of life.

98 Caesar's wife must be above suspicion.

99 Charity begins at home.

100 Christmas comes but once a year.

101 Civility costs nothing.

102 Cold hands, warm heart.

103 Constant dripping wears away the stone.

104 Curiosity killed the cat.

105 Cut your coat according to your cloth.

106 Dead men tell no tales.

107 Death defies the doctor.

108 Death is the great leveller.

109 Desperate cuts must have desperate cures.

110 Divide and rule.

111 Do as I say, not as I do.

112 Do as you would be done by.

113 Dog does not eat dog.

114 Doing is better than saying.

115 Don't count your chickens before they are hatched.

116 Don't cross the bridge till you get to it.

117 Don't cut off your nose to spite your face.

118 Don't meet troubles half-way.

119 Don't put all your eggs in one basket.

120 Don't spoil the ship for a ha'porth of tar.

121 Don't teach your grandmother to suck eggs.

122 Don't throw the baby out with the bathwater.

123 Don't wash your dirty linen in public.

124 Early to bed and early to rise, makes a man healthy, wealthy and wise.

125 Easier said than done.

126 East, west, home's best.

127 Easy come, easy go.

128 Eat to live and not live to eat.

129 Empty vessels make the greatest sound.

130 Even a worm will turn.

131 Every book must be chewed to get out its juice.
Chinese proverb

132 Every cloud has a silver lining.

133 Every dog has his day.

134 Every dog is allowed one bite.

135 Every family has a skeleton in the cupboard.

136 Every little helps.

137 Every man after his fashion.

138 Every man for himself, and the devil take the hindmost.

139 Every man is his own worst enemy.

140 Every man to his trade.

141 Every one is innocent until he is proved guilty.

142 Every one to his taste.

143 Every picture tells a story.

144 Everything comes to him who waits.

145 Experience is the best teacher.

146 Experience is the mother of wisdom.

147 Faith will move mountains.

148 Familiarity breeds contempt.

149 Fear of death is worse than death itself.

150 Fight fire with fire.

151 Finders keepers, losers seekers.

152 Fine feathers make fine birds.

153 Fine words butter no parsnips.

154 Fingers were made before forks, and hands before knives.

155 First come, first served.

156 First impressions are the most lasting.

157 First things first.

158 Fish and guests smell in three days.

159 Fools build houses, and wise men buy them.

160 Fools live poor to die rich.

161 Footprints on the sands of time are not made by sitting down.

162 Forbidden fruit is sweet.

163 Forewarned is forearmed.

164 Forgive and forget.

165 Fortune favours fools.

166 For want of a nail the shoe was lost; for want of a shoe the horse was lost; for want of a horse the rider was lost.

167 From clogs to clogs is only three generations.

168 From small beginnings come great things.

169 From the sublime to the ridiculous is only a step.

170 Garbage in, garbage out.

171 Genius is an infinite capacity for taking pains.

172 Give a dog a bad name and hang him.

173 Give a thief enough rope and he'll hang himself.

174 Give him an inch and he'll take a yard.

175 Give me a child for the first seven years, and you may do what you like with him afterwards.

176 God defend me from my friends; from my enemies I can defend myself.

177 God helps them that help themselves.

178 God is always on the side of the big battalions.

179 Good fences make good neighbours.

180 Go to bed with the lamb, and rise with the lark.

181 Great minds think alike.

182 Great oaks from little acorns grow.

183 Grey hairs are death's blossoms.

184 Half a loaf is better than no bread.

185 Handsome is as handsome does.

186 Haste makes waste.

187 Health is better than wealth.

188 He helps little that helps not himself.

189 He that fights and runs away, may live to fight another day.

190 He that has no children brings them up well.

191 He that has no wife, beats her oft.

192 He that is his own lawyer has a fool for a client.

193 He that knows little, often repeats it.

194 He that knows nothing, doubts nothing.

195 He that lives long suffers much.

196 He travels fastest who travels alone.

197 He was a bold man that first ate an oyster.

198 He who drinks a little too much drinks much too much.

199 He who hesitates is lost.

200 He who lives by the sword dies by the sword.

201 He who pays the piper calls the tune.

202 He who rides a tiger is afraid to dismount.

203 He who sups with the devil should have a long spoon.

204 History repeats itself.

205 Hoist your sail when the wind is fair.

206 Home is home, though it be never so homely.

207 Home is where the heart is.

208 Honesty is the best policy.

209 Hope for the best.

210 Hunger is the best sauce.

211 If a job's worth doing, it's worth doing well.

212 If anything can go wrong, it will.

213 If at first you don't succeed, try, try, try again.

214 If ifs and ans were pots and pans, there'd be no trade for tinkers.

215 If the mountain will not come to Mahomet, Mahomet must go to the mountain.

216 If wishes were horses, beggars would ride.

217 If you can't be good, be careful.

218 If you don't like the heat, get out of the kitchen.

219 If you play with fire you get burnt.

220 If you trust before you try, you may repent before you die.

221 If you want a thing well done, do it yourself.

222 Imitation is the sincerest form of flattery.

223 In for a penny, in for a pound.

224 In the country of the blind, the one-eyed man is king.

225 It is a long lane that has no turning.

226 It is better to be born lucky than rich.

227 It is easy to bear the misfortunes of others.

228 It is easy to be wise after the event.

229 It is no use crying over spilt milk.

230 It never rains but it pours.

231 It's an ill wind that blows nobody any good.

232 It's a small world.

233 It's too late to shut the stable door after the horse has bolted.

234 It takes all sorts to make a world.

235 It takes two to make a quarrel.

236 It takes two to tango.

237 It will all come right in the wash.

238 It will be all the same a hundred years.

239 Jack of all trades, master of none.

240 Keep something for a rainy day.

241 Keep your mouth shut and your eyes open.

242 Keep your weather-eye open.

243 Kill not the goose that lays the golden egg.

244 Knowledge is power.

245 Knowledge is the mother of all virtue; all vice proceeds from ignorance.

246 Know thyself.

247 Laugh and grow fat.

248 Laugh before breakfast, you'll cry before supper.

249 Laughter is the best medicine.

250 Learning is a treasure which accompanies its owner everywhere.
Chinese proverb

251 Least said soonest mended.

252 Leave well alone.

253 Lend only that which you can afford to lose.

254 Let bygones be bygones.

255 Let sleeping dogs lie.

256 Let the cobbler stick to his last.

257 Life begins at forty.

258 Life is just a bowl of cherries.

259 Life is not all beer and skittles.

260 Life is sweet.

261 Like breeds like.

262 Like father, like son.

263 Listeners never hear good of themselves.

264 Live and learn.

265 Long absent, soon forgotten.

266 Look after number one.

267 Look before you leap.

268 Look on the bright side.

269 Love conquers all.

270 Love is blind.

271 Love laughs at locksmiths.

272 Love makes the world go round.

273 Love me, love my dog.

274 Love will find a way.

275 Love your neighbour, yet pull not down your hedge.

276 Lucky at cards, unlucky in love.

277 Mackerel sky and mares' tails make lofty ships carry low sails.

278 Make hay while the sun shines.

279 Manners maketh man.

280 Man proposes, God disposes.

281 Many a mickle makes a muckle.

282 Many a true word is spoken in jest.

283 Many hands make light work.

284 Many irons in the fire, some must cool.

285 March comes in like a lion and goes out like a lamb.

286 March winds and April showers bring forth May flowers.

287 Marriages are made in heaven.

288 Marry in haste, and repent at leisure.

289 Marry in Lent, and you'll live to repent.

290 Marry in May, rue for aye.

291 Meet on the stairs and you won't meet in heaven.

292 Mind your own business.

293 Moderation in all things.

294 Monday's child is fair of face,
Tuesday's child is full of grace;
Wednesday's child is full of woe,
Thursday's child has far to go;
Friday's child is loving and giving,
Saturday's child works hard for
its living; and the child that's born
on the Sabbath day, is fair and
wise and good and gay.

295 More haste, less speed.

296 Music helps not the toothache.

297 Music is the food of love.

298 Necessity is the mother of invention.

299 Needs must when the devil drives.

300 Ne'er cast a clout till May be out.

301 Never do things by halves.

302 Never judge from appearances.

303 Never look a gift horse in the mouth.

304 Never put off till tomorrow what you can do today.

305 Never say die.

306 Never speak ill of the dead.

307 Never too late to learn.

308 Ninety per cent of inspiration is perspiration.

309 No bees, no honey; no work, no money.

310 No love like the first love.

311 No man is a hero to his valet.

312 No man is infallible.

313 No names, no pack-drill.

314 No news is good news.

315 No pleasure without pain.

316 Nothing is certain but death and taxes.

317 Nothing so bad but it might have been worse.

318 Nothing succeeds like success.

319 Nothing ventured, nothing gained.

320 No time like the present.

321 Old habits die hard.

322 Old sins cast long shadows.

323 Old soldiers never die, they simply fade away.

324 Once a parson always a parson.

325 One for sorrow, two for mirth;
three for a wedding, four for a
birth; five for silver, six for gold;
seven for a secret, not to be told;
eight for heaven, nine for hell;
and ten for the devil's own sel.
Referring to magpies or crows; there are numerous variants

326 One good turn deserves another.

327 One hour's sleep before midnight, is worth two after.

328 One joy scatters a hundred griefs.
Chinese proverb

329 One man's meat is another man's poison.

330 One swallow does not make a summer.

331 Opportunity seldom knocks twice.

332 Out of debt, out of danger.

333 Out of sight, out of mind.

334 Patience is a virtue.

335 Penny wise, pound foolish.

336 Pigs might fly, if they had wings.

337 Possession is nine points of the law.

338 Poverty is not a crime.

339 Practice makes perfect.

340 Practise what you preach.

341 Prevention is better than cure.

342 Promises are like pie-crust, made to be broken.

343 Punctuality is the politeness of princes.

344 Put an Irishman on the spit, and you can always get another Irishman to baste him.

345 Put off the evil hour as long as you can.

346 Rain before seven: fine before eleven.

347 Rain, rain, go away, come again another day.

348 Red sky at night, shepherd's delight; red sky in the morning, shepherd's warning.

349 Revenge is a dish that tastes better cold.

350 Revenge is sweet.

351 Rome was not built in a day.

352 Sailors have a port in every storm.

353 Salt water and absence wash away love.

354 Save your breath to cool your porridge.

355 Saying is one thing, and doing another.

356 Scratch my back and I'll scratch yours.

357 See a pin and pick it up, all the day you'll have good luck; see a pin and let it lie, you'll want a pin before you die.

358 Seeing is believing.

359 See Naples and die.

360 Self-praise is no recommendation.

361 Send a fool to the market and a fool he will return again.

362 Silence is golden.

363 Slow but sure wins the race.

364 Small is beautiful.

365 Soon learnt, soon forgotten.

366 Spare the rod and spoil the child.

367 Speak when you are spoken to.

368 Speech is silver, silence is golden.

369 Sticks and stones may break my bones, but words will never hurt me.

370 Still waters run deep.

371 Strike while the iron is hot.

372 St. Swithin's Day, if thou dost rain, for forty days it will remain; St. Swithin's Day, if thou be fair, for forty days 'twill rain no more.

373 Take a hair of the dog that bit you.

374 Take care of the pence, and the pounds will take care of themselves.

375 Take things as they come.

376 Talk of the devil, and he is bound to appear.

377 Tell the truth and shame the devil.

378 The best of friends must part.

379 The best things come in small parcels.

380 The best things in life are free.

381 The better the day, the better the deed.

382 The cuckoo comes in April, and stays the month of May; sings a song at midsummer, and then goes away.

383 The darkest hour is just before the dawn.

384 The devil finds work for idle hands to do.

385 The devil is not so black as he is painted.

386 The devil looks after his own.

387 The early bird catches the worm.

388 The end justifies the means.

389 The exception proves the rule.

390 The eye is bigger than the belly.

391 The eyes are the window of the soul.

392 The family that prays together stays together.

393 The first day a guest, the second day a guest, the third day a calamity.
Indian proverb

394 The first step is the hardest.

395 The first wife is matrimony, the second company, the third heresy.

396 The good die young.

397 The guest who outstays his fellow-guests loses his overcoat.
Chinese proverb

398 The hand that rocks the cradle rules the world.

399 The last straw breaks the camel's back.

400 The law does not concern itself about trifles.

401 The more the merrier; the fewer the better fare.

402 The nearer the bone, the sweeter the flesh.

403 The north wind does blow, and we shall have snow.

404 The old man has his death before his eyes; the young man behind his back.

405 There are more old drunkards than old doctors.

406 There are only twenty-four hours in the day.

407 There is a time and place for everything.

408 There is honour among thieves.

409 There is more than one way to skin a cat.

410 There is no accounting for tastes.

411 There is safety in numbers.

412 There's a black sheep in every flock.

413 There's always room at the top.

414 There's many a good tune played on an old fiddle.

415 There's many a slip 'twixt the cup and the lip.

416 There's no fool like an old fool.

417 There's no place like home.

418 There's no smoke without fire.

419 There's nowt so queer as folk.

420 There's one law for the rich, and another for the poor.

421 There's only one pretty child in the world, and every mother has it.

422 There will be sleeping enough in the grave.

423 The road to hell is paved with good intentions.

424 The shoemaker's son always goes barefoot.

425 The streets of London are paved with gold.

426 The style is the man.

427 The way to a man's heart is through his stomach.

428 The weakest goes to the wall.

429 Things are not always what they seem.

430 Third time lucky.

431 Throw dirt enough, and some will stick.

432 Throw out a sprat to catch a mackerel.

433 Time and tide wait for no man.

434 Time is a great healer.

435 Time will tell.

436 To deceive oneself is very easy.

437 To err is human.

438 Tomorrow is another day.

439 Tomorrow never comes.

440 Too many cooks spoil the broth.

441 Travel broadens the mind.

442 True love never grows old.

443 Truth fears no trial.

444 Truth is stranger than fiction.

445 Truth will out.

446 Two heads are better than one.

447 Two wrongs do not make a right.

448 Union is strength.

449 United we stand, divided we fall.

450 Vice is often clothed in virtue's habit.

451 Walls have ears.

452 Waste not, want not.

453 We must learn to walk before we can run.

454 What can't be cured, must be endured.

455 What must be, must be.

456 What's done cannot be undone.

457 What you don't know can't hurt you.

458 What you lose on the swings you gain on the roundabouts.

459 When one door shuts, another opens.

460 When poverty comes in at the door, love flies out of the window.

461 When the cat's away, the mice will play.

462 When the wine is in, the wit is out.

463 Where there's a will there's a way.

464 While there's life there's hope.

465 Whom the gods love dies young.

466 Who spits against the wind, it falls in his face.

467 Why buy a cow when milk is so cheap?

468 Why keep a dog and bark yourself?

469 You can have too much of a good thing.

470 You can lead a horse to the water, but you can't make him drink.

471 You cannot run with the hare and hunt with the hounds.

472 You can't get a quart into a pint pot.

473 You can't get blood out of a stone.

474 You can't make an omelette without breaking eggs.

475 You can't make bricks without straw.

476 You can't please everyone.

477 You can't take it with you when you go.

478 You can't teach an old dog new tricks.

479 You can't tell a book by its cover.

PROVIDENCE

See destiny

PROVOCATION

1 My wife hath something in her gizzard, that only waits an opportunity of being provoked to bring up.
Samuel Pepys (1633–1703) English diarist.
Diary, 17 June 1668

2 Ask you what provocation I have had?
The strong antipathy of good to bad.
Alexander Pope (1688–1744) British poet.
Epilogue to the Satires, Dialogue II

PRUDENCE

See also caution, wisdom

1 A bird in the hand is worth two in the bush.
Proverb

2 Forewarned is forearmed.
Proverb

3 For want of a nail the shoe was lost; for want of a shoe the horse was lost; for want of a horse the rider was lost.
Proverb

4 Prevention is better than cure.
Proverb

5 One does not insult the river god while crossing the river.
Anonymous Chinese proverb.

6 It is always good
When a man has two irons in the fire.
Francis Beaumont (1584–1616) English dramatist. *The Faithful Friends*, I:2

7 Put your trust in God, my boys, and keep your powder dry.
Valentine Blacker (1778–1823) British soldier. *Oliver Cromwell's Advice*

8 I'd much rather have that fellow inside my tent pissing out, than outside my tent pissing in.
Lyndon B. Johnson (1908–73) US statesman. When asked why he retained J. Edgar Hoover at the FBI. *Guardian Weekly*, 18 Dec 1971

9 One should oblige everyone to the extent of one's ability. One often needs someone smaller than oneself.
Jean de La Fontaine (1621–95) French poet. *Fables*, II, 'Le Lion et le Rat'

10 Any girl who was a lady would not

even think of having such a good time that she did not remember to hang on to her jewelry.
Anita Loos (1891–1981) US novelist. *Gentlemen Prefer Blondes,* Ch. 4

11 Be nice to people on your way up because you'll meet 'em on your way down.
Wilson Mizner (1876–1933) US writer and wit. Also attributed to Jimmy Durante. *A Dictionary of Catch Phrases* (Eric Partridge)

PRUDERY

See also censorship, pornography, puritanism

1 Would you allow your wife or your servant to read this book?
Mervyn Griffith-Jones (1909–78) British lawyer. As counsel for the prosecution in the *Lady Chatterley's Lover* trial

2 We have long passed the Victorian Era when asterisks were followed after a certain interval by a baby.
W. Somerset Maugham (1874–1965) British novelist. *The Constant Wife*

3 Age will bring all things, and everyone knows, Madame, that twenty is no age to be a prude.
Molière (Jean Baptiste Poquelin; 1622–73) French dramatist. *Le Misanthrope,* III:4

4 An orgy looks particularly alluring seen through the mists of righteous indignation.
Malcolm Muggeridge (1903–) British writer. *The Most of Malcolm Muggeridge,* 'Dolce Vita in a Cold Climate'

5 Obscenity is what happens to shock some elderly and ignorant magistrate.
Bertrand Russell (1872–1970) British philosopher. *Look* magazine

PSYCHIATRY

See also madness, neurosis, psychology

1 The new definition of psychiatry is the care of the id by the odd.
Anonymous

2 The psychiatrist is the obstetrician of the mind.
Anonymous

3 Just because you're paranoid doesn't mean you're not being followed.
Anonymous

4 I have myself spent nine years in a lunatic asylum and have never suffered from the obsession of wanting to kill myself; but I know that each conversation with a psychiatrist in the morning, made me want to hang myself because I knew I could not strangle him.
Antonin Artaud (1896–1948) French theater producer, actor, and theorist.

5 To us he is no more a person
Now but a climate of opinion.
W. H. Auden (1907–73) British poet. *In Memory of Sigmund Freud*

6 Of course, Behaviourism 'works'. So does torture. Give me a no-nonsense, down-to-earth behaviourist, a few drugs, and simple electrical appliances, and in six months I will have him reciting the Athanasian creed in public.
W. H. Auden *A Certain World,* 'Behaviourism'

8 Psychiatrist: A man who asks you a lot of expensive questions your wife asks you for nothing.
Sam Bardell (1915–)

9 No man is a hero to his wife's psychiatrist.
Dr. Eric Berne *Bartlett's Unfamiliar Quotations* (Leonard Louis Levinson)

10 Psychiatry's chief contribution to philosophy is the discovery that the toilet is the seat of the soul.
Alexander Chase (1926–) US journalist. *Perspectives*

11 I can think of no better step to signalize the inauguration of the National Health service than that a person who so obviously needs psychiatric attention should be among the first of its patients.
Winston Churchill (1874–1965) British statesman. Referring to Aneurin Bevan. Speech, July 1948

12 A mental stain can neither be blotted out by the passage of time nor washed away by any waters.
Cicero (106 BC–43 BC) Roman orator and statesman. *De Legibus,* Bk. II

13 In a disordered mind, as in a disordered body, soundness of health is impossible.
Cicero *Tusculanarum Disputationum,* Bk. III

14 The trouble with Freud is that he never played the Glasgow Empire Saturday night.
Ken Dodd (1931–) British comedian. TV interview, 1965

15 The psychic development of the individual is a short repetition of the course of development of the race.
Sigmund Freud (1856–1939) Austrian psychoanalyst. *Leonardo da Vinci*

16 Sometimes a cigar is just a cigar.
Sigmund Freud When asked by one of his students whether there was any symbolism in the large cigars that Freud smoked. Attrib.

17 Anybody who goes to see a psychiatrist ought to have his head examined.
Samuel Goldwyn (Samuel Goldfish; 1882–1974) Polish-born US film producer. Attrib.

18 Freud is the father of psychoanalysis. It has no mother.
Germaine Greer (1939–) Australian-born British writer and feminist. *The Female Eunuch*

19 If a patient is poor he is committed to a public hospital as 'psychotic'; if he can afford the luxury of a private sanitarium, he is put there with the diagnosis of 'neurasthenia'; if he is wealthy enough to be isolated in his own home under constant watch of nurses and physicians he is simply an indisposed 'eccentric'.
Pierre Marie Félix Janet (1859–1947) French psychologist and neurologist. *La Force et la faiblesse psychologiques*

20 The relation between psychiatrists and other kinds of lunatics is more or less the relation of a convex folly to a concave one.
Karl Kraus *Bartlett's Unfamiliar Quotations* (Leonard Louis Levinson)

21 Schizophrenic behaviour is a special strategy that a person invents in order to live in an unlivable situation.
R. D. Laing (1927–) British psychiatrist. *The Politics of Experience*

22 Schizophrenia cannot be understood without understanding despair.
R. D. Laing *The Divided Self,* Ch. 2

23 The mystic sees the ineffable, and the psychopathologist the unspeakable.
W. Somerset Maugham (1874–1965) British novelist. *The Moon and Sixpence,* Ch. 1

24 If the nineteenth century was the age of the editorial chair, ours is the century of the psychiatrist's couch.
Marshall McLuhan (1911–81) Canadian sociologist. *Understanding Media,* Introduction

25 They have a financial interest in being wrong; the more children

they can disturb, the larger their adult clientele.
Geoffrey Robinson *Hedingham Harvest*

26 The care of the human mind is the most noble branch of medicine.
Aloysius Sieffert (fl. 1858) *Medical and Surgical Practitioner's Memorandum*

27 One should only see a psychiatrist out of boredom.
Muriel Spark (1918–) British novelist.

28 A psychiatrist is a man who goes to the Folies-Bergère and looks at the audience.
Mervyn Stockwood (1913–) British churchman. *The Observer*, 'Sayings of the Week', 15 Oct 1961

29 Psychiatrists classify a person as neurotic if he suffers from his problems in living, and a psychotic if he makes others suffer.
Thomas Szasz (1920–) US psychiatrist. *The Second Sin 'Psychiatry'*

30 In the past, men created witches: now they create mental patients.
Thomas Szasz

31 We must remember that every 'mental' symptom is a veiled cry of anguish. Against what? Against oppression, or what the patient experiences as oppression. The oppressed speak a million tongues ....
Thomas Szasz

32 A neurotic is the man who builds a castle in the air. A psychotic is the man who lives in it. And a psychiatrist is the man who collects the rent.
Lord Robert Webb-Johnstone (1879–) *Collected Papers*

33 The ideas of Freud were popularized by people who only imperfectly understood them, who were incapable of the great effort required to grasp them in their relationship to larger truths, and who therefore assigned to them a prominence out of all proportion to their true importance.
Alfred North Whitehead (1861–1947) British philosopher and mathematician. *Dialogues*, Dialogue XXVIII (June 3, 1943)

34 He was meddling too much in my private life.
Tennessee Williams (1911–83) US dramatist. Explaining why he had given up visiting his psychoanalyst. Attrib.

35 He is always called a nerve specialist because it sounds better, but everyone knows he's a sort of janitor in a looney bin.
P. G. Wodehouse (1881–1975) British humorous novelist. *The Inimitable Jeeves*

PSYCHOANALYSIS

1 Who looks after the psychoanalyst's wife while the psychoanalyst is away being psychoanalysed.
Scarritt Adams *Bartlett's Unfamiliar Quotations* (Leonard Louis Levinson)

2 A psychoanalyst is one who pretends he doesn't know everything.
Anonymous

3 In today's highly complex society it takes years of training in rationalization, accommodation and compromise to qualify for the good jobs with the really big payoffs you need to retain a first-rate psychiatrist in today's world.
Russell Baker (1925–) US journalist. *The New York Times*, 21 Mar 1968

4 Psychoanalysts are not occupied with the minds of their patients; they do not believe in the mind but in a cerebral intestine.
Bernard Berenson (1865–1959) US art historian. *Conversations with Berenson* (Umberto Morra)

5 Self-contemplation is infallibly the symptom of disease.
Thomas Carlyle (1795–1881) Scottish historian and essayist. *Characteristics*

6 Psychoanalysis is confession without absolution.
G. K. Chesterton (1874–1936) British writer.

7 Psychoanalysis is spending 40 dollars an hour to squeal on your mother.
Mike Connolly *Bartlett's Unfamiliar Quotations* (Leonard Louis Levinson)

8 Or look at it this way. Psychoanalysis is a permanent fad.
Peter de Vries (1906–) US writer. *Forever Panting*, opening words

9 He formulated his ideas in extravagant and exclusive forms, which have since got quietly modified – I doubt whether psychoanalysts would now maintain that dreams of overcoats, staircases, ships, rooms, tables, children, landscapes, machinery, airships, and hats commonly represent the genitals.
Rosemary Dinnage Referring to Sigmund Freud. *Observer*, 20 July 1980

10 The poets and philosophers before me have discovered the unconscious; I have discovered the scientific method with which the unconscious can be studied.
Sigmund Freud (1856–1939) Austrian psychoanalyst. Letter

11 No doubt fate would find it easier than I do to relieve you of your illness. But you will be able to convince yourself that much will be gained if we succeed in transforming your hysterical misery into common unhappiness.
Sigmund Freud

12 The examined life has always been pretty well confined to a privileged class.
Edgar Z. Friedenberg (1921–) US sociologist. *The Vanishing Adolescent*, 'The Impact of the School'

13 The man who once cursed his fate, now, curses himself – and pays his psychoanalyst.
John W. Gardner (1912–) US public official. *No Easy Victories*, 1

14 Fortunately, analysis is not the only way to resolve inner conflicts. Life itself remains a very effective therapist.
Karen Horney (1885–)

15 Psychoanalysis cannot be considered a method of education if by education we mean the topiary art of clipping a tree into a beautiful artificial shape. But those who have a higher conception of education will prize most the method of cultivating a tree so that it fulfils to perfection its own natural conditions of growth.
C. G. Jung (1875–1961) Swiss psychologist.

16 Freud and his three slaves, Inhibition, Complex and Libido.
Sophie Kerr (1880–1965) *The Saturday Evening Post*, 9 Apr 1932

17 Psychoanalysis is the disease it purports to cure.
Karl Kraus (1874–1936)

18 Considered in its entirety, psychoanalysis won't do. It is an end product, moreover, like a dinosaur or a zeppelin; no better theory can ever by erected on its ruins, which will remain for ever one of the saddest and strangest of all landmarks in the history of twentieth century thought.
Peter Medawar (1915–87) British immunologist. *The Hope of Progress*

19 It is sometimes best to slip over thoughts and not go to the bottom of them.
Marie de Sévigné (1626–96) French letter-writer. Letter to her daughter

20 Psychoanalysts believe that the only 'normal' people are those who cause no trouble either to themselves or anyone else.
A. J. P. Taylor (1906–) British historian. *The Trouble Makers*, 1957

21 Like all analysts Randolph is interested only in himself. In fact, I have often thought that the analyst should pay the patient for allowing himself to be used as a captive looking-glass.
Gore Vidal (1925–) US novelist. *Myra Breckinridge*, Ch. 37

22 Daughters go into analysis hating their fathers, and come out hating their mothers. They never come out hating themselves.
Laurie Jo Wojcik

PSYCHOLOGY

See also mind, psychiatry

1 An animal psychologist is a man who pulls habits out of rats.
Anonymous

2 Behavioural psychology is the science of pulling habits out of rats.
Douglas Busch *Peter's Quotations* (Laurence J. Peter)

3 It seems a pity that psychology should have destroyed all our knowledge of human nature.
G. K. Chesterton (1874–1936) British essayist, novelist, and poet. *Observer*, 9 Dec 1934

4 Every day, in every way, I am getting better and better.
Emile Coué (1857–1926) French psychologist and pharmacist. Formula for a cure by autosuggestion used at his clinic in Nancy. *My Method*, Ch. 3

5 Popular psychology is a mass of cant, of slush and of superstition worthy of the most flourishing days of the medicine man.
John Dewey (1859–1952) US philosopher. *The Public and Its Problems*, Ch. 5

6 Psychology has a long past, but only a short history.
Hermann Ebbinghaus (1850–1909) German psychologist. *Summary of Psychology*

7 What progress we are making. In the Middle Ages they would have burned me. Now they are content with burning my books.
Sigmund Freud (1856–1939) Austrian psychoanalyst. Referring to the public burning of his books in Berlin. Letter to Ernest Jones, 1933

8 The separation of psychology from the premises of biology is purely artificial, because the human psyche lives in indissoluble union with the body.
C. G. Jung (1875–1961) Swiss psychoanalyst. *Factors Determining Human Behaviour*, 'Psychological Factors Determining Human Behaviour'

9 It is indeed high time for the clergyman and the psychotherapist to join forces.
Carl Jung *Modern Man in Search of a Soul*, Ch. 11

10 Psychology is as unnecessary as directions for using poison.
Karl Kraus (1874–1936)

11 Psychology which explains everything
explains nothing,
and we are still in doubt.
Marianne Moore (1887–1972) US poet. *Collected Poems*, 'Marriage'

12 Idleness is the parent of all psychology.
Friedrich Nietzsche (1844–1900) German philosopher. *Twilight of the Idols*, 'Maxims and Missiles'

13 I never saw a person's id
I hope I never see one.
But I can tell you if I did
I'd clamp an ego as a lid
Upon the id to keep it hid,
Which is, I gather, what God did
When he first saw a free one.
Helen Harris Perlman (1905–) *National Association of Social Workers News*, 9:2, 1964

14 I don't think the profession of historian fits a man for psychological analysis. In our work we have to deal only with simple feelings to which we give generic names such as Ambition and Interest.
Jean-Paul Sartre (1905–80) French writer. *Nausea*

15 I maintain that today many an inventor, many a diplomat, many a financier is a sounder philosopher than all those who practise the dull craft of experimental psychology.
Oswald Spengler (1880–1936) German philosopher. *Decline of the West*

16 A large part of the popularity and persuasiveness of psychology comes from its being a sublimated spiritualism: a secular, ostensibly scientific way of affirming the primacy of 'spirit' over matter.
Susan Sontag (1933–) US novelist and essayist. *Illness as Metaphor*, Ch. 7

17 There is no psychology; there is only biography and autobiography.
Thomas Szasz (1920–) US psychiatrist. *The Second Sin*, 'Psychology'

18 Man, by the very fact of being man, by possessing consciousness, is, in comparison with the ass or the crab, a diseased animal. Consciousness is a disease.
Miguel de Unamuno y Jugo (1864–1937) Spanish writer and philosopher. *The Tragic Sense of Life*, 1

19 The object of psychology is to give us a totally different idea of the things we know best.
Paul Valéry (1871–1945) French writer. *Tel quel*

PUBLIC

See also class, majority

1 *Vox populi, vox dei.*
The voice of the people is the voice of God.
Alcuin (c. 735–804) English theologian. Letter to Charlemagne

2 But that vast portion, lastly, of the working-class which, raw and half-developed, has long lain half-hidden amidst its poverty and squalor, and is now issuing from its hiding-place to assert an Englishman's heaven-born privilege of doing as he likes, and is beginning to perplex us by marching where it likes, meeting where it likes, bawling what it likes, breaking what it likes – to this vast residuum we may with great propriety give the name of Populace.
Matthew Arnold (1822–88) British poet and critic. *Culture and Anarchy*, Ch. 3

3 Our researchers into Public Opinion are content
That he held the proper opinions for the time of year;
When there was peace, he was for peace; when there was war, he went.
W. H. Auden (1907–73) British poet. *The Unknown Citizen*

4 You cannot make a man by standing a sheep on its hind legs. But by standing a flock of sheep in that

position you can make a crowd of men.
Max Beerbohm (1872–1956) British writer. *Zuleika Dobson*, Ch. 9

5 The great Unwashed.
Henry Peter Brougham (1778–1868) Scottish lawyer and politician. Attrib.

6 The people are the masters.
Edmund Burke (1729–97) British politician. *Speech on the Economical Reform* (House of Commons, 11 Feb 1780)

7 The public buys its opinions as it buys its meat, or takes in its milk, on the principle that it is cheaper to do this than to keep a cow. So it is, but the milk is more likely to be watered.
Samuel Butler (1835–1902) British writer. *Notebooks*

8 The Public is an old woman. Let her maunder and mumble.
Thomas Carlyle (1795–1881) Scottish historian and essayist. *Journal*, 1835

9 The people would be just as noisy if they were going to see me hanged.
Oliver Cromwell (1599–1658) English soldier and statesman. Referring to a cheering crowd.

10 If by the people you understand the multitude, the *hoi polloi*, 'tis no matter what they think; they are sometimes in the right, sometimes in the wrong; their judgement is a mere lottery.
John Dryden (1631–1700) British poet and dramatist. *Essay of Dramatic Poesy*

11 Nor is the Peoples Judgment always true:
The Most may err as grosly as the Few.
John Dryden *Absalom and Achitophel*, I

12 Ill fares the land, to hast'ning ills a prey,
Where wealth accumulates, and men decay;
Princes and lords may flourish, or may fade;
A breath can make them, as a breath has made;
But a bold peasantry, their country's pride,
When once destroy'd, can never be supplied.
Oliver Goldsmith (1728–74) Irish-born British writer. *The Deserted Village*

13 There is not a more mean, stupid, dastardly, pitiful, selfish, spiteful, envious, ungrateful animal than the public. It is the greatest of cowards, for it is afraid of itself.
William Hazlitt (1778–1830) British essayist. *On Living to Oneself*

14 Only constant repetition will finally succeed in imprinting an idea on the memory of the crowd.
Adolf Hitler (1889–1945) German dictator. *Mein Kampf*, Ch. 6

15 The people long eagerly for just two things – bread and circuses.
Juvenal (Decimus Junius Juvenalis; 60–130 AD) Roman satirist. *Satires*, X

16 They are only ten.
Lord Northcliffe (1865–1922) Irish-born British newspaper proprietor. Rumoured to have been a notice to remind his staff of his opinion of the mental age of the general public. Attrib.

17 The multitude is always in the wrong.
Earl of Roscommon (1633–85) Irish-born English poet. *Essay on Translated Verse*

18 Once the people begin to reason, all is lost.
Voltaire (François-Marie Arouet; 1694–1778) French writer. Letter to Damilaville, 1 Apr 1766

19 The century on which we are entering – the century which will come out of this war – can be and must be the century of the common man.
Henry Wallace (1888–1965) US economist and politician. Speech, 'The Price of Free World Victory', 8 May 1942

20 Our supreme governors, the mob.
Horace Walpole (1717–97) British writer. Letter to Sir Horace Mann, 7 Sept 1743

21 I have no concern for the common man except that he should not be so common.
Angus Wilson (1913–) British novelist. *No Laughing Matter*

PUBLIC HOUSES

See also alcohol, drunkenness

1 A tavern chair is the throne of human felicity.
Samuel Johnson (1709–84) British lexicographer. *Johnsonian Miscellanies* (ed. G. B. Hill), Vol. II

2 There is nothing which has yet been contrived by man, by which so much happiness is produced as by a good tavern or inn.
Samuel Johnson *Life of Johnson* (J. Boswell), Vol. II

3 Souls of poets dead and gone,
What Elysium have ye known,
Happy field or mossy cavern,
Choicer than the Mermaid Tavern?
Have ye tippled drink more fine
Than mine host's Canary wine?
John Keats (1795–1821) British poet. *Lines on the Mermaid Tavern*

4 The hands of the clock have stayed still at half past eleven for fifty years. It is always opening time in the Sailors Arms.
Dylan Thomas (1914–53) Welsh poet. *Under Milk Wood*

5 Come, Come, Come and have a drink with me
Down at the old 'Bull and Bush'.
Harry Tilzer (Albert von Tilzer; 1878–1956) British songwriter. *The Old Bull and Bush*

PUBLISHING

See also books, editors

1 Publication is the male equivalent of childbirth.
Richard Acland (1906–) British politician and writer. *The Observer*, 'Sayings of the Week', 19 May 1974

2 I'll publish, right or wrong:
Fools are my theme, let satire be my song.
Lord Byron (1788–1824) British poet. *English Bards and Scotch Reviewers*

3 Now Barabbas was a publisher.
Thomas Campbell (1777–1844) British poet. Attrib.

4 Gentlemen, you must not mistake me. I admit that he is the sworn foe of our nation, and, if you will, of the whole human race. But, gentlemen, we must be just to our enemy. We must not forget that he once shot a bookseller.
Thomas Campbell Excusing himself in proposing a toast to Napoleon at a literary dinner. *The Life and Letters of Lord Macaulay* (G. O. Trevelyan)

5 As repressed sadists are supposed to become policemen or butchers so those with irrational fear of life become publishers.
Cyril Connolly (1903–74) British journalist. *Enemies of Promise*, Ch. 3

6 Let it be kept till the ninth year, the manuscript put away at home: you may destroy whatever you haven't published; once out, what you've said can't be stopped.
Horace (Quintus Horatius Flaccus; 65–8 BC) Roman poet. *Ars Poetica*

7 My own motto is publish and be sued.
Richard Ingrams (1937–) British editor. Referring to his editorship of *Private Eye*. BBC radio broadcast, 4 May 1977

8 The booksellers are generous liberal-minded men.
Samuel Johnson (1709–84) British lexicographer. *Life of Johnson* (J. Boswell), Vol. I

9 Curse the blasted, jelly-boned swines, the slimy, the belly-wriggling invertebrates, the miserable sodding rutters, the flaming sods, the snivelling, dribbling, dithering, palsied, pulse-less lot that make up England today. They've got white of egg in their veins and their spunk is that watery it's a marvel they can breed.
D. H. Lawrence (1885–1930) British novelist. Letter to Edward Garnet, 3 July 1912, on Heinemann's rejection of *Sons and Lovers*

10 Publish and be damned!
Duke of Wellington (1769–1852) British general and statesman. On being offered the chance to avoid mention in the memoirs of Harriette Wilson by giving her money. Attrib.

11 Being published by the O.U.P. is rather like being married to a duchess; the honour is almost greater than the pleasure.
G. M. Young Letter to Rupert Hart-Davis, 20 Nov 1956

PUNCTUALITY

See promptness

PUNISHMENT

See also education, execution, imprisonment, retribution

1 Spare the rod and spoil the child.
Proverb

2 Wherefore putting away lying, speak every man truth with his neighbour: for we are members one of another.
Be ye angry, and sin not: let not the sun go down upon your wrath:
Neither give place to the devil.
Let him that stole steal no more: but rather let him labour, working with his hands the thing which is good, that he may have to give to him that needeth.
Bible: Ephesians 4:25–28

3 When thou tillest the ground, it shall not henceforth yield unto thee her strength; a fugitive and a vagabond shalt thou be in the earth.
And Cain said unto the Lord, My punishment is greater than I can bear.
Bible: Genesis 4:12–13

4 And surely your blood of your lives will I require; at the hand of every beast will I require it, and at the hand of man; at the hand of every man's brother will I require the life of man.
Whoso sheddeth man's blood, by man shall his blood be shed: for in the image of God made he man.
Bible: Genesis 9:5–6

5 Then the Lord rained upon Sodom and upon Gomorrah brimstone and fire from the Lord out of heaven.
Bible: Genesis 19:24

6 There is no peace, saith the Lord, unto the wicked.
Bible: Isaiah 48:22

7 He that spareth his rod hateth his son: but he that loveth him chasteneth him betimes.
Bible: Proverbs 13:24

8 Love is a boy, by poets styl'd,
Then spare the rod, and spoil the child.
Samuel Butler (1612–80) English satirist. *Hudibras*, Pt. II

9 Never under the most despotic of infidel governments did I behold such squalid wretchedness as I have seen since my return in the very heart of a Christian country.
Lord Byron (1788–1824) British poet. Speaking against the death penalty for machine wrecking. Speech, House of Lords, 27 Feb 1812

10 Quoth he, 'The man hath penance done,
And penance more will do.'
Samuel Taylor Coleridge (1772–1834) British poet. *The Rime of the Ancient Mariner*, V

11 As some day it may happen that a victim must be found
I've got a little list – I've got a little list
Of society offenders who might well be underground,
And who never would be missed – who never would be missed!
W. S. Gilbert (1836–1911) British dramatist. *The Mikado*, I

12 My object all sublime
I shall achieve in time –
To let the punishment fit the crime –
The punishment fit the crime.
W. S. Gilbert *The Mikado*, II

13 The billiard sharp whom any one catches,
His doom's extremely hard –
He's made to dwell –
In a dungeon cell
On a spot that's always barred.
And there he plays extravagant matches
In fitless finger-stalls
On a cloth untrue
With a twisted cue
And elliptical billiard balls.
W. S. Gilbert *The Mikado*, II

14 Something lingering, with boiling oil in it, I fancy.
W. S. Gilbert *The Mikado*, II

15 The door flew open, in he ran,
The great, long, red-legged scissor-man.
Heinrich Hoffman (1809–74) German writer. *Struwwelpeter*, 'The Little Suck-a-Thumb'

16 The only thing I really mind about going to prison is the thought of Lord Longford coming to visit me.
Richard Ingrams (1937–) British editor. Attrib.

17 Corporal punishment is as humiliating for him who gives it as for him who receives it; it is ineffective besides. Neither shame nor physical pain have any other effect than a hardening one . . .
Ellen Key (Karolina Sofia Key; 1849–1926) Swedish writer. *The Century of the Child*, Ch. 8

18 The refined punishments of the spiritual mode are usually much more indecent and dangerous than a good smack.
D. H. Lawrence (1885–1930) British novelist. *Fantasia of the Unconscious*, Ch. 4

19 Men are not hanged for stealing horses, but that horses may not be stolen.
George Saville (1633–95) English statesman. *Political, Moral and Miscellaneous Thoughts and Reflections*

20 And where the offence is let the great axe fall.
William Shakespeare (1564–1616) English dramatist. *Hamlet*, IV:5

21 Condemn the fault and not the actor of it?
William Shakespeare *Measure for Measure*, II:2

22 Nay, take my life and all; pardon not that:

You take my house when you do take the prop
That doth sustain my house; you take my life
When you do take the means whereby I live.

William Shakespeare *The Merchant of Venice,* IV:1

23 Eating the bitter bread of banishment.

William Shakespeare *Richard II,* III:1

24 Every child should have an occasional pat on the back, as long as it is applied low enough, and hard enough.

J. Fulton Sheen (1895–1979) US Roman Catholic archbishop. *On Children* (Frank Muir)

25 Whipping and abuse are like laudanum: You have to double the dose as the sensibilities decline.

Harriet Beecher Stowe (1811–96) US novelist. *Uncle Tom's Cabin,* Ch. 20

26 He must have known me had he seen me as he was wont to see me, for he was in the habit of flogging me constantly. Perhaps he did not recognize me by my face.

Anthony Trollope (1815–82) British novelist. *Autobiography,* Ch. 1

27 I'm all for bringing back the birch, but only between consenting adults.

Gore Vidal (1925–) US novelist. Said when asked by David Frost in a TV interview for his views about corporal punishment.

28 We spared the rod and wound up with the beat generation.

L. J. Wolf *Bartlett's Unfamiliar Quotations* (Leonard Louis Levinson)

29 The use of the birch is not to be deplored. All the best men in the country have been beaten, archbishops, bishops and even deans. Without sensible correction they could not be the men they are today.

Very Rev. Michael S. Carey (1913–) British churchman. Attrib.

PUNS

See also humor

1 When I am dead, I hope it may be said:
'His sins were scarlet, but his books were read.'

Hilaire Belloc (1870–1953) French-born British poet. *Epigrams,* 'On His Books'

2 VISITOR. Ah, Bottomley, sewing?
BOTTOMLEY. No, reaping.

Horatio William Bottomley (1860–1933) British newspaper editor. When found sewing mail bags. *Horatio Bottomley* (Julian Symons)

3 Like Webster's Dictionary
We're Morocco bound.

Johnny Burke (1908–64) US songwriter. Song, 'Road to Morocco' from the film *The Road to Morocco*

4 A man who could make so vile a pun would not scruple to pick a pocket.

John Dennis (1657–1734) British critic and dramatist. *The Gentleman's Magazine,* 1781

5 'In our case,' says the Frenchman, addressing the Englishman, 'we have 'goût' for the taste; in your case, you have 'gout' for the result!'

George Herman Ellwanger (fl. 1897) *Meditations on Gout,* 'The Theory'

6 Any stigma will do to beat a dogma.

Philip Guedalla (1889–1944) British writer. Attrib.

7 His death, which happen'd in his berth,
At forty-odd befell:
They went and told the sexton, and
The sexton toll'd the bell.

Thomas Hood (1799–1845) British poet. *Faithless Sally Brown*

8 The love that loves a scarlet coat
Should be more uniform.

Thomas Hood *Faithless Nelly Gray*

9 Ben Battle was a soldier bold,
And used to war's alarms:
But a cannon-ball took off his legs,
So he laid down his arms!

Thomas Hood *Faithless Nelly Gray*

10 For here I leave my second leg,
And the Forty-second Foot!

Thomas Hood *Faithless Nelly Gray*

11 For that old enemy the gout
Had taken him in toe!

Thomas Hood *Lieutenant Luff*

12 It is a pistol let off at the ear; not a feather to tickle the intellect.

Charles Lamb (1775–1834) British essayist. Referring to the nature of a pun. *Last Essays of Elia,* 'Popular Fallacies'

13 Thou canst not serve both cod and salmon.

Ada Beddington Leverson (1862–1933) British writer. Reply when offered a choice of fish at dinner. *The Times,* 7 Nov 1970

14 You know it's hard to hear what a bearded man is saying. He can't speak above a whisker.

Herman J. Mankiewicz (1897–1953) US journalist and screenwriter. *Wit's End* (R. E. Drennan)

15 What's a thousand dollars? Mere chicken feed. A poultry matter.

Groucho Marx (Julius Marx; 1895–1977) US comedian. *The Cocoanuts*

16 Contraceptives should be used on all conceivable occasions.

Spike Milligan (1918–) British comedian and humorous writer.

17 It has been said that a bride's attitude towards her betrothed can be summed up in three words: Aisle. Altar. Hymn.

Frank Muir (1920–) British writer and broadcaster. *Upon My Word!* (Frank Muir and Dennis Norden), 'A Jug of Wine'

18 A thing of duty is a boy for ever.

Flann O'Brien (Brian O'Nolan; 1911–66) Irish novelist and journalist. About policemen always seeming to be young-looking. *The Listener,* 24 Feb 1977

19 You can lead a whore to culture but you can't make her think.

Dorothy Parker (1893–1967) US writer. Speech to American Horticultural Society

20 You can't teach an old dogma new tricks.

Dorothy Parker *Wit's End* (R. E. Drennan)

21 I tried to resist his overtures, but he plied me with symphonies, quartettes, chamber music and cantatas.

S. J. Perelman (1904–79) US humorous writer. *Crazy Like a Fox,* 'The Love Decoy'

22 Mother always told me my day was coming, but I never realized that I'd end up being the shortest knight of the year.

Gordon Richards (1904–86) British champion jockey. Referring to his diminutive size, on learning of his knighthood. Attrib.

23 Private Means is dead,
God rest his soul,
Officers and fellow-rankers said.

Stevie Smith (Florence Margaret Smith; 1902–71) British poet. *Private Means is Dead*

24 That's right. 'Taint yours, and 'taint mine.

Mark Twain (Samuel Langhorne Clemens; 1835–1910) US writer. Agreeing with a friend's comment that the money of a particular rich industrialist was 'tainted'. Attrib.

25 To me Adler will always be Jung.

Max Wall (1908–) British comedian. Telegram to Larry Adler on his 60th birthday

PURITANISM

See also prudery

1 A puritan's a person who pours righteous indignation into the wrong things.
G. K. Chesterton (1874–1936) British writer. Attrib.

2 To the Puritan all things are impure, as somebody says.
D. H. Lawrence (1885–1930) British novelist. *Etruscan Places*, 'Cerveteri'

3 The Puritan hated bear-baiting, not because it gave pain to the bear, but because it gave pleasure to the spectators.
Lord Macaulay (1800–59) British historian. *History of England*, Vol. I, Ch. 2

4 Persecution produced its natural effect on them. It found them a sect; it made them a faction.
Lord Macaulay Referring to the early Puritans. *History of England*

5 Puritanism – The haunting fear that someone, somewhere, may be happy.
H. L. Mencken (1880–1956) US journalist. *A Book of Burlesques*

PURITY

1 Caesar's wife must be above suspicion.
Proverb

2 I'm as pure as the driven slush.
Tallulah Bankhead (1903–68) US actress. *The Observer*, 'Sayings of the Week', 24 Feb 1957

3 *Romance on the High Seas* was Doris Day's first picture; that was before she became a virgin.
Oscar Levant (1906–72) US pianist and actor. *Memoirs of an Amnesiac*

4 Lawn as white as driven snow.
William Shakespeare (1564–1616) English dramatist. *The Winter's Tale*, IV:3

5 A simple maiden in her flower
Is worth a hundred coats-of-arms.
Alfred, Lord Tennyson (1809–92) British poet. *Lady Clara Vere de Vere*, II

6 It is one of the superstitions of the human mind to have imagined that virginity could be a virtue.
Voltaire (François-Marie Arouet; 1694–1778) French writer. *Notebooks*

7 Age cannot wither her, nor custom stale her infinite virginity.
Daniel Webster (1782–1852) US statesman. Paraphrasing a line from Shakespeare's *Antony and Cleopatra* on hearing of Andrew Jackson's steadfast maintenance that his friend Peggy Eaton did not deserve her scandalous reputation. *Presidential Anecdotes* (P. Boller)

8 I used to be Snow White . . . but I drifted.
Mae West (1892–1980) US actress. *The Wit and Wisdom of Mae West* (ed. J. Weintraub)

PURPOSE

See also futility, motive

1 Everything's got a moral, if only you can find it.
Lewis Carroll (Charles Lutwidge Dodgson; 1832–98) British writer. *Alice's Adventures in Wonderland*, Ch. 9

2 What is the use of a new-born child?
Benjamin Franklin (1706–90) US scientist and statesman. Response when asked the same question of a new invention. *Life and Times of Benjamin Franklin* (J. Parton), Pt. IV

3 A useless life is an early death.
Goethe (1749–1832) German poet and dramatist. *Iphegenie*, I:2

4 A mission to explain.
Peter Jay (1937–) British journalist and broadcaster. Explaining his philosophy for a new breakfast-television company. Said on many occasions

5 Fortunately, in her kindness and patience, Nature has never put the fatal question as to the meaning of their lives into the mouths of most people. And where no one asks, no one needs to answer.
Carl Gustav Jung (1875–1961) Swiss psychoanalyst. *The Development of Personality*

6 I go among the fields and catch a glimpse of a stoat or a fieldmouse peeping out of the withered grass – the creature hath a purpose and its eyes are bright with it. I go amongst the buildings of a city and I see a man hurrying along – to what? the Creature has a purpose and his eyes are bright with it.
John Keats (1795–1821) British poet. Letter, 1819

7 Riddle of destiny, who can show
What thy short visit meant, or know
What thy errand here below?
Charles Lamb (1775–1834) British essayist. *On an Infant Dying as soon as Born*

8 The purpose of population is not ultimately peopling earth. It is to fill heaven.
Graham Leonard (1921–) British churchman (Bishop of London). Said during a debate on the Church and the Bomb. Speech, General Synod of the Church of England, 10 Feb 1983

9 If people want a sense of purpose they should get it from their archbishop. They should certainly not get it from their politicians.
Harold Macmillan (1894–1986) British politician and prime minister. *The Life of Politics* (H. Fairlie)

10 Yes there is a meaning; at least for me, there is one thing that matters – to set a chime of words tinkling in the minds of a few fastidious people.
Logan Pearsall Smith (1865–1946) US writer. Attrib.

11 It should not merely be useful and ornamental; it should preach a high moral lesson.
Lytton Strachey (1880–1932) British writer. Referring to Prince Albert's plans for the Great Exhibition. *Queen Victoria*, Ch. 4

Q

QUOTATIONS

1 It is a good thing for an uneducated man to read books of quotations.
Winston Churchill (1874–1965) British statesman. *My Early Life*, Ch. 9

2 Don't half-quote me to reinforce your own prejudices.
Brian Clark (1932–) British playwright. *Kipling*

3 We prefer to believe that the absence of inverted commas guarantees the originality of a thought, whereas it may be merely that the utterer has forgotten its source.
Clifton Fadiman (1904–) US writer. *Any Number Can Play*

4 When a thing has been said and said well, have no scruple. Take it and copy it.
Anatole France (Jacques Anatole François Thibault; 1844–1924) French writer. Copied from *The Routledge Dictionary of Quotations* (Robert Andrews)

5 Classical quotation is the *parole* of literary men all over the world.
Samuel Johnson (1709–84) British lexicographer. *Life of Johnson* (J. Boswell), Vol. IV

6 Every quotation contributes something to the stability or enlargement of the language.
Samuel Johnson *Dictionary of the English Language*

7 In England only uneducated people show off their knowledge; nobody quotes Latin or Greek authors in the course of conversation, unless he has never read them.
George Mikes (1912–87) Hungarian-born British writer. *How to be an Alien*

8 To be amused at what you read – that is the great spring of happy quotation
C. E. Montague (1867–1928) British editor and writer. *A Writer's Notes on his Trade*

9 Mr Blunden is no more able to resist a quotation than some people are to refuse a drink.
George Orwell (Eric Blair; 1903–50) British novelist. Reviewing a book by Edmund Blunden. *Manchester Evening News*, 20 Apr 1944

10 If with the literate I am
Impelled to try an epigram
I never seek to take the credit
We all assume that Oscar said it.
Dorothy Parker (1893–1967) US writer. *Oscar Wilde*

11 I might repeat to myself . . . a list of quotations from minds profound – if I can remember any of the damn things.
Dorothy Parker *The Little Hours*

12 A book that furnishes no quotations is, *me judice*, no book – it is a plaything.
Thomas Love Peacock (1785–1866) British novelist. *Crotchet Castle*, Ch. 9

13 A widely-read man never quotes accurately . . . Misquotation is the pride and privilege of the learned.
Hesketh Pearson (1887–1964) British biographer. *Common Misquotations*

14 Misquotations are the only quotations that are never misquoted.
Hesketh Pearson *Common Misquotations*

15 It is gentlemanly to get one's quotations very slightly wrong. In that way one unprigs oneself and allows the company to correct one.
Lord Ribblesdale (1854–1925) British aristocrat. *The Light of Common Day* (Lady D. Cooper)

16 To say that anything was a quotation was an excellent method, in Eleanor's eyes, for withdrawing it from discussion.
Saki (Hector Hugh Munro; 1870–1916) British writer. *The Jesting of Arlington Stringham*

17 The devil can cite Scripture for his purpose.
William Shakespeare (1564–1616) English dramatist. *The Merchant of Venice*, I:3

18 It's better to be quotable than to be honest.
Tom Stoppard (1937–) Czech-born British dramatist. *The Guardian*

19 In the dying world I come from quotation is a national vice. It used to be the classics, now it's lyric verse.
Evelyn Waugh (1903–66) British novelist. *The Loved One*

20 The nicest thing about quotes is that they give us a nodding acquaintance with the originator which is often socially impressive.
Kenneth Williams (1926–88) British comic actor. *Acid Drops*

R

RABBITS

See also animals

1 The rabbit has a charming face;
Its private life is a disgrace.
Anonymous *The Rabbit*

2 I shall tell you a tale of four little rabbits whose names were Flopsy, Mopsy, Cottontail and Peter.
Beatrix Potter (1866–1943) British children's writer. *The Tale of Peter Rabbit*

RABELAIS, François

(1483–1553) French humanist and satirist. He is best known for his *Pantagruel* (1532) and *Gargantua* (1534), which are renowned for their bawdiness.

Quotations about Rabelais

1 Rabelais is the wondrous mask of ancient comedy . . . henceforth a human living face, remaining enormous and coming among us to laugh at us and with us.
Victor Hugo (1802–85) French writer. Attrib.

Quotations by Rabelais

2 I drink for the thirst to come.
Gargantua, Bk. I, Ch. 5

3 Appetite comes with eating.
Gargantua, Bk. I, Ch. 5

4 In their rules there was only one clause: Do what you will.
Referring to the fictional Abbey of Thélème. *Gargantua*, Bk. I, Ch. 57

5 Man never found the deities so kindly
As to assure him that he'd live tomorrow.
Pantagruel, Bk. III, Ch. 2

6 Not everyone is a debtor who wishes to be; not everyone who wishes makes creditors.
Pantagruel, Bk. III, Ch. 3

7 Nature abhors a vacuum.
Attrib.

8 I owe much; I have nothing; the rest I leave to the poor.
Last words. Attrib.

9 Ring down the curtain, the farce is over.
Last words. Attrib.

10 I am going in search of a great perhaps.
Last words. Attrib.

RACE

See also equality, freedom, human rights, Jews, oppression, prejudice, racism, slavery

1 There was a young woman called Starkie,
Who had an affair with a darky.
The result of her sins
Was quadruplets, not twins –
One black, and one white, and two khaki.
Anonymous

2 Black is beautiful.
Anonymous US civil rights slogan

3 It is a great shock at the age of

five or six to find that in a world of Gary Coopers you are the Indian.

James Baldwin (1924–87) US writer. Speech, Cambridge Union, 17 Feb 1965

4 The future is . . . black.

James Baldwin *The Observer,* 'Sayings of the Week', 25 Aug 1963

5 My mother bore me in the southern wild.
And I am black, but O! my soul is white;
White as an angel is the English child,
But I am black, as if bereav'd of light.

William Blake (1757–1827) British poet. *Songs of Innocence,* 'The Little Black Boy'

6 I suffer from an incurable disease – colour blindness.

Joost de Blank (1908–68) Dutch-born British churchman. Attrib.

7 Say It Loud, 'I'm Black and I'm Proud.'

James Brown (1934–) US singer. Song title

8 I'm a colored, one-eyed Jew.

Sammy Davis Jnr (1925–) Black US singer. When asked what his handicap was during a game of golf. Attrib.

9 The so-called white races are really pinko-gray.

E. M. Forster (1879–1970) British novelist. *A Passage to India,* Ch. 7

10 When the white man came we had the land and they had the Bibles; now they have the land and we have the Bibles.

Dan George (1899–1982) Canadian Indian chief. Attrib.

11 I want to be the white man's brother, not his brother-in-law.

Martin Luther King (1929–68) US Black civil-rights leader. *New York Journal-American,* 10 Sept 1962

12 Take up the White Man's burden –
And reap his old reward:
The blame of those ye better,
The hate of those ye guard.

Rudyard Kipling (1865–1936) Indian-born British writer. *The White Man's Burden*

13 So 'ere's to you, Fuzzy-Wuzzy, at your 'ome in the Soudan;
You're a pore benighted 'eathen but a first-class fightin' man;
An' 'ere's to you, Fuzzy-Wuzzy, with your 'ayrick 'ead of 'air –
You big black boundin' beggar – for you broke a British square!

Rudyard Kipling *Fuzzy-Wuzzy*

14 When old settlers say 'One has to understand the country', what they mean is, 'You have to get used to our ideas about the native.' They are saying, in effect, 'Learn our ideas, or otherwise get out; we don't want you.'

Doris Lessing (1919–) British novelist. Referring specifically to South Africa. *The Grass is Singing,* Ch. 1

15 When a white man in Africa by accident looks into the eyes of a native and sees the human being (which it is his chief preoccupation to avoid), his sense of guilt, which he denies, fumes up in resentment and he brings down the whip.

Doris Lessing *The Grass is Singing,* Ch. 8

16 It's just like when you've got some coffee that's too black, which means it's too strong. What do you do? You integrate it with cream, you make it weak . . . It used to wake you up, now it puts you to sleep.

Malcolm X (1925–65) US Black leader. Referring to Black Power and the Civil Rights movement. *Malcolm X Speaks,* Ch. 14

17 He's really awfully fond of colored people. Well, he says himself, he wouldn't have white servants.

Dorothy Parker (1893–1967) US writer. *Arrangements in Black and White*

18 As I look ahead, I am filled with foreboding. Like the Roman, I seem to see 'the River Tiber foaming with much blood'.

Enoch Powell (1912–) British politician. Talking about immigration. Speech in Birmingham, 20 Apr 1968

19 He liked to patronise coloured people and treated them as equals because he was quite sure they were not.

Bertrand Russell (1872–1970) British philosopher. *The Autobiography of Bertrand Russell*

20 Never forget that two blacks do not make a white.

George Bernard Shaw (1856–1950) Irish dramatist and critic. *The Adventures of the Black Girl in her Search for God*

21 I don't believe in black majority rule ever in Rhodesia . . . not in a thousand years.

Ian Smith (1919–) Rhodesian (Zimbabwean) politician. Speech, Mar 1976

22 There are two kinds of blood, the blood that flows in the veins and the blood that flows out of them.

Julian Tuwim (1894–1954) Polish writer and poet. *We, the Polish Jews*

RACISM

See also equality, freedom, human rights, Jews, oppression, prejudice, race, slavery

1 To like an individual because he's black is just as insulting as to dislike him because he isn't white.

e. e. cummings (1894–1962) US poet. Attrib.

2 All those who are not racially pure are mere chaff.

Adolf Hitler (1889–1945) German dictator. *Mein Kampf,* Ch. 2

3 Sanctions are now the only feasible, non-violent way of ending apartheid. The other road to change is covered with blood.

Neil Kinnock (1942–) British politician. Speech, July 1988

4 A coloured man can tell, in five seconds dead, whether a white man likes him or not. If the white man *says* he does, he is instantly – and usually quite rightly – mistrusted.

Colin MacInnes (1914–76) British novelist. *England, Half English,* 'A Short Guide for Jumbles'

5 One of the things that makes a Negro unpleasant to white folk is the fact that he suffers from their injustice. He is thus a standing rebuke to them.

H. L. Mencken (1880–1956) US journalist. *Notebooks,* 'Minority Report'

6 We don't want apartheid liberalized. We want it dismantled. You can't improve something that is intrinsically evil.

Desmond Tutu (1931–) South African clergyman. *The Observer,* 'Sayings of the Week', 10 Mar 1985

7 It seems that the British Government sees black people as expendable.

Desmond Tutu Speech, June 1986

READING

See also books, criticism, fiction, literacy, literature, novels, writing

1 The middle brows like John Henry O'Hara because his books remind them of the lives they imagine themselves to be leading.

John W. Aldridge (1922–) Writer. *Time to Murder and Create*

2 We welcome sleepers here. A sleeping reader is less of a menace to the books than a waking one.

Anonymous Librarian at Cambridge University. *The Times*

3 Reading maketh a full man; conference a ready man; and writing an exact man.
Francis Bacon (1561–1626) English philosopher. *Essays*, 'Of Studies'

4 He has only half learned the art of reading who has not added to it the even more refined accomplishments of skipping and skimming.
Arthur Balfour (1848–1930) British statesman; Conservative prime minister (1902–05). *Mr. Balfour* (E. T. Raymond)

5 I read, much of the night, and go south in the winter.
T. S. Eliot (1888–1965) US-born British poet and dramatist. *The Waste Land*, 'The Burial of the Dead'

6 A lonesome man on a rainy day who does not know how to read.
Benjamin Franklin (1706–90) US scientist and statesman. On being asked what condition of man he considered the most pitiable. *Wit, Wisdom, and Foibles of the Great* (C. Shriner)

7 As writers become more numerous, it is natural for readers to become more indolent.
Oliver Goldsmith (1728–74) Irish-born British writer. *The Bee*, 'Upon Unfortunate Merit'

8 Reading is sometimes an ingenious device for avoiding thought.
Arthur Helps (1813–75) British historian. *Friends in Council*

9 ELPHINSTON. What, have you not read it through? . . .
JOHNSON. No, Sir, do *you* read books *through*?
Samuel Johnson (1709–84) British lexicographer. *Life of Johnson* (J. Boswell), Vol. II

10 A man ought to read just as inclination leads him; for what he reads as a task will do him little good.
Samuel Johnson *Life of Johnson* (J. Boswell), Vol. I

11 I love to lose myself in other men's minds. When I am not walking, I am reading; I cannot sit and think. Books think for me.
Charles Lamb (1775–1834) British essayist. *Last Essays of Elia*, 'Detached Thoughts on Books and Reading'

12 I'm re-reading it with a slow deliberate carelessness.
T. E. Lawrence (1888–1935) British soldier and writer. Letter to Edward Marsh, 18 Apr 1929

13 To read too many books is harmful.
Mao Tse-Tung (1893–1976) Chinese communist leader. *The New Yorker*, 7 Mar 1977

14 I have only read one book in my life and that is *White Fang*. It's so frightfully good I've never bothered to read another.
Nancy Mitford (1904–73) British writer. *The Pursuit Of Love*

15 There are two motives for reading a book: one, that you enjoy it, the other that you can boast about it.
Bertrand Russell (1872–1970) British philosopher. *The Conquest of Happiness*

16 People say that life is the thing, but I prefer reading.
Logan Pearsall Smith (1865–1946) US writer. *Afterthoughts*, 'Myself'

17 Reading is to the mind what exercise is to the body.
Richard Steele (1672–1729) Dublin-born British essayist. *The Tatler*, 147

18 Education . . . has produced a vast population able to read but unable to distinguish what is worth reading.
George Macaulay Trevelyan (1876–1962) British historian. *English Social History*, Ch. 18

19 I have led a life of business so long that I have lost my taste for reading, and now – what shall I do?
Horace Walpole (1717–97) British writer. *Thraliana* (K. Balderston)

20 Lady Peabury was in the morning room reading a novel; early training gave a guilty spice to this recreation, for she had been brought up to believe that to read a novel before luncheon was one of the gravest sins it was possible for a gentlewoman to commit.
Evelyn Waugh (1903–66) British novelist. *Work Suspended*, 'An Englishman's Home'

21 As in the sexual experience, there are never more than two persons present in the act of reading – the writer who is the impregnator, and the reader who is the respondent.
Elwyn Brooks White (1899–1985) US journalist and humorist. *The Second Tree from the Corner*

REAGAN, Ronald

(1911–) US Republican president (1981–89). He entered politics as governor of California (1966–74) after a career as a film actor.

Quotations about Reagan

1 That youthful sparkle in his eyes is caused by his contact lenses, which he keeps highly polished.
Sheilah Graham *The Times*, 22 Aug 1981

2 As the age of television progresses the Reagans will be the rule, not the exception. To be perfect for television is all a President has to be these days.
Gore Vidal (1925–) US novelist. Attrib.

3 A triumph of the embalmer's art.
Gore Vidal Attrib.

4 Ask him the time, and he'll tell you how the watch was made.
Jane Wyman First wife of Reagan. Attrib.

Quotations by Reagan

5 Please assure me that you are all Republicans!
Addressing the surgeons on being wheeled into the operating theater for an emergency operation after an assassination attempt. *Presidential Anecdotes* (P. Boller)

6 No one can kill Americans and brag about it. No one.
The Observer, 'Sayings of the Week', 27 Apr 1986

7 You know, by the time you reach my age, you've made plenty of mistakes if you've lived your life properly
The Observer, 'Sayings of the Week', 8 Mar 1987

8 They say hard work never hurt anybody, but I figure why take the chance.
Attrib.

REALISM

1 Mr Lely, I desire you would use all your skill to paint my picture truly like me, and not flatter me at all; but remark all these roughnesses, pimples, warts, and everything as you see me, otherwise I will never pay a farthing for it.
Oliver Cromwell (1599–1658) English soldier and statesman. The origin of the expression 'warts and all'. *Anecdotes of Painting* (Horace Walpole), Ch. 12

2 We must rediscover the distinction between hope and expectation.
Ivan Illich (1926–) Austrian sociologist. *Deschooling Society*, Ch. 7

3 If someone tells you he is going to make 'a realistic decision', you immediately understand that he has resolved to do something bad.
Mary McCarthy (1912–) US novelist. *On the Contrary*

4 Better by far

For Johnny-the-bright-star,
To keep your head
And see his children fed.

John Sleigh Pudney (1909–77) British poet and writer. *For Johnny*

REALITY

1 For I see now that I am asleep that I dream when I am awake.

Pedro Calderón de la Barca (1600–81) Spanish dramatist. *La Vida es Sueño,* II

2 He who confronts the paradoxical exposes himself to reality.

Friedrich Dürrenmatt (1921–) Swiss writer. *The Physicists*

3 Human kind
Cannot bear very much reality.

T. S. Eliot (1888–1965) US-born British poet and dramatist. *Four Quartets,* 'Burnt Norton'

4 Dear friend, theory is all grey,
And the golden tree of life is green.

Goethe (1749–1832) German poet and dramatist. *Faust,* Pt. I

5 The supreme reality of our time is . . . the vulnerability of this planet.

John Fitzgerald Kennedy (1917–63) US statesman. Speech, Dublin, 28 June 1963

6 I fancy, for myself, that they are rather out of touch with reality; by reality I mean shops like Selfridges, and motor buses, and the *Daily Express.*

T. E. Lawrence (1888–1935) British soldier and writer. Referring to expatriate authors living in Paris, such as James Joyce. Letter to W. Hurley, 1 Apr 1929

7 If this were play'd upon a stage now, I could condemn it as an improbable fiction.

William Shakespeare (1564–1616) English dramatist. *Twelfth Night,* III:4

REASON

See also motive

1 Some who had received a liberal education at the Colleges of Unreason, and taken the highest degrees in hypothetics, which are their principal study.

Samuel Butler (1835–1902) British writer. *Erewhon,* Ch. 9

2 Reason is itself a matter of faith. It is an act of faith to assert that our thoughts have any relation to reality at all.

G. K. Chesterton (1874–1936) British writer. *Orthodoxy,* Ch. 3

3 Fools give you reasons, wise men never try.

Oscar Hammerstein II (1895–1960) US lyricist. *South Pacific,* 'Some Enchanted Evening'

4 Come now, let us reason together.

Lyndon B. Johnson (1908–73) US Democratic president. Attrib., often used

5 My dear friend, clear your *mind* of cant . . . You may *talk* in this manner; it is a mode of talking in Society: but don't *think* foolishly.

Samuel Johnson (1709–84) British lexicographer. *Life of Johnson* (J. Boswell), Vol. IV

6 A man who does not lose his reason over certain things has none to lose.

Gotthold Ephraim Lessing (1729–81) German dramatist. *Emilia Galotti,* IV:7

7 There is occasions and causes why and wherefore in all things.

William Shakespeare (1564–1616) English dramatist. *Henry V,* V:1

REBELLION

See also revolution

1 In this king's time there was nothing but disturbance and wickedness and robbery, for forthwith the powerful men who were traitors rose against him

Anonymous Referring to the reign of Stephen, 1135–54. *Anglo-Saxon Chronicle*

2 The defiance of established authority, religious and secular, social and political, as a world-wide phenomenon may well one day be accounted the outstanding event of the last decade.

Hannah Arendt (1906–75) German-born US philosopher and historian. *Crises of the Republic,* 'Civil Disobedience'

3 Son of man, thou dwellest in the midst of a rebellious house, which have eyes to see, and see not; they have ears to hear, and hear not: for they are a rebellious house.

Bible: Ezekiel 12:2

4 What is a rebel? A man who says no.

Albert Camus (1913–60) French existentialist writer. *The Rebel*

5 No one can go on being a rebel too long without turning into an autocrat.

Lawrence Durrell (1912–) British novelist. *Balthazar,* II

6 The whole of the Welsh nation in these parts are concerned in this rebellion.

John Fairfield Receiver of Brecon. Referring to the rebellion of Owen Glendower. Letter to Henry IV

7 When the People contend for their Liberty, they seldom get anything by their Victory but new masters.

Lord Halifax (1633–95) English statesman. *Political, Moral, and Miscellaneous Thoughts and Reflections*

8 This is a standard of rebellion.

James II (1633–1701) King of England. Referring to a petition from seven bishops against his Declaration of Indulgence (1687; reissued 7 May 1688); the bishops were prosecuted for seditious libel, but acquitted. Remark, ?2 June 1688

9 A little rebellion now and then is a good thing.

Thomas Jefferson (1743–1826) US statesman. Letter to James Madison, 30 Jan 1787

10 A riot is at bottom the language of the unheard.

Martin Luther King (1929–68) US Black civil-rights leader. *Chaos or Community,* Ch. 4

11 In my opinion it is better that all of these peasants should be killed rather than that the sovereigns and magistrates should be destroyed, because the peasants take up the sword without God's authorization.

Martin Luther (1483–1546) German Protestant. Letter to Nicholas von Ansdorf, 30 May 1525

12 Angry Young Man.

Leslie Paul (1905–) British writer. Book title

13 You noble Diggers all, stand up now,
The waste land to maintain, seeing Cavaliers by name
Your digging do disdain and persons all defame.

Gerrard Winstanley (c. 1609–c. 1660) Leader of the Diggers. The Diggers were a radical group that believed in land reform and practiced a primitive agrarian communism. Important in 1649, they were dispersed by the Commonwealth government in 1650. *The Diggers' Song*

14 Seeing the common people of England by joint consent of person and purse have cast out Charles our Norman oppressor, we have by this victory recovered ourselves from under his Norman yoke.

Gerrard Winstanley Remark to Lord Fairfax, 8 Dec 1649

REGRET

See also apologies, memory, mourning, nostalgia, past, sorrow

1 It is no use crying over spilt milk.
Proverb

2 It's too late to shut the stable door after the horse has bolted.
Proverb

3 What's done cannot be undone.
Proverb

4 Then I said, Woe is me! for I am undone; because I am a man of unclean lips, and I dwell in the midst of a people of unclean lips: for mine eyes have seen the King, the Lord of hosts.
Then flew one of the seraphims unto me, having a live coal in his hand, which he had taken with tongs from off the altar:
And he laid it upon my mouth, and said, Lo, this hath touched thy lips; and thine iniquity is taken away, and thy sin purged.
Bible: Isaiah 6:5–7

5 I say unto you, that likewise joy shall be in heaven over one sinner that repenteth, more than over ninety and nine just persons, which need no repentance.
Bible: Luke 15:7

6 One doesn't recognize in one's life the really important moments – not until it's too late.
Agatha Christie (1891–1976) British detective-story writer. *Endless Night*, Bk. II, Ch. 14

7 This hand hath offended.
Thomas Cranmer (1489–1556) English churchman. *Memorials of Cranmer* (Strype)

8 All I have, I would have given gladly not to be standing here today.
Lyndon B. Johnson (1908–73) US Democratic president. Following the assassination of president Kennedy. Speech to Congress, 27 Nov 1963

9 Were it not better to forget
Than but remember and regret?
Letitia Landon (1802–38) British poet and novelist. *Despondency*

10 We might have been – These are but common words,
And yet they make the sum of life's bewailing.
Letitia Landon *Three Extracts from the Diary of a Week*

11 And so, I missed my chance with one of the lords
Of life.
And I have something to expiate;
A pettiness.
D. H. Lawrence (1885–1930) British novelist. *Snake*

12 Maybe it would have been better if neither of us had been born.
Napoleon I (Napoleon Bonaparte; 1769–1821) French emperor. Said while looking at the tomb of the philosopher Jean-Jacques Rousseau, whose theories had influenced the French Revolution. *The Story of Civilization* (W. Durant), Vol. II

13 It serves me right for putting all my eggs in one bastard.
Dorothy Parker (1893–1967) US writer and wit. On going into hospital for an abortion. *You Might As Well Live*, II, Ch. 3 (J. Keats)

14 Good-bye, I've barely said a word to you, it is always like that at parties, we never see the people, we never say the things we should like to say, but it is the same everywhere in this life. Let us hope that when we are dead things will be better arranged.
Marcel Proust (1871–1922) French novelist. *À la recherche du temps perdu: Sodome et Gomorrhe*

15 Had I been brighter, the ladies been gentler, the Scotch been weaker, had the gods been kinder, had the dice been hotter, this could have been a one-sentence story: Once upon a time I lived happily ever after.
Mickey Rooney (1920–) US actor. Attrib.

16 The follies which a man regrets most in his life are those which he didn't commit when he had the opportunity.
Helen Rowland (1876–1950) US writer. *Reflections of a Bachelor Girl*

17 But with the morning cool repentance came.
Walter Scott (1771–1832) Scottish novelist. *Rob Roy*, Ch. 12

18 Had I but serv'd my God with half the zeal
I serv'd my King, he would not in mine age
Have left me naked to mine enemies.
William Shakespeare (1564–1616) English dramatist. Said by Cardinal Wolsey. *Henry VIII*, III:2

19 O, pardon me, thou bleeding piece of earth,
That I am meek and gentle with these butchers!
Thou art the ruins of the noblest man
That ever lived in the tide of times.
William Shakespeare *Julius Caesar*, III:1

20 To mourn a mischief that is past and gone
Is the next way to draw new mischief on.
William Shakespeare *Othello*, I:3

21 Things sweet to taste prove in digestion sour.
William Shakespeare *Richard II*, I:3

22 O! call back yesterday, bid time return.
William Shakespeare *Richard II*, III:2

23 When to the sessions of sweet silent thought
I summon up remembrance of things past,
I sigh the lack of many a thing I sought,
And with old woes new wail my dear time's waste.
William Shakespeare *Sonnet 30*

24 What's gone and what's past help
Should be past grief.
William Shakespeare *The Winter's Tale*, III:2

25 The bitterest tears shed over graves are for words left unsaid and deeds left undone.
Harriet Beecher Stowe (1811–96) US novelist. *Little Foxes*, Ch. 3

26 I never wonder to see men wicked, but I often wonder to see them not ashamed.
Jonathan Swift (1667–1745) Irish-born Anglican priest and writer. *Thoughts on Various Subjects*

27 Though nothing can bring back the hour
Of splendour in the grass, of glory in the flower;
We will grieve not, rather find
Strength in what remains behind . . .
William Wordsworth (1770–1850) British poet. *Ode. Intimations of Immortality*, IX

28 Men are we, and must grieve when even the shade
Of that which once was great is passed away.
William Wordsworth *Sonnets*, 'Once did she hold'

RELIABILITY

1 He's the Man Who Delivers the Goods.
Walt Mason (1862–1939) Canadian poet and humorist. *The Man Who Delivers the Goods*

RELIGION

See also atheism, belief, Bible, Catholicism, Christianity, Christmas, Church, damnation, devil, doomsday, faith, God, heaven, hell, Jews, martyrdom, prayer, Protestantism, Sunday

1 Nearer, my God, to thee,
Nearer to thee!

Sarah F. Adams (1805–48) British poet and hymn writer. *Nearer My God to Thee*

2 . . . of middle stature, neither tall nor short. His complexion was rosy white; his eyes black; his hair, thick, brilliant, and beautiful, fell to his shoulders. His profuse beard fell to his breast . . . There was such sweetness in his visage that no one, once in his presence, could leave him. If I hungered, a single look at the Prophet's face dispelled the hunger. Before him all forgot their griefs and pains.

Ali (c. 600–661) Son-in-law of Mohammed and fourth caliph. Describing Mohammed (570–632). *Chronique* (Abu Jafar Mohammed al-Tabari), Pt. III, Ch. 46

3 He was of the faith chiefly in the sense that the church he currently did not attend was Catholic.

Kingsley Amis (1922–) British novelist. *One Fat Englishman*

4 There is no salvation outside the church.

St Augustine of Hippo (354–430) Bishop of Hippo. *De Bapt.*, IV

5 The Jews and Arabs should sit down and settle their differences like good Christians.

Warren Austin (1877–1962) US politician and diplomat. Attrib.

6 If the concept of God has any validity or use, it can only be to make us larger, freer, and more loving. If God cannot do this, then it is time we got rid of Him.

James Baldwin (1924–1987) US writer. *The Fire next Time*

7 I'm a Communist by day and a Catholic as soon as it gets dark.

Brendan Behan (1923–64) Irish playwright. Attrib.

8 Ye shall circumcise the flesh of your foreskin; and it shall be a token of the covenant betwixt me and you.

Bible: Genesis 17:11

9 Blessed are the pure in heart: for they shall see God.

Blessed are the peacemakers: for they shall be called the children of God.

Blessed are they which are persecuted for righteousness' sake: for theirs is the kingdom of heaven.

Bible: Matthew 5:8–10

10 *Saint, n.* a dead sinner revised and edited.

Ambrose Bierce (1842–?1914) US writer and journalist. *The Devil's Dictionary*

11 As for the British churchman, he goes to church as he goes to the bathroom, with the minimum of fuss and no explanation if he can help it.

Ronald Blythe (1922–) British writer. *The Age of Illusion*

12 Every day people are straying away from the church and going back to God. Really.

Lenny Bruce (1925–66) US comedian. *The Essential Lenny Bruce* (ed. J. Cohen), 'Religions Inc.'

13 This Ariyan Eightfold Path, that is to say: Right view, right aim, right speech, right action, right living, right effort, right mindfulness, right contemplation.

Buddha (Gautama Siddhartha; c. 563–c. 483 BC) Indian religious teacher. *Some Sayings of the Buddha* (F. L. Woodward)

14 Man is by his constitution a religious animal.

Edmund Burke (1729–97) British politician. *Reflections on the Revolution in France*

15 One religion is as true as another.

Robert Burton (1577–1640) English scholar and explorer. *Anatomy of Melancholy*, Pt. III

16 To be at all is to be religious more or less.

Samuel Butler (1835–1902) British writer. *Notebooks*

17 He no play-a da game. He no make-a da rules!

Earl Butz (1909–) US politician. Referring to the Pope's strictures against contraception. Remark, 1974

18 Not a religion for gentlemen.

Charles II (1630–85) King of England. Referring to Presbyterianism. *History of My Own Time* (Burnet), Vol. I, Bk. II, Ch. 2

19 Religion is by no means a proper subject of conversation in a mixed company.

Earl of Chesterfield (1694–1773) English statesman. Letter to his godson

20 When your ladyship's faith has removed them, I will go thither with all my heart.

Earl of Chesterfield Said to his sister, Lady Gertrude Hotham, when she suggested he go to a Methodist seminary in Wales to recuperate, recommending the views of the mountains. Attrib.

21 Talk about the pews and steeples
And the cash that goes therewith!
But the souls of Christian
peoples . . . .
Chuck it, Smith!

G. K. Chesterton (1874–1936) British writer. *Antichrist, or the Reunion of Christendom*

22 Men will wrangle for religion; write for it; fight for it; anything but – live for it.

Charles Caleb Colton (?1780–1832) British clergyman and writer. *Lacon*, Vol. I

23 Pray remember, Mr Dean, no dogma, no Dean.

Benjamin Disraeli (1804–81) British statesman. Attrib.

24 'Sensible men are all of the same religion.' 'And pray what is that?' inquired the prince. 'Sensible men never tell.'

Benjamin Disraeli *Endymion*, Bk. I, Ch. 81

25 I neglect God and his angels for the noise of a fly, for the rattling of a coach, for the whining of a door.

John Donne (1573–1631) English poet. *Sermons*, 80

26 In pious times, e'r Priest-craft did begin,
Before Polygamy was made a Sin.

John Dryden (1631–1700) British poet and dramatist. *Absalom and Achitophel*, I

27 It would be better to see the royal turban of the Turks in the midst of the city than the Latin mitre.

Michael Ducas (?1400–?70) Byzantine historian. Referring to Emperor Constantine XI's reunification of the Orthodox and Roman Churches (1452), in an attempt to save the Byzantine Empire from the Turks. Attrib.

28 Christian Science explains all cause and effect as mental, not physical.

Mary Baker Eddy (1821–1910) US religious leader. *Science and Health, with Key to the Scriptures*

29 Sickness, sin and death, being inharmonious, do not originate in God, nor belong to His government.

Mary Baker Eddy *Science and Health, with Key to the Scriptures*

30 Science without religion is lame, religion without science is blind.

Albert Einstein (1879–1955) German-born US physicist. *Out of My Later Years*

31 The whole religious complexion of the modern world is due to the absence from Jerusalem of a lunatic asylum.

Havelock Ellis (1859–1939) British sexologist. *Impressions and Comments*

32 The religions we call false were once true.

Ralph Waldo Emerson (1803–82) US poet and essayist. *Essays*, 'Character'

33 Religion is an illusion and it derives its strength from the fact that it falls in with our instinctual desires.

Sigmund Freud (1856–1939) Austrian psychoanalyst. *New Introductory Lectures on Psychoanalysis*, 'A Philosophy of Life'

34 Religion
Has made an honest woman of the supernatural,
And we won't have it kicking over the traces again.

Christopher Fry (1907–) British dramatist. *The Lady's Not for Burning*, II

35 There exists no politician in India daring enough to attempt to explain to the masses that cows can be eaten.

Indira Gandhi (1917–84) Indian stateswoman. *New York Review of Books*, 'Indira's Coup' (Oriana Fallaci)

36 The various modes of worship, which prevailed in the Roman world, were all considered by the people as equally true; by the philosopher, as equally false; and by the magistrate, as equally useful. And thus toleration produced not only mutual indulgence, but even religious concord.

Edward Gibbon (1737–94) British historian. *Decline and Fall of the Roman Empire*, Ch. 2

37 As I take my shoes from the shoemaker, and my coat from the tailor, so I take my religion from the priest.

Oliver Goldsmith (1728–74) Irish-born British writer. *Life of Johnson* (J. Boswell)

38 Decide for Christ.

Billy Graham (1918–) US evangelist. Slogan

39 Those who marry God . . . can become domesticated too – it's just as humdrum a marriage as all the others.

Graham Greene (1904–) British novelist. *A Burnt-Out Case*, Ch. 1

40 They illuminate our whole country with the bright light of their preaching and teaching.

Robert Grosseteste (c. 1175–1253) Bishop of Lincoln. Referring to the Franciscans. Letter to Pope Gregory IX, 1238

41 Pray, good people, be civil. I am the Protestant whore.

Nell Gwyn (1650–87) English actress. On being surrounded in her coach by an angry mob in Oxford at the time of the Popish Plot. The crowd, believing her to be the King's catholic mistress Louise de Kerouaille, shouted 'It's the Catholic whore!'. *Nell Gwyn* (Bevan), Ch. 13

42 But as I rav'd and grew more fierce and wild
At every word,
Methought I heard one calling, 'Child';
And I replied, 'My Lord.'

George Herbert (1593–1633) English poet. *The Collar*

43 The sedate, sober, silent, serious, sad-coloured sect.

Thomas Hood (1799–1845) British poet. Referring to the Quakers. *The Doves and the Crows*

44 To become a popular religion, it is only necessary for a superstition to enslave a philosophy.

Dean Inge (1860–1954) British churchman. *Outspoken Essays*

45 Many people believe that they are attracted by God, or by Nature, when they are only repelled by man.

Dean Inge *More Lay Thoughts of a Dean*

46 Many people think they have religion when they are troubled with dyspepsia.

Robert G. Ingersoll (1833–99) US lawyer and agnostic. *Liberty of Man, Woman and Child*, Section 3

47 There are as many miracles as there are articles of the *Summa*.

John XXII (Jacques d'Euse; c. 1249–1334) Pope. Referring to the *Summa Theologiae* of Thomas Aquinas, who was in the process of being canonized. Attrib.

48 Among all my patients in the second half of life . . . there has not been one whose problem in the last resort was not that of finding a religious outlook on life.

Carl Gustav Jung (1875–1961) Swiss psychoanalyst. *Modern Man in Search of a Soul*

49 The month of Ramadan shall ye fast, in which the Koran was sent down from heaven, a direction unto men, and declarations of direction, and the distinction between good and evil.

Koran Ch. II

50 But I suppose even God was born
too late to trust the old religion –
all those setting out
that never left the ground,
beginning in wisdom, dying in doubt.

Robert Lowell (1917–77) US poet. *Tenth Muse*

51 Here stand I. I can do no other. God help me. Amen.

Martin Luther (1483–1546) German Protestant. Speech at the Diet of Worms, 18 Apr 1521

52 Abide with me; fast falls the eventide;
The darkness deepens; Lord, with me abide;
When other helpers fail, and comforts flee,
Help of the helpless, O, abide with me.

Henry Francis Lyte (1793–1847) British hymn writer. *Abide with Me*

53 Religion . . . is the opium of the people.

Karl Marx (1818–83) German philosopher and revolutionary. *Criticism of the Hegelian Philosophy of Right*, Introduction

54 Things have come to a pretty pass when religion is allowed to invade the sphere of private life.

Lord Melbourne (1779–1848) British statesman. Attrib.

55 There are many who stay away from church these days because you hardly ever mention God any more.

Arthur Miller (1915–) US dramatist. *The Crucible*, I

56 New Presbyter is but old Priest writ large.

John Milton (1608–74) English poet. *Sonnet*: 'On the New Forcers of Conscience under the Long Parliament'

57 Man is quite insane. He wouldn't know how to create a maggot and he creates Gods by the dozen.

Michel de Montaigne (1533–92) French essayist. *Essais*, II

58 There is a very good saying that if triangles invented a god, they would make him three-sided.

Baron de Montesquieu (1688–1755) French writer. *Lettres persanes*

59 There's no reason to bring religion into it. I think we ought to have as great a regard for religion as we can, so as to keep it out of as many things as possible.

Sean O'Casey (1884–1964) Irish dramatist. *The Plough and the Stars*, I

60 The brotherhood of man under the fatherhood of God.

Nelson Rockefeller (1908–79) US Republican politician and Vice-President. Attrib.

61 We must reject a privatization of religion which results in its

reduction to being simply a matter of personal salvation.
Robert Runcie (1921–) British churchman (Archbishop of Canterbury). *The Observer*, 'Sayings of the Week', 17 Apr 1988

62 Unlike Christianity, which preached a peace that it never achieved, Islam unashamedly came with a sword.
Steven Runciman (1903–) British academic and diplomat. *A History of the Crusades*, 'The First Crusade'

63 I have been into many of the ancient cathedrals – grand, wonderful, mysterious. But I always leave them with a feeling of indignation because of the generations of human beings who have struggled in poverty to build these altars to the unknown god.
Elizabeth Stanton (1815–1902) US suffragette. *Diary*

64 Whenever a man talks loudly against religion, – always suspect that it is not his reason, but his passions which have got the better of his creed.
Laurence Sterne (1713–68) Irish-born British writer. *Tristram Shandy*

65 I believe in the Church, One Holy, Catholic and Apostolic, and I regret that it nowhere exists.
William Temple (1881–1944) British churchman. Attrib.

66 Alas, O Lord, to what a state dost Thou bring those who love Thee!
St Teresa of Ávila (1515–82) Spanish mystic. *The Interior Castle*, VI

67 It is spring, moonless night in the small town, starless and bible-black.
Dylan Thomas (1914–53) Welsh poet. *Under Milk Wood*

68 I fled Him, down the nights and down the days;
I fled Him, down the arches of the years;
I fled Him, down the labyrinthine ways
Of my own mind; and in the mist of tears
I hid from Him, and under running laughter.
Francis Thompson (1859–1907) British poet. *The Hound of Heaven*

69 Rock of ages, cleft for me,
Let me hide myself in Thee.
Augustus Montague Toplady (1740–78) British hymn writer. *Rock of Ages*

70 Beware when you take on the Church of God. Others have tried and have bitten the dust.
Desmond Tutu (1931–) South African clergyman. Speech, Apr 1987

71 In general the churches, visited by me too often on weekdays . . . bore for me the same relation to God that billboards did to Coca-Cola: they promoted thirst without quenching it.
John Updike (1932–) US novelist. *A Month of Sundays*, Ch. 2

72 Organized religion is making Christianity political rather than making politics Christian.
Laurens Van der Post (1906–) South African novelist. *The Observer*, 'Sayings of the Week', 9 Nov 1986

73 Jesus loves me – this I know,
For the Bible tells me so.
Susan Warner (1819–85) US novelist. *The Love of Jesus*

74 Lord, I ascribe it to Thy grace,
And not to chance, as others do,
That I was born of Christian race,
And not a Heathen, or a Jew.
Isaac Watts (1674–1748) English theologian and hymn writer. *Divine Songs for Children*, 'Praise for the Gospel'

75 Our God, our help in ages past,
Our hope for years to come,
Our shelter from the stormy blast,
And our eternal home.
Isaac Watts *Our God, Our Help in Ages Past*

76 I have noticed again and again since I have been in the Church that lay interest in ecclesiastical matters is often a prelude to insanity.
Evelyn Waugh (1903–66) British novelist. *Decline and Fall*, Pt. I, Ch. 8

77 There is a species of person called a 'Modern Churchman' who draws the full salary of a beneficed clergyman and need not commit himself to any religious belief.
Evelyn Waugh *Decline and Fall*, Pt. II, Ch. 4

78 Mrs. Ape, as was her invariable rule, took round the hat and collected nearly two pounds. 'Salvation doesn't do them the same good if they think it's free' was her favourite axiom.
Evelyn Waugh *Vile Bodies*

79 Religion is love; in no case is it logic.
Beatrice Webb (1858–1943) British economist and writer. *My Apprenticeship*, Ch. 2

80 I look upon all the world as my parish.
John Wesley (1703–91) British religious leader. *Journal*, 11 June 1739

81 Why do born-again people so often make you wish they'd never been born the first time?
Katherine Whitehorn (1926–) British journalist. *The Observer*, 20 May 1979

82 So many gods, so many creeds,
So many paths that wind and wind,
While just the art of being kind
Is all the sad world needs.
Ella Wheeler Wilcox (1850–1919) US poet. *The World's Need*

83 The itch of disputing will prove the scab of churches.
Henry Wotton (1568–1639) English poet and diplomat. *A Panegyric to King Charles*

84 The Ethiopians say that their gods are snub-nosed and black, the Thracians that theirs have light blue eyes and red hair.
Xenophanes (c. 560–c. 478 BC) Greek poet and philosopher. *Fragment 15*

85 No Jew was ever fool enough to turn Christian unless he was a clever man.
Israel Zangwill (1864–1926) British writer. *Children of the Ghetto*, Ch. 1

REMEDIES

See also doctors, illness, medicine

1 He's the best physician that knows the worthlessness of the most medicines.
Proverb

2 Many medicines, few cures.
Proverb

3 Visitors' footfalls are like medicine; they heal the sick.
Bantu proverb

4 A single untried popular remedy often throws the scientific doctor into hysterics.
Chinese proverb

5 Three remedies of the physicians of Myddfai: water, honey, and labour.
Welsh proverb

6 There is no curing a sick man who believes himself in health.
Henri Amiel (1821–81) Swiss writer and philosopher. *Journal*, 6 Feb 1877

7 Modern therapy, particularly of malignancy, makes good use of the

Borgia effect – two poisons are more efficacious than one.
Anonymous

8 Why should a man die who has sage in his garden?
Anonymous *Regimen Sanitatis, Salernitanum*

9 You give medicine to a sick man; the sick man hands you gold in return. You cure his disease, he cures yours.
Anonymous

10 Cure the disease and kill the patient.
Francis Bacon (1561–1626) English philosopher. *Essays*, 'Of Friendship'

11 The remedy is worse than the disease.
Francis Bacon *Essays*, 'Of Seditions and Troubles'

12 Then Peter said, Silver and gold have I none; but such as I have give I thee: In the name of Jesus Christ of Nazareth rise up and walk.
Bible: Acts 3:6

13 The Lord hath created medicines out of the earth; and he that is wise will not abhor them.
Bible: Ecclesiasticus 38:4

14 And besought him that they might only touch the hem of his garment: and as many as touched were made perfectly whole.
Bible: Matthew 14:36

15 My father invented a cure for which there was no disease and unfortunately my mother caught it and died of it.
Victor Borge (1909–) Danish-born US composer, actor, and musical comedian. *In Concert*

16 We all labour against our own cure, for death is the cure of all diseases.
Thomas Browne (1605–82) English physician and writer.

17 *Diseases* of their own Accord,
But *Cures* come difficult and hard.
Samuel Butler (1612–80) English poet and satirist. *Satyr upon the Weakness and Misery of Man*

18 Medical men all over the world . . . merely entered into a tacit agreement to call all sorts of maladies people are liable to, in cold weather, by one name; so that one sort of treatment may serve for all, and their practice be thereby greatly simplified.
Jane Welsh Carlyle (1801–66) The wife of Thomas Carlyle. Letter to John Welsh, 4 Mar 1837

19 A reckoning up of the cause often solves the malady.
Celsus (25 BC–50 AD) Roman scholar. *De Medicina*, Prooemium

20 Well, now, there's a remedy for everything except death.
Miguel de Cervantes (1547–1616) Spanish novelist. *Don Quixote*, Pt. II, Ch. 10

21 When a lot of remedies are suggested for a disease, that means it can't be cured.
Anton Chekhov (1860–1904) Russian dramatist. *The Cherry Orchard*, II

22 Men worry over the great number of diseases; doctors worry over the small number of remedies.
Pien Ch'iao (c. 225 BC)

23 When ill, indeed,
E'en dismissing the doctor don't *always* succeed.
George Colman, the Younger (1762–1836) British dramatist. *Lodgings for Single Gentlemen*

24 If you are too fond of new remedies, first you will not cure your patients; secondly, you will have no patients to cure.
Astley Paston Cooper (1768–1841)

25 What destroys one man preserves another.
Pierre Corneille (1606–84) French dramatist. *Cinna*, II:1

26 Every day, in every way, I am getting better and better.
Émile Coué (1857–1920) French doctor. Formula for a cure by autosuggestion

27 You see – he's got a perfectly new idea. He never sees his patients. He's not interested in individuals, he prefers to treat a crowd. And he's organized these mass cures . . . And he cures thirty thousand people every Thursday.
Ruth Draper *Doctors and Diets*

28 Then comes the question, how do drugs, hygiene and animal magnetism heal? It may be affirmed that they do not heal, but only relieve suffering temporarily, exchanging one disease for another.
Mary Baker Eddy (1821–1910) US religious leader. *Science and Health, with Key to the Scriptures*

29 The poisons are our principal medicines, which kill the disease and save the life.
Ralph Waldo Emerson (1803–82) US poet and essayist. *The Conduct of Life*, Ch. 7

30 Life as we find it is too hard for us; it entails too much pain, too many disappointments, impossible tasks. We cannot do without palliative remedies.
Sigmund Freud (1856–1939) Austrian psychoanalyst. *Civilization and Its Discontents*

31 Like cures like.
Samuel Hahnemann (1755–1843) Motto for homeopathy

32 Extreme remedies are most appropriate for extreme diseases.
Hippocrates (c. 460–c. 377 BC) Greek physician. *Aphorisms*, I

33 To do nothing is also a good remedy.
Hippocrates

34 By opposites opposites are cured.
Hippocrates *Deflatibus*, Vol. I

35 Like cures like.
Hippocrates Attrib.

36 One of the most successful physicians I have ever known, has assured me, that he used more bread pills, drops of colored water, and powders of hickory ashes, than of all other medicines put together. It was certainly a pious fraud.
Thomas Jefferson (1743–1826) US statesman. Letter to Dr. Caspar Wistar, 21 June 1807

37 The patient, treated on the fashionable theory, sometimes gets well in spite of the medicine. The medicine therefore restored him, and the young doctor receives new courage to proceed in his bold experiments on the lives of his fellow creatures.
Thomas Jefferson Letter to Dr. Caspar Wistar, 21 June 1807

38 Poisons and medicine are oftentimes the same substance given with different intents.
Peter Mere Latham (1789–1875) US poet and essayist. *General Remarks on the Practice of Medicine*, Ch. 7

39 Remedies, indeed, are our great analysers of disease.
Peter Mere Latham *General Remarks on the Practice of Medicine*, Ch. 7

40 You know that medicines when well used restore health to the sick: they will be well used when the doctor together with his understanding of their nature shall understand also what man is, what life is, and what constitution and health are. Know these well and you will know their opposites; and when this is the case you will know well how to devise a remedy.

Leonardo da Vinci (1452–1519) Italian artist, sculptor, architect, and engineer. *Codice Atlantico*, 270

41 Is getting well ever an art
Or art a way to get well.

Robert Lowell (1917–77) US poet. 'Unwanted'

42 Most men die of their remedies, and not of their illnesses.

Molière (1622–73) French dramatist. *Le Malade imaginaire*, III:3

43 We are more sensible of one little touch of a surgeon's lancet than of twenty wounds with a sword in the heat of fight.

Michel de Montaigne (1533–92) French essayist and moralist.

44 Medicines are only fit for old people.

Napoleon I (Napoleon Bonaparte; 1769–1821) French Emperor. *Napoleon in Exile* (Barry O'Meara)

45 The best of healers is good cheer.

Pindar (c. 522–443 BC) *Nemean Ode*, IV

46 As soon as he ceased to be mad he became merely stupid. There are maladies we must not seek to cure because they alone protect us from others that are more serious.

Marcel Proust (1871–1922) French novelist. *À la recherche du temps perdu: Le Côté de Guermantes*

47 Nothing hinders a cure so much as frequent change of medicine.

Seneca (c. 4 BC–65 AD) Roman writer. *Epistulae ad Lucilium*

48 It is medicine not scenery, for which a sick man must go searching.

Seneca *Epistulae ad Lucilium*

49 It is part of the cure to wish to be cured.

Seneca *Hippolytus*, 249

50 Our remedies oft in ourselves do lie,
Which we ascribe to heaven.

William Shakespeare (1564–1616) English dramatist and poet. *All's Well That Ends Well*, I:1

51 They all thought she was dead; but my father he kept ladling gin down her throat till she came to so sudden that she bit the bowl off the spoon.

George Bernard Shaw (1856–1950) Irish dramatist and critic. *Pygmalion*, III

52 Nicotinic acid cures pellagra, but a beefsteak prevents it.

Henry E. Sigerist (1891–1957) *Atlantic Monthly*, June 1939

53 I watched what method Nature might take, with intention of subduing the symptom by treading in her footsteps.

Thomas Sydenham (1624–89) *Medical Observations*, 5, Ch. 2

54 Our body is a machine for living. It is organized for that, it is its nature. Let life go on in it unhindered and let it defend itself, it will do more than if you paralyse it by encumbering it with remedies.

Leo Tolstoy (1828–1910) Russian writer. *War and Peace*, Bk. X, Ch. 29

55 Wonderful is the skill of a physician; for a rich man he prescribeth various admixtures and compounds, by which the patient is rought to health in many days at an expense of fifty pounds; while for a poor man for the same disease he giveth a more common name, and prescribeth a dose of oil, which worketh a cure in a single night charging fourpence therefor.

James Townley (1714–78)

56 We do not know the mode of action of almost all remedies. Why therefore fear to confess our ignorance? In truth, it seems that the words 'I do not know' stick in every physician's throat.

Armand Trousseau (1801–67) *Bulletin de l'académie impériale de médecine*, 25:733, 1860

57 Dr. Snow gave that blessed Chloroform & the effect was soothing, quieting & delightful beyond measure.

Victoria (1819–1901) Queen of England. Describing her labor. *Journal*

58 Sparrowhawks, Ma'am.

Duke of Wellington (1769–1852) British general and statesman. Advice when asked by Queen Victoria how to remove sparrows from the Crystal Palace. Attrib.

59 Saying 'Gesundheit' doesn't really help the common cold – but its about as good as anything the doctors have come up with.

Earl Wilson *Bartlett's Unfamiliar Quotations* (Leonard Louis Levinson)

60 There is only one cure for grey hair. It was invented by a Frenchman. It is called the guillotine.

P. G. Wodehouse (1881–1975) British humorous novelist. *The Old Reliable*

61 Some reckoned he killed himself with purgations.

Charles Wriothesley *Chronicle*, Vol. I

RENUNCIATION

See also dismissal

1 Renounce the devil and all his works.

The Book of Common Prayer *Publick Baptism of Infants*

2 I would rather be a brilliant memory than a curiosity.

Emma Eames (1865–1952) US opera singer. Referring to her retirement at the age of 47. *The Elephant that Swallowed a Nightingale* (C. Galtey)

3 You won't have Nixon to kick around any more, gentlemen. This is my last Press Conference.

Richard Milhous Nixon (1913–) US president. Press conference, after losing the election for the governorship of California, 2 Nov 1962

4 I'll break my staff,
Bury it certain fathoms in the earth,
And deeper than did ever plummet sound
I'll drown my book.

William Shakespeare (1564–1616) English dramatist. *The Tempest*, V:1

5 It is very simple. The artists retired. The British remained.

James Whistler (1834–1903) US painter. Explaining his resignation as president of the Royal Society of British Artists. *Whistler Stories* (D. Seitz)

REPARTEE

1 It hasn't taken Winston long to get used to American ways. He hadn't been an American citizen for three minutes before attacking an ex-secretary of state!

Dean Acheson (1893–1971) US lawyer and statesman. At a ceremony in 1963 to make Churchill an honorary American citizen, Churchill obliquely attacked Acheson's reference to Britain losing an empire. *Randolph Churchill* (K. Halle)

2 Because you're in Chatham.

Anonymous Heckler at an election meeting, when Harold Wilson asked 'Why do I emphasize the importance of the Royal Navy?'. Chatham was the home of the Royal Navy dockyards.

3 The house is well, but it is you,

Your Majesty, who have made me too great for my house.

Francis Bacon (1561–1626) English philosopher. Reply when Elizabeth I remarked on the smallness of his house. *After-dinner Stories and Anecdotes* (L. Meissen)

4 Christianity, of course but why journalism?

Arthur Balfour (1848–1930) British statesman. In reply to Frank Harris's remark, '. . . all the faults of the age come from Christianity and journalism'. *Autobiography* (Margot Asquith), Ch. 10

5 I rather think of having a career of my own.

Arthur Balfour When asked whether he was going to marry Margot Tennant. *Autobiography* (Margot Asquith), Ch. 9

6 Certainly not – if you don't object if I'm sick.

Thomas Beecham (1879–1961) British conductor. When asked whether he minded if someone smoked in a non-smoking compartment. Attrib.

7 I don't like your Christian name. I'd like to change it.

Thomas Beecham To his future wife. She replied, 'You can't, but you can change my surname.' Attrib.

8 I have known many an instance of a man writing a letter and forgetting to sign his name, but this is the only instance I have ever known of a man signing his name and forgetting to write the letter.

Henry Ward Beecher (1813–87) US Congregational minister. Said on receiving a note containing the single word: 'Fool'. *The Best Stories in the World* (T. Masson)

9 So who's in a hurry?

Robert Benchley (1889–1945) US humorist. When asked whether he knew that drinking was a slow death. Attrib.

10 The gentleman will please remember that when his half-civilized ancestors were hunting the wild boar in Silesia, mine were princes of the earth.

Judah Philip Benjamin (1811–84) US politician. Replying to a senator of Germanic origin who had made an antisemitic remark. Attrib.

11 I don't deserve this, but I have arthritis, and I don't deserve that either.

Jack Benny (Benjamin Kubelsky; 1894–1974) US actor. Said when accepting an award. Attrib.

12 Down South where I come from you don't go around hitting too many white keys.

Eubie Blake (1883–1983) US pianist and ragtime composer. When asked why his compositions contained so many sharps and flats. Attrib.

13 I can't say I was ever lost, but I was bewildered once for three days.

Daniel Boone (1734–1820) US pioneeer. Reply when asked if he had ever been lost. Attrib.

14 JOHNSON. Well, we had a good talk.
BOSWELL. Yes, Sir; you tossed and gored several persons.

James Boswell (1740–95) Scottish lawyer and writer. *Life of Johnson*, Vol. II

15 VISITOR. Ah, Bottomley, sewing?
BOTTOMLEY. No, reaping.

Horatio William Bottomley (1860–1933) British newspaper editor. When found sewing mail bags. *Horatio Bottomley* (Julian Symons)

16 Nothing grows well in the shade of a big tree.

Constantin Brancusi (1876–1957) Romanian sculptor. Refusing Rodin's invitation to work in his studio. *Compton's Encyclopedia*

17 ANDREA. Unhappy the land that has no heroes.
GALILEO. No, unhappy the land that needs heroes.

Bertolt Brecht (1898–1956) German dramatist. *Galileo*, 13

18 The King to Oxford sent a troop of horse,
For Tories own no argument but force:
With equal skill to Cambridge books he sent,
For Whigs admit no force but argument.

William Browne (1692–1774) English physician. A reply to TRAPP *Literary Anecdotes* (Nichols), Vol. III

19 This is very true: for my words are my own, and my actions are my ministers'.

Charles II (1630–85) King of Great Britain and Ireland. Replying to Lord ROCHESTER'S suggested epitaph. *King Charles II* (A. Bryant)

20 Make him a bishop, and you will silence him at once.

Earl of Chesterfield (1694–1773) English statesman. When asked what steps might be taken to control the evangelical preacher George Whitefield. Attrib.

21 When your ladyship's faith has removed them, I will go thither with all my heart.

Earl of Chesterfield Said to his sister, Lady Gertrude Hotham, when she suggested he go to a Methodist seminary in Wales to recuperate, recommending the views of the mountains. Attrib.

22 And you, madam, are ugly. But I shall be sober in the morning.

Winston Churchill (1874–1965) British statesman. Replying to Bessie Braddock MP, who told him he was drunk. Attrib.

23 I must point out that my rule of life prescribed as an absolutely sacred rite smoking cigars and also the drinking of alcohol before, after, and if need be during all meals and in the intervals between them.

Winston Churchill Said during a lunch with the Arab leader Ibn Saud, when he heard that the king's religion forbade smoking and alcohol. *The Second World War*

24 If you were my wife, I'd drink it.

Winston Churchill Replying to Lady Astor who had said, 'If you were my husband, I'd put poison in your coffee'. *Nancy Astor and Her Friends* (E. Langhorne)

25 Examinations are formidable even to the best prepared, for the greatest fool may ask more than the wisest man can answer.

Charles Caleb Colton (?1780–1832) British clergyman and writer. *Lacon*, Vol. II

26 'She still seems to me in her own way a person born to command,' said Luce . . .
'I wonder if anyone is born to obey,' said Isabel.
'That may be why people command rather badly, that
they have no suitable material to work on.'

Ivy Compton-Burnett (1892–1969) British novelist. *Parents and Children*, Ch. 3

27 Neither am I.

Peter Cook (1937–) British writer and entertainer. On being told that the person sitting next to him at a dinner party was 'writing a book'. Attrib.

28 He said he was against it.

Calvin Coolidge (1872–1933) US president. Reply when asked what a clergyman had said regarding sin in his sermon. Attrib.

29 How strange, when I saw you acting in *The Glorious Adventure* I laughed all the time.

Noël Coward (1899–1973) British dramatist. To Lady Diana Cooper, who said she had not laughed once at his comedy *The Young Idea*. *The Noel Coward Diaries*

30 Why didn't you bring him with you? I should be delighted to meet him.

Lady (Maud) 'Emerald' Cunard (1872–1948) American-born society figure in Britain. To Somerset Maugham, who said he was leaving a dinner party early 'to keep his youth'. *Emerald and Nancy* (D. Fielding)

31 I go to a better tailor than any of you and pay more for my clothes.

The only difference is that you probably don't sleep in yours.

Clarence Seward Darrow (1857–1938) US lawyer. Reply when teased by reporters about his appearance. *2500 Anecdotes* (E. Fuller)

32 With the newspaper strike on I wouldn't consider it.

Bette Davis (Ruth Elizabeth Davis; 1908–) US film star. When told that a rumor was spreading that she had died. *Book of Lists* (I. Wallace)

33 Stand a little less between me and the sun.

Diogenes (412–322 BC) Greek philosopher. When Alexander the Great asked if there was anything he wanted. *Life of Alexander* (Plutarch)

34 A majority is always the best repartee.

Benjamin Disraeli (1804–81) British statesman. *Tancred*, Bk. II, Ch. 14

35 Her Majesty is not a subject.

Benjamin Disraeli Responding to Gladstone's taunt that Disraeli could make a joke out of any subject, including Queen Victoria. Attrib.

36 I know he is, and he adores his maker.

Benjamin Disraeli Replying to a remark made in defense of John Bright that he was a self-made man. *The Fine Art of Political Wit* (L. Harris)

37 If I had a good quote, I'd be wearing it.

Bob Dylan (1941–) US singer and songwriter. When a French journalist asked him for a good quote. *The Times*, July 1981

38 REPORTER. If Mr Stalin dies, what will be the effect on international affairs?
EDEN. That is a good question for you to ask, not a wise question for me to answer.

Anthony Eden (1897–1977) British statesman. Interview on board the *Queen Elizabeth*, 4 Mar 1953

39 If thy heart fails thee, climb not at all.

Elizabeth I (1533–1603) Queen of England. Written on a window in reply to Walter RALEIGH's line. *Worthies of England* (Fuller), Vol. I

40 How odd
Of God
To choose
The Jews.

William Norman Ewer (1885–1976) British writer. For a reply see Cecil BROWNE *How Odd*

41 But not so odd
As those who choose
A Jewish God,
But spurn the Jews.

Cecil Browne In reply to EWER (above)

42 He has never been known to use a word that might send the reader to the dictionary.

William Faulkner (1897–1962) US novelist. Referring to Ernest HEMINGWAY Attrib.

43 I think it would be a good idea.

Mahatma Gandhi (Mohandas Karamchand Gandhi; 1869–1948) Indian national leader. On being asked for his view on Western civilization. Attrib.

44 Oh! he is mad, is he? Then I wish he would bite some other of my generals.

George II (1683–1760) King of Great Britain and Ireland. Replying to advisors who told him that General James Wolfe was mad. Attrib.

45 LEONTINE. An only son, sir, might expect more indulgence.
CROAKER. An only father, sir, might expect more obedience.

Oliver Goldsmith (1728–74) Irish-born British writer. *The Good-Natured Man*, I

46 Old Cary Grant fine. How you?

Cary Grant (Archibald Leach; 1904–86) British-born US film star. Replying to a telegram sent to his agent inquiring: 'How old Cary Grant?'. *The Filmgoer's Book of Quotes* (Leslie Halliwell)

47 Pray, good people, be civil. I am the Protestant whore.

Nell Gwyn (1650–87) English actress. On being surrounded in her coach by an angry mob in Oxford at the time of the Popish Plot. The crowd, believing her to be the King's catholic mistress Louise de Kerouaille, shouted 'It's the Catholic whore!'. *Nell Gwyn* (Bevan), Ch. 13

48 MASTER. They split the atom by firing particles at it, at 5,500 miles a second.
BOY. Good heavens. And they only split it?

Will Hay (1888–1949) British comedian. *The Fourth Form at St Michael's*

49 Poor Faulkner. Does he really think big emotions come from big words? He thinks I don't know the ten-dollar words. I know them all right. But there are older and simpler and better words, and those are the ones I use.

Ernest Hemingway (1899–1961) US novelist. In response to a jibe by William FAULKNER. Attrib.

50 I would like to throw an egg into an electric fan.

Oliver Herford (1863–1935) British-born US humorist. When asked if he really had no ambition beyond making people laugh. Attrib.

51 If it's a boy I'll call him John. If it's a girl I'll call her Mary. But if, as I suspect, it's only wind, I'll call it F. E. Smith.

Gordon Hewart (1870–1943) British lawyer. When F. E. Smith commented on the size of his stomach, saying 'What's it to be – a boy or a girl?'. Attrib.

52 Do you call that thing under your hat a head?

Ludwig Holberg (1684–1754) Danish dramatist. Reply to the jibe, 'Do you call that thing on your head a hat?'. *Anekdotenschatz* (H. Hoffmeister)

53 ?

Victor Hugo (1802–85) French writer. The entire contents of a telegram sent to his publishers asking how *Les Misérables* was selling; the reply was '!'. *The Literary Life* (R. Hendrickson)

54 I asserted – and I repeat – that a man has no reason to be ashamed of having an ape for his grandfather. If there were an ancestor whom I should feel shame in recalling it would rather be a *man* – a man of restless and versatile intellect – who, not content with an equivocal success in his own sphere of activity, plunges into scientific questions with which he has no real acquaintance, only to obscure them by an aimless rhetoric, and distract the attention of his hearers from the real point at issue by eloquent digressions and skilled appeals to religious prejudice.

T. H. Huxley (1825–95) British biologist. Replying to Bishop WILBERFORCE. No transcript was taken at the time; the version above is commonly quoted. After hearing Wilberforce's speech, and before rising himself, Huxley is said to have remarked, 'The Lord has delivered him into my hands!'

55 The difference between us is that my family begins with me, whereas yours ends with you.

Iphicrates (d. 353 BC) Athenian general. Reply to a descendant of Harmodius (an Athenian hero), who had derided Iphicrates for being the son of a cobbler. Attrib.

56 Madame, I would have given you another!

Alfred Jarry (1873–1907) French surrealist dramatist. On being reprimanded by a woman for firing his pistol in the vicinity of her child, who might have been killed. *Recollections of a Picture Dealer* (A. Vollard)

57 Never mind about my soul, just make sure you get my tie right.

James Joyce (1882–1941) Irish novelist. Responding to the painter Patrick Tuohy's assertion that he wished to capture Joyce's soul in his portrait of him. *James Joyce* (R. Ellmann)

58 Son, they are all my helicopters.

Lyndon B. Johnson (1908–73) US Democratic president. Johnson was moving towards the wrong helicopter and an officer said to him, 'Your helicopter is over there'. Attrib.

59 Ignorance, madam, pure ignorance.

Samuel Johnson (1709–84) British lexicographer. His reply on being questioned, by a lady reader of his *Dictionary*, why he had incorrectly defined 'pastern' as the 'knee' of a horse. *Life of Johnson* (J. Boswell), Vol. I

60 When the messenger who carried the last sheet to Millar returned, Johnson asked him, 'Well, what did he say?' – 'Sir (answered the messenger), he said, thank God I have done with him.' – 'I am glad (replied Johnson, with a smile) that he thanks God for anything.'

Samuel Johnson After the final page of his *Dictionary* had been delivered. *Life of Johnson* (J. Boswell)

61 BOSWELL. I do indeed come from Scotland, but I cannot help it . . .
JOHNSON. That, Sir, I find, is what a very great many of your countrymen cannot help.

Samuel Johnson *Life of Johnson* (J. Boswell), Vol. I

62 No, it did a lot of other things, too.

James Joyce (1882–1941) Irish novelist. When a young man asked, 'May I kiss the hand that wrote Ulysses?'. *James Joyce* (R. Ellman)

63 Today I dressed to meet my father's eyes; yesterday it was for my husband's.

Julia (39 BC–AD 14) Daughter of Augustus. On being complimented by her father, the emperor Augustus, on her choice of a more modest dress than the one she had worn the previous day. *Saturnalia* (Macrobius)

64 The baby doesn't understand English and the Devil knows Latin.

Ronald Knox (1888–1957) British Roman Catholic priest. Said when asked to conduct a baptism service in English. *Ronald Knox* (Evelyn Waugh), Pt. I, Ch. 5

65 Play us a medley of your hit.

Oscar Levant (1906–72) US pianist and actor. Replying to George Gershwin's barb 'If you had it all over again, would you fall in love with yourself?'. Attrib.

66 I can piss the old boy in the snow.

Max Liebermann (1847–1935) German painter. Remark to an artist who said he could not draw General Paul von Hindenburg's face. *Conversations with Stravinsky* (Igor Stravinsky and Robert Craft)

67 I cried all the way to the bank.

Liberace (Wladzin Valentino Liberace; 1919–87) US pianist and showman. Said when asked whether he minded being criticized. *Liberace: An Autobiography*, Ch. 2

68 Because it is there.

George Mallory (1886–1924) British mountaineer. Answer to the question 'Why do you want to climb Mt. Everest?'. *George Mallory* (D. Robertson)

69 Sir, you have the advantage of me.
– Not yet I haven't, but wait till I get you outside.

Groucho Marx (Julius Marx; 1895–1977) US comedian. *Monkey Business*

70 What I want is men who will support me when I am in the wrong.

Lord Melbourne (1779–1848) British statesman. Replying to someone who said he would support Melbourne as long as he was in the right. *Lord M.* (Lord David Cecil)

71 If I were the Archangel Gabriel, madam, I'm afraid you would not be in my constituency.

Robert Menzies (1894–1978) Australian prime minister. Replying to a heckler who shouted, 'I wouldn't vote for you if you were the Archangel Gabriel'. *The Wit of Sir Robert Menzies* (R. Robinson)

72 Considering the company I keep in this place, that is hardly surprising

Robert Menzies When accused of having a superiority complex in parliament. *Time*, 29 May 1978

73 JOURNALIST. Didn't you have anything on?
M. M. I had the radio on.

Marilyn Monroe (Norma-Jean Baker; 1926–62) US film star. Attrib.

74 The bullet that is to kill me has not yet been moulded.

Napoleon I (Napoleon Bonaparte; 1769–1821) French emperor. In reply to his brother Joseph, King of Spain, who had asked whether he had ever been hit by a cannonball. Attrib.

75 This vice brings in one hundred million francs in taxes every year. I will certainly forbid it at once – as soon as you can name a virtue that brings in as much revenue.

Napoleon III (1808–73) French emperor. Reply when asked to ban smoking. *Anekdotenschatz* (H. Hoffmeister)

76 What is your fortune, my pretty maid?
My face is my fortune, sir, she said.
Then I can't marry you, my pretty maid.
Nobody asked you, sir, she said.

Nursery Rhyme *Archaeologia Cornu-Britannica* (William Pryce)

77 Outspoken by whom?

Dorothy Parker (1893–1967) US writer. When told that she was 'very outspoken'. Attrib.

78 Where does she find them?

Dorothy Parker In reply to a remark, 'Anyway, she's always very nice to her inferiors'. *Lyttelton Hart-Davis Letters*

79 Pearls before swine.

Dorothy Parker Clare Booth Luce, going through a door with her, said, 'Age before beauty'. *You Might As Well Live* (J. Keats)

80 If I like it, I say it's mine. If I don't I say it's a fake.

Pablo Picasso (1881–1973) Spanish painter. When asked how he knew which paintings were his. *The Sunday Times*, 10 Oct 1965

81 Fain would I climb, yet fear I to fall.

Walter Raleigh (1554–1618) English explorer. Written on a window pane. For the reply *see* ELIZABETH I. Attrib.

82 How can I possibly dislike a sex to which Your Majesty belongs?

Cecil Rhodes (1853–1902) South African statesman. Replying to Queen Victoria's suggestion that he disliked women. *Rhodes* (Lockhart)

83 Here lies our sovereign lord the King
Whose promise none relies on;
He never said a foolish thing,
Or ever did a wise one.

John Wilmot, Earl of Rochester (1647–80) British poet. For a reply see CHARLES II *The King's Epitaph*

84 The people – could you patent the sun?

Jonas E. Salk (1914–) US virologist. On being asked who owned the patent on his polio vaccine. *Famous Men of Science* (S. Bolton)

85 CHIEF JUSTICE. God send the prince a better companion!
FALSTAFF. God send the companion a better prince! I cannot rid my hands of him.

William Shakespeare (1564–1616) English dramatist. *Henry IV, Part 2*, I:2

86 MACBETH. I bear a charmed life, which must not yield
To one of woman born.
MACDUFF. Despair thy charm;
And let the angel whom thou still hast serv'd
Tell thee Macduff was from his mother's womb
Untimely ripp'd.

William Shakespeare *Macbeth*, V:8

87 LORD NORTHCLIFFE. The trouble with you, Shaw, is that you look as if there were famine in the land.
G.B.S. The trouble with you, Northcliffe, is that you look as if you were the cause of it.

George Bernard Shaw (1856–1950) Irish dramatist and critic. Attrib.

88 The trouble, Mr Goldwyn is that you are only interested in art and I am only interested in money.
George Bernard Shaw Turning down Goldwyn's offer to buy the screen rights of his plays. *The Movie Moguls* (Philip French), Ch. 4

89 I quite agree with you, sir, but what can two do against so many?
George Bernard Shaw Responding to a solitary hiss heard among the applause at the first performance of *Arms and the Man* in 1894. *Oxford Book of Literary Anecdotes*

90 Mr. Speaker, I said the honorable member was a liar it is true and I am sorry for it. The honourable member may place the punctuation where he pleases.
Richard Brinsley Sheridan (1751–1816) British dramatist. On being asked to apologize for calling a fellow MP a liar. Attrib.

91 It is not my interest to pay the principal, nor my principle to pay the interest.
Richard Brinsley Sheridan To his tailor when he requested the payment of a debt, or of the interest on it at least. Attrib.

92 The Right Honourable gentleman is indebted to his memory for his jests, and to his imagination for his facts.
Richard Brinsley Sheridan Replying to a speech in the House of Commons. Attrib.

93 I'm sorry to hear that, sir, you don't happen to have the shilling about you now, do you?
Tom Sheridan (1775–1817) Son of the dramatist Richard Brinsley Sheridan. To his father, on being told that he was to be cut off in his will with a shilling. *The Fine Art of Political Wit* (L. Harris)

94 A pompous woman of his acquaintance, complaining that the head-waiter of a restaurant had not shown her and her husband immediately to a table, said, 'We had to tell him who we were.' Gerald, interested, enquired, 'And who were you?'
Edith Sitwell (1887–1964) British poet and writer. *Taken Care Of*, Ch. 15

95 JUDGE WILLIS. What do you suppose I am on the Bench for, Mr Smith?
SMITH. It is not for me to attempt to fathom the inscrutable workings of Providence.
F. E. Smith (1872–1930) British lawyer. *Frederick Elwin, Earl of Birkenhead* (Lord Birkenhead), Vol. I, Ch. 9

96 JUDGE WILLIS. You are extremely offensive, young man.
F. E. SMITH. As a matter of fact, we both are, and the only difference between us is that I am trying to be, and you can't help it.
F. E. Smith *Frederick Elwin, Earl of Birkenhead* (Lord Birkenhead), Vol. I, Ch. 9

97 Try taking a couple of aspirates.
F. E. Smith Replying to the Labour MP J. H. Thomas who had complained that he ''ad a 'eadache'. Attrib.

98 Possibly no wiser, My Lord, but far better informed.
F. E. Smith To a judge who complained that he had listened to Smith's argument but was still none the wiser. *Life of F. E. Smith* (Birkenhead)

99 The Pope! How many divisions has *he* got?
Joseph Stalin (J. Dzhugashvili; 1879–1953) Soviet statesman. When urged by Pierre Laval to tolerate Catholicism in the USSR to appease the Pope, 13 May 1935. When told of this by Churchill, the Pope (Pius XII) replied, 'Tell our brother Joseph that he will meet our divisions in Heaven'. *The Second World War* (W. S. Churchill), Vol. I, Ch. 8

100 Hurry! I never hurry. I have no time to hurry.
Igor Stravinsky (1882–1971) Russian-born US composer. Responding to his publisher's request that he hurry his completion of a composition. Attrib.

101 MILNE. No matter how imperfect things are, if you've got a free press everything is correctable, and without it everything is conceivable.
RUTH. I'm with you on the free press. It's the newspapers I can't stand.
Tom Stoppard (1937–) Czech-born British dramatist. *Night and Day*, I

102 'Are you not,' a Rugby master had asked him in discussing one of his essays, 'a little out of your depth here?' 'Perhaps, Sir,' was the confident reply, 'but I can swim.'
William Temple (1881–1944) British churchman. *William Temple* (F. A. Iremonger)

103 She was – but I assure you that she was a very bad cook.
Louis Adolphe Thiers (1797–1877) French statesman and historian. Defending his social status after someone had remarked that his mother had been a cook. Attrib.

104 With all my heart. Whose wife shall it be?
John Horne Tooke (1736–1812) British clergyman, politician, and etymologist. Replying to the suggestion that he take a wife. Attrib.

105 It's too late to apologize.
Arturo Toscanini (1867–1957) Italian conductor. Retort to the insult 'Nuts to you!' shouted at him by a player he had just ordered from the stage during rehearsal. *The Humor of Music* (L. Humphrey)

106 The King, observing with judicious eyes
The state of both his universities,
To Oxford sent a troop of horse, and why?
That learned body wanted loyalty;
To Cambridge books, as very well discerning
How much that loyal body wanted learning.
Joseph Trapp (1679–1747) English churchman and academic. Written after George I donated the Bishop of Ely's library to Cambridge; for a reply see BROWNE *Literary Anecdotes* (Nichols), Vol. III

107 That's right. 'Taint yours, and 'taint mine.
Mark Twain (Samuel Langhorne Clemens; 1835–1910) US writer. Agreeing with a friend's comment that the money of a particular rich industrialist was 'tainted'. Attrib.

108 Scarce, sir. Mighty scarce.
Mark Twain Responding to the question 'In a world without women what would men become?'. Attrib.

109 No, my dear, it is *I* who am surprised; you are merely astonished.
Noah Webster (1758–1843) US lexicographer. Responding to his wife's comment that she had been surprised to find him embracing their maid. Attrib.

110 Sparrowhawks, Ma'am.
Duke of Wellington (1769–1852) British general and statesman. Advice when asked by Queen Victoria how to remove sparrows from the Crystal Palace. Attrib.

111 Yes, about ten minutes.
Duke of Wellington Responding to a vicar's query as to whether there was anything he would like his forthcoming sermon to be about. Attrib.

112 Yes, and they went down very well too.
Duke of Wellington Replying to the observation that the French cavalry had come up very well during the Battle of Waterloo. *The Age of Elegance* (A. Bryant)

113 – My goodness those diamonds are lovely!
Goodness had nothing whatever to do with it.
Mae West (1892–1980) US actress. Used in 1959 as the title of the first volume of her autobiography. *Diamond Lil*

114 A LADY. This landscape reminds me of your work.
WHISTLER. Yes madam, Nature is creeping up.
James Whistler (1834–1903) US painter. *Whistler Stories* (D. Seitz)

115 Well, not bad, but there are decidedly too many of them, and they are not very well arranged. I would have done it differently.

James Whistler His reply when asked if he agreed that the stars were especially beautiful one night. Attrib.

116 No, I ask it for the knowledge of a lifetime.

James Whistler Replying to the taunt, during the Ruskin trial, that he was asking a fee of 200 guineas for two days' painting. *Lives of the Wits* (H. Pearson)

117 The explanation is quite simple. I wished to be near my mother.

James Whistler Explaining to a snobbish lady why he had been born in such an unfashionable place as Lowell, Massachusetts. Attrib.

118 Isn't it? I know in my case I would grow intolerably conceited.

James Whistler Replying to the pointed observaton that it was as well that we do not see ourselves as others see us. *The Man Whistler* (H. Pearson)

119 A LADY. I only know of two painters in the world: yourself and Velasquez.
WHISTLER. Why drag in Velasquez?

James Whistler *Whistler Stories* (D. Seitz)

120 I cannot tell you that, madam. Heaven has granted me no offspring.

James Whistler Replying to a lady who had inquired whether he thought genius hereditary. *Whistler Stories* (D. Seitz)

121 You will, Oscar, you will.

James Whistler Replying to Oscar Wilde's exclamation 'I wish I had said that!'. Attrib.

122 MRS ALLONBY. They say, Lady Hunstanton, that when good Americans die they go to Paris.
LADY HUNSTANTON. Indeed? And when bad Americans die, where do they go to?
LORD ILLINGWORTH. Oh, they go to America.

Oscar Wilde (1854–1900) Irish-born British dramatist. *A Woman of No Importance,* I

123 LORD ILLINGWORTH. The Book of Life begins with a man and a woman in a garden.
MRS ALLONBY. It ends with Revelations.

Oscar Wilde *A Woman of No Importance,* I

124 CECILY. When I see a spade I call it a spade.
GWENDOLEN. I am glad to say I have never seen a spade. It is obvious that our social spheres have been widely different.

Oscar Wilde *The Importance of Being Earnest,* II

125 Nothing, except my genius.

Oscar Wilde Replying to a US customs official on being asked if he had anything to declare. Attrib.

126 And when we open our dykes, the waters are ten feet deep.

Wilhelmina (1880–1962) Queen of the Netherlands. Replying to a boast by Wilhelm II that his guardsmen were all seven feet tall. Attrib.

127 LORD SANDWICH. You will die either on the gallows, or of the pox.
WILKES. That must depend on whether I embrace your lordship's principles or your mistress.

John Wilkes (1725–97) British politician. Sometimes attrib. to Samuel Foote. *Portrait of a Patriot* (Charles Chenevix-Trench), Ch. 3

REPENTANCE

See regret

REPRESENTATION

1 In Scotland there is no shadow even of representation. There is neither a representation of property for the counties, nor of population for the towns.

Charles James Fox (1749–1806) British politician. *Parliamentary History of England* (W. Cobbett), Vol. XXXIII

2 Taxation without representation is tyranny.

James Otis (1725–83) US political activist. As 'No taxation without representation' this became the principal slogan of the American Revolution. Attrib.

3 No annihilation without representation.

Arnold Toynbee (1889–1975) British historian. Urging the need for a greater British influence in the UN, 1947

REPUBLIC

See also democracy, State

1 Our object in the construction of the state is the greatest happiness of the whole, and not that of any one class.

Plato (429–347 BC) Greek philosopher. *Republic,* Bk. 4

2 As there was no form of government common to the peoples thus segregated, nor tie of language, history, habit, or belief, they were called a Republic.

Evelyn Waugh (1903–66) British novelist. *Scoop,* Bk. II, Ch. 1

REPUTATION

See also fame, posterity

1 For my name and memory, I leave it to men's charitable speeches, and to foreign nations, and the next ages.

Francis Bacon (1561–1626) English philosopher. Will, 19 Dec 1625

2 I hold it as certain, that no man was ever written out of reputation but by himself.

Richard Bentley (1662–1742) English academic. *The Works of Alexander Pope* (W. Warburton), Vol. IV

3 Dead flies cause the ointment of the apothecary to send forth a stinking savour: so doth a little folly him that is in reputation for wisdom and honour.

Bible: Ecclesiastes 10:1

4 The Doctor fared even better. The fame of his new case spread far and wide. People seemed to think that if he could cure an elephant he could cure anything.

Henry Cuyler Bunner (1855–96) *Short Sixes,* 'The Infidelity of Zenobia'

5 Die when I may, I want it said of me by those who know me best, that I have always plucked a thistle and planted a flower where I thought a flower would grow.

Abraham Lincoln (1809–65) US statesman. *Presidential Anecdotes* (P. Boller)

6 Until you've lost your reputation, you never realize what a burden it was or what freedom really is.

Margaret Mitchell (1909–49) US novelist. *Gone with the Wind*

7 This famous store needs no name on the door.

H. Gordon Selfridge (1856–1947) US businessman. Slogan

8 Reputation, reputation, reputation!
O, I have lost my reputation! I have lost the immortal part of myself, and what remains is bestial.

William Shakespeare (1564–1616) English dramatist. *Othello,* II:3

9 Good name in man and woman, dear my lord,
Is the immediate jewel of their souls:
Who steals my purse steals trash; 'tis something, nothing;

'Twas mine, 'tis his, and has been slave to thousands;
But he that filches from me my good name
Robs me of that which not enriches him
And makes me poor indeed.

William Shakespeare *Othello*, III:3

10 The purest treasure mortal times afford
Is spotless reputation; that away,
Men are but gilded loam or painted clay.

William Shakespeare *Richard II*, I:1

11 The king's name is a tower of strength.

William Shakespeare *Richard III*, V:3

12 Even the fact that doctors themselves die of the very diseases they profess to cure passes unnoticed. We do not shoot out our lips and shake our heads, saying, 'They save others: themselves they cannot save': their reputation stands, like an African king's palace, on a foundation of dead bodies.

George Bernard Shaw (1856–1950) Irish dramatist and critic. *The Doctor's Dilemma*, 'Preface on Doctors'

13 My reputation grew with every failure.

George Bernard Shaw Referring to his unsuccessful early novels. *Bernard Shaw* (Hesketh Pearson)

14 I'm called away by particular business. But I leave my character behind me.

Richard Brinsley Sheridan (1751–1816) British dramatist. *The School for Scandal*, II

15 Everything.

Mae West (1892–1980) US actress. When asked what she wanted to be remembered for. Attrib.

RESEARCH

1 We vivisect the nightingale
To probe the secret of his note.

T. B. Aldrich (1836–1907) US writer and editor.

2 I have yet to see any problem, however complicated, which, when looked at in the right way, did not become still more complicated.

Poul Anderson *New Scientist*, 1969

3 Research demands involvement. It cannot be delegated very far.

Anonymous

4 We must discover the laws on which our profession rests, and not invent them.

Anonymous

5 Celsus . . . tells us that the experimental part of medicine was first discovered, and that afterwards men philosophized about it; and hunted for and assigned causes; and not by an inverse process that philosophy and the knowledge of causes led to the discovery and development of the experimental part.

Francis Bacon (1561–1626) English philosopher. *Novum Organum*, 'Aphorisms', LXXIII

6 Man can learn nothing except by going from the known to the unknown.

Claude Bernard (1813–78) French physiologist. *An Introduction to the Study of Experimental Medicine*, Ch. 2

7 Behavioural psychology is the science of pulling habits out of rats.

Dr. Douglas Busch

8 I must begin with a good body of facts and not from a principle (in which I always suspect some fallacy) and then as much deduction as you please.

Charles Darwin (1809–82) British life scientist. Letter to J. Fiske, 8 Dec 1874

9 No amount of experimentation can ever prove me right; a single experiment can prove me wrong.

Albert Einstein (1879–1955) German physicist.

10 Don't despise empiric truth. Lots of things work in practice for which the laboratory has never found proof.

Martin H. Fischer (1879–1962) *Fischerisms* (Howard Fabing and Ray Marr)

11 Research has been called good business, a necessity, a gamble, a game. It is none of these – it's a state of mind.

Martin H. Fischer *Fischerisms* (Howard Fabing and Ray Marr)

12 I have been trying to point out that in our lives chance may have an astonishing influence and, if I may offer advice to the young laboratory worker, it would be this – never to neglect an extraordinary appearance or happening. It may be – usually is, in fact – a false alarm that leads to nothing, but it may on the other hand be the clue provided by fate to lead you to some important advance.

Alexander Fleming (1881–1955) Scottish bacteriologist. Lecture at Harvard

13 One does not discover new lands without consenting to lose sight of the shore for a very long time.

André Gide (1869–1951) French novelist. *The Counterfeiters*

14 The way to do research is to attack the facts at the point of greatest astonishment.

Celia Green *The Decline and Fall of Science*, 'Aphorisms'

15 If . . . an outbreak of cholera might be caused either by an infected water supply or by the blasphemies of an infidel mayor, medical research would be in confusion.

W. R. Inge (1860–1954) British clergyman. *Outspoken Essays*, 'Confessio Fidei'

16 Research! A mere excuse for idleness; it has never achieved, and will never achieve any results of the slightest value.

Benjamin Jowett (1817–93) British theologian. *Unforgotten Years* (Logan Pearsall Smith)

17 O speculator concerning this machine of ours let it not distress you that you impart knowledge of it through another's death, but rejoice that our Creator has ordained the intellect to such excellence of perception.

Leonardo da Vinci (1452–1519) Italian artist, architect, and engineer. *Quaderni d'Anatomia*, Vol. II

18 There are people who do not object to eating a mutton chop – people who do not even object to shooting a pheasant with the considerable chance that it may be only wounded and may have to die after lingering in pain, unable to obtain its proper nutriment – and yet who consider it something monstrous to introduce under the skin of a guinea pig a little inoculation of some microbe to ascertain its action. These seem to me to be most inconsistent views.

Joseph Lister, 1st Baron (1827–1912) British surgeon. *British Medical Journal*, 1:317, 1897

19 The aim of research is the discovery of the equations which subsist between the elements of phenomena.

Ernst Mach (1838–1916) Austrian physicist and philosopher. *Popular Scientific Lectures*

20 The human body is private property. We have to have a search warrant to look inside, and even then an investigator is confined to a few experimental tappings here and there, some gropings on the party wall, a torch flashed rather hesitantly into some of the dark corners.

Jonathan Miller (1936–) British writer and doctor. BBC TV program, *The Body in Question*, 'Perishable Goods', 15 Feb 1979

21 When you steal from one author, it's plagiarism; if you steal from many, it's research.

Wilson Mizner (1876–1933) US writer and wit. Attrib.

22 Always verify your references.

Martin Joseph Routh (1755–1854) British scholar. Attrib.

23 We haven't the money, so we've got to think.

Ernest Rutherford (1871–1937) British physicist. Attrib.

24 It is too bad that we cannot cut the patient in half in order to compare two regimens of treatment.

Béla Schick (1877–1967) Austrian pediatrician. *Aphorisms and Facetiae of Béla Schick*, 'Early Years' (I. J. Wolfe)

25 Research is fundamentally a state of mind involving continual reexamination of the doctrines and axioms upon which current thought and action are based. It is, therefore, critical of existing practices.

Theobald Smith (1859–1934) *American Journal of Medical Science*, 178:741, 1929

26 The outcome of any serious research can only be to make two questions grow where only one grew before.

Thorstein Bunde Veblen (1857–1929) US social scientist. *The Place of Science in Modern Civilization*

27 It requires a very unusual mind to undertake the analysis of the obvious.

A. N. Whitehead (1861–1947) British philosopher. *Science and the Modern World*

RESPECT

See also courtesy, self-respect

1 Let them hate, so long as they fear.

Lucius Accius (170–c. 85 BC) Roman tragic playwright. *Atreus*, 'Seneca'

2 One does not arrest Voltaire.

Charles De Gaulle (1890–1970) French general and statesman. Explaining why he had not arrested Jean-Paul Sartre for urging French soldiers in Algeria to desert. Attrib.

3 I hate victims who respect their executioners.

Jean-Paul Sartre (1905–80) French writer. *Altona*

4 We owe respect to the living; to the dead we owe only truth.

Voltaire (François-Marie Arouet; 1694–1778) French writer. *Oeuvres*, 'Première lettre sur Oedipe'

5 His indolence was qualified with enough basic bad temper to ensure the respect of those about him.

Evelyn Waugh (1903–66) British novelist. *Put Out More Flags*

6 The old-fashioned respect for the young is fast dying out.

Oscar Wilde (1854–1900) Irish-born British dramatist. *The Importance of Being Earnest*, I

RESPECTABILITY

1 Since when was genius found respectable?

Elizabeth Barrett Browning (1806–61) British poet. *Aurora Leigh*, Bk. VI

2 Let them cant about decorum
Who have characters to lose.

Robert Burns (1759–96) Scottish poet. *The Jolly Beggars*

3 Respectable means rich, and decent means poor. I should die if I heard my family called decent.

Thomas Love Peacock (1785–1866) British novelist. *Crotchet Castle*, Ch. 3

4 So live that you wouldn't be ashamed to sell the family parrot to the town gossip.

Will Rogers (1879–1935) US actor and humorist. Attrib.

RESPONSIBILITY

See also accusation

1 A bad workman always blames his tools.

Proverb

2 What the proprietorship of these papers is aiming at is power, and power without responsibility – the prerogative of the harlot through the ages.

Stanley Baldwin (1867–1947) British statesman. Attacking the press barons Lords Rothermere and Beaverbrook. It was first used by KIPLING *See also* DUKE OF DEVONSHIRE; STOPPARD Speech, election rally, 18 Mar 1931

3 Each man the architect of his own fate.

Appius Caecus (4th–3rd century BC) Roman statesman. *De Civitate* (Sallust), Bk. I

4 Everyone threw the blame on me. I have noticed that they nearly always do. I suppose it is because they think I shall be able to bear it best.

Winston Churchill (1874–1965) British statesman. *My Early Life*, Ch. 17

5 Perhaps it is better to be irresponsible and right than to be responsible and wrong.

Winston Churchill Party Political Broadcast, London, 26 Aug 1950

6 Good God, that's done it. He's lost us the tarts' vote.

Duke of Devonshire (1895–1950) Conservative politician. Referring to Stanley BALDWIN's attack on newspaper proprietors; recalled by Harold Macmillan. Attrib.

7 It matters not how strait the gate,
How charged with punishments the scroll,
I am the master of my fate:
I am the captain of my soul.

William Ernest Henley (1849–1903) British writer. *Echoes*, IV, 'Invictus. In Mem. R.T.H.B.'

8 It often happens that I wake at night and begin to think about a serious problem and decide I must tell the Pope about it. Then I wake up completely and remember I am the Pope.

John XXIII (1881–1963) Italian-born pope. Attrib.

9 Power without responsibility – the prerogative of the harlot throughout the ages.

Rudyard Kipling (1865–1936) Indian-born British writer. Better known for its subsequent use by BALDWIN Attrib.

10 Accuse not Nature, she hath done her part;
Do thou but thine.

John Milton (1608–74) English poet. *Paradise Lost*, Bk. VIII

11 *We can believe what we choose.* We are answerable for what we choose to believe.

Cardinal Newman (1801–90) British theologian. Letter to Mrs Froude, 27 June 1848

12 You become responsible, forever, for what you have tamed. You are responsible for your rose.

Antoine de Saint-Exupéry (1900–44) French novelist and aviator. *The Little Prince*, Ch. 21

13 What infinite heart's ease

Must kings neglect, that private men enjoy!
And what have kings that privates have not too,
Save ceremony, save general ceremony?

William Shakespeare (1564–1616) English dramatist. *Henry V*, IV:1

14 'Tis not the balm, the sceptre and the ball,
The sword, the mace, the crown imperial,
The intertissued robe of gold and pearl,
The farced title running 'fore the king,
The throne he sits on, nor the tide of pomp
That beats upon the high shore of this world,
No, not all these, thrice-gorgeous ceremony,
Can sleep so soundly as the wretched slave,
Who with a body fill'd and vacant mind
Gets him to rest, cramm'd with distressful bread;
Never sees horrid night, the child of hell,
But, like a lackey, from the rise to set
Sweats in the eye of Phoebus, and all night
Sleeps in Elysium.

William Shakespeare *Henry V*, IV:1

15 O God! methinks it were a happy life,
To be no better than a homely swain;
To sit upon a hill, as I do now,
To carve out dials, quaintly, point by point,
Thereby to see the minutes how they run,
How many make the hour full complete;
How many hours bring about the day;
How many days will finish up the year;
How many years a mortal man may live.

William Shakespeare *Henry VI*, Pt. 3, II:5

16 The salvation of mankind lies only in making everything the concern of all.

Alexander Solzhenitsyn (1918–) Soviet novelist. Nobel Lecture, 1970

17 The House of Lords, an illusion to which I have never been able to subscribe – responsibility without power, the prerogative of the eunuch throughout the ages.

Tom Stoppard (1937–) Czech-born British dramatist. *See also* BALDWIN *Lord Malquist and Mr Moon*, Pt. VI, Ch. 1

18 For man is man and master of his fate.

Alfred, Lord Tennyson (1809–92) British poet. *Idylls of the King*, 'The Marriage of Geraint'

19 The buck stops here.

Harry S. Truman (1884–1972) US statesman. Sign kept on his desk during his term as president. *Presidential Anecdotes* (P. Boller)

20 I don't know whether you fellows ever had a load of hay fall on you, but when they told me yesterday what had happened, I felt like the moon, the stars, and all the planets had fallen on me.

Harry S. Truman On succeeding Roosevelt as president. Attrib.

21 Every man who takes office in Washington either grows or swells, and when I give a man office I watch him carefully to see whether he is growing or swelling.

Woodrow Wilson (1856–1925) US statesman. Speech, 15 May 1916

22 In dreams begins responsibility.

W. B. Yeats (1865–1939) Irish poet. *Old Play, Epigraph, Responsibilities*

REST

See also bed, idleness, leisure, sleep

1 Will there be beds for me and all who seek?
Yea, beds for all who come.

Christina Rossetti (1830–74) British poet. *Up-Hill*

2 Unarm, Eros; the long day's task is done,
And we must sleep.

William Shakespeare (1564–1616) English dramatist. *Antony and Cleopatra*, IV:12

3 I enjoy convalescence. It is the part that makes the illness worth while.

George Bernard Shaw (1856–1950) Irish dramatist and critic. *Back to Methuselah*, Pt. II

4 It is well to lie fallow for a while.

Martin Farquhar Tupper (1810–89) British writer. *Proverbial Philosophy*, 'Of Recreation'

RESULTS

1 Desperate cuts must have desperate cures.

Proverb

2 The little bit (two inches wide) of ivory on which I work with so fine a brush as produces little effect after much labour.

Jane Austen (1775–1817) British novelist. Letter, 16 Dec 1816

3 Ye shall know them by their fruits. Do men gather grapes of thorns, or figs of thistles?
Even so every good tree bringeth forth good fruit; but a corrupt tree bringeth forth evil fruit.
A good tree cannot bring forth evil fruit, neither can a corrupt tree bring forth good fruit.
Every tree that bringeth not forth good fruit is hewn down, and cast into the fire.
Wherefore by their fruits ye shall know them.

Bible: Matthew 7:16–20

4 You have a row of dominoes set up; you knock over the first one, and what will happen to the last one is that it will go over very quickly.

Dwight D. Eisenhower (1890–1969) US general and statesman. The so-called 'domino effect'; said during the Battle of Dien Bien Phu, in which the French were defeated by the communist Viet-Minh. Press conference, 7 Apr 1954

5 You can do anything in this world if you are prepared to take the consequences.

W. Somerset Maugham (1874–1965) British novelist. *The Circle*

6 Our love of what is beautiful does not lead to extravagance; our love of the things of the mind does not make us soft.

Pericles (c. 495–429 BC) Greek statesman. Part of the funeral oration, 430 BC, for the dead of the first year of the Peloponnesian War. Attrib. in *Histories*, Bk. II, Ch. 40 (Thucydides)

7 What dire offence from am'rous causes springs,
What mighty contests rise from trivial things.

Alexander Pope (1688–1744) British poet. *The Rape of the Lock*, I

RETRIBUTION

See also punishment, revenge

1 Give a thief enough rope and he'll hang himself.

Proverb

2 *Nemo me impune lacessit.*
No one provokes me with impunity.

Anonymous Motto of the Crown of Scotland

3 And if any mischief follow, then thou shalt give life for life,

Eye for eye, tooth for tooth, hand for hand, foot for foot,
Burning for burning, wound for wound, stripe for stripe.
Bible: Exodus 21:23–25

4 Be not deceived: God is not mocked: for whatsoever a man soweth, that shall he also reap.
For he that soweth to his flesh shall of the flesh reap corruption; but he that soweth to the Spirit shall of the Spirit reap life everlasting.
And let us not be weary in well doing: for in due season we shall reap, if we faint not.
Bible: Galatians 6:7–9

5 For they have sown the wind, and they shall reap the whirlwind: it hath no stalk: the bud shall yield no meal: if so be it yield, the strangers shall swallow it up.
Bible: Hosea 8:7

6 For I say unto you, That except your righteousness shall exceed the righteousness of the scribes and Pharisees, ye shall in no case enter into the kingdom of heaven.
Bible: Matthew 5:20

7 And if thy right eye offend thee, pluck it out, and cast it from thee: for it is profitable for thee that one of thy members should perish, and not that thy whole body should be cast into hell.
Bible: Matthew 5:29

8 For thou shalt heap coals of fire upon his head, and the Lord shall reward thee.
Bible: Proverbs 25:22

9 But men never violate the laws of God without suffering the consequences, sooner or later.
Lydia M. Child (1802–80) US abolitionist campaigner. *The Freedmen's Book*, 'Toussaint L'Ouverture'

10 The Germans, if this Government is returned, are going to pay every penny; they are going to be squeezed, as a lemon is squeezed – until the pips squeak. My only doubt is not whether we can squeeze hard enough, but whether there is enough juice.
Eric Campbell Geddes (1875–1937) British politician. Speech, Cambridge, 10 Dec 1918

RETURN

1 Winston's back.
Anonymous Signal to all ships of the Royal Navy from the Admiralty when Churchill was reappointed First Sea Lord, 3 Sept 1939.

2 Poor wandering one!
Though thou hast surely strayed,
Take heart of grace,
Thy steps retrace,
Poor wandering one!
W. S. Gilbert (1836–1911) British dramatist. *The Pirates of Penzance*, I

3 Ten o'clock . . . and back he'll come.
I can just see him.
With vine leaves in his hair. Flushed and confident.
Henrik Ibsen (1828–1906) Norwegian dramatist. *Hedda Gabler*, II

4 The Spy Who Came In From the Cold.
John Le Carre (1931–) British novelist. Book title

5 Better lo'ed ye canna be,
Will ye no come back again?
Carolina Nairne (1766–1845) Scottish songwriter. Referring to Bonnie Prince Charlie. *Bonnie Charlie's now awa!*

REVENGE

See also retribution

1 Don't cut off your nose to spite your face.
Proverb

2 Revenge is a dish that tastes better cold.
Proverb

3 Revenge is sweet.
Proverb

4 Revenge is a kind of wild justice; which the more man's nature runs to, the more ought law to weed it out.
Francis Bacon (1561–1626) English philosopher. *Essays*, 'Of Revenge'

5 A man that studieth revenge keeps his own wounds green.
Francis Bacon *Essays*, 'Of Revenge'

6 Perish the Universe, provided I have my revenge.
Cyrano de Bergerac (1619–55) French writer. *La Mort d'Agrippine*, IV

7 And the Lord said unto him, Therefore whosoever slayeth Cain, vengeance shall be taken on him sevenfold. And the Lord set a mark upon Cain, lest any finding him should kill him.
And Cain went out from the presence of the Lord, and dwelt in the land of Nod, on the east of Eden.
Bible: Genesis 4:15–16

8 But I say unto you, That ye resist not evil; but whosoever shall smite thee on thy right cheek, turn to him the other also.
Bible: Matthew 5:39 *See also* HOLMES; KHRUSCHEV

9 I make war on the living, not on the dead.
Charles V (1500–58) Holy Roman Emperor. After the death of Martin Luther, when it was suggested that he hang the corpse on a gallows. Attrib.

10 Rome shall perish – write that word
In the blood that she has spilt.
William Cowper (1731–1800) British poet. *Boadicea*

11 Wisdom has taught us to be calm and meek,
To take one blow, and turn the other cheek;
It is not written what a man shall do
If the rude caitiff smite the other too!
Oliver Wendell Holmes (1809–94) US writer. *Non-Resistance*

12 No one delights more in vengeance than a woman.
Juvenal (Decimus Junius Juvenalis; 60–130 AD) Roman satirist. *Satires*, XIII

13 Don't get mad, get even.
Joseph P. Kennedy (1888–1969) US politician; father of president Kennedy. *Conversations with Kennedy* (B. Bradlee)

14 We had no use for the policy of the Gospels: if someone slaps you, just turn the other cheek. We had shown that anyone who slapped us on our cheek would get his head kicked off.
Nikita Khrushchev (1894–1971) Soviet statesman. *Khrushchev Remembers*, Vol. II

15 Revenge, at first though sweet,
Bitter ere long back on itself recoils.
John Milton (1608–74) English poet. *Paradise Lost*, Bk. IX

16 Revenge his foul and most unnatural murder.
William Shakespeare (1564–1616) English dramatist. *Hamlet*, I:5

17 Set you down this;
And say besides, that in Aleppo once,
Where a malignant and a turban'd Turk

Beat a Venetian and traduc'd the state,
I took by the throat the circumcised dog,
And smote him thus.

William Shakespeare *Othello,* V:2

18 I do begin to have bloody thoughts.

William Shakespeare *The Tempest,* IV:1

19 I'll be revenged on the whole pack of you.

William Shakespeare *Twelfth Night,* V:1

20 No more tears now; I will think upon revenge.

Mary Stuart (1542–87) Queen of Scots. Remark on hearing of the murder (9 Mar 1566) of her secretary, David Riccio, by her husband, Lord Darnley

21 Those who offend us are generally punished for the offence they give; but we so frequently miss the satisfaction of knowing that we are avenged!

Anthony Trollope (1815–82) British novelist. *The Small House at Allington,* Ch. 50

REVOLUTION

See also French Revolution, rebellion, Russian Revolution

1 Inferiors revolt in order that they may be equal and equals that they may be superior. Such is the state of mind which creates revolutions.

Aristotle (384–322 BC) Greek philosopher. *Politics,* Bk. V

2 One of the strangest catastrophes that is in any history. A great king, with strong armies and mighty fleets, a great treasure and powerful allies, fell all at once, and his whole strength, like a spider's web, was . . . irrecoverably broken at a touch.

Gilbert Burnet (1643–1715) English bishop and historian. Referring to the Glorious Revolution, 1688. *History of My Own Times*

3 All modern revolutions have ended in a reinforcement of the power of the State.

Albert Camus (1913–60) French existentialist writer. *The Rebel*

4 A revolution is not a bed of roses. A revolution is a struggle to the death between the future and the past.

Fidel Castro (1926–) Cuban statesman. Speech, Havana, Jan 1961 (2nd anniversary of Revolution)

5 I believe in the armed struggle as the only solution for those people who fight to free themselves, and I am consistent with my beliefs. Many will call me an adventurer – and that I am, only one of a different sort: one of those who risks his skin to prove his platitudes.

Che Guevara (Ernesto G.; 1928–67) Argentine revolutionary. On leaving Cuba to join guerrillas in the Bolivian jungle. Last letter to his parents (1965)

6 What is wrong with a revolution is that it is natural. It is as natural as natural selection, as devastating as natural selection, and as horrible.

William Golding (1911–) British novelist. *The Observer,* 'Sayings of the Year', 1974

7 'Liberty Mr Gumboil?' he said, 'you don't suppose any serious minded person imagines a revolution is going to bring liberty do you?'

Aldous Huxley (1894–1964) British novelist. *Antic Hay*

8 Revolution is delightful in the preliminary stages. So long as it's a question of getting rid of the people at the top.

Aldous Huxley *Eyeless in Gaza*

9 The uprising of the masses implies a fabulous increase of vital possibilities; quite the contrary of what we hear so often about the decadence of Europe.

José Ortega y Gasset (1883–1955) Spanish philosopher. *The Revolt of the Masses,* Ch. 2

10 Revolution is not the uprising against pre-existing order, but the setting-up of a new order contradictory to the traditional one.

José Ortega y Gasset *The Revolt of the Masses,* Ch. 6

11 We are dancing on a volcano.

Comte de Salvandy (1795–1856) French nobleman. A remark made before the July Revolution in 1830.

12 To attempt to export revolution is nonsense.

Joseph Stalin (J. Dzhugashvili; 1879–1953) Soviet statesman. Remark, 1 Mar 1936, to Roy Howard (US newspaper owner)

13 Insurrection is an art, and like all arts it has its laws.

Leon Trotsky (Lev Davidovich Bronstein; 1879–1940) Russian revolutionary. *History of the Russian Revolution,* Pt. III, Ch. 6

14 Revolutions are always verbose.

Leon Trotsky *History of the Russian Revolution,* Pt. II, Ch. 12

15 The fundamental premise of a revolution is that the existing social structure has become incapable of solving the urgent problems of development of the nation.

Leon Trotsky *History of the Russian Revolution,* Pt. III, Ch. 6

16 Revolution by its very nature is sometimes compelled to take in more territory than it is capable of holding. Retreats are possible – when there is territory to retreat from.

Leon Trotsky *Diary in Exile,* 15 Feb 1935

17 The word 'revolution' is a word for which you kill, for which you die, for which you send the labouring masses to their death, but which does not possess any content.

Simone Weil (1909–43) French philosopher. *Oppression and Liberty,* 'Reflections Concerning the Causes of Liberty and Social Oppression'

18 We invented the Revolution
but we don't know how to run it.

Peter Weiss (1916–82) German novelist and dramatist. *Marat Sade,* 15

19 Where the populace rise at once against the never-ending audacity of elected persons.

Walt Whitman (1819–92) US poet. *Song of the Broad Axe,* 5

REWARDS

1 Vice is its own reward.

Quentin Crisp (c. 1910–) Model, publicist, and writer. *The Naked Civil Servant*

2 The reward of a thing well done is to have done it.

Ralph Waldo Emerson (1803–82) US poet and essayist. *Essays,* 'New England Reformers'

3 In nature there are neither rewards nor punishments – there are consequences.

Robert G. Ingersoll (1833–99) US lawyer and agnostic. *Lectures & Essays,* 'Some Reasons Why'

4 To give and not to count the cost;
To fight and not to heed the wounds;
To toil and not to seek for rest;
To labour and not ask for any reward
Save that of knowing that we do Thy will.

St Ignatius Loyola (1491–1556) Spanish priest. *Prayer for Generosity*

5 Men are rewarded and punished not for what they do, but rather for how their acts are defined. This is why men are more interested in better justifying themselves than in better behaving themselves.

Thomas Szasz (1920–) US psychiatrist. *The Second Sin*

RICHES

See poverty and wealth, wealth

RIDICULE

See also contempt, satire

1 For what do we live, but to make sport for our neighbours, and laugh at them in our turn?
Jane Austen (1775–1817) British novelist. *Pride and Prejudice*, Ch. 57

2 Few women care to be laughed at and men not at all, except for large sums of money.
Alan Ayckbourn (1939–) British dramatist. *The Norman Conquests*, Preface

3 Ridicule often checks what is absurd, and fully as often smothers that which is noble.
Walter Scott (1771–1832) Scottish novelist. *Quentin Durward*

4 Had it pleas'd heaven
To try me with affliction, had he rain'd
All kinds of sores, and shames, on my bare head,
Steep'd me in poverty to the very lips,
Given to captivity me and my utmost hopes,
I should have found in some part of my soul
A drop of patience; but, alas! to make me
The fixed figure for the time of scorn
To point his slow and moving finger at;
Yet could I bear that too; well, very well.
William Shakespeare (1564–1616) English dramatist. *Othello*, IV:2

RIGHT

1 This the grave of Mike O'Day
Who died maintaining his right of way.
His right was clear, his will was strong.
But he's just as dead as if he'd been wrong.
Anonymous Epitaph

2 The more you are in the right the more natural that everyone else should be bullied into thinking likewise.
George Orwell (Eric Blair; 1903–50). British novelist. *The Road to Wigan Pier*

3 A child becomes an adult when he realizes that he has a right not only to be right but also to be wrong.
Thomas Szasz (1920–) US psychiatrist. *The Second Sin*

4 While I'd rather be right than president, at any time I'm ready to be both.
Norman M. Thomas (1884–1968) US politician. Referring to his lack of success in presidential campaigns. The expression 'I'd rather be right than president' is also attributed to the US politician Henry Clay (1777–1852). *Come to Judgment* (A. Whitman)

5 Always do right. This will gratify some people, and astonish the rest.
Mark Twain (Samuel Langhorne Clemens; 1835–1910) US writer. Speech to young people, Brooklyn, 16 Feb 1901

6 Right is more precious than peace.
Woodrow Wilson (1856–1925) US statesman. *Radio Times*, 10 Sept 1964

RIGHTEOUSNESS

See also good, integrity, morality, virtue

1 The eternal *not ourselves* that makes for righteousness.
Matthew Arnold (1822–88) British poet and critic. *Literature and Dogma*, Ch. 8

2 Righteous people terrify me . . .
Virtue is its own punishment.
Aneurin Bevan (1897–1960) British Labour politician. *Aneurin Bevan 1897–1945* (Michael Foot)

3 Neither do men light a candle, and put it under a bushel, but on a candlestick; and it giveth light unto all that are in the house.
Let your light so shine before men, that they may see your good works, and glorify your Father which is in heaven.
Bible: Matthew 5:15–16

4 And I saw heaven opened, and behold a white horse; and he that sat upon him was called Faithful and True, and in righteousness he doth judge and make war.
Bible: Revelations 19:11

5 Ye must leave righteous ways behind, not to speak of unrighteous ways.
Buddha (Gautama Siddhartha; c. 563–c. 483 BC) Indian religious teacher. *Some Sayings of the Buddha* (F. L. Woodward)

6 The man of life upright,
Whose guiltless heart is free
From all dishonest deeds
Or thought of vanity.
Thomas Campion (1567–1620) English poet. *The Man of Life Upright*

7 Good thoughts his only friends,
His wealth a well-spent age,
The earth his sober inn
And quiet pilgrimage.
Thomas Campion *The Man of Life Upright*

8 Perhaps it is better to be irresponsible and right than to be responsible and wrong.
Winston Churchill (1874–1965) British statesman. Party Political Broadcast, London, 26 Aug 1950

9 Looks the whole world in the face,
For he owes not any man.
Henry Wadsworth Longfellow (1807–82) US poet. *The Village Blacksmith*

10 Live among men as if God beheld you; speak to God as if men were listening.
Seneca (c. 4 BC–65 AD) Roman author. *Epistles*

RIVERS

1 I have seen the Mississippi. That is muddy water. I have seen the St Lawrence. That is crystal water. But the Thames is liquid history.
John Burns (1858–1943) British Labour politician. Attrib.

2 Ol' man river, dat ol' man river,
He must know sumpin', but don't say nothin',
He just keeps rollin', he keeps on rollin' along.
Oscar Hammerstein (1895–1960) US lyricist. From the musical *Show Boat*. *Ol' Man River*

3 riverrun, past Eve and Adam's, from swerve of shore to bend of bay.
James Joyce (1882–1941) Irish novelist. *Finnegan's Wake*

4 What is there to make so much of in the Thames? I am quite tired of it. Flow, flow, flow, always the same.
Duke of Queensberry (1724–1810) British peer. *Century of Anecdote* (J. Timbs)

5 *Die Wacht am Rhein.*
The Watch on the Rhine.
Max Schneckenburger (1819–49) German poet. Song title

6 Sweet Thames! run softly, till I end my Song.
Edmund Spenser (1552–99) English poet. *Prothalamion*, 18

7 I come from haunts of coot and hern,
I make a sudden sally
And sparkle out among the fern,

To bicker down a valley.

Alfred, Lord Tennyson (1809–92) British poet. *The Brook*

ROCHEFOUCAULD, François, Duc de la

(1613–80) French writer. His literary circle included Mme de Sévigné and the Comtesse de La Fayette. He is best known for his *Maximes*, published in five editions between 1665 and 1678.

1 Self-love is the greatest of all flatterers.
Maximes, 2

2 We are all strong enough to bear the misfortunes of others.
Maximes, 19

3 We need greater virtues to sustain good fortune than bad.
Maximes, 25

4 If we had no faults of our own, we would not take so much pleasure in noticing those of others.
Maximes, 31

5 Self-interest speaks all sorts of tongues, and plays all sorts of roles, even that of disinterestedness.
Maximes, 39

6 We are never so happy nor so unhappy as we imagine.
Maximes, 49

7 To succeed in the world, we do everything we can to appear successful.
Maximes, 50

8 There are very few people who are not ashamed of having been in love when they no longer love each other.
Maximes, 71

9 If one judges love by its visible effects, it looks more like hatred than like friendship.
Maximes, 72

10 The love of justice in most men is simply the fear of suffering injustice.
Maximes, 78

11 Silence is the best tactic for him who distrusts himself.
Maximes, 79

12 It is more shameful to distrust one's friends than to be deceived by them.
Maximes, 84

13 Everyone complains of his memory, but no one complains of his judgement.
Maximes, 89

14 In the misfortune of our best friends, we always find something which is not displeasing to us.
Maximes, 99

15 The intellect is always fooled by the heart.
Maximes, 102

16 One gives nothing so freely as advice.
Maximes, 110

17 One had rather malign oneself than not speak of oneself at all.
Maximes, 138

18 To refuse praise reveals a desire to be praised twice over.
Maximes, 149

19 Hypocrisy is the homage paid by vice to virtue.
Maximes, 218

20 The height of cleverness is to be able to conceal it.
Maximes, 245

21 There is scarcely a single man sufficiently aware to know all the evil he does.
Maximes, 269

22 We only confess our little faults to persuade people that we have no large ones.
Maximes, 327

23 The accent of one's birthplace lingers in the mind and in the heart as it does in one's speech.
Maximes, 342

24 We seldom attribute common sense except to those who agree with us.
Maximes, 347

25 Nothing prevents us from being natural so much as the desire to appear so.
Maximes, 431

26 Quarrels would not last so long if the fault were on only one side.
Maximes, 496

27 Most usually our virtues are only vices in disguise.
Maximes, added to the 4th edition

ROOSEVELT, Franklin D(elano)

(1882–1945) US Democratic president. Although partially paralysed by polio (from 1921), he was re-elected three times and became an effective war leader.

Quotations about Roosevelt

1 A chameleon on plaid.
Herbert Hoover (1874–1964) US statesman. Attrib.

2 The man who started more creations since Genesis – and finished none.
Hugh Johnson Attrib.

Quotations by Roosevelt

3 I murdered my grandmother this morning.
His habitual greeting to any guest at the White House he suspected of paying no attention to what he said. *Ear on Washington* (D. McClellan)

4 It is fun to be in the same decade with you.
After Churchill had congratulated him on his 60th birthday. *The Hinge of Fate* (Winston S. Churchill), Ch. 4

5 Stalin hates the guts of all your top people. He thinks he likes me better, and I hope he will continue to do so.
The Hinge of Fate (Winston S. Churchill), Ch. 11

6 Defeat of Germany means the defeat of Japan, probably without firing a shot or losing a life.
The Hinge of Fate (Winston S. Churchill), Ch. 25

7 The best immediate defence of the United States is the success of Great Britain defending itself.
At press conference, 17 Dec 1940. *Their Finest Hour* (Winston S. Churchill), Ch. 28

8 The forgotten man at the bottom of the economic pyramid.
Speech on radio, 7 Apr 1932

9 I pledge you, I pledge myself, to a new deal for the American people.
Speech accepting nomination for presidency, Chicago, 2 July 1932

10 Let me assert my firm belief that the only thing we have to fear is fear itself.
First Inaugural Address, 4 Mar 1933

11 In the field of world policy; I would dedicate this nation to the policy of the good neighbor.
First Inaugural Address, 4 Mar 1933

12 A radical is a man with both feet firmly planted in air.
Broadcast, 26 Oct 1939

13 We must be the great arsenal of democracy.
Broadcast address to Forum on Current Problems, 29 Dec 1940

14 We look forward to a world founded upon four essential human freedoms. The first is freedom of speech and expression – everywhere in the world. The second is freedom of every person to worship God in his own way – everywhere in the world. The third is freedom from want . . . everywhere in the world. The fourth is freedom from fear . . . anywhere in the world.
Speech to Congress, 6 Jan 1941

15 Never before have we had so little time in which to do so much.
Radio address, 23 Feb 1942

16 We all know that books burn – yet we have the greater knowledge that books cannot be killed by fire. People die, but books never die. No man and no force can abolish memory. . . In this war, we know, books are weapons.
Message to American Booksellers Association, 23 Apr 1942

17 More than an end to war, we want an end to the beginnings of all wars.
Speech broadcast on the day after his death (13 Apr 1945)

ROOSEVELT, Theodore

(1858–1919) US Republican president. His presidency (1901–09) is remembered for his Square Deal program for social reform and the construction of the Panama Canal.

Quotations about Roosevelt

1 I always enjoy his society, he is so hearty, so straightforward, outspoken and, for the moment, so absolutely sincere.
Mark Twain (Samuel Langhorne Clemens; 1835–1910) US writer. *Autobiography*

2 Father always wanted to be the bride at every wedding and the corpse at every funeral.
Nicholas Roosevelt *A Front Row Seat*

Quotations by Roosevelt

3 No man is justified in doing evil on the ground of expediency.
The Strenuous Life

4 Kings and such like are just as funny as politicians.
Mr Wilson's War (John Dos Passos), Ch. 1

5 A man who will steal *for* me will steal *from* me
Firing a cowboy who had applied Roosevelt's brand to a steer belonging to a neighboring ranch. *Roosevelt in the Bad Lands* (Herman Hagedorn)

6 I wish to preach, not the doctrine of ignoble ease, but the doctrine of the strenuous life.
Speech, Chicago, 10 Apr 1899

7 There is a homely adage which runs 'Speak softly and carry a big stick, you will go far'.
Speech, Minnesota State Fair, 2 Sept 1901

8 A man who is good enough to shed his blood for the country is good enough to be given a square deal afterwards. More than that no man is entitled to, and less than that no man shall have.
Speech at the Lincoln Monument, Springfield, Illinois, 4 June 1903

9 There is no room in this country for hyphenated Americanism.
Speech, New York, 12 Oct 1915

10 There can be no fifty-fifty Americanism in this country. There is room here for only one hundred per cent Americanism.
Speech, Saratoga, 19 July 1918

ROYALTY

See also monarchy

1 Be the Emperor, be Peter the Great, John the Terrible, the Emperor Paul – crush them all under you – Now don't you laugh, naughty one – but I long to see you so with those men who try to govern *you* and it must be the contrary.
Alexandra (1872–1918) Empress-Consort of Russia. Letter (in English) to Nicholas II, 27 Dec 1916

2 The personality conveyed by the utterances which are put into her mouth is that of a priggish schoolgirl, captain of the hockey team, a prefect, and a recent candidate for confirmation. It is not thus that she will be able to come into her own as an independent and distinctive character.
Lord Altrincham (John Grigg; 1924–) British writer. Referring to Queen Elizabeth II. *National and English Review*, Aug 1958

3 Your experience will be a lesson to all of us men to be careful not to marry ladies in very high positions.
Idi Amin (1925–) Ugandan soldier and president. Message to Lord Snowdon, on the break-up of his marriage to Princess Margaret. *International Gossip* (A. Barrow)

4 Bloody hell, Ma'am, what's he doing here?
Elizabeth Andrews Royal chambermaid. Discovering an intruder sitting on Queen Elizabeth II's bed. *Daily Mail*, July 1982

5 There is no romance between us. He is here solely to exercise the horses.
Anne (1950–) The Princess Royal, only daughter of Elizabeth II. Shortly before her engagement to Captain Phillips. Attrib.

6 One was presented with a small, hairy individual and, out of general curiosity, one climbed on.
Anne On her first horse ride. *Princess Anne and Mark Phillips Talking Horses with Genevieve Murphy*

7 It's a very boring time. I am not particularly maternal – it's an occupational hazard of being a wife.
Anne TV interview, talking about pregnancy. *Daily Express*, 14 Apr 1981

8 Why don't you naff off!
Anne To reporters. *Daily Mirror*, 17 Apr 1982

9 . . . his lieges who from their hearts entirely thank God who has given them such a lord and governor, who has delivered them from servitude to other lands and from the charges sustained by them in times past.
Anonymous A tribute by the Commons to Edward III. *Rotuli Parliamentorum*, Vol. II

10 It was not, as our enemies say, our intention to kill the king and his sons, but to make him the duke of Lancaster, which is what he ought to be.
Anonymous Referring to Henry IV; said by one of the Franciscans condemned for plotting (1402) to overthrow him. *Eulogium Historiarum*

11 In Hide Park he rides like a hog in armour,
In Whitehall he creeps like a country farmer,
Old England may boast of a godly reformer;

A dainty fine king indeed.

Anonymous Referring to William III. *The Faber Book of English History in Verse* (Kenneth Baker)

12 Good People come buy
The Fruit that I cry,
That now is in Season, tho' Winter is nigh;
'Twill do you all good
And sweeten your Blood,
I'm sure it will please when you've once understood
'tis an *Orange*.

Anonymous Referring to William III. *The Faber Book of English History in Verse* (Kenneth Baker)

13 Lost or strayed out of this house, a man who left a wife and six children on the parish; whoever will give any tidings of him to the churchwardens of St. James's Parish, so he may be got again, shall receive four shillings and sixpence. N.B. This reward will not be increased, nobody judging him to deserve a Crown.

Anonymous Referring to George II, whose frequent absences in Hanover made him unpopular. Notice posted on the gate of St. James's Palace

14 My Lord Archbishop, what a scold you are
And when a man is down, how bold you are,
Of Christian charity how scant you are
You auld Lang Swine, how full of cant you are!

Anonymous Archbishop Lang was one of the chief opponents of Edward VIII's marriage to Mrs Wallis Simpson. *The Faber Book of English History in Verse* (Kenneth Baker)

15 Hark the herald angels sing
Mrs Simpson's pinched our king.

Anonymous Referring to the abdication of Edward VIII.

16 We shall not pretend that there is nothing in his long career which those who respect and admire him would wish otherwise.

Anonymous On the accession of King Edward VII, referring to his lifestyle. *The Times*, Jan 1901

17 The King over the Water.

Anonymous Jacobite toast

18 How different, how very different from the home life of our own dear Queen!

Anonymous Remark about the character of Cleopatra as performed by Sarah Bernhardt, referring to Queen Victoria

19 Here lies Fred,
Who was alive and is dead:
Had it been his father,
I had much rather;
Had it been his brother,
Still better than another;
Had it been his sister,
No one would have missed her;
Had it been the whole generation,
Still better for the nation:
But since 'tis only Fred,
Who was alive and is dead, –
There's no more to be said.

Anonymous Referring to Frederick, Prince of Wales, eldest son of George II and father of George III. *Memoirs of George II* (Horace Walpole)

20 The King told me he would never have died if it had not been for that fool Dawson of Penn.

Margot Asquith (1865–1945) The second wife of Herbert Asquith. Referring to Lord Dawson of Penn. *George V* (K. Rose)

21 George, be a King.

Augusta of Saxe-Gotha, Princess of Wales (1719–72) Mother of King George III. Attrib.

22 The house is well, but it is you, Your Majesty, who have made me too great for my house.

Francis Bacon (1561–1626) English philosopher. Reply when Elizabeth I remarked on the smallness of his house. *After-dinner Stories and Anecdotes* (L. Meissen)

23 Throughout the greater part of his life George III was a kind of 'consecrated obstruction'.

Walter Bagehot (1826–1877) British economist and journalist. *The English Constitution*, 'The Monarchy'

24 Our cock won't fight.

Lord Beaverbrook (Maxwell Aitken; 1879–1964) Canadian-born politician and newspaper proprietor. To Winston Churchill referring to Edward VIII during the abdication crisis. *Edward VIII* (F. Donaldson)

25 So whether it is that the King, misled
By flattering talk to giving his consent,
And truly ignorant of their designs
Unknowingly approves such wrongs as these
Whose only end can be destruction, and
The ruin of his land; or whether he,
With malice in his heart, and ill-intent,
Commits these shameful crimes by raising up
His royal state and power far beyond
The reach of all his country's laws, so that
His whim is satisfied by the abuse
Of royal privilege and strength; if thus
Or otherwise this land of ours is brought
To total rack and ruin, and at last
The kingdom is left destitute, it is
The duty of the great and noble men
To rescue it, to purge the land of all
Corruption and all false authority.

Roger de Berksted Referring to Henry III. *The Song of Lewes*

26 The benefit of the King's Coronation depends under God upon . . . the faith, prayer and self-dedication of the King himself. . . . We hope that he is aware of this need. Some of us wish that he gave more positive signs of such awareness.

Alfred Blunt (1879–1957) British bishop. Referring to Edward VIII shortly before the abdication crisis. Address to diocesan conference, 1 Dec 1936

27 Speed, bonny boat, like a bird on the wing;
'Onward', the sailors cry;
Carry the lad that's born to be king
Over the sea to Skye.

H. E. Boulton (1859–1935) Scottish songwriter. Referring to Bonnie Prince Charlie. *Skye Boat Song*

28 It is neither fitting nor safe that all the keys should hang from the belt of one woman.

Thomas Brinton (c. 1320–89) Bishop of Rochester. Criticizing the influence of Alice Perrers over the ageing Edward III. Sermon, Westminister Abbey, 18 May 1376

29 Such grace had kings when the world begun!

Robert Browning (1812–89) British poet. *Pippa Passes*, Pt. I

30 Kings are naturally lovers of low company.

Edmund Burke (1729–97) British politician. *Speech on the Economical Reform* (House of Commons, 11 Feb 1780)

31 The Duke of Buckingham gave me once a short but severe character of the two brothers. It was the more severe, because it was true: the King (he said) could see things if he would, and the Duke would see things if he could.

Gilbert Burnet (1643–1715) English bishop and historian. Referring to Charles II and James II. *History of My Own Times*

32 . . . was apt to suffer things to run on till there was a great heap of papers laid before him, so then he

signed them a little too precipitately.
Gilbert Burnet Referring to William III; his authorization of the Glencoe Massacre (1692) may have been one consequence of this habit. *History of My Own Times*

33 A better farmer ne'er brushed dew from lawn,
A worse king never left a realm undone!
Lord Byron (1788–1824) British poet. Referring to George III. *The Vision of Judgment*, VIII

34 . . . by putting her hand to her head, when the King of Scots was named to succeed her, they all knew he was the man she desired should reign after her.
Sir Robert Carey (c. 1560–1639) English courtier. Referring to the death of Elizabeth I. *Memoirs*

35 I shall be an autocrat: that's my trade. And the good Lord will forgive me: that's his.
Catherine the Great (1729–96) Empress of Russia (1762–96). Attrib.

36 The sovereign is absolute; for, in a state whose expanse is so vast, there can be no other appropriate authority except that which is concentrated in him.
Catherine the Great *Nakaz*

37 Conquering kings their titles take.
John Chandler (1806–76) British clergyman and writer. Poem title

38 Brother, I am too old to go again to my travels.
Charles II (1630–85) King of England. Referring to his exile, 1651–60. *History of Great Britain (Hume)*, Vol. II, Ch. 7

39 The monarchy is the oldest profession in the world.
Charles, Prince of Wales (1948–) Eldest son of Elizabeth II. Attrib.

40 The one advantage about marrying a princess – or someone from a royal family – is that they do know what happens.
Charles, Prince of Wales Attrib.

41 One could forgive the fiend for becoming a torrent, but to become an earthquake was really too much.
Charles-Joseph, Prince de Ligne (1735–1814) Austrian diplomat. Referring to Napoleon I. Attrib.

42 His views and affections were singly confined to the narrow compass of the Electorate; England was too big for him.
Earl of Chesterfield (1694–1773) English statesman. Referring to George I. *Letters*

43 My lord, if this be so, why did we take up arms at first? This is against fighting ever hereafter.
Oliver Cromwell (1599–1658) English soldier and statesman. Reply to the Earl of MANCHESTER. Remark

44 Most excellent Royall Majesty, of our *Elizabeth* (sitting at the *Helm* of this Imperial Monarchy: or rather, at the Helm of the Imperiall Ship).
John Dee (1527–1608) English mathematician and astrologer. *General and Rare Memorials pertaining to the Perfect Arte of Navigation*

45 Her Majesty is not a subject.
Benjamin Disraeli (1804–81) British statesman. Responding to Gladstone's taunt that Disraeli could make a joke out of any subject, including Queen Victoria. Attrib.

46 The courtiers who surrounded him have forgotten nothing and learnt nothing.
Charles-François Dumouriez (1739–1823) French general. Referring to Louis XVIII. This remark is also attributed to Talleyrand. Attrib.

47 Royalty must think the whole country always smells of fresh paint.
Elizabeth Dunn *Sunday Times*

48 . . . the king of France, hardened in his malice, would assent to no peace or treaty, but called together his strong host to take into his hand the duchy of Aquitaine, declaring against all truth that it was forfeit to him.
Edward III (1312–77) King of England. Proclamation on the outbreak of the Hundred Years War. *Foedera* (ed. T. Rymer), Vol. IV

49 I know I have the body of a weak and feeble woman, but I have the heart and stomach of a King, and of a King of England too.
Elizabeth I (1533–1603) Queen of England. Speech at Tilbury on the approach of the Spanish Armada

50 Though God hath raised me high, yet this I count the glory of my crown: that I have reigned with your loves.
Elizabeth I *The Golden Speech*, 1601

51 The queen of Scots is this day leichter of a fair son, and I am but a barren stock.
Elizabeth I *Memoirs of Sir James Melville* (1549–93)

52 The daughter of debate, that eke discord doth sow.
Elizabeth I Referring to Mary Queen of Scots. *Sayings of Queen Elizabeth* (Chamberlin)

53 I will that a king succeed me, and who but my kinsman the king of Scots.
Elizabeth I Said shortly before she died, when pressed concerning the succession. *The Reign of Elizabeth* (J. D. Black), Ch. 13

54 I will make you shorter by a head.
Elizabeth I *Sayings of Queen Elizabeth* (Chamberlin)

55 I should like to be a horse.
Elizabeth II (1926–) Queen of the United Kingdom. When asked about her ambitions when a child. Attrib.

56 I think that everyone will conceed that – today of all days –I should begin by saying, 'My husband and I'.
Elizabeth II On her silver wedding. Speech, Guildhall, 1972

57 In the midst stood Prince Henry, who showed already something of royalty in his demeanour, in which there was a certain dignity combined with singular courtesy.
Erasmus (1466–1536) Dutch humanist, scholar, and writer. Remark on first meeting the future Henry VIII

58 . . . to long for and desire the landing of that Prince, whom they looked on as their deliverer from Popish tyranny, praying incessantly for an Easterly wind . . .
John Evelyn (1620–1706) English diarist. Referring to William III. Diary, 6 Oct 1688

59 She came into Whitehall laughing and jolly, as to a wedding, so as to seem quite transported.
John Evelyn Referring to Mary II's arrival in London. Diary, 21 Feb 1689

60 Your peoples die of hunger. Agriculture is almost stationary, industry languishes everywhere, all commerce is destroyed . . . You relate everything to yourself as though you were God on earth.
François Fénelon (1651–1715) French writer and prelate. Letter to Louis XIV

61 A crown is merely a hat that lets the rain in.
Frederick the Great (1712–86) King of Prussia. Remark

62 The King of England changes his ministers as often as he changes his shirts.
Frederick the Great Referring to George III. Attrib.

63 After I am dead the boy will ruin himself in twelve months.
George V (1865–1936) King of the United Kingdom Referring to the Prince of Wales, later Edward VIII; said to Stanley Baldwin. Attrib.

64 We're not a family; we're a firm.
George VI (1895–1952) King of the United Kingdom. *Our Future King* (Peter Lane)

65 . . . her face oblong, fair but wrinkled; her eyes small, yet black and pleasant; her nose a little hooked, her lips narrow and her teeth black (a defect the English seem subject to from their too great use of sugar) . . . She wore false hair and that red.
Paul Hentzner (fl. 1590s) German tutor. Referring to Elizabeth I. *Journey into England*

66 After all the stormy, tempestuous, and blustering windy weather of Queen Mary was overblown, the darksome clouds of discomfort dispersed, the palpable fogs and mist of the most intolerable misery consumed, and the dashing showers of persecution overpast: it pleased God to send England calm and quiet season, a clear and lovely sunshine, a quitsest from former broils of a turbulent estate, and a world of blessings by good Queen Elizabeth.
Raphael Holinshed (d. 1580) English chronicler. *Chronicles*

67 This delightful, blissful, wise, pleasurable, honourable, virtuous, true and immortal Prince was a violator of his word, a libertine over head and ears in debt and disgrace, and despiser of domestic ties, the companion of gamblers and demireps, a man who has just closed half a century without one single claim on the gratitude of his country or the respect of posterity.
Leigh Hunt (1784–1859) British poet. Referring to the Prince Regent. Hunt was imprisoned for two years for this libellous attack. *The Examiner*, 22 Mar 1812

68 A more virtuous man, I believe, does not exist, nor one who is more enthusiastically devoted to better the condition of mankind.
Thomas Jefferson (1743–1826) US statesman. Referring to Tsar Alexander I. Letter to William Duane, 20 July 1807

69 For, he said, albeit unworthy, he was a king's son and one of the greatest lords in the kingdom after the king: and what had been so evilly spoken of him could rightly be called plain treason . . . And if any man were so bold as to charge him with treason or other disloyalty or with anything prejudicial to the realm, he was ready to defend himself with his body as though he were the poorest bachelor in the land.
John of Gaunt (1340–99) Duke of Lancaster. Report of a speech to Richard II's first parliament. *Rotuli Parliamentorum*, Vol. III

70 George the First knew nothing, and desired to know nothing; did nothing, and desired to do nothing; and the only good thing that is told of him is, that he wished to restore the crown to its hereditary successor.
Samuel Johnson (1709–84) British lexicographer. *Life of Johnson* (J. Boswell)

71 I'm prepared to take advice on leisure from Prince Philip. He's a world expert on leisure. He's been practising for most of his adult life.
Neil Kinnock (1942–) British politician. *Western Mail*, 1981

72 Walk wide o' the Widow at Windsor,
For 'alf o' Creation she owns:
We have bought 'er the same with sword an' the flame,
An' we've salted it down with our bones.
Rudyard Kipling (1865–1936) Indian-born British writer. Referring to Queen Victoria. *The Widow at Windsor*

73 I don't mind your being killed, but I object to your being taken prisoner.
Lord Kitchener (1850–1916) British field marshal. Said to the Prince of Wales (later Edward VIII) when he asked to go to the Front. *Journal* (Viscount Esher), 18 Dec 1914

74 He contents the people where he goes best that ever did Prince, for many a poor man that hath suffered wrong many days has been relieved and helped by him.
Thomas Langton (c. 1440–1501) Bishop of St David's. Referring to Richard III. Remark

75 Ah, if I were not king, I should lose my temper.
Louis XIV (1638–1715) French king. Attrib.

76 Junker Henry means to be God and do as he pleases.
Martin Luther (1483–1546) German Protestant. Referring to Henry VIII's religious policy. *The Earlier Tudors* (J. D. Mackie)

77 . . . this haughty, vigilant, resolute, sagacious blue-stocking, half Mithridates and half Trissotin, bearing up against a world in arms.
Lord Macaulay (1800–59) British historian. Referring to Frederick the Great. *Historical Essays*, 'Frederick the Great'

78 If we beat the King ninety and nine times yet he is King still, and so will his posterity be after him; but if the King beat us once we shall all be hanged, and our posterity made slaves.
Earl of Manchester For reply see CROMWELL Remark

79 Well, Mr Baldwin! *this* is a pretty kettle of fish!
Queen Mary (1867–1953) Consort of George V. Referring to the abdication of Edward VIII. *Life of Queen Mary* (James Pope-Hennessy)

80 For God's sake, ma'am, let's have no more of that. If you get the English people into the way of making kings, you'll get them into the way of *un*making them.
Lord Melbourne (1779–1848) British statesman. Advising Queen Victoria against granting Prince Albert the title of King Consort. *Lord M.* (Lord David Cecil)

81 Of hearte couragious, politique in counsaile in adversitie nothynge abashed, in peace juste and mercifull, in warre sharpe and fyerce, in the fielde bolde and hardye and natheless no farther than wysedome woulde adventurouse. Whose warres whoso will consyder, hee shall no lesse commende hys wysedome where he voyded than hys mannehode where he vanquished. He was of visage louelye, of body myghtie, strong and cleane made.
Thomas More (1478–1535) English lawyer and scholar. Referring to Edward IV. *The Historie of Kyng Rycharde the Thirde*

82 The King has a way of making every man feel that he is enjoying his special favour, just as the London wives pray before the image of Our Lady by the Tower till each of them believes it is smiling upon her.
Thomas More Referring to Henry VIII. Letter to Bishop John Fisher, 1518

83 Oh, my Erasmus, if you could see how all the world here is rejoicing in the possession of so great a prince, how his life is all their desire, you could not contain your tears for joy. The heavens laugh, the earth exults, all things are full of milk, of honey and of nectar! Avarice is expelled the country.

Liberality scatters wealth with bounteous hand. Our king does not desire gold or gems or precious metals, but virtue, glory, immortality . . . The other day he wished he was more learned. I said, that is not what we expect of your Grace, but that you will foster and encourage learned men. Yea, surely, said he, for indeed without them we should scarcely exist at all.

Lord Mountjoy Referring to Henry VIII. Letter to Erasmus, 27 May 1509

84 Frumpish and banal.

Malcolm Muggeridge (1903–) British writer. Referring to Queen Elizabeth II. Magazine article, Oct 1957

85 I shall maintain the principle of autocracy just as firmly and unflinchingly as it was upheld by my own ever to be remembered dead father.

Nicholas II (1868–1918) Tsar of Russia. Declaration to representatives of Tver, 17 Jan 1896

86 Our dear King James is good and honest, but the most incompetent man I have ever seen in my life. A child of seven years would not make such silly mistakes as he does.

Duchess of Orleans (1652–1722) Sister-in-law to Louis XIV. Referring to James II, who was in exile in France. Letter to the Electress Sophia, 6 June 1692

87 He will go from resort to resort getting more tanned and more tired.

Westbrook Pegler (1894–1969) US journalist. On the abdication of Edward VIII. *Six Men* (Alistair Cooke), Pt. II

88 I'm self-employed.

Prince Philip (1921–) The consort of Queen Elizabeth II. Answering a query as to what nature of work he did. Attrib.

89 I know of no one in the realm who would not more fitly to come to me than I to him.

Richard, Duke of York (1411–60) Father of Edward IV. Reply when asked, in parliament, whether he wished to go and see the king; York formally claimed the throne six days later. Remark, 10 Oct 1460

90 To know how to dissimulate is the knowledge of kings.

Cardinal Richelieu (1585–1642) French statesman. *Testament Politique*, Maxims

91 Not least among the qualities in a great King is a capacity to permit his ministers to serve him.

Cardinal Richelieu *Testament Politique*, Maxims

92 A merry monarch, scandalous and poor.

Earl of Rochester (1647–80) English poet. Referring to Charles II. *A Satire on King Charles II*

93 Kings and such like are just as funny as politicians.

Theodore Roosevelt (1858–1919) US Republican president. *Mr Wilson's War* (John Dos Passos), Ch. 1

94 The sun does not set in my dominions.

Friedrich von Schiller (1759–1805) German dramatist. Said by Philip II. *Don Carlos*, I:6

95 I would not be a queen
For all the world.

William Shakespeare (1564–1616) English dramatist. *Henry VIII*, II:3

96 Ay, every inch a king.

William Shakespeare *King Lear*, IV:6

97 Kings are earth's gods; in vice their law's their will.

William Shakespeare *Pericles*, I:1

98 For God's sake let us sit upon the ground
And tell sad stories of the death of kings:
How some have been depos'd, some slain in war,
Some haunted by the ghosts they have depos'd,
Some poison'd by their wives, some sleeping kill'd,
All murder'd – for within the hollow crown
That rounds the mortal temples of a king
Keeps Death his court.

William Shakespeare *Richard II*, III:2

99 Albert was merely a young foreigner, who suffered from having no vices, and whose only claim to distinction was that he had happened to marry the Queen of England.

Lytton Strachey (1880–1932) British writer. *Queen Victoria*, Ch. 5

100 The king is incompetent to govern in person. Throughout his reign he has been controlled and governed by others who have given him evil counsel.

John de Stratford (d. 1348) Archbishop of Canterbury. Referring to Edward II. *Historiae Anglicanae Scriptores* (Twysden)

101 Authority forgets a dying king.

Alfred, Lord Tennyson (1809–92) British poet. *Idylls of the King*, 'The Passing of Arthur'

102 In this year King Edward of England made Lord Edward, his son and heir, Prince of Wales and Earl of Chester. When the Welsh heard this, they were overjoyed, thinking him their lawful master, as he was born in their lands.

Thomas of Walsingham (d. 1419) English monk and chronicler. Edward of Caernarfon, later Edward II, began the tradition that male heirs to the English throne were invested with these titles. *Historia Anglicana*

103 I'd punch him in the snoot.

William Hale 'Big Bill' Thompson (1867–1944) US politician and Mayor of Chicago. His reaction if ever King George V were to come to Chicago. Attrib.

104 He used towardes every men of highe and low degree more than mete famylyarytie which trade of life he never changed.

Polydore Vergil (c. 1470–c. 1555) Italian historian. Referring to Edward IV. *Anglica Historia*

105 We are not amused!

Victoria (1819–1901) Queen of the United Kingdom. Attrib.

106 I sat between the King and Queen. We left supper soon. My health was drunk. I then danced one more quadrille with Lord Paget. . . . I was *very* much amused.

Victoria Journal, 16 June 1833

107 It has none, your Highness. Its history dates from today.

James Whistler (1834–1903) US painter. Replying to a query from the Prince of Wales about the history of the Society of British Artists, which he was visiting for the first time. *Whistler Stories* (D. Seitz)

108 The Tsar is not treacherous but he is weak. Weakness is not treachery, but it fulfils all its functions.

Wilhelm II (1859–1941) King of Prussia and Emperor of Germany. Comment written on a despatch from the German ambassador to Russia, 16 Mar 1907. Referring to Nicholas II

109 Now what do I do with *this*?

Duke of Windsor (1894–1972) King of the United Kingdom; abdicated 1936. On being handed the bill after a lengthy stay in a luxury hotel. Attrib.

110 He is a prince of royal courage and hath a princely heart; and rather than he will miss or want part of his appetite, he will hazard the loss of one-half of his kingdom.

Cardinal Wolsey Referring to Henry VIII. Remark, Nov 1530

RUDENESS

See also impertinence, insults

1 I should never be allowed out in private.
Randolph Churchill (1911–68) British political journalist. Apologizing to a hostess whose dinner party he had ruined. *Randolph* (B. Roberts)

2 Abuse is in order, but it is best if it is supported by argument.
Robin Day (1923–) British TV and radio journalist. *Election Call* (BBC Radio)

3 The right people are rude. They can afford to be.
W. Somerset Maugham (1874–1965) British novelist. *Our Betters*, II

4 JUDGE WILLIS. You are extremely offensive, young man.
F. E. SMITH. As a matter of fact, we both are, and the only difference between us is that I am trying to be, and you can't help it.
F. E. Smith (1872–1930) British lawyer and politician. *Frederick Elwin, Earl of Birkenhead* (Lord Birkenhead), Vol. I, Ch. 9

RULES

1 The exception proves the rule.
Proverb

2 If anything can go wrong, it will.
Anonymous Commonly known as 'Murphy's Law'; various other forms exist. It is uncertain who Murphy was.

3 Rules and models destroy genius and art.
William Hazlitt (1778–1830) British essayist. *On Taste*

4 Orr was crazy and could be grounded. All he had to do was ask; and as soon as he did, he would no longer be crazy and would have to fly more missions . . . Yossarian was moved very deeply by the absolute simplicity of this clause of Catch-22 and let out a respectful whistle.
Joseph Heller (1923–) US novelist. *Catch-22*

5 The golden rule is that there are no golden rules.
George Bernard Shaw (1856–1950) Irish dramatist and critic. *Man and Superman*, 'Maxims for Revolutionists'

RUNYON, (Alfred) Damon

(1884–1946) US writer and journalist. His works include *Rhymes of the Firing Line* (1912), the collection of short stories *Guys and Dolls* (1932), and the play *A Slight Case of Murder* (1935).

1 All she has to do is to walk around and about Georgie White's stage with only a few light bandages on, and everybody considers her very beautiful, especially from the neck down.
Furthermore, 'A Very Honourable Guy'

2 My boy . . . always try to rub up against money, for if you rub up against money long enough, some of it may rub off on you.
Furthermore, 'A Very Honourable Guy'

3 More than somewhat.
Title of a collection of stories

4 And you cannot tell by the way a party looks or how he lives in this town, if he has any scratch, because many a party who is around in automobiles, and wearing good clothes, and chucking quite a swell is nothing but a phonus bolonus and does not have any real scratch whatever.
More than Somewhat, 'The Snatching of Bookie Bob'

5 She is a smart old broad. It is a pity she is so nefarious.
Runyon à la carte, 'Broadway Incident'

6 At such an hour the sinners are still in bed resting up from their sinning of the night before, so they will be in good shape for more sinning a little later on.
Runyon à la carte, 'The Idyll of Miss Sarah Brown'

7 I once knew a chap who had a system of just hanging the baby on the clothes line to dry and he was greatly admired by his fellow citizens for having discovered a wonderful innovation on changing a diaper.
Short Takes, 'Diaper Dexterity'

8 A free-loader is a confirmed guest. He is the man who is always willing to come to dinner.
Short Takes, 'Free-Loading Ethics'

9 He is without strict doubt a Hoorah Henry, and he is generally figured as nothing but a lob as far as doing anything useful in this world is concerned.
Short Takes, 'Tight Shoes'

10 These citizens are always willing to bet that what Nicely-Nicely dies of will be over-feeding and never anything small like pneumonia, for Nicely-Nicely is known far and wide as a character who dearly loves to commit eating.
Take it Easy, 'Lonely Heart'

RUSKIN, John

(1819–1900) British art critic and writer on sociology and economics. His books include *Modern Painters* (1843–60), *The Seven Lamps of Architecture* (1849), and *Munera Pulveris* (1862).

Quotations about Ruskin

1 A certain girlish petulance of style that distinguishes Ruskin was not altogether a defect. It served to irritate and fix attention where a more evenly judicial writer might have remained unread.
W. R. Sickert (1860–1942) British impressionist painter. *New Age*, 'The Spirit of the Hive'

2 I doubt that art needed Ruskin any more than a moving train needs one of its passengers to shove it.
Tom Stoppard (1937–) Czech-born British dramatist. *Times Literary Supplement*, 3 June 1977

Quotations by Ruskin

3 No person who is not a great sculptor or painter can be an architect. If he is not a sculptor or painter, he can only be a *builder*.
Lectures on Architecture and Painting

4 Life without industry is guilt, and industry without art is brutality.
Lectures on Art, 3, 'The Relation of Art to Morals', 23 Feb 1870

5 What is poetry? The suggestion, by the imagination, of noble grounds for the noble emotions.
Modern Painters, Vol. III

6 Mountains are the beginning and the end of all natural scenery.
Modern Painters, Vol. IV

7 If a book is worth reading, it is worth buying.
Sesame and Lilies, 'Of Kings' Treasuries'

8 All books are divisible into two classes, the books of the hour, and the books of all time.
Sesame and Lilies, 'Of Kings' Treasuries'

9 How long most people would look at the best book before they would give the price of a large turbot for it!
Sesame and Lilies, 'Of Kings' Treasuries'

10 When we build let us think that we build for ever.
The Seven Lamps of Architecture, Ch. 6, 'The Lamp of Memory'

11 Remember that the most beautiful things in the world are the most useless, peacocks and lilies for instance.
The Stones of Venice, Vol. I, Ch. 2

12 To make your children *capable of honesty* is the beginning of education.
Time and Tide, Letter VIII

13 Fine art is that in which the hand, the head, and the heart of man go together.
The Two Paths, Lecture II

14 Nobody cares much at heart about Titian, only there is a strange undercurrent of everlasting murmur about his name, which means the deep consent of all great men that he is greater than they.
The Two Paths, Lecture II

15 No human being, however great, or powerful was ever so free as a fish.
The Two Paths, Lecture V

16 Whereas it has long been known and declared that the poor have no right to the property of the rich, I wish it also to be known and declared that the rich have no right to the property of the poor.
Unto this Last, Essay III

17 I have seen, and heard, much of Cockney impudence before now; but never expected to hear a coxcomb ask two hundred guineas for flinging a pot of paint in the public's face.
On Whistler's painting 'Nocturne in Black and Gold'. Letter, 18 June 1877

18 What have we to say to India?
Referring to the completion of the British-Indian cable. Attrib.

RUSSELL, Bertrand Arthur William, Earl

(1872–1970) British philosopher. His many books include *Principia Mathematica* (with A. N. Whitehead; 1910) and *Our Knowledge of the External World* (1914). He was an ardent pacifist and campaigner for nuclear disarmament.

Quotations about Russell

1 In trying to recall his face I am able to see it only in profile – the sharp, narrow silhouette of an aggressive jester.
Arthur Koestler (1905–83) Hungarian-born British writer. *Stranger on the Square*

2 The beauty of Bertrand Russell's beautiful mathematical mind is absolute, like the third movement of Beethoven's A Minor Quartet . . .
Ethel Mannin *Confessions and Impressions*

Quotations by Russell

3 Three passions, simple but overwhelmingly strong, have governed my life: the longing for love, the search for knowledge, and unbearable pity for the suffering of mankind.
The Autobiography of Bertrand Russell, Prologue

4 I was told that the Chinese said they would bury me by the Western Lake and build a shrine to my memory. I have some slight regret that this did not happen, as I might have become a god, which would have been very *chic* for an atheist.
The Autobiography of Bertrand Russell, Vol. II, Ch. 3

5 One of the symptoms of approaching nervous breakdown is the belief that one's work is terribly important. If I were a medical man, I should prescribe a holiday to any patient who considered his work important.
The Autobiography of Bertrand Russell, Vol. II, Ch. 5

6 . . . the nuns who never take a bath without wearing a bathrobe all the time. When asked why, since no man can see them, they reply 'Oh, but you forget the good God.'
The Basic Writings, Pt. II, Ch. 7

7 The megalomaniac differs from the narcissist by the fact that he wishes to be powerful rather than charming, and seeks to be feared rather than loved. To this type belong many lunatics and most of the great men of history.
The Conquest of Happiness

8 There are two motives for reading a book: one, that you enjoy it, the other that you can boast about it.
The Conquest of Happiness

9 Man is not a solitary animal, and so long as social life survives, self-realization cannot be the supreme principle of ethics.
History of Western Philosophy, 'Romanticism'

10 The more you are talked about, the more you will wish to be talked about. The condemned murderer who is allowed to see the account of his trial in the Press is indignant if he finds a newspaper which has reported it inadequately. . . Politicians and literary men are in the same case.
Human Society in Ethics and Politics

11 Of all forms of caution, caution in love is perhaps the most fatal to true happiness.
Marriage and Morals

12 Mathematics may be defined as the subject in which we never know what we are talking about, nor whether what we are saying is true.
Mysticism and Logic, Ch. 4

13 Pure mathematics consists entirely of assertions to the effect that, if such and such a proposition is true of *anything*, then such and such another proposition is true of that thing. It is essential not to discuss whether the first proposition is really true, and not to mention what the anything is, of which it is supposed to be true.
Mysticism and Logic, Ch. 5

14 Organic life, we are told, has developed gradually from the protozoon to the philosopher, and this development, we are assured, is indubitably an advance. Unfortunately it is the philosopher, not the protozoon, who gives us this assurance.
Mysticism and Logic, Ch. 6

15 Brief and powerless is Man's life; on him and all his race the slow, sure doom falls pitiless and dark.
Mysticism and Logic, 'A Free Man's Worship'

16 No one gossips about other people's secret virtues.
On Education

17 Matter . . . a convenient formula for describing what happens where it isn't.
An Outline of Philosophy

18 It is undesirable to believe a proposition when there is no ground whatever for supposing it true.
Sceptical Essays

19 We have, in fact, two kinds of morality side by side; one which we preach but do not practise, and

another which we practise but seldom preach.
Sceptical Essays

20 Mathematics possesses not only truth, but supreme beauty – a beauty cold and austere, like that of sculpture.
The Study of Mathematics

21 In America everybody is of the opinion that he has no social superiors, since all men are equal, but he does not admit that he has no social inferiors.
Unpopular Essays

22 People don't seem to realize that it takes time and effort and preparation to think. Statesmen are far too busy making speeches to think.
Kenneth Harris Talking To: 'Bertrand Russell' (Kenneth Harris)

23 There's a Bible on that shelf there. But I keep it next to Voltaire – poison and antidote.
Kenneth Harris Talking To: 'Bertrand Russell' (Kenneth Harris)

24 Obscenity is what happens to shock some elderly and ignorant magistrate.
Look magazine

25 The collection of prejudices which is called political philosophy is useful provided that it is not called philosophy.
The Observer, 'Sayings of the Year', 1962

26 Not a gentleman; dresses too well
Referring to Anthony Eden. *Six Men* (A. Cooke)

27 Many people would sooner die than think. In fact they do.
Thinking About Thinking (A. Flew)

28 You may reasonably expect a man to walk a tightrope safely for ten minutes; it would be unreasonable to do so without accident for two hundred years.
On the subject of nuclear war between the USA and the Soviets. *The Tightrope Men* (D. Bagley)

29 Few people can be happy unless they hate some other person, nation or creed.
Attrib.

30 Patriots always talk of dying for their country, and never of killing for their country.
Attrib.

31 Of course not. After all, I may be wrong.
On being asked whether he would be prepared to die for his beliefs. Attrib.

32 Every time I talk to a savant I feel quite sure that happiness is no longer a possibility. Yet when I talk with my gardener, I'm convinced of the opposite.
Attrib.

RUSSIA

See also Cold War, oppression, Russian Revolution

1 I cannot forecast to you the action of Russia. It is a riddle wrapped in a mystery inside an enigma.
Winston Churchill (1874–1965) British statesman. Broadcast talk, 1 Oct 1939

2 The Soviet people want full-blooded and unconditional democracy.
Mikhail Gorbachov (1931–) Soviet statesman. Speech, July 1988

3 Russia will certainly inherit the future. What we already call the greatness of Russia is only her prenatal struggling.
D. H. Lawrence (1885–1930) British novelist. *Phoenix*, Preface to 'All Things are Possible' by Leo Shostov

4 Neither can you expect a revolution, because there is no new baby in the womb of our society. Russia is a collapse, not a revolution.
D. H. Lawrence *Phoenix*, 'The Good Man'

5 Scratch the Russian and you will find the Tartar.
Joseph de Maistre (1753–1821) French monarchist. Attributed also to Napoleon and Prince de Ligne

6 Absolutism tempered by assassination.
Ernst Friedrich Herbert Münster (1766–1839) Hanoverian statesman. Referring to the Russian Constitution. Letter

7 Gaiety is the most outstanding feature of the Soviet Union.
Joseph Stalin (J. Dzhugashvili; 1879–1953) Soviet statesman. Attrib.

8 It was the supreme expression of the mediocrity of the apparatus that Stalin himself rose to his position.
Leon Trotsky (Lev Davidovich Bronstein; 1879–1940) Russian revolutionary. *My Life*, Ch. 40

9 From being a patriotic myth, the Russian people have become an awful reality.
Leon Trotsky *History of the Russian Revolution*, Pt. III, Ch. 7

RUSSIAN REVOLUTION

See also revolution, Russia

1 Peace, Bread and Land.
Anonymous Slogan of workers in Petrograd (St Petersburg) during the February Revolution

2 All Power to the Soviets!
Anonymous Slogan of workers in Petrograd (St Petersburg) during the October Revolution

3 The Germans turned upon Russia the most grisly of all weapons. They transported Lenin in a sealed truck like a plague bacillus from Switzerland to Russia.
Winston Churchill (1874–1965) British statesman. *The World Crisis*

4 Of all tyrannies in history the Bolshevik tyranny is the worst, the most destructive, the most degrading
Winston Churchill Speech, London, 11 Apr 1919

5 Dear comrades, soldiers, sailors and workers! I am happy to greet in you the victorious Russian Revolution!
Lenin (Vladimir Ilich Ulyanov; 1870–1924) Russian revolutionary leader. Speech, Finland Station (Petrograd), 16 Apr 1917

6 The substitution of the proletarian for the bourgeois state is impossible without a violent revolution.
Lenin *State and Revolution*, Ch. 1

7 Ten Days that Shook the World.
John Reed (1887–1920) American journalist. Referring to the Bolshevik Revolution in Russia (Nov 1917). Book title

8 The 23rd of February was International Woman's Day. . . It had not occurred to anyone that it might become the first day of the revolution.
Leon Trotsky (Lev Davidovich Bronstein; 1879–1940) Russian revolutionary. *History of the Russian Revolution*, Pt. I, Ch. 7

9 The revolution does not choose its paths: it made its first steps towards victory under the belly of a Cossack's horse.
Leon Trotsky *History of the Russian Revolution*, Pt. I, Ch. 7

RUTHLESSNESS

1 Would that the Roman people had but one neck!

Caligula (Gaius Caesar; 12–41 AD) Roman Emperor. *Life of Caligula* (Suetonius), Ch. 30

2 What millions died – that Caesar might be great!

Thomas Campbell (1777–1844) British poet. *Pleasures of Hope*, II

3 I would walk over my grandmother if necessary to get Nixon re-elected!

Charles Colson (1931–) US Watergate conspirator. Talk to campaign staff. *Born Again*

4 Exterminate all brutes.

Joseph Conrad (Teodor Josef Konrad Korzeniowski; 1857–1924) Polish-born British novelist. *Heart of Darkness*

5 We are about to engage in a battle on which the fate of our country depends and it is important to remind all ranks that the moment has passed for looking to the rear; all our efforts must be directed to attacking and driving back the enemy. Troops that can advance no farther must, at any price, hold on to the ground they have conquered and die on the spot rather than give way. Under the circumstances which face us, no act of weakness can be tolerated.

Joseph Jacques Césaire Joffre (1852–1931) French soldier. *The Memoirs of Marshall Joffre*

6 I do not have to forgive my enemies, I have had them all shot.

Ramón Maria Narváez (1800–68) Spanish general and political leader. Said on his deathbed, when asked by a priest if he forgave his enemies. *Famous Last Words* (B. Conrad)

7 3RD FISHERMAN. Master, I marvel how the fishes live in the sea.
1ST FISHERMAN. Why, as men do a-land – the great ones eat up the little ones.

William Shakespeare (1564–1616) English dramatist. *Pericles*, II:1

8 The world continues to offer glittering prizes to those who have stout hearts and sharp swords.

F. E. Smith (1872–1930) British lawyer and politician. Speech, Glasgow University, 7 Nov 1923

9 It is not enough to succeed. Others must fail.

Gore Vidal (1925–) US novelist. *Antipanegyric for Tom Driberg* (G. Irvine)

S

SACRIFICE

1 You can't learn too soon that the most useful thing about a principle is that it can always be sacrificed to expediency.

W. Somerset Maugham (1874–1965) British novelist. *The Circle*, III

2 A woman will always sacrifice herself if you give her the opportunity. It is her favourite form of self-indulgence.

W. Somerset Maugham *The Circle*, III

3 I could not give my name to aid the slaughter in this war, fought on both sides for grossly material ends, which did not justify the sacrifice of a single mother's son. Clearly I must continue to oppose it, and expose it, to all whom I could reach with voice or pen.

Sylvia Pankhurst (1882–1960) British suffragette. *The Home Front*, Ch. 25

4 When men grow virtuous in their old age, they only make a sacrifice to God of the devil's leavings.

Alexander Pope (1688–1744) British poet. *Thoughts on Various Subjects*

SADNESS

See sorrow

SAILORS

See boats, sea

SAKI

(Hector Hugh Munro; 1870–1916) British writer. He is best-known for his collections of humorous short stories, including *Reginald* (1904), *The Chronicles of Clovis* (1911), and *Beasts and Super-Beasts* (1914).

1 By insisting on having your bottle pointing to the north when the cork is being drawn, and calling the waiter Max, you may induce an impression on your guests which hours of laboured boasting might be powerless to achieve. For this purpose, however, the guests must be chosen as carefully as the wine.

The Chaplet

2 Addresses are given to us to conceal our whereabouts.

Cross Currents

3 'I believe I take precedence,' he said coldly; 'you are merely the club Bore: I am the club Liar.'

A Defensive Diamond

4 Waldo is one of those people who would be enormously improved by death.

Referring to Ralph Waldo Emerson. *The Feast of Nemesis*

5 Children with Hyacinth's temperament don't know better as they grow older; they merely know more.

Hyacinth

6 The people of Crete unfortunately make more history than they can consume locally.

The Jesting of Arlington Stringham

7 To say that anything was a quotation was an excellent method, in Eleanor's eyes, for withdrawing it from discussion.

The Jesting of Arlington Stringham

8 He's simply got the instinct for being unhappy highly developed.

The Match-Maker

9 All decent people live beyond their incomes nowadays, and those who aren't respectable live beyond other people's. A few gifted individuals manage to do both.

The Match-Maker

10 Oysters are more beautiful than any religion . . . There's nothing in Christianity or Buddhism that quite matches the sympathetic unselfishness of an oyster.

The Match-Maker

11 His socks compelled one's attention without losing one's respect.

Ministers of Grace

12 The young have aspirations that never come to pass, the old have reminiscences of what never happened.

Reginald at the Carlton

13 There may have been disillusionments in the lives of the medieval saints, but they would scarcely have been better pleased if they could have foreseen that their names would be associated nowadays chiefly with racehorses and the cheaper clarets.

Reginald at the Carlton

14 The Western custom of one wife and hardly any mistresses.
Reginald in Russia

15 But, good gracious, you've got to educate him first.
You can't expect a boy to be vicious till he's been to a good school.
Reginald in Russia

16 The cook was a good cook, as cooks go; and as cooks go she went.
Reginald on Besetting Sins

17 People may say what they like about the decay of Christianity; the religious system that produced green Chartreuse can never really die.
Reginald on Christmas Presents

18 Even the Hooligan was probably invented in China centuries before we thought of him.
Reginald on House-Parties

19 Every reformation must have its victims. You can't expect the fatted calf to share the enthusiasm of the angels over the prodigal's return.
Reginald on the Academy

20 I think she must have been very strictly brought up, she's so desperately anxious to do the wrong thing correctly.
Reginald on Worries

21 I always say beauty is only sin deep.
Reginald's Choir Treat

22 In baiting a mouse-trap with cheese, always leave room for the mouse.
The Square Egg

23 Sherard Blaw, the dramatist who had discovered himself, and who had given so ungrudgingly of his discovery to the world.
The Unbearable Bassington, Ch. 13

SANITY

1 Sanity is very rare; every man almost, and every woman, has a dash of madness.
Ralph Waldo Emerson (1803–82) US poet and essayist.

2 Who, then, is sane?.
Horace (65 BC–8 BC) Roman poet.

3 Every man has a sane spot somewhere.
Robert Louis Stevenson (1850–94) Scottish writer. *Bartlett's Unfamiliar Quotations* (Leonard Louis Levinson)

SANTAYANA, George

(1863–1952) US philosopher and poet. His books include *Realms of Being* (1927–40), *Background of my Life* (1945), several volumes of poetry, and a novel.

Quotations about Santayana

1 He stood on the flat road to heaven and buttered slides to hell for all the rest.
Oliver Wendell Holmes (1809–94) US writer. Letter, 5 Dec 1913

Quotations by Santayana

2 The working of great institutions is mainly the result of a vast mass of routine, petty malice, self interest, carelessness, and sheer mistake. Only a residual fraction is thought.
The Crime of Galileo

3 The young man who has not wept is a savage, and the old man who will not laugh is a fool.
Dialogues in Limbo, Ch. 3

4 The Bible is literature, not dogma.
Introduction to the Ethics of Spinoza

5 Happiness is the only sanction of life; where happiness fails, existence remains a mad and lamentable experiment.
The Life of Reason

6 Progress, far from consisting in change, depends on retentiveness. Those who cannot remember the past are condemned to repeat it.
The Life of Reason

7 Because there's no fourth class.
On being asked why he always traveled third class. *Living Biographies of the Great Philosophers* (H. Thomas)

8 Life is not a spectacle or a feast; it is a predicament.
The Perpetual Pessimist (Sagittarius and George)

9 England is the paradise of individuality, eccentricity, heresy, anomalies, hobbies, and humors.
Soliloquies in England, 'The British Character'

10 Trust the man who hesitates in his speech and is quick and steady in action, but beware of long arguments and long beards.
Soliloquies in England, 'The British Character'

11 There is no cure for birth and death save to enjoy the interval.
Soliloquies in England, 'War Shrines'

12 It is a great advantage for a system of philosophy to be substantially true.
The Unknowable

13 For an idea ever to be fashionable is ominous, since it must afterwards be always old-fashioned.
Winds of Doctrine, 'Modernism and Christianity'

14 If all the arts aspire to the condition of music, all the sciences aspire to the condition of mathematics.
The Observer, 'Sayings of the Week', 4 Mar 1928

SARCASM

1 Sarcasm I now see to be, in general, the language of the devil.
Thomas Carlyle (1795–1881) Scottish historian and essayist. *Sartor Resartus*, Bk. II, Ch. 4

2 'Yes I have a pair of eyes,' replied Sam, 'and that's just it. If they was a pair o' patent double million magnifyin' gas microscopes of hextra power, p'raps I might be able to see through a flight o' stairs and a deal door; but bein' only eyes, you see, my vision's limited.'
Charles Dickens (1812–70) British novelist. *The Pickwick Papers*

3 If you don't want to use the army, I should like to borrow it for a while. Yours respectfully, A. Lincoln.
Abraham Lincoln (1809–65) US statesman. Letter to General George B. McClellan, whose lack of activity during the US Civil War irritated Lincoln.

4 Oh, life is a glorious cycle of song,
A medley of extemporanea;
And love is a thing that can never go wrong
And I am Marie of Roumania.
Dorothy Parker (1893–1967) US writer. *Enough Rope*, 'Comment'

SARTRE, Jean-Paul

(1905–80) French philosopher, dramatist, and novelist. The principal exponent of existentialism, he wrote a number of books on this subject, including *Critique de la raison dialectique* (1960). His novels include the trilogy *The Roads to Freedom* (1945–49), and *The Respectable Prostitute* (1946) is the best known of his plays.

1 I hate victims who respect their executioners.
Altona

2 An American is either a Jew, or an anti-Semite, unless he is both at the same time.
Altona

3 Man is condemned to be free.
Existentialism is a Humanism

4 Three o'clock is always too late or too early for anything you want to do.
Nausea

5 Things are entirely what they appear to be and *behind them* . . . there is nothing.
Nausea

6 My thought is *me*: that is why I can't stop. I exist by what I think . . . and I can't prevent myself from thinking.
Nausea

7 I know perfectly well that I don't want to do anything; to do something is to create existence – and there's quite enough existence as it is.
Nausea

8 I don't think the profession of historian fits a man for psychological analysis. In our work we have to deal only with simple feelings to which we give generic names such as Ambition and Interest.
Nausea

9 I think they do that to pass the time, nothing more. But time is too large, it refuses to let itself be filled up.
Nausea

10 You get the impression that their normal condition is silence and that speech is a slight fever which attacks them now and then.
Nausea

11 The poor don't know that their function in life is to exercise our generosity.
Words

12 A kiss without a moustache, they said then, is like an egg without salt; I will add to it: and it is like Good without Evil.
Words

13 She believed in nothing; only her scepticism kept her from being an atheist.
Words

14 There is no such thing as psychological. Let us say that one can improve the biography of the person.
The Divided Self (R. D. Laing), Ch. 8

15 In the first days of the revolt you must kill: to shoot down a European is to kill two birds with one stone, to destroy an oppressor and the man he oppresses at the same time: there remain a dead man, and a free man.
The Wretched of the Earth (F. Fanon), Preface

SATAN

See devil

SATIRE

See also ridicule, sarcasm

1 It's hard not to write satire.
Juvenal (Decimus Junius Juvenalis; 60–130 AD) Roman satirist. *Satires*, I

2 Satire should, like a polished razor keen,
Wound with a touch that's scarcely felt or seen.
Lady Mary Wortley Montagu (1689–1762) English writer. *To the Imitator of the First Satire of Horace*, Bk. II

3 Hush, hush
Nobody cares!
Christopher Robin
Has
  Fallen
    Down-
      Stairs.
J. B. Morton (1893–1979) British journalist. *By the Way*, 'Now We Are Sick'

4 As we get older we do not get any younger.
Seasons return, and today I am fifty-five,
And this time last year I was fifty-four,
And this time next year I shall be sixty-two.
Henry Reed (1914–86) British poet and dramatist. *A Map of Verona*, 'Chard Whitlow'

5 Satire is a sort of glass, wherein beholders do generally discover everybody's face but their own.
Jonathan Swift (1667–1745) Irish-born Anglican priest and writer. *The Battle of the Books*, 'Preface'

SATISFACTION

See also contentment

1 Youth will be served, every dog has his day, and mine has been a fine one.
George Henry Borrow (1803–81) British writer. *Lavengro*, Ch. 92

2 I wasna fou, but just had plenty.
Robert Burns (1759–96) Scottish poet. *Death and Doctor Hornbrook*

3 The reward of a thing well done is to have done it.
Ralph Waldo Emerson (1803–82) US poet and essayist. *Essays*, 'New England Reformers'

4 I can't get no satisfaction.
Mick Jagger (1943–) British rock musician and songwriter. 'Satisfaction' (With Keith Richard)

SAYINGS

See also quotations

1 A platitude is simply a truth repeated till people get tired of hearing it.
Stanley Baldwin (1867–1947) British statesman. Attrib.

2 The hunter for aphorisms on human nature has to fish in muddy water, and he is even condemned to find much of his own mind.
F. H. Bradley (1846–1924) British philosopher. *Aphorisms*

3 The great writers of aphorisms read as if they had all known each other well.
Elias Canetti (1905–) Bulgarian-born novelist. *The Human Province*

4 A proverb is much matter decorated into few words.
Thomas Fuller (1608–61) English historian. *The History of the Worthies of England*, Ch. 2

5 A new maxim is often a brilliant error.
Chrétien Guillaume de Lamoignonde Malesherbes (1721–94) French statesman. *Pensées et maximes*

6 A proverb is one man's wit and all men's wisdom.
Lord John Russell (1792–1878) British statesman. Attrib.

7 A truism is on that account none the less true.
Herbert Samuel (1870–1963) British Liberal statesman. *A Book of Quotations*

SCANDAL

1 In England there is only silence or scandal.

André Maurois (Émile Herzog; 1885–1967) French writer. Attrib.

2 It is a public scandal that gives offence, and it is no sin to sin in secret.

Molière (Jean Baptiste Poquelin; 1622–73) French dramatist. *Tartuffe*, IV:5

SCEPTICISM

See also doubt, proof

1 We don't believe in rheumatism and true love until after the first attack.

Marie Ebner von Eschenbach (1830–1916) Austrian writer. *Aphorism*

2 I am too much of a sceptic to deny the possibility of anything.

T. H. Huxley (1825–95) British biologist. Letter to Herbert Spencer, 22 Mar 1886

3 Truth, Sir, is a cow, which will yield such people no more milk, and so they are gone to milk the bull.

Samuel Johnson (1709–84) British lexicographer. Referring to sceptics. *Life of Johnson* (J. Boswell), Vol. I

4 It is undesirable to believe a proposition when there is no ground whatever for supposing it true.

Bertrand Russell (1872–1970) British philosopher. *Sceptical Essays*

5 She believed in nothing; only her scepticism kept her from being an atheist.

Jean-Paul Sartre (1905–80) French writer. *Words*

6 The temerity to believe in nothing.

Ivan Turgenev (1818–83) Russian novelist. *Fathers and Sons*, Ch. 14

SCHOOLTEACHERS

See education

SCHOPENHAUER, Arthur

(1788–1860) German philosopher. His books include *Die Welt als Wille und Vorstellung* (1819) and *Die Beiden Grundprobleme der Ethik* (1841).

1 To be alone is the fate of all great minds – a fate deplored at times, but still always chosen as the less grievous of two evils.

Aphorismen zur Lebensweisheit

2 Intellect is invisible to the man who has none.

Aphorismen zur Lebensweisheit

3 The fundamental fault of the female character is that it has no sense of justice.

Gedanken uber vielerlei Gegenstande, XXVII

4 Every parting gives a foretaste of death; every coming together again a foretaste of the resurrection.

Gedanken uber vielerlei Gegenstande, XXVI

5 The thing-in-itself, the will-to-live, exists whole and undivided in every being, even in the tiniest; it is present as completely as in all that ever were, are, and will be, taken together.

Parerga and Paralipomena

6 To expect a man to retain everything that he has ever read is like expecting him to carry about in his body everything that he has ever eaten.

Parerga and Paralipomena

7 After your death you will be what you were before your birth.

Parerga and Paralipomena

8 Wealth is like sea-water; the more we drink, the thirstier we become; and the same is true of fame.

Parerga and Paralipomena

SCIENCE

See also discovery, mathematics, Nature, progress, research, scientists, technology

1 On 13 September 1765 people in fields near Luce, in France, saw a stone-mass drop from the sky after a violent thunderclap. The great physicist Lavoisier, who knew better than any peasant that this was impossible, reported to the Academy of Science that the witnesses were mistaken or lying. The Academy would not accept the reality of meteorites until 1803.

Anonymous *Fortean Times*

2 *Eureka!*
I have found it!

Archimedes (c. 287–212 BC) Greek mathematician. An exclamation of joy supposedly uttered as, stepping into a bath and noticing the water overflowing, he saw the answer to a problem and began the train of thought that led to his principle of buoyancy. Attrib.

3 There are no such things as incurable, there are only things for which man has not found a cure.

Bernard Baruch (1870–1965) US financier and statesman. Quoting his father Simon Baruch, the pioneer surgeon, in a speech to the President's Committee on Employment of the Physically Handicapped, 30 Apr 1954

4 Science seldom renders men amiable; women, never.

Edmone-Pierre Chanvot de Beauchêne (1748–1824) *Maximes, réflexions et pensées diverses*

5 The Microbe is so very small
You cannot make him out at all,
But many sanguine people hope
To see him through a microscope.
His jointed tongue that lies beneath
A hundred curious rows of teeth;
His seven tufted tails with lots
Of lovely pink and purple spots,
On each of which a pattern stands,
Composed of forty separate bands;
His eyebrows of a tender green;
But Scientists, who ought to know,
Assure us that they must be so. . . .
Oh! let us never, never doubt
What nobody is sure about!

Hilaire Belloc (1870–1953) French-born British poet, essayist and historian. *Cautionary Verses*, 'The Microbe'

6 There are more microbes *per person* than the entire population of the world. Imagine that. Per person. This means that if the time scale is diminished in proportion to that of space it would be quite possible for the whole story of Greece and Rome to be played out between farts.

Alan Bennett (1934–) British dramatist and actor. *The Old Country*, II

7 Medical scientists are nice people, but you should not let them treat you.

August Bier (1861–1949) Attrib.

8 O Timothy, keep that which is committed to thy trust, avoiding profane and vain babblings, and oppositions of science falsely so called.

Bible: I Timothy 6:20

9 A first-rate laboratory is one in which mediocre scientists can produce outstanding work.

Patrick Maynard Stuart Blackett (1897–1974) Attrib.

10 It is my intent to beget a good understanding between the chymists and the mechanical philosophers who have hitherto been too little

acquainted with one another's learning.

Robert Boyle (1627–91) British scientist. *The Sceptical Chymist*

11 Private practice and marriage – those twin extinguishers of science.

Paul Broca (1824–80) Letter, 10 Apr 1851

12 That is the essence of science: ask an impertinent question, and you are on the way to the pertinent answer.

Jacob Bronowski (1908–74) British scientist, mathematician, and writer. *The Ascent of Man*, Ch. 4

13 Physics becomes in those years the greatest collective work of science – no, more than that, the great collective work of art of the twentieth century.

Jacob Bronowski Referring to the period around the turn of the century marked by the elucidation of atomic structure and the development of the quantum theory. *The Ascent of Man*, Ch. 10

14 Science has nothing to be ashamed of, even in the ruins of Nagasaki.

Jacob Bronowski *Science and Human Values*

15 No one should approach the temple of science with the soul of a money changer.

Thomas Browne (1605–82) English physician and writer.

16 There was a young lady named Bright,
Whose speed was far faster than light;
She set out one day
In a relative way,
And returned home the previous night.

Arthur Henry Reginald Buller (1874–1944) British botanist. *Limerick*

17 X-RAYS: Their moral is this – that a right way of looking at things will see through almost anything.

Samuel Butler (1835–1902) British writer. *Note-Books*, Vol. V

18 That is how the atom is split. But what does it mean? To us who think in terms of practical use it means – Nothing!

Ritchie Calder (1898–) US engineer and sculptor. *The Daily Herald*, 27 June 1932

19 It is, of course, a bit of a drawback that science was invented after I left school.

Lord Carrington (1919–) British statesman. *The Observer*, 23 Jan 1983

20 When a distinguished but elderly scientist states that something is possible, he is almost certainly right. When he states that something is impossible, he is very probably wrong.

Arthur C. Clarke (1917–) British science-fiction writer. *Profiles of the Future*

21 We have discovered the secret of life!

Francis Crick (1916–) British biophysicist. Excitedly bursting into a Cambridge pub with James Watson to celebrate the fact that they had unravelled the structure of DNA. *The Double Helix* (J. D. Watson)

22 I also suspect that many workers in this field and related fields have been strongly motivated by the desire, rarely actually expressed, to refute vitalism.

Francis H. C. Crick Referring to molecular biology. *British Medical Bulletin*, 21:183, 1965

23 After all, science is essentially international, and it is only through lack of the historical sense that national qualities have been attributed to it.

Marie Curie (1867–1934) Polish chemist. *Memorandum*, 'Intellectual Co-operation'

24 One never notices what has been done; one can only see what remains to be done. . . .

Marie Curie Letter to her brother, 18 Mar 1894

25 But in science the credit goes to the man who convinces the world, not to the man to whom the idea first occurs.

Francis Darwin (1848–1925) British scientist. *Eugenics Review*, 6:1, 1914

26 Every great advance in science has issued from a new audacity of imagination.

John Dewey (1859–1952) US philosopher and educator. *The Quest for Certainty*, Ch. 11

27 Putting on the spectacles of science in expectation of finding the answer to everything looked at signifies inner blindness.

J. Frank Dobie (1888–1964) *The Voice of Coyote*, Introduction

28 And new Philosophy calls all in doubt,
The Element of fire is quite put out;
The Sun is lost, and th' earth, and no man's wit
Can well direct him where to look for it.

John Donne (1573–1631) English poet. *An Anatomy of the World*, 205

29 The content of physics is the concern of physicists, its effect the concern of all men.

Friedrich Dürrenmatt (1921–) Swiss writer. *The Physicists*

30 Electrical force is defined as something which causes motion of electrical charge; an electrical charge is something which exerts electric force.

Arthur Eddington (1882–1944) British astronomer. *The Nature of the Physical World*

31 Man is slightly nearer to the atom than the stars. From his central position he can survey the grandest works of Nature with the astronomer, or the minutest works with the physicist.

Arthur Eddington *Stars and Atoms*

32 When you are courting a nice girl an hour seems like a second. When you sit on a red-hot cinder a second seems like an hour. That's relativity.

Albert Einstein (1879–1955) German-born US physicist. *News Chronicle*, 14 Mar 1949

33 The whole of science is nothing more than a refinement of everyday thinking.

Albert Einstein *Out of My Later Years*

34 Science without religion is lame, religion without science is blind.

Albert Einstein *Out of My Later Years*

35 I believe my theory of relativity to be true. But it will only be proved for certain in 1981, when I am dead.

Albert Einstein *Einstein: A Study in Simplicity*

36 God does not play dice.

Albert Einstein Einstein's objection to the quantum theory, in which physical events can only be known in terms of probabilities. It is sometimes quoted as 'God does not play dice with the Universe'. *Albert Einstein, Creator and Rebel* (B. Hoffman), Ch. 10

37 God is subtle but he is not malicious.

Albert Einstein Inscribed over the fireplace in the Mathematical Institute, Princeton. It refers to Einstein's objection to the quantum theory. *Albert Einstein* (Carl Seelig), Ch. 8

38 All the world is a laboratory to the inquiring mind.

Martin H. Fischer (1879–1962) *Fischerisms* (Howard Fabing and Ray Marr)

39 A vacuum can only exist, I imagine, by the things which enclose it.

Zelda Fitzgerald (1900–48) US writer. Journal, 1932

40 Thus I saw that most men only care for science so far as they get a living by it, and that they worship even error when it affords them a subsistence.

Johann Wolfgang von Goethe (1749–1832) German poet, dramatist, and scientist. *Conversations with Goethe* (Johann Peter Eckermann)

41 Science is not to be regarded merely as a storehouse of facts to be used for material purposes, but as one of the great human endeavours to be ranked with arts and religion as the guide and expression of man's fearless quest for truth.

Richard Arman Gregory (1864–1952) *The Harvest of a Quiet Eye* (Alan L. Mackay)

42 Discovery consists of seeing what everybody has seen and thinking what nobody has thought.

Albert Szent-Györgyi (1893–) Hungarian-born US biochemist. *The Scientist Speculates* (I. J. Good)

43 Shelley and Keats were the last English poets who were at all up to date in their chemical knowledge.

J. B. S. Haldane (1892–1964) British geneticist. *Daedalus or Science and the Future*

44 MASTER. They split the atom by firing particles at it, at 5,500 miles a second.
BOY. Good heavens. And they only split it?

Will Hay (1888–1949) British comedian. *The Fourth Form at St Michael's*

45 Oh, powerful bacillus,
With wonder how you fill us,
Every day!
While medical detectives,
With powerful objectives,
Watch your play.

William T. Helmuth (1833–1902) *Ode to the Bacillus*

46 Science has 'explained' nothing; the more we know the more fantastic the world becomes and the profounder the surrounding darkness.

Aldous Huxley (1894–1964) British novelist. *Views Of Holland*

47 Along with many scientists he considered the discovery of psychedelics one of the three major scientific break-throughs of the twentieth century, the other two being the splitting of the atom and the manipulation of genetic structures.

Laura Huxley Referring to Aldous Huxley. *This Timeless Moment*

48 Science is nothing but trained and organized common sense, differing from the latter only as a veteran may differ from a raw recruit: and its methods differ from those of common sense only as far as the guardsman's cut and thrust differ from the manner in which a savage wields his club.

T. H. Huxley (1825–95) British biologist. *Collected Essays*, Ch. VIII 'The Method of Zadig'

49 The great tragedy of Science – the slaying of a beautiful hypothesis by an ugly fact.

T. H. Huxley *Collected Essays*, 'Biogenesis and Abiogenesis'

50 Science . . . commits suicide when it adopts a creed.

T. H. Huxley *Darwiniana*, 'The Darwin Memorial'

51 Reason, Observation, and Experience – the Holy Trinity of Science.

Robert G. Ingersoll (1833–99) US lawyer and agnostic. *The Gods*

52 Many persons nowadays seem to think that any conclusion must be very scientific if the arguments in favor of it are derived from twitching of frogs' legs – especially if the frogs are decapitated – and that – on the other hand – any doctrine chiefly vouched for by the feelings of human beings – with heads on their shoulders – must be benighted and supersititious.

William James (1842–1910) US psychologist and philosopher. *Pragmatism*

53 Life exists in the universe only because the carbon atom possesses certain exceptional properties.

James Jeans (1877–1946) British scientist. *The Mysterious Universe*, Ch. 1

54 Science should leave off making pronouncements: the river of knowledge has too often turned back on itself.

James Jeans *The Mysterious Universe*, Ch. 5

55 Three quarks for Muster Mark!

James Joyce (1882–1941) Irish novelist. The word quark has since been adopted by physicists for hypothetical elementary particles. *Finnegans Wake*

56 Let both sides seek to invoke the wonders of science instead of its terrors. Together let us explore the stars, conquer the deserts, eradicate disease, tap the ocean depths, and encourage the arts and commerce.

John F. Kennedy (1917–63) US statesman. Inaugural Address, 20 Jan 1961

57 We have genuflected before the god of science only to find that it has given us the atomic bomb, producing fears and anxieties that science can never mitigate.

Martin Luther King (1929–68) US Black civil-rights leader. *Strength through Love*, Ch. 13

58 In everything that relates to science, I am a whole Encyclopaedia behind the rest of the world.

Charles Lamb (1775–1834) British essayist. *Essays of Elia*, 'The Old and the New Schoolmaster'

59 Water is H_2O, hydrogen two parts, oxygen one,
but there is also a third thing, that makes it water
and nobody knows what that is.

D. H. Lawrence (1885–1930) British novelist. *Pansies*, 'The Third Thing'

60 It is a good morning exercise for a research scientist to discard a pet hypothesis every day before breakfast.

Konrad Lorenz (1903–89) Austrian zoologist and pioneer of ethology. *On Aggression*, Ch. 2

61 Science conducts us, step by step, through the whole range of creation, until we arrive, at length, at God.

Marguerite of Valois (1553–1615) *Memoirs (1594–1600)*, Letter XII

62 Scientific discovery is a private event, and the delight that accompanies it, or the despair of finding it illusory does not travel.

Peter Medawar (1915–87) British immunologist. *Hypothesis and Imagination*

63 *Laboratorium est oratorium.* The place where we do our scientific work is a place of prayer.

Joseph Needham (1900–) British biochemist. *The Harvest of a Quiet Eye* (A. L. Mackay)

64 I do not know what I may appear to the world, but to myself I seem to have been only like a boy playing on the sea-shore, and diverting myself in now and then finding a smoother pebble or a prettier shell than ordinary, whilst the great ocean of truth lay all undiscovered before me.

Isaac Newton (1642–1727) British scientist. *Isaac Newton* (L. T. More)

65 O Diamond! Diamond! thou little knowest the mischief done!

Isaac Newton Said to a dog that set fire to some papers, representing several years' work, by knocking over a candle. *Wensley-Dale . . . a Poem* (Thomas Maude)

66 Do you really believe that the sciences would ever have originated and grown if the way had not been prepared by magicians, alchemists, astrologers and witches whose promises and pretensions first had to create a thirst, a hunger, a taste for *hidden* and *forbidden* powers? Indeed, infinitely more had to be *promised* than could ever be fulfilled in order that anything at all might be fulfilled in the realms of knowledge.

Friedrich Wilhelm Nietzsche (1844–1900) German philosopher. *The Gay Science*

67 There are no such things as applied sciences, only applications of science.

Louis Pasteur (1822–95) French scientist. Address, 11 Sept 1872

68 Traditional scientific method has always been at the very *best*, 20-20 hindsight. It's good for seeing where you've been.

Robert T. Pirsig (1928–) US writer. *Zen and the Art of Motorcycle Maintenance*, Pt. III, Ch. 24

69 We have no right to assume that any physical laws exist, or if they have existed up to now, that they will continue to exist in a similar manner in the future.

Max Planck (1858–1947) German physicist. *The Universe in the Light of Modern Physics*

70 Science must begin with myths, and with the criticism of myths.

Karl Popper (1902–) Austrian-born British philosopher. *British Philosophy in the Mid-Century* (ed. C. A. Mace)

71 Science may be described as the art of systematic over-simplification.

Karl Popper Remark, Aug 1982

72 Should we force science down the throats of those that have no taste for it? Is it our duty to drag them kicking and screaming into the twenty-first century? I am afraid that it is.

George Porter (1920–) British chemist. Speech, Sept 1986

73 A device which enables us to see how the bones in the back room are doing.

Don Quinn *Bartlett's Unfamiliar Quotations* (Leonard Louis Levinson)

74 Science without conscience is the death of the soul.

François Rabelais (c. 1494–1553) French writer.

75 The simplest schoolboy is now familiar with truths for which Archimedes would have sacrificed his life.

Ernest Renan (1823–92) French philosopher and theologian. *Souvenirs d'enfance et de jeunesse*

76 When we have found how the nucleus of atoms are built-up we shall have found the greatest secret of all – except life. We shall have found the basis of everything – of the earth we walk on, of the air we breathe, of the sunshine, of our physical body itself, of everything in the world, however great or however small – except life.

Ernest Rutherford (1871–1937) British physicist. *Passing Show 24*

77 The people – could you patent the sun?

Jonas E. Salk (1914–) US virologist. On being asked who owned the patent on his polio vaccine. *Famous Men of Science* (S. Bolton)

78 If all the arts aspire to the condition of music, all the sciences aspire to the condition of mathematics.

George Santayana (1863–1952) US philosopher. *The Observer*, 'Sayings of the Week', 4 Mar 1928

79 People must understand that science is inherently neither a potential for good nor for evil. It is a potential to be harnessed by man to do his bidding.

Glenn T. Seaborg (1912–) US physicist. Associated Press interview with Alton Blakeslee, 29 Sept 1964

80 Science is always wrong. It never solves a problem without creating ten more.

George Bernard Shaw (1856–1950) Irish dramatist and critic.

81 Science is the great antidote to the poison of enthusiasm and superstition.

Adam Smith (1723–90) Scottish economist. *The Wealth of Nations*, Bk. V, Ch. 1

82 Art and religion first; then philosophy; lastly science. That is the order of the great subjects of life, that's their order of importance.

Muriel Spark (1918–) British novelist. *The Prime of Miss Jean Brodie*, Ch. 2

83 Mystics always hope that science will some day overtake them.

Booth Tarkington (1869–1946) US novelist. *Looking Forward to the Great Adventure*

84 Her own mother lived the latter years of her life in the horrible suspicion that electricity was dripping invisibly all over the house.

James Thurber (1894–1961) US humorist. *My Life and Hard Times*, Ch. 2

85 Modern Physics is an instrument of Jewry for the destruction of Nordic science . . . True physics is the creation of the German spirit.

Rudolphe Tomaschek (20th century) German scientist. *The Rise and Fall of the Third Reich* (W. L. Shirer), Ch. 8

86 Science robs men of wisdom and usually converts them into phantom beings loaded up with facts.

Miguel de Unamuno y Jugo (1864–36) Spanish writer and philosopher. *Essays and Soliloques*

87 The term Science should not be given to anything but the aggregate of the recipes that are always successful. All the rest is literature.

Paul Valéry (1871–1945) French poet and writer. *Moralités*

88 Whenever science makes a discovery, the devil grabs it while the angels are debating the best way to use it.

Alan Valentine

89 As long as vitalism and spiritualism are open questions so long will the gateway of science be open to mysticism.

Rudolf Virchow (1821–1902) German pathologist. *Bulletin of the New York Academy of Medicine*, 4:994, 1928

90 Classical physics has been superseded by quantum theory: quantum theory is verified by experiments. Experiments must be described in terms of classical physics.

C. F. von Weizsäcker (1912–) German physicist and philosopher. Attrib.

91 If silicon had been a gas I should have been a major-general.

James Whistler (1834–1903) US painter. Referring to his failure in a West Point chemistry examination. *English Wits* (L. Russell)

92 A science which hesitates to forget its founders is lost.

A. N. Whitehead (1861–1947) British philosopher. Attrib.

93 The airplane stays up because it doesn't have the time to fall.
Orville Wright (1871–1948) US aviator. Explaining the principles of powered flight. Attrib.

94 With a microscope you see the surface of things. It magnifies them but does not show you reality. It makes things seem higher and wider. But do not suppose you are seeing things in themselves.
Feng-shen Yin-Te (1771–1810) *The Microscope*

SCIENTISTS

See also science

1 When I find myself in the company of scientists, I feel like a shabby curate who has strayed by mistake into a drawing-room full of dukes.
W. H. Auden (1907–73) British poet. *The Dyer's Hand*

2 The true men of action in our time, those who transform the world, are not the politicians and statesmen, but the scientists. Unfortunately, poetry cannot celebrate them, because their deeds are concerned with things, not persons and are, therefore, speechless.
W. H. Auden *The Dyer's Hand*

3 Sir Humphry Davy
Abominated gravy.
He lived in the odium
Of having discovered Sodium.
Edmund Clerihew Bentley (1875–1956) British writer. *Biography for Beginners*

4 I believe the souls of five hundred Sir Isaac Newtons would go to the making up of a Shakespeare or a Milton.
Samuel Taylor Coleridge (1772–1834) British poet. Letter to Thomas Poole, 23 Mar 1801

5 If you want to find out anything from the theoretical physicists about the methods they use, I advise you to stick closely to one principle: Don't listen to their words fix your attention on their deeds.
Albert Einstein (1879–1955) German-born US physicist. *The World As I See It*

6 Einstein – the greatest Jew since Jesus. I have no doubt that Einstein's name will still be remembered and revered when Lloyd George, Foch and William Hohenzollern share with Charlie Chaplin that ineluctable oblivion which awaits the uncreative mind.
J. B. S. Haldane (1892–1964) British geneticist. *Daedalus or Science and the Future*

7 Yet had Fleming not possessed immense knowledge and an unremitting gift of observation he might not have observed the effect of the hyssop mould. 'Fortune', remarked Pasteur, 'favours the prepared mind.'
André Maurois (Émile Herzog; 1885–1967) French writer. *Life of Alexander Fleming*

8 The physicists have known sin; and this is a knowledge which they cannot lose.
J. Robert Oppenheimer (1904–67) US physicist. Lecture, Massachusetts Institute of Technology, 25 Nov 1947

9 Nature, and Nature's laws lay hid in night:
God said, *Let Newton be!* and all was light.
Alexander Pope (1688–1744) British poet.
For a reply, *see* John Collings SQUIRE *Epitaphs*, 'Intended for Sir Isaac Newton'

10 It did not last: the Devil howling 'Ho!
Let Einstein be!' restored the status quo.
John Collings Squire (1884–1958) British journalist. Answer to POPE's Epitaph for Newton. *Epigrams*, 'The Dilemma'

11 He snatched the lightning shaft from heaven, and the sceptre from tyrants.
Anne-Robert-Jacques Turgot (1727–81) French economist. An inscription for a bust of Benjamin Franklin, alluding both to Franklin's invention of the lightning conductor and to his role in the American Revolution. *Vie de Turgot* (A. N. de Condorcet)

12 Already for thirty-five years he had not stopped talking and almost nothing of fundamental value had emerged.
James Dewey Watson (1928–) US geneticist. Referring to Francis Crick. *The Double Helix*, Ch. 8

13 He doubted the existence of the Deity but accepted Carnot's cycle, and he had read Shakespeare and found him weak in chemistry.
H. G. Wells (1866–1946) British writer. *Short Stories*, 'The Lord of the Dynamos'

SCOTLAND

See also Britain, Scots

1 O ye'll tak' the high road, and I'll tak' the low road,
And I'll be in Scotland afore ye,
But me and my true love will never meet again,
On the bonnie, bonnie banks o' Loch Lomon'.
Anonymous *The Bonnie Banks o' Loch Lomon'*

2 My heart's in the Highlands, my heart is not here;
My heart's in the Highlands a-chasing the deer;
Chasing the wild deer, and following the roe,
My heart's in the Highlands, wherever I go.
Robert Burns (1759–96) Scottish poet. *My Heart's in the Highlands*

3 *Oats*. A grain, which in England is generally given to horses, but in Scotland supports the people.
Samuel Johnson (1709–84) British lexicographer. *Dictionary of the English Language*

4 Norway, too, has noble wild prospects; and Lapland is remarkable for prodigious noble wild prospects. But, Sir, let me tell you, the noblest prospect which a Scotchman ever sees, is the high road that leads him to England!
Samuel Johnson *Life of Johnson* (J. Boswell), Vol. I

5 Seeing Scotland, Madam, is only seeing a worse England.
Samuel Johnson *Life of Johnson* (J. Boswell), Vol. III

6 Roamin' in the gloamin',
By the bonny banks of Clyde.
Harry Lauder (Hugh MacLennon; 1870–1950) Scottish music-hall artist. Song

7 O Caledonia! stern and wild,
Meet nurse for a poetic child!
Land of brown heath and shaggy wood,
Land of the mountain and the flood,
Land of my sires! what mortal hand
Can e'er untie the filial band
That knits me to thy rugged strand!
Walter Scott (1771–1832) Scottish novelist. *The Lay of the Last Minstrel*, VI

8 That knuckle-end of England – that land of Calvin, oat-cakes, and sulphur.
Sydney Smith (1771–1845) British clergyman and essayist. *Memoir* (Lady Holland)

SCOTS

See also British, Scotland

1 You've forgotten the grandest moral attribute of a Scotsman, Maggie,

that he'll do nothing which might damage his career.

J. M. Barrie (1860–1937) British novelist and dramatist. *What Every Woman Knows*, II

2 There are few more impressive sights in the world than a Scotsman on the make.

J. M. Barrie *What Every Woman Knows*, II

3 A Scotchman must be a very sturdy moralist who does not love Scotland better than truth.

Samuel Johnson (1709–84) British lexicographer. *Journey to the Western Islands of Scotland*, 'Col'

4 BOSWELL. I do indeed come from Scotland, but I cannot help it . . .
JOHNSON. That, Sir, I find, is what a very great many of your countrymen cannot help.

Samuel Johnson *Life of Johnson* (J. Boswell), Vol. I

5 Much may be made of a Scotchman, if he be *caught* young.

Samuel Johnson Referring to Lord Mansfield. *Life of Johnson* (J. Boswell), Vol. II

6 Their learning is like bread in a besieged town: every man gets a little, but no man gets a full meal.

Samuel Johnson Referring to education in Scotland. *Life of Johnson* (J. Boswell), Vol. II

7 I have been trying all my life to like Scotchmen, and am obliged to desist from the experiment in despair.

Charles Lamb (1775–1834) British essayist. *Essays of Elia*, 'Imperfect Sympathies'

8 In all my travels I never met with any one Scotchman but what was a man of sense. I believe everybody of that country that has any, leaves it as fast as they can.

Francis Lockier (1667–1740) English writer. *Anecdotes* (Joseph Spence)

9 Join a Highland regiment, me boy. The kilt is an unrivalled garment for fornication and diarrhoea.

John Masters (1914–) British writer. *Bugles and a Tiger*

10 It's ill taking the breeks aff a wild Highlandman.

Walter Scott (1771–1832) Scottish novelist. *The Fair Maid of Perth*, Ch. 5

11 It is never difficult to distinguish between a Scotsman with a grievance and a ray of sunshine.

P. G. Wodehouse (1881–1975) British humorous novelist. *Wodehouse at Work to the End* (Richard Usborne), Ch. 8

SCOTT, Sir Walter

(1771–1832) Scottish novelist. Originally a lawyer, he turned to writing for a living after the success of his narrative poem, *The Lay of the Last Minstrel* (1805). *Waverley* (1814) was the first of many successful historical novels, including *Rob Roy* (1817), *The Heart of Midlothian* (1818), *The Bride of Lammermoor* (1818), *Ivanhoe* (1819) and *The Talisman* (1825).

Quotations about Scott

1 It can be said of him, when he departed he took a Man's life with him. No sounder piece of British manhood was put together in that eighteenth century of time.

Thomas Carlyle (1795–1881) Scottish historian and essayist. *Essays*, 'Lockhart's Life of Scott'

2 Sir Walter Scott, when all is said and done, is an inspired butler.

William Hazlitt (1778–1830) British essayist. *Mrs Siddons*

Quotations by Scott

3 Look back, and smile at perils past.

The Bridal of Triermain, Introduction

4 It's ill taking the breeks aff a wild Highlandman.

The Fair Maid of Perth, Ch. 5

5 The Big Bow-Wow strain I can do myself like any now going; but the exquisite touch, which renders ordinary commonplace things and characters interesting, from the truth of the description and the sentiment, is denied to me.

In praise of Jane Austen. *Journal*, 14 Mar 1826

6 For ne'er
Was flattery lost on poet's ear:
A simple race! they waste their toil
For the vain tribute of a smile.

The Lay of the Last Minstrel, IV

7 True love's the gift which God has given
To man alone beneath the heaven.

The Lay of the Last Minstrel, V

8 Breathes there the man, with soul so dead,
Who never to himself hath said,
This is my own, my native land!
Whose heart hath ne'er within him burn'd,
As home his footsteps he hath turn'd
From wandering on a foreign strand!

The Lay of the Last Minstrel, VI

9 O Caledonia! stern and wild,
Meet nurse for a poetic child!
Land of brown heath and shaggy wood,
Land of the mountain and the flood,
Land of my sires! what mortal hand
Can e'er untie the filial band
That knits me to thy rugged strand!

The Lay of the Last Minstrel, VI

10 His morning walk was beneath the elms in the churchyard; 'for death,' he said, 'had been his next-door neighbour for so many years, that he had no apology for dropping the acquaintance.'

The Legend of Montrose, Introduction

11 There is a Southern proverb, – fine words butter no parsnips.

The Legend of Montrose, Ch. 3

12 To that dark inn, the grave!

The Lord of the Isles, VI

13 But search the land of living men,
Where wilt thou find their like agen?

Marmion, I

14 O, young Lochinvar is come out of the west,
Through all the wide Border his steed was the best.

Marmion, V

15 So faithful in love, and so dauntless in war,
There never was knight like the young Lochinvar.

Marmion, V

16 The stubborn spear-men still made good
Their dark impenetrable wood,
Each stepping where his comrade stood,
The instant that he fell.

Marmion, VI

17 Ridicule often checks what is absurd, and fully as often smothers that which is noble.

Quentin Durward

18 But with the morning cool repentance came.

Rob Roy, Ch. 12

19 See yon pale stripling! when a boy,
A mother's pride, a father's joy!

Rokeby, III

20 O, Brignal banks are wild and fair,
And Gretna woods are green,
And you may gather garlands there
Would grace a summer queen.

Rokeby, III

21 My heart's in the Highlands, my heart is not here,

My heart's in the Highlands a-chasing the deer.

Waverley, Ch. 28

22 No, this right hand shall work it all off.

Refusing offers of help following his bankruptcy in 1826. *Century of Anecdote* (J. Timbs)

SCULPTURE

See also art, artists

1 Sculptor Henry Moore has been asked not to leave any holes in which boys could trap their heads when he carves 'Family Group' for Harlow New Town.

Anonymous *The News Chronicle*

2 If people dug up the remains of this civilization a thousand years hence, and found Epstein's statues and that man Ellis, they would think we were just savages.

Doris Lessing (1919–) British novelist. *Martha Quest*, Pt. I, Ch. 1

3 Patriotism is the last refuge of the sculptor.

William Plomer (1903–73) British writer and poet. Attrib.

4 My god, they've shot the wrong person!

James Pryde (1866–1941) British artist. At the unveiling of a statue to Nurse Edith Cavell. Attrib.

5 See what will happen to you if you don't stop biting your fingernails.

Will Rogers (1879–1935) US actor and humorist. Message written on a postcard of the Venus de Milo that he sent to his young niece.

SEA

See also boats, Navy, seaside

1 The sea is calm to-night,
The tide is full, the moon lies fair
Upon the Straits.

Matthew Arnold (1822–88) British poet and critic. *Dover Beach*

2 For all at last return to the sea – to Oceanus, the ocean river, like the ever-flowing stream of time, the beginning and the end.

Rachel Carson (1907–64) US biologist. The closing words of the book. *The Sea Around Us*

3 The voice of the sea speaks to the soul. The touch of the sea is sensuous, enfolding the body in its soft, close embrace.

Kate Chopin (1851–1904) US writer. *The Awakening*, Ch. 6

4 The ice was here, the ice was there,
The ice was all around:
It cracked and growled, and roared and howled,
Like noises in a swound!

Samuel Taylor Coleridge (1772–1834) British poet. *The Rime of the Ancient Mariner*, I

5 We are as near to heaven by sea as by land.

Humphrey Gilbert (c. 1539–83) English navigator. Remark made shortly before he went down with his ship *Squirrel*. *A Book of Anecdotes* (D. George)

6 When men come to like a sea-life, they are not fit to live on land.

Samuel Johnson (1709–84) British lexicographer. *Life of Johnson* (J. Boswell), Vol. II

7 The snotgreen sea. The scrotumtightening sea.

James Joyce (1882–1941) Irish novelist. *Ulysses*

8 It keeps eternal whisperings around
Desolate shores, and with its mighty swell
Gluts twice ten thousand Caverns.

John Keats (1795–1821) British poet. *On the Sea*

9 'Wouldst thou' – so the helmsman answered –
'Learn the secret of the sea?
Only those who brave its dangers
Comprehend its mystery!'

Henry Wadsworth Longfellow (1807–82) US poet. *The Secret of the Sea*

10 I must down to the seas again, to the lonely sea and the sky,
And all I ask is a tall ship and a star to steer her by,
And the wheel's kick and the wind's song and the white sail's shaking,
And a grey mist on the sea's face and a grey dawn breaking.

John Masefield (1878–1967) British poet. Often quoted using 'sea' rather than 'seas', and 'I must go down' rather than 'I must down'. *Sea Fever*

11 Rocked in the cradle of the deep.

Emma Millard (1787–1870) British songwriter. Song

12 A life on the ocean wave,
A home on the rolling deep.

Epes Sargent (1813–80) US writer and dramatist. *A Life on the Ocean Wave*

13 O hear us when we cry to Thee
For those in peril on the sea.

William Whiting (1825–78) British hymn writer. *Eternal Father Strong to Save*

14 The sea! the sea!

Xenophon (430–354 BC) Greek historian. *Anabasis*, IV:7

SEASIDE

See also sea

1 The King bathes, and with great success; a machine follows the Royal one into the sea, filled with fiddlers, who play *God Save the King* as his Majesty takes his plunge.

Fanny Burney (Frances Burney D'Arblay; 1752–1840) British novelist. Referring to George III at Weymouth. Diary, 8 July 1789

2 The Walrus and the Carpenter
Were walking close at hand;
They wept like anything to see
Such quantities of sand:
'If this were only cleared away,'
They said, 'it *would* be grand!'

Lewis Carroll (Charles Lutwidge Dodgson; 1832–98) British writer. *Through the Looking-Glass*, Ch. 4

3 It is the drawback of all sea-side places that half the landscape is unavailable for purposes of human locomotion, being covered by useless water.

Norman Douglas (1868–1952) British novelist. *Alone*, 'Mentone'

4 I do Like to be Beside the Seaside.

John A. Glover-Kind (19th century) US songwriter. Song title

SEASONS

See also autumn, months, spring, summer, winter

1 I'll see you again,
Whenever spring breaks through again.

Noël Coward (1899–1973) British dramatist. *Bittersweet*

2 Four seasons fill the measure of the year;
There are four seasons in the mind of men.

John Keats (1795–1821) British poet. *Four Seasons*

3 No one thinks of winter when the grass is green!

Rudyard Kipling (1865–1936) Indian-born British writer. *A St Helena Lullaby*

4 If Winter comes, can Spring be far behind?

Percy Bysshe Shelley (1792–1822) British poet. *Ode to the West Wind*

SECRECY

See also gossip

1 Only the nose knows
Where the nose goes
When the door close.

Muhammad Ali (Cassius Clay; 1942–) US boxer. When asked whether a boxer should have sex before a big fight. Remark, reported by Al Silverman

2 Careless talk costs lives.

Anonymous British wartime slogan

3 Walls have ears.

Anonymous British wartime slogan

4 I have seldom spoken with greater regret, for my lips are not yet unsealed. Were these troubles over I would make a case, and I guarantee that not a man would go into the Lobby against us.

Stanley Baldwin (1867–1947) British statesman. Referring to the Abyssinian crisis; usually misquoted as 'My lips are sealed'. Speech, House of Commons, 10 Dec 1935

5 Curse not the king, no not in thy thought; and curse not the rich in thy bedchamber: for a bird of the air shall carry the voice, and that which hath wings shall tell the matter.

Bible: Ecclesiastes 10:20

6 If thou hast heard a word, let it die with thee; and be bold, it will not burst thee.

Bible: Ecclesiasticus 19:10

7 Stolen waters are sweet, and bread eaten in secret is pleasant.

Bible: Proverbs 9:17

8 Mum's the word.

George Colman the Younger (1762–1836) British dramatist. *The Battle of Hexham*, II:1

9 O fie miss, you must not kiss and tell.

William Congreve (1670–1729) British Restoration dramatist. *Love for Love*, II:10

10 I know that's a secret, for it's whispered every where.

William Congreve *Love for Love*, III:3

11 Three may keep a secret, if two of them are dead.

Benjamin Franklin (1706–90) US scientist and statesman. *Poor Richard's Almanack*

12 It is a secret in the Oxford sense: you may tell it to only one person at a time.

Oliver Franks (1905–) British philosopher and administrator. *Sunday Telegraph*, 30 Jan 1977

SEDUCTION

1 Candy
Is dandy
But liquor
Is quicker.

Ogden Nash (1902–71) US poet. *Hard Lines*, 'Reflection on Ice-Breaking'

SELF

See also self-confidence, etc.

1 Every man is his own worst enemy.

Proverb

2 God helps them that help themselves.

Proverb

3 He helps little that helps not himself.

Proverb

4 He travels fastest who travels alone.

Proverb

5 And now the end is near
And so I face the final curtain,
My friend, I'll say it clear,
I'll state my case of which I'm certain.
I've lived a life that's full, I've traveled each and evr'y high-way
And more, much more than this, I did it my way.

Paul Anka (1941–) US singer and songwriter. Based on the French composition, 'Comme d'habitude'. *My Way*

6 Lord, deliver me from myself.

Thomas Browne (1605–82) English physician and writer. *Religio Medici*, Pt. II

7 I have always disliked myself at any given moment; the total of such moments is my life.

Cyril Connolly (1903–74) British journalist. *Enemies of Promise*, Ch. 18

8 But I do nothing upon myself, and yet I am mine own Executioner.

John Donne (1573–1631) English poet. *Devotions*, 12

9 What we must decide is perhaps how we are valuable, rather than how valuable we are.

F. Scott Fitzgerald (1896–1940) US novelist. *The Crack-Up*

10 We never remark any passion or principle in others, of which, in some degree or other, we may not find a parallel in ourselves.

David Hume (1711–76) Scottish philosopher. *A Treatise of Human Nature*

11 Whenever I look inside myself I am afraid.

Cyril Joad (1891–1953) British writer and broadcaster. *The Observer*, 'Sayings of the Week', 8 Nov 1942

12 All censure of a man's self is oblique praise. It is in order to shew how much he can spare.

Samuel Johnson (1709–84) British lexicographer. *Life of Johnson* (J. Boswell), Vol. III

13 One should examine oneself for a very long time before thinking of condemning others.

Molière (Jean Baptiste Poquelin; 1622–73) French dramatist. *Le Misanthrope*, III:4

14 Self-love seems so often unrequited.

Anthony Powell (1905–) British novelist. *The Acceptance World*

15 Why, man, he doth bestride the narrow world
Like a Colossus; and we petty men
Walk under his huge legs, and peep about
To find ourselves dishonourable graves.
Men at some time are masters of their fates:
The fault, dear Brutus, is not in our stars,
But in ourselves that we are underlings.

William Shakespeare (1564–1616) English dramatist. *Julius Caesar*, I:2

16 Do not love your neighbour as yourself. If you are on good terms with yourself it is an impertinence; if on bad, an injury.

George Bernard Shaw (1856–1950) Irish dramatist and critic. *Man and Superman*, 'Maxims for Revolutionists'

17 Self-sacrifice enables us to sacrifice
Other people without blushing.

George Bernard Shaw *Man and Superman*

18 The unexamined life is not worth living.

Socrates (469–399 BC) Athenian philosopher. *Apology* (Plato)

19 I am always with myself, and it is I who am my tormentor.

Leo Tolstoy (1828–1910) Russian writer. *Memoirs of a Madman*

20 Meanwhile you will write an essay on 'self-indulgence'. There will be a prize of half a crown for the longest essay, irrespective of any possible merit.

Evelyn Waugh (1903–66) British novelist. *Decline and Fall*, Pt. I, Ch. 5

21 I can't quite explain it, but I don't believe one can ever be unhappy

for long provided one does just exactly what one wants to and when one wants to.
Evelyn Waugh *Decline and Fall*, Pt. I, Ch. 5

22 I celebrate myself, and sing myself,
And what I assume you shall assume.
Walt Whitman (1819–92) US poet. *Song of Myself*, 1

23 Behold, I do not give lectures or a little charity,
When I give I give myself.
Walt Whitman *Song of Myself*, 40

24 I have said that the soul is not more than the body,
And I have said that the body is not more than the soul,
And nothing, but God, is greater to one than one's self is.
Walt Whitman *Song of Myself*, 48

25 Do I contradict myself?
Very well then I contradict myself,
(I am large, I contain multitudes).
Walt Whitman *Song of Myself*, 51

26 Self-determination is not a mere phrase. It is an imperative principle which statesmen will henceforth ignore at their peril.
Woodrow Wilson (1856–1925) US statesman. Speech to Congress, 11 Feb 1918

SELF-CONFIDENCE

See also shyness

1 I know I'm not clever but I'm always right.
J. M. Barrie (1860–1937) British playwright. *Peter Pan*

2 Those who believe that they are exclusively in the right are generally those who achieve something.
Aldous Huxley (1894–1964) British novelist. *Proper Studies*

3 I can honestly say that I was never affected by the question of the success of an undertaking. If I felt it was the right thing to do, I was for it regardless of the possible outcome.
Golda Meir (1898–1978) Russian-born Israeli stateswoman. *Golda Meir: Woman with a Cause* (Marie Syrkin)

4 I wish I was as cocksure of anything as Tom Macaulay is of everything.
Lord Melbourne (1779–1848) British statesman. *Preface to Lord Melbourne's Papers* (Earl Cowper)

5 Bring me no more reports; let them fly all:
Till Birnam wood remove to Dunsinane
I cannot taint with fear.
William Shakespeare (1564–1616) English dramatist. *Macbeth*, V:3

6 Hang out our banners on the outward walls;
The cry is still, 'They come'; our castle's strength
Will laugh a siege to scorn.
William Shakespeare *Macbeth*, V:5

7 'Tis an ill cook that cannot lick his own fingers.
William Shakespeare *Romeo and Juliet*, IV:2

8 'Are you not,' a Rugby master had asked him in discussing one of his essays, 'a little out of your depth here?' 'Perhaps, Sir,' was the confident reply, 'but I can swim.'
William Temple (1881–1944) British churchman. *William Temple* (F. A. Iremonger)

9 I am certain that we will win the election with a good majority. Not that I am ever over-confident.
Margaret Thatcher (1925–) British politician and prime minister. *Evening Standard*, 1987

10 If I ever felt inclined to be timid as I was going into a room full of people, I would say to myself, 'You're the cleverest member of one of the cleverest families in the cleverest class of the cleverest nation in the world, why should you be frightened?'
Beatrice Webb (1858–1943) British economist and writer. *Portraits from Memory* (Bertrand Russell), 'Sidney and Beatrice Webb'

SELF-CONTROL

1 He that is slow to anger is better than the mighty; and he that ruleth his spirit than he that taketh a city.
Bible: Proverbs 16:32

2 No one who cannot limit himself has ever been able to write.
Nicolas Boileau (1636–1711) French writer. *L'Art poétique*, I

3 The highest possible stage in moral culture is when we recognize that we ought to control our thoughts.
Charles Darwin (1809–82) British life scientist. *Descent of Man*, Ch. 4

4 When things are steep, remember to stay level-headed.
Horace (Quintus Horatius Flaccus; 65–8 BC) Roman poet. *Odes*, II

5 If you can keep your head when all about you
Are losing theirs and blaming it on you.
Rudyard Kipling (1865–1936) Indian-born British writer. *If*

6 He that would govern others, first should be
The master of himself.
Philip Massinger (1583–1640) English dramatist. *The Bondman*, I

7 Never lose your temper with the Press or the public is a major rule of political life.
Christabel Pankhurst (1880–1958) British suffragette. *Unshackled*

SELF-DENIAL

See also abstinence, selflessness

1 Self-denial is not a virtue; it is only the effect of prudence on rascality.
George Bernard Shaw (1856–1950) Irish dramatist and critic. *Man and Superman*, 'Maxims for Revolutionists'

2 Thy need is yet greater than mine.
Philip Sidney (1554–86) English poet and courtier. Giving his own water bottle to a humble wounded soldier after he had himself been wounded. Attrib.

SELF-DESTRUCTION

1 Lie down, and stray no further.
Now all labour
Mars what it does; yea, very force entangles
Itself with strength . . .
William Shakespeare (1564–1616) English dramatist. *Antony and Cleopatra*, IV:12

2 ANTONY. Not Caesar's valour hath o'erthrown Antony
But Antony's hath triumphed on itself.
CLEOPATRA. So it should be, that none but Antony
Should conquer Antony.
William Shakespeare *Antony and Cleopatra*, IV:13

SELF-INDULGENCE

1 Meanwhile you will write an essay on 'self-indulgence'. There will be a prize of half a crown for the longest essay, irrespective of any possible merit.
Evelyn Waugh (1903–66) British novelist. *Decline and Fall*, Pt. I, Ch. 5

SELF-INTEREST

See also parochialism, selfishness

1 Every man for himself, and the devil take the hindmost.
Proverb

2 The land self-interest groans from shore to shore,
For fear that plenty should attain the poor.
Lord Byron (1788–1824) British poet. *The Age of Bronze*, XIV

3 Anyone informed that the universe is expanding and contracting in pulsations of eighty billion years has a right to ask, 'What's in it for me?'
Peter De Vries (1910–) US novelist. *The Glory of the Hummingbird*, Ch. 1

4 The least pain in our little finger gives us more concern and uneasiness than the destruction of millions of our fellow-beings.
William Hazlitt (1778–1830) British essayist. *American Literature*, 'Dr Channing'

5 It is difficult to love mankind unless one has a reasonable private income and when one has a reasonable private income one has better things to do than loving mankind.
Hugh Kingsmill (1889–1949) British writer. *God's Apology* (R. Ingrams)

6 Self-interest speaks all sorts of tongues, and plays all sorts of roles, even that of disinterestedness.
Duc de la Rochefoucauld (1613–80) French writer. *Maximes*, 39

SELFISHNESS

See also self-interest

1 I have been a selfish being all my life, in practice, though not in principle.
Jane Austen (1775–1817) British novelist. *Pride and Prejudice*, Ch. 58

2 And this the burthen of his song,
For ever us'd to be,
I care for nobody, not I,
If no one cares for me.
Isaac Bickerstaffe (c. 1735–c. 1812) Irish dramatist. *Love in a Village*, I

3 It's 'Damn you, Jack – I'm all right!' with you chaps.
David Bone (1874–1959) British sea captain and writer. *The Brassbounder*, Ch. 3

4 The proud, the cold untroubled heart of stone,
That never mused on sorrow but its own.
Thomas Campbell (1777–1844) British poet. *Pleasures of Hope*, I

SELF-KNOWLEDGE

1 Resolve to be thyself: and know, that he
Who finds himself, loses his misery.
Matthew Arnold (1822–88) British poet and critic. *Self-Dependence*

2 We confess our bad qualities to others out of fear of appearing naive or ridiculous by not being aware of them.
Gerald Brenan (Edward Fitzgerald Brenan; 1894–1987) British writer. *Thoughts in a Dry Season*

3 I always thought I was Jeanne d'Arc and Buonaparte–how little one knows oneself.
Charles de Gaulle (1890–1970) French general and president. On being compared with Robespierre. *Figaro Littéraire*, 1958

4 'I know myself,' he cried, 'but that is all.'
F. Scott Fitzgerald (1896–1940) US novelist. *This Side of Paradise*, Bk. II, Ch. 5

5 I do not know myself, and God forbid that I should.
Goethe (1749–1832) German poet and dramatist. *Conversations with Eckermann*, 10 Apr 1829

6 I have the true feeling of myself only when I am unbearably unhappy.
Franz Kafka (1883–1924) Czech novelist. *Diaries*

7 Know then thyself, presume not God to scan,
The proper study of Mankind is Man.
Alexander Pope (1688–1744) British poet. *An Essay on Man*, II

8 That true self-love and social are the same;
That virtue only makes our bliss below;
And all our knowledge is, ourselves to know.
Alexander Pope *An Essay on Man*, IV

9 You go not, till I set you up a glass
Where you may see the inmost part of you.
William Shakespeare (1564–1616) English dramatist. *Hamlet*, III:4

10 Speak no more;
Thou turn'st mine eyes into my very soul.
William Shakespeare *Hamlet*, III:4

11 Greatness knows itself.
William Shakespeare *Henry IV, Part 1*, IV:3

12 Self-knowledge is a dangerous thing, tending to make man shallow or insane.
Karl Shapiro (1913–) US poet, critic, and editor. *The Bourgeois Poet*, 3

13 Explore thyself. Herein are demanded the eye and the nerve.
Henry David Thoreau (1817–62) US writer. *Walden*, 'Conclusions'

SELFLESSNESS

See also charity, self-denial

1 Of gold she would not wear so much as a seal-ring, choosing to store her money in the stomachs of the poor rather than to keep it at her own disposal.
St Jerome (c. 347–c. 420) Italian monk and scholar. *Letter CXXVII*

2 The way to get things done is not to mind who gets the credit of doing them.
Benjamin Jowett (1817–93) British theologian. Attrib.

3 To give and not to count the cost;
To fight and not to heed the wounds;
To toil and not to seek for rest;
To labour and not ask for any reward
Save that of knowing that we do Thy will.
St Ignatius Loyola (1491–1556) Spanish priest. *Prayer for Generosity*

4 'I haven't got time to be sick!' he said. 'People need me.' For he was a country doctor, and he did not know what it was to spare himself.
Don Marquis (1878–1937) US journalist and writer. *Country Doctor*

5 There is nothing in Christianity or Buddhism that quite matches the sympathetic unselfishness of an oyster.
Saki (Hector Hugh Munro; 1870–1916) British writer. *Chronicles of Clovis*

6 O good old man! how well in thee appears
The constant service of the antique world,
When service sweat for duty, not for meed!
Thou art not for the fashion of these times,
Where none will sweat but for promotion,
And having that, do choke their service up
Even with the having.
William Shakespeare (1564–1616) English dramatist. *As You Like It*, II:3

SELF-MADE MEN

1 I know he is, and he adores his maker.

Benjamin Disraeli (1804–81) British statesman. Replying to a remark made in defense of John Bright that he was a self-made man. *The Fine Art of Political Wit* (L. Harris)

2 He was a self-made man who owed his lack of success to nobody.

Joseph Heller (1923–) US novelist. *Catch-22*, Ch. 3

3 A self-made man is one who believes in luck and sends his son to Oxford.

Christina Stead (1902–83) Australian novelist. *House of All Nations*, 'Credo'

SELF-PRESERVATION

See also survival

1 Look after number one.

Proverb

2 I want to get out with my greatness intact.

Muhammad Ali (Cassius Clay; 1942–) US heavyweight boxer. Announcing his retirement. *The Observer*, 4 July 1974

3 He that fights and runs away
May live to fight another day.

Anonymous *Musarum Deliciae*

4 This animal is very dangerous; when attacked it defends itself.

Anonymous *La Ménagerie* (P. K. Théodore), 1828

5 In good King Charles's golden days,
When loyalty no harm meant,
A zealous High Churchman was I,
And so I got preferment.

And this is law, that I'll maintain,
Unto my dying day, Sir,
That whatsoever King shall reign,
I'll be the Vicar of Bray, Sir.

Anonymous *The Vicar of Bray*

6 Kill the other guy before he kills you.

Jack Dempsey (1895–1983) US heavyweight boxer. *The Times*, 2 June 1983

7 There was only one catch and that was Catch-22, which specified that a concern for one's own safety in the face of dangers that were real and immediate was the process of a rational mind.

Joseph Heller (1923–) US novelist. *Catch-22*, Ch. 5

8 If a madman were to come into this room with a stick in his hand, no doubt we should pity the state of his mind; but our primary consideration would be to take care of ourselves. We should knock him down first, and pity him afterwards.

Samuel Johnson (1709–84) British lexicographer. *Life of Johnson* (J. Boswell), Vol. III

9 We intend to remain alive. Our neighbors want to see us dead. This is not a question that leaves much room for compromise.

Golda Meir (1898–1978) Russian-born Israeli stateswoman. *Reader's Digest* (July 1971), 'The Indestructible Golda Meir'

10 England has saved herself by her exertions, and will, as I trust, save Europe by her example.

William Pitt the Younger (1759–1806) British statesman. Speech, Guildhall, 1805

11 The better part of valour is discretion; in the which better part I have saved my life.

William Shakespeare (1564–1616) English dramatist. *Henry IV, Part One*, V:4

12 *J'ai vécu.*
I survived.

Abbé de Sieyès (1748–1836) French churchman. Replying to an enquiry concerning what he had done during the Terror. *Dictionnaire Encyclopédique* (E. Guérard)

13 Greater love hath no man than this, that he lay down his friends for his life.

Jeremy Thorpe (1929–) British politician. After Macmillan's 1962 Cabinet reshuffle. *The Pendulum Years* (Bernard Levin), Ch. 12

14 He was gifted with the sly, sharp instinct for self-preservation that passes for wisdom among the rich.

Evelyn Waugh (1903–66) British novelist. *Scoop*

15 Scheherazade is the classical example of a woman saving her head by using it.

Esme Wynne-Tyson (1898–) British writer. Attrib.

SELF-RELIANCE

See also independence

1 If you want a thing well done, do it yourself.

Proverb

2 The gods help them that help themselves.

Aesop (6th century BC) Reputed Greek writer of fables. *Fables*, 'Hercules and the Waggoner'

3 Be Prepared . . . the meaning of the motto is that a scout must prepare himself by previous thinking out and practising how to act on any accident or emergency so that he is never taken by surprise; he knows exactly what to do when anything unexpected happens.

Robert Baden-Powell (1857–1941) British soldier and founder of the Boy Scouts. Motto of the Scout movement. *Scouting for Boys*

4 I am the cat that walks alone.

Lord Beaverbrook (Maxwell Aitken; 1879–1964) Canadian-born politician and newspaper proprietor. *Beaverbrook* (A. J. P. Taylor)

5 They do most by Books, who could do much without them, and he that chiefly owes himself unto himself, is the substantial Man.

Thomas Browne (1605–82) English physician and writer. *Christian Morals*, Pt. II

6 Let the boy win his spurs.

Edward III (1312–77) King of England. Replying to a suggestion that he should send reinforcements to his son, the Black Prince, during the Battle of Crécy, 1346. Attrib.

7 I am your anointed Queen. I will never be by violence constrained to do anything. I thank God that I am endued with such qualities that if I were turned out of the Realm in my petticoat I were able to live in any place in Christome.

Elizabeth I (1533–1603) Queen of England. *Sayings of Queen Elizabeth* (Chamberlin)

8 Very well, alone.

David Low (1891–1963) British cartoonist. The cartoon showed a British soldier shaking his fist at a hostile sea and a sky full of war planes. Caption to cartoon, *Evening Standard*, 18 June 1940

9 The first rule in opera is the first rule in life: see to everything yourself.

Nellie Melba (Helen Porter Mitchell; 1861–1931) Australian soprano. *Melodies and Memories*

10 The greatest thing in the world is to know how to be self-sufficient.

Michel de Montaigne (1533–92) French essayist. *Essais*, I

11 I think it is about time we pulled our fingers out . . . The rest of the world most certainly does not owe us a living.

Prince Philip (1921–) The consort of Queen Elizabeth II. Speech, London, 17 Oct 1961

12 Our remedies oft in ourselves do lie,
Which we ascribe to heaven.

William Shakespeare (1564–1616) English dramatist. *All's Well that Ends Well*, I:1

13 I'll never

Be such a gosling to obey instinct, but stand
As if a man were author of himself
And knew no other kin.

William Shakespeare *Coriolanus*, V:3

14 Cassius from bondage will deliver Cassius.

William Shakespeare *Julius Caesar*, I:3

SELF-RESPECT

See also pride, respect

1 I will rather risk my Crown than do what I think personally disgraceful, and whilst I have no wish but for the good and prosperity of my country, it is impossible that the nation shall not stand by me; if they will not, they shall have another King.

George III (1738–1820) King of Great Britain and Ireland. Letter to Lord North, 17 Mar 1778

2 It is better to die on your feet than to live on your knees.

Dolores Ibarruri (1895–) Spanish politician. Speech, Paris, 1936

3 Self-respect – the secure feeling that no one, as yet, is suspicious.

H. L. Mencken (1880–1956) US journalist. *A Mencken Chrestomathy*

4 Whatever talents I possess may suddenly diminish or suddenly increase. I can with ease become an ordinary fool. I may be one now. But it doesn't do to upset one's own vanity.

Dylan Thomas (1914–53) Welsh poet. *Notebooks*

5 As for conceit, what man will do any good who is not conceited? Nobody holds a good opinion of a man who has a low opinion of himself.

Anthony Trollope (1815–82) British novelist. *Orley Farm*, Ch. 22

6 And, above all things, never think that you're not good enough yourself. A man should never think that. My belief is that in life people will take you very much at your own reckoning.

Anthony Trollope *The Small House at Allington*, Ch. 32

7 When people do not respect us we are sharply offended; yet deep down in his heart no man much respects himself.

Mark Twain (Samuel Langhorne Clemens; 1835–1910) US writer. *Notebooks*

SENSATION

1 O for a life of sensations rather than of thoughts!

John Keats (1795–1821) British poet. Letter to Benjamin Bailey, 22 Nov 1817

SENTIMENTALITY

See also emotion

1 They had been corrupted by money, and he had been corrupted by sentiment. Sentiment was the more dangerous, because you couldn't name its price. A man open to bribes was to be relied upon below a certain figure, but sentiment might uncoil in the heart at a name, a photograph, even a smell remembered.

Graham Greene (1904–) British novelist. *The Heart of the Matter*

2 Sentimentality is a superstructure covering brutality.

Carl Gustav Jung (1875–1961) Swiss psychoanalyst. *Reflections*

3 One may not regard the world as a sort of metaphysical brothel for emotions.

Arthur Koestler (1905–83) Hungarian-born British writer. *Darkness at Noon*, 'The Second Hearing'

4 Sentimentality is only sentiment that rubs you up the wrong way.

W. Somerset Maugham (1874–1965) British novelist. *A Writer's Notebook*

5 She likes stories that make her cry – I think we all do, it's so nice to feel sad when you've nothing particular to be sad about.

Annie Sullivan (1866–1936) US teacher of the handicapped. Referring to Helen Keller. Letter, 12 Dec 1887

SEPARATION

See also absence, parting

1 My Bonnie lies over the ocean,
My Bonnie lies over the sea,
My Bonnie lies over the ocean,
Oh, bring back my Bonnie to me.

Anonymous *My Bonnie*

2 If I should meet thee
After long years,
How should I greet thee? –
With silence and tears.

Lord Byron (1788–1824) British poet. *When we two parted*

3 Absence from whom we love is worse than death.

William Cowper (1731–1800) British poet. *'Hope, like the Short-lived Ray'*

4 As it will be the right of all, so it will be the duty of some, definitely to prepare for a separation, amicably if they can, violently if they must.

Josiah Quincy (1772–1864) US statesman. *Abridgement of Debates of Congress*, Vol. IV, 14 Jan 1811

5 Every parting gives a foretaste of death; every coming together again a foretaste of the resurrection.

Arthur Schopenhauer (1788–1860) German philosopher. *Gedanken über vielerlei Gegenstände*, XXVI

6 I do desire we may be better strangers.

William Shakespeare (1564–1616) English dramatist. *As You Like It*, III:2

SERMONS

See also brevity, speeches, verbosity

1 The British churchgoer prefers a severe preacher because he thinks a few home truths will do his neighbours no harm.

George Bernard Shaw (1856–1950) Irish dramatist and critic. Attrib.

2 They are written as if sin were to be taken out of man like Eve out of Adam – by putting him to sleep.

Sydney Smith (1771–1845) British clergyman and essayist. Referring to boring sermons. *Anecdotes of the Clergy* (J. Larwood)

3 I never quite forgave Mahaffy for getting himself suspended from preaching in the College Chapel. Ever since his sermons were discontinued, I suffer from insomnia in church.

George Tyrrell (1861–1909) Irish Catholic theologian. *As I Was Going Down Sackville Street* (Oliver St John Gogarty), Ch. 25

4 Yes, about ten minutes.

Duke of Wellington (1769–1852) British general and statesman. Responding to a vicar's query as to whether there was anything he would like his forthcoming sermon to be about. Attrib.

SERVANTS

1 His lord said unto him, Well done, thou good and faithful servant: thou hast been faithful over a few things, I will make thee ruler over many things: enter thou into the joy of thy lord.

Bible: Matthew 25:21

2 There they are cutting each other's throats, because one half of them prefer hiring their servants for life, and the other by the hour.

Thomas Carlyle (1795–1881) Scottish historian and essayist. Referring to the American Civil War. Attrib.

3 Servants should not be ill. We have quite enough illnesses of our own without them adding to the symptoms.

Lady Diana Cooper (1892–1986) Actress and writer. *Diana Cooper* (Philip Ziegler)

4 Many a man has been a wonder to the world, whose wife and valet have seen nothing in him that was even remarkable. Few men have been admired by their servants.

Michel de Montaigne (1533–92) French essayist. *Essais*, III

5 He's really awfully fond of colored people. Well, he says himself, he wouldn't have white servants.

Dorothy Parker (1893–1967) US writer. *Arrangements in Black and White*

6 A very large part of English middle-class education is devoted to the training of servants . . . In so far as it is, by definition, the training of upper servants, it includes, of course, the instilling of that kind of confidence which will enable the upper servants to supervise and direct the lower servants.

Raymond Henry Williams (1921–) British academic and writer. *Culture and Society*, Ch. 3

SERVICE

See also help

1 His lord said unto him, Well done, thou good and faithful servant: thou hast been faithful over a few things, I will make thee ruler over many things: enter thou into the joy of thy lord.

Bible: Matthew 25:21

2 He was caught
Red-handed with the silver and his Grace
Being short of staff at the time asked him to stay
And clean it.

Christopher Fry (1907–) British dramatist. *Venus Observed*

3 Oh that I were an orange-tree,
That busy plant!
Then I should ever laden be,
And never want
Some fruit for Him that dressed me.

George Herbert (1593–1633) English poet. *Employment*

4 All English shop assistants are Miltonists. All Miltonists firmly believe that 'they also serve who only stand and wait.'

George Mikes (1912–87) Hungarian-born British writer. *How to be Inimitable*

5 God doth not need
Either man's work or his own gifts. Who best
Bear his mild yoke, they serve him best: his state
Is kingly; thousands at his bidding speed,
And post o'er land and ocean without rest;
They also serve who only stand and wait.

John Milton (1608–74) English poet. *Sonnet*: 'On his Blindness'

6 Small service is true service, while it lasts.

William Wordsworth (1770–1850) British poet. *To a Child, Written in her Album*

SERVILITY

See also flattery, humility

1 Fine words and an insinuating appearance are seldom associated with true virtue.

Confucius (K'ung Fu-tzu; 551–479 BC) Chinese philosopher. *Analects*

2 I am well aware that I am the 'umblest person going . . . .My mother is likewise a very 'umble person. We live in a numble abode.

Charles Dickens (1812–70) British novelist. Said by Uriah Heep. *David Copperfield*, Ch. 16

3 Uriah, with his long hands slowly twining over one another, made a ghastly writhe from the waist upwards.

Charles Dickens *David Copperfield*, Ch. 17

4 A pious man is one who would be an atheist if the king were.

Jean de La Bruyère (1645–96) French satirist. *Les Caractères*

5 Wit that can creep, and pride that licks the dust.

Alexander Pope (1688–1744) British poet. *Epistle to Dr. Arbuthnot*

6 You know that nobody is strongminded around a President . . . it is always: 'yes sir', 'no sir' (the 'no sir' comes when he asks whether you're dissatisfied).

George Edward Reedy (1917–) US government official. *The White House* (ed. R. Gordon Hoxie)

7 Whenever he met a great man he grovelled before him, and my-lorded him as only a free-born Briton can do.

William Makepeace Thackeray (1811–63) British novelist. *Vanity Fair*, Ch. 13

SEX

See also abstinence, adultery, animalism, contraception, debauchery, illegitimacy, lust, pornography, promiscuity, prudery, purity, sexes

1 Is sex dirty? Only if it's done right.

Woody Allen (Allen Stewart Konigsberg; 1935–) US film actor, writer, and director. *All You've Ever Wanted to Know About Sex*

2 It was the most fun I ever had without laughing.

Woody Allen *Annie Hall*

3 Don't knock it, it's sex with someone you love.

Woody Allen Referring to masturbation. *Annie Hall*

4 WOMAN. You are the greatest lover I have ever known.
ALLEN. Well, I practice a lot when I'm on my own.

Woody Allen *Love and Death*

5 My brain: it's my second favorite organ.

Woody Allen *Sleeper*

6 Sex between a man and a woman can be wonderful – provided you get between the right man and the right woman.

Woody Allen Attrib.

7 Virginity is rather a state of mind.

Maxwell Anderson (1888–1959) *Elizabeth the Queen*, II:3

8 She sighed, she cried, she damned near died: she said 'What shall I do?'
So I took her into bed and covered up her head
Just to save her from the foggy, foggy dew.

Anonymous *Weaver's Song*

9 You are the first American to make sex funny.

Anonymous Said to Anita Loos by a friend on reading her *Gentlemen Prefer Blondes* (1928).

10 Writing about erotics is a perfectly respectable function of medicine, and about the way to make the

woman enjoy sex; these are an important part of reproductive physiology.

Avicenna (Ibn Sina; 980–1037) *Sex in Society* (Alex Comfort)

11 The Seven Year Itch.

George Axelrod (1922–) US screenwriter. Play and film title

12 It is called in our schools 'beastliness', and this is about the best name for it . . . should it become a habit it quickly destroys both health and spirits; he becomes feeble in body and mind, and often ends in a lunatic asylum.

Robert Baden-Powell (1857–1941) British soldier and founder of the Boy Scouts. Referring to masturbation. *Scouting for Boys*

13 The great and terrible step was taken. What else could you expect from a girl so expectant? 'Sex,' said Frank Harris, 'is the gateway to life.' So I went through the gateway in an upper room in the Cafe Royal.

Enid Bagnold (1889–1981) British playwright. *Enid Bagnold's Autobiography*

14 Money, it turned out, was exactly like sex, you thought of nothing else if you didn't have it and thought of other things if you did.

James Baldwin (1924–87) US writer. *Nobody Knows My Name*

15 I'll come and make love to you at five o'clock. If I'm late start without me.

Tallulah Bankhead (1903–68) US actress. *Somerset Maugham* (E. Morgan)

16 Sexuality is the lyricism of the masses.

Charles Baudelaire (1821–67) French poet. *Journaux intimes*, 93

17 My beloved put in his hand by the hole of the door, and my bowels were moved for him.

Bible: Song of Solomon 5:4

18 If God had meant us to have group sex, I guess he'd have given us all more organs.

Malcolm Bradbury (1932–) British academic and novelist. *Who Do You Think You Are?*, 'A Very Hospitable Person'

19 Sex and the Single Girl.

Helen Gurley Brown (1922–) US journalist. Book title

20 He said it was artificial respiration but now I find I'm to have his child.

Anthony Burgess (John Burgess Wilson; 1917–) British novelist. *Inside Mr. Enderby*

21 It doesn't matter what you do in the bedroom as long as you don't do it in the street and frighten the horses.

Mrs Patrick Campbell (Beatrice Stella Tanner; 1865–1940) British actress. *The Duchess of Jermyn Street* (Daphne Fielding), Ch. 2

22 The Summer hath his joys,
And Winter his delights.
Though Love and all his pleasures are but toys,
They shorten tedious nights.

Thomas Campion (1567–1620) English poet. *Now Winter Nights Enlarge*

23 I'll wager you that in 10 years it will be fashionable again to be a virgin.

Barbara Cartland (1902–) British romantic novelist. *The Observer*, 'Sayings of the Week', 20 June 1976

24 I answer 20 000 letters a year and so many couples are having problems because they are not getting the right proteins and vitamins.

Barbara Cartland *The Observer*, 'Sayings of the Week', 31 Aug 1986

25 I said 10 years ago that in 10 years time it would be smart to be a virgin. Now everyone is back to virgins again.

Barbara Cartland *The Observer*, 'Sayings of the Week', 12 July 1987

26 She gave me a smile I could feel in my hip pocket.

Raymond Chandler (1888–1959) US novelist. *Farewell, My Lovely*, Ch. 18

27 The pleasure is momentary, the position ridiculous and the expense damnable.

Earl of Chesterfield (1694–1773) English statesman. *Nature*, 1970, 227, 772

28 Dead birds don't fall out of their nests.

Winston Churchill (1874–1965) British statesman. When someone told him that his trouser fly-buttons were undone. Attrib.

29 When she raises her eyelids it's as if she were taking off all her clothes.

Colette (1873–1954) French novelist. *Claudine and Annie*

30 The doggie in front has suddenly gone blind, and the other one has very kindly offered to push him all the way to St Dunstan's.

Noël Coward (1899–1973) British dramatist. To a small child, who asked what two dogs were doing together in the street. St Dunstan's is a British institution for the blind. *Two Hands Clapping* (K. Tynan)

31 You notice that the tabetic has the power of holding water for an indefinite period. He also is impotent – in fact two excellent properties to possess for a quiet day on the river.

Dr. Dunlop (fl. early 20th century) Lecture at Charing Cross Hospital, London

32 No more about sex, it's too boring. Everyone's got one. Nastiness is a real stimulant though – but poor honest sex, like dying, should be a private matter.

Laurence Durrell (1912–) British novelist and poet. *Prospero's Cell*, Ch. 1

33 You think intercourse is a private act; it's not, it's a social act. Men are sexually predatory in life; and women are sexually manipulative. When two individuals come together and leave their gender outside the bedroom door, then they make love. If they take it inside with them, they do something else, because society is in the room with them.

Andrea Dworkin US feminist. *Intercourse*

34 He in a few minutes ravished this fair creature, or at least would have ravished her, if she had not, by a timely compliance, prevented him.

Henry Fielding (1707–54) British novelist. *Jonathan Wild*, Bk. III, Ch. 7

35 Older women are best because they always think they may be doing it for the last time.

Ian Fleming (1908–64) British journalist and author. *Life of Ian Fleming* (John Pearson)

36 The members of our secret service have apparently spent so much time looking under the beds for Communists, they haven't had time to look in the bed.

Michael Foot (1913–) British Labour politician and journalist. Referring to the Profumo affair. Attrib.

37 Personally I know nothing about sex because I've always been married.

Zsa Zsa Gabor (1919–) Hungarian-born US film star. *The Observer*, 'Sayings of the Week', 16 Aug 1987

38 Despite a lifetime of service to the cause of sexual liberation I have never caught a venereal disease, which makes me feel rather like an arctic explorer who has never had frostbite.

Germaine Greer (1939–) Australian-born British writer and feminist. *The Observer*, 'Sayings of the Week', 4 Mar 1973

39 For all the pseudo-sophistication of

twentieth-century sex theory, it is still assumed that a man should make love as if his principal intention was to people the wilderness.
Germaine Greer Attrib.

40 No sex is better than bad sex.
Germaine Greer Attrib.

41 Masturbation is the thinking man's television.
Christopher Hampton (1946–) British playwright. *The Philanthropist*

42 Prostitution gives her an opportunity to meet people. It provides fresh air and wholesome exercise, and it keeps her out of trouble.
Joseph Heller (1923–) US novelist. *Catch-22*, Ch. 33

43 But did thee feel the earth move?
Ernest Hemingway (1899–1961) US novelist. *For Whom the Bell Tolls*, Ch. 13

44 I am happy now that Charles calls on my bedchamber less frequently than of old. As it is, I now endure but two calls a week and when I hear his steps outside my door I lie down on my bed, close my eyes, open my legs and think of England.
Lady Alice Hillingdon (1857–1940) Wife of 2nd Baron Hillingdon. Often mistakenly attributed to Queen Victoria. *Journal* (1912)

45 My life with girls has ended, though till lately I was up to it and soldiered on not ingloriously; now on this wall will hang my weapons and my lyre, discharged from the war.
Horace (Quintus Horatius Flaccus; 65–8 BC) Roman poet. *Odes*, III

46 People will insist . . . on treating the *mons Veneris* as though it were Mount Everest.
Aldous Huxley (1894–1964) British novelist. *Eyeless in Gaza*, Ch. 30

47 A million million spermatozoa,
All of them alive:
Out of their cataclysm but one poor Noah
Dare hope to survive.
Aldous Huxley *Fifth Philosopher's Song*

48 'Bed,' as the Italian proverb succinctly puts it, 'is the poor man's opera.'
Aldous Huxley *Heaven and Hell*

49 The zipless fuck is the purest thing there is. And it is rarer than the unicorn. And I have never had one.
Erica Jong (1942–) US novelist. *Fear of Flying*

50 My response . . . was . . . to evolve my fantasy of the Zipless Fuck . . . Zipless because when you come together zippers fell away like petals.
Erica Jong *Fear of Flying*

51 The discussion of the sexual problem is, of course, only the somewhat crude beginning of a far deeper question, namely, that of the psychic of human relationship between the sexes. Before this later question the sexual problem pales into significance.
C. G. Jung (1875–1961) Swiss psychologist. *Bartlett's Unfamiliar Quotations* (Leonard Louis Levinson)

52 To be solemn about the organs of generation is only possible to someone who, like Lawrence, has deified the will and denied the spirit.
Hugh Kingsmill Referring to D. H. Lawrence. *Tread Softly for You Tread on My Jokes* (Malcolm Muggeridge)

53 Who would not be curious to see the lineaments of a man who, having himself been twice married wished that mankind were propagated like trees.
Charles Lamb (1775–1834) British essayist. Referring to Thomas Browne. *New Monthly Magazine*, Jan 1826

54 Sexual intercourse began
In nineteen sixty-three
(Which was rather late for me) –
Between the end of the *Chatterley* ban
And the Beatles' first LP.
Philip Larkin (1922–85) British poet. *High Windows*, 'Annus Mirabilis'

55 When Eve ate this particular apple, she became aware of her own womanhood, mentally. And mentally she began to experiment with it. She has been experimenting ever since. So has man. To the rage and horror of both of them.
D. H. Lawrence (1885–1930) British novelist. *Fantasia of the Unconscious*, Ch. 7

56 John Thomas says good-night to Lady Jane, a little droopingly, but with a hopeful heart.
D. H. Lawrence The closing words of the book. *Lady Chatterley's Lover*

57 You mustn't think I advocate perpetual sex. Far from it. Nothing nauseates me more than promiscuous sex in and out of season.
D. H. Lawrence Referring to *Lady Chatterley's Lover*. Letter to Lady Ottoline Morrell, 22 Dec 1928

58 Making love is the sovereign remedy for anguish.
Frédérick Leboyer (1918–) French obstetrician. *Birth without Violence*

59 The trouble with Ian is that he gets off with women because he can't get on with them.
Rosamond Lehmann (1901–) British writer. Referring to Ian Fleming. *The Life of Ian Fleming* (J. Pearson)

60 He was into animal husbandry – until they caught him at it.
Tom Lehrer (1928–) US songwriter and entertainer. *An Evening Wasted with Tom Lehrer*

61 No sex without responsibility.
Lord Longford (1905–) British politician and social reformer. *The Observer*, 'Sayings of the Week', 3 May 1954

62 The reproduction of mankind is a great marvel and mystery. Had God consulted me in the matter, I should have advised him to continue the generation of the species by fashioning them of clay.
Martin Luther (1483–1546) German Protestant reformer.

63 The Duke returned from the wars today and did pleasure me in his top-boots.
Sarah, Duchess of Marlborough (1660–1744) Wife of John Churchill, 1st Duke of Marlborough. Attributed to her in various forms; a more ambitious version goes '. . . pleasure me three times in his top-boots'.

64 FRIAR BARNARDINE. Thou hast committed –
BARABAS. Fornication: but that was in another country;
And beside the wench is dead.
Christopher Marlowe (1564–93) English dramatist. *The Jew of Malta*, IV:1

65 Whoever named it necking was a poor judge of anatomy.
Groucho Marx (Julius Marx; 1895–1977) US comedian. Attrib.

66 If sex is such a natural phenomenon, how come there are so many books on how to?
Bette Midler (1944–) US actress and comedienne.

67 Continental people have sex life; the English have hot-water bottles.
George Mikes (1912–) Hungarian-born British writer and humorist. *How to be an Alien*

68 Sex is one of the nine reasons for reincarnation . . . The other eight are unimportant.

Henry Miller (1891–1980) US novelist. *Big Sur and the Oranges of Hieronymus Bosch*

69 There was a little girl
Who had a little curl
Right in the middle of her forehead,
When she was good she was very very good
And when she was bad she was very very popular.

Max Miller (Harold Sargent; 1895–1963) British music-hall comedian. *The Max Miller Blue Book*

70 When she saw the sign 'Members Only' she thought of him.

Spike Milligan (1918–) British comic actor and author. *Puckoon*

71 The daughter-in-law of Pythagoras said that a woman who goes to bed with a man ought to lay aside her modesty with her skirt, and put it on again with her petticoat.

Michel de Montaigne (1533–92) French essayist. *Essais*, I

72 Two minutes with Venus, two years with mercury.

J. Earle Moore (1892–1957) US physician. Alluding to the former use of mercury compounds in the treatment of syphilis. Aphorism

73 Why do they put the Gideon Bibles only in the bedrooms where it's usually too late?

Christopher Darlington Morley (1890–1957) US writer. *Quotations for Speakers and Writers*

74 The orgasm has replaced the Cross as the focus of longing and the image of fulfilment.

Malcolm Muggeridge (1903–) British writer. *The Most of Malcolm Muggeridge*, 'Down with Sex'

75 It has to be admitted that we English have sex on the brain, which is a very unsatisfactory place to have it.

Malcolm Muggeridge *The Observer*, 'Sayings of the Decade', 1964

76 It's all any reasonable child can expect if the dad is present at the conception.

Joe Orton (1933–67) British dramatist. *Entertaining Mr Sloane*, III

77 If all the young ladies who attended the Yale promenade dance were laid end to end, no one would be the least surprised.

Dorothy Parker (1893–1967) US writer. *While Rome Burns* (Alexander Woollcott)

78 Tell him I've been too fucking busy – or vice versa.

Dorothy Parker When asked why she had not delivered her copy on time. *You Might As Well Live* (J. Keats)

79 There, but for a typographical error, is the story of my life.

Dorothy Parker At a Hallowe'en party, when someone remarked, 'They're ducking for apples'. *You Might As Well Live* (J. Keats)

80 I know it does make people happy but to me it is just like having a cup of tea.

Cynthia Payne (1934–) London housewife. After her acquittal on a charge of controlling prostitutes in a famous 'sex-for-luncheon-vouchers' case, 8 Nov 1987

81 Love is not the dying moan of a distant violin – it's the triumphant twang of a bedspring.

S. J. Perelman (1904–79) US humorous writer. *Quotations for Speakers and Writers* (A. Andrews)

82 I tend to believe that cricket is the greatest thing that God ever created on earth . . . certainly greater than sex, although sex isn't too bad either.

Harold Pinter (1930–) British playwright. *The Observer*, 5 Oct 1980

83 On a sofa upholstered in panther skin
Mona did researches in original sin.

William Plomer (1903–73) South African poet and novelist. *Mews Flat Mona*

84 A PUSHING LADY. What are your views on love?

MME LEROI. Love? I make it constantly but I never talk about it.

Marcel Proust (1871–1922) French novelist. *À la recherche du temps perdu: Le Côté de Guermantes*

85 One orgasm in the bush is worth two in the hand.

Robert Reisner *Graffiti*, 'Masturbation'

86 Everything You Always Wanted to Know About Sex But Were Afraid to Ask.

David Reuben (1933–) US doctor and author. Book title

87 The Christian view of sex is that it is, indeed, a form of holy communion.

John Robinson (1919–83) Bishop of Woolwich. Giving evidence in the prosecution of Penguin Books for publishing *Lady Chatterly's Lover*.

88 Love is two minutes fifty-two seconds of squishing noises. It shows your mind isn't clicking right.

Johnny Rotten (1957–) British punk musician. In the *Daily Mirror* in 1983 Rotten said that owing to a new-found technique, the time was now about five minutes. Attrib.

89 Love as a relation between men and women was ruined by the desire to make sure of the legitimacy of the children.

Bertrand Russell (1872–1970) British philosopher. *Marriage and Morals*

90 Civilized people cannot fully satisfy their sexual instinct without love.

Bertrand Russell *Marriage and Morals*, 'The Place of Love in Human Life'

91 His excessive emphasis on sex was due to the fact that in sex alone he was compelled to admit that he was not the only human being in the universe. It was so painful that he conceived of sex relations as a perpetual fight in which each is attempting to destroy the other.

Bertrand Russell Referring to D.H. Lawrence. *Autobiography*

92 Sex is something I really don't understand too hot. You never know *where* the hell you are. I keep making up these sex rules for myself, and then I break them right away.

J. D. Salinger (1919–) US novelist. *The Catcher in the Rye*, Ch. 9

93 Is it not strange that desire should so many years outlive performance?

William Shakespeare (1564–1616) English dramatist. *Henry IV, Part Two*, II:4

94 Even now, now, very now, an old black ram
Is tupping your white ewe.

William Shakespeare *Othello*, I:1

95 Your daughter and the Moor are now making the beast with two backs.

William Shakespeare *Othello*, I:1

96 Lechery, lechery! Still wars and lechery! Nothing else holds fashion.

William Shakespeare *Troilus and Cressida*, V:2

97 A determining point in the history of gynecology is to be found in the fact that sex plays a more important part in the life of woman than in that of man, and that she is more burdened by her sex.

Henry E. Sigerist (1891–1957) *American Journal of Obstetrics and Gynecology* 42:714, 1941

98 Someone asked Sophocles, 'How do

you feel now about sex? Are you still able to have a woman?' He replied, 'Hush, man; most gladly indeed am I rid of it all, as though I had escaped from a mad and savage master.'

Sophocles (c. 496–406 BC) Greek dramatist. *Republic* (Plato), Bk. I

99 Masturbation: the primary sexual activity of mankind. In the nineteenth century it was a disease; in the twentieth, it's a cure.

Thomas Szasz (1920–) US psychiatrist. *The Second Sin*

100 Traditionally, sex has been a very private, secretive activity. Herein perhaps lies its powerful force for uniting people in a strong bond. As we make sex less secretive, we may rob it of its power to hold men and women together.

Thomas Szasz *The Second Sin*

101 Chasing the naughty couples down the grassgreen gooseberried double bed of the wood.

Dylan Thomas (1914–53) Welsh poet. *Under Milk Wood*

102 Old Nat Burge sat . . . He was . . . watching the moon come up lazily out of the old cemetery in which nine of his daughters were lying, and only two of them were dead.

James Thurber (1894–1961) US humorist. *Let Your Mind Alone*, 'Bateman Comes Home'

103 Surely you don't mean by unartificial insemination!

James Thurber On being accosted at a party by a drunk woman who claimed she would like to have a baby by him. Attrib.

104 Is Sex Necessary?

James Thurber and E. B. White (1894–1961 and 1899–) US writers, humorists, and cartoonists. Title of a book

105 Familiarity breeds contempt – and children.

Mark Twain (Samuel Langhorne Clemens; 1835–1910) US writer. *Notebooks*

106 All this fuss about sleeping together. For physical pleasure I'd sooner go to my dentist any day.

Evelyn Waugh (1903–66) British novelist. *Vile Bodies*, Ch. 6

107 The mind can also be an erogenous zone.

Raquel Welch (1940–) US film star. *Colombo's Hollywood* (J.R. Colombo)

108 When women go wrong, men go right after them.

Mae West (1892–1980) US actress. *The Wit and Wisdom of Mae West* (ed. J. Weintraub)

109 It's not the men in my life that count; it's the life in my men.

Mae West Attrib.

110 When I'm good I'm very good, but when I'm bad I'm better.

Mae West Attrib.

111 I shall not say why and how I became, at the age of fifteen, the mistress of the Earl of Craven.

Harriette Wilson (1789–1846) British writer and courtesan. *Memoirs*, Opening

112 Freud found sex an outcast in the outhouse and left it in the living room an honored guest.

W. Beran Wolfe Referring to Sigmund Freud. *The Great Quotations* (George Seldes)

113 A mistress should be like a little country retreat near the town, not to dwell in constantly, but only for a night and away.

William Wycherley (1640–1716) English dramatist. *The Country Wife*, I:1

SEXES

See also feminism, marriage, men, sex, woman's role, women

1 Between man and woman there is little difference, but *vive la différence.*

French proverb

2 Physically, a man is a man for a much longer time than a woman is a woman.

Honoré de Balzac (1799–1850) French writer. *The Physiology of Marriage*

3 As men
Do walk a mile, women should talk an hour,
After supper. 'Tis their exercise.

Francis Beaumont (1584–1616) English dramatist. *Philaster*, II:4

4 And the man said, The woman whom thou gavest to be with me, she gave me of the tree, and I did eat.
And the Lord God said unto the woman, What is this that thou hast done? And the woman said, The serpent beguiled me, and I did eat.
And the Lord God said unto the serpent, Because thou hast done this, thou art cursed above all cattle, and above every beast of the field; upon thy belly shalt thou go, and dust shalt thou eat all the days of thy life:
And I will put enmity between thee and the woman, and between thy seed and her seed; it shall bruise thy head, and thou shalt bruise his heel.
Unto the woman he said, I will greatly multiply thy sorrow and thy conception; in sorrow thou shalt bring forth children; and thy desire shall be to thy husband, and he shall rule over thee.
And unto Adam he said, Because thou hast hearkened unto the voice of thy wife, and has eaten of the tree, of which I commanded thee, saying, Thou shalt not eat of it: cursed is the ground for thy sake; in sorrow shalt thou eat of it all the days of thy life.

Bible: Genesis 3:12–17

5 Mr. Darwin . . . has failed to hold definitely before his mind the principle that the difference of sex, whatever it may consist in, must itself be subject to natural selection and to evolution.

Antoinette Brown Blackwell (1825–1921) US feminist writer. *The Sexes Throughout Nature*

6 Man's love is of man's life a thing apart,
'Tis woman's whole existence.

Lord Byron (1788–1824) British poet. *Don Juan*, I

7 There is more difference within the sexes than between them.

Ivy Compton-Burnett (1892–1969) British novelist. *Mother and Son*

8 In the sex-war thoughtlessness is the weapon of the male, vindictiveness of the female.

Cyril Connolly (1903–74) British journalist. *The Unquiet Grave*

9 The average man is more interested in a woman who is interested in him than he is in a woman – any woman – with beautiful legs.

Marlene Dietrich (Maria Magdalene von Losch; 1904–) German-born film star. News item, 13 Dec 1954

10 Most women set out to try to change a man, and when they have changed him they do not like him.

Marlene Dietrich Attrib.

11 The reason that husbands and wives do not understand each other is because they belong to different sexes.

Dorothy Dix (Elizabeth Meriwether Gilmer; 1861–1951) US journalist and writer. News item

12 Where young boys plan for what they will achieve and attain, young girls plan for whom they will achieve and attain.

Charlotte Perkins Gilman (1860–1935) US writer. *Women and Economics*, Ch. 5

13 Man has his will, – but woman has her way.

Oliver Wendell Holmes (1809–94) US writer. *The Autocrat of the Breakfast Table*, Prologue

14 Boys will be boys – '
'And even that . . . wouldn't matter if we could only prevent girls from being girls.'

Anthony Hope (Anthony Hope Hawkins; 1863–1933) British novelist. *The Dolly Dialogues*

15 If Nature had arranged that husbands and wives should have children alternatively, there would never be more than *three* in a family.

Laurence Housman (1865–1959)

16 For men must work, and women must weep,
And there's little to earn, and many to keep,
Though the harbour bar be moaning.

Charles Kingsley (1819–75) British writer. *The Three Fishers*

17 The silliest woman can manage a clever man; but it needs a very clever woman to manage a fool.

Rudyard Kipling (1865–1936) Indian-born British writer. *Plain Tales from the Hills*, 'Three and – an Extra'

18 Men have broad and large chests, and small narrow hips, and more understanding than women, who have but small and narrow breasts, and broad hips, to the end they should remain at home, sit still, keep house, and bear and bring up children.

Martin Luther (1483–1546) German Protestant reformer. *Table-Talk*, 'Of Marriage and Celibacy'

19 The only really happy people are married women and single men.

H. L. Mencken (1880–1956) US journalist. Attrib.

20 Perhaps at fourteen every boy should be in love with some ideal woman to put on a pedestal and worship. As he grows up, of course, he will put her on a pedestal the better to view her legs.

Barry Norman (1933–) British cinema critic and broadcaster. *The Listener*

21 The seldom female in a world of males!

Ruth Pitter (1897–) British poet. *The Kitten's Eclogue*, IV

22 I often want to cry. That is the only advantage women have over men – at least they can cry.

Jean Rhys (1894–1979) Dominican-born British novelist. *Good Morning, Midnight*, Pt. II

23 Woman's virtue is man's greatest invention.

Cornelia Otis Skinner (1901–79) US stage actress. Attrib.

24 A man may sympathize with a woman in childbed, though it is impossible that he should conceive himself as suffering her pains in his own proper person and character.

Adam Smith (1723–90) Scottish economist. *The Theory of Moral Sentiments*, Pt. VII

25 Man is a creature who lives not upon bread alone, but principally by catchwords; and the little rift between the sexes is astonishingly widened by simply teaching one set of catchwords to the girls and another to the boys.

Robert Louis Stevenson (1850–94) Scottish writer. *Virginibus Puerisque*

26 Man is the hunter; woman is his game:
The sleek and shining creatures of the chase,
We hunt them for the beauty of their skins.

Alfred, Lord Tennyson (1809–92) British poet. *The Princess*, V

27 Man for the field and woman for the hearth:
Man for the sword and for the needle she:
Man with the head and woman with the heart:
Man to command and woman to obey;
All else confusion.

Alfred, Lord Tennyson *The Princess*, V

28 There are some meannesses which are too mean even for man – woman, lovely woman alone, can venture to commit them.

William Makepeace Thackeray (1811–63) British novelist. *A Shabby-Genteel Story*, Ch. 3

29 The War between Men and Women.

James Thurber (1894–1961) US humorist. Title of a series of cartoons

30 When a man confronts catastrophe on the road, he looks in his purse – but a woman looks in her mirror.

Margaret Turnbull (fl. 1920s–1942) US writer. *The Left Lady*

31 Instead of this absurd division into sexes they ought to class people as static and dynamic.

Evelyn Waugh (1903–66) British novelist. *Decline and Fall*, Pt. III, Ch. 7

32 All women become like their mothers. That is their tragedy. No man does. That's his.

Oscar Wilde (1854–1900) Irish-born British dramatist. *The Importance of Being Earnest*, I

33 Women represent the triumph of matter over mind, just as men represent the triumph of mind over morals.

Oscar Wilde *The Picture of Dorian Gray*, Ch. 4

34 Why are women . . . so much more interesting to men than men are to women?

Virginia Woolf (1882–1941) British novelist. *A Room of One's Own*

SEXISM

1 In this country a wife is regarded as a chattel, just as a thoroughbred mare or cow.

G. N. Butler (1930–) British circuit judge. Addressing a Dublin jury. *The Observer*, 'Sayings of the Week', 25 June 1972

SHAKESPEARE, William

(1564–1616) English dramatist and poet, universally acknowledged to be the greatest English writer of historical plays, comedies, and tragedies. His sonnets have love and friendship as their themes.

Quotations about Shakespeare

1 Others abide our question, Thou art free,
We ask and ask: Thou smilest and art still,
Out-topping knowledge.

Matthew Arnold (1822–88) British poet and critic. *Shakespeare*

2 When he killed a calf he would do it in a high style, and make a speech.

John Aubrey (1626–1697) English antiquary. *Brief Lives*, 'William Shakespeare'

3 Our myriad-minded Shakespeare.
Samuel Taylor Coleridge (1772–1834) British poet. *Biographia Literaria*, Ch. 15

4 I have tried lately to read Shakespeare, and found it so intolerably dull that it nauseated me.
Charles Darwin (1809–82) British life scientist. *Autobiography*

5 He was the man who of all modern, and perhaps ancient poets had the largest and most comprehensive soul.
John Dryden (1631–1700) British poet and dramatist. *Essay of Dramatic Poesy*

6 He was naturally learned; he needed not the spectacles of books to read nature; he looked inwards, and found her there.
John Dryden *Essay of Dramatic Poesy*

7 We can say of Shakespeare, that never has a man turned so little knowledge to such great account.
T. S. Eliot (1888–1965) US-born British poet and dramatist. *The Classics and the Man of Letters* (lecture)

8 The remarkable thing about Shakespeare is that he is really very good – in spite of all the people who say he is very good.
Robert Graves (1895–1985) British poet and novelist. *The Observer*, 'Sayings of the Week', 6 Dec 1964

9 Shakespeare never had six lines together without a fault. Perhaps you may find seven, but this does not refute my general assertion.
Samuel Johnson (1709–84) British lexicographer. *Life of Johnson* (J. Boswell), Vol. II

10 He was not of an age, but for all time!
Ben Jonson (1573–1637) English dramatist. *To the Memory of William Shakespeare*

11 Sweet Swan of Avon!
Ben Jonson *To the Memory of William Shakespeare*

12 When I read Shakespeare I am struck with wonder
That such trivial people should muse and thunder
In such lovely language.
D. H. Lawrence (1885–1930) British novelist. *When I Read Shakespeare*

13 Or sweetest Shakespeare, Fancy's child,
Warble his native wood-notes wild.
John Milton (1608–74) English poet. *L'Allegro*

14 Shakespeare – the nearest thing in incarnation to the eye of God.
Laurence Olivier (1907–) British actor. *Kenneth Harris Talking To*, 'Sir Laurence Olivier'

15 A man can be forgiven a lot if he can quote Shakespeare in an economic crisis.
Prince Philip (1921–) The consort of Queen Elizabeth II. Attrib.

16 Brush Up Your Shakespeare.
Cole Porter (1891–1964) US composer and lyricist. *Kiss Me Kate*

17 With the single exception of Homer, there is no eminent writer, not even Sir Walter Scott, whom I can despise so entirely as I despise Shakespeare when I measure my mind against his . . . It would positively be a relief to me to dig him up and throw stones at him.
George Bernard Shaw (1856–1950) Irish dramatist and critic. *Dramatic Opinions and Essays*, Vol. 2

18 Wonderful women! Have you ever thought how much we all, and women especially, owe to Shakespeare for his vindication of women in these fearless, high-spirited, resolute and intelligent heroines?
Ellen Terry (1847–1928) British actress. *Four Lectures on Shakespeare*, 'The Triumphant Women'

19 One of the greatest geniuses that ever existed, Shakespeare, undoubtedly wanted taste.
Horace Walpole (1717–97) British writer. Letter to Wren, 9 Aug 1764

Quotations by Shakespeare

20 Our remedies oft in ourselves do lie,
Which we ascribe to heaven.
All's Well that Ends Well, I:1

21 The web of our life is of a mingled yarn, good and ill together.
All's Well that Ends Well, IV:3

22 Th' inaudible and noiseless foot of Time.
All's Well that Ends Well, V:3

23 The triple pillar of the world transform'd
Into a strumpet's fool.
Antony and Cleopatra, I:1

24 There's beggary in the love that can be reckon'd.
Antony and Cleopatra, I:1

25 Where's my serpent of old Nile?
Antony and Cleopatra, I:5

26 My salad days,
When I was green in judgment, cold in blood,
To say as I said then!
Antony and Cleopatra, I:5

27 The barge she sat in, like a burnish'd throne,
Burn'd on the water. The poop was beaten gold;
Purple the sails, and so perfumed that
The winds were love-sick with them; the oars were silver,
Which to the tune of flutes kept stroke and made
The water which they beat to follow faster,
As amorous of their strokes. For her own person,
It beggar'd all description.
Antony and Cleopatra, II:2

28 Age cannot wither her, nor custom stale
Her infinite variety. Other women cloy
The appetites they feed, but she makes hungry
Where most she satisfies.
Antony and Cleopatra, II:2

29 I will praise any man that will praise me.
Antony and Cleopatra, II:6

30 Celerity is never more admir'd
Than by the negligent.
Antony and Cleopatra, III:7

31 To business that we love we rise betime,
And go to't with delight.
Antony and Cleopatra, IV:4

32 Unarm, Eros; the long day's task is done,
And we must sleep.
Antony and Cleopatra, IV:12

33 I am dying, Egypt, dying; only
I here importune death awhile, until
Of many thousand kisses the poor last
I lay upon thy lips.
Antony and Cleopatra, IV:13

34 O, wither'd is the garland of the war,
The soldier's pole is fall'n! Young boys and girls
Are level now with men. The odds is gone,
And there is nothing left remarkable

Beneath the visiting moon.
Antony and Cleopatra, IV:13

35 The bright day is done,
And we are for the dark.
Antony and Cleopatra, V:2

36 Dost thou not see my baby at my breast
That sucks the nurse asleep?
Holding the asp to her breast. *Antony and Cleopatra,* V:2

37 Well said; that was laid on with a trowel.
As You Like It, I:2

38 I had rather bear with you than bear you.
As You Like It, II:4

39 If thou rememb'rest not the slightest folly
That ever love did make thee run into,
Thou hast not lov'd.
As You Like It, II:4

40 Under the greenwood tree
Who loves to lie with me,
And turn his merry note
Unto the sweet bird's throat,
Come hither, come hither, come hither.
Here shall he see
No enemy
But winter and rough weather.
As You Like It, II:5

41 And so, from hour to hour, we ripe and ripe,
And then, from hour to hour, we rot and rot;
And thereby hangs a tale.
As You Like It, II:7

42 All the world's a stage,
And all the men and women merely players;
They have their exits and their entrances;
And one man in his time plays many parts,
His acts being seven ages.
As You Like It, II:7

43 Last scene of all,
That ends this strange eventful history,
Is second childishness and mere oblivion;
Sans teeth, sans eyes, sans taste, sans every thing.
As You Like It, II:7

44 Blow, blow, thou winter wind,
Thou art not so unkind
As man's ingratitude.
As You Like It, II:7

45 Most friendship is feigning, most loving mere folly.
As You Like It, II:7

46 He that wants money, means, and content, is without three good friends.
As You Like It, III:2

47 Do you not know I am a woman?
When I think, I must speak.
As You Like It, III:2

48 I do desire we may be better strangers.
As You Like It, III:2

49 The truest poetry is the most feigning.
As You Like It, III:3

50 Men have died from time to time, and worms have eaten them, but not for love.
As You Like It, IV:1

51 Your If is the only peace-maker; much virtue in If.
As You Like It, V:4

52 If it be true that good wine needs no bush, 'tis true that a good play needs no epilogue.
As You Like It, Epilogue

53 Custom calls me to't.
What custom wills, in all things should we do't,
The dust on antique time would lie unswept,
And mountainous error be too highly heap'd
For truth to o'erpeer.
Coriolanus, II:3

54 Like a dull actor now
I have forgot my part and I am out,
Even to a full disgrace.
Coriolanus, V:3

55 O, this life
Is nobler than attending for a check,
Richer than doing nothing for a bribe,
Prouder than rustling in unpaid-for silk.
Cymbeline, III:3

56 Society is no comfort
To one not sociable.
Cymbeline, IV:2

57 Fear no more the heat o' th' sun
Nor the furious winter's rages;
Thou thy worldly task hast done,
Home art gone, and ta'en thy wages.
Golden lads and girls all must,
As chimney-sweepers, come to dust.
Cymbeline, IV:2

58 For this relief much thanks. 'Tis bitter cold,
And I am sick at heart.
Hamlet, I:1

59 A little more than kin, and less than kind.
Hamlet, I:2

60 But I have that within which passes show –
these but the trappings and the suits of woe.
Hamlet, I:2

61 How weary, stale, flat, and unprofitable,
Seem to me all the uses of this world!
Hamlet, I:2

62 Frailty, thy name is woman!
Hamlet, I:2

63 It is not, nor it cannot come to good.
Hamlet, I:2

64 'A was a man, take him for all in all,
I shall not look upon his like again.
Hamlet, I:2

65 Do not, as some ungracious pastors do,
Show me the steep and thorny way to heaven,
Whiles, like a puff'd and reckless libertine,
Himself the primrose path of dalliance treads
And recks not his own rede.
Hamlet, I:3

66 Costly thy habit as thy purse can buy,
But not express'd in fancy; rich, not gaudy;
For the apparel oft proclaims the man.
Hamlet, I:3

67 Neither a borrower nor a lender be;
For loan oft loses both itself and friend,
And borrowing dulls the edge of husbandry.
This above all: to thine own self be true,
And it must follow, as the night the day,
Thou canst not then be false to any man.
Hamlet, I:3

68 But to my mind, though I am native here
And to the manner born, it is a custom
More honour'd in the breach than the observance.
Hamlet, I:4

69 Something is rotten in the state of Denmark.
Hamlet, I:4

70 Murder most foul, as in the best it is;
But this most foul, strange, and unnatural.
Hamlet, I:5

71 There are more things in heaven and earth, Horatio,
Than are dreamt of in your philosophy.
Hamlet, I:5

72 Brevity is the soul of wit.
Hamlet, II:2

73 To be honest, as this world goes, is to be one man pick'd out of ten thousand.
Hamlet, II:2

74 Though this be madness, yet there is method in't.
Hamlet, II:2

75 There is nothing either good or bad, but thinking makes it so.
Hamlet, II:2

76 What a piece of work is a man! How noble in reason! how infinite in faculties! in form and moving, how express and admirable! in action, how like an angel! in apprehension, how like a god! the beauty of the world! the paragon of animals! And yet, to me, what is this quintessence of dust? Man delights not me – no, nor woman neither.
Hamlet, II:2

77 The play, I remember, pleas'd not the million; 'twas caviare to the general.
Hamlet, II:2

78 Use every man after his desert, and who shall scape whipping?
Hamlet, II:2

79 The play's the thing
Wherein I'll catch the conscience of the King.
Hamlet, II:2

80 To be, or not to be – that is the question;
Whether 'tis nobler in the mind to suffer
The slings and arrows of outrageous fortune,
Or to take arms against a sea of troubles,
And by opposing end them? To die, to sleep –
No more; and by a sleep to say we end
The heart-ache and the thousand natural shocks
That flesh is heir to, 'tis a consummation
Devoutly to be wish'd. To die, to sleep;
To sleep, perchance to dream. Ay, there's the rub;
For in that sleep of death what dreams may come,
When we have shuffled off this mortal coil,
Must give us pause.
Hamlet, III:1

81 The dread of something after death –
The undiscover'd country, from whose bourn
No traveller returns.
Hamlet, III:1

82 Thus conscience does make cowards of us all;
And thus the native hue of resolution
Is sicklied o'er with the pale cast of thought.
Hamlet, III:1

83 Madness in great ones must not unwatch'd go.
Hamlet, III:1

84 It out-herods Herod.
Hamlet, III:2

85 Suit the action to the word, the word to the action; with this special observance, that you o'erstep not the modesty of nature.
Hamlet, III:2

86 The lady doth protest too much, methinks.
Hamlet, III:2

87 Very like a whale.
Hamlet, III:2

88 A king of shreds and patches.
Hamlet, III:4

89 Some craven scruple
Of thinking too precisely on th' event.
Hamlet, IV;4

90 When sorrows come, they come not single spies,
But in battalions!
Hamlet, IV:5

91 There's such divinity doth hedge a king
That treason can but peep to what it would.
Hamlet, IV:5

92 Alas, poor Yorick! I knew him, Horatio: a fellow of infinite jest, of most excellent fancy.
Hamlet, V:1

93 There's a divinity that shapes our ends,
Rough-hew them how we will.
Hamlet, V:2

94 If thou didst ever hold me in thy heart,
Absent thee from felicity awhile,
And in this harsh world draw thy breath in pain,
To tell my story.
Hamlet, V:2

95 The rest is silence.
Hamlet, V:2

96 If all the year were playing holidays, To sport would be as tedious as to work.
Henry IV, Part One, I:2

97 Falstaff sweats to death
And lards the lean earth as he walks along.
Henry IV, Part One, II:2

98 I have more flesh than another man, and therefore more frailty.
Henry IV, Part One, III:3

99 Honour pricks me on. Yea, but how if honour prick me off when I come on? How then? Can honour set to a leg? No. Or an arm? No. Or take away the grief of a wound? No. Honour hath no skill in surgery, then? No. What is honour? A word. What is in that word? Honour. What is that honour? Air.
Henry IV, Part One, V:1

100 But thoughts, the slaves of life, and life, time's fool,
And time, that takes survey of all the world,
Must have a stop.
Henry IV, Part One, V:4

101 The better part of valour is discretion; in the which better part I have saved my life.
Henry IV, Part One, V:4

102 I am not only witty in myself, but the cause that wit is in other men. I do here walk before thee like a sow that hath overwhelm'd all her litter but one.
Henry IV, Part Two, I:2

103 Well, I cannot last ever; but it was always yet the trick of our English nation, if they have a good thing, to make it too common.
Henry IV, Part Two, I:2

104 I can get no remedy against this consumption of the purse; borrowing only lingers and lingers it out, but the disease is incurable.
Henry IV, Part Two, I:2

105 He hath eaten me out of house and home.
Henry IV, Part Two, II:1

106 Is it not strange that desire should so many years outlive performance?
Henry IV, Part Two, II:4

107 Uneasy lies the head that wears a crown.
Henry IV, Part Two, III:1

108 We have heard the chimes at midnight.
Henry IV, Part Two, III:2

109 I care not; a man can die but once; we owe God a death.
Henry IV, Part Two, III:2

110 Care I for the limb, the thews, the stature, bulk, and big assemblance of a man! Give me the spirit.
Henry IV, Part Two, III:2

111 I dare not fight; but I will wink and hold out mine iron.
Henry V, II:1

112 Though patience be a tired mare, yet she will plod.
Henry V, II:1

113 His nose was as sharp as a pen, and 'a babbl'd of green fields.
Referring to Falstaff on his deathbed. *Henry V,* II:3

114 Once more unto the breach, dear friends, once more;
Or close the wall up with our English dead.
Henry V, III:1

115 Men of few words are the best men.
Henry V, III:2

116 I think the King is but a man as I am: the violet smells to him as it doth to me.
Henry V, IV:1

117 Every subject's duty is the King's; but every subject's soul is his own.
Henry V, IV:1

118 Old men forget; yet all shall be forgot,
But he'll remember, with advantages,
What feats he did that day.
Henry V, IV:3

119 There is occasions and causes why and wherefore in all things.
Henry V, V:1

120 Heat not a furnace for your foe so hot
That it do singe yourself. We may outrun
By violent swiftness that which we run at,
And lose by over-running.
Henry VIII, I:1

121 I would not be a queen
For all the world.
Henry VIII, II:3

122 Farewell, a long farewell, to all my greatness!
This is the state of man: to-day he puts forth
The tender leaves of hopes: tomorrow blossoms
And bears his blushing honours thick upon him;
The third day comes a frost, a killing frost,
And when he thinks, good easy man, full surely
His greatness is a-ripening, nips his root,
And then he falls, as I do.
Henry VIII, III:2

123 Had I but serv'd my God with half the zeal
I serv'd my King, he would not in mine age
Have left me naked to mine enemies.
Henry VIII, III:2

124 Men's evil manners live in brass: their virtues
We write in water.
Henry VIII, IV:2

125 Beware the ides of March.
Julius Caesar, I:2

126 Let me have men about me that are fat;
Sleek-headed men, and such as sleep o' nights.
Yond Cassius has a lean and hungry look;
He thinks too much. Such men are dangerous.
Julius Caesar, I:2

127 For mine own part, it was Greek to me.
Julius Caesar, I:2

128 Cowards die many times before their deaths:
The valiant never taste of death but once.
Julius Caesar, II:2

129 *Et tu, Brute?*
Julius Caesar, III:1

130 Why, he that cuts off twenty years of life
Cuts off so many years of fearing death.
Julius Caesar, III:1

131 O mighty Caesar! dost thou lie so low?
Are all thy conquests, glories, triumphs, spoils,
Shrunk to this little measure?
Julius Caesar, III:1

132 O, pardon me, thou bleeding piece of earth,
That I am meek and gentle with these butchers!
Thou art the ruins of the noblest man
That ever lived in the tide of times.
Julius Caesar, III:1

133 Cry 'Havoc!' and let slip the dogs of war.
Julius Caesar, III:1

134 Not that I lov'd Caesar less, but that I lov'd Rome more.
Julius Caesar, III:2

135 Friends, Romans, countrymen, lend me your ears
I come to bury Caesar, not to praise him.
The evil that men do lives after them;
The good is oft interred with their bones.
Julius Caesar, III:2

136 For Brutus is an honourable man;
So are they all, all honourable men.
Julius Caesar, III:2

137 Ambition should be made of sterner stuff.
Julius Caesar, III:2

138 If you have tears, prepare to shed them now.
Julius Caesar, III:2

139 For I have neither wit, nor words, nor worth,
Action, nor utterance, nor the power of speech,
To stir men's blood; I only speak right on.
Julius Caesar, III:2

140 A friend should bear his friend's infirmities,
But Brutus makes mine greater than they are.
Julius Caesar, IV:3

141 There is a tide in the affairs of men
Which, taken at the flood, leads on to fortune;
Omitted, all the voyage of their life
Is bound in shallows and in miseries.
On such a full sea are we now afloat,
And we must take the current when it serves,
Or lose our ventures.
Julius Caesar, IV:3

142 This was the noblest Roman of them all.
All the conspirators save only he
Did that they did in envy of great Caesar.
Julius Caesar, V:5

143 His life was gentle; and the elements
So mix'd in him that Nature might stand up
And say to all the world 'This was a man!'
Referring to Brutus. *Julius Caesar,* V:5

144 Well, whiles I am a beggar, I will rail
And say there is no sin but to be rich;
And being rich, my virtue then shall be
To say there is no vice but beggary.
King John, II:1

145 Bell, book, and candle, shall not drive me back,
When gold and silver becks me to come on.
King John, III:3

146 Life is as tedious as a twice-told tale
Vexing the dull ear of a drowsy man.
King John, III:4

147 To gild refined gold, to paint the lily,
To throw a perfume on the violet,
To smooth the ice, or add another hue
Unto the rainbow, or with taper-light
To seek the beauteous eye of heaven to garnish,
Is wasteful and ridiculous excess.
King John, IV:2

148 I beg cold comfort.
King John, V:7

149 Nothing will come of nothing. Speak again.
King Lear, I:1

150 This is the excellent foppery of the world, that, when we are sick in fortune, often the surfeits of our own behaviour, we make guilty of our disasters the sun, the moon, and stars.
King Lear, I:2

151 Ingratitude, thou marble-hearted fiend,
More hideous when thou show'st thee in a child
Than the sea-monster!
King Lear I:4

152 O, let me not be mad, not mad, sweet heaven!
Keep me in temper; I would not be mad!
King Lear, I:5

153 Thou whoreson zed! thou unnecessary letter!
King Lear, II:2

154 Down, thou climbing sorrow,
Thy element's below.
King Lear, II:4

155 O, reason not the need! Our basest beggars
Are in the poorest thing superfluous.
Allow not nature more than nature needs,
Man's life is cheap as beast's.
King Lear, II:4

156 Blow, winds, and crack your cheeks; rage, blow.
You cataracts and hurricanoes, spout
Till you have drench'd our steeples, drown'd the cocks.
King Lear, III:2

157 Rumble thy bellyful. Spit, fire; spout rain.
Nor rain, wind, thunder, fire, are my daughters
I tax not you, you elements, with unkindness.
King Lear, III:2

158 I am a man
More sinn'd against than sinning.
King Lear, III:2

159 Poor naked wretches, wheresoe'er you are,
That bide the pelting of this pitiless storm,
How shall your houseless heads and unfed sides,
Your loop'd and window'd raggedness, defend you
From seasons such as these?
King Lear, III:4

160 Take physic, pomp;
Expose thyself to feel what wretches feel.
King Lear, III:4

161 Poor Tom's a-cold.
King Lear, III:4

162 Out vile jelly!
Where is thy lustre now?
Spoken by Cornwall as he puts out Gloucester's remaining eye. *King Lear,* III:7

163 The worst is not
So long as we can say 'This is the worst'.
King Lear, IV:1

164 As flies to wanton boys are we to th' gods –
They kill us for their sport.
King Lear, IV:1

165 Ay, every inch a king.
King Lear, IV:6

166 The wren goes to't, and the small gilded fly
Does lecher in my sight.
King Lear, IV:6

167 Through tatter'd clothes small vices do appear;
Robes and furr'd gowns hide all.
King Lear, IV:6

168 Get thee glass eyes,
And, like a scurvy politician, seem
To see the things thou dost not.
King Lear, IV:6

169 When we are born, we cry that we are come
To this great stage of fools.
King Lear. IV:6

170 Thou art a soul in bliss; but I am bound

Upon a wheel of fire, that mine own tears
Do scald like molten lead.
King Lear, IV:7

171 Men must endure
Their going hence, even as their coming hither:
Ripeness is all.
King Lear, V:2

172 And my poor fool is hang'd! No, no, no life!
Why should a dog, a horse, a rat have life,
And thou no breath at all? Thou'lt come no more,
Never, never, never, never.
King Lear, V:3

173 At Christmas I no more desire a rose
Than wish a snow in May's newfangled shows.
Love's Labour's Lost, I:1

174 He hath never fed of the dainties that are bred in a book; he hath not eat paper, as it were; he hath not drunk ink; his intellect is not replenished.
Love's Labour's Lost, IV:2

175 For where is any author in the world
Teaches such beauty as a woman's eye?
Learning is but an adjunct to oneself.
Love's Labour's Lost, IV:3

176 A jest's prosperity lies in the ear
Of him that hears it, never in the tongue
Of him that makes it.
Love's Labour's Lost, V:2

177 When icicles hang by the wall,
And Dick the shepherd blows his nail,
And Tom bears logs into the hall,
And milk comes frozen home in pail,
When blood is nipp'd, and ways be foul,
Then nightly sings the staring owl:
'Tu-who;
Tu-whit, Tu-who' – A merry note,
While greasy Joan doth keel the pot.
Love's Labour's Lost, V:2

178 So foul and fair a day I have not seen.
Macbeth, I:3

179 This supernatural soliciting
Cannot be ill; cannot be good.
Macbeth, I:3

180 Come what come may,
Time and the hour runs through the roughest day.
Macbeth, I:3

181 Nothing in his life
Became him like the leaving it: he died
As one that had been studied in his death
To throw away the dearest thing he ow'd
As 'twere a careless trifle.
Macbeth, I:4

182 Yet do I fear thy nature;
It is too full o' th' milk of human kindness
To catch the nearest way.
Macbeth, I:5

183 If it were done when 'tis done, then 'twere well
It were done quickly.
Macbeth, I:7

184 That but this blow
Might be the be-all and the end-all here –
But here upon this bank and shoal of time –
We'd jump the life to come.
Macbeth, I:7

185 I have no spur
To prick the sides of my intent, but only
Vaulting ambition, which o'er-leaps itself,
And falls on th' other.
Macbeth, I:7

186 False face must hide what the false heart doth know.
Macbeth, I:7

187 Sleep that knits up the ravell'd sleave of care,
The death of each day's life, sore labour's bath,
Balm of hurt minds, great nature's second course,
Chief nourisher in life's feast.
Macbeth, II:2

188 It provokes the desire, but it takes away the performance. Therefore much drink may be said to be an equivocator with lechery.
Macbeth, II:3

189 I had else been perfect,
Whole as the marble, founded as the rock,
As broad and general as the casing air,
But now I am cabin'd, cribb'd, confin'd, bound in
To saucy doubts and fears.
Macbeth, II:4

190 Nought's had, all's spent,
Where our desire is got without content.
'Tis safer to be that which we destroy,
Than by destruction dwell in doubtful joy.
Macbeth, III:2

191 Stand not upon the order of your going,
But go at once.
Macbeth, III:4

192 I am in blood
Stepp'd in so far that, should I wade no more,
Returning were as tedious as go o'er.
Macbeth, III:4

193 Out, damned spot! out, I say!
Macbeth, V:1

194 Here's the smell of the blood still.
All the perfumes of Arabia will not sweeten this little hand.
Macbeth, V:1

195 I have liv'd long enough.
My way of life
Is fall'n into the sear, the yellow leaf;
And that which should accompany old age,
As honour, love, obedience, troops of friends,
I must not look to have.
Macbeth, V:3

196 I have supp'd full with horrors.
Macbeth, V:5

197 Tomorrow, and tomorrow, and tomorrow,
Creeps in this petty pace from day to day
To the last syllable of recorded time,
And all our yesterdays have lighted fools
The way to dusty death. Out, out, brief candle!
Life's but a walking shadow, a poor player,
That struts and frets his hour upon the stage,
And then is heard no more; it is a tale
Told by an idiot, full of sound and fury,

Signifying nothing.
Macbeth, V:5

198 I gin to be aweary of the sun,
And wish th' estate o' th' world were now undone.
Macbeth, V:5

199 MACBETH. I bear a charmed life, which must not yield
To one of woman born.
MACDUFF. Despair thy charm;
And let the angel whom thou still hast serv'd
Tell thee Macduff was from his mother's womb
Untimely ripp'd.
Macbeth, V:8

200 But man, proud man
Dress'd in a little brief authority,
Most ignorant of what he's most assur'd,
His glassy essence, like an angry ape,
Plays such fantastic tricks before high heaven
As makes the angels weep.
Measure for Measure, II:2

201 That in the captain's but a choleric word
Which in the soldier is flat blasphemy.
Measure for Measure, II:2

202 The miserable have no other medicine
But only hope.
Measure for Measure, III:1

203 Thou hast nor youth nor age;
But, as it were, an after-dinner's sleep,
Dreaming on both.
Measure for Measure, III:1

204 Ay, but to die, and go we know not where;
To lie in cold obstruction, and to rot;
This sensible warm motion to become
A kneaded clod; and the delighted spirit
To bathe in fiery floods or to reside
In thrilling region of thick-ribbed ice.
Measure for Measure, III:1

205 I am a kind of burr; I shall stick.
Measure for Measure, IV:3

206 Haste still pays haste, and leisure answers leisure;
Like doth quit like, and Measure still for Measure.
Measure for Measure, V:1

207 As who should say 'I am Sir Oracle,
And when I ope my lips let no dog bark'.
The Merchant of Venice, I:1

208 If to do were as easy as to know what were good to do, chapels had been churches, and poor men's cottages princes' palaces.
The Merchant of Venice, I:2

209 The devil can cite Scripture for his purpose.
The Merchant of Venice, I:3

210 It is a wise father that knows his own child.
The Merchant of Venice, II:2

211 But love is blind, and lovers cannot see
The pretty follies that themselves commit.
The Merchant of Venice, II:6

212 The ancient saying is no heresy:
Hanging and wiving goes by destiny.
The Merchant of Venice, II:9

213 Hath not a Jew eyes? Hath not a Jew hands, organs, dimensions, senses, affections, passions, fed with the same food, hurt with the same weapons, subject to the same diseases, healed by the same means, warmed and cooled by the same winter and summer, as a Christian is? If you prick us, do we not bleed? If you tickle us, do we not laugh? If you poison us, do we not die? And if you wrong us, shall we not revenge?
The Merchant of Venice, III:1

214 The quality of mercy is not strain'd;
It droppeth as the gentle rain from heaven
Upon the place beneath. It is twice blest;
It blesseth him that gives and him that takes.
The Merchant of Venice, IV:1

215 I am never merry when I hear sweet music.
The Merchant of Venice, V:1

216 The man that hath no music in himself,
Nor is not mov'd with concord of sweet sounds,
Is fit for treasons, stratagems, and spoils.
The Merchant of Venice, V:1

217 How far that little candle throws his beams!
So shines a good deed in a naughty world.
The Merchant of Venice, V:1

218 For a light wife doth make a heavy husband.
The Merchant of Venice, V:1

219 Why, then the world's mine oyster,
Which I with sword will open.
The Merry Wives of Windsor, II:2

220 They say there is divinity in odd numbers, either in nativity, chance, or death.
The Merry Wives of Windsor, V:1

221 For aught that I could ever read,
Could ever hear by tale or history,
The course of true love never did run smooth.
A Midsummer Night's Dream, I:1

222 Love looks not with the eyes, but with the mind;
And therefore is wing'd Cupid painted blind.
A Midsummer Night's Dream, I:1

223 I am slow of study.
A Midsummer Night's Dream, I:2

224 A lion among ladies is a most dreadful thing; for there is not a more fearful wild-fowl than your lion living.
A Midsummer Night's Dream, III:1

225 Lord, what fools these mortals be!
A Midsummer Night's Dream, III:2

226 The lunatic, the lover, and the poet,
Are of imagination all compact.
A Midsummer Night's Dream, V:1

227 The poet's eye, in a fine frenzy rolling,
Doth glance from heaven to earth, from earth to heaven;
And as imagination bodies forth
The forms of things unknown, the poet's pen
Turns them to shapes, and gives to airy nothing
A local habitation and a name.
A Midsummer Night's Dream, V:1

228 Would you have me speak after my custom, as being a professed tyrant to their sex?
Much Ado About Nothing, I:1

229 Friendship is constant in all other things

Save in the office and affairs of love.
Much Ado About Nothing, II:1

230 Silence is the perfectest herald of joy: I were but little happy if I could say how much.
Much Ado About Nothing, II:1

231 Doth not the appetite alter? A man loves the meat in his youth that he cannot endure in his age.
Much Ado About Nothing, II:3

232 To be a well-favoured man is the gift of fortune; but to write and read comes by nature.
Much Ado About Nothing, III:3

233 I thank God I am as honest as any man living that is an old man and no honester than I.
Much Ado About Nothing, III:5

234 Comparisons are odorous.
Much Ado About Nothing, III:5

235 Our watch, sir, have indeed comprehended two aspicious persons.
Much Ado About Nothing, III:5

236 Write down that they hope they serve God; and write God first; for God defend but God should go before such villains!
Much Ado About Nothing, IV:2

237 For there was never yet philosopher
That could endure the toothache patiently.
Much Ado About Nothing, V:1

238 To mourn a mischief that is past and gone
Is the next way to draw new mischief on.
Othello, I:3

239 Put money in thy purse.
Othello, I:3

240 For I am nothing if not critical.
Othello, II:1

241 To suckle fools and chronicle small beer.
Othello, II:1

242 Reputation, reputation, reputation! O, I have lost my reputation! I have lost the immortal part of myself, and what remains is bestial.
Othello, II:3

243 Good name in man and woman, dear my lord,
Is the immediate jewel of their souls:
Who steals my purse steals trash; 'tis something, nothing;
'Twas mine, 'tis his, and has been slave to thousands;
But he that filches from me my good name
Robs me of that which not enriches him
And makes me poor indeed.
Othello, III:3

244 O, beware, my lord, of jealousy;
It is the green-ey'd monster which doth mock
The meat it feeds on.
Othello, III:3

245 O curse of marriage,
That we can call these delicate creatures ours,
And not their appetites! I had rather be a toad,
And live upon the vapour of a dungeon,
Than keep a corner in the thing I love
For others' uses.
Othello, III:3

246 He that is robb'd, not wanting what is stol'n,
Let him not know't, and he's not robb'd at all.
Othello, III:3

247 Farewell the neighing steed and the shrill trump,
The spirit-stirring drum, th'ear piercing fife,
The royal banner, and all quality,
Pride, pomp, and circumstance, of glorious war!
Othello, III:3

248 Put out the light, and then put out the light.
If I quench thee, thou flaming minister,
I can again thy former light restore,
Should I repent me; but once put out thy light,
Thou cunning'st pattern of excelling nature,
I know not where is that Promethean heat
That can thy light relume.
Othello, V:2

249 Then must you speak
Of one that lov'd not wisely, but too well;
Of one not easily jealous, but, being wrought,
Perplexed in the extreme; of one whose hand,
Like the base Indian, threw a pearl away
Richer than all his tribe.
Othello, V:2

250 Crabbed age and youth cannot live together:
Youth is full of pleasure, age is full of care;
Youth like summer morn, age like winter weather;
Youth like summer brave, age like winter bare.
The Passionate Pilgrim, XII

251 Kings are earth's gods; in vice their law's their will.
Pericles, I:1

252 3rd fisherman. Master, I marvel how the fishes live in the sea.
1st fisherman. Why, as men do a-land – the great ones eat up the little ones.
Pericles, II:1

253 Beauty itself doth of itself persuade
The eyes of men without an orator.
The Rape of Lucrece, I

254 The purest treasure mortal times afford
Is spotless reputation; that away,
Men are but gilded loam or painted clay.
Richard II, I:1

255 Things sweet to taste prove in digestion sour.
Richard II, I:3

256 Teach thy necessity to reason thus:
There is no virtue like necessity.
Richard II, I:3

257 This royal throne of kings, this sceptred isle,
This earth of majesty, this seat of Mars,
This other Eden, demi-paradise,
This fortress built by Nature for herself
Against infection and the hand of war,
This happy breed of men, this little world,
This precious stone set in the silver sea,
Which serves it in the office of a wall,
Or as a moat defensive to a house,
Against the envy of less happier lands;
This blessed plot, this earth, this realm, this England,
This nurse, this teeming womb of royal kings,

Fear'd by their breed, and famous by their birth.
Richard II, II:1

258 Not all the water in the rough rude sea
Can wash the balm from an anointed king;
The breath of worldly men cannot depose
The deputy elected by the Lord.
Richard II, III:2

259 For God's sake let us sit upon the ground
And tell sad stories of the death of kings:
How some have been depos'd, some slain in war,
Some haunted by the ghosts they have depos'd,
Some poison'd by their wives, some sleeping kill'd,
All murder'd – for within the hollow crown
That rounds the mortal temples of a king
Keeps Death his court.
Richard II, III:2

260 How sour sweet music is
When time is broke and no proportion kept!
So is it in the music of men's lives.
Richard II, V:5

261 Now is the winter of our discontent
Made glorious summer by this sun of York.
Richard III, I:1

262 O Lord, methought what pain it was to drown,
What dreadful noise of waters in my ears,
What sights of ugly death within my eyes!
Richard III, I:4

263 A horse! a horse ! my kingdom for a horse.
Richard III, V:4

264 O Romeo, Romeo! wherefore art thou Romeo?
Romeo and Juliet, II:2

265 What's in a name? That which we call a rose
By any other name would smell as sweet.
Romeo and Juliet, II:2

266 O, swear not by the moon, th' inconstant moon,
That monthly changes in her circled orb,
Lest that thy love prove likewise variable.
Romeo and Juliet, II:2

267 Good night, good night! Parting is such sweet sorrow
That I shall say good night till it be morrow.
Romeo and Juliet, II:2

268 Wisely and slow; they stumble that run fast.
Romeo and Juliet, II:3

269 Therefore love moderately: long love doth so;
Too swift arrives as tardy as too slow.
Romeo and Juliet, II:6

270 A plague o' both your houses!
They have made worms' meat of me.
Romeo and Juliet, III:1

271 Thank me no thankings, nor proud me no prouds.
Romeo and Juliet, III:5

272 'Tis an ill cook that cannot lick his own fingers.
Romeo and Juliet, IV:2

273 From fairest creatures we desire increase,
That thereby beauty's rose might never die.
Sonnet 1

274 Shall I compare thee to a summer's day?
Thou art more lovely and more temperate.
Rough winds do shake the darling buds of May,
And summer's lease hath all too short a date.
Sonnet 18

275 A woman's face, with Nature's own hand painted,
Hast thou, the Master Mistress of my passion.
Sonnet 20

276 When in disgrace with fortune and men's eyes
I all alone beweep my outcast state,
And trouble deaf heaven with my bootless cries,
And look upon myself, and curse my fate,
Wishing me like to one more rich in hope
Featur'd like him, like him with friends possess'd,
Desiring this man's art, and that man's scope,
With what I most enjoy contented least.
Sonnet 29

277 When to the sessions of sweet silent thought
I summon up remembrance of things past,
I sigh the lack of many a thing I sought,
And with old woes new wail my dear time's waste.
Sonnet 30

278 Not marble, nor the gilded monuments
Of princes, shall outlive this powerful rhyme.
Sonnet 55

279 Like as the waves make towards the pebbled shore,
So do our minutes hasten to their end.
Sonnet 60

280 That time of year thou mayst in me behold
When yellow leaves, or none, or few, do hang
Upon those boughs which shake against the cold,
Bare ruin'd choirs, where late the sweet birds sang.
Sonnet 73

281 Farewell! thou art too dear for my possessing,
And like enough thou know'st thy estimate:
The charter of thy worth gives thee releasing;
My bonds in thee are all determinate.
Sonnet 87

282 For sweetest things turn sourest by their deeds:
Lilies that fester smell far worse than weeds.
Sonnet 94

283 When in the chronicle of wasted time
I see descriptions of the fairest wights.
Sonnet 106

284 Let me not to the marriage of true minds
Admit impediments. Love is not love
Which alters when it alteration finds,
Or bends with the remover to remove.

O, no! it is an ever-fixed mark,
That looks on tempests and is never shaken.
Sonnet 116

285 Love alters not with his brief hours and weeks,
But bears it out even to the edge of doom.
If this be error, and upon me prov'd,
I never writ, nor no man ever lov'd.
Sonnet 116

286 Th' expense of spirit in a waste of shame
Is lust in action; and till action, lust
Is perjur'd, murd'rous, bloody, full of blame,
Savage, extreme, rude, cruel, not to trust;
Enjoy'd no sooner but despised straight.
Sonnet 129

287 My mistress' eyes are nothing like the sun;
Coral is far more red than her lips' red.
Sonnet 130

288 And yet, by heaven, I think my love as rare
As any she belied with false compare.
Sonnet 130

289 Two loves I have, of comfort and despair,
Which like two spirits do suggest me still;
The better angel is a man right fair,
The worser spirit a woman colour'd ill.
Sonnet 144

290 No profit grows where is no pleasure ta'en;
In brief, sir, study what you most affect.
The Taming of the Shrew, I:1

291 This is a way to kill a wife with kindness.
The Taming of the Shrew, IV:1

292 Our purses shall be proud, our garments poor;
For 'tis the mind that makes the body rich;
And as the sun breaks through the darkest clouds,
So honour peereth in the meanest habit.
The Taming of the Shrew, IV:3

293 Full fathom five thy father lies;
Of his bones are coral made;
Those are pearls that were his eyes;
Nothing of him that doth fade
But doth suffer a sea-change
Into something rich and strange.
The Tempest, I:2

294 When they will not give a doit to relieve a lame beggar, they will lay out ten to see a dead Indian.
The Tempest, II:2

295 Misery acquaints a man with strange bedfellows.
The Tempest, II:2

296 He that dies pays all debts.
The Tempest, III:2

297 Our revels now are ended. These our actors,
As I foretold you, were all spirits, and
Are melted into air, into thin air;
And, like the baseless fabric of this vision,
The cloud-capp'd towers, the gorgeous palaces,
The solemn temples, the great globe itself,
Yea, all which it inherit, shall dissolve,
And, like this insubstantial pageant faded,
Leave not a rack behind. We are such stuff
As dreams are made on; and our little life
Is rounded with a sleep.
The Tempest, IV:1

298 I'll break my staff,
Bury it certain fathoms in the earth,
And deeper than did ever plummet sound
I'll drown my book.
The Tempest, V:1

299 How beauteous mankind is! O brave new world
That has such people in't!
The Tempest, V:1

300 That she belov'd knows nought that knows not this:
Men prize the thing ungain'd more than it is.
Troilus and Cressida, I:2

301 O, when degree is shak'd,
Which is the ladder of all high designs,
The enterprise is sick!
Troilus and Cressida, I:3

302 To be wise and love
Exceeds man's might.
Troilus and Cressida, III:2

303 Time hath, my lord, a wallet at his back,
Wherein he puts alms for oblivion,
A great-siz'd monster of ingratitudes.
Troilus and Cressida, III:3

304 Lechery, lechery! Still wars and lechery! Nothing else holds fashion.
Troilus and Cressida, V:2

305 If music be the food of love, play on,
Give me excess of it, that, surfeiting,
The appetite may sicken and so die.
Twelfth Night, I:1

306 Is it a world to hide virtues in?
Twelfth Night, I:3

307 Many a good hanging prevents a bad marriage.
Twelfth Night, I:5

308 Not to be abed after midnight is to be up betimes.
Twelfth Night, II:3

309 What is love? 'Tis not hereafter;
Present mirth hath present laughter;
What's to come is still unsure.
In delay there lies no plenty,
Then come kiss me, sweet and twenty;
Youth's a stuff will not endure.
Twelfth Night, II:3

310 Dost thou think, because thou art virtuous, there shall be no more cakes and ale?
Twelfth Night, II:3

311 She never told her love,
But let concealment, like a worm i' th' bud,
Feed on her damask cheek. She pin'd in thought;
And with a green and yellow melancholy
She sat like Patience on a monument,
Smiling at grief.
Twelfth Night, II:4

312 Some are born great, some achieve greatness, and some have greatness thrust upon 'em.
Twelfth Night, II:5

313 Love sought is good, but given unsought is better.
Twelfth Night, III:1

314 If this were play'd upon a stage now, I could condemn it as an improbable fiction.
Twelfth Night, III:4

315 Still you keep o' th' windy side of the law.
Twelfth Night, III:4

316 I hate ingratitude more in a man
Than lying, vainness, babbling drunkenness,
Or any taint of vice whose strong corruption
Inhabits our frail blood.
Twelfth Night, III:4

317 Home-keeping youth have ever homely wits.
The Two Gentlemen of Verona, I:1

318 I have no other but a woman's reason:
I think him so, because I think him so.
The Two Gentlemen of Verona, I:2

319 Who is Silvia? What is she,
That all our swains commend her?
Holy, fair, and wise is she.
The Two Gentlemen of Verona, IV:2

320 What's gone and what's past help
Should be past grief.
The Winter's Tale, III:2

321 I would there were no age between ten and three and twenty, or that youth would sleep out the rest; for there is nothing in the between but getting wenches with child, wronging the ancientry, stealing, fighting.
The Winter's Tale, III:3

322 *Exit, pursued by a bear.*
Stage direction. *The Winter's Tale,* III:3

323 A snapper-up of unconsidered trifles.
The Winter's Tale, IV:2

324 Though I am not naturally honest, I am so sometimes by chance.
The Winter's Tale, IV:3

325 Though authority be a stubborn bear, yet he is oft led by the nose with gold.
The Winter's Tale, IV:3

SHAW, George Bernard

(1856–1950) Irish dramatist and critic. His plays, with their long prefaces, established him as the leading British playwright of his time. Included among his prose works are *The Intelligent Woman's Guide to Socialism and Capitalism* (1928) and *The Black Girl in Search of God* (1932).

Quotations about Shaw

1 Shaw's works make me admire the magnificent tolerance and broadmindedness of the English.
James Joyce (1882–1941) Irish novelist. *The Wild Geese* (Gerald Griffin)

2 He writes like a Pakistani who has learned English when he was twelve years old in order to become a chartered accountant.
John Osborne (1929–) British dramatist. Attrib.

Quotations by Shaw

3 Whether you think Jesus was God or not, you must admit that he was a first-rate political economist.
Androcles and the Lion, Preface, 'Jesus as Economist'

4 All great truths begin as blasphemies.
Annajanska

5 You are a very poor soldier: a chocolate cream soldier!
Arms and the Man, I

6 Silence is the most perfect expression of scorn.
Back to Methuselah

7 When a stupid man is doing something he is ashamed of, he always declares that it is his duty.
Caesar and Cleopatra, III

8 A man of great common sense and good taste, – meaning thereby a man without originality or moral courage.
Referring to Julius Caesar. *Caesar and Cleopatra,* Notes

9 The British soldier can stand up to anything except the British War Office.
The Devil's Disciple, II

10 I never expect a soldier to think.
The Devil's Disciple, III

11 With the single exception of Homer, there is no eminent writer, not even Sir Walter Scott, whom I can despise so entirely as I despise Shakespeare when I measure my mind against his . . . It would positively be a relief to me to dig him up and throw stones at him.
Dramatic Opinions and Essays, Vol. 2

12 Physically there is nothing to distinguish human society from the farm-yard except that children are more troublesome and costly than chickens and women are not so completely enslaved as farm stock.
Getting Married, Preface

13 My way of joking is to tell the truth. It's the funniest joke in the world.
John Bull's Other Island, II

14 Cusins is a very nice fellow, certainly: nobody would ever guess that he was born in Australia.
Major Barbara, I

15 Nobody can say a word against Greek: it stamps a man at once as an educated gentleman.
Major Barbara, I

16 Alcohol is a very necessary article . . . It enables Parliament to do things at eleven at night that no sane person would do at eleven in the morning.
Major Barbara, II

17 He never does a proper thing without giving an improper reason for it.
Major Barbara, III

18 He knows nothing; and he thinks he knows everything. That points clearly to a political career.
Major Barbara, III

19 CUSINS. Do you call poverty a crime?
UNDERSHAFT. The worst of all crimes. All the other crimes are virtues beside it.
Major Barbara, IV

20 Give women the vote, and in five years there will be a crushing tax on bachelors.
Man and Superman, Preface

21 A lifetime of happiness: no man alive could bear it: it would be hell on earth.
Man and Superman, I

22 Very nice sort of place, Oxford, I should think, for people that like that sort of place.
Man and Superman, II

23 It is a woman's business to get married as soon as possible, and a

man's to keep unmarried as long as he can.
Man and Superman, II

24 There are two tragedies in life. One is to lose your heart's desire. The other is to gain it.
Man and Superman, IV

25 In heaven an angel is nobody in particular.
Man and Superman, 'Maxims for Revolutionists'

26 Beware of the man who does not return your blow: he neither forgives you nor allows you to forgive yourself.
Man and Superman, 'Maxims for Revolutionists'

27 Do not love your neighbour as yourself. If you are on good terms with yourself it is an impertinence; if on bad, an injury.
Man and Superman, 'Maxims for Revolutionists'

28 Titles distinguish the mediocre, embarrass the superior, and are disgraced by the inferior.
Man and Superman, 'Maxims for Revolutionists'

29 Self-denial is not a virtue; it is only the effect of prudence on rascality.
Man and Superman, 'Maxims for Revolutionists'

30 If you strike a child, take care that you strike it in anger, even at the risk of maiming it for life. A blow in cold blood neither can nor should be forgiven.
Man and Superman, 'Maxims for Revolutionists'

31 The golden rule is that there are no golden rules.
Man and Superman, 'Maxims for Revolutionists'

32 He who can, does. He who cannot, teaches.
Man and Superman, 'Maxims for Revolutionists'

33 Optimistic lies have such immense therapeutic value that a doctor who cannot tell them convincingly has mistaken his profession.
Misalliance, Preface

34 Heaven, as conventionally conceived, is a place so inane, so dull, so useless, so miserable, that nobody has ever ventured to describe a whole day in heaven, though plenty of people have described a day at the seaside.
Misalliance, Preface

35 The secret of being miserable is to have leisure to bother about whether you are happy or not.
Misalliance, Preface

36 The English have no respect for their language, and will not teach their children to speak it . . . It is impossible for an Englishman to open his mouth, without making some other Englishman despise him.
Pygmalion, Preface

37 They all thought she was dead; but my father he kept ladling gin down her throat till she came to so sudden that she bit the bowl off the spoon.
Pygmalion, III

38 Gin was mother's milk to her.
Pygmalion, III

39 Assassination is the extreme form of censorship.
The Shewing-Up of Blanco Posnet, 'The Limits of Toleration'

40 It is the sexless novel that should be distinguished: the sex novel is now normal.
Table-Talk of G.B.S.

41 It does not follow . . . that the right to criticize Shakespeare involves the power of writing better plays. And in fact . . . I do not profess to write better plays.
Three Plays for Puritans, Preface

42 We're from Madeira, but perfectly respectable, so far.
You Never Can Tell, I

43 Well, sir, you never can tell. That's a principle in life with me, sir, if you'll excuse my having such a thing, sir.
You Never Can Tell, II

44 I've been offered titles, but I think they get one into disreputable company.
Gossip (A. Barrow)

45 The thought of two thousand people crunching celery at the same time horrified me.
Explaining why he had turned down an invitation to a vegetarian gala dinner. *The Greatest Laughs of All Time* (G. Lieberman)

46 It's a funny thing about that bust. As time goes on it seems to get younger and younger.
Referring to a portrait bust sculpted for him by Rodin. *More Things I Wish I'd Said* (K. Edwards)

47 The trouble, Mr Goldwyn is that you are only interested in art and I am only interested in money.
Turning down Goldwyn's offer to buy the screen rights of his plays. *The Movie Moguls* (Philip French), Ch. 4

48 I quite agree with you, sir, but what can two do against so many?
Responding to a solitary hiss heard amongst the applause at the first performance of *Arms and the Man* in 1894. *Oxford Book of Literary Anecdotes*

49 Certainly, there is nothing else here to enjoy.
Said at a party when his hostess asked him whether he was enjoying himself. *Pass the Port* (Oxfam)

50 Far too good to waste on children.
Reflecting upon youth. *10,000 Jokes, Toasts, and Stories* (L. Copeland)

51 Better never than late.
Responding to an offer by a producer to present one of Shaw's plays, having earlier rejected it. *The Unimportance of Being Oscar* (Oscar Levant)

52 LORD NORTHCLIFFE. The trouble with you, Shaw, is that you look as if there were famine in the land.
G.B.S. The trouble with you, Northcliffe, is that you look as if you were the cause of it.
Attrib.

53 If all economists were laid end to end, they would not reach a conclusion.
Attrib.

SHELLEY, Percy Bysshe

(1792–1822) British poet. Most of his poetry was written in Italy, including *Prometheus Unbound* (1818–19), *Adonais* (1821), and much lyrical poetry.

Quotations about Shelley

1 In his poetry as well as in his life Shelley was indeed 'a beautiful and ineffectual angel', beating in the void his luminous wings in vain.
Matthew Arnold (1822–88) British poet and critic. *Literature and Drama*, 'Shelley'

2 Poor Shelley always was, and is, a kind of ghastly object; colourless, pallid, tuneless, without health or warmth or vigour.
Thomas Carlyle (1795–1881) Scottish historian and essayist. *Reminiscences*

Quotations by Shelley

3 I weep for Adonais – he is dead!
O, weep for Adonais! though our tears

Thaw not the frost which binds so dear a head!
Prompted by the death of Keats. *Adonais*, I

4 He hath awakened from the dream of life –
'Tis we, who lost in stormy visions, keep
With phantoms an unprofitable strife,
And in mad trance, strike with our spirit's knife
Invulnerable nothings.
Adonais, XXXIX

5 I wield the flail of the lashing hail,
And whiten the green plains under,
And then again I dissolve it in rain,
And laugh as I pass in thunder.
The Cloud

6 I am the daughter of Earth and Water,
And the nursling of the Sky;
I pass through the pores of the ocean and shores;
I change, but I cannot die,
For after the rain when with never a stain
The pavilion of Heaven is bare,
And the winds and sunbeams with their convex gleams
Build up the blue dome of air,
I silently laugh at my own cenotaph,
And out of the caverns of rain,
Like a child from the womb, like a ghost from the tomb,
I arise and unbuild it again.
The Cloud

7 Poetry is the record of the best and happiest moments of the happiest and best minds.
A Defence of Poetry

8 Life may change, but it may fly not;
Hope may vanish, but can die not;
Truth be veiled, but still it burneth;
Love repulsed, – but it returneth!
Hellas, I

9 Let there be light! said Liberty,
And like sunrise from the sea,
Athens arose!
Hellas, I

10 London, that great sea, whose ebb and flow
At once is deaf and loud, and on the shore
Vomits its wrecks, and still howls on for more.
Letter to Maria Gisborne, I

11 Have you not heard
When a man marries, dies, or turns Hindoo,
His best friends hear no more of him?
Referring to Thomas Love Peacock, who worked for the East India Company and had recently married. *Letter to Maria Gisborne*, I

12 Lift not the painted veil which those who live
Call life.
Lift not the Painted Veil

13 I met Murder on the way–
He had a mask like Castlereagh.
Viscount Castlereagh (1769–1822) was British foreign secretary (1812–22); he was highly unpopular and became identified with such controversial events as the Peterloo massacre of 1819. *The Mask of Anarchy*, 5

14 O Wild West Wind, thou breath of Autumn's being,
Thou, from whose unseen presence the leaves dead
Are driven, like ghosts from an enchanter fleeing,
Yellow, and black, and pale, and hectic red,
Pestilence-stricken multitudes.
Ode to the West Wind

15 If Winter comes, can Spring be far behind?
Ode to the West Wind

16 I met a traveller from an antique land
Who said: Two vast and trunkless legs of stone
Stand in the desert.
Referring to the legs of a broken statue of the Pharaoh Rameses II (1301–1234 BC; Greek name, Ozymandias). *Ozymandias*

17 'My name is Ozymandias, king of kings:
Look on my works, ye Mighty, and despair!'
Ozymandias

18 Sometimes
The Devil is a gentleman.
Peter Bell the Third

19 Teas,
Where small talk dies in agonies.
Peter Bell the Third

20 'Twas Peter's drift
To be a kind of moral eunuch.
Peter Bell the Third

21 Hell is a city much like London–
A populous and smoky city.
Peter Bell the Third

22 Death is the veil which those who live call life:
They sleep, and it is lifted.
Prometheus Unbound, III

23 It is a modest creed, and yet
Pleasant if one considers it,
To own that death itself must be,
Like all the rest, a mockery.
The Sensitive Plant, III

24 Hail to thee, blithe Spirit!
Bird thou never wert,
That from Heaven, or near it,
Pourest thy full heart
In profuse strains of unpremeditated art.
To a Skylark

25 Music, when soft voices die,
Vibrates in the memory –
Odours, when sweet violets sicken,
Live within the sense they quicken.
Rose leaves, when the rose is dead,
Are heaped for the beloved's bed;
And so thy thoughts, when thou art gone,
Love itself shall slumber on.
To –

26 For she was beautiful – her beauty made
The bright world dim, and everything beside
Seemed like the fleeting image of a shade.
The Witch of Atlas, XII

SHERIDAN, Richard Brinsley

(1751–1816) British dramatist. His best-known comedies are *The Rivals* (1775) and *School for Scandal* (1777). He was manager of the Drury Lane Theatre and a Whig MP (1780–1812).

Quotations about Sheridan

1 Good at a fight, but better at a play
God-like in giving, but the devil to pay.
Lord Byron (1788–1824) British poet. *On a Cast of Sheridan's Hand*

2 He could not make enemies. If anyone came to request the repayment of a loan from him he borrowed more. A cordial shake of his hand was a receipt in full for all demands.
William Hazlitt (1778–1830) British essayist. *New Monthly Magazine*, Jan 1824

Quotations by Sheridan

3 If it is abuse – why one is always sure to hear of it from one damned good-natured friend or other!
The Critic, I

4 A progeny of learning.
The Rivals, I

5 Illiterate him, I say, quite from your memory.
The Rivals, II

6 It gives me the hydrostatics to such a degree.
The Rivals, III

7 As headstrong as an allegory on the banks of the Nile.
The Rivals, III

8 He is the very pine-apple of politeness!
The Rivals, III

9 If I reprehend any thing in this world, it is the use of my oracular tongue, and a nice derangement of epitaphs!
The Rivals, III

10 You had no taste when you married me.
The School for Scandal, I

11 I'm called away by particular business. But I leave my character behind me.
The School for Scandal, II

12 Well, then, my stomach must just digest in its waistcoat.
On being warned that his drinking would destroy the coat of his stomach. *The Fine Art of Political Wit* (L. Harris)

13 What His Royal Highness most particularly prides himself upon, is the excellent harvest.
Lampooning George IV's habit of taking credit for everything good in England. *The Fine Art of Political Wit* (L. Harris)

14 My dear fellow, be reasonable; the sum you ask me for is a very considerable one, whereas I only ask you for twenty-five pounds.
On being refused a further loan of £25 from a friend to whom he already owed £500. *Literary and Scientific Anecdotes* (W. Keddie)

15 Whatsoever might be the extent of the private calamity, I hope it will not interfere with the public business of the country.
On learning, while in the House of Commons, that his Drury Lane Theatre was on fire. *Memoirs of Life of the Rt. Hon. Richard Brinsley Sheridan* (T. Moore)

16 A man may surely be allowed to take a glass of wine by his own fireside.
As he sat in a coffeehouse watching his Drury Lane Theatre burn down. *Memoirs of the Life of the Rt. Hon. Richard Brinsley Sheridan* (T. Moore)

17 Thank God, that's settled.
Handing one of his creditors an IOU. *Wit, Wisdom, and Foibles of the Great* (C. Shriner)

18 Won't you come into the garden? I would like my roses to see you.
Said to a young lady. Attrib. in *The Perfect Hostess*

19 It is not my interest to pay the principal, nor my principle to pay the interest.
To his tailor when he requested the payment of a debt, or of the interest on it at least. Attrib.

20 The Right Honourable gentleman is indebted to his memory for his jests, and to his imagination for his facts.
Replying to a speech in the House of Commons. Attrib.

21 Mr. Speaker, I said the honorable member was a liar it is true and I am sorry for it. The honourable member may place the punctuation where he pleases.
On being asked to apologize for calling a fellow MP a liar. Attrib.

SHIPS

1 In an English ship, they say, it is poor grub, poor pay, and easy work; in an American ship, good grub, good pay, and hard work. And this is applicable to the working populations of both countries.
Jack London (1876–1916) US novelist. *The People of the Abyss*, Ch. 20

SHYNESS

See also self-confidence

1 I'm really a timid person – I was beaten up by Quakers.
Woody Allen (Allen Stewart Konigsberg; 1935–) US film actor. *Sleeper*

2 A timid question will always receive a confident answer.
Lord Darling (1849–1936) British judge. *Scintillae Juris*

3 Why so shy, my pretty Thomasina?
Thomasin, O Thomasin,
Once you were so promisin'.
Christopher Fry (1907–) British dramatist. *The Dark Is Light Enough*, II

4 Shyness is just egotism out of its depth.
Penelope Keith British actress. Remark, July 1988

5 Had we but world enough, and time,
This coyness, lady, were no crime.
Andrew Marvell (1621–78) English poet. *To His Coy Mistress*

SICKNESS

See illness

SIGNATURES

1 Never sign a walentine with your own name.
Charles Dickens (1812–70) British novelist. Said by Sam Weller. *Pickwick Papers*, Ch. 33

2 There, I guess King George will be able to read that.
John Hancock (1737–93) US revolutionary. Referring to his signature, written in a bold hand, on the US Declaration of Independence. *The American Treasury* (C. Fadiman)

3 The hand that signed the treaty bred a fever,
And famine grew, and locusts came;
Great is the hand that holds dominion over
Man by a scribbled name.
Dylan Thomas (1914–53) Welsh poet. *The Hand that Signed the Paper*

SILENCE

See also speech

1 A still tongue makes a wise head.
Proverb

2 Speech is silver, silence is golden.
Proverb

3 No voice; but oh! the silence sank
Like music on my heart.
Samuel Taylor Coleridge (1772–1834) British poet. *The Rime of the Ancient Mariner*, VI

4 When you have nothing to say, say nothing.
Charles Caleb Colton (c. 1780–1832) British clergyman and writer. *Lacon*, Vol. I

5 For God's sake hold your tongue and let me love.
John Donne (1573–1631) English poet. *The Canonization*

6 Silence is become his mother tongue.
Oliver Goldsmith (1728–74) Irish-born British writer. *The Good-Natured Man*, II

7 That man's silence is wonderful to listen to.
Thomas Hardy (1840–1928) British novelist. *Under the Greenwood Tree*, Ch. 14

8 Silence is as full of potential wisdom

and wit as the unhewn marble of great sculpture.

Aldous Huxley (1894–1964) British novelist. *Point Counter Point*

9 Thou still unravish'd bride of quietness,
Thou foster-child of silence and slow time.

John Keats (1795–1821) British poet. *Ode on a Grecian Urn*

10 Silence is the best tactic for him who distrusts himself.

Duc de la Rochefoucauld (1613–80) French writer. *Maximes*, 79

11 You get the impression that their normal condition is silence and that speech is a slight fever which attacks them now and then.

Jean-Paul Sartre (1905–80) French writer. *Nausea*

12 Silence is the perfectest herald of joy: I were but little happy if I could say how much.

William Shakespeare (1564–1616) English dramatist. *Much Ado About Nothing*, II:1

13 Silence is the most perfect expression of scorn.

George Bernard Shaw (1856–1950) Irish dramatist and critic. *Back to Methuselah*

14 My personal hobbies are reading, listening to music, and silence.

Edith Sitwell (1887–1964) British poet and writer. Attrib.

15 The cruellest lies are often told in silence.

Robert Louis Stevenson (1850–94) Scottish writer. *Virginibus Puerisque*

16 Whereof one cannot speak, thereon one must remain silent.

Ludwig Wittgenstein (1889–1951) Austrian philosopher. *Tractatus Logico-Philosophicus*, Ch. 7

SIMILARITY

See also analogy, difference

1 Birds of a feather flock together.

Proverb

2 Great minds think alike.

Proverb

3 Like breeds like.

Proverb

4 Never mind, dear, we're all made the same, though some more than others.

Noël Coward (1899–1973) British dramatist. *The Café de la Paix*

5 I never knows the children. It's just six of one and half-a-dozen of the other.

Captain Frederick Marryat (1792–1848) British novelist. *The Pirate*, Ch. 4

SIMPLICITY

1 'Excellent!' I cried. 'Elementary,' said he.

Arthur Conan Doyle (1856–1930) British writer. Watson talking to Sherlock Holmes; Holmes's reply is often misquoted as 'Elementary, my dear Watson'. *The Crooked Man*

2 The ability to simplify means to eliminate the unnecessary so that the necessary may speak.

Hans Hofmann (1880–1966) German-born US painter. *Search for the Real*

3 O holy simplicity!

John Huss (Jan Hus; c. 1369–1415) Bohemian religious reformer. On noticing a peasant adding a faggot to the pile at his execution. *Apophthegmata* (Zincgreff-Weidner), Pt. III

4 The trivial round, the common task,
Would furnish all we ought to ask;
Room to deny ourselves; a road
To bring us, daily, nearer God.

John Keble (1792–1866) British poet and clergyman. *The Christian Year*, 'Morning'

5 A child of five would understand this.
Send somebody to fetch a child of five.

Groucho Marx (Julius Marx; 1895–1977) US comedian. *Duck Soup*

6 Entities should not be multiplied unnecessarily.
No more things should be presumed to exist than are absolutely necessary.

William of Okham (c. 1280–1349) English philosopher. 'Okham's Razor'. Despite its attribution to William of Okham, it was in fact a repetition of an ancient philosophical maxim.

7 An honest tale speeds best being plainly told.

William Shakespeare (1564–1616) English dramatist. *Richard III*, IV:4

8 Anybody can shock a baby, or a television audience. But it's too easy, and the effect is disproportionate to the effort.

Richard G. Stern (1928–) US writer. *Golk*, Ch. 4

9 Our life is frittered away by detail . . . Simplify, simplify.

Henry David Thoreau (1817–62) US writer. *Walden*, 'Where I Lived, and What I Lived for'

SIN

See also evil, vice

1 Old sins cast long shadows.

Proverb

2 All sin tends to be addictive, and the terminal point of addiction is what is called damnation.

W. H. Auden (1907–73) British poet. *A Certain World*

3 Wherefore putting away lying, speak every man truth with his neighbour: for we are members one of another.
Be ye angry, and sin not: let not the sun go down upon your wrath:
Neither give place to the devil.
Let him that stole steal no more: but rather let him labour, working with his hands the thing which is good, that he may have to give to him that needeth.

Bible: Ephesians 4:25–28

4 Afterward Jesus findeth him in the temple, and said unto him, Behold, thou art made whole: sin no more, lest a worse thing come unto thee.

Bible: John 5:14

5 She said, No man, Lord. And Jesus said unto her, Neither do I condemn thee: go, and sin no more.

Bible: John 8:11

6 So when they continued asking him, he lifted up himself, and said unto them, He that is without sin among you, let him first cast a stone at her.

Bible: John Often misquoted as 'cast the first stone'. 8:7

7 If we say that we have no sin, we deceive ourselves, and the truth is not in us.
If we confess our sins, he is faithful and just to forgive us our sins, and to cleanse us from all unrighteousness.

Bible: I John 1:8–9

8 Wherefore I say unto thee, Her sins, which are many, are forgiven; for she loved much: but to whom little is forgiven, the same loveth little.

Bible: Luke 7:47

9 But if ye will not do so, behold, ye have sinned against the Lord: and be sure your sin will find you out.

Bible: Numbers 32:23

10 Then said Saul, I have sinned: return, my son David: for I will no more do thee harm, because my soul was precious in thine eyes this

day: behold, I have played the fool, and have erred exceedingly.
Bible: I Samuel 26:21

11 This is a faithful saying, and worthy of all acceptation, that Christ Jesus came into the world to save sinners; of whom I am chief.
Bible: I Timothy 1:15

12 We have erred, and strayed from thy ways like lost sheep.
The Book of Common Prayer *Morning Prayer, General Confession*

13 We have left undone those things which we ought to have done; and we have done those things we ought not to have done.
The Book of Common Prayer *Morning Prayer, General Confession*

14 A private sin is not so prejudicial in the world as a public indecency.
Miguel de Cervantes (1547–1616) Spanish novelist. *Don Quixote*, Pt. II, Ch. 22

15 He said he was against it.
Calvin Coolidge (1872–1933) US president. Reply when asked what a clergyman had said regarding sin in his sermon. Attrib.

16 It is my belief, Watson, founded upon my experience, that the lowest and vilest alleys of London do not present a more dreadful record of sin than does the smiling and beautiful countryside.
Arthur Conan Doyle (1856–1930) English writer. *Copper Beeches*

17 I have never killed a man, but I have read many obituaries with a lot of pleasure.
Clarence Darrow (1857–1938) US lawyer. *Medley*

18 Did wisely from Expensive Sins refrain,
And never broke the Sabbath, but for Gain.
John Dryden (1631–1700) English poet and dramatist. *Absalom and Achitophel*, I

19 Sin brought death, and death will disappear with the disappearance of sin.
Mary Baker Eddy (1821–1910) US religious leader. *Science and Health, with Key to the Scriptures*

20 There's nothing so artificial as sinning nowadays. I suppose it once was real.
D. H. Lawrence (1885–1930) British novelist. *St. Mawr*

21 Of Man's first disobedience, and the fruit
Of that forbidden tree, whose mortal taste
Brought death into the World, and all our woe . . .
John Milton (1608–74) English poet. *Paradise Lost*, Bk. I

22 The only people who should really sin
Are the people who can sin with a grin.
Ogden Nash (1902–71) US poet. *I'm a Stranger Here Myself*

23 She holds that it were better for sun and moon to drop from heaven, for the earth to fail, and for all the many millions who are upon it to die of starvation in extremest agony, as far as temporal affliction goes, than that one soul, I will not say, should be lost, but should commit one single venial sin, should tell one wilful untruth, . . . or steal one poor farthing without excuse.
Cardinal Newman (1801–90) British theologian. Referring to the Roman Catholic Church. *Lectures on Anglican Difficulties*, VIII

24 At such an hour the sinners are still in bed resting up from their sinning of the night before, so they will be in good shape for more sinning a little later on.
Damon Runyon (1884–1946) US writer. *Runyon à la carte*, 'The Idyll of Miss Sarah Brown'

25 Commit
The oldest sins the newest kind of ways.
William Shakespeare (1564–1616) English dramatist. *Henry IV, Part 2*, IV:5

26 . . . I am a man
More sinned against than sinning.
William Shakespeare *King Lear*, III:2

27 Were't not for gold and women, there would be no damnation.
Cyril Tourneur (1575–1626) English dramatist. *The Revenger's Tragedy*, II:1

SINCERITY

See also frankness, honesty, integrity

1 Best be yourself, imperial, plain and true!
Robert Browning (1812–89) British poet. *Bishop Blougram's Apology*

2 What comes from the heart, goes to the heart.
Samuel Taylor Coleridge (1772–1834) British poet. *Table Talk*

3 Sincerity is all that counts. It's a wide-spread modern heresy. Think again. Bolsheviks are sincere. Fascists are sincere. Lunatics are sincere. People who believe the earth is flat are sincere. They can't all be right. Better make certain first you've got something to be sincere about and with.
Tom Driberg (1905–76) British politician, journalist and author. *Daily Express*, 1937

4 Some of the worst men in the world are sincere and the more sincere they are the worse they are.
Lord Hailsham (1907–) British Conservative politician. *The Observer*, 'Sayings of the Week', 7 Jan 1968

5 I'm afraid of losing my obscurity. Genuineness only thrives in the dark. Like celery.
Aldous Huxley (1894–1964) British novelist. *Those Barren Leaves*, Pt. I, Ch. 1

6 What's a man's first duty? The answer's brief: To be himself.
Henrik Ibsen (1828–1906) Norwegian dramatist. *Peer Gynt*, IV:1

7 It is dangerous to be sincere unless you are also stupid.
George Bernard Shaw (1865–1950) Irish dramatist and critic. *Man and Superman*

8 A little sincerity is a dangerous thing, and a great deal of it is absolutely fatal.
Oscar Wilde (1854–1900) Irish-born British dramatist. *The Critic as Artist*, Pt. 2

SINGERS

See also musicians, singing

1 Swans sing before they die –
'twere no bad thing,
Did certain persons die before they sing.
Samuel Taylor Coleridge (1772–1834) British poet. *Epigram on a Volunteer Singer*

2 A wandering minstrel I –
A thing of shreds and patches,
Of ballads, songs and snatches,
And dreamy lullaby!
W. S. Gilbert (1836–1911) British dramatist. *The Mikado*, I

3 The Last of the Red-Hot Mamas.
Sophie Tucker (Sophia Abuza; 1884–1966) Russian-born US singer. Description of herself. *Dictionary of Biographical Quotation* (J. Wintle and R. Kenin)

SINGING

See also music, opera, singers

1 You know whatta you do when you

shit? Singing, it's the same thing, only up!

Enrico Caruso (1873–1921) Italian tenor. *Whose Little Boy Are You?* (H. Brown)

2 I have a song to sing O!
Sing me your song, O!

W. S. Gilbert (1836–1911) British dramatist. *The Yeoman of the Guard*, I

3 Just a little more reverence, please, and not so much astonishment.

Malcolm Sargent (1895–1967) British conductor. Rehearsing the female chorus in 'For unto Us a Child is Born' from Handel's *Messiah*. *2500 Anecdotes* (E. Fuller)

SLAVERY

See also oppression

1 From the beginning all were created equal by nature, slavery was introduced through the injust oppression of worthless men, against the will of God; for, if God had wanted to create slaves, he would surely have decided at the beginning of the world who was to be slave and who master.

John Ball Sermon, Blackheath, 1381

2 The future is the only kind of property that the masters willingly concede to slaves.

Albert Camus (1913–60) French existentialist writer. *The Rebel*

3 There they are cutting each other's throats, because one half of them prefer hiring their servants for life, and the other by the hour.

Thomas Carlyle (1795–1881) Scottish historian and essayist. Referring to the American Civil War. Attrib.

4 Slaves cannot breathe in England; if their lungs
Receive our air, that moment they are free;
They touch our country, and their shackles fall.

William Cowper (1731–1800) English poet. A situation resulting from a judicial decision in 1772. *The Task*

5 The compact which exists between the North and the South is a covenant with death and an agreement with hell.

William Lloyd Garrison (1805–79) US abolitionist. Resolution, Massachusetts Anti-Slavery Society, 27 Jan 1843

6 No man should be a serf, nor do homage or any manner of service to any lord, but should give fourpence rent for an acre of land, and that no one should work for any man but as his own will, and on terms of a regular covenant.

Wat Tyler (d. 1381) English rebel. *Anonimalle Chronicle*

7 The whole commerce between master and slave is a perpetual exercise of the most boisterous passions, the most unremitting despotism on the one part, and degrading submissions on the other.

Thomas Jefferson (1743–1826) US statesman. *Notes on the State of Virginia*

SLEEP

See also bed, dreams

1 Sleep is better than medicine.

Proverb

2 One hour's sleep before midnight, is worth two after.

Proverb

3 The beginning of health is sleep.

Irish proverb

4 Now I lay me down to sleep,
I pray the Lord my soul to keep.
If I should die before I wake,
I pray the Lord my soul to take.

Anonymous *New England Primer*, 1781

5 The amount of sleep required by the average person is just five minutes more.

Anonymous

6 Lay your sleeping head, my love,
Human on my faithless arm.

W. H. Auden (1907–73) British poet. *Lullaby*

7 Rock-a-bye baby on the tree top,
When the wind blows the cradle will rock,
When the bough bends the cradle will fall,
Down comes the baby, cradle and all.

Charles Dupee Blake (1846–1903) British writer of nursery rhymes. Attrib.

8 Laugh and the world laughs with you; snore and you sleep alone.

Anthony Burgess (1917–) British novelist and critic. *Inside Mr. Enderby*

9 Oh sleep! it is a gentle thing,
Beloved from pole to pole!

Samuel Taylor Coleridge (1772–1834) British poet. *The Rime of the Ancient Mariner*, V

10 Golden slumbers kiss your eyes,
Smiles awake you when you rise.

Thomas Dekker (c. 1572–c. 1632) English dramatist. *Patient Grissil*, IV:2

11 Sleep is that golden chaine that ties health and our bodies together.

Thomas Dekker *The Guls Horn-Booke*, Ch. 2

12 Health is the first muse, and sleep is the condition to produce it.

Ralph Waldo Emerson (1803–82) US poet and essayist. *Uncollected Lectures*, 'Resources'

13 It appears that every man's insomnia is as different from his neighbor's as are their daytime hopes and aspirations.

F. Scott Fitzgerald (1896–1940) US writer. *The Crack-up*, 'Sleeping and Waking'

14 Try thinking of love, or something.
Amor vincit insomnia.

Christopher Fry (1907–) British dramatist. *A Sleep of Prisoners*

15 Sleep is when all the unsorted stuff comes flying out as from a dustbin upset in a high wind.

William Golding (1911–) British novelist. *Pincher Martin*

16 Sleep is gross, a form of abandonment, and it is impossible for anyone to awake and observe its sordid consequences save with a faint sense of recent dissipation, of minute personal disquiet and remorse.

Patrick Hamilton *Slaves of Solitude*

17 Sleep and watchfulness, both of them, when immoderate, constitute disease.

Hippocrates (c. 460 BC–c. 377 BC) Greek physician. *Aphorisms*, II

18 Three natural anaesthetics . . . sleep, fainting, death.

Oliver Wendell Holmes (1809–94) US writer and physician. *Medical Essays*, 'The Medical Profession in Massachusetts'

19 Insomnia never comes to a man who has to get up exactly at six o'clock. Insomnia troubles only those who can sleep any time.

Elbert G. Hubbard (1856–1915) *The Philistine*, 'In Re Muldoon'

20 He's a wicked man that comes after children when they won't go to bed and throws handfuls of sand in their eyes.

Ernst Hoffmann (1776–1822) German composer. *The Sandman*

21 Now deep in my bed I turn
And the world turns on the other side.

Elizabeth Jennings (1926–) British poet *In the Night*

22 O soft embalmer of the still midnight.
John Keats (1795–1821) British poet. *To Sleep*

23 Turn the key deftly in the oiled wards,
And seal the hushed casket of my soul.
John Keats *To Sleep*

24 How do people go to sleep? I'm afraid I've lost the knack. I might try busting myself smartly over the temple with the nightlight. I might repeat to myself, slowly and soothingly, a list of quotations beautiful from minds profound; if I can remember any of the damn things.
Dorothy Parker (1893–1967) US writer. *The Little Hours*

25 Slepe is the nouryshment and food of a sucking child.
Thomas Phaer (c. 1510–60) *The Boke of Chyldren*

26 Those no-sooner-have-I-touched-the-pillow people are past my comprehension. There is something bovine about them.
J. B. Priestley (1894–1984) British novelist. *All About Ourselves*

27 Our foster nurse of nature is repose.
William Shakespeare (1564–1616) English dramatist and poet. *King Lear*, IV

28 Sleep that knits up the ravell'd sleave of care,
The death of each day's life, sore labour's bath,
Balm of hurt minds, great nature's second course,
Chief nourisher in life's feast.
William Shakespeare *Macbeth*, II:2

29 Sleep's the only medicine that gives ease.
Sophocles (c. 496–406 BC) Greek dramatist. *Philoctetes*, 766

30 Of all the soft, delicious functions of nature this is the chiefest; what a happiness it is to man, when the anxieties and passions of the day are over.
Laurence Sterne (1713–68) Irish-born English novelist.

31 Sleep, Death's twin-brother, knows not Death,
Nor can I dream of thee as dead.
Alfred, Lord Tennyson (1809–92) British poet. *In Memoriam*, LXVIII

32 There ain't no way to find out why a snorer can't hear himself snore.
Mark Twain (Samuel Langhorne Clemens; 1835–1910) US writer. *Tom Sawyer Abroad*, Ch. 10

33 It was the time when first sleep begins for weary
mortals and by the gift of the gods creeps over them
most welcomely.
Virgil (Publius Vergilius Maro; 70–19 BC) Roman poet. *Aeneid*, Bk. II

34 That sweet, deep sleep, so close to tranquil death.
Virgil *Aeneid*, VI

35 I haven't been to sleep for over a year. That's why I go to bed early. One needs more rest if one doesn't sleep.
Evelyn Waugh (1903–66) British novelist. *Decline and Fall*, Pt. II, Ch. 3

36 I believe the greatest asset a head of state can have is the ability to get a good night's sleep.
Harold Wilson (1916–) British politician and prime minister. *The World Tonight*, BBC Radio, 16 Apr 1975

37 Dear God! the very houses seem asleep;
And all that mighty heart is lying still!
William Wordsworth (1770–1850) British poet. *Sonnets*, 'Composed upon Westminster Bridge'

SMALLNESS

See also triviality

1 The best things come in small parcels.
Proverb

2 The Microbe is so very small
You cannot make him out at all.
Hilaire Belloc (1870–1953) French-born British poet. *More Beasts for Worse Children*, 'The Microbe'

3 One cubic foot less of space and it would have constituted adultery.
Robert Benchley (1889–1945) US humorist. Describing an office shared with Dorothy Parker. Attrib.

4 Small is beautiful.
E. F. Schumacher (1911–77) German-born British economist. Title of book

SMITH, Sydney

(1771–1845) British clergyman, essayist, and wit. He helped to found the *Edinburgh Review* (1802), and published many of his sermons, essays, speeches, and letters.

1 Mankind are always happy for having been happy, so that if you make them happy now, you make them happy twenty years hence by the memory of it.
Elementary Sketches of Moral Philosophy

2 The moment the very name of Ireland is mentioned, the English seem to bid adieu to common feeling, common prudence, and common sense, and to act with the barbarity of tyrants, and the fatuity of idiots.
The Letters of Peter Plymley

3 They are written as if sin were to be taken out of man like Eve out of Adam – by putting him to sleep.
Referring to boring sermons. *Anecdotes of the Clergy* (J. Larwood)

4 Heat, madam! It was so dreadful that I found there was nothing for it but to take off my flesh and sit in my bones.
Discussing the hot weather with a lady acquaintance. *Lives of the Wits* (H. Pearson)

5 You never expected justice from a company, did you? They have neither a soul to lose nor a body to kick.
Memoir (Lady Holland)

6 What you don't know would make a great book.
Memoir (Lady Holland)

7 That knuckle-end of England – that land of Calvin, oat-cakes, and sulphur.
Memoir (Lady Holland)

8 How can a bishop marry? How can he flirt? The most he can say is, 'I will see you in the vestry after service.'
Memoir (Lady Holland)

9 You find people ready enough to do the Samaritan, without the oil and twopence.
Memoir (Lady Holland)

10 My definition of marriage : . . . .it resembles a pair of shears, so joined that they cannot be separated; often moving in opposite directions, yet always punishing anyone who comes between them.
Memoir (Lady Holland)

11 He has occasional flashes of silence, that make his conversation perfectly delightful.
Referring to Lord Macaulay. *Memoir* (Lady Holland)

12 Minorities . . . are almost always in the right.

The Smith of Smiths (H. Pearson), Ch. 9

13 I am just going to pray for you at St Paul's, but with no very lively hope of success.

On meeting an acquaintance. *The Smith of Smiths* (H. Pearson), Ch. 13

14 I look upon Switzerland as an inferior sort of Scotland.

Letter to Lord Holland, 1815

15 He who drinks a tumbler of London water has literally in his stomach more animated beings than there are men, women and children on the face of the globe.

Letter

16 You must not think me necessarily foolish because I am facetious, nor will I consider you necessarily wise because you are grave.

Letter to Bishop Blomfield

17 No furniture so charming as books.

Memoir (Lady Holland)

18 He rose by gravity; I sank by levity.

Comparing his career with that of his brother, Robert Percy Smith. Attrib.

SMOKING

See also abstinence

1 It is better to be without a wife for a bit than without tobacco for an hour.

Proverb

2 Tobacco hic,
Will make a man well if he be sick.

Proverb

3 Caution: Cigarette Smoking May Be Hazardous to Your Health.

Anonymous Statement required on cigarette packages and cartons by the 89th US Congress, 1st Session

4 The Elizabethan age might be better named the beginning of the smoking era.

J. M. Barrie (1860–1937) British novelist and dramatist. *My Lady Nicotine*

5 Certainly not – if you don't object if I'm sick.

Thomas Beecham (1879–1961) British conductor. When asked whether he minded if someone smoked in a non-smoking compartment. Attrib.

6 No matter what Aristotle and all philosophy may say, there's nothing like tobacco. 'Tis the passion of decent folk; he who lives without tobacco isn't worthy of living.

Molière (Jean Baptiste Poquelin; 1622–73) French dramatist. *Don Juan, ou le festin de Pierre*, I:1

7 Tobacco, divine, rare, superexcellent tobacco, which goes far beyond all their panaceas, potable gold, and philosopher's stones, a sovereign remedy to all diseases.

Robert Burton (1577–1640) English scholar and explorer. *Anatomy of Melancholy*

8 Jones – (who, I'm glad to say,
Asked leave of Mrs J. –)
Daily absorbs a clay
After his labours.

C. S. Calverley (1831–84) British poet. *Ode to Tobacco*

9 I must point out that my rule of life prescribed as an absolutely sacred rite smoking cigars and also the drinking of alcohol before, after, and if need be during all meals and in the intervals between them.

Winston Churchill (1874–1965) British statesman. Said during a lunch with the Arab leader Ibn Saud, when told that the king's religion forbade smoking and alcohol. *The Second World War*

10 Smokers, male and female, inject and excuse idleness in their lives every time they light a cigarette.

Colette (1873–1954) French novelist. *Earthly Paradise*, 'Freedom'

11 It is quite a three-pipe problem.

Arthur Conan Doyle (1856–1930) British writer. *The Red-Headed League*

12 I have seen many a man turn his gold into smoke, but you are the first who has turned smoke into gold.

Elizabeth I (1533–1603) Queen of England. Speaking to Sir Walter Raleigh

13 What smells so? Has somebody been burning a Rag, or is there a Dead Mule in the Back yard? No, the Man is Smoking a Five-Cent Cigar.

Eugene Field (1850–95) US poet and journalist. *The Tribune Primer*, 'The Five-Cent Cigar'

14 Tobacco surely was designed
To poison, and destroy mankind.

Philip Freneau (1752–1832) US poet. *Poems*, 'Tobacco'

15 What a blessing this smoking is! perhaps the greatest that we owe to the discovery of America.

Arthur Helps (1813–75) British historian. *Friends in Council*

16 Tobacco is a dirty weed. I like it.
It satisfies no normal need. I like it.
It makes you thin, it makes you lean,
It takes the hair right off your bean.
It's the worst darn stuff I've ever seen.
I like it.

Graham Lee Hemminger (1896–1949) *Penn State Froth*, Nov 1915

17 But when I don't smoke I scarcely feel as if I'm living. I don't feel as if I'm living unless I'm killing myself.

Russell Hoban *Turtle Diary*, Ch. 7

18 A custom loathsome to the eye, hateful to the nose, harmful to the brain, dangerous to the lungs, and in the black, stinking fume thereof, nearest resembling the horrible Stygian smoke of the pit that is bottomless.

James I (1566–1625) King of England. *A Counterblast to Tobacco*

19 Neither do thou lust after that tawney weed tobacco.

Ben Jonson (1573–1637) English dramatist. *Bartholomew Fair*, II:6

20 Ods me, I marvel what pleasure or felicity they have in taking their roguish tobacco. It is good for nothing but to choke a man, and fill him full of smoke and embers.

Ben Jonson *Every Man in His Humour*, III:5

21 Smoking . . . is a shocking thing, blowing smoke out of our mouths into other people's mouths, eyes and noses, and having the same thing done to us.

Samuel Johnson (1709–84) English lexicographer. *Tour to the Hebrides* (James Boswell)

22 The tobacco business is a conspiracy against womanhood and manhood. It owes its origin to that scoundrel Sir Walter Raleigh, who was likewise the founder of American slavery.

Dr. John Harvey Kellogg *Tobacco*

23 A woman is only a woman, but a good cigar is a smoke.

Rudyard Kipling (1865–1936) Indian-born British writer and poet. *The Betrothed*

24 It is now proved beyond doubt that smoking is one of the leading causes of statistics.

Fletcher Knebel *Reader's Digest*, Dec 1961

25 This very night I am going to leave off tobacco! Surely there must be some other world in which this unconquerable purpose shall be realized. The soul hath not her generous aspirings implanted in her in vain.

Charles Lamb (1775–1834) British essayist. Letter to Thomas Manning, 26 Dec 1815

26 Dr Parr . . . asked him, how he had acquired his power of smoking at such a rate? Lamb replied, 'I toiled after it, sir, as some men toil after virtue.'

Charles Lamb *Memoirs of Charles Lamb* (Talfourd)

27 This vice brings in one hundred million francs in taxes every year. I will certainly forbid it at once – as soon as you can name a virtue that brings in as much revenue.

Napoleon III (1808–73) French emperor. Reply when asked to ban smoking. *Anekdotenschatz* (H. Hoffmeister)

28 Cigarettes are killers that travel in packs.

Mary S. Ott *Bartlett's Unfamiliar Quotations* (Leonard Louis Levinson)

29 My doctor has always told me to smoke. He even explains himself: 'Smoke, my friend. Otherwise someone else will smoke in your place.'

Erik Satie (1866–1925) French composer. *Mémoires d'un amnésique*

30 I have every sympathy with the American who was so horrified by what he had read of the effects of smoking that he gave up reading.

Henry G. Strauss *Quotations for Speakers and Writers* (A. Andrews)

31 I asked a coughing friend of mine why he doesn't stop smoking. 'In this town it wouldn't do any good,' he explained. 'I happen to be a chain breather.'

Robert Sylvester (1907–75) US writer. *Bartlett's Unfamiliar Quotations* (Leonard Louis Levinson)

32 We shall not refuse tobacco the credit of being sometimes medical, when used temperately, though an acknowledged poison.

Jesse Torrey (1787–1834) *The Moral Instructor*, Pt. IV

33 When I was young, I kissed my first woman, and smoked my first cigarette on the same day. Believe me, never since have I wasted any more time on tobacco.

Arturo Toscanini (1867–1957) Italian conductor.

34 To cease smoking is the easiest thing I ever did. I ought to know because I've done it a thousand times.

Mark Twain (Samuel L. Clemens; 1835–1910) US writer.

35 There are people who strictly deprive themselves of each and every eatable, drinkable and smokable which has in any way acquired a shady reputation. They pay this price for health. And health is all they get for it.

Mark Twain (Samuel L. Clemens; 1835–1910) US writer.

36 Tobacco drieth the brain, dimmeth the sight, vitiateth the smell, hurteth the stomach, destroyeth the concoction, disturbeth the humors and spirits, corrupteth the breath, induceth a trembling of the limbs, exsiccateth the windpipe, lungs, and liver, annoyeth the milt, scorcheth the heart, and causeth the blood to be adjusted.

Tobias Venner (1577–1660) *Via Recta ad Vitam Longam*

37 A cigarette is the perfect type of a perfect pleasure. It is exquisite, and it leaves one unsatisfied. What more can one want?

Oscar Wilde (1854–1900) Irish-born British dramatist. *The Picture of Dorian Gray*, Ch. 6

SNOBBERY

See also aristocracy, class, one-upmanship

1 In our way we were both snobs, and no snob welcomes another who has risen with him.

Cecil Beaton (1904–80) British photographer. Referring to Evelyn Waugh. Attrib.

2 And this is good old Boston,
The home of the bean and the cod,
Where the Lowells talk only to Cabots,
And the Cabots talk only to God.

John Collins Bossidy (1860–1928) US writer. Toast at Holy Cross Alumni dinner, 1910

3 Of course they have, or I wouldn't be sitting here talking to someone like you.

Barbara Cartland (1902–) British romantic novelist. When asked in a radio interview whether she thought that British class barriers had broken down. *Class* (J. Cooper)

4 I've danced with a man, who's danced with a girl, who's danced with the Prince of Wales.

Herbert Farjeon (1887–1945) British writer. *Picnic*

5 His hatred of snobs was a derivative of his snobbishness, but made the simpletons (in other words, everyone) believe that he was immune from snobbishness.

Marcel Proust (1871–1922) French novelist. *À la recherche du temps perdu: Le côté de Guermantes*

6 Skullion had little use for contraceptives at the best of times. Unnatural, he called them, and placed them in the lower social category of things along with elastic-sided boots and made-up bow ties. Not the sort of attire for a gentleman.

Tom Sharpe (1928–) British novelist. *Porterhouse Blue*, Ch. 9

7 I mustn't go on singling out names. One must not be a name-dropper, as Her Majesty remarked to me yesterday.

Norman St John Stevas (1929–) British politician. Speech, Museum of the Year luncheon, 20 June 1979

8 He who meanly admires mean things is a Snob.

William Makepeace Thackeray (1811–63) British novelist. *The Book of Snobs*, Ch. 2

9 It is impossible, in our condition of society, not to be sometimes a Snob.

William Makepeace Thackeray *The Book of Snobs*, Ch. 3

10 She was – but I assure you that she was a very bad cook.

Louis Adolphe Thiers (1797–1877) French statesman and historian. Defending his social status after someone had remarked that his mother had been a cook. Attrib.

11 My dear – the people we should have been seen dead with.

Rebecca West (Cicely Isabel Fairfield; 1892–1983) British novelist and journalist. Cable sent to Noel Coward after learning they had both been on a Nazi death list. *Times Literary Supplement*, 1 Oct 1982

12 CECILY. When I see a spade I call it a spade.

GWENDOLEN. I am glad to say I have never seen a spade. It is obvious that our social spheres have been widely different.

Oscar Wilde (1854–1900) Irish-born British dramatist. *The Importance of Being Earnest*, II

13 Never speak disrespectfully of Society, Algernon. Only people who can't get into it do that.

Oscar Wilde *The Importance of Being Earnest*, III

14 I don't owe a penny to a single soul

– not counting tradesmen, of course.

P. G. Wodehouse (1881–1975) British humorous novelist. *My Man Jeeves*, 'Jeeves and the Hard-Boiled Egg'

SOBRIETY

See alcohol, drunkenness

SOCIALISM

See also Communism, Marxism

1 A divorced woman on the throne of the House of Windsor would be a pretty big feather in the cap of that bunch of rootless intellectuals, alien Jews and international pederasts who call themselves the Labour Party.

Alan Bennett (1934–) British playwright and actor. Parodying Bulldog Drummond. *Forty Years On*

2 Why is it always the intelligent people who are socialists?

Alan Bennett (1934–) British playwright and actor. *Forty Years On*

3 The language of priorities is the religion of Socialism.

Aneurin Bevan (1897–1960) British Labour politician. *Aneurin Bevan* (Vincent Brome), Ch. 1

4 Socialism in the context of modern society (means) the conquest of the commanding heights of the economy.

Aneurin Bevan Speech, Labour Party Conference, Nov 1959

5 . . . when internal and external forces that are hostile to socialism try to turn the development of some socialist country towards the restoration of a capitalist regime, when socialism in that country and the socialist community as a whole is threatened . . .

Leonid Brezhnev (1906–82) Soviet statesman. The 'Brezhnev doctrine', used to justify Russia's intervention in Czechoslovakia, stated the circumstances when Russia had a right to intervene.

6 The people's flag is deepest red;
It shrouded oft our martyred dead,
And ere their limbs grew stiff and cold,
Their heart's blood dyed its every fold.
Then raise the scarlet standard high!
Within its shade we'll live or die.
Tho' cowards flinch and traitors sneer,
We'll keep the red flag flying here.

James Connell (1852–1929) British socialist. Traditionally sung at the close of annual conferences of the British Labour Party. *The Red Flag*, in *Songs that Made History* (H. E. Piggot), Ch. 6

7 There is nothing in Socialismthat a little age or a little money will not cure.

Will Durant (1885–1982) US teacher, philosopher, and historian. Attrib.

8 Socialism can only arrive by bicycle.

José Antonio Viera Gallo (1943–) Chilean politician. *Energy and Equity* (Ivan Illich)

9 Only socialism would put up with it for so long. Capitalism would have gone bankrupt years ago.

Mikhail Gorbachov (1931–) Soviet statesman. Talking of sub-standard workmanship in the Soviet Union. TV documentary, 23 March 1987

10 The essence of perestroika lies in the fact that *it unites socialism with democracy* and revives the feminist concept of socialist construction both in theory and in practice.

Mikhail Gorbachov *Perestroika*

11 Well, what are you socialists going to do about me?

George V (1865–1936) King of the United Kingdom. To Ramsay MacDonald at his first meeting as prime minister. Attrib.

12 We are all Socialists now.

William Harcourt (1827–1904) British statesman. Attrib.

13 Compassion is not a sloppy, sentimental feeling for people who are underprivileged or sick . . . it is an absolutely practical belief that, regardless of a person's background, ability or ability to pay, he should be provided with the best that society has to offer.

Neil Kinnock (1942–) British politician. Maiden speech, House of Commons, 1970

14 It is inconceivable that we could transform this society without a major extension of public ownership.

Neil Kinnock *Marxism Today*, 1983

15 Under socialism *all* will govern in turn and will soon become accustomed to no one governing.

Lenin (Vladimir Ilich Ulyanov; 1870–1924) Russian revolutionary leader. *The State and Revolution*, Ch. 6

16 We shall now proceed to construct the socialist order.

Lenin First words to the Congress of Soviets after the capture of the Winter Palace, 26 Oct 1917

17 In so far as socialism means anything, it must be about the wider distribution of smoked salmon and caviar.

Richard Marsh (1928–) British businessman. Remark, Oct 1976

18 As with the Christian religion, the worst advertisement for Socialism is its adherents.

George Orwell (Eric Blair; 1903–50) British novelist. *The Road to Wigan Pier*, Ch. 11

19 To the ordinary working man, the sort you would meet in any pub on Saturday night, Socialism does not mean much more than better wages and shorter hours and nobody bossing you about.

George Orwell *The Road to Wigan Pier*, Ch. 11

20 The higher-water mark, so to speak, of Socialist literature is W. H. Auden, a sort of gutless Kipling.

George Orwell *The Road to Wigan Pier*, Ch. 11

21 I am a socialist – and I only wish the Labour Party was.

Donald Soper (1903–) British Methodist Minister and writer. *Any Questions* (radio program), 11 May 1979

22 In place of the conception of the Power-State we are led to that of the Welfare-State.

Archbishop William Temple (1881–1944) British churchman. *Citizen and Churchman*, Ch. 11

23 State socialism is totally alien to the British character.

Margaret Thatcher (1925–) British politician and prime minister. *The Times*, 1983

24 We are redefining and we are restating our socialism in terms of the scientific revolution . . . the Britain that is going to be forged in the white heat of this revolution will be no place for restrictive practices or out-dated methods on either side of industry.

Harold Wilson (1916–) British politician and prime minister. Speech, Labour Party Conference, 1 Oct 1963

25 . . . if there was one word I would use to identify modern socialism, it was 'Science'.

Harold Wilson (1916–) British politician and prime minister. Speech, 17 June 1967

SOCIETY

See also mankind

1 I am a sociable worker.
Brendan Behan (1923–64) Irish playwright. *The Hostage*, II

2 Man was formed for society.
William Blackstone (1723–80) British jurist. *Commentaries on the Laws of England*, Introduction

3 There are those who collect the refuse of the public streets, but in order to be received into the band it is necessary to have been born one of the Hereditary Confederacy of Superfluity Removers and Abandoned Oddment Gatherers.
Ernest Bramah (1869–1942) British writer. *Kai Lung Unrolls His Mat*

4 No man is an Island, entire of itself; every man is a piece of the Continent, a part of the main.
John Donne (1573–1631) English poet. *Devotions*, 17

5 They hated everybody, and abused everybody, and would sit together in White's bay window, or the pit boxes at the Opera, weaving tremendous crammers. They swore a good deal, never laughed, looked hazy after dinner, and had most of them been patronized at one time or other by Brummel and the Prince Regent.
Rees Howell Gronow (1795–1865) British MP and social observer. Referring to Regency 'dandies'. *Reminiscences*, Vol. I

6 The permissive society has been allowed to become a dirty phrase. A better phrase is the civilized society.
Roy Jenkins (1920–) British Liberal Democrat politician (formerly a Labour Home Secretary). Speech, Abingdon, 19 July 1969

7 The great society is a place where men are more concerned with the quality of their goods than the quantity of their goods.
Lyndon B. Johnson (1908–73) US statesman. Speech, 22 May 1964

8 If a free society cannot help the many who are poor, it cannot save the few who are rich.
John Fitzgerald Kennedy (1917–63) US statesman. Speech, 20 Jan 1961

9 People who need people are the luckiest people in the world.
Bob Merrill (Robert Merrill; 1890–1977) US lyricist and composer. *People Who Need People*

10 Our civilization . . . has not yet fully recovered from the shock of its birth – the transition from the tribal or 'closed society', with its submission to magical forces, to the 'open society' which sets free the critical powers of man.
Karl Popper (1902–) Austrian-born British philosopher. *The Open Society and Its Enemies*

11 Man is not a solitary animal, and so long as social life survives, self-realization cannot be the supreme principle of ethics.
Bertrand Russell (1872–1970) British philosopher. *History of Western Philosophy*, 'Romanticism'

12 Society is no comfort
To one not sociable.
William Shakespeare (1564–1616) English dramatist. *Cymbeline*, IV:2

13 The liberty the citizen enjoys is to be measured not by the governmental machinery he lives under, whether representative or other, but by the paucity of restraints it imposes on him.
Herbert Spencer (1820–1903) British philosopher. *Man versus the State*

14 Man is a social animal.
Benedict Spinoza (Baruch de Spinoza; 1632–77) Dutch philosopher. *Ethics*

15 What men call social virtues, good fellowship, is commonly but the virtue of pigs in a litter, which lie close together to keep each other warm. It brings men together in crowds and mobs in bar-rooms and elsewhere, but it does not deserve the name of virtue.
Henry David Thoreau (1817–62) US writer. *Journal*, 1852

SOCIOLOGY

1 Sociology is the science with the greatest number of methods and the least results.
J. H. Poincaré *Science and Method*

2 Those terrible sociologists who are the astrologers and alchemists of our twentieth century.
Miguel de Unamuno y Jugo (1864–1936) Spanish writer. *Fanatical scepticism*

SOLDIERS

See also army, officers, war

1 Some talk of Alexander, and some of Hercules,
Of Hector and Lysander, and such great names as these;
But of all the world's brave heroes there's none that can compare
With a tow, row, row, row, row, row for the British Grenadier.
Anonymous *The British Grenadiers*

2 The mounted knight is irresistable; he would bore his way through the walls of Babylon.
Anna Comnena Describing the French knights of the First Crusade, who passed through Constantinople in 1097. *The Alexiad*

3 It's Tommy this, an' Tommy that, an' 'Chuck him out, the brute!'
But it's 'Saviour of 'is country' when the guns begin to shoot.
Rudyard Kipling (1865–1936) Indian-born British writer. *Tommy*

4 Oh, it's Tommy this, an' Tommy that, an' 'Tommy, go away';
But it's 'Thank you, Mister Atkins,' when the band begins to play.
Rudyard Kipling *Tommy*

5 Lions led by donkeys.
Erich Ludendorff (1865–1937) German general. Referring to British troops in World War I. Attrib.

6 They're changing guard at Buckingham Palace
Christopher Robin went down with Alice.
Alice is marrying one of the guard.
'A soldier's life is terrible hard,'
Says Alice.
A. A. Milne (1882–1956) British writer. *When We Were Very Young*, 'Buckingham Palace'

7 Then was seen with what a strength and majesty the British soldier fights.
Sir William Napier (1785–1860) British general and historian. *History of the War in the Peninsula* Bk. XII, Ch. 6

8 Every French soldier carries in his cartridge-pouch the baton of a marshal of France.
Napoleon I (1769–1821) French emperor. *La Vie militaire sous l'empire* (E. Blaze)

9 It must have been a little trying to the colonel who came up to him and asked him if he was fond of horses to be told 'No but I adore giraffes.'
John Beverley Nichols (1898–1983) British writer. Referring to Osbert Sitwell. *Twenty Five*

10 Soldiers are citizens of death's grey land,
Drawing no dividend from time's tomorrows.
Siegfried Sassoon (1886–1967) British poet. *Dreamers*

11 The soldier's body becomes a stock

of accessories that are not his property.
Antoine de Saint-Exupéry (1900–44) French novelist and aviator. *Flight To Arras*

12 A soldier is better accommodated than with a wife.
William Shakespeare (1564–1616) English dramatist. *Henry IV, Part 2,* III:2

13 You are a very poor soldier: a chocolate cream soldier!
George Bernard Shaw (1856–1950) Irish dramatist and critic. *Arms and the Man,* I

14 I never expect a soldier to think.
George Bernard Shaw *The Devil's Disciple,* III

15 They're overpaid, overfed, oversexed and over here.
Tommy Trinder (1909–) British entertainer. Referring to the G.I.s. Attrib.

16 He (the recruiting officer) asked me 'Why tanks?' I replied that I preferred to go into battle sitting down.
Peter Ustinov (1921–) British actor. *Dear Me*

17 It all depends upon that article there.
Duke of Wellington (1769–1852) British general and statesman. Indicating a passing infantryman when asked if he would be able to defeat Napoleon. *The Age of Elegance* (A. Bryant)

SOLITUDE

See also loneliness

1 Whosoever is delighted in solitude is either a wild beast or a god.
Francis Bacon (1561–1626) English philosopher. *Essays,* 'Of Friendship'

2 Alone, alone, all, all alone,
Alone on a wide wide sea!
And never a saint took pity on
My soul in agony.
Samuel Taylor Coleridge (1772–1834) British poet. *The Rime of the Ancient Mariner,* IV

3 Oh for a lodge in some vast wilderness,
Some boundless contiguity of shade,
Where rumour of oppression and deceit,
Of unsuccessful or successful war,
Might never reach me more!
William Cowper (1731–1800) British poet. *The Task*

4 Society, friendship, and love,
Divinely bestowed upon man,
Oh, had I the wings of a dove,
How soon would I taste you again!
William Cowper *Verses Supposed to be Written by Alexander Selkirk*

5 I am monarch of all I survey,
My right there is none to dispute;
From the centre all round to the sea
I am lord of the fowl and the brute.
Oh, solitude! where are the charms
That sages have seen in thy face?
Better dwell in the midst of alarms,
Than reign in this horrible place.
William Cowper *Verses Supposed to be Written by Alexander Selkirk*

6 As *sickness* is the greatest misery so the greatest misery of sickness is *solitude. Solitude* is a torment which is not threatened in *hell* itselfe.
John Donne (1573–1631) English poet. *Awakenings* (Oliver W. Sacks)

7 I want to be alone.
Greta Garbo (1905–) Swedish-born US film star. Words spoken by Garbo in the film *Grand Hotel,* and associated with her for the rest of her career.

8 Far from the madding crowd's ignoble strife,
Their sober wishes never learn'd to stray;
Along the cool sequester'd vale of life
They kept the noiseless tenor of their way.
Thomas Gray (1716–71) British poet. *Elegy Written in a Country Churchyard*

9 One of the pleasantest things in the world is going on a journey; but I like to go by myself.
William Hazlitt (1778–1830) British essayist. *On Going a Journey*

10 It is a fine thing to be out on the hills alone. A man can hardly be a beast or a fool alone on a great mountain.
Francis Kilvert (1840–79) British diarist and clergyman. *Diary,* 29 May 1871

11 In solitude
What happiness? who can enjoy alone,
Or, all enjoying, what contentment find?
John Milton (1608–74) English poet. *Paradise Lost,* Bk. VIII

12 I want to be a movement
But there's no one on my side.
Adrian Mitchell (1932–) British writer and dramatist. *Loose Leaf Poem*

13 A man must keep a little back shop where he can be himself without reserve. In solitude alone can he know true freedom.
Michel de Montaigne (1533–92) French essayist. *Essais,* I

14 Solitude is the playfield of Satan.
Vladimir Nabokov (1899–1977) Russian-born US novelist. *Pale Fire*

15 I never found the companion that was so companionable as solitude.
Henry David Thoreau (1817–62) US writer. *Walden,* 'Solitude'

16 Alas, Lord, I am powerful but alone. Let me sleep the sleep of the earth.
Alfred de Vigny (1797–1863) French writer. *Moïse*

17 For oft, when on my couch I lie
In vacant or in pensive mood,
They flash upon that inward eye
Which is the bliss of solitude.
William Wordsworth (1770–1850) British poet. *I Wandered Lonely as a Cloud*

18 Behold her, single in the field,
Yon solitary Highland lass!
William Wordsworth *The Solitary Reaper*

19 I will arise and go now, and go to Innisfree,
And a small cabin build there, of clay and wattles made;
Nine bean rows will I have there, a hive for the honey bee,
And live alone in the bee-loud glade.
W. B. Yeats (1865–1939) Irish poet. *The Lake Isle of Innisfree*

SONG

1 Some of the songs making the rounds now will be popular when Bach, Beethoven and Wagner are forgotten – but not before.
Louis Sobel *Encyclopedia of Quotations About Music*

2 There are few moments during her recital when one can relax and feel confident that she will make her goal, which is the end of the song.
Paul Hume (1915–) US music critic. Referring to Margaret Truman. *Washington Post*

SORROW

See also despair, melancholy, mourning, regret

1 A wound heals but the scar remains.
Proverb

2 Every tear from every eye
Becomes a babe in Eternity.
William Blake (1757–1827) British poet. *Auguries of Innocence*

3 Do you hear the children weeping,
O my brothers,
Ere the sorrow comes with years?
Elizabeth Barrett Browning (1806–61) British poet. *The Cry of the Children*

4 Follow thy fair sun, unhappy shadow.
Thomas Campion (1567–1620) English poet. *Follow Thy Fair Sun*

5 One often calms one's grief by recounting it.
Pierre Corneille (1606–84) French dramatist. *Polyeucte*, I:3

6 Tears were to me what glass beads are to African traders.
Quentin Crisp (c. 1910–) Model, publicist, and writer. *The Naked Civil Servant*

7 There is no greater sorrow than to recall a time of happiness when in misery.
Dante (1265–1321) Italian poet. *Divine Comedy, Inferno*, V

8 *Adieu tristesse*
Bonjour tristesse
Tu es inscrite dans les lignes du plafond.
Farewell sadness
Good day sadness
You are written in the lines of the ceiling.
Paul Éluard (Eugène Grindel; 1895–1952) French surrealist poet. *La Vie immédiate*

9 A moment of time may make us unhappy for ever.
John Gay (1685–1732) English poet and dramatist. *The Beggar's Opera*

10 Sadness is almost never anything but a form of fatigue.
André Gide (1869–1951) French novelist. *Journals*, 1922

11 They say my verse is sad: no wonder;
Its narrow measure spans
Tears of eternity, and sorrow,
Not mine, but man's.
A. E. Housman (1859–1936) British scholar and poet. *Last Poems*, 'Fancy's Knell'

12 Then Sir Launcelot saw her visage, but he wept not greatly, but sighed!
Thomas Malory (1400–71) English writer. *Morte d'Arthur*, Bk. XXI, Ch. 11

13 Tears such as angels weep, burst forth.
John Milton (1608–74) English poet. *Paradise Lost*, Bk. I

14 Art thou weary, art thou languid,
Art thou sore distressed?
John Mason Neale (1818–66) British churchman. *Art thou Weary?*

15 Sorrow is tranquillity remembered in emotion.
Dorothy Parker (1893–1967) US writer. *Sentiment*

16 Line after line my gushing eyes o'erflow,
Led through a sad variety of woe.
Alexander Pope (1688–1744) British poet. *Eloisa to Abelard*

17 Not louder shrieks to pitying heav'n are cast,
When husbands, or when lap-dogs breathe their last.
Alexander Pope *The Rape of the Lock*, III

18 As soon as one is unhappy one becomes moral.
Marcel Proust (1871–1922) French novelist. *À la recherche du temps perdu: À l'ombre des jeunes filles en fleurs*

19 Happiness is beneficial for the body, but it is grief that develops the powers of the mind.
Marcel Proust *À la recherche du temps perdu: Le temps retrouvé*

20 It is such a secret place, the land of tears.
Antoine de Saint-Exupéry (1900–44) French novelist and aviator. *The Little Prince*, Ch. 7

21 He's simply got the instinct for being unhappy highly developed.
Saki (Hector Hugh Munro; 1870–1916) British writer. *The Match-Maker*

22 When sorrows come, they come not single spies,
But in battalions.
William Shakespeare (1564–1616) English dramatist. *Hamlet*, IV:5

23 If you have tears, prepare to shed them now.
William Shakespeare *Julius Caesar*, III:2

24 Down, thou climbing sorrow,
Thy element's below.
William Shakespeare *King Lear*, II:4

25 This sorrow's heavenly,
It strikes where it doth love.
William Shakespeare *Othello*, V:2

26 The secret of being miserable is to have leisure to bother about whether you are happy or not.
George Bernard Shaw (1856–1950) Irish dramatist and critic. *Misalliance*, Preface

27 'Tis held that sorrow makes us wise.
Alfred, Lord Tennyson (1809–92) British poet. *In Memoriam*, CXIII

28 My regret
Becomes an April violet,
And buds and blossoms like the rest.
Alfred, Lord Tennyson *In Memoriam*, CXV

29 Tears, idle tears, I know not what they mean,
Tears from the depth of some divine despair.
Alfred, Lord Tennyson *The Princess*, IV

30 Indescribable, O queen, is the grief you bid me to renew.
Virgil (Publius Vergilius Maro; 70–19 BC) Roman poet. The opening words of Aeneas' account to Dido of the fall of Troy. *Aeneid*, Bk. II

SOUL

1 The eyes are the window of the soul.
Proverb

2 We cannot kindle when we will
The fire which in the heart resides,
The spirit bloweth and is still,
In mystery our soul abides.
Matthew Arnold (1822–88) British poet and critic. *Morality*

3 And see all sights from pole to pole,
And glance, and nod, and bustle by;
And never once possess our soul
Before we die.
Matthew Arnold *A Southern Night*

4 Disease is in essence the result of conflict between soul and mind – So long as our souls and personalities are in harmony all is joy and peace, happiness and health. It is when our personalities are led astray from the path laid down by the soul, either by our own wordly desires or by the persuasion of others, that a conflict arises.
Dr. Edward Bach (1880–1936) British doctor; founder of Bach Flower Remedies. *The Alternative Health Guide* (Brian Inglis and Ruth West)

5 Man has no Body distinct from his Soul; for that called Body is a portion of Soul discerned by the five Senses, the chief inlets of Soul in this age.
William Blake (1757–1827) British poet. *The Marriage of Heaven and Hell*, 'The Voice of the Devil'

6 It seems to me . . . highly dishonourable for a Reasonable Soul to live in so Divinely built a Mansion, as the Body she resides in, altogether unacquainted with the exquisite Structure of it.
Robert Boyle (1627–91) Irish scientist. *The Usefulness of Natural Philosphy*, Pt. I

7 Leave the flesh to the fate it was fit for! the spirit be thine!
Robert Browning (1812–89) British poet. *Saul*, XIII

8 Diseases . . . crucify the soul of man, attenuate our bodies, dry them, wither them, rivel them up like old apples, make them as so many Anatomies.
Robert Burton (1577–1640) English scholar and explorer. *The Anatomy of Melancholy*, Pt. I, Sect. 2

9 Diseases of the soul are more dangerous and more numerous than those of the body.
Cicero (106 BC–43 BC) Roman orator and statesman. *Tusculanarum Disputationum*, Bk III, Ch. 3

10 In the real dark night of the soul it is always three o'clock in the morning.
F. Scott Fitzgerald (1896–1940) US novelist. *See* ST JOHN OF THE CROSS *The Crack-Up*

11 That night, that year
Of now done darkness I wretch lay
wrestling with (my God!) my God.
Gerard Manley Hopkins (1844–99) British Jesuit and poet. *Carrion Comfort*

12 The dark night of the soul.
St John of the Cross (Juan de Yepes y Alvarez; 1542–91) Spanish churchman and poet. English translation of *Noche obscura del alma*, the title of a poem; *see also* F. SCOTT FITZGERALD

13 Nor let the beetle, nor the death-moth be
Your mournful Psyche.
John Keats (1795–1821) British poet. *Ode on Melancholy*

14 The soul is subject to health and disease, just as is the body. The health and disease of both . . . undoubtedly depend upon beliefs and customs, which are peculiar to mankind. Wherefore I call senseless beliefs and degenerate customs . . . diseases of humanity.
Maimonides (Moses ben Maimon; 1135–1204) Jewish philosopher and physician. *Aphorisms According to Galen*

15 And looks commercing with the skies,
Thy rapt soul sitting in thine eyes.
John Milton (1608–74) English poet. *Il Penseroso*

16 Every subject's duty is the king's; but every subject's soul is his own.
William Shakespeare (1564–1616) English dramatist. *Henry V*, IV:1

17 I am positive I have a soul; nor can all the books with which materialists have pestered the world ever convince me of the contrary.
Laurence Sterne (1713–68) Irish-born British writer. *A Sentimental Journey*, 'Maria, Moulines'

18 The human body is the best picture of the human soul.
Ludwig Wittgenstein (1889–1951) Austrian philosopher. *Philosophical Investigations*

19 Fair seed-time had my soul, and I grew up
Fostered alike by beauty and by fear.
William Wordsworth (1770–1850) British poet. *The Prelude*, I

SPACE

See also astronomy, discovery, exploration, moon, science, stars, sun, technology, universe

1 Tranquillity Base here – the Eagle has landed.
Neil Armstrong (1930–) US astronaut. The first words spoken on touchdown of the space module Apollo XI on the moon.

2 That's one small step for man, one giant leap for mankind.
Neil Armstrong Remark, 21 July 1969 Said on stepping onto the moon. Often quoted as, 'small step for a man . . . ' (which is probably what he intended). Remark, 21 July 1969

3 Don't tell me that man doesn't belong out there. Man belongs wherever he wants to go; and he'll do plenty well when he gets there.
Wernher von Braun (1912–77) German rocket engineer. Referring to space flights

4 Outer space is no place for a person of breeding.
Violet Bonham Carter (1887–1969) British politician. *The New Yorker*

5 The World would be a safer place,
If someone had a plan,
Before exploring Outer Space,
To find the Inner Man.
E. Y. Harburg (1896–1981) US songwriter.

6 OK, Houston, we have had a problem here . . . Houston, we have a problem.
James Lovell (1928–) US astronaut. After explosion on board Apollo XIII, 11 Apr 1970

7 And this certainly has to be the most historic phone call ever made.
Richard Milhous Nixon (1913–) US President. Telephone call to astronauts on moon, 20 July 1969.

8 The Right Stuff.
Tom Wolfe (1931–) US writer. Referring to people involved in the early US space program. Book title

SPARSENESS

1 As for the grass, it grew as scant as hair
In leprosy.
Robert Browning (1812–89) British poet. *Childe Roland to the Dark Tower Came*, XIII

SPEAKING

1 Outspoken by whom?
Dorothy Parker (1893–1967) US writer. When told that she was 'very outspoken'. Attrib.

SPECIALISTS

1 An internist is someone who knows everything and does nothing.
A surgeon is someone who does everything and knows nothing.
A psychiatrist is someone who knows nothing and does nothing.
A pathologist is someone who knows everything and does everything too late.
Anonymous

2 Choose your specialist and you choose your disease.
Anonymous *The Westminster Review*, 18 May 1906

3 A medical chest specialist is long-winded about the short-winded.
Kenneth T. Bird (1917–)

4 Consultant specialists are a degree more remote (like bishops!); and therefore (again like bishops) they need a double dose of Grace to keep them sensitive to the personal and the pastoral.
Geoffrey Fisher, Archbishop of Canterbury (1887–1972) British churchman. *Lancet*, 2:775, 1949

5 The specialist is a man who fears the other subjects.
Martin H. Fischer (1879–1962) *Fischerisms* (Howard Fabing and Ray Marr)

6 Given one well-trained physician of the highest type he will do better work for a thousand people than ten specialists.
William J. Mayo (1861–1939) US surgeon.

7 A general practitioner can no more become a specialist than an old shoe can become a dancing slipper. Both have developed habits which are immutable.
Frank Kittredge Paddock (1841–1901) Aphorism

8 Pediatricians eat because children don't.
Meyer A. Perlstein (1902–)

9 No man can be a pure specialist without being in the strict sense an idiot.
George Bernard Shaw (1856–1950) Irish dramatist and critic.

SPECULATION

1 While to deny the existence of an unseen kingdom is bad, to pretend that we know more about it than its bare existence is no better.
Samuel Butler (1835–1902) British writer. *Erewhon*, Ch. 15

2 If the world were good for nothing else, it is a fine subject for speculation.
William Hazlitt (1778–1830) British essayist. *Characteristics*

SPEECH

See also silence, speeches, verbosity, words

1 Save your breath to cool your porridge.
Proverb

2 Speak when you are spoken to.
Proverb

3 This god-forsaken city, with a climate so evil that no self-respecting singer would ever set foot in it! It is a catarrhal place that has been the cause through the centuries of the nasal Liverpool accent.
Thomas Beecham (1879–1961) British conductor. *Beecham Stories* (Harold Atkins and Archie Newman)

4 Let your speech be alway with grace, seasoned with salt, that ye may know how ye ought to answer every man.
Bible: Colossians 4:6

5 Let thy speech be short, comprehending much in few words; be as one that knoweth and yet holdeth his tongue.
Bible: Ecclesiasticus 32:8

6 Even so the tongue is a little member, and boasteth great things. Behold, how great a matter a little fire kindleth!
Bible: James 3:5

7 But the tongue can no man tame; it is an unruly evil, full of deadly poison.
Bible: James 3:8

8 To know how to say what others only know how to think is what makes men poets or sages; and to dare to say what others only dare to think makes men martyrs or reformers – or both.
Elizabeth Charles (1828–96) British writer. *Chronicle of the Schönberg-Cotta Family*

9 No, Sir, because I have time to think before I speak, and don't ask impertinent questions.
Erasmus Darwin (1731–1802) British physician, biologist, and poet. Reply when asked whether he found his stammer inconvenient. *Reminiscences of My Father's Everyday Life* (Sir Francis Darwin)

10 The metaphor is probably the most fertile power possessed by man.
José Ortega y Gasset (1883–1955) Spanish philosopher. *The Dehumanization of Art*

11 The true use of speech is not so much to express our wants as to conceal them.
Oliver Goldsmith (1728–74) Irish-born British writer. *Essays*, 'The Use of Language'

12 Most men make little use of their speech than to give evidence against their own understanding.
Lord Halifax (1633–95) English statesman. *Political, Moral, and Miscellaneous Thoughts and Reflections*

13 Talking and eloquence are not the same: to speak, and to speak well, are two things.
Ben Jonson (1573–1637) English dramatist. *Timber, or Discoveries made upon Men and Matter*

14 Speech is civilisation itself. The word, even the most contradictory word, preserves contact – it is silence which isolates.
Thomas Mann (1875–1955) German novelist. *The Magic Mountain*

15 The most precious things in speech are pauses.
Ralph Richardson (1902–83) British actor. Attrib.

16 But words once spoke can never be recall'd.
Earl of Roscommon (1633–85) Irish-born English poet. *Art of Poetry*

17 Words may be false and full of art,
Sighs are the natural language of the heart.
Thomas Shadwell (1642–92) English dramatist. *Psyche*, III

18 I don't want to talk grammar, I want to talk like a lady.
George Bernard Shaw (1856–1950) Irish dramatist and critic. *Pygmalion*

19 Speech was given to man to disguise his thoughts.
Talleyrand (Charles Maurice de Talleyrand-Périgord; 1754–1838) French politician. Attrib.

SPEECHES

See also brevity, sermons, verbosity

1 Frankly a pain in the neck.
Lord Altrincham (John Grigg; 1924–) British writer. Referring to Queen Elizabeth II's public speaking. *National and English Review*, Aug 1958

2 Mr Lloyd George spoke for a hundred and seventeen minutes, in which period he was detected only once in the use of an argument.
Arnold Bennett (1867–1931) British writer. *Things That Have Interested Me*, 'After the March Offensive'

3 Listening to a speech by Chamberlain is like paying a visit to Woolworths; everything in its place and nothing over sixpence.
Aneurin Bevan (1897–1960) Welsh Labour politician. In *Tribune*

4 I take the view, and always have done, that if you cannot say what you have to say in twenty minutes, you should go away and write a book about it.
Lord Brabazon of Tara (1910–74) British businessman and Conservative politician. Attrib.

5 An after-dinner speech should be like a lady's dress – long enough to cover the subject and short enough to be interesting.
R. A. Butler (1902–82) British Conservative politician. Remark made at an Anglo-Jewish dinner

6 He is one of those orators of whom it was well said, 'Before they get up they do not know what they are going to say; when they are speaking, they do not know what they are saying; and when they sit down, they do not know what they have said'.
Winston Churchill (1874–1965) British statesman. Referring to Lord Charles Beresford. Speech, House of Commons, 20 Dec 1912

7 Haven't you learned yet that I put something more than whisky into my speeches.
Winston Churchill To his son Randolph. Attrib.

8 Call that a maiden speech? I call it a brazen hussy of a speech.
Winston Churchill To A. P. Herbert. *Immortal Jester* (L. Frewin)

9 I dreamt that I was making a speech in the House. I woke up, and by Jove I was!
Duke of Devonshire (1833–1908) Conservative politician. *Thought and Adventures* (W. S. Churchill)

10 Did y'ever think, Ken, that making a speech on economics is a lot like pissing down your leg? It seems hot to you, but it never does to anyone else.
Lyndon B. Johnson (1908–73) US Democratic president. *A Life in Our Times*

11 For I have neither wit, nor words, nor worth,
Action, nor utterance, nor the power of speech,
To stir men's blood; I only speak right on.
William Shakespeare (1564–1616) English dramatist. *Julius Caesar*, III:2

12 Don't quote Latin; say what you have to say, and then sit down.
Duke of Wellington (1769–1852) British general and statesman. Advice to a new Member of Parliament. Attrib.

13 If you want me to talk for ten minutes I'll come next week. If you want me to talk for an hour I'll come tonight.
Woodrow Wilson (1856–1925) US statesman. Answering an invitation to make a speech. Attrib.

SPELLING

See also language, pronunciation, words, writing

1 Put it down a we, my lord, put it down a we!
Charles Dickens (1812–70) British novelist. *Pickwick Papers*, Ch. 34

2 They spell it Vinci and pronounce it Vinchy; foreigners always spell better than they pronounce.
Mark Twain (Samuel Langhorne Clemens; 1835–1910) US writer. *The Innocents Abroad*, Ch. 19

SPONTANEITY

See also impetuosity

1 Spontaneity is only a term for man's ignorance of the gods.
Samuel Butler (1835–1902) British writer. *Erewhon*, Ch. 25

2 *L'acte gratuite.*
The unmotivated action.
André Gide (1869–1951) French novelist. *Les Caves du Vatican*

3 Away with all ideals. Let each individual act spontaneously from the for ever incalculable prompting of the creative wellhead within him. There is no universal law.
D. H. Lawrence (1885–1930) British novelist. *Phoenix*, Preface to 'All Things are Possible' by Leo Shostov

4 Nothing prevents us from being natural so much as the desire to appear so.
Duc de la Rochefoucauld (1613–80) French writer. *Maximes*, 431

SPOONERISMS

Sayings associated with the Oxford clergyman and academic William Archibald Spooner (1844–1930).

1 You will find as you grow older that the weight of rages will press harder and harder on the employer.
Spooner (Sir W. Hayter), Ch. 6

2 I remember your name perfectly, but I just can't think of your face.

3 Kinquering Congs their titles take.
A scrambled announcement of the hymn in New College Chapel (probably apocryphal)

4 Let us drink to the queer old Dean.

5 Sir, you have tasted two whole worms; you have hissed all my mystery lectures and have been caught fighting a liar in the quad; you will leave Oxford by the town drain.

6 Poor soul – very sad; her late husband, you know, a very sad death – eaten by missionaries – poor soul.
Spooner (Sir W. Hayter)

SPORT AND GAMES

See also cricket, fishing, football, golf, horses, hunting

1 Anyone for tennis?
Anonymous

2 Float like a butterfly
Sting like a bee.
Muhammad Ali (Cassius Clay; 1942–) US boxer. Describing his boxing style.

3 The game isn't over till it's over.
Yogi Berra (1925–) US baseball player. Attrib.

4 Follow up! Follow up! Follow up! Follow up! Follow up!
Till the field ring again and again,
With the tramp of the twenty-two men,
Follow up!
E. E. Bowen (1836–1901) British writer. *Forty Years On* (the Harrow school song)

5 Life's too short for chess.
Henry James Byron (1834–84) British dramatist and actor. *Our Boys*, I

6 There is plenty of time to win this game, and to thrash the Spaniards too.
Francis Drake (1540–96) British navigator and admiral. Referring to the sighting of the Armada during a game of bowls, 20 July 1588. Attrib.

7 Exercise is bunk. If you are healthy, you don't need it: if you are sick, you shouldn't take it.
Henry Ford (1863–1947) US car manufacturer. Attrib.

8 Bullfighting is the only art in which the artist is in danger of death and in which the degree of brilliance in the performance is left to the fighter's honor.
Ernest Hemingway (1899–1961) US novelist. *Death in the Afternoon*, Ch. 9

9 When in doubt, win the trick.
Edmond Hoyle (1672–1769) English writer on card games. *Hoyle's Games*, 'Whist, Twenty-four Short Rules for Learners'

10 The only athletic sport I ever mastered was backgammon.
Douglas William Jerrold (1803–57) British dramatist. *Douglas Jerrold* (W. Jerrold), Vol. I, Ch. 1

11 It is unbecoming for a cardinal to ski badly.
John Paul II (Karol Wojtyla; 1920–) Polish pope (1978–). Replying to the suggestion that it was inappropriate for him, a cardinal, to ski. *John Paul II*

12 I am sorry I have not learned to play at cards. It is very useful in life: it generates kindness and consolidates society.
Samuel Johnson (1709–84) British lexicographer. *Tour to the Hebrides* (J. Boswell)

13 At what time does the dissipation of energy begin?
Lord Kelvin (1824–1907) British physicist. On realizing that his wife was planning an afternoon excursion. *Memories of a Scientific Life* (A. Fleming)

14 Man is a gaming animal. He must

always be trying to get the better in something or other.
Charles Lamb (1775–1834) British essayist. *Essays of Elia*, 'Mrs Battle's Opinions on Whist'

15 O, he flies through the air with the greatest of ease,
This daring young man on the flying trapeze.
George Leybourne (?–1884) British songwriter. *The Man on the Flying Trapeze*

16 I don't like this game.
Spike Milligan (1918–) British comic actor and author. *The Goon Show*

17 Serious sport has nothing to do with fair play. It is bound up with hatred, jealousy, boastfulness, disregard of all rules and sadistic pleasure in witnessing violence; in other words it is war minus the shooting.
George Orwell (Eric Blair; 1903–50) British novelist. *The Sporting Spirit*

18 Gamesmanship or The Art of Winning Games Without Actually Cheating.
Stephen Potter (1900–69) British writer. Book title

19 For when the One Great Scorer comes
To write against your name,
He marks – not that you won or lost –
But how you played the game.
Grantland Rice (1880–1954) US sportswriter. *Alumnus Football*

20 Show me a good and gracious loser and I'll show you a failure.
Knute Rockne (1888–1931) US football coach. Attrib.

21 It was remarked to me by the late Mr Charles Roupell . . . that to play billiards well was a sign of an ill-spent youth.
Herbert Spencer (1820–1903) British philosopher. *Life and Letters of Spencer* (Duncan), Ch. 20

22 I wanted a play that would paint the full face of sensuality, rebellion and revivalism. In South Wales these three phenomena have played second fiddle only to the Rugby Union which is a distillation of all three.
Gwyn Thomas (1913–1981) British writer. *Jackie the Jumper* (Introduction), 'Plays and Players' 19 Jan 1963

23 There's no secret. You just press the accelerator to the floor and steer left.
Bill Vukovich (1918–55) US motor-racing driver. Explaining his success in the Indianapolis 500. Attrib.

SPRING

See also months, seasons

1 My beloved spake, and said unto me, Rise up, my love, my fair one, and come away.
For, lo, the winter is past, the rain is over and gone;
The flowers appear on the earth; the time of the singing of birds is come, and the voice of the turtle is heard in our land.
Bible: Song of Solomon 2:10–12

2 Now Spring, sweet laxative of Georgian strains,
Quickens the ink in literary veins,
The Stately Homes of England ope their doors
To piping Nancy-boys and Crashing Bores.
Roy Campbell (1901–57) South African poet. *The Georgiad*

3 Where are the songs of Spring? Ay, where are they?
John Keats (1795–1821) British poet. *To Autumn*

4 Yes, time heals all things,
So I needn't cling to this fear,
It's merely that Spring
Will be a little late this year.
Frank Loesser (1910–69) US songwriter. *Christmas Holiday*, 'Spring Will Be a Little Late This Year'

5 Spring has returned. The earth is like a child that knows poems.
Rainer Maria Rilke (1875–1926) Austrian poet. *Die Sonette an Orpheus*, I, 21

6 The country habit has me by the heart,
For he's bewitched for ever who has seen,
Not with his eyes but with his vision, Spring
Flow down the woods and stipple leaves with sun.
Vita Sackville-West (Victoria Sackville-West; 1892–1962) British poet and novelist. *The Land*, 'Winter'

7 When the hounds of spring are on winter's traces,
The mother of months in meadow or plain
Fills the shadows and windy places
With lisp of leaves and ripple of rain . . .
Algernon Charles Swinburne (1837–1909) British poet. *Atlanta in Calydon*

8 In the Spring a young man's fancy lightly turns to thoughts of love.
Alfred, Lord Tennyson (1809–92) British poet. *Locksley Hall*

9 Spring is come home with her world-wandering feet.
And all the things are made young with young desires.
Francis Thompson (1859–1907) British poet. *The Night of Forebeing*, 'Ode to Easter'

10 Like an army defeated
The snow hath retreated.
William Wordsworth (1770–1850) British poet. *Written in March*

STAGE

See theater

STARING

1 It is better to be looked over than overlooked.
Mae West (1892–1980) US actress. *The Wit and Wisdom of Mae West* (ed. J. Weintraub)

2 Don't go on looking at me like that, because you'll wear your eyes out.
Émile Zola (1840–1902) French novelist. *La Bête humaine*, Ch. 5

STARS

See also astronomy, moon, space, sun, universe

1 And God made two great lights: the greater light to rule the day, and the lesser light to rule the night: he made the stars also.
Bible: Genesis 1:16

2 Look at the stars! look, look up at the skies!
O look at all the fire-folk sitting in the air!
The bright boroughs, the circle-citadels there!
Gerard Manley Hopkins (1844–99) British Jesuit and poet. *The Starlight Night*

3 Bright star, would I were steadfast as thou art.
John Keats (1795–1821) British poet. *Bright Star*

4 Twinkle, twinkle, little star,
How I wonder what you are!
Up above the world so high,
Like a diamond in the sky!
Jane Taylor (1783–1824) British writer. *Rhymes for the Nursery* (with Ann Taylor), 'The Star'

5 For still I looked on that same star,
That fitful, fiery Lucifer,
Watching with mind as quiet as moss
Its light nailed to a burning cross.

Andrew John Young (1885–1971) Scottish poet. *The Evening Star*

6 Stars lay like yellow pollen
That from a flower has fallen;
And single stars I saw
Crossing themselves in awe;
Some stars in sudden fear
Fell like a falling tear.

Andrew John Young *The Stars*

STATE

See also democracy, government, republic

1 The only way to erect such a common power, as may be able to defend them from the invasion of foreigners, and the injuries of one another . . . is, to confer all their power and strength upon one man, or upon one assembly of men, that may reduce all their wills, by plurality of voices, unto one will . . . This is the generation of that great Leviathan, or rather (to speak more reverently) of that *Mortal God*, to which we owe under the *Immortal God*, our peace and defence.

Thomas Hobbes (1588–1679) English philosopher. *Leviathan*, Pt. II, Ch. 17

2 So long as the state exists there is no freedom. When there is freedom there will be no state.

Lenin (Vladimir Ilich Ulyanov; 1870–1924) Russian revolutionary leader. *The State and Revolution*, Ch. 5

3 In a free society the state does not administer the affairs of men. It administers justice among men who conduct their own affairs.

Walter Lippman (1889–1974) US editor and writer. *An Enquiry into the Principles of a Good Society*

4 The worth of a State in the long run is the worth of the individuals composing it.

John Stuart Mill (1806–73) British philosopher. *On Liberty*, Ch. 5

5 The state is an instrument in the hands of the ruling class for suppressing the resistance of its class enemies.

Joseph Stalin (J. Dzhugashvili; 1879–1953) Soviet statesman. *Stalin's Kampf* (ed. M. R. Werner)

STATELY HOMES

See also architecture, aristocracy, houses

1 One way a peer can make a bit of extra money is by letting the public into his house. Another way is by letting the public into his head. Either way, the dottier the contents the better.

Anonymous Referring to the Earl of Avon's column in *The Evening News*. *The Sunday Times*, 15 Jan 1967

2 An extraordinary aspect of running a stately home is that much of its success depends, not on how many Van Dycks you have, but how many loos. No amount of beautiful objects can compensate a visitor who is kept queuing in the cold.

Duchess of Bedford *Nicole Nobody*

3 Now Spring, sweet laxative of Georgian strains,
Quickens the ink in literary veins,
The Stately Homes of England ope their doors
To piping Nancy-boys and Crashing Bores.

Roy Campbell (1901–57) South African poet. *The Georgiad*

4 The Stately Homes of England
How beautiful they stand,
To prove the upper classes
Have still the upper hand.

Noël Coward (1899–1973) British dramatist. *Operette*, 'The Stately Homes of England'

5 And though the Van Dycks have to go
And we pawn the Bechstein grand,
We'll stand by the Stately Homes of England.

Noël Coward *Operette*, The Stately Homes of England

6 The stately homes of England,
How beautiful they stand!
Amidst their tall ancestral trees,
O'er all the pleasant land.

Felicia Dorothea Hemans (1793–1835) British poet. *The Homes of England*

7 Those comfortably padded lunatic asylums which are known, euphemistically, as the stately homes of England.

Virginia Woolf (1882–1941) British novelist. *The Common Reader*, 'Lady Dorothy Nevill'

STATISTICS

1 Medical statistics are like a bikini. What they reveal is interesting but what they conceal is vital.

Anonymous

2 A witty statesman said, you might prove anything by figures.

Thomas Carlyle (1795–1881) Scottish historian and essayist. *Critical and Miscellaneous Essays*, 'Chartism'

3 There are three kinds of lies: lies, damned lies and statistics.

Benjamin Disraeli (1804–81) British statesman. *Autobiography* (Mark Twain)

4 We are just statistics, born to consume resources.

Horace (Quintus Horatius Flaccus; 65–8 BC) Roman poet. *Epistles*, I

5 He uses statistics as a drunken man uses lamp-posts – for support rather than illumination.

Andrew Lang (1844–1912) Scottish writer and poet. *Treasury of Humorous Quotations*

6 You cannot feed the hungry on statistics.

David Lloyd George (1863–1945) British Liberal statesman. Advocating Tariff Reform. Speech, 1904

7 Statistics will prove anything, even the truth.

Noël Moynihan (1916–) British doctor and writer. Attrib.

8 To understand God's thoughts we must study statistics, for these are the measure of his purpose.

Florence Nightingale (1820–1910) British nurse. *Life . . . of Francis Galton* (K. Pearson), Vol. II, Ch. 13

9 I am one of the unpraised, unrewarded millions without whom Statistics would be a bankrupt science. It is we who are born, who marry, who die, in constant ratios.

Logan Pearsall Smith (1865–1946) US writer. *Trivia*

10 A single death is a tragedy; a million is a statistic.

Joseph Stalin (J. Dzhugashvili; 1879–1953) Soviet statesman. Attrib.

11 There are two kinds of statistics, the kind you look up and the kind you make up.

Rex Stout (1886–1975) US writer. *Death of a Doxy*, Ch. 9

12 Facts speak louder than statistics.

Geoffrey Streatfield (1897–1978) British lawyer. *The Observer*, 'Sayings of the Week', 19 Mar 1950

STEVENSON, Robert Louis

(1850–94) Scottish writer. His books include *Treasure Island* (1883), *Kidnapped* (1886), and *The Strange Case of Dr Jekyll and Mr Hyde* (1886).

Quotations about Stevenson

1 Stevenson seemed to pick the right word up on the point of his pen, like a man playing spillikins.

G. K. Chesterton (1874–1936) British writer. *The Victorian Age in Literature*

2 I think of Mr Stevenson as a consumptive youth weaving garlands of sad flowers with pale, weak hands.

George Moore (1852–1933) Irish writer and art critic. *Confessions of a Young Man*

Quotations by Stevenson

3 If your morals make you dreary, depend upon it, they are wrong.

Across the Plains

4 Politics is perhaps the only profession for which no preparation is thought necessary.

Familiar Studies of Men and Books, 'Yoshida-Torajiro'

5 Vanity dies hard; in some obstinate cases it outlives the man.

Prince Otto

6 Wealth I ask not; hope nor love,
Nor a friend to know me;
All I seek, the heaven above
And the road below me.

Songs of Travel, 'The Vagabond'

7 For my part, I travel not to go anywhere, but to go. I travel for travel's sake. The great affair is to move.

Travels with a Donkey, 'Cheylard and Luc'

8 Fifteen men on the dead man's chest
Yo-ho-ho, and a bottle of rum!
Drink and the devil had done for the rest –
Yo-ho-ho, and a bottle of rum!

Treasure Island, Ch. 1

9 Pieces of eight!

Treasure Island, Ch. 10

10 Many's the long night I've dreamed of cheese – toasted, mostly.

Treasure Island, Ch. 15

11 Of all my verse, like not a single line;
But like my title, for it is not mine.
That title from a better man I stole;
Ah, how much better, had I stol'n the whole!

Underwoods, Foreword

12 Under the wide and starry sky
Dig the grave and let me lie.
Glad did I live and gladly die,
– And I laid me down with a will.
This is the verse you grave for me:
'Here he lies where he longed to be;
Home is the sailor, home from sea,
And the hunter home from the hill.'

Underwoods, Bk. I, 'Requiem'

13 Even if we take matrimony at its lowest, even if we regard it as no more than a sort of friendship recognized by the police.

Virginibus Puerisque

14 Man is a creature who lives not upon bread alone, but principally by catchwords; and the little rift between the sexes is astonishingly widened by simply teaching one set of catchwords to the girls and another to the boys.

Virginibus Puerisque

15 The cruellest lies are often told in silence.

Virginibus Puerisque

16 When the torrent sweeps a man against a boulder, you must expect him to scream, and you need not be surprised if the scream is sometimes a theory.

Virginibus Puerisque

17 Old and young, we are all on our last cruise.

Virginibus Puerisque

18 Books are good enough in their own way, but they are a mighty bloodless substitute for life.

Virginibus Puerisque

19 Extreme *busyness*, whether at school or college, kirk or market, is a symptom of deficient vitality.

Virginibus Puerisque

20 There is no duty we so much underrate as the duty of being happy.

Virginibus Puerisque

21 Give me the young man who has brains enough to make a fool of himself!

Virginibus Puerisque

22 Lastly (and this is, perhaps, the golden rule), no woman should marry a teetotaller, or a man who does not smoke.

Virginibus Puerisque

23 Marriage is a step so grave and decisive that it attracts light-headed, variable men by its very awfulness.

Virginibus Puerisque

24 In marriage, a man becomes slack and selfish and undergoes a fatty degeneration of his moral being.

Virginibus Puerisque

25 Marriage is like life in this – that it is a field of battle, and not a bed of roses.

Virginibus Puerisque

26 To travel hopefully is a better thing than to arrive, and the true success is to labour.

Virginibus Puerisque

27 It's deadly commonplace, but, after all, the commonplaces are the great poetic truths.

Weir of Hermiston, Ch. 6

STRANGENESS

1 There is no excellent beauty that hath not some strangeness in the proportion.

Francis Bacon (1561–1626) English philosopher. *Essays*, 'Of Beauty'

2 'Tis strange – but true; for truth is always strange;
Stranger than fiction: if it could be told,
How much would novels gain by the exchange!

Lord Byron (1788–1824) British poet. *Don Juan*, XIV

3 But Lord! to see the absurd nature of Englishmen, that cannot forbear laughing and jeering at everything that looks strange.

Samuel Pepys (1633–1703) English diarist. *Diary*, 27 Nov 1662

STRENGTH

1 Be strong and of a good courage, fear not, nor be afraid of them: for the Lord thy God, he it is that doth go with thee; he will not fail thee, nor forsake thee.

Bible: Deuteronomy 31:6

2 Patience and passage of time do more than strength and fury.

Jean de La Fontaine (1621–95) French poet. *Fables*, II, 'Le Lion et le Rat'

3 *Kraft durch Freude.*

Strength through joy.
Robert Ley (1890–1945) German Nazi. German Labour Front slogan

4 Sorrow and silence are strong, and patient endurance is godlike.
Henry Wadsworth Longfellow (1807–82) US poet. *Evangeline*

5 Know how sublime a thing it is
To suffer and be strong.
Henry Wadsworth Longfellow *The Light of Stars*

6 We are all strong enough to bear the misfortunes of others.
Duc de la Rochefoucauld (1613–80) French writer. *Maximes*, 19

7 This is the Law of the Yukon, that only the strong shall thrive;
That surely the weak shall perish, and only the Fit survive.
Robert William Service (1874–1958) Canadian poet. *The Law of the Yukon*

8 My strength is as the strength of ten,
Because my heart is pure.
Alfred, Lord Tennyson (1809–92) British poet. *Sir Galahad*

9 We are not now that strength which in old days
Moved earth and heaven; that which we are, we are;
One equal temper of heroic hearts,
Made weak by time and fate, but strong in will
To strive, to seek, to find, and not to yield.
Alfred, Lord Tennyson *Ulysses*

STRIKES

See also industrial relations

1 The rights and interests of the laboring man will be protected and cared for, not by the labor agitators, but by the Christian men to whom God in His infinite wisdom has given control of the property interests of the country.
George Baer (1842–1914) American railroad magnate. Written during the Pennsylvania miners' strike. Letter to the press, Oct 1902

2 Constitutional Government is being attacked . . . The general strike is a challenge to Parliament, and is the road to anarchy and ruin.
Stanley Baldwin (1867–1947) British politician and prime minister. *The British Gazette*, 6 May 1926

3 Not a penny off the pay; not a minute on the day.
A. J. Cook (1885–1931) British trade-union leader. Slogan used in the miners' strike, 1925

4 There is no right to strike against the public safety by anybody, anywhere, any time.
Calvin Coolidge (1872–1933) US President. Referring to the Boston police strike. Remark, 14 Sept 1919

5 It is difficult to go on strike if there is no work in the first place.
Lord George-Brown (1914–85) British statesman. *The Observer*, 24 Feb 1980

6 Another fact of life that will not have escaped you is that, in this country, the twenty-four-hour strike is like the twenty-four-hour flu. You have to reckon on it lasting at least five days.
Frank Muir (1920–) British writer and broadcaster. *You Can't Have Your Kayak and Heat It* (Frank Muir and Dennis Norden), 'Great Expectations'

7 Have you noticed, the last four strikes we've had, it's pissed down? It wouldn't be a bad idea to check the weather reports before they pull us out next time.
Johnny Speight (1920–) British television scriptwriter. *Till Death Do Us Part*

STUBBORNNESS

See also determination, inflexibility, petulance

1 None so blind as those who won't see.
Proverb

2 You can lead a horse to the water, but you can't make him drink.
Proverb

3 Obstinate people can be divided into the opinionated, the ignorant, and the boorish.
Aristotle (384–322 BC) Greek philosopher. *Nicomachean Ethics*, Bk. VII

4 'Tis known by the name of perseverance in a good cause, – and of obstinacy in a bad one.
Laurence Sterne (1713–68) Irish-born British writer. *Tristram Shandy*

STUPIDITY

See also foolishness, ignorance

1 His mind is open; yes, it is so open that nothing is retained; ideas simply pass through him.
F. H. Bradley (1846–1924) British philosopher. Attrib.

2 The trouble with Senator Long is that he is suffering from halitosis of the intellect. That's presuming Emperor Long has an intellect.
Harold L. Ickes (1874–1952) US Republican politician. *The Politics of Upheaval* (A. M. Schlesinger Jnr), Pt. II, Ch. 14

3 Jerry Ford is so dumb that he can't fart and chew gum at the same time.
Lyndon B. Johnson (1908–73) US statesman. Sometimes quoted as '. . . can't walk and chew gum'. *A Ford, Not a Lincoln* (R. Reeves), Ch. 1

4 That fellow seems to me to possess but one idea, and that is a wrong one.
Samuel Johnson (1709–84) British lexicographer. *Life of Johnson* (J. Boswell), Vol. II

5 I've been married six months. She looks like a million dollars, but she only knows a hundred and twenty words and she's only got two ideas in her head. The other one's hats.
Eric Linklater (1889–1974) Scottish novelist. *Juan in America*, Pt. II, Ch. 5

STYLE

1 Style is the man himself.
Comte de Buffon (1707–88) French naturalist. *Discours sur le style*

2 Style, like sheer silk, too often hides eczema.
Albert Camus (1913–60) French existentialist writer. *The Fall*

3 An author arrives at a good style when his language performs what is required of it without shyness.
Cyril Connolly (1903–74) British journalist. *Enemies of Promise*, Ch. 3

4 He has never been known to use a word that might send the reader to the dictionary.
William Faulkner (1897–1962) US novelist. Referring to Ernest HEMINGWAY Attrib.

5 Poor Faulkner. Does he really think big emotions come from big words? He thinks I don't know the ten-dollar words. I know them all right. But there are older and simpler and better words, and those are the ones I use.
Ernest Hemingway (1899–1961) US novelist. In response to a jibe by William FAULKNER Attrib.

6 All styles are good except the tiresome sort.
Voltaire (François-Marie Arouet; 1694–1778) French writer. *L'Enfant prodigue*, Preface

7 In matters of grave importance, style, not sincerity, is the vital thing.
Oscar Wilde (1854–1900) Irish-born British dramatist. *The Importance of Being Earnest*, III

SUBJECTIVITY

See also objectivity, prejudice

1 She was one of the people who say, 'I don't know anything about music really, but I know what I like'.
Max Beerbohm (1872–1956) British writer. *Zuleika Dobson*, Ch. 16

2 An apology for the Devil – it must be remembered that we have only heard one side of the case. God has written all the books.
Samuel Butler (1835–1902) British writer. *Notebooks*

3 It is a general mistake to think the men we like are good for everything, and those we do not, good for nothing.
Lord Halifax (1633–95) English statesman. *Political, Moral and Miscellaneous Thoughts and Reflections*

4 He who knows only his own side of the case knows little of that.
John Stuart Mill (1806–73) British philosopher. *On Liberty*, Ch. 2

5 All the world is queer save thee and me, and even thou art a little queer.
Robert Owen (1771–1858) British social reformer. Referring to William Allen, his partner in business. Attrib., 1828

6 To observations which ourselves we make
We grow more partial for th' observer's sake.
Alexander Pope (1688–1744) British poet. *Moral Essays*, I

7 Partisanship is our great curse. We too readily assume that everything has two sides and that it is our duty to be on one or the other.
James Harvey Robinson (1863–1936) US historian and educator. *The Mind in the Making*

SUBURBIA

1 I come from suburbia, Dan, personally, I don't ever want to go back. It's the one place in the world that's further away than anywhere else.
Frederic Raphael (1931–) British author. *The Glittering Prizes: A Sex Life*, I:3

2 She was more than ever proud of the position of the bungalow, so almost in the country.
Angus Wilson (1913–) British novelist. *A Bit Off the Map*, 'A Flat Country Christmas'

SUCCESS

See also achievement, victory

1 Nothing succeeds like success.
Proverb

2 'Tis not in mortals to command success,
But we'll do more, Sempronius; we'll deserve it.
Joseph Addison (1672–1719) British essayist. *Cato*, I:2

3 The penalty of success is to be bored by people who used to snub you.
Nancy Astor (1879–1964) American-born British politician. *Sunday Express*, 12 Jan 1956

4 One's religion is whatever he is most interested in, and yours is Success.
J. M. Barrie (1860–1937) British novelist and dramatist. *The Twelve-Pound Look*

5 Ask, and it shall be given you; seek, and ye shall find; knock, and it shall be opened unto you:
For every one that asketh receiveth; and he that seeketh findeth; and to him that knocketh it shall be opened.
Bible: Matthew 7:7–8

6 The only infallible criterion of wisdom to vulgar minds – success.
Edmund Burke (1729–97) British politician. *Letter to a Member of the National Assembly*

7 Success is counted sweetest
By those who ne'er succeed.
Emily Dickinson (1830–86) US poet. *Success is Counted Sweetest*

8 Success is relative. It is what we can make of the mess we have made of things.
T. S. Eliot (1888–1965) US-born British poet and dramatist. *The Family Reunion*

9 There are two reasons why I am successful in show business and I am standing on both of them.
Betty Grable (1916–73) US actress. Attrib.

10 The moral flabbiness born of the bitch-goddess Success.
William James (1842–1910) US psychologist and philosopher. Letter to H. G. Wells, 11 Sept 1906

11 Victory has a thousand fathers but defeat is an orphan.
John Fitzgerald Kennedy (1917–63) US statesman. Attrib.

12 The shortest and best way to make your fortune is to let people see clearly that it is in their interests to promote yours.
Jean de La Bruyère (1645–96) French satirist. *Les Caractères*

13 Sweet Smell of Success.
Ernest Lehman (1920–) US screenwriter. Novel and film title

14 You write a hit the same way you write a flop.
Alan Jay Lerner (1918–86) US lyricist and playwright. Attrib.

15 We in this industry know that behind every successful screenwriter stands a woman. And behind her stands his wife.
Groucho Marx (Julius Marx; 1895–1977) US comedian. Attrib.

16 The secret of my success is that no woman has ever been jealous of me.
Elsa Maxwell (1883–1963) US songwriter, broadcaster, and actress. *The Natives were Friendly* (Noël Barber)

17 As is the case in all branches of art, success depends in a very large measure upon individual initiative and exertion, and cannot be achieved except by dint of hard work.
Anna Pavlova (1881–1931) Russian ballet dancer. *Pavlova: A Biography* (ed. A. H. Franks), 'Pages of My Life'

18 To succeed in the world, we do everything we can to appear successful.
Duc de la Rochefoucauld (1613–80) French writer. *Maximes*, 50

19 The only place where success comes before work is a dictionary.
Vidal Sassoon (1928–) British hair stylist. Quoting one of his teachers in a BBC radio broadcast

20 The only way to succeed is to make people hate you. That way, they remember you.
Joseph von Sternberg (1894–1969) US film director. *Autobiography (Fun in a Chinese Laundry)*

21 There are no gains without pains.
Adlai Stevenson (1900–65) US statesman. Speech, Chicago, 26 July 1952

SUFFERING

1 An hour of pain is as long as a day of pleasure.
Proverb

2 He that lives long suffers much.
Proverb

3 Time heals old pain, while it creates new ones.
Hebrew proverb

4 Man endures pain as an undeserved punishment; woman accepts it as a natural heritage.
Anonymous

5 There was a faith-healer of Deal,
Who said, 'Although pain isn't real,
If I sit on a pin
And it punctures my skin,
I dislike what I fancy I feel.'
Anonymous

6 The greatest evil is physical pain.
St Augustine (354–430) Bishop of Hippo in North Africa. *Soliloquies*, I

7 One does not love a place the less for having suffered in it unless it has all been suffering, nothing but suffering.
Jane Austen (1775–1817) British novelist. *Persuasion*, Ch. 20

8 And the name of the star is called Wormwood: and the third part of the waters became wormwood; and many men died of the waters, because they were made bitter.
Bible: Revelations 8:11

9 There is no point in being overwhelmed by the appalling total of human suffering; such a total does not exist. Neither poverty nor pain is accumulable.
Jorge Luis Borges (1899–1986) Argentinian writer. *Other Inquisitions*, 'A New Refutation of Time'

10 Once drinking deep of that divinest anguish,
How could I seek the empty world again?
Emily Brontë (1818–48) British novelist. *Remembrance*

11 I am convinced that we have a degree of delight, and that no small one, in the real misfortunes and pains of others.
Edmund Burke (1729–97) British politician. *On the Sublime and Beautiful*, Pt. I

12 What deep wounds ever closed without a scar?
Lord Byron (1788–1824) British poet. *Childe Harold's Pilgrimage*

13 I lead a most dyspeptic, solitary, self-shrouded *life*: consuming, if possible in silence, my considerable daily allotment of *pain*.
Thomas Carlyle (1795–1881) Scottish historian and essayist. Letter to Ralph Waldo Emerson, 8 Feb 1839

14 The horror! The horror!
Joseph Conrad (Teodor Josef Konrad Korzeniowski; 1857–1924) Polish-born British *Heart of Darkness*

15 Pain – has an Element of Blank –
It cannot recollect
When it begun – or if there were
A time when it was not –.
Emily Dickinson (1830–86) US poet. Poem

16 Much of your pain is self-chosen. It is the bitter potion by which the physician within you heals your sick self.
Kahlil Gibran (1888–1931) Lebanese mystic and poet. *The Prophet*, 'On Pain'

17 If suffer we must, let's suffer on the heights.
Victor Hugo (1802–85) French writer. *Contemplations*, 'Les Malheureux'

18 The music, yearning like a God in pain.
John Keats (1795–1821) British poet. *The Eve of Saint Agnes*, VII

19 Rather suffer than die is man's motto.
Jean de La Fontaine (1621–95) French poet. *Fables*, I, 'La Mort et le bûcheron'

20 It would be a great thing to understand Pain in all its meanings.
Peter Mere Latham (1789–1875) US physician. *General Remarks on the Practice of Medicine*, Ch. 14

21 The new-born child does not realize that his body is more a part of himself than surrounding objects, . . . and it is only by degrees, through pain, that he understands the fact of the body.
W. Somerset Maugham (1874–1965) British writer and doctor. *Of Human Bondage*, Ch. 13

22 I knew that suffering did not ennoble; it degraded. It made men selfish, mean, petty and suspicious. It absorbed them in small things . . . it made them less than men; and I wrote ferociously that we learn resignation not by our own suffering, but by the suffering of others.
W. Somerset Maugham *The Summing Up*

23 But pain is perfect miserie, the worst
Of evils, and excessive, overturnes
All patience.
John Milton (1608–74) English poet. *Paradise Lost*, Bk. VI

24 A man who fears suffering is already suffering from what he fears.
Michel de Montaigne (1533–92) French essayist. *Essais*, III

25 The mind grows sicker than the body in contemplation of its suffering.
Ovid (Publius Ovidius Naso; 43 BC–17 AD) Roman poet. *Tristia*, Bk. IV

26 There is nothing encourageth a woman sooner to be barren than hard travail in child bearing.
Pliny the Elder (Gaius Plinius Secundus; 23 AD–79 AD) Roman writer. *Natural History*

27 Every reformation must have its victims. You can't expect the fatted calf to share the enthusiasm of the angels over the prodigal's return.
Saki (Hector Hugh Munro; 1870–1916) British writer. *Reginald on the Academy*

28 We must all die. But that I can save him from days of torture, that is what I feel as my great and ever new privilege. Pain is a more terrible lord of mankind than even death himself.
Albert Schweitzer (1875–1965) French Protestant theologian, philosopher, and physician. *On the Edge of the Primeval Forest*, Ch. 5

29 Remember that pain has this most excellent quality: if prolonged it cannot be severe, and if severe it cannot be prolonged.
Seneca (c. 4 BC–65 AD) Roman author and statesman. *Epistulae ad Lucilium*, XCIV

30 Thou art a soul in bliss; but I am bound
Upon a wheel of fire, that mine own tears
Do scald like molten lead.
William Shakespeare (1564–1616) English dramatist. *King Lear*, IV:7

31 Oh! when I have the gout, I feel as if I was walking on my eyeballs.
Sydney Smith (1771–1845) English churchman, essayist, and wit. *A Memoir of the Rev. Sydney Smith*, Ch. 11 (Lady Holland)

32 Pain is the correlative of some species of wrong – some kind of

divergence from that course of action which perfectly fills all requirements.

Herbert Spencer (1820–1903) British philosopher and supporter of Darwinism. *The Data of Ethics,* Ch. 15

33 Pain of mind is worse than pain of body.

Publilius Syrus (1st century BC) Roman dramatist. *Sententiae*

34 Half the misery in the world is caused by ignorance. The other half is caused by knowledge.

Bonar Thompson (d. 1963) Hyde Park Orator. *The Black Hat*

35 Nothing begins and nothing ends
That is not paid with moan;
For we are born in others' pain.
And perish in our own.

Francis Thompson (1859–1907) British poet and critic. 'Daisy'

36 *Miseris succurrere disco.*
I learn to relieve the suffering.

Virgil (Publius Vergilius Maro; 70 BC–19 BC) Roman poet. Motto on the seal of the New Jersey College of Medicine. *Aeneid,* Bk. I

37 Pain with the thousand teeth.

William Watson (1858–1935) British poet. *The Dream of Man*

SUICIDE

See also death

1 To run away from trouble is a form of cowardice and, while it is true that the suicide braves death, he does it not for some noble object but to escape some ill.

Aristotle (384 BC–322 BC) Greek philosopher and scientist. *Nicomachean Ethics,* 3

2 If I had the use of my body I would throw it out of the window.

Samuel Beckett (1906–) Irish novelist and dramatist. *Malone Dies*

3 If you must commit suicide . . . always contrive to do it as decorously as possible; the decencies, whether of life or of death, should never be lost sight of.

George Borrow (1803–81) British writer. *Lavengro,* Ch. 23

4 There is but one truly serious philosophical problem, and that is suicide. Judging whether life is, or is not worth living amounts to answering the fundamental question of philosophy.

Albert Camus (1913–60) French existentialist writer. *The Myth of Sisyphus*

5 As soon as one does not kill oneself, one must keep silent about life.

Albert Camus *Notebooks 1935–1942,* 1

6 To attempt suicide is a criminal offense. Any man who, of his own will, tries to escape the treadmill to which the rest of us feel chained incites our envy, and therefore our fury. We do not suffer him to go unpunished.

Alexander Chase (1926–) US journalist. *Perspectives*

7 The strangest whim has seized me
. . . After all
I think I will not hang myself today.

G. K. Chesterton (1874–1936) British writer. *A Ballade of Suicide*

8 Not only is suicide a sin, it is the sin. It is the ultimate and absolute evil, the refusal to take the oath of loyalty to life. The man who kills a man, kills a man. The man who kills himself kills all men; as far as he is concerned he wipes out the world.

G. K. Chesterton *Orthodoxy*

9 Suicide is the worst form of murder, because it leaves no opportunity for repentance.

John Churton Collins (1848–1908) *Life and Memoirs of John Churton Collins,* Appendix VII (L. C. Collins)

10 There are many who dare not kill themselves for fear of what the neighbours might say.

Cyril Connolly (1903–74) British journalist. *The Unquiet Grave*

11 Self-destruction is the effect of cowardice in the highest extreme.

Daniel Defoe (c. 1659–1731) English journalist and writer. *An Essay Upon Projects,* 'Of Projectors'

12 My work is done. Why wait?

George Eastman (1854–1932) US inventor and industrialist. His suicide note

13 The prevalence of suicide is a test of height in civilization; it means that the population is winding up its nervous and intellectual system to the utmost point of tension and that sometimes it snaps.

Havelock Ellis (1859–1939) British psychologist.

14 Suicide is not a remedy.

James A. Garfield (1831–81) US statesman. Inaugural address, 4 Mar 1881

15 However great a man's fear of life . . . suicide remains the courageous act, the clear-headed act of a mathematician. The suicide has judged by the laws of chance – so many odds against one, that to live will be more miserable than to die. His sense of mathematics is greater than his sense of survival.

Graham Greene (1904–) British novelist. *The Comedians,* I

16 Hatred and the feeling of solidarity pay a high psychological dividend. The statistics of suicide show that, for noncombatants at least, life is more interesting in war than in peace.

W. R. Inge (1860–1954) British writer and churchman. *The End of an Age,* Ch. 3

17 I take it that no man is educated who has never dallied with the thought of suicide.

William James (1842–1910) US psychologist and philosopher.

18 Suicide is something on its own. It seems to me to be a flight by which man hopes to recover Paradise Lost instead of trying to deserve Heaven.

Paul-Louis Landsberg (1901–43) *The Experience of Death and the Moral Problem of Suicide*

19 Nature puts upon no man an unbearable burden; if her limits be exceeded, man responds by suicide. I have always respected suicide as a regulator of nature.

Emil Ludwig (1881–1948) *I Believe* (Clifton Fadiman)

20 The thought of suicide is a great source of comfort: with it a calm passage is to be made across many a bad night.

Friedrich Wilhelm Nietzsche (1844–1900) German philosopher. *Jenseits von Gut und Bose*

21 You fellows, in your business, you have a way of handling problems like this. Somebody leaves a pistol in the drawer. I don't have a pistol.

Richard Milhous Nixon (1913–) US President. To General Alexander Haig. *Final Days* (R. Woodward and C. Bernstein)

22 When you go to drown yourself always take off your clothes, they may fit your wife's next husband.

Gregory Nunn

23 Razors pain you
Rivers are damp;
Acids stain you;
And drugs cause cramp.
Guns aren't lawful;
Nooses give;
Gas smells awful;
You might as well live.

Dorothy Parker (1893–1967) US writer. *Enough Rope,* 'Resumé'

24 No one ever lacks a good reason for suicide.
Cesare Pavese (1908–50) Italian writer. *The Savage God* (A. Alvarez)

25 Amid the miseries of our life on earth, suicide is God's best gift to man.
Pliny the Elder (23–79 AD) Roman scholar. *Natural History*, II

26 When you're between any sort of devil and the deep blue sea, the deep blue sea sometimes looks very inviting.
Terence Rattigan (1911–77) British dramatist. *The Deep Blue Sea*

27 How many people have wanted to kill themselves, and have been content with tearing up their photograph!
Jules Renard (1864–1910) French writer. *Journal*

28 Next week, or next month, or next year I'll kill myself. But I might as well last out my month's rent, which has been paid up, and my credit for breakfast in the morning.
Jean Rhys (1894–1979) Dominican-born British novelist. *Good Morning, Midnight*, Pt. II

29 It is against the law to commit suicide in this man's town... although what the law can do to a guy who commits suicide I am never able to figure out.
Damon Runyon (1884–1946) US writer. *Guys and Dolls*

30 The miserable change now at my end
Lament nor sorrow at; but please your thoughts
In feeding them with those my former fortunes
Wherein I liv'd the greatest prince o' the world,
The noblest; and do now not basely die,
Not cowardly put off my helmet to
My countryman; a Roman by a Roman
Valiantly vanquished.
William Shakespeare (1564–1616) English dramatist. *Antony and Cleopatra*, IV:13

31 Dost thou not see my baby at my breast
That sucks the nurse asleep?
William Shakespeare Holding the asp to her breast. *Antony and Cleopatra*, V:2

32 My desolation does begin to make
A better life. 'Tis paltry to be Caesar;
Not being Fortune, he's but Fortune's knave,
A minister of her will; and it is great
To do that thing that ends all other deeds,
Which shackles accidents, and bolts up change,
Which sleeps, and never palates more the dug,
The beggar's nurse and Caesar's.
William Shakespeare *Antony and Cleopatra*, V:2

33 She hath pursu'd conclusions infinite
Of easy ways to die.
William Shakespeare *Antony and Cleopatra*, V:2

34 To be, or not to be – that is the question;
Whether 'tis nobler in the mind to suffer
The slings and arrows of outrageous fortune,
Or to take arms against a sea of troubles,
And by opposing end them? To die, to sleep –
No more; and by a sleep to say we end
The heart-ache and the thousand natural shocks
That flesh is heir to, 'tis a consummation
Devoutly to be wish'd. To die, to sleep;
To sleep, perchance to dream. Ay, there's the rub;
For in that sleep of death what dreams may come,
When we have shuffled off this mortal coil,
Must give us pause.
William Shakespeare *Hamlet*, III:1

35 A still small voice spake unto me,
'Thou art so full of misery,
Were it not better not to be?'
Alfred, Lord Tennyson (1809–92) British poet. *The Two Voices*

36 I am the only man in the world who cannot commit suicide.
Rev. Chad Varah (1911–) Founder of the Samaritans. Attrib.

37 Not that suicide always comes from madness. There are said to be occasions when a wise man takes that course: but, generally speaking, it is not in an access of reasonableness that people kill themselves.
Voltaire (François-Marie Arouet; 1694–1778) French writer and philosopher. Letter to James Marriott, 1767

38 There is no refuge from confession but suicide; and suicide is confession.
Daniel Webster (1782–1852) US statesman. *The Murder of Captain Joseph White: Argument on the Trial of John Francis Knapp*

39 Never murder a man who is committing suicide.
Woodrow Wilson (1856–1925) US statesman. *Mr Wilson's War* (John Dos Passos), Pt. II, Ch. 10

SUITABILITY

1 In seed time learn, in harvest teach, in winter enjoy.
William Blake (1757–1827) British poet. *The Marriage of Heaven and Hell*, 'Proverbs of Hell'

2 A cow is a very good animal in the field; but we turn her out of a garden.
Samuel Johnson (1709–84) British lexicographer. Responding to Boswell's objections to the expulsion of six Methodists from Oxford University. *The Personal History of Samuel Johnson* (C. Hibbert)

3 Today I dressed to meet my father's eyes; yesterday it was for my husband's.
Julia (39 BC–AD 14) Daughter of Augustus. On being complimented by her father, the emperor Augustus, on her choice of a more modest dress than the one she had worn the previous day. *Saturnalia* (Macrobius)

4 At Christmas I no more desire a rose
Than wish a snow in May's newfangled shows.
William Shakespeare (1564–1616) English dramatist. *Love's Labour's Lost*, I:1

SUMMER

See also months, seasons

1 Sumer is icumen in,
Lhude sing cuccu!
Groweth sed, and bloweth med,
And springth the wude nu.
Anonymous *Cuckoo Song*

2 All the live murmur of a summer's day.
Matthew Arnold (1822–88) British poet and critic. *The Scholar Gipsy*

3 It is time for the destruction of error.
The chairs are being brought in from the garden,
The summer talk stopped on that savage coast
Before the storms.
W. H. Auden (1907–73) British poet. *It is time*

4 Summer has set in with its usual severity.
Samuel Taylor Coleridge (1772–1834) British poet. Quoted in Lamb's letter to V. Novello, 9 May 1826

5 Summer afternoon – summer afternoon; to me those have always been the two most beautiful words in the English language.
Henry James (1843–1916) US novelist. *A Backward Glance* (Edith Wharton), Ch. 10

6 In a somer season, when soft was the sonne.
William Langland (c. 1330–c. 1400) English poet. *The Vision of Piers Plowman*, Prologue

7 The moans of doves in immemorial elms,
And murmuring of innumerable bees.
Alfred, Lord Tennyson (1809–92) British poet. *The Princess*, VII

8 The way to ensure summer in England is to have it framed and glazed in a comfortable room.
Horace Walpole (1717–97) British writer. Letter to Cole, 28 May 1774

SUMMONS

See also invitations

1 Go, for they call you, Shepherd, from the hill.
Matthew Arnold (1822–88) British poet and critic. *The Scholar Gipsy*

2 Whistle and she'll come to you.
Francis Beaumont (1584–1616) English dramatist. *Wit Without Money*, IV:4

3 Mr Watson, come here; I want you.
Alexander Graham Bell (1847–1922) Scottish scientist. The first telephone conversation, 10 Mar 1876, in Boston. Attrib.

4 Dauntless the slug-horn to my lips I set,
And blew. *Childe Roland to the Dark Tower came.*
Robert Browning (1812–89) British poet. *Childe Roland to the Dark Tower Came*, XXXIV

SUN

See also weather

1 The Sun came up upon the left,
Out of the sea came he!
And he shone bright, and on the right
Went down into the sea.
Samuel Taylor Coleridge (1772–1834) British poet. *The Rime of the Ancient Mariner*, I

2 Busy old fool, unruly Sun,
Why dost thou thus,
Through windows and through curtains call on us?
John Donne (1573–1631) English poet. *The Sun Rising*

3 I have a horror of sunsets, they're so romantic, so operatic.
Marcel Proust (1871–1922) French novelist. *À la recherche du temps perdu: Sodome et Gomorrhe*

4 Thank heavens, the sun has gone in, and I don't have to go out and enjoy it.
Logan Pearsall Smith (1865–1946) US writer. *Afterthoughts*

5 Hath Britain all the sun that shines?
William Shakespeare (1564–1616) English dramatist. *Cymbeline*, III:4

SUNDAY

1 And on the seventh day God ended his work which he had made; and he rested on the seventh day from all his work which he had made.
Bible: Genesis 2:2

2 And he said unto them, The sabbath was made for man, and not man for the sabbath: Therefore the Son of man is Lord also of the sabbath.
Bible: Mark 2:27–28

3 We give warning that a festival must be observed on Sunday and honoured with full intent from noon on Saturday until dawn on Monday, and that no person shall presume either to practise trade or attend any meeting on this Holy Day; and all men, poor and rich, shall go to their church and offer supplication for their sins and observe zealously every appointed fast and honour readily those saints whose feasts shall be commended by the priests.
Canute (995–1035) King of England, Denmark, and Norway. Letter to the Archbishops and people of England

4 Of all the days that's in the week
I dearly love but one day –
And that's the day that comes betwixt
A Saturday and Monday.
Henry Carey (c. 1690–1743) English poet and musician. *Sally in our Alley*

5 The boredom of Sunday afternoon, which drove De Quincey to opium also gave birth to surrealism; hours propitious to making bombs.
Cyril Connolly (1903–74) British journalist. *The Unquiet Grave*

6 The better day, the worse deed.
Matthew Henry (1662–1714) English nonconformist minister. *Exposition of the Old and New Testaments*

7 The feeling of Sunday is the same everywhere, heavy, melancholy, standing still. Like when they say, 'As it was in the beginning, is now, and ever shall be, world without end.'
Jean Rhys (1894–1979) Dominican-born British novelist. *Voyage in the Dark*, Ch. 4

SUPERIORITY

See also equality, excellence, one-upmanship, snobbery

1 My name is George Nathaniel Curzon,
I am a most superior person.
My face is pink, my hair is sleek,
I dine at Blenheim once a week.
Anonymous *The Masque of Balliol*

2 The slave begins by demanding justice and ends by wanting to wear a crown. He must dominate in his turn.
Albert Camus (1913–60) French existentialist writer. *The Rebel*

3 The superior man is satisfied and composed; the mean man is always full of distress.
Confucius (K'ung Fu-tzu; 551–479 BC) Chinese philosopher. *Analects*

4 The superior man is distressed by his want of ability.
Confucius *Analects*

5 When you meet someone better than yourself, turn your thoughts to becoming his equal. When you meet someone not as good as you are, look within and examine your own self.
Confucius *Analects*

6 And lo! Ben Adhem's name led all the rest.
Leigh Hunt (1784–1859) British poet. *Abou Ben Adhem and the Angel*

7 Though I've belted you an' flayed you,
By the livin' Gawd that made you,
You're a better man than I am, Gunga Din!
Rudyard Kipling (1865–1936) Indian-born British writer. *Gunga Din*

8 Sir, you have the advantage of me.
– Not yet I haven't, but wait till I get you outside.
Groucho Marx (Julius Marx; 1895–1977) US comedian. *Monkey Business*

9 What men value in this world is not rights but privileges.
H. L. Mencken (1880–1956) US journalist. *Minority Report*

10 Considering the company I keep in this place, that is hardly surprising.
Robert Menzies (1894–1978) Australian prime minister. When accused of having a superiority complex in parliament. *Time*, 29 May 1978

11 Above the vulgar flight of common souls.
Arthur Murphy (1727–1805) Irish dramatist, writer, and actor. *Zenobia*, V

12 I teach you the Superman. Man is something that is to be surpassed.
Friedrich Wilhelm Nietzsche (1844–1900) German philosopher. *Thus Spake Zarathustra*

13 It is brought home to you . . . that it is only because miners sweat their guts out that superior persons can remain superior.
George Orwell (Eric Blair; 1903–50) British novelist. *The Road to Wigan Pier*, Ch. 2

14 'I believe I take precedence,' he said coldly; 'you are merely the club Bore: I am the club Liar.'
Saki (Hector Hugh Munro; 1870–1916) British writer. *A Defensive Diamond*

15 In the Country of the Blind the One-eyed Man is King.
H. G. Wells (1866–1946) British writer. *The Country of the Blind*

SUPERNATURAL

See also fairies

1 From ghoulies and ghosties and long-leggety beasties
And things that go bump in the night,
Good Lord, deliver us!
Anonymous Cornish prayer

2 Open Sesame!
The Arabian Nights (c. 1500) A collection of tales from the East. *The History of Ali Baba*

3 Thou shalt not suffer a witch to live.
Bible: Exodus 22:18

4 For my part, I have ever believed, and do now know, that there are witches.
Thomas Browne (1605–82) English physician and writer. *Religio Medici*, Pt. I

5 This time it vanished quite slowly, beginning with the end of the tail, and ending with the grin, which remained some time after the rest of it had gone.
Lewis Carroll (Charles Lutwidge Dodgson; 1832–98) British writer. Describing the Cheshire Cat. *Alice's Adventures in Wonderland*, Ch. 6

6 A savage place! as holy and enchanted
As e'er beneath a waning moon was haunted
By woman wailing for her demon-lover!
Samuel Taylor Coleridge (1772–1834) British poet. *Kubla Khan*

7 Religion
Has made an honest woman of the supernatural,
And we won't have it kicking over the traces again.
Christopher Fry (1907–) British dramatist. *The Lady's Not for Burning*, II

8 Every old woman with a wrinkled face, a furr'd brow, a hairy lip, a gobber tooth, a squint eye, a squeaking voice, or a scolding tongue . . . a dog or cat by her side, is not only suspected but pronounced for a witch.
John Gaule (fl. 1660) Vicar of Great Stoughton (Huntingdonshire). *Sermons on Witchcraft*

9 All argument is against it; but all belief is for it.
Samuel Johnson (1709–84) British lexicographer. Of the ghost of a dead person. *Life of Johnson* (J. Boswell), Vol. III

10 La belle Dame sans Merci
Hath thee in thrall!
John Keats (1795–1821) British poet. *La Belle Dame Sans Merci*

11 That old black magic has me in its spell.
Johnny Mercer (1909–76) US lyricist and composer. *That Old Black Magic*

12 Once upon a midnight dreary, while I pondered, weak and weary,
Over many a quaint and curious volume of forgotten lore,
While I nodded, nearly napping, suddenly there came a tapping,
As of some one gently rapping, rapping at my chamber door.
Edgar Allan Poe (1809–49) US poet and writer. *The Raven*

13 My question is not whether there be witches or nay; but whether they can do such marvellous works as are imputed to them. Good Master Dean, is it possible for a man to break his fast with you at Rochester, and to dine that day at Durham with Master Doctor Matthew; or can your enemy maim you, when the Ocean sea is betwixt you? May a spiritual body become temporal at his pleasure? Or may a carnal body become invisible? . . . Alas, I am sorry and ashamed to see how many die, that being said to be bewitched, only seek for magical cures, whom wholesome diet and good medicines would have recovered.
Reginald Scot *The Discoverie of Witchcraft*

14 There are more things in heaven and earth, Horatio,
Than are dreamt of in your philosophy.
William Shakespeare (1564–1616) English dramatist. *Hamlet*, I:5

15 This supernatural soliciting
Cannot be ill; cannot be good.
William Shakespeare *Macbeth*, I:3

SUPERSTITION

See also luck

1 A dimple in the chin, a devil within.
Proverb

2 Meet on the stairs and you won't meet in heaven.
Proverb

3 One for sorrow, two for mirth; three for a wedding, four for a birth; five for silver, six for gold; seven for a secret, not to be told; eight for heaven, nine for hell; and ten for the devil's own sel.
Referring to magpies or crows; there are numerous variants. Proverb

4 See a pin and pick it up, all the day you'll have good luck; see a pin and let it lie, you'll want a pin before you die.
Proverb

5 Third time lucky.
Proverb

6 (For all the Athenians and strangers which were there spent their time in nothing else, but either to tell, or to hear some new thing.)
Then Paul stood in the midst of Mars' hill, and said, Ye men of Athens, I perceive that in all things ye are too superstitious.
For as I passed by, and beheld your devotions, I found an altar with this inscription, TO THE UNKNOWN GOD. Whom therefore ye ignorantly worship, him declare I unto you.
God that made the world and all things therein, seeing that he is Lord

of heaven and earth, dwelleth not in temples made with hands.
Bible: Acts 17:21–24

7 Of course I don't believe in it. But I understand that it brings you luck whether you believe in it or not.
Niels Bohr (1885–1962) Danish physicist. When asked why he had a horseshoe on his wall. Attrib.

8 Superstition is the religion of feeble minds.
Edmund Burke (1729–97) British politician. *Reflections on the Revolution in France*

9 Superstition is the poetry of life.
Goethe (1749–1832) German poet and dramatist. *Sprüche in Prosa*, III

10 And some of the bigger bears try to pretend
That they came round the corner to look for a friend;
And they'll try to pretend that nobody cares
Whether you walk on the lines or the squares.
A. A. Milne (1882–1956) British writer. *When We Were Very Young*, 'Lines and Squares'

11 They say there is divinity in odd numbers, either in nativity, chance, or death.
William Shakespeare (1564–1616) English dramatist. *The Merry Wives of Windsor*, V:1

12 Superstition sets the whole world in flames; philosophy quenches them.
Voltaire (François-Marie Arouet; 1694–1778) French writer. *Dictionnaire philosophique*, 'Superstition'

SUPPORT

See also loyalty

1 He found him in a desert land, and in the waste howling wilderness; he led him about, he instructed him, he kept him as the apple of his eye.
Bible: Deuteronomy 32:10

2 The finest plans have always been spoiled by the littleness of those that should carry them out. Even emperors can't do it all by themselves.
Bertolt Brecht (1898–1956) German dramatist. *Mother Courage*, VI

3 Either back us or sack us.
James Callaghan (1912–) British politician and prime minister. Speech, Labour Party Conference, Brighton, 5 Oct 1977

4 Give me your arm, old Toad;
Help me down Cemetery Road.
Philip Larkin (1922–85) British poet. *The Whitsun Weddings*, 'Toads Revisited'

5 What I want is men who will support me when I am in the wrong.
Lord Melbourne (1779–1848) British statesman. Replying to someone who said he would support Melbourne as long as he was in the right. *Lord M.* (Lord David Cecil)

6 While I cannot be regarded as a pillar, I must be regarded as a buttress of the church, because I support it from the outside.
Lord Melbourne Attrib.

7 And so, tonight – to you, the great silent majority of my fellow Americans – I ask for your support.
Richard Milhous Nixon (1913–) US President. On a plan for peace in Vietnam. Broadcast address, 3 Nov 1969

8 Ladies and gentleman, it takes more than one to make a ballet.
Ninette de Valois (Edris Stannus; 1898–) British ballet dancer and choreographer. *New Yorker*

SURGEONS

1 The best surgeon is he that has been well hacked himself.
Proverb

2 The egotistical surgeon is like a monkey; the higher he climbs the more you see of his less attractive features.
Anonymous

3 Tree surgeons are taught to wear safety belts so they won't fall out of patients.
Anonymous

4 The glory of surgeons is like that of actors, who exist only in their lifetime and whose talent is no longer appreciable once they have disappeared.
Honoré de Balzac (1799–1850) French novelist. *The Atheist's Mass*

5 I have made many mistakes myself; in learning the anatomy of the eye I dare say, I have spoiled a hatful; the best surgeon, like the best general, is he who makes the fewest mistakes.
Astley Paston Cooper (1768–1841) *Lectures on Surgery*

6 My lectures were highly esteemed, but I am of the opinion my operations rather kept down my practice.
Astley Paston Cooper *Bulletin of the New York Academy of Medicine*, 5:155, 1929 (F. H. Garrison)

7 A good surgeon operates with his hand, not with his heart.
Alexandre Dumas père (1802–70) French novelist and dramatist.

8 The first attribute of a surgeon is an insatiable curiosity.
Russell John Howard (1875–1942) *The Hip*, Ch. 2 (F. G. St. Clair Strange)

9 Speed in operating should be the achievement, not the aim, of every surgeon.
Russell John Howard (1875–1942) *The Hip*, Ch. 9 (F. G. St. Clair Strange)

10 In surgery eyes first and most fingers next and little; tongue last and least.
Sir George Murray Humphry (1820–96)

11 A possible apprehension now is that the surgeon be sometimes tempted to supplant instead of aiding Nature.
Henry Maudsley (1835–1918)

12 A vain surgeon is like a milking stool, of no use except when sat upon.
Robert Tuttle Morris (1857–1945)

13 Any fool can cut off a leg – it takes a surgeon to save one.
George G. Ross (1834–92)

14 In surgery all operations are recorded as successful if the patient can be got out of the hospital or nursing home alive, though the subsequent history of the case may be such as would make an honest surgeon vow never to recommend or perform the operation again.
George Bernard Shaw (1856–1950) Irish dramatist and critic. *The Doctor's Dilemma*, 'Preface on Doctors'

15 Now it cannot be too often repeated that when an operation is once performed, nobody can ever prove that it was unnecessary. If I refuse to allow my leg to be amputated, its mortification and my death may prove that I was wrong; but if I let the leg go, nobody can ever prove that it would not have mortified had I been obstinate. Operation is therefore the safe side for the surgeon as well as the lucrative side.
George Bernard Shaw *The Doctor's Dilemma*, 'Preface on Doctors'

16 When *I* take up assassination, I shall start with the surgeons in this city and work *up* to the gutter.
Dylan Thomas (1914–53) Welsh poet. *The Doctor and the Devils*, 88

SURVIVAL

See also evolution, self-preservation

1 I haven't asked you to make me young again. All I want is to go on getting older.
Konrad Adenauer (1876–1967) German statesman. Replying to his doctor. Attrib.

2 It isn't important to come out on top; what matters is to come out alive.
Bertolt Brecht (1898–1956) German dramatist. *Jungle of Cities*

3 People are inexterminable – like flies and bed-bugs. There will always be some that survive in cracks and crevices – that's us.
Robert Frost (1875–1963) US poet. *The Observer*, 29 Mar 1959

4 Ideal mankind would abolish death, multiply itself million upon million, rear up city upon city save every parasite alive, until the accumulation of mere existence is swollen to a horror.
D. H. Lawrence (1885–1930) British novelist. *St. Mawr*

5 The perpetual struggle for room and food.
Thomas Robert Malthus (1766–1834) British clergyman and economist. *Essays on the Principle of Population*

6 Species do not evolve toward perfection, but quite the contrary. The weak, in fact, always prevail over the strong, not only because they are in the majority, but also because they are the more crafty.
Friedrich Nietzsche (1844–1900) German philosopher. *The Twilight of the Idols*

7 When you get to the end of your rope, tie a knot and hang on.
Franklin D. Roosevelt (1882–1945) US Democratic president. Attrib.

8 The thing-in-itself, the will-to-live, exists whole and undivided in every being, even in the tiniest; it is present as completely as in all that ever were, are, and will be, taken together.
Arthur Schopenhauer (1788–1860) German philosopher. *Parerga and Paralipomena*

9 Survival of the fittest.
Herbert Spencer (1820–1903) British philosopher. *Principles of Biology*, Pt. III, Ch. 12

10 This is the Law of the Yukon, that only the strong shall thrive;
That surely the weak shall perish, and only the Fit survive.
Robert William Service (1874–1958) Canadian poet. *The Law of the Yukon*

11 One can survive everything nowadays, except death.
Oscar Wilde (1854–1900) Irish-born British dramatist. *A Woman of No Importance*, I

SUSPENSE

1 This suspense is terrible. I hope it will last.
Oscar Wilde (1854–1900) Irish-born British dramatist. *The Importance of Being Earnest*, III

SUSPICION

See also mistrust

1 Suspicions amongst thoughts are like bats amongst birds, they ever fly by twilight.
Francis Bacon (1561–1626) English philosopher. *Essays*, 'Of Suspicion'

2 He had the sort of convoluted mind that could attribute evil and devious motives to a bee-keeper offering him a pot of honey as a gift.
Hugh Cudlipp Referring to H. G. Bartholomew, editor of *The Daily Mirror*. *Walking on the Water*

3 I found a long gray hair on Kevin's jacket last night – If it's another woman's I'll kill him. If it's mine I'll kill myself.
Neil Simon (1927–) US playwright. *It Hurts Only When I Laugh*

4 By heaven, he echoes me,
As if there were some monster in his thought
Too hideous to be shown.
William Shakespeare (1564–1616) English dramatist. *Othello*, III:3

SWIFT, Jonathan

(1667–1745) Irish-born Anglican priest who became a poet and satirist in London. He is remembered for his *Journal to Stella* (1710–13) and *A Tale of A Tub* (1704), but best of all for *Gulliver's Travels* (1726), written after his return to Dublin as dean of St Patrick's.

Quotations about Swift

1 He delivered Ireland from plunder and oppression; and showed that wit, confederated with truth, had such force as authority was unable to resist.
Samuel Johnson (1709–84) British lexicographer. Attrib.

2 A monster gibbering, shrieking and gnashing imprecations against mankind.
William Makepeace Thackeray (1811–63) British novelist. Attrib.

Quotations by Swift

3 Satire is a sort of glass, wherein beholders do generally discover everybody's face but their own.
The Battle of the Books, 'Preface'

4 'Tis an old maxim in the schools,
That flattery's the food of fools;
Yet now and then your men of wit
Will condescend to take a bit.
Cadenus and Vanessa

5 It is folly of too many to mistake the echo of aLondon coffee-house for the voice of the kingdom.
The Conduct of the Allies

6 I have heard of a man who had a mind to sell his house, and therefore carried a piece of brick in his pocket, which he shewed as a pattern to encourage purchasers.
The Drapier's Letters, 2 (4 Aug 1724)

7 I cannot but conclude the bulk of your natives to be the most pernicious race of little odious vermin that nature ever suffered to crawl upon the surface of the earth.
Referring to the English. *Gulliver's Travels*, 'Voyage to Brobdingnag', Ch. 6

8 Whoever could make two ears of corn or two blades of grass to grow upon a spot of ground where only one grew before would deserve better of mankind and do more essential service to his country than the whole race of politicians put together.
Gulliver's Travels, 'Voyage to Brobdingnag', Ch. 7

9 So, naturalist observe, a flea
Hath smaller fleas that on him prey,
And these have smaller fleas to bite 'em.
And so proceed *ad infinitum*.
On Poetry

10 Promises and pie-crust are made to be broken.
Polite Conversation, Dialogue 1

11 Bachelor's fare; bread and cheese, and kisses.
Polite Conversation, Dialogue 1

12 He was a bold man that first eat an oyster.
Polite Conversation, Dialogue 2

13 I never saw, heard, nor read, that the clergy were beloved in any nation where Christianity was the religion of the country. Nothing can render them popular, but some degree of persecution.
Thoughts on Religion

14 When a true genius appears in the world, you may know him by this sign, that the dunces are all in confederacy against him.
Thoughts on Various Subjects

15 What they do in heaven we are ignorant of; what they do *not* we are told expressly, that they neither marry, nor are given in marriage.
Thoughts on Various Subjects

16 I never wonder to see men wicked, but I often wonder to see them not ashamed.
Thoughts on Various Subjects

17 Most sorts of diversion in men, children, and other animals, are an imitation of fighting.
Thoughts on Various Subjects

18 Laws are like cobwebs, which may catch small flies, but let wasps and hornets break through.
Similar remarks have been made by others. *A Tritical Essay upon the Faculties of the Mind*

19 For God's sake, madam, don't say that in England for if you do, they will surely tax it.
Responding to Lady Carteret's admiration for the quality of the air in Ireland. *Lives of the Wits* (H. Pearson)

20 I shall be like that tree; I shall die from the top.
Predicting his own mental decline on seeing a tree with a withered crown. *Lives of the Wits* (H. Pearson)

21 If Heaven had looked upon riches to be a valuable thing, it would not have given them to such a scoundrel.
Letter to Miss Vanhomrigh, 12–13 Aug 1720

22 Ah, a German and a genius! a prodigy, admit him!
Learning of the arrival of Handel; Swift's last words. Attrib.

SWITZERLAND

See also Europe

1 Since both its national products, snow and chocolate, melt, the cuckoo clock was invented solely in order to give tourists something solid to remember it by.
Alan Coren (1938–) British humorist and writer. *The Sanity Inspector*, 'And Though They Do Their Best'

2 The Swiss who are not a people so much as a neat clean quite solvent business.
William Faulkner (1897–1962) US novelist. *Intruder in the Dust*, Ch. 7

3 I look upon Switzerland as an inferior sort of Scotland.
Sydney Smith (1771–1845) British clergyman and essayist. Letter to Lord Holland, 1815

4 They say that if the Swiss had designed these mountains they'd be rather flatter.
Paul Theroux (1941–) US-born writer. Referring to the Alps. *The Great Railway Bazaar*, Ch. 28

5 In Italy for thirty years under the Borgias they had warfare, terror, murder, bloodshed – they produced Michelangelo, Leonardo da Vinci and the Renaissance. In Switzerland they had brotherly love, five hundred years of democracy and peace, and what did they produce . . . ? The cuckoo clock.
Orson Welles (1915–85) US film actor. *The Third Man*

SYMPATHY

See also comfort

1 Sympathy – for all these people, for being foreigners – lay over the gathering like a woolly blanket; and no one was enjoying it at all.
Malcolm Bradbury (1932–) British academic and novelist. *Eating People is Wrong*, Ch. 2

2 To be sympathetic without discrimination is so very debilitating.
Ronald Firbank (1886–1926) British novelist. *Vainglory*

3 This is for all ill-treated fellows
Unborn and unbegot,
For them to read when they're in trouble
And I am not.
A. E. Housman (1859–1936) British poet. Epigraph, *More Poems*

4 She was a machine-gun riddling her hostess with sympathy.
Aldous Huxley (1894–1964) British novelist. *Mortal Coils*, 'The Gioconda Smile'

5 I can sympathize with people's pains, but not with their pleasures. There is something curiously boring about somebody else's happiness.
Aldous Huxley *Limbo*, 'Cynthia'

6 To show pity is felt as a sign of contempt because one has clearly ceased to be an object of *fear* as soon as one is pitied.
Friedrich Wilhelm Nietzsche (1844–1900) German philosopher. *The Wanderer and His Shadow*

7 I can sympathize with everything, except suffering.
Oscar Wilde (1854–1900) Irish-born British dramatist. *The Picture of Dorian Gray*, Ch. 3

SZASZ, Thomas

(1920–) US psychiatrist and writer. His writings include *Pain and Pleasure* (1957) and *The Second Sin* (1974).

1 Men are rewarded and punished not for what they do, but rather for how their acts are defined. This is why men are more interested in better justifying themselves than in better behaving themselves.
The Second Sin

2 Traditionally, sex has been a very private, secretive activity. Herein perhaps lies its powerful force for uniting people in a strong bond. As we make sex less secretive, we may rob it of its power to hold men and women together.
The Second Sin

3 Formerly, when religion was strong and science weak, men mistook magic for medicine, now, when science is strong and religion weak, men mistake medicine for magic.
The Second Sin

4 A child becomes an adult when he realizes that he has a right not only to be right but also to be wrong.
The Second Sin

5 Happiness is an imaginary condition, formerly often attributed by the living to the dead, now usually attributed by adults to children, and by children to adults.
The Second Sin

6 The stupid neither forgive nor forget; the naive forgive and forget; the wise forgive but do not forget.
The Second Sin

7 Psychiatrists classify a person as neurotic if he suffers from his

problems in living, and a psychotic if he makes others suffer.
The Second Sin

8 If you talk to God, you are praying; if God talks to you, you have schizophrenia. If the dead talk to you, you are a spiritualist; if God talks to you, you are a schizophrenic.
The Second Sin

9 Masturbation: the primary sexual activity of mankind. In the nineteenth century it was a disease; in the twentieth, it's a cure.
The Second Sin

T

TACT

See also diplomacy

1 Leave well alone.
Proverb

2 Let sleeping dogs lie.
Proverb

3 Although there exist many thousand subjects for elegant conversation, there are persons who cannot meet a cripple without talking about feet.
Chinese proverb

4 One shouldn't talk of halters in the hanged man's house.
Miguel de Cervantes (1547–1616) Spanish novelist. *Don Quixote*, Pt. I, Ch. 25

5 Tact consists in knowing how far we may go too far.
Jean Cocteau (1889–1963) French poet and artist. *Treasury of Humorous Quotations*

6 Tact is a valuable attribute in gaining practice. It consists in telling a squint-eyed man that he has a fine, firm chin.
J. Chalmers Da Costa (1863–1933) *The Trials and Triumphs of the Surgeon*, Ch. 1

7 My advice was delicately poised between the cliché and the indiscretion.
Robert Runcie (1921–) British churchman (Archbishop of Canterbury). Comment to the press concerning his advice to the Prince of Wales and Lady Diana Spencer on their approaching wedding, 13 July 1981

TAFT, William Howard

(1857–1930) US statesman. He became president (1909–13), having been a judge and the secretary of war (1904–08). After his defeat for a second term as president he became professor of law at Yale.

1 Well, I have one consolation, No candidate was ever elected ex-president by such a large majority!
Referring to his disastrous defeat in the 1912 presidential election. Attrib.

TALENT

See also genius, talent and genius

1 The English instinctively admire any man who has no talent and is modest about it.
James Agate (1877–1947) British theater critic. Attrib.

2 Whom the gods wish to destroy they first call promising.
Cyril Connolly (1903–74) British journalist. *Enemies of Promise*, Ch. 3

3 I believe that since my life began
The most I've had is just
A talent to amuse.
Noël Coward (1899–1973) British dramatist. *Bitter Sweet*, 'If Love Were All'

4 Talent develops in quiet places, character in the full current of human life.
Goethe (1749–1832) German poet and dramatist. *Torquato Tasso*, I

5 Middle age snuffs out more talent than ever wars or sudden deaths do.
Richard Hughes (1900–) British writer. *The Fox in the Attic*

6 There is no substitute for talent. Industry and all the virtues are of no avail.
Aldous Huxley (1894–1964) British novelist. *Point Counter Point*

7 I think it's the most extraordinary collection of talent, of human knowledge, that has ever been gathered together at the White House – with the possible exception of when Thomas Jefferson dined alone.
John Fitzgerald Kennedy (1917–63) US statesman. Said at a dinner for Nobel Prizewinners, 29 Apr 1962.

8 It's not enough to be Hungarian, you must have talent too.
Alexander Korda (Sandor Kellner; 1893–1956) Hungarian-born British film director. *Alexander Korda* (K. Kulik)

9 Let our children grow tall, and some taller than others if they have it in them to do so.
Margaret Thatcher (1925–) British politician and prime minister. Speech, US tour, 1975

10 Talent is hereditary; it may be the common possession of a whole family (e.g., the Bach family); genius is not transmitted; it is never diffused, but is strictly individual.
Otto Weininger (1880–1903) *Sex and Character*, Pt. II, Ch. 4

TALENT AND GENIUS

See also genius, talent

1 It takes people a long time to learn the difference between talent and genius, especially ambitious young men and women.
Louisa May Alcott (1832–88) US novelist. *Little Women*, Pt. II

2 Mediocrity knows nothing higher than itself, but talent instantly recognizes genius.
Arthur Conan Doyle (1856–1930) British writer. *The Valley of Fear*

3 Genius does what it must, and Talent does what it can.
Owen Meredith (Robert Bulmer-Lytton, 1st Earl of Lytton; 1831–91) British statesman and poet. *Last Words of a Sensitive Second-rate Poet*

TASTE

See also difference, individuality

1 Between friends differences in taste or opinions are irritating in direct proportion to their triviality.
W. H. Auden (1907–73) British poet. *The Dyer's Hand*

2 Good taste is better than bad taste, but bad taste is better than no taste.
Arnold Bennett (1867–1931) British novelist. *The Observer*, 'Sayings of the Week', 24 Aug 1930

3 Taste is the feminine of genius.
Edward Fitzgerald (1809–83) British poet. Letter to J. R. Lowell, Oct 1877

4 Our tastes greatly alter. The lad does not care for the child's rattle, and the old man does not care for the young man's whore.
Samuel Johnson (1709–84) British lexicographer. *Life of Johnson* (J. Boswell), Vol. II

5 What is food to one man is bitter poison to others.
Lucretius (Titus Lucretius Carus; c. 99–55 BC) Roman philosopher. *On the Nature of the Universe*, IV

6 The kind of people who always go on about whether a thing is in good taste invariably have very bad taste.
Joe Orton (1933–67) British dramatist. Attrib.

7 The play, I remember, pleas'd not the million; 'twas caviare to the general.
William Shakespeare (1564–1616) English dramatist. *Hamlet*, II:2

8 Do not do unto others as you would they should do unto you. Their tastes may not be the same.
George Bernard Shaw (1856–1950) Irish dramatist and critic. *Man and Superman*, 'Maxims for Revolutionists'

9 You had no taste when you married me.
Richard Brinsley Sheridan (1751–1816) British dramatist. *The School for Scandal*, I

TAXATION

1 Neither will it be, that a people overlaid with taxes should ever become valiant and martial.
John Aubrey (1626–97) English antiquary. *Essays*, 'Of the True Greatness of Kingdoms'

2 And it came to pass in those days, that there went out a decree from Caesar Augustus, that all the world should be taxed.
Bible: Luke 2:1

3 They can't collect legal taxes from illegal money.
Al Capone (1899–1947) Italian-born US gangster. Objecting to the US Bureau of Internal Revenue claiming large sums in unpaid back tax. *Capone* (J. Kobler)

4 The hardest thing in the world to understand is income tax.
Albert Einstein (1879–1955) German-born US physicist. Attrib.

5 The greatest harm that cometh of a king's poverty is, that he shall by necessity be forced to find exquisite means of getting goods, as to put in default some of his subjects that be innocent, and upon the rich men more than the poor, because they may the better pay.
John Fortescue (c. 1394–1476) English jurist. *The Governance of England*

6 In this world nothing is certain but death and taxes.
Benjamin Franklin (1706–90) US scientist and statesman. Letter to Jean-Baptiste Leroy, 13 Nov 1789

7 I warn you there are going to be howls of anguish from the 80,000 people who are rich enough to pay over 75% on the last slice of their income.
Denis Healey (1917–) British Labour politician. Speech, Labour Party Conference, 1 Oct 1973

8 This would, at a stroke, reduce the rise in prices, increase productivity and reduce unemployment.
Edward Heath (1916–) British politician and prime minister. Press release from Conservative Central Office, 16 June 1970

9 You have gold and I want gold; where is it?
Henry IV (1367–1413) King of England. Said to merchants at a Great Council (Apr–June 1407) when trying to borrow money to pay the garrison at Calais, which had mutinied because of arrears in its wages. Attrib. in *Eulogium Historiarum*

10 When they fire a rocket at Cape Canaveral, I feel as if I own it.
William Holden US actor. *TV Times*, 25 Aug 1972

11 *Excise*. A hateful tax levied upon commodities.
Samuel Johnson (1709–84) British lexicographer. *Dictionary of the English Language*

12 Sir, I now pay you this exorbitant charge, but I must ask you to explain to her Majesty that she must not in future look upon me as a source of income.
Charles Kemble (1775–1854) British actor. On being obliged to hand over his income tax to the tax collector. *Humour in the Theatre* (J. Aye)

13 The avoidance of taxes is the only pursuit that still carries any reward.
John Maynard Keynes (1883–1946) British economist. Attrib.

14 The Chancellor of the Exchequer is a man whose duties make him more or less of a taxing machine. He is intrusted with a certain amount of misery which it is his duty to distribute as fairly as he can.
Robert Lowe (1811–92) British lawyer and politician. Speech, House of Commons, 11 Apr 1870

15 His taxes now prove
His great love for the people,
So wisely they're managed
To starve the poor souls.
Charles Morris (1745–1838) British songwriter. Referring to William Pitt the Younger. *The Faber Book of English History in Verse* (Kenneth Baker)

16 The British parliament has no right to tax the Americans . . . Taxation and representation are inseparably united.
Charles Pratt (1714–94) English Lord Chancellor. Speech, House of Lords, Dec 1765

17 The taxpayer is someone who works for the federal government but doesn't have to take a civil service examination.
Ronald Reagan (1911–) US politician and president. Attrib.

18 It has made more liars out of the American people than Golf.
Will Rogers (1879–1935) US actor and humorist. Referring to income tax. *Saturday Review*, 'A Rogers Thesaurus', 25 Aug 1962

19 There is no art which one government sooner learns of another than that of draining money from the pockets of the people.
Adam Smith (1723–90) Scottish economist. *The Wealth of Nations*

20 For God's sake, madam, don't say that in England for if you do, they will surely tax it.
Jonathan Swift (1667–1745) Irish-born Anglican priest and writer. Responding to Lady Carteret's admiration for the quality of the air in Ireland. *Lives of the Wits* (H. Pearson)

TEARS

1 Life is made up of sobs, sniffles, and smiles, with sniffles predominating.
O. Henry (William Sydney Porter; 1862–1910) US writer. *Gift of the Magi*

2 It's my party and I'll cry if I want to.
Herb Weiner US songwriter. Song title

TECHNOLOGY

See also progress, science

1 At sixty miles an hour the loudest noise in this new Rolls-Royce comes from the electric clock.
Anonymous Advertising slogan for Rolls-Royce

2 Give me a firm place to stand, and I will move the earth.
Archimedes (c. 287–212 BC) Greek mathematician. *On the Lever*

3 Man is a tool-using animal.
Thomas Carlyle (1795–1881) Scottish historian and essayist. *Sartor Resartus*, Bk. I, Ch. 5

4 Machines from the Maxim gun to the computer, are for the most part means by which a minority can keep free men in subjection.
Kenneth Clark (1903–83) British art historian. *Civilisation*

5 Any sufficiently advanced technology is indistinguishable from magic.
Arthur C. Clarke (1917–) British science-fiction writer. *The Lost Worlds of 2001*

6 Man is a tool-making animal.
Benjamin Franklin (1706–90) US scientist and statesman. *Life of Johnson* (J. Boswell), 7 Apr 1778

7 Our rockets can find Halley's comet and fly to Venus with amazing accuracy, but side by side with these scientific and technical triumphs is an obvious lack of efficiency in using scientific achievements for economic needs, and many Soviet household appliances are of poor quality.
Mikhail Gorbachov (1931–) Soviet statesman. *Perestroika*

8 One machine can do the work of fifty ordinary men. No machine can do the work of one extraordinary man.
Elbert Hubbard (1856–1915) US writer. *Roycroft Dictionary and Book of Epigrams*

9 The new electronic interdependence recreates the world in the image of a global village.
Marshall McLuhan (1911–81) Canadian sociologist. *The Gutenberg Galaxy*

10 For tribal man space was the uncontrollable mystery. For technological man it is time that occupies the same role.
Marshall McLuhan *The Mechanical Bride*, 'Magic that Changes Mood'

11 The machine threatens all achievement.
Rainer Maria Rilke (1875–1926) Austrian poet. *Die Sonette an Orpheus*, II, 10

12 The technology of medicine has outrun its sociology.
Henry E. Sigerist (1891–1957) *Medicine and Human Welfare*, Ch. 3

13 Pylons, those pillars
Bare like nude giant girls that have no secret.
Stephen Spender (1909–) British poet. *The Pylons*

14 No man . . . who has wrestled with a self-adjusting card table can ever quite be the man he once was.
James Thurber (1894–1961) US humorist. *Let Your Mind Alone*, 'Sex ex Machina'

15 Sir, I have tested your machine. It adds new terror to life and makes death a long-felt want.
Herbert Beerbohm Tree (1853–1917) British actor and theater manager. Referring to a gramophone. *Beerbohm Tree* (H. Pearson)

16 I see no reason to suppose that these machines will ever force themselves into general use.
Duke of Wellington (1769–1852) British general and statesman. Referring to steam locomotives. *Geoffrey Madan's Notebooks* (J. Gere)

TEETH

1 Removing the teeth will cure something, including the foolish belief that removing the teeth will cure everything.
Anonymous

2 DENTIST, n. A prestidigitator who, putting metal into your mouth, pulls coins out of your pocket.
Ambrose Bierce (1842–?1914) US writer and journalist. *The Devil's Dictionary*

3 Every Tooth in a Man's Head is more valuable than a Diamond.
Miguel de Cervantes (1547–1616) Spanish novelist. *Don Quixote*, Pt. I, Ch. 4

4 It is necessary to clean the teeth frequently, more especially after meals, but not on any account with a pin, or the point of a penknife, and it must never be done at table.
St. Jean Baptiste de la Salle (1651–1719) *The Rules of Christian Manners and Civility*, I

5 I find that most men would rather have their bellies opened for five hundred dollars than have a tooth pulled for five.
Martin H. Fischer (1879–1962) *Fischerisms* (Howard Fabing and Ray Marr)

6 For years I have let dentists ride roughshod over my teeth: I have been sawed, hacked, chopped, whittled, bewitched, bewildered, tattooed, and signed on again; but this is cuspid's last stand.
S. J. Perelman (1904–79) US humorous writer. *Crazy Like a Fox*, 'Nothing but the Tooth'

7 I'll dispose of my teeth as I see fit, and after they've gone, I'll get along. I started off living on gruel, and by God, I can always go back to it again.
S. J. Perelman *Crazy Like a Fox*, 'Nothing but the Tooth'

8 Certain people are born with natural false teeth.
Robert Robinson (1927–) British writer and broadcaster. BBC radio program, *Stop the Week*, 1977

9 He that sleeps feels no the toothache.
William Shakespeare (1564–1616) English dramatist and poet. *Cymbeline*

10 The man with toothache thinks everyone happy whose teeth are sound.
George Bernard Shaw (1856–1950) Irish dramatist and critic. *Man and Superman*, 'Maxims for Revolutionists'

11 Sweet things are bad for the teeth.
Jonathan Swift (1667–1746) Anglo-Irish priest, poet, and satirist. *Polite Conversation*, Dialogue II

12 Adam and Eve had many advantages, but the principal one was that they escaped teething.
Mark Twain (Samuel L. Clemens; 1835–1910) US writer. *The Tragedy of Pudd'nhead Wilson*, Ch. 4

13 To lose a lover or even a husband or two during the course of one's life can be vexing. But to lose one's teeth is a catastrophe.
Hugh Wheeler (1912–) British-born US writer. *A Little Night Music*

TELEGRAMS

1 To hell with you. Offensive letter follows.
Anonymous Telegram to Sir Alec Douglas-Home

2 Winston's back.
Anonymous Signal to all ships of the Royal Navy from the Admiralty when Churchill was reappointed First Sea Lord, 3 Sept 1939.

3 Streets full of water. Please advise.
Robert Benchley (1889–1945) US humorist. Telegram sent to his editor on arriving in Venice. Attrib.

4 Price of Herald three cents daily. Five cents Sunday. Bennett.
James Gordon Bennett (1841–1918) US editor. Telegram to William Randolph Hearst, when he heard that Hearst was trying to buy his paper. *The Life and Death of the Press Barons* (P. Brandon)

5 Nothing to be fixed except your performance.
Noël Coward (1899–1973) British dramatist. Replying to a telegram from the actress Gertrude Lawrence – 'Nothing wrong that can't be fixed' – referring to her part in Coward's play *Private Lives*. *Noël Coward and his Friends*

6 Dear Mrs A., hooray hooray,

At last you are deflowered
On this as every other day
I love you. Noël Coward.
Noël Coward Telegram to Gertrude Lawrence on her marriage to Richard S. Aldrich

7 ?
Victor Hugo (1802–85) French writer. The entire contents of a telegram sent to his publishers asking how *Les Misérables* was selling; the reply was '!'. *The Literary Life* (R. Hendrickson)

8 Have strong suspicions that Crippen London cellar murderer and accomplice are amongst saloon passengers moustache taken off growing beard accomplice dressed as boy voice manner and build undoubtedly a girl both travelling as Mr and Master Robinson.
Captain Kendall This was the first time a wireless telegraphy message from a ship at sea led to the arrest of criminals. Telegram to Scotland Yard, 22 July 1910

9 We have finished the job, what shall we do with the tools?
Haile Selassie (1892–1975) Emperor of Ethiopia. Telegram sent to Winston Churchill, mimicking his 'Give us the tools, and we will finish the job'. *Ambrosia and Small Beer*, Ch. 4 (Edward Marsh)

10 Reports of my death are greatly exaggerated.
Mark Twain (Samuel Langhorne Clemens; 1835–1910) US writer. On learning that his obituary had been published. Cable to the Associated Press

11 Nurse unupblown.
Evelyn Waugh (1903–66) British novelist. Cable sent after he had failed, while a journalist serving in Ethiopia, to substantiate a rumor that an English nurse had been blown up in an Italian air raid. *Our Marvelous Native Tongue* (R. Claiborne)

12 No, no, Oscar, you forget. When you and I are together we never talk about anything except me.
James Whistler (1834–1903) US painter. Cable replying to Oscar Wilde's message: 'When you and I are together we never talk about anything except ourselves'. *The Gentle Art of Making Enemies*

TELEVISION

See also media

1 That's the sixty-four thousand dollar question.
Anonymous Title of US TV quizzes

2 There is a bias in television journalism. It is not against any particular party or point of view – it is a bias against *understanding.*
John Birt (1944–) British TV executive. This launched a series of articles written jointly with Peter Jay. *The Times*, 28 Feb 1975

3 Some television programs are so much chewing gum for the eyes.
John Mason Brown (1900–69) US critic. Interview, 28 July 1955

4 Television is more interesting than people. If it were not, we should have people standing in the corners of our rooms.
Alan Coren (1938–) British humorist and writer. *The Times*

5 Television is for appearing on, not looking at.
Noël Coward (1899–1973) British dramatist. Attrib.

6 If any reader of this book is in the grip of some habit of which he is deeply ashamed, I advise him not to give way to it in secret but to do it on television. No-one will pass him with averted gaze on the other side of the street. People will cross the road at the risk of losing their own lives in order to say 'We saw you on the telly'.
Quentin Crisp (?1910–) Model, publicist, and writer. *How to Become a Virgin*

7 Television is an invention that permits you to be entertained in your living room by people you wouldn't have in your home.
David Frost (1939–) British television personality. Attrib., CBS television, 1971

8 Why should people go out and pay to see bad films when they can stay at home and see bad television for nothing?
Samuel Goldwyn (Samuel Goldfish; 1882–1974) Polish-born US film producer. *The Observer*, 9 Sept 1956

9 TV . . . is our latest medium – we call it a medium because nothing's well done.
Ace Goodman (1899–) US writer. Letter to Groucho Marx, 1954. *The Groucho Letters*

10 A medium, so called because it is neither rare nor well done.
Ernie Kovacs (1919–62) US entertainer. Referring to television. Attrib.

11 Television won't matter in your lifetime or mine.
Rex Lambert *The Listener*

12 Television brought the brutality of war into the comfort of the living room. Vietnam was lost in the living rooms of America – not on the battlefields of Vietnam.
Marshall McLuhan (1911–81) Canadian sociologist. Montreal *Gazette*, 16 May 1975

13 I have had my aerials removed – it's the moral equivalent of a prostate operation.
Malcolm Muggeridge (1903–) British writer. *Radio Times*, Apr 1981

14 Television? No good will come of this device. The word is half Greek and half Latin.
C. P. Scott (1846–1932) British journalist. Attrib.

TEMPERANCE

1 I prefer temperance hotels – although they sell worse kinds of liquor than any other kind of hotels.
Artemus Ward (Charles Farrar Browne; 1834–67) US humorous writer. *Artemus Ward's Lecture*

TEMPTATION

1 Forbidden fruit is sweet.
Proverb

2 If you can't be good, be careful.
Proverb

3 Saintliness is also a temptation.
Jean Anouilh (1910–87) French dramatist. *Becket*

4 I am not over-fond of resisting temptation.
William Beckford (1759–1844) British writer. *Vathek*

5 The Devil, having nothing else to do
Went off to tempt my Lady Poltagrue.
My Lady, tempted by a private whim
To his annoyance tempted him.
Hilaire Belloc (1870–1953) French-born British poet. *Epigrams*

6 Blessed is the man that endureth temptation: for when he is tried, he shall receive the crown of life, which the Lord hath promised to them that love him.
Bible: James 1:12

7 Then was Jesus led up of the Spirit into the wilderness to be tempted of the devil.
And when he had fasted forty days and forty nights, he was afterward an hungred.
And when the tempter came to him, he said, If thou be the Son of God, command that these stones be made bread.

But he answered and said, It is written, Man shall not live by bread alone, but by every word that proceedeth out of the mouth of God.
Bible: Matthew 4:1–4

8 Jesus said unto him, It is written again, Thou shalt not tempt the Lord thy God.
Again, the devil taketh him up into an exceeding high mountain, and sheweth him all the kingdoms of the world, and the glory of them.
Bible: Matthew 4:7–8

9 All the deceits of the world, the flesh, and the devil.
The Book of Common Prayer *Morning Prayer, Prayer of St Chrysostom*

10 She's not so pretty anyone would want to ruin her.
Bertolt Brecht (1898–1956) German dramatist. *Mother Courage and her Children*

11 Not all that tempts your wand'ring eyes
And heedless hearts, is lawful prize;
Nor all, that glisters, gold.
Thomas Gray (1716–71) British poet. *Ode on the Death of a Favourite Cat*

12 'You oughtn't to yield to temptation.'
'Well, somebody must, or the thing becomes absurd.'
Anthony Hope (Sir Anthony Hope Hawkins; 1863–1933) British novelist. *The Dolly Dialogues*

13 . . . with peaches and women, it's only the side next the sun that's tempting.
Ouida (Marie Louise de la Ramée; 1839–1908) British novelist. *Strathmore*

14 Is this her fault or mine?
The tempter or the tempted, who sins most?
William Shakespeare (1564–1616) English dramatist. *Measure for Measure*, II:2

15 O cunning enemy, that, to catch a saint,
With saints dost bait thy hook! Most dangerous
Is that temptation that doth goad us on
To sin in loving virtue; never could the strumpet,
With all her double vigour, art and nature,
Once stir my temper; but this virtuous maid
Subdues me quite. Ever till now
When men were fond, I smil'd and wonder'd how.
William Shakespeare *Measure for Measure*, II:2

16 I never resist temptation because I have found that things that are bad for me never tempt me.
George Bernard Shaw (1856–1950) Irish dramatist and critic. *The Apple Cart*

17 I can resist everything except temptation.
Oscar Wilde (1854–1900) Irish-born British dramatist. *Lady Windermere's Fan*, I

18 The only way to get rid of a temptation is to yield to it.
Oscar Wilde Repeating a similar sentiment expressed by Clementina Stirling Graham (1782–1877). *The Picture of Dorian Gray*, Ch. 2

19 She had no use for morals and always omitted 'Lead us not into temptation' from the Lord's Prayer. 'It's no business of His' she proclaimed.
Philip Ziegler (1929–) British biographer. *Diana Cooper*

TENNYSON, Alfred, Baron

(1809–92) British poet. He established his reputation with *Morte d'Arthur* (1842). Of his many other works, *In Memoriam* (1850), *The Charge of the Light Brigade* (1854), *Maud* (1855), and *The Idylls of the King* (1859) are outstanding. He became poet laureate in 1850.

Quotations about Tennyson

1 . . . there was little about melancholia that he didn't know; there was little else that he did.
W. H. Auden (1907–73) British poet. *Selected Poems of Tennyson*, Introduction

2 Let school-miss Alfred vent her chaste delight
On 'darling little rooms so warm and bright.'
Edward Bulwer-Lytton (1803–73) British novelist and politician. Attrib.

3 Alfred is always carrying a bit of chaos round with him, and turning it into cosmos.
Thomas Carlyle (1795–1881) Scottish historian and essayist.

4 Tennyson was not Tennysonian.
Henry James (1843–1916) US novelist. *The Middle Years*

Quotations by Tennyson

5 And the stately ships go on
To their haven under the hill;
But O for the touch of a vanish'd hand,
And the sound of a voice that is still!
Break, Break, Break

6 For men may come and men may go
But I go on for ever.
The Brook

7 I come from haunts of coot and hern,
I make a sudden sally
And sparkle out among the fern,
To bicker down a valley.
The Brook

8 Half a league, half a league,
Half a league onward,
All in the valley of Death
Rode the six hundred.
The Charge of the Light Brigade

9 'Forward the Light Brigade!'
Was there a man dismay'd?
Not tho' the soldier knew
Some one had blunder'd:
Their's not to make reply,
Their's not to reason why,
Their's but to do and die:
Into the valley of Death
Rode the six hundred.
The Charge of the Light Brigade

10 Into the jaws of Death,
Into the mouth of Hell.
The Charge of the Light Brigade

11 Come not, when I am dead,
To drop thy foolish tears upon my grave,
To trample round my fallen head,
And vex the unhappy dust thou wouldst not save.
Come Not, When I Am Dead

12 Sunset and evening star,
And one clear call for me!
And may there be no moaning of the bar
When I put out to sea.
Crossing the Bar

13 God made the woman for the man,
And for the good and increase of the world.
Edwin Morris

14 Half light, half shade,
She stood, a sight to make an old man young.
The Gardener's Daughter

15 That a lie which is all a lie may be met and fought with outright,
But a lie which is part a truth is a harder matter to fight.
The Grandmother

16 Dreams are true while they last,
and do we not live in dreams?
The Higher Pantheism

17 His honour rooted in dishonour
stood,
And faith unfaithful kept him falsely
true.
Idylls of the King, 'Lancelot and Elaine'

18 He makes no friend who never
made a foe.
Idylls of the King, 'Lancelot and Elaine'

19 For man is man and master of his
fate.
Idylls of the King, 'The Marriage of Geraint'

20 An arm
Rose up from out the bosom of the
lake,
Clothed in white samite, mystic,
wonderful.
Idylls of the King, 'The Passing of Arthur'

21 Authority forgets a dying king.
Idylls of the King, 'The Passing of Arthur'

22 For now I see the true old times
are dead,
When every morning brought a noble
chance,
And every chance brought out a noble knight.
Idylls of the King, 'The Passing of Arthur'

23 And slowly answer'd Arthur from
the barge:
'The old order changeth, yielding
place to new,
And God fulfils himself in many
ways.'
Idylls of the King, 'The Passing of Arthur'

24 If thou shouldst never see my face
again,
Pray for my soul. More things are
wrought by prayer
Than this world dreams of.
Idylls of the King, 'The Passing of Arthur'

25 I am going a long way
With these thou seest – if indeed I
go
(For all my mind is clouded with a
doubt) –
To the island-valley of Avilion;
Where falls not hail, or rain, or any
snow,
Nor ever wind blows loudly; but it
lies
Deep-meadow'd, happy, fair with
orchard lawns
And bowery hollows crown'd with
summer sea,
Where I will heal me of my grievous
wound.
Idylls of the King, 'The Passing of Arthur'

26 Our little systems have their day;
They have their day and cease to be.
In Memoriam A.H.H., Prologue

27 For words, like Nature, half reveal
And half conceal the Soul within.
In Memoriam A.H.H., V

28 I hold it true, whate'er befall;
I feel it, when I sorrow most;
'Tis better to have loved and lost
Than never to have loved at all.
In Memoriam A.H.H., XXVII

29 And so the Word had breath, and
wrought
With human hands the creed of
creeds
In loveliness of perfect deeds,
More strong than all poetic thought.
In Memoriam A.H.H., XXXVI

30 But what am I?
An infant crying in the night:
An infant crying for the light:
And with no language but a cry.
In Memoriam A.H.H., LIV

31 Are God and Nature then at strife
That Nature lends such evil dreams?
So careful of the type she seems,
So careless of the single life.
In Memoriam A.H.H., LV

32 Sleep, Death's twin-brother, knows
not Death,
Nor can I dream of thee as dead.
In Memoriam A.H.H., LXVIII

33 I dreamed there would be Spring no
more,
That Nature's ancient power was
lost.
In Memoriam A.H.H., LXIX

34 So many worlds, so much to do,
So little done, such things to be.
In Memoriam A.H.H., LXXIII

35 Ring out, wild bells, to the wild
sky,
The flying cloud, the frosty light:
The year is dying in the night;
Ring out, wild bells, and let him die.
In Memoriam A.H.H., CVI

36 'Tis held that sorrow makes us
wise.
In Memoriam A.H.H., CXIII

37 My regret
Becomes an April violet,
And buds and blossoms like the rest.
In Memoriam A.H.H., CXV

38 One God, one law, one element,
And one far-off divine event,
To which the whole creation moves.
In Memoriam A.H.H., CXXXI

39 A simple maiden in her flower
Is worth a hundred coats-of-arms.
Lady Clara Vere de Vere, II

40 Kind hearts are more than
coronets,
And simple faith than Norman blood.
Lady Clara Vere de Vere, VI

41 On either side the river lie
Long fields of barley and of rye,
That clothe the wold and meet the
sky;
And thro' the field the road runs by
To many-tower'd Camelot.
The Lady of Shalott, Pt. I

42 Willows whiten, aspens quiver,
Little breezes dusk and shiver.
The Lady of Shalott, Pt. I

43 Or when the moon was overhead,
Came two young lovers lately wed;
'I am half sick of shadows,' said
The Lady of Shalott.
The Lady of Shalott, Pt. II

44 She has heard a whisper say,
A curse is on her if she stay
To look down to Camelot.
The Lady of Shalott, Pt. II

45 A bow-shot from her bower-eaves,
He rode between the barley-
sheaves,
The sun came dazzling thro' the
leaves
And flamed upon the brazen graves
Of bold Sir Lancelot.
The Lady of Shalott, Pt. III

46 'The curse is come upon me,' cried
The Lady of Shalott.
The Lady of Shalott, Pt. III

47 But Lancelot mused a little space;
He said, 'She has a lovely face;
God in his mercy lend her grace,
The Lady of Shalott.'
The Lady of Shalott, Pt. IV

48 Ah God! the petty fools of rhyme
That shriek and sweat in pigmy
wars.
Literary Squabbles

49 Nourishing a youth sublime
With the fairy tales of science, and
the long result of Time.
Locksley Hall

50 In the Spring a young man's fancy
lightly turns to thoughts of love.
Locksley Hall

51 Such a one do I remember, whom
to look at was to love.
Locksley Hall

52 So I triumphed ere my passion, sweeping thro' me, left me dry,
Left me with the palsied heart, and left me with the jaundiced eye.
Locksley Hall

53 Not with blinded eyesight poring over miserable books.
Locksley Hall

54 Time driveth onward fast,
And in a little while our lips are dumb.
Let us alone. What is it that will last?
All things are taken from us, and become
Portions and parcels of the dreadful Past.
The Lotos-Eaters, 'Choric Song'

55 Music that gentlier on the spirit lies,
Than tir'd eyelids upon tir'd eyes.
The Lotos-Eaters, 'Choric Song'

56 Come into the garden, Maud,
For the black bat, night, has flown,
Come into the garden, Maud,
I am here at the gate alone.
Maud, I

57 The rose was awake all night for your sake,
Knowing your promise to me;
The lilies and roses were all awake,
They sighed for the dawn and thee.
Maud, I

58 I embrace the purpose of God and the doom assigned.
Maud, III

59 But the churchmen fain would kill their church,
As the churches have kill'd their Christ.
Maud, V

60 You must wake and call me early, call me early, mother dear;
To-morrow 'ill be the happiest time of all the glad New-year;
Of all the glad New-year, mother, the maddest merriest day;
For I'm to be Queen o' the May, mother, I'm to be Queen o' the May.
The May Queen

61 The splendour falls on castle walls
And snowy summits old in story.
The Princess, III

62 Tears, idle tears, I know not what they mean,
Tears from the depth of some divine despair.
The Princess, IV

63 Dear as remembered kisses after death,
And sweet as those by hopeless fancy feign'd
On lips that are for others: deep as love,
Deep as first love, and wild with all regret;
O Death in Life, the days that are no more.
The Princess, IV

64 O tell her, brief is life but love is long.
The Princess, IV

65 Man is the hunter; woman is his game:
The sleek and shining creatures of the chase,
We hunt them for the beauty of their skins.
The Princess, V

66 Man for the field and woman for the hearth:
Man for the sword and for the needle she:
Man with the head and woman with the heart:
Man to command and woman to obey;
All else confusion.
The Princess, V

67 Home they brought her warrior dead.
She nor swoon'd, nor utter'd cry:
All her maidens, watching said,
'She must weep or she will die.'
The Princess, VI

68 The moans of doves in immemorial elms,
And murmuring of innumerable bees.
The Princess, VII

69 Revolts, republics, revolutions, most
No graver than a schoolboy's barring out.
The Princess, Conclusion

70 And they blest him in their pain, that they were not left to Spain,
To the thumbscrew and the stake, for the glory of the Lord.
The Revenge, III

71 A day less or more
At sea or ashore,
We die – does it matter when?
The Revenge, XI

72 My strength is as the strength of ten,
Because my heart is pure.
Sir Galahad

73 How sweet are looks that ladies bend
On whom their favours fall!
Sir Galahad

74 Battering the gates of heaven with storms of prayer.
St Simeon Stylites

75 The woods decay, the woods decay and fall,
The vapours weep their burthen to the ground,
Man comes and tills the field and lies beneath,
And after many a summer dies the swan.
Tithonus

76 The Gods themselves cannot recall their gifts.
Tithonus

77 A life that moves to gracious ends
Thro' troops of unrecording friends,
A deedful life, a silent voice.
To – , after reading a Life and Letters

78 God gives us love. Something to love
He lends us; but, when love is grown
To ripeness that on which it throve
Falls off, and love is left alone.
To J.S.

79 A still small voice spake unto me,
'Thou art so full of misery,
Were it not better not to be?'
The Two Voices

80 All experience is an arch wherethro'
Gleams that untravelled world, whose margin fades
For ever and for ever when I move.
Ulysses

81 We are not now that strength which in old days
Moved earth and heaven; that which we are, we are;
One equal temper of heroic hearts,
Made weak by time and fate, but strong in will
To strive, to seek, to find, and not to yield.
Ulysses

82 Every moment dies a man,
Every moment one is born.
The Vision of Sin

TERROR

1 *Nacht und Nebel*
Night and Fog.
Adolf Hitler (1889–1945) German dictator. Hitler's euphemism for the way in which people suspected of crimes against occupying forces

would be dealt with. They would be spirited away into the night and fog. Title of decree, 1941

TERRORISM

1 The terrorist and the policeman both come from the same basket.
Joseph Conrad (Teodor Josef Konrad Korzeniowski; 1857–1924) Polish-born British novelist. *The Secret Agent*, Ch. 4

2 All terrorists, at the invitation of the Government, end up with drinks at the Dorchester.
Hugh Gaitskell (1906–63) British Labour politician. Letter to *The Guardian*, 23 Aug 1977 (Dora Gaitskell)

THATCHER, Margaret

(1925–) British politician, prime minister since 1979. Trained as a chemist and a barrister, she became a Conservative MP in 1959 and minister of education and science (1970–74).

Quotations about Thatcher

1 Mrs Thatcher is a woman of common views but uncommon abilities.
Julian Critchley (1930–) British Conservative politician. *The Times*, Profile: Margaret Thatcher

2 Attila the Hen.
Clement Freud (1924–) British Liberal politician and broadcaster. BBC Radio program, *The News Quiz*

3 She approaches the problems of our country with all the one-dimensional sublety of a comic-strip.
Denis Healey (1917–) British Labour politician. Speech, House of Commons, 22 May 1979

Quotations by Thatcher

4 I'm not hard – I'm frightfully soft. But I will not be hounded.
Daily Mail, 1972

5 Let our children grow tall, and some taller than others if they have it in them to do so.
Speech, US tour, 1975

6 Britain is no longer in the politics of the pendulum, but of the ratchet.
Speech, Institute of Public Relations, 1977

7 I love argument, I love debate. I don't expect anyone just to sit there and agree with me, that's not their job.
The Times, 1980

8 If a woman like Eva Peron with no ideals can get that far, think how far I can go with all the ideals that I have.
The Sunday Times, 1980

9 U-turn if you want to. The lady's not for turning.
Speech, Conservative Conference, 1980

10 No one would have remembered the Good Samaritan if he'd only had good intentions. He had money as well.
Television interview, 1980

11 The battle for women's rights has been largely won.
The Guardian, 1982

12 Pennies do not come from heaven. They have to be earned here on earth.
Sunday Telegraph, 1982

13 Victorian values . . . were the values when our country became great.
Television interview, 1982

14 Oh. I have got lots of human weaknesses, who hasn't?
The Times, 1983

15 State socialism is totally alien to the British character.
The Times, 1983

16 I am painted as the greatest little dictator, which is ridiculous – you always take some consultations.
The Times, 1983

17 We are the true peace movement.
The Times, 1983

18 And what a prize we have to fight for: no less than the chance to banish from our land the dark divisive clouds of Marxist socialism.
Speech, Scottish Conservative Conference, 1983

19 Young people ought not to be idle. It is very bad for them.
The Times, 1984

20 I love being at the centre of things.
Reader's Digest, 1984

21 I am certain that we will win the election with a good majority. Not that I am ever over-confident.
Evening Standard, 1987

22 I don't mind how much my ministers talk – as long as they do what I say.
The Times, 1987

23 I wasn't lucky. I deserved it.
Said after receiving a school prize, aged nine. Attrib.

THEATER

See also acting, actors, audiences, criticism, literature, plays, Shakespeare

1 The reason why Absurdist plays take place in No Man's Land with only two characters is primarily financial.
Arthur Adamov (1908–70) Russian-born French dramatist. Said at the Edinburgh International Drama Conference, 13 Sept 1963

2 It's one of the tragic ironies of the theater that only one man in it can count on steady work – the night watchman.
Tallulah Bankhead (1903–68) US actress. *Tallulah*, Ch. 1

3 Some of my plays peter out, and some pan out.
J. M. Barrie (1860–1937) British novelist and dramatist. Attrib.

4 There's No Business Like Show Business.
Irving Berlin (1888–) US composer and lyricist. Song title

5 Tragedy is if I cut my finger. Comedy is if I walk into an open sewer and die.
Mel Brooks (Melvyn Kaminsky; 1926–) US film director. *New Yorker*, 30 Oct 1978

6 All tragedies are finish'd by a death,
All comedies are ended by a marriage.
Lord Byron (1788–1824) British poet. *Don Juan*, III

7 You know, I go to the theatre to be entertained . . . I don't want to see plays about rape, sodomy and drug addiction . . . I can get all that at home.
Peter Cook (1937–) British writer and entertainer. *The Observer*, caption to cartoon, 8 July 1962

8 Don't put your daughter on the stage, Mrs Worthington.
Noël Coward (1899–1973) British dramatist. *Title of song*

9 Farce is the essential theatre. Farce refined becomes high comedy: farce brutalized becomes tragedy.
Gordon Craig (1872–1966) British actor. *The Story of my Days, Index*

10 I have knocked everything except the knees of the chorus girls. Nature anticipated us there.
Percy Hammond (1873–1936) US drama critic. Attrib.

11 We participate in a tragedy; at a comedy we only look.

Aldous Huxley (1894–1964) British novelist. *The Devils of Loudon*, Ch. 11

12 I never deliberately set out to shock, but when people don't walk out of my plays I think there is something wrong.

John Osborne (1929–) British dramatist. *The Observer*, 'Sayings of the Week', 19 Jan 1975

13 She's not going to walk in here . . . and turn it into a Golden Sanitary Towel Award Presentation.

John Osborne *Hotel in Amsterdam*

14 The Great White Way.

Albert Bigelow Paine (1861–1937) US writer. Later used as a name for Broadway. Book title

15 Popular stage-plays are sinful, heathenish, lewd, ungodly Spectacles and most pernicious Corruptions, condemned in all ages as intolerable Mischiefs to Churches, to Republics, to the manners, minds and souls of men.

William Prynne (1600–69) English Puritan. *Histriomastix*

16 Can this cockpit hold
The vasty fields of France? or may we cram
Within this wooden O the very casques
That did affright the air at Agincourt?

William Shakespeare (1564–1616) English dramatist. *Henry V*, Prologue

17 I depict men as they ought to be, but Euripides portrays them as they are.

Sophocles (c. 496–406 BC) Greek dramatist. *Poetics* (Aristotle)

18 The bad end unhappily, the good unluckily. That is what tragedy means.

Tom Stoppard (1937–) Czech-born British dramatist. *Rosencrantz and Guildenstern Are Dead*, II

19 It was the kind of show where the girls are not auditioned – just measured.

Irene Thomas (1920–) British writer. Attrib.

20 I would just like to mention Robert Houdin who in the eighteenth century invented the vanishing bird-cage trick and the theater matinée – may he rot and perish. Good afternoon.

Orson Welles (1915–85) US film actor. Addressing the audience at the end of a matinée performance. *Great Theatrical Disasters* (G. Brandreth)

THEFT

See also crime

1 The fault is great in man or woman
Who steals a goose from off a common;
But what can plead that man's excuse
Who steals a common from a goose?

Anonymous *The Tickler Magazine*, 1 Feb 1821

2 They will steal the very teeth out of your mouth as you walk through the streets. I know it from experience.

William Arabin (1773–1841) British judge. Referring to the people of Uxbridge. *Arabinesque at Law* (Sir R. Megarry)

3 Prisoner, God has given you good abilities, instead of which you go about the country stealing ducks.

William Arabin *Arabinesque at Law* (Sir R. Megarry)

4 I am laughing to think what risks you take to try to find money in a desk by night where the legal owner can never find any by day.

Honoré de Balzac (1799–1850) French novelist. Said on waking to find a burglar in the room. Attrib.

5 Stolen sweets are best.

Colley Cibber (1671–1757) British actor and dramatist. *The Rival Fools*, I

6 Travel light and you can sing in the robber's face.

Juvenal (Decimus Junius Juvenalis; 60–130 AD) Roman satirist. *Satires*, X

7 Stolen sweets are always sweeter,
Stolen kisses much completer,
Stolen looks are nice in chapels,
Stolen, stolen, be your apples.

Hunt Leigh (1784–1859) British poet. *Song of Fairies Robbing an Orchard*

THEORY

See also ideas

1 Medical theories are most of the time even more peculiar than the facts themselves.

August Bier (1861–1949) Aphorism

2 A thing may look specious in theory, and yet be ruinous in practice; a thing may look evil in theory, and yet be in practice excellent.

Edmund Burke (1729–97) British politician. Impeachment of Warren Hastings, 19 Feb 1788

3 A theory can be proved by experiment; but no path leads from experiment to the birth of a theory.

Albert Einstein (1879–1955) German-born US physicist. *The Sunday Times*, 18 July 1976

4 Don't confuse *hypothesis* and *theory*. The former is a possible explanation; the latter, the correct one. The establishment of theory is the very purpose of science.

Martin H. Fischer (1879–1962) *Fischerisms* (Howard Fabing and Ray Marr)

5 For hundreds of pages the closely-reasoned arguments unroll, axioms and theorems interlock. And what remains with us in the end? A general sense that the world can be expressed in closely-reasoned arguments, in interlocking axioms and theorems.

Michael Frayn (1933–) British journalist and writer. *Constructions*

6 Factual evidence can never 'prove' a hypothesis; it can only fail to disprove it, which is what we generally mean when we say, somewhat inexactly, that the hypothesis is 'confirmed' by experience.

Milton Friedman (1912–) US economist. *Essays in Positive Economics*

7 Dear friend, theory is all grey,
And the golden tree of life is green.

Goethe (1749–1832) German poet and dramatist. *Faust*, Pt. I

8 You know very well that unless you're a scientist, it's much more important for a theory to be shapely, than for it to be true.

Christopher Hampton (1946–) British writer and dramatist. *The Philanthropist*, Sc. 1

9 Those who are enamoured of practice without science are like a pilot who goes into a ship without rudder or compass and never has any certainty where he is going. Practice should always be based upon a sound knowledge of theory.

Leonardo da Vinci (1452–1519) Italian artist, sculptor, architect, and engineer. *The Notebooks of Leonardo da Vinci* (Edward MacCurdy)

10 A first rate theory predicts; a second rate theory forbids, and a third rate theory explains after the event.

A. I. Kitaigorodskii *Harvest of a Quiet Eye*

11 It is a good morning exercise for a research scientist to discard a pet hypothesis every day before breakfast. It keeps him young.

Konrad Lorenz (1903–89) Austrian zoologist. *On Aggression*, Ch. 2

12 Theory, glamorous mother of the drudge experiment.
Harlan Mayer, Jr. *Physics for the Inquiring Mind*

13 Physicians are inclined to engage in hasty generalizations. Possessing a natural or acquired distinction, endowed with a quick intelligence, an elegant and facile conversation . . . the more eminent they are . . . the less leisure they have for investigative work . . . Eager for knowledge . . . they are apt to accept too readily attractive but inadequately proven theories.
Louis Pasteur (1822–95) French scientist. *Études sur la bière*, Ch. 3

14 In making theories always keep a window open so that you can throw one out if necessary.
Béla Schick (1877–1967) Austrian pediatrician. *Aphorisms and Facetiae of Béla Schick* (I. J. Wolf)

15 When the torrent sweeps a man against a boulder, you must expect him to scream, and you need not be surprised if the scream is sometimes a theory.
Robert Louis Stevenson (1850–94) Scottish writer. *Virginibus Puerisque*

THINKING

See also intellect, intelligence, mind, philosophy

1 I have always found that the man whose second thoughts are good is worth watching.
J. M. Barrie (1860–1937) British novelist and dramatist. *What Every Woman Knows*, III

2 He can't think without his hat.
Samuel Beckett (1906–) Irish novelist and dramatist. *Waiting for Godot*

3 Mirrors should think longer before they reflect.
Jean Cocteau (1889–1963) French poet and artist. *The Sunday Times*, 20 Oct 1963

4 *Cogito, ergo sum.*
I think, therefore I am.
René Descartes (1596–1650) French philosopher. *Le Discours de la méthode*

5 It would not be at all a bad thing if the elite of the medical world would be a little less clever, and would adopt a more primitive method of thinking, and reason more as children do.
George Groddeck (1866–1934) *The Book of the It*, Letter XII

6 The most fluent talkers or most plausible reasoners are not always the justest thinkers.
William Hazlitt (1778–1830) British essayist. *On Prejudice*

7 Most of one's life . . . is one prolonged effort to prevent oneself thinking.
Aldous Huxley (1894–1964) British novelist. *Mortal Coils*, 'Green Tunnels'

8 Meditation is not a means to an end. It is both the means and the end.
Jiddu Krishnamurti (1895–) Indian Hindu philosopher. *The Penguin Krishnamurti Reader*

9 The brain has muscles for thinking as the legs have muscles for walking.
Julien Offroy de la Mettrie (1709–51) *L'Homme machine*

10 You can't think rationally on an empty stomach, and a whole lot of people can't do it on a full one either.
Lord Reith (1889–1971) British administrator. Attrib.

11 One of the worst diseases to which the human creature is liable is its disease of thinking.
John Ruskin (1819–1900) British art critic and social reformer. *The Political Economy of Art*, 'A Joy For Ever'

12 People don't seem to realize that it takes time and effort and preparation to think. Statesmen are far too busy making speeches to think.
Bertrand Russell (1872–1970) British philosopher. *Kenneth Harris Talking To:* 'Bertrand Russell' (Kenneth Harris)

13 Many people would sooner die than think. In fact they do.
Bertrand Russell *Thinking About Thinking* (A. Flew)

14 My thought is *me*: that is why I can't stop. I exist by what I think . . . and I can't prevent myself from thinking.
Jean-Paul Sartre (1905–80) French writer. *Nausea*

15 There is nothing either good or bad, but thinking makes it so.
William Shakespeare (1564–1616) English dramatist. *Hamlet*, II:2

16 Thinking is to me the greatest fatigue in the world.
John Vanbrugh (1664–1726) English architect and dramatist. *The Relapse*, II:1

17 Great thoughts come from the heart.
Marquis de Vauvenargues (1715–47) French soldier and writer. *Réflexions et maximes*

18 Thinking is the most unhealthy thing in the world, and people die of it just as they die of any other disease.
Oscar Wilde (1854–1900) Irish-born British writer and wit. *The Decay of Lying*

19 In order to draw a limit to thinking, we should have to be able to think both sides of this limit.
Ludwig Wittgenstein (1889–1951) Austrian philosopher. *Tractatus Logico-Philosophicus*, Preface

THIRST

See also alcohol, desire, drinks, hunger

1 There are two reasons for drinking; one is, when you are thirsty, to cure it; the other, when you are not thirsty, to prevent it . . . Prevention is better than cure.
Thomas Love Peacock (1785–1866) British novelist. *Melincourt*

2 I drink for the thirst to come.
François Rabelais (1483–1553) French satirist. *Gargantua*, Bk. I, Ch. 5

3 As pants the hart for cooling streams
When heated in the chase.
Nahum Tate (1652–1715) Irish-born English poet. *New Version of the Psalms*, 'As Pants the Hart'

THOMAS, Dylan

(1914–53) Welsh poet. His collections include *18 Poems* (1934) and *Deaths and Entrances* (1946). His radio play *Under Milk Wood* (1954) is also well known. His early death resulted from alcoholism.

Quotations about Thomas

1 The first time I saw Dylan Thomas I felt as if Rubens had suddenly taken it into his head to paint a youthful Silenus.
Edith Sitwell (1887–1964) British poet and writer. *Taken Care of: An Autobiography*

2 He was a detestable man. Men pressed money on him, and women their bodies. Dylan took both with equal contempt. His great pleasure was to humiliate people.
A. J. P. Taylor (1906–) British historian. *Autobiography*

Quotations by Thomas

3 I, born of flesh and ghost, was neither
A ghost nor man, but mortal ghost.
And I was struck down by death's feather.
Before I knocked

4 These poems, with all their crudities, doubts, and confusions, are written for the love of Man and in praise of God, and I'd be a damn' fool if they weren't.
Collected Poems, Note

5 Do not go gentle into that good night,
Old age should burn and rave at close of day;
Rage, rage, against the dying of the light.
Do not go gentle into that good night

6 The force that through the green fuse drives the flower
Drives my green age.
The force that through the green fuse drives the flower

7 The hand that signed the treaty bred a fever,
And famine grew, and locusts came;
Great is the hand that holds dominion over
Man by a scribbled name.
The hand that signed the paper

8 The hunchback in the park
A solitary mister
Propped between trees and water.
The hunchback in the park

9 And the wild boys innocent as strawberries.
The hunchback in the park

10 Light breaks where no sun shines;
Where no sea runs, the waters of the heart
Push in their tides.
Light breaks where no sun shines

11 I missed the chance of a lifetime, too. Fifty lovelies in the rude and I'd left my Bunsen burner home.
Portrait of the Artist as a Young Dog, 'One Warm Saturday'

12 After the first death, there is no other.
A Refusal to Mourn the Death, by Fire, of a Child in London

13 This bread I break was once the oat,
This wine upon a foreign tree
Plunged in its fruit;
Man in the day or wind at night
Laid the crops low, broke the grape's joy.
This bread I break

14 Mr Pritchard. I must dust the blinds and then I must raise them.
Mrs Ogmore-Pritchard. And before you let the sun in, mind it wipes its shoes.
Under Milk Wood

15 Gomer Owen who kissed her once by the pig-sty when she wasn't looking and never kissed her again although she was looking all the time.
Under Milk Wood

16 Sleeping as quiet as death, side by wrinkled side, toothless, salt and brown, like two old kippers in a box.
Under Milk Wood

17 The hands of the clock have stayed still at half past eleven for fifty years. It is always opening time in the Sailors Arms.
Under Milk Wood

18 Chasing the naughty couples down the grassgreen gooseberried double bed of the wood.
Under Milk Wood

19 Every night of her married life she has been late for school.
Under Milk Wood

20 Oh, isn't life a terrible thing, thank God?
Under Milk Wood

21 Oh I'm a martyr to music.
Under Milk Wood

22 . . . his nicotine eggyellow weeping walrus Victorian moustache worn thick and long in memory of Doctor Crippen.
Under Milk Wood

23 Portraits of famous bards and preachers, all fur and wool from the squint to the kneecaps.
Under Milk Wood

24 It is a winter's tale
That the snow blind twilight ferries over the lakes
And floating fields from the farm in the cup of the vales.
A Winter's Tale

25 The land of my fathers. My fathers can have it.
Referring to Wales. *Dylan Thomas* (John Ackerman)

26 Somebody's boring me, I think it's me.
Remark made after he had been talking continuously for some time. *Four Absentees* (Rayner Heppenstall)

27 Too many of the artists of Wales spend too much time about the position of the artist of Wales. There is only one position for an artist anywhere: and that is, upright.
New Statesman, 18 Dec 1964

THOREAU, Henry David

(1817–62) US writer. He is best known for *Walden* (1854), an account of his year spent as a recluse in the Walden woods in Massachusetts. He also wrote poetry and many essays, including one on *Civil Disobedience.*

Quotations about Thoreau

1 Whatever question there may be of his talent, there can be none I think of his genius. It was a slim and crooked one, but it was eminently personal.
Henry James (1843–1916) US novelist. *Hawthorne*

2 I love Henry, but I cannot like him; and as for taking his arm, I should as soon think of taking the arm of an elm tree.
Remark by an unknown friend

Quotations by Thoreau

3 Under a government which imprisons any unjustly, the true place for a just man is also a prison.
Civil Disobedience

4 The most attractive sentences are not perhaps the wisest, but the surest and soundest.
Journal, 1842

5 Whatever sentence will bear to be read twice, we may be sure was thought twice.
Journal, 1842

6 Some circumstantial evidence is very strong, as when you find a trout in the milk.
Journal, 1850

7 What men call social virtues, good fellowship, is commonly but the virtue of pigs in a litter, which lie close together to keep each other warm. It brings men together in crowds and mobs in bar-rooms and

elsewhere, but it does not deserve the name of virtue.
Journal, 1852

8 As if you could kill time without injuring eternity.
Walden, 'Economy'

9 The mass of men lead lives of quiet desperation.
Walden, 'Economy'

10 I have lived some thirty years on this planet, and I have yet to hear the first syllable of valuable or even earnest advice from my seniors.
Walden, 'Economy'

11 There are now-a-days professors of philosophy but not philosophers.
Walden, 'Economy'

12 As for doing good, that is one of the professions which are full.
Walden, 'Economy'

13 Beware of all enterprises that require new clothes.
Walden, 'Economy'

14 I never found the companion that was so companionable as solitude.
Walden, 'Solitude'

15 The three-o'-clock in the morning courage, which Bonaparte thought was the rarest.
Walden, 'Sounds'

16 Our life is frittered away by detail . . . Simplify, simplify.
Walden, 'Where I lived, and What I Lived For'

17 Time is but the stream I go a-fishing in.
Walden, 'Where I Lived, and What I Lived For'

18 I once had a sparrow alight upon my shoulder for a moment while I was hoeing in a village garden, and I felt that I was more distinguished by that circumstance than I should have been by any epaulet I could have worn.
Walden, 'Winter Visitors'

19 It takes two to speak the truth – one to speak, and another to hear.
A Week on the Concord and Merrimack Rivers

20 Not that the story need be long, but it will take a long while to make it short.
Letter, 16 Nov 1867

21 One world at a time.
On being asked his opinion of the hereafter. Attrib.

22 I did not know that we had ever quarrelled.
On being urged to make his peace with God. Attrib.

23 Yes – around Concord.
On being asked whether he had traveled much. Attrib.

THREATS

1 Today we were unlucky. But remember, we have only to be lucky once. You will have to be lucky always.
Anonymous Telephone call from the IRA following their unsuccessful attempt to blow up Margaret Thatcher and other ministers at the Grand Hotel, Brighton, in 1984

2 We have ways of making men talk.
Anonymous Film catchphrase, often repeated as 'We have ways of making you talk'. *Lives of a Bengal Lancer*

3 Not while I'm alive, he ain't.
Ernest Bevin (1881–1951) British Labour politician. When told that Aneurin Bevan was 'his own worst enemy'. Also attributed to others. *Aneurin Bevan* (M. Foot)

4 Violet Elizabeth dried her tears. She saw that they were useless and she did not believe in wasting her effects. 'All right,' she said calmly, 'I'll thcream then. I'll thcream, an' thcream, an' thcream till I'm thick.'
Richmal Crompton (Richmal Crompton Lamburn; 1890–1969) British writer. Violet Elizabeth Bott, a character in the *William* books, had both a lisp and an exceptional ability to get her own way. *Just William*

5 He will give him seven feet of English ground, or as much more as he may be taller than other men.
Harold II (1022–66) King of England (1066). Offer to Harald, King of Norway, who invaded England immediately before William the Conqueror (1066). *Heimskringla* (Snorri Sturluson)

6 If you start throwing hedgehogs under me, I shall throw two porcupines under you.
Nikita Khrushchev (1894–1971) Soviet statesman. *The Observer*, 'Sayings of the Week', 10 Nov 1963

7 My solution to the problem would be to tell them . . . they've got to draw in their horns or we're going to bomb them into the Stone Age.
Curtis E. LeMay (1906–) US general and air-force chief. On the North Vietnamese. *Mission with LeMay*

8 I shall not hesitate to issue writs for libel and slander if scandalous allegations are made or repeated outside the House.
John Profumo (1915–) British politician. Speech, House of Commons, 22 Mar 1963

9 He's a businessman. I'll make him an offer he can't refuse.
Mario Puzo (1920–) US novelist. *The Godfather*

10 After I die, I shall return to earth as a gatekeeper of a bordello and I won't let any of you – not a one of you – enter!
Arturo Toscanini (1867–1957) Italian conductor. Rebuking an incompetent orchestra. *The Maestro: The Life of Arturo Toscanini* (Howard Taubman)

THRIFT

See also extravagance, money

1 A penny saved is a penny earned.
Proverb

2 Keep something for a rainy day.
Proverb

3 Many a mickle makes a muckle.
Proverb

4 Penny wise, pound foolish.
Proverb

5 I knew once a very covetous, sordid fellow, who used to say, 'Take care of the pence, for the pounds will take care of themselves.'
Earl of Chesterfield (1694–1773) English statesman. Possibly referring to William Lowndes. Letter to his son, 6 Nov 1747

6 . . . we owe something to extravagance, for thrift and adventure seldom go hand in hand.
Jennie Jerome Churchill (1854–1921) US-born British hostess and writer. *Pearson's*, 'Extravagance'

7 Everybody is always in favour of general economy and particular expenditure.
Anthony Eden (1897–1977) British statesman. *The Observer*, 'Sayings of the Week', 17 June 1956

8 Economy is going without something you do want in case you should, some day, want something you probably won't want.
Anthony Hope (Sir Anthony Hope Hawkins; 1863–1933) British novelist. *The Dolly Dialogues*

9 What! Can't a fellow even enjoy a biscuit any more?
Duke of Portland (1857–1943) British peer. On being informed that as one of several

measures to reduce his own expenses he would have to dispense with one of his two Italian pastry cooks. *Their Noble Lordships* (S. Winchester)

10 A hole is the accident of a day, while a darn is premeditated poverty.
Edward Shuter (1728–76) British actor. Explaining why he did not mend the holes in his stocking. *Dictionary of National Biography*

11 I belong to a generation that don't spend until we have the money in hand.
Margaret Thatcher (1925–) British politician and prime minister. *The Observer*, 'Sayings of the Week', 13 Feb 1977

12 Beware of all enterprises that require new clothes.
Henry David Thoreau (1817–62) US writer. *Walden*, 'Economy'

THURBER, James

(1894–1961) US writer, humorist, and cartoonist. A contributor to the *New Yorker*, he published a number of collected writings, including *The Thurber Carnival* (1945).

Quotations about Thurber

1 A tall, thin, spectacled man with the face of a harassed rat.
Russell Maloney *Saturday Review*, 'Tilley the Toiler'

Quotations by Thurber

2 'Joe,' I said, 'was perhaps the first great nonstop literary drinker of the American nineteenth century. He made the indulgences of Coleridge and De Quincey seem like a bit of mischief in the kitchen with the cooking sherry.'
Alarms and Diversions, 'The Moribundant Life . . . '

3 I was seized by the stern hand of Compulsion, that dark, unseasonable Urge that impels women to clean house in the middle of the night.
Alarms and Diversions, 'There's a Time for Flags'

4 It is better to have loafed and lost than never to have loafed at all.
Fables for Our Time, 'The Courtship of Arthur and Al'

5 You can fool too many of the people too much of the time.
Fables for Our Time, 'The Owl Who Was God'

6 Early to rise and early to bed makes a male healthy and wealthy and dead.
Fables for Our Time, 'The Shrike and the Chipmunks'

7 Old Nat Burge sat . . . He was . . . watching the moon come up lazily out of the old cemetery in which nine of his daughters were lying, and only two of them were dead.
Let Your Mind Alone, 'Bateman Comes Home'

8 No man . . . who has wrestled with a self-adjusting card table can ever quite be the man he once was.
Let Your Mind Alone, 'Sex ex Machina'

9 I suppose that the high-water mark of my youth in Columbus, Ohio, was the night the bed fell on my father.
My Life and Hard Times, Ch. 1

10 Her own mother lived the latter years of her life in the horrible suspicion that electricity was dripping invisibly all over the house.
My Life and Hard Times, Ch. 2

11 Then, with that faint fleeting smile playing about his lips, he faced the firing squad; erect and motionless, proud and disdainful, Walter Mitty, the undefeated, inscrutable to the last.
My World and Welcome to It, 'The Secret Life of Walter Mitty'

12 A man should not insult his wife publicly, at parties. He should insult her in the privacy of the home.
Thurber Country

13 The difference between our decadence and the Russians' is that while theirs is brutal, ours is apathetic.
The Observer, 'Sayings of the Week', 5 Feb 1961

14 The War between Men and Women.
Title of a series of cartoons

15 Well, if I called the wrong number, why did you answer the phone?
Cartoon caption

16 You wait here and I'll bring the etchings down.
Cartoon caption

17 I said the hounds of spring are on winter's traces – but let it pass, let it pass!
Cartoon caption

18 Why do you have to be a nonconformist like everybody else?
Attrib. Actually a cartoon caption by Stan Hunt in the *New Yorker*

19 Surely you don't mean by unartificial insemination!
On being accosted at a party by a drunk woman who claimed she would like to have a baby by him. Attrib.

20 It had only one fault. It was kind of lousy.
Remark made about a play. Attrib.

21 God bless . . . God damn.
His last words. Attrib.

TIME

See also eternity, future, life, past, present, transience

1 An hour in the morning is worth two in the evening.
Proverb

2 There are only twenty-four hours in the day.
Proverb

3 There is a time and place for everything.
Proverb

4 Time and tide wait for no man.
Proverb

5 Time cures the sick man, not the ointment.
Proverb

6 Time is a great healer.
Proverb

7 Time will tell.
Proverb

8 To choose time is to save time.
Francis Bacon (1561–1626) English philosopher. *Essays*, 'Of Dispatch'

9 VLADIMIR. That passed the time.
ESTRAGON. It would have passed in any case.
VLADIMIR. Yes, but not so rapidly.
Samuel Beckett (1906–) Irish novelist and dramatist. *Waiting for Godot*, I

10 I believe the twenty-four hour day has come to stay.
Max Beerbohm (1872–1956) British writer. *A Christmas Garland*, 'Perkins and Mankind'

11 Time is a great teacher, but unfortunately it kills all its pupils.
Hector Berlioz (1803–69) French composer. *Almanach des lettres françaises*

12 To every thing there is a season, and a time to every purpose under the heaven:
A time to be born, and a time to die; a time to plant, and a time to pluck up that which is planted;
A time to kill, and a time to heal; a time to break down, and a time to build up;
A time to weep, and a time to laugh;

a time to mourn, and a time to dance;
A time to cast away stones, and a time to gather stones together; a time to embrace, and a time to refrain from embracing;
A time to get, and a time to lose; a time to keep, and a time to cast away;
A time to rend, and a time to sew; a time to keep silence, and a time to speak;
A time to love, and a time to hate; a time of war, and a time of peace.

Bible: Ecclesiastes 3:1–8

13 Men talk of killing time, while time quietly kills them.

Dion Boucicault (Dionysius Lardner Boursiquot; 1820–90) Irish-born US actor and dramatist. *London Assurance*, II:1

14 I recommend you to take care of the minutes: for hours will take care of themselves.

Earl of Chesterfield (1694–1773) English statesman. Letter to his son, 6 Nov 1747

15 Time is a physician that heals every grief.

Diphilius (4th century BC)

16 Time is the great physician.

Benjamin Disraeli (1804–81) British statesman. *Henrietta Temple*, Bk. VI, Ch. 9

17 Time present and time past
Are both perhaps present in time future
And time future contained in time past.

T. S. Eliot (1888–1965) US-born British poet and dramatist. *Four Quartets*

18 Come, fill the Cup, and in the Fire of Spring
The Winter Garment of Repentance fling:
The Bird of Time has but a little way
To fly – and Lo! the Bird is on the Wing.

Edward Fitzgerald (1809–83) British poet. *The Rubáiyát of Omar Khayyám*

19 Ah, fill the Cup: – what boots it to repeat
How Time is slipping underneath our Feet:
Unborn TOMORROW, and dead YESTERDAY,
Why fret about them if TODAY be sweet!

Edward Fitzgerald *The Rubáiyát of Omar Khayyám*

20 Dost thou love life? Then do not squander time, for that's the stuff life is made of.

Benjamin Franklin (1706–90) US scientist and statesman. *Poor Richard's Almanack*

21 In order to be utterly happy the only thing necessary is to refrain from comparing this moment with other moments in the past, which I often did not fully enjoy because I was comparing them with other moments of the future.

André Gide (1869–1951) French novelist. *Journals*

22 You must remember this;
A kiss is just a kiss,
A sigh is just a sigh –
The fundamental things apply
As time goes by.

Herman Hupfeld (20th century) US songwriter. From the film *Casablanca*. *As Time Goes By*

23 The now, the here, through which all future plunges to the past.

James Joyce (1882–1941) Irish novelist. *Ulysses*

24 O aching time! O moments big as years!

John Keats (1795–1821) British poet. *Hyperion*, I

25 We must use time as a tool, not as a couch.

John Fitzgerald Kennedy (1917–63) US statesman. *The Observer*, 'Sayings of the Week', 10 Dec 1961

26 They shut the road through the woods
Seventy years ago.
Weather and rain have undone it again,
And now you would never know
There was once a road through the woods.

Rudyard Kipling (1865–1936) Indian-born British writer. *The Way Through the Woods*

27 The Future is something which everyone reaches at the rate of sixty minutes an hour, whatever he does, whoever he is.

C. S. Lewis (1898–1963) British academic and writer. *The Screwtape Letters*

28 Yes, time heals all things,
So I needn't cling to this fear,
It's merely that Spring
Will be a little late this year.

Frank Loesser (1910–69) US songwriter. *Christmas Holiday*, 'Spring Will Be a Little Late This Year'

29 I stood on the bridge at midnight,
As the clocks were striking the hour.

Henry Wadsworth Longfellow (1807–82) US poet. *The Bridge*

30 The man is killing time – there's nothing else.

Robert Lowell (1917–77) US poet. *The Drinker*

31 Time wounds all heels.

Groucho Marx (Julius Marx; 1895–1977) US comedian. Attrib.

32 'Twenty-three and a quarter minutes past', Uncle Matthew was saying furiously, 'in precisely six and three-quarter minutes the damned fella will be late.'

Nancy Mitford (1904–73) British writer. *Love in a Cold Climate*

33 A physician can sometimes parry the scythe of death, but has no power over the sand in the hourglass.

Hester Lynch Piozzi (Mrs. Henry Thrale; 1741–1821) British writer. Letter to Fanny Burney, 22 Nov 1781

34 They do that to pass the time, nothing more. But Time is too large, it refuses to let itself be filled up.

Jean-Paul Sartre (1905–80) French writer. *Nausea*

35 The physician's best remedy is *Tincture of Time!*

Béla Schick (1877–1967) Austrian pediatrician. *Aphorisms and Facetiae of Béla Schick* (I. J. Wolf)

36 Time heals what reason cannot.

Seneca (c. 4 BC–65 AD) Roman writer and statesman. *Agamemnon*, 130

37 Ah! the clock is always slow;
It is later than you think.

Robert William Service (1874–1958) Canadian poet. *It is Later than You Think*

38 Th' inaudible and noiseless foot of Time.

William Shakespeare (1564–1616) English dramatist and poet. *All's Well that Ends Well*, V:3

39 Come what come may,
Time and the hour runs through the roughest day.

William Shakespeare *Macbeth*, I:3

40 I wasted time, and now doth time waste me.

William Shakespeare *Richard II*, V:5

41 Like as the waves make towards the pebbled shore,

So do our minutes hasten to their end.
William Shakespeare *Sonnet 60*

42 Time's thievish progress to eternity.
William Shakespeare *Sonnet 77*

43 Time's glory is to calm contending kings,
To unmask falsehood, and bring truth to light.
William Shakespeare *The Rape of Lucrece*, Dedication

44 Time hath, my lord, a wallet at his back,
Wherein he puts alms for oblivion,
A great-siz'd monster of ingratitudes.
William Shakespeare *Troilus and Cressida*, III:3

45 Beauty, wit,
High birth, vigour of bone, desert in service,
Love, friendship, charity, are subjects all
To envious and calumniating time.
One touch of nature makes the whole world kin,
That all with one consent praise new-born gawds,
Though they are made and moulded of things past,
And give to dust that is a little gilt
More laud than gilt o'er-dusted.
William Shakespeare *Troilus and Cressida*, III:3

46 The end crowns all,
And that old common arbitrator, Time,
Will one day end it.
William Shakespeare *Troilus and Cressida*, IV:5

47 Thus the whirligig of time brings in his revenges.
William Shakespeare *Twelfth Night*, V:1

48 In reality, *killing time*
Is only the name for another of the multifarious ways
By which Time kills us.
Osbert Sitwell (1892–1969) British writer. *Milordo Inglese*

49 Time driveth onward fast,
And in a little while our lips are dumb.
Let us alone. What is it that will last?
All things are taken from us, and become
Portions and parcels of the dreadful Past.
Alfred, Lord Tennyson (1809–92) British poet. *The Lotos-Eaters*, 'Choric Song'

50 Time held me green and dying
Though I sang in my chains like the sea.
Dylan Thomas (1914–53) Welsh poet. *Fern Hill*

51 Time is but the stream I go a-fishing in.
Henry David Thoreau (1817–62) US writer. *Walden*, 'Where I Lived, and What I Lived For'

52 As if you could kill time without injuring eternity.
Henry David Thoreau *Walden*, 'Economy'

53 Times carries all things, even our wits, away.
Virgil (Publius Vergilius Maro; 70 BC–19 BC) Roman poet. *Eclogues*, Bk. IX

54 But meanwhile it is flying, irretrievable time is flying.
Virgil *Georgics*, Bk. III

55 Time drops in decay,
Like a candle burnt out.
W. B. Yeats (1865–1939) Irish poet. *The Moods*

56 The bell strikes one. We take no note of time
But from its loss.
Edward Young (1683–1765) British poet. *Night Thoughts*

57 Time flies, death urges, knells call, heaven invites,
Hell threatens.
Edward Young *Night Thoughts*

TITLES

See also aristocracy, courtesy, honor, nobility

1 As far as the 14th Earl is concerned, I suppose Mr Wilson, when you come to think of it, is the 14th Mr Wilson.
Alec Douglas-Home (1903–) British statesman. On renouncing his peerage (as 14th Earl of Home) to become prime minister. TV interview, 21 Oct 1963

2 Madam I may not call you; mistress I am ashamed to call you; and so I know not what to call you; but howsoever, I thank you.
Elizabeth I (1533–1603) Queen of England. Writing to the wife of the Archbishop of Canterbury, expressing her disapproval of married clergy. *Brief View of the State of the Church* (Harington)

3 Tyndall, I must remain plain Michael Faraday to the last; and let me now tell you, that if I accepted the honour which the Royal Society desires to confer upon me, I would not answer for the integrity of my intellect for a single year.
Michael Faraday (1791–1867) British scientist. Said when Faraday was offered the Presidency of the Royal Society. *Faraday as a Discoverer* (J. Tyndall), 'Illustrations of Character'

4 Pooh-Bah (Lord High Everything Else)
W. S. Gilbert (1836–1911) British dramatist. *The Mikado, Dramatis Personae*

5 I like the Garter; there is no damned merit in it.
Lord Melbourne (1779–1848) British statesman. *Lord Melbourne* (H. Dunckley), 'On the Order of the Garter'

6 When I want a peerage, I shall buy one like an honest man.
Lord Northcliffe (1865–1922) Irish-born British newspaper proprietor. Attrib.

7 Call me madame.
Francis Perkins (1882–1965) US social worker and politician. Deciding the term of address she would prefer when made the first woman to hold a cabinet office in the USA. *Familiar Quotations* (J. Bartlett)

8 A person seeking a quiet life is greatly helped by not having a title.
Captain Mark Phillips (1948–) Husband of Princess Anne. Attrib.

9 Mother always told me my day was coming, but I never realized that I'd end up being the shortest knight of the year.
Gordon Richards (1904–86) British champion jockey. Referring to his diminutive size, on learning of his knighthood. Attrib.

10 Members rise from CMG (known sometimes in Whitehall as 'Call me God') to the KCMG ('Kindly Call me God') to . . . The GCMG ('God Calls me God').
Anthony Sampson (1926–) British writer and journalist. *Anatomy of Britain*, Ch. 18

11 Titles distinguish the mediocre, embarrass the superior, and are disgraced by the inferior.
George Bernard Shaw (1856–1950) Irish dramatist and critic. *Man and Superman*, 'Maxims for Revolutionists'

12 I've been offered titles, but I think they get one into disreputable company.
George Bernard Shaw *Gossip* (A. Barrow)

13 After half a century of democratic advance, the whole process has ground to a halt with a 14th Earl.
Harold Wilson (1916–) British politician and prime minister. Speech, Manchester, 19 Oct 1963

TOLERANCE

1 There is, however, a limit at which forbearance ceases to be a virtue.
Edmund Burke (1729–97) British politician. *Observations on a Publication, 'The Present State of the Nation'*

2 Of this you may be assured, that you shall none of you suffer for your opinions or religion, so long as you live peaceably, and you have the word of a king for it.
Charles II (1630–85) King of England. Said to a deputation of Quakers. *Works* (R. Hubberthorn)

3 I respect only those who resist me; but I cannot tolerate them.
Charles de Gaulle (1890–1970) French general and statesman. *New York Times magazine,* 12 May 1966

4 The various modes of worship, which prevailed in the Roman world, were all considered by the people as equally true; by the philosopher, as equally false; and by the magistrate, as equally useful. And thus toleration produced not only mutual indulgence, but even religious concord.
Edward Gibbon (1737–94) British historian. *Decline and Fall of the Roman Empire,* Ch. 2

5 It is flattering some men to endure them.
Lord Halifax (1633–95) English statesman. *Political, Moral and Miscellaneous Thoughts and Reflections*

6 . . . we are moved to grant the right of private worship to the Lutheran, Calvinist and non-Uniat Greek religions everywhere.
Joseph II (1741–90) Holy Roman Emperor. Edict of Toleration, 13 Oct 1781

7 If you cannot mould yourself as you would wish, how can you expect other people to be entirely to your liking?
Thomas à Kempis (Thomas Hemmerken; c. 1380–1471) German monk. *The Imitation of Christ,* I

8 In university they don't tell you that the greater part of the law is learning to tolerate fools.
Doris Lessing (1919–) British novelist. *Martha Quest,* Pt. III, Ch. 2

9 We must respect the other fellow's religion, but only in the sense and to the extent that we respect his theory that his wife is beautiful and his children smart.
H. L. Mencken (1880–1956) US journalist. *Notebooks,* 'Minority Report'

10 A cough is something that you yourself can't help, but everybody else does on purpose just to torment you.
Ogden Nash (1902–71) US poet. *You Can't Get There from Here,* 'Can I Get You a Glass of Water? Or Please Close the Glottis After You'

11 Steven's mind was so tolerant that he could have attended a lynching every day without becoming critical.
Thorne Smith (1892–1934) US humorist. *The Jovial Ghosts,* Ch. 11

12 So long as a man rides his hobby-horse peaceably and quietly along the king's highway, and neither compels you or me to get up behind him, – pray, Sir, what have either you or I to do with it?
Laurence Sterne (1713–68) Irish-born British writer. *Tristram Shandy*

13 It is because we put up with bad things that hotel-keepers continue to give them to us.
Anthony Trollope (1815–82) British novelist. *Orley Farm,* Ch. 18

14 Every dog is allowed one bite, but a different view is taken of a dog that goes on biting all the time. He may not get his licence returned when it falls due.
Harold Wilson (1916–) British politician and prime minister. Referring to opposition within his own party. Speech, 2 Mar 1967

15 Once lead this people into war and they'll forget there ever was such a thing as tolerance.
Woodrow Wilson (1856–1924) US statesman. *Mr Wilson's War* (John Dos Passos), Pt. III, Ch. 2

TONGUE

1 Even so the tongue is a little member, and boasteth great things. Behold, how great a matter a little fire kindleth!
Bible: James 3:5

2 But the tongue can no man tame; it is an unruly evil, full of deadly poison.
Bible: James 3:8

3 In me the need to talk is a primary impulse, and I can't help saying right off what comes to my tongue.
Miguel de Cervantes (1547–1616) Spanish novelist. *Don Quixote,* Pt. I, Ch. 30

4 A tart temper never mellows with age, and a sharp tongue is the only edged tool that grows keener with constant use.
Washington Irving (1783–1859) US writer. *The Sketch Book,* 'Rip Van Winkle'

5 I have neither eye to see, nor tongue to speak here, but as the House is pleased to direct me.
William Lenthall (1591–1662) English parliamentarian. Said on 4 Jan 1642 in the House of Commons when asked by Charles I if he had seen five MPs whom the King wished to arrest. It was a succinct restatement of the Speaker's traditional role. *Historical Collections* (Rushworth)

TOURISTS

1 The tourists who come to our island take in the Monarchy along with feeding the pigeons in Trafalgar Square.
William Hamilton (1917–) Scottish MP. *My Queen and I,* Ch. 9

2 Of all noxious animals, too, the most noxious is a tourist. And of all tourists the most vulgar, ill-bred, offensive and loathsome is the British tourist.
Francis Kilvert (1840–79) British diarist and clergyman. *Diary,* 5 Apr 1870

TRAFFIC

1 *Rush hour:* that hour when traffic is almost at a standstill.
J. B. Morton (1893–1979) British journalist. *Morton's Folly*

TRAGEDY

1 One of Edward's Mistresses was Jane Shore, who has had a play written about her, but it is a tragedy and therefore not worth reading.
Jane Austen (1775–1817) British novelist. *The History of England*

2 Tragedy is if I cut my finger. Comedy is if I walk into an open sewer and die.
Mel Brooks (Melvyn Kaminsky; 1926–) US film director. *New Yorker,* 30 Oct 1978

3 Farce is the essential theatre. Farce refined becomes high comedy: farce brutalized becomes tragedy.
Gordon Craig (1872–1966) British actor. *The Story of my Days, Index*

4 We participate in a tragedy; at a comedy we only look.
Aldous Huxley (1894–1964) British novelist. *The Devils of Loudon,* Ch. 11

5 The bad end unhappily, the good unluckily. That is what tragedy means.
Tom Stoppard (1937–) Czech-born British dramatist. *Rosencrantz and Guildenstern Are Dead,* II

6 The world is a comedy to those who think, a tragedy to those who feel.
Horace Walpole (1717–97) British writer. Letter to Sir Horace Mann, 1769

7 All women become like their mothers. That is their tragedy. No man does. That's his.
Oscar Wilde (1854–1900) Irish-born British dramatist. *The Importance of Being Earnest,* I

TRANSIENCE

See also life, mortality, time

1 So passes the glory of the world.
Anonymous Referring to the large number of ruined castles in England, Normandy, and Anjou, which had been demolished after the rebellion (1173–74) against Henry II. *Histoire de Guillaume le Maréchal*

2 Everything is only for a day, both that which remembers and that which is remembered.
Marcus Aurelius (121–180 AD) Roman emperor. *Meditations,* Bk. IV, Ch. 35

3 Time is like a river made up of the events which happen, and its current is strong; no sooner does anything appear than it is swept away, and another comes in its place, and will be swept away too.
Marcus Aurelius *Meditations,* Bk. IV, Ch. 43

4 Faith, Sir, we are here to-day, and gone tomorrow.
Aphra Behn (1640–89) English novelist and dramatist. *The Lucky Chance,* IV

5 Vanity of vanities, saith the Preacher, vanity of vanities; all is vanity.
What profit hath a man of all his labour which he taketh under the sun?
One generation passeth away, and another generation cometh: but the earth abideth for ever.
Bible: Ecclesiastes 1:2–4

6 And I gave my heart to seek and search out by wisdom concerning all things that are done under heaven: this sore travail hath God given to the sons of man to be exercised therewith.
I have seen all the works that are done under the sun; and, behold, all is vanity and vexation of spirit.
Bible: Ecclesiastes 1:13–14

7 Whatsoever thy hand findeth to do, do it with thy might; for there is no work, nor device, nor knowledge, nor wisdom, in the grave, whither thou goest.
Bible: Ecclesiastes 9:10

8 And behold joy and gladness, slaying oxen, and killing sheep, eating flesh, and drinking wine: let us eat and drink; for tomorrow we shall die.
Bible: Isaiah 22:13 A similar sentiment is expressed in Corinthians 15:32–33. Often misquoted as 'let us eat, drink, and be merry'.

9 Heaven and earth shall pass away, but my words shall not pass away.
Bible: Matthew 24:35

10 Suddenly, as rare things will, it vanished.
Robert Browning (1812–89) British poet. *One Word More,* IV

11 Now the peak of summer's past, the sky is overcast
And the love we swore would last for an age seems deceit.
C. Day Lewis (1904–72) British poet. *Hornpipe*

12 They are not long, the days of wine and roses.
Ernest Dowson (1867–1900) British lyric poet. *Vitae Summa Brevis Spem Nos Vetat Incohare Longam*

13 A little rule, a little sway,
A sunbeam in a winter's day,
Is all the proud and mighty have
Between the cradle and the grave.
John Dyer (1700–58) British poet. *Grongar Hill*

14 The Worldly Hope men set their Hearts upon
Turns Ashes – or it prospers; and anon,
Like Snow upon the Desert's dusty face,
Lighting a little Hour or two – is gone.
Edward Fitzgerald (1809–83) British poet. *The Rubáiyát of Omar Khayyám,* XIV

15 Fair daffodils, we weep to see
You haste away so soon:
As yet the early-rising sun
Has not attain'd his noon.
Stay, stay,
Until the hasting day
Has run
But to the even-song;
And, having pray'd together, we
Will go with you along.

We have short time to stay, as you,
We have as short a Spring;
As quick a growth to meet decay,
As you or any thing.
Robert Herrick (1591–1674) English poet. *Hesperides,* 'To Daffodils'

16 Not to hope for things to last for ever, is what the year teaches and even the hour which snatches a nice day away.
Horace (Quintus Horatius Flaccus; 65–8 BC) Roman poet. *Odes,* IV

17 Ships that pass in the night, and speak each other in passing;
Only a signal shown and a distant voice in the darkness;
So on the ocean of life we pass and speak one another,
Only a look and a voice; then darkness again and a silence.
Henry Wadsworth Longfellow (1807–82) US poet. *Tales of a Wayside Inn,* 'The Theologian's Tale. Elizabeth'

18 But she was of the world where the fairest things have the worst fate. Like a rose, she has lived as long as roses live, the space of one morning.
François de Malherbe (1555–1628) French poet. *Consolation à M. du Périer*

19 Gone With the Wind.
Margaret Mitchell (1909–49) US novelist. From the poem *Non Sum Qualis Eram* (Ernest Dowson): 'I have forgot much, Cynara! Gone with the wind . . . '. Book title

20 O ruin'd piece of nature! This great world
Should so wear out to nought.
William Shakespeare (1564–1616) English dramatist. *King Lear,* IV:4

21 The painful warrior famoused for fight,
After a thousand victories once foil'd,
Is from the book of honour razed quite,
And all the rest forgot for which he toil'd.
William Shakespeare *Sonnet 25*

22 What's past, and what's to come is strew'd with husks
And formless ruin of oblivion.
William Shakespeare *Troilus and Cressida,* IV:5

23 Our little systems have their day;
They have their day and cease to be.
Alfred, Lord Tennyson (1809–92) British poet. *In Memoriam A.H.H.,* Prologue

24 Will anyone, a hundred years from

now, consent to live in the houses the Victorians built, travel by their roads or railways, value the furnishings they made to live among or esteem, except for curious or historial reasons, their prevalent art and the clipped and limited literature that satisfied their souls?

H. G. Wells (1866–1946) British writer. *The New Machiavelli*

TRANSLATION

1 The original is unfaithful to the translation.

Jorge Luis Borges (1899–1986) Argentinian writer. Referring to Henley's translation of Beckford's *Vathek*. *Sobre el 'Vathek' de William Beckford*

2 Translations (like wives) are seldom faithful if they are in the least attractive.

Roy Campbell (1901–57) South African poet. *Poetry Review*

3 Poetry is what gets lost in translation.

Robert Frost (1875–1963) US poet. Attrib.

4 An idea does not pass from one language to another without change.

Miguel de Unamuno y Jugo (1864–1936) Spanish writer. *The Tragic Sense of Life*

5 Humour is the first of the gifts to perish in a foreign tongue.

Virginia Woolf (1882–1941) British novelist. *The Common Reader*

TRANSPORT

1 No other form of transport in the rest of my life has ever come up to the bliss of my pram.

Osbert Lancaster (1908–86) British cartoonist. *The Obsever*, 'Sayings of the Week', 25 Jan 1976

TRAVEL

See also boats, flying

1 Travel broadens the mind.

Proverb

2 The time to enjoy a European tour is about three weeks after you unpack.

George Ade (1866–1944) US dramatist and humorist. *Forty Modern Fables*

3 Is your journey really necessary?

Anonymous British wartime slogan

4 If It's Tuesday, This Must be Belgium.

Anonymous Title of film about US tourists in Europe

5 This is the Night Mail crossing the Border
Bringing the cheque and the postal order.

W. H. Auden (1907–73) British poet. Commentary for Post Office documentary film. *Night Mail*

6 Travel, in the younger sort, is a part of education; in the elder, a part of experience.

Francis Bacon (1561–1626) English philosopher. *Essays*, 'Of Travel'

7 Second to the right, and straight on till morning.

J. M. Barrie (1860–1937) British playwright. *Peter Pan*

8 I have recently been all round the world and have formed a very poor opinion of it.

Thomas Beecham (1879–1961) British conductor. Speech at the Savoy. *The News Review*, 22 Aug 1946

9 Rumbling under blackened girders,
Midland, bound for Cricklewood,
Puffed its sulphur to the sunset
where the Land of Laundries stood.
Rumble under, thunder over, train
and tram alternate go.

John Betjeman (1906–84) British poet. *Parliament Hill Fields*

10 May not and ought not the children of these fathers rightly say: 'Our fathers were Englishmen which came over this great ocean, and were ready to perish in this wilderness.'

William Bradford (1590–1657) Pilgrim Father. Referring to the Pilgrim Fathers, after their arrival at Cape Cod. *Of Plymouth Plantation*, Ch. 10

11 Before the Roman came to Rye or
out to Severn strode,
The rolling English drunkard made
the rolling English road.

G. K. Chesterton (1874–1936) British writer. *The Rolling English Road*

12 The only way to be sure of catching a train is to miss the one before it.

G. K. Chesterton *Vacances à tous prix*, 'Le Supplice de l'heure' (P. Daninos)

13 Travelling is almost like talking with men of other centuries.

René Descartes (1596–1650) French philosopher. *Le Discours de la méthode*

14 How does it feel
To be without a home
Like a complete unknown
Like a rolling stone?

Bob Dylan (Robert Allen Zimmerman; 1941–) US popular singer. *Like a Rolling Stone*

15 I read, much of the night, and go south in the winter.

T. S. Eliot (1888–1965) US-born British poet and dramatist. *The Waste Land*, 'The Burial of the Dead'

16 The woods are lovely, dark, and deep,
But I have promises to keep,
And miles to go before I sleep,
And miles to go before I sleep.

Robert Frost (1875–1963) US poet. *Stopping by Woods on a Snowy Evening*

17 He gave the impression that very many cities had rubbed him smooth.

Graham Greene (1904–) British novelist. *A Gun for Sale*, Ch. 4

18 Follow the Yellow Brick Road.

E. Y. Harburg (1898–1981) US lyricist. *The Wizard of Oz*, Title of song

19 One of the pleasantest things in the world is going on a journey; but I like to go by myself.

William Hazlitt (1778–1830) British essayist. *On Going a Journey*

20 They change their clime, not their frame of mind, who rush across the sea. We work hard at doing nothing: we look for happiness in boats and carriage rides. What you are looking for is here, is at Ulubrae, if only peace of mind doesn't desert you.

Horace (Quintus Horatius Flaccus; 65–8 BC) Roman poet. *Epistles*, I

21 A man who has not been in Italy, is always conscious of an inferiority, from his not having seen what it is expected a man should see. The grand object of travelling is to see the shores of the Mediterranean.

Samuel Johnson (1709–84) British lexicographer. *Life of Johnson* (J. Boswell), Vol. III

22 Much have I travell'd in the realms of gold,
And many goodly states and kingdoms seen.

John Keats (1795–1821) British poet. *On first looking into Chapman's Homer*

23 Of all noxious animals, too, the most noxious is a tourist. And of all tourists the most vulgar, ill-bred, offensive and loathsome is the British tourist.

Francis Kilvert (1840–79) British diarist and clergyman. *Diary*, 5 Apr 1870

24 Like Brighton pier, all right as far as it goes, but inadequate for getting to France.

Neil Kinnock (1942–) British politician. Speech, House of Commons, 1981

25 Give me your arm, old Toad;
Help me down Cemetery Road.

Philip Larkin (1922–85) British poet. *The Whitsun Weddings*, 'Toads Revisited'

26 Oh, mister porter, what shall I do?
I wanted to go to Birmingham, but they've carried me on to Crewe.

Marie Lloyd (1870–1922) British music-hall singer. *Oh, Mister Porter*

27 Americans are people who prefer the Continent to their own country but refuse to learn its languages.

E. V. Lucas (1868–1938) British publisher and writer. *Wanderings and Diversions*

28 The great and recurrent question about abroad is, is it worth getting there?

Rose Macaulay (1889–1958) British writer. Attrib.

29 Whenever I prepare for a journey I prepare as though for death. Should I never return, all is in order. This is what life has taught me.

Katherine Mansfield (1888–1923) New-Zealand-born British writer. *The Journal of Katherine Mansfield*, 1922

30 The car has become the carapace, the protective and aggressive shell, of urban and suburban man.

Marshall McLuhan (1911–81) Canadian sociologist. *Understanding Media*, Ch. 22

31 SEAGOON. I want you to accompany me on the safari.
BLOODNOCK. Gad sir, I'm sorry, I've never played one.

Spike Milligan (1918–) British comic actor and author. *The Goon Show*

32 It is the overtakers who keep the undertakers busy.

William Ewart Pitts (1900–) British chief constable. *The Observer*, 'Sayings of the Week', 22 Dec 1963

33 A trip to the moon on gossamer wings.

Cole Porter (1891–1964) US composer and lyricist. *Jubilee*, 'Just One of Those Things'

34 Travel is the most private of pleasures. There is no greater bore than the travel bore. We do not in the least want to hear what he has seen in Hong-Kong.

Vita Sackville-West (Victoria Sackville-West; 1892–1962) British poet and novelist. *Passenger to Tehran*, Ch. 1

35 A man should know something of his own country, too, before he goes abroad.

Laurence Sterne (1713–68) Irish-born British writer. *Tristram Shandy*

36 Wealth I ask not; hope nor love,
Nor a friend to know me;
All I seek, the heaven above
And the road below me.

Robert Louis Stevenson (1850–94) Scottish writer. *Songs of Travel*, 'The Vagabond'

37 For my part, I travel not to go anywhere, but to go. I travel for travel's sake. The great affair is to move.

Robert Louis Stevenson *Travels with a Donkey*, 'Cheylard and Luc'

38 Travel is glamorous only in retrospect.

Paul Theroux (1941–) US-born writer. *The Observer*, 'Sayings of the Week', 7 Oct 1979

39 Ever since childhood, when I lived within earshot of the Boston and Maine, I have seldom heard a train go by and not wished I was on it.

Paul Theroux *The Great Railway Bazaar*

40 Yes – around Concord.

Henry David Thoreau (1817–62) US writer. On being asked whether he had traveled much. Attrib.

41 He travelled in order to come home.

William Trevor (1928–) British writer. *Matilda's England*

42 If you ever plan to motor west,
Travel my way, take the highway, that's the best,
Get your kicks on Route 66.

Bobby Troup (1919–) US songwriter. *Route 66*

43 Commuter – one who spends his life
In riding to and from his wife;
A man who shaves and takes a train,
And then rides back to shave again.

Elwyn Brooks White (1899–1985) US journalist and humorist. *The Commuter*

44 The Victorians had not been anxious to go away for the weekend. The Edwardians, on the contrary, were nomadic.

T. H. White (1906–64) British novelist. *Farewell Victoria*, Ch. 4

TREACHERY

1 Where we are,
There's daggers in men's smiles: the near in blood,
The nearer bloody.

William Shakespeare (1564–1616) English dramatist. *Macbeth*, II:3

TREASON

See also betrayal

1 Please to remember the Fifth of November,
Gunpowder Treason and Plot.
We know no reason why gunpowder treason
Should ever be forgot.

Anonymous Traditional

2 . . . in general sorrow that so monstrous a wickedness should be found harboured within the breast of any of their religion.

Charles Cornwallis (c. 1580–1629) British ambassador in Madrid. Describing Spanish reaction to the Gunpowder Plot. Letter to Lord Salisbury, Nov 1605

3 During his Office, Treason was no Crime.
The Sons of Belial had a Glorious Time.

John Dryden (1631–1700) British poet and dramatist. *Absalom and Achitophel*, I

4 A desperate disease requires a dangerous remedy.

Guy Fawkes (1570–1606) English conspirator. In justification of the Gunpowder Plot; said when questioned by the King and council immediately after his arrest (5 Nov 1605). *Dictionary of National Biography*

5 . . . to blow the Scots back again into Scotland.

Guy Fawkes One of his professed objectives for the Gunpowder Plot, referring to the Scottish-born King James I; said when questioned by the King and council immediately after his arrest (5 Nov 1605). *Dictionary of National Biography*

6 Treason doth never prosper: what's the reason?
For if it prosper, none dare call it treason.

John Harington (1561–1612) English writer. *Epigrams*, 'Of Treason'

7 He maintained his denial. He was offered immunity from prosecution. He sat in silence for a while. He got up, looked out of the window, poured himself a drink and after a few minutes confessed. Later he co-operated, and he continued to co-operate. That is how the immunity was given and how Blunt responded.

Michael Havers (1923–) British lawyer and Conservative politician. On the immunity from prosecution offered to the spy, Sir Anthony Blunt, in 1964. Speech, House of Commons, 21 Nov 1979

8 Germany calling, Germany calling.

'Lord Haw-Haw' (William Joyce; 1906–46) US-born propagandist for German Nazis. Radio broadcasts to Britain, during World War II

9 Caesar had his Brutus – Charles

the First, his Cromwell – and George the Third – ('Treason,' cried the Speaker) . . . *may profit by their example*. If *this* be treason, make the most of it.
Patrick Henry (1736–99) US statesman. Speech, Virginia Convention, May 1765

10 On the 5th of November we began our Parliament, to which the King should have come in person, but refrained, through a practice but that morning discovered. The plot was to have blown up the King.
Edward Hoby (1560–1617) English politician. Letter to Sir Thomas Edmondes, 19 Nov 1605

11 Any service rendered to the temporal king to the prejudice of the eternal king is, without doubt, an act of treachery.
Stephen Langton (c. 1150–1228) Archbishop of Canterbury. Letter to the barons of England, 1207

12 Gives not the hawthorn bush a sweeter shade
To shepherds, looking on their silly sheep,
Than doth a rich embroider'd canopy
To kings that fear their subjects' treachery?
William Shakespeare (1564–1616) English dramatist. *Henry VI*, Pt. 3, II:5

13 O villains, vipers, damn'd without redemption!
Dogs, easily won to fawn on any man!
Snakes, in my heart-blood warm'd, that sting my heart!
Three Judases, each one thrice worse than Judas!
Would they make peace? terrible hell make war
Upon their spotted souls for this offence!
William Shakespeare *Richard II*, III:2

14 Mine eyes are full of tears, I cannot see:
And yet salt water blinds them not so much
But they can see a sort of traitors here.
Nay, if I turn my eyes upon myself,
I find myself a traitor with the rest.
William Shakespeare *Richard II*, IV:1

15 Talk'st thou to me of 'ifs'? Thou art a traitor:
Off with his head!
William Shakespeare *Richard III*, III:4

TREES

See also countryside, Nature

1 And the Lord God took the man, and put him into the garden of Eden to dress it and to keep it. And the Lord God commanded the man, saying, Of every tree of the garden thou mayest freely eat:
Bible: Genesis 2:15–16

2 But of the tree of the knowledge of good and evil, thou shalt not eat of it: for in the day that thou eatest thereof thou shalt surely die.
Bible: Genesis 2:17

3 O leave this barren spot to me!
Spare, woodman, spare the beechen tree.
Thomas Campbell (1777–1844) British poet. *The Beech-Tree's Petition*

4 The poplars are felled, farewell to the shade,
And the whispering sound of the cool colonnade!
William Cowper (1731–1800) British poet. *The Poplar Field*

5 On Wenlock Edge the wood's in trouble;
His forest fleece the Wrekin heaves;
The gale, it plies the saplings double,
And thick on Severn snow the leaves.
A. E. Housman (1859–1936) British scholar and poet. *A Shropshire Lad*, 'The Welsh Marches'

6 Loveliest of trees, the cherry now
Is hung with bloom along the bough,
And stands about the woodland ride
Wearing white for Eastertide.
A. E. Housman *A Shropshire Lad*, '1887'

7 I'm replacing some of the timber used up by my books. Books are just trees with squiggles on them.
Hammond Innes (1913–) British novelist. Interview in *Radio Times*, 18 Aug 1984

8 As when, upon a trancèd summer-night,
Those green-rob'd senators of mighty woods,
Tall oaks, branch-charmèd by the earnest stars,
Dream, and so dream all night without a stir.
John Keats (1795–1821) British poet. *Hyperion*, I

9 I think that I shall never see
A poem lovely as a tree.
Alfred Joyce Kilmer (1886–1918) US poet. *Trees*

10 Poems are made by fools like me,
But only God can make a tree.
Alfred Joyce Kilmer *Trees*

11 Yet once more, O ye laurels, and once more,
Ye myrtles brown, with ivy never sere,
I come to pluck your berries harsh and crude,
And with forced fingers rude
Shatter your leaves before the mellowing year.
John Milton (1608–74) English poet. *Lycidas*

12 Woodman, spare that tree!
Touch not a single bough!
In youth it sheltered me,
And I'll protect it now.
George Pope Morris (1802–64) US journalist. *Woodman, Spare That Tree*

13 I think that I shall never see
A billboard lovely as a tree.
Perhaps unless the billboards fall,
I'll never see a tree at all.
Ogden Nash (1902–71) US poet. *Song of the Open Road*

14 The difference between a gun and a tree is a difference of tempo. The tree explodes every spring.
Ezra Pound (1885–1972) US poet. *Criterion*, July 1937

TRIVIALITY

See also insignificance

1 Nothing matters very much, and very few things matter at all.
Arthur Balfour (1848–1930) British statesman. Attrib.

2 A Storm in a Teacup.
W. B. Bernard (1807–75) British dramatist. Play title

3 It beareth the name of Vanity Fair, because the town where 'tis kept is lighter than vanity.
John Bunyan (1628–88) English writer. *The Pilgrim's Progress*, Pt. I

4 As she frequently remarked when she made any such mistake, it would be all the same a hundred years hence.
Charles Dickens (1812–70) British novelist. Said by Mrs Squeers. *Martin Chuzzlewit*, Ch. 9

5 Little things affect little minds.
Benjamin Disraeli (1804–81) British statesman. *Sybil*, Bk. III, Ch. 2

6 You know my method. It is founded upon the observance of trifles.
Arthur Conan Doyle (1856–1930) British writer. *The Boscombe Valley Mystery*

7 It has long been an axiom of mine that the little things are infinitely the most important.
Arthur Conan Doyle *A Case of Identity*

8 Depend upon it, there is nothing so unnatural as the commonplace.
Arthur Conan Doyle *A Case of Identity*

9 'Is there any point to which you would wish to draw my attention?'
'To the curious incident of the dog in the night-time.'
'The dog did nothing in the night-time.'
'That was the curious incident,' remarked Sherlock Holmes.
Arthur Conan Doyle *The Silver Blaze*

10 To great evils we submit; we resent little provocations.
William Hazlitt (1778–1830) British essayist. *On Great and Little Things*

11 Little minds are interested in the extraordinary; great minds in the commonplace.
Elbert Hubbard (1856–1915) US writer. *Roycroft Dictionary and Book of Epigrams*

12 What should I do? I think the best thing is to order a new stamp to be made with my face on it.
Charles Francis Joseph (1887–1922) Emperor of Austria. On hearing of his accession as emperor. *Anekdotenschatz* (H. Hoffmeister)

13 To suckle fools and chronicle small beer.
William Shakespeare (1564–1616) English dramatist. *Othello*, II:1

14 It's deadly commonplace, but, after all, the commonplaces are the great poetic truths.
Robert Louis Stevenson (1850–94) Scottish writer. *Weir of Hermiston*, Ch. 6

15 Ah God! the petty fools of rhyme
That shriek and sweat in pigmy wars.
Alfred, Lord Tennyson (1809–92) British poet. *Literary Squabbles*

TROLLOPE, Anthony

(1815–82) British novelist. He established his reputation with the Barsetshire series of novels, including *The Warden* (1855) and *Barchester Towers* (1857). Later books include *Phineas Finn* (1869).

Quotations about Trollope

1 He has a gross and repulsive face but appears *bon enfant* when you talk to him. But he is the dullest Briton of them all.
Henry James (1843–1916) US novelist. Letter to his family, 1 Nov 1875

Quotations by Trollope

2 He must have known me had he seen me as he was wont to see me, for he was in the habit of flogging me constantly. Perhaps he did not recognize me by my face.
Autobiography, Ch. 1

3 Three hours a day will produce as much as a man ought to write.
Autobiography, Ch. 15

4 No man thinks there is much ado about nothing when the ado is about himself.
The Bertrams, Ch. 27

5 Those who have courage to love should have courage to suffer.
The Bertrams, Ch. 27

6 And, above all things, never think that you're not good enough yourself. A man should never think that. My belief is that in life people will take you very much at your own reckoning.
The Small House at Allington, Ch. 32

7 In these days a man is nobody unless his biography is kept so far posted up that it may be ready for the national breakfast-table on the morning after his demise.
Doctor Thorne, Ch. 25

8 The comic almanacs give us dreadful pictures of January and February; but, in truth, the months which should be made to look gloomy in England are March and April. Let no man boast himself that he has got through the perils of winter till at least the seventh of May.
Doctor Thorne, Ch. 47

9 It's dogged as does it. It ain't thinking about it.
Last Chronicle of Barset, Ch. 61

10 With many women I doubt whether there be any more effectual way of touching their hearts than ill-using them and then confessing it. If you wish to get the sweetest fragrance from the herb at your feet, tread on it and bruise it.
Miss Mackenzie, Ch. 10

11 We cannot bring ourselves to believe it possible that a foreigner should in any respect be wiser than ourselves. If any such point out to us our follies, we at once claim those follies as the special evidences of our wisdom.
Orley Farm, Ch. 18

12 It is because we put up with bad things that hotel-keepers continue to give them to us.
Orley Farm, Ch. 18

13 As for conceit, what man will do any good who is not conceited? Nobody holds a good opinion of a man who has a low opinion of himself.
Orley Farm, Ch. 22

14 Mr Turnbull had predicted evil consequences . . . and was now doing the best in his power to bring about the verification of his own prophecies.
Phineas Finn, Ch. 25

15 I doubt whether any girl would be satisfied with her lover's mind if she knew the whole of it.
The Small House at Allington, Ch. 4

16 Those who offend us are generally punished for the offence they give; but we so frequently miss the satisfaction of knowing that we are avenged!
The Small House at Allington, Ch. 50

TROUBLE

1 A trouble shared is a trouble halved.
Proverb

2 Don't meet troubles half-way.
Proverb

3 What's the use of worrying?
It never was worth while,
So, pack up your troubles in your old kit-bag,
And smile, smile, smile.
George Asaf (George H. Powell; 1880–1951) US songwriter. *Pack up Your Troubles in Your Old Kit-bag*

4 Man that is born of a woman is of few days, and full of trouble.
Bible: Job 14:1

5 There remaineth a rest for the people of God:
And I have had troubles enough, for one.
Robert Browning (1812–89) British poet. *Old Pictures in Florence*, XVII

6 Now one of the great reasons why so many husbands and wives make shipwreck of their lives together is because a man is always seeking for happiness, while a woman is on a perpetual still hunt for trouble.
Dorothy Dix (Elizabeth Meriwether Gilmer; 1861–1951) US journalist and writer. *Dorothy Dix, Her Book*, Ch. 1

7 Our ingress into the world
Was naked and bare;
Our progress through the world
Is trouble and care.
Henry Wadsworth Longfellow (1807–82) US poet. *Tales of A Wayside Inn*, 'The Student's Tale'

8 To be, or not to be – that is the question;
Whether 'tis nobler in the mind to suffer
The slings and arrows of outrageous fortune,
Or to take arms against a sea of troubles,
And by opposing end them? To die, to sleep –
No more; and by a sleep to say we end
The heart-ache and the thousand natural shocks
That flesh is heir to, 'tis a consummation
Devoutly to be wish'd. To die, to sleep;
To sleep, perchance to dream. Ay, there's the rub;
For in that sleep of death what dreams may come,
When we have shuffled off this mortal coil,
Must give us pause.
William Shakespeare *Hamlet*, III:1

TRUMAN, Harry S.

(1884–1972) US statesman. He became president (1945–53) after the death of Roosevelt and ordered the dropping of the atom bombs on Hiroshima and Nagasaki. His administration also established NATO.

Quotations about Truman

1 The captain with the mighty heart.
Dean Acheson (1893–1971) US lawyer and statesman. *Present at the Creation*

2 Truman is short, square, simple, and looks one straight in the face.
Harold Nicolson (1886–1968) British writer. *Diaries*, 8 Aug 1945

Quotations by Truman

3 If you can't stand the heat, get out of the kitchen.
Perhaps proverbial in origin, possibly echoes the expression 'kitchen cabinet'. *Mr Citizen*, Ch. 15

4 If we see that Germany is winning the war we ought to help Russia, and if Russia is winning we ought to help Germany, and in that way let them kill as many as possible.
New York Times, 24 July 1941, when Russia was invaded by Germany

5 A politician is a man who understands government, and it takes a politician to run a government. A statesman is a politician who's been dead ten or fifteen years.
New York World Telegram and Sun, 12 Apr 1958

6 The President spends most of his time kissing people on the cheek in order to get them to do what they ought to do without getting kissed.
The Observer, 'Sayings of the Week', 6 Feb 1949

7 It's a recession when your neighbor loses his job; it's a depression when you lose your own.
The Observer, 'Sayings of the Week', 6 Apr 1958

8 I didn't fire him because he was a dumb son of a bitch, although he was, but that's not against the law for generals. If it was, half to three-quarters of them would be in jail.
Referring to General MacArthur. *Plain Speaking* (Merle Miller)

9 Give me a one-handed economist! All my economists say, 'on the one hand . . . on the other.
Presidential Anecdotes (P. Boller)

10 The buck stops here.
Sign kept on his desk during his term as president. *Presidential Anecdotes* (P. Boller)

TRUST

See also faith, mistrust

1 Trust ye not in a friend, put ye not confidence in a guide: keep the doors of thy mouth from her that lieth in thy bosom.
Bible: Micah 7:5

2 Never trust the man who hath reason to suspect that you know he hath injured you.
Henry Fielding (1707–54) British novelist. *Jonathan Wild*, Bk. III, Ch. 4

3 Some patients, though conscious that their condition is perilous, recover their health simply through their contentment with the goodness of the physician.
Hippocrates (c. 460–c. 377 BC) Greek physician. *Precepts*, VI

4 We are inclined to believe those whom we do not know because they have never deceived us.
Samuel Johnson (1709–84) British lexicographer. *The Idler*

5 Never trust a husband too far, nor a bachelor too near.
Helen Rowland (1876–1950) US writer. *The Rubaiyat of a Bachelor*

6 Would you buy a second-hand car from this man?
Mort Sahl (1926–) US political comedian. Referring to President Nixon. Attrib.

TRUTH

See also facts, frankness, honesty, lying, sincerity

1 Better a lie that heals than a truth that wounds.
Proverb

2 Many a true word is spoken in jest.
Proverb

3 Tell the truth and shame the devil.
Proverb

4 Truth fears no trial.
Proverb

5 Truth is stranger than fiction.
Proverb

6 Truth will out.
Proverb

7 The truth that makes men free is for the most part the truth which men prefer not to hear.
Herbert Sebastian Agar (1897–1980) US writer. *A Time for Greatness*

8 Plato is dear to me, but dearer still is truth.
Aristotle (384–322 BC) Greek philosopher. Attrib.

9 Truth sits upon the lips of dying men.
Matthew Arnold (1822–88) British poet and critic. *Sohrab and Rustum*

10 What is truth? said jesting Pilate, and would not stay for an answer.
Francis Bacon (1561–1626) English philosopher. *Essays*, 'Of Truth'

11 And ye shall know the truth, and the truth shall make you free.
Bible: John 8:32

12 Pilate saith unto him, What is truth?

And when he had said this, he went out again unto the Jews, and saith unto them, I find in him no fault at all.
Bible: John 18:38

13 A truth that's told with bad intent
Beats all the lies you can invent.
William Blake (1757–1827) British poet. *Auguries of Innocence*

14 To treat your facts with imagination is one thing, to imagine your facts is another.
John Burroughs (1837–1921) US naturalist. *The Heart of Burroughs Journals*

15 Some men love truth so much that they seem to be in continual fear lest she should catch a cold on overexposure.
Samuel Butler (1835–1902) British writer. *Notebooks*

16 Agree to a short armistice with truth.
Lord Byron (1788–1824) British poet. *Don Juan*, III

17 'Tis strange – but true; for truth is always strange;
Stranger than fiction: if it could be told,
How much would novels gain by the exchange!
Lord Byron *Don Juan*, XIV

18 Before you tell the 'truth' to the patient, be sure you know the 'truth,' and that the patient wants to hear it.
Richard Clarke Cabot (1868–1939) *Journal of Chronic Diseases*, 16:443, 1963

19 What I tell you three times is true.
Lewis Carroll (Charles Lutwidge Dodgson; 1832–98) British writer. *The Hunting of the Snark*

20 You can only find truth with logic if you have already found truth without it.
G. K. Chesterton (1874–1936) British writer. *The Man who was Orthodox*

21 Much truth is spoken, that more may be concealed.
Lord Darling (1849–1936) British judge. *Scintillae Juris*

22 Perjury is often bold and open. It is truth that is shamefaced – as, indeed, in many cases is no more than decent.
Lord Darling *Scintillae Juris*

23 It is an old maxim of mine that when you have excluded the impossible, whatever remains, however improbable, must be the truth.
Arthur Conan Doyle (1856–1930) British writer. *The Beryl Coronet*

24 Errors, like Straws, upon the surface flow;
He who would search for Pearls must dive below.
John Dryden (1631–1700) British poet and dramatist. *All for Love*, Prologue

25 A man is to be cheated into passion, but to be reasoned into truth.
John Dryden *Religio Laici*, Preface

26 Ethical axioms are found and tested not very differently from the axioms of science. Truth is what stands the test of experience.
Albert Einstein (1879–1955) German-born US physicist. *Out of My Later Years*

27 Truth, like a torch, the more it's shook it shines.
William Hamilton (1788–1856) Scottish philosopher. *Discussions on Philosophy*, title page

28 The great glory of modern medicine is that it regards nothing as essential but the truth.
Burton J. Hendrick (1870–1949)

29 True and False are attributes of speech, not of things. And where speech is not, there is neither Truth nor Falsehood.
Thomas Hobbes (1588–1679) English philosopher. *Leviathan*, Pt. I, Ch. 4

30 Truth is the breath of life to human society. It is the food of the immortal spirit. Yet a single word of it may kill a man as suddenly as a drop of prussic acid.
Oliver Wendell Holmes (1809–94) US writer and physician. Valedictory address, Harvard Commencement, 10 Mar 1858

31 It's easy to make a man confess the lies he tells to himself; it's far harder to make him confess the truth.
Geoffrey Household (1900–) British writer. *Rogue Male*

32 There is no worse lie than a truth misunderstood by those who hear it.
William James (1842–1910) US psychologist and philosopher. *The Varieties of Religious Experience*

33 I am certain of nothing but the holiness of the heart's affections and the truth of imagination – what the imagination seizes as beauty must be truth – whether it existed before or not.
John Keats (1795–1821) British poet. Letter to Benjamin Bailey, 22 Nov 1817

34 I never can feel certain of any truth but from a clear perception of its beauty.
John Keats Letter to George and Georgiana Keats, 16 Dec 1818–4 Jan 1819

35 'Beauty is truth, truth beauty,' – that is all
Ye know on earth, and all ye need to know.
John Keats *Ode on a Grecian Urn*

36 Truths without exception are not the truths most commonly met with in medicine.
Peter Mere Latham (1789–1875) US physician. *Diseases of the Heart*, Lecture III

37 How is it that in medicine Truth is thus measured out to us in fragments, and we are never put in trust of it *as a whole*?
Peter Mere Latham *General Remarks on the Practice of Medicine*, Ch. 13

38 It is one thing to show a man that he is in an error, and another to put him in possession of truth.
John Locke (1632–1704) English philosopher. *An Essay Concerning Human Understanding*, Bk. IV, Ch. 7

39 Let her and Falsehood grapple; who ever knew Truth put to the worse, in a free and open encounter?
John Milton (1608–74) English poet. *Areopagitica*

40 Let us begin by committing ourselves to the truth, to see it like it is and to tell it like it is, to find the truth, to speak the truth and live with the truth. That's what we'll do.
Richard Milhous Nixon (1913–) US president. Nomination acceptance speech, Miami, 8 Aug 1968

41 There can be no whitewash at the White House.
Richard Milhous Nixon Referring to the Watergate scandal. *The Observer*, 'Sayings of the Week', 30 Dec 1973

42 Truth has no special time of its own. Its hour is now – always.
Albert Schweitzer (1875–1965) French Protestant theologian, philosopher, physician, and musician. *Out of My Life and Thought*

43 Truth will come to light; murder cannot be hid long.
William Shakespeare (1564–1616) English dramatist and poet. *The Merchant of Venice*, II:2

44 Truth telling is not compatible with the defence of the realm.
George Bernard Shaw (1856–1950) Irish dramatist and critic. *Heartbreak House*

45 My way of joking is to tell the truth. It's the funniest joke in the world.
George Bernard Shaw *John Bull's Other Island*, II

46 When truth is discovered by someone else, it loses something of its attractiveness.
Alexander Solzhenitsyn (1918–) Soviet novelist. *Candle in the Wind*, 3

47 It takes two to speak the truth – one to speak, and another to hear.
Henry David Thoreau (1817–62) US writer. *A Week on the Concord and Merrimack Rivers*

48 I never give them hell. I just tell the truth and they think it is hell.
Harry S. Truman (1884–1972) US statesman. *Look magazine*, 3 Apr 1956

49 The only truths which are universal are those gross enough to be thought so.
Paul Valéry (1871–1945) French poet and writer. *Mauvaises Pensées et autres*

50 But not even Marx is more precious to us than the truth.
Simone Weil (1909–43) French philosopher. *Oppression and Liberty*, 'Revolution Proletarienne'

51 There are no whole truths; all truths are half-truths. It is trying to treat them as whole truths that plays the devil.
A. N. Whitehead (1861–1947) British philosopher. *Dialogues*, 16

52 I believe that in the end the truth will conquer.
John Wycliffe (1329–84) English religious reformer. Said to John of Gaunt, Duke of Lancaster, 1381. *Short History of the English People* (J. R. Green)

53 Truth is on the march; nothing can stop it now.
Émile Zola (1840–1902) French novelist. Referring to the Dreyfus scandal. Attrib.

TWAIN, Mark

(Samuel Langhorne Clemens; 1835–1910) US writer. A steamboat pilot, he wrote a novel, *The Adventures of Huckleberry Finn* (1884), which established his reputation as a writer.

Quotations about Twain

1 The average American loves his family. If he has any love left over for some other person, he generally selects Mark Twain.
Thomas Edison (1847–1931) US inventor. Attrib.

2 Mark Twain and I are in the same position. We have to put things in such a way as to make people, who would otherwise hang us, believe that we are joking.
George Bernard Shaw (1856–1950) Irish dramatist and critic. Attrib.

Quotations by Twain

3 There was things which he stretched, but mainly he told the truth.
The Adventures of Huckleberry Finn, Ch. 1

4 There are three kinds of lies: lies, damned lies, and statistics.
Autobiography

5 Soap and education are not as sudden as a massacre, but they are more deadly in the long run.
The Facts concerning the Recent Resignation

6 It takes your enemy and your friend, working together, to hurt you to the heart; the one to slander you and the other to get the news to you.
Following the Equator

7 It is by the goodness of God that in our country we have those three unspeakably precious things: freedom of speech, freedom of conscience, and the prudence never to practice either of them.
Following the Equator, heading of Ch. 20

8 Man is the only animal that blushes. Or needs to.
Following the Equator, heading of Ch. 27

9 I must have a prodigious quantity of mind; it takes me as much as a week, sometimes, to make it up.
The Innocents Abroad, Ch. 7

10 They spell it Vinci and pronounce it Vinchy; foreigners always spell better than they pronounce.
The Innocents Abroad, Ch. 19

11 The radical invents the views. When he has worn them out, the conservative adopts them.
Notebooks

12 Familiarity breeds contempt – and children.
Notebooks

13 When people do not respect us we are sharply offended; yet deep down in his heart no man much respects himself.
Notebooks

14 Good breeding consists in concealing how much we think of ourselves and how little we think of other persons.
Notebooks

15 Adam was but human – this explains it all. He did not want the apple for the apple's sake, he wanted it only because it was forbidden.
Pudd'nhead Wilson's Calendar, Ch. 2

16 There ain't no way to find out why a snorer can't hear himself snore.
Tom Sawyer Abroad, Ch. 10

17 Something that everybody wants to have read and nobody wants to read.
Definition of a classic of literature. Speech at Nineteenth Century Club, New York, 20 Nov 1900

18 Reports of my death are greatly exaggerated.
On learning that his obituary had been published. Cable to the Associated Press

19 That's right. 'Taint yours, and 'taint mine.
Agreeing with a friend's comment that the money of a particular rich industrialist was 'tainted'. Attrib.

20 Scarce, sir. Mighty scarce.
Responding to the question 'In a world without women what would men become?'. Attrib.

21 I've done it a hundred times!
Referring to giving up smoking. Attrib.

TYRANNY

See also authoritarianism, oppression

1 Churchill on top of the wave has in him the stuff of which tyrants are made.
Lord Beaverbrook (1879–1964) Canadian-born British newspaper proprietor. *Politicians and the War*

2 He is an ordinary human being after all! . . . now he will put himself above everyone else and become a tyrant.
Ludwig van Beethoven (1770–1827) German composer. Referring to Napoleon, on hearing that he had declared himself emperor. Remark to Ferdinand Ries, a pupil

3 To tell the truth, Napoleon is a dangerous man in a free country.

He seems to me to have the makings of a tyrant.
Lucien Bonaparte (1775–1840) Brother of Napoleon I. Letter to Joseph Bonaparte, 1790

4 Nature has left this tincture in the blood,
That all men would be tyrants if they could.
Daniel Defoe (1660–1731) British journalist and writer. *The Kentish Petition*, Addenda

5 'Twixt kings and tyrants there's this difference known;
Kings seek their subjects' good: tyrants their own.
Robert Herrick (1591–1674) English poet. *Hesperides*, 'Kings and Tyrants'

6 So long as men worship the Caesars and Napoleons, Caesars and Napoleons will arise to make them miserable.
Aldous Huxley (1894–1964) British novelist. *Ends and Means*

7 A country governed by a despot is an inverted cone.
Samuel Johnson (1709–84) British lexicographer. *Life of Johnson* (J. Boswell), Vol. III

8 It is better that a man should tyrannize over his bank balance than over his fellow citizens.
John Maynard Keynes (1883–1946) British economist. *The General Theory of Employment, Interest and Money*, Bk. VI, Ch. 24

9 . . . whenever kingship approaches tyranny it is near its end, for by this it becomes ripe for division, change of dynasty, or total destruction, especially in a temperate climate . . . where men are habitually, morally and naturally free.
Nicholas of Oresme (c. 1320–82) Chaplain to Charles V of France. *De Moneta*

10 Where laws end, tyranny begins.
William Pitt the Elder (1708–78) British statesman. Speech, House of Lords, referring to the Wilkes case, 9 Jan 1770

11 The only tyrannies from which men, women and children are suffering in real life are the tyrannies of minorities.
Theodore Roosevelt (1858–1919) US Republican president. Speech, 22 Mar 1912

12 The laity found him more than a king, the clergy more than a pope, and both an intolerable tyrant.
William of Newburgh (1136–c. 1198) English monk and historian. Referring to William Longchamp, Justiciar and Chancellor of England during Richard I's absence on Crusade. *Historia Rerum Anglicarum*, Bk. IV, Ch. 14

U

UNCERTAINTY

See also doubt, indecision

1 If ifs and ans were pots and pans, there'd be no trade for tinkers.
Proverb

2 I have known uncertainty: a state unknown to the Greeks.
Jorge Luis Borges (1899–1986) Argentinian writer. *Ficciones*, 'The Babylonian Lottery'

3 Without measureless and perpetual uncertainty the drama of human life would be destroyed.
Winston Churchill (1874–1965) British statesman. *The Gathering Storm*

4 Of course not. After all, I may be wrong.
Bertrand Russell (1872–1970) British philosopher. On being asked whether he would be prepared to die for his beliefs. Attrib.

UNDERSTANDING

See also intelligence, wisdom

1 And come hither, and I shall light a candle of understanding in thine heart, which shall not be put out, till the things be performed which thou shalt begin to write.
Bible: II Esdras 14:25

2 It is good to know what a man is, and also what the world takes him for. But you do not understand him until you have learnt how he understands himself.
F. H. Bradley (1846–1924) British philosopher. *Aphorisms*

3 The people may be made to follow a course of action, but they may not be made to understand it.
Confucius (K'ung Fu-tzu; 551–479 BC) Chinese philosopher. *Analects*

4 Only one man ever understood me. . . . And he didn't understand me.
Hegel (1770–1831) German philosopher. Said on his deathbed. *Famous Last Words* (B. Conrad)

5 Even when poetry has a meaning, as it usually has, it may be inadvisable to draw it out . . . Perfect understanding will sometimes almost extinguish pleasure.
A. E. Housman (1859–1936) British scholar and poet. *The Name and Nature of Poetry*

6 Thought must be divided against itself before it can come to any knowledge of itself.
Aldous Huxley (1894–1964) British novelist. *Do What You Will*

7 She did her work with the thoroughness of a mind that reveres details and never quite understands them.
Sinclair Lewis (1885–1951) US novelist. *Babbitt*, Ch. 18

8 I used to tell my husband that, if he could make *me* understand something, it would be clear to all the other people in the country.
Eleanor Roosevelt (1884–1962) US writer and lecturer. Newspaper column, 'My Day', 12 Feb 1947

9 I have striven not to laugh at human actions, not to weep at them, nor to hate them, but to understand them.
Benedict Spinoza (Baruch de Spinoza; 1632–77) Dutch philosopher. *Tractatus Theologico-Politicus*, Ch. 1

10 All, everything that I understand, I understand only because I love.
Leo Tolstoy (1828–1910) Russian writer. *War and Peace*, Bk. VII, Ch. 16

UNEMPLOYMENT

See also idleness, work

1 Giz a job.
Alan Bleasdale Said by his character Yosser Hughes. *Boys From the Blackstuff*

2 When a great many people are unable to find work, unemployment results.
Calvin Coolidge (1872–1933) US president. *City Editor*

3 My father did not wait around . . . he got on his bike and went out looking for work.
Norman Tebbitt (1931–) British Conservative politician. Speech, Conservative Party conference, 1981

4 It's a recession when your neighbor

loses his job; it's a depression when you lose your own.

Harry S. Truman (1884–1972) US statesman. *The Observer*, 'Sayings of the Week', 6 Apr 1958

5 Something must be done.

Duke of Windsor (1894–1972) King of the United Kingdom; abdicated 1936. Said while visiting areas of high unemployment in South Wales during the 1930s. Attrib.

UNFAITHFULNESS

See also adultery

1 Early one morning, just as the sun was rising,
I heard a maid sing in the valley below
'Oh, don't deceive me; Oh, never leave me!
How could you use a poor maiden so?'

Anonymous *Early One Morning*

2 Frankie and Johnny were lovers, my gawd, how they could love,
Swore to be true to each other, true as the stars above;
He was her man, but he done her wrong.

Anonymous *Frankie and Johnny*

3 It would take a far more concentrated woman than Amanda to be unfaithful every five minutes.

Noël Coward (1899–1973) British dramatist. *Private Lives*

4 But I kissed her little sister,
And forgot my Clementine.

Percy Montrose (19th century) US songwriter. *Clementine*

5 One man's folly is another man's wife.

Helen Rowland (1876–1950) US writer. *A Guide to Men*

6 O, swear not by the moon, th' inconstant moon,
That monthly changes in her circled orb,
Lest that thy love prove likewise variable.

William Shakespeare (1564–1616) English dramatist. *Romeo and Juliet*, II:2

7 His honour rooted in dishonour stood,
And faith unfaithful kept him falsely true.

Alfred, Lord Tennyson (1809–92) British poet. *Idylls of the King*, 'Lancelot and Elaine'

8 No man worth having is true to his wife, or can be true to his wife, or ever was, or ever will be so.

John Vanbrugh (1664–1726) English architect and dramatist. *The Relapse*, III:2

UNITED STATES

Quotations about the United States

1 The second day of July 1776 will be the most memorable epoch in the history of America . . . It ought to be solemnized with pomp and parade, with shows, games, sports, guns, bells, bonfires and illuminations from one end of this continent to the other, from this time forward, for ever more.

John Adams (1735–1826) Second president of the USA. The Continental Congress voted for independence from Britain on 2 July. Letter to his wife, 3 July 1776

2 Superman, disguised as Clark Kent, mild-mannered reporter for a great metropolitan newspaper, fights a never-ending battle for truth, justice, and the American way.

Anonymous Hence the description 'Mild-mannered Clark Kent'. Introduction to radio series

3 Our society distributes itself into Barbarians, Philistines, and Populace; and America is just ourselves, with the Barbarians quite left out, and the Populace nearly.

Matthew Arnold (1822–88) British poet and critic. *Culture and Anarchy*, Preface

4 God bless the USA, so large,
So friendly, and so rich.

W. H. Auden (1907–73) British poet. *On the Circuit*

5 Yankee Doodle came to town
Riding on a pony;
Stuck a feather in his cap
And called it Macaroni.

Edward Bangs (fl. 1775) US songwriter. *Yankee Doodle; or Father's Return to Camp*

6 O beautiful for spacious skies,
For amber waves of grain,
For purple mountain majesties
Above the fruited plain!
America! America!
God shed His grace on thee
And crown thy good with brotherhood
From sea to shining sea!

Katharine Lee Bates (1859–1929) US writer and poet. *America the Beautiful*

7 The United States is the best and fairest and most decent nation on the face of the earth.

George Bush (1924–) US statesman. Speech, May 1988

8 I called the New World into existence to redress the balance of the Old.

George Canning (1770–1827) British statesman. Speech, 12 Dec 1826

9 This is virgin territory for whorehouses.

Al Capone (1899–1947) Italian-born US gangster. Talking about suburban Chicago. *The Bootleggers* (Kenneth Allsop), Ch. 16

10 You will have heard of our taking of New Amsterdam . . . It did belong to England heretofore, but the Dutch by degrees drove our people out and built a very good town, but we have got the better of it, and 'tis now called New York.

Charles II (1630–85) King of England. Letter, 24 Oct 1664

11 How beautiful it would be for someone who could not read.

G. K. Chesterton (1874–1936) British writer. Referring to the lights on Broadway. Attrib.

12 I hope to see the day when the American flag will float over every square foot of the British North American possessions clear to the North Pole.

James Beauchamp Clark (1850–1921) Speaker of US House of Representatives. Speech, House of Representatives, June 1911

13 America is the only nation in history which miraculously has gone directly from barbarism to degeneration without the usual interval of civilization.

Georges Clemenceau (1841–1929) French statesman. Attrib.

14 Patriotism is easy to understand in America; it means looking out for yourself while looking out for your country.

Calvin Coolidge (1872–1833) US president. Attrib.

15 The business of America is business.

Calvin Coolidge Speech, Washington, 17 Jan 1925

16 Poor Mexico, so far from God and so near to the United States!

Porfirio Diaz (1830–1915) Mexican general and statesman. Attrib.

17 Whatever America hopes to bring to pass in this world must first come to pass in the heart of America.

Dwight D. Eisenhower (1890–1969) US general and statesman. Inaugural address, 1953

18 America is a country of young men.
Ralph Waldo Emerson (1803–82) US poet and essayist. *Society and Solitude*, 'Old Age'

19 Long Island represents the American's idea of what God would have done with Nature if he'd had the money.
Peter Fleming (1907–1971) British writer. Letter to his brother Rupert, 29 Sept 1929

20 Our country is the world – our countrymen are all mankind.
William Lloyd Garrison (1805–79) US abolitionist. *The Liberator*, 15 Dec 1837

21 I can never suppose this country so far lost to all ideas of self-importance as to be willing to grant America independence; if that could ever be adopted I shall despair of this country being ever preserved from a state of inferiority and consequently falling into a very low class among the European States.
George III (1738–1820) King of Great Britain and Ireland. Letter to Lord North, 7 Mar 1780

22 . . . New York . . . that unnatural city where every one is an exile, none more so than the American.
Charlotte Perkins Gilman (1860–1935) US writer. *The Living of Charlotte Perkins Gilman*

23 The United States is like a gigantic boiler. Once the fire is lighted under it there is no limit to the power it can generate.
Lord Grey (1862–1933) British statesman. *Their Finest Hour* (Winston S. Churchill), Ch. 32

24 Let Americans disdain to be the instruments of European greatness. Let the Thirteen States, bound together in a strict and indissoluble union, concur in erecting one great American system.
Alexander Hamilton (1755–1804) American statesman. *Federalist Papers*, XI

25 America's present need is not heroics but healing, not nostrums but normalcy.
Warren G. Harding (1865–1923) US President. Speech, Boston, May 1920

26 For the Colonies in the Indies, they are yet babes that cannot live without sucking the breasts of their mother-Cities, but such as, I mistake, if when they come of age they do not wean themselves.
James Harrington (1611–77) English political writer. *The Commonwealth of Oceana*

27 Many, if not most, of our Indian wars have had their origin in broken promises and acts of injustice on our part.
Rutherford B. Hayes (1822–93) US president. Message to Congress, 4 Dec 1877

28 Everything about the behavior of American society reveals that it is half judaised and half negrified. How can one expect a state like that to hold together?
Adolf Hitler (1889–1945) German dictator. Attrib.

29 The United States, I believe, are under the impression that they are twenty years in advance of this country; whilst, as a matter of actual verifiable fact, of course, they are just about six hours behind it.
Harold Hobson (1904–) British theater critic and writer. *The Devil in Woodford Wells*, Ch. 8

30 The American system of rugged individualism.
Herbert Clark Hoover (1874–1964) US statesman. Speech, New York, 22 Oct 1928

31 . . . I have no fears for the future of our country. It is bright with hope.
Herbert Clark Hoover Inaugural address, 4 Mar 1929

32 America is not a blanket woven from one thread, one color, one cloth.
Jesse Jackson (1941–) US politician. Speech, Democratic Party Convention, Atlanta, July 1988

33 There is not a single crowned head in Europe whose talents or merits would entitle him to be elected a vestryman by the people of any parish in America.
Thomas Jefferson Written from Paris. Letter to George Washington, 2 May 1788

34 The United States has to move very fast to even stand still.
John Fitzgerald Kennedy (1917–63) US statesman. *The Observer*, 'Sayings of the Week', 21 July 1963

35 'Tis the star-spangled banner; O long may it wave
O'er the land of the free, and the home of the brave!
Francis Scott Key (1779–1843) US lawyer. *The Star-Spangled Banner*

36 Give me your tired, your poor,
Your huddled masses yearning to breathe free,
The wretched refuse of your teeming shore,
Send these, the homeless, tempest-tossed to me,
I lift my lamp beside the golden door!
Emma Lazarus (1849–87) US poet and philanthropist. Used as an inscription on the Statue of Liberty. *The New Colossus*

37 That these United Colonies are, and of right ought to be, free and independent states.
Richard Henry Lee (1732–94) US Revolutionary patriot and Senator. Motion, Continental Congress, Philadelphia, 7 June 1776

38 In other countries, art and literature are left to a lot of shabby bums living in attics and feeding on booze and spaghetti, but in America the successful writer or picture-painter is indistinguishable from any other decent business man.
Sinclair Lewis (1885–1951) US novelist. *Babbitt*, Ch. 14

39 This country, with its institutions, belongs to the people who inhabit it. Whenever they shall grow weary of the existing government, they can exercise their constitutional right of amending it, or their revolutionary right to dismember or overthrow it.
Abraham Lincoln (1809–65) US statesman. First Inaugural Address, 4 Mar 1861

40 In an English ship, they say, it is poor grub, poor pay, and easy work; in an American ship, good grub, good pay, and hard work. And this is applicable to the working populations of both countries.
Jack London (1876–1916) US novelist. *The People of the Abyss*, Ch. 20

41 First the sweetheart of the nation, then the aunt, woman governs America because America is a land of boys who refuse to grow up.
Salvador de Madariaga y Rogo (1886–1978) Spanish diplomat and writer. *The Perpetual Pessimist* (Sagitarius and George)

42 If there is any country on earth where the course of true love may be expected to run smooth, it is America.
Harriet Martineau (1802–76) British writer. *Society in America*, Vol. III, 'Marriage'

43 When you become used to never being alone you may consider yourself Americanised.
André Maurois (Émile Herzog; 1885–1967) French writer. Attrib.

44 The immense popularity of American movies abroad demonstrates that Europe is the

unfinished negative of which America is the proof.
Mary McCarthy (1912–) US novelist. *On the Contrary*

45 This country needs good farmers, good businessmen, good plumbers.
Richard Milhouse Nixon (1913–) US President. Farewell address, 9 Aug 1974

46 I rejoice that America has resisted. Three millions of people, so dead to all the feelings of liberty, as voluntarily to submit to be slaves, would have been fit instruments to make slaves of the rest.
William Pitt the Elder (1708–78) British statesman. Speech, House of Commons, 14 Jan 1766

47 You cannot conquer America.
William Pitt the Elder Speech, House of Lords, 18 Nov 1777

48 I invoke the genius of the Constitution.
William Pitt the Elder Referring to the American Revolution. Speech, House of Lords, 18 Nov 1777

49 I know only two words of American slang, 'swell' and 'lousy'. I think 'swell' is lousy, but 'lousy' is swell.
J. B. Priestley (1894–1984) British novelist. Interview, US radio

50 The national dish of America is menus.
Robert Robinson (1927–) British writer and broadcaster. BBC TV program, *Robinson's Travels*, Aug 1977

51 I pledge you, I pledge myself, to a new deal for the American people.
Franklin D. Roosevelt (1882–1945) US Democratic president. Speech accepting nomination for presidency, Chicago, 2 July 1932

52 I see one-third of a nation ill-housed, ill-clad, ill-nourished.
Franklin D. Roosevelt Second Inaugural Address, 20 Jan 1937

53 The first requisite of a good citizen in this Republic of ours is that he shall be able and willing to pull his weight.
Theodore Roosevelt (1858–1919) US Republican president. Speech, New York, 11 Nov 1902

54 In the Western hemisphere the adherence of the United States to the Monroe Doctrine may force the United States, however reluctantly, in flagrant cases of wrongdoing or impotence, to the exercise of an international police power.
Theodore Roosevelt Message to Congress, 6 Dec 1904

55 America . . . where law and customs alike are based on the dreams of spinsters.
Bertrand Russell (1872–1970) British philosopher. *Marriage and Morals*

56 In America everybody is of the opinion that he has no social superiors, since all men are equal, but he does not admit that he has no social inferiors.
Bertrand Russell *Unpopular Essays*

57 England and America are two countries separated by the same language.
George Bernard Shaw (1856–1950) Irish dramatist and critic. Attrib.

58 New York . . . is not Mecca. It just smells like it.
Neil Simon (1927–) US playwright. *California Suite*

59 In the United States there is more space where nobody is than where anybody is. That is what makes America what it is.
Gertrude Stein (1874–1946) US writer. *The Geographical History of America*

60 I like to walk around Manhattan, catching glimpses of its wild life, the pigeons and cats and girls.
Rex Todhunter Stout (1886–1975) US writer. *Three Witnesses*, 'When a Man Murders'

61 I found there a country with thirty-two religions and only one sauce.
Talleyrand (Charles Maurice de Talleyrand-Périgord; 1754–1838) French politician. *Autant en apportent les mots* (Pedrazzini)

62 America is a large, friendly dog in a very small room. Every time it wags its tail it knocks over a chair.
Arnold Toynbee (1889–1975) British historian. Broadcast news summary, 14 July 1954

63 By the waters of Babylon we sit down and weep, when we think of thee, O America!
Horace Walpole (1717–97) British writer. On the eve of the American Revolution. Letter to Mason, 12 June 1775

64 Up from the meadows rich with corn,
Clear in the cool September morn,

The clustered spires of Frederick stand
Green-walled by the hills of Maryland.
John Greenleaf Whittier (1807–92) US poet. *Barbara Frietchie*

65 There exists in the world today a gigantic reservoir of good will toward us, the American people.
Wendell Lewis Willkie (1892–1944) US lawyer and businessman. *One World*, Ch. 10

66 I want to take this occasion to say that the United States will never again seek one additional foot of territory by conquest.
Woodrow Wilson (1856–1924) US statesman. Speech, Mobile, 27 Oct 1913.

67 The United States must be neutral in fact as well as in name during these days that are to try men's souls. We must be impartial in thought as well as in action.
Woodrow Wilson Message to the Senate, 19 Aug 1914

68 America cannot be an ostrich with its head in the sand.
Woodrow Wilson Speech, Des Moines, 1 Feb 1916

69 Sometimes people call me an idealist. Well, that is the way I know I am an American. America is the only idealistic nation in the world.
Woodrow Wilson Speech, Sioux Falls, 8 Sept 1919

70 America . . . is the prize amateur nation of the world. Germany is the prize professional nation.
Woodrow Wilson Speech, Aug 1917. *Mr Wilson's War* (John Dos Passos), Pt. III, Ch. 13

71 New York is a small place when it comes to the part of it that wakes up just as the rest is going to bed.
P. G. Wodehouse (1881–1975) British humorous novelist. *My Man Jeeves*, 'The Aunt and the Sluggard'

72 America is God's Crucible, the great Melting-Pot where all the races of Europe are melting and re-forming!
Israel Zangwill (1864–1926) British writer. *The Melting Pot*, I

Quotations about Americans

73 Any gum, chum?
Anonymous Children's cry in Britain to US GIs.

74 Good Americans, when they die, go to Paris.
Thomas Gold Appleton (1812–84) US writer. *Autocrat of the Breakfast Table* (O. W. Holmes), Ch. 6

75 A Boston man is the east wind made flesh.
Thomas Gold Appleton Attrib.

76 Americans have a perfect right to

exist. But he did often find himself wishing Mr. Rhodes had not enabled them to excercise that right at Oxford.
Max Beerbohm (1872–1936) British writer. *Zuleika Dobson*

77 The English are polite by telling lies. The Americans are polite by telling the truth.
Malcolm Bradbury (1932–) British academic and novelist. *Stepping Westward*, Bk. II, Ch. 5

78 There is nothing the matter with Americans except their ideals. The real American is all right; it is the ideal American who is all wrong.
G. K. Chesterton (1874–1936) British writer. *New York Times*, 1 Feb 1931

79 The Americans cannot build aeroplanes. They are very good at refrigerators and razor blades.
Hermann Goering (1893–1946) German leader. Assurance to Hitler. *America* (Alistair Cooke)

80 Scratch an American and you get a Seventh Day Adventist every time.
Lord Hailsham (1907–) British Conservative politician. *The Observer*, 'Sayings of the Week', 1 June 1969

81 I am not a Virginian, but an American.
Patrick Henry (1736–99) US statesman. Speech, Continental Congress, 5 Sept 1774

82 I am willing to love all mankind, *except an American.*
Samuel Johnson (1709–84) British lexicographer. *Life of Johnson* (J. Boswell), Vol. III

83 Americans have plenty of everything and the best of nothing.
John C. Keats (1920–) US writer. *You Might As Well Live*

84 Does that mean that because Americans won't listen to sense, you intend to talk nonsense to them?
John Maynard Keynes (1883–1946) British economist. Said before a monetary conference, 1944 or 1945.

85 No one ever went broke underestimating the intelligence of the American people.
H. L. Mencken (1880–1956) US journalist. Attrib.

86 There won't be any revolution in America . . . The people are too clean. They spend all their time changing their shirts and washing themselves. You can't feel fierce and revolutionary in a bathroom.
Eric Linklater (1889–1974) Scottish novelist. *Juan in America*, Pt. V, Ch. 3

87 No one can kill Americans and brag about it. No one.
Ronald Reagan (1911–) US politician and president. *The Observer*, 'Sayings of the Week', 27 Apr 1986

88 An American is either a Jew, or an anti-Semite, unless he is both at the same time.
Jean-Paul Sartre (1905–80) French writer. *Altona*

89 I wish all Americans were as blind as you.
George Bernard Shaw (1856–1950) Irish dramatist and critic. Speaking to Helen Keller. *Bernard Shaw* (H. Pearson)

90 An asylum for the sane would be empty in America.
George Bernard Shaw

91 That strange blend of the commercial traveller, the missionary, and the barbarian conqueror, which was the American abroad.
Olaf Stapledon (1886–1950) British philosopher and science-fiction writer. *Last and First Men*, Ch. 3

92 Americans have been conditioned to respect newness, whatever it costs them.
John Updike (1932–) US novelist. *A Month of Sundays*, Ch. 18

93 American writers want to be not good but great; and so are neither.
Gore Vidal (1925–) US novelist. *Two Sisters*

94 MRS ALLONBY. They say, Lady Hunstanton, that when good Americans die they go to Paris.
LADY HUNSTANTON. Indeed? And when bad Americans die, where do they go to?
LORD ILLINGWORTH. Oh, they go to America.
Oscar Wilde (1854–1900) Irish-born British dramatist. *See* Thomas Gold APPLETON *A Woman of No Importance*, I

95 Like so many substantial Americans, he had married young and kept on marrying, springing from blonde to blonde like the chamois of the Alps leaping from crag to crag.
P. G. Wodehouse (1881–1975) British humorous novelist. *Wodehouse at Work to the End* (Richard Usborne), Ch. 2

UNITY

1 A chain is no stronger than its weakest link.
Proverb

2 Union is strength.
Proverb

3 United we stand, divided we fall.
Proverb

4 That typically English characteristic for which there is no English name – *esprit de corps*.
Frank Ezra Adcock (1886–1968) British classicist. Presidential address

5 And if one prevail against him, two shall withstand him; and a threefold cord is not quickly broken.
Bible: Ecclesiastes 4:12

6 And the whole earth was of one language, and of one speech.
Bible: Genesis 11:1

7 When bad men combine, the good must associate; else they will fall one by one, an unpitied sacrifice in a contemptible struggle.
Edmund Burke (1729–97) British politician. *Thoughts on the Cause of the Present Discontents*

8 All for one, and one for all.
Alexandre Dumas père (1802–70) French novelist and dramatist. *The Three Musketeers*

9 We must indeed all hang together, or most assuredly, we shall all hang separately.
Benjamin Franklin (1706–90) US scientist and statesman. Remark on signing the Declaration of Independence, 4 July 1776

10 Everyone has observed how much more dogs are animated when they hunt in a pack, than when they pursue their game apart. We might, perhaps, be at a loss to explain this phenomenon, if we had not experience of a similar in ourselves.
David Hume (1711–76) Scottish philosopher. *A Treatise of Human Nature*

11 It is true that a house divided against itself is a house that cannot stand. There is a division in the American house now and believing this as I do, I have concluded that I should not permit the Presidency to become involved in the partisan divisions that are developing in this political year. Accordingly, I shall not seek, and I will not accept, the

nomination of my party for another term as your President.

Lyndon B. Johnson (1908–73) US Democratic president. Announcing his intention not to stand again. Broadcast address, 31 Mar 1968

12 Now, is it to lower the price of corn, or isn't it? It is not much matter which we say, but mind, we must all say *the same.*

Lord Melbourne (1779–1848) British statesman. Said at a cabinet meeting. *The English Constitution* (Bagehot), Ch. 1

UNIVERSE

See also astronomy, moon, space, stars, sun, world

1 Had I been present at the Creation, I would have given some useful hints for the better ordering of the universe.

Alfonso the Wise (c. 1221–84) King of Castile and Léon. Referring to the complicated Ptolemaic model of the universe. Often quoted as, 'Had I been consulted I would have recommended something simpler'. Attrib.

2 The visible universe was an illusion or, more precisely, a sophism. Mirrors and fatherhood are abominable because they multiply it and extend it.

Jorge Luis Borges (1899–1986) Argentinian writer. *Ficciones,* 'Tlön, Uqbar, Orbis Tertius'

3 In this unbelievable universe in which we live there are no absolutes. Even parallel lines, reaching into infinity, meet somewhere yonder.

Pearl Buck (1892–1973) US novelist. *A Bridge for Passing*

4 I don't pretend to understand the Universe – it's a great deal bigger than I am . . . People ought to be modester.

Thomas Carlyle (1795–1881) Scottish historian and essayist. Attrib.

5 MARGARET FULLER. I accept the universe.

CARLYLE. Gad! she'd better!

Thomas Carlyle Attrib.

6 The cosmos is about the smallest hole that a man can hide his head in.

G. K. Chesterton (1874–1936) British writer. *Orthodoxy,* Ch. 1

7 There is no reason to assume that the universe has the slightest interest in intelligence – or even in life. Both may be random accidental by-products of its operations like the beautiful patterns on a butterfly's wings. The insect would fly just as well without them.

Arthur C. Clarke (1917–) British science-fiction writer. *The Lost Worlds of 2001*

8 I am very interested in the Universe – I am specializing in the universe and all that surrounds it.

Peter Cook (1937–) British writer and entertainer. *Beyond the Fringe*

9 Listen; there's a hell of a good universe next door: let's go.

e. e. cummings (1894–1962) US poet. *Pity this Busy Monster, Mankind*

10 My own suspicion is that the universe is not only queerer than we suppose, but queerer than we *can* suppose.

J. B. S. Haldane (1892–1964) British geneticist. *Possible Worlds,* 'On Being the Right Size'

11 The universe is not hostile, nor yet is it friendly. It is simply indifferent.

John Haynes Holmes (1879–1964) US clergyman. *A Sensible Man's View of Religion*

12 The universe begins to look more like a great thought than like a great machine.

James Jeans (1877–1946) British scientist. *The Mysterious Universe*

13 In my youth I regarded the universe as an open book, printed in the language of physical equations, whereas now it appears to me as a text written in invisible ink, of which in our rare moments of grace we are able to decipher a small fragment.

Arthur Koestler (1905–83) Hungarian-born British writer. *Bricks to Babel,* Epilogue

14 Out of all possible universes, the only one which can exist, in the sense that it can be known, is simply the one which satisfies the narrow conditions necessary for the development of intelligent life.

Bernard Lovell (1913–) British astronomer and writer. *In the Centre of Immensities*

15 The universe ought to be presumed too vast to have any character.

C. S. Peirce (1839–1914) US physicist. *Collected Papers,* VI

UNKNOWN

1 And I said to the man who stood at the gate of the year: 'Give me a light that I may tread safely into the unknown'. And he replied: 'Go out into the darkness and put your hand into the hand of God. That shall be to you better than light and safer than a known way.'

Minnie Louise Haskins (1875–1957) US writer. Remembered because it was quoted by George VI in his Christmas broadcast, 1939. *The Desert,* Introduction

2 In other words, apart from the known and the unknown, what else is there?

Harold Pinter (1930–) British dramatist. *The Homecoming,* II

3 There is not any book
Or face of dearest look
That I would not turn from now
To go into the unknown
I must enter, and leave, alone,
I know not how.

Edward Thomas (1878–1917) British poet. *Lights Out*

V

VANITY

See conceit

VEGETARIANISM

1 Vegetarianism is harmless enough, though it is apt to fill a man with wind and self righteousness.

Robert Hutchinson President, Royal College of Physicians. Attrib.

2 There are millions of vegetarians in the world but only one Bernard Shaw. You do not obtain eminence quite so cheaply as by eating macaroni instead of mutton chops.

George Bernard Shaw (1856–1950) Irish dramatist and critic. Replying to a suggestion, during the meat shortage of the 1914–18 war, that he should be cited as an example of the advantages of vegetarianism.

3 A man of my spiritual intensity does not eat corpses.
George Bernard Shaw Attrib.

VENICE

See also Europe

1 Streets full of water. Please advise.
Robert Benchley (1889–1945) US humorist. Telegram sent to his editor on arriving in Venice. Attrib.

2 Venice is like eating an entire box of chocolate liqueurs at one go.
Truman Capote (1924–84) US novelist. *The Observer,* 'Sayings of the Week', 26 Nov 1961

3 Venice, the eldest Child of Liberty.
She was a maiden City, bright and free.
William Wordsworth (1770–1850) British poet. Venice, a republic since the Middle Ages, was conquered by Napoleon in 1797 and absorbed into his Kingdom of Italy in 1805. *Sonnets,* 'Once did she hold'

4 Once did she hold the gorgeous east in fee;
And was the safeguard of the west.
William Wordsworth *Sonnets,* 'Once did she hold'

5 When she took unto herself a mate,
She must espouse the everlasting sea.
William Wordsworth *Sonnets,* 'Once did she hold'

VERBOSITY

See also brevity, sermons, speech, speeches, writing

1 There was a young man of Japan
Whose limericks never would scan;
When they said it was so,
He replied, 'Yes, I know,
But I always try to get as many words into the last line as ever I possibly can.'
Anonymous

2 As far as I can see, you have used every cliché except 'God is love' and 'Please adjust your dress before leaving'.
Winston Churchill (1874–1965) British statesman. Complaining about a memorandum from Anthony Eden. *The Mirror: A Political History* (M. Edelman)

3 A sophistical rhetorician inebriated with the exuberance of his own verbosity.
Benjamin Disraeli (1804–81) British statesman. Referring to Gladstone. Speech, 27 July 1878

4 But far more numerous was the Herd of such,
Who think too little, and who talk too much.
John Dryden (1631–1700) British poet and dramatist. *Absalom and Achitophel,* I

5 Nothing is more despicable than a professional talker who uses his words as a quack uses his remedies.
Franççois Fénelon (1651–1715) French writer and prelate. Letter to M. Dacier

6 I have made this letter longer than usual, only because I have not had the time to make it shorter.
Blaise Pascal (1623–62) French philosopher and mathematician. *Lettres provinciales,* XVI

7 Words are like leaves; and where they most abound,
Much fruit of sense beneath is rarely found.
Alexander Pope (1688–1744) British poet. *An Essay on Criticism*

VICE

See also crime, evil, sin, virtue and vice

1 When vice prevails, and impious men bear sway,
The post of honour is a private station.
Joseph Addison (1672–1719) British essayist. *Cato,* IV:1

2 We make ourselves a ladder out of our vices if we trample the vices themselves underfoot.
St Augustine of Hippo (354–430) Bishop of Hippo. *Sermons,* Bk. III, 'De Ascensione'

3 And when Jehu was come to Jezreel, Jezebel heard of it; and she painted her face, and tired her head, and looked out at a window.
Bible: II Kings 9:30

4 Often the fear of one evil leads us into a worse.
Nicolas Boileau (1636–1711) French writer. *L'Art poétique,* I

5 The wickedness of the world is so great you have to run your legs off to avoid having them stolen from under you.
Bertolt Brecht (1898–1956) German dramatist. *The Threepenny Opera,* I:3

6 Vice itself lost half its evil, by losing all its grossness.
Edmund Burke (1729–97) British politician. *Reflections on the Revolution in France*

7 Half the vices which the world condemns most loudly have seeds of good in them and require moderate use rather than total abstinence.
Samuel Butler (1835–1902) British writer. *The Way of All Flesh*

8 Vice is its own reward.
Quentin Crisp (c. 1910–) Model, publicist, and writer. *The Naked Civil Servant*

9 In my time, the follies of the town crept slowly among us, but now they travel faster than a stagecoach.
Oliver Goldsmith (1728–74) Irish-born British writer. *She Stoops to Conquer,* I

10 It is the restrictions placed on vice by our social code which makes its pursuit so peculiarly agreeable.
Kenneth Grahame (1859–1932) Scottish writer. *Pagan Papers*

11 We have become, Nina, the sort of people our parents warned us about.
Augustus John (1878–1961) British artist. To Nina Hamnet. Attrib.

12 She was too fond of her most filthy bargain.
William Shakespeare (1564–1616) English dramatist. *Othello,* V:2

13 Vice is waste of life. Poverty, obedience and celibacy are the canonical vices.
George Bernard Shaw (1856–1950) Irish dramatist and critic. *Man and Superman*

14 Wrongdoing can only be avoided if those who are not wronged feel the same indignation at it as those who are.
Solon (6th century BC) Athenian statesman. *Greek Wit* (F. Paley)

15 Whenever I'm caught between two evils, I take the one I've never tried.
Mae West (1892–1980) US actress. Attrib.

16 Never support two weaknesses at the same time. It's your combination sinners – your lecherous liars and your miserly drunkards – who dishonor the vices and bring them into bad repute.
Thornton Wilder (1897–1975) US novelist and dramatist. *The Matchmaker,* III

VICTORY

See also war

1 *Veni, vidi, vici.*
I came, I saw, I conquered.
Julius Caesar (100–44 BC) Roman general and statesman. *The Twelve Caesars* (Suetonius)

2 I came, I saw, God conquered.
Charles V (1500–58) Holy Roman Emperor. Remark after the Battle of Mühlberg, 23 Apr 1547

3 Victory at all costs, victory in spite of all terror, victory however long and hard the road may be; for without victory there is no survival.
Winston Churchill (1874–1965) British statesman. Speech, House of Commons, 13 May 1940

4 This is *your* victory.
Winston Churchill Speech, London, 8 May 1945

5 As always, victory finds a hundred fathers, but defeat is an orphan.
Count Galeazzo Ciano (1903–44) Italian Foreign Minister. Diary entry, 9 Sept 1942

6 We triumph without glory when we conquer without danger.
Pierre Corneille (1606–84) French dramatist. *Le Cid*, II:2

7 The most important thing in the Olympic Games is not winning but taking part . . . The essential thing in life is not conquering but fighting well.
Pierre de Coubertin (1863–1937) French educator and sportsman. Speech, Banquet to Officials of Olympic Games, London, 24 July 1908

8 A game which a sharper once played with a dupe, entitled 'Heads I win, tails you lose.'
John Wilson Croker (1780–1857) British Tory politician. *Croker Papers*

9 The happy state of getting the victor's palm without the dust of racing.
Horace (Quintus Horatius Flaccus; 65–8 BC) Roman poet. *Epistles*, I

10 They talk about who won and who lost. Human reason won. Mankind won.
Nikita Khrushchev (1894–1971) Soviet statesman. Referring to the Cuban missiles crisis. *The Observer*, 'Sayings of the Week', 11 Nov 1962

11 Winning isn't everything, but wanting to win is.
Vince Lombardi (1913–70) US football coach.

12 I have not time to say more, but to beg you will give my duty to the Queen, and let her know her army has had a glorious victory. Monsieur Tallard and two other generals are in my coach, and I am following the rest . . .
Duke of Marlborough (1650–1722) British military commander. Referring to the Battle of Blenheim, 13 Aug 1704. Note to his wife, written on a tavern bill

13 How vainly men themselves amaze
To win the palm, the oak, or bays.
Andrew Marvell (1621–78) English poet. *The Garden*

14 Who overcomes
By force, hath overcome but half his foe.
John Milton (1608–74) English poet. *Paradise Lost*, Bk. I

15 See, the conquering hero comes!
Sound the trumpets, beat the drums!
Thomas Morell (1703–84) British classicist. The libretto for Handel's oratorio. *Joshua*, Pt. III

16 We have met the enemy, and they are ours.
Oliver Hazard Perry (1785–1819) US naval officer. Message sent reporting his victory in a naval battle on Lake Erie. *Familiar Quotations* (J. Bartlett)

17 Now indeed with God's help the final stone has been laid in the foundation of St Petersburg.
Peter the Great (1672–1725) Tsar of Russia. Referring to his victory over Charles XII of Sweden at the Battle of Poltava (28 June 1709). Letter to Admiral Apraksin, 27 June 1709

18 Such another victory and we are ruined.
Pyrrhus (319–272 BC) King of Epirus. Commenting upon the costliness of his victory at the Battle of Asculum, 279 BC *Life of Pyrrhus* (Plutarch)

19 For when the One Great Scorer comes
To write against your name,
He marks – not that you won or lost –
But how you played the game.
Grantland Rice (1880–1954) US sportswriter. *Alumnus Football*

20 Thus we have defeated the king of France at Gisors but it is not we who have done it, but God and our right through us.
Richard I (1157–99) King of England. Letter to the Bishop of Durham, 1198

21 The earth is still bursting with the dead bodies of the victors.
George Bernard Shaw (1856–1950) Irish dramatist and critic. *Heartbreak House*, Preface

22 'And everybody praised the Duke,
Who this great fight did win.'
'But what good came of it at last?'
Quoth little Peterkin.
'Why that I cannot tell,' said he,
'But 'twas a famous victory.'
Robert Southey (1774–1843) British poet. *The Battle of Blenheim*

23 Since it is neither right nor natural for Frenchmen to be subject to Englishmen, but rather for Englishmen to be subject to Frenchmen, the outcome of the event mocked his vile expectation.
Suger, Abbot of St Denis (1081–1152) French monk and diplomat. Referring to William II of England's campaigns in Normandy. *Life of Louis VI*

24 Just rejoice at that news and congratulate our forces and the Marines. Goodnight. Rejoice!
Margaret Thatcher (1925–) British politician and prime minister. On the recapture of South Georgia, to newsmen outside 10 Downing Street. TV news coverage, 25 Apr 1982

25 It was easier to conquer it than to know what to do with it.
Horace Walpole (1717–97) British writer. Referring to the East. Letter to Sir Horace Mann, 27 Mar 1772

26 The next greatest misfortune to losing a battle is to gain such a victory as this.
Duke of Wellington (1769–1852) British general and statesman. *Recollections* (S. Rogers)

27 I always say that, next to a battle lost, the greatest misery is a battle gained.
Duke of Wellington *Diary* (Frances, Lady Shelley)

28 By the splendour of God I have taken possession of my realm; the earth of England is in my two hands.
William the Conqueror (1027–87) King of England. Said after falling over when coming ashore at Pevensey with his army of invasion. Attrib.

VIOLENCE

See also cruelty, force

1 You know I hate fighting. If I knew how to make a living some other way, I would.
Muhammad Ali (Cassius Clay; 1942–) US boxer. *The Observer*, 'Sayings of the Week', 21 Nov 1971

2 A bit of shooting takes your mind off your troubles – it makes you forget the cost of living.
Brendan Behan (1923–64) Irish playwright. *The Hostage*

3 Violence is the repartee of the illiterate.
Alan Brien (1925–) British journalist. *Punch*, 7 Feb 1973

4 So soon as the man overtook me, he was but a word and a blow.
John Bunyan (1628–88) English writer. *The Pilgrim's Progress*, Pt. I

5 Two lovely black eyes,
Oh, what a surprise!
Only for telling a man he was wrong.
Two lovely black eyes!
Charles Coborn (1852–1945) US songwriter. *Two Lovely Black Eyes*

6 It is better to be violent, if there is violence in our hearts, than to put on the cloak of non-violence to cover impotence.
Mahatma Gandhi (Mohandas Karamchand Gandhi; 1869–1948) Indian national leader. *Non-Violence in Peace and War*

7 Let the Turks now carry away their abuses in the only possible manner, namely by carrying off themselves. Their Zaptiehs and their Mudirs, their Bimbashis and their Yuzbachis, their Kaimakans and their Pashas, one and all, bag and baggage, shall, I hope, clear out from the province they have desolated and profaned.
William Ewart Gladstone (1809–98) British statesman. Reaction to the massacres of Bulgarians committed by Turkish Bashi-Bazouks (irregular troops). *The Bulgarian Horrors and the Question of the East* (pamphlet, 6 Sept 1876)

8 It's possible to disagree with someone about the ethics of non-violence without wanting to kick his face in.
Christopher Hampton (1946–) British writer and dramatist. *Treats*, Sc. 4

9 We are effectively destroying ourselves by violence masquerading as love.
R. D. Laing (1927–) British psychiatrist. *The Politics of Experience*, Ch. 13

10 If someone puts his hand on you, send him to the cemetery.
Malcolm X (1925–65) US Black leader. *Malcolm X Speaks*

11 Remove your pants before resorting to violence.
Yoko Ono (1933–) Japanese-born US rock musician and composer. Attrib.

12 Today violence is the rhetoric of the period.
José Ortega y Gasset (1883–1955) Spanish philosopher. *The Revolt of the Masses*

13 Every puny whipster gets my sword.
William Shakespeare (1564–1616) English dramatist. *Othello*, V:2

14 If you strike a child, take care that you strike it in anger, even at the risk of maiming it for life. A blow in cold blood neither can nor should be forgiven.
George Bernard Shaw (1856–1950) Irish dramatist and critic. *Man and Superman*, 'Maxims for Revolutionists'

VIRGIL

(Publius Vergilius Maro; 70–19 bc) Roman poet. His *Eclogues* (42–37 bc) were followed by the *Georgics* (36–29 bc), works that expressed his pastoral and agricultural interests. His national epic in 12 books, the *Aeneid*, led to his veneration by subsequent generations.

Quotations about Virgil

1 Thou art my master and my author, thou art he from whom alone I took the style whose beauty has done me honour.
Dante (1265–1321) Italian poet. *Divine Comedy*, 'Inferno', I

2 Virgil's great judgement appears in putting things together, and in his picking gold out of the dunghills of old Roman writers.
Alexander Pope (1688–1744) British poet. *Observations, Anecdotes and Characters* (Rev. Joseph Spence)

Quotations by Virgil

3 Anger supplies the arms.
Aeneid, Bk. I

4 I sing of arms and the man who first from the shores of Troy came destined an exile to Italy and the Lavinian beaches, much buffeted he on land and on the deep by force of the gods because of fierce Juno's never-forgetting anger.
Referring to Aeneas. *Aeneid*, Bk. I

5 O you who have borne even heavier things, God will grant an end to these too.
Aeneid, Bk. I

6 Maybe one day we shall be glad to remember even these hardships
Aeneid, Bk. I

7 A grief too much to be told, O queen, you bid me renew.
The opening words of Aeneas' account to Dido of the fall of Troy. *Aeneid*, Bk. II

8 *Equo ne credite, Teucri.*
Quidquid id est timeo Danaos et dona ferentis.
Do not trust the horse, Trojans. Whatever it is, I fear the Greeks even when they bring gifts.
Aeneid, Bk. II

9 It was the time when first sleep begins for weary mortals and by the gift of the gods creeps over them most welcomely.
Aeneid, Bk. II

10 What do you not drive human hearts into, cursed
craving for gold!
Aeneid, Bk. III

11 Woman is always fickle and changing.
Aeneid, Bk. IV

12 The way down to Hell is easy.
Aeneid, Bk. VI

13 I see wars, horrible wars, and the Tiber foaming with much blood.
Part of the Sibyl's prophecy to Aeneas, foretelling his difficulties in winning a home in Italy. *Aeneid*, Bk. VI

14 Fear lent wings to his feet.
Aeneid, Bk. VIII

15 Everyone is dragged on by their favourite pleasure.
Eclogue, Bk. II

16 There's a snake hidden in the grass.
Eclogue, Bk. III

17 Love conquers all things: let us too give in to Love.
Eclogue, Bk. X

18 But meanwhile it is flying, irretrievable time is flying.
Georgics, Bk. III

VIRGINITY

See purity, sex

VIRTUE

See also good, morality, purity, righteousness, virtue and vice

1 Virtue is like a rich stone, best plain set.
Francis Bacon (1561–1626) English philosopher. *Essays,* 'Of Beauty'

2 As in nature things move violently to their place and calmly in their place, so virtue in ambition is violent, in authority settled and calm.
Francis Bacon *Essays,* 'Of Great Place'

3 A good name is better than precious ointment; and the day of death than the day of one's birth.
It is better to go to the house of mourning, than to go to the house of feasting: for that is the end of all men; and the living will lay it to his heart.
Bible: Ecclesiastes 7:1–2

4 Enter ye in at the strait gate: for wide is the gate, and broad is the way, that leadeth to destruction, and many there be which go in thereat:
Because strait is the gate, and narrow is the way, which leadeth unto life, and few there be that find it.
Bible: Matthew 7:13–14

5 Then shall the King say unto them on his right hand, Come, ye blessed of my Father, inherit the kingdom prepared for you from the foundation of the world:
For I was an hungred, and ye gave me meat: I was thirsty, and ye gave me drink: I was a stranger, and ye took me in:
Naked, and ye clothed me: I was sick, and ye visited me: I was in prison, and ye came unto me.
Bible: Matthew 25:34–36

6 Finally, brethren, whatsoever things are true, whatsoever things are honest, whatsoever things are just, whatsoever things are pure, whatsoever things are lovely, whatsoever things are of good report; if there be any virtue; and if there be any praise, think on these things.
Bible: Philippians 4:8

7 But the path of the just is as the shining light, that shineth more and more unto the perfect day.
Bible: Proverbs 4:18

8 Whenever there are tremendous virtues it's a sure sign something's wrong.
Bertolt Brecht (1898–1956) German dramatist. *Mother Courage*

9 Virtue consisted in avoiding scandal and venereal disease.
Robert Cecil (1913–) British writer. *Life in Edwardian England*

10 My virtue's still far too small, I don't trot it out and about yet.
Colette (1873–1954) French novelist. *Claudine at School*

11 To be able to practise five things everywhere under heaven constitutes perfect virtue . . . gravity, generosity of soul, sincerity, earnestness, and kindness.
Confucius (K'ung Fu-tzu; 551–479 BC) Chinese philosopher. *Analects*

12 Good, but not religious-good.
Thomas Hardy (1840–1928) British novelist. *Under the Greenwood Tree,* Ch. 2

13 The greatest offence against virtue is to speak ill of it.
William Hazlitt (1778–1830) British essayist. *On Cant and Hypocrisy*

14 Only a sweet and virtuous soul,
Like season'd timber, never gives;
But though the whole world turn to coal,
Then chiefly lives.
George Herbert (1593–1633) English poet. *Virtue*

15 Be good, sweet maid, and let who can be clever;
Do lovely things, not dream them, all day long;
And so make Life, and Death, and that For Ever,
One grand sweet song.
Charles Kingsley (1819–75) British writer. *A Farewell. To C. E. G.*

16 To be discontented with the divine discontent, and to be ashamed with the noble shame, is the very germ and first upgrowth of all virtue.
Charles Kingsley *Health and Education*

17 Most men admire
Virtue, who follow not her lore.
John Milton (1608–74) English poet. *Paradise Regained,* Bk. I

18 When men grow virtuous in their old age, they only make a sacrifice to God of the devil's leavings.
Alexander Pope (1688–1744) British poet. *Thoughts on Various Subjects*

VIRTUE AND VICE

See also good and evil, vice, virtue

1 Good girls go to heaven, bad girls go everywhere.
Helen Gurley Brown (1922–) US journalist. *Cosmopolitan* magazine

2 It is the function of vice to keep virtue within reasonable bounds.
Samuel Butler (1835–1902) British writer. *Notebooks*

3 Our virtues and vices couple with one another, and get children that resemble both their parents.
Lord Halifax (1633–95) English statesman. *Political, Moral and Miscellaneous Thoughts and Reflections*

4 Most usually our virtues are only vices in disguise.
Duc de la Rochefoucauld (1613–80) French writer. *Maximes,* added to the 4th edition

5 Vice and virtues are products like sulphuric acid and sugar.
Hippolyte Adolphe Taine (1828–93) French writer and philosopher. *Histoire de la littérature anglaise,* Introduction

VIVISECTION

1 I would rather that any white rabbit on earth should have the Asiatic cholera twice than that I should have it just once.
Irvin S. Cobb (1876–1944)

2 Vivisection . . . is justifiable for real investigations on physiology; but not for mere damnable and detestable curiosity.
Charles Darwin (1809–22) British life scientist. Letter, 22 Mar 1871

3 There are a few honest antivivisectionists . . . I have not met any of them, but I am quite prepared to believe that they exist.
J. B. S. Haldane (1892–1964) British geneticist. *Possible Worlds,* 'Some Enemies of Science'

4 I know not, that by living dissections any discovery has been made by which a single malady is more easily cured.
Samuel Johnson (1709–84) English lexicographer and writer. *The Idler,* No. 17, 5 Aug 1758

5 Like following life through creatures you dissect,
You lose it in the moment you detect.
Alexander Pope (1688–1744) English poet. *Moral Essays,* I

VOLTAIRE

(François-Marie Arouet; 1694–1778) French writer and philosopher. A fearless campaigner against injustice, he was imprisoned in the Bastille, exiled to England, Germany, and Switzerland, and later became a hero of French culture. His works include *Lettres philosophiques* (1734), the fable *Candide* (1759), and the *Dictionnaire philosophique* (1764).

Quotations about Voltaire

1 When he talked our language he was animated with the soul of a Briton. He had bold flights. He had humour. He had an extravagance.
James Boswell (1740–95) Scottish lawyer and writer. *Boswell on the Grand Tour* (ed. by F. A. Pottle)

2 I was born much too soon, but I do not regret it; I have seen Voltaire.
Frederick the Great (1712–86) King of Prussia. Attrib.

Quotations by Voltaire

3 If we do not find anything pleasant, at least we shall find something new.
Candide, Ch. 17

4 *Dans ce pay-ci, il est bon de tuer de temps en temps un amiral pour encourager les autres.*
In this country it is good to kill an admiral from time to time, to encourage the others.
Referring to England: Admiral Byng was executed for failing to defeat the French at Minorca (1757). *Candide*, Ch. 23

5 All is for the best in the best of possible worlds.
Candide, Ch. 30

6 'That is well said,' replied Candide, 'but we must cultivate our garden.'
Candide, Ch. 30

7 Work banishes those three great evils, boredom, vice, and poverty.
Candide, Ch. 30

8 . . . use thought only to justify their injustices, and speech only to conceal their thoughts.
Referring to men. *Dialogue*, 'Le Chapon et la poularde'

9 The best is the enemy of the good.
Dictionnaire philosophique, 'Art dramatique'

10 Superstition sets the whole world in flames; philosophy quenches them.
Dictionnaire philosophique, 'Superstition'

11 If God did not exist, it would be necessary to invent Him.
Épîtres, 'À' l'auteur du livre des trois Imposteurs'

12 The secret of the arts is to correct nature.
Épîtres, 'À M. de Verrière'

13 This agglomeration which was called and which still calls itself the Holy Roman Empire was neither holy, nor Roman, nor an empire.
Essai sur les moeurs et l'esprit des nations, LXX

14 All our ancient history, as one of our wits remarked, is no more than accepted fiction.
Jeannot et Colin

15 All styles are good except the tiresome sort.
L'Enfant prodigue, Preface

16 If God made us in His image, we have certainly returned the compliment.
Le Sottisier

17 Indeed, history is nothing more than a tableau of crimes and misfortunes.
L'Ingénu, Ch. 10

18 It is one of the superstitions of the human mind to have imagined that virginity could be a virtue.
Notebooks

19 Governments need to have both shepherds and butchers.
Notebooks

20 God is on the side not of the heavy battalions, but of the best shots.
Notebooks

21 We owe respect to the living; to the dead we owe only truth.
Oeuvres, 'Première lettre sur Oedipe'

22 Faith consists in believing when it is beyond the power of reason to believe. It is not enough that a thing be possible for it to be believed.
Questions sur l'encyclopédie

23 Marriage is the only adventure open to the cowardly.
Thoughts of a Philosopher

24 Never having been able to succeed in the world, he took his revenge by speaking ill of it.
Zadig, Ch. 4

25 There are two things for which animals are to be envied: they know nothing of future evils, or of what people say about them.
Letter, 1739

26 Men will always be mad and those who think they can cure them are the maddest of all.
Letter, 1762

27 The great consolation in life is to say what one thinks.
Letter, 1765

28 Once the people begin to reason, all is lost.
Letter to Damilaville, 1 Apr 1766

29 I am not like a lady at the court of Versailles, who said: 'What a dreadful pity that the bother at the tower of Babel should have got language all mixed up, but for that, everyone would always have spoken French.
French was the dominant language in the educated circles of 18th-century Europe. Letter to Catherine the Great, Empress of Russia, 26 May 1767

30 The man who leaves money to charity in his will is only giving away what no longer belongs to him.
Letter, 1769

31 Men of England! You wish to kill me because I am a Frenchman. Am I not punished enough in not being born an Englishman?
Addressing an angry London mob who desired to hang him because he was a Frenchman. Attrib.

32 I think it must be so, for I have been drinking it for sixty-five years and I am not dead yet.
On learning that coffee was considered a slow poison. Attrib.

33 He was a great patriot, a humanitarian, a loyal friend – provided, of course, that he really is dead.
Giving a funeral oration. Attrib.

34 I do not think this poem will reach its destination.
Reviewing Rousseau's poem 'Ode to Posterity'. Attrib.

35 Once: a philosopher; twice: a pervert!
Turning down an invitation to an orgy, having attended one the previous night for the first time. Attrib.

36 I disapprove of what you say, but I will defend to the death your right to say it.
Attrib.

VULGARITY

See also humor

1 You gotta have a swine to show you where the truffles are.
Edward Albee (1928–) US dramatist. *Who's Afraid of Virginia Woolf?*, I

2 The aristocratic pleasure of displeasing is not the only delight that bad taste can yield. One can love a certain kind of vulgarity for its own sake.
Aldous Huxley (1894–1964) British novelist. *Vulgarity in Literature*, Ch. 4

3 That fellow would vulgarize the day of judgment.
Douglas William Jerrold (1803–57) British dramatist. *Wit and Opinions of Douglas Jerrold*, 'A Comic Author'

4 It is disgusting to pick your teeth. What is vulgar is to use a gold toothpick.
Louis Kronenberger (1904–80) US writer and literary critic. *The Cat and the Horse*

5 With our James vulgarity begins at home, and should be allowed to stay there.
Oscar Wilde (1854–1900) Irish-born British dramatist. Referring to the artist James Whistler. Letter to the *World*

6 I can't stand a naked light bulb, any more than I can a rude remark or a vulgar action.
Tennessee Williams (1911–83) US dramatist. *A Streetcar Named Desire*, II:3

W

WALES

See also Britain, Welsh

1 The thing I value about Wales and Welsh background is that it has always been a genuinely more classless society than many people present England as being.
Geoffrey Howe (1926–) British politician. *The Observer*, 'Sayings of the Week', 9 Nov 1986

2 The land of my fathers. My fathers can have it.
Dylan Thomas (1914–53) Welsh poet. Referring to Wales. *Dylan Thomas* (John Ackerman)

3 Too many of the artists of Wales spend too much time about the position of the artist of Wales. There is only one position for an artist anywhere: and that is, upright.
Dylan Thomas *New Statesman*, 18 Dec 1964

4 Make me content
With some sweetness
From Wales
Whose nightingales
Have no wings.
Edward Thomas (1878–1917) British poet. *Words*

5 We can trace almost all the disasters of English history to the influence of Wales.
Evelyn Waugh (1903–66) British novelist. *Decline and Fall*, Pt. I, Ch. 8

WALKING

1 He walks as if balancing the family tree on his nose.
Raymond Morley (1908–) British actor.

WANT

1 The great question . . . which I have not been able to answer, despite my thirty years of research into the feminine soul, is 'What does a woman want?'
Sigmund Freud (1856–1939) Austrian psychoanalyst. *Psychiatry in American Life* (Charles Rolo)

2 So have I loitered my life away, reading books, looking at pictures, going to plays, hearing, thinking, writing on what pleased me best. I have wanted only one thing to make me happy, but wanting that have wanted everything.
William Hazlitt (1778–1830) British essayist. *English Literature*, Ch. XVII, 'My First Acquaintance with Poets'

3 Economy is going without something you do want in case you should, some day, want something you probably won't want.
Anthony Hope (Sir Anthony Hope Hawkins; 1863–1933) British novelist. *The Dolly Dialogues*

4 We look forward to a world founded upon four essential human freedoms. The first is freedom of speech and expression – everywhere in the world. The second is freedom of every person to worship God in his own way – everywhere in the world. The third is freedom from want . . . everywhere in the world. The fourth is freedom from fear . . . anywhere in the world.
Franklin D. Roosevelt (1882–1945) US Democratic president. Speech to Congress, 6 Jan 1941

5 As if a woman of education bought things because she wanted 'em.
John Vanbrugh (1664–1726) English architect and dramatist. *The Confederacy*, II:1

WAR

See also army, Cold War, defeat, navy, nuclear weapons, officers, patriotism, soldiers, victory, war and peace, weapons, World War II

1 We have suffered the inevitable consequences of a combination of unpreparedness and feeble counsel.
Julian Amery (1919–) British Conservative politician. Referring to Argentina's seizure of the Falkland Islands. Speech, House of Commons, 3 Apr 1982

2 *Flavit deus et dissipati sunt.*
God blew and they were scattered.
Anonymous Inscription on the medallion minted to commemorate the defeat of the Spanish Armada.

3 They did not, in all their sailing round about England, so much as sink or take one ship, bark, pinnace, or cockboat of ours, or even burn so much as one sheepcote in this land.
Anonymous Referring to the Spanish Armada. *The Reign of Elizabeth* (J. D. Black), Ch. 10

4 Oh! the grand old Duke of York
He had ten thousand men;
He marched them up to the top of the hill,
And he marched them down again.
And when they were up they were up,
And when they were down they were down,
And when they were only half way up,
They were neither up nor down.
Anonymous Referring to Frederick Augustus, son of George III and Duke of York, who commanded two unsuccessful campaigns against the French (1793 and 1799). Traditional

5 Your country needs YOU.
Anonymous British recruiting poster featuring Lord Kitchener

6 Oh, my dear fellow, the noise . . . and the people!
Anonymous A soldier describing battle conditions.

7 Here on 11 November 1918 succumbed the criminal pride of the German Reich, vanquished by the

free peoples which it tried to enslave.
Anonymous In the forest of Compiègne, France, where the Armistice was signed at the end of World War I.

8 It became necessary to destroy the town of Ben Tre to save it.
Anonymous Said by a US Major in Vietnam. *The Observer*, 'Sayings of the Week', 11 Feb 1968

9 Hell no, we won't go!
Anonymous US anti-war chant during the time of the Vietnam war

10 Give them the cold steel, boys!
Lewis Addison Arminstead (1817–63) US general. Exhortation given to his troops during the US Civil War. Attrib.

11 And we are here as on a darkling plain
Swept with confused alarms of struggle and flight,
Where ignorant armies clash by night.
Matthew Arnold (1822–88) British poet and critic. *Dover Beach*

12 We shall never sheathe the sword which we have not lightly drawn until Belgium receives in full measure all and more than all that she has sacrificed, until France is adequately secured against the menace of aggression, until the rights of the smaller nationalities of Europe are placed upon an unassailable foundation, and until the military domination of Prussia is wholly and finally destroyed.
Herbert Henry Asquith (1852–1928) British statesman. Speech, Guildhall, 9 Nov 1914

13 To save your world you asked this man to die:
Would this man, could he see you now, ask why?
W. H. Auden (1907–73) British poet. *Epitaph for an Unknown Soldier*

14 Well, if you knows of a better 'ole, go to it.
Bruce Bairnsfather (1888–1959) British cartoonist. *Fragments from France*

15 I think it is well also for the man in the street to realise that there is no power on earth that can protect him from being bombed. Whatever people may tell him, the bomber will always get through, and it is very easy to understand that, if you realise the area of space.
Stanley Baldwin (1867–1947) British statesman. Speech, House of Commons, 10 Nov 1932

16 The only defence is in offence, which means that you have to kill more women and children more quickly than the enemy if you want to save yourselves.
Stanley Baldwin Speech, Nov 1932

17 From the point of view of sexual morality the aeroplane is valuable in war in that it destroys men and women in equal numbers.
Ernest William Barnes (1874–1953) British clergyman and mathematician. *Rise of Christianity*

18 It takes twenty years or more of peace to make a man, it takes only twenty seconds of war to destroy him.
King Baudouin of Belgium (1930–) Addressing US Congress, 12 May 1959

19 I have never understood this liking for war. It panders to instincts already catered for within the scope of any respectable domestic establishment.
Alan Bennett (1934–) British playwright. *Forty Years On*, I

20 And ye shall hear of wars and rumours of wars: see that ye be not troubled: for all these things must come to pass, but the end is not yet.
For nation shall rise against nation, and kingdom against kingdom: and there shall be famines, and pestilences, and earthquakes, in divers places.
All these are the beginning of sorrows.
Bible: Matthew 24:6–8

21 Then said Jesus unto him, Put up again thy sword into his place: for all they that take the sword shall perish with the sword.
Bible: Matthew Often misquoted as 'They that live by the sword shall die by the sword'. 26:52

22 If there is ever another war in Europe, it will come out of some damned silly thing in the Balkans.
Otto von Bismarck (1815–98) German statesman. Remark to Ballen, shortly before Bismarck's death

23 The Falklands thing was a fight between two bald men over a comb.
Jorge Luis Borges (1899–1986) Argentinian novelist. Referring to the war with the UK over the Falklands (1982). *Time*, 14 Feb 1983

24 *C'est magnifique, mais ce n'est pas la guerre.*
It is magnificent, but it is not war.
Pierre Bosquet (1810–61) French marshal. Referring to the Charge of the Light Brigade at the Battle of Balaclava, 25 Oct 1854. Attrib.

25 The wrong war, at the wrong place, at the wrong time, and with the wrong enemy.
Omar Nelson Bradley (1893–1981) US general. Said in evidence to a Senate inquiry, May 1951, over a proposal by MacArthur that the Korean War should be extended into China

26 What they could do with round here is a good war.
Bertolt Brecht (1898–1956) German dramatist. *Mother Courage*, I

27 A war of which we could say it left nothing to be desired will probably never exist.
Bertolt Brecht *Mother Courage*, VI

28 War is like love, it always finds a way.
Bertolt Brecht *Mother Courage*, VI

29 The Angel of Death has been abroad throughout the land: you may almost hear the beating of his wings.
John Bright (1811–89) British radical politician. Referring to the Crimean War. Speech, House of Commons, 23 Feb 1855

30 If I should die, think only this of me:
That there's some corner of a foreign field
That is forever England.
Rupert Brooke (1887–1915) British poet. *The Soldier*

31 Now, God be thanked who has matched us with His hour,
And caught our youth, and wakened us from sleeping.
Rupert Brooke *Peace*

32 War knows no power. Safe shall be my going,
Secretly armed against all death's endeavour;
Safe though all safety's lost; safe where men fall;
And if these poor limbs die, safest of all.
Rupert Brooke *Safety*

33 Scots, wha hae wi' Wallace bled,
Scots, wham Bruce has aften led,
Welcome to your gory bed,
Or to victorie.
Robert Burns (1759–96) Scottish poet. *Scots, Wha Hae*

34 When civil fury first grew high,

And men fell out they knew not why.
Samuel Butler (1612–80) English satirist. *Hudibras*, Pt. I

35 War, war is still the cry, 'War even to the knife!'
Lord Byron (1788–1824) British poet. *Childe Harold's Pilgrimage*, I

36 When was a war not a war? When it was carried on by methods of barbarism.
Henry Campbell-Bannerman (1836–1908) British statesman. Referring to the Boer War. Speech, National Reform Union Dinner, 14 June 1901

37 Tweedledum and Tweedledee
Agreed to have a battle;
For Tweedledum said Tweedledee
Had spoiled his nice new rattle.
Lewis Carroll (Charles Lutwidge Dodgson; 1832–98) British writer. *Through the Looking-Glass*, Ch. 4

38 I wanted the experience of war. I thought there would be no more wars.
Joyce Cary (1888–1957) British novelist. Reason for going to the Balkan War in 1912.

39 Carthage must be destroyed.
Cato the Elder (Marcius Porcius C; 234–149 BC) Roman statesman. *Life of Cato* (Plutarch)

40 In war, whichever side may call itself the victor, there are no winners, but all are losers.
Neville Chamberlain (1869–1940) British statesman. Speech, Kettering, 3 July 1938

41 Wars, conflict, it's all business. One murder makes a villain. Millions a hero. Numbers sanctify.
Charlie Chaplin (Sir Charles Spencer C.; 1889–1977) British film actor. *Monsieur Verdoux*

42 The redress of the grievances of the vanquished should precede the disarmament of the victors.
Winston Churchill (1874–1965) British statesman. *The Gathering Storm*, Ch. 3

43 I said that the world must be made safe for at least fifty years. If it was only for fifteen to twenty years then we should have betrayed our soldiers.
Winston Churchill *Closing the Ring*, Ch. 20

44 No one can guarantee success in war, but only deserve it.
Winston Churchill *Their Finest Hour*

45 War is the continuation of politics by other means.
Karl von Clausewitz (1780–1831) Prussian general. The usual misquotation of 'War is nothing but a continuation of politics with the admixture of other means'. *Vom Kriege*

46 My home policy? I wage war. My foreign policy? I wage war. Always, everywhere, I wage war . . . And I shall continue to wage war until the last quarter of an hour.
Georges Clemenceau (1841–1929) French statesman. Speech, Chamber of Deputies, 8 Mar 1918

47 Now, gentlemen, let us do something today which the world may talk of hereafter.
Lord Collingwood (1750–1810) British admiral. Said before Trafalgar, 21 Oct 1805. *Correspondence and Memoir of Lord Collingwood* (G. L. Newnham; ed. Collingwood)

48 Our troops are all moving from this place at present. Lord Wellington was at the ball tonight as composed as ever.
Thomas Creevey (1768–1838) British politician and diarist. Written at Brussels. *Journal*, 16 June 1815

49 *C'est une drôle de guerre.*
It is a phoney war.
Edouard Daladier (1884–1970) French prime minister. Speech, Chamber of Deputies, 22 Dec 1939

50 Come on, you sons of bitches! Do you want to live for ever?
Dan Daly (20th century) Sergeant in the US Marines. Remark during Allied resistance at Belleau Wood, June 1918. *See also* FREDERICK THE GREAT. Attrib.

51 If we lose this war, I'll start another in my wife's name.
Moshe Dayan (1915–81) Israeli general. Attrib.

52 There is plenty of time to win this game, and to thrash the Spaniards too.
Francis Drake (1540–96) English navigator. Referring to the sighting of the Armada during a game of bowls, 20 July 1588. Attrib.

53 I have singed the Spanish king's beard.
Francis Drake Referring to the raid on Cadiz harbor, 1587. Attrib.

54 The advantage of time and place in all practical actions is half a victory; which being lost is irrecoverable.
Francis Drake Letter to Elizabeth I, 1588

55 We are not at war with Egypt. We are in an armed conflict.
Anthony Eden (1897–1977) British statesman. Speech, House of Commons, 4 Nov 1956

56 There is nothing that war has ever achieved that we could not better achieve without it.
Havelock Ellis (1859–1939) British sexologist. *The Philosophy of Conflict*

57 My centre is giving way, my right is in retreat; situation excellent. I shall attack.
Marshal Foch (1851–1929) French soldier. Message sent during the second battle of the Marne, 1918. *Biography of Foch* (Aston), Ch. 13

58 Praise the Lord and pass the ammunition!
Howell Maurice Forgy (1908–) US naval lieutenant. Remark made during the Japanese attack on Pearl Harbor, 7 Dec 1941. Attrib. in *The Los Angeles Times*

59 I got there fustest with the mostest.
Nathan Bedford Forrest (1821–77) Confederate general. Popular misquotation of his explanation of his success in capturing Murfreesboro; his actual words were, 'I just took the short cut and got there first with the most men'. *A Civil War Treasury* (B. Botkin)

60 Rascals, would you live for ever?
Frederick the Great (1712–86) King of Prussia. Addressed to reluctant soldiers at the Battle of Kolin, 18 June 1757. *See also* DALY.

61 Madam, I am the civilization they are fighting to defend.
Heathcote William Garrod (1878–1960) British classical scholar. Replying to criticism that he was not fighting to defend civilization, during World War I. *Oxford Now and Then* (D. Balsdon)

62 France has lost a battle, but France has not lost the war!
Charles de Gaulle (1890–1970) French general and statesman. Proclamation, 18 June 1940

63 I have many times asked myself whether there can be more potent advocates of peace upon earth through the years to come than this massed multitude of silent witnesses to the desolation of war.
George V (1865–1936) King of the United Kingdom. Referring to the massed World War I graves in Flanders, 1922. *Silent Cities* (ed. Gavin Stamp)

64 He kept us out of war!
Martin H. Glynn (1891–1924) Governor of New York State. Referring to President Wilson. Speech, Democratic Convention, St Louis, 15 June 1916

65 The English do not treat very kindly the men who conduct their wars for them.
Joseph Goebbels (1897–1945) German politician. *Diaries*

66 You've got to forget about this civilian. Whenever you drop bombs, you're going to hit civilians.
Barry Goldwater (1904–) US politician. Speech, New York, 23 Jan 1967

67 We can now look forward with something like confidence to the time when war between civilized nations will be considered as antiquated as a duel.

George Peabody Gooch (1873–1968) English historian and Liberal MP. *History of Our Time*

68 No terms except unconditional and immediate surrender can be accepted. I propose to move immediately upon your works.

Ulysses Simpson Grant (1822–85) US general. Message to opposing commander, Simon Bolivar Buckner, during siege of Fort Donelson, 16 Feb 1862.

69 When the days of rejoicing are over,
When the flags are stowed safely away,
They will dream of another wild 'War to End Wars'
And another wild Armistice day.

But the boys who were killed in the trenches,
Who fought with no rage and no rant,
We left them stretched out on their pallets of mud
Low down with the worm and the ant.

Robert Graves (1895–1985) British poet and novelist. *Armistice Day, 1918*

70 Every position must be held to the last man: there must be no retirement. With our backs to the wall, and believing in the justice of our cause, each one of us must fight on to the end.

Earl Haig (1861–1928) British general. Order to the British Army, 12 Apr 1918

71 I'm not allowed to say how many planes joined the raid but I counted them all out and I counted them all back.

Brian Hanrahan (1949–) British journalist. Reporting a British air attack in the opening phase of the Falklands War. BBC broadcast, 1 May 1982

72 Gentlemen of the French Guard, fire first!

Lord Charles Hay (d. 1760) British soldier. Said at the Battle of Fontenoy, 1745. Attrib.

73 I'd like to see the government get out of war altogether and leave the whole feud to private industry.

Joseph Heller (1923–) US novelist. *Catch 22*

74 In starting and waging a war it is not right that matters, but victory.

Adolf Hitler (1889–1945) German dictator. *The Rise and Fall of the Third Reich* (W. L. Shirer), Ch. 16

75 War? War is an organized bore.

Oliver Wendell Holmes Jnr (1841–1935) US jurist. *Yankee from Olympus* (C. Bowen)

76 Older men declare war. But it is youth that must fight and die.

Herbert Clark Hoover (1874–1964) US statesman. Speech, Republican National Convention, Chicago, 27 June 1944

77 East and west on fields forgotten
Bleach the bones of comrades slain,
Lovely lads and dead and rotten;
None that go return again.

A. E. Housman (1859–1936) British scholar and poet. *A Shropshire Lad*, 'The Welsh Marches'

78 Elevate them guns a little lower.

Andrew Jackson (1767–1845) US statesman. Order given while watching the effect of the US artillery upon the British lines at the Battle of New Orleans. Attrib.

79 I had always to remember that I could have lost the war in an afternoon.

Lord Jellicoe (1859–1935) British admiral. Referring to the Battle of Jutland

80 We are about to engage in a battle on which the fate of our country depends and it is important to remind all ranks that the moment has passed for looking to the rear; all our efforts must be directed to attacking and driving back the enemy. Troops that can advance no farther must, at any price, hold on to the ground they have conquered and die on the spot rather than give way. Under the circumstances which face us, no act of weakness can be tolerated.

Joseph Jacques Césaire Joffre (1852–1931) French soldier. *The Memoirs of Marshall Joffre*

81 War should belong to the tragic past, to history: it should find no place on humanity's agenda for the future.

John Paul II (Karol Wojtyla; 1920–) Polish pope (1978–). Speech, 1982

82 The first casualty when war comes is truth.

Hiram Warren Johnson (1866–1945) US politician. Speech, U.S. Senate, 1917

83 Some men are killed in a war and some men are wounded, and some men never leave the country . . . Life is unfair.

John Fitzgerald Kennedy (1917–63) US statesman. *Robert Kennedy and His Times* (A. M. Schlesinger)

84 Formerly, a nation that broke the peace did not trouble to try and prove to the world that it was done solely from higher motives . . . *Now war has a bad conscience.* Now every nation assures us that it is bleeding for a human cause, the fate of which hangs in the balance of its victory. . . . No nation dares to admit the guilt of blood before the world.

Ellen Key (Karolina Sofia Key; 1849–1926) Swedish writer. *War, Peace, and the Future*, Preface

85 Everything, everything in war is barbaric . . . But the worst barbarity of war is that it forces men collectively to commit acts against which individually they would revolt with their whole being.

Ellen Key *War, Peace, and the Future*, Ch. 6

86 Our scientific power has outrun our spiritual power. We have guided missiles and misguided men.

Martin Luther King (1929–68) US Black civil-rights leader. *Strength to Love*

87 The conventional army loses if it does not win. The guerrilla wins if he does not lose.

Henry Kissinger (1923–) German-born US politician and diplomat. *Foreign Affairs*, XIII (Jan 1969), 'The Vietnam Negotiations'

88 The most persistent sound which reverberates through men's history is the beating of war drums.

Arthur Koestler (1905–83) Hungarian-born British writer. *Janus: A Summing Up*, Prologue

89 Napoleon is a torrent which as yet we are unable to stem. Moscow will be the sponge that will suck him dry.

Mikhail Kutuzov (1745–1813) Russian marshal. Address to the commanders of the Russian army, 13 Sept 1812

90 If, therefore, war should ever come between these two countries, which Heaven forbid! it will not, I think, be due to irresistible natural laws, it will be due to the want of human wisdom.

Bonar Law (1858–1923) British statesman. Referring to the UK and Germany. Speech, House of Commons, 27 Nov 1911

91 We have all lost the war. All Europe.

D. H. Lawrence (1885–1930) British novelist. *The Ladybird*, 'The Ladybird'

92 It is well that war is so terrible; else we would grow too fond of it.

Robert E. Lee (1807–70) US general. Speaking to another general during the battle of Fredericksburg. *The American Treasury* (C. Fadiman)

93 My solution to the problem would

be to tell them . . . they've got to draw in their horns or we're going to bomb them into the Stone Age.

Curtis E. LeMay (1906–) US general and air-force chief. On the North Vietnamese. *Mission with LeMay*

94 This war, like the next war, is a war to end war.

David Lloyd George (1863–1945) British Liberal statesman. Referring to the popular opinion that World War I would be the last major war.

95 In war there is no substitute for victory.

Douglas MacArthur (1880–1964) US general. Speech, US Congress, 19 Apr 1951

96 'War is the continuation of politics'. In this sense war is politics and war itself is a political action.

Mao Tse-Tung (1893–1976) Chinese communist leader. *See also* CLAUSEWITZ. *Quotations from Chairman Mao Tse-Tung*, Ch. 5

97 We are advocates of the abolition of war, we do not want war; but war can only be abolished through war, and in order to get rid of the gun it is necessary to take up the gun.

Mao Tse-Tung *Quotations from Chairman Mao Tse-Tung*, Ch. 5

98 Television brought the brutality of war into the comfort of the living room. Vietnam was lost in the living rooms of America – not on the battlefields of Vietnam.

Marshall McLuhan (1911–81) Canadian sociologist. Montreal *Gazette*, 16 May 1975

99 War will never cease until babies begin to come into the world with larger cerebrums and smaller adrenal glands.

H. L. Mencken (1880–1956) US journalist. *Notebooks*, 'Minority Report'

100 War is the national industry of Prussia.

Comte de Mirabeau (1749–91) French statesman. Attrib.

101 Fighting is like champagne. It goes to the heads of cowards as quickly as of heroes. Any fool can be brave on a battle field when it's be brave or else be killed.

Margaret Mitchell (1909–49) US novelist. *Gone with the Wind*

102 *La quinta columna.*
The Fifth Column.

Emilio Mola (1887–1937) Spanish Nationalist General. Reply when asked (Oct 1937) which of four Nationalist armies would capture Madrid; Mola was referring to Nationalist elements within the city.

103 War hath no fury like a non-combatant.

C. E. Montague (1867–1928) British editor and writer. *Disenchantment*, Ch. 15

104 An empire founded by war has to maintain itself by war.

Baron de Montesquieu (1688–1755) French writer. *Considérations sur les causes de la grandeur et de la décadence des romains*, Ch. 8

105 The U.S. has broken the second rule of war. That is, don't go fighting with your land army on the mainland of Asia. Rule One is don't march on Moscow. I developed these two rules myself.

Lord Montgomery (1887–1976) British field marshal. Referring to the Vietnam War. *Montgomery of Alamein* (Chalfont)

106 The Minstrel Boy to the war has gone,
In the ranks of death you'll find him;
His father's sword he has girded on,
And his wild harp slung behind him.

Thomas Moore (1779–1852) Irish poet. *Irish Melodies*, 'The Minstrel Boy'

107 War alone brings up to their highest tension all human energies and imposes the stamp of nobility upon the peoples who have the courage to make it.

Benito Mussolini (1883–1945) Italian dictator. *Encyclopedia Italiane*

108 It's the most beautiful battlefield I've ever seen.

Napoleon I (Napoleon Bonaparte; 1769–1821) French emperor. Referring to carnage on the field of Borodino, near Moscow, after the battle (7 Sept 1812). Attrib.

109 There rises the sun of Austerlitz.

Napoleon I Said at the Battle of Borodino (7 Sept 1812), near Moscow; the Battle of Austerlitz (2 Dec 1805) was Napoleon's great victory over the Russians and Austrians.

110 I don't care for war, there's far too much luck in it for my liking.

Napoleon III (1808–73) French emperor. Said after the narrow but bloody French victory at Solferino (24 June 1859). *The Fall of the House of Habsburg* (E. Crankshaw)

111 In case signals can neither be seen nor perfectly understood, no captain can do very wrong if he places his ship alongside that of an enemy.

Lord Nelson (1758–1805) British admiral. Memorandum before Trafalgar, 9 Oct 1805

112 The sand of the desert is sodden red, –
Red with the wreck of a square that broke; –
The gatling's jammed and the colonel dead,
And the regiment blind with the dust and smoke.
The river of death has brimmed its banks
And England's far and honour a name.
But the voice of a schoolboy rallies the ranks:
'Play up! play up! and play the game!'

Henry John Newbolt (1862–1938) British poet. *Vitai Lampada*

113 Drake he's in his hammock till the great Armadas come.
(Capten, art tha sleepin' there below?)
Slung atween the round shot, listenin' for the drum,
An dreamin' arl the time o' Plymouth Hoe.

Henry John Newbolt *Drake's Drum*

114 War is war. The only good human being is a dead one.

George Orwell (Eric Blair; 1903–50) British novelist. *Animal Farm*, Ch. 4

115 Probably the Battle of Waterloo *was* won on the playing-fields of Eton, but the opening battles of all subsequent wars have been lost there.

George Orwell *The Lion and the Unicorn*, 'England, Your England'

116 The quickest way of ending a war is to lose it.

George Orwell *Second Thoughts on James Burnham*

117 The pallor of girls' brows shall be their pall;
Their flowers the tenderness of patient minds,
And each slow dusk a drawing-down of blinds.

Wilfred Owen (1893–1918) British poet. *Anthem for Doomed Youth*

118 Red lips are not so red
As the stained stones kissed by the English dead.

Wilfred Owen *Greater Love*

119 I could not give my name to aid the slaughter in this war, fought on both sides for grossly material ends, which did not justify the sacrifice of a single mother's son. Clearly I must continue to oppose it, and expose it, to all whom I could reach with voice or pen.

Sylvia Pankhurst (1882–1960) British suffragette. *The Home Front,* Ch. 25

120 Stand your ground. Don't fire unless fired upon, but if they mean to have a war, let it begin here!

John Parker (1729–75) US general. Command given at the start of the Battle of Lexington. *Familiar Quotations* (J. Bartlett)

121 This is how war is begun: such is my advice. First destroy the land, deal after with the foe.

Philip, Count of Flanders Advice to William, King of Scotland. *Chronique de la guerre entre les Anglois et les Ecossois en 1173 et 1174* (Jordan Fantosme)

122 Don't cheer, boys; the poor devils are dying.

John Woodward Philip (1840–1900) US naval officer. Restraining his victorious crew during the naval battle off Santiago in the Spanish-American War. Attrib.

123 If sunbeams were weapons of war, we would have had solar energy long ago.

George Porter (1920–) British chemist. *The Observer,* 'Sayings of the Week', 26 Aug 1973

124 Don't fire until you see the whites of their eyes.

William Prescott (1726–95) US revolutionary soldier. Command given at the Battle of Bunker Hill

125 War is, after all, the universal perversion. We are all tainted: if we cannot experience our perversion at first hand we spend our time reading war stories, the pornography of war; or seeing war films, the blue films of war; or titillating our senses with the imagination of great deeds, the masturbation of war.

John Rae (1931–) British schoolmaster and writer. *The Custard Boys,* Ch. 6

126 In a civil war, a general must know – and I'm afraid it's a thing rather of instinct than of practice – he must know exactly when to move over to the other side.

Henry Reed (1914–) British poet and dramatist. *Not a Drum was Heard: The War Memoirs of General Gland*

127 And the various holds and rolls and throws and breakfalls
Somehow or other I always seemed to put
In the wrong place. And as for war, my wars
Were global from the start.

Henry Reed *A Map of Verona,* 'Lessons of the War', III

128 All Quiet on the Western Front.

Erich Maria Remarque (1898–1970) German novelist. Title of novel

129 All wars are planned by old men
In council rooms apart.

Grantland Rice (1880–1954) US sportswriter. *Two Sides of War*

130 (Fire – without hatred.)

Antonio Rivera (d. 1936) Spanish Nationalist hero. Giving the order to open fire at the siege of the Alcázar. *The Siege of the Alcázar* (C. Eby)

131 More than an end to war, we want an end to the beginnings of all wars.

Franklin D. Roosevelt (1882–1945) US Democratic president. Speech broadcast on the day after his death (13 Apr 1945)

132 I discovered to my amazement that average men and women were delighted at the prospect of war. I had fondly imagined what most pacifists contended, that wars were forced upon a reluctant population by despotic and Machiavellian governments.

Bertrand Russell (1872–1970) British philosopher. *The Autobiography of Bertrand Russell*

133 They dashed on towards that *thin red line tipped with steel.*

William Howard Russell (1820–1907) British journalist. Description of the Russian charge against the British at the Battle of Balaclava, 1854. *The British Expedition to the Crimea*

134 War is not an adventure. It is a disease. It is like typhus.

Antoine de Saint-Exupéry (1900–44) French novelist and aviator. *Flight to Arras*

135 Sometime they'll give a war and nobody will come.

Carl Sandburg (1878–1967) US author and poet. *The People, Yes*

136 Man, it seemed, had been created to jab the life out of Germans.

Siegfried Sassoon (1886–1967) British poet. *Memoirs of an Infantry Officer,* Pt. I, Ch 1

137 Safe with his wound, a citizen of life,
He hobbled blithely through the garden gate,
And thought: 'Thank God they had to amputate!'

Siegfried Sassoon *The One-Legged Man*

138 If I were fierce and bald and short of breath,
I'd live with scarlet Majors at the Base,
And speed glum heroes up the line to death.

Siegfried Sassoon *Base Details*

139 And when the war is done and youth stone dead
I'd toddle safely home and die – in bed.

Siegfried Sassoon *Base Details*

140 'Good morning; good morning!' the general said
When we met him last week on our way to the line.
Now the soldiers he smiled at are most of 'em dead,
And we're cursing his staff for incompetent swine.

Siegfried Sassoon *The General*

141 I am making this statement as a wilful defiance of military authority because I believe that the War is being deliberately prolonged by those who have the power to end it.

Siegfried Sassoon *Memoirs of an Infantry Officer,* Pt. X, Ch. 3

142 All wars are popular for the first thirty days.

Arthur Schlesinger Jnr (1917–) US historian, educator, and author. Attrib.

143 When you march into France, let the last man on the right brush the Channel with his sleeve.

Alfred Graf von Schlieffen (1833–1913) German general. Referring to the Schlieffen plan. *August 1914* (Barbara Tuchman), Ch. 2

144 Wars come because not enough people are sufficiently afraid.

Hugh Schonfield (1901–) British writer and editor. *The News Review,* 26 Feb 1948

145 The Cavaliers (wrong but Wromantic) and the Roundheads (Right but Repulsive).

W. C. Sellar (1898–1951) British humorous writer. *1066 And All That*

146 When we, the Workers, all demand: 'What are we fighting for?
...
Then, then we'll end that stupid crime, that devil's madness – War.

Robert William Service (1874–1958) Canadian poet. *Michael*

147 Cry 'Havoc!' and let slip the dogs of war.

William Shakespeare (1564–1616) English dramatist. *Julius Caesar*, III:1

148 Farewell the neighing steed and the shrill trump,
The spirit-stirring drum, th'ear piercing fife,
The royal banner, and all quality,
Pride, pomp, and circumstance, of glorious war!

William Shakespeare *Othello*, III:3

149 Nothing is ever done in this world until men are prepared to kill each other if it is not done.

George Bernard Shaw (1856–1950) Irish dramatist and critic. *Major Barbara*

150 The British soldier can stand up to anything except the British War Office.

George Bernard Shaw *The Devil's Disciple*, II

151 I am tired and sick of war. Its glory is all moonshine . . . War is hell.

General William Sherman (1820–91) US general. Attrib. in address, Michigan Military Academy, 19 June 1879

152 Who live under the shadow of a war,
What can I do that matters?

Stephen Spender (1909–) British poet. *Who Live under the Shadow*

153 To win in Vietnam, we will have to exterminate a nation.

Dr Benjamin Spock (1903–) US pediatrician and psychiatrist. *Dr Spock on Vietnam*, Ch.7

154 Yonder are the Hessians. They were bought for seven pounds and tenpence a man. Are you worth more? Prove it. Tonight the American flag floats from yonder hill or Molly Stark sleeps a widow!

John Stark (1728–1822) US general. Urging on his troops at the Battle of Bennington in 1777. *The American Treasury* (C. Fadiman)

155 That's what you are. That's what you all are. All of you young people who served in the war. You are a lost generation.

Gertrude Stein (1874–1946) US writer. *A Moveable Feast* (E. Hemingway)

156 War is capitalism with the gloves off.

Tom Stoppard (1937–) Czech-born British dramatist. *Travesties*

157 Most sorts of diversion in men, children, and other animals, are an imitation of fighting.

Jonathan Swift (1667–1745) Irish-born Anglican priest and writer. *Thoughts on Various Subjects*

158 The guerrilla fights the war of the flea, and his military enemy suffers the dog's disadvantages: too much to defend; too small, ubiquitous, and agile an enemy to come to grips with.

Robert Taber (20th century) US writer. *The War of the Flea*, Ch. 2

159 They make a wilderness and call it peace.

Tacitus (c. 55–c. 120 AD) Roman historian. *Agricola*, 30

160 Now all roads lead to France
And heavy is the tread
Of the living; but the dead
Returning lightly dance.

Edward Thomas (1878–1917) British poet. *Roads*

161 Dead battles, like dead generals, hold the military mind in their dead grip.

Barbara W. Tuchman (1912–) US editor and writer. *August 1914*, Ch. 2

162 They now *ring* the bells, but they will soon *wring* their hands.

Robert Walpole (1676–1745) British statesman. Said when war was declared in 1739 with Spain, against Walpole's wishes. *Memoirs of Sir Robert Walpole* (W. Coxe)

163 I heard the bullets whistle, and believe me, there is something charming in the sound.

George Washington (1732–99) US statesman. Referring to a recent skirmish in the French and Indian War. *Presidential Anecdotes* (P. Boller)

164 When the war broke out she took down the signed photograph of the Kaiser and, with some solemnity, hung it in the menservants' lavatory; it was her one combative action.

Evelyn Waugh (1903–66) British novelist. *Vile Bodies*, Ch. 3

165 Like German opera, too long and too loud.

Evelyn Waugh Giving his opinions of warfare after the Battle of Crete, 1941. Attrib.

166 It has been a damned serious business – Blücher and I have lost 30,000 men. It has been a damned nice thing – the nearest run thing you ever saw in your life . . . By God! I don't think it would have done if I had not been there.

Duke of Wellington (1769–1852) British general and statesman. Referring to the Battle of Waterloo. *Creevey Papers*, Ch. X

167 Yes, and they went down very well too.

Duke of Wellington Replying to the observation that the French cavalry had come up very well during the Battle of Waterloo. *The Age of Elegance* (A. Bryant)

168 A battle of giants.

Duke of Wellington Referring to the Battle of Waterloo; said to Samuel Rogers. Attrib.

169 Up, Guards, and at 'em.

Duke of Wellington Order given at the battle of Waterloo, 18 June 1815. Attrib.

170 The military don't start wars. The politicians start wars.

William Westmorland (1914–) US army officer. Attrib.

171 As long as war is regarded as wicked, it will always have its fascination. When it is looked upon as vulgar, it will cease to be popular.

Oscar Wilde (1854–1900) Irish-born British dramatist. *The Critic as Artist*, Pt. 2

172 You will be home before the leaves have fallen from the trees.

Wilhelm II (1859–1941) King of Prussia and Emperor of Germany. Said to troops leaving for the Front, Aug 1914. *August 1914* (Barbara Tuchman), Ch. 9

173 We draw the sword with a clear conscience and with clean hands.

Wilhelm II Speech, Berlin, 4 Aug 1914

174 It is my Royal and Imperial Command that you . . . exterminate first the treacherous English, and . . . walk over General French's contemptible little Army.

Wilhelm II Referring to the British Expeditionary Force; veterans of this force became known as 'Old Contemptibles'. *The Times*, 1 Oct 1914

175 There is such a thing as a man being too proud to fight.

Woodrow Wilson (1856–1925) US statesman. Address to foreign-born citizens, 10 May 1915

176 The war we have just been through, though it was shot through with terror, is not to be compared with the war we would have to face next time.

Woodrow Wilson *Mr Wilson's War* (John Dos Passos), Pt. V, Ch. 22

177 Once lead this people into war and

they'll forget there ever was such a thing as tolerance.
Woodrow Wilson *Mr Wilson's War* (John Dos Passos), Pt. III, Ch. 2

178 It takes only one gramme of explosive to kill a man, so why waste five tons?
Solly Zuckerman (1904–) South African-born British anatomist. *From Apes to War Lords*

WAR AND PEACE

See also peace, war

1 Since wars begin in the minds of men, it is in the minds of men that the defences of peace must be constructed.
Anonymous Constitution of UNESCO

2 And he shall judge among the nations, and shall rebuke many people: and they shall beat their swords into plowshares, and their spears into pruning-hooks: nation shall not lift up sword against nation, neither shall they learn war any more.
Bible: Isaiah 2:4

3 In war, resolution; in defeat, defiance; in victory, magnanimity; in peace, goodwill.
Winston Churchill (1874–1965) British statesman. Epigram used by Sir Edward Marsh after World War II; used as 'a moral of the work' in Churchill's book. *The Second World War*

4 Those who can win a war well can rarely make a good peace and those who could make a good peace would never have won the war.
Winston Churchill *My Early Life*, Ch. 26

5 It is far easier to make war than to make peace.
Georges Clemenceau (1841–1929) French statesman. *Speech*, 14 July 1919

6 We have won the war: now we have to win the peace, and it may be more difficult.
Georges Clemenceau *Clemenceau* (D. R. Watson)

7 My pacifism is not based on any intellectual theory but on a deep antipathy to every form of cruelty and hatred.
Albert Einstein (1879–1955) German-born US physicist. Said on the outbreak of World War I. Attrib.

8 There never was a good war or a bad peace.
Benjamin Franklin (1706–90) US scientist and statesman. Letter to Josiah Quincy, 11 Sept 1783

9 My argument is that War makes rattling good history; but Peace is poor reading.
Thomas Hardy (1840–1928) British novelist and poet. *The Dynasts*, II:5

10 He that makes a good war makes a good peace.
George Herbert (1593–1633) English poet. *Outlandish Proverbs*, 420

11 The statistics of suicide show that, for non-combatants at least, life is more interesting in war than in peace.
Dean Inge (1860–1954) British churchman. *The End of an Age*

12 Peace hath her victories
No less renowned than war.
John Milton (1608–74) English poet. *Sonnet*: 'To the Lord General Cromwell, May 1652'

13 Unquestionably there never was a time in the history of this country when, from the situation of Europe, we might more reasonably expect fifteen years of peace, than we may at this present moment.
William Pitt the Younger (1759–1806) British statesman. Revolutionary France declared war on Britain on 1 Feb 1793. Speech, House of Commons, 17 Feb 1792

14 Let me have war, say I; it exceeds peace as far as day does night; it's spritely, waking, audible, and full of vent. Peace is a very apoplexy, lethargy: mulled, deaf, sleepy, insensible; a getter of more bastard children than war's a destroyer of men.
William Shakespeare (1564–1616) English dramatist. *Coriolanus*, IV:5

15 Keep up your bright swords, for the dew will rust them.
William Shakespeare *Othello*, I:2

16 Peace is not only better than war, but infinitely more arduous.
George Bernard Shaw (1856–1950) Irish dramatist and critic. *Heartbreak House* (Preface)

17 Let him who desires peace, prepare for war.
Vegetius (Flavius Vegetius Renatus; 4th century AD) Roman writer. *Epitoma Rei Militaris*, 3, 'Prologue'

18 We sauntered through the crowd to Trafalgar Square where Labour, socialist, pacifist demonstrators — with a few trade union flags — were gesticulating from the steps of the monuments to a mixed crowd of admirers, hooligan warmongers and merely curious holidaymakers. It was an undignified and futile exhibition, this singing of the Red Flag and passing of well-worn radical resolutions in favour of universal peace.
Beatrice Webb (1858–1943) British economist and writer. Referring to an anti-war demonstration, 2 Aug 1914. *Diary*, 4 Aug 1914; war was declared on Germany at 11 p.m.

19 When you're at war you think about a better life; when you're at peace you think about a more comfortable one.
Thornton Wilder (1897–1975) US novelist and dramatist. *The Skin of Our Teeth*, III

20 The world must be safe for democracy. Its peace must be planted upon trusted foundations of political liberty.
Woodrow Wilson (1856–1924) US statesman. Speech to Congress, 2 Apr 1917

21 What we demand in this war is nothing peculiar to ourselves. It is that the world be made fit and safe to live in.
Woodrow Wilson Preamble to his 'Fourteen Points' for ensuring world peace. Speech to Congress, 8 Jan 1918

WASHINGTON, George

(1732–99) US statesman and first president of the USA (1789–97). Commander in chief of the American forces in the American Revolution, he presided over the Constitutional Convention (1787) and was elected president of the new republic.

Quotations about Washington

1 First in war, first in peace, first in the hearts of his countrymen.
Henry Lee Addressing the House of Representatives, Dec 1799

2 The crude commercialism of America, its materialising spirit are entirely due to the country having adopted for its natural hero a man who could not tell a lie.
Oscar Wilde (1854–1900) Irish-born British dramatist. *The Decay of Lying*

Quotations by Washington

3 Associate yourself with men of good quality if you esteem your own reputation; for 'tis better to be alone than in bad company.
Rules of Civility

4 I heard the bullets whistle, and

believe me, there is something charming in the sound.

Referring to a recent skirmish in the French and Indian War. *Presidential Anecdotes* (P. Boller)

5 Father, I cannot tell a lie. I did it with my little hatchet.

Attrib.

WASTE

See also extravagance

1 Waste not, want not.

Proverb

2 Full many a gem of purest ray serene,
The dark unfathom'd caves of ocean bear:
Full many a flower is born to blush unseen,
And waste its sweetness on the desert air.

Thomas Gray (1716–71) British poet. *Elegy Written in a Country Churchyard*

3 The world is too much with us; late and soon,
Getting and spending, we lay waste our powers:
Little we see in Nature that is ours.

William Wordsworth (1770–1850) British poet. *Sonnets*, 'The world is too much with us'

WATER

See also drinks

1 Well, the principle seems the same. The water still keeps falling over.

Winston Churchill (1874–1965) British statesman. When asked whether the Niagara Falls looked the same as when he first saw them. *Closing the Ring*, Ch. 5

2 Water, water, every where,
And all the boards did shrink;
Water, water, every where,
Nor any drop to drink.

Samuel Taylor Coleridge (1772–1834) British poet. *The Rime of the Ancient Mariner*, II

3 Fish fuck in it.

W. C. Fields (1880–1946) US actor. His reason for not drinking water. Attrib.

4 For any ceremonial purposes the otherwise excellent liquid, water, is unsuitable in colour and other respects.

A. P. Herbert (1890–1971) British writer and politician. *Uncommon Law*

5 If you believe Cratinus from days of old, Maecenas, (as you must know) no verse can give pleasure for long, nor last, that is written by drinkers of water.

Horace (Quintus Horatius Flaccus; 65–8 BC) Roman poet. *Epistles*, I

6 The biggest waste of water in the country by far. You spend half a pint and flush two gallons.

Prince Philip (1921–) The consort of Queen Elizabeth II. Speech, 1965

7 Human beings were invented by water as a device for transporting itself from one place to another.

Tom Robbins (1936–) US novelist. *Another Roadside Attraction*

8 He who drinks a tumbler of London water has literally in his stomach more animated beings than there are men, women and children on the face of the globe.

Sydney Smith (1771–1845) British clergyman and essayist. Letter

WAUGH, Evelyn

(1903–66) British novelist. He established his reputation with *Decline and Fall* (1928) and *Vile Bodies* (1930). Later books, after his conversion to Catholicism, include *Brideshead Revisited* (1945) and the war trilogy *Sword of Honour* (1952–61).

Quotations about Waugh

1 I expect you know my friend Evelyn Waugh, who, like you, your Holiness, is a Roman Catholic.

Randolph Churchill (1911–68) British political journalist. Remark made during an audience with the Pope

2 Mr. Waugh, I always feel, is an antique in search of a period, a snob in search of a class, perhaps even a mystic in search of a beatific vision.

Malcolm Muggeridge (1903–) British writer. *The Most of Malcolm Muggeridge*

Quotations by Waugh

3 I expect you'll be becoming a schoolmaster sir. That's what most of the gentlemen does sir, that gets sent down for indecent behaviour.

Decline and Fall, Prelude

4 The sound of the English county families baying for broken glass.

Decline and Fall, Prelude

5 We class schools you see, into four grades: Leading School, First-rate School, Good School, and School.

Decline and Fall, Pt. I, Ch. 1

6 We schoolmasters must temper discretion with deceit.

Decline and Fall, Pt. I, Ch. 1

7 Very hard for a man with a wig to keep order.

Decline and Fall, Pt. I, Ch. 3

8 That's the public-school system all over. They may kick you out, but they never let you down.

Decline and Fall, Pt. I, Ch. 3

9 Meanwhile you will write an essay on 'self-indulgence'. There will be a prize of half a crown for the longest essay, irrespective of any possible merit.

Decline and Fall, Pt. I, Ch. 5

10 I can't quite explain it, but I don't believe one can ever be unhappy for long provided one does just exactly what one wants to and when one wants to.

Decline and Fall, Pt. I, Ch. 5

11 Nonconformity and lust stalking hand in hand through the country, wasting and ravaging.

Decline and Fall, Pt. I, Ch. 5

12 For generations the British bourgeoisie have spoken of themselves as gentlemen, and by that they have meant, among other things, a self-respecting scorn of irregular perquisites. It is the quality that distinguishes the gentleman from both the artist and the aristocrat.

Decline and Fall, Pt. I, Ch. 6

13 There aren't many left like him nowadays, what with education and whisky the price it is.

Decline and Fall, Pt. I, Ch. 7

14 'The Welsh,' said the Doctor, 'are the only nation in the world that has produced no graphic or plastic art, no architecture, no drama. They just sing,' he said with disgust, 'sing and blow down wind instruments of plated silver.'

Decline and Fall, Pt. I, Ch. 8

15 We can trace almost all the disasters of English history to the influence of Wales.

Decline and Fall, Pt. I, Ch. 8

16 I have noticed again and again since I have been in the Church that lay interest in ecclesiastical matters is often a prelude to insanity.

Decline and Fall, Pt. I, Ch. 8

17 I have often observed in women of

her type a tendency to regard all athletics as inferior forms of fox-hunting.
Decline and Fall, Pt. I, Ch. 10

18 I haven't been to sleep for over a year. That's why I go to bed early. One needs more rest if one doesn't sleep.
Decline and Fall, Pt. II, Ch. 3

19 There is a species of person called a 'Modern Churchman' who draws the full salary of a beneficed clergyman and need not commit himself to any religious belief.
Decline and Fall, Pt. II, Ch. 4

20 I came to the conclusion many years ago that almost all crime is due to the repressed desire for aesthetic expression.
Decline and Fall, Pt. III, Ch. 1

21 He stood twice for Parliament, but so diffidently that his candidature passed almost unnoticed.
Decline and Fall, Pt. III, Ch. 1

22 Anyone who has been to an English public school will always feel comparatively at home in prison.
Decline and Fall, Pt. III, Ch. 4

23 He was greatly pained at how little he was pained by the events of the afternoon.
Decline and Fall, Pt. III, Ch. 4

24 Instead of this absurd division into sexes they ought to class people as static and dynamic.
Decline and Fall, Pt. III, Ch. 7

25 We are all American at puberty; we die French.
Diaries, 'Irregular Notes', 18 Jul 1961

26 Punctuality is the virtue of the bored.
Diaries, 'Irregular Notes', 26 Mar 1962

27 Assistant masters came and went .... Some liked little boys too little and some too much.
A Little Learning

28 You never find an Englishman among the underdogs – except in England of course.
The Loved One

29 In the dying world I come from quotation is a national vice. It used to be the classics, now it's lyric verse.
The Loved One

30 Enclosing every thin man, there's a fat man demanding elbow-room.
Similar sentiments have been expressed by others. *Officers and Gentlemen*, Interlude

31 Feather-footed through the plashy fen passes the questing vole.
Scoop, Bk. I, Ch. 1

32 '*The Beast* stands for strong mutually antagonistic governments everywhere', he said. Self-sufficiency at home, self-assertion abroad.
Scoop, Bk. I, Ch. 1

33 Yes, cider and tinned salmon are the staple diet of the agricultural classes.
Scoop, Bk. I, Ch. 1

34 Pappenhacker says that every time you are polite to a proletarian you are helping to bolster up the capitalist system.
Scoop, Bk. I, Ch. 5

35 'I will not stand for being called a woman in my own house,' she said.
Scoop, Bk. I, Ch. 5

36 News is what a chap who doesn't care much about anything wants to read. And it's only news until he's read it. After that it's dead.
Scoop, Bk. I, Ch. 5

37 As there was no form of government common to the peoples thus segregated, nor tie of language, history, habit, or belief, they were called a Republic.
Scoop, Bk. II, Ch. 1

38 The better sort of Ishmaelites have been Christian for many centuries and will not publicly eat human flesh uncooked in Lent, without special and costly dispensation from their bishop.
Scoop, Bk. II, Ch. 1

39 Other nations use 'force'; we Britons alone use 'Might'.
Scoop, Bk. II, Ch. 5

40 Up to a point, Lord Copper.
A euphemism for 'No'. *Scoop*, passim

41 Particularly against books the Home Secretary is. If we can't stamp out literature in the country, we can at least stop it being brought in from outside.
Vile Bodies, Ch. 2

42 When the war broke out she took down the signed photograph of the Kaiser and, with some solemnity, hung it in the menservants' lavatory; it was her one combative action.
Vile Bodies, Ch. 3

43 She had heard someone say something about an Independent Labour Party, and was furious that she had not been asked.
Vile Bodies, Ch. 4

44 All this fuss about sleeping together. For physical pleasure I'd sooner go to my dentist any day.
Vile Bodies, Ch. 6

45 Lady Peabury was in the morning room reading a novel; early training gave a guilty spice to this recreation, for she had been brought up to believe that to read a novel before luncheon was one of the gravest sins it was possible for a gentlewoman to commit.
Work Suspended, 'An Englishman's Home'

46 I wouldn't give up writing about God at this stage, if I was you. It would be like P. G. Wodehouse dropping Jeeves half-way through the Wooster series.
Said to Grahame Greene, who proposed to write a political novel. *Evelyn Waugh* (Christopher Sykes)

47 Simply a radio personality who outlived his prime.
Referring to Winston Churchill. *Evelyn Waugh* (Christopher Sykes)

48 Manners are especially the need of the plain. The pretty can get away with anything.
The Observer, 'Sayings of the Year,' 1962

49 No writer before the middle of the 19th century wrote about the working classes other than as grotesque or as pastoral decoration. Then when they were given the vote certain writers started to suck up to them.
Interview. *Paris Review*, 1963

50 Nurse unupblown.
Cable sent after he had failed, while a journalist serving in Ethiopia, to substantiate a rumor that an English nurse had been blown up in an Italian air raid. *Our Marvelous Native Tongue* (R. Claiborne)

51 A typical triumph of modern science to find the only part of Randolph that was not malignant and remove it.
Remarking upon the news that Randolph Churchill had had a noncancerous lung removed. Attrib.

52 Like German opera, too long and too loud.
Giving his opinions of warfare after the Battle of Crete, 1941. Attrib.

53 I put the words down and push them a bit.
Obituary, *New York Times*, 11 Apr 1966

WAY

1 Jesus saith unto him, I am the way, the truth, and the life: no man cometh unto the Father, but by me.
Bible: John 14:6

2 Wandering in a vast forest at night, I have only a faint light to guide me. A stranger appears and says to me: 'My friend, you should blow out your candle in order to find your way more clearly.' This stranger is a theologian.
Denis Diderot (1713–84) French writer. *Addition aux pensées philosophiques*

3 The Curfew tolls the knell of parting day,
The lowing herd winds slowly o'er the lea,
The plowman homeward plods his weary way,
And leaves the world to darkness and to me.
Thomas Gray (1716–71) British poet. *Elegy Written in a Country Churchyard*

4 Look for me by moonlight;
Watch for me by moonlight;
I'll come to thee by moonlight, though hell should bar the way!
Alfred Noyes (1880–1958) British poet. *The Highwayman*

5 Yet do I fear thy nature;
It is too full o' th' milk of human kindness
To catch the nearest way.
William Shakespeare (1564–1616) English dramatist. *Macbeth*, I:5

WEAKNESS

See also imperfection, yielding

1 The weakest goes to the wall.
Proverb

2 Oh, your precious 'lame ducks'!
John Galsworthy (1867–1933) British novelist. *The Man of Property*, Pt. II, Ch. 12

3 A sheep in sheep's clothing.
Edmund Gosse (1849–1928) British writer and critic. Referring to T. Sturge Moore. Sometimes attributed to Winston Churchill, referring to Clement Attlee. *Under the Bridge* (Ferris Greenslet), Ch. 12

4 My brother John is not the man to conquer a country if there is anyone to offer even the feeblest resistance.
Richard I (1157–99) King of England. *From Domesday Book to Magna Carta* (A. L. Poole)

5 Frailty, thy name is woman!
William Shakespeare (1564–1616) English dramatist. *Hamlet*, I:2

6 Thou knowest in the state of innocency Adam fell; and what should poor Jack Falstaff do in the days of villany. Thou seest I have more flesh than another man, and therefore more frailty.
William Shakespeare *Henry IV, Part 1*, III:3

WEALTH

See also capitalism, extravagance, materialism, money, ostentation, poverty and wealth

1 A good wife and health are a man's best wealth.
Proverb

2 The best things in life are free.
Proverb

3 You can't take it with you when you go.
Proverb

4 A rich man is one who isn't afraid to ask the salesman to show him something cheaper.
Anonymous *Ladies Home Journal*, Jan 1946

5 Rich men's houses are seldom beautiful, rarely comfortable, and never original. It is a constant source of surprise to people of moderate means to observe how little a big fortune contributes to Beauty.
Margot Asquith (1865–1945) The second wife of Herbert Asquith. *The Autobiography of Margot Asquith*, Ch. 17

6 A man who has a million dollars is as well off as if he were rich.
John Jacob Astor (1763–1848) US millionaire. Attrib.

7 Being a king that loved wealth and treasure, he could not endure to have trade sick.
Francis Bacon (1561–1626) English philosopher. Referring to Henry VII. *The Life of Henry VII*

8 For the Lord thy God bringeth thee into a good land, a land of brooks of water, of fountains and depths that spring out of valleys and hills;
A land of wheat, and barley, and vines, and fig trees, and pomegranates; a land of oil olive, and honey;
A land wherein thou shalt eat bread without scarceness, thou shalt not lack any thing in it; a land whose stones are iron, and out of whose hills thou mayest dig brass.
When thou hast eaten and art full, then thou shalt bless the Lord thy God for the good land which he hath given thee.
Bible: Deuteronomy 8:7–10

9 So the Lord blessed the latter end of Job more than his beginning: for he had fourteen thousand sheep, and six thousand camels, and a thousand yoke of oxen, and a thousand she asses.
Bible: Job 42:12

10 For what shall it profit a man, if he shall gain the whole world, and lose his own soul? Or what shall a man give in exchange for his soul?
Bible: Mark 8:36–37

11 Lay not up for yourselves treasures upon earth, where moth and rust doth corrupt, and where thieves break through and steal:
But lay up for yourselves treasures in heaven, where neither moth nor rust doth corrupt, and where thieves do not break through nor steal:
For where your treasure is, there will your heart be also.
Bible: Matthew 6:19–21

12 Then said Jesus unto his disciples, Verily I say unto you, That a rich man shall hardly enter into the kingdom of heaven.
And again I say unto you, It is easier for a camel to go through the eye of a needle, than for a rich man to enter into the kingdom of God.
Bible: Matthew 19:23–24

13 For we brought nothing into this world, and it is certain we carry nothing out.
Bible: I Timothy 6:7

14 The rich are the scum of the earth in every country.
G. K. Chesterton (1874–1936) British writer. *The Flying Inn*

15 People don't resent having nothing nearly as much as too little.
Ivy Compton-Burnett (1892–1969) British novelist. *A Family and a Fortune*

16 Poor Little Rich Girl.
Noël Coward (1899–1973) British dramatist. *Title of song*

17 Riches have wings, and grandeur is a dream.
William Cowper (1731–1800) British poet. *The Task*

18 FITZGERALD. The rich are different from us.
HEMINGWAY. Yes, they have more money.
F. Scott Fitzgerald (1896–1940) US novelist. *The Crack-Up*, 'Notebooks, E'

19 Wealth is not without its advantages, and the case to the contrary, although it has often been made, has never proved widely persuasive.
John Kenneth Galbraith (1908–) US economist. *The Affluent Society*, Ch. 1

20 The meek shall inherit the earth but not the mineral rights.
J. Paul Getty (1892–1976) US oil magnate. Attrib.

21 If you can actually count your money you are not really a rich man.
J. Paul Getty *Gossip* (A. Barrow)

22 As I walk along the Bois Bou-long,
With an independent air,
You can hear the girls declare,
'He must be a millionaire',
You can hear them sigh and wish to die,
You can see them wink the other eye
At the man who broke the Bank at Monte Carlo.
Fred Gilbert (1850–1903) British songwriter. The Bois de Boulogne was a fashionable recreational area on the outskirts of Paris. *The Man who Broke the Bank at Monte Carlo* (song)

23 The rich hate signing cheques. Hence the success of credit cards.
Graham Greene (1904–) British novelist. *Dr. Fischer of Geneva*

24 Sir, the insolence of wealth will creep out.
Samuel Johnson (1709–84) British lexicographer. *Life of Johnson* (J. Boswell), Vol. III

25 I don't know how much money I've got... I did ask the accountant how much it came to. I wrote it down on a bit of paper. But I've lost the bit of paper.
John Lennon (1940–80) British rock musician. *The Beatles* (Hunter Davies)

26 Those in the cheaper seats clap. The rest of you rattle your jewellery.
John Lennon Remark, Royal Variety Performance, 15 Nov 1963

27 Your lord the King of England, who lacks nothing, has men, horses, gold, silk, jewels, fruits, game and everything else. We in France have nothing but bread and wine and gaiety.
Louis VII (c. 1120–80) King of France. By 'France' Louis meant the comparatively small area around Paris that he ruled directly. Remark to Walter Map; cited in *Richard the Lionheart* (J. Gillingham), Ch. 4

28 So our Lord God commonly gives riches to those gross asses to whom he vouchsafes nothing else.
Martin Luther (1483–1546) German Protestant. *Colloquia* (J. Aurifaber), Ch. XX

29 Most of our people have never had it so good.
Harold Macmillan (1894–1986) British politician and prime minister. Speech, Bedford Football Ground, 20 July 1957

30 They gave me star treatment because I was making a lot of money. But I was just as good when I was poor.
Bob Marley (1945–81) Jamaican reggae singer. *The Radio Times*, 18 Sept 1981

31 And, as their wealth increaseth, so inclose
Infinite riches in a little room.
Christopher Marlowe (1564–93) English dramatist. *The Jew of Malta*, I:1

32 He must have killed a lot of men to have made so much money.
Molière (Jean Baptiste Poquelin; 1622–73) French dramatist. *Le Malade imaginaire*, I:5

33 I am rich beyond the dreams of avarice.
Edward Moore (1712–57) British dramatist. *The Gamester*, II

34 God shows his contempt for wealth by the kind of person he selects to receive it.
Austin O'Malley (1858–1932) US writer.

35 Gout is not relieved by a fine shoe nor a hangnail by a costly ring nor migraine by a tiara.
Plutarch (46 AD–120 AD) Greek biographer and essayist. *Moralia*, 'Contentment'

36 Who Wants to Be a Millionaire? I don't.
Cole Porter (1893–1964) US songwriter. *Who Wants to be a Millionaire?*, title song

37 I am a millionaire. That is my religion.
George Bernard Shaw (1856–1950) Irish dramatist and critic. *Major Barbara*

38 With the great part of rich people, the chief employment of riches consists in the parade of riches.
Adam Smith (1723–90) Scottish economist. *The Wealth of Nations*

39 It is the wretchedness of being rich that you have to live with rich people.
Logan Pearsall Smith (1865–1946) US writer. *Afterthoughts*, 'In the World'

40 If Heaven had looked upon riches to be a valuable thing, it would not have given them to such a scoundrel.
Jonathan Swift (1667–1745) Irish-born Anglican priest and writer. Letter to Miss Vanhomrigh, 12–13 Aug 1720

41 I have had no real gratification or enjoyment of any sort more than my neighbor on the next block who is worth only half a million.
William Henry Vanderbilt (1821–85) US railroad chief. *Famous Last Words* (B. Conrad)

42 One can never be too thin or too rich.
Duchess of Windsor (Wallis Warfield Simpson; 1896–1986) The wife of the Duke of Windsor (formerly Edward VIII). Attrib.

43 Just what God would have done if he had the money.
Alexander Woollcott (1887–1943) US journalist. On being shown round Moss Hart's elegant country house and grounds. Attrib.

WEAPONS

See also nuclear weapons, power politics, war

1 I put before the whole House my own view with appalling frankness ... supposing I had gone to the country and said ... that we must rearm, does anybody think that this pacific democracy would have rallied to that cry at that moment? I cannot think of anything that would have made the loss of the election from my point of view more certain.
Stanley Baldwin (1867–1947) British Conservative prime minister. Speech, House of Commons, 12 Nov 1936

2 If you carry this resolution and follow out all its implications and do not run away from it, you will send a Foreign Secretary, whoever he may be, naked into the conference chamber.
Aneurin Bevan (1897–1960) British Labour politician. Referring to unilateral disarmament. Speech, Labour Party Conference, 2 Oct 1957

3 In Place of Fear.
Aneurin Bevan Title of book about disarmament

4 It was very successful, but it fell on the wrong planet.
Wernher von Braun (1912–77) German rocket engineer. Referring to the first V2 rocket to hit London during World War II. Attrib.

5 We may find in the long run that tinned food is a deadlier weapon than the machine-gun.
George Orwell (Eric Blair; 1903–50) British novelist. *The Road to Wigan Pier*, Ch. 6

6 Today we have naming of parts.
Yesterday,
We had daily cleaning. And tomorrow morning
We shall have what to do after firing.
But today,
Today we have naming of parts.
Henry Reed (1914–) British poet and dramatist. *Naming of Parts*

7 They call it easing the Spring: it is perfectly easy
If you have any strength in your thumb: like the bolt,
And the breech, and the cocking-piece, and the point of balance,
Which in our case we have not got.
Henry Reed *Naming of Parts*

8 Though loaded firearms were strictly forbidden at St Trinian's to all but Sixth-Formers . . . one or two of them carried automatics acquired in the holidays, generally the gift of some indulgent relative.
Ronald Searle (1920–) British cartoonist. *The Terror of St Trinian's*, Ch. 3

9 But bombs *are* unbelievable until they actually fall.
Patrick White (1912–) British-born Australian novelist. *Riders in the Chariot*, I:4

WEATHER

See also sun

1 Mackerel sky and mares' tails make lofty ships carry low sails.
Proverb

2 Rain before seven: fine before eleven.
Proverb

3 Rain, rain, go away, come again another day.
Proverb

4 Red sky at night, shepherd's delight; red sky in the morning, shepherd's warning.
Proverb

5 St. Swithin's Day, if thou dost rain, for forty days it will remain; St. Swithin's Day, if thou be fair, for forty days 'twill rain no more.
Proverb

6 The north wind does blow, and we shall have snow.
Proverb

7 What dreadful hot weather we have! It keeps me in a continual state of inelegance.
Jane Austen (1775–1817) British novelist. Letter, 18 Sept 1796

8 Hath the rain a father? or who hath begotten the drops of dew?
Bible: Job 38:28

9 I like the weather, when it is not rainy,
That is, I like two months of every year.
Lord Byron (1788–1824) British poet. *Beppo*

10 This is a London particular . . . A fog, miss.
Charles Dickens (1812–70) British novelist. *Bleak House*, Ch. 3

11 The yellow fog that rubs its back upon the window panes.
T. S. Eliot (1888–1965) American-born poet. *The Love Song of J. Alfred Prufrock*

12 It ain't a fit night out for man or beast.
W. C. Fields (1880–1946) US actor. *The Fatal Glass of Beer*

13 I'm singing in the rain, just singing in the rain;
What a wonderful feeling, I'm happy again.
Arthur Freed (1894–1973) US film producer and songwriter. From the musical, *Hollywood Revue of 1929*. *Singing in the Rain*

14 This is the weather the cuckoo likes,
And so do I;
When showers betumble the chestnut spikes,
And nestlings fly:
And the little brown nightingale bills his best,
And they sit outside at 'The Travellers' Rest'.
Thomas Hardy (1840–1928) British novelist. *Weathers*

15 This is the weather the shepherd shuns,
And so do I.
Thomas Hardy *Weathers*

16 When two Englishmen meet, their first talk is of the weather.
Samuel Johnson (1709–84) British lexicographer. *The Idler*

17 A snake came to my water-trough
On a hot, hot day, and I in pyjamas for the heat,
To drink there.
D. H. Lawrence (1885–1930) British novelist. *Snake*

18 The British, he thought, must be gluttons for satire: even the weather forecast seemed to be some kind of spoof, predicting every possible combination of weather for the next twenty-four hours without actually committing itself to anything specific.
David Lodge (1935–) British author. *Changing Places*, Ch. 2

19 The first fall of snow is not only an event, it is a magical event. You go to bed in one kind of world and wake up in another quite different, and if this is not enchantment then where is it to be found?
J. B. Priestley (1894–1984) British novelist. *Apes and Angels*

20 Who has seen the wind?
Neither you nor I:
But when the trees bow down their heads,
The wind is passing by.
Christina Rossetti (1830–74) British poet. *Who Has Seen the Wind?*

21 Blow, winds, and crack your cheeks; rage, blow.
You cataracts and hurricanoes, spout
Till you have drench'd our steeples, drown'd the cocks.
William Shakespeare (1564–1616) English dramatist. *King Lear*, III:2

22 Rumble thy bellyful. Spit, fire; spout rain.
Nor rain, wind, thunder, fire, are my daughters
I tax not you, you elements, with unkindness.
William Shakespeare *King Lear*, III:2

23 Poor naked wretches, wheresoe'er you are,
That bide the pelting of this pitiless storm,
How shall your houseless heads and unfed sides,
Your loop'd and window'd raggedness, defend you

From seasons such as these?
William Shakespeare *King Lear*, III:4

24 So foul and fair a day I have not seen.
William Shakespeare *Macbeth*, I:3

25 I am the daughter of Earth and Water,
And the nursling of the Sky;
I pass through the pores of the ocean and shores;
I change, but I cannot die,
For after the rain when with never a stain
The pavilion of Heaven is bare,
And the winds and sunbeams with their convex gleams
Build up the blue dome of air,
I silently laugh at my own cenotaph,
And out of the caverns of rain,
Like a child from the womb, like a ghost from the tomb,
I arise and unbuild it again.
Percy Bysshe Shelley (1792–1822) British poet. *The Cloud*

26 I wield the flail of the lashing hail,
And whiten the green plains under,
And then again I dissolve it in rain,
And laugh as I pass in thunder.
Percy Bysshe Shelley *The Cloud*

27 O Wild West Wind, thou breath of Autumn's being,
Thou, from whose unseen presence the leaves dead
Are driven, like ghosts from an enchanter fleeing,
Yellow, and black, and pale, and hectic red,
Pestilence-stricken multitudes.
Percy Bysshe Shelley *Ode to the West Wind*

28 Still falls the Rain –
Dark as the world of man, black as our loss –
Blind as the nineteen hundred and forty nails
Upon the cross.
Edith Sitwell (1887–1964) British poet and writer. *Still Falls the Rain*

29 Heat, madam! It was so dreadful that I found there was nothing for it but to take off my flesh and sit in my bones.
Sydney Smith (1771–1845) British clergyman and essayist. Discussing the hot weather with a lady acquaintance. *Lives of the Wits* (H. Pearson)

30 Willows whiten, aspens quiver,
Little breezes dusk and shiver.
Alfred, Lord Tennyson (1809–92) British poet. *The Lady of Shalott*, Pt. I

WEBSTER, Daniel

(1782–1852) US statesman. A senator and renowned orator, he became secretary of state (1841–43; 1850–52) and an unsuccessful presidential candidate.

Quotations about Webster

1 Daniel Webster struck me much like a steam engine in trousers.
Sydney Smith (1771–1845) British clergyman and essayist. *A Memoir of the Reverend Sydney Smith* (Lady Holland)

2 God is the only president of the day, and Webster is his orator.
Henry David Thoreau (1817–62) US writer. Attrib.

Quotations by Webster

3 Age cannot wither her, nor custom stale her infinite virginity.
Paraphrasing a line from Shakespeare's *Antony and Cleopatra* on hearing of Andrew Jackson's steadfast maintenance that his friend Peggy Eaton did not deserve her scandalous reputation. *Presidential Anecdotes* (P. Boller)

4 The people's government, made for the people, made by the people, and answerable to the people.
Second speech on Foote's resolution, Jan 26 1830

5 The past, at least, is secure.
Speech, US Senate, 26 Jan 1830

6 I was born an American; I will live an American; I shall die an American.
Speech, US Senate, 17 July 1850

7 There is always room at the top.
When advised not to become a lawyer because the profession was overcrowded. Attrib.

WELLINGTON, Arthur Wellesley, Duke of

(1769–1852) British general and statesman. He defeated the French in the Peninsular War and Napoleon at Waterloo. Known as the 'Iron Duke', he became Tory prime minister (1828–30). Under Peel he served as foreign secretary (1834–35).

Quotations about Wellington

1 He accepted peace as if he had been defeated.
Napoleon I (Napoleon Bonaparte; 1769–1821) French emperor. Attrib.

2 The Duke of Wellington has exhausted nature and exhausted glory. His career was one unclouded longest day.
The Times, Obituary, 16 Sept 1852

Quotations by Wellington

3 It all depends upon that article there.
Indicating a passing infantryman when asked if he would be able to defeat Napoleon. *The Age of Elegance* (A. Bryant)

4 Yes, and they went down very well too.
Replying to the observation that the French cavalry had come up very well during the Battle of Waterloo. *The Age of Elegance* (A. Bryant)

5 In my situation as Chancellor of the University of Oxford, I have been much exposed to authors.
Collections and Recollections (G. W. E. Russell)

6 Not upon a man from the colonel to the private in a regiment – both inclusive. We may pick up a marshal or two perhaps; but not worth a damn.
Said during the Waterloo campaign, when asked whether he anticipated any desertions from Napoleon's army. *Creevey Papers*, Ch. X

7 It has been a damned serious business – Blücher and I have lost 30,000 men. It has been a damned nice thing – the nearest run thing you ever saw in your life... By God! I don't think it would have done if I had not been there.
Referring to the Battle of Waterloo. *Creevey Papers*, Ch. X

8 I always say that, next to a battle lost, the greatest misery is a battle gained.
Diary (Frances, Lady Shelley)

9 I see no reason to suppose that these machines will ever force themselves into general use.
Referring to steam locomotives. *Geoffrey Madan's Notebooks* (J. Gere)

10 I hate the whole race... There is no believing a word they say – your professional poets, I mean – there never existed a more worthless set than Byron and his friends for example.
Lady Salisbury's diary, 26 Oct 1833

11 I used to say of him that his presence on the field made the difference of forty thousand men.
Referring to Napoleon. *Notes of Conversations with the Duke of Wellington* (Stanhope), 2 Nov 1831

12 The next greatest misfortune to

losing a battle is to gain such a victory as this.
Recollections (S. Rogers)

13 The greatest tragedy in the world, Madam, except a defeat.
In reply to the remark, 'What a glorious thing must be a victory'. *Recollections* (S. Rogers)

14 You must build your House of Parliament upon the river: so . . . that the populace cannot exact their demands by sitting down round you.
Words on Wellington (Sir William Fraser)

15 I don't know what effect these men will have on the enemy, but, by God, they frighten me.
Referring to his generals. Attrib.

16 It is not the business of generals to shoot one another.
Refusing an artillery officer permission to fire upon Napoleon himself during the Battle of Waterloo, 1815. Attrib.

17 Up, Guards, and at 'em.
Order given at the battle of Waterloo, 18 June 1815. Attrib.

18 The battle of Waterloo was won on the playing fields of Eton.
Attrib.

19 Yes, about ten minutes.
Responding to a vicar's query as to whether there was anything he would like his forthcoming sermon to be about. Attrib.

20 Very well, then I shall not take off my boots.
Responding to the news, as he was going to bed, that the ship in which he was traveling seemed about to sink. Attrib.

21 Ours is composed of the scum of the earth.
Of the British army. Remark, 4 Nov 1831

22 Publish and be damned!
On being offered the chance to avoid mention in the memoirs of Harriette Wilson by giving her money. Attrib.

23 I don't care a twopenny damn what becomes of the ashes of Napoleon Bonaparte.
Attrib.

24 Don't quote Latin; say what you have to say, and then sit down.
Advice to a new Member of Parliament. Attrib.

25 A battle of giants.
Referring to the Battle of Waterloo; said to Samuel Rogers. Attrib.

26 Sparrowhawks, Ma'am.
Advice when asked by Queen Victoria how to remove sparrows from the Crystal Palace. Attrib.

WELLS, H(erbert) G(eorge)

(1866–1946) British writer. After studying science, he won a literary reputation with *The Time Machine* (1895) and *Kipps* (1905). His other books included *An Outline of History* (1920) and *The Shape of Things to Come* (1933).

Quotations about Wells

1 Whatever Wells writes is not only alive, but kicking.
Henry James (1843–1916) US novelist. Attrib.

2 I doubt whether in the whole course of our history, any one individual has explored as many avenues, turned over so many stones, ventured along so many culs-de-sac. Science, history, politics, all were within his compass.
Malcolm Muggeridge (1903–) British writer. *The Observer*, 11 Sep 1966

Quotations by Wells

3 The cat is the offspring of a cat and the dog of a dog, but butlers and lady's maids do not reproduce their kind. They have other duties.
Bealby, Pt I, Ch. 1

4 He was quite sure that he had been wronged. Not to be wronged is to forgo the first privilege of goodness.
Bealby, Pt. IV, Ch. 1

5 Miss Madeleine Philips was making it very manifest to Captain Douglas that she herself was a career; that a lover with any other career in view need not – as the advertisements say – apply.
Bealby, Pt. V, Ch. 5

6 He began to think the tramp a fine, brotherly, generous fellow. He was also growing accustomed to something –shall I call it an olfactory bar – that had hitherto kept them apart.
Bealby, Pt. VI, Ch. 3

7 The army ages men sooner than the law and philosophy; it exposes them more freely to germs, which undermine and destroy, and it shelters them more completely from thought, which stimulates and preserves.
Bealby, Pt. VIII, Ch. 1

8 He had one peculiar weakness; he had faced death in many forms but he had never faced a dentist. The thought of dentists gave him just the same sick horror as the thought of Socialism.
Bealby, Pt. VIII, Ch. 1

9 In the Country of the Blind the One-eyed Man is King.
The Country of the Blind

10 '*Language*, man!' roared Parsons; 'why, it's LITERATURE!'
The History of Mr Polly, Pt. I, Ch. 3

11 'You're a Christian?' 'Church of England,' said Mr Polly. 'Mm,' said the employer, a little checked. 'For good all round business work, I should have preferred a Baptist.'
The History of Mr Polly, Pt. III, Ch. 1

12 Arson, after all, is an artificial crime . . . A large number of houses deserve to be burnt.
The History of Mr Polly, Pt. X, Ch. 1

13 'It's giving girls names like that', said Buggins, 'that nine times out of ten makes 'em go wrong. It unsettles 'em. If ever I was to have a girl, if ever I was to have a dozen girls, I'd call 'em all Jane.'
Referring to the name Euphemia. *Kipps*, Bk. I, Ch. 4

14 It's 'aving 'ouses built by men, I believe, makes all the work and trouble.
Kipps, Bk. III, Ch. 1

15 Everybody hates house-agents because they have everybody at a disadvantage. All other callings have a certain amount of give and take; the house-agent simply takes.
Kipps, Bk. III, Ch. 1

16 We were taught as the chief subjects of instruction Latin and Greek. We were taught very badly because the men who taught us did not habitually use either of these languages.
The New Machiavelli, Bk. I., Ch. 3

17 Cynicism is humour in ill-health.
Short Stories, 'The Last Trump'

18 He doubted the existence of the Deity but accepted Carnot's cycle, and he had read Shakespeare and found him weak in chemistry.
Short Stories, 'The Lord of the Dynamos'

19 Bricklayers kick their wives to death, and dukes betray theirs; but it is among the small clerks and shopkeepers nowadays that it

comes most often to the cutting of throats.
Short Stories, 'The Purple Pileus'

20 The War to End War.
Book title

21 If Max gets to Heaven he won't last long. He will be chucked out for trying to pull of a merger between Heaven and Hell . . . after having secured a controlling interest in key subsidiary companies in both places, of course.
Referring to Lord Beaverbrook. *Beaverbrook* (A. J. P. Taylor)

22 One thousand years more. That's all *Homo sapiens* has before him.
Diary (Harold Nicolson)

WELSH

See also British, Wales

1 Eddy was a tremendously tolerant person, but he wouldn't put up with the Welsh. He always said, surely there's enough English to go round.
John Mortimer (1923–) British lawyer and dramatist. *Two Stars for Comfort*, I:2

2 There are still parts of Wales where the only concession to gaiety is a striped shroud.
Gwyn Thomas (1913–81) British writer. *Punch*, 18 June 1958

3 . . . an impotent people,
Sick with inbreeding,
Worrying the carcase of an old song.
R. S. Thomas (1913–) Welsh poet. *Welsh Landscape*

4 'The Welsh,' said the Doctor, 'are the only nation in the world that has produced no graphic or plastic art, no architecture, no drama. They just sing,' he said with disgust, 'sing and blow down wind instruments of plated silver.'
Evelyn Waugh (1903–66) British novelist. *Decline and Fall*, Pt. I, Ch. 8

WEST, Mae

(1892–1980) US actress, sex symbol, and comedienne. She made her reputation in the theater with *Diamond Lil* (1928). Her films included *She Done Him Wrong* (1933) and *I'm No Angel* (1933).

Quotations about West

1 In a non-permissive age, she made remarkable inroads against the taboos of her day, and did so without even lowering her neckline.
Leslie Halliwell *The Filmgoer's Book of Quotes*

2 She stole everything but the cameras.
George Raft (1895–1980) US actor. Attrib.

Quotations by West

3 A man in the house is worth two in the street.
Belle of the Nineties, film 1934

4 – My goodness those diamonds are lovely!
Goodness had nothing whatever to do with it.
Used in 1959 as the title of the first volume of her autobiography. *Diamond Lil*, film 1932

5 I have a lot of respect for that dame. There's one lady barber that made good.
Referring to Delilah. *Going to Town*, film 1934

6 Beulah, peel me a grape.
I'm No Angel, film 1933

7 A gold rush is what happens when a line of chorus girls spot a man with a bank roll.
Klondike Annie, film 1936

8 I always did like a man in uniform. And that one fits you grand. Why don't you come up sometime and see me?
Often misquoted as 'Come up and see me some time'. *She Done Him Wrong*, film 1933

9 You're a fine woman, Lou. One of the finest women that ever walked the streets.
She Done Him Wrong, film 1933

10 You can say what you like about long dresses, but they cover a multitude of shins.
Peel Me a Grape (J. Weintraub)

11 It's hard to be funny when you have to be clean.
The Wit and Wisdom of Mae West (ed. J. Weintraub)

12 It is better to be looked over than overlooked.
The Wit and Wisdom of Mae West (ed. J. Weintraub)

13 I used to be Snow White . . . but I drifted.
The Wit and Wisdom of Mae West (ed. J. Weintraub)

14 When women go wrong, men go right after them.
The Wit and Wisdom of Mae West (ed. J. Weintraub)

15 I'm glad you like my Catherine. I like her too. She ruled thirty million people and had three thousand lovers. I do the best I can in two hours.
After her performance in *Catherine the Great*. Speech from the stage

16 Everything.
When asked what she wanted to be remembered for. Attrib.

17 When I'm good I'm very good, but when I'm bad I'm better.
Attrib.

18 Whenever I'm caught between two evils, I take the one I've never tried.
Attrib.

WHISTLER, James Abbott McNeill

(1834–1903) US painter. Living mostly in Europe, he established his reputation with *The Artist's Mother* and *Nocturne in Blue and Gold*. He was also the author of *The Gentle Art of Making Enemies* (1890).

Quotations about Whistler

1 I have seen, and heard, much of cockney impudence before now, but never expected to hear a coxcomb ask two hundred guineas for flinging a pot of paint in the public's face.
John Ruskin (1819–1900) British art critic and writer. *Fors Clavigera*, 2 Jul 1877

2 That he is indeed one of the very greatest masters of painting, is my opinion. And I may add that in this opinion Mr. Whistler himself entirely concurs.
Oscar Wilde (1854–1900) Irish-born British dramatist. *Pall Mall Gazette*, 21 Feb 1885

Quotations by Whistler

3 I am not arguing with you–I am telling you.
The Gentle Art of Making Enemies

4 Nature is usually wrong.
The Gentle Art of Making Enemies

5 No, no, Oscar, you forget. When you and I are together we never talk about anything except me.
Cable replying to Oscar Wilde's message: 'When you and I are together we never talk about anything except ourselves'. *The Gentle Art of Making Enemies*

6 If silicon had been a gas I should have been a major-general.
Referring to his failure in a West Point chemistry examination. *English Wits* (L. Russell)

7 No, I ask it for the knowledge of a lifetime.
Replying to the taunt, during the Ruskin trial, that he was asking a fee of 200 guineas for two days' painting. *Lives of the Wits* (H. Pearson)

8 Isn't it? I know in my case I would grow intolerably conceited.
Replying to the pointed observation that it was as well that we do not not see ourselves as others see us. *The Man Whistler* (H. Pearson)

9 A LADY. I only know of two painters in the world: yourself and Velasquez.
WHISTLER. Why drag in Velasquez?
Whistler Stories (D. Seitz)

10 You shouldn't say it is not good. You should say you do not like it; and then, you know, you're perfectly safe.
Whistler Stories (D. Seitz)

11 A LADY. This landscape reminds me of your work.
WHISTLER. Yes madam, Nature is creeping up.
Whistler Stories (D. Seitz)

12 Perhaps not, but then you can't call yourself a great work of nature.
Responding to a sitter's complaint that his portrait was not a great work of art. *Whistler Stories* (D. Seitz)

13 I cannot tell you that, madam. Heaven has granted me no offspring.
Replying to a lady who had inquired whether he thought genius hereditary. *Whistler Stories* (D. Seitz)

WHISTLING

See also fear

1 You know you don't have to act with me, Steve. You don't have to say anything, and you don't have to do anything. Not a thing. Oh, maybe just whistle. You know how to whistle, don't you, Steve? You just put your lips together and blow.
Lauren Bacall (1924–) US film actress. *To Have and Have Not*

2 The schoolboy, with his satchel in his hand,
Whistling aloud to bear his courage up.
Robert Blair (1699–1746) Scottish poet. *The Grave*

3 I Whistle a Happy Tune.
Oscar Hammerstein (1895–1960) US lyricist. From the musical *The King and I*. Song title

WHITMAN, Walt

(1819–92) US poet. His first verse collection, *Leaves of Grass* (1855), was poorly received at first, although it went through nine editions in his lifetime. Other books include *Democratic Vistas* (1871), *November Boughs* (1888), and *Goodbye, My Fancy* (1891).

Quotations about Whitman

1 Walt Whitman who laid end to end words never seen in each other's company before outside of a dictionary.
David Lodge (1935–) British author. *Changing Places*, Ch. 5

2 He is a writer of something occasionally like English, and a man of something occasionally like genius.
Algernon Charles Swinburne (1837–1909) British poet. *Whitmania*

Quotations by Whitman

3 No one will ever get at my verses who insists upon viewing them as a literary performance.
A Backward Glance O'er Travel'd Roads

4 I hear it was charged against me that I sought to destroy institutions,
But really I am neither for nor against institutions.
I Hear It was Charged against Me

5 If anything is sacred the human body is sacred.
I Sing the Body Electric, 8

6 I celebrate myself, and sing myself,
And what I assume you shall assume.
Song of Myself, 1

7 I think I could turn and live with animals, they're so placid and self-contained,
I stand and look at them long and long.
Song of Myself, 32

8 Behold, I do not give lectures or a little charity,
When I give I give myself.
Song of Myself, 40

9 I have said that the soul is not more than the body,
And I have said that the body is not more than the soul,
And nothing, but God, is greater to one than one's self is.
Song of Myself, 48

10 Do I contradict myself?
Very well then I contradict myself,
(I am large, I contain multitudes).
Song of Myself, 51

11 Where the populace rise at once against the never-ending audacity of elected persons.
Song of the Broad Axe, 5

12 A great city is that which has the greatest men and women.
Song of the Broad Axe, 5

13 After you have exhausted what there is in business, politics, conviviality, and so on–have found that none of these finally satisfy, or permanently wear–what remains? Nature remains.
Specimen Days, 'New Themes Entered Upon'

14 The earth does not argue,
Is not pathetic, has no arrangements,
Does not scream, haste, persuade, threaten, promise,
Makes no discriminations, has no conceivable failures,
Closes nothing, refuses nothing, shuts none out.
To the sayers of words

WIFE

See marriage

WILDE, Oscar Fingal O'Flahertie Wills

(1856–1900) Irish-born British poet and dramatist. His comedies *Lady Windermere's Fan* (1892), *An Ideal Husband* (1895), and *The Importance of Being Earnest* (1895) made him a leading figure in London society. However he was ruined by a trial (1895) arising from his homosexual relationships, especially with Lord Alfred Douglas. During his imprisonment he wrote *De Profundis* (1905) and the *The Ballad of Reading Gaol* (1898).

Quotations about Wilde

1 From the beginning Wilde performed his life and continued to do so even after fate had taken the plot out of his hands.
W. H. Auden (1907–73) British poet. *Forewords and Afterwords*

2 If with the literate I am
Impelled to try an epigram
I never seek to take the credit
We all assume that Oscar said it.
Dorothy Parker (1893–1967) US writer. Attrib.

3 He was over-dressed, pompous,

snobbish, sentimental and vain. But he had an undeniable *flair* for the possibilities of commercial theatre.
Evelyn Waugh (1903–66) British novelist.
Harper's Bazaar, Nov 1930

Quotations by Wilde

4 I never saw a man who looked
With such a wistful eye
Upon that little tent of blue
Which prisoners call the sky.
The Ballad of Reading Gaol, I:3

5 Yet each man kills the thing he loves,
By each let this be heard,
Some do it with a bitter look,
Some with a flattering word.
The coward does it with a kiss,
The brave man with a sword!
The Ballad of Reading Gaol, I:7

6 The Governor was strong upon
The Regulations Act:
The Doctor said that Death was but
A scientific fact:
And twice a day the Chaplain called,
And left a little tract.
The Ballad of Reading Gaol, III:3

7 Something was dead in each of us,
And what was dead was Hope.
The Ballad of Reading Gaol, III:31

8 For he who lives more lives than one
More deaths than one must die.
The Ballad of Reading Gaol, III:37

9 I know not whether Laws be right,
Or whether Laws be wrong;
All that we know who lie in gaol
Is that the wall is strong;
And that each day is like a year,
A year whose days are long.
The Ballad of Reading Gaol, V:1

10 As long as war is regarded as wicked, it will always have its fascination. When it is looked upon as vulgar, it will cease to be popular.
The Critic as Artist, Pt. 2

11 The man who sees both sides of a question is a man who sees absolutely nothing at all.
The Critic as Artist, Pt. 2

12 A little sincerity is a dangerous thing, and a great deal of it is absolutely fatal.
The Critic as Artist, Pt. 2

13 Ah! don't say you agree with me. When people agree with me I always feel that I must be wrong.
The Critic as Artist, Pt. 2

14 There is no sin except stupidity.
The Critic as Artist, Pt. 2

15 There is much to be said in favour of modern journalism. By giving us the opinions of the uneducated, it keeps us in touch with the ignorance of the community.
The Critic as Artist, Pt. 2

16 Art never expresses anything but itself.
The Decay of Lying

17 To love oneself is the beginning of a lifelong romance.
An Ideal Husband, III

18 Other people are quite dreadful. The only possible society is oneself.
An Ideal Husband, III

19 Really, if the lower orders don't set us a good example, what on earth is the use of them?
The Importance of Being Earnest, I

20 I have invented an invaluable permanent invalid called Bunbury, in order that I may be able to go down into the country whenever I choose.
The Importance of Being Earnest, I

21 All women become like their mothers. That is their tragedy. No man does. That's his.
The Importance of Being Earnest, I

22 The amount of women in London who flirt with their own husbands is perfectly scandalous. It looks so bad. It is simply washing one's clean linen in public.
The Importance of Being Earnest, I

23 The old-fashioned respect for the young is fast dying out.
The Importance of Being Earnest, I

24 In married life three is company and two is none.
The Importance of Being Earnest, I

25 Ignorance is like a delicate exotic fruit; touch it, and the bloom is gone.
The Importance of Being Earnest, I

26 To lose one parent, Mr Worthing, may be regarded as a misfortune; to lose both looks like carelessness.
The Importance of Being Earnest, I

27 I hope you have not been leading a double life, pretending to be wicked and being really good all the time. That would be hypocrisy.
The Importance of Being Earnest, II

28 On an occasion of this kind it becomes more than a moral duty to speak one's mind. It becomes a pleasure.
The Importance of Being Earnest, II

29 CECILY. When I see a spade I call it a spade.
GWENDOLEN. I am glad to say I have never seen a spade. It is obvious that our social spheres have been widely different.
The Importance of Being Earnest, II

30 I never travel without my diary. One should always have something sensational to read in the train.
The Importance of Being Earnest, II

31 In matters of grave importance, style, not sincerity, is the vital thing.
The Importance of Being Earnest, III

32 Three addresses always inspire confidence, even in tradesmen.
The Importance of Being Earnest, III

33 Never speak disrespectfully of Society, Algernon. Only people who can't get into it do that.
The Importance of Being Earnest, III

34 No woman should ever be quite accurate about her age. It looks so calculating.
The Importance of Being Earnest, III

35 This suspense is terrible. I hope it will last.
The Importance of Being Earnest, III

36 It is a terrible thing for a man to find out suddenly that all his life he has been speaking nothing but the truth.
The Importance of Being Earnest, III

37 Please do not shoot the pianist. He is doing his best.
Impressions of America, 'Leadville'

38 I can resist everything except temptation.
Lady Windermere's Fan, I

39 It is absurd to divide people into good and bad. People are either charming or tedious.
Lady Windermere's Fan, I

40 I am the only person in the world I should like to know thoroughly.
Lady Windermere's Fan, II

41 We are all in the gutter, but some of us are looking at the stars.
Lady Windermere's Fan, III

42 There is nothing in the whole world so unbecoming to a woman as a Nonconformist conscience.
Lady Windermere's Fan, III

43 A man who knows the price of everything and the value of nothing.
A cynic. *Lady Windermere's Fan*, III

44 There is no such thing as a moral or an immoral book. Books are well written, or badly written.
The Picture of Dorian Gray, Preface

45 All Art is quite useless.
The Picture of Dorian Gray, Preface

46 There is only one thing in the world worse than being talked about, and that is not being talked about.
The Picture of Dorian Gray, Ch. 1

47 The only way to get rid of a temptation is to yield to it.
The Picture of Dorian Gray, Ch. 2

48 It is only shallow people who do not judge by appearances.
The Picture of Dorian Gray, Ch. 2

49 I can sympathize with everything, except suffering.
The Picture of Dorian Gray, Ch. 3

50 Women represent the triumph of matter over mind, just as men represent the triumph of mind over morals.
The Picture of Dorian Gray, Ch. 4

51 A cigarette is the perfect type of a perfect pleasure. It is exquisite, and it leaves one unsatisfied. What more can one want?
The Picture of Dorian Gray, Ch. 6

52 Anybody can be good in the country.
The Picture of Dorian Gray, Ch. 19

53 As for the virtuous poor, one can pity them, of course, but one cannot possibly admire them.
The Soul of Man under Socialism

54 Democracy means simply the bludgeoning of the people by the people for the people.
See LINCOLN. *The Soul of Man under Socialism*

55 Art is the most intense mode of individualism that the world has known.
The Soul of Man Under Socialism

56 Twenty years of romance makes a woman look like a ruin; but twenty years of marriage make her something like a public building.
A Woman of No Importance, I

57 MRS ALLONBY. They say, Lady Hunstanton, that when good Americans die they go to Paris.
LADY HUNSTANTON. Indeed? And when bad Americans die, where do they go to?
LORD ILLINGWORTH. Oh, they go to America.
See APPLETON, Thomas Gold. *A Woman of No Importance*, I

58 The English country gentleman galloping after a fox – the unspeakable in full pursuit of the uneatable.
A Woman of No Importance, I

59 One should never trust a woman who tells one her real age. A woman who would tell one that, would tell one anything.
A Woman of No Importance, I

60 LORD ILLINGWORTH. The Book of Life begins with a man and a woman in a garden.
MRS ALLONBY. It ends with Revelations.
A Woman of No Importance, I

61 Moderation is a fatal thing, Lady Hunstanton. Nothing succeeds like excess.
A Woman of No Importance, III

62 Ah, every day dear Herbert becomes *de plus en plus Oscarié*. It is a wonderful case of nature imitating art.
Referring to Beerbohm Tree's unconscious adoption of some of the mannerisms of a character he was playing in one of Wilde's plays. *Great Theatrical Disasters* (G. Brandreth)

63 I suppose that I shall have to die beyond my means.
When told that an operation would be expensive. He is also believed to have said 'I am dying beyond my means' on accepting a glass of champagne as he lay on his deathbed. *Life of Wilde* (Sherard)

64 One would have to have a heart of stone to read the death of Little Nell without laughing.
Lecturing upon Dickens. *Lives of the Wits* (H. Pearson)

65 A thing is not necessarily true because a man dies for it.
Oscariana

66 He hasn't an enemy in the world, and none of his friends like him.
Said of G. B. Shaw. *Sixteen Self Sketches* (Shaw), Ch. 17

67 With our James vulgarity begins at home, and should be allowed to stay there.
Referring to the artist James Whistler. Letter to the *World*

68 The man who can dominate a London dinner-table can dominate the world.
Attrib. by R. Aldington in his edition of Wilde

69 The gods bestowed on Max the gift of perpetual old age.
Referring to Max Beerbohm. Attrib.

70 The play was a great success, but the audience was a disaster.
Referring to a play that had recently failed. Attrib.

71 Who am I to tamper with a masterpiece?
Refusing to make alterations to one of his own plays. Attrib.

72 It requires one to assume such indecent postures.
Explaining why he did not play cricket. Attrib.

73 If this is the way Queen Victoria treats her prisoners, she doesn't deserve to have any.
Complaining at having to wait in the rain for transport to take him to prison. Attrib.

74 Grief has turned her fair.
Referring to the fact that a recently bereaved lady friend had dyed her hair blonde. Attrib.

75 Work is the curse of the drinking classes.
Attrib.

76 Nothing, except my genius.
Replying to a US customs official on being asked if he had anything to declare. Attrib.

77 I should be like a lion in a cave of savage Daniels.
Explaining why he would not be attending a function at a club whose members were hostile to him. Attrib.

78 Dear Frank, we believe you; you have dined in every house in London – *once*.
Interrupting Frank Harris's interminable account of the houses he had dined at. Attrib.

79 Either that wall paper goes, or I do.
Last words, as he lay dying in a drab Paris bedroom. *Time*, 16 Jan 1984

WILDER, Thornton

(1897–1975) US novelist and dramatist. His works include the novel *The Bridge of San Luis Rey* (1927) and the plays *Our Town* (1938) and *The Skin of Our Teeth* (1942).

1 A living is made, Mr Kemper, by selling something that everybody needs at least once a year. Yes, sir! And a million is made by producing something that everybody needs every day. You artists produce something that nobody needs at any time.
The Matchmaker, II

2 The best part of married life is the fights. The rest is merely so-so.
The Matchmaker, II

3 Never support two weaknesses at the same time. It's your combination sinners – your lecherous liars and your miserly drunkards – who dishonor the vices and bring them into bad repute.
The Matchmaker, III

4 But there comes a moment in everybody's life when he must decide whether he'll live among human beings or not – a fool among fools or a fool alone.
The Matchmaker, IV

5 My advice to you is not to inquire why or whither, but just enjoy your ice-cream while it's on your plate, – that's my philosophy.
The Skin of Our Teeth, I

6 When you're at war you think about a better life; when you're at peace you think about a more comfortable one.
The Skin of Our Teeth, III

7 Literature is the orchestration of platitudes.
Time magazine

WILDERNESS

1 As I walked through the wilderness of this world.
John Bunyan (1628–88) English writer. *The Pilgrim's Progress*, Pt. I

2 Oh for a lodge in some vast wilderness,
Some boundless contiguity of shade,
Where rumour of oppression and deceit,
Of unsuccessful or successful war,
Might never reach me more!
William Cowper (1731–1800) British poet. *The Task*

3 Here with a Loaf of Bread beneath the Bough,
A Flask of Wine, a Book of Verse – and Thou
Beside me singing in the Wilderness –
And Wilderness is Paradise enow.
Edward Fitzgerald (1809–83) British poet. *The Rubáiyát of Omar Khayyám*

4 I have a garden of my own,
But so with roses overgrown,
And lilies, that you would it guess
To be a little wilderness.
Andrew Marvell (1621–78) English poet. *The Nymph Complaining for the Death of her Fawn*

WILLIAMS, Tennessee

(1911–83) US dramatist. He established his reputation with *The Glass Menagerie* (1945). Subsequent successes include *A Streetcar Named Desire* (1947) and *Cat on a Hot Tin Roof* (1955).

1 My suit is pale yellow. My nationality is French, and my normality has been often subject to question.
Camino Real, Block 4

2 You can be young without money but you can't be old without it.
Cat on a Hot Tin Roof, I

3 That Europe's nothin' on earth but a great big auction, that's all it is.
Cat on a Hot Tin Roof, I

4 I can't stand a naked light bulb, any more than I can a rude remark or a vulgar action.
A Streetcar Named Desire, II:3

5 I have always depended on the kindness of strangers.
A Streetcar Named Desire, II:3

6 If people behaved in the way nations do they would all be put in straitjackets.
BBC interview

7 He was meddling too much in my private life.
Explaining why he had given up visiting his psychoanalyst. Attrib.

WILLS

1 The man who leaves money to charity in his will is only giving away what no longer belongs to him.
Voltaire (François-Marie Arouet; 1694–1778) French writer. Letter, 1769

WILSON, (Thomas) Woodrow

(1856–1925) US statesman. He became Democratic president in 1913 and declared war on Germany in 1917. He negotiated the peace treaty in 1918, making the League of Nations a part of the treaty. For this measure he received no support in the Senate.

Quotations about Wilson

1 The spacious philanthropy which he exhaled upon Europe stopped quite sharply at the coasts of his own country.
Winston Churchill (1874–1965) British statesman. *World Crisis*

2 Like Odysseus, he looked wiser when seated.
John Maynard Keynes (1883–1946) British economist. *The Worldly Philosophers* (R. Heilbron)

Quotations by Wilson

3 Never murder a man who is committing suicide.
Mr Wilson's War (John Dos Passos), Pt. II, Ch. 10

4 Once lead this people into war and they'll forget there ever was such a thing as tolerance.
Mr Wilson's War (John Dos Passos), Pt. III, Ch. 2

5 America . . . is the prize amateur nation of the world. Germany is the prize professional nation.
Speech, Aug 1917. *Mr Wilson's War* (John Dos Passos), Pt. III, Ch. 13

6 The war we have just been through, though it was shot through with terror, is not to be compared with the war we would have to face next time.
Mr Wilson's War (John Dos Passos), Pt. V, Ch. 22

7 Right is more precious than peace.
Radio Times, 10 Sept 1964

8 Business underlies everything in our national life, including our spiritual life. Witness the fact that in the Lord's Prayer the first petition is for daily bread. No one can worship God or love his neighbor on an empty stomach.
Speech, New York, 1912

9 No nation is fit to sit in judgement upon any other nation.
Address, Apr 1915

10 There is such a thing as a man being too proud to fight.
Address to foreign-born citizens, 10 May 1915

11 The world must be made safe for democracy.
Address to Congress, asking for a declaration of war 2 Apr 1917

12 Sometimes people call me an idealist. Well, that is the way I know I am an American. America is the only idealistic nation in the world.
Speech, Sioux Falls, 8 Sept 1919

WIND

1 It's an ill wind that blows nobody any good.
Proverb

2 Mock on, mock on, Voltaire, Rousseau;
Mock on, mock on; 'tis all in vain!
You throw the sand against the wind,
And the wind blows it back again.
William Blake (1757–1827) British poet. *Mock on, mock on, Voltaire, Rousseau*

3 Absence is to love what wind is to fire; it extinguishes the small, it inflames the great.
Bussy-Rabutin (Roger de Rabutin, Comte de Bussy; 1618–93) French soldier and writer. *Histoire amoureuse des Gaules*

4 I have forgot much, Cynara! gone with the wind,
Flung roses, roses riotously with the throng.
Ernest Dowson (1867–1900) British lyric poet. *Non Sum Qualis Eram Bonae Sub Regno Cynarae*

5 Yes, 'n' how many years can some people exist
Before they're allowed to be free?
Yes, 'n' how many times can a man turn his head,
Pretending he just doesn't see?
The answer, my friend, is blowin' in the wind.
Bob Dylan (Robert Allen Zimmerman; 1941–) US popular singer. *Blowin' in the Wind*

6 I came like Water, and like Wind I go.
Edward Fitzgerald (1809–83) British poet. *The Rubáiyát of Omar Khayyám* (1st edn.), XXVIII

7 *Nullius addictus iurare in verba magistri,*
Quo me cumque rapit tempestas, deferor hospes.
Not bound to swear allegiance to any master, wherever the wind takes me I travel as a visitor.
Horace (Quintus Horatius Flaccus; 65–8 BC) Roman poet. *Nullius in verba* is the motto of the Royal Society. *Epistles*, I

8 Who has seen the wind?
Neither you nor I:
But when the trees bow down their heads,
The wind is passing by.
Christina Rossetti (1830–74) British poet. *Who Has Seen the Wind?*

9 Blow, blow, thou winter wind,
Thou art not so unkind
As man's ingratitude.
William Shakespeare (1564–1616) English dramatist. *As You Like It*, II:7

10 Blow, winds, and crack your cheeks; rage, blow.
You cataracts and hurricanoes, spout
Till you have drench'd our steeples, drown'd the cocks.
William Shakespeare *King Lear*, III:2

11 I wield the flail of the lashing hail,
And whiten the green plains under,
And then again I dissolve it in rain,
And laugh as I pass in thunder.
Percy Bysshe Shelley *The Cloud*

WINTER

See also months, seasons

1 Many human beings say that they enjoy the winter, but what they really enjoy is feeling proof against it.
Richard Adams (1920–) British novelist. *Watership Down*, Ch. 50

2 St Agnes' Eve – Ah, bitter chill it was!
The owl, for all his feathers, was a-cold;
The hare limp'd trembling through the frozen grass,
And silent was the flock in woolly fold.
John Keats (1795–1821) British poet. *The Eve of Saint Agnes*, I

3 Russia has two generals in whom she can confide – Generals Janvier and Février.
Nicholas I (1796–1855) Tsar of Russia. Referring to the Russian winter. Nicholas himself succumbed to a February cold in 1855 – the subject of the famous *Punch* Cartoon, 'General Février turned traitor', 10 Mar 1855. Attrib.

4 Winter is icummen in,
Lhude sing Goddamm,
Raineth drop and staineth slop
And how the wind doth ramm!
Sing: Goddamm.
Ezra Pound (1885–1972) US poet. *Ancient Music*

5 In the bleak mid-winter
Frosty wind made moan,
Earth stood hard as iron,
Water like a stone;
Snow had fallen, snow on snow,
Snow on snow,
In the bleak mid-winter,
Long ago.
Christina Rossetti (1830–74) British poet. *Mid-Winter*

6 When icicles hang by the wall,
And Dick the shepherd blows his nail,
And Tom bears logs into the hall,
And milk comes frozen home in pail,
When blood is nipp'd, and ways be foul,
Then nightly sings the staring owl:
'Tu-who;
Tu-whit, Tu-who' – A merry note,
While greasy Joan doth keel the pot.
William Shakespeare (1564–1616) English dramatist. *Love's Labour's Lost*, V:2

7 It is a winter's tale
That the snow blind twilight ferries over the lakes
And floating fields from the farm in the cup of the vales.
Dylan Thomas (1914–53) Welsh poet. *A Winter's Tale*

8 The comic almanacs give us dreadful pictures of January and February; but, in truth, the months which should be made to look gloomy in England are March and April. Let no man boast himself that he has got through the perils of winter till at least the seventh of May.
Anthony Trollope (1815–82) British novelist. *Doctor Thorne*, Ch. 47

WISDOM

See also intelligence, knowledge, prudence, wisdom and foolishness

1 It is easy to be wise after the event.
Proverb

2 For in much wisdom is much grief: and he that increaseth knowledge increaseth sorrow.
Bible: Ecclesiastes 1:18

3 The words of wise men are heard

in quiet more than the cry of him that ruleth among fools.
Bible: Ecclesiastes 9:17

4 The wisdom of a learned man cometh by opportunity of leisure: and he that hath little business shall become wise.
How can he get wisdom that holdeth the plough, and that glorieth in the goad, that driveth oxen, and is occupied in their labours, and whose talk is of bullocks?
Bible: Ecclesiasticus 38:24–25

5 With the ancient is wisdom; and in length of days understanding.
Bible: Job 12:12

6 No mention shall be made of coral, or of pearls: for the price of wisdom is above rubies.
Bible: Job 28:18

7 A wise man will hear, and will increase learning; and a man of understanding shall attain unto wise counsels:
To understand a proverb, and the interpretation; the words of the wise, and their dark sayings.
The fear of the Lord is the beginning of knowledge: but fools despise wisdom and instruction.
Bible: Proverbs 1:5–7

8 Wisdom is the principal thing; therefore get wisdom: and with all thy getting get understanding.
Bible: Proverbs 4:7

9 Wisdom hath builded her house, she hath hewn out her seven pillars.
Bible: Proverbs 9:1

10 For wisdom is more moving than any motion: she passeth and go through all things by reason of her pureness.
For she is the breath of the power of God, and a pure influence flowing from the glory of the Almighty: therefore can no defiled thing fall into her.
Bible: Wisdom 7:24–25

11 Wisdom reacheth from one end to another mightily: and sweetly doth she order all things.
Bible: Wisdom 8:1

12 Does the Eagle know what is in the pit
Or wilt thou go ask the Mole?
Can Wisdom be put in a silver rod,
Or love in a golden bowl?
William Blake (1757–1827) British poet. *The Book of Thel,* 'Thel's Motto'

13 I care not whether a man is Good or Evil; all that I care
Is whether he is a Wise Man or a Fool. Go! put off Holiness,
And put on Intellect.
William Blake *Jerusalem*

14 Be wiser than other people if you can, but do not tell them so.
Earl of Chesterfield (1694–1773) English statesman. Letter to his son, 19 Nov 1745

15 A sadder and a wiser man,
He rose the morrow morn.
Samuel Taylor Coleridge (1772–1834) British poet. *The Rime of the Ancient Mariner,* VII

16 If one is too lazy to think, too vain to do a thing badly, too cowardly to admit it, one will never attain wisdom.
Cyril Connolly (1903–74) British journalist. *The Unquiet Grave*

17 Knowledge dwells
In heads replete with thoughts of other men;
Wisdom in minds attentive to their own.
William Cowper (1731–1800) British poet. *The Task*

18 Some are weather-wise, some are otherwise.
Benjamin Franklin (1706–90) US scientist and statesman. *Poor Richard's Almanack*

19 Self-reflection is the school of wisdom.
Baltasar Gracián (1601–58) Spanish writer and Jesuit. *The Art of Worldly Wisdom,* 69

20 Knowledge can be communicated but not wisdom.
Hermann Hesse (1877–1962) German novelist and poet. *Siddhartha*

21 It is the province of knowledge to speak and it is the privilege of wisdom to listen.
Oliver Wendell Holmes (1809–94) US writer. *The Poet at the Breakfast Table,* Ch. 10

22 Vain wisdom all, and false philosophy.
John Milton (1608–74) English poet. *Paradise Lost,* Bk. II

23 There is more wisdom in your body than in your deepest philosophy.
Friedrich Nietzsche (1844–1900) German philosopher. *Human, All Too Human,* Pt. II

24 The young man who has not wept is a savage, and the old man who will not laugh is a fool.
George Santayana (1863–1952) US philosopher. *Dialogues in Limbo,* Ch. 3

25 Thou speakest wiser than thou art ware of.
William Shakespeare (1564–1616) English dramatist. *As You Like It,* II:4

26 I never knew so young a body with so old a head.
William Shakespeare *The Merchant of Venice,* IV:1

27 This fellow's wise enough to play the fool,
And to do that well craves a kind of wit.
William Shakespeare *Twelfth Night,* III:1

28 Possibly no wiser, My Lord, but far better informed.
F. E. Smith (1872–1930) British lawyer and politician. To judge who complained that he had listened to Smith's argument but was still none the wiser. *Life of F. E. Smith* (Birkenhead)

29 Some folk are wise, and some are otherwise.
Tobias Smollett (1721–71) British novelist. *Roderick Random,* Ch. 6

30 An ounce of a man's own wit is worth a ton of other people's.
Laurence Sterne (1713–68) Irish-born British writer. *Tristram Shandy*

31 Sciences may be learned by rote, but Wisdom not.
Laurence Sterne *Tristram Shandy*

32 Oh, Vanity of vanities!
How wayward the decrees of Fate are;
How very weak the very wise,
How very small the very great are!
William Makepeace Thackeray (1811–63) British novelist. *Vanitas Vanitatum*

33 It is never wise to try to appear to be more clever than you are. It is sometimes wise to appear slightly less so.
William Whitelaw (1918–) British politician. *The Observer,* 'Sayings of the Year', 1975

WISDOM AND FOOLISHNESS

1 Then I saw that wisdom excelleth folly, as far as light excelleth darkness.
The wise man's eyes are in his head; but the fool walketh in darkness: and I myself perceived also that one event happeneth to them all.
Bible: Ecclesiastes 2:13–14

2 But God hath chosen the foolish things of the world to confound the wise; and God hath chosen the weak things of the world to

confound the things which are mighty.
Bible: I Corinthians 1:27

3 For ye suffer fools gladly, seeing ye yourselves are wise.
Bible: II Corinthians 11:19

4 Therefore whosoever heareth these sayings of mine, and doeth them, I will liken him unto a wise man, which built his house upon a rock:
And the rain descended, and the floods came, and the winds blew, and beat upon that house; and it fell not: for it was founded upon a rock.
And every one that heareth these sayings of mine, and doeth them not, shall be likened unto a foolish man, which built his house upon the sand:
And the rain descended, and the floods came, and the winds blew, and beat upon that house; and it fell: and great was the fall of it.
Bible: Matthew 7:24–27

5 And at midnight there was a cry made, Behold, the bridegroom cometh; go ye out to meet him.
Then all those virgins arose, and trimmed their lamps.
And the foolish said unto the wise, Give us of your oil; for our lamps are gone out.
Bible: Matthew 25:6–8

6 A fool sees not the same tree that a wise man sees.
William Blake (1757–1827) British poet. *The Marriage of Heaven and Hell*, 'Proverbs of Hell'

7 Many have been the wise speeches of fools, though not so many as the foolish speeches of wise men.
Thomas Fuller (1608–61) English historian. *The Holy State and the Profane State*

8 Give me the young man who has brains enough to make a fool of himself!
Robert Louis Stevenson (1850–94) Scottish writer. *Virginibus Puerisque*

WIT

See humor

WODEHOUSE, Sir P(elham) G(renville)

(1881–1975) British humorous novelist. His books feature the 1920s upper-class bachelor Bertie Wooster and his immaculate manservant Jeeves. He lived abroad, becoming a US citizen in 1955.

Quotations about Wodehouse

1 P. G. Wodehouse, whose works I place a little below Shakespeare's and any distance you like above anybody else's.
James Agate (1877–1947) British theater critic. *P. G. Wodehouse* (David A. Jasen)

2 English Literature's performing flea.
Sean O'Casey (1884–1964) Irish dramatist. Attrib.

Quotations by Wodehouse

3 All the unhappy marriages come from the husbands having brains. What good are brains to a man? They only unsettle him.
The Adventures of Sally

4 It is no use telling me that there are bad aunts and good aunts. At the core they are all alike. Sooner or later, out pops the cloven hoof.
The Code of the Woosters

5 He spoke with a certain what-is-it in his voice, and I could see that, if not actually disgruntled, he was far from being gruntled.
The Code of the Woosters

6 Big chap with a small moustache and the sort of eye that can open an oyster at sixty paces.
The Code of the Woosters

7 Jeeves coughed one soft, low, gentle cough like a sheep with a blade of grass stuck in its throat.
The Inimitable Jeeves, Ch. 13

8 It was my Uncle George who discovered that alcohol was a food well in advance of modern medical thought.
The Inimitable Jeeves, Ch. 16

9 It is a good rule in life never to apologize. The right sort of people do not want apologies, and the wrong sort take a mean advantage of them.
The Man Upstairs

10 New York is a small place when it comes to the part of it that wakes up just as the rest is going to bed.
My Man Jeeves, 'The Aunt and the Sluggard'

11 His ideas of first-aid stopped short at squirting soda-water.
My Man Jeeves, 'Doing Clarence a Bit of Good'

12 I don't owe a penny to a single soul – not counting tradesmen, of course.
My Man Jeeves, 'Jeeves and the Hard-Boiled Egg'

13 She fitted into my biggest armchair as if it had been built round her by someone who knew they were wearing armchairs tight about the hips that season.
My Man Jeeves, 'Jeeves and the Unbidden Guest'

14 I spent the afternoon musing on Life. If you come to think of it, what a queer thing Life is! So unlike anything else, don't you know, if you see what I mean.
My Man Jeeves, 'Rallying Round Old George'

15 If I had had to choose between him and a cockroach as a companion for a walking-tour, the cockroach would have had it by a short head.
My Man Jeeves, 'The Spot of Art'

16 There is only one cure for grey hair. It was invented by a Frenchman. It is called the guillotine.
The Old Reliable

17 I can honestly say that I always look on Pauline as one of the nicest girls I was ever engaged to.
Thank You Jeeves, Ch. 6

18 The Right Hon. was a tubby little chap who looked as if he had been poured into his clothes and had forgotten to say 'When!'
Very Good Jeeves!, 'Jeeves and the Impending Doom'

19 The stationmaster's whiskers are of a Victorian bushiness and give the impression of having been grown under glass.
Wodehouse at Work to the End (Richard Usborne), Ch. 2

20 Like so many substantial Americans, he had married young and kept on marrying, springing from blonde to blonde like the chamois of the Alps leaping from crag to crag.
Wodehouse at Work to the End (Richard Usborne), Ch. 2

21 Unlike the male codfish which, suddenly finding itself the parent of three million five hundred thousand little codfish, cheerfully resolves to love them all, the British aristocracy is apt to look with a

somewhat jaundiced eye on its younger sons.
Wodehouse at Work to the End (Richard Usborne), Ch. 5

22 He was either a man of about a hundred and fifty who was rather young for his years or a man of about a hundred and ten who had been aged by trouble.
Wodehouse at Work to the End (Richard Usborne), Ch. 6

23 It is never difficult to distinguish between a Scotsman with a grievance and a ray of sunshine.
Wodehouse at Work to the End (Richard Usborne), Ch. 8

WOMAN'S ROLE

See also feminism, housework, marriage, women, sexes

1 God could not be everywhere and therefore he made mothers.
Jewish proverb

2 What they say of us is that we have a peaceful time
Living at home, while they do the fighting in war.
How wrong they are! I would very much rather stand
Three times in the front of battle than bear one child.
Euripides (484 BC–406 BC) Greek tragic dramatist. *Medea*, 248

3 Mother is the dead heart of the family, spending father's earnings on consumer goods to enhance the environment in which he eats, sleeps and watches the television.
Germaine Greer (1939–) Australian-born British writer and feminist. *The Female Eunuch*

4 She-who-must-be-obeyed.
Henry Rider Haggard (1856–1925) British novelist. *She*

5 These are rare attainments for a damsel, but pray tell me, can she spin?
James I (1566–1625) King of England. On being introduced to a young girl proficient in Latin, Greek, and Hebrew. Attrib.

6 A man is in general better pleased when he has a good dinner upon his table, than when his wife talks Greek.
Samuel Johnson (1709–84) British lexicographer. *Johnsonian Miscellanies* (ed. G. B. Hill), Vol. II

7 To promote a Woman to bear rule, superiority, dominion or empire, above any Realm, Nation, or City, is repugnant to Nature; contumely to God, a thing most contrarious to his revealed will and approved ordinance, and finally it is the subversion of good Order, of all equity and justice.
John Knox (c. 1514–72) Scottish religious reformer. Opening words. *First Blast of the Trumpet against the Monstrous Regiment of Women*

8 Women exist in the main solely for the propagation of the species.
Arthur Schopenhauer (1788–1860) German philosopher.

9 Vain man is apt to think we were merely intended for the world's propagation and to keep its humane inhabitants sweet and clean; but, by their leaves, had we the same literature he would find our brains as fruitful as our bodies.
Hanna Woolley *Gentlewoman's Companion*, 1675

WOMEN

See also feminism

1 A man of straw is worth a woman of gold.
Proverb

2 A woman's place is in the home.
Proverb

3 A woman's work is never done.
Proverb

4 Six men give a doctor less to do than one woman.
Proverb

5 The hand that rocks the cradle rules the world.
Proverb

6 An ailing woman lives forever.
Spanish proverb

7 Old-fashioned ways which no longer apply to changed conditions are a snare in which the feet of women have always become readily entangled.
Jane Addams (1860–1935) US social worker. In *Newer Ideals of Peace*, 'Utilization of Women in City Government'

8 The woman that deliberates is lost.
Joseph Addison (1672–1719) British essayist. *Cato*, IV:1

9 A woman seldom asks advice until she has bought her wedding clothes.
Joseph Addison *The Spectator*, 475

10 . . . girls are so queer you never know what they mean. They say No when they mean Yes, and drive a man out of his wits for the fun of it . . .
Louisa May Alcott (1832–88) US novelist. *Little Women*, Pt. II

11 Votes for Women.
Anonymous Slogan

12 It is almost a pity that a woman has a womb.
Anonymous *Woman and Nature* (Susan Griffin)

13 The sort of woman who, if accidentally locked in alone in the National Gallery, would start rearranging the pictures.
Anonymous

14 A woman, especially if she have the misfortune of knowing anything, should conceal it as well as she can.
Jane Austen (1775–1817) British novelist. *Northanger Abbey*, Ch. 14

15 A lady's imagination is very rapid; it jumps from admiration to love, from love to matrimony in a moment.
Jane Austen *Pride and Prejudice*, Ch. 6

16 Next to being married, a girl likes to be crossed in love a little now and then.
Jane Austen *Pride and Prejudice*, Ch. 24

17 Women – one half the human race at least – care fifty times more for a marriage than a ministry.
Walter Bagehot (1826–77) British economist and journalist. *The English Constitution*, 'The Monarchy'

18 Every man who is high up likes to feel that he has done it himself; and the wife smiles, and lets it go at that. It's our only joke. Every woman knows that.
J. M. Barrie (1860–1937) British playwright. *Peter Pan*

19 One is not born a woman, one becomes one.
Simone de Beauvoir (1908–86) French writer. *Le Deuxième Sexe* (trans. *The Second Sex*)

20 It is in great part the anxiety of being a woman that devastates the feminine body.
Simone de Beauvoir *Womansize* (Kim Chernin)

21 You will find that the woman who is really kind to dogs is always one who has failed to inspire sympathy in men.
Max Beerbohm (1872–1956) British writer. *Zuleika Dobson*, Ch. 6

22 And the Lord God caused a deep

sleep to fall upon Adam, and he slept: and he took one of his ribs, and closed up the flesh instead thereof;
And the rib, which the Lord God had taken from man, made he a woman, and brought her unto the man.
And Adam said, This is now bone of my bones, and flesh of my flesh: she shall be called Woman, because she was taken out of Man.
Therefore shall a man leave his father and his mother, and shall cleave unto his wife: and they shall be one flesh.
And they were both naked, the man and his wife, and were not ashamed.

Bible: Genesis 2:21–25

23 For the lips of a strange woman drop as an honeycomb, and her mouth is smoother than oil:
But her end is bitter as wormwood, sharp as a two-edged sword.

Bible: Proverbs 5:3–4

24 Who can find a virtuous woman? for her price is far above rubies
The heart of her husband doth safely trust in her, so that he shall have no need of spoil.
She will do him good and not evil all the days of her life.

Bible: Proverbs 31:10–12

25 Intimacies between women often go backwards, beginning in revelations and ending in small talk without loss of esteem.

Elizabeth Bowen (1899–1973) Irish novelist. *The Death of the Heart*

26 Why need the other women know so much?

Robert Browning (1812–89) British poet. *Any Wife to any Husband*

27 The souls of women are so small,
That some believe they've none at all.

Samuel Butler (1612–80) English satirist. *Miscellaneous Thoughts*

28 Brigands demand your money or your life; women require both.

Samuel Butler Attrib.

29 I thought it would appear
That there had been a lady in the case.

Lord Byron (1788–1824) British poet. *Don Juan*, V

30 Do you know why God withheld the sense of humour from women?
That we may love you instead of laughing at you.

Mrs Patrick Campbell (1865–1940) British actress. To a man. *The Life of Mrs Pat* (M. Peters)

31 Women are much more like each other than men: they have, in truth, but two passions, vanity and love; these are their universal characteristics.

Earl of Chesterfield (1694–1773) English statesman. Letter to his son, 19 Dec 1749

32 There is no fury like an ex-wife searching for a new lover.

Cyril Connolly (1903–74) British journalist. *The Unquiet Grave*

33 Certain women should be struck regularly, like gongs.

Noël Coward (1899–1973) British dramatist. *Private Lives*

34 Mother love, particularly in America, is a highly respected and much publicised emotion and when exacerbated by gin and bourbon it can become extremely formidable.

Noël Coward *Future Indefinite*

35 What is woman? – only one of Nature's agreeable blunders.

Hannah Cowley (1743–1809) British poet and dramatist. *Who's the Dupe?*, II

36 Here's to the lot of them, murderer, thief,
Forger and lunatic too, Sir –
Infants, and those who get parish relief,
And women, it's perfectly true, Sir –
Please to take note, they are in the same boat:
They have not a chance of recording the vote.

H. Crawford Referring to the women's suffrage movement. *In the Same Boat*

37 Women never have young minds. They are born three thousand years old.

Shelagh Delaney (1939–) British dramatist. *A Taste of Honey*, I:1

38 'She's the sort of woman now,' said Mould, . . . 'one would almost feel disposed to bury for nothing: and do it neatly, too!'

Charles Dickens (1812–70) British novelist. *Martin Chuzzlewit*, Ch. 25

39 Women are most fascinating between the ages of thirty-five and forty, after they have won a few races and know how to pace themselves. Since few women ever pass forty, maximum fascination can continue indefinitely.

Christian Dior (1905–57) French couturier. *Colliers Magazine*, 10 June 1955

40 Girls bored me – they still do. I love Mickey Mouse more than any woman I've ever known.

Walt Disney (1901–66) US film-maker. *You Must Remember This* (W. Wagner)

41 It is only the women whose eyes have been washed clear with tears who get the broad vision that makes them little sisters to all the world.

Dorothy Dix (Elizabeth Meriwether Gilmer; 1861–1951) US journalist and writer. *Dorothy Dix, Her Book*, Introduction

42 There are only three things to be done with a woman. You can love her, you can suffer for her, or you can turn her into literature.

Lawrence Durrell (1912–) British novelist. *Justine*

43 All Berkshire women are very silly. I don't know why women in Berkshire are more silly than anywhere else.

Claude Duveen (1903–) British judge. Said in Reading County Court, July 1972.

44 She takes just like a woman, yes, she does
She makes love just like a woman, yes, she does
And she aches just like a woman
But she breaks just like a little girl.

Bob Dylan (Robert Allen Zimmerman; 1941–) US popular singer. *Just Like a Woman*

45 I should like to know what is the proper function of women, if it is not to make reasons for husbands to stay at home, and still stronger reasons for bachelors to go out.

George Eliot (Mary Ann Evans; 1819–80) British novelist. *The Mill on the Floss*, Ch. 6

46 In the room the women come and go
Talking of Michelangelo.

T. S. Eliot (1888–1965) US-born British poet and dramatist. *The Love Song of J. Alfred Prufrock*

47 When a woman behaves like a man, why doesn't she behave like a nice man?

Edith Evans (1888–1976) British actress. *The Observer*, 'Sayings of the Week', 30 Sept 1956

48 A woman should be an illusion.

Ian Fleming (1908–64) British writer. *Life of Ian Fleming* (John Pearson)

49 The great question . . . which I have not been able to answer, despite my thirty years of research into the feminine soul, is 'What does a woman want?'

Sigmund Freud (1856–1939) Austrian psychoanalyst. *Psychiatry in American Life* (Charles Rolo)

50 Women are equal because they are not different any more.

Erich Fromm (1910–80) US writer. *The Art of Loving*

51 How, like a moth, the simple maid
Still plays about the flame!

John Gay (1685–1732) English poet and dramatist. *The Beggar's Opera*

52 Fighting is essentially a masculine idea; a woman's weapon is her tongue.

Hermione Gingold (1897–1987) British actress. Attrib.

53 I know you do not make the laws but I also know that you are the wives and mothers, the sisters and daughters of those who do . . .

Angelina Grimké (1805–79) US writer and reformer. *The Anti-Slavery Examiner* (Sep 1836), 'Appeal to the Christian Women of the South'

54 There Is Nothin' Like a Dame.

Oscar Hammerstein II (1895–1960) US lyricist. *South Pacific*, Title of song

55 If men knew how women pass their time when they are alone, they'd never marry.

O. Henry (William Sidney Porter; 1862–1910) US short-story writer. *The Four Million Memoirs of a Yellow Dog*

56 O! men with sisters dear,
O! men with mothers and wives!
It is not linen you're wearing out,
But human creatures' lives!

Thomas Hood (1799–1845) British poet. *The Song of the Shirt*

57 Why should human females become sterile in the forties, while female crocodiles continue to lay eggs into their third century?

Aldous Huxley (1894–1964) British writer. *After Many a Summer*, I, Ch. 5

58 A woman's preaching is like a dog's walking on his hinder legs. It is not done well; but you are surprised to find it done at all.

Samuel Johnson (1709–84) British lexicographer. *Life of Johnson* (J. Boswell), Vol. I

59 No one delights more in vengeance than a woman.

Juvenal (Decimus Junius Juvenalis; 60–130 AD) Roman satirist. *Satires*, XIII

60 He play'd an ancient ditty, long since mute,
In Provence call'd, 'La belle dame sans mercy'.

John Keats (1795–1821) British poet. *The Eve of Saint Agnes*, XXXIII

61 When the Himalayan peasant meets the he-bear in his pride,
He shouts to scare the monster, who will often turn aside.
But the she-bear thus accosted rends the peasant tooth and nail
For the female of the species is more deadly than the male.

Rudyard Kipling (1865–1936) Indian-born British writer. *The Female of the Species*

62 And a woman is only a woman, but a good cigar is a smoke.

Rudyard Kipling *The Betrothed*

63 The First Blast of the Trumpet Against the Monstrous Regiment of Women.

John Knox (c. 1514–72) Scottish religious reformer. Title of Pamphlet, 1558

64 Women run to extremes; they are either better or worse than men.

Jean de La Bruyère (1645–96) French satirist. *Les Caractères*

65 Nobody can have the soul of me. My mother has had it, and nobody can have it again. Nobody can come into my very self again, and breathe me like an atmosphere.

D. H. Lawrence (1885–1930) British novelist. *Letters*

66 Thank heaven for little girls,
For little girls get bigger every day.

Alan Jay Lerner (1918–86) US lyricist and playwright. *Gigi*, 'Thank Heaven for Little Girls'

67 The female breast has been called 'the badge of feminity'. In order for the breast to be aesthetically pleasing, it should be a relatively firm, full breast which stands out from the chest wall and states with certainty, 'I am feminine'.

John Ransom Lewis Jnr M.D. *Atlas of Aesthetic Plastic Surgery*

68 I see some rats have got in; let them squeal, it doesn't matter.

David Lloyd George (1863–1945) British Liberal statesman. Said when suffragettes interrupted a meeting. *The Faber Book of English History in Verse* (Kenneth Baker)

69 So this gentleman said a girl with brains ought to do something else with them besides think.

Anita Loos (1891–1981) US novelist. *Gentlemen Prefer Blondes*, Ch. 1

70 Women do not find it difficult nowadays to behave like men; but they often find it extremely difficult to behave like gentlemen.

Compton Mackenzie (1883–1972) British writer. *On Moral Courage*

71 If you educate a man you educate a person, but if you educate a woman you educate a family.

Ruby Manikan (20th century) Indian Church leader. *The Observer*, 'Sayings of the Week', 30 Mar 1947

72 A woman should open everything to a man except her mouth.

Derek Marlowe *A Dandy in Aspic*

73 The Professor of Gynaecology began his course of lectures as follows: Gentlemen, woman is an animal that micturates once a day, defecates once a week, menstruates once a month, parturates once a year and copulates whenever she has the opportunity.

W. Somerset Maugham (1874–1965) British novelist. *A Writer's Notebook*

74 American women expect to find in their husbands a perfection that English women only hope to find in their butlers.

W. Somerset Maugham *A Writer's Notebook*

75 A woman will always sacrifice herself if you give her the opportunity. It is her favourite form of self-indulgence.

W. Somerset Maugham *The Circle*, III

76 Because women can do nothing except love, they've given it a ridiculous importance.

W. Somerset Maugham *The Moon and Sixpence*, Ch. 41

77 Thousands of American women know far more about the subconscious than they do about sewing.

H. L. Mencken (1880–1956) US journalist. *Prejudices*

78 When women kiss, it always reminds me of prize-fighters shaking hands.

H. L. Mencken Attrib.

79 I expect that Woman will be the last thing civilized by Man.

George Meredith (1828–1909) British novelist. *The Ordeal of Richard Feverel*, Ch. 1

80 One tongue is sufficient for a woman.

John Milton (1608–74) English poet. On being asked whether he would allow his daughters to learn foreign languages. Attrib.

81 I shrug my shoulders in despair at women who moan at the lack of opportunities and then take two weeks off as a result of falling out with their boyfriends.
Sophie Mirman British business woman. On receiving the *Business Woman of the Year Award.*

82 The moral world of the sick-bed explains in a measure some of the things that are strange in daily life, and the man who does not know sick women does not know women.
S. Weir Mitchell (1829–1914) *Doctor and Patient,* Introduction

83 Women would rather be right than reasonable.
Ogden Nash (1902–71) US poet. *Frailty, Thy Name is a Misnomer*

84 God created woman. And boredom did indeed cease from that moment – but many other things ceased as well! Woman was God's *second* mistake.
Friedrich Wilhelm Nietzsche (1844–1900) German philosopher. *The Antichrist*

85 When I think of women, it is their hair which first comes to my mind. The very idea of womanhood is a storm of hair . . . .
Friedrich Nietzsche *My Sister and I*

86 When a woman becomes a scholar there is usually something wrong with her sexual organs.
Friedrich Nietzche *Bartlett's Unfamiliar Quotations* (Leonard Louis Levinson)

87 If women didn't exist, all the money in the world would have no meaning.
Aristotle Onassis (1906–75) Greek businessman. Attrib.

88 The surgical cycle in woman: Appendix removed, right kidney hooked up, gall-bladder taken out, gastro-enterostomy, clean sweep of uterus and adnexa.
William Osler (1849–1919) Canadian physician. *Sir William Osler: Aphorisms* (William B. Bean)

89 Whether a pretty woman grants or withholds her favours, she always likes to be asked for them.
Ovid (Publius Ovidius Naso; 43 BC–17 AD) Roman poet. *Ars Amatoria*

90 So greatly did she care for freedom that she died for it. So dearly did she love women that she offered her life as their ransom. That is the verdict given at the great Inquest of the Nation on the death of Emily Wilding Davison.
Christabel Pankhurst (1880–1958) British suffragette. Emily Davison threw herself under the King's horse in protest at the imprisoning of suffragettes. *The Suffragette,* 13 June 1913

91 Most good women are hidden treasures who are only safe because nobody looks for them.
Dorothy Parker (1893–1967) US writer. Obituary, *The New York Times,* 8 June 1967

92 My wife, who, poor wretch, is troubled with her lonely life.
Samuel Pepys (1633–1703) English diarist. *Diary,* 19 Dec 1662

93 There are two kinds of women – goddesses and doormats.
Pablo Picasso (1881–1973) Spanish painter. Attrib.

94 Most women have no characters at all.
Alexander Pope (1688–1744) British poet. *Moral Essays,* II

95 Men, some to business, some to pleasure take;
But every woman is at heart a rake.
Alexander Pope *Moral Essays,* II

96 Woman's at best a contradiction still.
Alexander Pope *Moral Essays,* II

97 Bah! I have sung women in three cities,
But it is all the same;
And I will sing of the sun.
Ezra Pound (1885–1972) US poet. *Cino*

98 In a matriarchy men should be encouraged to take it easy, for most women prefer live husbands to blocks of shares and seats on the board.
J. B. Priestley (1894–1984) British novelist. *Thoughts in the Wilderness*

99 . . . it being natural and comely to women to nourish their hair, which even God and nature have given them for a covering, a token of subjection, and a natural badge to distinguish them from men.
William Prynne (1600–69) English Puritan. *Histriomastix*

100 The doctors said at the time that she couldn't live more than a fortnight, and she's been trying ever since to see if she could. Women are so opinionated.
Saki (Hector Hugh Munro; 1870–1916) British writer. *Reginald on Women*

101 The fundamental fault of the female character is that it has no sense of justice.
Arthur Schopenhauer (1788–1860) German philosopher. *Gedanken über vielerlei Gegenstände,* XXVII

102 Do you not know I am a woman? When I think, I must speak.
William Shakespeare (1564–1616) English dramatist. *As You Like It,* III:2

103 I know that a woman is a dish for the gods, if the devil dress her not.
William Shakespeare *Antony and Cleopatra,* V:2

104 Frailty, thy name is woman!
William Shakespeare *Hamlet,* I:2

105 She's beautiful and therefore to be woo'd;
She is a woman therefore to be won.
William Shakespeare *Henry VI,* Pt. 1, V:3

106 O tiger's heart wrapp'd in a woman's hide!
William Shakespeare *Henry VI,* Pt. 3, I:4

107 Would it not grieve a woman to be over-mastered with a piece of valiant dust? to make an account of her life to a clod of wayward marl?
William Shakespeare *Much Ado About Nothing,* II:1

108 I have no other but a woman's reason:
I think him so, because I think him so.
William Shakespeare *The Two Gentlemen of Verona,* I:2

109 This Englishwoman is so refined
She has no bosom and no behind.
Stevie Smith (Florence Margaret Smith; 1902–71) British poet. *This Englishwoman*

110 Womanhood is the great fact in her life; wifehood and motherhood are but incidental relations.
Elizabeth Stanton (1815–1902) US suffragette. *History of Woman Suffrage* (with Susan B. Anthony and Mathilda Gage), Vol. I

111 A ship is sooner rigged than a gentlewoman made ready.
Philip Stubbs *The Anatomie of Abuses*

112 The really original woman is the one who first imitates a man.
Italo Svevo (Ettore Schmitz; 1861–1928) Italian writer. *A Life,* Ch. 8

113 God made the woman for the man,
And for the good and increase of the world.
Alfred, Lord Tennyson (1809–92) British poet. *Edwin Morris*

114 How sweet are looks that ladies bend
On whom their favours fall!
Alfred, Lord Tennyson *Sir Galahad*

115 I've got woman's ability to stick to a job and get on with it when everyone else walks off and leaves it.
Margaret Thatcher (1925–) British politician and prime minister. *The Observer*, 'Sayings of the Week', 16 Feb 1975

116 It is a great glory in a woman to show no more weakness than is natural to her sex, and not be talked of, either for good or evil by men.
Thucydides (c. 460–c. 400 BC) Greek historian and general. *History of the Peloponnesian War*, Bk. II, Ch. 45

117 I was seized by the stern hand of Compulsion, that dark, unseasonable Urge that impels women to clean house in the middle of the night.
James Thurber (1894–1961) US humorist. *Alarms and Diversions*, 'There's a Time for Flags'

118 I am a source of satisfaction to him, a nurse, a piece of furniture, a *woman* – nothing more.
Sophie Tolstoy (1844–1919) Russian writer. *A Diary of Tolstoy's Wife, 1860–1891*

119 With many women I doubt whether there be any more effectual way of touching their hearts than ill-using them and then confessing it. If you wish to get the sweetest fragrance from the herb at your feet, tread on it and bruise it.
Anthony Trollope (1815–82) British novelist. *Miss Mackenzie*, Ch. 10

120 Scarce, sir. Mighty scarce.
Mark Twain (Samuel Langhorne Clemens; 1835–1910) US writer. Responding to the question 'In a world without women what would men become?'. Attrib.

121 Woman is unrivaled as a wet nurse.
Mark Twain Attrib.

122 As if a woman of education bought things because she wanted 'em.
John Vanbrugh (1664–1726) English architect and dramatist. *The Confederacy*, II:1

123 Once a woman has given you her heart you can never get rid of the rest of her.
John Vanbrugh *The Relapse*, II:1

124 Woman is always fickle and changing.
Virgil (Publius Vergilius Maro; 70–19 BC) Roman poet. *Aeneid*, Bk. IV

125 I have often observed in women of her type a tendency to regard all athletics as inferior forms of fox-hunting.
Evelyn Waugh (1903–66) British novelist. *Decline and Fall*, Pt. I, Ch. 10

126 'I will not stand for being called a woman in my own house,' she said.
Evelyn Waugh *Scoop*, Bk. I, Ch. 5

127 There is nothing in the whole world so unbecoming to a woman as a Nonconformist conscience.
Oscar Wilde (1854–1900) Irish-born British dramatist. *Lady Windermere's Fan*, III

128 I would venture to guess that Anon, who wrote so many poems without signing them, was often a woman.
Virginia Woolf (1882–1941) British novelist. *A Room of One's Own*

129 Women have served all these centuries as looking-glasses possessing the magic and delicious power of reflecting the figure of man at twice its natural size.
Virginia Woolf *A Room of One's Own*

WOMEN'S LIB

1 I owe nothing to Women's Lib.
Margaret Thatcher (1925–) British politician and prime minister. *The Observer*, 'Sayings of the Week', 1 Dec 1974

2 Opening the door is a political act. The door-opening ceremony represents a non-obtrusive measure of authority. The hand that holds the door-knob rules the world.
Professor Laurel Richardson Walum US university professor. Referring to Women's Lib. *The Observer*, 'Sayings of the Week', 9 Sept 1973

WONDER

See also admiration, curiosity

1 For all knowledge and wonder (which is the seed of knowledge) is an impression of pleasure in itself.
Francis Bacon (1561–1626) English philosopher. *The Advancement of Learning*, Bk. I, Ch. 1

2 To see a World in a grain of sand,
And a Heaven in a wild flower,
Hold Infinity in the palm of your hand,
And Eternity in an hour.
William Blake (1757–1827) British poet. *Auguries of Innocence*

3 Two things fill the mind with ever new and increasing wonder and awe, the more often and the more seriously reflection concentrates upon them: the starry heaven above me and the moral law within me.
Immanuel Kant (1724–1804) German philosopher. *Critique of Practical Reason*, Conclusion

4 . . . now in Ireland, now in England, now in Normandy, he must fly rather than travel by horse or ship.
Louis VII (c. 1120–80) King of France. Referring to Henry II of England. *Imagines Historiarum* (Ralph de Diceto)

5 Philosophy is the product of wonder.
A. N. Whitehead (1861–1947) British philosopher. *Nature and Life*, Ch. 1

WORDS

See also language, speech, verbosity

1 Actions speak louder than words.
Proverb

2 In the beginning was the Word, and the Word was with God, and the Word was God.
Bible: John 1:1

3 He said true things, but called them by wrong names.
Robert Browning (1812–89) British poet. *Bishop Blougram's Apology*

4 Oaths are but words, and words but wind.
Samuel Butler (1612–80) English satirist. *Hudibras*, Pt. II

5 Be not the slave of Words.
Thomas Carlyle (1795–1881) Scottish historian and essayist. *Sartor Resartus*, Bk I, Ch. 8

6 We must have a better word than 'prefabricated'. Why not 'ready-made'?
Winston Churchill (1874–1965) British statesman. *Closing the Ring*, Appendix C

7 Words as is well known, are great foes of reality.
Joseph Conrad (Teodor Josef Konrad Korzeniowski; 1857–1924) Polish-born British novelist. *Under Western Eyes*

8 When a diplomat says yes, he means perhaps. When he says perhaps he means no. When he says no, he is not a diplomat. When a lady says no, she means perhaps. When she says perhaps, she means yes. But when she says yes, she is no lady.
Lord Denning (1899–) British lawyer. Speech, 14 Oct 1982

9 Ad-i-ad-o-cho-kin-e-sis

Is a term that will bolster my thesis
That 'tis idle to seek
Such precision in Greek
When confusion it only increases.

Horace B. and Ava C. English (1892–1961; fl. 20th century) *A Comprehensive Dictionary of Psychological and Psychoanalytical Terms*

10 When there is no explanation, they give it a name, which immediately explains everything.

Martin H. Fischer (1879–1962) *Fischerisms* (Howard Fabing and Ray Marr)

11 Whenever ideas fail, men invent words.

Martin H. Fischer *Fischerisms* (Howard Fabing and Ray Marr)

12 You can stroke people with words.

F. Scott Fitzgerald (1896–1940) US novelist. *The Crack-up*

13 It was in the barbarous, gothic times when words had a meaning; in those days, writers expressed thoughts.

Anatole France (Jacques Anatole François Thibault; 1844–1924) French writer. *The Literary Life*, 'M. Charles Morice'

14 Some seventy years ago a promising young neurologist made a discovery that necessitated the addition of a new word to the English vocabulary. He insisted that this should be *knee-jerk*, and *knee-jerk* it has remained, in spite of the efforts of *patellar reflex* to dislodge it. He was my father; so perhaps I have inherited a prejudice in favour of home-made words.

Ernest Gowers (1880–1966) *Plain Words*, Ch. 5

15 The Spanish doctor who treated Yeats in Majorca reported to his Irish colleague. 'We have here an antique cardio-sclerotic of advanced years.' Gogarty tried to slur over the death sentence. 'Read it slowly and distinctly,' Yeats ordered. He inclined his head. He followed the cadence with his finger. As the sound died away he exclaimed, 'Do you know, I would rather be called 'Cardio-Sclerotic' than Lord of Lower Egypt.'

T. R. Henn *The Lonely Tower*

16 Many terms which have now dropped out of favour, will be revived, and those that are at present respectable will drop out, if usage so choose, with whom resides the decision and the judgement and the code of speech.

Horace (Quintus Horatius Flaccus; 65–8 BC) Roman poet. *Ars Poetica*

17 Thanks to words, we have been able to rise above the brutes; and thanks to words, we have often sunk to the level of the demons.

Aldous Huxley (1894–1964) British novelist. *Adonis and the Alphabet*

18 *Net.* Anything reticulated or decussated at equal distances, with interstices between the intersections.

Samuel Johnson (1709–84) British lexicographer. *Dictionary of the English Language*

19 He mobilized the English language and sent it into battle.

John Fitzgerald Kennedy (1917–63) US statesman. At a ceremony to confer honorary US citizenship on Winston Churchill. Speech, 9 Apr 1963

20 Words are, of course, the most powerful drug used by mankind.

Rudyard Kipling (1865–1936) Indian-born British writer. Speech, 14 Feb 1923

21 Words are men's daughters, but God's sons are things.

Samuel Madden (1686–1765) Irish writer. *Boulter's Monument*

22 Until we learn the use of living words we shall continue to be waxworks inhabited by gramophones.

Walter De La Mare (1873–1956) British poet. *The Observer*, 'Sayings of the Week', 12 May 1929

23 I am a Bear of Very Little Brain, and long words Bother me.

A. A. Milne (1882–1956) British writer. *Winnie-the-Pooh*, Ch. 4

24 It is an important general rule always to refer to your friend's country establishment as a 'cottage'.

Stephen Potter (1900–69) British writer. *Lifemanship*, Ch. 2

25 My father still reads the dictionary every day. He says your life depends on your power to master words.

Arthur Scargill (1941–) British trades union leader. *Sunday Times*, 10 Jan 1982

26 There is a Southern proverb, – fine words butter no parsnips.

Walter Scott (1771–1832) Scottish novelist. *The Legend of Montrose*, Ch. 3

27 POLONIUS. What do you read, my lord?
HAMLET. Words, words, words.

William Shakespeare (1564–1616) English dramatist. *Hamlet*, II:2

28 Let me be cruel, not unnatural;
I will speak daggers to her, but use none.

William Shakespeare *Hamlet*, III:2

29 My words fly up, my thoughts remain below:
Words without thoughts never to heaven go.

William Shakespeare *Hamlet*, III:3

30 But words are words; I never yet did hear
That the bruis'd heart was pierced through the ear.

William Shakespeare *Othello*, I:3

31 For words, like Nature, half reveal
And half conceal the Soul within.

Alfred, Lord Tennyson (1809–92) British poet. *In Memoriam*, V

32 One forgets words as one forgets names. One's vocabulary needs constant fertilisation or it will die.

Evelyn Waugh (1903–66) British novelist. *Diaries*

33 No, my dear, it is *I* who am surprised; you are merely astonished.

Noah Webster (1758–1843) US lexicographer. Responding to his wife's comment that she had been surprised to find him embracing their maid. Attrib.

WORDSWORTH, William

(1770–1850) British poet. His reputation was based on his *Lyrical Ballads* (1798), written with Samuel Taylor Coleridge. After settling in the Lake District with his wife and sister he produced *The Prelude*, a verse autobiography published posthumously, and much other verse.

Quotations about Wordsworth

1 Time may restore us in his course
Goethe's sage mind and Byron's force:
But where will Europe's latter hour
Again find Wordsworth's healing power?

Matthew Arnold (1822–88) British poet and critic. *Memorial Verses*

2 Wordsworth went to the Lakes, but he never was a lake poet. He found in stones the sermons he had already put there.

Oscar Wilde (1854–1900) Irish-born British dramatist. *The Decay of Lying*

Quotations by Wordsworth

3 Strongest minds
Are often those of whom the noisy world
Hears least.
The Excursion

4 The good die first,
And they whose hearts are dry as summer dust
Burn to the socket.
The Excursion

5 The wiser mind
Mourns less for what age takes away
Than what it leaves behind.
The Fountain

6 I travelled among unknown men
In lands beyond the sea;
Nor, England! did I know till then
What love I bore to thee.
I Travelled among Unknown Men

7 I wandered lonely as a cloud
That floats on high o'er vales and hills,
When all at once I saw a crowd,
A host, of golden daffodils.
I Wandered Lonely as a Cloud

8 For oft, when on my couch I lie
In vacant or in pensive mood,
They flash upon that inward eye
Which is the bliss of solitude.
I Wandered Lonely as a Cloud

9 That best portion of a good man's life,
His little, nameless, unremembered acts
Of kindness and of love.
Lines composed a few miles above Tintern Abbey

10 That blessed mood,
In which the burthen of the mystery,
In which the heavy and the weary weight
Of all this unintelligible world,
Is lightened.
Lines composed a few miles above Tintern Abbey

11 We are laid asleep
In body, and become a living soul:
While with an eye made quiet by the power
Of harmony, and the deep power of joy,
We see into the life of things.
Lines composed a few miles above Tintern Abbey

12 I have learned
To look on nature, not as in the hour
Of thoughtless youth; but hearing often-times
The still, sad music of humanity.
Lines composed a few miles above Tintern Abbey

13 Nature never did betray
The heart that loved her.
Lines composed a few miles above Tintern Abbey

14 Nor greetings where no kindness is, nor all
The dreary intercourse of daily life,
Shall e'er prevail against us, or disturb
Our cheerful faith, that all which we behold
Is full of blessings.
Lines composed a few miles above Tintern Abbey

15 A power is passing from the earth
To breathless Nature's dark abyss;
But when the great and good depart,
What is it more than this –

That Man who is from God sent forth,
Doth yet again to God return? –
Such ebb and flow must ever be,
Then wherefore should we mourn?
Referring to Charles James Fox, the hero of the liberal Whigs, who died in 1806. *Lines on the Expected Dissolution of Mr. Fox*

16 If this belief from heaven be sent,
If such be Nature's holy plan,
Have I not reason to lament
What man has made of man?
Lines written in Early Spring

17 The sweetest thing that ever grew
Beside a human door!
Lucy Gray

18 There neither is, nor can be, any *essential* difference between the language of prose and metrical composition.
Lyrical Ballads, Preface

19 Poetry is the spontaneous overflow of powerful feelings: it takes its origin from emotion recollected in tranquillity.
Lyrics Ballads, Preface

20 Every great and original writer, in proportion as he is great and original, must himself create the taste by which he is to be relished.
Lyrical Ballads, Preface

21 There is a comfort in the strength of love;
'Twill make a thing endurable, which else
Would overset the brain, or break the heart.
Michael, 448

22 Why art thou silent! Is thy love a plant
Of such weak fibre that the treacherous air
Of absence withers what was once so fair?
Miscellaneous Sonnets, III

23 My heart leaps up when I behold
A rainbow in the sky:
So was it when my life began;
So is it now I am a man;
So be it when I shall grow old,
Or let me die!
The Child is Father of the Man;
And I could wish my days to be
Bound each to each by natural piety.
My Heart Leaps Up

24 There was a time when meadow, grove, and stream,
The earth, and every common sight,
To me did seem
Apparelled in celestial light,
The glory and the freshness of a dream.
Ode. Intimations of Immortality, I

25 Whither is fled the visionary gleam?
Where is it now, the glory and the dream?
Our birth is but a sleep and a forgetting:
The Soul that rises with us, our life's Star,
Hath had elsewhere its setting,
And cometh from afar;
Not in entire forgetfulness,
And not in utter nakedness,
But trailing clouds of glory do we come
From God, who is our home:
Heaven lies about us in our infancy!
Shades of the prison-house begin to close
Upon the growing boy.
Ode. Intimations of Immortality, IV

26 Earth fills her lap with pleasures of her own:
Yearnings she hath in her own natural kind.
Ode. Intimations of Immortality, VI

27 Provoke
The years to bring the inevitable yoke.
Ode. Intimations of Immortality, VIII

28 Hence in a season of calm weather
Though inland far we be,
Our souls have sight of that immortal sea
Which brought us hither . . .
Ode. Intimations of Immortality, IX

29 Though nothing can bring back the hour
Of splendour in the grass, of glory in the flower;

We will grieve not, rather find
Strength in what remains behind . . .
Ode. Intimations of Immortality, IX

30 Another race hath been, and other palms are won.
Thanks to the human heart by which we live,
Thanks to its tenderness, its joys and fears,
To me the meanest flower that blows can give
Thoughts that do often lie too deep for tears.
Ode. Intimations of Immortality, IX

31 Those obstinate questionings
Of sense and outward things,
Fallings from us, vanishings;
Blank misgivings of a Creature
Moving about in worlds not realised,
High instincts before which our mortal nature
Did tremble like a guilty thing surprised.
Ode. Intimations of Immortality, IX

32 The clouds that gather round the setting sun
Do take a sober colouring from an eye
That hath kept watch o'er man's mortality.
Ode. Intimations of Immortality, XI

33 Me this unchartered freedom tires;
I feel the weight of chance-desires:
My hopes no more must change their name,
I long for a repose that ever is the same.
Ode to Duty

34 O Nightingale, thou surely art
A creature of a 'fiery heart'.
O Nightingale

35 Fair seed-time had my soul, and I grew up
Fostered alike by beauty and by fear.
The Prelude, I

36 Brothers all
In honour, as in one community,
Scholars and gentlemen.
The Prelude, IX

37 Bliss was it in that dawn to be alive,
But to be young was very heaven!
Referring to the French Revolution. *The Prelude*, XI

38 That which sets
. . . The budding rose above the rose full blown.
Referring to the French Revolution. *The Prelude*, XI

39 Not in Utopia, – subterranean fields, –
Or some secreted island, Heaven knows where!
But in the very world, which is the world
Of all of us, – the place where, in the end,
We find our happiness, or not at all!
Referring to the French Revolution. *The Prelude*, XI

40 There is
One great society alone on earth:
The noble living and the noble dead.
The Prelude, XI

41 The pious bird with the scarlet breast,
Our little English robin.
The Redbreast Chasing the Butterfly

42 Still glides the Stream, and shall for ever glide;
The Form remains, the Function never dies.
The River Duddon, 'After-Thought'

43 The good old rule
Sufficeth them, the simple plan,
That they should take, who have the power,
And they should keep who can.
Rob Roy's Grave

44 A youth to whom was given
So much of earth – so much of heaven,
And such impetuous blood.
Ruth

45 She dwelt among the untrodden ways
Beside the springs of Dove,
A maid whom there were none to praise
And very few to love . . .
She Dwelt Among the Untrodden Ways

46 A slumber did my spirit seal;
I had no human fears:
She seemed a thing that could not feel
The touch of earthly years.

No motion has she now, no force;
She neither hears nor sees;
Rolled round in earth's diurnal course,
With rocks, and stones, and trees.
A Slumber Did my Spirit Seal

47 Behold her, single in the field,
Yon solitary Highland lass!
The Solitary Reaper

48 Another year! – another deadly blow!
Another mighty empire overthrown!
And we are left, or shall be left, alone.
Napoleon defeated Prussia at the Battles of Jena and Anerstädt, 14 Oct 1806. *Sonnets*, 'Another year!'

49 Earth has not anything to show more fair:
Dull would he be of soul who could pass by
A sight so touching in its majesty:
The City now doth, like a garment, wear
The beauty of the morning; silent, bare,
Ships, towers, domes, theatres, and temples lie
Open unto the fields, and to the sky;
All bright and glittering in the smokeless air.
Sonnets, 'Composed upon Westminster Bridge'

50 Dear God! the very houses seem asleep;
And all that mighty heart is lying still!
Sonnets, 'Composed upon Westminster Bridge'

51 We must be free or die, who speak the tongue
That Shakspeare spake; the faith and morals hold
Which Milton held.
Sonnets, 'It is not to be thought of'

52 Milton! thou shouldst be living at this hour:
England hath need of thee; she is a fen
Of stagnant waters: altar, sword, and pen,
Fireside, the heroic wealth of hall and bower,
Have forfeited their ancient English dower
Of inward happiness.
Sonnets, 'Milton! thou shouldst'

53 Thy soul was like a star, and dwelt apart.
Sonnets, 'Milton! thou shouldst'

54 Plain living and high thinking are no more.
Sonnets, 'O friend! I know not'

55 Once did she hold the gorgeous east in fee;
And was the safeguard of the west.
Sonnets, 'Once did she hold'

56 Venice, the eldest Child of Liberty.
She was a maiden City, bright and free.
Venice, a republic since the Middle Ages, was conquered by Napoleon in 1797 and absorbed into his Kingdom of Italy in 1805. *Sonnets*, 'Once did she hold'

57 When she took unto herself a mate,
She must espouse the everlasting sea.
Sonnets, 'Once did she hold'

58 Men are we, and must grieve when even the shade
Of that which once was great is passed away.
Sonnets, 'Once did she hold'

59 Thou hast great allies;
Thy friends are exultations, agonies,
And love, and man's unconquerable mind.
Sonnets, 'Toussaint, the most unhappy man'

60 Two voices are there; one is of the sea,
One of the mountains; each a mighty voice:
In both from age to age thou didst rejoice,
They were thy chosen music, Liberty!
Sonnets, 'Two voices are there'

61 The world is too much with us; late and soon,
Getting and spending, we lay waste our powers:
Little we see in Nature that is ours.
Sonnets, 'The world is too much with us'

62 I'd rather be
A Pagan suckled in a creed outworn;
So might I, standing on this pleasant lea,
Have glimpses that would make me less forlorn;
Have sight of Proteus rising from the sea;
Or hear Old Triton blow his wreathed horn.
Sonnets, 'The world is too much with us'

63 Strange fits of passion have I known:
And I will dare to tell,
But in the lover's ear alone,
What once to me befell.
Strange Fits of Passion

64 Come forth into the light of things,
Let Nature be your Teacher.
The Tables Turned

65 One impulse from a vernal wood
May teach you more of man,
Of moral evil and of good,
Than all the sages can.
The Tables Turned

66 Three years she grew in sun and shower,
Then Nature said, 'A lovelier flower
On earth was never sown;
This child I to myself will take;
She shall be mine, and I will make
A Lady of my own.
Three Years she Grew

67 'Tis said that some have died for love.
'Tis Said that some have Died

68 Sweet childish days, that were as long
As twenty days are now.
To a Butterfly, I've Watched you now

69 Small service is true service, while it lasts.
To a Child, Written in her Album

70 Ethereal minstrel! pilgrim of the sky!
Dost thou despise the earth where cares abound?
To a Skylark

71 Thrice welcome, darling of the spring!
Even yet thou art to me
No bird, but an invisible thing,
A voice, a mystery.
To the Cuckoo

72 Thou unassuming common-place
Of Nature.
To the Daisy

73 Pleasures newly found are sweet
When they lie about our feet.
To the Small Celandine

74 Like an army defeated
The snow hath retreated.
Written in March

WORK

See also effort, unemployment

1 All work and no play makes Jack a dull boy.
Proverb

2 No bees, no honey; no work, no money.
Proverb

3 In work the greatest satisfaction lies – the satisfaction of stretching yourself, using your abilities and making them expand, and knowing that you have accomplished something that could have been done only by you using your unique apparatus. This is really the centre of life, and those who never orientate themselves in this direction are missing more than they ever know.
Kenneth Allsop (1920–73) British writer and broadcaster. *Letters to His Daughter*

4 Whatsoever thy hand findeth to do, do it with thy might; for there is no work, nor device, nor knowledge, nor wisdom, in the grave, whither thou goest.
Bible: Ecclesiastes 9:10

5 For even when we were with you, this we commanded you, that if any would not work, neither should he eat.
Bible: II Thessalonians 3:10

6 There is dignity in work only when it is work freely accepted.
Albert Camus (1913–60) French existentialist writer. *Notebooks*, 1935–42

7 Work is the grand cure of all the maladies and miseries that ever beset mankind.
Thomas Carlyle (1795–1881) Scottish historian and essayist. Speech, Edinburgh, 2 Apr 1886

8 Work is much more fun than fun.
Noël Coward (1899–1973) British dramatist. *The Observer*, 'Sayings of the Week', 21 June 1963

9 By working faithfully eight hours a day you may eventually get to be a boss and work twelve hours a day.
Robert Frost (1875–1963) US poet. Attrib.

10 The brain is a wonderful organ. It starts working the moment you get up in the morning, and does not stop until you get into the office.
Robert Frost Attrib.

11 Employment is nature's physician, and is essential to human happiness.
Galen (fl. 2nd century) Greek physician and scholar.

12 When work is a pleasure, life is a joy! When work is a duty, life is slavery.
Maxim Gorky (Aleksei Maksimovich Peshkov; 1868–1936) Russian writer. *The Lower Depths*

13 Idleness begets ennui, ennui the hypochondriac, and that a diseased body. No laborious person was ever yet hysterical.
Thomas Jefferson (1743–1826) US statesman. Letter to Martha Jefferson, 28 Mar 1787

14 That one must do some work seriously and must be independent and not merely amuse oneself in life – this our mother has told us always, but never that science was the only career worth following.
Irène Joliot-Curie (1897–1956) French scientist. Recalling the advice of her mother, Marie Curie. *A Long Way from Missouri* (Mary Margaret McBride), Ch. 10

15 Horny-handed sons of toil.
Denis Kearney (1847–1907) US Labor leader. Speech, San Francisco, c. 1878

16 Why should I let the toad *work*
Squat on my life?
Can't I use my wit as a pitchfork
And drive the brute off?
Philip Larkin (1922–85) British poet. *The Less Deceived*, 'Toads'

17 There must be love
Without love you will be merely skilful.
Frédérick Leboyer (1918–) French obstetrician. *Entering the World* (M. Odent)

18 It's been a hard day's night.
John Lennon (1940–80) British rock musician. *A Hard Day's Night* (with Paul McCartney)

19 . . . she had always found occupation to be one of the best medicines for an afflicted mind . . .
Eliza Leslie (1787–1858) *Pencil Sketches; or, Outlines of Character and Manners*, 'Constance Allerton; or the Mourning Suits'

20 Life is too short to do anything for oneself that one can pay others to do for one.
W. Somerset Maugham (1874–1965) British novelist. *The Summing Up*

21 Few men of action have been able to make a graceful exit at the appropriate time.
Malcolm Muggeridge (1903–) British writer. *Chronicles Of Wasted Time*

22 The rise in the total of those employed is governed by Parkinson's Law and would be much the same whether the volume of work were to increase, diminish or even disappear.
Cyril Northcote Parkinson (1919–) British historian and writer. *Parkinson's Law*, Ch. 1

23 Work expands so as to fill the time available for its completion.
Cyril Northcote Parkinson *Parkinson's Law*, Ch. 1

24 Work is necessary for man. Man invented the alarm clock.
Pablo Picasso (1881–1973) Spanish painter. Attrib.

25 They say hard work never hurt anybody, but I figure why take the chance.
Ronald Reagan (1911–) US Republican president. Attrib.

26 If you have great talents, industry will improve them: if you have but moderate abilities, industry will supply their deficiency.
Joshua Reynolds (1723–92) British portrait painter. Discourse to Students of the Royal Academy, 11 Dec 1769

27 I wish to preach, not the doctrine of ignoble ease, but the doctrine of the strenuous life.
Theodore Roosevelt (1858–1919) US Republican president. Speech, Chicago, 10 Apr 1899

28 Temperance and labour are the two real physicians of man: labour sharpens his appetite and temperance prevents his abusing it.
Jean Jacques Rousseau (1712–78) French philosopher. *Émile*, Bk. I

29 One of the symptoms of approaching nervous breakdown is the belief that one's work is terribly important. If I were a medical man, I should prescribe a holiday to any patient who considered his work important.
Bertrand Russell (1872–1970) British philosopher. *The Autobiography of Bertrand Russell*, Vol. II, Ch. 5

30 The only place where success comes before work is a dictionary.
Vidal Sassoon (1928–) British hair stylist. Quoting one of his teachers in a BBC radio broadcast

31 Pennies do not come from heaven. They have to be earned here on earth.
Margaret Thatcher (1925–) British politician and prime minister. *Sunday Telegraph*, 1982

32 I should have worked just long enough to discover that I didn't like it.
Paul Theroux (1941–) US-born writer. *The Observer Magazine*, 1 Apr 1979

33 Work banishes those three great evils, boredom, vice, and poverty.
Voltaire (François-Marie Arouet; 1694–1778) French writer. *Candide*, Ch. 30

34 How doth the little busy bee
Improve each shining hour,
And gather honey all the day
From every opening flower!
Isaac Watts (1674–1748) English theologian and hymn writer. *Divine Songs for Children*, 'Against Idleness and Mischief'

35 Work is the curse of the drinking classes.
Oscar Wilde (1854–1900) Irish-born British dramatist. Attrib.

36 I haven't got time to be tired.
Wilhelm I (1797–1888) King of Prussia and Emperor of Germany. Said during his last illness

WORLD

See also confusion

1 For the world, I count it not an inn, but an hospital, and a place, not to live, but to die in.
Thomas Browne (1605–82) English physician and writer. *Religio Medici*, Pt. II

2 As I walked through the wilderness of this world.
John Bunyan (1628–88) English writer. *The Pilgrim's Progress*, Pt. I

WORLD WAR I

1 And when they ask us, how dangerous it was,
We never will tell them, we never will tell them:
How we fought in some café
With wild women night and day,
'Twas the wonderfulest war you ever knew.'
Cole Porter (1891–1964) US composer and lyricist. *War Song*

2 . . . we mutally agreed to call it *The First World War* in order to prevent the millennium folk from forgetting that the history of the world was the history of war.
Lieut-Col. Charles A'Court Repington (1858–1925) British soldier and journalist. Diary, 10 Sept 1918

WORLD WAR II

See also Churchill, Germany, Hitler, Nazism, war

1 World War II began last week at 5.20 a.m. (Polish time) Friday, September 1, when a German bombing plane dropped a projectile on Puck, fishing village and air base in the armpit of the Hel Peninsula.
Anonymous *Time*, 11 Sept 1939

2 Hitler
Has only got one ball!
Goering
Has two, but very small!
Himmler
Has something similar,
But poor old Goebbels
Has no balls at all!
Anonymous World War II song (to the tune of 'Colonel Bogey')

3 Any gum, chum?
Anonymous Children's cry in Britain to US GIs.

4 You wear no uniforms and your weapons differ from ours – but they are not less deadly. The fact that you wear no uniforms is your

strength. The Nazi official and the German soldier don't know you. But they fear you . . . The night is your friend. The 'V' is your sign.
Colonel Britton (Douglas Ritchie; 1905–67) British propagandist. Broadcast to the resistance movement in occupied Europe. Radio broadcast, 1941

5 How horrible, fantastic, incredible, it is that we should be digging trenches and trying on gas-masks here because of a quarrel in a far-away country between people of whom we know nothing.
Neville Chamberlain (1869–1940) British statesman. Referring to Germany's annexation of the Sudetenland. Radio broadcast, 27 Sept 1938

6 This morning I had another talk with the German Chancellor, Herr Hitler, and here is the paper which bears his name upon it as well as mine . . . 'We regard the agreement signed last night – and the Anglo-German Naval Agreement – as symbolic of the desire of our two peoples never to go to war with one another again.'
Neville Chamberlain On returning from signing the Munich agreement. Speech, Heston airport, 30 Sept 1938

7 This morning the British Ambassador in Berlin handed the German Government a final note stating that, unless we heard from them by eleven o'clock that they were prepared at once to withdraw their troops from Poland, a state of war would exist between us. I have to tell you that no such undertaking has been received, and that consequently this country is at war with Germany.
Neville Chamberlain Radio broadcast from Downing Street, London, 3 Sept 1939

8 Hitler has missed the bus.
Neville Chamberlain Speech, House of Commons, 4 Apr 1940

9 We have sustained a defeat without a war.
Winston Churchill (1874–1965) British statesman. Speech, House of Commons, 5 Oct 1938

10 We shall not flag or fail. We shall fight in France, we shall fight on the seas and oceans, we shall fight with growing confidence and growing strength in the air, we shall defend our island, whatever the cost may be, we shall fight on the beaches, we shall fight on the landing grounds, we shall fight in the fields and in the streets, we shall fight in the hills; we shall never surrender.
Winston Churchill Speech, House of Commons, 4 June 1940

11 This was their finest hour.
Winston Churchill Referring to the Dunkirk evacuation. Speech, House of Commons, 18 June 1940

12 If we can stand up to Hitler, all Europe may be free and the life of the world may move forward into broad, sunlit uplands.
Winston Churchill Speech, House of Commons, 18 June 1940

13 The battle of Britain is about to begin.
Winston Churchill Speech, House of Commons, 1 July 1940

14 Never in the field of human conflict was so much owed by so many to so few.
Winston Churchill Referring to the Battle of Britain pilots. Speech, House of Commons, 20 Aug 1940

15 We are waiting for the long-promised invasion. So are the fishes.
Winston Churchill Radio broadcast to the French people, 21 Oct 1940

16 Give us the tools, and we will finish the job.
Winston Churchill Referring to Lend-lease, which was being legislated in the USA. Radio broadcast, 9 Feb 1941

17 You do your worst, and we will do our best.
Winston Churchill Addressed to Hitler. Speech, 14 July 1941

18 Do not let us speak of darker days; let us rather speak of sterner days. These are not dark days: these are great days – the greatest days our country has ever lived.
Winston Churchill Address, Harrow School, 29 Oct 1941

19 When I warned them that Britain would fight on alone whatever they did, their Generals told their Prime Minister and his divided Cabinet: 'In three weeks England will have her neck wrung like a chicken.'
Some chicken! Some neck!
Winston Churchill Referring to the French Government; see WEYGAND Speech, Canadian Parliament, 30 Dec 1941

20 This is not the end. It is not even the beginning of the end. But it is, perhaps, the end of the beginning.
Winston Churchill Referring to the Battle of Egypt. Speech, Mansion House, 10 Nov 1942

21 Wars are not won by evacuations.
Winston Churchill Referring to Dunkirk. *Their Finest Hour*

22 Before Alamein we never had a victory. After Alamein we never had a defeat.
Winston Churchill *The Hinge of Fate*, Ch. 33

23 Peace with Germany and Japan on our terms will not bring much rest. . . . As I observed last time, when the war of the giants is over the wars of the pygmies will begin.
Winston Churchill *Triumph and Tragedy*, Ch. 25

24 This whipped jackal . . . is frisking up by the side of the German tiger.
Winston Churchill Referring to Mussolini. Speech, House of Commons, Apr 1941

25 This is *your* victory.
Winston Churchill Speech, London, 8 May 1945

26 I, General de Gaulle, now in London, call on all French officers and men who are at present on British soil, or who may be in the future . . . to get in touch with me. Whatever happens the flame of French resistance must not and shall not be extinguished.
Charles De Gaulle (1890–1970) French general and statesman. Broadcast, 18 June 1940

27 Now we can look the East End in the face.
Elizabeth the Queen Mother (1900–) The wife of King George VI. Surveying the damage caused to Buckingham Palace by a bomb during the Blitz in World War II. Attrib.

28 This was the Angel of History! We felt its wings flutter through the room. Was that not the fortune we awaited so anxiously?
Joseph Goebbels (1897–1945) German politician. Referring to Roosevelt's death. *Diary*

29 They entered the war to prevent us from going into the East, not to have the East come to the Atlantic.
Hermann Goering (1893–1946) German Nazi leader. Referring to the war aims of the British in World War II. *Nuremberg Diary* (G. M. Gilbert)

30 The little ships, the unforgotten Homeric catalogue of *Mary Jane* and *Peggy IV*, of *Folkestone Belle*, *Boy Billy*, and *Ethel Maud*, of *Lady Haig* and *Skylark* . . . the little ships of England brought the Army home.
Philip Guedalla (1889–1944) British writer. Referring to the evacuation of Dunkirk. *Mr. Churchill*

31 Our ships have been salvaged and

are retiring at high speed toward the Japanese fleet.
W. C. Halsey (1882–1959) US admiral. Following Japanese claims that most of the American Third Fleet had been sunk or were retiring. Radio message, Oct 1944

32 Germany calling, Germany calling.
'Lord Haw-Haw' (William Joyce; 1906–46) US-born propagandist for German Nazis. Radio broadcasts to Britain, during World War II

33 The war situation has developed not necessarily to Japan's advantage.
Hirohito (1901–89) Japanese head of state. Announcing Japan's surrender, 15 Aug 1945

34 Before us stands the last problem that must be solved and will be solved. It is the last territorial claim which I have to make in Europe, but it is the claim from which I will not recede.
Adolf Hitler (1889–1945) German dictator. Referring to the Sudetenland (Czechoslovakia). Speech, Berlin, 26 Sept 1938

35 Well, he seemed such a nice old gentleman, I thought I would give him my autograph as a souvenir.
Adolf Hitler Referring to Neville Chamberlain. Attrib.

36 When Barbarossa commences, the world will hold its breath and make no comment.
Adolf Hitler Referring to the planned invasion of the USSR, Operation Barbarossa, which began on 22 June 1941. Attrib.

37 If we are going in without the help of Russia we are walking into a trap.
David Lloyd George (1863–1945) British Liberal statesman. Speech, House of Commons, 3 Apr 1939

38 And here we are – just as before – safe in our skins;
Glory to God for Munich.
And stocks go up and wrecks
Are salved and politicians' reputations
Go up like Jack-on-the-Beanstalk; only the Czechs
Go down and without fighting.
Louis Macneice (1907–63) Irish-born British poet. *Autumn Journal*

39 This Berlin–Rome connection is not so much a diaphragm as an axis, around which can revolve all those states of Europe with a will towards collaboration and peace.
Benito Mussolini (1883–1945) Italian dictator. Speech, Milan, 1 Nov 1936

40 Dear Ike, Today I spat in the Seine.
General George Patton (1885–1945) US general. Message sent to Eisenhower reporting his crossing of the Seine in World War II. *The American Treasury* (C. Fadiman)

41 To make a union with Great Britain would be fusion with a corpse.
Marshal Pétain (1856–1951) French marshal. On hearing Churchill's suggestion for an Anglo-French union, 1940. *Their Finest Hour* (Winston S. Churchill), Ch. 10

42 Our great-grandchildren, when they learn how we began this war by snatching glory out of defeat . . . may also learn how the little holiday steamers made an excursion to hell and came back glorious.
J. B. Priestley (1894–1984) British novelist. Referring to the British Expeditionary Force's evacuation from Dunkirk. Broadcast, 5 June 1940

43 The best immediate defense of the United States is the success of Great Britain defending itself.
Franklin D. Roosevelt (1882–1945) US Democratic president. At press conference, 17 Dec 1940. *Their Finest Hour* (Winston S. Churchill), Ch. 28

44 Defeat of Germany means the defeat of Japan, probably without firing a shot or losing a life.
Franklin D. Roosevelt *The Hinge of Fate* (Winston S. Churchill), Ch. 25

45 A date that shall live in infamy.
Franklin D. Roosevelt Referring to 7 Dec 1941, when Japan attacked Pearl Harbor. Message to Congress, 8 Dec 1941

46 We have finished the job, what shall we do with the tools?
Haile Selassie (1892–1975) Emperor of Ethiopia. Telegram sent to Winston Churchill, mimicking his 'Give us the tools, and we will finish the job'. *Ambrosia and Small Beer*, Ch. 4 (Edward Marsh)

47 This war is not as in the past; whoever occupies a territory also imposes on it his own social system. Everyone imposes his own system as far as his army has power to do so. It cannot be otherwise.
Joseph Stalin (J. Dzhugashvili; 1879–1953) Soviet statesman. *Conversations with Stalin* (Milovan Djilas)

48 If we see that Germany is winning the war we ought to help Russia, and if Russia is winning we ought to help Germany, and in that way let them kill as many as possible.
Harry S. Truman (1884–1972) US statesman. *New York Times*, 24 July 1941, when Russia was invaded by Germany

49 In three weeks England will have her neck wrung like a chicken.
Maxime Weygand (1867–1965) French general. Said at the fall of France; see CHURCHILL. *Their Finest Hour* (Winston S. Churchill)

50 I fear we have only awakened a sleeping giant, and his reaction will be terrible.
Isoroku Yamamoto (1884–1943) Japanese admiral. Said after the Japanese attack on Pearl Harbor, 1941.

WORLD-WEARINESS

1 Bankrupt of Life, yet Prodigal of Ease.
John Dryden (1631–1700) British poet and dramatist. *Absalom and Achitophel*, I

2 Spare all I have, and take my life.
George Farquhar (1678–1707) Irish dramatist. *The Beaux' Stratagem*, V:2

3 Death is a delightful hiding-place for weary men.
Herodotus (c. 484–c. 424 BC) Greek historian. *Histories*, VII, 46

4 I am sick of this way of life. The weariness and sadness of old age make it intolerable. I have walked with death in hand, and death's own hand is warmer than my own. I don't wish to live any longer.
W. Somerset Maugham (1874–1965) British novelist. Said on his ninetieth birthday. *Familiar Medical Quotations* (M. B. Strauss)

5 If it be a short and violent death, we have no leisure to fear it; if otherwise, I perceive that according as I engage myself in sickness, I do naturally fall into some disdain and contempt of life.
Michel de Montaigne (1533–92) French essayist and moralist. *Essais*

6 Stop the World, I Want to Get Off.
Anthony Newley (1931–) British actor, composer, singer, and comedian. With Leslie Bricusse. Title of musical

7 If thus thou vanishest, thou tell'st the world
It is not worth leave-taking.
William Shakespeare (1564–1616) English dramatist. *Antony and Cleopatra*, V:2

8 How weary, stale, flat, and unprofitable,
Seem to me all the uses of this world!
William Shakespeare *Hamlet*, I:2

9 Vex not his ghost: O! let him pass; he hates him
That would upon the rack of this tough world

Stretch him out longer.
William Shakespeare *King Lear,* V:3

10 I have supp'd full with horrors.
William Shakespeare *Macbeth,* V:5

11 I gin to be aweary of the sun,
And wish th' estate o' th' world were now undone.
William Shakespeare *Macbeth,* V:5

12 Death is not the greatest of ills; it is worse to want to die, and not be able to.
Sophocles (c. 496–406 BC) Greek dramatist. *Electra,* 1007

WORRY

See also misfortune

1 A trouble shared is a trouble halved.
Proverb

2 Don't meet troubles half-way.
Proverb

3 Every little yielding to anxiety is a step away from the natural heart of man.
Japanese proverb

4 It will be all the same in a hundred years.
Proverb

5 Take things as they come.
Proverb

6 Begone, dull care! I prithee begone from me!
Begone, dull care, you and I shall never agree.
Anonymous *Begone Dull Care*

7 'Life's too short for worrying.'
'Yes, that's what worries me.'
Anonymous

8 Behold the fowls of the air: for they sow not, neither do they reap, nor gather into barns; yet your heavenly Father feedeth them. Are ye not much better than they?
Which of you by taking thought can add one cubit unto his stature?
And why take ye thought for raiment? Consider the lilies of the field, how they grow; they toil not, neither do they spin:
And yet I say unto you, That even Solomon in all his glory was not arrayed like one of these.
Wherefore, if God so clothe the grass of the field, which today is, and tomorrow is cast into the oven, shall he not much more clothe you, O ye of little faith?
Therefore take no thought, saying, What shall we eat? or, What shall we drink? or, Wherewithal shall we be clothed?
Bible: Matthew 6:26–31

9 But seek ye first the kingdom of God, and his righteousness; and all these things shall be added unto you.
Take therefore no thought for the morrow: for the morrow shall take thought for the things of itself. Sufficient unto the day is the evil thereof.
Bible: Matthew 6:33–34

10 Just when we are safest, there's a sunset-touch,
A fancy from a flower-bell, some one's death,
A chorus-ending from Euripides, –
And that's enough for fifty hopes and fears
As old and new at once as Nature's self,
To rap and knock and enter in our soul.
Robert Browning (1812–89) British poet. *Bishop Blougram's Apology*

11 Before the cherry orchard was sold everybody was worried and upset, but as soon as it was all settled finally and once for all, everybody calmed down, and felt quite cheerful.
Anton Chekhov (1860–1904) Russian dramatist. *The Cherry Orchard,* IV

12 When I look back on all these worries I remember the story of the old man who said on his deathbed that he had had a lot of trouble in his life, most of which had never happened.
Winston Churchill (1874–1965) British statesman. *Their Finest Hour*

13 But Jesus, when you don't have any money, the problem is food. When you have money, it's sex. When you have both, it's health, you worry about getting ruptured or something. If everything is simply jake then you're frightened of death.
J. P. Donleavy (1926–) US writer.

14 Worry affects circulation, the heart and the glands, the whole nervous sytem, and profoundly affects the heart. I have never known a man who died from overwork, but many who died from doubt.
Charles H. Mayo (1865–1939) US physician. *Bartlett's Unfamiliar Quotations* (Leonard Louis Levinson)

15 Care
Sat on his faded cheek.
John Milton (1608–74) English poet. *Paradise Lost,* Bk. I

16 Worrying is the most natural and spontaneous of all human functions. It is time to acknowledge this, perhaps even to learn to do it better.
Lewis Thomas (1913–) US pathologist. *More Notes of a Biology Watcher,* 'The Medusa and the Snail'

WORSHIP

1 This is the temple of Providence where disciples still hourly mark its ways and note the system of its mysteries. Here is the one God whose worshippers prove their faith by their works and in their destruction still trust in Him.
F. H. Bradley (1846–1924) British philosopher. Referring to Monte Carlo. *Aphorisms*

2 O worship the King, all glorious above!
O gratefully sing his power and his love!
Our Shield and Defender – the Ancient of Days,
Pavilioned in splendour, and girded with praise.
Robert Grant (1779–1838) British hymn writer. Hymn

3 We look forward to a world founded upon four essential human freedoms. The first is freedom of speech and expression – everywhere in the world. The second is freedom of every person to worship God in his own way – everywhere in the world. The third is freedom from want . . . everywhere in the world. The fourth is freedom from fear . . . anywhere in the world.
Franklin D. Roosevelt (1882–1945) US Democratic president. Speech to Congress, 6 Jan 1941

4 Business underlies everything in our national life, including our spiritual life. Witness the fact that in the Lord's Prayer the first petition is for daily bread. No one can worship God or love his neighbor on an empty stomach.
Woodrow Wilson (1856–1925) US statesman. Speech, New York, 1912

WRITERS

See also criticism, Dickens, poets, Shakespeare, writing

1 A reader seldom peruses a book with pleasure until he knows whether the writer of it be a black man or a fair man, of a mild or choleric disposition, married or a bachelor.
Joseph Addison (1672–1719) British essayist. *The Spectator*, 1

2 Writers, like teeth, are divided into incisors and grinders.
Walter Bagehot (1826–77) British economist and journalist. *Estimates of some Englishmen and Scotchmen*, 'The First Edinburgh Reviewers'

3 Because he shakes hands with people's hearts.
Lord Beaverbrook (Maxwell Aitken; 1879–1964) Canadian-born politician and newspaper proprietor. On being asked why the sentimental writer Godfrey Winn was paid so much. *Somerset Maugham* (E. Morgan)

4 I have been told by hospital authorities that more copies of my works are left behind by departing patients than those of any other author.
Robert Benchley (1889–1945) US humorist. *Chips off the Old Benchley*, 'Why Does Nobody Collect Me?'

5 Miller is not really a writer but a non-stop talker to whom someone has given a typewriter.
Gerald Brenan (Edward Fitzgerald Brenan; 1894–1987) British writer. Referring to Henry Miller. *Thoughts in a Dry Season*, 'Literature'

6 The idea that it is necessary to go to a university in order to become a successful writer, or even a man or woman of letters (which is by no means the same thing), is one of those phantasies that surround authorship.
Vera Brittain (1893–1970) British writer and feminist. *On Being an Author*, Ch. 2

7 And, Robert Browning, you writer of plays,
Here's a subject made to your hand!
Robert Browning (1812–89) British poet. *A Light Woman*, XIV

8 Literary men are . . . a perpetual priesthood.
Thomas Carlyle (1795–1881) Scottish historian and essayist. *Critical and Miscellaneous Essays*, 'The State of German Literature'

9 Mr Shaw is (I suspect) the only man on earth who has never written any poetry.
G. K. Chesterton (1874–1936) British writer. Referring to George Bernard Shaw. *Orthodoxy*, Ch. 3

10 The faults of great authors are generally excellences carried to an excess.
Samuel Taylor Coleridge (1772–1834) British poet. *Miscellanies*, 149

11 I believe the souls of five hundred Sir Isaac Newtons would go to the making up of a Shakespeare or a Milton.
Samuel Taylor Coleridge Letter to Thomas Poole, 23 Mar 1801

12 The only way for writers to meet is to share a quick pee over a common lamp-post.
Cyril Connolly (1903–74) British journalist. *The Unquiet Grave*

13 He would not blow his nose without moralizing on conditions in the handkerchief industry.
Cyril Connolly Referring to George Orwell. *The Evening Colonnade*

14 A great writer creates a world of his own and his readers are proud to live in it. A lesser writer may entice them in for a moment, but soon he will watch them filing out.
Cyril Connolly *Enemies of Promise*, Ch. 1

15 Talent alone cannot make a writer. There must be a man behind the book.
Ralph Waldo Emerson (1803–82) US poet and essayist. *Goethe*

16 Creative writers are always greater than the causes that they represent.
E. M. Forster (1879–1970) British novelist. *Gide and George*

17 There is no arguing with Johnson; for when his pistol misses fire, he knocks you down with the butt end of it.
Oliver Goldsmith (1728–74) Irish-born British writer. *Life of Johnson* (J. Boswell)

18 The work of Henry James has always seemed divisible by a simple dynastic arrangement into three reigns: James I, James II, and the Old Pretender.
Philip Guedalla (1889–1944) British writer. *Collected Essays*, 'Men of Letters: Mr. Henry James'

19 His worst is better than any other person's best.
William Hazlitt (1778–1830) British essayist. *English Literature*, Ch. XIV, 'Sir Walter Scott'

20 He writes as fast as they can read, and he does not write himself down.
William Hazlitt *English Literature*, Ch. XIV, 'Sir Walter Scott'

21 Dr Johnson's sayings would not appear so extraordinary, were it not for his *bow-wow way*.
Henry Herbert (1734–94) British general. *Life of Johnson* (J. Boswell)

22 Mr. James' cosmopolitanism is, after all, limited; to be really cosmopolitan, a man must be at home even in his own country.
Thomas Wentworth Higginson (1823–1911) US churchman and writer. Referring to Henry James. *Short Studies of American Authors*

23 For Lawrence, existence was one continuous convalescence; it was as though he was newly reborn from a mortal illness every day of his life. What these convalescent eyes saw, his most casual speech would reveal.
Aldous Huxley (1894–1964) British writer. *The Olive Tree*, 'D. H. Lawrence'

24 He was unperfect, unfinished, inartistic; he was worse than provincial – he was parochial.
Henry James (1843–1916) US novelist. Referring to Thoreau. *Life of Nathaniel Hawthorne*, Ch. 4

25 Whatever Wells writes is not only alive, but kicking.
Henry James Referring to H. G. Wells. Attrib.

26 The reciprocal civility of authors is one of the most risible scenes in the farce of life.
Samuel Johnson (1709–84) British lexicographer. *Life of Sir Thomas Browne*

27 He is the richest author that ever grazed the common of literature.
Samuel Johnson Referring to Dr John Campbell. *Life of Johnson* (J. Boswell), Vol. I

28 Authors are easy to get on with – if you're fond of children.
Michael Joseph (1897–1958) British publisher. *The Observer*, 1949

29 One man is as good as another until he has written a book.
Benjamin Jowett (1817–93) British theologian. *Letters of B. Jowett* (Abbott and Campbell)

30 My God, what a clumsy *alla patrida* James Joyce is! Nothing but old fags and cabbage stumps of quotations from the Bible and the rest, stewed

in the juice of deliberate, journalistic dirty-mindedness.

D. H. Lawrence (1885–1930) British novelist. Letter to Aldous Huxley

31 The trouble with Ian is that he gets off with women because he can't get on with them.

Rosamond Lehmann (1901–) British writer. Referring to Ian Fleming. *The Life of Ian Fleming* (J. Pearson)

32 A good man fallen among Fabians.

Lenin (Vladimir Ilich Ulyanov; 1870–1924) Russian revolutionary leader. Referring to George Bernard Shaw. Attrib.

33 The last gentleman in Europe.

Ada Beddington Leverson (1862–1933) British writer. Said of Oscar Wilde. *Letters to the Sphinx* (Wilde), 'Reminiscences', 2

34 He was a writer who drank, not, as so many have believed, a drunk who wrote.

James Lundquist (1941–) US writer. *A Guide to Sinclair Lewis*

35 The contraction of his obicular, the lateral obtusion of his sense centres, his night fears, his stomach trouble, the polyencephalitic condition of his youth, and above all the heredity of his old father and young mother, combined to make him an hysterico-epileptic type, traceable in the paranoic psychoses evident in all he wrote.

Cesare Lombroso (1853–1909) Italian criminologist. Referring to Emile Zola. *Paris Was Yesterday* (Janet Flanner)

36 Our principal writers have nearly all been fortunate in escaping regular education.

Hugh MacDiarmid (Christopher Murray Grieve; 1892–1978) Scottish poet. *The Observer*, 'Sayings of the Week', 29 Mar 1953

37 The trouble with our younger authors is that they are all in the sixties.

W. Somerset Maugham (1874–1965) British novelist. *The Observer*, 'Sayings of the Week', 14 Oct 1951

38 A novelist is, like all mortals, more fully at home on the surface of the present than in the ooze of the past.

Vladimir Nabokov (1899–1977) Russian-born US novelist. *Strong Opinions*, Ch. 20

39 English literature's performing flea.

Sean O'Casey (1884–1964) Irish dramatist. Referring to P. G. Wodehouse. Attrib.

40 He is pretty certain to come back into favour. One of the surest signs of his genius is that women dislike his books.

George Orwell (Eric Blair; 1903–50) British novelist. Referring to Conrad. *New English Weekly*, 23 Jul 1936

41 The poor son-of-a-bitch!

Dorothy Parker (1893–1967) US writer. Quoting from *The Great Gatsby* on paying her last respects to F. Scott Fitzgerald. *Thalberg: Life and Legend* (B. Thomas)

42 A list of authors who have made themselves most beloved and therefore, most comfortable financially, shows that it is our national joy to mistake for the first-rate, the fecund rate.

Dorothy Parker *Wit's End* (R. E. Drennan)

43 Now that the old lion is dead, every ass thinks he may kick at him.

Samuel Parr (1747–1825) British writer and scholar. Referring to Dr Johnson. *Life of Johnson* (J. Boswell)

44 A novelist who writes nothing for 10 years finds his reputation rising. Because I keep on producing books they say there must be something wrong with this fellow.

J. B. Priestley (1894–1984) British novelist. *The Observer*, 'Sayings of the Week', 21 Sept 1969

45 There are plenty of clever young writers. But there is too much genius, not enough talent.

J. B. Priestley *The Observer*, 'Sayings of the Week', 29 Sept 1968

46 Everybody writes a book too many.

Mordecai Richler (1931–) Canadian novelist. *The Observer*, 'Sayings of the Week', 9 Jan 1985

47 Among the many problems which beset the novelist, not the least weighty is the choice of the moment at which to begin his novel.

Vita Sackville-West (Victoria Sackville-West; 1892–1962) British poet and novelist. *The Edwardians*, Ch. 1

48 Waldo is one of those people who would be enormously improved by death.

Saki (Hector Hugh Munro; 1870–1916) British writer. Referring to Ralph Waldo Emerson. *The Feast of Nemesis*

49 Sherard Blaw, the dramatist who had discovered himself, and who had given so ungrudgingly of his discovery to the world.

Saki *The Unbearable Bassington*, Ch. 13

50 The Big Bow-Wow strain I can do myself like any now going; but the exquisite touch, which renders ordinary commonplace things and characters interesting, from the truth of the description and the sentiment, is denied to me.

Walter Scott (1771–1832) Scottish novelist. In praise of Jane Austen. *Journal*, 14 Mar 1826

51 For where is any author in the world
Teaches such beauty as a woman's eye?
Learning is but an adjunct to oneself.

William Shakespeare (1564–1616) English dramatist. *Love's Labour's Lost*, IV:3

52 I enjoyed talking to her, but thought *nothing* of her writing. I considered her 'a beautiful little knitter'.

Edith Sitwell (1887–1964) British poet and writer. Referring to Virginia Woolf. Letter to G. Singleton

53 I do not want Miss Mannin's feelings to be hurt by the fact that I have never heard of her . . . At the moment I am debarred from the pleasure of putting her in her place by the fact that she has not got one.

Edith Sitwell Referring to the novelist Ethel Mannin. *Façades* (J. Pearson)

54 That great Cham of literature, Samuel Johnson.

Tobias Smollett (1721–71) British novelist. Letter to John Wilkes, 16 Mar 1759

55 No regime has ever loved great writers, only minor ones.

Alexander Solzhenitsyn (1918–) Soviet novelist. *The First Circle*, Ch. 57

56 William Congreve is the only sophisticated playwright England has produced; and like Shaw, Sheridan, and Wilde, his nearest rivals, he was brought up in Ireland.

Kenneth Tynan (1927–80) British theater critic. *Curtains*, 'The Way of the World'

57 I wouldn't give up writing about God at this stage, if I was you. It would be like P. G. Wodehouse dropping Jeeves half-way through the Wooster series.

Evelyn Waugh (1903–66) British novelist. Said to Graham Greene, who proposed to write a political novel. *Evelyn Waugh* (Christopher Sykes)

58 In my situation as Chancellor of the University of Oxford, I have been much exposed to authors.

Duke of Wellington (1769–1852) British general and statesman. *Collections and Recollections* (G. W. E. Russell)

59 I think it's good for a writer to think he's dying; he works harder.
Tennessee Williams (1911–83) US dramatist. *The Observer*, 'Sayings of the Week', 31 Oct 1976

60 Of all the great Victorian writers, he was probably the most antagonistic to the Victorian age itself.
Edmund Wilson (1895–1972) US critic and writer. Referring to Dickens. *The Wound and the Bow*, 'The Two Scrooges'

61 Literature is strewn with the wreckage of men who have minded beyond reason the opinions of others.
Virginia Woolf (1882–1941) British novelist. *A Room of One's Own*

62 A combination of Little Nell and Lady Macbeth.
Alexander Woollcott (1887–1943) US journalist. Referring to Dorothy Parker. *While Rome Burns*

63 At 83 Shaw's mind was perhaps not quite as good as it used to be. It was still better than anyone else's.
Alexander Woollcott Referring to George Bernard Shaw. *While Rome Burns*

64 It's not a writer's business to hold opinions.
W. B. Yeats (1865–1939) Irish poet. Speaking to playwright, Denis Johnston. *The Guardian*, 5 May 1977

WRITING

See also books, criticism, fiction, inspiration, letter-writing, literacy, literature, novels, plays, poetry, poetry and prose, prose, reading, style, writers

1 Every book must be chewed to get out its juice.
Chinese proverb

2 The style is the man.
Proverb

3 Most people enjoy the sight of their own handwriting as they enjoy the smell of their own farts.
W. H. Auden (1907–73) British poet. *The Dyer's Hand*, 'Writing'

4 It is all very well to be able to write books, but can you waggle your ears?
J. M. Barrie (1860–1937) British playwright. Speaking to H. G. Wells. *Barrie: The Story of A Genius* (J. A. Hamerton)

5 Sapper, Buchan, Dornford Yates, practitioners in that school of Snobbery with Violence that runs like a thread of good-class tweed through twentieth-century literature.
Alan Bennett (1934–) British playwright and actor. Obituary in *The Times* for Colin Watson, 21 Jan 1983

6 Beneath the rule of men entirely great,
The pen is mightier than the sword.
Edward Bulwer-Lytton (1803–73) British novelist and politician. *Richelieu*, II:2

7 From this it is clear how much more cruel the pen is than the sword.
Robert Burton (1577–1640) English scholar and explorer. *Anatomy of Melancholy*, Pt. I

8 That's not writing, that's typing.
Truman Capote (1924–84) US writer. Referring to the writer Jack Kerouac. Attrib.

9 NINA. Your play's hard to act, there are no living people in it.
TREPLEV. Living people! We should show life neither as it is nor as it ought to be, but as we see it in our dreams.
Anton Chekhov (1860–1904) Russian dramatist. *The Seagull*, I

10 Better to write for yourself and have no public, than write for the public and have no self.
Cyril Connolly (1903–74) British journalist. *Turnstile One* (ed. V. S. Pritchett)

11 Neither am I.
Peter Cook (1937–) British writer and entertainer. On being told that the person sitting next to him at a dinner party was 'writing a book'. Attrib.

12 All good writing is *swimming under water* and holding your breath.
F. Scott Fitzgerald (1896–1940) US novelist. Letter to Frances Scott Fitzgerald

13 No tears in the writer, no tears in the reader.
Robert Frost (1875–1963) US poet. *Collected Poems*, Preface

14 Another damned, thick, square book! Always scribble, scribble, scribble! Eh! Mr Gibbon?
William, Duke of Gloucester (1743–1805) The brother of George III. Addressing Edward Gibbon, author of *The History of the Decline and Fall of the Roman Empire*. *Literary Memorials* (Best)

15 You must write for children in the same way as you do for adults, only better.
Maxim Gorky (Aleksei Maksimovich Peshkov; 1868–1936) Russian writer. Attrib.

16 You will have written exceptionally well if, by skilful arrangement of your words, you have made an ordinary one seem original.
Horace (Quintus Horatius Flaccus; 65–8 BC) Roman poet. *Ars Poetica*

17 A bad book is as much a labour to write as a good one; it comes as sincerely from the author's soul.
Aldous Huxley (1894–1964) British novelist. *Point Counter Point*

18 A man will turn over half a library to make one book.
Samuel Johnson (1709–84) British lexicographer. *Life of Johnson* (J. Boswell), Vol. II

19 What is written without effort is in general read without pleasure.
Samuel Johnson *Johnsonian Miscellanies* (ed. G. B. Hill), Vol. II

20 Read over your compositions, and where ever you meet with a passage which you think is particularly fine, strike it out.
Samuel Johnson Recalling the advice of a college tutor. *Life of Johnson* (J. Boswell), Vol. II

21 No man but a blockhead ever wrote, except for money.
Samuel Johnson *Life of Johnson* (J. Boswell), Vol. III

22 Many suffer from the incurable disease of writing, and it becomes chronic in their sick minds.
Juvenal (Decimus Junius Juvenalis; 60–130 AD) Roman satirist. *Satires*, VII

23 Clear writers, like clear fountains, do not seem so deep as they are; the turbid look the most profound.
Walter Savage Landor (1775–1864) British poet and writer. *Imaginary Conversations*, 'Southey and Porson'

24 I like to write when I feel spiteful: it's like having a good sneeze.
D. H. Lawrence (1885–1930) British novelist. Letter to Lady Cynthia Asquith, Nov 1913

25 Nothing but old fags and cabbage-stumps of quotations from the Bible and the rest, stewed in the juice of deliberate, journalistic dirty-mindedness.
D. H. Lawrence Referring to James Joyce. Letter to Aldous Huxley, 15 Aug 1928

26 When once the itch of literature comes over a man, nothing can cure it but the scratching of a pen.
Samuel Lover (1797–1868) Irish novelist. *Handy Andy*, Ch. 36

27 I shall not be satisfied unless I produce something that shall for a few days supersede the last

fashionable novel on the tables of young ladies.
Lord Macaulay (1800–59) British historian. Letter to Macvey Napier, 5 Nov 1841

28 There is an impression abroad that everyone has it in him to write one book; but if by this is implied a good book the impression is false.
W. Somerset Maugham (1874–1965) British novelist. *The Summing Up*

29 When you steal from one author, it's plagiarism; if you steal from many, it's research.
Wilson Mizner (1876–1933) US writer and wit. Attrib.

30 I suffer from the disease of writing books and being ashamed of them when they are finished.
Baron de Montesquieu (1688–1755) French writer. *Pensées diverses*

31 Writing is like getting married. One should never commit oneself until one is amazed at one's luck.
Iris Murdoch (1919–) Irish-born British novelist. *The Black Prince*, 'Bradley Pearson's Foreword'

32 Poor Knight! he really had two periods, the first – a dull man writing broken English, the second – a broken man writing dull English.
Vladimir Nabokov (1899–1977) Russian-born US novelist. *The Real Life of Sebastian Knight*, Ch. 1

33 True ease in writing comes from art, not chance,
As those move easiest who have learn'd to dance.
'Tis not enough no harshness gives offence,
The sound must seem an echo to the sense.
Alexander Pope (1688–1744) British poet. *An Essay on Criticism*

34 What is the future of my kind of writing? . . . Perhaps in retirement . . . a quieter, narrower kind of life can be worked out and adopted. Bounded by English literature and the Anglican Church and small pleasures like sewing and choosing dress material for this uncertain summer.
Barbara Pym (1928–80) British novelist. Diary, 6 Mar 1972

35 Make 'em laugh; make 'em cry; make 'em wait.
Charles Reade (1911–77) British novelist and dramatist. Advice to an aspiring writer. Attrib.

36 The profession of letters is, after all, the only one in which one can make no money without being ridiculous.
Jules Renard (1894–1910) French writer. *Journal*

37 My scribbling pays me zero francs per line – not including the white spaces.
Marquis de Rochefort (1830–1913) French journalist. Referring to his salary as a writer. *Autant en apportent les mots* (Pedrazzini)

38 I have a certain hesitation in starting my biography too soon for fear of something important having not yet happened. Suppose I should end my days as President of Mexico; the biography would seem incomplete if it did not mention this fact.
Bertrand Russell (1872–1970) British philosopher. Letter to Stanley Unwin, Nov 1930

39 No, this right hand shall work it all off.
Walter Scott (1771–1832) Scottish novelist. Refusing offers of help following his bankruptcy in 1826. *Century of Anecdote* (J. Timbs)

40 Writing, when properly managed, (as you may be sure I think mine is) is but a different name for conversation.
Laurence Sterne (1713–68) Irish-born British writer. *Tristram Shandy*

41 Whatever sentence will bear to be read twice, we may be sure was thought twice.
Henry David Thoreau (1817–62) US writer. *Journal*, 1842

42 Not that the story need be long, but it will take a long while to make it short.
Henry David Thoreau Letter, 16 Nov 1867

43 Three hours a day will produce as much as a man ought to write.
Anthony Trollope (1815–82) British novelist. *Autobiography*, Ch. 15

44 I put the words down and push them a bit.
Evelyn Waugh (1903–66) British novelist. Obituary, *New York Times*, 11 Apr 1966

45 The fact that – these books – two novels, a book of travel, a biography, a work of contemporary history – never got beyond the first ten thousand words was testimony to the resilience of his character.
Evelyn Waugh *Put Out More Flags*

46 All my novels are an accumulation of detail. I'm a bit of a bower-bird.
Patrick White (1912–) British-born Australian novelist. *Southerly*, 139

47 Every great and original writer, in proportion as he is great and original, must himself create the taste by which he is to be relished.
William Wordsworth (1770–1850) British poet. *Lyrical Ballads*, Preface

Y

YEATS, W(illiam) B(utler)

(1865–1939) Irish poet and dramatist. His verse collections include *The Tower* (1928) and *The Winding Stair* (1929). With Lady Gregory, he founded the Abbey Theatre in Dublin, for which he wrote many plays.

Quotations about Yeats

1 Willie Yeats stood for enchantment.
G. K. Chesterton (1874–1936) British writer. *Autobiography*

2 Yeats is not a man of this world; and when you hurl an enormous, smashing chunk of it at him, he dodges it, small blame to him.
George Bernard Shaw (1856–1950) Irish dramatist and critic. Letter to Sean O'Casey

Quotations by Yeats

3 That William Blake
Who beat upon the wall
Till Truth obeyed his call.
An Acre of Grass

4 O chestnut tree, great rooted blossomer,
Are you the leaf, the blossom or the bole?
O body swayed to music; O brightening glance,
How can we know the dancer from the dance?
Among School Children

5 When I think of all the books I have read, and of the wise words I have heard spoken, and of the anxiety I have given to parents and grandparents, and of the hopes that

I have had, all life weighed in the scales of my own life seems to me preparation for something that never happens.
Autobiography

6 Now that my ladder's gone
I must lie down where all the ladders start,
In the foul rag-and-bone shop of the heart.
The Circus Animals' Desertion

7 Though leaves are many, the root is one;
Through all the lying days of my youth
I swayed my leaves and flowers in the sun;
Now I may wither into the truth.
The Coming of Wisdom with Time

8 But Love has pitched his mansion in
The place of excrement.
Crazy Jane Talks with the Bishop

9 Wine comes in at the mouth
And love comes in at the eye;
That's all we shall know for truth
Before we grow old and die.
A Drinking Song

10 All changed, changed utterly:
A terrible beauty is born
Easter 1916

11 Out of the quarrel with others we make rhetoric; out of the quarrel with ourselves we make poetry.
Essay

12 When I play on my fiddle in Dooney,
Folk dance like a wave of the sea.
The Fiddler of Dooney

13 For the good are always the merry,
Save by an evil chance,
And the merry love the fiddle,
And the merry love to dance
The Fiddler of Dooney

14 One that is ever kind said yesterday:
'Your well-belovèd's hair has threads of grey,
And little shadows come about her eyes.'
The Folly of Being Comforted

15 I have drunk ale from the Country of the Young
And weep because I know all things now.
He Thinks of his Past Greatness

16 Nor law, nor duty bade me fight,
Nor public men, nor cheering crowds,
A lonely impulse of delight
Drove to this tumult in the clouds;
I balanced all, brought all to mind,
The years to come seemed waste of breath,
A waste of breath the years behind
In balance with this life, this death.
An Irish Airman Foresees his Death

17 I will arise and go now, and go to Innisfree,
And a small cabin build there, of clay and wattles made;
Nine bean rows will I have there, a hive for the honey bee,
And live alone in the bee-loud glade.
The Lake Isle of Innisfree

18 And I shall have some peace there, for peace comes dropping slow,
Dropping from the veils of the morning to where the cricket sings.
The Lake Isle of Innisfree

19 The wind blows out of the gates of the day,
The wind blows over the lonely of heart,
And the lonely of heart is withered away.
The Land of Heart's Desire

20 I shudder and I sigh to think
That even Cicero
And many-minded Homer were
Mad as the mist and snow.
Mad as the Mist and Snow

21 Time drops in decay,
Like a candle burnt out.
The Moods

22 Never to have lived is best, ancient writers say;
Never to have drawn the breath of life,
never to have looked into the eye of day
The second best's a gay goodnight and quickly turn away.
Oedipus at Colonus

23 In dreams begins responsibility.
Old Play, Epigraph, Responsibilities

24 Where, where but here have Pride and Truth,
That long to give themselves for wage,
To shake their wicked sides at youth
Restraining reckless middle age?
On hearing that the Students of our New University have joined the Agitation against Immoral Literature

25 A pity beyond all telling
Is hid in the heart of love.
The Pity of Love

26 An intellectual hatred is the worst.
A Prayer for My Daughter

27 That is no country for old men. The young
In one another's arms, birds in the trees
– Those dying generations – at their song,
The salmon-falls, the mackerel-crowded seas,
Fish, flesh, or fowl, commend all summer long
Whatever is begotten, born, and dies.
Sailing to Byzantium, I

28 Things fall apart; the centre cannot hold;
Mere anarchy is loosed upon the world,
The blood-dimmed tide is loosed, and everywhere
The ceremony of innocence is drowned;
The best lack all conviction, while the worst
Are full of passionate intensity.
The Second Coming

29 A woman of so shining loveliness
That men threshed corn at midnight by a tress,
A little stolen tress.
The Secret Rose

30 And pluck till time and times are done
The silver apples of the moon
The golden apples of the sun.
The Song of Wandering Aengus

31 But was there ever dog that praised his fleas?
To a Poet, who would have me Praise certain Bad Poets, Imitators of His and Mine

32 Under bare Ben Bulben's head
In Drumcliff churchyard Yeats is laid . . .
On limestone quarried near the spot
By his command these words are cut: *Cast a cold eye On life, on death. Horseman, pass by!*
Under Ben Bulben, VI

33 When you are old and gray and full of sleep,
And nodding by the fire, take down this book,
And slowly read, and dream of the soft look
Your eyes had once, and of their shadows deep . . .
When you are Old

34 Love fled

And paced upon the mountains overhead
And hid his face amid a crowd of stars.
When you are Old

35 But I, being poor, have only my dreams;
I have spread my dreams under your feet;
Tread softly because you tread on my dreams.
He Wishes for the Cloths of Heaven

36 It's not a writer's business to hold opinions.
Speaking to playwright, Denis Johnston. *The Guardian*, 5 May 1977

37 He is all blood, dirt and sucked sugar stick.
Referring to Wilfred Owen. *Letters on Poetry to Dorothy Wellesley*, Letter, 21 Dec 1938

38 O'CONNOR. How are you?
W.B.Y. Not very well, I can only write prose today.
Attrib.

YIELDING

See also determination, weakness

1 The concessions of the weak are the concessions of fear.
Edmund Burke (1729–97) British politician. *Speech on Conciliation with America* (House of Commons, 22 Mar 1775)

2 He that complies against his will,
Is of his own opinion still.
Samuel Butler (1612–80) English satirist. *Hudibras*, Pt. III

YOUTH

See also age, children

1 The younger members of our society are not different from what they have always been . . . . At the time of the world when there were only two young people, Cain and Abel, one of them was a delinquent.
Lord Aberdare (1919–) *The Observer*, 'Sayings of the Week', 25 Feb 1968

2 A stage between infancy and adultery.
Anonymous

3 Better is a poor and a wise child than an old and foolish king, who will no more be admonished.
Bible: Ecclesiastes 4:13

4 It is good for a man that he bear the yoke in his youth.
Bible: Lamentations 3:27

5 Youth is something very new: twenty years ago no one mentioned it.
Coco Chanel (1883–1971) French dress designer. *Coco Chanel, Her Life, Her Secrets* (Marcel Haedrich)

6 This day I am thirty years old. Let me now bid a cheerful adieu to my youth. My young days are now surely over, and why should I regret them? Were I never to grow old I might be always here, and might never bid farewell to sin and sorrow.
Janet Colquhoun (1781–1846) Diary, 17 Apr 1811

7 I remember my youth and the feeling that will never come back any more – the feeling that I could last for ever, outlast the sea, the earth, and all men; the deceitful feeling that lures us on to perils, to love, to vain effort – to death . . .
Joseph Conrad (Teodor Josef Konrad Korzeniowski; 1857–1924) Polish-born British novelist. *Youth*

8 The young always have the same problem – how to rebel and conform at the same time. They have now solved this by defying their parents and copying one another.
Quentin Crisp (?1910–) Model, publicist, and writer. *The Naked Civil Servant*

9 Almost everything that is great has been done by youth.
Benjamin Disraeli (1804–81) British statesman. *Coningsby*, Bk. III, Ch. 1

10 'And youth is cruel, and has no remorse
And smiles at situations which it cannot see.'
I smile of course,
And go on drinking tea.
T. S. Eliot (1888–1965) US-born British poet and dramatist. *Portrait of a Lady*

11 I never dared be radical when young, for fear it would make me conservative when old.
Robert Frost (1875–1963) US poet. *Precaution*

12 *Les enfants terribles.*
The embarrassing young.
Paul Gavarni (1801–66) French illustrator. Title of a series of prints

13 No young man believes he shall ever die.
William Hazlitt (1778–1830) British essayist. *The Monthly Magazine*, Mar 1827

14 Is is the malady of our age that the young are so busy teaching us that they have no time left to learn.
Eric Hoffer (1902–) US writer.

15 A majority of young people seem to develop mental arteriosclerosis forty years before they get the physical kind.
Aldous Huxley (1894–1964) British writer. Interview. *Writers at Work: Second Series*

16 Youth will come here and beat on my door, and force its way in.
Henrik Ibsen (1828–1906) Norwegian dramatist. *The Master Builder*, I

17 Young men make great mistakes in life; for one thing, they idealize love too much.
Benjamin Jowett (1817–93) British theologian. *Letters of B. Jowett* (Abbott and Campbell)

18 When all the world is young, lad,
And all the trees are green;
And every goose a swan, lad,
And every lass a queen;
Then hey for boot and horse, lad,
And round the world away:
Young blood must have its course, lad,
And every dog his day.
Charles Kingsley (1819–75) British writer. *Songs from The Water Babies*, 'Young and Old'

19 Youth is a malady of which one becomes cured a little every day.
Benito Mussolini (1883–1945) Italian dictator. Said on his 50th birthday.

20 One starts to get young at the age of sixty and then it is too late.
Pablo Picasso (1881–1973) Spanish painter. *Sunday Times*, 20 Oct 1963

21 The atrocious crime of being a young man . . . I shall neither attempt to palliate nor deny.
William Pitt the Elder (1708–78) British statesman. Speech, House of Commons, 27 Jan 1741

22 He whom the gods love dies young, while he has his strength and senses and wits.
Plautus (c. 254 BC–184 BC) Roman dramatist. *Bacchides*, IV:8

23 One of the pleasures of middle age is to *find out* that one WAS right, and that one was much righter than one knew at say 17 or 23.

Ezra Pound (1885–1972) US poet. *ABC of Reading,* Ch. 1

24 Youth is in itself so amiable, that were the soul as perfect as the body, we could not forbear adoring it.

Marie de Sévigné (1626–96) French letter-writer. Letter to her daughter

25 My salad days,
When I was green in judgment, cold in blood,
To say as I said then!

William Shakespeare (1564–1616) English dramatist. *Antony and Cleopatra,* I:5

26 Crabbed age and youth cannot live together:
Youth is full of pleasure, age is full of care;
Youth like summer morn, age like winter weather;
Youth like summer brave, age like winter bare.

William Shakespeare *The Passionate Pilgrim,* XII

27 I would there were no age between ten and three and twenty, or that youth would sleep out the rest; for there is nothing in the between but getting wenches with child, wronging the ancientry, stealing, fighting.

William Shakespeare *The Winter's Tale,* III:3

28 Far too good to waste on children.

George Bernard Shaw (1856–1950) Irish dramatist and critic. *10,000 Jokes, Toasts, and Stories* (L. Copeland)

29 Live as long as you may, the first twenty years are the longest half of your life.

Robert Southey (1774–1843) British poet. *The Doctor,* Ch. 130

30 Proficiency at billiards is proof of a misspent youth.

Herbert Spencer (1820–1903) British philosopher. Attrib.

31 No wise man ever wished to be younger.

Jonathan Swift (1667–1745) Anglo-Irish priest, satirist, and poet. *Thoughts on Various Subjects, Moral and Diverting*

32 Young people ought not to be idle. It is very bad for them.

Margaret Thatcher (1925–) British politician and prime minister. *The Times,* 1984

• INDEXES

KEYWORD INDEX

A

infancy, childhood, a. and obsolescence AGE, 46
maturity is only a short break in a. AGE, 32
Adonais I weep for A. MOURNING, 14
adored a. once too LOVE, 166
adores he a. his maker CONCEIT, 8
The ignorant man always a. IGNORANCE, 15
adorned as a bride a. for her husband BIBLICAL QUOTATIONS, 601
adornment What time he can spare from the a. of his person NEGLECT, 4
adrenal larger cerebrums and smaller a. glands WAR, 99
adult A child becomes an a. when RIGHT, 3
the larger their a. clientele PSYCHIATRY, 25
What is an a. AGE, 11
adultery and gods a. ADULTERY, 1
between infancy and a. YOUTH, 2
commit a. at one end ADULTERY, 3
I've committed a. in my heart ADULTERY, 2
rather be taken in a. than in provincialism FASHION, 7
the Tasmanians, who never committed a. ADULTERY, 5
thou shalt not commit a. BIBLICAL QUOTATIONS, 147
would have constituted a. SMALLNESS, 3
adulthood a. . . . now eat dessert without eating her vegetables CHILDREN, 3
adults The value of marriage is . . . that children produce a. MARRIAGE, 52
advance Every great a. in science SCIENCE, 26
advanced years behind the a. countries PROGRESS, 22
advantage a. of time and place . . . is half a victory WAR, 54
not necessarily to Japan's a. DEFEAT, 8
The a. of doing one's praising PRAISE, 6
you have the a. of me REPARTEE, 69
advantages Wealth is not without its a. WEALTH, 19
adventure extravagance, . . . thrift and a. ADVENTURE, 2
Marriage is the only a. open to the cowardly ADVENTURE, 3
To die will be an awfully big a. ADVENTURE, 1
adventures A good critic . . . narrates the a. of his mind CRITICS, 4
adversity a. doth best discover virtue MISFORTUNE, 4
the bread of a. BIBLICAL QUOTATIONS, 267
advertise It pays to a. ADVERTISING, 2
advertised Wealth . . . must be a. OSTENTATION, 3
advertisement the worst a. for Socialism is its adherents CHRISTIANITY, 49
advertisers as the a. don't object to ADVERTISING, 5
advertising A. . . . most fun . . . with your clothes on ADVERTISING, 3
Half the money I spend on a. is wasted ADVERTISING, 4
advice A. is seldom welcome ADVICE, 8
a. . . . poised between the cliché TACT, 7
earnest a. from my seniors ADVICE, 22
how ready people always are with a. ADVICE, 21
intended to give you some a. ADVICE, 13
No one wants a. ADVICE, 20
nothing so freely as a. ADVICE, 15
woman seldom asks a. WOMEN, 9
advocaat a., a drink made from lawyers ALCOHOL, 28
advocate the soul of a martyr with the intellect of an a. POLITICIANS, 11
aeroplane a. is valuable . . . destroys men and women EQUALITY, 4
Aesculapius we owe a cock to A. LAST WORDS, 81
Aesop prettily devised of A. CONCEIT, 3
aesthetic the degree of my a. emotion CRITICISM, 7
afar a. and asunder PARTING, 4
affair The great a. is to move TRAVEL, 37
affairs tide in the a. of men OPPORTUNITY, 18
affectation Universities incline wits to sophistry and a. EDUCATION, 10
affection a. is too strong a word POLITICS, 131
affections different taste in jokes is a . . . strain on the a. HUMOR, 22
affliction feed him with bread of a. BIBLICAL QUOTATIONS, 404
the water of a. BIBLICAL QUOTATIONS, 267
affluent the a. society LUXURY, 3
The a. society . . . made everyone dislike work IDLENESS, 9
afford purest treasure mortal times a. REPUTATION, 10
afraid A. of Virginia Woolf BOOK TITLES, 1
be not a. to do thine office EXECUTION, 26
Englishman . . . is a. to feel EDUCATION, 29
Men not a. of God, a. of me PRIDE, 7
Whenever I look inside myself I am a. SELF, 11
Afric Where A.'s sunny fountains PLACES, 18
Africa more familiar with A. than my own body BODY, 18
something new out of A. AFRICA, 2
When a white man in A. AFRICA, 1
after-dinner an a.'s sleep AGE, 68
afterlife that the a. will be any less exasperating AFTERLIFE, 3
afternoon could lose the war in an a. OFFICERS, 4
I could have lost the war in an a. WAR, 79
Summer a. – summer a. SUMMER, 5
against A. whom EGOTISM, 1
He said he was a. it REPARTEE, 28
neither for nor a. institutions INDIFFERENCE, 7
This is a. fighting ever hereafter ROYALTY, 43
who's for you and who's a. you POLITICS, 77
Agamemnon I have looked upon the face of A. HISTORY, 31
Many brave men . . . before A.'s time OBLIVION, 1
age A child blown up by a. AGE, 11
A. cannot wither her ADMIRATION, 16
A. . . . nor custom stale her infinite virginity PURITY, 7
a. of chivalry is gone EUROPE, 3
A. only matters when one is ageing OLD AGE, 73
A. seldom arrives smoothly or quickly OLD AGE, 78
A. shall not weary them MEMORIALS, 6
A. will bring all things PRUDERY, 3
A. will not be defied AGE, 8
an a. in which useless knowledge KNOWLEDGE, 22
And now in a. I bud again OLD AGE, 51
an old a. of cards OLD AGE, 74
a sign of a. if you feel like the day after the night before OLD AGE, 13
A tart temper never mellows with a. CHARACTER, 13
at my a. I have to hold on to something OLD AGE, 26
At twenty years of a. AGE, 34
Cool'd a long a. in the deep-delved earth ALCOHOL, 46
Crabbed a. and youth AGE, 70
Damn the a.. I'll write for antiquity POSTERITY, 8
do not necessarily improve with a. AGE, 38
Do you think at your a., it is right OLD AGE, 28
gift of perpetual old a. OLD AGE, 100
He hath not forgotten my a. GOD, 52
He prays for a long life, and he fears an old a. OLD AGE, 4
how I have achieved such a ripe a. LONGEVITY, 5
I prefer old a. to the alternative OLD AGE, 31
I summon a. /To grant youth's heritage AGE, 17
I think middle a. is the best time AGE, 42
It is . . . at my a. I now begin to see things as they really are LAST WORDS, 34
I was born . . . at an extremely tender a. BIRTH, 13
lady of a certain a. AGE, 19
Lo, Hudled up, together Lye /Gray A., Grene youth, White Infancy ANONYMOUS, 54
Man arrives as a novice at each a. of his life AGE, 20
no a. between ten and three and twenty YOUTH, 27
nothing in thy youth, how canst thou find any thing in thine a. AGE, 12
No woman should ever be quite accurate about her a. AGE, 82
Old-a., a second child OLD AGE, 32
Old a. . . . gives us what we have earned OLD AGE, 25
old a. is . . . older than I am OLD AGE, 16
Old a. is the most unexpected OLD AGE, 98
Old a. is the out-patients' department OLD AGE, 30
old a. . . . the fear that it may go on too long OLD AGE, 96
Our parents' a. . . . has produced us AGE, 41
Socialism . . . a. or a little money will not cure SOCIALISM, 7
Some people reach the a. of 60 OLD AGE, 52
Thou has nor youth nor a. AGE, 68
treat . . . her a. with ambiguity AGE, 64
what a. takes away OLD AGE, 103
When men grow virtuous in their old a. SACRIFICE, 4
when Mozart was my a. AGE, 44
who tells one her real a. AGE, 83
Years hence, perhaps, may dawn an a. FUTURE, 2
aged a. diplomats . . . bored than for young men to die DIPLOMACY, 3
a man of about a hundred and ten who had been a. OLD AGE, 102
An a. man is but a paltry thing OLD AGE, 106
the beauty /Of an a. face OLD AGE, 27
ageing Age only matters when one is a. OLD AGE, 73
Like so many a. college people ACADEMICS, 6
The a. man of the middle twentieth century OLD AGE, 54
agenda Our a. is now exhausted AGREEMENT, 5
the a. winks at me BUREAUCRACY, 8
agent prime a. of all human perception IMAGINATION, 1
ages His acts being seven a. HUMAN CONDITION, 22
Our God, our help in a. past RELIGION, 75
Rock of a., cleft for me RELIGION, 69
the a. of other women AGE, 25
aggregate the a. of the recipes SCIENCE, 87
aggressor whole world should be ranged against an a. POLITICS, 10
aging A. . . . the only . . . way to live a long time LONGEVITY, 3
agitate to a. a bag of wind FOOTBALL, 13
Agnes St A.' Eve – Ah, bitter chill it was WINTER, 2
agnostic rather a compliment to be called an a. HUMILITY, 3
agony a lonely spasm of helpless a. DEATH, 84
agree colours will a. in the dark DARKNESS, 2
don't say you a. with me AGREEMENT, 6
If two men on the same job a. AGREEMENT, 7
those who a. with us AGREEMENT, 4
Two of a trade can ne'er a. ARGUMENTS, 5
agreeable I do not want people to be very a. NASTINESS, 2
My idea of an a. person AGREEMENT, 3
agreement My people and I have come to an a. FREEDOM, 15
Whenever you accept our views we shall be in full a. INFLEXIBILITY, 1
agrees a person who a. with me AGREEMENT, 3
agricultural the a. labourers . . . commute from London COUNTRYSIDE, 9
aid One who is ill has . . . the duty to seek medical a. ILLNESS, 44
Aids to stop them catching A. ILLNESS, 20
ail what can a. thee, knight at arms ILLNESS, 37
ailment An imaginary a. is worse than a disease HYPOCHONDRIA, 2
a symptom of some a. in the spiritual part HOLISTIC MEDICINE, 2
ailments our a. are the same ILLNESS, 65
ain't bet you a hundred bucks he a. in here ESCAPE, 2
air cat is a diagram and pattern of subtle a. CATS, 5
Fresh a. impoverishes the doctor HEALTHY LIVING, 6
Get your room full of good a. LONGEVITY, 11
my spirit found outlet in the a. FLYING, 3
Patients should have rest, food, fresh a., and exercise HEALTHY LIVING, 33
the castles I have, are built with a. DREAMS, 10
to the Germans that of the a. EMPIRE, 5
waste its sweetness on the desert a. WASTE, 2
Water, a., and cleanliness are the chief articles in my pharmacopeia HEALTHY LIVING, 32
airplane The a. stays up because it doesn't have the time to fall SCIENCE, 93
airplanes a. . . . are wonderful things for other people to FLYING, 4
I feel about a. the way I feel about diets FLYING, 4
airth Let them bestow on every a. a limb EXECUTION, 13
aisle A.. Altar. Hymn MARRIAGE, 99
aitches We have nothing to lose but our a. CLASS, 32
Alamein Before A. we never had a victory WORLD WAR II, 22
alarm The tocsin you hear today is not an a. but an alert PATRIOTISM, 11
alarms confused a. of struggle and flight WAR, 11
albatross I shot the a. BIRDS, 5

analyzed Everything has been discussed and a. BOOKS, 2
analysis a. is not the only way to resolve inner conflicts PSYCHOANALYSIS, 14
Daughters go into a. hating their fathers PSYCHOANALYSIS, 22
historian fits a man for psychological a. PSYCHOLOGY, 14
analyst the a. should pay the patient PSYCHOANALYSIS, 21
analysts Like all a. . . . interested only in himself PSYCHOANALYSIS, 21
anarchist I am a Tory A. POLITICS, 11
anarchy a well-bred sort of emotional a. CAMBRIDGE, 3
grieved under a *democracy*, call it *a.* ANARCHY, 1
anathema A. Maranatha BIBLICAL QUOTATIONS, 50
anatomies make them so many a. DISEASE, 14
anatomists There is no counting the names, that surgeons and a. give KNOWLEDGE, 32
We a. are like the porters DOCTORS, 40
anatomy A. is destiny DESTINY, 12
A. is to physiology MEDICINE, 28
he has studied a. and dissected at least one woman MARRIAGE, 18
in a. it is better to have learned and lost LEARNING, 13
ancestor I am my own a. ANCESTRY, 1
ancestors a. on either side of the Battle of Hastings ANCESTRY, 4
when his half-civilized a. were hunting the wild boar EARTH, 3
ancestry I can trace my a. back to a . . . globule ANCESTRY, 2
I can trace my a. back to a protoplasmal primordic atomic globule EVOLUTION, 14
ancient with the a. is wisdom BIBLICAL QUOTATIONS, 301
anecdotage man fell into his a. OLD AGE, 41
anesthesiologists whiff of a. LANGUAGE, 3
angel An a. writing in a book of gold DREAMS, 8
A. of Death has been abroad WAR, 29
A. of the Lord came down CHRISTMAS, 20
career that made the Recording A. think seriously about . . . shorthand EPITAPHS, 5
gave you manna . . . a.s' bread BIBLICAL QUOTATIONS, 120
in action, how like an a. DELIGHT, 10
in comparison with which . . . I am a A. EVIL, 10
In heaven an a. is nobody in particular ANGELS, 2
Is man an ape or an a. EVOLUTION, 12
Look Homeward, A. BOOK TITLES, 24
This was the A. of History WORLD WAR II, 28
woman yet think him an a. LOVE, 177
You may not be an a. LOVE, 61
angels a little lower than the a. CHARACTER, 17
fools rush in where a. fear to tread HASTE, 8
I . . . am on the side of the a. EVOLUTION, 12
Its visits, /Like those of a. ANGELS, 1
Not Angles, but a. ENGLISH, 17
One more devils'-triumph and sorrow for a. DAMNATION, 1
People are not fallen a. CRITICISM, 33
Tears such as a. weep SORROW, 13
There were a. dining at the Ritz BIRDS, 12
the tongues of men and of a. BIBLICAL QUOTATIONS, 44
anger A. is one of the sinews of the soul ANGER, 6
a. makes us all stupid ANGER, 9
A. supplies the arms ANGER, 10
Grief and disappointment give rise to a. EMOTION, 3
he that is slow to a. is better than the mighty BIBLICAL QUOTATIONS, 575
Juno's never-forgetting a. ENDURANCE, 27
Angles Not A., but angels ENGLISH, 17
Angli the *Saxones, A.*, and *Iutae* ENGLISH, 6
angling A. is somewhat like poetry FISHING, 2
A. may be said to be . . . like the mathematics FISHING, 5
lovers of virtue . . . and go a-A. FISHING, 4
We may say of a. as Dr Boteler said of strawberries FISHING, 3
Anglo-Catholic Becoming an A. must . . . be a sad business CATHOLICISM, 13
Anglo-Saxon Come in, you A. swine INSULTS, 15
those are A. attitudes ENGLISH, 11
angry A. Young Man ALIENATION, 3
The man who gets a. . . . in the right way . . . is commended ANGER, 2
anguish drinking deep of that divinest a. SUFFERING, 10
every 'mental' symptom is a veiled cry of a. PSYCHIATRY, 31
Making love is the sovereign remedy for a. SEX, 58
there are going to be howls of a. POLITICS, 62
angular an oblong a. figure HUMOR, 33
animal He was into a. husbandry SEX, 60
information vegetable, a. and mineral KNOWLEDGE, 16
Man is a gaming a. SPORT AND GAMES, 14
man is and will always be a wild a. MANKIND, 21
Man is an intellectual a. INTELLECT, 5
Man is a noble a. MANKIND, 13
man is . . . a religious a. RELIGION, 14
Man is a social a. SOCIETY, 14
Man is by nature a political a. POLITICS, 9
Man is the only a. . . . on friendly terms with the victims . . . he eats HYPOCRISY, 7
MAN, n. An a. so lost in rapturous contemplation MANKIND, 9
This a. is very bad ANONYMOUS, 101
This a. is very dangerous SELF-PRESERVATION, 4
true to your a. instincts ANIMALISM, 3
Whenever you observe an a. closely ANIMALS, 10
animality its own a. either objectionable or funny HUMOR, 34
animals All a. are equal EQUALITY, 21
all a. were created . . . for the use of man ANIMALS, 20
all there is to distinguish us from other a. MANKIND, 7
A. are such agreeable friends ANIMALS, 13
a. . . . know nothing . . . of what people say about them ANIMALS, 23
But if we stop loving a. LOVE, 169
differs in no respect from the ovules of other a. EVOLUTION, 7
I could . . . live with a. ANIMALS, 26
love a. and children too much LOVE, 127
Man, when perfected, is the best of a. MANKIND, 4
My music . . . understood by children and a. MUSIC, 47
Never work with a. or children ACTING, 2
paragon of a. DELIGHT, 10
some a. are more equal than others EQUALITY, 21
The a. went in one by one ANONYMOUS, 79
There are two things for which a. are . . . envied ANIMALS, 23
Wild a. never kill for sport HUNTING, 4
Anna great A.! whom three realms obey DRINKS, 16
annals short and simple a. of the poor POVERTY, 15
Anne Move Queen A.? Most certainly not MEMORIALS, 17
Annie for bonnie A. Laurie LOVE AND DEATH, 1
annihilating A. all that's made OBLIVION, 3
annihilation No a. REPRESENTATION, 3
anno A. domini . . . the most fatal complaint DEATH, 79
annual A. income twenty pounds ECONOMICS, 8
annuity Buy an a. cheap MONEY 18
anomaly Poverty is an a. to rich people HUNGER, 2
anon I would . . . guess that A. . . . was often a woman WOMEN, 128
another A. year! – a. deadly blow DEFEAT, 18
He who would do good to a. GOOD, 2
I would have given you a. CHIVALRY, 5
Life is just one damned thing after a. LIFE, 43
No man can . . . condemn a. JUDGMENT, 7
answer a. a fool according to his folly ANSWERS, 3
A timid question will . . . receive a confident a. ANSWERS, 6
But a. came there none ANSWERS, 4
give a. as need requireth ANSWERS, 2
I do not a. questions like this without being paid MASCULINITY, 1
more than the wisest man can a. ANSWERS, 5
The a. . . . is blowin' in the wind ANSWERS, 7
the inquisitive mind can . . . receive no a. ANSWERS, 8
we are not careful to a. thee in this matter BIBLICAL QUOTATIONS, 58
where no one asks, no one needs to a. ANSWERS, 9
would not stay for an a. ANSWERS, 1
antagonistic the most a. to the Victorian age WRITERS, 60
antan *les neiges d'a.* NOSTALGIA, 27
anthology a. is like all the plums and orange peel BOOKS, 34
A well chosen a. is a complete dispensary of medicine MEDICINE, 32
antic dance an a. hay DANCING, 8
anticipation the intelligent a. of facts JOURNALISM, 17
anti-clerical it makes me understand a. things CLERGY, 1
anti-climax everything afterward savors of a. PRECOCITY, 2
antidote the a. to desire DESIRE, 6
antipathy dislike the French from . . . vulgar a. FRANCE, 18
strong a. of good to bad PROVOCATION, 2
antiquated war . . . will be considered as a. as a duel WAR, 67
antiquity Damn the age. I'll write for a. POSTERITY, 8
anti-Semite An American is either a Jew, or an a. UNITED STATES, 88
hated /by every a. /as if I were a Jew PREJUDICE, 16
antiseptic Since the a. treatment CLEANNESS, 5
antivivisectionists There are a few honest a. VIVISECTION, 3
anvil My sledge and a. lie declined ANONYMOUS, 61
anxiety Every little yielding to a. WORRY, 3
groundless a. on the score of future misfortunes HYPOCHONDRIA, 11
the Age of A., the age of the neurosis NEUROSIS, 6
the a. of being a woman WOMEN, 20
anxious a. to do the wrong thing correctly ETIQUETTE, 8
piles to give him an A. Expression DOCTORS, 13
anybody A. can be Pope ACHIEVEMENT, 7
who you are, you aren't a. FAME, 20
anyone A. for tennis INVITATIONS, 1
a. here whom I have not insulted INSULTS, 20
anywhere go a. I damn well please FREEDOM, 4
apartheid Sanctions are now the only . . . way of ending a. RACISM, 3
We don't want a. liberalized RACISM, 6
apathy sheer a. and boredom DISCOVERY, 10
ape An a. is ne'er so like an a. EVOLUTION, 1
having an a. for his grandfather REPARTEE, 54
How like us is that ugly brute, the a. EVOLUTION, 13
Is man an a. or an angel EVOLUTION, 12
It is not the a., nor the tiger HUMAN NATURE, 26
Man . . . is halfway between an a. and a god MANKIND, 32
the a. from which he is descended EVOLUTION, 25
The exception is a naked a. MANKIND, 41
ape-like The a. virtues without which EDUCATION, 24
aphorisms The great writers of a. SAYINGS, 3
The hunter for a. . . . has to fish in muddy water SAYINGS, 2
aphrodisiac Fame is a powerful a. FAME, 14
Power is the ultimate a. PRESIDENTS, 8
The moon is nothing /But a circumambulating a. FERTILITY, 1
apologize a good rule in life never to a. APOLOGIES, 7
It's too late to a. INSULTS, 119
apology Friends . . . God's a. for relations FRIENDS, 10
Never make a defence or a. ACCUSATION, 2
apoplexy A. is an affection of the head NAMES, 14
apostates that peculiar malignity . . . characteristic of a. BETRAYAL, 9
great a. of the Philistines PHILISTINISM, 2
the a. of class-hatred MARXISM, 5
Apostles The Septuagint minus the A. NUMBERS, 6
apothecary A, n. The physician's accomplice DRUGS, 4
apothicaries A good Kitchen is a good A. shop FOOD, 18
apparatus *Brain*, n. An a. with which we think BRAIN, 1
apparel a. oft proclaims the man CLOTHES, 20
appeal The whole of art is an a. to a reality ARTS, 7
appealed hast thou a. unto Caesar BIBLICAL QUOTATIONS, 19

appear Things are . . . what they a. to be APPEARANCES, 24
appearance secret of a successful a. APPEARANCE, 56
appearances A. are deceptive APPEARANCES, 2
A. are not . . . a clue to the truth APPEARANCES, 14
Keep up a. APPEARANCES, 12
shallow people . . . do not judge by a. APPEARANCES, 38
you must preserve a. APPEARANCES, 15
appearing Television is for a. on TELEVISION, 5
appeasement internal equilibrium and a limitation of armaments by political a. EUROPE, 10
appeaser An a. is one who feeds a crocodile DIPLOMACY, 6
appendicitis chronic remunerative a. ILLNESS, 51
appetite A. comes with eating DESIRE, 13
a. may sicken and so die MUSIC, 43
Doth not the a. alter OLD AGE, 87
Illness isn't the only thing that spoils the a. FOOD, 68
the desire of satisfying a voracious a. LUST, 4
apple An a. a day HEALTHY LIVING, 2
as the a. of his eye BIBLICAL QUOTATIONS, 71
I raised thee up under the a. tree BIBLICAL QUOTATIONS, 640
My a. trees will never get across NEIGHBORS, 3
want the a. for the a.'s sake PERVERSITY, 6
When Eve ate this particular a. SEX, 55
apple-pie An a. without some cheese FOOD, 2
apples comfort me with a. BIBLICAL QUOTATIONS, 623
The silver a. of the moon DESIRE, 17
applications only a. of science SCIENCE, 67
applied no such things as a. sciences SCIENCE, 67
appointment a. by the corrupt few DEMOCRACY, 20
appreciate I never 'a.' BEAUTY, 29
appreciation total dependence on the a. of others CHARM, 2
apprehend Intelligence is quickness to a. ABILITY, 2
apprehensions elations and a. of growth AGE, 48
approve They that a. . . . call it opinion OPINIONS, 3
approved I never a. either the errors of his book, or the trivial truths FREEDOM, 60
April And after A., when May follows MONTHS, 6
A. is the cruellest month MONTHS, 8
gloomy in England are March and A. WINTER, 8
My regret /Becomes an A. violet SORROW, 28
Now that A.'s there ENGLAND, 12
Sweet A. showers MONTHS, 12
Aprille Whan that A. with his shoures sote MONTHS, 7
Arab I shook hands with a friendly A. PLACES, 26
Arabia All the perfumes of A. GUILT, 17
Arabs The Jews and A. should . . . settle their differences GOLDWYNISMS, 26
arbitrator the a. of the affairs of Christendom POLITICIANS, 51
arch All experience is an a. EXPERIENCE, 22
archaeologist An a. is the best husband MARRIAGE, 40
Archangel Gabriel If I were the A. REPARTEE, 71
archbishop the sign of an a. is a double-cross CLERGY, 4
arch-enemy love . . . has one a. – and that is life LOVE, 16
arches Underneath the a. DREAMS, 7
Archimedes The . . . schoolboy is now familiar with truths for which A. SCIENCE, 75
architect Each man the a. of his own fate FATE, 6
from the point of view of the hygienist, the physician, the a. . . . and the nurse HOSPITALS, 3
not a great sculptor or painter can be an a. ARCHITECTURE, 12
the a. can only advise MISTAKES, 22
The a. is a servant, a tailor ARCHITECTURE, 17
architecture A. has its political use ARCHITECTURE, 20
A. in general is frozen music ARCHITECTURE, 14
Fashion is a. FASHION, 3
modern, harmonic and liveiy a. ARCHITECTURE, 6
What has happened to a. . . . that the only passers-by who can contemplate it ARCHITECTURE, 8
ardua *Per a. ad astra* AMBITION, 2
'arf An' rather less than '. CLOTHES, 13
arguing I am not a. with you ARGUMENTS, 18
In a. too, the parson own'd his skill KNOWLEDGE, 17
argument All a. is against it SUPERNATURAL, 9
I have found you an a. ARGUMENTS, 9
I love a., I love debate ARGUMENTS, 15
work of art must start an a. ART, 32
arguments At social gatherings he was liable to engage in heated and noisy a. OBITUARIES, 8
beware of long a. and long beards BREVITY, 7
the world can be expressed in . . . a. THEORY, 5
Arian In three sips the A. frustrate DRINKS, 7
arise A., O Lord, plead Thine own cause PRAYER, 24
shall . . . a. with healing in his wings BIBLICAL QUOTATIONS, 455
aristocracy an absentee a. IRELAND, 7
An a. in a republic is like a chicken ARISTOCRACY, 16
a. . . . government by the badly educated ARISTOCRACY, 9
a. to what is decent CLASS, 20
displeased with *a.*, call it *oligarchy* ANARCHY, 1
If human beings could be propagated . . . a. would be . . . sound ARISTOCRACY, 12
Unlike the male codfish . . . the British a. is ARISTOCRACY, 22
aristocrat the gentleman from both the artist and the a. CLASS, 49
aristocratic To be a. in Art ART, 19
to distinguish . . . the a. class from the Philistines CLASS, 4
arithmetic different branches of A. EDUCATION, 19
Music is the a. of sounds MUSIC, 16
ark an a. of bulrushes BIBLICAL QUOTATIONS, 129
into the a., two and two BIBLICAL QUOTATIONS, 197
arm An a. /Rose up from . . . the lake ARTHURIAN LEGEND, 2
Don't carry away that a. till I have . . . my ring PRACTICALITY, 5
Human on my faithless a. SLEEP, 6
Armageddon a place called . . . A. BIBLICAL QUOTATIONS, 594
A. will be at our door PROPHECY, 12
armaments internal equilibrium and a limitation of a. by political appeasement EUROPE, 10
armchair She fitted into my biggest a. OBESITY, 18
arm'd a. with more than complete steel JUSTICE, 21
Armenteers A mademoiselle from A. FRANCE, 16
armies ignorant a. clash by night WAR, 11
not a. . . . but flocks of sheep DELUSION, 3
armistice a short a. with truth TRUTH, 16
dream of . . . another wild A. day WAR, 69
armor Conceit is the finest a. CONCEIT, 13
Prayer makes the Christian's a. bright PRAYER, 14
arms Anger supplies the a. ANGER, 10
Building up a. is not a substitute for diplomacy NUCLEAR WEAPONS, 19
For the theatre one needs long a. ACTING, 4
I never would lay down my a. PATRIOTISM, 32
I sing of a. and the man ENDURANCE, 27
opening time in the Sailors A. PUBLIC HOUSES, 4
So he laid down his a. PUNS, 9
army An a. is a nation within a nation ARMY, 4
An a. marches on its stomach FOOD, 56
Chief of the A. LAST WORDS, 57
contemptible little A. WAR, 174
her a. has had a glorious victory VICTORY, 12
If you don't want to use the a., I should like to borrow it SARCASM, 3
little ships of England brought the A. home BOATS, 8
no longer have an a. DEFEAT, 5
terrible as an a. with banners BIBLICAL QUOTATIONS, 635
The a. ages men sooner than the law ARMY, 7
The conventional a. loses if it does not win WAR, 87
arrest My father didn't create you to a. me POLICE, 9
arrest One does not a. Voltaire RESPECT, 2
arrested Christ . . . would quite likely have been a. OPPRESSION, 2
arrive To travel hopefully is . . . better . . . than to a. ANTICIPATION, 7
arrow Every a. . . . feels the attraction of earth AMBITION, 15
I, said the Sparrow, /With my bow and a. NURSERY RHYMES, 68
I shot an a. into the air CHANCE, 4
arse a politician is an a. POLITICIANS, 34
Sit on your a. for fifty years INDIFFERENCE, 4
arsenal a. of democracy DEMOCRACY, 18
arson A., after all, is an artificial crime FIRE, 6
art All a. deals with the absurd ART, 20
All A. is quite useless ART, 35
An a. can only be learned LEARNING, 5
A. and religion first; then philosophy IMPORTANCE, 4
A. . . . can go on mattering ART, 5
a. constantly aspires towards . . . music ART, 21
A. for art's sake ART, 6
A. is a jealous mistress ART, 7
A. is long, and Time is fleeting GRAVE, 10
A. is not a mirror . . . but a hammer ART, 17
A. is not a special sauce ART, 13
a. is not a weapon ART, 11
A. is ruled . . . by the imagination IMAGINATION, 3
A. is the imposing of a pattern ART, 33
A. is the most intense mode ART, 36
A. is . . . the transmission of feeling ART, 30
a. is to give life a shape ART, 2
A. never expresses anything ART, 34
a. of pleasing consists PLEASURE, 13
aspires . . . to the condition of a. LITERATURE, 2
A work of a. . . . has something which is anonymous ARTS, 11
A work of a. . . . seen through a temperament ARTS, 5
Bullfighting is the only a. SPORT AND GAMES, 8
Desiring this man's a. DISCONTENT, 8
Dying /is an a. DEATH, 116
excellence of every a. is its intensity ARTS, 6
Fine a. is that in which the hand ART, 26
great parables, . . . but false a. CRITICISM, 33
half a trade and half an a. LITERATURE, 9
I have discovered the a. . . . lost for two thousand years DANCING, 4
industry without a. is brutality ART, 25
Insurrection is an a. REVOLUTION, 13
It's clever but is it a. ART, 12
Medicine is a natural a. MEDICINE, 84
Mr Goldwyn . . . you are only interested in a. ART, 27
nature imitating a. ACTORS, 13
nature is the a. of God NATURE, 2
Nature's handmaid, a. NATURE, 11
Politics is not a science . . . but an a. POLITICS, 22
princes learn no a. truly, but . . . horsemanship HORSES, 7
Rules and models destroy genius and a. RULES, 3
Science and a. are only too often a superior kind of dope NARCOTICS, 6
sombre enemy of good a. BABIES, 2
the a. of the possible POLITICS, 27
The whole of a. is an appeal to a reality ARTS, 7
To be aristocratic in A. ART, 19
True ease in writing comes from a. WRITING, 33
work of a. must start an argument ART, 32
arteries A man is as old as his a. OLD AGE, 95
arteriosclerosis young people seem to develop mental a. YOUTH, 15
artery the a. ceases to beat DEATH, 75
artful The a. Dodger NAMES, 5
article It all depends upon that a. there SOLDIERS, 17
articles to pay for a. . . . they do not want BORROWING, 4
artificial All things are a. NATURE, 2
nothing so a. as sinning nowadays SIN, 20
artist An amateur is an a. who supports himself ARTISTS, 10
As an a., a man has no home PARIS, 5
Beware of the a. who's an intellectual ARTISTS, 5
God is really only another a. GOD, 48
No a. is ahead of his time ART, 9
only one position for an a. anywhere WALES, 3
Remember I'm an a. ARTISTS, 3
the gentleman from both the a. and the aristocrat CLASS, 49
What is an a. ARTISTS, 11
artistic a. temperament . . . afflicts amateurs ARTS, 2
There never was an a. period PHILISTINISM, 8
artists A. are not engineers of the soul ART, 11
Great a. have no country NATIONALITY, 9
The a. retired. The British remained RENUNCIATION, 5
art-loving an A. nation PHILISTINISM, 8
arts If all the a. aspire to the condition of music SCIENCE, 78
Murder . . . one of the Fine A. MURDER, 6

B

the tower of B. should have got language all mixed up LANGUAGE, 43
babes b. shall rule over them BIBLICAL QUOTATIONS, 248
babies bit the b. in the cradles ANIMALS, 7
If men had to have b. BIRTH, 9
Other people's b. BABIES, 5
putting milk into b. BABIES, 1
War will never cease until b. WAR, 99
You breed b. and you eat chips FOOD, 72
baby Anybody can shock a b. SIMPLICITY, 8
Don't throw the b. out HASTE, 1
Every b. born into the world BABIES, 3
Hanging head downwards between cliffs of bone, was the b. BIRTH, 2
hanging the b. on the clothes line to dry INNOVATION, 2
Hush-a-bye, b., on the tree top NURSERY RHYMES, 19
my b. at my breast SUICIDE, 31
no new b. in the womb of our society RUSSIA, 4
Rock-a-bye b. on the tree top SLEEP, 7
Walking My B. Back Home LOVE, 182
Babylon B. the great BIBLICAL QUOTATIONS, 596
By the waters of B. we sit down and weep UNITED STATES, 63
How many miles to B. NURSERY RHYMES, 17
Bach J. S. B. CRITICISM, 4
Some of the songs . . . will be popular when B., Beethoven and Wagner are forgotten SONG, 1
you play B. *your* way INSULTS, 80
bachelor A b. . . . dies like a beggar MARRIAGE, 90
B.'s fare BACHELORS, 3
die a b. MARRIAGE, 116
Never trust . . . a b. too near BACHELORS, 2
Now I am a b., I live by myself ANONYMOUS, 63
bachelors reasons for b. to go out BACHELORS, 1
bacillus Oh, powerful b. SCIENCE, 45
back any of you at the b. who do not hear me DISABILITY, 1
But at my b. I always hear AGE, 49
Either b. us or sack us SUPPORT, 3
I sit on a man's b. HYPOCRISY, 21
the credit belongs to the boys in the b. rooms GRATITUDE, 1
turn your b. upon the world PERFECTION, 5
Will ye no come b. again RETURN, 5
Winston's b. RETURN, 1
backs With our b. to the wall . . . each . . . must fight on to the end FIGHT, 11
backward In a country economically b., the proletariat can take power earlier CAPITALISM, 19
Bacon When their lordships asked B. BRIBERY, 1
bacteriologists staff of b. LANGUAGE, 3
bad a b. man must have brains GOOD AND EVIL, 5
a b. novel tells us the truth about its author NOVELS, 2
A b. penny LUCK, 1
a brave b. man OBITUARIES, 4
A truth that's told with b. intent TRUTH, 13
b. die late GOOD AND EVIL, 4
B. girls don't have the time DIARIES, 2
b. taste is better than no taste TASTE, 2
Defend the b. against the worse DECLINE, 3
It is as b. as b. can be FOOD, 40
never was a b. peace WAR AND PEACE, 8
nothing either good or b. THINKING, 15
Nothing so b. but it might have been worse OPTIMISM, 7
put up with b. things TOLERANCE, 13
resolved to do something b. DECISION, 4
she was a very b. cook REPARTEE, 103
so much b. in the best of us ANONYMOUS, 89
strong antipathy of good to b. PROVOCATION, 2
the b. die late GOOD AND EVIL, 4
the name of . . . obstinacy in a b. one STUBBORNNESS, 4
There's no such thing as a b. Picasso INFERIORITY, 4
what I feel really b. about LIBERALISM, 2
When b. men combine UNITY, 7
when I'm b. I'm better SEX, 110
badge Red B. of Courage COURAGE, 9
badly If you want to do a thing b. EFFORT, 6
bag b. and baggage VIOLENCE, 7
Bailey When will you pay me? /Say the bells of Old B. LONDON, 18
baker The butcher, the b., /The candlestick-maker NURSERY RHYMES, 44
balanced b. state of well-modulated dis-satisfaction POLITICS, 137
Food is an important part of a b. diet FOOD, 46
balances thou art weighed in the b., and art found wanting BIBLICAL QUOTATIONS, 63
bald being b. – one can hear snowflakes APPEARANCE, 17
Can't act, can't sing, slightly b. ACTING, 3
Falklands . . . a fight between two b. men over a comb WAR, 23
baldness There is more felicity on the far side of b. APPEARANCE, 57
There's one thing about b. APPEARANCE, 24
Baldwin not quite forget . . . B. till we're out of debt POLITICIANS, 54
Balfour Mr B.'s Poodle HOUSES OF PARLIAMENT, 15
Balkans some damned silly thing in the B. WAR, 22
ball B. . . . how very singular NAMES, 1
Hitler /Has only got one b. WORLD WAR II, 2
ballet it takes more than one to make a b. SUPPORT, 8
To enter the . . . B. is to enter a convent DANCING, 10
balloon the moon's /a b. BOOK TITLES, 20
ballot The b. is stronger than the bullet DEMOCRACY, 12
balm wash the b. from an anointed king MONARCHY, 23
baloney it's still b. POLITICS, 127
banal Frumpish and b. ROYALTY, 84
banality The fearsome . . . *b. of evil* EVIL, 3
bananas hanging around like clumps of b. INSULTS, 77
Banbury Ride a cock-horse to B. Cross NURSERY RHYMES, 41
bandages to walk around . . . with only a few light b. on BEAUTY, 32
bands Brass b. are all very well in their place MUSIC, 4
ladies who pursue·Culture in b. CULTURE, 4
bang bigger b. for a buck NUCLEAR WEAPONS, 24
Not with a b. but a whimper ENDING, 3
banish to b. . . . the dark divisive clouds of Marxist socialism MARXISM, 16
banishment bitter bread of b. PUNISHMENT, 23
bank a b. that would lend money to such a poor risk BANKS, 2
b. and shoal of time ENDING, 7
better that a man should tyrannize over his b. balance BANKS, 4
I cried all the way to the b. BANKS, 5
the b. was mightier than the sword BANKS, 6
the man who broke the B. at Monte Carlo WEALTH, 22
bankrupt B. of Life WORLD-WEARINESS, 1
banks cashiers of the Musical B. BANKS, 3
Got no check books, got no b. GRATITUDE, 2
Ye b. and braes NATURE, 4
banned any book should be b. BOOKS, 50
banner A b. with the strange device, /Excelsior AMBITION, 14
banners terrible as an army with b. BIBLICAL QUOTATIONS, 635
Baptist For good all round business work, I should have preferred a B. PROTESTANTISM, 7
bar an olfactory b. FAMILIARITY, 5
Into the B. ALCOHOL, 85
no moaning of the b. DUTY, 5
though hell should b. the way DETERMINATION, 17
When I went to the B. as a very young man LAW, 15
Barabbas B. was a publisher PUBLISHING, 3
now B. was a robber BIBLICAL QUOTATIONS, 360
Barbara Her name was B. Allen ANONYMOUS, 49
barbarians society distributes itself into B., Philistines, and Populace UNITED STATES, 3
barbarism methods of b. PLACES, 6
barbarity the . . . b. of war . . . forces men . . . to commit acts WAR, 85
the English seem . . . to act with the b. of tyrants IRELAND, 21
barbarous the invention of a b. age POETRY, 40
bard This goat-footed b. POLITICIANS, 67
bards Portraits of famous b. and preachers PAINTING, 19
bare Our ingress . . . /Was naked and b. CARE, 7
Pylons, those pillars /B. TECHNOLOGY, 13
barefoot b. and wearing coarse wool, he stood pitifully HUMILITY, 5
bargains rule for b. BUSINESS, 6
barge The b. she sat in, like a burnish'd throne ADMIRATION, 15
baritones b. are born villains in opera OPERA, 11
bark to hear the watch-dog's honest b. DOGS, 5
barking B. dogs ACTION, 1
Barnum the celebrated B.'s circus POLITICIANS, 27
barrage chemical b. has been hurled against the fabric of life ECOLOGY, 2
barrel drowned in a b. of malvesye EXECUTION, 10
you won't intoxicate with one glass someone who has . . . drunk . . . a . . . b. EXPERIENCE, 11
barren I am but a b. stock ROYALTY, 51
most b. country I have seen DISCOVERY, 5
There is nothing encourageth a woman sooner to be b. SUFFERING, 26
barrenness quarrels which vivify its b. LOVE, 72
barricade At some disputed b. DEATH, 130
barring a schoolboy's b. out POLITICS, 138
bar-rooms It brings men together in crowds and mobs in b. SOCIETY, 15
bars Nor iron b. a cage IMPRISONMENT, 7
barter All government . . . is founded on compromise and b. COMPROMISE, 4
base doing good to b. fellows CHARITY, 12
It takes a certain courage . . . to be truly b. EVIL, 2
scorning the b. degrees / . . . he did ascend AMBITION, 19
Why brand they us /With b. PREJUDICE, 9
baseball as sensible as b. in Italian OPERA, 7
prefer cricket, b. . . . to books BASEBALL, 1
based All progress is b. EXTRAVAGANCE, 2
basement interviewing a faded female in a damp b. INSULTS, 56
basing b. morals on myth MORALITY, 15
basket Have you ever taken anything out of the clothes b. CLEANNESS, 11
bastard Because I am a b. NASTINESS, 4
I hope you will not publicly call me a b. INSULTS, 129
It serves me right for putting all my eggs in one b. ILLEGITIMACY, 3
one lucky b. who's the artist ARTISTS, 11
we knocked the b. off ACHIEVEMENT, 6
bastards It is a pity . . . that more politicians are not b. POLITICIANS, 124
that'll hold the little b. CHILDREN, 20
bat black b., night, has flown INVITATIONS, 5
They came to see me b. not to see you bowl CRICKET, 3
Twinkle, twinkle, little b. NONSENSE, 5
bath a female llama surprised in her b. INSULTS, 32
B. . . . once a week to avoid being a public menace CLEANNESS, 3
b. with a friend ECONOMICS, 2
Oh! who can ever be tired of B. ENGLAND, 3
the nuns who never take a b. MODESTY, 9
bathe B. early every day and sickness will avoid you CLEANNESS, 1
bathes The King b. SEASIDE, 1
bathing caught the Whigs b. POLITICS, 44
something between a large b. machine BOATS, 6
bathroom fierce and revolutionary in a b. UNITED STATES, 86
he goes to church as he goes to the b. RELIGION, 11
bats b. in the belfry MADNESS, 29
battering B. the gates of heaven EXCESS, 15
battle A b. of giants WAR, 168
France has lost a b. FRANCE, 6
greatest misery is a b. gained MISERY, 4
next greatest misfortune to losing a b. VICTORY, 26
preferred to go into b. sitting down SOLDIERS, 16
The b. of Britain WORLD WAR II, 13
battlefield the most beautiful b. WAR, 108
we survive amongst the dead and the dying as on a b. OLD AGE, 93
battles Dead b., like dead generals GENERALS, 4
bauble that fool's b., the mace DISMISSAL, 5
bay we discovered a b. DISCOVERY, 6
baying b. for broken glass ARISTOCRACY, 21
bays To win the palm, the oak, or b. VICTORY, 13
be If you want to b. happy, b. HAPPINESS, 30
Let It B. IDEALISM, 6
To b., or not to b. FORTUNE, 6
What must b., must b. DESTINY, 1
beaches we shall fight on the b. WORLD WAR II, 10
beacons Logical consequences are the scarecrows of fools and the b. of wise men LOGIC, 6
beadle a b. on boxin' day POETRY, 16

except that the b. might eat them DRUGS, 8
I see all the b. are flown HOUSES OF PARLIAMENT, 7
no b. sing ILLNESS, 37
No fruits, no flowers, no leaves, no b. MONTHS, 10
spring now comes unheralded by the return of the b. ECOLOGY, 1
that make fine b. CLOTHES, 2
Two little dicky b., /Sitting on a wall NURSERY RHYMES, 63
where late the sweet b. sang OLD AGE, 89
Birmingham Am in B. MEMORY, 5
One has no great hopes from B. ENGLAND, 4
birth an environment equally fit for b., growth work, healing, and dying HEALTHY LIVING, 25
B., and copulation, and death LIFE AND DEATH, 13
B. may be a matter of a moment BIRTH, 12
From b. to age eighteen, a girl needs good parents AGE, 78
Man's main task in life is to give *b.* to himself BIRTH, 11
no credentials . . . not even . . . a certificate of b. ARISTOCRACY, 14
no cure for b. and death LIFE, 70
Our b. is but a sleep BIRTH, 18
The history of man for the nine months preceding his b. BIRTH, 8
The memory of b. LIFE AND DEATH, 15
To hinder a b. is merely speedier man-killing ABORTION, 4
what you were before your b. AFTERLIFE, 9
birthday A diplomat . . . always remembers a woman's b. AGE, 35
If one doesn't get b. presents GIFTS, 5
is it my b. or am I dying LAST WORDS, 5
birthplace accent of one's b. lingers HOMESICKNESS, 5
biscuit Can't a fellow even enjoy a b. THRIFT, 9
bishop a b. . . . must be blameless BIBLICAL QUOTATIONS, 647
another B. dead CLERGY, 10
been a b. so long CLERGY, 6
blonde to make a b. kick a hole APPEARANCE, 13
How can a b. marry CLERGY, 11
Make him a b., and you will silence him CLERGY, 3
May you be the mother of a b. BLESSING, 3
No B., no King CHURCH, 4
the symbol of a b. is a crook CLERGY, 4
bisier he semed b. than he was APPEARANCES, 11
bit He b. his lip in a manner HUMOR, 45
The dog . . . /Went mad and b. the man DOGS, 7
bitch an old b. gone in the teeth EPITAPHS, 32
The son of a b. isn't going to resign on me DISMISSAL, 11
bitches Now we are all sons of b. NUCLEAR WEAPONS, 3
bite b. the hand that fed them INGRATITUDE, 2
Every dog is allowed one b. POLITICS, 147
would b. some other of my generals GENERALS, 2
'You should not b. the hand that feeds you.' HEALTHY LIVING, 42
bites when a man b. a dog that is news JOURNALISM, 13
biting See what will happen . . . if you don't stop b. your fingernails SCULPTURE, 5
bitter Oh! how b. a thing it is to look into happiness through another man's eyes HAPPINESS, 24
bivouac an armed camp of Blackshirts, a b. for corpses FASCISM, 10
black A lady asked me why . . . , I wore b. MOURNING, 15
an old b. ram /Is tupping your white ewe SEX, 94
Any color, so long as it's b. CHOICE, 1
B. is beautiful RACE, 2
coffee that's too b. . . . You integrate it with cream RACE, 16
I am b., as if bereav'd of light RACE, 5
I am b., but comely BIBLICAL QUOTATIONS, 621
I don't believe in b. majority rule RACE, 21
'I'm B. and I'm Proud.' RACE, 7
looking for a b. hat DARKNESS, 6
One b., and one white, and two khaki ANONYMOUS, 96
sees b. people as expendable RACISM, 7
Take that b. box away CINEMA, 15
That old b. magic SUPERNATURAL, 11
The Ethiopians say that their gods are . . . b. RELIGION, 84
The future is . . . b. RACE, 4
There's a b. sheep FAMILY, 5
To like an individual because he's b. RACISM, 1
Two lovely b. eyes VIOLENCE, 5
Who art as b. as hell, as dark as night APPEARANCE, 54
blackbird When down came a b. NURSERY RHYMES, 47
blacker you the b. devil GOOD AND EVIL, 8
Blackpool With my little stick of B. rock FOOD, 33
blacks two b. do not make a white RACE, 20
Blackshirt Before the organization of the B. movement FASCISM, 6
Blackshirts an armed camp of B., a bivouac for corpses FASCISM, 10
bladder master of his soul, /Is servant to his b. OLD AGE, 9
Blake That William B. /Who beat upon the wall POETS, 38
blame Everyone threw the b. on me RESPONSIBILITY, 4
blank Pain – has an Element of B. SUFFERING, 15
Where were you fellows when the paper was b. EDITORS, 1
blanket not a b. woven from one thread, one color, one cloth UNITED STATES, 32
blankets the rough male kiss of b. BED, 4
blanks historians left b. in their writings HISTORIANS, 6
blasphemies All great truths begin as b. NOVELTY, 9
blasted Curse the b., jelly-boned swines CURSES, 2
bleed If you prick us, do we not b. EQUALITY, 26
bleeds My nose b. for you INSINCERITY, 6
blemish Christianity . . . the one immortal b. of mankind CHRISTIANITY, 48
lamb . . . without b. BIBLICAL QUOTATIONS, 138
Blenheim I dine at B. once a week ANONYMOUS, 60
God b. us, every one BLESSING, 6
blessed all generations shall call me b. BIBLICAL QUOTATIONS, 413
B. are the meek HUMILITY, 1
b. are the poor in spirit BIBLICAL QUOTATIONS, 472
b. are they that have not seen, and yet have believed BIBLICAL QUOTATIONS, 372
b. is he that cometh in the name of the Lord BIBLICAL QUOTATIONS, 522
b. is the man that endureth temptation BIBLICAL QUOTATIONS, 281
B. is the man who expects nothing EXPECTATION, 6
blessing a b. that money cannot buy HEALTH, 23
a b., . . . very well disguised DEFEAT, 1
health! the b. of the rich! the riches of the poor HEALTH, 15
Let the b. . . . be . . . upon all that are lovers of virtue FISHING, 4
blessings all which we behold /Is full of b. OPTIMISM, 40
a world of b. by good Queen Elizabeth ROYALTY, 66
The trained nurse has become one of the great b. of humanity NURSES, 7
blest It is twice b. MERCY, 4
The bed be b. BLESSING, 1
this b. man, let his just praise be given COMPLIMENTS, 37
blind A b. man in a dark room DARKNESS, 6
all the discomforts that will accompany my being b. BLINDNESS, 14
b. as those who won't see STUBBORNNESS, 1
b. in their own cause BLINDNESS, 2
Booth died b. FAITH, 19
Country of the B. BLINDNESS, 16
It is not miserable to be b. ENDURANCE, 11
I was eyes to the b. BIBLICAL QUOTATIONS, 308
love is b. LOVE, 161
Painting is a b. man's profession PAINTING, 14
The doggie in front has suddenly gone b. EXPLANATIONS, 2
union of a deaf man to a b. woman MARRIAGE, 41
whereas I was b., now I see BIBLICAL QUOTATIONS, 338
wing'd Cupid painted b. LOVE, 136
wish all Americans . . . as b. as you UNITED STATES, 89
blinded with b. eyesight BOOKS, 47
blindness it is miserable to be incapable of enduring b. ENDURANCE, 11
My b. is my sight BLINDNESS, 5
the . . . world was stumbling . . . in social b. BLINDNESS, 6
blinked the other fellow just b. POLITICS, 123
blinking The portrait of a b. idiot FOOLISHNESS, 20
bliss B. was it in that dawn to be alive FRENCH REVOLUTION, 11
where ignorance is b., /'Tis folly to be wise IGNORANCE, 9
blithe Hail to thee, b. Spirit BIRDS, 16
No lark more b. than he HAPPINESS, 4
blitz A b. of a boy is Timothy Winters APPEARANCE, 12
block a chip of the old b. PRIME MINISTERS, 7
there's a statue inside every b. of stone OBESITY, 12
blockhead No man but a b. ever wrote WRITING, 21
blocks philosophy ought to . . . unravel people's mental b. PHILOSOPHY, 13
blonde A b. to make a bishop kick a hole APPEARANCE, 13
blondes Gentlemen always seem to remember b. APPEARANCE, 34
blood be his b. on your own conscience GUILT, 4
B. is thicker FAMILY, 1
B. sport is brought to its ultimate refinement JOURNALISM, 24
b., toil, tears and sweat EFFORT, 3
critics . . . desire our b., not our pain CRITICS, 11
He is all b., dirt and sucked sugar stick CRITICISM, 68
his b. be on us BIBLICAL QUOTATIONS, 547
How does the heart pump b. BODY, 9
humble and meek are thirsting for b. HUMILITY, 8
I am in b. /Stepp'd in so far GUILT, 15
it touches a man that his b. is sea water ENVIRONMENT, 7
leeches have red b. LAST WORDS, 23
men with our own real body and b. MANKIND, 25
my b. of the new testament BIBLICAL QUOTATIONS, 540
rather have b. on my hands COMMITMENT, 4
Seas of B. CHRISTIANITY, 55
shed his b. for the country JUSTICE, 28
The b. of the martyrs is the seed of the Church CHRISTIANITY, 60
the b. that she has spilt REVENGE, 10
the old savage England, whose last b. flows still ENGLAND, 28
There are two kinds of b. RACE, 22
the River Tiber foaming with much b. PROPHECY, 14
thy brother's b. crieth unto me BIBLICAL QUOTATIONS, 191
trading on the b. of my men EXPLOITATION, 3
washed their robes . . . in the b. of the lamb BIBLICAL QUOTATIONS, 590
without shedding of b. is no remission BIBLICAL QUOTATIONS, 238
You can't get b. FUTILITY, 3
your b. of your lives will I require BIBLICAL QUOTATIONS, 200
bloodiness The sink is the great symbol of the b. of family life FAMILY, 36
bloody All the faces . . . seem to be b. Poms ENGLISH, 12
My head is b., but unbowed ENDURANCE, 6
not half b. enough JUSTICE, 16
to have b. thoughts REVENGE, 18
bloom It's a sort of b. on a woman CHARM, 1
lilac is in b. FLOWERS, 2
blossom Love's perfect b. ERROR, 10
the desert shall . . . b. as the rose BIBLICAL QUOTATIONS, 268
blot b. me . . . out of thy book BIBLICAL QUOTATIONS, 156
blow A b. in cold blood VIOLENCE, 14
Another year! – another deadly b. DEFEAT, 18
Beware of the man who does not return your b. FORGIVENESS, 18
B., b., thou winter wind INGRATITUDE, 4
b. the Scots back again into Scotland TREASON, 5
B. . . . till you burst CONTEMPT, 2
B., winds, and crack your cheeks WEATHER, 21
but a word and a b. VIOLENCE, 4
He would not b. his nose without moralizing WRITERS, 13
themselves must strike the b. FREEDOM, 9
this b. /Might be the be-all and the end-all here ENDING, 7

You know how to whistle . . . just put your lips together and b. WHISTLING, 1
bloweth the wind b. where it listeth BIBLICAL QUOTATIONS, 323
bludgeoning the b. of the people DEMOCRACY, 24
blue Little Boy B., /Come blow your horn NURSERY RHYMES, 28
that little tent of b. IMPRISONMENT, 13
The b. ribbon of the turf HORSES, 5
The essence of any b. material HUMOR, 32
What are those b. remembered hills NOSTALGIA, 11
blues Twentieth-Century B. MELANCHOLY, 4
blue-vested short, b. people FRANCE, 3
bluffed Winston Churchill has b. them all POLITICIANS, 53
blunder poverty . . . is a b. POVERTY, 21
worse than a crime, it is a b. MISTAKES, 4
Youth is a b. AGE, 26
blunders b. usually do more to shape history than . . . wickedness MISTAKES, 19
escaped making the b. that he has made POLITICIANS, 59
The b. of a doctor DOCTORS, 15
blush a b. to the cheek of a young person EMBARRASSMENT, 1
b. to find it fame GOOD, 14
flower is born to b. unseen WASTE, 2
blushes Man is the only animal that b. EMBARRASSMENT, 4
take away the candle and spare my b. MODESTY, 3
Boadicea some bargain-basement B. POLITICIANS, 57
boar the b. out of the wood doth waste it PRAYER, 24
when his half-civilized ancestors were hunting the wild b. EARTH, 3
boarding-house Any two meals at a b. FOOD, 44
boat a beautiful pea-green b. HONEY, 3
Do they allow tipping on the b. MONEY, 29
in the same b. . . . not a chance of recording the vote WOMEN, 36
It was involuntary. They sank my b. MODESTY, 4
On a slow b. to China BOATS, 11
boating Jolly b. weather BOATS, 4
boats b. against the current FUTILITY, 7
messing about in b. BOATS, 7
we look for happiness in b. and carriage rides TRAVEL, 20
Bobby B. Shafto's gone to sea NURSERY RHYMES, 5
bob-tail I bet my money on the b. nag HORSES, 6
bodies I will abstain from . . . abusing the b. of man or woman MEDICINE, 37
many b. of the saints which slept arose BIBLICAL QUOTATIONS, 549
Minds like b., will often fall into a pimpled, ill-conditioned state MIND, 6
our dead b. must tell the tale ENDURANCE, 17
Our minds are lazier than our b. MIND, 28
Sleep is that golden chaine that ties health and our b. together SLEEP, 11
well-developed b., fairly developed minds EDUCATION, 30
what happens in our b. is directed toward a useful end BODY, 8
You may house their b. but not their souls CHILDREN, 29
body A b. seriously out of equilibrium MENTAL ILLNESS, 5
A healthy b. is the guest-chamber of the soul BODY, 1
All there is of you is your b. OPERATIONS, 8
A man ought to handle his b. like the sail of a ship HEALTHY LIVING, 36
an intimate knowledge of the human b. MEDICINE, 47
a sound mind in a sound b. BODY, 12
B. and mind, . . . , do not always agree to die together OLD AGE, 39
B. and soul cannot be separated for purposes of treatment HOLISTIC MEDICINE, 7
b. of a weak and feeble woman ROYALTY, 49
by whom it is impossible to make ourselves understood: our b. BODY, 20
company, . . . have neither a soul to lose nor a b. to kick BUSINESS, 24
cure the infirmities of the b. DIAGNOSIS, 6
Disease is not of the b. DISEASE, 40
diseases as isolated disturbances in a healthy b. DISEASE, 3
fear made manifest on the b. ILLNESS, 23
Happiness is beneficial for the b. BODY, 19
Her b. dissected by fiendish men EPITAPHS, 43
her long struggle between mind and b. ILLNESS, 49
If I had the use of my b. SUICIDE, 2
If the b. be feeble, the mind will not be strong HOLISTIC MEDICINE, 5
It is fear made manifest on the b. DISEASE, 19
it leaves them nothing but b. ILLNESS, 45
Man has no B. distinct from his Soul BODY, 7
medicine may be regarded generally as the knowledge of the loves and desires of the b. MEDICINE, 78
men with our own real b. and blood MANKIND, 25
mind and b. must develop in harmonious proportions HEALTHY LIVING, 28
mind that makes the b. rich APPEARANCES, 36
more familiar with Africa than my own b. BODY, 18
Our b. is a machine for living BODY, 24
Pain of mind is worse than pain of b. SUFFERING, 33
Safeguard the health both of b. and soul HEALTH, 6
So long as the b. is affected through the mind FAITH, 16
take, eat; this is my b. BIBLICAL QUOTATIONS, 540
The b. is not a permanent dwelling BODY, 21
The b. is truly the garment of the soul BODY, 6
The b. must be repaired HOLISTIC MEDICINE, 10
The human b. is a machine BODY, 16
The human b. is like a bakery HOLISTIC MEDICINE, 11
The human b. is private property RESEARCH, 20
the human b. is sacred BODY, 26
The human b. is the best picture of the human soul SOUL, 18
The human b. is the only machine BODY, 4
the human psyche lives in indissoluble union with the b. PSYCHOLOGY, 8
The mind grows sicker than the b. SUFFERING, 25
The mind has great influence over the b. MIND, 22
the most abhorrent is b. without mind MIND, 15
the mysteries of the human b. MEDICINE, 36
the observations of the b. in health and disease NATURE, 17
the physicians separate the soul from the b. HOLISTIC MEDICINE, 8
There is more wisdom in your b. WISDOM, 23
the secrets of the structure of the human b. DEATH, 64
the soul is not more than the b. BODY, 27
We have rudiments of reverence for the human b. MIND, 11
Well in b. /But sick in mind HOLISTIC MEDICINE, 9
when the soul is oppressed so is the b. MELANCHOLY, 9
Why be given a b. if you . . . keep it shut up BODY, 14
your b. is the temple of the Holy Ghost BIBLICAL QUOTATIONS, 32
body-snatcher B, . . . One who supplies the young physicians DOCTORS, 22
Bogart B.'s a helluva nice guy till 11.30 p.m ACTORS, 4
Bognor Bugger B. LAST WORDS, 39
bogus genuinely b. APPEARANCES, 19
boil b. at different degrees INDIVIDUALITY, 5
boiler The United States is like a gigantic b. UNITED STATES, 23
bold He was a b. man PROVERBS 197
boldness B., and again b., and always b. BOLDNESS, 1
bomb Ban the b. NUCLEAR WEAPONS, 1
draw in their horns or . . . b. them into the Stone Age THREATS, 7
god of science . . . has given us the atomic b. SCIENCE, 57
bombed no power on earth that can protect him from being b. WAR, 15
bombing begin b. in five minutes PRESIDENTS, 13
bombs b. *are* unbelievable until they . . . fall WEAPONS, 9
Come, friendly b., and fall on Slough ENGLAND, 5
drop b. . . . hit civilians WAR, 66
Ears like b. APPEARANCE, 12
test the Russians, not the b. NUCLEAR WEAPONS, 8
bon to produce an occasional *b. mot* HUMOR, 6
Bonaparte The three-o'-clock in the morning courage, which B. thought was the rarest COURAGE, 28
Bonar Poor B. can't bear being called a liar POLITICIANS, 73
Bonar Law all the politicians . . . least significant was B. POLITICIANS, 12
bond I will have my b. DETERMINATION, 21
Let him look to his b. LAW, 31
bondage Cassius from b. will deliver Cassius SELF-RELIANCE, 14
Of Human B. BOOK TITLES, 16
bone b. to his b. BIBLICAL QUOTATIONS, 165
The nearer the b. FOOD, 5
boneless the b. wonder POLITICIANS, 27
bones Bleach the b. of comrades slain WAR, 77
Heat, madam! . . . to take off my flesh and sit in my b. WEATHER, 29
how the b. in the back room are doing SCIENCE, 73
Of his b. are coral made DEATH, 148
O ye dry b. BIBLICAL QUOTATIONS, 164
bonhomie Overcame his natural b. ECONOMICS, 3
bonjour *B. tristesse* SORROW, 8
bonkers If the British public falls for this . . . it will be . . . b. POLITICS, 58
bonnie *By the b. milldams o' Binnorie* ANONYMOUS, 98
My B. lies over the ocean ANONYMOUS, 58
Oh, bring back my B. to me ANONYMOUS, 58
bonny the child that is born on the Sabbath day /Is b. and blithe, and good and gay CHARACTER, 19
bonum *Summum b.* GOOD, 3
Boojum Snark *was* a B. NONSENSE, 6
book A b. may be amusing BOOKS, 21
A b.'s a b., although there's nothing in't BOOKS, 11
a b. . . . sealed with seven seals BIBLICAL QUOTATIONS, 586
A b. that furnishes no quotations is, . . . a plaything QUOTATIONS, 12
a b. that is a b. flowers once BOOKS, 25
a b. to kill time CRITICISM, 40
A good b. is the best of friends BOOKS, 48
A good b. is the precious life-blood BOOKS, 31
An angel writing in a b. of gold DREAMS, 8
Another damned, thick, square b. WRITING, 14
any b. should be banned BOOKS, 50
Bell, b., and candle MATERIALISM, 23
blot me . . . out of thy b. BIBLICAL QUOTATIONS, 156
b. is not harmless . . . consciously offended BOOKS, 18
b. where men /May read strange matters APPEARANCE, 51
dainties that are bred in a b. IGNORANCE, 19
do not throw this b. about BOOKS, 7
Everybody writes a b. too many WRITERS, 46
Every b. must be chewed PROVERBS, 131
go away and write a b. about it SPEECHES, 4
Go, litel b. BOOKS, 14
half a library to make one b. WRITING, 18
he who destroys a good b., kills reason BOOKS, 30
If a b. is worth reading BOOKS, 38
I have only read one b. READING, 14
I'll drown my b. RENUNCIATION, 4
moral or an immoral b. BOOKS, 51
never got around to reading the b. CRITICISM, 41
Never judge a cover by its b. BOOKS, 26
that everyone has it in him to write one b. WRITING, 28
The number one b. . . . was written by a committee BIBLE, 10
The possession of a b. OSTENTATION, 2
There are two motives for reading a b. BOASTS, 7
There is not any b. /Or face DEATH, 169
There must be a man behind the b. WRITERS, 15
unprintable b. that is readable BOOKS, 33
What is the use of a b. BOOKS, 13
What you don't know would make a great b. IGNORANCE, 21
When a b. is boring, they yawn openly BOOKS, 42
without mentioning a single b. BOOKS, 35
Would you allow your wife . . . to read this b. PRUDERY, 1
You can't tell a b. APPEARANCES, 7
books against b. the Home Secretary is PHILISTINISM, 7
All b. are divisible into two classes BOOKS, 39
An author who speaks about his own b. EGOTISM, 5
be not swallowed up in b. KNOWLEDGE, 37
between a man of sense and his b. BOOKS, 15
B. and friends BOOKS, 1
B. are a load of crap BOOKS, 24
B. are . . . a mighty bloodless substitute for life BOOKS, 45
B. are made . . . like pyramids BOOKS, 19

boyhood The smiles, the tears, /Of b.'s years NOSTALGIA, 17
boys As flies to wanton b. DESTINY, 22
B. and girls come out to play NURSERY RHYMES, 6
B. are capital fellows in their own way CHILDREN, 40
B. do not grow up gradually CHILDREN, 23
B. will be b. SEXES, 14
Claret is the liquor for b. ALCOHOL, 42
the credit belongs to the b. in the back rooms GRATITUDE, 1
Where are the b. of the Old Brigade NOSTALGIA, 28
Where . . . b. plan for what . . . young girls plan for whom SEXES, 12
Written by office b. for office b. NEWSPAPERS, 12
bra Burn your b. FEMINISM, 4
bracelet diamond and safire b. lasts forever MATERIALISM, 18
I had b. on my teeth and got high marks APPEARANCE, 35
braes Ye banks and b. NATURE, 4
brain a Bear of Very Little B. WORDS, 23
b. attic stocked with all the furniture that he is likely to use BRAIN, 4
B., n. An apparatus with which we think BRAIN, 1
If it is for mind that we are seaching the b. BRAIN, 7
It is good to rub and polish our b. MIND, 23
Let schoolmasters puzzle their b. ALCOHOL, 36
My b.: it's my second favorite organ SEX, 5
our b. is a mystery MIND, 4
Pure symmetry of the b. MIND, 19
that most perfect and complex of computers the human b. MEDICINE, 79
the biggest b. of all the primates MANKIND, 42
The b. has muscles for thinking THINKING, 9
The b. is a wonderful organ WORK, 10
The b. is not an organ to be relied upon MIND, 3
The b. is the organ of longevity LONGEVITY, 12
the human b. is a device to keep the ears from grating BRAIN, 3
the universe, the reflection of the structure of the b. MIND, 4
Tobacco drieth the b. SMOKING, 36
we are supposing the b. . . . more than a telephone-exchange BRAIN, 7
with no deep researches vex the b. CLARITY, 1
brains a girl with b. ought to do something else BRAIN, 5
a good reliable set of bowels is worth more to a man than any quantity of b. BODY, 5
b. enough to make a fool of himself BRAIN, 8
I mix them with my b. BRAIN, 6
many b. and many hands are needed DISCOVERY, 14
our b. as fruitful as our bodies WOMAN'S ROLE, 9
something better than our b. to depend upon ARISTOCRACY, 8
sometimes his b. go to his head INTELLIGENCE, 1
What good are b. to a man BRAIN, 9
brainsick folly of one b. Pole POLITICS, 42
braking British civil service . . . effective b. mechanism BUREAUCRACY, 9
branch Cut is the b. that might have grown DEATH, 102
brandy I am not well; pray get me . . . b. FIRST IMPRESSIONS, 3
brass B. bands are all very well in their place MUSIC, 4
Make it compulsory for a doctor using a b. plate DOCTORS, 87
Men's evil manners live in b. MEMORIALS, 15
sounding b. BIBLICAL QUOTATIONS, 44
brat than it is to turn one b. into a decent human being CHILDREN, 39
brave Any fool can be b. on a battle field WAR, 101
b. new world . . . such people in't MANKIND, 57
Fortune favours the b. COURAGE, 27
land of the free, and the home of the b. UNITED STATES, 35
Many b. men . . . before Agamemnon's time OBLIVION, 1
the B. deserves the Fair COURAGE, 11
we could never learn to be b. . . . if there were only joy COURAGE, 18
bravery man of the greatest honour and b. CHARACTER, 23
Brazil B., where the nuts come from PLACES, 38
breach a custom more honour'd in the b. CUSTOM, 4
Once more unto the b. COURAGE, 21
breache lay the b. at their door DIPLOMACY, 1
bread b. and cheese, and kisses BACHELORS, 3
b. and circuses BREAD, 7
b. eaten in secret is pleasant BIBLICAL QUOTATIONS, 572
b. enough and to spare BIBLICAL QUOTATIONS, 439
B. is the staff of life FOOD, 3
cast thy b. upon the waters BIBLICAL QUOTATIONS, 96
I am the b. of life BIBLICAL QUOTATIONS, 331
if his son ask b., will he give him a stone BIBLICAL QUOTATIONS, 489
Jesus took b., and blessed it BIBLICAL QUOTATIONS, 540
known of them in breaking of b. BIBLICAL QUOTATIONS, 451
Loaf of B. beneath the Bough BREAD, 4
man shall not live by b. alone BIBLICAL QUOTATIONS, 468
One swears by wholemeal b. HEALTHY LIVING, 24
Peace, B. and Land RUSSIAN REVOLUTION, 2
that b. should be so dear BREAD, 5
Their learning is like b. in a besieged town BREAD, 6
the living b. BIBLICAL QUOTATIONS, 333
This b. I break was once the oat AGRICULTURE, 5
break sucker an even b. FAIRNESS, 1
breakdown One of the symptoms of approaching nervous b. WORK, 29
breakfast b.. I told Jeeves to drink it himself ALCOHOL, 86
she must not reheat his sins for b. FORGIVENESS, 12
breakfast-table ready for the national b. OBITUARIES, 10
breakfast-time critical period in matrimony is b. MARRIAGE, 77
breaking B. the mould POLITICS, 76
known of them in b. of bread BIBLICAL QUOTATIONS, 451
break-throughs discovery of psychedelics one of the three major scientific b. SCIENCE, 47
breast charms to soothe a savage b. MUSIC, 14
my baby at my b. SUICIDE, 31
The female b. has been called 'the badge of feminity' WOMEN, 67
breast-feeding atheism, b., circumcision INDULGENCE, 3
breastplate the b. of righteousness BIBLICAL QUOTATIONS, 119
breasts they add weight to the b. EATING, 6
women, who have but small and narrow b. SEXES, 18
breath blow hot and cold with the same b. INDECISION, 1
Can storied urn . . . /Back to its mansion call the fleeting b. DEATH, 73
He reaps the bearded grain at a b. DEATH, 98
in this harsh world draw thy b. in pain HEART, 19
such is the b. of kings POWER, 20
The first b. is the beginning of death LIFE AND DEATH, 1
The years to come seemed waste of b. FIGHT, 19
wish the night /Had borne my b. away NIGHT, 7
world will hold its b. WORLD WAR II, 36
breathed God . . . b. into his nostrils BIBLICAL QUOTATIONS, 181
God . . . b. into his nostrils GARDENS, 3
breather I happen to be a chain b. SMOKING, 31
breathing Keep b. LONGEVITY, 17
breed happy b. of men EARTH, 16
more careful of the b. of their horses and dogs than of their children FAMILY, 42
breeding formed by a different b. POVERTY AND WEALTH, 4
God-like in our . . . b. of . . . plants and animals EVOLUTION, 24
Good b. consists in concealing how . . . we think of ourselves MANNERS, 6
breeks taking the b. aff a wild Highlandman SCOTS, 10
breeze The fair b. blew EXPLORATION, 1
breezes spicy b. /Blow soft o'er Ceylon's isle MISANTHROPY, 1
brethren the least of these my b. BIBLICAL QUOTATIONS, 538
brevity B. is the soul of lingerie BREVITY, 6
B. is the soul of wit BREVITY, 8
brewery O take me to a b. ALCOHOL, 11
The b. is the best drugstore ALCOHOL, 7
bribe doing nothing for a b. CONTENTMENT, 9
The man who offers a b. BRIBERY, 4
You cannot hope to b. or twist JOURNALISM, 43
bribes How many b. he had taken BRIBERY, 1
bribing Money is good for b. yourself MONEY, 35
brick carried a . . . b. in his pocket BUSINESS, 25
he found it b. IMPROVEMENT, 1
He is a man of b. CHARACTER, 29
the Yellow B. Road TRAVEL, 18
bricklayers B. kick their wives to death CLASS, 51
bricks You can't make b. PROVERBS, 475
bride a b.'s attitude towards her betrothed MARRIAGE, 99
as a b. adorned for her husband BIBLICAL QUOTATIONS, 601
It helps . . . to remind your b. that you gave up a throne for her MARRIAGE, 154
unravish'd b. of quietness SILENCE, 9
bridegroom behold, the b. cometh BIBLICAL QUOTATIONS, 532
like the b. on the wedding cake APPEARANCE, 33
the friend of the b. . . . rejoiceth BIBLICAL QUOTATIONS, 326
bridge A B. Too Far BOOK TITLES, 22
Beautiful Railway B. of the Silv'ry Tay BRIDGE, 3
I am not going to speak to the man on the b. DEPARTURE, 3
I stood on the b. at midnight BRIDGE, 2
Like a b. over troubled water BRIDGE, 5
London B. is broken down BRIDGE, 4
over the B. of Sighs into eternity BRIDGE, 1
brief I strive to be b., and I become obscure BREVITY, 3
Out, out, b. candle LIFE, 76
'Tis b., my lord. /HAMLET: As woman's love LOVE, 138
briefcase A lawyer with his b. can steal more LAWYERS, 9
briers O, how full of b. is this working-day world LIFE, 72
brigade Forward the Light B. OBEDIENCE, 6
Where are the boys of the Old B. NOSTALGIA, 28
brigands B. demand your money WOMEN, 28
bright b. with hope UNITED STATES, 31
her beauty made /The b. world dim BEAUTY, 38
I've got B.'s disease and he's got mine ILLNESS, 54
Look on the b. side OPTIMISM, 5
the creature hath a purpose and its eyes are b. with it PURPOSE, 6
Tiger! burning b. ANIMALS, 6
young lady named B. LIGHT, 7
brightening He died when his prospects seemed to be b. ANONYMOUS, 27
brighter Had I been b. EXCUSES, 5
brightness To pass away ere life hath lost its b. DEATH, 76
Brighton Like B. pier, . . . inadequate for getting to France TRAVEL, 24
bright-star Johnny-the-b. REALISM, 4
brilliance No b. is needed in the law LAW, 24
brilliant a b. mind until he makes it up INTELLIGENCE, 2
a far less b. pen than mine CONCEIT, 4
b. men . . . will come to a bad end GREATNESS, 2
The dullard's envy of b. men GREATNESS, 2
brillig Twas b., and the slithy toves NONSENSE, 7
brimstone b. and fire BIBLICAL QUOTATIONS, 210
bring thou knowest not what a day may b. forth BIBLICAL QUOTATIONS, 582
Why didn't you b. him with you HOMOSEXUALITY, 6
brink scared to go to the b. COURAGE, 13
Britain a time when B. had a savage culture CIVILIZATION, 2
battle of B. is about to begin WORLD WAR II, 13
B. . . . Fabian Society writ large BRITAIN, 7
B. fit country for heroes to live in GOVERNMENT, 20
B. is no longer in the politics of the pendulum POLITICS, 139
B. is not . . . easily rocked by revolution BRITAIN, 7
to help B. to become a Third Programme BRITAIN, 15
When B. first, at heaven's command BRITAIN, 14
Britannia Rule, B., rule the waves BRITAIN, 14
British but we are B. – thank God HOMOSEXUALITY, 12
I would rather be B. than just BRITISH, 10
less known by the B. than these selfsame B. Islands BRITISH, 2
socialism . . . alien to the B. character SOCIALISM, 23

No shade, no shine, no b., no bees MONTHS, 10
butterfly a man dreaming I was a b. DREAMS, 4
Float like a b. SPORT AND GAMES, 2
Happiness is like a b. HAPPINESS, 17
buttocks Two b. of one bum FRIENDSHIP, 29
buttress a b. of the church SUPPORT, 6
buy American heiress wants to b. a man MATERIALISM, 19
I could b. back my introduction INTRODUCTIONS, 2
I will b. with you PREJUDICE, 10
would never b. my pictures PAINTING, 9
bygones Let b. be b. FORGIVENESS, 2
Byron a more worthless set than B. POETS, 36

C

cabbages c. and kings NONSENSE, 9
The c. are coming now ENGLAND, 5
cabbage-stumps Nothing but old fags and c. CRITICISM, 34
cabin'd c., cribb'd, confin'd, bound in FEAR, 16
cabs busy driving c. and cutting hair GOVERNMENT, 9
Caesar *Ave C., morituri te salutant* ANONYMOUS, 9
C.! dost thou lie so low CAESAR, 4
C. had his Brutus – Charles the First, his Cromwell CAESAR, 3
C.'s laurel crown CAESAR, 2
C.'s wife INTEGRITY, 2
hast thou appealed unto C. BIBLICAL QUOTATIONS, 19
I always remember that I am C.'s daughter EXTRAVAGANCE, 3
I come to bury C. EVIL, 19
Not that I lov'd C. less PATRIOTISM, 37
Regions C. never knew ENGLAND, 17
render . . . unto C. the things which are C.'s BIBLICAL QUOTATIONS, 525
Rose . . . where some buried C. bled FLOWERS, 5
that C. might be great RUTHLESSNESS, 2
Caesars
So long as men worship the C. and Napoleons TYRANNY, 6
cage keep such a bird in a c. IMPRISONMENT, 5
Marriage is like a c. MARRIAGE, 97
Nor iron bars a c. IMPRISONMENT, 7
robin redbreast in a c. BIRDS, 3
She's only a bird in a gilded c. BIRDS, 10
caged We think c. birds sing, when indeed they cry BIRDS, 17
Cain the Lord set a mark upon C. BIBLICAL QUOTATIONS, 193
caitiff If the rude c. smite the other too REVENGE, 11
cake Bake me a c. as fast as you can NURSERY RHYMES, 37
certain sized c. to be divided up ECONOMICS, 6
enough white lies to ice a wedding c. LYING, 4
Let them eat c. HUNGER, 10
like the bridegroom on the wedding c. APPEARANCE, 33
my face looks like a wedding c. left out in the rain APPEARANCE, 7
cakes no more c. and ale MERRYMAKING, 4
Calais 'C.' lying in my heart DEFEAT, 11
calamities C. are of two kinds MISFORTUNE, 5
the c. of life CLASS, 12
calamity thou are wedded to c. LOVE AND DEATH, 9
Whatsoever . . . the private c., I hope it will not interfere with the public business of the country FIRE, 4
calculating A dessicated c. machine POLITICIANS, 18
Calcutta Oh, C. PLACES, 39
Caledonia C.! stern and wild SCOTLAND, 7
calf a molten c. BIBLICAL QUOTATIONS, 153
but the c. won't get much sleep MISTRUST, 3
the fatted c. BIBLICAL QUOTATIONS, 440
call one clear c. for me DUTY, 5
called c. a cold a cold ILLNESS, 11
calling Germany c. TREASON, 8
calm sea is c. to-night SEA, 1
Wisdom has taught us to be c. and meek REVENGE, 11
calories the only thing that matters is c. HEALTHY LIVING, 24
calumnies C. are answered best INSULTS, 76
Calvary the place, which is called C. BIBLICAL QUOTATIONS, 446
Calvin land of C., oat-cakes, and sulphur SCOTLAND, 8
Cambridge C. as a little town and Oxford OXFORD, 16
C. people rarely smile PLACES, 8
Oxford is on the whole more attractive than C. CAMBRIDGE, 1
Spring and summer did happen in C. CAMBRIDGE, 4
The young C. group CAMBRIDGE, 3
To C. books CAMBRIDGE, 6
With equal skill to C. books he sent CAMBRIDGE, 2
came I c., I saw, God conquered VICTORY, 2
I c., I saw, I conquered VICTORY, 1
I c. like Water LIFE AND DEATH, 14
camel easier for a c. to go through the eye of a needle BIBLICAL QUOTATIONS, 520
Camelot many-tower'd C. ARTHURIAN LEGEND, 3
there was a spot . . . known /As C. PLACES, 24
To look down to C. CURSES, 7
camels the c. and the sand CINEMA, 14
camera The c. cannot lie. But . . . PHOTOGRAPHY, 3
camp an armed c. of Blackshirts, a bivouac for corpses FASCISM, 10
Campbells The C. are comin' ANONYMOUS, 80
Campland This is C., an invisible country IMPRISONMENT, 11
campus three major administrative problems on a c. EDUCATION, 50
can Talent does what it c. TALENT AND GENIUS, 3
Canada what street C. is on IGNORANCE, 6
cancel to c. half a Line DESTINY, 8
cancels debt which c. all others OBLIGATION, 1
cancer a patient has terminal c. DISEASE, 6
c. . . . close to the Presidency CORRUPTION, 2
C.'s a Funny Thing DISEASE, 24
there are several chronic diseases more destructive to life than c., none is more feared DISEASE, 31
to give up everything that scientists have linked to c. HYPOCHONDRIA, 3
candid save me, from the c. friend FRANKNESS, 1
candidates C. should not attempt more than six BIBLE, 2
candle a c. of understanding BIBLICAL QUOTATIONS, 126
Bell, book, and c. MATERIALISM, 23
blow out your c. . . . to find your way ATHEISM, 6
It is burning a farthing c. at Dover CRITICISM, 25
light a c., and put it under a bushel BIBLICAL QUOTATIONS, 473
light a c. to the sun FUTILITY, 11
Like a c. burnt out TIME, 55
little c. throws his beams GOOD, 16
My c. burns at both ends PLEASURE, 23
Out, out, brief c. LIFE, 76
take away the c. and spare my blushes MODESTY, 3
we shall this day light such a c. EXECUTION, 21
candle-light Can I get there by c. NURSERY RHYMES, 17
candles Night's c. are burnt out DAY AND NIGHT, 21
She would rather light c. than curse the darkness COMPLIMENTS, 35
candlestick The butcher, the baker, /The c.-maker NURSERY RHYMES, 44
candy C. /Is dandy SEDUCTION, 1
canem *Cave c.* DOGS, 1
canker killing as the c. to the rose CORRUPTION, 7
Cannes C. . . . lie on the beach FAME, 21
cannibal Better sleep with a sober c. than a drunken Christian DRUNKENNESS, 21
cannon-ball c. took off his legs PUNS, 9
cannot I c. pardon him because I dare not GUILT, 4
canoe every man paddle his own c. INDEPENDENCE, 4
Canossa We will not go to C. DETERMINATION, 6
cant auld Lang Swine, how full of c. you are ROYALTY, 14
'C.' will be the epitaph of the British Empire BRITISH EMPIRE, 6
clear your *mind* of c. . . . REASON, 5
love – all the wretched c. of it LOVE, 72
Popular psychology is a mass of c. PSYCHOLOGY, 5
where the Greeks had modesty, we have c. CANT, 1
capability Negative C. DOUBT, 7
capable c. of being well set to music MUSIC, 2
capers run into strange c. LOVE, 132
capital Boys are c. fellows in their own way CHILDREN, 40
capitalism C. is the exploitation of man by man CAPITALISM, 1
C. re-creates POLITICS, 117
c. . . . : the process whereby American girls turn into American women CAPITALISM, 6
I am going to fight c. CAPITALISM, 15
imperialism is the monopoly stage of c. POLITICS, 87
Lenin was the first to discover that c. 'inevitably' caused war CAPITALISM, 18
militarism . . . is one of the chief bulwarks of c. CAPITALISM, 9
not just here to manage c. POLITICIANS, 15
the acceptable face of c. CAPITALISM, 8
unacceptable face of c. CAPITALISM, 7
We cannot remove the evils of c. CAPITALISM, 10
capitalist C. production begets . . . its own negation CAPITALISM, 13
Not every problem someone has with his girlfriend is . . . due to . . . c. . . . production CAPITALISM, 12
capitulate I will be conquered; I will not c. DETERMINATION, 12
Capricorn Lady C., . . . was . . . keeping open bed PROMISCUITY, 2
captain C. of the *Pinafore* CONCEIT, 10
captain's c. LEADERSHIP, 11
I am the c. of my soul FATE, 10
captains C. of industry LEADERSHIP, 4
Capten C., art tha sleepin' there below WAR, 113
captive Beauty stands . . . Led c. BEAUTY, 28
captivity such as are for the c., to the c. BIBLICAL QUOTATIONS, 293
car I thought I told you to wait in the c. GREETINGS, 3
The c. has become the carapace TRAVEL, 30
Would you buy a used c. from this man POLITICIANS, 4
carapace The car has become the c. TRAVEL, 30
carbon c. atom possesses certain exceptional properties SCIENCE, 53
carbuncle Like a c. on the face of an old and valued friend ARCHITECTURE, 4
carcinoma To sing of rectal c. DISEASE, 24
card wrestled with a self-adjusting c. table TECHNOLOGY, 14
cardinal This c. is the person who rules POLITICIANS, 50
unbecoming for a c. to ski badly SPORT AND GAMES, 11
cardio-sclerotic We have here an antique c. WORDS, 15
cards an old age of c. OLD AGE, 74
I have not learned to play at c. SPORT AND GAMES, 12
Never play c. with a man called Doc ADVICE, 5
care age is full of c. AGE, 70
Begone, dull c. ANONYMOUS, 10
can c. intelligently for the future of England ENGLAND, 25
C. /Sat on his faded cheek CARE, 8
Effective health c. depends on self-c. PATIENTS, 9
For want of timely c. ILLNESS, 7
I c. for nobody CARE, 2
I don't c. for war WAR, 110
Our progress . . . /Is trouble and c. CARE, 7
People who are always taking c. of their health are like misers HYPOCHONDRIA, 12
pleasures are their only c. CARE, 5
Sleep that knits up the ravell'd sleave of c. CARE, 9
so vain . . . c. for the opinion of those we don't c. for CARE, 6
take c. of the minutes CARE, 4
Take c. of the pence CARE, 3
The first C. in building of Cities ENVIRONMENT, 2
what is past my help is past my c. INDIFFERENCE, 1
career a lover with any other c. in view COMMITMENT, 6
c. that made the Recording Angel think seriously about . . . shorthand EPITAPHS, 5
having a c. of my own MARRIAGE, 15
Miss Madeleine Philips . . . was a c. COMMITMENT, 6
nothing in his long c. which those . . . would wish otherwise ROYALTY, 16
nothing which might damage his c. SCOTS, 1
science was the only c. worth following WORK, 14
careers The best c. advice to give to the young OCCUPATIONS, 21
careful be very c. o' vidders CAUTION, 11

we are not c. to answer thee in this matter BIBLICAL QUOTATIONS, 58
careless C. talk costs lives SECRECY, 2
first fine c. rapture BIRDS, 4
carelessness To lose one parent, . . . a misfortune; to lose both looks like c. CARELESSNESS, 1
with a slow deliberate c. READING, 12
cares the earth where c. abound BIRDS, 18
careth he that is married c. . . . how he may please his wife BIBLICAL QUOTATIONS, 36
cargo , With a c. of ivory BOATS, 13
With a c. of Tyne coal BOATS, 14
caring take millions off the c. services PATRIOTISM, 25
Carnation C. milk is the best in the land FOOD, 8
carpe *C. diem* PRESENT, 8
Carpenter Walrus and the C. SEASIDE, 2
carpet a Turkey c. bears to a picture CRITICISM, 38
only men in rags . . . /Mistake themselves for c. bags ETIQUETTE, 6
carriage Go together like a horse and c. LOVE AND MARRIAGE, 1
very small second-class c. BOATS, 6
we look for happiness in boats and c. rides TRAVEL, 20
carriages when they think they are alone in railway c. HABIT, 5
carry certain we can c. nothing out BIBLICAL QUOTATIONS, 650
cars the selling of c. in Great Portland Street COMPLIMENTS, 10
carter how a c., a common sailor, a beggar is still . . . an Englishman ENGLAND, 35
Carthage C. must be destroyed WAR, 39
Casbah Come with me to the C. INVITATIONS, 2
case If ever there was a c. of clearer evidence NONSENSE, 2
in our c. we have not got WEAPONS, 7
It is not a c. we are treating PATIENTS, 3
the c. is still before the courts ARGUMENTS, 6
the reason of the c. LAW, 26
there had been a lady in the c. WOMEN, 29
The world is everything that is the c. LOGIC, 7
casements Charm'd magic c. BIRDS, 9
cases a narrative of the special c. of his patients MEDICINE, 6
cash Nothing links man to man like . . . c. MONEY, 42
One cannot assess in terms of c. . . . a church tower ENVIRONMENT, 3
only the poor who pay c. MONEY, 20
take the C. in hand MONEY, 19
cashiers c. of the Musical Banks BANKS, 3
casino I have come to regard . . . courts . . . as a c. JUSTICE, 15
cask A c. of wine ALCOHOL, 1
casket seal the hushed c. of my soul SLEEP, 23
Cassius C. has a lean and hungry look MISTRUST, 10
cassock C., band, and hymn-book too CLERGY, 15
cassowary If I were a c. CLERGY, 15
cast c. thy bread upon the waters BIBLICAL QUOTATIONS, 96
he that is without sin . . . let him first c. a stone BIBLICAL QUOTATIONS, 334
him that cometh to me I will in no wise c. out BIBLICAL QUOTATIONS, 332
pale c. of thought CONSCIENCE, 7
set my life upon a c. CHANCE, 7
The die is c. IRREVOCABILITY, 1
caste measure the social c. of a person CLASS, 3
casteth perfect love c. out fear BIBLICAL QUOTATIONS, 379
casting It is no good c. out devils DEVIL, 12
castle A c. called Doubting Castle DESPAIR, 4
A neurotic is the man who builds a c. in the air PSYCHIATRY, 32
The house of every one is to him as his c. PRIVACY, 2
Castlereagh Murder . . . had a mask like C. MURDER, 12
castles C. in the air DREAMS, 9
Pale Death kicks his way . . . into . . . the c. of kings EQUALITY, 31
the c. I have, are built with air DREAMS, 10
casualty except the c. list of the World War MURDER, 3
The first c. when war comes WAR, 82
cat A c. has nine lives LUCK, 2
A c. may look EQUALITY, 1
a C. of such deceitfulness CATS, 2
c. is a diagram and pattern of subtle air CATS, 5
God . . . a cosmic Cheshire c. GOD, 31
Had Tiberius been a c. CATS, 1
He bought a crooked c., which caught a crooked mouse NURSERY RHYMES, 53
he is a very fine c. CATS, 4
Hey diddle diddle, /The c. and the fiddle NURSERY RHYMES, 14
I am the c. that walks alone INDEPENDENCE, 2
I'll bell the c. COURAGE, 10
More ways of killing a c. CHOICE, 3
That tossed the dog, /That worried the c. NURSERY RHYMES, 57
The C., the Rat, and Lovell our dog INSULTS, 36
What c.'s averse to fish MATERIALISM, 12
When I play with my c. CATS, 6
When the c.'s away ABSENCE, 3
cataclysm Out of their c. but one poor Noah / Dare hope to survive SEX, 47
catastrophe to lose one's teeth is a c. TEETH, 13
When a man confronts c. . . . a woman looks in her mirror SEXES, 30
catch Go, and c. a falling star NONSENSE, 11
Catch-22 moved very deeply by . . . this clause of C. LOGIC, 5
only one catch and that was C. OBSTRUCTION, 4
catchwords Man is a creature who lives . . . by c. SEXES, 25
categorical This imperative is C. MORALITY, 8
cathedrals the ancient c. – grand, wonderful, mysterious RELIGION, 63
Catherine I'm glad you like my C. PROMISCUITY, 10
Catholic A C. layman who has never been averse INSULTS, 84
I am a C.. . . . I go to Mass every day PREJUDICE, 1
I have a C. soul, but a Lutheran stomach CATHOLICISM, 4
I'm still a C. CATHOLICISM, 14
One cannot . . . be a C. and grown-up CATHOLICISM, 10
quite lawful for a C. woman to avoid pregnancy by . . . mathematics CONTRACEPTION, 9
Roman C. women must keep taking the *Tablet* CONTRACEPTION, 13
who, like you, your Holiness, is a Roman C. CATHOLICISM, 3
Catholics C. and Communists have committed great crimes COMMITMENT, 4
they may be C. but they are not Christians INSULTS, 97
We know these new English C. CATHOLICISM, 8
cats All c. are gray EQUALITY, 2
A lotta c. copy the Mona Lisa IMITATION, 1
what c. most appreciate . . . is . . . entertainment value CATS, 3
cattle Actors should be treated like c. ACTORS, 6
O Mary, go and call the c. home AGRICULTURE, 4
cause A c. is like champagne and high heels BELIEF, 3
A reckoning up of the c. often solves the malady REMEDIES, 19
Arise, O Lord, plead Thine own c. PRAYER, 24
for what high c. /This darling of the Gods DESTINY, 16
has to know the c. of the ailment before he can cure it DIAGNOSIS, 18
the great c. of cheering us all up.' HUMOR, 9
the name of perseverance in a good c. STUBBORNNESS, 4
to attribute to a single c. that which is the product of several DIAGNOSIS, 14
causes Home of lost c. OXFORD, 1
they should declare the c. which impel them to . . . separation INDEPENDENCE, 3
cavaliero a perfect c. HEROISM, 5
Cavaliers
C. (Wrong but Wromantic) HISTORY, 33
cave *C. canem* DOGS, 1
I should be like a lion in a c. of savage Daniels ENEMIES, 10
Caverns Gluts twice ten thousand C. SEA, 8
Through c. measureless to man PLEASURE, 9
caves be c. . . . in which his shadow will be shown GOD, 45
sunny pleasure-dome with c. of ice MIRACLES, 1
caviar c. to the general TASTE, 7
cavity John Brown is filling his last c. ANONYMOUS, 74
cease have their day and c. to be TRANSIENCE, 23
I will not c. from mental fight ENGLAND, 6
restless Cromwell could not c. POLITICIANS, 80
ceases forbearance c. to be a virtue TOLERANCE, 1
celebrate I c. myself SELF, 22
poetry cannot c. them SCIENTISTS, 2
celebrity A c. . . . works hard . . . to become known FAME, 2
The c. . . . known for his well-knownness FAME, 5
celerity C. is never more admir'd IMPETUOSITY, 3
celery Genuineness . . . Like c. DARKNESS, 12
two thousand people crunching c. at the same time FOOD, 64
Celia Come, my C., let us prove LOVE, 85
celibacy c. is . . . a muddy horse-pond MARRIAGE, 103
cello The c. is not one of my favourite instruments MUSIC, 50
cells These little grey c. INTELLECT, 1
cemetery Help me down C. Road SUPPORT, 4
old c. in which nine of his daughters were lying SEX, 102
send him to the c. VIOLENCE, 10
censor Deleted by French c. NEWSPAPERS, 3
censorship Assassination . . . the extreme form of c. ASSASSINATION, 7
C. . . . depraving and corrupting CENSORSHIP, 8
censure All c. of a man's self SELF, 12
center I love being at the c. of things COMMITMENT, 5
century The c. on which we are entering . . . must be the c. of the common man PUBLIC, 19
The great man . . . walks across his c. INFLUENCE, 7
the twentieth c. will be . . . the c. of Fascism FASCISM, 8
The twentieth c. will be remembered HEALTHY LIVING, 44
cereal Do you *know* what breakfast c. is made of FOOD, 25
cerebral they do not believe in the mind but in a c. intestine PSYCHOANALYSIS, 4
cerebrums larger c. and smaller adrenal glands WAR, 99
certain I am c. that we will win the election with a good majority SELF-CONFIDENCE, 9
Nothing is c. but death DEATH, 12
One thing is c. LIFE, 35
certainties begin with c. CERTAINTY, 1
His doubts are better than . . . c. DOUBT, 6
cesspit I see increasing evidence of people swirling about in a human c. DISEASE, 4
cesspool London, that great c. LONDON, 9
Ceylon spicy breezes /Blow soft o'er C.'s isle MISANTHROPY, 1
chaff An editor . . . separates the wheat from the c. EDITORS, 4
Editor: . . . to separate the wheat from the c. JOURNALISM, 23
chain A c. is no stronger PROVERBS, 9
the flesh to feel the c. IMPRISONMENT, 3
chains c. that tie /The hidden soul of harmony MUSIC, 30
It's often safer to be in c. FREEDOM, 30
Man . . . everywhere he is in c. FREEDOM, 52
nothing to lose but their c. MARXISM, 12
chair Give Dayrolles a c. LAST WORDS, 18
Inspiration is the act of drawing up a c. INSPIRATION, 3
the nineteenth century was the age of the editorial c. PSYCHIATRY, 24
chairs The c. are being brought in from the garden ERROR, 1
chaise All in a c. and pair MARRIAGE, 48
chaise-longue Wedlock – the . . . deep peace of the double bed after the . . . c. MARRIAGE, 37
chalices In old time we had treen c. and golden priests CLERGY, 8
Cham That great C. of literature, Samuel Johnson WRITERS, 54
chamber rapping at my c. door SUPERNATURAL, 12
Upstairs and downstairs /And in my lady's c. NURSERY RHYMES, 13
Chamberlain a speech by C. is like . . . Woolworths INSULTS, 17

C.'s umbrella on the cobblestones of Munich POLITICS, 114
chambermaid a man would be as happy in the arms of a c. IMAGINATION, 6
chamois springing from blonde to blonde like the c. of the Alps UNITED STATES, 95
champagne Fighting is like c. WAR, 101
I get no kick from c. COMPLIMENTS, 23
like a glass of c. that has stood HOUSES OF PARLIAMENT, 2
water flowed like c. ABSTINENCE, 4
chance every c. brought out a noble knight NOSTALGIA, 25
Grab a c. OPPORTUNITY, 17
in our lives c. may have an astonishing influence RESEARCH, 12
time and c. happeneth to them all BIBLICAL QUOTATIONS, 90
We have had our last c. PROPHECY, 12
chancellor C. of the Exchequer TAXATION, 14
change c. . . . due to truths being in and out of favor CHANGE, 9
C. is not made without inconvenience CHANGE, 12
I c., but I cannot die WEATHER, 25
If you leave a thing alone you leave it to a torrent of c. CONSERVATISM, 2
Most of the c. we think we see NOVELTY, 2
Most women set out to try to c. a man CHANGE, 5
Plus ça c. CONSTANCY, 3
Popularity? . . . glory's small c. POPULARITY, 4
The miserable c. now at my end /Lament nor sorrow at SUICIDE, 30
The more things c. CONSTANCY, 3
There is a certain relief in c. CHANGE, 13
The wind of c. CHANGE, 16
changed All c., c. utterly BEAUTY, 43
changeth The old order c. CHANGE, 21
changez *C. vos amis* FRIENDS, 6
changing c. scenes of life CHANGE, 20
Woman is always fickle and c. WOMEN, 124
Channel dream you are crossing the C. BOATS, 6
let the last man . . . brush the C. with his sleeve WAR, 143
chaos a perfectly possible means of overcoming c. POETRY, 46
The grotesque c. of a Labour council – a *Labour* council INCOMPETENCE, 2
the view that there is mounting c. POLITICS, 29
when I love thee not, /C. is come again LOVE, 145
chapel Devil always builds a c. there DEVIL, 10
chapels c. had been churches ACTION, 13
chaplain twice a day the C. called IMPRISONMENT, 14
Chaplin C. is no business man ACTORS, 5
chaps Biography is about C. BIOGRAPHY, 1
chapter c. of accidents MISFORTUNE, 9
c. of accidents is the longest . . . in the book ACCIDENTS, 9
character I had become a woman of . . . c. CHARACTER, 5
I leave my c. behind REPUTATION, 14
What is c. but the determination of incident CHARACTER, 14
characteristic typically English c. ENGLISH, 3
characters a talent for describing the involvements and feelings and c. AUSTEN, JANE, 2
c. in one of my novels FICTION, 2
Most women have no c. WOMEN, 94
charge Electrical force . . . causes motion of electrical c. SCIENCE, 30
charged it was c. against me INDIFFERENCE, 7
charges who goeth a warfare . . . at his own c. BIBLICAL QUOTATIONS, 38
Charing Cross between Heaven and C. HEAVEN, 14
I went out to C., to see Major-general Harrison hanged EXECUTION, 29
the full tide of human existence is at C. LONDON, 16
chariot a c. . . . of fire BIBLICAL QUOTATIONS, 405
Swing low sweet c. ANONYMOUS, 76
the dust beneath thy c. wheel DUST, 5
Time's winged c. AGE, 49
charity C. begins at home CHARITY, 1
C. is the power of defending that which we know to be indefensible CHARITY, 13
c. never faileth BIBLICAL QUOTATIONS, 44
c. offers to the poor the gains in medical skill CHARITY, 17
c. suffereth long, and is kind BIBLICAL QUOTATIONS, 44
In c. there is no excess CHARITY, 4
knowledge puffeth up, but c. edifieth BIBLICAL QUOTATIONS, 37
lectures or a little c. SELF, 23
now abideth faith, hope, c. BIBLICAL QUOTATIONS, 44
the greatest of these is c. BIBLICAL QUOTATIONS, 44
The house which is not opened for c. CHARITY, 24
The living need c. CHARITY, 3
The man who leaves money to c. in his will BEQUESTS, 3
without c. are nothing worth BOOK OF COMMON PRAYER, THE, 2
Charles Caesar had his Brutus – C. the First, his Cromwell CAESAR, 3
cast out C. our Norman oppressor REBELLION, 14
There were gentlemen and . . . seamen in the navy of C. the Second NAVY, 8
Charley I'm C.'s aunt from Brazil PLACES, 38
Charlie C. is my darling ADMIRATION, 11
charm Conversation has a kind of c. CONVERSATION, 9
Oozing c. . . . He oiled his way CHARM, 3
the c. . . . of a nomadic existence CAMPING, 1
charming c. people have something to conceal CHARM, 2
I heard the bullets whistle, . . . c. in the sound WAR, 163
It is c. to totter into vogue AGE, 80
charms Whose c. all other maids surpass ADMIRATION, 9
Charon C., seeing, may forget LUST, 7
charter This c. . . . constitutes an insult to the Holy See FREEDOM, 26
chartreuse religious system that produced green C. ALCOHOL, 66
chaste godly poet must be c. himself POETRY, 14
chastity Give me c. and continence CHASTITY, 1
Give me c. and continence PRAYER, 4
Chatham Because you're in C. REPARTEE, 2
Chatterley Put thy shimmy on, Lady C. PARTING, 7
cheap flesh and blood so c. BREAD, 5
Pile it high, sell it c. BUSINESS, 4
send me some good actors – c. ACTORS, 1
cheating *Peace . . . a period of c.* PEACE, 5
check Any general statement is like a c. GENERALIZATIONS, 4
C. enclosed MONEY, 34
dreadful is the c. IMPRISONMENT, 3
Got no c. books, got no banks GRATITUDE, 2
Mrs Claypool's c. will come back to you HUMOR, 39
checker-board a C. of Nights and Days DESTINY, 7
checks The rich hate signing c. WEALTH, 23
cheek Care /Sat on his faded c. CARE, 8
the c. that doth not fade APPEARANCE, 27
turn the other c. REVENGE, 11
whosoever shall smite thee on thy right c. BIBLICAL QUOTATIONS, 477
cheeks Blow, winds, and crack your c. WEATHER, 21
cheer cups, /That c. but not inebriate DRINKS, 10
Don't c., boys; the poor devils are dying WAR, 122
cheerful God loveth a c. giver BIBLICAL QUOTATIONS, 52
cheerfulness Health and c. mutually beget each other HEALTHY LIVING, 9
No warmth, no c., no healthful ease MONTHS, 10
cheering the great cause of c. us all up. HUMOR, 9
cheese 265 kinds of c. FRANCE, 8
bread and c., and kisses BACHELORS, 3
c. – toasted, mostly DREAMS, 16
when the c. is gone NONSENSE, 4
chef the resurrection of a French c. FOOD, 32
Cheltenham Here lie I . . . /Killed by drinking C. waters ANONYMOUS, 25
chemical c. barrage has been hurled against the fabric of life ECOLOGY, 2
Shelley and Keats were . . . up to date in . . . c. knowledge POETS, 20
chemistry he had read Shakespeare and found him weak in c. SCIENTISTS, 13
chemotherapy under the influence of modern c. DISEASE, 47
cherish to love and to c. BOOK OF COMMON PRAYER, THE, 15
Cherith the brook C. BIBLICAL QUOTATIONS, 401
cherry Before the c. orchard was sold WORRY, 11
C. ripe, ripe, ripe BUSINESS, 14
Loveliest of trees, the c. TREES, 6
Till 'C. ripe' themselves do cry ADMIRATION, 4
chess Life's too short for c. SPORT AND GAMES, 5
the devil played at c. with me EXPLOITATION, 1
chess-board c. is the world; the pieces . . . the phenomena of the universe GOD, 32
chest Fifteen men on the dead man's c. ALCOHOL, 77
He may have hair upon his c. MEN, 11
separating disorders of the c. from disorders of the bowels BODY, 2
chestnut O c. tree NATURE, 40
Under the spreading c. tree IRON, 3
chestnuts warmongers who . . . have others pull the c. out of the fire POLITICS, 130
chests Men have broad and large c. SEXES, 18
chew he can't fart and c. gum at the same time INSULTS, 69
chewing c. little bits of String FOOD, 11
television programs are so much c. gum TELEVISION, 3
chic very *c.* for an atheist MEMORIALS, 13
chicken a c. in his pot every Sunday POVERTY, 17
England will have her neck wrung like a c. WORLD WAR II, 49
Some c. WORLD WAR II, 19
chickens children are more troublesome and costly than c. MANKIND, 59
count their c. ere they're hatched ANTICIPATION, 5
Don't count your c. ANTICIPATION, 4
If I didn't start painting, I would have raised c. OCCUPATIONS, 17
You don't set a fox to watching the c. EXPERIENCE, 23
chief C. Defect of Henry King FOOD, 11
C. of the Army LAST WORDS, 57
child A c. becomes an adult when RIGHT, 3
A c. deserves the maximum respect CHILDREN, 36
A c.'s a plaything for an hour CHILDREN, 41
A c. . . . would have no more idea of death than a cat or a plant DEATH, 174
all any reasonable c. can expect SEX, 76
better . . . a poor and a wise c. than an old and foolish king BIBLICAL QUOTATIONS, 85
C.! do not throw this book about BOOKS, 7
c. of five would understand this SIMPLICITY, 5
Every c. should have an occasional pat on the back PUNISHMENT, 24
flourish in a c. of six CHILDREN, 10
getting wenches with c. YOUTH, 27
give her the living c. BIBLICAL QUOTATIONS, 398
Give me a c. for the first seven years PROVERBS, 175
hard travail in c. bearing SUFFERING, 26
He who shall teach the c. to doubt DOUBT, 4
If you strike a c. VIOLENCE, 14
institute for the study of c. guidance CHILDREN, 39
I would . . . stand /Three times in the front of battle than bear one c. WOMAN'S ROLE, 2
nobody's c. LONELINESS, 1
One stops being a c. when . . . telling one's trouble does not make it better DISILLUSION, 5
receive one such little c. in my name BIBLICAL QUOTATIONS, 515
spoil the c. INDULGENCE, 1
The business of being a c. CHILDREN, 32
The C. is Father of the Man AGE, 85
The mother-c. relationship is paradoxical FAMILY, 20
The new-born c. does not realize that his body is more a part of himself than surrounding objects SUFFERING, 21
There are only two things a c. will share willingly CHILDREN, 51
Think no more of it, John; you are only a c. FORGIVENESS, 16
unless the play is stopped, the c. cannot . . . go on AUDIENCES, 4
unto us a c. is born BIBLICAL QUOTATIONS, 256
What is the use of a new-born c. PURPOSE, 2
when I was a c., I spake as a c. BIBLICAL QUOTATIONS, 44
wise father that knows his own c. FAMILY, 48
childbearing Common morality now treats c. as an aberration CHILDREN, 30
childbed A man may sympathize with a woman in c. SEXES, 24

childbirth At the moment of c., every woman has the same aura of isolation LONELINESS, 7
Death and taxes and c. INCONVENIENCE, 1
Mountains will heave in c. DISAPPOINTMENT, 3
the male equivalent of c. PUBLISHING, 1
childe C. Roland to the Dark Tower SUMMONS, 4
childhood infancy, c., adolescence and obsolescence AGE, 46
The books one reads in c. . . . create in one's mind a . . . false map BOOKS, 32
childish I put away c. things BIBLICAL QUOTATIONS, 44
Sweet c. days NOSTALGIA, 29
childishness second c. OLD AGE, 82
children a Friend for little c. /Above the bright blue sky GOD, 42
Anybody who hates c. and dogs CHILDREN, 26
Are the c. all in bed? It's past eight o'clock NURSERY RHYMES, 64
as c. fear to go in the dark DARKNESS, 3
a wicked man that comes after c. SLEEP, 20
c. are more troublesome and costly than chickens MANKIND, 59
C. aren't happy with nothing to ignore FAMILY, 38
c. are true judges of character CHILDREN, 5
C. do not give up their innate imagination, curiosity, dreaminess easily IMAGINATION, 8
c. – especially when they cry CHILDREN, 44
C. have never been very good at listening CHILDREN, 7
C. . . . have no use for psychology. They detest sociology BOOKS, 42
C., in general, are overclothed and overfed INDULGENCE, 2
c., obey your parents BIBLICAL QUOTATIONS, 118
C. should acquire . . . heroes and villains from fiction HISTORY, 2
C. sweeten labours CHILDREN, 6
C. with Hyacinth's temperament . . . merely know more CHARACTER, 22
Come dear c. DEPARTURE, 1
desire not a multitude of unprofitable c. BIBLICAL QUOTATIONS, 106
Do you hear the c. weeping SORROW, 3
except ye . . . become as little c. BIBLICAL QUOTATIONS, 514
Familiarity breeds . . . c. SEX, 105
Far too good to waste on c. YOUTH, 28
He that has no c. ADVICE, 3
He that loves not his wife and c. MARRIAGE, 138
his wife is beautiful and his c. smart TOLERANCE, 9
I love all my c. FAMILY, 13
in sorrow thou shalt bring forth c. BIBLICAL QUOTATIONS, 188
I've lost one of my c. this week LOSS, 9
Let our c. grow tall TALENT, 9
like a c.'s party taken over by the elders AGE, 33
little c., keep yourselves from idols BIBLICAL QUOTATIONS, 381
love animals and c. too much LOVE, 127
make your c. *capable of honesty* is the beginning of education HONESTY, 6
Men are but c. of a larger growth AGE, 28
more careful of the breed of their horses and dogs than of their c. FAMILY, 42
Most of the people . . . will be c. FUNERALS, 1
My music . . . understood by c. and animals MUSIC, 47
Never have c. CHILDREN, 53
Never work with animals or c. ACTING, 2
Old men are twice c. OLD AGE, 6
our c. can give it ten or fifteen minutes HEALTHY LIVING, 28
Parents learn a lot from their c. CHILDREN, 50
provoke not your c. BIBLICAL QUOTATIONS, 25
She had so many c. she didn't know what to do FAMILY, 40
that husbands and wives should have c. alternatively SEXES, 15
the c. I might have had CHILDREN, 43
the early marriages of silly c. MARRIAGE, 93
the more c. they can disturb PSYCHIATRY, 25
the Revolution may . . . devour each of her c. FRENCH REVOLUTION, 10
The value of marriage is . . . that c. produce adults MARRIAGE, 52
to avoid having c. CONTRACEPTION, 14
To bear many c. is considered . . . an investment CHILDREN, 27
to seyn, to syngen and to rede, /As smale c. doon EDUCATION, 20
We have no c., except me CHILDREN, 8
Were we closer to the ground as c. NOSTALGIA, 1
We want far better reasons for having c. CONTRACEPTION, 11
when they started life as c. CHILDREN, 4
write for c. . . . as you do for adults WRITING, 15
You can do anything with c. if you only play with them CHILDREN, 18
you can get it from your c. MADNESS, 24
Chile Small earthquake in C. NEWSPAPERS, 8
chill St Agnes' Eve – Ah, bitter c. it was WINTER, 2
chilled c. into a selfish prayer for light DAY AND NIGHT, 5
chime to set a c. of words tinkling in . . . a few fastidious people PURPOSE, 10
chimes c. at midnight MERRYMAKING, 3
chimney sixty horses wedged in a c. JOURNALISM, 32
chimney-sweepers As c., come to dust DUST, 9
China Even the Hooligan was probably invented in C. PLACES, 32
On a slow boat to C. BOATS, 11
The infusion of a C. plant DRINKS, 1
Chinese Nothing . . . can destroy the C. people PLACES, 9
chip c. of the old block PRIME MINISTERS, 7
chips You breed babies and you eat c. FOOD, 72
chirche-dore Housbondes at c. MARRIAGE, 39
chivalry age of c. is gone EUROPE, 3
The age of c. is never past CHIVALRY, 6
truant been to c. CHIVALRY, 11
Chi Wen Tzu C. always CAUTION, 10
Chloë In the spring . . . your lovely C. APPEARANCE, 50
chloroform that blessed C. & the effect was soothing REMEDIES, 57
chocolate a c. cream soldier SOLDIERS, 13
both its national products, snow and c., melt SWITZERLAND, 1
Venice is like eating . . . c. liqueurs VENICE, 2
choice he makes a c. PHILOSOPHY, 20
choir Sweet singing in the c. ANONYMOUS, 82
choirs Bare ruin'd c. OLD AGE, 89
cholera If . . . an outbreak of c. RESEARCH, 15
I would rather that any white rabbit on earth should have the Asiatic c. VIVISECTION, 1
choose I do not c. to run POLITICS, 40
I will not c. what many men desire INDIVIDUALITY, 6
We can believe what we c. RESPONSIBILITY, 11
Chopin to bridge the awful gap between Dorothy and C. MUSIC, 3
chord c. of music MUSIC, 36
chorus a dozen are only a c. BEAUTY, 18
knocked everything except the knees of the c. girls THEATER, 10
chose *plus c'est la même c.* CONSTANCY, 3
chosen a c. vessel BIBLICAL QUOTATIONS, 8
but few are c. BIBLICAL QUOTATIONS, 524
ye have not c. me, but I have c. you BIBLICAL QUOTATIONS, 352
Christ C. is all, and in all BIBLICAL QUOTATIONS, 23
C. . . . would quite likely have been arrested OPPRESSION, 2
churches have kill'd their C. CLERGY, 14
Decide for C. RELIGION, 38
I beseech you, in the bowels of C. MISTAKES, 7
The Jews have produced . . . C., Spinoza, and myself CONCEIT, 18
We're more popular than Jesus C. POPULARITY, 6
Who dreamed that C. has died in vain CHRISTIANITY, 55
Christendom Of the two lights of C. DEFEAT, 14
wisest fool in C. FOOLISHNESS, 13
Christian A C. . . . feels /Repentance on a Sunday CHRISTIANITY, 63
any man . . . who could not bear another's misfortunes . . . like a C. MISFORTUNE, 14
Better sleep with a sober cannibal than a drunken C. DRUNKENNESS, 21
C. glories in the death of a pagan CHRISTIANITY, 5
C. Science explains all cause and effect as mental RELIGION, 28
How very hard . . . /To be a C. CHRISTIANITY, 31
I die a C. EXECUTION, 6
in what peace a C. can die LAST WORDS, 3
I was born of C. race RELIGION, 74
No Jew was ever fool enough to turn C. JEWS, 21
object . . . to form C. men EDUCATION, 7
Onward, C. soldiers CHRISTIANITY, 3
several young women . . . would render the C. life intensely difficult CHRISTIANITY, 44
The C. religion not only was at first attended with miracles CHRISTIANITY, 42
Christianity C. accepted as given a metaphysical system CHRISTIANITY, 43
C., . . . but why journalism CHRISTIANITY, 2
C. has done a great deal for love CHRISTIANITY, 37
C. has made of death a terror CHRISTIANITY, 50
C. is part of the Common Law of England CHRISTIANITY, 39
C. is the most materialistic of all great religions CHRISTIANITY, 58
C. . . . says that they are all fools MANKIND, 17
C. the one great curse CHRISTIANITY, 48
C. . . . the one immortal blemish of mankind CHRISTIANITY, 48
decay of C. ALCOHOL, 66
His C. was muscular CHRISTIANITY, 36
local cult called C. CHRISTIANITY, 41
loving C. better than Truth CHRISTIANITY, 34
nothing in C. or Buddhism that quite matches FISH, 2
Rock and roll or C. POPULARITY, 6
single friar who goes counter to all C. PROTESTANTISM, 2
Christians C. awake, salute the happy morn CHRISTMAS, 13
Onward, C., onward go ENDURANCE, 28
settle their differences like good C. GOLDWYNISMS, 26
these C. love one another CHRISTIANITY, 61
they may be Catholics but they are not C. INSULTS, 97
Christian Science C. will cure imaginary diseases, and they can not MEDICINE, 14
Christ-like C. heroes and woman-worshipping Don Juans MEN, 8
Christmas At C. I no more desire a rose SUITABILITY, 4
C. comes but once a year CHRISTMAS, 21
C. should fall out in the Middle of Winter CHRISTMAS, 1
Eating a C. pie NURSERY RHYMES, 29
I'm dreaming of a white C. CHRISTMAS, 6
I'm walking backwards till C. NONSENSE, 24
perceive C. through its wrapping CHRISTMAS, 22
The first day of C., /My true love sent to me CHRISTMAS, 16
'Twas the night before C. CHRISTMAS, 14
Christopher C. Robin /Has / Fallen / Down- / Stairs SATIRE, 3
C. Robin went down with Alice SOLDIERS, 6
chronicle c. small beer TRIVIALITY, 13
the c. of wasted time HISTORY, 38
chum Any gum, c. UNITED STATES, 73
church an alien C. IRELAND, 7
Beware when you take on the C. of God RELIGION, 70
But get me to the c. on time MARRIAGE, 89
custom of the Roman C. CATHOLICISM, 5
he'd go to c., start a revolution – *something* MATERIALISM, 20
he goes to c. as he goes to the bathroom RELIGION, 11
I believe in the C. RELIGION, 65
I should never have entered the c. on that day MODESTY, 2
straying away from the c. RELIGION, 12
The blood of the martyrs is the seed of the C. CHRISTIANITY, 60
The C. exists CHURCH, 10
the c. he . . . did not attend was Catholic RELIGION, 3
The C.'s one foundation CHRISTIANITY, 56
The farther you go from the c. of Rome PROTESTANTISM, 8
There are many who stay away from c. RELIGION, 55
There is no salvation outside the c. RELIGION, 4
There was I, waiting at the c. MARRIAGE, 88
where MCC ends and the C. of England begins CHURCH, 8
churches chapels had been c. ACTION, 13

After that you just take the girl's c. off ALCOHOL, 25
as if she were taking off all her c. SEX, 29
bought her wedding c. WOMEN, 9
enterprises that require new c. THRIFT, 12
Fine c. are good CLOTHES, 12
hanging the baby on the c. line to dry INNOVATION, 2
Have you ever taken anything out of the c. basket CLEANNESS, 11
if it be our c. alone which fit us for society CLOTHES, 6
more leisure, better c., better food HEALTHY LIVING, 39
Nothing to wear but c. PESSIMISM, 10
No woman so naked as . . . underneath her c. NAKEDNESS, 7
walked away with their c. POLITICS, 44
wrapped him in swaddling c. BIBLICAL QUOTATIONS, 418
cloud a c. received him out of their sight BIBLICAL QUOTATIONS, 1
a pillar of a c. BIBLICAL QUOTATIONS, 141
Every c. has a silver lining OPTIMISM, 2
fiend hid in a c. BIRTH, 5
I wandered lonely as a c. FLOWERS, 14
clouds But trailing c. of glory METAPHYSICS, 6
c. that gather round the setting sun MORTALITY, 21
clout Ne'er cast a c. MONTHS, 2
clown I remain . . . a c. CLOWNS, 1
clowns Send in the C. CLOWNS, 2
club any c. that will accept me as a member CLUBS, 4
Mankind is a c. CLUBS, 1
takes you so far from the c. house CLUBS, 3
the best c. in London CLUBS, 2
the most exclusive c. there is CLUBS, 5
cluster The human face is . . . a whole c. of faces MANKIND, 46
Clyde the bonny banks of C. SCOTLAND, 6
CMG Members rise from C. TITLES, 10
coach c. and six horses through the Act of Settlement IRELAND, 18
indifference and a c. and six LOVE, 49
coal best sun . . . made of Newcastle c. BUSINESS, 28
having a live c. in his hand BIBLICAL QUOTATIONS, 252
though the whole world turn to c. VIRTUE, 14
coals heap c. of fire upon his head BIBLICAL QUOTATIONS, 579
coarse barefoot and wearing c. wool, he stood pitifully HUMILITY, 5
coaster Dirty British c. BOATS, 14
coat a c. of many colours BIBLICAL QUOTATIONS, 219
cobbler Let the c. stick CLASS, 1
cobwebs Laws are like c. LAW, 36
laws were like c. LAW, 7
Coca-Cola the churches . . . bore for me the same relation to God that billboards did to C. RELIGION, 71
cocaine C. isn't habit-forming ADDICTION, 1
there still remains the c. bottle ADDICTION, 4
cock before the c. crow, thou shalt deny me BETRAYAL, 2
He was like a c. ARROGANCE, 3
Our c. won't fight ROYALTY, 24
That kept the c. that crowed in the morn NURSERY RHYMES, 57
waiting for the c. to crow BETRAYAL, 8
we owe a c. to Aesculapius LAST WORDS, 81
cockles Crying, C. and mussels! alive, alive, O ANONYMOUS, 47
cockpit Can this c. hold THEATER, 16
cockroach to choose between him and a c. as a companion INSULTS, 134
cockroaches The huge laughing c. APPEARANCE, 36
cocksure as c. of anything SELF-CONFIDENCE, 4
cocktail Mona Lisa c. . . . can't get the silly grin ALCOHOL, 12
weasel under the c. cabinet PLAYS, 8
cod piece of c. passes all understanding FOOD, 50
serve both c. and salmon PUNS, 13
the c.'s wallop is always fresh made COMMUNISM, 11
The home of the bean and the c. BOSTON, 2
codfish Unlike the male c. . . . the British aristocracy is ARISTOCRACY, 22
coffee c. that's too black . . . You integrate it with cream RACE, 16
C. which makes the politician wise DRINKS, 15
if this is c., I want tea DRINKS, 3
measured out my life with c. spoons LIFE, 33
coffee-house It is folly . . . to mistake the echo of a . . . c. for the . . . kingdom KINGS AND KINGDOMS, 15
coffin the silver plate on a c. INSULTS, 100
coffins ignoring the price of c. IMMORTALITY, 2
cogito *C., ergo sum* THINKING, 4
coil shuffled off this mortal c. FORTUNE, 6
coke Happiness is like c. HAPPINESS, 12
Colbert I can pay some of my debt with this gift – C. BETRAYAL, 10
cold a period of c. peace COLD WAR, 3
blow hot and c. with the same breath INDECISION, 1
C. hands, warm heart PROVERBS, 102
C. Pastoral ETERNITY, 3
Feed a c. ILLNESS, 1
I beg c. comfort COMFORT, 4
If you think that you have caught a c., call in a good doctor DOCTORS, 21
It leapt straight past the common c. DISCOVERY, 3
Saying 'Gesundheit' doesn't really help the common c. REMEDIES, 59
she should catch a c. on overexposure TRUTH, 15
The Irish, . . . are needed in this c. age IRISH, 4
The Spy Who Came In From the C. RETURN, 4
we are . . . in the midst of a c. war COLD WAR, 1
We called a c. a c. ILLNESS, 11
Whiskey is the most popular of . . . remedies that won't cure a c. ALCOHOL, 83
coldly c. she turns from their gaze, and weeps GRAVE, 12
colic One physician cures you of the c. DOCTORS, 12
Coliseum While stands the C., Rome shall stand EUROPE, 4
collapse Russia is a c., not a revolution RUSSIA, 4
collapses Force . . . c. through its own mass JUDGMENT, 11
collar no shirt or c. ever comes back twice NEGLECT, 2
collections those mutilators of c. BOOKS, 23
collective the greatest c. work of science SCIENCE, 13
college I am Master of this c. ACADEMICS, 2
Like so many ageing c. people ACADEMICS, 6
colleges a liberal education at the C. of Unreason REASON, 1
colonel The gatling's jammed and the c. dead WAR, 112
colonies C. in the Indies, . . . are yet babes UNITED STATES, 26
these United C. are, . . . free and independent states UNITED STATES, 37
colonnade whispering sound of the cool c. TREES, 4
color an incurable disease – c. blindness DISEASE, 13
not a blanket woven from one thread, one c., one cloth UNITED STATES, 32
colored I'm a c., one-eyed Jew DISABILITY, 2
water, is unsuitable in c. WATER, 4
colorless C. green ideas NONSENSE, 10
colors a coat of many c. BIBLICAL QUOTATIONS, 219
All c. will agree in the dark DARKNESS, 2
column The Fifth C. WAR, 102
coma shuffle off in a c. DEATH, 83
comb Falklands . . . a fight between two bald men over a c. WAR, 23
combine When bad men c. UNITY, 7
combustion the Immaculate Conception was spontaneous c. CATHOLICISM, 11
come C. what come may TIME, 39
I c. as a thief BIBLICAL QUOTATIONS, 594
I do not say the French cannot c. NAVY, 7
mine hour is not yet c. BIBLICAL QUOTATIONS, 319
Mr Watson, c. here; I want you SUMMONS, 3
O c. all ye faithful CHRISTMAS, 18
Our day will c. IRELAND, 3
that thou wouldest c. down BIBLICAL QUOTATIONS, 278
Thou'lt c. no more MOURNING, 13
Whistle and she'll c. to you SUMMONS, 2
Why don't you c. up sometime and see me INVITATIONS, 6
Will ye no c. back again RETURN, 5
comedian A c. can only last HUMOR, 51
comedies c. are ended by a marriage THEATER, 6
comedy All I need to make a c. COMEDY, 2
All I need to make a c. HUMOR, 13
at a c. we only look COMEDY, 6
C. is if I walk into an open sewer and die COMEDY, 1
C. is medicine MEDICINE, 33
C., like sodomy, is an unnatural act COMEDY, 5
C., we may say, is society COMEDY, 7
Farce refined becomes high c. COMEDY, 4
Life is . . . a c. in long-shot COMEDY, 3
What a fine c. this world would be LIFE, 30
world is a c. to those who think LIFE, 87
comely I am black, but c. BIBLICAL QUOTATIONS, 621
comes Everything c. to him who waits PATIENCE, 2
cometh he c. with clouds BIBLICAL QUOTATIONS, 584
him that c. to me I will in no wise cast out BIBLICAL QUOTATIONS, 332
comfort carrion c., Despair, not feast on thee DESPAIR, 6
c. me with apples BIBLICAL QUOTATIONS, 623
c. ye, c. ye my people BIBLICAL QUOTATIONS, 270
From ignorance our c. flows IGNORANCE, 18
He supplies the perennial demand for c. DOCTORS, 97
I beg cold c. COMFORT, 4
thought of suicide is a great . . . c. NIGHT, 9
Two loves I have, of c. and despair CONFLICT, 7
until his friends came to c. him ENDURANCE, 8
comfortable something more c. CLOTHES, 8
to be baith grand and c. LUXURY, 1
comfortably Are you sitting c.? Then I'll begin BEGINNING, 13
comforted he refused to be c. BIBLICAL QUOTATIONS, 221
comforter another C., that he may abide BIBLICAL QUOTATIONS, 348
if I go not . . . the C. will not come BIBLICAL QUOTATIONS, 355
comforters miserable c. are ye all BIBLICAL QUOTATIONS, 304
comforts Increase of material c. . . . moral growth MATERIALISM, 11
comic It is so c. to hear oneself called old OLD AGE, 55
comic strip the one-dimensional subtlety of a c. INSULTS, 58
coming C. through the rye LOVE, 40
he . . . c. after me is preferred before me BIBLICAL QUOTATIONS, 317
who may abide the day of his c. BIBLICAL QUOTATIONS, 454
command but to c. LEADERSHIP, 12
mortals to c. success SUCCESS, 2
one of those born neither to obey nor to c. NASTINESS, 5
people c. rather badly OBEDIENCE, 2
commandments fear God, and keep his c. BIBLICAL QUOTATIONS, 99
fear God, and keep his c. GOD, 13
if ye love me, keep my c. BIBLICAL QUOTATIONS, 348
Where there aren't no Ten C. DESIRE, 9
commands Every good servant does not all c. OBEDIENCE, 5
commas absence of inverted c. guarantees . . . originality QUOTATIONS, 3
commend forced to c. her highly INSINCERITY, 4
into thy hands I c. my spirit BIBLICAL QUOTATIONS, 449
commended The man who gets angry . . . in the right way . . . is c. ANGER, 2
commendeth obliquely c. himself CRITICISM, 12
comment C. is free but facts are sacred FACTS, 6
commentators rather give me c. plain CLARITY, 1
commerce Friendship is a disinterested c. between equals LOVE AND FRIENDSHIP, 2
honour sinks where c. long prevails BUSINESS, 13
commercing looks c. with the skies SOUL, 15
commission A Royal C. is a broody hen BUREAUCRACY, 5
Each bullet has got its c. MORTALITY, 4
commit woman alone, can . . . c. them SEXES, 28
committee A c. is a cul-de-sac BUREAUCRACY, 3
A c. is an animal DEMOCRACY, 3
A c. should consist of three men DEMOCRACY, 22
The number one book . . . was written by a c. BIBLE, 10

commodity *C., Firmness,* and *Delight* ARCHITECTURE, 19
common All the realm shall be in c. LAWYERS, 10
C. Law of England LAW, 20
C. sense is the collection of prejudices PREJUDICE, 4
good thing, to make it too c. ENGLAND, 45
He nothing c. did or mean EXECUTION, 22
lose the c. touch IDEALISM, 3
seldom attribute c. sense AGREEMENT, 4
the happiness of the c. man GOVERNMENT, 8
The trivial round, the c. task SIMPLICITY, 4
'Tis education forms the c. mind EDUCATION, 70
trained and organized c. sense SCIENCE, 48
common-looking The Lord prefers c. people APPEARANCE, 31
common man I have no concern for the c. PUBLIC, 21
commonplace nothing so unnatural as the c. TRIVIALITY, 8
renders . . . c. things and characters interesting WRITERS, 50
unassuming c. /Of Nature FLOWERS, 15
commonplaces c. are the great poetic truths TRIVIALITY, 14
Commons The C., faithful to their system GOVERNMENT, 22
common sense Soap and water and c. CLEANNESS, 9
Commonwealth a C. of Nations BRITISH EMPIRE, 8
turn to the wider vision of the C. POLITICS, 92
communications evil c. corrupt good manners BIBLICAL QUOTATIONS, 47
communism arrested under the Suppression of C. Act OPPRESSION, 2
C. continued to haunt Europe as a spectre COMMUNISM, 18
C. is in fact the completion of Socialism COMMUNISM, 12
C. is like prohibition COMMUNISM, 13
C. is Soviet power plus the electrification COMMUNISM, 8
C. with a human face COMMUNISM, 4
For us in Russia c. is a dead dog COMMUNISM, 15
Russian c. is the illegitimate child COMMUNISM, 2
communist Every c. has a fascist frown COMMUNISM, 16
I'm a C. by day RELIGION, 7
your grandson will . . . be a C. COMMUNISM, 6
communists Catholics and C. have committed great crimes COMMITMENT, 4
In Germany, the Nazis came for the C. NAZISM, 6
looking under the beds for C. SEX, 36
community journalism. . . . keeps us in touch with the ignorance of the c. JOURNALISM, 42
Marriage . . . a c. . . . making in all two MARRIAGE, 30
the c. of Europe EUROPE, 15
commute the agricultural labourers . . . c. from London COUNTRYSIDE, 9
commuter C. . . . riding to and from his wife TRAVEL, 43
compact the damned, c., liberal majority MAJORITY, 6
companion God send the c. a better prince REPARTEE, 85
to choose between him and a cockroach as a c. INSULTS, 134
companionable so c. as solitude SOLITUDE, 15
companions Boys . . . are unwholesome c. for grown people CHILDREN, 40
c. for middle age MARRIAGE, 13
company better to be alone than in bad c. FRIENDS, 16
c., . . . have neither a soul to lose nor a body to kick BUSINESS, 24
C., villainous company COMPANY, 1
Considering the c. . . . hardly surprising REPARTEE, 72
Crowds without c. LONDON, 13
I've been offered titles . . . get one into disreputable c. TITLES, 12
pleasure of your c. MOUNTAINS, 2
Take the tone of the c. CONFORMITY, 4
Tell me what c. thou keepest FRIENDS, 4
You never expected justice from a c. BUSINESS, 24
comparative progress is simply a c. PROGRESS, 8
compare any she belied with false c. ANALOGY, 5
c. thee to a summer's day COMPLIMENTS, 31
Learn, c., collect the facts EDUCATION, 68
compared The war we have just been through, . . . is not to be c. WAR, 176
comparisons c. are odious ANALOGY, 2
C. are odorous MALAPROPISMS, 2
compass my heart shall be /The faithful c. FAITHFULNESS, 4
compassion But a certain Samaritan . . . had c. on him BIBLICAL QUOTATIONS, 433
C. is not a sloppy, sentimental feeling COMPASSION, 2
The purpose of human life is to serve and to show c. KINDNESS, 8
complacency c. and satisfaction . . . in . . . a new-married couple MARRIAGE, 85
complain Never c. and never explain COMPLAINTS, 1
one hardly knows to whom to c. COMPLAINTS, 3
complaint Anno domini . . . the most fatal c. DEATH, 79
how is the old c. MEMORY, 6
I want to register a c. COMPLAINTS, 9
Life is a fatal c. LIFE, 42
complaints The imaginary c. of indestructible old ladies HYPOCHONDRIA, 14
complete now I feel like a c. idiot INFERIORITY, 1
complex Freud and his three slaves, Inhibition, C. and Libido PSYCHOANALYSIS, 16
Wherever an inferiority c. exists, there is . . . reason INFERIORITY, 2
complexes A man should not strive to eliminate his c. NEUROSIS, 3
complexion Mislike me not for my c. PREJUDICE, 12
There should be no doubt . . . as to . . . the meaning of c. and pulse DIAGNOSIS, 19
compliance by a timely c. SEX, 34
compliment returned the c. GOD, 57
compose Never c. . . . unless . . . not composing . . . becomes a positive nuisance MUSIC, 21
composed When I c. that, I was . . . inspired by God MUSIC, 8
composer A good c. . . . steals COMPOSERS, 9
demands of a c. is that he be dead COMPOSERS, 5
composers The greatest c. since Beethoven COMPOSERS, 4
composition difference between . . . prose and metrical c. POETRY AND PROSE, 7
comprehended c. two aspicious persons MALAPROPISMS, 1
compromise All government . . . is founded on c. and barter COMPROMISE, 4
C. used to mean that half a loaf COMPROMISE, 5
not a question that leaves much room for c. SELF-PRESERVATION, 9
compulsion seized by the stern hand of C. WOMEN, 117
compulsory c. and irreproachable idleness ARMY, 3
comrade stepping where his c. stood COURAGE, 20
comrades Bleach the bones of c. slain WAR, 77
Dear c., soldiers, sailors and workers RUSSIAN REVOLUTION, 5
conceal Addresses . . . c. our whereabouts ADDRESSES, 1
height of cleverness is . . . to c. it CLEVERNESS, 5
speech only to c. their thoughts HUMAN NATURE, 27
concealed Much truth is spoken, . . . more . . . c. TRUTH, 21
concealing Good breeding consists in c. how . . . we think of ourselves MANNERS, 6
concealment c., like a worm i' th' bud LOVE, 167
conceit C. is the finest armour CONCEIT, 13
public school . . . an appalling and impregnable c. MODESTY, 7
conceited I would grow intolerably c. CONCEIT, 22
what man will do any good who is not c. SELF-RESPECT, 5
concept If the c. of God has RELIGION, 6
conception if the dad is present at the c. SEX, 76
the Immaculate C. was spontaneous combustion CATHOLICISM, 11
concepts walks up the stairs of his c. MANKIND, 60
concerned great society . . . men are more c. with the quality of their goods SOCIETY, 7
concessions The c. of the weak are the c. of fear YIELDING, 1
conclusions Life is the art of drawing . . . c. LIFE, 19
concord toleration produced . . . religious c. RELIGION, 36
Yes – around C. TRAVEL, 40
concurrence fortuitous c. of atoms CHANCE, 5
condemn No man can justly censure or c. another JUDGMENT, 7
condemned If God were suddenly c. to live the life HUMAN CONDITION, 7
I have . . . taken his side when absurd men have c. him FREEDOM, 60
Man is c. to be free FREEDOM, 54
condemning One should examine oneself . . . before . . . c. others SELF, 13
condition fools decoyed into our c. MARRIAGE, 105
hopes for the human c. PESSIMISM, 4
The c. of man . . . is a c. of war HUMAN CONDITION, 12
the Jews have made a contribution to the human c. JEWS, 19
To be a poet is a c. POETS, 18
wearisome c. of humanity HUMAN CONDITION, 11
conditioned Americans have been c. to respect newness UNITED STATES, 92
conditions my people live in such awful c. POVERTY, 14
conduct C. . . . to the prejudice of good order and military discipline ANONYMOUS, 14
conductor dare look back lest . . . the c. DEPARTURE, 9
The c. . . . advantage of not seeing the audience MUSICIANS, 3
conference naked into the c. chamber WEAPONS, 2
confess It's easy to make a man c. . . . lies TRUTH, 31
Men will c. HUMOR, 15
only c. our little faults IMPERFECTION, 11
We c. our bad qualities . . . out of fear SELF-KNOWLEDGE, 2
confessed poured himself a drink and . . . c. TREASON, 7
confessing I am ashamed of c. INNOCENCE, 1
women . . . ill-using them and then c. it WOMEN, 119
confession There is no refuge from c. but suicide SUICIDE, 38
confidence never dedicated to something you have complete c. in FANATICISM, 3
one cannot really have c. in doctors DOCTORS, 49
Three addresses always inspire c. ADDRESSES, 2
confident There are two things which I am c. I can do very well CRITICISM, 24
confin'd cabin'd, cribb'd, c., bound in FEAR, 16
conflict We are in an armed c. WAR, 55
conform how to rebel and c. at the same time YOUTH, 8
conformable Nature is very consonant and c. NATURE, 27
confound the weak things of the world to c. the . . . mighty BIBLICAL QUOTATIONS, 28
confused Anyone who isn't c. here doesn't really understand CONFUSION, 1
confusion C. is a word we have invented CONFUSION, 8
congratulate rejoice at that news and c. our forces VICTORY, 24
Congreve C. is the only sophisticated playwright WRITERS, 56
Congs Kinquering C. their titles take SPOONERISMS, 3
conked John Le Mesurier . . . c. out on November 15th OBITUARIES, 6
connect Only c. COMMUNICATION, 1
conquer Antony /Should c. Antony SELF-DESTRUCTION, 2
easier to c. it VICTORY, 25
in the end the truth will c. TRUTH, 52
not the man to c. a country WEAKNESS, 4
They will c., but . . . not convince PERSUASION, 4
We'll fight and we'll c. COURAGE, 14
when we c. without danger VICTORY, 6
conquered I came, I saw, God c. VICTORY, 2
I came, I saw, I c. VICTORY, 1
I will be c.; I will not capitulate DETERMINATION, 12
the English seem . . . to have c. and peopled half the world BRITISH EMPIRE, 9
conquering C. kings ROYALTY, 37
not c. but fighting well VICTORY, 7
See, the c. hero comes VICTORY, 15
conquest Socialism . . . the c. of the . . . economy SOCIALISM, 4

correction It is a stupidity . . . to busy oneself with the c. of the world IMPROVEMENT, 3
correctly anxious to do the wrong thing c. ETIQUETTE, 8
corroboration c. . . . in the records of Somerset House HUMILITY, 12
corrupt Among a people generally c. CORRUPTION, 1
appointment by the c. few DEMOCRACY, 20
Power tends to c. POWER, 3
corrupted They had been c. by money SENTIMENTALITY, 1
corruptible born again, not of c. seed BIBLICAL QUOTATIONS, 560
corruption C., the most infallible symptom of constitutional liberty CORRUPTION, 4
I have said to c., thou art my father BIBLICAL QUOTATIONS, 305
purge the land of all /C. ROYALTY, 25
the foul dregs of his power, the tools of despotism and c. POLITICS, 146
corruptly O! that estates, degrees, and offices / Were not deriv'd c. CORRUPTION, 13
corrupts lack of power c. absolutely PRESIDENTS, 16
corse As his c. to the rampart FUNERALS, 13
cosmetics In the factory we make c. COSMETICS, 4
cosmopolitan I was told I am a true c. MELANCHOLY, 12
to be really c., a man must be at home WRITERS, 22
cosmos c. is about the smallest hole UNIVERSE, 6
cost To give and not to count the c. FIGHT, 14
Why so large c. . . . upon thy fading mansion spend APPEARANCE, 53
cottage Love and a c. LOVE, 49
poorest man may in his c. bid defiance to . . . the Crown DEFIANCE, 4
to refer to your friend's country establishment as a 'c.' WORDS, 24
cottages Pale Death kicks his way equally into the c. of the poor EQUALITY, 31
couch the century of the psychiatrist's c. PSYCHIATRY, 24
time as a tool not as a c. TIME, 25
when on my c. I lie SOLITUDE, 17
cough A c. is something that you yourself can't help TOLERANCE, 10
Jeeves coughed one soft, low, gentle c. ANALOGY, 6
coughing keeping people from c. ACTING, 11
coughs C. and sneezes spread diseases ILLNESS, 6
were less troubled with C. when they went naked HEALTHY LIVING, 14
council The grotesque chaos of a Labour c. INCOMPETENCE, 2
counsel consequences of . . . unpreparedness and feeble c. WAR, 1
C. of her country's gods BRITAIN, 6
give me that c. that you think best ADVICE, 12
sometimes c. take – and sometimes Tea DRINKS, 16
count Don't c. your chickens ANTICIPATION, 4
If you can . . . c. your money you are not . . . rich man WEALTH, 21
One has to be able to c. MATHEMATICS, 10
To give and not to c. the cost FIGHT, 14
counted I c. them all out and I c. them all back JOURNALISM, 21
countenance his c. was as the sun BIBLICAL QUOTATIONS, 584
the Lord lift up his c. upon thee BIBLICAL QUOTATIONS, 553
counter-democratic Proportional Representation . . . is fundamentally c. POLITICS, 83
counterpoint Too much c.; what is worse, Protestant c. CRITICISM, 4
counties see the coloured c. COUNTRYSIDE, 7
countries preferreth all c. before his own DISCONTENT, 7
country absolved from all duty to his c. MARRIAGE, 104
a c. diversion COUNTRYSIDE, 1
A c. governed by a despot TYRANNY, 7
a c. of young men UNITED STATES, 18
affections must be confined . . . to a single c. PATRIOTISM, 13
A man should know something of his own c. TRAVEL, 35
An everyday story of c. folk MEDIA, 3
an honest man sent to lie abroad for . . . his c. DIPLOMACY, 26
Anybody can be good in the c. COUNTRYSIDE, 13
Anyone who loves his c., follow me PATRIOTISM, 14
Counsel of her c.'s gods BRITAIN, 6
c. from whose bourn no traveller returns AFTERLIFE, 10
God made the c. COUNTRYSIDE, 2
go down into the c. DECEPTION, 11
good news from a far c. BIBLICAL QUOTATIONS, 580
Great artists have no c. NATIONALITY, 9
How I leave my c. LAST WORDS, 64
I have but one life to lose for my c. PATRIOTISM, 17
I love thee still, My c. PATRIOTISM, 10
In the c. of the blind PROVERBS, 224
I vow to thee, my c. PATRIOTISM, 40
I would die for my c. PATRIOTISM, 26
loathe the c. COUNTRYSIDE, 1
My c., right or wrong PATRIOTISM, 8
nothing good . . . in the c. COUNTRYSIDE, 5
Our c. is the world UNITED STATES, 20
our c., right or wrong PATRIOTISM, 12
proud of the position of the bungalow, . . . in the c. SUBURBIA, 2
she is my c. still PATRIOTISM, 9
supposing I had gone to the c. and said . . . rearm WEAPONS, 1
That is no c. for old men MORTALITY, 23
The history of every c. begins in the heart HISTORY, 8
The idiot who praises . . . every c. but his own DISCONTENT, 2
The past is a foreign c. PAST, 5
The undiscover'd c. AFTERLIFE, 10
This c. . . . belongs to the people who inhabit it DEMOCRACY, 13
this House . . . fight for its King and C. PATRIOTISM, 6
This isn't going to be a good c. EQUALITY, 20
to leave his c. as good as he had found it DUTY, 1
understanding the problems of running a c. POLITICS, 142
we can die but once to serve our c. PATRIOTISM, 1
what was good for our c. BUSINESS, 30
When I am in the c. I wish to vegetate COUNTRYSIDE, 6
where they're living it's peacetime, and we're all in the same c. DISEASE, 29
Your c. needs you PATRIOTISM, 5
countryside a more dreadful record of sin than . . . c. SIN, 16
county The sound of the English c. families ARISTOCRACY, 21
couple A married c. are well suited MARRIAGE, 109
Splendid c. – slept with both MARRIAGE, 32
couples so many c. . . . not getting the right proteins SEX, 24
courage be strong and of a good c. BIBLICAL QUOTATIONS, 70
be strong and of a good c. GOD, 12
C. is the price . . . for granting peace COURAGE, 12
c. to love . . . courage to suffer LOVE, 180
good deal of physical c. to ride a horse ALCOHOL, 52
prince of royal c. ROYALTY, 110
screw your c. to the sticking-place AMBITION, 22
tale . . . of . . . c. of my companions ENDURANCE, 17
The Red Badge of C. COURAGE, 9
three o'clock in the morning c. COURAGE, 28
Whistling aloud to bear his c. up WHISTLING, 2
couragious Of hearte c., politique in counsaile ROYALTY, 81
course c. of true love never did run smooth LOVE, 135
court The history of the World is the World's c. HISTORY, 30
courteous If a man be . . . c. to strangers COURTESY, 2
courtesy C. is not dead BRITISH, 7
courtier Here lies a noble c. /Who never kept his word ANONYMOUS, 28
courtiers c. . . . forgotten nothing and learnt nothing ROYALTY, 46
courting When you are c. a nice girl SCIENCE, 32
courts I have come to regard . . . c. . . . as a casino JUSTICE, 15
the case is still before the c. ARGUMENTS, 6
courtship C. to marriage MARRIAGE, 43
covenant a c. between me and the earth BIBLICAL QUOTATIONS, 201
a c. with death SLAVERY, 5
covenants C. without the sword are but words POWER POLITICS, 3
Coventry putting him into a moral C. IRELAND, 16
cover I . . . will c. thee with my hand BIBLICAL QUOTATIONS, 158
Never judge a c. by its book BOOKS, 26
covet thou shalt not c. BIBLICAL QUOTATIONS, 147
covetousness A physician ought to be extremely watchful against c. ENVY 7
cow A c. is a very good animal in the field SUITABILITY, 2
That milked the c. with the crumpled horn NURSERY RHYMES, 57
The c. is of the bovine ilk ANIMALS, 19
The c. jumped over the moon NURSERY RHYMES, 14
till the c. comes home ETERNITY, 1
Truth, Sir, is a c. SCEPTICISM, 3
Why buy a c. FUTILITY, 1
Coward a very Noel C. sort of person FAME, 28
coward better to be the widow of a hero than the wife of a c. COURAGE, 16
Conscience is a c. CONSCIENCE, 4
No c. soul is mine COURAGE, 4
None but a c. . . . has never known fear COWARDICE, 2
The c. does it with a kiss KILLING, 10
Cowardice guilty of Noël C. COWARDICE, 1
cowardly Marriage is the only adventure open to the c. ADVENTURE, 3
took a grip on c. Marxism NAZISM, 3
cowards C. die many times COWARDICE, 10
the future . . . makes c. of us PRESENT, 3
Thus conscience does make c. of us all CONSCIENCE, 7
cowboy easier to get an actor to be a c. ACTING, 8
cows daring . . . to explain . . . that c. can be eaten RELIGION, 35
'Horses' should have read 'C.' MISTAKES, 12
The c. in the corn NURSERY RHYMES, 28
coxcomb to hear a c. ask two hundred guineas CRITICISM, 56
coyness This c., lady, were no crime SHYNESS, 5
compassion C. is not a sloppy, sentimental feeling SOCIALISM, 13
cracked The c. looking glass of a servant IRELAND, 12
cradle Between the c. and the grave GRAVE, 4
Rocked in the c. of the deep SEA, 11
The hand that rocks the c. INFLUENCE, 12
cradles bit the babies in the c. ANIMALS, 7
craft the c. so long to lerne MORTALITY, 3
The life so short, the c. so long to learn MORTALITY, 12
craftsmanship Skill without imagination is c. ART, 29
crafty too c. a woman to invent a new lie LYING, 13
cranny We seek . . . In every c. but the right PERVERSITY, 3
crap Books are a load of c. BOOKS, 24
Craven why and how I became . . . mistress of the Earl of C. SEX, 111
cream coffee that's too black . . . You integrate it with c. RACE, 16
create I c. new heavens and a new earth BIBLICAL QUOTATIONS, 280
My father didn't c. you to arrest me POLICE, 9
created God c. . . . the earth BIBLICAL QUOTATIONS, 174
man alone leaves traces of what he c. MANKIND, 12
Man, . . . had been c. to jab the life out of Germans WAR, 136
Thou hast c. us for Thyself HUMAN CONDITION, 2
we cannot be c. for this sort of suffering AFTERLIFE, 7
creates he c. Gods by the dozen RELIGION, 57
creation C. /To produce my foot, each feather CREATION, 12
Had I been present at the C. MISQUOTATION, 1
Science conducts us, . . . through the whole range of c. SCIENCE, 61
The art of c. /is older CREATION, 17
creator All right, my lord c., Don Miguel DEATH, 172
Man . . . hasn't been a c., only a destroyer ECOLOGY, 3

D

every victory turns into a d. DISILLUSION, 2
God's will to lead . . . South Africa through d. and humiliation PLACES, 36
In d. unbeatable OFFICERS, 3
we are not interested in the possibilities of d. DEFEAT, 17
defeated Like an army d. /The snow hath retreated SPRING, 10
man can be destroyed . . . not d. DEFEAT, 6
defect Chief D. of Henry King FOOD, 11
England's chief d. depends upon the navy NAVY, 9
defend I will d. to the death your right to say it FREEDOM, 60
defense Never make a d. or apology ACCUSATION 2
Preparing for suicide . . . means of d. DEFENSE, 2
the d. of England BOUNDARIES, 1
The only d. is in offence DEFENSE, 1
Truth telling is not compatible with the d. of the realm DEFENSE, 4
defiance in defeat, d. DEFIANCE, 2
poorest man may in his cottage bid d. to . . . the Crown DEFIANCE, 4
The d. of established authority DEFIANCE, 1
deficiencies The d. which I think good to note MEDICINE, 6
defied Age will not be d. AGE, 8
defiled Hell itself is d. by . . . King John EPITAPHS, 28
defined There are things which will not be d. ILLNESS, 40
defining Language is . . . a d. framework LANGUAGE, 45
definition This d. . . . would not do for a policeman NURSES, 6
deflowered At last you are d. MARRIAGE, 46
deformity Another great Advantage of D. is, that it tends to the Improvement of the Mind INTELLECT, 4
His modesty amounts to d. MODESTY, 1
defying by d. their parents and copying one another YOUTH, 8
degenerates everything d. in the hands of man MANKIND, 49
degeneration fatty d. of his moral being MARRIAGE, 134
the fatty d. of the conscience AGE, 42
degradation a . . . sense of intellectual d. after an interview with a doctor DOCTORS, 56
degree d. of delight DELIGHT, 5
The heaven themselves, . . . /Observe d. ORDER, 5
when d. is shak'd ORDER, 4
degrees Crime, like virtue, has its d. CRIME, 6
We boil at different d. INDIVIDUALITY, 5
deid Gey few, and they're a' d. ANONYMOUS, 36
deities the d. so kindly DESTINY, 19
Deity to distinguish between the D. and the Drains GOD, 54
Delacroix The recipe for making a man like D. ARTISTS, 7
deleted D. by French censor NEWSPAPERS, 3
deliberate with a slow d. carelessness READING, 12
deliberates woman that d. is lost WOMEN, 8
deliberation D. is the work of many men ACTION, 9
delicacy the talent of flattering with d. FLATTERY, 2
delicious delightful, it's d., it's de-lovely PLEASURE, 28
delight a degree of d. DELIGHT, 5
Commodity, Firmness, and *D.* ARCHITECTURE, 19
Energy is Eternal D. DELIGHT, 4
go to't with d. DELIGHT, 9
Studies serve for d. DELIGHT, 3
Teach us d. in simple things DELIGHT, 8
The leaping light for your d. discovers DELIGHT, 1
very temple of d. DELIGHT, 7
wept with d. when you gave her a smile DELIGHT, 6
delighted Whosoever is d. in solitude DELIGHT, 2
You have d. us long enough DISMISSAL, 2
delightful d., it's delicious, it's de-lovely PLEASURE, 28
make his conversation perfectly d. DELIGHT, 11
What a d. thing this perspective is ART, 31
delights Man d. not me DELIGHT, 10
delirious he is said to be d. MENTAL ILLNESS, 3
deliver d. me from myself SELF, 6
deliverer their d. from Popish tyranny ROYALTY, 58
delivers the Man Who D. the Goods RELIABILITY, 1
de-lovely delightful, it's delicious, it's d. PLEASURE, 28
deluge After us the d. PROPHECY, 13
Après nous le d. PROPHECY, 13
delusion he who can analyze his d. is called a philosopher PHILOSOPHERS, 1
delusions Many people have d. of grandeur DELUSION, 5
delusive Decades have a d. edge CLASSIFICATION, 3
delved When Adam d. CLASS, 5
demagogues the vilest specimens of human nature are . . . found among d. POLITICS, 90
demands the populace cannot exact their d. HOUSES OF PARLIAMENT, 22
demented shrill d. choirs of wailing shells MEMORIALS, 12
demigod wherever life is dear he is a d. MEDICINE, 27
democracies d. . . . think that a stupid man is more likely to be honest POLITICIANS, 96
democracy arsenal of d. DEMOCRACY, 18
D. . . . government by the uneducated ARISTOCRACY, 9
D. is only an experiment in government DEMOCRACY, 8
D. is the wholesome and pure air DEMOCRACY, 6
D. means government by discussion DEMOCRACY, 1
D. passes into despotism DEMOCRACY, 16
d. . . . recognises the subjecting of the minority DEMOCRACY, 10
D. resumed her reign POLITICS, 13
D. substitutes election by the incompetent many DEMOCRACY, 20
extreme d. or absolute oligarchy . . . will come GOVERNMENT, 5
grieved under a *d.*, call it *anarchy* ANARCHY, 1
In Switzerland they had . . . five hundred years of d. and peace SWITZERLAND, 5
Man's capacity for evil makes d. necessary DEMOCRACY, 15
not the voting that's d. DEMOCRACY, 21
unites socialism with d. SOCIALISM, 10
world . . . made safe for d. DEMOCRACY, 25
world must be safe for d. WAR AND PEACE, 20
democratic thoroughly d. and patronise everybody CLASS, 40
demon woman wailing for her d.-lover SUPERNATURAL, 6
demons We have often sunk to the level of the d. WORDS, 17
den a d. of thieves BIBLICAL QUOTATIONS, 523
denial the highest praise of God consists in the d. of Him ATHEISM, 12
denies spirit that always d. DENIAL, 1
Denmark rotten in the state of D. CORRUPTION, 11
denounce We thus d. . . . the arms race NUCLEAR WEAPONS, 9
dentist D., n. A prestidigitator TEETH, 2
fuss about sleeping together . . . sooner go to my d. SEX, 106
like going to the d. CINEMA, 20
dentists gratitude to most benefactors is the same as . . . for d. INGRATITUDE, 3
I have let d. ride roughshod over my teeth TEETH, 6
The thought of d. gave him just the same sick horror FEAR, 22
dentopedology D. is . . . opening your mouth and putting your foot EMBARRASSMENT, 3
deny before the cock crow, thou shalt d. me thrice BETRAYAL, 2
let him d. himself BIBLICAL QUOTATIONS, 513
Those who d. freedom FREEDOM, 34
depart D., . . . and let us have done with you DISMISSAL, 1
lettest thou thy servant d. in peace BIBLICAL QUOTATIONS, 422
when the great and good d. MORTALITY, 20
departure the time of my d. is at hand BIBLICAL QUOTATIONS, 656
depends It all d. upon that article there SOLDIERS, 17
depraved No one . . . suddenly became d. DEBAUCHERY, 7
depression Recession . . . a neighbor loses . . . d. . . . you lose ECONOMICS, 19
deprivation D. is for me what daffodils were INSPIRATION, 6
depth out of your d. REPARTEE, 102
derangement a nice d. of epitaphs MALAPROPISMS, 8
derision Ambition, Distraction, Uglification, and D. EDUCATION, 19
dermatologists a rash of d. LANGUAGE, 3
dermatology D. is the best speciality MEDICINE, 3
descend Never d. to the ways of those above you EQUALITY, 18
descendants The day your d., /Outnumber your friends OLD AGE, 72
descended D. from the apes . . . hope it is not true EVOLUTION, 2
we are d. not only from monkeys but from monks EVOLUTION, 18
descent of pre-Adamite ancestral d. EVOLUTION, 14
description beggar'd all d. ADMIRATION, 15
descriptions d. of the fairest wights HISTORY, 38
desert The sand of the d. is sodden red WAR, 112
Use every man after his d. MERIT, 6
deserts D. of vast eternity AGE, 49
wandered in d. . . . dens and caves BIBLICAL QUOTATIONS, 236
deserve I have arthritis, and I don't d. that either MERIT, 2
deserved I wasn't lucky. I d. it MERIT, 7
deserves At 50, everyone has the face he d. AGE, 54
the government it d. GOVERNMENT, 23
designing I am d. St Paul's ARCHITECTURE, 1
desire antidote to d. DESIRE, 6
a universal innate d. EXTRAVAGANCE, 2
d. is got without content CONTENTMENT, 10
D. is the very essence of man DESIRE, 16
d. should so many years outlive performance SEX, 93
d. to be praised twice over PRAISE, 8
I am my beloved's, and his d. is toward me BIBLICAL QUOTATIONS, 639
It provokes the d. ALCOHOL, 68
nothing like d. for preventing the thing one says DESIRE, 12
not really d. the things they failed to obtain AMBITION, 16
The D. of Man being Infinite INFINITY, 1
Those who restrain D. DESIRE, 2
to have few things to d. FEAR, 2
to lose your heart's d. DESIRE, 15
desired war which . . . left nothing to be d. WAR, 27
desires He who d. but acts not ACTION, 7
made young with young d. SPRING, 9
Man's D. are limited by his Perceptions DESIRE, 4
Strong enough to answer back to d. CHARACTER, 12
than nurse unacted d. DESIRE, 3
desiring pessimists end up by d. the things they fear PESSIMISM, 12
desist to d. from the experiment in despair SCOTS, 7
desk what risks you take . . . to find money in a d. THEFT, 4
desks Stick . . . to your d. and never go to sea OFFICERS, 7
desolate d. and sick of an old passion LOVE, 60
desolated from the province they have d. and profaned VIOLENCE, 7
desolation My d. does begin to make /A better life SUICIDE, 32
despair carrion comfort, D., not feast on thee DESPAIR, 6
D. is better treated with hope, not dope DESPAIR, 1
Don't d., not even over . . . d. DESPAIR, 7
Patience, n. A minor form of d. PATIENCE, 8
some divine d. SORROW, 29
Somewhere on the other side of d. MADNESS, 11
to desist from the experiment in d. SCOTS, 7
without understanding d. PSYCHIATRY, 22
despairs He who d. over an event is a coward PESSIMISM, 4
desperate D. cuts PROVERBS, 109
desperation lives of quiet d. DESPAIR, 10
despicable this formidable Kingdom is . . . a province of a d. Electorate ENGLAND, 40
despise some other Englishman d. him CLASS, 43

despised A poor man is d. the whole world over POVERTY, 21
I doubt if the philosopher lives . . . who could know himself . . . d. by a street boy PHILOSOPHERS, 5
despises A woman d. a man for loving her LOVE, 170
despond name of the slough was D. DESPAIR, 3
despot A country governed by a d. TYRANNY, 7
despotism Democracy passes into d. DEMOCRACY, 16
d. tempered by casualness GOVERNMENT, 3
extreme democracy or absolute oligarchy or d. will come GOVERNMENT, 5
France was a long d. FRANCE, 2
the foul dregs of his power, the tools of d. and corruption POLITICS, 146
dessicated A d. calculating machine POLITICIANS, 18
destination I do not think this poem will reach its d. CRITICISM, 62
destinies in determining the future d. of mankind BRITISH EMPIRE, 1
destiny Anatomy is d. DESTINY, 12
I were walking with d. DESTINY, 5
Riddle of d. ERROR, 7
destroy Doth the wingèd life d. PLEASURE, 5
He would like to d. his old diaries CONCEIT, 20
necessary to d. the town . . . to save it WAR, 8
sought to d. institutions INDIFFERENCE, 7
they shall not hurt nor d. in all my holy mountain BIBLICAL QUOTATIONS, 258
Whom God wishes to d. MADNESS, 1
Whom the gods wish to d. TALENT, 2
destroy'd a bold peasantry . . . /When once d. PUBLIC, 12
destroyed man can be d. . . . not defeated DEFEAT, 6
destroyer I am become death, the d. of worlds NUCLEAR WEAPONS, 16
Man . . . hasn't been a creator, only a d. ECOLOGY, 3
destroying simplifying something by d. nearly everything CIVILIZATION, 4
destroys he who d. a good book, kills reason BOOKS, 30
What d. one man preserves another REMEDIES, 25
destruction broad is the way, that leadeth to d. BIBLICAL QUOTATIONS, 490
It is time for the d. of error ERROR, 1
detail life is frittered away by d. SIMPLICITY, 9
details with the thoroughness of a mind that reveres d. UNDERSTANDING, 7
detective The d. novel is NOVELS, 14
deterrent the d. is a phallic symbol NUCLEAR WEAPONS, 23
detest they d. at leisure LOVE AND HATE, 1
detested D. sport HUNTING, 3
Deutschland *D., D. über alles* GERMANY, 3
device A banner with the strange d., /Excelsior AMBITION, 14
devil Abashed the d. . . . felt how awful goodness is GOOD, 12
between any sort of d. and the deep blue sea SUICIDE, 26
cleft the D.'s foot NONSENSE, 11
D. always builds a chapel there DEVIL, 10
d. can cite Scripture DEVIL, 14
d.'s walking parody ANIMALS, 11
given up believing in the d. DEVIL, 11
I do not see . . . why the d. should have all the good tunes MUSIC, 20
nickname is the heaviest stone that the d. can throw NAMES, 7
Renounce the d. BOOK OF COMMON PRAYER, THE, 12
resist the d., and he will flee BIBLICAL QUOTATIONS, 287
sacrifice . . . of the d.'s leavings SACRIFICE, 4
Sarcasm . . . the language of the d. SARCASM, 1
the d. did not play in tempting of me PROSE, 2
The d. finds work PROVERBS, 384
The D. is a gentleman DEVIL, 15
The d. is not so black DEVIL, 2
the D. knows Latin LANGUAGE, 26
The d. looks after his own LUCK, 5
the d. played at chess with me EXPLOITATION, 1
world, the flesh, and the d. BOOK OF COMMON PRAYER, THE, 8
devils It is no good casting out d. DEVIL, 12
many d. would set on me in Worms PROTESTANTISM, 4
One more d.'-triumph and sorrow for angels DAMNATION, 1
devoted definition of . . . a nurse . . . 'd. and obedient.' NURSES, 6
devotion The almighty dollar . . . object of universal d. MATERIALISM, 15
devour he shall d. the prey BIBLICAL QUOTATIONS, 230
shed tears when they would d. HYPOCRISY, 2
the Revolution may . . . d. each of her children FRENCH REVOLUTION, 10
dew his body was wet with the d. of heaven BIBLICAL QUOTATIONS, 61
Just to save her from the foggy, foggy d. ANONYMOUS, 63
dexterity Your d. seems a happy compound INSULTS, 42
diabetic Many a d. has stayed alive DISEASE, 23
diagnose d. the present DIAGNOSIS, 11
diagnoses than to make d. DIAGNOSIS, 4
diagnosis A smart mother makes often a better d. DIAGNOSIS, 3
D, n. A physician's forecast of disease DIAGNOSIS, 5
D. precedes treatment DIAGNOSIS, 12
does not prove that your d. was correct DIAGNOSIS, 16
In d. think of the easy first DIAGNOSIS, 7
The medicalization of early d. PATIENTS, 9
There is no royal road to d. DIAGNOSIS, 17
diagram cat is a d. and pattern of subtle air CATS, 5
dialect a d. I understand very little HUNTING, 7
D. words – those terrible marks of the beast CLASS, 19
diamond An imitation rough d. INSULTS, 5
D.! D. ACCIDENTS, 7
more of rough than polished d. BRITISH, 4
diamonds D. Are MATERIALISM, 22
D. Are Forever BOOK TITLES, 8
My goodness those d. are lovely GOOD, 18
to give him d. back MATERIALISM, 10
Diana great is D. of the Ephesians BIBLICAL QUOTATIONS, 15
diaphragm D, n. A muscular partition BODY, 2
diaries He would like to destroy his old d. CONCEIT, 20
Let d., therefore DIARIES, 1
Only good girls keep d. DIARIES, 2
diary I never travel without my d. DIARIES, 7
keep a d. . . . keep you DIARIES, 6
To write a d. . . . returning to one's own vomit DIARIES, 4
What is a d. as a rule DIARIES, 5
dictation God wrote it. I merely did his d. INSPIRATION, 8
dictator and finally a single d. substitutes himself COMMUNISM, 19
I am painted as the greatest little d. AUTHORITARIANISM, 7
dictators D. ride to and fro upon tigers AUTHORITARIANISM, 4
dictatorship The d. of the proletariat MARXISM, 13
dictionaries To make d. is dull work LEXICOGRAPHY, 7
dictionary send the reader to the d. INSULTS, 47
The responsibility of a d. LEXICOGRAPHY, 3
this is the first time I ever made the d. LEXICOGRAPHY, 8
words never seen . . . before outside of a d. POETS, 26
diddle Hey d. d., /The cat and the fiddle NURSERY RHYMES, 14
die A man can d. DEATH, 2
argue that I shall some day d. DEATH, 97
As long as men are liable to d. DOCTORS, 25
better to d. on your feet than to live on your knees COURAGE, 17
Body and mind . . . do not always agree to d. together OLD AGE, 39
but to do and d. OBEDIENCE, 6
curse God, and d. BIBLICAL QUOTATIONS, 297
d. on the spot rather than give way RUTHLESSNESS, 5
D. . . . the last thing I shall do LAST WORDS, 62
D. when I may . . . I have always plucked a thistle and planted a flower REPUTATION, 5
easy ways to d. SUICIDE, 33
either do, or d. ACTION, 6
Everybody has got to d. . . . . Now what LAST WORDS, 76
expedient that one man should d. for the people BIBLICAL QUOTATIONS, 358
for me to d., for you to go on living GOD, 51
have to d. beyond my means LAST WORDS, 91
'How hard it is that we have to d.' LIFE AND DEATH, 33
How often are we to d. DEATH, 119
I am ready to d. for my Lord LAST WORDS, 7
I d. a Christian EXECUTION, 6
I d. because I do not d. DEATH, 85
I d. happy LAST WORDS, 36
I do not want to d. . . . until I have . . . cultivated the seed ACHIEVEMENT, 8
If a man hasn't discovered something that he would d. for IDEALISM, 2
If I should d. WAR, 30
If it were now to d., /'Twere now to be most happy LOVE, 144
I have been learning how to d. DEATH, 173
in what peace a Christian can d. LAST WORDS, 3
I shall be like that tree; I shall d. from the top DECLINE, 13
I suppose I shall have to d. beyond my means OPERATIONS, 16
It is as natural to d. as to be born LIFE AND DEATH, 6
It is natural to d. BIRTH, 1
it is worse to want to d. WORLD-WEARINESS, 12
it is youth that must fight and d. WAR, 76
it was not easy for me to d. OBITUARIES, 7
I will d. in peace LAST WORDS, 93
I will d. in the last ditch PATRIOTISM, 44
I would d. for my country PATRIOTISM, 26
let me d. drinking in an inn ALCOHOL, 54
Let us determine to d. here DETERMINATION, 4
Let us do or d. ACTION, 8
let us eat and drink; for tomorrow we d. BIBLICAL QUOTATIONS, 47
live for ever or d. in the attempt IMMORTALITY, 4
man can d. but once DEATH, 137
Many people would sooner d. than think THINKING, 13
me . . . who is going to d. . . . DEATH, 100
More d. in the United States GREED, 9
Never say d. PERSISTENCE, 2
No young man believes he shall ever d. IMMORTALITY, 3
one may d. without ever laughing LAUGHTER, 8
pie in the sky when you d. AFTERLIFE, 5
place . . . to d. in WORLD, 1
Rather suffer than d. SUFFERING, 19
Ring out, wild bells, and let him d. ENDING, 10
save your world you asked this man to d. WAR, 13
she only wants to be let d. in peace HOSPITALS, 7
sometimes they d. DOCTORS, 57
Spend all you have before you d. HEALTHY LIVING, 38
The dead don't d. DEATH, 96
The d. is cast IRREVOCABILITY, 1
The human race is the only one that knows it must d. DEATH, 174
the only decent thing . . . is to d. at once BEQUESTS, 1
those who are about to d. salute you ANONYMOUS, 9
to d., and go we know not where DEATH, 142
To d. will be an awfully big adventure ADVENTURE, 1
to live will be more miserable than to d. SUICIDE, 15
trains all night groan on the rail /To men that d. at morn EXECUTION, 16
we can d. but once to serve our country PATRIOTISM, 1
We d. – does it matter when DEATH, 164
We must all d. SUFFERING, 28
we must live as though . . . never going to d. ACHIEVEMENT, 11
We must love one another or d. LOVE, 20
we shall d. as usual DEATH, 64
when good Americans d. they go to Paris REPARTEE, 122
Will tell me that I have to d. DOCTORS, 17
wisdom says: 'We must d.,' LIFE AND DEATH, 34
died A piece of each of us d. at that moment ASSASSINATION, 6
dog it was that d. DOGS, 8
He d. as he lived – at sea EPITAPHS, 42
I d. . . . of my physician DISEASE, 36
Men have d. from time to time LOVE AND DEATH, 7

there were people who d. of dropsies ALCOHOL, 43
'Tis said that some have d. for love LOVE AND DEATH, 10
What can you say about a 25-year-old girl who d. EPITAPHS, 35
diem *Carpe d.* PRESENT, 8
dies A bachelor . . . d. like a beggar MARRIAGE, 90
a young person, who . . . marries or d., is sure to be kindly spoken of HUMAN NATURE, 2
Every moment d. a man LIFE AND DEATH, 5
He d. every day who lives a lingering life ILLNESS, 59
He d. from his whole life LIFE AND DEATH, 26
he d. in pain LIFE AND DEATH, 20
He that d. pays all debts DEATH, 149
It matters not how a man d. DEATH, 87
king never d. MONARCHY, 6
One d. only once DEATH, 110
Whatever is begotten, born, and d. MORTALITY, 23
diet A little with quiet is the only d. HEALTHY LIVING, 1
cured only with d. and tendering HEALTH, 3
D. away your stress HEALTHY LIVING, 34
D. cures more than the lancet HEALTHY LIVING, 10
Doctor D., /Doctor Quiet and Doctor Merryman DOCTORS, 94
Food is an important part of a balanced d. FOOD, 46
I told my doctor I get very tired . . . on a d. FOOD, 47
dietitians The death of all d. FOOD, 32
diets I feel about airplanes the way I feel about d. FLYING, 4
Dieu *D. et mon droit* FAITH, 27
difference Because there is no d. LIFE AND DEATH, 32
Between man and woman there is little d. SEXES, 1
d. between . . . prose and metrical composition POETRY AND PROSE, 7
made the d. of forty thousand men OFFICERS, 16
more d. within the sexes than between them SEXES, 7
differences If we cannot now end our d. DIFFERENCE, 9
The Jews and Arabs should . . . settle their d. GOLDWYNISMS, 26
different rich are d. WEALTH, 18
differently I would have done it d. ARROGANCE, 9
differeth one star d. from another . . . in glory ASTRONOMY, 1
difficult D. do you call it, Sir CRITICISM, 31
It is d. to be humble HUMILITY, 4
It is very d. to get up resentment BITTERNESS, 2
When a piece gets d. MUSICIANS, 7
difficulties settle up these little local d. POLITICS, 92
difficulty A d. for every solution BUREAUCRACY, 6
I feel . . . a certain d. in continuing to exist LAST WORDS, 35
digest It's that confounded cucumber /I've eat and can't d. FOOD, 9
mark, learn, and inwardly d. BOOK OF COMMON PRAYER, THE, 1
my stomach must just d. in its waistcoat ALCOHOL, 74
To eat is human, to d. divine FOOD, 24
digestion d. is the great secret of life HEALTHY LIVING, 40
the good or bad d. of a prime minister POLITICIANS, 121
Things sweet to taste prove in d. sour REGRET, 21
digestions Few radicals have good d. POLITICS, 28
Diggers You noble D. all REBELLION, 13
digitalis I use d. in doses the text books say are dangerous DRUGS, 18
dignity All human beings are born free and equal in d. and rights ANONYMOUS, 3
a paunch to give him D. DOCTORS, 13
d. and greatness and peace again DRINKS, 9
human beings are born free . . . d. and rights HUMAN RIGHTS, 1
Official d. . . . in inverse ratio to . . . importance DIPLOMACY, 13
dike February, fill the d. MONTHS, 11
dikes our d., . . . are ten feet deep REPARTEE, 126
our d., the waters are ten feet deep BOASTS, 8
diligently Had I . . . served God as d. as I have served the king LOYALTY, 15
dim My eyes are d. BLINDNESS, 3
my lamp burns low and d. ENVY, 3
dime Brother, can you spare a d. MISQUOTATION, 16
dimensions sickness enlarges the d. of a man's self ILLNESS, 38
diminished ought to be d. MONARCHY, 10
dimmed The eyes that shone, /Now d. and gone NOSTALGIA, 17
dimple A d. in the chin, a devil within PROVERBS, 13
dine wretches hang that jury-men may d. JUSTICE, 26
dined More d. against than dining FOOD, 17
when Thomas Jefferson d. alone TALENT, 7
you have d. in every house in London – *once* BORES, 9
diners-out d. from whom we guard our spoons MISTRUST, 8
ding D. dong, bell, /Pussy's in the well NURSERY RHYMES, 9
dinkum a 'd. hard-swearing Aussie' PATRIOTISM, 19
dinky Hinky, d., par-lee-voo FRANCE, 16
dinner A d. lubricates business BUSINESS, 19
A man is . . . better pleased when he has a good d. upon his table WOMAN'S ROLE, 6
Breakfast, D., Lunch and Tea FOOD, 10
people . . . would ask him to d. BELIEF, 5
This was a good d. enough FOOD, 39
dinner-table dominate a London d. INFLUENCE, 14
diplomacy All d. is a continuation of war DIPLOMACY, 17
Building up arms is not a substitute for d. NUCLEAR WEAPONS, 19
diplomat A d. . . . always remembers a woman's birthday AGE, 35
d. these days is nothing but a head-waiter DIPLOMACY, 23
diplomatic d. history is . . . what one clerk said to another clerk HISTORY, 43
diplomats aged d. to be bored DIPLOMACY, 3
Dirce With D. in one boat conveyed LUST, 7
direction God knows how you Protestants . . . have any sense of d. CATHOLICISM, 14
directions rode madly off in all d. NONSENSE, 16
director Every d. bites the hand MIXED METAPHORS, 2
Theatre d.: a person ACTING, 1
dirt After the first four years the d. doesn't get any worse HOUSEWORK, 3
he begins as d. and departs as stench MANKIND, 65
Throw d. enough GOSSIP, 6
dirtiness the other half is d. CLEANNESS, 2
dirty A rather d. Wykehamist EDUCATION, 13
Is sex d. SEX, 1
The permissive society has . . . become a d. phrase LIBERALISM, 3
You d. double-crossing rat INSULTS, 25
disadvantage d. of merely counting votes DEMOCRACY, 8
disagree Who shall decide when doctors d. DOCTORS, 78
disappointment Grief and d. give rise to anger EMOTION, 3
disapprove I d. of what you say FREEDOM, 60
disarm Let no one expect us to d. unilaterally POWER POLITICS, 1
disarmament precede the d. of the victors WAR, 42
disaster the audience was a d. PLAYS, 17
disasters the middle station had the fewest d. CLASS, 12
trace . . . the d. of English history to . . . Wales WALES, 5
disbelief willing suspension of d. POETRY, 15
discandy do d., melt their sweets /On blossoming Caesar INCONSTANCY, 1
disciple a d. . . . of the fiend, called the Pucelle ACCUSATION, 3
disciples d. . . . mark its ways and note . . . its mysteries GAMBLING, 1
one of his d., whom Jesus loved BIBLICAL QUOTATIONS, 345
discomfiture We're in the Embassy residence, subject . . . to some . . . d. DIPLOMACY, 2
discomforts all the d. that will accompany my being blind BLINDNESS, 14
discommendeth He who d. others CRITICISM, 12
discontent lent /To youth and age . . . – d. DISCONTENT, 1
To be discontented with the divine d. VIRTUE, 16
winter of our d. OPTIMISM, 33
discontents the family . . . source of all our d. FAMILY, 31
discord what d. follows ORDER, 6
discourse their d. was about hunting HUNTING, 7
discover not d. new lands RESEARCH, 13
discovered We have d. the secret of life DISCOVERY, 8
discoverer differentiating the brilliant d. from the . . . plodder GENIUS, 6
discoverers They are ill d. that think there is no land DISCOVERY, 4
discoveries d. are usually not made by one man alone DISCOVERY, 14
Many a man who is brooding over alleged mighty d. DISCOVERY, 7
None of the great d. DISCOVERY, 9
discovery behind the d. of America JEWS, 16
D. consists of seeing what everybody has seen DISCOVERY, 15
he who never made a mistake never made a d. MISTAKES, 18
Scientific d. is a private event SCIENCE, 62
that philosophy and the knowledge of causes led to the d. RESEARCH, 5
Whenever science makes a d. SCIENCE, 88
discretion better part of valour is d. DISCRETION, 2
temper d. with deceit DISCRETION, 3
the years of d. AGE, 16
discrimination sympathetic without d. SYMPATHY, 2
discussed Everything has been d. and analysed BOOKS, 2
discussion D. in class, which means EDUCATION, 63
more time for d. . . . more mistakes MISTAKES, 21
disdains He d. all things above his reach DISCONTENT, 7
disease A bodily d., . . . whole and entire within itself HOLISTIC MEDICINE, 2
a cure for which there was no d. REMEDIES, 15
a d. in which death and life are so strangely blended DISEASE, 17
A d. known is half cured DISEASE, 1
a d. which medicine never cured DISEASE, 17
All interest in d. and death LIFE, 53
amusing the patient while Nature cures the d. DISEASE, 46
and so, it seems, is perfect d. HEALTH, 16
An imaginary ailment is worse than a d. HYPOCHONDRIA, 2
an incurable d. – colour blindness DISEASE, 13
a poor man for the same d. he giveth a more common name REMEDIES, 55
Choose your specialist and you choose your d. SPECIALISTS, 2
Confront d. at its first stage ILLNESS, 55
Consciousness is a d. PSYCHOLOGY, 18
Cur'd . . . of my d. DISEASE, 36
Cure the d. DISEASE, 9
Decay and d. are often beautiful DISEASE, 45
desperate d. requires a dangerous remedy TREASON, 4
Despite a lifetime of service . . . venereal d. SEX, 38
D. can carry its ill-effects no farther than mortal mind ILLNESS, 23
D. creates poverty POVERTY, 35
D. has social as well as physical, chemical, and biological causes HOLISTIC MEDICINE, 12
D. is an experience of mortal mind DISEASE, 19
D. is an image of thought externalized ILLNESS, 23
d. is connected only with immediate causes DISEASE, 43
D. is not of the body DISEASE, 40
d. is the result of sin MEDICINE, 76
D. is . . . the result of conflict between soul and mind SOUL, 4
D. is very old PROGRESS, 7
D. makes men more physical ILLNESS, 45
each civilization has a pattern of d. ENVIRONMENT, 6
Evil comes . . . like the d.; good . . . like the doctor DISEASE, 15
Half of the secret of resistance to d. is cleanliness CLEANNESS, 2
Have a chronic d. and take care of it LONGEVITY, 9
he does not die from the d. alone LIFE AND DEATH, 26
he is a d. of the dust MANKIND, 18

I am suffering from the particular d. HYPOCHONDRIA, 9
I'd make health catching instead of d. HEALTH, 13
if the physician had the same d. upon him that I have DISEASE, 39
I have Bright's d. DISEASE, 34
it separates the patient from his d. OPERATIONS, 6
I've got Bright's d. and he's got mine ILLNESS, 54
let us . . . , eradicate d. SCIENCE, 56
Life is a d. LIFE, 78
Life is an incurable d. DISEASE, 16
Medicine, to produce health, has to examine d. MEDICINE, 80
Natural forces are the healers of d. HOLISTIC MEDICINE, 3
Nature cures the d. MEDICINE, 104
Old age is a d. OLD AGE, 81
Only those in the last stage of d. CHILDREN, 5
Remedies, . . . are our great analysers of d. REMEDIES, 39
remedies . . . suggested for a d. REMEDIES, 21
remedy is worse than the d. DISEASE, 10
Self-contemplation is . . . the symptom of d. PSYCHOANALYSIS, 5
Sleep and watchfulness . . . when immoderate, constitute d. SLEEP, 17
strange d. of modern life DISEASE, 7
The aim of medicine is to prevent d. MEDICINE, 62
the d. ceases without the use of any kind of medicine ENVIRONMENT, 1
The d. of an evil conscience is beyond the practice of all the physicians EVIL, 12
the d. of writing books DISEASE, 33
the d., the patient, and physician MEDICINE, 39
the god of physic and sender of d. DOCTORS, 95
the incurable d. of writing DISEASE, 28
The medicine increases the d. ILLNESS, 66
the observations of the body in health and d. NATURE, 17
the only d. you don't look forward to being cured of DEATH, 101
The prevention of d. today is one of the most important factors MEDICINE, 61
'There is no cure for this d..' DOCTORS, 19
the relief of d. MEDICINE, 44
The soul is subject to health and d. SOUL, 14
The treatment of a d. may be entirely impersonal PATIENTS, 16
this long d., my life DISEASE, 35
tied to d. HOLISTIC MEDICINE, 4
when the cause of d. is discovered ILLNESS, 18
You cure his d. REMEDIES, 9
diseases All d. run into one OLD AGE, 46
Coughs and sneezes spread d. ILLNESS, 6
death is the cure of all d. DEATH, 41
D. are the tax on pleasures DISEASE, 37
d. as isolated disturbances in a healthy body DISEASE, 3
D. crucify the soul of man DISEASE, 14
d. may also colour the moods of civilizations DISEASE, 18
D. of their own Accord REMEDIES, 17
D. of the soul are more dangerous SOUL, 9
doctors themselves die of the very d. they profess to cure REPUTATION, 12
Extreme remedies . . . for extreme d. REMEDIES, 32
for doctors imagine d. ILLNESS, 43
Hungry Joe collected lists of fatal d. ILLNESS, 29
In acute d. it is not quite safe to prognosticate . . . death DIAGNOSIS, 10
Man is a museum of d. MANKIND, 65
Medicine can only cure curable d. MEDICINE, 2
Medicine heals doubts as well as d. MEDICINE, 60
Men worry over the great number of d. REMEDIES, 22
new-fangled names to d. ILLNESS, 56
Not even remedies can master incurable d. DISEASE, 41
Occupational d. are socially different from other d. DISEASE, 42
The cure of many d. is unknown HOLISTIC MEDICINE, 8
The deviation of man . . . seems to have proved . . . a prolific source of d. HEALTHY LIVING, 26
The d. which destroy a man DISEASE, 38
disgrace a d. to our family name of Wagstaff DISHONOR, 2
disgracefully The world is d. managed COMPLAINTS, 3
disguise virtues are . . . vices in d. VIRTUE AND VICE, 4
disguised a blessing, . . . very well d. DEFEAT, 1
dish And the d. ran away with the spoon NURSERY RHYMES, 14
a side d. he hadn't ordered CONTEMPT, 4
butter in a lordly d. BIBLICAL QUOTATIONS, 390
The national d. of America UNITED STATES, 50
dishes Thou shalt not wash d. NURSERY RHYMES, 8
dishonor honour rooted in d. DISHONOR, 3
who fears d. more than death DISHONOR, 1
disillusionments d. in the lives of the medieval saints DECLINE, 9
disinclination d. to inflict pain upon oneself GOOD, 11
disinfectants the best d. CLEANNESS, 9
disinterested D. intellectual curiosity . . . life blood of . . . civilisation CURIOSITY, 8
dislike I d. what I fancy I feel. ANONYMOUS, 91
that *my* statue should be moved, which I should much d. MEMORIALS, 17
The law of d. for the unlike JEWS, 20
disliked I have always d. myself SELF, 7
dismal the D. Science ECONOMICS, 4
dismissed Shakespeare . . . is d. in a page carelessly HISTORY, 17
Disney D. the most significant figure . . . since Leonardo ART, 15
disobedience Of Man's first d. SIN, 21
disorder A sweet d. in the dress CLOTHES, 10
dispepsia d. is the apparatus of illusions ILLNESS, 48
disposes God d. GOD, 34
dispute Many a long d. among divines ARGUMENTS, 4
disputing The itch of d. . . . the scab of churches RELIGION, 83
disreputable I've been offered titles . . . get one into d. company TITLES, 12
disrespectfully Never speak d. of Society SNOBBERY, 13
dis-satisfaction balanced state of well-modulated d. POLITICS, 137
dissect Like following life through creatures you d. VIVISECTION, 5
dissections I know not, that by living d. VIVISECTION, 4
dissimulate how to d. is the knowledge of kings ROYALTY, 90
dissipated still keep looking so d. DEBAUCHERY, 2
dissipation At what time does the d. of energy begin SPORT AND GAMES, 13
d. without pleasure LONDON, 13
other things than d. . . . thicken the features APPEARANCE, 64
dissolve Fade far away, d. HUMAN CONDITION, 14
distance The d. doesn't matter BEGINNING, 6
distempers infectious D. must necessarily be propagated ENVIRONMENT, 2
disthressful She's the most d. country that iver yet was seen ANONYMOUS, 46
distinguish all there is to d. us from other animals MANKIND, 7
distinguished a sparrow alight upon my shoulder . . . I was more d. by that HONOR, 9
So it has come at last, the d. thing LAST WORDS, 52
When a d. but elderly scientist states SCIENCE, 20
distraction Ambition, D., Uglification, and Derision EDUCATION, 19
distress All pray in their d. DISTRESS, 1
the mean man is always full of d. DISTRESS, 2
distribution the wider d. of smoked salmon SOCIALISM, 17
distrust shameful to d. one's friends DISTRUST, 3
stay together, but we d. one another DISTRUST, 1
distrusts him who d. himself DISTRUST, 2
disturb What isn't part of ourselves doesn't d. us HATE, 6
ditchwater Is d. dull NATURE, 7
diver a d. poised in albumen BIRTH, 2
diversion Most sorts of d. . . . are an imitation of fighting WAR, 157
'tis a country d. COUNTRYSIDE, 1
diversity make the world safe for d. DIFFERENCE, 9
divide D. and rule POWER, 1
divided in their death they were not d. BIBLICAL QUOTATIONS, 615
Obstinate people can be d. into STUBBORNNESS, 3
Thought must be d. against itself UNDERSTANDING, 6
divine attain to the d. perfection PERFECTION, 5
The Hand that made us is d. CREATION, 1
The right d. of kings to govern wrong MONARCHY, 18
To be discontented with the d. discontent VIRTUE, 16
To err is human, to forgive, d. ERROR, 11
divines Many a long dispute among d. ARGUMENTS, 4
divinity a d. that shapes our ends DESTINY, 20
a piece of d. in us DIVINITY, 1
d. in odd numbers DIVINITY, 4
There is surely a piece of d. in us MANKIND, 14
There's such d. doth hedge a king DIVINITY, 2
divisions How many d. has *he* got CATHOLICISM, 12
divorce D.? Never. But murder often MARRIAGE, 144
do D. as you would be done by EXAMPLE, 3
D. other men BUSINESS, 6
d. what the mob d. MAJORITY, 3
either d., or die ACTION, 6
for they know not what they d. BIBLICAL QUOTATIONS, 447
go, and d. thou likewise BIBLICAL QUOTATIONS, 434
I am to d. what I please FREEDOM, 15
Let us d. or die ACTION, 8
Nature . . . hath done her part; D. thou but thine RESPONSIBILITY, 10
Now what d. I d. with *this* ROYALTY, 109
Preachers say, D. as I say, not as I d. DISEASE, 39
so much to d., /So little done ACTION, 14
they would d. you BUSINESS, 6
to d. something is to create existence EXISTENCE, 5
dobest Dowel, Dobet and D. GOOD, 10
Doc Never play cards with a man called D. ADVICE, 5
What's up, D. CINEMA, 3
doctor A country d. needs more brains to do his work DOCTORS, 77
A d. . . . is a patient half-cured OCCUPATIONS, 19
A d. is . . . licensed to make grave mistakes DOCTORS, 58
A d. must work eighteen hours a day DOCTORS, 38
a d. who has gone into lonely and discouraged homes DOCTORS, 59
After all, a d. is just to put your mind at rest DOCTORS, 75
After death the d. DEATH, 1
A man who cannot work without his hypodermic needle is a poor d. DRUGS, 7
a man who drinks more than his own d. DRUNKENNESS, 8
a . . . sense of intellectual degradation after an interview with a d. DOCTORS, 56
A young d. makes a humpy graveyard DOCTORS, 1
by stealing the bread denied him by his d. DISEASE, 23
D. Foster went to Gloucester NURSERY RHYMES, 10
E'en dismissing the d. don't *always* succeed REMEDIES, 23
Even if the d. does not give you a year DETERMINATION, 22
Evil comes . . . like the disease; good . . . like the d. DISEASE, 15
Foolish the d. who despises the knowledge DOCTORS, 55
For he was a country d., and he did not know what it was to spare himself SELFLESSNESS, 4
Fresh air impoverishes the d. HEALTHY LIVING, 6
Give me a d. partridge-plump DOCTORS, 17
God and the D. we alike adore FAITH, 25
God is forgotten, and the D. slighted FAITH, 25
He has been a d. a year now DOCTORS, 99
he would never have died but for that vile d. DOCTORS, 16
I do not love thee, D. Fell HATE, 1
If you are too smart to pay the d. ILLNESS, 5
It is the duty of a d. to prolong life DEATH, 81
I told my d. I get very tired . . . on a diet FOOD, 47
Knocked down a d.? With an ambulance ACCIDENTS, 8
look for a d. who is hated by the best doctors DOCTORS, 104
Make it compulsory for a d. using a brass plate DOCTORS, 87
Nature is better than a middling d. NATURE, 1

Never believe what a patient tells you his d. has said PATIENTS, 11
No d. takes pleasure in the health even of his friends DOCTORS, 62
no one ever considered the d. a gentleman CLASS, 27
not even a d. can kill you DOCTORS, 73
Our d. would never really operate unless it was necessary DOCTORS, 90
Passion . . . can be destroyed by a d. PASSION, 8
People pay the d. for his trouble KINDNESS, 9
popular remedy often throws the scientific d. into hysterics REMEDIES, 4
seek out a bright young d. DOCTORS, 104
Six men give a d. less to do than one woman WOMEN, 4
Some d. full of phrase and fame ILLNESS, 8
Than fee the d. for a nauseous draught HEALTHY LIVING, 20
The best d. in the world is the Veterinarian DOCTORS, 81
The d. fainted HUMOR, 3
The D. fared even better REPUTATION, 4
The d. found . . . /Her last disorder mortal DOCTORS, 50
the d. must always be a student LEARNING, 14
The d. occupies a seat in the front row of the stalls of the human drama DOCTORS, 84
The D. said that Death was but /A scientific fact FACTS, 8
The d. says there is no hope HOPE, 22
the d. takes the fee DOCTORS, 3
The essential unit of medical practice is the occasion when . . . a person . . . seeks the advice of a d. PATIENTS, 18
the inferior d. treats those who are ill DOCTORS, 31
The most tragic thing in the world is a sick d. DOCTORS, 88
The older a d. is and the more venerated he is DOCTORS, 104
The presence of the d. is the beginning of the cure DOCTORS, 6
The real work of a d. . . . is not an affair of health centres PATIENTS, 18
There is not a d. who desires the health of his friends DOCTORS, 76
The silent d. shook his head DOCTORS, 47
The skilful d. treats those who are well DOCTORS, 31
the successful d. was said to need three things DOCTORS, 13
The superior d. prevents sickness DOCTORS, 7
'What sort of d. is he?' DOCTORS, 35
When a d. does go wrong DOCTORS, 34
doctors a meeting of d. DOCTORS, 60
Call in three good d. and play bridge DOCTORS, 21
d. and patients MANKIND, 33
D. and undertakers /Fear epidemics of good health DOCTORS, 18
D. are generally dull dogs DOCTORS, 105
D. are just the same as lawyers DOCTORS, 30
D. are mostly impostors DOCTORS, 104
D., . . . know men as thoroughly as if they had made them MANKIND, 52
d. rob you and kill you, too DOCTORS, 30
d. themselves die of the very diseases they profess to cure REPUTATION, 12
for d. imagine diseases ILLNESS, 43
I have two d. HEALTHY LIVING, 11
Most of those evils . . . /From d. and imagination flow ILLNESS, 17
one cannot really have confidence in d. DOCTORS, 49
sitting in the midst of the d. BIBLICAL QUOTATIONS, 423
The best d. in the world DOCTORS, 94
The d. allow one to die DOCTORS, 26
The d. are always changing their opinions DOCTORS, 48
The d. found, when she was dead DEATH, 72
The d. were very brave about it DOCTORS, 71
the duty of training the rising generation of d. EDUCATION, 41
The great d. all got their education off dirt pavements EDUCATION, 28
There are more old drunkards than old d. DOCTORS, 41
We d. have always been a simple trusting folk DOCTORS, 66
when he wears a d. cape EVOLUTION, 1
While d. consult, the patient dies DOCTORS, 8
Who are the greatest deceivers? The d. DOCTORS, 101
Who shall decide when d. disagree DOCTORS, 78
You, as d., will be in a position to see the human race stark naked DOCTORS, 37
doctrine a d. so illogical and so dull MARXISM, 6
any d. . . . vouched for by . . . human beings . . . must be benighted and supersititious SCIENCE, 52
doctrines he should resist the fascination of d. and hypotheses MEDICINE, 11
What makes all d. plain MONEY, 13
documents sign d. which they do not read BORROWING, 4
Dodger artful D. NAMES, 5
Dodgers Giants three, D. nothing BASEBALL, 5
doers be ye d. of the word BIBLICAL QUOTATIONS, 283
does It's dogged as d. it ACTION, 15
dog A door is what a d. is . . . on the wrong side of DOGS, 11
A good d. MERIT, 1
America is a large, friendly d. UNITED STATES, 62
And every d. his day YOUTH, 18
as though my d. has just died POLITICIANS, 120
A woman's preaching is like a d.'s walking on his hinder legs WOMEN, 58
Beware of the d. DOGS, 1
D. does not eat d. LOYALTY, 1
d. that praised his fleas PARASITES, 4
end up eating our d. ECOLOGY, 7
Every d. has his day OPPORTUNITY, 2
Every d. is allowed LAW, 2
Give a d. a bad name INJUSTICE, 1
I am His Highness' d. at Kew DOGS, 13
If a d. jumps . . . but if a cat CATS, 7
I ope my lips let no d. bark EGOTISM, 8
passers-by who can contemplate it . . . are those . . . with a white stick and a d. ARCHITECTURE, 8
That tossed the d., /That worried the cat NURSERY RHYMES, 57
The d. it was that died DOGS, 8
The d. . . . /Went mad and bit the man DOGS, 7
The great pleasure of a d. DOGS, 4
The little d. laughed /To see such sport NURSERY RHYMES, 14
The world regards such a person as . . . an unmuzzled d. CLASSIFICATION, 1
whose d. are you DOGS, 13
Why keep a d. FUTILITY, 2
You ain't nothin' but a hound d. DOGS, 10
dogged It's d. as does it ACTION, 15
doggie The d. in front has suddenly gone blind EXPLANATIONS, 2
dogging A case of the tail d. the wag HUMOR, 47
dogma Any stigma . . . to beat a d. PUNS, 6
no d., no Dean RELIGION, 23
You can't teach an old d. CONSERVATISM, 7
dogmas these d. or goals are in doubt FANATICISM, 3
dogs And dancing d. and bears ANIMALS, 15
Anybody who hates children and d. CHILDREN, 26
Doctors are generally dull d. DOCTORS, 105
d. delight to bark and bite ANIMALS, 24
D., like horses, are quadrupeds ANIMALS, 18
how much more d. are animated when they hunt in a pack UNITY, 10
I loathe people who keep d. DOGS, 15
let slip the d. of war WAR, 147
like asking a lamp-post . . . about d. CRITICS, 6
more careful of the breed of their horses and d. than of their children FAMILY, 42
Rats . . . fought the d. ANIMALS, 7
Stop . . . those d. . . . peeing on my cheapest rug DOGS, 9
The woman who is really kind to d. DOGS, 2
doing Anything that is worth d. ORIGINALITY, 1
D. is better than saying ACTION, 2
Find out what you like d. best and get someone to pay you for d. it OCCUPATIONS, 21
let us not be weary in well d. BIBLICAL QUOTATIONS, 173
we learn by d. LEARNING, 2
Whatever is worth d. EXCELLENCE, 1
doings All our d. without charity BOOK OF COMMON PRAYER, THE, 2
dollar The almighty d. . . . object of universal devotion MATERIALISM, 15
dollars What's a thousand d. MONEY, 28
dolls The fifth week, he cut out paper d. HYPOCHONDRIA, 3
dominate d. the world INFLUENCE, 14
dominion Death Shall Have No D. DEATH, 168
dominions The sun does not set in my d. ROYALTY, 94
dominoes a row of d. set up; you knock over the first RESULTS, 4
dona *timeo Danaos et d. ferentis* MISTRUST, 12
done bright day is d. DARKNESS, 17
Do as you would be d. by EXAMPLE, 3
d. those things we ought not BOOK OF COMMON PRAYER, THE, 4
If it were d. when 'tis d. HASTE, 10
Justice should . . . be seen to be d. JUSTICE, 14
Let justice be d. JUSTICE, 11
long day's task is d. REST, 2
One never notices what has been d. ACHIEVEMENT, 4
so little d. ACTION, 14
the dread of doing what has been d. before IMMATURITY, 3
The way to get things d. is not to mind who gets the credit SELFLESSNESS, 2
thy worldly task hast d. DUST, 9
What's d. cannot be undone IRREVOCABILITY, 2
What you do not want d. to yourself EXAMPLE, 4
Dong The D. with a luminous Nose NONSENSE, 18
Don Juan *D.* when anger is subsiding into indifference LITERATURE, 16
Don Juans Christ-like heroes and woman-worshipping D. MEN, 8
donkeys Lions led by d. LEADERSHIP, 7
Don Miguel All right, my lord creator, D. DEATH, 172
Don Quixote the only absolutely original creation . . . is D. FICTION, 5
dons If the D. sight Devon PATRIOTISM, 29
It is the little d. I complain about CRITICS, 13
donsmanship D. . . . the art of criticizing INATTENTION, 3
don't-knows One day the d. will get in GOVERNMENT, 25
Doodle Yankee D. came to town NURSERY RHYMES, 69
doom bears it out even to the edge of d. DOOM, 3
purpose of God and the d. assigned DESTINY, 28
regardless of their d. DOOM, 1
slow, sure d. falls pitiless and dark DARKNESS, 16
door A d. is what a dog is . . . on the wrong side of DOGS, 11
I am the d. BIBLICAL QUOTATIONS, 340
sweetest thing that ever grew /Beside a human d. ADMIRATION, 20
the judge standeth before the d. BIBLICAL QUOTATIONS, 288
When one d. shuts OPTIMISM, 10
world will make a beaten path to his d. FAME, 10
Youth will come . . . beat on my d. YOUTH, 16
doors the d. of perception were cleansed PERCEPTION, 1
dope Despair is better treated with hope, not d. DESPAIR, 1
Science and art are only too often a superior kind of d. NARCOTICS, 6
Dorchester All terrorists . . . end up with drinks at the D. POLITICS, 48
doses A hundred d. of happiness are not enough DRUGS, 12
dots those damned d. MATHEMATICS, 3
double But the horrible d.-entendre ANONYMOUS, 93
down the grassgreen gooseberried d. bed SEX, 101
make that a d. LAST WORDS, 45
double-entendre But the horrible d. INNUENDO, 1
doublethink D. . . . holding two contradictory beliefs DOUBLETHINK, 2
doubt a life of d. diversified by faith DOUBT, 5
all my mind is clouded with a d. AFTERLIFE, 11
faith without d. is nothing but death FAITH, 30
Humility is only d. HUMILITY, 2
new Philosophy calls all in d. SCIENCE, 28
No . . . shadow of d. CERTAINTY, 2
O thou of little faith, wherefore didst thou d. BIBLICAL QUOTATIONS, 510
these dogmas or goals are in d. FANATICISM, 3
Through the night of d. and sorrow ENDURANCE, 5
When a man is in d. about . . . his writing POSTERITY, 5

Not a d. was heard FUNERALS, 13
Take my d. to England PATRIOTISM, 29
drums the beating of war d. WAR, 88
drunk Bowen's Beer Makes You D. DRINKS, 2
If, d. with sight of power, we loose BOASTS, 4
Lord George-Brown d. is a better man DRUNKENNESS, 4
man . . . must get d. DRUNKENNESS, 13
Most British statesmen have either d. too much or womanized too much POLITICIANS, 21
My mother, d. or sober PATRIOTISM, 8
not so think as you d. DRUNKENNESS, 27
this meeting is d. DRUNKENNESS, 14
you won't intoxicate with one glass someone who has . . . d. . . . a . . . barrel EXPERIENCE, 11
drunkards There are more old d. DOCTORS, 41
drunken Better sleep with a sober cannibal than a d. Christian DRUNKENNESS, 21
d., but not with wine BIBLICAL QUOTATIONS, 266
He uses statistics as a d. man uses lamp-posts STATISTICS, 5
What shall we do with the d. sailor ANONYMOUS, 106
drunkenness A branch of the sin of d. DRUNKENNESS, 19
D. is never anything but a substitute for happiness DRUNKENNESS, 17
D. is simply voluntary insanity DRUNKENNESS, 26
D. is temporary suicide DRUNKENNESS, 24
D. . . . spoils health DRUNKENNESS, 22
D., the ruin of reason DRUNKENNESS, 9
If . . . 'feeling good' could decide, d. would be . . . supremely valid DRUNKENNESS, 18
there is more drinking . . . less d. ALCOHOL, 22
dry old man in a d. month AGE, 30
out of these wet clothes and into a d. Martini ALCOHOL, 88
O ye d. bones BIBLICAL QUOTATIONS, 164
the midst of the sea upon d. ground BIBLICAL QUOTATIONS, 142
Dublin D., though . . . much worse than London PLACES, 19
In D.'s fair city, where the girls are so pretty ANONYMOUS, 47
ducats My daughter! O my d.! O my daughter LOSS, 7
Duce The D. is always right FASCISM, 1
duck looks like a d. COMMUNISM, 10
duckling The Ugly D. BOOK TITLES, 3
ducks you go about the country stealing d. THEFT, 3
your precious 'lame d.' WEAKNESS, 2
duel war . . . will be considered as antiquated as a d. WAR, 67
duke A . . . D. costs as much . . . as two Dreadnoughts ARISTOCRACY, 15
a naked D. of Windlestraw addressing a naked House of Lords NAKEDNESS, 5
How very mean a thing's a D. PRIDE, 10
dukes a drawing-room full of d. SCIENTISTS, 1
dulce Died some . . . /non 'd.' non 'et decor' EPITAPHS, 33
D. et decorum est PATRIOTISM, 18
dull a doctrine so illogical and so d. MARXISM, 6
as d. as ditch water DULLNESS, 1
a very d. Play MARRIAGE, 43
Heaven . . . is a place so inane, so d. HEAVEN, 13
He was d. in a new way POETS, 24
not only d. in himself DULLNESS, 2
The prospect of a lot /Of d. MPs POLITICIANS, 49
To make dictionaries is d. work LEXICOGRAPHY, 7
dullard The d.'s envy of brilliant men GREATNESS, 2
dullness the cause of d. in others DULLNESS, 2
dumplings I am the emperor, and I want d. PETULANCE, 3
dunces the d. are all in confederacy against him GENIUS, 9
dung no grass there groweth, /Only their engines' d. ENGLAND, 7
dupe The d. of friendship, and the fool of love BITTERNESS, 1
dusk In the d., with a light behind her AGE, 36
slow d. a drawing-down of blinds WAR, 117
dusky Midnight brought on the d. hour DAY AND NIGHT, 17
dust A heap of d. alone remains DUST, 7
As chimney-sweepers, come to d. DUST, 9
d. shalt thou eat BIBLICAL QUOTATIONS, 188
d. thou art BIBLICAL QUOTATIONS, 189
fear in a handful of d. DUST, 4
fly . . . said, what a d. do I raise CONCEIT, 3
he is a disease of the d. MANKIND, 18
not worth the d. INSULTS, 111
pride that licks the d. DUST, 8
raised a d. COMPLAINTS, 2
The d. and silence of the upper shelf DUST, 6
the d. beneath thy chariot wheel DUST, 5
The d. of great persons' graves DUST, 3
this quintessence of d. DELIGHT, 10
Dutch my dear old D. LOVE, 47
duties he devotes to the neglect of his d. NEGLECT, 4
One of the first d. of the physician DOCTORS, 68
Property has its d. CAPITALISM, 5
the d. of a physician DOCTORS, 10
duty absolved from all d. to his country MARRIAGE, 104
a stupid man . . . always declares that it is his d. DUTY, 4
A thing of d. is a boy for ever POLICE, 6
Do your d. and leave the rest to the Gods DUTY, 2
d. of an opposition OPPOSITION, 2
England expects every man will do his d. DUTY, 3
give my d. to the Queen VICTORY, 12
It is my d. to warn you that it will be used against you JUSTICE, 9
It is the d. of a doctor to prolong life DEATH, 81
more than a moral d. to speak one's mind FRANKNESS, 5
Nor law, nor d. bade me fight FIGHT, 19
Patriotism . . . is a revolutionary d. PATRIOTISM, 41
right of all . . . d. of some SEPARATION, 4
the d. of being happy HAPPINESS, 28
this is the whole d. of man BIBLICAL QUOTATIONS, 99
What's a man's first d. SINCERITY, 6
when constabulary d.'s to be done POLICE, 3
dwarfs A number of anxious d. POLITICIANS, 92
dwell d. among scorpions BIBLICAL QUOTATIONS, 159
he that sitteth on the throne shall d. among them BIBLICAL QUOTATIONS, 590
Let other pens d. on guilt and misery OPTIMISM, 14
dwelt She d. among the untrodden ways LONELINESS, 13
dyb D.-d.-d. ADVICE, 7
dyin' 'Young man, I think you're d.!' ANONYMOUS, 49
dying alike are the groans of love to . . . d. LOVE AND DEATH, 4
All men are afraid of d. DEATH, 124
an environment equally fit for birth, growth work, healing, and d. HEALTHY LIVING, 25
Death must be distinguished from d. DEATH, 156
Don't cheer, boys; the poor devils are d. WAR, 122
D. /is an art DEATH, 116
D. for an idea MARTYRDOM, 3
D. is as natural as living LIFE AND DEATH, 2
D. is a very dull, dreary affair DEATH, 106
D. is the most hellishly boresome experience in the world DEATH, 107
D. while young is a boon in old age OLD AGE, 7
Ever since d. came into fashion DEATH, 9
For a priest to turn a man when he lies a-d. PERSUASION, 2
good for a writer to think he's d. WRITERS, 59
He had been, he said, a most unconscionable time d. DEATH, 47
Here am I, d. DEATH, 118
I cannot forgive my friends for d. DEATH, 154
If this is d. LAST WORDS, 83
is it my birthday or am I d. LAST WORDS, 5
it is not death, but d., which is terrible DEATH, 62
It is not his duty to prolong the act of d. DEATH, 81
poor honest sex, like d., should be a private matter SEX, 32
she cheats the sick and the d. with illusions NATURE, 19
There is a dignity in d. DEATH, 22
Time held me green and d. TIME, 50
'Tis not the d. for a faith FAITH, 29
Truth sits upon the lips of d. men TRUTH, 9
we survive amongst the dead and the d. as on a battlefield OLD AGE, 93
dynamic class people as static and d. SEXES, 31
play is a d. thing NOVELS, 17
dyspepsia GLUTTON, n. A person . . . committing d. GREED, 6
when they are troubled with d. RELIGION, 46
dyspeptic I lead a most d., solitary, self-shrouded *life* SUFFERING, 13

E

Eagle Tranquillity Base here – the E. has landed SPACE, 1
ear a pistol let off at the e. PUNS, 12
I took the right sow by the e. INFLUENCE, 13
jest's prosperity lies in the e. HUMOR, 56
more is meant than meets the e. INNUENDO, 3
nor e. heard BIBLICAL QUOTATIONS, 29
the e. begins to hear IMPRISONMENT, 3
Earl As far as the 14th E. is concerned TITLES, 1
Life is much easier, being an E. ARISTOCRACY, 3
the whole process has ground to a halt with a 14th E. TITLES, 13
early A useless life is an e. death PURPOSE, 3
E. to bed BED, 1
E. to rise and early to bed BED, 12
good die e. GOOD AND EVIL, 4
nobody who does not rise e. BED, 6
The e. bird ANTICIPATION, 3
too e. to form a final judgement on the French Revolution FRENCH REVOLUTION, 9
you have to get up e. if you want to get out of bed BED, 8
earn this is the week I e. my salary MERIT, 5
earned Old age . . . gives us what we have e. OLD AGE, 25
earning learning, e. and yearning LIFE, 60
ears A hungry stomach has no e. HUNGER, 8
can you waggle your e. ACHIEVEMENT, 2
device to keep the e. from grating BRAIN, 3
e. to hear, let him hear BIBLICAL QUOTATIONS, 502
Romans, countrymen, lend me your e. EVIL, 19
the seven thin e. BIBLICAL QUOTATIONS, 223
Walls have e. SECRECY, 3
earth a covenant between me and the e. BIBLICAL QUOTATIONS, 201
a new heaven and a new e. BIBLICAL QUOTATIONS, 601
axis of the e. sticks out visibly through . . . every town or city NATURE, 20
But did thee feel the e. move EARTH, 10
Cool'd . . . in the deep-delved e. ALCOHOL, 46
E. fills her lap with pleasures EARTH, 21
E. has not anything to show more fair EARTH, 20
from whose face the e. and the heaven fled BIBLICAL QUOTATIONS, 600
God called the dry land E. BIBLICAL QUOTATIONS, 176
God created . . . the e. BIBLICAL QUOTATIONS, 174
heaven and e. shall pass away BIBLICAL QUOTATIONS, 531
heav'n on e. EARTH, 13
hell upon e. . . . in a melancholy man's heart MELANCHOLY, 3
I will move the e. EARTH, 1
lards the lean e. as he walks EARTH, 14
let all the e. keep silence before him BIBLICAL QUOTATIONS, 231
mine were princes of the e. EARTH, 3
more things in heaven and e. EARTH, 15
so much of e. . . . of heaven EARTH, 19
the cool flowery lap of e. EARTH, 2
The e. does not argue EARTH, 17
the e. is free for every son and daughter of mankind HUMAN RIGHTS, 8
the e. is the Lord's, and the fulness BIBLICAL QUOTATIONS, 41
the e. of England is in my two hands EARTH, 18
the e. where cares abound BIRDS, 18
The Lord hath created medicines out of the e. REMEDIES, 13
The meek do not inherit the e. EARTH, 12
This e. of majesty EARTH, 16
what fault they commit, the e. covereth DOCTORS, 79
When e. was nigher heaven EARTH, 9
earthquake Small e. in Chile NEWSPAPERS, 8
ear trumpet blowing all those shrimps through her e. PARTIES, 4
ease done with so much e. CHARACTER, 6
Joys in another's loss of e. LOVE, 34
No warmth, no cheerfulness, no healthful e. MONTHS, 10

Has anyone here been raped and speaks E. INSENSITIVITY, 1
hearts at peace, under an E. heaven ENGLAND, 11
He uses the E. language like a truncheon INSULTS, 14
I do love cricket – it's so very E. CRICKET, 2
If the E. language had been properly organized LANGUAGE, 30
If you get the E. people into the way of making kings ROYALTY, 80
my own heart to be entirely E. PATRIOTISM, 3
one of the few E. novels for grown up people CRITICISM, 67
Opera in E. OPERA, 7
our E. nation, if they have a good thing, to make it too common ENGLAND, 45
part of E. middle-class education is devoted to the training of servants CLASS, 54
stones kissed by the E. dead WAR, 118
The attitude of the E. . . . toward E. history ENGLISH, 19
The baby doesn't understand E. LANGUAGE, 26
The E. . . . are rather a foul-mouthed nation ENGLISH, 21
the E. are . . . the least a nation of pure philosophers ENGLISH, 5
the E. have hot-water bottles ENGLISH, 27
The E. have no respect for their language CLASS, 43
The E. instinctively admire ENGLISH, 4
The E. may not like music MUSIC, 5
The E. nation . . . has successfully regulated the power of its kings GOVERNMENT, 40
the E. seem . . . to have conquered and peopled half the world BRITISH EMPIRE, 9
The E. take their pleasures ENGLAND, 47
The E. want *inferiors* PRIDE, 11
ther is so greet diversitee /in E. LANGUAGE, 12
This is the sort of E. GRAMMAR, 4
To Americans E. manners are . . . frightening MANNERS, 4
to the E. that of the sea EMPIRE, 5
two most beautiful words in the E. language SUMMER, 5
typically E. characteristic ENGLISH, 3
Englishman Am I not punished enough in not being born an E. NATIONALITY, 11
An E. . . . forms an orderly queue of one ENGLISH, 26
an E.'s heaven-born privilege of doing as he likes PUBLIC, 2
An E.'s way of speaking CLASS, 23
An E.'s word ENGLISH, 2
an . . . young E. of our upper class ARISTOCRACY, 1
E. . . . is afraid to feel EDUCATION, 29
E. never enjoys himself except for a noble purpose ENGLISH, 22
E. . . . weighs up the birth, the rank, . . . the wealth of the people he meets CLASS, 36
He was born an E. NATIONALITY, 2
how a carter, a common sailor, a beggar is still . . . an E. ENGLAND, 35
If I were an American, as I am an E. PATRIOTISM, 32
in spite of all temptations . . . He remains an E. NATIONALITY, 7
it takes a great deal to produce ennui in an E. ENGLISH, 18
never find an E. among the underdogs ENGLAND, 50
Remember that you are an E. ENGLISH, 34
some other E. despise him CLASS, 43
tale . . . which would have stirred . . . E. ENDURANCE, 17
there are fifty thousand men slain . . . , and not one E. DIPLOMACY, 24
To be an E. CLUBS, 5
to behold the E. at his *best* ENGLISH, 16
You may be the most liberal Liberal E. CLASS, 21
Englishmen E. to be subject to Frenchmen VICTORY, 23
Our fathers were E. TRAVEL, 10
the future E. must take business as seriously as their grandfathers had done BUSINESS, 16
to create Frenchmen in the image of E. NATIONALITY, 6
to see the absurd nature of E. ENGLISH, 33
When two E. meet, their first talk is of the weather ENGLISH, 23
Englishwoman This E. is so refined WOMEN, 109
enigma a riddle wrapped in a mystery inside an e. RUSSIA, 1
enjoy Better to e. and suffer PRAYER, 23
Certainly, there is nothing else here to e. PARTIES, 8
He knew everything about literature except how to e. it LITERATURE, 6
Since God has given us the papacy . . . e. it CATHOLICISM, 9
to e. the interval LIFE, 70
enjoyment I do not eat for the sake of e. FOOD, 34
ennui e. the hypochondriac WORK, 13
Idleness begets e. WORK, 13
it takes a great deal to produce e. in an Englishman ENGLISH, 18
enough It comes soon e. FUTURE, 8
patriotism is not e. LAST WORDS, 14
enrage e. his antagonists . . . own impotence to e. him ANGER, 1
entente *La cordiale e.* DIPLOMACY, 18
enter but the King of England cannot e. DEFIANCE, 4
entered I should never have e. the church on that day MODESTY, 2
entereth he that e. in by the door is the shepherd BIBLICAL QUOTATIONS, 339
enterprises e. that require new clothes THRIFT, 12
entertained Television . . . permits you to be e. in your living room TELEVISION, 7
entertainment what cats most appreciate . . . is . . . e. value CATS, 3
enthusiasm Nothing great was ever achieved without e. ENTHUSIASM, 4
We were as nearly bored as e. would permit CRITICISM, 23
enthusiastic Latins are tenderly e. PLACES, 16
enthusiasts so few e. can be trusted ENTHUSIASM, 3
entities E. should not be multiplied SIMPLICITY, 6
entitled bill of rights is what the people are e. to HUMAN RIGHTS, 4
entrance all men have one e. into life BIBLICAL QUOTATIONS 662
entrances the e. of this world made narrow BIBLICAL QUOTATIONS, 124
envied Better be e. ENVY, 1
There are two things for which animals are . . . e. ANIMALS, 23
environment an e. equally fit for birth, growth work, healing, and dying HEALTHY LIVING, 25
a standing-room-only e. ENVIRONMENT, 10
President Robbins was so well adjusted to his e. ADAPTABILITY, 3
the response of man to his total e. ENVIRONMENT, 6
envy 2 percent moral, 48 percent indignation and 50 percent e. INDIGNATION, 2
e. is a kind of praise ENVY, 6
prisoners of addiction and . . . prisoners of e. MATERIALISM, 14
The dullard's e. of brilliant men GREATNESS, 2
the upbringing a nun would e. BODY, 18
Ephesians great is Diana of the E. BIBLICAL QUOTATIONS, 15
Epicurus one of E.' herd of pigs PRESENT, 7
epidemic they feel snubbed if an e. overlooks them DISEASE, 26
We're all going to go crazy, living this e. every minute DISEASE, 29
epidemics Doctors and undertakers /Fear e. of good health DOCTORS, 18
E. have often been more influential than statesmen DISEASE, 18
epigrams long despotism tempered by e. FRANCE, 2
epilogue good play needs no e. PLAYS, 13
Epipsychidion You understand *E.* best when you are in love LITERATURE, 16
epitaph 'Can't' will be the e. of the British Empire BRITISH EMPIRE, 6
epitaphs a nice derangement of e. MALAPROPISMS, 8
epithet *Bourgeois*, . . . is an e. CLASS, 20
epitome all Mankind's E. HUMAN NATURE, 9
epoch From today . . . there begins a new e. in the history of the world BEGINNING, 9
Epp There's Gert and there's E. and there's Ein ANONYMOUS, 90
Epsom Had we but stick to E. salts ANONYMOUS, 25
Epstein If people . . . a thousand years hence . . . found E.'s statues SCULPTURE, 2
equal All animals are e. EQUALITY, 21
all men are created e. EQUALITY, 16
All shall e. be CLASS, 17
all were created e. by nature SLAVERY, 1
Everybody should have an e. chance EQUALITY, 29
Inferiors revolt . . . that they may be e. REVOLUTION, 1
some animals are more e. than others EQUALITY, 21
That all men are e. is a proposition EQUALITY, 11
When you meet someone better . . . turn your thoughts to becoming his e. SUPERIORITY, 5
equality E. may perhaps be a right, but no . . . fact EQUALITY, 3
E. must yield EQUALITY, 6
e. . . . with our superiors EQUALITY, 5
Freedom! E.! Brotherhood ANONYMOUS, 51
never be e. in the servants' hall CLASS, 6
equally I hate everyone e. HATE, 4
It comes e. to us all DUST, 3
Pale Death kicks his way e. into the cottages of the poor EQUALITY, 31
That all who are happy, are e. happy HAPPINESS, 13
equals the Republic of E. FRENCH REVOLUTION, 1
equanimity an e. bordering on indifference INDIFFERENCE, 3
equilibrium internal e. and a limitation of armaments by political appeasement EUROPE, 10
equipping e. us with a neck BOLDNESS, 3
equitable some greater and more e. system PROPHECY, 12
equivalent musical e. of . . . St Pancras CRITICISM, 5
erect he faced the firing squad; e. and motionless EXECUTION, 38
erection Then we must rate the cost of the e. ARCHITECTURE, 15
ergo *Cogito, e. sum* THINKING, 4
erogenous The mind can also be an e. zone MIND, 34
Eros Unarm, E. REST, 2
erotics e. is a perfectly respectable function of medicine SEX, 10
err The Most may e. as grosly ERROR, 6
those /Who e. each other must respect ERROR, 10
To e. is human IMPERFECTION, 3
To e. is human, to forgive, divine ERROR, 11
errand What thy e. here below ERROR, 7
erred We have e., and strayed from thy ways BOOK OF COMMON PRAYER, THE, 3
error A new maxim is often a brilliant e. ERROR, 9
but for a typographical e., . . . the story of my life HUMAN CONDITION, 18
Ignorance is preferable to e. IGNORANCE, 12
It is time for the destruction of e. ERROR, 1
show a man that he is in an e. ERROR, 8
the e. of his way BIBLICAL QUOTATIONS, 289
errors E., like Straws, upon the surface flow ERROR, 5
few e. they have ever avoided ERROR, 4
I never approved either the e. of his book, or the trivial truths FREEDOM, 60
the e. of those who think they are strong ERROR, 2
The medical e. of one century MISTAKES, 6
Esau E. . . . a hairy man BIBLICAL QUOTATIONS, 215
escape Gluttony is an emotional e. GREED, 8
Let no guilty man e. JUSTICE, 13
escaped e. from a mad and savage master SEX, 98
escaping fortunate in e. regular education WRITERS, 36
esprit English characteristic . . . *e. de corps* ENGLISH, 3
essay an over-ambitious e. by a second-year student CRITICS, 13
essence Desire is the very e. of man DESIRE, 16
The poet gives us his e. POETRY AND PROSE, 6
essential liberty as an e. condition of excellence OXFORD, 9
establishment to refer to your friend's country e. as a 'cottage' WORDS, 24
estate a fourth e. of the realm JOURNALISM, 29
at no time stand so highly in our e. royal GOVERNMENT, 16
e. o' th' world were now undone WORLD-WEARINESS, 11

F

a pillar of f. BIBLICAL QUOTATIONS, 141
Billy . . . /Fell in the f. FIRE, 3
bound /Upon a wheel of f. SUFFERING, 30
cloven tongues like as of f. BIBLICAL QUOTATIONS, 2
F. – without hatred WAR, 130
four men . . . walking in the midst of the f. BIBLICAL QUOTATIONS, 60
French Guard, f. first WAR, 72
heap coals of f. upon his head BIBLICAL QUOTATIONS, 579
heretic that makes the f. MARTYRDOM, 6
how great a matter a little f. kindleth BIBLICAL QUOTATIONS, 285
Ideas that enter the mind under f. INDOCTRINATION, 3
It is with our passions as it is with f. and water PASSION, 5
it is your business, when the wall next door catches f. NEIGHBORS, 4
I warmed both hands before the f. of life LIFE AND DEATH, 21
that deplorable f. near Fish Street in London LONDON, 11
the bush burned with f. BIBLICAL QUOTATIONS, 131
the f. next time PROPHECY, 2
The f. . . . walks in a broader gross FIRE, 2
The f. which in the heart resides HEART, 2
two irons in the f. PRUDENCE, 6
what wind is to f. ABSENCE, 6
firearms Though loaded f. were strictly forbidden at St Trinian's WEAPONS, 8
fire-folk the f. sitting in the air STARS, 2
fireirons Saint Preux never kicked the f. IMPERFECTION, 5
fires Husbands are like f. MARRIAGE, 67
Keep the Home F. Burning HOME, 9
fireside A man may surely be allowed to take a glass of wine by his own f. FIRE, 5
firing he faced the f. squad; erect and motionless EXECUTION, 38
firm not a family; we're a f. ROYALTY, 64
firmness *Commodity, F.,* and *Delight* ARCHITECTURE, 19
first Because of my title, I was the f. COURAGE, 1
British navy always travels f. class NAVY, 6
F. come HASTE, 2
F. impressions FIRST IMPRESSIONS, 1
F. things first PATIENCE, 3
If at f. you don't succeed PERSISTENCE, 5
many that are f. shall be last BIBLICAL QUOTATIONS, 521
The constitution . . . f. and second class citizens CLASS, 55
The f. day a guest HOSPITALITY, 4
the last shall be f. MERIT, 3
there is no last or f. EQUALITY, 7
which came f., the Greeks or the Romans IGNORANCE, 8
Who ever loved, that loved not at f. sight FIRST IMPRESSIONS, 6
first-aid His ideas of f. INCOMPETENCE, 6
firstborn I . . . will smite all the f. BIBLICAL QUOTATIONS, 139
firstfruits first of the f. BIBLICAL QUOTATIONS, 150
first-rate the powers of a f. man and the creed of a second-rate man POLITICIANS, 10
to mistake for the f., the fecund rate WRITERS, 42
fish a great f. to swallow up Jonah BIBLICAL QUOTATIONS, 383
a recently dead f. before it has had time to stiffen APPEARANCE, 42
F. and guests HOSPITALITY, 2
F. die belly-upward and rise . . . their way of falling FISH, 1
F. fuck in it WATER, 3
I have my own f. to fry EATING, 5
No human being, . . . was ever so free as a f. FREEDOM, 53
Phone for the f. knives Norman ETIQUETTE, 1
This man . . . is a poor f. MARRIAGE, 51
What cat's averse to f. MATERIALISM, 12
white wine came up with the f. ETIQUETTE, 4
fishbone The monument sticks like a f. MEMORIALS, 10
fishermen a bite every time for f. HUMOR, 42
fishers f. of men BIBLICAL QUOTATIONS, 471
fishes f. live in the sea EATING, 11
five barley loaves, and two small f. BIBLICAL QUOTATIONS, 330
So are the f. WORLD WAR II, 15
fishing Time is but the stream I go a-f. in TIME, 51
fishmonger She was a f., but sure 'twas no wonder ANONYMOUS, 47
fishy something f. about the French FRANCE, 4
fist You cannot shake hands with a clenched f. INFLEXIBILITY, 2
fit a pleasing f. of melancholy MELANCHOLY, 10
It is not f. that you should sit here DISMISSAL, 4
let the punishment f. the crime PUNISHMENT, 12
news that's f. to print NEWSPAPERS, 10
only the F. survive STRENGTH, 7
fitly no one in the realm . . . f. to come to me ROYALTY, 89
fits periodical f. of morality MORALITY, 10
Strange f. of passion PASSION, 11
fittest Survival of the f. SURVIVAL, 9
five child of f. would understand this SIMPLICITY, 5
F. for the symbol at your door ANONYMOUS, 45
F. gold rings CHRISTMAS, 17
If you don't find a God by f. o'clock this afternoon ATHEISM, 9
practise f. things VIRTUE, 11
The formula 'Two and two make f.' PHILOSOPHY, 3
five-pound get a f. note as . . . a light for a cigarette GENEROSITY, 3
five-year-old real menace in dealing with a f. CHILDREN, 37
fixed Nothing to be f. except your performance ACTING, 6
flabbiness The moral f. born of . . . Success SUCCESS, 10
flag But spare your country's f. PATRIOTISM, 43
futile exhibition, this singing of the Red F. WAR AND PEACE, 18
keep the red f. flying here SOCIALISM, 6
Tonight the American f. floats from yonder hill WAR, 154
flagons stay me with f. BIBLICAL QUOTATIONS, 623
flame like a moth, the simple maid /Still plays about the f. WOMEN, 51
flames Commit it then to the f. ILLUSIONS, 3
Superstition sets the whole world in f. SUPERSTITION, 12
Flanders In F. fields MEMORIALS, 11
You have sent me a F. mare FIRST IMPRESSIONS, 4
flash the f. cut him, and he lies in the stubble ANONYMOUS, 27
flashing His f. eyes, his floating hair CAUTION, 9
flat Very f., Norfolk ENGLAND, 16
Vile snub-nose, f.-nosed ass APPEARANCE, 49
flatter not f. me REALISM, 1
We f. those we scarcely know HURT, 4
flattered He that loves to be f. is worthy o' the flatterer FLATTERY, 9
flatterer the brave beast is no f. HORSES, 7
flatterers f. live at the expense of those who listen FLATTERY, 6
Self-love . . . greatest of all f. CONCEIT, 15
flattering It is f. some men to endure them TOLERANCE, 5
the talent of f. with delicacy FLATTERY, 2
flattery consider whether . . . your f. is worth his having FLATTERY, 5
F. is all right FLATTERY, 10
f.'s the food of fools FLATTERY, 11
Imitation is the sincerest form of f. IMITATION, 2
ne'er /Was f. lost POETS, 30
woman . . . to be gained by . . . f. FLATTERY, 4
flaunt if you've got it, f. it OSTENTATION, 1
flautists f. . . . know something we don't know MUSICIANS, 2
flea English literature's performing f. WRITERS, 39
man's whole frame is obvious to a f. CLARITY, 3
The guerrilla fights the war of the f. WAR, 158
the point of precedency between a louse and a f. INSULTS, 73
fleas dog that praised his f. PARASITES, 4
F. . . . upon the body of a giant PERSPECTIVE, 3
the f. in my bed were as good COMPLIMENTS, 8
The f. that tease in the high Pyrenees NONSENSE, 3
these have smaller f. to bite 'em PARASITES, 3
fled I f. Him, down the nights RELIGION, 68
fleet The F.'s lit up. It is like fairyland NAVY, 11
Fleming had F. not possessed immense knowledge and an unremitting gift of observation SCIENTISTS, 7
flesh all f. is as grass BIBLICAL QUOTATIONS, 560
a thorn in the f. BIBLICAL QUOTATIONS, 55
f. and blood so cheap BREAD, 5
f. to feel the chain IMPRISONMENT, 3
Heat, madam! . . . to take off my f. and sit in my bones WEATHER, 29
I, born of f. and ghost DEATH, 165
I have more f. than another man OBESITY, 15
Ishmaelites . . . will not publicly eat human f. uncooked in Lent CANNIBALISM, 3
I wants to make your f. creep FEAR, 11
Leave the f. to the fate it was fit for FATE, 5
more f. than another man, and therefore more frailty WEAKNESS, 6
Rehearsing a play is making the word f. PLAYS, 12
that which is born of the f. is f. BIBLICAL QUOTATIONS, 322
the f. is weak BIBLICAL QUOTATIONS, 543
the f. lusteth against the Spirit BIBLICAL QUOTATIONS, 171
the lust of the f. BIBLICAL QUOTATIONS, 377
the way of all f. DEATH, 51
the way of all f. . . . towards the kitchen FOOD, 71
the word was made f. BIBLICAL QUOTATIONS, 316
the world, the f., and the devil JOURNALISM, 33
we do not war after the f. BIBLICAL QUOTATIONS, 53
world, the f., and the devil BOOK OF COMMON PRAYER, THE, 8
fleshly The F. School of Poetry POETS, 8
flies As f. to wanton boys DESTINY, 22
certain, that Life f. LIFE, 35
dead f. cause the ointment . . . to send forth a stinking savour BIBLICAL QUOTATIONS, 92
Time f., death urges TIME, 57
flight Above the vulgar f. of common souls SUPERIORITY, 11
fling I'll have a f. FREEDOM, 3
flirt f. with their own husbands LOVE AND MARRIAGE, 7
float rather be an opportunist and f. EXPEDIENCY, 6
flock he shall feed his f. BIBLICAL QUOTATIONS, 271
keeping watch over their f. by night BIBLICAL QUOTATIONS, 419
flogging There is now less f. in our great schools EDUCATION, 48
flood the f. was forty days upon the earth BIBLICAL QUOTATIONS, 197
Which, taken at the f. OPPORTUNITY, 18
floor stood ninety years on the f. CLOCKS, 3
flop You write a hit the same way you write a f. SUCCESS, 14
flowed water f. like champagne ABSTINENCE, 4
flower A lovelier f. / . . . was never sown DEATH, 178
I have always plucked a thistle and planted a f. REPUTATION, 5
just miss the prizes at the f. show MEDIOCRITY, 2
many a f. is born to blush unseen WASTE, 2
The F. that once has blown LIFE, 35
the meanest f. . . . can give /Thoughts NATURE, 38
flowers a book that is a book f. once BOOKS, 25
Do spring May f. MONTHS, 12
Gather the f., but spare the buds FLOWERS, 9
Letting a hundred f. blossom FREEDOM, 38
No fruits, no f., no leaves, no birds MONTHS, 10
Say it with f. FLOWERS, 11
The f. that bloom in the spring APPEARANCE, 22
Their f. the tenderness of patient minds WAR, 117
Too late for fruit, too soon for f. ILLNESS, 21
When people come together, f. always flourish NEW YORK, 3
Where have all the f. gone LOSS, 5
flowery A little thin, f. border GARDENS, 9
flown I see all the birds are f. HOUSES OF PARLIAMENT, 7
flows Everything f. and nothing stays CHANGE, 10
flung he f. himself from the room NONSENSE, 16
fly A f., Sir, may sting a stately horse CRITICS, 9
Do not remove a f. . . . with a hatchet FORCE, 1
f. . . . said, what a dust do I raise CONCEIT, 3
said a spider to a f. INVITATIONS, 3
small gilded f. /Does lecher ANIMALISM, 7
Who saw him die? /I, said the F. NURSERY RHYMES, 68
flying Days and moments quickly f. DEATH, 46
There is no f. without wings NARCOTICS, 1
foam the f. /Of perilous seas BIRDS, 9
the white f. flew EXPLORATION, 1
foe Heat not a furnace for your f. EXCESS, 13

G

The chairs are being brought in from the g. ERROR, 1
the g. of Eden BIBLICAL QUOTATIONS, 182
There are fairies at the bottom of our g. FAIRIES, 4
gardener Every time I talk to . . . my g., I'm convinced of the opposite HAPPINESS, 21
Nor does a . . . g. scent his roses POETS, 11
Oh, Adam was a g. GARDENS, 8
supposing him to be the g. BIBLICAL QUOTATIONS, 369
gardens a fountain of g. BIBLICAL QUOTATIONS, 630
closing time in the g. of the West CAPITALISM, 4
garland wither'd is the g. of the war MOURNING, 9
garlands gather g. there COUNTRYSIDE, 10
Garter I like the G. TITLES, 5
gas If silicon had been a g. I should have been a major-general EXAMINATIONS, 3
gaslight Fanny by G. BOOK TITLES, 23
gas-masks digging trenches and trying on g. WORLD WAR II, 5
gate I am here at the g. alone INVITATIONS, 5
I said to the man who stood at the g. of the year FAITH, 15
matters not how strait the g. FATE, 10
the g. of heaven BIBLICAL QUOTATIONS, 217
gatekeeper After I die, I shall return to earth as a g. of a bordello THREATS, 10
gates Battering the g. of heaven EXCESS, 15
the g. of the day HEART, 23
the iron g. of life LOVE, 101
the twelve g. were twelve pearls BIBLICAL QUOTATIONS, 603
thou leadest to the g. of hell BIBLICAL QUOTATIONS, 665
gateway 'Sex,' . . . 'is the g. to life.' SEX, 13
gather G. the flowers . . . FLOWERS, 9
G. ye rosebuds while ye may PRESENT, 6
If thou may not continually g. thyself together PRAYER, 22
gathered where two or three are g. together BIBLICAL QUOTATIONS, 516
gatling The g.'s jammed and the colonel dead WAR, 112
gaudy round, neat, not g. GARDENS, 9
Gaul G. is divided into three FRANCE, 1
Gaulle I, General de G., now in London WORLD WAR II, 26
Gaullist I . . . have become a G. . . . little by little POLITICS, 43
gave God . . . g. his only begotten Son BIBLICAL QUOTATIONS, 324
the Lord g., and the Lord hath taken away BIBLICAL QUOTATIONS, 296
gay g. without frivolity FUTURE, 2
I love the g. Eastertide PLEASURE, 19
Gaza Eyeless in G. BLINDNESS, 7
gazelle never nurs'd a dear g. ANIMALS, 17
general caviare to the g. TASTE, 7
In a civil war, a g. must know WAR, 126
was good for G. Motors BUSINESS, 30
generalizations All g. are dangerous GENERALIZATIONS, 2
Physicians are inclined to engage in hasty g. THEORY, 13
generalize To g. is to be an idiot GENERALIZATIONS, 1
generals at the age of four with paper hats and wooden swords we're all G. AUTHORITARIANISM, 9
Dead battles, like dead g. GENERALS, 4
It is not the business of g. to shoot one another GENERALS, 6
that's not against the law for g. GENERALS, 3
to be left to the g. GENERALS, 1
wish he would *bite* . . . my g. GENERALS, 2
generation a g. that don't spend THRIFT, 11
Each g. imagines itself . . . more intelligent AGE, 55
he suffered . . . the neurotic ills of an entire g. NEUROSIS, 4
to continue the g. of the species by fashioning them of clay SEX, 62
You are a lost g. GENERATIONS, 3
generations all g. shall call me blessed BIBLICAL QUOTATIONS, 413
g. . . . have struggled in poverty to build these altars RELIGION, 63
g. . . . pass in a short time GENERATIONS, 1
No hungry g. tread thee down BIRDS, 9
generosity The poor . . . their function . . . is to exercise our g. POVERTY, 32
generous a loyal, a gallant, a g., an ingenious, and good-temper'd people FRANCE, 17
genetics biologists studied g. and natural selection EVOLUTION, 16
genius a country full of g., but with absolutely no talent IRELAND, 13
A g.! For thirty-seven years I've practiced . . . and now they call me a g. GENIUS, 8
a German and a g. COMPOSERS, 10
G. . . . capacity of taking trouble GENIUS, 2
G. does what it must TALENT AND GENIUS, 3
G. is an infinite capacity GENIUS, 1
g. is not transmitted TALENT, 10
G. is one per cent inspiration GENIUS, 4
I invoke the g. of the Constitution UNITED STATES, 48
Milton, Madam, was a g. POETS, 25
Nothing, except my g. CONCEIT, 25
Only an organizing g. INCOMPETENCE, 1
Rules and models destroy g. and art RULES, 3
Since when was g. . . . respectable RESPECTABILITY, 1
talent instantly recognizes g. MEDIOCRITY, 3
Taste is the feminine of g. TASTE, 3
the difference between talent and g. TALENT AND GENIUS, 1
there is too much g., not enough talent WRITERS, 45
true g. is a mind of large general powers GENIUS, 7
True g. walks along a line GENIUS, 5
Unless one is a g. COMMUNICATION, 2
When a true g. appears GENIUS, 9
gent what a man is to a g. INTELLIGENCE, 3
gentil parfit, g. knyght CHIVALRY, 4
Gentiles a light to lighten the G. BIBLICAL QUOTATIONS, 422
gentleman A g. need not know Latin EDUCATION, 57
a g. . . . never inflicts pain CHIVALRY, 8
A g. . . . wouldn't hit a woman with his hat on CHIVALRY, 1
Every other inch a g. INSULTS, 127
g. of leisure MATERIALISM, 25
g. . . . robbing the poor CLASS, 41
God is a g. GOD, 46
Not a g.; dresses too well CLOTHES, 18
The Devil is a g. DEVIL, 15
the English country g. galloping after a fox HEALTH, 26
the g. is an *attorney* INSULTS, 71
Who was then the g. CLASS, 5
gentlemanly secondly, g. conduct EDUCATION, 8
gentlemen by g. for g. NEWSPAPERS, 13
extremely difficult to behave like g. WOMEN, 70
g., let us do something today WAR, 47
G. . . . remember blondes APPEARANCE, 34
God rest you merry, g. ANONYMOUS, 21
Good-morning, g. both INSULTS, 45
one of Nature's G. CHIVALRY, 7
religion for g. RELIGION, 18
Scholars and g. HONOR, 10
the British bourgeoisie have spoken of themselves as g. CLASS, 49
There were g. and . . . seamen in the navy of Charles the Second NAVY, 8
the seamen were not g. NAVY, 8
gentlewoman a g. made ready WOMEN, 111
gravest sins it was possible for a g. to commit READING, 20
genuinely g. bogus APPEARANCES, 19
genuineness G. only thrives in the dark DARKNESS, 12
geographical India is a g. term PLACES, 12
geography G. is about Maps BIOGRAPHY, 1
geometrical Population, . . . increases in a g. ratio ECONOMICS, 17
geometricians we are g. only by chance PHILOSOPHY, 5
geometry G. is not true MATHEMATICS, 14
Poetry is as exact a science as g. POETRY, 19
There is no 'royal road' to g. MATHEMATICS, 7
George *Death of King G. V* HUNTING, 2
G., be a King ROYALTY, 21
G. III was a kind of 'consecrated obstruction' ROYALTY, 23
G. the First knew nothing ROYALTY, 70
G. the Third . . . . . . *may profit by their example* CAESAR, 3
King G. will be able to read that SIGNATURES, 2
Lloyd G. POWER, 6
Georgia marching through G. GLORY, 7
Georgie G. Porgie, pudding and pie NURSERY RHYMES, 12
German a G. and a genius COMPOSERS, 10
I speak . . . G. to my horse LANGUAGE, 11
Life is too short to learn G. LANGUAGE, 33
The G. army was stabbed in the back DEFEAT, 7
The G. Empire has become a world empire GERMANY, 7
the G. text of French operas OPERA, 13
Germans Don't let's be beastly to the G. GERMANY, 2
How . . . thorough these G. always managed to be GERMANY, 5
Man, . . . had been created to jab the life out of G. WAR, 136
The G., . . . are going to be squeezed, as a lemon RETRIBUTION, 10
to the G. that of the air EMPIRE, 5
Germany Defeat of G. means WORLD WAR II, 44
G. calling TREASON, 8
G., G. before all else GERMANY, 3
G. was the cause of Hitler LAST WORDS, 94
G. will be . . . a world power GERMANY, 4
If we see that G. is winning WORLD WAR II, 48
In G., the Nazis came for the Communists NAZISM, 6
Nazi G. had become a menace to all mankind NAZISM, 5
Gert G.'s poems are bunk ANONYMOUS, 90
There's G. and there's Epp and there's Ein ANONYMOUS, 90
gesture g. by the individual to himself BUSINESS, 11
get a round of G. the Guests PARTIES, 1
I thought it was a pity to g. up BED, 9
getting a secret way . . . of g. at a boy EVIL, 10
G. and spending WASTE, 3
ghost I, born of flesh and g. DEATH, 165
oh that I had given up the g. BIBLICAL QUOTATIONS, 300
the G. in the Machine MIND, 29
The Papacy is not other than the G. of the deceased Roman Empire CATHOLICISM, 6
There is a g. /That eats handkerchiefs LOSS, 4
yielded up the g. BIBLICAL QUOTATIONS, 549
ghoulies From g. and ghosties and long-leggety beasties ANONYMOUS, 19
giant Fleas . . . upon the body of a g. PERSPECTIVE, 3
owner whereof was G. Despair DESPAIR, 4
we have only awakened a sleeping g. WORLD WAR II, 50
giants A battle of g. WAR, 168
G. three, Dodgers nothing BASEBALL, 5
it is by standing on the shoulders of g. PROGRESS, 17
not g. but windmills DELUSION, 2
there were g. in the earth BIBLICAL QUOTATIONS, 195
war of the g. is over WORLD WAR II, 23
gibes a great master of g. POLITICIANS, 41
Gideon Why do they put the G. Bibles SEX, 73
gift Never look a g. horse INGRATITUDE, 1
The g. of broadcasting MEDIA, 8
the timeliness of the g. PROMPTNESS, 1
True love's the g. which God has given /To man alone LOVE, 128
worth more than the g. GIFTS, 4
gifts deserves the name of happy who knows how to use the gods' g. wisely DISHONOR, 1
God's g. put man's best g. GOD, 19
I fear the Greeks even when they bring g. MISTRUST, 12
The Gods themselves cannot recall their g. IRREVOCABILITY, 3
gild To g. refined gold EXCESS, 12
gilded A best-seller is the g. tomb of a mediocre talent BOOKS, 43
She's only a bird in a g. cage BIRDS, 10
gin G. was mother's milk ALCOHOL, 73
No man is genuinely happy, married, who has to drink worse g. ALCOHOL, 57
Of all the g. joints in all the towns in all the world CHANCE, 3
she was dead; but my father he kept ladling g. REMEDIES, 51
The shortest way out of Manchester is . . . g. DRINKS, 6
giraffes No but I adore g. SOLDIERS, 9

if triangles invented a g., they would make him three-sided RELIGION, 58
If you don't find a G. by five o'clock this afternoon ATHEISM, 9
If you talk to G., you are praying MADNESS, 40
I know I am G. GOD, 6
I'll die young, but it's like kissing G. ADDICTION, 3
I neglect G. and his angels RELIGION, 25
In the Nineteenth Century men lost their fear of G. FEAR, 1
Isn't G. a shit BIBLE, 4
It takes a long while for a . . . trustful person to reconcile himself to . . . G. FAITH, 22
I wouldn't give up writing about G. WRITERS, 57
I wretch lay wrestling with . . . my G. SOUL, 11
justify the ways of G. to men DARKNESS, 15
Just what G. would have done if he had the money WEALTH, 43
Kill everyone, and you are a g. KILLING, 9
Know then thyself, presume not G. to scan SELF-KNOWLEDGE, 7
Live among men as if G. beheld you RIGHTEOUSNESS, 10
Man . . . is halfway between an ape and a g. MANKIND, 32
Many people believe that they are attracted by G. PEOPLE, 5
May G. deny you peace GLORY, 3
nature is the art of G. NATURE, 2
Nearer, my G., to thee RELIGION, 1
none deny there is a G. ATHEISM, 3
One does not insult the river g. PRUDENCE, 5
One G., one law, one element DESTINY, 27
One on G.'s side is a majority GOD, 47
only G. can make a tree TREES, 10
Our G., our help in ages past RELIGION, 75
poems . . . for the love of Man and in praise of G. POETRY, 60
proof that G. is a bore PROTESTANTISM, 6
prose for G. LANGUAGE, 21
put your hand into the hand of G. FAITH, 15
Sickness, sin and death . . . do not originate in G. RELIGION, 29
Since G. has given us the papacy . . . enjoy it CATHOLICISM, 9
speak to G. as if men were listening RIGHTEOUSNESS, 10
that G. is interested only . . . in religion GOD, 55
that great Leviathan, or rather . . . that *Mortal G.* STATE, 1
The Act of G. designation ACCIDENTS, 2
the dear G. who loveth us PRAYER, 12
the electric display of G. the Father LIFE, 64
the highest praise of G. consists in the denial of Him ATHEISM, 12
the nearer you are to G. PROTESTANTISM, 8
The noblest work of G.? Man MANKIND, 66
the one G. whose worshippers . . . still trust in Him GAMBLING, 1
There, but for the Grace of G., goes G. ARROGANCE, 5
There once was a man who said 'G. EXISTENCE, 4
The true G., . . . God of ideas INSPIRATION, 9
Those who marry G. . . . can become domesticated too RELIGION, 39
to the unknown g. BIBLICAL QUOTATIONS, 12
To understand G.'s thoughts STATISTICS, 8
we come /From G., who is our home METAPHYSICS, 6
we owe G. a death DEATH, 137
What G. does, He does well GOD, 38
When I composed that, I was . . . inspired by G. MUSIC, 8
when one has loved a man it is very different to love G. LOVE, 126
Which is, I gather, what G. did PSYCHOLOGY, 13
Whom G. wishes to destroy MADNESS, 1
yearning like a G. in pain SUFFERING, 18
you hardly ever mention G. any more RELIGION, 55
you must believe in G. FAITH, 18
goddamm Lhude sing G. WINTER, 4
godlike patient endurance is g. ENDURANCE, 9
gods by force of the g. ENDURANCE, 27
deserves the name of happy who knows how to use the g.' gifts wisely DISHONOR, 1
for what high cause /This darling of the G. DESTINY, 16
G. help them SELF-RELIANCE, 2
Kings are earth's g. ROYALTY, 97
leave the rest to the G. DUTY, 2
Live with the g. CONTENTMENT, 1
man's ignorance of the g. SPONTANEITY, 1
no other g. before me BIBLICAL QUOTATIONS, 147
So many g., so many creeds KINDNESS, 12
The Ethiopians say that their g. are . . . black RELIGION, 84
The G. themselves cannot recall their gifts IRREVOCABILITY, 3
we're forbidden to know – what end the g. have in store DESTINY, 15
Whom the g. love DEATH, 109
Whom the g. wish to destroy TALENT, 2
goe to morowe longe I to g. to God EXECUTION, 24
Gog G. and Magog BIBLICAL QUOTATIONS, 599
going I am just g. outside LAST WORDS, 61
Men must endure /Their g. hence ENDURANCE, 20
Stand not upon the order of your g. DISMISSAL, 9
gold A g. rush is what happens when MATERIALISM, 28
all the g. that the goose could give MATERIALISM, 2
An angel writing in a book of g. DREAMS, 8
cursed /craving for g. MATERIALISM, 26
For g. in phisik is a cordial MATERIALISM, 8
gild refined g. EXCESS 12
Good morning to the day: and next my g. MATERIALISM, 16
I have seen many a man turn his g. into smoke SMOKING, 12
I stuffed their mouths with g. BRIBERY, 2
Nor all that glisters g. TEMPTATION, 11
silver and g. have I none BIBLICAL QUOTATIONS, 4
Silver threads among the g. OLD AGE, 77
The ring so worn . . . is yet of g. APPEARANCE, 16
the sick man hands you g. in return REMEDIES, 9
To a shower of g. BRIBERY, 3
travell'd in the realms of g. TRAVEL, 22
Were't not for g. and women SIN, 27
What female heart can g. despise MATERIALISM, 12
When every . . . thing you hold /Is made of silver, or of g. ECONOMICS, 10
You have g. and I want g. TAXATION, 9
golden G. slumbers kiss your eyes SLEEP, 10
In good King Charles's g. days ANONYMOUS, 48
In old time we had treen chalices and g. priests CLERGY, 8
Jerusalem the g. PLACES, 28
perhaps, the g. rule ABSTINENCE, 9
The g. apples of the sun DESIRE, 17
the G. Road to Samarkand KNOWLEDGE, 15
there are no g. rules RULES, 5
Goldwyn knew where you were with G. GOLDWYNISMS, 1
Mr G. . . . you are only interested in art ART, 27
golf an earnest protest against g. CRICKET, 1
G. . . . a form of moral effort GOLF, 3
G. is a good walk spoiled GOLF, 5
more satisfying to be a bad player at g. GOLF, 2
G.O.M The G.., when his life ebbs out POLITICIANS, 1
Gomorrah Sodom and . . . G. BIBLICAL QUOTATIONS, 210
gone g. with the wind BOOK TITLES, 19
gongs women should be struck . . . like g. WOMEN, 33
good a gigantic reservoir of g. will UNITED STATES, 65
A g. man fallen among Fabians WRITERS, 32
A g. novel tells us the truth NOVELS, 2
A G. Time Was Had by All PLEASURE, 33
All g. writing WRITING, 12
Anybody can be g. in the country COUNTRYSIDE, 13
as gods, knowing g. and evil BIBLICAL QUOTATIONS, 186
Be g., sweet maid, and let who can be clever CLEVERNESS, 3
being really g. all the time HYPOCRISY, 22
dedicate this nation to the policy of the g. neighbor CHARITY, 19
Do g. by stealth GOOD, 14
doing g. . . . professions which are full CHARITY, 26
doing g. to base fellows CHARITY, 12
dull prospect of a distant g. PLEASURE, 12
every creature of God is g. BIBLICAL QUOTATIONS, 648
Every g. servant does not all commands OBEDIENCE, 5
every man at the beginning doth set forth g. wine ALCOHOL, 17
Every man loves what he is g. at ENTHUSIASM, 7
Evil, be thou my G. EVIL, 15
Evil comes . . . like the disease; g. . . . like the doctor DISEASE, 15
Far too g. to waste on children YOUTH, 28
General G. is the plea of the scoundrel GOOD, 2
God saw that it was g. BIBLICAL QUOTATIONS, 176
G., but not religious-good VIRTUE, 12
G. girls go to heaven VIRTUE AND VICE, 1
g. in everything GOOD, 15
G. isn't the word CRITICISM, 22
g. shepherd giveth his life for the sheep BIBLICAL QUOTATIONS, 341
G. things, when short, are twice as good BREVITY, 2
g. tidings of great joy BIBLICAL QUOTATIONS, 419
good wine is a g. familiar creature if it be well used ALCOHOL, 70
greatest g. GOOD, 3
happiness makes them g. GOOD, 9
He who would do g. to another GOOD, 2
hold fast that which is g. BIBLICAL QUOTATIONS, 644
how *can* they become g. people PREJUDICE, 14
how can ye, being evil, speak g. BIBLICAL QUOTATIONS, 504
How g. is man's life, the mere living LIFE, 17
If . . . 'feeling g.' could decide, drunkenness would be DRUNKENNESS, 18
If to do were as easy as to know what were g. ACTION, 13
If you can't be g. PROVERBS, 217
I have fought a g. fight BIBLICAL QUOTATIONS, 656
it cannot come to g. PESSIMISM, 14
It is g. to know what a man is UNDERSTANDING, 2
It is seldom . . . one parts on g. terms PARTING, 9
little of what you fancy does you g. PLEASURE, 21
Men have never been g. GOOD, 1
never was a g. war WAR AND PEACE, 8
no hint throughout the universe /Of g. or ill NECESSITY, 11
Nothing can harm a g. man GOOD, 17
nothing either g. or bad THINKING, 15
nothing g. to be had in the country COUNTRYSIDE, 5
on earth peace, g. will toward men BIBLICAL QUOTATIONS, 420
One man is as g. as another WRITERS, 29
Only g. girls keep diaries DIARIES, 2
our people have never had it so g. WEALTH, 29
Roman Conquest . . . a G. Thing HISTORY, 35
science is . . . neither a potential for g. nor for evil SCIENCE, 79
strong antipathy of g. to bad PROVOCATION, 2
suppose the people g. CORRUPTION, 10
The g. die early GOOD AND EVIL, 4
The g. die first GOOD AND EVIL, 9
The g. die young DEATH, 13
The g. is oft interred with their bones EVIL, 19
The g. is the beautiful GOOD, 13
the g. must associate UNITY, 7
The g. of the people LAW, 9
The 'g. old times NOSTALGIA, 5
The king has been very g. to me MARTYRDOM, 1
the name of perseverance in a g. cause STUBBORNNESS, 4
The only g. Indians I ever saw were dead ENEMIES, 8
There is so much g. in the worst of us ANONYMOUS, 89
the thing which is g. BIBLICAL QUOTATIONS, 117
those who go about doing g. CHARITY, 14
thou g. and faithful servant BIBLICAL QUOTATIONS, 534
three ingredients in the g. life LIFE, 60
to write g. prose is an affair of g. manners POETRY AND PROSE, 4
'Well done thou g. and faithful servant' ANONYMOUS, 70
we looked for peace, but no g. came BIBLICAL QUOTATIONS, 291
what g. came of it at last VICTORY, 22
What's the g. of a home ABSENCE, 7
Whenever two g. people argue over principles PRINCIPLES, 4
When I'm g. I'm very g. SEX, 110
when the great and g. depart MORTALITY, 20
Why care for grammar as long as we are g. GRAMMAR, 9
You shouldn't say it is not g. GOOD, 19

How very small the very g. FATE, 17
If I am a g. man GREATNESS, 9
many of the g. men of history are frauds GREATNESS, 9
No g. man lives in vain GREATNESS, 6
On earth there is nothing g. but man MANKIND, 30
Some are born g. GREATNESS, 12
the g. break through LAW, 34
The g. man . . . walks across his century INFLUENCE, 7
the g. ones eat up the little ones EATING, 11
the shade /Of that which once was g. REGRET, 28
those who were truly g. HEROISM, 9
To be g. is to be misunderstood GREATNESS, 7
when the g. and good depart MORTALITY, 20
you, . . . who have made me too g. for my house REPARTEE, 3
great-aunt A person may be indebted for a nose or an eye, . . . to a g. FAMILY, 25
Great Britain G. could say that she supported both sides DIPLOMACY, 20
G. has lost an Empire BRITAIN, 1
To make a union with G. WORLD WAR II, 41
greater g. love hath no man BIBLICAL QUOTATIONS, 351
The g. the power POWER, 8
Thy need is yet g. than mine SELF-DENIAL, 2
greatest great city . . . has the g. men and women GREATNESS, 15
I'm the g. CONCEIT, 1
the g. deeds require a certain insensitiveness INSENSITIVITY, 4
The g. happiness of the g. number HAPPINESS, 3
the g. of these is charity BIBLICAL QUOTATIONS, 44
great-grandfathers Classicism, . . . the literature that gave . . . pleasure to their g. LITERATURE, 22
greatness dignity and g. and peace again DRINKS, 9
get out with my g. intact SELF-PRESERVATION, 2
long farewell to all my g. HUMAN CONDITION, 23
Men who have g. . . . don't go in for politics PRIME MINISTERS, 9
some have g. thrust upon 'em GREATNESS, 12
Greece Athens holds sway over all G. INFLUENCE, 11
greedy be not g. to add money to money BIBLICAL QUOTATIONS, 658
Greek I . . . impress upon you the study of G. literature CLASSICS, 4
it was G. to me CONFUSION, 11
neither Jew nor G. BIBLICAL QUOTATIONS, 169
Nobody can say a word against G. CLASSICS, 9
prefers to describe in G. what he can't LANGUAGE, 4
small Latin and less G. CLASSICS, 6
the intrigue of a G. of the lower empire INSULTS, 42
The word is half G. and half Latin LATIN, 5
We were taught . . . Latin and G. CLASSICS, 10
Greeks G. Had a Word LANGUAGE, 1
G. seek after wisdom BIBLICAL QUOTATIONS, 27
I fear the G. even when they bring gifts MISTRUST, 12
The Romans and G. found everything human ANTHROPOMORPHISM, 1
To the G. the Muse gave native wit CLASSICS, 5
uncertainty: a state unknown to the G. UNCERTAINTY, 2
where the G. had modesty, we have cant CANT, 1
which came first, the G. or the Romans IGNORANCE, 8
green a g. thought in a g. shade OBLIVION, 3
Anything g. that grew out of the mould NATURE, 25
for the wearin' o' the G. ANONYMOUS, 46
G. grow the rashes O LOVE, 38
I was g. in judgment YOUTH, 25
religious system that produced g. Chartreuse ALCOHOL, 66
There is a g. hill far away CHRISTIANITY, 1
Time held me g. and dying TIME, 50
tree of life is g. REALITY, 4
When the g. woods laugh HAPPINESS, 5
green-ey'd jealousy . . . g. monster JEALOUSY, 8
Greenland From G.'s icy mountains PLACES, 18
green-rob'd g. senators of mighty woods TREES, 8
Greensleeves G. was all my joy ANONYMOUS, 22
greenwood Under the g. tree COUNTRYSIDE, 12
greeting the sort of g. a corpse would give to an undertaker GREETINGS, 2
greetings g. where no kindness is OPTIMISM, 40
perhaps the g. are intended for me POPULARITY, 1
grenadier With a tow, . . . row for the British G. ANONYMOUS, 73
grew Three years she g. DEATH, 178
grief calms one's g. by recounting it GRIEF, 3
G. and disappointment give rise to anger EMOTION, 3
G. has turned her fair APPEARANCE, 65
in much wisdom is much g. BIBLICAL QUOTATIONS, 78
it is g. that develops the powers of the mind MIND, 27
Should be past g. GRIEF, 5
The heart which g. hath cankered ALCOHOL, 24
griefs But not my g.; still am I king of those DECLINE, 12
grievances redress of the g. of the vanquished WAR, 42
grieve G. not that I die young DEATH, 76
Men are we, and must g. REGRET, 28
grill be careful not to look like a mixed g. APPEARANCE, 15
grimace the only pianist . . . who did not g. MUSICIANS, 9
grin All Nature wears one universal g. NATURE, 12
ending with the g., which remained some time SUPERNATURAL, 5
grind g. the faces of the poor BIBLICAL QUOTATIONS, 249
mills of God g. slowly GOD, 40
yet they g. exceeding small GOD, 40
grinders Writers, like teeth, are divided into incisors and g. WRITERS, 2
grip took a g. on cowardly Marxism NAZISM, 3
grist All's g. that comes to the mill OPPORTUNITY, 1
groan men sit and hear each other g. HUMAN CONDITION, 14
groans How alike are the g. of love to those of the dying LOVE AND DEATH, 4
Gromyko the G. of the Labour party POLITICIANS, 58
grooves specialists . . . tend to think in g. EXPERTS, 8
grope they g. in the dark BIBLICAL QUOTATIONS, 302
gross reconciling my g. habits with my net income DEBAUCHERY, 6
Groucho had Marx been G. instead of Karl HUMOR, 10
No, G. is not my real name NAMES, 9
ground he spills his seed on the g. BIRDS, 15
group A g. of closely related persons FAMILY, 33
grovelled Whenever he met a great man he g. SERVILITY, 7
groves And seek for truth in the g. of Academe EDUCATION, 40
grow Green g. the rashes O LOVE, 38
make two ears of corn . . . g. . . . where only one grew before POLITICIANS, 106
make two questions g. where only one RESEARCH, 26
some of us never g. out AUTHORITARIANISM, 9
They shall g. not old MEMORIALS, 6
grow'd 'I 'spect I g..' CREATION, 14
groweth no grass there g., /Only their engines' dung ENGLAND, 7
growing G. old is like being increasingly penalized OLD AGE, 75
growl I hate a fellow . . . who does nothing . . . but sit and *g.* PETULANCE, 4
grown Boys . . . are unwholesome companions for g. people CHILDREN, 40
one of the few English novels for g. up people CRITICISM, 67
grown-ups g. . . . have forgotten what it is like to be a child CHILDREN, 34
grows Nothing g. well in the shade GREATNESS, 5
growth an environment equally fit for birth, g. work, healing, and dying HEALTHY LIVING, 25
as short a Spring; /As quick a g. to meet decay TRANSIENCE, 15
elations and apprehensions of g. AGE, 48
G. is a greater mystery than death AGE, 48
grub it is poor g., poor pay, and easy work ENGLAND, 30
grudge feed fat the ancient g. I bear him BUSINESS, 21
grumbler I have always been a g. COMPLAINTS, 10
grumbling the muttering grew to a g. ANIMALS, 8
gruntled far from feeling g. DISCONTENT, 9
he was far from being g. HUMOR, 60
guarantee No one can g. success in war WAR, 44
guard That g. our native seas NAVY, 3
guardian As g. of His Majesty's conscience MONARCHY, 25
when health is restored, he is a g. DOCTORS, 11
guards Up, G., and at 'em WAR, 169
Who is to guard the g. themselves MISTRUST, 7
gudeman Robin Gray, he was g. to me MARRIAGE, 19
guerre *ce n'est pas la g.* WAR, 24
une drôle de g. WAR, 49
guerrilla The g. fights the war of the flea WAR, 158
The g. wins if he does not lose WAR, 87
guest A free-loader is a confirmed g. PARASITES, 2
Earth, receive an honoured g. POETS, 5
The g. who outstays HOSPITALITY, 3
guests a round of Get the G. PARTIES, 1
the g. must be chosen as carefully as the wine ALCOHOL, 67
guide Custom, then, is the great g. of human life CUSTOM, 2
Everyman, I will go with thee, and be thy g. ANONYMOUS, 17
I have only a faint light to g. me ATHEISM, 6
guiding little onward lend thy g. hand GUIDANCE, 3
guillotine There is only one cure for grey hair. . . . the g. REMEDIES, 60
guilt fills his mind with the blackest horrors of g. HYPOCHONDRIA, 8
Let other pens dwell on g. and misery OPTIMISM, 14
Life without industry is g. ART, 25
put on a dress of g. GUILT, 8
guiltless Whose g. heart is free RIGHTEOUSNESS, 6
guilty g. of Noël Cowardice COWARDICE, 1
I declare myself g. GUILT, 6
It is quite gratifying to feel g. GUILT, 1
Let no g. man escape JUSTICE, 13
Suspicion always haunts the g. mind GUILT, 13
ten g. persons escape than one innocent suffer JUSTICE, 4
tremble like a g. thing surprised DOUBT, 9
guinea a round disc of fire somewhat like a g. PERCEPTION, 3
I would not give half a g. to live under one form of government GOVERNMENT, 18
there go two-and-forty sixpences . . . to one g. MERIT, 4
guinea pig consider it something monstrous to introduce under the skin of a g. RESEARCH, 18
guineas I have only five g. in my pocket GENEROSITY, 4
gulphs whelm'd in deeper g. than he DEATH, 52
gum Any g., chum UNITED STATES, 73
gun it is necessary to take up the g. WAR, 97
The difference between a g. and a tree TREES, 14
we have got /The Maxim G., and they have not POWER POLITICS, 2
gunfire Thanks to the movies, g. has always sounded unreal CINEMA, 16
Gunga Din You're a better man than I am, G. SUPERIORITY, 7
gunpowder G., Printing, and the Protestant Religion CIVILIZATION, 3
guns But it's 'Saviour of 'is country' when the g. SOLDIERS, 3
Elevate them g. a little lower WAR, 78
gutless W. H. Auden, a sort of g. Kipling SOCIALISM, 20
gutter We are all in the g. OPTIMISM, 38
gynecology A determining point in the history of g. SEX, 97
gypsies My mother said that I never should /Play with the

H

habit a h. the pleasure of which increases with practice LETTER-WRITING, 1
H. is a great deadener HABIT, 2
honour peereth in the meanest h. APPEARANCES, 36
some h. of which he is deeply ashamed TELEVISION, 6
habitation to airy nothing /A local h. POETRY, 51
habits An animal psychologist is a man who pulls h. out of rats PSYCHOLOGY, 1
Curious things, h. HABIT, 3

h. that carry them far apart HABIT, 4
Old h. die hard HABIT, 1
hack Do not h. me EXECUTION, 23
had you h. it in you EXPECTATION, 5
hae Scots, wha h. WAR, 33
ha-ha Funny peculiar, or funny h. HUMOR, 25
hail All h., the power of Jesus' name CHRISTIANITY, 51
h. and farewell GREETINGS, 4
the flail of the lashing h. WEATHER, 26
hair A h, in the head HUMOR, 26
busy driving cabs and cutting h. GOVERNMENT, 9
He may have h. upon his chest MEN, 11
if a woman have long h. APPEARANCE, 9
I think of women, it is their h. WOMEN, 85
long gray h. on Kevin's jacket SUSPICION, 3
Man can have only a certain number of teeth, h. and ideas OLD AGE, 99
never get on in politics, my dear, with *that* h. POLITICIANS, 8
part my h. behind OLD AGE, 44
scant as h. /In leprosy SPARSENESS, 1
Take a h. of the dog ALCOHOL, 6
there shall not one h. of his head fall BIBLICAL QUOTATIONS, 611
To Crystal, h. was the most important APPEARANCE, 40
Wash That Man Right Out of My H. DECISION, 1
you have lovely h. BEAUTY, 15
hairy a small, h. individual ROYALTY, 6
Esau . . . a h. man BIBLICAL QUOTATIONS, 215
half And when they were only h. way up ARMY, 2
H. a loaf COMPROMISE, 5
I am only h. there when I am ill ILLNESS, 41
I have not told h. of what I saw LAST WORDS, 66
longest h. of your life YOUTH, 29
One h. . . . cannot understand . . . the other PLEASURE, 3
There is an old saying 'well begun is h. done' BEGINNING, 11
half-a-dozen six of one and h. of the other SIMILARITY, 5
half-developed the working-class which, raw and h. PUBLIC, 2
half-naked striding h. up the steps of the vice-regal palace CONTEMPT, 3
half-quote Don't h. me to reinforce your own prejudices PREJUDICE, 3
half-wits a wit out of two h. FOOLISHNESS, 16
halitosis h. of the intellect INSULTS, 66
hall one of the sparrows . . . flew . . . through the h. LIFE, 9
We met . . . Dr H. in such very deep mourning MOURNING, 1
hallelujah Here lies my wife, / . . . /H. ANONYMOUS, 31
hallowed The place of justice is a h. place JUSTICE, 1
halt the whole process has ground to a h. with a 14th Earl TITLES, 13
halters talk of h. in the hanged man's house TACT, 4
halves Never do things by h. COMMITMENT, 2
Hamelin H. Town's in Brunswick GERMANY, 1
hammer Art is not a mirror . . . but a h. ART, 17
hand bite the h. that fed them INGRATITUDE, 2
educate with the head instead of with the h. EDUCATION, 51
fingers of a man's h., and wrote BIBLICAL QUOTATIONS, 62
h. that signed the treaty bred a fever SIGNATURES, 3
he wouldn't lay a h. on you DOCTORS, 90
I . . . will cover thee with my h. BIBLICAL QUOTATIONS, 158
little onward lend thy guiding h. GUIDANCE, 3
No, this right h. shall work it all off WRITING, 39
one of those parties which got out of h. CHRISTIANITY, 32
put your h. into the h. of God FAITH, 15
sweeten this little h. GUILT, 17
The H. that made us is divine CREATION, 1
The h. that rocks the cradle PROVERBS, 398
This h. hath offended REGRET, 7
touch his weaknesses with a delicate h. IMPERFECTION, 8
'You should not bite the h. that feeds you.' HEALTHY LIVING, 42
handbook have used the Bible as if it was a constable's h. BIBLE, 8
handful for a h. of silver he left us BETRAYAL, 5
handicraft Art is not a h. ART, 30
handkerchiefs There is a ghost /That eats h. LOSS, 4
handle I polished up the h. of the big front door OFFICERS, 6
polished up the h. of the big front door OFFICERS, 6
touch not; taste not; h. not BIBLICAL QUOTATIONS, 22
hands don't raise your h. because I am also nearsighted DISABILITY, 1
Farewell, my poor h. LAST WORDS, 71
He hath shook h. with time DEATH, 65
he shakes h. with people's hearts JOURNALISM, 8
into thy h. I commend my spirit BIBLICAL QUOTATIONS, 449
Licence my roving h. LUST, 3
many brains and many h. are needed DISCOVERY, 14
Many h. make light work HELP, 2
Pale h. I loved beside the Shalimar LOVE, 78
Pilate . . . washed his h. BIBLICAL QUOTATIONS, 547
Pilate . . . washed his h. GUILT, 3
temples made with h. BIBLICAL QUOTATIONS, 12
the earth of England is in my two h. EARTH, 18
To be played with both h. in the pocket MUSIC, 39
Tomorrow my h. will be bound EXECUTION, 2
We draw the sword . . . with clean h. WAR, 173
You cannot shake h. with a clenched fist INFLEXIBILITY, 2
handsaw I know a hawk from a h. MADNESS, 32
handsome H. is as handsome does APPEARANCE, 3
handsomest h. man in England POETS, 39
handwriting Most people enjoy the sight of their own h. WRITING, 3
hang if you want to kill a picture all you have to do is to h. it beautifully PAINTING, 15
I will find something . . . to h. him EXECUTION, 34
I will neither go nor h. DETERMINATION, 5
I will not h. myself today SUICIDE, 7
They h. us now in Shrewsbury jail EXECUTION, 16
We must indeed all h. together UNITY, 9
wretches h. that jury-men may dine JUSTICE, 26
hanged h. privily by night INJUSTICE, 3
if the King beat us once we shall all be h. ROYALTY, 78
if they were going to see me h. PUBLIC, 9
I went out to Charing Cross, to see Major-general Harrison h. EXECUTION, 29
Men are not h. for stealing EXAMPLE, 6
resolved to be h. with the Bible EXECUTION, 1
talk of halters in the h. man's house TACT, 4
to be h. for nonsense EXECUTION, 9
when a man knows he is to be h. in a fortnight EXECUTION, 18
hangin' they're h. Danny Deever in the mornin' EXECUTION, 20
hanging H. and wiving goes by destiny DESTINY, 24
h. prevents a bad marriage MARRIAGE, 122
hangman if I were a grave-digger, or . . . a h. OCCUPATIONS, 11
Hansard H. is history's ear GOVERNMENT, 35
happen poetry makes nothing h. POETRY, 5
happened most of which had never h. WORRY, 12
happening h. to somebody else HUMOR, 52
happens Everything that h. h. as it should DESTINY, 3
I don't give a shit what h. POLITICS, 107
I just don't want to be there when it h. DEATH, 16
life . . . seems to me preparation for something that never h. LIFE, 89
Nothing h. BOREDOM, 1
happiest h. time of all the glad New-year MERRYMAKING, 5
Poetry is the record of the best and h. moments POETRY, 54
happiness A lifetime of h. . . . hell on earth HAPPINESS, 25
a man is always seeking for h. MARRIAGE, 56
curiously boring about . . . h. SYMPATHY, 5
Drunkenness is never anything but a substitute for h. DRUNKENNESS, 17
Good health is an essential to h. HEALTH, 17
greatest h. of the greatest number HAPPINESS, 3
h. fails, existence remains . . . experiment HAPPINESS, 23
h. gives us the energy HEALTH, 2
H. in marriage MARRIAGE, 11
H. is a mystery like religion HAPPINESS, 7
h. is an essential to good citizenship HEALTH, 17
H. is an imaginary condition HAPPINESS, 29
H. is beneficial for the body BODY, 19
H. is like a butterfly HAPPINESS, 17
H. is like coke HAPPINESS, 12
H. is no laughing matter HAPPINESS, 31
h. is not an ideal of reason HAPPINESS, 14
H. is not best achieved HAPPINESS, 20
H. is no vague dream HAPPINESS, 22
H. is the only sanction of life HAPPINESS, 23
h. makes them good GOOD, 9
h. of man that he be mentally faithful INTEGRITY, 5
In Hollywood, if you don't have h. CINEMA, 13
In solitude /What h. SOLITUDE, 11
I thought that success spelled h. HAPPINESS, 17
It is of no moment to the h. of an individual GOVERNMENT, 18
life, liberty, and the pursuit of h. HUMAN RIGHTS, 3
nothing . . . by which so much h. is produced as by a good tavern PUBLIC HOUSES, 2
Oh! how bitter a thing it is to look into h. through another man's eyes HAPPINESS, 24
one may fail to find h. in theatrical life DANCING, 10
our friends are true and our h. OPTIMISM, 16
Poverty is a great enemy to human h. POVERTY, 23
recall a time of h. when in misery SORROW, 7
result h. ECONOMICS, 8
the greatest h. for the greatest numbers HAPPINESS, 11
the greatest h. of the whole REPUBLIC, 1
the h. of the common man GOVERNMENT, 8
where . . . We find our h. FRENCH REVOLUTION, 13
Who never knew the price of h. HAPPINESS, 33
you'll give h. and joy to many other people COMPOSERS, 2
you take away his h. DELUSION, 4
happy Ask . . . whether you are h. HAPPINESS, 16
be h. later on, but it's much harder HAPPINESS, 2
Few people can be h. unless they hate HATE, 8
Goodness does not . . . make men h. GOOD, 9
H. Days HAPPINESS, 32
h. families resemble each other FAMILY, 54
H. the hare at morning HUNTING, 1
H. the Man PRESENT, 4
If it were now to die, /'Twere now to be most h. LOVE, 144
If you want to be h., be HAPPINESS, 30
I have wanted only one thing to make me h. DISCONTENT, 3
I've had a h. life LAST WORDS, 44
I were but little h. JOY, 6
laugh before one is h. LAUGHTER, 8
Let us all be h., and live within our means BORROWING, 12
Lucid intervals and h. pauses MADNESS, 2
man is h. so long as he chooses to be h. HAPPINESS, 27
Mankind are always h. for having been h. HAPPINESS, 26
Not the owner of many possessions will you be right to call h. DISHONOR, 1
One is h. as a result of one's own efforts HAPPINESS, 22
only really h. people SEXES, 19
policeman's lot is not a h. one POLICE, 3
Puritanism – The haunting fear that someone . . . may be h. PURITANISM, 5
That all who are h., are equally h. HAPPINESS, 13
the duty of being h. HAPPINESS, 28
. . . the one and only thing . . . that can make a man h. . . . HAPPINESS, 8
There is a h. land HEAVEN, 16
to have been h. HAPPINESS, 6
To make men h. ADMIRATION, 12
utterly h. . . . refrain from comparing this moment TIME, 21
We are never so h. nor so unhappy as we imagine HAPPINESS, 19
what it is that makes a Scotchman h. ALCOHOL, 44
hard Don't clap too h. ENTHUSIASM, 6
H. and high to the stars ANONYMOUS, 68
I'm not h. – I'm frightfully soft CHARACTER, 28
It's been a h. day's night WORK, 18
Saturday's child works h. for his living CHARACTER, 19
hard-faced A lot of h. men HOUSES OF PARLIAMENT, 4
hardly the summit of Everest was h. the place PHOTOGRAPHY, 4

hoist H. your sail OPPORTUNITY, 3
hold always keep a h. of Nurse COMFORT, 1
damn'd be him that first cries, 'H., enough!' COURAGE, 23
h. fast that which is good BIBLICAL QUOTATIONS, 644
h. your tongue and let me love SILENCE, 5
To have and to h. BOOK OF COMMON PRAYER, THE, 15
When every . . . thing you h. /Is made of silver, or of gold ECONOMICS, 10
holder office sanctifies the h. POWER, 3
hole A h. is the accident THRIFT, 10
if you knows of a better h. WAR, 14
In a h. in the ground there lived a hobbit FAIRIES, 5
smallest h. . . . man can hide his head in UNIVERSE, 6
What happens to the h. when the cheese is gone NONSENSE, 4
holiday the little h. steamers made an excursion to hell WORLD WAR II, 42
The living . . . the dead on h. LIFE, 52
holier h. than thou BIBLICAL QUOTATIONS, 279
holiness put off H. WISDOM, 13
the h. of the heart's affections HEART, 11
who, like you, your H., is a Roman Catholic CATHOLICISM, 3
Holland H. . . . lies so low they're only saved by being dammed EUROPE, 7
hollow We are the h. men INSIGNIFICANCE, 2
within the h. crown ROYALTY, 98
holly The h. and the ivy ANONYMOUS, 82
The h. bears the crown ANONYMOUS, 82
Hollywood H. – a place where people from Iowa CINEMA, 1
H. . . . the personality of a paper cup CINEMA, 5
In H., if you don't have happiness CINEMA, 13
I should not have been invited to H. CINEMA, 4
Strip the phoney tinsel off H. APPEARANCES, 21
the attitude of a H. director toward love ENGLISH, 19
holy everything that lives is h. HOLINESS, 2
h., h., h., is the Lord of hosts BIBLICAL QUOTATIONS, 252
H., h., h., Lord God Almighty GOD, 28
the H. Roman Empire was neither h., nor Roman, nor an empire EMPIRE, 6
'Twas on a H. Thursday CHILDREN, 19
unite in some h. confederacy CHRISTIANITY, 35
Holy See This charter . . . constitutes an insult to the H. FREEDOM, 26
home against books the H. Secretary is PHILISTINISM, 7
A House Is Not a H. HOME, 3
Charity begins at h. CHARITY, 11
Comin' for to carry me h. ANONYMOUS, 76
Despair abroad . . . pleasant thoughts of h. NOSTALGIA, 9
eaten me out of house and h. GREED, 13
English should give Ireland h. rule IRELAND, 19
Father, . . . come h. with me now ALCOHOL, 89
for de old folks at h. HOMESICKNESS, 3
For h. is best HOME, 12
For the old Kentucky H. far away HOMESICKNESS, 2
give me a h. where the buffalo roam HOMESICKNESS, 4
h. his footsteps he hath turn'd HOMESICKNESS, 6
H. is heaven DEBAUCHERY, 10
H. is home HOME, 4
H. is the sailor, h. from sea DEATH, 160
H. is where HOME, 2
H. of lost causes OXFORD, 1
H. . . . where . . . they have to take you in HOME, 5
I can get all that at h. THEATER, 7
Irish H. Rule is conceded IRELAND, 20
Keep the H. Fires Burning HOME, 9
Managing is . . . h. runs someone else hits BASEBALL, 8
Many a man who thinks to found a h. PARASITES, 1
no h. . . . save in Paris PARIS, 5
permits you to be entertained . . . by people you wouldn't have in your h. TELEVISION, 7
Pleasure never is at h. DISCONTENT, 5
She's leaving h. DEPARTURE, 8
The Life and Soul, the man who will never go h. PARTIES, 11
there's no place like h. HOME, 10
till the cow comes h. ETERNITY, 1
We are all H. Rulers today IRELAND, 4
we come /From God, who is our h. METAPHYSICS, 6
What's the good of a h. ABSENCE, 7
home-keeping h. youth HOME, 11
homely A h. face . . . aided many women heavenward APPEARANCE, 5
be never so h. HOME, 4
h. wits HOME, 11
homeopathy H. . . . a mingled mass of perverse ingenuity MEDICINE, 41
H. is insignificant as an act of healing MEDICINE, 26
Homer Cicero /And . . . H. were /*Mad as the mist and snow* MADNESS, 45
even excellent H. nods IMPERFECTION, 9
Mr Gladstone read H. for fun CLASSICS, 3
Seven cities warr'd for H., being dead POVERTY, 18
The author of that poem is either H. ARGUMENTS, 7
homes go back to thy stately h. of England PARTING, 7
Healthy people are those who live in healthy h. HEALTHY LIVING, 25
the Stately H. of England DECLINE, 1
home-sickness In h. you must keep moving HOMESICKNESS, 7
homeward Look H., Angel BOOK TITLES, 24
homo ecce h. BIBLICAL QUOTATIONS, 362
The 'h.' is the legitimate child HOMOSEXUALITY, 10
homos one of the stately h. of England HOMOSEXUALITY, 4
homosexuals h. . . . set out to win the love of a 'real' man HOMOSEXUALITY, 5
honest An h. broker DIPLOMACY, 4
An h. God GOD, 33
an h. man sent to lie abroad for . . . his country DIPLOMACY, 26
An h. man's word HONESTY, 1
give me six lines . . . by the most h. man EXECUTION, 34
h. tale SIMPLICITY, 7
I am as h. as any man living HONESTY, 8
It's better to be quotable than . . . h. QUOTATIONS, 18
liars and swearers enow to beat the h. men GOOD AND EVIL, 7
not an h. man HONESTY, 13
She was poor but she was h. ANONYMOUS, 71
then they get h. DOCTORS, 82
thinks men h. that but seem to be so INNOCENCE, 9
Though I am not naturally h. HONESTY, 10
Though I be poor, I'm h. HONESTY, 5
To be direct and h. is not safe HONESTY, 9
honestly If possible h., if not, somehow, make money MONEY, 22
honesty H. is the best policy HONESTY, 2
make your children *capable of h.* is the beginning of education HONESTY, 6
Philosophers never balance between profit and h. PHILOSOPHERS, 4
what a fool H. is HONESTY, 11
honey a land flowing with milk and h. BIBLICAL QUOTATIONS, 133
a land of oil olive, and h. BIBLICAL QUOTATIONS, 66
gather h. all the day HONEY, 4
h. still for tea HONEY, 2
They took some h., and plenty of money HONEY, 3
water, h., and labour REMEDIES, 5
what is sweeter than h. BIBLICAL QUOTATIONS, 393
honey'd the h. middle of the night LOVE, 88
honey-dew on h. hath fed CAUTION, 9
honi *H. soit qui mal y pense* ANONYMOUS, 39
honor All is lost save h. DEFEAT, 4
a prophet is not without h. BIBLICAL QUOTATIONS, 507
Brothers all /In h. HONOR, 10
could not love thee . . . /Loved I not H. HONOR, 3
His h. rooted in dishonour DISHONOR, 3
h. all men BIBLICAL QUOTATIONS, 561
H. pricks me on HONOR, 5
h. sinks where commerce long prevails BUSINESS, 13
h. thy father and thy mother BIBLICAL QUOTATIONS, 147
if I accepted the h. . . . I would not answer for the integrity of my intellect TITLES, 3
I like not such grinning h. as Sir Walter hath HONOR, 6
Let us h. if we can POSTERITY, 3
man of the greatest h. and bravery CHARACTER, 23
only h. and life have been spared DEFEAT, 4
peace I hope with h. PEACE, 10
So h. peereth in the meanest habit APPEARANCES, 36
That chastity of h. HONOR, 2
then they get *h.* DOCTORS, 82
There is h. among thieves LOYALTY, 2
To h. we call you COURAGE, 14
Wealth has never been a sufficient source of h. OSTENTATION, 3
we're fighting for this woman's h. HONOR, 4
honorable His designs were strictly h. MARRIAGE, 64
honored h. in their generations BIBLICAL QUOTATIONS, 114
hoof I see many h.-marks going in MISTRUST, 2
hook canst thou draw out leviathan with an h. BIBLICAL QUOTATIONS, 314
Hooligan Even the H. was probably invented in China PLACES, 32
hoorah He is without strict doubt a H. Henry ARISTOCRACY, 17
hoo-ray H. and up she rises ANONYMOUS, 106
hope Abandon h., all ye who enter here HELL, 2
a faint h. that he will die HUMAN NATURE, 10
Always give the patient h. HOPE, 18
And what was dead was H. IMPRISONMENT, 15
bright with h. UNITED STATES, 31
Confidence and h. do be more good than physic HOPE, 12
green the colour of h. FRENCH REVOLUTION, 2
He that lives upon h. HOPE, 11
H. for the best HOPE, 2
H. is necessary in every condition HOPE, 15
h. is . . . the dream of those that wake HOPE, 20
H. is the physician of each misery HOPE, 5
H. is the power of being cheerful CHARITY, 13
H. may vanish, but can die not OPTIMISM, 34
H. springs eternal in the human breast HOPE, 19
I do not h. to turn DESPAIR, 5
'Is there no h.?' the sick man said DOCTORS, 47
it cuts off h. HOPE, 14
Land of H. and Glory BRITAIN, 3
no other medicine but only h. HOPE, 21
Not to h. for things to last for ever, is what the year teaches TRANSIENCE, 16
now abideth faith, h., charity BIBLICAL QUOTATIONS, 44
Our h. for years to come RELIGION, 75
the distinction between h. and expectation REALISM, 2
The doctor says there is no h. HOPE, 22
The triumph of h. over experience MARRIAGE, 80
The Worldly H. men set their Hearts upon TRANSIENCE, 14
unconquerable h. HOPE, 7
What a strange thing is memory, and h. MEMORY, 13
While there's life there's h. HOPE, 4
Without all h. of day BLINDNESS, 9
hopefulness The first qualification for a physician is h. HOPE, 16
hopeless that controversy is either superfluous or h. ARGUMENTS, 11
hopes enough for fifty h. and fears WORRY, 10
Life's short span forbids us to enter on far-reaching h. MORTALITY, 13
My h. no more must change their name FREEDOM, 62
The h. and prayers of liberty-loving people FREEDOM, 14
Horatius brave H. COURAGE, 19
horde Society is now one polish'd h. BORES, 2
horizontal perpendicular expression of a h. desire DANCING, 11
we value none /But the h. one POSTERITY, 3
horizontally one who has ceased to grow vertically but not h. AGE, 3
Horner Little Jack H. /Sat in the corner NURSERY RHYMES, 29
Hornie Auld H., Satan, Nick DEVIL, 9
horns draw in their h. or . . . bomb them into the Stone Age THREATS, 7
Memories are hunting h. MEMORY, 1
When you take the bull by the h. . . . CHANCE, 6
horny-handed H. sons of toil WORK, 15
Horowitz Vladimir H. MUSICIANS, 7
horrible A strange, h. business, . . . good enough for Shakespeare's day CRITICISM, 61
horrid are they all h. NASTINESS, 1
horror I have a h. of sunsets HORROR, 2
mere existence is swollen to a h. HORROR, 1
The h.! The h. SUFFERING, 14
The thought of dentists gave him just the same sick h. FEAR, 22
horrors I have supp'd full with h. HORROR, 3
horse A fly, Sir, may sting a stately h. CRITICS, 9

own up to a lack of h. HUMOR, 15
Total absence of h. HUMOR, 17
hump A woman . . . without a positive h., may marry whom she likes MARRIAGE, 141
Humpty H. Dumpty sat on a wall NURSERY RHYMES, 18
hunchback The h. in the park LONELINESS, 12
hundred a h. schools of thought contend FREEDOM, 38
bet you a h. bucks he ain't in here ESCAPE, 2
it would be all the same a h. years hence TRIVIALITY, 4
Letting a h. flowers blossom FREEDOM, 38
Lloyd George spoke for a h. and seventeen minutes POLITICIANS, 17
of all this host of men not one will still be alive in a h. years' time MORTALITY, 22
to trade a h. contemporary readers for POSTERITY, 7
Hungarian It's not enough to be H. EUROPE, 8
hunger best sauce . . . is h. HUNGER, 4
H. is the best sauce HUNGER, 1
The war against h. HUNGER, 7
to banish h. by rubbing the belly HUNGER, 5
hungred h., and ye gave me meat BIBLICAL QUOTATIONS, 537
hungry A h. stomach has no ears HUNGER, 8
h. as a hunter HUNGER, 9
H. Joe collected lists of fatal diseases ILLNESS, 29
h. sheep look up, and are not fed CORRUPTION, 6
she makes h. /Where most she satisfies ADMIRATION, 16
You cannot feed the h. on statistics STATISTICS, 6
hunt how much more dogs are animated when they h. in a pack UNITY, 10
people who h. are the right people HUNTING, 8
hunted tell the others by their h. expression CHARITY, 18
hunter hungry as a h. HUNGER, 9
Man is the h. SEXES, 26
Miss J. H. Dunn, Miss J. H. Dunn ADMIRATION, 1
My heart is a lonely h. HEART, 13
Nimrod the mighty h. BIBLICAL QUOTATIONS, 202
The Heart Is a Lonely H. BOOK TITLES, 18
hunting Memories are h. horns MEMORY, 1
their discourse was about h. HUNTING, 7
when his half-civilized ancestors were h. the wild boar EARTH, 3
hurrah h.! we bring the Jubilee GLORY, 7
The Last H. ENDING, 5
hurricanoes You cataracts and h. WEATHER, 21
hurries h. to the main event PLAYS, 7
hurry An old man in a h. PRIME MINISTERS, 14
He sows h. and reaps indigestion HASTE, 12
H.! I never h.. I have no time to h. HASTE, 13
So who's in a h. ALCOHOL, 14
hurrying I see a man h. along – to what PURPOSE, 6
hurt it h. too much to laugh DISAPPOINTMENT, 8
It takes your enemy and your friend . . . to h. you HURT, 3
Those have most power to h. HURT, 1
wish to h. CRUELTY, 1
hurting Art . . . can go on mattering once it has stopped h. ART, 5
husband An archaeologist is the best h. MARRIAGE, 40
at all times yr faithful h. MARRIAGE, 130
Being a h. is a whole-time job MARRIAGE, 22
easier to be a lover than a h. HUMOR, 6
happened unawares to look at her h. MARRIAGE, 12
h. render unto the wife due benevolence BIBLICAL QUOTATIONS, 33
in love with . . . Her own h. LOVE AND MARRIAGE, 2
light wife doth make a heavy h. MARRIAGE, 118
My h. and I' ROYALTY, 56
My h. is dead DEATH, 105
Never trust a h. too far BACHELORS, 2
she must have a h. JEALOUSY, 12
that monstrous animal a h. and wife MARRIAGE, 65
The h. frae the wife despises MARRIAGE, 35
trust my h. not to fall asleep POLITICS, 140
You may have my h., but not my horse MASCULINITY, 2
husbandman my Father is the h. BIBLICAL QUOTATIONS, 350
husbandry borrowing dulls the edge of h. BORROWING, 8
He was into animal h. SEX, 60
husbands American women expect to find in their h. WOMEN, 74
flirt with their own h. LOVE AND MARRIAGE, 7
h. and wives . . . belong to different sexes SEXES, 11
h. and wives make shipwreck of their lives MARRIAGE, 56
H. are like fires MARRIAGE, 67
h., love your wives BIBLICAL QUOTATIONS, 24
h. remind me of an orangutang MARRIAGE, 17
h. to stay at home BACHELORS, 1
that h. and wives should have children alternatively SEXES, 15
hush a breathless h. in the Close tonight CRICKET, 5
somebody ought to have said 'h.' PRECOCITY, 1
husks the h. that the swine did eat BIBLICAL QUOTATIONS, 439
hussy a brazen h. of a speech SPEECHES, 8
hut Love in a h. LOVE, 87
The Arab who builds . . . a h. out of . . . a temple MUSEUMS, 1
Hyacinth Children with H.'s temperament . . . merely know more CHARACTER, 22
every H. the Garden wears FLOWERS, 5
hydrostatics It gives me the h. MALAPROPISMS, 5
hygiene how do drugs, h. and animal magnetism heal REMEDIES, 28
h. . . . , is not much good CLEANNESS, 4
H. is the corruption of medicine by morality CLEANNESS, 6
hygienist from the point of view of the h., the physician, the architect, the tax-payer, the superintendents, and the nurse HOSPITALS, 3
hymn Aisle. Altar. H. MARRIAGE, 99
hymn-book Cassock, band, and h. too CLERGY, 15
hymns I moved from Schumann to folk songs, then to h. MUSIC, 22
My poems are h. of praise POETRY, 56
hyper-thyroid Shelley had a h. face APPEARANCE, 59
hyphenated h. Americanism PATRIOTISM, 33
hypochondria H. torments us not only with causeless irritation HYPOCHONDRIA, 11
hypochondriac ennui the h. WORK, 13
the h. affection in men, and the hysteric in women HYPOCHONDRIA, 8
hypochondriacs 'hopeless, hysterical h. of history.' MEDIA, 2
H. squander large sums of time HYPOCHONDRIA, 5
hypocrisy an organized h. POLITICS, 45
H. . . . is a whole-time job HYPOCRISY, 12
H. is the homage paid by vice to virtue HYPOCRISY, 14
H. is the most . . . nerve-racking vice HYPOCRISY, 12
neither man nor angel can discern /H. HYPOCRISY, 13
That would be h. HYPOCRISY, 22
hypocrite No man is a h. in his pleasures PLEASURE, 16
see . . . into a h. HYPOCRISY, 9
hypocritical Man . . . learns by being h. HYPOCRISY, 11
hypotheses he should resist the fascination of doctrines and h. MEDICINE, 11
hypothesis discard a pet h. every day before breakfast SCIENCE, 60
Factual evidence can never 'prove' a h. THEORY, 6
I have no need of that h. ATHEISM, 10
the slaying of a beautiful h. by an ugly fact SCIENCE, 49
to discard a pet h. every day THEORY, 11
hysteria I cultivate my h. with joy and terror MADNESS, 3
hysteric the hypochondriac affection in men, and the h. in women HYPOCHONDRIA, 8
hysterical No laborious person was ever yet h. WORK, 13

I

I I also had my hour ANIMALS, 12
I am not what I am APPEARANCES, 31
in the infinite I AM IMAGINATION, 1
I would have done it differently ARROGANCE, 9
ice A Shape of I. BOATS, 9
skating over thin i. HASTE, 6
The i. was all around SEA, 4
iceberg as the smart ship grew . . . grew the I. too BOATS, 9
ice-cream just enjoy your i. while it's on your plate PHILOSOPHY, 23
iced three parts i. over AGE, 7
icicles When i. hang by the wall WINTER, 6
id I never saw a person's i. PSYCHOLOGY, 13
put the i. back in yid JEWS, 17
the care of the i. by the odd PSYCHIATRY, 1
idea An i. does not pass from one language TRANSLATION, 4
An i. isn't responsible for the people IDEAS, 7
constant repetition . . . in imprinting an i. PUBLIC, 14
Dying for an i. MARTYRDOM, 3
I think it would be a good i. CIVILIZATION, 6
'Mad' is . . . a man who is obsessed with one i. OBSESSIONS, 2
no stand can be made against invasion by an i. IDEAS, 3
That fellow seems to me to possess but one i. STUPIDITY, 4
the i. of death as an individual NUCLEAR WEAPONS, 11
they will end by ruining our i. FASCISM, 7
ideal at fourteen every boy should be in love with some i. woman . . . on a pedestal SEXES, 20
the i. American UNITED STATES, 78
idealist An i. . . . , on noticing that a rose smells better than a cabbage IDEALISM, 7
people call me an i. UNITED STATES, 69
ideals Away with all i. SPONTANEITY, 3
think how far I can go with all the i. that I have IDEALISM, 11
ideas down which i. are lured and . . . strangled BUREAUCRACY, 3
i. are of more importance than values INTELLECTUALS, 5
i. simply pass through him STUPIDITY, 1
I. that enter the mind under fire INDOCTRINATION, 3
I stopped . . . to exchange i. INFERIORITY, 1
Learn our i., or otherwise get out RACE, 14
Man can have only a certain number of teeth, hair and i. OLD AGE, 99
Many i. grow better when transplanted into another mind IDEAS, 4
Morality which is based on i. MORALITY, 9
no i. . . . not a nuisance PRESIDENTS, 11
she's only got two i. in her head STUPIDITY, 5
the addiction of political groups to the i. POLITICS, 51
There are no poetic i. POETRY, 62
The true God, . . . God of i. INSPIRATION, 9
Whenever i. fail, men invent words WORDS, 11
ides Beware the i. of March PROPHECY, 15
idiot now I feel like a complete i. INFERIORITY, 1
tale told by an i. LIFE, 76
The i. who praises . . . every country but his own DISCONTENT, 2
To generalize is to be an i. GENERALIZATIONS, 1
idiots the English seem . . . to act with . . . the fatuity of i. IRELAND, 21
idle As i. as a painted ship BOATS, 3
I am happiest when I am i. IDLENESS, 11
Satan finds . . . mischief . . . /For i. hands IDLENESS, 12
thousands of i. persons are within this realm IDLENESS, 5
We would all be i. IDLENESS, 8
Young people ought not to be i. IDLENESS, 10
idleness compulsory and irreproachable i. ARMY, 3
i. and indifference CHANGE, 3
I. begets ennui WORK, 13
I. is the parent of all psychology PSYCHOLOGY, 12
I. . . . the refuge of weak minds IDLENESS, 2
Research! A mere excuse for i. RESEARCH, 16
idling It is impossible to enjoy i. IDLENESS, 6
idol one-eyed yellow i. to the north of Khatmandu MOURNING, 5
idolatry There is no i. in the Mass CATHOLICISM, 7
idols little children, keep yourselves from i. BIBLICAL QUOTATIONS, 381
if I. you can keep your head SELF-CONTROL, 5
much virtue in I. POSSIBILITY, 2
ifs If i. and ans PROVERBS, 214
ignominious History is full of i. getaways by the great COWARDICE, 5
ignoramus *I.*, . . . person unacquainted with . . . knowledge familiar to yourself IGNORANCE, 5
ignorance for i. is never better than knowledge NATURE, 13
From i. our comfort flows IGNORANCE, 18
his chosen mode of i. EXPERTS, 6

His i. was an Empire State Building of i. IGNORANCE, 17
I. is like a delicate exotic fruit IGNORANCE, 23
I. is preferable to error IGNORANCE, 12
I. is Strength DOUBLETHINK, 1
I., madam, pure i. IGNORANCE, 13
I. of the law excuses LAW, 29
journalism. . . . keeps us in touch with the i. of the community JOURNALISM, 42
knowledge increases . . . i. unfolds KNOWLEDGE, 27
Lawyers are the only persons in whom i. . . . is not punished LAWYERS, 4
man's i. of the gods SPONTANEITY, 1
no sin but i. IGNORANCE, 16
opinion breeds i. OPINIONS, 2
Somebody else's i. is bliss IGNORANCE, 22
where i. is bliss, /'Tis folly to be wise IGNORANCE, 9
Why therefore fear to confess our i. REMEDIES, 56
Your i. cramps my conversation IGNORANCE, 11
ignorant Let no one i. of mathematics enter here MATHEMATICS, 15
The i. man always adores IGNORANCE, 15
the opinionated, the i., and the boorish STUBBORNNESS, 3
To confess that you are totally I. about the Horse HORSES, 9
what may follow it, or what preceded it, we are absolutely i. LIFE, 9
you can go through the wards of a hospital and be as i. HOSPITALS, 5
ill being i. as one of the greatest pleasures of life ILLNESS, 16
Cannot be i.; cannot be good SUPERNATURAL, 15
give /The i. he cannot cure a name ILLNESS, 8
he usually discovers that he is i. HYPOCHONDRIA, 7
human i. does not dawn seem . . . an alternative HUMAN CONDITION, 28
I am only half there when I am i. ILLNESS, 41
If . . . someone is speaking i. of you CRITICISM, 18
no hint throughout the universe /Of good or i. NECESSITY, 11
One who is i. has . . . the duty to seek medical aid ILLNESS, 44
PHYSICIAN, n. One upon whom we set our hopes when i. DOCTORS, 23
the inferior doctor treats those who are i. DOCTORS, 31
the Prince . . . is restrained from doing i. GOVERNMENT, 40
very fine country to be acutely i. BRITAIN, 11
We're all of us i. in one way or another HEALTH, 9
When people's i., they comes to I DOCTORS, 57
woman colour'd i. CONFLICT, 7
you had better be too smart to get i. ILLNESS, 5
illegal collect legal taxes from i. money TAXATION, 3
the things I really like . . . are either immoral, i., or fattening PLEASURE, 35
illegitimate There are no i. children ILLEGITIMACY, 4
ill-health Cynicism is humour in i. CYNICISM, 3
ill-housed one-third of a nation i. UNITED STATES, 52
illiteracy The ratio of literacy to i. LITERACY, 1
illiterate I. him . . . from your memory MALAPROPISMS, 4
Violence is the repartee of the i. VIOLENCE, 3
illness A long i. seems to be placed between life and death ILLNESS, 15
Considering how common i. is ILLNESS, 69
he was newly reborn from a mortal i. WRITERS, 23
I. is in part what the world has done to a victim ILLNESS, 47
I. isn't the only thing that spoils the appetite FOOD, 68
I. is the night-side of life ILLNESS, 64
I. makes a man a scoundrel ILLNESS, 36
I. of any kind is hardly a thing to be encouraged in others ILLNESS, 67
In i. the physician is a father DOCTORS, 11
It is the part that makes the i. worth while REST, 3
No doubt fate would find it easier than I do to relieve you of your i. PSYCHOANALYSIS, 11
Prolonged and costly i. in later years OLD AGE, 58
sooner or later have to find time for i. HEALTHY LIVING, 16
strange indeed that i. has not taken its place with love ILLNESS, 69
The doctor may also learn more about the i. DIAGNOSIS, 9
The most important thing in i. is never to lose heart ILLNESS, 42
To be too conscious is an i. ILLNESS, 22
Too much health, the cause of i. HEALTH, 11
illnesses Most men die of their remedies, and not of their i. REMEDIES, 42
illogical Faith . . . an i. belief in . . . the improbable FAITH, 21
ills sharp remedy . . . for all i. EXECUTION, 33
ill-spent sign of an i. youth SPORT AND GAMES, 21
ill-treated all i. fellows /Unborn and unbegot SYMPATHY, 3
illuminate i. our whole country with the bright light of their preaching RELIGION, 40
illumine What in me is dark /I. DARKNESS, 15
illusion it can contain nothing but sophistry and i. ILLUSIONS, 3
Religion is an i. ILLUSIONS, 2
The House of Lords, an i. HOUSES OF PARLIAMENT, 21
visible universe was an i. ILLUSIONS, 1
illusions dispepsia is the apparatus of i. ILLNESS, 48
It's life's i. I recall ILLUSIONS, 4
ill-will I bear no i. against those responsible for this FORGIVENESS, 20
image any graven i. BIBLICAL QUOTATIONS, 147
any graven i. GOD, 14
A photograph is not only an i. IMAGE, 4
fall down and worship the golden i. BIBLICAL QUOTATIONS, 57
If God made us in His i. GOD, 57
make man in our own i. BIBLICAL QUOTATIONS, 179
Why should I consent to the perpetuation of the i. of this i. IMAGE, 3
imaginary Happiness is an i. condition HAPPINESS, 29
imagination A lady's i. is very rapid WOMEN, 15
a new audacity of i. SCIENCE, 26
Art is ruled . . . by the i. IMAGINATION, 3
Children do not give up their innate i., curiosity, dreaminess easily IMAGINATION, 8
I. and fiction . . . three quarters of our real life IMAGINATION, 12
I.! . . . I put it first years ago ACTING, 14
I. is more important than knowledge IMAGINATION, 4
I. without skill gives us modern art ART, 29
indebted to his . . . i. for his facts POLITICIANS, 100
Most of those evils . . . /From doctors and i. flow ILLNESS, 17
no i. and . . . no compassion IMAGINATION, 5
not an ideal of reason but of i. HAPPINESS, 14
of i. all compact LOVE, 137
The primary i. IMAGINATION, 1
treat your facts with i. is one thing TRUTH, 14
truth of i. HEART, 11
imagine I. there's no heaven IDEALISM, 5
never so happy . . . as we i. HAPPINESS, 19
imagined What is now proved was . . . i. PROOF, 3
imagining How reconcile this world . . . with . . . my i. BLINDNESS, 6
imitate An original writer is . . . one whom nobody can i. ORIGINALITY, 2
never failed to i. CHILDREN, 7
obliged to i. himself, and to repeat IMITATION, 5
people . . . usually i. each other IMITATION, 3
imitates Photography can never grow up if it i. PHOTOGRAPHY, 1
imitation An i. rough diamond INSULTS, 5
every i. from 'Eton and Oxford' PARTIES, 12
I. is the sincerest form of flattery FLATTERY, 1
Man . . . is an i. MANKIND, 44
Immaculate the I. Conception was spontaneous combustion CATHOLICISM, 11
Immanuel call his name I. BIBLICAL QUOTATIONS, 253
immature the i. man . . . wants to die nobly for a cause AGE, 74
immaturity common symptom of i. IMMATURITY, 3
the executive expression of human i. IMMATURITY, 1
immoral moral or an i. book BOOKS, 51
the things I really like . . . are either i., illegal, or fattening PLEASURE, 35
worse than i. MISTAKES, 2
immorality the most rigid code of i. ENGLISH, 7
immortal I have lost the i. part REPUTATION, 8
make me i. with a kiss BEAUTY, 25
Our souls have sight of that i. sea METAPHYSICS, 7
Why are you weeping? Did you imagine that I was i. LAST WORDS, 56
immortality I . . . want to achieve i. . . . through not dying IMMORTALITY, 1
just ourselves /And I. DEATH, 55
immutable Few things are as i. POLITICS, 51
impediment cause, or just i. BOOK OF COMMON PRAYER, THE, 13
imperative This i. is Categorical MORALITY, 8
imperfection i. itself may have its . . . perfect state IMPERFECTION, 7
imperial be yourself, i., plain and true SINCERITY, 1
imperialism i. is the monopoly stage of capitalism POLITICS, 87
Their Europeanism is . . . i. with an inferiority complex POLITICS, 61
impersonal In the philosopher there is nothing whatever i. PHILOSOPHERS, 7
impertinent ask an i. question SCIENCE, 12
impetuous such i. blood EARTH, 19
importance Official dignity . . . in inverse ratio to . . . i. DIPLOMACY, 13
important One doesn't recognize . . . the really i. moments . . . until it's too late REGRET, 6
that basic weekendmanship should contain . . . I. Person Play ONE-UPMANSHIP, 3
the little things are infinitely the most i. TRIVIALITY, 7
imposed wish to be i. on, and then are CARE, 5
impossibility a physical and metaphysical i. POETS, 9
impossible complete sorrow is as i. EMOTION, 6
I believe because it is i. BELIEF, 11
It's either easy or i. PAINTING, 6
something is i., he is . . . wrong SCIENCE, 20
when you have excluded the i. IMPROBABILITY, 1
impostors Doctors are mostly i. DOCTORS, 104
impotent an i. people, /Sick with inbreeding WELSH, 3
He also is i. SEX, 31
impregnator the writer . . . is the i. READING, 21
impressed all the more i. because of the delay DIAGNOSIS, 2
impression knowledge and wonder . . . is an i. of pleasure KNOWLEDGE, 5
impressionable Give me a girl at an i. age IMPRESSIONABILITY, 5
impressions i. . . . lasting as . . . an oar upon the water INSIGNIFICANCE, 1
imprisonment Thirty years' i. is IMPRISONMENT, 4
improbable an i. fiction IMPROBABILITY, 3
Faith . . . an illogical belief in . . . the i. FAITH, 21
whatever remains, however i., must be the truth IMPROBABILITY, 1
improper I only hope it is not i. ETIQUETTE, 3
impropriety I. is the soul of wit HUMOR, 41
There was no i. whatsoever DENIAL, 5
improved enormously i. by death WRITERS, 48
improvement most schemes of political i. are very laughable POLITICS, 79
improvised A master of i. speech and i. policies POLITICIANS, 108
impulse the i. of the moment FLATTERY, 2
the need to talk is a primary i. IMPETUOSITY, 1
impulses Mistrust first i. FIRST IMPRESSIONS, 7
impure To the Puritan all things are i. PURITANISM, 2
in you had it i. you EXPECTATION, 5
inactivity wise and masterly i. GOVERNMENT, 22
inadequate Like Brighton pier, . . . i. for getting to France TRAVEL, 24
inarticulate speak for the i. and the submerged JOURNALISM, 7
inartistic He was imperfect, unfinished, i. WRITERS, 24
inbreeding an impotent people, /Sick with i. WELSH, 3
incest except i. and folk-dancing EXPERIENCE, 8
inch every i. a king ROYALTY, 96
Give him an i. GREED, 1
inches They that die by famine die by i. HUNGER, 6
incident What is i. but the illustration of character CHARACTER, 14
incisors Writers, like teeth, are divided into i. and grinders WRITERS, 2

inclination A man ought to read just as i. leads him READING, 10
incoherent I'm not i. CONFUSION, 10
income Annual i. twenty pounds ECONOMICS, 8
difficult to love mankind . . . private i. SELF-INTEREST, 5
hardest thing . . . to understand is i. tax TAXATION, 4
her Majesty . . . must not . . . look upon me as a source of i. TAXATION, 12
live beyond its i. EXTRAVAGANCE, 2
incomes people live beyond their i. EXTRAVAGANCE, 4
incompetence Work . . . by those employees who have not yet reached . . . i. INCOMPETENCE, 4
incompetent a tax on pianos for the i. MUSIC, 44
Democracy substitutes election by the i. many DEMOCRACY, 20
God is the immemorial refuge of the i. GOD, 41
i. swine WAR, 140
incomplete A man in love is i. until . . . married MARRIAGE, 68
incomprehensible an old, wild, and i. man POLITICIANS, 118
inconvenience Change is not made without i. CHANGE, 12
gangrene is pain and i. NAMES, 14
inconveniences A good many i. attend play-going PLAYS, 15
inconvenient i. to be poor POVERTY, 7
incorruptible seagreen I. INCORRUPTIBILITY, 2
the dead shall be raised i. BIBLICAL QUOTATIONS, 49
increase from fairest creatures we desire i. BEAUTY, 36
he must i., but I must decrease BIBLICAL QUOTATIONS, 326
increased influence of the Crown has i. MONARCHY, 10
incredibly I., . . . adorably beautiful BEAUTY, 11
incurable Not even medicine can master i. diseases MEDICINE, 89
the i. disease of writing DISEASE, 28
There are no such things as i. SCIENCE, 3
Ind Outshone the wealth of Ormus and of I. DEVIL, 13
indecency perfectly ordinary little case of a man charged with i. HOMOSEXUALITY, 8
prejudicial . . . as a public i. INDECENCY, 1
The older one grows the more one likes i. AGE, 84
indecent It requires one to assume such i. postures CRICKET, 7
much more i. . . . than a good smack PUNISHMENT, 18
sent down for i. behaviour EDUCATION, 85
indefatigable i. and unsavoury engine of pollution DOGS, 14
indefensible political speech and writing are largely the defence of the i. POLITICS, 109
independent an I. Labour Party PARTIES, 10
An i. . . . wants to take the politics out of politics POLITICS, 134
these United Colonies are, . . . free and i. states UNITED STATES, 37
to become fully i. FAMILY, 20
To be poor and i. POVERTY, 6
indescribable I., O queen GRIEF, 6
India From I.'s coral strand PLACES, 18
I. is a geographical term PLACES, 12
I. . . . the strength and the greatness of England BRITISH EMPIRE, 4
What have we to say to I. COMMUNICATION, 5
Indian base I., threw a pearl away LOVE, 143
in a world of Gary Coopers you are the I. RACE, 3
I. wars have had their origin in broken promises UNITED STATES, 27
lay out ten to see a dead I. CHARITY, 20
Indians The only good I. I ever saw were dead ENEMIES, 8
indictment an i. against an whole people ACCUSATION, 1
indifference and cold i. came INDIFFERENCE, 5
equanimity bordering on i. INDIFFERENCE, 3
idleness and i. CHANGE, 3
i. and a coach and six LOVE, 49
Nothing is so fatal to religion as i. INDIFFERENCE, 2
indigestion An i. is an excellent common-place CONVERSATION, 4
Don't tell your friends about your i. MANNERS, 3
He sows hurry and reaps i. HASTE, 12
I. is charged by God ILLNESS, 31
I, n. A disease which the patient and his friends frequently mistake for deep religious conviction ILLNESS, 14
indignation Moral i. is in most cases 2 percent moral INDIGNATION, 2
puritan pours righteous i. INDIGNATION, 1
the mists of righteous i. INDIGNATION, 3
Wrongdoing can only be avoided if those who are not wronged feel the same i. INDIGNATION, 4
indignity ultimate i. is to be given a bedpan MEDICINE, 51
indiscretion lover without i. LOVE, 75
poised between a cliché and an i. POLITICS, 91
indispensables She was one of those i. INSIGNIFICANCE, 3
indistinct and makes it i., /As water is in water CHANGE, 19
indistinguishable in America the successful writer or picture-painter is i. from any other decent business man ART, 14
individual gesture by the i. to himself BUSINESS, 11
It is of no moment to the happiness of an i. GOVERNMENT, 18
the idea of death as an i. NUCLEAR WEAPONS, 11
The liberty of the i. must be thus far limited FREEDOM, 39
The psychic development of the i. PSYCHIATRY, 15
individualism American system of rugged i. POLITICS, 69
Art is the most intense mode of i. ART, 36
individuality England is the paradise of i. ENGLAND, 43
indolence i. . . . qualified with . . . bad temper RESPECT, 5
Your daily task of i. LAZINESS, 7
indoors God having given us i. and out-of-doors NATURE, 26
indulgence An only son, sir, might expect more i. FAMILY, 24
sign of the cross . . . an i. for all the sins CHRISTIANITY, 6
industrial I. relations are like sexual relations INDUSTRIAL RELATIONS, 2
industry Captains of i. LEADERSHIP, 4
i. will supply their deficiency WORK, 26
Life without i. is guilt ART, 25
national i. of Prussia WAR, 100
inebriated i. with . . . his own verbosity PRIME MINISTERS, 20
inelegance a continual state of i. WEATHER, 7
ineligible honourably i. for the struggle of life ARISTOCRACY, 10
inequalities only i. that matter begin in the mind DIFFERENCE, 8
inequality There is always i. . . . Life is unfair INEQUALITY, 1
inevitable ACCIDENT N. AN I. OCCURRENCE ACCIDENTS, 1
Nothing is i. INEVITABILITY, 1
inexactitude terminological i. LYING, 10
inexperience I. is what makes a young man AGE, 59
infallible an i. sign of the second-rate INFALLIBILITY, 3
No man is i. IMPERFECTION, 2
The only i. criterion of wisdom INFALLIBILITY, 2
We are none of us i. IMPERFECTION, 14
infamous I have got an i. army ARMY, 5
infamy A date that shall live in i. WORLD WAR II, 45
infancy between i. and adultery YOUTH, 2
Heaven lies about us in our i. METAPHYSICS, 6
i., childhood, adolescence and obsolescence AGE, 46
Lo, Hudled up, together Lye /Gray Age, Grene youth, White I. ANONYMOUS, 54
infant a mixed i. CHILDREN, 9
An i. crying in the night HUMAN CONDITION, 26
Sooner murder an i. in its cradle DESIRE, 3
infanticide as indefensible as i. BOOKS, 50
infants I. do not cry without some legitimate cause BABIES, 4
infection gazing into that happy future when the i. will be banished ILLNESS, 62
inferior No one can make you feel i. without your consent INFERIORITY, 6
Switzerland . . . an i. sort of Scotland SWITZERLAND, 3
inferiority minds so impatient of i. GRATITUDE, 3
Their Europeanism is . . . imperialism with an i. complex POLITICS, 61
Wherever an i. complex exists, there is . . . reason INFERIORITY, 2
inferiors I. revolt in order that they may be equal REVOLUTION, 1
The English want i. PRIDE, 11
inferno A man who has not passed through the i. of his passions PASSION, 3
infidelity I. . . . consists in professing to believe INTEGRITY, 5
infinite both are i. LOVE, 152
The Desire of Man being I. INFINITY, 1
The sight . . . gave me i. pleasure EXECUTION, 28
infinitive When I split an i. GRAMMAR, 2
infinity I cannot help it; . . . i. torments me INFINITY, 2
I. in the palm of your hand WONDER, 2
infirmities friend should bear his friend's i. FRIENDS, 14
infirmity last i. of noble mind FAME, 17
they desire but prolonged i. OLD AGE, 15
inflation a little i. is like being a little pregnant ECONOMICS, 11
I. in the Sixties was a nuisance ECONOMICS, 16
influence guard against . . . unwarranted i. INFLUENCE, 3
How to . . . I. People INFLUENCE, 2
i. of the Crown has increased MONARCHY, 10
unable to i. events . . . do not have the power BRITAIN, 9
influenza call it i. if ye like ILLNESS, 11
inform not to i. the reader ACHESON, DEAN GOODERHAM, 7
informed far better i. REPARTEE, 98
infortune The worst kinde of i. is this MISFORTUNE, 8
infringement Necessity is the plea for every i. of human freedom NECESSITY, 5
infusion The i. of a China plant DRINKS, 1
ingenious a loyal, a gallant, a generous, an i., and good-temper'd people FRANCE, 17
inglorious the i. arts of peace POLITICIANS, 80
ingratitude Austria will astound the world with . . . her i. DIPLOMACY, 22
I hate i. more in a man INGRATITUDE, 6
I., thou marble-hearted fiend INGRATITUDE, 5
man's i. INGRATITUDE, 4
ingress Our i. . . . /Was naked and bare CARE, 7
inherit Russia will certainly i. the future RUSSIA, 3
inherited infinitely fragile and never directly i. HUMAN NATURE, 18
inhibition Freud and his three slaves, I., Complex and Libido PSYCHOANALYSIS, 16
inhumanity Man's i. to man CRUELTY, 2
initiative success depends . . . upon individual i. and exertion EFFORT, 5
injured Never trust the man who . . . hath i. you TRUST, 2
injury An i. is much sooner forgotten INSULTS, 30
Recompense i. with justice KINDNESS, 3
injustice A lawyer has no business with . . . justice or i. JUSTICE, 18
fear of suffering i. JUSTICE, 27
threatened with a great i. INJUSTICE, 5
what a man still plans . . . shows the . . . i. in his death DEATH, 45
injustices thought only to justify their i. HUMAN NATURE, 27
ink an optimist . . . fills up his crossword puzzle in i. OPTIMISM, 35
inmost Where you may see the i. part of you SELF-KNOWLEDGE, 9
inn no room for them in the i. BIBLICAL QUOTATIONS, 418
To that dark i., the grave DEATH, 128
inner Conscience is the i. voice CONSCIENCE, 6
exploring Outer Space, /To find the I. Man SPACE, 5
strengthened . . . in the i. man BIBLICAL QUOTATIONS 116
Innisfree I will arise and . . . go to I. SOLITUDE, 19
innocence it is . . . our business to lose i. FATE, 4
my i. begins to weigh me down INNOCENCE, 2
Ralph wept for the end of i. INNOCENCE, 5
innocent Every one is i. LAW, 3
ten guilty persons escape than one i. suffer JUSTICE, 4
innocently i. employed than in getting money MONEY, 24

innovator time is the greatest i. INNOVATION, 1
inquiry The world is but a school of i. CURIOSITY, 5
inquisitive the i. mind can . . . receive no answer ANSWERS, 8
insane he is pronounced i. by all smart doctors MENTAL ILLNESS, 3
if we tried to shut up the i. MADNESS, 42
Man is quite i. RELIGION, 57
Ordinarily he is i. MADNESS, 19
insanity Drunkenness is simply voluntary i. DRUNKENNESS, 26
I. in individuals is something rare MADNESS, 27
I. is hereditary MADNESS, 24
I. is often the logic of an accurate mind overtaxed MADNESS, 20
lay interest in ecclesiastical matters . . . often a prelude to i. RELIGION, 76
Where does one go from a world of i. MADNESS, 11
inscrutable Dumb, i. and grand CATS, 1
fathom the i. workings of Providence REPARTEE, 95
insect the Egyptians worshipped an i. POLITICIANS, 43
insemination Surely you don't mean by unartificial i. SEX, 103
insensitiveness the greatest deeds require a certain i. INSENSITIVITY, 4
inseparably Taxation and representation are i. united TAXATION, 16
inside attention to the i. . . . contempt for the outside BOOKS, 15
insight moment's i. . . . worth a life's experience EXPERIENCE, 17
insignificance A man of . . . the utmost i. INSULTS, 40
insignificant as i. men as any in England ARISTOCRACY, 20
insolence a wretch who supports with i. INSOLENCE, 1
i. is not invective IMPERTINENCE, 2
the i. of wealth INSOLENCE, 2
insolent their i. and unfounded airs of superiority FRANCE, 18
insomnia *Amor vincit i.* LOVE, 67
every man's i. is as different from his neighbor's SLEEP, 13
I. troubles only those who can sleep any time SLEEP, 19
inspiration Genius is one per cent i. GENIUS, 4
I. is the act of drawing up a chair INSPIRATION, 3
Ninety per cent of i. INSPIRATION, 2
instinct the i. for being unhappy SORROW, 21
institution Any i. which does not suppose the people good CORRUPTION, 10
more than a game. It's an i. CRICKET, 4
institutions working of great i. BUREAUCRACY, 7
instructed the worst i. ARISTOCRACY, 6
instruction The most essential part of a student's i. EDUCATION, 39
instrument An i. to tickle human ears MUSIC, 9
there you sit with that magnificent i. between your legs INCOMPETENCE, 5
The state is an i. . . . of the ruling class STATE, 5
insufferable It is Oxford that has made me i. EDUCATION, 12
insult adding i. to injuries AGGRAVATION, 1
A man should not i. his wife publicly MARRIAGE, 145
One does not i. the river god PRUDENCE, 5
sooner forgotten than an i. INSULTS, 30
insulted anyone here whom I have not i. INSULTS, 20
insured you cannot be i. for the accidents . . . most likely to happen ACCIDENTS, 2
insurrection I. is an art REVOLUTION, 13
integrate I i. the current export drive BUSINESS, 3
integrity if I accepted the honour . . . I would not answer for the i. of my intellect TITLES, 3
I. without knowledge is weak INTEGRITY, 4
intellect a feather to tickle the i. PUNS, 12
a mark of superior i. PESSIMISM, 7
a road . . . that does not go through the i. EMOTION, 1
halitosis of the i. INSULTS, 66
his i. is not replenished IGNORANCE, 19
i. is . . . fooled by the heart EMOTION, 4
I. is invisible INTELLECT, 9
put on I. WISDOM, 13
take care not to make the i. our god INTELLECT, 2
the soul of a martyr with the i. of an advocate POLITICIANS, 11
The voice of the i. is a soft one INTELLECT, 3
we cannot exclude the i. from . . . any of our functions INTELLECT, 6
intellects highest i., like the tops of mountains INTELLECT, 7
There is a wicked inclination . . . to suppose an old man decayed in his i. OLD AGE, 56
intellectual an i. . . . mind watches itself INTELLECTUALS, 6
artist who's an i. ARTISTS, 5
Every i. attitude is latently political POLITICS, 96
i., but I found it too difficult HUMILITY, 10
i. . . . doesn't know how to park a bike INTELLECTUALS, 1
I've been called many things, but never an i. INTELLECTUALS, 3
Man is an i. animal INTELLECT, 5
The word I. suggests INTELLECTUALS, 2
thirdly, i. ability EDUCATION, 8
intellectuals impudent snobs who characterize themselves as i. MEDIA, 1
i.' chief cause of anguish INTELLECTUALS, 4
Pointy-headed i. INTELLECTUALS, 15
vanishing race. . . . the i. INTELLECTUALS, 12
intelligence a story of amazing foolishness and amazing i. MEDICINE, 101
I. is quickness to apprehend ABILITY, 2
i. is the great polluter ENVIRONMENT, 9
i. of the American people INTELLIGENCE, 6
The more i. . . . the more . . . one finds original INTELLIGENCE, 8
intelligent A really i. man feels what other men . . . know INTELLIGENCE, 7
Each generation imagines itself . . . more i. AGE, 55
i. people . . . are socialists SOCIALISM, 2
stupid are cocksure . . . i. full of doubt DOUBT, 8
The i. are to the intelligentsia INTELLIGENCE, 3
intelligentsia intelligent are to the i. INTELLIGENCE, 3
intelligible to aim at being i. COMMUNICATION, 2
intended i. to give you some advice ADVICE, 13
intensity excellence of every art is its i. ARTS, 6
intent A truth that's told with bad i. TRUTH, 13
prick the sides of my i. AMBITION, 21
intercourse dreary i. of daily life OPTIMISM, 40
i. is . . . a social act SEX, 33
Sexual i. began /In nineteen sixty-three SEX, 54
interest How can I take an i. in my work ENTHUSIASM, 2
It is not my i. to pay the principal, nor my principle to pay the i. BORROWING, 10
interested always been i. in people MISANTHROPY, 2
The average man is . . . i. in a woman who is i. in him SEXES, 9
interests all these great i. entrusted to the shaking hand POLITICIANS, 118
intérieur 'Vive l'i. HISTORY, 36
intermarriage By i. and by every means in his power DIPLOMACY, 21
intermission Pleasure is . . . i. of pain PAIN, 8
international I. Woman's Day RUSSIAN REVOLUTION, 8
science is essentially i. SCIENCE, 23
internist An i. is someone who knows everything SPECIALISTS, 1
interns scrub of i. LANGUAGE, 3
interrupted Mr Wordsworth is never i. INTERRUPTIONS, 3
interval an opera without an i., or an i. without an opera OPERA, 8
interviewing i. a faded female in a damp basement INSULTS, 56
intolerably I would grow i. conceited CONCEIT, 22
intolerant what is dangerous about extremists is . . . that they are i. POLITICS, 82
intoxicate you won't i. with one glass someone who has . . . drunk . . . a . . . barrel EXPERIENCE, 11
intoxicated A man who exposes himself when he is i. DRUNKENNESS, 20
No, thank you, I was born i. DRUNKENNESS, 25
intoxication best of life is . . . i. DRUNKENNESS, 13
intrigue the i. of a Greek of the lower empire INSULTS, 42
introduce let me i. you to that leg of mutton INTRODUCTIONS, 1
introduction I could buy back my i. INTRODUCTIONS, 2
intrudes society, where none i. NATURE, 5
invade when religion is allowed to i. . . . private life RELIGION, 54
invalid an invaluable permanent i. called Bunbury DECEPTION, 11
Every i. is a physician PATIENTS, 1
invalids the modern sympathy with i. ILLNESS, 67
invasion no stand can be made against i. by an idea IDEAS, 3
the long-promised i. WORLD WAR II, 15
invective insolence is not i. IMPERTINENCE, 2
invent it would be necessary to i. Him GOD, 56
inventing Prolonged . . . reviewing of books involves constantly *i.* reactions CRITICISM, 46
invention A long poem is a test of i. POETRY, 30
i. . . . arises directly from idleness IDLENESS, 3
Woman's virtue is man's greatest i. SEXES, 23
inventions All one's i. are true POETRY, 19
investment There is no finer i. for any community BABIES, 1
To bear many children is considered . . . an i. CHILDREN, 27
inviolable the i. shade HOPE, 7
invisible no i. means of support ATHEISM, 4
the only evil that walks /I. HYPOCRISY, 13
invisibly electricity was dripping i. SCIENCE, 84
invited People were not i. – they went there PARTIES, 6
involuntary It was i.. They sank my boat MODESTY, 4
inward They flash upon that i. eye SOLITUDE, 17
Iowa Hollywood – a place where people from I. CINEMA, 1
Ireland a picture of a relief map of I. APPEARANCE, 6
English should give I. home rule IRELAND, 19
'How's poor ould I., and how does she stand?' ANONYMOUS, 46
I'll not forget old I. HOMESICKNESS, 1
I never met anyone in I. who understood the Irish question IRELAND, 8
I. is the old sow IRELAND, 11
I would have liked to go to I. IRELAND, 22
Now I. has her madness POETRY, 5
The moment . . . I. is mentioned IRELAND, 21
The problem with I. IRELAND, 13
Irish All races have . . . economists, with the exception of the I. ECONOMICS, 9
answer to the I. Question IRISH, 9
as I. as Black Americans IRISH, 6
historic inability in Britain to comprehend I. feelings IRELAND, 9
I. . . . devotion to higher arts ECONOMICS, 9
I. might do very good Service IRISH, 10
That is the I. Question IRELAND, 7
The English and Americans dislike only *some* I. IRISH, 3
The I. and the Jews have a psychosis IRISH, 2
The I. are a fair people IRISH, 7
The I., . . . are needed in this cold age IRISH, 4
The I. don't know what they want IRISH, 8
Irishman Put an I. on the spit IRISH, 1
iron An i. curtain COLD WAR, 2
muscles . . . /Are strong as i. bands IRON, 3
rule them with a rod of i. BIBLICAL QUOTATIONS, 585
the i. enter into his soul BITTERNESS, 4
the i. has entered his soul INSULTS, 88
The I. Lady of British politics POLITICIANS, 2
the I. Lady of the Western World APPEARANCES, 37
will wink and hold out mine i. COWARDICE, 9
ironies Life's Little I. LIFE, 40
irons Many i. in the fire PROVERBS, 284
two i. in the fire PRUDENCE, 6
irrelevant the most i. thing in nature FAMILY, 29
irreproachable compulsory and i. idleness ARMY, 3
irresponsible better to be i. and right RESPONSIBILITY, 5
Isaac the God of I. BIBLICAL QUOTATIONS, 132
Ishmaelites I. . . . will not publicly eat human flesh uncooked in Lent CANNIBALISM, 3
Islam In some remote regions of I. MODESTY, 5
I. unashamedly came with a sword ISLAM, 1
island No man is an I. SOCIETY, 4
wealth of our i. may be diminished ENGLISH, 14
islands less known by the British than these selfsame British I. BRITISH, 2
isle Kelly from the I. of Man ABSENCE, 8

this sceptred i. EARTH, 16
isolating by i. him . . . as if he were a leper IRELAND, 16
isolation At the moment of childbirth, every woman has the same aura of i. LONELINESS, 7
our splendid i. DIPLOMACY, 10
Israel When I. was in Egypt land, /Let my people go ANONYMOUS, 108
Italian as sensible as baseball in I. OPERA, 7
I speak . . . I. to women, French to men LANGUAGE, 11
The crafty, cold-blooded, black-hearted I. FASCISM, 2
italics 'I adore i., don't you?' LITERATURE, 21
Italy A man who has not been in I. TRAVEL, 21
I. a paradise for horses NATIONALITY, 5
itch The i. of disputing . . . the scab of churches RELIGION, 83
the i. of literature WRITING, 26
The Seven Year I. SEX, 11
What used to be merely an i. is now an allergy PROGRESS, 1
iteration i. of nuptials MARRIAGE, 44
itself Love seeketh not i. to please LOVE, 33
Iutae the *Saxones, Angli,* and *I.* ENGLISH, 6

J

jab Man, . . . had been created to j. the life out of Germans WAR, 136
Jack Damn you, J. – I'm all right SELFISHNESS, 3
J. and Jill went up the hill /To fetch a pail of water NURSERY RHYMES, 24
J. of all trades OCCUPATIONS, 3
J. Sprat could eat no fat NURSERY RHYMES, 25
Little J. Horner /Sat in the corner NURSERY RHYMES, 29
the house that J. built NURSERY RHYMES, 57
jackal This whipped j. WORLD WAR II, 24
jackals J. piss at their foot BOOKS, 19
Jackson J. standing like a stone wall DETERMINATION, 4
Jacob Talk to him of J.'s ladder PRACTICALITY, 4
the God of J. BIBLICAL QUOTATIONS, 132
the traffic of J.'s ladder HEAVEN, 14
Jael J. the wife of Heber BIBLICAL QUOTATIONS, 390
jail being in a ship is being in a j. BOATS, 10
jam J. today, and men aren't at their most exciting PROMISES, 7
The rule is, j. tomorrow and j. yesterday PROMISES, 4
James King J. is good and honest ROYALTY, 86
The work of Henry J. has always seemed divisible WRITERS, 18
James Joyce J. . . . Nothing but old fags and cabbage stumps of quotations WRITERS, 30
Jane if ever I was to have a dozen girls, I'd call 'em all J. NAMES, 15
John Thomas says good-night to Lady J. SEX, 56
Time's up for Sir John, an' for little Lady J. PARTING, 7
jangled j. in every ale-house and tavern BIBLE, 7
January dreadful pictures of J. and February WINTER, 8
Janvier Generals J. and Février WINTER, 3
Japan not necessarily to J.'s advantage DEFEAT, 8
There was a young man of J. ANONYMOUS, 95
Japanese The J. have perfected good manners PLACES, 37
jargon Murder with j. where his medicine fails DOCTORS, 45
The j. of scientific terminology LANGUAGE, 19
jaundiced with the j. eye PASSION, 10
jawbone with the j. of an ass BIBLICAL QUOTATIONS, 395
jaw-jaw To j. is better than to war-war DIPLOMACY, 5
jazz J. . . . people hear it through their feet JAZZ, 3
J. will endure POPULAR MUSIC, 11
The basic difference between classical music and j. JAZZ, 2
the J. Age . . . became less and less an affair of youth AGE, 33
jealous a j. God BIBLICAL QUOTATIONS, 147
a j. God GOD, 14
Art is a j. mistress ART, 7
j. for they are j. JEALOUSY, 10
jealousy J. . . . feeling alone among smiling enemies JEALOUSY, 2
J.'s rife in heroes' hall POLITICIANS, 53
of j.; /It is the green-ey'd monster JEALOUSY, 8
the ear of j. heareth all things BIBLICAL QUOTATIONS, 660
Jeepers J. Creepers EYES, 6
jeering laughing and j. at everything . . . strange ENGLISH, 33
jeers j. at Fate ENVY, 2
Jeeves J. coughed one soft, low, gentle cough ANALOGY, 6
like P. G. Wodehouse dropping J. WRITERS, 57
Jefferson Thomas J. – when he said, not less than two hours a day should be devoted to exercise HEALTHY LIVING, 28
when Thomas J. dined alone TALENT, 7
jelly Out vile j. EYES, 8
the way he eats j. beans CHARACTER, 21
jelly-boned Curse the blasted, j. swines CURSES, 2
Jemmy Young J. Grove on his death-bed lay ANONYMOUS, 49
Jenny J. kissed me when we met KISSING, 3
Jericho by faith the walls of J. fell down BIBLICAL QUOTATIONS, 235
Jerusalem J. ENGLAND, 6
J. the golden PLACES, 28
J. . . . the mother of us all BIBLICAL QUOTATIONS, 170
that great city, the holy J. BIBLICAL QUOTATIONS, 602
the holy city, new J. BIBLICAL QUOTATIONS, 601
Till we have built J. ENGLAND, 6
jest a fellow of infinite j. MISQUOTATION, 21
A j.'s prosperity lies in the ear HUMOR, 56
glory, j., and riddle of the world HUMAN CONDITION, 19
Life is a j. LIFE, 38
jesting j. Pilate ANSWERS, 1
Jesus All hail, the power of J.' name CHRISTIANITY, 51
Gentle J. HUMILITY, 14
If J. Christ were to come to-day BELIEF, 5
J. loves me – this I know RELIGION, 73
J. picked up twelve men from the bottom ranks CHRISTIANITY, 4
J. was . . . a first-rate political economist CHRISTIANITY, 54
J. was not . . . marrying sort MARRIAGE, 98
more popular than J. Christ POPULAR MUSIC, 8
when J. was born in Bethlehem of Judaea BIBLICAL QUOTATIONS, 463
jeunesse *Si j. savait* AGE, 31
Jew An American is either a J., or an anti-Semite UNITED STATES, 88
difficult for a J. to be converted JEWS, 8
Einstein – the greatest J. since Jesus SCIENTISTS, 6
hated /by every anti-semite /as if I were a J. PREJUDICE, 16
Hath not a J. eyes EQUALITY, 26
I'm a colored, one-eyed J. DISABILITY, 2
I'm not really a J.; just J.-ish HALF MEASURES, 2
I was born of Christian race, /And not a Heathen, or a J. RELIGION, 74
neither J. nor Greek BIBLICAL QUOTATIONS, 169
no intellectual society can flourish where a J. feels . . . uneasy JEWS, 10
No J. was ever fool enough to turn Christian JEWS, 21
Pessimism is a luxury that a J. never can allow himself JEWS, 13
jewel that most precious j., the Word of God BIBLE, 7
jewelry Don't ever wear artistic j. JEWELRY, 1
j. . . . wrecks a woman's reputation JEWELRY, 1
she did not remember . . . her j. PRUDENCE, 10
The rest of you rattle your j. AUDIENCES, 5
jewels a capital bosom to hang j. upon APPEARANCE, 19
Jewish A J. man with parents alive JEWS, 18
a *total solution* of the J. question NAZISM, 2
best that is in the J. blood JEWS, 11
I'm not really a Jew; just J. HALF MEASURES, 2
only half-J. JEWS, 12
Jewry Modern Physics is an instrument of J. ANTISEMITISM, 1
Jews But spurn the J. JEWS, 7
J. require a sign BIBLICAL QUOTATIONS, 27
King of the J. BIBLICAL QUOTATIONS, 463
not enough prisons . . . in Palestine to hold all the J. JEWS, 14
The Irish and the J. have a psychosis IRISH, 2
The J. and Arabs should . . . settle their differences GOLDWYNISMS, 26
the J. bring the unlike into the heart of *every milieu* JEWS, 20
the J. have made a contribution to the human condition JEWS, 19
The J. have produced . . . Christ, Spinoza, and myself CONCEIT, 18
To choose /The J. JEWS, 6
Jezebel J. . . . painted her face BIBLICAL QUOTATIONS, 406
Jill Jack and J. went up the hill NURSERY RHYMES, 24
Jim Lucky J. BOOK TITLES, 2
jingo We don't want to fight, but, by j. if we do FIGHT, 12
jo John Anderson my j. NOSTALGIA, 4
Joan greasy J. doth keel the pot WINTER, 6
Job hast thou considered my servant J. BIBLICAL QUOTATIONS, 295
J. endured everything – until his friends came ENDURANCE, 8
the Lord answered J. out of the whirlwind BIBLICAL QUOTATIONS, 310
the Lord blessed the latter end of J. BIBLICAL QUOTATIONS, 315
job Being a husband is a whole-time j. MARRIAGE, 22
Giz a j. UNEMPLOYMENT, 1
If two men on the same j. agree AGREEMENT, 7
We have finished the j. TELEGRAMS, 9
we will finish the j. WORLD WAR II, 16
woman's ability to stick to a j. WOMEN, 115
jockey the . . . cup is given to the j. INJUSTICE, 7
Joe Hungry J. collected lists of fatal diseases ILLNESS, 29
John D'ye ken J. Peel HUNTING, 5
Hell itself is defiled by . . . King J. EPITAPHS, 28
J. Anderson my jo NOSTALGIA, 4
J. Brown's body GRAVE, 6
Matthew, Mark, Luke and J. BLESSING, 1
Think no more of it, J.; you are only a child FORGIVENESS, 16
Time's up for Sir J., an' for little Lady Jane PARTING, 7
Johnny J. head-in-air IDEALISM, 9
J.-the-bright-star REALISM, 4
J. underground IDEALISM, 9
Johnson Dr J.'s morality was as English . . . as a beefsteak ENGLAND, 24
Dr J.'s sayings WRITERS, 21
That great Cham of literature, Samuel J. WRITERS, 54
There is no arguing with J. WRITERS, 17
join He's gone to j. the majority DEATH, 24
will you j. the dance DANCING, 2
joined what . . . God hath j. together, let not man put asunder BIBLICAL QUOTATIONS, 518
joke A j.'s a very serious thing HUMOR, 14
a j. with a double meaning HUMOR, 7
A rich man's j. is always funny FLATTERY, 3
good deed to forget a poor j. HUMOR, 11
Housekeeping ain't no j. HOUSEWORK, 1
The coarse j. proclaims HUMOR, 34
jokes different taste in j. is a . . . strain on the affections HUMOR, 22
Forgive . . . my little j. on Thee JOKES, 4
He cannot bear old men's j. JOKES, 3
I don't make j. GOVERNMENT, 34
joking My way of j. is to tell the truth TRUTH, 45
jolly There was a j. miller HAPPINESS, 4
Jonah a great fish to swallow up J. BIBLICAL QUOTATIONS, 383
and the lot fell upon J. BIBLICAL QUOTATIONS, 382
Joneses drag the J. down to my level ONE-UPMANSHIP, 1
Jordan the people were passed clean over J. BIBLICAL QUOTATIONS, 384
Joseph Here lies J., who failed in everything he undertook EPITAPHS, 19
jot one j. or one tittle BIBLICAL QUOTATIONS, 474
journal *Punch* – the official j. JOURNALISM, 1
journalism Christianity, . . . but why j. CHRISTIANITY, 2
J. is the only job that requires no degrees JOURNALISM, 14
j.. . . . keeps us in touch with the ignorance of the community JOURNALISM, 42

K

The man is k. time TIME, 30
To save a man's life against his will is . . . k. him KILLING, 5
kills Time is a great teacher, but . . . k. all its pupils TIME, 11
time quietly k. them TIME, 13
Who k. a man k. a reasonable creature BOOKS, 30
Yet each man k. the thing he loves KILLING, 10
kilt Is anything worn beneath the k. CLOTHES, 15
The k. is an unrivalled garment for fornication SCOTS, 9
kin, author of himself /And knew no other k. SELF-RELIANCE, 13
kind a k. parent . . . or a merciless step-mother NATURE, 28
be cruel only to be k. CRUELTY, 5
being k. /Is all the sad world needs KINDNESS, 12
charity suffereth long, and is k. BIBLICAL QUOTATIONS, 44
He was a vicious man, but very k. CHARACTER, 15
I love thee for a heart that's k. HEART, 7
Too k., too k. GRATITUDE, 7
try to be *k.* ACADEMICS, 5
kindle the sole purpose of human existence is to k. a light EXISTENCE, 3
a young person, who . . . marries or dies, is sure to be k. spoken of HUMAN NATURE, 2
the deities so k. DESTINY, 19
kindness a cup o' k. yet FRIENDSHIP, 17
A word of k. is better than a fat pie KINDNESS, 1
for his k. they still remain in his debt KINDNESS, 9
full o' th' milk of human k. KINDNESS, 10
greetings where no k. is OPTIMISM, 40
its unembarrassed k., its insight into life KINDNESS, 7
kill a wife with k. KINDNESS, 11
recompense k. with k. KINDNESS, 3
set a high value on spontaneous k. FRIENDSHIP, 25
the k. of strangers CHARITY, 27
True k. presupposes the faculty KINDNESS, 6
unremembered acts /Of k. and of love KINDNESS, 13
Woman Killed with K. BOOK TITLES, 11
you will find light and help and human k. HOSPITALS, 9
kindred Like k. drops, been mingled MOUNTAINS, 1
king A constitutional k. must learn to stoop MONARCHY, 15
A k. is a thing MONARCHY, 19
a k. may make a nobleman CHIVALRY, 3
A k. of shreds and patches INFERIORITY, 7
All the k.'s horses, /And all the k.'s men NURSERY RHYMES, 18
an atheist if the k. were KINGS AND KINGDOMS, 9
and Northcliffe has sent for the K. EDITORS, 2
a new k. over Egypt BIBLICAL QUOTATIONS, 128
An unlettered k. is a crowned ass MONARCHY, 1
Authority forgets a dying k. ROYALTY, 101
A worse k. never left a realm undone ROYALTY, 33
better . . . a poor and a wise child than an old and foolish k. BIBLICAL QUOTATIONS, 85
better have one K. than five hundred GOVERNMENT, 10
But not my griefs; still am I k. of those DECLINE, 12
but the K. of England cannot enter DEFIANCE, 4
curse not the k., no not in thy thought BIBLICAL QUOTATIONS, 95
every inch a k. ROYALTY, 96
Every man a k. EQUALITY, 17
Every subject's duty is the K.'s MONARCHY, 22
George, be a K. ROYALTY, 21
God save our Gracious K. BRITAIN, 5
great k., . . . fell all at once REVOLUTION, 2
half the zeal I serv'd my K. REGRET, 18
harm that cometh of a k.'s poverty TAXATION, 5
heart and stomach of a K. ROYALTY, 49
He played the K. as though CRITICISM, 19
Here lies our sovereign lord the K. EPITAPHS, 37
if I were not k., I should lose my temper ROYALTY, 75
I'm the k. of the castle NURSERY RHYMES, 23
I think the K. is but a man EQUALITY, 23
I wanted to be an up-to-date k. KINGS AND KINGDOMS, 16
I will that a k. succeed me ROYALTY, 53
k. is always a k. FEMINISM, 45
k. is incompetent to govern ROYALTY, 100
K. of England changes his ministers ROYALTY, 62
K. of Scots was named to succeed her ROYALTY, 34
k. reigns, but does not govern MONARCHY, 27
k.'s council . . . chosen of the great princes, and of the greatest lords of the land GOVERNMENT, 12
Mrs Simpson's pinched our k. ROYALTY, 15
No Bishop, no K. CHURCH, 4
rather hew wood than be . . . K. of England MONARCHY, 7
service rendered to the temporal k. to the prejudice of the eternal k. TREASON, 11
such divinity doth hedge a k. DIVINITY, 2
That whatsoever K. shall reign, /I'll be the Vicar of Bray, Sir ANONYMOUS, 48
the faith, prayer and self-dedication of the K. ROYALTY, 26
the k. can do no wrong MONARCHY, 5
the K. . . . could see things if he would ROYALTY, 31
The k. has been very good to me MARTYRDOM, 1
The k. never dies MONARCHY, 6
The K. of Spain's daughter /Came to visit me NURSERY RHYMES, 20
The K. over the Water ANONYMOUS, 83
The k. reigns, and the people govern themselves MONARCHY, 24
The k. sits in Dunfermline town ANONYMOUS, 84
The k. was in his counting-house, /Counting out his money NURSERY RHYMES, 47
The present life of men on earth, O k. LIFE, 9
this House . . . fight for its K. and Country ANONYMOUS, 78
wash the balm from an anointed k. MONARCHY, 23
kingdom glory of your k. EDUCATION, 3
It is folly . . . to mistake the echo of a . . . coffee-house for the . . . k. KINGS AND KINGDOMS, 15
k. and the priesthood, are brought together by divine mystery POLITICS, 112
my k. for a horse HORSES, 10
No k. has . . . had as many . . . wars as the k. of Christ CHRISTIANITY, 47
Our k. . . . we place at your disposal DIPLOMACY, 12
remember me when thou comest into thy k. BIBLICAL QUOTATIONS, 448
repent: for the k. of heaven is at hand BIBLICAL QUOTATIONS, 470
the k. of God is not in word, but in power BIBLICAL QUOTATIONS, 30
the k. of God is within you BIBLICAL QUOTATIONS, 442
this formidable K. is . . . a province of a despicable Electorate ENGLAND, 40
kingfish I'm the K. POWER, 15
kings Conquering k. their titles take ROYALTY, 37
Grammar, which can govern even k. GRAMMAR, 6
how to dissimulate is the knowledge of k. ROYALTY, 90
If you get the English people into the way of making k. ROYALTY, 80
K. are earth's gods ROYALTY, 97
K. . . . are just as funny ROYALTY, 93
K. are naturally lovers of low company ROYALTY, 30
k. enough in England HOUSES OF PARLIAMENT, 12
K. govern by . . . assemblies only when MONARCHY, 12
Or walk with K. IDEALISM, 3
Pale Death kicks his way . . . into . . . the castles of k. EQUALITY, 31
sad stories of the death of k. ROYALTY, 98
Such grace had k. ROYALTY, 29
teeming womb of royal k. EARTH, 16
The English nation . . . has successfully regulated the power of its k. GOVERNMENT, 40
the K. of England, Diamonds, Hearts, Spades and Clubs MONARCHY, 11
The power of k. and magistrates POWER, 17
This royal throne of k. EARTH, 16
till philosophers become k. PHILOSOPHY, 12
'Twixt k. and tyrants there's this difference KINGS AND KINGDOMS, 6
kingship k. approaches tyranny it is near its end TYRANNY, 9
kinquering K. Congs their titles take SPOONERISMS, 3
Kipling W. H. Auden, a sort of gutless K. SOCIALISM, 20
kippers like two old k. in a box OLD AGE, 97
Kish that is come into the son of K. BIBLICAL QUOTATIONS, 609
kiss A k. without a moustache KISSING, 6
come let us k. and part PARTING, 6
effrontery to k. me on the lips ETIQUETTE, 2
Every time we k. he says 'Murder!' LOVE, 97
Killing myself to die upon a k. LOVE AND DEATH, 8
K. me, Hardy LAST WORDS, 59
K. me Kate, we will be married o' Sunday MARRIAGE, 119
make me immortal with a k. BEAUTY, 25
spend that k. /Which is my heaven to have JEALOUSY, 6
stop his mouth with a k. LOVE, 139
The coward does it with a k. KILLING, 10
The k. of sun for pardon GARDENS, 7
Then come k. me, sweet and twenty PRESENT, 13
the rough male k. of blankets BED, 4
Without a single k. or a good-bye PARTING, 8
you must not k. and tell SECRECY, 9
You must remember this; /A k. is just a k. TIME, 22
kissed Being k. by a man who didn't wax his moustache KISSING, 4
hail, master; and k. him BETRAYAL, 3
I k. her little sister UNFAITHFULNESS, 4
Jenny k. me when we met KISSING, 3
k. her once by the pig-sty EXPECTATION, 8
K. the girls and made them cry NURSERY RHYMES, 12
Wherever one wants to be k. COSMETICS, 2
kisses bread and cheese, and k. BACHELORS, 3
remembered k. after death NOSTALGIA, 26
Stolen sweets are always sweeter, /Stolen k. much completer THEFT, 7
kissing it was made /For k. CONTEMPT, 6
K. don't last FOOD, 52
The President spends most of his time k. PERSUASION, 3
when the k. had to stop BOOK TITLES, 7
kit-bag pack up your troubles in your old k. OPTIMISM, 13
kitchen A good K. is a good Apothecaries shop FOOD, 18
can't stand the heat, get out of the k. ENDURANCE, 24
the way of all flesh . . . towards the k. FOOD, 71
Kitchener If K. was not a great man, he was . . . a great poster OFFICERS, 2
K-K-K-Katy K., beautiful Katy LOVE, 109
knackery end up in the Tory k. POLITICIANS, 68
knave The K. of Hearts /He stole the tarts NURSERY RHYMES, 52
knaves world is made up . . . of fools and k. FOOLISHNESS, 11
knee at the name of Jesus every k. should bow BIBLICAL QUOTATIONS, 563
He insisted that this should be *k.-jerk* WORDS, 14
knee-cap The soul started at the k. ANIMALISM, 5
knees die on your feet than to live on your k. COURAGE, 17
knew I k. him, Horatio MISQUOTATION, 21
much righter than one k. at say 17 or 23 AGE, 58
O! that she k. she were LOVE, 148
what we once k. is of little consequence MATHEMATICS, 22
knife I had a k. and two forks left ETIQUETTE, 7
it keeps them on the k. ANONYMOUS, 41
last twist of the k. LIFE, 32
stuck a k. in the Queen.' OPERATIONS, 12
War even to the k. WAR, 35
knight every chance brought out a noble k. NOSTALGIA, 25
I never realized that I'd end up being the shortest k. of the year PUNS, 22
mounted k. is irresistable SOLDIERS, 2
Poor K.! he really had two periods WRITING, 32
There came a k. to be their wooer ANONYMOUS, 98
what can ail thee, k. at arms ILLNESS, 37
knights gives me great joy to see . . . k. and horses in battle array PLEASURE, 19
sorrier for my good k.' loss than for . . . my fair queen LOSS, 3
knitter a beautiful little k. INSULTS, 112
knives Night of the Long K. FASCISM, 4
Phone for the fish k. Norman ETIQUETTE, 1
knock Don't k. it SEX, 3
k., and it shall be opened unto you BIBLICAL QUOTATIONS, 488
k. him down first, and pity him afterwards PITY, 2
Three, four, /K. at the door NUMBERS, 4
knocked k. everything except the knees of the chorus girls THEATER, 10
we k. the bastard off ACHIEVEMENT, 6
know all /Ye k. on earth BEAUTY, 24

A really intelligent man feels what other men . . . k. INTELLIGENCE, 7
Children with Hyacinth's temperament . . . merely k. more CHARACTER, 22
for they k. not what they do BIBLICAL QUOTATIONS, 447
I do not k. myself SELF-KNOWLEDGE, 5
I k. as much as God knew MATHEMATICS, 23
I k. I am God GOD, 6
I k. myself SELF-KNOWLEDGE, 4
I k. that my redeemer liveth BIBLICAL QUOTATIONS, 306
I k. thee not, old man OLD AGE, 84
I k. what I like SUBJECTIVITY, 1
Jesus I k., and Paul I k. BIBLICAL QUOTATIONS, 14
K. then thyself, presume not God to scan SELF-KNOWLEDGE, 7
K. thyself PROVERBS, 246
Not many people k. that KNOWLEDGE, 9
scarcely hate any one that we k. HATE, 5
Teach thy tongue to say 'I do not k..' KNOWLEDGE, 31
the gentleman in Whitehall really does k. better POLITICS, 73
the only person . . . I should like to k. EGOTISM, 11
the words 'I do not k.' stick in every physician's throat REMEDIES, 56
To k. how to say what others only . . . think SPEECH, 8
tragedy of the world that no one knows what he doesn't k. IGNORANCE, 7
we k. not where they have laid him BIBLICAL QUOTATIONS, 368
we should occupy our minds only with what we continue to k. MATHEMATICS, 22
What we k. of the past HISTORY, 19
What you don't k. IGNORANCE, 3
What you don't k. would make a great book IGNORANCE, 21
You k. . . . what you are KNOWLEDGE, 20
knowed The clever men at Oxford /Know all that there is to be k. KNOWLEDGE, 18
knowest thou k. all things BIBLICAL QUOTATIONS, 374
knowing A woman, especially if she have the misfortune of k. anything WOMEN, 14
knowledge a k. of nothing KNOWLEDGE, 13
All k. is of itself of some value KNOWLEDGE, 23
all k. to be my province KNOWLEDGE, 4
all our k. is, ourselves to know SELF-KNOWLEDGE, 8
an age in which useless k. KNOWLEDGE, 22
an intimate k. of its ugly side DISILLUSION, 1
civilizations . . . abandon the quest for k. KNOWLEDGE, 28
Foolish the doctor who despises the k. DOCTORS, 55
for ignorance is never better than k. NATURE, 13
he giveth . . . k. to them that know understanding BIBLICAL QUOTATIONS, 56
how to dissimulate is the k. of kings ROYALTY, 90
If a little k. is dangerous, where is the man . . . out of danger KNOWLEDGE, 21
if a little k. was a dangerous thing KNOWLEDGE, 35
if education is . . . a mere transmission of k. EDUCATION, 61
Integrity without k. is weak INTEGRITY, 4
K. advances by steps KNOWLEDGE, 29
k. and wonder . . . is an impression of pleasure KNOWLEDGE, 5
K. can be communicated but not wisdom WISDOM, 20
K. dwells /In heads replete KNOWLEDGE, 12
K. indeed is a desirable HOLISTIC MEDICINE, 5
K. is of two kinds KNOWLEDGE, 26
K. is power PROVERBS, 244
K. is proportionate to being KNOWLEDGE, 20
K. is the mother KNOWLEDGE, 1
K. itself is power KNOWLEDGE, 3
k. puffeth up BIBLICAL QUOTATIONS, 37
lawyers . . . have taken away the key of k. BIBLICAL QUOTATIONS, 435
let him receive the new k. HEAVEN, 4
light of k. in their eyes KNOWLEDGE, 36
No, I ask it for the k. of a lifetime ARTISTS, 16
only uneducated people show off their k. QUOTATIONS, 7
Our k. can only be finite KNOWLEDGE, 34
province of k. to speak KNOWLEDGE, 19
Science is the father of k. OPINIONS, 2
the river of k. has too often turned back on itself SCIENCE, 54
the search for k. PHILOSOPHERS, 10
the tree of the k. of good and evil BIBLICAL QUOTATIONS, 181
the tree of the k. of good and evil GARDENS, 3
What I don't know isn't k. ACADEMICS, 2
worth a pound of k. KNOWLEDGE, 37
you impart k. of it through another's death RESEARCH, 17
known apart from the k. and the unknown METAPHYSICS, 5
going from the k. to the unknown RESEARCH, 6
knows a woman who k. all . . . that can be taught INSULTS, 29
Greatness k. itself SELF-KNOWLEDGE, 11
He that k. little IGNORANCE, 1
He that k. nothing IGNORANCE, 2
he thinks he k. everything POLITICIANS, 99
He who k. only his own side . . . k. little SUBJECTIVITY, 4
how little one k. oneself SELF-KNOWLEDGE, 3
Only the nose k. . . . SECRECY, 1
knuckle-end k. of England SCOTLAND, 8
knyf The smyler with the k. HYPOCRISY, 8
knyght parfit, gentil k. CHIVALRY, 4
Kodak painted . . . by the great artist K. PHOTOGRAPHY, 6
Kubla In Xanadu did K. Khan PLEASURE, 9

L

labor all ye that l. and are heavy laden BIBLICAL QUOTATIONS, 503
A mountain in l. shouted so loud DISAPPOINTMENT, 4
l. of love BIBLICAL QUOTATIONS, 642
little effect after much l. LABOR, 1
Man . . . can only find relaxation from one . . . l. by taking up another CHANGE, 8
Medical practice is not knitting and weaving and the l. of the hands MEDICINE, 58
Temperance and l. are the two real physicians of man WORK, 28
the l. having been . . . rather in a circle than in progression MEDICINE, 8
To l. and not ask for any reward FIGHT, 14
water, honey, and l. REMEDIES, 5
laboratorium *L. est oratorium* SCIENCE, 63
laboratory A first-rate l. is one SCIENCE, 9
All the world is a l. SCIENCE, 38
if I may offer advice to the young l. worker RESEARCH, 12
I see there are l. men here.' DOCTORS, 60
the l. has never found proof RESEARCH, 10
We're all of us guinea pigs in the l. of God MANKIND, 71
laborer the l. is worthy of his hire BIBLICAL QUOTATIONS, 430
laboring rights and interests of the l. man STRIKES, 1
labors absorbs a clay /After his l. LABOR, 4
Children sweeten l. CHILDREN, 6
labor-saving inventing l. devices . . . manufactured an abyss of boredom BOREDOM, 8
Labour
an Independent L. Party PARTIES, 10
disastrous element in the L. party POLITICS, 37
England elects a L. Government POLITICS, 119
genius the L. Party has for cutting itself in half POLITICS, 31
L. is not fit to govern POLITICS, 32
model L. voter POLITICS, 84
pederasts who call themselves the L. Party SOCIALISM, 1
political leader for the L. Party is a desiccated calculating machine LEADERSHIP, 1
the Gromyko of the L. party POLITICIANS, 58
The grotesque chaos of a L. council – a *L.* council INCOMPETENCE, 2
labyrinthine I fled Him, down the l. ways RELIGION, 68
lack l. of power corrupts absolutely PRESIDENTS, 16
own up to a l. of humor HUMOR, 15
lad many a lightfoot l. NOSTALGIA, 12
ladder behold a l. set up on earth BIBLICAL QUOTATIONS, 216
Talk to him of Jacob's l. PRACTICALITY, 4
the traffic of Jacob's l. HEAVEN, 14
We make ourselves a l. out of our vices VICE, 2
ladies How sweet are looks that l. bend WOMEN, 114
lion among l. FEAR, 19
lady Dance, dance, dance little l. DANCING, 3
I want to talk like a l. SPEECH, 18
L. Bountiful CHARITY, 15
l. doth protest too much EXCESS, 9
l. of a certain age AGE, 19
l. of Christ's College POETS, 4
My fair l. BRIDGE, 4
O lang will his L. /Look owre the Castle Downe ANONYMOUS, 110
The Iron L. of British politics POLITICIANS, 2
the Iron L. of the Western World APPEARANCES, 37
the L. Is a Tramp DECLINE, 2
The l.'s not for turning INFLEXIBILITY, 3
there had been a l. in the case WOMEN, 29
There is a l. sweet and kind ANONYMOUS, 87
When a l. says no . . . means perhaps WORDS, 8
young l. named Bright LIGHT, 7
ladybird L., l., /Fly away home NURSERY RHYMES, 26
Lady Chatterley *L.'s Lover* . . . all Christians might read with profit PORNOGRAPHY, 6
Put thy shimmy on, L. PARTING, 7
Lady Macbeth A combination of Little Nell and L. WRITERS, 62
ladyship When your l.'s faith has removed them RELIGION, 20
Lafayette L., we are here GREETINGS, 7
lag a comfortable time l. . . . between the perception PROGRESS, 23
lag-end entertain the l. of my life /With quiet hours OLD AGE, 83
laid all the young ladies who attended the Yale promenade dance were l. end to end SEX, 77
get rich, get famous and get l. FAME, 13
l. on with a trowel EXCESS, 11
we know not where they have l. him BIBLICAL QUOTATIONS, 368
laissez *L. faire* FREEDOM, 49
L. faire, laissez passer FREEDOM, 17
lake An arm /Rose up from . . . the l. ARTHURIAN LEGEND, 2
Marriage may often be a stormy l. MARRIAGE, 103
sedge is wither'd from the l. ILLNESS, 37
lamb a l. as it had been slain BIBLICAL QUOTATIONS, 587
as a l. to the slaughter BIBLICAL QUOTATIONS, 276
Did he who made the L. make thee CREATION, 8
l. . . . without blemish BIBLICAL QUOTATIONS, 138
Little L., who made thee CREATION, 9
Mary had a little l. ANIMALS, 14
one little ewe l. ANIMALS, 5
Pipe a song about a L. MUSIC, 12
the l. is the light thereof BIBLICAL QUOTATIONS, 603
the L. of God BIBLICAL QUOTATIONS, 318
to make the lion lie down with the l. HUMAN NATURE, 17
washed . . . in the blood of the l. BIBLICAL QUOTATIONS, 590
worthy is the l. that was slain BIBLICAL QUOTATIONS, 588
Lambeth doin' the L. walk DANCING, 5
lambs feed my l. BIBLICAL QUOTATIONS, 373
send you forth as l. among wolves BIBLICAL QUOTATIONS, 430
We're poor little l. DEBAUCHERY, 8
lame your precious 'l. ducks' WEAKNESS, 2
lament reason to l. /What man has made of man MANKIND, 72
lamp my l. burns low and dim ENVY, 3
To keep a l. burning CHARITY, 25
lampada *vitai l.* GENERATIONS, 1
lamp-post I'm leaning on a l. LOVE, 66
like asking a l. . . . about dogs CRITICS, 6
share a quick pee over a common l. WRITERS, 12
lamp-posts He uses statistics as a drunken man uses l. STATISTICS, 5
lamps l. are going out all over Europe PROPHECY, 9
new l. for old ones BUSINESS, 2
the people are forbidden to light l. INJUSTICE, 12
trimmed their l. BIBLICAL QUOTATIONS, 532
Ye living l. BIRDS, 11
Lancelot bold Sir L. CHIVALRY, 13
lancet Diet cures more than the l. HEALTHY LIVING, 10

lawyers L. are the only persons in whom ignorance . . . is not punished LAWYERS, 4
let's kill all the l. LAWYERS, 10
woe unto you, l. BIBLICAL QUOTATIONS, 435
laxative be afraid to commit themselves to the doctrine that castor oil is a l. DIAGNOSIS, 8
sweet l. of Georgian strains SPRING, 2
lay I never would l. down my arms PATRIOTISM, 32
L. your sleeping head SLEEP, 6
Lazarus L. . . . laid at his gate, full of sores BIBLICAL QUOTATIONS, 441
lazy be efficient if you're going to be l. LAZINESS, 3
There are no ugly women, only l. ones BEAUTY, 31
lead L., kindly Light FAITH, 23
leader A l. who doesn't hesitate . . . is not fit to be a l. LEADERSHIP, 9
I have to follow them, I am their l. LEADERSHIP, 6
one man in a thousand is a l. of men LEADERSHIP, 8
One Realm, One People, One L. NAZISM, 1
political l. for the Labour Party is a desiccated calculating machine LEADERSHIP, 1
Take me to your l. GREETINGS, 1
leadership men do not approach to l. LEADERSHIP, 2
the very stuff of political l. LEADERSHIP, 13
leap a great l. in the dark DARKNESS, 11
A l. over the hedge PRAYER, 10
And twenty-nine in each l. year NURSERY RHYMES, 56
It isn't the ecstatic l. across BED, 3
one giant l. for mankind MISQUOTATION, 3
leapt Into the dangerous world I l. BIRTH, 5
learn always ready to l. LEARNING, 7
know enough who know how to l. EDUCATION, 2
L., compare, collect the facts EDUCATION, 68
l. from mistakes, not from example LEARNING, 10
The life so short, the craft so long to l. MORTALITY, 12
we could never l. to be brave . . . if there were only joy COURAGE, 18
What we have to l. to do LEARNING, 2
youth now in England . . . be set to l. EDUCATION, 4
learned A l. man is an idler EDUCATION, 75
I am . . . of the opinion with the l. AGREEMENT, 2
the l. roast an egg FOOD, 60
learning A little l. is a dangerous thing KNOWLEDGE, 33
A progeny of l. MALAPROPISMS, 3
beauty and the lust for l. BEAUTY, 7
I have been l. how to die DEATH, 173
I thought that I was l. how to live DEATH, 173
l., earning and yearning LIFE, 60
L. hath gained most BOOKS, 20
L. is a treasure KNOWLEDGE, 2
L. is but an adjunct LEARNING, 16
L. is good in and of itself EDUCATION, 17
L. without thought is labour lost KNOWLEDGE, 11
public school, where . . . l. was painfully beaten into him EDUCATION, 69
Their l. is like bread in a besieged town BREAD, 6
learnt
child must say something that he has merely l. LEARNING, 8
I l. just by going around LEARNING, 1
I only remember what I've l. KNOWLEDGE, 38
people . . . never have l. anything from history EXPERIENCE,
Soon l. EDUCATION, 1
least death . . . the l. of all evils DEATH, 27
L. said soonest mended ARGUMENTS, 2
Strongest minds / . . . the noisy world /Hears l. MIND, 36
the l. of these my brethren BIBLICAL QUOTATIONS, 538
leave Fare thee well, for I must l. thee ANONYMOUS, 88
How I l. my country LAST WORDS, 64
If you l. a thing alone you l. it to a torrent of change CONSERVATISM, 2
L. well alone PROVERBS, 252
to l. his country as good as he had found it DUTY, 1
leaves before the l. have fallen WAR, 172
If poetry comes not . . . as l. to a tree POETRY, 32
No fruits, no flowers, no l., no birds MONTHS, 10
the l. . . . were for the healing of the nations BIBLICAL QUOTATIONS, 604
Though l. are many, the root is one AGE, 88
With vine l. in his hair RETURN, 3
Words are like l. VERBOSITY, 7
leave-taking thou tell'st the world /It is not worth l. WORLD-WEARINESS, 7
leaving became him like the l. it DEATH, 141
She's l. home DEPARTURE, 8
leavings sacrifice . . . of the devil's l. SACRIFICE, 4
lecher small gilded fly does l. ANIMALISM, 7
lechery drink . . . an equivocator with l. ALCOHOL, 68
Still wars and l. SEX, 96
lectures l. or a little charity SELF, 23
led l. by the nose with gold BRIBERY, 5
leech A skilful l. is better far DOCTORS, 27
leeches l. have red blood LAST WORDS, 23
left a handful of silver he l. us BETRAYAL, 5
And we are l., or shall be l., alone DEFEAT, 18
better to be l. than never to have been loved LOVE, 52
man who l. a wife and six children on the parish ROYALTY, 13
You just press the accelerator to the floor and steer l. SPORT AND GAMES, 23
leg Any fool can cut off a l. SURGEONS, 13
here I leave my second l. PUNS, 10
Lose a l. rather than life OPERATIONS, 1
legal collect l. taxes from illegal money TAXATION, 3
legality do not let so great an achievement suffer from . . . l. LAW, 22
legs cannon-ball took off his l. PUNS, 9
close my eyes, open my l. and think of England MISQUOTATION, 17
there you sit with that magnificent instrument between your l. INCOMPETENCE, 5
You were born with your l. apart PROMISCUITY, 6
Leicester Square Good-bye Piccadilly, Farewell L. HOMESICKNESS, 8
leisure gentleman of l. MATERIALISM, 25
I am interested in l. . . . can't get enough of it LEISURE, 4
Men . . . detest at l. LOVE AND HATE, 1
more l., better clothes, better food HEALTHY LIVING, 39
Prince Philip. . . . a world expert on l. ROYALTY, 71
The secret of being miserable is to have l. SORROW, 26
Very few people can endure much l. LEISURE, 2
wisdom . . . cometh by opportunity of l. BIBLICAL QUOTATIONS, 112
lemon The Germans . . . are going to be squeezed, as a l. RETRIBUTION, 10
lend I would not l. my pony now, /For all the lady's hire NURSERY RHYMES, 21
L. only that PROVERBS, 253
lender Neither a borrower nor a l. be BORROWING, 8
lene As l. was his hors as is a rake HORSES, 4
Lenin L.'s method leads to this COMMUNISM, 19
L. was the first to discover that capitalism 'inevitably' caused war CAPITALISM, 18
transported L. . . . like a plague bacillus RUSSIAN REVOLUTION, 3
Lent Ishmaelites . . . will not publicly eat human flesh uncooked in L. CANNIBALISM, 3
Leonardo Disney the most significant figure . . . since L. ART, 15
leopard or the l. his spots BIBLICAL QUOTATIONS, 292
leper by isolating him . . . as if he were a l. IRELAND, 16
leprosy It is full of l. PRACTICALITY, 2
scant as hair /In l. SPARSENESS, 1
lerne gladly wolde he l. CHARACTER, 4
less found it l. exciting COWARDICE, 3
I love not Man the l. NATURE, 5
l. in this than meets the eye CRITICISM, 3
L. is more ARCHITECTURE, 9
Specialist – A man who knows more and more about l. and l. EXPERTS, 7
the l. they have . . . the more noise they make CHARACTER, 20
let I l. down my friends BETRAYAL, 11
kick you out, but . . . never l. you down EDUCATION, 88
L. It Be IDEALISM, 6
L. it be, l. it pass FREEDOM, 49
Lethe go not to L. OBLIVION, 2
wait upon the tedious shores of L. INSIGNIFICANCE, 4
letter I have made this l. longer VERBOSITY, 6
Offensive l. follows INSULTS, 3
Someone . . . wants a l. from you LETTER-WRITING, 2
thou unnecessary l. INSULTS, 110
writing a l. and forgetting to sign his name INSULTS, 12
letters His sayings are generally like women's l. LETTER-WRITING, 4
The profession of l. . . . in which one can make no money without being ridiculous WRITING, 36
the republic of l. MANKIND, 1
When I pass my name in such large l. FAME, 27
level-headed When things are steep, remember to stay l. SELF-CONTROL, 4
levellers Your l. wish to level *down* as far as themselves EQUALITY, 14
leviathan canst thou draw out l. with an hook BIBLICAL QUOTATIONS, 314
that great L., or rather . . . that *Mortal God* STATE, 1
lexicographer L. . . . harmless drudge LEXICOGRAPHY, 6
to wake a l. LEXICOGRAPHY, 4
liaison partly a l. man and partly P.R.O BUSINESS, 3
liar A l. is worse LYING, 1
He did not feel a l. LYING, 16
Mr. Speaker, I said the honorable member was a l. APOLOGIES, 6
Poor Bonar can't bear being called a l. POLITICIANS, 73
you are . . . the club Bore: I am the club L. SUPERIORITY, 14
liars It has made more l. LYING, 19
l. and swearers enow to beat the honest men GOOD AND EVIL, 7
the Cretians are alway l. BIBLICAL QUOTATIONS, 657
Lib I owe nothing to Women's L. FEMINISM, 36
libel writs for l. and slander THREATS, 8
Liberal either a little L. POLITICS, 55
liberal a l. education at the Colleges of Unreason REASON, 1
ineffectual l.'s problem LIBERALISM, 2
Just like an old l. /Between the wars BANKS, 6
the damned, compact, l. majority MAJORITY, 6
When a l. is abused, he says LIBERALISM, 4
liberality L. lies less in giving liberally PROMPTNESS, 1
liberal-minded booksellers are generous l. men PUBLISHING, 8
Liberals L. think that goats are just sheep from broken homes LIBERALISM, 1
liberation truly mankind's war of l. HUNGER, 7
liberté *L.! Égalité! Fraternité* ANONYMOUS, 51
liberties government will protect all l. but one FREEDOM, 44
libertine Prince was . . . a l. over head and ears in debt ROYALTY, 67
liberty condition upon which God hath given l. FREEDOM, 12
Corruption . . . symptom of constitutional l. CORRUPTION, 4
don't suppose . . . a revolution is going to bring l. REVOLUTION, 7
extremism in the defence of l. is no vice EXCESS, 5
give me l. or give me death FREEDOM, 21
If men are to wait for l. FREEDOM, 35
It is true that l. is precious FREEDOM, 32
King still stands between us and l. FRENCH REVOLUTION, 7
l. as an essential condition of excellence OXFORD, 9
l. cannot long exist CORRUPTION, 1
l. for one person is constrained only EQUALITY, 12
L. is so much latitude as the powerful FREEDOM, 19
L. is the hardest test FREEDOM, 59
L. is the right to do everything FREEDOM, 42
l. . . . is to be measured not by the governmental machinery SOCIETY, 13
L. means responsibility FREEDOM, 55
L. . . . not . . . mere declarations of the rights of man FREEDOM, 61
L. of action FREEDOM, 17
L., too, must be limited FREEDOM, 8
l. . . . what on earth would they do COMMUNISM, 9
life, l., and the pursuit of happiness HUMAN RIGHTS, 3
love of l. is the love of others FREEDOM, 20
Oh l.! . . . What crimes are committed in thy name EXECUTION, 35
Power . . . and L. . . . are seldom upon good Terms FREEDOM, 18

All that is l. seeks to communicate power BOOKS, 17
All the rest is l. SCIENCE, 87
American professors like their l. . . . dead LITERATURE, 14
great deal of history to produce a little l. HISTORY, 20
He knew everything about l. except how to enjoy it LITERATURE, 6
If we can't stamp out l. PHILISTINISM, 7
I . . . impress upon you the study of Greek l. CLASSICS, 4
itch of l. WRITING, 26
Language, man! . . . it's L. LITERATURE, 24
L. and butterflies are the two sweetest passions BUTTERFLIES, 1
L. flourishes best LITERATURE, 9
L. is mostly about having sex LITERATURE, 15
L. is news LITERATURE, 19
L. is simply language charged with meaning LITERATURE, 20
L. is strewn with the wreckage of men WRITERS, 61
L. is the orchestration of platitudes LITERATURE, 25
l. . . . poisoned by its own secretions LANGUAGE, 8
L. . . . something that will be read twice JOURNALISM, 16
no l. can outdo the cynicism of real life EXPERIENCE, 11
Renaissance is a mere ripple on the surface of l. LITERATURE, 13
That great Cham of l., Samuel Johnson WRITERS, 54
The Bible is l. BIBLE, 12
the chief difference between l. and life LITERATURE, 8
litter What men call social virtues, . . . is . . . but the virtue of pigs in a l. SOCIETY, 15
little Every l. helps HELP, 1
He who knows only his own side . . . knows l. SUBJECTIVITY, 4
it was a very l. one EXCUSES, 2
L. things affect little minds TRIVIALITY, 5
Man wants but l. MORTALITY, 9
So l. done, so much to do LAST WORDS, 73
the l. things are infinitely the most important TRIVIALITY, 7
'These l. grey cells INTELLECT, 1
Little Nell A combination of L. and Lady Macbeth WRITERS, 62
the death of L. without laughing INSENSITIVITY, 5
littleness the l. of those that should carry them out SUPPORT, 2
the long l. of life LIFE, 27
liv'd And they that L. and Lov'd Either, /Should Dye and Lye and Sleep together ANONYMOUS, 54
live All would l. long, but none would be old OLD AGE, 3
anything but l. for it RELIGION, 22
better to die on your feet than to l. on your knees SELF-RESPECT, 2
Come l. with me LOVE, 56
die on your feet than to l. on your knees COURAGE, 17
Do not try to l. forever LONGEVITY, 13
Do you want to l. for ever WAR, 50
eat to l., not l. to eat EATING, 8
from the mouths of people who have had to l. LIFE AND DEATH, 33
he forgets to l. LIFE AND DEATH, 20
hence its name – liver, the thing we l. with BODY, 3
He that would l. for aye, must eat sage in May LONGEVITY, 2
Houses are built to l. in HOUSES, 1
I eat to l. FOOD, 34
If God were suddenly condemned to l. the life HUMAN CONDITION, 7
If you l. long enough, the venerability factor creeps in LONGEVITY, 15
I have learned to l. each day as it comes PRESENT, 3
in him we l., and move, and have our being BIBLICAL QUOTATIONS, 13
in order to l. in an unlivable situation MENTAL ILLNESS, 4
in Rome, l. as the Romans CONFORMITY, 2
I thought that I was learning how to l. DEATH, 173
I want to love first, and l. incidentally LOVE, 64
Like a rose, she has lived as long as roses l. FATE, 14
L. all you can; it's a mistake not to LIFE, 45
L. among men as if God beheld you RIGHTEOUSNESS, 10
L. and learn EXPERIENCE, 5
l. beyond its income EXTRAVAGANCE, 2
l. dangerously DANGER, 6
l. for ever or die in the attempt IMMORTALITY, 4
L. Now, Pay Later FUTURE, 13
L. that thou mayest desire to live again AFTERLIFE, 8
Live that thou mayest desire to l. again AFTERLIFE, 8
L. this day, as . . . thy last PRESENT, 12
l. to fight another day ANONYMOUS, 38
L. with the gods CONTENTMENT, 1
One can't l. on love alone LOVE, 179
People do not l. nowadays LIFE, 31
people l. beyond their incomes EXTRAVAGANCE, 4
Rascals, would you l. for ever WAR, 60
Science says: 'We must l.' LIFE AND DEATH, 34
self-willed determination to l. LIFE AND DEATH, 19
Sometimes they l. DOCTORS, 57
Teach me to l. DEATH, 92
than to l. up to them PRINCIPLES, 1
there shall no man see me, and l. BIBLICAL QUOTATIONS, 157
They l. ill LONGEVITY, 16
those who l. . . . believe . . . to be the truth HONESTY, 4
Those who l. by . . . a lie, and those who l. by . . . the truth HONESTY, 4
To l. is like love LIFE, 20
to l. will be more miserable than to die SUICIDE, 15
To l. with thee, and be thy love LOVE, 120
we l. but to make sport RIDICULE, 1
We l. in stirring times PRESENT, 11
we l. not alone BODY, 20
we must l. as though . . . never going to die ACHIEVEMENT, 11
wish to l., . . . first attend your own funeral LIFE AND DEATH, 23
You might as well l. SUICIDE, 23
you will l. to ninety-nine LONGEVITY, 1
lived Never to have l. is best LIFE, 91
no man . . . hath l. better than I ACHIEVEMENT, 9
She . . . has never l. LOVE, 69
slimy things L. on GUILT, 5
livelihood slave for l. ENVY, 3
liver L, n. a large red organ BODY, 3
the positions of the l. and the heart MEDICINE, 67
Liverpool L. is the pool of life PLACES, 20
This god-forsaken city . . . L. SPEECH, 3
lives He that l. long PROVERBS, 195
He who l. by the sword CONFLICT, 3
he who l. more l. than one DEATH, 176
l. of quiet desperation DESPAIR, 10
men devote the greater part of their l. MANKIND, 34
no man loses any other life than . . . he now l. LIFE, 7
the stage of the disease at which he l. LIFE, 78
You medical people will have more l. to answer for DOCTORS, 24
liveth their name l. for evermore BIBLICAL QUOTATIONS, 115
living A house is a machine for l. in HOUSES, 3
A l. is made . . . by selling something that everybody needs ARTISTS, 17
a proper way of l. be adopted ENVIRONMENT, 1
are you yet l. CONVERSATION, 10
Civilization is a method of l. CIVILIZATION, 1
Dying is as natural as l. LIFE AND DEATH, 2
Evolution is far more important than l. EVOLUTION, 20
he who lives without tobacco isn't worthy of l. SMOKING, 6
History is . . . the wrong way of l. HISTORY, 10
How good is man's life, the mere l. LIFE, 17
I make war on the l. REVENGE, 9
It does not then concern either the l. or the dead DEATH, 60
let the earth bring forth the l. creature ANIMALS, 3
life had prepared Podduyev for l. DEATH 157
L. frugally, . . . he died early ABSTINENCE, 2
L. is a sickness LIFE, 23
l. need charity CHARITY, 3
L. well and beautifully and justly LIFE, 80
no one has yet found a way to drink for a l. ALCOHOL, 48
search the land of l. men ADMIRATION, 14
Television . . . permits you to be entertained in your l. room TELEVISION, 7
the l. are the dead on holiday LIFE, 52
the l. bread BIBLICAL QUOTATIONS, 333
The noble l. and the noble dead NOBILITY, 8
two people l. together for 25 years without having a cross word MARRIAGE, 76
Vietnam was lost in the l. rooms of America TELEVISION, 12
We owe respect to the l. RESPECT, 4
why seek ye the l. among the dead BIBLICAL QUOTATIONS, 450
Livingstone Dr L., I presume EXPLORATION, 5
llama a female l. surprised in her bath INSULTS, 32
Lloyd George L. could not see a belt . . . hitting below it INSULTS, 4
loaf half a l. is better than a whole l. COMPROMISE, 5
loafed It is better to have l. and lost LAZINESS, 9
loathe I l. the country COUNTRYSIDE, 1
loaves five barley l., and two small fishes BIBLICAL QUOTATIONS, 330
lobby not a man would go into the L. against us MISQUOTATION, 4
local settle up these little l. difficulties POLITICS, 92
Lochinvar young L. CHIVALRY, 9
locusts l. and wild honey BIBLICAL QUOTATIONS, 465
lodge a l. in some vast wilderness SOLITUDE, 3
log-cabin L. to White House ACHIEVEMENT, 10
logic L. must take care of itself LOGIC, 8
L., . . . thinking . . . with the limitations . . . of the human understanding LOGIC, 1
That's l. LOGIC, 2
the l. of our times DECLINE, 3
The principles of l. and metaphysics are true PHILOSOPHY, 1
You can only find truth with l. LOGIC, 4
logical consequences L. are the scarecrows of fools LOGIC, 6
logik un-to l. hadde longe y-go LOGIC, 3
loitered I l. my life away, reading books DISCONTENT, 3
loitering Alone and palely l. ILLNESS, 37
Lolita L., light of my life LUST, 8
Lomon' On the bonnie, . . . banks o' Loch L. ANONYMOUS, 67
London dominate a L. dinner-table INFLUENCE, 14
Dublin, though . . . much worse than L. PLACES, 19
great city of L. LONDON, 15
Hell is a city much like L. HELL, 7
I don't know what L.'s coming to LONDON, 8
I, General de Gaulle, now in L. WORLD WAR II, 26
I've been to L. to look at the queen NURSERY RHYMES, 40
I would sell L. LONDON, 20
L. . . . Clearing-house of the World ECONOMICS, 5
L. is a splendid place to live in LONDON, 3
L., that great cesspool LONDON, 9
L., that great sea LONDON, 21
L., thou art the flour of Cities all LONDON, 10
Nobody is healthy in L. LONDON, 2
the agricultural labourers . . . commute from L. COUNTRYSIDE, 9
the best club in L. CLUBS, 2
the lowest and vilest alleys of L. SIN, 16
When a man is tired of L. LONDON, 17
you have dined in every house in L. – *once* BORES, 9
You will hear more good things on . . . a stagecoach from L. to Oxford INTELLECTUALS, 10
Londoner spirit of the L. stands resolute LONDON, 12
loneliest the l. job in the world OCCUPATIONS, 10
loneliness L. . . . is the most terrible poverty LONELINESS, 11
l. may spur you into finding something LONELINESS, 3
l. of my country and my God LONELINESS, 9
lonely All the l. people LONELINESS, 4
l. of heart is withered away HEART, 23
None But the L. Heart BOOK TITLES, 15
She left l. for ever DEPARTURE, 2
the l. sea and the sky SEA, 10
Lonelyhearts Write to Miss L. ADVICE, 23
lonesome A l. man . . . who does not know how to read READING, 6
one, that on a l. road FEAR, 9
long a l., l. way to Tipperary HOMESICKNESS, 8

M

Ma'am Bloody hell, M. ROYALTY, 4
macaroni And called it M. NURSERY RHYMES, 69
Macaulay apostle of the Philistines, Lord M. PHILISTINISM, 2
Lord M. DELIGHT, 11
Macavity there's no one like M. CATS, 2
MacDonald Ramsay M. POLITICIANS, 82
mace that fool's bauble, the m. DISMISSAL, 5
machine a taxing m. TAXATION, 14
cannot endow . . . m. with initiative IDEAS, 5
Man is a beautiful m. MANKIND, 38
One m. can do the work of fifty ordinary men MACHINES, 1
Our body is a m. for living BODY, 24
the Ghost in the M. MIND, 29
The human body is a m. BODY, 16
The m. is running away with *him* POWER, 23
The m. threatens MACHINES, 2
machine-gun a m. riddling her hostess SYMPATHY, 4
machinery liberty . . . is to be measured not by the governmental m. SOCIETY, 13
machines M. . . . keep free men in subjection TECHNOLOGY, 4
no reason . . . these m. will ever force themselves into general use MACHINES, 4
mackerel M. sky and mares' tails PROVERBS, 277
Macmillan M. seemed . . . to embody the national decay DECLINE, 5
MacWonder M. one moment and MacBlunder the next POLITICIANS, 77
mad All of us are m. MADNESS, 5
being m. among madmen MADNESS, 9
Don't get m., get even REVENGE, 13
escaped from a m. and savage master SEX, 98
Every one is more or less m. on one point MADNESS, 22
half of the nation is m. ENGLISH, 36
he ceased to be m. he became merely stupid MALADIES, 3
he first makes m. MADNESS, 1
I am but m. north-north-west MADNESS, 32
I said of laughter, it is m. BIBLICAL QUOTATIONS, 79
let me not be m. MADNESS, 35
M. about the boy LOVE, 53
M. as the Mist and Snow MADNESS, 45
'M.' is . . . a man who is obsessed with one idea OBSESSIONS, 2
Men are so necessarily m. MADNESS, 28
Men will always be m. MADNESS, 43
Never go to bed m. ANGER, 4
The dog . . . /Went m. and bit the man DOGS, 7
There is a pleasure sure /In being m. MADNESS, 10
We all are born m. MADNESS, 4
We want a few m. people now MADNESS, 37
When we remember that we are all m. MADNESS, 41
Whom Fortune wishes to destroy she first makes m. MADNESS, 39
who turns m. for a reason MADNESS, 6
madam M. I may not call you TITLES, 2
madame Call me m. TITLES, 7
Madame Bovary All I could think of . . . was: *M.* NOVELS, 12
maddest those who think they can cure them are the m. MADNESS, 43
made Annihilating all that's m. OBLIVION, 3
Don't you think I was m. for you LOVE, 63
Do you know who m. you CREATION, 14
Little Lamb, who m. thee CREATION, 9
many a gentle person m. a Jack CLASS, 38
My father m. . . . you . . . out of nothing DEFIANCE, 3
we're all m. the same SIMILARITY, 4
Madeira We're from M. EUROPE, 16
madeleine The taste was that of the little crumb of m. MEMORY, 14
mademoiselle A m. from Armenteers FRANCE, 16
Madison How were the receipts today in M. Square Garden LAST WORDS, 6
madman frightens us in a m. MADNESS, 14
If a m. were to come into this room PITY, 2
The m. . . . has lost everything except his reason MADNESS, 7
The m. thinks the rest of the world crazy MADNESS, 38
Thou call'st me m. INSULTS, 19
madmen The world is so full of simpletons and m. MADNESS, 18
madness a dash of m. SANITY, 1
destroyed by m., starving hysterical naked MADNESS, 17
devil's m. – War WAR, 146
every man . . . , and every woman, has a dash of m. MADNESS, 12
Great Wits . . . to M. near alli'd GENIUS, 3
I felt pass over me a breath of wind from the wings of m. MADNESS, 3
M. and suffering can set themselves no limit MENTAL ILLNESS, 5
M. in great ones MADNESS, 34
M. is part of all of us MADNESS, 15
M. need not be all breakdown MADNESS, 23
Much M. is divinest Sense MADNESS, 8
Much Sense – the starkest M. MADNESS, 8
Now Ireland has her m. POETRY, 5
Our occasional m. is less wonderful MADNESS, 31
Sanity is m. put to good uses MADNESS, 30
The great proof of m. MADNESS, 26
What is m. /To those who only observe MADNESS, 16
What is m. MADNESS, 44
maestro Music, M., Please MUSIC, 27
maggot how to create a m. RELIGION, 57
magic men mistook m. for medicine MEDICINE, 100
That old black m. SUPERNATURAL, 11
magicians if the way had not been prepared by m. SCIENCE, 66
magistrate Obscenity . . . happens to shock some elderly . . . m. PRUDERY, 5
suppose . . . the m. corruptible CORRUPTION, 10
magistrates rather than that the sovereigns and m. should be destroyed REBELLION, 11
The power of kings and m. POWER, 17
Magna Charta M. is such a fellow MONARCHY, 9
magnanimity in victory, m. DEFIANCE, 2
magnetism how do drugs, hygiene and animal m. heal REMEDIES, 28
magnificent some m. myth PROPAGANDA, 6
there you sit with that m. instrument between your legs INCOMPETENCE, 5
magnifique *c'est m., mais* WAR, 24
magnify my soul doth m. the Lord BIBLICAL QUOTATIONS, 413
Magog Gog and M. BIBLICAL QUOTATIONS, 599
Mahomet If the hill will not come to M. ADAPTABILITY, 2
maid Being an old m. is like death by drowning MARRIAGE, 61
like a moth, the simple m. WOMEN, 51
The m. was in the garden, /Hanging out the clothes NURSERY RHYMES, 47
Where are you going to, my pretty m. NURSERY RHYMES, 67
maiden A m. at college, named Breeze EDUCATION, 6
A simple m. in her flower PURITY, 5
How could you use a poor m. so?' ANONYMOUS, 16
I've a neater, sweeter m. DISCONTENT, 6
many a rose-lipt m. NOSTALGIA, 12
That kissed the m. all forlorn NURSERY RHYMES, 57
maids And pretty m. all in a row GARDENS, 1
Three little m. from school CHILDREN, 28
mail the Night M. crossing the Border TRAVEL, 5
maintenance Zen and the Art of Motorcycle M. PHILOSOPHY, 11
majesty A sight so touching in its m. EARTH, 20
deck thyself . . . with m. and excellency BIBLICAL QUOTATIONS, 313
Her M. is not a subject REPARTEE, 35
her M. . . . must not . . . look upon me as a source of income TAXATION, 12
Her M.'s Opposition OPPOSITION, 1
How can I . . . dislike a sex to which Your M. belongs MISOGYNY, 2
If Her M. stood for Parliament POLITICS, 128
Ride on! ride on in m. CHRISTIANITY, 45
This earth of m. EARTH, 16
When I invented the phrase 'His M.'s Opposition' OPPOSITION, 3
major-general very model of a modern M. KNOWLEDGE, 16
majority A m. is always the best repartee MAJORITY, 4
Fools are in a terrible . . . m. FOOLISHNESS, 15
great changes occur in history . . . the m. are wrong MAJORITY, 2
He's gone to join the m. DEATH, 24
I am certain that we will win the election with a good m. SELF-CONFIDENCE, 9
No candidate . . . elected ex-president by such a large m. DEFEAT, 15
One on God's side is a m. GOD, 47
the damned, compact, liberal m. MAJORITY, 6
the great silent m. MAJORITY, 7
The m. has the might MAJORITY, 5
the tyranny of the m. MAJORITY, 1
majors scarlet M. WAR, 138
make a Scotsman on the m. SCOTS, 2
Love? I m. it constantly SEX, 84
The white man knows how to m. everything CHARITY, 22
maker he adores his m. CONCEIT, 8
I am ready to meet my M. DEATH, 48
Whether my M. is ready for . . . meeting me DEATH, 49
makes either m. me or fordoes me quite DECISION, 5
making He is very fond of m. things FUTILITY, 8
If you get the English people into the way of m. kings ROYALTY, 80
mal *Honi soit qui m. y pense* ARISTOCRACY, 13
maladies all the m. and miseries MALADIES, 2
Heavy thoughts bring on physical m. MELANCHOLY, 9
m. often have their origin there MIND, 22
Medical men . . . call all sorts of m. . . . by one name MALADIES, 1
The dreary . . . tale /Our mortal m. is worn and stale HEALTH, 25
There are m. we must not seek to cure MALADIES, 3
to call all sorts of m. people are liable to . . . , by one name REMEDIES, 18
malady A reckoning up of the cause often solves the m. REMEDIES, 19
a single m. is more easily cured VIVISECTION, 4
Is is the m. of our age YOUTH, 14
not only the m. . . . , but also his habits when in health HOLISTIC MEDICINE, 1
malaise Wembley, adj. Suffering from a vague *m.* HUMOR, 28
male especially the m. of the species MEN, 7
In the sex-war thoughtlessness is the weapon of the m. SEXES, 8
m. and female created he them BIBLICAL QUOTATIONS, 179
more deadly than the m. WOMEN, 61
preserve one last m. thing MASCULINITY, 2
malefactions They have proclaim'd their m. GUILT, 10
malice M. is like a game of poker NASTINESS, 9
malicious God is subtle but he is not m. GOD, 25
malign rather m. oneself EGOTISM, 7
malignant the only part of Randolph that was not m. INSULTS, 124
malignity that peculiar m. . . . characteristic of apostates BETRAYAL, 9
malingering Neurosis has an absolute genius for m. NEUROSIS, 10
malt M. does more than Milton ALCOHOL, 40
malvesye drowned in a barrel of m. EXECUTION, 10
mama the m. of dada NONSENSE, 12
mamas The Last of the Red-Hot M. SINGERS, 3
mammal Like the skins of some small m. APPEARANCE, 8
Mammon M. wins his way where Seraphs might despair MATERIALISM, 7
ye cannot serve God and m. BIBLICAL QUOTATIONS, 482
man A 'Grand Old M.' OLD AGE, 60
all animals were created . . . for the use of m. ANIMALS, 20
a m. after his own heart BIBLICAL QUOTATIONS, 610
a m. can die but once DEATH, 137
a m. has no reason to be ashamed of having an ape for his grandfather REPARTEE, 54
A m. in the house is worth two MEN, 14
a m. is always seeking for happiness MARRIAGE, 56
a m. is a m. for a much longer time SEXES, 2
A m. is as old as he feels PROVERBS, 44
A m. is as old as he's feeling OLD AGE, 38
A m. is as old as his arteries OLD AGE, 95
A m. is not completely born LIFE AND DEATH, 16
A m. is only as old as the woman AGE, 50
A m. . . . is *so* in the way MEN, 4
A m. must serve his time to every trade CRITICS, 2

when a man should m. MARRIAGE, 14
When you see what some girls m. MARRIAGE, 111
while ye may, go m. MARRIAGE, 78
marry'd M. in haste MARRIAGE, 42
marrying Jesus was not . . . m. sort MARRIAGE, 98
Mars Now all labour /M. what it does SELF-DESTRUCTION, 1
seat of M. EARTH, 16
marshal We may pick up a m. or two OFFICERS, 15
Martini out of these wet clothes and into a dry M. ALCOHOL, 88
martyr a m. to music MUSIC, 49
Now he will raise me to be a m. MARTYRDOM, 1
the soul of a m. with the intellect of an advocate POLITICIANS, 11
martyrdom M. is the test FREEDOM, 28
martyrs I look on m. as mistakes MARTYRDOM, 4
The blood of the m. is the seed of the Church CHRISTIANITY, 60
marvel To m. at nothing is just about the one and only thing HAPPINESS, 8
Marx had M. been Groucho instead of Karl HUMOR, 10
M. is a case in point ILLNESS, 27
not even M. is more precious . . . than the truth TRUTH, 50
Marxian M. Socialism must always remain a portent MARXISM, 6
Marxism M. is like a classical building that followed the Renaissance MARXISM, 8
took a grip on cowardly M. NAZISM, 3
Marxist I am not a M. MARXISM, 14
The M. analysis . . . like blaming Jesus Christ for the Inquisition MARXISM, 1
to banish . . . M. socialism MARXISM, 16
wasn't a M. all the time MARXISM, 3
Mary Hail M., full of grace ANONYMOUS, 24
I'm sitting on the stile, M. NOSTALGIA, 8
M. had a little lamb ANIMALS, 14
M., M., quite contrary GARDENS, 1
O M., go and call the cattle home AGRICULTURE, 4
Maryland the hills of M. UNITED STATES, 64
masculine Fighting is essentially a m. idea WOMEN, 52
It makes me feel m. to tell you MASCULINITY, 1
Masefield M.'s sonnets? . . . Yes. Pure M. POETRY, 11
Mass I am a Catholic. . . . I go to M. every day PREJUDICE, 1
Paris is worth a m. PARIS, 3
There is no idolatry in the M. CATHOLICISM, 7
massage plastic surgery . . . combines . . . psychoanalysis, m., and a trip to the beauty salon OPERATIONS, 14
masses Give me your tired, . . . /Your huddled m. UNITED STATES, 36
I will back the m. against the classes CLASS, 18
The uprising of the m. REVOLUTION, 9
master A m. is dead COMPOSERS, 3
commerce between m. and slave is . . . exercise of . . . boisterous passions SLAVERY, 7
Man is the m. of things MANKIND, 61
m., is it I BETRAYAL, 1
m. of himself SELF-CONTROL, 6
m. of his soul, /Is servant to his bladder OLD AGE, 9
Not bound to swear allegiance to any m. FREEDOM, 24
One for the m. NURSERY RHYMES, 4
the M. Mistress of my passion LOVE, 156
the m. of my fate FATE, 10
the morals of a whore, and the manners of a dancing m. CRITICISM, 28
masterpiece Man is Heaven's m. MANKIND, 47
the m. of Nature FRIENDS, 8
Who am I to tamper with a m. CONCEIT, 27
masters an ambitious man has as many m. as . . . may be useful AMBITION, 13
Assistant m. . . . liked little boys EDUCATION, 90
Buy old m. PAINTING, 2
By studying the m. EXPERTS, 1
good servants, but bad m. PASSION, 5
no man can serve two m. BIBLICAL QUOTATIONS, 482
people are the m. PUBLIC, 6
that the m. willingly concede to slaves SLAVERY, 2
mastication EAT, v.i. To perform successively . . . the functions of m. FOOD, 16
masturbation M. is the thinking man's television SEX, 41
m. of war WAR, 125
M.: the primary sexual activity SEX, 99
match man who had missed the last home m. FOOTBALL, 10
mate Healthy people need no bureaucratic interference to m. HEALTHY LIVING, 25
material Increase of m. comforts . . . moral growth MATERIALISM, 11
that which was most m. in the postscript LETTER-WRITING, 3
materialistic Christianity is the most m. of all great religions CHRISTIANITY, 58
only really m. people . . . Europeans MATERIALISM, 19
materialists all the books with which m. have pestered the world SOUL, 17
mates moves, and m., and slays DESTINY, 7
mathematician m. . . . highest rung on the ladder MATHEMATICS, 6
mathematics All science requires m. MATHEMATICS, 1
Angling may be said to be . . . like the m. FISHING, 5
As far as the laws of m. refer to reality MATHEMATICS, 4
How are you at M. MATHEMATICS, 12
I like m. because it is *not* human MATHEMATICS, 21
Let no one ignorant of m. enter here MATHEMATICS, 15
M. may be defined as the subject MATHEMATICS, 18
m. . . . most inhuman of all human activities MATHEMATICS, 5
M. . . . possesses . . . supreme beauty MATHEMATICS, 17
M. . . . sphere of complete abstraction MATHEMATICS, 25
Pure m. consists entirely of assertions MATHEMATICS, 19
quite lawful for a Catholic woman to avoid pregnancy by . . . m. CONTRACEPTION, 9
spirit of delight . . . in m. MATHEMATICS, 16
Matilda You'll come a-waltzing, M. PLACES, 30
matinée Robert Houdin who . . . invented the . . . theater m. THEATER, 20
mating Only in the m. season ANIMALISM, 6
matriarchy In a m. men should be encouraged to take it easy WOMEN, 98
matrimony critical period in m. is breakfast-time MARRIAGE, 77
it jumps from . . . love to m. WOMEN, 15
m., which I always thought a highly overrated performance MARRIAGE, 60
matter It is not much m. which we say UNITY, 12
M. . . . a convenient formula PHILOSOPHY, 14
Mind over m. MIND, 32
proverb is much m. decorated SAYINGS, 4
We die – does it m. when DEATH, 164
Women represent . . . m. over mind SEXES, 33
mattering Art . . . can go on m. once it has stopped hurting ART, 5
matters Nothing m. very much TRIVIALITY, 1
Matthew M., Mark, Luke and John BLESSING, 1
maturing Do you think my mind is m. late AGE, 53
maturity m. is only a short break in adolescence AGE, 32
Maud Come into the garden, M. INVITATIONS, 5
maunder m. and mumble PUBLIC, 8
mausoleums designing m. for his enemies HATE, 7
Max If M. gets to Heaven BUSINESS, 29
maxim A new m. is often a brilliant error ERROR, 9
we have got /The M. Gun POWER POLITICS, 2
May And after April, when M. follows MONTHS, 6
as fresh as is the month of M. CHARACTER, 3
darling buds of M. COMPLIMENTS, 31
Do spring M. flowers MONTHS, 12
got through the perils of winter till at least the seventh of M. WINTER, 8
Here we come gathering nuts in M. ANONYMOUS, 37
I'm to be Queen o' the M. MERRYMAKING, 5
the merry month of M. ANONYMOUS, 86
wish a snow in M. SUITABILITY, 4
maze Life is a m. LIFE, 26
mazes The melting voice through m. running MUSIC, 30
MCC where M. ends and the Church of England begins CHURCH, 8
McCarthyism M. is Americanism POLITICS, 99
McGregor Don't go into Mr M.'s garden ANIMALS, 21
M.D.s Weighed down by B.A.s and M. EDUCATION, 6
me Besides Shakespeare and m., who do you think there is CONCEIT, 17
between m. and the sun REPARTEE, 33
My thought is m. THINKING, 14
we never talk about anything except m. CONCEIT, 21
Whether my Maker is ready for . . . meeting m. DEATH, 49
meal A m. without flesh FOOD, 1
meals Any two m. at a boarding-house FOOD, 44
I was born . . . because my mother needed a fourth at m. BIRTH, 13
mean a more m., stupid . . . ungrateful animal than the public PUBLIC, 13
Down these m. streets COURAGE, 7
He nothing common did or m. EXECUTION, 22
He who meanly admires m. things is a Snob SNOBBERY, 8
it means just what I choose it to m. MEANING, 3
She was a woman of m. understanding INSULTS, 7
whatever that may m. LOVE, 46
'you should say what you m.', the March Hare went on MEANING, 1
meaner A patronizing disposition . . . has its m. side CHARACTER, 7
motives m. than your own MOTIVE, 1
meanest the m. . . . deeds require spirit and talent INSENSITIVITY, 4
the m. of his creatures /Boasts two soul-sides HYPOCRISY, 6
meaning Even when poetry has a m. POETRY, 26
Literature is simply language charged with m. LITERATURE, 20
Nature has never put the fatal question as to the m. of their lives ANSWERS, 9
The least of things with a m. is worth more . . . than the greatest MEANING, 5
meannesses some m. . . . too mean even for man SEXES, 28
means Errors look so very ugly in persons of small m. FORTUNE, 2
I shall have to die beyond my m. EXTRAVAGANCE, 5
Let us all be happy, and live within our m. BORROWING, 12
m. just what I choose it to mean MEANING, 3
Private M. is dead PUNS, 23
We are living beyond our m. ECOLOGY, 5
measle he Wont let his Little Baby have More than One M. at a time DISEASE, 22
measles Love is like the m. LOVE, 81
Love's like the m. LOVE, 82
measure M. still for M. JUSTICE, 29
Shrunk to this little m. CAESAR, 4
measureless caverns m. to man PLEASURE, 9
meat man loves the m. in his youth AGE, 69
one man is appointed to buy the m. MONARCHY, 19
One man's m. DIFFERENCE, 3
out of the eater came forth m. BIBLICAL QUOTATIONS, 392
Some hae m., and canna eat BURNS, ROBERT, 19
The public buys its opinions as it buys its m. PUBLIC, 7
meats m. for the belly BIBLICAL QUOTATIONS, 31
Mecca New York . . . is not M. UNITED STATES, 58
meddling He was m. too much in my private life PSYCHIATRY, 34
media M. . . . come to mean bad journalism MEDIA, 6
medical A m. revolution has extended the life of our elder citizens OLD AGE, 57
an unfair burden upon the m. profession ILLNESS, 61
if the elite of the m. world would be a little less clever THINKING, 5
m. attention – a dog licked me MEDICINE, 96
M. practice is not knitting and weaving and the labor of the hands MEDICINE, 58
the cost of m. care MEDICINE, 49
two objects of m. education EDUCATION, 58
We shall not refuse tobacco the credit of being . . . m. SMOKING, 32
You m. people will have more lives to answer for DOCTORS, 24
medicalization The m. of early diagnosis PATIENTS, 9
medically Who lives m. lives miserably HEALTHY LIVING, 12

great city . . . has the greatest m. and women GREATNESS, 15
Great m. are almost always bad m. . . . POWER, 3
great m. have not commonly been great scholars GREATNESS, 8
happy breed of m. EARTH, 16
honour all m. BIBLICAL QUOTATIONS, 561
It brings m. together in crowds and mobs in bar-rooms SOCIETY, 15
It's not the m. in my life that count SEX, 109
Many m. would take the death-sentence FATE, 11
m. about me that are fat MISTRUST, 10
m. and sea interpenetrate ENGLAND, 15
M. are but children of a larger growth AGE, 28
M. are m., but Man is a woman MANKIND, 20
M. are . . . more careful of the breed of their horses and dogs FAMILY, 42
M. are not hanged for stealing horses EXAMPLE, 6
M. are we, and must grieve REGRET, 28
m. . . . capable of every wickedness EVIL, 9
M. come of age at sixty AGE, 75
m. devote the greater part of their lives MANKIND, 34
m. everywhere could be free FREEDOM, 33
M. fear death DARKNESS, 3
M. have broad and large chests SEXES, 18
M. have never been good GOOD, 1
M. of few words are the best men BREVITY, 9
m. represent . . . mind over morals SEXES, 33
M.'s natures are alike HABIT, 4
m. think all m. mortal ARROGANCE, 11
M. will always be mad MADNESS, 43
M. will confess HUMOR, 15
Most m. admire /Virtue VIRTUE, 17
O! m. with sisters dear WOMEN, 56
rich m. rule the law LAW, 18
schemes o' mice an' m. DISAPPOINTMENT, 2
Science seldom renders m. amiable SCIENCE, 4
So many m., so many opinions OPINIONS, 8
Such m. are dangerous MISTRUST, 10
than M. now in Chambers and Feather-beds HEALTHY LIVING, 14
That all m. are equal EQUALITY, 11
The many m., so beautiful GUILT, 5
The mass of m. lead lives DESPAIR, 10
the m. who borrow, and the m. who lend BORROWING, 5
the only advantage women have over m. – . . . they can cry SEXES, 22
the race of m. is almost extinct in Europe MEN, 8
the tongues of m. and of angels BIBLICAL QUOTATIONS, 44
The War between M. and Women SEXES, 29
those m. have their price CORRUPTION, 15
tide in the affairs of m. OPPORTUNITY, 18
To famous m. all the earth is a sepulchre FAME, 25
to form Christian m. EDUCATION, 7
We are the hollow m. INSIGNIFICANCE, 2
we cannot instruct women as we do m. in the science of medicine MEDICINE, 22
We live under a government of m. and . . . newspapers GOVERNMENT, 31
when m. and mountains meet GREATNESS, 4
Why are women . . . so much more interesting to m. SEXES, 34
Women . . . are either better or worse than m. WOMEN, 64
menace Nazi Germany had become a m. to all mankind NAZISM, 5
mend God won't, and we can't m. it CONFUSION, 5
If every man would m. a man MEDICINE, 4
mendacity clergyman whose mendicity is only equalled by their m. CLERGY, 13
mended then all the world would be m. MEDICINE, 4
mental A m. stain can neither be blotted out PSYCHIATRY, 12
Christian Science explains all cause and effect as m. RELIGION, 28
every 'm.' symptom is a veiled cry of anguish PSYCHIATRY, 31
my m. edge BLINDNESS, 11
now they create m. patients PSYCHIATRY, 30
philosophy ought to . . . unravel people's m. blocks PHILOSOPHY, 13
to infer or guess how the m. apparatus is constructed MIND, 9
When a man lacks m. balance in pneumonia MENTAL ILLNESS, 3
mentally happiness of man that he be m. faithful INTEGRITY, 5
if you are m. sick, you are lucky if the janitor comes around MENTAL ILLNESS, 2
merci La belle Dame sans M. SUPERNATURAL, 10
mercies For his m. ay endure GOD, 43
merciless a kind parent . . . or a m. step-mother NATURE, 28
mercury 'Twas a chilly day for Willie /When the m. went down ANONYMOUS, 52
Two minutes with Venus, two years with m. SEX, 72
mercy And that is M.'s door MERCY, 2
For M. has a human heart MANKIND, 10
God ha' m. on such as we DEBAUCHERY, 8
La belle dame sans m. WOMEN, 60
m. unto you . . . be multiplied BIBLICAL QUOTATIONS, 387
quality of m. is not strain'd MERCY, 4
To M., Pity, Peace, and Love DISTRESS, 1
merit no damned m. in it TITLES, 5
Satan exalted sat, by m. raised DEVIL, 13
meritocracy The Rise of the M. MERIT, 8
mermaid Choicer than the M. Tavern PUBLIC HOUSES, 3
mermaids I have heard the m. singing OLD AGE, 44
merry For tonight we'll m., m. be ANONYMOUS, 12
I am never m. when I hear sweet music MUSIC, 41
I commended mirth . . . to eat . . . to drink, and to be m. BIBLICAL QUOTATIONS, 88
merryman Doctor Diet, /Doctor Quiet and Doctor M. DOCTORS, 94
It's a song of a m. LOVE, 70
merry monarch A m. ROYALTY, 92
Mersey quality of M. ENGLAND, 1
mess another fine m. ACCIDENTS, 5
message the electric m. came ILLNESS, 9
The medium is the m. COMMUNICATION, 3
Messiah He was the M. of the new age POLITICIANS, 102
messing m. about in boats BOATS, 7
Mesurier John Le M. . . . conked out on November 15th OBITUARIES, 6
met I m. a man who wasn't there NONSENSE, 23
We have m. too late INFLUENCE, 5
metaphor all m. is poetry LANGUAGE, 14
m. . . . most fertile power possessed by man SPEECH, 10
metaphysical a physical and m. impossibility POETS, 9
a sort of m. brothel for emotions SENTIMENTALITY, 3
metaphysics M. is the finding of bad reasons METAPHYSICS, 2
The unrest which keeps . . . m. going METAPHYSICS, 4
meteorites The Academy would not accept the reality of m. until 1803 SCIENCE, 1
meter Poetry is opposed to science, . . . prose to m. POETRY AND PROSE, 1
without . . . understanding what m. POETS, 13
method madness, yet there is m. in't MADNESS, 33
Traditional scientific m. has always been SCIENCE, 68
You know my m. TRIVIALITY, 6
methods m. of barbarism PLACES, 6
Methuselah all the days of M. AGE, 13
metrical difference between . . . prose and m. composition POETRY AND PROSE, 7
Mexico Poor M. UNITED STATES, 16
mice schemes o' m. an' men DISAPPOINTMENT, 2
Three blind m., see how they run NURSERY RHYMES, 59
Michael Angelo last words . . . name of – M. ARTISTS, 8
Michelangelo If M. had been straight HOMOSEXUALITY, 13
Talking of M. WOMEN, 46
Mickey Mouse I love M. more than any woman WOMEN, 40
mickle Many a m. makes a muckle PROVERBS, 281
microbe The M. is so very small SCIENCE, 5
microbes acquired a fear of m. FEAR, 1
There are more m. *per person* SCIENCE, 6
microscope It is only in the m. that our life looks so big LIFE, 71
With a m. you see the surface of things SCIENCE, 94
middle a whole is that which has a beginning, a m., and an end PLAYS, 1
Bow, bow, ye lower m. classes CLASS, 15
I like a film to have a beginning, a m. and an end CINEMA, 7
In a man's m. years there is scarcely a part of the body AGE, 81
M. age is when your age starts to show AGE, 40
M. age is youth without its levity AGE, 24
no m. course between the throne and the scaffold MONARCHY, 8
One of the pleasures of m. age is to *find out* that one WAS right AGE, 58
people who stay in the m. of the road COMPROMISE, 2
Senescence begins /And m. age ends OLD AGE, 72
the dead center of m. age AGE, 5
the ease . . . move into the m. class CLASS, 47
The m. brows like John Henry O'Hara READING, 1
the right wing of the m. of the road POLITICIANS, 16
You've reached m. age when all you exercise is caution AGE, 4
middle-aged a m. man . . . is half dead AGE, 23
middle-class part of English m. education is devoted to the training of servants CLASS, 54
respectable, m., . . . lady AUDIENCES, 7
the healthy type that was essentially m. CLASS, 14
Midland M., bound for Cricklewood TRAVEL, 9
midnight chimes at m. MERRYMAKING, 3
I stood on the bridge at m. BRIDGE, 2
It came upon the m. clear CHRISTMAS, 19
M. brought on the dusky hour DAY AND NIGHT, 17
m. never come DAMNATION, 3
Not to be abed after m. BED, 11
Once upon a m. dreary SUPERNATURAL, 12
See her on the bridge at m. ANONYMOUS, 71
soft embalmer of the still m. SLEEP, 22
To cease upon the m. with no pain DEATH, 90
mid-stream best to swap horses in m. CHANGE, 14
mid-winter In the bleak m. WINTER, 5
might Fight the good fight with all thy m. CHRISTIANITY, 46
The majority has the m. MAJORITY, 5
we Britons . . . use 'M.' BRITISH, 12
We m. have been REGRET, 10
might-have-been Look in my face; my name is M. DISAPPOINTMENT, 6
mightier pen is m. than the sword WRITING, 6
mighty Another m. empire overthrown DEFEAT, 18
How are the m. fallen BIBLICAL QUOTATIONS, 616
put down the m. BIBLICAL QUOTATIONS, 414
share in the good fortunes of the m. INJUSTICE, 4
the weak things of the world to confound the . . . m. BIBLICAL QUOTATIONS, 28
migraine nor m. by a tiara WEALTH, 35
mike I'm being amplified by the m. OBESITY, 5
Milan he wants M., and so do I AGREEMENT, 1
miles m. to go before I sleep TRAVEL, 16
militant I am an optimist, unrepentant and m. OPTIMISM, 36
militarism m. . . . is one of the chief bulwarks of capitalism CAPITALISM, 9
military The chief attraction of m. service ARMY, 3
milk a kid in his mother's m. BIBLICAL QUOTATIONS, 150
a land flowing with m. and honey BIBLICAL QUOTATIONS, 133
as when you find a trout in the m. PROOF, 7
drunk the m. of Paradise CAUTION, 9
Gin was mother's m. ALCOHOL, 73
putting m. into babies CHILDREN, 22
too full o' th' m. of human kindness KINDNESS, 10
milking A vain surgeon is like a m. stool SURGEONS, 12
Mill John Stuart M. /By a mighty effort of will ECONOMICS, 3
miller There was a jolly m. HAPPINESS, 4
million Fifty m. Frenchmen can't be wrong PROOF, 2
I have had no real gratification . . . more than my neighbor . . . who is worth only half a m. LAST WORDS, 88
man who has a m. dollars WEALTH, 6
million m. spermatozoa, /All of them alive SEX, 47
Son, here's a m. dollars ADVICE, 14
millionaire He must be a m. WEALTH, 22
I am a m.. That is my religion WEALTH, 37
Who Wants to Be a M. WEALTH, 36
millions take m. off the caring services PATRIOTISM, 25
unrewarded m. without whom Statistics would be a bankrupt science STATISTICS, 9

mills m. of God grind slowly GOD, 40
millstone a m. . . . hanged about his neck BIBLICAL QUOTATIONS, 515
Milton Malt does more than M. can ALCOHOL, 40
M., Madam, was a genius POETS, 25
M.! thou shouldst be living at this hour DECLINE, 18
the faith and morals hold /Which M. held FREEDOM, 63
the making up of a Shakespeare or a M. SCIENTISTS, 4
mimsy All m. were the borogoves NONSENSE, 7
min' never brought to m. FRIENDSHIP, 16
mince dined on m., and slices of quince FOOD, 45
mind A dagger of the m. DELUSION, 6
A fat paunch never bred a subtle m. OBESITY, 2
After all, a doctor is just to put your m. at rest DOCTORS, 75
A good critic . . . narrates the adventures of his m. CRITICS, 4
an exaggerated stress on not changing one's m. DECISION, 3
Another great Advantage of Deformity is, that it tends to the Improvement of the M. INTELLECT, 4
an unseemly exposure of the m. NASTINESS, 3
A physician is . . . a consoler of the m. DOCTORS, 14
A short neck denotes a good m. APPEARANCE, 58
A sick m. cannot endure any harshness MIND, 24
a sound m. in a sound body BODY, 12
At 83 Shaw's m. MIND, 35
Beauty in things exists in the m. which contemplates them BEAUTY, 21
Body and m., . . . , do not always agree to die together OLD AGE, 39
Canst thou not minister to a m. diseas'd MADNESS, 36
change their clime, not their frame of m., who rush across the sea TRAVEL, 20
clear your *m.* of cant . . . REASON, 5
Disease is . . . the result of conflict between soul and m. SOUL, 4
Do you think my m. is maturing late AGE, 53
fills his m. with the blackest horrors of guilt HYPOCHONDRIA, 8
her long struggle between m. and body ILLNESS, 49
If it is for m. that we are seaching the brain BRAIN, 7
If the body be feeble, the m. will not be strong HOLISTIC MEDICINE, 5
if we would preserve the m. in all its vigour HOLISTIC MEDICINE, 10
it is grief that develops the powers of the m. MIND, 27
It is none of these – it's a state of m. RESEARCH, 11
it's all in the m. ILLNESS, 68
making things plain to uninstructed people was . . . best means of clearing . . . one's own m. EDUCATION, 43
Many ideas grow better when transplanted into another m. IDEAS, 4
men represent . . . m. over morals SEXES, 33
m. and body must develop in harmonious proportions HEALTHY LIVING, 28
M. is ever the ruler of the universe MIND, 26
M. over matter MIND, 32
m. that makes the body rich APPEARANCES, 36
M. your own business PROVERBS, 292
natural course of the human m. is . . . from credulity to scepticism MIND, 14
never to ransack any m. but his own IMITATION, 5
No m. is thoroughly well organized HUMOR, 16
only inequalities that matter begin in the m. DIFFERENCE, 8
our love . . . of the m. does not make us soft RESULTS, 6
Pain of m. is worse than pain of body SUFFERING, 33
Physicians must discover the weaknesses of the human m. DIAGNOSIS, 6
prodigious quantity of m. INDECISION, 4
Reading is to the m. READING, 17
So long as the body is affected through the m. FAITH, 16
someone whose m. watches itself INTELLECTUALS, 6
spirit . . . of a sound m. BIBLICAL QUOTATIONS, 654
That's the classical m. at work MIND, 25
the best medicines for an afflicted m. . . . WORK, 19
The care of the human m. is the most noble branch of medicine PSYCHIATRY, 26
The conscious m. may be compared to a fountain MIND, 8
The highest function of *m.* MIND, 18
the inquisitive m. can . . . receive no answer ANSWERS, 8
The m. can also be an erogenous zone MIND, 34
The m. . . . Can make a Heaven of Hell MIND, 21
The m. grows sicker than the body SUFFERING, 25
The m. has great influence over the body MIND, 22
The m. is an iceberg MIND, 7
The m. is its own place MIND, 21
The m. like a sick body can be healed MIND, 20
the m. must sweat a poison MIND, 19
the most abhorrent is body without m. MIND, 15
The pendulum of the m. oscillates between sense and nonsense MIND, 16
the prison of our m. MIND, 31
The psychiatrist is the obstetrician of the m. PSYCHIATRY, 2
There is in the British Museum an enormous m. MUSEUMS, 3
The remarkable thing about the human m. MIND, 10
The tendency of the casual m. GENERALIZATIONS, 3
they do not believe in the m. but in a cerebral intestine PSYCHOANALYSIS, 4
'Tis education forms the common m. EDUCATION, 70
to change your m. ADAPTABILITY, 1
To know the *m.* of a woman LOVE, 92
true genius is a m. of large general powers GENIUS, 7
unless your m. is in a splint DISABILITY, 3
we consider as nothing the rape of the human m. MIND, 11
Well in body /But sick in m. HOLISTIC MEDICINE, 9
Women represent . . . matter over m. SEXES, 33
You should pray for a healthy m. in a healthy body MIND, 17
minds All things can corrupt perverted m. CORRUPTION, 9
great m. in the commonplace MIND, 12
Great m. think alike PROVERBS, 181
Little m. are interested in the extraordinary EXTRAORDINARY, 1
many open m. should be closed for repairs MIND, 2
marriage of true m. LOVE, 158
M. are not ever craving BOOKS, 16
M. like beds always made up INFLEXIBILITY, 4
M. like bodies, will often fall into a pimpled, ill-conditioned state MIND, 6
m. so impatient of inferiority GRATITUDE, 3
Old age puts more wrinkles in our m. than on our faces OLD AGE, 68
Our m. are lazier than our bodies MIND, 28
Strongest m. / . . . the noisy world /Hears least MIND, 36
Superstition is the religion of feeble m. SUPERSTITION, 8
the hobgoblin of little m. CONSTANCY, 1
the m. of the people are closed HOLISTIC MEDICINE, 4
To be alone is the fate of all great m. GREATNESS, 11
to lead ignorant and prejudic'd m. into more happy and successful methods LEARNING, 11
well-developed bodies, fairly developed m. EDUCATION, 30
When people will not weed their own m. MIND, 33
miner Dwelt a m., Forty-niner, /And his daughter, Clementine MOURNING, 7
miners it is only because m. sweat their guts out SUPERIORITY, 13
mingled Like kindred drops, been m. MOUNTAINS, 1
minister safety of a m. lies in his having the approbation of this House POLITICIANS, 122
the Prime M. has to be a butcher POLITICIANS, 22
ministers I don't mind how much my m. talk AUTHORITARIANISM, 8
King of England changes his m. ROYALTY, 62
my actions are my m.' REPARTEE, 19
ministries *The Times* has made many m. NEWSPAPERS, 2
ministry Women . . . care fifty times more for a marriage than a m. WOMEN, 17
minorities M. . . . are almost always in the right MINORITY, 3
we are all m. now POLITICS, 144
minority not enough people to make a m. MINORITY, 1
The m. is always right MAJORITY, 5
minstrel A wandering m. I SINGERS, 2
Ethereal m. BIRDS, 18
The M. Boy WAR, 106
minute m. hand of history JOURNALISM, 28
M. Particulars GOOD, 2
not a m. on the day STRIKES, 3
sucker born every m. GULLIBILITY, 1
To a philosopher no circumstance, . . . is too m. PHILOSOPHERS, 3
minutes at the rate of sixty m. an hour TIME, 27
some of them are about ten m. long POPULAR MUSIC, 7
take care of the m. CARE, 4
Yes, about ten m. REPARTEE, 111
miracle A m. is an event which creates faith FAITH, 28
a m. of rare device MIRACLES, 1
man prays . . . for a m. MIRACLES, 5
m. cannot fix INSULTS, 135
miracles before we *know* he is a saint, there will have to be m. MIRACLES, 3
M. are laughed at by a nation MIRACLES, 2
The Christian religion not only was at first attended with m. CHRISTIANITY, 42
There are as many m. RELIGION, 47
mirror A novel is a m. NOVELS, 16
Art is not a m. . . . but a hammer ART, 17
Look not in my eyes, for fear /They m. true the sight I see LOVE, 79
When a man confronts catastrophe . . . a woman looks in her m. SEXES, 30
mirrors M. and fatherhood are abominable ILLUSIONS, 1
M. should think longer THINKING, 3
mirth I commended m. . . . to eat . . . to drink, and to be merry BIBLICAL QUOTATIONS, 88
I love such m. as does not make friends ashamed MERRYMAKING, 6
to fence against the infirmities of ill health . . . by m. LAUGHTER, 11
miscarriage procure thee m. ABORTION, 5
success and m. are empty sounds DISILLUSION, 4
they induce herbs . . . to cause m. ABORTION, 1
miscast George Bernard Shaw is sadly m. CRITICISM, 59
mischief If you want to make m. . . . papers JOURNALISM, 5
Satan finds . . . m. . . . /For idle hands IDLENESS, 12
thou little knowest the m. done ACCIDENTS, 7
To mourn a m. that is past REGRET, 20
mischievous what a m. devil Love is LOVE, 42
miserable m. have no other medicine HOPE, 21
poring over m. books BOOKS, 47
The secret of being m. is to have leisure SORROW, 26
miserie y-fallen out of heigh degree. Into m. MISFORTUNE, 7
miseries all the maladies and m. MALADIES, 2
makes men's m. of alarming brevity LONGEVITY, 6
misery certain amount of m. . . . to distribute as fairly as he can TAXATION, 14
greatest m. is a battle gained MISERY, 4
Half the m. . . . caused by ignorance SUFFERING, 34
he /Who finds himself, loses his m. MISERY, 1
if we succeed in transforming your hysterical m. into common unhappiness PSYCHOANALYSIS, 11
Let other pens dwell on guilt and m. OPTIMISM, 14
Man hands on m. to man CHILDREN, 42
M. acquaints a man with strange bedfellows MISERY, 2
Thou art so full of m. MISERY, 3
misfortune In the m. of our best friends HUMAN NATURE, 19
next greatest m. to losing a battle VICTORY, 26
the most unhappy kind of m. HAPPINESS, 6
worst m. was his birth POLITICIANS, 24
misfortunes any man . . . who could not bear another's m. MISFORTUNE, 14
history . . . a tableau of crimes and m. HISTORY, 41
history . . . the register of the . . . m. of mankind HISTORY, 16
if a man talks of his m. MISFORTUNE, 12
strong enough to bear the m. of others MISFORTUNE, 15
The m. of poverty POVERTY, 24
the real m. and pains of others DELIGHT, 5
misguided We have guided missiles and m. men WAR, 86

For years politicians have promised the m. MOON, 5
I got the sun in the mornin' and the m. at night GRATITUDE, 2
I saw the new m. late yestreen ANONYMOUS, 84
I see the m., /And the m. sees me BLESSING, 2
moving M. went up the sky MOON, 2
nothing left remarkable beneath the . . . m. MOURNING, 9
only a paper m. FAITH, 14
shine on, shine on, harvest m. MOON, 6
The M. and Sixpence BOOK TITLES, 17
The m. doth shine as bright as day NURSERY RHYMES, 6
The m. is nothing /But a circumambulating aphrodisiac FERTILITY, 1
the m.'s /a balloon BOOK TITLES, 20
They danced by the light of the m. FOOD, 45
th' inconstant m. UNFAITHFULNESS, 6
We're very wide awake, /The m. and I APPEARANCES, 18

moonlight Look for me by m. DETERMINATION, 17

moons So sicken waning m. too near the sun MOON, 4

moral All universal m. principles are idle fancies MORALITY, 14
each man must struggle, lest the m. law become . . . separated MORALITY, 1
Everything's got a m. PURPOSE, 1
it should preach a high m. lesson PURPOSE, 11
Let us be m. EXISTENCE, 2
Love is m. even without . . . marriage LOVE AND MARRIAGE, 3
m. attribute of a Scotsman SCOTS, 1
M. indignation is in most cases 2 percent m. INDIGNATION, 2
m. is what you feel good after MORALITY, 6
m. or an immoral book BOOKS, 51
more than a m. duty to speak one's mind FRANKNESS, 5
one is unhappy one becomes m. SORROW, 18
profoundly m. and packed with deep spiritual significance NOVELS, 8
putting him into a m. Coventry IRELAND, 16
The highest possible stage in m. culture SELF-CONTROL, 3
the m. law WONDER, 3
The worst government is the most m. GOVERNMENT, 24

moralist A Scotchman must be a very sturdy m. SCOTS, 3
no sterner m. than Pleasure PLEASURE, 8

morality Dr Johnson's m. was as English . . . as a beefsteak ENGLAND, 24
live for others . . . middle class m. CLASS, 45
M. consists in suspecting MORALITY, 16
M. . . . is herd-m. MORALITY, 12
M.'s a gesture. . . . learnt from books MORALITY, 3
M.'s not practical MORALITY, 3
M. which is based on ideas MORALITY, 9
new m. . . . the old immorality condoned MORALITY, 18
No m. can be founded on authority MORALITY, 2
periodical fits of m. MORALITY, 10
there is such a thing as physical m. HEALTHY LIVING, 41
This imperative may be called that of M. MORALITY, 8
two kinds of m. MORALITY, 13

moralizing He would not blow his nose without m. WRITERS, 13

morals basing m. on myth MORALITY, 15
If your m. make you dreary MORALITY, 20
men represent . . . mind over m. SEXES, 33
M. are an acquirement MORALITY, 22
She had no use for m. TEMPTATION, 19
the faith and m. hold /Which Milton held FREEDOM, 63
the m. of a whore, and the manners of a dancing master CRITICISM, 28

mordre M. wol out MURDER, 4

more As I know m. of mankind EXPECTATION, 3
Less is m. ARCHITECTURE, 9
m. will mean worse EDUCATION, 5
Oliver Twist has asked for m. BOLDNESS, 2
Specialist – A man who knows m. and m. about less and less EXPERTS, 7
take *m.* than nothing LANGUAGE, 9
The m. the merrier PROVERBS, 401

mores *O tempora! O m.* CUSTOM, 1

morn From m. /To noon he fell DECLINE, 4
From m. to night, my friend ENDURANCE, 16
He rose the morrow m. WISDOM, 15
the opening eye-lids of the m. DAY AND NIGHT, 15

mornin' nice to get up in the m. BED, 7

morning Early one m., just as the sun was rising ANONYMOUS, 16
I awoke one m. FAME, 7
I'm getting married in the m. MARRIAGE, 89
M. in the Bowl of Night DAY AND NIGHT, 8
m. larked and crowed and belling DAY AND NIGHT, 22
Oh, what a beautiful m. DAY AND NIGHT, 11
she has lived . . . the space of one m. FATE, 14
straight on till m. TRAVEL, 7
that . . . turneth the shadow of death into the m. BIBLICAL QUOTATIONS, 20
the m. cometh, and also the night BIBLICAL QUOTATIONS, 261
'Tis always m. somewhere BEGINNING, 10

Morocco We're M. bound LEXICOGRAPHY, 2

morphia have yourself squirted full of m. DEATH, 83

morrow take . . . no thought for the m. BIBLICAL QUOTATIONS, 484

mortal All men are m. MORTALITY, 1
Her last disorder m. DEATH, 72
I was not unaware that I had begotten a m. MORTALITY, 8
men think all men m. ARROGANCE, 11
'Remember that I too am m.' DOCTORS, 87
that M. God STATE, 1
The doctor found . . . /Her last disorder m. DOCTORS, 50
we have been m. enemies ever since ENEMIES, 5

mortality kept watch o'er man's m. MORTALITY, 21
M., behold and fear MORTALITY, 2

mortals A novelist is, like all m. WRITERS, 38
We m. cross the ocean HUMAN CONDITION, 5
what fools these m. be FOOLISHNESS, 18

Moscow don't march on M. WAR, 105

Moses he saw his role as being that of M. LEADERSHIP, 5
M. was very meek BIBLICAL QUOTATIONS, 554
there arose not a prophet . . . like unto M. BIBLICAL QUOTATIONS, 73

most The M. may err as grosly ERROR, 6

mostest I got there fustest with the m. MISQUOTATION, 13

mote the m. that is in thy brother's eye BIBLICAL QUOTATIONS, 486

moth like a m., the simple maid WOMEN, 51
The desire of the m. for the star HUMOR, 30

mother And Her M. Came Too FAMILY, 39
as is the m., so is her daughter BIBLICAL QUOTATIONS, 161
A smart m. makes often a better diagnosis DIAGNOSIS, 3
behold thy m. BIBLICAL QUOTATIONS, 364
Dead! and . . . never called me m. DEATH, 177
Don't tell my m. I'm in politics POLITICS, 5
English girl hates . . . her m. FAMILY, 49
Eve . . . the m. of all living BIBLICAL QUOTATIONS, 189
I am old enough to be – in fact am – your m. AGE, 51
If poverty is the m. of crime, stupidity is its father CRIME, 5
I was born . . . because my m. needed a fourth at meals BIRTH, 13
I wished to be near my m. BIRTH, 17
Jerusalem . . . the m. of us all BIBLICAL QUOTATIONS, 170
May you be the m. of a bishop BLESSING, 3
M. is far too clever to understand PREJUDICE, 2
M. is the dead heart of the family WOMAN'S ROLE, 3
M. love . . . is a highly respected and much publicised emotion WOMEN, 34
M. of the Free BRITAIN, 3
My m., drunk or sober PATRIOTISM, 8
the most intense love on the m.'s side FAMILY, 20
The m.-child relationship is paradoxical FAMILY, 20
the m. of parliaments ENGLAND, 9
this war . . . which did not justify the sacrifice of a single m.'s son SACRIFICE, 3
worse consequences than . . . a really affectionate m. FAMILY, 35

motherhood wifehood and m. are but incidental relations WOMEN, 110

mother-in-law as the man said when his m. died FAMILY, 27

The sort of place everyone should send his m. FAMILY, 11
What a marvellous place to drop one's m. FAMILY, 19

mothers Come m. and fathers /Throughout the land CHANGE, 6
O! men with m. and wives WOMEN, 56
therefore he made m. WOMAN'S ROLE, 1
unfair not only to the m. and ancestors MEDICINE, 94
women become like their m. SEXES, 32

mothers-in-law Two m. FAMILY, 47

motives m. meaner than your own MOTIVE, 1

motorcycle Zen and the Art of M. Maintenance PHILOSOPHY, 11

motors was good for General M. BUSINESS, 30

mountain A m. in labour shouted so loud DISAPPOINTMENT, 4
hardly be a beast or a fool alone on a great m. SOLITUDE, 10
If the m. will not come to Mohammed ADAPTABILITY, 2
Land of the m. and the flood SCOTLAND, 7
never see another m. MOUNTAINS, 2

mountains all faith, so that I could remove m. BIBLICAL QUOTATIONS, 44
England's m. green ENGLAND, 6
highest intellects, like the tops of m. INTELLECT, 7
how beautiful upon the m. are the feet BIBLICAL QUOTATIONS, 275
if the Swiss had designed these m. MOUNTAINS, 4
M. interposed /Make enemies of nations MOUNTAINS, 1
M. . . . the beginning and the end of all natural scenery MOUNTAINS, 3
M. will heave in childbirth DISAPPOINTMENT, 3
Two voices . . . one is of the sea, /One of the m. FREEDOM, 64
when men and m. meet GREATNESS, 4

mounting the view that there is m. chaos POLITICS, 29

mourn countless thousands m. CRUELTY, 2
it is chiefly our own deaths that we m. for FUNERALS, 3
To m. a mischief that is past REGRET, 20

mourning I'm in m. for my life MOURNING, 4
in m. . . . for the world MOURNING, 15
tedium is the very basis of m. BOREDOM, 6
We met . . . Dr Hall in such very deep m. MOURNING, 1
What we call m. for our dead MOURNING, 6
with my m. . . . and new periwig APPEARANCE, 47

mouse a silly little m. will be born DISAPPOINTMENT, 3
He bought a crooked cat, which caught a crooked m. NURSERY RHYMES, 53
leave room for the m. EXCESS, 7
she brought forth a m. DISAPPOINTMENT, 4
The m. ran up the clock NURSERY RHYMES, 15

mouse-trap If a man make a better m. FAME, 10

mouth A politician is a statesman . . . with an open m. POLITICIANS, 105
butter wouldn't melt in her m. ACTORS, 8
Dentopedology is . . . opening your m. and putting your foot EMBARRASSMENT, 3
God be in my m., /And in my speaking ANONYMOUS, 20
Keep your m. shut and your eyes open CAUTION, 6
need not look in your m. APPEARANCE, 1
out of thine own m. will I judge thee BIBLICAL QUOTATIONS, 444

mouth-brothels Great restaurants are . . . nothing but m. FOOD, 63

move But did thee feel the earth m. EARTH, 10
in him we live, and m., and have our being BIBLICAL QUOTATIONS, 13
I will m. the earth EARTH, 1
The great affair is to m. TRAVEL, 37

movement I want to be a m. SOLITUDE, 12
We are the true peace m. PEACE, 21

moves m., and mates, and slays DESTINY, 7
Yet it m. ASTRONOMY, 3

movie don't like his m., you're dead CINEMA, 21
This is a m., not a lifeboat EQUALITY, 28

movies Thanks to the m., gunfire has always sounded unreal CINEMA, 16

moving In home-sickness you must keep m. HOMESICKNESS, 7
m. Moon went up the sky MOON, 2

people under suspicion are better m. JUDGMENT, 12
The M. Finger writes DESTINY, 8
Mozart The sonatas of M. are unique MUSIC, 40
when M. was my age AGE, 44
MPs The prospect of a lot /Of dull M. POLITICIANS, 49
much m. . . . said on both sides OBJECTIVITY, 2
So little done, so m. to do LAST WORDS, 73
so m. owed by so many to so few WORLD WAR II, 14
muchness Much of a m. MEDIOCRITY, 9
muck Money is like m. MONEY, 6
sing 'em m. PLACES, 25
mud One sees the m., and one the stars OPTIMISM, 29
muddle a beginning, a m., and an end NOVELS, 9
muddle-headed He's a m. fool FOOLISHNESS, 12
muddy The hunter for aphorisms . . . has to fish in m. water SAYINGS, 2
Mudirs Their Zaptiehs and their M. VIOLENCE, 7
Muffet Little Miss M. /Sat on a tuffet NURSERY RHYMES, 30
multiplied Entities should not be m. SIMPLICITY, 6
mercy unto you . . . be m. BIBLICAL QUOTATIONS, 387
multiply be fruitful and m. BIBLICAL QUOTATIONS, 179
multitude a m. of sins BIBLICAL QUOTATIONS, 289
long dresses, . . . cover a m. of shins CLOTHES, 23
The m. is always in the wrong PUBLIC, 17
this massed m. of silent witnesses to . . . war WAR, 63
multitudes I contain m. SELF, 25
mum M.'s the word SECRECY, 8
They fuck you up, your m. and dad FAMILY, 30
mumble maunder and m. PUBLIC, 8
mundi *Sic transit gloria m.* GLORY, 4
Munich Glory to God for M. WORLD WAR II, 38
murder Divorce? Never. But m. often MARRIAGE, 144
Every time we kiss he says 'M.!' LOVE, 97
love and m. will out LOVE, 50
m. back into its rightful setting – in the home MURDER, 7
M. considered as one of the Fine Arts MURDER, 6
M. . . . had a mask like Castlereagh MURDER, 12
M., like talent, seems . . . to run in families MURDER, 9
M. most foul MURDER, 10
m. shrieks out MURDER, 13
Never m. a man who is committing suicide SUICIDE, 39
So it was m. DEATH, 105
Sooner m. an infant in its cradle DESIRE, 3
murdered I m. my grandmother this morning INATTENTION, 4
murderer Kill a man, and you are a m. KILLING, 9
strong suspicions that Crippen London cellar m. TELEGRAMS, 8
murmur live m. of a summer's day SUMMER, 2
Murray And the bonny Earl of M., /O he might hae been a king ANONYMOUS, 110
muscles a network of nerves and m. and tissues inflamed by disease BODY, 25
muscular His Christianity was m. CHRISTIANITY, 36
Muse The M. prefers the liars POETRY, 68
To the Greeks the M. gave native wit CLASSICS, 5
mused Lancelot m. a little space BEAUTY, 41
museum the m. of this world MASCULINITY, 2
museums more philosophical than . . . curators of the m. MUSEUMS, 1
mushroom a supramundane m. NUCLEAR WEAPONS, 13
Fame is sometimes like unto a . . . m. FAME, 12
to stuff a m. HOUSEWORK, 2
music A Dance to the M. of Time BOOK TITLES, 21
a martyr to m. MUSIC, 49
Architecture . . . is frozen m. ARCHITECTURE, 14
art constantly aspires towards . . . m. ART, 21
capable of being well set to m. MUSIC, 2
chord of m. MUSIC, 36
food in m. MUSIC, 26
God tells me how he wants this m. played MUSIC, 51
Having verse set to m. POETRY, 61
how potent cheap m. is MUSIC, 15
How sour sweet m. is ORDER, 3
I don't write modern m. MUSIC, 46
If all the arts aspire to the condition of m. SCIENCE, 78
If m. be the food of love MUSIC, 43
I'll set it to m. MUSIC, 38
In m., the punctuation is absolutely strict ACTING, 12
making m. throatily and palpitatingly sexual MUSIC, 23
man that hath no m. in himself MUSIC, 42
M. and women I cannot but give way to MUSIC, 34
M. begins to atrophy ARTS, 9
M. . . . confirm human loneliness MUSIC, 17
M. creates order out of chaos MUSIC, 29
m. critics. . . . small and rodent-like with padlocked ears CRITICS, 18
M. has charms to soothe MUSIC, 14
M. helps not MUSIC, 1
M. is not written in red, white and blue MUSIC, 28
M. is the arithmetic of sounds MUSIC, 16
M. is the food of love PROVERBS, 297
M. is your own experience MUSIC, 33
M., Maestro, Please MUSIC, 27
M. that gentlier on the spirit lies MUSIC, 48
M., when soft voices die MEMORY, 21
never merry when I hear sweet m. MUSIC, 41
no more m. in them MUSICIANS, 1
Poetry . . . set to more or less lascivious m. POETRY, 37
silence sank like m. SILENCE, 3
The English may not like m. MUSIC, 5
The hills are alive with the sound of m. MUSIC, 19
the line that fits the m. POPULAR MUSIC, 10
The m. teacher came twice each week MUSIC, 3
thy chosen m., Liberty FREEDOM, 64
Van Gogh's ear for m. INSULTS, 131
musical cashiers of the M. Banks BANKS, 3
Most m., most melancholy BIRDS, 14
music-lovers Thank-you, m. GRATITUDE, 5
musicologist A m. . . . can read music but can't hear it MUSIC, 7
Mussolini Herr Hitler and Signor M. had been at Oxford OXFORD, 11
Hitler was a nuisance. M. was bloody POLITICS, 95
must Genius does what it m. TALENT AND GENIUS, 3
Is *m.* a word to be addressed to princes IMPERTINENCE, 3
mustache A kiss without a m. KISSING, 6
a man outside with a big black m. APPEARANCE, 38
Being kissed by a man who didn't wax his m. KISSING, 4
his nicotine eggyellow weeping walrus Victorian m. APPEARANCE, 60
muttering the m. grew to a grumbling ANIMALS, 8
mutton Alice – M.; M. – Alice INTRODUCTIONS, 1
I could no longer stand their eternal cold m. ENGLAND, 41
people who do not object to eating a m. chop RESEARCH, 18
myriad There died a m., /And of the best EPITAPHS, 32
myrrh gathered my m. with my spice BIBLICAL QUOTATIONS, 632
myself deliver me from m. SELF, 6
I am always with m. SELF, 19
I follow but m. LOYALTY, 10
I have always disliked m. SELF, 7
I know m. SELF-KNOWLEDGE, 4
I like to go by m. SOLITUDE, 9
I've over-educated m. DEBAUCHERY, 5
not only witty in m. HUMOR, 55
The Jews have produced . . . Christ, Spinoza, and m. CONCEIT, 18
mysteries disciples . . . mark its ways and note . . . its m. GAMBLING, 1
mysterious God moves in a m. way GOD, 23
the ancient cathedrals – grand, wonderful, m. RELIGION, 63
mystery a riddle wrapped in a m. inside an enigma RUSSIA, 1
Growth is a greater m. than death AGE, 48
Happiness is a m. like religion HAPPINESS, 7
In m. our soul abides HEART, 2
mystic The m. sees the ineffable PSYCHIATRY, 23
mystical to stimulate the m. faculties of human nature ALCOHOL, 41
mystics M. always hope that science SCIENCE, 83
myth A m. is, of course, not a fairy story MYTHS, 2
basing morals on m. MORALITY, 15
some magnificent m. PROPAGANDA, 6

N

Nabob A savage old N. POLITICIANS, 76
nabobs nattering n. of negativism MEDIA, 2
naff Why don't you n. off ROYALTY, 8
nailed n. up the doors of Parliament FASCISM, 10
nails I used to bite my n. FAME, 19
naive the n. forgive FORGIVENESS, 19
naked a n. Duke of Windlestraw addressing a n. House of Lords NAKEDNESS, 5
a pretty girl who n. is NAKEDNESS, 6
I can't stand a n. light bulb VULGARITY, 6
n., and ye clothed me BIBLICAL QUOTATIONS, 537
n. into the conference chamber NUCLEAR WEAPONS, 4
No woman so n. as . . . underneath her clothes NAKEDNESS, 7
Our ingress . . . /Was n. and bare CARE, 7
Poor n. wretches WEATHER, 23
The exception is a n. ape MANKIND, 41
they were both n. BIBLICAL QUOTATIONS, 184
who told thee that thou wast n. BIBLICAL QUOTATIONS, 187
nakedness N. is uncomely NAKEDNESS, 2
name a good n. is better than precious ointment BIBLICAL QUOTATIONS, 87
And lo! Ben Adhem's n. led all the rest SUPERIORITY, 6
Arm, arm, my n. POWER, 21
as long as you spell my n. right FAME, 8
Bossom? What an extraordinary n. NAMES, 4
Good n. in man and woman REPUTATION, 9
his n. shall be called, Wonderful, Counsellor BIBLICAL QUOTATIONS, 256
How I loathe that other with my n. DENIAL, 2
I don't like your Christian n. NAMES, 2
I remember your n. perfectly SPOONERISMS, 2
king's n. REPUTATION, 11
local habitation and a n. POETRY, 51
No, Groucho is not my real n. NAMES, 9
no n. on the door REPUTATION, 7
Oh liberty! . . . What crimes are committed in thy n. EXECUTION, 35
People you know, yet can't quite n. OLD AGE, 59
rose by any other n. NAMES, 13
signing his n. and forgetting to write the letter INSULTS, 12
that was the n. thereof BIBLICAL QUOTATIONS, 183
their n. liveth for evermore BIBLICAL QUOTATIONS, 115
the n. of which was Beautiful ARCHITECTURE, 2
thou shalt not take the n. of . . . God in vain BIBLICAL QUOTATIONS, 147
to call all sorts of maladies people are liable to . . . , by one n. REMEDIES, 18
two or three . . . gathered together in my n. BIBLICAL QUOTATIONS, 516
What's in a n. NAMES, 13
When I pass my n. in such large letters FAME, 27
When there is no explanation, they give it a n. WORDS, 10
you fall asleep halfway through her n. INSULTS, 16
name-dropper One must not be a n. SNOBBERY, 7
names new-fangled n. to diseases ILLNESS, 56
No n., no pack-drill GOSSIP, 4
There is no counting the n., that surgeons and anatomists give KNOWLEDGE, 32
naming Today we have n. of parts WEAPONS, 6
Naples See N. and die PLACES, 2
Napoleon ashes of N. INDIFFERENCE, 6
Comrade N. is always right PROPAGANDA, 5
N. OFFICERS, 16
N. is a dangerous man TYRANNY, 3
N. is a torrent WAR, 89
the N. of crime CRIME, 4
Napoleons So long as men worship the Caesars and N. TYRANNY, 6
narcotic The amount of n. you use is inversely proportional to your skill DRUGS, 7
narcotics Two great European n. NARCOTICS, 7
nastier she could have found anything n. to say NASTINESS, 7
nasty how n. the nice people can be NASTINESS, 6
Something n. in the woodshed EVIL, 11
nation America became top n. HISTORY, 37
An army is a n. within a n. ARMY, 4
A n. is not in danger ECONOMICS, 18
a n. of amateurs BRITISH, 11
dedicate this n. to the policy of the good neighbor CHARITY, 19

England is a n. of shopkeepers ENGLISH, 31
he is the sworn foe of our n. PUBLISHING, 4
I will make of thee a great n. BIBLICAL QUOTATIONS, 205
n. . . . fall victim to a big lie LYING, 12
n. shall not lift up sword against n. BIBLICAL QUOTATIONS, 247
n. shall rise against n. BIBLICAL QUOTATIONS, 529
N. shall speak peace PEACE, 18
No n. is fit to sit in judgement DIPLOMACY, 25
No n. was ever ruined by trade BUSINESS, 8
right to fix the boundary of . . . a n. IRELAND, 17
the English are . . . the least a n. of pure philosophers ENGLISH, 5
the kind of n. . . . President Kennedy died for AMBITION, 12
the kind of n. that President Roosevelt hoped for AMBITION, 12
the Third Estate contains . . . a n. FRENCH REVOLUTION, 8
ventured my life in defence of this n. PATRIOTISM, 22
national as clear as a crystal, the synthesis – German N. Socialism NAZISM, 3
Our long n. nightmare is over POLITICS, 47
nationalism N. is . . . the measles of mankind NATIONALISM, 1
wind of n. and freedom blowing FREEDOM, 2
nationality My n. is French NORMALITY, 2
Other people have a n. IRISH, 2
nations Commonwealth of N. BRITISH EMPIRE, 8
extends over many n. and three continents EXPERIENCE, 13
If people behaved in the way n. do GOVERNMENT, 44
languages are the pedigree of n. LANGUAGE, 25
The day of small n. has long passed away EMPIRE, 2
The great n. have always acted like gangsters DIPLOMACY, 16
the healing of the n. BIBLICAL QUOTATIONS, 604
The n. which have put mankind and posterity most in their debt NATIONS, 3
three very powerful n. of the Germans ENGLISH, 6
Two n. POVERTY AND WEALTH, 4
native My n. Land – Good Night DEPARTURE, 5
my own, my n. land HOMESICKNESS, 6
to appear considerable in his n. place FAME, 15
white man . . . looks into the eyes of a n. AFRICA, 1
natives Britons were only n. HISTORY, 35
natural First feelings are always the most n. FIRST IMPRESSIONS, 5
It is n. to die BIRTH, 1
n. false teeth TEETH, 8
N. Selection EVOLUTION, 10
Nothing prevents us from being n. SPONTANEITY, 4
'twas N. to please CHARACTER, 6
What is wrong with a revolution . . . n. REVOLUTION, 6
naturally Though I am not n. honest HONESTY, 10
nature Accuse not N., she hath done her part RESPONSIBILITY, 10
All N. wears one universal grin NATURE, 12
Allow not n. more than n. needs NECESSITY, 6
a noble n., . . . treats . . . a serious subject POETRY, 3
but N. more NATURE, 5
Consistency is contrary to n. CONSTANCY, 2
drive out n. with a pitchfork HUMAN NATURE, 11
fortress built by N. EARTH, 16
Friend . . . masterpiece of N. FRIENDS, 8
God and N. then at strife NATURE, 31
go into partnership with n. NATURE, 14
Human n. is so well disposed HUMAN NATURE, 2
I got disappointed in human n. HUMAN NATURE, 8
I have always respected suicide as a regulator of n. SUICIDE, 19
I have learned /To look on n. EXPERIENCE, 24
In n. there are neither rewards nor punishments NATURE, 24
I watched what method N. might take REMEDIES, 53
Let N. be your Teacher NATURE, 39
Little we see in N. that is ours WASTE, 3
Man has wrested from n. NUCLEAR WEAPONS, 22
Man is N.'s sole mistake MANKIND, 28
N. abhors a vacuum NATURE, 29
N. admits no lie NATURE, 6
N. can do more than physicians NATURE, 9
N. has always had more power than education NATURE, 32
N. has left this tincture TYRANNY, 4
N. has never put the fatal question as to the meaning of their lives ANSWERS, 9
N. has no cure for this sort of madness COMMUNISM, 14
N. heals, under the auspices of the medical profession MEDICINE, 24
n. imitating art ACTORS 13
N., in medical language MEDICINE, 44
N. is a benevolent old hypocrite NATURE, 19
n. is a conjugation of the verb to eat NATURE, 23
N. is better than a middling doctor NATURE, 1
N. is but a name for an effect NATURE, 8
N. is creeping up ARROGANCE, 8
N. is often hidden HUMAN NATURE, 5
n. is the art of God NATURE, 2
N. is usually wrong NATURE, 33
N. is very consonant and conformable NATURE, 27
N. made him, and then broke the mould COMPLIMENTS, 1
N., . . . must be obeyed HUMAN NATURE, 6
N. never did betray HEART, 22
N. puts upon no man an unbearable burden SUICIDE, 19
N. remains NATURE, 34
N.'s ancient power was lost DECLINE, 14
N.'s handmaid, art NATURE, 11
n.'s law HELP, 8
N.'s laws lay hid in night SCIENTISTS, 9
N., time and patience are the three great physicians MEDICINE, 1
N. . . . wasteful of promising young men NATURE, 22
new sights of N. made me rejoice NATURE, 10
not formed by n. to bear ENDURANCE, 4
o'erstep not the modesty of n. ACTION, 11
Of all the soft, delicious functions of n. this is the chiefest SLEEP, 30
one of N.'s Gentlemen CHIVALRY, 7
one of the forces of n. GREATNESS, 10
Our foster nurse of n. is repose SLEEP, 27
rules of the game are what we call the laws of N. GOD, 32
science . . . is . . . the interplay between n. and ourselves NATURE, 16
secret of the arts is to correct n. ARTS, 10
The art of healing comes from n. MEDICINE, 73
the encroachment of n. NATURE, 18
the most irrelevant thing in n. FAMILY, 29
the physician must start from n. MEDICINE, 73
the surgeon be sometimes tempted to supplant instead of aiding N. SURGEONS, 11
Though you drive away N. NATURE, 21
to see the absurd n. of Englishmen ENGLISH, 33
True wit is n. to advantage dress'd HUMOR, 49
unassuming common-place /Of N. FLOWERS, 15
until n. kills him or cures him MEDICINE, 63
vacuum . . . better . . . stuff that n. replaces NATURE, 35
We must turn to n. itself NATURE, 17
We need more understanding of human n. HUMAN NATURE, 13
Whatever N. has in store for mankind NATURE, 13
you can't call yourself a great work of n. INSULTS, 128
natures Men's n. are alike HABIT, 4
naught N. so sweet as Melancholy MELANCHOLY, 2
nauseate I n. walking COUNTRYSIDE, 1
Navee Ruler of the Queen's N. OFFICERS, 6
navel thy n. is like a round goblet BIBLICAL QUOTATIONS, 637
navy British n. always travels first class NAVY, 6
England's chief defence depends upon the n. NAVY, 9
There were gentlemen and . . . seamen in the n. of Charles the Second NAVY, 8
The Royal N. of England . . . its greatest defence NAVY, 2
upon the n. . . . safety, honour, and welfare . . . chiefly attend NAVY, 4
We joined the N. to see the world EXPECTATION, 1
Nazi N. Germany had become a menace to all mankind NAZISM, 5
Nazis In Germany, the N. came for the Communists NAZISM, 6
near I wished to be n. my mother BIRTH, 17
nearer N., my God, to thee RELIGION, 1
the n. you are to God PROTESTANTISM, 8
nearest the n. run thing you ever saw WAR, 166
nearsighted don't raise your hands because I am also n. DISABILITY, 1
neat round, n., not gaudy GARDENS, 9
Nebuchadnezzar N. . . . did eat grass as oxen BIBLICAL QUOTATIONS, 61
necessary Government, . . . is but a n. evil GOVERNMENT, 28
necessities disregard for the n. of existence CIVILIZATION, 10
we will dispense with its n. LUXURY, 4
necessity I am sworn brother, sweet, /To grim N. NECESSITY, 9
I find alone N. Supreme NECESSITY, 11
N. hath no law NECESSITY, 4
N. is the mother NECESSITY, 2
N. is the plea for every infringement of human freedom NECESSITY, 5
N. knows no law NECESSITY, 10
no virtue like n. NECESSITY, 8
neck a pain in the n. SPEECHES, 1
A short n. denotes a good mind APPEARANCE, 58
England will have her n. wrung like a chicken WORLD WAR II, 49
equipping us with a n. BOLDNESS, 3
go to the bottom with my principles round my n. EXPEDIENCY, 6
my n. is very short EXECUTION, 26
Some n. WORLD WAR II, 19
the Roman people had but one n. RUTHLESSNESS, 1
necking me and Morpheus off in a corner, n. BOASTS, 6
Whoever named it n. SEX, 65
neckties men wore their beards, like they wear their n. APPEARANCE, 28
Ned no more work for poor old N. DEATH, 67
need All You N. Is Love LOVE, 94
An artist . . . produces things that people don't n. ARTISTS, 15
reason not the n. NECESSITY, 6
Thy n. is yet greater than mine SELF-DENIAL, 2
needle easier for a camel to go through the eye of a n. BIBLICAL QUOTATIONS, 520
needs N. must NECESSITY, 3
to each according to his n. MARXISM, 9
Your country n. YOU WAR, 5
negation Capitalist production begets . . . its own n. CAPITALISM, 13
negative Europe is the unfinished n. UNITED STATES, 44
N. Capability DOUBT, 7
negativism nattering nabobs of n. MEDIA, 2
neglect A little n. may breed mischief NEGLECT, 1
he devotes to the n. of his duties NEGLECT, 4
negligent Celerity . . . admired . . . by the n. IMPETUOSITY, 3
negligible the work is n. CRITICISM, 1
Negro One of the things that makes a N. unpleasant to white folk RACISM, 5
Negroes revenge by the culture of the N. MUSIC, 32
neiges *les n. d'antan* NOSTALGIA, 27
neighbor better mouse-trap than his n. FAME, 10
death . . . had been his next-door n. DEATH, 129
Death is my n. now DEATH, 61
Do not love your n. as yourself SELF, 16
I have had no real gratification . . . more than my n. LAST WORDS, 88
It's a recession when your n. UNEMPLOYMENT, 4
love thy n. as thyself BIBLICAL QUOTATIONS, 526
they helped every one his n. BIBLICAL QUOTATIONS, 272
told men to love their n. HUNGER, 3
neighbors fear of what the n. might say SUICIDE, 10
improper thoughts about n. MORALITY, 4
make sport for our n. RIDICULE, 1
neither better if n. of us had been born EPITAPHS, 25
N. am I REPARTEE, 27
Nell Pretty witty N. COMPLIMENTS, 21
the death of Little N. without laughing INSENSITIVITY, 5
Nelly let not poor N. starve LAST WORDS, 16
Nelson N., born in a fortunate hour OFFICERS, 11
The N. touch OFFICERS, 10
nerve called a n. specialist because it sounds better PSYCHIATRY, 35
Herein are demanded the eye and the n. SELF-KNOWLEDGE, 13

Those people . . . are making such a n. AUDIENCES, 6
noises Like n. in a swound SEA, 4
noisy Strongest minds / . . . the n. world /Hears least MIND, 36
The people would be just as n. PUBLIC, 9
noli n. me tangere BIBLICAL QUOTATIONS, 370
nomadic the charm . . . of a n. existence CAMPING, 1
nomenclature even the learned ignorance of a n. LEARNING, 9
nominated I will not accept if n. POLITICIANS, 101
nomination I will not accept, the n. UNITY, 11
No-more I am also called N. DISAPPOINTMENT, 6
non-being Neurosis is the way of avoiding n. NEUROSIS, 14
non-combatant War hath no fury like a n. WAR, 103
nonconformist a N. conscience WOMEN, 127
man must be a n. CONFORMITY, 5
Why do you have to be a n. CONFORMITY, 6
nonconformity N. and lust stalking hand in hand LUST, 11
none N. but the Brave COURAGE, 11
nonsense you intend to talk n. UNITED STATES, 84
Non-U U and N. CLASS, 37
non-violence to disagree . . . about . . . n. without wanting to kick VIOLENCE, 8
noon From morn /To n. he fell DECLINE, 4
from n. to dewy eve DECLINE, 4
O dark, dark, dark, amid the blaze of n. BLINDNESS, 9
Norfolk bear him up the N. sky HUNTING, 2
Very flat, N. ENGLAND, 16
Norgay Tenzing N. PHOTOGRAPHY, 4
Norma Jean Goodbye N. ACTORS, 12
normal the n. is so . . . interesting NORMALITY, 1
normalcy not nostrums but n. POLITICS, 60
Normans The Saxon is not like us N. NATIONALITY, 8
north The n. wind does blow PROVERBS, 403
nose A custom loathsome to the eye, hateful to the n. SMOKING, 18
A person may be indebted for a n. . . . to a great-aunt FAMILY, 25
Dong with a luminous N. NONSENSE, 18
Had Cleopatra's n. been shorter APPEARANCE, 46
led by the n. with gold BRIBERY, 5
My n. bleeds for you INSINCERITY, 6
My n. is huge APPEARANCE, 49
Only the n. knows SECRECY, 1
This fellow did not see further than his . . . n. PAROCHIALISM, 1
will it come without warning /Just as I'm picking my n. LOVE, 19
nostrils God . . . breathed into his n. BIBLICAL QUOTATIONS, 181
nostrums not n. but normalcy POLITICS, 60
not Believe it or n. BELIEF, 10
how n. to do it BUREAUCRACY, 4
I am n. what I am APPEARANCES, 31
note The world will little n., nor long remember MEMORIALS, 9
notes the pauses between the n. MUSICIANS, 8
nothin' N. Like a Dame WOMEN, 54
You ain't heard n. yet PROPHECY, 10
You ain't n. but a hound dog DOGS, 10
nothing Blessed is the man who expects n. EXPECTATION, 6
Certainly, there is n. else here to enjoy PARTIES, 8
certain we can carry n. out BIBLICAL QUOTATIONS, 650
Children aren't happy with n. to ignore FAMILY, 38
Death is n. AFTERLIFE, 6
doing n. for each other FRIENDSHIP, 21
from n. to a state of extreme poverty POVERTY, 30
George the First knew n. ROYALTY, 70
God made everything out of n. CREATION, 16
have n. whatever to do with it DEATH, 106
It is very good, sometimes, to have n. POVERTY, 39
I (Who Have N.) POVERTY, 29
N. FRENCH REVOLUTION, 5
N. can be created out of nothing NOTHING, 1
n. can bring back the hour REGRET, 27
n. either good or bad THINKING, 15
N., except my genius CONCEIT, 25
N. happens BOREDOM, 1
n. if not critical CRITICISM, 57
n. is /But what is not APPEARANCES, 30
n. is certain but death and taxes TAXATION, 6
n., . . . is greater . . . than one's self BODY, 27
n. is had for n. EFFORT, 4
n. is law that is not reason LAW, 26
N. long HUMAN NATURE, 9
N. matters very much TRIVIALITY, 1
N. to do but work PESSIMISM, 10
n. to do with the case APPEARANCE, 22
N. will come of nothing NOTHING, 2
opened it only to find – n. MATERIALISM, 2
People don't resent having n. WEALTH, 15
Signifying n. LIFE, 76
sooner read a time-table . . . than n. NOVELS, 11
take *more* than n. LANGUAGE, 9
The House of Peers, . . . Did n. HOUSES OF PARLIAMENT, 13
the sort of woman now, . . . said Mould, ... one would almost feel disposed to bury for n. WOMEN, 38
The temerity to believe in n. SCEPTICISM, 6
those who were up to n. INTRIGUE, 2
To be thus is n. FEAR, 17
To marvel at n. is just about the one and only thing HAPPINESS, 8
We are n.; less than n., and dreams INSIGNIFICANCE, 4
When you have n. to say, say n. SILENCE, 4
Where some people are very wealthy and others have n. GOVERNMENT, 5
nothingness the n. shows through CREATION, 16
notice The State, in choosing men . . . takes no n. of their opinions LOYALTY, 6
notices One never n. what has been done ACHIEVEMENT 4
nought N.'s had, all's spent CONTENTMENT, 10
This great world /Should so wear out to n. TRANSIENCE, 20
nourisher a n. of thine old age BIBLICAL QUOTATIONS, 607
Chief n. in life's feast CARE, 9
novel Among the many problems . . . the choice of the moment . . . to begin his n. WRITERS, 47
A n. is a mirror NOVELS, 16
A n. is a static thing NOVELS, 17
because a n.'s invented, it isn't true NOVELS, 13
good n. tells us the truth NOVELS, 2
I'm going to write the Great Australian N. AMBITION, 26
not a n. to be tossed aside lightly CRITICISM, 49
scrofulous French n. NOVELS, 1
The detective n. is NOVELS, 14
the last fashionable n. on the tables of young ladies WRITING, 27
The n. being dead NOVELS, 18
the n. tells a story NOVELS, 4
The only obligation to which . . . we may hold a n. NOVELS, 7
the sex n. is now normal NOVELS, 15
to read a n. before luncheon was one of the gravest sins READING, 20
When I want to read a n. NOVELS, 3
novelist A n. is, like all mortals WRITERS, 38
n. who writes nothing for 10 years WRITERS, 44
novelists n. the story of the present NOVELS, 6
There are many reasons why n. write FICTION, 3
novels characters in one of my n. FICTION, 2
one of the few English n. for grown up people CRITICISM, 67
novelty N., n., n. NOVELTY, 3
November N. MONTHS, 10
Please to remember the Fifth of N. ANONYMOUS, 69
Thirty days hath N. MONTHS, 9
novice Man arrives as a n. at each age of his life AGE, 20
now Are you n. or have you ever been a member COMMUNISM, 1
The n., the here, through which TIME, 23
We are all Socialists n. SOCIALISM, 12
nowhere All dressed up, with n. to go FUTILITY, 13
He's a real N. Man FUTILITY, 9
noxious the most n. is a tourist BRITISH, 9
nuclear Wars cannot be fought with n. weapons NUCLEAR WEAPONS, 15
nude skied down Mount Everest in the n. LOVE, 104
The trouble with n. dancing DANCING, 6
To keep one from going n. PESSIMISM, 10
nudging fed up with fudging and n. POLITICS, 108
nudity you don't need the n. CINEMA, 19
nuisance exchange of one n. for another n. PROGRESS, 10
Inflation in the Sixties was a n. ECONOMICS, 16
Never compose . . . unless . . . not composing . . . becomes a positive n. MUSIC, 21
no ideas . . . not a n. PRESIDENTS, 11
nuisances a change of n. is as good as a vacation CHANGE, 15
number *abstract reasoning concerning quantity or n.* ILLUSIONS, 3
a very interesting n. NUMBERS, 5
Look after n. one PROVERBS, 266
numbers divinity in odd n. DIVINITY, 4
N. . . . only universal language MATHEMATICS, 24
Round n. NUMBERS, 2
the greatest happiness for the greatest n. HAPPINESS, 11
up in the high n. NUMBERS, 3
numble We live in a n. abode SERVILITY, 2
numbness drowsy n. pains /My sense HEART, 12
nun the upbringing a n. would envy BODY, 18
nuns the n. who never take a bath MODESTY, 9
nuptials prone to any iteration of n. MARRIAGE, 44
nurse a good n. is of more importance than a physician NURSES, 4
always keep a hold of N. COMFORT, 1
definition of . . . a n. . . . 'devoted and obedient.' NURSES, 6
from the point of view of the hygienist, the physician, the architect, the tax-payer, the superintendents, and the n. HOSPITALS, 3
If ye had a good n. NURSES, 2
It's better to be sick than n. the sick NURSES, 3
N. unupblown BREVITY, 10
Our foster n. of nature is repose SLEEP, 27
Talk of the patience of Job, said a Hospital n. NURSES, 8
That person alone is fit to n. or to attend the bedside of a patient NURSES, 9
The trained n. has become one of the great blessings of humanity NURSES, 7
The trained n. has given nursing the human . . . touch NURSES, 5
nurseries n. of all vice EDUCATION, 27
nurses a giggle of n. LANGUAGE, 3
old men's n. MARRIAGE, 13
nursing n. means vexation of the mind NURSES, 3
nut I had a little n. tree, /Nothing would it bear NURSERY RHYMES, 20
nut-brown the spicy n. ale ALCOHOL, 58
nutmeg But a silver n. NURSERY RHYMES, 20

O

oak Absalom hanged in an o. BIBLICAL QUOTATIONS, 619
Heart of o. are our ships COURAGE, 14
To win the palm, the o., or bays VICTORY, 13
oar impressions . . . lasting as . . . an o. upon the water INSIGNIFICANCE, 1
oat This bread I break was once the o. AGRICULTURE, 5
oat-cakes land of Calvin, o., and sulphur SCOTLAND, 8
oaths God pardon all o. that are broke FAITHFULNESS, 6
O. are but words WORDS, 4
o. are straws DISTRUST, 4
obedience The reluctant o. of distant provinces DIPLOMACY, 19
obedient definition of . . . a nurse . . . 'devoted and o..' NURSES, 6
o. unto death BIBLICAL QUOTATIONS, 563
obesity O. is a mental state OBESITY, 7
obey born to o. OBEDIENCE, 2
children, o. your parents BIBLICAL QUOTATIONS, 118
one of those born neither to o. nor to command NASTINESS, 5
safer to o. than to rule OBEDIENCE, 3
obeyed Nature, . . . must be o. HUMAN NATURE, 6
She-who-must-be-o. WOMAN'S ROLE, 4
obituaries I have read many o. with a lot of pleasure SIN, 17
were my o. good OBITUARIES, 7
object o. will be, if possible to form Christian men EDUCATION, 7
objectionable its own animality either o. or funny HUMOR, 34

tell the o. by their hunted expression CHARITY, 18
to encourage the o. EXAMPLE, 10
otherwise nothing in his long career which those . . . would wish o. ROYALTY, 16
Some folk . . . are o. WISDOM, 29
Otis Miss O. regrets APOLOGIES, 4
ounce An o. of a man's own wit WISDOM, 30
ours We have met the enemy, and they are o. VICTORY, 16
ourselves all our knowledge is, o. to know SELF-KNOWLEDGE, 8
By persuading others we convince o. PERSUASION, 1
In every friend we lose a part of o. DEATH, 119
remedies oft in o. do lie SELF-RELIANCE, 12
'tis in o. that we are thus, or thus HUMAN NATURE, 24
we but praise o. in other men PRAISE, 7
What isn't part of o. doesn't disturb us HATE, 6
'ousemaids I walks with fifty 'o. outer Chelsea to the Strand DISCONTENT, 6
'ouses It's 'aving 'o. built by men HOUSES, 5
out Mordre wol o. MURDER, 4
once o., what you've said can't be stopped PUBLISHING, 6
O., damned spot GUILT, 16
outer exploring O. Space, /To find the Inner Man SPACE, 5
out-herods it o. Herod ACTING, 13
outlive do not o. yourself HEALTHY LIVING, 38
o. this powerful rhyme POETRY, 53
outlook religious o. on life RELIGION, 48
out-of-doors God having given us indoors and o. NATURE, 26
outrun We may o. EXCESS, 13
outside I am just going o. LAST WORDS, 61
I support it from the o. SUPPORT, 6
outspoken O. by whom REPARTEE, 77
outward I may not hope from o. forms APPEARANCES, 13
over Nothing is more fatal to *Health*, than an *o. care* of it HYPOCHONDRIA, 6
Now the day is o. DAY AND NIGHT, 1
The game isn't o. till it's o. SPORT AND GAMES, 3
overboard throw the occasional man o. POLITICS, 56
overcome I have o. the world BIBLICAL QUOTATIONS, 357
overcomes Who o. /By force VICTORY, 14
over-confident Not that I am ever o. SELF-CONFIDENCE, 9
over-educated I've o. myself in all the things DEBAUCHERY, 5
overexposure she should catch a cold on o. TRUTH, 15
overfed They're overpaid, o., oversexed and over here SOLDIERS, 15
over-feeding what Nicely-Nicely dies of will be o. GREED, 11
overlooked better to be looked over than o. STARING, 1
overpaid They're o., overfed, oversexed and over here SOLDIERS, 15
overrated matrimony, which I always thought a highly o. performance MARRIAGE, 60
overrun apt to be o. with nettles MIND, 33
over-running and lose by o. EXCESS, 13
oversexed They're overpaid, overfed, o. and over here SOLDIERS, 15
overtakers It is the o. who TRAVEL, 32
overthrown Another mighty empire o. DEFEAT, 18
o. /More than your enemies LOVE, 131
overtures I tried to resist his o. PUNS, 21
ovule Man is developed from an o. EVOLUTION, 7
ovules differs in no respect from the o. of other animals EVOLUTION, 7
owe I don't o. a penny to a single soul BORROWING, 13
I o. nothing to Women's Lib FEMINISM, 36
owed so much o. by so many to so few WORLD WAR II, 14
owes A nation is not in danger . . . because it o. itself money ECONOMICS, 18
he o. not any man RIGHTEOUSNESS, 9
oweth woman o. to her husband MARRIAGE, 120
owl The O. and the Pussy-Cat went to sea HONEY, 3
owls Two O. and a Hen APPEARANCE, 29
own mine o. Executioner SELF, 8
ownership its source of power: o. CAPITALISM, 10
personal o. is in harmony with . . . British people MATERIALISM, 17
transform this society without . . . extension of public o. SOCIALISM, 14
ox This dumb o. will fill the whole world EXPECTATION, 4
When he stands like an o. in the furrow NATIONALITY, 8
Oxenford Clerk . . . of O. LOGIC, 3
Oxford a secret in the O. sense OXFORD, 7
Cambridge as a little town and O. OXFORD, 16
every imitation from 'Eton and O.' PARTIES, 12
Herr Hitler and Signor Mussolini had been at O. OXFORD, 11
It is O. that has made me insufferable EDUCATION, 12
nice sort of place, O. OXFORD, 13
O. . . . full of a particular non-social snobbiness OXFORD, 15
O. is on the whole more attractive than Cambridge CAMBRIDGE, 1
The clever men at O. /Know all that there is to be knowed KNOWLEDGE, 18
The King to O. sent a troop of horse CAMBRIDGE, 2
To O. sent a troop of horse CAMBRIDGE, 6
To the University of O. I acknowledge no obligation EDUCATION, 34
You will hear more good things on . . . a stagecoach from London to O. INTELLECTUALS, 10
you will leave O. by the town drain SPOONERISMS, 5
oyster bold man that first eat an o. COURAGE, 24
sympathetic unselfishness of an o. FISH, 2
the sort of eye that can open an o. at sixty paces APPEARANCE, 66
world's mine o. OPPORTUNITY, 19
oysters Poverty and o. POVERTY, 8

P

pace this petty p. from day to day LIFE, 76
Pacific salutes the Admiral of the P. ARROGANCE, 10
pacifism My p. is not based on . . . intellectual theory WAR AND PEACE, 7
pack how much more dogs are animated when they hunt in a p. UNITY, 10
the human p. is shuffled and cut EDUCATION, 53
paddle every man p. his own canoe INDEPENDENCE, 4
paddling p. palms and pinching fingers LOVE, 163
padlocked music critics. . . . small and rodent-like with p. ears CRITICS, 18
pagan A P. suckled in a creed outworn DISCONTENT, 10
Christian glories in the death of a p. CHRISTIANITY, 5
pageant insubstantial p. faded MORTALITY, 17
paid I do not answer questions like this without being p. MASCULINITY, 1
paiementz Daily many warantis come to me of p. ECONOMICS, 7
pain a gentleman . . . never inflicts p. CHIVALRY, 8
Although p. isn't real ANONYMOUS, 91
a p. in the neck SPEECHES, 1
But p. is perfect miserie SUFFERING, 23
critics . . . desire our blood, not our p. CRITICS, 11
disinclination to inflict p. upon oneself GOOD, 11
For we are born in others' p. SUFFERING, 35
gangrene is p. and inconvenience NAMES, 14
He that is uneasy at every little p. HYPOCHONDRIA, 1
hour of p. is as long SUFFERING, 1
I feel no p., dear mother, now ALCOHOL, 11
if it did not involve giving p. OCCUPATIONS, 7
it entails too much p. REMEDIES, 30
it is only by degrees, through p., that he understands the . . . body SUFFERING, 21
It would be a great thing to understand P. SUFFERING, 20
Man endures p. as an undeserved punishment SUFFERING, 4
momentary intoxication with p. CRUELTY, 1
Much of your p. is self-chosen SUFFERING, 16
my considerable daily allotment of *p.* SUFFERING, 13
Neither poverty nor p. is accumulable SUFFERING, 9
Neither shame nor physical p. have any . . . effect PAIN, 5
owes its pleasures to another's p. HUNTING, 3
P. and death are a part of life LIFE, 34
P. – has an Element of Blank SUFFERING, 15
P. is a more terrible lord of mankind than even death himself SUFFERING, 28
P. is life – the sharper, the more evidence of life LIFE, 47
P. is the correlative of some species of wrong SUFFERING, 32
P. of mind is worse than p. of body SUFFERING, 33
P. was my portion EPITAPHS, 56
P. with the thousand teeth SUFFERING, 37
People will not . . . bear p. unless there is hope HOPE, 10
Pleasure is . . . intermission of p. PAIN, 8
Remember that p. has this most excellent quality SUFFERING, 29
The art of life is the art of avoiding p. LIFE, 46
The first cry of p. . . . was the first call for a physician MEDICINE, 84
The greatest evil is physical p. SUFFERING, 6
The least p. in our little finger SELF-INTEREST, 4
the momentary intoxication with p. MENTAL ILLNESS, 1
The p. passes, but the beauty remains ART, 23
Time heals old p. SUFFERING, 3
what p. it was to drown DROWNING, 2
yearning like a God in p. SUFFERING, 18
painful the one is as p. as the other LIFE AND DEATH, 6
pains He therefore was at strenuous p. POLITICIANS, 13
no gains without p. ENDURANCE, 23
suffering her p. in his own proper person and character SEXES, 24
With what shift and p. we come into the World DEATH, 43
paint A professional is someone whose wife works to enable him to p. ARTISTS, 10
flinging a pot of p. in the public's face CRITICISM, 56
I p. objects as I think them PAINTING, 13
My business is to p. . . . what I see PAINTING, 20
to p. the lily EXCESS, 12
painted As idle as a p. ship BOATS, 3
I am p. as the greatest little dictator AUTHORITARIANISM, 7
Most women are not so young as they are p. COSMETICS, 1
p. . . . by the great artist Kodak PHOTOGRAPHY, 6
painter A p. should not paint what he sees ARTISTS, 13
I am married to Beatrice Salkeld, a p. CHILDREN, 8
I could have become a real p. LAST WORDS, 50
memory is a p. MEMORY, 13
not a great sculptor or p. can be an architect ARCHITECTURE, 12
painters Good p. imitate nature PAINTING, 4
P. and poets . . . licence to dare anything FREEDOM, 23
p., poets and builders have very high flights ARTS, 8
Poets and p. are outside the class system ARTISTS, 2
painting a great difference between p. a face APPEARANCE, 21
If I didn't start p., I would have raised chickens OCCUPATIONS, 17
If people only knew . . . about p. PAINTING, 9
I just keep p. till I feel like pinching. Then I know it's right PAINTING, 17
P. is a blind man's profession PAINTING, 14
P., . . . protecting flat surfaces from the weather PAINTING, 3
pair A p. so famous LOVE AND DEATH, 6
pajamas I shot an elephant in my p. HUMOR, 35
palace Love in a p. LOVE, 87
striding half-naked up the steps of the vice-regal p. CONTEMPT, 3
palaces Mid pleasures and p. though we may roam HOME, 10
pale a p. horse BIBLICAL QUOTATIONS, 589
Palestine not enough prisons . . . in P. to hold all the Jews JEWS, 14
pall The pallor of girls' brows shall be their p. WAR, 117
Palladium Liberty of the press is the *P.* of . . . rights FREEDOM, 29
pallor The p. of girls' brows shall be their pall WAR, 117
palm happy state of getting the victor's p. without the dust of racing VICTORY, 9
To win the p., the oak, or bays VICTORY, 13
palms p. before my feet ANIMALS, 12

they found no more of her than . . . the p. of her hands BIBLICAL QUOTATIONS, 407
palsied with the p. heart PASSION, 10
Pan Forty years ago he was Slightly in Peter P. INSULTS, 121
Put on the p.; /Says Greedy Nan NURSERY RHYMES, 7
Pancras musical equivalent of . . . St P. CRITICISM, 5
Pandora open that P.'s Box . . . Trojan 'orses will jump out MIXED METAPHORS, 1
Panjandrum the grand P. NONSENSE, 13
pantheist The modern p. not only PHOTOGRAPHY, 5
pants There were times my p. were so thin POVERTY, 40
Your eyes shine like the p. COMPLIMENTS, 18
papacy Since God has given us the p. . . . enjoy it CATHOLICISM, 9
The P. is not other than the Ghost of the deceased Roman Empire CATHOLICISM, 6
paper only a p. moon FAITH, 14
reactionaries are p. tigers POLITICS, 97
The atom bomb is a p. tiger NUCLEAR WEAPONS, 14
This p. will no doubt be found interesting CRITICISM, 17
Where were you fellows when the p. was blank EDITORS, 1
papers a great heap of p. ROYALTY, 32
fornicated and read the p. MANKIND, 15
only two posh p. on a Sunday NEWSPAPERS, 11
papists revenged to the utmost upon all P. ASSASSINATION, 1
papyromania *P.* – compulsive accumulation OBSESSIONS, 3
papyrophobia *P.* – abnormal desire OBSESSIONS, 3
parables great p., . . . but false art CRITICISM, 33
parade solemnized with pomp and p. UNITED STATES, 1
the chief employment of riches consists in the p. of riches OSTENTATION, 6
paradise A p. for a sect FANATICISM, 2
drunk the milk of P. CAUTION, 9
England is a p. for women NATIONALITY, 5
England is the p. of women ENGLAND, 21
England is the p. of individuality ENGLAND, 43
Grant me p. in this world HEAVEN, 15
If a man could pass through P. PROOF, 4
Same old glimpse of /P. MARRIAGE, 86
the p. of fools is not an unpleasant abode HEAVEN, 6
to hope for P. is to live in P. HEAVEN, 10
we go to P. by way of Kensal Green EXPECTATION, 2
Wilderness is P. enow BREAD, 4
paradoxes P. are useful IDEAS, 1
paradoxical He who confronts the p. REALITY, 2
paragon the p. of animals DELIGHT, 10
parallel We never remark any passion . . . in others, of which, . . . we may not find a p. SELF, 10
parallelogram The landlady . . . is a p. HUMOR, 33
paralysis p. is nervousness NAMES, 14
paralyze p. it by encumbering it with remedies BODY, 24
paranoid Even a p. can have enemies ENEMIES, 4
Just because you're p. PSYCHIATRY, 3
parasite save every p. alive SURVIVAL, 4
The sick man is a p. of society PATIENTS, 15
parcels Portions and p. of the dreadful Past TIME, 49
pardon God may p. you, but I never can FORGIVENESS, 13
God will p. me. It is His trade LAST WORDS, 47
the government that should ask me for a p. FORGIVENESS, 11
pardoned The women p. all FORGIVENESS, 10
parent a kind p. . . . or a merciless step-mother NATURE, 28
To lose one p., . . . a misfortune; to lose both looks like carelessness CARELESSNESS, 1
parenthood p. . . . feeding the mouth that bites you FAMILY, 16
parents A Jewish man with p. alive JEWS, 18
by defying their p. and copying one another YOUTH, 8
children, obey your p. BIBLICAL QUOTATIONS, 118
Don't hold your p. up to contempt FAMILY, 58
From birth to age eighteen, a girl needs good p. AGE, 78
joys of p. are secret FAMILY, 8
necessary precautions to avoid having p. FAMILY, 14
P. . . . a disappointment to their children FAMILY, 43
P. are strange FAMILY, 57
P. are the last people on earth FAMILY, 12
P. . . . bones on which children sharpen their teeth FAMILY, 56
P. learn a lot from their children CHILDREN, 50
Possessive p. rarely live long enough to see FAMILY, 21
sort of people our p. warned us about VICE, 11
the way p. obey their children FAMILY, 59
what p. were created for FAMILY, 38
Paris delivered of a city bigger than P. DISAPPOINTMENT, 4
Good Americans, when they die, go to P. UNITED STATES, 74
I love P. PARIS, 6
Is P. burning PARIS, 4
no home . . . save in P. PARIS, 5
P. is worth a mass PARIS, 3
P. Loves Lovers PARIS, 7
The last time I saw P. PARIS, 1
when good Americans die they go to P. REPARTEE, 122
parish all the world as my p. RELIGION, 80
He was born, bred, and hanged, all in the same p. ANONYMOUS, 34
man who left a wife and six children on the p. ROYALTY, 13
park The hunchback in the p. LONELINESS, 12
Parkinson The rise in the . . . employed is governed by P.'s Law WORK, 22
par-lee-voo Hinky, dinky, p. FRANCE, 16
parliament a regular income from his p. INSINCERITY, 3
build your House of P. upon the river HOUSES OF PARLIAMENT, 22
If Her Majesty stood for P. POLITICS, 128
more fit for a grammar school than a Court of P. HOUSES OF PARLIAMENT, 6
nailed up the doors of P. FASCISM, 10
no reference to fun in any Act of P. PLEASURE, 14
P. is the longest running farce GOVERNMENT, 36
the full-hearted consent of the P. POLITICS, 63
The rights of p. should be preserved GOVERNMENT, 26
parliaments England . . . mother of p. ENGLAND, 9
P. are the great lie of our time GOVERNMENT, 32
parlor Will you walk into my p. INVITATIONS, 3
parochial worse than provincial – he was p. WRITERS, 24
parody devil's walking p. ANIMALS, 11
parole Classical quotation is the *p.* of literary men QUOTATIONS, 5
parrot to sell the family p. RESPECTABILITY, 4
parsnips fine words butter no p. WORDS, 26
parson If P. lost his senses ANIMALS, 15
In arguing too, the p. own'd his skill KNOWLEDGE, 17
Once a p. OCCUPATIONS, 5
parsons Our dourest p. PRAYER, 26
part A stage where every man must play a p. LIFE, 77
If you're not p. of the solution CONFORMITY, 3
I have forgot my p. FAILURE, 7
In every friend we lose a p. of ourselves DEATH, 119
it is a little flesh and breath, and the ruling p. MANKIND, 5
let us kiss and p. PARTING, 6
till death us do p. BOOK OF COMMON PRAYER, THE, 15
We only p. to meet again FAITHFULNESS, 4
particular a London p. . . . A fog WEATHER, 10
did nothing in p. HOUSES OF PARLIAMENT, 13
particulars Minute P. GOOD, 2
parties it is always like that at p. REGRET, 14
one of those p. which got out of hand CHRISTIANITY, 32
parting Every p. gives a foretaste of death SEPARATION, 5
P. is all we know of heaven PARTING, 5
P. is such sweet sorrow PARTING, 10
partisanship P. is our great curse SUBJECTIVITY, 7
partly Man p. is AMBITION, 5
partridge A p. in a pear tree CHRISTMAS, 16
well-shot woodcock, p., snipe HUNTING, 2
parts It is seldom . . . one p. on good terms PARTING, 9
one man in his time plays many p. HUMAN CONDITION, 22
there are no spare p. BODY, 4
Today we have naming of p. WEAPONS, 6
part-time p. nihilist COMMITMENT, 3
parturition P. is a physiological process BIRTH 7
party A great p. is not to be brought down POLITICS, 59
Any p. which takes credit for the rain POLITICS, 102
best number for a dinner p. is two FOOD, 36
Englishman has to have a P. POLITICS, 124
Heard there was a p. ACCIDENTS, 6
I always voted at my p.'s call POLITICIANS, 48
It's my p. TEARS, 2
p. is a political evil POLITICS, 23
the Conservative P. at prayer CHURCH 9
The p. is the rallying-point for the . . . working class COMMUNISM, 17
The sooner every p. breaks up the better PARTIES, 2
Well, did you evah! What a swell p. PARTIES, 7
pass ideas simply p. through him STUPIDITY, 1
I shall not p. this way again MORTALITY, 11
no delight to p. away the time APPEARANCE, 52
p. for forty-three AGE, 36
Praise the Lord and p. the ammunition WAR, 58
They shall not p. DETERMINATION, 19
To p. away ere life hath lost its brightness DEATH, 76
passage a fair and easie p. for it to go out LIFE AND DEATH, 17
calm p. . . . across many a bad night NIGHT, 9
Patience and p. of time FURY, 4
passageways smell of steaks in p. FOOD, 29
passed p. by on the other side BIBLICAL QUOTATIONS, 432
p. from death unto life BIBLICAL QUOTATIONS, 329
That p. the time TIME, 9
the people were p. clean over Jordan BIBLICAL QUOTATIONS, 384
passengers fools and p. drink at sea BOATS, 16
passeront *Ils ne p. pas* DETERMINATION, 19
passes Men seldom make p. APPEARANCE, 43
passeth know the love of Christ, which p. knowledge BIBLICAL QUOTATIONS, 116
the fashion of this world p. away BIBLICAL QUOTATIONS, 35
the peace of God, which p. all understanding BIBLICAL QUOTATIONS, 565
passion All breathing human p. far above PASSION, 4
Asthma is a disease that has practically the same symptoms as p. PASSION, 1
cheated into p., but . . . reasoned into truth TRUTH, 25
Culture is the p. for sweetness and light CULTURE, 2
desolate and sick of an old p. LOVE, 60
Master Mistress of my p. LOVE, 156
one master-p. . . . /swallows up the rest PASSION, 6
p. and party blind our eyes EXPERIENCE, 12
P. . . . can be destroyed by a doctor PASSION, 8
p. in the human soul MUSIC, 26
So I triumphed ere my p. PASSION, 10
Strange fits of p. PASSION, 11
The p. and the life, whose fountains are within APPEARANCES, 13
The ruling p. conquers reason still PASSION, 7
We never remark any p. . . . in others, of which, . . . we may not find a parallel SELF, 10
you say you're his . . . his p. is /Infinite, . . . One of you is lying LYING, 18
passions A man who has not passed through the inferno of his p. PASSION, 3
It is with our p. as it is with fire and water PASSION, 5
Literature and butterflies are the two sweetest p. BUTTERFLIES, 1
not his reason, but his p. RELIGION, 64
that man /That is not p. slave PASSION, 9
The man who is master of his p. PASSION, 2
Three p., simple but overwhelmingly strong, have governed my life PHILOSOPHERS, 10
passover it is the Lord's p. BIBLICAL QUOTATIONS, 139
past Even God cannot change the p. PAST, 1
half of you belongs to the p. OLD AGE, 14

We are the true p. movement PEACE, 21
we looked for p., but no good came BIBLICAL QUOTATIONS, 291
we might more reasonably expect fifteen years of p. WAR AND PEACE, 13
We wanted p. on earth PEACE, 16
When p. has been broken anywhere PEACE, 19
When there was p., he was for p. PUBLIC, 3
you buy a pill and buy p. DRUGS, 13
peacetime where they're living it's p., and we're all in the same country DISEASE, 29
peach dare to eat a p. OLD AGE, 44
'Fan vaulting' . . . belongs to the 'Last-supper-carved-on-a-p.-stone' ARCHITECTURE, 7
peaches poetry in p. POETRY, 23
with p. and women, it's . . . the side next the sun that's tempting TEMPTATION, 13
peak One sees . . . only small things from the p. PERSPECTIVE, 2
Silent, upon a p. in Darien DISCOVERY, 11
peanuts pay p., . . . get monkeys BUSINESS, 12
pear And a golden p. NURSERY RHYMES, 20
pearl base Indian, threw a p. away LOVE, 143
pearls He who would search for P. ERROR, 5
p. before swine BIBLICAL QUOTATIONS, 487
p. that were his eyes DEATH, 148
the twelve gates were twelve p. BIBLICAL QUOTATIONS, 603
peas I always eat p. with honey ANONYMOUS, 41
peasantry a bold p. . . . /When once destroy'd PUBLIC, 12
peasants If the French noblesse had been capable of playing cricket with their p. ARISTOCRACY, 19
it is better that all of these p. should be killed REBELLION, 11
peck Peter Piper picked a p. of pickled pepper NURSERY RHYMES, 38
peculiar a tense and p. family, the Oedipuses CLASSICS, 1
Funny p., or funny ha-ha HUMOR, 25
pederasts p. who call themselves the Labour Party SOCIALISM, 1
pedestal at fourteen every boy should be in love with some ideal woman . . . on a p. SEXES, 20
pediatricians P. eat because children don't SPECIALISTS, 8
pedigree languages are the p. of nations LANGUAGE, 25
pee share a quick p. over a common lamp-post WRITERS, 12
Peel D'ye ken John P. HUNTING, 5
P.'s smile INSULTS, 100
Sir Robert P. POLITICIANS, 10
peer A life p. is like a mule HOUSES OF PARLIAMENT, 19
peerage When I want a p., I shall buy one TITLES, 6
peers Fears, prejudices, misconceptions – those are the p. HOUSES OF PARLIAMENT, 16
pelican A fashionable surgeon like a p. DOCTORS, 33
pellagra Nicotinic acid cures p. REMEDIES, 52
pen how much more cruel the p. WRITING, 7
less brilliant p. than mine CONCEIT, 4
nothing can cure it but the scratching of a p. WRITING, 26
p. is mightier than the sword WRITING, 6
penance The man hath p. done PUNISHMENT, 10
pence Take care of the p. CARE, 3
pendulum politics of the p., but of the ratchet POLITICS, 139
The p. of the mind oscillates between sense and nonsense MIND, 16
penetrablé most things are p. BRIBERY, 3
penis he also has the biggest p. MANKIND, 42
pennies P. do not come from heaven WORK, 31
P. from Heaven OPTIMISM, 20
penny A p. saved PROVERBS, 58
Hot cross buns! / . . . /One a p., two a p. NURSERY RHYMES, 16
I don't owe a p. to a single soul BORROWING, 13
In for a p. COMMITMENT, 1
Not a p. off the pay STRIKES, 3
P. wise PROVERBS, 335
pens Let other p. dwell on guilt and misery OPTIMISM, 14
pense *Honi soit qui mal y p.* ARISTOCRACY, 13
Pentecost when the day of P. was fully come BIBLICAL QUOTATIONS, 2
people a loyal, a gallant, a generous, an ingenious, and good-temper'd p. FRANCE, 17
always been interested in p. MISANTHROPY, 2
Be nice to p. on your way up PRUDENCE, 11
bill of rights is what the p. are entitled to HUMAN RIGHTS, 4
Boys . . . are unwholesome companions for grown p. CHILDREN, 40
good of the p. LAW, 9
government . . . must be built upon the rights of the p. GOVERNMENT, 38
government of the p., by the p., and for the p. DEMOCRACY, 14
Hell is other p. HELL, 6
How do p. go to sleep SLEEP, 24
If p. behaved in the way nations do GOVERNMENT, 44
if the p. . . . can be reached with the truth DEMOCRACY, 17
indictment against an whole p. ACCUSATION, 1
in trust from the p. to the common good of them all POWER, 17
It is with . . . p. as with . . . bottles CHARACTER, 20
Most of the p. . . . will be children FUNERALS, 1
my p. live in such awful conditions POVERTY, 14
Once the p. begin to reason PUBLIC, 18
One Realm, One P., One Leader NAZISM, 1
p. . . . are attracted by God PEOPLE, 5
P. are not fallen angels CRITICISM, 33
p. are the masters PUBLIC, 6
p. may be made to follow a course of action UNDERSTANDING, 3
P. must help one another HELP, 8
p.'s government GOVERNMENT, 43
p. standing in the corners of our rooms TELEVISION, 4
p. under suspicion are better moving JUDGMENT, 12
p. . . . usually imitate each other IMITATION, 3
P. who like this sort of thing CRITICISM, 37
P. who need people are the luckiest PEOPLE, 10
p. whose company is coveted OSTENTATION, 4
p. who stay in the middle of the road NONCOMMITMENT, 1
P. will cross the road . . . to say 'We saw you on the telly' TELEVISION, 6
Religion . . . is the opium of the p. RELIGION, 53
show my head to the p. EXECUTION, 7
sort of p. our parents warned us about VICE, 11
the bludgeoning of the p. DEMOCRACY, 24
The Lord prefers common-looking p. APPEARANCE, 31
the noise . . . and the p. WAR, 6
the p. are forbidden to light lamps INJUSTICE, 12
The p. – could you patent the sun DISCOVERY, 13
The p.'s flag is deepest red SOCIALISM, 6
the p. we should have been seen dead with SNOBBERY, 11
The p. would be just as noisy PUBLIC, 9
there are no unimportant p. IMPORTANCE, 5
The right p. are rude PEOPLE, 9
The Swiss . . . are not a p. so much as a . . . business SWITZERLAND, 2
They didn't act like p. ACTORS, 11
This country . . . belongs to the p. who inhabit it DEMOCRACY, 13
thy p. shall be my p. BIBLICAL QUOTATIONS, 606
two kinds of p. in the world ARISTOCRACY, 2
two p. with one pulse LOVE, 99
we are not a small p. BRITAIN, 8
What kind of p. do they think we are NATIONS, 2
When . . . it becomes necessary for one p. to dissolve . . . political bonds INDEPENDENCE, 3
When p. come together, flowers always flourish NEW YORK, 3
When the P. contend for their Liberty PEOPLE, 3
You can fool too many of the p. DECEPTION, 10
pepper Peter Piper picked a peck of pickled p. NURSERY RHYMES, 38
Pepper's Sergeant P. Lonely Hearts Club Band BOOK TITLES, 14
perception any truth but from a clear p. TRUTH, 34
doors of p. were cleansed PERCEPTION, 1
prime agent of all human p. IMAGINATION, 1
perceptions Man's Desires are limited by his P. DESIRE, 4
perestroika essence of p. SOCIALISM, 10
Russian word 'p.' has easily entered the international lexicon PROGRESS, 13
perfect A cigarette is . . . a p. pleasure SMOKING, 37
be ye therefore p. BIBLICAL QUOTATIONS, 479
p. in a short time BIBLICAL QUOTATIONS, 661
p. love casteth out fear BIBLICAL QUOTATIONS, 379
perfection attain to the divine p. PERFECTION, 5
Finality is death. P. is finality PERFECTION, 10
one does not seek p. PERFECTION, 7
P. has one grave defect PERFECTION, 6
Species do not evolve toward p. SURVIVAL, 6
The pursuit of p. PERFECTION, 1
performance desire should . . . outlive p. SEX, 93
it takes away the p. ALCOHOL, 68
Nothing to be fixed except your p. ACTING, 6
verses . . . as a literary p. POETRY, 64
performing English literature's p. flea WRITERS, 39
perfume As a p. doth remain MEMORY, 23
perfumes All the p. of Arabia GUILT, 17
No p., but very fine linen FASHION, 2
perhaps I am going in search of a great p. LAST WORDS, 70
The grand P. POSSIBILITY, 1
When a lady says no . . . means p. WORDS, 8
peril an imperative principle which statesmen . . . ignore at their p. SELF, 26
For those in p. on the sea SEA, 13
perils all p. and dangers of this night BOOK OF COMMON PRAYER, THE, 7
smile at p. past PAST, 8
period Never neglect the history of a missed menstrual p. EVOLUTION, 22
periods Decades . . . are not . . . really p. at all CLASSIFICATION, 3
perish Cause thy fruit to p. ABORTION, 5
P. the Universe REVENGE, 6
they that take the sword shall p. with the sword BIBLICAL QUOTATIONS, 545
though the world p. JUSTICE, 11
weak shall p. STRENGTH, 7
periwig with my mourning . . . and new p. APPEARANCE, 47
perjury P. . . . is truth that is shamefaced TRUTH, 22
permanence love p. more than . . . beauty BRITISH, 3
permissive The p. society has . . . become a dirty phrase LIBERALISM, 3
pernicious the most p. race ENGLISH, 37
Peron If a woman like Eva P. with no ideals IDEALISM, 11
If I had not been born P. CONTENTMENT, 6
perpendicular p. expression of a horizontal desire DANCING, 11
perpetual gift of p. old age OLD AGE, 100
Literary men are . . . a p. priesthood WRITERS, 8
perpetuation Why should I consent to the p. of the image of this image IMAGE, 3
persecutest Saul, why p. thou me BIBLICAL QUOTATIONS, 6
persecution P. produced its natural effect PURITANISM, 4
perseverance the name of p. in a good cause STUBBORNNESS, 4
persistent The most p. sound . . . through men's history WAR, 88
person A p. may be indebted for a nose or an eye, . . . to a great-aunt FAMILY, 25
My idea of an agreeable p. AGREEMENT, 3
the only p. . . . I should like to know EGOTISM, 11
the only thing that can exist is an uninterested p. CURIOSITY, 4
The world regards such a p. as . . . an unmuzzled dog CLASSIFICATION, 1
to the cheek of a young p. EMBARRASSMENT, 1
personal They do those little p. things HABIT, 5
personalities all great events and p. in . . . history reappear HISTORY, 23
personality Hollywood . . . the p. of a paper cup CINEMA, 5
Simply a radio p. INSULTS, 125
persons God is no respecter of p. BIBLICAL QUOTATIONS, 10
I am made up of several p. CHARACTER, 18
perspective What a delightful thing this p. is ART, 31
perspire he never seemed to p. CLASS, 14
persuade Beauty . . . doth . . . p. the eyes of men BEAUTY, 37

The p. are here, too DOCTORS, 60
The p. are the natural attorneys of the poor DOCTORS, 100
The p. best remedy is *Tincture of Time* TIME, 35
the p. separate the soul from the body HOLISTIC MEDICINE, 8
the p. with their art, know . . . how to make it still shorter DOCTORS, 74
the p. words will be received with just that much more attention DIAGNOSIS, 2
The sick man is the garden of the p. PATIENTS, 2
Three remedies of the p. of Myddfai REMEDIES, 5
two p. cure you of the medicine DOCTORS, 12
physicist The great p. Lavoisier, who knew better than any peasant SCIENCE, 1
physicists The p. have known sin SCIENTISTS, 8
to find out anything from the theoretical p. SCIENTISTS, 5
physics Classical p. . . . superseded by quantum theory SCIENCE, 90
Modern P. is an instrument of Jewry ANTISEMITISM, 1
The content of p. is the concern SCIENCE, 29
physiology an important part of reproductive p. SEX, 10
pianist do not shoot the p. EFFORT, 7
not so much . . . a p., but a vampire MUSICIANS, 6
the only p. . . . who did not grimace MUSICIANS, 9
Piatigorsky Gregor P. EGOTISM, 6
Picardy Roses are flowering in P. COMPLIMENTS, 38
Picasso Nothing divides them like P. ART, 18
There's no such thing as a bad P. INFERIORITY, 4
Piccadilly Crossing P. Circus AFRICA, 3
Good-bye P., Farewell Leicester Square HOMESICKNESS, 8
pick Whenever you fall, p. up something OPPORTUNITY, 8
pickle weaned on a p. APPEARANCE, 32
picnic futile to attempt a p. in Eden FATE, 4
picture Every p. tells a story PROVERBS, 143
If you want a p. of the future OPPRESSION, 4
It's no go the p. palace INDIFFERENCE, 4
One p. is worth ten thousand words PAINTING, 1
pictures book . . . without p. BOOKS, 13
dearth of bad p. GOLDWYNISMS, 24
would never buy my p. PAINTING, 9
pidgin-English I include 'p.' LANGUAGE, 32
pie Amblongus P. NONSENSE, 22
A word of kindness is better than a fat p. KINDNESS, 1
p. in the sky when you die AFTERLIFE, 5
piece A p. of each of us died at that moment ASSASSINATION, 6
p. of cod passes all understanding FOOD, 50
p. of divinity in us DIVINITY, 1
Prologues precede the p. PLAYS, 4
What a p. of work is a man DELIGHT, 10
When a p. gets difficult MUSICIANS, 7
pieces P. of eight MONEY, 43
pie-crust Promises and p. are made to be broken PROMISES, 8
pieman Simple Simon met a p. NURSERY RHYMES, 46
pier Like Brighton p. . . . TRAVEL, 24
Pierian Drink deep, or taste not the P. spring KNOWLEDGE, 33
pies I could eat one of Bellamy's veal p. EATING, 9
pig p. of a Henry VIII BETRAYAL, 13
pigeons tourists . . . take in the Monarchy . . . with . . . the p. LONDON, 14
piggy This little p. went to market NURSERY RHYMES, 58
pigmy That shriek and sweat in p. wars TRIVIALITY, 15
pigs And whether p. have wings NONSENSE, 9
one of Epicurus' herd of p. PRESENT, 7
P. might fly PROVERBS, 336
What men call social virtues, . . . is . . . but the virtue of p. in a litter SOCIETY, 15
pig-sty kissed her once by the p. EXPECTATION, 8
Pilate jesting P. ANSWERS, 1
P. . . . washed his hands BIBLICAL QUOTATIONS, 547
rather have blood on my hands . . . P. COMMITMENT, 4
pile P. it high, sell it cheap BUSINESS, 4
piles p. to give him an Anxious Expression DOCTORS, 13
pilgrim p. of the sky BIRDS, 18
pilgrims strangers and p. on the earth BIBLICAL QUOTATIONS, 240
pill buy a p. and buy peace with it MEDICINE, 55
Protestant women may take the P. CONTRACEPTION, 13
you buy a p. and buy peace DRUGS, 13
pillar a p. of a cloud BIBLICAL QUOTATIONS, 141
a p. of salt BIBLICAL QUOTATIONS, 211
the lie has become . . . a p. of the State LYING, 23
triple p. of the world LOVE, 129
pillars wisdom . . . hath hewn out her seven p. BIBLICAL QUOTATIONS, 571
pillow no-sooner-have-I-touched-the-p. people SLEEP, 26
pills It is an age of p. DRUGS, 14
I will lift up mine eyes unto the p. DRUGS, 14
One of the most successful physicians . . . , has . . . used more bread p. REMEDIES, 36
pilot Dropping the p. DISMISSAL, 10
Pimpernel That damned elusive P. ABSENCE, 9
pin If I sit on a p. /And it punctures my skin ANONYMOUS, 91
See a p. and pick it up PROVERBS, 357
you are like a p., but without . . . head or . . . point BORES, 3
pinafore Captain of the *P.* CONCEIT, 10
pinch time for me to enjoy another p. of snuff EXECUTION, 2
pinching I just keep painting till I feel like p.. Then I know it's right PAINTING, 17
pine-apple p. of politeness MALAPROPISMS, 7
pinko-gray white races are . . . p. RACE, 9
pint one cannot put a quart in a p. cup IMPOSSIBILITY, 2
You spend half a p. and flush two gallons WATER, 6
pious A p. man . . . would be an atheist KINGS AND KINGDOMS, 9
p. bird with the scarlet breast BIRDS, 20
p. frauds of friendship FRIENDSHIP, 23
pipe Blow your p. there CONTEMPT, 2
piped their fountains p. an answer ANTHROPOMORPHISM, 1
Piper Peter P. picked a peck of pickled pepper NURSERY RHYMES, 38
pipers Wi' a hundred p. an' a', an' a' GLORY, 5
piping Helpless, naked, p. loud BIRTH, 5
P. down the valleys wild MUSIC, 11
pips squeezed – until the p. squeak RETRIBUTION, 10
piss I can p. the old boy BOASTS, 5
pissed the last four strikes we've had, it's p. down STRIKES, 7
pissing inside my tent p. out PRUDENCE, 8
making a speech on economics is a lot like p. ECONOMICS, 12
pistol a p. let off at the ear PUNS, 12
Somebody leaves a p. in the drawer SUICIDE, 21
pit And wretched, blind, p. ponies ANIMALS, 15
pitcher a p. of warm spit POLITICS, 53
pitchfork drive out nature with a p. . . . she'll be constantly running back HUMAN NATURE, 11
pith all the p. is in the postscript LETTER-WRITING, 4
pitied one has . . . ceased to be an object of *fear* as soon as one is p. PITY, 3
pitifully barefoot and wearing coarse wool, he stood p. HUMILITY, 5
pitiless slow, sure doom falls p. and dark DARKNESS, 16
pits You are the p. INSULTS, 96
Pitt P. . . . given by the people to the King POLITICIANS, 64
P. is to Addington PRIME MINISTERS, 10
pity A p. beyond all telling LOVE, 193
I thought it was a p. to get up BED, 9
knock him down first, and p. him afterwards PITY, 2
My subject is War, and the p. of War PITY, 4
no soul will p. me DESPAIR, 9
P. a human face MANKIND, 10
p. for the suffering of mankind PHILOSOPHERS, 10
The Poetry is in the p. PITY, 4
'Tis P. She's a whore BOOK TITLES, 9
To marry a man out of p. is folly MARRIAGE, 8
To show p. is felt as a sign of contempt PITY, 3
place A p. for everything ORDER, 7
everything in its p. ORDER, 7
firm p. to stand EARTH, 1
give p. to better men DISMISSAL, 4
Home is the p. where HOME, 5
I go to prepare a p. for you BIBLICAL QUOTATIONS, 346
In P. of Fear WEAPONS, 3
Never the time and the p. PERVERSITY, 2
putting her in her p. INSULTS, 113
running . . . to keep in the same p. NONSENSE, 8
there's no p. like home HOME, 10
the summit of Everest was hardly the p. PHOTOGRAPHY, 4
this is an awful p. PLACES, 33
Upon the p. beneath MERCY, 4
plague A p. o' both your houses CURSES, 4
plagues of all p. with which mankind are curst CHURCH, 3
plain be p. and simple PROSE, 2
be yourself, imperial, p. and true SINCERITY, 1
making things p. to uninstructed people was . . . best means of clearing . . . one's own mind EDUCATION, 43
Manners are . . . the need of the p. MANNERS, 8
plainness perfect p. of speech . . . perfect nobleness BIBLE, 1
plaisir *P. d'amour* LOVE, 65
plan save the p. POLITICS, 107
plane only two emotions in a p.: boredom and terror FLYING, 6
planet I have lived some thirty years on this p. ADVICE, 22
it fell on the wrong p. WEAPONS, 4
The human race will be the cancer of the p. MANKIND, 31
When a new p. swims into his ken DISCOVERY, 11
planets felt like the moon, the stars, and all the p. had fallen RESPONSIBILITY, 20
plans Life . . . happens . . . while you're busy making other p. LIFE, 50
The finest p. have always been spoiled SUPPORT, 2
what a man still p. . . . shows the . . . injustice in his death DEATH, 45
plant Is thy love a p. /Of such weak fibre ABSENCE, 10
The infusion of a China p. DRINKS, 1
Plantagenet the winding ivy of a P. should kill the . . . tree DESTINY, 4
plants bottinney means a knowledge of p. EDUCATION, 25
p. left over from the Edwardian Wilderness CHANGE, 18
tend to make us forget the medicinal value of p. NATURE, 15
plashy p. fen passes the questing vole ANIMALS, 25
plastic surgery everyone thought I'd had it fixed by p. PHOTOGRAPHY, 2
plate clean your p. POLITICS, 121
the silver p. on a coffin INSULTS, 100
platitude A longitude with no p. MEANING, 4
A p. is simply a truth repeated SAYINGS, 1
platitudes Literature is the orchestration of p. LITERATURE, 25
Plato P. is dear to me TRUTH, 8
platonic I know nothing about p. love LOVE, 80
plausible rat-like cunning, a p. manner JOURNALISM, 40
play a good p. needs no epilogue PLAYS, 13
a p. is a dynamic thing NOVELS, 17
behold the Englishman . . . p. tip-and-run ENGLISH, 16
Better than a p. HOUSES OF PARLIAMENT, 8
If you p. with fire DANGER, 2
Judge not the p. JUDGMENT, 10
p., I remember, pleas'd not the million TASTE, 7
p.'s the thing PLAYS, 14
P. up! p. up! and p. the game WAR, 112
Rehearsing a p. is making the word flesh PLAYS, 12
The little victims p. DOOM, 1
unless the p. is stopped, the child cannot . . . go on AUDIENCES, 4
writing a good p. is difficult PLAYS, 10
playboy p. of the western world LOSS, 8
played I have p. the fool BIBLICAL QUOTATIONS, 614
player poor p., /That struts and frets his hour LIFE, 76
players men and women merely p. HUMAN CONDITION, 22
to conceal the fact that the p. cannot act ACTING, 1
play-going A good many inconveniences attend p. PLAYS, 15

The p. and philosophers . . . have discovered the unconscious PSYCHOANALYSIS, 10
point you are like a pin, but without . . . head or . . . p. BORES, 3
poison food to one man is bitter p. to others TASTE, 5
it is always easy to p. and to kill KILLING, 1
Neither will I administer a p. to anybody MEDICINE, 37
Psychology is as unnecessary as directions for using p. PSYCHOLOGY, 10
strongest p. ever known CAESAR, 2
The treatment with p. medicines comes from the West DRUGS, 17
wounds and abscesses no longer p. the atmosphere CLEANNESS, 5
poisons P. and medicine are oftentimes the same substance REMEDIES, 38
The p. are our principal medicines REMEDIES, 29
two p. are more efficacious than one REMEDIES, 7
poker Malice is like a game of p. NASTINESS, 9
pokers Wreathe iron p. into true-love knots POETS, 12
Pole folly of one brainsick P. POLITICS, 42
pole And see all sights from p. to p. SOUL, 3
Beloved from p. to p. SLEEP, 9
One step beyond the p. EXPLORATION, 3
polecat A semi-house-trained p. INSULTS, 48
Poles few virtues . . . the P. do not possess ERROR, 4
police P. State . . . always regards all opposition as a crime OPPOSITION, 6
Reading isn't an occupation we encourage among p. officers POLICE, 7
the exercise of an international p. power UNITED STATES, 54
The South African P. would leave no stone unturned PLACES, 34
policeman A p.'s lot is not a happy one POLICE, 3
park, a p. and a pretty girl COMEDY, 2
so dismal that a p. couldn't make it worse POLICE, 1
the air of someone who is lying . . . to a p. POLICE, 10
The p. isn't there to *create* disorder POLICE, 2
The terrorist and the p. EQUALITY, 8
This definition . . . would not do for a p. NURSES, 6
policemen how young the p. look AGE, 39
P. are numbered POLICE, 5
P., like red squirrels, must be protected POLICE, 8
repressed sadists . . . become p. or butchers PUBLISHING, 5
policy My home p.? I wage war WAR, 46
polished p. up the handle of the big front door OFFICERS, 6
Satire should, like a p. razor keen SATIRE, 2
whole man in himself, p. and well-rounded CHARACTER, 12
polite it costs nothing to be p. DIPLOMACY, 7
p. by telling lies COURTESY, 3
time to be p. ENGLISH, 29
too p. to ask POLITENESS, 2
politeness pine-apple of p. MALAPROPISMS, 7
P. is organised indifference MANNERS, 7
Punctuality is the p. of kings PROMPTNESS, 2
political addiction of p. groups to ideas POLITICS, 51
After all, we are not p. whores POLITICS, 103
All p. lives . . . , end in failure POLITICS, 113
a man who was lucky enough to have discovered a p. theory MARXISM, 2
Every intellectual attitude is latently p. POLITICS, 96
Jesus was . . . a first-rate p. economist CHRISTIANITY, 54
most schemes of p. improvement are very laughable POLITICS, 79
one of these is the history of p. power HISTORY, 27
p. speech and writing are largely the defence of the indefensible POLITICS, 109
That points clearly to a p. career POLITICIANS, 99
the formation of the p. will of the nation POLITICS, 68
When in the course of human events, it becomes necessary for one people to dissolve . . . p. bonds INDEPENDENCE, 3
politician a bit of a murderer, to be a p. POLITICS, 101
a p. is an arse POLITICIANS, 34
A p. is a statesman . . . with an open mouth POLITICIANS, 105
A p. rises on the backs POLITICIANS, 63
A statesman is a p. who POLITICIANS, 89
A statesman is a p. who's been dead POLITICIANS, 116
at home you're just a p. POLITICIANS, 79
Coffee which makes the p. wise DRINKS, 15
every Labour p. feels more at home attacking his own POLITICS, 7
like a scurvy p. POLITICIANS, 98
p. never believes what he says POLITICIANS, 38
the p. poses as the servant POLITICIANS, 39
The proper memory for a p. POLITICIANS, 84
unfair to expect a p. to live . . . up to the statements he makes in public POLITICIANS, 81
politicians All p. have vanity POLITICIANS, 103
all the p. . . . least significant was Bonar Law POLITICIANS, 12
It is a pity . . . that more p. are not bastards POLITICIANS, 124
P. . . . can never forgive being ignored POLITICIANS, 123
P. neither love nor hate POLITICIANS, 46
P. . . . promise to build bridges POLITICIANS, 69
P. tend to live *in character* POLITICS, 88
politics are too serious . . . to be left to the p. POLITICIANS, 40
There is just one rule for p. POLITICS, 52
politics An independent . . . wants to take the p. out of p. POLITICS, 134
Britain is no longer in the p. of the pendulum POLITICS, 139
can't adopt p. . . . and remain honest POLITICS, 71
Don't tell my mother I'm in p. POLITICS, 5
his amusements, like his p., are essentially destructive POLITICIANS, 23
History is past p. HISTORY, 32
I am not made for p. POLITICS, 30
I gave up p. when I discovered POLITICS, 110
In p., . . . ask a woman POLITICIANS, 112
in p. there is no heart, only head HEART, 15
making p. Christian RELIGION, 72
Men who have greatness . . . don't go in for p. PRIME MINISTERS, 9
never get on in p., my dear, with *that* hair POLITICIANS, 8
Never judge a country by its p. POLITICS, 67
P. are now nothing more than POLITICS, 80
p. are too serious . . . to be left to the politicians POLITICIANS, 40
P. is a blood sport POLITICS, 15
P. is not an exact science POLITICS, 21
P. is not a science . . . but an art POLITICS, 22
P. is the art of preventing people from taking part POLITICS, 145
P. is . . . the only profession POLITICS, 135
P., . . . the systematic organisation of hatreds POLITICS, 3
p. was the second lowest profession POLITICS, 115
Practical p. . . . ignoring facts POLITICS, 2
that men enter local p. MARRIAGE, 102
The more you read about p. POLITICS, 118
The P. of Joy HAPPINESS, 10
There are times in p. POLITICS, 50
they can at least pretend that p. is a game HOUSES OF PARLIAMENT, 17
War is the continuation of p. MISQUOTATION, 11
polloi the multitude, the *hoi p.* PUBLIC, 10
polluter intelligence is the great p. ENVIRONMENT, 9
pollution indefatigable and unsavoury engine of p. DOGS, 14
Polly P. put the kettle on NURSERY RHYMES, 39
polygamy P. was made a Sin RELIGION, 26
pomp Hath not old custom made this life more sweet /Than that of painted p. COUNTRYSIDE, 11
In lowly p. ride on to die CHRISTIANITY, 45
Pride, p., and circumstance WAR, 148
solemnized with p. and parade UNITED STATES, 1
Take physic, p. HUMILITY, 11
pompous A p. woman . . . complaining that the head-waiter EGOTISM, 9
p. in the grave MANKIND, 13
Poms All the faces . . . seem to be bloody P. ENGLISH, 12
ponces The wriggling p. of the spoken word MEDIA, 5
pondered Mary . . . p. them in her heart BIBLICAL QUOTATIONS, 421
ponies And wretched, blind, pit p. ANIMALS, 15
pontifical royal power takes all its reputation . . . from the p. power POWER, 11
pony I had a little p., /His name was Dapple Grey NURSERY RHYMES, 21
poodle Mr Balfour's P. HOUSES OF PARLIAMENT, 15
Pooh-Bah P. (Lord High Everything Else) TITLES, 4
pool Liverpool is the p. of life PLACES, 20
poor A p. man is despised the whole world over POVERTY, 21
a p. society cannot be too p. POVERTY AND WEALTH, 8
ask of the p. that they get up and act POVERTY, 16
choosing to store her money in the stomachs of the p. SELFLESSNESS, 1
cynical gestures of the p. POVERTY, 36
decent means p. RESPECTABILITY, 3
Few, save the p., feel for the p. POVERTY, 28
give to the p. BIBLICAL QUOTATIONS, 519
great men have their p. relations FAMILY, 17
grind the faces of the p. BIBLICAL QUOTATIONS, 249
Hard to train to accept being p. POVERTY, 20
health! the blessing of the rich! the riches of the p. HEALTH, 15
I, being p., have only my dreams POVERTY, 42
I can dare to be p. POVERTY, 13
If a free society cannot help the . . . p. SOCIETY, 8
If a patient is p. he is committed . . . as 'psychotic' PSYCHIATRY, 19
I have nothing; the rest I leave to the p. LAST WORDS, 68
inconvenient to be p. POVERTY, 7
it is p. grub, p. pay, and easy work ENGLAND, 30
It's the p. wot gets the blame ANONYMOUS, 71
Laws grind the p. LAW, 18
many a p. man . . . has been relieved and helped by him ROYALTY, 74
only the p. . . . are forbidden to beg POVERTY, 11
only the p. who pay cash MONEY, 20
p. have no right to the property of the rich POVERTY AND WEALTH, 6
P. Little Rich Girl WEALTH, 16
p. relation FAMILY, 29
Resolve not to be p. POVERTY, 23
She was p. but she was honest ANONYMOUS, 71
short and simple annals of the p. POVERTY, 15
that art most rich, being p. APPEARANCES, 26
that plenty should attain the p. SELF-INTEREST, 2
the p. are our brothers and sisters POVERTY, 37
the p. devils in the hospital I am bound to take care of CHARITY, 2
the p. . . . need love, . . . need care, . . . have to be wanted POVERTY, 37
the p. person . . . thinks money would help MONEY, 25
The p. . . . their function . . . is to exercise our generosity POVERTY, 32
Though I be p., I'm honest HONESTY, 5
To be p. and independent POVERTY, 6
very p. are unthinkable POVERTY, 10
What fun it would be to be p. EXCESS, 3
'You speak of –' . . . /'the rich and the p..' POVERTY AND WEALTH, 4
poorer for richer for p. BOOK OF COMMON PRAYER, THE, 15
poorest p. . . . hath a life to live as the greatest HUMAN RIGHTS, 5
p. man may in his cottage bid defiance to . . . the Crown DEFIANCE, 4
pop In England, p. art and fine art ART, 16
Pope Anybody can be P. ACHIEVEMENT, 7
I wake up . . . and remember I am the P. RESPONSIBILITY, 8
Popery No P., No Slavery POLITICS, 6
Popish their deliverer from P. tyranny ROYALTY, 58
poplars The p. are felled TREES, 4
poppies the p. blow MEMORIALS, 11
populace society distributes itself into Barbarians, Philistines, and P. UNITED STATES, 3
the p. cannot exact their demands HOUSES OF PARLIAMENT, 22
this vast residuum we may . . . give the name of P. PUBLIC, 2
popular Nothing can render them p. CLERGY, 12
The worse I do, the more p. I get POPULARITY, 5
We're more p. than Jesus Christ POPULARITY, 6
popularity P.? . . . glory's small change POPULARITY, 4

prison an extraordinarily pleasant p. LEXICOGRAPHY, 1
Anyone who has been to . . . public school will . . . feel . . . at home in p. EDUCATION, 89
a sick, its p. BODY, 1
compare /This p. where I live unto the world IMPRISONMENT, 10
In a wall'd p. IMPRISONMENT, 9
P. . . . start sending a better class of people CLASS, 34
Stone walls do not a p. make IMPRISONMENT, 7
The only thing I really mind about going to p. PUNISHMENT, 16
the p. of our mind MIND, 31
the true place for a just man is also a p. JUSTICE, 31
The world . . . is but a large p. EXECUTION, 30
prisoner I object to your being taken p. ROYALTY, 73
P., God has given you good abilities THEFT, 3
p. sees the door of his dungeon open he dashes IMPETUOSITY, 4
prisoners If this is the way Queen Victoria treats her p. COMPLAINTS, 11
p. of addiction and . . . p. of envy MATERIALISM, 14
prisons not enough p. . . . in Palestine to hold all the Jews JEWS, 14
P. are built with stones of Law HYPOCRISY, 5
privacy a right to share your p. in a public place PRIVACY, 5
That should assure us of . . . forty-five minutes of undisturbed p. INATTENTION, 2
private heart's ease /Must kings neglect, that p. men enjoy EQUALITY, 24
He was meddling too much in my p. life PSYCHIATRY, 34
I should never be allowed out in p. APOLOGIES, 2
most beautiful in Britain . . . in p. hands BRITAIN, 13
P. faces in public places PRIVACY, 1
P. Means is dead PUNS, 23
P. practice and marriage SCIENCE, 11
Scientific discovery is a p. event SCIENCE, 62
sex has been a very p., secretive activity SEX, 100
The grave's a fine and p. place DEATH, 103
The human body is p. property RESEARCH, 20
Travel is the most p. of pleasures TRAVEL, 34
Whatsoever . . . the p. calamity, I hope it will not interfere with the public business of the country FIRE, 4
when religion is allowed to invade . . . p. life RELIGION, 54
privilege a defender of p. PESSIMISM, 2
an Englishman's heaven-born p. of doing as he likes PUBLIC, 2
The accursed power which stands on P. POLITICS, 13
privileges men value . . . not rights but p. SUPERIORITY, 9
privily hanged p. by night INJUSTICE, 3
prize in a race run all, but one receiveth the p. BIBLICAL QUOTATIONS, 39
Men p. the thing ungain'd DESIRE, 14
Not all that tempts your wand'ring eyes . . . is lawful p. TEMPTATION, 11
prize-fighters p. shaking hands WOMEN, 78
prizes just miss the p. at the flower show MEDIOCRITY, 2
The world continues to offer glittering p. RUTHLESSNESS, 8
P.R.O partly a liaison man and partly P. BUSINESS, 3
problem Houston, we have a p. SPACE, 6
ineffectual liberal's p. LIBERALISM, 2
Not every p. someone has with his girlfriend is . . . due to . . . capitalist . . . production CAPITALISM, 12
problems Among the many p. . . . the choice of the moment . . . to begin his novel WRITERS, 47
There are two p. in my life POLITICIANS, 44
procession A torchlight p. ALCOHOL, 60
proctologists pile of p. LANGUAGE, 3
prodigal P. of Ease WORLD-WEARINESS, 1
producing Man . . . consumes without p. CAPITALISM, 14
production Capitalist p. begets . . . its own negation CAPITALISM, 13
productivity reduce the rise in prices, increase p. and reduce unemployment POLITICS, 64
profaned from the province they have desolated and p. VIOLENCE, 7
professed Medicine is a science which hath been . . . more p. than laboured MEDICINE, 8
profession Politics is . . . the only p. POLITICS, 135
The price . . . for pursuing any p. DISILLUSION, 1
professional A p. is someone whose wife works to enable him to paint ARTISTS, 10
professor A p. is a gentleman who has a different opinion ACADEMICS, 3
A p. is one who talks in someone else's sleep ACADEMICS, 1
professors American p. like their literature clear and cold and pure and very dead LITERATURE, 14
As to religion, . . . duty of government to protect all . . . p. thereof GOVERNMENT, 29
Culture is an instrument wielded by p. CULTURE, 3
If there weren't so many p. ACADEMICS, 4
now-a-days p. of philosophy but not philosophers PHILOSOPHERS, 14
profit Drop . . . what tomorrow may bring . . . count as p. every day that Fate allows you PRESENT, 9
No p. grows where is no pleasure EDUCATION, 74
Philosophers never balance between p. and honesty PHILOSOPHERS, 4
profound turbid look the most p. WRITING, 23
progeny A p. of learning MALAPROPISMS, 3
progress All p. is based EXTRAVAGANCE, 2
Man's 'p.' is but a gradual discovery PROGRESS, 20
Our p. . . . /Is trouble and care CARE, 7
P. . . . depends on retentiveness HISTORY, 29
P. is /The law of life PROGRESS, 5
'p.' is simply a comparative PROGRESS, 8
the things which government does . . . social p. GOVERNMENT, 42
thievish p. TIME, 42
What p. . . . In the Middle Ages PSYCHOLOGY, 7
What we call p. is PROGRESS, 10
progression the labour having been, . . . , rather in a circle than in p. MEDICINE, 8
Without Contraries is no p. CONFLICT, 4
prohibition Communism is like p. COMMUNISM, 13
proletarian substitution of the p. for the bourgeois state RUSSIAN REVOLUTION, 6
proletariat In a country economically backward, the p. can take power earlier CAPITALISM, 19
The dictatorship of the p. MARXISM, 13
the p. will . . . wage a class struggle for Socialism CLASS, 22
prologues P. precede the piece PLAYS, 4
prolonged the War is being deliberately p. WAR, 141
promise A p. made is a debt unpaid PROMISES, 6
rarely . . . one can see in a little boy the p. of a man CHILDREN, 25
promised Only do always in health what you have often p. to do when you are sick ADVICE, 18
promises Indian wars have had their origin in broken p. UNITED STATES, 27
P. and pie-crust are made to be broken PROMISES, 8
P. are like pie-crust PROVERBS, 342
young man of p. INSULTS, 8
promisin' Once you were so p. SHYNESS, 3
promotion Thou art not for the fashion of these times, /Where none will sweat but for p. SELFLESSNESS, 6
promptly He gives twice who gives p. PROMPTNESS, 4
pronounce foreigners . . . spell better than they p. PRONUNCIATION, 5
p. foreign names as he chooses PRONUNCIATION, 2
spell it Vinci and p. it Vinchy PRONUNCIATION, 5
pronounced not only suspected but p. for a witch SUPERNATURAL, 8
pronouncements Science should leave off making p. SCIENCE, 54
pronunciation To correct an Englishman's p. PRONUNCIATION, 3
proof feeling p. against it WINTER, 1
The great p. of madness MADNESS, 26
propaganda P. . . . consists in nearly deceiving your friends PROPAGANDA, 1
p. . . . successful when it stirs up hatred PROPAGANDA, 7
propagandist The p.'s purpose PROPAGANDA, 3
propagated If human beings could be p. . . . aristocracy would be . . . sound ARISTOCRACY, 12
wished that mankind were p. like trees SEX, 53
propagation we were merely intended for the world's p. WOMAN'S ROLE, 9
Women exist . . . solely for the p. of the species WOMAN'S ROLE, 8
propensities the silk stockings and white bosoms . . . excite my amorous p. LUST, 5
proper He never does a p. thing without . . . an improper reason MORALITY, 17
The p. study of Mankind is Man SELF-KNOWLEDGE, 7
property Government has no other end but the preservation of p. GOVERNMENT, 21
poor have no right to the p. of the rich POVERTY AND WEALTH, 6
P. has its duties CAPITALISM, 5
P. is organised robbery CAPITALISM, 17
P. is theft CAPITALISM, 16
The future is the only kind of p. SLAVERY, 2
the right of governing was not p. but a trust GOVERNMENT, 13
Thieves respect p. CRIME, 3
prophecies bring about the verification of his own p. PROPHECY, 19
prophet A historian is a p. in reverse HISTORIANS, 7
a p. is not without honour BIBLICAL QUOTATIONS, 507
single look at the P.'s face RELIGION, 2
there arose not a p. . . . like unto Moses BIBLICAL QUOTATIONS, 73
the sole qualification to be a p. PROPHECY, 4
The sons of the p. were brave men and bold ANONYMOUS, 99
proportion strangeness in the p. BEAUTY, 6
Proportional Representation P. . . . fundamentally counter-democratic POLITICS, 83
proposes Man p. GOD, 34
proposition undesirable to believe a p. SCEPTICISM, 4
propriety The p. of . . . having improper thoughts about . . . neighbours MORALITY, 4
prose anything except bad p. PROSE, 3
difference between . . . p. and metrical composition POETRY AND PROSE, 7
good p. should resemble the conversation PROSE, 5
I can only write p. today POETRY AND PROSE, 8
I have been talking p. for over forty years PROSE, 6
no one hears his own remarks as p. PROSE, 1
Poetry is opposed to science, . . . p. to metre POETRY AND PROSE, 1
Poetry is to p. POETRY AND PROSE, 5
poetry sinks and swoons under . . . p. POETRY AND PROSE, 3
P. . . . can bear a great deal of poetry POETRY AND PROSE, 3
p. = words in their best order POETRY AND PROSE, 2
the cradle of English p. PROSE, 4
the p. for God LANGUAGE, 21
to write good p. is an affair of good manners POETRY AND PROSE, 4
prosper Treason doth never p. TREASON, 6
prosperitee A man to have ben in p. MISFORTUNE, 8
him that stood in greet p. MISFORTUNE, 7
prosperity P. doth best discover vice MISFORTUNE, 4
prostate moral equivalent of a p. operation TELEVISION, 13
prostitutes the small nations like p. DIPLOMACY, 16
prostitution P. . . . keeps her out of trouble SEX, 42
P. . . . provides fresh air and wholesome exercise SEX, 42
protect countries of western Europe . . . no longer . . . p. themselves EUROPE, 1
p. the writer BUREAUCRACY, 1
protection Every man who comes to England is entitled to the p. of the English law EQUALITY, 19
protest doth p. too much EXCESS, 9
Protestant A P. with a horse NATIONALITY, 3
Gunpowder, Printing, and the P. Religion CIVILIZATION, 3
I am the P. whore RELIGION, 41
P. women may take the Pill CONTRACEPTION, 13
Too much counterpoint; what is worse, P. counterpoint CRITICISM, 4
Protestantism The chief contribution of P. to human thought PROTESTANTISM, 6
Protestants God knows how you P. . . . have any sense of direction CATHOLICISM, 14
P. protesting against Protestantism CATHOLICISM, 8
Proteus P. rising from the sea DISCONTENT, 10

protozoon Organic life . . . has developed . . . from the p. to the philosopher PROGRESS, 19
proud Death be not p. DEATH, 57
He who does not need to lie is p. LYING, 17
'I'm Black and I'm P..' RACE, 7
no guarantee . . . you will not be p. of the feat HUMILITY, 4
p. me no prouds GRATITUDE, 8
scattered the p. BIBLICAL QUOTATIONS, 414
too p. to fight FIGHT, 18
Yes; I am p. PRIDE, 7
proudest the moment of greatest humiliation is . . . when the spirit is p. FIGHT, 16
prove p. anything by figures STATISTICS, 2
proved p. upon our pulses PHILOSOPHY, 9
What is now p. was . . . imagined PROOF, 3
Which was to be p. MATHEMATICS, 8
proverb A p. is much matter SAYINGS, 4
no p. to you till your life has illustrated it EXPERIENCE, 19
p. is one man's wit and all men's wisdom SAYINGS, 6
provided Add: 'p. he is really dead' ADMIRATION, 8
providence a kind of P. will . . . end . . . the acts of God DISASTER, 2
fathom the inscrutable workings of P. REPARTEE, 95
that P. dictates with the assurance of a sleepwalker DESTINY, 14
This is the temple of P. GAMBLING, 1
providential a case /of P. interference LUCK, 13
province all knowledge to be my p. KNOWLEDGE, 4
from the p. they have desolated and profaned VIOLENCE, 7
provinces The reluctant obedience of distant p. DIPLOMACY, 19
provincial worse than p. – he was parochial WRITERS, 24
provincialism rather be taken in adultery than . . . p. FASHION, 7
provocations To great evils we submit; we resent little p. TRIVIALITY, 10
provoke P. /The years OLD AGE, 104
p. not your children BIBLICAL QUOTATIONS, 25
provoked an opportunity of being p. PROVOCATION, 1
provokes No one p. me with impunity ANONYMOUS, 62
prude twenty is no age to be a p. PRUDERY, 3
prudence freedom of speech, freedom of conscience, and the p. never to practice . . . them FREEDOM, 58
Prussia military domination of P. is . . . destroyed WAR, 12
psyche the human p. lives in indissoluble union with the body PSYCHOLOGY, 8
Your mournful P. SOUL, 13
psychedelics discovery of p. one of the three major scientific break-throughs SCIENCE, 47
psychiatric a person who so obviously needs p. attention PSYCHIATRY, 11
psychiatrist And a p. is the man who collects the rent PSYCHIATRY, 32
Anybody who goes to see a p. PSYCHIATRY, 17
A p. is a man who goes to the Folies-Bergère PSYCHIATRY, 28
A p. is someone who knows nothing SPECIALISTS, 1
I know that each conversation with a p. PSYCHIATRY, 4
No man is a hero to his wife's p. PSYCHIATRY, 9
One should only see a p. out of boredom PSYCHIATRY, 27
P.: A man who asks you a lot of expensive questions PSYCHIATRY, 8
the century of the p.'s couch PSYCHIATRY, 24
The p. is the obstetrician of the mind PSYCHIATRY, 2
you need to retain a first-rate p. in today's world PSYCHOANALYSIS, 3
psychiatrists P. classify a person as neurotic PSYCHIATRY, 29
The relation between p. and other kinds of lunatics PSYCHIATRY, 20
psychiatry P.'s chief contribution to philosophy PSYCHIATRY, 10
The new definition of p. PSYCHIATRY, 1
psychic p. development of the individual PSYCHIATRY, 15
the p. of human relationship between the sexes SEX, 51
psychoanalysis Considered in its entirety, p. won't do PSYCHOANALYSIS, 18
Freud is the father of p. PSYCHIATRY, 18
plastic surgery . . . combines . . . p., massage, and a trip to the beauty salon OPERATIONS, 14
P. cannot be considered a method of education PSYCHOANALYSIS, 15
P. is a permanent fad PSYCHOANALYSIS, 8
P. is confession PSYCHOANALYSIS, 6
P. is spending 40 dollars an hour PSYCHOANALYSIS, 7
P. is the disease it purports to cure PSYCHOANALYSIS, 17
psychoanalyst A p. is one who pretends he doesn't know everything PSYCHOANALYSIS, 2
The man who once cursed his fate, now, curses himself – and pays his p. PSYCHOANALYSIS, 13
psychoanalysts I doubt whether p. would now maintain PSYCHOANALYSIS, 9
P. are not occupied with the minds of their patients PSYCHOANALYSIS, 4
Who looks after the p. wife PSYCHOANALYSIS, 1
psychological historian fits a man for p. analysis PSYCHOLOGY, 14
There is no such thing as p. CHARACTER, 24
psychologist An animal p. is a man who pulls habits out of rats PSYCHOLOGY, 1
psychology Behavioural p. is . . . pulling habits out of rats PSYCHOLOGY, 2
Children . . . have no use for p.. They detest sociology BOOKS, 42
Idleness is the parent of all p. PSYCHOLOGY, 12
Popular p. is a mass of cant PSYCHOLOGY, 5
P. is as unnecessary as directions for using poison PSYCHOLOGY, 10
P. . . . long past, . . . short history PSYCHOLOGY, 6
p. should have destroyed . . . human nature PSYCHOLOGY, 3
P. which explains everything PSYCHOLOGY, 11
the dull craft of experimental p. PSYCHOLOGY, 15
The object of p. is to give us a totally different idea PSYCHOLOGY, 19
the popularity and persuasiveness of p. PSYCHOLOGY, 16
There is no p. PSYCHOLOGY, 17
The separation of p. from the premises of biology PSYCHOLOGY, 8
psychopathologist the p. the unspeakable PSYCHIATRY, 23
psychotherapist time for the clergyman and the p. to join forces PSYCHOLOGY, 9
psychotic A p. is the man who lives in it PSYCHIATRY, 32
If a patient is poor he is committed . . . as 'p.' PSYCHIATRY, 19
Psychiatrists classify a person as . . . p. PSYCHIATRY, 29
p. means he's even worse than my brother-in-law NEUROSIS, 8
The p. person knows that two and two make five NEUROSIS, 1
puberty We are all American at p. NATIONALITY, 12
public a more mean, stupid . . . ungrateful animal than the p. PUBLIC, 13
Anyone who has been to . . . p. school will . . . feel . . . at home in prison EDUCATION, 89
a right to share your privacy in a p. place PRIVACY, 5
enjoy a p. school EDUCATION, 24
false to his friends . . . true to the p. FALSENESS, 1
flinging a pot of paint in the p.'s face CRITICISM, 56
give the p. what they want to see and they'll come out for it FUNERALS, 10
If the British p. falls for this . . . it will be . . . bonkers POLITICS, 58
I hope it will not interfere with the p. business of the country FIRE, 4
Keats's vulgarity with a P. school accent CRITICISM, 35
Never lose your temper with . . . the p. SELF-CONTROL, 7
not describe holding p. office GOVERNMENT, 1
Not even a p. figure INSULTS, 40
Private faces in p. places PRIVACY, 1
p. school . . . an appalling and impregnable conceit MODESTY, 7
p. schools are the nurseries of all vice EDUCATION, 27
p. school, where . . . learning was painfully beaten into him EDUCATION, 69
strike against p. safety STRIKES, 4
The p. be damned. I am working for my stockholders CAPITALISM, 20
The p. buys its opinions as it buys its meat PUBLIC, 7
The p. doesn't give a damn AUDIENCES, 3
The P. is an old woman PUBLIC, 8
the p.-school system all over EDUCATION, 88
three things . . . the p. will always clamour for NOVELTY, 3
transform this society without a major extension of p. ownership SOCIALISM, 14
twenty years of marriage make her . . . like a p. building MARRIAGE, 150
publicity Any p. ADVERTISING, 1
publish I'll p., right or wrong PUBLISHING, 2
P. and be damned PUBLISHING, 10
p. and be sued PUBLISHING, 7
published Being p. by the O.U.P. is rather like being married to a duchess PUBLISHING, 11
not so much p. as carried screaming NEWSPAPERS, 16
you may destroy whatever you haven't p. PUBLISHING, 6
publisher Barabbas was a p. PUBLISHING, 3
publishers those with irrational fear of life become p. PUBLISHING, 5
Puccini Wagner is the P. of music COMPOSERS, 7
Pucelle a disciple . . . of the fiend, called the P. ACCUSATION, 3
puffeth knowledge p. up, but charity edifieth BIBLICAL QUOTATIONS, 37
pulled about time we p. our fingers out SELF-RELIANCE, 11
pulse A p. in the eternal mind ENGLAND, 11
The fingers should be kept on the p. DIAGNOSIS, 2
There are worse occupations in the world than feeling a woman's p. DOCTORS, 92
There should be no doubt . . . as to . . . the meaning of complexion and p. DIAGNOSIS, 19
two people with one p. LOVE, 99
pulseless p. lot that make up England CURSES, 2
pulses proved upon our p. PHILOSOPHY, 9
pumpkin coach has turned into a p. DISILLUSION, 3
pun A man who could make so vile a p. PUNS, 4
punch I'd p. him in the snoot POLITICIANS, 114
P. – the official journal JOURNALISM, 1
punctuality P. is the politeness PROMPTNESS, 2
P. is the virtue of the bored PROMPTNESS, 5
punished Am I not p. enough in not being born an Englishman NATIONALITY, 11
Men are rewarded and p. not for what they do MOTIVE, 6
Those who offend us are generally p. REVENGE, 21
punishing p. anyone who comes between them MARRIAGE, 129
punishment Corporal p. is . . . humiliating for him who gives it PAIN, 5
let the p. fit the crime PUNISHMENT, 12
Virtue is its own p. RIGHTEOUSNESS, 2
punishments In nature there are neither rewards nor p. NATURE, 24
puny Every p. whipster gets my sword VIOLENCE, 13
pupils Time is a great teacher, but . . . kills all its p. TIME, 11
puppy Frogs and snails /And p.-dogs' tails NURSERY RHYMES, 65
purchasers a pattern to encourage p. BUSINESS, 25
pure All those who are not racially p. RACISM, 2
a p. river of water of life BIBLICAL QUOTATIONS, 604
Because my heart is p. HEART, 20
p. as the driven slush PURITY, 2
purest The zipless fuck is the p. thing SEX, 49
purgations he killed himself with p. REMEDIES, 61
purgatory the p. of men ENGLAND, 21
purge I'll p., and leave sack HEALTHY LIVING, 37
p. the land of all /Corruption ROYALTY, 25
puritan A p.'s a person who pours righteous indignation INDIGNATION, 1
The P. hated bear-baiting PURITANISM, 3
To the P. all things are impure PURITANISM, 2
puritanism P. – The haunting fear that someone . . . may be happy PURITANISM, 5
purity I have laboured to refine our language to grammatical p. LANGUAGE, 24
purple-stained And p. mouth ALCOHOL, 47
purpose I want . . . art /To speak and p. not DECEPTION, 6
p. of God and the doom assigned DESTINY, 28
sense of p. . . . from their archbishop POLITICIANS, 78

the creature hath a p. and its eyes are bright with it PURPOSE, 6
You seem to have no real p. in life AMBITION, 6
purse consumption of the p. MONEY, 38
Put money in thy p. MONEY, 39
restore a man to his health, his p. lies open to thee HEALTH, 4
Sickness soaks the p. ILLNESS, 3
pushing P. forty AGE, 22
pussy Ding dong, bell, /P.'s in the well NURSERY RHYMES, 9
P. cat, p. cat, where have you been NURSERY RHYMES, 40
put I p. away childish things BIBLICAL QUOTATIONS, 44
p. down the mighty BIBLICAL QUOTATIONS, 414
p. up with bad things TOLERANCE, 13
To p. an antic disposition on HYPOCRISY, 16
pygmies wars of the p. will begin WORLD WAR II, 23
pyjamas I in p. for the heat WEATHER, 17
pylons P., those pillars /Bare TECHNOLOGY, 13
pyramid bottom of the economic p. POVERTY, 31
pyramids Books are made . . . like p. BOOKS, 19
summit of these p., forty centuries look down HISTORY, 25
Pyrenees The fleas that tease in the high P. NONSENSE, 3

Q

quack By q. I mean imposter DOCTORS, 103
uses his words as a q. uses his remedies VERBOSITY, 5
quackery Q. gives birth to nothing MEDICINE, 20
quacks But modern q. have lost the art DOCTORS, 28
Q. are the greatest liars in the world DOCTORS, 42
Q. in medicine, . . . know this, and act upon that knowledge GULLIBILITY, 3
The practice of physic is jostled by q. on the one side MEDICINE, 53
quad *I* am always about in the Q. ANONYMOUS, 15
no one about in the Q. EXISTENCE, 4
quadrangle the q. of health HEALTHY LIVING, 33
quadrupeds Dogs, like horses, are q. ANIMALS, 18
quaffing Long q. maketh a short lyfe ALCOHOL, 53
Quakers I was beaten up by Q. SHYNESS, 1
qualities Almost every man . . . attempts to display q. which he does not possess DECEPTION, 3
q. . . . necessary for success upon the stage ACTING, 14
quality great society . . . men are more concerned with the q. of their goods SOCIETY, 7
quantity *abstract reasoning concerning q. or number* ILLUSIONS, 3
a prodigious q. of mind INDECISION, 4
quarks Three q. for Muster Mark NONSENSE, 15
quarrel a q. in a far-away country WORLD WAR II, 5
a q. in the streets is . . . to be hated ARGUMENTS, 10
It takes . . . one to make a q. ARGUMENTS, 8
Out of the q. . . . we make rhetoric POETRY, 67
q. at the same time MARRIAGE, 109
q. . . . energies displayed in it are fine ARGUMENTS, 10
The justice of my q. JUSTICE, 21
quarrelled I did not know that we had ever q. ARGUMENTS, 16
I have q. with my wife MARRIAGE, 104
quarrels q. which vivify its barrenness LOVE, 72
Q. would not last ARGUMENTS, 12
quart one cannot put a q. in a pint cup IMPOSSIBILITY, 2
You can't get a q. PROVERBS, 472
quarter wage war until the last q. of an hour WAR, 46
Quebec I would rather have written those lines than take Q. POETRY, 65
Queen 'Fella belong Mrs Q.' LANGUAGE, 32
give my duty to the Q. VICTORY, 12
he . . . happened to marry the Q. ROYALTY, 99
how very different from the home life of our own dear Q.! ANONYMOUS, 40
I am your anointed Q. SELF-RELIANCE, 7
isn't a bad bit of goods, the Q. COMPLIMENTS, 8
I've been to London to look at the q. NURSERY RHYMES, 40
I would not be a q. /For all the world ROYALTY, 95
Move Q. Anne? Most certainly not MEMORIALS, 17
sorrier for my good knights' loss than for . . . my fair q. LOSS, 3
the British warrior q. BRITAIN, 6
the Q. of England /Lay in may arms DESIRE, 1
The Q. of Hearts FOOD, 20
The Q. of Hearts /She made some tarts NURSERY RHYMES, 52
the q. of Sheba BIBLICAL QUOTATIONS, 399
The q. was in the parlour, /Eating bread and honey NURSERY RHYMES, 47
queenly She keeps on being Q. AFFECTATION, 2
queens for q. I might have enough LOSS, 3
queer All the world is q. SUBJECTIVITY, 5
girls are so q. WOMEN, 10
the q. old Dean SPOONERISMS, 4
There's nowt so q. DIFFERENCE, 6
thou art a little q. SUBJECTIVITY, 5
queerer the universe is . . . q. than we *can* suppose UNIVERSE, 10
questing plashy fen passes the q. vole ANIMALS, 25
question a good q. for you to ask REPARTEE, 38
A timid q. will . . . receive a confident answer ANSWERS, 6
Nature has never put the fatal q. as to the meaning of their lives ANSWERS, 9
No q. is ever settled /Until ARGUMENTS, 19
not a wise q. for me to answer REPARTEE, 38
q. . . . which I have not been able to answer WANT, 1
That is the Irish Q. IRELAND, 7
that is the q. FORTUNE, 6
That's the sixty-four thousand dollar q. TELEVISION, 1
the q. that we do not know KNOWLEDGE, 30
questioning Q. is not the mode of conversation CONVERSATION, 5
questionings Those obstinate q. DOUBT, 9
questions all q. are open OBJECTIVITY, 3
I do not answer q. like this without being paid MASCULINITY, 1
make two q. grow where only one RESEARCH, 26
queue An Englishman . . . forms an orderly q. of one ENGLISH, 26
quicker liquor /Is q. SEDUCTION, 1
quiet Anythin' for a q. life PEACE, 9
a revolution so q. and yet so total POLITICS, 65
Doctor Diet, /Doctor Q. and Doctor Merryman DOCTORS, 94
Here, where the world is q. PEACE, 20
quietness unravish'd bride of q. SILENCE, 9
quince dined on mince, and slices of q. FOOD, 45
quintessence this q. of dust DELIGHT, 10
quit I don't believe I ought to q. DETERMINATION, 18
quo q. vadis BIBLICAL QUOTATIONS, 354
quod *Q. erat demonstrandum* MATHEMATICS, 8
quotable It's better to be q. than . . . honest QUOTATIONS, 18
quotation Classical q. is the *parole* of literary men QUOTATIONS, 5
Every q. contributes something QUOTATIONS, 6
no more able to resist a q. than . . . a drink CRITICISM, 47
q. is a national vice QUOTATIONS, 19
the great spring of happy q. QUOTATIONS, 8
To say that anything was a q. QUOTATIONS, 16
quotations A book that furnishes no q. is, . . . a plaything QUOTATIONS, 12
a list of q. QUOTATIONS, 11
good thing . . . to read books of q. QUOTATIONS, 1
It needs no dictionary of q. EYES, 3
q. very slightly wrong QUOTATIONS, 15
quote good q., I'd be wearing it REPARTEE, 37
quotes A widely-read man never q. accurately MISQUOTATION, 20
q. . . . give us a nodding acquaintance with the originator QUOTATIONS, 20

R

rabbit r.-like in our unplanned breeding of ourselves EVOLUTION, 24
The r. has a charming face ANONYMOUS, 85
rabbits a tale of four little r. RABBITS, 2
except to shoot r. and hit his father on the jaw NASTINESS, 5
race A loftier r. KNOWLEDGE, 36
Christians . . . humanity without r. CHRISTIANITY, 53
in a r. run all, but one receiveth the prize BIBLICAL QUOTATIONS, 39
I wish I loved the Human R. MANKIND, 48
my opinion of the human r. MANKIND, 37
Slow and steady wins the r. HASTE, 7
races human species . . . composed of two distinct r. BORROWING, 5
the r. of Europe are melting UNITED STATES, 72
Rachmaninov R.'s immortalizing totality was his scowl COMPOSERS, 8
racially those who are not r. pure RACISM, 2
racing happy state of getting the victor's palm without the dust of r. VICTORY, 9
rack Leave not a r. behind MORTALITY, 17
r. of this tough world WORLD-WEARINESS, 9
radical A r. is a man IDEALISM, 10
A r. is a man with both feet . . . in the air POLITICS, 120
I never dared be r. when young YOUTH, 11
The r. invents the views. . . . the conservative adopts them CONSERVATISM, 8
radicals Few r. have good digestions POLITICS, 28
radio I had the r. on NAKEDNESS, 10
Simply a r. personality INSULTS, 125
rage all Heaven in a r. BIRDS, 3
R., r., against the dying of the light DEATH, 167
rages the weight of r. SPOONERISMS, 1
rags no scandal like r. POVERTY, 9
only men in r. . . . /Mistake themselves for carpet bags ETIQUETTE, 6
railing R. at life, and yet afraid of death OLD AGE, 32
railway when they think they are alone in r. carriages HABIT, 5
raiment they parted his r., and cast lots BIBLICAL QUOTATIONS, 447
rain A Hard R.'s A-Gonna Fall PESSIMISM, 5
a hat that lets the r. in ROYALTY, 61
drop of r. maketh a hole in the stone PERSISTENCE, 7
droppeth as the gentle r. MERCY, 4
falls not hail, or r., or any snow AFTERLIFE, 11
hath the r. a father BIBLICAL QUOTATIONS, 311
He comes in the terrible R. CHRISTIANITY, 55
R. before seven PROVERBS, 346
R., r., go away PROVERBS, 347
singing in the r. WEATHER, 13
Still falls the R. WEATHER, 28
rainbow A r. in the morning PROVERBS, 62
Somewhere over the r. DESIRE, 8
the R. gave thee birth BIRDS, 6
raineth it r. on the just JUSTICE, 5
rains It never r. but it pours MISFORTUNE, 3
rainy Keep something for a r. day PROVERBS, 240
when it is not r. WEATHER, 9
raise My God shall r. me up EXECUTION, 31
Now he will r. me to be a martyr MARTYRDOM, 1
rake every woman is at heart a r. WOMEN, 95
lene . . . as is a r. HORSES, 4
rallying-point The party is the r. for the . . . working class COMMUNISM, 17
Ralph R. wept for the end of innocence INNOCENCE, 5
ram a r. caught in a thicket BIBLICAL QUOTATIONS, 213
Ramadan month of R. shall ye fast RELIGION, 49
Randolph the only part of R. that was not malignant INSULTS, 124
rank Englishman . . . weighs up the birth, the r., . . . the wealth of the people he meets CLASS, 36
O! my offence is r., it smells to heaven GUILT, 12
raped Has anyone here been r. and speaks English INSENSITIVITY, 1
rapidly but not so r. TIME, 9
rapists All men are r. MEN, 3
rapping r. at my chamber door SUPERNATURAL, 12
rapture a r. on the lonely shore NATURE, 5
The first fine careless r. BIRDS, 4
rare as r. things will, it vanished TRANSIENCE, 10
keep it shut up . . . like a r., r. fiddle BODY, 14
neither r. nor well done TELEVISION, 10
Sanity is very r. MADNESS, 12
rascal Get down you dirty r. NURSERY RHYMES, 23
rascals R., would you live for ever WAR, 60
rash It is too r. LOVE, 151
rat Mr Speaker, I smell a r. MIXED METAPHORS, 4
r., but you can't re-r. BETRAYAL, 6
That killed the r. NURSERY RHYMES, 57
You dirty double-crossing r. INSULTS, 25

ratchet politics of the pendulum, but of the r. POLITICS, 139
rather It's all been r. lovely LAST WORDS, 55
rationalized Happiness . . . should never be r. HAPPINESS, 7
rat-like r. cunning, a plausible manner JOURNALISM, 40
rats I see some r. have got in WOMEN, 68
R.! /They fought the dogs ANIMALS, 7
rattle The rest of you r. your jewellery AUDIENCES, 5
ravages What do the r. of time not injure AGE, 41
raven Quoth the R., 'Nevermore' EVIL, 16
ravens I have commanded the r. to feed thee there BIBLICAL QUOTATIONS, 401
There were three r. sat on a tree ANONYMOUS, 97
ravish You can't r. a tin of sardines DEBAUCHERY, 9
ravished He . . . r. this fair creature SEX, 34
raw the working-class which, r. and half-developed PUBLIC, 2
razor my skin bristles so that the r. ceases to act POETRY, 27
Satire should, like a polished r. keen SATIRE, 2
razors R. pain you SUICIDE, 23
reach a man's r. should exceed his grasp AMBITION, 4
reactionaries r. are paper tigers POLITICS, 97
read A lonesome man . . . who does not know how to r. READING, 6
A man ought to r. just as inclination leads him READING, 10
beautiful . . . for someone who could not r. UNITED STATES, 11
books. . . . criticized and r. by people who don't understand them BOOKS, 27
do *you* r. books *through* READING, 9
Education . . . has produced a vast population able to r. EDUCATION, 82
everybody wants to have r. LITERATURE, 23
Hares have no time to r. HUMAN CONDITION, 4
he had r. of the effects of smoking SMOKING, 30
He writes as fast as they can r. WRITERS, 20
His books were r. BOOKS, 6
In my early years I r. very hard KNOWLEDGE, 25
I've just r. that I am dead OBITUARIES, 5
King George will be able to r. that SIGNATURES, 2
R., mark, learn and inwardly digest BOOK OF COMMON PRAYER, THE, 1
sooner r. a time-table . . . than nothing NOVELS, 11
When I want to r. a novel NOVELS, 3
will bear to be r. twice, . . . was thought twice WRITING, 41
reader A r. seldom peruses a book with pleasure WRITERS, 1
A sleeping r. is less of a menace to the books READING, 2
not to inform the r. BUREAUCRACY, 1
send the r. to the dictionary INSULTS, 47
the writer . . . is the impregnator, . . . the r. . . . is the respondent READING, 21
readers his r. are proud to live in it WRITERS, 14
The human race, . . . many of my r. HUMAN CONDITION, 6
to trade a hundred contemporary r. for POSTERITY, 7
Was there ever yet anything written . . . that was wished longer by its r. LITERATURE, 11
reading as much pleasure in the r. PLEASURE, 29
a substitute for r. it OSTENTATION, 2
a tragedy and therefore not worth r. PLAYS, 2
but I prefer r. READING, 16
half learned the art of r. READING, 4
If a book is worth r. BOOKS, 38
I have led a life of business so long that I have lost my taste for r. READING, 19
I loitered my life away, r. books DISCONTENT, 3
I shall lose no time in r. it INATTENTION, 1
Peace is poor r. WAR AND PEACE, 9
R. . . . ingenious device for avoiding thought READING, 8
R. isn't an occupation we encourage among police officers POLICE, 7
R. is to the mind READING, 17
R. maketh a full man READING, 3
The r. of all good books LITERATURE, 3
There are two motives for r. a book BOASTS, 7
When I am not walking, I am r. READING, 11
ready critics all are r. made CRITICS, 2
I have but ninepence in r. money CONVERSATION, 1
ready made Why not . . . r. WORDS, 6
Reagan disastrous fire in President R.'s library both books were destroyed INSULTS, 64
real I could have become a r. painter LAST WORDS, 50
Nothing ever becomes r. till it is experienced EXPERIENCE, 19
whether Zelda and I are r. FICTION, 2
realistic he is going to make 'a r. decision' DECISION, 4
reality art . . . r. which is . . . in our minds ARTS, 7
As far as the laws of mathematics refer to r. MATHEMATICS, 4
by r. I mean shops like Selfridges REALITY, 6
Cannot bear very much r. REALITY, 3
He had surrendered all r. DOCTORS, 36
statesmen of the world . . . are far more dangerous, and far more estranged from 'r.' NUCLEAR WEAPONS, 12
The Academy would not accept the r. of meteorites until 1803 SCIENCE, 1
The whole of art is an appeal to a r. ARTS, 7
realize I saw it, but I did not r. it PERCEPTION, 4
realm A worse king never left a r. undone ROYALTY, 33
no one in the r. . . . fitly to come to me ROYALTY, 89
One R., One People, One Leader NAZISM, 1
realms travell'd in the r. of gold TRAVEL, 22
reap sow . . . in righteousness, r. in mercy BIBLICAL QUOTATIONS, 243
sown the wind . . . r. the whirlwind BIBLICAL QUOTATIONS, 242
whatsoever a man soweth, that shall he also r. BIBLICAL QUOTATIONS, 173
reaper a R. whose name is Death DEATH, 98
reaping No, r. PUNS, 2
reappear all great events and personalities in . . . history r. HISTORY, 23
rearm supposing I had gone to the country and said . . . r. WEAPONS, 1
reason always with right r. dwells FREEDOM, 41
A man who does not lose his r. REASON, 6
Faith consists in believing when it is beyond the power of r. to believe FAITH, 32
happiness is not an ideal of r. HAPPINESS, 14
He never does a proper thing without . . . an improper r. MORALITY, 17
he who destroys a good book, kills r. BOOKS, 30
Human r. won. Mankind won VICTORY, 10
it was neither rhyme nor r. CRITICISM, 45
let us r. together REASON, 4
man . . . is R.'s slave PASSION, 2
nothing is law that is not r. LAW, 26
not to r. why OBEDIENCE, 6
Once the people begin to r. PUBLIC, 18
Only r. can convince us OBJECTIVITY, 3
R. is itself a matter of faith REASON, 2
r. not the need NECESSITY, 6
R., Observation, and Experience SCIENCE, 51
right deed for the wrong r. MOTIVE, 2
The madman . . . has lost everything except his r. MADNESS, 7
the r. of the case LAW, 26
The ruling passion conquers r. still PASSION, 7
who turns mad for a r. MADNESS, 6
woman's r. WOMEN, 108
reasonable Act of God . . . *something which no r. man could have expected* DISASTER, 3
figure of 'The R. Man' LAW, 20
It is his r. conversation MADNESS, 14
We are r. FAIRNESS, 2
Who kills a man kills a r. creature BOOKS, 30
reasoners most plausible r. THINKING, 6
reasoning *abstract r. concerning quantity or number* ILLUSIONS, 3
reasons Fools give you r. REASON, 3
Metaphysics is the finding of bad r. METAPHYSICS, 2
never give your r. JUDGMENT, 13
r. for not printing any list of subscribers FRANKNESS, 2
The heart has its r. HEART, 16
two r. for drinking THIRST, 1
rebel how to r. and conform at the same time YOUTH, 8
What is a r. ALIENATION, 2
rebellion A little r. now and then REBELLION, 9
a standard of r. REBELLION, 8
recall The Gods themselves cannot r. their gifts IRREVOCABILITY, 3
receipts How were the r. today in Madison Square Garden LAST WORDS, 6
receive whoso shall r. one such little child BIBLICAL QUOTATIONS, 515
received a cloud r. him out of their sight BIBLICAL QUOTATIONS, 1
freely ye have r., freely give BIBLICAL QUOTATIONS, 499
receiver your wife . . . is a r. of stolen goods INSULTS, 72
reception men that . . . hinder the r. of every work CRITICS, 8
recession r. when . . . neighbour loses his job ECONOMICS, 19
reckon'd beggary in the love that can be r. LOVE, 130
reckoning No man gets away from his r. FATE, 9
take you . . . at your own r. SELF-RESPECT, 6
recognize did not r. me by my face PUNISHMENT, 26
recognized The true system of the World has been r. BOOKS, 2
recoils Revenge . . . back on itself r. REVENGE, 15
recompense R. injury with justice KINDNESS, 3
reconcile How r. this world . . . with . . . my imagining BLINDNESS, 6
It takes a long while for a . . . trustful person to r. himself to . . . God FAITH, 22
reconnaissance Exploratory operation: a remunerative r. OPERATIONS, 2
recounting calms one's grief by r. it GRIEF, 3
recovery Despair of all r. LONGEVITY, 6
recreation woman accepted cooking . . . but man . . . made of it a r. FOOD, 61
red Better r. than dead NUCLEAR WEAPONS, 2
Coral is far more r. ANALOGY, 4
his eyes shall be r. with wine BIBLICAL QUOTATIONS, 227
it's not even r. brick, but white tile CLASS, 33
. . . leeches have r. blood LAST WORDS, 23
R. Badge of Courage COURAGE, 9
R. lips are not so r. WAR, 118
R. sky at night PROVERBS, 348
She wore false hair and that r. ROYALTY, 65
The people's flag is deepest r. SOCIALISM, 6
The sand of the desert is sodden r. WAR, 112
thin r. line tipped with steel WAR, 133
redeemed he hath visited and r. his people BIBLICAL QUOTATIONS, 415
redeemer I know that my r. liveth BIBLICAL QUOTATIONS, 306
redemption married past r. MARRIAGE, 59
red-handed R. with the silver SERVICE, 2
Red-Hot The Last of the R. Mamas SINGERS, 3
redundancy hiring taxis . . . handing out r. notices to its own workers INCOMPETENCE, 2
redwood Nixon . . . would cut down a r. tree POLITICIANS, 104
reeling R. and Writhing EDUCATION, 19
references Always verify your r. RESEARCH, 22
refined One of those r. people CLASS, 9
reflection a r. of the British Museum Reading Room INTELLECTUALS, 13
reform All r. . . . will prove unavailing CHANGE, 2
Any attempt to r. the university EDUCATION, 44
reformation Every r. must have its victims SUFFERING, 27
refreshed The tree of liberty must be r. FREEDOM, 27
refuge God is the immemorial r. of the incompetent GOD, 41
Idleness . . . the r. of weak minds IDLENESS, 2
Patriotism is the last r. PATRIOTISM, 23
refuse an offer he can't r. BUSINESS, 18
those who collect the r. of the public streets SOCIETY, 3
To r. praise PRAISE, 8
refused She r. to begin the 'Beguine' PETULANCE, 1
refute I r. it *thus* PHILOSOPHY, 6
regardless r. of their doom DOOM, 1
R. of what they say DOGS, 12
regime No r. has ever loved great writers WRITERS, 55
regimen R. is superior to medicine HEALTHY LIVING, 45

regiment led his r. from behind COWARDICE, 3
register history . . . the r. of the . . . misfortunes of mankind HISTORY, 16
I want to r. a complaint COMPLAINTS, 9
regret My r. /Becomes an April violet SORROW, 28
remember and r. REGRET, 9
wild with all r. NOSTALGIA, 26
regrets the Cup that clears /TO-DAY of past R. PRESENT, 5
The follies which a man r. REGRET, 16
regulated The English nation . . . has successfully r. the power of its kings GOVERNMENT, 40
regulator I have always respected suicide as a r. of nature SUICIDE, 19
rehearsing R. a play is making the word flesh PLAYS, 12
Reich *Ein R., Ein Volk, Ein Führer* NAZISM, 1
the criminal pride of the German R. WAR, 7
reigned I have r. with your loves ROYALTY, 50
reigns king r., but does not govern MONARCHY, 27
reject If you r. me on account of my religion PREJUDICE, 1
rejoice new sights of Nature made me r. NATURE, 10
r. at that news and congratulate our forces VICTORY, 24
r. in the Lord alway BIBLICAL QUOTATIONS, 564
r. with joy unspeakable BIBLICAL QUOTATIONS, 559
rejoiced my spirit hath r. in God my Saviour BIBLICAL QUOTATIONS, 413
related A group of closely r. persons FAMILY, 33
relation If a man's character is to be abused . . . there's nobody like a r. to do the business FAMILY, 53
relations Fate chooses your r. FAMILY, 15
great men have their poor r. FAMILY, 17
Personal r. . . . important thing LIFE, 36
relationship a special r. POLITICS, 35
relativity I believe my theory of r. SCIENCE, 35
relaxation Man . . . can only find r. from one . . . labour by taking up another CHANGE, 8
relief For this r. much thanks COMFORT, 3
There is a certain r. in change CHANGE, 13
thou wilt give thyself r. LIFE, 54
religion a feeling of inward tranquillity which r. is powerless to bestow CLOTHES, 7
Art and r. first; then philosophy IMPORTANCE, 4
As to r., . . . duty of government to protect all . . . professors thereof GOVERNMENT, 29
brothels with bricks of R. HYPOCRISY, 5
Fascism is a r. FASCISM, 8
I am of the same r. as all those who are brave and true CONSCIENCE, 5
If you reject me on account of my r. PREJUDICE, 1
Love is my r. LOVE AND DEATH, 3
Many people think they have r. RELIGION, 46
Men will wrangle for r. RELIGION, 22
monstrous a wickedness . . . within . . . their r. TREASON, 2
none of you suffer for your opinions or r. TOLERANCE, 2
no reason to bring r. into it RELIGION, 59
Not a r. for gentlemen RELIGION, 18
Nothing is so fatal to r. as indifference INDIFFERENCE, 2
One r. is as true as another RELIGION, 15
One's r. . . . yours is Success SUCCESS, 4
R. /Has made an honest woman of the supernatural RELIGION, 34
R. is an illusion ILLUSIONS, 2
R. is by no means a proper subject RELIGION, 19
R. is love RELIGION, 79
R. . . . is the opium of the people RELIGION, 53
r. of feeble minds SUPERSTITION, 8
r. of Socialism SOCIALISM, 3
R.'s in the heart PRAYER, 19
Science without r. is lame RELIGION, 30
Sensible men are all of the same r. RELIGION, 24
talks loudly against r. RELIGION, 64
that God is interested only . . . in r. GOD, 55
To become a popular r. RELIGION, 44
To die for a r. is easier than to live it absolutely MARTYRDOM, 2
when r. is allowed to invade . . . private life RELIGION, 54
when r. was strong . . . men mistook magic for medicine MEDICINE, 100
religions a country with thirty-two r. and only one sauce UNITED STATES, 61
sixty different r., and only one sauce ENGLAND, 14
The r. we call false were once true FALSENESS, 3
religious a r. animal RELIGION, 14
first, r. and moral principles EDUCATION, 8
INDIGESTION, n. A disease which the patient and his friends frequently mistake for deep r. conviction ILLNESS, 14
not r.-good VIRTUE, 12
r. outlook on life RELIGION, 48
skilled appeals to r. prejudice REPARTEE, 54
To be at all is to be r. RELIGION, 16
relished the taste by which he is . . . r. WRITING, 47
reluctant The r. obedience of distant provinces DIPLOMACY, 19
remarkable nothing left r. /Beneath the visiting moon MOURNING, 9
remedies amusing him with r. good or bad MEDICINE, 63
doctors worry over the small number of r. REMEDIES, 22
Extreme r. . . . for extreme diseases REMEDIES, 32
he that will not apply new r., must expect new evils PROGRESS, 2
He that will not apply new r. INNOVATION, 1
If you are too fond of new r. REMEDIES, 24
Most men die of their r., and not of their illnesses REMEDIES, 42
Not even r. can master incurable diseases DISEASE, 41
Our r. oft in ourselves do lie REMEDIES, 50
paralyse it by encumbering it with r. BODY, 24
R., . . . are our great analysers of disease REMEDIES, 39
r. . . . suggested for a disease REMEDIES, 21
We cannot do without palliative r. REMEDIES, 30
We do not know the mode of action of almost all r. REMEDIES, 56
Whiskey is the most popular of . . . r. that won't cure a cold ALCOHOL, 83
remedy a r. for everything except death REMEDIES, 20
a sovereign r. to all diseases SMOKING, 7
Force is not a r. FORCE, 2
I never think of finding a r. ILLNESS, 52
popular r. often throws the scientific doctor into hysterics REMEDIES, 4
r. is worse than the disease DISEASE, 10
Tis a sharp r., but a sure one EXECUTION, 33
To do nothing is also a good r. REMEDIES, 33
remember I only r. what I've learnt KNOWLEDGE, 38
I r., I r. INNOCENCE, 6
I r. it well MEMORY, 10
Oh! don't you r. sweet Alice, Ben Bolt DELIGHT, 6
one man to r. me LAST WORDS, 74
r. and regret REGRET, 9
r. Lot's wife BIBLICAL QUOTATIONS, 443
R. me when I am gone away MEMORY, 17
r. me when thou comest into thy kingdom BIBLICAL QUOTATIONS, 448
r. what I must be now DESPAIR, 8
she did not r. . . . her jewelry PRUDENCE, 10
The world will little note, nor long r. MEMORIALS, 9
we shall be glad to r. even these hardships ENDURANCE, 26
We will r. them MEMORIALS, 6
When I meet a man whose name I can't r. MEMORY, 6
Who will r., . . . /The unheroic dead MEMORIALS, 14
remembered By this may I r. be /When I should be forgotten ANONYMOUS, 107
I r. my God GOD, 52
remembers r. /The beauty of fire from . . . embers OLD AGE, 62
remembrance r. of things past REGRET, 23
there is no r. of former things BIBLICAL QUOTATIONS, 76
reminiscences the old have r. AGE, 65
remorse r. for what you have thought about your wife MARRIAGE, 110
remove all faith, so that I could r. mountains BIBLICAL QUOTATIONS, 44
Renaissance R. is a mere ripple on the surface of literature LITERATURE, 13
the R. was . . . the green end of one of civilization's hardest winters CIVILIZATION, 5
render husband r. unto the wife due benevolence BIBLICAL QUOTATIONS, 33
r. . . . unto Caesar BIBLICAL QUOTATIONS, 525
rendezvous a r. with Death DEATH, 130
renegades Political r. always start their career of treachery POLITICIANS, 68
renewal urban r. in New York City EDUCATION, 44
rent they r. out my room EXPEDIENCY, 5
repair the landlord does not intend to r. LAST WORDS, 2
repartee A majority is always the best r. MAJORITY, 4
Violence is the r. of the illiterate VIOLENCE, 3
repast A new r., or an untasted spring PLEASURE, 2
repay whatsoever thou spendest more . . . I will r. BIBLICAL QUOTATIONS, 433
repeal the r. of bad or obnoxious laws LAW, 19
repeat History does not r. itself HISTORY, 5
obliged to imitate himself, and to r. IMITATION, 5
repeated A platitude is simply a truth r. SAYINGS, 1
repent Do you . . . Never, my Love, r. PARTING, 8
r. at leisure MARRIAGE, 42
r.: for the kingdom of heaven is at hand BIBLICAL QUOTATIONS, 470
repentance A Christian . . . feels /R. on a Sunday CHRISTIANITY, 63
There's no r. in the grave DEATH, 175
with the morning cool r. REGRET, 17
repented it r. the Lord that he had made man BIBLICAL QUOTATIONS, 196
repenteth joy . . . over one sinner that r. BIBLICAL QUOTATIONS, 438
repetition constant r. will finally succeed in imprinting an idea PUBLIC, 14
History is an endless r. HISTORY, 10
replenished His intellect is not r. IGNORANCE, 19
replied And I r., 'My Lord.' RELIGION, 42
report A drug is that substance which . . . will produce a scientific r. DRUGS, 2
reporter A r. is a man who has renounced everything JOURNALISM, 33
I am a r. ATHEISM, 8
reporting Language is not simply a r. device for experience LANGUAGE, 45
repose Joy and Temperance and R. HEALTHY LIVING, 30
Our foster nurse of nature is r. SLEEP, 27
reprehend If I r. any thing MALAPROPISMS, 8
representation In Scotland there is no shadow even of r. REPRESENTATION, 1
Proportional R. . . . is fundamentally counter-democratic POLITICS, 83
Taxation and r. are inseparably united TAXATION, 16
Taxation without r. REPRESENTATION, 2
reproduction The r. of mankind is a great marvel and mystery SEX, 62
reproductions accurate r. of Anne Hathaway's cottage HOUSES, 2
I've seen color r. PHILISTINISM, 5
republic An aristocracy in a r. is like a chicken ARISTOCRACY, 16
the r. of letters MANKIND, 1
Republican The R. form of Government POLITICS, 129
Republicans Please assure me that you are all R. POLITICS, 116
republication Every twenty years one sees a r. of the same ideas MEDICINE, 88
republics Revolts, r., revolutions POLITICS, 138
repugnant Woman to bear rule . . . is r. to Nature WOMAN'S ROLE, 7
repulsive Roundheads (Right but R.) HISTORY, 33
reputability Conspicuous consumption . . . is a means of r. MATERIALISM, 25
reputation ever written out of r. but by himself REPUTATION, 2
it is better for the r. ORTHODOXY, 3
it wrecks a woman's r. JEWELRY, 1
O, I have lost my r. REPUTATION, 8
r. grew with every failure REPUTATION, 13
spotless r. REPUTATION, 10
their r. stands . . . on a foundation of dead bodies REPUTATION, 12
Until you've lost your r., you never realize . . . what freedom really is REPUTATION, 6
requests thou wilt grant their r. BOOK OF COMMON PRAYER, THE, 6
requires all the Human Frame r. FOOD, 10
re-rat rat, but you can't r. BETRAYAL, 6

the choice between smoked s. and tinned s. FOOD, 73
salon plastic surgery . . . psychoanalysis, massage, and a trip to the beauty s. OPERATIONS, 14
salt a pillar of s. BIBLICAL QUOTATIONS, 211
nobody likes having s. rubbed into their wounds AGGRAVATION, 2
S. water and absence LOVE, 9
speech . . . seasoned with s. BIBLICAL QUOTATIONS, 26
the s. of the earth BIBLICAL QUOTATIONS, 473
salvage Is a man a s. at heart MANKIND, 6
salvaged Our ships have been s. WORLD WAR II, 31
salvagery is s. but a faint taint in the natural man's gentility MANKIND, 6
salvation S. doesn't do them the same good RELIGION, 78
s. . . . in the hands of the creatively maladjusted PROGRESS, 15
the helmet of s. BIBLICAL QUOTATIONS, 119
There is no s. outside the church RELIGION, 4
The s. of mankind RESPONSIBILITY, 16
water out of the wells of s. BIBLICAL QUOTATIONS, 259
Sam Play it, S. MISQUOTATION, 9
Samaritan But a certain S. . . . had compassion on him BIBLICAL QUOTATIONS, 433
No one would have remembered the Good S. MONEY, 45
ready enough to do the S. CHARITY, 23
Samarkand the Golden Road to S. KNOWLEDGE, 15
same he is much the s. ILLNESS, 9
It will be all the s. PROVERBS, 238
it would be all the s. a hundred years hence TRIVIALITY, 4
principle seems the s. WATER, 1
the s. is my brother BIBLICAL QUOTATIONS, 505
we must all say *the s.* UNITY, 12
we're all made the s. SIMILARITY, 4
samite Clothed in white s. ARTHURIAN LEGEND, 2
Samuel When they circumcised Herbert S. INSULTS, 86
sanction Happiness is the only s. of life HAPPINESS, 23
sanctions S. are now the only . . . way of ending apartheid RACISM, 3
sand a foolish man, which built his house upon the s. BIBLICAL QUOTATIONS, 493
and throws . . . s. in their eyes SLEEP, 20
The s. of the desert is sodden red WAR, 112
They wept . . . to see /Such quantities of s. SEASIDE, 2
throw the s. against the wind FUTILITY, 4
World in a grain of s. WONDER, 2
sane An asylum for the s. would be empty in America UNITED STATES, 90
being s. all by oneself MADNESS, 9
Every man has a s. spot somewhere SANITY, 3
See where the s. ones have landed us MADNESS, 37
Show me a s. man and I will cure him for you MADNESS, 21
the asylums can hold the s. people MADNESS, 42
Who, then, is s. SANITY, 2
sanitarium if he can afford the luxury of a private s. PSYCHIATRY, 19
sanitary Golden S. Towel Award Presentation THEATER, 13
Sanity S. is madness put to good uses MADNESS, 30
S. is very rare MADNESS, 12
sank Tallulah Bankhead barged down the Nile last night and s. CRITICISM, 11
sans S. teeth, s. eyes, s. taste, s. every thing OLD AGE, 82
Sarah and S. shall have a son BIBLICAL QUOTATIONS, 208
sarcasm petulance is not s. IMPERTINENCE, 2
S. . . . the language of the devil SARCASM, 1
sardines Life is . . . like a tin of s. LIFE, 10
You can't ravish a tin of s. DEBAUCHERY, 9
Sargent He's a kind of musical Malcolm S. COMPOSERS, 1
sat The . . . gentleman has s. so long on the fence INSULTS, 88
Satan And S. trembles PRAYER, 14
beheld S. as lightning fall from heaven BIBLICAL QUOTATIONS, 431
S. answered the Lord DEVIL, 6
S. exalted sat, by merit raised DEVIL, 13
S. finds . . . mischief . . . /For idle hands IDLENESS, 12
S., Nick, or Clootie DEVIL, 9
satire hard not to write s. SATIRE, 1
S. is a sort of glass SATIRE, 5
S. should, like a polished razor keen SATIRE, 2
satirists S. should be heard and not seen CRITICISM, 59
satisfaction complacency and s. . . . in . . . a new-married couple MARRIAGE, 85
I can't get no s. SATISFACTION, 4
In work the greatest s. lies WORK, 3
the s. of knowing that we are avenged REVENGE, 21
satisfied his soul is s. with what is assigned to him CONTENTMENT, 1
The superior man is s. DISTRESS, 2
Saturday betwixt /A S. and Monday SUNDAY, 4
Died on S. HUMAN CONDITION, 17
S.'s child works hard for his living CHARACTER, 19
what he did on S. CHRISTIANITY, 63
satyr man is . . . either a stoic or a s. AGE, 56
sauce a country with thirty-two religions and only one s. UNITED STATES, 61
Art is not a special s. ART, 13
sixty different religions, and only one s. ENGLAND, 14
The best s. in the world HUNGER, 4
Saul S. hath slain his thousands BIBLICAL QUOTATIONS, 613
savage A s. old Nabob POLITICIANS, 76
a time when Britain had a s. culture CIVILIZATION, 2
s. place! as holy and enchanted SUPERNATURAL, 6
soothe a s. breast MUSIC, 14
The young man who has not wept is a s. AGE, 66
savaged s. by a dead sheep INSULTS, 57
savait *Si jeunesse s.* AGE, 31
save Christ Jesus came into the world to s. sinners BIBLICAL QUOTATIONS, 646
s. the plan POLITICS, 107
S. your breath PROVERBS, 354
To s. a man's life against his will is . . . killing him KILLING, 5
saved he that endureth to the end shall be s. BIBLICAL QUOTATIONS, 500
they only s. the world HEROISM, 3
thy faith hath s. thee BIBLICAL QUOTATIONS, 429
You might have s. him if you would GUILT, 4
saviour But it's 'S. of 'is country' when the guns SOLDIERS, 3
savor Filths s. but themselves EVIL, 20
saw I came, I s., God conquered VICTORY, 2
I came, I s., I conquered VICTORY, 1
I s. it, but I did not realize it PERCEPTION, 4
Saxon The S. is not like us Normans NATIONALITY, 8
Saxones the *S., Angli,* and *Iutae* ENGLISH, 6
say cannot s. what you have to s. in twenty minutes SPEECHES, 4
Do as I s. PROVERBS, 111
if we s. that we have no sin, we deceive BIBLICAL QUOTATIONS, 376
If you haven't anything nice to s. about anyone CONVERSATION, 6
I have nothing to s., I am saying it POETRY, 13
Preachers s., Do as I s., not as I do DISEASE, 39
Regardless of what they s. DOGS, 12
S. it with flowers FLOWERS, 11
s. what you have to s., and then sit down LATIN, 7
The great consolation . . . is to s. what one thinks FRANKNESS, 4
They are to s. what they please FREEDOM, 15
they do not know what they are going to s. SPEECHES, 6
What have we to s. to India COMMUNICATION, 5
When you have nothing to s. SILENCE, 4
When you take your family on holiday, do you s. LANGUAGE, 5
saying S. is one thing ACTION, 5
when . . . speaking, they do not know what they are s. SPEECHES, 6
sayings Dr Johnson's s. WRITERS, 21
His s. are generally like women's letters LETTER-WRITING, 4
scab The itch of disputing . . . the s. of churches RELIGION, 83
scaffold no middle course between the throne and the s. MONARCHY, 8
scalpel You can't probe for faith with a s. DOCTORS, 39
scandal In England there is only silence or s. ENGLAND, 32
It is a public s. that gives offence MORALITY, 11
s. by a woman . . . proved liar POLITICS, 59
There's no s. like rags POVERTY, 9
scape who shall s. whipping MERIT, 6
scarce S., sir. Mighty s. REPARTEE, 108
scare A good s. is worth more ADVICE, 1
scarecrow We must not make a s. of the law LAW, 30
scarecrows Logical consequences are the s. of fools LOGIC, 6
scarlet His sins were s. BOOKS, 6
pious bird with the s. breast BIRDS, 20
though your sins be as s. BIBLICAL QUOTATIONS, 244
scatter We plough the fields, and s. AGRICULTURE, 1
scattered God blew and they were s. WAR, 2
s. the proud BIBLICAL QUOTATIONS, 414
scenery Mountains . . . the beginning and the end of all natural s. MOUNTAINS, 3
S. is fine HUMAN NATURE, 15
scenes I'll come no more behind your s., David LUST, 5
sceptic too much of a s. to deny the possibility of anything SCEPTICISM, 2
scepticism natural course of the human mind is . . . from credulity to s. MIND, 14
s. kept her from being an atheist SCEPTICISM, 5
sceptred this s. isle EARTH, 16
Scheherazade S. . . . a woman saving her head SELF-PRESERVATION, 15
schemes best laid s. o' mice an' men DISAPPOINTMENT, 2
schizophrenia if God talks to you, you have s. MADNESS, 40
S. cannot be understood PSYCHIATRY, 22
schizophrenic S. behaviour is a special strategy MENTAL ILLNESS, 4
scholar ills the s.'s life assail EDUCATION, 49
the last humiliation of an aged s. OLD AGE, 37
scholars great men have not commonly been great s. GREATNESS, 8
S. and gentlemen HONOR, 10
S. dispute ARGUMENTS, 6
school A good clinical teacher is himself a Medical S. EDUCATION, 37
enjoy a public s. EDUCATION, 24
Example is the s. of mankind EXAMPLE, 2
fleshly s. of Poetry POETS, 8
If every day in the life of a s. EDUCATION, 52
more fit for a grammar s. than a Court of Parliament HOUSES OF PARLIAMENT, 6
never gone to s. may steal from a freight car CRIME, 7
nothing on earth . . . so horrible as a s. EDUCATION, 76
public s. . . . an appalling and impregnable conceit MODESTY, 7
public s., where . . . learning was painfully beaten into him EDUCATION, 69
the public-s. system all over EDUCATION, 88
The Stealthy S. of Criticism CRITICISM, 54
The world is but a s. of inquiry CURIOSITY, 5
Three little maids from s. CHILDREN, 28
till he's been to a good s. EDUCATION, 72
schoolboy a s.'s barring out POLITICS, 138
every s. repeating my words POSTERITY, 9
schoolboys 'tis the s. that educate my son EDUCATION, 26
schoolgirl a priggish s., captain of the hockey team, a prefect ROYALTY, 2
schoolmaster Every s. after the age of 49 EDUCATION, 64
Nothing is more hideous than an old s. EDUCATION, 54
schoolmasters Let s. puzzle their brain ALCOHOL, 36
schools a hundred s. of thought contend FREEDOM, 38
Public s. are the nurseries of all vice EDUCATION, 27
There is now less flogging in our great s. EDUCATION, 48
We class s. . . . into four grades EDUCATION, 86
schoolteacher The s. . . . ludicrously overpaid as an educator EDUCATION, 65

Schumann I moved from S. to folk songs, then to hymns MUSIC, 22
science All s. requires mathematics MATHEMATICS, 1
A man of true s. . . . uses but few hard words LANGUAGE, 29
A s. which hesitates to forget SCIENCE, 92
Christian S. explains all cause and effect as mental RELIGION, 28
drawback that s. . . . invented after I left school SCIENCE, 19
Ethics and S. need to shake hands PRINCIPLES, 2
Experience is the mother of s. EXPERIENCE, 3
Facts are not s. FACTS, 2
god of s. . . . has given us the atomic bomb SCIENCE, 57
great tragedy of S. SCIENCE, 49
guy in a s. fiction movie INSULTS, 50
In everything that relates to s. SCIENCE, 58
invoke the wonders of s. instead of its terrors SCIENCE, 56
its hold on s. KINDNESS, 7
Language is only the instrument of s. LANGUAGE, 23
lastly s. IMPORTANCE, 4
Learn to innure yourself to drudgery in s. EDUCATION, 68
Medical s. is . . . imperfectly differentiated from . . . witchcraft MEDICINE, 92
men only care for s. so far as they get a living by it SCIENCE, 40
No one should approach the temple of s. SCIENCE, 15
not to trust any evidence except that . . . of physical s. MEDICINE, 79
one word . . . to identify modern socialism, it was 'S.' SOCIALISM, 25
only applications of s. SCIENCE, 67
oppositions of s. falsely so called BIBLICAL QUOTATIONS, 653
Poetry is opposed to s. . . . prose to metre POETRY AND PROSE, 1
Politics is not an exact s. POLITICS, 21
Politics is not a s. . . . but an art POLITICS, 22
Putting on the spectacles of s. SCIENCE, 27
S. and art are only too often a superior kind of dope NARCOTICS, 6
s. and faith exclude one another FAITH, 31
s. . . . a refinement of everyday thinking SCIENCE, 33
S. . . . art of systematic over-simplification SCIENCE, 71
s. can wait, research can wait PATIENTS, 17
S. . . . commits suicide when it adopts a creed SCIENCE, 50
S. conducts us . . . through the whole range of creation SCIENCE, 61
S. fiction is no more written for scientists FICTION, 1
S. has 'explained' nothing SCIENCE, 46
S. has nothing to be ashamed of SCIENCE, 14
S. is always wrong SCIENCE, 80
s. is essentially international SCIENCE, 23
s. is . . . neither a potential for good nor for evil SCIENCE, 79
S. is nothing but trained and organized common sense SCIENCE, 48
S. is not to be regarded merely as a storehouse of facts SCIENCE, 41
S. is the father of knowledge OPINIONS, 2
S. is the great antidote SCIENCE, 81
s. . . . is . . . the interplay between nature and ourselves NATURE, 16
S. is what you know PHILOSOPHY, 17
S. made man feel small NEUROSIS, 7
S. must begin with myths MYTHS, 1
S. robs men of wisdom SCIENCE, 86
S. says: 'We must live,' LIFE AND DEATH, 34
S. seldom renders men amiable SCIENCE, 4
S. should leave off making pronouncements SCIENCE, 54
s. was the only career worth following WORK, 14
S. without conscience SCIENCE, 74
S. without religion is lame RELIGION, 30
Should we force s. down the throats SCIENCE, 72
ten dollars' worth of medical s. KINDNESS, 5
the department of witchcraft called medical s. MEDICINE, 93
the essence of s. SCIENCE, 12
The establishment of theory is the very purpose of s. THEORY, 4
the fairy tales of s. EXPERIENCE, 21
the greatest collective work of s. SCIENCE, 13
The highest wisdom has but one s. MANKIND, 64
the Holy Trinity of S. SCIENCE, 51
the laws of physical s. are positive MEDICINE, 10
The term S. should not be given to anything SCIENCE, 87
those twin extinguishers of s. SCIENCE, 11
to advance the s. EDUCATION, 58
Whenever s. makes a discovery SCIENCE, 88
when religion was strong and s. weak MEDICINE, 100
sciences Books must follow s. BOOKS, 5
Do you . . . believe that the s. would . . . have . . . grown SCIENCE, 66
no such things as applied s. SCIENCE, 67
S. may be learned by rote WISDOM, 31
s. were transmitted into the Arabic language LANGUAGE, 2
scientific any conclusion must be very s. SCIENCE, 52
I have discovered the s. method PSYCHOANALYSIS, 10
it's not very s., but it helps ALCOHOL, 32
lack of efficiency in using s. achievements for economic needs TECHNOLOGY, 7
no longer an individual man but a jumble of s. data PATIENTS, 19
restating our socialism in terms of the s. revolution SOCIALISM, 24
S. discovery is a private event SCIENCE, 62
Traditional s. method has always been SCIENCE, 68
scientist I consider myself superior to the saint, the s. NOVELS, 10
It is a good morning exercise for a research s. SCIENCE, 60
When a distinguished but elderly s. states SCIENCE, 20
scientists in the company of s., I feel like a shabby curate SCIENTISTS, 1
Medical s. are nice people SCIENCE, 7
The true men of action . . . are . . . s. SCIENTISTS, 2
scissor-man The great, long, red-legged s. PUNISHMENT, 15
scope this man's art, and that man's s. DISCONTENT, 8
scorer when the One Great S. comes SPORT AND GAMES, 19
scorn Silence is the . . . perfect expression of s. SILENCE, 13
to make me /The fixed figure . . . of s. RIDICULE, 4
scorned fury like a woman s. FURY, 1
scorning Job . . . drinketh up s. BIBLICAL QUOTATIONS, 309
scorpions dwell among s. BIBLICAL QUOTATIONS, 159
scotch single s. is nothing more than a dirty glass INFLATION, 1
Scotchman A S. must be a very sturdy moralist SCOTS, 3
Much may be made of a S. SCOTS, 5
never met with any one S. but what was a man of sense SCOTS, 8
the noblest prospect which a S. ever sees SCOTLAND, 4
what it is that makes a S. happy ALCOHOL, 44
Scotchmen trying . . . to like S. SCOTS, 7
Scotland blow the Scots back again into S. TREASON 5
I do indeed come from S. REPARTEE, 61
I'll be in S. afore ye ANONYMOUS, 67
In S. there is no shadow even of representation REPRESENTATION, 1
Seeing S., Madam SCOTLAND, 5
Switzerland . . . an inferior sort of S. SWITZERLAND, 3
Scots blow the S. back again into Scotland TREASON, 5
S., wha hae wi' Wallace bled WAR, 33
Scotsman A young S. of your ability BRITISH, 1
S. on the make SCOTS, 2
the grandest moral attribute of a S. SCOTS, 1
to distinguish between a S. with a grievance SCOTS, 11
Scott C. P. S. EDITORS, 3
scoundrel given them to such a s. WEALTH, 40
scourge whore, and the whoremonger, shall ye s. PROMISCUITY, 4
Scout A S. smiles and whistles OPTIMISM, 15
scowl Rachmaninov's immortalizing totality was his s. COMPOSERS, 8
scratch S. an actor ACTORS, 10
S. my back HELP, 4
S. the Russian and . . . find the Tartar RUSSIA, 5
screen A wide s. . . . makes a bad film twice as bad CINEMA, 10
screenwriter behind every successful s. SUCCESS, 15
scribble Always s., s., s. WRITING, 14
scribbling My s. pays me zero francs per line WRITING, 37
Scripture devil can cite S. DEVIL, 14
Scriptures I believe firmly what I read in the holy S. BELIEF, 7
scrofulous s. French novel NOVELS, 1
sculptor not a great s. or painter can be an architect ARCHITECTURE, 12
Patriotism is the last refuge of the s. SCULPTURE, 3
S. . . . asked not to leave any holes in which boys SCULPTURE, 1
scum of the s. of the earth ARMY, 6
The rich are the s. of the earth WEALTH, 14
scutcheon I bear no other s. JOURNALISM, 19
sea all the s. were ink ANONYMOUS, 42
Alone on a wide wide s. SOLITUDE, 2
change their clime . . . who rush across the s. TRAVEL, 20
Down to a sunless s. PLEASURE, 9
espouse the everlasting s. VENICE, 5
fishes live in the s. EATING, 11
For all at last return to the s. SEA, 2
For those in peril on the s. SEA, 13
He died as he lived – at s. EPITAPHS, 42
Jesus . . . walking on the s. BIBLICAL QUOTATIONS, 509
kings of the s. DEPARTURE, 2
Learn the secret of the s. SEA, 9
like throwing water into the s. CHARITY, 12
Man has in him the silence of the s. MANKIND, 62
men and s. interpenetrate ENGLAND, 15
Out of the s. came he SUN, 1
Over the s. to Skye ROYALTY, 27
Owl and the Pussy-Cat went to s. HONEY, 3
precious stone set in the silver s. EARTH, 16
Stick . . . to your desks and never go to s. OFFICERS, 7
the midst of the s. upon dry ground BIBLICAL QUOTATIONS, 142
The s. is calm to-night SEA, 1
The s.! the s.! SEA, 14
The voice of the s. speaks to the soul SEA, 3
to the English that of the s. EMPIRE, 5
Two voices . . . one is of the s. FREEDOM, 64
We are as near to heaven by s. as by land LAND, 4
when they can see nothing but s. DISCOVERY, 4
why the s. is boiling hot NONSENSE, 9
sea-change doth suffer a s. DEATH, 148
seagreen The s. Incorruptible INCORRUPTIBILITY, 2
seal you heard a s. bark BELIEF, 12
sealed My lips are s. MISQUOTATION, 4
sea-life When men come to like a s. SEA, 6
seals sealed with seven s. BIBLICAL QUOTATIONS, 586
seam And sew a fine s. NURSERY RHYMES, 8
seamen There were gentlemen and . . . s. in the navy of Charles the Second NAVY, 8
search in s. of a great perhaps LAST WORDS, 70
s. for knowledge PHILOSOPHERS, 10
s. the land of living men ADMIRATION, 14
We have to have a s. warrant to look inside RESEARCH, 20
seas I must down to the s. again SEA, 10
That guard our native s. NAVY, 3
the waters called he S. BIBLICAL QUOTATIONS, 176
seaside Beside the S. SEASIDE, 4
the drawback of all s. places SEASIDE, 3
season a perfectly ghastly s. . . . for you Spanish dancers CHARITY, 5
Only in the mating s. ANIMALISM, 6
to every thing there is a s. BIBLICAL QUOTATIONS, 81
seasoned speech . . . s. with salt BIBLICAL QUOTATIONS, 26
seasons a man for all s. ADAPTABILITY, 4
four s. in the mind of men SEASONS, 2
seat the pleasure of offering my s. to three ladies OBESITY, 4
seatbelts Fasten your s. PROPHECY, 6
seated S. . . . at the organ MUSIC, 36
sea-water Wealth is like s. GREED, 12
second The constitution . . . first and s. class citizens CLASS, 55

second-hand Would you buy a s. car PRESIDENTS, 15
second-rate an infallible sign of the s. INFALLIBILITY, 3
nor even booksellers have put up with poets being s. POETS, 22
the creed of a s. man POLITICIANS, 10
secrecy S. is the first essential GOVERNMENT, 33
secret a s. in the Oxford sense OXFORD, 7
a s. way . . . of getting at a boy EVIL, 10
bread eaten in s. is pleasant BIBLICAL QUOTATIONS, 572
I know that's a s. SECRECY, 10
it is no sin to sin in s. MORALITY, 11
joys of parents are s. FAMILY, 8
Learn the s. of the sea SEA, 9
not to give way to it in s. TELEVISION, 6
s. of reaping the greatest fruitfulness . . . from life DANGER, 6
Three may keep a s. SECRECY, 11
We have discovered the s. of life DISCOVERY, 8
when it ceases to be a s. LOVE, 23
secreted Not in Utopia . . . /Or some s. island FRENCH REVOLUTION, 13
secretive As we make sex less s., we may rob it of its power SEX, 100
secrets Conversation . . . elicits s. from us CONVERSATION, 9
sect paradise for a s. FANATICISM, 2
sedate, sober, silent, serious, sad-coloured s. RELIGION, 43
secure only place where a man can feel . . . s. MEN, 5
The past, at least, is s. PAST, 11
security only freedom can make s. secure FREEDOM, 47
sedan in a flood of tears and a S. chair HUMOR, 20
sedge s. has wither'd from the lake ILLNESS, 37
seditious s. person is an outlaw before God PROTESTANTISM, 5
seducers evil men and s. BIBLICAL QUOTATIONS, 655
see change we think we s. NOVELTY, 2
complain we cannot s. COMPLAINTS, 2
eyes to s., and s. not BIBLICAL QUOTATIONS, 160
I now begin to s. things as they really are LAST WORDS, 34
I s. but as one sees after an operation BLINDNESS, 4
I s. none coming out MISTRUST, 2
My business is to paint . . . what I s. PAINTING, 20
s. . . . into a hypocrite HYPOCRISY, 9
seem to s. things thou dost not POLITICIANS, 98
the day I was meant not to s. ASSASSINATION, 8
there shall no man s. me, and live BIBLICAL QUOTATIONS, 157
we received from that S. our Crown OBLIGATION, 2
whereas I was blind, now I s. BIBLICAL QUOTATIONS, 338
Why don't you come up sometime and s. me INVITATIONS, 6
seed Fair s.-time had my soul SOUL, 19
he spills his s. on the ground BIRDS, 15
I do not want to die . . . until I have . . . cultivated the s. ACHIEVEMENT, 8
In s. time learn, in harvest teach SUITABILITY, 1
Onan knew that the s. should not be his BIBLICAL QUOTATIONS, 222
s. time and harvest BIBLICAL QUOTATIONS, 199
you have the fruit already in its s. ABORTION, 4
seeing do not suppose you are s. things in themselves SCIENCE, 94
S. is believing BELIEF, 2
seek I will undoubtedly have to s. . . . gainful employment GOVERNMENT, 1
s., and ye shall find BIBLICAL QUOTATIONS, 488
To toil and not to s. for rest FIGHT, 14
We s. him here, we s. him there ABSENCE, 9
We s. it, ere it comes to light PERVERSITY, 3
why s. ye the living among the dead BIBLICAL QUOTATIONS, 450
seem s. a saint when most I play the devil APPEARANCES, 33
Things are not always what they s. APPEARANCES, 5
thinks men honest that but s. to be so INNOCENCE, 9
seeming beguile /The thing I am by s. otherwise APPEARANCES, 32
The s. truth . . . entrap the wisest APPEARANCES, 35
seen blessed are they that have not s., and yet have believed BIBLICAL QUOTATIONS, 372
eye hath not s. BIBLICAL QUOTATIONS, 29
Justice must . . . be s. to be believed JUSTICE, 23
Who has s. the wind WEATHER, 20
sees fool s. not the same tree WISDOM AND FOOLISHNESS, 6
What, when drunk, one s. in other women COMPLIMENTS, 36
Seine Today I spat in the S. WORLD WAR II, 40
seize S. the day PRESENT, 8
seldom s. attribute common sense AGREEMENT, 4
selection biologists studied genetics and natural s. EVOLUTION, 16
Natural S. EVOLUTION, 10
self All censure of a man's s. SELF, 12
nothing . . . is greater . . . than one's s. BODY, 27
sickness enlarges the dimensions of a man's s. ILLNESS, 38
to thine own s. be true BORROWING, 8
self-adjusting No man . . . who has wrestled with a s. card table TECHNOLOGY, 14
self-assertion Self-sufficiency at home, s. abroad NEWSPAPERS, 14
self-conceit the uncouth gravity and supercilious s. of a physician DOCTORS, 91
self-contemplation S. is . . . the symptom of disease PSYCHOANALYSIS, 5
self-dedication the faith, prayer and s. of the King ROYALTY, 26
self-denial S. is not a virtue SELF-DENIAL, 1
self-destruction S. is the effect of cowardice in the highest extreme SUICIDE, 11
self-determination S. is not a mere phrase SELF, 26
self-employed I'm s. ROYALTY, 88
self-indulgence her favourite form of s. SACRIFICE, 2
write an essay on 's.' SELF, 20
self-interest S. speaks all sorts of tongues SELF-INTEREST, 6
selfish all Governments are s. GOVERNMENT, 11
a man becomes slack and s. MARRIAGE, 134
French governments more s. than most GOVERNMENT, 11
I have been a s. being all my life SELFISHNESS, 1
self-knowledge S. is a dangerous thing SELF-KNOWLEDGE, 12
self-love S. is the greatest of all flatterers CONCEIT, 15
S. seems so often unrequited CONCEIT, 14
true s. and social are the same SELF-KNOWLEDGE, 8
self-made A s. man . . . believes in luck SELF-MADE MEN, 3
a s. man who owed his lack of success to nobody SELF-MADE MEN, 2
self-praise S. is no recommendation PRAISE, 1
self-preservation gifted with the . . . instinct for s. SELF-PRESERVATION, 14
self-reflection S. is the school of wisdom WISDOM, 19
self-respect S. – the secure feeling that SELF-RESPECT, 3
Selfridges by reality I mean shops like S. REALITY, 6
self-sacrifice S. enables us to sacrifice SELF, 17
self-sufficiency S. at home, self-assertion abroad NEWSPAPERS, 14
self-sufficient know how to be s. SELF-RELIANCE, 10
self-will now is the time to get rid of s. in him CHILDREN, 47
selling A best-seller . . . because it was s. well BOOKS, 9
A living is made . . . by s. something that everybody needs ARTISTS, 17
the s. of cars in Great Portland Street COMPLIMENTS, 10
semed he s. bisier than he was APPEARANCES, 11
semi-apes We are very slightly changed /From the s. EVOLUTION, 21
senators Do you pray for the s., Dr Hale POLITICIANS, 56
green-rob'd s. of mighty woods TREES, 8
senescence S. begins /And middle age ends OLD AGE, 72
senile a paralytic stroke which was followed by s. decay OLD AGE, 42
a sign that they now consider him s. OLD AGE, 37
seniors earnest advice from my s. ADVICE, 22
sensations life of s. rather than of thoughts SENSATION, 1
sense because Americans won't listen to s. UNITED STATES, 84
between a man of s. and his books BOOKS, 15
Common s. is in medicine the master workman INTELLIGENCE, 5
Common s. is the collection of prejudices PREJUDICE, 4
drowsy numbness pains my s. HEART, 12
Horse s. is a good judgement GAMBLING, 2
Let's talk s. to the American people ENDURANCE, 23
Money is like a sixth s. MONEY, 30
Much Madness is divinest S. MADNESS, 8
seldom attribute common s. AGREEMENT, 4
Take care of the s. MEANING, 2
The sound must seem an echo to the s. WRITING, 33
trained and organized common s. SCIENCE, 48
senses If Parson lost his s. ANIMALS, 15
sensible S. men are all of the same religion RELIGION, 24
sensitive more s. one is to great art ART, 3
sensual The only s. pleasure without vice MUSIC, 24
sent If this belief from heaven be s. MANKIND, 72
sentence S. first – verdict afterwards INJUSTICE, 6
structure of the . . . British s. GRAMMAR, 3
sentences Backward ran s. JOURNALISM, 20
The most attractive s. are not perhaps the wisest LANGUAGE, 42
sentiment Sentimentality is only s. SENTIMENTALITY, 4
sentimentality S. is a superstructure covering brutality SENTIMENTALITY, 2
sentiments high s. always win in the end NOBILITY, 4
sentinels men . . . who stand as s. in the avenues of fame CRITICS, 8
separation prepare for a s. SEPARATION, 4
they should declare the causes which impel them to . . . s. INDEPENDENCE, 3
September Clear in the cool S. morn UNITED STATES, 64
Thirty days hath S., /April, June, and November NURSERY RHYMES, 56
Septuagint The S. minus the Apostles NUMBERS, 6
sepulchre a new s., wherein was never man yet laid BIBLICAL QUOTATIONS, 367
no man knoweth of his s. BIBLICAL QUOTATIONS, 72
the stone taken away from the s. BIBLICAL QUOTATIONS, 368
To famous men all the earth is a s. FAME, 25
sepulchres whited s. BIBLICAL QUOTATIONS, 527
seraphims the s.: each one had six wings BIBLICAL QUOTATIONS, 252
Seraphs Mammon wins his way where S. might despair MATERIALISM, 7
serf No man should be a s. SLAVERY, 6
sergeant S. Pepper's Lonely Hearts Club Band BOOK, SONG, AND PLAY TITLES, 14
serious a damned s. business WAR, 166
A joke's a very s. thing HUMOR, 14
a noble nature, . . . treats . . . a s. subject POETRY, 3
Mix a little foolishness with your s. plans FOOLISHNESS, 14
they are too *s.* FRANCE, 17
seriously Everything must be taken s., nothing tragically PERSPECTIVE, 4
sermons Ever since his s. were discontinued SERMONS, 3
He that takes pleasure to hear s. PLEASURE, 31
serpent sharper than a s.'s tooth DULLNESS, 1
that old s. BIBLICAL QUOTATIONS, 592
the s. beguiled me BIBLICAL QUOTATIONS, 188
the s. was more subtil ANIMALS, 4
servant for the last time in my life, Your Humble S. ARGUMENTS, 17
speak, Lord; for thy s. heareth BIBLICAL QUOTATIONS, 608
The cracked looking glass of a s. IRELAND, 12
the politician poses as the s. POLITICIANS, 39
thou good and faithful s. BIBLICAL QUOTATIONS, 534
servants Few men have been admired by their s. ADMIRATION, 10
good s., but bad masters PASSION, 5

half of them prefer hiring their s. for life SERVANTS, 2
he wouldn't have white s. RACE, 17
part of English middle-class education is devoted to the training of s. CLASS, 54
S. should not be ill CLASS, 10
Socialists treat their s. with respect POLITICS, 136
We teachers can only help . . . as s. EDUCATION, 62
serve capacity to permit his ministers to s. him ROYALTY, 91
if thou . . . s. the Lord, prepare . . . for temptation BIBLICAL QUOTATIONS, 100
They also s. who only stand and wait SERVICE, 5
served I must have things daintily s. ETIQUETTE, 1
Youth will be s. SATISFACTION, 1
service I will see you in the vestry after s. CLERGY, 11
Small s. is true s. SERVICE, 6
services Sometimes give your s. for nothing PHILANTHROPY, 1
serviettes kiddies have crumpled the s. ETIQUETTE, 1
servitude delivered them from s. to other lands ROYALTY, 9
Sesame Open S. SUPERNATURAL, 2
sessions s. of sweet silent thought REGRET, 23
set best plain s. VIRTUE, 1
s. thine house in order BIBLICAL QUOTATIONS, 408
sets on which the sun never s. BRITISH EMPIRE, 7
setter up Proud s. and puller down of kings INFLUENCE, 9
setting clouds that gather round the s. sun MORTALITY, 21
settled No question is ever s. /Until ARGUMENTS, 19
Thank God, that's s. BORROWING, 9
Settlement coach and six horses through the Act of S. IRELAND, 18
seven his acts being s. ages HUMAN CONDITION, 22
sealed with s. seals BIBLICAL QUOTATIONS, 586
S. for the s. stars in the sky ANONYMOUS, 45
S. swans a-swimming CHRISTMAS, 17
the s. pillared worthy house LOVE, 93
The S. Year Itch SEX, 11
wisdom . . . hath hewn out her s. pillars BIBLICAL QUOTATIONS, 571
seventh God . . . rested on the s. day BIBLICAL QUOTATIONS, 180
seventy Being over s. is like being engaged in a war OLD AGE, 93
Being s. is not a sin OLD AGE, 67
Oh, to be s. again LUST, 6
sever a tie that only death can s. MARRIAGE, 95
severe if prolonged it cannot be s. SUFFERING, 29
severity Summer has set in with its usual s. SUMMER, 4
sewage piped growing volumes of s. into the sea ENVIRONMENT, 4
sewer s. in a glass-bottomed boat CORRUPTION, 14
sex As we make s. less secretive, we may rob it of its power SEX, 100
Christian view of s. SEX, 87
Continental people have s. life ENGLISH, 27
Everything . . . Wanted to Know About S. SEX, 86
farmyard world of s. ANIMALISM, 2
For all the pseudo-sophistication of twentieth-century s. theory SEX, 39
Freud found s. an outcast in the outhouse SEX, 112
have s. or appear on television OPPORTUNITY, 22
His excessive emphasis on s. SEX, 91
How can I . . . dislike a s. to which Your Majesty belongs MISOGYNY, 2
If s. is such a natural phenomenon SEX, 66
if there was a third s. MEN, 13
In the s.-war thoughtlessness is the weapon of the male SEXES, 8
Is s. dirty SEX, 1
Is S. Necessary SEX, 104
it's s. with someone you love SEX, 3
Literature is mostly about having s. LITERATURE, 15
make s. funny SEX, 9
meant us to have group s. SEX, 18
Money, it turned out, was exactly like s. MONEY, 7
much more fundamental than s. MONEY, 17
No more about s. SEX, 32
no more weakness than is natural to her s. WOMEN, 116
No s. is better than bad s. SEX, 40
No s. without responsibility SEX, 61
Nothing nauseates me more than promiscuous s. PROMISCUITY, 5
People should be very free with s. HOMOSEXUALITY, 9
Personally I know nothing about s. SEX, 37
poor honest s., like dying, should be a private matter SEX, 32
Pornography is the attempt to insult s. PORNOGRAPHY, 3
professed tyrant to their s. MISOGYNY, 3
promiscuous s. in and out of season SEX, 57
S. and the Single Girl SEX, 19
S. between a man and a woman SEX, 6
s. has been a very private, secretive activity SEX, 100
S. is one of the nine reasons for reincarnation SEX, 68
S. is something I really don't understand SEX, 92
'S.,' . . . 'is the gateway to life.' SEX, 13
s. . . . must itself be subject . . . to evolution SEXES, 5
s. plays a more important part in the life of woman SEX, 97
the s. novel is now normal NOVELS, 15
To defend society from s. is no one's business CENSORSHIP, 2
we English have s. on the brain ENGLISH, 30
You mustn't think I advocate perpetual s. PROMISCUITY, 5
sexes husbands and wives . . . belong to different s. SEXES, 11
more difference within the s. than between them SEXES, 7
the psychic of human relationship between the s. SEX, 51
the . . . rift between the s. is . . . widened SEXES, 25
sexton went and told the s. PUNS, 7
sexual avowed purpose is to excite s. desire PORNOGRAPHY, 5
Civilized people cannot fully satisfy their s. instinct without love SEX, 90
Industrial relations are like s. relations INDUSTRIAL RELATIONS, 2
music throatily . . . s. MUSIC, 23
The discussion of the s. problem SEX, 51
sexuality S. is the lyricism of the masses SEX, 16
shabby For tamed and s. tigers ANIMALS, 15
shade a green thought in a green s. OBLIVION, 3
inviolable s. HOPE, 7
No s., no shine, no butterflies, no bees MONTHS, 10
Nothing grows well in the s. GREATNESS, 5
the s. /Of that which once was great REGRET, 28
shadow be caves . . . in which his s. will be shown GOD, 45
lose the substance by grasping at the s. GREED, 5
unhappy s. SORROW, 4
Who live under the s. of a war WAR, 152
Your s. at morning DUST, 4
shadows brooding tragedy and its dark s. can be lightened HISTORY, 14
half sick of s. MARRIAGE, 139
s. to-night /Have struck more terror FEAR, 20
The s. that I feared so long BLINDNESS, 5
shak'd when degree is s. ORDER, 4
shake I will s. my little finger – and there will be no more Tito INFLUENCE, 10
Shakespeare A strange, horrible business, . . . good enough for S.'s day CRITICISM, 61
Besides S. and me, who do you think there is CONCEIT, 17
he had read S. and found him weak in chemistry SCIENTISTS, 13
reading S. by flashes of lightning CRITICISM, 14
S., I come LAST WORDS, 26
the making up of a S. or a Milton SCIENTISTS, 4
the right to criticize S. CRITICISM, 58
shaking After s. hands with a Greek MISTRUST, 1
all these great interests entrusted to the s. hand POLITICIANS, 118
Shakspeare who speak the tongue /That S. spake FREEDOM, 63
Shalimar Pale hands I loved beside the S. LOVE, 78
shambles Our civilization is founded on the s. DEATH, 84
shame expense of spirit in a waste of s. LUST, 9
Neither s. nor physical pain have any . . . effect PAIN, 5
shamefaced Perjury . . . is truth that is s. TRUTH, 22
shape The S. of Things to Come FUTURE, 15
shapely it's . . . more important for a theory to be s., than . . . true THEORY, 8
share s. in the good fortunes of the mighty INJUSTICE, 4
shares Fair S. for All EQUALITY, 13
Sharon the rose of S. BIBLICAL QUOTATIONS, 622
sharp those who have stout hearts and s. swords RUTHLESSNESS, 8
sharper the word of God is . . . s. than any two-edged sword BIBLICAL QUOTATIONS, 234
shaves man who s. and takes a train TRAVEL, 43
Shaw G. B. S. POPULARITY, 8
George Bernard S. is sadly miscast CRITICISM, 59
Mr S. . . . has never written any poetry WRITERS, 9
S.'s mind . . . was still better than anyone else's WRITERS, 63
she s. is my country still PATRIOTISM, 9
S.-who-must-be-obeyed WOMAN'S ROLE, 4
shears marriage . . . resembles a pair of s. MARRIAGE, 129
sheathe never s. the sword WAR, 12
Sheba the queen of S. BIBLICAL QUOTATIONS, 399
shed s. . . . for the remission of sins BIBLICAL QUOTATIONS, 540
shedding without s. of blood is no remission BIBLICAL QUOTATIONS, 238
sheep as a shepherd divideth his s. from the goats BIBLICAL QUOTATIONS, 536
A s. in s.'s clothing WEAKNESS, 3
Baa, baa, black s. NURSERY RHYMES, 4
feed my s. BIBLICAL QUOTATIONS, 374
good shepherd giveth his life for the s. BIBLICAL QUOTATIONS, 341
hungry s. look up, and are not fed CORRUPTION, 6
I have found my s. which was lost BIBLICAL QUOTATIONS, 438
like lost s. BOOK OF COMMON PRAYER, THE, 3
make a man by standing a s. PUBLIC, 4
not armies . . . but flocks of s. DELUSION, 3
savaged by a dead s. INSULTS, 57
s.'s clothing BIBLICAL QUOTATIONS, 491
The mountain s. are sweeter GREED, 10
the s. . . . know his voice BIBLICAL QUOTATIONS, 339
The s.'s in the meadow NURSERY RHYMES, 28
the wolf in the s.'s clothing APPEARANCES, 8
useless for the s. to pass resolutions in favour of vegetarianism ARGUMENTS, 8
shelf The dust and silence of the upper s. DUST, 6
Shelley S. and Keats were . . . up to date in . . . chemical knowledge POETS, 20
S. had a hyper-thyroid face APPEARANCE, 59
the right sphere for S.'s genius POETS, 1
shells shrill demented choirs of wailing s. MEMORIALS, 12
With silver bells and cockle s. GARDENS, 1
shelter Our s. from the stormy blast RELIGION, 75
Shenandoah O, S., I long to hear you ANONYMOUS, 66
shepherd Go, for they call you, S., from the hill SUMMONS, 1
he that entereth in by the door is the s. BIBLICAL QUOTATIONS, 339
I am the good s. BIBLICAL QUOTATIONS, 341
This is the weather the s. shuns WEATHER, 15
shepherds Governments needs to have both s. and butchers GOVERNMENT, 41
s. abiding in the field BIBLICAL QUOTATIONS, 419
s. watch'd their flocks CHRISTMAS, 20
Sherard S. Blaw, the dramatist who had discovered himself WRITERS, 49
sherry With first-rate s. flowing into second-rate whores MEDIOCRITY, 7
shield the s. of faith BIBLICAL QUOTATIONS, 119
shift for coming down let me s. for myself EXECUTION, 25
shilling you don't happen to have the s. about you now BEQUESTS, 2
Shiloh until S. come BIBLICAL QUOTATIONS, 226
shimmy Put thy s. on, Lady Chatterley PARTING, 7
shine s. on, s. on, harvest moon MOON, 6
shining A woman of so s. loveliness BEAUTY, 42
shins long dresses, . . . cover a multitude of s. CLOTHES, 23

ship as the smart s. grew . . . grew the Iceberg too BOATS, 9
A whale s. was my Yale College EDUCATION, 59
being in a s. is being in a jail BOATS, 10
Don't give up the s. LAST WORDS, 54
I have not been on a s. . . . they still call me 'Admiral' INSULTS, 2
places his s. alongside that of an enemy WAR, 111
S. me somewheres east of Suez DESIRE, 9
The s. follows Soviet custom CLASS, 48
They did not, . . . so much as sink . . . one s. WAR, 3
ships Heart of oak are our s. COURAGE, 14
I spied three s. come sailing by ANONYMOUS 8
little s. of England brought the Army home BOATS, 8
S. that pass in the night NIGHT, 8
something wrong with our bloody s. BOATS, 1
stately s. go on NOSTALGIA, 24
the face that launch'd a thousand s. BEAUTY, 25
We've got the s., we've got the men, we've got the money too FIGHT, 12
shipwreck husbands and wives make s. of their lives MARRIAGE, 56
Old age is a s. OLD AGE, 40
shirt no s. or collar ever comes back twice NEGLECT, 2
shit a s. about the lira POLITICS, 106
I could . . . *s.* better lyrics CRITICISM, 43
I don't give a s. what happens POLITICS, 107
Isn't God a s. BIBLE, 4
the sun shining ten days a year and s. in the streets ENGLAND, 26
when you s.? Singing, it's the same thing SINGING, 1
shock Anybody can s. a baby SIMPLICITY, 8
deliberately set out to s. THEATER, 12
shocked how to be amused rather than s. AGE, 18
shocking little man wears a s. bad hat CLOTHES, 25
shocks s. /That flesh is heir to FORTUNE, 6
shoemaker I take my shoes from the s. RELIGION, 37
The s.'s son EXPEDIENCY, 3
shoes before you let the sun in, mind it wipes its s. CLEANNESS, 10
I take my s. from the shoemaker RELIGION, 37
s. and ships and sealing wax NONSENSE, 9
shook Ten Days that S. the World RUSSIAN REVOLUTION, 7
shoot do not s. the pianist EFFORT, 7
except to s. rabbits and hit his father on the jaw NASTINESS, 5
It is not the business of generals to s. one another GENERALS, 6
S., if you must, this old gray head PATRIOTISM, 43
they could s. me in my absence JUSTICE, 2
shooting A bit of s. takes your mind off VIOLENCE, 2
war minus the s. SPORT AND GAMES, 17
shop All English s. assistants are Miltonists SERVICE, 4
A man must keep a little back s. SOLITUDE, 13
shop-keepers A nation of s. BRITAIN, 2
England is a nation of s. ENGLISH, 31
shopping Today you're unhappy? . . . Go s. MATERIALISM, 20
shore adieu! my native s. DEPARTURE, 4
riverrun, past Eve and Adam's, from swerve of s. RIVERS, 3
waves make towards the pebbled s. TIME, 41
Shoreditch When I grow rich, /Say the bells of S. LONDON, 18
shores eternal whisperings around Desolate s. SEA, 8
short Good things, when s., are twice as good BREVITY, 2
Is not life . . . too s. . . . to bore ourselves BOREDOM, 9
it will take a long while to make it s. WRITING, 42
Life, . . . is much too s. to be taken seriously LIFE, 13
Life is too s. to do anything . . . one can pay others to do WORK, 20
make the beat keep time with s. steps FUNERALS, 1
s. and simple annals of the poor POVERTY, 15
the life of man, solitary, poor, nasty, brutish, and s. HUMAN CONDITION, 13
short We have s. time to stay, as you TRANSIENCE, 15
shortage a s. of coal and fish . . . at the same time INCOMPETENCE, 1
shorter not had the time to make it s. VERBOSITY, 6
s. by a head ROYALTY, 54
shortest I never realized that I'd end up being the s. knight of the year PUNS, 22
the s. works are always the best BREVITY, 5
shorthand career that made the Recording Angel think seriously about . . . s. EPITAPHS, 5
shot had them all s. LAST WORDS, 58
he once s. a bookseller PUBLISHING, 4
they've s. the wrong person INSULTS, 107
shots They really are bad s. ASSASSINATION, 4
shoulder-blade I have a left s. CONCEIT, 11
shoulders it is by standing on the s. of giants PROGRESS, 17
shout S. with the largest MAJORITY, 3
show I have that within which passes s. MOURNING, 10
I often wish they would s. off a little more OSTENTATION, 4
showers Sweet April s. MONTHS, 12
shows All my s. are great BOASTS, 3
shreds A thing of s. and patches MANKIND, 26
Shrewsbury They hang us now in S. jail: /The whistles blow forlorn EXECUTION, 16
shriek That s. and sweat in pigmy wars TRIVIALITY, 15
shrimp a s. learns to whistle COMMUNISM, 7
shrine Melancholy has her . . . s. DELIGHT, 7
shrink all the boards did s. WATER, 2
shuffled s. off this mortal coil FORTUNE, 6
the human pack is s. and cut EDUCATION, 53
Shulamite return, return, O S. BIBLICAL QUOTATIONS, 636
shut when I was there it seemed to be s. PLACES, 17
shy Why so s., my pretty Thomasina SHYNESS, 3
shyness S. is just egotism out of its depth SHYNESS, 4
sick A person seldom falls s. HUMAN NATURE, 10
Are you s., or are you sullen HOLISTIC MEDICINE, 6
a s., its prison BODY, 1
being s. with other people singing PARTIES, 9
Be not slow to visit the s. ILLNESS, 12
Dante makes me s. LAST WORDS, 13
Every man who feels well is a s. man ILLNESS, 60
He that eats till he is s. GREED, 4
I am s. at heart COMFORT, 3
I deny the lawfulness of telling a lie to a s. man FRANKNESS, 3
If you are physically s. MENTAL ILLNESS, 2
if you don't object if I'm s. REPARTEE, 6
In the old-fashioned days when a man got s. MEDICINE, 54
I only take money from s. people HYPOCHONDRIA, 4
It is dainty to be s. ILLNESS, 25
it is useless to tell him what he or his s. child needs is not medicine HEALTHY LIVING, 39
I will use treatment to help the s. MEDICINE, 37
make any man s. to hear her INSINCERITY, 4
medicines when well used restore health to the s. REMEDIES, 40
she cheats the s. and the dying with illusions NATURE, 19
S. minds must be healed as well as sick bodies HOLISTIC MEDICINE, 7
so many poor s. people in the streets full of sores ILLNESS, 53
The multitude of the s. ILLNESS, 24
The prayer that . . . heals the s. FAITH, 13
There is no curing a s. man REMEDIES, 6
The s. are the greatest danger for the healthy ILLNESS, 50
the s. man hands you gold in return REMEDIES, 9
The s. man is a parasite of society PATIENTS, 15
The s. man is the garden of the physicians PATIENTS, 2
the very first requirement in a Hospital that it should do the s. no harm HOSPITALS, 8
the wary fox said . . . to the s. lion MISTRUST, 5
'Tis healthy to be s. sometimes HEALTH, 22
Tobacco hic, /Will make a man well if he be s. SMOKING, 2
To be s. is to enjoy monarchal prerogatives ILLNESS, 39
To heal the s. EDUCATION, 58
Treat the man who is s. PATIENTS, 10
We have on our hands a s. man DECLINE, 7
you usually find that you are s. ILLNESS, 28
sickness As *s.* is the greatest misery SOLITUDE, 6
Bathe early every day and s. will avoid you CLEANNESS, 1
He learns to depend on the physician in s. and in health PATIENTS, 9
in s. and in health BOOK OF COMMON PRAYER, THE, 15
In s., respect health principally HEALTH, 3
Love is a s. LOVE, 54
s. enlarges the dimensions of a man's self ILLNESS, 38
S. is felt ILLNESS, 2
S. is single trouble for the sufferer NURSES, 3
S., sin and death . . . do not originate in God RELIGION, 29
S. soaks the purse ILLNESS, 3
S. tells us what we are ILLNESS, 4
Study s. while you are well MEDICINE, 30
the greatest misery of s. is *solitude* SOLITUDE, 6
The problem of economic loss due to s. ILLNESS, 61
The superior doctor prevents s. DOCTORS, 7
To avoid s., eat less HEALTHY LIVING, 17
weary thing is s. ILLNESS, 26
Sidcup If only I could get down to S. PROOF, 6
side A door is what a dog is . . . on the wrong s. of DOGS, 11
a s. dish he hadn't ordered CONTEMPT, 4
He who knows only his own s. . . . knows little SUBJECTIVITY, 4
passed by on the other s. BIBLICAL QUOTATIONS, 432
Time is on our s. FIGHT, 9
sides Do not . . . write on both s. of the paper EXAMINATIONS, 2
said on both s. OBJECTIVITY, 2
We . . . assume that everything has two s. SUBJECTIVITY, 7
sighed They s. for the dawn and thee LOVE, 174
sighs over the Bridge of S. into eternity BRIDGE, 1
S. are the natural language of the heart SPEECH, 17
sight a s. to make an old man young BEAUTY, 40
Out of s. ABSENCE, 2
should I not bear gently the deprivation of s. BLINDNESS, 11
s. is the most perfect and most delightful of all our senses EYES, 2
we walk by faith, not by s. BIBLICAL QUOTATIONS, 51
Who ever loved, that loved not at first s. FIRST IMPRESSIONS, 6
sightless clapped the glass to his s. eye BLINDNESS, 13
When I was s. I cared for nothing BLINDNESS, 4
sights And see all s. from pole to pole SOUL, 3
few more impressive s. in the world SCOTS, 2
sign Jews require a s. BIBLICAL QUOTATIONS, 27
Never s. a walentine SIGNATURES, 1
s. of an ill-spent youth SPORT AND GAMES, 21
the s. 'Members Only' SEX, 70
writing a letter and forgetting to s. his name INSULTS, 12
signal I really do not see the s. BLINDNESS, 12
significance profoundly moral and packed with deep spiritual s. NOVELS, 8
significant s. form ART, 4
signifying S. nothing LIFE, 76
signing I am s. my death warrant PROPHECY, 5
silence a period of s. on your part would be welcome POLITICIANS, 9
Come to me in the s. of the night NOSTALGIA, 22
foster-child of s. and slow time SILENCE, 9
In England there is only s. or scandal ENGLAND, 32
let all the earth keep s. before him BIBLICAL QUOTATIONS, 231
Make him a bishop, and you will s. him CLERGY, 3
My personal hobbies . . . s. SILENCE, 14
occasional flashes of s. DELIGHT, 11
S. is as full of potential wisdom SILENCE, 8
S. is become his mother tongue SILENCE, 6
S. is golden PROVERBS, 362
S. is the best tactic DISTRUST, 2
S. is the perfectest herald of joy JOY, 6
S. is the . . . perfect expression of scorn SILENCE, 13
s. sank /Like music SILENCE, 3
Sorrow and s. are strong ENDURANCE, 9
That man's s. is wonderful to listen to SILENCE, 7
The cruellest lies are . . . told in s. SILENCE, 15
The dust and s. of the upper shelf DUST, 6

snub Vile s.-nose, flat-nosed ass APPEARANCE, 49
snuff time for me to enjoy another pinch of s. EXECUTION, 2
so It is s.. It is not s. ARGUMENTS, 4
soap Man does not live by s. alone CLEANNESS, 4
S. and education . . . are more deadly EDUCATION, 83
S. and water and common sense CLEANNESS, 9
soar to run, though not to s. CRITICISM, 39
sober a s. colouring from an eye MORTALITY, 21
as s. as a Judge DRUNKENNESS, 15
Better sleep with a s. cannibal than a drunken Christian DRUNKENNESS, 21
England should be compulsorily s. FREEDOM, 36
he that will go to bed s. ALCOHOL, 34
How do you look when I'm s. CLOTHES, 14
My mother, drunk or s. PATRIOTISM, 8
one sees in Garbo s. COMPLIMENTS, 36
sedate, s., silent, serious, sad-coloured sect RELIGION, 43
Tomorrow we'll be s. ANONYMOUS, 12
sociable I am a s. worker SOCIETY, 1
Society is no comfort to one not s. SOCIETY, 12
social a great s. and economic experiment ALCOHOL, 39
At s. gatherings he was liable to engage in heated and noisy arguments OBITUARIES, 8
Man is a s. animal SOCIETY, 14
our s. spheres have been widely different REPARTEE, 124
the things which government does . . . s. progress GOVERNMENT, 42
the . . . world was stumbling . . . in s. blindness BLINDNESS, 6
to enter s. life on tiptoe FOOTBALL, 10
true self-love and s. are the same SELF-KNOWLEDGE, 8
socialism as clear as a crystal, the synthesis – German National S. NAZISM, 3
Communism is in fact the completion of S. COMMUNISM, 12
Marxian S. must always remain a portent MARXISM, 6
one word . . . to identify modern s., it was 'Science' SOCIALISM, 25
Only s. would put up with it SOCIALISM, 9
religion of S. SOCIALISM, 3
restating our s. in terms of the scientific revolution SOCIALISM, 24
S. . . . age or a little money will not cure SOCIALISM, 7
s. . . . alien to the British character SOCIALISM, 23
s. . . . as a whole is threatened SOCIALISM, 5
S. can only arrive by bicycle SOCIALISM, 8
S. . . . the conquest of the . . . economy SOCIALISM, 4
the proletariat will . . . wage a class struggle for S. CLASS, 22
the worst advertisement for S. is its adherents CHRISTIANITY, 49
to banish . . . the dark divisive clouds of Marxist s. MARXISM, 16
To the ordinary working man, . . . S. SOCIALISM, 19
Under s. *all* will govern SOCIALISM, 15
unites s. with democracy SOCIALISM, 10
socialist construct the s. order SOCIALISM, 16
I am a s. . . . wish the Labour Party was SOCIALISM, 21
socialists For s., going to bed with the Liberals is POLITICS, 148
intelligent people . . . are s. SOCIALISM, 2
S. treat their servants with respect POLITICS, 136
We are all S. now SOCIALISM, 12
what are you s. going to do about me SOCIALISM, 11
societies range of human s. in time, the other in space MANKIND, 35
society a free s. . . . where it is safe to be unpopular FREEDOM, 57
an age in which human s. dared to think of the health of the whole human race HEALTHY LIVING, 44
a poor s. cannot be too poor POVERTY AND WEALTH, 8
A s. . . . of individuals . . . capable of original thought would probably be unendurable IDEAS, 8
Comedy, we may say, is s. COMEDY, 7
great s. . . . men are more concerned with the quality of their goods SOCIETY, 7
if it be our clothes alone which fit us for s. CLOTHES, 6
impossible, in our condition of s., not to be sometimes a Snob SNOBBERY, 9
In a consumer s. there are . . . two kinds of slaves MATERIALISM, 14
it proved that I was in a civilized s. EXECUTION, 28
Mankind is a closed s. MANKIND, 54
Man was formed for s. SOCIETY, 2
Never speak disrespectfully of S. SNOBBERY, 13
no intellectual s. can flourish where a Jew feels . . . uneasy JEWS, 10
no new baby in the womb of our s. RUSSIA, 4
nothing to distinguish human s. from the farm-yard MANKIND, 59
only possible s. is oneself MISANTHROPY, 5
S., friendship, and love SOLITUDE, 4
S. goes on and on and on IDEAS, 6
S. is no comfort /To one not sociable SOCIETY, 12
S. is now one polish'd horde BORES, 2
s. . . . pays a harlot 25 times as much as it pays its Prime Minister INJUSTICE, 16
s., where none intrudes NATURE, 5
so famous, that it would permit me . . . to break wind in s. FAME, 4
The history of all . . . s. is the history of class struggles CLASS, 26
the opportunity to move . . . upward to the Great S. CIVILIZATION, 8
There are two classes in good s. CLASS, 39
The sick man is a parasite of s. PATIENTS, 15
the transition from the . . . 'closed s.', . . . to the 'open s.' SOCIETY, 10
to change s. and to define its finer values POLITICIANS, 15
transform this s. without a major extension of public ownership SOCIALISM, 14
sociology Children . . . have no use for psychology. They detest s. BOOKS, 42
The technology of medicine has outrun its s. TECHNOLOGY, 12
socks His s. compelled one's attention CLOTHES, 19
sodium Of having discovered S. SCIENTISTS, 3
Sodom S. and . . . Gomorrah BIBLICAL QUOTATIONS, 210
the men of S. were wicked BIBLICAL QUOTATIONS, 206
sodomy Comedy, like s., is an unnatural act COMEDY, 5
rum, s., and the lash NAVY, 5
sofa rather lie on a s. than sweep beneath it LAZINESS, 3
soft I'm not hard – I'm frightfully s. CHARACTER, 28
our love . . . of the mind does not make us s. RESULTS, 6
solar the whole s. and stellar systems COMFORT, 2
soldier a chocolate cream s. SOLDIERS, 13
Ben Battle was a s. bold PUNS, 9
Every French s. carries in his cartridge-pouch SOLDIERS, 8
I never expect a s. to think SOLDIERS, 14
in the s. is flat blasphemy INJUSTICE, 14
strength and majesty the British s. fights SOLDIERS, 7
The s.'s body . . . a stock of accessories SOLDIERS, 11
The summer s. and the sunshine patriot COWARDICE, 6
Tinker, /Tailor, /S., /Sailor NURSERY RHYMES, 60
soldiers Dear comrades, s., sailors and workers RUSSIAN REVOLUTION, 5
English s. fight like lions OFFICERS, 8
Old s. never die OCCUPATIONS, 4
S. are citizens of death's grey land SOLDIERS, 10
when staring at our s. drilling in Berlin ENGLAND, 35
soliciting supernatural s. SUPERNATURAL, 15
solitary Life is for each man a s. cell LIFE, 62
Man is not a s. animal MANKIND, 50
Only s. men know the full joys of friendship FRIENDSHIP, 18
solitude In s. /What happiness SOLITUDE, 11
In s. alone can he know true freedom SOLITUDE, 13
so companionable as s. SOLITUDE, 15
S. is the playfield of Satan SOLITUDE, 14
s.! where are the charms SOLITUDE, 5
the bliss of s. SOLITUDE, 17
the greatest misery of sickness is *s.* SOLITUDE, 6
Whosoever is delighted in s. DELIGHT, 2
Solomon S. Grundy, /Born on a Monday HUMAN CONDITION, 17
S. loved many strange women BIBLICAL QUOTATIONS, 400
the song of songs, which is S.'s BIBLICAL QUOTATIONS, 621
solution A difficulty for every s. BUREAUCRACY, 6
a *total* s. of the Jewish question NAZISM, 2
If you're not part of the s. CONFORMITY, 3
The final s. FASCISM, 5
some I . . . may be s. time LAST WORDS, 61
s. more than others SIMILARITY, 4
You can fool s. of the people all the time DECEPTION, 4
somebody s. may be looking CONSCIENCE, 6
someone I wouldn't be . . . talking to s. like you SNOBBERY, 3
like sleeping with s. else's wife NEWSPAPERS, 5
somer In a s. season SUMMER, 6
Somerset corroboration . . . in the records of S. House HUMILITY, 12
something Everybody was up to s. INTRIGUE, 2
I too hope to become 's.' AMBITION, 11
S. must be done UNEMPLOYMENT, 5
S. nasty in the woodshed EVIL, 11
sometime Why don't you come up s. and see me INVITATIONS, 6
somewhere 'Tis always morning s. BEGINNING, 10
son and Sarah shall have a s. BIBLICAL QUOTATIONS, 208
An only s., sir, might expect more indulgence FAMILY, 24
O Absalom, my s. BIBLICAL QUOTATIONS, 620
the earth is free for every s. and daughter of mankind HUMAN RIGHTS, 8
the form of the fourth is like the S. of God BIBLICAL QUOTATIONS, 60
the S. of man coming . . . with power BIBLICAL QUOTATIONS, 530
the S. of man hath not where to lay his head BIBLICAL QUOTATIONS, 495
the s. of peace BIBLICAL QUOTATIONS, 430
woman, behold thy s. BIBLICAL QUOTATIONS, 364
sonatas The s. of Mozart are unique MUSIC, 40
song I have a s. to sing O SINGING, 2
she will make her goal, which is the end of the s. SONG, 2
the s. of songs, which is Solomon's BIBLICAL QUOTATIONS, 621
the s. that is sung in our hearts MUSIC, 31
they shall not drink wine with a s. BIBLICAL QUOTATIONS, 263
Who loves not wine, woman and s. PLEASURE, 22
songs Sing no sad s. DEATH, 123
Some of the s. . . . will be popular when Bach, Beethoven and Wagner are forgotten SONG, 1
Where are the s. of Spring SPRING, 3
son-in-law The s. also rises NEPOTISM, 1
sonne when soft was the s. SUMMER, 6
sonnet I have three phobias which . . . would make my life as slick as a s. OBSESSIONS, 1
s. is a moment's monument POETRY, 47
son-of-a-bitch The poor s. WRITERS, 41
sons I have a wife, I have s. FAMILY, 32
my four s. who cease not to persecute me CHILDREN, 31
Now we are all s. of bitches NUCLEAR WEAPONS, 3
S. of Belial had a Glorious Time TREASON, 3
soon day returns too s. LOVE, 43
soothe put you to sleep, wake you up, stimulate and s. you all in one DRUGS, 14
sophistry it can contain nothing but s. and illusion ILLUSIONS, 3
Universities incline wits to s. and affectation EDUCATION, 10
sorcery false enchantments and s. ACCUSATION, 3
sores Lazarus . . . laid at his gate, full of s. BIBLICAL QUOTATIONS, 441
sorrow Down, thou climbing s. SORROW, 24
in s. thou shalt bring forth children BIBLICAL QUOTATIONS, 188
Much in s., oft in woe ENDURANCE, 28
One for s. BIRDS, 1
Parting is such sweet s. PARTING, 10
Pure and complete s. is as impossible EMOTION, 6
S. and silence are strong ENDURANCE, 9
S. is tranquillity remembered in emotion SORROW, 15
s. makes us wise SORROW, 27
Tears of eternity and s. SORROW, 11
the Lord . . . give thee joy for this thy s. BIBLICAL QUOTATIONS, 659

There is no greater s. SORROW, 7
Through the night of doubt and s. ENDURANCE, 5
sorrows When s. come, they come not single spies MISFORTUNE, 17
sort that like that s. of place OXFORD, 13
Soudan to you, Fuzzy-Wuzzy, at your 'ome in the S. RACE, 13
soufflé can't make a s. rise twice FOOD, 49
sought by night on my bed I s. him whom my soul loveth BIBLICAL QUOTATIONS, 628
Love s. is good LOVE, 168
Pleasure is . . . seldom found where it is s. PLEASURE, 15
soul A healthy body is the guest-chamber of the s. BODY, 1
And never once possess our s. SOUL, 3
Anger is one of the sinews of the s. ANGER, 6
Artists are not engineers of the s. ART, 11
a . . . s. like season'd timber VIRTUE, 14
become a living s. DEATH, 179
Body and s. cannot be separated for purposes of treatment HOLISTIC MEDICINE, 7
company, . . . have neither a s. to lose nor a body to kick BUSINESS, 24
Disease is . . . the result of conflict between s. and mind SOUL, 4
education is a leading out of what is . . . in the pupil's s. EDUCATION, 81
Education is . . . the s. of a society EDUCATION, 22
every subject's s. is his own SOUL, 16
Fair seed-time had my s. SOUL, 19
His s. is marching on GRAVE, 6
his s. is satisfied with what is assigned to him CONTENTMENT, 1
I am positive I have a s. SOUL, 17
I am the captain of my s. FATE, 10
Impropriety is the s. of wit HUMOR, 41
In mystery our s. abides HEART, 2
I pray the Lord my s. to keep ANONYMOUS, 64
it must be inspired with s. MEDICINE, 58
Man has no Body distinct from his S. BODY, 7
my s. doth magnify the Lord BIBLICAL QUOTATIONS, 413
My s. in agony SOLITUDE, 2
my s. is exceeding sorrowful BIBLICAL QUOTATIONS, 542
My s. is full of whispered song BLINDNESS, 5
my s. is white RACE, 5
Never mind about my s. . . . get my tie right PAINTING, 8
Nobody can have the s. of me WOMEN, 65
No coward s. is mine COURAGE, 4
Nowhere can man find a quieter . . . retreat than in his own s. PRAYER, 25
passion in the human s. MUSIC, 26
possessive outrage done to a free solitary human s. FAMILY, 45
Raises from Hell a human s. HELL, 1
real dark night of the s. SOUL, 10
Safeguard the health both of body and s. HEALTH, 6
seal the hushed casket of my s. SLEEP, 23
than that one s. . . . should commit one single venial sin SIN, 23
The body is truly the garment of the s. BODY, 6
The British postgraduate student is a lonely forlorn s. EDUCATION, 53
The dark night of the s. DARKNESS, 13
the . . . essence of a human s. BOOKS, 12
the eyes are the windows of the s. EYES, 3
The human body is the best picture of the human s. SOUL, 18
the iron enter into his s. BITTERNESS, 4
the iron has entered his s. INSULTS, 88
The Life and S., the man who will never go home PARTIES, 11
the physicians separate the s. from the body HOLISTIC MEDICINE, 8
The s. hath not her generous aspirings SMOKING, 25
the s. is not more than the body BODY, 27
The s. is subject to health and disease SOUL, 14
the s. of a martyr with the intellect of an advocate POLITICIANS, 11
The s. started at the knee-cap ANIMALISM, 5
The S. that rises with us, our life's Star METAPHYSICS, 6
The voice of the sea speaks to the s. SEA, 3
Thy rapt s. sitting in thine eyes SOUL, 15
Thy s. was like a star, and dwelt apart NOBILITY, 9
turn'st mine eyes into my very s. SELF-KNOWLEDGE, 10
when the s. is oppressed so is the body MELANCHOLY, 9
souls Above the vulgar flight of common s. SUPERIORITY, 11
a follower of hounds to become a shepherd of s. CHARACTER, 11
damp s. of the housemaids MELANCHOLY, 5
Our s. have sight of that immortal sea METAPHYSICS, 7
So long as our s. and personalities are in harmony all is joy and peace SOUL, 4
S. of poets dead and gone PUBLIC HOUSES, 3
their s. dwell in the house of tomorrow CHILDREN, 29
the s. of five hundred . . . Newtons SCIENTISTS, 4
The s. of women are so small WOMEN, 27
Two s. dwell, alas! in my breast CONFLICT, 6
Two s. with but a single thought LOVE, 98
You may house their bodies but not their s. CHILDREN, 29
soul-sides the meanest of his creatures /Boasts two s. HYPOCRISY, 6
sound full of s. and fury LIFE, 76
s. of a great Amen MUSIC, 36
The hills are alive with the s. of music MUSIC, 19
The most persistent s. . . . through men's history WAR, 88
The s. must seem an echo to the sense WRITING, 33
the s. of many waters BIBLICAL QUOTATIONS, 584
The s. of the English county families ARISTOCRACY, 21
the trumpet shall s. BIBLICAL QUOTATIONS, 49
whispering s. of the cool colonnade TREES, 4
sounded last one s. kinda high BASEBALL, 6
sounding s. brass BIBLICAL QUOTATIONS, 44
sounds Music is the arithmetic of s. MUSIC, 16
the s. will take care of themselves MEANING, 2
soup concludes that it will . . . make better s. IDEALISM, 7
S. of the evening, beautiful S. FOOD, 21
Take the s. away FOOD, 38
sour How s. sweet music is ORDER, 3
I am sure the grapes are s. ENVY, 4
source her Majesty . . . must not . . . look upon me as a s. of income TAXATION, 12
sourest sweetest things turn s. CORRUPTION, 12
south beaker full of the warm S. ALCOHOL, 47
go s. in the winter READING, 5
hardly be a town in the S. of England ENGLAND, 37
South Africa God's will to lead . . . S. through defeat and humiliation PLACES, 36
Three words made peace and union in S. PLACES, 6
South African The S. Police would leave no stone unturned PLACES, 34
southern mother bore me in the s. wild RACE, 5
souvenir give him my autograph as a s. WORLD WAR II, 35
sovereign A Subject and a S. are clean different things LAST WORDS, 15
Here lies our s. lord the King EPITAPHS, 37
he will have no s. MONARCHY, 9
The S. has, under a constitutional monarchy . . . three rights MONARCHY, 3
The s. is absolute ROYALTY, 36
When I forget my s. LOYALTY, 14
sovereigns rather than that the s. and magistrates should be destroyed REBELLION, 11
Soviet Communism is S. power plus the electrification COMMUNISM, 8
S. people want full-blooded . . . democracy RUSSIA, 2
The ship follows S. custom CLASS, 48
Soviets All Power to the S. RUSSIAN REVOLUTION, 1
sow Ireland is the old s. IRELAND, 11
I took the right s. by the ear INFLUENCE, 13
like a s. that hath overwhelm'd all her litter HUMOR, 55
s. . . . in righteousness, reap in mercy BIBLICAL QUOTATIONS, 243
that man hath the s. by the right ear POLITICS, 66
soweth whatsoever a man s., that shall he also reap BIBLICAL QUOTATIONS, 173
sown A lovelier flower / . . . was never s. DEATH, 178
space annihilate but s. and time LOVE, 113
In the United States there is more s. UNITED STATES, 59
Outer s. is no place SPACE, 4
range of human societies in time, the other in s. MANKIND, 35
spade When I see a s. I call it a s. REPARTEE, 124
Spain Farewell and adieu to you, Ladies of S. ANONYMOUS, 18
spam he wanted steak and they offered s. DISAPPOINTMENT, 5
span Life's short s. forbids us . . . far-reaching hopes MORTALITY, 13
Spaniards the S. seem wiser than they are APPEARANCES, 9
time to win this game, and to thrash the S. SPORT AND GAMES, 6
spaniel the cur dog of Britain and s. of Spain POLITICIANS, 107
Spanish I speak S. to God LANGUAGE, 11
singed the S. king's beard WAR, 53
spare bread enough and to s. BIBLICAL QUOTATIONS, 439
Brother, can you s. a dime MISQUOTATION, 16
I can't s. this man; he fights OFFICERS, 9
S. all I have WORLD-WEARINESS, 2
s. the rod CHILDREN, 1
Woodman, s. that tree TREES, 12
spareth he that s. his rod hateth his son BIBLICAL QUOTATIONS, 573
sparkling scorn ride s. in her eyes CONTEMPT, 5
sparrow a s. alight upon my shoulder . . . I was more distinguished by that HONOR, 9
I, said the S., /With my bow and arrow NURSERY RHYMES, 68
It is a city where you can see a s. fall IRELAND, 15
sparrowhawks S., Ma'am REMEDIES, 58
sparrows five s. . . . not one of them is forgotten BIBLICAL QUOTATIONS, 436
one of the s. . . . flew . . . through the hall LIFE, 9
spasm a lonely s. of helpless agongy DEATH, 84
statesmanship. I call it an emotional s. POLITICS, 18
spat So he stood up and s. on the ceiling ANONYMOUS, 92
Today I s. in the Seine WORLD WAR II, 40
speak I didn't s. up NAZISM, 6
I'll s. for the man POLITICS, 105
I only s. right on SPEECHES, 11
I want . . . art /To s. and purpose not DECEPTION, 6
Let him now s. BOOK OF COMMON PRAYER, THE, 14
more than a moral duty to s. one's mind FRANKNESS, 5
Never s. ill of the dead DEATH, 11
province of knowledge to s. KNOWLEDGE, 19
some . . . s. . . . before they think IMPETUOSITY, 2
s., Lord; for thy servant heareth BIBLICAL QUOTATIONS, 608
s. to God as if men were listening RIGHTEOUSNESS, 10
S. when you're spoken to MANNERS, 2
time to think before I s. SPEECH, 9
When I think, I must s. WOMEN, 102
Whereof one cannot s. SILENCE, 16
speaking An Englishman's way of s. CLASS, 23
People talking without s. FUTILITY, 12
when . . . s., they do not know what they are saying SPEECHES, 6
special a s. relationship POLITICS, 35
I only smoke on s. occasions EXCUSES, 1
specialist A general practitioner can no more become a s. SPECIALISTS, 7
A medical chest s. is long-winded about the short-winded SPECIALISTS, 3
called a nerve s. because it sounds better PSYCHIATRY, 35
Choose your s. and you choose your disease SPECIALISTS, 2
No man can be a pure s. SPECIALISTS, 9
S. – A man who knows more and more about less and less EXPERTS, 7
The s. is a man who fears the other subjects SPECIALISTS, 5
specialists Given one well-trained physician . . . than ten s. SPECIALISTS, 6
s. . . . tend to think in grooves EXPERTS, 8
species Pain is the correlative of some s. of wrong SUFFERING, 32
S. do not evolve toward perfection SURVIVAL, 6
the idea of its death as a s. NUCLEAR WEAPONS, 11
the one s. I wouldn't mind seeing vanish DOGS, 3
Women exist . . . solely for the propagation of the s. WOMAN'S ROLE, 8

s. waters are sweet BIBLICAL QUOTATIONS, 572
your wife . . . is a receiver of s. goods INSULTS, 72
stomach A hungry s. has no ears HUNGER, 8
a little wine for thy s.'s sake DRINKS, 5
An army marches on its s. FOOD, 56
my s. must just digest in its waistcoat ALCOHOL, 74
No one can worship God . . . on an empty s. BUSINESS, 31
The way to a man's heart is through his s. FOOD, 30
use a little wine for thy s.'s sake ALCOHOL, 21
with enforcing morality on the s. ILLNESS, 31
You can't think rationally on an empty s. THINKING, 10
stomachs Napoleon's armies used to march on their s. HISTORY, 36
stone and youth s. dead WAR, 139
a s. most precious BIBLICAL QUOTATIONS, 602
Constant dripping hollows out a s. PERSISTENCE, 10
draw in their horns or . . . bomb them into the S. Age THREATS, 7
Dripping water hollows out a s. PERSISTENCE, 11
he that is without sin . . . let him first cast a s. BIBLICAL QUOTATIONS, 334
if his son ask bread, will he give him a s. BIBLICAL QUOTATIONS, 489
Jackson standing like a s. wall DETERMINATION, 4
Like a rolling s. TRAVEL, 14
not be left here one s. upon another BIBLICAL QUOTATIONS, 528
precious s. set in the silver sea EARTH, 16
raised not a s. FUNERALS, 14
tables of s., and a law AUTHORITARIANISM, 3
the final s. . . . in the foundation of St Petersburg VICTORY, 17
the s. taken away from the sepulchre BIBLICAL QUOTATIONS, 368
Virtue is like a rich s. VIRTUE, 1
Stonehenge bring S. to Nyasaland CIVILIZATION, 2
stones s. kissed by the English dead WAR, 118
the s. would immediately cry out BIBLICAL QUOTATIONS, 445
stony fell upon s. places BIBLICAL QUOTATIONS, 506
stood We should have s. in bed DEFEAT, 9
stoop A constitutional king must learn to s. MONARCHY, 15
stoops When lovely woman s. to folly GULLIBILITY, 2
stop come to the end: then s. ORDER, 1
s. everyone from doing it PERVERSITY, 4
S. the World, I Want to Get Off WORLD-WEARINESS, 6
time . . . must have a s. DEATH, 136
when the kissing had to s. BOOK TITLES, 7
stopped man has s. moving EVOLUTION, 5
s. short – never to go again CLOCKS, 4
stops The buck s. here RESPONSIBILITY, 19
storage A library is thought in cold s. BOOKS, 41
stories She likes s. that make her cry SENTIMENTALITY, 5
storm After a s. comes a calm OPTIMISM, 1
a mighty s. . . . to freshen us up CHANGE, 3
lovers fled away into the s. DEPARTURE, 7
S. in a Teacup TRIVIALITY, 2
storms greater s. in politics than you'll ever find at sea OCCUPATIONS, 13
s. of prayer EXCESS, 15
The summer talk stopped . . . /Before the s. ERROR, 1
story A cruel s. runs on wheels CRUELTY, 4
brother-in-law wrote an unusual murder s. BOOKS, 46
Not that the s. need be long WRITING, 42
novel tells a s. NOVELS, 4
Tell me the old, old s. CHRISTIANITY, 40
stout those who have s. hearts and sharp swords RUTHLESSNESS, 8
stoutness I see no objection to s. OBESITY, 11
straight If Michelangelo had been s. HOMOSEXUALITY, 13
the street which is called S. BIBLICAL QUOTATIONS, 7
straight-jacket the discredited s. of the past POLITICS, 133
strain'd quality of mercy is not s. MERCY, 4
strait matters not how s. the gate FATE, 10
s. is the gate BIBLICAL QUOTATIONS, 490
straitened to face s. circumstances at home POVERTY, 25
Strand I walk down the S. FASHION, 6
Let's all go down the S. LONDON, 6
wandering on a foreign s. HOMESICKNESS, 6
strange A s., horrible business, . . . good enough for Shakespeare's day CRITICISM, 61
I perish through great grief in a s. land BIBLICAL QUOTATIONS, 452
it's a jolly s. world CONFUSION, 2
laughing and jeering at everything . . . s. ENGLISH, 33
pass my declining years saluting s. women OLD AGE, 71
The Law of England is a very s. one LAW, 11
truth is always s. STRANGENESS, 2
strangeness s. in the proportion BEAUTY, 6
stranger a s. in a strange land ALIENATION, 1
Look, s., at this island now DELIGHT, 1
S. than fiction STRANGENESS, 2
strangers better s. SEPARATION, 6
s. and pilgrims on the earth BIBLICAL QUOTATIONS, 240
the kindness of s. CHARITY, 27
strangled down which ideas are lured and . . . s. BUREAUCRACY, 3
Stratford S., . . . suggests powdered history ENGLAND, 23
S. trades on Shakespeare EUROPE, 2
straw Headpiece filled with s. INSIGNIFICANCE, 2
strawberries innocent as s. INNOCENCE, 11
We may say of angling as Dr Boteler said of s. FISHING, 3
strawberry My good man, I'm not a s. ACCIDENTS, 4
straws Errors, like S. ERROR, 5
strayed s. from thy ways BOOK OF COMMON PRAYER, THE, 3
straying s. away from the church RELIGION, 12
stream Still glides the S. CONSTANCY, 5
Time is but the s. I go a-fishing in TIME, 51
street don't do it in the s. SEX, 21
I doubt if the philosopher lives . . . who could know himself . . . despised by a s. boy PHILOSOPHERS, 5
the s. which is called Straight BIBLICAL QUOTATIONS, 7
streets a quarrel in the s. is . . . to be hated ARGUMENTS, 10
grass will grow in the s. POLITICS, 70
S. full of water TELEGRAMS, 3
The s. of London LONDON, 1
strength Credulity is . . . the child's s. INNOCENCE, 7
Ignorance is S. DOUBLETHINK, 1
My s. is as the s. of ten HEART, 20
s. and fury FURY, 4
S. through joy NAZISM, 4
We are not now that s. DETERMINATION, 23
strengthened s. . . . in the inner man BIBLICAL QUOTATIONS, 116
strenuous doctrine of the s. life WORK, 27
stress Diet away your s. HEALTHY LIVING, 34
stretched things which he s. LYING, 26
stricken old, and well s. in age BIBLICAL QUOTATIONS, 214
strife God and Nature then at s. NATURE, 31
With phantoms an unprofitable s. LIFE AND DEATH, 29
strike difficult to go on s. STRIKES, 5
If you s. a child VIOLENCE, 14
no right to s. against the public safety STRIKES, 4
S. while the iron is hot OPPORTUNITY, 7
The general s. . . . is the road to anarchy STRIKES, 2
themselves must s. the blow FREEDOM, 9
the twenty-four-hour s. STRIKES, 6
where ever you meet with a passage . . . s. it out WRITING, 20
strikes the last four s. we've had, it's pissed down STRIKES, 7
Strindberg S. when you have a temperature LITERATURE, 16
string chewing little bits of S. FOOD, 11
strings 'There are s.', said Mr Tappertit, 'in the human heart . . . ' EMOTION, 2
stripling yon pale s. EXPECTATION, 7
strive I s. to be brief, and I become obscure BREVITY, 3
needst not s. / . . . to keep alive KILLING, 4
To s., to seek, to find, and not to yield DETERMINATION, 23
strives s. to touch the stars AMBITION, 24
stroke man fears . . . only the s. of death DEATH, 28
none so fast as s. BOATS, 2
strong a s. ass BIBLICAL QUOTATIONS, 228
be s. and of a good courage BIBLICAL QUOTATIONS, 70
be s. in the Lord BIBLICAL QUOTATIONS, 119
disarm the s. and arm the weak INJUSTICE, 8
how sublime . . . /To suffer and be s. ENDURANCE, 10
Sorrow and silence are s. ENDURANCE, 9
S. enough to answer back to desires CHARACTER, 12
s. enough to bear the misfortunes of others MISFORTUNE, 15
the errors of those who think they are s. ERROR, 2
the s. shall thrive STRENGTH, 7
the wall is s. IMPRISONMENT, 16
The weak, . . . always prevail over the s. SURVIVAL, 6
waxed s. in spirit BIBLICAL QUOTATIONS, 416
woe unto them that . . . follow s. drink ALCOHOL, 16
strongest He who was s. got most INJUSTICE, 2
S. minds / . . . the noisy world /Hears least MIND, 36
strongminded nobody is s. around a President PRESIDENTS, 14
strove I s. with none LIFE AND DEATH, 21
struck Certain women should be s. regularly WOMEN, 33
structure s. of the . . . British sentence GRAMMAR, 3
struggle each man must s., lest the moral law become . . . separated MORALITY, 1
I believe in the armed s. as the only solution REVOLUTION, 5
manhood a s. AGE, 26
The perpetual s. for room and food SURVIVAL, 5
the s. for existence EVOLUTION, 9
struggles The history of all . . . society is the history of class s. CLASS, 26
your s., your dreams, your telephone number LOVE, 18
struggling the greatness of Russia is only her pre-natal s. RUSSIA, 3
strumpet a s.'s fool LOVE, 129
struts player that s. and frets LIFE, 76
stubborn s. spear-men COURAGE, 20
student an over-ambitious essay by a second-year s. CRITICS, 13
a s. to the end of my days LEARNING, 6
GRAVE, N. A PLACE . . . TO AWAIT THE COMING OF THE MEDICAL S. MEDICINE, 13
He is a senior s. anxious to help his juniors ACADEMICS, 7
He was . . . – a s. of history EXPERIENCE, 20
I have learned since to be a better s. EDUCATION, 67
In teaching the medical s. EDUCATION, 45
students Half of what you are taught as medical s. will in ten years have been shown to be wrong EDUCATION, 16
If you want to get out of medicine . . . be s. all your lives DOCTORS, 80
I taught medical s. in the wards EDUCATION, 66
studies S. serve for delight DELIGHT, 3
study much s. is a weariness of the flesh BIBLICAL QUOTATIONS, 98
s. at small cost and short wayfaring EDUCATION, 32
s. what you most affect EDUCATION, 74
The proper s. of Mankind is Man SELF-KNOWLEDGE, 7
the result of previous s. FLATTERY, 2
studying By s. the masters EXPERTS, 1
stuff Ambition should be made of sterner s. AMBITION, 20
such s. as dreams are made on MORTALITY, 17
The future is made of the same s. FUTURE, 14
the s. of which tyrants are made TYRANNY, 1
to s. a mushroom HOUSEWORK, 2
stuffed We are the s. men INSIGNIFICANCE, 2
stumble they s. that run fast HASTE, 11
stumbled s. when I saw BLINDNESS, 15
stumbling the . . . world was s. . . . in social blindness BLINDNESS, 6
stupid a more mean, s. . . . ungrateful animal than the public PUBLIC, 13
anger makes us all s. ANGER, 9
clever man . . . came of . . . s. people CLEVERNESS, 1
he ceased to be mad he became merely s. MALADIES, 3
Living in England, . . . must be like being married to a s. . . . wife ENGLAND, 22
s. are cocksure . . . intelligent full of doubt DOUBT, 8

The s. neither forgive FORGIVENESS, 19
To be clever enough to get . . . money, one must be s. MATERIALISM, 9
stupidity If poverty is the mother of crime, s. is its father CRIME, 5
It is a s. . . . to busy oneself with the correction of the world IMPROVEMENT, 3
Nothing . . . more dangerous . . . conscientious s. IGNORANCE, 14
Stygian resembling the horrible S. smoke of the pit SMOKING, 18
ye S. set LUST, 7
style s. is the man himself STYLE, 1
s., not sincerity, is the vital thing STYLE, 7
s. . . . often hides eczema STYLE, 2
the grand s. arises in poetry POETRY, 3
The s. is the man PROVERBS, 426
styles All s. are good except the tiresome sort STYLE, 6
subconscious American women know far more about the s. WOMEN, 77
subject a noble nature . . . treats . . . a serious s. POETRY, 3
A S. and a Sovereign are clean different things LAST WORDS, 15
Every s.'s duty is the King's MONARCHY, 22
Her Majesty is not a s. REPARTEE, 35
the individual s. . . . 'has nothing to do with the laws but to obey them.' LAW, 21
subjects Although there exist many thousand s. PROVERBS, 42
subjunctive S. to the last, he preferred GRAMMAR, 10
sublime a step from the s. to the ridiculous DECLINE, 6
Beethoven's Fifth Symphony is the most s. noise MUSIC, 18
From the s. to the ridiculous PROVERBS, 169
how s. . . . /To suffer and be strong ENDURANCE, 10
The s. and the ridiculous OPPOSITES, 4
submerged speak for the inarticulate and the s. JOURNALISM, 7
submit To great evils we s.; we resent little provocations TRIVIALITY, 10
subscribers reasons for not printing any list of s. FRANKNESS, 2
substance faith is the s. of things hoped for BIBLICAL QUOTATIONS, 239
lose the s. by grasping at the shadow GREED, 5
substantial he that chiefly owes himself . . . is the s. Man SELF-RELIANCE, 5
substantives tell the s. from the adjectives POLITICS, 95
substitute a s. for reading it OSTENTATION, 2
no s. for talent TALENT, 6
substitutes and finally a single dictator s. himself COMMUNISM, 19
subtil the serpent was more s. ANIMALS, 4
subtle Time, the s. thief of youth AGE, 52
suburbia I come from s. SUBURBIA, 1
subverts a continued miracle in his own person, which s. all the principles of his understanding CHRISTIANITY, 42
succeed If at first you don't s. PERSISTENCE, 5
If they s., they fail HOMOSEXUALITY, 5
I'm . . . ugly enough to s. on my own INDEPENDENCE, 1
It is not enough to s. RUTHLESSNESS, 9
Never having been able to s. in the world ENVY, 10
those who ne'er s. SUCCESS, 7
to s. unconventionally ORTHODOXY, 3
way to s. is to make people hate you SUCCESS, 20
succeeds Nothing s. PROVERBS, 318
Whenever a friend s. ENVY, 9
success a self-made man who owed his lack of s. to nobody SELF-MADE MEN, 2
I thought that s. spelled happiness HAPPINESS, 17
I was never affected by the question of the s. SELF-CONFIDENCE, 3
Never let s. hide its emptiness DESTINY, 13
no s. like failure FAILURE, 4
not in mortals to command s. SUCCESS, 2
no very lively hope of s. PRAYER, 27
only place where s. comes before work SUCCESS, 19
religion . . . yours is S. SUCCESS, 4
secret of my s. JEALOUSY, 5
s. and miscarriage are empty sounds DISILLUSION, 4
s. . . . by dint of hard work EFFORT, 5
s. depends . . . upon individual initiative and exertion EFFORT, 5
S. is counted sweetest SUCCESS, 7
S. is relative SUCCESS, 8
Sweet Smell of S. SUCCESS, 13
The moral flabbiness born of . . . S. SUCCESS, 10
The penalty of s. SUCCESS, 3
two to make a marriage a s. MARRIAGE, 114
what s. . . . they have, the world proclaimeth DOCTORS, 79
successful It was very s. WEAPONS, 4
two reasons why I am s. in show business SUCCESS, 9
we do everything we can to appear s. SUCCESS, 18
sucker a s. born every minute GULLIBILITY, 1
s. an even break FAIRNESS, 1
suckle To s. fools TRIVIALITY, 13
sucks s. the nurse asleep SUICIDE, 31
suddenly No one . . . s. became depraved DEBAUCHERY, 7
sued publish and be s. PUBLISHING, 7
Suez Ship me somewheres east of S. DESIRE, 9
the S. Canal was flowing through my drawing room POLITICS, 46
suffer courage to love . . . courage to s. LOVE, 180
how sublime . . . /To s. and be strong ENDURANCE, 10
If s. we must, let's s. on the heights SUFFERING, 17
Rather s. than die SUFFERING, 19
s. fools gladly BIBLICAL QUOTATIONS, 54
sufferance s. is the badge of all our tribe ENDURANCE, 21
suffered he s. . . . the neurotic ills of an entire generation NEUROSIS, 4
love a place the less for having s. SUFFERING, 7
suffering A man who fears s. SUFFERING, 24
I knew that s. did not ennoble SUFFERING, 22
I learn to relieve the s. SUFFERING, 36
imagining as one's own the s. and joy of others KINDNESS, 6
Madness and s. can set themselves no limit MENTAL ILLNESS, 5
Neurosis is always a substitute for legitimate s. NEUROSIS, 5
pity for the s. of mankind PHILOSOPHERS, 10
sympathize with everything, except s. SYMPATHY, 7
the appalling total of human s. SUFFERING, 9
The prime goal is to alleviate s., and not to prolong life MEDICINE, 9
we cannot be created for this sort of s. AFTERLIFE, 7
sufficient s. unto the day is the evil thereof BIBLICAL QUOTATIONS, 484
sugar like sulphuric acid and s. VIRTUE AND VICE, 5
S. and spice /And all that's nice NURSERY RHYMES, 65
suggestion They'll take s. IMPRESSIONABILITY, 3
suicide committed s. 25 years after his death DIARIES, 3
if her limits be exceeded, man responds by s. SUICIDE, 19
If you must commit s. SUICIDE, 3
I have always respected s. as a regulator of nature SUICIDE, 19
it is true that the s. braves death SUICIDE, 1
Never murder a man who is committing s. SUICIDE, 39
No one ever lacks a good reason for s. SUICIDE, 24
Not only is s. a sin SUICIDE, 8
Not that s. always comes from madness SUICIDE, 37
one truly serious philosophical problem, . . . s. SUICIDE, 4
s. in this man's town SUICIDE, 29
s. is God's best gift to man SUICIDE, 25
S. is not a remedy SUICIDE, 14
S. is something on its own SUICIDE, 18
S. is the worst form of murder SUICIDE, 9
s. remains the courageous act SUICIDE, 15
the only man . . . who cannot commit s. SUICIDE, 36
The prevalence of s. is a test of height in civilization SUICIDE, 13
There is no refuge from confession but s. SUICIDE, 38
The statistics of s. show SUICIDE, 16
thought of s. is a great . . . comfort NIGHT, 9
To attempt s. is a criminal offense SUICIDE, 6
who has never dallied with the thought of s. SUICIDE, 17
suit in a light so dim he would not have chosen a s. by it LOVE, 48
My s. is pale yellow. My nationality is French NORMALITY, 2
suitable no s. material to work on OBEDIENCE, 2
Sukey S. take it off again NURSERY RHYMES, 39
sulfur land of Calvin, oat-cakes, and s. SCOTLAND, 8
Puffed its s. to the sunset TRAVEL, 9
sulfuric like s. acid and sugar VIRTUE AND VICE, 5
sullen Are you sick, or are you s. HOLISTIC MEDICINE, 6
sultry common where the climate's s. ADULTERY, 1
sum *Cogito, ergo s.* THINKING, 4
Sumer S. is icumen in ANONYMOUS, 75
summer after many a s. dies the swan MORTALITY, 19
All on a s. day FOOD, 20
Beauty sat with me all the s. day BEAUTY, 10
Before the war . . . it was s. all the year round NOSTALGIA, 19
choosing dress material for this uncertain s. WRITING, 34
Made glorious s. OPTIMISM, 33
Now the peak of s.'s past TRANSIENCE, 11
Spring and s. did happen in Cambridge CAMBRIDGE, 4
S. afternoon – s. afternoon SUMMER, 5
S. has set in with its usual severity SUMMER 4
the last rose of s. FLOWERS, 10
Warm s. sun shine kindly here ANONYMOUS, 105
way to ensure s. in England SUMMER, 8
summit the s. of Everest was hardly the place PHOTOGRAPHY, 4
summons when Fate s. FATE, 7
summum *S. bonum* GOOD, 3
sun aweary of the s. WORLD-WEARINESS, 11
before you let the s. in, mind it wipes its shoes CLEANNESS, 10
better is he . . . who hath not seen the evil work under the s. BIBLICAL QUOTATIONS, 82
between me and the s. REPARTEE, 33
Busy old fool, unruly S. SUN, 2
Fear no more the heat o' th' s. DUST, 9
Follow thy fair s. SORROW, 4
Furnish'd and burnish'd by Aldershot s. ADMIRATION, 1
Hath Britain all the s. that shines SUN, 5
his countenance was as the s. BIBLICAL QUOTATIONS, 584
I got the s. in the mornin' and the moon at night GRATITUDE, 2
it were better for s. and moon to drop from heaven SIN, 23
I will sing of the s. WOMEN, 97
let not the s. go down upon your wrath BIBLICAL QUOTATIONS, 117
Light breaks where no s. shines EMOTION, 5
My s. sets OPTIMISM, 17
nothing like the s. ANALOGY, 4
on which the s. never sets BRITISH EMPIRE, 7
So sicken waning moons too near the s. MOON, 4
s. came dazzling thro' the leaves CHIVALRY, 13
s. had risen to hear him crow ARROGANCE, 3
S. remains fixed in the centre ASTRONOMY, 2
Thank heavens the s. has gone in LAST WORDS, 80
The bright s. was extinguished DAY AND NIGHT, 5
The kiss of s. for pardon GARDENS, 7
The people – could you patent the s. DISCOVERY, 13
there is no new thing under the s. BIBLICAL QUOTATIONS, 75
There rises the s. of Austerlitz WAR, 109
The S. came up upon the left SUN, 1
The s. does not set in my dominions ROYALTY, 94
the s. shining ten days a year and shit in the streets ENGLAND, 26
this s. of York OPTIMISM, 33
To have enjoy'd the s. LIFE, 4
we cannot make our s. /Stand still LOVE, 101
with peaches and women, it's . . . the side next the s. that's tempting TEMPTATION, 13
sunburn S. is very becoming APPEARANCE, 15
Sunday A Christian . . . feels /Repentance on a S. CHRISTIANITY, 63
Buried on S. HUMAN CONDITION, 17
festival must be observed on S. SUNDAY, 3
only two posh papers on a S. NEWSPAPERS, 11
The boredom of S. afternoon SUNDAY, 5
The feeling of S. is the same everywhere SUNDAY, 7

sundry God, who at s. times . . . spake BIBLICAL QUOTATIONS, 233
sung I have s. women in three cities WOMEN, 97
sunk thanks to words, we have often s. to the level of the demons WORDS, 17
sunless Down to a s. sea PLEASURE, 9
sunlit broad, s. uplands WORLD WAR II, 12
sunset a s.-touch WORRY, 10
Puffed its sulphur to the s. TRAVEL, 9
S. and evening star DUTY, 5
s. breezes shiver BOATS, 15
sunsets I have a horror of s. HORROR, 2
superfluous that controversy is either s. or hopeless ARGUMENTS, 11
superintendents from the point of view of the hygienist, the physician, the architect, the tax-payer, the s., and the nurse HOSPITALS, 3
superior I consider myself s. to the saint, the scientist NOVELS, 10
One is not s. . . . because one sees the world in an odious light CYNICISM, 1
The French want no-one to be their *s.* PRIDE, 11
young man with so s. a voice OXFORD, 4
superiority their insolent and unfounded airs of s. FRANCE, 18
The s. of one man's opinion over another's OPINIONS, 4
superiors equality . . . with our s. EQUALITY, 5
In America everybody is of the opinion that he has no social s. EQUALITY, 22
Super-jew I'm S. JEWS, 5
superlative we have not settled the s. PROGRESS, 8
Super-Mac Introducing S. POLITICIANS, 117
Superman I teach you the S. SUPERIORITY, 12
supernatural Religion /Has made an honest woman of the s. RELIGION, 34
This s. soliciting SUPERNATURAL, 15
supersititious any doctrine . . . vouched for by . . . human beings . . . must be benighted and s. SCIENCE, 52
superstition necessary for a s. to enslave a philosophy RELIGION, 44
S. is the poetry of life SUPERSTITION, 9
S. is the religion of feeble minds SUPERSTITION, 8
S. sets the whole world in flames SUPERSTITION, 12
superstitions new truths . . . end as s. NOVELTY, 4
s. of the human mind PURITY, 6
superstitious men of Athens . . . ye are too s. BIBLICAL QUOTATIONS, 12
superstructure Sentimentality is a s. covering brutality SENTIMENTALITY, 2
supp'd I have s. full with horrors HORROR, 3
supper Better lose a s. than have a hundred physicians HEALTHY LIVING, 8
support atheist . . . no invisible means of s. ATHEISM, 4
s. me when I am . . . wrong REPARTEE, 70
the great silent majority of my fellow Americans – I ask for your s. SUPPORT, 7
supposing s. him to be the gardener BIBLICAL QUOTATIONS, 369
supreme Our s. governors, the mob PUBLIC, 20
sups He who s. with the devil CAUTION, 4
surgeon A fashionable s. like a pelican DOCTORS, 33
A good s. operates with his hand SURGEONS, 7
A s. is someone who does everything SPECIALISTS, 1
A vain s. is like a milking stool SURGEONS, 12
it takes a s. to save one SURGEONS, 13
one little touch of a s.'s lancet REMEDIES, 43
The best s. is he that has been well hacked himself SURGEONS, 1
the best s., . . . , is he who makes the fewest mistakes SURGEONS, 5
The egotistical s. is like a monkey SURGEONS, 2
The first attribute of a s. is an insatiable curiosity SURGEONS, 8
the s. be sometimes tempted to supplant instead of aiding Nature SURGEONS, 11
surgeons Human beings, yes, but not s. MEDICINE, 102
start with the s. . . . and work *up* to the gutter SURGEONS, 16
The glory of s. is like that of actors SURGEONS, 4
There is no counting the names, that s. and anatomists give KNOWLEDGE, 32
'The s. have arrived.' DOCTORS, 60
Tree s. are taught to wear safety belts SURGEONS, 3
surgery In s. all operations are recorded as successful SURGEONS, 14
In s. eyes first and most SURGEONS, 9
plastic s. . . . combines . . . psychoanalysis, massage, and a trip to the beauty salon OPERATIONS, 14
S. does the ideal thing OPERATIONS, 6
S. is the ready motion of steady and experienced hands OPERATIONS, 10
The greatest triumph of s. today . . . lies in finding ways for avoiding s. OPERATIONS, 13
the practice of s. a plumber's OPERATIONS, 9
surgical take a s. operation OPERATIONS, 8
surmise with a wild s. DISCOVERY, 11
surpassed Man is something that is to be s. SUPERIORITY, 12
surprise Life is a great s. LIFE AND DEATH, 24
surprised it is *I* who am s.; you are merely astonished REPARTEE, 109
the audience want to be s. . . . by things that they expect PLAYS, 3
surrender No terms except . . . s. WAR, 68
we shall never s. WORLD WAR II, 10
survey When I s. the wondrous Cross HUMILITY, 13
survival S. of the fittest EVOLUTION, 11
without victory there is no s. VICTORY, 3
survive always be some that s. SURVIVAL, 3
as fitted to s. . . . as a tapeworm EVOLUTION, 15
only the Fit s. STRENGTH, 7
Out of their cataclysm but one poor Noah /Dare hope to s. SEX, 47
that far down you have to struggle to s. FAMILY, 28
What will s. of us is love LOVE, 89
survived I s. SELF-PRESERVATION, 12
survives Education is what s. EDUCATION, 80
suspect I rather s. her of being in love LOVE AND MARRIAGE, 2
suspected New opinions are always s. NOVELTY, 5
not only s. but pronounced for a witch SUPERNATURAL, 8
suspense This s. is terrible SUSPENSE, 1
suspension willing s. of disbelief POETRY, 15
suspicion Caesar's wife must be above s. INTEGRITY, 2
people under s. are better moving JUDGMENT, 12
S. always haunts the guilty mind GUILT, 13
suspicions S. amongst thoughts SUSPICION, 1
swagman Once a jolly s. camped by a billy-bong PLACES, 30
swains all our s. commend her ADMIRATION, 18
swallow One s. does not make a summer PROOF, 1
swallowed death is s. up in victory BIBLICAL QUOTATIONS, 49
swallows I hate a man who s. it FOOD, 42
one master-passion . . . /s. up the rest PASSION, 6
swan after many a summer dies the s. MORTALITY, 19
What time is the next s. MISTAKES, 17
Swanee 'Way down upon de S. Ribber HOMESICKNESS, 3
swans his own geese are s. ARTISTS, 14
S. sing before they die SINGERS, 1
sway A little rule, a little s. GRAVE, 4
swear s. not by the moon UNFAITHFULNESS, 6
swear-word A foreign s. is LANGUAGE, 41
sweat blood, toil, tears and s. EFFORT, 3
it is only because miners s. their guts out SUPERIORITY, 13
That shriek and s. in pigmy wars TRIVIALITY, 15
sweats Falstaff s. to death EARTH, 14
sweet Heard melodies are s. MUSIC, 25
How s. are looks that ladies bend WOMEN, 114
if TODAY BE S. TIME, 19
Is trifle sufficient for s. FOOD, 12
Pleasures newly found are s. PLEASURE, 36
Revenge, at first though s. REVENGE, 15
so s. as Melancholy MELANCHOLY, 2
S. childish days NOSTALGIA, 29
S. day, so cool, so calm DAY AND NIGHT, 12
S. Smell of Success SUCCESS, 13
s. will be the flower PATIENCE, 9
that bitter beer that tastes s. IMMORTALITY, 6
sweeter The mountain sheep are s. GREED, 10
what is s. than honey BIBLICAL QUOTATIONS, 393
sweetest Success is counted s. SUCCESS, 7
s. things turn sourest CORRUPTION, 12
s. thing that ever grew /Beside a human door ADMIRATION, 20
sweetness Culture is the passion for s. and light CULTURE, 2
He who works for s. and light PERFECTION, 1
waste its s. on the desert air WASTE, 2
sweets Stolen s. are always sweeter, /Stolen kisses much completer THEFT, 7
Stolen s. are best THEFT, 5
swerve riverrun, past Eve and Adam's, from s. of shore RIVERS, 3
swift s. to hear BIBLICAL QUOTATIONS, 283
Too s. arrives as tardy as too slow LOVE, 154
swimming s. under water WRITING, 12
swine a s. to show you where the truffles are VULGARITY, 1
Come in, you Anglo-Saxon s. INSULTS, 15
pearls before s. BIBLICAL QUOTATIONS, 487
the husks that the s. did eat BIBLICAL QUOTATIONS, 439
swines Curse the blasted, jelly-boned s. CURSES, 2
swing S., s. together BOATS, 4
swings we pulls up on the s. LOSS, 2
Swiss if the S. had designed these mountains MOUNTAINS, 4
The S. . . . are not a people so much as a . . . business SWITZERLAND, 2
Swithin St. S.'s Day, if thou dost rain PROVERBS, 372
Switzerland Austria is S. . . . with history added EUROPE, 12
In S. they had brotherly love SWITZERLAND, 5
S. . . . an inferior sort of Scotland SWITZERLAND, 3
swollen mere existence is s. to a horror HORROR, 1
sword Covenants without the s. are but words POWER POLITICS, 3
his sore and great and strong s. BIBLICAL QUOTATIONS, 264
Islam unashamedly came with a s. ISLAM, 1
more cruel . . . the pen than the s. WRITING, 7
nation shall not lift up s. against nation BIBLICAL QUOTATIONS, 247
not to send peace, but a s. BIBLICAL QUOTATIONS, 501
pen is mightier than the s. WRITING, 6
s. sleep in my hand ENGLAND, 6
the bank was mightier than the s. BANKS, 6
the s. of the Spirit BIBLICAL QUOTATIONS, 119
the word of God is . . . sharper than any two-edged s. BIBLICAL QUOTATIONS, 234
they smote the city with the edge of the s. BIBLICAL QUOTATIONS, 388
they that take the s. shall perish with the s. BIBLICAL QUOTATIONS, 545
We draw the s. with a clear conscience WAR, 173
swords beat their s. into plowshares BIBLICAL QUOTATIONS, 247
Keep up your bright s. WAR AND PEACE, 15
those who have stout hearts and sharp s. RUTHLESSNESS, 8
swound Like noises in a s. SEA, 4
Sydney There was the vast town of S. PLACES, 23
symmetry S. is tedious BOREDOM, 6
thy fearful s. ANIMALS, 6
sympathetic To be s. without discrimination SYMPATHY, 2
sympathize s. with everything, except suffering SYMPATHY, 7
sympathy failed to inspire s. in men WOMEN, 21
machine-gun riddling her hostess with s. SYMPATHY, 4
S. . . . lay over the gathering like a woolly blanket SYMPATHY, 1
This basis of medicine is s. and the desire to help others MEDICINE, 75
symptom a s. of some ailment in the spiritual part HOLISTIC MEDICINE, 2
common s. of immaturity IMMATURITY, 3
symptoms Here am I dying of a hundred good s. ILLNESS, 58
One of the s. of approaching nervous breakdown WORK, 29
please have all your s. ready DIAGNOSIS, 1
syne For auld lang s. FRIENDSHIP, 17
synthesis as clear as a crystal, the s. – German National Socialism NAZISM, 3
Syrian The S. stars look down DEATH, 26
system Christianity accepted . . . a metaphysical s. CHRISTIANITY, 43

I'm not interested in the bloody s. CHARITY, 16
some greater and more equitable s. PROPHECY, 12
The true s. of the World has been recognized BOOKS, 2
systems Our little s. have their day TRANSIENCE, 23
the whole solar and stellar s. COMFORT, 2

T

table A man is . . . better pleased when he has a good dinner upon his t. WOMAN'S ROLE, 6
crumbs which fell from the rich man's t. BIBLICAL QUOTATIONS, 441
patient etherized upon a t. DEPARTURE, 6
put them at a t. together FEAR, 8
tableau history . . . a t. of crimes and misfortunes HISTORY, 41
tables It is not your trade to make t. CRITICISM, 26
t. of stone, and a law AUTHORITARIANISM, 3
tablet Roman Catholic women must keep taking the *T.* CONTRACEPTION, 13
tact T. consists in knowing TACT, 5
tactic Silence is the best t. DISTRUST, 2
tae Here's t. us wha's like us ANONYMOUS, 36
tail A case of the t. dogging the wag HUMOR, 47
The only man who really needs a t. coat CLOTHES, 22
tailor I go to a better t. than any of you CLOTHES, 5
Tinker, /T., /Soldier, /Sailor NURSERY RHYMES, 60
tails t. you lose VICTORY, 8
'taint That's right. 'T. yours, and 't. mine PUNS, 24
tainted the supply is not t. FACTS, 6
take T. care of the sense MEANING, 2
T. things as they come PROVERBS, 375
They have to t. you in HOME, 5
You can't t. it with you PROVERBS, 477
taken from him that hath not shall be t. away BIBLICAL QUOTATIONS, 535
the Lord gave, and the Lord hath t. away BIBLICAL QUOTATIONS, 296
takes It t. all sorts OPPOSITES, 1
taking not winning but t. part VICTORY, 7
tale a t. /Told by an idiot LIFE, 76
A t. never loses GOSSIP, 1
Life is as tedious as a twice-told t. LIFE, 75
t. to tell of the hardihood, endurance, and courage of my companions ENDURANCE, 17
thereby hangs a t. LIFE, 73
talent A best-seller is the gilded tomb of a mediocre t. BOOKS, 43
a country full of genius, but with absolutely no t. IRELAND, 13
any man who has no t. ENGLISH, 4
A t. to amuse TALENT, 3
Middle age snuffs out more t. TALENT, 5
T. alone cannot make a writer WRITERS, 15
T. develops in quiet places CHARACTER, 9
T. does what it can TALENT AND GENIUS, 3
t. instantly recognizes genius MEDIOCRITY, 3
the difference between t. and genius TALENT AND GENIUS, 1
the meanest . . . deeds require spirit and t. INSENSITIVITY, 4
the most extraordinary collection of t. TALENT, 7
There is no substitute for t. TALENT, 6
There is no such thing as a great t. without great will-power DETERMINATION, 3
the t. of flattering with delicacy FLATTERY, 2
talents If you have great t., industry will improve them WORK, 26
the difference between our t. and our expectations DISAPPOINTMENT, 1
talk If you can t. with crowds and keep your virtue IDEALISM, 3
If you want me to t. for ten minutes SPEECHES, 13
my ministers t. – as long as they do what I say AUTHORITARIANISM, 8
T. of the devil DEVIL, 1
Teas, /Where small t. dies CONVERSATION, 12
the need to t. is a primary impulse IMPETUOSITY, 1
think too little . . . t. too much VERBOSITY, 4
Two may t. . . . yet never really meet FRIENDSHIP, 19
ways of making men t. MISQUOTATION, 2
we never t. about anything except me CONCEIT, 21
when I hear anyone t. of Culture PHILISTINISM, 4
When two Englishmen meet, their first t. is of the weather ENGLISH, 23
women should t. an hour SEXES, 3
you wished him to t. on for ever COMPLIMENTS, 12
talked He t. on for ever COMPLIMENTS, 12
The more you are t. about, the more you . . . wish to be t. about FAME, 22
There is only one thing . . . worse than being t. about FAME, 30
talker A good listener is a good t. with a sore throat CONVERSATION, 14
a non-stop t. to whom someone has given a typewriter WRITERS, 5
Nothing is more despicable than a professional t. VERBOSITY, 5
talkers fluent t. THINKING, 6
talking for thirty-five years he had not stopped t. SCIENTISTS, 12
Frenchman must be always t. FRANCE, 11
good newspaper, . . . is a nation t. to itself JOURNALISM, 31
if you ain't t. about him, ain't listening ACTORS, 2
I wouldn't be . . . t. to someone like you SNOBBERY, 3
People t. without speaking FUTILITY, 12
T. and eloquence are not the same SPEECH, 13
T. of Michelangelo WOMEN, 46
While we're t., time will have meanly run on PRESENT, 10
talks Garbo T. CINEMA, 2
tall Let our children grow t. TALENT, 9
Tallulah T. Bankhead barged down the Nile last night and sank CRITICISM, 11
tambourine Hey! Mr T. Man LEISURE, 3
tame the tongue can no man t. BIBLICAL QUOTATIONS, 286
tamper Who am I to t. with a masterpiece CONCEIT, 27
tangere noli me t. BIBLICAL QUOTATIONS, 370
tangerine t. trees and marmalade skies IMAGINATION, 9
tankard heart which grief hath cankered / . . . remedy – the T. ALCOHOL, 24
tanned getting more t. and more tired ROYALTY, 87
tapeworm as fitted to survive . . . as a t. EVOLUTION, 15
Tara's through T. halls IRELAND, 14
tarnished neither t. nor afraid COURAGE, 7
tarry having lost . . . your prime, /You may for ever t. MARRIAGE, 78
Tartar Scratch the Russian and . . . find the T. RUSSIA, 5
tarts He's lost us the t.' vote JOURNALISM, 18
The Queen of Hearts /She made some t. FOOD, 20
Tarzan Me? T. CINEMA, 17
task No t. is a long one but the t. on which one dare not start BEGINNING, 4
The trivial round, the common t. SIMPLICITY, 4
Tasmanians the T. . . . are now extinct ADULTERY, 5
taste bad t. is better than no t. TASTE, 2
Between friends differences in t. TASTE, 1
different t. in jokes is a . . . strain on the affections HUMOR, 22
Drink deep, or t. not the Pierian spring KNOWLEDGE, 33
Every one to his t. DIFFERENCE, 2
great common sense and good t. CHARACTER, 27
I suspect his t. in higher matters FOOD, 42
no t. when you married me TASTE, 9
people who always go on about . . . good t. TASTE, 6
T. is the feminine of genius TASTE, 3
the bouquet is better than the t. ALCOHOL, 64
the t. by which he is . . . relished WRITING, 47
The t. was that of the little crumb of madeleine MEMORY, 14
Things sweet to t. prove . . . sour REGRET, 21
willing to t. any drink once DRINKS, 8
tasted Sir, you have t. two whole worms SPOONERISMS, 5
Some books are to be t. BOOKS, 4
tastes It is like a cigar. . . . it never t. quite the same LOVE, 185
Our t. greatly alter TASTE, 4
t. may not be the same TASTE, 8
There is no accounting for t. DIFFERENCE, 5
taught a woman who knows all . . . that can be t. INSULTS, 29
I forget what I was t. KNOWLEDGE, 38
tavern A t. chair is the throne PUBLIC HOUSES, 1
he has . . . opened a t. for his friends PARASITES, 1
jangled in every ale-house and t. BIBLE, 7
nothing . . . by which so much happiness is produced as by a good t. PUBLIC HOUSES, 2
There is a t. in the town ANONYMOUS, 88
tawney that t. weed tobacco SMOKING, 19
tax A hateful t. TAXATION, 11
For God's sake, madam, don't say that in England for . . . they will surely t. it TAXATION, 20
hardest thing . . . to understand is income t. TAXATION, 4
taxation T. and representation are inseparably united TAXATION, 16
T. without representation REPRESENTATION, 2
taxed all the world should be t. BIBLICAL QUOTATIONS, 417
taxes collect legal t. from illegal money TAXATION, 3
Death and t. and childbirth INCONVENIENCE, 1
His t. . . . starve the poor souls TAXATION, 15
people overlaid with t. TAXATION, 1
The avoidance of t. . . . still carries . . . reward TAXATION, 13
taxi done almost every human activity inside a t. BOASTS, 1
taxis hiring t. . . . handing out redundancy notices to its own workers INCOMPETENCE, 2
I don't take whores in t. PROMISCUITY, 8
tax-payer from the point of view of the hygienist, the physician, the architect, the t., the superintendents, and the nurse HOSPITALS, 3
The t. is someone who works for the federal government TAXATION, 17
Tay Beautiful Railway Bridge of the Silv'ry T. BRIDGE, 3
tea Dinner, Lunch and T. FOOD, 10
honey still for t. HONEY, 2
If I had known there was no Latin word for t. DRINKS, 4
if this is coffee, I want t. DRINKS, 3
it is just like having a cup of t. SEX, 80
sometimes counsel take – and sometimes T. DRINKS, 16
Take some more t. LANGUAGE, 9
T. for Two, and Two for T. DRINKS, 12
we drink too much t. DRINKS, 17
When I makes t. I makes t. HUMOR, 31
teach Don't t. your grandmother ADVICE, 2
For every person wishing to t. EDUCATION, 73
He who shall t. the child to doubt DOUBT, 4
It is no matter what you t. them first EDUCATION, 47
the time had passed . . . merely to t. foreigners BUSINESS, 16
they cannot t. students clinical medicine MEDICINE, 98
You can't t. an old dog OLD AGE, 2
teacher A good clinical t. is himself a Medical School EDUCATION, 37
A t. is paid to teach EDUCATION, 33
Experience is a good t. EXPERIENCE, 7
the qualities of a good t. of medicine MEDICINE, 5
Time is a great t., but . . . kills all its pupils TIME, 11
teachers We t. can only help . . . as servants EDUCATION, 62
teaches He who cannot, t. EDUCATION, 77
teaching it is easily possible for t. to be too 'up to date' EDUCATION, 41
the true center of medical t. EDUCATION, 38
teacup Storm in a T. TRIVIALITY, 2
team Is my t. ploughing AGRICULTURE, 3
team games The British, being brought up on t. HOUSES OF PARLIAMENT, 17
tear Every t. from every eye SORROW, 2
Some stars . . . Fell like a falling t. STARS, 6
tears blood, toil, t. and sweat EFFORT, 3
foolish t. upon my grave HYPOCRISY, 20
God shall wipe away all t. BIBLICAL QUOTATIONS, 590
He spoke, and loos'd our heart in t. EARTH, 2
his t. are salt ENVIRONMENT, 7
If you have t., prepare to shed them SORROW, 23
in a flood of t. and a Sedan chair HUMOR, 20
mine own t. /Do scald SUFFERING, 30
No more t. now REVENGE, 20

No t. in the writer WRITING, 13
our t. /Thaw not the frost MOURNING, 14
shed t. when they would devour HYPOCRISY, 2
T., idle tears SORROW, 29
T. such as angels weep SORROW, 13
T. were to me SORROW, 6
The bitterest t. . . . are for words . . . unsaid and deeds . . . undone REGRET, 25
the land of t. SORROW, 20
The smiles, the t., /Of boyhood's years NOSTALGIA, 17
the women whose eyes have been washed . . . with t. WOMEN, 41
Violet Elizabeth dried her t. THREATS, 4
wash his feet with t. BIBLICAL QUOTATIONS, 427
With silence and t. SEPARATION, 2
teas T., /Where small talk dies CONVERSATION, 12
tease The fleas that t. in the high Pyrenees NONSENSE, 3
tea-stirring t. times PRESENT, 11
teatray Like a t. in the sky NONSENSE, 5
teche gladly wolde he lerne, and gladly t. CHARACTER, 4
technological For t. man it is time TECHNOLOGY, 10
technology t. . . . indistinguishable from magic TECHNOLOGY, 5
The t. of medicine has outrun its sociology TECHNOLOGY, 12
Teddy T. Bear to the Nation BETJEMAN, SIR JOHN, 1
tedious They shorten t. nights NIGHT, 5
tedium t. is the very basis of mourning BOREDOM, 6
teeth an old bitch gone in the t. EPITAPHS, 32
everyone happy whose t. are sound TEETH, 10
her lips narrow and her t. black ROYALTY, 65
I had braces on my t. and got high marks APPEARANCE, 35
I have let dentists ride roughshod over my t. TEETH, 6
I'll dispose of my t. as I see fit TEETH, 7
It is necessary to clean the t. frequently TEETH, 4
Man can have only a certain number of t., hair and ideas OLD AGE, 99
natural false t. TEETH, 8
nice smile, but . . . iron t. POLITICIANS, 55
Pain with the thousand t. SUFFERING, 37
removing the t. will cure everything TEETH, 1
Removing the t. will cure something TEETH, 1
Sweet things are bad for the t. TEETH, 11
take the bull between the t. MIXED METAPHORS, 3
taking out his false t. and hurling them at his wife MARRIAGE, 57
They will steal the very t. out of your mouth THEFT, 2
to lose one's t. is a catastrophe TEETH, 13
teething they escaped t. TEETH, 12
teetotaller a beer t., not a champagne t. ALCOHOL, 71
no woman should marry a t. ABSTINENCE, 9
teetotallers T. lack the sympathy ABSTINENCE, 3
telephone He really needs to t. EMBARRASSMENT, 2
I don't know his t. number NUMBERS, 3
your struggles, your dreams, your t. number LOVE, 18
telephone-exchange we are supposing the brain . . . more than a t. BRAIN, 7
television but to do it on t. TELEVISION, 6
eats, sleeps and watches the t. WOMAN'S ROLE, 3
have sex or appear on t. OPPORTUNITY, 22
Masturbation is the thinking man's t. SEX, 41
stay at home and see bad t. for nothing CINEMA, 9
T. brought the brutality of war TELEVISION, 12
T. is for appearing on TELEVISION, 5
T. is more interesting than people TELEVISION, 4
T.? No good will come LATIN, 5
T. . . . permits you to be entertained in your living room TELEVISION, 7
t. programs are so much chewing gum TELEVISION, 3
There is a bias in t. journalism JOURNALISM, 12
tell do not t. them so WISDOM, 14
How could they t. POLITICIANS, 88
people who love to t. us what to do ENGLISH, 25
T. the truth PROVERBS, 377
you must not kiss and t. SECRECY, 9
you never can t.. That's a principle PRINCIPLES, 5
telly People will cross the road . . . to say 'We saw you on the t.' TELEVISION, 6
You don't get any pornography . . . on the t. PORNOGRAPHY, 7
Téméraire She's the Fighting T. BOATS, 15
temper A tart t. never mellows with age CHARACTER, 13
if I were not king, I should lose my t. ROYALTY, 75
Never lose your t. with the Press SELF-CONTROL, 7
temperament artistic t. is a disease ARTS, 2
temperance Exercise and t. can preserve something of our early strength HEALTHY LIVING, 18
I prefer t. hotels ALCOHOL, 84
Joy and T. and Repose HEALTHY LIVING, 30
T. is the love of health MODERATION, 10
tempests On whom Thy t. fell all night OLD AGE, 51
That looks on t. LOVE, 158
temple in the very t. of delight DELIGHT, 7
The Arab who builds . . . a hut out of . . . a t. . . . is more philosophical MUSEUMS, 1
the veil of the t. was rent in twain BIBLICAL QUOTATIONS, 549
This is the t. of Providence GAMBLING, 1
who is there . . . would go into the t. to save his life BIBLICAL QUOTATIONS, 552
your body is the t. of the Holy Ghost BIBLICAL QUOTATIONS, 32
temples t. made with hands BIBLICAL QUOTATIONS, 12
tempora *O t.! O mores* CUSTOM, 1
temporal service rendered to the t. king to the prejudice of the eternal king TREASON, 11
temporary force alone is but *t.* FORCE, 3
tempt The Devil, having nothing else to do /Went off to t. TEMPTATION, 5
thou shalt not t. the Lord thy God BIBLICAL QUOTATIONS, 469
temptation blessed is the man that endureth t. BIBLICAL QUOTATIONS, 281
I never resist t. TEMPTATION, 16
lead us not into t. BIBLICAL QUOTATIONS, 480
over-fond of resisting t. TEMPTATION, 4
prepare thy soul for t. BIBLICAL QUOTATIONS, 100
resist everything except t. TEMPTATION, 17
The last t. MOTIVE, 2
The only way to get rid of a t. TEMPTATION, 18
You oughtn't to yield to t.. TEMPTATION, 12
temptations in spite of all t. . . . He remains an Englishman NATIONALITY, 7
tempted The tempter or the t., who sins most TEMPTATION, 14
tempter The t. or the tempted, who sins most TEMPTATION, 14
tempting the devil did not play in t. of me PROSE, 2
with peaches and women, it's . . . the side next the sun that's t. TEMPTATION, 13
ten only t. PUBLIC, 16
our dykes, the waters are t. feet deep BOASTS, 8
T. Days that Shook the World RUSSIAN REVOLUTION, 7
Ten for the t. commandments ANONYMOUS, 45
T. pipers piping CHRISTMAS, 17
The good Lord has only t. POLITICS, 38
Yes, about t. minutes REPARTEE, 111
tender I was born . . . at an extremely t. age BIRTH, 13
T. Is the Night BOOK TITLES, 6
tendering cured only with diet and t. HEALTH, 3
tenderness Their flowers the t. of patient minds WAR, 117
ten-dollar He thinks I don't know the t. words REPARTEE, 49
tenement I inhabit a weak, frail, decayed t. LAST WORDS, 2
tennis Anyone for t. INVITATIONS, 1
playing t. with the net down POETRY, 21
tennis-balls We are merely the stars' t. DESTINY, 29
tent inside my t. pissing out PRUDENCE, 8
tentacles dear octopus from whose t. we never quite escape FAMILY, 50
tents Those who have never dwelt in t. CAMPING, 1
term Is a t. that will bolster my thesis WORDS, 9
terminological t. inexactitude LYING, 10
terminology The jargon of scientific t. LANGUAGE, 19
terms No t. except . . . surrender WAR, 68
terrible It is well that war is so t.; . . . WAR, 92
t. as an army with banners BIBLICAL QUOTATIONS, 635
t. thing for a man to find out HONESTY, 14
This suspense is t. SUSPENSE, 1
terribles *Les enfants t.* YOUTH, 12
territorial the last t. claim which I have to make in Europe WORLD WAR II, 34
territory the United States will never again seek one additional foot of t. by conquest UNITED STATES, 66
terror added another t. to death BIOGRAPHY, 4
Christianity has made of death a t. CHRISTIANITY, 50
new t. to life TECHNOLOGY, 15
terrorist The t. and the policeman EQUALITY, 8
terrorists All t. . . . end up with drinks at the Dorchester POLITICS, 48
test Martyrdom is the t. FREEDOM, 28
text great t. in Galatians BIBLE, 3
Thackeray W. M. T. CLERGY, 15
Thames Sweet T.! run softly RIVERS, 6
the T. is liquid history RIVERS, 1
What is there to make so much of in the T. RIVERS, 4
thank Don't bother to t. me CHARITY, 5
T. me no thankings GRATITUDE, 8
thankful I am . . . t. for not having married MARRIAGE, 92
thanks For this relief much t. COMFORT, 3
I am glad . . . he t. God for anything GRATITUDE, 4
T. MEMORY, 15
thanksgiving With proud t. MOURNING, 3
thank-you T., music-lovers GRATITUDE, 5
that 1066 And All T. HISTORY, 34
Goodbye to All T. BOOK TITLES, 10
Thatcher Blimpish patriotism in the mode of Margaret T. PATRIOTISM, 25
Margaret T.'s great strength CLASS, 52
thcream I'll t., an' t., . . . till I'm thick THREATS, 4
theater Farce is the essential t. COMEDY, 4
For the t. one needs long arms ACTING, 4
nobody goes to the t. unless he . . . has bronchitis AUDIENCES, 1
T. director: a person ACTING, 1
the t. of events MEDICINE, 28
theatrical one may fail to find happiness in t. life DANCING, 10
theft Property is t. CAPITALISM, 16
theologian This stranger is a t. ATHEISM, 6
theorems About binomial t. MATHEMATICS, 9
the world can be expressed in . . . arguments, . . . axioms and t. THEORY, 5
theories In making t. always keep a window open THEORY, 14
Medical t. are most of the time even more peculiar THEORY, 1
the bewitching delusions of their t. EDUCATION, 46
theory A t. can be proved by experiment THEORY, 3
a thing may look evil in t. THEORY, 2
Don't confuse *hypothesis* and *t.* THEORY, 4
it's . . . more important for a t. to be shapely, than . . . true THEORY, 8
no path leads from experiment to . . . t. THEORY, 3
Philosophy is not a t. PHILOSOPHY, 25
Practice should always be based upon a sound knowledge of t. THEORY, 9
The establishment of t. is the very purpose of science THEORY, 4
t. is all grey REALITY, 4
the scream is sometimes a t. THEORY, 15
therapeutic have such immense t. value MEDICINE, 91
therapist Life itself remains a very effective t. PSYCHOANALYSIS, 14
therapy how much valuable t. the profession has cast on the dump PRAYER, 16
thesis Is a term that will bolster my t. WORDS, 9
thick Through t. and thin FAITHFULNESS, 2
thicken other things than dissipation . . . t. the features APPEARANCE, 64
thickens plot t. INTRIGUE, 1
thief as a t. in the night BIBLICAL QUOTATIONS, 643
I come as a t. BIBLICAL QUOTATIONS, 594
Time, the subtle t. of youth AGE, 52
which is the justice, which is the t. APPEARANCES, 27
thieves a den of t. BIBLICAL QUOTATIONS, 523

fell among t. BIBLICAL QUOTATIONS, 432
T. respect property CRIME, 3
thigh he smote them hip and t. BIBLICAL QUOTATIONS, 394
thighs thy t. are like jewels BIBLICAL QUOTATIONS, 637
thin Enclosing every t. man, there's a fat man APPEARANCE, 62
in every fat man a t. one OBESITY, 6
One can never be too t. WEALTH, 42
Outside every t. girl LUST, 12
The one way to get t. OBESITY, 8
there's a t. man inside every fat man OBESITY, 12
There were times my pants were so t. POVERTY, 40
T. people . . . should . . . never take exercise on an empty stomach HEALTHY LIVING, 22
t. red line tipped with steel WAR, 133
Through thick and t. FAITHFULNESS, 2
thing call that t. under your hat a head INSULTS, 62
good t., to make it too common ENGLAND, 45
It is a far, far, better t. that I do EXECUTION, 8
something between a t. and a thought PAINTING, 11
sooty bosom /Of such a t. as thou PREJUDICE, 13
The play's the t. PLAYS, 14
the t. which is good BIBLICAL QUOTATIONS, 117
thing-in-itself The t., the will-to-live, exists . . . in every being SURVIVAL, 8
things all t. were made by him BIBLICAL QUOTATIONS, 316
Glorious t. of thee are spoken HEAVEN, 9
T. are entirely what they appear to be APPEARANCES, 24
To talk of many t. NONSENSE, 9
think apparatus with which we t. BRAIN, 1
He can't t. without his hat THINKING, 2
I cannot sit and t. READING, 11
I exist by what I t. THINKING, 14
If you start to t. about your physical or moral condition ILLNESS, 28
I never t. of the future FUTURE, 8
I t. him so, because I t. him so WOMEN, 108
I t. therefore I am THINKING, 4
Many people would sooner die than t. THINKING, 13
not so t. as you drunk DRUNKENNESS, 27
some . . . speak . . . before they t. IMPETUOSITY, 2
There exist some evils so terrible . . . that we dare not t. of them MISFORTUNE, 13
T. of your posterity POSTERITY, 1
t. only this of me WAR, 30
t. too little . . . talk too much VERBOSITY, 4
time to t. before I speak SPEECH, 9
To know how to say what others only . . . t. SPEECH, 8
We haven't the money, so we've got to t. RESEARCH, 23
When I t. of all the books I have read LIFE, 89
You can't t. rationally on an empty stomach THINKING, 10
thinkers not always the justest t. THINKING, 6
thinking In order to draw a limit to t. THINKING, 19
It ain't t. about it ACTION, 15
its disease of t. THINKING, 11
one prolonged effort to prevent oneself t. THINKING, 7
Plain living and high t. are no more DECLINE, 17
Power of Positive T. OPTIMISM, 31
T. is the most unhealthy thing in the world THINKING, 18
T. is to me the greatest fatigue in the world THINKING, 16
t. makes it so THINKING, 15
try t. of love LOVE, 67
We are t. beings INTELLECT, 6
thinks He t. too much . . . dangerous MISTRUST, 10
never t. of me ANONYMOUS, 88
The great consolation . . . is to say what one t. FRANKNESS, 4
third if there was a t. sex MEN, 13
the T. Estate contains . . . a nation FRENCH REVOLUTION, 8
T. time lucky PROVERBS, 430
to help Britain to become a T. Programme BRITAIN, 15
third-rate And t. conversation MEDIOCRITY, 7
thirst the t. to come THIRST, 2
whosoever drinketh of this water shall t. again BIBLICAL QUOTATIONS, 327
thirsty He that goes to bed t. rises healthy ALCOHOL, 37
t., and ye gave me drink BIBLICAL QUOTATIONS, 537
thirteen the clocks were striking t. CLOCKS, 1
thirty Don't trust anyone over t. AGE, 63
T. days hath November MONTHS, 9
T. days hath September, /April, June, and November ANONYMOUS, 100
T. millions, mostly fools ENGLISH, 10
t. pieces of silver BETRAYAL, 4
thirty-five for t. years he had not stopped talking SCIENTISTS, 12
thistle I have always plucked a t. and planted a flower REPUTATION, 5
Thomas John T. says good-night to Lady Jane SEX, 56
Thomasina Why so shy, my pretty T. SHYNESS, 3
thorn A rose without a t. ADMIRATION, 9
a t. in the flesh BIBLICAL QUOTATIONS, 55
thorough How . . . t. these Germans always managed to be GERMANY, 5
thoroughness with the t. of a mind that reveres details UNDERSTANDING, 7
thou Book of Verse – and T. BREAD, 4
thought a green t. in a green shade OBLIVION, 3
A library is t. in cold storage BOOKS, 41
A society . . . of individuals . . . capable of original t. would probably be unendurable IDEAS, 8
A t. is often original ORIGINALITY, 3
conversation must be an exchange of t. CONVERSATION, 8
Disease is an image of t. externalized ILLNESS, 23
evil is wrought by want of t. EVIL, 13
Learning without t. is labour lost KNOWLEDGE, 11
monster in his t. /Too hideous to be shown SUSPICION, 4
My t. is *me* THINKING, 14
Only a residual fraction is t. BUREAUCRACY, 7
pale cast of t. CONSCIENCE, 7
Reading . . . ingenious device for avoiding t. READING, 8
sessions of sweet silent t. REGRET, 23
silent form, dost tease us out of t. ETERNITY, 3
something between a thing and a t. PAINTING, 11
T. must be divided against itself UNDERSTANDING, 6
t. only to justify their injustices HUMAN NATURE, 27
t. without learning is perilous KNOWLEDGE, 11
Two souls with but a single t. LOVE, 98
What was once t. IDEAS, 2
will bear to be read twice, . . . was t. twice WRITING, 41
thoughtlessness In the sex-war t. is the weapon of the male SEXES, 8
thoughts Great t. come from the heart HEART, 21
Heavy t. bring on physical maladies MELANCHOLY, 9
Keep off your t. from things that are past PAST, 10
man whose second t. are good THINKING, 1
my t. remain below WORDS, 29
our life is what our t. make it LIFE, 8
sensations rather than of t. SENSATION, 1
speech only to conceal their t. HUMAN NATURE, 27
Speech . . . to disguise . . . t. SPEECH, 19
Suspicions amongst t. SUSPICION, 1
the meanest flower . . . can give /T. NATURE, 38
To understand God's t. STATISTICS, 8
we ought to control our t. SELF-CONTROL, 3
your love but not your t. CHILDREN, 29
thousand I can draw for a t. pounds CONVERSATION, 1
I could be a good woman if I had five t. MONEY, 44
if I were a t. years old MEMORY, 2
One picture is worth ten t. words PAINTING, 1
One t. years more. That's all *Homo sapiens* has MANKIND, 68
the face that launch'd a t. ships BEAUTY, 25
The thought of two t. people crunching celery FOOD, 64
Victory has a t. fathers SUCCESS, 11
We are not about to send American boys nine or ten t. miles DIPLOMACY, 14
What's a t. dollars MONEY, 28
thread from eternity spinning the t. of your being DESTINY, 2
not a blanket woven from one t., one color, one cloth UNITED STATES, 32
threads well-belovèd's hair has t. of grey AGE, 86
threat one can . . . see in a little girl the t. of a woman CHILDREN, 25
three A committee should consist of t. men DEMOCRACY, 22
There are only t. events in a man's life LIFE AND DEATH, 20
there are only t. things to see PHILISTINISM, 5
thought t. times before taking action CAUTION, 10
T. for the rivals ANONYMOUS, 45
T. French hens CHRISTMAS, 17
t. fundamental truths OBJECTIVITY, 3
T. little maids from school CHILDREN, 28
t. o'clock in the morning courage COURAGE, 28
T. o'clock is always too late or too early DAY AND NIGHT, 18
t. things . . . the public will always clamour for NOVELTY, 3
T. years she grew DEATH, 178
we galloped all t. HORSES, 3
who sneaked into my room at t. o'clock this morning COMPLAINTS, 9
threefold a t. cord is not quickly broken BIBLICAL QUOTATIONS, 84
three-pipe a t. problem SMOKING, 11
three-sided if triangles invented a god, they would make him t. RELIGION, 58
thrice before the cock crow, thou shalt deny me t. BETRAYAL, 2
thrift extravagance, . . . t. and adventure ADVENTURE, 2
thrive strong shall t. STRENGTH, 7
throat A good listener is a good talker with a sore t. CONVERSATION, 14
grips him warmly by the t. POLITICIANS, 125
the second act and the child's t. CHILDREN, 24
throats cutting each other's t. SERVANTS, 2
throne A tavern chair is the t. PUBLIC HOUSES, 1
barge . . . like a burnished t. ADMIRATION, 15
he that sitteth on the t. shall dwell among them BIBLICAL QUOTATIONS, 590
High on a t. of royal state DEVIL, 13
It helps . . . to remind your bride that you gave up a t. for her MARRIAGE, 154
no middle course between the t. and the scaffold MONARCHY, 8
royal t. of kings EARTH, 16
something behind the t. MONARCHY, 17
throve that on which it t. /Falls off LOVE, 176
throw t. an egg into an electric fan AMBITION, 10
t. away the dearest thing he ow'd DEATH, 141
thrush That's the wise t. BIRDS, 4
Thucydides the historical works of T. NEWSPAPERS, 7
Thummim Urim and . . . T. BIBLICAL QUOTATIONS, 152
thunder laugh as I pass in t. WEATHER, 26
Thurlow No man . . . so wise as T. looked APPEARANCES, 16
Thursday T.'s child has far to go CHARACTER, 19
Took ill on T. HUMAN CONDITION, 17
'Twas on a Holy T. CHILDREN, 19
thyself Be so true to t. INTEGRITY, 1
Know then t., presume not God to scan SELF-KNOWLEDGE, 7
Resolve to be t. MISERY, 1
Tiber married to the only man north of the T. . . . untidier than I am MARRIAGE, 149
the River T. foaming with much blood PROPHECY, 14
Tiberius Had T. been a cat CATS, 1
tickle a feather to t. the intellect PUNS, 12
ticky-tacky They're all made out of t. HOUSES, 4
tide a t. in the affairs of men OPPORTUNITY, 18
ever lived in the t. of times REGRET, 19
the full t. of human existence is at Charing-Cross LONDON, 16
The t. is full SEA, 1
The western t. crept up DROWNING, 1
t. in the affairs of men DESTINY, 21
tides the waters of the heart /Push in their t. EMOTION, 5
tidings good t. of great joy BIBLICAL QUOTATIONS, 419
tie Never mind about my soul . . . get my t. right PAINTING, 8
tied t. to the stake ENDURANCE, 18
tiger It is not the ape, nor the t. HUMAN NATURE, 26
The atom bomb is a paper t. NUCLEAR WEAPONS, 14
T.! T.! burning bright ANIMALS, 6

U

understood Only one man ever u. me LAST WORDS, 46
undertaker the sort of greeting a corpse would give to an u. GREETINGS, 2
undertakers Doctors and u. /Fear epidemics of good health DOCTORS, 18
I have nothing against u. personally OCCUPATIONS, 16
undertaking no such u. has been received WORLD WAR II, 7
The love of life is necessary to . . . any u. ENTHUSIASM, 5
undiscovered whilst the great ocean of truth lay all u. before me DISCOVERY, 12
undone estate o' th' world were now u. WORLD-WEARINESS, 11
left u. those things BOOK OF COMMON PRAYER, THE, 4
Things hitherto u. should be given . . . a wide berth ORIGINALITY, 1
What's done cannot be u. IRREVOCABILITY, 2
uneasy U. lies the head that wears a crown MONARCHY, 21
uneatable the unspeakable in full pursuit of the u. HEALTH, 26
uneducated Democracy . . . government by the u. ARISTOCRACY, 9
unemployment reduce the rise in prices, increase productivity and reduce u. POLITICS, 64
When a great many people . . . , u. results UNEMPLOYMENT, 2
unendurable A society . . . of individuals . . . capable of original thought would probably be u. IDEAS, 8
unequal Men are made by nature u. EQUALITY, 10
unexamined The u. life SELF, 18
unexpected Old age is the most u. OLD AGE, 98
unfaithful a far more concentrated woman . . . to be u. UNFAITHFULNESS, 3
better to be u. FAITHFULNESS, 1
original is u. to the translation TRANSLATION, 1
unfortunates one of those u. to whom death is EXPLANATIONS, 4
ungain'd Men prize the thing u. more DESIRE, 14
ungrateful a more mean, stupid . . . u. animal than the public PUBLIC, 13
one u. person and a hundred with a grievance PROMOTION, 3
unhappily The bad end u. THEATER, 18
unhappiness if we succeed in transforming your hysterical misery into common u. PSYCHOANALYSIS, 11
unhappy A moment of time may make us u. for ever SORROW, 9
don't believe one can ever be u. for long SELF, 21
each u. family is u. in its own way FAMILY, 54
It is better that some should be u. EQUALITY, 15
making their remaining years u. MANKIND, 34
most u. kind of misfortune HAPPINESS, 6
one is u. one becomes moral SORROW, 18
only when I am unbearably u. SELF-KNOWLEDGE, 6
the instinct for being u. SORROW, 21
Today you're u.? . . . Go shopping MATERIALISM, 20
U. the land that has no heroes HEROISM, 4
unheralded spring now comes u. by the return of the birds ECOLOGY, 1
unicorn The lion and the u. NURSERY RHYMES, 51
uniform love that loves a scarlet coat /Should be more u. PUNS, 8
The u. 'e wore CLOTHES, 13
uniformity let use be preferred before u. HOUSES, 1
uninstructed making things plain to u. people was . . . best means of clearing . . . one's own mind EDUCATION, 43
uninteresting no . . . u. subject CURIOSITY, 4
union To make a u. with Great Britain WORLD WAR II, 41
U. is strength PROVERBS, 448
unionist most conservative man . . . is the British Trade U. CONSERVATISM, 1
unite u. in some holy confederacy CHRISTIANITY, 35
Workers of the world, u. MARXISM, 12
united U. we stand PROVERBS, 449
United Nations U. is not . . . equivalent of our own legal system LAW, 13
United States adherence . . . to the Monroe Doctrine may force the U. UNITED STATES, 54
In the U. there is more space UNITED STATES, 59
so near to the U. UNITED STATES, 16
The best immediate defense of the U. DEFENSE, 3
The U., . . . are twenty years in advance of this country UNITED STATES, 29
The U. has to move very fast UNITED STATES, 34
The U. is like a gigantic boiler UNITED STATES, 23
The U. . . . six hours behind . . . UNITED STATES, 29
the U. will never again seek one additional foot of territory by conquest UNITED STATES, 66
U. is the best and fairest . . . nation UNITED STATES, 7
U. of Europe EUROPE, 5
universal Aunt Edna is u. AUDIENCES, 7
There is no u. law SPONTANEITY, 3
universe a hell of a good u. next door UNIVERSE, 9
chess-board is the world; the pieces . . . the phenomena of the u. GOD, 32
I accept the u. UNIVERSE, 5
I don't pretend to understand the U. UNIVERSE, 4
In this unbelievable u. . . . no absolutes UNIVERSE, 3
I regarded the u. as an open book UNIVERSE, 13
Life exists in the u. SCIENCE, 53
Man's the bad child of the u. MANKIND, 43
Mind is ever the ruler of the u. MIND, 26
no hint throughout the u. /Of good or ill NECESSITY, 11
no reason to assume that the u. has the slightest interest UNIVERSE, 7
Perish the U. REVENGE, 6
take his attention away from the u. PRAYER, 15
the better ordering of the u. MISQUOTATION, 1
the u. and all that surrounds it UNIVERSE, 8
the u. is expanding and contracting SELF-INTEREST, 3
The u. is not hostile UNIVERSE, 11
the u. is . . . queerer than we *can* suppose UNIVERSE, 10
The u. is transformation LIFE, 8
The u. . . . more like a great thought UNIVERSE, 12
The u. ought to be presumed too vast UNIVERSE, 15
the u., the reflection of the structure of the brain MIND, 4
The visible u. was an illusion ILLUSIONS, 1
universes Out of all possible u., the only one which can exist UNIVERSE, 14
universities mortifying fate of most English u. FATE, 12
The King, observing . . . the state of both his u. CAMBRIDGE, 6
U. incline wits to sophistry and affectation EDUCATION, 10
university Any attempt to reform the u. EDUCATION, 44
it is necessary to go to a u. . . . to become a successful writer WRITERS, 6
u., where it was carefully taken out EDUCATION, 69
unjust he that is u., let him be u. still BIBLICAL QUOTATIONS, 605
The u. steals the just's umbrella JUSTICE, 5
unkind Thou art not so u. INGRATITUDE, 4
unkindness I tax not you, you elements, with u. WEATHER, 22
unknown apart from the known and the u. METAPHYSICS, 5
Give me a light that I may tread safely into the u. FAITH, 15
going from the known to the u. RESEARCH, 6
I travelled among u. men HOMESICKNESS, 9
the U. Prime Minister POLITICIANS, 6
To go into the u. DEATH, 169
to the u. god BIBLICAL QUOTATIONS, 12
unmourned and u. OBLIVION, 1
unlabeled One of the unpardonable sins . . . is . . . to go about u. CLASSIFICATION, 1
unlettered An u. king is a crowned ass MONARCHY, 1
unlike the Jews bring the u. into the heart of *every milieu* JEWS, 20
The law of dislike for the u. JEWS, 20
unluckily the good u. THEATER, 18
unmarried to keep u. MARRIAGE, 125
unmotivated The u. action SPONTANEITY, 2
unmuzzled The world regards such a person as . . . an u. dog CLASSIFICATION, 1
unnatural so u. as the commonplace TRIVIALITY, 8
unobtrusive Poetry should be great and u. POETRY, 31
unofficial An u. English rose FLOWERS, 3
unpaid A promise made is a debt u. PROMISES, 6
unpardonable One of the u. sins, . . . , is . . . to go about unlabelled CLASSIFICATION, 1
unperfect He was u., unfinished, inartistic WRITERS, 24
unpleasant Cynicism is an u. way of saying the truth CYNICISM, 2
without mentioning a single book, or *in fact anything u.* BOOKS, 35
unpopular a free society . . . where it is safe to be u. FREEDOM, 57
unprofitable How weary, stale, flat, and u. WORLD-WEARINESS, 8
unreason a liberal education at the Colleges of U. REASON, 1
unrecording troops of u. friends LIFE, 84
unremembered u. acts /Of kindness and of love KINDNESS, 13
unrequited Self-love seems so often u. CONCEIT, 14
unsaid The bitterest tears . . . are for words . . . u. and deeds . . . undone REGRET, 25
unsatisfied It is exquisite, and it leaves one u. SMOKING, 37
unsavory indefatigable and u. engine of pollution DOGS, 14
unsealed my lips are not yet u. MISQUOTATION, 4
unseemly an u. exposure of the mind NASTINESS, 3
unseen to deny the existence of an u. kingdom is bad SPECULATION, 1
unselfishness sympathetic u. of an oyster SELFLESSNESS, 5
unsex u. me here, /And fill me . . . full /Of direst cruelty EVIL, 22
unshriven I am curious to see what happens . . . to one who dies u. LAST WORDS, 63
unsoundness no person can be a poet . . . without . . . u. of mind POETRY, 35
unspeakable the psychopathologist the u. PSYCHIATRY, 23
the u. in full pursuit of the uneatable HEALTH, 26
unspoiled utterly u. by failure FAILURE, 3
unstoned I wouldn't have left a turn u. CRITICISM, 64
untidier married to the only man north of the Tiber . . . u. than I am MARRIAGE, 149
untraveled Gleams that u. world EXPERIENCE, 22
untruth The camera . . . an accessory to u. PHOTOGRAPHY, 3
unupblown Nurse u. BREVITY, 10
unused left over from last year u. ADVICE, 13
unvaccinated let his children go u. ILLNESS, 32
unwashed The great U. PUBLIC, 5
unwholesome Boys . . . are u. companions for grown people CHILDREN, 40
up *How to be one u.* ONE-UPMANSHIP, 2
I saw it at a disadvantage – the curtain was u. CRITICISM, 65
u. with which I will not put GRAMMAR, 4
What's u., Doc CINEMA, 3
upbringing the u. a nun would envy BODY, 18
uplands broad, sunlit u. WORLD WAR II, 12
upper Like many of the u. class ARISTOCRACY, 4
the person that . . . has the u. hand will inevitably give place to another CHARACTER, 18
the u. classes /Have still the u. hand ARISTOCRACY, 11
upper-middle Shirley Williams . . . a member of the u. class CLASS, 52
upright man of life u. RIGHTEOUSNESS, 6
upstairs U. and downstairs /And in my lady's chamber NURSERY RHYMES, 13
Uriah U., . . . made a ghastly writhe SERVILITY, 3
Urim U. and . . . Thummim BIBLICAL QUOTATIONS, 152
urine nose-painting, sleep, and u. ALCOHOL, 69
What is man . . . a . . . machine for turning . . . the red wine of Shiraz into u. MANKIND, 11
urn Can storied u. . . . /Back to its mansion call the fleeting breath DEATH, 73
urologists flood of u. LANGUAGE, 3
usage if u. so choose, with whom resides the decision WORDS, 16
use let u. be preferred before uniformity HOUSES, 1
no reason . . . these machines will ever force themselves into general u. MACHINES, 4
what is the u. of a book BOOKS, 13
What is the u. of a new-born child PURPOSE, 2

W

war-war To jaw-jaw is better than to w. DIPLOMACY, 5
wary the w. fox said . . . to the sick lion MISTRUST, 5
wash Don't w. your dirty linen GOSSIP, 2
W. That Man Right Out of My Hair DECISION, 1
W. your hands often, your feet seldom, and your head never HEALTHY LIVING, 5
washed Pilate . . . w. his hands BIBLICAL QUOTATIONS, 547
w. their robes . . . in the blood of the lamb BIBLICAL QUOTATIONS, 590
washing painting a face and not w. APPEARANCE, 21
wasps w. and hornets break through LAW, 36
waste Far too good to w. on children YOUTH, 28
The years to come seemed w. of breath FIGHT, 19
W. not, want not PROVERBS, 452
wasted Half the money I spend on advertising is w. ADVERTISING, 4
most w. of all days LAUGHTER, 7
wasting she did not believe in w. her effects THREATS, 4
watch Either he's dead or my w. has stopped DEATH, 104
keeping w. over their flock by night BIBLICAL QUOTATIONS, 419
The W. on the Rhine RIVERS, 5
w. and pray BIBLICAL QUOTATIONS, 543
why not carry a w. CLOCKS, 2
watch-dog to hear the w.'s honest bark DOGS, 5
watched A w. pot PATIENCE, 1
watches 'Tis with our judgments as our w. OPINIONS, 5
watchmaker I should have become a w. NUCLEAR WEAPONS, 7
watchman only one man . . . can count on steady work – the night w. NIGHT, 1
watch-tower To hear the lark . . . From his w. in the skies BIRDS, 13
water a pure river of w. of life BIBLICAL QUOTATIONS, 604
better deeds /Shall be in w. writ MEMORIALS, 3
biggest waste of w. in the country WATER, 6
Dripping w. hollows out a stone PERSISTENCE, 11
half the landscape is . . . covered by useless w. SEASIDE, 3
He who drinks a tumbler of London w. WATER, 8
Human beings were invented by w. WATER, 7
I came like W. LIFE AND DEATH, 14
if I were under w. I would scarcely kick MELANCHOLY, 6
impressions . . . lasting as . . . an oar upon the w. INSIGNIFICANCE, 1
It is with our passions as it is with fire and w. PASSION, 5
Like a bridge over troubled w. BRIDGE, 5
like throwing w. into the sea CHARITY, 12
no verse can give pleasure . . . that is written by drinkers of w. WATER, 5
Soap and w. and common sense CLEANNESS, 9
Streets full of w. TELEGRAMS, 3
The first possibility of rural cleanliness lies in *w. supply.* CLEANNESS, 8
the w. that was made wine ALCOHOL, 17
virtues we write in w. MEMORIALS, 15
W., air, and cleanliness are the chief articles in my pharmacopeia HEALTHY LIVING, 32
w. flowed like champagne ABSTINENCE, 4
w., honey, and labour REMEDIES, 5
W. is H_2O, hydrogen two parts, oxygen one SCIENCE, 59
w., is unsuitable in colour WATER, 4
w. still keeps falling over WATER, 1
W., w., every where WATER, 2
when I makes w. I makes w. HUMOR, 31
when I touch wine, it turns into w. ALCOHOL, 49
watering a-w. the last year's crop FUTILITY, 6
Waterloo Battle of W. WAR, 168
Every man meets his W. DEFEAT, 13
the Battle of W. *was* won on the playing-fields of Eton WAR, 115
waters dreadful noise of w. in my ears DROWNING, 2
stolen w. are sweet BIBLICAL QUOTATIONS, 572
the earth shall be full . . . as the w. cover the sea BIBLICAL QUOTATIONS, 258
the sound of many w. BIBLICAL QUOTATIONS, 584
the Spirit of God moved upon . . . the w. BIBLICAL QUOTATIONS, 174
the w. of the heart /Push in their tides EMOTION, 5
w. flowed over mine head BIBLICAL QUOTATIONS, 411
water-trough A snake came to my w. WEATHER, 17
Watson Mr W., come here; I want you SUMMONS, 3
wave Churchill on top of the w. TYRANNY, 1
waves the w. make towards the pebbled shore TIME, 41
wax Skin is like w. paper BODY, 13
waxworks w. inhabited by gramophones WORDS, 22
way A man . . . is *so* in the w. MEN, 4
blow out your candle . . . to find your w. ATHEISM, 6
catch the nearest w. KINDNESS, 10
Great White W. PLACES, 29
I am the w., the truth, and the life BIBLICAL QUOTATIONS, 347
I did it my w. SELF, 5
I go my w. to him that sent me BIBLICAL QUOTATIONS, 353
in every war they kill you a new w. PROGRESS, 18
plowman homeward plods his weary w. DAY AND NIGHT, 10
the error of his w. BIBLICAL QUOTATIONS, 289
The w. to a man's heart LOVE, 10
The w. to dusty death LIFE, 76
though hell should bar the w. DETERMINATION, 17
w. of all flesh DEATH, 51
woman has her w. SEXES, 13
wayfaring study at small cost and short w. EDUCATION, 32
Wayne John W. is dead ANONYMOUS, 50
ways consider your w. BIBLICAL QUOTATIONS, 232
She dwelt among the untrodden w. LONELINESS, 13
w. of making men talk MISQUOTATION, 2
wayside If you see anybody fallen by the w. CHARITY, 21
wayward She was an open, w. . . . sensuous human being BANKHEAD, TALLULAH, 3
we put it down a w. SPELLING, 1
weak Beauty stands /In the admiration . . . of w. minds BEAUTY, 28
concessions of the w. YIELDING, 1
disarm the strong and arm the w. INJUSTICE, 8
Idleness . . . the refuge of w. minds IDLENESS, 2
I inhabit a w., frail, decayed tenement LAST WORDS, 2
Is thy love a plant /Of such w. fibre ABSENCE, 10
Like all w. men . . . an exaggerated stress DECISION, 3
surely the w. shall perish STRENGTH, 7
The w., . . . always prevail over the strong SURVIVAL, 6
The w. have one weapon ERROR, 2
they are w. men ADDICTION, 5
weaker the w. vessel BIBLICAL QUOTATIONS, 562
weakest The w. goes to the wall PROVERBS, 428
weakness no act of w. can be tolerated RUTHLESSNESS, 5
no more w. than is natural to her sex WOMEN, 116
private universe of physical w. and mental decay OLD AGE, 54
weaknesses I have got lots of human w. IMPERFECTION, 13
Never support two w. VICE, 16
touch his w. with a delicate hand IMPERFECTION, 8
weal I will govern according to the common w. MONARCHY, 14
wealth All health is better than w. HEALTH, 21
God shows his contempt for w. WEALTH, 34
Health is better than w. HEALTH, 1
His w. a well-spent age RIGHTEOUSNESS, 7
Outshone the w. of Ormus and of Ind DEVIL, 13
the insolence of w. INSOLENCE, 2
W. has never been a sufficient source of honor OSTENTATION, 3
W. I ask not TRAVEL, 36
W. is like sea-water GREED, 12
W. is not without its advantages WEALTH, 19
Where w. and freedom reign, contentment fails BUSINESS, 13
wealthy Where some people are very w. and others have nothing GOVERNMENT, 5
weaned w. on a pickle APPEARANCE, 32
weapon art is not a w. ART, 11
In the sex-war thoughtlessness is the w. of the male SEXES, 8
The weak have one w. ERROR, 2
tinned food is a deadlier w. WEAPONS, 5
weapons books are w. BOOKS, 37
If sunbeams were w. ENVIRONMENT, 8
on this wall will hang my w. and my lyre, discharged from the war SEX, 45
wear I . . . chose my wife . . . for . . . such qualities as would w. well MARRIAGE, 73
I want you to w. me LOVE, 63
you'll w. your eyes out STARING, 2
weariest The w. nights . . . must . . . end ENDURANCE, 12
weariness much study is a w. of the flesh BIBLICAL QUOTATIONS, 98
The w., the fever, and the fret HUMAN CONDITION, 14
wearing good quote, I'd be w. it REPARTEE, 37
weary Art thou w. SORROW, 14
let us not be w. in well doing BIBLICAL QUOTATIONS, 173
weasel w. under the cocktail cabinet PLAYS, 8
weather even the w. forecast seemed to be some kind of spoof WEATHER, 18
Give me books, fruit, French wine and fine w. PLEASURE, 18
I like the w. WEATHER, 9
This is the w. the cuckoo likes WEATHER, 14
This is the w. the shepherd shuns WEATHER, 15
When two Englishmen meet, their first talk is of the w. ENGLISH, 23
weather-eye Keep your w. open CAUTION, 7
weather-wise Some are w. WISDOM, 18
web The w. of our life is of a mingled yarn GOOD AND EVIL, 6
webs Laws are like spider's w. LAW, 35
weddings w. is sadder than funerals MARRIAGE, 21
Wednesday Married on W. HUMAN CONDITION, 17
W.'s child is full of woe CHARACTER, 19
wee W. . . . tim'rous beastie ANIMALS, 9
weed that tawney w. tobacco SMOKING, 19
What is a w. GOOD, 5
weeds Lilies that fester smell far worse than w. CORRUPTION, 12
nature runs either to herbs, or to w. HUMAN NATURE, 3
Worthless as wither'd w. BELIEF, 4
week Of all the days that's in the w. SUNDAY, 4
see what can be accomplished in a w. DETERMINATION, 22
World War II began last w. WORLD WAR II, 1
weekendmanship that basic w. should contain . . . Important Person Play ONE-UPMANSHIP, 3
weep By the waters of Babylon we sit down and w. UNITED STATES, 63
weep Fair daffodils, we w. to see TRANSIENCE, 15
For men must work, and women must w. SEXES, 16
not to w. at them, nor to hate them, but to understand them UNDERSTANDING, 9
She must w. or she will die MOURNING, 16
so that I do not w. LAUGHTER, 5
Tears such as angels w. SORROW, 13
w. for her sins at the other ADULTERY, 3
W. no more, my lady HOMESICKNESS, 2
weeping Do you hear the children w. SORROW, 3
Why are you w.? Did you imagine that I was immortal LAST WORDS, 56
weigh my innocence begins to w. me down INNOCENCE, 2
weighed thou art w. in the balances, and art found wanting BIBLICAL QUOTATIONS, 63
weight the w. of rages SPOONERISMS, 1
welcome Advice is seldom w. ADVICE, 8
a period of silence on your part would be w. POLITICIANS, 9
Love bade me w. GUILT, 7
Thrice w., darling of the spring BIRDS, 21
welfare-state led to that of the W. SOCIALISM, 22
well as w. off as if he were rich WEALTH, 6
At last I am going to be w. LAST WORDS, 77
do not speak w. of yourself MODESTY, 6
eat wisely but not too w. ETIQUETTE, 5
Every man who feels w. is a sick man ILLNESS, 60
fast till he is w. GREED, 4
I am not w.; pray get me . . . brandy FIRST IMPRESSIONS, 3
Is getting w. ever an art REMEDIES, 41
Living w. and beautifully and justly LIFE, 80

w.'s whole existence SEXES, 6
W. to bear rule . . . is repugnant to Nature WOMAN'S ROLE, 7
W. was God's *second* mistake WOMEN, 84
w. who . . . locked in alone in the National Gallery WOMEN, 13
W. will be the last thing civilized by Man WOMEN, 79
wrecks a w.'s reputation JEWELRY, 1
You're a fine w., Lou INSULTS, 126
womanhood The tobacco business is a conspiracy against w. and manhood SMOKING, 22
W. is the great fact in her life WOMEN, 110
womanized Most British statesmen have either drunk too much or w. too much POLITICIANS, 21
womb How does a child live in the w. BODY, 9
It is almost a pity that a woman has a w. WOMEN, 12
mother's w. /Untimely ripp'd BIRTH, 15
no new baby in the w. of our society RUSSIA, 4
teeming w. of royal kings EARTH, 16
wombs when they feel the life of a child in their w. ABORTION, 1
women a few more w. in parliament POLITICS, 141
A homely face . . . aided many w. heavenward APPEARANCE, 5
All Berkshire w. are very silly WOMEN, 43
all w. do MARRIAGE, 9
American w. expect to find in their husbands WOMEN, 74
An experience of w. EXPERIENCE, 13
a snare in which the feet of w. have always become readily entangled WOMEN, 7
Because w. can do nothing except love LOVE, 103
comely to w. to nourish their hair WOMEN, 99
Few w. care to be laughed at RIDICULE, 2
great city . . . has the greatest men and w. GREATNESS, 15
he gets off with w. because he can't get on SEX, 59
If men knew how w. pass their time WOMEN, 55
If w. didn't exist, . . . money . . . no meaning WOMEN, 87
I have sung w. in three cities WOMEN, 97
Intimacies between w. WOMEN, 25
in w. nine out of ten abdominal swellings are the pregnant uterus BIRTH, 14
I owe nothing to W.'s Lib FEMINISM, 36
I think of w., it is their hair WOMEN, 85
made love to ten thousand w. PROMISCUITY, 9
Monstrous Regiment of W. WOMEN, 63
Most good w. are hidden treasures WOMEN, 91
Most w. have no characters WOMEN, 94
Most w. set out to try to change a man CHANGE, 5
Music and w. I cannot but give way to MUSIC, 34
Older w. are best SEX, 35
proper function of w. BACHELORS, 1
several young w. . . . would render the Christian life intensely difficult CHRISTIANITY, 44
souls of w. are so small WOMEN, 27
Suffer the w. whom ye divorce MARRIAGE, 84
Surgeons and anatomists see no beautiful w. BODY, 25
the man who does not know sick w. does not know w. WOMEN, 82
the only advantage w. have over men – . . . they can cry SEXES, 22
There are two kinds of w. WOMEN, 93
The War between Men and W. SEXES, 29
the w. come and go WOMEN, 46
the w. whose eyes have been washed . . . with tears WOMEN, 41
Votes for W. WOMEN, 11
we cannot instruct w. as we do men in the science of medicine MEDICINE, 22
Were't not for gold and w. SIN, 27
When w. go wrong SEX, 108
Why are w. . . . so much more interesting to men SEXES, 34
Why need . . . w. know so much WOMEN, 26
with peaches and w., it's . . . the side next the sun that's tempting TEMPTATION, 13
W. . . . are either better or worse than men WOMEN, 64
W. are equal because . . . not different WOMEN, 50
W. are most fascinating between the ages of thirty-five and forty WOMEN, 39
W. are much more like each other WOMEN, 31
W. are so opinionated WOMEN, 100
w. become like their mothers SEXES, 32
W. . . . care fifty times more for a marriage than a ministry WOMEN, 17
w. dislike his books WRITERS, 40
W. exist . . . solely for the propagation of the species WOMAN'S ROLE, 8
W. have served . . . as looking-glasses WOMEN, 129
w. . . . ill-using them and then confessing it WOMEN, 119
w., never SCIENCE, 4
W. never have young minds WOMEN, 37
w. . . . not so young as . . . painted COSMETICS, 1
W. represent . . . matter over mind SEXES, 33
w. require both WOMEN, 28
w. should be struck . . . like gongs WOMEN, 33
W. who love the same man LOVE, 22
w. who moan at the lack of opportunities WOMEN, 81
W. would rather be right than reasonable WOMEN, 83
Women's Lib I owe nothing to W. WOMEN'S LIB, 1
womman worthy w. al hir lyve MARRIAGE, 39
won Human reason w.. Mankind w. VICTORY, 10
therefore to be w. WOMEN, 105
wonder knowledge and w. . . . is an impression of pleasure KNOWLEDGE, 5
Many a man has been a w. to the world ADMIRATION, 10
Philosophy is the product of w. PHILOSOPHY, 21
the common w. of all men APPEARANCE, 10
wonderful It is a w. case of nature imitating art ACTORS, 13
the ancient cathedrals – grand, w., mysterious RELIGION, 63
wonderfulest 'Twas the w. war you ever knew.' WORLD WAR I, 1
wonders His w. to perform GOD, 23
wondrous When I survey the w. Cross HUMILITY, 13
wont seen me as he was w. to see me PUNISHMENT, 26
woo the . . . only thing that I ever did wrong /Was to w. a fair young maid ANONYMOUS, 63
wood about the dreadful w. /Of conscious evil GUILT, 2
hewers of w. BIBLICAL QUOTATIONS, 386
the boar out of the w. doth waste it PRAYER, 24
therefore to be w. WOMEN, 105
woman in this humour w. LOVE, 146
would rather hew w. than be a king MONARCHY, 7
woodcock well-shot w., partridge, snipe HUNTING, 2
wooden this w. O THEATER, 16
woodman W., spare that tree TREES, 12
w. spare the beechen tree TREES, 3
woods fresh w., and pastures new CHANGE, 17
Spring /Flow down the w. SPRING, 6
The w. are lovely TRAVEL, 16
the w. decay and fall MORTALITY, 19
They shut the road through the w. TIME, 26
We'll to the w. no more ENDING, 4
When the green w. laugh HAPPINESS, 5
woodshed Something nasty in the w. EVIL, 11
woodworm the w. obligingly held hands HUMOR, 21
Woolworths a speech by Chamberlain is like . . . W. INSULTS, 17
word better w. than prefabricated WORDS, 6
be ye doers of the w. BIBLICAL QUOTATIONS, 283
but a w. and a blow VIOLENCE, 4
every w. stabs CONVERSATION, 11
Good isn't the w. CRITICISM, 22
Greeks had a W. for It LANGUAGE, 1
in the beginning was the w. BIBLICAL QUOTATIONS, 316
in the captain's but a choleric w. INJUSTICE, 14
I would never use a long w. LANGUAGE, 22
Rehearsing a play is making the w. flesh PLAYS, 12
that most precious jewel, the W. of God BIBLE, 7
the addition of a new w. to the English vocabulary WORDS, 14
the kingdom of God is not in w., but in power BIBLICAL QUOTATIONS, 30
the W. had breath CHRISTIANITY, 59
The w. is half Greek and half Latin LATIN, 5
the w. of God is . . . sharper than any two-edged sword BIBLICAL QUOTATIONS, 234
the w. was made flesh BIBLICAL QUOTATIONS, 316
What is honour? A w. HONOR, 5
when *I* use a w. MEANING, 3
words A man of true science . . . uses but few hard w. LANGUAGE, 29
Be not the slave of W. WORDS, 5
best w. in the best order POETRY AND PROSE, 2
big emotions come from big w. REPARTEE, 49
But w. are w. WORDS, 30
by skilful arrangement of your w. WRITING, 16
Covenants without the sword are but w. POWER POLITICS, 3
Don't listen to their w. fix your attention on their deeds SCIENTISTS, 5
Fine w. and an insinuating appearance SERVILITY, 1
Fine w. butter no parsnips PROVERBS, 153
For w., like Nature, half reveal WORDS, 31
I always try to get as many w. ANONYMOUS, 95
I put the w. down WRITING, 44
It wasn't the w. /That frightened the birds ANONYMOUS, 93
learn the use of living w. WORDS, 22
life depends on your power to master w. WORDS, 25
Men of few w. are the best BREVITY, 9
my w. are my own REPARTEE, 19
neither wit, nor w., nor worth SPEECHES, 11
One picture is worth ten thousand w. PAINTING, 1
Thanks to w., we . . . rise above the brutes . . . sunk to the level of the demons WORDS, 17
the barbarous, gothic times when w. had a meaning WORDS, 13
to set a chime of w. tinkling in . . . a few fastidious people PURPOSE, 10
uses his w. as a quack uses his remedies VERBOSITY, 5
use the most common, . . . w. LANGUAGE, 44
Whenever ideas fail, men invent w. WORDS, 11
W. . . . , are great foes of reality WORDS, 7
W. are like leaves VERBOSITY, 7
W. are men's daughters WORDS, 21
w. are the daughters of earth LANGUAGE, 23
W. are . . . the most powerful drug WORDS, 20
w. but wind WORDS, 4
w. left unsaid and deeds left undone REGRET, 25
W. may be false and full of art SPEECH, 17
w. never seen . . . before outside of a dictionary POETS, 26
w. once spoke . . . never be recall'd SPEECH, 16
Words, w., w. WORDS, 27
You can stroke people with w. WORDS, 12
Wordsworth Mr W. is never interrupted INTERRUPTIONS, 3
W.'s healing power POETS, 3
wore w. enough for modesty CLOTHES, 4
work All w. and no play PROVERBS, 41
an environment equally fit for birth, growth w., healing, and dying HEALTHY LIVING, 25
dignity in w. WORK, 6
Every man's w. . . . is always a portrait of himself ARTS, 1
For men must w., and women must weep SEXES, 16
How can I take an interest in my w. ENTHUSIASM, 2
if any would not w., neither should he eat BIBLICAL QUOTATIONS, 645
I like w.; it fascinates me IDLENESS, 7
In w. the greatest satisfaction lies WORK, 3
it is poor grub, poor pay, and easy w. ENGLAND, 30
My Nails are Drove, My W. is done ANONYMOUS, 61
No, this right hand shall w. it all off WRITING, 39
no w., nor device, nor knowledge . . . in the grave BIBLICAL QUOTATIONS, 89
one must do some w. seriously . . . and not merely amuse oneself WORK, 14
only place where success comes before w. SUCCESS, 19
prejudice against w. CHANGE, 3
success . . . by dint of hard w. EFFORT, 5
the w. comes out more beautiful ARTS, 4
the w. is negligible CRITICISM, 1
the world's w., . . . is done by men who do not feel . . . well ILLNESS, 27
they must hate to w. for a living MARRIAGE, 111
To sport would be as tedious as to w. LEISURE, 5
When w. is a pleasure WORK, 12
Why should I let the toad *w.* WORK, 16
W. and love – these are the basics NEUROSIS, 13
W. banishes those three great evils WORK, 33
W. . . . by those employees who have not yet reached . . . incompetence INCOMPETENCE, 4
W. expands so as to fill the time WORK, 23
W. is much more fun than fun WORK, 8
W. is necessary for man WORK, 24

W. is the curse of the drinking classes WORK, 35
W. is the grand cure MALADIES, 2
you can't call yourself a great w. of nature INSULTS, 128
worked should have w. just long enough WORK, 32
worker a sociable w. SOCIETY, 1
a standardised w. with interchangeable parts INDUSTRIAL RELATIONS, 3
workers Dear comrades, soldiers, sailors and w. RUSSIAN REVOLUTION, 5
He is used to dealing with estate w. POLITICIANS, 45
hiring taxis . . . handing out redundancy notices to its own w. INCOMPETENCE, 2
W. of the world, unite MARXISM, 12
worketh according to the power that w. in us BIBLICAL QUOTATIONS, 116
working God as a w. hypothesis GOD, 17
No writer before the . . . 19th century wrote about the w. classes CLASS, 50
The party is the rallying-point for the . . . w. class COMMUNISM, 17
the w.-class which, raw and half-developed PUBLIC, 2
To the ordinary w. man, . . . Socialism SOCIALISM, 19
worst fault of the w. classes CLASS, 30
workman A bad w. PROVERBS, 2
tell a British w. by his hands LAZINESS, 1
works all his w. BOOK OF COMMON PRAYER, THE, 12
faith, if it hath not w., is dead BIBLICAL QUOTATIONS, 284
more copies of my w. are left behind WRITERS, 4
they were judged every man according to their w. BIBLICAL QUOTATIONS, 600
W. done least rapidly PERFECTION, 4
workshop England . . . the w. of the world ENGLAND, 20
worktime the bustle of man's w. OPTIMISM, 18
world a citizen of the w. NATIONALITY, 10
A great writer creates a w. of his own WRITERS, 14
A lie can be halfway round the w. LYING, 9
All's right with the w. PERFECTION, 3
all the uses of this w. WORLD-WEARINESS, 8
all the w. as my parish RELIGION, 80
All the w. is queer SUBJECTIVITY, 5
All the w. loves a lover LOVE, 2
All the w.'s a stage HUMAN CONDITION, 22
all the w. should be taxed BIBLICAL QUOTATIONS, 417
a man for whom the outside w. exists CHARACTER, 8
A man travels the w. over HOME, 8
as good be out of the w. FASHION, 4
a W. in a grain of sand WONDER, 2
brave new w. /That has such people in't MANKIND, 57
brought nothing into this w. BIBLICAL QUOTATIONS, 650
chess-board is the w.; the pieces . . . the phenomena of the universe GOD, 32
citizen of the w. COURTESY, 2
compare /This prison where I live unto the w. IMPRISONMENT, 10
Dear W., I am leaving you because I am bored LAST WORDS, 75
dominate the w. INFLUENCE, 14
excellent foppery of the w. MISFORTUNE, 18
Germany will be . . . a w. power GERMANY, 4
glory, jest, and riddle of the w. HUMAN CONDITION, 19
God so loved the w. BIBLICAL QUOTATIONS, 324
good deed in a naughty w. GOOD, 16
Grant me paradise in this w. HEAVEN, 15
Had we but w. enough, and time SHYNESS, 5
he could not avoid making Him set the w. in motion CREATION, 13
he must view the man in his w. ENVIRONMENT, 5
I am the light of the w. BIBLICAL QUOTATIONS, 336
I called the New W. into existence UNITED STATES, 8
If all the w. were paper ANONYMOUS, 42
If the w. were good for . . . speculation SPECULATION, 2
If you were the only girl in the w. LOVE, 73
I have . . . been all round the w. TRAVEL, 8
I have overcome the w. BIBLICAL QUOTATIONS, 357
in mourning . . . for the w. MOURNING, 15
in the w. . . . and the w. knew him not BIBLICAL QUOTATIONS, 316
in this harsh w. HEART, 19
Into the dangerous w. I leapt BIRTH, 5
I . . . pass through this w. but once MORTALITY, 11
it's a jolly strange w. CONFUSION, 2
It's the same the whole w. over ANONYMOUS, 71
joy that a man is born into the w. BIBLICAL QUOTATIONS, 356
little sisters to all the w. WOMEN, 41
Looks the whole w. in the face RIGHTEOUSNESS, 9
Many a man has been a wonder to the w. ADMIRATION, 10
Never having been able to succeed in the w. ENVY, 10
now shall the prince of this w. be cast out BIBLICAL QUOTATIONS, 344
One w. at a time AFTERLIFE, 12
Our country is the w. UNITED STATES, 20
queen for all the w. ROYALTY, 95
say to all the w. 'This was a man' CHARACTER, 26
Stop the W., I Want to Get Off WORLD-WEARINESS, 6
Superstition sets the whole w. in flames SUPERSTITION, 12
Ten Days that Shook the W. RUSSIAN REVOLUTION, 7
the credit goes to the man who convinces the w. SCIENCE, 25
the entrances of this w. made narrow BIBLICAL QUOTATIONS, 124
The German Empire has become a w. empire GERMANY, 7
the hand that rules the w. INFLUENCE, 12
The history of the W. is the W.'s court HISTORY, 30
The madman thinks the rest of the w. crazy MADNESS, 38
The true system of the W. has been recognized BOOKS, 2
The wickedness of the w. VICE, 5
the w. hath lost his youth BIBLICAL QUOTATIONS, 125
The w. is becoming like a lunatic asylum MADNESS, 25
The w. . . . is but a large prison EXECUTION, 30
The w. is but a school of inquiry CURIOSITY, 5
The w. is disgracefully managed COMPLAINTS, 3
The w. is everything that is the case LOGIC, 7
The w. is made of people who MEDIOCRITY, 2
The w. is made up for the most part of fools FOOLISHNESS, 11
The w. is too much with us WASTE, 3
the w. may talk of hereafter WAR, 47
the w. must be made safe for . . . fifty years WAR, 43
the w.'s mine oyster OPPORTUNITY, 19
the w., the flesh, and the devil BOOK OF COMMON PRAYER, THE, 8
The W. would be a safer place SPACE, 5
the w. would not be the same NUCLEAR WEAPONS, 17
they only saved the w. HEROISM, 3
This is the way the w. ends ENDING, 3
this little w. EARTH, 16
This w. is very odd we see CONFUSION, 5
This w. nis but a thurghfare LIFE AND DEATH, 12
though the w. perish JUSTICE, 11
triple pillar of the w. LOVE, 129
turn your back upon the w. PERFECTION, 5
We joined the Navy to see the w. EXPECTATION, 1
What a fine comedy this w. would be LIFE, 30
When all the w. dissolves DOOMSDAY, 5
When all the w. is young, lad YOUTH, 18
where in this small-talking w. MEANING, 4
which taketh away the sin of the w. BIBLICAL QUOTATIONS, 318
wilderness of this w. WILDERNESS, 1
with how little wisdom the w. is governed GOVERNMENT, 27
w. be made fit and safe to live in WAR AND PEACE, 21
w., I count it . . . but an hospital WORLD, 1
w. is a beautiful place HUMAN CONDITION, 9
w. is a comedy to those who think LIFE, 87
w. is charged with the grandeur of God GOD, 29
w. . . . made safe for democracy DEMOCRACY, 25
w. will make a . . . path to his door FAME, 10
w. without end BOOK OF COMMON PRAYER, THE, 5
w. would go round . . . faster INTERFERING, 1
worldly Mr W. Wiseman MATERIALISM, 6
The W. Hope men set their Hearts upon TRANSIENCE, 14
worlds best of possible w. OPTIMISM, 37
I am become death, the destroyer of w. NUCLEAR WEAPONS, 16
So many w. ACTION, 14
Wandering between two w. LIMBO, 1
we live in the best of all possible w. OPTIMISM, 21
worm a w. at one end and a fool at the other FISHING, 1
Even a w. will turn ENDURANCE, 1
The cut w. FORGIVENESS, 9
the w., thou art my mother BIBLICAL QUOTATIONS, 305
To tread by chance upon a w. DEATH, 114
worms eaten of w. BIBLICAL QUOTATIONS, 11
many devils would set on me in W. PROTESTANTISM, 4
Sir, you have tasted two whole w. SPOONERISMS, 5
w. have eaten them, but not for love LOVE AND DEATH, 7
wormwood her end is bitter as w. BIBLICAL QUOTATIONS, 570
the name of the star is called W. BIBLICAL QUOTATIONS, 591
the w. and the gall BIBLICAL QUOTATIONS, 409
worry W. affects circulation, the heart and the glands WORRY, 14
worrying W. is the most natural and spontaneous of . . . functions WORRY, 16
worse Defend the bad against the w. DECLINE, 3
Dublin, though . . . much w. than London PLACES, 19
for better for w. BOOK OF COMMON PRAYER, THE, 15
If my books had been any w. CINEMA, 4
MORE WILL MEAN W. EDUCATION, 5
sin no more, lest a w. thing come unto thee BIBLICAL QUOTATIONS, 328
The w. I do, the more popular I get POPULARITY, 5
who ever knew Truth put to the w. TRUTH, 39
worship external public w. of God, . . . might be preserved CHURCH, 5
freedom . . . to w. HUMAN RIGHTS, 6
grant the right of private w. TOLERANCE, 6
No one can w. God . . . on an empty stomach BUSINESS, 31
O w. the King GOD, 27
worshippers the one God whose w. . . . still trust in Him GAMBLING, 1
worst His w. is better than any other person's best COMPLIMENTS, 13
it was the w. of times FRENCH REVOLUTION, 3
no surer way of calling the w. HUMAN NATURE, 7
The w. is not, /So long as we can say ENDURANCE, 19
They . . . like to be told the w. BRITISH, 6
we can say 'This is the w.' OPTIMISM, 32
w. kinde of infortune MISFORTUNE, 8
You do your w. WORLD WAR II, 17
worth A man's w. something CONFLICT, 5
If a job's w. doing EFFORT, 1
Paris is w. a mass PARIS, 3
The w. of a State STATE, 4
Whatever is w. doing EXCELLENCE, 1
W. seeing? yes IRELAND, 10
worthless a more w. set than Byron POETS, 36
Our parents' age . . . has produced us, more w. still AGE, 41
worthy the labourer is w. of his hire BIBLICAL QUOTATIONS, 430
w. is the lamb that was slain BIBLICAL QUOTATIONS, 588
would He w., wouldn't he DENIAL, 4
You might have saved him if you w. GUILT, 4
wound A w. heals but the scar remains SORROW, 1
To w. thy lord, thy king, thy governor BITTERNESS, 3
W. with a touch SATIRE, 2
wounds Bind up their w. HELP, 7
Millions have died of medicable w. ILLNESS, 7
To fight and not to heed the w. FIGHT, 14
What deep w. ever closed without a scar SUFFERING, 12
w. and abscesses no longer poison the atmosphere CLEANNESS, 5
wrapp'd O tiger's heart w. in a woman's hide WOMEN, 106
wrapped w. him in swaddling clothes BIBLICAL QUOTATIONS, 418
wrapping perceive Christmas through its w. CHRISTMAS, 22
wrath let not the sun go down upon your w. BIBLICAL QUOTATIONS, 117
trampling out the vintage where the grapes of w. GOD, 30
wreathe W. iron pokers into true-love knots POETS, 12

BIOGRAPHICAL INDEX

References are to the thematic headings under which an author or speaker appears. Entries set in bold captials (e.g. **SHAKESPEARE**) indicate biographical entires in the main part of the dictionary. These are listed in their normal alphabetical position.

Gilman, Charlotte Perkins FEMINISM, 12, IMPOSSIBILITY, 2; NEW YORK, 2, SEXES, 12, UNITED STATES, 22
Gilmour, Ian POLITICS, 56
Gingold, Hermione WOMEN, 52
Ginsberg, Allen MADNESS, 17
Giraudoux, Jean CLARITY, 2, INDUSTRIAL RELATIONS, 3, LAW, 17, MANKIND, 29, MEDIOCRITY, 4
Gisborne, Thomas ENVY, 7
Giustiniani, Sebastian POLITICIANS, 50, 51
Gladstone, William Ewart CLASS, 18, EVIL, 12, FIGHT, 9, OXFORD, 9; PROGRESS, 12, VIOLENCE, 7
Glasse, Hannah FOOD, 35, MISQUOTATION, 15
Gloucester, William, Duke of WRITING, 14
Glover-Kind, John A. SEASIDE, 4
Glynn, Martin H. WAR, 64
Godard, Jean-Luc CINEMA, 7, 8
Goebbels, Joseph WAR, 65; WORLD WAR II, 28
Goering, Hermann NAZISM, 2, 3, PHILISTINISM, 4, UNITED STATES, 79; WORLD WAR II, 29
Goethe BEGINNING, 9, CHARACTER, 9, CONFLICT, 6, DENIAL, 1; DISCOVERY, 10, DOCTORS, 49, HYPOCHONDRIA, 7; ILLNESS, 28, LAST WORDS, 42; LIFE, 39; MADNESS, 18, MEDICINE, 31, MORTALITY, 8, OLD AGE, 48, PURPOSE, 3, REALITY, 4, SCIENCE, 40, SELF-KNOWLEDGE, 5, SUPERSTITION, 9; TALENT, 4; THEORY, 7
Golding, William EVOLUTION, 15, INNOCENCE, 5, INSULTS, 53, REVOLUTION, 6, SLEEP, 15
Goldsmith, James BUSINESS, 12, MARRIAGE, 71
GOLDSMITH, Oliver
Goldwater, Barry EXCESS, 5; GOVERNMENT, 15, POLITICS, 57, WAR, 66
GOLDWYN, Samuel
Goncourt, Edmond de NOVELS, 6
Gonne, Maud POETS, 17
Gooch, George Peabody WAR, 67
Goodman, Ace TELEVISION, 9
Goodman, Edward H. DOCTORS, 51
Gorbachov, Mikhail DEMOCRACY, 6, 7, PROGRESS, 13, RUSSIA, 2, SOCIALISM, 9, 10, TECHNOLOGY, 7
Gordon, Adam Lindsay MISFORTUNE, 11
Gorer, Geoffrey MARRIAGE, 74
Gorky, Maxim GOOD AND EVIL, 5; MARRIAGE, 75; MATHEMATICS, 10, WORK, 12, WRITING, 15
Goschen, George Joachim DIPLOMACY, 10
Gosse, Edmund CRITICISM, 23, WEAKNESS, 3
Gourmont, Remy de OPERATIONS, 11
Gournay, Jean Claude Vincent de FREEDOM, 17
Gove, Philip Babcock LEXICOGRAPHY, 3
Gowers, Ernest WORDS, 14
Grable, Betty SUCCESS, 9
Grace, W. G. CRICKET, 3
Gracián, Baltasar BREVITY, 2; WISDOM, 19
Grade, Lew BOASTS, 3, CHRISTIANITY, 38, CONCEIT, 12, GOLDWYNISMS, 27, 28; PLAYS, 5
Grafton, Richard MONTHS, 9
Graham, Dr. Billy RELIGION, 38
Graham, Harry FIRE, 3, INSENSITIVITY, 3
Graham, James EXECUTION, 13
Graham, Martha ART, 9
Graham, Sheilah EYES, 5
Grahame, Kenneth BOATS, 7, KNOWLEDGE, 18, OXFORD, 10, VICE, 10
Grange, Red FOOTBALL, 4
Grant, Cary AGE, 37, REPARTEE, 46
Grant, Robert GOD, 27, WORSHIP, 2
GRANT, Ulysses Simpson
Granville-Barker, Harley ANIMALISM, 2, LANGUAGE, 21; POETRY, 23
Graves, John Woodcock HUNTING, 5
Graves, Robert BOOK TITLES, 10, HUMOR, 24, LOVE, 71; MEDICINE, 32; POETS, 18, 19, WAR, 69
Gray, Thomas DAY AND NIGHT, 10, DEATH, 73, 74, DOOM, 1, EPITAPHS, 13, 14, 15; GRAVE, 5, IGNORANCE, 9, 10; LONELINESS, 2, MATERIALISM, 12; MORTALITY, 10, POVERTY, 15, SOLITUDE, 8; TEMPTATION, 11, WASTE, 2, WAY, 3
Grayson, Victor EXPLANATIONS, 3
Greeley, Horace EXPLORATION, 2
Green, Celia MIND, 10; RESEARCH, 14
Green, Kensal POLITICIANS, 52, 53, 54
Greene, Graham ATHEISM, 8, BEAUTY, 19, BRIBERY, 4, CLERGY, 7, COMMITMENT, 4, FAME, 14, LITERATURE, 5, MEDIA, 6; MIRACLES, 3, OLD AGE, 49; PROOF, 5; RELIGION, 39; SENTIMENTALITY, 1; SUICIDE, 15, TRAVEL, 17, WEALTH, 23
Greer, Germaine CHILDREN, 30, FEMINISM, 13, 14, HUMAN CONDITION, 10, LOVE, 72, MEN, 5, PSYCHIATRY, 18; SEX, 38, 39, 40; WOMAN'S ROLE, 3
Gregg, Alan CHARITY, 17, GENIUS, 6
Gregory I ENGLISH, 17
Gregory VII CATHOLICISM, 5, HUMILITY, 5
Gregory, Richard Arman SCIENCE, 41
Gregory, William EXECUTION, 14
Grellet, Stephen MORTALITY, 11
Greville, Fulke HUMAN CONDITION, 11
Grey, Lord PROPHECY, 9; UNITED STATES, 23
Griffith-Jones, Mervyn HOMOSEXUALITY, 8, PRUDERY, 1
Griffiths, Trevor MEDICINE, 33
Grimké, Angelina FEMINISM, 15; WOMEN, 53
Groddeck, George THINKING, 5
Groener, Wilhelm DEFEAT, 5
Gromyko, Andrei POLITICIANS, 55
Gronow, Rees Howell SOCIETY, 5
Gropius, Walter ARCHITECTURE, 6
Grosseteste, Robert RELIGION, 40
Grossmith, George ABSENCE, 7, HOME, 6, LOVE, 73
Guedalla, Philip BOATS, 8, HISTORIANS, 3, PUNS, 6, WORLD WAR II, 30, WRITERS, 18
Guevara, Che REVOLUTION, 5
Guiterman, Arthur MANNERS, 3
Guitry, Sacha JEALOUSY, 4
Gulbenkian, Nubar FOOD, 36, GOLF, 2
Gull, William Withey MEDICINE, 34, PATIENTS, 4
Gunn, Neil FATE, 9
Gurney, Dorothy GARDENS, 7
Gwenn, Edmund ACTING, 9, LAST WORDS, 43
Gwyn, Nell RELIGION, 41, REPARTEE, 47
Hadrian DOCTORS, 52
Haeser, Heinrich MEDICINE, 35
Haggard, Henry Rider WOMAN'S ROLE, 4
Hahnemann, Samuel REMEDIES, 31
Haig, Earl FIGHT, 11; WAR, 70
Hailsham, Lord BOREDOM, 5, LANGUAGE, 20, POLITICS, 58, 59, SINCERITY, 4, UNITED STATES, 80
Hakluyt, Richard IDLENESS, 5
Haldane, J. B. S. ARISTOCRACY, 12, DISEASE, 24, EVOLUTION, 16, POETS, 20; SCIENCE, 43, SCIENTISTS, 6, UNIVERSE, 10, VIVISECTION, 3
Hale, Edward Everett POLITICIANS, 56
Hale, Matthew CHRISTIANITY, 39
Hale, Nathan PATRIOTISM, 17
Hale, Sarah Josepha ANIMALS, 14, LAMBS, 3
Halicarnassus, Dionysius of HISTORY, 9
Halifax, Lord FREEDOM, 18, PEOPLE, 3, POPULARITY, 3, PROMOTION, 2, REBELLION, 7, SPEECH, 12, SUBJECTIVITY, 3, TOLERANCE, 5, VIRTUE AND VICE, 3
Halifax, Viscount OXFORD, 11
Hall, Charles Sprague EPITAPHS, 16, GRAVE, 6; MEMORIALS, 7
Hall, Peter AGE, 38
Haller, Albrecht von DEATH, 75
Halliwell, Leslie FICTION, 4
Halsey, Margaret ENGLAND, 22, 23, ENGLISH, 18, 19, 20
Halsey, W. C. WORLD WAR II, 31
Hamilton, Alexander UNITED STATES, 24
Hamilton, Patrick SLEEP, 16
Hamilton, William BRITAIN, 7, LONDON, 14, MANKIND, 30, TOURISTS, 1, TRUTH, 27
Hammarskjold, Dag DESTINY, 13, DETERMINATION, 11, LONELINESS, 3, OLD AGE, 50, PRAYER, 20 WHISTLING, 3
Hammerstein, Oscar DAY AND NIGHT, 11, DECISION, 1, LOVE, 74, MEN, 6, MUSIC, 19; OPTIMISM, 27, PARIS, 1, REASON, 3, RIVERS, 2, WHISTLING, 3, WOMEN, 54
Hammond, Percy THEATER, 10
Hampton, Christopher CAPITALISM, 6, CRITICS, 6, HONESTY, 4; SEX, 41, THEORY, 8; VIOLENCE, 8
Hancock, John SIGNATURES, 2
Hand, Judge Learned FREEDOM, 19
Hankey, Katherine CHRISTIANITY, 40
Hanrahan, Brian JOURNALISM, 21, WAR, 71
Harbach, Otto DRINKS, 12, INDECISION, 2
Harbord, James Guthrie DIPLOMACY, 11, INSULTS, 55
Harburg, E. Y. DESIRE, 7, 8, FAITH, 14, MISQUOTATION, 16, SPACE, 5, TRAVEL, 18
Harcourt, William SOCIALISM, 12
Harding, Gilbert INSULTS, 56, MEDIA, 7
Harding, Warren G. POLITICS, 60, UNITED STATES, 25
Hardwicke, Lord DOUBT, 6
Hardy, Oliver ACCIDENTS, 5
Hardy, Thomas BOATS, 9; CHRISTIANITY, 41, CLASS, 19, LIFE, 40, LOVE, 75; POETRY, 24, SILENCE, 7, VIRTUE, 12, WAR AND PEACE, 9, WEATHER, 14, 15
Hargreaves, W. F. BED, 5, FASHION, 6
Harington, John TREASON, 6
Harlow, Jean CLOTHES, 8
Harold II THREATS, 5
Harrington, James UNITED STATES, 26
Harrington, Michael POVERTY, 16
Harris, Frank HISTORY, 17
Harris, George ADVICE, 13
Hart, Lorenz CONFUSION, 6, DECLINE, 2
Hartley, L. P. PAST, 5
Harvey, William BODY, 11, EVOLUTION, 17
Haskell, Arnold PATRIOTISM, 19
Haskins, Minnie Louise FAITH, 15, LIGHT, 9, UNKNOWN, 1
Hassall, Christopher APPEARANCES, 19, CHARACTER, 10
Hastings, Lady Flora DEATH, 76
Haughey, Charles IRELAND, 9
Havers, Michael TREASON, 7
Haw-Haw, Lord TREASON, 8; WORLD WAR II, 32
Hawker, R. S. EXECUTION, 15
Hawkes, Jacquetta DIFFERENCE, 8
Hawthorne, Nathaniel AFTERLIFE, 4, DISEASE, 25, ENGLAND, 24, HOLISTIC MEDICINE, 2
Hay, Ian HUMOR, 25
Hay, Lord Charles WAR, 72
Hay, Will INTELLECT, 4, REPARTEE, 48, SCIENCE, 44
Hayes, J. Milton MOURNING, 5
Hayes, Rutherford B. UNITED STATES, 27
HAZLITT, William
Healey, Denis INSULTS, 57, 58, 59, POLITICIANS, 57, 58, POLITICS, 61, 62, PRIME MINISTERS, 22, TAXATION, 7
Hearst, William Randolph DOGS, 9
Heath, Edward BRITAIN, 8, CAPITALISM, 7, 8, POLITICS, 63, 64, 65, TAXATION, 8
Heath, Neville LAST WORDS, 45
Heber, Reginald GOD, 28; MISANTHROPY, 1, PLACES, 18
Heberden, William HYPOCHONDRIA, 8
Hecht, Ben MEDICINE, 36
Hegel EXPERIENCE, 16, LAST WORDS, 46, UNDERSTANDING, 4
Heifetz, Jascha EGOTISM, 6, INSULTS, 60
Heine, Heinrich CENSORSHIP, 3, INFERIORITY, 1, JEWS, 8, LAST WORDS, 47, MADNESS, 19, PESSIMISM, 8
Heisenberg, Werner EXPERTS, 4, NATURE, 16
Heller, Joseph ILLNESS, 29, IMMORTALITY, 4, LITERATURE, 6, LOGIC, 5, MEDIOCRITY, 5, OBSTRUCTION, 4, RULES, 4, SELF-MADE MEN, 2, SELF-PRESERVATION, 7, SEX, 42; WAR, 73
Hellman, Lillian CYNICISM, 2, INTEGRITY, 3, MASCULINITY, 1
Helmuth, William T. SCIENCE, 45
Helpmann, Robert DANCING, 6, NAKEDNESS, 8
Helps, Arthur POLITICIANS, 59, READING, 8, SMOKING, 15
Helvétius, Claude-Adrien EDUCATION, 36
Hemans, Felicia Dorothea COURAGE, 15, STATELY HOMES, 6
HEMINGWAY, Ernest
Hemminger, Graham Lee SMOKING, 16
Henderson, Leon ECONOMICS, 11
Henderson, Nicholas BRITAIN, 9
Hendrick, Burton J. DOCTORS, 53, TRUTH, 28
Hendrix, Jimi DEATH, 77; GOLDWYNISMS, 29
Henley, William Ernest ENDURANCE, 6, FATE, 10, RESPONSIBILITY, 7
Henn, T. R. WORDS, 15
Henri IV CONSCIENCE, 5, FOOLISHNESS, 13, PARIS, 3, POVERTY, 17
Henry II ASSASSINATION, 5, CHILDREN, 31, CORRUPTION, 5, DIPLOMACY, 12, GUILT, 6
Henry IV MONARCHY, 13; TAXATION, 9
Henry V MERCY, 3
Henry VIII BIBLE, 7, FIRST IMPRESSIONS, 4, GOVERNMENT, 16; INSULTS, 61, OBLIGATION, 2, POLITICS, 66
Henry, Prince of Wales IMPRISONMENT, 5
Henry, Matthew HUNGER, 6, SUNDAY, 6
Henry, O. APPEARANCE, 23, DARKNESS, 10, LAST WORDS, 48, LIFE, 41; TEARS, 1, WOMEN, 55
Henry, Patrick CAESAR, 3; FREEDOM, 21, TREASON, 9, UNITED STATES, 81
Hentzner, Paul ROYALTY, 65
Hepworth, Barbara ART, 10
Heraclitus CHANGE, 10, 11
Herbert, A. P. BABIES, 5, DISASTER, 3, ENGLISH, 22, LAW, 20, MARRIAGE, 76, 77; PERVERSITY, 4, PLEASURE, 14, POETRY, 25, WATER, 4
Herbert, George ALCOHOL, 37, DAY AND NIGHT, 12; DEATH, 78, FREEDOM, 22; GRAVE, 7, GUILT, 7, LOVE, 76; OLD AGE, 51, RELIGION, 42, SERVICE, 3, VIRTUE, 14, WAR AND PEACE, 10
Herbert, Henry WRITERS, 21
Herford, Oliver AMBITION, 10; HUMOR, 26, REPARTEE, 50
Herodotus WORLD-WEARINESS, 3
Herold, Don APPEARANCE, 24
Herophilus DRUGS, 10
Herrick, James B. DIAGNOSIS, 9
Herrick, Robert BUSINESS, 14, CLOTHES, 10, 11, KINGS AND KINGDOMS, 6, MARRIAGE, 78, PRESENT, 6, TRANSIENCE, 15, TYRANNY, 5
Hervey, Lord LYING, 11
Hesse, Hermann HATE, 6, LIFE AND DEATH, 19, WISDOM, 20
Hewart, Gordon APPEARANCE, 25; JUSTICE, 14; REPARTEE, 51
Heywood, Thomas BOOK TITLES, 11, POVERTY, 18
Hicks, Seymour AGE, 39
Hickson, William Edward PERSISTENCE, 5
Higginson, Thomas Wentworth WRITERS, 22
Higley, Brewster HOMESICKNESS, 4
Hill, Aaron DECISION, 2
Hill, Joe AFTERLIFE, 5; HEAVEN, 5
Hill, Rowland MUSIC, 20
Hillary, Edmund ACHIEVEMENT, 6, CIVILIZATION, 7, PHOTOGRAPHY, 4

Low, David ART, 15; DETERMINATION, 14, SELF-RELIANCE, 8
Lowe, Robert TAXATION, 14
Lowell, Robert MEMORIALS, 10; PESSIMISM, 11; RELIGION, 50, REMEDIES, 41, TIME, 30
Lowry, L. S. MARRIAGE, 90
Lowry, Malcolm CHILDREN, 43, CONTRACEPTION, 7, LOVE AND DEATH, 4
Loyola, St Ignatius CHURCH, 6, FIGHT, 14, LABOR, 6, REWARDS, 4, SELFLESSNESS, 3
Lucan FAMILY, 32; FATE, 13
Lucas, E. V. TRAVEL, 27
Lucretius GENERATIONS, 1, MIND, 20, MORTALITY, 15, NOTHING, 1, PERSISTENCE, 10; TASTE, 5
Ludendorff, Erich LEADERSHIP, 7, SOLDIERS, 5
Ludwig, Emil SUICIDE, 19
Lundquist, James WRITERS, 34
Luther, Martin FAITH, 20, ILLNESS, 43, MEDICINE, 57, MELANCHOLY, 9, PLEASURE, 22; PROTESTANTISM, 3, 4, 5, REBELLION, 11, RELIGION, 51, ROYALTY, 76; SEX, 62, SEXES, 18; WEALTH, 28
Lutyens, Edwin FOOD, 50, INSULTS, 91
Lyly, John ALCOHOL, 53
Lynch, Jack CONTRACEPTION, 8
Lyte, Henry Francis RELIGION, 52
Lyttelton, G. W. EDUCATION, 54
Macarthur, Douglas DETERMINATION, 15, OPPORTUNITY, 15; PROPHECY, 12, WAR, 95
Macarthy, Desmond JOURNALISM, 28
Macaulay, Lord BETRAYAL, 9; BIBLE, 9, CIVILIZATION, 9; COURAGE, 19, CRITICISM, 38, 39, DIPLOMACY, 19; DUST, 6, FREEDOM, 35; IMAGINATION, 11; INTELLECT, 7; JOURNALISM, 29, KNOWLEDGE, 29, MISTRUST, 8, MORALITY, 10, NAVY, 8, NEGLECT, 3; PAROCHIALISM, 2, POETRY, 35, POLITICIANS, 76, POLITICS, 90; PRECOCITY, 3, PURITANISM, 3, 4, ROYALTY, 77; WRITING, 27
Macaulay, Rose BOOKS, 28, CLASSIFICATION, 3, CRITICISM, 40, FAMILY, 33, NATURE, 26, POETRY, 36, TRAVEL, 28
MacCarthy, Desmond ARTS, 7, LITERATURE, 16, OSTENTATION, 4
MacDiarmid, Hugh KILLING, 7; LOVE AND DEATH, 5, WRITERS, 36
MacDonald, Betty APPEARANCE, 35
MacDonald, Ramsey DIPLOMACY, 20, IDEAS, 6
Mach, Ernst RESEARCH, 19
Machiavelli CHURCH, 7, OBLIGATION, 3
MacInnes, Colin ART, 16, ENGLISH, 25, RACISM, 4
Mackenzie, Compton WOMEN, 70
Mackintosh, James GOVERNMENT, 22
MacLeish, Archibald KNOWLEDGE, 30
Macleod, Fiona HEART, 13, LONELINESS, 6
Macleod, Iain HISTORIANS, 5; OPPORTUNITY, 16
Macmillan, Harold CHANGE, 16, MARXISM, 8, POLITICIANS, 77, 78, 79, POLITICS, 91, 92, 93, 94; POWER, 16, PURPOSE, 9, WEALTH, 29
MacNally, Leonard ADMIRATION, 9, COMPLIMENTS, 16
MacNeice, Louis INDIFFERENCE, 4, LOVE, 99, WORLD WAR II, 38
Madariaga y Rogo, Salvador de POLITICS, 95, UNITED STATES, 41
Madden, Samuel WORDS, 21
Maeterlinck, Maurice LIFE, 52
Magee, William Connor FREEDOM, 36
Magidson, Herb MUSIC, 27
Magnus, Albertus EXPECTATION, 4
Mailer, Norman AGE, 48, FACTS, 5, JOURNALISM, 30, MARRIAGE, 91
Maimonides ILLNESS, 44; KNOWLEDGE, 31, MEDICINE, 58, SOUL, 14
Maistre, Joseph de GOVERNMENT, 23, RUSSIA, 5
Makarios OBITUARIES, 7
Malamud, Bernard DISAPPOINTMENT, 5
Malcolm X RACE, 16; VIOLENCE, 10
Malesherbes, Chrétien Guillaume de Lamoignonde ERROR, 9, SAYINGS, 5
Malherbe, François de FATE, 14, TRANSIENCE, 18
Mallaby, George EQUALITY, 18
Mallet, Robert PESSIMISM, 12
Mallory, George MOTIVE, 3, REPARTEE, 68
Malmesbury, William of EXCESS, 17
Malory, Thomas ACHIEVEMENT, 9, LOSS, 3; NOSTALGIA, 16, SORROW, 12
Malraux, André DEATH, 100
Malthus, Thomas Robert ECONOMICS, 17, SURVIVAL, 5
Manchester, Earl of ROYALTY, 78
Mancroft, Lord LAZINESS, 6
Mandela, Nelson FREEDOM, 37
Mandelstam, Osip APPEARANCE, 36, DENIAL, 2, POSTERITY, 9
Manikan, Ruby EDUCATION, 55, WOMEN, 71
Mankiewicz, Herman J. ARROGANCE, 5; DEATH, 101, DISEASE, 30, ETIQUETTE, 4, INSULTS, 92, PUNS, 14
Mann, Thomas ILLNESS, 45; LIFE, 53, MOURNING, 6, POLITICS, 96, SPEECH, 14
Mansfield, Katherine APPEARANCE, 37, BODY, 14, LIFE AND DEATH, 23, NAKEDNESS, 9, TRAVEL, 29
Mansfield, Lord EQUALITY, 19, JUDGMENT, 13, PATIENTS, 12
Mansfield, Michael J. ASSASSINATION, 6
MAO TSE-TUNG
Map, Walter ALCOHOL, 54, CHARACTER, 17, DIPLOMACY, 21, EDUCATION, 56
Maradona, Diego FOOTBALL, 7
Marcuse, Herbert CAPITALISM, 12
Mare, Walter De La FOOD, 26, ILLNESS, 21, LAST WORDS, 24, WORDS, 22
Marets, Jean Nicolas Corvisart des MEDICINE, 59
Marguerite of Valois SCIENCE, 61
Marie-Antoinette HUNGER, 10
Marie de Sévigné PSYCHOANALYSIS, 19 YOUTH, 24
Mark, Robert POWER POLITICS, 4
Markstein, David LITERATURE, 17
Marlborough, Duke of VICTORY, 12
Marlborough, Sarah, Duchess of ARTS, 8; SEX, 63
Marley, Bob WEALTH, 30
Marlowe, Christopher BEAUTY, 25, 26, COMPLIMENTS, 17, DAMNATION, 3, 4, DANCING, 8, DEATH, 102, DOOMSDAY, 5; FIRST IMPRESSIONS, 6, FLOWERS, 8, IGNORANCE, 16, JUSTICE, 21, LOVE, 100, SEX, 64, WEALTH, 31
Marlowe, Derek LIFE, 55, WOMEN, 72
Marquis, Don HAPPINESS, 15, IDEAS, 7, LAZINESS, 7, OPTIMISM, 30, SELFLESSNESS, 4
Marryat, Captain Frederick EXCUSES, 2, ILLEGITIMACY, 2, INDEPENDENCE, 4, SIMILARITY, 5
Marsh, Edward Howard CRITICS, 10
Marsh, Richard SOCIALISM, 17
Marshall, Alfred BUSINESS, 16
Martial LIFE, 56
Martineau, Harriet ENGLAND, 31, FEMINISM, 21, LOVE AND MARRIAGE, 5, MARRIAGE, 92, 93, 94, UNITED STATES, 42
Marvell, Andrew AGE, 49, BIRDS, 11, DEATH, 103, DESTINY, 16, EXECUTION, 22, FLOWERS, 9, GARDENS, 10, GRAVE, 11, LOVE, 101, OBLIVION, 3, POLITICIANS, 80, SHYNESS, 5, VICTORY, 13, WILDERNESS, 4
Marx, Chico EXCUSES, 3, KISSING, 5
Marx, Groucho AGE, 50; APPEARANCE, 38, 39; BEAUTY, 27, BED, 8, CLUBS, 4, COMPLAINTS, 9, COMPLIMENTS, 18, CRITICISM, 41, DEATH, 104, 105, DISHONOR, 2, DISMISSAL, 6, FAMILY, 34, HONOR, 4, HUMOR, 35, 36, 37, 38, 39, 40, INSULTS, 93, 94, INTRODUCTIONS, 2; JEWS, 12, LEADERSHIP, 8, LOVE, 102, MEMORY, 11, MONEY, 28, 29, NAMES, 9, POVERTY, 30, PREJUDICE, 7, PUNS, 15, REPARTEE, 69, SEX, 65, SIMPLICITY, 5, SUCCESS, 15, SUPERIORITY, 8, TI M E, 31
Marx, Karl CAPITALISM, 13, CLASS, 26, HISTORY, 23, MARXISM, 9, 10, 11, 12, 13, 14, MEDICINE, 60, PHILOSOPHERS, 6, RELIGION, 53
Mary ROYALTY, 79
Mary I DEFEAT, 11, DEFIANCE, 3
Maschwitz, Eric BIRDS, 12, MEMORY, 12
Masefield, John ANIMALS, 16, BOATS, 13, 14, MARTYRDOM, 4, NASTINESS, 5, OLD AGE, 62, SEA, 10
Mason, Walt RELIABILITY, 1
Masor, Nathan ALCOHOL, 55
Massinger, Philip SELF-CONTROL, 6
Masters, John SCOTS, 9
Mathew, James JUSTICE, 22
Matson, Carlton K. DOCTORS, 59
Matthews, Brander EDUCATION, 57, LATIN, 4
Maudling, Reginald DISMISSAL, 7
Maudsley, Henry SURGEONS, 11
Maugham, W. Somerset ACTION, 10, ADULTERY, 5, BED, 9, BOOK TITLES, 16, 17, CHARACTER, 18, CIVILIZATION, 10, CLASS, 27, COMPLIMENTS, 19, CRITICISM, 42, DAY AND NIGHT, 14, DEATH, 106, 107, DECISION, 3 EATING, 7, ETIQUETTE, 5, EXPEDIENCY, 9, FAMILY, 35, FICTION, 5, FOOD, 51, FUTURE, 11, HOSPITALS, 5, HUMOR, 41, HYPOCRISY, 12, LEARNING, 13, LOVE, 103, LYING, 13, MANKIND, 37, MARRIAGE, 95, MISANTHROPY, 2, MONEY, 30, NOVELS, 11, OLD AGE, 63, 64, 65, PEOPLE, 8, 9, PERFECTION, 6, POETRY AND PROSE, 4, POLITICIANS, 81, POLITICS, 98, PROSE, 5, PRUDERY, 2, PSYCHIATRY, 23, RESULTS, 5, RUDENESS, 3, SACRIFICE, 1, 2, SENTIMENTALITY, 4, SUFFERING, 21, 22, WOMEN, 73, 74, 75, 76, WORK, 20, WORLD-WEARINESS, 4, WRITERS, 37; WRITING, 28
Maurier, Daphne du DREAMS, 6, HUMOR, 21
Maurier, George du DOCTORS, 35
Maurois, André AMBITION, 16, ENGLAND, 32, OLD AGE, 66, SCANDAL, 1, SCIENTISTS, 7 UNITED STATES, 43
Maxton, James POLITICIANS, 82
Maxwell, Elsa JEALOUSY, 5, SUCCESS, 16
Mayakovsky, Vladimir ART, 17
Mayer, Louis B. BIBLE, 10
Maynard, John INSULTS, 95
Mayo, Charles H. DISEASE, 31, EDUCATION, 58, HEALTH, 17, HOSPITALS, 6, LEARNING, 14, MEDICINE, 61, NURSES, 5, WORRY, 14
Mayo, William J. DIAGNOSIS, 15, DOCTORS, 60, EXPERTS, 7, ILLNESS, 46, MEDICINE, 62, SPECIALISTS, 6
Mazarin, Cardinal BETRAYAL, 10
McCarthy, Joseph R. COMMUNISM, 10, POLITICS, 99
McCarthy, Mary DECISION, 4; INSULTS, 97; MATERIALISM, 19; NEUROSIS, 7; NOVELS, 12, NOVELTY, 7, REALISM, 3, UNITED STATES, 44
McCartney, Paul PEACE, 16
McCrae, John MEMORIALS, 11
McCullers, Carson BOOK TITLES, 18
McEnroe, John INSULTS, 96
McGahern, John PORNOGRAPHY, 4
McGonagall, William BRIDGE, 3, DEATH, 108, DISASTER, 4
McGough, Roger GUILT, 8
McKinney, Joyce LOVE, 104
McLuhan, Marshall COMMUNICATION, 3, PSYCHIATRY, 24; TECHNOLOGY, 9, 10, TELEVISION, 12, TRAVEL, 30; WAR, 98
Mead, Margaret ECOLOGY, 5, FEMINISM, 22, HUMAN NATURE, 18; MEDIOCRITY, 6
Mearns, Hughes NONSENSE, 23
Medawar, Peter PSYCHOANALYSIS, 18, SCIENCE, 62
Meir, Golda FEMINISM, 23, JEWS, 13, 14, KILLING, 8, LEADERSHIP, 9, OLD AGE, 67, SELF-CONFIDENCE, 3, SELF-PRESERVATION, 9
Melba, Nellie FAME, 16, MUSIC, 28, PLACES, 25, SELF-RELIANCE, 9
MELBOURNE, Lord
Mellon, Andrew William ECONOMICS, 18
Meltzer, Samuel J. DIAGNOSIS, 16
Melville, Herman BODY, 15; DRUNKENNESS, 21, EDUCATION, 59, KNOWLEDGE, 32, LANGUAGE, 29
Ménage, Gilles MEDICINE, 63
Menander DEATH, 109
Mencken, H. L. ALCOHOL, 56, 57, BUSINESS, 17, CANNIBALISM, 2; CLEANNESS, 6, CONSCIENCE, 6, CONTRACEPTION, 9, FAITH, 21, 22, GOD, 41, GOVERNMENT, 24, IDEALISM, 7, IDEAS, 8, IMPROBABILITY, 2, INTELLIGENCE, 6, LYING, 14, MANKIND, 38, MARRIAGE, 96, MEDICINE, 64, OPERA, 7, POETRY, 37, 38, POETS, 27, PRESIDENTS, 11, PROTESTANTISM, 6, PURITANISM, 5, RACISM, 5, SELF-RESPECT, 3, SEXES, 19, SUPERIORITY, 9, TOLERANCE, 9, UNITED STATES, 85, WAR, 99; WOMEN, 77, 78
Mendes, Francisco ECOLOGY, 6
Menninger, Karl ILLNESS, 47, NEUROSIS, 8
Menon, V. K. Krishna POLITICS, 100
Menuhin, Yehudi MUSIC, 29
Menzies, Robert REPARTEE, 71, 72, SUPERIORITY, 10
Mercer, Johnny CRITICISM, 43, EYES, 6, SUPERNATURAL, 11
Merck, George MEDICINE, 65
Meredith, George FOOD, 52, GOOD, 11, ILLNESS, 48, PAIN, 6, WOMEN, 79
Meredith, Owen TALENT AND GENIUS, 3
Merrill, Bob PEOPLE, 10; SOCIETY, 9
Mettrie, Julien Offroy de la BODY, 16, THINKING, 9
Meynell, Alice HEART, 14, LOVE, 105
Michelet, Jules GREATNESS, 10
Middleton, Thomas HONESTY, 5
Midlane, Albert GOD, 42
Midler, Bette SEX, 66
Mies Van Der Rohe, Ludwig ARCHITECTURE, 9
Mikes, George CLASS, 28, ENGLAND, 33, 34, ENGLISH, 26, 27, MANNERS, 5, QUOTATIONS, 7, SERVICE, 4, SEX, 67
Mill, John Stuart FEMINISM, 24, FREEDOM, 39, HAPPINESS, 16, ORIGINALITY, 4, STATE, 4, SUBJECTIVITY, 4
Millard, Emma SEA, 11
Millay, Edna St Vincent LIFE, 57, PLEASURE, 23
Miller, Arthur EUROPE, 11, FUNERALS, 9, JOURNALISM, 31; MATERIALISM, 20; MISTRUST, 9, POPULARITY, 7, RELIGION, 55
Miller, C. Jeff HOLISTIC MEDICINE, 7
Miller, Henry BOOKS, 29; CLASSICS, 8, CONFUSION, 8, CRITICISM, 44, LIFE, 58, POLITICS, 101, SEX, 68
Miller, Jonathan HABIT, 5, HALF MEASURES, 2, JEWS, 15; MEDICINE, 66; RESEARCH, 20
Miller, Max SEX, 69
Milligan, Spike ANIMALISM, 6, CLASS, 29, CLOTHES, 15, CONTRACEPTION, 10, GOVERNMENT, 25, HEROISM, 7, MATHEMATICS, 12, MONEY, 31, NONSENSE, 24, PHOTOGRAPHY, 6, PLACES, 26, POLICE, 5, PUNS, 16, SEX, 70, SPORT AND GAMES, 16, TRAVEL, 31
Mills, Hugh ART, 18
Milman, Henry Hart CHRISTIANITY, 45
Milne, A. A. AGE, 51, FOOD, 53; LANGUAGE, 30, LAZINESS, 8, SOLDIERS, 6, SUPERSTITION, 10, WORDS, 23
MILTON, John
Mirabeau, Comte de FRENCH REVOLUTION, 6, WAR, 100
Mirman, Sophie WOMEN, 81
Mitchell, Adrian SOLITUDE, 12
Mitchell, Joni ILLUSIONS, 4, LIFE, 59
Mitchell, Julian FAMILY, 36, NEUROSIS, 9
Mitchell, Margaret BOOK TITLES, 19; HOPE, 17, INCONVENIENCE, 1, REPUTATION, 6, TRANSIENCE, 19; WAR, 101
Mitchell, S. Weir WOMEN, 82
Mitford, Jessica OCCUPATIONS, 16
Mitford, Mary Russell MEN, 10